ONTARIO SMALL CLAIMS COURT PRACTICE

2015

Justice MARVIN A. ZUKER
Ontario Court of Justice

J. SEBASTIAN WINNY
Small Claims Court

CARSWELL®

ISSN 1191-1581
ISSN 1191-159X
ISBN 978-0-7798-6176-7 (2015 edition)

A cataloguing record for this publication is available from Library and Archives Canada.

Printed in the United States by Thomson Reuters.

 **THOMSON REUTERS**

CARSWELL, A DIVISION OF THOMSON REUTERS CANADA LIMITED

One Corporate Plaza
2075 Kennedy Road
Toronto, Ontario
M1T 3V4

Customer Relations
Toronto 1-416-609-3800
Elsewhere in Canada/U.S. 1-800-387-5164
Fax 1-416-298-5082
www.carswell.com
Contact www.carswell.com/contact

*Thank you to everyone for the
past 36 years and counting*

PREFACE

Now into the fifth year after the $25,000 monetary limit came into effect, the Small Claims Court continues to handle the increased variety and complexity of cases that the increased monetary limit has produced. A greater proportion of litigants in Small Claims Court are represented by lawyers and paralegals, and there are a greater number of longer trials, requiring a full day or more, and fewer short trials, requiring under half a day.

The statistic continues to be that about 45% of civil claims in Ontario proceed in the Small Claims Court, making it the face of justice for a great many litigants. In virtually every public statement made in recent years by the leaders of our court system, including Chief Justice Heather Smith and recently retired Chief Justice Warren Winkler, access to justice is emphasized as a key and essential underpinning of the civil justice system. If the system is not accessible, it is not meaningful, and it is nothing but a weak and watered-down version of a justice system. The Small Claims Court deals with small and simple civil matters and involves less pre-trial procedures and much shorter trials, compared to matters in the Superior Court of Justice. The Small Claims Court should be, and is, the people's court. It provides the simplest and most user-friendly process for litigious disputes.

Reporting of Small Claims Court decisions has increased significantly in the past year. The increased monetary jurisdiction has probably played its part in producing written decisions more often, given the possibility of appeal is more real when more money is at stake. The online reporting services have taken to more frequent reporting of Small Claims Court decisions, despite the limited precedential value they possess as decisions of a statutory court of inferior jurisdiction. The appellate decisions of the Divisional Court on appeal from the Small Claims Court, despite the low incidence of such appeals, are often reported online and are significant in defining legal issues which arise in Small Claims Court.

There are currently approximately 380 deputy judges in Ontario. That is down from about 420 as of five years ago, which may be due primarily to the effect of the new mandatory retirement provisions under the *Courts of Justice Act* s. 32. It remains true that the majority of deputy judges, almost all of whom practice as lawyers full-time and as deputy judges only part-time, preside as deputy judges only two days a month on average.

Continuing Professional Development for deputy judges has been made available on a formal and regular basis thanks to the excellent work of the Deputy Judges Council. In that regard (and without in any way downplaying the contributions of others), two now retired judges whose contributions to the work of the Deputy Judges Council and in particular to the annual Caswell Seminars have been specially appreciated are Associate Chief Justice Douglas Cunningham and Justice James Carnwath. Recently, the Ontario Deputy Judges Association, under the leadership of Deputy Judge Marcel Mongeon, has became another source of Continuing Legal Education for deputy judges, providing webinars which are well-attended and well-received.

The result is that deputy judges now have a solid and regular base of CPD materials on subjects specific to their court. This promotes a degree of consistency in the application of law across Ontario by the deputy judges of the Small Claims Court. CPD is of course mandatory for lawyers and paralegals under Law Society rules enacted several years ago, which promotes education among advocates appearing in Small Claims Court.

In this edition of Ontario Small Claims Court Practice, we have as usual added annotations of appropriate caselaw, and we have added to the commentaries and provided a new section on recent developments in the legislation and caselaw relevant to the court. We have adjusted formatting in some respects to enhance readability, including streamlining of the Table of Contents. We hope this edition will continue to assist readers in understanding and using the people's court.

Many thanks are due to Susan Goodman at Carswell for all her help and encouragement with this work, and also Heather Kerr, and to all those at Carswell without whose assistance this would not be possible. Recognition is also due to the staff of the court across Ontario, without whose efforts the court would quickly grind to a standstill.

Marvin A. Zuker
Toronto, Ontario
April 2014

J. Sebastian Winny
Waterloo, Ontario
April 2014

ACKNOWLEDGEMENTS

I could not have written this book without a lot of help along the way from so many people. I recall the Preface to the 1981 Supplement to McKeon's *Small Claims Court Handbook*. That was 36 years ago.

History

"For too long, Small Claims Courts were the victims of judicial, academic and governmental neglect. Many people tended to regard Small Claims Courts as a marginal part of the administration of justice. It has now become apparent, at least in Ontario, that the rightful place of these courts as a vital and integral part of the administration of justice has been recognized.

During the Fall of 1980 the first Canadian National Small Claims Courts Seminar, under the sponsorship of the Canadian Institute for the Administration of Justice, was held in Toronto. The Seminar was very well attended, with representation from Small Claims Courts from across Canada and the United States.

It was also during the Fall of 1980 that the Department of Continuing Education of the Law Society of Upper Canada sponsored another 'first,' this time a seminar on Small Claims Court actions in Metropolitan Toronto under the *Provincial Court (Civil Division) Project Act, 1979*. Again the response was nothing less than overwhelming.

The new wave of the 1980s may well be Provincial (Civil Division) Courts with monetary jurisdictions approaching if not exceeding the present $6,000 limit of the Quebec Provincial Courts.

The high cost of justice demands nothing less.

The monetary jurisdiction of Ontario's Small Claims Courts was increased from $400 to $1,000 in 1977. The new *Provincial Court (Civil Division) Project Act* creates in the Municipality of Metropolitan Toronto, a Court of Record as of June 30th, 1980. The courts operating under the legislation have all the jurisdiction that the Small Claims Courts of Metropolitan Toronto previously had, and in addition, have monetary jurisdiction over civil claims up to $3,000 in amount. The Judges are all provincially appointed Small Claims Court Judges."

"In Utopia, as described by Sir Thomas More, there are few laws and they are comprehensible by everyone. There are no lawyers in Utopian courts. More states that:

> They think it better for each man to plead his own cause, and tell the judge the same story as he'd otherwise tell his lawyer. Under such conditions, the point at issue is less likely to be obscured, and it's easier to get at the truth — for, if nobody's telling the sort of lies that one learns from lawyers, the judge can apply all his shrewdness to weighing the facts of the case, and protecting simpleminded characters against the unscrupulous attacks of clever ones.

In Utopia it seems, all courts will be Small Claims Courts."

Toronto, Ontario
December 31, 1980

The Provincial Court (Civil Division) project in Metropolitan Toronto had its origin in the *Provincial Court (Civil Division) Project Act, 1979*, enacted in June 1979. In introducing the Bill, then Attorney General, the Honourable R. Roy McMurtry, Q.C., said that its goals were to provide more speedy and less expensive procedures for the resolution of disputes over fairly small amounts of money, to increase the accessibility of Ontario citizens to the courts, and to assist the County Court of the Judicial District of York in decreasing its caseload.

Acknowledgements

To quote the Attorney General in his introductory statement on 25th November 1982 during first reading of the *Provincial Court (Civil Division) Project Amendment Act, 1982*, c. 58:

> Mr. Speaker, I am pleased to move first reading of an Act to amend the *Provincial Court (Civil Division) Project Act*, the *Civil Division Act* is due to expire on January 1, 1983 and the purpose of this Bill is to provide for that court to be made permanent in Metropolitan Toronto.
>
> In Metropolitan Toronto, the Provincial Court (Civil Division) has assumed the civil jurisdiction previously exercised by the small claims court and has, in addition, jurisdiction over civil claims up to $3,000. Rules of court, specially designed for the Provincial Court (Civil Division), provide the necessary procedural structure without sacrificing the informality of small claims court procedures.
>
> The court has been very favourably received by the public and by the legal profession in the Toronto area and I am confident that its continuation on a permanent basis will be wholeheartedly welcomed.

The goals of the Provincial Court (Civil Division) project may be broadly stated:

- to make courts accessible to ordinary citizens,
- to reduce the expense of litigation involving relatively small amounts of money,
- to reduce delay in litigation.

Can the project be said to have met these goals?

The answer is "yes."

Effective January 1, 1983, this court became the Provincial Court (Civil Division), no longer a *project* court. In October 1983, all eleven small claims court judges, including yours truly, were sworn in as Provincial Court Judges by the Chief Justice of Ontario.

The Attorney General, in a statement to the legislature on October 27, 1983, introduced the *Courts of Justice Act* as a significant step in the reform of civil procedure in Ontario.

> The *Courts of Justice Act* will provide the framework for the new rules. In addition, it is intended to revise and consolidate the many statutes that establish courts and regulate their procedures. Some of these statutes date back many decades and contain numerous archaic and obscure provisions. The *Courts of Justice Act* is intended to modernize this legislation.

Sections 1, 73, 76, 85, 89, 90, 221 and 222 of the *Courts of Justice Act*, S.O. 1984, c. 11 were proclaimed in force June 1, 1984; the remaining sections came into force on proclamation, January 1, 1985.

Three editions to McKeon's *Small Claims Court Handbook* were published in 1953, 1965 and in 1975. With respect to the small claims courts of Ontario, "new" rules in 1985 represented the first complete revision of the court this century. The 1985 Rules were similar to the former rules of the Provincial Court (Civil Division) in Metropolitan Toronto.

In 1985 all Small Claims Courts became Provincial Court (Civil Division) courts, presided over by Provincial Court judges and lawyers appointed as deputy judges on a part-time basis, and also presided over by then District Court judges.

The Honourable T.G. Zuber of the Ontario Court of Appeal recognized in his 1987 *Report of the Ontario Court Inquiry* the desire to make our judicial system more accessible, convenient, and basically simpler. Justice Zuber recommended that the civil jurisdiction of the Provincial Court be increased to $10,000 throughout the Province of Ontario.

Pursuant to the amendments of the *Courts of Justice Act, 1984*, enacted on November 15, 1989, and December 14, 1989, and in force September 1, 1990, substantial changes were made to the structure of the Ontario courts. There was a new court called the Ontario Court of Justice composed of two divisions — the General Division (combining the jurisdiction now exercised by the High Court, the District Court and the surrogate courts) and the Provincial Court (combining the jurisdiction of the Provincial Court (Criminal Division), the Provincial Court (Family Division) and the Provincial Offences Court).

Acknowledgements

Conspicuous by its absence was the Provincial Court (Civil Division). This Division, created in 1980, no longer exists as a separate division. It became part of the Ontario Court (General Division). The Small Claims Court is but a branch of the Ontario Court (General Division).

On April 21, 1992 then Attorney General for Ontario, Howard Hampton, announced that, effective July 1, 1992, the monetary jurisdiction of Small Claims Courts outside the Municipality of Metropolitan Toronto would increase to $3,000, with a further increase for all courts to $6,000, effective April 1, 1993.

The first *Report of Civil Justice Review* was submitted for consideration in March 1995. One of the specific areas addressed was that of the Small Claims Court in Ontario.

The bottom line was access to Justice and costs as a possible barrier associated with litigation. Recommendations were made in Chapter 17.1 to the Small Claims Court including the procedure for appeals from this Court to the General Division as well as possibly increasing the threshold amount for appeals from $500.00 to $1,200.00.

As a result of lengthy work by the then Small Claims Court Sub-Committee of the Ontario Civil Rules Committee chaired by Justice Peter Jarvis, amendments were made to simplify language and improve the administrative operation of the Small Claims Court Rules. These were gazetted on June 13, 1998, filed as O. Reg. 258/98, and implemented on September 1, 1998.

The *Courts of Justice Act* was further amended to incorporate changes made to Ontario court names and court officials, effective April 19, 1999. Section 1.1(1) of the *Courts of Justice Act* stated that a reference to a former name of a court or court official "shall be deemed, unless a contrary intention appears, to be a reference to the new name of that court or the new title of that official."

On December 22, 2000, then Attorney General Jim Flaherty announced that the monetary limit in the Small Claims Courts for Ontario would be increased to $10,000 effective April 2, 2001 (see O. Reg. 626/00). Ontario Regulation 92/93 was accordingly revoked. According to the Attorney General, ". . . . The Small Claims Court is the busiest civil court in Ontario, receiving approximately 85,000 claims each year. . . ." *Inter alia*, claims involving amounts of up to $10,000 commenced in the Superior Court could be transferred to the Small Claims Court after April 2, 2001. Where a claim was for $10,000 or less, and involved the payment of money or recovery of personal property, parties, on consent, could transfer their actions to the Small Claims Court.

The continuing need to regulate paralegals was reflected in the report on paralegals prepared by Justice Peter Cory for the Ontario Ministry of the Attorney General. In his report entitled, "A Framework for Regulating Paralegal Practice," Justice Cory stated that paralegals have a significant role to play in increasing access to legal services. Attorney General Flaherty affirmed the Ministry's priority of ensuring that the justice system continues to be accessible to ordinary people. "Paralegals perform important advocacy services for clients appearing before specialized boards and tribunals such as the Ontario Rental Housing Tribunal and in the Ontario Small Claims Court. The disputes and amounts involved in the proceedings may not justify the retention of a lawyer, but are significant enough to require proper, efficient representation. Accordingly, paralegals are part of the solution in ensuring meaningful access to justice."

The Law Society of Upper Canada more recently prepared its own report on paralegal regulation after interviewing 500 stakeholders, including consumers, business people and 200 paralegals. The vast majority of those surveyed favour paralegal regulation and defining permitted areas of practice. Justice Cory also had recommended a system for regulating and licensing independent paralegals, including qualifying examinations for different areas of practice.

The Canadian Bar Association in August 2000, suggested that advantages such as more efficient use of time and increased competitiveness due to cost saving might spark future interest in the use of paralegals by law firms. Their report stated "this use of paralegals should be uncontroversial and encouraged." The Canadian Bar Association Special Committee on the Status of Paralegals (the "Strauss Report") specifically recommended that CBA members utilize, where appropriate, the services of paralegals in law firms in order to pass along the cost-saving to the legal services consuming public. Certainly if the U.S. experience is any indication of what could happen in Canada, there are enormous future opportunities for paralegals. "In the U.S., the demand for paralegals is exploding. There are currently about 100,000 paralegals nationally and the U.S. Bureau of Labour predicts that the job market will double in size in the next decade (source: www.law.net *The Paralegal Profession*)."

Justice Cory stated that licensed paralegals must attain an adequate level of education and achieve competence in the fields in which they wish to practice. He recognized that experience is important, but stated that experience must be based on a solid educational foundation. He recommended that such education should take place within a community college. The National Federation of Paralegal Associations, a non-profit, professional association made up of state and local paralegal associations throughout the United States and Canada, "recommended that based upon current hiring trends, future practitioners should have a four-year degree to enter the paralegal profession (*Quality Paralegal Education, Part 3; Curriculum*. www.aafpe.org/curriculum.html)."

The Ontario Bar Association supports the position that paralegals can be a useful and effective addition to our justice system, but they need to be properly trained and regulated to protect the public, according to *Regulation of Paralegals*, Ontario Bar Association (see www.oba.org/current issues en/paralegals.asp). "Untrained representation in court can also result in huge personal costs such as unnecessary incarceration, deportation, or loss of access to ones' children or home." The OBA approved a resolution on September 24, 2000 outlining the services that could be provided by paralegals with the appropriate education and regulation.

The proclamation of the *Post-secondary Education Choice and Excellence Act, 2000*, S.O. 2000, c. 36 made it possible for the Minister of Training, Colleges and Universities to authorize a college of applied arts and technology to offer applied degree programs. The Post-secondary Education Quality Assessment Board (PEQAB) was established for the purpose of assessing proposed applied degree programs and other matters referred to it by the Minister.

On March 27, 2002 it was announced that among twelve pilot projects approved, Humber College was approved to offer a Bachelor of Applied Arts in Paralegal Studies, effective September, 2003. The curriculum is designed in keeping with the concerns of the Law Society. According to Humber College, once paralegal regulation is in place, the curriculum will be modified, if necessary, to conform to the areas of practice specified in the regulatory regime. Thus Humber College became the first post-secondary institution in Ontario, if not Canada, to offer such a degree program.

The monetary limit of small claims courts in the Province of Alberta was raised to $25,000 effective November 1, 2002. British Columbia raised its monetary jurisdiction also to $25,000, effective September 1, 2005.

The Law Society of Upper Canada Task Force on Paralegal Regulations was established by Law Society Treasurer, Frank Marrocco, Q.C., following the January 2004 Convocation, at which Ontario Attorney General Michael Bryant stated his support of the Law Society as the regulator of paralegals, and asked the Society to assume this responsibility.

Access to Justice Act

Bill 14, the Ontario *Access to Justice Act, 2006*, received royal assent on October 27, 2005. The legislation is intended to increase openness, improve accountability, and reinforce the public's confidence in the justice system.

This new Act reformed the justice of the peace system, regulated paralegals, amended the *Courts of Justice Act* and *Limitations Act*, as well as created a single source for rules about Ontario's laws called the *Legislation Act*.

Under the legislation paralegals are:

- required to complete an approved college program including a field placement, and pass a licensing examination;
- required to adhere to a code of conduct, carry insurance and contribute to a compensation fund;
- subject to the governance of the Law Society and in particular regulated by the Law Society.

The new legislation expands the public interest mandate of the Law Society to regulate all legal service providers including independent paralegals.

The regulatory model outlined in the *Access to Justice Act, 2006* shares many common features with the current regulatory system for lawyers and reflects the recommendations included in the Law Society's report submitted to the Attorney General in September 2004. The Attorney General has made clear his view that the Law Society is able to extend its mandate to protect consumers of all legal services.

> Paralegals have an important role to play in increasing access to justice, however, there is currently no regulation of paralegals respecting fees equivalent to that applicable to lawyers. Consequently, the need for regulation to avoid the abuses inherent in contingency fees may be more pressing for paralegals. This is not so because paralegals are inherently less trustworthy than lawyers, but because most individuals who retain paralegals are particularly vulnerable because of their social and/or economic circumstances. Unless and until paralegals are brought within a regulatory scheme that permits oversight of the terms and conditions of contingency fee arrangements, the benefit/risk analysis favours maintaining the absolute prohibition against contingency fee agreements. The appropriate response to this problem lies in the enactment of legislation recognizing the valuable role of paralegals in the justice system and regulating that role.

"The need to preserve public policy by not enforcing illegal agreements must be balanced with the need to prevent unjust enrichment. In this case, the contingency fee agreement was created in fair circumstances where both parties were fully aware of what they bargained for." See *Koliniotis v. Tri Level Claims Consultants Ltd.* (August 12, 2005) McMurtry C.J.O., Doherty and LaForme JJ.A. (By the Court).

Justice Pamela Thomson was appointed Chair of the most recent Small Claims Court Rules Subcommittee by Chief Justice Roy McMurtry in January 2002. The Committee has met continuously since March 2002. Its work was completed in the Fall of 2005 in terms of a revision of the present Small Claims Court Rules and Court Forms. These major changes took effect on July 1, 2006.

Thank You

Where does one begin? With Ontario Chief Justice Roy McMurtry, then Attorney General who appointed me to the Small Claims Court on July 1, 1978? Then Chief Judge Bill Coulter of the County and District Courts for Ontario, a great person and wonderful supporter of this court? Two unbelievable colleagues, Doug Turner, the first and only Chief Judge of this Court, a role model and mentor for all who knew him? Justice Moira Carswell whose enthusiasm, warmth, and just plain caring remained long after she was appointed to the then General Division? With all my colleagues on this Bench over the years, in particular amongst equals, Pam Thomson, whose leadership, support and determination on behalf of everyone in this Court is legendary, and deservedly so.

To so many others throughout the years who have provided assistance and direction, Steve McCann, Ron McFarland, Tony Bridges, Ross Flowers, Mitch Saunders, John Twohig, Guy Attisano, Mary Macri, still going strong, Marg White, Rick Soderberg, Bob Shore, Linda

Acknowledgements

Groen, Jennifer Francisco, Ted Tjaden, and Ali Maqbool. The secretarial and support services I have had, has been second to none, Pauline Geddes, Marie Lowe, Chris Elie, Jackie Crawford, Sharon Rosenberg, Catherine Gelman, Doreen Meadley, Nancy Mayes, Lynne Howard, Gayle Grisdale, Jean Brown, Jayne Poyner, Vicki Charles, and Laurel Campbell, who is the point guard for this edition. I am eternally indebted to so many at Carswell, who have read all the manuscripts with great care and made terrific suggestions, Bill Rankin, Dwight Richardson, Bernie Aron, Jeff Maddison, David Keeshan, Julia Gulej, Laura Spicer-Kush, Lorraine Aston, Carol MacKay, Karol Roseman, Ruth Epstein, Ainsley Davison, Robert Jarovi, Seán DaCosta, Marja Appleford, Heather Kerr, Ken Mathies, Steve Iseman, and Susan Goodman, my current batting manager.

Finally, I have to thank my wife, Brenda, for putting up with me all these many years and many hours, working often and mostly at home, raiding the fridge far too frequently. Our children, Paul, Michael, and Pam, and grandchildren, Rebecca and Jenna and Michael's other half, Leslie, have all made me a very lucky man.

If there has been one singular inspiration along the way, it was June Callwood, with whom I had the great good fortune to collaborate on two publications. June was a jewel, a bright light and everything the word good stands for. Thank you again from the bottom of my heart.

Marvin A. Zuker
April 2011

KEY TOPICS

TABLE OF CONTENTS

CHAPTER 1 — A SELF-HELP OVERVIEW

CHAPTER 2 — COURTS OF JUSTICE ACT

Table of Contents

CHAPTER 3 — RULES OF THE SMALL CLAIMS COURT

Table of Contents

Table of Contents

Table of Contents

CHAPTER 4 — COURT FEES

CHAPTER 5 — COURT FORMS IN SMALL CLAIMS COURT

CHAPTER 6 — SMALL CLAIMS COURT JUDGES AND COURT OFFICES

CHAPTER 7 — APPEALS

RECENT AMENDMENTS TO THE SMALL CLAIMS COURT RULES

Service

The rule for alternative service by service on a lawyer was amended to provide for service on a lawyer or paralegal, or an employee of the lawyer or paralegal: see rules 8.03(5) & (6), effective January 31, 2014.

Representation

New rule 1.08 was enacted effective January 11, 2014, stating that nothing in the rules allows the court to permit representation by a person not authorized to do so under the *Law Society Act* (and under the *Courts of Justice Act* s. 26). The intention of that change is to eliminate representation by unauthorized persons and to discourage judges from allowing such representation on an *ad hoc* basis.

A series of rules amendments came into force on July 1, 2014, including the following:

Forms

The Forms for Plaintiff's Claim (Form 7A), Defence (Form 9A), and Defendant's Claim (Form 10A) have been amended.

Electronic Filing

New rule 1.05.1 provides for electronic filing and issuance of court documents in the Small Claims Court using software authorized by the Ministry of the Attorney General for specific court offices. While the rule comes into force on July 1, 2014, the question of whether and when it in fact applies at any given court office would have to be determined by inquiring with the relevant court office. It is likely to start as a pilot project in specific larger centres and may then be expanded if the system works satisfactorily. There are consequential amendments to rule 7 (plaintiff's claim — see new rules 7.02 & 7.04) and to rule 20.07 (writ of seizure and sale of land).

Defences

Previously, defendants had to file a Defence with enough copies for the clerk to serve the other parties. Defences will no longer be served by the clerk but must be served by the defendant and then filed with proof of service. That brings the Small Claims Court in line with the practice under other procedural codes. See amended rules 9.01 & 10.03.

Motions for Judgment

Rule 12.02 (motions for judgment) has been amended to clarify that the court may stay or dismiss an action on its own motion, in which case the rule provides for written submissions from the parties. See new rules 12.02(3), (4), (5) & (6).

Rule 12.02 has been further amended to provide that the court may, on its own motion, stay or dismiss a motion. See new rules 12.02(7), (8) & (9). There is also an amendment dealing with stays or dismissals of proceedings commenced or continued without leave despite a vexatious litigant order having been made pursuant to the *Courts of Justice Act* s. 140. See new rule 12.03.

These amendments to rule 12.02 clarify and codify aspects of the court's practice under a pilot project by which administrative deputy judges, in locations where such judges have been appointed (currently Toronto, Ottawa, Brampton, and Hamilton), review all new files with a view to the possible need for orders to be made at an early juncture.

Settlement Conference

The settlement conference rule has been amended to provide that a settlement conference judge may stay or dismiss an action, with written reasons for decision: see amended rule 13.05(2)(a)(iii). The rule previously contained no express requirement for reasons.

SURVEY OF RECENT CASELAW AFFECTING SMALL CLAIMS COURT

1. — Discovery-Type Motions

The mandate of the Small Claims Court is to hear and determine cases in a summary manner, under the *Courts of Justice Act* s. 25. Consistent with that mandate, the extent of pre-trial procedures in Small Claims Court is modest compared with those in other courts. The basic three steps in a Small Claims Court action are pleadings, settlement conference, and trial. At present, the *Small Claims Court Rules* are made up of 22 rules, compared to 77 under the *Rules of Civil Procedure*.

The court continues to see attempts by some litigants to inject discovery-type steps into Small Claims Court. Most often these take the form of motions for discovery of documents, but the creativity of some parties and their willingness to spend a lot of money on pre-trial motions can produce an array of different strategies. This line of cases has continued to develop over the past year.

The Court of Appeal for Ontario held in *Van de Vrande v. Butkowsky*, 2010 ONCA 230, 2010 CarswellOnt 1777, 99 O.R. (3d) 648, 99 O.R. (3d) 641, 85 C.P.C. (6th) 205, 319 D.L.R. (4th) 132, 260 O.A.C. 323, [2010] O.J. No. 1239 (Ont. C.A.); additional reasons 2010 ONCA 400, 2010 CarswellOnt 3629, 85 C.P.C. (6th) 212 (Ont. C.A.), that motion procedure in Small Claims Court is found in the *Small Claims Court Rules*. A motion for judgment is available under rule 12.02 of those rules and the court cannot resort to Rules 20 or 21 of the *Rules of Civil Procedure* because those rules don't apply in Small Claims Court. That decision should have laid to rest the occasional suggestion that procedures from the *Rules of Civil Procedure* could freely apply in Small Claims Court where desired.

The position adopted in *Van de Vrande v. Butkowsky*, *supra*, was foresaged by Deputy Judge Searle in *Fountain v. Ford*, 2009 CarswellOnt 705, [2009] O.J. No. 562 (Ont. Sm. Cl. Ct.), who described examination for discovery and cross-examinations on affidavits as some of the procedures under the *Rules of Civil Procedure* that are alien to the Small Claims Court. In his view, attempts to expand procedure in this court had been consistently rejected. *Fountain v. Ford*, *supra*, has been followed by a number of deputy judges, including Deputy Judge Bale (as he then was) in *Caprio v. Caprio*, 2009 CarswellOnt 8270, 97 O.R. (3d) 312 (Ont. Sm. Cl. Ct.). As he pointed out, if procedures under the *Rules of Civil Procedure* could be freely imported into Small Claims Court, why stop at Rule 20? Why not import documentary and oral examinations for discovery, security for costs, cross-examination on affidavits, requests to admit, etc?

Deputy Judge Searle addressed the question of pre-trial motions for production of documents and held that there was no such thing as such a motion in Small Claims Court. Parties could ask a settlement conference judge to order production of documents because the Small Claims Court Rules provide for such orders at a settlement conference. But there is no such thing as a motion for production of documents in Small Claims Court: *Norquay Developments Ltd. v. Oxford County Housing Corp.*, 2010 CarswellOnt 366, [2010] O.J. No. 274 (Ont. Sm. Cl. Ct.). That decision was followed by Deputy Judge Winny in *Petrykowski v. 553562 Ontario Ltd.*, 2010 CarswellOnt 11112, [2010] O.J. No. 1048 (Ont. Sm. Cl. Ct.), and most recently by Deputy Judge Rose in *Cathers v. RBC Dominion Securities Inc.*, 2013 CarswellOnt 15726, [2013] O.J. No. 5119 (Ont. Sm. Cl. Ct.).

The position that procedures from the *Rules of Civil Procedure* should not be applied in Small Claims Court is not consistently followed however. In *National Service Dog Training*

Centre Inc. v. Hall, 2013 CarswellOnt 9429, [2013] O.J. No. 3216 (Ont. Sm. Cl. Ct.), the plaintiff claimed the recovery of possession of a dog. The case was hard-fought, with senior counsel on both sides. In September 2012 the plaintiff brought a pre-trial motion for interim recovery of possession. Deputy Judge Lannan ruled (without reported reasons) that the court had jurisdiction to make such an order but he found that interim recovery of possession was inappropriate and a trial was required. Then at what was supposed to be the start of trial in April 2013, the plaintiff brought a motion for inspection of the dog on certain terms designed to produce expert evidence concerning the dog's condition. As a result the trial was adjourned and the hearing of that and related motions took two days over a period of two months. In written reasons, Deputy Judge McGill held that the court had jurisdiction to make the requested order for inspection, that the request for possession of the dog for purposes of inspection was different than the earlier motion for interim possession, and that the order should be granted.

Deputy Judge McGill distinguished *Van de Vrande v. Butkowsky, supra*, and other authorities rejecting attempts to import procedures from the *Rules of Civil Procedure* into Small Claims Court. She held that the court's jurisdiction to make specific discovery-type orders was not foreclosed and that the court could apply Rule 32 (Inspection of Property) of the *Rules of Civil Procedure* because the *Small Claims Court Rules* contained a legislative gap on the question of interim inspection. She granted an order that the plaintiff was entitled to possession of the dog on six occasions for the purpose of veterinary and other assessments.

The decision of Deputy Judge McGill conflicts with *Solylo v. Lamontagne*, 2008 CarswellOnt 4440, [2008] O.J. No. 2959 (Ont. Sm. Cl. Ct.), holding that the court has no jurisdiction to order an independent veterinary examination of a dog, and with *Ever Fresh Direct Foods Inc. v. Schindler* (August 11, 2011), Doc. Court File No. 315/11, [2011] O.J. No. 3634 (Ont. Small Cl. Ct.), holding that the court has no jurisdiction to award interim recovery of personal property. The latter decision was followed in *Gunn v. Gunn*, 2013 CarswellOnt 235, [2013] O.J. No. 30 (Ont. Sm. Cl. Ct.).

The latest and perhaps most comprehensive decision to date on the question of pretrial document discovery motions is the decision of Deputy Judge McNulty in *Crocker v. Ventawood Management Inc.* (September 26, 2013), Doc. SC-11-00007447-0000, [2013] O.J. No. 4588 (Ont. Sm. Cl. Ct.). In that case the plaintiff, on what was supposed to be the trial date, brought a motion for document discovery and for particulars. The specific items requested are helpfully reproduced as an addendum to Deputy Judge McNulty's reasons for decision. There were 51 specific requests including requests for existing documents, documents which would have to be created by the defendant, and various pieces of information requested as "particulars". The plaintiff's request could only be characterized as a request for discovery of both documents and information.

Deputy Judge McNulty dismissed the motion. He followed several authorities holding that there is no discovery in the Small Claims Court, including *Norquay Developments, supra*. He specifically agreed with the proposition that while orders for production of documents may be requested of a settlement conference judge, there is no such thing as a pretrial motion for production of documents in Small Claims Court.

These recent decisions illustrate that, perhaps like any other court made up of several hundred judges, some difference of judicial opinion can be expected. But it is submitted that three observations fall from the recent developments:

1. *Van de Vrande v. Butkowsy, supra*, is a decision of the Court of Appeal and it instructs that procedure in the Small Claims Court must be found in the *Small Claims Court Rules* and cannot freely be supplemented by importing procedure from the *Rules of Civil Procedure*;

2. Apart from that binding authority, the weight of the cases from the Small Claims Court itself, as observed by Deputy Judge Searle in *Fountain v. Ford, supra*, is against

importing procedures from the *Rules of Civil Procedure* which are alien to and dispro-portionately costly in the context of Small Claims Court litigation; and

3. There is good reason to resist attempts to import alien procedures into Small Claims Court. In *Crocker, supra*, the discovery motion supplanted what was supposed to be the trial (and trial had been adjourned twice before on consent) with a two-day motion which must have delayed the eventual trial by at least six months. In *National Service Dog Training Centre Inc., supra*, the parties underwent three days of motion litigation and the trial was delayed by about 12 months as a result, all of which over a dog whose monetary value must be less than the cost of even one day in court.

One aspect of this debate is that pretrial discovery-type motions generally produce orders which are interlocutory in nature and not subject to appeal under the *Courts of Justice Act* s. 31. The potential for binding resolution of these issues may lie with judicial review on a point of jurisdiction or natural justice, which the Divisional Court has accepted as a proper avenue for review of interlocutory orders of the Small Claims Court. That topic is addressed in the next section.

2. — Judicial Review of Interlocutory Orders

Appeals from the Small Claims Court are only available from final orders and subject to the minimum appealable limit under the *Courts of Justice Act* s. 31, which is $2,500 exclusive of costs. Only final orders in actions for the payment of money in excess of that limit, or for recovery of possession of personal property valued in excess of that limit, may be appealed to a single judge of the Divisional Court. Interlocutory orders of the Small Claims Court are not subject to appeal under s. 31: see *Grainger v. Windsor-Essex Children's Aid Society*, 2009 CarswellOnt 4000, 96 O.R. (3d) 711 (Ont. S.C.J.). That decision was followed in *Cudini v. 1704405 Ontario Inc.*, 2012 ONSC 6645, 2012 CarswellOnt 15146, [2012] O.J. No. 5620 (Ont. Div. Ct.), and *Full Line Construction v. Harvey & Dennis* (October 4, 2013), Doc. D.C. 12-0079-00, [2013] O.J. No. 4720 (Ont. Div. Ct.).

Only final orders in excess of the minimum appealable limit may be appealed to the Divisional Court, and such appeals are heard by one judge of that court. While it may seem counter-intuitive, it appears that interlocutory orders and other orders of the Small Claims Court may be reviewed by a panel of three judges of that court by way of application for judicial review. It was *Peck v. Residential Property Management Inc.*, 2009 CarswellOnt 4330, [2009] O.J. No. 3064 (Ont. Div. Ct.), which first held that such review was available, albeit the court said it was reluctant to exercise that jurisdiction absent error of jurisdiction or breach of the principles of natural justice.

The point was confirmed in *ThyssenKrupp Elevator (Canada) Ltd. v. 1147335 Ontario Inc.*, 2012 ONSC 4139, 2012 CarswellOnt 9698, 43 Admin. L.R. (5th) 61, 18 C.L.R. (4th) 82, 295 O.A.C. 71, [2012] O.J. No. 3674 (Ont. Div. Ct.), where Justice Nordheimer (for the court) reviewed the authorities dealing with whether judicial officers other than judges of the Superior Court of Justice were subject to judicial review. In that case the question was judi-cial review of the interlocutory order of a master. The court concluded that judicial review was available but should not be invoked routinely, nor as an avenue to avoid statutory re-strictions on the right of appeal. Judicial review is available where the conduct of the judicial officer is brought into serious question such as an assertion of bias. See also *Ellins v. Mc-Donald*, 2012 ONSC 4831, 2012 CarswellOnt 12001, [2012] O.J. No. 4556 (Ont. Div. Ct.).

More recently in *Stewart v. Toronto Standard Condominium Corp. No. 1591*, 2014 ONSC 795, 2014 CarswellOnt 1377 (Ont. Div. Ct.), the court followed *1147335 Ontario Inc. v. Thyssen Krupp Elevator (Canada) Inc., supra*, accepting that an interlocutory order of the

Small Claims Court could be judicially reviewed. But Justice Nordheimer (for the court) was careful to describe such review in this way (at para. 2):

> This jurisdiction is, however, a "limited and narrow" one that will generally only arise in exceptional circumstances such as bias, a breach of the principles of natural justice or an excess of jurisdiction.

In *Millard v. Di Carlo*, 2014 ONSC 1218, 2014 CarswellOnt 2438 (Ont. Div. Ct.), a deputy judge dismissed a motion to dismiss the claim. In part she ruled on a question of jurisdiction, but in the result left that issue to be determined at trial. The Divisional Court dismissed an application for judicial review of that interlocutory order, holding that such review is available only in a narrow range of circumstances such as when the court acts without jurisdiction. Although the deputy judge provisionally determined a question of jurisdiction, she did not finally determine that question.

In *Zeppieri & Associates v. Jabbari*, 2014 ONSC 818, 2014 CarswellOnt 1414 (Ont. Div. Ct.), a deputy judge refused to permit the plaintiff to proceed with its judgment-debtor examination because in the deputy judge's view such an examination could not proceed once the debtor said she was a recipient of social assistance. The application for judicial review was granted and a further examination before a different deputy judge was ordered. The court held that the deputy judge was wrong in law to terminate the examination and she exceeded her jurisdiction by doing so.

This line of cases appears firmly established at the Divisional Court level. Since that court generally takes the position that it is bound to follow its own precedents, it would take a contrary decision by the Court of Appeal to change the position that interlocutory orders of the Small Claims Court can be judicially reviewed on the limited and narrow basis described by Justice Nordheimer. This means, for example, that the debate over the availability of discovery-type motion orders discussed above could in theory be resolved by judicial review as it involves a question of jurisdiction.

3. — Adjournments

Adjournments are an ongoing concern in Small Claims Court given the cost they impose on the litigants and the system. Part of the problem is that in some places, Small Claims Court lists have in the past been so dramatically overburdened that the judges cannot possibly hear all the cases on the list, giving rise to the perception that anyone asking for an adjournment is likely to get it, regardless of the reason. But overburdened trial lists are not the norm and in any event, while practical realities may intervene they do not change the law. The court has a discretion to grant or deny adjournment requests and parties who take it for granted that adjournments will always be granted do so at their peril.

In *Holtzman v. Suite Collections Canada Inc.*, 2013 ONSC 4240, 2013 CarswellOnt 9010, 310 O.A.C. 243 (Ont. Div. Ct.), Justice Grace confirmed that adjournment decisions of the Small Claims Court are discretionary and on appeals from such decisions, appellate deference applies. The defendants' appeal from the denial of their request for adjournment of the trial was dismissed. What happened was the trial date was set several months in advance for a date one year after the proceeding was commenced. Both parties attended the trial date with paralegals; however, the defence paralegal advised that the defendants had retained a lawyer five days earlier and he was unavailable for that date. Deputy Judge Yeates heard submissions and denied the adjournment request. The defence paralegal then requested and was granted permission to leave, since she was not prepared for trial. Trial proceeded in the absence of the defence.

On appeal, Justice Grace reviewed the law of adjournments and confirmed that adjournments are discretionary and fact-specific decisions calling for consideration of both the interests of the parties and the interests of the administration of justice. Justice Grace stated succinctly (at para. 42) that litigants in the Small Claims Court "cannot simply assume that an adjournment request will be granted: even if the trial has not been adjourned before."

Notably, Justice Grace clarified that the Practice Direction entitled "Trial Dates in the Superior Court of Justice and the Ontario Court of Justice" dated June 8, 1999, applies in the Small Claims Court. It provides that where a trial date has been set, the trial is expected to proceed on that date. While the Small Claims Court is a branch of the Superior Court of Justice, that Practice Direction did not specifically mention the Small Claims Court. Justice Grace has clarified the applicability of that Practice Direction and has confirmed that decisions on adjournment requests will be treated with deference by the appeal court. There is no rule that a first adjournment request in Small Claims Court will always be granted.

In *Bond v. Deeb*, 2013 CarswellOnt 3769, [2013] O.J. No. 1524 (Ont. Sm. Cl. Ct.), the court dismissed a motion by the plaintiff to set aside an earlier order dismissing her claim after she failed to attend for the third scheduled trial date, which had been made peremptory on all parties. Peremptory means there will be no more adjournments. The court accepted that a peremptory trial could be adjourned in exceptional circumstances, but was not persuaded by the plaintiff's argument that she was unable to attend court for trial due to her mother's health. The justice of the case did not favour setting aside the dismissal of the plaintiff's claim.

4. — Default Judgments

Two undefended claims resulted in notable decisions from the Divisional Court in 2013.

The case of *Capital One Bank v. Wright*, 2013 ONSC 5440, 313 ONSC 5440, 2013 CarswellOnt 12424, (sub nom. *Capital One Bank v. Toogood)* 313 O.A.C. 49, [2013] O.J. No. 4023 (Ont. Div. Ct.) (*"Toogood"*), involved a claim on a credit card debt for $7,101, plus prejudgment and postjudgment interest claimed at a contractual rate of 21.7%. The defendant was served but failed to defend and the plaintiff proceeded to an assessment hearing. It relied on the credit card agreement and the monthly statements for the month when the last payment was made through to when the account was closed, which set out the balance and the current interest rate. The deputy judge dismissed the claim, holding that the plaintiff was obliged to present evidence which would permit the court to identify the amount claimed for purchases made by the defendant and the amount of contractual interest already included in the principal amount of $7,101. He found the contractual interest rate to be inconsistent with the notion of good conscience set out in the *Courts of Justice Act* s. 25.

On appeal the decision was set aside and judgment granted for the plaintiff in the amount due as at the last payment, plus prejudgment and postjudgment interest at the contractual rate. Justice M.L. Edwards held that the debt was a liquidated demand and there was no requirement for the plaintiff to prove a breakdown of the purchases and interest charges as at the date of last payment. Proof of the amount owing at that juncture was sufficient to support the judgment requested and the contractual rate applied to prejudgment and postjudgment interest.

It might be thought that *Toogood* simply deals with a straightforward error by a deputy judge concerning the sufficiency of evidence at an assessment hearing. But the result at first instance could reflect judicial resistance to the high-interest rates of some credit companies and the prospect of unfortunate debtors becoming liable for large interest amounts. The larger issue is that the Small Claims Court is a court of law like any other and is duty-bound to apply the law. The appellate authorities for the past 80 years have consistently held that the Small Claims Court's mandate to conduct summary hearings and to make "such order as is considered just and agreeable to good conscience" (under what is now *Courts of Justice Act* s. 25) does not authorize the court to make decisions that are contrary to law: see *Sereda v. Consolidated Fire & Casualty Insurance Co.*, 1934 CarswellOnt 37, [1934] O.R. 502, [1934] 3 D.L.R. 504, [1934] O.W.N. 394 (Ont. C.A.); *Smith v. Galin*, 1956 CarswellOnt 253, 3 D.L.R. (2d) 302, [1956] O.W.N. 432 (Ont. C.A.); *Travel Machine Ltd. v. Madore*, 1983 CarswellOnt 901, 143 D.L.R. (3d) 94 (Ont. H.C.); *R. v. Bennett*, 1992 CarswellOnt

1108, 8 O.R. (3d) 651, 54 O.A.C. 321 (Ont. Div. Ct.); *O'Shanter Development Corp. v. Separi*, 1996 CarswellOnt 1701, [1996] O.J. No. 1589 (Ont. Div. Ct.).

The law relating to contractual interest claims and the court's limited discretion to depart from such rates is set out in *Bank of America Canada v. Mutual Trust Co.*, 2002 SCC 43, 2002 CarswellOnt 1114, 2002 CarswellOnt 1115, REJB 2002-30907, [2002] 2 S.C.R. 601, 211 D.L.R. (4th) 385, 49 R.P.R. (3d) 1, 287 N.R. 171, 159 O.A.C. 1, [2002] S.C.J. No. 44 (S.C.C.). Generally, unless high interest amounts to a criminal interest rate, such rates will be enforced in a civil court judgment. The court's discretion to depart from the contractual rate is limited to exceptional circumstances, but the court in that case did not elaborate on what might constitute such circumstances and left it to the lower courts to grapple with that question in future cases. But clearly, and as *Toogood* illustrates, for a deputy judge to decline to apply a legal rule merely because it does not appear just to the particular judge is not likely to assist the Divisional Court in finding a legally-valid route to the resulting judgment.

Another notable default judgment case involved a car leasing company: *Action Auto Leasing & Gallery Inc. v. Crawford*, 2013 ONSC 6299, 2013 CarswellOnt 14270, [2013] O.J. No. 4684 (Ont. S.C.J.). In *Crawford*, the plaintiff brought a motion for default judgment on its claim for $9,185. The deputy judge, on his own initiative, embarked on a detailed review of the *Consumer Protection Act, 2002*. In the result he found the plaintiff guilty of various violations of that *Act* and he dismissed the motion and the claim. On appeal the decision was set aside and the matter was sent back for a new assessment hearing before a different deputy judge. Justice Nightingale held that the deputy judge was wrong to ignore the fact that liability was deemed to be admitted, to have embarked on an analysis of an unpleaded defence, and to have done so without notice to the plaintiff.

Crawford is perhaps indicative of the temptation that may arise in Small Claims Court, given the high incidence of self-represented parties, for judges to analyze cases that come before them without regard to the state of the pleadings. Sometimes the court can decide unpleaded issues, as was held in *936464 Ontario Ltd. v. Mungo Bear Ltd.*, 2003 CarswellOnt 8091, 74 O.R. (3d) 45, 258 D.L.R. (4th) 754, [2003] O.J. No. 3795 (Ont. Div. Ct.). But whether it should do so in any given situation requires consideration of whether it would be fair to do so. One aspect of that analysis is whether it will give the appearance that the judge has descended into the arena or is helping one party or another in a way that compromises the appearance of impartiality. The general rule is that positive defences may be pleaded but the court has no business giving effect to potentially-available positive defences when the case is undefended: see *Panza v. Bayaty* (October 6, 2009), Doc. 78072/08, [2009] O.J. No. 4163 (Ont. Small Cl. Ct.); *Contact Resource Services Inc. v. Fletcher*, 2013 CarswellOnt 4369, [2013] O.J. No. 1685 (Ont. Sm. Cl. Ct.).

5. — Defective Real Property Cases

The Small Claims Court continues to see a steady flow of real estate cases in which purchasers sue vendors after finding problems with the real property they have purchased. Examples of recent decisions are *Leech v. Dietrich*, 2012 CarswellOnt 13011, [2012] O.J. No. 4944 (Ont. S.C.J.); *Merola v. Miller* (August 16, 2013), Doc. File No. SC-12-28566-00, [2013] O.J. No. 3784 (Ont. S.C.J.); *Vivian v. Ferreira*, 2013 CarswellOnt 10814, [2013] O.J. No. 3509 (Ont. S.C.J.), and *Robb-Sim v. Solomes*, 2013 CarswellOnt 9432, [2013] O.J. No. 3217 (Ont. S.C.J.).

The state of the authorities may leave some uncertainty on whether vendors are under a positive duty to disclose known defects in the property. It is submitted that the appellate authorities provide that there is in law no positive duty on sellers to disclose defects in the property and that in the absence of any representations which could support a claim of negligent or fraudulent misrepresentation, *caveat emptor* remains the governing principle.

The root case on the duty on a vendor to disclose defects in real property to a prospective purchaser is *McGrath v. MacLean*, 1979 CarswellOnt 1426, 22 O.R. (2d) 784, 95 D.L.R.

(3d) 144, 27 Chitty's L.J. 58, [1979] O.J. No. 4039 (Ont. C.A.). In that case the majority assumed for the sake of argument that buyers were under a legal duty to disclose defects which rendered the property uninhabitable or inherently unsafe, and found that the evidence did not support the plaintiff's claim. In *Tony's Broadloom & Floor Covering Ltd. v. NMC Canada Inc.*, 1996 CarswellOnt 4926, 31 O.R. (3d) 481, 141 D.L.R. (4th) 394, 6 R.P.R. (3d) 143, 95 O.A.C. 358, [1996] O.J. No. 4372 (Ont. C.A.), the vendor of commercial property did not disclose the fact of ground contaminant of which it was aware. The buyer's claim was dismissed by summary judgment which was upheld by the Court of Appeal. Doherty J.A. found that the purchaser received what it bargained for, namely industrial land.

Guglielmi v. Russo, 2010 ONSC 833, 2010 CarswellOnt 1172, 92 R.P.R. (4th) 117, [2010] O.J. No. 1145 (Ont. Div. Ct.); additional reasons 2010 ONSC 2618, 2010 CarswellOnt 4018 (Ont. Div. Ct.), was an appeal from Small Claims Court. Justice Swinton upheld the dismissal of the buyer's claim and in her reasons indicated that in any event, the seller could only be liable for known defects if they rendered the property unsafe or uninhabitable.

In *Outaouais Synergest Inc. v. Keenan*, 2013 ONCA 526, 2013 CarswellOnt 11723, (sub nom. *Outsouais Synergest Inc. v. Lang Michener LLP)* 116 O.R. (3d) 742, 32 R.P.R. (5th) 169, 12 M.P.L.R. (5th) 173, 310 O.A.C. 120 (Ont. C.A.) at para. 76, the court confirmed that ". . . in Ontario, as a general proposition, a vendor is, apart from express contract, under no general duty to disclose defects going to title or to quality . . ." The court also confirmed at para. 77 that if a vendor breaks his or her silence, the doctrine of *caveat emptor* can give way to liability for negligent or fraudulent misrepresentation. The court made no reference to the position which was accepted only for purposes of argument in *McGrath v. MacLean, supra,* that a duty of disclose existed as to defects which rendered the property uninhabitable or inherently unsafe.

Another specific aspect of the defective real estate cases is the question of "stigmatized property". There are some, including many realtors, who believe there is a legal duty on sellers to disclose the fact of prior events on a property such as death, suicide, murder, or even ghosts. It is argued that any material fact which might affect what the buyer is willing to pay for the property should be subject to mandatory disclosure. From a contract law perspective it is difficult to argue in favour of the existence of any such duty. The standard Agreement of Purchase and Sale contains an "entire agreement" clause by which the parties agree that there are no terms, warranties or representations concerning the property other than the terms of the Agreement of Purchase and Sale. Unless the contract contains an applicable warranty or term, *caveat emptor* applies (as was held in *McGrath v. MacLean, supra*).

There are only two "stigmatized property" cases in Canada to date. In *Knight c. Dionne,* 2006 QCCQ 1260, 2006 CarswellQue 3297, 2006 CarswellQue 14207, EYB 2006-104073, [2006] R.D.I. 398, [2006] J.Q. No. 3671, [2006] Q.J. No. 3671 (C.Q.), the purchaser's claim for damages alleging that the seller ought to have disclosed the fact of his son's suicide in the property ten years earlier. The court held that there was no duty on a seller to disclose such things.

In *1784773 Ontario Inc. v. K-W Labour Assn. Inc.*, 2013 ONSC 5401, 2013 CarswellOnt 13500 (Ont. S.C.J.); affirmed 2014 ONCA 288, 2014 CarswellOnt 4675 (Ont. C.A.), released August 21, 2013, the plaintiff purchaser claimed damages based on an allegation that the seller ought to have disclosed to it the fact of a rumour that a ghost haunted the property. The claim against the seller was dismissed by summary judgment. Sloan J. found that there was no legal duty on a seller to disclose the fact of prior death on a property and there was in that case no evidence of any prior death having occurred and no way of proving the existence of a ghost. That decision, which is under appeal to the Court of Appeal, is the only Ontario decision to date dealing with "stigmatized property".

One very basic problem with claims based on theories of stigmatization is the rule that the law does not inquire into the sufficiency of consideration exchanged for a contract. If the sufficiency or fairness of the price, measured objectively, cannot be questioned in court, how can it be questioned from the purchaser's subjective after-the-fact perspective? The cases in this area have yet to address that problem.

For further discussion of stigmatized property, there are a number of interesting American cases — although care must be taken that such authorities are not binding on any Canadian court and, also, may turn on legislation in specific states which has no parallel in Ontario. The most recent appellate case is *Milliken v. Jacono*, 2012 PA Super 284. In that case a 9-judge panel ruled 6:3 in favour of summary judgment dismissing the plaintiff's claim that the seller had a legal duty to disclose the fact that a murder-suicide had occurred in the property one year before the sale. That case is under further appeal to the Pennsylvania Supreme Court, which reserved decision on November 19, 2013.

6. — Admission of Documents Under Rule 18.02

Many practitioners continue to take the position that documents not served at least 30 days before trial are inadmissible or require leave of the trial judge, by virtue of rule 18.02. That is not what the rule says. As the Divisional Court clarified in *O'Connell v. Custom Kitchen & Vanity*, 1986 CarswellOnt 414, 56 O.R. (2d) 57, 11 C.P.C. (2d) 295, 17 O.A.C. 157 (Ont. Div. Ct.), rule 18.02 is only one method to admit documents in Small Claims Court without the need for a live witness to identify the documents. Documents which are not admitted under rule 18.02 may nevertheless be admitted either through a live witness or through the court's general discretion to admit evidence under the *Courts of Justice Act* s. 27: see *Fakhoury v. Gurguis*, 2013 CarswellOnt 4390, [2013] O.J. No. 1688 (Ont. S.C.J.) at para. 5.

Equally, documents which may be qualified for admission under rule 18.02 (i.e. served at least 30 days before trial and containing the required witness information) may nevertheless be excluded where appropriate grounds for exclusion exist. The rule gives the court a discretion to admit eligible documents without formal identification evidence from a live witness, but does not require the court to accept all such documents as evidence: *MBK Services Inc. v. PowerForward Inc.*, 2013 ONSC 4506, 2013 CarswellOnt 9211, [2013] O.J. No. 3115 (Ont. Div. Ct.).

In *Suganthan v. Calexico Holdings Inc.* (August 30, 2012), Doc. SC-11-88015-00, [2012] O.J. No. 6612 (Ont. S.C.J.), Deputy Judge Goldstein held that modern forms of photographic and video evidence storage such as DVD, memory sticks, and USB drives can all be admitted as evidence subject to the traditional criteria of accuracy, fairness, and absence of any intention to mislead, and verification under oath by a person capable to do so.

7. — Monetary Jurisdiction

The Divisional Court has reconfirmed the long-standing principle that the monetary limit of the Small Claims Court is a limit on the amount which may be claimed and awarded, but does not limit the amount of damages which may be alleged and assessed by the court prior to any deduction of a set-off amount: *2146100 Ontario Ltd. v. 2052750 Ontario Inc.*, 2013 ONSC 2483, 2013 CarswellOnt 5148, 115 O.R. (3d) 636, 308 O.A.C. 8 (Ont. Div. Ct.).

8. — Motions for Judgment

Since *Van de Vrande v. Butkowsky*, 2010 ONCA 230, 2010 CarswellOnt 1777, 99 O.R. (3d) 648, 99 O.R. (3d) 641, 85 C.P.C. (6th) 205, 319 D.L.R. (4th) 132, 260 O.A.C. 323, [2010] O.J. No. 1239 (Ont. C.A.); additional reasons 2010 ONCA 400, 2010 CarswellOnt 3629, 85 C.P.C. (6th) 212 (Ont. C.A.), motions for judgment under rule 12.02 of the *Small Claims Court Rules* are consistently decided in accordance with that decision, holding that the jurisprudence developed under Rule 20 and 21 of the *Rules of Civil Procedure*, including concepts such as "no genuine issue for trial", should not be applied under rule 12.02. The Divisional Court has found that judgment under rule 12.02 is appropriately granted where the claim or defence has "no meaningful chance of success." See *O'Brien v. Ottawa Hospital*, 2011 ONSC 231, 2011 CarswellOnt 88, [2011] O.J. No. 66 (Ont. Div. Ct.).

The summary judgment law under Rule 20 of the *Rules of Civil Procedure* was significantly changed by the decision of the Supreme Court of Canada in *Combined Air Mechanical Services Inc. v. Flesch*, 2014 CSC 7, 2014 SCC 7, 2014 CarswellOnt 640, 2014 CarswellOnt 641, 12 C.C.E.L. (4th) 1, 27 C.L.R. (4th) 1, 46 C.P.C. (7th) 217, *(*sub nom. *Hryniak v. Mauldin)* 366 D.L.R. (4th) 641, 37 R.P.R. (5th) 1, *(*sub nom. *Hryniak v. Mauldin)* 453 N.R. 51, *(*sub nom. *Hryniak v. Mauldin)* 314 O.A.C. 1, [2014] S.C.J. No. 7 (S.C.C.). That case makes no reference to civil procedure in the Small Claims Court.

In *Tuka v. Butt*, 2014 CarswellOnt 2035, [2014] O.J. No. 852 (Ont. S.C.J.), it was held that neither *Hryniak v. Mauldin, supra*, nor *Petersen v. Matt*, 2014 ONSC 896, 2014 CarswellOnt 1868, [2014] O.J. No. 745 (Ont. Div. Ct.), affect the law stated by the Court of Appeal in *Van de Vrande, supra*. The test of "no genuine issue requiring a trial" under Rule 20 of the *Rules of Civil Procedure* does not apply in Small Claims Court.

TABLE OF CASES

Table of Cases

Table of Cases

Table of Cases

Table of Cases

Table of Cases

Table of Cases

Table of Cases

Table of Cases

Table of Cases

Table of Cases

MONETARY LIMITS — COMPARATIVE CHART
Small Claims in Canada

The following chart summarizes the current monetary limits and adjudication in the small claims courts in Canada.

Jurisdiction	Monetary Limit
British Columbia	$25,000
Alberta	$25,000
Saskatchewan[1]	$20,000
Manitoba	$10,000
Ontario[2]	$25,000 with a $2,500 appeal minimum
Quebec[3]	$7,000
New Brunswick[4]	$12,500
Nova Scotia	$25,000
Prince Edward Island	$8,000
Newfoundland and Labrador	$25,000
Northwest Territories	$10,000
Yukon Territories	$25,000
Nunavut	$20,000

Notes:

1   *Small Claims Regulations, 1998*, R.R.S. c. S-50.11 Reg. 1. Saskatchewan continues to increase the monetary limit of cases heard in small claims court to the desired maximum of $25,000. Effective November 2007, the limit was increased to $20,000.

2   O. Reg. 626/00, *Small Claims Court Jurisdiction and Appeal Limit*. Effective January 1, 2010.

3   *Code of Civil Procedure*, Art. 953(a).

4   Rule 80 of the *Rules of Court of New Brunswick*. In force July 15, 2010. Repealed 2012, c. 15, c. 47(2), in force January 1, 2013.

The Canadian Bar Association has recommended that all jurisdictions should consider raising the monetary limit in Small Claims Court to $10,000. See Resolution 97-15-M: *Systems of Civil Justice* (1997 Mid-Winter Meeting), Schedule 1.

British Columbia increased its monetary jurisdiction of the Small Claims Court from $3,000 to $10,000 in February of 1991. In 1992, a study was carried out to determine what effect the change had on the use of the court. The study's authors concluded:

> The program has answered a need or provided *access* to significantly more people in the province than was true under the former version of Small Claims Court. The increase in Small Claims volumes [of 42.2%] is thought to be entirely in claims within the $3,000 to $10,000 range.

> Little of the increased volume of claims in Small Claims Court since the start of the new program was observed to have transferred from the Supreme Court. The cases that have "*come out of the woodwork*" are cases that were not previously served by either court. See Adams, C.

Getz, J. Valley and S. Jani, *Evaluation of the Small Claims Program*, vol. 1 (British Columbia, Ministry of Attorney General, 1992) ii.

The reality, of course, is that the "real" limit in these courts has been reduced substantially by inflation alone, as the Consumer Price Index increased by 35.6% between 1986 and 1996.

Small Claims Courts in Alberta

The Provincial Court of Alberta has concurrent civil jurisdiction with the Queen's Bench in civil matters involving debt or damages (including damages for breach of contract) to a maximum of $25,000 effective November 1, 2002 as a result of the *Justice Statutes Amendment Act*, R.S.A. 2000, c. 16 (Supp.). The Court also has concurrent jurisdiction in landlord and tenant matters under the *Residential Tenancies Act* (R.S.A. 2000, c. R-17) and the *Mobile Home Sites Tenancies Act* (R.S.A. 2000, c. M-20).

In 1996 the Court established a system of pre-trial conferences in Edmonton and Calgary. It has established a program of court ordered mediation in both cities in 1998, with a success rate of approximately 70% in resolving disputes. This was expanded to Red Deer and Lethbridge in 2002.

Small Claims Courts in British Columbia

The monetary jurisdiction is $25,000. The government may consider a jurisdiction of $30,000. All Small Claims matters are mediated at what is called a "settlement conference". Thirty minutes are set aside for each settlement conference. Non-judicial staff handle the mediation. This occurs only where both parties consent. Approximately two-thirds of cases are settled during mediation.

Manitoba Courts

The Small Claims Court is under the jurisdiction of the Manitoba Court of Queen's Bench regarding monetary disputes that do not exceed $10,000.

Nova Scotia Small Claims Court

The Small Claims Court provides a quick, informal and cost-effective method for deciding claims up to $25,000 (not including interest). It is not necessary for the person making the claim (claimant) and the person whom the claim is against (defendant) to have lawyers.

Small Claims Court of New Brunswick

New Brunswick has reinstated its Small Claims Court, under the *Small Claims Act*, SNB 2012, c. 15. As of January 1, 2013, claims up to $12,500 in debt, damages, or for recovery of possession of personal property valued at not more than that amount proceed in Small Claims Court. Procedure in that court is established by N.B. Reg. 2012-103.

The Supreme Court of P.E.I.

The Trial Division deals with pre-trial matters and hears trials in general civil matters including small claims.

Provincial Courts of Saskatchewan

Small Claims Court is within the Civil Division of the Saskatchewan Provincial Court. Claims cannot exceed $20,000 in value. Dispute involving title to land, slander, libel, bankruptcy, false imprisonment or malicious prosecution must be handled at Queen's Bench.

Small Claims Courts in Newfoundland and Labrador

The Small Claims Court of Newfoundland is part of the Provincial Court and all the Provincial Court judges have Small Claims jurisdiction.

The first Small Claims Act (*Small Claims Act, 1979*, R.S.N. 1979, c. 34) for Newfoundland was enacted in 1979 and was proclaimed in force that same year. The upper claim limit has been increased to $25,000 in 2010.

The Court has been held to be confined to award money damages only. In the case of *Popular Shoe Stores Ltd. v. Simoni* (1998), 163 Nfld. & P.E.I.R. 100, 503 A.P.R. 100 (Nfld. C.A.) the Newfoundland Court of Appeal held that a Small Claims Court judge did not have the authority to order the return of items (in that particular case, shoes). There is no limitation requiring that a party claim only liquidated damages and general damage claims up to $3,000 as held in *Collins v. Aylward's (1975) Ltd.* (1995), 134 Nfld. & P.E.I.R. 195, 417 A.P.R. 195 (Nfld. Prov. Ct.).

Small Claims Courts in Quebec

Quebec is the only province in Canada to have a provincial court with vast jurisdiction in civil matters, a jurisdiction up to $70,000, including hypothecary recourse. The Small Claims Division deals with all claims for $7,000 or less. Judgments are final and without appeal.

Territorial Court of the Northwest Territories

The Territorial Court of the Northwest Territories has pursuant to legislation, jurisdiction in civil matters where the amount in dispute is $5,000 or less, supported by Rules of Court and procedures designed by the Territorial Court.

Small Claims Courts in Saskatchewan

Saskatchewan law governing small claims matters is found in the *Small Claims Act, 1997*, S.S. 1997, c. S-50.11. Among the changes were provisions broadening the jurisdiction, modernizing service, empowering mediation and allowing by regulation changes in the monetary limit. The monetary limit in Saskatchewan is $20,000. See Sask. Reg. S-50.11, Reg. 1. Although there has been discussion about the advantages of creating small claims court rules, at the moment no such rules exist. The Provincial Court hears all claims under *The Small Claims Act*.

Yukon Courts

The Small Claims Court hears civil cases in which the amount of money or the value of personal property being claimed is $25,000 or less. It does not have jurisdiction over actions concerning land, actions against a personal representative of a deceased person, or actions for libel or slander. The Small Claims Court sits in the same locations as the Territorial Court and can hear cases as part of court circuits to the communities. Every judge of the Territorial Court is a judge of the Small Claims Court.

1 — A SELF-HELP OVERVIEW[1]

1

1. — Developments in Small Claims Court

On December 22, 2000, then Attorney General Jim Flaherty announced that, effective April 2, 2001, Ontarians would be able to pursue claims of up to $10,000 in Small Claims Court. "Increasing the monetary limit from $6,000 to $10,000 will increase access to justice by allowing individuals and businesses with higher value claims to resolve legal disputes within a reasonable time and at a reasonable cost," said Flaherty.

The limit for Small Claims Court was changed in 1993 from $3,000 in Metropolitan Toronto ($1,000 for the rest of the province) to $6,000, and before that in 1979. According to a press release from the Office of the Attorney General on December 22, 2000:

> A recent survey of Small Claims Court customers found that more than 81 per cent of users were pleased with the service of the court. This supports the claims limit increase as the Small Claims Court clearly has the expertise to handle it. The Small Claims Court provides a forum where litigants can make or defend claims involving relatively small amounts of money quickly, simply and inexpensively. Litigants can present their own cases without professional legal representation. The Small Claims Court is the busiest civil court in Ontario, receiving approximately 85,000 claims each year. There are 87 Small Claims Court offices in the province.

Monetary Jurisdiction

The monetary jurisdiction of the Small Claims Court is set by regulation under the *Courts of Justice Act* (*Small Claims Court Jurisdiction and Appeal Limit*, O. Reg. 626/00). As of January 1, 2010, the monetary jurisdiction of the Small Claims Court is $25,000 (Canadian), excluding interest and costs.

A claim cannot be divided into two or more actions for the purpose of bringing it within the court's jurisdiction [rule 6.02]. A claim in excess of $25,000 can be reduced to comply with the monetary jurisdiction of the court.

Where a plaintiff files more than one claim against the same defendant, the total of which exceeds the monetary jurisdiction of the Small Claims Court, while default will be noted against a defendant who fails to file a Defence (Form 9A), default judgment will NOT be entered. The plaintiff will need to either file a motion in writing for an assessment of damages or file a Request to Clerk to schedule an assessment hearing for both claims.

Where a person obtains an order to enforce an obligation in a foreign currency, including orders for default judgment, the orders are to be signed for the foreign currency amount claimed. Conversion of the foreign currency amount to Canadian dollars takes place when the judgment is being paid. Subject to any other order of the court pursuant to section 121(3) and section 121(4), section 121(1) of the *Courts of Justice Act* should form part of the order. Section 121 provides:

> Subject to subsections (3) and (4), where a person obtains an order to enforce an obligation in a foreign currency, the order shall require payment of an amount in Canadian currency sufficient to purchase the amount of the obligation in the foreign currency at a bank in Ontario listed in Schedule I to the *Bank Act* (Canada) at the close of business on the first day on which the bank

---

[1]The Self-help Overview reflects the court as it is today and how it has been historically.

quotes a Canadian dollar rate for purchase of the foreign currency before the day payment of the obligation is received by the creditor.

Since the monetary limit of the Small Claims Court is set at $25,000, there is no authority to issue a default judgment above that amount. Therefore, if the value of a default judgment expressed in foreign currency exceeds $25,000 once it has been converted into Canadian funds, the creditor is deemed to have abandoned the excess amount. This principle must be reflected in the text of the default judgment, in order to ensure that the order does not exceed the jurisdiction of the Small Claims Court.

The Right to Counsel and Self-Representation

I believe the legal system has five major obligations to the public:

1. Justice must be understandable;
2. Justice must be efficient;
3. Justice must be affordable;
4. Justice must be accessible to all; and
5. Justice must be equal under the law.

In the interests of accessibility, and affordability, more and more do-it-yourself litigants are heading to our courts than ever before. Thus, at the top of any litigator's Small Claims Court checklist must be the determination of whether or not the other party is represented.

The right to be heard in court is, in many cases, of little avail if it does not comprehend the right to be represented by counsel. Even the intelligent and educated layman has small, and sometimes no, skill in the science of law. He or she is unfamiliar with the rules of evidence and, unrepresented, stands to lose his or her case based on incompetent evidence, irrelevant evidence, or evidence which should otherwise be inadmissible.

Fundamentally, however, everyone has the right to represent him- or herself (as long as it is not disruptive of orderly procedures), and may do so for any one, or a combination, of reasons. Often the reason is the desire to conserve modest resources. But the trend towards self-help litigation in Small Claims Court, while understandable, challenges us to examine the underlying reasons people are choosing to self-represent and to consider the efficacy of policies that may impede the help which lawyers and judges can provide these litigants.

Clearly, some people with legal issues choose to represent themselves because they want to retain control of their case, or because they have a disdain for lawyers. But the predominant reason for proceeding on a pro se basis is lack of resources. Many people in low-and moderate-income households ignore their legal problems while others try to resolve them on their own.

Small claims courts allow litigants to adjudicate legal matters that are worthy of their time, but may not be worthy of a lawyer's time. The misplaced or damaged clothes from the dry cleaners, the improperly repaired television, the broken window caused by the errant baseball . . . these are the types of matters pursued regularly where even the wealthiest person would not find it of value to hire a lawyer.

Many litigants in Small Claims Court represent themselves. However, a party may also be represented in Small Claims Court by a lawyer or by a person authorized under the *Law Society Act*, R.S.O. 1990, G. L-8, such as a law student or a paralegal. If you wish to contact a paralegal in your area, you may consult the *Paralegal Directory*, established by the Law Society of Upper Canada.

If you wish to hire an Ontario lawyer, you can contact the Lawyer Referral Service operated by the Law Society of Upper Canada. The Lawyer Referral Service will provide the name of a lawyer who practices in your area, and who provides a free consultation of up to 30 minutes. The Lawyer Referral Service is available by telephone only at 1-800-268-8326 (or in the Greater Toronto Area at 416-947-3330). If you are calling from outside the province, you can reach the Lawyer Referral Service by dialing 1-416-947-3330. A half-hour consultation is not guaranteed if you do not have an Ontario lawyer and their contact information, which may be accessed through the Law Society of Upper Canada website at: www.lsuc.on.ca.

An interpreter translates communication from one language to another. Small Claims Court provides interpretation services for all court proceedings and written documents from English to French and French to English. If you or your witnesses will need language interpretation in court from French to English or English to French, notify the court office at the outset of the case.

Interpretation from English or French to any other language must be arranged for and paid by the party who requires the interpretation. The interpreter must be accredited as being capable of performing that function. The court office will pay for "in-court" interpretation in any language for individuals who qualify for fee waiver.

The Poor Person's Court

In the case of *Polewsky v. Home Hardware Stores Ltd.* (2003), [2003] O.J. No. 2908, 2003 CarswellOnt 2755, 229 D.L.R. (4th) 308, 174 O.A.C. 358, 66 O.R. (3d) 600, 109 C.R.R. (2d) 189, 34 C.P.C. (5th) 334 (Ont. Div. Ct.); leave to appeal allowed 2004 CarswellOnt 763, [2004] O.J. No. 954 (Ont. C.A.), the Divisional Court of Ontario decided that poor people with meritorious cases should not be denied their day in small claims court simply because they could not afford filing fees. The Court ordered the Ontario government to change the law so judges could waive court costs when necessary.

There is a common law right of access to the courts, the panel of the court ruled.

The current inability of judges to reduce fees in cases where poverty is a proven barrier to bringing a small claims case forward breaches the rule of law and is a "constitutional defect that must be cured." The court gave the province up to 12 months to amend small claims court regulations so judges have the power to waive the mandatory court fees, which include $50 for filing or defending a lawsuit and another $100 for setting a trial.

The message coming out of this case is that access to justice and legal services is itself an important value.

Destitute Litigants

Larabie v. Montfils (2004), 2004 CarswellOnt 186, 44 C.P.C. (5th) 66, (sub nom. *J.-P.L. v. Montfils*) 181 O.A.C. 239 (Ont. C.A. [In Chambers]) was a tort case brought by a plaintiff from outside Ontario for damages for sexual and physical assaults he allegedly suffered half a century earlier while a resident at an Ontario training school during the early 1950s. His first action, filed eight years earlier, apparently named the wrong individuals and he brought a motion to add the correct persons. His motion failed. He moved to amend his statement of claim. That motion also failed. He then launched a string of appeals of that second motion, all of which failed and all of which leveled further costs against him.

The defendants made a successful motion to strike out this new statement of claim as an abuse of process, with further costs against him. He then appealed to the Court of Appeal, by which time he faced a total of $27,500 in unpaid costs. The defendants brought a motion before the Court of Appeal for an order (a) to stay the plaintiff's case for non-payment of cost orders; and (b) for security for costs on the appeal.

A single judge of the Court of Appeal (sitting in chambers) dismissed the defendants' motion. The appeal judge explained:

[16] I am satisfied on the record that Mr. Larabie is an impecunious plaintiff. His income is limited to approximately $840 per month in the form of a disability pension from the federal government and he becomes eligible for the old age pension this month. He has no assets save for basic clothing and a few personal belongings. He simply has no means of satisfying the outstanding costs orders or posting any meaningful amount as security for costs. To accede to the moving parties' requests would end the proceeding for all practical purposes and, in effect, bar him from the judicial process without his having had a final chance to persuade the court that he should be permitted to have his claims adjudicated on the merits.

[17] There is ample authority for the proposition that the courts are reluctant to deprive a worthy but impecunious litigant of the opportunity to have his or her claim adjudicated when it is not plainly devoid of merit . . .

[18] The problem here is that Mr. Larabie has never had the opportunity to have his case considered on the merits. In hindsight, of course, it might have been better if the original order of Manton J. had been appealed. When that was not done, the substance of his claim was overshadowed by procedural questions whether the matter had become *res judicata* and thereafter whether the various requisites for appeal or leave to appeal had been met.

The appeal judge also noted that there was some basis for the plaintiff's claim on its merits, if his case could ever get heard on those merits. He remarked:

[21] I am not unmindful of the moving parties' arguments outlined above, nor am I unsympathetic towards the position in which they find themselves. Litigants are not free to ignore or flout orders of the court awarding costs against them or to re-litigate matters that truly have been litigated and decided before. Having considered all of the circumstances, however, and having weighed and balanced the various competing interests and factors in relation to this matter, I conclude that I should exercise my discretion in favour of permitting Mr. Larabie to proceed with the appeal, and to do so without having to post security for costs. I expect that he will do so in a reasonably expeditious fashion.

By contrast, *Susin v. Chapman* (2004), [2004] O.J. No. 123, 2004 CarswellOnt 143 (Ont. C.A.); affirming (2002), [2002] O.J. No. 4755, 2002 CarswellOnt 4213 (Ont. S.C.J.) was a tort case (one of several) where the plaintiff sued in negligence against a lawyer. The plaintiff had the habit of "cherry-picking" only those cost orders that he felt would allow him to carry on with his various claims and to ignore other costs orders. In this case, the lawyer finally moved to dismiss the lawsuit because of the plaintiff's failure to pay a long outstanding debt of costs of $2,300. The motions judge rejected the plaintiff's protestations of poverty, noting that other judges had done so as well and that the plaintiff was two-faced on the issue — raising poverty as an excuse when trying to escape an order for costs but denying poverty whenever an opposite party moved to have him post security for costs. In dismissing the plaintiff's action for his non-payment of costs, the motions judge stated:

Although the court does not wish to prevent litigants from pursuing claims, it cannot allow litigation to continue in the face of the clear non-payment of outstanding costs *without any justification* (emphasis added).

The plaintiff appealed, having in the interim paid the outstanding costs in issue, although he still had other costs orders that remained unpaid. A three-judge panel of the Court of Appeal dismissed his appeal. With respect to the issue of a motion judge's discretion, the appeal court stated:

[6] Finally, the appellant submits that the motion judge erred in the exercise of her discretion in dismissing an action, in which the appellant claimed damages for millions of dollars, for failure to pay costs of $2,200. We have not been persuaded that the motion judge erred in principle in the exercise of her discretion. The appellant attempts to pursue litigation without paying the costs orders made by various courts. He picks and chooses those orders that he will pay. We are satisfied that the motion judge was entitled to make the order she did, given the lengthy history of these proceedings and the material that was before her.

Waiver of Fees

Vandenelsen v. Merkley (2003), [2003] O.J. No. 3577, 2003 CarswellOnt 3483 (Ont. C.A.) was another case involving an impecunious litigant. The Superior Court of Stratford dismissed the mother's application to vary custody. The mother made a motion to a single judge of the Court of Appeal on various procedural matters. The single judge dismissed the mother's motion. The judge refused to waive the requirement that the mother pay court administration fees ($225 for filing a notice of appeal and $175 for perfecting an appeal). The judge doubted that she had the authority to waive payment but, even if she did have that power, she found no evidence to persuade her that payment of those fees would prejudice the mother's right to pursue her appeal.

The mother moved to have that ruling reviewed by a three-judge panel of the Court of Appeal. She failed. The court agreed with the single judge and added this additional observation:

> [3] Subsequent to the argument of the [mother's] motion, a panel of the Divisional Court held in the context of a proceeding in the Small Claims Court that the absence of a statutory mechanism for the waiver or reduction of fees in limited circumstances was a breach of the rule of law and was unconstitutional: *Polewsky v. Home Hardware Stores Ltd.*, [2003] O.J. No. 2908. The court held that, as at common law, there is a constitutional right of access to the courts, indigent persons should not be denied access to the Small Claims court when their claims or defences are meritorious and their inability to pay the prescribed fees is proven on a balance of probabilities. However, on the facts of the case, the court found that Mr. Polewsky had failed to demonstrate that, but for the reduction or waiver of fees, he would not be able to access the court.

> [4] Assuming, without deciding, that the principles discussed in *Polewsky* apply to proceedings in the Court of Appeal, we are of the opinion that, had the *Polewsky* decision been available to Charron J.A., she would have come to the same decision on the basis of her findings of fact.

It is evident that the Court of Appeal did not actually endorse the ruling in *Polewsky v. Home Hardware*, and the current small claims court regulations are silent on whether fees can be waived. It is to be noted that small claims court judges are lawyer working part-time as judges, who must adhere strictly to court rules laid out by statute, with no inherent jurisdiction to dispense with fees. Thus, the issue whether small claims court fees may be waived for an impecunious litigant, in the interests of access to justice, remains open.

See Fee Waiver information on page 1034.

Challenges in Judging

Judges face significant challenges in providing the people they serve with appropriate access to the courts. The first is the increasing number of people who come to court without counsel. Judges understand that to understand and support the rule of law, everyone must have access to courts when needed. For many, however, it is a question of cost.

The increasing number of self-represented litigants places an additional burden on judges in their courtrooms and mediation rooms. Generally, self-represented litigants do not know or understand the applicable substantive law and process to prosecute or defend a claim. As a result, judges have additional responsibilities to explain the process and law to the self-represented litigant at the same time as remaining and appearing to remain impartial.

Another challenge for judges is the significant changes in technology that have occurred. Some have improved access to justice. Witnesses in remote communities can testify by video-conference, easily accessible electronic materials can be made available to self-represented litigants to assist them in preparing for court, and courtrooms are less burdened with paper. The challenge comes in the increased access that the public has to the judiciary.

What has not changed is the collegiality that I have seen throughout 36 years. Judges want to help each other so that they collectively can serve in the best possible way.

Unrepresented Litigants

In *Cicciarella v. Cicciarella*, 2009 CarswellOnt 3972, [2009] O.J. No. 2906, 72 R.F.L. (6th) 319, 252 O.A.C. 156 (Ont. Div. Ct.), the Court wrote:

> The extent to which judges should afford an unrepresented litigant additional "leeway" with respect to court procedures and the rules of evidence is an increasingly vexing problem for courts at all levels. It is generally recognized that the court should provide some assistance to an unrepresented litigant, as occurred in Barrett. See as well *A.C.M. v. P.F.M.*, 2003 MBQB 244 (CanLII); [2003] M.J. No. 386, 2003 MBQB 244. *But at the same time, this must be done in such a way as not to breach either the appearance or reality of judicial neutrality.* See *Selmeci v. Canada*, 2002 FCA 293 (CanLII); [2002] F.C.J. No. 1086, 2002 FCA 293. How to balance the sometimes competing imperatives of helping a litigant who is in need of assistance while maintaining impartiality is a recurring dilemma for both trial and appellate courts. [Emphasis added.]

> It does require that the trial judge treat the litigant fairly and attempt to accommodate unrepresented litigants' unfamiliarity with the process so as to permit them to present their case. *In doing so, the trial judge must, of course, respect the rights of the other party.* [Emphasis added.]

As Platana J. noted at para. 18 of *Baziuk v. BDO Dunwoody Ward Mallette* (1997), [1997] O.J. No. 2374, 34 O.T.C. 53, 13 C.P.C. (4th) 156, 1997 CarswellOnt 2507 (Ont. Gen. Div.):

> *Notwithstanding the difficulty with such parties attempting to properly represent themselves, courts must also balance the issues of fairness and be mindful of both or all parties.* Issues of fairness, of course, must always be determined in accordance with accepted legal principles and the law which has developed. *A sense of fairness and understanding granted to unrepresented parties ought never to extend to the degree where courts do not give effect to the existing law, or where the issue of fairness to an unrepresented litigant is permitted to override the rights of a defendant party.* [Emphasis added.]

In 2006 the Canadian Judicial Council adopted a "Statement of Principles on Self-represented Litigants and Accused Persons." The advisory statement refers to a number of responsibilities expected of judges, such as the responsibility to promote opportunities for all persons to understand and meaningfully present their case, regardless of representation and to promote access to the justice system for all persons on an equal basis, regardless of representation.

The Principles refer to an expectation that judges will do whatever is possible to provide a fair and impartial process and to prevent an unfair disadvantage to self-represented persons.

Self-represented Litigants

> "Unrepresented litigants are entitled to justice, but they are not entitled to command disproportionate amounts of court resources to remedy their inability or unwillingness to retain counsel. If they seek free lunch, they should not complain about the size of the helpings."
>
> (*Broda v. Broda* (2001), 2001 ABCA 151, 2001 CarswellAlta 865, 253 W.A.C. 120, 286 A.R. 120, [2001] A.J. No. 800 (Alta. C.A.))

And my own observation about self-litigants (apologies to Shakespeare, who may or may not owe the same to Bacon):
"Some are born reasonable; some can achieve reasonableness; and others must have reasonableness thrust upon them."
-Francis Bacon

"I never met a man I didn't like": Will Rogers

"One impulse from a vernal wood may teach you more of man, of moral evil and of good, than all the sages can":
William Wordsworth

What do Will Rogers and William Wordsworth have in common?

"It's life, Jim, but not as we know it." (Dr. McCoy, *Star Trek*)

- Or do we recognize and remember it?
- The life form needs to be recognized.
- The life form needs to be identified.
- Can it evolve to acquire a more recognized shape and form so it will be recognized by others?

Neither spent enough time with self-represented litigants.

Self-Represented Persons

Self-represented persons are generally uninformed about their rights and about the consequences of choosing the options available to them; they may find court procedures complex, confusing and intimidating; and they may not have the knowledge or skills to participate actively and effectively in their own litigation. See Hann, *et al. A Study of Unrepresented Accused in Nine Canadian Court* (Ottawa: Department of Justice, 2003).

Self-represented persons may have limited literacy skills and many speak Canada's official languages as a second language, if at all. As a result, many self-represented persons tend to access information about the courts through means other than the written word.

Judges must exercise diligence in ensuring that the law is applied in an even-handed way to all, regardless of representation. The Canadian Judicial Council's statement of *Ethical Principles for Judges* (1998) has already established the principle of equality in principles governing judicial conduct. The document states: "Judges should conduct themselves and proceedings before them so as to ensure equality according to law."

Treating all persons alike does not necessarily result in equal justice. The *Ethical Principles for Judges* also cites *Eldridge v. British Columbia (Attorney General)* (1997), 38 B.C.L.R. (3d) 1, [1997] 3 S.C.R. 624, 3 B.H.R.C. 137, 46 C.R.R. (2d) 189, [1997] S.C.J. No. 86, 155 W.A.C. 81, 96 B.C.A.C. 81, 218 N.R. 161, [1998] 1 W.W.R. 50, 1997 CarswellBC 1940, 1997 CarswellBC 1939, 151 D.L.R. (4th) 577 (S.C.C.), *per* LaForest, J. for the court at 667, on a judge's duty to "rectify and prevent" discriminatory effects against particular groups.

Self-represented persons, like all other litigants, are subject to the provisions whereby courts maintain control of their proceedings and procedures. In the same manner as with other litigants, self-represented persons may be treated as vexatious or abusive litigants where the administration of justice requires it. The ability of judges to promote access may be affected by the actions of self-represented litigants themselves.

Self-represented persons are expected to familiarize themselves with the relevant legal practices and procedures pertaining to their case. Self-represented persons are expected to prepare their own case. Self-represented persons are required to be respectful of the court process and the officials within it. Vexatious litigants will not be permitted to abuse the process.

Members of the bar are expected to be respectful of self-represented persons and to adjust their behaviour accordingly when dealing with self-represented persons, in accordance with their professional obligations.

A Fair Hearing

Decisions reflect the view that self-represented litigants should, as a matter of consistent practice, be afforded some accommodations to ensure they understand the issues in dispute and have an opportunity to address those issues, despite their inexperience or lack of knowledge or skill.

Determining the appropriate standard of fairness should not involve comparing the self-represented litigant's own abilities to those of a lawyer. Rather, it is important to assist self-represented litigants in understanding the legal process and relevant legal issues so that the case may be presented to the best of the litigant's ability.

The most common area of debate involves rulings on the admissibility of evidence. Most self-represented litigants have difficulty grasping the concepts of "relevance" and "admissibility" of evidence, and tend to assume that any document, conversation, or testimony should be considered by the court. These concepts must be carefully explained to self-represented litigants, and, in some cases, "borderline" evidence may be admitted.

Flexibility extended to one party because of a "structural vulnerability" (i.e., their lack of legal representation) should not translate into a corresponding rigorousness or over-vigilance with respect to the other "represented" party. Any special treatment must not yield an unfair and unintended advantage to the self-represented litigant.

In *Lieb v. Smith* (1994), [1994] N.J. No. 199, 1994 CarswellNfld 176, 373 A.P.R. 201, 120 Nfld. & P.E.I.R. 201 (Nfld. T.D.), a self-represented plaintiff was suing for defamation and harassment. On the defendants' motion to strike the pleadings, the plaintiff argued that the court should be lenient in judging the materials, as the Rules of Court specifically permit parties to represent themselves. The court rejected that argument. While the court must take into account the lack of experience and training of the self-represented litigant, that person must also realize that implicit in the decision to act as his or her own counsel, is the willingness to accept the consequences that may flow from such lack of experience or training.

In *Butler v. Kronby* (1996), 1996 CarswellOnt 4781, [1996] O.J. No. 4434 (Ont. Gen. Div.), a self-represented plaintiff faced a motion dismissing her statement of claim at the instance of the defendant. The court expressed an understanding of how difficult it was for the plaintiff to grapple with the intricacies of such a motion without the benefit of legal expertise, even though she was highly-educated and intelligent. At para. 5, Wilkins J. stated:

> It is very difficult not to consider the application of a more relaxed set of standards when the pleadings and the affidavit material of the personam litigant lack the direction, form and structure which might ordinarily be expected. However, Rule 20 has no place for the exercise of such discretion.

There are other examples of trial judges refusing to allow their concern for the disadvantage faced by a self-represented litigant to outweigh the court's duty to uphold the Rules of Practice, for example, in *Angel v. Angel* (1997), 38 O.T.C. 377, 1997 CarswellOnt 3796, [1997] O.J. No. 3976 (Ont. Gen. Div.), Ferrier J. states (at para. 8):

> I am mindful of the fact that the plaintiff was unrepresented and was unfamiliar with the rules of evidence and the rules of procedure of this court. A trial judge should bear in mind when a trial is conducted by an unrepresented litigant [it should], to every reasonable degree, grant the litigant understanding and assistance. This is, of course, subject to the overriding proviso that the trial judge must be absolutely impartial, must not play the role of advocate, and must apply the rules of evidence and procedure equally to all litigants. The fact that a litigant is unrepresented does not entitle a trial judge to fail to apply the rules of procedure or ignore the law.

There are, however, decisions in which the court appears to have somewhat tempered the Rules or legislation in order to accommodate unrepresented litigants. *Rogers v. Barry* (2002), 2002 CarswellNfld 113, [2002] N.J. No. 115, *(sub nom. Barry v. Rogers)* 640 A.P.R. 239, *(sub nom. Barry v. Rogers)* 213 Nfld. & P.E.I.R. 239 (Nfld. T.D.) (Handrigan J.), a self-represented father was successful in applying to vary a child support order, Handrigan J. stated at para. 8:

> As well, it would appear that the Applicant has only recently understood the impact that a shared custody arrangement might have on his support obligation. It would be unfair, especially because he is unrepresented, not to afford him an opportunity to address the matte on its merits. The otherwise rigorous requirements of the legislation must be tempered to accommodate parties who find themselves in these circumstances.

The issue of fairness and the necessity of providing some accommodation is further addressed in the Ontario decision *Davids v. Davids* (1999), 1999 CarswellOnt 3304, [1999] O.J. No. 3930, 125 O.A.C. 375 (Ont. C.A.) (Labrosse, Doherty and O'Connor JJ.A.) in which a self-represented husband unsuccessfully appealed a support order. At para. 36, the Ontario Court of appeal states as follows:

> The fairness of this trial is not measured by comparing the appellant's conduct of his own case with the conduct of that case by a competent lawyer . . . Fairness does not demand that the unrepresented litigant be able to present his case as effectively as a competent lawyer. Rather, it demands that he have a fair opportunity to present his case to the best of his ability. Nor does fairness dictate that the unrepresented litigant have a lawyer's familiarity with procedures and forensic tactics. It does require that the trial judge treat the litigant fairly and attempt to accommodate unrepresented litigants' unfamiliarity with the process so as to permit them to present their case. In doing so, the trial judge must, of course, respect the rights of the other party.

Some past observations from the Bench:

> If Mr. Powell wants to remove his inflamed appendix he can do so, but he will botch the job. If he wants to drill and fill his aching tooth he can do so, but he will botch the job. If he wants to act for himself in this lawsuit he can do so, but he will botch the job. He has.
>
> *Alberta Treasury Branches v. Supreme Green Ltd.*, 1998 ABQB 253 (Alta. Master), per Master Funduk, (March 31, 1998).

Strategies for the Court

The following are possible strategies in dealing with self-represented litigants at a settlement conference. Some may also be helpful during motions and trials.

1) Ensure the presence of a court reporter. It is important to have a record when individuals are self-represented to avoid the suggestion of pressure or misdirection.

2) If a self-represented litigant fails to appear, verify proper service.

3) It is also helpful to set the ground rules, i.e., who is going to speak and when; one person speaks at a time; no one is to interrupt. The time that it will take to complete can be provided.

4) Determine language of choice and arrange for a translator if necessary. The literacy level should also be determined, if possible.

5) In listening to the self-represented litigant's outline of the issues and facts, frequently paraphrase what is said to demonstrate you are listening and ask more questions than might otherwise be appropriate. More helpful to use questions and not assertions. Rhetorical questions can be quite effective.

6) It is important to avoid dialogue or conduct with opposing counsel that could give rise to a perception that there may be some personal relationship or friendship. This could lead to a reasonable apprehension of bias. Self-represented litigants are very vigilant in this regard.

7) Address each issue raised by the self-represented litigant. Focus on the proof or evidence that will be necessary for the party to succeed and ask how the self-represented litigant plans to prove their case. This can help focus preparation and it may also enable the party to acknowledge that without an ability to obtain evidence, the court will not be able to rule in their favour on a particular point.

Management of Self-Represented Persons

1. Self-represented persons may be unable to perform the role expected of them. "Access to the courtroom does not necessarily mean access to the legal system." David Luban

2. It may cause stress for opposing party, both emotional and financial (e.g., cross-examination by an adversary)

3. The judge may appear biased as he or she assists the self-represented person

4. It may create difficulties for opposing counsel trying to represent client and adapt to self-represented opponent

5. It may delay the process, creating backlog

6. On the other hand, may speed up the process, but at the expense of the self-represented person's rights. "Cases involving unrepresented accused typically take less time overall to resolve than do cases involving private counsel": Robert G. Hann, Colin Meredith, Joan Nuffield and Mira Svoboda

7. Demands on court staff to assist the self-represented person

If self-represented persons are here to stay, should we only worry about how to assist them in conforming to our established processes, or should we try to simplify our processes and make them more accessible?

Measures to Assist the Self-represented

- Good public legal education, guidelines, protocols and other assistance

- Good alternative, front-end procedures to divert cases from the system where possible

• Well-trained court staff

UNREPRESENTED LITIGANTS:

A PERSPECTIVE

GROUNDS FOR APPEAL

Complaints

• Order doesn't reflect settlement terms

• I didn't know I needed to testify

• The judge made up his or her mind before we began

• The judge didn't understand what I was saying

• The judge was a friend of the lawyer

• The judge didn't take the proceeding seriously

• Judge was biased

• Judge was in a hurry

• Judge pressured me to settle

• Decision leaves out key evidence

• Mistakes in the decision

Reasonable Apprehension of Bias

Public confidence in our legal system "is rooted in the fundamental belief that those who adjudicate must always do so without bias or prejudice and must be perceived to do so" (See *Roberts v. R.*, 2003 CarswellNat 2822, 2003 CarswellNat 2823, REJB 2003-47809, (sub nom. *Wewaykum Indian Band v. Canada)* [2003] S.C.J. No. 50, 2003 SCC 45, 19 B.C.L.R. (4th) 195, [2004] 2 W.W.R. 1, (sub nom. *Wewaykum Indian Band v. Canada)* 309 N.R. 201, (sub nom. *Wewaykum Indian Band v. Canada)* [2003] 2 S.C.R. 259, 231 D.L.R. (4th) 1, 7 Admin. L.R. (4th) 1, 40 C.P.C. (5th) 1, (sub nom. *Wewaykum Indian Band v. Canada)* [2004] 1 C.N.L.R. 342 at para. 57 (S.C.C.)).

The Ontario Court of Appeal stated in *Rando Drugs Ltd. v. Scott*, 86 O.R. (3d) 653, 86 O.R. (3d) 641, 229 O.A.C. 1, 284 D.L.R. (4th) 756, [2007] O.J. No. 2999, 2007 CarswellOnt

4888, 2007 ONCA 553, 42 C.P.C. (6th) 23 (Ont. C.A.); leave to appeal refused (2008), 2008 CarswellOnt 354, 2008 CarswellOnt 353 (S.C.C.), at paragraph 29:

> ... the different contexts and in particular, the strong presumption of judicial impartiality that applies in the context of disqualification of a judge. There is no such presumption in cases of allegations of conflict of interest against a lawyer because of a firm's previous involvement in the case. To the contrary, as explained by Sopinka J., in *MacDonald Estate v. Martin* (1990), 77 D.L.R. (4th) 249 (S.C.C.), for sound policy reasons there is a presumption of a disqualifying interest that can rarely be overcome. In particular, a conclusory statement from the lawyer that he or she had no confidential information about the case will never be sufficient. The case is the opposite were the allegation of bias is made against a trial judge. His or her statement that he or she knew nothing about the case and had no involvement in it will ordinarily be accepted at face value unless there is good reason to doubt it. (See Paul Perrell, "The Disqualification of Judges and Judgments on the Grounds of Bias or the Reasonable Apprehension of Bias" (2004), 29 The Advocates' Quarterly 102, at pages 106 to 107).

It is important to distinguish between the concepts of impartiality and independence (impartiality relates to individual judges while independence is primarily a constitutional requirement, see *Ruffo c. Québec (Conseil de la magistrature)*, 1995 CarswellQue 183, 1995 CarswellQue 184, [1995] S.C.J. No. 100, EYB 1995-67891, (sub nom. *Ruffo v. Conseil de la magistrature)* 190 N.R. 1, (sub nom. *Ruffo v. Conseil de la magistrature)* [1995] 4 S.C.R. 267, 35 Admin. L.R. (2d) 1, (sub nom. *Ruffo v. Conseil de la magistrature)* 130 D.L.R. (4th) 1, (sub nom. *Ruffo v. Conseil de la magistrature)* 33 C.R.R. (2d) 269 (S.C.C.)).

In *R. v. S. (R.D.)*, [1997] 3 S.C.R. 484, [1997] S.C.J. No. 84, 1 Admin. L.R. (3d) 74, 218 N.R. 1, 10 C.R. (5th) 1, 1997 CarswellNS 302, 1997 CarswellNS 301, 118 C.C.C. (3d) 353, 151 D.L.R. (4th) 193, 477 A.P.R. 241, 161 N.S.R. (2d) 241 (S.C.C.), impartiality was described "as a state of mind in which the adjudicator is disinterested in the outcome, and is open to persuasion by the evidence and submissions" while bias was defined as "a state of mind that is in some way predisposed to a particular result, or that is closed with regard to particular issues." In *Arsenault-Cameron v. Prince Edward Island*, [1999] S.C.J. No. 75, [1999] 3 S.C.R. 851, 605 A.P.R. 1, 201 Nfld. & P.E.I.R. 1, 267 N.R. 386, 1999 CarswellPEI 96, 1999 CarswellPEI 87 (S.C.C.), at paragraph 3, the Court indicated that "true impartiality" does not "require that the judge have no sympathies or opinions. It requires that the judge nevertheless be free to entertain and act upon different points of view with an open mind."

In *Boardwalk Reit LLP v. Edmonton (City)*, [2008] A.J. No. 515, 2008 CarswellAlta 646, 91 Alta. L.R. (4th) 49, [2008] 8 W.W.R. 251, 57 C.P.C. (6th) 1, 433 W.A.C. 199, 437 A.R. 199, 2008 ABCA 176 (Alta. C.A.); leave to appeal refused (2008), 2008 CarswellAlta 2024, 2008 CarswellAlta 2025, 392 N.R. 399 (note) (S.C.C.), the Alberta Court of Appeal listed a number of instances, in which it was concluded that a reasonable apprehension of bias had *not* been established. See paragraph 26:

> (a) Counsel is someone with whom the trial judge sometimes socializes, but he does not do so around the time of an actual case and did not around the time of this case, and never mentions his cases with that lawyer: *Wellesley L. Trophy Lodge v. BLD Silviculture*, 2006 BCCA 328, [2006] 10 W.W.R. 82.

> (b) The judge is a close neighbour and social friend of counsel's parents, and is the father of a classmate of counsel: *Banyay v. I.C.B.C. (Actton Petr. Sales)* (1995), 17 B.C.L.R. (3d) 216 (C.A.).

> (c) Even in a large city, where the judge's brother is a member of the large law firm appearing for one side; one cannot bar a judge from hearing any cases involving a large firm in his or her city: *G.W.L. Property v. W.R. Grace Ins. Co. of Canada* (1992), 74 B.C.L.R. (2d) 283 288-89 (B.C. C.A.).

(d) One party's firm of lawyers also acts for the trial judge in drafting and holding the judge's will, even if the firm is revising the will about the same time as the trial: *Taylor v. Lawrence*, [2002] EWCA Civ. 90, [2003] Q.B. 528, [2002] 2 All E.R. 353.

(e) Two lawyers are in a big firm. One (a partner) is retained to defend a suit against a small law firm. The plaintiff in that suit is the respondent in a probate proceeding (a separate suit) being tried by a judge married to the other lawyer (an employee) in the big firm: *Re Serdahaly Est. (Popke v. Bolt)*, 2005 ABQB 861, 392 A.R. 220.

(f) Counsel for the accused is from the same law firm which had previously defended the son of the trial judge on a somewhat similar criminal charge: *R. v. Nicol*, 2006 BCCA 370, 211 C.C.C. (3d) 33.

(g) A statutory tribunal retains a lawyer as its adviser who had previously advised it with respect to other matters with which one party before it had been involved (which had been overturned on appeal), irrespective of the lawyers' personal views: *Ayangma v. Human Rts. Comm.*, 2005 PESCAD 18, 248 N. & P.E.I.R. 79 at para. 19-20.

(h) The trial judge was divorced from a lawyer practising with one of the firms in the lawsuit in question, but no longer has any relationship with him: *Middlekamp v. Fraser Valley Real Est. Bd.*, [1993] B.C.J. No. 2695 at para. 7-8 (S.C. June 10); affd. (1993), 83 B.C.L.R. (2d) 257, 20 C.P.C. (3d) 27 (C.A.).

(i) The trial judge's present spouse was represented in unrelated litigation by one of the big law firms acting on the present trial, and the trial judge was an inactive officer of the spouse's management company (which was not a party): *Middlekamp v. Fraser Valley Real Est. Bd.*, *supra* (S.C.) (paras. 9–15).

(j) The trial judge's son is a lawyer employed in a firm of over 50 lawyers and is not a partner and was not involved on the file, but his firm acts for one side: *Makowsky v. Doe*, 2007 BCSC 1231, [2007] B.C.J. No. 1809 at para. 4, 5, 9, 20, 29, 35; affirmed 2008 BCCA 112, [2008] B.C.A.C. Uned. 22, [2008] B.C.J. 576 (B.C. C.A.).

In *Kelly v. Palazzo*, 2008 CarswellOnt 564, 2008 ONCA 82, 233 O.A.C. 160, 290 D.L.R. (4th) 315, 89 O.R. (3d) 111, 168 C.R.R. (2d) 256 (Ont. C.A.); leave to appeal refused 2008 CarswellOnt 3741, 2008 CarswellOnt 3742 (S.C.C.), the Ontario Court of Appeal pointed out that it "takes much more than a demonstration of judicial impatience with counsel or even downright rudeness to dispel the strong presumption of impartiality" (at para. 21):

> It takes much more than a demonstration of judicial impatience with counsel or even downright rudeness to dispel the strong presumption of impartiality. While litigants may not appreciate that presumption and thus may misread judicial conduct, lawyers are expected to appreciate that presumption and, where necessary, explain it to their client. Baseless allegations of bias or of a reasonable apprehension of a bias founded on a perceived slight or discourtesy that occurred during a trial, will not assist the client's cause and do a disservice to the administration of justice.

If counsel indicates that they found a comment made to them by a judge to be improper or demeaning, then the judge should apologize for having left that impression and this should cure any apprehension of bias that may have arisen (See *Kelly v. Palazzo* at paragraph 33).

In addition to making intemperate comments to counsel during a proceeding, occasions arise where our previous dealings with a specific counsel have been less than ideal.

The mere fact that a judge has had prior dealings with counsel that are of a negative nature is not sufficient to require a recusal. However, a personal relationship, with counsel, the accused, or a witness, depending on the nature and extent of it, can constitute a basis for disqualification.

In *Makowsky v. John Doe*, 2007 BCSC 1231, 2007 CarswellBC 1874, [2007] B.C.J. No. 1809 (B.C. S.C.); affirmed 2008 BCCA 112, 2008 CarswellBC 652, [2008] B.C.J. No. 576

(B.C. C.A.), the trial judge was asked to recuse himself because the law firm who represented one of the defendants employed his son. In rejecting the application, the trial judge concluded that an "informed, reasonable and right minded person viewing the matter realistically and practically, and having thought through the matter, would not conclude that it is more likely than not that I would consciously or unconsciously not decide the case fairly because my son is associated with one of the law firms." See *Frambordeaux Developments Inc. v. Romandale Farms Ltd.* (2007), [2007] O.J. No. 4483, 2007 CarswellOnt 7455 (Ont. S.C.J.) and *Marshall v. British Columbia (Public Guardian & Trustee)*, [2007] B.C.J. No. 1962, 2007 CarswellBC 2054, 2007 BCSC 1338 (B.C. S.C.).

In *Foto v. Jones* (1974), 1974 CarswellOnt 884, 45 D.L.R. (3d) 43, 3 O.R. (2d) 238 (Ont. C.A.), a reasonable apprehension of bias was found to exist based upon the trial judge having said that he did not believe the evidence of the plaintiff and that: "I regret to have to say that too many newcomers to our country have as yet not learned the necessity of speaking the whole truth...They have not learned that frankness is essential to our system of law and justice."

In *R. v. S. (R.D.)*, [1997] 3 S.C.R. 484, [1997] S.C.J. No. 84, 1 Admin. L.R. (3d) 74, 218 N.R. 1, 10 C.R. (5th) 1, 1997 CarswellNS 302, 1997 CarswellNS 301, 118 C.C.C. (3d) 353, 151 D.L.R. (4th) 193, 477 A.P.R. 241, 161 N.S.R. (2d) 241 (S.C.C.), the trial judge's remarks (concerning racism and police officers) were described as "worrisome and come very close to the line," but not sufficient to establish a reasonable apprehension of bias.

The Supreme Court of Canada dealt with the issue of reasonable apprehension of bias in *R. v. S. (R.D.)*, [1997] 3 S.C.R. 484, [1997] S.C.J. No. 84, 1 Admin. L.R. (3d) 74, 218 N.R. 1, 10 C.R. (5th) 1, 1997 CarswellNS 302, 1997 CarswellNS 301, 118 C.C.C. (3d) 353, 151 D.L.R. (4th) 193, 477 A.P.R. 241, 161 N.S.R. (2d) 241 (S.C.C.). The Court adopted the wording of de Grandpre J. in *Committee for Justice & Liberty v. Canada (National Energy Board)* (1976), 1976 CarswellNat 434, 1976 CarswellNat 434F, [1976] S.C.J. No. 118, [1976] A.C.S. No. 118, [1978] 1 S.C.R. 369, 68 D.L.R. (3d) 716, 9 N.R. 115 (S.C.C.) at para. 394:

> The apprehension of bias must be a reasonable one, held by reasonable and right minded persons applying themselves to the question and obtaining thereon the required information ... the test is "what would an informed person, viewing the matter realistically and practically, and having thought the matter through — conclude?"

In *R. v. S. (R.D.)*, *supra*, the court concluded that judicial officers are to be presumed to be impartial and stated at paras. 60-61:

> Thus, reviewing courts have been hesitant to make a finding of bias or to perceive a reasonable apprehension of bias on the part of a judge, in the absence of convincing evidence to that effect.

The Ontario Court of Appeal has further dealt with reasonable apprehension of bias in the following circumstances: the trial judge intervened and adopted an adversarial position: *Shoppers Mortgage & Loan Corp. v. Health First Wellington Square Ltd.* (1995), 1995 CarswellOnt 350, [1995] O.J. No. 1268, 38 C.P.C. (3d) 8, 23 O.R. (3d) 362, 124 D.L.R. (4th) 440, 80 O.A.C. 346 (Ont. C.A.); additional reasons at (1995), 1995 CarswellOnt 351, 124 D.L.R. (4th) 440 at 448, 38 C.P.C. (3d) 18, 25 O.R. (3d) 95 (Ont. C.A.); the trial judge usurped the role of counsel and descended into the arena: *Stein v. Sandwich West (Township)* (1995), [1995] O.J. No. 423, 77 O.A.C. 40, 25 M.P.L.R. (2d) 170, 1995 CarswellOnt 160 (Ont. C.A.); the trial judge engaged in extensive cross-examination of two witnesses and challenged their credibility: *Lennox v. Arbor Memorial Services Inc.* (2001), 56 O.R. (3d) 795, 151 O.A.C. 297, 16 C.C.E.L. (3d) 157, 2001 CarswellOnt 4248 (Ont. C.A.). The Canadian Judicial Council in its publication *Ethical Principles for Judges* has provided the following guidance to judges on the subject of conflict of interest at page 46:

> ... the general principle that a judge should disqualify him or herself if aware of any interest or relationship which, to a reasonable, fair minded and informed person would rise to reason suspicion of lack of impartiality.

It is well established that the test to be applied on the review of a Small Claims Court deputy judge's decision is as follows:

(a) Findings of fact or inferences of fact cannot be reversed unless the trial judge has made a palpable and overriding error;

(b) The trial judge's interpretation of the evidence as a whole should not be overturned absent palpable and overriding error; and,

(c) If the matter is one of law that is deemed to be vital to the disposition of the law suit, the test should be one of correctness.

As the Supreme Court of Canada stated in *Housen v. Nikolaisen*, 2002 CarswellSask 178, 2002 CarswellSask 179, [2002] S.C.J. No. 31, REJB 2002-29758, 10 C.C.L.T. (3d) 157, 211 D.L.R. (4th) 577, 286 N.R. 1, [2002] 7 W.W.R. 1, 2002 SCC 33, 30 M.P.L.R. (3d) 1, 219 Sask. R. 1, 272 W.A.C. 1, [2002] 2 S.C.R. 235 (S.C.C.) at page 3:

> It is argued that the trial judge enjoys numerous advantages over appellant judges which bear on all conclusions of fact, and, even in the absence of these advantages, there are other compelling policy reasons supporting a deferential approach to inferences of fact. We conclude, therefore, by emphasizing that there is one, and only one standard of review applicable to all factual conclusions made by the trial judge — that of palpable and overriding error.

As Smith J. said in *Savin v. McKay* (1984), 1984 CarswellOnt 404, 44 C.P.C. 192 (Ont. Div. Ct.) at pages 192-193:

> Since it is an appellate court which is not designed for retrial of the action, an error of law must be shown before the appeal will succeed.

A Civil Hearing

There is always a need to reach an acceptable balance between zealous advocacy and ethical argument. As one judge has observed, "There's nothing wrong with strong advocacy in the case of your client . . . but it has to be done with respect for . . . counsel and respect for the court." Along the same lines, one decision states, "To be aggressive is not a license to ignore the rules of evidence and to decorum; and to be zealous is not to be uncivil." When counsel intentionally drive an otherwise routine case to the margins by infecting the trial with personal issues or by purposefully seeking to supercharge emotions, alert observers quickly recognize that the object is not justice, but victory. The courtroom is a forum for the presentation of evidence and rational argument, not a stage for overt melodrama. The responsibility of a lawyer is to raise issues, not scenes. Invective, with all its theatrics, has no place in the language of law. Uncivil communication by lawyers adversely affects public perception of the profession and legal system. A lawyer who exhibits a lack of civility, good manners and common courtesy tarnishes the image of the legal profession.

The personal attack, or argument *ad hominem* ("against the person"), attempts to undercut a claim by drawing unfavourable attention to the person making it. An opponent's thesis is asserted to be wrong or unworthy of attention because of the opponent's character or situation. Such reasoning is fallacious because it does not address the trust or falsity of the proposition itself.

Diffusing litigants or lawyers who push the limits of decorum unfortunately can often bait judges, and each judge develops his or her own method to deal with these moments. Some may address the existence of the anger through direct observation, while others may take a recess or simply get up and leave the bench. The craft comes into play in assessing the technique that will not only diffuse the anger of the parties or their lawyers, but also the anger of the judge. It is rarely advisable for judges to engage in an arugment about power with parties or lawyers. Judges, through their positions, have authority over the participants in the courtroom and the corresponding responsibility to exercise that authority in a manner that maintains the appropriate tone and respect for the law and the dispute in question.

Interpretation Services

The Ontario Ministry of the Attorney General provides court interpretation services in any language in Small Claims Court matters *if* the litigant qualifies for the fee waiver and in French and in sign language in all Small Claims Court matters. Section 126 of the *Courts of Justice Act* details the requirements for holding a bilingual proceeding.

Visual language interpreters in Small Claims Court for all litigants are provided, if required. Visual language interpretation includes American Sign Language, deaf-blind interpreter services, deaf interpreter services, text-based services, and Langue des Signes du Québec. The Ministry will also provide visual language interpretation at counters in Small Claims Court.

Persons with Disabilities

Ontario has passed two statutes to help implement the right of people with disabilities to live in a barrier-free society. These laws apply to our courts. They provide for the systematic identification, removal and prevention of barriers.

The first, the *Ontarians with Disabilities Act*, 2001, focuses on barriers in the public sector. It obliges all public sector organizations including provincial ministries (such as the Ontario Ministry of the Attorney General) each year to make public an annual accessibility plan. These plans must spell out steps the organization took in the past year, and the steps it will take in the next year to remove and prevent barriers against persons with disabilities. The preamble declares, among other things:

> Ontarians with disabilities experience barriers to participating in the mainstream of Ontario society ... The Government of Ontario is committed to working with every sector of society to build on what it has already achieved together with those sectors to move towards a province in which no new barriers are created and existing ones removed. This responsibility rests with every social and economic association, and every person in Ontario.

The *Accessibility Standards for Customer Service Ontario Regulation 429/07* came into force on January 1, 2008. It is the first accessibility standard created under the *Accessibility for Ontarians with Disabilities Act, 2005* and is a significant step toward the overarching goals of achieving a barrier-free Ontario by 2025. The Ministry is required to comply with the regulation by January 1, 2010.

Deputy judges and judges should always:

- Talk directly to the person with a disability, not to a third party.

- If someone appears not to understand, consider that:
  - She may be suffering from traumatic shock;
  - She may be hearing impaired;
  - English may not be her first language;
  - Your voice or accent may be difficult for her to follow;
  - She may have an intellectual, cognitive or psychiatric disability.

- If someone appears to be intoxicated, consider that:
  - He may have a neurological condition such as cerebral palsy;
  - He may have a medical condition such as diabetes.

- Avoid being overly sensitive or self-conscious about using words such as "walking" or "running."

- People who are non-speaking sometimes use a symbolic communication system, such as a bliss board, as an alternative to speech. The person may need an interpreter, someone who knows the person well, since each person who uses such symbolic communication may do so in a different way.

- When talking to someone who is blind, use a normal tone and speed of voice. Blindness does not affect hearing or comprehension.

- Do not prejudge the mental condition of any person. A person who has been given a psychiatric label may not be functionally impaired.

The right to a fair trial, including the right to make full answer and defence, is dependent on the ability to understand the evidence. For those who require interpretation, that right to a fair trial can be compromised significantly if the interpretation is not accurate. It is the responsibility of the trial judge to ensure that the interpreter possesses the appropriate qualifications before proceeding.

If you have a hearing impairment and need an interpreter, you can make a request at the Small Claims Court office. The staff will first ask whether written communication would satisfy your needs. If written communication would not be satisfactory, then a visual language interpreter can be used. You can either bring an interpreter with you or ask to have one arranged for you. The court will pay visual language interpreters the standard Ministry interpreter rate or a requested fee (whichever is less).

Section 7 of the *Ontarians with Disabilities Act* provides:

> Within a reasonable time after receiving a request by or on behalf of a person with disabilities, the Government of Ontario shall make an Ontario Government publication available in a format that is accessible to the person, unless it is not technically feasible to do so.

If you want to request a publication in a different format, please contact Service Ontario Publications at:

Service Ontario Publications

50 Grosvenor Street

Toronto, ON M7A 1N8

Toll Free: 1-800-668-9938

TTY Toll Free: 1-800-268-7095

Accessibility Tips for Judges

It is an ideal of every judge that their courtroom be accessible for everyone who needs to use it. There is always a need for judges to identify accessibility issues in a case at the earliest possible opportunity.

It is important to address accessibility needs as early as possible to avoid unnecessary adjournments. If you learn at the last minute that a witness has a significant hearing loss and can't hear the evidence, or a witness who is in a wheelchair can't get into the courtroom, you might not have time to accommodate the accessibility need and might lose the trial time.

Addressing accessibility needs at an early stage allows for the following:

a. Proper scheduling of the trial, since you can allocate more trial time to address the accessibility need.

b. The ability to organize when to call a witness with accessibility needs; for instance, some witnesses will function best first thing in the morning.

c. Sufficient time to book an accessible courtroom for the hearing.

d. Sufficient time to obtain accessible devices, such as captioning equipment that might be necessary on the return date.

More important, accommodating persons with disabilities is the right thing to do in order to ensure that everyone has full access to our courtrooms.

Flag each file to determine if:

a. Dedicated court time will be required.

b. A specialized courtroom will be required.

c. Assistive devices will be needed on the return date.

d. Additional time will have to be scheduled for the hearing.

How to accomplish this?

a. Provide dedicated time for the case.

b. Find out if the person with the accessibility need functions better at a certain time of the day and schedule the case accordingly.

c. Alert the court clerk to call the case first.

d. Close the court to eliminate distractions.

e. Talk more slowly.

f. Break down concepts into short bites and use short sentences.

g. Repeat positions and evidence and ask the person if they understand it properly.

h. Ask the person to repeat what has been said to ensure that everything has been properly understood.

If you treat people with respect and communicate that you care about understanding their evidence or argument, they will not perceive this approach as condescending.

a. Enforce the rule that no one can speak over anyone else.

b. Model respectful and calm behaviour.

c. Smile a lot, making eye contact and providing a lot of validation and reassurance, where appropriate.

d. Permit a support person to sit beside the party.

There should be an Accessibility Co-ordinator at every court site. The Accessibility Co-ordinator should be able to give you the following information:

a. A list of accessibility services and devices which are available at your court site and in your region.

b. How long it will take to obtain accessibility services and devices that are not on site. For instance, you might need a lot of lead time to obtain captioning equipment (used for hearing and learning disabilities or American Sign Language interpreters).

c. How much lead time you will need to schedule an accessible courtroom.

d. What accessibility services the accessible courtroom offers and what services it might lack.

People might be afraid to speak up about accessibility needs in the courtroom. To address this issue:

a. Try to create a comfortable environment so that parties will feel more willing to let you know about any accessibility need.

b. Ask counsel if there are any accessibility needs that will have to be accommodated for a *party, witness, counsel or any member of the public that they expect to attend at court*. Most lawyers aren't attuned to this issue until it is raised. If counsel is unaware of any accessibility needs, ask them to look into the issue and to advise the court's Accessibility Co-ordinator.

We must be alert to the fact that persons with disabilities might require assistance outside of the courtroom. Some courts will have a bed and a calm room where the person can lie down and rest. Check with your Accessibility Co-ordinator to see if your court has this accommodation.

If a person has a hearing disability:

a. Consider turning off heavy machinery or air conditioning in the courtroom.

b. Be sure that the person with a hearing disability has a clean line of sight to whoever is speaking.

c. Don't cover your mouth or look down while you are speaking.

d. Look at and talk to the person with the disability, not their interpreter.

e. The interpreter requires a direct line of sight with the person for whom they are interpreting. They might need to try out different positions before court starts. Make sure that counsel conducting an examination is not blocking this line of sight.

f. If someone will be using an assisted listening device, it is a good idea to test out this equipment before court starts. Arrange for the party and counsel to come in early, so that court time is not wasted.

g. Book sign-language interpreters well in advance. If they are needed for more than two hours they might need relief, as this type of interpretation is an exhausting process.

If you are dealing with a person with a visual disability:

a. Identify the person by name when you are talking with them. They may not be aware that you are looking at them when you are speaking. Don't take this for granted.

b. If a physical gesture is important in the evidence, articulate what the physical gesture is for the benefit of the person with the disability.

c. At many court sites, you can ask court services to reformat documents in an accessible format. Most scanners have optical recognition technology that lets a printed document be quickly scanned and converted to an accessible electronic format. You will be able to have these documents reformatted very quickly (same day). Check and see if your court has this capability. If not, find out from your Accessibility Co-ordinator how long it would take to obtain the documents in an accessible format.

If a person has speech issues:

a. Be patient.

b. If you are having difficulty understanding the witness, ask them to repeat what they are saying.

c. Restate your understanding of their evidence and have them confirm its accuracy.

d. Don't finish their sentences.

If a person has a mobility issue, find this out early so that an accessible courtroom can be arranged. Be aware that persons with mobility issues will require longer recesses for washroom breaks.

If a person has fibromyalgia or incontinence issues, schedule frequent breaks. It might also be wise to only book hearings for a half-day.

Civility

While their duties to clients are often paramount, lawyers and paralegals also have duties to others that might temper the zeal with which they are permitted to act on behalf of their clients. The lawyers' *Rules of Professional Conduct* and the *Paralegal Rules of Conduct* require lawyers and paralegals to be courteous and civil and to act in good faith when dealing with other persons in relation to his or her law or legal services practice. See subrule 6.03(1) and subrule 2.01(3), respectively.

In particular, lawyers and paralegals must agree to *"reasonable requests concerning trial dates, adjournments, the waiver of procedural formalities and similar matters that do not prejudice the rights of the client"* [subrule 6.03(2) and subrule 7.01(2), respectively]. Therefore, you may not accept these instructions from your client and must advise them of this.

Even if permitted by law, both lawyers and paralegals are prohibited from recording a conversation with a client or another lawyer or paralegal, unless the client or the other lawyer or paralegal is first informed that they will be recorded. See subrule 6.03(4) of the lawyers' *Rules of Professional Conduct* and subrule 7.01(7) of the *Paralegal Rules of Conduct*. Though the other party does not need to consent to being recorded, advising the party allows him or her to refuse to talk under those circumstances. Neither lawyer nor paralegal may surreptitiously record another lawyer, paralegal or client.

When representing a client in a contentious matter where oral communications between opposing sides may or has become difficult, lawyers and paralegals may wish to consider obtaining the client's consent to use written communications (e.g., via mail, e-mail or fax) to limit hostility, misunderstanding and cost.

The need for courtesy and civility in the practice of law and the provision of legal services is for the benefit of both the public and the legal professions. As outlined in the commentary to subrule 6.03(1) of the lawyers' *Rules of Professional Conduct*:

> The public interest demands that matters entrusted to a lawyer be dealt with effectively and expeditiously, and fair and courteous dealing on the part of each lawyer engaged in a matter will contribute materially to this end. The lawyer who behaves otherwise does a disservice to the client, and neglect of the rule will impair the ability of lawyers to perform their function properly.

The Parental Responsibility Act

- holds parents financially responsible for property loss, damage or destruction intentionally caused by their children who are under 18 years of age;

- allows property owners, renters and lessees whose property has been intentionally damaged, destroyed or stolen by minors to bring a claim for a maximum of $10,000 against parents through Small Claims Court (as of January 1, 2010, a maximum of $25,000). This amount includes costs incurred by the victim such as lost wages or profits and car rental costs arising from the property damage or loss; and

- permits victims to use documents under the federal *Young Offenders Act* and *Youth Criminal Justice Act* to help prove their case where the youth has been found guilty of that property offence in youth court.

Victims of property crimes committed by minors follow the standard Small Claims Court process. This process starts by the victim filing a claim for damages against the parent(s) of the child. The parent(s) then have an opportunity to file a defence. This may be followed by a pre-trial conference requested by the victim or the parent(s) or ordered by the court. This meeting can help resolve the dispute before a trial.

If the case goes to trial, the victim provides evidence before a Small Claims Court judge to prove his or her case. This evidence may include documentation and/or the testimony of witnesses. Since Small Claims Court is a civil court, police charges or a police report are not required to start or prove the case.

Parents who choose to defend the case would then have an opportunity to show that they exercised reasonable supervision and tried to stop the damage from happening, or to show that their child's act was *not* intentional.

Examples of property loss or damage valued at under $25,000

Examples of property crime may include, but are not limited to:

- Damage to windows, doors, and interiors or exteriors of homes, apartments, cottages, or businesses,
- Theft of contents such as jewellery, televisions, computers, and merchandise,
- Damage to automobiles, and
- Losses from shoplifting.

Under the *Parental Responsibility Act*, victims need prove:

- That the child caused the property damage or loss,
- That the defendant(s) are the parent(s) of the child, and
- The amount of the damage.

The burden then shifts to the young person's parent(s) to establish why they should not be found liable for their children's property offences.

The *Parental Responsibility Act* also helps victims obtain access to documents under the *Youth Criminal Justice Act* to use in their cases. Where a youth had been found guilty of a property offence in youth court, the *Parental Responsibility Act* has special rules allowing access to proof of guilt. Access to this information is otherwise restricted.

What do parents of minors accused of property damage have to prove in court?

Parents can be held liable for property loss, destruction, or damage caused by their children, who are under 18 years of age, unless the parents can prove:

- The loss or damage caused was not intentional; or
- They exercised reasonable supervision of the child and made reasonable efforts to prevent the damage from occurring.

Under the *Parental Responsibility Act* the court may consider the following factors:

- The youth's age,
- The youth's prior conduct,
- The potential danger of the activity,
- The youth's mental or physical capacity,

- Any psychological disorders affecting the youth,
- Whether the youth was under direct supervision of the parent at the time when the damage or loss was caused,
- Whether a parent had made reasonable arrangements for supervision,
- Whether a parent had sought to improve his/her parenting skills,
- Whether a parent had sought professional assistance for the youth, and
- Any other factor that the judge believes is relevant to the case.

The court may order the parent to make payments to the victim in fixed instalments in cases where the full payment ordered by the court cannot be made immediately.

The victim can take the steps needed to enforce an unpaid judgment.

Checklist for Small Claims Court

The following represents a list of issues to consider:

1. Has a demand been made?[2]
2. Is leave of the court required?[3]
3. Is notice required?[4]
4. Is there a limitation period issue?[5]
5. Claims for interest[6]
6. Party under legal disability[7]
7. Proceedings in different courts[8]
8. Alternatives to personal service[9]
9. Amending pleadings[10]
10. Default proceedings[11]

---

[2]*Solicitors Act*, R.S.O. 1990, c. S.15, s. 2.

[3]*Courts of Justice Act*, R.S.O. 1990, c. C.43, s. 140.

[4]See, e.g., *Libel and Slander Act*, R.S.O. 1990, c. L-12, s. 5(1); *Proceedings Against the Crown Act*, R.S.O. 1990, c. P-27, s. 7; and *Public Authorities Protection Act*, R.S.O. 1990, c. P-38, s. 6.

[5]See *Limitations Act* 2002, S.O. 2002, c. 24, Sched. B.

[6]*Courts of Justice Act*, R.S.O. 1990, c. C.43, ss. 128, 130.

[7]*Small Claims Court Rules*, Rule 4.

[8]*Courts of Justice Act*, R.S.O. 1990, c. C.43, ss. 107, 110.

[9]Rule 8.

[10]Rule 12.

[11]Rule 11.

11. Third party claims[12]
12. Pre-trial procedures[13]
13. Offers to settle[14]
14. Witnesses[15]
15. Documents[16]

What of the Future?

Small Claims courts will continue to be busy, although the "Next Society"[17] may change the mix and the nature of the disputes decided in these courts. Knowledge-worker disputes will increase in number and take the place of traditional employment disputes that progressively will be diverted into private arbitration. Furthermore, such disputes no longer will be mostly local: co-operative working relationships will — due to instant internet communication — become global. Court ADR will be institutionalized.[18]

Torts committed over the internet will be a burgeoning new category of nonrelational disputes. Resident plaintiffs will file claims against cyberspace communicators for anything and maybe everything. Whether our courts will extend their jurisdiction over residents for such keyboard assaults will depend on the degree of internet interactivity between the parties and whether court view its citizens' interests as significantly offended . . . a flexible standard, indeed.[19]

Private Judging

The move toward court specialization on the civil side will be even more stimulated by the rise of the private judge industry. These alternative dispute resolution (ADR) providers, staffed largely by retired judges, provide arbitration and mediation services to litigants who may be dissatisfied with the public courts. The litigants who stipulate that their disputes may be decided by a private judge find various advantages: the perceived expertise or even-handedness of the judge they have selected; the confidentiality of the non-public proceeding; and often, the flexibility and convenience of the process. Private judging may take away from the public court some of the more significant disputes. The public courts, to accommodate, will create courts geared for particular disputes and may identify, early in their careers, judges with suitable skills for those courts.

Many litigants in Small Claims Court represent themselves. However, a party may also be represented in small Claims Court by a lawyer or by a person authorized under the *Law*

---

[12]Rule 10.04(3).

[13]Rule 13.

[14]Rule 14.

[15]There is no property in a witness: see *Ward v. Magna International Inc.* (1994), 28 C.P.C. (3d) 327, 1994 CarswellOnt 543, 21 C.C.L.T. (2d) 178 (Ont. Gen. Div.); additional reasons at (1994), 1994 CarswellOnt 4559, 21 C.C.L.T. (2d) 178 at 197, 28 C.P.C. (3d) 327 at 346 (Ont. Gen. Div.). Regarding failure to testify, see *Royal Trust Co. v. Toronto Transportation Commission*, [1935] S.C.R. 671, 1935 CarswellOnt 120, 44 C.R.C. 90, [1935] 3 D.L.R. 420 (S.C.C.).

[16]*Evidence Act*, R.S.O. 1990, c. E-23.

[17]See Dr. Peter Drucker, "The Next Society," *The Economist*, November 3, 2001.

[18]See Roselle L. Wissler, "Mediation and Adjudication in Small Claims Court," 29 *Law and Society Review* 323 (1995). Also see 17 Ohio State University on Dispute Resolution (2002), and Pepperdine Dispute Resolution Law Journal (2002).

[19]See *Zippo Manufacturing Co. v. Zippo Dot Com Inc.* (1997), 952 F. Supp. 1119, 65 U.S.L.W. 2551, 42 U.S.P.Q.2d 1062 (U.S. W.D. Pa.).

Society Act, R.S.O. 1990, G. L-8, such as a law student or a paralegal. If you wish to contact a paralegal in your area, you may consult the Paralegal Directory, established by the Law Society of Upper Canada.

The Law Society Referral Service will provide the name of a lawyer or paralegal who practices in the area, who provides a free consultation of up to 30 minutes. The Law Society Referral Service is available by telephone only at 1-800-268-8326 (or in the Greater Toronto Area at 416-947-3330). If calling from outside the province, the Law Society Referral Service can be reached by dialling 1-416-947-3330. A party can advise the operator that he or she is calling from outside the province. A half-hour consultation is not guaranteed if a party does not have an Ontario number. The Law Society of Upper Canada also maintains a list of lawyers and paralegals in Ontario and their contact information, which may be accessed through the Law Society of Upper Canada website at: http://lrs.lsuc.on.ca/lsrs/.

A party may wish to contact a local Community Legal Clinic which may provide services in the party's geographic area for information about eligibility for services.

A party may also wish to contact Justice Net, which is a program of Lawyers Aid Canada, a federally incorporated not-for profit organization whose aim is to complement legal aid and pro bono law programs in making justice more accessible to Canadians. Under Justice Net, lawyers reduce their hourly fees on a portion of their practice to address the unmet legal needs of low and middle income members of their communities. For more information, the Justice Net website may be accessed at www.justicenet.ca or call 1-866-919-3219.

An Interpreter

Small Claims Court provides interpretation services for all court proceedings and written documents from English to French and French to English.

Interpretation from English or French to any other language must be arranged for, and paid by, the party who requires the interpretation. The interpreter must be accredited as being capable of performing that function. The court office will pay for "in-court" interpretation in any language for individuals who qualify for fee waiver.

Visual language interpretation

Anyone who has a hearing impairment that needs an interpreter can request this at the Small Claims Court office. A visual language interpreter can be used. You can either bring an interpreter with you or ask to have one arranged for you.

Section 7 of the *Ontarians with Disabilities Act* provides:

> Within a reasonable time after receiving a request by or on behalf of a person with disabilities, the Government of Ontario shall make an Ontario Government publication available in a format that is accessible to the person, unless it is not technically feasible to do so.

Interest

Prejudgment interest rate is defined in the *Courts of Justice Act* (s.127(1)). These rates are posted quarterly in the Ontario Gazette. It is the responsibility of the claimant to indicate prejudgment interest to the date the claim was prepared. Prejudgment interest may be claimed in accordance with the *Courts of Justice Act* or payable by agreement. Principal judgment amount × prejudgment interest rate %, 365 days per year × number of days from the date the claim arose, or the claim was issued if the date the claim arose is not indicated, to date of judgment.

The Act states that prejudgment interest will not be awarded on the following [s.128(3), *CJA*]:

- interest accruing under this section;

- an award of costs in the proceeding;

- an advance payment that has already been made, from the date the payment was made;

- an order made on consent, except by consent of the debtor; and/or

- where interest is payable by a right (e.g. contractual right) other than under Section 128, *Courts of Justice Act*

What happens if prejudgment interest is claimed but the date the cause of action arose is not set out in the claim and the claimant does not specify in the claim a date from which interest is to commence?

In that case, in signing default judgment, interest would be calculated from the date that the claim was issued and at the contractual rate indicated or at the applicable rate under the *Courts of Justice Act.*

What happens if a judge at an assessment or trial does not make an order with respect to prejudgment interest?

No prejudgment interest may be allowed.

If a default judgment is sent in by mail, how are claimants to determine the date of judgment for the purpose of calculating prejudgment interest?

Claimants electing to submit default judgments by mail must calculate prejudgment interest by using the date of mailing as the date of judgment.

Section 127(1) of the *Courts of Justice Act* provides that the prejudgment interest rate is determined by the quarter in which the proceeding was commenced.

Section 128(1) of the *Courts of Justice Act* provides that prejudgment interest is calculated from the date the cause of action arose to the date of the order.

Therefore, the rate of prejudgment interest is determined by the date the claim is issued and the amount is calculated from the date of the debt to the date of the order. For example, the cause of action arose on February 1, 2011, the claim was issued on October 30, 2011 and the judgment was received and entered on May 1, 2012. The 2011, fourth quarter pre-judgment interest rate would apply and it would be calculated from February 1, 2011 to May 1, 2012.

Section 128(4)(g) provides for interest payable by a right other than under section 128 of the *Courts of Justice Act* (for example by way of a contract between the parties). In such cases, the rates are determined and calculated at the stated contractual rate even if a judge has not specified the rate.

Default Judgment

If a Defence (Form 9A) has been filed for a debt or liquidated demand in money, the clerk may sign Default Judgment (Form 11B) on the undefended part of the liquidated claim.

If a defence has been filed in which the defendant makes a proposal of terms of payment (and the plaintiff did not dispute the proposal), and if the defendant fails to make payment in accordance with the proposal, then the plaintiff will file an Affidavit of Default of Payment (Form 20M) indicating that the Notice of Default of Payment (Form 20L) was served on the defendant.

The clerk will sign default judgment for the unpaid balance of the undisputed amount as long as:

- the affidavit of default of payment indicates that the defendant failed to make payment in accordance with the proposal;

- 15 days have passed since the defendant was served with the notice of default of payment;

- the amount paid by the defendant and the unpaid balance [r. 9.03(2)(c)]; and

- the parties have not filed a written consent to waive the default of payment.

A default judgment may **not** be issued in the following circumstances:

1. In a Defendant's Claim (Form 10A) where the plaintiff in the defendant's claim wishes to obtain judgment against a defendant who has been noted in default with respect to a defendant's claim, judgment may only be obtained at trial or on motion to a judge [r.11.04];

2. In an action in which the Crown in Right of Ontario is a party, leave of the court is required before default judgment may be issued [s.18, *Proceedings Against the Crown Act*];

3. In an action in which Her Majesty in right of Canada is a party, leave of the court is required before default judgment may be issued [s.25, *Crown Liability and Proceedings Act*]; and

4. In an action in which the defendant is a person under disability, unless leave of the court has been given to note the defendant in default [r.11.01(2)].

2. — What Is The Small Claims Court?

In Ontario, the Division Courts' name was changed to the Small Claims Court, with the enactment of the *Small Claims Court Act*, R.S.O. 1970, c. 439. This Act empowered the province to appoint full-time judges to hear disputes. The federally-appointed County and District Court Judges continued to adjudicate nominal small claims. However, the *Small Claims Court Act* provided that County and District Court Judges could appoint part-time deputy judges who had to be lawyers.

By 1977 the jurisdiction of the Small Claims Court had increased to $1,000.

In 1979, the Small Claims Court in Toronto became a division of the Provincial Court. Initially established on a three-year trial basis, it was called the *Provincial Court (Civil Division)*, and was presided over by full-time, provincially appointed judges with the status and terms of office of Provincial Court Judges. The Court was continued on a permanent basis in 1982. It applied only to Metropolitan Toronto and had the jurisdiction up to $3,000. Elsewhere in the province the small claims jurisdiction remained at the $1,000.

In 1984, the Provincial Court (Civil Division) and the Small Claims Court were amalgamated under the revision of Ontario's *Courts of Justice Act*. In 1985, all Small Claims Courts became Provincial Courts (Civil Division). The Court in Toronto retained a jurisdiction at $1,000. Deputy Judges could hear claims up to $1,000. Only full-time Provincial Court Judges could hear claims between $1,000 and $3,000.

In 1990, major changes were made to the structure of the courts in Ontario. The former High Court of Justice and the District Court were merged to create one superior trial court for the province, and the new Court was regionalized. These changes also affected the Small Claims Court, which became a branch of the General Division. The names of the Ontario Court (General Division) and the Ontario Court (Provincial Division) were changed to the Superior Court of Justice and the Ontario Court of Justice, repectively, as of April 19, 1999. For further information concerning court name changes, please see page xi.

The Small Claims Court consists of the Chief Justice of the Superior Court of Justice, and such other Superior Court of Justice Judges as the Chief Justice may designate from time to time. All Superior Court of Justice Judges have jurisdiction to be Small Claims Court Judges.

Parties often represent themselves in Small Claims Court proceedings. Alternatively, they may be represented by counsel or by a representative. The Small Claims Court has the jurisdiction to bar a representative, who is not a solicitor, from the proceedings if the court finds that the paralegal is not properly competent to represent the party, or if the representative does not comply with the duties and responsibilities of an advocate.

The Small Claims Court is not a building or a courtroom, but a special procedure, established by provincial statute, that simplifies the court process for a specific monetary range of small civil disputes. In his seminal work, *Justice and the Poor*, published in 1909, Reginald Heber Smith concluded that "the splendid thing" about this court is "it does Justice where before there was no Justice at all." In provinces that have "special" small claims procedures, the Small Claims Court is a division or a part of an existing lower court of general jurisdiction. The maximum dollar amount varies from province to province.

The Small Claims Court is an informal, convenient and inexpensive forum for settling disputes and the collection of debts. The monetary jurisdiction of the court is $25,000 exclusive of interest and costs. You may sue for any cause not otherwise prohibited by law. Some examples are arrears of rent; unpaid accounts for services rendered or goods sold and delivered; NSF cheques; damage to property; failure to repay a loan; breach of contract; failure to pay for goods bought on credit; refund of a deposit and recovery of personal property in someone else's possession. A final decision in favour of a party is called a judgment. An unpaid judgment can be enforced through the court by seizure and sale of goods or property; attachment of monies owing to the debtor from a third party such as wages, a bank account or money owing on a contract; and where no information is available to assist in collection the debtor, by way of a notice of examination, may be examined as to his or her assets and ability to pay the judgment.

3. — How Do Small Claims Courts Differ From Other Courts?

Small Claims Courts originated in response to a perception that the complex and technical regular civil procedure made it virtually impossible for wage earners and small businessmen to use the court system to collect wages or accounts which they were owed. The basic problem was perceived to be caused by cumbersome formal civil court procedures that resulted in unreasonable delay and expense, since a lawyer was a virtual necessity to enable litigants to find their way through the complex procedural requirements. The primary aim was to reduce delay by simplifying the court process by reducing the need for litigants to be represented by a lawyer.

While the adversary process was retained, in the sense that each side to a dispute was responsible for presenting the arguments and facts in its favour, it was envisioned that the judge in a small claims proceeding would play an active role at trial — assisting litigants in bringing out relevant facts and clarifying the legal issues involved. Trial procedures and rules of evidence were to be "informal" and were left largely to the discretion of the trial judge. Generally, a small claims judgment was still required to accord to the rules of substantive law, although in some jurisdictions the small claims judge was directed, in addition, to do "substantial justice" between the parties.

The crux of the small claims procedure is informality and simplicity, in the sense that little paperwork is required beyond a brief initial claim commencing the action. Formal rules of trial procedure and rules of evidence are often waived. In some jurisdictions, no formal answer is required of the defendant beyond appearing in court on the trial date to explain his or her side of the case.

Small claims are defined as civil claims that can be satisfied by money damages below a specified dollar amount.

Over the years, a number of goals have been identified for the small claims process. Early reformers emphasized providing accessibility to the machinery of law for all classes — specifically, working and tradespeople. Since the primary problem with existing civil procedure was seen to be its complexity with resulting delay and expense, early goals were simplicity, speed and low cost. By simplifying the process of adjudication, early reformers also hoped to maximize self-representation by litigants. Small claims decisions were intended to be "fair," in that judges were required to arrive at even-handed decisions by applying the regular substantive law to the facts of a case.

Generally, all Small Claims Courts share the basic characteristics of informal adjudication set out in the proceeding section: most procedural steps and paperwork are eliminated, and informal rules of procedure and informal rules of evidence are often used at trial. Small claims jurisdiction is almost always limited to a specified monetary range of civil claims that can be satisfied in money damages. Beyond these common features, however, several other procedural features have evolved as different paths of moving closer to the goals of the small claims process.

4. — The Role of the Clerk

An important development in the small claims process is using Small Claims Court clerks to assist litigants in filing (such as filling out a claims form) and to provide information on what types of proof will be needed at trial, or when supporting witnesses may be required and how to subpoena them. Some courts presently permit court clerks to give quasi-legal advice to litigants, such as how to determine the correct defendant, how to sue business defendants, and so on.

Small Claims Courts are organized administratively around the small claims clerk's office. The Small Claims Manual of Administration defines the clerk's role as follows:

> The clerk has a more responsible role in the Small Claims Court than in other courts. As well as filing, recording and issuing processes, the clerk should endeavour to assist the public through the court process. This does not mean giving out legal advice. It does mean explaining procedures, advising as to correct procedures and assisting the public competently and efficiently. The clerk must remember that he or she is not the judge. It is not the clerk's role to reject documents that may differ from the procedure set out in the manual. However, in some specific cases, the clerk has a quasi-judicial as well as a clerical role. In these particular instances, the clerk has a duty to refuse to sign a default judgment where there is non-compliance with the rules of the court. For example, a clerk may be asked to sign a default judgment where there is some question as to whether or not the claim was entered in the proper court. If the clerk is in some doubt, the matter should be referred to a judge.

In some courts a clerk will also sit in the courtroom with a judge to call the calendar of cases, pass case files to the judge as each case is called, and record the judgments. In some courts, court clerks issue default judgments. Clerk's office staffing can range from one to a dozen or more, depending on the volume of cases that a particular court handles.

The clerk's office in each Small Claims Court provides some assistance to litigants in the form of information about how to file a claim, the cost of filing, how long it would take to reach trial, evidence needed for trial, and the collection of judgments. Providing information and assistance within the court process is not unique, for court clerks have been providing this service to lawyers since the beginnings of our justice system. Any student or lawyer who is unsure about a particular step in the procedural paperwork of litigation can rely on a court clerk to provide help on time limits for filing, necessary forms, information on who must be served and by when, and so forth. Thus, the advice to litigants provided in Small Claims Court is unique only in that it is provided to non-lawyers as well as to lawyers, and that it may extend in some cases to legal or evidentiary aspects of preparing a case that have traditionally been under the exclusive purview of lawyers.

With few exceptions, clerks are very knowledgeable about the small claims process and have accumulated a substantial amount of training, either formally or on the job. Providing first class in-court assistance to lay persons requires patience, training and the undivided attention of the staff — in other words, specialization.

One aspect of legal advice to litigants deserves mention: case screening, or giving litigants some idea of whether they have a good cause of action. As a general rule court clerks are hesitant to discourage filings, even if they feel they are clearly groundless, because of the unauthorized practice of law.

When a claim is filed, the clerk examines it to determine

1. if it is within the jurisdiction of the court where the cause of action arose;

2. when the action took place;

3. that there are sufficient copies of all documents attached or filed; and

4. if the plaintiff is suing the correct person, although legal advice as such is not given.

The clerk must ensure that documents filed with the court comply with the rules, that notices of any proceeding are issued and served upon any person entitled to same and that monies received by the court are promptly disbursed. The clerk must be prepared to explain the rules of the court to any party requiring assistance.

An action shall be commenced by filing a claim together a copy.

In the case of company, the proper name of the company, whether a proprietorship, partnership or limited company, should be set out. The plaintiff should file his or her claim with proper given names and not initials.

Where a claim is based in whole or in part on a document, a copy of the document shall be attached to each copy of the claim. If the document cannot be produced, the claim shall state the reason why it has not been attached.

If you wish pre-judgment interest you must claim it, unlike post-judgment interest. Section 128 of the *Courts of Justice Act* provides for pre-judgment interest for the payment of money at the pre-judgment interest rate calculated from the date the cause of action arose to the date of the order. This applies to causes of action arising after October 23, 1989. If you have a contract which provides for interest at a rate higher than that set out under section 128 or 129, then pursuant to section 130, the court may exercise its discretion and award you interest at the higher rate. Where a plaintiff is claiming interest based on a contract, etc., the clerk will ensure that a copy of the document outlining the interest rate is filed with the claim. In the case of an unrepresented litigant, the clerk will normally assist in determining the amount of interest.

Once the claim has been prepared and the required issuing fee has been paid, the clerk will issue the claim by dating, signing and sealing it and assigning a court number. The plaintiff will be advised of the normal waiting period which will follow to permit service of the claim and filing of a defence. The plaintiff need do nothing until further written advice is received from the court. That does not mean you should not phone the court and inquire if there has been a long delay.

The clerk will check the certificate or affidavit of service to ensure that the claim has been served properly before permitting the action to proceed further. Where the claim is not served within a six month period, the party issuing the claim should ask to have the claim renewed before re-service is attempted. The claim may be renewed even after six months have elapsed.

If no defence has been entered by the defendant, the clerk will enter judgment for claim, costs and pre-judgment interest, provided the claim is for a liquidated amount. The solicitor, representative or plaintiff will prepare a notice of judgment and the clerk will sign them. The plaintiff should then attend at the court office to commence enforcement proceedings. If the plaintiff's claim is for damages, or a non-liquidated claim, the plaintiff must ask the clerk to note the defendant in default and will issue a notice of trial only to the plaintiff, so that the plaintiff's damages might be proven.

Where a defendant admits liability for all or part of the plaintiff's claim in the defence, the defendant may request a hearing to arrange terms of payment. The clerk will then list the matter for a hearing before the referee or any other person designated by the court. If the defendant fails to appear at the hearing and the plaintiff appears, judgment may be entered by the clerk, who will forward notices of judgment to both the plaintiff and defendant. The case may also be adjourned. Where an order for payment has been made and the defendant defaults, judgment may be entered by the clerk upon the filing of an affidavit swearing to the default. As long as the defendant abides by the order for payment, judgment may not be signed by the clerk.

Any party may also request a pre-trial by filing a request. The clerk will forward the request to a judge and notify the party requesting same of the outcome. The clerk may advise the parties of any documents, etc. which should be brought to the pre-trial hearing.

A summons to witness must be personally served and cannot be left with an adult at the person's place or residence. Any requests for a summons to witness are handled promptly.

With the exception of a Writ of Seizure and Sale of Land, any enforcement proceedings should be commenced in the territorial division in whose jurisdiction the defendant resides or carries on business. Unless specifically requested, there is no stay of proceedings after judgment. This applies to judgments given in court as well as default judgments signed by the clerk.

Post judgment interest flows with any judgment unless otherwise ordered by the judge. However, the *Courts of Justice Act* provides that interest shall not be awarded where interest is payable by a right other than under this section (that is, where a promissory note stipulates an annual percentage rate of, for example, 24 per cent, the plaintiff may be entitled to post judgment interest at this rate).

Certificates of Judgment are used to transfer judgments from one territorial Small Claims Court to another. A request, together with a written statement in support, must be filed with the clerk in whose jurisdiction the judgment is registered along with the required fee. The plaintiff must now take the necessary steps to forward the certificates. The party requesting the transfer may ask the clerk to include enforcement instructions with the certificate or, in the alternative, may forward them directly to the receiving court.

Any enforcement proceedings will be commenced *only* at the request of the judgment creditor.

Where a party commences an action for the return of personal property and desires to have the property in question held by the court pending disposition of the claim, he may have the claim issued and commence an *ex parte* notice of motion for a writ of delivery along with the original claim to the bailiff who will seize the property and effect service of the claim. The property will remain with the bailiff pending on order of the court for its release. Where the court has previously ordered the return of personal property and the order is not complied with, the party in whose favour the order was made may file a request for a writ of delivery along with an affidavit stating that the property has not been delivered. If the property cannot be found or delivered, the creditor or his or her representative may proceed by way of a notice of motion and supporting affidavit for an order to seize other personal property of the debtor.

A writ of seizure and sale of personal property is commenced by affidavit and payment of the proper fees. The writ must set out the amount of judgment, any subsequent costs and/or credits, plus post judgment interest to the date of issuing of the writ of seizure. The bailiff is responsible for the enforcement of same and any monies realized will be returned to the clerk for subsequent distribution to the judgment creditor. The writ of seizure and sale of personal property remains in force for six months. The request for renewal may be made by Motion.

The writ of seizure and sale of land may be issued in the court where the judgment is situated regardless of where the defendant resides or carries on business. It is commenced by filing a written request with the clerk who will prepare the writ of seizure and sale of land and deliver same to the judgment credit for filing with the proper sheriff. The writ must set out the amount of judgment, subsequent costs and/or credits plus the applicable post judgment interest rate.

A notice of garnishment is commenced by filing with the clerk an affidavit setting out the particulars of the judgment as well as the names and addresses of the persons to whom the notice of garnishment are to be directed. The garnishment must be issued in the division where the defendant resides or carries on business regardless of where the garnishee company is situated. Any funds realized from the notice of garnishment will be promptly paid out to the judgment creditor unless one of the parties has requested a hearing. Where notices of garnishment have been issued at the request of more than one creditor, the clerk will divide the monies equally among the creditors who have filed a notice of garnishment. Garnishments remain in force for a period of twelve months or until the outstanding amount shown on the notice of garnishment is paid, whichever comes first. If the judgment is not satisfied within the twelve month period, the judgment creditor must file a fresh affidavit with the clerk stating the current outstanding balance. Where a request is received to place the matter on the list, the clerk will forward notices of trial to all parties named in the garnishment by registered mail. Monies standing in court will be held by the clerk, pending a judge's order.

A judgment debtor who has two or more outstanding orders for the payment of money against him/her may apply for a consolidation order. The application is commenced by notice of motion and supporting affidavit which should contain the following information:

1. the names and addresses of creditors who have obtained an order for payment of monies;

2. the amount owing to each creditor; and

3. the defendant's current financial position, including details of the defendant's income and expenses.

The defendant must serve each creditor with a copy of the notice of motion and affidavit at least seven days prior to the hearing if served personally or twelve days if served by mail. Service may be made by mail or by personal service or an alternative to personal service. Monies paid into court pursuant to a consolidation order will be distributed every six months and will be divided equally among the creditors rather than on a pro-rated basis, as was the case under previous rules. Where a defendant falls in arrears for a period of 21 days, the clerk will terminate the consolidation order and notify the creditors in writing. A further consolidation order cannot issue for one year from the date of termination.

An examination of a debtor must issue out of the division in which the defendant resides or carries on business and is commenced by the filing of an affidavit containing the following information:

1. amount of judgment, including pre-judgment interest;

2. any subsequent costs and/or credits; and

3. the amount of post-judgment interest.

Examination is served by the plaintiff with the date and time. The clerk will notify the judgment creditor of the date and time of the hearing. If a person to whom a notice of examination has been served fails to attend court in response to a notice of examination or attends and refuses to answer questions, the court may order the person to attend. If the judge permits the creditor and/or his representative to attend the hearing, the clerk will forward a notice of hearing. As this practice may not be followed in all jurisdictions, the clerk should be consulted. If the person appears, the judge may order that the warrant be enforced, order the debtor to appear at a future examination hearing or make an order as to payment. If the judge orders a warrant of committal, the clerk will direct it to the police who are responsible for its enforcement. The creditor or his/her representative should maintain contact with the clerk to determine the progress of the warrant as the police do not provide status reports to parties. Where applicable, a Motion may be served by fax before 5:00 p.m.

5. — What Does it Cost to Sue or Defend a Case?

One important goal of the small claims process is to provide an inexpensive mechanism for resolving disputes.

One important measure of the real cost of the case to a person involved in a small claims action is the total cost as a percentage of claim amount, since that ratio helps decide whether the decision to pursue a case is economically justified. At the very least, if plaintiffs stand to incur costs of as much or more than they could win, then the Small Claims Court does not serve its purpose.

It is a reasonable assumption that the bulk of lost wages reported primarily results from having to go to court to appear for trial. The reduction of waiting time on trial day is thus an important target for reducing the costs to litigants in pursuing a small claims case. Evening small claims sessions provide another means of reducing lost wages for many litigants.

6. — Do I Need a Lawyer?

A major component of costs, legal fees, can be reduced in several ways. First, lawyers are certainly not mandatory in these courts and in some jurisdictions not allowed to appear. Second, increased court-provided assistance in trial preparation to both plaintiffs and defendants could make formal legal assistance less necessary. Better court-provided pre-trial advice and devices available to judges at trial can help compensate for poor pre-trial preparation by unrepresented litigants.

The fact that a small claim is simply filed may often result in settlement of the dispute or payment of a claim before the scheduled trial date. To the extent that this happens, this is also a solution produced by using the small claims process. In those cases, then, the small claims process produces a resolution for just the cost of processing the filing of a claim and having it served.

Help

Court staff cannot provide legal advice. They also cannot fill out forms. A lawyer may be in the best position to advise someone about their legal rights and responsibilities. Consultations with a lawyer are private and confidential.

The Law Referral Service operated by the Law Society of Upper Canada charges $6 for each telephone call to use this service.

For information on how to search a corporation or registered business name, you may contact the Companies Helpline, Ministry of Government Services. Please note that there is a fee for the search and the search will not be conducted over the phone. The Helpline can be reached at (416) 314-8880 or toll-free in Ontario at 1-800-361-3223. Before requesting a search, you must have the exact name of the corporation or the Ontario corporation number, or the exact name of the registered business.

If you need to find a lawyer, you can call the Lawyer Referral Service of the Law Society at 1-900-565-4577. A LRS member lawyer will provide up to 30 minutes of free consultation. A $6.00 chare is billed to your phone bill. See also Legalline at *www.Legalline.ca*. From 416-314-8880 to 416-326-8555 (www.gov.on.ca/MGS).

7. — Fee Waivers

Generally, you must pay a fee to start a civil or small claims court proceeding. There are also fees for other steps, such as filing documents and scheduling a hearing.

If you cannot afford to pay court or enforcement fees, you may request a fee waiver.

For more information on fee waiver, you should contact your local court or enforcement office. A listing of the court addresses can be found on the Ministry website at: www.attorneygeneral.jus.gov.on.ca.

Request to Court

If you do not qualify for a fee waiver under the financial eligibility criteria, and feel that your fees should be waived, you may make a request to the court by completing the required form and attaching the necessary documents. The court will review your request and decide whether you should get fee waiver even though you do not qualify under the financial eligibility criteria.

Complete a Fee Waiver Request to Court form and attach required documents, if:

- You know you do not qualify for fee waiver under the financial eligibility criteria, or
- You have submitted a Fee Waiver Request to Registrar, Clerk or Sheriff that has not been approved.

If you are eligible for fee waiver, you will be given a Fee Waiver Certificate. To get a fee waived, you must present the Fee Waiver Certificate to court or enforcement office staff when a fee is payable. Staff cannot waive your fees if you have not received a fee waiver certificate.

The Fee Waiver Certificate is valid to waive fees payable from the day you get it through the rest of your case, including enforcement. However, if your case is appealed, you need to request a new fee waiver from the appeal court.

If you are not eligible for fee waiver, you may request fee waiver again if your financial situation changes.

What are the Financial Eligibility Criteria?

The financial eligibility criteria are:

1. Your primary source of household income is one or more of:
   - income assistance from Ontario Works;
   - income support from the Ontario Disability Support Program;
   - *Family Benefits Act* allowance;
   - Old Age Security Pension together with the Guaranteed Income Supplement;
   - War Veterans Allowance; or
   - Canada Pension Plan benefits.

OR

2. Your household income and assets are below the following cut-offs:

Number of people in household	Gross monthly household income
1	$1,500
2	$2,250
3	$2,583
4	$3,083
5 or more	$3,583
Household liquid assets:	$1,500
Household net worth:	$6,000

The waivers are a result of amendments to the *Administration of Justice Act* and Ontario Regulation 2/05, and took effect Jan. 28, 2005.

The fee waiver does apply to: fees for court reporters, court monitors' fees, official examiners' fees, fees payable by parties to witnesses, and mediators' fees for civil mediation not criminal or quasi-criminal fees.

Those covered by Legal Aid Ontario or who have a contingency-fee agreement with their lawyers are exempt from the fee waiver.

8. — Where Do You Find Your Local Court?

To use a court, you must first find that court.

Once a dispute arises, many people who have heard of the Small Claims Court need to know where the court is and what is required to file a claim. A common response is to look in the phone book under "S" for "Small Claims Court." The results are not always encouraging.

Traditionally, courts have not paid much attention to the convenience of the public which uses them. Courts just exist, and it is up to the public to seek them out. (See List of Courts for Ontario)

In the conventional civil court process several important steps in initiating a law suit are generally left to counsel: advising on whether a dispute is worth pursuing in court, filing the papers initiating the action, and identifying and mustering both evidence and witnesses necessary to prove (or to defend) a claim. Small Claims Court is presently unique in that it is the only area of the judicial system in which it is assumed that a significant number of people will attempt to pursue a claim themselves and in which the judicial system recognizes an obligation to assist ligitants.

Small Claims Court Offices:

Ottawa	613-239-1560	*www.ontariocourts.on.ca*
St. Catharines	905-988-6200	*www.ontariocourts.on.ca*
Toronto	416-326-3554	*www.ontariocourts.on.ca*
Windsor	519-973-6620	*www.ontariocourts.on.ca*

The jurisdiction of the Small Claims Court is $10,000 until January 1, 2010 when it increases to $25,000.

9. — Who Can Sue and Be Sued?

Who Can Sue and Be Sued?

Who has access to the courts in Ontario? Who can be sued in an Ontario court?

- All adults, regardless of their citizenship.

- Minors, who require a litigation guardian if the claim is for a sum exceeding $500

- Other parties under disability, who require a litigation guardian in all cases

- Partnerships and sole proprietorships

- Corporations, even if they are incorporated outside of Ontario. (Remember that the law treats corporations as legal persons for some purposes.)

- Trade unions.

Unincorporated organizations, such as clubs, amateur teams, and community groups, are generally not recognized in law as "persons." Thus, these organizations cannot sue or be sued as an organization. If you want to sue a club, you must sue individual members of the club. If members of a club wish to pursue legal action against another party, they must bring their legal action as individuals. They cannot sue in the name of the club or organization. Trade unions, however, are an important exception to this rule.

Historically, it was not possible to sue the government. However, legislation has now made it possible to sue the government under some circumstances.

10. — What Cases will the Small Claims Court Hear?

The most common types of claims are actions for debt recovery or damages. A debt is a sum of money due by certain and expressed agreement where the amount is fixed and specified and does not depend on any subsequent valuation by the court to settle it. Examples of debt actions include those for services rendered, goods sold and delivered, promissory notes or dishonoured cheques. Damage claims are those for loss, injury or deterioration caused by the negligence, design or accident of one person to another, the amount claimed being a sum which must be evaluated by the court.

The following can be used as a framework for most particulars of a claim:

1. cause of action;

2. particulars of debt or damage;

3. the plaintiff claims against the defendant for:

    (a) damages (or debt) in the amount of $..........;

    (b) costs of this action;

    (c) pre-judgment interest; or

    (d) such further and other relief as to this Honourable Court may seem just; and

4. the cause of action arose within the jurisdiction of this Honourable Court; (or) the defendant resides within the jurisdiction of this Honourable Court; (or) the defendant carries on business within the jurisdiction of this Honourable Court.

Examples of particulars of claim:

1. An Action for Debt — Monies Owing for Goods Sold or Services Rendered

    The Plaintiff's claim is for debt in the amount of $.......... being the amount due and owing to the Plaintiff on an account for (or being the price of, as the case may be) goods sold and delivered (or services rendered) by the Plaintiff to the Defendant at his request.

The goods sold and delivered (or the services rendered) were: (a description of the goods or services) and were delivered (or rendered) on or about the .... day of .... A.D. 2011, at .... in the .... of ...., Province of Ontario.

2. Motor Vehicle Accident

(a) The Plaintiff's claim is for the sum of $.........., for damages sustained by the Plaintiff resulting from a motor vehicle collision on or about the .... day of .... A.D. 2013, at or near the intersection of .... and .... in the .... of ...., Province of Ontario, when a motor vehicle owned by .... and negligently operated by .... with the consent of the Defendant .... struck the Plaintiff's vehicle causing damages in the above amount.

If the Plaintiff's claim is only for the deductible of his insurance coverage, the above claim can be reworded as:

(b) The Plaintiff's claim is for damages in the amount of $ (deductible) being the amount unpaid of damages sustained ... etc. as above — causing damages of $ (whole amount).

NOTE: The *Insurance Act*, R.S.O. 1990, c. I.8 states in part:

> 263 (5)(a) an insured has no right of action against any person involved in the incident other than the insured's insurer for damages to the insured's automobile or its contents or for loss of use;
>
> . . . . .
>
> 281 (2) No person may bring a proceeding in any court, refer the issues in dispute to an arbitrator under section 282 or agree to submit an issue for arbitration in accordance with the *Arbitration Act, 1991* unless mediation was sought, mediation failed and, if the issues in dispute were referred for an evaluation under section 280.1, the report of the person who performed the evaluation has been given to the parties.
>
> 1996, c. 21, s. 37.

3. Improper Repairs

The Plaintiff's claim is for damages in the amount of $......... sustained by the Plaintiff by reason of the defendant's breach of contract to repair the Plaintiff's motor vehicle. The said contract was an oral contract made between the Plaintiff and the Defendant on or about the .... day of ...., 2013. The Defendant breached the said contract by failing to repair the said vehicle in a proper and workmanlike manner. The repairs were to take place at the Defendant's place of business at .... Alternatively, the Plaintiff claims the said amount as damages sustained by reason of the Defendant's negligent repair of the Plaintiff's motor vehicle, as aforesaid. The negligent repair occurred at the Defendant's place of business at .... on or about ....

4. Dishonoured Cheques

The Plaintiff's claim is for debt in the amount of $......... being the amount of a cheque drawn by the Defendant on the (name and Branch of bank), dated the .... day of .... A.D. 2013, payable to the Plaintiff and delivered by the .... day of .... A.D. 2011, which cheque was dishonoured by the bank and returned to the Plaintiff. The Defendant has been advised of the said dishonour and has neglected and/or refused to rectify same.

5. Promissory Note

The Plaintiff's claim is for a debt in the amount $......... being the amount due on a promissory note signed by the Defendant and delivered to the plaintiff on the .... day of .... A.D. 2013 and made payable to the Plaintiff on the .... day of ....

A.D. 2013. The Plaintiff has demanded payment of the said debt and the defendant has refused and/or neglected to pay.

Note: The best way to determine jurisdiction in a promissory note claim is to file the claim within the jurisdiction in which the defendant resides. If it is not filed within this jurisdiction, there may be some problem if the defendant files a defence.

6. Wrongful Seizure of a Motor Vehicle

The Plaintiff's claim is for damages of $.........., for the wrongful seizure and detention of the Plaintiff's motor vehicle, a .... The Defendant (name of Bailiff) wrongfully seized the Plaintiff's motor vehicle on or about the .... day of .... A.D. 2013 at .... in the Province of Ontario. In so seizing the Defendant (Bailiff) purported to act under instruction from the Defendant (name of workman).

7. *Repair and Storage Liens Act*

A bailiff may act as a bailiff in a county other than the county for which he or she is appointed. See the *Bailiffs Act*, R.S.O. 1990, c. B.2, s. 4; 2000, c. 26, Sched. B, s. 1(1).

Application Under Section 23 of the *Repair and Storage Liens Act* ("RSLA") in the Small Claims Court — Form 12

Subsection 23(1) of the RSLA allows any person to apply to the court for a determination of the rights of the parties where questions arise as to:

(a) the seizure of the article under Part II of the RSLA (Non-possessory Liens), or any other right to seizure in respect of the article;

(b) the sale of the article under Part III of the RSLA (Redemption, Sale or Other Disposition);

(c) the distribution of the proceeds of sale under Part III of the RSLA;

(d) the amount of a lien or the right of any person to a lien; and

(e) any other matter arising out of the application of the RSLA.

The section gives the court the authority to make such order as it considers necessary to give effect to the rights of the parties. The only limitation provided in section 23 is in subsection (2), which prohibits an application under section 23(1)(d) where an application has been made under section 24.

Where a party wishes to commence an application under section 23 of the RSLA, *a party will*:

1. Provide at least two copies of a completed Application Under Section 23 Small Claims Court, Form 12 (one copy for the court file and ensure the applicant inserts the court file number on all other copies.)

2. Pay the appropriate filing fee in accordance with the SCC Schedule of Fees for filing an RSLA Application.

Note: If the respondent is an incorporated company, the name of the company must be exact. The applicant may obtain this information from the Companies Helpline, Ministry of Government Services, Companies and Personal Property Security Branch at 416-314-8880, or toll free at 1-800-361-3223.

24. (1) Return of article when dispute — Where a claimant claims a lien against an article under Part I (Possessory Liens) and refuses to surrender possession of the article to its owner or any other person entitled to it and where one of the circumstances described in subsection (1.2) exists, the owner or other person lawfully entitled to the article may apply to the court in accordance with the procedure set out in this section to have the dispute resolved and the article returned.

2000, c. 26, Sched. B, s. 18(2).

(1.1) **Same, non-possessory lien** — Where a claimant claims a lien against an article under Part II (Non-Possessory Liens), where the person who has possession of the article refuses to surrender it to its owner or any other person entitled to it and where one of the circumstances described in subsection (1.2) exists, the owner or other person lawfully entitled to the article may apply to the court in accordance with the procedure set out in this section to have the dispute resolved and the article returned.

2000, c. 26, Sched. B, s. 18(2).

. . . . .

25. An application under this Part may be brought in any court of appropriate monetary jurisdiction.

R.S.O. 1990, c. R.25, s. 25.

The Act deals with the availability of a lien when there is a sub-bailment. Suppose that an owner leaves an article for repair with A. A delivers the article to B who carries out the repairs. The Act provides that A is deemed to have performed the services and may claim a lien, and that B does not have a lien. However, if A agreed to act as agent for the owner in forwarding the article to an identified repairer or storer, then B may claim a lien.

The Small Claims Court's main involvement is in respect to "Part IV — Dispute Resolution" (see section 23) which is a procedure established to allow persons to recover possession of their articles when there is a dispute as to the price of the repair, storage or repair and storage services. In the past a person usually had to pay the repairer's or storer's bill in full in order to obtain the release of their articles and then commence civil court proceedings for recovery of all or part of the monies which they felt was overpaid. Section 24 provides an alternate dispute resolution process.

Subsecs. (1) and (2) repealed and the following substituted 2000, c. 26, Sched. B, s. 18(2):

(1) Where a claimant claims a lien against an article under Part I (Possessory Liens) and refuses to surrender possession of the article to its owner or other person entitled to it and where one of the circumstances described in subsection (1.2) exists, the owner or other person lawfully entitled to the article may apply to the court in accordance with the procedure set out in this section to have the dispute resolved and the article returned.

(1.1) Where a claimant claims a lien against an article under Part II (Non-Possessory Liens), where the person who has possession of the article refuses to surrender it to its owner or any other person entitled to it and where one of the circumstances described in subsection (1.2) exists, the owner or other person lawfully entitled to the article may apply to the court in accordance with the procedure set out in this section to have the dispute resolved and the article returned.

(1.2) Subsection (1) or (1.1) applies if there is,

(a) a dispute concerning the amount of the lien of the lien claimant including any question relating to the quality of the repair, storage or storage and repair;

(b) in the case of a repair, a dispute concerning the amount of work that was authorized to be made to the article; or

(c) a dispute concerning the right of the lien claimant to retain possession of the article.

(2) The application shall name, as the respondents, the lien claimant and, in the case of a non-possessory lien, the person who has possession of the article.

The application and initial certificate is based on the monetary jurisdiction of the court. Unlike a writ of delivery, the outstanding amount of the repairer's or storer's bill and not the value of the article determines monetary jurisdiction. The application may be commenced in the territorial jurisdiction of either the respondent's address or the address where the repairs or storage took place.

8. A Claim for Property Damage under the *Parental Responsibility Act, 2000*

The *Parental Responsibility Act, 2000* deals with claims for damages against a parent of a child (under 18 years of age) who intentionally takes, damages or destroys property.

The person bringing this kind of claim to court (the plaintiff) must prove that a child caused the property damage suffered, that the defendant is the child's parent, and prove the loss suffered.

The Act provides that the parent (defendant) is liable for the damages, unless the parent can prove that the child's activity that caused the loss was not intentional; or that the parent exercised reasonable supervision over the child and made reasonable efforts to prevent or discourage the child from engaging in the kind of activity that resulted in the loss or damage.

O. Reg. 212/03 under the *Parental Responsibility Act, 2000*, which makes changes to Form 2 of the *Parental Responsibility Act, 2000* came into force effective May 22, 2003. The changes were due to the implementation of the *Youth Criminal Justice Act*, which came into force on April 1, 2003.

9.

(a) Claim for Rent Arrears

The Plaintiff's claim is against the Defendant for debt in the sum of $.......... as the sum owed by the Defendant to the Plaintiff for rent on residential premises located at .... in the .... of ...., Province of Ontario, for the period of .... to .... A.D. 2013. The said rent was due and payable pursuant to a (verbal or written) agreement between the Plaintiff and the Defendant for the rental of the said premises made on or about the .... day of .... A.D. 2013 at .... The Plaintiff has demanded payment of the said sum of $.......... from the Defendant, however, the Defendant has refused and/or neglected to pay same and the whole of the said sum of $.......... remains justly due and owing to the Plaintiff by the Defendant.

(b) Claim for Damages to Rental Premises

The Plaintiff's claim is for damages in the sum of $.........., for damages to (residental or commercial) rental premises at ...., in the .... of ...., Province of Ontario, due to the Defendant's wilful, default or negligent conduct or that of a person permitted on the premises by him, between the period of .... and .... A.D. 2013 being the Defendant's tenancy period. The contract between the Plaintiff and the Defendant for the Defendant's rental of the mentioned premises was a (verbal/written) contract made on or about the .... day of .... A.D. 2013 at ...., in the Judicial District of York.

10. Abandoning the Excess

The following statement may be added after the particulars:

The Plaintiff has agreed to reduce his claim to $25,000 to bring it within the jurisdiction of this Honourable Court.

11. — How Do I Take Action?

If you consider that you have a claim against someone, attempt to settle the dispute before resorting to court action.

To initiate an action, you have to file a claim in the manner previously set out and thereafter describe your claim.

The style of cause refers to the way the plaintiff and defendant are named on the claim. It is important to determine the correct legal description of both since the action may be disputed if parties are named incorrectly.

When a claim is filed, the clerk will examine the claim to ensure that the court has both territorial and monetary jurisdiction to issue the claim, that there are sufficient copies of all documents attached or filed and that the party is sure he or she is suing the right person. The clerk has no right to refuse to accept and issue a claim for any reason as the refusal to accept a claim could deprive a party of a right to which the court might subsequently hold he or she is entitled. These are judicial functions which are beyond the authority of a clerk.

Types of Claims

The most common type of claim processed in the Small Claims Court is a claim for a debt up to $25,000. A liquidated claim is a sum of money owed by an express agreement where the amount owed is fixed and specified and does not require any valuation by the court.

Examples of liquidated claims are the following:

1. unpaid accounts for goods supplied or sold and delivered;
2. services;
3. unpaid loans;
4. rent; and
5. NSF cheques.

A claim where the amount in dispute is not fixed and specified is known as an unliquidated claim (damages). This type of claim must be put before the court to determine the amount a plaintiff is entitled to receive.

Examples of unliquidated claims (damages) are the following:

1. property damage;
2. clothes damaged by a dry cleaner;
3. personal injury; and
4. breach of contract.

If the claim is based on a document, you must ensure that sufficient copies of the document are filed (see subrule 7.01(2)). If a document cannot be produced, you should include in the particulars of the claim the reasons it cannot be produced. The appropriate filing fee is set out in Schedule 1 of the Tariff of Fees.

See Rule 7.01(2).

Cases involving some areas of law are dealt with by specialized bodies or are governed by specialized procedures.

- Does your dispute relate the building of a new home? Contact the Ministry of Government Services regarding the *Ontario New Home Warranties Plan Act* at www.gov.on.ca/MGS.
- Does your dispute relate to your lawyer's bill? Assessments of lawyers' bills may be conducted by an assessment officer. You may find further information about this process from the Law Society of Upper Canada at www.lsuc.on.ca.
- Are you having a dispute with your residential landlord or tenant? Contact the Ontario Rental Housing Tribunal regarding your rights and responsibilities under the *Tenant Protection Act* at www.ltb.gov.on.ca.

- Do you have a complaint regarding insurance? Contact the Financial Services Commission of Ontario for information regarding insurance and insurance complaints at www.fsco.gov.on.ca.

- Are you considering declaring bankruptcy or does someone who is declaring bankruptcy owe you money? You can contact the Bankruptcy Branch — Industry Canada at 416-973-6441 or 613-941-2863. See also www.strategiis.ic.gc.ca.

- Do you have a complaint against a private bailiff? The *Bailiff's Act* sets out a procedure for complaints against private bailiffs. Contact the Ministry of Government Services for more information at www.gov.on.ca/MGS.

- Do you have a complaint against a lawyer? Contact the Law Society of Upper Canada at www.lsuc.on.ca.

- Do you have a complaint against a judicial official? Visit the Ontario Courts website for more information at:

    www.ontariocourts.on.ca./ontario_judicial_council/complaint.htm.

12. — Limitation Periods

Limitation periods are the period of time within which an action must be started. Legal claims must be made within a certain period of time or the court will not allow the claim to proceed. In Ontario, the general limitation period is two years from "discovery" of the claim: see ss. 4 & 5 of the *Limitations Act, 2002.*

If the plaintiff fails to start a claim before expiry of the applicable limitation period, the claim may still be pursued but limitation would be a complete defence available to the defendant. If a debtor acknowledges a debt, the acknowledgment re-starts the limitation period and effectively extends the time available for commencement of an action on the balance due.

13. — How Do I Defend Myself?

When you receive a claim, read it carefully. The facts of the claim will tell you who is suing you (you are the defendant) and in which court the action was started. It will also show the amount claimed by the plaintiff and the total amount to be paid. The total amount equals the amount claimed plus the costs paid by the plaintiff for filing and service and may also include interest.

Once you have read the particulars of the claim you may possibly agree that you owe the money. If you have funds to pay, the claim can be paid only by cash, certified cheque or money order. The certified cheque or money order should be made payable to the court. It is unnecessary to go to the court to pay the claim. A certified cheque or money order may be mailed; the address of the court should appear on the bottom of the face of the claim. When you mail the remittance enclose either a copy of the claim or a letter stating the number of the action so the clerk will know where the money is to be applied.

If you admit owing the plaintiff's claim but you do not have funds to pay, you should go to the court of filing and ask to file a defence. This must be done within 20 days after you receive the claim. You can file your defence even after the 20-day period is up, but leave of the court is *now* required. Please refer to new Rule 10 for a more detailed discussion of the Defence Rule and, where service has been by mail, when claims may be filed in some cases up to forty days from the date of mailing. After the defence is filed, the action, upon payment of the appropriate fee, is set for hearing and, at that time, you present your reasons for not being able to pay the debt. The judge or referee *may* grant an order for you to arrange terms of payment. You may also dispute part of the plaintiff's claim and admit the remainder and again seek to arrange terms of payment.

If you fail to make payments in accordance with the schedule, the plaintiff may have default judgment entered. To do so requires an affidavit swearing that you have not made the required payments. After the affidavit is filed, the clerk can sign default judgment and both parties are notified, after which enforcement can be taken. A notice of default judgment (Form 11B) would be mailed to the parties or their representatives.

Where you fail to file a defence within the prescribed time, the clerk will automatically enter default judgment, provided the claim was for a debt or liquidated amount, with proof the claim was served within the territorial jurisdiction. Where the claim is for damages, the clerk may *note* you in default, but *not* sign default judgment. If you filed a defence in respect of part of the claim, default judgment can be signed for the balance and the disputed amount still has to be listed for trial. Notices are then sent out. At the trial, the plaintiff need prove the monetary amount of the claim. This is commonly known as an "assessment."

If you have a valid excuse (illness, vacation, death in family, etc.) as to why you did not file a defence within the prescribed limit, you may bring a motion asking that the default judgment be set aside.

If you believe you do not owe the money claimed, you must file a defence. The defence is filed at the court where the claim was filed. If you file a defence and the case is proved against you, you may render yourself liable for further costs, including the costs of witnesses called to prove the plaintiff's claim. Any claim by you against the plaintiff will be included in the defendant's claim. See subrule 10.03(1) and 10.04(3).

The results of a court action are only binding between the parties to that action. Therefore, if there is some other person who you feel should be wholly or partly responsible for the plaintiff's claim or for any damage caused to you pursuant to the plaintiff's claim, you may want to make sure he or she is a party to this action.

Under Rule 9.03(7) referees or mediators have the authority to make orders as to terms of payment. The process under subrule 9.03 for dealing with defaults in proposals for periodic payments has been modified as of July 1, 2006. Referees can conduct settlement conferences under Rule 13, make consolidation orders under subrule 20.09, and can assist local clerks in assessing disbursements, the latter authority effective July 1, 2006.

Before determining the course of action, a judge will review the pleadings and will order any corrections, additions, etc. that may be required. As this could result in re-service of documents, additional costs and time delays, the importance of proper completion in the first instance becomes apparent.

Some things to keep in mind in preparing your defence are listed below.

1. Do not waste the court's time by disputing things with which you really do not disagree.

2. Check that the correct parties have been named. A mistake in your name in the claim will not usually be an effective defence unless the plaintiff fails to identify you as the person with whom he dealt. However, if you are the president of a limited company and the plaintiff may be suing you personally for a company debt, that is a defence as the plaintiff is suing the wrong party.

3. The amount of the claim should be examined. Some things to check are:

(a) Is the plaintiff seeking compensation for an amount which could have been reduced? A plaintiff must do what is reasonable to keep his damages to a minimum after suffering the initial loss (for example, a landlord usually should attempt to re-rent the premises even if the tenants vacated improperly).

(b) Are similar items of quality of workmanship readily available at lower prices than those being demanded by the plaintiff?

(c) Is the plaintiff claiming an amount which exceeds fair compensation? For example, if old and used property were lost and damaged, the owner cannot ask for an amount equivalent to the market value of new goods.

14. — Bankruptcy

When a trustee in bankruptcy provides written notice to the court to the Small Claims Court of a stay of proceedings against a particular debtor under the *Bankruptcy and Insolvency Act* ("BIA"), the court will assume that all steps in the proceeding against that debtor are stayed unless an order of the Bankruptcy Court provides otherwise. Written notice of the stay may be received by: notice of intention to make a proposal; proposal; consumer proposal; receiving order; or by an assignment in bankruptcy. If a party to the proceedings want to take steps against the debtor, the party should apply to Bankruptcy Court for leave to do so, or for an order that the stay does not apply. If there is a dispute about the stay, the party should take the matter to the to the Bankruptcy Court for resolution.

See in particular, Part IV, Property of the Bankrupt, Stay of Proceedings, section 69 of the *Bankruptcy and Insolvency Act*, R.S.C. 1985, c. B-3.

By virtue of s. 71(2) of the *Bankruptcy and Insolvency Act*, R.S.C. 1985, c. B-3, when a receiving order is made or an assignment filed, a bankrupt ceases to have any capacity to dispose of or otherwise deal with his or her property. Subject to the provisions of the *Bankruptcy and Insolvency Act* and the rights of secured creditors, the bankrupt's property forthwith passes to and vests in the trustee in bankruptcy. It should be noted, however, that the operation of this section may be waived by the trustee (*Heine v. Century 21 Professional Real Estate Services Ltd. (Trustee of)* (1991), 118 A.R. 176 (Alta. Master)). See also section 69.3 of the Act, *Tucker v. Jollimore*, 1978 CarswellNS 37, 29 C.B.R. (N.S.) 198, 34 N.S.R. (2d) 187, 59 A.P.R. 187 (N.S. T.D.), *Neufeld v. Wilson*, [1997] B.C.J. No. 279, 1997 CarswellBC 281, 86 B.C.A.C. 109, 142 W.A.C. 109, 45 C.B.R. (3d) 180 (B.C. C.A.) and *Long Shong Pictures (H.K.) Ltd. v. NTC Entertainment Ltd.*, [2000] F.C.J. No. 1813, 2000 CarswellNat 899, 18 C.B.R. (4th) 233, 6 C.P.R. (4th) 506, 190 F.T.R. 257 (Fed. T.D.).

15. — Do I Need an Interpreter?

The Ministry of the Attorney General through its court interpretation and translation services (416-326-4059 for general inquiry and translation and 416-327-5014 for an interpreter) may provide and pay for a court interpreter for a French language trial in Small Claims Court. The Ministry has two branches that provide written translation services: 1) Court Interpretation and Translation Services; and 2) French Language Services. The Ministry has no legal obligation to provide written translations involving any other language, and therefore does not provide this service. It is up to the parties to have translations involving languages other than English and French done at their own expense. Unless it is considered a Ministry service, translation is the responsibility (legal and financial) of the parties. Bilingual proceedings pursuant to the *Courts of Justice Act* are covered by regulation (*e.g.*, see O. Reg. 53/01, in force June 1, 2001). The following are guidelines developed by the Ministry.

The Ministry of the Attorney General has an extensive list of accredited court interpreters in roughly one hundred languages throughout the province. The Ministry will provide court interpreters in *any* language required in all criminal (including domestic violence) courts and in all Provincial Offences courts, which the Municipalities have not yet taken over jurisdiction. In civil matters, the Ministry provides French/English interpretation only. Those who speak other languages are required to provide their own interpreters in civil cases. The only exception to this are: 1) in Small Claims Court, where the Ministry also provides Sign Language Interpreters; and 2) in Family matters, where child welfare or placement of children are at stake.

No person shall act as an interpreter in any proceeding in which he or she, will appear as counsel, agent, or a witness or has an interest. No person who has been convicted of an indictable offence and is under sentence shall act as an interpreter in any proceeding. The spouse, child, brother, sister, parent or other close relative of an accused, witness, counsel in, or party to a proceeding is excluded from acting as an interpreter in such proceeding, unless the judge after due inquiry authorizes such person to act as interpreter in the proceeding.

Where a person is called upon to act as an interpreter for a friend or acquaintance in a proceeding, the presiding judge shall be advised by the person of the relationship and after due inquiry, if the judge is satisfied that a fair and impartial interpretation will not be rendered, the person shall be excluded from acting as an interpreter in the proceeding. Where the presiding judge was originally satisfied that an interpreter could render a fair and impartial translation, he or she may choose to disqualify that interpreter if it appears that the individual is unable to interpret fairly and impartially. Where a person believes that he or she will have difficulty rendering a fair or impartial interpretation for any reason such as religious or political beliefs, he or she has a duty to state the reason and to decline to act as an interpreter in the proceeding.

Effective September 15th, 2005, court interpreters in Small Claims Court cases will be provided for those who have been given a Fee Waiver Certificate and who indicate the need for an interpreter either themselves or for their witness(es), for all court appearances.

Amendments to the *Administration of Justice Act* Fee Waiver regulation (O. Reg. 2/05) came into effect December 28, 2005.

16. — Settlement Conferences

Rule 13 of the rules of this court provide for the conducting of a settlement conference or hearing. Whether your case will be pretried or not depends on many factors. How much money are you suing for? Is there a clerk or referee in your territorial jurisdiction who hears pre-trials? Has your case been reviewed by a judge or court official to determine whether you should have a pre-trial, since it is not mandatory and you can request a settlement conference?

If you represent yourself or if you are totally unfamiliar with the court process, nothing is more important than a pre-trial hearing. It is not only forced (by a judge or referee) bargaining, which is a contradiction in terms, but if you have, for example, sued the wrong person or not sued someone you should have, if you do not understand the rules of evidence and what is required at trial or if you do not know how to proceed to trial, then these things should be explained to you. Finally, of course, many cases are settled at a pre-trial. (See also Rule 14.)

17. — Building a Better Case, Being Better Prepared

Effective preparation should begin with initial contact with a litigant, either through the intake interview or the assignment of the file (depending on whether you are initiating or defending the action).

The foundation of the evidence available to be marshalled at trial laid by the early gathering and sifting of important details, the preservation of information that assists your case and the early warning of evidence that does not. Having as clear an understanding of the evidence, as early in the game as possible, allows you to be in the best possible position to assess your case, anticipate its weakness, build on its strengths and ensure a more effective interaction with opposing parties. Whether you are bringing or defending an action, proper preparation will ultimately lead to enhancing your skills and both the frequency and quality of your settlements.

In many cases the plaintiff is in the best position to obtain information first and to use it to their advantage. Regardless of which party you represent in a case, early interaction with witnesses and the timely review of available evidence becomes potent ammunition in the hands of skilled counsel to address issues of liability and damages. The party who is best able to marshal their evidence and to clarify their understanding of the case first can often influence both what their opponent should think and what they should think about.

As stated by Sopinka, Houston and Sopinka in *The Trial of an Action* (2nd ed.): "The brilliant orator who is unprepared will seldom prevail over a well-prepared but less articulate adversary."

In an age in which our legal system has increasingly moved towards the encouragement of mediated intervention, it is no surprise that fewer and fewer cases proceed to trial.

It is trite to say that you cannot marshal evidence that you do not have or scrutinize facts that you do not know. It is simply not possible for a client, who more often than not is inexperienced and fearful of the litigation process, to appreciate the importance of their evidence or how it impacts upon the theory of the case. Many otherwise good cases can turn bad quickly due to counsel's failure to fully review, appreciate and respond to new or changing evidence.

The benefit of getting your ducks in order early will not only save you countless hours of review and preparation later on, but will likely pay dividends in the long run both in terms of your reputation and the ultimate disposition of the matter at hand.

In a paper prepared for the Canadian Bar Association, entitled *Trial Preparation*, David Broad suggests formulating an early checklist addressing:

- issues of fact and law;

- documents;

- potential witnesses and witness statements;

- identification of issues requiring expert opinion;

- legal memoranda;

- and a concise chronology of the events.

The pleadings in an action effectively set the parameters of what can and cannot be canvassed in addition to merely identifying the proper parties to the action. In order to draft effective pleadings, you must have a good appreciation of your case. There is little more embarrassing than discovering that your pleading misidentifies the incident giving rise to the claim, the identity of your client or some basic undisputed fact. Equally annoying is a pleading that is clearly a boilerplate document, which provides no useful information relevant to the actual claim.

"If you have a good case, produce everything you have. Leave no stone unturned . . . The most dangerous plaintiff is the one who has nothing to hide."

It is often useful to provide an explanation of the process and a list of "do's" and "don'ts" in bullet form. Examples of some of those considerations are set out below.

- Relax.

- Listen to each question and make sure you understand it.

- Answer the question directly. The best answer is "yes," "no" or "I don't know".

- If you don't know an answer, don't guess.

- Don't be afraid to admit that you don't know or can't recall.

- If you can't answer yes or no, try to be brief and answer only the question asked.

- Do not volunteer information that was not asked for.
- If you don't understand a question, ask that it be repeated or clarified.
- Don't interrupt.
- Don't make speeches.
- Be courteous and polite.
- Don't argue or lose your cool.
- Always tell the truth.

Effective Oral Argument

The substance of what you argue is dictated by the strengths and weaknesses of your case.

The central reality is that lengthy trial lists limit the time argument.

Rehearsing can be an invaluable part of preparation.

Unless you are intimately familiar with the small claims court before which you are appearing, if possible, arrive early and observe a session of the court.

If you can observe the deputy judge who will hear your case, you may also pick up valuable clues to questions he or she might ask. Any "local knowledge" you can gain about the court can help eliminate the element of surprise.

When it comes to what counsel brings to the podium with them, it really varies. Some bring nothing, others a page or at most two of notes, still others bring carefully constructed notebooks. With whatever you are comfortable, keep these rules in mind:

1. Don't lose whatever you intend to bring.

2. Make certain whatever you bring fits on the lectern.

3. Finally, ignore whatever you bring. Notes are crutches, and when you look down you lose the attention of the court.

Try to have one opening sentence that ties up the issues in an advantageous way, and then proceed immediately to the meat of your case. Most judges today are well prepared, will be bored by a recitation of the facts and will move you to the heart of the case with questions if you tarry on background. Much better to get there on your own terms, right away, rather than have even your first point dictated by a question.

Rejoice when the judge asks questions because it: (1) shows that you have not yet put him or her to sleep; and (2) allows you to focus on precisely what the judge is interested in. You should have prepared very concise answers to every question you can reasonably anticipate. But be sure to listen carefully to the question before delivering one of your prepared replies; don't assume the judge is asking a question you're ready for, just because that makes the answering easier. And don't assume that the question is hostile; don't fire on the lifeboats coming to save you.

Many lawyers react too defensively to questioning in general, as if the judge is trying to trip them up.

Standard of Proof

In a civil case, the plaintiff must establish its allegation on the balance of probabilities. Where allegations carry increased moral stigma for the defendant, such as fraud, professional negligence, or sexual misconduct, they argue that courts should exercise increased caution before finding for a plaintiff. In *C. (R.) v. McDougall*, 2008 SCC 53, 2008 CarswellBC 2041,

2008 CarswellBC 2042, (sub nom. *F.H. v. McDougall)* [2008] 3 S.C.R. 41, 83 B.C.L.R. (4th) 1, 60 C.C.L.T. (3d) 1, 61 C.P.C. (6th) 1, 61 C.R. (6th) 1, (sub nom. *H. (F.) v. McDougall)* 297 D.L.R. (4th) 193, [2008] 11 W.W.R. 414, (sub nom. *F.H. v. McDougall)* 260 B.C.A.C. 74, (sub nom. *F.H. v. McDougall)* 380 N.R. 82, (sub nom. *F.H. v. McDougall)* 439 W.A.C. 74, [2008] A.C.S. No. 54, [2008] S.C.J. No. 54 (S.C.C.), the Supreme Court of Canada rejected this approach. Justice Rothstein spoke for the Court as follows at para. 49:

> [I] would reaffirm that in civil cases there is only one standard of proof that is proof on the balance of probabilities. In all civil cases, the trial judge must scrutinize the relevant evidence with care to determine whether it is more likely than not that an alleged event occurred. In *Merck Frosst Canada Ltée c. Canada (Ministre de la Santé)*, 2012 SCC 3, 2012 CarswellNat 148, 2012 CarswellNat 149, [2012] 1 S.C.R. 23, (sub nom. *Merck Frosst Canada Ltd. v. Canada (Minister of Health))* 99 C.P.R. (4th) 65, (sub nom. *Merck Frosst Canada Ltd. v. Canada (Minister of Health))* 342 D.L.R. (4th) 257, (sub nom. *Merck Frosst Canada Ltd. v. Canada (Minister of Health))* 426 N.R. 200, [2012] A.C.S. No. 3, [2012] S.C.J. No. 3 (S.C.C.) the Court reiterated that it is settled law that there is but one standard of proof in civil cases and that is on a balance of probabilities: "However, what evidence will be required to reach that standard will be affected by the nature of the proposition the third party seeks to establish and the particular context of the case." [at para. 94]

One Party Represented

There is no reason to believe that the phenomenon of self-representation is going to go away. On the contrary, it will increase. The vast majority of the self-represented make that choice for simple economic reasons.

The self-represented are a fact of life.

I would identify the best practices as follows:

- Framing the subject matter of the hearing
- Explaining the process that will be followed or guiding the process
- Eliciting needed information from the litigants by:
    - Allowing litigants to make initial presentations to the court
    - Breaking the hearing into topics
    - Moving back and forth between the parties
    - Paraphrasing
    - Maintaining control of the courtroom
    - Giving litigants an opportunity to be heard while constraining the scope and length of their presentations, and
    - Giving litigants a last opportunity to add information before any decision
- Engaging the litigants in the decision-making
- Articulating the decision from the bench
- Explaining the decision
- Summarizing the terms of any order or decision
- Anticipating and resolving issues with compliance

The theoretical label that has been given to this approach to judging is "engaged neutrality," with the phrase intended to convey that judges can be deeply engaged with the case without threatening, in any way, the neutrality of the court.

This more engaged form of judging is likely to mean that when there is counsel on only one side, the judge will do a much more complete job of exploring the self-represented litigant's position in all its implications. It will mean that the lawyer will still be able to present his or her own case and to cross-examine the self-represented litigant. The judge may put in place a more flexible procedure, but without prejudice to the represented party. The impact should be that the courtroom process will be more predictable and controlled, with the lawyer less likely to be put in difficult strategic and tactical positions as to how aggressive or deferential they should be in dealing with the self-represented litigant. That the self-represented litigant is likely to leave the courtroom satisfied with the process (although not necessarily with the result) should lead to greater compliance with ultimate orders, as well as courtroom services (order, support, etc.). Greater respect for the legal process can only assist the legal profession in its protection of its unique role.

What happens in the courtroom is also impacted by those beyond the judge.

It is important that litigants not be given the feeling that the justice system is diverting their cases away from the judicial attention they want and need. The selection of diversion protocols should take into account the importance to the public's and litigants' perception of judicial accessibility, and should take into account the legitimacy and transparency of any decision that cases should be processed by anyone other than a judge. More specifically, conflict cases should go to judges, unless the parties want otherwise.

I often find that lawyers are anxious about self-represented cases, in part fearing that the judge may take over the case, rendering them irrelevant (particularly in the eyes of the client), and in part fearing that the judge may "lean over the bench" to help the self-represented party.

It is helpful to explain what will happen, including that the lawyer will play the traditional role, including that of presenting evidence and cross-examining, and the self-represented litigant's right to be heard will be protected.

The judge normally may ask questions about the direct testimony presented by the party with counsel, treat testimony as objected to, and rule on these objections. This does not put the judge on the side of the self-represented litigant. Unless there has been formal objection to this direct testimony, the judge may evaluate the answers without formally ruling on the evidence. It is fairer to be explicit, however.

Concise objections are likely to confuse the self-represented litigant. Judges can request greater specificity and explanation, ask additional questions about the evidence, explain the process and the ruling, and possibly indicate another way to make the point.

Sometimes lawyers disrupt the self-represented litigant's presentation with repeated objections. Initial objections should be treated respectfully, but if counsel appears to be making objections for tactical purposes rather than to exclude inappropriate evidence, permit a standing objection and warn counsel to limit the frequency of objections, stating the reason for this instruction. Giving the lawyer or paralegal an opportunity at the end of that phase of the proceeding to identify any particular harm that the modified proceeding has caused should then fully protect the record.

Counsel is entitled to be exploratory in cross-examination and to make helpful factual points, not to humiliate or deter a witness. Judges should put counsel on notice of the problems with their approach and escalate their interventions. The judge can request that the basis of cross-examination or representation questions be based on a good-faith belief in the possibility of their leading to relevant testimony. (Similar techniques are appropriate with a self-represented party who is engaging in similar behaviour.)

A clear, early explanation of what is being done will make it more likely that the lawyer/paralegal is not caught unawares and that he or she will go along without objection.

Many counsel do not initially understand that the rules and practices give judges flexibility to modify procedure where appropriate. An explanation may well mollify counsel. A record is critical to protect all parties.

For those for whom all the world is a frightening place, the courtroom is even more so, with its rituals, power, and risk of sudden life-changing outcomes.

Seriously disturbed litigants may bring issues over which the court has no real-world jurisdiction, such as the assertion that the landlord is beaming radio waves into their teeth. In other situations, the litigant's mental health may make it hard for them to understand the limitations upon judicial power. In either situation, being explicit about what the court can and cannot do, and being respectful of the litigant's emotions, may help at least to move forward. A calm understanding will help litigants get over their anxiety and focus on the substance.

Many litigants are highly anxious. The more anxious the litigant, the more important is a case structure that is manageable and understandable for all. Breaking the case into small steps and explaining each one while repeating where necessary can be very helpful. The litigant is less likely to lose track of the issue at hand, and the other parties will be better able to understand and address the anxious litigant's position.

With a disturbed or challenged litigant, the risk of unintentional noncompliance after the court's decision may be greater. Judges have found it helpful to make sure that such litigants understand both what has happened and their obligations. It can be helpful to ask them to restate what they understand their obligations to be and to suggest the possibility of getting help from family or friends.

Maintaining a respectful environment in the face of a litigant's out-of-control, or nearly out-of-control, anger is, of course, much harder when the judge does not have the lawyer to rely on to restrain the litigant. Appealing to the litigant's sense of fairness may be of help. Similarly, expressing sympathy with the intensity of the emotion may reduce the litigant's alienation. Such statements may help the litigant feel less anger at the judge as a person, thus helping the litigant focus on the process as a whole.

If nothing works, the judge can offer a brief "cooling off" period, like a child's "timeout," to let the litigant get a grip and then participate fully in the process.

More stringent measures include adjournment, which must, of course, not be allowed to prejudice the non-responsible party, or a range of sanctions for noncompliance, including the drawing of adverse inferences against the responsible party, particularly for behaviour that threatens the integrity of the process and summary contempt. Some judges use a three-step process of first explaining the concept of contempt, then the sanctions authorized, and only then imposing the sanction (which can later be waived if the litigant then complies).

When litigants become dismayed because a judge does not follow their requests, it is usually helpful to explain that there are requests to which a court cannot accede if it is to remain neutral. It can be helpful to remind the litigant that the court cannot be a particular party's counsel. Litigants will normally be respectful of refusals when explained in terms to which the litigant can relate, such as the need for neutrality.

The judge has to maintain accessibility and the dignity of the courtroom and avoid abuse of the legal system. Limiting the focus of the proceedings to those appropriate to the particular court, while maintaining a respectful and non-confrontational attitude to the litigant, is the best policy. Even after explaining that the court cannot grant the party's judgment as requested, it may be helpful to ask why the party seeks that relief or thing as he/she does.

Pretrial Conferences

Pretrial conferences allow questions of admissibility, organization of evidence, and court-room procedure to be resolved without the formality pressure and time of the courtroom. The conference can resemble a "dress rehearsal" of the trial, going over the principal elements of testimony beforehand. Discussion during the conference of the witnesses and expected testimony can help ensure the relevance and admissibility of testimony. Such conferences may also play a discovery role and help to simplify proceedings.

Evidence that requires foundation — documents and hearsay — seems to produce the most time-wasting confusion in trials. A focus on the required foundations in a pretrial conference will improve trial efficiency.

The more complicated the case, the more important it is that self-represented litigants understand the governing law and procedure. Increasingly, resources are available. Law librarians can assist the self-represented with research into the more complicated areas of law with which self-help centre staff are not necessarily familiar.

The use of pretrial forms can organize testimony. Such forms help judges identify and resolve problems in advance.

The form might ask for the points that the litigant intends to prove, a list of witnesses and what they would testify to, a list of the documentary evidence to be introduced and where it came from, and a list of problems that the self-represented party would like the judge to resolve.

Through pretrial orders, courts can simplify, minimizing the requirements on both parties. They can also include an approach to the handling of sensitive information that might normally be restricted to the counsel, but in which the judge might have to play a more assertive role.

18. — The Small Claims Judge

Since a key distinguishing characteristic of the small claims process is its informality and lack of rigid trial procedures, small claims trials are much more influenced by individual practices and attitudes of the trial judge than are formal civil trials. Small claims trial procedures can vary widely, even within a given court, depending on the individual judge conducting the trial.

In order to simplify and speed up the process of getting to trial, the focusing and clarification of issues is often left to the trial. This requires a more judicially active role at trial. Even in courts which permit lawyers, in a significant number of cases the judge will still have to assist the parties without a lawyer to explain their side of the controversy and to identify the relevant facts in a case.

The inquisitorial trial procedure used in small claims court is much more efficient than rigid formal trial procedure in getting quickly to the heart of a dispute, since the judge has more control over the trial and can question litigants and witnesses to draw out relevant facts and clarify conflicting testimony.

Typically, small claims trials are conducted as follows. The judge summarizes the small claims complaint in his or her case file, identifying the plaintiff and defendant and describing the alleged cause of action and the amount claimed as damages. The plaintiff is then asked if this is correct in order to verify the claim. The plaintiff is then sworn in and told to tell his story in his own words. Testifying parties are directed to sit in a witness chair in front of the judge's bench or to stand in front of the bench. Generally, judges do not permit any interruptions or questions by the other side or by a solicitor while a litigant is testifying; also, judges assist the testifying party in laying out the facts and examining receipts or other documents which the plaintiff has brought to court. If the plaintiff has brought any witnesses, these witnesses are then sworn in and testify after the plaintiff. Finally, the defendant tells his story and presents witnesses, if any. Judges then permit the plaintiff and defendant to cross-examine each other, or their witnesses.

The degree of judicial activism observed in small claims trials is usually reflected in the extent to which judges "control" the trial process. More active judges, many "inquisitorial" or "investigatory," move from a brief review of the case to questioning the plaintiff to establishing the necessary cause of action and proof of damages. They then shift to questioning the defendant to clarify his side of the case to bring out any defences or any facts indicated by the plaintiff. After an opportunity for questions by the litigants, the judge announces a decision, explaining how he arrived at the dollar amount of the award. Judges who use this inquisitorial approach justify it on the grounds that it speeds up trials, enabling the judge to skip over or to cut short rambling or extraneous testimony and take the burden off inexperienced litigants.

Judges with a strong background in litigation may find it difficult to resist the urge to step into the "arena" as an inexperienced litigant starts to flounder in the unfamiliar waters of civil procedure, evidence and substantive law.

It is possible for a judge to intervene in a courteous manner. Some cases have suggested that this courtesy amounts to a duty in respect of an unrepresented litigant. *R. v. Taubler* (1987), 20 O.A.C. 64 (C.A.), was admittedly a criminal case, but the advice set out by Appeals Justice Donald Thorson at page 71 is instructive and certainly applicable to a broader range of cases:

> While it is undoubtedly true that a trial judge has a duty to see that an unrepresented accused person is not denied a fair trial because he is not familiar with court procedure, the duty must necessarily be circumscribed by what is reasonable. Clearly it cannot and does not extend to his providing to the accused at each stage of his trial the kind of advice that counsel could be expected to provide if the accused were represented by counsel. If it did, the trial judge would quickly find himself in the impossible position of being both advocate and impartial arbiter at one and the same time.

In *Borden & Elliot v. Deer Home Investments* (1992), 14 C.P.C. (3d) 269 (Ont. Gen. Div.), a case involving costs, Justice Sandra Chapnick remarked:

> In order to implement that principle, judicial officers hearing such cases (as indeed, any case where a party is unrepresented) must exhibit more patience and courtesy than might otherwise be required. Procedures and rules of evidence may well have to be explained more than once, regardless of whether the time allotted for the hearing is thereby expanded. That is not to say, of course, that an inordinate amount of time need be spent on relatively minor matters or that rulings and instructions must be repeated many times over. The court is certainly not expected to represent a party.

> It should be understood, however, that the procedure may become more cumbersome and protracted than ordinarily, in order to provide not only a full and fair hearing, but also, the perception of fairness when the public is involved.

> . . . . .

> May I also take the liberty of pointing out that the obligation to be helpful to an unrepresented client also extends to opposing counsel.

Almost all judges take notes during the trial, which often includes calculation of the damages and sometimes include necessary elements of the cause of action alleged (if complex), the witnesses testifying and the relevant points being made.

Every judge recognizes a therapeutic function in small claims trials and they often let litigants explain their side of the story long past the point where the judge had enough facts to decide the case.

"Ineptitude, inherent in almost any case of self-representation, is a constitutionally protected prerogative." See *People v. Schoolfield* (1994), 196 A.2d 111 and *People v. Romero* (1986), 694 P.2d 1256. But see also *R. v. Tran* (2001), 149 O.A.C. 120, 2001 CarswellOnt 2706, [2001] O.J. No. 3056, 156 C.C.C. (3d) 1, 44 C.R. (5th) 12, 55 O.R. (3d) 161, 14 M.V.R. (4th) 1 (Ont. C.A.).

Some judges feel that for many plaintiffs the real function of a small claims trial is not primarily the recovery of money damages, although that is always important, but rather it is a chance to tell their story at their "day in court" before a real judge. Small claims hearings help to "clear the air" in festering disputes. Parties must be treated politely and fairly and the judge must be a good listener in order for a small claims trial to be conducted well. Many judges make an effort to put parties at ease and reassure them with occasional words of encouragement during their testimony to keep them moving along to all the points they should touch on.

All Small Claims Courts are courts of law, in that the judge's decision must be decided by established principles of law.

Small claims judges apply the regular civil burden of proof in small claims trials. This so-called "preponderance of the evidence rule" means that the burden of going forward is first placed on the plaintiff to establish his or her cause of action by a preponderance of the evidence (sometimes described as 51 per cent). Once the plaintiff does so, he or she has established a *prima facie* case and the burden of disproving it shifts to the defendant. If the defendant does not then produce evidence which reduces the plaintiff's level of proof to less than 51 per cent, the plaintiff wins.

The plaintiff puts his proof on one side and the defendant puts his proof on the other. If the plaintiff's side is heavier, the plaintiff wins. If the defendant's side is heavier or if the scales are evenly balanced, the plaintiff loses. If a plaintiff in a Small Claims Court cannot establish that he has a cause of action under law by 51 per cent of the weight of the evidence, generally he gets nothing.

Plaintiffs rarely lose because of lack of proof of damages or missing evidence, since evidentiary defects can be remedied by granting a continuance at trial for the plaintiff to bring in missing evidence or witnesses or the judge can grant what he feels are fair damages if he believes the plaintiff. Usually, plaintiffs lose because their case lacked a legal cause of action. Plaintiffs may have been wronged in some way, or felt that they had been wronged, but the defendant was not liable under the law.

Often, judges will accept any and all evidence so long as it seems relevant to a case. The key function of the judge at trial is to sort out the truth, and judges believe it is easier to do this if as much evidence as possible is available.

In provinces which permit lawyers, judges are troubled by the situation of unrepresented litigant facing a represented litigant on the other side. While judges actively intervene in such a situation to assist an unrepresented party, intervention usually takes the form of limiting efforts by the lawyer to rattle a lay person with objections to evidence or with sharp cross-examination techniques, rather than of acting as lawyer for the unrepresented litigant.

"When one side is without a lawyer, the natural tendency of a judge is to favour the underdog — and when the judge is acting as the lawyer for one side, as well as the judge, you can imagine the judge's client will not lose too often." Some judges feel that a lawyer might be at a real disadvantage against a layman in a small claims trial. As one judge says "You have to remember that all judges are lawyers too, and their natural instinct is to oppose anyone making lawyer-like noises."

A good Small Claims Court requires good judges. The entire fabric of trial procedure, including provisions for dealing with unprepared or inexperienced litigants, is left up to the judge. Because of this situation, this individual plays a key role in achieving even-handed and just results, particularly where litigants of widely disparate backgrounds or abilities are involved.

The most important qualities for small claims judges are likely to be more subtle qualities, such as patience, sensitivity and a desire to achieve a just result, rather than the amount of "control" which a judge exercises at trial.

Literacy

Because our justice system is so heavily text-based, courts may be accused of *systemic discrimination* against those with low literacy skills. The everyday demands of the justice system, like those of society may well require an ability to read and write. We may take it for granted that those who appear in our courts have that ability.

If we ever doubt a person or party's literacy skills, we should take the initiative to find out whether he or she can read and write well enough to understand the court process.

We must slow down and do as much orally as possible. We should speak clearly and repeat important information. Most people who cannot use printed material must rely on memory. Repeating important information can help increase and/or reinforce knowledge and understanding. We could supplement oral information with a written note so that someone with low literacy can take it away and go over it in private, or ask someone to read it for them later.

Plain language plays a key role in fulfilling the justice system's task of helping people understand and cope with the law. Plain language focuses on the needs of the reader or listener, not those of the writer or speaker, and is based on the premise that readers or speakers should be able to understand text or speech without having to struggle.

In some cases, courts have ordered a stay of proceedings where there was evidence that a particular litigant lacked the ability to represent him/herself and would therefore be denied the right to a fair trial. In the decision of *New Brunswick (Minister of Health & Community Services) v. G. (J.)*, 26 C.R. (5th) 203, [1999] S.C.J. No. 47, 177 D.L.R. (4th) 124, 244 N.R. 276, 1999 CarswellNB 306, 1999 CarswellNB 305, REJB 1999-14250, 7 B.H.R.C. 615, [1999] 3 S.C.R. 46, 552 A.P.R. 25, 216 N.B.R. (2d) 25, 50 R.F.L. (4th) 63, 66 C.R.R. (2d) 267 (S.C.C.), the Supreme Court of Canada emphasized the need for state funded counsel in child protection hearings where, as noted by the Court, the litigants often have low literacy skills and the matters are complex.

Judicial Notice

In what circumstances can a court take judicial notice of facts?

Judicial notice is the acceptance by a court, without the requirement of proof, of any fact or matter that is so generally known and accepted in the community that it cannot be reasonably questioned, or any fact or matter that can readily be determined or verified by resort to sources whose accuracy cannot reasonably be questioned.

Judicial notice dispenses with the need for proof of facts that are clearly uncontroversial or beyond reasonable dispute. Facts judicially noticed are not proved by evidence under oath. Nor are they tested by cross-examination. Therefore, the threshold for judicial notice is strict. A court may properly take judicial notice of facts that are either:

1. so notorious or generally accepted as not to be the subject of debate among reasonable persons; or

2. capable of immediate and accurate demonstration by resort to readily accessible sources of indisputable accuracy.

"A judge may be entitled to consult court record that are not directly before him or her and may be entitled to use them as evidence to decide a case. He or she should not normally do so, however, without advising the parties of his or her intentions and without giving them an opportunity to address the issue. In this way, the documents, even without formal proof, can properly be said to have become part of the evidence in the case". *Petrelli v. Lindell Beach Holiday Resort Ltd.* (2011), 2011 BCCA 367, 2011 CarswellBC 2331, 24 B.C.L.R. (5th) 4, 340 D.L.R. (4th) 733, [2012] 1 W.W.R. 720, 310 B.C.A.C. 196, 526 W.A.C. 196 (B.C. C.A.) at [42].

19. — Writing Judgments

The Supreme court of Canada in *R. v. Sheppard*, 2002 SCC 26, [2002] S.C.J. No. 30, 2002 CarswellNfld 74, 2002 CarswellNfld 75, 162 C.C.C. (3d) 298, 210 D.L.R. (4th) 608, 50 C.R. (5th) 68, 284 N.R. 342, 211 Nfld. & P.E.I.R. 50, 633 A.P.R. 50, [2002] 1 S.C.R. 869 (S.C.C.) confirmed the obligation of a trial judge to give reasons for judgment. The judge's reasons can be delivered either in writing or orally and the reasons must not be so deficient that: "deficiencies in the reasons prevent meaningful appellate review of the correctness of the decision." At the end of the evidence if the judge concludes that he or she can orally provide reasons they should do so. It is generally preferable to deliver an oral judgment as it provides a speedy result for the litigants and avoids adding to any backlog of outstanding judgments. There are also benefits to delivering a written judgment.

In small claims litigation (particularly with unrepresented parties), there may be an advantage to providing a written judgment as it may diffuse tension and avoid confrontation between the parties and judge. Any judge who has had the experience of trying to deliver a judgment orally in small claims court with the unsuccessful litigant arguing everything can appreciate the value of providing a written judgment. A written judgment allows the parties to leave the courtroom peacefully and confident they have been heard and their arguments considered.

It is important that a judgment be presented in an objective manner. Many legal tests may appear to litigants to be somewhat elastic. In applying legal tests (e.g., an air of reality, clearest of cases or the reasonable person), it does not help understanding if the style is vague or oblique. Long unnecessary descriptive passages should be avoided, as should attempts at humour. Humour is often too subjective to have any place in a judgment. It is a distraction and diminishes the appearance of objectivity.

My own experience is to give decisions orally at the conclusion of a trial, but if that is not possible I look at my calendar and set a date for putting the decision on the record, taking into account everyone's convenience, as well as my own, so that I have enough time to write the decision, but not so much time that it will get put on the back burner or forgotten. Try to avoid reserving judgments. If I reserve it is usually because I need to do research or, occasionally, because I want to think about credibility issues in a lengthy trial. However, even for an oral decision, you should recess to review the evidence and write a brief basis for what you will give from the bench, just to ensure that you have not missed anything. Written decisions may, of course, simply be mailed to the parties or their counsel.

A well-written trial judgment will explain to both the litigants and possibly an appellate court, in understandable language, the rationale of your decision. They may disagree with both the rationale and the outcome, but to do either they must first have understood it. Usually, no embarrassment follows a reversal by an appellate court on those occasions when that court disagrees with a trial judgment. But double embarrassment flows when it confesses to not understanding either what you said or how your conclusion was reached.

Begin by first introducing the case to the reader with a broad statement of the litigation, then move on to an identification of the main issue or sub-issues, progressing to the material facts as found by the trier after resolving any credibility problems. Finally, an application of the relevant statue law or jurisprudence leads to an almost inevitable conclusion.

Trial judgments are usually fact-oriented. The central purpose of the trial, after all, is to ascertain the facts. The written decision will usually analyze the testimony of the individual witnesses in sufficient detail to support finding of fact. The reasoning by which the facts are arrived at should resolve questions of credibility.

Findings of credibility should be explained with sufficient clarity to permit an appeals court to determine whether the process was valid or faulty. Resist the temptation to 'personalize' the judgment by first-person references. Referring to 'the court' will keep the writing on a higher plane.

Latin maxims and arcane terms of art should be avoided unless absolutely necessary to the decision. If they are used, explain them. After all, if Cicero did, why shouldn't we?

The judgment should be long enough to cover all essential elements. That's it. A judgment need not be eternal in length to be immortal in content. Do not state personal, as opposed to judicial, opinions about matters, in particular gratuitous observations about 'how things have changed since the good old days.' To do so invites labelling of 'fuddy-duddy-ism.' Adhere to the maxim: If it is not necessary to say it, then it is necessary *not* to say it! Remember also, a written judgment is not intended to be a work of literary achievement, Lord Denning notwithstanding.

20. — Costs

Costs Overview

Like other civil courts, the Small Claims Court has a "loser pay" costs system. The general rule is that the unsuccessful party can expect to be liable to pay to the successful party an amount as compensation for the costs of the dispute. Therefore, if a trial results in a judgment for the plaintiff, the defendant will generally be liable to pay to the plaintiff not only the amount of damages awarded, but also costs. If judgment is granted for the defendant, the claim will be dismissed, and costs will generally be payable by the plaintiff to the defendant.

The court has a general discretion over costs, pursuant to *Courts of Justice Act* section 131(1), but that discretion is significantly tempered for Small Claims Court proceedings. There are three aspects to the law of costs as applicable in the Small Claims Court: the *prima facie* limit under *Courts of Justice Act* section 29, the specific costs rules under the *Small Claims Court Rules*, and the common law, to the extent that common law principles are not ousted by the legislative scheme.

Prima Facie Limit on Costs

The extent of potential costs liability is more limited in Small Claims Court than in other courts. The overriding limitation on the court's costs power is the *prima facie* limit created by *Courts of Justice Act* section 29, which provides:

> 29. Limit on costs — An award of costs in the Small Claims Court, other than disbursements, shall not exceed 15 per cent of the amount claimed or the value of the property sought to be recovered unless the court considers it necessary in the interests of justice to penalize a party or a party's representative for unreasonable behaviour in the proceeding.

Section 29 is the so-called "15% rule". It means that unless the penalty costs proviso is applied, no costs order, apart from disbursements, can exceed 15% of the amount claimed: *Twan v. Zellers Inc.*, 2008 CarswellOnt 8803, 93 O.R. (3d) 582 (Ont. Div. Ct.). The rule applies to fees and does not limit the amount of disbursements which may be awarded: *Allison v. Street Imports Ltd.* (May 14, 2009), Doc. 03 DV 000953, [2009] O.J. No. 1979 (Ont. Div. Ct.).

The maximum award in an action in which $25,000 is claimed is $3,750 plus disbursements. If the amount claimed is a lesser amount, the limit is 15% of that amount, plus disbursements.

The 15% rule applies to each potential order for costs in an action, so for example if a claim is dismissed against two separately-represented defendants, the defendants are not limited to sharing the 15%: see *681638 Ontario Ltd. v. UGT Ltd.*, 2009 CarswellOnt 4477, 252 O.A.C. 285 (Ont. Div. Ct.); additional reasons at 2009 CarswellOnt 6473 (Ont. Div. Ct.); additional reasons at 2009 CarswellOnt 8141 (Ont. Div. Ct.).

In cases involving a defendant's claim, the amount claimed in the defendant's claim and the amount claimed in the plaintiff's claim are added to determine the "amount claimed" for purposes of section 29: *King v. K-W Homes Ltd.*, 2006 CarswellOnt 8358, [2006] O.J. No. 5104 (Ont. Sm. Cl. Ct.); *Nerdahl v. Sun Life Financial Distributors (Canada) Inc.* (May 11, 2010), Doc. Kitchener 1421/08; 1421D1/08, [2010] O.J. No. 1954 (Ont. Sm. Cl. Ct.).

By its terms, section 29 is only a *prima facie* limit. In appropriate cases that limit may be displaced if the court considers it necessary to penalize a party for unreasonable behaviour in the proceeding. Where the penalty costs proviso is applied, the 15% rule does not limit the amount of the potential costs order.

However, even where the penalty costs proviso is applied, the court's discretion remains limited by the principle of indemnity. Any costs award cannot be more than the costs actually incurred by the party who is entitled to costs as a result of the unreasonable behaviour. The proviso does not create a general power to impose a fine or to punish a party for contempt: *West End Tree Service Inc. v. Stabryla*, 2010 ONSC 68, 2010 CarswellOnt 12, 257 O.A.C. 265, [2010] O.J. No. 7 (Ont. Div. Ct.).

If a court applies the proviso, it must be based on a finding of unreasonable conduct in the proceeding. A court's failure to make such a finding may justify a reduction of the costs award by the appeal court: *West End Tree Service Inc. v. Stabryla*, 2010 ONSC 68, 2010 CarswellOnt 12, 257 O.A.C. 265, [2010] O.J. No. 7 (Ont. Div. Ct.); *Prevost v. Gilmour*, 2009 CarswellOnt 2188, [2009] O.J. No. 1681 (Ont. Div. Ct.); *Schaer v. Barrie Yacht Club*, 2003 CarswellOnt 5233, (sub nom. *Stacey v. Barrie Yacht Club*) [2003] O.J. No. 5278, 108 O.A.C. 95 (Ont. Div. Ct.); leave to appeal refused 2004 CarswellOnt 3007 (Ont. C.A.).

An example of a large costs award resulting from application of the penalty costs proviso is *Jones v. LTL Contracting Ltd.* (May 5, 1995), Doc. 987-94, [1995] O.J. No. 4927 (Ont. Sm. Cl. Ct.); leave to appeal costs order denied (July 20, 1995), Doc. 987/94, [1995] O.J. No. 4928 (Ont. Gen. Div.). In that case the court applied the penalty costs proviso and awarded costs on a substantial indemnity scale. The claim took several days for trial, was unnecessarily prolonged, complicated, and complex, and required the defendants to present expert evidence. One set of defendants were awarded total costs of $11,015 and another defendant was awarded $6,715.

Costs under the Small Claims Court Rules

Courts of Justice Act section 29 creates a *prima facie* maximum amount of costs, but does not guide the court's determination of how to fix the amount of costs: in other words it provides a maximum but not necessarily an appropriate amount for the specific case. Subject to the limitation imposed by section 29, costs are fixed pursuant to the *Small Claims Court Rules*.

The two most important costs rules are Rule 19 dealing with costs generally and rule 14.07 dealing with the costs consequences of offers to settle.

The representation fee under rule 19.04 is the largest single costs item in most cases where the party entitled to costs is represented by a professional advocate. If the successful party is represented by a lawyer, student-at-law, or paralegal, a reasonable representation fee may be awarded at trial or at an assessment hearing. There is no specific limit, other than reasonableness, on the amount of such a fee, but it is subject to the actual cost incurred by the successful party.

Previous versions of this rule contained a cap on the amount of a representation fee and limited the amount for a student-at-law or paralegal to 7.5% of the amount claimed. A repealed version of the rule was considered in *Bird v. Ireland*, 2005 CarswellOnt 6945, [2005] O.J. No. 5125, 205 O.A.C. 1 (Ont. Div. Ct.). The current rule contains no limit on the amount of a representation fee — other than section 29 itself.

Subject to section 29, and subject to the discretion of the court, a representation fee to a party represented by a lawyer will often be in a range from $500 to $2,500. The actual amount may be influenced by the length of trial, the complexity of the issues, and the seniority of counsel, among other factors.

Self-represented parties are not entitled to a representation fee, but may be entitled to an amount of up to $500 for inconvenience and expense under rule 19.05. Such awards are not routinely granted. The same is true of awards under rule 19.06 for compensation for unreasonable behaviour.

The offer to settle rule can have a significant impact on costs because the right offer can produce an award of double costs. Rules 14.07(1) and (2) deal with offers to settle by plaintiffs and offers to settle by defendants, respectively. To qualify for the potential cost consequences, the offer must be made in writing at least seven days before the trial and must have remained open until the start of trial. Double costs may be awarded where: (i) in the case of a plaintiff's offer, the plaintiff obtains a judgment as favourable as or more favourable than the terms of the offer; or (ii) in the case of a defendant's offer, the plaintiff obtains a judgment as favourable as or less favourable than the terms of the offer.

If the plaintiff is entitled to cost consequences under rule 14.07(1), the court may award the plaintiff up to double the costs of the action.

If the defendant is entitled to cost consequences under rule 14.07(2), the court may award the defendant up to double the costs awardable to a successful party from the date the offer was served (which would include a doubled representation fee). However, the defendant's cost consequences are not triggered if the plaintiff's claim is dismissed, since the plaintiff did not obtain a judgment as required by the rule: see *S & A Strasser Ltd. v. Richmond Hill (Town)*, 1990 CarswellOnt 435, [1990] O.J. No. 2321, 1 O.R. (3d) 243, 49 C.P.C. (2d) 234, 45 O.A.C. 394 (Ont. C.A.).

Where double costs are awarded under rule 14.07, it is the fees but not the disbursements which are doubled: *Ohler v. Pye* (March 25, 2009), [2009] O.J. No. 3434, Doc. 991/08 (Ont. Sm. Cl. Ct.).

The potential for double costs awards means that parties have a particular incentive to make the right offer to settle, keeping in mind rule 14.07.

The interaction of the rule 14.07 cost consequences with the *prima facie* limit on costs under *Courts of Justice Act* section 29 has been considered in a number of cases. If an award of double costs under rule 14.07 would produce an award in excess of the *prima facie* limit, the court must decide whether there is a proper basis to apply the penalty costs proviso. In the absence of such grounds, the double costs award under rule 14.07 would offend the statutory limitation on costs.

A number of cases have held that a party's failure to accept an offer to settle, which triggers rule 14.07 cost consequences, can itself constitute unreasonable behaviour within the meaning of section 29 and support application of the penalty costs proviso. If so the double costs award under rule 14.07 can be made in tandem with a penalty costs award under section 29 and there is no contravention of the statutory limitation: see *Kakamin v. Hasan*, 2005 Cars-wellOnt 4066, [2005] O.J. No. 2778 (Ont. Sm. Cl. Ct.); *Beatty v. Reitzel Insulation Co.*, 2008 CarswellOnt 1364, [2008] O.J. No. 953 (Ont. Sm. Cl. Ct.); *Melara-Lopez v. Richarz*, 2009 CarswellOnt 6459, [2009] O.J. No. 6313 (Ont. Sm. Cl. Ct.); affirmed 2009 CarswellOnt 6333, [2009] O.J. No. 4362, 255 O.A.C. 160 (Ont. Div. Ct.); *Barrie Trim & Mouldings Inc. v. Country Cottage Living Inc.*, 2010 ONSC 2598, 2010 CarswellOnt 2783, [2010] O.J. No. 1836, 93 C.L.R. (3d) 166 (Ont. Div. Ct.); *Propane Levac Propane Inc. v. Macauley*, 2010 ONSC 293, 2011 CarswellOnt 108, 2011 ONSC 293, 2011 CarswellOnt 108, [2011] O.J. No. 105 (Ont. Div. Ct.); *1604966 Ontario Ltd. v. Andsign International Management Inc.*, 2013 CarswellOnt 6783, [2013] O.J. No. 2401 (Ont. S.C.J.). Any party seeking rule 14.07 cost consequences which would result in more than the *prima facie* limit on costs, and any court considering such an award, should address whether there has been unreasonable beha-viour within the meaning of section 29. In the absence of such behaviour, the *prima facie* limit applies.

Costs of motions and settlement conferences are specifically addressed by the *Small Claims Court Rules*. Rule 15.07 provides that motion costs shall not exceed $100 plus disbursements unless there are special circumstances, and rule 13.10 provides the same limitation for settle-ment conference costs orders.

Disbursements may be claimed in full by a successful party under rule 19.01(1). The dis-bursements must be reasonable; the only specific limitation on a court's determination of the amount of disbursements to be awarded is that the amount for service shall not exceed $60 for each person served, unless there are special circumstances: rule 19.01(3). Disbursements in most cases simply involve the court filing fees, but where other disbursements are in-curred by the successful party they may be recovered. The larger items typically seen in-volve expert reports or expert testimony, and travel cost, where such disbursements have been incurred. In *Moore v. Brazeau Seller LLP*, Doc. SC-07SC101675-0000, [2011] O.J. No. 3171 (Ont. Sm. Cl. Ct.), the successful defendant was awarded disbursements of $13,581 based primarily on expert evidence which was required to defend a complex lawyer malprac-tice claim.

The *Small Claims Court Rules* do not apply to appeals from the Small Claims Court. Costs of such appeals are determined pursuant to Rule 57 of the *Rules of Civil Procedure*.

Common Law Costs Rules

Various common law costs rules may apply in Small Claims Court — assuming they are not ousted by *Courts of Justice Act* section 29 or by the *Small Claims Court Rules*. Here are some examples.

Perhaps most broadly, there is the common law rule that costs are intended as an indemnity only. That rule was applied in *West End Tree Service Inc. v. Stabryla*, 2010 ONSC 68, 2010 CarswellOnt 12, 257 O.A.C. 265, [2010] O.J. No. 7 (Ont. Div. Ct.).

Costs are discretionary, as is confirmed by *Courts of Justice Act* s. 131(1).

In cases of evenly divided success, there may be no costs awarded.

Bullock or Sanderson costs orders (special costs orders where a plaintiff succeeds against one defendant and fails against the other) may be made in Small Claims Court: *Fovant Farms Ltd. v. West Elgin Mutual Insurance Co.*, 2009 CarswellOnt 3332, 74 C.C.L.I. (4th) 236 (Ont. Div. Ct.).

21. — Enforcement of a Judgment

Once judgment is given in your favour, you are called the "judgment creditor." This applies to both judgment obtained by default as well as judgment following a trial. The party against whom judgment is given is called the "judgment debtor." You can become a judgment creditor whether it is to enforce a claim or you may wish to enforce judgment on a counterclaim.

Once you have judgment, the defendant is obliged to pay you the amount of the judgment immediately, unless the judge has ordered a payment schedule or you have agreed on a payment schedule with the judgment debtor.

Your first step to collect the judgment should be to send the judgment debtor a copy of the judgment, together with a request for payment. This lets him know the exact amount he is obliged to pay. If this demand is not successful, you will have to take further proceedings. *It is up to you to collect the judgment. This is not the court's responsibility.* Proceedings to enforce a judgment are called "execution proceedings."

Enforcement proceedings will only commence by the court office on the receipt of written instructions from the creditor or his or her representative.

A claim is not resolved until the judgment has been enforced. Since small claims judgments usually represent money damages, these judgments are enforced by collecting the money.

A structural problem inherent in the collection process is that it is often fragmented. No one agency is responsible for all of the elements of collection.

A variable in the process is the judgment debtor. Once the defendant(s) has left the court (if appearing at all), the court's jurisdiction over the party ends unless the judgment creditor initiates procedures of requesting the court to summon the debtor into court for an examination of his assets.

Securing a judgment in the Small Claims Court can turn out to be a hollow victory if the judgment cannot be enforced. All too often creditors become frustrated because of the time and money spent trying to recover money awarded by the court, often with no positive results. While enforcement can never be guaranteed the chances of success are visibly improved if one understands the system and can avoid the common pitfalls. It is hoped that the information contained in the following sections will provide the necessary insight to help you be a winner.

When considering your options, you should be aware of the following points which are common to all enforcements:

- Enforcement proceedings can be taken as soon as judgment has been given (this applies to both default judgments and judgments given following a full trial).

- Enforcement proceedings will only be initiated by the court office on the receipt of written instructions from the creditor or his or her representative.

- The instructions must be in the form of a written request or affidavit and must include a breakdown of the outstanding amount.

Rule 20 "Enforcement of Orders" addresses service of documents connected to the enforcement process.

With the exception of writs of seizure and sale against lands and writs of delivery, enforcement proceedings are normally issued in the territorial division where the debtor resides or carries on business. It may, therefore, be necessary to have the judgment transferred from one Small Claims Court office to another before issuing enforcement instructions.

Pitfalls await a judgment creditor trying to use collection remedies. The most common first step is to use garnishment to have the judgment taken out of the debtor's bank account (if any) or deducted in installments from the debtor's wages (if any). However, to do this, the creditor must know where the debtor's bank or employer is. Again, a creditor or his or her representative should maintain contact with the court office to ensure that payments are being regularly received. Joint debts are garnishable to a maximum of 50 per cent pursuant to new Rule 20.08(2) which conforms with the *Rules of Civil Procedure.*

Further steps include trying to attach the debtor's personal property (car, t.v., personal effects, and so on). This can be risky; the property may not belong to the debtor, other creditors may have secured interests in the property, or the property may be statutorily protected or exempted from attachment under law (such as a vehicle needed to get to work or tools used in a trade).

Many defendants do not realize that the plaintiff's court costs are added to the judgment amount and pay only the amount of damages announced in court.

Unpaid judgments can produce serious secondary consequences, including loss of a driver's licence, garnishment, and liens on real estate owned by the debtor. In addition, since in many courts commercial credit rating agencies check the judgment files daily, any judgment not marked paid may adversely affect a judgment debtor's credit rating.

If you are a creditor, you may issue a notice of examination, directed to the debtor accompanied by an affidavit setting out the particulars of your judgment, the rate of post judgment interest, any amount received since the judgment was given, and the final amount owing. The notice of examination shall be served on the debtor personally or by alternative service 14 days in advance of the examination. Notices of garnishment (where personal service is requested), notices of examination, warrant letters and all documents ordered by a judge are required to be served by the bailiff; but again, see section 141 of the *Courts of Justice Act*. At the examination, you can ask the debtor

1. the reason for nonpayment;

2. their income and property;

3. debts, disposal of any property;

4. their ability to satisfy the judgment; and

5. if they intend to obey the order in the future.

Other ways of trying to enforce a judgment against a debtor include; a notice of garnishment; seizure and sale of personal property; seizure and sale of lands; and a writ of delivery.

Seizing of personal property is also used as a method of enforcement if the creditor knows where the debtor's assets or personal property are.

The creditor may also apply (through the clerk of the court) to the Sheriff for a writ preventing the debtor from selling off or disposing of any land until the judgment is satisfied. The creditor may also apply (through the clerk of the court) to the Sheriff for a writ preventing the debtor from selling off or disposing of any land until the judgment is satisfied. Where a person wishes to obtain a writ of delivery, he or she is required to file a claim. The claim should not be given out for the service. Together with the request for the writ of delivery, the claim shall be brought before the court by way of an *ex parte* notice of motion and supporting affidavit. The affidavit should describe clearly and concisely the property to be delivered, the value of the property and set out the rights to recovery. After the order has been given by the court, the writ of delivery is to be forwarded to the appropriate bailiff for enforcement.

The court may also order the defendant to return personal property to the plaintiff by means of a writ of delivery. The creditor also may apply to the Registrar of Motor Vehicles to have the debtor's driver's licence suspended if the outstanding judgment is not paid. In order to do this, however, one would need a certificate of judgment and the action must have involved damages as a result of a motor vehicle accident.

22. — Is the Court's Judgment the End of the Road?

There are two types of appeals which may be made from a Small Claims Court judgment: 1) an application for a new trial and 2) an appeal to the Divisional Court in the region in which the order appealed from was made, unless the parties agree otherwise. See section 31 of the *Courts of Justice Act*, R.S.O. 1990, c. C.43.

A "new trial" proceeds as if the first trial had never taken place. In certain cases, it may be obvious after a trial that justice was not done. Such cases might arise where the defendant had failed to appear at the trial through no fault of his own, or where some crucial piece of evidence, such as a lost cancelled cheque or receipt, becomes available after the original trial. A new trial is a useful and inexpensive way of correcting the original judgment in such cases.

An appeal from a final order or judgment of the Small Claims Court in an action for the payment of money in excess of $2,500, exclusive of costs, lies as indicated to the Divisional Court. This type of appeal should generally be used where a question of law or mixed question of fact and law is involved. The appeal court may dismiss the appeal, give the judgment that in its opinion ought to have been given at trial, or, in some circumstances, order a new trial.

23. — Set Asides

A notice of motion is a document which tells the judge and the other party to the action when the person applying for an order will be appearing in court, what type of order the person wants to obtain, and what evidence will be used to support the application.

See subrule 11.06 setting out the grounds for setting aside default judgment and the noting in default.

An affidavit is a document which sets out certain facts which you swear under oath to be true. The affidavit which you prepare must contain the following:

1. a statement that you are the defendant;

2. a statement that a judgment was granted against you;

3. a statement of why you failed to file a defence or why you failed to appear on the date set for trial;

4. a statement that you are bringing on the application at the first possible opportunity (explain the reason for any prolonged delay in bringing up the application);

5. a statement of the facts on which your defence is based; and

6. a statement of why the affidavit has been prepared.

Service is necessary on all parties who have filed a claim or defence (subrule 15.01(2)). It is the responsibility of the party initiating the notice of motion to effect service. You may also have to serve Motion on parties even where no defence filed. The date for the hearing is inserted in the notice of motion. Finally, the notice of motion and supporting documents where served personally (at least seven days before the motion is to be heard) or by mail (at least twelve days before the motion is to be heard). Service, therefore, must be made at least seven days prior to the hearing if served personally or must be made at least twelve days prior to the hearing where service is made by either regular lettermail or registered mail (see subrule 8.07(2)).

On the date which has been set for you to appear in court you should be sure to arrive on time.

Stand when you speak to the judge and address him or her as "Your Honour." You should say the following:

> Your Honour, I am making an application to have a default judgment entered against me set aside.

The judge may ask you some questions about your case. He will then either grant the order you are seeking, tell you what further things you must do to obtain your order, or dismiss it.

If the judge does grant the order you are seeking, he may at the same time award costs to the plaintiff. This is because a judge may feel that the plaintiff should be compensated for the inconvenience he or she has been put through.

24. — Warrants in Small Claims Court

General Information

There are two types of warrants in Small Claims Court: A Warrant for Arrest of Defaulting Witness (Form 18B) and a Warrant of Committal (Form 20J) following a Contempt Hearing. These warrants are to be directed to all police officers in Ontario and not to the bailiff for enforcement.

Warrant for Arrest of Defaulting Witness

(a) Generally: A Warrant for Arrest of Defaulting Witness is used to arrest a witness who has been served with a summons to witness and has failed to attend or remain in attendance at trial as required. This type of warrant enables the police to apprehend the witness and bring him/her promptly before the court. The witness may be detained in custody until his/her presence is no longer required or he/she is released on such terms as the court deems just. Costs may be awarded against the witness, arising from failure to attend (Rule 18.03(6) and (7)).

18.03 (6) **Failure to Attend or Remain in Attendance** — If a witness whose evidence is material to the conduct of an action fails to attend at the trial or to remain in attendance in accordance with the requirements of a summons to witness served on him or her, the trial judge may, by warrant (Form 18B) directed to all police officers in Ontario, cause the witness to be apprehended anywhere within Ontario and promptly brought before the court.

(7) On being apprehended, the witness may be detained in custody until his or her presence is no longer required or released on such terms as are just, and may be ordered to pay the costs arising out of the failure to attend or remain in attendance.

(b) Process: See new subrule 8.03(6.1) and the filing of an Identification Form (Form 20K).

25. — DOs and DON'Ts in Court

1) Do be on time. If you cannot avoid being late, tell someone so that the judge can be made aware. As soon as you arrive, apologize to the Court.

2) Do dress for court. Dress professionally for all court appearances.

3) Do be courteous and respectful in the courtroom.

4) Don't interrupt the Court or other counsel. If you have an objection to what other counsel is saying, stand up, say "objection", and wait for the judge to call on you. If you disagree with something the judge is saying, wait for the judge to finish on that point, stand up and advise that you respectfully take issue with what has been said.

5) Do be prepared.

6) Don't waste time: the Court's, your client's, other counsel's, or your own. Have your necessary discussions with opposite counsel and your client before Court starts; make submissions efficiently; and adhere to any time restrictions the Court has imposed.

7) Don't use electronic devices (laptop, blackberry, iPad) when your matter is being dealt with, unless you first request and receive permission from the Court.

8) Don't take or make a telephone call in court.

9) Do be a good loser or a good winner.

10) Don't take the Court's decision personally.

11) Do keep it simple.

12) Do keep it brief.

13) Do be respectful.

14) Don't make a fool of yourself.

15) Don't be your own lawyer or you will have a fool for a client.

16) Don't argue against someone; argue for your case.

17) Don't forget image, it is everything.

18) Do argue the facts, they won't go away.

19) Do know the law; ignorance of the law is no excuse.

20) Don't argue with the judge: he/she is never wrong.

21) Don't refer to witnesses as being old or to their age; look at the judge first.

22) Don't wait for the judge to compliment you, it usually means you lost.

23) Don't keep jumping up and down and saying, "I object." Too much of Perry Mason is not a good thing.

24) Don't try to fill a sack that is full of holes.

25) Don't wake up the judge. He/she may wink a while, but will see in the end.

26) Don't keep saying, "It is the truth, it is the truth." Truth and falsehoods are often indistinguishable.

27) Don't forget to call all your witnesses. One eyewitness is worth more than ten who tell what they have heard.

28) Don't use too many words, especially one, et cetera, et cetera. You don't want to have to eat them.

29) Don't forget that sweet words to a judge are like honey; a little may refresh, but too much may bloat the stomach.

30) Don't forget, if you have a good case, try to settle; if you have a bad one, don't take it to court.

31) Don't forget that cases can be like a fruit tree planted in your garden, except that many judges are not gardeners.

32) Don't be scared of a courtroom. Judges are there to interpret and apply the law, not make it.

33) Don't forget that your success or failure or your death trap may be between your teeth.

34) Don't worry if the judge refers to you as a donkey; more than once, start to worry, three times, get a saddle.

35) Don't forget that preparation is the be-all and end-all of good trial work. It is after all, the resolution of a dispute.

36) Don't forget, if all else fails, call the judge "Your Majesty."

26.

MOVIE	SPEAKING OUT
ANATOMY OF A MURDER (1959) Directed by Otto Preminger Written by Wendell Mayes	"A witness that cannot talk will be a welcome relief." (The judge, referring to Laura Manion's dog.)
A FEW GOOD MEN (1992) Directed by Rob Reiner Written by Aaron Sorkin	"He is dead because he had no honor." Kiefer Sutherland's character (referring to Santiago.)
GHOSTS OF MISSISSIPPI (1996) Directed by Rob Reiner Written by Lewis Colick	"I did not kill him, but he sho is dead." (Byron De La Beckwith in a television interview.)
INHERIT THE WIND (1960) Directed by Stanley Kramer Written by Nathan E. Douglas and Harold Jacob Smith	"Where did Cain's wife come from?" (Spencer Tracy, as the defence lawyer, to Frederic March, as the prosecutor, questioning literal interpretations of the Book of Genesis.)
THE JUROR (1996) Directed by Brian Gibson Written by Ted Tally	"You could do nothing but make art for the rest of your life." (Hit man to Annie, offering big money for her cooperation.)
JURY DUTY (1995) Directed by John Fortenberry Written by Neil Tolkin, Barbara Williams and Samantha Adams	"So this whole thing had nothing to do with justice, did it?" (Monica, a fellow juror played by Tia Carrere, to Tommy.)
TRIAL BY JURY (1994) Directed by Heywood Gould Written by Jordan Katz and Mr. Gould	"We're out of your life forever." (William Hurt, as a gum chewing ex-cop who now works for the mob, to Valerie.)
TWELVE ANGRY MEN (1957) Directed by Sidney Lumet Written by Reginald Rose	"They're no good. There's not a one of them that's any good." (Ed Begley, as Juror No. 10, about "those people," as he refers to the defendant and the victim.)
THE VERDICT (1982) Directed by Sidney Lumet Written by David Mamet	"I came here to take your money." (Paul Newman, as a washed-up lawyer once accused of jury-tampering, to church officials.)
WITNESS FOR THE PROSECUTION (1957) Directed by Billy Wilder Written by Larry Marcus and Harry Kurnitz	"They don't like her, but they believed her." (An associate of the judge on the juror's opinion of Marlene Dietrich's character.)
TAKE A GUESS	

MOVIE	SPEAKING OUT
(read the paper) Thank you very much and good litigating.	

If privacy is a concern, the Court can order that parties be identified only by initials, or seal its files. The test is whether such an order is necessary to achieve justice. Simple convenience or the potential for embarrassment (see *R.K. v. Bride*, [1994] B.C.J. No. 27) will not suffice to displace the public interest in an open process, and the onus is on the applicant to demonstrate necessity. For a discussion of the policy considerations involved, see *R. v. Moozhayil*, 2004 BCSC 976, 2004 CarswellBC 1639, [2004] B.C.J. No. 1499 (B.C. S.C.) and *B. (A.) v. D. (C.)*, 2010 BCSC 1530, 2010 CarswellBC 2912 (B.C. S.C.).

Jurisdiction

Areas of law often falling outside the jurisdiction of the Small Claims Court are divorce, trusts, wills (i.e. probate), prerogative writs, and bankruptcy. However, the court may have jurisdiction over cases where these areas of law are involved only circumstantially — where the pith and substance of the case does fall within the court's jurisdiction. Where the dispute is contractual, the existence of a "forum selection clause" may provide jurisdictional difficulties. Forum selection clauses try to prevent conflicts between the parties from being adjudicated except for in the named jurisdiction. Such clauses will generally be upheld absent a finding of "strong cause" to hear the matter in the jurisdiction of another court. Courts will generally not enforce illegal contracts or dishonest transactions. However, *Transport North American Express Inc. v. New Solutions Financial Corp.*, 2004 SCC 7, 2004 CarswellOnt 512, 2004 CarswellOnt 513, REJB 2004-53611, [2004] 1 S.C.R. 249, 70 O.R. (3d) 255 (note), 40 B.L.R. (3d) 18, 18 C.R. (6th) 1, 235 D.L.R. (4th) 385, 17 R.P.R. (4th) 1, 316 N.R. 84, 183 O.A.C. 342, [2004] S.C.J. No. 9 (S.C.C.) states that a court may enforce legal portions of a contract, thus effectively severing the illegal portion. A common example involves contracts purporting to charge interest rates prohibited under s. 347 of the *Criminal Code*. The court will not enforce a term in a contract purporting to charge such a rate. (However, section 347.1 exempts payday loans from criminal sanctions, if certain conditions are met.)

Claims Over $25,000

For claims exceeding $25,000, the claimant must "abandon the excess", if the claim is to be heard in small claims court. For example: "The claimant abandons the excess amount to bring this claim within the jurisdiction of this court". Is an abandonment of the amount in excess of $25,000 irrevocable?

Settlement Conference

Parties should prepare a brief, clear, and chronological summary of their case, with supporting evidence on hand. Be able to summarize your case for the judge at the settlement conference and break down your case into each of its elements and to bring documents to prove each element of the case.

A judge may dismiss a case if it is outside the court's jurisdiction, the claimant presents no evidence, or if the limitation period at the date of filing has expired. A judge should not dismiss a case at the settlement conference on the basis of issues relating to the credibility of witness or evidence. A judge may also order that multiple claims be heard at the same time, or consolidated into one claim. The distinction is important.

If the parties cannot reach a settlement, the focus will turn to trial preparation. To be well prepared for trial, you must know you have to meet. Therefore, you want full disclosure from the other side well in advance of the trial. The judge at a settlement conference has the power to order production of documents and you can assist with a list of what you believe is in the possession of the other parties.

At a settlement conference, each party must disclose the number of witnesses that party intends to call, indicate what evidence each witness will give, and provide an estimate of time required. If expert evidence will be used, it is helpful if a written report (or at least a draft copy) is available for the settlement conference. Often, the "threat" of an expert report provides the impetus for a settlement proposal.

If a party does not comply with a disclosure order, a judge may adjourn the trial or settlement conference and order that party to pay expenses, order the trial to proceed without allowing that evidence to be used, or dismiss the action.

Consider writing to the other side after the settlement conference to confirm the deadline, the documents you require and which remedy you will pursue if there is no disclosure. When you send documents, it is important to include a list or outline of hat material is enclosed.

Judge's Summary of the Issue

The settlement/ conference judge will often include a summary on the record sheet of the issues in dispute or agreed facts for the information of the trial judge. If it is clear that some issues are not contentious, one should seek admissions at the settlement/ trial conference, so proof will not be at trial. That may reduce the number of witnesses required. Also, if a party is in a position to offer admissions, it will save time and allow the trial to focus only on the points in issue. To save trial time, suggest compiling an agreed statement of facts by a certain deadline.

Agreement Reached

If an agreement reached at a settlement conference includes payment, and if a party does not comply, the agreement can be cancelled.

After filing an affidavit describing the non-compliance, the person entitled to payment may file a payment order for either the amount agreed to by the parties as the default amount and note on the record as the default amount endorsed by the judge at the settlement conference or the full amount of the original claim if there was no default amount endorsed by the judge.

If the settlement pertains to an action against a lawyer for which a complaint has been filed with the Law Society, you should not use complaint withdrawal as a bargaining technique; it is improper during settlement negations to offer to withdraw a complaint against a lawyer as a part of the settlement.

It is also in appropriate for a lawyer to threaten to initiate or proceed with a criminal charge, make a complaint to a regulatory body or threaten disciplinary procedures with the Law Society to further a client's civil claim against another.

Trial Preparation

Expert Witnesses

An expert witness, although not a witness to the actual event, is allowed to give an opinion about what happened — if expertise is required to help the court better understand the issues (for case law on the admissibility of expert evidence see *R. v. Mohan*, 1994 CarswellOnt 1155, 1994 CarswellOnt 66, EYB 1994-67655, [1994] 2 S.C.R. 9, 18 O.R. (3d) 160 (note),

89 C.C.C. (3d) 402, 29 C.R. (4th) 243, 114 D.L.R. (4th) 419, 166 N.R. 245, 71 O.A.C. 241, [1994] S.C.J. No. 36 (S.C.C.))

Evidence may be given by an expert at trial or through a written report (note: expert reports must be the opinion of one person).

Expert witness testimony may be inadmissible if it is used merely to lay out possible scenarios or to advance arguments in relation to commonplace issues that the court is able to analyze itself.

An expert witness report would include the resume or qualifications of the expert, a brief discussion of the facts of the case supporting the opinion or conclusion, the opinion or conclusion itself, and what was done to arrive at that conclusion.

An exception to the "in person" rule for expert witnesses is permitted for estimates and quotes. The claimant may bring a written estimate for the repair of damage or a written estimate of the property value and present it as evidence at trial without calling the person who gave the estimate or quote. Estimates of repairs or value of goods are not considered to be expert evidence.

Order of Proceedings at Trial

Once a trial is ready to proceed and the court clerk calls the parties to the litigants' table, most trials are conducted as follows:

a) opening statement by claimant;

b) one of the counsel should be sure to ask for an order excluding all witnesses who are to be called in the case, excepting the parties involved;

c) direct and cross-examination of claimant;

d) direct and cross-examination of claimant's witnesses;

e) claimant has a right to re-examine their witness, but only if something new arises from cross-examination;

f) opening statement by defendant;

g) direct and cross-examination of defendant;

h) direct and cross-examination of defendant's witnesses;

i) defendant has a right to re-examine their witnesses, but only if something new arises during cross-examination;

j) claimant's closing argument;

k) defendant's closing argument;

l) claimant has a right of reply; and

m) judgment.

Objections may arise at any point during the trial.

Conduct During the Trial

- Be on time. If you are late, apologize and be prepared to give an excellent explanation.

- Do not argue directly with opposing counsel. Make submissions only to the judge and have him or her ask questions to opposing counsel.

- Never call witnesses by their given name. Use Mr., Ms., Miss, or Mrs. And their last name.

- While you may be trying to get a witness to relax, courtrooms are not casual settings and most judges will try to maintain considerable decorum. It will not help you to relax if you are reprimanded for being too casual in addressing a witness.

- A judge of the Provincial Court is referred to as "Your Honour" and opposing counsel as "my friend". The clerk is referred to as "Madame Clerk" or "Mr. Clerk".

- Focus on the main issues in the trial and what evidence on each issue you expect from each witness. You should be able to predict the weakness in your opponent's case and also how he or she might try to correct hose problems. That will help you choose your battles and your objections should focus mostly on those issues. There may be other reasons for objecting, but generally you should limit objections. If you have an objection, stand up quickly and make sure you are heard. If you do not want the witness to hear the question or the judge to hear the answer you must act quickly and effectively — then fumble, if you must with articulating your reason.

Caselaw

Interpretation

Section 14 of the *Charter* guaranteed accused the right to an interpreter — Without an interpreter, she could not have a fair trial — The usual remedy for a breach of s. 14 is a rehearing of the proceeding: *R. v. Tran*, 1994 CarswellNS 24, 1994 CarswellNS 435, EYB 1994-67408, [1994] 2 S.C.R. 951, 133 N.S.R. (2d) 81, 92 C.C.C. (3d) 218, 32 C.R. (4th) 34, 117 D.L.R. (4th) 7, 380 A.P.R. 81, 23 C.R.R. (2d) 32, 170 N.R. 81, [1994] S.C.J. No. 16 (S.C.C.) — Trial judge failed to apply proper test for a stay.

Costs

An appropriate costs order balances two conflicting principles; namely, that:

> 1. A blameless litigant who is successful in a proceeding should not be required to bear the costs of prosecuting or defending the proceeding.

> 2. Parties should not be made to feel unduly hesitant to assert or defend their rights in court by the prospect that, if unsuccessful, they will be required to bear all the costs of their opponent.

The Supreme Court of Canada has held that the ultimate objective in balancing these two principles is to ensure that the justice system works fairly and efficiently. *British Columbia (Minister of Forests) v. Okanagan Indian Band* (2003), 2003 SCC 71, 2003 CarswellBC 3040, 2003 CarswellBC 3041, [2003] 3 S.C.R. 371, 21 B.C.L.R. (4th) 209, 43 C.P.C. (5th) 1, 233 D.L.R. (4th) 577, [2004] 2 W.W.R. 252, 189 B.C.A.C. 161, [2004] 1 C.N.L.R. 7, 114 C.R.R. (2d) 108, 313 N.R. 84, 309 W.A.C. 161, [2003] S.C.J. No. 76 (S.C.C.) at paras. 25 and 26 [*Okanagan*].

The entitlement to costs and the amount to be paid are "within the court's discretion." *Courts of Justice Act*, s. 131.

The Court of Appeal for Ontario in *1465778 Ontario Inc. v. 1122077 Ontario Ltd.*, 2006 CarswellOnt 6582, 82 O.R. (3d) 757, 38 C.P.C. (6th) 1, 275 D.L.R. (4th) 321, 216 O.A.C. 339, [2006] O.J. No. 4248 (Ont. C.A.) at para. 45) held that the courts, in awarding costs, should also consider a further objective, in the need to preserve access to justice. While historically, courts reserved costs awards exclusively to litigants who were represented by lawyers, and tied the amounts of costs awards to the fees paid to the lawyers, courts more recently have recognized that allowing self-represented litigants to recover costs helps attain the broader objectives of costs awards and advances access to justice.

Self-represented lay litigants are also not bound by the rules of professional conduct or by the strictures applying to "officers of the court." Judges presiding at hearings where one party is represented and the other is not must constantly reconcile the expectations designed for legal professionals with the limited ability that the self-represented litigant may have to meet them.

Wildman J. assessed the self-represented litigant's costs in *Rashid v. Shaher*, 2011 ONSC 852, 2011 CarswellOnt 738, 97 R.F.L. (6th) 213, Wildman J. (Ont. S.C.J. [In Chambers])

Both a litigant's failure to make reasonable efforts to settle and a grossly excessive claim, whether by a lawyer or a self-represented litigant, are factors properly considered in reducing the rate, as well as the time, allowed in a costs assessment.

In *Izyuk v. Bilousov*, 2011 ONSC 7476, 2011 CarswellOnt 14392, 7 R.F.L. (7th) 358, [2011] O.J. No. 5814 (Ont. S.C.J.). Pazaratz J. applied an hourly rate of $100 to the successful self-represented litigant (against a litigant whose lawyer's hourly rate was $325 on a substantial indemnity scale, or $200 on a partial indemnity scale), although he reduced what would have been the resulting award of $30,000 to $10,000 based on the payer's limited ability to pay. In *Rodriguez v. Sing*, 2012 ONCJ 797, 2012 CarswellOnt 16843 (Ont. C.J.). Curtis J. awarded a successful self-represented litigant costs at approximately the same hourly rate ($100).

In *Spettigue v. Varcoe*, 2012 ONSC 925, 2012 CarswellOnt 1422 (Ont. S.C.J.) at para. 52), Chappel J. awarded the self-represented litigant's costs at $100 on a substantial indemnity scale, and $75 on a partial indemnity scale. She stated:

> The case-law is clear that in valuing a self-represented litigant's work on the case, the court should consider not only the income loss that the litigant experienced, but also the value of the work to the court. Having considered this principle and the factors discussed above, I conclude that Mr. Spettigue's time should be valued at $100 per hour on a full indemnity basis, and $75 per hour on a partial indemnity basis.

Courts — Bias

Court of Appeal found that judge had failed to weigh submission carefully and contextually and to take account of all relevant circumstances — In this case, properly informed reasonable person would only conclude that connection of judge's wife to disputed property was deep and current and multi-layered — Appellant had met high threshold to establish reasonable apprehension of bias — New trial ordered before different judge. *Bailey v. Barbour*, 2012 ONCA 325, 2012 CarswellOnt 6026, 110 O.R. (3d) 161, 21 C.P.C. (7th) 260, 17 R.P.R. (5th) 49, 291 O.A.C. 344, [2012] O.J. No. 2178 (Ont. C.A.).

Trial judge also made seemingly gratuitous statement midway through trial that single inaccuracy in plaintiff's *curriculum vitae* spoke to her credibility — He also labelled it as a "falsification" of document — Defendants had never raised this point in their cross-examination of plaintiff and it was not part of their defence — Judge's comments "out of the blue" before the end of trial were inappropriate — They raised serious issue about his impartiality and raised reasonable apprehension of bias, especially in context of his previous fixation on fraud and its apparent impact on his perception of the plaintiffs' case — New trial ordered. *Lloyd v. Bush*, 2012 ONCA 349, 2012 CarswellOnt 6490, 110 O.R. (3d) 781, 350 D.L.R. (4th) 81, 292 O.A.C. 251, [2012] O.J. No. 2343 (Ont. C.A.).

Ontario Deputy Judges' Association v. Ontario (Attorney General), 2012 ONCA 437, 2012 CarswellOnt 7932, 23 C.P.C. (7th) 1, [2012] O.J. No. 2865 (Ont. C.A.)

We agree with the application judge that the process for renewing the appointments of Deputy Judges of the Small Claims Court ("Deputy Judges") does not infringe the principles of judicial independence.

Pursuant to s. 32(1) of the *Courts of Justice Act*, R.S.O. 1990, c. C-43, as amended (the "*CJA*"), a Regional Senior Judge of the Superior Court may, with the approval of the Attorney General, appoint a lawyer to act as a Deputy Judge of the Small Claims Court for a period of three years.

A reasonable and well informed observer would conclude that the Deputy Judges and the Ontario Small Claims Court are sufficiently independent so as to satisfy constitutional requirements.

We also endorse the application judge's comment as follows (at para. 62):

> Without doubt, the [Small Claims Court] plays an important and unique role in the justice system. It is absolutely essential that the [Small Claims Court] institutionally and the [Deputy Judges] personally, be regarded as independent.

Appeal dismissed

Costs for Self Represented Parties

The costs claimed by self-represented litigants has been dealt with by Justice D. G. Price in *Jahn-Cartwright v. Cartwright*, 2010 ONSC 2263, 2010 CarswellOnt 5657, 91 R.F.L. (6th) 301, [2010] O.J. No. 3307 (Ont. S.C.J.) and *Cassidy v. Cassidy*, 2011 ONSC 791, 2011 CarswellOnt 1541, 89 C.C.P.B. 294, 92 R.F.L. (6th) 120 (Ont. S.C.J.).

Justice Price made the following observations of the Ontario Court of Appeal decision in *Fong v. Chan*, 1999 CarswellOnt 3955, 46 O.R. (3d) 330, 181 D.L.R. (4th) 614, 128 O.A.C. 2, [1999] O.J. No. 4600 (Ont. C.A.):

a. The Court of Appeal confirmed a self-represented litigant's entitlement to costs.

b. The Court gave some guidance on the method of quantifying those costs, but did not elaborate as to the methodology to be used.

c. Self-represented litigants are not entitled to costs calculated on the same basis as litigants who retain counsel.

d. The self-represented litigant should not recover costs for the time and effort that any litigant would have to devote to the case.

e. Costs should only be awarded to those lay litigants who can demonstrate they devoted time and effort to do the work ordinarily done by a lawyer retained to conduct the litigation.

f. The trial judge is particularly well-placed to assess the appropriate allowance, if any, for a self-represented litigant.

In *Jahn-Cartwright* and *Cassidy*, Justice Price expanded the analysis:

a. The entitlement to costs and the appropriate amount to be paid is within the court's discretion.

b. Rule 24(1) of the Family Law Rules creates a presumption of costs in favour of the successful party.

c. In setting the amount of costs, the court must try to indemnify the successful party while avoiding an overly onerous costs burden for the unsuccessful party which would jeopardize access to justice.

d. For many years indemnification of a successful party was considered the only objective, and this was held to preclude an award of costs to a successful self-represented litigant who had not paid fees for which they needed to be indemnified. But while indemnification remains a paramount consideration in awarding costs, it is not the only one.

e. In both *Fong v. Chan* and more recently in *Serra v. Serra*, 2009 ONCA 395, 2009 CarswellOnt 2475, 66 R.F.L. (6th) 40, [2009] O.J. No. 1905 (Ont. C.A.), the Ontario

Court of Appeal confirmed that costs rules are designed to foster three important principles:

1. To partially indemnify successful litigants for the cost of litigation;

2. To encourage settlement; and

3. To discourage and sanction inappropriate behaviour by litigants.

f. Access to justice has been recognized as a further objective that the court should seek to achieve when awarding costs. (*1465778 Ontario Inc. v. 1122077 Ontario Ltd.*, 2006 CarswellOnt 6582, 82 O.R. (3d) 757, 38 C.P.C. (6th) 1, 275 D.L.R. (4th) 321, 216 O.A.C. 339, [2006] O.J. No. 4248 (Ont. C.A.)).

g. A party with counsel, opposite an unrepresented litigant, should not perceive that they are immune from a costs award merely because such opposite party is unrepresented. They should be discouraged from presuming they will face only nominal costs.

If a self-represented litigant, in performing the tasks that would normally have been performed by a lawyer, lost the opportunity to earn income elsewhere, this may be a relevant factor. But costs for self-represented parties are not the same as damages for lost income. Remunerative loss is not a "condition precedent" to an award of costs. To require proof of lost income would disqualify litigants who are homemakers, retirees, students, unemployed, unemployable, and disabled; and deprive courts of a tool required re administration of justice.

In considering the appropriate hourly rate, the court should consider what the lay litigant's reasonable expectations were as to the costs he would pay if unsuccessful. (*Boucher v. Public Accountants Council (Ontario)*, 2004 CarswellOnt 2521, 71 O.R. (3d) 291, 48 C.P.C. (5th) 56, 188 O.A.C. 201, [2004] O.J. No. 2634 (Ont. C.A.)).

Self-represented litigants may be held to the standards of civility expected of lawyers and a proper reprimand for failure to do so is an award of costs on a substantial indemnity basis. Where either a litigant or his/her lawyer acts unreasonably, by incivility or otherwise, it is a factor that may result in discounting the costs that should otherwise be awarded. This discounting is a necessary part of quantifying costs and is consistent with the overall purpose of costs awards in improving the efficiency of the administration of justice.

The *Jahn-Cartwright* analysis was accepted by Wildman, J. in *Rashid v. Shaher*, 2011 ONSC 852, 2011 CarswellOnt 738, 97 R.F.L. (6th) 213 (Ont. S.C.J. [In Chambers]) in which a successful self-represented party was awarded $10,000.00 in costs for an 11 day trial.

Rule 14.07

The purpose of Rule 14.07 is to encourage parties to make reasonable offers to settle or to contribute by imposing costs consequences on those who do not reasonable assess the actual value of the case in advance of trial.

Cost consequences are result oriented. The terms of the offer are measured not against the claim advanced, but rather against the judgment obtained in order to determine whether such offer is "as favourable as", "more favourable than" or "less favourable than" the judgment.

For the purpose of comparing the offer with the judgment, the court considers the amount finally awarded by the trial judge plus prejudgment interest: see *Pilon v. Janveaux*, 2006 CarswellOnt 1211, 29 M.V.R. (5th) 172, 211 O.A.C. 19, [2006] O.J. No. 887 (Ont. C.A.). This is the amount contained in the formal judgment that finally disposed of the action.

Van Breda v. Village Resorts Ltd., 2012 SCC 17, 2012 CarswellOnt 4268, 2012 CarswellOnt 4269, (sub nom. *Club Resorts Ltd. v. Van Breda*) [2012] 1 S.C.R. 572, (sub nom. *Charron Estate v. Village Resorts Ltd.*) 114 O.R. (3d) 79 (note), 91 C.C.L.T. (3d) 1, 17 C.P.C. (7th)

223, 343 D.L.R. (4th) 577, 10 R.F.L. (7th) 1, 429 N.R. 217, 291 O.A.C. 201, [2012] A.C.S. No. 17, [2012] S.C.J. No. 17 (S.C.C.)

Respondents injured while vacationing in Cuba — Actions for damages brought in Ontario. Defendants bringing motion to stay actions on grounds that Ontario court lacks jurisdiction, or alternatively, should decline to exercise jurisdiction on basis of forum non conveniens. Whether Ontario court can assume jurisdiction over actions. If so, whether Ontario court should decline to exercise its jurisdiction on ground that court of another jurisdiction is clearly a more appropriate forum for hearing of actions.

Motion judges found that the Ontario courts had jurisdiction with respect to the actions against Club Resorts. In considering *forum non conveniens*, it was also held that the Ontario court was clearly a more appropriate forum. The two cases were heard together in the Court of Appeal. The appeals were both dismissed. The appeals should be dismissed.

In a case concerning a tort, the factors are presumptive connecting factors that, *prima facie*, entitle a court to assume jurisdiction over a dispute:

(a) the defendant is domiciled or resident in the province;

(b) the defendant carries on business in the province;

(c) the tort was committed in the province; and

(d) a contract connected with the dispute was made in the province.

Colavecchia v. Berkeley Hotel Ltd., 2012 ONSC 4747, 2012 CarswellOnt 10313, 112 O.R. (3d) 287, 353 D.L.R. (4th) 343 (Ont. S.C.J.); additional reasons 2012 ONSC 5868, 2012 CarswellOnt 12806 (Ont. S.C.J.)

Defendant was a boutique hotel located in London, England. The female plaintiff booked a room at the hotel through the TD Visa Travel Rewards website and paid by redeeming travel points. The male plaintiff was injured when he slipped and fell in the bathroom of their hotel room. The plaintiffs sued the defendant in Ontario for damages for negligence. The defendant brought a motion to dismiss the action for lack of jurisdiction.

The website was nothing more than a search engine for those who wanted to use their travel points.

Right to counsel — No right of access to affordable justice — Plaintiff argued that Law Society's regulation of paralegals violated constitutional right of access to affordable justice, but could point to no provision of *Canadian Charter of Rights and Freedoms* that enshrined this alleged right — Court relied on A.G. for *Christie v. British Columbia (Attorney General)*, 2007 SCC 21, 2007 CarswellBC 1117, 2007 CarswellBC 1118, (sub nom. *British Columbia (Attorney General) v. Christie*) [2007] 1 S.C.R. 873, 66 B.C.L.R. (4th) 1, 280 D.L.R. (4th) 528, [2007] 8 W.W.R. 64, 240 B.C.A.C. 1, (sub nom. *British Columbia (Attorney General) v. Christie*) 155 C.R.R. (2d) 366, (sub nom. *British Columbia (Attorney General) v. Christie*) 2007 D.T.C. 5525 (Eng.), (sub nom. *British Columbia (Attorney General) v. Christie*) 2007 D.T.C. 5229 (Fr.), (sub nom. *British Columbia (Attorney General) v. Christie*) 2007 G.T.C. 1493 (Fr.), (sub nom. *British Columbia (Attorney General) v. Christie*) 2007 G.T.C. 1488 (Eng.), 361 N.R. 322, 398 W.A.C. 1, [2007] S.C.J. No. 21 (S.C.C.), to reject plaintiff's position.

Pleadings — Striking out pleadings — Grounds — Pleadings disclose no cause of action — Where claim not only failed to disclose cause of action but was also doomed to fail, no matter how cleverly drafted, court allowed defendant's motion to strike plaintiff's pleadings without permission to amend those pleadings. *Kopyto v. Law Society of Upper Canada*, 2012 ONCA 833, 2012 CarswellOnt 15010 (Ont. C.A.); affirming 2012 ONSC 4050, 2012 CarswellOnt 8759, 218 A.C.W.S. (3d) 766, [2012] O.J. No. 3221 (Ont. S.C.J.), *per* Justice Darla A. Wilson.

COURTS OF JUSTICE ACT

An Act to revise and consolidate the Law respecting the Organization, Operation and Proceedings of Courts of Justice in Ontario

R.S.O. 1990, c. C.43, as am. S.O. 1991 (Vol. 2), c. 46; 1993, c. 27, Sched. (Fr.); O. Reg. 922/93 [Amended O. Reg. 441/97]; 1994, c. 12, ss. 1–48 [s. 9 not in force at date of publication. Repealed 1999, c. 12, Sched. B, s. 5.]; 1994, c. 27, s. 43; 1996, c. 25, ss. 1, 9; 1996, c. 31, ss. 65, 66; 1997, c. 19, s. 32; 1997, c. 23, s. 5; 1997, c. 26, Sched.; 1998, c. 4, s. 2; 1998, c. 18, Sched. B, s. 5, Sched. G, s. 48; 1998, c. 20, s. 2, Sched. A; 1999, c. 6, s. 18; 1999, c. 12, Sched. B, ss. 4, 5; 2000, c. 26, Sched. A, s. 5; 2000, c. 33, s. 20 [Not in force at date of publication. Amended 2002, c. 18, Sched. A, s. 6(8). Repealed 2009, c. 11, s. 21.]; 2001, c. 9, Sched. B, s. 6 [Not in force at date of publication. Repealed 2006, c. 21, Sched. F, s. 10.1(1).]; 2002, c. 13, s. 56; 2002, c. 14, Sched., s. 9; 2002, c. 17, Sched. F, s. 1; 2002, c. 18, Sched. A, s. 4; 2004, c. 17, s. 32, Table; 2005, c. 5, s. 17; 2006, c. 1, s. 4; 2006, c. 19, Sched. D, s. 5; 2006, c. 21, Sched. A, Sched. C, s. 105, Sched. F, ss. 106, 136(1), Table 1; 2006, c. 35, Sched. C, s. 20; 2009, c. 11, ss. 19, 20; 2009, c. 33, Sched. 2, s. 20, Sched. 6, s. 50 [Sched. 2, s. 20(1), (12)–(14) not in force at date of publication.].

[Editor's note: please see transitional provision from Courts Improvement Act, 1996 *regarding court name changes below*

> *10. Transition, seals and forms — (1) A reference in a court seal or printed court form to the name of a court or the title of an official changed by section 8 does not prevent the form or seal from being used during the one year period following the date the change to the name or title becomes effective.*
>
> *(2) This section applies only to court seals and printed court forms in existence on the date the changes to the names of the courts and the titles of the officials becomes effective.]*

Key sections of the *Courts of Justice Act* include:

Role of sheriff	Section 141(1) states that unless an Act provides otherwise, orders of a court arising out of a civil proceeding and enforceable in Ontario shall be directed to a sheriff for enforcement.
Enlisting Police	Section 141(2) states that a sheriff who believes that the execution of an order may give rise to a breach of the peace may require a police officer to accompany the sheriff and assist in the execution of the order.
Contempt	Section 143 states that the sheriff shall proceed immediately to carry out writs to enforce a fine for contempt or a bond or recognizance from a civil proceeding, without a direction to enforce.
Security in Respect of Proceedings	Section 115 states that where a person is required to give security in respect of a proceeding in a court, a bond of an insurer licensed under the *Insurance Act* to write surety and fidelity insurance is sufficient, unless the court orders otherwise.

Organization of the Courts of Ontario: The development of the *Courts of Justice Act, 1984* can be divided into three major phases:

Phase 1: The original *Courts of Justice Act, 1984*, S.O. 1984, c. 11 replaced the former *Judicature Act*, R.S.O. 1980, c. 223. The Act brought major changes to the court structure: it consolidated all Acts relating to the courts of Ontario; it amalgamated all the county and district courts into the District Court; and it came into force together with the *Rules of Civil Procedure*.

Phase 2: The Courts of *Justice Amendment Act, 1989*, S.O. 1989, c. 55, introduced further significant changes in the court structure by merging the former Supreme Court of Ontario, the District Court of Ontario and the Provincial Court (Civil Division) into a single court called the Ontario Court of Justice.

Phase 3: The *Courts of Justice Act*, R.S.O. 1990, c. C.43, substantially renumbered the predecessor Act. In 1996, the Legislative Assembly made further efforts to improve the administration of justice in Ontario by enacting the *Courts Improvement Act, 1996*, S.O. 1996, c. 25. The *Courts Improvement Act* amended certain sections of the *Courts of Justice Act*, *Evidence Act*, *Children's Law Reform Act*, and the *Freedom of Information Act*. Part IV of the Act came into force on April 19, 1999 and changed the name of the Ontario Court of Justice to Court of Ontario, the name of the Ontario Court (General Division) to the Superior Court of Justice, and the name of the Ontario Court (Provincial Division) to the Ontario Court of Justice.

Divisional Court

By s. 18 of the Act, the branch of the High Court of Justice formerly known as the Divisional Court was continued as a branch of the Superior Court of Justice under the same name. The Divisional Court has as its head the Chief Justice of the Superior Court of Justice, who is the president of the court. Every judge of the Superior Court of Justice is also a judge of the Divisional Court, and the Chief Justice is responsible for designating judges to that court as required.

By s. 20 of the Act, an appeal to the Divisional Court shall be heard in the region in which the order appealed from was made, unless the parties agree otherwise or the Chief Justice of the Superior Court of Justice orders otherwise. Any other proceedings in the Divisional Court may be brought in any region.

Small Claims Court

Like the Divisional Court, the Small Claims Court is a branch of the Superior Court of Justice and has as its judicial head the Chief Justice of the Superior Court of Justice, who is also the president of the Court of Justice, who is also the president of the court and who is responsible for assigning the judges to the court. Every judge of the Superior Court of Justice is also a judge of the Small Claims Court.

The Small Claims Court's jurisdiction is governed by s. 23 of the Act. This section provides that the court has jurisdiction in any action for the payment of money or the recovery of personal property where the amount claimed or the value of the property does not exceed the prescribed amount, which was increased to $25,000 effective January 1, 2010.

A proceeding in the Small Claims Court shall be heard and determined by one judge of the Superior Court of Justice: s. 24(1). However, a proceeding may also be determined by a provincial judge who was assigned to the former Provincial Court (Civil Division) immediately before the new *Courts of Justice Act, 1984* came into force, or by a deputy judge appointed under s. 32 of the Act. A deputy judge is a barrister and solicitor who has been appointed to act as a deputy judge by a regional senior judge of the Superior Court of Justice with the approval of the Attorney General. Deputy judges are appointed for a term of three years and cannot hear and determine an action for the payment of money or the recovery of personal property exceeding the prescribed amount of $25,000. The Small Claims Court has no jurisdiction to try actions that exceed these monetary limits, or to grant equitable relief: s. 96.

The Small Claims Court is required to hear and determine all questions of law and act in a summary way and make such order as it considers "just and agreeable to good conscience." To ensure that the court meets its statutory mandate to hear and determine cases in a summary way, s. 27 of the Act empowers the court to admit as evidence any oral testimony and any document or other thing so long as the evidence is relevant to the subject matter of the proceeding. The only exceptions to this rule are that the court will not admit into evidence testimony, documents or other things that would otherwise be inadmissible by reason of any privilege under the law of evidence or that are inadmissible by any statute.

An appeal lies to the Divisional Court from a final order of the Small Claims Court in an action for the payment of money or the recovery of personal property exceeding $2,500 in value: s. 31.

1. (1) Definitions — In this Act,

"action" means a civil proceeding that is not an application and includes a proceeding commenced by,

    (a) claim,

    (b) statement of claim,

    (c) notice of action,

    (d) counterclaim,

    (e) crossclaim,

    (f) third or subsequent party claim, or

    (g) divorce petition or counterpetition;

"application" means a civil proceeding that is commenced by notice of application or by application;

"defendant" means a person against whom an action is commenced;

"hearing" includes a trial;

"motion" means a motion in a proceeding or an intended proceeding;

"order" includes a judgment or decree;

"plaintiff" means a person who commences an action;

"region" means a region prescribed under section 79.1.

(2) Application to other Acts — This section applies to all other Acts affecting or relating to the courts and the administration of justice.

2006, c. 21, Sched. A, s. 1, Sched. F, s. 106

1.1 (1) References to former names of courts — A reference in an Act, rule or regulation to a court or official by the former name of that court or the former title of that official set out in column 1 of the following table or by a shortened version of that name or title shall be deemed, unless a contrary intention appears, to be a reference to the new name of that court or the new title of that official set out in column 2.

Column 1/Colonne 1 Former names and titles Anciennes appellations et anciens titres	Column 2/ Colonne 2 New names and titles Nouvelles appellations et nouveaux titres
Ontario Court of Justice Cour de justice de l'Ontario	Court of Ontario Cour de l'Ontario
Ontario Court (General Division) Cour de l'Ontario (Division générale)	Superior Court of Justice Cour supérieure de justice
Ontario Court (Provincial Division) Cour de l'Ontario (Division provinciale)	Ontario Court of Justice Cour de justice de l'Ontario
Chief Justice of the Ontario Court of Justice Juge en chef de la Cour de justice de l'Ontario	Chief Justice of the Superior Court of Justice Juge en chef de la Cour supérieure de justice
Associate Chief Justice of the Ontario Court of Justice Juge en chef adjoint de la Cour de justice de l'Ontario	Associate Chief Justice of the Superior Court of Justice Juge en chef adjoint de la Cour supérieure de justice
Associate Chief Justice (Family Court) of the Ontario Court of Justice Juge en chef adjoint (Cour de la famille) de la Cour de justice de l'Ontario	Associate Chief Justice (Family Court) of the Superior Court of Justice Juge en chef adjoint (Cour de la famille) de la Cour supérieure de justice
Chief Judge of the Ontario Court (Provincial Division) Juge en chef de la Cour de l'Ontario (Division provinciale)	Chief Justice of the Ontario Court of Justice Juge en chef de la Cour de justice de l'Ontario
Associate Chief Judge of the Ontario Court (Provincial Division) Juge en chef adjoint de la Cour de l'Ontario (Division provinciale)	Associate Chief Justice of the Ontario Court of Justice Juge en chef adjoint de la Cour de justice de l'Ontario
Associate Chief Judge-Co-ordinator of Justices of the Peace Juge en chef adjoint-coordonnateur des juges de paix	Associate Chief Justice Co-ordinator of Justices of the Peace Juge en chef adjoint et coordonnateur des juges de paix
Accountant of the Ontario Court Comptable de la Cour de l'Ontario	Accountant of the Superior Court of Justice Comptable de la Cour supérieure de justice

(2) **Same** — Subsection (1) does not apply to references to the Ontario Court of Justice enacted or made on or after the date this section comes into force.

1996, c. 25, s. 9(1)

PART I — COURT OF APPEAL FOR ONTARIO

2. (1) **Court of Appeal** — The Court of Appeal for Ontario is continued as a superior court of record under the name Court of Appeal for Ontario in English and Cour d'appel de l'Ontario in French.

(2) **Idem** — The Court of Appeal has the jurisdiction conferred on it by this or any other Act, and in the exercise of its jurisdiction has all the powers historically exercised by the Court of Appeal for Ontario.

3. (1) Composition of court — The Court of Appeal shall consist of,

    (a) the Chief Justice of Ontario, who shall be president of the court;

    (b) the Associate Chief Justice of Ontario; and

    (c) fourteen other judges.

(2) Idem — The Lieutenant Governor in Council may by regulation increase the number of judges of the Court of Appeal who are in addition to the Chief Justice and the Associate Chief Justice.

(3) Additional judges — There shall be such additional offices of judge of the Court of Appeal as are from time to time required, to be held by Chief Justices of Ontario and Associate Chief Justices of Ontario who have elected under the *Judges Act* (Canada) to perform only the duties of a judge of the Court of Appeal.

(4) Supernumerary judges — There shall be such additional offices of supernumerary judge of the Court of Appeal as are from time to time required, to be held by judges of the Court of Appeal who have elected under the *Judges Act* (Canada) to hold office only as a supernumerary judge of the court.

4. (1) Assignment of judges from Superior Court of Justice — The Chief Justice of Ontario, with the concurrence of the Chief Justice of the Superior Court of Justice, may assign a judge of the Superior Court of Justice to perform the work of a judge of the Court of Appeal.

(2) Superior Court of Justice judges — A judge of the Superior Court of Justice is, by virtue of his or her office, a judge of the Court of Appeal and has all the jurisdiction, power and authority of a judge of the Court of Appeal.

                                          1996, c. 25, s. 9(14), (17)

5. (1) Powers and duties of Chief Justice — The Chief Justice of Ontario has general supervision and direction over the sittings of the Court of Appeal and the assignment of the judicial duties of the court.

(2) Absence of Chief Justice — If the Chief Justice of Ontario is absent from Ontario or is for any reason unable to act, his or her powers and duties shall be exercised and performed by the Associate Chief Justice of Ontario.

(3) Absence of Associate Chief Justice — If the Chief Justice of Ontario and the Associate Chief Justice of Ontario are both absent from Ontario or for any reason unable to act, the powers and duties of the Chief Justice shall be exercised and performed by a judge of the Court of Appeal designated by the Chief Justice or Associate Chief Justice.

6. (1) Court of Appeal jurisdiction — An appeal lies to the Court of Appeal from,

    (a) an order of the Divisional Court, on a question that is not a question of fact alone, with leave of the Court of Appeal as provided in the rules of court;

    (b) a final order of a judge of the Superior Court of Justice, except an order referred to in clause 19(1)(a) or an order from which an appeal lies to the Divisional Court under another Act;

    (c) a certificate of assessment of costs issued in a proceeding in the Court of Appeal, on an issue in respect of which an objection was served under the rules of court.

(2) **Combining of appeals from other courts** — The Court of Appeal has jurisdiction to hear and determine an appeal that lies to the Divisional Court or the Superior Court of Justice if an appeal in the same proceeding lies to and is taken to the Court of Appeal.

(3) **Idem** — The Court of Appeal may, on motion, transfer an appeal that has already been commenced in the Divisional Court or the Superior Court of Justice to the Court of Appeal for the purpose of subsection (2).

1994, c. 12, s. 1; 1996, c. 25, s. 9(17)

Case Law: *Laczko v. Alexander*, 2012 ONCA 803, 2012 CarswellOnt 14480, Weiler J.A. (Ont. C.A. [In Chambers]); additional reasons 2012 ONCA 872, 2012 CarswellOnt 17256 (Ont. C.A.)

The moving parties seek an order to extend the time for filing a notice of appeal from an order striking out their statement of defence.

In deciding whether to extend the time, the following factors are relevant: (1) whether the moving parties formed an intention to appeal within the relevant period; (2) the length of and explanation for the delay; (3) any prejudice to the responding party; (4) the merits of the appeal; and (5) whether the justice of the case requires it: *Kefeli v. Centennial College of Applied Arts & Technology*, 2002 CarswellOnt 2539, 23 C.P.C. (5th) 35, [2002] O.J. No. 3023 (Ont. C.A. [In Chambers]); additional reasons 2002 CarswellOnt 6212, 20 C.P.C. (6th) 25 (Ont. C.A. [In Chambers]).

An order striking out a statement of defence is final for purposes of appeal: *Four Seasons Travel Ltd. v. Laker Airways Ltd.*, 1974 CarswellOnt 876, 6 O.R. (2d) 453 (Ont. Div. Ct.).

Court prepared to accept moving parties formed intention to appeal within the time for bringing an appeal, and that a satisfactory explanation for the delay in filing a notice of appeal has been given.

A solicitor is an agent of his client: *Birjasingh v. Coseco Insurance Co.* (1999), 1999 CarswellOnt 3899, 182 D.L.R. (4th) 751, [2000] I.L.R. I-3822, [1999] O.J. No. 4546 (Ont. S.C.J.) at para. 11. This principle is often invoked in support of a lawyer's capacity to act on behalf of his or her client. However, it also means that, vis-a-vis the other party, it is generally the client who is responsible for the actions of the client's lawyer. This is not an overly harsh approach, especially in the circumstances of this case. As noted by this court in *Machacek v. Ontario Cycling Assn.*, 2011 ONCA 410, 2011 CarswellOnt 3624, [2011] O.J. No. 2379 (Ont. C.A.) at para. 10, "the appellants are not left without a remedy as they still have recourse through an action in solicitor's negligence.".

To grant the relief requested by the moving parties would cause prejudice to the responding party. There is little merit to the appeal, and justice of the case does not require that leave be granted. Accordingly, motion to extend the time to appeal dismissed.

Massoudinia v. Volfson, 2013 ONCA 29, 2013 CarswellOnt 256 (Ont. C.A. [In Chambers]), Weiler J.A.

On a motion for an extension to file a notice of motion for leave to appeal from the judgment of Justice M. McKelvey, sitting as a single judge of the Divisional Court, dated September 19, 2012.

Moving party formed a *bona fide* intention to appeal within the prescribed appeal period. I also accept her explanation for the delay. However, the appeal has no merit.

Appellate courts recognize that oral reasons ordinarily cannot be as thorough and detailed as written reasons. As Carthy J.A. said, in *R. v. Richardson*, 1992 CarswellOnt 830, 9 O.R. (3d) 194, 74 C.C.C. (3d) 15, 57 O.A.C. 54, [1992] O.J. No. 1498 (Ont. C.A.) at para. 13, "[i]n moving under pressure from case to case it is expected that oral judgments will contain much less than the complete line of reasoning leading to the result.".

Baldwin v. Baldwin, 2013 BCCA 35, 2013 CarswellBC 455, 333 B.C.A.C. 148, 571 W.A.C. 148 (B.C. C.A.).

Ms. Baldwin appeals the dismissal of her application for judicial review of the decision of a Provincial Court judge dismissing her small claims action against her brother, Mr. Baldwin.

The jurisprudence of this Court is clear that litigants may seek judicial review of decisions made by Provincial Court judges in small claims actions that may not be appealed under s.5: see, for example, *Shaughnessy v. Roth*, 2006 BCCA 547, 2006 CarswellBC 2963, 61 B.C.L.R. (4th) 268, 233 B.C.A.C. 212, 386 W.A.C. 212, [2006] B.C.J. No. 3125 (B.C. C.A.), which involved an order transferring an action from the Provincial Court to the Supreme Court, and *Hubbard v. Acheson*, 2009 BCCA 251, 2009 CarswellBC 1439, 93 B.C.L.R. (4th) 315, 271 B.C.A.C. 215, 458 W.A.C. 215 (B.C. C.A.), which involved an order dismissing an application to set aside a default judgment.

Although delay is a factor that may be taken into account in judicial review proceedings, there is no specific deadline for the bringing of such a proceeding.

It is preferable for the judicial review to be conducted by the Supreme Court.

Appeal allowed and remit petition to the Supreme Court.

Enbridge Gas Distribution Inc. v. Froese, 2013 ONCA 131, 2013 CarswellOnt 2423, 114 O.R. (3d) 636 (Ont. C.A.)

A motion for an extension of time to seek leave to appeal from an order of the Divisional Court, allowing an appeal from the Small Claims Court, was denied. In general, the Divisional Court's determination of an appeal is intended to be final. A further appeal is exceptional. In this case the court found the proposed further appeal was largely fact-based and raised no legal issue of public importance.

7. (1) Composition of court for hearings — A proceeding in the Court of Appeal shall be heard and determined by not fewer than three judges sitting together, and always by an uneven number of judges.

(2) Idem, motions — A motion in the Court of Appeal and an appeal under clause 6(1)(c) shall be heard and determined by one judge.

(3) Idem — Subsection (2) does not apply to a motion for leave to appeal, a motion to quash an appeal or any other motion that is specified by the rules of court.

(4) Idem — A judge assigned to hear and determine a motion may adjourn the motion to a panel of the Court of Appeal.

(5) Idem — A panel of the Court of Appeal may, on motion, set aside or vary the decision of a judge who hears and determines a motion.

8. (1) References to Court of Appeal — The Lieutenant Governor in Council may refer any question to the Court of Appeal for hearing and consideration.

(2) Opinion of court — The court shall certify its opinion to the Lieutenant Governor in Council, accompanied by a statement of the reasons for it, and any judge who differs from the opinion may certify his or her opinion and reasons in the same manner.

(3) Submissions by Attorney General — On the hearing of the question, the Attorney General of Ontario is entitled to make submissions to the court.

(4) Idem — The Attorney General of Canada shall be notified and is entitled to make submissions to the court if the question relates to the constitutional validity or constitutional applicability of an Act, or of a regulation or by-law made under an Act, of the Parliament of Canada or the Legislature.

(5) Notice — The court may direct that any person interested, or any one or more persons as representatives of a class of persons interested, be notified of the hearing and be entitled to make submissions to the court.

(6) Appointment of counsel — If an interest affected is not represented by counsel, the court may request counsel to argue on behalf of the interest and the reasonable expenses of counsel shall be paid by the Minister of Finance.

(7) Appeal — The opinion of the court shall be deemed to be a judgment of the court and an appeal lies from it as from a judgment in an action.

2006, c. 21, Sched. A, s. 2

9. (1) Meeting of judges — The judges of the Court of Appeal shall meet at least once in each year, on a day fixed by the Chief Justice of Ontario, in order to consider this Act, the rules of court and the administration of justice generally.

(2) Idem — The judges shall report their recommendations to the Attorney General.

Proposed Repeal — 9(2)

(2) [Repealed 2009, c. 33, Sched. 2, s. 20(1). Not in force at date of publication.]

PART II — COURT OF ONTARIO

10. (1) Court of Ontario — The Ontario Court of Justice is continued under the name Court of Ontario in English and Cour de l'Ontario in French.

(2) Divisions — The Court of Ontario shall consist of two divisions, the Superior Court of Justice (formerly the Ontario Court (General Division)) and the Ontario Court of Justice (formerly the Ontario Court (Provincial Division)).

(3) President — The person who is the Chief Justice of the Superior Court of Justice shall also be the president of the Court of Ontario.

1996, c. 25, s. 9(2)

Superior Court of Justice

11. (1) Superior Court of Justice — The Ontario Court (General Division) is continued as a superior court of record under the name Superior Court of Justice in English and Cour supérieure de justice in French.

Commentary

(2) Idem — The Superior Court of Justice has all the jurisdiction, power and authority historically exercised by courts of common law and equity in England and Ontario.

1996, c. 25, s. 9(3), (17)

12. (1) Composition of Superior Court of Justice — The Superior Court of Justice consists of,

(a) the Chief Justice of the Superior Court of Justice who shall be president of the Superior Court of Justice;

(b) the Associate Chief Justice of the Superior Court of Justice;

(c) a regional senior judge of the Superior Court of Justice for each region.

(d) the Senior Judge of the Family Court; and

(e) such number of judges of the Superior Court of Justice as is fixed under clause 53(1)(a).

(1.1) [Repealed 1998, c. 20, Sched. A, s. 1(2).]

(1.2) [Repealed 1998, c. 20, Sched. A, s. 1(2).]

(1.3) [Repealed 1998, c. 20, Sched. A, s. 1(2).]

(2) Additional judges — There shall be such additional offices of judge of the Superior Court of Justice as are from time to time required, to be held by Chief Justices of the Superior Court of Justice, Associate Chief Justices of the Superior Court of Justice and regional senior judges of the Superior Court of Justice who have elected under the *Judges Act* (Canada) to perform only the duties of a judge of the Superior Court of Justice.

(3) Supernumerary judges — There shall be such additional offices of supernumerary judge of the Superior Court of Justice as are from time to time required, to be held by judges of the Superior Court of Justice who have elected under the *Judges Act* (Canada) to hold office only as a supernumerary judge of that court.

1994, c. 12, s. 2; 1996, c. 25, s. 9(4), (14), (15), (17); 1998, c. 20, Sched. A, ss. 1, 22

13. (1) Assignment of judges from Court of Appeal — The Chief Justice of Ontario, with the concurrence of the Chief Justice of the Superior Court of Justice, may assign a judge of the Court of Appeal to perform the work of a judge of the Superior Court of Justice.

(2) Court of Appeal judges — A judge of the Court of Appeal is, by virtue of his or her office, a judge of the Superior Court of Justice and has all the jurisdiction, power and authority of a judge of the Superior Court of Justice.

1996, c. 25, s. 9(14), (17)

14. (1) Powers and duties of Chief Justice of Superior Court of Justice — The Chief Justice of the Superior Court of Justice shall direct and supervise the sittings of the Superior Court of Justice and the assignment of its judicial duties.

Case Law: *Webb v. 3584747 Canada Inc.*, 2004 CarswellOnt 325, [2004] O.J. No. 215, 183 O.A.C. 155, 69 O.R. (3d) 502, 41 C.P.C. (5th) 98 (Ont. C.A.) — Appeal whether Divisional Court erred when it held that the motion judge exercised the power reserved to the Chief Justice under s. 14(1) of the *Courts of Justice Act* when he appointed judicial officers to conduct references under s. 25(1)(b) of the *Class Proceedings Act*, 1992, S.O. 1992, c. 6.

(2) Regional senior judges, Superior Court of Justice — A regional senior judge of the Superior Court of Justice shall, subject to the authority of the Chief Justice of the Superior Court of Justice, exercise the powers and perform the duties of the Chief Justice in respect of the Superior Court of Justice in his or her region.

(3) Delegation — A regional senior judge of the Superior Court of Justice may delegate to a judge of the Superior Court of Justice in his or her region the authority to exercise specified functions.

(4) Absence of Chief Justice of Superior Court of Justice — If the Chief Justice of the Superior Court of Justice is absent from Ontario or is for any reason unable to act, his or her powers and duties shall be exercised and performed by the Associate Chief Justice of the Superior Court of Justice.

(5) Senior Judge of Family Court — The Senior Judge of the Family Court shall,

    (a) advise the Chief Justice of the Superior Court of Justice with regard to,

        (i) the education of judges sitting in the Family Court,

        (ii) practice and procedure, including mediation, in the Family Court,

        (iii) the expansion of the Family Court, and

        (iv) the expenditure of funds budgeted for the Family Court;

    (b) meet from time to time with the community liaison committees and community resources committees established under sections 21.13 and 21.14; and

    (c) perform other duties relating to the Family Court assigned to the Senior Judge of the Family Court by the Chief Justice.

(6) Absence of regional senior judge or Senior Judge of Family Court — The powers and duties of a regional senior judge of the Superior Court of Justice and the Senior Judge of the Family Court when he or she is absent from Ontario or is for any reason unable to act shall be exercised and performed by a judge of the Superior Court of Justice designated by the Chief Justice of the Superior Court of Justice.

(7) Meetings with Associate Chief Justice, regional senior judges and Senior Judge of Family Court — The Chief Justice of the Superior Court of Justice may hold meetings with the Associate Chief Justice, the regional senior judges and the Senior Judge of the Family Court in order to consider any matters concerning sittings of the Superior Court of Justice and the assignment of its judicial duties.

1994, c. 12, s. 3; 1998, c. 20, Sched. A, s. 22(3)

15. (1) Judges assigned to regions — The Chief Justice of the Superior Court of Justice shall assign every judge of the Superior Court of Justice to a region and may reassign a judge from one region to another.

(2) At least one judge in each county — There shall be at least one judge of the Superior Court of Justice assigned to each county and district.

(3) High Court and District Court judges — No judge of the Superior Court of Justice who was a judge of the High Court of Justice or the District Court of Ontario before the 1st day of September, 1990 shall be assigned without his or her consent to a region other than the region in which he or she resided immediately before that day.

(4) Idem — Subsections (1) to (3) do not prevent the temporary assignment of a judge to a location anywhere in Ontario.

1996, c. 25, s. 9(14), (17)

16. Composition of court for hearings — A proceeding in the Superior Court of Justice shall be heard and determined by one judge of the Superior Court of Justice.

1996, c. 25, s. 9(16), (17)

17. Appeals to Superior Court of Justice — An appeal lies to the Superior Court of Justice from,

(a) an interlocutory order of a master or case management master;

(b) a certificate of assessment of costs issued in a proceeding in the Superior Court of Justice, on an issue in respect of which an objection was served under the rules of court.

1996, c. 25, ss. 1(1), 9(17)

Divisional Court

18. (1) Divisional Court — The branch of the Superior Court of Justice known as the Divisional Court is continued under the name Divisional Court in English and Cour divisionnaire in French.

(2) Same — The Divisional Court consists of the Chief Justice of the Superior Court of Justice, who is president of the Divisional Court, the associate chief justice and such other judges as the Chief Justice designates from time to time.

(3) Jurisdiction of judges — Every judge of the Superior Court of Justice is also a judge of the Divisional Court.

1994, c. 12, s. 5; 1996, c. 25, s. 9(14), (17); 1998, c. 20, Sched. A, s. 3

19. (1) Divisional Court jurisdiction — An appeal lies to the Divisional Court from,

(a) a final order of a judge of the Superior Court of Justice, as described in subsections (1.1) and (1.2);

(b) an interlocutory order of a judge of the Superior Court of Justice, with leave as provided in the rules of court;

(c) a final order of a master or case management master.

Case Law: *Sepe v. Monteleone*, 2006 CarswellOnt 234, 262 D.L.R. (4th) 105, 78 O.R. (3d) 676, 207 O.A.C. 38, 22 C.P.C. (6th) 323 (Ont. C.A.).

The *Courts of Justice Act*, R.S.O. 1990, c. C.43, s. 19(1)(a), provided that appeal lay to Divisional Court for an award or dismissal of a claim for a single payment of not more than $25,000. The Divisional Court held that the combination of payments ordered and claims dismissed totalled more than $25,000. Amount beyond jurisdiction of Divisional Court and should be appealed to the Ontario Court of Appeal. The plaintiff appealed to the Ontario Court of Appeal.

Matter within the jurisdiction of the Divisional Court. Appeal allowed.

Shuter v. Toronto Dominion Bank (2007), 2007 CarswellOnt 8302 (Ont. Div. Ct.), Jennings J.

Orders for security for costs treated as being interlocutory. See, e.g., *Valu Healthcare Realty Inc. v. Zellers Inc.*, 2004 CarswellOnt 5039, [2004] O.J. No. 4939 (Ont. S.C.J.) and *Padnos v. Luminart Inc.*, 1996 CarswellOnt 4860, [1996] O.J. No. 4549, 35 C.P.C. (4th) 202, 21 O.T.C. 155, 32 O.R. (3d) 120 (Ont. Gen. Div.).

Security for costs provided for in Rule 56.01. See *Websports Technologies Inc. v. Cryptologic Inc.*, [2005] O.J. No. 1320, 2005 CarswellOnt 1327, 15 C.P.C. (6th) 340 (Ont. Master). The order from which the appeal is taken was interlocutory, court has no jurisdiction to entertain appeal.

(1.1) Same — If the notice of appeal is filed before October 1, 2007, clause (1)(a) applies in respect of a final order,

(a) for a single payment of not more than $25,000, exclusive of costs;

(b) for periodic payments that amount to not more than $25,000, exclusive of costs, in the 12 months commencing on the date the first payment is due under the order;

(c) dismissing a claim for an amount that is not more than the amount set out in clause (a) or (b); or

(d) dismissing a claim for an amount that is more than the amount set out in clause (a) or (b) and in respect of which the judge or jury indicates that if the claim had been allowed the amount awarded would have been not more than the amount set out in clause (a) or (b).

(1.2) Same — If the notice of appeal is filed on or after October 1, 2007, clause (1)(a) applies in respect of a final order,

(a) for a single payment of not more than $50,000, exclusive of costs;

(b) for periodic payments that amount to not more than $50,000, exclusive of costs, in the 12 months commencing on the date the first payment is due under the order;

(c) dismissing a claim for an amount that is not more than the amount set out in clause (a) or (b); or

(d) dismissing a claim for an amount that is more than the amount set out in clause (a) or (b) and in respect of which the judge or jury indicates that if the claim had been allowed the amount awarded would have been not more than the amount set out in clause (a) or (b).

(2) Combining of appeals from Superior Court of Justice — The Divisional Court has jurisdiction to hear and determine an appeal that lies to the Superior Court of Justice if an appeal in the same proceeding lies to and is taken to the Divisional Court.

(3) Idem — The Divisional Court may, on motion, transfer an appeal that has already been commenced in the Superior Court of Justice to the Divisional Court for the purpose of subsection (2).

(4) Appeal from interlocutory orders — No appeal lies from an interlocutory order of a judge of the Superior Court of Justice made on an appeal from an interlocutory order of the Ontario Court of Justice.

1994, c. 12, s. 6; 1996, c. 25, ss. 1(2), 9(17), (18); 2006, c. 21, Sched. A, s. 3; 2009, c. 33, Sched. 2, s. 20(2), (3)

20. (1) Place for hearing appeals — An appeal to the Divisional Court shall be heard in the region where the hearing or other process that led to the decision appealed from took place, unless the parties agree otherwise or the Chief Justice of the Superior Court of Justice orders otherwise because it is necessary to do so in the interests of justice.

Commentary: This subsection is amended to require Divisional Court appeals to take place in the region where the *trial or hearing* took place, rather than where the decision was made. It is amended to also permit the Chief Justice of the Superior Court of Justice to order the appeal to be held other than in the region where it is necessary to do so in the interests of justice.

(2) Other proceedings in any region — Any other proceeding in the Divisional Court may be brought in any region.

1994, c. 12, s. 7; 1996, c. 25, s. 9(14)

21. (1) Composition of court for hearings — A proceeding in the Divisional Court shall be heard and determined by three judges sitting together.

(2) Idem — A proceeding in the Divisional Court may be heard and determined by one judge where the proceeding,

(a) is an appeal under clause 19(1)(c);

(b) is an appeal under section 31 from a provincial judge or a deputy judge presiding over the Small Claims Court; or

(c) is in a matter that the Chief Justice of the Superior Court of Justice or a judge designated by the Chief Justice is satisfied, from the nature of the issues involved and the necessity for expedition, can and ought to be heard and determined by one judge.

(3) Idem, motions — A motion in the Divisional Court shall be heard and determined by one judge, unless otherwise provided by the rules of court.

(4) Idem — A judge assigned to hear and determine a motion may adjourn it to a panel of the Divisional Court.

(5) Idem — A panel of the Divisional Court may, on motion, set aside or vary the decision of a judge who hears and determines a motion.

1996, c. 25, s. 9(14)

Commentary: NOTE: R. 61.02 of the *Rules of Civil Procedure*, R. 63.01(1) as well as R. 103.9.

Family Court

21.1 (1) Family Court — There shall be a branch of the Superior Court of Justice known as the Family Court in English and Cour de la famille in French.

(2) Unified Family Court — The Unified Family Court is amalgamated with and continued as part of the Family Court.

(3) Same — The Family Court has the jurisdiction conferred on it by this or any other Act.

(4) Jurisdiction — The Family Court has jurisdiction in the City of Hamilton and in the additional areas named in accordance with subsection (5).

(5) Proclamation — The Lieutenant Governor in Council may, by proclamation, name additional areas in which the Family Court has jurisdiction.

1994, c. 12, s. 8; 1996, c. 25, s. 9(17); 2002, c. 17, Sched. F

21.2 (1) Composition of Family Court — The Family Court consists of,

(a) the Chief Justice of the Superior Court of Justice, who shall be president of the Family Court;

(b) the Associate Chief Justice;

(c) the Senior Judge of the Family Court.

(d) the five judges and one supernumerary judge of the Superior Court of Justice assigned to the Unified Family Court on June 30, 1993;

(e) the judges of the Superior Court of Justice appointed to be members of the Family Court, the number of whom is fixed by regulation under clause 53(1)(a.1);

(f) the judges of the Superior Court of Justice assigned to the Family Court by the Chief Justice from time to time.

(2) **Supernumerary judges** — There shall be such additional offices of supernumerary judge of the Superior Court of Justice and member of the Family Court as are from time to time required, to be held by judges referred to in clauses (1)(d) and (e) who have elected under the *Judges Act* (Canada) to hold office only as supernumerary judges.

(3) **Jurisdiction of judges** — Every judge of the Superior Court of Justice is also a judge of the Family Court.

(4) **Temporary assignments** — The Chief Justice of the Superior Court of Justice may, from time to time, temporarily assign a judge referred to in clause (1)(d) or (e) to hear matters outside the jurisdiction of the Family Court.

(5) [Repealed 1998, c. 20, Sched. A, s. 4(2).]

(6) [Repealed 1998, c. 20, Sched. A, s. 4(2).]

1994, c. 12, s. 8; 1996, c. 25, s. 9(14), (17); 1998, c. 20, Sched. A, ss. 4, 22(4)

21.3 (1) **Transitional measure** — All proceedings referred to in the Schedule to section 21.8 or in section 21.12 that are pending in the Superior Court of Justice or the Ontario Court of Justice in an area named under subsection 21.1(5) as an area in which the Family Court has jurisdiction shall be transferred to and continued in the Family Court.

(2) **Same** — If a judge sitting in the Ontario Court of Justice is seized of a matter in a proceeding that is the subject of a transfer under subsection (1), the judge may complete that matter.

1994, c. 12, s. 8; 1998, c. 20, Sched. A, ss. 5, 22(5)

21.4 [Repealed 1998, c. 20, Sched. A, s. 5.]

21.5 [Repealed 1998, c. 20, Sched. A, s. 5.]

21.6 [Repealed 1998, c. 20, Sched. A, s. 5.]

21.7 **Composition of court for hearings** — A proceeding in the Family Court shall be heard and determined by one judge.

1994, c. 12, s. 8; 2009, c. 33, Sched. 2, s. 20(4)

21.8 (1) **Proceedings in Family Court** — In the parts of Ontario where the Family Court has jurisdiction, proceedings referred to in the Schedule to this section, except appeals and prosecutions, shall be commenced, heard and determined in the Family Court.

(2) **Motions for interlocutory relief** — A motion for interim or other interlocutory relief in a proceeding referred to in the Schedule that is required or permitted by

the rules or an order of a court to be heard and determined in a part of Ontario where the Family Court has jurisdiction shall be heard and determined in the Family Court.

(3) Same — A motion for interim or other interlocutory relief in a proceeding referred to in the Schedule that is required or permitted by the rules or an order of the Family Court to be heard and determined in a part of Ontario where the Family Court does not have jurisdiction shall be heard and determined in the court that would have had jurisdiction if the proceeding had been commenced in that part of Ontario.

Schedule

1. Proceedings under the following statutory provisions:

   Change of Name Act

   Child and Family Services Act, Parts III, VI and VII

   Children's Law Reform Act, except sections 59 and 60

   Divorce Act (Canada)

   Family Law Act, except Part V

   Interjurisdictional Support Orders Act, 2002

   Family Responsibility and Support Arrears Enforcement Act, 1996

   Marriage Act, section 6

1.1 [Repealed 2009, c. 11, s. 19.]

2. Proceedings for the interpretation, enforcement or variation of a marriage contract, cohabitation agreement, separation agreement, paternity agreement, family arbitration agreement or family arbitration award.

3. Proceedings for relief by way of constructive or resulting trust or a monetary award as compensation for unjust enrichment between persons who have cohabited.

4. Proceedings for annulment of a marriage or for a declaration of validity or invalidity of a marriage.

5. Appeals of family arbitration awards under the *Arbitration Act, 1991*.

> 1994, c. 12, s. 8; 1996, c. 31, s. 65; 1999, c. 6, s. 18(1); 2002, c. 13, s. 56; 2002, c. 14, Sched., s. 9; 2005, c. 5, s. 17(1); 2006, c. 1, s. 4; 2009, c. 11, s. 19

21.9 Other jurisdiction — Where a proceeding referred to in the Schedule to section 21.8 is commenced in the Family Court and is combined with a related matter that is in the judge's jurisdiction but is not referred to in the Schedule, the court may, with leave of the judge, hear and determine the combined matters.

> 1994, c. 12, s. 8

21.9.1 Certain appeals — A statutory provision referred to in the Schedule to section 21.8 or in section 21.12 that provides for appeals from decisions of the Ontario Court of Justice to the Superior Court of Justice shall be deemed to provide for appeals from decisions of the Family Court to the Divisional Court.

> 1996, c. 25, ss. 1(4), 9(17), (18); 1998, c. 20, Sched. A, s. 6

21.10 (1) Orders of predecessor court — The Family Court may hear and determine an application under an Act to discharge, vary or suspend an order made by the Provincial Court (Family Division), the Ontario Court of Justice, the Superior Court of Justice or the Unified Family Court.

(2) Same — The Family Court may enforce orders made by the Provincial Court (Family Division), the Ontario Court of Justice, the Superior Court of Justice or the Unified Family Court.

1994, c. 12, s. 8; 1996, c. 25, s. 9(17), (18)

21.11 (1) Place where proceeding commenced — Proceedings referred to in the Schedule to section 21.8 may be commenced in the Family Court if the applicant or the respondent resides in a part of Ontario where the Family Court has jurisdiction.

(2) Custody and access — An application under Part III of the *Children's Law Reform Act* in respect of a child who ordinarily resides in a part of Ontario where the Family Court has jurisdiction may be commenced in the Family Court in that part of Ontario.

(3) Transfer to other court — A judge presiding over the Family Court may, on motion, order that a proceeding commenced in the Family Court be transferred to the appropriate court in a place where the Family Court does not have jurisdiction if, in the judge's opinion, the preponderance of convenience favours having the matter dealt with by that court in that place.

(4) Transfer from other court — A judge of a court having jurisdiction in a proceeding referred to in the Schedule to section 21.8 in an area where the Family Court does not have jurisdiction may, on motion, order that the proceeding be transferred to the Family Court in a particular place if, in the judge's opinion, the preponderance of convenience favours having the matter dealt with by that court in that place.

(5) Directions — A judge making an order under subsection (3) or (4) may give such directions for the transfer as are considered just.

1994, c. 12, s. 8

21.12 (1) Enforcement of orders — A judge presiding over the Family Court shall be deemed to be a judge of the Ontario Court of Justice for the purpose of prosecutions under Part III (Child Protection) and Part VII (Adoption) of the *Child and Family Services Act*, the *Children's Law Reform Act*, the *Family Law Act* and the *Family Responsibility and Support Arrears Enforcement Act, 1996*.

(2) [Repealed 2009, c. 33, Sched. 2, s. 20(5).]

(3) [Repealed 2009, c. 33, Sched. 2, s. 20(5).]

1994, c. 12, s. 8; 1996, c. 31, s. 66; 1998, c. 20, Sched. A, ss. 7, 22(6); 2009, c. 33, Sched. 2, s. 20(5)

21.13 (1) Community liaison committee — There shall be one or more community liaison committees, as determined by the Chief Justice of the Superior Court of Justice, or by a person he or she designates for the purpose, for each area in which the Family Court has jurisdiction.

(2) Composition — A community liaison committee consists of judges, lawyers, persons employed in court administration and other residents of the community, appointed by the Chief Justice of the Superior Court of Justice or by a person he or she designates for the purpose.

(3) **Function** — A community liaison committee shall consider matters aff
general operations of the court in the municipality and make recommendatioₙₛ
appropriate authorities.

> 1994, c. 12, s. 8; 1998, c. 20, Sched. A, ss. 8, 22(7); 2009, c. 33, Sched. 2, s. 20(6)

21.14 (1) Community resources committee — There shall be one or more community resources committees, as determined by the Chief Justice of the Superior Court of Justice, or by a person he or she designates for the purpose, for each area in which the Family Court has jurisdiction.

(2) **Composition** — A community resources committee consists of judges, lawyers, members of social service agencies, persons employed in court administration and other residents of the community, appointed by the Chief Justice of the Superior Court of Justice or by a person whom he or she designates for the purpose.

(3) **Function** — A community resources committee shall develop links between the court and social service resources available in the community, identify needed resources and develop strategies for putting them in place.

> 1994, c. 12, s. 8; 1998, c. 20, Sched. A, ss. 9, 22(8); 2009, c. 33, Sched. 2, s. 20(7)

21.15 Dispute resolution service — A service for the resolution of disputes by alternatives to litigation may be established, maintained and operated as part of the Family Court.

> 1994, c. 12, s. 8

Small Claims Court

22. (1) Small Claims Court — The Small Claims Court is continued as a branch of the Superior Court of Justice under the name Small Claims Court in English and Cour des petites créances in French.

(2) **Idem** — The Small Claims Court consists of the Chief Justice of the Superior Court of Justice who shall be president of the court and such other judges of the Superior Court of Justice as the Chief Justice designates from time to time.

(3) **Jurisdiction of judges** — Every judge of the Superior Court of Justice is also a judge of the Small Claims Court.

> 1996, c. 25, s. 9(14), (17)

Commentary: The Small Claims Court (SCC) is a branch of the Superior Court of Justice.

The Small Claims Court is designed to provide a simple and inexpensive forum for people to settle their civil claims. It is generally perceived as a "do-it-yourself" court. People may choose to represent themselves, or to be represented by counsel or an agent.

Every justice of the Superior Court of Justice is also a justice of the Small Claims Court. As well, justices of the Provincial Court (Civil Division) sit in Small Claims Court. Small Claims Court matters are also heard by deputy judges. Deputy judges are lawyers appointed by the Regional Senior Justice to hear these cases.

The Small Claims Court has jurisdiction in any action for the payment of money or the recovery of possession of personal property where the amount claimed does not exceed $25,000 (excluding interest and costs). The monetary jurisdiction of this court is fixed by regulation under the *Courts of Justice Act*.

Section 96 of the *Constitution Act, 1867* requires that judges of the superior courts be appointed by the Governor-General and although subsection 22(3) of the *Courts of Justice Act* provides that the judges of the Superior Court of Justice are judges of the Small Claims Court, there are judges of the Small Claims Court appointed by the Lieutenant Governor. Subsection 32(1) of the *Courts of Justice Act* makes provision for the appointment of deputy judges by a regional senior judge of the Superior Court of Justice and although the jurisdiction of deputy judges is limited by subsection 24(3) of the Act, their appointments are also clearly not consistent with the requirement of section 96.

If as a branch of the Superior Court of Justice, the Small Claims Court is a superior court, then the Lieutenant Governor would have no authority to appoint judges to the Court. (See, *McEvoy v. New Brunswick (Attorney General)*, [1983] 1 S.C.R. 704 at 721, 14 C.C.C. (2d) 219, 46 N.B.R. (2d) 219, 121 A.P.R. 219, 48 N.R. 228, where the Court said *inter alia*: "New Brunswick cannot exercise an appointing power in respect of courts with s. 96 jurisdiction ..."). Also of course, its jurisdiction is limited, both monetarily and otherwise. Such limited jurisdiction is at variance with the status of a superior court which traditionally exercises a jurisdiction without monetary limits.

Motion by plaintiffs who were unrepresented that they be provided with legal aid or other legal assistance in filing a claim against individuals associated with province plaintiffs were dismissed from employment with province in special care homes. Although courts ordinarily hesitate to interfere with process in which legal aid is administered, it was appropriate here to request the Minister of Justice and the Attorney General to cover reasonable legal fees of plaintiffs. *Gallant v. Fenety* (1999), 221 N.B.R. (2d) 146, 567 A.P.R. 146, 1999 CarswellNB 491 (N.B. Q.B.); *Gallant v. Fenety* (February 15, 2000), Doc. 8/2000/CA (N.B. C.A.).

Case Law: *Western Irrigation District v. Craddock*, 267 A.R. 297, 2000 CarswellAlta 649, [2000] A.J. No. 738 (Alta. Q.B.) — The Provincial Court was the court of inferior jurisdiction and its powers were limited to those granted to it by Statute. Finding bylaw approval without benefit of judicial review, which was beyond the judge's jurisdiction.

R. v. Romanowicz (1999), 26 C.R. (5th) 246, 45 M.V.R. (3d) 294, 124 O.A.C. 100, 138 C.C.C. (3d) 225, 178 D.L.R. (4th) 466, 45 O.R. (3d) 506, (sub nom. *R. c. Romanowicz)* 45 O.R. (3d) 532 (Fr.), 1999 CarswellOnt 2671, [1999] O.J. No. 3191 (Ont. C.A.) — Is there a constitutional right to effective assistance where the accused is represented by an agent, not a lawyer? There is no constitutional right to competent representation. However, constitutional right to a fair trial remained in full force and absence of legally trained counsel put added obligation on the trial judge to protect that right.

Gallant v. Fenety (1999), 221 N.B.R. (2d) 146, 567 A.P.R. 146, 1999 CarswellNB 491 (N.B. Q.B.) — A motion by the plaintiffs, who were unrepresented, that they be provided with civil legal aid or other legal assistance. It was appropriate in this case, which appeared meritorious, to request the Minister of Justice and Attorney General to cover reasonable legal fees of the plaintiffs.

Polewsky v. Home Hardware Stores Ltd. (2000), 71 C.R.R. (2d) 330, 2000 CarswellOnt 72 (Ont. S.C.J.) — This case concerned an application for leave to appeal decision, which held that tariff fees charged to pursue Small Claims Court actions did not violate s. 7 guarantee of life, liberty and security of person unless in accordance with principles of fundamental justice.

R. v. Sheppard, 2002 SCC 26, [2002] S.C.J. No. 30, 2002 CarswellNfld 74, 2002 CarswellNfld 75, 162 C.C.C. (3d) 298, 210 D.L.R. (4th) 608, 50 C.R. (5th) 68, 284 N.R. 342, 211 Nfld. & P.E.I.R. 50, 633 A.P.R. 50, [2002] 1 S.C.R. 869 (S.C.C.) — Reasons for judgment. Duty on trial judge to give reasons. Trial judge's generic reasons amounted to no reasons at all and precluded proper appellate scrutiny of whether verdict was unreasonable. Trial judge erred in law in failing to give functional reasons.

Clarke v. Regency Frobisher Inn (2000), 2000 CarswellNun 2 (Nun. C.J.) — The plaintiff's claim statute barred and no genuine issue to be tried. With regard to costs, the Nunavut Court of Justice created on April 1st, 1999, the date Nunavut became a new territory in Canada. The Nunavut Court of Justice is first single level trial Court in Canada where the Territorial Court (Provincial Court) and the Superior Court are combined into on level of Court where Justices have jurisdiction over all matters. At the time of creation of the new territory and amalgamation of the levels of court, the small claims procedure disappeared. To date, the small claims procedure available in Canada not available in Nunavut.

Battiste v. Chapel Island Band, 2005 CarswellNS 661, 2005 NSSM 14, 6 N.S.R. (2d) 6, 789 A.P.R. 6 (N.S. Small Cl. Ct.).

Preliminary hearing held regarding impartiality of Small Claims Court. Small Claims Court was not improper venue. Small Claims Court could provide fair hearing. Court capable of meting out natural justice in that government representatives would be treated impartially. Judges of Small Claims Court were independent and impartial. No reasonable apprehension of bias existed as to court as a whole.

Palkowski v. Ivancic, 84 R.P.R. (4th) 226, 2009 ONCA 705, 2009 CarswellOnt 5950, 76 C.P.C. (6th) 204 (Ont. C.A.).

"Simply because a matter is dealt with in a judge's chambers does not mean the hearing is not open to the public . . . [C]ourtrooms, and by courtroom mean anywhere where judicial business is conducted, are presumed to be open to the public.

. . . the requirements of s. 135(1) of the *Courts of Justice Act* [R.S.O. 1990, c. C-43] were met because there was nothing in the record to suggest that "anyone was excluded from the judge's chambers. No one requested that the appellants personally be permitted to attend on the motion judge with their counsel.".

Legislative Amendments

Amendment to statute restricting appeals in cases in which sum in dispute over $500. Action commenced before amendment. Judgment delivered after amendment. Right of appeal substantive. Right of appeal vesting at commencement of action. Amendment not retroactive. Right of appeal subsisting. *Small Claims Courts Amendment Act*, S.O. 1977, c. 52, s. 10. *Petrofina Canada Ltd. v. Lynn*, 1978 CarswellOnt 400, 19 O.R. (2d) 97, 6 C.P.C. 94, 84 D.L.R. (3d) 129 (Ont. Div. Ct.).

"Retroactive" legislation changes the past effects of past situations, whereas "retrospective" legislation changes the future effects of past situations: See Ruth Sullivan, *Sullivan & Dreidger on the Construction of Statutes* (Markham: Butterworths Canada Ltd., 2002) at p. 548:

> . . . the negative effects of discrimination can be felt for generations. That does not mean, however, that the descendants of past victims of discrimination are entitled to relief under section 15 [of the *Canadian Charter of Rights and Freedoms*], when such relief depends on a retroactive application of the Charter.

There is a strong presumption against the retroactive operation of legislation, and that presumption is not rebutted by the wording of the [*Canadian Bill of Rights*, S.C. 1960, c. 44 [reprinted R.S.C. 1985, Appendix III]].

Veleta v. Canada (Minister of Citizenship & Immigration), 2005 CarswellNat 3145, 2005 CarswellNat 1220, 254 D.L.R. (4th) 484, 46 Imm. L.R. (3d) 303, 2005 CF 572, 2005 FC 572 (F.C.), Mactavish J.

23. (1) Jurisdiction — The Small Claims Court,

(a) has jurisdiction in any action for the payment of money where the amount claimed does not exceed the prescribed amount exclusive of interest and costs; and

(b) has jurisdiction in any action for the recovery of possession of personal property where the value of the property does not exceed the prescribed amount.

Commentary: This replaces s. 78(1) of the *Courts of Justice Act, 1984*. The monetary limit of the Small Claims Court is prescribed by regulation, O. Reg. 626/00. See s. 53(1)(e), *Courts of Justice Act*.

O. Reg. 626/00, made under the *Courts of Justice Act*, as amended by O. Reg. 439/08, in force January 1, 2010, reads as follows:

> 1. (1) The maximum amount of a claim is $25,000.
>
> (2) The maximum amount of a claim over which a deputy judge may preside is $25,000.

Parental Responsibility Act

A claim for damages may be brought against the parent of a child under 18 years of age who intentionally takes, damages or destroys property as a result of the parent's failure to exercise reasonable supervision over the child and make reasonable efforts to prevent the damages [s. 2, *PRA*].

A claim may be brought by an owner or person entitled to possession of the property that was taken, damaged or destroyed. A claimant may be an individual or corporation who suffered the property loss or damage, that person's litigation guardian, or that person's insurer.

Where a claim is being made against the parent for property damage, loss or destruction caused by a child under 18 years of age who has been found guilty and sentenced for the offence in Youth Court, the claimant may file the sentence order (or where no sentence order is available, the probation order) under the *Youth Criminal Justice Act* (Canada) obtained from the Youth Justice Court where the child was sentenced by completing and filing a prescribed form, Request for a Copy of a Youth Criminal Justice Act Sentence Order [s. 3(3), *PRA*] in the Youth Justice Court.

Authority for the inspection and use of the sentence order in a claim for property damage, loss or destruction under the *Parental Responsibility Act, 2000* is made by Order of the Lieutenant Governor under para. 119(1)(r) of the *Youth Criminal Justice Act* (Canada).

A claimant who does present a sentence order obtained under the *Youth Criminal Justice Act* (Canada) in a claim for property damage, loss or destruction against a parent of a child under 18 years of age brought under the *Parental Responsibility Act, 2000* must first give the court notice in the prescribed form, Notice About Evidence Obtained Under the Youth Criminal Justice Act (Canada), Form 2 [s. 3(4), *PRA*].

Bankruptcy

The *Bankruptcy and Insolvency Act* (BIA) creates a national system of bankruptcy courts by vesting bankruptcy jurisdiction in the Superior Court of each province.

Bankruptcy is the formal legal status of a person who has become bankrupt under the BIA. Insolvency is a condition, short of bankruptcy, in which a person is unable to meet his or her liabilities or has an excess of liabilities over assets. Determining whether someone is, or was, bankrupt can be easily accomplished with certainty by performing a bankruptcy search. A bankruptcy search can be obtained by fax at a cost of $8 from the Superintendent of Bankruptcy at (613) 941-2863, fax (613) 941-9490. It may be necessary first to set up an account.

Stay of Proceedings

BIA s. 69.3(1) states:

> 69.3 (1) Stay of proceedings — bankruptcies — [Subject to the rights of secured creditors
> and any order the bankruptcy court may make to declare inoperable the stay of proceedings],
> on the bankruptcy of any debtor, no creditor has any remedy against the debtor or the debtor's
> property, or shall commence or continue any action, execution or other proceedings, for the
> recovery of a claim provable in bankruptcy, until the trustee has been discharged.

It can be dangerous to ignore a bankruptcy stay. See *General Motors of Canada Ltd. v. Hoffer Estate*, 1994 CarswellMan 23, 29 C.B.R. (3d) 163, 97 Man. R. (2d) 210, 79 W.A.C. 210 (Man. C.A.): "Ordinarily a bankruptcy trustee who has been brought into proceedings unnecessarily when there are no assets in the estate is entitled to solicitor and client costs." [p. 167 C.B.R.].

Bankruptcy does not stay proceedings for contempt, provided that the purpose of the contempt proceeding is not to collect a debt that is stayed by the bankruptcy. See *Pankhurst v. Kwan*, [1999] O.J. No. 41, 1999 CarswellOnt 31 (Ont. Gen. Div.), Hawkins J. Creditor sought costs re debtor's non-attendance at judgment debtor examination. The defaulting debtor went bankrupt. Judge has jurisdiction to fix costs despite stay: "I cannot imagine that the act of making an assignment in bankruptcy would stay the hand of a judge of this court in proceedings which were based upon contempt of court any more than an assignment in bankruptcy could bring a criminal prosecution to a halt." [Para. 9]. The contempt power must not be used, however, to coerce payment of a debt which has been extinguished by the bankruptcy.

Claims of a spouse or common-law partner, or former spouse or common-law partner, for wages, salary, commission or compensation for work done or services rendered in connection with the bankrupt's business, are subordinated to the claims of all other creditors: BIA s. 137(2). Under s. 138, the wage claims of other relatives are treated equally with all other creditors, but lose the special priority otherwise granted under s. 136(1)(d).

The bankrupt's discharge does not release any debt or liability for alimony or under a support, maintenance or affiliation order or under an agreement for maintenance and support of a spouse, former spouse, former common-law partner or child living apart from the bankrupt: BIA s. 178(1)(b), (c). If such claims are payable under an order or agreement made *before* the date of bankruptcy and at a time when the claimant was living apart from the bankrupt, they are both provable in the bankruptcy [BIA s. 121(4)] and entitled to a limited degree of priority over other creditors: BIA s. 136(1)(d.1). The priority, "in fifth position," applies to any lump sum that is payable together with any periodic amounts that accrued in the year before the date of bankruptcy. The bankruptcy stay of proceedings does not apply to such claims, save that no enforcement may be made against the bankrupt's property that has vested in the trustee or against any surplus portion of the bankrupt's wages that is payable to the trustee: BIA s. 69.41.

Case Law: *Lemoine v. Lemoine* (1990), 80 Nfld. & P.E.I.R. 339 (Nfld. T.D.) — The wife sued in Small Claims Court to enforce terms of a separation agreement with regards to the division of assets, i.e. the sale of a motorcycle. Section 7 of the *Unified Family Court Act* conferred exclusive jurisdiction on the Unified Family Court.

Murday v. Schmidt (1992), 6 C.P.C. 389 (Ont. Gen. Div.) — O. Reg. 706/89, which prescribes a maximum jurisdiction of $3,000 for Small Claims Courts in the Toronto Region and a $1,000 maximum in all other regions, does not violate the equality provisions of the Canadian Charter of Rights and Freedoms.

Brightwood Golf & Country Club Ltd. v. Pelham (1990), 98 N.S.R. (2d) 222, 263 A.P.R. 222 (Co. Ct.) — Legislation provides for $100 limit for general damages. The loss in question did not predate the hearing and was not quantifiable. Therefore the adjudicator exceeded his jurisdiction.

Beardsley v. Baecker, 1993 CarswellNS 72, 20 C.P.C. (3d) 235, 125 N.S.R. (2d) 61, 349 A.P.R. 61 (N.S. S.C.) — The Small Claims Court does not have jurisdiction to hear a dispute between a landlord and a tenant regardless of whether the tenancy is commercial or residential. Ss. 9 and 10 of the *Small Claims Court Act*, R.S.N.S. 1989, c. 430, deal with jurisdiction and the court is limited to the jurisdiction therein defined.

Valley Rite-Mix Ltd. v. Storrie (1993), 86 B.C.L.R. (2d) 312 (B.C. S.C.) — A Small Claims Court Judge ruled that he had no jurisdiction to hear a claim under the *Builder's Lien Act* (B.C.) as jurisdiction was reserved exclusively to the Supreme Court of British Columbia. Where the term "court" was used in the Act, that court was the Supreme Court. However, in s. 2(1) which creates trusts, no reference is made to a court. Exclusive jurisdiction was confined to the lien itself. There was no statutory obstruction to a claim based on trust provisions of the section being heard in the Small Claims Court.

West v. Saskatchewan (Provincial Court Judge) (1994), 27 C.P.C. (3d) 198 (Sask. C.A.) — The Provincial Court had jurisdiction to deal with a solicitor's claim for unpaid legal account, despite provisions for taxation of such accounts contained in the *Legal Profession Act, 1990* (Sask.).

Kelly v. Markey (1993), 98 D.L.R. (4th) 729 (N.B. C.A.) — Small Claims Court without jurisdiction to hear counterclaim in excess of maximum provided.

Shoppers Trust Co. v. Mann Taxi Management Ltd. (1993), 16 O.R. (3d) 196, 19 C.P.C. (3d) 7 (Gen. Div.) — The plaintiff, who had commenced an action in the General Division when the monetary jurisdiction of the Small Claims Court was $3,000 sought to have the action transferred to the Small Claims Court after the jurisdiction was raised to $6,000 on April 1, 1993. The transfer was allowed given the wording of section 23 of the *Courts of Justice Act*.

Grand Bay (Town) v. Fox (1993), 136 N.B.R. (2d) 44, 347 A.P.R. 44 (C.A.) — A counterclaim in Small Claims Court cannot exceed the monetary limit(here $3,000) unless the "counterclaimant" abandons the excess.

Quenville v. Carpentier (July 22, 1993), Doc. S3316 (B.C. S.C.) — Monetary jurisdiction of the B.C. Small Claims Court cannot be greater than that conferred by the *Small Claims Act*, S.B.C., c. 38, s. 12.

Smith v. Zimmermann (1993), 84 B.C.L.R. (2d) 142, 18 C.P.C. (3d) 271 (Master) — A plaintiff may be justified in bringing an action in the superior court notwithstanding that it has turned out that the sum awarded, or accepted, is within the jurisdiction of an inferior court.

ARS Trucking & Welding Ltd. v. Greco (1987), 23 C.P.C. (2d) 95, 1987 CarswellAlta 354 (Alta. Q.B.) — An inferior court does not have jurisdiction for an amount in excess of the jurisdiction merely by reason of the existence of a set-off.

Campbell v. Tsui (1994), 52 A.C.W.S. (3d) 262 (B.C. S.C.) — The plaintiff was awarded $5,640 plus interest on income loss as a result of a motor vehicle action brought in the Supreme Court. Judgment was within jurisdiction of the Provincial Court and substance of claim was firm and known to the plaintiff six months after the collision. Sufficient reason had not been shown for bringing action in the Supreme Court. The plaintiff's recovery of costs was limited to disbursements.

Hall v. New Breton Homes Ltd. (1994), 25 C.B.R. (3d) 307, 131 N.S.R. (2d) 218, 371 A.P.R. 218 (N.S. S.C.) — A bankrupt appealed from the decision of the adjudicator, claiming that the adjudicator had exceeded his jurisdiction or erred in law by deciding that the debt owed to the respondent was not extinguished by the appellant's absolute discharge from bankruptcy.

The appeal was allowed, but without costs. There is nothing in the *Small Claims Court Act* which entitles and adjudicator to deal with matters touching on bankruptcy. Having been advised that the appellant had gone bankrupt after the debt had been incurred, the adjudicator had no authority to deal with the respondent's claim. By deciding the debt is still collectible, the adjudicator erred in law and exceeded his jurisdiction.

Hynes v. Hynes (January 10, 1995) (Nfld. Small Claims Ct.), Orr, Prov. Ct. J. — This was a Small Claims Court action for recovery of damages for clothes claimed by the plaintiff to have been removed. Other property division issues had been dealt with by the Unified Family Court. At issue was the court's jurisdiction to deal with the clothing claim. The parties agreed the clothes were solely the plaintiff's and not a matrimonial asset. Action was allowed in part. The defendant had become a bailee by requiring or ordering the plaintiff to leave the home.

Mailman Publishing v. Century 21 — Georges Bank Realty Ltd. (1993), 21 C.P.C. (3d) 6 (N.S. S.C.) — A court adjudicator erred in finding that the counterclaim advanced was in excess of $25,000, therefore he was without jurisdiction to proceed when hearing. The plaintiff by counterclaim was bound by its solicitor's consent that both the claim and counterclaim would be heard and adjudicated in the Small Claims Court — implicit in that agreement was that monetary jurisdiction was limited to $5,000. The appeal was allowed — the matter was remitted to the Small Claims Court.

Moore v. Shay (1994), 30 C.P.C. (3d) 309 (N.S. S.C.) — This was an appeal from a Small Claims Court judgment. In a divorce order, minutes of settlement included terms the appellant pay certain family debts and that each party would have title to vehicles registered in their names. The appellant did not pay the loan and the respondent's vehicle was seized by the creditor as a result. The adjudicator awarded the respondent the value of the vehicle. The appellant argued this was beyond his jurisdiction as an attempt to enforce a divorce order.

The appeal was dismissed. The Small Claims Court could enforce a contract. Incorporation of the minutes into the order did not oust this jurisdiction per se.

Pachini v. Pietramala, 1995 CarswellBC 294, 7 B.C.L.R. (3d) 266, 38 C.P.C. (3d) 122, 54 A.C.W.S. (3d) 19 (B.C. S.C.) — The plaintiff was awarded non-pecuniary damages of $7,500 which was within the jurisdiction of the Small Claims Court. As there was sufficient reason to bring the action in the Supreme Court, the plaintiff was not to be denied costs pursuant to the Supreme Court Rules (B.C.), r. 57(10). Had the defence applied to move the matter to the Small Claims Court, the application would likely have been denied.

Parris v. Reber (1994), 28 C.P.C. (3d) 398, 22 Alta. L.R. (3d) 78 (Alta. Prov. Ct.) — A plaintiff's motion to vary her relief claimed in a Small Claims Court action to the amount of $4,000 for damages and $2,100 for debt, plus interest, was granted. Conjunctive reading of s. 36(1) of the *Provincial Court Act* (Alta.) regarding monetary jurisdiction of court resulted in cases where relief claimed for damages and debt were as high as $8,000.

The definition of the word "and" in monetary jurisdiction s. 36(1) should be given its normal conjunctive meaning, limiting claims for debt to $4,000 and claims for damages to $4,000, but resulting in some instances in relief claimed for damages and debt as high as $8,000.

Holden Day Wilson v. Ashton (1993), 14 O.R. (3d) 306, 104 D.L.R. (4th) 266, 64 O.A.C. 4 (Div. Ct.) — Trial judge found Ministry policy whereby court clerks were not to sign default judgment in the case of solicitors' accounts was incorrect pursuant to Rule 10.02. On appeal decision was reversed, (June 2, 1993), Doc. No. 697 (Ont. Div. Ct.).

Cox Downie v. Patterson (1992), 9 C.P.C. (3d) 21 (N.S. T.D.) — Small Claims Court does not have jurisdiction to grant a Solicitor's application for declaration of entitlement to solicitor's lien against client's property that solicitor recovered or preserved for client.

Naffouj v. D.E. Wilson Management Co. (1991), 5 O.R. (3d) 424 (Ont. Small Cl. Ct.) — Regulation setting monetary jurisdiction in Toronto higher than in other regions of Ontario contrary to the Charter of Rights and Freedoms.

Beairsto v. Roper Aluminum Products Inc. (1994), 29 C.P.C. (3d) 400 (N.S. S.C.) — The Small Claims Court adjudicator found claim for wrongful dismissal damages was a claim for general damages and was not the type of matter the court was intended to deal with since general damages awards were deemed not to exceed $100. On appeal, the court found claim for damages up to trial was for claim for special damages and fell within the Small Claims Court's jurisdiction. Appeal was allowed and the matter was sent back to adjudicator for trial on merits.

Parth v. Andrews (1995), 28 Alta. L.R. (3d) 55 (Q.B.) — Action in Provincial Court involving restructive covenant was an action involving negligent misrepresentation and breach of contract, not "title" and therefore could be heard in the Provincial Court. See also *Re Emery* (1858), 140 E.R. 1149 (C.P.) at 1152 and *R. v. Everett* (1852), 118 E.R. 439 (Q.B.) at 441.

Morton v. Harper Gray Easton, 1995 CarswellBC 306, [1995] B.C.J. No. 1356, 8 B.C.L.R. (3d) 53 (B.C. S.C.) — Former client of respondent (defendant) law firm appealed successfully for damages for loss of accumulated child support and mortgage payments caused by delay of her solicitors.

858579 Ontario Inc. v. QAP Parking Enforcement Ltd. (1994), 7 P.P.S.A.C. (2d) 201 (Ont. Gen. Div.) — The legislature did not intend the Repair and *Storage Liens Act* to extend to parking security.

Vacation Brokers Inc. v. Espinoza (October 25, 1995), Doc. 01822/90U (Ont. Gen. Div.) — Procedure and policy instituted by the court where some 160 other actions all involving same plaintiff dealt with. *Whiteoak Lincoln Mercury Sales Ltd. v. C.P. Ltd.* (1982), 30 C.P.C. 136 (Ont. H.C.) referred to.

Hutson v. Versteeg, [1995] W.D.F.L. 1675 (Ont. Small Cl. Ct.) — Small Claims Court had jurisdiction to decide contract between the parties for arrears of child support. Children no longer dependants. *Decree Nisi* did not oust jurisdiction of court to deal with claim.

Albert Bloom Ltd. v. Cumming (June 14, 1995), Doc. 94-LT-82905 (Ont. Gen. Div.) — The tenant brought an action in Landlord and Tenant Court for punitive damages against the landlord. The tenant claimed that the landlord in obtaining default judgment without notice to the tenant constituted an abuse of process. The landlord brought his application to have the tenant's claim transferred to the Small Claims Court. The motion was dismissed. The court held that it was appropriate for the Landlord and Tenant Court to adjudicate upon the process taken under the *Act* and the appropriate remedy for deficiency in the process rather than for it to require a separate proceeding in another court.

Weiss v. Prentice Hall Canada Inc. (1995), 1995 CarswellOnt 729, [1995] O.J. No. 4188, 66 C.P.R. (3d) 417, 7 W.D.C.P. (2d) 99 (Ont. Small Cl. Ct.) — There is concurrent jurisdiction of provincial courts and the Federal Court: s. 37 of the *Copyright Act*. That Act of the Federal Parliament makes every provincial court a *curia designata* to enforce civil remedies provided by that Act. The application of Rule 20.03 of the Small Claims Court Rules with its maximum counsel fee $300 is inconsistent with the discretion in s. 25 of the *Courts of Justice Act*. The court referred to s. 29 of the *Courts of Justice Act*. Section 29 is in conflict with Rule 20.03 of the Small Claims Rules. Any conflict must be resolved in favour of the *Act*.

Stockey v. Peel Condominium Corp. No. 174 (1996), 5 C.P.C. (4th) 246, 30 O.R. (3d) 464, 94 O.A.C. 26 (Ont. Div. Ct.) — Did Deputy Judge of Small Claims Court have jurisdiction to determine issues in this action? Important nature of provincial tribunals such as the Small Claims Court is reflected by the words of Chief Justice Lamer in *Reference re An Act to Amend Chapter 401 of the Revised Statutes, 1989, the Residential Tenancies Act, R.S.N.S.*,

[1996] 193 N.R. 1 (S.C.C.), who stated at p. 1 of his Reasons for Judgment: "the need for efficient and speedy dispute resolution has become an important goal of provincial administration". Deputy Judges are judges of a branch of the General Division, subject to the limitations of appointment and monetary jurisdiction. Section 49 of the *Condominium Act*, R.S.O. 1990, c. C.26, does not contain an express statutory requirement that such disputes shall be heard by a judge appointed under s. 96 of the *Constitution Act, 1867* (U.K.), 30 & 31 Vict., c. 3.

O'Shanter Development Corp. v. Separi (1996), 7 W.D.C.P. (2d) 267 (Ont. Div. Ct.) — Small Claims Court has no jurisdiction to determine amount of money owing and whether or not retroactive rent increase payable in action for arrears of rent.

Black v. Bautista (1995), 13 B.C.L.R. (3d) 275 (S.C.) — Court allowed claimant's application for an order for production of tape recording of evidence taken at trial in Small Claims Court.

Russell v. Maritime Life Assurance Co. (1996), 175 N.B.R. (2d) 317, 446 A.P.R. 317 (C.A.) — Queen's Bench Judge presented with motion requesting an order that numerous Rules of Court were applicable in small claims court action. Judge ruled he did not have jurisdiction to hear motion. On appeal, court ruled judge had jurisdiction to hear application.

V. & M. Gratton Enterprises Ltd. v. Ontario (Workers' Compensation Board) (April 9, 1997), Doc. No. 641/96 (Ont. Sm. Cl. Ct.), Searle, Deputy J. — Court has one jurisdiction to deal with matters over which administrative bodies have exclusive jurisdiction such as s. 69 of the *Workers' Compensation Act*, R.S.O. 1990, c. W.11.

Crews v. College of Physicians & Surgeons (Ontario) (February 29, 1996), Doc. Toronto T15853/95, T15855/95 (Ont. Sm. Cl. Ct.) — Court has no jurisdiction to deal with claim pursuant to s. 38 of the *Regulated Health Professions Act*, S.O. 1991, c. 18 as amended.

Holliday v. Barnes (February 6, 1996), Doc. Toronto T10827/1995 (Ont. Sm. Cl. Ct.) — Although a trade union may be made a party to an action, action dismissed since brought in the wrong division of the Ontario Court (General Division).

Paul Revere Life Insurance Co. v. Herbin, 1996 CarswellNS 101, [1996] N.S.J. No. 88, 149 N.S.R. (2d) 200, 432 A.P.R. 200, [1996] I.L.R. 1-3321 (N.S. S.C.) — Applicant prohibited from suing for disability benefits in Small Claims Court. Court has an inherent jurisdiction to protect its own integrity and prevent an abuse of process. Plaintiff directed to file in higher court.

McCubbing Trucking Ltd. v. Andre Blais Holdings Ltd. (1996), 149 Sask. R. 161 (Sask. Q.B.) — Only claim properly before Provincial Court judge was that of appellant and such claim did not bring title of land into question. Provincial Court judge erred in deciding he had no jurisdiction to proceed with appellant's claim. Respondent could not make idle threat to counterclaim for specific performance with sole purpose of ousting the appellant from the jurisdiction of the small claims court. Matter remitted back to small claims court.

Chediac v. Desmond (1996), 148 N.S.R. (2d) 198, 429 A.P.R. 198 (C.A.) — Small claims adjudicator granted judgment against appellant upon being satisfied appellant had been served with notice, not filed defence and time for filing defence had lapsed. Appeal court found adjudicator's decision was within her jurisdiction pursuant to *Small Claims Court Act*. Appeal dismissed.

Haines, Miller & Associates Inc. v. Foss, 1996 CarswellNS 301, 153 N.S.R. (2d) 53, 450 A.P.R. 53, 3 C.P.C. (4th) 349 (N.S. S.C. [In Chambers]); additional reasons at (1996), 158 N.S.R. (2d) 389, 466 A.P.R. 389, 1999 CarswellNS 304 (N.S. S.C.) — Employee brought small claims action to recover loan to employer. Employer counterclaiming for damages in excess of monetary jurisdiction of small claims court. Employer bringing action on same facts in Supreme Court and applying for a stay of small claims action. Application dismissed. *Small Claims Court Act* does not ouster the Supreme Court in matters properly brought under Act. Supreme Court cautious to exercise inherent jurisdiction to intervene in matters within small claims jurisdiction. Small claims action severable from counterclaim. No prejudice if counterclaim severed.

Luo v. Canada (Attorney General), 1997 CarswellOnt 1577, 145 D.L.R. (4th) 457, 28 C.C.E.L. (2d) 304, 33 O.R. (3d) 300, 9 C.P.C. (4th) 343 (Ont. Div. Ct.) — Small Claims Court has jurisdiction to entertain suits against the Crown. The combined effect of section 21 *Crown Liability and Proceedings Act* and *Interpretation Act* read in light of *Courts of Justice Act*, confers jurisdiction on small claims court in actions against the federal Crown.

Royal Insurance Co. of Canada v. Legge, 1996 CarswellNS 233, 36 C.C.L.I. (2d) 210, 152 N.S.R. (2d) 283, 442 A.P.R. 283, 7 C.P.C. (4th) 96 (N.S. S.C.) — Insured started action in small claims court for arrears of benefits relating to car accident. Insurance company filed statement of Defence and did not challenge jurisdiction. Insurance company brought application for declaration that N.S. S.C. was proper court. Application dismissed. Small Claims Court being tribunal clearly established by legislature as having own authority. N.S. S.C. owed curial deference to Small Claims Court.

O'Brien v. Rideau Carleton Raceway Holdings Ltd. (1998), 34 C.C.E.L. (2d) 199, 109 O.A.C. 173 (Ont. Div. Ct.) — Unsuccessful defendant in Small Claims Court complained on appeal that no real trial had taken place nor evidence heard because no witness asked to swear or affirm prior to giving evidence at the hearing. Court rejected the complaint because ss. 27(1) and 27(2) of the *Courts of Justice Act*, R.S.O. 1990, c. C.43, allowed the Small Claims Court to admit relevant evidence and act upon it whether or not the evidence was given or proven under oath, or affirmation, or admissible as evidence in any other court.

Ricciuto v. Chin (June 30, 1997), Doc. CP-02407-97MO (Ont. Sm. Cl. Ct.) — Claim was for malicious prosecution and slander in the Small Claims Court. Defendant successfully brought a motion to strike the plaintiff's claims. In its decision the Court stated that the defendant entered a peace bond which in itself denies the plaintiff any cause of action for malicious prosecution. In addition, any statements made to the police by defendant are privileged and do not create a cause of action. Finally, any statements made by the defendant in court (criminal court) are privileged and do not create a cause of action.

Patel v. Claire's Canada Corp. (August 28, 1997), Doc. 3103/96 (Ont. Sm. Cl. Ct.) — The Small Claims Court ordered damages to four minors for false arrest and imprisonment by security guards at a shopping mall. The damages awarded were for loss of liberty, indignity, humiliation and mental anguish. No punitive damages were awarded.

Jones v. Canada (Attorney General) (January 31, 1997), Doc. Ottawa 92140195 (Ont. Gen. Div.) — Action for wrongful dismissal struck out in Federal Court without prejudice to commencement of new action. Plaintiff then brought second action on identical basis in Ontario court, which was also struck out. "New action" contemplated by first order did not merely mean commencing same action in another court.

Patrie v. Royal Bank of Canada (January 31, 1997), Doc. Peterborough 11017195 (Ont. Gen. Div.) — Where plaintiff had brought separate successful application to have lien removed from original vehicle, but did not claim damages at that time, damage issue was *res judicata* since it arose out of same transaction.

Lochner v. Ontario (Workers' Compensation Appeals Tribunal), 1997 CarswellOnt 5264 (Ont. Sm. Cl. Ct.) — Plaintiff claimed expenses incurred by her and her witnesses in connection with appearances before Workers' Compensation Appeals Tribunal. Claim arose out of misrepresentation allegations against case worker of defendant, who allegedly stated to plaintiff that expenses would be paid. Small Claims Court had jurisdiction to hear plaintiff's claim for damages for misrepresentation.

Roberts v. Canada Post Corporation (October 31, 1997), Doc. T-929-96, T-969-96 (Fed. T.D.); affirmed (March 31, 1998), Doc. A-232-97, A-233-97 (Fed. C.A.) — Statement of Claim which contained allegations in tort against defendant was struck out on basis of lack of jurisdiction. Federal courts had no jurisdiction both on basis of claim in tort which was within provincial jurisdiction, and no jurisdiction where claim was one governed by collective agreement.

Imperial Life Financial v. Langille (1997), 166 N.S.R. (2d) 46, 498 A.P.R. 46, 2 C.C.L.I. (3d) 117, 21 C.P.C. (4th) 170 (N.S. S.C. [In chambers]) — Can an insured's claim for disability benefits be prosecuted in Small Claims Court on a piecemeal basis so as not to exceed that Court's monetary jurisdiction? Is it an actual claim that may be advanced from time to time, or is it the total potential claim? The reference to "claim" in s. 9 of the *Small Claims Court Act*, R.S.N.S. 1989, c. 430, refers to "claim" in the global sense. To circumvent the discovery process by allowing claims like this to go forward on a piecemeal basis in Small Claims Court would represent a potential disservice to both sides and would be contrary to the stated purpose of the *Small Claims Court Act*. See Saunders, J., in *Paul Revere Life Insurance Co. v. Herbin*, 1996 CarswellNS 101, [1996] N.S.J. No. 88, 149 N.S.R. (2d) 200, 432 A.P.R. 200, [1996] I.L.R. 1-3321 (N.S. S.C.). There is no legislation or case law that takes away the Supreme Court's jurisdiction for all claims regardless of the amount involved. See *Haines, Miller & Associates Inc. v. Foss* (1996), 158 N.S.R. (2d) 389 (N.S. S.C. [In Chambers]).

Manitoba Public Insurance Corp. v. Sundstrom, [1998] I.L.R. I-3529, 16 C.P.C. (4th) 353, 125 Man. R. (2d) 268, 2 C.C.L.I. (3d) 167 (Man. Q.B.) — Position of insurance company was that nature and extent of repairs must be determined by appraisal process set out in Manitoba Regulation 290/88, s. 70(1), passed under *Manitoba Public Insurance Corporation Act, R.S.M. 1987*, regardless of whether coverage was admitted and that, given obligatory nature of procedure, no jurisdiction to court.

Ziegler v. Sherkston Resorts Inc. (1996), 30 O.R. (3d) 375, 4 C.P.C. (4th) 225, 15 O.T.C. 92 (Ont. Gen. Div.); additional reasons at (1997), 13 C.P.C. (4th) 177 (Ont. Gen. Div.) — Cause of action for illegal rent created and governed by *Rent Control Act* (Ont.). Chief Rent Officer had jurisdiction to determine whether illegal rent had been paid and facts necessarily incidental thereto. Action in Ontario Court of Justice (General Division) was dismissed.

Piko v. Hudson's Bay Co. (January 27, 1997), Doc. C34503/95 (Ont. Gen. Div.) — Plaintiff sued for malicious prosecution and mental distress. Defendant argued court had no jurisdiction to deal with dispute since it arose under collective agreement. Matter was still within employment context even though criminal charge had been laid. Claim was dismissed.

Corley v. Rathbone (March 4, 1997), Doc. Kamloops 24256 (B.C. S.C.) — Provincial court had set aside arbitrator's decision in residential tenancy dispute and ordered matter tried in provincial court. Provincial court did not have jurisdiction to adjudicate merits of residential tenancy dispute. Court only had power to return matter to Residential Tenancy Branch.

Maber v. Wilson (1998), (sub nom. *Wilson v. Maber*) 198 N.B.R. (2d) 247, 506 A.P.R. 247, 22 C.P.C. (4th) 108, [1998] N.B.J. No. 71 (N.B. C.A.) — Appeal from the dismissal of an action. Appeal dismissed. An action for libel or slander where the claim was not for more than $3,000 had to be conducted under Rule 75 unless a judge ordered otherwise or the parties agreed.

Popular Shoe Store Ltd. v. Simoni, 1998 CarswellNfld 48, [1998] N.J. No. 57, 163 Nfld. & P.E.I.R. 100, 503 A.P.R. 100, 24 C.P.C. (4th) 10 (Nfld. C.A.) — Appeal from the dismissal of an appeal from a Small Claims Court decision. The appeal was allowed. *Small Claims Act*, R.S.N. 1990, c. S-16, did not include any jurisdiction to grant non-monetary remedies. Appellate court could only grant the relief which was within the jurisdiction of the trial court to grant in the first instance.

Ostafiow Estate v. Lukinuk & McKenzie (January 19, 1999), Doc. Thunder Bay 98-0952 (Ont. Gen. Div.) — Application by the client for order referring the solicitor's account to an assessment officer. At issue was whether special circumstances existed to justify the referral of legal account to an assessment officer. The client had also brought an action in Small Claims Court for recovery of the funds. Application allowed. Small Claims Court was not the appropriate forum for the assessment of legal fees. As a result, special circumstances existed to justify the referral of the account to an assessment officer.

Carby-Samuels v. Royal Bank of Canada (September 3, 1998), Doc. Toronto CP-08847-98 (Ont. Sm. Cl. Ct.) — Action dismissed. The Small Claims Court had no jurisdiction under the *Class Proceedings Act*, S.O. 1992, c. 6. It was clear from claim that Samuels did not seek money but other equitable remedies that court had no jurisdiction to grant or declare.

MacLeod v. Ziengenhagel (June 25, 1998), Doc. 970339, [1998] A.J. No. 849 (Alta. Prov. Ct.), LeGrandeur J. — Action allowed. Counterclaim allowed in part. Although neither party was entitled to judgment for more than $4,000 given the jurisdictional limitation of the court, the court could consider the total amount of each party's claim when setting off one claim against the other.

McDonald v. Ontario (1999), 118 O.A.C. 394 (Ont. C.A.); leave to appeal refused (March 2, 2000), Doc. 27365 (S.C.C.) — Defendants moved for order striking out the statement of claim and dismissing the action. Judicial immunity is not something restricted solely to the *Courts of Justice Act*, R.S.O. 1990, c. C.43. See also Lord Justice Denning in *Sirros v. Moore*, [1975] 1 Q.B. 118. Applicants granted costs fixed at $650. Unrepresented plaintiff, Marion Elaine McDonald, allowed to represent limited company, A.C.E. Paralegals Ltd. See *419212 Ontario Ltd. v. Astrochrome Crankshaft Toronto Ltd.* (1991), 3 O.R. (3d) 116 (Ont. Master).

Carruth v. Singleton Murphy (1998), 169 N.S.R. (2d) 170, 508 A.P.R. 170, 25 C.P.C. (4th) 69 (N.S. S.C.) — Client contended she was given inadequate representation by law firm and that Small Claims Court adjudicator could not tax law firm's account without jurisdiction pursuant to the *Barristers and Solicitors Act*, R.S.N.S. 1989, c. 30. Appeal allowed. Section 42 of Act provided accounts by barristers and solicitors for fees, costs, charges or disbursements had to be taxed either before a taxing master or judge of Supreme Court. The *Rules of Civil Procedure* did not affect this section though a taxing officer for purposes of the Rules included adjudicator of the Small Claims Court.

B.M.W.E. v. Litke, 1998 CarswellMan 588, [1998] M.J. No. 569, 40 C.C.E.L. (2d) 203, (sub nom. *Brotherhood of Maintenance of Way Employees v. Litke)* 133 Man. R. (2d) 146, [1999] 8 W.W.R. 619 (Man. Q.B.); affirmed 1999 CarswellMan 446, [2000] 1 W.W.R. 383, (sub nom. *Brotherhood of Maintenance of Way Employees v. Litke)* 138 Man. R. (2d) 266, (sub nom. *Brotherhood of Maintenance of Way Employees v. Litke)* 202 W.A.C. 266, 181 D.L.R. (4th) 188 (Man. C.A.) — Challenge by defendant of jurisdiction of court to entertain claim of plaintiff. Plaintiff was union, but not registered under the *Trade Unions Act*, R.S.C. 1985, c. T-14. *Bonsor v. Musician's Union* (1955), [1956] A.C. 104 (U.K. H.L.) at 135-136 referenced similar proscription in English Act against court enforcement of penalties imposed by trade unions. Further, the $5,000.00 amount claimed was a penalty and not enforceable by the court. The court has no jurisdiction.

Lee v. Yeung (January 29, 1999), Doc. Edmonton 9803-08861 (Alta. Q.B.) — Appeal from judgment striking out Plaintiff's claim on basis that pursuant to s. 10 of the *Proceedings Against the Crown Act*, R.S.A. 1980, c. P-18, the Provincial Court, insofar as the claim, had no jurisdiction. In the case of *Nelles v. Ontario*, EYB 1989-67463, 1989 CarswellOnt 963, 1989 CarswellOnt 415, [1989] S.C.J. No. 86, 69 O.R. (2d) 448 (note), [1989] 2 S.C.R. 170, 60 D.L.R. (4th) 609, 98 N.R. 321, 35 O.A.C. 161, 41 Admin. L.R. 1, 49 C.C.L.T. 217, 37 C.P.C. (2d) 1, 71 C.R. (3d) 358, 42 C.R.R. 1 (S.C.C.), majority of Court held that immunity was not justified "in the interests of public policy". Historical immunity of the Crown does not extend to the protection of a Crown servant from personal responsibility for his tortuous acts. See: *Mostyn v. Fabrigas* (1775), 98 E.R. 1021 (Eng. K.B.); *Feather v. R.* (1865), 122 E.R. 1191 (Eng. K.B.). See also *Canada (National Harbours Board) v. Langelier*, [1969] S.C.R. 60 (S.C.C.). Provincial Court of Alberta does have jurisdiction.

Associates Financial Services of Canada Ltd. v. Campbell (1998), 8 C.B.R. (4th) 187, 1998 CarswellOnt 5089 (Ont. Sm. Cl. Ct.) — The Small Claims Court had no jurisdiction to lift a stay of proceedings and grant the plaintiff leave to continue execution of default judgment against defendant who was an undischarged bankrupt. The stay of proceedings was created by s. 69(1) of the *Bankruptcy and Insolvency Act* (Canada). Only the superior court had authority to proceed under s. 183 of Act. The motion was dismissed with costs of $50.

Lopes v. Mohammed (September 7, 1998), Doc. North York ET 10051/95 (Ont. Sm. Cl. Ct.) — Pursuant to the *Workplace Safety and Insurance Act* (Ontario), the employee of a Schedule 1 employer is not permitted to sue another employee. The Court did not have jurisdiction to determine whether statutory criteria for ousting jurisdiction of court had been met. Action in Small Claims Court was stayed pending determination by the Act's Appeal Tribunal on whether the plaintiff had a right to sue in court.

Sabine v. University of New Brunswick (1999), 210 N.B.R. (2d) 86, 536 A.P.R. 86 (N.B. C.A.) — The case involved an appeal from a decision that referred the plaintiff's four actions to the Trial Division on the basis of complexity. The plaintiff's claim was for alleged negligence in the treatment of the plaintiff as a student. The plaintiff was authorized to continue. Four actions were to be consolidated and conducted in accordance with the Rules of Court (N.B.).

O'Brien v. 718458 Ontario Inc. (1999), 25 R.P.R. (3d) 57 (Ont. Gen. Div.) — The plaintiff brought an action for $16,000. The defendant sought to strike out the action due to improper venue. The Ontario Court (General Division) was the proper venue as it has jurisdiction to hear all matters of substantive law pursuant to the *Courts of Justice Act* (Ontario), s. 11. The *Tenant Protection Act* (Ontario) does not govern all relationships between landlords and tenants. Here, the claim exceeded the tribunal's limit of $10,000.

Ortiz v. Patrk, 99 C.L.L.C. 220-006, 40 C.C.E.L. (2d) 84, 26 C.P.C. (4th) 56, [1998] L.V.I. 2986-1 (Ont. Gen. Div.) — The employee grieved termination through a collective agreement. The grievance was referred to arbitration. The employee brought action. The dispute as to whether the employee uttered death threats was within the provisions of the collective agreement. The Court lacked jurisdiction. The motion was granted, the action dismissed.

Nedeljkovic v. Helliwell (1999), 176 Sask. R. 135 (Sask. Q.B.) — The provisions of the Residential Tenancies Act, R.S.S. 1978, limit monetary jurisdiction of the Rentalsman to claims that do not exceed monetary limit of *The Small Claims Act, 1997* (Saskatchewan). The jurisdiction of the Rentalsman is governed by claim, not amount ultimately found by the Rentalsman to be due and owing. If monetary amount of claim, reasonably understood and considered on its face exceeds $5,000, the matter must be referred to the Court of Queen's Bench.

Greer v. Co-operators General Insurance Co. (1999), [2000] I.L.R. I-3785, 13 C.C.L.I. (3d) 255 (Ont. S.C.J.) — The determination of a disputed value of loss mandated in an appraisal mechanism under the *Insurance Act* and court actions to resolve same was stayed.

Pino v. Van Roon (1998), 28 C.P.C. (4th) 274 (Ont. Gen. Div.) — A solicitor was granted a charging order and solicitor's lien on any funds that might become payable to a former client from two actions instituted and pursued by the solicitor. The right to sue is a choice in action, which is property, and the right of the client to sue had clearly been preserved by his former solicitor's efforts.

Robinson v. Cooney (1999), 29 C.P.C. (4th) 72 (Ont. Gen. Div.) — A retainer providing for a contingent percentage fee was illegal and unenforceable, also there was no recovery on a *quantum meruit* basis. However, the law appears ripe for reform and if the legislature does not do so, the court might.

At the time the amended claim was filed, this was an outstanding judgment of the Ontario Housing Rental Tribunal. This Court is not an Appeal Court from Ontario Housing Rental Tribunal. Pursuant to the *Tenant Protection Act*, the Order of the Ontario Housing Rental Tribunal is deemed to be a Judgment of Court and the plaintiff may enforce it if monies ordered are not paid. Defence struck in so far as it is an appeal and deals with issues of the Ontario Housing Rental Tribunal. *Karn v. MacKay* (March 2, 2000), Doc. CP-16774-99 (Ont. Ct.).

The Ontario Rental Housing Tribunal has exclusive authority concerning the issues raised in the defence (notice given, inconvenience). Section 184 of the *Tenant Protection Act* provides that the *Statutory Powers Procedure Act* applies to all proceedings. Section 19(1) allows the Ontario Rental Housing Tribunal Order of Decision to be filed. The Order is deemed to be an Order of the Superior Court and may be enforced as such. The garnishment issued will not be stayed. The defendant's remedies are under the *Tenant Protection Act*. Monies in court to the plaintiff. *Petrik v. Mohammed* (August 17, 1999), Doc. Toronto CP-16218/99 (Ont. Sm. Cl. Ct.).

The *Tenant Protection Act*, S.O. 1997, c. 24 provides that the Ontario Rental Housing Tribunal has exclusive jurisdiction to determine all applications with respect to all matters conferred on it by the Act. See *inter alia*, ss. 32(1), 35 and 193(1). The plaintiff argues action one of conversion and trespass over which court has jurisdiction and not the Ontario Rental Housing Tribunal. Relationship arises out of one in which the plaintiff is a former tenant. Only the Tribunal has jurisdiction to deal with tenancy matters.

Dismissal of the plaintiff's claim would seriously prejudice the plaintiff because the time for applying under the *Tenant Protection Act* is one year. The Court does not have jurisdiction. Pursuant to s. 110(1), the matter was transferred to the Ontario Housing Tribunal as if it commenced on June 25, 1998. *Sood v. Ontario (Ministry of Municipal Affairs & Housing)* (March 2, 1999), Doc. Toronto T10984-98 (Ont. Sm. Cl. Ct.).

Bower v. Rosicky, 2000 BCSC 1235, 2000 CarswellBC 2396 (B.C. S.C.) — The defendants accidentally trespassed and cut down trees. Action should have been brought in provincial court. The plaintiffs were entitled to disbursements only: *Rules of Court* (B.C.), r. 57(10).

Arbutus Leasing Ltd v. Deghati, 2000 ABQB 831, 2000 CarswellAlta 1305 (Alta. Master); additional reasons at 2000 ABQB 876, 2000 CarswellAlta 1382 (Alta. Master); further additional reasons at 2001 ABQB 472, 2001 CarswellAlta 773 (Alta. Master) — The defendants leased equipment from the plaintiff and defaulted on the lease. The plaintiff applied for summary judgment. The law did not prohibit a lawsuit in Queen's Bench just because the cause of action was within the Provincial Court's jurisdiction.

5L Farms Ltd. v Miniota (Rural Municipality), 2000 MBQB 240, 2000 CarswellMan 664 (Man. Master) — The municipality that appealed the decision was not entitled to order adding third parties prior to the hearing of the appeal by trial *de novo*. The decision of the Small Claims Court was sufficient to support a plea of *res judicata*. The municipality was not permitted to make a motion to add third parties until hearing of the trial *de novo* itself.

R. v. Devgan (1999), 121 O.A.C. 265, 44 O.R. (3d) 161, 136 C.C.C. (3d) 238, 26 C.R. (5th) 307, 1999 CarswellOnt 1534 (Ont. C.A.); leave to appeal refused (2000), 254 N.R. 393 (note), 134 O.A.C. 396 (note), 2000 CarswellOnt 911, 2000 CarswellOnt 912 (S.C.C.) — Compensation order: civil judgment against the accused not precluding granting of compensation order; compensation order may not be granted for legal fees, disbursements or interest: *Criminal Code*, R.S.C. 1985, c. C-46, s. 725(1).

Kizemchuk v. Kizemchuk (2000), 135 O.A.C. 263, 2000 CarswellOnt 2547 (Ont. Div. Ct.) — The appellants appeared unrepresented to defend application to terminate tenancy. The Divisional Court held fairness required opportunity for the appellants to obtain counsel to address issues. The Tribunal erred in law by failing to accord natural justice to appellants. The Court remitted the matter for further hearing before a different adjudicator.

Graves v. Hughes, 2001 CarswellNS 168, 2001 NSSC 68, 25 C.B.R. (4th) 255, 194 N.S.R. (2d) 51, 606 A.P.R. 51 (N.S. S.C.) — Small Claims Court had jurisdiction to make determination as to whether judgment obtained by respondents against appellant, now discharged bankrupt, survived bankruptcy on grounds of fraud.

Leader School Division No. 24 v. Fisher, 2001 CarswellSask 341, 2001 SKQB 209, (sub nom. *Board of Education of Leader School Division No. 24 v. Fisher*) 206 Sask. R. 207 (Sask. Q.B.) — Any grievance with respect to a collective agreement entered into pursuant to the *Education Act, 1995*, S.S. 1995, c. E-0.2, must be submitted to arbitration. Issues relating to salary arose under agreement. The Court did not have concurrent jurisdiction to decide disputes.

A. (A.M.) (Litigation Guardian of) v. Toronto District School Board (2001), 2001 CarswellOnt 3305 (Ont. S.C.J.) — Child suspended from school. He had been yelled at by principal in absence of parents. Claims relating to statutory duty to discipline and to educate student within exclusive jurisdiction of *Education Act*, R.S.O. 1990, c. E-2. Claims struck out. Claim in tort against principal to proceed.

Athabasca Chipewyan First Nation v. Canada (Minister of Indian Affairs & Northern Development), [2001] 8 W.W.R. 419, 2001 CarswellAlta 576, 2001 ABCA 112, 199 D.L.R. (4th) 452, 281 A.R. 38, 248 W.A.C. 38, 30 Admin. L.R. (3d) 87, 7 C.P.C. (5th) 1, 93 Alta. L.R. (3d) 1, (sub nom. *Athabasca Chipewyan First Nation v. British Columbia*) [2001] 3 C.N.L.R. 8 (Alta. C.A.) — Practice and procedure involving Crown in right of Canada. Forum for proceedings. In proceedings against Crown. Statutory jurisdiction of provincial courts. Under s. 2(c) of *Crown Proceedings Act*, R.S.B.C. 1996, c. 89, province was subject to same liabilities as it would be if it were person. Section 4(1) of Act requires that action against province be brought in British Columbia Supreme Court.

Djukic v. Canada (Attorney General) (2000), 52 O.R. (3d) 348, 2000 CarswellOnt 4872, 4 C.P.C. (5th) 205 (Ont. C.A.) — Action against Federal Crown. Jurisdiction requirement is s. 21(1)(a) of *Crown Liability and Proceedings Act*, R.S.C. 1985, c. C-50, that claim has arisen in province applying equally to s. 21(1)(b) of Act. Superior Court of province not having jurisdiction to hear claim against Crown where claim did not arise in province.

Crooks v. Levine (2001), 148 O.A.C. 44, 2001 CarswellOnt 2541 (Ont. Div. Ct.) — A tenant brought a small claims action against her former landlord for damages for wrongful conversion of goods *inter alia*. Landlord asserted Rental Housing Tribunal had exclusive jurisdiction over disputes in residential tenancies. Divisional Court dismissed the appeal, stating that the claim for damages was properly within the jurisdiction of Small Claims Court.

Qubti v. Ontario Jockey Club (2002), 166 O.A.C. 179, 2002 CarswellOnt 4218, 62 O.R. (3d) 290, 29 C.P.C. (5th) 94 (Ont. Div. Ct.) — Plaintiff commenced action under the simplified procedure provided by Civil Procedure Rule 76. He claimed damages of $25,000 plus pre-judgment interest and costs. The trial judge held defendant negligent. However, she found the plaintiff 50 per cent liable. She assessed the plaintiff's damages at $34,933.14. She applied the contributory negligence to the assessed damages and awarded judgment for $17,466.57. The defendant appealed. The Divisional Court dismissed the appeal. The Court stated that by making a claim under the simplified procedure a plaintiff abandons "the amount of the claim for which judgment is awarded in excess of $25,000.".

Helsberg v. Sutton Group Achievers's Reality Inc. (2002), 165 O.A.C. 122, 2002 CarswellOnt 4640, [2002] O.J. No. 2311 (Ont. Div. Ct.) — On June 4, 1998, the plaintiff issued a claim for $6,644.26, post judgment interest and costs. On October 8, 1999 judgment for the plaintiff given for $5,522.46, postjudgment interest and disbursements. On April 2, 2001, the maximum amount of a claim in the Small Claims Court was increased from $6,000 to $10,000, exclusive of interest and costs. On April 17, 2001, the defendant's appeal factum was filed. It raised jurisdictional issues for the first time. The Ontario Divisional Court held that the Small Claims Court lacked jurisdiction to hear the matter because the amount claimed exceeded its jurisdictional limit of $6,000. The amendment raising the jurisdiction limit to $10,000 was not procedural and did not have retrospective application.

Mack v. Canada (Attorney General) (2002), 165 O.A.C. 17, 2002 CarswellOnt 2927, 217 D.L.R. (4th) 583, 96 C.R.R. (2d) 254, 60 O.R. (3d) 737, 60 O.R. (3d) 756, 24 Imm. L.R. (3d) 1, [2002] O.J. No. 3488 (Ont. C.A.); leave to appeal refused (2003), 2003 CarswellOnt 1455, 2003 CarswellOnt 1456, 319 N.R. 196 (note), 101 C.R.R. (2d) 375 (note) (S.C.C.) — The *Chinese Immigration Act 1885 (Can.)*, imposed a "head tax" or duty on persons of Chinese origin who immigrated to Canada. The plaintiffs, as class representatives, sought the return of monies paid as head tax etc. The Attorney General of Canada moved to have the claim struck on the ground that it disclosed no reasonable cause of action. The Ontario Court of Appeal dismissed appeal, affirming that the action was properly struck. Action could not proceed because of the principle that customary international law may be ousted for domestic purposes by contrary domestic legislation, which occurred in this case.

Hunt v. C. (K.), 19 C.P.C. (5th) 221, 2002 CarswellAlta 525, 2002 ABPC 57, [2002] 7 W.W.R. 767, 3 Alta. L.R. (4th) 400, 314 A.R. 303 (Alta. Prov. Ct.) — Accused young offender was convicted of vandalism regarding fleet of vehicles owned by plaintiff. Compensation order did not restrict plaintiff from pursuing claim. As plaintiff already had compensation order for $3,000, remaining amount of $8,840 had to be considered. Due to limits of court, plaintiff had to abandon excess over $7,500 resulting in plaintiff abandoning $1,340.

Guenette v. Canada (Attorney General) (2002), 162 O.A.C. 371, 2002 CarswellOnt 2554, [2002] O.J. No. 3062, 2002 C.L.L.C. 220-038, 19 C.C.E.L. (3d) 36, 216 D.L.R. (4th) 410, 60 O.R. (3d) 601 (S.C.C.) — Complaints brought by employees not subject to, and could not be adjudicated under, adjudication process established by collective agreement and Act. There was no reason for the Court to decline to exercise its jurisdiction.

M. Tucci Construction Ltd. v. Lockwood (2002), 2002 CarswellOnt 365 (Ont. C.A.) — Cause of action estoppel did not apply because same cause action not determined in earlier proceedings by court of competent jurisdiction. Earlier Small Claims Court action resolved in settlement. No determination by court and no releases. Sufficient to dispose of this ground of appeal. May have been separate causes of action. Respondent not required to assert complaint with counterclaim, especially since the counterclaim would have exceeded the monetary jurisdiction of the court and could only be moved to the Superior Court of Justice with appellant's consent. Appeal dismissed with costs.

Swire v. Walleye Trailer Park Ltd. (2001), 2001 CarswellOnt 2832, 203 D.L.R. (4th) 402, 149 O.A.C. 108, 44 R.P.R. (3d) 120 (Ont. Div. Ct.) — Appellant purchased trailer from former tenant in trailer park who assigned lease in park without respondent landlord's consent. Respondent obtained judgment. Small Claims Court had no jurisdiction to deal with matter applying to mobile home tenancy in relation to tax, evidenced by section 29 of Ontario Regulations 194/98 that dealt specifically with property taxes. Judgment set aside.

Ritchie v. Edmonton Eskimo Football Club, 2003 ABQB 59, 2003 CarswellAlta 57 (Alta. Q.B.) — Award in favour of Ritchie of $10,400 (2002 CarswellAlta 1591, 2002 ABQB 1078 (Alta. Q.B.)) exceeded small claims limit until limit changed about one month before trial. Plaintiff entitled to total bill of costs. See Rule 605(7). Amendments to the *Provincial Court Act* did not purport to give jurisdiction to that court unless cause of action rose after proclamation of increased limits.

Harvey v. Matacheskie, 2003 BCPC 8, 2003 CarswellBC 88 (B.C. Prov. Ct.). Application brought by defendant, for order pursuant to Small Claims *Rule 7(14)(ii)* dismissing Claim of John Harvey. Questioning if all issues in the within lawsuit have already been determined in another lawsuit?.

Principle of law that a party is prevented from re-litigating a question which has been fairly decided against him. Exceptions such as fraud or other misconduct in earlier proceedings or the discovery of decisive fresh evidence. (See *Saskatoon Credit Union Ltd. v. Central Park Enterprises Ltd.* (1988), [1988] B.C.J. No. 49, 1988 CarswellBC 16, 22 B.C.L.R. (2d) 89, 47 D.L.R. (4th) 431 (B.C. S.C.)).

No appeal was taken by Harvey from earlier decision. His counsel submitted no appeal from decision possible as section 5 of *The Small Claims Act* states that no appeal lies from an Order except after trial. Appeals from decisions upon Applications or at Settlement Conferences are made to the Supreme Court see: *Artisan Floor Co. v. Lam* (1993), [1993] B.C.J. No. 518, 1993 CarswellBC 42, 76 B.C.L.R. (2d) 384 (B.C. S.C.), and *Cohen v. Kirkpatrick* (1993), 1993 CarswellBC 2106 (B.C. S.C.).

Second action merely an attempt by Harvey to re-litigate issue which already determined by the Court.

Alberta Tractor Ltd. v. Noralta Clearing Ltd., 2003 CarswellAlta 260, 2003 ABPC 39, 333 A.R. 249, 14 Alta. L.R. (4th) 150 (Alta. Prov. Ct.). Defendant argued Plaintiff limited by the monetary jurisdiction of court of $7,500.

McDonald, J. in *Kondro v. Parker*, 49 A.R. 332, 1983 CarswellAlta 146, [1983] A.J. No. 27, [1983] 6 W.W.R. 380, 27 Alta. L.R. (2d) 285, 37 C.P.C. 272 (Alta. Q.B.) stated "Provincial Court has jurisdiction to try and to adjudicate claim even if the Plaintiff alleges in the body of his summons, that debt in excess of $1,000 or the damage or injury was of a value in an amount in excess of $1,000. It is the form of the claim for judgment itself which determines the jurisdiction of the court.".

Berger J. as he then was, in *ARS Trucking & Welding Ltd. v. Greco* (1987), 23 C.P.C. (2d) 95, 1987 CarswellAlta 354 (Alta. Q.B.) disagreed with *Kondro* as did Dixon, J. in *Swainson Trucking Ltd. v. E.V. Snow Holdings* (1985), 38 Alta. L.R. (2d) 286, 1985 CarswellAlta 109 (Alta. Q.B.). Berger, J. held that a Provincial Judge could not set off the value of the counterclaim against the total charges in that case. The Court must connect the counterclaim to the claim as a true set off.

See also *Anderson v. Parney*, [1930] 4 D.L.R. 833, 66 O.L.R. 112 (Ont. C.A.). Majority of Court found that a judgment could be entered for no more than the amount claimed, but that in ascertaining that amount it may be necessary to give evidence of damages exceeding the amount claimed. The dissenting judgment of Orde J.A., and in particular his reference to the limit upon the Courts jurisdiction being "upon the amount recoverable" was later unanimously adopted by the Supreme Court of Canada in the subsequent decision of *Burkhardt v. Beder* (1962), 36 D.L.R. (2d) 313, 1962 CarswellOnt 78, [1963] S.C.R. 86 (S.C.C.). The decision of the Supreme Court of Canada was then followed in *Kondro v. Parker, supra.*

Plaintiff awarded net judgment based upon $13,175.27 which was owed to it less damages to the Defendant by way of set off of $7,294.08. Judgment for the Plaintiff granted totaling $5,881.19 plus GST of $411.69.

Bohatti & Co. v. DeBartolo (2003), 2003 CarswellOnt 4887 (Ont. Div. Ct.) Appeal from judgment of the Small Claims Court.

Landlord submitted trial judge both allowed the Defendant a set-off from the landlord's judgment in the amount of approximately $10,000 and granted him a judgment for a further $10,000 thereby giving him relief worth a total of $20,000, far beyond the monetary jurisdiction of the Small Claims Court. See *ARS Trucking & Welding Ltd. v. Greco* (1987), 23

C.P.C. (2d) 95, 1987 CarswellAlta 354 (Alta. Q.B.) for the authority that a combined set-off and judgment may not exceed the monetary jurisdiction of the Court. Trial judge found there had been a breach by landlord. Appeal dismissed.

Easy Home v. Rogalski, 2004 CarswellOnt 475, 46 C.P.C. (5th) 318 (Ont. Sm. Cl. Ct.). Reasons dealt with procedure to be followed in obtaining a Writ of Delivery for return of personal property in Small Claims Court.

A Writ of Delivery (Form 20B) is a direction from the Court to the bailiff instructing the bailiff to seize certain goods specified from the Defendant and to deliver them to the Plaintiff in accordance with an Order of the Court made on a particular date. issues pursuant to *Rule 20.05(1)*. Under s. 23(1)(b) of the *Courts of Justice Act* the Court has jurisdiction *in any action* for the recovery of possession of personal property where the value of the property does not exceed the prescribed amount.

Plaintiff must first commence an action by issuing a claim for the return of the goods in question. Plaintiff must then obtain a judgment either by default or otherwise for the return of the goods. It is only when judgment or Order not complied with that Plaintiff may file affidavit setting out the non-compliance and obtain a Writ of Delivery for the forcible return of the goods.

Small Claims Court silent as to the procedure to be followed in obtaining interim Order as those pursuant to Section 104 of the *Courts of Justice Act*. Motion dismissed.

J. Connelly Rental Ltd. v. Lefebvre (2003), 2003 CarswellOnt 4393, 178 O.A.C. 246 (Ont. Div. Ct.). The Small Claims court litigant who decides to take the successful party to appeal in Divisional Court runs risk of substantial costs. Award of $3,000 on a substantive indemnity basis appropriate.

Gerhardt v. Scotia Best Christmas Tree Ltd., 2004 CarswellNS 83, 221 N.S.R. (2d) 227, 697 A.P.R. 227, 2004 NSSC 53 (N.S. S.C.). Appeal from Small Claims Court decision. Appellants claimed there was not a fair hearing because they were not given opportunity to cross-examine witness who testified for Plaintiff.

The right to cross-examine a fundamental. Basic that each party has right to cross-examine witnesses put forward by other. The parties must be informed of their basic procedural rights, including as a minimum method available to them to present their case.

Those without counsel as self-represented litigants should not be expected to know the procedure or to realize that they have a right to cross-examine, unless so advised. Appeal allowed. New hearing Ordered.

Osterbauer v. Ash Temple Ltd. (2003), 169 O.A.C. 301, 2003 CarswellOnt 866, 2003 C.L.L.C. 210-047, 63 O.R. (3d) 697 (Ont. C.A.). Test for reasonable apprehension of bias is well-established by the Supreme Court of Canada in *R. v. S. (R.D.)*, 1997 CarswellNS 301, 1997 CarswellNS 302, [1997] S.C.J. No. 84, 151 D.L.R. (4th) 193, 118 C.C.C. (3d) 353, 10 C.R. (5th) 1, 218 N.R. 1, 161 N.S.R. (2d) 241, 477 A.P.R. 241, [1997] 3 S.C.R. 484, 1 Admin. L.R. (3d) 74 (S.C.C.). See also *Committee for Justice & Liberty v. Canada (National Energy Board)*, 1976 CarswellNat 434, 1976 CarswellNat 434F, [1978] 1 S.C.R. 369, 68 D.L.R. (3d) 716, 9 N.R. 115 (S.C.C.). "The apprehension of bias must be a reasonable one, held by reasonable and right-minded persons, applying themselves to the question and obtaining thereon the required information.".

Bohatti & Co. v. DeBartolo (2003), 2003 CarswellOnt 4887 (Ont. Div. Ct.) Small Claims court jurisdiction at issue. Tenant found not entitled to terminate or rent abatement but entitled on ground of wrongful refusal to consent to assignment. Amount of dismissed claim for rent of $10,000 not deemed to be added to award of damages of $10,000. Award not above jurisdiction. Landlord's appeal dismissed.

Kalevar v. Mihevc (2003), 2003 CarswellOnt 4666 (Ont. S.C.J.). Small Claims Court jurisdictional issue stating that defendant had been misrepresenting his academic status while running for municipal office. Small Claims Court had no power to enact standards for municipal politicians. Claim dismissed.

British Columbia (Minister of Forests) v. Okanagan Indian Band (2003), 2003 CarswellBC 3040, 2003 CarswellBC 3041, 2003 SCC 71, 43 C.P.C. (5th) 1, [2003] 3 S.C.R. 371, 313 N.R. 84, [2004] 2 W.W.R. 252, 21 B.C.L.R. (4th) 209, 233 D.L.R. (4th) 577, [2004] 1 C.N.L.R. 7, 189 B.C.A.C. 161, 309 W.A.C. 161 (S.C.C.). Public interest litigation. Courts had discretionary power in its equitable jurisdiction to award interim costs. No other realistic option for bringing issues to trial available, and meritorious case made out.

Funk, Re, 2003 CarswellSask 677, 2003 SKPC 150, 242 Sask. R. 78 (Sask. Prov. Ct.). Plaintiff in Saskatchewan sought to issue claim against Ontario tow truck operator arising out of vehicle accident in Ontario, and against British Columbia trailer sales company and its Manitoba resident manager. Claims should be brought in respective provinces connected to claims. Issue of summons refused.

Klein v. R. (2003), 2003 CarswellNat 3365, 2003 TCC 700, 2003 D.T.C. 1427, [2004] 1 C.T.C. 2814 (T.C.C. [General Procedure]). K. retired lawyer, represented himself throughout conduct of successful appeal from assessment. K. awarded costs. K's bill of costs included fees for counsel. K. to be treated as self-represented litigant. Self-represented litigant could not render service to himself. Not entitled to fees for services of counsel.

MacKenzie v. MacKenzie, 2003 CarswellNS 391, 2003 NSCA 120, 47 R.F.L. (5th) 104, 218 N.S.R. (2d) 306, 687 A.P.R. 306 (N.S. C.A.). Applicant's application to admit fresh evidence on appeal of order of child support denied. Appeal not opportunity for second trial. Court cannot condone Applicant's disregard of his legal obligation at trial stage.

Lam v. Scintrex Trace Corp. (2003), 2003 CarswellOnt 3048 (Ont. S.C.J.). Plaintiff commenced action in Toronto. Defendant's action in Ottawa stayed. Defendant's main witness in New Jersey. Plaintiff located near Toronto. Balance of convenience favoured trial in Toronto.

Pearl v. Sovereign Management Group Inc. (2003), [2003] O.J. No. 2161, 2003 CarswellOnt 2010, 37 C.P.C. (5th) 143 (Ont. S.C.J.). Plaintiff purchased 30 vending machines from Defendant. Plaintiff resided in Toronto. Defendant located in British Columbia. Bulk of evidence in Ontario. Jurisdiction clause indicated interpretation in British Columbia. Jurisdiction clause only applied 5 of 30 machines. Ontario proper forum as defendant had office in Ontario, had employees in Ontario.

Underhay v. MacDonald, 2003 CarswellPEI 53, 2003 PESCAD 14, 38 R.F.L. (5th) 225, 224 Nfld. & P.E.I.R. 320, 669 A.P.R. 320 (P.E.I. C.A.). Settlement allegedly reached at conference declared enforceable. Trial judge could not have reached decision without improper use of documents and communications not contained in memorandum. Decision based on prohibited disclosures and was set aside.

Sinardi Hair Design v. Knifton (2003), 2003 CarswellOnt 1547 (Ont. Div. Ct.). Appellants moved to extend time for filing their appeal from decision of Small Claims Court. Decision in question interlocutory in nature. Appeal only available from final order of Small Claims Court under s.31 of *Courts of Justice Act (Ont.)*. No common law right of appeal. Motion to extend time dismissed.

Bank of Nova Scotia v. Pelley, 2003 CarswellNS 92, 2003 NSSC 53, 213 N.S.R. (2d) 210, 667 A.P.R. 210 (N.S. S.C.). Adjournment granted four days before trial where Defendant produced letter from psychiatrist indicating that Defendant apt to be severely destabilized by trial.

Turner (Litigation Guardian of) v. Court, 2003 CarswellSask 7, 2003 SKQB 10 (Sask. Q.B.). Defendants applied to file defence after noted in default. Defendants served with claim on November 5, 2002, and noted in default on November 29, 2002. Application brought in timely fashion once default known. There was no question that meritorious defence was made out in draft defence. Application granted to set aside default.

Canada Trust Co. v. Menzies, 2002 CarswellSask 733, 2002 SKQB 386 (Sask. Q.B.). Defendants were husband and wife and signed MasterCard acceptance form, which stated that parties were jointly and severally liable. Defendants separated. Male defendant used card for his own personal use. Defendants both liable to Plaintiff.

Serco Facilities Management Inc. v. A & E Precision Fabricating & Machine Shop Inc., 2004 CarswellNfld 131, 2004 NLSCTD 86 (N.L. T.D.), Robert A. Fowler, J. Serco filed counterclaim which exceeded the $3,000 monetary jurisdiction of Court and sought to transfer proceedings to the Supreme Court Trial Division. S. 6 of *Small Claims Act* intended to move borderline jurisdictional cases along and where the plaintiff's claim within jurisdiction of Court, to permit the respondent to automatically move to the Trial Division on basis that the counterclaim exceeds the jurisdiction of the Provincial Court would not serve the purpose of that section of Act. Costs determined by Provincial Court Judge hearing matter. Motion dismissed.

Harron Enterprises Inc. v. Von Pfahlenburg, 2004 CarswellBC 1768, 2004 BCPC 264, Romilly, J. Application to Court for Order for release of file in Residential Tenancy Branch. Only jurisdiction given to Small Claims Court is power of enforcement if judgment of Arbitrator registered with Court. No other jurisdiction in residential tenancy matters conferred to Court under the *Residential Tenancy Act.* Court without jurisdiction to grant Order sought.

New Brunswick Assn. of Real Estate Appraisers v. Poitras, 2005 CarswellNB 1, [2005] N.B.J. No. 1, 2005 NBQB 8, 286 N.B.R. (2d) 131, 748 A.P.R. 131 (N.B. Q.B.), Lucie A. LaVigne, J. Application for appeal by trial *de novo* under the *Small Claims Act.* Discipline Committee of Association ordered Poitras to pay a fine of $500 and 70 per cent of costs of hearing for total of $3,055. He argued this is a penalty, not a debt, and therefore Court should not issue judgment as requested. No authority for the Court to enforce payments of fines and costs ordered by the Association's Discipline Committee by giving a judgment for such amount. Claim dismissed without costs.

Boulet v. Aspen Interiors Inc., 2004 CarswellSask 893, 2004 SKPC 80, 41 C.L.R. (3d) 141 (Sask. Prov. Ct.), Dirauf, H.G. The monetary limit of Court is $5,000. Counterclaim is defined as including a set-off. Nothing in provisions state that a "counterclaimant" can bring counterclaim for more than $5,000. Not intention of legislature to place a claimant on a different footing than a counterclaimant.

Counterclaim must be reduced to $5,000 before it is applied to the plaintiff's claim to give the court jurisdiction.

Pierce v. Canada (Customs & Revenue Agency), 2004 CarswellBC 1923, 2004 BCPC 307 (B.C. Prov. Ct.), J.F. Galati, P.C.J. Does Provincial Court have inherent jurisdiction over matter covered by s. 21(1) of the *Crown Liability and Proceedings Act,* which authorizes a claim against the federal Crown *only* in the Federal Court or the superior court of a province, here the Supreme Court of British Columbia? If there is no statute, federal or provincial, which provides jurisdiction to the Provincial Court, then it has no jurisdiction. No such statute that confers jurisdiction for the Provincial Court in British Columbia. Notice of Claim dismissed.

Accent Leasing & Sales Ltd. v. Parsons, 2004 CarswellBC 1200, 7 P.P.S.A.C. (3d) 151, 2004 BCPC 140 (B.C. Prov. Ct.), Judge E.D. Schmidt. Defendants defaulted on lease payments. Claimant seized vehicle and brought action in Provincial Court claiming for lease payments for the 16 months remaining of the lease, arrears of lease payments, kilometre charge and Bailiff fees, all of which exceeded $10,000. Claimant abandoned excess of their claim that exceeds $10,000 in order to fall within monetary jurisdiction of the Provincial Court.

Personal Property Security Act defines "court" as the Supreme Court in s. 1(1). Legislators excluded jurisdiction of Provincial Court either expressly or by definition, regardless of the monetary amount of the claim, in a number of Acts of Parliament or of the Provincial Legislatures. The *Crown Proceedings Act*, the *Bankruptcy and Insolvency Act*, the *Residential Tenancy Act*, the *Commercial Arbitration Act*, and the *Builders Lien Act* are examples, where often amount in issue less than $10,000. Provincial Court not the forum for hearing the dispute. Court does not have jurisdiction.

Hudson v. Flowers By The Dozen Inc., 2005 CanLII 1724 (Ont. L.R.B.), Brian McLean, Vice-Chair. Applicant sued the company in Small Claims Court. Flowers by the Dozen defended the lawsuit by relying on s. 97 of Act.

The Court dismissed the applicant's lawsuit.

Wray v. Best G.I.S. Co., 2004 CarswellBC 2238, 2004 BCSC 1247 (B.C. S.C.), Curtis, J. Wray applied for order setting aside decision of arbitrator made pursuant to the *Residential Tenancy Act*, R.S.B.C. 1996, c. 406. Wray brought action in Small Claims Court. Section 84 of the Act prohibits the bringing of an action in Provincial Court for debt or damages which arises out of a right or obligation under Act or tenancy agreement. Section dependent on preliminary finding valid tenancy agreement formed between the parties. No valid tenancy agreement created by Best. The arbitrator's order set aside.

Anani v. Ismail, 2004 CarswellBC 1451, 2004 BCCA 370 (B.C. C.A.). In 2002, Malaspina Coach Lines Ltd. et al brought small claims action and was successful in recovering $2,945.31 against the Ananis in that action. Ananis' counterclaim dismissed and their later appeal to the Supreme Court was unsuccessful. They then filed a writ of summons in Supreme Court claiming damages and other relief for alleged perjury, etc. during testimony in the action in small claims court.

Mr. Justice Williams ordered that venue of Ananis' new action be moved from New Westminster to Powell River and ordered that they post security for costs.

Kagal v. Tessler, 2004 CarswellOnt 3772, 190 O.A.C. 77, 41 C.L.R. (3d) 1, 36 C.C.E.L. (3d) 105 (Ont. C.A.). It may be that punitive damages are generally available in commercial relations if there is an abuse of power. In the Court of Appeal decision, recognition of the vulnerability of Kagal but no reference to specific independent actionable wrong.

Lazarof v. Trimart Trillion Corp., 2005 CarswellOnt 6440 (Ont. S.C.J.), Frank J. Defendants, relying on alleged attempt to pay plaintiff $4,100 prior to the institution of action and Offer to Settle in amount of $4,839.82, seeks costs of $33,185.69. The plaintiff, who recovered $3,769.55 plus prejudgment interest seeks costs of $37,622.85.

Claim, as of pre-trial, was for amount barely more than $20,000. Judge not prepared to find that this action should have proceeded in Small Claim Court.

The factors to be considered in determining costs are set out in Rule 58.06. See *Boucher v. Public Accountants Council (Ontario)*, 2004 CarswellOnt 2521, [2004] O.J. No. 2634, (sub nom. *Boucher v. Public Accountants Council for the Province of Ontario)* 71 O.R. (3d) 291, 48 C.P.C. (5th) 56, 188 O.A.C. 201 (Ont. C.A.). Resulting fee does not meet the overriding test of reasonableness.

Plaintiff awarded costs of $1,500 together with disbursements of $930.75 plus GST.

Saskatchewan Government Insurance v. Valliere, 2005 CarswellSask 669, 27 C.C.L.I. (4th) 236, 24 C.P.C. (6th) 236, 2005 SKQB 430 (Sask. Q.B.), Krueger J. Saskatchewan Government Insurance appeals from the decision of a Small Claims Court judge who found that the

Small Claims Court has jurisdiction to hear and determine liability issue in a single vehicle accident.

In *Canson Enterprises Ltd. v. Boughton & Co.*, EYB 1991-67056, 1991 CarswellBC 269, 1991 CarswellBC 925, [1991] S.C.J. No. 91, [1992] 1 W.W.R. 245, 9 C.C.L.T. (2d) 1, 39 C.P.R. (3d) 449, 131 N.R. 321, 85 D.L.R. (4th) 129, 61 B.C.L.R. (2d) 1, 6 B.C.A.C. 1, 13 W.A.C. 1, [1991] 3 S.C.R. 534, 43 E.T.R. 201 (S.C.C.), La Forest J. defined damages as being a "monetary payment awarded for the invasion of a right at common law.".

The respondent's only financial obligation is a liability to pay a $25 surcharge. That is not an insured's financial liability for damages. Remedy sought by respondent of a declaratory nature. Matters subject to Highway Traffic Board. Appeal allowed and claim dismissed.

New Brunswick Assn. of Real Estate Appraisers v. Poitras, 2005 CarswellNB 751, 2005 CarswellNB 752, 2005 NBCA 112, 294 N.B.R. (2d) 312, 765 A.P.R. 312 (N.B. C.A.). Issue whether appellant, the New Brunswick Association of Real Estate Appraisers, entitled to resort to the *Small Claims Act*, S.N.B. 1997, c. S-9.1 for purposes of recovering fines and costs imposed on one of its members, the respondent, Poitras. Adjudicator and Court of Queen's Bench answered in the negative. Appeal allowed.

De novo judge held that as the amount being sought did not qualify as a claim for "debt" or "damage" within the meaning of the Act, Court lacked jurisdiction to grant judgment for the amount claimed. See 2005 CarswellNB 1, [2005] N.B.J. No. 1, 2005 NBQB 8, 286 N.B.R. (2d) 131, 748 A.P.R. 131 (N.B. Q.B.).

No legal basis for denying Association right to resort to courts to compel payment of monies owing. Judge hearing *de novo* appeal concluded amount claimed by Association as costs and an unpaid fine did *not* qualify as a "debt" or "damages" consistent with earlier decision involving another self-regulating profession: *Cosmetology Assn. (New Brunswick) v. Ouellette*, 2001 CarswellNB 412, 2001 NBQB 215, 244 N.B.R. (2d) 69, 634 A.P.R. 69 (N.B. Q.B.).

Unpaid fine and costs qualify as a debt at common law. In the absence of clear and explicit language, presumed legislature did *not* intend to depart from common law meaning.

"Debt" as found in the Act not to be given restricted meaning. Judgment in favour of appellant for $2,705. Applying *Beaulieu v. Day & Ross Inc.*, 2005 CarswellNB 98, 2005 CarswellNB 99, 280 N.B.R. (2d) 201, 734 A.P.R. 201, 2005 NBCA 25, 250 D.L.R. (4th) 533 (N.B. C.A.) and *Naderi v. Strong*, [2005] N.B.J. No. 67, 2005 CarswellNB 89, 2005 CarswellNB 90, 280 N.B.R. (2d) 379, 734 A.P.R. 379, 2005 NBCA 10 (N.B. C.A.) not a case for costs.

Shukster [c.o.b. Del Norte Construction] v. Heglin, 2005 CarswellMan 519, 2005 MBQB 300 (Man. Q.B.), Schulman, J. Appeal under *Court of Queen's Bench Small Claims Practices Act*, R.S.M. 1987, c. C285. What judgment or remedy should be rendered of the claim and counterclaim in this statutory proceeding?.

Nothing contained in S.C.P.A. [*Court of Queen's Bench Small Claims Practices Act*] restricts scope of s. 4 T.C.N.A. [*Tortfeasors and Contributory Negligence Act*]. Nothing in S.C.P.A. prohibits plaintiff from adducing evidence of a loss greater than $7,500. Section 5 permits a defendant to assert a counterclaim in excess of $7,500 by separate action. Two statutes may be interpreted in a harmonious manner, reduction in claim for contributory negligence can be based on actual loss adjudged by court or agreed by parties. Plaintiff's claim dismissed. Defendants awarded $14,445 less $4,242, or $10,203, being the difference between the amount of loss and unpaid portion of contract, capped at $7,500 under statute.

Roach and Adamson et al, No. 7880/78 (Ont. Small Cl. Ct.), Toronto Small Claims Court (Zuker, Small Claims Court Judge). Claims for false arrest and false imprisonment struck out for want of prosecution. Judgment for Plaintiff lawyer dated February 25, 1980 for assault and exemplary damages. Judgment set aside. No. 151/80 (Ont. Div. Ct.) July 9, 1981. Appeal allowed, order of Divisional Court set aside (Ont. C.A.) January 28, 1982 (No. 749/81). Trial judgment restored.

Castle v. Toronto Harbour Commissioners, 1987 CarswellOnt 464, 20 C.P.C. (2d) 266 (Ont. Prov. Ct.). Action transferred to Supreme Court of Ontario. No jurisdiction in Provincial Court (Civil Division) to hear matters of maritime law.

Hutley v. Great West Life Assurance Co., 1982 CarswellOnt 516, 40 O.R. (2d) 34, 30 C.P.C. 305 (Ont. H.C.). Fact that action fit to be tried in Supreme Court not meaning it ought to be if also fit for Small Claims Court. Declaration of total disablement sought by plaintiff limited to given point in time. Not having ongoing effect. Claim not exceeding monetary jurisdiction of lower Court. *Small Claims Court Act*, R.S.O. 1970, c. 439, ss. 61, 63.

Mackin v. Strange, 1996 CarswellNB 162, [1996] N.B.J. No. 188, (sub nom. *Strange v. Mackin*) 134 D.L.R. (4th) 243, (sub nom. *Strange, C.J.P.C. v. Mackin*) 176 N.B.R. (2d) 321, (sub nom. *Strange, C.J.P.C. v. Mackin*) 447 A.P.R. 321 (N.B. C.A.); leave to appeal to S.C.C. refused (1996), (sub nom. *Strange v. Mackin*) 139 D.L.R. (4th) vii (note), (sub nom. *Strange, C.J.P.C. v. Mackin, P.C.J.*) 206 N.R. 314, (sub nom. *Strange, C.J.P.C. v. Mackin, P.C.J.*) 183 N.B.R. (2d) 320 (note), (sub nom. *Strange, C.J.P.C. v. Mackin, P.C.J.*) 465 A.P.R. 320 (note) (S.C.C.). Appellant Provincial Court Judge began proceedings against the province, claiming that legislative amendments infringed on the independence of the judiciary. Application for injunction dismissed. Judge then declared that he was without jurisdiction to hear cases until his dispute with the province resolved. Judge had a public duty to act pursuant to the *Provincial Court Act* and duty owed to the Chief Judge under the Act. As the Judge was not hearing a case when he declared he lacked jurisdiction, it was a unilateral declaration and not a judicial pronouncement. Appropriate remedy was an order in the nature of mandamus directing Judge to perform his duties.

705589 Alberta Ltd. v. Cameron, 2005 CarswellAlta 941, 2005 ABPC 150, 14 C.P.C. (6th) 153 (Alta. Prov. Ct.). Provincial Court is statutory court without inherent jurisdiction. Nature of claim for unjust enrichment claim for debt or damages. Unjust enrichment created debt. Claim for recovery of such debt arises under category of quasi-contract or restitution. Solicitor's claim for unjust enrichment is liquidated claim recoverable by action and is debt within meaning of Act for which court has jurisdiction to grant equitable relief.

Plaintiff was retired social assistance recipient under *Family Income Security Act* receiving payment net of monthly annuity payments of $105 from employer pension. Recipient filed claim against defendant province in small claims court for withheld portion of income assistance. Action dismissed. Small claims court lacked jurisdiction to review decision of appeals board. Court's jurisdiction was limited to claims for debt, damages or recovery of possession of personal property. *Bernard v. New Brunswick*, 2004 CarswellNB 1, 2004 NBQB 3, 270 N.B.R. (2d) 83, 710 A.P.R. 83, 48 C.P.C. (5th) 228 (N.B. Q.B.). See also *Petrella v. Westwood Chev Olds (1993) Ltd.*, 2004 CarswellOnt 364, [2004] O.J. No. 491 (Ont. S.C.J.); *Dolmage v. Erskine*, 2003 CarswellOnt 161, 23 C.P.R. (4th) 495 (Ont. S.C.J.); *Cormier v. Saint John (City)* (2001), 233 N.B.R. (2d) 81, 601 A.P.R. 81, 2001 CarswellNB 23 (N.B. Q.B.).

Leader School Division No. 24 v. Fisher, 2001 CarswellSask 341, 2001 SKQB 209, (sub nom. *Board of Education of Leader School Division No. 24 v. Fisher*) 206 Sask. R. 207 (Sask. Q.B.). Plaintiff employee alleged that school division owed her pay for work done. Action struck. Appropriately dealt with under dispute resolution provisions of *Education Act*, rather than small claims court.

Bank of Montreal v. Gardner, 1998 CarswellOnt 89 (Ont. Sm. Cl. Ct.). No prohibition in Act or Rules against awarding costs to litigant represented by agent. Neither Act nor Rules conferred jurisdiction to, or expressed prohibition against, making such award. Common law does not allow for such award. *Courts of Justice Act*, R.S.O. 1990, c. C.43. *Rules of the Small Claims Court*, R.R.O. 1990, Reg. 201.

Lochner v. Ontario (Workers' Compensation Appeals Tribunal), 1997 CarswellOnt 5264 (Ont. Sm/ Cl. Ct.). Claims for damages for misrepresentation not claims contemplated to be included in those dealt with under *Workers' Compensation Act*. Small Claims Court had jurisdiction to hear plaintiff's claim for damages from misrepresentation.

Luo v. Canada (Attorney General), 1997 CarswellOnt 1577, 145 D.L.R. (4th) 457, 28 C.C.E.L. (2d) 304, 33 O.R. (3d) 300, 9 C.P.C. (4th) 343 (Ont. Div. Ct.); affirming 1996 CarswellOnt 3936 (Ont. Sm. Cl. Ct.). Section 21(1) of the *Crown Liability and Proceedings Act* provides that provincial superior courts have jurisdiction over claims against the federal Crown, and s. 35(1) of federal *Interpretation Act* established Ontario Court (General Division) as superior court for Ontario. Section 22 of *Courts of Justice Act* makes all judges of the General Division, judges of the Small Claims Court. The combined effect of these provisions is to confer jurisdiction on the Small Claims Court in suits against the federal Crown.

Sabine v. University of New Brunswick, 1996 CarswellNB 80, 174 N.B.R. (2d) 65, 444 A.P.R. 65 (N.B. Q.B.). Actions dismissed as beyond the jurisdiction of the Small Claims Court. Pursuant to R. 75, court has discretion to refuse to hear cases that are too complex and not satisfactorily defined.

Jumbo Motor Express Ltd. v. Hilchie, 1988 CarswellNS 224, 89 N.S.R. (2d) 222, 227 A.P.R. 222 (N.S. Co. Ct.). Right to overtime wages statutory, not contractual. Employee limited to recovery under Code and Small Claims Court not having jurisdiction to adjudicate claim.

N.A.P.E. v. Drake, 2002 CarswellNfld 24, (sub nom. *Newfoundland Association of Public Employees v. Drake*) 209 Nfld. & P.E.I.R. 330, (sub nom. *Newfoundland Association of Public Employees v. Drake*) 626 A.P.R. 330, 82 C.L.R.B.R. (2d) 207 (Nfld. T.D.). Provincial Court judge did not err in holding that fines levied against respondents not debts or liquidated damages within meaning *Small Claims Court Act*. Parties to agreement cannot give court jurisdiction it does not otherwise possess simply by classifying fine as debt. Debts under Act are those which are fixed and ascertainable at time of occurrence.

B.M.W.E. v. Litke, 1999 CarswellMan 446, [2000] 1 W.W.R. 383, (sub nom. *Brotherhood of Maintenance of Way Employees v. Litke*) 138 Man. R. (2d) 266, (sub nom. *Brotherhood of Maintenance of Way Employees v. Litke*) 202 W.A.C. 266, 181 D.L.R. (4th) 188 (Man. C.A.); affirming 1998 CarswellMan 588, [1998] M.J. No. 569, 40 C.C.E.L. (2d) 203, (sub nom. *Brotherhood of Maintenance of Way Employees v. Litke*) 133 Man. R. (2d) 146, [1999] 8 W.W.R. 619 (Man. Q.B.); leave to appeal refused 2000 CarswellMan 438, 2000 CarswellMan 439, (sub nom. *Brotherhood of Maintenance of Way Employees v. Litke*) 260 N.R. 397 (note), (sub nom. *Brotherhood of Maintenance of Way Employees v. Litke*) 160 Man. R. (2d) 40 (note), (sub nom. *Brotherhood of Maintenance of Way Employees v. Litke*) 262 W.A.C. 40 (note) (S.C.C.). Union had no right to turn to civil courts to enforce fines. *Trade Unions Act*, R.S.C. 1985, c. T-14.

Johnston v. Smith, 1928 CarswellSask 124, [1928] 3 W.W.R. 495, [1928] 4 D.L.R. 774 (Sask. C.A.). Action involved a question of title to land. Beyond jurisdiction of the District Court.

Sinclair v. Sharpe (1924), 26 O.W.N. 134 (Ont. H.C.). The right to the flow of water in a natural watercourse constitutes an easement. Action for the obstruction of such flow, in which right or title comes in question beyond jurisdiction of the Division Court under s. 61(a) of the Act.

Caranci v. Ford Credit Canada Leasing Ltd., 2002 CarswellOnt 4882 (Ont. S.C.J.); reversing 2001 CarswellOnt 2916, 17 M.V.R. (4th) 200 (Ont. S.C.J.). Appeal allowed. Trial judge made award on basis of unjust enrichment and principle of restitution, both of which are equitable remedies and not within power of small claims courts to grant.

Fantasy Construction Ltd. v. Condominium Plan No. 9121612, 1998 CarswellAlta 1007, 26 C.P.C. (4th) 311, (sub nom. *Owners-Condominium Plan No. 9121612 v. Fantasy Construction Ltd.*) 235 A.R. 147 (Alta. Q.B.). Defendant wished to counterclaim for amount in excess of provincial court jurisdiction. Defendant requested adjournment in order to bring application to transfer action to Court of Queen's Bench. Judge granted adjournment on condition that defendant pay full amount of claim into court. Defendant appealed. Appeal allowed. Payment of full amount of claim was not security for costs. Judge had no jurisdiction under *Provincial Court Act* to impose condition to satisfy judgment.

Owen Bird v. Nanaimo Shipyards Ltd., 1996 CarswellBC 2742 (B.C. S.C.). Appeal allowed. Provincial Court did not have jurisdiction to make award of costs arising out of Supreme Court action. The claim made in the Provincial Court as damages could not be characterized as damages but rather was for costs of the litigation in the Supreme Court. Provincial Court acted without jurisdiction.

Beardsley v. Baecker, 1993 CarswellNS 72, 20 C.P.C. (3d) 235, 125 N.S.R. (2d) 61, 349 A.P.R. 61 (N.S. S.C.); additional reasons to 1993 CarswellNS 642, 20 C.P.C. (3d) 235 at 237 (N.S. S.C.). Reading of ss. 9 and 10 of the Act led to conclusion that Small Claims Court does not have jurisdiction to hear a dispute between a landlord and a tenant, regardless of whether the tenancy is a commercial or residential.

Smith v. Harbour Authority of Port Hood, 1993 CarswellNS 59, 16 C.P.C. (3d) 192, (sub nom. *Smith v. Port Hood Harbour Authority*) 123 N.S.R. (2d) 225, (sub nom. *Smith v. Port Hood Harbour Authority*) 340 A.P.R. 225 (N.S. S.C.). Harbour authority leased land from Crown including government wharf facilities. Harbour authority sued successfully for berthage fees in Small Claims Court. Appellants appealed. Appeal allowed. Action dismissed. Small Claims Court did not have jurisdiction to hear and determine claim for berthage fees because it was a statutory right and not one based on contract or tort or any other enumerated in s. 9 of the *Small Claims Court Act*.

Teitel v. Theriault, 1983 CarswellOnt 866, 44 O.R. (2d) 127 (Ont. Div. Ct.). Provincial Court (Civil Division) has jurisdiction in action for false arrest and false imprisonment. S. 57 of *Judicature Act* inapplicable to Provincial Court (Civil Division). *Judicature Act*, R.S.O. 1980, c. 223, s. 57.

Reddick v. Traders' Bank (1892), 22 O.R. 449 (Ont. C.A.). The words "all personal actions" include personal actions of an equitable nature where claim "a purely money demand," as well as common law actions. According to current legislation which flows towards increasing rather than curtailing jurisdiction of inferior Courts.

Bernard v. New Brunswick, 2006 CarswellNB 277, 2006 CarswellNB 278, 2006 NBCA 57 (N.B. C.A.) 2006-03-29.

Appellant sought to obtain the deductions Province made to his monthly social assistance payments, represented by the amount of a monthly annuity payment he received as a pension from his former employer.

The Court of Queen's Bench correctly determined the jurisdiction of the Small Claims Court as follows:

> The Small Claims Court was established by the *Small Claims Act*, S.N.B. 1997, c. S-9.1. Section 3 of that *Act* states:
>
> > 3. There is hereby established a court of record to be known as the Small Claims Court of New Brunswick which shall hear and determine in a summary way all questions of law and fact and may make such decision or order as is considered just and reasonable in the circumstances.

Because the Small Claims Court was established by an *Act* of the Legislature, it can only hear and decide cases within the jurisdiction that is given to it by that *Act*.

Appeal dismissed.

Neil v. Equifax Canada Inc., 2006 CarswellSask 161, 2006 SKQB 169 (Sask. Q.B.) 2006-04-07.

Appeal from Small Claims damage award in favour of Neil, on October 31, 2005. Appropriate test for punitive damages provided in *Hill v. Church of Scientology of Toronto*, EYB 1995-68609, 1995 CarswellOnt 396, 1995 CarswellOnt 534, [1995] S.C.J. No. 64, 25 C.C.L.T. (2d) 89, 184 N.R. 1, (sub nom. *Manning v. Hill)* 126 D.L.R. (4th) 129, 24 O.R. (3d) 865 (note), 84 O.A.C. 1, [1995] 2 S.C.R. 1130, (sub nom. *Hill v. Church of Scientology)* 30 C.R.R. (2d) 189, 1995 SCC 67 (S.C.C.). Small Claims Court judge referred to breaches of the *Credit Reporting Agencies Act* and in particular to s. 25(5). See also McIntyre J., in *Woelk v. Halvorson*, 1980 CarswellAlta 277, 1980 CarswellAlta 317, [1980] 2 S.C.R. 430, [1981] 1 W.W.R. 289, 14 C.C.L.T. 181, 24 A.R. 620, 114 D.L.R. (3d) 385, 33 N.R. 232 (S.C.C.). Conduct of appellant, while negligent and insensitive, not so malicious, oppressive or high-handed as to justify award of punitive damages.

Brown v. Godfrey, 2006 CarswellOnt 3091, 210 O.A.C. 156 (Ont. Div. Ct.) 2006-05-18.

Appeal from decision of Tierney J. in which he awarded damages to Brown, the plaintiff (respondent on appeal).

Trial judge erred in awarding damages for mental distress. No reference to a claim for such damages in pleadings, and plaintiff cannot recover for claims not pleaded, since the defendants not given proper notice of the issue so as to be able to respond adequately. See *Rodaro v. Royal Bank*, 2002 CarswellOnt 1047, [2002] O.J. No. 1365, 22 B.L.R. (3d) 274, 157 O.A.C. 203, 49 R.P.R. (3d) 227, 59 O.R. (3d) 74 (Ont. C.A.) at para. 61.

Such damages rarely awarded for breach of contract, and this is not an appropriate case in which to award them. See *Turczinski Estate v. Dupont Heating & Air Conditioning Ltd.*, 2004 CarswellOnt 4532, (sub nom. *Turczinski v. Dupont Heating & Air Conditioning Ltd.)* 191 O.A.C. 350, 38 C.L.R. (3d) 123, 246 D.L.R. (4th) 95 (Ont. C.A.) at para. 27.

Trial judge erred in awarding damages for the legal costs incurred in contemplation of litigation. Costs recoverable in a proceeding are a matter of procedural law governed by the *Small Claims Court Rules* and the *Courts of Justice Act*, R.S.O. 1990, c. C.43.

Pursuant to s. 134(1) of the *Courts of Justice Act*, an appellate court may make any order or decision that ought to or could have been made by the court appealed from.

Appeal allowed, award of $8,723.07 set aside, and an order will go awarding the respondent $5,000, the amount of the forfeited deposit.

Marina v. Malecek, 2006 CarswellBC 812, 2006 BCPC 139 (B.C. Prov. Ct.) 2006-04-06.

While claims for damage to ships are specifically within the Federal Court's jurisdiction under section 22(2)(e) of the *Federal Court Act*, the section speaks of concurrent jurisdiction and does not make the Federal Court the only forum where actions for damage may be brought.

In order to award punitive damages "the act of the wrongdoer must have been consciously directed against the . . . property of the plaintiff": see *Moore v. Borg-Warner Acceptance Canada Ltd.*, [1980] B.C.J. No. 2256 (B.C. Co. Ct.) at para. 18, citing *Kaytor v. Lion's Driving Range Ltd.*, 1962 CarswellBC 130, 40 W.W.R. 173, 35 D.L.R. (2d) 426 (B.C. S.C.).

Conduct falls short of that which would warrant punitive damages. Claim dismissed.

Canadian Tire Bank v. Roach, 2006 CarswellBC 735, 2006 BCPC 120 (B.C. Prov. Ct.) 2006-03-24.

The Claimant alleges that the totality of conduct of Defendant ("Total Credit Recovery") towards her, amounted to the tort of harassment. She alleges that she suffered by virtue of Total Credit Recovery's actions.

Roach is a debtor and Total Credit Recovery is a collection agency.

Roach complained about specific violations of the provincial *Debt Collection Act* ("DCA"), which was in place at that time. Some, but not all, of the specific violations complained of, as conduct specifically constituting "harassment" under the DCA, was repeated in the provisions of the *Business Practices Act and Consumer Protection Act* ("BPACPA") which came into effect on July 4, 2004. She was entitled to a damage award to compensate her for both heads of damage.

Brighton Heating & Air Conditioning Ltd. v. Savoia, 2006 CarswellOnt 340, 49 C.L.R. (3d) 235, 79 O.R. (3d) 386, 207 O.A.C. 1 (Ont. Div. Ct.) 2006-01-16.

The plaintiff brought an action in Small Claims Court. The issue of a trust claim under the *Construction Lien Act* ("CLA") was not pleaded by the plaintiff, but was raised by the trial judge during closing arguments.

The Small Claims Court has jurisdiction to hear a trust claim under the *CLA*, provided that the amount of the claim is within the monetary jurisdiction of the court. A trust claim under the *CLA* is not a claim for a declaratory remedy. Orders under ss. 8 and 13 of the *CLA* are not truly declaratory in nature. Any declaration is incidental to the substantive remedy of damages. The court makes findings that a trust exists and that moneys are owed. The judgment obtained is a money judgment.

In the Small Claims Court, a liberal, non-technical approach should be taken to pleadings. Unpled relief may be granted, and an unpled defence allowed, so long as supporting evidence is not needed beyond what was adduced at trial, or what reasonably should have been adduced in support of the relief or defence that was pled, provided that it is not unfair to grant such relief, or allow such defence. In the circumstances of this case, it was unfair to the defendant for judgment to be awarded against him upon a trust claim that was not pleaded. As the unfairness rose to the level of a substantial wrong or miscarriage of justice, a new trial was ordered.

Section 50(2) of the *CLA* states that trust claims may be brought in any court of competent jurisdiction:

> 50. (2) A trust claim shall not be joined with a lien claim but may be brought in any court of competent jurisdiction.

"Court" in s. 50(2) means the Superior Court of Justice: see s. 1(1) of the *CLA*, as amended. And, the Small Claims Court is a branch of the Superior Court of Justice: see s. 22(1) of the *Courts of Justice Act*. Therefore, the Small Claims Court is a "court of competent jurisdiction.".

Associates Financial Services of Canada Ltd. v. Campbell (1998), 8 C.B.R. (4th) 187, 1998 CarswellOnt 5089 (Ont. Sm. Cl. Ct.), Thomson J.

Creditor brought motion for removal of stay of proceedings. Motion dismissed. Stay created by s. 69(1) of *Bankruptcy and Insolvency Act* not imposed under *Courts of Justice Act*. Only superior court sitting in bankruptcy has authority to lift stay of proceedings created by s. 69(1). Small Claims Court has no jurisdiction to grant leave to continue execution of judgment in action as court has not jurisdiction under Act. Execution of default judgment could proceed only with leave of bankruptcy court. After bankrupt had been discharged, creditor could seek leave from Small Claims Court to continue, subject to s. 178(1) of Act. See *382231 Ontario Ltd. v. Wilanson Resources Ltd.* (1982), 43 C.B.R. (N.S.) 153 (Ont. S.C.).

New Brunswick Assn. of Real Estate Appraisers v. Poitras, 2005 CarswellNB 751, 2005 CarswellNB 752, 2005 NBCA 112, 294 N.B.R. (2d) 312, 765 A.P.R. 312 (N.B. C.A.).

Discipline committee of New Brunswick Association of Real Estate Appraisers suspended an appraiser and ordered him to pay a $500 fine and 70 per cent of the costs of the hearing, for a total of $3,055. Association commenced a small claims action, seeking to have judgment entered for the outstanding amount plus costs.

Action dismissed for lack of jurisdiction. Court of Appeal allowed appeal. The *Small Claims Act* gave the Small Claims Court jurisdiction in an action for debt. The unpaid fines and costs constituted a debt under the Act.

Sier Bath Deck Gear Corp. v. Polymotion Ltd. (1996), 30 O.R. (3d) 736, 1996 CarswellOnt 3873, 42 C.B.R. (3d) 1, 15 O.T.C. 323 (Ont. Gen. Div.), Taliano J.

Appeal from judgement of Deputy Judge who awarded $6,000 to the plaintiff for goods supplied and delivered.

Appeal allowed. It has been held in *McNamara v. Pagecorp Inc.*, [1989] O.J. No. 1461, 1989 CarswellOnt 183, 76 C.B.R. (N.S.) 97, 38 C.P.C. (2d) 117 (Ont. C.A.), at 119, that an undischarged bankrupt cannot bring an action to enforce property claims even where the property is allegedly sold by the trustee to the bankrupt prior to his discharge. *Small Claims Court Rules* silent with respect to the right of an undischarged bankrupt to sue for the recovery of property rights, and in that circumstance.

LaFleur v. Canadian Bond Credits Ltd., 2003 CarswellOnt 6338, 68 O.R. (3d) 754 (Ont. Small Cl. Ct.).

Collection agency breaching *Collections Agencies Act* by harassing telephone calls to relative of debtor. Judgment for plaintiffs. Plaintiffs entitled to punitive damages to accomplish the objectives of retribution, deterrence and denunciation.

John Carten Personal Law Corp. v. British Columbia (Attorney General), 1997 CarswellBC 2290, [1997] B.C.J. No. 2460, 153 D.L.R. (4th) 460, [1998] 3 W.W.R. 571, 40 B.C.L.R. (3d) 181, 48 C.R.R. (2d) 12, 98 B.C.A.C. 1, 161 W.A.C. 1, 98 G.T.C. 6053 (B.C. C.A.).

Applicant applying for declaration that tax on legal services inconsistent with *Charter*. Applicant not adducing any evidence that rights of access to courts or to legal services or justice denied because of tax. Court not entitled to speculate that existence of tax would necessarily prevent someone from going to court. Evidence insufficient to provide basis for conclusion that tax unconstitutional. Application dismissed.

936464 Ontario Ltd. v. Mungo Bear Ltd., [2003] O.J. No. 3795, 2003 CarswellOnt 8091, 74 O.R. (3d) 45, 258 D.L.R. (4th) 754 (Ont. Div. Ct.).

Deputy Judge not lacking jurisdiction to award damages based on *quantum meruit*, common law rather than equitable remedy. Small Claims Court specifically empowered to grant equitable relief in forms of orders for payment of money and orders for recovery of possession of personal property. See *Courts of Justice Act*, R.S.O. 1990, c. C.43, ss. 23(1), 96(1), (3).

Courts authorized under s. 96(1) to concurrently administer all rules of equity and the common law. Small Claims Court not empowered to grant any forms of equitable relief, such as injunctions, declarations and specific performance (unless, perhaps, the performance involves nothing beyond the payment of money or the delivery of possession of personal property, within the applicable limits).

JPMorgan Chase Bank, N.A. v. Petrovici, 2006 CarswellNS 530, 2006 NSSM 29, 249 N.S.R. (2d) 297, 792 A.P.R. 297 (N.S. Small Cl. Ct.), 2006-11-27, Adjudicator David T.R. Parker.

Section 5(1) states in part:

> 5. (1) . . . no corporation may succeed upon a claim pursuant to this Act in respect of a debt or liquidated demand unless the claimant is one of the original parties to the contract or tort upon which the claim is based or unless the claim is raised by way of set-off or counterclaim.

Application not going to succeed at this stage for the following reasons: issue if contract with Defendant was with Sears Canada Bank or Sears Canada Inc. Whether JPMorgan Chase Bank, N.A. original party to the contract.

Purpose of section 5(1) of the *Small Claims Court Act* may well be to avoid having the court turn into a debt collection court. Application denied.

Accent Leasing & Sales Ltd. v. Parsons, 2004 CarswellBC 1200, 7 P.P.S.A.C. (3d) 151, 2004 BCPC 140 (B.C. Prov. Ct.), Schmidt Prov. J.

Small Claims Court of British Columbia not having jurisdiction over litigation involving *Personal Property Security Act*. Definition of "court" within Act referring to Supreme Court.

Tabingo v. Bitton, 2006 CarswellOnt 1774, 36 C.C.L.I. (4th) 121 (Ont. S.C.J.), Thomson J.

Defendants claimed that because the jurisdiction of court was $10,000 and there was a $30,000 deductible under the Regulations of the *Insurance Act* the court lacked jurisdiction. Plaintiffs claimed that their damages were over $30,001 but under $100,000. There was never a limit put on the judges of the court as to the amount of damages that could be assessed. Amount that a plaintiff could claim and the amount that a judge could award was limited by the *Courts of Justice Act* but not the amount that could be proven. *Insurance Act*, R.S.O. 1990, c. I.8; *Courts of Justice Act*, R.S.O. 1990, c. C.43.

Reischer v. Insurance Corp. of British Columbia, 2006 CarswellBC 270, [2006] B.C.J. No. 235, 2006 BCSC 198 (B.C. S.C. [In Chambers]), Macaulay J.

Plaintiff accepted offer to settle for amount within monetary jurisdiction of Small Claims Court. Master dismissed plaintiff's claim to entitlement of costs other than disbursements. Plaintiff appealed. Plaintiff could have sued in either Provincial or Supreme Court. Cost consequence as set out in Rule 37(37) of the *Rules of Court* (B.C.). Plaintiff decided to accept offer for amount within jurisdiction of Provincial Court with respect to proceeding that could have been brought in that court.

Matyjaszczyk v. Peel Condominium Corp. No. 17, 2006 CarswellOnt 469 (Ont. S.C.J.), Wein J.

Applicant owned a residential unit in the respondent condominium corporation. He applied for damages, compensation and reimbursement on various grounds. Application subject matter of Small Claims Court trial in which applicant generally unsuccessful. Application by respondent to dismiss application on basis that it was a duplicate process and an abuse of process allowed.

Lone Cypress Woodworking Ltd. v. Manabe, 2006 CarswellNS 43, 240 N.S.R. (2d) 302, 763 A.P.R. 302, 29 C.P.C. (6th) 261, 2006 NSSM 2, 58 C.L.R. (3d) 108 (N.S. Sm. Cl. Ct.).

Counterclaim alleged to be in excess of jurisdiction of Small Claims Court does not deny claimant's *prima facie* right to have its claim heard in Small Claims Court and does not entitle defendant as of right to force transfer to Supreme Court. Small Claims Court does not have jurisdiction over claim where issues in dispute are already before another court unless that proceeding is withdrawn, abandoned, struck out or transferred in accordance with *Small Claims Court Act*. Small Claims Court adjudicator faced with counterclaim outside of court's jurisdiction may inquire into circumstances of counterclaim to prevent it from frustrating desire of claimant to proceed in Small Claims Court. Adjudicator may determine whether to hear two claims together. Adjudicator may sever counterclaim and proceed to hear claim.

Manitoba Public Insurance Corp. v. Day & Ross Inc., 2004 CarswellMan 592, 197 Man. R. (2d) 161, 24 C.P.C. (6th) 94, 2004 MBQB 277, 33 C.C.L.I. (4th) 281 (Man. Q.B.), Schulman J.

Plaintiff, who sued for $7,500 damages after waiving portion of his claim, contributory negligent. Plaintiff should suffer reduction of his claim, based on his actual loss of $8,281, not based on less amount actually claimed in small claim proceeding, namely $7,500.

Saskatchewan Government Insurance v. Valliere, 2005 CarswellSask 669, 27 C.C.L.I. (4th) 236, 24 C.P.C. (6th) 236, 2005 SKQB 430 (Sask. Q.B.), Krueger J.

Respondent operator of vehicle involved in a single motor vehicle accident. Appellant made finding that respondent more than 50 per cent responsible for the accident and imposed $25 penalty. Before the Small Claims Court could assume jurisdiction plaintiff must seek remedy enumerated in the *Small Claims Act, 1997*, S.S. 1997, c. S-50.11. The respondent's only financial obligation was to pay a $25 surcharge. Small Claims Court judge erred when ruling that Court had jurisdiction.

Prince Edward Island v. Canada (Minister of Fisheries & Oceans), 2006 CarswellPEI 72, 2006 PESCAD 27 (P.E.I. C.A.), 2006-12-29.

Appellant argued that issues raised in respondents' statement of claim within sole jurisdiction of Federal Court because they dealt with decisions of the Minister in relation to fisheries licences and quotas.

Test for striking out a statement of claim set out in *Hunt v. T & N plc*, 1990 CarswellBC 759, 1990 CarswellBC 216, (sub nom. *Hunt v. Carey Canada Inc.*) [1990] S.C.J. No. 93, 4 C.C.L.T. (2d) 1, 43 C.P.C. (2d) 105, 117 N.R. 321, 4 C.O.H.S.C. 173 (headnote only), (sub nom. *Hunt v. Carey Canada Inc.*) [1990] 6 W.W.R. 385, 49 B.C.L.R. (2d) 273, (sub nom. *Hunt v. Carey Canada Inc.*) 74 D.L.R. (4th) 321, [1990] 2 S.C.R. 959 (S.C.C.), Wilson J.

Part of claim with respect to constitutional challenge to s. 7 of the *Fisheries Act* struck out as disclosing no reasonable cause of action. The claim for breach of the Terms of Union also discloses no reasonable cause of action. Supreme Court of Prince Edward Island has no jurisdiction to hear s. 36 constitutional claim, the s. 15 *Charter* claim or breach of public trust claim. Appeal allowed.

New Brunswick Assn. of Real Estate Appraisers v. Poitras, 2005 CarswellNB 751, 2005 CarswellNB 752, 2005 NBCA 112, 294 N.B.R. (2d) 312, 765 A.P.R. 312 (N.B. C.A.); reversing 2005 CarswellNB 1, [2005] N.B.J. No. 1, 2005 NBQB 8, 286 N.B.R. (2d) 131, 748 A.P.R. 131 (N.B. Q.B.).

No legal basis for denying Association right to resort to courts to compel payment of monies that were owing unconditionally. Unpaid fine and costs in issue in present case qualified as debt at common law. Term "debt" in *Small Claims Court Act* does not derogate from common law meaning.

Kaur v. Deopaul, 2006 CarswellOnt 6388, 216 O.A.C. 247 (Ont. Div. Ct.), Cameron J.

Deputy Judge Iacono dismissed Plaintiff's action as being statute barred.

Plaintiff appealed that judgment be set aside and matter set down for trial.

Three issues in appeal:

    1.   Is motion for summary judgment permissible in the Small Claims Court?

    2.   When did the limitation period start to run?

    3.   Did the Defendant waive the limitation period?

There is no rule in the *Small Claims Court Rules* that allows a motion for summary judgment.

See *Clayton v. Zorn*, Claim No. T96340/04, a medical malpractice action, commenced 20 months after expiry of the limitation period. The court said:

> There is no provision in the Rules of the Small Claims Court to bring a motion for summary judgment. See *Wolf v. Goldenberg*, [2003] O.J. No. 3067, Maefs, Deputy Judge set out the

interrelationship between Rules 1.03(2) and 12.02(2) of the Rules of the Small Claim Court and Rule 21.01(1) dismissing an action on a point of law.

Defendant should be able to bring a motion for summary judgment similar to Rule 20.01(3) of the *Rules of Civil Procedure* for summary judgment.

Jurisdiction in Small Claims Court to dismiss the action, notwithstanding the absence of a specific provision, if the limitation period has clearly expired.

Small Claims Court action out of time. No waiver or estoppel. Claim dismissed.

Saskatchewan Government Insurance v. Valliere, 2005 CarswellSask 669, 27 C.C.L.I. (4th) 236, 24 C.P.C. (6th) 236, 2005 SKQB 430 (Sask. Q.B.).

Section 3(2) of *Small Claims Act, 1997* gave small claims court discretion in resolving disputes between insurers and their customers. However, if s. 3(2) was interpreted as suggested by small claims court judge, jurisdiction would be extended to granting declaratory relief in disputes between insurers and their customers. Such interpretation was inconsistent with overall framework of Act. Section 3(2) confined to situations where insurer and insured disagree as to assessed financial liability of insured, amount of damages, or some other remedy.

Manitoba Public Insurance Corp. v. Day & Ross Inc., 2004 CarswellMan 592, 197 Man. R. (2d) 161, 24 C.P.C. (6th) 94, 2004 MBQB 277, 33 C.C.L.I. (4th) 281 (Man. Q.B.).

Insurer brought action against defendant in Small Claims Court under *Court of Queen's Bench Small Claims Practices Act* ("SCPA") for $7,500 waiving additional $981. Defendant counterclaimed for $3,746. Trial of issue of liability found three drivers all equally negligent. Issue arose as to whether insurer was entitled to one-third of damages claimed in Small Claims Court or total of damages claimed. Insurer's claim was limited by provision of *SPCA*.

Seaside Chevrolet Oldsmobile Ltd. v. VFC Inc., 2005 CarswellNB 397, 2005 NBQB 233, 22 C.P.C. (6th) 374, 761 A.P.R. 61, 292 N.B.R. (2d) 61 (N.B. Q.B.).

Fact that *Small Claims Act* and regulations do not contain provision comparable to R. 30.13 of *Rules of Court* does not leave Small Claims Court without jurisdiction to hear fourth or subsequent party claims. Claim was for $6,000 which was amount within jurisdiction of court. Parties agreed that action not complex and not rendered complex by participation of counsel and addition of fourth party.

Small Claims Court has jurisdiction to hear fourth-party claims.

Sullivan v. Draper-Sereda, 2006 CarswellOnt 7402, [2006] O.J. No. 4671 (Ont. Sm. Cl. Ct.), Pickell D.J.

Essence of Plaintiff's claim contained in the following paragraphs of her amended Claim, which read as follows:

31. On or about January 18, 2005, the Defendant informed Leslie Allen, a Children's Aid Society Worker that 'Mark Sereda and Samantha Sullivan are having an affair.'.

32. On or about November 18, 2004, the Defendant informed Lori Laprise, a Children's Aid Society Worker that 'Mark Sereda and Samantha Sullivan are having an affair.'.

33. On or about October 22, 2004, the Defendant informed the Law Society in writing that 'she had reasonable grounds to believe that Samantha Sullivan is carrying on an affair with Mark Sereda.'

Plaintiff says that allegations made in these not true. As a result, Plaintiff made claim against Defendant for defamation as well as for intentional infliction of nervous shock.

The written submissions on behalf of the Defendant state (in paragraph 30):

An absolute privilege, or in effect an immunity, extends to all utterances and/or communications which take place incidental to and in the course of or furtherance of judicial proceedings.

Defamatory statement Defendant made in her complaint to Law Society protected by absolute privilege. Accordingly, Plaintiff's claim arising from paragraph 32 of Claim dismissed.

Defamatory statements protected by qualified privilege. Accordingly, Plaintiff's claims arising from paragraph 30 and 31 of Claim also dismissed.

Sauve v. Paglione, 2006 CarswellOnt 5322 (Ont. Sm. Cl. Ct.).

Threshold issue on motion whether Small Claims Court has jurisdiction to grant relief sought
by plaintiff.

In the "Type of Claim" portion of his Claim form commencing this action the plaintiff seeks:

> Damages under the *Condominium Act, 1998, Ontario*, known as the Act s. 55(8), (9) and (10).

The plaintiff sought order prohibiting the defendants from expending the corporation's funds
in defending action and order that such funds already expended be returned to the
corporation.

Section 55 of the *Condominium Act* reads in part:

> If a corporation without reasonable excuse does not permit an owner or an agent of an owner to
> examine records or to copy them under this section, the Small Claims Court may order the
> corporation to produce the records for examination.

Section 130 permits the Superior Court of Justice, upon the application of certain persons, to
appoint an inspector to, *inter alia*, "investigate the corporation's records mentioned in subsection 55(1)." The fact that the legislature has granted apparently full Superior Court jurisdiction for certain purposes does not derogate from the power granted to the Small Claims
Court for the limited purpose set out in s. 55.

Motion dismissed.

Christie v. British Columbia (Attorney General), 2006 CarswellBC 1202, 225 B.C.A.C. 285,
371 W.A.C. 285, 141 C.R.R. (2d) 363, 2006 BCCA 241, 270 D.L.R. (4th) 697 (B.C. C.A.).

Case involves the constitutionality of a tax on legal services that was introduced by the B.C.
government in 1993. The late Dugald Christie challenged the tax, alleging that it denied
access to justice, and was contrary to the rule of law and the *Charter*. The B.C. Court of
Appeal agreed that the tax is unconstitutional.

CBA granted leave to intervene. Principle to be argued that access to the courts means more
than physical access.

R. v. Gioronda, 2006 CarswellOnt 6980, 2006 ONCJ 425 (Ont. C.J.), Harpur J.

Former counsel ordered to deliver disclosure to new counsel, despite solicitor's lien on accused's file. New counsel requested disclosure in former counsel's possession, which he declined to give, citing a solicitor's lien on files. Court's jurisdiction to control its process
extends to these circumstances. Absent specific words in s. 13 of Ontario's *Solicitor's Act*
negating the court's jurisdiction to deal with such an application by accused, the provision
does not have that effect.

Baird v. R., 2006 CarswellNat 1729, 2006 CarswellNat 3599, 2006 FCA 183, 2006 CAF 183
(F.C.A.), Pelletier J.A.

Self-represented appellant had no sense of relevance or proportion in preparation of material
which he filed in support of his various proceedings. Appellant's conduct not so egregious
that court should gag him by order for security for costs.

Sulz v. Canada (Attorney General), 2006 CarswellBC 141, 2006 C.L.L.C. 230-005, 54
B.C.L.R. (4th) 328, 2006 BCSC 99, 48 C.C.E.L. (3d) 92, 263 D.L.R. (4th) 58, 37 C.C.L.T.
(3d) 271 (B.C. S.C.), Lamperson J.

Plaintiff, former female member of RCMP, brought action against Crown and former superior officers for harassment and mental suffering. Defendants submitted that court lacked

jurisdiction or ought to decline jurisdiction because plaintiff's claims would be more appropriately resolved by Human Rights Commission or by internal grievance process of RCMP. Court ruled that it had jurisdiction. Plaintiff had advanced claim in contract. Because these proceedings now plaintiff's only opportunity to seek redress, wrong for court to decline jurisdiction.

Hare v. Hare, [2006] O.J. No. 4955, 2006 CarswellOnt 7859, 24 B.L.R. (4th) 230, 277 D.L.R. (4th) 236, 218 O.A.C. 164, 83 O.R. (3d) 766 (Ont. C.A.).

Lender of demand loan making demand for payment after six-year limitation period expired and after new Act came into effect. Transitional provisions of new Act applied. Loan matured on delivery of note or last payment on loan, not on day of refusal to pay after demand. Old limitation period applied. Action barred. See *Limitations Act*, R.S.O. 1990, c. L.15, s. 45(1)(g). *Limitations Act*, 2002, S.O. 2002, c. 24, Sch. B., ss. 1, definition "claim," 4, 5, 15(2), (6)(c), 24(1), (2), (5).

Wu v. Chen, 2006 CarswellOnt 5983 (Ont. Sm. Cl. Ct.); additional reasons at 2006 CarswellOnt 5984 (Ont. S.C.J.), Krawchenko D.J. Jurisdiction. Small Claims or other inferior courts. General principles. Rental Housing Tribunal.

R. v. Daley, 2007 CarswellNB 104, 806 A.P.R. 16, 312 N.B.R. (2d) 16, 2007 NBPC 11 (N.B. Prov. Ct.); reversed 2008 CarswellNB 18, 2008 NBQB 21, 841 A.P.R. 156, 328 N.B.R. (2d) 156, 58 M.V.R. (5th) 199 (N.B. Q.B.), R.L. Jackson Prov. J. Jurisdiction. Small Claims or other inferior courts. Provincial courts.

Melnikov v. Bazarsky (2007), 2007 CarswellOnt 3522 (Ont. Div. Ct.), S.E. Greer J. Jurisdiction. Small Claims or other inferior courts. General principles. Standard of review on appeal.

Findology Interactive Media Inc. v. Revquest Technologies Inc., 2007 CarswellNS 198, 2007 NSSM 13, 851 A.P.R. 282, 266 N.S.R. (2d) 282 (N.S. Sm. Cl. Ct.), M.J. O'Hara Adjud. Jurisdiction. Small Claims or other inferior courts.

Barabonoff v. Saskatchewan Government Insurance, 2007 CarswellSask 446, 52 C.C.L.I. (4th) 61, [2007] I.L.R. I-4630, (sub nom. *Saskatchewan Government Insurance v. Barabonoff*) 300 Sask. R. 188, 2007 SKQB 273 (Sask. Q.B.), T.C. Zarzeczny J.

Insured exercised his right to refer disagreement to arbitration pursuant to s. 39 of *Automobile Accident Insurance Act*. Provincial Court judge failed to correctly identify nature and scope of his jurisdiction as consequence of interpretation and application of applicable provisions of Act. Act confers exclusive jurisdiction to determine issues with respect to payment of comprehensive insurance benefits to Court of Queen's Bench.

Hannah v. Industrial Alliance Insurance & Financial Services Inc., 2007 CarswellSask 225, 296 Sask. R. 5, 2007 SKPC 15 (Sask. Prov. Ct.), S.C. Carter Prov. J.

The plaintiff alleged that insurance premiums would be $2,400 per year. He has commenced this action pursuant to the *Small Claims Act*, 1977, c-s 50.11, as amended (the Act). On December 18, 2006, at what was to be a case management conference, the defendants brought this application urging the court to transfer the claim pursuant to s. 11(1) of the Act.

The defendants' position was that the plaintiff's claim against the defendants will arise each and every year until the contract of insurance is cancelled or payment is triggered by the plaintiff's death. This will have a cumulative effect of exceeding the monetary limit imposed by Act.

Clear what is really being sought is refund from defendants from what plaintiff says is overpayment on his life insurance policy.

If, in the final analysis, the court rules that the defendants are correctly interpreting the contract, then the plaintiff will have to accept that decision. If a court rules that the defendants are incorrect in their interpretation, they will surely not continue to over-charge the plaintiff year after year despite the ruling of the court. Application to transfer claim to Court of Queen's Bench dismissed.

Grant v. V & G Realty Ltd., 2007 CarswellNS 333, 2007 NSSM 37, 262 N.S.R. (2d) 207, 839 A.P.R. 207 (N.S. Sm. Cl. Ct.); reversed 2008 CarswellNS 303, 2008 NSSC 180, 869 A.P.R. 3, 272 N.S.R. (2d) 3, 58 C.P.C. (6th) 26 (N.S. S.C.).

Matter first came before Supreme Court of Nova Scotia and claimant elected to have action transferred to Small Claims Court.

Prior to hearing, claimant made application requesting court to make a determination of whether the Implied Undertaking Rule applied to matters before the Small Claims Court.

Section 2 of the *Small Claims Court Act* states that the purpose of the Act is as follows:

> 2. It is the intent and purpose of this act to constitute a Court wherein claims up to but not exceeding the monetary jurisdiction of the Court are adjudicated informally and inexpensively.
>
> But in accordance with established principles of law and natural justice.

Fact that Small Claims Court procedure more informal and streamlined makes no difference. Similar to rationale applied to the court in *Scaraveilli & Associates v. Quinlan*, 2005 CarswellNS 616, [2005] N.S.J. No. 575, 2005 NSSM 7, 241 N.S.R. (2d) 64, 767 A.P.R. 64 (N.S. Small Cl. Ct.), where it was held that court had authority to issue orders for discovery in aid of execution.

The Small Claims Court is a creature of statute and its jurisdiction comes from the *Small Claims Court Act*, regulations and other statutes pertaining to the court. It does not have the inherent jurisdiction provided to the Supreme Court of Nova Scotia or the Nova Scotia Court of Appeal.

The Small Claim Court does not have the authority to provide injunctive relief, make declaratory orders, hold parties in contempt of court and it does not have inherent jurisdiction to dismiss an action for abuse of process all of which are afforded to the Supreme Court of Nova Scotia. The Implied Undertaking Rule does not apply to the Small Claims Court.

Krawchuk v. Carpick Estate, 2007 CarswellMan 372, 2007 MBQB 232 (Man. Q.B.), 2007-09-17, Sinclair J.

Appeal by plaintiff from decision of Small Claims hearing officer dismissing his claim. The plaintiff is a solicitor who acted as executor and legal counsel for the estate of Mary Claire Carpick. Defendant executor, Carpick, maintains plaintiff unable to sue for his executor's fees until he has passed his final accounts. The plaintiff maintains that the Small Claims Court has jurisdiction to pass his accounts and that he is prepared to do so in Small Claims Court.

Section 90(1) of the *Trustee Act*, R.S.M. 1987, c. T160, specifically sets out that a judge or master may make allowances for the personal representative of an estate. The plaintiff's claim is premature. He must first pass his accounts as executor. Claim dismissed without prejudice to right to bring a further claim once accounts passed should it remain unpaid.

Pereversoff v. Behie, 2007 CarswellNS 404, 2007 NSSM 55 (N.S. Sm. Cl. Ct.), 2007-07-27, P.L. Casey Adjud.

Issue of jurisdiction of court in the *Small Claims Court Act*, R.S.N.S. 1989, c. 430. Under section 9 a person may seek a monetary award in respect of any matter arising under contract or tort where the claim does not exceed $25,000 inclusive of general damages but exclusive of interest.

Jurisdiction limited by exclusions contained in section 10. Also, section 15 of the Act precludes court from proceeding with claim where issues in dispute already before another court unless that proceeding withdrawn or abandoned or transferred in accordance with section 19 of the Act. Other claims dismissed as matters are before the Supreme Court of Nova Scotia (Family Division).

Amex Bank of Canada v. Golovatcheva, 2007 CarswellBC 2833, 39 C.B.R. (5th) 34, 2007 BCPC 369 (B.C. Prov. Ct.), 2007-11-16, P. Meyers J.

Settlement Conference scheduled. Both parties notified. Defendant attended in person. Claimant failed to have representative or counsel attend in person or by telephone. Claim dismissed May 1, 2007. Shortly thereafter, claimant filed application to set aside dismissal order. Claimant had not wilfully failed to attend Settlement Conference and timely in filing application to set aside dismissal order.

Assignment in Bankruptcy took place. Defendant subsequently discharged. The charges to her American Express card came to the attention of the claimant after the discharge. The claimant sued.

Claimant's argument was that under the *Bankruptcy and Insolvency Act*, an order of discharge does not release the bankrupt from any debt or liability incurred if they had obtained property or money by false pretences. [See s. 178 of the *Bankruptcy and Insolvency Act*.].

The Provincial Court of B.C. has the statutory jurisdiction to hear case, notwithstanding that s. 3 of the *Small Claims Act* excludes bankruptcy and insolvency cases from the jurisdiction of the Provincial Court of B.C. The case is not really a bankruptcy or insolvency case, but rather a claim in debt and, of course, the Provincial Court of B.C. has jurisdiction to decide claims in debt. See, e.g., *Amex Bank of Canada v. Johnson*, 2007 CarswellAlta 664, [2007] A.J. No. 567, 42 C.P.C. (6th) 284, 33 C.B.R. (5th) 290, 2007 ABPC 130, 75 Alta. L.R. (4th) 387, [2007] 11 W.W.R. 732, 418 A.R. 321 (Alta. Prov. Ct.).

It is simply an action expressly unaffected by the *Bankruptcy and Insolvency Act*.

The proper procedure to recover a debt not released by discharge is for creditor to bring an action in the "ordinary civil courts." The ordinary civil courts have jurisdiction to determine whether debt or liability incurred through fraud and therefore not released by an order of discharge. See *Beneficial Finance v. Durward*, 1961 CarswellOnt 40, 2 C.B.R. (N.S.) 173 (Ont. Bktcy.) and *Graves v. Hughes*, 2001 CarswellNS 168, 2001 NSSC 68, 25 C.B.R. (4th) 255, 194 N.S.R. (2d) 51, 606 A.P.R. 51 (N.S. S.C.). See also *Smith, Re*, 1985 CarswellSask 68, 43 Sask. R. 27, 59 C.B.R. (N.S.) 272 (Sask. Q.B.); affirmed 1986 CarswellSask 449, 45 Sask. R. 240 (Sask. C.A.) and *Berthold v. McLellan*, 1994 CarswellAlta 340, [1994] A.J. No. 275, 25 C.B.R. (3d) 45, 19 Alta. L.R. (3d) 28 (Alta. C.A.). In her dissenting judgment in *Canada (Attorney General) v. Bourassa (Trustee of)*, [2002] A.J. No. 1091, 2002 Carswell-Alta 1109, 2002 ABCA 205, 36 C.B.R. (4th) 181, [2002] 11 W.W.R. 285, 219 D.L.R. (4th) 32, 6 Alta. L.R. (4th) 223, 312 A.R. 19, 281 W.A.C. 19 (Alta. C.A.), Chief Justice Fraser of the Court of Appeal of Alberta stated that focusing on who must make the finding of fraud without addressing the substantive issue of whether the debt or liability was incurred through fraud can lead to error.

See further *Sears Canada Inc. v. Edwards*, [2006] O.J. No. 2914, 2006 CarswellOnt 4436 (Ont. S.C.J.) (Hamilton Small Claims Court); *Sears Canada Inc. v. Jirjis* (October 25, 2005), Doc. 04-SC-007002 (Ont. S.C.J.) (Windsor Small Claims Court). Judge O'Ferrall, in the *Amex Bank of Canada v. Johnson* case, *supra*, at page 6, dealt with the distinctive relation in Ontario between Small Claims Court and the Superior Court of Justice, in Ontario, as it related to bankruptcy cases. Ontario cases supportive of the same reasoning used to find that the Alberta Small Claims Courts had jurisdiction to hear debt cases after bankruptcy and discharge. Accordingly, the Dismissal Order dated May 1, 2007 set aside.

Valliere v. Saskatchewan Government Insurance, 2007 CarswellSask 663, 2007 SKPC 126, 55 C.C.L.I. (4th) 296, 305 Sask. R. 148, [2007] S.J. No. 624 (Sask. Prov. Ct.), D.J. Kaiser Prov. J., November 7, 2007.

Specific grant of jurisdiction over safety rating reviews to the Highway Traffic Board exclusive. No provision in the *Automobile Accident Insurance Act* authorizing review of driver safety ratings by the Small Claims Court or any other court. Section 6(8) does not grant court jurisdiction to review and vary driver safety rating itself. Small Claims Court is a statutory body and, as such, its jurisdiction to hear matters and grant remedies is limited to the authority given by statute.

T.W.U., Local 202 v. MacMillan, 2008 CarswellAlta 144, (sub nom. *Telecommunications Workers Union Local 202 v. MacMillan)* 438 A.R. 280, 2008 ABPC 38, [2008] 7 W.W.R. 170, 89 Alta. L.R. (4th) 116 (Alta. Prov. Ct.); affirmed (2008), 2008 CarswellAlta 1614, [2009] 3 W.W.R. 342, 2009 C.L.L.C. 220-029, 97 Alta. L.R. (4th) 393, 2008 ABQB 657, 63 C.P.C. (6th) 250, (sub nom. *Telecommunications Workers Union Local 202 v. Macmillan)* 458 A.R. 367 (Alta. Q.B.); leave to appeal refused (2009), 2009 CarswellAlta 664, 2009 CarswellAlta 665 (S.C.C.), J.N. LeGrandeur Prov. J., February 1, 2008.

Defendants dispute right of TWU to obtain judgment against them and bring before court preliminary application seeking dismissal of plaintiff's claims. See *Berry v. Pulley*, 2002 CarswellOnt 1111, 2002 CarswellOnt 1112, [2002] S.C.J. No. 41, REJB 2002-30870, 2002 C.L.L.C. 220-022, 287 N.R. 303, 211 D.L.R. (4th) 651, 82 C.L.R.B.R. (2d) 161, 59 O.R. (3d) 159 (note), 158 O.A.C. 329, 11 C.C.L.T. (3d) 157, 2002 SCC 40, 20 C.P.C. (5th) 205, [2002] 2 S.C.R. 493 (S.C.C.). TWU argued *Berry* stands for proposition that trade unions are entities possessing legal personality that enables them to enter and enforce contract relations with union members.

Jurisdiction of Provincial Court is set out in s. 9.6 of the *Provincial Court Act*.

Fines plaintiff seeks to be made into judgments of court not debts within meaning of that word as used in the *Provincial Court Act* or as broadly understood at common law. The enforcement of fines imposed by the union as discipline do not constitute debts.

Plaintiff's claim not enforceable as a claim in liquidated damages. Ogus in his text *The Law of Damages* published by Butterworths, 1973 at page 41, declared:

> This requires little comment. The notion that a party may be punished for failing to perform his contractual obligations is repugnant to a system of law which subscribes to a general compensatory principle of damages.

Plaintiff's claim dismissed against defendants.

TeleZone Inc. v. Canada (Attorney General) (2007), [2007] O.J. No. 4766, 2007 CarswellOnt 7847, 88 O.R. (3d) 173 (Ont. S.C.J.); leave to appeal allowed (2008), 2008 CarswellOnt 610 (Ont. Div. Ct.); affirmed 2008 CarswellOnt 7826, [2008] O.J. No. 5291, 245 O.A.C. 91, 40 C.E.L.R. (3d) 183, 86 Admin. L.R. (4th) 163, (sub nom. *G-Civil Inc. v. Canada (Minister of Public Works & Government Services))* 303 D.L.R. (4th) 626, 2008 ONCA 892, 94 O.R. (3d) 19 (Ont. C.A.); additional reasons at 2009 CarswellOnt 426, 77 C.L.R. (3d) 153, 40 C.E.L.R. (3d) 229, 2009 ONCA 91 (Ont. C.A.); leave to appeal allowed (2009), 2009 CarswellOnt 3492, 2009 CarswellOnt 3493, [2009] S.C.C.A. No. 77 (S.C.C.); leave to appeal allowed (2009), 2009 CarswellOnt 3534, 2009 CarswellOnt 3535 (S.C.C.); leave to appeal allowed (2009), 2009 CarswellOnt 3536, 2009 CarswellOnt 3537 (S.C.C.).

Under s. 21 of the *Crown Liability and Proceedings Act*, R.S.C. 1985, c. C-50, the Ontario Superior Court has concurrent jurisdiction to hear claims against the federal Crown, except where the Federal Court has exclusive jurisdiction. The exclusive jurisdiction provision of the *Federal Courts Act* ("FCA"), s. 18(1), focuses on the relief that is sought in the claim. Section 18(1) of the FCA does not contain clear and explicit language precluding the Superior Court from hearing a civil action against the federal Crown that engages, but does not seek to disturb, a decision taken pursuant to a federal grant of power.

J.P. Morgan Chase Bank, N.A. v. McCann, 2008 CarswellNS 61, 2008 NSSM 10 (N.S. Sm. Cl. Ct.).

Claim by J.P. Morgan Chase Bank on a credit card account. Issue whether s. 5(1) of the *Nova Scotia Small Claims Court Act* applies. Section 5(1) reads as follows:

> 5 (1) To better effect the intent and purpose of this Act and to prevent the procedure provided by this Act being used by a corporate person to collect a debt or a liquidated demand where there is no dispute, no partnership within the meaning of the *Partnership and Business Names Registration Act* and no corporation may succeed upon a claim pursuant to this Act in respect of a debt or liquidated demand unless the claimant is one of the original parties to the contract or tort upon which the claim is based or unless the claim is raised by way of set-off or counterclaim.

Sears Canada Inc. sold its credit and financial services operations to J.P. Morgan Chase Bank, N.A.

J.P. Morgan Chase Bank, N.A. cannot assert that it is one of the ". . . original parties to the contract" as required by s. 5. Claim dismissed. Court statutory creation and therefore bound, jurisdictionally, to *Nova Scotia Small Claims Court Act*.

Ryan v. 30 Plus Club Inc., 2008 CanLII 8011 (N.L. Prov. Ct.), Hon. Robert B. Hyslop.

Plaintiff sought legal advice. He incurred fees of $756, costs of $44 and photocopying fees of $20. He also sought recovery of costs of filing action.

Court is a statutory court and one with circumscribed jurisdiction. Section 3 of the *Small Claims Act* reads:

> A judge has jurisdiction to try and adjudicate upon a claim for debt, whether payable in money or otherwise, or for damages, including damages for breach of contract, where the amount claimed does not exceed $5,000.00 . . . .

Costs of individual legal fees not a debt owed to defendant. When one embarks on litigation, one cannot generally count on indemnification for his or her legal fees unless they receive an order allowing solicitor and client costs. In effect, plaintiff expects defendant to give him a blank cheque for legal services.

Action dismissed.

Tulloch v. AmeriSpec Home Inspection Services, 2006 CarswellNS 623, 2006 NSSM 48, 47 C.P.C. (6th) 337, 253 N.S.R. (2d) 37, 807 A.P.R. 37 (N.S. Sm. Cl. Ct.).

Arbitration clause in contract provided that dispute concerning interpretation of agreement or arising from services and report to be resolved by arbitration and that decision of arbitrator final, binding and not subject to appeal. Claimant may elect to proceed to arbitration by consent or apply to court to have issues resolved. Small Claims Court does not have jurisdiction to stay claims but may grant adjournment. Pursuant to s. 14(1)(a) of *Small Claims Court Act*, such provision is severable from agreement. Arbitration clause void and severed from agreement because it was designed to limit jurisdiction of Small Claims Court.

Tennis v. Stracuzza, 2007 CarswellBC 2464, 246 B.C.A.C. 291, 2007 BCCA 480, 72 B.C.L.R. (4th) 106, 406 W.A.C. 291 (B.C. C.A.).

Petitioner brought Small Claims action against respondents. Liability issue decided in petitioner's favour. Respondents applied for production of petitioner's medical records before provincial Small Claims Court judge. Provincial Court judge granted production order without affording petitioner a chance to be heard. Appeal allowed. Although extent to which Provincial Court judge can order production in Small Claims matter appeared to be unsettled, this was not issue that should be resolved on present appeal.

Ontario (Attorney General) v. Pembina Exploration Canada Ltd, EYB 1989-67481, 1989 CarswellOnt 970, 1989 CarswellOnt 970F, [1989] 1 S.C.R. 206, 57 D.L.R. (4th) 710, *(sub nom. *William Siddall & Sons Fisheries v. Pembina Exploration Can. Ltd.)* 92 N.R. 137, *(sub nom. *William Siddall & Sons Fisheries v. Pembina Exploration Can. Ltd.)* 33 O.A.C. 321 (S.C.C.), Dickson C.J., McIntyre, Le Dain, La Forest and L'Heureux-Dubé JJ.

Plaintiff brought an action in Small Claims Court for the negligence involving the law of the sea and admiralty. The trial judge dismissed the motion for want of jurisdiction. Plaintiff appealed. The Divisional Court dismissed the plaintiff's action. Further appeal was allowed. A provincial legislature has power to grant jurisdiction to an inferior court to hear a matter falling within federal legislative jurisdiction. Such power limited. Section 55 of the *Small Claims Courts Act* ought to be interpreted to include federal matters and s. 22 of the *Federal Court Act* ought to be read as allowing this. Section 96 of the *Constitution Act* did not preclude the exercise of maritime law jurisdiction by provincial inferior courts.

Sobeys Stores Ltd. v. Yeomans, EYB 1989-67394, 1989 CarswellNS 388, 1989 CarswellNS 113, 89 C.L.L.C. 14,017, 92 N.R. 179, [1989] 1 S.C.R. 238, 57 D.L.R. (4th) 1, 90 N.S.R. (2d) 271, 230 A.P.R. 271, 25 C.C.E.L. 162 (S.C.C.).

Appeal from decision of the Nova Scotia Court of Appeal that s. 67A of the *Labour Standards Code* was unconstitutional because it conferred the power of a court on a provincially appointed tribunal. The provision in question provided for the establishment of a system whereby non-unionized employees who were discharged from their employment could bring a complaint against the employer. The Nova Scotia Court of Appeal found that legislation had conferred superior court jurisdiction upon an inferior tribunal.

Appeal allowed. The Labour Standards Tribunal exercised jurisdiction that broadly conformed to that of superior courts at the time of Confederation and performed a judicial function in so doing. However, it did so only as a necessarily incidental aspect of the broader goal of the social policy of providing protection for non-unionized employees.

Bernard v. New Brunswick, 2006 CarswellNB 277, 2006 CarswellNB 278, 299 N.B.R. (2d) 198, 778 A.P.R. 198, 2006 NBCA 57 (N.B. C.A.), Turnbull J.A.

According to the *Small Claims Act*, Small Claims Court jurisdiction is limited to actions for debt, damages or the recovery of personal property.

Fantasy Construction Ltd., Re, 2007 CarswellAlta 1049, [2007] A.J. No. 909, *(sub nom. Fantasy Construction Ltd. (Bankrupt), Re)* 420 A.R. 120, 2007 ABQB 502, 78 Alta. L.R. (4th) 121, 35 C.B.R. (5th) 86, [2007] 12 W.W.R. 327, 66 Admin. L.R.(4th) 247 (Alta. Q.B.), Topolniski J.; leave to appeal refused (2007), 2007 CarswellAlta 1849, [2007] A.J. No. 1182, 2007 ABCA 335, [2008] 5 W.W.R. 475, *(sub nom. Fantasy Construction Ltd. (Bankrupt), Re)* 410 W.A.C. 255, *(sub nom. Fantasy Construction Ltd. (Bankrupt), Re)* 417 A.R. 255, 40 C.B.R. (5th) 212, 89 Alta. L.R. (4th) 93 (Alta. C.A.).

Jurisdiction to determine vires and application of *Superintendent of Bankruptcy's Directive No. 10* rests with the Bankruptcy Court. The Federal Court could not entertain proceedings in respect of bankruptcy matters unless *Bankruptcy and Insolvency Act* had expressly conferred jurisdiction on it. Aside from s. 14.02(5), jurisdiction in bankruptcy matters was not otherwise expressly conferred on Federal Court.

British Columbia v. Zastowny, 2008 CarswellBC 214, 2008 CarswellBC 215, [2008] S.C.J. No. 4, *(sub nom. Zastowny v. MacDougall)* 290 D.L.R. (4th) 219, [2008] 1 S.C.R. 27, 53 C.C.L.T. (3d) 161, *(sub nom. X v. R.D.M.)* 250 B.C.A.C. 3, 2008 SCC 4, [2008] 4 W.W.R. 381, 76 B.C.L.R. (4th) 1, *(sub nom. X. v. R.D.M.)* 370 N.R. 365, *(sub nom. X v. R.D.M.)* 416 W.A.C. 3 (S.C.C), Rothstein J.

The appeal raised a question whether plaintiff can be compensated for time spent in prison after he became eligible for parole. Whether recovery for past wage loss while incarcerated barred by application of *ex turpi causa non oritur actio* doctrine.

The Supreme Court of Canada held that a person is not entitled to compensation for periods of unemployment due to incarceration for conduct which the criminal law has determined worthy of punishment, except for exceptional circumstances such as a wrongful conviction. The doctrine of *ex turpi causa non oritur actio* precludes damage awards that allow a person to profit from illegal or wrongful conduct or that permit evasion or rebate of a penalty prescribed by the criminal law. It does not preclude damages for personal injury.

Canada (Attorney General) v. Ketenjian (March 4, 2008), Doc. Toronto 471/07 (Ont. Div. Ct.), Cumming J.

Appellant had an outstanding integrated Ontario Canada student loan. Respondent, Attorney General was awarded $3,167.82 in Small Claims Court. Appellant sought $850,460.85 as special damages, $580,405 as general damages and $10 million in punitive damages.

On appeal to the Divisional Court, dismissing the appeal, it was held that Deputy Judge had jurisdiction to make the endorsement she made since the appellant failed to request to transfer the proceedings to the Superior Court of Justice under s. 107(1)(d) of the *Court of Justice Act*. However, this failure was not important to the determination of the jurisdiction of the court, as the plaintiff (Attorney General of Canada), whose consent was mandatory requirement under s. 107(2) of the *Courts of Justice Act*, would not consent to such transfer.

Cunning v. Whitehorse, 2008 CarswellYukon 84, 2008 YKSM 3 (Y.T. Sm. Cl. Ct.), Faulkner J.

Plaintiff commenced two concurrent actions in the Supreme Court of Yukon seeking damages and other relief from the defendant and in the Small Claims Court for damages limited to $25,000. The defendant moved to dismiss or stay the plaintiff's Small Claims Court action on two grounds: (1) the Court has no jurisdiction to award declaration or an injunction; (2) it is unfair that it should have to defend two suits in two different courts based on the same cause of action. Motion granted. The Court has no power to grant equitable relief. The plaintiff can not concurrently sue the defendant in two courts. She has to elect to proceed with one suit or the other.

Grant v. V & G Realty Ltd., 2008 CarswellNS 303, 2008 NSSC 180, 869 A.P.R. 3, 272 N.S.R. (2d) 3, 58 C.P.C. (6th) 26 (N.S. S.C.).

Appeal involved the applicability of the "Implied Undertaking Rule" (the IUR) in the Small Claims Court. The Adjudicator decided that the IUR did not apply to the Small Claims Court, as those powers of Superior Courts were necessary in order to apply or enforce the IUR. Defendants appealed.

Appeal allowed in part. Small claims court is general law mandated and qualified to apply common law, of which IUR was part. However, it is appropriate to provide relief from the Rule in the circumstances of this case which involves litigation of serious public issues.

Michell v. Emond, 2008 CarswellBC 162, 2008 BCSC 111, 77 Admin. L.R. (4th) 282 (B.C. S.C.).

Plaintiff commenced action in Small Claims Court against RCMP office. Officer brought unsuccessful motion challenging court's jurisdiction to adjudicate claim against servant of federal Crown. Motion judge found that Small Claims Court had jurisdiction in action in which only Crown servant is named as defendant. The officer brought application for judicial review. Application dismissed. Provincial court had jurisdiction to hear claim as it was framed, as the plaintiff chose not to name Crown as defendant.

Nepogodin v. Austin Contracting Ltd., 2008 CarswellNS 159, 2008 NSSM 17, 72 C.L.R. (3d) 276 (N.S. Sm. Cl. Ct.), Parker. Adj.

The plaintiff brought two actions against the defendants. With consent of parties and pursuant these actions were dealt with together. The defendant brought motion that the second claim should not proceed under s. 13 of Act. Motion dismissed as the purpose of having two claims in this case was not to obtain amount in excess of $25,000. The plaintiff was prepared to combine both claims and reduce global amount of claims to $25,000.

Parker v. Cox, 2008 CarswellNS 245, 2008 NSSM 29 (N.S. Sm. Cl. Ct.), Slone Adj.

Nothing in *Small Claims Court Act* or *Probate Act*, expressly or by necessary implication, would prohibit court from hearing claim by executor of estate that could properly be described as arising from contract or tort. The defendant did not object to jurisdiction and nothing in law stood in way.

Cunning v. Whitehorse (City), 2009 CarswellYukon 7, 2009 YKSM 1, [2009] Y.J. No. 2 (Y.T. Sm. Cl. Ct.), Faulkner J.; affirmed 2009 CarswellYukon 90, 2009 YKSC 48, 74 C.P.C. (6th) 141 (Y.T. S.C.).

Application by defendant to dismiss plaintiff's claim on ground claim not within jurisdiction of Small Claims Court.

Allegation that developers of subdivision, who had purchased area from Federal government, were allowed by City to fob off responsibility to upgrade water and sewer system. The device used was a "transfer of easement agreement.".

An interest in land "comes in question" in a lawsuit if, and only if, the judgment the court makes could affect an interest in land.

In *Lou Guidi Construction Ltd. v. Fedick* (1994), [1994] B.C.J. No. 2409, 1994 CarswellBC 2818 (B.C. Prov. Ct.), the Court held there was no bar to the Small Claims Court considering interests in land in a case for damages within the court's jurisdiction so long as the remedies sought by the claimant did not in any way purport to affect an interest in land.

Can a *lis pendens* be issued? See *Tkalych v. Tkalych*, 208 Sask. R. 19, 2001 CarswellSask 305, 2001 SKQB 208 (Sask. Q.B.).

Defendant's application dismissed.

Schwartz v. Ingenious Ideas Inc., 2009 CarswellNS 456, 2009 NSSC 255, (sub nom. *Ingenious Ideas Inc. v. Schwartz*) 893 A.P.R. 233, (sub nom. *Ingenious Ideas Inc. v. Schwartz*) 281 N.S.R. (2d) 233 (N.S. S.C.).

Adjudicator found SCCA did not exclude Small Claims Court from hearing claims as copyright infringement not expressly mentioned within exclusions of claims set out in s. 20 of SCCA. Certain defendants appealed. Appeal allowed. No provision in *Copyright Act* authorizing or directing Small Claims Court to determine matters pursuant to that Act. Alleged copyright infringement had to be with respect of or arise under tort. Pleadings did not raise issue of tort law.

Weah v. Weah, [2009] M.J. No. 331, 2009 CarswellMan 447, 2009 MBQB 246 (Man. Q.B.), Schulman J.

The Small Claims Court has jurisdiction to hear a spouse's claim against other spouse for claim that does not involve determination of questions appropriate to a family proceeding.

Bagaco v. Union Energy Ltd. Partnership, 2009 CarswellOnt 900, [2009] O.J. No. 673, 76 C.P.C. (6th) 314 (Ont. S.C.J.).

Thirty-five plaintiffs brought action for negligence and breach of contract. The defendant brought motion for order severing plaintiffs' claims. Motion granted. The claims were improperly joined. Severance would result in significant savings of costs and time for parties. Twenty-seven claims within Small Claims Court jurisdiction, that could be conducted pursuant to summary procedures. Trial scheduling would be easier without having to coordinate all plaintiffs. Each plaintiff required to assert claim in separate proceeding.

The right to join the claims of different plaintiffs is subject to the Court's overriding discretionary power to sever claims where it appears that joinder will cause undue complication or delay, or cause prejudice to one of the parties.

Schwartz v. Ingenious Ideas Inc., 2009 NSSC 255, 2009 CarswellNS 456, (sub nom. *Ingenious Ideas Inc. v. Schwartz*) 281 N.S.R. (2d) 233, (sub nom. *Ingenious Ideas Inc. v. Schwartz*) 893 A.P.R. 233, 82 C.P.C. (6th) 111 (N.S. S.C.).

The claimant filed notices of claim, claiming copyright infringement. The Small Claims Court adjudicator determined, *inter alia*, that Small Claims Court had jurisdiction to hear claims. The adjudicator erred in determining Small Claims Court had jurisdiction to adjudicate claim for copyright infringement arising out of or with respect to tort. There was no allegation or issue that the alleged copyright infringement arose out of a contract. There was no provision contained in the *Copyright Act*, R.S.C. 1985, c-42, authorizing or directing the Small Claims Court to determine matters pursuant to the Act. Protection against copyright infringement is a statutory right created pursuant to the *Copyright Act*. A person cannot be held liable in tort for copyright infringement. See *Compo Co. v. Blue Crest Music Inc.* (1979), 1979 CarswellNat 640F, 29 N.R. 296, 105 D.L.R. (3d) 249, 45 C.P.R. (2d) 1, 1979 CarswellNat 640, [1980] 1 S.C.R. 357 (S.C.C.).

Williams v. Kameka, 2009 NSCA 107, 2009 CarswellNS 553, 282 N.S.R. (2d) 376, 895 A.P.R. 376, 85 M.V.R. (5th) 157, 77 C.P.C. (6th) 218 (N.S. C.A.).

The plaintiff brought action in Small Claims Court and obtained judgment against driver of van. The plaintiff then brought action against owner of van in Nova Scotia Supreme Court. The defendants brought unsuccessful application to dismiss claim on basis of *res judicata*. The defendants appealed. The appeal was allowed. There is only one cause of action for single wrongful or negligent act. Monetary or jurisdictional limits do not preclude the application of doctrine of *res judicata*. No basis to conclude that Small Claims Court is *not* court of competent jurisdiction to hear and decide allegations of negligence. There are well-established principles that require plaintiffs not to litigate in instalments. Plaintiff's claim for general damages for personal injuries became merged into Small Claims Court judgment. Plaintiff therefore stopped from proceeding with same cause of action again.

The remedy plaintiff sought in Supreme Court action available in Small Claims Court.

The legislature intended that the order of the Small Claims Court would discharge all demands, in any court, for the balance that exceeded the Small Claims Court's jurisdiction. Doctrine of *res judicata*'s long-standing existence was commented on by Binnie J., in *Danyluk v. Ainsworth Technologies Inc.*, 2001 SCC 44, 2001 CarswellOnt 2434, 2001 CarswellOnt 2435, REJB 2001-25003, [2001] S.C.J. No. 46, [2001] 2 S.C.R. 460, 54 O.R. (3d) 214 (headnote only), 201 D.L.R. (4th) 193, 10 C.C.E.L. (3d) 1, 2001 C.L.L.C. 210-033, 272 N.R. 1, 149 O.A.C. 1, 7 C.P.C. (5th) 199, 34 Admin. L.R. (3d) 163 (S.C.C.).

Zammit Semple LLP v. Attar, [2009] O.J. No. 5044, 2009 CarswellOnt 7369 (Ont. S.C.J.).

The plaintiff obtained default judgment against the defendant. The defendant brought the motion to set aside default judgment. Motion dismissed. The plaintiff waited over one-and-a-half years. The circumstances were not obstacle to granting the defendant relief sought. The defendant met test, being whether motion brought forthwith after default judgment came to the defendant's attention. The defendant failed, however, to meet branch of test, whether the defendant could present viable defence on merits.

MacDonald v. Myra, 2009 CarswellNS 454, 2009 NSSM 33, 281 N.S.R. (2d) 354, 893 A.P.R. 354 (N.S. Sm. Cl. Ct.), Michael J. O'Hara Adjud.

Grandparents brought action in Small Claims Court for damages for breach of fiduciary duties. Granddaughter brought counterclaim for reimbursement of amount paid for caregiver services. Small Claims Court did not have jurisdiction to deal with claims based on breach of fiduciary duties. Jurisdiction of Small Claims Court limited to claims arising under contract or tort. Authorities indicated Small Claims Court had jurisdiction to deal with unjust enrichment distinguishable. Furthermore, *Powers of Attorney Act* granted exclusive jurisdiction to Supreme Court for claims made against attorneys.

Pyramid Properties Ltd. v. Johnston, 2010 NSSC 53, 2010 CarswellNS 79 (N.S. S.C.).

The adjudicator did not err in finding that PJ, who was party to several claims against PP Ltd. that in total amounted to more than monetary jurisdiction of Small Claims Court, did not split his claim for purpose of bringing it before court. Goal of Small Claims Court in effecting cost-effective and expeditious resolution of claims was achieved by addressing all claims in single hearing, which was done with the consent of all parties and in accordance with the *Small Claims Court Act*.

Gradek v. DaimlerChrysler Financial Services Canada Inc./Services Financiers DaimlerChrysler Canada Inc., 2010 BCCA 256, 2010 CarswellBC 1278 (B.C. C.A. [In Chambers]).

Plaintiff recovered $9,685.87 in damages of which $8,000 represented general damages, below Provincial Court jurisdictional of $25,000.

Costs awarded under r. 66(29)(b) in the amount of $6,600, which is the statutory amount for a two-day trial. Rule 66(29)(b) expressly made subject to r. 57(10) which provides:

> A plaintiff who recovers a sum within the jurisdiction of the Provincial Court under the *Small Claims Act* is not entitled to costs, other than disbursements, unless the court finds that there was sufficient reason for bringing the proceeding in the Supreme Court and so orders.

In general, on applications for leave to appeal, the court will take into account considerations set out in *Chavez v. Sundance Cruises Corp.*, [1993] B.C.J. No. 577, 1993 CarswellBC 74, 15 C.P.C. (3d) 305, 77 B.C.L.R. (2d) 328 (B.C. C.A.). Those are:

1. whether the appeal is *prima facie* meritorious or, on the other hand, frivolous;

2. the significance of the point on appeal to the litigants;

3. the significance of the point on appeal to practice generally; and

4. the question of whether the appeal will delay or hinder the progress of the action.

Issue of how Supreme Court determines whether matter is brought in that court for "sufficient reason" is a matter of general importance in litigation, particularly given that the monetary limit for Small Claims Court $25,000.

Leave granted and a division of the Court should hear matter.

Aschenbrenner v. Yahemech, 2010 BCSC 1541, 2010 CarswellBC 2930 (B.C. S.C.).

Should the plaintiffs' costs be limited to disbursements since award within the jurisdiction of Small Claims Court? Were plaintiffs substantially successful? If the plaintiffs were entitled to costs, is it fair and equitable to award costs if they exceed the damages the plaintiffs were awarded at trial?.

In this case, there was sufficient reason for plaintiffs to bring action in B.C. Supreme Court as neither an injunction nor damages for defamation were available in the Provincial Court of British Columbia. Plaintiffs' costs not limited to disbursements only. [See *Bhanji v. Quezada*, 303 W.A.C. 301, 185 B.C.A.C. 301, [2003] B.C.J. No. 1883, 2003 CarswellBC 1986, 2003 BCCA 445 (B.C. C.A.); *Reimann v. Aziz*, 72 B.C.L.R. (4th) 1, 2007 BCCA 448, 406 W.A.C. 143, 246 B.C.A.C. 143, [2007] B.C.J. No. 2025, 286 D.L.R. (4th) 330, 47 C.P.C. (6th) 351, 2007 CarswellBC 2190 (B.C. C.A.); *Icecorp International Cargo Express Corp. v. Nicolaus*, 2007 BCCA 97, 2007 CarswellBC 444, 38 C.P.C. (6th) 26, 390 W.A.C. 294, 236 B.C.A.C. 294 (B.C. C.A.); *Kuehne v. Probstl*, [2004] B.C.J. No. 1383, 2004 BCSC 865, 2004 CarswellBC 1515 (B.C. Master)].

Substantial success not determined by counting up the number of issues and allocating success on each, or by comparing the dollar amounts, but by assessing success in the major issues of substance. See *Cohen v. Cohen*, [1995] B.C.J. No. 1370, 1995 CarswellBC 608, 15 R.F.L. (4th) 84 (B.C. C.A.); *Reilly v. Reilly*, 1996 CarswellBC 1279, [1996] B.C.J. No. 1244 (B.C. S.C.); and *Rattenbury v. Rattenbury*, [2001] B.C.J. No. 889, 2001 CarswellBC 875, 2001 BCSC 593 (B.C. S.C.).

Balance of fairness will not be disrupted by allowing the plaintiffs their costs on the usual scale including the costs of this hearing, less a 20% reduction of the plaintiffs' total costs and disbursements. The "good reason" for the deduction is the plaintiffs' decision to withhold from the defendant, until the first day of trial, their intent to abandon the injunction application.

Lindhorst v. Cornwall (City), 2010 CarswellOnt 6846, 2010 ONSC 5044 (Ont. S.C.J.).

The plaintiff's claim dismissed for reasons delivered July 7, 2010, following the defendant's motion for summary judgment heard June 25, 2010. Award of costs governed by r. 57 and section 131 of the *Courts of Justice Act*.

The defendant would be fully indemnified by award of $16,682.00.

Self-represented persons expected to familiarize themselves with relevant legal practices and procedures pertaining to case. The plaintiff initiated this action in Toronto. He brought it without regard to the Small Claims Court option. The plaintiff was alerted to costs exposure every time the file came before court.

The rules are guideline for litigants intended to achieve the most expeditious and least expensive determination of every civil proceeding on its merits (r. 1.04(1)). Proportionality to the importance and complexity of the issues is one of the driving features of how parties and the court are to interpret rules.

The interface between legal professionals and self-represented litigants can become inefficient when respective expectations are frustrated. Lawyers are generally trained to proceed with a view to expedient application of the Rules. Self-represented litigants do not have that training.

Costs consequences imposed primarily on the party who avers the forum subject to the general principles and factors. Here the plaintiff selected the forum and is responsible for the consequences. The Court does not hold the plaintiff to a standard to attract sanction under sub paragraphs 57.01(1)(e)(f)(g). Proper case for partial indemnity costs. The defendant shall have costs of $10,600.00 against the plaintiff.

Zale v. Colwell, 2010 BCSC 1040, 2010 CarswellBC 1991 (B.C. S.C.).

The plaintiff's total award of $10,635.89 within the jurisdiction of the Provincial Court, Small Claims Division.

The plaintiff applied for costs if the Court "finds there was sufficient reason for bringing the proceeding in Supreme Court and so orders." The counsel for plaintiff submits sufficient reason for bringing the proceeding in Supreme Court such that an order for costs should be made. In the circumstances, it was ultimately reasonable for plaintiff to make the decision to have the matter heard in Supreme Court.

Impey v. Thompson, 2002 CarswellSask 618, 2002 SKQB 410, 229 Sask. R. 244 (Sask. Q.B.).

The Provincial Court is a court of limited jurisdiction which can only hear and decide matters within its statutory jurisdiction. The Provincial Court does not have jurisdiction to vary, enforce, or otherwise interpret existing judgments made pursuant to the *Family Property Act* by the Court of Queen's Bench. Judgment of Provincial Court quashed and set aside.

Laurentide Cabinet Corp. v. Beyond Flooring, 2010 ONSC 3609, 323 D.L.R. (4th) 475, 86 C.P.R. (4th) 303, 2010 CarswellOnt 5553 (Ont. Div. Ct.).

What is the jurisdiction of the Small Claims Court? See *Courts of Justice Act*, R.S.O. 1990, c. C.43, s. 22(1). The trial judge found continued display of the plaintiffs' logo violation of section 7 of the *Trade-marks Act*, R.S.C. 1985, c. T-13. The plaintiffs awarded $2,500 in damages. Appeal allowed.

Effect of legislation that created Small Claims Court as a branch of the Superior Court of Justice meant proceeding was before the Superior Court as defined by section 52 of the *Trade-marks Act*. Reading the *Trade-marks Act* with the *Courts of Justice Act*, and the *Interpretation Act*, R.S.C. 1985, c. I-21, established the Small Claims Court as the Superior Court within the meaning of the *Trade-marks Act* with the jurisdiction to hear actions arising out of the *Trade-marks Act* that fell within the Small Claims Court's monetary limit. Nothing to suggest defendant violated section 7(b) of the *Trade-marks Act*.

Tercon Contractors Ltd. v. British Columbia (Minister of Transportation & Highways), 100 B.C.L.R. (4th) 201, [2010] 3 W.W.R. 387, 65 B.L.R. (4th) 1, 86 C.L.R. (3d) 163, 2010 SCC 4, 2010 CarswellBC 297, 2010 CarswellBC 296, [2010] S.C.J. No. 4, 315 D.L.R. (4th) 385, 475 W.A.C. 245, 281 B.C.A.C. 245, [2010] 1 S.C.R. 69, 397 N.R. 331 (S.C.C.). *Tercon* unanimously held that the application of a limitation of liability provision involves a three-stage analysis:

> i. As a matter of ordinary contractual interpretation, does the exclusion clause apply to the circumstances established in the evidence?

> ii. If yes, was the exclusion clause unconscionable at the time the contract was made?

> iii. If no, should the court decline to enforce the exclusion clause because of an overriding public policy concern which outweighs the very strong public interest in the enforcement of contracts?

Reasonable interpretations of exclusion clauses led to enforceability in *Calder v. Jones*, 2010 CarswellBC 1556, 2010 BCPC 77, 75 C.C.L.T. (3d) 144, [2010] B.C.J. No. 1030 (B.C. Prov. Ct.), *Campbell v. 0698900 B.C. Ltd.*, 2010 BCPC 136, 2010 CarswellBC 1808 (B.C. Prov. Ct.), *Arnold v. Bekkers Pet Care Inc.* (May 21, 2010), [2010] O.J. No. 2153, Doc. 08-SC-105438 (Ont. S.C.J.) and *Dennis v. Ontario Lottery & Gaming Corp.*, 2010 CarswellOnt 1975, 2010 ONSC 1332, 101 O.R. (3d) 23, 92 C.P.C. (6th) 119, [2010] O.J. No. 1223, 318 D.L.R. (4th) 110 (Ont. S.C.J.); affirmed 2011 ONSC 7024, 2011 CarswellOnt 13514, 19 C.P.C. (7th) 32, 344 D.L.R. (4th) 65, 286 O.A.C. 329 (Ont. Div. Ct.); affirmed 2013 ONCA 501, 2013 CarswellOnt 10539, 116 O.R. (3d) 321, 37 C.P.C. (7th) 268, 365 D.L.R. (4th) 145, 307 O.A.C. 377 (Ont. C.A.); leave to appeal refused 2014 CarswellOnt 1724, 2014 CarswellOnt 1725 (S.C.C.). Somewhat strained interpretations adopted in order to find exclusion clauses inapplicable in *Schiltroth v. RDS Enterprises*, 2010 SKPC 47, 2010 CarswellSask 261, 355 Sask. R. 192, [2010] S.J. No. 244 (Sask. Prov. Ct.). *Calder, Campbell* and *Arnold* are small claims court cases in which exclusion clauses in standard-form contracts entered into in consumer-type settings found to be enforceable.

For example, *Arnold* involved the death of a beloved pet dog while the pet was in the care of a kennel: "It seems reasonable to me that, through a relatively simple [exclusion] clause in a contract such as the one here, such a kennel should be able to try to avoid potential costly exposure to prolonged litigation about the standard of care in relation to the loss of someone's pet.".

Hodgins v. Grover, 2011 ONCA 72, 2011 CarswellOnt 336, [2011] O.J. No. 310, *(sub nom. Grover v. Hodgins)* 103 O.R. (3d) 721, *(sub nom. Grover v. Hodgins)* 275 O.A.C. 96, *(sub nom. Grover v. Hodgins)* 330 D.L.R. (4th) 712, 5 C.P.C. (7th) 33 (Ont. C.A.); leave to appeal refused 2012 CarswellOnt 825, 2012 CarswellOnt 826, 432 N.R. 392 (note), (sub nom. *Grover v. Hodgins)* 295 O.A.C. 398 (note), [2011] S.C.C.A. No. 142 (S.C.C.).

Small Claims Court action was based in contract or, in the alternative, unjust enrichment. The claim in contract failed. Trial judge found appellants (the respondents in the cross-appeal) liable to the respondents for a share in legal fees, based on unjust enrichment. Does a deputy judge of the Small Claims Court have jurisdiction to grant equitable relief? The Small Claims Court has jurisdiction to grant such relief *when* the order involves the return of personal property or a monetary payment within the limit of the Small Claims Court. Respondents' claims both in contract and in unjust enrichment must fail.

The Small Claims Court is a statutory court that derives its jurisdiction solely through the *Courts of Justice Act*, R.S.O. 1990, c. C.43; see sections 23 and 96.

The Divisional Court in *936464 Ontario Ltd. v. Mungo Bear Ltd.*, 2003 CarswellOnt 8091, 258 D.L.R. (4th) 754, 74 O.R. (3d) 45, [2003] O.J. No. 3795 (Ont. Div. Ct.), in which a remedy based on *quantum meruit* was in issue at paras. 12–15, concluded that notwithstanding that *quantum meruit* is part of the restitutionary group of remedies, its origins can be found in the common law and therefore the court does *not* need equitable jurisdiction to award it.

While section 96(3) specifically excludes the Small Claims Court from the list of courts able to grant equitable relief, it does so with the proviso found in the words "*unless otherwise provided.*" Section 23(1)(a) provides otherwise in the words "any action," wording sufficiently broad so as to encompass both common law claims and equitable claims.

See also *311874 Ontario Ltd. v. 1461763 Ontario Ltd.*, [2006] O.J. No. 2779, 2006 CarswellOnt 8660 (Ont. S.C.J.) and *Tang v. Jarrett*, 251 O.A.C. 123, 2009 CarswellOnt 1656 (Ont. Div. Ct.).

According to *Rizzo & Rizzo Shoes Ltd., Re*, 98 C.L.L.C. 210-006, 106 O.A.C. 1, 221 N.R. 241, 36 O.R. (3d) 418 (headnote only), 154 D.L.R. (4th) 193, [1998] S.C.J. No. 2, 33 C.C.E.L. (2d) 173, [1998] 1 S.C.R. 27, 50 C.B.R. (3d) 163, 1998 CarswellOnt 2, 1998 CarswellOnt 1 (S.C.C.), the analysis must focus on the words of the relevant statutory provisions, read in their entire context and in their grammatical and ordinary sense, interpreted harmoniously with the scheme and the object of the *Act* and with the legislature's intention.

With the passage of Bill 2, *An Act to amend the Courts of Justice Act, 1984*, 2d Sess., 34th Leg., Ontario, 1989 (assented November 15, 1989), S.O. 1989, c. 55, the Small Claims Court became a branch of the newly-created Ontario Court (General Division), part of the province's superior court.

The cause of action for unjust enrichment has three elements: (1) an enrichment of the defendant; (2) a corresponding deprivation of the plaintiff; and (3) an absence of any juristic reason for the enrichment. See *Becker v. Pettkus*, 19 R.F.L. (2d) 165, 8 E.T.R. 143, 34 N.R. 384, 117 D.L.R. (3d) 257, [1980] 2 S.C.R. 834, [1980] S.C.J. No. 103, 1980 CarswellOnt 644, 1980 CarswellOnt 299 (S.C.C.).

The claim in unjust enrichment must fail.

Trial judge overlooked the difference between unjust enrichment through the provision of money and unjust enrichment through the provision of services. See Laskin J.A. in *Sharwood & Co. v. Municipal Financial Corp.*, 2001 CarswellOnt 749, 53 O.R. (3d) 470, 142 O.A.C. 350, 12 B.L.R. (3d) 219, 197 D.L.R. (4th) 477 (Ont. C.A.), at para. 26: "The receipt of money is always a benefit to the defendant. The receipt of services may not be a benefit because the defendant may not have wanted the services or may not have wanted them if it had to pay for them.".

Appeal allowed and cross-appeal dismissed. Decision of Divisional Court set aside and judgment of deputy judge of the Small Claims Court set aside. Action dismissed.

Szpakowsky v. Kramar, 2012 ONCA 77, 2012 CarswellOnt 1320, 19 C.P.C. (7th) 274, [2012] O.J. No. 446 (Ont. C.A.); additional reasons at 2012 ONCA 136, 2012 CarswellOnt 2087 (Ont. C.A.).

This case contains security for costs, as the case may be a waste of time or nuisance. The Court does not need to be satisfied that a case is without merit and frivolous, vexatious, or otherwise an abuse of the court's process. The Court needs only to have "good reason to believe" that a case has those characteristics. The appellant's history of re-litigating this case brought it within those characteristics. For this and other grounds, the appeal court ordered the appellant to pay $15,000 into the court as security for the costs of appeal.

With respect to the second arm of the test in clause 61.06(1)(a) of *Rules of Civil Procedure*, the appellant conceded that she was impecunious. Impecunious litigants are not entitled to litigate with impunity, causing their opponents to run up significant costs and without having to face normal consequences of costs if they (impecunious litigants) were unsuccessful. The Court was unwilling to make an order for security for costs of more than $43,000 and instead settled upon a sum of $15,000 as security for costs. The appeal has been stayed pending the appellant's compliance with this order.

Indcondo Building Corp. v. Sloan, 2012 ONCA 83, 2012 CarswellOnt 1742, 18 C.P.C. (7th) 223, 347 D.L.R. (4th) 119 (Ont. C.A. [In Chambers]); affirmed 2012 ONCA 502, 2012 CarswellOnt 9030, 91 C.B.R. (5th) 324, 22 C.P.C. (7th) 22, 352 D.L.R. (4th) 235, 293 O.A.C. 392 (Ont. C.A.); additional reasons 2012 ONCA 619, 2012 CarswellOnt 11697 (Ont. C.A.); leave to appeal refused 2013 CarswellOnt 8, 2013 CarswellOnt 9, 446 N.R. 391 (note), 309 O.A.C. 399 (note) (S.C.C.).

The respondents sought an order requiring the law firm for the appellant to pay into court security for the costs of an action, which was dismissed as an abuse of process, and to pay into court security for costs of the appeal.

The appellant corporation and its principal were impecunious. The appellant had insufficient assets in Ontario to pay the costs below and the costs of appeal. The appellant's law firm was retained on a contingency basis.

The issue was addressed by Nordheimer J. in *Intellibox Concepts Inc. v. Intermec Technologies Canada Ltd.*, 2005 CarswellOnt 1603, [2005] O.J. No. 1087, [2005] O.T.C. 310, 14 C.P.C. (6th) 339 at para. 12 (Ont. S.C.J.):

> As I have noted, the logical extension of ordering security for costs to be posted by an impecunious corporate plaintiff by reason of the fact that its solicitors are operating on a contingency fee basis is, in effect, to require those solicitors to provide the security. Solicitors who make legal services available based on contingency fee arrangements with clients, who could not otherwise afford to litigate a claim, assume the risk that they may not be paid for their work unless a favourable result is achieved. To require those solicitors to assume the additional burden of posting security for costs, with the concomitant risk of losing those funds (in addition to going unpaid for their own services), would impose a significant disincentive to contingency fee arrangements and would run contrary to the very rationale by which they are permitted. In my view, it would be incongruous to interpret the *Rules of Civil Procedure* in such a fashion.

It may be that in some future case, a basis will be established upon which such an order is justified. That said, I do not see this as such a case. The motion was dismissed without costs.

Hodgins v. Grover, 2011 ONCA 72, 2011 CarswellOnt 336, [2011] O.J. No. 310, (sub nom. *Grover v. Hodgins*) 103 O.R. (3d) 721, (sub nom. *Grover v. Hodgins*) 275 O.A.C. 96, (sub nom. *Grover v. Hodgins*) 330 D.L.R. (4th) 712, 5 C.P.C. (7th) 33 (Ont. C.A.); leave to appeal refused 2012 CarswellOnt 825, 2012 CarswellOnt 826, 432 N.R. 392 (note), (sub nom. *Grover v. Hodgins*) 295 O.A.C. 398 (note), [2011] S.C.C.A. No. 142 (S.C.C.).

There was an appeal and cross-appeal of the decision of a deputy judge granting judgment in favour of the respondents (who were the appellants in the cross-appeal).

An important issue was raised over the jurisdiction of a deputy judge of the Small Claims Court to grant equitable relief. The Court was concerned with the issue of whether a trial judge has power to grant relief based on unjust enrichment.

The decision of the Divisional Court contains no reference to the case being decided. It does not permit any meaningful appellate review and therefore constitutes legal error: see *R. v. Brown*, 2002 CarswellOnt 3368, [2002] O.J. No. 3882, 61 O.R. (3d) 619, 165 O.A.C. 36, 170 C.C.C. (3d) 37, 7 C.R. (6th) 129 at para. 30 (Ont. C.A.).

The Small Claims Court is a statutory court that derives its jurisdiction solely through the *Courts of Justice Act*, R.S.O. 1990, c. C.43. Section 23 is of primary relevance in this appeal, while section 96 is also informative to the analysis.

In the decision of the Divisional Court in *936464 Ontario Ltd. v. Mungo Bear Ltd.*, 2003 CarswellOnt 8091, [2003] O.J. No. 3795, 74 O.R. (3d) 45, 258 D.L.R. (4th) 754 (Ont. Div. Ct.), a remedy based on quantum meruit was in issue. Heeney J., at paras. 12–15, concluded that, notwithstanding, quantum meruit is part of the restitutionary group of remedies, its origins can be found in the common law, and therefore the court does not need equitable jurisdiction to award it.

Heeney J. noted that while section 96(3) specifically excludes the Small Claims Court from the list of courts able to grant equitable relief, it does so with the proviso found in the words "unless otherwise provided." He reasoned that section 23(1)(a) provides otherwise in the words "any action" — wording sufficiently broad so as to encompass both common law claims and equitable claims.

Two subsequent decisions adopted the reasoning of Heeney J. in relation to the jurisdiction of the Small Claims Court to grant equitable relief, although, as in the case of *Mungo Bear*, the analysis was not necessary for either decision: *311874 Ontario Ltd. v. 1461763 Ontario Ltd.*, 2006 CarswellOnt 8660, [2006] O.J. No. 2779 (Ont. S.C.J.) and *Tang v. Jarrett*, 2009 CarswellOnt 1656, 251 O.A.C. 123, [2009] O.J. No. 1282 (Ont. Div. Ct.).

Court has been operating on the basis that it has jurisdiction to consider claims for equitable relief and, in appropriate cases, to grant it. See *Szeib v. Team Truck Centres — Freightliner*, 2001 CarswellOnt 2026, [2001] O.J. No. 2208, [2001] O.T.C. 439 (Ont. Sm. Cl. Ct.), where Searle Deputy J. specifically considered the jurisdictional issue and held that the Small Claims Court has jurisdiction to grant relief from forfeiture, a form of equitable relief. In a myriad of other cases, the Small Claims Court has, without any analysis of jurisdiction, considered and awarded (or rejected after consideration) remedies in equity, particularly based on unjust enrichment. See, for example, *P & G Electronics Ltd. v. Scottish & York Insurance Co.* (June 23, 1992), Doc. NY 13603/89, [1992] O.J. No. 2707 (Ont. Gen. Div.); *Gula v. Ontario Hydro*, [1995] O.J. No. 2392, 1995 CarswellOnt 4519 (Ont. Sm. Cl. Ct.); *Michael Davies Plymouth Chrysler Ltd. v. Shabsove*, 1995 CarswellOnt 3605, [1995] O.J. No. 5017 (Ont. Gen. Div.); *Bell, Baker v. Wong* (March 28, 1996), Doc. 32258/94, [1996] O.J. No. 5443 (Ont. Gen. Div.); *Canada Post Corp. v. Asquith* (April 15, 1999), Doc. 2383/98, [1999] O.J. No. 5583 (Ont. Gen. Div.); *1346597 Ontario Ltd. v. Riddiford* (June 8, 2007), Doc. SM-02-00048643, [2007] O.J. No. 5502 (Ont. S.C.J.); *Causeway View Road South Assn. v. Foster*, 2009 CarswellOnt 8841, 91 R.P.R. (4th) 314 (Ont. S.C.J.).

The resolution of whether the Small Claims Court has jurisdiction to grant equitable relief involves basic statutory interpretation. According to *Rizzo & Rizzo Shoes Ltd., Re*, 1998 CarswellOnt 1, 1998 CarswellOnt 2, [1998] S.C.J. No. 2, [1998] 1 S.C.R. 27, 36 O.R. (3d) 418 (headnote only), 50 C.B.R. (3d) 163, 33 C.C.E.L. (2d) 173, 154 D.L.R. (4th) 193, (sub nom. *Rizzo & Rizzo Shoes Ltd. (Bankrupt), Re*) 221 N.R. 241, (sub nom. *Rizzo & Rizzo Shoes Ltd. (Bankrupt), Re*) 106 O.A.C. 1, (sub nom. *Adrien v. Ontario Ministry of Labour*) 98 C.L.L.C. 210-006 (S.C.C.), at para. 21, the analysis must focus on the words of the relevant statutory provisions, read in their entire context, in their grammatical and ordinary sense, and interpreted harmoniously with the scheme and the object of the Act and with the legislature's intention.

The wording of "any action" is sufficiently broad so as to encompass both common law and equitable claims.

See Heeney J. at para. 29 of *Mungo Bear* that section 23, section 96(1) and section 96(3) are to be read as a "coherent package." Under section 96(1), the courts, including the Small Claims Court, are authorized to concurrently administer all rules of equity and the common law.

Interpretation of the *Courts of Justice Act* provisions is relevant to the jurisdiction of the Small Claims Court that is in keeping with the wording of the *Act* . . . is that the Small Claims Court has jurisdiction to award legal or equitable relief.

The appeal was allowed and the cross-appeal was dismissed. The action was dismissed.

Cunning v. Whitehorse (City), 2009 YKSM 1, 2009 CarswellYukon 7 (Y.T. Sm. Cl. Ct.); affirmed 2009 YKSC 48, 2009 CarswellYukon 90, 74 C.P.C. (6th) 141 (Y.T. S.C.).

The Application by the defendant to dismiss the plaintiff's claim on ground claim was not within the jurisdiction of the Small Claims Court.

Cunning, in an earlier decision, elected to proceed in Small Claims Court and discontinued her participation in the Supreme Court action.

The City argued that the Small Claims Court had no jurisdiction because the action was one in which "an interest in land comes in question." The topic of easements featured prominently in the case.

An interest in land "comes in question" in a lawsuit if, and only if, the judgment the court makes could affect an interest in land. In *Chilliwack (Township), Re*, 1984 CarswellBC 142, [1984] B.C.J. No. 2935, 53 B.C.L.R. 391 (B.C. S.C.), the Small Claims Court judge had held he had no jurisdiction in a nuisance case because the defendant municipality disputed the claim that it owned the lands from whence that notorious coastal scourge, runaway blackberry bushes, had escaped. The British Columbia *Small Claim Act*, R.S.B.C. 1979, c.387, at that time provided that the Small Claims Court lacked jurisdiction "where the title to land comes into question.".

On appeal, Proudfoot J. (as she then was) held that although ownership of the lands in question was a factual matter that needed to be decided in order to determine who was liable for any nuisance proved, that did not mean that the title to the land was in question. Whatever judgment the court gave, it could not affect the title to the land in any way.

See also Stansfield J. (as he then was) in *Lou Guidi Construction Ltd. v. Fedick*, 1994 CarswellBC 2818, [1994] B.C.J. No. 2409 (B.C. Prov. Ct.). The suit dealt with damages claimed in regard to an uncompleted sale of real property. The Court held that there was no bar to the Small Claims Court considering interests in land in a case for damages within the court's jurisdiction so long as the remedies sought by the claimant did not in any way purport to affect an interest in land:

> . . . the focus of the jurisdictional inquiry is the nature of the relief sought, not whether the matter touches upon certain issues. (para. 18).

An issue is whether or not a *lis pendens* can be issued. See e.g., *Tkalych v. Tkalych*, 2001 SKQB 208, 2001 CarswellSask 305, 208 Sask. R. 19 (Sask. Q.B.).

The defendant's Application was dismissed.

Pictou Landing Indian Band v. Clark, 2011 NSSC 270, 2011 CarswellNS 491, (sub nom. *Clark v. Pictou Landing Indian Band*) 305 N.S.R. (2d) 297, (sub nom. *Clark v. Pictou Landing Indian Band*) 966 A.P.R. 297 (N.S. S.C.).

There was a jurisdictional issue as to whether the Small Claims Court had jurisdiction to hear the claim. An adjudicator determined that the Small Claims Court had jurisdiction.

The respondent commenced an action in Small Claims Court against the appellant for a breach of fiduciary and trust obligations. An adjudicator of Small Claims Court found the Court had jurisdiction to hear the matter, as the claim was one of the tort of negligence.

Clark submitted that a breach of fiduciary duty and a breach of trust are torts and, therefore, within the Small Claims Court jurisdiction. See *Canada Building Materials Co. v. Olser Paving & Construction Ltd. (Trustee of)*, 2009 CarswellOnt 926, 95 O.R. (3d) 448, 80 C.L.R. (3d) 295 (Ont. Master).

See LaForest, J., in *M. (K.) v. M. (H.)*, 1992 CarswellOnt 998, 1992 CarswellOnt 841, EYB 1992-67549, [1992] S.C.J. No. 85, *(sub nom. M. c. M.)* [1992] 3 S.C.R. 6, 142 N.R. 321, 96 D.L.R. (4th) 289, 57 O.A.C. 321, 14 C.C.L.T. (2d) 1 (S.C.C.), as to the distinction between a tort and fiduciary duty.

A breach of fiduciary duty or a breach of trust are breaches of equitable duties, not torts. Clark's claim is not under a contract.

Breaches of fiduciary duty or trust are breaches of equitable duties, not torts. The claim was not within the jurisdiction of the Small Claims Court. The appeal was allowed. LaForest, J., in giving the majority judgment in *M. (K.) v. M. (H.)*, 1992 CarswellOnt 998, 1992 CarswellOnt 841, EYB 1992-67549, [1992] S.C.J. No. 85, *(sub nom. M. c. M.)* [1992] 3 S.C.R. 6, 142 N.R. 321, 96 D.L.R. (4th) 289, 57 O.A.C. 321, 14 C.C.L.T. (2d) 1 (S.C.C.), indicated the distinction between a tort and fiduciary duty at paras. 68 and 70. A breach of fiduciary duty or breach of trust is a breach of equitable duties, not torts. Clark's claim was not under a contract. The claim of Clark, not being under a contract or a tort, but rather pursuant to equitable claims of breach of trust and/or breach of fiduciary duty, was not within the jurisdiction of the Small Claims Court.

The claim, not being under a contract or a tort, but rather pursuant to equitable claims of breach of trust and/or breach of fiduciary duty, was not within the jurisdiction of the Small Claims Court. The appeal was allowed.

Laurentide Cabinet Corp. v. Beyond Flooring, 2010 ONSC 3609, 2010 CarswellOnt 5553, 86 C.P.R. (4th) 303, 323 D.L.R. (4th) 475 (Ont. Div. Ct.).

The Small Claims Court is the Superior Court under the *Trade-marks Act*.

An effect of the legislation that created the Small Claims Court as a branch of the Superior Court of Justice meant that this proceeding was before the Superior Court of the province of Ontario as defined by section 52 of the *Trade-marks Act*. Reading the *Trade-marks Act* with the *Courts of Justice Act*, R.S.O. 1990, c. C.43, and the *Interpretation Act*, R.S.C. 1985, c. I-21, established the Small Claims Court as the Superior Court within the meaning of the *Trade-marks Act* with the jurisdiction to her actions arising out of the *Trade-marks Act* that fell within the Small Claims Court's monetary limit.

The purpose of the Small Claims Court is to improve access to justice and alleviate the burden on the courts, and on the parties, by enabling parties to bring forward a claim, as was done here, in person, quickly and expeditiously and at little cost. See Sharpe J. (as he then was) in *Luo v. Canada (Attorney General)*, 1997 CarswellOnt 1577, 33 O.R. (3d) 300, 9 C.P.C. (4th) 343, 28 C.C.E.L. (2d) 304, 145 D.L.R. (4th) 457 (Ont. Div. Ct.). See also *Brighton Heating & Air Conditioning Ltd. v. Savoia*, 2006 CarswellOnt 340, [2006] O.J. No. 250, 79 O.R. (3d) 386, 49 C.L.R. (3d) 235, 207 O.A.C. 1 (Ont. Div. Ct.).

Hodgins v. Grover, 2011 ONCA 72, 2011 CarswellOnt 336, [2011] O.J. No. 310, *(sub nom. Grover v. Hodgins)* 103 O.R. (3d) 721, *(sub nom. Grover v. Hodgins)* 275 O.A.C. 96, *(sub nom. Grover v. Hodgins)* 330 D.L.R. (4th) 712, 5 C.P.C. (7th) 33 (Ont. C.A.); leave to appeal refused 2012 CarswellOnt 825, 2012 CarswellOnt 826, 432 N.R. 392 (note), (sub nom. *Grover v. Hodgins)* 295 O.A.C. 398 (note), [2011] S.C.C.A. No. 142 (S.C.C.).

Section 23 of the *Courts of Justice Act (Ont.)* sets out the jurisdiction of the Small Claims Court, while section 96 deals with the equitable jurisdiction of all courts. The Court of Appeal held that section 23 was a wide grant of jurisdiction. The wording "any action" was sufficiently broad enough to include the jurisdiction to grant equitable remedies. Sections 23, 96(1) and 96(3) are to be read as a "coherent package." Section 23 was broad enough to allow the Small Claims Court to deal with claims in common law and equity. Under section 96(1), the courts, including the Small Claims Court, is authorized to concurrently administer all rules of equity and the common law.

This court has been operating on the basis that it has jurisdiction to consider claims for equitable relief and, in appropriate cases, to grant it.

See *Szeib v. Team Truck Centres — Freightliner*, [2001] O.T.C. 439, [2001] O.J. No. 2208, 2001 CarswellOnt 2026 (Ont. Sm. Cl. Ct.), Searle Deputy, J., specifically considered the jurisdictional issue and held that the Small Claims Court has jurisdiction to grant relief from forfeiture, a form of equitable relief. See *Rizzo & Rizzo Shoes Ltd., Re*, 1998 CarswellOnt 1, 1998 CarswellOnt 2, [1998] S.C.J. No. 2, [1998] 1 S.C.R. 27, 36 O.R. (3d) 418 (headnote only), 50 C.B.R. (3d) 163, 33 C.C.E.L. (2d) 173, 154 D.L.R. (4th) 193, (sub nom. *Rizzo & Rizzo Shoes Ltd. (Bankrupt), Re)* 221 N.R. 241, (sub nom. *Rizzo & Rizzo Shoes Ltd. (Bankrupt), Re)* 106 O.A.C. 1, (sub nom. *Adrien v. Ontario Ministry of Labour)* 98 C.L.L.C. 210-006 at para. 21 (S.C.C.). Analysis must focus on the words of the relevant statutory provisions, read in their entire context and interpreted harmoniously with the scheme and the object of the *Act* and with the legislature's intention.

Grover v. Canada (Attorney General), 2011 ONSC 4025, 2011 CarswellOnt 5692 (Ont. Master), Master MacLeod.

A civil action for a remedy under the Canadian *Charter of Rights and Freedoms* is not precluded by proceedings before a human rights tribunal or a labour relations board.

Dennis v. Gray, 2011 ONSC 1567, 2011 CarswellOnt 1757, 105 O.R. (3d) 546, 333 D.L.R. (4th) 376 (Ont. S.C.J.), Hoy J.

The defendants brought a motion for an order dismissing an action against them by the plaintiffs. The motion was dismissed. It was not plain and obvious that the plaintiffs' action was certain to fail. The plaintiffs' claim was novel and raised policy issues.

Beaman v. Renwick, 2011 BCPC 70, 2011 CarswellBC 737 (B.C. Prov. Ct.), J. O'C. Wingham Prov. J.

The provincial court had jurisdiction to hear a nuisance claim despite the possible need for injunctive relief.

Pictou Landing Indian Band v. Clark, 2011 NSSC 270, 2011 CarswellNS 491, (sub nom. *Clark v. Pictou Landing Indian Band)* 305 N.S.R. (2d) 297, (sub nom. *Clark v. Pictou Landing Indian Band)* 966 A.P.R. 297 (N.S. S.C.), Justice C. Richard Coughlan.

The Small Claims Court jurisdiction is limited to those matters set out in its enabling legislation.

> Section 9(a): seeking a monetary award in respect of a matter or thing arising under a contract or a tort where the claim does not exceed twenty-five thousand dollars inclusive of any claim for general damages but exclusive of interest.

Clark submitted that a breach of fiduciary duty and a breach of trust are torts and, therefore, within the Small Claims Court jurisdiction.

She referred to *Canada Building Materials Co. v. Olser Paving & Construction Ltd. (Trustee of)*, 2009 CarswellOnt 926, 95 O.R. (3d) 448, 80 C.L.R. (3d) 295 (Ont. Master), although in that case Master Dash found at para. 43:

> I am of the view however., that the breach of trust under the *Construction Lien Act* allegedly committed by the defendants was not a tort, but is rather that field of "legal liability calling for demarcation from tort" as described by Fleming as liability based on "restitution of unintended benefits so as to prevent unjust enrichment." . . ..

Incest constitutes not only a tort, but is also a breach of the fiduciary relationship between parent and child. LaForest, J., in giving the majority judgment in *M. (K.) v. M. (H.)*, 1992 CarswellOnt 998, 1992 CarswellOnt 841, EYB 1992-67549, [1992] S.C.J. No. 85, *(sub nom. M. c. M.)* [1992] 3 S.C.R. 6, 142 N.R. 321, 96 D.L.R. (4th) 289, 57 O.A.C. 321, 14 C.C.L.T. (2d) 1 (S.C.C.), indicated the distinction between tort and fiduciary duty. A breach of fiduciary duty or breach of trust are breaches of equitable duties, not torts.

Claims, not being under a contract or a tort but rather pursuant to equitable claims of breach of trust and/or breach of fiduciary duty, are not within the jurisdiction of Small Claims Court. The appeal was allowed.

Chrysler Financial Services Canada Inc. v. Misner, 2012 ONSC 4609, 2012 CarswellOnt 9805, 19 P.P.S.A.C. (3d) 246 (Ont. S.C.J.), Healey J.

Appeal by Chrysler Financial (the "appellant") from the Judgment of Small Claims Court on July 29, 2011. Appellant's claim was dismissed on basis of the lack of jurisdiction in the Small Claims Court to grant relief under *Part V* of the *Personal Property Security Act*, R.S.O. c. P.10 (the "PPSA").

The test for introducing fresh evidence on appeal was reviewed by Bellamy J. in *Dew Point Insulation Systems Inc. v. JV Mechanical Ltd.*, 2009 CarswellOnt 8064, 87 C.L.R. (3d) 138, 84 C.P.C. (6th) 297, 259 O.A.C. 179, [2009] O.J. No. 5446 (Ont. Div. Ct.), where at para. 16 he adopted what is referred to as the "*Palmer* test" as being as an appropriate test to apply in civil matters, it having been adopted by both the Court of Appeal and the Divisional Court in the cases reviewed by him. The *Palmer* test is a four-part test articulated in *R. v. Palmer* (1979), 1979 CarswellBC 533, 1979 CarswellBC 541, [1980] 1 S.C.R. 759, 50 C.C.C. (2d) 193, 14 C.R. (3d) 22, 17 C.R. (3d) 34 (Fr.), 106 D.L.R. (3d) 212, 30 N.R. 181, [1979] S.C.J. No. 126 (S.C.C.).

The evidence could not have been adduced at trial through due diligence because the respondent gave no prior notice to the appellant that he was challenging the sale on this technical ground, and so the appellant had not included the Notice of Sale in its documentary disclosure in advance of trial.

Deputy Judge identified sections 57(2), 56(4), 56(6), and 57(2) as provisions within the *PPSA* that could give the Small Claims Court jurisdiction as each of those provisions refers to a "court of competent jurisdiction".

Section 22(1) of the *Courts of Justice Act* provides:

> 22. (1) the Small Claims Court is continued as a branch of the Superior Court of Justice under the name Small Claims Court in English and Cour des petites creances in French.

In *Luo v. Canada (Attorney General)*, 1997 CarswellOnt 1577, 33 O.R. (3d) 300, 28 C.C.E.L. (2d) 304, 9 C.P.C. (4th) 343, 145 D.L.R. (4th) 457 (Ont. Div. Ct.) it was held that reference to the Superior Court in s.21(1) of the *Crown Liability and Proceedings Act* included the Small Claims Court. Similarly, in *Laurentide Cabinet Corp. v. Beyond Flooring*, 2010 ONSC 3609, 2010 CarswellOnt 5553, 86 C.P.R. (4th) 303, 323 D.L.R. (4th) 475 (Ont. Div. Ct.), the Divisional Court held that the Small Claims Court was a branch of the Superior Court of Justice and therefore had authority to adjudicate on a claim arising under s. 52 of the *Canadian Trade-marks Act*.

As stated by the court in *Laurentide*, at para. 15:

> This is consistent with the purpose of the Small Claims Court to improve access to justice and alleviate the burden on the courts, and on the parties, by enabling parties to bring forward claim, as was done here, in person, quickly and expeditiously and at little cost. . . ..

Left unexamined, the ruling of the Deputy Judge would require every litigant in Ontario to attend in the Superior Court of Justice to request relief on any claim or defence that requires adjudication on the procedure or rights established by *Part V* of the *PPSA*. Particularly for financing companies, the increased costs associated with proceedings in the Superior Court of Justice, as opposed to the Small Claims Court, will impose a significant financial burden.

Accordingly, appeal allowed and judgment shall issue to the appellant.

Ellins v. McDonald, 2012 ONSC 4831, 2012 CarswellOnt 12001 (Ont. Div. Ct.).

The applicants seek judicial review of a decision of the Small Claims Court which stayed the action in order to permit the Ontario Labour Relations Board (the OLRB) to determine whether it has jurisdiction to deal with this dispute.

The claim in the Small Claims Court was brought after the Respondents cancelled the health and welfare benefits of the individual applicants and refused to reimburse them.

Court has jurisdiction to review decisions of the Small Claims Court including interlocutory orders (see *Peck v. Residential Property Management Inc.*, 2009 CarswellOnt 4330, [2009] O.J. No. 3064 (Ont. Div. Ct.)).

Small Claims Court judge had jurisdiction to make the Order he did and that there is no suggestion it offended principles of natural justice. Matter should be first brought to the attention of the OLRB. The OLRB should be given the opportunity of determining whether indeed it has jurisdiction in this case.

This application is dismissed.

Lahrkamp v. Metropolitan Toronto Condominium Corp. No. 932, 2012 ONSC 6326, 2012 CarswellOnt 15878, 300 O.A.C. 323, Lederer J. (Ont. Div. Ct.)

The appellant sought election as a candidate to the Board of Directors of the corporation. The appellant was not elected. The appellant brought an action in the Small Claims Court for an order requiring their production (see: *Condominium Act, 1998, supra*, at s. 55(10)).

A Small Claims Court trial was conducted over the course of three days. Justice Godfrey, the presiding judge, issued reasons and a judgment on October 29, 2010. The judge ordered that the proxies and ballots used in the election, as well as other records of the corporation be produced to the appellant.

It was said on behalf of the corporation that this Court has no jurisdiction to consider this appeal.

The problem is that the original judgment is not the order from which an appeal is now being taken. The Notice of Appeal makes clear that the order being appealed is the one which varied the trial judgment to allow for the redaction of the proxies. This order makes no reference to any amount of money, other than costs, which are specifically excluded from any consideration of jurisdiction for an appeal.

Insofar as it applies here, substance is given to this direction by Rule 15.01(6) of the *Small Claims Court Rules* which provides that motions can be made after judgment has been signed. This is added to by Rule 1.04 of the *Small Claims Court Rules* which, contrary to the submissions of counsel on behalf of the appellant, makes clear that the Small Claims Court can impose conditions on the orders which it makes. Even if this were not so, Rule 1.03(2) provides that where the *Small Claims Court Rules* do not adequately cover a matter, if the court considers it appropriate, it may consider it by reference the *Rules of Civil Procedure*.

This would include reference to Rule 59.06 of the *Rules of Civil Procedure* which deals with "amending, setting aside or varying" orders.

Court without jurisdiction to deal with this appeal. The order appealed from is essentially a procedural matter meant to clarify the judgment which had been made and from which no appeal was taken.

The Small Claims Court judge had the jurisdiction to clarify the order. There is no reason why the clarification should be set aside.

For oral reasons delivered, the appeal is dismissed.

On this basis costs would be $5,432.38. As a matter of policy, the *Condominium Act, 1998* suggests that condominium corporations should not be put to unnecessary expense. In effect these applications are lawsuits among owners of, in part, a shared asset.

On the other hand, disputes do arise and sometimes have to come to court. Costs to the respondent in the amount of $7,932.38.

Giannaris v. Toronto (City), 2012 ONSC 5183, 2012 CarswellOnt 11747, [2012] O.J. No. 4460, Lax J. (Ont. Div. Ct.)

The appellant, Mr. Giannaris, has been involved in an ongoing dispute with the City of Toronto regarding his property taxes for his property in the City of Toronto at 983 Pape Avenue.

Giannaris wants Court to declare that his calculation is the correct one but Thomson J. correctly found that the Small Claims Court has no jurisdiction to issue a declaratory order.

The *Assessment Act*, the *Municipal Acts* and/or the *City of Toronto Act, 2006* form a comprehensive code for property assessment and taxation. This legislative scheme contains numerous appeal provisions by which a taxpayer can seek to correct errors or pursue property tax or refunds or other relief. None of these are through a claim at Small Claims Court. The equitable doctrine of unjust enrichment is ousted by this comprehensive statutory scheme. See *Zaidan Group Ltd. v. London (City)*, 1990 CarswellOnt 474, 71 O.R. (2d) 65, 64 D.L.R. (4th) 514, 35 E.T.R. 162, 47 M.P.L.R. 1, 36 O.A.C. 384, [1990] O.J. No. 33 (Ont. C.A.) at para. 3; ; affirmed 1991 CarswellOnt 550, 1991 CarswellOnt 1030, EYB 1991-67634, [1991] 3 S.C.R. 593, 5 O.R. (3d) 384, 85 D.L.R. (4th) 448, 44 E.T.R. 193, 7 M.P.L.R. (2d) 235, 129 N.R. 227, 50 O.A.C. 1, [1991] S.C.J. No. 92 (S.C.C.), see also *Alcorn v. Bayham (Municipality)*, 2002 CarswellOnt 3809, 33 M.P.L.R. (3d) 132, 166 O.A.C. 78, [2002] O.J. No. 4288 (Ont. Div. Ct.).

Appeal dismissed.

Collett v. Reliance Home Comfort Limited Partnership, 2012 ONCA 822, 2012 CarswellOnt 14921 (Ont. C.A.), Gillese J.A.; leave to appeal refused 2013 CarswellOnt 4860, 2013 CarswellOnt 4861, [2013] S.C.C.A. No. 38 (S.C.C.).

This appeal, like the companion case of *Szilvasy v. Reliance Home Comfort Limited Partnership*, 2012 ONCA 821, 2012 CarswellOnt 14920, 299 O.A.C. 119, [2012] O.J. No. 5555 (Ont. C.A.); leave to appeal refused 2013 CarswellOnt 4858, 2013 CarswellOnt 4859 (S.C.C.) (*Szilvasy*), involves the application of s. 9(2) of the *Consumer Protection Act, 2002*, S.O. 2002, c. 30, Schedule A (the *CPA*) to the rental of a hot water heater.

The Colletts brought a subrogated claim in Small Claims Court for the property damages arising from the leak. They succeeded at trial and were awarded damages in the amount of $3,994.15, plus disbursements, costs and interest.

Reliance's appeal to the Divisional Court was dismissed.

The factual differences between this case and *Szilvasy* do not affect the outcome. For the reasons given in *Szilvasy*, this appeal must fail.

Arshinoff c. Warner, 2012 QCCQ 5769 (Que. Sm. Cl. Ct.), Suzanne Handman, J.C.Q.

The Court of Quebec, Small Claims Division only has jurisdiction if Defendant is domiciled in Quebec, has a residence or establishment in this province or if the contract was formed in Quebec or if the cause of action arose in Quebec (article 958 of the Code of civil procedure).

Defendant is not domiciled in Quebec; he has no residence or establishment in this province.

In light of the evidence, the Court concludes that the contract was formed in Ontario, where Defendant received Plaintiff's acceptance.

In sum, the formation of the contract and the cause of action took place in Ontario, which is the Defendant's domicile and residence and the place where he has an establishment. Quebec does not have competence over the present action or cross demand. Plaintiff must therefore institute his action in Ontario.

Cooper v. Advanced Glazing Technologies Ltd., 2012 NSSM 2, 2012 CarswellNS 5 (N.S. Sm. Cl. Ct.), Adjudicator: David TR Parker.

This matter came before the Small Claims Court on a preliminary matter whether or not court had jurisdiction in this particular case to hear the taxation.

The Small Claims Court has jurisdiction to hear taxation matters that pertain to equitable notions, including breaches of conduct by solicitors related to their fiduciary duties to the client.

There are two overriding concerns that are to be dealt with in a taxation of Solicitor's account. So the most expeditious route would be to have the statements of account taxed by that court if the court decides in favour of the respondent in The Supreme Court Action. Of course the Supreme Court of Nova Scotia can always send it back to the Small Claims Court here for taxation if it so chooses and of course if the Solicitor's account as lawful.

Taxation stayed.

R. v. Blackwood, 2010 ONSC 2202, 2010 CarswellOnt 2554, [2010] O.J. No. 1736 (Ont. S.C.J.)

Applicant sought order that court recuse itself and declare mistrial because of a reasonable apprehension of bias. The test set out in the dissenting reasons of de Grandpre J. in *Committee for Justice & Liberty v. Canada (National Energy Board)* (1976), 1976 CarswellNat 434, 1976 CarswellNat 434F, [1978] 1 S.C.R. 369, 68 D.L.R. (3d) 716, 9 N.R. 115, [1976] A.C.S. No. 118, [1976] S.C.J. No. 118 (S.C.C.).) and thereafter adopted in (*R. v. S. (R.D.)*, 1997 CarswellNS 301, 1997 CarswellNS 302, [1997] 3 S.C.R. 484, 161 N.S.R. (2d) 241, 1 Admin. L.R. (3d) 74, 118 C.C.C. (3d) 353, 10 C.R. (5th) 1, 151 D.L.R. (4th) 193, 477 A.P.R. 241, 218 N.R. 1, [1997] S.C.J. No. 84 (S.C.C.) at para. 31):

> The apprehension of bias must be a reasonable one, held by reasonable and right-minded persons, applying themselves to the question and obtaining thereon the required information . . .
> The test is "what would an informed person, viewing the matter realistically and practically —
> and having thought the matter through — conclude."

Roberts v. R. (2003), 2003 SCC 45, 2003 CarswellNat 2822, 2003 CarswellNat 2823, REJB 2003-47809, (sub nom. *Wewayakum Indian Band v. Canada*) [2003] 2 S.C.R. 259, 7 Admin. L.R. (4th) 1, 19 B.C.L.R. (4th) 195, 40 C.P.C. (5th) 1, 231 D.L.R. (4th) 1, [2004] 2 W.W.R. 1, (sub nom. *Wewaykum Indian Band v. Canada*) [2004] 1 C.N.L.R. 342, (sub nom. *Wewayakum Indian Band v. Canada*) 309 N.R. 201, (sub nom. *Wewayakum Indian Band v. Canada*) [2003] S.C.J. No. 50 (S.C.C.). and *Taylor Ventures Ltd. (Trustee of) v. Taylor*, 2005 BCCA 350, 2005 CarswellBC 1499, 49 B.C.L.R. (4th) 134, 214 B.C.A.C. 7, 353 W.A.C. 7, [2005] B.C.J. No. 1380 (B.C. C.A.) at para. 7 and *Makowsky v. John Doe*, 2007 BCSC 1231, 2007 CarswellBC 1874, [2007] B.C.J. No. 1809 (B.C. S.C.) at paras. 14 and 18; ; affirmed 2008 BCCA 112, 2008 CarswellBC 652, [2008] B.C.J. No. 576 (B.C. C.A.)) the following principles were enunciated:

    i. a judge's impartiality is presumed;

ii. a party arguing for disqualification must establish that the circumstances justify a finding that the judge must be disqualified;

iii. the criterion of disqualification is the reasonable apprehension of bias;

iv. the question is what would an informed, reasonable and right minded person, reviewing the matter realistically and practically and having thought the matter through, conclude;

v. the test for disqualification is not satisfied unless it is proved that the informed, reasonable and right minded person would think that it is more likely than not that the judge, whether consciously or unconsciously, would not decide fairly;

vi. the test requires demonstration of serious grounds on which to base the apprehension; and

vii. each case must be examined contextually and the inquiry is fact specific.

In *R. v. H. (G)[26]*, 2002 CarswellOnt 3080, 165 O.A.C. 56, [2002] O.J. No. 3635 (Ont. C.A.) at para. 6.), the court held that, "Trial judges are constantly called upon to assess credibility in making rulings on pre-trial motions and *voir dires* during the trial. It is a necessary and accepted part of the judicial role and of the administration of justice that those conclusions will not impermissibly flow through to the trial proper."

2146100 Ontario Ltd. v. 2052750 Ontario Inc., 2013 ONSC 2483, 2013 CarswellOnt 5148, 115 O.R. (3d) 636, 308 O.A.C. 8, Boswell, J. (Ont. Div. Ct.).

Trial judge in Small Claims Court action finding that plaintiff owed defendant amount in excess of court's monetary jurisdiction of $25, 000 and that defendant owed plaintiff lesser amount. Trial judge setting those amounts off and awarding judgment to defendant in amount of $21, 538.85. Trial judge not exceeding monetary jurisdiction of Small Claims Court Monetary limits being restriction on amount of recoverable by judgment and not on reasoning process utilized to arrive at that amount.The jurisdiction of the Small Claims Court is established by s. 23 of the *Courts of Justice Act*, R.S.O. 1990, c. C.43, which provides, in part, as follows:

> 23. (1) The Small Claims Court,
>
> > (a) has jurisdiction in any action for the payment of money where the amount claimed does not exceed the prescribed amount exclusive of interest and costs.

The prescribed amount referred to in s. 23(1)(a) is currently $25,000, in accordance with O. Reg. 626/00 (*Courts of Justice Act*). Section 1 of the Regulation provides as follows:

> 1. (1) The maximum amount of a claim in the Small Claims Court is $25,000.
>
> (2) The maximum amount of a claim over which a deputy judge may preside is $25,000.

Lippa v. R., 2013 ONSC 4424, 2013 CarswellOnt 8884, (sub nom. *R. v. Lippa)* 116 O.R. (3d) 354, (sub nom. *R. v. Lippa)* 289 C.R.R. (2d) 301, Fuerst, J. (Ont. S.C.J.)

Application, brought by paralegal Marian Lippa, sought reconsideration of an order in which the court called matters. Lippa took issue with a judicial officer's order to hear matters brought by senior counsel before those of paralegals.

"The order about the manner in which cases would be called in court did not impinge on Ms. Lippa's life, liberty or security of the person. It may have impinged on her economic interest, but that is not an interest protected by s.7", wrote Fuerst.

The justice of the peace was not exceeding her jurisdiction or breaching principles of fundamental justice in ordering that licensed paralegals remain behind bar in the courtroom until their cases were called or in directing the Crown to call cases involving lawyers ahead of those involving paralegals.

Application dismissed.

Determining where individuals sit in a courtroom falls within the jurisdiction of a judicial officer to maintain order in the courtroom and the dignity of the proceedings.

The *Barristers Act*, R.S.O. 1990, c. B.3 does not explicitly require the Crown to give precedence to senior counsel. Because the *Act* refers to "members of the bar", it necessarily excludes licensed paralegals from its application. The *Act* does not prevent a judicial officer from controlling the process in his or her own court.

Canada (Attorney General) v. Khawaja (2007), 2007 CF 490, 2007 FC 490, 2007 CarswellNat 1129, 2007 CarswellNat 2337, [2008] 1 F.C.R. 547, 312 F.T.R. 217 (Eng.), 219 C.C.C. (3d) 305, 47 C.R. (6th) 346, [2007] F.C.J. No. 622 (F.C.); reversed 2007 CAF 342, 2007 FCA 342, 2007 CarswellNat 3603, 2007 CarswellNat 5652, 228 C.C.C. (3d) 1, 52 C.R. (6th) 107, 370 N.R. 128, [2007] F.C.J. No. 1473 (F.C.A.)

The *ex parte* affidavits filed with the Court identify and categorize in detail the nature of the risks of injury claimed by the Attorney General with specific reference to [. . .] In a small claims action its importance might not easily prevail over that of the public interest in national security or international relations.

Matteau v. Johnson, 2012 ONSC 1179, 2012 CarswellOnt 2216, [2012] O.J. No. 763, Wilcox, J. (Ont. S.C.J.)

The Respondent appealed from order of Deputy Judge.

The claim was for payment of moneys allegedly owed by the Appellant to the Respondent under an oral agreement between them, together with some living expense debts. The Appellant's defence was based solely on procedural grounds.

In *Hodgins v. Grover*, 2011 ONCA 72, 2011 CarswellOnt 336, (sub nom. *Grover v. Hodgins*) 103 O.R. (3d) 721, 5 C.P.C. (7th) 33, (sub nom. *Grover v. Hodgins*) 330 D.L.R. (4th) 712, (sub nom. *Grover v. Hodgins*) 275 O.A.C. 96, [2011] O.J. No. 310 (Ont. C.A.); leave to appeal refused (2012), 2012 CarswellOnt 825, 2012 CarswellOnt 826, 432 N.R. 392 (note), (sub nom. *Grover v. Hodgins*) 295 O.A.C. 398 (note), [2011] S.C.C.A. No. 142 (S.C.C.), a decision of the Court of Appeal for Ontario dated January 27, 2011, Epstein J. A., writing for the court, after a lengthy analysis concluded that the Small Claims Court does have jurisdiction to award legal or equitable relief where the relief requested is a monetary payment under the limit of $25,000 or the return of personal property valued within that limit. The claim discloses a common law cause of action. The claim could be characterized as one based in contract for the repayment of moneys lent. The Respondent appears to have waived the excess in order to bring the claim within the monetary jurisdiction of the Small Claims Court. The appeal is dismissed.

Ellins v. McDonald, 2012 ONSC 4831, 2012 CarswellOnt 12001, [2012] O.J. No. 4556 (Ont. Div. Ct.).

The applicants seek judicial review of a decision of the Small Claims Court which stayed the action in order to permit the Ontario Labour Relations Board (the OLRB) to determine whether it has jurisdiction to deal with this dispute. The claim in the Small Claims Court was brought after the Respondents cancelled the health and welfare benefits of the individual applicants and refused to reimburse them.

We have jurisdiction to review decisions of the Small Claims Court including interlocutory orders (see *Peck v. Residential Property Management Inc.*, 2009 CarswellOnt 4330, [2009] O.J. No. 3064 (Ont. Div. Ct.)). The Small Claims Court judge had jurisdiction to make the Order he did and there is no suggestion that it offended principles of natural justice. This matter should be first brought to the attention of the OLRB, the body with exclusive jurisdiction to hear labour relations issues.

Application dismissed.

Grimaldi v. Bomben Plumbing & Heating Ltd., 2013 HRTO 1935 (Ont. Human Rights Trib.).

Application filed on October 1, 2013 under section 34 of Part IV of the *Human Rights Code*, R.S.O. 1990, c. H.19. The applicant states that there is a court action based on the same facts as the Application although no remedy is sought based on the discrimination. Section 45 of the *Code* confirms the Tribunal's authority to defer consideration of an application. A deferral to Small Claims Court action was appropriate.

Hasselsjo v. CBI Home Health Care, 2013 ONSC 2684, 2013 CarswellOnt 5630, Nightingale, J. (Ont. S.C.J.) — The Deputy Judge found that as the consolidated claim exceeded the monetary jurisdiction, the Small Claims Court had no jurisdiction pursuant to Section 23(1) of the *Courts of Justice Act*. He accordingly dismissed the consolidated claim. The appellant advised the Court that she has since commenced an action in the Superior Court of Justice for the same relief against the same defendants. The Deputy Judge made an order that the appellant pay the respondents' fees of $1000 with a brief endorsement "which I consider special circumstances at $1000" and then referred to Rule 13.05[1] and [2] of the *Small Claims Court Rules*, which the latter subrule included his authority to make an order regarding costs after dismissing an action.

The order for costs was the subject matter of the appellant's application for a leave to appeal under Section 133 of the *Courts of Justice Act*. Leave to appeal a costs order should be sparingly granted and only if there has been an error in principle or if the costs award is clearly wrong. Proposed appeal should raise issue of some importance to the administration of justice that goes beyond interest of parties, *Bougadis Chang LLP v. 1231238 Ontario Inc.*, 2012 ONSC 6409, 2012 CarswellOnt 14490, 300 O.A.C. 363, [2012] O.J. No. 5433 (Ont. Div. Ct.); *Gale v. Gale*, 2006 CarswellOnt 6263, [2006] O.J. No. 4121 (Ont. Div. Ct.). The appellant's application for a leave to appeal was dismissed.

Inside Outside Home Services Inc. v. Einstein Design, 2013 ONSC 2753, 2013 CarswellOnt 5946, Van Melle, J. (Ont. S.C.J.)

Defendant submits allegations in Claim that demonstrate damages sought totaled $28,013 inclusive of GST and plaintiff should have given up the small amount by which quantum exceeded Small Claims Court jurisdiction of $25,000. The plaintiff was not obliged to forgo amount over $25,000. However, the fact that the judgment was within the jurisdiction of the Small Claims Court is relevant. It is the amount recovered, not the amount claimed that is relevant. The plaintiff was successful at trial and thus was entitled to a portion of its costs and was successful in obtaining more than the defendant's offer at trail. The lien was valid. The plaintiff was justified in proceeding in the Superior Court. The appropriate amount for costs inclusive is $5000.

Raymond v. Royal & Sun Alliance Insurance Co. of Canada, 2014 NSCA 13, 2014 CarswellNS 72, 340 N.S.R. (2d) 290, 50 C.P.C. (7th) 57, 1077 A.P.R. 290, Bryson, J.A. (N.S. C.A.)

Trial judge could not make award for amounts in the future as they had not yet arisen. "All claims" must be read as confined to existing causes of action. Decisions disallowing disability claims in the Small Claims Court were clearly distinguishable, based on statutory and procedural differences. The Small Claims Court cases are distinguishable.

(2) Transfer from Superior Court of Justice — **An action in the Superior Court of Justice may be transferred to the Small Claims Court by the local registrar of the Superior Court of Justice on requisition with the consent of all parties filed before the trial commences if,**

    (a) the only claim is for the payment of money or the recovery of possession of personal property; and

(b) the claim is within the jurisdiction of the Small Claims Court.

Commentary: Most proceedings in the Small Claims Court are started and completed in that court. From time to time cases may be transferred either from the Superior Court of Justice to the Small Claims Court, or *vice versa*. The various potential means by which transfer may be accomplished are reviewed below.

Consent Transfer from the Superior Court of Justice to the Small Claims Court

Where the parties, on consent, wish to transfer a case from the Superior Court of Justice to the Small Claims Court, this can be accomplished on an over-the-counter basis, without a judge's order. *Courts of Justice Act* section 23(2) provides for such transfers, on consent, so long as the relief requested in the statement of claim (and counterclaim if any) is for the payment of money or the recovery of possession of personal property, and is within the monetary jurisdiction of the Small Claims Court.

If the damages claimed exceed $25,000 and a transfer to the Small Claims Court is desired, the claim must first be amended down to $25,000, and transfer under section 23(2) may be requisitioned after the amendment is effected. In cases involving claims for the return of possession of personal property, the value of the property cannot exceed $25,000. Any claims for declaratory, injunctive, or other relief which the Small Claims Court cannot grant are disqualified from transfer and should be deleted by amendment prior to transfer under section 23(2).

Consent transfer under section 23(2) therefore involves a simple procedure, by requisition, subject only to the possible need for amendment to the relief requested prior to transfer. There is currently a court fee of $75 to transfer a court file.

There is no requirement to convert the pleadings in an action which is transferred from the Superior Court of Justice to the Small Claims Court into the forms used in that court. Transferred cases simply carry on using the pleadings filed in the Superior Court of Justice, unless an amendment is needed for some reason other than the transfer.

Transfer by Order of the Superior Court of Justice to the Small Claims Court

An action in the Superior Court of Justice may in some circumstances be transferred to the Small Claims Court by order of a judge of the Superior Court of Justice. A judge of the Small Claims Court has no jurisdiction to transfer an action from the Superior Court of Justice to the Small Claims Court.

Where an action in the Superior Court of Justice involves a claim that is within the jurisdiction of the Small Claims Court, or that is amended to come within that jurisdiction, it may be ordered transferred to the Small Claims Court. As discussed below, such a transfer could raise the question of costs incurred prior to transfer.

It should be noted that the civil justice reforms in force January 1, 2010 make no provision for the automatic transfer of proceedings in the Superior Court of Justice which are pending at that date and in which the relief claimed falls within the increased jurisdiction of the Small Claims Court. Such actions remain in the Superior Court of Justice unless transferred either by the parties on consent under section 23(2), or by order of a judge of the Superior Court of Justice.

A transfer order may be made at a pretrial conference. In *Shoppers Trust Co. v. Mann Taxi Management Ltd.*, 1993 CarswellOnt 437, 16 O.R. (3d) 192, 19 C.P.C. (3d) 7 (Ont. Gen. Div.), it was held that a judge of the Ontario Court (General Division) has an inherent jurisdiction to transfer to the Small Claims Court a case that is within that court's monetary jurisdiction. A pretrial conference judge transferred a case involving a claim for damages of $3,239 to the Small Claims Court, where the pretrial conference took place after the monetary jurisdiction of the Small Claims Court was increased from $3,000 to $6,000. The decision did not address the matter of costs.

Similarly, in *Graves v. Avis Rent A Car System Inc.*, 1993 CarswellOnt 472, [1993] O.J. No. 2771, 21 C.P.C. (3d) 391 (Ont. Gen. Div.), the claim in the Ontario Court (General Division) was for damages that fell within the monetary jurisdiction of the Small Claims Court after that jurisdiction was increased. After the defendant refused consent under section 23(2), on motion by the plaintiff the action was transferred to the Small Claims Court. The judge reserved the issue of costs to date to be determined by the trial judge.

The situation was different in *McGinty v. Toronto Transit Commission*, 1996 CarswellOnt 288, [1996] O.J. No. 320 (Ont. Div. Ct.). In that case, a pretrial judge of the Ontario Court (General Division) transferred an action to the Small Claims Court based on his expectation that the damages, although pleaded in excess of that court's monetary jurisdiction, would not in fact exceed that amount. The plaintiff had not abandoned the amount of damages in excess of the monetary jurisdiction of the Small Claims Court. Leave to appeal that transfer order to the Divisional Court was granted.

A transfer order in the circumstances of *McGinty, supra*, where the plaintiff does not abandon the damages claimed in excess of the monetary jurisdiction of the Small Claims Court, represents an error of jurisdiction. Since the excess damages amount was not abandoned, the Small Claims Court would have no jurisdiction to hear the case: see *Helsberg v. Sutton Group Achievers's Realty Inc.*, 2002 CarswellOnt 4640, [2002] O.J. No. 2311, 165 O.A.C. 122 (Ont. Div. Ct.), holding that the Small Claims Court has no jurisdiction to hear a claim for an amount exceeding its monetary jurisdiction, even if the amount actually awarded falls within that monetary jurisdiction.

It may be inappropriate to transfer a case to the Small Claims Court after the proceedings are sufficiently underway, as was recently held in *Capano v. Rahm*, 2010 ONSC 3241, 2010 CarswellOnt 4760, [2010] O.J. No. 2866 (Ont. S.C.J.); additional reasons at 2010 ONSC 4131, 2010 CarswellOnt 6013 (Ont. S.C.J.); leave to appeal refused 2010 CarswellOnt 7425 (Ont. Div. Ct.). On the other hand, the transfer may be granted on terms such as payment by the plaintiff of the costs of steps taken in the Superior Court of Justice which would not have been required in the Small Claims Court: *Ali v. Schrauwen*, 2011 ONSC 2158, 2011 CarswellOnt 3201, 18 C.P.C. (7th) 425, [2011] O.J. No. 1671 (Ont. Master). It should be noted that the matter of costs to date in the Superior Court of Justice, where a case is transferred to the Small Claims Court, cannot be reserved to the trial judge in the Small Claims Court: *Pietrangelo v. Lundrigan*, 1999 CarswellOnt 3062, 44 O.R. (3d) 71, 43 C.P.C. (4th) 157 (Ont. Div. Ct.). The costs to date should be addressed, if they are in issue, at the time of transfer from the Superior Court of Justice. Such costs could be reserved for later determination on motion to the Superior Court of Justice, after the matter has proceeded to judgment in the Small Claims Court.

With the increase to the monetary jurisdiction of the Small Claims Court to $25,000, more cases in the Superior Court of Justice will produce the situation where transfer to the Small Claims Court is desired — often when the plaintiff determines, after the case has started, that the damages claim can be reduced to $25,000 or less. Unless transfer is agreed between the parties, a motion to a judge or master of the Superior Court of Justice will be required to address whether a transfer should be ordered, and if so on what terms. Each case will be determined based on its own circumstances.

Transfer from the Small Claims Court to the Superior Court of Justice

In unusual cases, a plaintiff who has commenced a claim in the Small Claims Court could later decide to increase the damages claimed to an amount which exceeds the monetary jurisdiction of that court. In those situations, the plaintiff should bring a motion to a judge of the Superior Court of Justice asking for both the amendment and a transfer to that court. That judge could at the same time address any incidental question of costs incurred to date in the

Small Claims Court, or other procedural points arising from the proposed transfer such as the form of pleadings, discovery, and the future course of the proceeding.

On the other hand, occasionally claims are started in Small Claims Court even though the damages claimed exceed $25,000. Such actions may be ordered transferred to the Superior Court of Justice under section 110 of the *Courts of Justice Act*, on the basis that they are in the wrong court. However it should be noted that the Small Claims Court is not the "wrong court" within the meaning of section 110 where the amount of damages alleged exceeds the monetary jurisdiction, but the amount actually claimed is within the monetary jurisdiction: *Alexandrov v. Csanyi*, 2009 CarswellOnt 1325, 247 O.A.C. 228 (Ont. Div. Ct.).

Exemption from Small Claims Court

There have been a small number of decisions in which cases are transferred from the Small Claims Court to the Superior Court of Justice even though the amount claimed falls within the monetary jurisdiction of the Small Claims Court. Such cases usually involve defence arguments that the issues are sufficiently complex that to proceed without discoveries would be inappropriate. Often the defendants proposing such transfers are represented by counsel and the plaintiffs responding to such a proposal are self-represented and have made a decision to proceed in the Small Claims Court.

Orders transferring actions in these situations are more accurately described as exemption orders rather than transfer orders. It is submitted that the availability of such exemption orders as a matter of law is debatable. However the existing caselaw endorses the availability of exemption orders in exceptional cases.

In *Vigna v. Toronto Stock Exchange*, 1998 CarswellOnt 4560, [1998] O.J. No. 4924, 115 O.A.C. 393, 28 C.P.C. (4th) 318 (Ont. Div. Ct.); reversing 1997 CarswellOnt 4515, 155 D.L.R. (4th) 504, 18 C.P.C. (4th) 170 (Ont. Gen. Div.), the Divisional Court was satisfied that a judge of the Ontario Court (General Division) had a discretion, in rare cases, to transfer an action from the Small Claims Court without the plaintiff's consent. The case involved complex issues arising from negligence allegations against a stock exchange. There were six related actions in the Ontario Court (General Division), which were the subject of a pending request for certification as a class action. A motions judge had denied the requested transfer but, on appeal, the Divisional Court held that full discovery was required to "deal fairly and fully with the issues raised" and that "the summary procedures available in Small Claims Court are inappropriate for the fair and just determination of the issues raised here." The Divisional Court transferred the case to the Ontario Court (General Division) and stayed it for one year. In addition, and for essentially the same reasons which supported the transfer, the court also ordered that the action was exempted from the simplified procedure (which at the time did not permit examinations for discovery) and would proceed under the ordinary procedure, with full discovery rights.

In *Crane Canada Co. v. Montis Sorgic Associates Inc.*, [2005] O.J. No. 6247, 2005 CarswellOnt 9989 (Ont. S.C.J.); affirmed [2006] O.J. No. 1999, 2006 CarswellOnt 3051 (Ont. C.A.), a series of subrogated product liability claims all brought by one insurer were ordered transferred from the Small Claims Court to the Superior Court of Justice. The respondents on the motion conceded that transfer would be appropriate for a product liability case of sufficient complexity. The motions judge found that given the centrality and complexity of the expert evidence involved, "the claims would be more appropriately dealt with in the Superior Court." The judge declined to order that, despite the transfer, the matter would continue under the *Small Claims Court Rules*. Since the reasons do not suggest otherwise, presumably the proceedings were then subject to the simplified procedure, which at the time provided for document discovery but no examinations for discovery.

In a very brief endorsement, the Court of Appeal upheld that order, finding that it was "a proper exercise of discretion that should be rarely exercised." However the Court of Appeal felt that the key factor was "that all the claims are subrogated claims brought by one insurer." It therefore appears that while the motions judge's decision turned on factual and evidentiary complexity, the Court of Appeal upheld the result based on judicial economy, while emphasizing that such transfer orders should rarely be granted. The endorsement does not suggest that the existence of the discretion to exempt a case from the Small Claims Court was an issue on the appeal.

Another exemption order was recently granted in *Farlow v. Hospital for Sick Children*, 2009 CarswellOnt 7124, [2009] O.J. No. 4847, 100 O.R. (3d) 213, 83 C.P.C. (6th) 290 (Ont. S.C.J.). That was a medical malpractice claim for damages of $10,000 brought in the Small Claims Court by self-represented plaintiffs. The motions judge granted a motion by the defendants to both transfer the case to the Superior Court of Justice and exempt it from the simplified procedure. Justice Herman cited both *Vigna, supra*, and her own decision in *Crane Canada, supra*, for the proposition that transfer out of the Small Claims Court may ordered based on consideration of the complexity of the issues, the importance of expert evidence, the need for discovery, whether the case involved issues of general importance, and the desire for a just and fair determination. The transfer was ordered despite the court's acknowledgment that such a transfer raised access to justice concerns.

None of these authorities appear to have considered the effect of the repeal in 1984 of a statutory discretion to remove a case from the Small Claims Court and direct that it be tried in what was then the branch of the Supreme Court of Ontario known as the High Court of Justice. The former *Small Claims Courts Act*, R.S.O. 1980, c. 439, s. 62, provided as follows:

> 62. If it appears to a judge of the Supreme Court that an action is a fit one to be tried in the Supreme Court, he may order that it be transferred to the Supreme Court upon such terms as to payment of costs or otherwise as he thinks fit.

That provision was very rarely invoked. One such instance is the decision of Reid J. in *Livingston v. Ould*, 1976 CarswellOnt 321, [1976] O.J. No. 953, 2 C.P.C. 41 (Ont. H.C.). His Lordship granted the transfer order, finding the action in that case to be sufficiently "serious, novel and complicated" that a transfer was appropriate. In part the decision turned on the apparent reality at the time that the quality of trial transcripts used on appeals from the Small Claims Court was "frequently wanting." Reid J. found that rather than have a case of general importance proceed to trial in the Small Claims Court, followed by an appeal based on a poor-quality transcript to a single judge of the Supreme Court of Ontario (sitting as the Divisional Court), it was more expeditious to have the trial before a judge of the Supreme Court sitting as a judge of the High Court of Justice.

The result and reasoning in *Livingston v. Ould, supra*, may be contrasted with *Rajakaruna v. Air France*, 1979 CarswellOnt 430, 25 O.R. (2d) 156, 11 C.P.C. 172 (Ont. H.C.). In that case, four members of the same family each commenced actions in the Small Claims Court for damages of $1,000, being that court's monetary limit at the time. The plaintiffs each alleged negligence and breach of contract in booking or overbooking flights. The defendants moved to transfer the cases to the Supreme Court, based on the alleged complexity of the case and their desire for discovery. Grange J. (as he then was), while accepting the existence of the discretion to transfer under former section 62, denied the defendants' request, stating in part:

> ... [I]t appears to me of the utmost importance that the plaintiffs should be permitted, save in exceptional circumstances, to take their claims to the Small Claims Court when it is within the jurisdiction of that Court. I accept ... that the policy of one of permitting and even extending access to these informal Courts ...
>
> I am satisfied that to move the case to the Supreme Court without very stringent terms being imposed upon the defendants would effectively destroy the opportunity for these plaintiffs to have their day in Court and to seek redress for what they claim are the wrongs of the defend-

> ants. Counsel for the defendants have pointed out to me that the issues raised may involve very difficult considerations of law and fact and may well involve issues concerning the conflict of laws, the custom of the trade and the *Carriage by Air Act*, R.S.C. 1970, c. C-14. Certainly these would be considerations, but they are not sufficient, in my view, to justify the transfer . . .
>
> . . .
>
> Counsel have also pointed out to me that in view of the claims made, discovery would be desirable. I agree that discovery would indeed be desirable but it is not available in the Small Claims Court because of the desire to avoid formality and delay and its absence is justified because of the limitation of the amounts that can be claimed. It is also to be remembered that there is an appeal if a substantial amount should be awarded and protection is thus given to the defendants if they are, as they obviously are, worried that a dangerous legal precedent might be established.
>
> For these reasons, I would dismiss the application . . .

Based on the cases interpreting section 62, the discretion to transfer a case from the Small Claims Court to the Supreme Court of Ontario, even while that provision was in force, was reserved for only the most rare and exceptional cases. But section 62 of the *Small Claims Courts Act* was repealed by the *Courts of Justice Act, 1984*, S.O. 1984, c. 11, s. 213. The 1984 amendments to the *Courts of Justice Act* also repealed a similar provision permitting a judge of the Supreme Court of Ontario to refer a question of law directly to the Court of Appeal (*Judicature Act*, R.S.O. 1980, c. 223, s. 34): *Courts of Justice Act, 1984*, s. 187(1).

It is submitted that the repeal of former section 62 must be given meaning. If, despite that repeal, cases can nevertheless be removed from the Small Claims Court to the Superior Court of Justice, one could argue that cases can still be referred by judges of the Superior Court of Justice directly to the Court of Appeal. That is clearly not so.

Assistance is available by analogy from cases in which the use of the simplified procedure has been challenged. In *Baker v. Chrysler Canada Ltd.*, 1998 CarswellOnt 526, 38 O.R. (3d) 729, 18 C.P.C. (4th) 36, 53 O.T.C. 230 (Ont. Gen. Div.); leave to appeal refused 1998 CarswellOnt 1614, [1998] O.J. No. 1709, 112 O.A.C. 277 (Ont. Div. Ct.), the defendants moved for an order that the action commenced under the simplified procedure proceed under the ordinary procedure, based on the alleged complexity of the case. Each of the plaintiffs claimed less than the monetary limit of the simplified procedure. Justice Ellen Macdonald dismissed the motion, holding that the identical claims of 50 claims could be dealt with expeditiously and economically by a single judge. The number of plaintiffs did not displace the application of the simplified procedure.

In his reasons for denying leave to appeal in *Baker v. Chrysler Canada Ltd.*, *supra*, Farley J. observed that the monetary limit for mandatory use of the simplified procedure (which at the time was $25,000) was not defined on the basis of complexity or credibility or other reasons. Justice Farley went on to reject a submission that the superior court should relieve against the use of the simplified procedure because precluding discoveries would amount to compromising the quality of justice. Justice Farley stated in part (at para. 7):

> If [the court were to do] so, then many parties to many cases under R. 76 would want discovery. Neither do I see this as amenable to inherent jurisdiction since the Rules here are quite specific as to this present case coming under the Simplified Procedure and thus there is no gap to be filled by inherent jurisdiction . . .

To like effect is the decision of McDermid J. in *Gibbons v. York Fire & Casualty Insurance Co.*, 1997 CarswellOnt 4246, [1997] O.J. No. 4125, 47 O.T.C. 200 (Ont. Gen. Div.). The defendant argued that it would be unjust to preclude discoveries and therefore it asked that the claim be exempted from the simplified procedure. Justice McDermid was satisfied that Rule 76 showed that the drafters considered what types of actions should be excluded and that if all cases in which credibility issues were central should be excluded, the rules drafters could quite easily have said so. The motions judge continued (at para. 8):

> 8. There is no doubt that the simplified procedure removes from the arsenal of the litigants some of the traditional armament of battle. However, that is exactly what it was meant to do in the interests of expediting and reducing the cost of trials where the amount in issue is less than $25,000. In my opinion, the policy underlying the simplified procedure rules is sound and ought not to be rendered impotent by creating so many exceptions to its application that these rules are left without any force or effect.

Justice Wein made the same point in *Kurnell v. 910938 Ontario Inc.*, 2002 CarswellOnt 4524, 29 C.P.C. (5th) 311, 25 C.C.E.L. (3d) 126 (Ont. S.C.J.). In dismissing a motion by the defendant asking that the simplified procedure action proceed under the ordinary procedure, Wein J. stated (at para. 5):

> 5. It is quite clear that the policy underlying the enactment of Rule 76 is to reduce the cost of litigating claims of relatively modest sums by streamlining the procedure available in such cases. Even where issues of credibility arise or where the legal issues are complex, if the amounts are within the scope of the rule, the simplified procedure was intended to apply . . . [citations omitted]

Similarly, in *Egbeocha v. Brampton (City)*, 1998 CarswellOnt 1485, 38 O.R. (3d) 94 (Ont. Master), Master Peterson rejected an argument that a plaintiff's request to amend a claim into the simplified procedure should be denied because the defendant would be prejudiced by the resulting loss of discovery rights. The master held that the loss of discovery rights was simply a policy which had been adopted under Rule 76.

It is submitted that the reasoning in this line of cases applies with equal force to the argument that cases of a certain complexity, or in which credibility is central, may be exempted from the Small Claims Court and transferred to the Superior Court of Justice to proceed under the *Rules of Civil Procedure*. There is no legislative basis for such a discretion, and moreover a provision which provided for precisely such a discretion was repealed in 1984. The allocation of cases to the Small Claims Court is defined by the amount claimed and not by complexity or other characteristics of the particular litigation.

This position is now fortified under the *Rules of Civil Procedure* by the enhanced emphasis on proportionality and access to justice which is seen in the recent civil justice reforms, and particularly the new interpretation rule 1.04(1.1) and new Rule 29.1 — Proportionality in Discovery. There is no "legislative gap" which leaves the court a general discretion to move cases between the three legislatively-defined tiers of (non-family) civil procedure in Ontario — Small Claims Court, Simplified Procedure, and ordinary procedure: see *Baker v. Chrysler Canada, supra* (*per* Farley J.); *Kovach (Litigation Guardian of) v. Kovach*, 2010 ONCA 126, 2010 CarswellOnt 846, [2010] O.J. No. 643, 100 O.R. (3d) 608, (sub nom. *Kovach v. Kovach*) 261 O.A.C. 190, 316 D.L.R. (4th) 341, 92 M.V.R. (5th) 39, 80 C.P.C. (6th) 40 (Ont. C.A.); leave to appeal refused 2010 CarswellOnt 4831, 2010 CarswellOnt 4832, [2010] S.C.C.A. No. 165, (sub nom. *Kovach v. Kovach*) 276 O.A.C. 399 (note), (sub nom. *Kovach v. Kovach*) 409 N.R. 399 (note) (S.C.C.).

Properly understood, both *Vigna v. Toronto Stock Exchange, supra*, and the Court of Appeal's decision in *Crane Canada, supra*, turn on considerations of judicial economy rather than the competence or streamlined procedure of the Small Claims Court. It may be that in rare cases it is appropriate to order that a case in the Small Claims Court be tried along with related proceedings in the Superior Court of Justice. In such cases, the Small Claims Court proceeding would not be exempted from Small Claims Court procedure, but would simply be heard by a judge of the Superior Court of Justice presiding over that case as a judge of the Small Claims Court. That would not represent an exemption from the Small Claims Court but would simply permit a single trial judge to determine related cases where trial together is appropriate and where one of those cases happens to be a Small Claims Court case, in the interests of judicial economy.

In *Ontario Deputy Judges Assn. v. Ontario*, 2006 CarswellOnt 3137, [2006] O.J. No. 2057, 80 O.R. (3d) 481, 268 D.L.R. (4th) 86, 28 C.P.C. (6th) 1, 210 O.A.C. 94, (sub nom. *Ontario Deputy Judges' Assn. v. Ontario (Attorney General))* 141 C.R.R. (2d) 238 (Ont. C.A.), it was held that the deputy judges, although part-time, fully assume the judicial role when sitting as judges. In law, judges of all courts are presumed to be fit for office, to know the law, and to discharge their duties with reasonable skill, diligence, and competence. It would be anomalous to suggest that an entire branch of the Superior Court of Justice might be presumed unable to properly discharge its duties in cases of perceived comparative complexity. The *Courts of Justice Act* contains no such limitation on the jurisdiction of the Small Claims Court.

There is a right of appeal to protect against the possibility that particular trial judges of any court may commit occasional errors in simple and complex cases alike. It is submitted that there is no need to supplant or supplement the discipline of appellate review with a separate power to exempt particular cases from proceeding before the Small Claims Court at first instance. It is submitted that the *Vigna* line of cases, dealing with the inherent jurisdiction of the Superior Court of Justice to effectively exempt cases from the Small Claims Court, is ripe for appellate reconsideration.

Transfer Where Several Proceedings Pending

Courts of Justice Act section 107 deals with various procedural options where two or more related proceedings are pending in two or more different courts. Proceedings may be transferred to one court to be heard together or one after the other or consolidated, or a proceeding may be stayed until after another is determined, or a proceeding may be required to be asserted by way of counterclaim in another proceeding.

The scope of section 107 is limited, where a Small Claims Court proceeding is concerned. A proceeding in the Small Claims Court shall not be transferred to the Superior Court of Justice to be consolidated with or heard together with or after a proceeding in that court, without the consent of the plaintiff in the proceeding in the Small Claims Court: section 107(2). Similarly, a proceeding in the Small Claims Court shall not be required to be asserted by way of counterclaim in a proceeding in the Superior Court of Justice without the consent of the plaintiff in the proceeding in the Small Claims Court: section 107(3).

Those limitations signal a legislative intention that plaintiffs should not be forced out of the Small Claims Court if they choose to remain there despite the existence of related pending proceedings in the Superior Court of Justice. The limitations do not prevent a judge of the Superior Court of Justice from ordering that several related proceedings be heard together in the Superior Court of Justice by a judge of that court who would sit as a judge of the Small Claims Court when hearing the proceeding from that court. Such a procedure would not involve a transfer out of the Small Claims Court, since every judge of the Superior Court of Justice is also a judge of the Small Claims Court: see *Courts of Justice Act* s. 22(3).

Possibly the limitations in section 107 do not prevent a stay of a proceeding in the Small Claims Court pending determination of a proceeding in the Superior Court of Justice. However any motion under section 107 must be to a judge of the Superior Court of Justice. The Small Claims Court has no jurisdiction to make an order under section 107.

Case Law: *32262 B.C. Ltd. v. 271617 B.C. Ltd.*, [1995] B.C.W.L.D. 1674 (B.C. S.C.) — Plaintiff brought motion for summary judgment. Defendant brought two motions. Judgment awarded but court did *not* award costs, commenting that judgment could have been obtained and maybe more cheaply in the Small Claims Court.

McGinty v. Toronto Transit Commission (1996), 7 W.D.C.P. (2d) 101 (Ont. Div. Ct.) — The pre-trial judge, on his own motion, ordered action transferred to the Small Claims Court. The endorsement transferring the action allowed for the possibility that the plaintiff's damages could exceed the Small Claims Court limit. In granting motion, the Court found that there was reason to doubt the correctness of the pre-trial judge's decision. Neither ss. 23(2) or 110(1) of the *Courts of Justice Act*, R.S.O. 1990, c. C.43, Rule 50.02(1)(b) nor the judge's inherent jurisdiction afforded authority for ordering the transfer of the action under those terms. Pre-trial judges were not to make significant, contentious rulings without clear notice and an opportunity to respond. The Court also found that the matter transcended the interests of the particular litigants.

McCubbing Trucking Ltd. v. Andre Blais Holdings Ltd. (1996), 149 Sask. R. 161 (Sask. Q.B.) — Only claim properly before court was that of appellant, and claim did not bring title to land in question. Respondent could not threaten counterclaim for specific performance for sole purpose of ousting appellant from jurisdiction of Small Claims Court. Remitted back to Small Claims Court for trial.

See also *Maber v. Wilson* (1998), (sub nom. *Wilson v. Maber)* 198 N.B.R. (2d) 247, 506 A.P.R. 247, 22 C.P.C. (4th) 108, [1998] N.B.J. No. 71 (N.B. C.A.) — Small Claims actions are presently provided for in New Brunswick by Rule 75 of the *Rules of Court*.

An action for damages, which would include actions for libel and slander, not exceeding $3,000 shall be conducted under Rule 75.

Despite s. 57 of the *Judicature Act*, R.S.O. 1990, c. 223, which provides that actions for libel and slander shall be tried by a jury unless the parties waive such a trial, libel and slander actions within the monetary jurisdiction of the Small Claims Court are tried in that Court. See *Suedfeld v. Lancia* (July 13, 1993), Doc. Barrie 9/93 (Ont. Gen. Div.), *Bhaduria v. Standard Broadcasting*, [1996] O.J. No. 2853 (Q.L.) and *Kopyto v. Ontario*, [1995] O.J. No. 601 (Q.L.).

By s. 4(2) of the *Small Claims Act*, S.N.B. 1997, S-9.1, which is not yet proclaimed, libel and slander actions are excluded from the jurisdiction of the Small Claims Court.

Rule 75 should be respected and the action tried as a Small Claim.

Mariotto v. Waterman (1998), 54 B.C.L.R. (3d) 364 (B.C. Master) — Cross-application by plaintiff to transfer the proceedings to the Provincial Court for all purposes pursuant to s. 13.1 of the *Supreme Court Act* of B.C., S.B.C. 1989, c. 40. While this is a proper case for the consideration of a jury, a jury trial would be expensive and lengthy and out of proportion to the probable amount involved. Order transferring case to the Provincial Court. Costs in the Supreme Court reserved until proceedings in Small Claims Court are disposed of.

Canadian Imperial Bank of Commerce v. Vold Jones & Vold Auction Co. (1999), 240 A.R. 20, 1999 CarswellAlta 48 (Alta. Q.B.) — Appeal from a decision of Provincial Court Judge refusing to transfer matter to Queen's Bench. To compel the plaintiff to conduct trial in Queen's Bench so defendant can have indemnity action tried with plaintiff's claim was an unwarranted and unreasonable denial of plaintiff's right to quick and inexpensive trial. Appellation for transfer refused.

Clearnet Inc. v. Blue Line Distribution Ltd. (April 7, 1999), Doc. 97-CT-004150, 98-CU-140427 (Ont. Gen. Div.) — The case involved an application to continue stay ordered in respect of a Small Claims Court action until all of discoveries in the General Division action were completed. The action was complex and involved many parties and issues. The Small Claims Court action involved the same parties and raised similar issues. Allowing the Small Claims Court action to proceed could give rise to issue estoppel.

Peitrangelo v. Lundrigan (1999), 44 O.R. (3d) 71 (Ont. Div. Ct.) — When an order is made transferring an action to the Small Claims Court, there is no jurisdiction to order that the costs of the action to the date of the transfer be paid to the successful party at trial.

Miranda v. Bossio (2000), 2000 CarswellOnt 3761 (Ont. C.J.) — Claim for support started in General Division, but on consent transferred to Provincial Division Court. Provincial Division had authority to assess costs for entire matter. Costs were to be assessed under both new and old Rules depending upon when the specific conduct that was subject to cost order arose.

Osadca v. Cadillac Fairview Corp. (2000), 2000 CarswellOnt 3158 (Ont. S.C.J.) — An action transferred to Small Claims Court was ordered returned to the Ontario Supreme Court under Simplified Rules. Claim in the cross-claim was for $6,200, which exceeded the monetary jurisdiction of the Small Claims Court.

Cohen v. Thomas Hinds Tobacconist (2000), 2000 CarswellOnt 3643 (Ont. Div. Ct.) — A claim was not transferred from Small Claims Court to Superior Court. The plaintiff offered no evidence to warrant a transfer. The defendant would suffer prejudice that was not reasonably compensable in costs.

Cormier v. Saint John (City) (2001), 233 N.B.R. (2d) 81, 601 A.P.R. 81, 2001 CarswellNB 23 (N.B. Q.B.) — Small Claims Court had jurisdiction over an action for false arrest: *Small Claims Act*, S.N.B. 1997, c. S-9.1, s. 4(2).

Pappin v. Continental Insurance Co., 1999 CarswellBC 2996 (B.C. Master) — The defendant moved to have the matter transferred to Small Claims Court. There was no evidence that the plaintiff would succeed on a claim exceeding $10,000. There were no other compelling reasons to keep matter in Supreme Court. The motion was allowed.

Polish National Union of Canada Inc. v. Dopke, 2001 CarswellOnt 2896, 55 O.R. (3d) 728 (Ont. S.C.J.) — Plaintiff commencing action under simplified procedure for damages in excess of the monetary jurisdiction of simplified procedure. Plaintiff not abandoning any claims. Plaintiff recovering judgment within the monetary jurisdiction of simplified procedure. Plaintiff not entitled to recover costs. *Rules of Civil Procedure*, R.R.O. 1990, Reg. 194, Rule 7.10(2).

Goodyear v. Bidgood (2000), 1 C.P.C. (5th) 303, 2000 CarswellNfld 225, 193 Nfld. & P.E.I.R. 240, 582 A.P.R. 240 (Nfld. T.D.) — Plaintiffs issued claim out of Supreme Court alleging breach of agreement. Amount of claim was $3,168.50 related to cost of repair of roof. Plaintiffs granted consent order transferring matter to Small Claims Court. After hearing evidence, Small Claims Court judge determined that he did not have jurisdiction to make award over $3,000. Plaintiffs discovered serious damage occurred inside their house in amount of additional $8,688.63. Plaintiffs claimed extent of damage not known at time of issuance of claim. Plaintiffs brought application to transfer action back to Supreme Court. Application granted. Small Claims Court had not adjudicated upon matter and plaintiffs had not abandoned portion of claim that was in excess of monetary jurisdiction. Nothing in consent order stated in writing that excess claim was abandoned. Statement of claim issued in Supreme Court was not amended to abandon excess, nor was any such amendment made in Small Claims Court.

Mayo v. Veenstra (2003), 2003 CarswellOnt 9, 63 O.R. (3d) 194 (Ont. S.C.J.) — Applicant sought in Superior Court to stay order of Small Claims Court requiring her to submit to a cross-examination, failing which her motion to set aside the "Noting in Default" against her would be dismissed. No authority to order submission within 30 days of motion. Endorsed over to Superior Court judge.

Bains v. Mattu, 2002 CarswellBC 2397, 2002 BCSC 1437 (B.C. S.C.) — Plaintiff succeeded on claim on loan for $15,000, and defendant succeeded on claim for $6,250 on promissory note. Transactions separate. Two separate judgments issued, and claim of plaintiff reduced to $10,000 monetary jurisdiction limit before set-off of claim of defendant.

Rai Trucking Ltd. v. Barakat Industries Ltd., 2002 CarswellAlta 1508, 2002 ABQB 1057 (Alta. Master); reversed 2003 CarswellAlta 240, 2003 ABQB 177 (Alta. Q.B.) — Plaintiff brought action for $12,957. Plaintiff sought summary judgment for $5,174 and requested balance to be referred to Provincial Court Civil Division. Summary judgment granted to plaintiff for $5,174. If parties agreed that remaining matters be transferred, application could be made to clerk of provincial court to do so.

Dhya Transport Ltd. v. Barakat Industries Ltd., 2002 CarswellAlta 1507, 2002 ABQB 1056 (Alta. Master) — Defendant admitted in discovery that $5,382 held back from payment to plaintiff. Summary judgment granted to plaintiff for $5,382. If parties agreed remaining matters be transferred, application could be made to clerk of provincial court to do so.

Akitt v. McColl, 2002 CarswellBC 1817, 2002 BCSC 1086 (B.C. S.C.) — Plaintiffs recovered general damages in personal injury action of $2,090 and $3,500 respectively. First plaintiff had undisclosed pre-existing medical condition, and second plaintiff failed to show inability to work. Plaintiffs failed to show good reason for bringing claims in Supreme Court. Disentitled to costs by the Rules of Court (B.C.), Rule 57(10).

Moncton Chrysler Dodge (1990) Ltd., Re, 2003 CarswellNB 412, 264 N.B.R. (2d) 198, 691 A.P.R. 198, 2003 NBCA 66 (N.B. C.A.) — Appellant not entitled to adjournment because of unavailability of counsel. Counsel knowing about unavailability several months before hearing date set.

Cook v. Webb, 2004 CarswellBC 1212, 2004 BCSC 715 (B.C. S.C.), R.D. Wilson, J. — Damages assessed at $1,375. Defendants say plaintiff is not entitled to costs, other than disbursements, pursuant to Rule 57(10) of the *Rules of Court*. At settlement conference, order made "that file be transferred to Supreme Court for all further proceedings by consent." No application made to transfer proceedings to the Provincial Court pursuant to s. 15 of the *Supreme Court Act*. Therefore plaintiff entitled to costs of Supreme Court trial.

Kurylo v. Rai, 2006 CarswellBC 982, 28 C.P.C. (6th) 28, 2006 BCCA 176, 53 B.C.L.R. (4th) 214 (B.C. C.A.).

Small Claims Division judge ordered transfer of matter to Supreme Court. Defendants made offer to settle. Following five-day jury trial, plaintiff was awarded judgment in amount within jurisdiction of Small Claims Court. Defendants contended that they should be awarded costs on basis that verdict within monetary jurisdiction of Small Claim Court and that plaintiff should be denied costs other than disbursements. Plaintiff applied for costs. Application dismissed on other grounds. Appeal allowed. Judge of Small Claims Division erred in costs order. Rule 37(27) of *Rules of Court, 1990* makes it clear that consideration can only be at time available to accept offer not anything other than that.

Koo v. Wong, 2004 CarswellBC 613, 2004 BCSC 397 (B.C. S.C.), Burnyeat, J. A plaintiff who recovers a sum within the jurisdiction of the Provincial Court under the *Small Claims Act* is not entitled to costs unless court finds sufficient reason for bringing proceeding in Supreme Court. Order to go.

There are no pleadings and no provision for discovery.

Matter is complicated. The original Claim requested punitive damages.

Walia v. Ulmer, 2005 CarswellBC 946, 12 C.P.C. (6th) 313, 2005 BCSC 601 (B.C. S.C.), Sigurdson J. Application concerns question of costs where plaintiff's judgment within jurisdiction of Small Claims Court.

Defendants argue that plaintiff should only recover disbursements. Rule 57(10) provides:

> A plaintiff who recovers a sum within the jurisdiction of the Provincial Court under the *Small Claims Act* is not entitled to costs other than disbursements, unless the court finds that there was sufficient reason for bringing the proceeding in the Supreme Court and so orders.

Leading authority *Bhanji v. Quezada*, [2003] B.C.J. No. 1883, 2003 CarswellBC 1986, 185 B.C.A.C. 301, 303 W.A.C. 301, 2003 BCCA 445 (B.C. C.A.). There jury awarded $1,400. Mr. Justice Low for the Court of Appeal, in allowing the appeal from a costs order in favour of the plaintiff, said at para. 8:

> [The trial judge] did not articulate any basis on which it could be said that the plaintiff might reasonably expect damages to exceed the Provincial Court jurisdiction. . . . It was for the plaintiff to justify his choice of forum when the resulting monetary judgment fell well below the threshold.

He continued at para. 19:

> The purpose of R. 57(10) is to encourage actions to be brought and continued in Provincial Court when there is no sufficient reason to expect that the claim might give rise to damages in excess of $10,000.

Issue not only with respect to commencing action but continuing claim.

No sufficient reason to bring the action in Supreme Court. Plaintiff only entitled to disbursements.

Kasey v. Royal Drake Investments Ltd., 2005 CarswellBC 2022, 2005 BCPC 368 (B.C. Prov. Ct.), Judge M.E. Rae. Reviewing the *Residential Tenancy Act*, this Court does not have jurisdiction.

Under *Small Claims Act* no jurisdiction to adjudicate on any issues arising from a landlord tenant relationship.

Axiom Services Ltd. v. Weigert, 2005 CarswellBC 1076, 2005 BCSC 665 (B.C. S.C.), Groberman J. Rule 57(10) provides that where a plaintiff recovers a sum within jurisdiction of Provincial Court under the *Small Claims Act*, no costs other than disbursements will be awarded unless the court finds that there was sufficient reason for bringing the proceedings in the Supreme Court.

Plaintiffs could not reasonably have known, prior to conclusion of discoveries (at the earliest) that award would be within jurisdiction of the Small Claims Court.

Plaintiffs are entitled to costs on scale 3.

Royal Insurance Co. of Canada v. Legge, 1996 CarswellNS 233, 36 C.C.L.I. (2d) 210, 152 N.S.R. (2d) 283, 442 A.P.R. 283, 7 C.P.C. (4th) 96 (N.S. S.C.). Insurance company brought application for declaration that Supreme Court of Nova Scotia proper court for any action brought by insured against them for total disability benefits and for stay of Small Claims Court action, arguing that the subject matter inappropriate for the Small Claims Court, and that matters raised sufficiently complex so as to require protections of Civil Procedure Rules. Application dismissed. Not for the Supreme Court to decide at present stage whether subject matter of action beyond the monetary limits of Small Claims Court. Nothing in *Small Claims Court Act* excluded complex matters from jurisdiction of the Act.

Squamish Ford Sales Ltd. v. Doll, 1997 CarswellBC 1311 (B.C. Master). Plaintiff commenced action seeking damages for defamation. Defendants counterclaimed for rescission of contract of sale and damages. Plaintiff's application to transfer proceedings to Provincial Court dismissed. Plaintiff could not conclusively establish that defendants' counterclaim would not exceed monetary jurisdiction.

Webb v. 3584747 Canada Inc., 2004 CarswellOnt 325, [2004] O.J. No. 215, 183 O.A.C. 155, 69 O.R. (3d) 502, 41 C.P.C. (5th) 98 (Ont. C.A.).

Relevant part of motion judge's order:

> 31. This Court orders that where a class member residing in Ontario has a claim for $25,000 or less, exclusive of interest and costs, a Deputy Judge of the Ontario Small Claims Court shall be appointed as Referee.

If the motion judge had appointed Small Claims Court judges as individuals in their private capacity to be paid in accordance with direction of referee rather than by the government, s. 14(1) of the *Courts of Justice Act* would not have been contravened.

Redekop v. Partridge, 2006 CarswellBC 3145, 2006 BCSC 1878 (B.C. Master), 2006-12-18, Master Baker.

Section 15 of the *Supreme Court Act* provides for the transfer of proceedings from this court to the Provincial Court. Several cases have encouraged transfer. See, e.g., *Pachini v. Pietramala*, 1995 CarswellBC 294, 7 B.C.L.R. (3d) 266, 38 C.P.C. (3d) 122, 54 A.C.W.S. (3d) 19 (B.C. S.C.) at para. 16, or *Manley v. Burns Lake Community Development Assn.*, 1996 CarswellBC 2490, [1996] B.C.J. No. 2236 (B.C. Master). Should the proceedings be transferred, any existing Supreme Court orders would survive, and funds currently in court would remain there until lower court's proceedings are done. The parties could then request the release of payment of the Supreme Court funds in accordance with the result in the Provincial Court.

Matter may continue in this court, but parties are encouraged to consider transferring matter to the Provincial Court, Small Claims.

Spalding v. Carr Estate, 2006 CarswellNB 595, (sub nom. *Barry Spalding v. Cornish)* 800 A.P.R. 86, (sub nom. *Barry Spalding v. Cornish)* 310 N.B.R. (2d) 86, 2006 NBQB 337, 34 C.P.C. (6th) 356 (N.B. Q.B.), P.S. Glennie J.

Law firm sought to have action transferred to Small Claims Court under s. 8(1) of *Small Claims Act*. Application dismissed. Determination of whether to transfer action from Court of Queen's Bench to Small Claims Court involved more than consideration of Small Claims Court monetary jurisdiction and that law firm was prepared to abandon portion of claim to fit within jurisdiction of Small Claims Court. Allegation of breach of trust serious. Party entitled to avail herself of discovery and documentary production in Court of Queen's Bench.

In *Hayes v. Maritime Life Assurance Co.* (2000), 45 C.P.C. (4th) 333, 225 N.B.R. (2d) 133, 578 A.P.R. 133, 2000 CarswellNB 163 (N.B. Q.B.), Russell J. ordered a Small Claims action to be transferred to the Court of Queen's Bench because of the potential for complexity and corresponding necessity of discovery procedures and because of the possibility of multiplicity of actions.

In *CGU Insurance Co. Canada v. Mulrooney*, [2002] N.B.J. No. 420, 2002 CarswellNB 461, 44 C.C.L.I. (3d) 299, 2002 NBQB 384, 255 N.B.R. (2d) 61, 668 A.P.R. 61 (N.B. Q.B.), the court ordered that the plaintiff's action for Section B benefits be transferred to the Court of Queen's Bench because the plaintiff's pre-existing health problems were an issue and the litigation could become complex.

Gale v. Knapp, 2006 CarswellBC 2190, 2006 BCSC 1225 (B.C. S.C.), E.A. Bennett J.

Plaintiff commenced action for damages arising out of motor vehicle accident. Action allowed. Not inappropriate for plaintiff to continue action in Supreme Court rather than transfer it to Small Claims Court. Costs dealt with according to *Supreme Court Rules*. Court had discretion whether or not to order double costs. Offer was reasonable because offer was made less than two weeks prior to trial and award was significantly higher than offer. Plaintiff entitled to double his costs for period from when offer was made up to and including trial. Plaintiff awarded $7,200 in costs, exclusive of disbursements.

Reimann v. Aziz, 2007 CarswellBC 2190, [2007] B.C.J. No. 2025, 47 C.P.C. (6th) 351, 286 D.L.R. (4th) 330, 246 B.C.A.C. 143, 406 W.A.C. 143, 2007 BCCA 448, 72 B.C.L.R. (4th) 1 (B.C. C.A.), 2007-09-18, Chiasson J.

Does a party have an ongoing obligation in relation to costs to assess the reasonableness of pursuing an action in the Supreme Court where recoverable damages may be within jurisdiction of the Small Claims Court?.

At time action initiated, the maximum jurisdiction of the Small Claims Court was $10,000. This was increased to $25,000 on September 1, 2006. Respondent's defence filed November 9, 2006. Case dealt with on fast-track basis pursuant to Rule 66 of the *Supreme Court Rules*, B.C. Reg. 221/90 and set for a one-day trial for February 20, 2007. Examinations for discovery took place and the parties prepared for trial.

Appellants argued judge "erred by failing to exercise his discretion . . . in a judicial manner by awarding the respondent costs pursuant to Rule 66(29) . . . instead of applying Rule 57(10) of the *Supreme Court Rules*." Policy underlying Rule 57(10) was to encourage litigants to bring and maintain actions in the Small Claims Division of the Provincial Court when there is not sufficient reason to expect that the recoverable amount will exceed the monetary jurisdiction of that court. See *Icecorp International Cargo Express Corp. v. Nicolaus*, 2007 CarswellBC 444, 236 B.C.A.C. 294, 390 W.A.C. 294, 38 C.P.C. (6th) 26, 2007 BCCA 97 (B.C. C.A.), which considered the issue of costs in the context of offers to settle where the amount accepted was within the jurisdiction of the Small Claims Court.

Section 15 of the *Supreme Court Act* states:

> 15 A judge or master may transfer proceedings to the Provincial Court of British Columbia if
>
>> (a) the proceedings are within the jurisdiction of the Provincial Court under the *Small Claims Act*,
>>
>> (b) a party to the proceedings applies to the judge or master, or all parties to the proceedings agree to the transfer, and
>>
>> (c) the judge or master considers it appropriate to do so.

The court has discretion to transfer when it considers it appropriate to do so. Nothing in section requiring transfer merely because claim may be within jurisdiction of Provincial Court. Obligation to assess quantum of claim. Point in time to consider whether plaintiff had sufficient reason for bringing a proceeding in Supreme Court is time of initiation of the action. Appeal dismissed.

Fawcett v. Bayview Credit Union Ltd., 2007 CarswellNB 456, 2007 NBQB 303 (N.B. Q.B.), 2007-08-27, P.S. Glennie J.

Application by claimant in Small Claims Court to transfer an action from the Small Claims Court to the Court of Queen's Bench.

Section 9(2) of the *Small Claims Act* provides as follows:

> 9 (2) Any party to an action in the court may apply to the Court of Queen's Bench of New Brunswick to have the matter transferred to that court and the Court of Queen's Bench of New Brunswick may order that the matter be transferred.

In exercising its discretion to transfer a Small Claims action to the Court of Queen's Bench, the court must determine whether issues involved are complex and may require discovery procedures which are not available under the *Small Claims Act*. Nothing complex about claim and it should not require discovery procedures. Application to transfer dismissed without costs.

Reimann v. Aziz, 72 B.C.L.R. (4th) 1, 2007 BCCA 448, 406 W.A.C. 143, 246 B.C.A.C. 143, [2007] B.C.J. No. 2025, 286 D.L.R. (4th) 330, 47 C.P.C. (6th) 351, 2007 CarswellBC 2190 (B.C. C.A.).

The respondent began action in Supreme Court claiming damages. The appellants' application to transfer proceedings to Small Claims Court dismissed. The respondent awarded damages below Small Claims Court limit. The appellants submitting respondent should only recover disbursements because judgment was within monetary jurisdiction of Small Claims Court. Plaintiff entitled to Supreme Court costs if sufficient reason to bring claim in Supreme Court at time of its commencement. Plaintiff did not have ongoing obligation to assess quantum of claim. No palpable or overriding error in judge's finding of fact that respondent's choice of forum reasonable.

If sufficient reason for bringing proceeding in Supreme Court, plaintiff was entitled to be in that forum. Nothing required a transfer merely because claim may be within jurisdiction of the Provincial Court.

The point in time for a consideration of whether a plaintiff had sufficient reason for bringing a proceeding in the Supreme Court was the time of the initiation of the action.

See *McGrath v. Scriven*, 1920 CarswellNS 25, 52 D.L.R. 342, 33 C.C.C. 70, 54 N.S.R. 1 (N.S. C.A.); affirmed (1920), 56 D.L.R. 117, 35 C.C.C. 93, [1921] 1 W.W.R. 1075 (S.C.C.), the Nova Scotia Court of Appeal considered a statutory provision that stated "no action . . . shall be brought" and at p. 345 referred to United States' authority (*Hames v. Judd* (1890), 18 Civ. Pro. Rep. (N.Y.) 324) to support its conclusion:

> The phrase "to bring an action" has a settled customary legal as well as general meaning and refers to the initiation of legal proceedings in the suit.
>
> The action was brought in this case when the writ was issued. . . ..

McGrath followed in *Kemp v. Metzner*, 229 W.A.C. 242, 140 B.C.A.C. 242, 2000 CarswellBC 1616, 2000 BCCA 462, 190 D.L.R. (4th) 388, 78 B.C.L.R. (3d) 187 (B.C. C.A.); additional reasons at 241 W.A.C. 9, 147 B.C.A.C. 9, 194 D.L.R. (4th) 760, 83 B.C.L.R. (3d) 101, 2000 CarswellBC 2534, 2000 BCCA 694 (B.C. C.A.). Court was considering whether the phrase "bring an action" includes filing and service of the writ or just the filing of it.

Toronto Dominion Bank v. Thind, 2010 ONSC 6974, 2010 CarswellOnt 9651 (Ont. S.C.J.), Gray, J.

Two motions were before the court, motion by defendant to transfer action to the Small Claims Court and cross-motion by the plaintiff for summary judgment.

The plaintiff sued on three separate claims, based on different credit facilities. The total claims, apart from interest, were for $22,049.90, within the jurisdiction of the Small Claims Court.

Plaintiff's counsel submits that, where no adequate defence is pleaded or shown, the summary judgment procedure is available in the Superior Court. No corresponding procedure is available under the *Small Claims Court Rules*, albeit the Court of Appeal, in *Van de Vrande v. Butkowsky*, 319 D.L.R. (4th) 132, 2010 CarswellOnt 1777, 2010 ONCA 230, 99 O.R. (3d) 641, 99 O.R. (3d) 648, [2010] O.J. No. 1239, 260 O.A.C. 323, 85 C.P.C. (6th) 205 (Ont. C.A.); additional reasons at 2010 CarswellOnt 3629, 2010 ONCA 400, 85 C.P.C. (6th) 212 (Ont. C.A.), suggested that there appear to be mechanisms within the *Small Claims Court Rules* that would allow motions to be brought to deal with claims expeditiously where inadequate claims or defences have been pleaded.

Since no real defence pleaded, no sense to transfer action to the Small Claims Court. For the same reason, summary judgment should issue on the plaintiff's claim, but there must be costs consequences for the plaintiff's decision to bring the matter in Superior Court, even though it is clear action is within the jurisdiction of the Small Claims Court. See statement of

Justice Nolan in *Lore v. Tortola*, 2008 CarswellOnt 1054, [2008] O.J. No. 769 (Ont. S.C.J.), at para. 17:

> The Superior Court of Justice is currently overburdened with cases. Parties should not be rewarded with costs in matters that should have been properly brought in another forum designed to handle claims of a specific magnitude or monetary value, such as the Ontario Small Claims Court.

Rule 57.05(1) permits the Court to order that a plaintiff not recover any costs if the plaintiff recovers an amount within the monetary jurisdiction of the Small Claims Court. Here the plaintiff has not only recovered an amount within the monetary jurisdiction of the Small Claims Court, the plaintiff made a deliberate decision to commence this action in the Superior Court when it was clear that the action was within the jurisdiction of the Small Claims Court.

Defendant's motion to transfer action to Small Claims Court dismissed. The plaintiff's cross-motion for summary judgment granted.

Spencer v. Popham, 2010 BCSC 683, 2010 CarswellBC 1221 (B.C. S.C. [In Chambers]), Punnett, J.

Plaintiff commenced action in Supreme Court but then settled for an amount within the Small Claim Court's jurisdiction. Is she entitled to costs in the Supreme Court? Was there "sufficient reason" for her to commence the claim in Supreme Court?.

At time action commenced, plaintiff had not obtained any medical records or medical opinions. Parties settled the claim for $13,500.

Rule 57(10) of the *Rules of Court* states:

> A plaintiff who recovers a sum within the jurisdiction of the Provincial Court under the *Small Claims Act* is not entitled to costs, other than disbursements, unless the court finds that there was sufficient reason for bringing the proceeding in the Supreme Court and so orders.

Rule encourages persons to bring actions in Small Claims Court when a claim falls within that court's monetary jurisdiction. It is an example of "proportionality"; the judicial process should match the amount in dispute. However, the court must also respect a party's "legitimate choice" of forum: see *Reimann v. Aziz*, 72 B.C.L.R. (4th) 1, 2007 BCCA 448, 406 W.A.C. 143, 246 B.C.A.C. 143, [2007] B.C.J. No. 2025, 286 D.L.R. (4th) 330, 47 C.P.C. (6th) 351, 2007 CarswellBC 2190 (B.C. C.A.) at para. 35.

Burden on claimants to evaluate their claims prior to commencement and to justify their decision if they recover less than the Small Claims Court limit of $25,000.

See also *Gradek v. DaimlerChrysler Financial Services Canada Inc./Services Financiers DaimlerChrysler Canada Inc.*, 2010 CarswellBC 665, 2010 BCSC 356, 95 C.P.C. (6th) 375 (B.C. S.C. [In Chambers]), at para. 19; affirmed 2011 BCCA 136, 2011 CarswellBC 588, 100 C.P.C. (6th) 12, (sub nom. *Gradek v. DaimlerChrysler Financial Services Canada Inc.*) 307 B.C.A.C. 7, (sub nom. *Gradek v. DaimlerChrysler Financial Services Canada Inc.*) 519 W.A.C. 7 (B.C. C.A.), R. 57(10) contemplates the possibility that factors other than quantum must be considered.

Factors that can give rise to "sufficient reason" set out in *Kuehne v. Probstl*, [2004] B.C.J. No. 1383, 2004 BCSC 865, 2004 CarswellBC 1515 (B.C. Master) at para. 22, and accepted in *Icecorp International Cargo Express Corp. v. Nicolaus*, 2007 BCCA 97, 2007 CarswellBC 444, 38 C.P.C. (6th) 26, 390 W.A.C. 294, 236 B.C.A.C. 294 (B.C. C.A.) at para. 27. They include:

> i. The legal or factual complexity of the case;
>
> ii. The need for discovery of documents and examinations for discovery;
>
> iii. The need for a judgment enforceable outside of British Columbia;

iv. A *bona fide* preference for a jury trial; and

v. Access to the summary trial procedure available in Supreme Court.

Other factors can be the need for the plaintiff to have legal counsel (*Faedo v. Dowell*, 2007 BCSC 1985, 2007 CarswellBC 3479 (B.C. S.C.) at para. 36; *Ostovic v. Foggin*, 2009 BCSC 58, 2009 CarswellBC 114, [2009] B.C.J. No. 85 (B.C. S.C.) at para. 42; *Gradek* at para. 43), and the defendant's denial of liability, causation, and injury or loss and allegations of contributory negligence, pre-existing conditions, previous causes, and a failure to mitigate (*Ostovic* at paras. 39-40; *Gradek* at para. 35). In Supreme Court, *Johannson v. National Car Rental (Canada) Inc./National Location D'Autos (Canada) Inc.*, 2009 BCSC 1284, 2009 CarswellBC 2529 (B.C. S.C.) at para. 5.

> Defendants created situation giving rise to motion. Pleadings raised multitude of issues in their defence. Those issues raised complex questions of fact and law. Unlikely that a layperson could address them competently. Sufficient reason for the plaintiff to bring the action in Supreme Court regardless of the quantum at the time of commencement.

Capano v. Rahm, 2010 CarswellOnt 4760, 2010 ONSC 3241, [2010] O.J. No. 2866 (Ont. S.C.J.); additional reasons at 2010 ONSC 4131, 2010 CarswellOnt 6013 (Ont. S.C.J.); leave to appeal refused 2010 CarswellOnt 7425 (Ont. Div. Ct.), Pitt J.

The motion was brought pursuant to the rr. 1.04(1), (1.1) and 48.04(1) of the *Rules of Civil Procedure*, R.R.O. 1990, Reg. 194, and sections 23(2) and 110 of the *Courts of Justice Act*, R.S.O. 1990, c. C.43 by the plaintiffs, for order moving matter *to* the Small Claims Court, in light of the increase in the Small Claims Court's monetary jurisdiction to $25,000 from $10,000 as of January 1, 2010.

Section 23(2) of the *Courts of Justice Act* makes it clear that an action in the Superior Court of Justice may be transferred to the Small Claims Court before the trial commences only on the consent of *all* parties. The defendant refused to consent.

Court may draw on its inherent powers over its own process to transfer an action from one judicial forum to another: see *Vigna v. Toronto Stock Exchange* (1998), 28 C.P.C. (4th) 318, [1998] O.J. No. 4924, 115 O.A.C. 393, 1998 CarswellOnt 4560 (Ont. Div. Ct.) at para. 7. However, particular facts of this case do not warrant its exercise.

Master has jurisdiction to decide whether to move an action in the Superior Court to the Small Claims Court. Section 107(4) of the *Courts of Justice Act* states that where there are two or more proceedings pending in two or more different courts, a request to transfer must be made to a judge of the Superior Court. In other words, judges of the Superior Court have the exclusive jurisdiction to hear motions for consolidation, hearing together, or hearing one after the other of *existing* proceedings. By implication, requests for transfer *simpliciter* can be dealt with by either a judge or a master.

On February 22, 2010, pretrial adjourned to a date after August 1, 2010. Plaintiffs had benefit of mediation, two motions and the assessment of Master Haberman. Pretrial to proceed without need for expert evidence. It was too late to transfer case to another court. Motion dismissed.

A & A Steelseal Waterproofing Inc. v. Kalovski, 2010 CarswellOnt 3455, 2010 ONSC 2652 (Ont. S.C.J.).

The action commenced in January 2005 pursuant to the *Construction Lien Act*, R.S.O. 1990, as a result of the defendant's failure to pay for work done.

The plaintiff sought costs on a substantial indemnity basis in the sum of $41,661.47. The defendants submit plaintiff's costs should be on a Small Claims Court basis only, given the amount recovered at trial. Alternatively, proportionality must be considered.

Justice is best served when costs are awarded to successful litigants and the principle of indemnity is paramount: *Waterloo (City) v. Ford*, 2008 CarswellOnt 2692 (Ont. S.C.J. [Commercial List]).

Rule 57.05(1) of the *Rules of Civil Procedure*, R.S.O. 1990, provides that where a judgment is obtained which is within the jurisdiction of the Small Claims Court, the court may, in its discretion, order that the plaintiff shall not recover any costs. This is neither a proper case for the denial of costs to the plaintiff, nor for an award of costs in favour of the plaintiff on a Small Claims Court basis.

The plaintiff, while advancing a modest claim for payment of its account in the deposit amount was also required to defend a substantial counterclaim in the sum of $150,000.00. That claim was outstanding until the commencement of the trial.

The plaintiff entitled to costs in the circumstances. An award of costs on a substantial indemnity basis was appropriate.

It is not the case that the mere fact that costs exceed damages awarded renders such an award inappropriate: see *Bonaiuto v. Pilot Insurance Co.*, 81 C.C.L.I. (4th) 213, 2010 ONSC 1248, 2010 CarswellOnt 1039, 101 O.R. (3d) 157, 81 C.C.L.I. (4th) 213, [2010] O.J. No. 745 (Ont. S.C.J.). As noted by Lane J. in *163972 Canada Inc. v. Isacco*, 1997 CarswellOnt 636, [1997] O.J. No. 838 (Ont. Gen. Div.): "to reduce the plaintiff's otherwise reasonable costs on this basis would simply encourage the kind of intransigence displayed by the defendants in this case.".

Sum of $41,661.47, inclusive of disbursements and GST, on a substantial indemnity basis, fair and reasonable in circumstances.

1000728 Ontario Ltd. v. Kakish, 2010 ONSC 538, 2010 CarswellOnt 599, 88 C.P.C. (6th) 108 (Ont. S.C.J.).

The consignee brought motion to transfer action from Small Claims Court to Superior Court of Justice. Motion granted. Case complex and expert evidence required to assess interrelationship of invoices, purchase orders, bills of lading and other documents as well as their legal relationship. Small Claims Court lacked procedure for exchange of expert reports prior to trial. Full discovery was required.

Cases may be moved from the Small Claims Court on a motion and with the order of a Superior Court judge. See *Alexandrov v. Csanyi*, 247 O.A.C. 228, 2009 CarswellOnt 1325 (Ont. Div. Ct.); *Csanyi v. Alexandrov*, 2009 CarswellOnt 5446 (Ont. S.C.J.), and *Haines, Miller & Associates Inc. v. Foss*, 1996 CarswellNS 301, 3 C.P.C. (4th) 349, 450 A.P.R. 53, 153 N.S.R. (2d) 53 (N.S. S.C. [In Chambers]); additional reasons at 1996 CarswellNS 304, 466 A.P.R. 389, 158 N.S.R. (2d) 389 (N.S. S.C. [In Chambers]).

In *Alexandrov*, the Court stated that the jurisprudence on transfer is that a plaintiff may be forced, in very exceptional cases, into the Superior Court against the actual wishes of the plaintiff. In *Farlow v. Hospital for Sick Children*, 2009 CarswellOnt 7124, 83 C.P.C. (6th) 290, [2009] O.J. No. 4847, 100 O.R. (3d) 213 (Ont. S.C.J.), Court held that on a motion to transfer an action from Small Claims Court to the Superior Court of Justice, there must be a balancing of the various factors enumerated in that decision.

The Small Claims Court does *not* have procedural framework similar to rr. 53.03 and 76.10(4) of the *Rules of Civil Procedure*, R.R.O. 1990, Reg. 194 for the timely exchange of expert reports in advance of the trial. In *Crane Canada Co. v. Montis Sorgic Associates Inc.*, 2005 CarswellOnt 9989, [2005] O.J. No. 6247 (Ont. S.C.J.); affirmed 2006 CarswellOnt 3051, [2006] O.J. No. 1999 (Ont. C.A.), the Court found that expert evidence would be central to the determination of the claims and that such evidence would likely be complex, and decided accordingly that claims would be more appropriately dealt with in the Superior Court.

Quartey-Harrison v. Klusiewich, 2011 BCSC 1744, 2011 CarswellBC 3420 (B.C. S.C.). The plaintiff was awarded special damages of $910.56 and general damages of $18,000.

Rule 14-1(10) of the B.C. *Supreme Court Civil Rules* provides that a plaintiff who recovers a monetary judgment within the jurisdiction of the Provincial Court under the *Small Claims Act* is not entitled to costs, other than disbursements, unless the court finds that there was sufficient reason for bringing the proceeding in the Supreme Court and orders it done. The burden is on the plaintiff to justify his choice of forum. The court must also consider circumstances at the time the action was commenced.

A mild whiplash-type injury suffered was unlikely to result in an award in excess of the $25,000 monetary limit in Small Claims Court. The right to recover disbursements should not be nullified by the offer. Each party was to bear its own costs, but the plaintiff was entitled to recover his disbursements from the defendants.

Westerhof v. Gee Estate, 2011 ONSC 7437, 2011 CarswellOnt 14465, [2012] I.L.R. I-5233 (Ont. S.C.J.).

The jury awarded the plaintiff $22,000 in non-pecuniary general damages, $13,000 in loss of income to the date of the trial, and zero dollars for future loss of economic opportunity or earning capacity. The plaintiff's total recovery prior to statutory deduction was $35,000, a sum in excess of the monetary jurisdiction of the Small Claims Court. Neither party made a Rule 49 Offer to Settle.

Rider v. Dydyk, 2007 ONCA 687, 2007 CarswellOnt 6394, [2007] O.J. No. 3837, 87 O.R. (3d) 507, 231 O.A.C. 169, [2007] I.L.R. I-4649, 286 D.L.R. (4th) 517, 53 C.C.L.I. (4th) 188 (Ont. C.A.); leave to appeal refused (2008), 2008 CarswellOnt 1226, 2008 CarswellOnt 1227, [2007] S.C.C.A. No. 594, 385 N.R. 400 (note), 252 O.A.C. 398 (note) (S.C.C.) provides that the present statutory deduction of $30,000 from a court award of non-pecuniary general damages is not considered when determining the issue of costs in the face of a defendant's Rule 49 offer of settlement. *Rider* rules that a defendant, in making an offer to settle non-pecuniary general damages, must consider what a court would award under that heading, prior to the statutory deduction, when formulating the quantum of the offer to settle.

The statutory deduction has rendered the non-pecuniary general damage award to nil.

To determine costs, the recovery by the plaintiff is $22,000 in general damages and nil for loss of income. This results in the award for costs purposes to be within the monetary jurisdiction of the Small Claims Court.

In *Rider (supra)*, the court stated in part in that paragraph:

> The statutory deductions from a plaintiff's *assessed damages* are not to be considered in determining a party's entitlement to costs.

In the result, the plaintiff has recovered a nil judgment for the consideration of costs consequences. Westerhof has no realistic prospect to pay costs to the defendant.

The result for the defendants is a nil judgment against it after deduction of the benefits paid to Westerhof by his own insurer and the effect of the provisions of the *Insurance Act*. Justice would be done on the basis that the principle of costs following the event be observed by an award of costs fixed in the sum of $10,000 in favour of the defendant.

Saskatchewan Government Insurance v. Williams, 2011 SKCA 66, 2011 CarswellSask 361, [2011] I.L.R. I-5151, (sub nom. *Williams v. Saskatchewan Government Insurance*) 371 Sask. R. 305, (sub nom. *Williams v. Saskatchewan Government Insurance*) 518 W.A.C. 305 (Sask. C.A.).

The insured brought an action for damages to her vehicle. The insurer denied coverage, arguing, inter alia, that the claim was statute-barred since it was brought outside the two-year limitation period set out in section 5 of the *Limitations Act*.

The issue concerning the limitation period proceeded by way of a preliminary hearing. A provincial court judge held that the action was statute-barred. The plaintiff successfully appealed. A Queen's Bench judge held the action was not statute-barred and ordered that the claim be returned for trial. The insurer appealed. The appeal was allowed.

A provincial court has jurisdiction to determine a point of law that does not dispose of an action in its entirety. The point of law relating to the limitation period did not dispose of the action. Liability and damages were yet to be determined. It was apparent by use of the words "decide a claim" in section 24(1) of *Small Claims Act* that all issues must be determined in order to utilize this provision. Regardless of the outcome of the appeal, liability and damages were live issues to be dealt with at the trial.

Slipcon USA Inc. v. Pfeiffer, 2011 ONSC 6876, 2011 CarswellOnt 13722 (Ont. S.C.J.), Justice P.B. Hambly.

Slipcon obtained a judgment against Pfeiffer and 155 for $23,281.25.

Slipcon served an offer to settle its claim against Pfeiffer and 155.

Slipcon commenced its claim on June 19, 2009, when the monetary limit in Small Claims Court was $10,000. On January 1, 2010, the monetary limit of claims in Small Claims Court was increased to $25,000. The relevant *Rules of Civil Procedure* in these circumstances is as follows:

> 57.05 (1) If a plaintiff recovers an amount within the monetary jurisdiction of the Small Claims Court, the court may order that the plaintiff shall not recover any costs.
>
> (2) Subrule (1) does not apply to an action transferred to the Superior Court of Justice under section 107 of the *Courts of Justice Act*.

This is not a proper case to deny the plaintiff costs on the Superior Court scale.

In a simplified procedure case, the principle of proportionality must be applied even where the plaintiff obtained a judgment in excess of an offer to settle (see *Culligan Springs Ltd. v. Dunlop Lift Truck (1994) Inc.*, 2006 CarswellOnt 2516, [2006] O.J. No. 1667, 211 O.A.C. 65 at para. 29 (Ont. Div. Ct.)). The Court, in fixing costs, must apply the principle of reasonableness (see the judgment of Justice Armstrong in *Boucher v. Public Accountants Council (Ontario)*, 2004 CarswellOnt 2521, [2004] O.J. No. 2634, 71 O.R. (3d) 291, 48 C.P.C. (5th) 56, 188 O.A.C. 201 at para. 37 (Ont. C.A.)).

The conduct of Pfeiffer was outrageous. Costs were awarded to Slipcon in the main action for $16,000.

Ali v. Schrauwen, 2011 ONSC 2158, 2011 CarswellOnt 3201, 18 C.P.C. (7th) 425, [2011] O.J. No. 1671 (Ont. Master), Master MacLeod.

The action was commenced under the simplified procedure in Rule 76 seeking damages of $31,000. The plaintiff sought to transfer the action to Small Claims Court and to limit the claim to $25,000.

The action commenced in November of 2008, when the Small Claims Court limit was $10,000 and the Rule 76 limit was $50,000. Now, the Small Claims limit is $25,000 and the Rule 76 limit is $100,000. It is open to the court to order this matter transferred to Small Claims Court even when *not* on consent under section 23(2) of the *Courts of Justice Act*. See *Shoppers Trust Co. v. Mann Taxi Management Ltd.*, 1993 CarswellOnt 437, 16 O.R. (3d) 192, 19 C.P.C. (3d) 7 (Ont. Gen. Div.). The power to transfer a case to Small Claims Court over an objection of a party is grounded in the inherent jurisdiction of the court to supervise its own process, and a master may exercise that jurisdiction. See *Capano v. Rahm*, 2010 ONSC 3241, 2010 CarswellOnt 4760, [2010] O.J. No. 2866 (Ont. S.C.J.); additional reasons at 2010 ONSC 4131, 2010 CarswellOnt 6013 (Ont. S.C.J.); leave to appeal refused 2010 CarswellOnt 7425 (Ont. Div. Ct.).

The defendant has incurred roughly $13,000 in costs defending this action to date. See *Pietrangelo v. Lundrigan*, 1999 CarswellOnt 3062, 44 O.R. (3d) 71, 43 C.P.C. (4th) 157 (Ont. Div. Ct.). There is no jurisdiction to direct the judge or deputy judge at trial on how to apply the Small Claims Court rules on costs or power to direct the court to ignore the provisions of the *Courts of Justice Act*.

An Order transferred the action to Small Claims Court. The original pleadings were to be used as pleadings in the Small Claims Court, except the statement of claim was amended to limit it to $25,000. There was no further settlement conference in Small Claims Court. The plaintiff was to pay costs to the defendant fixed at $2,800 for costs incurred by the defendant that would not have been necessary had the transfer occurred in January of 2010.

The plaintiff was successful on the motion, though ordered to pay costs as a term of the relief. The plaintiff was to have the costs of motion fixed at $2,500.

Lamarche v. ING Insurance Co. of Canada, 2012 ONSC 4111, [2012] I.L.R. I-5317, [2012] O.J. No. 3248 (Ont. S.C.J.), Master MacLeod (Ont. Master).

The plaintiff was served with a notice of examination for discovery in November of 2010. He did not attend. He brought a motion to limit his claim to $25,000 and to transfer the action to Small Claims Court.

The fees and disbursements incurred by the defendant were not recoverable in Small Claims Court. Court cannot make an order either fettering or expanding the limited costs jurisdiction of the Deputy Judge. Costs can only be awarded prior to the transfer as a term of my order.

Motion to transfer dismissed. Leave to amend claim to under $100,000.00 in which case action shall proceed under Rule 76.

Noël et Associés, s.e.n.c.r.l. v. Sincennes, 2012 ONSC 3770, 2012 CarswellOnt 9810, (sub nom. *Noël et Associés, S.E.N.C.R.L. v. Sincennes*) 112 O.R. (3d) 138, 41 C.P.C. (7th) 175, Kane J. (Ont. S.C.J.)

Is the holder of a foreign judgment for the payment of money entitled to seek the enforcement of that judgment in Ontario by way of declaratory relief in an application under rule 14.05(3)(h) of the Ontario *Rules of Civil Procedure*, R.R.O. 1990, Reg. 194 or, should the matter proceed by action, and;.

Where the foreign judgment is for the payment of money in an amount within the monetary jurisdiction of the Ontario Small Claims Court, should the proceeding be brought in the Small Claims Court or the Superior Court of Justice?.

Quebec is not a reciprocating state. A Quebec judgment may not be registered in and enforced here as if obtained in Ontario. The holder of that Quebec judgment must commence an Ontario proceeding.

The availability of an application requires consideration as to the nature of the rights held by the Quebec judgment holder seeking Ontario enforcement.

Canadian courts, as in *Rutledge v. United States Savings & Loan Co.*, 1906 CarswellYukon 34, 37 S.C.R. 546 (S.C.C.) and *Livesley v. E. Clemens Horst Co.* (1924), 1924 CarswellBC 115, [1924] S.C.R. 605, [1925] 1 D.L.R. 159 (S.C.C.) at pp. 609 and 610 [S.C.R.], have, for limitations purposes, traditionally treated a foreign judgment as an action upon a simple contract debt.

The *Rules of Civil Procedure*, including rule 76.02, do not prohibit an action for a debt below $25,000 being brought in the Superior Court of Justice. This court however doubts that the Province of Ontario would intentionally duplicate and incur the costs of parallel court systems up to the level of $25,000. Most actions for the recovery of debt below that limit however are presumably brought in the Small Claims Court.

Section 23(2) of the *Courts of Justice Act*, states that where the only claim is for the payment of money up to $25,000, such an action commenced in the Superior Court may be transferred to the Small Claims Court on consent, by motion or pursuant to the inherent jurisdiction of a Superior Court Judge: see *McGinty v. Toronto Transit Commission*, 1996 CarswellOnt 288, [1996] O.J. No. 320 (Ont. Div. Ct.) at para. 15. This court has repeatedly held that such actions should customarily be transferred to the Small Claims Court: see *Shoppers Trust Co. v. Mann Taxi Management Ltd.*, 1993 CarswellOnt 437, 16 O.R. (3d) 192, 19 C.P.C. (3d) 7 (Ont. Gen. Div.); *Graves v. Avis Rent A Car System Inc.*, 1993 CarswellOnt 472, 21 C.P.C. (3d) 391, [1993] O.J. No. 2771 (Ont. Gen. Div.) and *Ali v. Schrauwen*, 2011 ONSC 2158, 2011 CarswellOnt 3201, 18 C.P.C. (7th) 425, [2011] O.J. No. 1671 (Ont. Master) at para. 2. The direction in these decisions places into context the jurisdiction of this court and the right of claimants to present their claim in the Superior Court where the sole remedy is judgment for debt owing below $25,000.

Proceedings in Ontario for debt owing in the amount of $25,000 or less, based on a foreign judgment from a non-reciprocating state, should be brought by action in the Small Claims Court.

Application dismissed without costs.

Ecolab Co. v. SAVD Holdings Inc., 2012 ONSC 2358, 2012 CarswellOnt 5122 (Ont. S.C.J.), Fragomeni J.

The plaintiff seeks the following relief:

1. An interim order for the recovery of property.

2. An order transferring the balance of this action to the Brampton Small Claims Court.

.

Court not satisfied that matter ought to be transferred to Small Claims Court. The defendants strongly oppose a transfer to Small Claims Court. See Section 23(1)(a)(b) of the *Courts of Justice Act*.

Nothing in the evidentiary record setting out the value of the equipment. Matter to continue under the simplified procedure provided in Rule 76 as brought by the plaintiff in its Statement of Claim. The plaintiff's motion is dismissed as the issues to be determined require a trial.

Toronto Dominion Bank v. Thind, 2010 ONSC 6974, 2010 CarswellOnt 9651, Gray, J. (Ont. S.C.J.)

There were two motions before the court: a motion by the defendant to transfer action to the Small Claims Court, and a cross-motion by the plaintiff for summary judgment.

Where no adequate defence is pleaded or shown, the summary judgment procedure is available in the Superior Court. No corresponding procedure is available under the *Small Claims Court Rules*, albeit the Court of Appeal, in *Van de Vrande v. Butkowsky*, 2010 ONCA 230, 2010 CarswellOnt 1777, 99 O.R. (3d) 648, 99 O.R. (3d) 641, 85 C.P.C. (6th) 205, 319 D.L.R. (4th) 132, 260 O.A.C. 323, [2010] O.J. No. 1239 (Ont. C.A.); additional reasons 2010 ONCA 400, 2010 CarswellOnt 3629, 85 C.P.C. (6th) 212 (Ont. C.A.), it was suggested that there appears to be mechanisms within the *Small Claims Court Rules* that would allow motions to be brought to deal with claims expeditiously where inadequate claims or defences have been pleaded. It is the policy of the legislature and Rules Committee that cases worth $25,000 or less be heard in the Small Claims Court. As reflected in rule 57.05, there are costs consequences where the plaintiff recovers an amount within the monetary jurisdiction of the Small Claims Court.

Since no real defence is pleaded, it makes no sense to transfer this action to the Small Claims Court.

There must be costs consequences for the plaintiff's decision to bring the matter in this Court, even though it is clear that this action is within the jurisdiction of the Small Claims Court. See Nolan, J., in *Lore v. Tortola*, 2008 CarswellOnt 1054, [2008] O.J. No. 769 (Ont. S.C.J.) at para. 17:

> The Superior Court of Justice is currently overburdened with cases. Parties should not be rewarded with costs in matters that should have been properly brought in another forum designed to handle claims of a specific magnitude or monetary value, such as the Ontario Small Claims Court.

The business decision made by the plaintiff to bring the action in this Court should carry with it the business decision that it will likely receive no costs if it is successful.

No order as to costs.

The defendant's motion to transfer this action to the Small Claims Court was dismissed. The plaintiff's cross-motion for summary judgment was granted.

Shakur v. Mitchell Plastics, 2012 ONSC 1780, 2012 CarswellOnt 3626, 1 C.C.E.L. (4th) 149, [2012] O.J. No. 1345, D. A. Broad, J. (Ont. S.C.J.); leave to appeal refused 2012 ONSC 4500, 2012 CarswellOnt 9681 (Ont. S.C.J.)

The plaintiff awarded $12,514, an amount within the jurisdiction of the Small Claims Court. Although action commenced prior to the increase in the jurisdiction of the Small Claims Court, it was evident no consideration was given during proceeding to moving the action to that Court. The Plaintiff seeks costs in the sum of $21,409.07. Rule 57.05(1) provides that if a plaintiff recovers an amount within the monetary jurisdiction of the Small Claims Court, the court may order that the Plaintiff shall not recover any costs. There does not appear to be any exception for cases which were commenced prior to the increase in the jurisdiction of the Small Claims Court. No order as to costs.

Vallie Construction Inc. v. Minaker, 2012 ONSC 4577, 2012 CarswellOnt 9802, 21 C.L.R. (4th) 333, Master Sandler (Ont. S.C.J.).

The cases of *Shoppers Trust Co. v. Mann Taxi Management Ltd.*, 1993 CarswellOnt 437, 16 O.R. (3d) 192, 19 C.P.C. (3d) 7 (Ont. Gen. Div.) and *Graves v. Avis Rent A Car System Inc.*, 1993 CarswellOnt 472, 21 C.P.C. (3d) 391, [1993] O.J. No. 2771 (Ont. Gen. Div.) hold that a judge of the Superior Court has inherent jurisdiction to transfer a Superior Court action to the S.C.C. without the consent of all parties, i.e., where one party objects. But in both those cases, the amount actually claimed was within the jurisdiction of the Superior Court when the actions were commenced but thereafter, the jurisdiction of the S.C.C. was increased to exceed the amounts being claimed and so, the courts there held that the actions should be transferred.

Lamarche v. ING Insurance Co. of Canada, 2012 ONSC 4111, [2012] I.L.R. I-5317, [2012] O.J. No. 3248, Master MacLeod (Ont. S.C.J.).

Assuming that it would be appropriate to transfer a claim to Small Claims Court over the objection of the opposing party (See *Ali v. Schrauwen*, 2011 ONSC 2158, 2011 CarswellOnt 3201, 18 C.P.C. (7th) 425, [2011] O.J. No. 1671 (Ont. Master), I decline to do so in this case. The fees and disbursements incurred by the defendant in defending the action to date exceed $7,000. These costs would not be recoverable in Small Claims Court as I cannot make an order either fettering or expanding the limited costs jurisdiction of the Deputy Judge. See *Pietrangelo v. Lundrigan*, 1999 CarswellOnt 3062, 44 O.R. (3d) 71, 43 C.P.C. (4th) 157 (Ont. Div. Ct.). Accordingly, costs can only be awarded if I award them prior to the transfer as a term of my order.

There is a parallel tort action before court. Though it may not be necessary to order the matters tried together there remains a possibility this may be so. In that case the action would have to be retrieved from Small Claims Court or the Small Claims trial would have to proceed before a judge of this court. That would be inefficient. Motion to transfer the action to Small Claims Court dismissed. Plaintiff has leave to amend the statement of claim to reduce the damages to under $100,000 in which case the action shall proceed under Rule 76.

(3) Idem — **An action transferred to the Small Claims Court shall be titled and continued as if it had been commenced in that court.**

1996, c. 25, s. 9(17)

Commentary

Transferring a Case from Superior Court of Justice to Small Claims Court

Claim started in Superior Court valued at $25,000 or less

↓	↓
↓	↓

Parties agree to transfer Case to Small Claims Court.   Parties do *not* agree to transfer case to Small Claims Court.

One party asks the Registrar Superior Court of Justice to transfer case to Small Claims Court.

One party brings a motion in Superior Court of Justice to transfer the case to Small Claims Court.

No motion to transfer. Case proceeds in Superior Court of Justice.

The party asking for the transfer:

1. Files with the court a Form 4E and the written consent of the parties;

2. Pays court fee to transfer the court file to Small Claims Court ($75 fee).

For the steps, see *Small* Claims Court — Increase in monetary limit from $10,000 to $25,000.

Moving party pays court fee for filing a Notice of Motion ($127 fee).

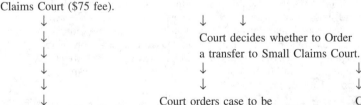

Court decides whether to Order a transfer to Small Claims Court.

Court orders case to be

Court refuses to order

Claim started in Superior Court valued at $25,000 or less

↓	transferred to Small	transfer. Case proceeds in
↓	Claims Court.	Superior Court of Justice.
↓	↓	
↓	Moving party pays court fee to transfer court	
↓	file to the Small Claims Court ($75 fee).	
↓	↓	
↓	↓	
↓	↓	

Registrar transfers the case to   Court transfers the case to
Small Claims Court.   Small Claims Court.

Case Law: *Chymyshyn v. Aldinger Construction Ltd.* (1994), 27 C.P.C. (3d) 391 (Man. Q.B.) — The amount of claim was $120,000. The plaintiff was awarded $6,000 at trial. The defendant was awarded costs in the amount of $27,000. The plaintiff claimed a substantial amount of damages but the vast majority of the plaintiff's claims were completely unsubstantiated. The plaintiff's conduct tended to unnecessarily lengthen the proceedings. Offers to settle were made but were not accepted. All factors considered, it would be unconscionable to deprive the defendants of costs, notwithstanding the plaintiff's limited success.

Mak v. Hlinomaz (1994), 1 B.C.L.R. (3d) 360 (B.C. S.C.) — The plaintiff applied under s. 13.1 of the *Supreme Court Act* to transfer a minor motor vehicle personal injury action to the Small Claims Court before the defendant served jury notice. The defendant, seeking a trial by jury, opposed the application. Application to transfer to the Small Claims Court was allowed. Factors weighed in favour of the defendant's position. However, those circumstances had to be weighed against the obvious merit in having the trial heard in the Small Claims Court. In these circumstances, it was appropriate to transfer the matter to the Small Claims Court.

Waymark v. Barnes (1994), 98 B.C.L.R. (2d) 352 (B.C. S.C.); leave to appeal refused (1995), 3 B.C.L.R. (3d) 354 (B.C. C.A.) — The plaintiff, in minor personal injury action, wanted to transfer the case to the Small Claims Court under s. 13.1 of the Supreme Court Act. The defendant opposed the transfer and wanted a jury trial. (A 5-day trial before a jury was estimated). The case was singularly appropriate to be heard in the Small Claims Court. Application to transfer was appropriate where amount of personal injury claim would not exceed the monetary limit of $10,000. The defendant's intention to file jury notice did not bar the transfer where the notice was not yet filed. The plaintiff's application was made with the aim of saving the inordinately high costs which would be incurred in the Supreme Court.

Wright v. Uchida (1994), 1 B.C.L.R. (3d) 252 (B.C. S.C.) — The plaintiff sued for damages arising out of a motor vehicle accident. The defendant filed and served jury notice. The plaintiff then decided his claim would not exceed the monetary jurisdiction of the Small Claims Court and applied to transfer the action to that Court under s. 13.1 of the *Supreme Court Act*. The Master dismissed the application and the plaintiff appealed. The plaintiff lost the right to transfer the case to the Small Claims Court where not filing the application to transfer before delivery of notice of trial and notice requiring trial by jury. Referred to *Kirk v. Ciceri*, Melvin J. [reported 99 B.C.L.R. (2d) 26 (S.C.)].

Yuen v. Regency Lexus Toyota Inc. (1994), 30 C.P.C. (3d) 315 (B.C. S.C.) — The plaintiff sued for rescission and, alternatively, for damages in excess of $10,000 in respect of a vehicle purchased from the defendant. The plaintiff only recovered $6,000. The judgment was within the monetary jurisdiction of the Provincial Court. The plaintiff was not entitled to costs other than disbursements. Assuming, without deciding that the remedy of rescission was not available in the Provincial Court, the inclusion of a claim for rescission was not a good ground for awarding costs because that claim failed.

Lau v. Chisholm (1995), 6 W.D.C.P. (2d) 402 (Ont. Gen. Div.) — Plaintiff failed to demonstrate triable issue. Plaintiff previously lost case against hospital in Small Claims Court. He then sued doctor in General Division. Defendant entitled to costs on a solicitor and client basis.

Hiebert v. Brown, [1995] B.C.W.L.D. 2656 (Master) — Defendant sought trial by judge and jury. Plaintiff allowed to transfer to Small Claims Court since parties agreed quantum within jurisdiction of Provincial Court. Court noted situations where transfer would not be allowed.

Stewart v. Manitoba Opera Assn. Inc. (1995), 104 Man. R. (2d) 159 (Q.B.) — Amount awarded at trial in Queen's Bench within jurisdiction of Small Claims Court. Court awarded costs of $1,500, not $100 set out in Small Claims tariff. Discoveries had been held prior to trial.

Andrews v. North Burnaby Towing Ltd., [1996] B.C.W.L.D. 013 (Master) — The test applied to transfer case "down" was whether or not plaintiff had an arguable case. Unless the court concluded that the plaintiff could not possibly succeed on the claim to an extent beyond the monetary jurisdiction of Provincial Court, the motion would be denied.

McGinty v. Toronto Transit Commission (1996), 7 W.D.C.P. (2d) 101 (Ont. Div. Ct.) — Pre-trial judge, on his own motion, decided to transfer action from the General Division to the Small Claims Court. If it were clear that the plaintiff's claim was for $6,000 or less, then under s. 23(2) of the *Courts of Justice Act* with consent of all parties, the action could have been transferred to the Small Claims Court. If it were also clear that the plaintiff's claim was for $6,000 or less, even without a motion made by a party the pre-trial judge could exercise his inherent jurisdiction and, without necessary recourse to either s. 23(2) or s. 110(1), could have made an order transferring the action to the Small Claims Court. See *Shoppers Trust Co. v. Mann Taxi Management Ltd.* (1993), 16 O.R. (3d) 192 (Gen. Div.), just as an action brought in the Small Claims Court could be transferred to the General Division where the value of the claim exceeds that of the Small Claims Court. See *Tawfik v. Baker* (1992), 10 O.R. (3d) 569 (Gen. Div.). Jurisprudence governing pre-trials followed in *Essa (Township) v. Guergis* (1993), 15 O.R. (3d) 573 (Div. Ct.).

Shibley v. Harris, [1995] B.C.W.L.D. 2724 (B.C. S.C.) — Offer to settle in Supreme Court rejected by plaintiff. Damages awarded of $4,400. Plaintiff *only* entitled to disbursements up to date offer made. Defendant entitled to costs and disbursements thereafter.

Mohsen v. Watson, 1995 CarswellOnt 2198 (Ont. Gen. Div.) — Plaintiff recovered $1,600 at trial where original claim was $13,587.97. Plaintiff awarded one-half party and party costs fixed at $5,061.45. Defendant made no offer to settle and neither party applied to transfer case to Small Claims Court. Rule 57.05(1) of *Rules of Civil Procedure* applied.

Purcell v. Taylor (1994), 120 D.L.R. (4th) 161 (Ont. Gen. Div.) — Monetary recovery of $2,500 within jurisdiction of Small Claims Court, trial in General Division. Rule 57.05(1) of *Rules of Civil Procedure* did not apply re default judgment against dog owner, costs assessed pursuant to Rule 57.05(3) and Small Claims Court tariff. Successful defendant home owner awarded costs of $2,000. Plaintiff should have transferred case down to Small Claims Court.

32262 B.C. Ltd. v. Trans Western Express Inc. (1995), 38 C.P.C. (3d) 201 (B.C. S.C.) — Section 13 of the *Small Claims Act* (B.C.) allowed the Supreme Court of British Columbia to award costs to any party to an appeal, in accordance with the rules of court. A party who failed on an appeal should be subject to an award of costs from the appeal. A defendant who succeeded on an appeal had a moral claim to costs of the appeal, having been brought into litigation at the instance of the plaintiff. A plaintiff who has rightly chosen the Provincial

Court as the proper forum for his claim but has been denied victory wrongly should, succeeding on appeal, ordinarily be entitled to an award of costs. That general rule was subject to the recognized exception where the case was won in the Supreme Court on the basis of evidence or a submission not presented in the Provincial Court.

Perret v. Pappas (1995), 13 B.C.L.R. (3d) 166 (Master) — The plaintiff sued for damages. After pleadings were filed, documents exchanged, discovery completed and motion heard, the plaintiff applied successfully to transfer action to Provincial Court — Small Claims Division. The defendant applied for costs of proceedings in the Supreme Court. The plaintiff had availed himself of procedures, such as examinations for discovery, not available in the Provincial Court. Defendant entitled to costs, including disbursements of $1,800.

Yee v. Tight Spot Rentals Ltd. (1995), 11 B.C.L.R. (3d) 291 (S.C.) — The plaintiff sued for damages for a mild injury. Despite liability being clear, the defendants disputed it and delivered a notice requiring trial by jury. Plaintiff awarded non-pecuniary damages of $1,000. The defendants applied for an order limiting the costs recoverable by the plaintiff to those available in the Provincial Court — Small Claims Division. The application was dismissed on the basis that the plaintiff was prevented from transferring his action to the Provincial Court by the Defendant's insistence on a jury trial. The view that costs are awarded solely to indemnify a successful litigant for legal fees and disbursements is outdated.

Eades v. Kootnikoff (1995), 13 B.C.L.R. (3d) 182 (S.C.) — Whether a claim can be identified as a "liquidated demand" such that, upon default of appearance, final judgment may be taken for the amount of the claim depends upon whether the amount to which the plaintiff is entitled can be ascertained from the contract itself or by calculation or fixed by a scale of charges agreed upon by the contract or implied by it. Some lawyers' accounts for legal services may be liquidated demands and others may not. Where the pleadings do not claim that there was an agreement as to the amount the lawyer was to be paid or as to the method of calculation of the lawyer's fee, a lawyer's claim for legal services is not a liquidated demand. *Holden Day Wilson v. Ashton* (1993), 14 O.R. (3d) 306, 104 D.L.R. (4th) 266, 64 O.A.C. 4 (Div. Ct.) applied.

U.C. Home Equity Development Ltd. v. British Columbia (Provincial Court Judge) (1996), 24 B.C.L.R. (3d) 135 (S.C.) — Supreme Court of British Columbia, on appeal from order of Provincial court under *Small Claims Court Act*, did not have jurisdiction to remit claim for retrial in Provincial Court. Appeal was by way of new trial in Supreme Court.

Martin v. Tom (1996), 27 B.C.L.R. (3d) 268 (S.C.) — Master transferring action to Provincial Court and ordering costs up to and including transfer application payable to successful litigant. Defendant appealing ruling on costs. Master erred in awarding costs. Plaintiff was not required to justify why she had commenced action in Supreme Court. In the circumstances, no costs were awarded.

Samain v. Roman (1996), 62 A.C.W.S. 65 (B.C. Master) — Plaintiff commenced action in Supreme Court claiming damages for motor vehicle accident. Action settled in part and releases executed. Claim for punitive, aggravated and exemplary damages continued and would be less than $10,000. Defendant claimed plaintiff's application for transfer to Provincial Court was improper splitting of case. Application for transfer granted on terms providing for right of discoveries.

Meanley v. Dicky (1996), 64 A.C.W.S. 785 (B.C. Master) — Plaintiff injured in motor vehicle accident and elected to receive worker's compensation. Workers' compensation board as subrogated to plaintiff rights, brought action in supreme court against defendants. After discoveries, board determined size of claim was within small claims court jurisdiction and brought motion for transfer. Court held that in view of number of witnesses and procedures unavailable in small claims court, balance of prejudice lay in favour of keeping matter in

Supreme Court where defendants would have more complete opportunity to present defence. Motion dismissed.

Wexford Communications Ltd. v. Buildrite Centres Inc. (1996), 156 N.S.R. (2d) 78, 461 A.P.R. 78 (S.C.) — Appellants initiated action in Supreme Court but then elected to transfer to small claims court. That there was no provision in *Small Claims Court Act* or Regulations for discovery did not constitute breach of natural justice. When appellants transferred, they must be taken to have known about absence of statutory authority for discovery and to have weighed impact of that fact upon presentation of their case.

Manley v. Burns Lake Community Development Assn., 1996 CarswellBC 2490, [1996] B.C.J. No. 2236 (B.C. Master) — Plaintiff commenced action in supreme court for damages for breach of confidence. Discoveries had not occurred. Application brought seven months after notice of trial. Legal issues and facts were complex. Damages over $10,000 waived.

Norman v. Ontario (Human Rights Commission) (December 13, 1996), Doc. 96-CU-107224 (Ont. Gen. Div.) — Application for summary dismissal of claim for relocation was dismissed as there was conflict of evidence. As claim was for less than $6,000, court directed claim to be considered by Small Claims Court.

Barnstead v. Ramsay, [1996] B.C.W.L.D. 1528 (B.C. S.C.); additional reasons at [1996] B.C.W.L.D. 2489 (B.C. S.C.) — Plaintiffs awarded damages of $6,700 in Supreme Court action. Award was within jurisdiction of provincial court. Plaintiffs should have transferred action to provincial court after examinations for discovery. Costs awarded up to and including date of examinations for discovery. No costs were awarded from examinations date forward.

Sutcliffe v. Jessen, [1997] B.C.W.L.D. 101 (B.C. S.C.) — Proceeding in Supreme Court instead of in Small Claims Court. Plaintiff awarded damages of $2,000 in action arising from motor vehicle accident. Although sum recovered within jurisdiction of Small Claims Court, plaintiff had sufficient reason for bringing action in Supreme Court. Plaintiff entitled to her costs. Certainty of sum was test as to validity of offer to settle. There was no uncertainty as to offer.

Global Experience v. 855983 Ontario Ltd. (January 30, 1998), Doc. Thunder Bay 95/0266 (Ont. Gen. Div.) — Although plaintiff was awarded judgment for amount within jurisdiction of Small Claims Court and General Division court had discretion to deny plaintiff costs, General Division awarded plaintiff party-and-party costs after date of their offer to change court venue to Thunder Bay Small Claims Court.

Bulmer v. 770011 Ontario Inc. (December 7, 1998), Doc. Windsor 95-GD-34495 (Ont. Gen. Div.); was additional reasons to (June 30, 1998), Doc. Windsor 95-GD-34495 (Ont. Gen. Div) — Trial lasted almost five days, with both liability and general damages contested. Plaintiff's injuries and complaints exaggerated. Plaintiff's recovery was $2,000 together with prejudgment interest. Was plaintiff entitled to any award of costs, or should Rule 57.05(1) of the *Rules of Civil Procedure*, R.R.O. 1990, Reg. 194, be implemented? Not a situation where the action was transferred from the Small Claims Court. Plaintiff's counsel, at least at time of discovery, should have considered the Small Claims Court or, at minimum, defense counsel, who by then had assessed the plaintiff's claim. While every citizen is entitled to his day in court, the issues must be considered in the proper forum. It is the plaintiff who should suffer the costs consequence. It is proper to invoke Rule 57.05(1). No costs ordered for either party.

Cox v. Robertson (January 28, 1999), Doc. Vancouver C976553 (B.C. S.C.) — Damages were awarded to the plaintiff in the jurisdiction of Provincial Court under the *Small Claims Act* (B.C.). So long as action was properly brought in Supreme Court, Rules of Court (B.C.), Rule 37(24) applied to determine costs. The plaintiff had sufficient reason to bring action in the Supreme Court. There was reasonable prospect that the plaintiff would succeed on issue of mitigation. Rule 37(24) applied in this case.

Sangster v. Musil (March 3, 1999), Doc. Vancouver B972110 (B.C. Master) — The action was brought in B.C. Supreme Court, but the settlement was made for amount within the jurisdiction of the B.C. Provincial Court. The plaintiff was not entitled to costs. There was no discretion under Rule 37(47) of the Supreme Court Rules (B.C.). The defendant was entitled to costs. Each party was to bear its own costs for motion.

Sterrett v. MKA Leasing Inc. (June 14, 1999), Doc. Vancouver B964301 (B.C. S.C.) — An action was brought in Supreme Court (B.C.). The recovery was within the jurisdiction of the Provincial court. It was open to the plaintiff to transfer the claim to Provincial Court. After examination for discovery it would have been reasonable to do so. The plaintiff was only entitled to her disbursements.

Williams (Litigation Guardian of) v. Barnett (2001), 2001 CarswellOnt 92 (Ont. S.C.J.) — The respondent sought costs for an unsuccessful motion by the applicant to transfer proceeding from Small Claims Court to Superior Court. Modest costs were awarded.

Pietrangelo v. Lundrigan (1999), 44 O.R. (3d) 71, 43 C.P.C. (4th) 157, 1999 CarswellOnt 3062 (Ont. Div. Ct.) — The plaintiff commenced an action for damages in Superior Court. The defendant brought a motion to transfer the action to Small Claims Court. The motion was granted. The Motions Judge ordered costs of action to date of transfer in the cause following trial. The defendant appealed from pre-transfer costs order; the appeal was allowed. The costs order unlawfully fettered already limited discretion of Deputy Judge in Small Claims Court. The Motions Judge lacked the jurisdiction to make an order awarding costs of action in Small Claims Court.

Wharton v. Tom Harris Chevrolet Oldsmobile Cadillac Ltd., 163 B.C.A.C. 122, 2002 CarswellBC 137, 2002 BCCA 78, 97 B.C.L.R. (3d) 307, [2002] 3 W.W.R. 629, 267 W.A.C. 122 (B.C. C.A.) — Plaintiff awarded $7,257.17 damages at trial, plus costs. Defendant disputed costs on ground recovery within the jurisdiction of the Small Claims Court, precluding costs under Rule 57(10). Court of Appeal refused to interfere with the Court's discretion in awarding costs, noting that the plaintiff's claim of over $30,000 brought her within the jurisdiction of Supreme Court.

Lowe v. Redding, 2003 CarswellBC 778, 2003 BCSC 356, 14 B.C.L.R. (4th) 192 (B.C. S.C. [In Chambers]) — Plaintiff suing for defamation. Defendant making offer to settle for zero dollars and costs. Plaintiff seeking award of costs. Application allowed. While amount within jurisdiction of Small Claims Court, action for defamation not permitted in Small Claims Court.

Biddles v. Ellsworth, 2002 CarswellAlta 1796, 2002 ABPC 151, 331 A.R. 397 (Alta. Prov. Ct.) — Plaintiff's action for damages resulting from motor vehicle accident within jurisdiction of Provincial Court. Court had no further jurisdiction under section 56 of Act to consider defendant's request to transfer action to Court of Queen's Bench to be joined with defendant's action.

Shaughnessy v. Roth, 2006 CarswellBC 806, 2006 BCSC 531 (B.C. S.C.) 2006-04-03.

Petitioner applied for judicial review of decision of Provincial Court judge sitting in Small Claims, that entire action be transferred to the Supreme Court.

Petitioner seeks order under *Judicial Review Procedure Act*, R.S.B.C. 1996, c. 241, setting aside order of the Provincial Court judge.

On September 1, 2005, the monetary jurisdiction of the Small Claims Court was increased to $25,000 by B.C. Regulation 179/2005.

As of September 1, 2005 the amounts in Rule 1 and 4 were increased to $25,000 and Rule 8(7) requires that a claimant who filed a notice of claim before September 1, 2005 may change the notice of claim to increase the amount of the claim to an amount that is more than $10,000 and not more than $25,000. Rule 8(9) requires the change to be made by changing the notice of claim in which the claim was first made.

The authority of a Provincial Court judge to transfer a Small Claims action to Supreme Court is found within Rule 7.1 of the *Small Claims Rules*, B.C. Reg. 261/193, as amended, which states as of September 1, 2005:

> (1) If satisfied that the monetary outcome of claim (not including interest and expenses) may exceed $25,000, a judge must transfer the claim to the Supreme Court
>
>> (a) on application at any time, or
>>
>> (b) on the judge's own motion at the settlement conference or trial.

Provincial Court judge did not have jurisdiction to make the order transferring the petitioner's claim to Supreme Court.

Provincial Court to reconsider and determine whether the petitioner's claim by itself has a monetary outcome that might exceed $25,000, and if so whether the petitioner chooses to abandon the amount of $25,000 to maintain the claim within Provincial Court.

Nesbitt v. James Western Star Sterling Ltd., 2006 CarswellBC 1147, 32 M.V.R. (5th) 12, 2006 BCSC 740 (B.C. S.C.) 2006-05-11.

Plaintiff was successful in action for deceit: 2006 CarswellBC 713, 2006 BCSC 473; damages assessed at $21,509.47, which included $5,000 for punitive damages. The plaintiff seeks special costs. The defendant takes the position that the plaintiff should receive disbursements only because amount of damages within Small Claims limit.

Not unreasonable to bring claim in Supreme Court. Not obviously a Small Claims action, notwithstanding eventual award.

Menna v. Toronto Humane Society, 2006 CarswellOnt 3170 (Ont. S.C.J.) 2006-05-25.

Plaintiff was successful and therefore is presumptively entitled to costs. Defendant argues that provisions of Rule 57.05 should operate to deprive the Plaintiff of costs in view of assertion that value of the Plaintiff's recovery falls within the $10,000 limit of the monetary jurisdiction of the Small Claims Court.

Monetary value of "Chrissy" not subject of specific evidence at trial. Discretion to decline to give effect to Rule 57.05 in this case. Written offer to settle delivered by Plaintiff on May 8, 2006, some two weeks prior to trial. The fair and reasonable sum to award to Plaintiff for her costs $10,000.

Radovici v. Toronto Police Services Board (2007), 2007 CarswellOnt 4317, 86 O.R. (3d) 691 (Ont. S.C.J.), Lax J.

Damages assessed at $7,500.

Royal Oak v. Quality, 2013 ONSC 7135, D. L. Edwards, J. (Ont. S.C.J.)

In Judgment, the Court ordered that Quality Engineered Homes Ltd ("QEH") pay to Kirsteen Dies and David William Dies ("Dies") the sum of $8,820. Dies seek a cost award in the amount of $26,072.17 on a partial indemnity basis.

QEH submits that the divided success favoured it and it should receive costs on a partial indemnity basis of $14,752.13. Appropriate case for each party to bear its own costs. Contract dispute could have been pursued through the Small Claims Court.

As per Rule 57.05 discretion to order that the plaintiff not recover its costs.

Once lien action dismissed, matter could have gone by way of the simplified procedure.

Goulding v. Street Motor Sales Ltd., 2013 ONSC 1904, 2013 CarswellOnt 3648, Beaudoin, J. (Ont. S.C.J.)

Following a two-day trial total recovery below amount recoverable in Small Claims Court. See Rule 57.05(1) regarding cost submissions. Damages were arguably above the jurisdiction of the Small Claims Court. Case law where it could not reasonable by known until the conclusion of the matter that damages would be within a lesser jurisdiction. See *Wicken (Litigation Guardian of) v. Harssar*, 2002 CarswellOnt 2410, 24 C.P.C. (5th) 164, [2002] O.T.C. 1067, [2002] O.J. No. 2843 (Ont. S.C.J.); leave to appeal allowed 2003 CarswellOnt 106 (Ont. Div. Ct.); affirmed 2004 CarswellOnt 1858, 73 O.R. (3d) 600, 11 C.C.L.I. (4th) 150, 49 C.P.C. (5th) 76, 240 D.L.R. (4th) 520, (sub nom. *Wicken v. Harssar)* 186 O.A.C. 344 (Ont. Div. Ct.) and *Hunt v. TD Securities Inc.*, 2003 CarswellOnt 4971, 40 B.L.R. (3d) 156, 43 C.P.C. (5th) 211, [2003] O.J. No. 4868 (Ont. C.A.).

Plaintiff not entitled to costs not withstanding modest success at trial. Only issue whether to award any costs to the defendants. Inflammatory pleadings drafted to expand issues and drive up costs unnecessarily. The defendants were dragged to Ottawa. The defendants did not beat their Rule 49 offer to settle, the court can consider under Rule 57.01(1). Rule 57.01(2) allows for an award of costs against a successful party "in a proper case". This is such a case. Plaintiff to pay defendants $10,000 plus HST disbursements for a total of $11,571.20.

24. (1) Composition of court for hearings — A proceeding in the Small Claims Court shall be heard and determined by one judge of the Superior Court of Justice.

(2) Provincial judge or deputy judge may preside — A proceeding in the Small Claims Court may also be heard and determined by,

(a) a provincial judge who was assigned to the Provincial Court (Civil Division) immediately before the 1st day of September, 1990;

(b) a deputy judge appointed under section 32.

Commentary: This permits a Small Claims Court referee, on consent of all parties to the proceeding, to have the proceeding heard and determined by the referee. This section has *not* yet been proclaimed in force.

(3) Where deputy judge not to preside — A deputy judge shall not hear and determine an action,

(a) for the payment of money in excess of the prescribed amount; or

(b) for the recovery of possession of personal property exceeding the prescribed amount in value.

1996, c. 25, s. 9(17)

Commentary: Deputy judges are clearly appointed to preside over matters in the Small Claims Court. These are also arguably bound by s. 123 of the *Courts of Justice Act* and the protocol pursuant to s. 136.

Case Law: *Lippé c. Charest*, [1991] S.C.J. No. 128, 1990 CarswellQue 98, (sub nom. *R. v. Lippé)* 61 C.C.C. (3d) 127, (sub nom. *R. c. Lippé)* [1991] 2 S.C.R. 114, 5 M.P.L.R. (2d) 113, 5 C.R.R. (2d) 31, (sub nom. *Lippé v. Québec (Procureur général))* 128 N.R. 1 (S.C.C.); *R. v. Lippé* (1990), 1991 CarswellQue 45, REJB 1990-95652, 64 C.C.C. (3d) 513 (S.C.C.) — Does the Quebec system of permitting part-time Municipal Court Judges to practise law infringe the guarantee of judicial impartiality under s. 11(d) of the *Canadian Charter of Rights and Freedoms* and s. 23 of the Quebec *Charter of Human Rights and Freedoms*? The Supreme Court of Canada said no by a vote of 7-0 and issued two concurring judgments.

That Judges were part-time did not per se raise a reasonable apprehension of bias on an institutional level, but certain activities or professions in which they engaged might be incompatible with their duties as Judges and raise such a bias.

The occupation of practising law was per se incompatible with the function of a Judge because it gave rise to a reasonable apprehension of bias in the mind of a fully informed person in a substantial number of cases. However, having regard to the safeguards in place, the risk of bias had been minimized. The safeguards included the oath sworn by the Judges, the Code of ethics to which they were subject and the restrictions set out in s. 608.1 of the *Cities and Towns Act*, R.S.Q. c. C-19. The safeguards all combined to alleviate the apprehension of bias. A person reasonably well-informed about the Quebec Municipal Court system should not have an apprehension of bias in a substantial number of cases.

Lupton v. Tamin (2000), 2000 CarswellOnt 218 (Ont. S.C.J.) — The question was whether a deputy judge had erred by recommending to unrepresented plaintiffs that they amend their claim to include alternate claim for damages for tile repair. The appeal was dismissed. The plaintiffs were not legally trained. It is important that the Small Claims Court judge ensures that issues are decided on merits and not on procedural technicalities.

Webb v. 3584747 Canada Inc., 2002 CarswellOnt 2125, (sub nom. *Webb v. 3574747 Canada Inc.*) 161 O.A.C. 244, (sub nom. *Webb v. 3574747 Canada Inc.*) 24 C.P.C. (5th) 76 (Ont. Div. Ct.); affirmed 2004 CarswellOnt 325, [2004] O.J. No. 215, 183 O.A.C. 155, 69 O.R. (3d) 502, 41 C.P.C. (5th) 98 (Ont. C.A.); leave to appeal refused [2004] S.C.C.A. No. 114, 2004 CarswellOnt 2988, 2004 CarswellOnt 2989, 331 N.R. 399 (note) (S.C.C.) — In a class action proceeding, the managing judge directed that certain claims be heard before deputy judges of the Small Claims Court who consented to conduct hearings. The defendant in action obtained leave to appeal on the issue of whether, in making the order, the managing judge had exercised the power reserved to the Chief Justice under section 14(1) of the Courts of Justice Act to direct and supervise the sittings of the Superior Court of Justice and the assignment of its judicial duties. The Ontario Divisional Court allowed the appeal. The direction could not stand. If the deputy judges were appointed as persons, whose attributes included that holding of an office, then they could not bring with them their court staff, offices or support, or the right to remuneration as if sitting in court. The Divisional Court commented that "whether a Deputy Judge of the Small Claims Court is an officer of the Superior Court, or is a judge of the court within Rule 54.03, was not argued before us and we can express no final opinion on such an issue. However, we have serious reservations about both propositions.".

Reference re Territorial Court Act (Northwest Territories) (1997), 1997 CarswellNWT 24, 152 D.L.R. (4th) 132, 12 C.P.C. (4th) 7, [1998] 1 W.W.R. 733, [1997] N.W.T.R. 377 (N.W.T. S.C.) — Constitutional validity of appointment of deputy Territorial Judge full-time or part-time, for a fixed period of two years or less. Interesting 38-page decision, unlimited discretion reposed in executive to appoint or reappoint deputy judges incompatible with the principles of independence, both individual and institutional leads to the perception of a lack of impartiality. It results in deputy judges being subject to different legislative regime than full territorial judges. Results in two classes of judges. *Lippé c. Charest*, [1991] S.C.J. No. 128, 1990 CarswellQue 98, (sub nom. *R. v. Lippé*) 61 C.C.C. (3d) 127, (sub nom. *R. c. Lippé*) [1991] 2 S.C.R. 114, 5 M.P.L.R. (2d) 113, 5 C.R.R. (2d) 31, (sub nom. *Lippé v. Québec (Procureur général)*) 128 N.R. 1 (S.C.C.). While the Charter does not prohibit part-time judges, it does not guarantee they will not engage in activities incompatible with their duties as a judge distinguished. There are a few professions that if engaged in by part-time judges, may raise an apprehension of bias on an institutional level.

Dolmage v. Erskine, 2003 CarswellOnt 161, 23 C.P.R. (4th) 495 (Ont. S.C.J.). Pursuant to provisions of *Copyright Act*, R.S.C., 1985, c. C-42 the Plaintiff claimed declarations, a permanent injunction *inter alia*. Small Claims Court has jurisdiction to hear claim for damages for infringement of copyright or moral rights. See Section 37 of *Copyright Act* See also: Section 20(2) of the *Federal Court Act* R.S.C. 1985, c.F-70 as amended. Damages assessed at $3,000 for indignation and diminution of reputation.

Liu Estate v. Chau, 2004 CarswellOnt 442, 69 O.R. (3d) 756, 236 D.L.R. (4th) 711, 182 O.A.C. 366 (Ont. C.A.). Trial judge excluded female defendant (Chau) from the courtroom while the male defendant (Chau's husband) testified. Trial judge breached *Civil Procedure Rule 52.06(2)* which provided, in part, that an order for exclusion of witnesses could not be made in respect of a party. Although a serious procedural error, the Court denied a new trial, holding no substantial wrong or miscarriage of justice.

Hubley v. Nissan, 2003 NSSC 236, 2003 CarswellNS 490, 219 N.S.R. (2d) 165, 692 A.P.R. 165 (N.S. S.C.). Denial of adjournment to beef farmer unable to attend for trial during calving season denial of natural justice.

Boer v. Cairns (2003), 2003 CarswellOnt 5455, [2003] O.J. No. 5466, 21 C.C.L.T. (3d) 95 (Ont. S.C.J.), Molloy, J. Plaintiff obtained judgment for $5,000. Defendant made initial offer under Rule 49 of *Rules of Civil Procedure* (Ont.) to pay $20,000 to settle action. Defendant's subsequent offer to pay $56,000 was not *Rule 49* offer. Second offer could not constitute implied revocation of *Rule 49* offer. Costs consequences triggered by initial offer.

Cloverdale Paint Inc. v. Duchesne, 2003 CarswellBC 2181, 2003 BCSC 1375 (B.C. S.C.). Defendant served with default judgment on February 11th. Defendant applying to set judgment aside on April 10th. Application dismissed. Defendant failing to take steps without good reason. No justifiable reason for delay.

Ibranovic v. Advanced Servo Technologies (2003), 2003 CarswellOnt 3565 (Ont. S.C.J.). Plaintiff obtaining judgment for $916.75 more than offer to settle amount. Entitled to substantial indemnity costs from date of offer to settle. In the absence of special circumstances, the entitlement to increased costs pursuant to *Rule 49.10* for an offer to settle applied to an action governed by simplified procedure under *Rule 76*.

O'Brien v. O'Brien (2003), 2003 CarswellOnt 2761 (Ont. S.C.J.). Unrepresented litigant sought costs of $45,000. Litigant successful. $10,000 paid into Court earlier. Costs limited to $10,000 paid into Court.

Michalakis v. Nikolitsas, 2002 CarswellBC 3258, 2002 BCSC 1708 (B.C. S.C.). Settlement conference was to take place but petitioner ill and could not attend, so rescheduled. Petitioner did not attend rescheduled settlement conference because he did not receive notice of it. Settlement judge noted petitioner in default. Petitioner applied to set aside default judgment. Application granted.

Children's Aid Society of Niagara Region v. P. (D.) (2002), 2002 CarswellOnt 4418, 62 O.R. (3d) 668, 16 O.F.L.R. 145 (Ont. S.C.J.). Test for allowing representation by unpaid, non-lawyer agent-friend. Agent, like self-represented litigant, must act, with courtesy and respect towards all and not create undue delay in proceedings. Representation by unpaid, non-lawyer agent-friend does not violate s. 50(1) (*Solicitors Act*).

Korhani v. Bank of Montreal (2002), 2002 CarswellOnt 4223, [2002] O.J. No. 4785 (Ont. S.C.J.). Claim against self-represented Defendant dismissed as part of settlement of action by other parties. Defendant not employed and not entitled to compensation for her time spent, or that of husband who assisted her. However, defendant entitled to generous disbursements of $6,990 including fees paid to solicitors who assisted, travel costs for obtaining documents, and child care costs for attendance times, payable jointly by plaintiff and other defendant.

Ravka v. Ravka (2002), 2002 CarswellOnt 3081, 165 O.A.C. 44, 35 R.F.L. (5th) 176 (Ont. C.A.). Judge intervened 101 times in 218 pages of transcript, during presentation of parties' case in application for variation of spousal support. Intervention excessive. Decision set aside.

Sidlofsky v. Crown Eagle Ltd. (2002), 2002 CarswellOnt 3620, [2002] O.J. No. 4152 (Ont. S.C.J.). Plaintiffs purchased vacation package in Ontario from Defendant S, Ontario corporation. Accommodation was at Holiday Inn in Jamaica. Holiday Inn was Tennessee corporation. Plaintiff fell and was injured at hotel. Ontario had both jurisdiction and was *forums conveniens*.

Petrella v. Westwood Chev Olds (1993) Ltd., 2004 CarswellOnt 364, [2004] O.J. No. 491 (Ont. S.C.J.), Durno, RSJ. On appeal from the decision of Deputy Judge Warren McCrea. Motion to have the defendant's counsel removed from case because he was a Deputy Judge in Toronto. Motion to be heard by Superior Court Judge, because any Deputy Judge would have a pecuniary interest in the motion, thereby creating a reasonable apprehension of bias? Deputy Judge exceeded his jurisdiction when he ordered application to be heard by a Judge of the Superior Court. Deputy Judges do not have inherent jurisdiction. The Small Claims Court is a branch of the Superior Court of Justice, s. 22(1) of the *CJA*.

Ontario Deputy Judges Assn. v. Ontario, 2005 CarswellOnt 6638, 18 C.P.C. (6th) 324, 78 O.R. (3d) 504, 139 C.R.R. (2d) 38 (Ont. S.C.J.), M. Dambrot J. Deputy Judges of the Ontario Small Claims Court paid $232 per day since 1982.

Deputy Judges are judges by history, appointment, function and jurisdiction. They are referred to as "Your Honour" by virtue of a Ministry of the Attorney General directive. They swear the same oath of office as every other judge of a court in Ontario. They have judicial immunity. Proceedings of the Small Claims Court commence with a formal opening read by the Clerk. The Small Claims Court is a court of record.

Salaries of the Deputy Judges of the Small Claims Court have fallen below a minimum acceptable level. They do not have sufficient financial security to meet the legal test for judicial independence.

Respondents shall, within six months of the release of this judgment, provide recourse to the Deputy Judges of the Small Claims Court to a commission for determining judicial remuneration that is independent, efficient and objective.

Ontario Deputy Judges Assn. v. Ontario, 2006 CarswellOnt 3137, 268 D.L.R. (4th) 86, 28 C.P.C. (6th) 1, 80 O.R. (3d) 481, 210 O.A.C. 94, *(sub nom. Ontario Deputy Judges' Assn. v. Ontario (Attorney General))* 141 C.R.R. (2d) 238 (Ont. C.A.).

Remuneration of Deputy Judges of Small Claims Court. Application judge found appropriate order that Commission be struck to advise Governor in Council of appropriate remuneration package. Attorney General appealed. Appeal allowed in part; aspects of order dealing with constitutional minimum set aside; Attorney General ordered to establish independent, effective and objective process within four months.

Roskam v. Rogers Cable (2008), [2008] O.J. No. 2049, 2008 CarswellOnt 2958, *(sub nom. Roskam v. Rogers Cable (A Business))* 173 C.R.R. (2d) 157 (Ont. Div. Ct.), DiTomaso J.

Deputy Judges are allowed to practice law while adjudicating claims and this does not infringe Appellants Charter rights either in respect of section 15 or section 11(d) of the Charter.

Provincial courts do not have jurisdiction to review abuse of licence issue (here, broadcasting licence) which is regulatory matter and thus, shall be decided by a specialized body.

Prefontaine v. Minister of National Revenue (2001), 257 W.A.C. 369, 293 A.R. 369, 97 Alta. L.R. (3d) 37, [2001] A.J. No. 1444, [2002] 1 W.W.R. 647, 13 C.P.C. (5th) 230, *(sub nom. Prefontaine v. M.N.R.)* 88 C.R.R. (2d) 373, 2001 CarswellAlta 1508, 2001 ABCA 288 (Alta. C.A.), Berger J.A.

Rule 505(6) of Alberta Rules of Court, which prevents judgment given or order made by one justice of appeal from being subject to any appeal, except by leave of justice giving judgment or making order violated section 7 of the *Canadian Charter of Rights and Freedoms*. Notwithstanding the presumption of neutrality and the oath of office taken by judges, a reasonable person would apprehend bias on the part of a judge called upon to decide whether his or her judgment should be appealed.

Ontario Deputy Judges Assn. v. Ontario, 2009 CarswellOnt 3976, 251 O.A.C. 241, 98 O.R. (3d) 89 (Ont. Div. Ct.), Swinton J.; additional reasons at 2010 ONSC 3570, 2010 Carswell-Ont 5012 (Ont. Div. Ct.).

Application made by the Ontario Deputy Judges Association to quash Ontario government's response to recommendations made by the First Deputy Judges Remuneration Commission. Application dismissed. The standard of review applicable to the government's response was rationality. The government provided legitimate reasons for departing from the Commissioner's recommendations. There was no evidence the government's response was based on political or discriminatory considerations or any improper motive. It properly relied on economic data that the Commission had ignored.

Ontario Deputy Judges Assn. v. Ontario (Attorney General), 2011 ONSC 6956, 2011 Carswell-Ont 13192, 108 O.R. (3d) 429 (Ont. S.C.J.); affirmed 2012 ONCA 437, 2012 Carswell-Ont 7932, 23 C.P.C. (7th) 1, [2012] O.J. No. 2865 (Ont. C.A.).

An application as to whether deputy judges ("DJs") in the Ontario Small Claims Court (the "OSCC") are sufficiently independent.

The Ontario Small Claims Court

The OSCC is a branch of the Superior Court of Justice. The OSCC deals with civil disputes where the claim is for less than $25,000 dollars or $50,000 where there is a cross-claim. The OSCC has a limited power to imprison in civil contempt matters (up to five days, section 30(4) of the CJA).

The Chief Justice of the Superior Court of Justice is the President of the OSCC.

Regional Senior Justices ("RSJs"), in their region, carry out those duties and responsibilities delegated by the Chief Justice.

There are over 400 DJs in 90 locations throughout the province. Most work an average of less than two days a month. Typically, DJs earn their income mainly from the private practice of law.

The jurisprudence is replete with references to the important and demanding role played by the OSCC in our province's justice system. The OSCC is often referred to as the "face of justice" for most citizens (see *Ontario Deputy Judges Assn. v. Ontario*, 2006 CarswellOnt 3137, [2006] O.J. No. 2057, 80 O.R. (3d) 481, 268 D.L.R. (4th) 86, 28 C.P.C. (6th) 1, 210 O.A.C. 94, (sub nom. *Ontario Deputy Judges' Assn. v. Ontario (Attorney General)*) 141 C.R.R. (2d) 238 at paras. 26 and 27 (Ont. C.A.)).

DJs "fully assume the judicial role" when sitting in the OSCC.

The Use of Comparators

When one compares the subject matter of the OSSC, it is clear that it is qualitatively different — in terms of monetary value and in dealing with issues of personal liberty — from the work done by Judges and Justices of the Peace in the Ontario Court of Justice, and Masters in the Superior Court.

There is simply no basis for comparing the work of Judges and Justices of the Peace in the Ontario Court of Justice and Masters in the Superior Court. The model of part time fixed term judicial appointments renders the entire underpinning of the OSCC qualitatively different.

As the courts have repeatedly said, the features in support of independence are not required to be ideal, but rather, sufficient given the particular work of the court in question. Independence is a flexible concept that must be understood contextually.

A reasonable and well-informed observer would conclude that DJs and the OSCC are sufficiently independent in their work, so as to satisfy constitutional requirements.

Without doubt, the OSCC plays an important and unique role in the justice system. It is absolutely essential that the OSCC institutionally, and the DJs personally, be regarded as independent.

While it is clear that the principles of judicial independence apply to DJs in the OSCC it is also clear that these principles must be flexibly applied in a manner that takes into consideration the unique features of the work of the court and the breadth of its jurisdiction. I reject the suggestion that the OSCC will be a diminished court in the absence of the requested relief.

The Application was dismissed.

25. Summary hearings — The Small Claims Court shall hear and determine in a summary way all questions of law and fact and may make such order as is considered just and agreeable to good conscience.

Commentary: The Small Claims Court hears and determines matters in a summary way. There is no discovery in the Small Claims Court: *Phillips v. Dis-Management*, 1995 CarswellOnt 865, 24 O.R. (3d) 435 (Ont. Gen. Div.). This eliminates the bulk of pre-trial procedure normally required in civil proceedings.

Trials in Small Claims Court tend to be quite short and usually not more than half a day. Trial procedure is generally the same as in other courts although the rules of evidence under significantly relaxed, under s. 27 of the *Courts of Justice Act*.

The court's mandate to hear and determine cases in a summary way and to make such order as appears just and agreeable to good conscience does not change its nature as a court of law. Decisions of the court must be made in accordance with applicable legal principles; the fact that a case is in the Small Claims Court does not change the substantive law which applies to that case. A number of appellate cases have consistently held that it is an error for the Small Claims Court to fail to apply the substantive law: see *Sereda v. Consolidated Fire & Casualty Insurance Co.*, 1934 CarswellOnt 37, [1934] O.R. 502, [1934] 3 D.L.R. 504, [1934] O.W.N. 394 (Ont. C.A.); *Smith v. Galin*, 1956 CarswellOnt 253, 3 D.L.R. (2d) 302, [1956] O.W.N. 432 (Ont. C.A.); *Travel Machine Ltd. v. Madore*, 1983 CarswellOnt 901, 143 D.L.R. (3d) 94 (Ont. H.C.); *R. v. Bennett*, 1992 CarswellOnt 1108, 8 O.R. (3d) 651, 54 O.A.C. 321 (Ont. Div. Ct.); *O'Shanter Development Corp. v. Separi*, 1996 CarswellOnt 1701, [1996] O.J. No. 1589 (Ont. Div. Ct.); *Grant v. V & G Realty Ltd.*, 2008 NSSC 180, 2008 CarswellNS 303, 272 N.S.R. (2d) 3, 58 C.P.C. (6th) 26, 869 A.P.R. 3 (N.S. S.C.).

A motion for a non-suit can be made at trial in Small Claims Court; however, the plaintiff who wants such a motion decided at the conclusion of the plaintiff's case must elect, as in other civil courts, to call no evidence if the motion is dismissed: *Consumers' Gas Co. and Pierce (c.o.b. Beard Bulldozing and Grading), Re* (September 19, 1980), [1980] O.J. No. 1326, Cromarty J. (Ont. Div. Ct.); *Fine Art Painting and Decorating Inc. v. Rob Piroli Construction Inc.*, 2013 CarswellOnt 4681, [2013] O.J. No. 1789 (Ont. Sm. Cl. Ct.); *Bu v. Xie*, 2013 ONSC 6365, 2013 CarswellOnt 14577, [2013] O.J. No. 4761 (Ont. Div. Ct.).

The court should not decide cases based on a party's oral motion for judgment at the start of trial, but should hear evidence and submissions in the normal course: *Oakes v. Stevenson* (October 7, 2008), Doc. 129/07, [2008] O.J. No. 5842 (Ont. S.C.J.); *Bear v. Pitvor*, 2010 CarswellOnt 11081, [2010] O.J. No. 3690 (Ont. S.C.J.).

Case Law: *Field v. Menuck* (1985), 2 W.D.C.P. 219 (Ont. Prov. Ct.) — Although the Rules of this Court do not deal with notices of withdrawal or discontinuance, the *Courts of Justice Act* does reserve the use of discretion for the court with respect to its own procedure. A plaintiff cannot withdraw an action at whim or with immunity, where notice is served two days before trial. Leave or consent is necessary. The defendants were prepared for trial and thus an order as to costs is proper. See also Rule 20.

Amendments to the *Line Fences Act*, S.O. 1986, c. 47, ss. 1 to 13, were proclaimed in force on July 1, 1988. As a result, appeals that were formerly heard by a Small Claims Court Judge are now referred to a referee appointed by the Lieutenant Governor in Council. Notices of appeal filed with the Civil Division prior to July 1, 1988, will have been referred to a Small Claims Court Judge for disposition. In the event that any notice or appeal was filed on or after July 1, 1988, you should be aware of the procedural change. Any party who may have been served in error with a notice of hearing by a Small Claims Court should realize that it has been cancelled and any deposit that may have been paid should be refunded.

Smith v. Harbour Authority of Port Hood, 1993 CarswellNS 59, 16 C.P.C. (3d) 192, (sub nom. *Smith v. Port Hood Harbour Authority*) 123 N.S.R. (2d) 225, (sub nom. *Smith v. Port Hood Harbour Authority*) 340 A.P.R. 225 (N.S. S.C.) — Since the claim here was based on the provisions of the *Fishing and Recreational Harbours Act*, R.S.C. 1985, c. F-24, a Federal statute and there was no implied contract to pay, the Small Claims Court did not have jurisdiction over the matter. See also *Jumbo Motor Express Ltd. v. Hilchie*, 1988 CarswellNS 224, 89 N.S.R. (2d) 222, 227 A.P.R. 222 (N.S. Co. Ct.) where the court held that the Small Claims Court had no jurisdiction to deal with a claim for wages based on a Federal statute (*Canada Labour Code*), because this was a statutory right.

Ontario (Attorney General) v. Pembina Exploration Canada Ltd., [1989] 1 S.C.R. 206, 57 D.L.R. (4th) 710, 92 N.R. 137, (sub nom. *William Siddall & Sons Fisheries v. Pembina Exploration Can. Ltd.*) 33 O.A.C. 321 (S.C.C.) — Provided that actions are brought within the monetary limits of the Small Claims Court, this court has jurisdiction to deal with admiralty or maritime matters.

Grant v. Sehdev (1987), 3 A.C.W.S. (3d) 421 (Ont. Prov. Ct.) — The Provincial Court (Civil Division) does not have jurisdiction to hear cases where the amount of alleged damages exceeds the monetary jurisdiction of the court, notwithstanding that the amount claimed is within the courts monetary jurisdiction.

Dalhousie University v. Chapman (1988), 88 N.S.R. (2d) 439 (N.S. Co. Ct.), 225 A.P.R. 439 — The relationship between a university and its students is one of licensor and licensee and not landlord and tenant, and therefore this action falls within the jurisdiction of the small claims court.

Minielly v. Kristjanson (1989), 34 C.P.C. (2d) 120, 75 Sask. R. 317 (Sask. Q.B.) — The Provincial Court trial judge heard a motion for non-suit without explaining its meaning to the plaintiffs. The plaintiffs were, therefore, not given their day in court having regard to the spirit of the legislation.

R. v. Bennett (1992), 8 O.R. (3d) 651, 54 O.A.C. 321 (Div. Ct.) — The *Public Authorities Protection Act* limitation period, R.S.O. 1990, c. P.38, s. 7(1) applies to Small Claims Court actions. See also *Kim v. Smarte*, summarized at 28 A.C.W.S. (3d) 505 and *Dowson v. Yaworski* (1985), 12 Admin. L.R. 133, 8 O.A.C. 344 (Div. Ct.).

Span-Co. Mechanical & General Contractors v. Kournetas (November 16, 1992), Greer J. — The judgment at trial was set aside on the basis that the trial judge made findings of fact inconsistent with the evidence.

Todd v. Canada (Solicitor General) (1993), 4 W.D.C.P. (2d) 506 — An action against the Queen in right of Canada can be maintained in the Small Claims Court. Section 23(1) of the *Crown Liability & Proceedings Act*, R.S.C. 1985, c. C-50 as amended does not affect the jurisdiction of the Small Claims Court in spite of the words "superior court" since the Small Claims Court is a branch of the General Division. Reference was made to the decision in *Ontario (Attorney General) v. Pembina Exploration Canada Ltd.*, [1989] 1 S.C.R. 206, 57

D.L.R. (4th) 710, 92 N.R. 137, (sub nom. *William Siddall & Sons Fisheries v. Pembina Exploration Can. Ltd.)* 33 O.A.C. 321 (S.C.C.), where it was held that an admiralty law matter that was otherwise within the monetary jurisdiction of this Court could be heard.

Haas v. Grinyer (September 13, 1994), Doc. Kitchener 1192/94 (Ont. Gen. Div.) — Motion to strike out pleadings allowed. All matters raised clearly an attempt to relitigate issues, proceedings abuse of process. *Trendsetter Developments v. Ottawa Financial Corp.* (1989), 33 C.P.C. (2d) 16 (Ont. C.A.) followed. Rules 21.01(3)(d) and 25.11 of *Rules of Civil Procedure* applied.

Subadar v. Manerowiski (January 29, 1997), Doc. 95-CU-90990CM (Ont. Gen. Div.) — Defendants sought to have plaintiff's action dismissed for failure to pay costs previously ordered. Plaintiff admitted there had never been order made in his favour for costs payable forthwith by any defendant. Action dismissed.

R. v. Lord Chancellor, [1997] 2 All E.R. 781, [1998] Q.B. 575, [1998] 2 W.L.R. 849 (Eng. Q.B.) — Applicant wished to bring proceedings in the court but could not afford to pay the applicable court fees. He applied for judicial review, asking for a declaration that the Act which set forth the fee schedule was *ultra vires* and unlawful on the ground that it breached the implied limitation in that section that fees could not be prescribed in such a way as to deprive a citizen of his constitutional right of access to the courts. Court held that a citizen's right of access to the courts is a common law constitutional right which could only be abrogated by specific statutory authority which specifically conferred the power to abrogate that right. In this instance, the effect was to bar many persons from seeking justice in the courts, and as such the provision was held to be unlawful.

Breeze v. Ontario (Attorney General) (December 10, 1997) (Ont. Gen. Div.), Southey J. — The Court held that the Lieutenant Governor in Council, pursuant to the *Administration of Justice Act,* R.S.O. 1990, c. A.6, and its regulations, has the power to make regulations requiring the payment of fees in respect of proceedings in any court and to prescribe the amount thereof. For this reason, the applicant's argument that a filing fee of $75.00 to file a motion in Landlord and Tenant Court should not be required was rejected.

Mattick Estate v. Ontario (Minister of Health) (1999), 46 O.R. (3d) 613, 1999 CarswellOnt 4271 (Ont. S.C.J.); reversed (2001), 195 D.L.R. (4th) 540, 52 O.R. (3d) 221, 139 O.A.C. 149, 2001 CarswellOnt 1, [2001] O.J. No. 21, 8 C.P.C. (5th) 39 (Ont. C.A.) — A claim was statute-barred because notice was given 55 days before the claim was issued and not at least 60 days. See s. 7(1) of *Proceedings Against the Crown Act,* R.S.O. 1990, c. P.27. Earlier letter from plaintiff to Ministry expressing concern over care given to the deceased did not constitute notice of claim.

The recent decision of the Supreme Court in *R. v. Starr,* 2000 SCC 40, 36 C.R. (5th) 1, 147 C.C.C. (3d) 449, 190 D.L.R. (4th) 591, [2000] 11 W.W.R. 1, 148 Man. R. (2d) 161, 224 W.A.C. 161, 258 N.R. 250, [2000] 2 S.C.R. 144, 2000 CarswellMan 449, 2000 CarswellMan 450 (S.C.C.) dramatically changes the approach to hearsay and exceptions to the hearsay rule. *Starr* arises in a criminal context, but the analysis is not limited to criminal law. Justice Iacobucci makes it clear that Starr applies to both civil and criminal matters. The decision in Starr would tend to suggest the hearsay exclusionary rule is alive and well in both civil and criminal contexts.

Garry v. Pohlmann, 2001 CarswellBC 1893, [2001] B.C.J. No. 1804, 2001 BCSC 1234, 12 C.P.C. (5th) 107 (B.C. S.C.) — Requirements of Small Claims process involving unrepresented litigants compelled trial judge to play somewhat more interventionist role in proceedings. Specific interventions by trial judge intended to control proceedings to prevent argument and direct parties away from irrelevant considerations.

Newell v. Ziegemen, 2003 SKPC 159, 2003 CarswellSask 899, 242 Sask. R. 273 (Sask. Prov. Ct.). The Plaintiffs' claim was for the cost of removal and replacement of carpets in a house purchased from the Defendant in Prince Albert in October 2002.

In *Peel (Regional Municipality) v. Canada*, [1992] 3 S.C.R. 762, 1992 CarswellNat 15, 1992 CarswellNat 659, (sub nom. *Peel (Regional Municipality) v. Ontario)* 144 N.R. 1, 12 M.P.L.R. (2d) 229, 98 D.L.R. (4th) 140, 59 O.A.C. 81, 55 F.T.R. 277 (note) (S.C.C.), McLachlin, J., quoting the American Restatement of the Law of Restitution, 1937 as follows:

> A person who has been unjustly enriched at the expense of another is required to make restitution to the other. Where the legal tests for recovery are clearly not met, can recovery be rewarded on the basis of justice or fairness alone? If courts can grant judgment on the basis on justice alone, does justice so require in this case?

The first question, on a review of authorities, was answered in the negative. Courts have chosen a "middle course" between the extremes of inflexible rules and case by case "palm tree justice." Recovery cannot be based upon a bare assertion that "fairness" so requires. There must in addition be at least a general congruence with accepted legal principle.

There does not appear to be any justification in law or equity to allow claim. Claim dismissed.

Polewsky v. Home Hardware Stores Ltd. (2003), [2003] O.J. No. 2908, 2003 CarswellOnt 2755, 229 D.L.R. (4th) 308, 174 O.A.C. 358, 66 O.R. (3d) 600, 109 C.R.R. (2d) 189, 34 C.P.C. (5th) 334 (Ont. Div. Ct.); leave to appeal allowed 2004 CarswellOnt 763, [2004] O.J. No. 954 (Ont. C.A.). Appeal from motion whereby Judge dismissed motion for a declaration that the Small Claims Court tariff fees are unconstitutional. Fees are contained in the regulations established by the *Administration of Justice Act*, R.S.O. 1990, c. A.6, s. 5c. The regulations set the fees and *Rule 13.01(7)* of the *Small Claims Court Rules* O. Reg. 258/98, r. 1.01, compels the payment of the prescribed fee to set a matter down for trial.

Neither the *Administration of Justice Act* nor Ontario Regulation 432/93 (*Small Claims Court — Fees and Allowances*) make any provision for the waiving of the prescribed fees in any circumstances.

There is a common law constitutional right of access to the Small Claims Court. It must be subject to the exercise of judicial discretion on issues of merit and financial circumstances that trigger the right to proceed in *forma pauperis*. There will have to be a statutory adendment to give effect to the findings of this Court. It should be done within a reasonable period of time and not later than 12 months. Appellant would not have met the requirements because of the evidentiary deficiencies. Appeal allowed in accordance with reasons.

Larabie v. Montfils (2004), 2004 CarswellOnt 186, 44 C.P.C. (5th) 66, (sub nom. *J.-P.L. v. Montfils)* 181 O.A.C. 239 (Ont. C.A. [In Chambers]). Defendants moved for Order staying action because of non-payment of cost Orders made against the Plaintiff in prior proceedings related to same allegations *and* for an Order for security for costs respecting the appeal. Motion dismissed. Courts are reluctant to deprive a worthy but impecunious litigant of the opportunity to have his or her claim adjudicated when it is not plainly devoid of merits. This should apply in appeals as well as in the lower courts.

Qualico Developments (Vancouver) Inc. v. Scott, 2004 CarswellBC 162, 2004 BCSC 108 (B.C. S.C.). Plaintiff in small claims proceeding awarded $10,000. Defendant appealing to Supreme Court. Appeal successful. Defendant entitled to costs and double costs from date of formal offer.

Ring Contracting Ltd. v. PCL Constructors Canada Inc., 2003 CarswellBC 2276, 2003 BCCA 492 (B.C. C.A.). Appellant's lawyer retiring. Appellant seeking adjournment of appeal. Application granted. Appellant should have acted with more diligence to find other counsel but no prejudice to Respondent.

Travel Machine Ltd. v. Madore, 1983 CarswellOnt 901, 143 D.L.R. (3d) 94 (Ont. H.C.). Judge bound to apply statutes and ordinary rules of law notwithstanding provisions of s. 57 of Act. *Small Claims Court Act*, R.S.O. 1980, c. 476, s. 57. Provisions of s. 57 of Act empowering a Judge to "make such order or judgment as appears to him just and agreeable to equity and good conscience" does not mean that a Judge acting under the Act is not required to apply the rules of law, or that he can decide an issue contrary to law.

Canada (Attorney General) v. Strachan, 2006 CarswellNat 888, 2006 CarswellNat 3240, 348 N.R. 302, 2006 FCA 135, 2006 CAF 135 (F.C.A.).

Rule 45 gave court discretion to order that an inmate be physically brought before the court. Judge made order under rule 45 that an inmate seeking judicial review of his mandatory release revocation be physically brought before the court to argue his application. Federal Court of Appeal held trial judge erred in exercising her discretion by stating that inmate had a right to be physically present and placing an onus on Crown to establish that interests of justice did not require physical attendance.

Gardiner v. Mulder (2007), 2007 CarswellOnt 1411 (Ont. Div. Ct.); additional reasons at (2007), 2007 CarswellOnt 2829, 224 O.A.C. 156 (Ont. Div. Ct.), March 9, 2007, Cusinato J.

Appeal by Plaintiff from a Small Claims Court judgment arising from dismissal of Plaintiffs' claims against the Defendants collectively for breach of contract and damages.

Although these are not proceedings where parties not totally self-represented, see s. 25 of the *Courts of Justice Act*, R.S.O. 1990, c. C.43, which applies to both represented and unrepresented parties. See Heeney J. in *936464 Ontario Ltd. v. Mungo Bear Ltd.*, [2003] O.J. No. 3795, 2003 CarswellOnt 8091, 74 O.R. (3d) 45, 258 D.L.R. (4th) 754 (Ont. Div. Ct.) in reference to precise pleadings relative to claimed relief. See *Popular Shoe Store Ltd. v. Simoni*, 1998 CarswellNfld 48, [1998] N.J. No. 57, 163 Nfld. & P.E.I.R. 100, 503 A.P.R. 100, 24 C.P.C. (4th) 10 (Nfld. C.A.) at 106 (Nfld. & P.E.I.R.).

Even where there is a failure of the Plaintiff to properly plead and frame claim, it is for the court "to make such order as is considered just and agreeable to good conscience" and the evidence. This principle is subject, however, to the considerations of fairness, surprise and amendment if required.

Appeal allowed in part for damages relative to the hot tub. Issue of costs awarded to the Defendants set aside.

Histed v. Law Society (Manitoba) (2007), 2007 CarswellMan 504, [2007] M.J. No. 460, 165 C.R.R. (2d) 137, 287 D.L.R. (4th) 577, 225 Man. R. (2d) 74, 419 W.A.C. 74, 49 C.P.C. (6th) 257, [2008] 2 W.W.R. 189, 2007 MBCA 150 (Man. C.A.), Steel J.; leave to appeal refused (2008), 2008 CarswellMan 206, 2008 CarswellMan 207, 387 N.R. 380 (note) (S.C.C.).

Appellant, a lawyer, whom the Disciplinary Committee of the Law Society of Manitoba found had breached the Code of Professional Conduct by sending a letter to opposing counsel in which he called a judge a "bigot," claimed that the letter should have not been admitted as evidence to settlement privilege.

Appeal dismissed. The letter was not part of a settlement negotiation and was in the hands of the Law Society with the consent of the letter's recipient. In this case, the purpose of the letter was not to attempt to effect a settlement and thus, settlement privilege did not attach to the letter.

Lawyers are not precluded from criticizing judiciary; however lawyers are required to avoid use of abusive or offensive statements, irresponsible allegations of partiality ad communications that are abusive, offensive or inconsistent with proper tone of communication.

Rose v. Roderick, 2009 CarswellBC 2178, 2009 BCPC 253 (B.C. Prov. Ct.), Morgan Prov. J.

Matter dismissed on basis that parties' unreasonable conduct in refusing to bridge the r monetary gap resulted in the matter becoming both frivolous and an abuse of Court's settlement process. The claimant's conduct towards defendant during settlement conference condescending, disrespectful and counterproductive. Parties refused to bridge $25.00 gap in proposed settlement of $275.00. To allow the parties to consume full day of court time over such a minor gap counter to legislative directive set out in s. 2 of *Small Claims Act*.

United States v. Bari, Docket No. 09-1074-cr (decided March 22, 2010).

A recent decision by the U.S. Second Circuit Court of Appeals raises questions about the propriety of trial court judges using the Internet to confirm their "hunches" when taking judicial notice.

In *United States v. Bari*, the Second Circuit Court of Appeals held it was not reversible error for the district court to consider information it confirmed through its own Internet search in deciding to revoke a defendant's supervised release.

To emphasize the similarities between the hat found in the garage and the one worn by the robber, the Court said "[o]ne can Google yellow rain hats and find lots of different yellow rain hats." The district court judge also noted that he had done a Google search to confirm this observation.

Bari argued that the district court judge's observations from an Internet search violated the Federal Rule of Evidence 605, which prohibits a judge presiding over a trial from testifying in the trial as a witness.

On appeal, the Second Circuit disagreed. It reasoned that "if a fact is of a kind that a judge may properly take judicial notice," the judge is not improperly testifying by noting the fact.

"If, after all, a judge was improperly testifying at trial each time he took judicial notice of a fact, it would be effectively impermissible to take judicial notice of any fact," the Second Circuit opined.

The district court's Internet search "served only to confirm [a] common sense supposition," the Second Circuit concluded.

"Twenty years ago, to confirm an intuition about the variety of rain hats, a trial judge may have needed to travel to a local department store to survey the rain hats on offer. Rather than expend that time, he likely would have relied on his common sense to take judicial notice of the fact that not all rain hats are alike," the Second Circuit observed. "Today, however, a judge need only take a few moments to confirm his intuition by conducting a basic Internet search," the court said.

"[W]ith so much information at our fingertips (almost literally), we all likely confirm hunches with a brief visit to our favorite search engine that in the not-so-distant past would have gone unconfirmed," the court said. "As the cost of confirming one's intuition decreases, we would expect to see more judges doing just that," the court opined.

"As Gen-X and Gen-Y lawyers are appointed to the bench, is it inevitable that judges will be turning to the Internet as they ponder questions of judicial notice? Internet searches are a prime method for gathering information. We all have to learn how to verify that information." See *United States v. Bari*, Docket No. 09-1074-cr (decided March 22, 2010).

26. Representation — **A party may be represented in a proceeding in the Small Claims Court by a person authorized under the *Law Society Act* to represent the party, but the court may exclude from a hearing anyone, other than a person licensed under the *Law Society Act*, appearing on behalf of the party if it finds that such person is not competent properly to represent the party, or does not understand and comply at the hearing with the duties and responsibilities of an advocate.**

1994, c. 12, s. 10; 2006, c. 21, Sched. C, s. 105(1)

Commentary: The provision in subsection 50(1) of the *Law Society Act*, R.S.O. 1990, c. L-8, prohibiting others from acting as a barrister, is prefaced by the words "Except where otherwise provided by law." Even a magistrate's court has the "inherent" discretionary authority to allow lay persons to present a case on behalf of a party; *O'Toole v. Scott*, [1965] A.C. 939, [1965] 2 All E.R. 240, [1965] 2 W.L.R. 1160 (New South Wales P.C.).

Law Society (Prince Edward Island) v. Nova Collections (P.E.I.) Ltd. (1998), (sub nom. *Law Society of Prince Edward Island Society v. Nova Collections (P.E.I.)*) 170 Nfld. & P.E.I.R. 62, (sub nom. *Law Society of Prince Edward Island Society v. Nova Collections (P.E.I.) Ltd.*) 522 A.P.R. 62, 26 C.P.C. (4th) 326 (P.E.I. T.D. [In Chambers]) — The application by the Prince Edward Island Law Society was for an injunction to restrain the respondent collection service from practicing law in Small Claims Court and in particular, from performing certain services within the domain of barristers and solicitors, for a fee. The application was granted.

Paralegals in Court

The *Law Society Act* [as amended by the *Access to Justice Act*] and Law Society by-laws 4 and 7 require, with exceptions, one to have a licence to appear or act for another in the Ontario Court of Justice. Paralegals with a licence and those within the exceptions may appear in *Provincial Offences Act* proceedings and *Criminal Code* summary conviction matters, including those subject to maximum terms of imprisonment longer than six months: s. 6(2) by-law 4.

Exceptions

"Grandfather Provision": The experience of paralegals operating prior to May 1, 2007 is recognized in two ways.

    1.   Licensed: s. 11(1) by-law 4.

        Provided legal services on a full-time basis for a total of three years in the five years prior to May 1, 2007.

        Applied prior to November 1, 2007, and

        Passed the licensing examination.

    2.   Unlicensed: s. 30(1) para. 8 by-law 4, s. 30(2) by-law 4.

        Providing legal services prior to May 1, 2007 [no minimum period] and

        Applied by October 31, 2007.

        May continue to operate without a licence until the earlier of

        April 30, 2008

        Final denial of application for a licence.

Articling students when acting under supervision of an approved licensed lawyer: s. 34 by-law 4.

Lawyers' employees may set dates: s. 5(1)(b) by-law 7.1.

Exceptions outside legal profession: s. 30(1) by-law 4.

    1.   In-house legal services provider

    2.   Legal clinics

    3.   Student legal aid services societies

    4.   Not-for-profit organizations

    5.   Acting for family, friend or neighbour

    6.   Constituency assistants

7.   Other — occasional provision of legal services only as ancillary part of occupation and member of

   a)   Human Resources Professionals Association of Ontario,

   b)   Ontario Professional Planners Institute,

   c)   Board of Canadian Registered Safety Professionals, or

   d)   Appraisal Institute of Canada.

Criminal Code *Summary Conviction Proceedings*

A licence is required for summary conviction proceedings where the maximum prison term is over six months: s. 802.1.

However, the *Code* has no restrictions as to who may appear as agent for other summary conviction matters.

Provincial Offences Act *Proceedings*

Only those in compliance with the new licensing regime are permitted to appear: s. 1(1) and 50(1) *POA*. No obligation is placed on presiding judicial officer to ascertain whether agent is in compliance.

Unlicensed agents appearing pursuant to one of the exceptions remain subject to the court's jurisdiction to bar them for

   Incompetence, s. 50(3), 94

   Contempt, s. 91(7).

Paralegals are permitted to practice in previously permitted areas of practice, in matters before Small Claims Court and administrative tribunals, and Boards, such as the Financial Services Commission and the Workplace Safety Insurance Board.

Paralegals are not permitted to represent someone in Family Court.

Case Law: *Re Milligan* (1991), 1 C.P.C. (3d) 12 (Ont. Gen. Div.) — The inherent right to control one's own process does not carry with it the right of a trial judge to choose which counsel were to appear before him.

Fortland Realty Inc. v. London Life Insurance Co. (September 19, 1995), Doc. 95-CU-877-91 (Ont. Gen. Div.) — Leave granted to allow non-lawyer to present case on behalf of plaintiff subject to the defendant's being at liberty to seek the intervention of the court. Case involved several million dollars. See *419212 Ontario Ltd. v. Astrochrome Crankshaft Toronto Ltd.* (1991), 3 O.R. (3d) 116 at 120 (Master).

Jackson v. Ontario (Attorney General) (April 12, 1995), Doc. 463/94 (Ont. Gen. Div.) — But for the authority granted by statute, the applicant, a paralegal, would be unable to appear on behalf of a litigant in the Ontario Court, General Division. Finding having regard to Rule 15 of the Rules of Civil Procedure, s. 1 of the *Solicitors Act*, R.S.O. 1990, c. S.15, and s. 50(1) of the *Law Society Act*, R.S.O. 1990, c. L.8. It is not unconstitutional that applicant cannot appear on behalf of client in the Divisional Court.

R. v. Gregoire (November 18, 1994) (Ont. Prov. Div.), Allen J. — Client, charged with an offence under the *Highway Traffic Act*, was represented in Provincial Court by HK, a former lawyer who had been disbarred for dishonesty. On behalf of HK, client's mother appeared before the court requesting an adjournment, as HK was not available on the date set for appeal. The judge refused to entertain the application for an adjournment, stating the client was free to be represented by any type of agent, but that he would not allow an appearance by HK in his court. The appeal was to go ahead as scheduled unless another basis for adjournment could be found.

Manufacturer's Life v. Molyneux (January 9, 1995), Doc. 868/94 (Ont. Div. Ct.) — Application pursuant to section 114 of the *Landlord and Tenant Act* dismissed. Successful landlord, respondent on appeal represented by agent. Costs awarded in the sum of $250. See also *Bonshaw-Estates Inc. and Indrakumaran et al.*, unreported, File No. 421/92 where agent awarded $750.00 in costs (Ont. Div. Ct.).

Banyasz v. Galbraith (1996), 94 O.A.C. 75, 7 C.P.C. (4th) 307 (Ont. Div. Ct.) — Issue was right of party to be represented by agent on appeal from order made on application under the *Landlord and Tenant Act*, R.S.O. 1990, c. L.7 (now the *Commercial Tenancies Act*). Divisional Court held that there being no statutory authority allowing parties to such an appeal to be represented by agents, a party was not permitted to appear by agent except with leave under special circumstances. No such special circumstances in this case. Divisional Court should not have heard the agent for the appellant. *Gotlibowicz v. Gillespie* (1996), 90 O.A.C. 251; 28 O.R. (3d) 402 referred to. *O'Shanter Development Corp. v. Separi* (May 7, 1996), Doc. 761/94 (Ont. Div. Ct.) found that there was no authority for an agent to appear on an appeal from the Small Claims Court.

Karach v. Karach (1995), 35 Alta. L.R. (3d) 311, [1996] 3 W.W.R. 297, 177 A.R. 100 (Q.B.) — When a litigant asks to be represented by an untrained and uninsured agent, the court must then balance the competing objectives of protecting the litigant and society and respecting the litigant's choice. Accordingly, if a litigant wishes to be represented by someone other than a solicitor, it is reasonable to require the litigant to make application to the court, which will then have the opportunity of reviewing the public interest issues that such a request raises.

Kobetek Systems Ltd. v. Canada, [1998] 1 C.T.C. 308 (Fed. T.D.) — Application by corporation to be represented by officer of corporation denied as "special circumstances," contemplated by *Federal Court Rules* (Can.), Rule 300(2), did not exist. Officer's sole ground was that he considered himself capable. This was not "special circumstance.".

Bank of Montreal v. Gardner, 1998 CarswellOnt 89 (Ont. Sm. Cl. Ct.) — Failure by plaintiff to pay monies into court in timely manner was oversight and not deliberate act. Request for contempt relief was dismissed. Law firm did not obtain any advantage from actions of deputy judge but appearance of impartiality was required. Law firm was restrained from acting for plaintiff in this matter. Section 15 did not cover discrimination in terms of right to recover costs as between litigants represented or not represented by counsel. There was no expressed jurisdiction in *Courts of Justice Act* or Rules of Small Claims Court to award costs to litigant represented by agent nor was there expressed prohibition to make such award. Agent had sent unsolicited letter to judge while matter was before judge. Affidavit of agent contained scandalous assertions. Court sanctioned improper conduct of agent by denying defendants costs.

Kopyto v. Ontario (Attorney General) (1997), 104 O.A.C. 128, 14 C.P.C. (4th) 169, 152 D.L.R. (4th) 572 (Ont. Div. Ct.) — Kopyto, a disbarred lawyer, applied to represent client in a family law matter. Family Court Judge acting in his judicial capacity when he made order and thus s. 82 of the *Courts of Justice Act* applicable. Application is dismissed.

R. v. Lemonides (1997), 151 D.L.R. (4th) 546, 35 O.R. (3d) 611, 10 C.R. (5th) 135 (Ont. Gen. Div.) — The issue in this case was that of agents. The waiver by an accused of the right to counsel must be unequivocal and fully informed. The mere fact that an accused's legal representative refers to himself as "an agent" does not absolve the trial judge from the duty to ensure that the accused understands that he/she is entitled to be represented by counsel, and understands the inherent limitations in the agent's status. As the accused was unaware of his agent's status (*i.e.*, did not understand the agent was not a lawyer) and specifically his lack of understanding of his new agent's role, his constitutional right to counsel was infringed. A new trial was ordered.

Trillium Investment Group of Companies Inc. and Harvey Dennis and 1078105 Ontario Inc. (October 29, 1997) (Ont. Gen. Div.), Ferrier, J. — Order that 1078105 Ontario Inc. carrying on business as Citywide Paralegal Services be prohibited from appearing as agent in any court in the Province of Ontario until the amount due to the said judgment is paid and the costs of motion are paid.

Fortin c. Chrétien, 1998 CarswellQue 3769, REJB 1998-09966, [1998] Q.J. No. 4010 (Que. C.A.); affirmed 2000 CarswellQue 2211, 2000 CarswellQue 2212 (S.C.C.); additional reasons 2001 CarswellQue 1395, 2001 CarswellQue 1396, REJB 2001-25001, *(*sub nom. *Fortin v. Chrétien)* 201 D.L.R. (4th) 223, *(*sub nom. *Fortin v. Barreau du Québec)* 272 N.R. 359, 2001 SCC 45, [2001] 2 S.C.R. 500 (S.C.C.) — Section 61 of the Quebec *Code of Civil Procedure* allowed plaintiffs to sign and present applications for injunction themselves and defend their case without a lawyer. Applications in irreceivability were incorrectly allowed. Applications for injunctions should proceed on merit.

Turner v. American Bar Association (1975), 407 F. Supp. 451 — The regulation of the practice of law by the legislature and the judicial branches is constitutionally acceptable and does not give rise to the cause of action on behalf of the plaintiff.

Strilets v. Vicom Multimedia Inc., 2000 ABQB 598, 2000 CarswellAlta 897 (Alta. Q.B.) — The agent was below the standard of an average articling student but possessed more ability and understanding than a typical lay person. Given the relatively small amount of money involved, improbable plaintiff would find lawyer to represent him. If the agent was not granted standing, the plaintiff would have no representation.

Petsinis v. Escalhorda (2000), 2000 CarswellOnt 3166, [2000] O.J. No. 3324 (Ont. S.C.J.) — *Tenant Protection Act, 1997*, S.O. 1997, c. 24. There was nothing in the *Tenant Protection Act* that purported to oust the application of Rules. Unclear whether agents were to appear in s. 193(2) proceedings. The former *Landlord and Tenant Act* (Ontario) expressly permitted the party to appear by agent on application authorized to be brought before the Superior Court. Provision was absent in the present Act.

Carroll v. Carroll (2000), 2000 CarswellOnt 3768, [2000] O.J. No. 3969 (Ont. C.J.) — The agent failed to show adequate understanding of court structure, procedure or case law, or ability to provide adequate representation, particularly in complex issues. Extraordinary circumstances for grant of leave under *Family Law Rules*, O. Reg. 114/99, s. 4(1)(c), not shown.

Gill v. Residential Property Management Inc. (2000), 50 O.R. (3d) 752, 2000 CarswellOnt 3507, [2000] O.J. No. 3709 (Ont. S.C.J.) — Residential tenancy matters. The *Rules of Civil Procedure* apply to proceedings under s. 193(2) of the *Tenant Protection Act, 1997* (Ontario). It is necessary for agents to seek leave to appear before the court.

Equiprop Management Ltd. v. Harris (2000), [2000] O.J. No. 4552, 2000 CarswellOnt 4398, 51 O.R. (3d) 496, 195 D.L.R. (4th) 680, 140 O.A.C. 1, 9 C.P.C. (5th) 323 (Ont. Div. Ct.) — On motion to lift stay pending appeal, an issue arose as to whether the tenants were entitled to be represented by a paralegal on appeal before the Divisional Court. The provisions did not permit representation of parties by paralegals. Representation by a paralegal was not permitted in proceedings governed by Rules.

Todd v. Chevalier (2000), 2000 CarswellOnt 5029 (Ont. S.C.J.); additional reasons at (2001), 2001 CarswellOnt 773 (Ont. S.C.J.) — Tenant's agent commenced an action in Superior Court under *Tenant Protection Act, 1997* (Ontario). The application was dismissed. Agent refused standing. *Rules of Civil Procedure* (Ontario) and not *Statutory Powers Procedure Act*, R.S.O. 1990, c. S.22 applied to proceedings before the court even where the tribunal had declined jurisdiction.

Sidhu c. Canada (Ministre de la Citoyenneté & de l'Immigration) (2000), 2000 CarswellNat 1434 (Fed. T.D.) — Immigration agent or paralegal had no authority, under Federal Court

Rules, 1998, to represent the plaintiff. Application indicated that the plaintiff was represented by a consultant. Application for leave to appeal dismissed.

Bhatti c. Canada (Ministre de la Citoyenneté & de l'Immigration) (2000), 2000 CarswellNat 1433 (Fed. T.D.) — Agent acting on the plaintiff's behalf was not qualified to represent him: *Federal Court Rules*, 1998, Rule 119.

Parmar c. Canada (Ministre de la Citoyenneté & de l'Immigration) (2000), 12 Imm. L.R. (3d) 178, 2000 CarswellNat 1432, 2000 CarswellNat 3429 (Fed. T.D.) — Agent acting on the plaintiff's behalf was not qualified to represent him. The judicial review application was dismissed.

Skrdla v. Graham, 2000 BCSC 1613, 81 B.C.L.R. (3d) 335, 2000 CarswellBC 2188 (B.C. S.C. [In Chambers]) — The *Legal Services Society Act*, R.S.B.C. 1996, c. 256 did not provide for a definition of "services ordinarily provided by a lawyer." Implied society must exercise some discretion in determining what services it would provide. Refusal of funding was within its jurisdiction and discretion.

O'Toole v. Scott, [1965] A.C. 939, [1965] 2 All E.R. 240, [1965] 2 W.L.R. 1160 (New South Wales P.C.) — Subsection 50(1) of the *Law Society Act* prohibits any non-lawyer from acting "as a barrister or solicitor" "except where otherwise provided by law." The case sets out the common law rule that even inferior court has the 'inherent' power to give a non-barrister the right of audience.

Gotlibowicz v. Gillespie (1996), 47 C.P.C. (3d) 96, 28 O.R. (3d) 402, 90 O.A.C. 251, 1996 CarswellOnt 1283 (Ont. Div. Ct.) — Inappropriate for the court to ignore section 1 of the Solicitors Act and section 50 of the *Law Society Act* and, in effect, condone activity that legislature characterizes as contempt of court and prohibits under penalty of prosecution.

R. v. Romanowicz (1999), 26 C.R. (5th) 246, 45 M.V.R. (3d) 294, 124 O.A.C. 100, 138 C.C.C. (3d) 225, 178 D.L.R. (4th) 466, 45 O.R. (3d) 506, (sub nom. *R. c. Romanowicz)* 45 O.R. (3d) 532 (Fr.), 1999 CarswellOnt 2671, [1999] O.J. No. 3191 (Ont. C.A.) — Broad discretion to authorize agents to appear in this court, subject only to the court's ensuring that the party wishing to be represented has made informed decision to proceed without counsel by an agent.

R. v. Lawrie & Pointts Ltd. (1987), 59 O.R. (2d) 161, 1987 CarswellOnt 42, 48 M.V.R. 189, 19 O.A.C. 81, 32 C.C.C. (3d) 549 (Ont. C.A.) — Effect of the 1970 revision of the Statutes was to transfer control of unauthorized practice to the *Law Society Act*. Section 1 of the *Solicitors Act* is merely an ancillary provision. It does not prohibit unauthorized practice.

Smith v. Smith (2000), 43 C.P.C. (4th) 293, 2000 CarswellOnt 1182, [2000] O.J. No. 1236 (Ont. S.C.J.) — The husband brought a motion seeking leave of court pursuant to clause 4(1)(c) of the *Family Law Rules* to permit him to be represented by a person who was not a lawyer. The motion was dismissed. The husband failed to discharge the onus to establish special circumstances to permit an agent.

Wainio v. Ontario Teachers' Pension Plan Board, [2000] 2 C.T.C. 513, 24 C.C.P.B. 175, 2000 CarswellOnt 1135, [2000] O.J. No. 1175 (Ont. S.C.J.) — Endorsement — A Justice of the Peace had jurisdiction pursuant to s. 50(3) of the *Provincial Offences Act*, R.S.O. 1990, c. P.33 to bar any person from appearing as an agent under certain conditions.

Stone v. Stone (1999), 4 R.F.L. (5th) 433, 1999 CarswellOnt 4584, [1999] O.J. No. 5266 (Ont. S.C.J.) — Representation by non-lawyer. Despite pleas of poverty, the wife was not entitled to order permitting her to be represented by paralegal. *Family Court Rules*, O. Reg. 144/99, s. 4(1)(c), permitted representation of parties by non-lawyers if the court permitted.

West v. Eisner, 1999 CarswellOnt 4017, [1999] O.J. No. 4705, 48 C.C.L.T. (2d) 274, 41 C.P.C. (4th) 378 (Ont. S.C.J.) — A paralegal operating a legal clinic through a corporation admitted liability. The client was entitled to damages comprising cost of obtaining reinstatement of compensation benefits, return of fees, wasted costs, and general damages of $3,500 for emotional distress.

Szebenyi v. R., 2001 CarswellNat 2061, 2001 FCA 277, (sub nom. *Szebenyi v. Canada)* 215 F.T.R. 159 (note) (Fed. C.A.); leave to appeal refused (2002), 2002 CarswellNat 1167, 2002 CarswellNat 1168, (sub nom. *Szebenyi v. Canada)* 300 N.R. 197 (note) (S.C.C.) — On appeal from decision of Motions Judge who refused to permit S to represent his mother at trial, no error shown. Open to S to reapply before trial judge for permission to speak for mother at trial, should matter proceed. Appeal dismissed.

Nirvair Transport Ltd. v. Dhillon (2001), 2001 CarswellOnt 4424 (Ont. Master) — Master strongly condemned practice of appointing paralegal as corporate director of corporate litigant, for purpose of having the paralegal apply to court for leave to represent the corporation pursuant to Rule 15.01(2) of *Rules of Civil Procedure* on basis of financial hardship.

Law Society (British Columbia) v. Gravelle, 154 B.C.A.C. 25, 2001 CarswellBC 1103, [2001] 7 W.W.R. 15, 2001 BCCA 383, 89 B.C.L.R. (3d) 187, 200 D.L.R. (4th) 82, 252 W.A.C. 25 (B.C. C.A.); leave to appeal refused (2002), 2002 CarswellBC 11, 2002 CarswellBC 12, 286 N.R. 198 (note), 171 B.C.A.C. 46 (note), 280 W.A.C. 46 (note) (S.C.C.) — The Law Society petitioned for a declaration that a notary public engaged in the unauthorized practice of law by giving legal advice to and offering to assist a member of the public with respect to the probate or letters of administration of the estate of a deceased person for or in the expectation of a fee, gain or reward. A permanent injunction against the notary was also sought. The British Columbia Court of Appeal dismissed the appeal. The Court affirmed that notaries were not probating wills in England on November 18, 1958. Therefore, the notary here engaged in the unauthorized practice of law.

Pellikaan v. R., 2001 CarswellNat 2951, [2001] F.C.J. No. 1923, 2001 FCT 1415 (Fed. T.D.) — Motion to allow lay person to act as agent or as representative of plaintiff denied. Antics and attitude and absence of any reasonable approach of proposed lay person made him untenable as lay representative.

R. v. Tran (2001), 149 O.A.C. 120, 2001 CarswellOnt 2706, [2001] O.J. No. 3056, 156 C.C.C. (3d) 1, 44 C.R. (5th) 12, 55 O.R. (3d) 161, 14 M.V.R. (4th) 1 (Ont. C.A.) — After representing himself at trial, Tran convicted on a number of charges. Tran appealed, arguing trial judge erred by failing to conduct inquiry into admissibility of evidence of his impairment. The Ontario Court of Appeal agreed. It noted that the trial judge did little to assist Tran and the *voir dires* he conducted concerning the qualifications of experts were questionable. Moreover, trial judge failed to explain the course which trial would take, knew that Tran needed an interpreter and was ignorant of the most basic stages of a trial.

Law Society (British Columbia) v. Siegel, 76 B.C.L.R. (3d) 381, 2000 CarswellBC 1182, 2000 BCSC 875 (B.C. S.C.) — Law society brought petition for declaration that notary public engages in unlawful practice of law when he or she prepares for fee, usual corporate documents and resolutions to maintain company in good standing. Petition granted. Sections 17 and 18 of *Notaries Act*, R.S.B.C. 1996, c. 334 do not permit notaries to prepare normal corporate documents necessary to keep company in good standing.

Simmons v. Boutlier (2000), 5 R.F.L. (5th) 149, 2000 CarswellOnt 492 (Ont. S.C.J.) — Judge dismissed wife's motion to allow paralegal to represent her in family law proceedings. Rule 4(1) intended to codify existing discretion of judges to permit non-lawyers to represent parties in court in very limited circumstances, perhaps where special expertise was required. Wife applied for leave to appeal. Application dismissed.

Clarke v. Clarke (2001), 2001 CarswellOnt 3381 (Ont. S.C.J.) — Paralegal acting as a solicitor contrary to s. 50(1) of the *Law Society Act*, R.S.O. 1990, c. L.8 and s. 1 of the *Solicitors Act*, R.S.O. 1990, c. S.15. As he did not have prior permission to represent parties, "representation" of parties was in violation of s. 4 of the *Family Law Rules* (O. Reg. 144/99). The paralegal must stop his practice of preparing and processing uncontested divorces without application to the court for permission pursuant to Rule 4(1).

Leung v. Rotstein, 2002 CarswellBC 2615, 2002 BCSC 1470, 25 C.P.C. (5th) 370, 8 B.C.L.R. (4th) 385 (B.C. S.C. [In Chambers]) — No bar to lawyer representing him- or herself before court. Self-represented lawyer had to act in manner consistent with Professional Conduct Handbook. No rule of law preventing lawyer from giving evidence and continuing as counsel. No authority to compel litigant to choose alternate counsel if chosen counsel was required to give evidence in case. Litigant chose himself to act as counsel.

786372 Alberta Ltd. v. Mohawk Canada Ltd., 2002 CarswellAlta 1047, 2002 ABQB 785, 22 C.P.C. (5th) 9, 3 Alta. L.R. (4th) 380, 324 A.R. 192 (Alta. Master) — The individual plaintiff was sole shareholder and director of the corporate plaintiff. The individual plaintiff was a non-lawyer who wished to appear on behalf of corporation. The defendant sought order requiring counsel to be appointed. Application granted. The Court had discretion to allow corporation to be represented by one of its officers or directors.

Law Society (British Columbia) v. Mangat (2001), 2001 CarswellBC 2168, 2001 CarswellBC 2169, [2001] S.C.J. No. 66, 2001 SCC 67, 16 Imm. L.R. (3d) 1, 205 D.L.R. (4th) 577, 157 B.C.A.C. 161, 256 W.A.C. 161, 96 B.C.L.R. (3d) 1, 276 N.R. 339, [2002] 2 W.W.R. 201, [2001] 3 S.C.R. 113 (S.C.C.) — Immigration consultants entitled to represent immigrants under *Immigration Act*, R.S.C., 1985, c. 1.2, ss. 30, 69(1), notwithstanding prohibition in section 26 of *Legal Profession Act*, S.B.C. 1987, c. 25. Non-lawyers entitled to act for fees despite a prohibition in provincial statute regulating the legal profession.

Gagnon v. Pritchard (2002), 2002 CarswellOnt 750, [2002] O.J. No. 928, 58 O.R. (3d) 557, 17 C.P.C. (5th) 297, 26 B.L.R. (3d) 216 (Ont. S.C.J.) — Grantees of powers of attorney could not act for their grantor in court proceedings pursuant to Rule 15.01(3) of *Rules of Civil Procedure*. Section 50(1) of the *Law Society Act*, R.S.O. 1990, c. L.8 stated that except where otherwise provided by law, no person other than a member should act as a lawyer or practice as a lawyer.

U.S. v. Johnson (2003), 327 F.3d 554 (U.S. 7th Circ. Ill.) — Review of NLPA National Legal Professional Associates and the unauthorized practice of law. Key among the inherent powers incidental to all courts is the authority to "control admission to its bar and to discipline attorneys who appear before it," id. at 43, 111 S.Ct. 2123 (citing *Ex parte Burr*, 22 (9 Wheat.) 529, 6 L.Ed. 152 (1824)), and, as we have noted previously, "a federal court has the inherent power to sanction for conduct which abuses the judicial process." *Barnhill v. United States*, 11 F.3d 1360(1367), 7th Cir.1993. It follows that a federal court's power to regulate and discipline attorneys extends to conduct by non-lawyers amounting to practicing law without a license. This logical extension of the inherent powers is consistent with the Supreme Court's reasoning in *Roadway Express, Inc. v. Piper* (1980), 447 U.S. 752 and 766, 100 S.Ct. 2455, 65 L.Ed.2d 488 ("The power of a court over the members of its bar is at least as great as its authority over litigants.").

Law Society of Upper Canada v. Stoangi (2003), 2003 CarswellOnt 1112, [2003] O.J. No. 1110, 64 O.R. (3d) 122 (Ont. C.A.) — Appeal related to the definition of legal services under the Law Society Act, R.S.O. 1990, c. L.8. Appellant disbarred in 1984. Section 50(1) of the Act provides that "except where otherwise provided by law" no person other than a member of the Law Society shall act or practice as a barrister or solicitor. The exception-"where otherwise provided by law"-refers to statutes that specifically provide that agents who are not barristers or solicitors may appear and represent another person before designated adjudicative bodies and tribunals: see *R. v. Lawrie & Pointts Ltd.* (1987), 59 O.R. (2d) 161, 1987 CarswellOnt 42, 48 M.V.R. 189, 19 O.A.C. 81, 32 C.C.C. (3d) 549 (Ont. C.A.). Long-standing case law interpreting "practising as a solicitor" to include advising another on legal questions: *R. v. Mitchell* (1952), 102 C.C.C. 307, 1952 CarswellOnt 221, [1953] 1

D.L.R. 143, [1952] O.W.N. 248 (Ont. Co. Ct.); affirmed (1952), 104 C.C.C. 247, 1952 CarswellOnt 389, 1952 CarswellOnt 85, [1952] O.R. 896, [1952] O.W.N. 808, [1953] 1 D.L.R. 700 (Ont. C.A.); *R. v. Zaza* (May 1, 1974), Ont. Co. Ct.; affirmed (November 20, 1975), [1975] O.J. No. 1113 (Ont. Div. Ct.), Galligan J., Osler J., Reid J.; *R. v. Engel* (1976), 11 O.R. (2d) 343, 29 C.C.C. (2d) 135 (Ont. Prov. Ct.); *R. v. Brunet* (July 13, 1987), Doc. Ottawa 85-7202700 (Ont. Prov. Ct.). The impugned conduct must be carried out "frequently, customarily, or habitually": *R. v. Ott*, [1950] O.R. 493, 1950 CarswellOnt 60, 97 C.C.C. 302, [1950] 4 D.L.R. 426 (Ont. C.A.), at 493-503 [O.R.]; *Apothecaries Co. v. Jones*, [1893] 1 Q.B. 89, 17 Cox C.C. 588; and *R. v. Campbell* (1974), 3 O.R. (2d) 402, 17 C.C.C. (2d) 400, 45 D.L.R. (3d) 522 (Ont. Prov. Ct.).

R. v. Morden (2000), 2000 CarswellOnt 1037, [2000] O.J. No. 873 (Ont. C.J.) — Duties of justice of the peace to person represented by agent. Duty to protect administration of justice. See also *R. v. Romanowicz* (1999), 26 C.R. (5th) 246, 45 M.V.R. (3d) 294, 124 O.A.C. 100, 138 C.C.C. (3d) 225, 178 D.L.R. (4th) 466, 45 O.R. (3d) 506, *(sub nom. R. c. Romanowicz)* 45 O.R. (3d) 532 (Fr.), 1999 CarswellOnt 2671, [1999] O.J. No. 3191 (Ont. C.A.).

Ontario (Attorney General) v. Fleet Rent-A-Car Ltd., 2002 CarswellOnt 4286, 29 C.P.C. (5th) 315, [2002] O.J. No. 4693 (Ont. S.C.J.) — Motion granted to exclude Melvin Deutsch from appearing as agent before the Superior Court of Justice, Toronto Small Claims Court, pursuant to sections 25, 26, 96 and 106 of the *Courts of Justice Act*, and Rule 1.03.

Potvin v. Gionet (January 24, 2003) (Ont. S.C.J.), Nadeau J. — Is paralegal authorized to represent parties in "basket divorce" cases? Public policy best served with legal representation by those trained in the law, qualified as to academic standards and character by a governing body, and responsible and accountable as officers of the Court. In this case, Tom Martin did not seek leave of the court by way of notice of motion with supporting affidavits as specified in *Equiprop Management Ltd. v. Harris* (2000), [2000] O.J. No. 4552, 2000 CarswellOnt 4398, 51 O.R. (3d) 496, 195 D.L.R. (4th) 680, 140 O.A.C. 1, 9 C.P.C. (5th) 323 (Ont. Div. Ct.). In the August 16, 2002 decision of *Clarke v. Clarke*, [2002] O.J. No. 3223, 2002 CarswellOnt 2759, 32 R.F.L. (5th) 282, [2002] O.T.C. 611 (Ont. S.C.J.), Olah J. determined that "given the absence of the Rules and Practice Directions addressing unrepresented basket divorces, what remains is the ability of the individual trial judge to exercise his or her inherent jurisdiction regarding matters of procedure and process on a case by case basis . . ." (at para. 61). The Court may therefore impose further requirements pursuant to its inherent jurisdiction, as long as requirements do not contradict applicable Rules or Practice Directions.

Fortin c. Chrétien, 1998 CarswellQue 3769, REJB 1998-09966, [1998] Q.J. No. 4010 (Que. C.A.); affirmed 2000 CarswellQue 2211, 2000 CarswellQue 2212 (S.C.C.); additional reasons 2001 CarswellQue 1395, 2001 CarswellQue 1396, REJB 2001-25001, *(sub nom. Fortin v. Chrétien)* 201 D.L.R. (4th) 223, *(sub nom. Fortin v. Barreau du Québec)* 272 N.R. 359, 2001 SCC 45, [2001] 2 S.C.R. 500 (S.C.C.) — Parties representing themselves after using disbarred advocate to draw up legal proceedings. Contract null. Invalidity of contract did not render subsequent proceedings void. *Act respecting the Barreau du Québec*, R.S.Q., c. B-1, s. 128(1)(b). *Civil Code of Quebec*, S.Q. 1991, c. 64, arts. 1411, 1417, 1438. *Code of Civil Procedure*, R.S.Q., c. C-25, art. 61. Applying the principle of simple nullity of the agreement was consistent with the intent of art. 61 of the CCP, which establishes a right of access to the courts and which cannot be rendered ineffective by the provisions of the ABQ. Recognition of the right of persons to represent themselves in legal proceedings should not be regarded as a matter of access to justice. Further, use of non-qualified persons to assist such persons may often affect their interests adversely. In contrast, advocates as officers of the court play an important role in representing the rights of litigants before the courts. It is desirable for all litigants to retain the services of an advocate.

Avance Venture Corp. v. Noram Relations Group Corp., 2002 CarswellBC 3033, 2002 BCSC 327 (B.C. S.C.) — Respondent corporation (in B.C.) sought order allowing Alberta lawyer to act for it. Alberta lawyer under suspension in Alberta. He was not director or officer of respondent. Lawyer under order dated June 1996 to disclose not licensed to practice in B.C. He failed to inform respondent. Application dismissed.

Children's Aid Society of Niagara Region v. P. (D.) (2002), 2002 CarswellOnt 4418, 62 O.R. (3d) 668, 16 O.F.L.R. 145 (Ont. S.C.J.) — Subrule 4(1)(c) of the Family Law Rules, O. Reg. 114/99, provides that a party may be represented "by a person who is not a lawyer, but only if the court gives permission in advance." "Permission in advance" means nothing more than permission in advance of the non-lawyer representation. A distinction should be made between paid, non-lawyer agents, such as paralegals, and unpaid, non-lawyer agent-friends. Neither section 1 of the Solicitors Act nor section 50(1) of the *Law Society Act* affects the inherent jurisdiction of the court to allow an unpaid, non-lawyer agent-friend to assist a litigant. The test, does the litigant honestly believe that he or she would benefit from the assistance of his friend and does that belief appear to be reasonable in all the circumstances? "Special circumstances" do not apply to unpaid, non-lawyer agent-friends.

Zenkewich v. Eremko, 2002 CarswellSask 785, 2002 SKQB 494 (Sask. Q.B.). Appellant ordered to pay respondent $2,500. This was an appeal. Trial judge exercised discretion not to grant adjournment that he had at law and that discretion was exercised judiciously.

Leung v. Rotstein, 2002 CarswellBC 2615, 2002 BCSC 1470, 25 C.P.C. (5th) 370, 8 B.C.L.R. (4th) 385 (B.C. S.C. [In Chambers]). Lawyer representing self in legal proceeding. Opposing party applying for order that lawyer not permitted to act as both party and advocate. Application dismissed. No rule of law preventing lawyer from representing self in legal proceedings.

Jessa v. Future Shop Ltd., 2002 CarswellBC 2639, 2002 BCSC 1531 (B.C. S.C. [In Chambers]). Defendant applying to set aside default judgment. Defendant not having notice of trial date. Likely that Defendant would have attended trial if advised of date. Application allowed.

Lamond v. Smith, 2004 CarswellOnt 3213 (Ont. S.C.J.), J.W. Quinn, J. Cases decided under Subrule 15.01(2) of *Rules of Civil Procedure* that discourage granting permission for non-lawyer to represent corporation do not apply to case of small, one-man company.

Inquiry into non-lawyer's qualifications whether proposed representative of corporation could fulfil duties under rules of court was unimportant. In era when self-represented litigants abounded no sense to worry whether non-lawyer could carry out responsibilities of litigation. Absent proven mental incompetence his intelligence and litigious capabilities irrelevant.

Order made on motion. Order obtained on incomplete and misleading evidence. Where party secured order on motion by means of affidavit evidence that he knew to be materially incomplete and that had misled court, court entitled, upon learning of deception, to set order aside on its own initiative.

Law Society of Upper Canada v. Boldt, 2006 CarswellOnt 1754 (Ont. S.C.J.) 2006-03-22.

Motion for contempt against Maureen Boldt for breaching injunction Order of Bolan J. dated September 1, 2000.

Order of Bolan J. included the following terms:

1. A finding that Maureen Boldt had been acting as a barrister and solicitor in contravention of s. 50 of the *Law Society Act* in contravention of the 1998 Agreement.

2. A permanent injunction restraining Maureen Boldt from acting or practising as a barrister or solicitor.

Bolan J. relied on the definition of "acting as a solicitor" drawn from *R. v. Campbell* (1974), 3 O.R. (2d) 402, 17 C.C.C. (2d) 400, 45 D.L.R. (3d) 522 (Ont. Prov. Ct.) at 411 (O.R.):

> A person who 'acts as a solicitor' is one who conducts an action or other legal proceeding on behalf of another, or advises that other persons on legal matters, or frames documents intended to have a legal operation, or generally assists that other person in matters affecting his legal position.

The law on contempt was stated in *B.C.G.E.U., Re*, EYB 1988-67021, 1988 CarswellBC 762, 1988 CarswellBC 363, [1988] S.C.J. No. 76, (sub nom. *B.C.G.E.U. v. British Columbia (Attorney General))* [1988] 6 W.W.R. 577, 30 C.P.C. (2d) 221, [1988] 2 S.C.R. 214, 220 A.P.R. 93, 53 D.L.R. (4th) 1, 87 N.R. 241, 31 B.C.L.R. (2d) 273, 71 Nfld. & P.E.I.R. 93, 44 C.C.C. (3d) 289, 88 C.L.L.C. 14,047 (S.C.C.) at 234 (S.C.R.):

> Contempt . . . embraces 'where a person, whether a party to a proceeding or not, does any act which may tend to hinder the course of justice or show disrespect to the court's authority', 'interfering with the business of the court on the part of a person who has no right to do so' . . . The overriding concept of contempt is that of public respect for the orders of our courts.

The mediation process is not a shield for those who are illegally providing legal advice. Where individuals seek advice, they are entitled to that advice *only* from lawyers who are regulated in the public interest.

You cannot ignore an injunction simply by changing the title of a document.

Boldt in contempt of court.

Winkelman v. Parma City School District, 05-983.

On February 27, 2007, the U.S. Supreme Court heard oral arguments as to whether parents who are not lawyers have a right to represent their child with disabilities, or themselves, in a federal court action under the U.S. federal *Individuals with Disabilities Education Act*.

The appeal stems from a lawsuit by Jeff and Sandee Winkelman, two Ohio parents who challenged the appropriateness of a school's educational plan for their son, Jacob, who has autism spectrum disorder.

A non-lawyer parent can only represent himself or herself and not the parent's child, according to the U.S. Sixth Circuit. There is a three-way split among the First, Second, Third, Sixth, Seventh and Eleventh U.S. Circuit Courts of Appeal. In Ontario, of course, legal aid would not be provided as a matter of course, let alone self-representation.

Baird v. R., 2006 CarswellNat 1729, 2006 CarswellNat 3599, 2006 FCA 183, 2006 CAF 183 (F.C.A.), J.D.D. Pelletier J.A.

Motion for order for financial aid for self-represented impecunious litigant. Impecuniosity and belief in justness of cause not sufficient grounds.

Kemp v. Prescesky, [2006] N.S.J. No. 174, 2006 CarswellNS 175, 244 N.S.R. (2d) 67, 744 A.P.R. 67, 28 C.P.C. (6th) 361, 2006 NSSC 122 (N.S. S.C.).

Small Claims Court created to provide forum for informal, simple, efficient, and independent adjudication of claims. Requirements for natural justice in Small Claims Court system have increased with increase in monetary jurisdiction. Same principles of fairness as exist in Supreme Court should apply in Small Claims Court.

Elliott v. Chiarelli, 2006 CarswellOnt 6261, 83 O.R. (3d) 226 (Ont. S.C.J.), 2006-10-06, Baltman J.

Appeal from judgment of Deputy Judge dismissing appellant's malpractice claim against the respondent. The appellant "hired" respondent, Vince Chiarelli, a paralegal. Claim in Small Claims Court against Chiarelli to recover money paid him, based on professional negligence and breach of contract. Appeal allowed.

Issue of standard of care applicable to a paralegal: see *West v. Eisner*, 1999 CarswellOnt 4017, [1999] O.J. No. 4705, 48 C.C.L.T. (2d) 274, 41 C.P.C. (4th) 378 (Ont. S.C.J.), Stinson J.; and *ter Neuzen v. Korn*, 1995 CarswellBC 593, 1995 CarswellBC 1146, [1995] S.C.J. No. 79, EYB 1995-67069, [1995] 10 W.W.R. 1, 64 B.C.A.C. 241, 105 W.A.C. 241, 188 N.R. 161, 11 B.C.L.R. (3d) 201, [1995] 3 S.C.R. 674, 127 D.L.R. (4th) 577 (S.C.C.).

Standard of review is palpable and overriding error. Deputy Judge erred in construing relationship between parties and contract too narrowly. Standard based on common sense and ordinary understanding appropriate. Respondent's advice clearly wrong. Respondent misled appellant. Respondent acted unconscionably.

R. v. Gouchie, 2006 CarswellNS 442, 2006 NSCA 109, 213 C.C.C. (3d) 250, 248 N.S.R. (2d) 167, 789 A.P.R. 167 (N.S. C.A.).

Issues as to limitations on legal aid funding and paralegal representation.

How can someone of such disreputable antecedents be allowed to address the Court? In Ontario clinics assist inmates in presenting appeals but this issue is likely to continue to be significant. Nova Scotia court adopted Ontario caselaw and applied it to the appeal situation. It quoted, with approval, *R. v. Romanowicz* (1999), 26 C.R. (5th) 246, 45 M.V.R. (3d) 294, 124 O.A.C. 100, 138 C.C.C. (3d) 225, 178 D.L.R. (4th) 466, 45 O.R. (3d) 506, *(sub nom. R. c. Romanowicz)* 45 O.R. (3d) 532 (Fr.), 1999 CarswellOnt 2671, [1999] O.J. No. 3191 (Ont. C.A.):

> Surely, representation by an agent who has been shown to be incompetent or disreputable can imperil the accused's right to a fair trial and can undermine the integrity of the proceedings just as much as if an accused who was incapable of representing himself were required to proceed without counsel . . .

Deevy v. Canada (Minister of Social Development), 2006 CarswellNat 688, 2006 CarswellNat 2268, 2006 FCA 115, 2006 CAF 115, 350 N.R. 91 (F.C.A.).

Applicant in judicial review proceedings moved for an order permitting her to be represented by Fraser who was a registered nurse and a non-lawyer. The Federal Court of Appeal, per Sexton, J.A., stated that it had been recognized that court might have inherent jurisdiction required to permit representation by a non-lawyer, if the interests of justice so required. However, the court dismissed application where Fraser did not appreciate the nature of judicial review or the procedures that were to be followed.

Chancey v. Dharmadi (2007), [2007] O.J. No. 2852, 2007 CarswellOnt 4664, 44 C.P.C. (6th) 158, 86 O.R. (3d) 612 (Ont. Master), Master Dash.

Defendant in civil action arising out of motor vehicle action retained paralegal to defend her on *Highway Traffic Act* charges arising out of same accident. Communications between defendant and paralegal privileged on application of Wigmore criteria.

Communications between defendant and the paralegal originated in a confidence that they would not be disclosed. The confidentiality was essential to the full and satisfactory maintenance of the relation between the defendant and the paralegal. The relation was one which in the opinion of the community ought to be sedulously fostered. Paralegals fill an affordability gap in the justice system. Access to justice is a goal to be sedulously fostered.

The Government of Ontario has recognized in the *Access to Justice Act* that paralegals play a pivotal role in the justice system. The Act imposes upon the Law Society in its development of rules for the regulation of paralegals "a duty to act so as to facilitate access to justice for the people of Ontario" (*Access to Justice Act, supra*, s. 7; amended *Law Society Act* s. 4.2(2)). The *Paralegal Rules of Conduct* provide that the Rules be interpreted in a way that recognizes that "a paralegal, as a provider of legal services, has an important role to play in a free and democratic society and in the administration of justice" (*Paralegal Rules of Conduct*, rule 1.03(b)). The failure of the court to protect as confidential communications between paralegal and client sends a message to the public that there is a "two-tier" justice system in effect.

Rockwood v. Newfoundland & Labrador, 2007 CarswellNfld 341, 826 A.P.R. 65, 2007 NLCA 68, 287 D.L.R. (4th) 471, 271 Nfld. & P.E.I.R. 65, 46 C.P.C. (6th) 86, [2007] N.J. No. 382, (sub nom. *R. v. Rockwood*) 164 C.R.R. (2d) 345 (N.L. C.A.).

[A Rule of Court holding that corporations must be represented by solicitors in court actions does not violate s. 15 of the *Charter*. Corporations are not "individuals" under s. 15. In any event, nothing of human dignity or stereotype is involved in such a rule, even if the corporation is closely held. The choice of a person to claim the benefits of incorporation means the person takes the disadvantages of doing so, as well.].

Respondent had challenged a rule of court that prevented a corporation from proceeding with an action otherwise than by a solicitor as a violation of s. 15(1) of the *Charter*.

See *Kosmopoulos v. Constitution Insurance Co. of Canada*, 1987 CarswellOnt 132, 1987 CarswellOnt 1054, [1987] S.C.J. No. 2, EYB 1987-68613, 22 C.C.L.I. 296, [1987] 1 S.C.R. 2, (sub nom. *Constitution Insurance Co. of Canada v. Kosmopoulos*) 34 D.L.R. (4th) 208, 74 N.R. 360, 21 O.A.C. 4, (sub nom. *Kosmopoulos v. Constitution Insurance Co.*) 36 B.L.R. 233, [1987] I.L.R. 1-2147 (S.C.C.) at page 11 (S.C.R.). Does s. 15(1) of the *Charter* apply to corporations? See *Edmonton Journal v. Alberta (Attorney General)*, [1989] S.C.J. No. 124, EYB 1989-66926, 1989 CarswellAlta 198, 1989 CarswellAlta 623, 1989 SCC 133, [1990] 1 W.W.R. 577, [1989] 2 S.C.R. 1326, 64 D.L.R. (4th) 577, 102 N.R. 321, 71 Alta. L.R. (2d) 273, 103 A.R. 321, 41 C.P.C. (2d) 109, 45 C.R.R. 1 (S.C.C.) in part. *Law v. Canada (Minister of Employment & Immigration)*, 1999 CarswellNat 359, 1999 CarswellNat 360, [1999] S.C.J. No. 12, 170 D.L.R. (4th) 1, (sub nom. *Law v. Canada (Minister of Human Resources Development))* 60 C.R.R. (2d) 1, 236 N.R. 1, [1999] 1 S.C.R. 497, 43 C.C.E.L. (2d) 49, (sub nom. *Law v. Minister of Human Resources Development*) 1999 C.E.B. & P.G.R. 8350 (headnote only) (S.C.C.) refers to the violation of essential human dignity and freedom through the imposition of disadvantage, stereotyping, or political or social prejudice.

Hill v. Toronto (City), [2007] O.J. No. 2232, 2007 CarswellOnt 3578, (sub nom. *Toronto (City) v. Hill)* 221 C.C.C. (3d) 189, 2007 ONCJ 253, 48 M.V.R. (5th) 55 (Ont. C.J.), Libman J.

Paralegal agent on appeal should only bring allegations of incompetence against trial agent after personal investigation.

Trial agent should be provided with notice of allegations and given fair opportunity to respond. Accused entitled to effective assistance of paralegal practitioner where such representation chosen. Here there was absence of proper notice to trial agents and lack of proper supporting materials in further of allegations.

Elliott v. Chiarelli, 2006 CarswellOnt 6261, 83 O.R. (3d) 226 (Ont. S.C.J.), Baltman J.

Plaintiff consulted defendant paralegal after receiving eviction notice for non-payment of rent. Competent legal advisor would have attempted to negotiate repayment schedule with landlord or would have advised plaintiff to use her money for first and last month's rent for new apartment. Defendant fell below standard of care of ethical and competent paralegal. Defendant liable to plaintiff in negligence.

The trial judge decided the case on contract principles, and did not consider the negligence claim. The plaintiff appealed. Appeal allowed.

The defendant was liable in both negligence and breach of contract. The defendant's advice was bad.

In *West v. Eisner*, 1999 CarswellOnt 4017, [1999] O.J. No. 4705, 48 C.C.L.T. (2d) 274, 41 C.P.C. (4th) 378 (Ont. S.C.J.), Stinson J. assessed damages for malpractice against a paralegal. He suggested it made sense to apply a standard based on common sense and ordinary understanding, relying on commentary by the Supreme Court of Canada in *ter Neuzen v. Korn*, 1995 CarswellBC 593, 1995 CarswellBC 1146, [1995] S.C.J. No. 79, EYB 1995-67069, [1995] 10 W.W.R. 1, 64 B.C.A.C. 241, 105 W.A.C. 241, 188 N.R. 161, 11 B.C.L.R. (3d) 201, [1995] 3 S.C.R. 674, 127 D.L.R. (4th) 577 (S.C.C.), at p. 701 S.C.R., p. 595 D.L.R.

Christie v. British Columbia (Attorney General), [2007] S.C.J. No. 21, 2007 CarswellBC 1117, 2007 CarswellBC 1118, (sub nom. *British Columbia (Attorney General) v. Christie*) 2007 D.T.C. 5525 (Eng.), (sub nom. *British Columbia (Attorney General) v. Christie*) 2007 D.T.C. 5229 (Fr.), 240 B.C.A.C. 1, 398 W.A.C. 1, (sub nom. *British Columbia (Attorney General) v. Christie*) 2007 G.T.C. 1493 (Fr.), 66 B.C.L.R. (4th) 1, 361 N.R. 322, (sub nom. *British Columbia (Attorney General) v. Christie*) 2007 G.T.C. 1488 (Eng.), 2007 SCC 21, 280 D.L.R. (4th) 528, [2007] 8 W.W.R. 64, (sub nom. *British Columbia (Attorney General) v. Christie*) [2007] 1 S.C.R. 873, (sub nom. *British Columbia (Attorney General) v. Christie*) 155 C.R.R. (2d) 366 (S.C.C.).

Appeal allowed. The alleged right to be represented by a lawyer in legal proceedings in which legal rights or obligations are in issue is a broad right that, if recognized, would lead to a constitutionally mandated legal aid scheme for almost all legal proceedings. Recognition of such a right would involve a significant change in the delivery of legal services and would impose a considerable burden on taxpayers.

The alleged right to be represented by counsel in legal proceedings cannot be based on the rule of law contained in the preamble to the *Canadian Charter of Rights and Freedoms*. The rule of law is explicitly and implicitly a foundational principle recognized as an aspect of the rule of law and it should not be so recognized in this case.

Dublin v. Montessori Jewish Day School of Toronto, 2007 CarswellOnt 1663, [2007] O.J. No. 1062, 38 C.P.C. (6th) 312, 281 D.L.R. (4th) 366, 85 O.R. (3d) 511 (Ont. S.C.J.); additional reasons at (2007), 2007 CarswellOnt 2338 (Ont. S.C.J.); leave to appeal allowed (2007), 2007 CarswellOnt 6097 (Ont. Div. Ct.), Perell J.

Appeal allowed. E-mail message between client and lawyer who was acting in his professional capacity as a lawyer, sent in the context of obtaining legal advice, and was intended to be confidential. But for its content, it would be a communication for the purpose of obtaining legal advice and would therefore be protected by solicitor-client privilege. However, there was an exception to solicitor-client privilege for communications in furtherance of an illegal purpose. This exception included communications perpetrating tortuous conduct that might become the subject of civil proceedings. The exception to privilege for communications in furtherance of unlawful conduct was applicable to the message. It should have been disclosed to the plaintiffs in the first place and did not have to be returned.

Law Society (Manitoba) v. Pollock, [2007] M.J. No. 67, 2007 CarswellMan 80, 213 Man. R. (2d) 81, 2007 MBQB 51, 37 C.P.C. (6th) 125, [2007] 5 W.W.R. 147, 153 C.R.R. (2d) 131 (Man. Q.B.); affirmed 2008 CarswellMan 238, 2008 MBCA 61, [2008] 7 W.W.R. 493, 54 C.P.C. (6th) 4, 427 W.A.C. 273, 228 Man. R. (2d) 273 (Man. C.A.), Monnin C.J.Q.B.

Paralegal advertised himself as agent who could help people with their court cases for fee. Law Society brought application for declaration paralegal not entitled to practise as lawyer and for injunction preventing him from doing so. Application granted in part. Section 20(2) of *Legal Profession Act* prohibited practice of law by person not member of Law Society except as permitted under other Act. Paralegal permitted under s. 802.1 of *Criminal Code* to act as agent in summary conviction proceedings under *Code* where maximum penalty was term of six months in prison or less. Use of term "advocate" in s. 9 of *Divorce Act* did not authorize individuals not licensed as lawyers to represent individuals in divorce proceedings. *Small Claims Practice Act* permitted filing of claim by someone other than party but did not permit appearing in court on behalf of party, nor did it permit provision of legal service to small claims litigants on commercial fee basis. *Human Rights Code* did not permit paralegal to act on behalf of other claimants in human rights matters. Section 20 of *Legal Profession Act* did not breach paralegal's rights under s. 2 or 7 of *Canadian Charter of Rights and Freedoms*.

R. v. Gouchie, 2006 CarswellNS 442, 2006 NSCA 109, 213 C.C.C. (3d) 250, 248 N.S.R. (2d) 167, 789 A.P.R. 167 (N.S. C.A.).

Accused sought to have F represent him as agent on application for appointment of counsel. F in prison and not lawyer. F not qualified to represent accused on application. Fact that F was inmate did not automatically bar him from assisting accused. F admitted to perjuring himself in other proceedings. Obvious from rambling and largely irrelevant submissions advanced by F that he would be entirely ineffective as accused's agent.

R. v. Kubinski, 2006 CarswellAlta 1817, 2006 ABPC 172 (Alta. Prov. Ct.), C.M. Skene Prov. J.

Agent did not have any formal legal training. Many judges refused in past to allow this agent to represent clients at trial, but this fact was not communicated to accused. Agent exhibited questionable judgment in past cases by misrepresenting facts to court. Unethical and disreputable acts could imperil accused's right to fair trial and undermine integrity of proceedings.

Christie v. British Columbia (Attorney General), [2007] S.C.J. No. 21, 2007 CarswellBC 1117, 2007 CarswellBC 1118, (sub nom. *British Columbia (Attorney General) v. Christie)* 2007 D.T.C. 5525 (Eng.), (sub nom. *British Columbia (Attorney General) v. Christie)* 2007 D.T.C. 5229 (Fr.), 240 B.C.A.C. 1, 398 W.A.C. 1, (sub nom. *British Columbia (Attorney General) v. Christie)* 2007 G.T.C. 1493 (Fr.), 66 B.C.L.R. (4th) 1, 361 N.R. 322, (sub nom. *British Columbia (Attorney General) v. Christie)* 2007 G.T.C. 1488 (Eng.), 2007 SCC 21, 280 D.L.R. (4th) 528, [2007] 8 W.W.R. 64, (sub nom. *British Columbia (Attorney General) v. Christie)* [2007] 1 S.C.R. 873, (sub nom. *British Columbia (Attorney General) v. Christie)* 155 C.R.R. (2d) 366 (S.C.C.).

Is tax on legal services unconstitutional because it infringes right to access to justice of low-income persons? Is general constitutional right to counsel in court or tribunal proceedings dealing with a person's rights and obligations?.

There is no general constitutional right to counsel in proceedings before courts and tribunals dealing with rights and obligations. The right to access the courts is not absolute and a legislature has the power under s. 92(14) of the *Constitution Act, 1867* to impose at least some conditions on how and when people have a right to access the courts. General access to legal services is also not a currently recognized aspect of, or a precondition to, the rule of law. The fact that s. 10(b) does not exclude a finding of a constitutional right to legal assistance in other situations, notably under s. 7 of the *Charter*, does not support a general right to legal assistance whenever a matter of rights and obligations is before a court or tribunal. The right to counsel outside the s. 10(b) context is a case-specific multi-factored enquiry.

The general right to be represented by a lawyer in a court or tribunal proceedings where legal rights or obligations are at stake is a broad right. This court is not in a position to assess the cost to the public that the right would entail.

It is argued that access to justice is a fundamental constitutional right that embraces the right to have a lawyer in relation to court and tribunal proceedings. See *B.C.G.E.U., Re*, EYB 1988-67021, 1988 CarswellBC 762, 1988 CarswellBC 363, [1988] S.C.J. No. 76, (sub nom. *B.C.G.E.U. v. British Columbia (Attorney General))* [1988] 6 W.W.R. 577, 30 C.P.C. (2d) 221, [1988] 2 S.C.R. 214, 220 A.P.R. 93, 53 D.L.R. (4th) 1, 87 N.R. 241, 31 B.C.L.R. (2d) 273, 71 Nfld. & P.E.I.R. 93, 44 C.C.C. (3d) 289, 88 C.L.L.C. 14,047 (S.C.C.). The right affirmed in *B.C.G.E.U.* is not absolute.

General access to legal services is not a currently recognized aspect of the rule of law. The S.C.C. has repeatedly emphasized the important role that lawyers play in ensuring access to justice and upholding the rule of law. See *Andrews v. Law Society (British Columbia)*, EYB 1989-66977, 1989 CarswellBC 16, 1989 CarswellBC 701, [1989] S.C.J. No. 6, 10 C.H.R.R. D/5719, [1989] 2 W.W.R. 289, 56 D.L.R. (4th) 1, 91 N.R. 255, 34 B.C.L.R. (2d) 273, 25 C.C.E.L. 255, 36 C.R.R. 193, [1989] 1 S.C.R. 143 (S.C.C.), at p. 187 (S.C.R.); *MacDonald Estate v. Martin*, 1990 CarswellMan 384, [1990] S.C.J. No. 41, 1990 CarswellMan 233, EYB 1990-68602, [1991] 1 W.W.R. 705, 77 D.L.R. (4th) 249, 121 N.R. 1, (sub nom. *Martin v. Gray)* [1990] 3 S.C.R. 1235, 48 C.P.C. (2d) 113, 70 Man. R. (2d) 241, 285 W.A.C. 241 (S.C.C.), at p. 1265 (S.C.R.); *Fortin c. Chrétien*, 2001 CarswellQue 1395, 2001 CarswellQue 1396, REJB 2001-25001, (sub nom. *Fortin v. Chrétien)* 201 D.L.R. (4th) 223, (sub nom. *Fortin v. Barreau du Québec)* 272 N.R. 359, 2001 SCC 45, [2001] 2 S.C.R. 500 (S.C.C.), at para. 49; *Law Society (British Columbia) v. Mangat* (2001), 2001 CarswellBC 2168, 2001 CarswellBC 2169, [2001] S.C.J. No. 66, 2001 SCC 67, 16 Imm. L.R. (3d) 1, 205 D.L.R. (4th) 577, 157 B.C.A.C. 161, 256 W.A.C. 161, 96 B.C.L.R. (3d) 1, 276 N.R. 339, [2002] 2 W.W.R. 201, [2001] 3 S.C.R. 113 (S.C.C.), at para. 43; *R. v. Lavallee, Rackel & Heintz*, [2002] S.C.J. No. 61, 2002 CarswellAlta 1818, 2002 CarswellAlta 1819, REJB 2002-33795, 216 D.L.R. (4th) 257, (sub nom. *Lavallee, Rackel & Heintz v. Canada (Attorney General))* 167 C.C.C. (3d) 1, 4 Alta. L.R. (4th) 1, (sub nom. *Lavallee, Rackel & Heintz v. Canada (Attorney General))* 164 O.A.C. 280, 2002 SCC 61, (sub nom. *Lavallee, Rackel & Heintz v. Canada (Attorney General))* 96 C.R.R. (2d) 189, [2002] 11 W.W.R. 191, (sub nom. *Lavallee, Rackel & Heintz v. Canada (Attorney General))* [2002] 3 S.C.R. 209, 2002 D.T.C. 7267 (Eng.), 2002 D.T.C. 7287 (Fr.), 3 C.R. (6th) 209, [2002] 4 C.T.C. 143, 292 N.R. 296, 312 A.R. 201, 281 W.A.C. 201, (sub nom. *Lavallee, Rackel & Heintz v. Canada (Attorney General))* 217 Nfld. & P.E.I.R. 183, (sub nom. *Lavallee, Rackel & Heintz v. Canada (Attorney General))* 651 A.P.R. 183 (S.C.C.), at paras. 64-68, per LeBel J. (dissenting in part but not on this point). This is only fitting. Lawyers are a vital conduit through which citizens access the courts, and the law. They help maintain the rule of law by working to ensure that unlawful private and unlawful state action in particular do no got unaddressed. The role that lawyers play in this regard is so important that the right to counsel in some situations has been given constitutional status.

Section 10(b) does not exclude a finding of a constitutional right to legal assistance in other situations. Section 7 of the *Charter*, for example, has been held to imply a right to counsel as an aspect of procedural fairness where life, liberty and security of the person are affected. See *Dehghani v. Canada (Minister of Employment & Immigration)*, 1993 CarswellNat 57, 1993 CarswellNat 1380, EYB 1993-67290, [1993] S.C.J. No. 38, 18 Imm. L.R. (2d) 245, 101 D.L.R. (4th) 654, [1993] 1 S.C.R. 1053, 150 N.R. 241, 14 C.R.R. (2d) 1, 10 Admin. L.R. (2d) 1, 20 C.R. (4th) 34 (S.C.C.), at p. 1077 (S.C.R.); *New Brunswick (Minister of Health & Community Services) v. G. (J.)*, REJB 1999-14250, 1999 CarswellNB 305, 1999 CarswellNB 306, [1999] S.C.J. No. 47, 66 C.R.R. (2d) 267, 50 R.F.L. (4th) 63, 216 N.B.R. (2d) 25, 552 A.P.R. 25, [1999] 3 S.C.R. 46, 7 B.H.R.C. 615, 244 N.R. 276, 177 D.L.R. (4th) 124, 26 C.R. (5th) 203 (S.C.C.). But this does not support a general right to legal assistance whenever a matter of rights and obligations is before a court or tribunal. Thus in *New Brunswick*, the court was at pains to state that the right to counsel outside of the s. 10(b) context is a case-specific multi-factored enquiry (see para. 86).

Law Society (British Columbia) v. Bryfogle, 2007 CarswellBC 2526, [2007] B.C.J. No. 2289, 73 B.C.L.R. (4th) 237, 2007 BCCA 511, 409 W.A.C. 283, 247 B.C.A.C. 283 (B.C. C.A.), Prowse J.

The Law Society of British Columbia sought an order to restrain the defendant from engaging in activities that constituted the practice of law and to prevent him from acting on his own behalf or on behalf of others in litigation without leave of court. Trial judge granted the order. Defendant appealed claiming that he was entitled to appear for clients for a fee as of right pursuant to a power of attorney and in fact in some of those proceedings, he had been given permission by the court to speak on behalf of others.

Appeal dismissed. Acting pursuant to a power of attorney did not permit a person who was not a lawyer to engage in conduct which constituted the practice of law The fact that the defendant was granted right of audience before one or more judges in the past did not preclude finding that he was unlawfully engaged in the practice of law on those occasions.

Law Society (Manitoba) v. Pollock, 2008 CarswellMan 238, 2008 MBCA 61, [2008] 7 W.W.R. 493, 54 C.P.C. (6th) 4, 427 W.A.C. 273, 228 Man. R. (2d) 273 (Man. C.A.).

Appeal from judge's decision granting permanent injunction against appellant in relation to various activities determined to amount to the unauthorized practice of law.

Appellant argued that ss. 6(1) and 11(1) of the *Small Claims Practices Act* permits "another person" or "someone" to act for a party and that because statute does not expressly state a non-lawyer cannot appear for a fee, s. 20 of *The Legal Profession Act* will not prevent him from providing representation on a commercial basis.

Appellant relied on decision in *Law Society (British Columbia) v. Mangat* (2001), REJB 2001-26158, [2001] 3 S.C.R. 113, 96 B.C.L.R. (3d) 1, [2002] 2 W.W.R. 201, 276 N.R. 339, 2001 CarswellBC 2169, 2001 CarswellBC 2168, 2001 SCC 67, 205 D.L.R. (4th) 577, 16 Imm. L.R. (3d) 1, 256 W.A.C. 161, 157 B.C.A.C. 161, [2001] S.C.J. No. 66 (S.C.C.), where it stated, ". . . Had Parliament wanted to declare that 'other counsel' means only unpaid persons, it would have said so by using distinctive terms in ss. 30 and 69(1)" (at para. 65). Unlike legislation in *Mangat*, the *Small Claims Practices Act* does not contain a provision authorizing non-lawyers to appear for a fee. No provision in *The Legal Profession Act* or the *Small Claims Practices Act* that authorizes non-lawyers to appear on a commercial basis before that court. No provision in the *Small Claims Practices Act* relating to expenses for such representation.

Law Society of Upper Canada v. Canada (Minister of Citizenship & Immigration), 2008 CarswellNat 5012, 2008 CarswellNat 2487, 295 D.L.R. (4th) 488, 383 N.R. 200, 2008 CAF 243, 2008 FCA 243, 72 Imm. L.R. (3d) 26 (F.C.A.).

The Regulations were introduced by the federal government in 2004 to regulate immigration consultants. Representation of clients in matters before the Immigration and Refugee Board for a fee had been limited to lawyers, notaries, students-at-law, and members of the Canadian Society of Immigration Consultants (CSIC). The court found that the Regulations did not discriminate where they did not permit lawyers' employees, including paralegals, to provide representation as the Parliament has power to create self-governing profession through regulations.

R. v. Toutissani, 2008 CarswellOnt 1688, [2008] O.J. No. 1174, 2008 ONCJ 139, Casey J. (Ont. C.J.); leave to appeal refused (2008), 2008 CarswellOnt 5424, 2008 CarswellOnt 5425, 390 N.R. 390 (note) (S.C.C.).

Application was made by the Crown for an order removing a non-lawyer as agent for the accused. The agent acknowledged that he was not a person licensed by the Law Society to provide legal services, but submitted that ss. 800 and 802 of the *Criminal Code* permitted him to appear as agent, notwithstanding the provisions of the Act.

Ontario Court of Justice held that Parliament's purpose in enacting sections 800(2), 802(2) and 802.1 of the *Criminal Code* was to permit defendants, in summary conviction proceedings, to be represented by either by counsel or by non-lawyer agents. This purpose is not frustrated by the *Law Society Act* which attempts to ensure that non-lawyers who are hired for a fee and appear for defendants in summary conviction matters are competent and qualified. Person could comply with both provisions of Act and Code and thus, application allowed.

Warner v. Balsdon (2008), 2008 CarswellOnt 2847, 237 O.A.C. 317, 63 C.C.L.I. (4th) 293, 91 O.R. (3d) 124 (Ont. Div. Ct.), Ferrier J.

Appeal by defendant from order refusing to strike out cross-claim. The plaintiff sued the defendant for injuries and also sued paralegal for negligence in having settled her claim against defendant. The paralegal cross-claimed against the defendant, alleging that the defendant owed the plaintiff duty of care to negotiate fairly. Cross-claim dismissed.

If the release was upheld, then by its terms the plaintiff was barred from bringing an action against anyone who might claim contribution and indemnity from the defendant. The cross-claim was moot as the only damages claimed against paralegal were the damages received had release not been executed. The paralegal breached s. 398(1) of the *Insurance Act* which prohibited anyone from negotiating a settlement of a personal injury claim on behalf of a plaintiff or potential plaintiff.

Turner v. Rogers et al., Certiorari to the Supreme Court of South Carolina. Decided June 20, 2011.

The U.S. Supreme Court decision in *Turner v. Rogers* may greatly influence the judicial handling of civil self-represented litigation.

In *Turner*, a custodial maternal grandparent asked the court to penalize the father for failure to pay child support. Neither party had counsel, nor was the state a party. The judge imposed a 12-month civil contempt order, upheld on appeal to the South Carolina Supreme Court. At the urging of the United States, as *amicus curiae*, Justice Stephen Breyer's majority opinion reversed on the ground that in the absence of counsel, the judge's failure to provide procedural safeguards *sua sponte* constituted a violation of the father's due process rights.

Law Society of Upper Canada v. Ernest Guiste, 2011 ONLSHP 24.

A hearing panel of the Law Society ruled that lawyers' conduct during the mediation process is subject to the *Rules of Professional Conduct*. The panel found that the provisions of confidentiality contained in an agreement to mediate was for the benefit of the parties and was not intended to protect lawyers from allegations of misconduct.

The lawyer, who was the subject of findings of professional misconduct, was alleged to have committed six acts of professional misconduct.

The allegation with respect to the conduct during mediation is:

> 1. On June 21, 2007, during a mediation in the matter of *D.L. v. N. Ltd. et al.*, the respondent failed to be courteous, civil, and act in good faith by using sexually explicit, rude, and profane language, and raising his voice at a mediation session, contrary to Rule 4.01(6) of the *Rules of Professional Conduct*:

.

(6) A lawyer shall be courteous, civil, and act in good faith to the tribunal and with all persons with whom the lawyer has dealings in the course of litigation.

Sahyoun v. Ho, 2011 BCSC 567, 2011 CarswellBC 1050 (B.C. S.C.).

The plaintiffs sought state-funded counsel under section 7 of the *Canadian Charter of Rights and Freedoms*. See *New Brunswick (Minister of Health & Community Services) v. G. (J.)*, 1999 CarswellNB 305, 1999 CarswellNB 306, REJB 1999-14250, [1999] S.C.J. No. 47, [1999] 3 S.C.R. 46, 216 N.B.R. (2d) 25, 66 C.R.R. (2d) 267, 50 R.F.L. (4th) 63, 552 A.P.R. 25, 7 B.H.R.C. 615, 244 N.R. 276, 177 D.L.R. (4th) 124, 26 C.R. (5th) 203 (S.C.C.), in support of this assertion. Right to state-funded counsel arising under the Chapter is *R. v. Rowbotham*, 1988 CarswellOnt 58, [1988] O.J. No. 271, 25 O.A.C. 321, 35 C.R.R. 207, 41 C.C.C. (3d) 1, 63 C.R. (3d) 113 (Ont. C.A.).

In *Christie v. British Columbia (Attorney General)*, 2007 SCC 21, 2007 CarswellBC 1117, 2007 CarswellBC 1118, [2007] S.C.J. No. 21, (sub nom. *British Columbia (Attorney General) v. Christie)* [2007] 1 S.C.R. 873, (sub nom. *British Columbia (Attorney General) v. Christie)* 2007 D.T.C. 5525 (Eng.), (sub nom. *British Columbia (Attorney General) v. Christie)* 2007 D.T.C. 5229 (Fr.), 240 B.C.A.C. 1, 398 W.A.C. 1, (sub nom. *British Columbia (Attorney General) v. Christie)* 2007 G.T.C. 1493 (Fr.), 66 B.C.L.R. (4th) 1, 361 N.R. 322, (sub nom. *British Columbia (Attorney General) v. Christie)* 2007 G.T.C. 1488 (Eng.), 280 D.L.R. (4th) 528, [2007] 8 W.W.R. 64, (sub nom. *British Columbia (Attorney General) v. Christie)* 155 C.R.R. (2d) 366 (S.C.C.), in a constitutional challenge to the *Social Service Tax Amendment Act (No. 2), 1993*, S.B.C. 1993, c. 24 based upon unwritten constitutional principles such as the rule of law and "access to justice," the Court said:

> 25. Section 10(b) does not exclude a finding of a constitutional right to legal assistance in other situations, Section 7 of the *Charter*, for example, has been held to imply a right to counsel as an aspect of procedural fairness where life, liberty and security of the person are affected: see *Dehghani v. Canada (Minister of Employment and Immigration)*, [1993] 1 S.C.R. 1053 at p. 1077; *New Brunswick (Minister of Health and Community Services) v. G.(J.)*, [1999] 3 S.C.R. 46. But this does not support a general right to legal assistance whenever a matter of rights and obligations is before a court or tribunal. Thus, in *New Brunswick*, the Court was at pains to state that the right to counsel outside of the s. 10(b) context is a case-specific multi-factored enquiry (see para. 86).

See further *Holland (Guardian ad litem of) v. Marshall*, 2008 BCSC 1899, 2008 CarswellBC 3288 (B.C. S.C. [In Chambers]); affirmed 2010 BCCA 164, 2010 CarswellBC 912, 3 B.C.L.R. (5th) 352 (B.C. C.A.); leave to appeal refused 2010 CarswellBC 2645, 2010 CarswellBC 2646, [2010] S.C.C.A. No. 224, (sub nom. *Holland v. Marshall)* 410 N.R. 395 (note), (sub nom. *Holland v. Marshall)* 300 B.C.A.C. 320 (note), (sub nom. *Holland v. Marshall)* 509 W.A.C. 320 (note) (S.C.C.). See also *D. (P.) v. British Columbia*, 2010 BCSC 290, 2010 CarswellBC 571, [2010] B.C.J. No. 405, 7 B.C.L.R. (5th) 312, 82 R.F.L. (6th) 180, 210 C.R.R. (2d) 1 (B.C. S.C.).

Present action does not involve any state action or involvement. The fact that some of the defendants are bodies or individuals that represent various levels of government does not change this. Section 7 is not engaged and provides no support for the plaintiffs' application for state-funded counsel.

Section 15(1) of the *Charter* provides:

> Every individual is equal before and under the law and has the right to the equal protection and equal benefit of the law without discrimination and, in particular, without discrimination based on race, national or ethnic origin, colour, religion, sex, age or mental or physical disability.

Poverty is not one of the enumerated grounds listed in section 15. In *Affordable Energy Coalition, Re*, 2009 NSCA 17, 2009 CarswellNS 79, (sub nom. *Boulter v. Nova Scotia Power Inc.)* 275 N.S.R. (2d) 214, (sub nom. *Boulter v. Nova Scotia Power Inc.)* 877 A.P.R. 214, (sub nom. *Boulter v. Nova Scotia Power Inc.)* 307 D.L.R. (4th) 293 (N.S. C.A.), Fichaud J.A.; leave to appeal refused 2009 CarswellNS 485, 2009 CarswellNS 486, (sub nom. *Boulter v. Nova Scotia Power Inc.)* 293 N.S.R. (2d) 400 (note), (sub nom. *Boulter v. Nova Scotia Power Inc.)* 199 C.R.R. (2d) 375 (note), (sub nom. *Boulter v. Nova Scotia Power Inc.)* 400 N.R. 394 (note), (sub nom. *Boulter v. Nova Scotia Power Inc.)* 928 A.P.R. 400 (note) (S.C.C.), for the court, at paras. 32–44, determined that poverty is not an analogous ground under section 15(1).

There is no legal basis for the section 15 submission that Dr. Sahyoun seeks to advance.

Specific orders made:

i) The present action is stayed;

ii) The plaintiffs' application for state-funded counsel is dismissed;

iii) The plaintiffs' application for advance or interim costs is dismissed; and

iv) The plaintiffs' challenge to the validity of Rule 20-2(4) is dismissed.

Jacob v. Pool, 2011 ABPC 321, 2011 CarswellAlta 2282, 514 A.R. 114 (Alta. Prov. Ct.), Judge J.L. Skitsko.

The case involved the purchase and sale of a property. The plaintiffs were the buyers.

Damages totalling $1,150 were awarded to the plaintiffs.

The trial took place over three days. The court observed a certain lack of decorum and courtesy between the parties. The court was required to chide both sides when each would display a lack of courtesy to the other. The plaintiffs would regularly interrupt witnesses, even their own, and would on occasion not allow the witnesses to finish their answers before purporting to ask further questions.

The court was particularly concerned with the plaintiffs' demeanour during their cross-examination of witnesses, as they would prove to be argumentative with the witnesses. Questions were often posed without the facts necessary to support the question. See Williston and Rolls in their text, *The Conduct of an Action*, (1982, Butterworths, Toronto). Pages 119 to 120 make it clear:

> ... that a party may cross-examine any witness not called by him on all facts in issue and on all matters subsequently relevant to the credibility of the witness, and on such cross-examination, may ask the witness leading questions, but the section goes on to provide that a party shall not allege or assume facts on cross-examination unless he is in a position to substantiate them.

While self-represented non-legally-trained people will be given full access to dispute resolution by the Courts, this does not mean that the trial process and the rules associated with the conduct of a trial will be waived or ignored.

The remaining claims against the defendants were dismissed.

Pardar v. McKoy, 2011 ONSC 2549, 2011 CarswellOnt 3059, [2011] O.J. No. 2092 (Ont. Div. Ct.).

The respondent commenced proceedings in Small Claims Court against the applicant. The respondent's representative was a paralegal. The applicant's motion to prevent the respondent's representative from representing the respondent in proceedings was dismissed. The applicant sought judicial review. The application was dismissed. There was no breach of natural justice. Small Claims Court has jurisdiction to determine who can appear before it.

Divisional Court has jurisdiction to hear appeal from a final order of the Small Claims Court pursuant to section 31 of the *Courts of Justice Act*. Court also has jurisdiction to judicially review decisions of a Small Claims Court judge, *including* interlocutory orders. However, as per *Peck v. Residential Property Management Inc.*, 2009 CarswellOnt 4330, [2009] O.J. No. 3064 (Ont. Div. Ct.):

> [T]his Court is reluctant to interfere with a decision of a Small Claims Court judge on judicial review unless it is an order made without jurisdiction or in breach of principles of natural justice. (para. 3).

This is, in essence, an appeal.

> The purpose of Small Claims Court is to provide expeditious and low-cost settlement of monetary disputes. That purpose is reflected in the legislation that does not permit an appeal from interlocutory orders.

Application for judicial review dismissed. Costs fixed at $5,000.

Law Society of Upper Canada v. David Robert Conway, 2011 ONLSHP 33 (Ont. L.S.H.P.).

Lawyer found guilty of professional misconduct for practicing while suspended.

Fact that Lawyer had applied for a P1 licence did not allow him to continue to provide l ⌣ services as a paralegal in Small Claims Court while application pending.

By-Law 4 amendment of January 24, 2008 (Exhibit 14) which provides the following:

> Applicants for a paralegal licence may *not* also be licensed as a lawyer.

By-Law 4 amended to provide that lawyer licensees, including those whose licences are suspended, may not also be licensed as a paralegal. This reflects the new licensing regime whereby a licence to practise law (for lawyers) and a licence to provide legal services (for paralegals) are separate.

Under the new paralegal regulatory scheme, anyone who did not hold an L1 licence and who wished to provide or to continue to provide legal services was required to apply for a P1 licence. Those that applied and had no impediment to their application going forward, were granted a P1 licence. Those that declared some prior conduct that raised issues of good character were put in the good character hearing process. Those that had an impediment to even being considered, like the suspended Lawyer, were advised that their applications would not be processed unless and until they had surrendered their L1 licences.

The panel is also of the view that when the Law Society advised the suspended Lawyer of its position, his remedy was by way of Judicial Review of its refusal to process his application for a P1 licence.

27. (1) Evidence — **Subject to subsections (3) and (4), the Small Claims Court may admit as evidence at a hearing and act upon any oral testimony and any document or other thing so long as the evidence is relevant to the subject-matter of the proceeding, but the court may exclude anything unduly repetitious.**

(2) Idem — **Subsection (1) applies whether or not the evidence is given or proven under oath or affirmation or admissible as evidence in any other court.**

(3) Idem — **Nothing is admissible in evidence at a hearing,**

> **(a) that would be inadmissible by reason of any privilege under the law of evidence; or**
>
> **(b) that is inadmissible by any Act.**

(4) Conflicts — **Nothing in subsection (1) overrides the provisions of any Act expressly limiting the extent to or purposes for which any oral testimony, documents or things may be admitted or used in evidence in any proceeding.**

Commentary [S. 27(1)]: The Small Claims Court has its own rules of evidence, which are significantly more flexible than the evidence law which applies in other courts. The general rule is section 27(1) of the *Courts of Justice Act*, which provides a very broad discretion for the court to admit and act upon "any oral testimony and any document or other thing." The only categories of evidence which are not subject to the broad discretion under section 27(1), are (a) evidence that is protected by the law of privilege; and (b) evidence that is inadmissible by statute: see s. 27(3).

The most common example of how section 27 operates is hearsay evidence. By virtue of section 27(1), hearsay may be admitted as evidence in Small Claims Court proceedings: *Central Burner Service Inc. v. Texaco Canada Inc.*, 1989 CarswellOnt 1427, 36 O.A.C. 239 (Ont. Div. Ct.). If admitted, because it is less reliable, hearsay is usually entitled to less weight than other evidence. The court must decide the facts and in some cases hearsay evidence may be determinative: *Sathaseevan v. Suvara Travel Canada Inc.*, 1998 CarswellOnt 880, [1998] O.J. No. 1055 (Ont. Div. Ct.).

Section 27 applies specifically to the Small Claims Court and it may displace other rules dealing with the admissibility of evidence. For example, documents which do not qualify for admission as business records under section 35 of the *Evidence Act*, R.S.O. 1990, c. E.23, may nevertheless be admitted under section 27: see *VFC Inc. v. Balchand*, 2008 CarswellOnt 909, 233 O.A.C. 359, 291 D.L.R. (4th) 367 (Ont. Div. Ct.).

Section 27(2) provides that section 27(1) applies whether or not the evidence is given under oath or affirmation or is admissible in any other court. In *O'Brien v. Rideau Carleton Raceway Holdings Ltd.*, 1998 CarswellOnt 293, [1998] O.J. No. 500, 34 C.C.E.L. (2d) 199, 109 O.A.C. 173 (Ont. Div. Ct.), the court dismissed an appeal from a judgment after a trial at which none of the witnesses were placed under oath or affirmation. While the failure to administer the oath or affirmation is unusual and does not reflect the court's usual practice, that case illustrates the flexibility of the Small Claims Court's discretion over the admissibility of evidence.

Admission of Documents under Rule 18.02

The most commonly-used method to admit documents in the Small Claims Court is under rule 18.02. Any document or thing may be admitted under rule 18.02, if it was served at least 30 days before trial, and if certain information about the author was provided. That procedure avoids the need to introduce documents through a witness who provides the necessary background evidence to explain the nature, origin, and content of a document.

Rule 18.02 is often misinterpreted. The rule provides a procedure for the admission of documents which have been served on the other parties at least 30 days before trial, without the need for an in-person witness. It does not say that no document can be admitted at trial unless it was disclosed at least 30 days before trial: see *O'Connell v. Custom Kitchen & Vanity*, 1986 CarswellOnt 414, 56 O.R. (2d) 57, 11 C.P.C. (2d) 295, 17 O.A.C. 157 (Ont. Div. Ct.). Rule 18.02 is an enabling provision and not a prohibition. It enables the admission of documents which might otherwise be excluded as hearsay. Documents not admitted under rule 18.02 may be admitted by other means such as through an in-person witness.

Under rule 18.02(3), documents must include or have appended to them the name, telephone number, and address for service of the witness or author of the document, and, if the witness or author is to give expert evidence, a summary of his or her qualifications. If that information is not provided, then even if the document was served 30 days before trial the rule does not apply. Theoretically the trial judge could dispense with compliance with the information requirements, or could adjourn the trial if necessary.

A party who receives a document served under rule 18.02 and who wishes to cross-examine that witness or author at trial has the option to serve a summons on that person, with payment or tender of attendance money: rules 18.02(4) and (6). A copy of the summons must also be served on the other parties: rule 18.02(5).

Rule 18.02 is an enabling rule which facilitates the admission of documents which would be hearsay in the absence of a live witness to identify them. It serves to avoid the cost to the tendering parties of calling witnesses in addition to presenting the documents themselves. A party who invokes rule 18.02 effectively elects not to call the author of the document for examination-in-chief. The other party may elect to cross-examine the witness, but if so that party bears the onus and the expense to summons the person and to pay the necessary attendance money.

No Documents are Admitted Prior to Trial

Because copies of various documents are often attached to the pleadings and/or attached to the List of Proposed Witnesses (Form 13A) filed for the settlement conference, some parties assume that those copies of documents are part of the evidence at trial simply because they are already in the court file before the trial starts. That is wrong. Until the trial starts, nothing has been admitted as evidence. Documents which are intended by a party to become evidence must be tendered to the trial judge as such, and once admitted they are marked as exhibits. Documents are not evidence at trial merely because they have been placed in the court file prior to trial: see *Maguire v. Maguire*, 2003 CarswellOnt 1671, [2003] O.J. No. 1760, 38 R.F.L. (5th) 300 (Ont. Div. Ct.), dealing with an analogous point under the *Family Law Rules*, O.Reg. 114/99.

List of Proposed Witnesses

The List of Proposed Witnesses (Form 13A) that is required for the settlement conference under rule 13.03(2) does not limit a party's right to call witnesses at trial. Some parties misinterpret the rules as precluding a party from calling any witness not named on a List of Proposed Witnesses. However the *Small Claims Court Rules* contain no such limitation: see *Kungl v. Fallis*, 1988 CarswellOnt 360, 26 C.P.C. (2d) 102 (Ont. H.C.), dealing with a similar issue under the *Rules of Civil Procedure*.

Expert Evidence

As noted above, expert evidence may be admitted under rule 18.02 in the form of an expert's report, without calling the expert to testify in person. All that is required is compliance with the procedural requirements of that rule, including service of the report at least 30 days before trial.

Apart from rule 18.02, unlike some other procedural codes, the *Small Claims Court Rules* contain no requirement for service of an expert report in advance of trial as a prerequisite to calling the expert to give in-person opinion evidence at trial: *Steckley v. Haid* (May 19, 2009), Doc. 1494/07, [2009] O.J. No. 2014 (Ont. Sm. Cl. Ct.). A party who wishes to present expert evidence through in-person testimony is not required to serve an expert report prior to trial; however, any potential surprise or unfairness where expert evidence is tendered without prior notice could be grounds for an adjournment request.

Agreed Facts

Although the *Small Claims Court Rules* make no such provision, it is always open to the parties to agree to facts which are admitted or uncontested, so as to shorten their trial and focus the presentation of evidence — and their trial judge's attention — on the real factual issues. Agreed facts can be written out, signed by the parties, and made an exhibit. Less formally, parties may sometimes state or stipulate agreed facts at the start of trial during opening statements. Such agreements can be most helpful in ensuring a focused and expeditious trial. The quality of the parties' presentations is likely to affect the quality of the judgment that results.

(5) Copies — A copy of a document or any other thing may be admitted as evidence at a hearing if the presiding judge is satisfied as to its authenticity.

Commentary [S. 27(5)]

Hearsay

The principled approach to the hearsay rule has two key components. This first is the *Khan* exception to the hearsay rule. See *R. v. Khan*, [1990] S.C.J. No. 81, 1990 CarswellOnt 1001, 1990 CarswellOnt 108, EYB 1990-67557, 59 C.C.C. (3d) 92, [1990] 2 S.C.R. 531, 41 O.A.C. 353, 79 C.R. (3d) 1, 113 N.R. 53 (S.C.C.). This exception permits hearsay evidence to be admitted, regardless of whether any of the traditional fixed hearsay exceptions apply, where the twin principles of necessity and reliability are met and where judges choose not to exercise their residual exclusionary discretion. The second is the obligation of courts, identified in *R. v. Starr* (2000), REJB 2000-20233, [1998] S.C.C.A. No. 141, 258 N.R. 250, 224 W.A.C. 161, 148 Man. R. (2d) 161, 147 C.C.C. (3d) 449, [2000] 11 W.W.R. 1, [2000] 2 S.C.R. 144, 190 D.L.R. (4th) 591, 2000 SCC 40, 36 C.R. (5th) 1, [2000] S.C.J. No. 40, 2000

CarswellMan 450, 2000 CarswellMan 449 (S.C.C.), to revise or refuse to apply traditional fixed hearsay exceptions where they fail to satisfy the principles of necessity and reliability.

The hearsay rule is a rule meant to improve the ability of courts to come to accurate determinations by excluding evidence that can distort their ability to reach factually correct decisions. The rule is, in the words of the Supreme Court of Canada, "intended to enhance the accuracy of the court's findings of fact, not impede its truth-seeking function." See *R. v. Khelawon*, [2006] S.C.J. No. 57, 215 C.C.C. (3d) 161, 2006 SCC 57, 2006 CarswellOnt 7826, 2006 CarswellOnt 7825, 42 C.R. (6th) 1, [2006] 2 S.C.R. 787, 220 O.A.C. 338, 274 D.L.R. (4th) 385, 355 N.R. 267 (S.C.C.). As the Court explained in *R. v. Khelawon*:

> Without the maker of the statement in court, it may be impossible to inquire into the person's perception, memory, narration or sincerity. The statement itself may not be accurately recorded. Mistakes, exaggerations or deliberate falsehoods may go undetected and lead to unjust verdicts.

In tribunals that are unbridled by rules of admissibility, there is no forced attention given to reliability issues. Of course, there are examples in small claims court matters. See e.g., *Morris v. Cameron* (2006), [2006] N.S.J. No. 19, 2006 CarswellNS 18, 2006 NSSC 9, (sub nom. *Cameron v. Morris*) 763 A.P.R. 123, (sub nom. *Cameron v. Morris*) 240 N.S.R. (2d) 123 (N.S. S.C.) (and the decisions cited therein).

Clark v. Horizon Holidays Ltd. (1993), 1993 CarswellOnt 929, [1993] O.J. No. 4348, 45 C.C.E.L. 244 (Ont. Gen. Div.) involved an issue about what was said between the plaintiff Clark and Slichter, an employee of Horizon Holidays Ltd., concerning Clark's "dismissal." By the time of trial, Slichter had died, but he had "recorded" details of that conversation and of a conversation he had had with another employee. The documents were arguably admissible as business records but there was some contest about this. The Court admitted the records. Adams J. noted when rendering his decision that the case involved a wrongful dismissal claim: a context in which informal alternative dispute resolutions are common, and where hearsay is freely admitted in the name of informality, expediency and reduction of cost.

"Expedience and convenience" are criteria according to which the civil context of the case can impact on the court's ultimate decision. If requiring the "best evidence" would be prohibitively expensive or burdensome, given the role the evidence would play in the case, it may not be reasonable to expect the party to produce it. Reasonableness should be measured contextually, including by considering the public interest in preserving the relevance, accessibility, and fairness of the civil litigation process. See e.g., *Ethier v. Royal Canadian Mounted Police Commissioner*, 1993 CarswellNat 220, 1993 CarswellNat 220F, [1993] F.C.J. No. 183, 63 F.T.R. 29 (note), 151 N.R. 374, (sub nom. *Éthier v. Canada (RCMP Commissioner)*) [1993] 2 F.C. 659 (Fed. C.A.). While it may be hypothetically possible for parties to identify and call individual authors, given the range of documents and lengthy period over which they were created it is impractical and unproductive to do so.

While physical, legal or practical unavailability of witnesses may meet the necessity requirement, it is important to appreciate that necessity does not require the unavailability of the witness *per se*. Indeed, the proper focus of the necessity inquiry is on the availability of the *testimony* of the witness.

There is no closed list of features that indicate trustworthiness, more familiar factors relied upon include identifying whether the statement was made, e.g.

- spontaneously;
- naturally;
- without suggestion;

- reasonably contemporaneously with the event;

- by a person who had no motive to fabricate;

- and who was capable of making the observation

- was against the person's interest in whole or in part;

- was by a young person who would be unlikely to have the knowledge of the acts alleged.

Other safeguards often invoked include:

- that the person was under a duty;

- that the statement was made to public officials;

- that the person knew the statement was being publicized.

Electronic Records

There is no doubt that today many documents are stored electronically. Accordingly, most of the jurisdictions have enacted specific legislation to deal with electronic documents. See the *Ontario Evidence Act*, s. 34.1.

The legislation does not create any new hearsay exception. Rather, the concern with electronic records is authenticity and maintaining confidence in the integrity of the stored information. Electronic documents, therefore, need to be admitted under existing common law and statutory hearsay exceptions. For example, a deceased's online diary — if admissible for its truth — is still hearsay. What this does mean is that business records, electronically stored, will need to comply with the business record exception, in terms of hearsay, and meet statutory or common law requirements in terms of authenticity. See, e.g., *McGarry v. Co-operators Life Insurance Co.*, 2011 BCCA 214, 2011 CarswellBC 998, 18 B.C.L.R. (5th) 353, 93 C.C.E.L. (3d) 179, 96 C.C.L.I. (4th) 169, 333 D.L.R. (4th) 533, [2011] 8 W.W.R. 653, 304 B.C.A.C. 238, 2011 C.E.B. & P.G.R. 8434, [2011] I.L.R. I-5139, 513 W.A.C. 238 (B.C. C.A.) at [54–77]; ; additional reasons (2011), 2011 BCCA 272, 2011 CarswellBC 3719, 29 B.C.L.R. (5th) 356, 99 C.C.E.L. (3d) 37, 5 C.C.L.I. (5th) 267, 342 D.L.R. (4th) 685, [2012] 6 W.W.R. 429 (B.C. C.A.).

Adding Parties

Sloan v. Sauve Heating Ltd., 2011 ONCA 91, 2011 CarswellOnt 515, [2011] O.J. No. 402 (Ont. C.A.)

The Court of Appeal held that the plaintiff's application to add the independent contractor and truck driver should be dismissed. The only step the plaintiff took was to question Sauve Heating Ltd. on discovery. The plaintiff failed to provide a reasonable explanation as to why proposed defendants were not identifiable and therefore not named prior to the expiry of the *Limitations Act, 2002*.

Lockett v. Boutin, 2011 ONSC 2098, 2011 CarswellOnt 2261, [2011] O.J. No. 1530 (Ont. S.C.J.); affirmed 2011 ONCA 809, 2011 CarswellOnt 14466, [2011] O.J. No. 5844 (Ont. C.A.)

There was no evidence of any effort by plaintiffs, prior to expiry of the limitation period, to determine identity and potential liability of persons who owned, supplied, installed, or maintained the water heater.

Trench v. Parmat Investments Ltd., 2010 ONSC 1564, 2010 CarswellOnt 1416 (Ont. S.C.J.)

The plaintiff tripped and fell at her community mailbox. She moved to add Canada Post as a defendant two and one half years after the accident. The impetus was a letter from the defendant in Brampton suggesting that Canada Post be sued as the "occupier." The application was dismissed. The plaintiff failed to demonstrate she could not have discovered Canada Post's liability with the exercise of due diligence.

Felker v. Gateway Property Management Corp., 2010 ONSC 4513, 2010 CarswellOnt 5917 (Ont. S.C.J.)

The plaintiff was injured in a slip and fall accident on a condominium property in December, 2005. The plaintiff slipped on debris. The plaintiff sued the condominium's manager. The defendant third party worked for the Toronto Star. The plaintiff moved in late 2009 to have the Toronto Star and its paper carrier as defendants. The newspaper carrier argued that his identity could have been discovered long before 2009.

The Court held that the plaintiff, with reasonable diligence, could *not* have been expected to know about the newspapers or the carrier before the third party notice was filed in February, 2009.

What is or is not a new cause of action?

Dee Ferraro Ltd. v. Pellizzari, 2012 ONCA 55, 2012 CarswellOnt 816, 346 D.L.R. (4th) 624, [2012] O.J. No. 355 (Ont. C.A.); reversing 2011 ONSC 3995, 2011 CarswellOnt 8211 (Ont. S.C.J.)

This judgment illustrates the difference between amending a statement of claim to allege a new cause of action (impermissible if the new claim is stature barred), and amending the statement of claim to add new remedies or heads of damages (permissible), provided there is no non-compensable prejudice.

The original pleading contained all the facts necessary to support the amendments. The amendments simply claimed additional forms of relief, or clarified the relief sought, based on the same facts as originally pleaded. The Court relied on *Canadian National Railway v. Canadian Industries Ltd.*, 1940 CarswellOnt 213, [1940] 4 D.L.R. 629, 52 C.R.T.C. 31, [1940] O.W.N. 452, [1940] O.J. No. 266 (Ont. C.A.); affirmed 1941 CarswellOnt 84, [1941] S.C.R. 591, [1941] 4 D.L.R. 561, 53 C.R.T.C. 162 (S.C.C.), and distinguished *Frohlick v. Pinkerton Canada Ltd.*, 2008 ONCA 3, 2008 CarswellOnt 66, 88 O.R. (3d) 401, 62 C.C.E.L. (3d) 161, 49 C.P.C. (6th) 209, 289 D.L.R. (4th) 639, 232 O.A.C. 146, [2008] O.J. No. 17 (Ont. C.A.).

This was not a case in which new and unrelated causes of action were being asserted based on new facts. The claims flow directly from the facts previously pleaded. Therefore, the claims were not statute-barred and the amendments should have been permitted, since there was no evidence of non-compensable prejudice.

Misnomer

Streamline Foods Ltd. v. Jantz Canada Corp., 2012 ONCA 174, 2012 CarswellOnt 3333, [2012] O.J. No. 1213 (Ont. C.A.); affirming 2011 ONSC 1630, 2011 CarswellOnt 1674, 6 C.P.C. (7th) 399, 280 O.A.C. 152 (Ont. Div. Ct.); affirming 2010 ONSC 6393, 2010 CarswellOnt 8790, [2010] O.J. No. 4988 (Ont. Master).

This judgment establishes that s. 21(1) of the *Limitations Act, 2002 does* apply to plaintiffs (as opposed, as some have argued, only to defendants). The Court refused to allow for the plaintiff's parent corporation to be added as a party plaintiff after the limitation period had expired.

This was not a misnomer. The plaintiffs sought to add the parent corporation of the original plaintiff because it was the parent corporation which incurred certain losses, not the original plaintiff. The plaintiffs were not seeking to correct the name of a party; rather, they were seeking to add a party and to pursue that party's claims.

Livingston v. Williamson, 2011 ONSC 3849, 2011 CarswellOnt 5872, 107 O.R. (3d) 75, 99 C.C.L.I. (4th) 331 (Ont. Master)

The plaintiff sued the TTC in its capacity as owner of the bus, employer of the driver, and provider of uninsured motorist coverage.

The TTC was not the insurer. The plaintiff was unaware that TTC Insurance was a separate company. The plaintiff brought a motion to correct the name of the insurer by adding TTC Insurance as a party defendant. TTC Insurance took the position that this was a motion to add a party after the limitation period had expired. Motion allowed both the TTC legal department and TTC Insurance operated from the same building, had identical postal codes and were represented by the same lawyer on the argument of the motion. Master Hawkins found that a representative of the TTC Insurance would have known immediately that insofar as unidentified motorist coverage was concerned, TTC Insurance was intended. Neither TTC nor TTC Insurance suffered any actual prejudice.

Stekel v. Toyota Canada Inc., 2011 ONSC 6507, 2011 CarswellOnt 11971, 107 O.R. (3d) 431 (Ont. S.C.J.); leave to appeal refused 2012 ONSC 2572, 2012 CarswellOnt 5718 (Ont. Div. Ct.); affirming 2011 ONSC 2211, 2011 CarswellOnt 2378, [2011] O.J. No. 1591 (Ont. Master)

Plaintiff injured due to an apparent mechanical malfunction in Lexus vehicle she was driving. She sued Toyota Canada Inc., believing it was both the distributor and manufacturer of the vehicle. More than two years after the accident, the plaintiff learned that the vehicle was in fact manufactured by Toyota Motors Canada. She moved to add Toyota Manufacturers Canada (TMC) as a party defendant in the action.

While the limitation period in respect of the plaintiff's claim against TMS has expired, s. 21(2) of the *Limitations Act 2002* permitted the plaintiffs to correct their "misnomer" with respect to the manufacturer of their vehicle and add TMC as a defendant to the litigation. The plaintiffs had always intended to include the manufacturer of the vehicle as a defendant in their action. Equally importantly, TMC knew that the plaintiffs were pointing at the manufacturer of the vehicle, even though they had misnamed the manufacturer.

Ontario (Attorney General) v. Pembina Exploration Canada Ltd., 1989 CarswellOnt 970, 1989 CarswellOnt 970F, EYB 1989-67481, [1989] 1 S.C.R. 206, 57 D.L.R. (4th) 710, (sub nom. *William Siddall & Sons Fisheries v. Pembina Exploration Can. Ltd.*) 92 N.R. 137, (sub nom. *William Siddall & Sons Fisheries v. Pembina Exploration Can. Ltd.*) 33 O.A.C. 321 (S.C.C.)

Appeal raised the question whether a province may grant jurisdiction to a small claims court to hear a case involving an admiralty or maritime matter.

Case Law: *Mullins v. Morgan*, 2010 ONSC 5722, 2010 CarswellOnt 8681 (Ont. Div. Ct.)

Although hearsay may be admitted in Small Claims Court, there is no requirement that it be admitted. Section 27 gives the court a discretion to admit such evidence.

Central Burner Service Inc. v. Texaco Canada Inc. (1989), 36 O.A.C. 239 (Ont. Div. Ct.) — Section 80 permits the admission of hearsay evidence, provided it is relevant. There is no distinction between critical issues and more peripheral issues. Where the trial judge states that appropriate weight is to be given to the evidence, an appeal from the judgment was dismissed even though there was little or no other evidence to support the plaintiff's case.

Wilson, King & Co. v. Torabian, Doc. SMC 21328/89 (B.C. Prov. Ct.); reversed 1991 CarswellBC 21, 45 C.P.C. (2d) 238, 53 B.C.L.R. (2d) 251 (B.C. S.C.) — The plaintiff sued the defendant for a legal account. The court brought up the question of Solicitor/Client privilege. Provincial Judge R.S. Murro stated that the provincial court had no inherent jurisdiction to order a Solicitor's bill to be taxed. If the defendant client refuses to waive his right to privilege, the plaintiff cannot adduce evidence and therefore the claim must fail.

Sathaseevan v. Suvara Travel Canada Inc., 1998 CarswellOnt 880, [1998] O.J. No. 1055 (Ont. Div. Ct.) — Appeal from decision of Small Claims Court awarding plaintiff damages.

All evidence from the plaintiff was hearsay from the people who actually booked flight. The Small Claims Court is, pursuant to section 27 of the *Courts of Justice Act*, entitled to admit and act upon any oral testimony or document whether or not admissable in any other court. *Central Burner Service Inc. v. Texaco Canada Inc.* (1989), 36 O.A.C. 239 (Ont. Div. Ct.) held that the Small Claims Court may decide cases entirely on the basis of hearsay evidence. The test is whether the trial judge was clearly wrong. Given the power of the trial judge to rely on hearsay evidence pursuant to the Act, appeal court not satisfied that he was.

Levin, Re (1997), 217 N.R. 393 (H.L.) — Levin claimed, *inter alia*, a print-out produced respecting fraud allegedly generated from Levin's computer should not have been admitted because of hearsay. The House of Lords stated that print-outs were tendered "to prove the transfers of funds, not that such transfers took place. Evidential status of print-outs no different from that of a photocopy of a forged cheque.".

VFC Inc. v. Balchand (2007), 2007 CarswellOnt 6344, [2007] O.J. No. 3793 (Ont. Div. Ct.), Archibald J., 2007-10-02.

Issue of jurisdiction of Small Claims Court to admit hearsay into evidence on the central issue in dispute. Since 1989 weight of authority, commencing with Justice Steele's decision in *Central Burner Service Inc. v. Texaco Canada Inc.* (1989), 36 O.A.C. 239 (Ont. Div. Ct.), is in favour of the admissibility of hearsay in a Small Claims Court proceeding pursuant to s. 80 (now s. 27) of the *Courts of Justice Act*, R.S.O. 1990, c. C-43. See also *Sathaseevan v. Suvara Travel Canada Inc.*, 1998 CarswellOnt 880, [1998] O.J. No. 1055 (Ont. Div. Ct.).

Hearsay evidence permitted under the *Rules of the Small Claims Court*, O. Reg. 258/98. Rule 18.02(1) grants a discretion to the trial judge with respect to admitting documents or other evidence: "A document or written statement or an audio or visual record that has been served, at least 30 days before the trial date, on all parties who were served with the notice of trial, shall be received in evidence, unless the trial judge orders otherwise.".

Section 27(3)(b) of the *Courts of Justice Act* reads: "Nothing is admissible in evidence at a hearing that is inadmissible by any Act." Section 27(3)(b) would appear to qualify s. 27(1).

Section 2 of the *Evidence Act*, R.S.O. 1990, c. E-23, reads as follows: "This Act applies to all actions and other matters whatsoever respecting which the Legislature has jurisdiction.".

The issue therefore becomes: What is the relationship between s. 2 of the *Evidence Act* and s. 27 of the *Courts of Justice Act*? Is hearsay admissible in a Small Claims Court case absent compliance with the *Evidence Act*?.

Neither the appellant nor the respondent addressed this issue in their factums. They have both asked for additional time to amend their factums accordingly. A new date for the appeal to be set with concurrence of the Registrar of the Divisional Court, once factums amended.

VFC Inc. v. Balchand, 2008 CarswellOnt 909, 233 O.A.C. 359, 291 D.L.R. (4th) 367 (Ont. Div. Ct.), M. Dambrot J.

Appeal to Divisional Court by defendant, now appellant, pursuant to s. 31(a) of the *Courts of Justice Act* from the judgment of the Toronto Small Claims Court.

Appeal originally came on for hearing before Archibald J. Appellant argued trial judge wrongly relied on hearsay evidence to find appellant liable to respondent under a Conditional Sales Contract. Respondent pointed to s. 27(1) of the *Courts of Justice Act* and a line of decisions commencing with judgment of Steele J. in *Central Burner Service Inc. v. Texaco Canada Inc.* (1989), 36 O.A.C. 239 (Ont. Div. Ct.). Section 27(1) permits the Small Claims Court to admit as evidence at a hearing and act upon any oral testimony and any document or other thing, so long as the evidence is relevant. In *Central Burner*, Steele J. concluded that s. 80(1) of the *Courts of Justice Act*, the predecessor of s. 27(1), allows relevant hearsay evidence to be admitted and relied upon in a Small Claims Court trial even in relation to a critical issue. His decision has been followed in a number of cases, including the judgment of Lane J. in *Sathaseevan v. Suvara Travel Canada Inc.*, 1998 CarswellOnt 880, [1998] O.J. No. 1055 (Ont. Div. Ct.).

Archibald J. was concerned, however, that none of the cases had considered the significance of s. 27(3)(b) of the *Courts of Justice Act*. He went on to note that s. 2 of the *Ontario Evidence Act* provides, "This Act applies to all actions and other matters whatsoever respecting which the Legislature has jurisdiction.".

Nothing in the *Ontario Evidence Act* to call into question the admissibility of hearsay at a Small Claims Court trial, even when the hearsay is contained in business records. Appeal dismissed.

Sparks v. Benteau, 2008 CarswellNS 42, 2008 NSSM 3 (N.S. Small Cl. Ct.), E.K. Slone Adjud.

Issue of Benteau coming to court with witnesses other than himself.

Written statements purely hearsay, second hand evidence, letters or documents stating what a person would say if he or she were in court.

The right to cross-examine a cornerstone of our system of justice, and while many self-represented litigants exercise this right sparingly, still a vital right. Having the witness in court also would allow the Adjudicator to ask pointed questions that might help decide the issue. See, e.g., *L.A. Oakes Resource Systems Inc. v. Metex Corp.*, 2007 CarswellNS 471, 260 N.S.R. (2d) 186, 831 A.P.R. 186, 2007 NSSM 71 (N.S. Small Cl. Ct.). See also *Malloy v. Atton*, [2004] N.S.J. No. 217, 2004 CarswellNS 218, 50 C.P.C. (5th) 176, 2004 NSSC 110, 225 N.S.R. (2d) 201, 713 A.P.R. 201 (N.S. S.C.) where the Adjudicator received affidavits, with no opportunity for cross-examination. In allowing the appeal and overturning the decision, the learned Justice said:

> I interpret [the *Small Claims Court Act*] as giving an Adjudicator the discretion to admit or exclude affidavit evidence, provided there is compliance with the rules of natural justice.

> The Nova Scotia Civil Procedure Rules, although not directly applicable in Small Claims Court, may be consulted for guidance in the absence of an applicable Small Claims Court rule. Civil Procedure Rule 38.10 provides that the deponent of an affidavit to be used at trial may be examined, cross-examined, and re-examined.

The claim here seeks damages close to the $25,000 maximum allowed. To relax such a fundamental rule of natural justice as the right to cross-examine witnesses in a case of this size would, in my opinion, be a gross failure to provide natural justice to the claimant.

Only credible quote produced by claimant.

Aberdeen v. Langley (Township), 2006 CarswellBC 3634, 2006 BCSC 2064 (B.C. S.C.), J.R. Groves.

Plaintiff's witness made prior written inconsistent statement, which was admitted in evidence. Defendants sought to admit as evidence various police documents that were created by the police for statistical and investigative purposes and were based on hearsay discussions with the Plaintiff's witness.

Ruling was made that under principled approach, it was not necessary for police officer to introduce hearsay evidence about what was already before court in written form. Inconsistent statement was written; in such cases, Court of Appeal has held that further evidence of statement's contents is inadmissible.

Lombard Insurance Co. v. Stock Transportation Ltd., 2007 CarswellNS 607, [2007] N.S.J. No. 540, 2007 NSSM 83, 261 N.S.R. (2d) 12, 835 A.P.R. 12 (N.S. Small Cl. Ct.), Parker Adjud.

Issue arose as to admissibility of an unsworn recorded statement to insurance adjuster. The court held that such statement is admissible, except for parts that might have been tainted by leading questions. Although hearsay is presumptively inadmissible, functional approach and need for flexibility applies in dealing with exceptions to hearsay evidence. The fact that author of the statement was named as defendant in actions did not detract from admissibility. Statement could be tested against others who provided evidence.

Petti v. George Coppel Jewellers Ltd. (2008), 2008 CarswellOnt 1324, 234 O.A.C. 85 (Ont. Div. Ct.), Quinn J.

Propriety of relying on polygraph evidence in legal proceedings. In legal proceedings, polygraph tests may be approached from three perspectives: (1) whether the taking of the polygraph test was volunteered or, if offered, rejected; (2) the questions asked and the answers given on the test; and, (3) the results of the test.

With respect to (1) above, the fact that a litigant volunteered to take a polygraph test is relevant (See e.g. *R. v. B. (S.C.)* (1997), 36 O.R. (3d) 516 at para. 29 (Ont. C.A.)).

The questions and answers on a polygraph test — (2) above — may be admissible where, for example, the answers constitute an admission against interest.

The results of a polygraph test — (3) above — are not admissible in an Ontario court, as those results "usurp the very function of the trier of fact". And, if the results are tendered by a litigant who passed the test, they are tantamount to oath helping.

Appeal allowed as trial judge relied on the results of the polygraph tests, at least in part, when reaching his decision to dismiss the claim. Results of polygraph test should not be used to help decide the truth of the facts in dispute.

Boisvert v. Régie de l'assurance-maladie du Québec, 2004 CarswellQue 1341, 2004 CarswellQue 1342, REJB 2004-65745, (sub nom. *Bibaud v. Quebec (Régie de l'assurance maladie))* 240 D.L.R. (4th) 244, 50 C.P.C. (5th) 1, 2004 SCC 35, (sub nom. *Bibaud v. Quebec (Régie de l'assurance maladie))* 321 N.R. 273, [2004] 2 S.C.R. 3 (S.C.C.).

Appellant wished to intervene, pursuant to art. 208 C.C.P., to represent her husband in an action brought by him against the respondents, on the ground that he was incapable of representing himself because of his physical and mental state. Appeal dismissed. The legislative framework in the Quebec courts set out in the *Code of Civil Procedure* and in the *Act respecting the Barreau du Québec*. Representation by spouses, relatives, in-laws or friends is only allowed in cases falling within the jurisdiction of the small claims division of the Court of Québec (art. 959 C.C.P.). Representatives of other persons must themselves be represented in the courts, for acts covered by the monopoly granted to the legal profession, by members of the Barreau in good standing.

R. v. L. (G.Y.) (2009), [2009] O.J. No. 3089, 246 C.C.C. (3d) 112, 2009 CarswellOnt 4350 (Ont. S.C.J.), J.D. McCombs J.

Paralegal licensed and insured by the Law Society of Upper Canada may appear in the Ontario Court of Justice pursuant to a duly executed designation under s. 650. *Criminal Code* for the purpose of routine remands for indictable offences. Designation appointed lawyer as his counsel of choice, and designated his "counsel, articling student, or agent acting on his behalf to appear for all proceedings where [his] attendance is not required by law or the direction of the Ontario Court of Justice.".

Law Society (Manitoba) v. Pollock, 228 Man. R. (2d) 273, 427 W.A.C. 273, 54 C.P.C. (6th) 4, [2008] 7 W.W.R. 493, 2008 MBCA 61, 2008 CarswellMan 238 (Man. C.A.).

Appeal from judge's decision granting permanent injunction against appellant in relation to various activities determined to amount to the unauthorized practice of law. Appeal dismissed with costs.

Appellant relied on Supreme Court of Canada decision in *Law Society (British Columbia) v. Mangat* (2001), REJB 2001-26158, [2001] 3 S.C.R. 113, 96 B.C.L.R. (3d) 1, [2002] 2

W.W.R. 201, 276 N.R. 339, 2001 CarswellBC 2169, 2001 CarswellBC 2168, 2001 SCC 67, 205 D.L.R. (4th) 577, 16 Imm. L.R. (3d) 1, 256 W.A.C. 161, 157 B.C.A.C. 161, [2001] S.C.J. No. 66 (S.C.C.), where it stated, ". . . Had Parliament wanted to declare that 'other counsel' means only unpaid persons, it would have said so by using distinctive terms in ss. 30 and 69(1)" (at para. 65).

The Supreme Court of Canada concluded in *Mangat* that the terms "counsel" and "person's own expense" found in ss. 30 and 69(1) of the *Immigration Act* were to be interpreted as authorizing non-lawyers to appear for a fee. It stated (at para. 64):

> The *Immigration Act* and the Rules and Regulations made thereunder make no distinction between barrister and solicitor who could act for a fee and other counsel who could not. If parliament had intended to limit the meaning of "other counsel" to unpaid non-lawyers, the section would have been drafted differently so as to make it clear that the phrase "at [that] person's own expense" only referred to barristers and solicitors and not to other counsel.

VFC Inc. v. Balchand, 291 D.L.R. (4th) 367, 233 O.A.C. 359, 2008 CarswellOnt 909 (Ont. Div. Ct.).

Defendant appealed judgment of Small Claims Court finding her liable under a bill of sale and conditional sales contract for purchase of motor vehicle. The only witness called by plaintiff was the supervisor of the legal department, not present when bill of sale and conditional sales contract signed but saw documents when forwarded to plaintiff.

Trial judge dismissed defendant's motion for a non-suit, bill of sale and conditional sales contract bearing apparent signature of defendant, in the absence of evidence to the contrary, established defendant was a party to the contract and liable for the amount owing. Appeal dismissed.

Nothing in the *Evidence Act*, R.S.O. 1990, c. E.23, calls into question the admissibility of hearsay at a Small Claims Court trial, even when the hearsay is contained in business records. Section 35 of the *Evidence Act* provides a statutory mechanism for the admission of business records into evidence and section 27(1) of the *Courts of Justice Act*, R.S.O. 1990, c. C.43, permits hearsay evidence to be admitted into evidence. A consideration of these provisions leads to the conclusion that the trial judge did *not* err in law in admitting into evidence the oral and documentary hearsay of the plaintiff's witness. See *Central Burner Service Inc. v. Texaco Canada Inc.*, 1989 CarswellOnt 1427, 36 O.A.C. 239 (Ont. Div. Ct.). Section 27(1) permits the Small Claims Court to admit as evidence at a hearing and act upon any oral testimony and any document or other thing, so long as the evidence is relevant. In *Central Burner*, Steele J. concluded that section 80(1) of the *Courts of justice Act, 1984*, S.O. 1984, c. 11, the predecessor of section 27(1), allows relevant hearsay evidence to be admitted and relied upon in a Small Claims Court trial even in relation to a critical issue. See also *Sathaseevan v. Suvara Travel Canada Inc.*, [1998] O.J. No. 1055, 1998 CarswellOnt 880 (Ont. Div. Ct.).

Section 27(1) is, by its terms, subject to subsections (3) and (4). Section 2 of the *Ontario Evidence Act*, R.S.O. 1990, c. E.23, provides, "This Act applies to all actions and other matters whatsoever respecting which the Legislature has jurisdiction.".

Section 35 of the *Evidence Act* deals with business records.

If a party to any proceeding governed by the *Ontario Evidence Act* proposes that a business record be received in evidence pursuant to section 35(2), the proponent of the evidence must comply with the section. The record must be made in the usual and ordinary course of business as described in section 35(2), and notice must be given in accordance with section 35(3).

Prior to the liberalizing impact of the decision in *Ares v. Venner*, 14 D.L.R. (3d) 4, 73 W.W.R. 347, 12 C.R.N.S. 349, [1970] S.C.R. 608, 1970 CarswellAlta 142, [1970] S.C.J. No. 26, 1970 CarswellAlta 80 (S.C.C.), the common law rules governing the admissibility of business records were widely felt to be completely out of line with the every-increasing complexity of business organizations.

The object of section 80(1) of the *Courts of Justice Act*, the predecessor of section 27(1) of the *Act*, was remedial. As stated in *Central Burner*, "The object of s. 80 is to avoid technical procedures and the additional cost of calling extra witnesses in cases involving small claims.".

A *prima facie* case is one that covers the allegations made and which, if they are believed, is complete and sufficient to justify a verdict in the complainant's favour in the absence of an answer from the respondent. See *Montreuil c. Forces canadiennes*, 2009 CarswellNat 5464, 2009 CarswellNat 5463, 2009 CHRT 28, 2009 TCDP 28 (Can. Human Rights Trib.), at para. 45 Deschamps (Member).

Stone's Jewellery Ltd. v. Arora (2009), 2009 ABQB 656, 2009 CarswellAlta 1883, 484 A.R. 286, 90 R.P.R. (4th) 90, 314 D.L.R. (4th) 166, [2010] 5 W.W.R. 297, 20 Alta. L.R. (5th) 50, [2009] G.S.T.C. 168, [2010] 2 C.T.C. 139 (Alta. Q.B.).

An exhibit relating to meeting between parties marked "without prejudice" should not be considered. Document stated on face it was without prejudice, providing *prima facie* evidence that meeting held on that basis. No evidentiary basis to rebut *prima facie* evidence.

Parkway Collision awarded judgment for a towing bill paid on behalf of Ryan and charges for storage of vehicle for $1,298.50. Ryan appealed, arguing trial judge erred in rejecting the evidence of bylaw tow rates in surrounding areas because bylaw not produced. Divisional Court, per Stong J., stated that: "In rejecting oral evidence of By-laws of other municipalities, which By-laws were not in fact presented to the court, the trial judge rejecting collateral and hearsay evidence the acceptance of which would have been simply opinion of a third party and not subject to cross-examination": *Parkway Collision Ltd. v. Ryan*, 2009 CarswellOnt 6266, 255 O.A.C. 74 (Ont. Div. Ct.).

Ring v. Canada (Attorney General), 2010 NLCA 20, 2010 CarswellNfld 86, [2010] N.J. No. 107, 297 Nfld. & P.E.I.R. 86, 918 A.P.R. 86, 86 C.P.C. (6th) 8, 72 C.C.L.T. (3d) 161 (N.L. C.A.); leave to appeal refused 2010 CarswellNfld 304, 2010 CarswellNfld 305, 410 N.R. 399 (note), 309 Nfld. & P.E.I.R. 362 (note), 962 A.P.R. 362 (note) (S.C.C.).

The application judge admitted affidavit of plaintiff's expert. Appeal allowed. It was error in law to admit affidavit of plaintiff's expert for purpose of proof of content of published texts or papers discussed by her. All such papers and texts remained inadmissible hearsay in absence of author of work or expert in proper field who was prepared to adopt work. Findings could not be made on basis of published scientific treatises discovered on research of judge or bibliographer.

The hearing officer erred in law in purporting to take judicial notice that combined effects of consumption of alcohol and percocets would negatively impact on an individual's ability to perceive and recall experienced events. Subject was neither notorious nor within any specialized knowledge of tribunal, and properly the subject of expert evidence: *McCormick v. Greater Sudbury Police Service*, 2010 CarswellOnt 1871, 2010 ONSC 270, 259 O.A.C. 226, 6 Admin. L.R. (5th) 79 (Ont. Div. Ct.).

. . . the plain meaning of "independent evidence" is evidence other than that of the claimant which does not emanate from a spouse or dependant relative. If the drafters of the policy intended to further reduce the categories of individuals capable of providing corroborative evidence, they could have done so. See *Pepe v. State Farm Mutual Automobile Insurance Co.*, 85 C.C.L.I. (4th) 315, 2010 CarswellOnt 3422, 2010 ONSC 2977, [2010] I.L.R. I-4996, 101 O.R. (3d) 547 (Ont. S.C.J.); affirmed 2011 ONCA 341, 2011 CarswellOnt 2889, [2011] O.J. No. 2011, 105 O.R. (3d) 794, 98 C.C.L.I. (4th) 1, 282 O.A.C. 157 (Ont. C.A.).

Canada (Privacy Commissioner) v. Air Canada, [2010] F.C.J. No. 504, 2010 Carsw 1052, 2010 FC 429, 367 F.T.R. 76 (Eng.), 2010 CarswellNat 2898, 2010 CF 429 (I

A passenger requested a personal file from an airline. The airline asserted privilege over reports of flight attendant, witness and other airline personnel. Privacy commissioner (PC) alleged documents were not privileged. PC brought application for order regarding privilege of documents and requiring airline to provide passenger with documents. The application was granted in part. Day-to-day work done by unlicensed paralegal under supervision of lawyer could still be privileged.

Delano v. Craig, 2010 CarswellNS 264, 2010 NSSC 60 (N.S. S.C.), Glen G. McDougall J.

The plaintiff brought claim in small claims court concerning dispute over lawn mower. Mechanic was not present in court in spite of fact that he had been subpoenaed. The plaintiff did not want opportunity to enforce subpoena, due to circumstances making it difficult for mechanic to attend. The letter had not been provided to defendants prior to court. The adjudicator did not admit letter into evidence. The plaintiff's claim was dismissed. The plaintiff appealed. Appeal dismissed.

Fullerton v. Poirier, 2012 PECA 22, 2012 CarswellPEI 49, 329 Nfld. & P.E.I.R. 54, 1022 A.P.R. 54 (P.E.I. C.A.).

Appeal from decision dated March 23, 2012, of Justice Campbell of the Supreme Court of Prince Edward Island sitting in Small Claims Court. The trial judge dismissed the appellant's claim and awarded costs of $100. to the respondent.

We recognize that the Small Claims Court Rules of Civil Procedure may be somewhat relaxed in that any evidence that is relevant may be admitted. However, any decision relating to the admission of evidence is an exercise of discretion by the trial judge, and this court cannot intervene in the exercise of a trial judge's discretion unless the trial judge exercised his discretion arbitrarily, capriciously or upon an incorrect or inapplicable principle of law.

The trial judge found that no aspect of the claim was proven.

The trial judge assessed the evidence before him and he made findings which are amply supported by the evidence.

Appeal dismissed with costs in the amount of $500.

28. Instalment orders — The Small Claims Court may order the times and the proportions in which money payable under an order of the court shall be paid.

Commentary: This provision is often overlooked. The court may make an instalment order at trial. The defendant may simply ask for such an order and give his or her reasons. In some cases an instalment order may facilitate satisfaction of a judgment in a way that is preferable, from both parties' perspectives, to spending time and money on enforcement steps if such steps are not truly necessary.

29. Limit on costs — An award of costs in the Small Claims Court, other than disbursements, shall not exceed 15 per cent of the amount claimed or the value of the property sought to be recovered unless the court considers it necessary in the interests of justice to penalize a party or a party's representative for unreasonable behaviour in the proceeding.

2006, c. 21, Sched. C, s. 105(2)

Commentary: For commentary on costs in the Small Claims Court, please refer to the earlier chapter entitled A Self-Help Overview, starting at p. 56.

See *Kakamin v. Hasan* (2005), 2005 CarswellOnt 4066, [2005] O.J. No. 2778 (Ont. Sm. Cl. Ct.).

> Failure to accept a reasonable offer to settle, made at least seven days before trial and not withdrawn before trial, is evidence of unreasonable behaviour in the conduct of the proceeding, for which the maximum penalty is double costs: Small Claims Court Rule 14.07(1).

> The whole scheme is that the Small Claims Court has the authority to fix costs in its discretion (s. 131, CJA), but only to a maximum of 15% of the value of the claim (s. 29 CJA), unless there is a finding of unreasonable behaviour in the conduct of the proceeding (s. 29, CJA), of which failure to accept a reasonable offer to settle is one example (Rule 14.07), whether the award is characterized as counsel fee, compensation for inconvenience and expense, or costs (Rule 19).

See *King v. K-W Homes Ltd.* (2006), [2006] O.J. No. 5104, 2006 CarswellOnt 8358 (Ont. Sm. Cl. Ct.), N.B. Pickell, Deputy J., which dealt with the issue of costs.

Deputy Judge Pickell then turned his mind to the question of representation fee. He first looked at s. 29 and its 15 per cent limit, if it was not necessary to penalize a party, counsel or agent for unreasonable behaviour in the proceeding, and indicated that he did not find it reasonable to penalize anyone for unreasonable behaviour in the case.

He allowed the defendant a representation fee of $2,400.00.

See *Williams v. Roberge* (2007), [2007] O.J. No. 2567, 2007 CarswellOnt 4182, D.J. Lange, Deputy J. (Ont. Sm. Cl. Ct.)

Deputy Judge Lange interpreted the phrase "representation fee at trial" (in R.19.04) to mean the daily representation fee. A reasonable representation fee at trial for this action was the $1,000.00 as submitted by the defendants.

See *Dalton v. MacKinnon* (2007), [2007] O.J. No. 1712, 2007 CarswellOnt 2766, D.J. Lange, Deputy J. (Ont. Sm. Cl. Ct.)

The objective is to fix an amount that is fair and reasonable for the unsuccessful party to pay in the particular proceeding rather than an amount fixed by the actual costs incurred by the successful party. In his view, a reasonable representation fee at trial was $750.00 on a partial indemnity basis before a consideration of R.14.07(1). He then went on to double the amount to $1,500.00, based upon R.14.

See *McCallister v. Wiegand* (March 16, 2009), Doc. 0251/05, [2009] O.J. No. 1097, D.J. Lange, Deputy J. (Ont. Sm. Cl. Ct.)

There were no reasons for imposition of a penalty in this case.

He looked at Rule 57.01 of the Rules of Civil Procedure as identifying as a factor the "amount of costs that an unsuccessful party could reasonably be expected to pay." Considering the costs submission of the defendant Grace Wiegand, and the straightforward nature of the proceeding, a partial indemnity rate of $250.00 should apply, and that accordingly the total representation fee at trial was to be $500.00.

See *Georgina Collision Specialists Inc. v. Okjan* (November 8, 2007), Doc. 18084/03, 18084/03A, [2007] O.J. No. 4327, P. Gollom, Deputy J. (Ont. Sm. Cl. Ct.)

The trial had taken two and a half days. Deputy Judge Gollom fixed the Defendant's costs at $2,000.00, and allowed the Defendant's disbursements in the amount of $1,071.26.

See *Beatty v. Reitzel Insulation Co.* (2008), 2008 CarswellOnt 1364, [2008] O.J. No. 953, Winny, Deputy J. (Ont. Sm. Cl. Ct.)

Unreasonable behaviour should permit rule 14.07 to operate in tandem with the court's discretion under the proviso in section 29.

Plaintiff had sued for $10,000.00, and was awarded $200.00. The defendant's claim of $1,897.11 was allowed.

Deputy Judge Winny stated that the cost consequences of a party's failure to accept a reasonable offer should be meaningful consequences. To interpret section 29 as if it were a *de facto* bar or effective cap on the operation of rule 14.07 is undesirable and unwarranted.

Deputy Judge Winny concluded that section 29 was *not* intended to cap the costs at 15% in such circumstances, and awarded costs of $1,000.00, which he then doubled to $2,000.00.

See *Bird v. Ireland* (2005), 2005 CarswellOnt 6945, [2005] O.J. No. 5125, 205 O.A.C. 1 (Ont. Div. Ct.), R.A. Clark J., an appeal from a Small Claims Court trial which included an appeal of the costs award of the deputy judge. Decision revolved around wording of rule 19.04, which at that time provided maximum costs award to counsel was $300.00.

Justice Clark found that the maximum costs award was a daily award of $300.00.

Justice Clark found that rule 19 was subject to section 29 of the *Courts of Justice Act*. Section 29 provides that an award of costs in the Small Claims Court shall not exceed 15% of the amount claimed, unless the court considers it necessary to penalize a party for unreasonable behaviour in the proceeding.

See *Dunbar v. Helicon Properties Ltd.* (2006), [2006] O.J. No. 2992, 213 O.A.C. 296, 2006 CarswellOnt 4580 (Ont. Div. Ct.), J.R. McIsaac J., an appeal from a Small Claims Court decision that dealt in part with costs. A costs award of $500.00 for counsel fee did not exceed that permitted by rule 19.04 (which would have to have been the earlier version of the rule, pre-July 1, 2006) that which allowed for $300.00 maximum representation fee as the award was a daily one.

See *Biggins v. Bovan* (February 10, 2005), Doc. 1078/04, [2005] O.J. No. 1000, J.D. Searle, Deputy J. (Ont. Sm. Cl. Ct.) There were three defendants represented by one counsel. The trial took three days and argument, apart from costs, a further half-day. The plaintiff was found to have brought these actions in a vindictive fashion.

Deputy Judge Searle awarded costs of $2,500.00 for counsel fee, preparation and disbursements.

The Lawyer as Witness

A lawyer should not express personal opinions or beliefs or assert as a fact anything that is properly subject to legal proof, cross-examination, or challenge. The lawyer should not in effect appear as an unsworn witness or put the lawyer's own credibility in issue. The lawyer who is a necessary witness should testify and entrust the conduct of the case to another lawyer. There are no restrictions on the advocate's right to cross-examine another lawyer, however, and the lawyer who does appear as a witness should not expect to receive special treatment because of professional status.

Appeals

> (3) A lawyer who is a witness in proceedings shall not appear as advocate in any appeal from the decision in those proceedings.

Case Law: *Serodio v. White* (1994), 5 W.D.C.P. (2d) 153 (Ont. Sm. Cl. Ct.) — Section 29 of the *Courts of Justice Act* permits a Judge or a Deputy Judge of the Small Claims Court to award costs personally against a counsel or agent similar to that permitted by section 57.07 of the *Rules of Civil Procedure*.

Weiss v. Prentice Hall Canada Inc. (1995), 1995 CarswellOnt 729, [1995] O.J. No. 4188, 66 C.P.R. (3d) 417, 7 W.D.C.P. (2d) 99 (Ont. Sm. Cl. Ct.) — There is concurrent jurisdiction of provincial courts and the Federal Court: s. 37 of the *Copyright Act*. That Act of the Federal Parliament makes every provincial court a *curia designata* to enforce civil remedies provided by that Act. The application of Rule 20.03 of the Small Claims Court Rules with its maximum counsel fee $300 is inconsistent with the discretion in s. 25 of the *Courts of Jus-*

tice Act. The court referred to s. 29 of the *Courts of Justice Act.* Section 29 is in conflict with Rule 20.03 of the Small Claims Rules. Any conflict must be resolved in favour of the Act.

Manufacturer's Life v. Molyneux (January 9, 1995), Doc. 868/94 (Ont. Div. Ct.) — Application pursuant to section 114 of the *Landlord and Tenant Act* dismissed. Successful landlord, respondent on appeal represented by agent. Costs awarded in the sum of $250. See also *Bonshaw-Estates Inc. and Indrakumaran et al.,* unreported, File No. 421/92 where agent awarded $750 in costs (Ont. Div. Ct.).

Jones v. LTL Contracting Ltd., [1995] O.J. No. 4928 (Ont. Gen. Div.), Cosgrove J. — Appeal from Halabisky, Deputy Judge, where costs awarded totalled $17,730.09. Costs awarded on appeal of $4,000.

Barrons v. Hyundai Auto Canada Inc. (October 7, 1993), Doc. C14201 (Ont. C.A.); leave to appeal refused (1994), *(sub nom. Barrons v. Ontario Automobile Dealers Assn.)* 72 O.A.C. 239 (note), 174 N.R. 319 (note) (S.C.C.) — The inequality of resources between the parties is not a ground to deviate from the ordinary rule that costs follow the event.

Mosely v. Spray Lakes Sawmills (1980) Ltd. (1994), 33 C.P.C. (3d) 382, 26 Alta. L.R. (3d) 359, [1995] 4 W.W.R. 367, 164 A.R. 76 (Q.B.) — Financial hardship, in itself, does not justify an application to split or sever trial issues.

Brown v. McLeod (1997), [1998] 3 W.W.R. 385, 123 Man. R. (2d) 176, 159 W.A.C. 176 (Man. C.A.) — Trial judge erred in refusing adjournment unless appellant agreed to pay costs of $250. Maximum allowance for costs was $100 in absence of exceptional circumstances. Adjournment should have been granted where there was no ineptitude of counsel or prejudice to respondent. Appeal allowed and new trial ordered.

F. (J.M.) v. Chappell (1998), 106 B.C.A.C. 128, 172 W.A.C. 128 (B.C. C.A.) — Ruling respecting the entitlement to costs. The judgment awarded at trial was well below the Small Claims limit, but on appeal her award for damages for breach of privacy was increased to $18,000. The plaintiff was awarded party and party costs throughout. Both causes of action depended on the same body of evidence and costs should follow the overall outcome.

Global Experience v. 855983 Ontario Ltd. (January 30, 1998), Doc. Thunder Bay 95/0266 (Ont. Gen. Div.) — Plaintiff obtained judgment for $4,200, an amount within the jursidiction of the Small Claims Court. Application was allowed in part. The plaintiff was not entitled to any costs to the date of the first offer under Rule 57.05 since the amount recovered fell within the jurisdiction of the Small Claims Court. Matter fell within the territorial jurisdiction of the Small Claims Court in Thunder Bay under Rule 6 of the *Small Claims Court Rules,* R.R.O. 1990, Reg. 201, where the plaintiff would have been entitled to commence the action.

Breton v. Lindsey Morden Claim Services Ltd. (March 10, 1998), Doc. Kamloops 22042 (B.C. S.C.), Gill J. — This was a hearing to determine costs in connection with a wrongful dismissal action. The plaintiff, Breton, was awarded damages at trial of $6,800. This proceeding was properly brought within the Supreme Court. It was not an appropriate case for Small Claims Court. There was divided success at trial. Costs were apportioned accordingly.

Pang v. Westfair Properties Pacific Ltd. (1998), 25 C.P.C. (4th) 180 (B.C. S.C.) — Jury verdict apportioned liability 70 per cent to the plaintiff for her injuries. What percentage, if any, of her taxable costs and disbursements should the plaintiff recover? Awarded an amount below jurisdictional limit of the Small Claims Court. Justice achieved with order that plaintiff recover 30 per cent of her costs from the defendant, commensurate with the apportionment of liability.

Martin v. Heier (March 23, 1998), Doc. Edmonton 9703-24138 (Alta. Q.B.) — Necessary to provide full and fair hearing. The Civil Division is basically the only forum for which these litigants can have such a hearing. Appellant not given a full opportunity to state his case. Appeal allowed.

Ladies Dress & Sportswear Industry Advisor v. M.W. Pressing Co. (May 27, 1998), Doc. Toronto CP 07471/97 (Ont. Small Cl. Ct.), Thomson J. — Costs awarded against the Defendant under Rule 16 and under s. 29 of the *Courts of Justice Act*, against the Defendant's solicitor personally. Counsel has clearly ignored and delayed the orders of Court as well as the concerns of counsel throughout this matter. Costs against the Defendant in favour of the Attorney General under Rule 16.02(2) and under s. 29 of the *Courts of Justice Act* and costs to the Plaintiff under Rule 16.02(2) and s. 29 of the *Courts of Justice Act* as against the Defendant solicitor personally.

Dugas v. Page (1998), 512 A.P.R. 68, 200 N.B.R (2d) 68 (N.B. Q.B.) — The conduct of a lawyer in making a claim for that extra $1,000.00 and maintaining it until two days before the trial is so "unreasonable . . . as to attract costs under rule 75", to use the words of the Court of Appeal in *Kelly v. Markey* (1992), 130 N.B.R. (2d) 155 (N.B. C.A.) at 167. Defendant allowed costs of $250.00.

Pace v. Floral Studio Ltd. (1998), 56 O.T.C. 210 (Ont. Gen. Div.); additional reasons at (March 23, 1998), Doc. Toronto 96-CU-103670CM (Ont. Gen. Div.) — Judgment found in favour of plaintiff for $3,333.33. Defendant argued plaintiff should have commenced action in the Small Claims Court. The defendant relied on Rule 57.05 of the *Rules of Civil Procedure*, R.R.O. 1990, Reg. 194, to argue that plaintiff should not recover any costs and Rule 57.01(2) to seek costs awarded to the defendant. There should be no order as to costs. Plaintiff should have brought action in the Small Claims Court. The defendant should also have provided the plaintiff with some quantification of costs as well as some indication of a profit margin.

MacDonald v. Huckin (March 31, 1998), Doc. Victoria 96/1921 (B.C. S.C.) — Plaintiff awarded $12,000.00 non-pecuniary damages and divided liability 50 per cent/50 per cent. Should plaintiff be denied his costs because amount of judgment fell within jurisdiction of Provincial Court (B.C. Reg. 221/90, R. 57(10))? Plaintiff should recover 50 per cent of his costs. See *Flatley v. Denike* (1997), 32 B.C.L.R. (3d) 97 at 103 (B.C. C.A.). There was sufficient reason for plaintiff to bring proceedings in Supreme Court. Estimating the amount of damages a court might award in a personal injury claim is not always easy, partly because amount of damages question of fact.

Byers v. Prince George (City) Downtown Parking Commission (1998), 111 B.C.A.C. 144, 181 W.A.C. 144, (sub nom. *Byers v. Prince George Downtown Parking Commission)* 98 C.L.L.C. 210-033, 38 C.C.E.L. (2d) 83, 53 B.C.L.R. (3d) 345, [1999] 2 W.W.R. 335 (B.C. C.A.) — The plaintiff who was deprived of costs at trial since action ought to have been brought in Small Claims Court in view of limited entitlement to damages for wrongful dismissal was reversed on appeal. The Appeal Court increased damages to eight months from four months' salary. The plaintiff was entitled to costs of trial and appeal.

Minhas v. Canada (Minister of Citizenship & Immigration) (September 25, 1998), Doc. IMM-3860-97 (Fed. T.D.) — Show cause hearing why costs of $2,000 should not be payable personally by solicitor, for failure to attend scheduled hearing, leaving client without representation. The agent for the solicitor indicated that he advised counsel that he was unable to attend on date scheduled. Little regard was shown for client. Arrangements were vague and uncertain. There was no valid reason why her client was not represented at the hearing, and was ordered to pay costs.

Teed v. Langlais (1999), 47 M.V.R. (3d) 85 (N.B. C.A.) — The plaintiff appealed from a Small Claims decision apportioning liability for a car accident. The judge's conclusion was unreasonable. There was no legal basis to award of costs. The appeal was allowed, and full liability was assessed against the defendant. The awards for the defendant's counterclaim and costs were set aside.

Wacowich v. Wacowich (1999), 248 A.R. 350 at 368 (Alta. Q.B.) — The plaintiff engaged in self-help remedies that created further litigation. The order for costs reflected the court's disapproval for self-help remedies and for actions tending to lengthen litigation. The plaintiff was ordered to pay the defendant's cost throughout.

Niskanen Builders Ltd. v. Rodin (1996), 3 C.P.C. (4th) 166, 10 O.T.C. 248 (Ont. Gen. Div.) — Where a client was not notified of the increase in her solicitor's hourly rate, the court held that the account was to be based on the original hourly rate.

St. Laurent v. Burchak (2000), 2000 CarswellAlta 670 (Alta. Q.B.) — The defendants made a formal offer of judgment for $2,000, which the plaintiff did not accept. The plaintiff was awarded $673. Costs were at issue. The application was granted; matter should never have come to court. As the defendants failed to pay the plaintiff her vacation pay in accordance with the law, they contributed to the matter coming to court and were not entitled to costs.

Oxford Condominium Corp. No. 16 v. Collins (2000), 2000 CarswellOnt 4060 (Ont. Small Cl. Ct.) — A condominium corporation succeeded in a claim against unit owners for the full amount of $267. The plaintiff was entitled to costs based on contractual relationship. Tariff of Small Claims Court was not applicable to cap the amount recoverable.

Ganderton v. Marzen Artistic Aluminum Ltd., 2000 BCSC 1726, 2000 CarswellBC 2607 (B.C. S.C.) — The plaintiff's award was within the jurisdiction of the Provincial Court. The plaintiff was entitled to costs. It was not inappropriate for the plaintiff to bring an action in Supreme Court and to take advantage of summary trial procedure.

Royal Lepage Commercial Inc. v. Achievor Recycling Services Ltd. (October 12, 2000), Doc. 99-CV-166733 (Ont. S.C.J.) — Costs claimed by the plaintiff were excessive. The total fees awarded were $9,000. Although the amount recovered at trial was less than the jurisdiction of the Small Claims Court, the judge found the Small Claims Court scale not appropriate.

Bergel & Edson v. Wolf (2000), 50 O.R. (3d) 777, 49 C.P.C. (4th) 131, 2000 CarswellOnt 3388 (Ont. S.C.J.) — Rules of Professional Conduct did not explicitly render contingency fee agreements unenforceable at common law. It was also clearly unjust to deny lawyers the right to have their bills assessed where ample evidence before the assessment officer to permit an assessment. Fees assessed at $5,000.

Carmichael v. Stathshore Industrial Park Ltd. (1999), 121 O.A.C. 289, 1999 CarswellOnt 1838 (Ont. C.A.) — Rule 57.07 of the *Rules of Civil Procedure* provide for the assessment of costs against solicitors. In *Young v. Young*, EYB 1993-67111, [1993] S.C.J. No. 112, 1993 CarswellBC 264, 1993 CarswellBC 1269, [1993] 8 W.W.R. 513, 108 D.L.R. (4th) 193, 18 C.R.R. (2d) 41, [1993] 4 S.C.R. 3, 84 B.C.L.R. (2d) 1, 160 N.R. 1, 49 R.F.L. (3d) 117, 34 B.C.A.C. 161, 56 W.A.C. 161, [1993] R.D.F. 703 (S.C.C.), the Supreme Court of Canada advised, *inter alia*, that courts must be extremely cautious in awarding costs personally against solicitors.

Fong v. Chan (1999), 46 O.R. (3d) 330, 1999 CarswellOnt 3955, [1999] O.J. No. 4600, 181 D.L.R. (4th) 614, 128 O.A.C. 2 (Ont. C.A.) — The Ontario Court of Appeal discussed the extent to which self-represented lawyers are entitled to recover costs in litigation to which they were parties. The Court held that the firm's claim to an allowance for the salaried employees was justified by s. 36 of the *Solicitors Act* (Ontario), and that the claim for the partner's work was allowable at common law. All litigants suffer a loss of time through their involvement in the legal process. Costs should only be awarded to those lay litigants who can demonstrate that they devoted time and effort to do the work ordinarily done by a lawyer retained to conduct the litigation.

Canaccord Capital Corp. v. Clough, 2000 BCSC 410, 48 C.P.C. (4th) 359, 2000 CarswellBC 505 (B.C. S.C.) — The plaintiff obtained a judgment in Supreme Court for $8,250. The trial judge awarded the plaintiff costs on a small claims scale, including only disbursements. The plaintiff's disbursements totaled $2,279. The defendant claimed that the plaintiff should be allowed only those disbursements that would have been incurred in Small Claims Court. The plaintiff was entitled to recover the full amount. The disbursements meant money actually spent.

Brownell v. Stelter, 2001 CarswellAlta 636, 2001 ABQB 355, [2001] A.J. No. 564 (Alta. Master) — Impecunious plaintiff moved from Alberta to Ontario. Defendants' application for security for costs dismissed.

Crocker-McEwing v. Drake (2001), 2001 CarswellAlta 917, 2001 ABQB 592, [2002] 1 W.W.R. 354, 290 A.R. 365, 96 Alta. L.R. (3d) 301 (Alta. Q.B.) — Defendants awarded security for costs on a slip-and-fall lawsuit of doubtful strength where the plaintiff, who resided in Newfoundland, had no assets available sufficient to compensate defendants in costs if action failed. Action dismissed. Plaintiff had not met the requirements of original order.

Swire v. Walleye Trailer Park Ltd. (2001), 2001 CarswellOnt 2832, 203 D.L.R. (4th) 402, 149 O.A.C. 108, 44 R.P.R. (3d) 120 (Ont. Div. Ct.) — Appellant purchased trailer from former tenant in trailer park who assigned lease in park without respondent landlord's consent. Respondent obtained judgment. Small Claims Court had no jurisdiction to deal with matter applying to mobile home tenancy in relation to tax, evidenced by s. 29 of O. Reg. 194/98 that dealt specifically with property taxes. Judgment set aside.

Polish National Union of Canada Inc. v. Dopke, 2001 CarswellOnt 2896, 55 O.R. (3d) 728 (Ont. S.C.J.) — Plaintiff granted judgment for 1.5% of amount sought. Judgment against three defendants fell within monetary jurisdiction of Small Claims Court. Plaintiff did not prove fraud. Plaintiff awarded punitive damages for defendant's conduct. Plaintiff deprived of costs by Rule 76.10(2) of *Rules of Civil Procedure*. Defendant awarded costs because of wrongful conduct and award of punitive damages.

Krackovitch v. Scherer Leasing Inc. (2001), 2001 CarswellOnt 2938 (Ont. S.C.J.) — Defendant succeeded on most substantive claims, but had withdrawn settlement offer. Plaintiff recovered amount less than claimed and was within jurisdiction of Small Claims Court. No costs ordered.

Catalanotto v. Nina D'Aversa Bakery Ltd. (2001), 2001 CarswellOnt 4058 (Ont. S.C.J.) — Issues at trial not complex and matter ultimately within jurisdiction of Small Claims Court. Plaintiff acted unreasonably in not offering settlement. Failure of plaintiff to continue proceeding under simplified rules in Ontario justified that plaintiff pay defendant's party-and-party costs.

Young v. Young, EYB 1993-67111, [1993] S.C.J. No. 112, 1993 CarswellBC 264, 1993 CarswellBC 1269, [1993] 8 W.W.R. 513, 108 D.L.R. (4th) 193, 18 C.R.R. (2d) 41, [1993] 4 S.C.R. 3, 84 B.C.L.R. (2d) 1, 160 N.R. 1, 49 R.F.L. (3d) 117, 34 B.C.A.C. 161, 56 W.A.C. 161, [1993] R.D.F. 703 (S.C.C.) — (Per McLachlin J.) "The basic principal on which costs are awarded is as *compensation* for the successful party, not in order to punish a barrister. Any member of the legal profession might be subject to a compensatory order for costs if it is shown that repetitive and irrelevant material, and excessive motions and applications, characterized the proceedings in which they were involved, and that the lawyer acted in bad faith encouraging this abuse and delay. It is clear that the courts possess jurisdiction to make such an award, often under statute and, in any event, as part of their inherent jurisdiction to control abuse of process and contempt of court.".

Twaits v. Monk (2000), 8 C.P.C. (5th) 230, 2000 CarswellOnt 1685, [2000] O.J. No. 1699, 132 O.A.C. 180 (Ont. C.A.) — Trial judge erred in principle in awarding solicitor-client costs to the respondent. Solicitor-client costs may be ordered in cases where allegations of fraud are shown to be totally unfounded, see *131843 Canada Inc. v. Double "R" (Toronto) Ltd.* (1992), 7 C.P.C. (3d) 15, 1992 CarswellOnt 437, [1992] O.J. No. 3879 (Ont. Gen. Div.); additional reasons at (February 28, 1992), Doc. 18781/84 (Ont. Gen. Div.) and *Procor Ltd. v. U.S.W.A.* (1989), 71 O.R. (2d) 410, 1989 CarswellOnt 873, 65 D.L.R. (4th) 287 (Ont. H.C.); additional reasons at (1990), 65 D.L.R. (4th) 287 at 310, 71 O.R. (2d) 410 at 434 (Ont. H.C.) — While these allegations were not established at trial, they were made with some justification.

Groupe Essaim Inc. v. Village Pharmacy Minto Inc. (2000), 10 C.P.C. (5th) 364, 2000 CarswellNB 274, 227 N.B.R. (2d) 276, 583 A.P.R. 276 (N.B. Q.B.) — Costs award not appropriate since confusion was occasioned by ambiguity in wording of *Small Claims Act* (S.N.B. 1997, c. S-9.1) and Regulations.

Nuttall v. Thunder Bay (City) (2002), 163 O.A.C. 187, 2002 CarswellOnt 2113 (Ont. C.A.) — A woman sued the City for damages for personal injuries as a result of a fall on a city sidewalk. At trial she offered expert evidence. The trial judge discussed the criteria for the admission of expert evidence. The Court of Appeal affirmed the trial judge's decision to hear the expert evidence.

Stuart v. Hoffman Feeds Ltd. (2002), 2002 CarswellOnt 3255 (Ont. S.C.J.); additional reasons at (2002), 2002 CarswellOnt 3899 (Ont. S.C.J.) — Unsuccessful plaintiff's request to be relieved from award of costs due to financial hardship refused. Issues at trial difficult and there was basis for litigation, given opinions provided to plaintiff. Defendant awarded costs on party-and-party basis until date of defendant's offer to settle, and solicitor-and-client costs thereafter.

Connolly v. Canada Post Corp., 2002 CarswellNat 815, 2002 CarswellNat 1832, 2002 FCT 398, 2002 CFPI 398 (Fed. T.D.) — Lay litigant conducting unsuccessful judicial review application that resulted in extra work for respondent. Costs fixed to avoid further expense of assessment. *Federal Court Rules*, Rule 400(4).

Nelson v. Nelson, 2000 CarswellBC 2721, 2000 BCSC 1276 (B.C. S.C.) — Self-represented litigant interrupting and insulting counsel in court. Litigant ignored directions of Court to stop. Litigant persisting in rude behaviour. Special costs justified.

Spur Valley Improvement District v. Csokonay, 2001 CarswellBC 2780, 2001 BCSC 1615 (B.C. S.C.) — Proceeding focused on realty and whether one party or other owned water system. Case complex and would have been difficult to settle. Success divided. Plaintiff introduced evidence attacking defendants and prolonged case unnecessarily. Costs against plaintiff set at 15 per cent of actual costs.

Mansfield v. Hawkins, 2002 CarswellBC 3100, 2002 BCSC 1723 (B.C. S.C.) — Solicitor failed to keep time dockets. No evidence of time expended. Bill assessed on basis of quantum meruit. Solicitor not permitted to charge bonus unless client made aware of bonus at time retainer agreement entered into.

Hunt v. TD Securities Inc. (2003), 2003 CarswellOnt 4971, 43 C.P.C. (5th) 211, 40 B.L.R. (3d) 156 (Ont. C.A.). Hunt's recovered $9,374 in damages, $2,281.86 for prejudgment interest and costs and disbursements of approximately $14,000 in the Superior Court.

Bank's contention that Hunts not entitled to any costs because amount recovered within the monetary jurisdiction of the Small Claims Court and/or because the Hunts ought to have used the simplified procedures rejected. In light of complexity and unsettled law, not reasonably known damage award would be within the monetary jurisdiction of the Small Claims Court. Moreover, some of the claims equitable in nature.

Johnson v. Hogarth, 2004 BCPC 32, 2004 CarswellBC 364 (B.C. Prov. Ct.). Defendant sought to have the trial transferred to Victoria on Vancouver Island. Only connection anyone had to North Vancouver was that defendant Hogarth's solicitor there. Counsel for Plaintiff had business in Vancouver. Under *The Small Claims Act* (2.1) R.S.B.C. 1996 c. 430, the intent is to have claims resolved in as just and speedy and inexpensive manner as reasonable. This includes determination on "balance of convenience" where trial will be heard.

Fair to all parties to conduct litigation nearest event that resulted in the claim, i.e., the closest Court Registry to Sidney, British Columbia. File transferred to Victoria for trial.

Clark v. Canzio, 2003 NSSC 252, 2003 CarswellNS 465, 220 N.S.R. (2d) 256, 694 A.P.R. 256 (N.S.S.C.). Clark advanced claim in Small Claims Court. Issue whether Court should exercise its discretion to extend the time for filing of the notice of appeal and serving it on the claimant.

The Court is to be satisfied that (a) the Applicant had a *bona fide* intention to appeal while the right to appeal existed; (b) the Applicant had a reasonable excuse for the delay in not launching the appeal within the prescribed time; and (c) the appeal has sufficient merit in the sense of raising a reasonably arguable ground.

The Supreme Court has inherent jurisdiction to correct an error.

The Small Claims Court does not have any inherent jurisdiction except for enabling statute. The *Small Claims Court Act* does not provide for application of The *Civil Procedure Rules* to proceedings in Small Claims Court. In proceedings in the Small Claims Court, the *Nova Scotia Rules of Practice* apply except where there is a contrary intent shown by the *Small Claims Court Act*. Bona fide error on the part of the solicitor for the Plaintiff. Application granted for leave to extend the time.

J. Connelly Rental Ltd. v. Lefebvre (2003), 2003 CarswellOnt 4393, 178 O.A.C. 246 (Ont. Div. Ct.). Costs in Small Claims Court trials kept to modest levels so as not to impede acces to justice at that level. When successful litigant required to defend on appeal to Divisional Court award of costs more closely approximating the litigant's actual legal costs required. Court awarded Plaintiff costs of $3,000 on substantive indemnity basis.

MacEwan v. Henderson, 2003 CarswellNS 424, 2003 NSCA 133, 219 N.S.R. (2d) 183, 692 A.P.R. 183 (N.S. C.A.). Appeal from dismissal of appeal from Small Claims Court judgment where claim dismissed. Plaintiff claimed adjudicator in conflict of interest and should have recused himself. Application for recusal properly heard by judge being asked to withdraw. Appeal dismissed.

Koller v. Desnoyers (2003), 2003 CarswellOnt 2941 (Ont. S.C.J.). Plaintiffs were self-repre-sented and as such not entitled to costs. However, in early stages of litigation plaintiffs in-curred legal costs from their then solicitor and those expenses should be indemnified. Total costs payable to Plaintiff awarded at $9,987.

Benlolo v. Barzakay (2003), 2003 CarswellOnt 658, 169 O.A.C. 39 (Ont. Div. Ct.); addi-tional reasons at (2003), 2003 CarswellOnt 1260, 170 O.A.C. 115 (Ont. Div. Ct.). Registrar did not have jurisdiction to sign default judgment where amount of claim was unliquidated sum. Defendants not required to establish meritorious defence. Appeal allowed.

Susin v. Chapman (2004), [2004] O.J. No. 123, 2004 CarswellOnt 143 (Ont. C.A.). Appeal from Order of Bain J. dismissing appellant's action for non-payment of costs. Open to mo-tion judge to make the finding that appellant is not impecunious. The appellant argued he is impecunious when required to pay costs but denied impecuniosity when an opposite party sought security for costs. Appeal dismissed.

Johnston v. Morris, 2004 CarswellBC 3163, 2004 BCPC 511 (B.C. Prov. Ct.), P.M. Doherty, P.C.J. A claimant unprepared to prove loss has no reasonable prospect of success. Costs allowed at $3,133.21 for the clients of Clee. Morris entitled to $500.

Ogoki Frontier Inc. v. All A.I.R. Ltd., 2005 CanLII 614 (Ont. S.C.J.), Patrick Smith, J. Costs are at the discretion of the Court. General rule that costs follow the event. Misconduct of the parties. Miscarriage in the procedure. Oppressive and vexatious conduct of proceedings.

Painter v. Waddington, McLean & Co., 2004 CarswellOnt 279 (Ont. S.C.J.), Ditomaso, J. (1) Are self-represented lay plaintiffs entitled to costs? (2) If so, what is the appropriate measure of those costs?.

The plaintiffs commenced their action on October 27, 1999, when monetary jurisdiction of the Small Claims Court was $6,000. They recovered in excess of that amount at trial. No reason to exercise discretion to award no costs on the basis of r. 57.05.

Plaintiff relied on *Fellowes, McNeil v. Kansa General International Insurance Co.* (1997), 37 O.R. (3d) 464, 1997 CarswellOnt 5013, 17 C.P.C. (4th) 400 (Ont. Gen. Div.); *Fong v. Chan* (1999), 46 O.R. (3d) 330, 1999 CarswellOnt 3955, [1999] O.J. No. 4600, 181 D.L.R. (4th) 614, 128 O.A.C. 2 (Ont. C.A.); *Skidmore v. Blackmore*, 122 D.L.R. (4th) 330, 1995 CarswellBC 23, [1995] B.C.J. No. 305, 2 B.C.L.R. (3d) 201, [1995] 4 W.W.R. 524, 27 C.R.R. (2d) 77, 55 B.C.A.C. 191, 90 W.A.C. 191, 35 C.P.C. (3d) 28 (B.C. C.A.).

In *Fong*, Sharpe, J.A. considered both the *Fellowes* and *Skidmore* decisions. On reviewing the case law, Sharpe, J.A. found: ". . . the preponderance of modern authority supports the contention that both self-represented lawyers and self-represented lay litigants may be awarded costs and that such costs may include allowances for counsel fees." See *Fong* para. 23.

While a self-represented litigant may be entitled to costs, there is no automatic right of entitlement to recover costs. The trial judge maintains a discretion to make the appropriate costs award, including denial of costs. See *Fong* para. 27.

On the other hand, the cases show that an award to a lay litigant is not on the same basis as to the one represented by a solicitor, but is generally modest. Plaintiffs entitled to their costs throughout proceedings. Defence counsel offered to settle costs issue by only paying plaintiffs' disbursements with nothing allowed for fees. Costs awarded in the amount of $4,000, plus disbursements in the amount of $2,771.24.

TSP-Intl Ltd. v. Mills, 2005 CarswellOnt 2339 (Ont. S.C.J.), Wilson J. Cost awards under the Simplified Procedures have been significantly lower than they would be under the ordinary procedure.

Costs incurred under the Simplified Procedures, and in all cases, must be reasonable and proportionate to amount recovered.

An action conducted under Simplified Procedure meant to be cost effective. As a general rule, this process not intended to be as expensive as trial by ordinary procedure.

In *Glazman v. Toronto (City)*, 2002 CarswellOnt 2280, [2002] O.J. No. 2767 (Ont. S.C.J.), Lane J. noted at para. 10 that the costs grid does not alter a judge's discretion with respect to fixing costs that are reasonable. Rule 57.01(1) continues to apply. When determining costs, the judge must take into account all of the relevant factors.

The defendants refused disclosure.

Tri Level Claims Consultant Ltd. v. Koliniotis, 2005 CarswellOnt 3528, (sub nom. *Koliniotis v. Tri Level Claims Consultant Ltd.)* 201 O.A.C. 282, 15 C.P.C. (6th) 241, 257 D.L.R. (4th) 297 (Ont. C.A.). An appeal from the order of Justice John H. Jenkins of the Superior Court of Justice sitting as a single judge of the Divisional Court dismissing appeal from judgment of Deputy Judge A. Fisher of the Small Claims Court.

Whether the law permits paralegals and their clients to enter into contingency fee agreements? Can a paralegal recover in *quantum meruit* for services provided under a contingency fee agreement that is found to be champertous?.

If the law prohibits paralegal contingency agreements, the prohibition lies in *An Act Respecting Champerty*, R.S.O. 1897, c. 327 ("*Champerty Act*").

Leading authority in Ontario re contingency fees is the decision of O'Connor A.C.J.O. in *McIntyre Estate v. Ontario (Attorney General)*, 2002 CarswellOnt 2880, [2002] O.J. No. 3417, 23 C.P.C. (5th) 59, 218 D.L.R. (4th) 193, 61 O.R. (3d) 257, 164 O.A.C. 37 (Ont. C.A.). Reasonableness of lawyer's fee factor for court to consider in assessing whether a contingency fee arrangement champertous.

Paralegals have an important role to play in increasing access to justice. The role of paralegals in increasing access to justice has been recognized in several reports on paralegal activity in Ontario.

There is no regulation of paralegals equivalent to that applicable to lawyers. The need for regulation to avoid the abuses inherent in contingency fees may be more pressing for paralegals.

Several factors demonstrate that an absolute bar on *quantum meruit* recovery creates an injustice that is unacceptable when considered in light of the public policy informing the statutory prohibition against champertous agreements.

The sum of $1,300 would be reasonable compensation on a *quantum meruit* basis.

Decision of Divisional Court set aside and amount awarded in judgment of Fisher D.J. reduced to $1,300.

Culligan Springs Ltd. v. Dunlop Lift Truck (1994) Inc., 2005 CarswellOnt 4301 (Ont. S.C.J.), Shaughnessy, RSJ. In recent cases, the Ontario Court of Appeal has emphasized that there is an "overriding principle of reasonableness" that must govern the judicial exercise of fixing costs. (*Boucher v. Public Accountants Council (Ontario)*, 2004 CarswellOnt 2521, [2004] O.J. No. 2634, (sub nom. *Boucher v. Public Accountants Council for the Province of Ontario)* 71 O.R. (3d) 291, 48 C.P.C. (5th) 56, 188 O.A.C. 201 (Ont. C.A.); *Moon v. Sher*, [2004] O.J. No. 4651, 2004 CarswellOnt 4702, 246 D.L.R. (4th) 440, 192 O.A.C. 222 (Ont. C.A.); *Coldmatic Refrigeration of Canada Ltd. v. Leveltek Processing LLC*, 2005 CarswellOnt 189, [2005] O.J. No. 160, 5 C.P.C. (6th) 258, 75 O.R. (3d) 638 (Ont. C.A.).).

Trial Judge exercised his discretion and assessed costs applying principles in Rule 57.01(1) as well as the cost grid and whether "the result is fair and reasonable" (para. 16). But, not plain and obvious that he applied the "proportionately" principle as detailed in the *Trafalgar* case.

Leave granted, pursuant to s. 133 of the *Courts of Justice Act* to appeal the Order awarding Defendant its costs in amount of $60,267.39.

Bird v. Ireland, 2005 CarswellOnt 6945, [2005] O.J. No. 5125, 205 O.A.C. 1 (Ont. Div. Ct.), Clark J. Appeal from Small Claims Court trial.

Appellant argued trial judge erred in part:

> . . .
>
> (iv)   by fixing an amount for costs that was excessive and beyond his jurisdiction, by virtue of misapplying Rules 14.07 and 19.04 of the *Small Claims Court Rules* and section 29 of the *Courts of Justice Act*.

This was a one-day trial. Amount recovered $6,628.65, plus prejudgment interest of $1,551.84. The trial Judge awarded costs of $2,000. Purporting to apply s. 29 of the *Courts of Justice Act* ["CJA"], he took 15 per cent of $6,665, the principal amount awarded to the plaintiff at trial, namely, $994.28 and, purporting to apply Rule 14.07 of the *Small Claims Court Rules* he doubled that amount to arrive at $1,998.56. He then rounded this figure upward to $2,000. He erred in several respects.

Power to award costs conferred by Rule 19 limited by s. 29 of the CJA. The award, before the application of Rule 14.07, would be $300. Section 29 intended by the legislature to limit the power of the Small Claims Court to award costs, not to increase it. The purpose of s. 29

is to keep costs awards in proportion to the amounts recovered. If it had been the intention of the legislature to simply impose a general rule whereby costs awards were to be 15 per cent of the amount sued for, R. 19.04 would be superfluous. The Deputy Judge used s. 29 to increase the amount of costs he could award and ignored Rule 19.04.

Appeal allowed, judgments of trial court on both liability and costs set aside.

Respondent cannot succeed on a new trial. Judgment for appellant and respondent's claim for commission dismissed.

Hodson & Hodson Construction Ltd. v. Harrison, 2005 CarswellBC 1513, 2005 BCSC 905, 14 C.P.C. (6th) 179 (B.C. S.C.), Taylor J. Issue of costs that followed reasons issued May 12, 2004, 2004 CarswellBC 1087, 2004 BCSC 649 (B.C. S.C.) in which plaintiffs' claims against defendants in construction dispute dismissed save for a monetary judgment that was as a consequence of an accounting of materials charged to plaintiffs by defendants. Defendants sought special costs on basis that plaintiffs having plead but not proven fraud should be punished by such an order against them. Special costs are punitive in nature reflecting the opprobrium of the court as to a party's conduct.

See *Garcia v. Crestbrook Forest Industries Ltd.*, 1994 CarswellBC 1184, [1994] B.C.J. No. 2486, 119 D.L.R. (4th) 740, 9 B.C.L.R. (3d) 242, 14 C.C.E.L. (2d) 84, 41 C.P.C. (3d) 298, (sub nom. *Garcia v. Crestbrook Forest Industries Ltd. (No. 2))* 45 B.C.A.C. 222, (sub nom. *Garcia v. Crestbrook Forest Industries Ltd. (No. 2))* 72 W.A.C. 222 (B.C. C.A.) *[Garcia]* where Lambert J.A. considered the basis upon which special costs might be ordered. He reviewed *Young v. Young*, EYB 1993-67111, [1993] S.C.J. No. 112, 1993 CarswellBC 264, 1993 CarswellBC 1269, [1993] 8 W.W.R. 513, 108 D.L.R. (4th) 193, 18 C.R.R. (2d) 41, [1993] 4 S.C.R. 3, 84 B.C.L.R. (2d) 1, 160 N.R. 1, 49 R.F.L. (3d) 117, 34 B.C.A.C. 161, 56 W.A.C. 161, [1993] R.D.F. 703 (S.C.C.), in which the Supreme Court of Canada discussed the award of solicitor-client costs (now special costs) as being appropriate when there had been reprehensible, scandalous or outrageous conduct by a party.

Allegations of fraud as an assertion of criminal conduct in a civil case are not an automatic justification for special costs. Such an award requires a further examination of the course of conduct of the parties in the context of litigation.

Incumbent upon a party to demonstrate that he has attained "substantial success" at trial: See *Fotheringham v. Fotheringham*, 2001 CarswellBC 2148, [2001] B.C.J. No. 2083, 2001 BCSC 1321, 13 C.P.C. (5th) 302 (B.C. S.C.).

Actual time spent on an issue is but one factor to be considered along with the weight or value of an issue including the relative importance of the issues.

Rule 57(10) provides costs in cases within small claims jurisdiction.

Plaintiffs had sufficient reason to bring these proceedings in Supreme Court.

Reischer v. Insurance Corp. of British Columbia, 2006 CarswellBC 270, [2006] B.C.J. No. 235, 2006 BCSC 198 (B.C. S.C. [In Chambers]), Macaulay J.

Plaintiff accepted offer to settle for amount within monetary jurisdiction of Small Claims Court. Master dismissed plaintiff's claim to entitlement of costs other than disbursements. Plaintiff appealed. Plaintiff could have sued in either Provincial or Supreme Court. Cost consequence as set out in Rule 37(37) of the *Rules of Court* (B.C.). Plaintiff decided to accept offer for amount within jurisdiction of Provincial Court with respect to proceeding that could have been brought in that court.

Walford v. Stone & Webster Canada LP, 2006 CarswellOnt 6873, 217 O.A.C. 166 (Ont. Div. Ct.), 2006-11-06, Power J.

Plaintiff appealed judgment of Deputy Judge E.M. Osborne wherein she dismissed claim of Dr. Walford for damages arising out of alleged wrongful dismissal.

Appellant failed to appreciate proceeding one of appeal, not opportunity to retry case.

Trial judge's decision was a correct one.

Rule 61.03(7) applicable. Notwithstanding requirement for formal request for leave to appeal, Dr. Walford granted relief from his failure to seek leave.

The issue as to whether leave to appeal should be granted under s. 133(b) of the *Courts of Justice Act* from an order of the Small Claims Court judge not subject to Rule 62.02.

Section 29 of the *Courts of Justice Act* deals with costs awards made in the Small Claims Court.

There is no conflict between Rule 19(4) and s. 29 of the *Courts of Justice Act.*

Even if Rule amendment does not have retroactive effect, I would find that Statute takes priority over the old rule. In any event, s. 29 speaks of costs other than disbursements, whereas the old Rule 19.04 speaks of counsel fees. They are different things. In addition, Rule 19.02 now provides that "any power under this rule to award costs is subject to s. 29 of the *Courts of Justice Act.*".

An award of costs not exceeding 15 per cent of the amount claimed is not, in and of itself, an illegal award. The only issue to be considered on this appeal is whether, in all the circumstances, the award was appropriate.

No basis to substitute discretion of the trial judge with respect to her award of costs of $1,500. Appeal with respect to costs dismissed.

Cosentino v. Roiatti, 2007 CarswellOnt 104 (Ont. Div. Ct.), 2007-01-11, G.P. DiTomaso J.

Appeal heard December 6, 2006, detailed reasons for decision released on December 13, 2006. Costs determined by way of written submissions. The appellant was unsuccessful at trial before Winer D.J. to recover solicitor's fees claimed in the amount of $6,879.35. On appeal, all issues raised were decided against the appellant. See *Culligan Springs Ltd. v. Dunlop Lift Truck (1994) Inc.*, 2006 CarswellOnt 2516, [2006] O.J. No. 1667, 211 O.A.C. 65 (Ont. Div. Ct.).

In determining costs the result must be fair, reasonable and within the reasonable expectation of the parties. Determination of costs is not simply a mathematical exercise or mechanical calculation. See *Moon v. Sher*, [2004] O.J. No. 4651, 2004 CarswellOnt 4702, 246 D.L.R. (4th) 440, 192 O.A.C. 222 (Ont. C.A.) and *Boucher v. Public Accountants Council (Ontario)*, 2004 CarswellOnt 2521, [2004] O.J. No. 2634, (sub nom. *Boucher v. Public Accountants Council for the Province of Ontario)* 71 O.R. (3d) 291, 48 C.P.C. (5th) 56, 188 O.A.C. 201 (Ont. C.A.).

Costs in favour of successful respondent of $3,500 inclusive fair and reasonable. This award gives effect to the principles of reasonableness, proportionality and reasonable expectations of the parties in my view.

Pierlot Family Farm Ltd. v. Polstra, 2006 CarswellPEI 27, 2006 PESCAD 13, 271 D.L.R. (4th) 525, 766 A.P.R. 169, 257 Nfld. & P.E.I.R. 169 (P.E.I. C.A.).

Lay litigant entitled to costs taking into account only lost opportunity, not actual hours spent, and at lower rate than counsel. Costs of trial and appeal claimed at over $14,000. Some evidence was led at trial from which one could infer that litigant lost business income by reason of his involvement in acting as counsel. On partial indemnity basis, 40 hours of preparation reasonable, at $20 per hour, for total preparation fee of $800, plus disbursements, for total of $2,486.

Lunenburg Industrial Foundry & Engineering Ltd. v. Commercial Union Assurance Co. of Canada, 2006 CarswellNS 137, 2006 NSSC 105, 770 A.P.R. 282, 242 N.S.R. (2d) 282 (N.S. S.C.), Warner J.

Successful plaintiff had discharged lawyers six months prior to trial. Defendant contended that plaintiff L was self represented and therefore not entitled to legal costs. Plaintiffs represented from time of loss until eve of trial and had paid significant legal fees up to the point they became self represented. Not appropriate to compare L with other self-represented litigants who incurred little if any legal expenses. Party and party costs payable to L.

Burchell Hayman Parish v. Sirena Canada Inc., 2006 CarswellNS 520, 2006 NSSM 28 (N.S. Small Cl. Ct.), 2006-11-21, W. Augustus Richardson, Adjudicator.

Taxation of legal fees.

Time spent as set out in two accounts totalled 44.1 hours, too high for work done. Reason lawyer spent so much time is that, as a young lawyer just starting out, she lacked the knowledge, experience and confidence of a more senior lawyer.

Client should not be required to pay for the learning experience of a junior: see *Goodman & Carr v. Tempra Management Ltd.* (1991), 25 A.C.W.S. (3d) 169 (Ont Assess. O.), and *Canada Trustco Mortgage Co. v. Homburg*, 1999 CarswellNS 354, [1999] N.S.J. No. 382, 44 C.P.C. (4th) 103, 180 N.S.R. (2d) 258, 557 A.P.R. 258 (N.S. S.C.) at paras. 17-18. Test simply whether charge for a new lawyer's time is "fair and reasonable and stand the test of taxation, if requested": *Toulany v. McInnes, Cooper & Robertson*, [1989] N.S.J. No. 99, 1989 CarswellNS 298, 90 N.S.R. (2d) 256, 230 A.P.R. 256, (sub nom. *Toulany, Re*) 57 D.L.R. (4th) 649 (N.S. T.D.) at p. 4.

Colosimo v. Geraci, 2005 CarswellBC 2729, 2005 BCSC 1603 (B.C. S.C.), Ralph J.

Plaintiff sued for over $20,000, judgment for $8,000. Plaintiff seeking costs despite fact that judgment within limits of small claims court. Application allowed. Plaintiff having case for larger amount and appropriate that trial be brought in Supreme Court.

Euteneier v. Lee, 2005 CarswellOnt 6906, 260 D.L.R. (4th) 145, 204 O.A.C. 287, 139 C.R.R. (2d) 55 (Ont. C.A.).

The case raised complex issues of general public importance relating to the standard of care owed by the police to persons whose liberty is constrained in a police lock-up facility. Plaintiff's financial resources very modest. Exceptional case where costs should not be awarded against the unsuccessful litigant.

To do otherwise in all the circumstances would visit an unfair and onerous human and financial hardship on the respondent, resulting in fundamental injustice.

Guindon v. Ontario (Minister of Natural Resources), 2006 CarswellOnt 3173, 212 O.A.C. 207 (Ont. Div. Ct.).

Divisional Court rejected applicant's assertion that no costs be awarded given the public interest nature of the litigation. Applicants had not acted solely as public interest litigants. Nevertheless, the amount fixed should be fair and reasonable and within applicants' reasonable expectations.

Triple 3 Holdings Inc. v. Jan, 2006 CarswellOnt 5373, 274 D.L.R. (4th) 741, 214 O.A.C. 301, 32 C.P.C. (6th) 193, 82 O.R. (3d) 430 (Ont. C.A.).

Trial judge awarded respondents costs on a substantial indemnity basis of $140,000. He also ordered lawyer be jointly and severally liable with his clients for those costs because he found that lawyer's relationship with his clients placed him in conflict of interest. Lawyer appealed costs order. Appeal allowed.

Trial judge failed to find that lawyer caused costs to be incurred without reasonable cause or wasted by undue delay, negligence or other default (Rule 47.07(1)). Finding of common financial interest palpably wrong.

Williams (Litigation Guardian of) v. Bowler, 2006 CarswellOnt 3518, 81 O.R. (3d) 209 (Ont. S.C.J.), Roaccamo J.

Section 28.1(8) of the *Solicitor's Act* (Ont.) referred to. Exceptional circumstances existed where counsel assumed great responsibility and took on a very significant financial risk in a complicated personal injury action. Counsel entitled to contingency fees and legal costs.

Kerr v. Danier Leather Inc., 2005 CarswellOnt 2704, 76 O.R. (3d) 354, 18 C.P.C. (6th) 268 (Ont. S.C.J.).

Costs on party and party basis in favour of plaintiff appropriate if requested before orders finalized. Issue arose as to whether plaintiff entitled to costs in light of failure to raise issue prior to finalization of order. Rule 49.06 of *Rules of Civil Procedure* (Rules) allowed for amendment to orders, as court previously dealt not with ancillary, discrete issue costs of either motion, but with substantive issues of motions.

Bird v. Ireland, 2005 CarswellOnt 6945, [2005] O.J. No. 5125, 205 O.A.C. 1 (Ont. Div. Ct.), Clark J.

Plaintiff successfully sued to recover commission. Defendant appealed. Appeal allowed. Plaintiff not entitled to claim commission. Trial judge's findings based on misapprehension of evidence. Costs award set aside. Costs awarded exceeded maximum permitted by *Small Claims Court Rules* (Ont.) and s. 29 of *Courts of Justice Act* (Ont.). Section 29 of Act was to limit powers of Small Claims Court to award costs, not to increase it.

Chinese Business Chamber of Canada v. R., 2006 CarswellNat 1311, 2006 CarswellNat 2433, 54 Imm. L.R. (3d) 1, (sub nom. *Chinese Business Chamber of Canada v. Canada (Minister of Citizenship & Immigration)*) 349 N.R. 388, 2006 FCA 178, 2006 CAF 178 (F.C.A.).

Plaintiffs sought order staying enforcement of regulations that limited who could act for a fee in immigration matters before the Minister of Citizenship and Immigration. Motion for interim injunction denied and order for costs was made against them. Plaintiffs appealed, arguing that having regard to the nature of the application and the public importance of the issues raised, no costs should have been awarded against them. Appeal dismissed. The plaintiffs did not demonstrate that order founded on an error of principle or was plainly wrong.

R. v. Jedynack, 1994 CarswellOnt 826, [1994] O.J. No. 29, 16 O.R. (3d) 612, 20 C.R.R. (2d) 335 (Ont. Gen. Div.).

Costs order interlocutory and Appellate court had no jurisdiction to hear appeal from it under s. 830 of the *Criminal Code*.

Judge of Ontario Court (Provincial Division) had jurisdiction, as trial judge, to make order for costs against the Crown under s. 24(1) of the *Canadian Charter of Rights and Freedoms*. Such order should only be made where the acts or failures to act amount to something beyond inadvertent or careless failure to discharge a duty.

In this case, accused put to clear-cut extra and unnecessary expense by reason of the Crown's failure to comply fully with disclosure order. The Crown failed to act with due diligence.

Dunbar v. Helicon Properties Ltd., 2006 CarswellOnt 4580, [2006] O.J. No. 2992, 213 O.A.C. 296 (Ont. Div. Ct.), 2006-07-25, McIsaac J.

Appellants allege trial judge made two errors in assessment of damages for breach of contract.

Appellants argue that because monetary jurisdiction of the Small Claims Court is $10,000, the trial judge should have deducted the amounts set off in their favour from that amount instead of the total damages alleged by the respondent, an amount found to exceed $15,000. Appellants failed to satisfy appeal court that trial judge exceeded monetary limit of the Small Claims Court. He awarded the respondent $10,000, which complied with the applicable regulation: see O. Reg. 626/00.

Trial judge awarded respondent costs of $750 inclusive of approximately $250 in disbursements. The appellants argue that this $500 costs award exceeds the maximum provided for by way of counsel fee pursuant to R. 19.04(a) by $200. However, this provision has been interpreted as a daily counsel fee award: see *Bird v. Ireland*, 2005 CarswellOnt 6945, [2005] O.J. No. 5125, 205 O.A.C. 1 (Ont. Div. Ct.).

Appeal dismissed. Respondent awarded costs in fixed amount of $3,000.

Kennedy v. Kiss, [2006] B.C.J. No. 404, 2006 CarswellBC 453, 54 B.C.L.R. (4th) 151, 2006 BCSC 296 (B.C. S.C.), February 21, 2006, Williams J.

Plaintiff self-represented lawyer in fast-track personal injury litigation. Plaintiff made offer to settle in amount of $26,000 in July 2005. Plaintiff recovered judgment at trial in October 2005 in amount of $30,007.64. Parties made submissions on costs. Plaintiff awarded double costs capped at $7,200. As self-represented lawyer, plaintiff was entitled to costs. As well, plaintiff did bring counsel to lead his evidence and that was substantial component of evidence. Trial almost one and one-half days and should be treated as two-day trial for purpose of assessing costs.

Caselaw supports contention that self-represented lawyers may be awarded costs: *London Scottish Benefit Society v. Chorley* (1884), 13 Q.B.D. 872, [1881-1885] All E.R. 1111, 53 L.J.Q.B. 551, 51 L.T. 100, (sub nom. *London Permanent Building Society v. Thorley*) 32 W.R. 781 (Eng. C.A.). See *Fong v. Chan* (1999), 46 O.R. (3d) 330, 1999 CarswellOnt 3955, [1999] O.J. No. 4600, 181 D.L.R. (4th) 614, 128 O.A.C. 2 (Ont. C.A.).

Nazir v. Western Union Financial Services (Canada) Inc., 2007 CarswellOnt 5989 (Ont. Sm. Cl. Ct.), P.A. Thomson J.

Judgment in the amount of $85 being $62 plus interest from October 5, 2005 at 17 per cent per annum. Plaintiff entitled to costs of $245 under Rule 19.

Defendant submitted a brief requesting costs of $3,000.

Plaintiff sued for $10,000 damages including return of $62 paid to defendant and $9,938 for contract and tort damages. Defendant made an offer after the July 2006 Settlement Conference by formally serving an Offer to Settle under Rule 14 [Form 14A].

Plaintiff presented sincere issue to court and did not engage in unreasonable behaviour. No cause to penalize the plaintiff under s. 29. The Offer to Settle required the plaintiff to sign a release drafted by the defendant. The plaintiff was self-represented. This requirement takes the offer outside the purview of Rule 14. To award costs to the defendant would be to penalize the plaintiff.

1465778 Ontario Inc. v. 1122077 Ontario Ltd., 2006 CarswellOnt 6582, [2006] O.J. No. 4248, 216 O.A.C. 339, 38 C.P.C. (6th) 1, 275 D.L.R. (4th) 321, 82 O.R. (3d) 757 (Ont. C.A.).

There should be no prohibition on an award of costs in favour of a *pro bono* counsel in appropriate cases. Costs could serve purposes other than indemnity, including objectives of encouraging settlement, preventing frivolous or vexatious litigation, and discouraging unnecessary steps. Purpose of costs awards should also include access to justice in order to encourage counsel to take on *pro bono* work. Courts have scope to respond to any potential unfairness that might arise as a result of parties' unequal abilities to pay costs. The *pro bono* party was not paying a lawyer. Where costs were awarded in favour of a party, the costs belonged to that party.

Gook Country Estates Ltd. v. Quesnel (City), [2007] B.C.J. No. 246, 2007 CarswellBC 267, 68 B.C.L.R. (4th) 192, 2007 BCSC 171, 30 M.P.L.R. (4th) 307, 51 R.P.R. (4th) 310 (B.C. S.C. [In Chambers]), N.H. Smith J.

Public interest litigation. Action dismissed. Parties made submissions on costs. Costs awarded to defendants. Criteria for refusing to award costs in public interest litigation not met.

Order eventually entered, including costs, dated September 13, 2006. Unfair to expose plaintiff to additional costs that would be payable because of rule change on January 1, 2007. Costs payable by plaintiff would likely be significantly increased under new rules. Party should not be prejudiced by actions that were entirely those of court.

Ezer v. Yorkton Securities Inc., 2006 CarswellBC 2936, 2006 BCCA 548, 233 B.C.A.C. 161, 386 W.A.C. 161 (B.C. C.A.).

Unsuccessful appellant (Ezer) ordered to pay special costs. Matter proceeded to assessment. Ezer objected to charges for computer research, asserting that counsel had to demonstrate why charges for computer research were necessary and reasonable in the circumstances. Court deleted the amounts for research that it could not link to a claim in the fees.

Little Sisters Book & Art Emporium v. Canada (Commissioner of Customs & Revenue Agency), 2007 CarswellBC 78, 2007 CarswellBC 79, [2007] S.C.J. No. 2, 2007 SCC 2, 215 C.C.C. (3d) 449, 62 B.C.L.R. (4th) 40, 53 Admin. L.R. (4th) 153, 150 C.R.R. (2d) 189, 275 D.L.R. (4th) 1, (sub nom. *Little Sisters Book & Art Emporium v. Canada)* [2007] 1 S.C.R. 38, (sub nom. *Little Sisters Book & Art Emporium v. Minister of National Revenue)* 235 B.C.A.C. 1, (sub nom. *Little Sisters Book & Art Emporium v. Minister of National Revenue)* 388 W.A.C. 1, (sub nom. *Little Sisters Book and Art Emporium v. Minister of National Revenue)* 356 N.R. 83, 37 C.P.C. (6th) 1 (S.C.C.).

"A trial judge enjoys considerable discretion in fashioning a costs award. . . . While the general rule is that costs follow the cause, this need not always be the case. . . . A judge's decision on costs will generally be insulated from appellate review. . . . In exercising their discretion regarding costs, trial judges must, especially in making an order as exceptional as one awarding advance costs, be careful to stay within recognized boundaries.

. . . . .

.

"Bringing an issue of public importance to the courts will not automatically entitle a litigant to preferential treatment with respect to costs . . . By the same token, however, a losing party that raises a serious legal issue of public importance will not necessarily bear the other party's costs . . . Each case must be considered on its merits, and the consequences of an award for each party must be weighed seriously . . .".

Young v. Borzoni, 2007 CarswellBC 119, [2007] B.C.J. No. 105, 2007 BCCA 16, 388 W.A.C. 220, 277 D.L.R. (4th) 685, 235 B.C.A.C. 220, 64 B.C.L.R. (4th) 157 (B.C. C.A.).

Several paragraphs in claim alleged intolerance, deceit, harassment, intimidation, writing malicious letters, falsifying documents and, in general, disrupting the Youngs' lives. The motions judge held claim abuse of the court's process and that the Youngs were "using the court system as a plaything to harass others they do not like." The Court of Appeal affirmed findings. The court awarded Borzoni special costs. While the Youngs' frivolous and vexatious litigiousness might not amount to scandalous or outrageous conduct, it was reprehensible misconduct deserving of reproof or rebuke.

Miller v. Boxall, 2007 CarswellSask 7, 2007 SKQB 9, 30 M.P.L.R. (4th) 33, 291 Sask. R. 113, [2007] 3 W.W.R. 119 (Sask. Q.B.), R.L. Barclay J.

Party and party costs fixed at $5,000 awarded against applicant. Action not characterized as public interest litigation. Certain criteria did not apply in this case. In particular, proceedings did not invoke issues, importance of which extended beyond immediate interest of parties involved; applicant had as ratepayer interest in outcome of proceedings and respondents were not in clearly superior position to bear costs of proceedings.

1465778 Ontario Inc. v. 1122077 Ontario Ltd., 2006 CarswellOnt 6582, [2006] O.J. No. 4248, 216 O.A.C. 339, 38 C.P.C. (6th) 1, 275 D.L.R. (4th) 321, 82 O.R. (3d) 757 (Ont. C.A.).

In private action not involving public law or *Canadian Charter of Rights and Freedom* or similar issues of general public importance, court can make costs orders in favour of party represented by *pro bono* counsel. Court has discretion to make costs orders under s. 131 of *Courts of Justice Act* and r. 57.01 of *Rules of Civil Procedure*. Costs are to indemnify, to promote settlement, to deter frivolous actions and defences, to discourage unnecessary steps, and to promote access to justice. Litigants represented by *pro bono* counsel should not be denied access to costs regime. Losing party reimbursing *pro bono* counsel not inappropriate and not derogating from charitable purpose of volunteerism.

Clear Comfort Windows Inc. v. Newhook, 2006 CarswellOnt 8898, [2006] O.J. No. 5504 (Ont. Sm. Cl. Ct.); additional reasons to 2006 CarswellOnt 6306 (Ont. Sm. Cl. Ct.), D.J. Lange D.J. Costs in Small Claims Court.

Masih v. Janjic, 2005 CarswellOnt 9196 (Ont. S.C.J.); additional reasons to 2005 Carswell-Ont 9195 (Ont. S.C.J.), Criger D.J. Costs in Small Claims Court.

Martin v. Martin (2007), 2007 CarswellOnt 1574 (Ont. S.C.J.); additional reasons to (2007), 2007 CarswellOnt 683, [2007] O.J. No. 467 (Ont. S.C.J.), M. Linhares de Sousa J.

Husband ordered to pay wife's costs fixed at $40,000. Husband given much flexibility throughout trial because of his lack of legal representation and legal knowledge. Husband must have reasonably anticipated that he would be liable for wife's costs in event that he was unsuccessful in litigation.

Routhier v. Borris, 2007 CarswellOnt 1948 (Ont. S.C.J.); additional reasons to (2006), 2006 CarswellOnt 7458 (Ont. Div. Ct.), R.J. Smith J. Persons entitled to or liable for costs. Unrepresented party.

Bystedt (Guardian ad litem of) v. Bagdan, 2003 CarswellBC 812, 2003 BCSC 520 (B.C. S.C.); additional reasons to 2001 CarswellBC 2966, [2001] B.C.J. No. 2769 (B.C. S.C.), D. Smith J.

Normal rule is that costs follow event. Defendant had to instruct counsel, attend at discovery, and testify at trial. Defendant's participation was more than being witness.

Katish v. Mergaert, 2006 CarswellAlta 1418, 2006 ABQB 794 (Alta. Q.B.); additional reasons to 2006 CarswellAlta 880, 2006 ABQB 508 (Alta. Q.B.), D. Lee J. Particular items of costs. Witness fee and expenses. Expert witness.

Rendek v. Dufresne, 2006 CarswellAlta 1869, 414 A.R. 371, 2006 ABQB 822 (Alta. Q.B.); additional reasons to 2006 CarswellAlta 1212, [2006] A.J. No. 1167, 2006 ABQB 663 (Alta. Q.B.), B.R. Burrows J. Costs. Plaintiffs not entitled to reimbursement of personal representatives' travel costs to otherwise attend trial.

Crane Canada Co. v. Montis Sorgic Associates Inc., 2006 CarswellOnt 3051 (Ont. C.A.); affirming 2005 CarswellOnt 9989 (Ont. S.C.J.), Herman J.

Defendants applied successfully for relief including transfer of claims from Small Claims Court to Superior Court of Justice. Claims more appropriately dealt with in Superior Court of Justice. Plaintiffs appealed. Appeal dismissed. Court aware of access to justice concerns that were raised. Fact that all claims were subrogated claims brought by one insurer worthy of consideration.

MRSB Chartered Accountants v. Cardinal Packaging Ltd., [2006] P.E.I.J. No. 16, 2006 CarswellPEI 64, 46 C.P.C. (6th) 335, 773 A.P.R. 61, 256 Nfld. & P.E.I.R. 61, 2006 PESCTD 16 (P.E.I. S.C.), B.B. Taylor J.

Accountants brought Small Claims action for recovery of fees for accounting work done. Following pre-trial conference, plaintiff discontinued action. Section 53 of *Supreme Court Act* provides jurisdiction to Small Claims "Section" of Trial Division of Supreme Court of Prince Edward Island to award costs on substantial indemnity or partial indemnity basis. Rule 19.02 of *Small Claims Section Rules* provides that award of costs in Small Claims Section, other than disbursements, shall not exceed 15 per cent of amount claimed, unless court considers it necessary in interests of justice to penalize party, counsel or agent for unreasonable behaviour in proceeding. Rule 19.02 does not override authority in s. 53(1) of Act.

R. v. Maleki, 2007 CarswellOnt 6209, 2007 ONCJ 430 (Ont. C.J.), M. Lane J.

Accused convicted and sentenced to fine of $7,500. Neither party awarded costs. Criteria for making costs order against Crown not met. Crown fulfilled its professional responsibilities throughout proceeding. Even if provincial court judge had jurisdiction to order costs against accused and/or his agent, case at bar not analogous to decision where court held that its inherent power gave it jurisdiction to make such award. Section 131 of *Courts of Justice Act* and ss. 809 and 840 of *Criminal Code* did not persuasively provide jurisdiction to make meaningful costs order against accused.

Milne v. Columbia Health Centre Inc., 2007 CarswellAlta 590, 2007 ABQB 299, 416 A.R. 323 (Alta. Q.B.), P.A. Rowbotham J. Costs. Unrepresented party.

Celebre v. 1082909 Ontario Ltd. (2007), 2007 CarswellOnt 6249, 64 C.L.R. (3d) 211 (Ont. Div. Ct.), 2007-10-02, Lane Acting R.S.J.

Appeal dismissed on July 17, 2007. Appeal from Small Claims Court which had awarded the plaintiffs $9,148.58 and costs of $175 for the negligence of the defendant. After appeal launched defendant offered on March 13, 2007 to pay plaintiffs $500 for dismissal of appeal on consent and without costs. On May 14, 2007, the plaintiffs offered to accept $8,000 inclusive of costs and interest. The appeal would be dismissed and releases exchanged. Neither offer was accepted.

The plaintiffs claim partial indemnity costs up to May 14, 2007 and substantial indemnity costs thereafter, pursuant to r. 49.10. Their Bill of Costs claims for 17.7 hours charged by a lawyer of 14 years' experience at $225 if partial and $300 if substantial indemnity costs, for totals of $3,982.50 if partial and $5,310 if substantial.

Counsel for the defendant/appellant submits that:

a) Such an award is so large as to discourage litigants from using the court system; it is unreasonable and beyond the expectations of reasonable parties that the costs should exceed half of the amount of the judgment; Small Claims Court cases should carry only very small costs: *Roach v. Adamson*, 1982 CarswellOnt 934, [1982] O.J. No. 3346, 37 O.R. (2d) 547 (Ont. Assess. O.); and

b) Rule 49.10 does not apply to appeals: *Niagara Structural Steel (St. Catharines) Ltd. v. W.D. LaFlamme Ltd.* (1987), 1987 CarswellOnt 440, [1987] O.J. No. 2239, 58 O.R. (2d) 773, 19 O.A.C. 142, 19 C.P.C. (2d) 163 (Ont. C.A.).

Small cases cannot carry big fees. The costs award should not be so low that it deprives the successful party of the fruits of the judgment. A fair figure, within the reasonable expectations of the parties to a litigation at the appeal level involving about $10,000, and taking into account the offers, is $4,000 all-inclusive.

Kuzev v. Roha Sheet Metal Ltd. (2007), 2007 CarswellOnt 4338, 227 O.A.C. 3 (Ont. Div. Ct.), Lane J.

On March 22, 2007, court dismissed the defendant's appeal from the trial judge's award of $4,000 to plaintiff. The plaintiff sought costs on substantial indemnity scale of $7,691, or on the partial indemnity costs scale, $6,223.87. The basis for request is twofold: a) the defendant must be taken to know that the cost of responding to the appeal would be significantly more than the award; and b) the appellant's factum was unfocused which increased the cost for the respondent.

Even if a case has little merit, that alone does not justify substantial indemnity costs: *Young v. Young*, EYB 1993-67111, [1993] S.C.J. No. 112, 1993 CarswellBC 264, 1993 CarswellBC 1269, [1993] 8 W.W.R. 513, 108 D.L.R. (4th) 193, 18 C.R.R. (2d) 41, [1993] 4 S.C.R. 3, 84 B.C.L.R. (2d) 1, 160 N.R. 1, 49 R.F.L. (3d) 117, 34 B.C.A.C. 161, 56 W.A.C. 161, [1993] R.D.F. 703 (S.C.C.).

Is the total for fees and disbursements a fair and reasonable amount to be paid by the unsuccessful parties in the particular circumstances of this case? See *Murano v. Bank of Montreal* (1998), [1998] O.J. No. 2897, 1998 CarswellOnt 2841, 111 O.A.C. 242, 163 D.L.R. (4th) 21, 22 C.P.C. (4th) 235, 41 B.L.R. (2d) 10, 41 O.R. (3d) 222, 5 C.B.R. (4th) 57 (Ont. C.A.), at page 247 (O.R.); and *Zesta Engineering Ltd. v. Cloutier*, 2002 CarswellOnt 4020, [2002] O.J. No. 4495, 21 C.C.E.L. (3d) 161 (Ont. C.A.), Nov. 27, 2002. This is the major guiding principle in the fixing of costs, as reiterated by Borins J.A. for the Court of Appeal in *Moon v. Sher*, [2004] O.J. No. 4651, 2004 CarswellOnt 4702, 246 D.L.R. (4th) 440, 192 O.A.C. 222 (Ont. C.A.), at para. 30, where he observed that the case law established that such an award must:

> . . . reflect 'more what the court views as a fair and reasonable amount that should be paid by the unsuccessful parties rather than any exact measure of the actual costs to the successful litigant.' This is a fundamental concept in fixing or assessing costs.

An award of $2,500 plus disbursements of $351.47 reflects these principles.

Ibrahim v. Kadhim (2007), 2007 CarswellOnt 5606, 86 O.R. (3d) 728 (Ont. S.C.J.), 2007-09-10, Tulloch J.

The respondent sought costs in accordance with Rule 49.10 following success on an appeal of the Small Claims Court decision. The respondent requested costs of $12,940.90 plus disbursements of $637.96.

The objective of a costs order is to fix an amount that is fair and reasonable for the unsuccessful party to pay in the particular proceeding, rather than an amount fixed by the actual costs incurred by the successful party. See *Boucher v. Public Accountants Council (Ontario)*, 2004 CarswellOnt 2521, [2004] O.J. No. 2634, (sub nom. *Boucher v. Public Accountants Council for the Province of Ontario)* 71 O.R. (3d) 291, 48 C.P.C. (5th) 56, 188 O.A.C. 201 (Ont. C.A.). Costs fixed at $3,000 inclusive of GST and disbursements.

Jung v. Toronto Community Housing Corp., 2008 CarswellOnt 224 (Ont. Div. Ct.).

During submissions at the appeal and in his written submissions as to costs, counsel for Jung said that he was acting on a *pro bono* basis because his client was impecunious. Relying on *1465778 Ontario Inc. v. 1122077 Ontario Ltd.*, 2006 CarswellOnt 6582, [2006] O.J. No. 4248, 216 O.A.C. 339, 38 C.P.C. (6th) 1, 275 D.L.R. (4th) 321, 82 O.R. (3d) 757 (Ont. C.A.), counsel for the respondent argued that there was never an expectation that appellant would be able to pay costs if unsuccessful on appeal.

The Court of Appeal in the above case concluded that there should be no prohibition of an award of costs in favour of *pro bono* counsel in appropriate cases because the law now recognizes that costs awards may serve purposes other than indemnity.

Such an award is not mandatory and will depend on the rule 57.01 factors, considerations of access to justice and the need to maintain a level playing field between the parties.

Walsh v. 1124660 Ontario Ltd. (2007), 2007 CarswellOnt 4459, [2007] O.J. No. 2773, 59 C.C.E.L. (3d) 238 (Ont. S.C.J.), Lane J.

Jury trial resulted in verdict for defendants and action dismissed. Normal order would be defendants recover partial indemnity costs from plaintiff.

Plaintiff single mother with no employment-related skills. Costs always in discretion of court.

Myers v. Metropolitan Toronto (Municipality) Police Force, 1995 CarswellOnt 152, [1995] O.J. No. 1321, 37 C.P.C. (3d) 349, *(sub nom. Myers v. Metropolitan Toronto (Municipality) Chief of Police)* 125 D.L.R. (4th) 184, *(sub nom. Myers v. Metropolitan Toronto Chief of Police)* 84 O.A.C. 232 (Ont. Div. Ct.), paras. 19-22, determined that a rule based on impecuniosity would defy consistent application; would be difficult to administer as the court would have difficulty with the truthfulness of claims; and would allow impecunious litigants a means to ignore the rules of court. This would be even more troublesome when coupled with the contingency fee system developing in our litigation.

On the civil side, where the individual is a plaintiff, one can argue that it is a matter of choice whether to bring a particular lawsuit. Impecunious people do not have freedom of choice in the same degree that wealthy people do because they cannot afford to lose. In the case of dismissed employees or injured persons, there is often no redress without a legal action so the choice is to sue, running the unacceptable risk of a ruinous costs award, or go uncompensated. Defendants do not even have that limited degree of choice.

Not in the public interest to deter people from using their own courts for fear of costs consequences if they lose case. No order as to costs.

Paulus v. Murray (2007), 2007 CarswellOnt 1329 (Ont. Master), Master Lou Ann M. Pope.

Defendants' motion for security for costs under Rules 56.01(a) and (d). Paulus's evidence that he resides in Michigan.

Case law provides that impecuniosity is something more than having no assets, and in case of corporate plaintiff requires that it establish "impecuniosity beyond the mere evidence that it has no assets or income." See *Trottier Foods Ltd. v. Leblond*, 1987 CarswellOnt 549, [1987] O.J. No. 1246, 24 C.P.C. (2d) 272 (Ont. Master). Moreover, it must demonstrate that monies are not available from its shareholder or other sources by way of security. See also *1056470 Ontario Inc. v. Goh*, 1997 CarswellOnt 2434, [1997] O.J. No. 2545, 13 C.P.C. (4th) 120, 34 O.R. (3d) 92, 32 O.T.C. 225 (Ont. Gen. Div.).

See *O'Callaghan v. Lloyd's Underwriters*, 2002 CarswellOnt 3650, [2002] O.J. No. 4194 (Ont. Master), which followed *Hallum v. Canadian Memorial Chiropractic College*, [1989] O.J. No. 1399, 1989 CarswellOnt 896, 70 O.R. (2d) 119 (Ont. H.C.) at p. 125: "The plaintiff has a heavy burden to discharge in order to prove impecuniosity. He must do more than adduce some evidence of impecuniosity. He must show that he is impecunious.".

Having not proven impecuniosity, order for security for costs in the amount of $8,000 Canadian to be posted in stages considering the early stage of proceeding.

Christian Jew Foundation v. Christian Jew Outreach (2007), 2007 CarswellOnt 3446, [2007] O.J. No. 2140 (Ont. S.C.J.), Perell J. additional reasons at (2007), 2007 CarswellOnt 4580 (Ont. S.C.J.).

Defendants brought motion for leave to appeal an award of costs made by Master. At the heart of motion for leave to appeal and request court consider new evidence is allegation defendants are impecunious. Defendants' motion should be dismissed.

No appeal as of right of a Master's award. See M.M. Orkin, *The Law of Costs* (2nd ed.) (Canada Law Book: Aurora, looseleaf), para. 801.1.

Test for granting leave to appeal of discretionary costs award set out in *Rona Inc. v. Sevenbridge Developments Ltd.*, [2002] O.J. No. 3983, 2002 CarswellOnt 3361 (Ont. S.C.J.).

Section 4.02 of the *Rules of Professional Conduct* states:

> (1) Subject to any contrary provision of the law or the discretion of the tribunal before which a lawyer is appearing, a lawyer who appears as advocate shall not submit his or her own affidavit to the tribunal.

> **Submission of Testimony**

> (2) Subject to any contrary provisions of the law or the discretion of the tribunal before which a lawyer is appearing, a lawyer who appears as advocate shall not testify before the tribunal unless permitted to do so by the rules of court or the rules of procedure of the tribunal, or unless the matter is purely formal or uncontroverted.

Impecuniosity will not insulate a party from liability of costs otherwise payable and impecuniosity cannot be used as a justification for failure to obey a court order. See *Myers v. Metropolitan Toronto (Municipality) Police Force*, 1995 CarswellOnt 152, [1995] O.J. No. 1321, 37 C.P.C. (3d) 349, (sub nom. *Myers v. Metropolitan Toronto (Municipality) Chief of Police)* 125 D.L.R. (4th) 184, (sub nom. *Myers v. Metropolitan Toronto Chief of Police)* 84 O.A.C. 232 (Ont. Div. Ct.); *Abbott v. Reuter-Stokes Canada Ltd.*, 1988 CarswellOnt 520, 32 C.P.C. (2d) 161 (Ont. H.C.); *Schaer v. Barrie Yacht Club*, [2003] O.J. No. 4171, 2003 CarswellOnt 4009 (Ont. S.C.J.); *Baksh v. Sun Media (Toronto) Corp.*, 2003 CarswellOnt 24, [2003] O.J. No. 68, 63 O.R. (3d) 51 (Ont. Master); *Heu v. Forder Estate*, [2004] O.J. No. 705, 2004 CarswellOnt 729 (Ont. Master); *Scavarelli v. Bank of Montreal*, 2004 CarswellOnt 2083, [2004] O.J. No. 2175, 23 C.C.L.T. (3d) 306 (Ont. S.C.J.); *Cossette v. Gojit (Brampton) Inc.*, [2005] O.J. No. 6098 (Ont. Master); and *Kirwan v. Silver Brooke Golf Course Inc.*, 2006 CarswellOnt 2382, [2006] O.J. No. 1571, 46 R.P.R. (4th) 104 (Ont. S.C.J.).

Courts are reluctant to deprive a worthy but impecunious litigant of opportunity to have his or her claim adjudicated when it is not plainly devoid of merit. See, for example, *Rackley v. Rice*, [1992] O.J. No. 253, 1992 CarswellOnt 1092, 56 O.A.C. 349, 89 D.L.R. (4th) 62, 8 O.R. (3d) 105 (Ont. Div. Ct.); *John Wink Ltd. v. Sico Inc.*, 1987 CarswellOnt 370, [1987] O.J. No. 5, 57 O.R. (2d) 705, 15 C.P.C. (2d) 187 (Ont. H.C.); *Solcan Electric Corp. v. Viewstar Canada Inc.*, 1994 CarswellOnt 505, 25 C.P.C. (3d) 181 (Ont. Gen. Div.); *1056470 Ontario Inc. v. Goh*, 1997 CarswellOnt 2434, [1997] O.J. No. 2545, 13 C.P.C. (4th) 120, 34 O.R. (3d) 92, 32 O.T.C. 225 (Ont. Gen. Div.).

Motion for leave to appeal dismissed.

Walker v. Ritchie, 2006 CarswellOnt 6185, 2006 CarswellOnt 6186, [2006] S.C.J. No. 45, 2006 SCC 45, 353 N.R. 265, 33 C.P.C. (6th) 1, 43 C.C.L.I. (4th) 161, 43 C.C.L.T. (3d) 1, 273 D.L.R. (4th) 240, 217 O.A.C. 374, [2006] 2 S.C.R. 428 (S.C.C.).

Plaintiffs' counsel carrying lengthy personal injury litigation without remuneration because plaintiffs lacked financial resources to pay. Defendants not admitting liability. Whether plaintiffs' costs award payable by unsuccessful defendants may be increased to take into account risk of non-payment to plaintiffs' counsel. See *Rules of Civil Procedure*, R.R.O. 1990, Reg. 194, rr. 49, 57.01(1).

Risk of non-payment to the plaintiffs' lawyer not a relevant factor under costs scheme in r. 57.01(1) at time costs fixed in case.

The opportunity for counsel to charge his or her own client a risk premium, or now a contingency fee, encourages competent counsel to take on the cases of impecunious clients.

Costs awards made by trial judges should be accorded a high degree of deference. See *British Columbia (Minister of Forests) v. Okanagan Indian Band* (2003), 2003 CarswellBC 3040, 2003 CarswellBC 3041, 2003 SCC 71, 43 C.P.C. (5th) 1, [2003] 3 S.C.R. 371, 313

N.R. 84, [2004] 2 W.W.R. 252, 21 B.C.L.R. (4th) 209, 233 D.L.R. (4th) 577, [2004] 1 C.N.L.R. 7, 189 B.C.A.C. 161, 309 W.A.C. 161 (S.C.C.), at paras. 42-43; *Hamilton v. Open Window Bakery Ltd.*, [2003] S.C.J. No. 72, 2003 CarswellOnt 5591, 2003 CarswellOnt 5592, REJB 2004-54076, 2004 SCC 9, 316 N.R. 265, 235 D.L.R. (4th) 193, 2004 C.L.L.C. 210-025, 184 O.A.C. 209, [2004] 1 S.C.R. 303, 70 O.R. (3d) 255 (note), 40 B.L.R. (3d) 1 (S.C.C.), at para. 27. However, as LeBel J. stated in *Okanagan Indian Band*, at para. 43: "An appellate court may and should intervene where it finds that the trial judge has misdirected himself as to the applicable law." In this case, the court must look to the law governing costs in Ontario.

Legislation now permits counsel to charge contingency fees: See the *Solicitors Act* and the *Class Proceedings Act, 1992*, S.O. 1992, c. 6.

MRSB Chartered Accountants v. Cardinal Packaging Ltd., [2006] P.E.I.J. No. 16, 2006 CarswellPEI 64, 46 C.P.C. (6th) 335, 773 A.P.R. 61, 256 Nfld. & P.E.I.R. 61, 2006 PESCTD 16 (P.E.I. S.C.), B.B. Taylor J.

Accountants brought small claims action for recovery of fees. Accountants had no grounds to claim against CM Inc., L and G. Small Claims Rule 19 and general discretion under s. 53 of *Supreme Court Act* provide jurisdiction to Small Claims Section of Trial Division of Supreme Court of Prince Edward Island to award more than usual costs in exceptional cases. Necessary in interests of justice to penalize accountants for having made unfounded allegations of fraud, deceit and acting in bad faith.

In *Biggins v. Bovan*, [2005] O.J. No. 1000 (Ont. S.C.J.) at para. 9, Searle D.J. interpreted the phrase "in the proceeding" in "unreasonable behaviour in the proceeding" to include the commencement of a proceeding. I agree with this interpretation.

Court award substantial indemnity costs against such plaintiffs to punish the plaintiffs' reprehensible conduct in making the allegations, discourage other plaintiffs from making false and harmful assertions about defendants' character, and compensate the defendants for the expense incurred in answering the baseless attack on the defendants' integrity (*Twaits v. Monk* (2000), 8 C.P.C. (5th) 230, 2000 CarswellOnt 1685, [2000] O.J. No. 1699, 132 O.A.C. 180 (Ont. C.A.) at paras. 2 to 5).

Motion by defendants for costs against plaintiff on full indemnity basis following plaintiff's discontinuance of action, and for order fixing amount of costs.

Brace v. Canada (Customs & Revenue Agency), 2007 CarswellNfld 267, 47 C.P.C. (6th) 276, 822 A.P.R. 332, 2007 NLTD 149, 270 Nfld. & P.E.I.R. 332 (N.L. T.D.), A.E. Faour J.

As successful litigant, B awarded lump-sum amount of $1,750 on party and party basis. Costs awarded for hearing, all relevant pre-trial applications, and in recognition of CRA's claim for costs on two withdrawal applications and costs of current application. Costs not justified on solicitor and client scale. No evidence that any conduct had been reprehensible, scandalous or outrageous. CRA was only pursuing its statutory responsibility in instructing sheriff to make seizure. No basis for awarding costs at higher level as B was unrepresented.

Kuzev v. Roha Sheet Metal Ltd. (2007), 2007 CarswellOnt 4338, 227 O.A.C. 3 (Ont. Div. Ct.), Lane J.

Small Claims Court awarded plaintiff $4,000. Plaintiff claimed costs of $7,691 on a substantial indemnity scale or, alternatively, $6,223.87 on the partial indemnity scale. Divisional Court awarded costs on partial indemnity scale in amount of $2,500 plus $351.47 for disbursements. The paying party must not be faced with an award that did not reasonably reflect the amount of time and effort that was warranted by proceedings.

Even if a case has little merit, that alone does not justify substantial indemnity costs. See *Young v. Young*, EYB 1993-67111, [1993] S.C.J. No. 112, 1993 CarswellBC 264, 1993 CarswellBC 1269, [1993] 8 W.W.R. 513, 108 D.L.R. (4th) 193, 18 C.R.R. (2d) 41, [1993] 4

S.C.R. 3, 84 B.C.L.R. (2d) 1, 160 N.R. 1, 49 R.F.L. (3d) 117, 34 B.C.A.C. 161, 56 W.A.C. 161, [1993] R.D.F. 703 (S.C.C.).

MRSB Chartered Accountants v. Cardinal Packaging Ltd., [2006] P.E.I.J. No. 16, 2006 CarswellPEI 64, 46 C.P.C. (6th) 335, 773 A.P.R. 61, 256 Nfld. & P.E.I.R. 61, 2006 PESCTD 16 (P.E.I. S.C.), Taylor J.

The three defendants were awarded costs in discontinued small claims action against the plaintiff on a substantial indemnity basis in the amount of $15,000 plus taxes and disbursements. The plaintiff's allegations that the defendants were guilty of fraud, deceit and acting in bad faith were utterly false, and the court found that was necessary in interests of justice to penalize them for unreasonable behaviour.

Reimann v. Aziz, 2007 CarswellBC 2190, [2007] B.C.J. No. 2025, 47 C.P.C. (6th) 351, 286 D.L.R. (4th) 330, 246 B.C.A.C. 143, 406 W.A.C. 143, 2007 BCCA 448, 72 B.C.L.R. (4th) 1 (B.C. C.A.), Chiasson J.A.

Appeal related to the costs award dismissed. While action was tried in the Supreme Court appellants submitted that the respondent should only recover his disbursements because the judgment was within the jurisdiction of the Small Claims Court. The British Columbia Court of Appeal concluded that a plaintiff did not have an ongoing obligation to assess the quantum of a claim and that the point in time for a consideration of whether a plaintiff had sufficient reason for bringing a proceeding in the Supreme Court was the time of the initiation of the action.

Harrison v. British Columbia (Information & Privacy Commissioner), 2008 CarswellBC 1542, 60 C.P.C. (6th) 58, 2008 BCSC 979, 72 C.C.E.L. (3d) 103 (B.C. S.C.), Registrar Bouck.

Hearing related to assessment of plaintiff's costs flowing from successful judicial review. Self-represented plaintiff submitted bill of costs for $6,339 based on 51 units of work. Plaintiff based his bill on what would have been claimed if represented by counsel. Registrar found no requirement to discount costs because litigant was self-represented. Plaintiff was not required to demonstrate opportunity loss to claim costs. The plaintiff was awarded $4,750.

Kelly v. Aliant Telecom/Island Tel, 2008 CarswellPEI 11, [2008] P.E.I.J. No. 12, 833 A.P.R. 177, 2008 PESCTD 12, 273 Nfld. & P.E.I.R. 177 (P.E.I. T.D.).

The case involved an important issue of the assessment of costs where the amount of damages was small. Although the Rules of Civil Procedure provide that award of costs in Small Claims Section shall not exceed 15% of amount claimed, the court has discretion to depart from this rule if it is in interests of justice. It was not appropriate to do so in this case, as the amount of damages was small, but there were significant and costly pre-trial proceedings, the trial was not lengthy, and the plaintiff was not successful in the majority of her claims.

Silco Electric Ltd. v. Giammaria (2008), 2008 CarswellOnt 1637 (Ont. Div. Ct.) (Ont. Div. Ct), Maranger J.

$1,750.00 is the amount that a party might reasonably expect to receive or have to pay, depending on the result, in a Small Claims Court appeal where the matter is uncomplicated.

Belanger v. Belanger (2005), [2005] O.J. No. 3659, 2005 CarswellOnt 3991 (Ont. S.C.J.)

[11] I am guided, ultimately, by the Court of appeal reasoning in *Boucher v. Public Accountants Council (Ontario)* (2004), 71 O.R. (3d) 291 (Ont. C.A.), which moderated the indemnity principle reflected in the costs grid. The court held that the computation of billable hours multiplied by a lawyer's hourly rate is but one consideration in fixing costs. Overriding principle is that the fixed costs should be fair and reasonable to the litigant required to pay them. Although the costs grid is not applicable in family law litigation, the aforesaid overriding principle that costs should be fair and reasonable is applicable universally.

Butsky-Plekan v. Plekan (2005), 2005 CarswellOnt 3084 (Ont. S.C.J.), Joseph C.L. Scime J.

The objective of the court is to fix an amount for costs that is fair and reasonable for the unsuccessful party to pay in this particular proceeding, rather than an amount fixed by the actual costs incurred by the successful litigant. In fixing costs, the overriding principle is reasonableness so as to not produce a result that is contrary to the fundamental objective of access to justice. (Authority: *Boucher v. Public Accountants Council (Ontario)* (2004), [2004] O.J. No. 2634, 71 O.R. (3d) 291, 188 O.A.C. 201, 2004 CarswellOnt 2521, 48 C.P.C. (5th) 56 (Ont. C.A.)).

Blake v. Chen (2009), 2009 CarswellOnt 5693, 85 C.L.R. (3d) 81 (Ont. Div. Ct.); additional reasons at (2009), 2009 CarswellOnt 6724 (Ont. Div. Ct.), D.R. Aston J.

Appropriate scale of costs is partial indemnity. Most significant factor in determining quantum is amount in issue in proceeding. That said, plaintiff's Offer to Settle for $6,000 before significant appeal costs were incurred also significant. Rule 49.10 does not apply to appeals. However, Offers to Settle are the primary means by which successful Small Claims Court plaintiffs can protect themselves from Pyrrhic victories.

Datta v. Datta (2009), 2009 CarswellOnt 7650 (Ont. S.C.J.).

Claim for costs pursuant to Rule 38.08(3) of the *Rules of Civil Procedure*, where applications are abandoned or are deemed to be abandoned. Arguably, of course, costs are in the court's discretion under s. 131 of the *Court of Justice Act*, and Rule 57.01(1) of the *Rules of Civil Procedure*.

Substantial indemnity costs rewards appropriate where party has behaved in abusive manner, brought proceedings wholly devoid of merit, and unnecessarily run up the costs of litigation; in short, where a party has misconducted himself or herself in the course of the litigation, or behaved unreasonably in the litigation. See *Standard Life Assurance Co. v. Elliot* (2007), 2007 CarswellOnt 3236, [2007] O.J. No. 2031, 86 O.R. (3d) 221, 50 C.C.L.I. (4th) 288 (Ont. S.C.J.), and *Hunt v. TD Securities Inc.* (2003), 2003 CarswellOnt 3141, [2003] O.J. No. 3245, 66 O.R. (3d) 481, 229 D.L.R. (4th) 609, 175 O.A.C. 19, 36 B.L.R. (3d) 165, 39 C.P.C. (5th) 206 (Ont. C.A.); additional reasons at (2003), 2003 CarswellOnt 4971, 43 C.P.C. (5th) 211, 40 B.L.R. (3d) 156 (Ont. C.A.); leave to appeal refused (2004), 2004 CarswellOnt 1610, 2004 CarswellOnt 1611, [2003] S.C.C.A. No. 473, 330 N.R. 198 (note), 196 O.A.C. 399 (note) (S.C.C.). Applicant behaved unreasonably. Costs awarded on a substantial indemnity basis.

Ellis v. J & J Concrete Floors Ltd. (2009), 2009 CarswellOnt 3861 (Ont. S.C.J.), D.J. Lange D.J; additional reasons to (2009), 2009 CarswellOnt 3860 (Ont. S.C.J.), D.J. Lange D.J.

WE and BE brought unsuccessful action for amount of $4,507.82. Costs submissions were made by TJ. Costs awarded to TJ in amount of $440. TJ entitled to representation fee, determined to be $100 per hour for paralegal that attended for 3.5 hours. Additional fees were for preparation and filing.

K.N. Umlah Insurance Agency Ltd. v. Christie, 2009 CarswellNS 286, 2009 NSSM 15, 886 A.P.R. 285, 278 N.S.R. (2d) 285 (N.S. Small Cl. Ct.); additional reasons to 2009 CarswellNS 110, 2009 NSSM 7 (N.S. Small Cl. Ct.), Richardson Adjud..

Plaintiff claimed $16,194. Jurisdiction of Small Claims Court increased to $25,000. Action transferred to Small Claims Court. Claim dismissed in its entirety. Word "costs" in s. 15(1)(e) meant only costs incurred in Supreme Court prior to transfer in nature of disbursements and did not include costs referable to cost of retaining lawyer. Order made awarding costs of $360.73 plus whatever defendant paid in respect of discovery service's attendance and transcription costs.

McAllister v. Wiegand (2009), 2009 CarswellOnt 1529 (Ont. Sm. Cl. Ct.), Lange D.J.

Section 29 of *Courts of Justice Act*, capping costs in Small Claims Court at 15 percent of amount claimed, did not entitle plaintiff to maximum award. Fifteen percent rule did not prevail over R. 19.04 of Small Claims Court Rules as regards representation fee and should not be applied as matter of course. Delays in proceeding were not undue warranting penalty under R. 19.06 and did not constitute special situation justifying 15 percent rule. Delays mostly due to defendants, but some were bona fide and consented to by plaintiff without court attendance. Plaintiff's unrevoked offer to settle was more favourable to defendants than judgment. No special circumstances warranted suspension of costs consequences.

Mohamadi v. Tremblay, 2009 CarswellBC 1775, 2009 BCSC 898 (B.C. S.C.); additional reasons at 2009 CarswellBC 3120, 2009 BCSC 1583 (B.C. S.C.).

Plaintiff injured in motor vehicle accident. Defendant admitted liability. Plaintiff awarded general damages of $10,000. Plaintiff awarded special damages of $690. Plaintiff not entitled to costs. Sum plaintiff recovered within jurisdiction of Provincial Court under *Small Claims Act*.

Nazir v. Western Union Financial Services (Canada) Inc. (2008), 2008 CarswellOnt 8998 (Ont. Div. Ct.); affirming (2007), 2007 CarswellOnt 9351 (Ont. S.C.J.); additional reasons to (2007), 2007 CarswellOnt 5989 (Ont. S.C.J.).

Plaintiff brought action for $10,000 against defendant for return of $62 paid to Western Union, and damages of $9,938 for breach of contract. Action allowed. Plaintiff entitled to costs of $245, reflecting claim of $75, trial fee of $100, service fee of $20 and pleading fee of $50. Amount requested, totalling 30 per cent of claim twice maximum in *Courts of Justice Act*. Trial lasted one day. Awarding costs to defendant would penalize plaintiff. Defendant appealed costs order. Appeal dismissed. Trial judge not in error.

Prince Edward Island School Board, Regional Administrative Unit No. 3 v. Morin, 2009 CarswellPEI 41, 2009 PECA 18, (sub nom. *Morin v. Prince Edward Island Regional Administrative Unit No. 3)* 288 Nfld. & P.E.I.R. 85, (sub nom. *Morin v. Prince Edward Island Regional Administrative Unit No. 3)* 888 A.P.R. 85, 74 C.P.C. (6th) 8 (P.E.I. C.A.); additional reasons at 2009 CarswellPEI 45, 2009 PECA 20 (P.E.I. C.A.); leave to appeal refused 2010 CarswellPEI 7, 2010 CarswellPEI 8, (sub nom. *Morin v. Board of Education of Regional Unit No. 3)* 298 Nfld. & P.E.I.R. 287 (note), (sub nom. *Morin v. Board of Education of Regional Unit No. 3)* 921 A.P.R. 287 (note), (sub nom. *Morin v. Prince Edward Island Regional Administrative Unit No. 3)* 405 N.R. 394 (note) (S.C.C.).

Appellant awarded 100 percent of his costs on partial indemnity basis as lay litigant for entire action. Costs assessed by prothonotary pursuant to R. 57.01(3.1) of Rules of Civil Procedure. Appellant claimed he was entitled to lost opportunity costs because he was unable to attain or retain employment due to burden of carrying litigation by himself. Appeal allowed in part. Appellant not employed throughout most of litigation and therefore unable to claim time spent on litigation.

Sutherland v. Manulife Financial (2009), 2009 CarswellOnt 4489 (Ont. S.C.J.); additional reasons at (2009), 2009 CarswellOnt 4991 (Ont. S.C.J.).

Plaintiff Sutherland, self-represented, had two actions dismissed by Registrar's orders. Sutherland requests that any costs against her be in the cause. She was not in a position to afford to pay any costs until her claim was heard.

Although, technically, Ms. Sutherland was successful on her motions, the motions would not have been necessary had she taken timely steps to advance her actions. Fairest order is to make the costs of motions, $1,800 for each set of defendants, be payable to the defendants in any event of the cause.

Tripodi v. 434916 Ontario Ltd. (2009), 2009 CarswellOnt 6962 (Ont. S.C.J.), Romain Pitt J.; additional reasons at (2009), 2009 CarswellOnt 8112 (Ont. S.C.J.).

Solicitor's bill was for $10,590.67. Assessment Officer reduced it to $2,000.00. Client had changed counsel solely because the first counsel's fees were considered either beyond the client's means or not warranted by amount in issue. The lawyer should have: (a) made sure that his estimate of fees was realistic, that is, as near as possible to the actual fees; (b) kept the client constantly aware of potential increases in fees; and (c) got written instructions to proceed when it became clear that the costs would in fact be disproportionate to the amount involved in the litigation. None of these things was done.

White v. Ritchie (2009), 2009 CarswellOnt 3268 (Ont. S.C.J. [Commercial List]).

White claims disbursements and for time spent by him as a self-represented litigant dating back to October 1, 2008. White claims taxi and air expenses for his trip to Toronto. Disbursements supported by copies of invoices. Disbursements to be paid by defendants. Self-represented lay litigant may be awarded costs. Within discretion of the judge. See *Fong v. Chan* (1999), 46 O.R. (3d) 330, 128 O.A.C. 2, 181 D.L.R. (4th) 614, [1999] O.J. No. 4600, 1999 CarswellOnt 3955 (Ont. C.A.).

Self-represented litigant should not recover costs for time and effort that any litigant would have to devote to case. Lay litigants must demonstrate they devoted time and effort to do work ordinarily done by a lawyer retained to conduct litigation and therefore they incurred an opportunity cost by foregoing remunerative activity. White claimed approximately 240 hours for preparation of materials. A reasonable allowance for work done by White is Cdn. $15,000.

Wilson v. Bourbeau (2009), 249 O.A.C. 122, 2009 CarswellOnt 2583 (Ont. Div. Ct.), L.L. Gauthier J.

Applicant sought to seal portions of record of judicial review. Motion dismissed. In general, person's discomfort must yield to strong public policy in favour of openness. Applicant's desire to protect her identity and medical information did not raise question of serious risk to important public interest. No important societal value was involved in applicant's request for sealing order.

Woolner v. D'Abreau (2009), 2009 CarswellOnt 664, 70 C.P.C. (6th) 290, 50 E.T.R. (3d) 59, [2009] O.J. No. 1746 (Ont. S.C.J.), Brown J.; reversed (2009), 2009 CarswellOnt 6479, 53 E.T.R. (3d) 18 (Ont. Div. Ct.).

Court allowed two lawyers of elderly client to keep legal fees but for only a portion of services rendered to client that resulted in value to her. It disallowed other costs incurred because lawyers breached their fiduciary duties to client which included a duty to provide client with full disclosure of all relevant and material information that pertained to her interests and, after a certain point in litigation, incurred costs without reasonable cause.

383501 Alberta Ltd. v. Rangeland Truck & Crane Ltd., 2009 CarswellAlta 201, 2009 ABQB 87, 67 C.P.C. (6th) 358 (Alta. Q.B.).

Trial judge allowed recovery for filing fee and costs of service, but declined to award full indemnity costs. Plaintiff appealed. Appeal dismissed. While award of costs need not be pleaded, there is line of authority that suggests that notice should be given, presumably in pleadings, of party's intention to seek solicitor client costs. Plaintiff entitled to costs based on its relative success at trial. Provincial Court proceeds in terms of its mandate. Exercise of discretion, in this case, appeared to accord with generally applied rules, different than those applied in Court of Queen's Bench.

Bérubé v. Rational Entertainment Ltd., 2010 ONSC 894, 2010 CarswellOnt 725 (Ont. Div. Ct.).

Bérubé appealed decision of Tierney J. of the Small Claims Court dismissing her action. Appeal was dismissed. Each party sought costs.

General rule that costs should follow the success in the cause.

Respondent claims the amount of $5,529.31 on a partial indemnity scale, inclusive of disbursements of $457.81.

Amount claimed in appellant's statement of claim was $7,200. Award of costs on the appeal must take into consideration amount in issue.

Appropriate award on a partial indemnity basis is $3,500 inclusive of GST and disbursements.

LeBlanc v. Lalonde, 2010 ONSC 927, 2010 CarswellOnt 810 (Ont. Div. Ct.), Maranger, J.

Appeal of Small Claims Court judgment dismissed. Respondent seeking $9,052.81 in costs. The Appellant has suggested that $2,500.00 is a fair and reasonable costs award in this case. Judgment and award received in this case totalled $5,300.00. A costs award should be proportionate to the complexity and importance of the issues and to the amount involved. See also *Boucher v. Public Accountants Council (Ontario)* (2004), 2004 CarswellOnt 2521, [2004] O.J. No. 2634, 48 C.P.C. (5th) 56, 188 O.A.C. 201, 71 O.R. (3d) 291 at para. 26 (Ont. C.A.).

1465778 Ontario Inc. v. 1122077 Ontario Ltd., [2006] O.J. No. 4248, 82 O.R. (3d) 757, 275 D.L.R. (4th) 321, 2006 CarswellOnt 6582, 38 C.P.C. (6th) 1, 216 O.A.C. 339 (Ont. C.A.).

Plaintiffs' counsel was acting *pro bono* and sought costs from losing party. The defendants argued lawyers acting *pro bono* in commercial matters should not be awarded costs. The purpose of costs awards should include access to justice. There is no prohibition on award of costs to *pro bono* counsel in appropriate cases. Costs awarded. Costs could serve purposes other than indemnity, including the objectives of encouraging settlement, preventing frivolous or vexatious litigation, and discouraging unnecessary steps. In this case, plaintiffs impecunious, and it was because they were unable to pay a costs order that the case initially dismissed. No reason why the losing party should not be ordered to pay costs of the appeal.

See Major J. in a speech titled "Lawyers' Obligation to Provide Legal Services" delivered to the National Conference on the Legal Profession and Professional Ethics at the University of Calgary in 1994 (33 Alta. L. Rev. 719) where he said:

> It has long been part of the duty and tradition of the legal profession to provide services gratuitously for those who require them but cannot afford them. The profession, recognizing its commitment to the larger principle of justice, has traditionally not let such cases go unanswered merely because the individual is impecunious. Instead, the profession has collectively accepted the burden of such cases, thereby championing the cause of justice while at the same time sharing the cost that such cases entail. This is a tradition which dates to the very inception of the profession in medieval Europe in the thirteenth century.

Costs have been awarded in cases where the litigant was self-represented (*Skidmore v. Blackmore*, 122 D.L.R. (4th) 330, 35 C.P.C. (3d) 28, 90 W.A.C. 191, 55 B.C.A.C. 191, 27 C.R.R. (2d) 77, [1995] 4 W.W.R. 524, 2 B.C.L.R. (3d) 201, [1995] B.C.J. No. 305, 1995 CarswellBC 23 (B.C. C.A.)); where the winning party was a law firm represented by one of its partners who was not charging fees (*Fellowes, McNeil*); where counsel was salaried (*Solicitors Act*, R.S.O. 1990, c. S.15, s. 36); and, where the responsibility for a party's legal fees was undertaken by a third party (*Lavigne v. O.P.S.E.U.*, 1987 CarswellOnt 1074, 41 D.L.R. (4th) 86, 60 O.R. (2d) 486, 87 C.L.L.C. 14,044 (Ont. H.C.)).

Costs have also been awarded to counsel acting *pro bono* in *Charter* or public interest cases. See *Rogers v. Greater Sudbury (City) Administrator of Ontario Works*, 57 O.R. (3d) 467, [2001] O.J. No. 3346, 2001 CarswellOnt 2934 (Ont. S.C.J.).

In non-public interest cases, see e.g. *Mackay Homes v. North Bay (City)*, [2005] O.J. No. 3263, 2005 CarswellOnt 3367 (Ont. S.C.J.), *Spatone v. Banks*, [2002] O.J. No. 4647, 2002 CarswellOnt 4143 (Ont. S.C.J.), and *Jacks v. Victoria Amateur Swimming Club*, [2005] B.C.J. No. 2086, 2005 CarswellBC 2300, 2005 BCSC 1378 (B.C. S.C. [In Chambers]). In *Ontario (Human Rights Commission) v. Brockie*, 2004 CarswellOnt 1231, 185 O.A.C. 366

(Ont. C.A.), court reversed a decision of the Divisional Court that denied costs to *pro bono* counsel, holding that "[s]uch a policy would act as a severe penalty to lawyers acting in the public interest by making it possible for litigants of modest means to access the courts.".

Davies v. Clarington (Municipality), 254 O.A.C. 356, 77 C.P.C. (6th) 1, 2009 CarswellOnt 6185, 2009 ONCA 722, 100 O.R. (3d) 66, [2009] O.J. No. 4236, 312 D.L.R. (4th) 278 (Ont. C.A.).

Court of Appeal stated that while fixing costs was a discretionary exercise, attracting a high level of deference, it must be on a principled basis. Judicial discretion under rr. 49.13 and 57.01 not so broad as to permit a fundamental change to the law that governed the award of an elevated level of cost (full or substantial indemnity costs). Apart from the operation of r. 49.10, elevated costs should only be awarded on a clear finding of reprehensible conduct on the. part of the party against which the cost award being made.

681638 Ontario Ltd. v. UGT Ltd., 252 O.A.C. 285, 2009 CarswellOnt 4477 (Ont. Div. Ct.); additional reasons at 2009 CarswellOnt 6473 (Ont. Div. Ct.); additional reasons at 2009 CarswellOnt 8141 (Ont. Div. Ct.).

The plaintiff applied for leave to appeal costs awarded to three defendants against which the plaintiff had discontinued small claims action. The Divisional Court noted that trial judge made no reference to either of the two relevant statutory provisions, specifically, section 29 of the *Courts of Justice Act*, and r. 19.04(1) of the *Small Claims Court Rules*. Section 29 provided an award of costs, other than disbursements, was not to exceed 15 per cent of the amount claimed unless it was "necessary in the interests of justice to penalize a party . . . for unreasonable behaviour in the proceeding." The trial judge made no finding "of unreasonable behaviour" on the part of the plaintiff. Section 29, in the context of this case, limited any single award of costs to any one of the defendants to 15 percent of $1,000, namely, $1,500. That interpretation was supported by the use of "award" (singular) in section 29 and by public policy. There was a separate issue of costs between the plaintiff and each of the defendants. The trial judge required to consider each one separately and make a separate award to *each* defendant. If a judge invoked the "unreasonable behaviour" sanction against one of several unsuccessful defendants, that should affect only the additional amount for costs that could be awarded against only that defendant. However, if unsuccessful plaintiff engaged in "unreasonable behaviour," it might be that more than one of the successful defendants could be found to be entitled to costs in excess of 15 percent maximum.

Kurdina v. Gratzer, 2009 CarswellOnt 7700 (Ont. S.C.J.), Perell J.; was additional reasons to 2009 CarswellOnt 6772 (Ont. S.C.J.); affirmed 2010 ONCA 288, 2010 CarswellOnt 2251[2010] O.J. No. 1551 (Ont. C.A.); leave to appeal refused 2010 CarswellOnt 6875, 2010 CarswellOnt 6876, (sub nom. *Kurdina v. Dief)* 410 N.R. 391 (note), (sub nom. *Kurdina v. Dief)* 277 O.A.C. 402 (note), [2010] S.C.C.A. No. 199 (S.C.C.).

Defendant doctor's motion for summary judgment granted. The plaintiff's issue was income disability benefits. The defendant incurred legal expenses totalling $16,000, but sought costs of $500. No order for costs made. The plaintiff's experience of having to incur expenses related to expert testimony and toxicology reports provided more meaningful deterrent than nominal costs award.

A & A Steelseal Waterproofing Inc. v. Kalovski, 2010 CarswellOnt 3455, 2010 ONSC 2652 (Ont. S.C.J.).

The action commenced in January 2005 pursuant to the *Construction Lien Act*, R.S.O. 1990, as a result of the defendant's failure to pay for work done.

The plaintiff sought costs on a substantial indemnity basis in the sum of $41,661.47. The defendants submit plaintiff's costs should be on a Small Claims Court basis only, given the amount recovered at trial. Alternatively, proportionality must be considered.

Justice is best served when costs are awarded to successful litigants and the principle of indemnity is paramount: *Waterloo (City) v. Ford*, 2008 CarswellOnt 2692 (Ont. S.C.J. [Commercial List]).

Rule 57.05(1) of the *Rules of Civil Procedure*, R.S.O. 1990, provides that where a judgment is obtained which is within the jurisdiction of the Small Claims Court, the court may, in its discretion, order that the plaintiff shall not recover any costs. This is neither a proper case for the denial of costs to the plaintiff, nor for an award of costs in favour of the plaintiff on a Small Claims Court basis.

The plaintiff, while advancing a modest claim for payment of its account in the deposit amount was also required to defend a substantial counterclaim in the sum of $150,000.00. That claim was outstanding until the commencement of the trial.

The plaintiff entitled to costs in the circumstances. An award of costs on a substantial indemnity basis was appropriate.

Carleton v. Beaverton Hotel, 2009 CarswellOnt 6303, [2009] O.J. No. 2409, 96 O.R. (3d) 391, 314 D.L.R. (4th) 566 (Ont. Div. Ct.).

After ordering plaintiff to re-attend for examination for discovery and ordering production of various documents, motions judge made order for costs against solicitor personally. There is a danger in awarding costs personally against solicitor for professional misconduct as opposed to conduct that created unnecessary costs. Award of costs against solicitor personally set aside. Two-part test set out in r. 57.07. Principles in awarding costs personally against a lawyer set out in *Young v. Young*, 1993 CarswellBC 1269, 1993 CarswellBC 264, EYB 1993-67111, [1993] S.C.J. No. 112, [1993] R.D.F. 703, 56 W.A.C. 161, 34 B.C.A.C. 161, 49 R.F.L. (3d) 117, 160 N.R. 1, 84 B.C.L.R. (2d) 1, [1993] 4 S.C.R. 3, 18 C.R.R. (2d) 41, 108 D.L.R. (4th) 193, [1993] 8 W.W.R. 513 (S.C.C.) at para. 254.

See also *Walsh v. 1124660 Ontario Ltd.*, [2007] O.J. No. 639, 2007 CarswellOnt 982 (Ont. S.C.J.); additional reasons at [2007] O.J. No. 2773, 2007 CarswellOnt 4459, 59 C.C.E.L. (3d) 238 (Ont. S.C.J.), where Lane J. refused to order costs against a lawyer personally where the primary complaint was unprofessional conduct, where such conduct was unrelated to delay.

It is not the case that the mere fact that costs exceed damages awarded renders such an award inappropriate: see *Bonaiuto v. Pilot Insurance Co.*, 81 C.C.L.I. (4th) 213, 2010 ONSC 1248, 2010 CarswellOnt 1039, 101 O.R. (3d) 157, 81 C.C.L.I. (4th) 213, [2010] O.J. No. 745 (Ont. S.C.J.). As noted by Lane J. in *163972 Canada Inc. v. Isacco*, 1997 CarswellOnt 636, [1997] O.J. No. 838 (Ont. Gen. Div.): "to reduce the plaintiff's otherwise reasonable costs on this basis would simply encourage the kind of intransigence displayed by the defendants in this case.".

Sum of $41,661.47, inclusive of disbursements and GST, on a substantial indemnity basis, fair and reasonable in circumstances.

Blow v. Brethet, 92 C.C.L.I. (4th) 45, 2010 CarswellOnt 8819, 2010 ONSC 6332 (Ont. S.C.J.) McIsaac J.

The plaintiff sought costs award of approximately $64,000 in case where he was awarded $21,218.72, including pre-judgment interest. The action began in May 2009, under the *Simplified Procedure*. The trial took place over three days in May 2010, some four months after the monetary jurisdiction of the Small Claims Court increased to $25,000. Case cried out for immediate removal to the Small Claims Court as of January 2010. Defendants sought order of no costs to the plaintiff pursuant to r. 57.05(1). Costs to plaintiff fixed at $6,000 inclusive.

Mustang Investigations Inc. v. Ironside, 2010 CarswellOnt 5398, 2010 ONSC 3444, 267 O.A.C. 302, 321 D.L.R. (4th) 357, 103 O.R. (3d) 633, 98 C.P.C. (6th) 105, [2010] O.J. No. 3184 (Ont. Div. Ct.).

The plaintiff moved for leave to discontinue action. One of the defendants (Ironside), who was self-represented, opposed motion on the ground that he required his day in court in order to vindicate his reputation. The motions judge allowed the motion on the condition that the plaintiff pay Ironside $20,000 for counsel fee on a partial indemnity basis plus disbursements of $1,051.40. Divisional Court affirmed the award for disbursements of $1,051.40, but set aside the $20,000 award. The costs should only be awarded to self-represented litigants who demonstrated that they devoted time and effort to the work ordinarily done by a lawyer retained and that as a result they incurred an opportunity cost by foregoing remunerative activity. A self-represented litigant should only receive a moderate or reasonable allowance for the loss of time devoted to preparing and presenting the case.

Leading authority on costs to be awarded to unrepresented litigants, in *Fong v. Chan*, 46 O.R. (3d) 330, 128 O.A.C. 2, 181 D.L.R. (4th) 614, [1999] O.J. No. 4600, 1999 CarswellOnt 3955 (Ont. C.A.). *Fong* followed in *Izzard v. Goldreich*, 2002 CarswellOnt 1533, 159 O.A.C. 365 (Ont. Div. Ct.); additional reasons at [2002] O.J. No. 2931, 2002 CarswellOnt 4780 (Ont. Div. Ct.) (para. 3). *Fong* applied in *Logtenberg v. ING Insurance Co.*, 2008 CarswellOnt 2930 (Ont. S.C.J.).

See *White v. Ritchie*, 2009 CarswellOnt 3268, [2009] O.J. No. 2360 (Ont. S.C.J. [Commercial List]), Newbould, J. re *Fong*, at paragraph 15 that "Mr. White has not shown that he has a current job or other income sources that he has had to forego in order to spend time preparing his case. He has not worked for some considerable period of time.".

In *Henderson v. Pearlman*, 2010 ONSC 149, 2010 CarswellOnt 75 (Ont. S.C.J.), Hennessy J., after alluding to *Fong*, agreed with Newbould J., in *White v. Ritchie* and without making reference to whether or not lost opportunity costs established, awarded unrepresented litigant 120 hours of time spent at $20 per hour.

Propane Levac Propane Inc. v. Macauley, 2010 ONSC 293, 2011 CarswellOnt 108, [2011] O.J. No. 105 (Ont. Div. Ct.).

The appeal from judgment of deputy judge awarding costs of $1,650 to respondent following trial. If the defendant had not returned the plaintiff's propane tank within 20 days, the defendant was to pay the plaintiff the sum of $2,000. The appellant argued that deputy judge erred in awarding an amount of costs that exceeds 15 percent of the claim without directing himself to the criteria under section 29 of the *Courts of Justice Act*.

Interplay between r. 14.07 of the *Rules of the Small Claims Court* and section 29 of the *Courts of Justice Act*. See *Melara-Lopez v. Richarz*, 2009 CarswellOnt 6459 (Ont. S.C.J.); affirmed 2009 CarswellOnt 6333, 255 O.A.C. 160 (Ont. Div. Ct.), where deputy judge awarded costs in excess of 15 percent of the amount claimed in reliance on the rejection by the plaintiff of two offers and referred to section 29 of the *Courts of Justice Act*. Rule 14.07 can be applied to award double costs, even if that amount then exceeds the 15 percent limit under section 29. See also *Beatty v. Reitzel Insulation Co.*, [2008] O.J. No. 953, 2008 CarswellOnt 1364 (Ont. S.C.J.). Rules need to be read in a manner consistent with statute, and it is improper to hold that rule can trump statute.

Award of costs in this case does not prevent a party from proceeding to court to obtain a ruling on a legal matter. Rather it encourages litigants to have regard to the applicable law and to the principle of proportionality in their litigation, including at the Small Claims Court level. Hospital identified in its notice of motion that it was relying on r. 1.0-3 and 12.02 of the *Rules of Small Claims Court*. Respondents were entitled to have action dismissed. The claims were waste of time within meaning of r. 12.02 because no meaningful chance of success at trial.

Transport Training Centres of Canada v. Wilson, 2010 ONSC 2099, 2010 CarswellOnt 2155, (sub nom. *Wilson v. Transport Training Centres of Canada*) 261 O.A.C. 301 (Ont.

Div. Ct.); additional reasons at 2010 ONSC 2714, 2010 CarswellOnt 3549, (sub nom. *Wilson v. Transport Training Centres of Canada*) 263 O.A.C. 226 (Ont. Div. Ct.).

The trial judge awarded employee $7,000 in general damages for undue mental distress instead of claimed amount of $1,000, amending her statement of claim accordingly, and fixing her costs at $1,500. The employer appealed. Appeal allowed. The trial judge erred in awarding damages to employee. Interaction of r. 19.04(2) of *Small Claims Court Rules* and section 29 of *Courts of Justice Act* meant that award of costs with respect to employee's agent could not exceed half of statutory maximum of 15 percent of amount claimed. No evidence of unreasonable behaviour by employer, so as to justify under section 29 of *Act* amount exceeding statutory maximum amount. Costs award exceeded trial judge's discretion and was set aside.

West End Tree Service Inc. v. Stabryla, 2010 CarswellOnt 12, 2010 ONSC 68, 257 O.A.C. 265, [2010] O.J. No. 7 (Ont. Div. Ct.).

The defendant in small claims action paid money into court pursuant to notice of garnishment. The plaintiff obtained default judgment. The defendant obtained order setting aside judgment, but garnished money had already been paid out to the plaintiff. The endorsement stated, "Provided the defendant complies with my order, then, on or before 15 February 2008, the plaintiff is ordered to return the monies to the court to be held pending trial." When trial commenced, the plaintiff had not paid the money into court. Trial judge dismissed action and awarded defendant $1,500 in costs, where the plaintiff had neither paid the money into court nor undertaken to do so. Divisional Court allowed appeal. The court stated that had it not allowed the appeal on the merits, it would have set aside the costs order. Contrary to the judge's finding, the plaintiff had indicated at the outset of trial that if it had to pay, it would do so that day. Order required payment by February 15, 2008, but not sent to the plaintiff's lawyer until February 22, 2008. Even if unreasonable behaviour, judge gave no explanation as to how he arrived at $1,500. Costs pursuant to section 29 should logically bear some relationship to costs incurred by recipient as a result of other party's unreasonable behaviour. Costs would have been $375. Even if elevated costs warranted, no principled basis to arrive at $1,500.

Vigna v. Levant, 2011 CarswellOnt 357, 2011 ONSC 629, 2011 CarswellOnt 2592 (Ont. S.C.J.).

Factors to be considered when fixing costs set out in r. 57 of the *Rules of Civil Procedure* and include, in addition to success, the amount claimed and recovered, the complexity and importance of the matter and the principle of proportionality, the conduct of any party which unduly lengthened the proceeding, whether any step was improper, vexatious or unnecessary, or taken through negligence, mistake or excessive caution, a party's denial or refusal to admit anything, any offer to settle, the principle of indemnity, scale of costs, hourly rate claimed in relation to the partial indemnity rate set out in the Information to the Profession effective July 1, 2005, the time spent, and the amount that a losing party would reasonably expect to pay.

The plaintiff claims substantial indemnity costs for the law firm of Heenan Blaikie of $26,434.54. The plaintiff claims substantial indemnity fees in the amount of $68,250 for himself as a self-represented lawyer.

Vigna is a lawyer who was called to the Bar of Québec in 1992. Vigna is not engaged in private practice and has no overhead expenses.

In *Fong v. Chan*, 1999 CarswellOnt 3955, [1999] O.J. No. 4600, 46 O.R. (3d) 330, 181 D.L.R. (4th) 614, 128 O.A.C. 2 (Ont. C.A.), the court held that the issue the right to recover award costs to a self-represented litigant remains within the discretion of the trial judge. The Court of Appeal held that self-represented litigants, whether legally trained or not, are not entitled to costs on the same basis as those of a litigant retaining private counsel. Losing party would reasonably expect to pay the sum of $30,000 plus disbursement in costs.

Mennes v. Burgess, 2011 ONSC 5515, 2011 CarswellOnt 10570 (Ont. S.C.J.), McDermot, J.

Mennes is an inmate at a federal penitentiary and has very limited resources with which to pay a costs award.

Notwithstanding that the applicant is, in effect, an indigent litigant and costs are effectively uncollectable, this does not mean that costs should not be ordered in a reasonable amount. The costs payable by the applicant to the Crown are in the amount of $4,000.

Propane Levac Propane Inc. v. Macauley, 2010 ONSC 293, 2011 CarswellOnt 108, [2011] O.J. No. 105 (Ont. Div. Ct.), J. Mackinnon J.

Macaulay appealed from the judgment of the deputy judge, which awarded costs of $1,650 to the respondent following the trial. The judge ordered that if the defendant had not returned the plaintiff's propane tank within 20 days, then the defendant was to pay the Plaintiff the sum of $2,000. The appellant says that the deputy judge erred in awarding an amount of costs that exceeds 15 percent of the claim without directing himself to the criteria under section 29 of the *Courts of Justice Act* ("*CJA*").

The appellant argued that the leave to appeal costs award was not required because section 133 of the *Courts of Justice Act* only requires leave where the costs award has involved an exercise of discretion.

It was desirable that the court comment upon the interplay between rule 14.07 of the *Rules of the Small Claims Court* and section 29 of the *CJA*.

The appeal lies from the award of the trial judge, not from the reasons given. If the award was supportable of the facts as the judge found them to be, in accordance with the applicable statutory criteria, then it should not be set aside simply for the lack of reference to a particular section.

See *Melara-Lopez v. Richarz*, 2009 CarswellOnt 6459 (Ont. S.C.J.); affirmed 2009 CarswellOnt 6333, [2009] O.J. No. 4362, 255 O.A.C. 160 (Ont. Div. Ct.), where the deputy judge awarded costs in excess of 15 percent of the amount claimed, in reliance on the rejection by the plaintiff of two offers, both of which were more favourable to him than the trial judgment. He referred to section 29 of the *CJA* and held that the plaintiff's failure to accept the offers was deemed to be unreasonable behaviour for the purposes of section 29 of the *CJA*. Rule 14.07 can be applied to award double costs, even if that amount then exceeds the 15 percent limit under section 29: See *Beatty v. Reitzel Insulation Co.*, 2008 CarswellOnt 1364, [2008] O.J. No. 953 (Ont. S.C.J.). The court cannot agree with that ruling. The rules must be read in a manner consistent with the statute, and it is improper in this context to hold in effect that the rule can trump the statute. See Ruth Sullivan, *Sullivan on the Construction of Statutes*, 5th ed. (Canada: LexisNexis Canada Inc., 2008) at 341.

Mustang Investigations Inc. v. Ironside, 2010 ONSC 3444, 2010 CarswellOnt 5398, 103 O.R. (3d) 633, 98 C.P.C. (6th) 105, 321 D.L.R. (4th) 357, 267 O.A.C. 302, [2010] O.J. No. 3184 (Ont. Div. Ct.).

The defendant had previously worked for the plaintiff. Following the termination of the defendant's employment the plaintiff sued him, alleging that he had unlawfully taken confidential information. The plaintiff brought a motion to discontinue the proceedings. The motions judge granted the leave to discontinue proceedings and awarded the defendant costs of $21,051. The costs award could be made to the self-represented litigant if it was demonstrated that, as result of lawyer-like work put in on file, remunerative activity was foregone. The costs award was calculated based on an error in principle and was plainly wrong.

See *Fong v. Chan*, 1999 CarswellOnt 3955, [1999] O.J. No. 4600, 46 O.R. (3d) 330, 181 D.L.R. (4th) 614, 128 O.A.C. 2 (Ont. C.A.), at para. 10 of costs endorsement, where the motions judge correctly set forth principles enunciated by the Court of Appeal in that case.

A leave to appeal a costs award is rarely granted because of the deference due to a judge in exercising his or her discretion. If the leave is granted, the standard of review to be applied is high, and the reviewing court may only set aside an award of costs if the trial judge has made an error in principle or if the costs award is plainly wrong (*Duong v. NN Life Insurance Co. of Canada*, 2001 CarswellOnt 483, [2001] O.J. No. 641, 25 C.C.L.I. (3d) 22, [2001] I.L.R. I-3963, 141 O.A.C. 307 (Ont. C.A.)). *Fong v. Chan* (*supra*) seminal case in this area of the law. See paras. 25 and 26 of reasons, Sharpe J.A.

See also *Izzard v. Goldreich*, 2002 CarswellOnt 4780, (sub nom. *Izzard v. Friedberg*) [2002] O.J. No. 2931 at para. 3 (Ont. Div. Ct.). Some six months later, Lane J. revisited the issue in *Korhani v. Bank of Montreal*, [2002] O.J. No. 4785, 2002 CarswellOnt 422 (Ont. S.C.J.). *Fong* applied by Gauthier J. in *Logtenberg v. ING Insurance Co.*, 2008 CarswellOnt 2930 (Ont. S.C.J.). See further *Huard v. Hydro One Networks Inc.*, 2002 CarswellOnt 3996, [2002] O.J. No. 4547, 30 C.P.C. (5th) 164 (Ont. Master).

The appeal was allowed. An award of $20,000 for counsel fees on a partial indemnity basis was set aside. The award for disbursements was confirmed at $1,541, against which may be set off the $200 awarded by the Master.

Carleton v. Beaverton Hotel, 2009 CarswellOnt 6303, [2009] O.J. No. 2409, 96 O.R. (3d) 391, 314 D.L.R. (4th) 566 (Ont. Div. Ct.).

After ordering the plaintiff to re-attend for examination for discovery and ordering production of various documents, the motions judge made an order for costs against the solicitor personally. There is a danger in awarding costs personally against solicitor for professional misconduct, as opposed to awarding costs for conduct that created unnecessary costs.

The motions judge had ordered the plaintiff to produce several records and to pay costs, but the order was not complied with. The motions judge ordered the plaintiff to re-attend for examination for discovery, and ordered the production of various documents. The defendants were awarded costs of $15,000. The motions judge made an order for costs personally against the appellant, the plaintiff's solicitor, under rule 57.07 of the *Rules of Civil Procedure*, R.R.O. 1990, Reg. 194. An appeal was allowed. The motions judge was primarily concerned with the solicitor's professionalism and demeanour. The test, however, under rule 57.07, involved costs unreasonably incurred and not with professional conduct generally. The motions judge's observation that the solicitor had been conducting the litigation in an unreasonable manner did not permit an identification of what conduct might have contributed to delay proceedings and incur unnecessary costs.

The two-part test is as follows: In the first step, it must be tested whether the lawyer's conduct fell within rule 57.07(1) in the sense of causing costs to be unnecessarily incurred. The second step is whether, in the circumstances, the imposition of costs against the solicitor personally was warranted.

Governing principles in awarding costs personally against a lawyer were set out by the Supreme Court of Canada in *Young v. Young*, 1993 CarswellBC 264, 1993 CarswellBC 1269, EYB 1993-67111, [1993] S.C.J. No. 112, [1993] 4 S.C.R. 3, [1993] 8 W.W.R. 513, 108 D.L.R. (4th) 193, 18 C.R.R. (2d) 41, 84 B.C.L.R. (2d) 1, 160 N.R. 1, 49 R.F.L. (3d) 117, 34 B.C.A.C. 161, 56 W.A.C. 161, [1993] R.D.F. 703 at para. 254 (S.C.C.). See also Lane J. in *Walsh v. 1124660 Ontario Ltd.*, 2007 CarswellOnt 982, [2007] O.J. No. 639 (Ont. S.C.J.); additional reasons at 2007 CarswellOnt 4459, [2007] O.J. No. 2773, 59 C.C.E.L. (3d) 238 (Ont. S.C.J.), wherein the learned judge refused to order costs against a lawyer personally where the primary complaint was unprofessional conduct, where such conduct was not related to delay.

Taucar v. University of Western Ontario, 2011 ONSC 6593, 2011 CarswellOnt 8833, [2011] O.J. No. 66 (Ont. Div. Ct.); additional reasons to 2011 ONSC 3069, 2011 CarswellOnt 5210, 336 D.L.R. (4th) 305, 281 O.A.C. 1 (Ont. Div. Ct.).

Costs. Scale and quantum of costs. Quantum of costs. The respondent university was entitled to recover costs, fixed on a partial indemnity basis at $15,000, all-inclusive, from the applicant, payable forthwith. The amount awarded was fair and reasonable having regard to general principles set out in R. 57.01(1) of *Rules of Civil Procedure*. The Application served no public benefit, but was brought only to advance the personal interests of the applicant. The applicant's counsel's approach consumed extensive time that added significantly to the costs of this litigation of the university. There was no good reason why the applicant should be spared from monetary consequences of risks that she should have taken into account before she embarked on this futile exercise.

Imineo v. Price, 2012 ONCJ 55, 2012 CarswellOnt 1036, 14 R.F.L. (7th) 235, [2012] O.J. No. 450 (Ont. C.J.), Justice R. Zisman.

The self-represented litigant's own time and expenses resulted in lost income-earning opportunities. The Court relied on *Fong v. Chan*, 1999 CarswellOnt 3955, [1999] O.J. No. 4600, 46 O.R. (3d) 330, 181 D.L.R. (4th) 614, 128 O.A.C. 2 (Ont. C.A.) and on *Korhani v. Bank of Montreal*, [2002] O.J. No. 4785, 2002 CarswellOnt 4223 (Ont. S.C.J.) to conclude that a self-represented litigant should not get costs for time and effort that any litigant would have had to devote to a case even if represented by lawyer. Costs should only be awarded to lay litigants who can show they have spent time and effort on work normally done by a lawyer hired to conduct the case and that, as a result, they suffered a cost by having to forego their regular remunerative activity, such as in this case where the self-represented natural father had taken days off work to prepare for the trial and had therefore lost wages. The unsuccessful mother and stepfather should compensate the natural father for some of his lost wages as a result of the unnecessary trial. The father should be reimbursed for various other out-of-pocket expenses, such as his share of the cost assessment report, the cost of process servers, the cost to summon witnesses, photocopy expenses, etc.

Hodgins v. Grover, 2011 ONCA 72, 2011 CarswellOnt 336, [2011] O.J. No. 310, (sub nom. *Grover v. Hodgins*) 103 O.R. (3d) 721, (sub nom. *Grover v. Hodgins*) 275 O.A.C. 96, (sub nom. *Grover v. Hodgins*) 330 D.L.R. (4th) 712, 5 C.P.C. (7th) 33 (Ont. C.A.); leave to appeal refused 2012 CarswellOnt 825, 2012 CarswellOnt 826, 432 N.R. 392 (note), (sub nom. *Grover v. Hodgins*) 295 O.A.C. 398 (note), [2011] S.C.C.A. No. 142 (S.C.C.).

Hodgins and Dorans commenced an action in the Small Claims Court. When the matter was heard, Hodgins and Dorans were self-represented, but Grovers had legal counsel. The deputy judge granted the claim for a one-thirteenth share of the legal fees plus additional relief. The Superior Court dismissed an appeal and a cross-appeal. The C.A. granted the Grovers' appeal but dismissed the cross-appeal.

The Application for leave to appeal to the Supreme Court of Canada was dismissed with costs.

C & F Industrial Parts Co. v. Wastecorp Pumps Canada Inc., 2011 ONSC 7499, 2011 CarswellOnt 14408 (Ont. S.C.J.).

The Court granted the defendant's motion to dismiss the plaintiff's action under Rule 21.0(3)(b) of the *Rules of Civil Procedure*, on the grounds that the plaintiff was without legal capacity to commence or continue the action. The defendant sought costs of $22,926.62.

The defendant relied on the offer to settle, which was rejected by the plaintiff. The defendant submitted it was entitled to its costs on a partial indemnity scale up to July 1, 2011 and thereafter on a substantial indemnity scale, by reason of Rules 49.02(2) and 49.10 of the *Rules of Civil Procedure*.

The plaintiff submits costs sought by the defendant were not proportional to the amount of the claim made by the plaintiff and the complexity of the action, and cited Rule 1.04(1.1) of the *Rules of Civil Procedure*. A fair and reasonable amount of $12,000 was awarded.

Guelph (City) v. Wellington-Dufferin-Guelph Health Unit, 2011 ONSC 7523, 2011 CarswellOnt 15131, 97 M.P.L.R. (4th) 105 (Ont. S.C.J.).

Costs are in the absolute discretion of court. The overall objective is "to fix an amount that is fair and reasonable for the unsuccessful party to pay in the particular proceeding, rather than an amount fixed by the actual costs incurred by the successful litigant." This is a "fundamental concept in fixing or assessing costs." See *Boucher v. Public Accountants Council (Ontario)*, 2004 CarswellOnt 2521, [2004] O.J. No. 2634, 71 O.R. (3d) 291, 48 C.P.C. (5th) 56, 188 O.A.C. 201 at paras. 24 and 26 (Ont. C.A.). See also *Gratton-Masuy Environmental Technologies Inc. v. Ontario (Building Materials Evaluation Commission)*, 2003 CarswellOnt 1564, [2003] O.J. No. 1658, 170 O.A.C. 388 at para. 16 (Ont. Div. Ct.).

A further objective is that, in appropriate circumstances, a costs order may be broadly described as in the public interest. See *Mahar v. Rogers Cablesystems Ltd.*, 1995 CarswellOnt 4279, [1995] O.J. No. 3711, 25 O.R. (3d) 690 (Ont. Gen. Div.) at p. 702 [O.R.]. Justice Sharpe exercised his discretion in favour of the unsuccessful applicant in a case involving the eligible capital expenditure portion of the fee charged for cable TV services. The city should be relieved of obligation to pay costs. Rule 57.01(1) sets out a non-exhaustive checklist of factors that should guide the Court in this regard. Each party shall bear its own costs.

Sioufi v. Yogeswaran, 2011 ONSC 6501, 2011 CarswellOnt 12405 (Ont. S.C.J.), J.P.L. McDermot, J.

The defendants were entitled to their costs of motion based on a dismissal of the plaintiff's motion. The issue was whether costs should be assessed on a substantial indemnity basis, or if they should be less than that.

Rule 20.06 of the *Rules of Civil Procedure*, R.R.O. 1990, Reg. 194 allows costs to be assessed on a substantial indemnity basis.

The only ground for substantial indemnity costs would be if the plaintiff "acted unreasonably" in bringing the motion. This was not the case. The defendants were entitled to their costs, but on a partial indemnity basis.

The court considered that this was an action under the simplified rules for only $30,000, just over the present limit of the Small Claims Court. The issues were not complex but only evidentiary. It was an uncomplicated motion for a relatively minor amount. The partial indemnity costs being claimed by the defendants were excessive. The costs to the defendants of the motion were set at $3,250.

Thomas v. Advantagewon Inc., 2011 ONSC 5309, 2011 CarswellOnt 9286 (Ont. Div. Ct.), Parayeski, J.

The appellant was entitled to costs. Rule 57 of the *Rules of Civil Procedure* sets out a number of factors that the court may consider in respect of reasonableness of costs being sought. The action was properly commenced and heard in Small Claims Court. The amount claimed was $10,000. Reasonable costs were $5,000, all-inclusive. The $17,185.79 that the appellant sought was anything but reasonable or appropriate.

Asco Construction Ltd. v. Epoxy Solutions Inc., 2011 ONSC 4464, 2011 CarswellOnt 7211, 2 C.L.R. (4th) 287, Lalonde J. (Ont. S.C.J.); reversed 2013 ONSC 4001, 2013 CarswellOnt 7940, [2013] O.J. No. 2699 (Ont. Div. Ct.)

Following a one-week trial, Epoxy, Plaintiff by Counterclaim, received a judgment for $23,230. Asco's claim for a breach of contract was dismissed.

In *Job v. Re/Max Metro-City Realty Ltd.*, [2000] O.J. No. 1449, 2000 CarswellOnt 1544 (Ont. S.C.J.), Mr. Justice Panet, at paras. 9 and 10, explained:

> Section 131(1) of the *Courts of Justice Act* provides that the costs of and incidental to a proceeding are in the discretion of the court and the court may determine by whom and to what extent the costs shall be paid. Rule 57.01(3) of the *Rules of Civil Procedure* provide that, in awarding costs, the court may fix all or part of the costs with or without reference to the Tariffs instead of referring them for assessment.
>
> The power to fix costs should only be resorted to when the judge, having received the parties submissions, is satisfied that he or she is in a position to do procedural and substantive justice in fixing the costs instead of directing an assessment (see *Murano v. Bank of Montreal*, [1988] O.J. No. 2897). Further, where possible, a trial judge should fix costs at the conclusion of trial or as soon thereafter as it is possible to do so. (See *Coughlin v. Mutual of Omaha Ins. Co.* (1992), 10 O.R. (93d) 787).

Zesta Engineering Ltd. v. Cloutier, 2002 CarswellOnt 4020, [2002] O.J. No. 4495, 21 C.C.E.L. (3d) 161 (Ont. C.A.) at para. 4 held as follows:

> In our view, the costs award should reflect more what the Court views as a fair and reasonable amount that should be paid by the unsuccessful parties rather than any exact measure of the actual costs to the successful litigant.

Further, in the Divisional Court's decision in *Gratton-Masuy Environmental Technologies Inc. v. Ontario (Building Materials Evaluation Commission)*, 2003 CarswellOnt 1564, [2003] O.J. No. 1658, 170 O.A.C. 388 (Ont. Div. Ct.) at para. 17 Justices Lane, Lax, and Power noted that:

> The amount at which costs are to be fixed is not simply an arithmetic function dependant on the number of hours worked and the hourly rate employed but rather, the party paying the costs should be subjected to an order which is fair and predictable. In other words, the party required to pay costs must not be faced with an award that does not reasonably reflect the amount of time and effort that was warranted by the proceedings.

The Ontario Court of Appeal in *Boucher v. Public Accountants Council (Ontario)*, 2004 CarswellOnt 2521, [2004] O.J. No. 2634, 71 O.R. (3d) 291, 48 C.P.C. (5th) 56, 188 O.A.C. 201 (Ont. C.A.) has directed that the parties engaged in litigation should pay the costs that they contemplated as being reasonable in the event one of them becomes an unsuccessful litigant. Armstrong J.S., speaking for the Court, pointed out in para. 26 of the decision that:

> [T]he express language of Rule 57.03(3) makes it clear that the fixing of costs is not simply a mechanical exercise. In particular, the Rule makes it clear that the fixing of costs does not begin and end with a calculation of hours, time and rates.

Asco had no other option but to commence an action in the Superior Court of Justice, given Epoxy's failure to dismiss its Claim for Lien. Asco was clearly successful in its declaratory relief as Epoxy finally agreed to discharge its Claim for Lien and allow the return of the security.

While costs must be fair and reasonable, it is not the case that the mere fact that costs exceed the damages awarded renders such an award inappropriate: see *Dybongco-Rimando Estate v. Jackiewicz,* (sub nom. *Dybongco-Rimando Estate v. Lee*) [2003] O.J. No. 534, 2003 CarswellOnt 546 (Ont. S.C.J.); see also *Monks v. ING Insurance Co. of Canada*, 2005 CarswellOnt 4155, [2005] O.J. No. 3749, 80 O.R. (3d) 609, 30 C.C.L.I. (4th) 55 (Ont. S.C.J.); additional reasons at 2005 CarswellOnt 4385, [2005] O.J. No. 3945, 30 C.C.L.I. (4th) 87 (Ont. S.C.J.); affirmed 2008 ONCA 269, 2008 CarswellOnt 2036, [2008] O.J. No. 1371, 90 O.R. (3d) 689, [2008] I.L.R. I-4694, 235 O.A.C. 1, 61 C.C.L.I. (4th) 1, 66 M.V.R. (5th) 38 (Ont. C.A.). As Lane J. wrote in *163972 Canada Inc. v. Isacco*, [1997] O.J. No. 838, 1997 CarswellOnt 636 (Ont. Gen. Div.):

> That the costs significantly exceed the amounts at stake in the litigation is regrettable, but it is a common experience and is well-known to counsel as one of the risks involved in pursuing or

defending a case such as this to a bitter end rather than finding a compromise solution. To reduce the plaintiff's otherwise reasonable costs on this basis would simply encourage the kind of intransigence displayed by the defendants in this case.

Asco ignored Epoxy's offer to settle, and presented evidence at trial that was untrue. Epoxy had to call witnesses summoned while the trial was ongoing because Asco failed to produce documents to counter Epoxy's evidence. The documents Epoxy needed were requested months prior to trial, and Asco's failure to produce the documents definitely lengthened the trial time.

Court allowed $20,000 in fees for work before and after the Offer to Settle and $15,000 for trial counsel fees, as well as $100 for settling the judgment and $1,000 for the cost submissions.

Shakur v. Mitchell Plastics, 2012 ONSC 4500, 2012 CarswellOnt 9681 (Ont. S.C.J.), D.J. Taliano J.

Following a three day trial, held on February 6, 7, and 8, 2012, plaintiff awarded the sum of $12,000 in a wrongful dismissal case. Since the amount awarded was within the jurisdiction of the Small Claims Court, no costs awarded pursuant to the discretion vested in the trial judge under Rule 57.05(1) of the Rules of Civil Procedure, which permits a trial judge to deny costs to a successful plaintiff under such circumstances.

It was argued on the appellant's behalf that at the time of the institution of the plaintiff's action in August 2010, the Small Claims Court's monetary jurisdiction was only $10,000. It was increased in January 2011 to $25,000. However, this case was never transferred to the Small Claims Court.

The policy considerations underlying Ontario's legislation was expressed by Nolan J. in *Lore v. Tortola*, 2008 CarswellOnt 1054, [2008] O.J. No. 769 (Ont. S.C.J.) at para. 17 where she states that:

> The Superior Court of Justice is currently overburdened with cases. Parties should not be rewarded with costs in matters that should have been properly brought in another forum designed to handle claims of a specific magnitude or monetary value, such as the Ontario Small Claims Court.

As Steele J. put it in *Yakabuski v. Yakabuski Estate*, 1988 CarswellOnt 537, 36 C.P.C. (2d) 189, 31 O.A.C. 257, [1988] O.J. No. 2870 (Ont. Div. Ct.), leave to appeal a costs order "should be granted sparingly and only in very obvious cases". This is not such a case.

Leave to appeal denied.

Coffey v. Horizon Utilities Corp., 2012 ONSC 2870, 2012 CarswellOnt 5944 (Ont. S.C.J.), J.A. Milanetti J.

Section 29 of the *Courts of Justice Act* refers to "unreasonable behaviour". The defendant submits that the plaintiff acted unreasonably in this action. There was unreasonable behaviour on the part of the plaintiff due to her lengthy and unproductive cross-examination of Mr. Hart. A self-represented litigant should not be expected to bear responsibility for fees of $2,100.00 per day when their claim was less than $1,000 on its best day. Costs of $300 plus HST plus $100 disbursements shall be payable to Horizon.

Dechene v. Dr. Khurrum Ashraf Dentistry, 2012 ONSC 5856, 2012 CarswellOnt 14226, 10 C.C.E.L. (4th) 57, D.A. Broad J. (Ont. Div. Ct.)

Under section 131 of the Courts of *Justice Act*, R.S.O. 1990, c. C. 43, the court has discretion with respect to the costs of and incidental to a proceeding.

The overriding principle in fixing costs is fairness and reasonableness (see *L. (A.) v. Ontario (Minister of Community & Social Services)*, 2006 CarswellOnt 3283, 35 C.P.C. (6th) 55, 32 R.F.L. (6th) 390, 211 O.A.C. 247, [2006] O.J. No. 2158 (Ont. Div. Ct.)).

Court would not allow a partial indemnity hourly rate of $350, being the maximum for counsel with more than 20 years experience in the guideline published by the Rules Committee. A small claims court appeal would not attract the maximum, absent unusual circumstances.

No disbursements for document filing and travel/mileage as they are not provided for in the tariff.

Respondent's costs of the appeal, payable by the appellant $8,500.00 plus HST.

Elliot v. Waterloo Regional Police Services, 2012 ONSC 2881, 2012 CarswellOnt 5956 (Ont. S.C.J.), Justice J. A. Milanetti.

In this action plaintiff successful.

The plaintiff seeks fees of $34,406.25 plus disbursements of $1,146.58.

Court must assess what a reasonable litigant would expect to pay if unsuccessful. Compensating for legal fees of 147 hours on such a relatively small claim is not reasonable. Similarly, a partial indemnity rate of $200 per hour (roughly two-thirds of a substantial indemnity rate which would therefore be approximately $300 per hour) is excessive for a lawyer with three years experience.

It is not within the reasonable expectation of an unsuccessful litigant that the trial preparation (including preparation of a factum) should be three times the actual time spent at trial for instance.

Fees of $12,500 plus disbursements and HST.

Oskar United Group Inc. v. Chee, 2012 ONSC 2939, 2012 CarswellOnt 6640 (Ont. S.C.J.), Justice J.R. McCarthy.

The Plaintiffs submit that they should be awarded substantial indemnity costs throughout. Defendants submit that the Plaintiffs' costs should, at best, be limited to 15 per cent of the amount recovered since the monetary amount recovered was within the monetary jurisdiction of the Small Claims Court.

Rule 49 will not apply to an offer that includes a fixed amount for costs instead of costs as assessed, as the court should not enter into an *ad hoc* assessment of costs as of the date of the offer: see *Noyes v. Attfield*, 1994 CarswellOnt 549, 19 O.R. (3d) 319, 29 C.P.C. (3d) 184 (Ont. Gen. Div.); affirmed 1997 CarswellOnt 4658, [1997] O.J. No. 4671 (Ont. C.A.).

The wording employed results in an escalating offer, which would be different on each successive day. That being the case, it is the kind of escalating offer which the Ontario Court of Appeal rejected as being inconsistent with rule 49: see *Rooney (Litigation Guardian of) v. Graham*, 2001 CarswellOnt 887, 53 O.R. (3d) 685, 9 C.P.C. (5th) 50, 198 D.L.R. (4th) 1, (sub nom. *Rooney v. Graham*) 144 O.A.C. 240, [2001] O.J. No. 1055 (Ont. C.A.). Offers of this kind do not comply with the rule: see *Yepremian v. Weisz*, 1993 CarswellOnt 462, 16 O.R. (3d) 121, 20 C.P.C. (3d) 357 (Ont. Gen. Div.).

Conduct that is reprehensible, scandalous or outrageous, either giving rise to the action or in the proceedings themselves, is grounds for costs on a substantial indemnity basis. Breach of trust supports an award of substantial indemnity costs: see *Young v. Young*, 1993 CarswellBC 264, 1993 CarswellBC 1269, EYB 1993-67111, [1993] 4 S.C.R. 3, 84 B.C.L.R. (2d) 1, 108 D.L.R. (4th) 193, 49 R.F.L. (3d) 117, [1993] 8 W.W.R. 513, 34 B.C.A.C. 161, 18 C.R.R. (2d) 41, 160 N.R. 1, [1993] R.D.F. 703, 56 W.A.C. 161, [1993] S.C.J. No. 112 (S.C.C.); *York Region Condominium Corp. No. 890 v. RPS Resource Property Services Ltd.*, 2011 ONSC 1509, 2011 CarswellOnt 1798, [2011] O.J. No. 1185 (Ont. S.C.J.). The conduct of Peter Chee was deceitful, reprehensible, scandalous and outrageous. It was that conduct which led to the action being brought.

Having considered all relevant factors under rule 57.01(1) and having regard to the Costs Summary of Fees and Disbursements filed by the Plaintiffs, I order that the Plaintiffs are entitled to costs against the Defendants fixed and payable in the amount of $50,000 (fifty thousand dollars), inclusive of fees, HST and disbursements. That amount is payable forthwith.

1258917 Ontario Inc. v. Daimler Truck Financial, 2012 ONSC 4094, 2012 CarswellOnt 8970 (Ont. Div. Ct.), Justice R. Smith.

417 Truck Centre ("417") was a successful respondent in this appeal and seeks its costs on a partial indemnity basis of $15,961.25 ($11,875.00 for fees plus disbursements of $2,250.00 plus HST of $1,836.25).

The appellant submits that the amount under appeal in this matter was only $9,129.02 and involved an appeal from a decision of the Small Claims Court. Daimler submits that it would be unfair and unreasonable to award costs in the amount of $15,961.25 based on the small amount that was in issue.

With regards to proportionality, the amount claimed for costs is greater than the amount at issue in the appeal, which was approximately $9,000.00. However, the issues involved were complex and counsel referred to approximately 12 cases, none of which had identical facts to the circumstances involved in this case.

Successful respondent on appeal should be indemnified for their reasonable costs which they were forced to incur in order to adequately respond to an appeal. An order that Daimler pay costs to 417 in the amount of $7,500.00 plus HST plus disbursements of $2,000.00 for a total of $9,500.00 plus HST.

Kipiniak v. Ontario Judicial Council, 2012 ONSC 5866, 2012 CarswellOnt 14214, 298 O.A.C. 389, [2012] O.J. No. 5299 (Ont. Div. Ct.).

This is an application for judicial review of a decision of the Ontario Judicial Council (OJC). It arises from a complaint that the applicant, Mr. Kipiniak, made to the OJC about the conduct of a Justice of the Toronto Small Claims Court.

Mr. Kipiniak's complaint was investigated by a complaint subcommittee of the OJC appointed for that purpose in accordance with the procedure mandated by the *Courts of Justice Act*, R.S.O. 1990 c. C.43 (CJA) and the OJC's Procedures Document.

Mr. Kipiniak understands that the issue raised in the application for judicial review became moot once the OJC had dealt with the complaint.

This relates to questions of law subject to appeal and is not an allegation about conduct engaging the jurisdiction of the OJC. In any event, these errors were corrected on appeal.

Court unable to grant Mr. Kipiniak any of the remedies he seeks and the application for judicial review must be dismissed. These are circumstances where Court would deny costs to the successful party. Costs to Kipiniak in the amount of $382.00 representing the filing fee of $181.00 for the judicial review application and the fee of $201.00 for perfecting the application.

Application dismissed.

Gowling Lafleur Henderson LLP v. Springer, 2013 ONSC 923, 2013 CarswellOnt 1627 (Ont. S.C.J.), Himel J.

Gowling Lafleur Henderson LLP brought action against Springer to collect unpaid accounts in the amount of $219,697.07. Springer filed a statement of defence pleading equitable set-off. Gowlings filed a reply. Gowlings now brings a motion under Rule 21.01(1)(a). Springer asks that motion be dismissed and that action proceed to trial.

The issue is whether the limitation period in the *Solicitors' Act*, R.S.O. 1990, c. S.15, applies and whether it bars a claim for equitable set-off.

The defendants argue that both proceedings are actions commenced by Gowlings to reco、 unpaid fees and are not applications under the *Solicitors Act* for an order referring the accounts for assessment. Counsel takes the position that the *Solicitors Act* does not apply.

16142 Yukon Inc. v. Bergeron General Contracting Ltd., 2012 YKSM 5, 2012 CarswellYukon 68 (Y.T. Sm. Cl. Ct.), Judge Ruddy.

The Yukon Territorial Court, from which the Small Claims Court is constituted, is a statutory court. Its jurisdiction is defined by statute, and its costs jurisdiction is therefore limited to what is contemplated by the *Small Claims Court Act*, R.SY. 2002, c. 204 and *Regulations*.

Counsel for the defendant seeking increased counsel fees pursuant to s. 58 of the *Small Claims Court Regulations*, OIC 1995/152 as amended by OIC 2011/04.

As a general rule, where legislation fixes a new scale of costs, the scale of costs applicable is that in place at the date of the assessment: *Assn. of Professional Engineers & Geoscientists (British Columbia) v. Mah*, 1995 CarswellBC 354, 9 B.C.L.R. (3d) 224, 61 B.C.A.C. 287, 100 W.A.C. 287, [1995] B.C.J. No. 1442 (B.C. C.A.). The jurisdiction of a Small Claims Court judge to award increased legal fees in special circumstances is analogous to the broad jurisdiction of a superior court to award special costs. Rather, it means that a Small Claims Court judge may look to superior court case law relating to special costs awards for guidance in determining what may amount to special circumstances sufficient to justify an award of increased legal fees pursuant to s. 58(2).

In general, an adverse finding of credibility, alone, would be insufficient to warrant an award of special costs. See *O'Cadlaigh v. Madiuk* (1994), 33 C.P.C. (3d) 116, 1994 CarswellBC 759, [1994] B.C.J. No. 2521 (B.C. S.C.) and *Creed v. Creed*, 2003 BCSC 1425, 2003 CarswellBC 2306 (B.C. S.C.).

Cases of fabricated evidence or document falsification, particularly where intended to mislead the court, have resulted in special costs awards (see e.g. *Hundley v. Garnier*, 2011 BCSC 1317, 2011 CarswellBC 2515 (B.C. S.C.)). Counsel for the plaintiff relies on *Olive Hospitality Inc. v. Woo*, 2008 BCSC 615, 2008 CarswellBC 971 (B.C. S.C.) to argue that, in order to attract a special costs award, the documents in question must be fundamental to a question at issue or create or perpetuate a dispute, and she says that the falsified documents here do not meet that threshold.

$5,000 is the appropriate amount to be awarded to the defendant pursuant to sections 58(2) and 74(1) of the *Regulations*.

Panesso v. Corporate Image Building Maintenance (June 26, 2013), Doc. 11-10979, 11-10979D15, Criger, Dep. J. (Ont. S.C.J.)

Matters tried together.

One representation fee is appropriate, and that representation fee must reflect the general purposes and mandate of the Small Claims Court, to make orders that are "considered just and agreeable to good conscience" (*Courts of Justice Act*, R.S.O. 1990, c. C. 43, s. 25).

In reasons for Judgment, court awarded a $2,500 representation fee absent Offers to Settle, and specified a $5,000 representation fee if Offers to Settle had been made. The $5,000 award: 1) Represents 20% of the amount awarded to Mr. Panesso and 2) Exceeds the 15% limit imposed by Section 29 of the Courts of Justice Act, because 3) A valid Rule 14 Offer to Settle was made and was not accepted by the losing party.

30. (1) Contempt hearing for failure to attend examination — The Small Claims Court may, in accordance with the rules of court, order a debtor or other person who is required to and fails to attend an examination respecting a default by the debtor under an order of the court for the payment or recovery of money, to attend before the court for a contempt hearing.

(2) **Finding of contempt** — The Small Claims Court may find a person to be in contempt of court at a hearing referred to in subsection (1), if the court is satisfied that,

(a) the person was required to attend the examination;

(b) the person was served, in accordance with the rules of court, with a notice to attend the examination;

(c) the person failed to attend the examination; and

(d) the failure to attend was wilful.

(3) **Power conferred** — For greater certainty, the power of the Small Claims Court to order, hear and determine a contempt hearing under this section is conferred on and may be exercised by the persons referred to in clauses 24(2)(a) and (b).

(4) **Limit on imprisonment in certain cases** — If a contempt hearing under subsection (1) is heard and determined by a person referred to in clause 24(2)(a) or (b), the court may make such orders respecting the person in contempt as are specified by the rules of court, but the court shall not make an order that the person be imprisoned for a period of more than five days.

(5) **Authority unaffected** — Nothing in this section affects the authority of the Small Claims Court to order, hear and determine contempt hearings where it is otherwise authorized by law.

1994, c. 12, s. 11; 2009, c. 33, Sched. 2, s. 20(8)

31. Appeals — An appeal lies to the Divisional Court from a final order of the Small Claims Court in an action,

(a) for the payment of money in excess of the prescribed amount, excluding costs; or

(b) for the recovery of possession of personal property exceeding the prescribed amount in value.

2009, c. 33, Sched. 2, s. 20(9), (10)

Commentary

Appeal limit

2. (1) For the purposes of clause 31 (a) of the Act, the prescribed amount is $2,500. O. Reg. 317/11, s. 1.

(2) For the purposes of clause 31 (b) of the Act, the prescribed amount is $2,500. O. Reg. 317/11, s. 1.

3. Omitted (provides for coming into force of provisions of this Regulation). O. Reg. 626/00, s. 3.

The minimum appealable limit under O.Reg. 244/10, in force July 1, 2010, was amended following the decision of Justice Heeney in *Action Auto Leasing & Gallery Inc. v. Robillard*, 2011 ONSC 3264, 2011 CarswellOnt 4105, 106 O.R. (3d) 281, 22 C.P.C. (7th) 414, 335 D.L.R. (4th) 439, 278 O.A.C. 293, [2011] O.J. No. 2453 (Ont. Div. Ct.), to correct a drafting error which erroneously implied that the amount of the order or judgment in question determined the right of appeal. As s. 31 plainly states, it is the amount claimed in the action which determines whether the minimum appealable limit is met, and not the amount of the order or judgment.

It should also be noted that the minimum appealable limit is exclusive of costs. This means, looking to caselaw dealing with the analogously-worded right of appeal under s. 19(1.2), that the appealable limit is inclusive of the amount of prejudgment interest claimed: see *Medis Health & Pharmaceutical Services Inc. v. Belrose*, 1994 CarswellOnt 486, 17 O.R. (3d) 265,

23 C.P.C. (3d) 273, 72 O.A.C. 161, [1994] O.J. No. 457 (Ont. C.A.); *Watson v. Boundy*, 2000 CarswellOnt 905, 49 O.R. (3d) 134, 130 O.A.C. 328 (Ont. C.A.).

In *Matlin v. Crane Canada Inc.* (2004), [2004] O.J. No. 3497, 2004 CarswellOnt 3648 (Ont. S.C.J.), at para. 6, Hockin J. stated, "There is no inherent appellate jurisdiction. A right to appeal can only be provided by statute or regulation."

In *Kourtessis v. Minister of National Revenue*, EYB 1993-67101, [1993] 1 C.T.C. 301, 1993 CarswellBC 1213, [1993] S.C.J. No. 45, 1993 CarswellBC 1259, 20 C.R. (4th) 104, [1993] 4 W.W.R. 225, 45 W.A.C. 81, 27 B.C.A.C. 81, 14 C.R.R. (2d) 193, 78 B.C.L.R. (2d) 257, 81 C.C.C. (3d) 286, 102 D.L.R. (4th) 456, [1993] 2 S.C.R. 53, 153 N.R. 1, 93 D.T.C. 5137 (S.C.C.), LaForest J. explained at paras. 15-16:

> Appeals are solely creatures of statute . . . There is no inherent jurisdiction in any appeal court. Nowadays, however, this basic proposition tends at times to be forgotten.
>
> There are various policy reasons for enacting a procedure that limits rights of appeal. Sometimes the opportunity for more opinions does not serve the ends of justice . . . This is especially applicable to interlocutory matters which can ultimately be decided at trial; see *Mills v. The Queen*, [1986] 1 S.C.R. 863. On this point, McLachlin J., speaking for the majority in *R. v. Seaboyer*, [1991] 2 S.C.R. 577, noted that there was a valid policy concern to control the "plethora of interlocutory appeals and the delays which inevitably flow from them" (p. 641).

The Superior Court of Justice provisions are grouped in sections 11–17. The Divisional Court provisions are grouped in sections 18–21. The Small Claims Court provisions are grouped in sections 22–33.1. These groupings provide a measure of insight into what the legislature intended when they drafted the *Courts of Justice Act*. The legislature chose to deal with appeals from the Small Claims Court in its own section, namely, section 31, separate and distinct from the other appeal routes leading to the Divisional Court, namely, those contained in section 19.

See e.g. *Gelber v. Allstate Insurance Co. of Canada* (1983), 1983 CarswellOnt 457, 35 C.P.C. 324, 41 O.R. (2d) 318, Krever J. (Ont. Div. Ct.)

In *Foster Printing & Lithographing v. Pack-Tech Industries Ltd.* (1997), 1997 CarswellOnt 4575, [1997] O.J. No. 4462 (Ont. Div. Ct.), MacPherson J. stated:

> By virtue of s. 31 of the *Courts of Justice Act*, the Divisional Court has jurisdiction with respect to a final order of the Small Claims Court. It cannot hear an appeal of an interlocutory order made by a judge of that court: see *Gelber v. Allstate Insurance* (1983), 41 O.R. (2d) 318 at 320 (A.C.J., per Krever J.).

In *Razavi v. Queen's University* (March 6, 2003), Doc. 02-SC-078395, 03-DV-000839, [2003] O.J. No. 903 (Ont. Div. Ct.), Kealey J. stated:

> The parties agree the order in question is interlocutory and it seems clear from a number of decisions to which I've been referred that the Divisional Court has no jurisdiction to hear an appeal from such an order.

See further *Sinardi Hair Design v. Knifton* (2003), [2003] O.J. No. 1666, 2003 CarswellOnt 1547, Lane, J. (Ont. Div. Ct.)

The test of whether an order is final or interlocutory is set forth in *Hendrickson v. Kallio*, [1932] O.R. 675, [1932] 4 D.L.R. 580 (Ont. C.A.). The Ontario Court of Appeal stated:

> The interlocutory order from which there is no appeal is an order which does not determine the real matter in dispute between the parties — the very subject matter of the litigation, but only some matter collateral. It may be final in the final in the sense that it determines the very question raised by the applications, but it is interlocutory if the merits of the case remain to be determined.

See further *V.K. Mason Construction Ltd. v. Canadian General Insurance Group Ltd. / Groupe d'assurance canadienne generale Ltée* (1998), 1998 CarswellOnt 4909, [1998] O.J. No. 5291, 42 C.L.R. (2d) 241, (sub nom. *Mason (V.K.) Construction Ltd. v. Canadian*

General Insurance Group Ltd.) 116 O.A.C. 272, *(*sub nom. *V.K. Mason Construction Ltd. v. Canadian General Insurance Group Ltd.)* 42 O.R. (3d) 618 (Ont. C.A.).

In *Matlin, supra,* Hockin J., sitting as a judge of the Small Claims Court, declined to quash an order made by Deputy Judge McDonald, also sitting in the Small Claims Court. Justice Hockin stated at para. 10, "My jurisdiction on this motion is the same jurisdiction as that of Judge McDonald; the jurisdiction of the Small Claims Court. Justice Hockin dismissed the appeal on the grounds that it lacked jurisdiction; the appeal should have been to the Divisional Court.

Judicial Bias

Lawyers do encounter judges who appear to be biased against them, their clients, or their causes. Judges are no less human than anyone else, and neither their legal training nor their best intentions can completely eliminate biases and preconceptions from their thinking. Judicial bias may be conscious or unconscious and may take many forms.

One antidote to potential judicial bias can be summed up in a single word: Listen. This is so very hard for lawyers to do, especially trial lawyers. After all, even if they are God's gift to the uninformed and the last great breed of orators, orators must know their audience if they want to be great. Many times hostile judges will signal — if not flat out tell you — what they do or do not want to happen in their court. Lawyers, however, are often too busy talking (or arguing) to pick up on these vital, and sometimes obvious, clues. Slow down and listen, and you may just learn something.

Sometimes the best victory is the one that is never fought.

There is no dishonour in reaching an agreement with the opposing side that might be better than a result you would get from the judge.

If you are not careful, however, persistence before a biased judge can turn you into the legal equivalent of the Washington Generals. You may know that the Washington Generals are the foils for the antics and victories of the Harlem Globetrotters. Each day the Washington Generals put on their uniforms, play in front of a hostile crowd, and get humiliated by the Globetrotters. This is not what any of us aspire to.

You learn from losing by focusing on what you did right, what you did wrong, how to keep doing the things you did right, and how to avoid doing the things you did wrong.

Be a professional. Be careful not to lose your integrity when you lose a hearing. Whatever you do, do not return a negative ruling or attitude from a trial judge with a negative comment or attitude. Rather, try to raise your professionalism each time the court is hostile. And self-reflection is important: what did you do right, what did you do wrong, what can you do to cure these mistakes, what other approach should you take with the court?

The Divisional Court

In the Divisional Court, you may represent yourself or be represented by a lawyer. If you wish to hire an Ontario lawyer, you can contact the Lawyer Referral Service operated by the Law Society of Upper Canada. The Lawyer Referral Service will provide the name of a lawyer who practices in the relevant legal area and will provide a free half-hour consultation. The telephone number for the service is 1-900-565-4577. Please note there is a charge of $6.00 to use this service. If you are calling from outside the province, you can reach the Lawyer Referral Service by dialing 1-416-947-3330.

If you are not in a financial position to retain the services of a lawyer, you may wish to contact the Legal Aid Ontario office closest to you to see if you qualify for legal aid. For more information, you may visit Legal Aid Ontario's website at <http://www.legalaid.on.ca.>

For information about the rights of French-speaking individuals in the Ontario justice system, refer to the brochure Justice in Both Languages, available in French and English on the Ministry of the Attorney General website at <http://www.attorneygeneral.jus.gov.on.ca.>

The Court office will pay for "in court" interpretation in any language other than French only if you apply for and are given a fee waiver certificate.

How to Conduct an Appeal

An appeal differs significantly from a trial and is *not* a rehearing of a case. There are no witnesses. In an appeal, the person whose case was not successful in the lower court argues that the trial judge made a mistake; for example, the judge may have applied the wrong law to the facts of the case. A person or party who appeals must identify the mistake he or she believes the judge made.

The appeal court does not change the trial judge's decision just because the Appeal judge(s) disagrees with it. The lower court is entitled to hear the evidence and come to its own decision. The appeal court may only change that decision if the lower court made a mistake as to the law or significantly misunderstood the evidence. It is important to note that not all errors in law will affect or change the outcome of a case on appeal.

Only people who were parties in the case in the lower court may appeal.

An appeal takes a considerable amount of time, effort, and money. Paperwork must be done correctly, and documents must be prepared and "served" on the relevant parties. Your interests may be served by hiring a lawyer; however, you can represent yourself in almost all circumstances. Remember that court staff are not permitted or trained to provide legal advice.

Before the hearing, the appeal judge(s) reviews the reasons for the decision of the judge appealed from, some or all of the evidence presented in the lower court, and the written arguments set out in the factums.

At the hearing, the judges hear oral arguments from the parties. These arguments are about the law and how it is to be applied to the evidence in the case (as outlined in the factums). You go first, then the respondent. You have the right to reply, but not to repeat anything already said. The purpose of reply is only to address issues raised by the respondent that were not addressed during your initial submissions. The judge(s) will usually ask questions as the appeal is presented.

Sometimes judges will give the decision without hearing the respondent's oral argument. Other times, the judges will give the decision orally after both sides have argued. Quite often the judges will "reserve" their decision. This means that they will take time to think about the arguments and provide written reasons later, in the form of a judgment.

The Court should contact you before the judgment is released so that you will know where and when you can pick it up.

Once the judgment is given, the parties must prepare an order.

Sometimes the judges will give directions about who should prepare the order. The Court may dismiss the appeal (which means that it confirms the decision of the lower court), allow the appeal and order a new trial, or allow the appeal and change the order of the lower court. The decision is final unless the Ontario Court of Appeal agrees to hear your case.

The remedy (relief) is what you want the court to do. The appeal must clearly state whether all or only specified parts of the order appealed from are in issue in the appeal, and whether you want the court to allow the appeal and overturn or vary (change) the decision.

It is common for the successful party to recover a portion of the expenses incurred. If the appeal is dismissed, you will usually have to pay the respondent's costs. Whether to award costs is in the discretion of the judges.

‿ːnerally, costs become payable following the judgment.

Once a final judgment is obtained, different steps can be taken, as noted by analogy to Rule 20 of the Small Claims Court.

A judgment creditor has no priority status. If the person who owes you money has few or no assets, you may find it impossible to collect the money owing under the judgment.

Divisional Court Appeals

Document	Required to serve the other party(ies)	Required to file with court	Copies filed with court	Fee for filing	Deadlines	Rule	Form
Notice of Appeal	Yes	Yes	1	Yes	Serve within 30 days of final order; file within 10 days of service.	61.04	61A
Appellant's Certificate Respecting evidence	Yes	No, but preferred.	1	No	Same as above	61.05	61C
Respondent's Certificate Respecting Evidence	Only required to serve if filed	No, unless further evidence is sought.	1	No	If needed, within 15 days after service of the Appellant's Certificate.	61.05	61D
Appeal Book and Compendium	Yes	Yes	1 or 3*	No	*No transcript*: within 30 days after filing the Notice of Appeal. *Transcript*: within 60 days after notice of completion of transcript.	61.10	61H
Exhibit Book	Yes, unless parties agree	Yes, unless parties agree otherwise.	1	No	Same as above	61.10.1	
Appellant's Factum	Yes	Yes, plus an electronic version.	1 or 3*	No	Same as above	61.11	

Divisional Court Appeals

Document	Required to serve the other party(ies)	Required to file with court	Copies filed with court	Fee for filing	Deadlines	Rule	Form
Transcript of Evidence	Yes, if transcript required.	Yes, if transcript required, plus electronic version if available.	1	No	A Certificate of Ordering a Transcript for Appeal must be filed within 30 days after filing the Notice of Appeal. Transcript itself must be served and filed within 60 days after notice of completion.	4.09 61.05 61.09	
Certificate of Perfection	No	Yes	1	Yes	*No transcript*: within 30 days after filing Notice of Appeal. *Transcript*: within 60 days after service of appeal book and compendium, exhibit book, transcript of evidence (if any) and appellant's factum.	61.12 61.12	
Respondent's Factum	Yes	Yes, plus electronic version.	1 or 3*	No	Serve and file within 60 days after service of appeal book and compendium, exhibit book, transcript of evidence (if any) and appellant's factum.	61.12	
Respondent's Compendium	Yes, if there is one	Yes, if there is one.	1 or 3*	No	Same as above	61.12	
Appellant's book of authorities	No	No	1 or 3*	No	With the factum or not later than the Monday of the week preceding the hearing.	n/a	
Respondent's book of authorities	No	No	1 or 3*	No	Same as above	n/a	

Notes:

*   For hearings before single judge, one copy required. For hearings before panel of three judges, three copies required.

Principle of Deference

The principle of deference means that an appellate court may substitute its own view of the evidence and draw its own inferences only if the trial judge committed a palpable and overriding error or made findings of fact or drew inferences that are unreasonable or unsupported by the evidence. See *L. (H.) v. Canada (Attorney General)*, 2005 CarswellSask 268, 2005 CarswellSask 273, REJB 2005-89538, [2005] S.C.J. No. 24, EYB 2005-89538, 2005 SCC 25, 333 N.R. 1, 8 C.P.C. (6th) 199, 24 Admin. L.R. (4th) 1, 262 Sask. R. 1, 347 W.A.C. 1, [2005] 8 W.W.R. 1, 29 C.C.L.T. (3d) 1, 251 D.L.R. (4th) 604, [2005] 1 S.C.R. 401 (S.C.C.) at para. 4.

See also *Housen v. Nikolaisen*, REJB 2002-29758, 2002 CarswellSask 178, [2002] S.C.J. No. 31, 2002 SCC 33, 286 N.R. 1, 10 C.C.L.T. (3d) 157, 211 D.L.R. (4th) 577, [2002] 7 W.W.R. 1, 219 Sask. R. 1, 272 W.A.C. 1, 30 M.P.L.R. (3d) 1, [2002] 2 S.C.R. 235 (S.C.C.), *Equity Waste Management of Canada Corp. v. Halton Hills (Town)* (1997), 35 O.R. (3d) 321, 1997 CarswellOnt 3270, [1997] O.J. No. 3921, 40 M.P.L.R. (2d) 107, 103 O.A.C. 324 (Ont. C.A.), *Gottardo Properties (Dome) Inc. v. Toronto (City)*, [1998] O.J. No. 3048, 1998 CarswellOnt 3004, (sub nom. *Gottardo Properties (Dome) Inc. v. Regional Assessment Commissioner, Region No. 9)* 111 O.A.C. 272, 162 D.L.R. (4th) 574, 46 M.P.L.R. (2d) 309 (Ont. C.A.), and *Waxman v. Waxman*, 2004 CarswellOnt 1715, [2004] O.J. No. 1765, 44 B.L.R. (3d) 165, 186 O.A.C. 201 (Ont. C.A.). The principle of appellate deference to a trial judge's fact-finding and inference-drawing applies even when the entire trial record is in writing. Deference recognizes that even on a written record, the trial judge "lives through" the trial while a court of appeal reviews the record only through the lens of appellate review. Deference also preserves the integrity of the trial process.

Case Law: *Cudini v. 1704405 Ontario Inc.*, 2012 ONSC 6645, 2012 CarswellOnt 15146, [2012] O.J. No. 5620 (Ont. Div. Ct.), K. van Rensburg J..

This is a decision in two appeals to the Divisional Court and a separate application proceeding commenced in the Superior Court. The respondent seeks an order quashing the appeals and dismissing the application.

Section 31 of the *Courts of Justice Act* is exhaustive with respect to the rights to appeal a decision of the Small Claims Court: *Grainger v. Windsor-Essex Children's Aid Society*, 2009 CarswellOnt 4000, 96 O.R. (3d) 711 (Ont. S.C.J.) at para. 12.

The prescribed amount pursuant to O. Reg. 244/10 is $2,500.

As Granger J. concluded through his careful analysis in the *Grainger* case (at paras. 12 through 22), there is no right to appeal an order of the Small Claims Court other than pursuant to s. 31. There is no right to appeal an interlocutory order of that court, and there is no right to request leave to appeal an order of the Small Claims Court to the Divisional Court or to the Superior Court. Section 31 is the sole source of appeal jurisdiction for an order of the Ontario Small Claims Court.

The order that Ms. Cudini seeks to appeal is the order of Deputy Judge Latimer dated September 8, 2011, dismissing her motion for a new trial under rule 17.04. Mr. Smith argues that since this is not a judgment for an amount greater than $2,500 there is no right to appeal. Even if the appeal could be considered to relate to the original judgment of Deputy Judge Boguski, the amount of the judgment was only $1,155.

See *Action Auto Leasing & Gallery Inc. v. Robillard*, 2011 ONSC 3264, 2011 CarswellOnt 4105, 106 O.R. (3d) 281, 22 C.P.C. (7th) 414, 335 D.L.R. (4th) 439, 278 O.A.C. 293, [2011] O.J. No. 2453 (Ont. Div. Ct.), Heeney J. Heeney J. concluded that it was the amount at issue in the action, and not the amount of the judgment that determined the plaintiff's right of appeal. He distinguished the decision in *Lambert v. Clarke* (1904), 7 O.L.R. 130, [1904] O.J. No. 116 (Ont. C.A.), where the defendant had sought to appeal a judgment for less than the then prescribed limit of $100, where the plaintiff had sued for a greater amount, on the basis that the only number that mattered in an appeal by a *defendant* was the amount of the judgment against him. The "matter in dispute" in the appeal was a judgment for less than the prescribed limit.

To the extent that Ms. Cudini's notices of motion and other materials filed in respect of this matter seek relief other than already addressed, her claims are dismissed. There is no basis for the interlocutory relief she has requested in the form of a "supervision order," or for an order that the two Divisional Court appeals be heard together. There is also no evidentiary foundation for an order to prevent Mr. Smith from bringing further proceedings against her.

Bougadis Chang LLP v. 1231238 Ontario Inc., 2012 ONSC 6409, 2012 CarswellOnt 14490, 300 O.A.C. 363, [2012] O.J. No. 5433, Justice Swinton (Ont. Div. Ct.)

Assuming that I have jurisdiction to grant leave to appeal a "no costs" order in the Small Claims Court pursuant to s. 133 of the *Courts of Justice Act*, R.S.O. 1990, c. C.43 ("CJA"), I would, nevertheless, refuse to grant leave to appeal.

Leave to appeal a costs order should be sparingly granted, and only if there has been an error in principle, or the costs award is clearly wrong. Moreover, the proposed appeal should raise an issue of some importance to the administration of justice that goes beyond the interests of the parties (*Poulin v. Poulin*, 2007 CarswellOnt 8268, 48 R.F.L. (6th) 196, [2007] O.J. No. 4987 (Ont. S.C.J.) at para. 22). Appeal of a final order of the Small Claims Court can be brought only if amount in dispute exceeds $2,500 excluding costs (see s. 31 of the *Courts of Justice Act*, and O. Reg. 626/00, s. 2).

The Deputy Judge should have given the parties an opportunity to make submissions on costs. However, I am not satisfied that a "no costs" award for the motion was wrong or based on an error in principle. Rule 15.07 of the *Small Claims Court Rules* provides that the costs of a motion shall be $100 exclusive of disbursements, absent special circumstances.

Proposed appeal does not raise any issue of public importance that warrants consideration on an appeal.

Accordingly, the motion for leave to appeal the costs order is dismissed.

Annis v. Barbieri, 2012 ONSC 6479, 2012 CarswellOnt 14504 (Ont. Div. Ct.), Justice Swinton.

The appellant appeals from a decision of a Deputy Judge dated June 17, 2011, which dismissed her claim for damages against the respondent Barbieri arising after she purchased a home from him.

Appeal dismissed.

Standard of review on appeal from a trial judge is correctness with respect to questions of law. Standard is palpable and overriding error (*Housen v. Nikolaisen*, 2002 SCC 33, 2002 CarswellSask 178, 2002 CarswellSask 179, REJB 2002-29758, [2002] 2 S.C.R. 235, 10 C.C.L.T. (3d) 157, 211 D.L.R. (4th) 577, 30 M.P.L.R. (3d) 1, [2002] 7 W.W.R. 1, 286 N.R. 1, 219 Sask. R. 1, 272 W.A.C. 1, [2002] S.C.J. No. 31 (S.C.C.) at paras. 8 and 10).

The respondent seeks costs of the appeal on a substantial indemnity basis because of the unproved allegations of fraud. Respondent has not been as forthright and open as he could have been.

The amount of $5,000.00 inclusive of HST and disbursements would be reasonable and fair.

Zeh v. Ricciuti, [1946] 1 W.W.R. 687 (Alta. T.D.) — The existence of a right of appeal does not oust the jurisdiction of the superior court to grant certiorari unless there are exceptional and extraordinary circumstances.

Kerr v. Raso c.o.b. Eagle Couriers (February 28, 1983) (Ont. H.C.), Krever J. — The court will entertain an appeal with respect to a refusal to set aside a default judgment because "the circumstances of the case define that the issues between the parties be determined on their merits.".

Ron Robinson Ltd. v. Canadian Indemnity Co., 1984 CarswellOnt 1354, 45 O.R. (2d) 124, 2 O.A.C. 359 (Ont. Div. Ct.) — No right of appeal exists from pre-trial proceedings.

Gelber v. Allstate Insurance Co. of Canada, 1983 CarswellOnt 457, 41 O.R. (2d) 318, 35 C.P.C. 324 (Ont. Div. Ct.) — "An order adjourning a trial on terms prior to its commencement is an interlocutory order. The Divisional Court is without jurisdiction to hear an appeal from same.".

Petrofina Canada Ltd. v. Lynn, 1978 CarswellOnt 400, 19 O.R. (2d) 97, 6 C.P.C. 94, 84 D.L.R. (3d) 129 (Ont. Div. Ct.) — The right of appeal under this section is substantive rather than procedural. Accordingly, where an action had been commenced before an amendment limiting appeals to decisions in which the sum in dispute exceeded $500 (1977, c. 52, s. 10) became effective, and where the sum in dispute was less than $500, the defendant's right of appeal survived the amendment, which was not intended to have retroactive effect.

394705 Ont. Ltd. v. Moerenhout, 1983 CarswellOnt 452, 35 C.P.C. 258, 41 O.R. (2d) 637 (Ont. Co. Ct.) — An application for a new trial in an action involving $500 or less should be made to the original trial judge.

Gillman v. Vic Tanny Holdings (July 8, 1983) (Ont. Div. Ct.), Krever J. — There is no appeal from an order granting a new trial, but the court will entertain an appeal from an order refusing to grant a new trial.

Savin v. McKay (1984), 44 C.P.C. 192 (Ont. Div. Ct.) — Findings of credibility are not to be disturbed on appeal as a general rule as long as there is some evidence upon which the judgment is based. Since this is an appellate court which is not designated for a retrial of the action, an error of law must be shown before the appeal will succeed.

Lawry v. Eggett (July 7, 1978) (Ont. Div. Ct.) — "What is the 'sum in dispute'? The 'sum in dispute' for the purpose of an appeal is the amount of the judgment appealed from and the amount of the original claim is immaterial whether the appeal is by the plaintiff or the defendant," per Craig J.

Buckler v. Earthwood Mfg. Ltd. (1980), 18 C.P.C. 223 (B.C. Co. Ct.) — Where to a claim for debt is added a claim for prejudgment interest, the total amount claimed must be considered in determining whether the amount claimed is within the jurisdiction of the Small Claims Court and, therefore, outside the jurisdiction of the County Court.

McClellan's Sand & Gravel Ltd. v. Rueter (1982), 140 D.L.R. (3d) 679 (Ont. Div. Ct.) — The *Small Claims Courts Act*, R.S.O. 1980, c. 476, s. 108, provides that an appeal from a judgment of the court is available only where the sum in dispute exceeds $500. In the case of a judgment in favour of the plaintiff for less than $500 for the value of work and services performed and dismissing the defendant's counterclaim for over payment for such work, the amount of the claim and counterclaim are not to be aggregated and, accordingly, no appeal lies from such a judgment.

Wager & Wager Ltd. v. Fraser (1981), 23 C.P.C. 5 (Ont. Div. Ct.) — In this case the claim for interest is totally dependent upon the success or failure of the claim for commission and it is a claim which would be in the discretion of the court. The appeal provisions of the Act do not entitle the appellant herein to engrafton the sum in dispute the interest claim in order to bring that claim within the provisions of s. 108. The sum in dispute herein does not exceed $500 exclusive of costs. To permit a claimant to engraft a claim for interest on the amount in dispute and thereby bring the matter within the appellate jurisdiction of this court would be inconsistent with the policy of the Act and the scheme thereof as evidenced by the wording of ss. 54 and 108 as amended.

Lewis v. Todd, [1980] 2 S.C.R. 694 (S.C.C.) — "This important case in part stresses the paramount role of the trial Judge in assessing damages.".

Texaco Can. v. Deganais (1983), 40 C.P.C. 64 (Ont. Div. Ct.) — For the purposes of this section, the "sum of dispute" was the amount of the judgment appealed against, where the "sum in dispute" excluded $500. Upon an appeal in garnishee proceedings, the amount was determined by reference to the actual amount of the judgment in the garnishee proceedings, not to the debt itself.

Auto Gallery Inc. v. Hook (February 4, 1994), Doc. No. Regina Q.B.350/93 (Sask. Q.B.) — Following a trial in a Small Claims Court, the respondent/plaintiff was awarded judgment. The appellant/defendant submitted in this appeal that the trial judge erred in admitting parole evidence.

The appeal was dismissed. The dispute findings were factual and supported by evidence. There was no error of law.

Faye v. Dureault's Allied Sales Ltd. (January 6, 1995), Doc. No. Regina Q.B.M. 262/94 (Sask. Q.B.) — The appeal was based on questions of facts. Determination whether a motor engine is "old" or "new" is a question of fact.

The application and appeal was dismissed. The appellant did not meet the tests for introducing new evidence on appeal, as he had failed to explain why the evidence was not adduced at trial. The issue before the trial judge was one of fact, namely whether the appellant's tractor had a new motor. The trial judge's finding on this issue should not be disturbed unless it was unreasonable.

Hiebert v. Peters (1994), 27 C.P.C. (3d) 369 (Man. C.A.) — Application for leave to appeal from an order dismissing a claim for $1,052 and bodily injury damages on two questions of law.

Application granted and appeal allowed on both questions with an order that the action be returned to the Small Claims Court for rehearing on its merits without prejudice to the Crown's right to re-argue its defence under s. 2(3). The appellant had not been permitted to give his evidence under oath on all points or to make answer to the preliminary objection concerning lack of notice.

The tendency of the law of recent times is to ameliorate the rigours of absolute rules and absolulte duty in the sense indicated as contrary to natural justice.

Roscoe Construction Ltd. v. North Hills Nursing Home Ltd. (1994), 25 C.P.C. (3d) 315 (N.S. S.C.) — The appellant had failed to comply with Regulations 17(2) and (3) with respect to service of the Notice of Appeal. In that circumstance, the Court may dismiss summarily or exercise discretion and consider equities. Proceed "as may be just".

An appeal is on the basis of the "record". In Small Claims Court matters, the record consists of the summary Report of the adjudicator and, where filed, the Decision and exhibits. The appellant may have a restatement by the adjudicator added to the "record".

Popa v. Thorpe (1994), 119 Sask. R. 304 (Sask. Q.B.) — An appeal from the Small Claims Court had to accept facts as found unless a palpable and overriding error present. Appeal allowed on assessment of damages. The case was returned to the Provincial Court for a new trial to damages.

Tapscott v. Marshview Foundations & Construction Ltd. (February 15, 1994), Doc. No. SAM 2197/94 (N.S. S.C.) — Application to set aside the decision of an adjudicator. The adjudicator had estimated the amount of deficiencies in a contract for work and based his award on the estimate without giving the appellant the benefit of adducing evidence.

Application allowed. The decision was set aside on the ground that it constituted a denial of natural justice against the appellant.

Natural justice is nothing more than fair play. The parameters of natural justice must be determined in each case, having regard to the specific circumstances therein. The fact that the adjudicator did not state a time frame within which the appellant was to provide the additional documentation and the fact that the decision was rendered without further notice to the appellant resulted in a failure to follow the requirements of natural justice.

Mandel v. The Permanent (1985), 7 O.A.C. 365 (Ont. Div. Ct.) — In a small claims trial, the trial judge intervened to manage the trial where there was unacceptable conduct by a party, to elicit the party's story to enable her to obtain further legal advice if necessary, and to clarify her evidence and to assist her when she appeared in person on the second day of the trial. The Divisional Court cautioned against the intervention of a trial judge on such a scale but found nothing in this case to justify a new trial. A judge may certainly assist a party, but not be unfair to the other party at the same time.

Shanks v. J.D. Irving Ltd. c.o.b. Irving Equipment Ltd. (1986), 7 C.P.C. (2d) 96 (N.S. S.C.) — The plaintiffs sued the defendant in Small Claims Court for damages. The defendant did not defend. The plaintiffs then commenced action against the defendant in the Supreme Court, Trial Division claiming damages arising out of the same transaction. The Small Claims Court had jurisdiction over the claim and pronounced a final judgment. Accordingly, the subsequent Supreme Court action was *res judicata*.

Air Canada v. Reilly (1989), 89 N.S.R. (2d) 217 (T.D.) — The applicant was entitled to judicial review even in light of the "privative" clause contained in section 32(2) of the Nova Scotia Statute, i.e., S.N.S. 1982, s. 2, which states "32(2) . . . The order or decision of the county court is final and is not subject to appeal . . .". Such clauses do not preclude review by way of judicial review by the courts.

Carrier v. Cameron, [1985] O.J. No. 1357, 1985 CarswellOnt 637, 6 C.P.C. (2d) 208, 11 O.A.C. 369 (Ont. Div. Ct.) — On an appeal, a new trial should not be directed unless some substantial wrong or miscarriage of justice has occurred. (See s. 144(6) [now s. 134(6)] of the *Courts of Justice Act*.) Having regard to the nature of this claim and the manner in which it was presented to the trial judge and his ultimate disposition thereof, it could not be said that such a miscarriage has occurred in this case. The Small Claims Court is required to provide a speedy and expeditious method for resolving claims of this nature and has a mandate to do so in a "summary way." (See *Small Claims Court Act*, R.S.O. 1980, c. 476, s. 57). While the trial judge clearly did err in failing to call on the parties for argument, that error in the circumstances of this case did not result in a substantial wrong or miscarriage of justice.

Burchill v. Yukon Travel (1997), 28 B.C.L.R. (3d) 95 (Y.T. C.A.) — Defendant appealing from small claims court judgment to Supreme Court. Supreme Court dismissing appeal. Defendant appealing to Court of Appeal. Section 2 of *Court of Appeal Act* allowing for appeal to Court of Appeal from every order of Supreme Court. Legislature not intending that appeal lie to Court of Appeal from small claims matter. Court of Appeal having no jurisdiction to hear appeal.

Mooney v. Cariboo Regional District (December 9, 1996), Doc. Quesnel 5363 (B.C. S.C.) — Plaintiff did not appear at trial some five and one-half years before and did not appeal order. Court had no jurisdiction to determine issues again. Action dismissed.

Sier Bath Deck Gear Corp. v. Polymotion Ltd. (1996), 30 O.R. (3d) 736, 1996 CarswellOnt 3873, 42 C.B.R. (3d) 1, 15 O.T.C. 323 (Ont. Gen. Div.) — Defendant appealed judgment awarding plaintiff $6,000, on ground that plaintiff, Indiana corporation, was undischarged bankrupt and had sued to recover debt created before bankruptcy. Trial judge concluded effect of order permitted action to proceed as framed. Abandonment not assignment. Small Claims Court Rules silent as to right of undischarged bankrupt to sue for recovery of property rights. Appeal allowed and claim dismissed.

De Vos v. Robertson (1997), 103 O.A.C. 231, 14 C.P.C. (4th) 105 (Ont. C.A.) — The trial judge owes it to the parties to make clear his findings of credibility and fact, and to address the issues so that each of the parties would know that his or her case has been understood and carefully dealt with. This is particularly so after judgment has been reserved for such a long time. See *R. v. Richardson* (1992), 9 O.R. (3d) 194 at 201 (Ont. C.A.), Sopinka J. in *R. v. Feeney* (1997), 212 N.R. 83 at 105–6 (S.C.C.); *Koschman v. Hay* (1977), 17 O.R. (2d) 557 (Ont. C.A.) and *Mitro v. Mitro* (1977), 1 R.F.L. (2d) 382 (Ont. C.A.); *All Nations Trading Corp. v. Lumbermen's Mutual Casualty Co.* (1982), 37 O.R. (2d) 12 (Ont. C.A.); and the decision of Sopinka J. in *Hollis v. Dow Corning Corp.*, [1995] 4 S.C.R. 634 (S.C.C.).

New Brunswick (Department of Health & Community Services) v. Clark (October 16, 1998), Doc. 281/97/CA (N.B. C.A.) — Appeal dismissed. The grounds for appeal were of findings of fact and, therefore, could not be appealed.

J.J. Nichvolodov & Co. v. Brandon (July 2, 1998), Doc. Yorkton Q.B. 397/97 (Sask. Q.B.), Rice, Turnbull and Larlee JJ.A. — Appeal by the defendant. Appellant argued that trial judge was biased in favour of the respondent due to certain remarks he made during trial and that the trial judge slept during portions of the cross-examination of the respondent. Appeal dismissed. The trial judge's interjections at trial were justified in order to keep the questions relevant. There was no evidence that the trial judge slept through portions of the trial.

Kay v. Tynio (April 28, 1998), Doc. Toronto 588/97 (Ont. Div. Ct.) — Appeal by the plaintiff from trial judgment in Small Claims Court dismissing her action against the defendant dentist. Appeal dismissed. There was evidence to support the trial judge's conclusions, and he made reference to most of the evidence before him in his reasons for judgment.

Manz v. Loewen (March 12, 1999), Doc. Regina Q.B.G. 2759/98 (Sask. Q.B.), Armstrong J. — Manz was unrepresented by counsel at trial. Appeal dismissed. In Small Claims Court mistakes that could have been avoided in the presence of counsel did not by themselves afford a right of appeal. Nothing suggested that there would have been a different result if Manz had been specifically directed that she had an opportunity to cross-examine.

Salem v. Air Canada (January 4, 1999), Doc. S.H. 149810/98 (N.S. S.C.), Nathanson J. — Appeal from dismissal of Small Claims Court action. Salem claimed that the adjudicator displayed bias by grimacing during the hearing. She exceeded her jurisdiction, and she failed to heed the requirements of natural justice by delivering a summary of facts and reasons outside the 30-day time limit required by the Act. Appeal dismissed. The trial judge's grimace did not necessarily indicate bias. No jurisdictional error was made, and the requirements of natural justice were met.

Kowalsky v. Baker (1998), 107 O.A.C. 297 (Ont. Div. Ct.) — Plaintiff appealed from the dismissal of small claims action, asserting judge excessively intervened in defendant's cross-examination. Defendant was self-represented. Divisional Court rejected the plaintiff's argument. The judge's interventions were for purpose of controlling the proceedings and clarifying the evidence and nature of cross-examination. The court rejected defendant's argument that it was appropriate for a trial judge to intervene to assist an unrepresented litigant. Trial judge appeared to have participated in an expectation that trial would proceed in a certain manner. Appeal allowed.

Pavlovic v. Pav's Complete Excavating & Landscaping Services Ltd. (December 10, 1998), Doc. Kamloops 26806 (B.C. S.C.) — Appellant sought order to have appeal from Small Claims Court heard by way of trial *de novo*. Courts of Appeal are generally reluctant to order new trials. See *Kralj v. Murray* (1953), [1954] 1 D.L.R. 781 (Ont. C.A.) at 784 *per* Hope J.A. The requirements for the admission of fresh evidence are: 1. That the evidence was not discoverable by reasonable diligence before the end of the trial; 2. That the evidence is wholly credible; and 3. That the evidence would be practically conclusive of an issue before the court. Appellants did not satisfy conditions. Application dismissed.

Hilson v. Richmond Chandler Investments Ltd. (1999), 117 O.A.C. 297 (Ont. C.A); reversing (1996), 25 C.C.E.L. (2d) 75, 20 O.T.C. 22 (Ont. Gen. Div.) — Interventions by the trial judge. The law is clear "that not only should justice be done, but should manifestly and undoubtedly be seen to be done". *R. v. Justices of Sussex* (1923), [1924] 1 K.B. 256 *per* Lord Hewitt at 259. *R. v. Valley* (1986), 26 C.C.C. (3d) 207 (Ont. C.A.), Martin J.A. at 232. In *R. v. S. (R.D.)*, 1997 CarswellNS 301, 1997 CarswellNS 302, [1997] S.C.J. No. 84, 151 D.L.R. (4th) 193, 118 C.C.C. (3d) 353, 10 C.R. (5th) 1, 218 N.R. 1, 161 N.S.R. (2d) 241, 477 A.P.R. 241, [1997] 3 S.C.R. 484, 1 Admin. L.R. (3d) 74 (S.C.C.), L'Heureux-Dubé and McLachlin J. at 503 [S.C.R.]. As said in *Sorger v. Bank of Nova Scotia*, 1998 CarswellOnt 2108, 109 O.A.C. 130, 160 D.L.R. (4th) 66, 39 O.R. (3d) 1 (Ont. C.A.) at 2: "There is a reasonable apprehension of a judicial mind which was closed to the appellant's case rather than one which addressed that case with fairness and impartiality." Appeal allowed.

Waddell v. Dover Industries Ltd. (October 29, 1998), Doc. 107/98/CA (N.B. C.A.) — Appeal refused because it was not on a question of law alone, as required by Rule 75.18 (1) of the Rules of Court, N.B. Reg. 82-73.

Smith v. Harbour Authority of Port Hood (1998), 20 C.P.C. (4th) 277, (sub nom. *Smith v. Port Hood Harbour Authority)* 169 N.S.R. (2d) 323, 508 A.P.R. 323 (N.S. C.A.) — Section 39 of the *Court and Administrative Reform Act*, S.N.S. 1996, c. 23, added s-s. (6) to s. 32 of the *Small Claims Court Act*, R.S.N.S. 1989, c. 430, making a decision of the Supreme Court on appeal from the Small Claims Court final and not subject to further appeal. This section extinguishing the right of appeal was proclaimed in force by the Lieutenant Governor on April 1, 1997. The Supreme Court of Canada has ruled that a right of appeal crystallized on the day the proceedings are instituted in the lower courts and not on the day of judgment or the day on which deliberation begins. The Small Claims Court is constituted pursuant to the Province's power to legislate by virtue of s. 92(14) of the *Constitution Act, 1982* — administration of justice in the Province — does not alone preclude that Court from hearing matters which fall within federal jurisdiction. See *Ontario (Attorney General) v. Pembina Exploration Canada Ltd.*, [1989] 1 S.C.R. 206, 57 D.L.R. (4th) 710, 92 N.R. 137, (sub nom. *William Siddall & Sons Fisheries v. Pembina Exploration Can. Ltd.)* 33 O.A.C. 321 (S.C.C.) at 228 (S.C.R.). It is immaterial that s. 55 of the *Small Claims Court Act* of Ontario considered by the Supreme Court in *Pembina, supra*, conferred wider jurisdiction upon the court than does the *Small Claims Court Act* in this Province.

United Lumber & Building Supplies Co. v. 1104483 Ontario Inc. (May 27, 1998), Doc. Barrie G20769/97 (Ont. Gen. Div.) — Appeal on grounds of apprehension of bias by the deputy judge. The presumption which faced the appellant not rebutted. Court found that a reasonable person would conclude that the judge acted fairly to both sides in identifying possible conflicts of interest for the parties and proceeding only after both sides agreed to continue.

Stewart v. Strutt, 1998 CarswellBC 565, [1998] B.C.J. No. 636 (B.C. S.C.) — Appeal brought on record pursuant to Part 2 of the *Small Claims Act*, R.S.B.C. 1996, c. 430. The reasons for a new trial are not defined in the *Small Claims Act*, but I conclude that there must be more than just evidentiary oversights or omissions before the parties can be put to the expense of a new trial. Court reluctant to disturb findings of fact based on the evidence and court's assessment of the witnesses who appeared for both the claimants and the respondent.

Kendall v. Rankin (November 24, 1998), Doc. Vancouver A981638, 95-20844 (B.C. S.C.) — Appeal under the *Small Claims Act*, arises from dismissal of claim for the payment of the appellants' legal account for services rendered. Appellants' appeal relied on basis of *quantum meruit*. See *Peel (Regional Municipality) v. Canada*, (sub nom. *Peel (Regional Municipality) v. Ontario)*, [1992] 3 S.C.R. 762 (S.C.C.). *Quantum meruit* is a category even though no contract.

Sorger v. Bank of Nova Scotia, 1998 CarswellOnt 2108, 109 O.A.C. 130, 160 D.L.R. (4th) 66, 39 O.R. (3d) 1 (Ont. C.A.) — Trial judge requested plaintiffs lead evidence that they had attempted to recover from third parties. He repeatedly commented plaintiffs' case wasting court's time. He also prejudged the credibility of the plaintiffs' key witness. His reasons for judgment were only a compilation of parties' written submissions and 29 bald findings taken verbatim from the defendants' material. No analysis of evidence and no consideration of jurisprudence. Court of Appeal held that cumulative effect of trial judge's actions raised a reasonable apprehension of bias.

Hebert v. Morris (June 30, 1998), Doc. AI 98-30-03766 (Man. C.A. [In Chambers]) — The applicant sought leave to appeal from the decision of a Queen's Bench judge on a small claims matter. The appeal was dismissed. Leave to appeal may only be granted if the question of law has been identified of such sufficient importance to warrant review by the court. Other evidence on record of a contradictory nature did not constitute error in law. At most it would be an error of fact, from which there was no right of appeal.

Tsaoussis (Litigation Guardian of) v. Baetz (1998), (sub nom. *Tsaoussis v. Baetz)* 112 O.A.C. 78, 165 D.L.R. (4th) 268, 41 O.R. (3d) 257, 27 C.P.C. (4th) 223 (Ont. C.A.); leave to appeal refused (1999), (sub nom. *Tsaoussis v. Baetz)* 236 N.R. 189 (note), (sub nom. *Tsaoussis v. Baetz)* 122 O.A.C. 199 (note) (S.C.C.) — A three-year-old child was injured in 1990. The settlement for $5,420 was approved in 1992. In 1994 the mother commenced an action for $2 million. The defendant relied on the settlement. Inaccuracy alone did not justify setting aside judgments. New action was based on evidence developed after the settlement, but which could have been obtained earlier.

Wan v. R.I. Van Norman Ltd. (December 7, 1998), Doc. Saskatoon Q.B.G. 1525/98 (Sask. Q.B.) — The appeal court can intervene only if the trial judge erred in law or if he or she made a palpable and overriding error in findings of fact that are not reasonably supported by evidence. The appellant failed to establish that the trial judge made an appealable error.

Saskatchewan Kodokan Black Belt Assn. v. Bergey (1999), (sub nom. *Saskatchewan Kodokan Black Belt Association Inc. v. Bergey)* 183 Sask. R. 270 (Sask. Q.B.) — The applicant obtained a judgment against the respondent in small claims action. The respondent appealed but neglected to requisition the transcript of evidence presented at trial. Curative provision of s. 47 of *Small Claims Act* (Saskatchewan) did not override the deemed dismissal provision in s. 39(6) when the transcript was not filed before the end of the extension period.

Higgins v. Saunders (November 24, 1998), Doc. C.A. 145737 (N.S. C.A.) — The Small Claims Court adjudicator was found to have met the requirements by simply providing copy of a seven-page decision. The decision revealed a finding of law and fact. This enabled the Supreme Court to reach a conclusion whether or not any grounds for appeal listed in s. 32(1) existed.

Specht v. Yeo, 1999 BCCA 499, 130 B.C.A.C. 12, 211 W.A.C. 12 (B.C. C.A.) — The plaintiff recovered damages less than had actually been paid to the plaintiff by the defendant's insurer prior to trial. The defendant's appeal of the trial judge's ruling on costs was allowed. The plaintiff's claim was dismissed and the defendant was entitled to costs.

Delgamuukw v. British Columbia (1997), 153 D.L.R. (4th) 193, 220 N.R. 161, 99 B.C.A.C. 161, 162 W.A.C. 161, [1997] 3 S.C.R. 1010, [1998] 1 C.N.L.R. 14, [1999] 10 W.W.R. 34, 66 B.C.L.R. (3d) 285 (S.C.C.) — The Court was reluctant to interfere with findings of fact made at trial, when it was based on assessment of testimony. The appellate courts should not substitute their own findings of fact for those of the trial judge. See *Stein v. "Kathy K." (The)*, 1975 CarswellNat 385, 1975 CarswellNat 385F, [1976] 1 Lloyd's Rep. 153, 6 N.R. 359, 62 D.L.R. (3d) 1, [1976] 2 S.C.R. 802 (S.C.C.), per Ritchie J., at 808 and *N.V. Bocimar S.A. v. Century Insurance Co. of Canada*, [1987] 1 S.C.R. 1247 (S.C.C.). The policy reason underlying this rule is protection of "[t]he autonomy and integrity of the trial process":

Schwartz v. R., 1996 CarswellNat 422F, 1996 CarswellNat 2940, 17 C.C.E.L. (2d) 141, (sub nom. *Minister of National Revenue v. Schwartz)* 193 N.R. 241, (sub nom. *Schwartz v. Canada)* 133 D.L.R. (4th) 289, 96 D.T.C. 6103, 10 C.C.P.B. 213, [1996] 1 C.T.C. 303, (sub nom. *Schwartz v. Canada)* [1996] 1 S.C.R. 254 (S.C.C.) at 278.

Strilets v. Vicom Multimedia Inc. (2000), [2001] 1 W.W.R. 342, 49 C.P.C. (4th) 347, 85 Alta. L.R. (3d) 168, 274 A.R. 6, 2000 CarswellAlta 946 (Alta. Q.B.) — The plaintiff applied to extend time for filing transcript. The Civil Claims division of the provincial court established to promote a cost efficient resolution of relatively minor claims. Stringent time limits would defeat the purpose of allowing parties not versed with in legal system to have their day in court. The criteria was set out in *Cairns v. Cairns*, [1931] 4 D.L.R. 819, 26 Alta. L.R. 69, [1931] 4 D.L.R. 819, 1931 CarswellAlta 52 (Alta. C.A.).

Marchand v. Public General Hospital Society of Chatham (1993), 20 C.P.C. (3d) 68, 1993 CarswellOnt 455 (Ont. Gen. Div.) — None of the conduct complained about established judicial bias nor gave rise to reasonable apprehension of bias. The trial judge conducted the case fairly and thoroughly.

Suckling v. Peacey, 2000 BCSC 1397, 2000 CarswellBC 1933 (B.C. S.C.) — Appeal from Small Claims Court was allowed as the trial judge misapprehended facts.

Ivens v. Automodular Assemblies Inc. (2000), 2000 CarswellOnt 3146 (Ont. S.C.J.) — The plaintiff claimed $8,000 in costs after receiving a judgment of approximately $600. The claim for costs was out of proportion to the worth of the case. Costs of $2,500 were awarded. The plaintiff tried to enhance her common law damages by emphasizing human rights grounds to attract significant damages.

Brett Motors Leasing Ltd. v. Welsford (1999), 181 N.S.R. (2d) 76, 560 A.P.R. 76, 1999 CarswellNS 410 (N.S. S.C.) — An Appeal Court judge does not have the authority to go outside the facts as found by the adjudicator and determine own findings of fact.

S. (M.L.) v. Dorran, 1999 BCCA 769, 131 B.C.A.C. 187, 214 W.A.C. 187, 1999 CarswellBC 2877 (B.C. C.A. [In Chambers]); affirmed 2000 BCCA 125, 2000 CarswellBC 440 (B.C. C.A.) — The plaintiff sued the defendant in Small Claims Court for harassment. The claim was dismissed. The application for judicial review was dismissed and further application was brought to file application to extend time to appeal the dismissal. The plaintiff had no right of appeal under the *Judicial Review Procedure Act*, R.S.B.C. 1996, c. 241.

Chong v. MacKinnon (1989), 93 N.S.R. (2d) 361, 242 A.P.R. 361 (N.S. Co. Ct.) — Since the plaintiff appellant did not avail himself of the procedures available to him, his appeal failed.

G. v. B.S. Inc. and Di Paola (June 23, 1989) (Div. Ct.) — A new trial was granted where the trial judge participated too much in the examination of witnesses and denied the right of cross-examination.

Creditel of Canada Ltd. v. Hamilton Builders' Supply Inc. (May 19, 1989) (Div. Ct.) — A new trial was ordered where the trial judge erred in applying the principle of res judicata without a proper hearing of the plaintiff's case.

Furnell v. Whangarei High School Board, [1973] A.C. 660 at 679. — The denial of "natural justice" has been defined to be nothing more than "fair play in action".

Bissoondatt v. Arzadon (October 13, 1992), Doc. No. 252/92 (Ont. Div. Ct.) — An appellate court will not intervene unless it un mistakenly appears from the evidence that the trial judge has not taken proper advantage of having heard and seen the witnesses.

C.V.B.S. v. DiPaola (April 30, 1993), Montgomery, J. — The appeal was allowed on the basis that the trial judge entered into the arena and intervened too far in the examination of witnesses. He also denied the right to cross-examine.

Rivas v. Groumoutis (1994), 45 A.C.W.S. (3d) 10 (B.C. S.C.) — Appellant failed to comply with the provisions of ss. 8 and 11 of the *Small Claims Court Act* (B.C.), The Act did not contain provision which the court could apply to grant relief from strict compliance with the Act, even in extraordinary circumstances. Appeal was dismissed.

Happy Valley Mobile Home Park Ltd. v. Coutu (1994), 45 A.C.W.S.(3d) 628 (B.C. S.C.) — Judgment was granted against the company and not the principal shareholder, but the company had not been named as the defendant. Appeal by the company on the basis of lack of jurisdiction of court,was allowed. The matter was remitted to the Small Claims Court.

Ideal Concrete Ltd. v. Rhyno (1993), 118 N.S.R. (2d) 118 (N.S. Co. Ct.) — Denial of natural justice shown where defendant arrived for trial 13 minutes late and was not allowed to present its case.

Dunlop v. Anchor Towing & Recovery Ltd. (1994), 21 C.P.C. (3d) 147 (N.S. C.A.) — The respondent appellant had filed a notice of appeal to the Nova Scotia Court of Appeal from a decision of the Nova Scotia Supreme Court. The Supreme Court decision was an appeal from adjudication of the Small Claims Court action. The applicant applied to quash the notice of appeal alleging that no right of appeal existed. When the action was commenced, legislation was provided for the appeal to the County Court which was the final appeal. Subsequent to the commencement of the Small Claims Court action but prior to a decision being rendered, the *Court Reform Act*, S.N.S. 1992, c. 16, was passed, absorbing the County Court into the Supreme Court and allowing appeals from the Supreme Court to the Court of Appeal. The Court held that the plaintiff's right of appeal had crystallized on the day the action was commenced and that it would not be extended by a subsequent passage of new legislation. An extension of right of appeal, apparently allowed by the new Act, was a substantive right, but could not have retroactive effect unless it was purely beneficial which it was not. The notice of Appeal was quashed.

The change in jurisdiction from the County to the Supreme Court provided by the Act was procedural in nature. The resulting extension of right of appeal in the Small Claims Court cases was a substantive right, but did not have the retroactive effect, as the charge was not purely beneficial to all parties.

Estevan Motors Ltd. v. Anderson, 1995 CarswellSask 132, 129 Sask. R. 70 (Sask. Q.B.) — Section 40 of the Saskatchewan *Small Claims Enforcement Act* permits the court (on appeal) to give judgment that the trial judge should have given. The appeal court will not retry the case, but will confine itself to correcting errors of law and reversing unreasonable findings of fact.

Currie v. Fundy Computer Services Ltd. (1994), 33 C.P.C. (3d) 359 (N.B. C.A.) — The defendant appealed from a small claims judgment on the ground that he had been denied natural justice in the conduct of the hearing. The defendant's representative at the hearing had the opportunity to conduct an examination of his witnesses and cross-examination of the plaintiff's witness, to make representations on behalf of the defendant and, in fact, had made a brief summary of the position of the defendant at the close of the hearing. The practice of swearing all prospective witnesses as a group was not a denial of a fair hearing.

32262 B.C. Ltd. v. Trans Western Express Inc. (1995), 38 C.P.C. (3d) 201 (B.C. S.C.) — Section 13 of the *Small Claims Act* (B.C.) allowed the Supreme Court of British Columbia to award costs to any party to an appeal, in accordance with the rules of court. A party who failed on an appeal should be subject to an award of costs from the appeal. A defendant who succeeded on an appeal had a moral claim to costs of the appeal, having been brought into litigation at the instance of the plaintiff. A plaintiff who has rightly chosen the Provincial Court as the proper forum for his claim but has been denied victory wrongly should, succeeding on appeal, ordinarily be entitled to an award of costs. That general rule was subject to the recognized exception where the case was won in the Supreme Court on the basis of evidence or a submission not presented in the Provincial Court.

Shoppers Mortgage & Loan Corp. v. Health First Wellington Square Ltd. (1995), 38 C.P.C. (3d) 8 (Ont. C.A.) — During examination-in-chief and cross-examination of witnesses, the trial judge intervened on numerous occasions, adopting an adversarial position inimical to the co-defendant and his counsel. The trial judge refused to hear evidence on the agency issue and refused to hear evidence from expert witnesses on the issue of mitigation, admonishing defence counsel for "wasting my time" and "clutching at straws". A reasonable litigant in the co-defendant's position or any reasonable observer would have had some apprehension as to whether the agency and mitigation issues had been prejudged and rejected before all the evidence was in. The test was not prejudice to the co-defendant's case, but whether the image of impartiality, the absence of which deprived the court of jurisdiction, was destroyed.

Cassels v. Here & Now Picture Framing & Gallery Ltd. (January 6, 1997), Doc. No. 595/96 (Ont. Div. Ct.) — Notice of Appeal and service of same from Small Claims Court judgment did not comply with Rule 61.04(1) and Rule 16.03(5)(a) and 16.03(5)(b). Appeal quashed.

Pathak v. British Columbia (Public Service Commission) (1995), 3 B.C.L.R. (3d) 46 (B.C. S.C.); affirmed (1996), 26 B.C.L.R. (3d) 138, 83 B.C.A.C. 86, 136 W.A.C. 86 (B.C. C.A) — Appellant's counsel advised Commission appellant could not attend on scheduled date because he was on holidays. Persons who had filled positions would be prejudiced by application long after appointment. Chambers judge did not err in denying application for judicial review.

Diep v. Rollins (December 29, 1997), Doc. Nanaimo 13556 (B.C. Master) — Plaintiff appealed dismissal of Small Claims Court action for damages for personal injuries, following no evidence motion by defendant. Fact that appeal comprised new trial did not entitle defendant to serve jury notice.

Murphy v. Dennis McKay Ltd. (May 28, 1997), Doc. 25/96 (N.B. C.A.) — Appeal from small claims judgment in favour of respondent contractor. No error made by trial judge in her interpretation of written guarantee, which was for workmanship, not results.

Shewfelt v. Crawford (1997), 101 B.C.A.C. 95, 164 W.A.C. 95 (B.C. C.A. [In Chambers]) — Supreme Court Justice dismissed appeal from Small Claims Court order. Supreme Court subsequently dismissed application to reopen and reconsider judgment. Appeal from latter order dismissed. Court of Appeal had no jurisdiction to hear matter on basis that it arose out of small claims action. Appeal nullity.

Zeller v. Hetland (April 21, 1997), Doc. Melfort Q.B. 272/96 (Sask. Q.B.) — Provincial Court judge erred in allowing defendant's counterclaim where uncontradicted evidence at trial supported plaintiff's version of facts.

Ertel Manufacturing Corp. v. Florence (June 12, 1997), Doc. Peterborough 77976/97 (Ont. Div. Ct.); leave to appeal refused (October 14, 1997), Doc. CA M21021 (Ont. C.A.) — Trial judge did not err in finding that all goods were delivered as statement of defence never denied that goods were not delivered. Trial judge erred in dismissing defendant's counterclaim for set off for his additional expenses due to defective goods as trial judge misapprehended defendant's evidence.

Goudy v. Fenwick (June 5, 1997), Doc. Regina Q.B.G. 3143/96 (Sask. Q.B.) — Appeal dismissed from Small Claims Court judgment finding plaintiff driver liable for motor vehicle accident. There was no palpable error in that plaintiff's evidence was clearly inculpatory.

Hamon Design Group Inc. v. Jivov (November 15, 1996), Doc. Newmarket 37271/95 (Ont. Div. Ct.) — Trial judge failed to rule on counterclaim, nor did he make any finding of credibility on issues critical to outcome of case. Appeal allowed, judgment set aside.

Brown v. McLeod, [1997] 7 W.W.R. 553, 118 Man. R. (2d) 161 (Man. C.A.) — Small Claims Court judge refused to grant applicant's request for adjournment when his counsel was forced to withdraw during course of trial, upon realizing that he was in potential conflict position. Refusal to adjourn could, in circumstances of this case, be considered as error in law. Leave to appeal granted.

City Motors Ltd. v. Victor (1997), 9 C.P.C. (4th) 62 (N.S. S.C.) — Summary report prepared by adjudicator did not properly state findings of fact and basis for those findings. Adjudicator had apparently relied on inadmissible hearsay. Appeal was allowed and new hearing was ordered.

Foster Printing & Lithographing v. Pack-Tech Industries Ltd. (June 17, 1997), Doc. Toronto 573/96 (Ont. Div. Ct.) — Court held that the Divisional Court has jurisdiction with respect to a final order of the Small Claims Court. It cannot hear an appeal of an interlocutory order made by a judge of that court.

Madgett v. Jenkins (1997), 96 O.A.C. 396 (Ont. Div. Ct.) — Defendant sought validation of service of Notice of Appeal and other documentation. Court not prepared to exercise in favour of the applicant the discretion given to it by Rule 16.08 of the *Rules of Civil Procedure*. Court not satisfied the appellant is entitled to equitable relief.

Stein v. Sandwich West Township (1995), 25 M.P.L.R. (2d) 170, 77 O.A.C. 40 (Ont. C.A.) — The Ontario Court of Appeal discussed interventions by the trial judge in a nonjury civil trial. The case law was quite clear to the effect that the presiding judge must not deny a party the opportunity to present its full case, either by usurping the role of counsel or descending into the arena. See *Jones v. National Coal Board*, [1957] 2 All E.R. 155, [1957] 2 Q.B. 55 (Eng. C.A.); *Phillips v. Ford Motor Co. of Canada*, [1971] 2 O.R. 637 (Ont. C.A.); *Majcenic v. Natale* (1967), [1968] 1 O.R. 189 (Ont. C.A.).

Samuels v. Herald Insurance Co. (April 24, 1998), Doc. CA C22250 (Ont. C.A.) — Appellant argues that trial judge demonstrated an appearance of bias. Interventions of trial judge justified for the proper conduct of the trial. It cannot be said that a reasonable person hearing his comments would conclude trial judge might not be impartial. See *R. v. S. (R.D.)*, 1997 CarswellNS 301, 1997 CarswellNS 302, [1997] S.C.J. No. 84, 151 D.L.R. (4th) 193, 118 C.C.C. (3d) 353, 10 C.R. (5th) 1, 218 N.R. 1, 161 N.S.R. (2d) 241, 477 A.P.R. 241, [1997] 3 S.C.R. 484, 1 Admin. L.R. (3d) 74 (S.C.C.) at 540 [S.C.R.].

Brouse v. Factory Direct Flooring (June 12, 1998), Doc. Sudbury D.V. 309/97 (Ont. Gen. Div.) — Appeal from a judgment in the Ontario Court (Small Claims Division). Notice of appeal suggested that there has been new evidence found subsequent to the trial. There is a high onus on people wishing to produce new evidence after trials because society has an interest in putting an end to the trial process as quickly as possible. Keeping in mind the difficulties the judge had with both parties being unrepresented, trial Judge made no demonstrable error.

Larry Hart v. Investors Property Services Ltd. (June 26, 1996), Doc. 7325/94, 372/95 (Div. Ct) — The appeal was dismissed. The obvious error in addition contained in the judgment can be worked out between the parties.

Esther Tiwaah v. KLM Royal Dutch Airlines (February 24, 1998), Doc. 465/97 (Div. Ct) — There was evidence to support the findings of fact and no legal error that controlled the result. The appeal was dismissed although the costs at trial were reduced from $1,800 to the maximum allowable of $900.

Verret v. Carrier (2000), 2000 CarswellNB 220 (N.B. C.A.) — Appeal available only on question of law. Appeal dismissed.

Severson v. Nickel (Trustee of), 2000 SKQB 237, 2000 CarswellSask 357 (Sask. Q.B.) — Application by tenant to set aside writ of possession dismissed. The matter was dealt with at an earlier Small Claims Court hearing.

King v. Holker, 2000 BCSC 64, 2000 CarswellBC 1435 (B.C. S.C.) — Trial *de novo* not available to litigant simply because he or she wants to present case in a different manner second time around - Small Claims Act (B.C.), s.12.

Groupe Essaim Inc. v. Village Pharmacy Minto Inc. (2000), 10 C.P.C. (5th) 364, 2000 CarswellNB 274, 227 N.B.R. (2d) 276, 583 A.P.R. 276 (N.B. Q.B.) — The party was not permitted to apply under s. 37 of *Small Claims Act* (N.B.) for appeal of decision since it did not allow for the respondent to raise issues. The party was required to bring notice of appeal by trial *de novo*.

Potter v. R.W. Nelson Seed Farms Ltd., 2000 SKQB 289, 2000 CarswellSask 529 (Sask. Q.B.) — The trial judge awarded damages to the respondent. The appellant appealed. No palpable or overriding error that justified interfering with findings based on credibility.

Evans v. Bliss, 2000 SKQB 380, 2000 CarswellSask 530 (Sask. Q.B.) — The trial judge made no error in interpreting the law. Findings were supported by evidence.

Khan v. Calverley (2000), 2000 CarswellOnt 3970 (Ont. Div. Ct.) — Appeal from a Small Claims Court judgment that held the landlord liable to account to the plaintiff who owned goods seized by landlord when the tenant left premises. Despite occasional payment by the plaintiff of the share of the tenant's rent, no landlord and tenant relationship created. There was no error by the trial judge. The appeal was dismissed.

S. (R.) v. H. (R.) (2000), 195 D.L.R. (4th) 345, 52 O.R. (3d) 152, 139 O.A.C. 378, 2000 CarswellOnt 4864 (Ont. C.A.); affirming (2000), 187 D.L.R. (4th) 762, 8 R.F.L. (5th) 199, 49 O.R. (3d) 451, 2000 CarswellOnt 1994 (Ont. S.C.J.) — The interlocutory order from which there is no appeal is an order that does not determine the real matter in dispute but only some collateral matter. No pleading should be struck out unless it is obvious it discloses no reasonable cause of action or defence. The Motions Judge gave clear reasons that the statement of claim disclosed a valid cause of action but still dismissed the motion on the basis that the burden of establishing no cause of action had not been met.

Coldmatic Refrigeration of Canada Ltd. v. Atlantic Aluminum Inc. (2000), 2000 CarswellOnt 4499 (Ont. Div. Ct.) — In absence of palpable and overriding error, an appeal court should not interfere with the trial judge's findings of fact.

Walters v. MacDonald, 2001 BCCA 41, 2001 CarswellBC 85 (B.C. C.A. [In Chambers]) — The parties were lay litigants. The appellant seeking leave to extend time to appeal. The Court granted application. Merit to appeal existed. The issue was whether the formal order as drawn up by parties accurately reflected the decision of the judge.

Davids v. Davids (1999), 125 O.A.C. 375, 1999 CarswellOnt 3304, [1999] O.J. No. 3930 (Ont. C.A.) — The husband appealed the divorce judgment, seeking it be set aside. A new trial was ordered. He argued that the trial was unfair and a miscarriage of justice. He argued that he could not represent himself effectively in complex litigation. Fairness demanded that he have a fair opportunity to present his case to the best of his ability. The trial judge had to treat the litigant fairly and attempt to accommodate unrepresented litigants' unfamiliarity with the process so as to permit them to present case.

Thoms v. Hack, 2000 SKQB 133, 2000 CarswellSask 250 (Sask. Q.B.) — Notice of appeal of a Small Claims Court decision was sent by registered mail to respondent in 18 days but not delivered. Attempts at personal service after 30-day period were unsuccessful. The materials were insufficient to show arguable case on merits. Leave granted to file further material and reapply.

Pitre v. Law Society (Prince Edward Island), 2000 PESCAD 10, 187 Nfld. & P.E.I.R. 44, 566 A.P.R. 44, 8 C.P.C. (5th) 45, 2000 CarswellPEI 38 (P.E.I. C.A.) — A transcript was not required for appeal from judicial review where no evidence was given. There was a delay by the appellants acting through a non-lawyer and misunderstanding of the materials to be filed did not justify dismissal of appeal, but justified extension.

MacDonald v. Murphy (2000), 2000 CarswellNB 72 (N.B. C.A.). The Court raised questions of fact. As there was no question of law involved, the appeal was dismissed.

Hamm v. Frostland Commodities Ltd. (2000), 143 Man. R. (2d) 260, 2000 CarswellMan 24 (Man. Q.B.) — The plaintiff won a small claims award against the defendant, which the defendant appealed. The defendant failed to appear at the appeal and the appeal was dismissed. The defendant brought a motion to set aside the dismissal order. The motion was dismissed on the basis that the defendant had no reasonable excuse for not appearing.

Khalil v. Ontario College of Art (1999), 183 D.L.R. (4th) 186, 129 O.A.C. 294, 1999 CarswellOnt 4413 (Ont. Div. Ct.); additional reasons at (2001), 147 O.A.C. 216, 2001 CarswellOnt 1745 (Ont. Div. Ct.) — Material in possession of appellant since 1992 did not qualify as fresh evidence, based upon three-pronged criteria prescribed by the Supreme Court. See *R. v. Palmer*, 1979 CarswellBC 533, 1979 CarswellBC 541, [1980] 1 S.C.R. 759, 30 N.R. 181, 14 C.R. (3d) 22, 17 C.R. (3d) 34 (Fr.), 50 C.C.C. (2d) 193, 106 D.L.R. (3d) 212 (S.C.C.).

Hunt v. Hunt, 2001 CarswellBC 999, 2001 BCSC 328 (B.C. S.C.) — Reached proposed settlement. Defendant acting in person advised by judge to seek legal advice. He decided not to settle. Plaintiff applied for order judge had disqualified himself on ground of reasonable apprehension of bias. Dismissed.

R. v. Rose (2001), 143 O.A.C. 163, 2001 CarswellOnt 955, [2001] O.J. No. 1150, 153 C.C.C. (3d) 225, 42 C.R. (5th) 183, 53 O.R. (3d) 417 (Ont. C.A.) — The Ontario Appeal Court allowed appeal, set aside convictions and ordered a new trial. Accused argued that trial judge made disparaging and unwarranted comments about defence counsel that jeopardized the appearance of impartiality and fairness of trial. Court of Appeal rejected this ground of appeal.

Smyth v. Waterfall, 2000 CarswellOnt 3324, [2000] O.J. No. 3494, 50 O.R. (3d) 481, 136 O.A.C. 348, 4 C.P.C. (5th) 58 (Ont. C.A.) — The trial judge granted the defendant's motion for summary judgment dismissing plaintiff's claim. No reasons for judgment provided. The Ontario Court of Appeal stated that "this court has emphasized the desirability of trial judges giving the meaningful reasons, however brief, for their decisions." This is a principle that also applies, to decisions rendered by motions and applications judges. Parties are entitled to know why Court reached its decision. Failure to provide a reasoned decision tends to undermine confidence in the administration of justice as the absence of reasons may give the appearance of an arbitrary decision, particularly in the eyes of the unsuccessful party.

Capilano Fishing Ltd. v. "Qualicum Producer" (The), 150 B.C.A.C. 273, 2001 CarswellBC 611, 2001 BCCA 244, 87 B.C.L.R. (3d) 154, [2001] 4 W.W.R. 752, 198 D.L.R. (4th) 267, 245 W.A.C. 273 (B.C. C.A.); additional reasons at 2001 CarswellBC 1128, 2001 BCCA 381, 198 D.L.R. (4th) 766 (B.C. C.A.); leave to appeal refused (2001), 2001 CarswellBC 2215, 2001 CarswellBC 2216, 285 N.R. 394 (note), 167 B.C.A.C. 320 (note), 274 W.A.C. 320 (note) (S.C.C.) — The British Columbia Court of Appeal held that a trial judge did not err in prohibiting the plaintiffs from calling rebuttal evidence in response to surprise defence evidence.

Marchand (Litigation Guardian of) v. Public General Hospital Society of Chatham (2000), 138 O.A.C. 201, 2000 CarswellOnt 4362, [2000] O.J. No. 4428, 51 O.R. (3d) 97 (Ont. C.A.); leave to appeal refused 2001 CarswellOnt 3412, 2001 CarswellOnt 3413, [2001] S.C.C.A. No. 66, 282 N.R. 397 (note), (sub nom. *Marchand v. Public General Hospital Society of Chatham*) 156 O.A.C. 358 (note) (S.C.C.) — The Ontario Court of Appeal dismissed plaintiff's appeal without costs. The Court noted that trial judge intervened when needed in order to control what was a difficult trial and also to understand the evidence.

King v. McLennan, 2001 CarswellSask 252, 2001 SKQB 179, 208 Sask. R. 14 (Sask. Q.B.) — The Court on appeal had no power to retry case unless trial judge guilty of palpable or overriding error. Trial judge properly exercised discretion to allow respondent to proceed in negligence and bailment though bailment, not specifically pleaded.

Bruneski v. Fowell, 2001 CarswellBC 1591, 2001 BCSC 991 (B.C. Master) — Plaintiff refused to sign draft order dismissing action, alleging that consent was obtained by duress. As plaintiff had consented, plaintiff's approval of order dispensed with. Validity of consent to be determined on appeal.

Armour Group Ltd. v. Nova Scotia (Attorney General), 2001 CarswellNS 327, 2001 NSCA 135 (N.S. C.A.) — Appellant claimed judge misapprehended evidence in reaching conclusions. Judge made no error in law.

Nor-Villa Hotal Ltd. v. Maleschuk, 2001 CarswellSask 629, 2001 SKQB 433 (Sask. Q.B.) — Trial judge's findings were not so unreasonable that they should be reversed.

Prestige Closets & Cabinets Ltd. v. Finn (May 16, 2000), Doc. 634/99 (Ont. Div. Ct.) — Motion by appellant under Rule 61.16(5) to set aside order of registrar (Rule 61.13) dismissing appeal for delay. Delay can be "corrected" by interest and costs. Ten days given to perfect appeal.

Banfill Holovaci v. Zsoldos (2000), 2000 CarswellOnt 1552 (Ont. Div. Ct.); leave to appeal refused (2000), 2000 CarswellOnt 5281 (Ont. C.A.); leave to appeal refused (2001), 2001 CarswellOnt 1906, 2001 CarswellOnt 1907, 276 N.R. 393 (note), 152 O.A.C. 198 (note) (S.C.C.) — Appeal from Small Claims Court dismissed. Test of bias set out in *R. v. S. (R.D.)*, 1997 CarswellNS 301, 1997 CarswellNS 302, [1997] S.C.J. No. 84, 151 D.L.R. (4th) 193, 118 C.C.C. (3d) 353, 10 C.R. (5th) 1, 218 N.R. 1, 161 N.S.R. (2d) 241, 477 A.P.R. 241, [1997] 3 S.C.R. 484, 1 Admin. L.R. (3d) 74 (S.C.C.) at 530 [S.C.R.] and *Committee for Justice & Liberty v. Canada (National Energy Board)*, 1976 CarswellNat 434, 1976 CarswellNat 434F, [1978] 1 S.C.R. 369, 68 D.L.R. (3d) 716, 9 N.R. 115 (S.C.C.) at 394 [S.C.R.]. No reason to interfere with trial judge. Costs of appeal fixed at $3,000.

Four Seasons Greenhouses Canada v. Matlow (2000), 2000 CarswellOnt 4817, 140 O.A.C. 293 (Ont. Div. Ct.) — Appeal dismissed. Standard of appellate renew set out in *Equity Waste Management of Canada Corp. v. Halton Hills (Town)* (1997), 35 O.R. (3d) 321, 1997 CarswellOnt 3270, [1997] O.J. No. 3921, 40 M.P.L.R. (2d) 107, 103 O.A.C. 324 (Ont. C.A.); *Canada (Director of Investigation & Research) v. Southam Inc.*, [1997] 1 S.C.R. 748, 1997 CarswellNat 368, 1997 CarswellNat 369, 144 D.L.R. (4th) 1, 71 C.P.R. (3d) 417, 209 N.R. 20, 50 Admin. L.R. (2d) 199 (S.C.C.) and *Wilbur v. Wilbur* (1983), 41 O.R. (2d) 565, 1983 CarswellOnt 261, 33 R.F.L. (2d) 49, 147 D.L.R. (3d) 69 (Ont. C.A.).

Club Epiphany v. Robinson (March 1, 2001), Doc. 505/99 (Ont. Div. Ct.) — Appeal from Small Claims Court dismissed. Notice requirement contemplated in s. 5(1) of the *Libel and Slander Act*, R.S.O. 1990, c. L.12 must be pleaded, which it was not.

Shewan v. Canada (Attorney General) (2001), 2001 CarswellOnt 3049 (Ont. C.A.) — Impecunious appellant unable to pay for production of transcriptions and unable to provide Court with any indication when or how he could obtain funds. Application to extend time to review order dismissing appeal denied.

385268 B.C. Ltd. v. Alberta Treasury Branches, 2001 CarswellAlta 1572, 2001 ABCA 289, 29 C.B.R. (4th) 315, 299 A.R. 194, 266 W.A.C. 194 (Alta. C.A.) — Appeal dismissed as argument that findings of fact were unreasonable without merit. Complaint that case management role of Chambers Judge intruded upon adjudicative fairness without merit.

Kalevar v. Liberal Party of Canada, 2001 CarswellNat 2640, 2001 FCT 1261 (Fed. T.D.); affirmed 2002 CarswellNat 1398, 2002 FCA 246, 2002 CarswellNat 3018, 2002 CAF 246, 228 F.T.R. 159 (note) (Fed. C.A.); leave to appeal refused (2003), 2003 CarswellNat 91, 2003 CarswellNat 92, 307 N.R. 399 (note) (S.C.C.) — Prothonotary dismissed application for judicial review of lay litigant for delay. Applicant delaying over one month before appealing. Delay unjustified and appeal without merit. Rules of Court apply equally whether lay litigant or where counsel retained. Federal Court Rules, 1998 (SOR/98-106).

Oliveira v. Zhang (2000), 2000 CarswellOnt 692 (Ont. Div. Ct.) — Appeal from Small Claims Court dismissed. Ample evidence, trial judge made findings of fact. *Fletcher v. Manitoba Public Insurance Corp.*, [1990] 3 S.C.R. 191, 1990 CarswellOnt 1009, 1990 CarswellOnt 56, 5 C.C.L.T. (2d) 1, 74 D.L.R. (4th) 636, 116 N.R. 1, 44 O.A.C. 81, 1 C.C.L.I. (2d) 1, 71 Man. R. (2d) 81, 30 M.V.R. (2d) 260, 75 O.R. (2d) 373 (note), [1990] R.R.A. 1053 (headnote only), [1990] I.L.R. 1-2672 (S.C.C.) referred to.

Prentice v. Dharamshi, 6 B.C.L.R. (4th) 39, 2002 CarswellBC 2220, 2002 BCCA 490, 179 B.C.A.C. 200, 295 W.A.C. 200 (B.C. C.A.) — Action tried by judge and jury, trial judge refused to permit plaintiff's counsel to reply to jury after defendant's counsel completed his address. Plaintiff appealed, appeal allowed. Trial judge had no discretion to refuse plaintiff's right to reply, as plaintiff was "party who began." New trial ordered.

Rudd v. Hayward, 91 B.C.L.R. (3d) 227, 2001 CarswellBC 1463, 2001 BCCA 454, 12 M.V.R. (4th) 200, 156 B.C.A.C. 27, 255 W.A.C. 27 (B.C. C.A.) — Plaintiff's case did not require expert evidence, but it was logical and appropriate to allow him to call expert to reply to defendant's expert. Trial judge's decision to deny defendant opportunity to call second expert following testimony of plaintiff's expert was within his discretion. Restrictions on questioning represented proper enforcement of usual rule regarding evidence in reply.

Whitehorn v. Wallden, 90 B.C.L.R. (3d) 275, 2001 CarswellBC 1278, 2001 BCCA 419, 156 B.C.A.C. 317, 255 W.A.C. 317 (B.C. C.A.) — Defendant conceded that trial judge had erred in law by limiting plaintiff's ability to question expert witness. Properly instructed jury in possession of excluded evidence could have reached different verdict.

Law Society (British Columbia) v. Gravelle, 154 B.C.A.C. 25, 2001 CarswellBC 1103, [2001] 7 W.W.R. 15, 2001 BCCA 383, 89 B.C.L.R. (3d) 187, 200 D.L.R. (4th) 82, 252 W.A.C. 25 (B.C. C.A.); leave to appeal refused (2002), 2002 CarswellBC 11, 2002 CarswellBC 12, 286 N.R. 198 (note), 171 B.C.A.C. 46 (note), 280 W.A.C. 46 (note) (S.C.C.) — The Law Society petitioned for a declaration that a notary public engaged in the unauthorized practice of law by giving legal advice and offering to assist a member of the public with respect to the probate or letters of administration of the estate of a deceased person for, or in, the expectation of a fee, gain or reward. A permanent injunction against the notary was also sought. The British Columbia Court of Appeal dismissed the appeal. The Court affirmed that notaries were not probating wills in England on November 18, 1958. Therefore, the notary here engaged in the unauthorized practice of law.

Alcorn v. Bayham (Municipality) (2002), 2002 CarswellOnt 3809, 33 M.P.L.R. (3d) 132, 166 O.A.C. 78 (Ont. Div. Ct.) — The trial judge intervened to prevent defence questioning of the hierarchical superior of a highway patrolman. Interventions not so one-sided or without reason that a reasonable and fully informed observer would conclude that trial judge had lost his judicial impartiality.

Danyluk v. Ainsworth Technologies Inc., REJB 2001-25003, 2001 CarswellOnt 2434, 2001 CarswellOnt 2435, [2001] S.C.J. No. 46, 2001 SCC 44, 54 O.R. (3d) 214 (headnote only), 201 D.L.R. (4th) 193, 10 C.C.E.L. (3d) 1, 7 C.P.C. (5th) 199, 272 N.R. 1, 149 O.A.C. 1, 2001 C.L.L.C. 210-033, 34 Admin. L.R. (3d) 163, [2001] 2 S.C.R. 460 (S.C.C.) — Denial of natural justice by employment standards officer did not deprive standards officer's decision of its judicial character. Errors made by standards officer rendered decision voidable, not void. Employee's decision not to apply for review by director was not fatal to employee's action for $3,000 of unpaid wages and commissions. Court of Appeal concluded that the standards officer's decision was final on the grounds that neither party exercised its right of internal appeal. It confirmed that the standards officer's decision was judicial for the purpose of issue estoppel. The standards officer's failure to observe procedural fairness did not prevent the operation of issue estoppel.

De Fehr v. De Fehr, 156 B.C.A.C. 240, 2001 CarswellBC 1716, 2001 BCCA 485, 255 W.A.C. 240, 11 C.P.C. (5th) 195 (B.C. C.A. [In Chambers]) — Husband applied for indigent status. The term "indigent" is not defined in the Rules of Court, but its meaning has been considered in a number of cases. Indigent status ought to be granted to the applicant.

671122 Ontario Ltd. v. Sagaz Industries Canada Inc. (2001), 150 O.A.C. 12, 2001 Carswell-Ont 3357, 2001 CarswellOnt 3358, [2001] S.C.J. No. 61, 2001 SCC 59, 11 C.C.E.L. (3d) 1, [2001] 4 C.T.C. 139, 204 D.L.R. (4th) 542, 274 N.R. 366, 17 B.L.R. (3d) 1, 55 O.R. (3d) 782 (headnote only), 12 C.P.C. (5th) 1, 8 C.C.L.T. (3d) 60, [2001] 2 S.C.R. 983, 2002 C.L.L.C. 210-013 (S.C.C.); reconsideration refused (2001), 2001 CarswellOnt 4155, 2001 CarswellOnt 4156, 55 O.R. (3d) 782 (headnote only), 18 B.L.R. (3d) 159, 10 C.C.L.T. (3d) 292 (S.C.C.) — Trial judge refused plaintiff's motion to re-open the trial to hear evidence on the ground that the evidence in question available at trial. The plaintiff made a tactical decision not to call the owner. The Supreme Court of Canada allowed appeal from Court of Appeal and restored the trial judge's decision.

Barbeau-Lafacci v. Holmgren, 173 B.C.A.C. 280, 283 W.A.C. 280, 2002 CarswellBC 2343, [2002] B.C.J. No. 2295, 2002 BCCA 553 (B.C. C.A. [In Chambers]); additional reasons at 2003 CarswellBC 2533, 2003 BCCA 549 (B.C. C.A.) — The plaintiff applied for leave to extend the time for filing a notice of appeal. The plaintiff also sought indigent status and an order that the Crown provide her with a transcript of the summary proceedings. Court of Appeal, per Ryan, J.A., dismissed the application. Court held that the words "lacks merit" in Rule 56(a) of the Court of Appeal Rules, which equated to "has no reasonable prospect of success.".

Vernon v. General Motors of Canada Ltd. (2002), 163 O.A.C. 182, 2002 CarswellOnt 2846 (Ont. C.A.) — The appellant moved to augment record on appeal by including a certain document. The Court of Appeal treated the motion as a motion for leave to admit fresh evidence. Even accepting, without deciding, that the appellant could not satisfy the Palmer test, the Court stated that it had an overriding discretion to admit fresh evidence where the interests of justice required it. The document read to lower court judge during oral argument, though not marked as an exhibit. The Court admitted the document, holding it was in the interest of justice that appellant to be permitted to rely on document.

R. v. Messenger (2002), 160 O.A.C. 193, 2002 CarswellOnt 1749, 94 C.R.R. (2d) 355, [2002] O.J. No. 2031 (Ont. C.A.) — After counsel successfully applied to be removed as solicitor of record, Messenger represented himself at his trial. On day of trial, he sought adjournment on basis that he had been unable to obtain a copy of the Crown disclosure from his former counsel. The trial judge refused his request. On the third day of trial, he applied for prohibition, arguing that his Charter right to a fair trial had been infringed by the denial of adjournment and late disclosure. The Court of Appeal held that Messenger "should have waited until the end of the trial to appeal the ruling to which he objected.. . . Prerogative remedies are discretionary in nature. Only in exceptional circumstances should they be sought, or granted, during the course of a trial. The criminal trial process cannot be subject to unwarranted disruption at the unilateral election of an accused.".

Jumbo Systems Inc. v. Short (2002), 154 O.A.C. 49, 2002 CarswellOnt 30 (Ont. C.A.) — Appeal dismissed. Despite apparent unfairness to defendants from plaintiffs' omission to plead waiver, defendants were alerted to issue by trial judge's comments prior to argument.

No objection was raised by the defendants' counsel and submissions were made on the question. No substantial wrong or miscarriage of justice.

Lennox v. Arbor Memorial Services Inc. (2001), 56 O.R. (3d) 795, 2001 CarswellOnt 4248, 151 O.A.C. 297, 16 C.C.E.L. (3d) 157 (Ont. C.A.) — Trial judge's conduct of the trial created an appearance of unfairness. Trial judge appeared to assist the respondent:

- redirected lines of questioning that respondent's counsel sought to pursue and which the trial judge viewed as unhelpful to the respondent and strategically ill-advised;.

- engaged in extensive cross-examination of two of Arbor's witnesses and challenged their credibility;.

- required production of the appellant's policy manual, not part of the pleadings or productions, and therefore not part of the case before the Court as prepared and conducted by counsel;.

- and sought more than an explanation or clarification of evidence brought out by counsel, by questioning two witnesses extensively about the policy manual.

Grudich v. Babington, 2002 CarswellPEI 93, 2002 PESCAD 20, 217 Nfld. & P.E.I.R. 271, 651 A.P.R. 271 (P.E.I. C.A. [In Chambers]) — Appellant from small claims decision obtained transcript but failed to serve or file. *Civil Procedure Rule 74.19* (P.E.I.) did not set time-limit. Remedy of quashing not available. Proper remedy was to set matter for hearing, and order immediate compliance with Rule 74.19(5).

Morrison v. Rosser (Rural Municipality), 2002 CarswellMan 97, 2002 MBQB 26 (Man. C.A. [In Chambers]) — Order granting leave to appeal to two Small Claims Court actions that had been consolidated. Confirmation that order could be taken out in both proceedings not intended to have unlimited time. Time limits were specified. Supplementary reasons to decision at 2001 CarswellMan 443, 2001 MBCA 149 (Man. C.A. [In Chambers]).

Harris Floors Ltd. v. Eversen Enterprise Ltd., 2001 CarswellAlta 1602, 2001 ABQB 1013 (Alta. Q.B.) — Trial judge awarded plaintiff judgment on invoices. The defendant appealed. Appeal allowed. New trial ordered. As this appeal was a trial *de novo* defendant provided some new evidence. Defendant satisfied Court her evidence might have been inadvertently overlooked or not fully understood by trial judge.

Briand v. Coachman Insurance, 2003 NSCA 39, 2003 CarswellNS 124, [2003] N.S.J. No. 116 (N.S. C.A.) — Appeal from decision on October 10, 2002 dismissing application to extend time to file notice of appeal from July 16, 2001 decision of Small Claims Court adjudicator. No error in law resulting in an injustice, no *bona fide* intention to appeal and no reasonable cause for the delay. Hard to recreate a record after 14 months since Small Claims Court proceedings not recorded.

Sinardi Hair Design v. Knifton (2003), 2003 CarswellOnt 1547 (Ont. Div. Ct.) — By order of Judge Bromstein dated October 31, 2002, made by failure of third party (Greenwin) to attend pre-trial, Greenwin ordered to pay costs to other parties on or before December 15, 2002 or have pleading struck. It did not pay the costs. Instead, it moved to set aside the order, but did not appear on the return date. After pleadings struck, Greenwin brought a further motion for relief against the October 31 order, before Deputy Judge Libman on January 23, 2003. He ordered that Greenwin's pleadings be reinstated and that the cost order of Judge Bromstein be set aside. Order of Deputy Judge clearly an interlocutory order. Section 31 of the Courts of Justice Act provides for an appeal from a "final order of the Small Claims Court." No provision for an appeal from an interlocutory order of Small Claims Court. See *Gelber v. Allstate Insurance Co. of Canada*, 1983 CarswellOnt 457, 41 O.R. (2d) 318, 35 C.P.C. 324 (Ont. Div. Ct.); no appeal lies from a decision unless a right of appeal is granted by statute. There is no common law right of appeal. Motions dismissed with costs.

Kallinikos v. Wong (2003), 2003 CarswellOnt 632 (Ont. Div. Ct.) — Appeal from Thomson J. of Small Claims Court dismissed. Appeal based solely on findings of fact and no misapprehension of evidence.

Hallok v. Toronto Hydro Electric System Ltd. (2003), 2003 CarswellOnt 976 (Ont. Div. Ct.) — Appeal by Toronto Hydro and Park Lawn from decision of Deputy Judge allowed. Standard of appellate review in questions of mixed fact and law set out in *Housen v. Nikolaisen*, REJB 2002-29758, 2002 CarswellSask 178, [2002] S.C.J. No. 31, 2002 SCC 33, 286 N.R. 1, 10 C.C.L.T. (3d) 157, 211 D.L.R. (4th) 577, [2002] 7 W.W.R. 1, 219 Sask. R. 1, 272 W.A.C. 1, 30 M.P.L.R. (3d) 1, [2002] 2 S.C.R. 235 (S.C.C.), at paras. 36-37 [S.C.J. No.]. New Trial ordered pursuant to subsections 134(1) and (6) of the CJA.

R. v. Sheppard, 2002 SCC 26, [2002] S.C.J. No. 30, 2002 CarswellNfld 74, 2002 CarswellNfld 75, 162 C.C.C. (3d) 298, 210 D.L.R. (4th) 608, 50 C.R. (5th) 68, 284 N.R. 342, 211 Nfld. & P.E.I.R. 50, 633 A.P.R. 50, [2002] 1 S.C.R. 869 (S.C.C.) — Reasons for judgment. Duty on trial judge to give reasons. Trial judge's generic reasons amounted to no reasons at all and precluded proper appellate scrutiny of whether verdict was unreasonable. Trial judge erred in law in failing to give functional reasons.

R. v. Brown (2003), 2003 CarswellOnt 1312, 9 C.R. (6th) 240, [2003] O.J. No. 1251, 105 C.R.R. (2d) 132, 36 M.V.R. (4th) 1, 173 C.C.C. (3d) 23, 64 O.R. (3d) 161, 170 O.A.C. 131 (Ont. C.A.) — Trial judge's conduct created reasonable apprehension of bias. Comments reflected tendency to prejudge merits of application. Reasonable observer would have felt trial judge showed antipathy, resistance to application. Trial judge unable to hear application with open, dispassionate mind. Evidence before trial judge capable of supporting finding of racial profiling. Racial profiling can be demonstrated through circumstantial evidence.

Kutsogiannis v. Saskatoon Ceramic Tile (1984) Ltd., 2002 CarswellSask 731, 2002 SKQB 476, 226 Sask. R. 214 (Sask. Q.B.) — Appeal pursuant to section 39(1) of the *Small Claims Act*, 1997, S.S. 1997, c. S-50.11, as amended. Appeal dismissed. The Court not entitled to substitute its view of findings of fact of trial judge. Evidence before trial judge upon which he could reach conclusions that he did. The trial judge did not commit an error of law or make some palpable or overriding error in the process.

Ali v. Triple 3 Holdings Inc. (2002), 2002 CarswellOnt 3986 (Ont. C.A.) — Reasons of trial judge silent as to the burden of proof. Appeal dismissed. An appellate court should not presume that the judge of the first instance was not aware of or failed to apply the appropriate legal test (*i.e.*, fraudulent misrepresentation) merely because the test was not explicitly set out in the judge's reasons.

Earthcraft Landscape Ltd. v. Clayton, 2002 CarswellNS 497, [2002] N.S.J. No. 516, 2002 NSSC 259, 210 N.S.R. (2d) 101, 659 A.P.R. 101 (N.S. S.C.) — Adjudicator failing to advise unrepresented party that letter tendered in evidence would have less weight than oral testimony and that party had right to secure attendance of letter writer to provide oral evidence. Failure to advise party of this constituted denial of natural justice. [New hearing ordered in Small Claims Court.].

Byers (Litigation Guardian of) v. Pentex Print Master Industries Inc. (2003), 62 O.R. (3d) 647, 2003 CarswellOnt 18, [2003] O.J. No. 6, 167 O.A.C. 159, 28 C.P.C. (5th) 258 (Ont. C.A.); additional reasons at (2003), 2003 CarswellOnt 2476 (Ont. C.A.) — Judgment on merits and judgment with respect to costs separate appealable judgments. Different procedures for appeal of judgment on merits and appeal with respect to costs. Judgment on merits effective from time pronounced unless substantial matter remaining to be determined. Judgment as to costs collateral and not substantial matter that extends time for delivering notice of appeal. Judgment on merits appealable before court makes judgment as to costs. Leave may be granted to extend time for appeal. *Courts of Justice Act*, R.S.O. 1990, c. C.43, ss.

6(1)(a), (b), 131(1) and 133(b). *Rules of Civil Procedure*, R.R.O. 1990. Reg. 194, Rules 61.03.1(1), (16), (17), (18) and 61.04(1).

Welna v. Nolting (1999), 1999 CarswellNWT 104 (N.W.T. S.C.) — Appeal of judgment issued in Small Claims Court. Defendant did not appear and alleged on appeal that he did not receive Notice of Trial until after judgment issued and sheriff seized his goods. Defendant had filed defence to claim indicating intention to defend matter. Judgment set aside. Appellant to pay $5,400 in Court pending matter reheard in Territorial Court.

Dancovich v. Rast (2002), 2002 CarswellAlta 1298, 2002 ABQB 907, [2003] 2 W.W.R. 557, 8 Alta. L.R. (4th) 368 (Alta. Q.B.) — Rast, the plaintiff, respondent on the appeal, fell within the exception to the general rule that a party cannot recover what he has given another party under an illegal contract, in this case, a pyramid scheme. Appeal dismissed. Standard of review on appeal one of correctness on a question of law. Standard of review on a question of fact demonstrable unreasonableness. Not found in this case.

Antoniuk v. Edmonton (City), 2002 ABQB 918, 2002 CarswellAlta 1281, 33 M.P.L.R. (3d) 138, 325 A.R. 286 (Alta. Master) — Eighteen-month delay alone is sufficient application to appeal. Test seeking more time (i.e., beyond 30 days as set out in section 46(1) of the *Provincial Court Act*) not met by the plaintiff. Orders are decisions just as much as judgments are decisions. That is when 30-day appeal time period applies.

Addison v. Naqvi (2003), 2003 CarswellOnt 1775 (Ont. Div. Ct.). Appeal of judgment of Small Claims Court.

No transcript of the assessment on that date was filed by the *Appellant*. None was ordered by the *Appellant*. Appeal dismissed. For adequate reasons, the trier of fact may depart from requirement for payment of interest as per section 130(1) of *The Courts of Justice Act*. Given Applicant did not file transcripts of proceedings, reasons for judgment not available for review by Court.

Marta v. Francis Home Environment Centre (2004), 2004 CarswellOnt 61 (Ont. Div. Ct.). Appeal dismissed. Respondent entitled to award of costs. A litigant who loses in the Small Claims Court and takes his opponent on appeal to the Divisional Court, must expect to pay more substantial costs if unsuccessful. Award of $1,500 payable to the Respondent in addition to costs at trial appropriate.

Atlantic Auto Body v. Boudreau, 2004 CarswellOnt 649 (Ont. Div. Ct.). Issue whether Court has jurisdiction to hear motion to have appeal dismissed for delay.

February 28th, 2003 — Appellant served with copy of notice of examination by registered mail. March 13th, 2003 — Motion to be set aside dismissed. April 10th, 2003 — Notice of Appeal filed. January 21st, 2004 — Notice of Motion by Respondent to dismiss appeal for delay filed, returnable January 29th, 2004. January 27th, 2004 — Service of factum, book of authorities, and appeal book by Appellant.

Appellant, in responding to the motion, took position that a dismissal for delay of an appeal to the Divisional Court from the Small Claims Court is to be heard on motion to the Registrar under *Rule 61.13(1)(b)*. An appeal from a decision made by the Registrar lies to this Court under *Rule 61.16(5)*. Court does not have jurisdiction at this stage. Motion must be heard before the Registrar of the Divisional Court. See *Rule 61.13(1)*. See *McGlynn v. McGlynn*, [2002] O.J. No. 2047, 2002 CarswellOnt 5795 (Ont. Div. Ct.).

Under *Rule 61* Appellant must perfect his appeal and if not Respondent may move to the Registrar to have appeal dismissed for delay.

Bruvels v. Miller, 2004 CarswellOnt 1180 (Ont. Div. Ct.). Appeal from judgment of Justice Tierney in Ottawa dated June 17, 2002.

Plaintiff initiated proceedings before the Ontario Residential Housing Tribunal. These failed for want of jurisdiction.

Divisional Court has jurisdiction to hear appeal based on s.31 of The *Courts of Justice Act*. The standard of review for appeals from the Order of a judge is widely accepted to be whether the decision of judge was "clearly wrong". Standard applies to both to findings of fact and to legal principles.

Even when no oral evidence heard, and judge's findings not based on credibility, still entitled to deference from an Appellate Court. See *Equity Waste Management of Canada Corp. v. Halton Hills (Town)* (1997), 35 O.R. (3d) 321, 1997 CarswellOnt 3270, [1997] O.J. No. 3921, 40 M.P.L.R. (2d) 107, 103 O.A.C. 324 (Ont. C.A.) per Laskin J.A.

Judicial descretion should not be interfered with unless apparent trial judge applied erroneous principles that rendered the result "clearly wrong". On questions of law, standard of review is correctness. Appeal dismissed, save and except no award for punitive damages.

Painter v. Waddington, McLean & Co., 2004 CarswellOnt 279 (Ont. S.C.J.). Self-represented Plaintiffs successful at trial recovering judgment against the Defendants in the amount of $6,384.50 plus prejudgment and postjudgment interest as prescribed by *The Courts of Justice Act*. Are self-represented lay Plaintiffs entitled to costs?.

Plaintiffs commenced action when monetary jurisdiction of Court was $6,000. They recovered in excess of that amount at trial. No reason to no costs on the basis of r. 57.05 of the *Rules of Civil Procedure*.

Plaintiffs relied upon: *Fellowes, McNeil v. Kansa General International Insurance Co.* (1997), 37 O.R. (3d) 464, 1997 CarswellOnt 5013, 17 C.P.C. (4th) 400 (Ont. Gen. Div.); *Fong v. Chan* (1999), 46 O.R. (3d) 330, 1999 CarswellOnt 3955, [1999] O.J. No. 4600, 181 D.L.R. (4th) 614, 128 O.A.C. 2 (Ont. C.A.); *Skidmore v. Blackmore*, 122 D.L.R. (4th) 330, 1995 CarswellBC 23, [1995] B.C.J. No. 305, 2 B.C.L.R. (3d) 201, [1995] 4 W.W.R. 524, 27 C.R.R. (2d) 77, 55 B.C.A.C. 191, 90 W.A.C. 191, 35 C.P.C. (3d) 28 (B.C. C.A.).

Cases show award to lay litigant not on same basis as to party represented by a solicitor, but generally modest.

Plaintiffs entitled to their costs.

Trafalgar Industries of Canada Ltd. v. Pharmax Ltd. (2003), [2003] O.J. No. 1602, 2003 CarswellOnt 1535, 64 O.R. (3d) 288 (Ont. S.C.J.). Judgment for $26,978.84.

Plaintiff prepared a Bill of Costs requesting $63,710.55 for fees and disbursements. Simplified procedures introduced to promote affordable access to justice.

Costs incurred under the Simplified Procedures, *and in all cases*, must be reasonable *and* proportionate to the amount recovered. These principles underpin the important issue of access to justice. See: *Vokey v. Edwards* (1999), [1999] O.J. No. 2304, 1999 CarswellOnt 1919 (Ont. S.C.J.), *Rakoon Impex v. Nasr Foods Inc.* (1999), [1999] O.J. No. 3360, 1999 CarswellOnt 2855 (Ont. S.C.J.), and *McLean v. 721244 Ontario Ltd.* (2000), [2000] O.J. No. 3507, 2000 CarswellOnt 3305 (Ont. S.C.J.). *Rule 57.01(1)* provides guidance in imposing costs.

Costs to Applicant fixed at $12,000.

Sable Offshore Energy Inc. v. Bingley, 2003 NSSC 20, 2003 CarswellNS 46, 211 N.S.R. (2d) 15, 662 A.P.R. 15, [2003] N.S.J. No. 33 (N.S. S.C.). Appeal from decision of adjudicator in Small Claims Court.

Nova Scotia Civil Procedure *Rule 62.23(2)* states that:

> The powers of the Court may be exercised in respect of all or any part of the judgment or proceedings appealed from, notwithstanding that the notice of appeal states that only part of the judgment is complained of.

Duty owed by adjudicator to examine the pleadings and determine whether a cause of action exists. Despite informality of Small Claims Court, neither party should be held to have waived their rights to rely on arguments not raised in their pleadings. Adjudicator erred in law by awarding damages *without* considering these issues.

Small Claims Court here is not a court of record and there are no transcripts to provide a record of the evidence of what transpired at trial. The hearing is an appeal and thus it is not place of Court to consider the new evidence that will undoubtedly be presented. I must find an error in law and I am restricted by section 32(1) of the *Small Claims Court Act*.

Surrette Battery Co. v. McNutt, 2003 NSSC 6, 2003 CarswellNS 15, [2003] N.S.J. No. 20, 211 N.S.R. (2d) 294, 662 A.P.R. 294, 29 C.P.C. (5th) 215 (N.S.S.C.). Claimant appealed decision of adjudicator denying its request for a quick judgment pursuant to s. 23(1) of *The Small Claims Act*, and s. 14 of *The Small Claims Court Forms* and *Procedures Regulations*.

The standard of review is correctness. There is no requirement that evidence be adduced under oath or otherwise in proof of the claim where the Defendant does not appear nor is it necessary that a hearing or a trial be held. Where an assessment of damages is required undoubtedly it would be necessary for an adjudicator to hear evidence under oath.

Court found, based on documentary evidence accompanying claim, that claim would result in judgment if a trial held consistent with invoices, etc., and supporting affidavit on application. Quick Judgment to the Plaintiff.

Hubley v. Nissan, 2003 NSSC 236, 2003 CarswellNS 490, 219 N.S.R. (2d) 165, 692 A.P.R. 165 (N.S. S.C.). Appeal of Small Claims Court decision, where adjudicator refused appellant's request for a 4-month adjournment.

On the morning of June 13, 2003, the date of hearing, Plaintiff sought adjournment. By fax, he notified adjudicator he was unable to attend hearing because his cows were in labour.

Appeal subject to section 32(1) of *The Small Claims Court Act*, R.S.N.S. 1989, c. 430 as amended (*"Small Claims Court Act"*). It was in the interests of justice to adjourn the hearing. New hearing Ordered.

MacEwan v. Henderson, 2003 NSSC 120, 2003 CarswellNS 195 (N.S. S.C.); affirmed 2003 CarswellNS 424, 2003 NSCA 133, 219 N.S.R. (2d) 183, 692 A.P.R. 183 (N.S. C.A.). Appeal from Order of Small Claims Court.

No pre-trial disclosure process provided in *Act*. No requirement for Defendant at any stage to give disclosure of documents.

No requirements for filing pre-trial briefs and, accordingly, no established time limits for filing of briefs or for service on opposing party.

Appeal dismissed. Statutory $50 limit.

Benard v. New Brunswick, 2004 NBQB 3, 2004 CarswellNB 1 (N.B. Q.B.). Plaintiff learned that there were certain exemptions under the Regulations to the *Family Income Security Act*, S.N.B. 1994, c. F-2.01, (*"the Act"*). He requested a review of his social assistance payments and specifically the deduction of the $105.98 per month.

Bernard filed claim against Province in Small Claims Court claiming $5,087.04 plus costs and interest against the Province for withholding a portion of his income assistance.

The Small Claims Act does not provide Court with. Claim dismissed.

MacIntyre v. Nichols, 2004 CarswellNS 76, 221 N.S.R. (2d) 137, 697 A.P.R. 137, 2004 NSSC 36 (N.S. S.C.). Appeal from decision of adjudicator, in Small Claims Court, allowing respondents' claim for negligent misrepresentation. Appellants argued that no basis for finding of negligent misrepresentation, as it was not pleaded, and fraudulent misrepresentation was not found.

If a Claimant by his or her pleading or evidence states facts which, if accepted by the trier of fact, constitute a cause of action known to the law, the Claimant should *prima facie* be entitled to the remedy claimed if that is appropriate to vindicate that cause of action.

A Small Claims Court judge has a duty, on being presented with facts that fall broadly within the umbrella of the circumstances described in the Claim, to determine whether those facts constitute a cause of action known to the law, regardless of whether Claimant has asserted that or any other particular cause of action. Appeal dismissed with costs.

Auto List of Canada Inc. v. Sumner, 2004 CarswellMan 169, 184 Man. R. (2d) 155, 318 W.A.C. 155, 2004 MBCA 59 (Man. C.A. [In Chambers]). Applicant sought leave to appeal decision of Queen's Bench. Respondent had filed a small claim against Applicant, claiming the maximum permitted under *The Court of Queen's Bench Small Claims Practice Act*, C.C.S.M. c. C285 (*The Act*) of $7,500 plus interest and costs.

The Applicant served but failed to appear. The *Act* provides in s.15 that party may, with leave, appeal to the Court of Appeal on question of law only. Motion for extension of time to file application for leave to appeal granted, and leave to appeal is granted.

Bay One Glass Distributors Ltd. v. Funk, 2004 BCSC 516, 2004 CarswellBC 830 (B.C. S.C.). Defendants appealed the decision of Small Claims Court.

Applicable law with respect to court's function sitting as an appellate court, pursuant to the provisions of the *Small Claims Act*, set out by Supreme Court of Canada in *Housen v. Nikolaisen*, REJB 2002-29758, 2002 CarswellSask 178, [2002] S.C.J. No. 31, 2002 SCC 33, 286 N.R. 1, 10 C.C.L.T. (3d) 157, 211 D.L.R. (4th) 577, [2002] 7 W.W.R. 1, 219 Sask. R. 1, 272 W.A.C. 1, 30 M.P.L.R. (3d) 1, [2002] 2 S.C.R. 235 (S.C.C.). There is limited scope for appellate review when findings of fact, and inferences drawn from those facts, are challenged on appeal.

Presumption underlying the structure of court system is that a trial judge is competent to decide the case before him or her. Where trial judge mistaken then appellant must demonstrate mistake played essential part in the reasoning process resulting in liability being found. Appeal dismissed with costs.

Webb v. 3584747 Canada Inc., 2004 CarswellOnt 325, [2004] O.J. No. 215, 183 O.A.C. 155, 69 O.R. (3d) 502, 41 C.P.C. (5th) 98 (Ont. C.A.); leave to appeal refused [2004] S.C.C.A. No. 114, 2004 CarswellOnt 2988, 2004 CarswellOnt 2989, 331 N.R. 399 (note) (S.C.C.). In a class action proceeding, the managing judge directed certain issues be determined by way of references conducted by a deputy judge of the Small Claims Court, *inter alia*, "Absent a direction from the Chief Justice, the consent of individual judicial officers to serve in the manner specified in the Order did not satisfy the requirements of s.14(1) of *The Courts of Justice Act*.".

Markham School for Human Development v. Ghods (2002), 165 O.A.C. 173, 2002 Carswell-Ont 2672, [2002] O.J. No. 3153, 216 D.L.R. (4th) 202, 60 O.R. (3d) 624, 23 C.P.C. (5th) 279 (Ont. Div. Ct.) Appeal raised issue of effect of tendering postdated cheque in repayment of debt on commencement of limitation period. Defendants acknowledged debt when they provided four postdated cheques to the Plaintiff and the Defendants again acknowledged the debt by part payments on each of the dates. Action brought within limitation period.

Mitchell v. Noakes (2003), 2003 CarswellOnt 143, 167 O.A.C. 347 (Ont. Div. Ct.). Small claims trial. Judge requested written submissions. No specific directions given for written submissions No submissions filed on behalf of Defendant. Submissions should have been submitted within a reasonable time.

Brandt v. Armour (Township) (2002), 167 O.A.C. 308, 2002 CarswellOnt 2629 (Ont. Div. Ct.) *Rule 21(3)* of the *Courst of Justice Act* provided motion in Divisional Court should be heard and determined by one judge, unless otherwise provided *Rule 1.03* defined "motion" as a motion in a proceeding or an intended proceeding.

Farrar v. Farrar (2003), 167 O.A.C. 313, 2003 CarswellOnt 195, [2003] O.J. No. 181, 32 R.F.L. (5th) 35, 222 D.L.R. (4th) 19, 35 C.C.P.B. 14, 63 O.R. (3d) 141 (Ont. C.A.). The trial judge's intervention usurped the function of counsel and was impermissible. Additional evidence requested by trial judge could only benefit the husband, husband represented by counsel. No basis for the trial judge to intervene on his behalf. Equalization payment raised.

Magnish v. Steeves (2002), 167 O.A.C. 202, 2002 CarswellOnt 3074 (Ont. C.A.). Defendants moved to amend their defence. The motions judge refused leave to amend defence. No basis upon which to refuse leave to amend under *Rule 26.01 of Civil Rules.*

Hilton v. Norampac Inc. (2003), 176 O.A.C. 309, 2003 CarswellOnt 3111, 26 C.C.E.L. (3d) 179, 2004 C.L.L.C. 210-030 (Ont. C.A.); leave to appeal refused (2004), 2004 CarswellOnt 1608, 2004 CarswellOnt 1609 (S.C.C.). Before Plaintiff cross-examined, the trial judge gave parties "some comments" on what he had heard so far. Comments would have been far better left unsaid but they did *not* show he had prejudged the case. Views tentative and he had *not* closed his mind to the employer's position.

Khan v. Metroland Printing, Publishing & Distributing Ltd. (2003), 178 O.A.C. 201, 2003 CarswellOnt 4087, 68 O.R. (3d) 135, 44 C.P.C. (5th) 110 (Ont. Div. Ct.); additional reasons at (2004), 2004 CarswellOnt 564, 183 O.A.C. 317 (Ont. Div. Ct.); leave to appeal allowed (2004), 2004 CarswellOnt 1403 (S.C.C.). Motions judge ordered Plaintiffs to post security for costs under *Civil Procedure Rule 56.* Section 12 of *Libel and Slander Act* provided for security for costs in libel actions *Rule 1.02(1)3* provided that the Rules did not apply if a statute provided for a different procedure. Court rejected argument that the *Rules* could supplement s.12.

Toronto Dominion Bank v. Preston Springs Gardens Inc. (2003), 175 O.A.C. 312, 2003 CarswellOnt 3425, 43 C.P.C. (5th) 236, 47 C.B.R. (4th) 136 (Ont. Div. Ct.). Defendants appealed, asserting, *inter alia*, that: the Practice Direction should not take precedence over The *Rules of Civil Procedure.* Argued Practice Direction conflicted with *Rule 37.03.* Appeal dismissed.

Polewsky v. Home Hardware Stores Ltd. (2003), [2003] O.J. No. 2908, 2003 CarswellOnt 2755, 229 D.L.R. (4th) 308, 174 O.A.C. 358, 66 O.R. (3d) 600, 109 C.R.R. (2d) 189, 34 C.P.C. (5th) 334 (Ont. Div. Ct.); leave to appeal allowed 2004 CarswellOnt 763, [2004] O.J. No. 954 (Ont. C.A.). The Ontario Superior Court, in a decision reported at [1999] O.T.C. 109, 1999 CarswellOnt 3500, [1999] O.J. No. 4151, 68 C.R.R. (2d) 330, 40 C.P.C. (4th) 330 (Ont. S.C.J.), held the Small Claims Court did not have discretion to waive fees. Further, the Court held no constitutional right to unrestricted access to civil courts. Divisional Court allowed the appeal. Court affirmed that Small Claims Court did not have a discretion to waive the fees. Plaintiff failed to establish a breach of the Charter. However, the Court held common law constitutional right to access to the Small Claims Court. Court ordered statutory amendment within 12 months to provide for such discretion. The Plaintiff failed to meet the requirements to proceed in *forma pauperis* because of evidentiary deficiencies.

Currie v. Halton Regional Police Services Board (2003), 179 O.A.C. 67, 2003 CarswellOnt 4674, [2003] O.J. No. 4516, 233 D.L.R. (4th) 657 (Ont. C.A.). Motions judge dismissed action under *Rule 21.01 (3)(d)* on basis it was frivolous, vexatious and an abuse of process of the Court. Any action for which there is clearly no merit may qualify for classification as frivolous, vexatious or an abuse of process.

Obsessions Dress Designs Ltd. v. Tully (2004), 2004 CarswellOnt 868 (Ont. C.A.). Self-represented defendants appealed on grounds of failure to grant adjournment to obtain counsel, and failure to impress that evidence from counsel table not admissible. Adjournment not requested, and warnings as to evidence given. Appeal dismissed.

Stabile v. Milani Estate (2004), 2004 CarswellOnt 831 (Ont. C.A.). Proper procedure for dealing with issue of alleged bias was appeal from judgment. Comments by trial judge unfortunate but made in dealing with costs after giving judgment. Appeal dismissed.

Brooks v. Preckel, 2004 CarswellBC 402, 2004 BCCA 93 (B.C. C.A. [In Chambers]). Respondent in family law appeal self-represented. Child of parties very ill. Respondent caring for child on daily basis. Appropriate to grant adjournment of appeal. Difficult for mother to focus on appeal.

Barrett v. Layton (2003), 2003 CarswellOnt 5602, 69 O.R. (3d) 384 (Ont. S.C.J.) summarized procedures at outset. Reminded her of matters during Defendant's cross-examination and pointed to certain issues in defence. Adversarial system required modification in case of one party being unrepresented by counsel on principle that trial must be fair and must appeal to be fair. Conduct of judge met duty of fairness without overstepping bounds of adversarial process.

Jeffrys v. Veenstra, 2004 CarswellMan 26, 2004 MBCA 6 (Man. C.A. [In Chambers]). Default judgment entered in small claims court. Leave to appeal refused on ground that Defendant willfully failed to appear. Defendant raised arguable issue of law that Court erred in failing to consider whether meritorious defence was raised. Leave granted.

Petrella v. Westwood Chev Olds (1993) Ltd., 2004 CarswellOnt 364, [2004] O.J. No. 491 (Ont. S.C.J.). Plaintiff brought motion at start of trial in Small Claims Court to have Defendant's counsel removed from case. Deputy Judge did not have jurisdiction to order Superior Court Judge to hear application to remove counsel. Superior Court Judge did not have to hear application.

Rogacki v. Belz, [2003] O.J. No. 3809, 2003 CarswellOnt 3717, 232 D.L.R. (4th) 523, 177 O.A.C. 133, 67 O.R. (3d) 330, 41 C.P.C. (5th) 78 (Ont. C.A.); additional reasons at (2004), 2004 CarswellOnt 785, 236 D.L.R. (4th) 87, 183 O.A.C. 320 (Ont. C.A.). Conviction of contempt of Court set aside. Violation of confidentiality agreement not an order of the court that could be punished by a contempt of court order pursuant to *Rule 60*. A contempt of court order based on the Court's inherent jurisdiction available.

Insurance Corp. of British Columbia v. Phung, 2003 CarswellBC 2602, 2003 BCSC 1619, 7 C.C.L.I. (4th) 48 (B.C. S.C. [In Chambers]). Plaintiff obtained default judgment against defendant. Defendant applying to set judgment aside. Application dismissed. Defendant failed to show any meritorious defence.

Schaer v. Barrie Yacht Club, 2003 CarswellOnt 2531, [2003] O.J. No. 2673 (Ont. S.C.J.). Self-represented Plaintiff used status to support arrogant and vexatious manner of conducting action. Conduct justified award of $10,000 costs, based on substantial indemnity claim of $12,298.

Heartland Credit Union v. Lamping, 2003 CarswellSask 109, 2003 SKCA 15 (Sask. C.A.). Solicitor refused to consent to adjournment. Order requiring solicitor to refresh himself as to normal courtesies had no jurisdictional or substantive basis. Appeal allowed. Order struck out.

Roberts v. R. (2003), 2003 SCC 45, (sub nom. *Wewaykum Indian Band v. Canada*) [2003] S.C.J. No. 50, 2003 CarswellNat 2822, 2003 CarswellNat 2823, 231 D.L.R. (4th) 1, 19 B.C.L.R. (4th) 195, (sub nom. *Wewayakum Indian Band v. Canada*) 309 N.R. 201, [2004] 2 W.W.R. 1, (sub nom. *Wewaykum Indian Band v. Canada*) [2003] 2 S.C.R. 259, 40 C.P.C. (5th) 1, 7 Admin. L.R. (4th) 1, (sub nom. *Wewaykum Indian Band v. Canada*) [2004] 1 C.N.L.R. 342 (S.C.C.). A judge's impartiality is presumed and a party arguing for disqualification must establish that the circumstances justify a finding that the judge must be disqualified. The criterion of disqualification is the reasonable apprehension of bias. The question is what would an informed, reasonable and right-minded person, viewing the matter realistically and practically, and having thought the matter through, conclude.

Larabie v. Montfils (2004), 2004 CarswellOnt 186, 44 C.P.C. (5th) 66, (sub nom. *J.-P.L. v. Montfils*) 181 O.A.C. 239 (Ont. C.A. [In Chambers]). Larabie, a non-resident of Ontario, had insufficient assets in Ontario to pay costs or costs of pending appeal. Outstanding costs totalled $27,495.26. Ample authority for proposition that courts are reluctant to deprive a worthy but impecunious litigant of opportunity to have his or her claim adjudicated when not plainly devoid of merit. No good reason to believe that Larabie's appeal is frivolous and vexatious.

Larabie permitted to proceed with appeal without having to post security for costs. Motion dismissed.

Hansen v. Purdue, 2005 CarswellBC 582, 2005 BCSC 352 (B.C. S.C.), Meiklem, J. Costs of appeals from Small Claims Court acknowledge general rule that costs follow the event often applied. Statutory discretion in s. 13 of the *B.C. Act* and in Rule 57(9) of *Supreme Court Rules*. Each party to bear own costs. S. 12 of the Act provides expressly that an appeal not be heard as a new trial unless this court orders such.

Respondents at liberty to amend their notice of claim and are not required to abandon the part of their claim exceeding $10,000. *Rules of Supreme Court* apply.

Poitras v. Bossé, 2005 CanLII 4927 (N.B. C.A.), J.C. Marc Richard, J.A. Appellant sought to appeal decision of Court of Queen's Bench dismissing appeal by trial *de novo* of small claims action. Appeal to Court of Appeal grounded solely on questions of fact. Section 38 of Regulation 98-84 under *Small Claims Act*, S.N.B. 1997 c. S-9.1 provides that decision of Court of Queen's Bench following trial *de novo* may only be appealed with leave on question of law alone. Leave to appeal denied.

Shaw Cablesystems Ltd. v. Er-Conn Development Inc., 2004 CarswellBC 2381, 203 B.C.A.C. 262, 332 W.A.C. 262, 2004 BCCA 542 (B.C. C.A. [In Chambers]), Rowles, Madam J. Based on s. 13(2) of the *B.C. Act*, clear Court has no jurisdiction to hear appeal from order made by a Supreme Court judge when appeal brought from order made in Small Claims Court after a trial. Appeal sought was appeal of order made in Supreme Court on a procedural matter arising under s. 12(b) of Act, that is, whether appeal ought to be heard as a new trial.

No purpose served by granting leave to appeal. Leave dismissed.

Mitchell v. Schonmann, 2005 CarswellNB 51 (N.B. C.A.), Turnbull, J.A. Leave to appeal decision of judge of Court of Queen's Bench refusing application to extend time to appeal a small claims adjudicator's decision and, if leave granted extension of time to file a Notice of Appeal. In *Naderi v. Strong*, [2005] N.B.J. No. 67, 2005 CarswellNB 89, 2005 CarswellNB 90, 280 N.B.R. (2d) 379, 734 A.P.R. 379, 2005 NBCA 10 (N.B. C.A.), rendered January 27, 2005, Court decided small claims appeal concerning refusal of Queen's Bench judge to extend time to appeal (the same issue as here) without leave to appeal having been first obtained.

Intended Appellants formed intention to appeal within time prescribed and had been misinformed about procedure they had to follow. Extension of time necessary to do justice: see *Naderi v. Strong*, paras. 12 and 13.

1029822 Ontario Inc. v. Smith, 2005 CarswellOnt 906 (Ont. C.A.). Appeal from Superior Court Justice Power's dismissal of Superior Court action. Dismissal determined that action abuse of process because it raised the same *lis* already determined in earlier Small Claims Court action. Issues not identical, not substantially the same. Appeal allowed. Dismissal of Superior Court action set aside.

Matlin v. Crane Canada Inc., 2004 CarswellOnt 3648 (Ont. S.C.J.), Hocklin, J. Motion by defendant Crane on grounds Small Claims Court lacks jurisdiction and Court at Stratford not *forum conveniens*. Motion to Judge of Superior Court sitting as a Judge of the Small Claims Court. On December 15, 2003 Crane moved by Notice of Motion before Deputy Judge H. McDonald for identical relief when Judge McDonald, for written reasons, dismissed motion.

This motion dismissed. Order of Judge McDonald is a final order. See *M.J. Jones Inc. v. Kingsway General Insurance Co.*, 2003 CarswellOnt 4594, [2003] O.J. No. 4388, 178 O.A.C. 351, 68 O.R. (3d) 131, 233 D.L.R. (4th) 285, 41 C.P.C. (5th) 52 (C.A.), Sharpe, J.A. See also *Morguard Investments Ltd. v. DeSavoye*, EYB 1990-67027, 1990 CarswellBC 283, 1990 CarswellBC 767, [1990] S.C.J. No. 135, 46 C.P.C. (2d) 1, 15 R.P.R. (2d) 1, 76 D.L.R. (4th) 256, 122 N.R. 81, [1991] 2 W.W.R. 217, 52 B.C.L.R. (2d) 160, [1990] 3 S.C.R. 1077 (S.C.C.); *McNichol Estate v. Woldnik*, 2001 CarswellOnt 3342, [2001] O.J. No. 3731, 150 O.A.C. 68, 13 C.P.C. (5th) 61 (Ont. C.A.); *Muscutt v. Courcelles* (2002), 60 O.R. (3d) 20, 2002 CarswellOnt 1756, [2002] O.J. No. 2128, 213 D.L.R. (4th) 577, 160 O.A.C. 1, 13 C.C.L.T. (3d) 161, 26 C.P.C. (5th) 206 (Ont. C.A.); compare *Lemmex v. Bernard*, 2002 CarswellOnt 1812, [2002] O.J. No. 2131, 213 D.L.R. (4th) 627, 160 O.A.C. 31, 60 O.R. (3d) 54, 13 C.C.L.T. (3d) 203, 26 C.P.C. (5th) 259 (Ont. C.A.). There is no inherent appellate jurisdiction. A right to appeal can only be provided by statute or regulation. See *Gelber v. Allstate Insurance Co. of Canada*, 1983 CarswellOnt 457, 41 O.R. (2d) 318, 35 C.P.C. 324 (Ont. Div. Ct.) at p. 319 per Krever, J. Jurisdiction on motion same as that of Judge McDonald; the jurisdiction of the Small Claims Court. Court cannot sit in appeal of a judge at the same level or jurisdiction.

Gerhardt v. Scotia Best Christmas Tree Ltd., 2004 CarswellNS 83, 221 N.S.R. (2d) 227, 697 A.P.R. 227, 2004 NSSC 53 (N.S. S.C.), John D. Murphy, J. Appellants claimed there was not a fair hearing because they were not given an opportunity to cross examine witness who testified for the Plaintiff.

No official record of what happened at the Small Claims Court hearing. The right to cross examine is a fundamental part of the trial process. When citizens participate in Small Claims Court proceedings without counsel as self-represented litigants, they should not be expected to know the procedure or to realize that they have a right to cross examine, unless they are so advised.

Appeal allowed. New hearing.

Malloy v. Atton, [2004] N.S.J. No. 217, 2004 CarswellNS 218, 50 C.P.C. (5th) 176, 2004 NSSC 110, 225 N.S.R. (2d) 201, 713 A.P.R. 201 (N.S. S.C.), John D. Murphy, J. Affidavit filed by Mr. Atton to supplement oral testimony given by Ms. Atton. Adjudicator received affidavit without cross examination. No official record of what happened at Small Claims Court hearing. Cases involving up to $15,000 are very important to litigants. The right to cross examine is a fundamental part of the trial process. There will be situations where affidavit evidence will be accepted without cross examination, such as where the affidavit has been provided to the opposing party in advance and the affiant is not requested to attend, where the evidence is not disputed or does not address a crucial issue. Denial of natural justice at Small Claims court hearing. Appeal allowed. New hearing.

Jeffrys v. Veenstra, 2004 CarswellMan 26, 2004 MBCA 6 (Man. C.A. [In Chambers]), Twaddle, J.A. Application for leave to appeal to court from decision of Queen's Bench Judge in a small claims proceeding.

Question to be argued must be limited to one of law, as required by Statute. Question must also be one of sufficient public importance to warrant the attention of court. Applicant has an arguable case that the default judgment against her was for much too large an amount.

As a general rule, no appeal lies from a denial of leave to appeal. Another exception to the general rule is where, on a proper construction of the statute under which leave sought, the Legislature did not intend a denial of leave to be unappealable. Leave to appeal granted.

Bhaduria v. National Post, 2005 CarswellOnt 827, [2005] O.J. No. 809 (Ont. C.A.). Appellant appeals from summary judgment dismissing his claim that respondents defamed him. Appellant failed to raise any evidence on motion for summary judgment to support his position that there was genuine issue for trial. Appeal dismissed.

Dzourelov v. T.B. Bryk Management & Development Ltd., 2004 CarswellOnt 4052, 190 O.A.C. 321, 40 C.L.R. (3d) 301 (Ont. Div. Ct.), Dawson, J. Ground of appeal raised in relation to Deputy Judge's decision not to consider *quantum meruit* and unjust enrichment because they had not been pleaded. Not a case where party taken by surprise or failed to develop an evidential record to address the issue: see *Kalkinis (Litigation Guardian of) v. Allstate Insurance Co. of Canada*, 1998 CarswellOnt 4255, [1998] O.J. No. 4466, 41 O.R. (3d) 528, (sub nom. *Kalkinis v. Allstate Insurance Co. of Canada)* 117 O.A.C. 193 (Ont. C.A.). The evidence at trial in this case would have been no different had there been specific reference to these doctrines in the pleadings by name. Pleadings not prepared by counsel. Subject to considerations of fairness and surprise to the other side, if a cause of action has been established, the appropriate remedy, within the subject-matter jurisdiction of the court, ought to be granted. Appeal allowed. Plaintiff's claim dismissed, finding for the defendants.

Furlong v. Avalon Bookkeeping Services Ltd., 2004 CarswellNfld 237, 2004 NLCA 46, 243 D.L.R. (4th) 153, 49 C.P.C. (5th) 225, 6 M.V.R. (5th) 79, 239 Nfld. & P.E.I.R. 197, 709 A.P.R. 197 (N.L. C.A.). Central issue on appeal whether trial Judge erred in law applying doctrine of *res judicata* to facts of this case. No evidence, in the Small Claims action, Furlong elected to abandon her claim either in whole or in part. Nothing in Claim that Furlong had submitted her claim to the Small Claims Court subject to the $3,000 limit on damages by the *Small Claims Act*. Clear case where cause of action in the Supreme Court same as Provincial Court.

Trial Judge erred in not striking Furlong's claim. Appeal allowed, claim struck.

Fraser v. Woodland Building Supplies Ltd., 2004 CarswellNS 78, 222 N.S.R. (2d) 84, 701 A.P.R. 84, 2004 NSSC 44 (N.S. S.C.), Frank Edwards, J. In rejecting evidence of Claimant because it was not expert evidence or supported by expert evidence, Adjudicator committed legal error. Referred back to Small Claims Court for rehearing before different Adjudicator.

Trull v. Midwest Driveways Ltd., 2004 CarswellSask 857, [2004] S.J. No. 800, 2004 SKQB 528, 4 C.P.C. (6th) 324, 256 Sask. R. 314 (Sask. Q.B.), Baynton, J. Midwest does not take issue with the judgment but wants the opportunity to present a defence. Under new provisions, application to set aside judgment must be made to the Provincial Court, not Queen's Bench Court. Although Midwest brought an appeal, it is in essence an application to set aside the "default" judgment so that Midwest can present its defence at a new trial. Appeal dismissed.

Harpestad v. Hughes Agencies Ltd., 2005 CarswellSask 151, 2005 SKQB 121 (Sask. Q.B.), Kovach, J. Trial Judge erred in law in taking "judicial notice" of key finding of fact. Only evidence led at trial was that it was not common for this to occur. Supreme Court of Canada had occasion as to the standard of appellate review; see *Housen v. Nikolaisen*, REJB 2002-29758, 2002 CarswellSask 178, [2002] S.C.J. No. 31, 2002 SCC 33, 286 N.R. 1, 10 C.C.L.T. (3d) 157, 211 D.L.R. (4th) 577, [2002] 7 W.W.R. 1, 219 Sask. R. 1, 272 W.A.C. 1, 30 M.P.L.R. (3d) 1, [2002] 2 S.C.R. 235 (S.C.C.).

2304606 Nova Scotia Ltd. v. Taylor, 2004 CarswellNS 456, 2004 NSSC 218 (N.S. S.C.), Arthur J. LeBlanc, J. Applicant sought extension of time to file notice of appeal from decision of Small Claims Court. "Ultimately, it comes down to question of whether or not justice requires that discretion be exercised in favour of granting application": *Hanna v. Maritime Life Assurance Co.*, 1995 CarswellNS 284, 150 N.S.R. (2d) 34, 436 A.P.R. 34 (N.S. C.A. [In Chambers]) at para. 17. Applicant had *bona fide* intention to appeal adjudicator's decision. Illness of applicant's solicitor, a sole practitioner, sufficient excuse for delay. Application granted.

Atlantic Auto Body v. Boudreau, 2004 CarswellOnt 649 (Ont. Div. Ct.), Wein, J. Issue whether court has jurisdiction to hear motion to have the appeal dismissed for delay. Appellant, in responding to motion, took position dismissal for delay of appeal to the Divisional

Court from the Small Claims Court to be heard on motion to the Registrar under Rule 61.13(1)(b). Court does not have jurisdiction at this stage. See also, *McGlynn v. McGlynn*, [2002] O.J. No. 2047, 2002 CarswellOnt 5795 (Ont. Div. Ct.).

Auto Trim Shop v. Preston, 2005 CarswellOnt 577 (Ont. S.C.J.), J.E. Ferguson, J. Two issues on appeal. Whether trial Judge erred when he so intervened to give the appearance of bias? Trial ignored aspect of claim and provisions of the *Consumer Protection Act* S.O. 2002 and, if so, the effect of same? See *Garry v. Pohlmann*, 2001 CarswellBC 1893, [2001] B.C.J. No. 1804, 2001 BCSC 1234, 12 C.P.C. (5th) 107 (B.C. S.C.) as to the nature of Small Claims proceedings, "appellate courts have recognized that the role of trial judges in small claims court is often, by necessity, more interventionist...," and *R. v. S. (R.D.)*, 1997 CarswellNS 301, 1997 CarswellNS 302, [1997] S.C.J. No. 84, 151 D.L.R. (4th) 193, 118 C.C.C. (3d) 353, 10 C.R. (5th) 1, 218 N.R. 1, 161 N.S.R. (2d) 241, 477 A.P.R. 241, [1997] 3 S.C.R. 484, 1 Admin. L.R. (3d) 74 (S.C.C.) set out the grounds for a successful apprehension of bias at paragraph 113. Appeal denied with costs.

Strikaitis v. RBC Travel Insurance Co., 2005 CarswellBC 202, 2005 BCSC 103 (B.C. S.C.), Williams, J. Principles governing awarding of punitive damages, particularly in the context of an insurance claim, found in *Whiten v. Pilot Insurance Co.*, 2002 CarswellOnt 537, 2002 CarswellOnt 538, [2002] S.C.J. No. 19, 2002 SCC 18, [2002] I.L.R. I-4048, 20 B.L.R. (3d) 165, 209 D.L.R. (4th) 257, 283 N.R. 1, 35 C.C.L.I. (3d) 1, 156 O.A.C. 201, [2002] 1 S.C.R. 595 (S.C.C.) and *Fidler v. Sun Life Assurance Co. of Canada*, 2004 CarswellBC 1086, 239 D.L.R. (4th) 547, 13 C.C.L.I. (4th) 25, 27 B.C.L.R. (4th) 199, [2004] 8 W.W.R. 193, 196 B.C.A.C. 130, 322 W.A.C. 130, 2004 BCCA 273, [2004] I.L.R. I-4299 (B.C. C.A.). Not justified on the basis of a mere denial. The conduct of the insurer must be significantly improper or egregious. Award of punitive damages set aside.

Reynolds v. Spence, 2004 CarswellNS 499, 228 N.S.R. (2d) 199, 2004 NSSC 233 (N.S. S.C.), Donald M. Hall, Justice. Appeal as to whether denial of natural justice on ground bias or a reasonable apprehension of bias on the part of adjudicator? "Bias goes to the jurisdiction of the tribunal. In other words, if an Adjudicator is biased then the Adjudicator loses jurisdiction." See *R. v. Curragh Inc.*, [1997] S.C.J. No. 33, 1997 CarswellNS 88, 1997 CarswellNS 89, 113 C.C.C. (3d) 481, 159 N.S.R. (2d) 1, 144 D.L.R. (4th) 614, [1997] 1 S.C.R. 537, 5 C.R. (5th) 291, 209 N.R. 252, 468 A.P.R. 1 (S.C.C.) at paragraph 6.

See also *R. v. S. (R.D.)*, 1997 CarswellNS 301, 1997 CarswellNS 302, [1997] S.C.J. No. 84, 151 D.L.R. (4th) 193, 118 C.C.C. (3d) 353, 10 C.R. (5th) 1, 218 N.R. 1, 161 N.S.R. (2d) 241, 477 A.P.R. 241, [1997] 3 S.C.R. 484, 1 Admin. L.R. (3d) 74 (S.C.C.).

Test for reasonable apprehension of bias set out by de Grandpré, J. in *Committee for Justice & Liberty v. Canada (National Energy Board)*, 1976 CarswellNat 434, 1976 CarswellNat 434F, [1978] 1 S.C.R. 369, 68 D.L.R. (3d) 716, 9 N.R. 115 (S.C.C.). Though he wrote dissenting reasons, de Grandpré, J's articulation of test for bias has been consistently endorsed by this Court in the intervening decades: see, for example, *R. v. Valente (No. 2)*, 1985 CarswellOnt 948, 1985 CarswellOnt 129, [1985] S.C.J. No. 77, (sub nom. *Valente v. R.)* [1985] 2 S.C.R. 673, (sub nom. *Valente v. R.)* 37 M.V.R. 9, 64 N.R. 1, 14 O.A.C. 79, (sub nom. *Valente v. R.)* 23 C.C.C. (3d) 193, (sub nom. *Valente v. R.)* 19 C.R.R. 354, 52 O.R. (2d) 779, (sub nom. *Valente c. R.)* [1986] D.L.Q. 85, (sub nom. *Valente v. R.)* 24 D.L.R. (4th) 161, (sub nom. *Valente v. R.)* 49 C.R. (3d) 97 (S.C.C.); *Lippé c. Charest*, [1991] S.C.J. No. 128, 1990 CarswellQue 98, (sub nom. *R. v. Lippé)* 61 C.C.C. (3d) 127, (sub nom. *R. c. Lippé)* [1991] 2 S.C.R. 114, 5 M.P.L.R. (2d) 113, 5 C.R.R. (2d) 31, (sub nom. *Lippé v. Québec (Procureur général))* 128 N.R. 1 (S.C.C.); *Ruffo c. Québec (Conseil de la magistrature)*, 1995 CarswellQue 183, 1995 CarswellQue 184, [1995] S.C.J. No. 100, (sub nom. *Ruffo v. Conseil de la magistrature)* 190 N.R. 1, (sub nom. *Ruffo v. Conseil de la magistrature)* [1995] 4 S.C.R. 267, 35 Admin. L.R. (2d) 1, (sub nom. *Ruffo v. Conseil de la magistrature)*

130 D.L.R. (4th) 1, (sub nom. *Ruffo v. Conseil de la magistrature)* 33 C.R.R. (2d) 269 (S.C.C.). Appeal dismissed.

MacIntyre v. Nichols, 2004 CarswellNS 76, 221 N.S.R. (2d) 137, 697 A.P.R. 137, 2004 NSSC 36 (N.S. S.C.), Arthur J. Leblanc, J. Appeal from decision of adjudicator in Small Claims Court, allowing respondents' claim for negligent misrepresentation in purchase of a house. Appeal in part that adjudicator erred in law in deciding case on basis of negligent misrepresentation when claim made on basis of fraudulent misrepresentation. Appellants referred to decision of Newfoundland Court of Appeal in *Popular Shoe Store Ltd. v. Simoni,* 1998 CarswellNfld 48, [1998] N.J. No. 57, 163 Nfld. & P.E.I.R. 100, 503 A.P.R. 100, 24 C.P.C. (4th) 10 (Nfld. C.A.). Subject to considerations of fairness and surprise to the other side, if cause of action established, appropriate remedy, within the subject matter jurisdiction of the court, ought to be granted. Appeal dismissed with costs.

Auto List of Canada Inc. v. Sumner, 2004 CarswellMan 169, 184 Man. R. (2d) 155, 318 W.A.C. 155, 2004 MBCA 59 (Man. C.A. [In Chambers]), Freedman, J.A. Applicant sought leave to appeal decision of Queen's Bench judge and extension of time to file application for leave to appeal.

Person seeking extension of time must demonstrate: (1) continuous intention to appeal from a time within the period when the appeal should have been commenced; (2) that there is a reasonable explanation for the delay; and (3) arguable grounds of appeal. (See *Bohemier v. CIBC Mortgages Inc.,* 2001 CarswellMan 504, 2001 MBCA 161, 160 Man. R. (2d) 39, 262 W.A.C. 39 (Man. C.A.).) Leave to appeal granted.

Moffatt v. Sanchez, 2004 CarswellOnt 599, [2004] O.J. No. 558, 42 B.L.R. (3d) 96, 182 O.A.C. 361 (Ont. Div. Ct.), Sproat, J. Appeal by Sanchez from judgment of Deputy Judge awarding plaintiff $10,000 in damages plus prejudgment interest and costs for breach of a non-competition agreement. Reasonable basis not to reduce damage award on basis of $509 counterclaim. Appeal dismissed with costs.

Boodhoo v. Monaghan, 2004 CarswellSask 754, 2004 SKQB 460, 9 M.V.R. (5th) 128, 255 Sask. R. 103 (Sask. Q.B.), Sandomirsky, J. Appeal from judgment of Moxley, P.C.J. under provisions of the *Small Claims Act,* 1997, S.S. 1997, c. S-50.11.

Appellate function of Court not to retry case, but to confine itself to correcting errors of law and reversing unreasonable findings of fact. See *Estevan Motors Ltd. v. Anderson,* 1995 CarswellSask 132, 129 Sask. R. 70 (Sask. Q.B.). Findings of fact by trial judge on evidence adduced so clearly wrong as to make the decision unreasonable. Appeal allowed.

Greywall v. Sekhon, 2005 CarswellBC 169, 2005 BCSC 101 (B.C. S.C.), Rogers, J. Appeal of small claims matter. Appellants argued that trial judge erred by accepting evidence from witnesses who were present in courtroom during portion of respondent's testimony at trial.

Issue of evidence from witness who had seen another person testify is a question of weight, not admissibility. Trial judge carefully canvassed the evidence adduced at trial, and made findings of credibility and weight based on his observation of the witnesses on the stand. Appeal dismissed with costs.

Wilde v. Fraser Milner Casgrain LLP, 2004 CarswellOnt 4026 (Ont. S.C.J.), Wein, J. Wilde's legal costs for defending an appeal concerning a $7,000 judgment he won in Small Claims Court amounted to close to $35,000. Application for an order referring the cost accounts for assessment.

Wilde had $20,000 at risk on the appeal, including the $7,000 judgment he was awarded, the $3,000 costs judgment that had been separately appealed by way of an Amended Notice of Appeal and the Counterclaim for $10,000. Wilde retained Mr. de Vries whose hourly rate was $400 at the time.

Decision to refer a bills of costs for assessment must be considered in the context of sections 4(1) and 11 of the *Solicitors Act*. Preliminary determination must be made concerning nature of first four accounts. See *Enterprise Rent-A-Car Co. v. Shapiro, Cohen, Andrews, Finlayson*, 1998 CarswellOnt 707, [1998] O.J. No. 727, 157 D.L.R. (4th) 322, (sub nom. *Shapiro, Cohen, Andrews, Finlayson v. Enterprise Rent-A-Car Co.)* 107 O.A.C. 209, 38 O.R. (3d) 257, 80 C.P.R. (3d) 214, 18 C.P.C. (4th) 20 (Ont. C.A.). Reference of last two bills to be made for assessment. Application allowed in part.

PIN Services Ltd. v. Oehler, 2004 CarswellSask 775, 2004 SKQB 470 (Sask. Q.B.), Zarzezny, J. Notice of appeal filed by the self-represented plaintiff. The conclusions explicitly and implicitly reached by trial judge clearly supported by facts he found and law he applied and his judgment does not disclose reversible error.

Moslitho Inc. v. 1293423 Ontario Inc., 2004 CarswellOnt 1434 (Ont. S.C.J.), Weekes, J. Moslitho recovered a judgment for an amount only slightly in excess of the monetary jurisdiction of the Small Claims Court, $11,500. Moslitho's claim was for $57,351. One Twenty Nine advanced a counterclaim for $65,169. Moslitho awarded one half of its costs on a partial indemnity basis.

967686 Ontario Ltd. v. Burlington (City), 2005 CanLII 9334 (Ont. Div. Ct.), Mackenzie, J. An appeal from judgment of Deputy Judge. Supreme Court of Canada in *Housen v. Nikolaisen*, REJB 2002-29758, 2002 CarswellSask 178, [2002] S.C.J. No. 31, 2002 SCC 33, 286 N.R. 1, 10 C.C.L.T. (3d) 157, 211 D.L.R. (4th) 577, [2002] 7 W.W.R. 1, 219 Sask. R. 1, 272 W.A.C. 1, 30 M.P.L.R. (3d) 1, [2002] 2 S.C.R. 235 (S.C.C.) has set out the standards of appellate review.

(1) The standard of review for questions of law is correctness; (2) The standard of review for findings of fact and inferences from such findings is that of palpable and over-riding error; (3) Findings of mixed fact and law are also accorded deference and, absent legal error or palpable and over-riding factual error, are not to be disturbed on appeal.

Appeal against liability dismissed. Appeal as to damages award allowed, in part. Trial costs awarded by Deputy Judge be set off in their entirety against costs of appellant fixed at $350, plus court costs.

Maple View Building Corp. v. Tran, 2004 CarswellOnt 1811 (Ont. S.C.J.), Madam Justice R. Boyko. Plaintiff's appeal order of Deputy Judge. Appeal dismissed. Costs fixed at $2,500 to the respondents.

Deonarine v. Lachman, 2004 CarswellOnt 1807 (Ont. S.C.J.), Swinton, J. In accordance with Rule 49.10(1), Plaintiff entitled to costs on a partial indemnity scale. While costs awarded Lachman in jurisdiction of Small Claims Court, not a case where Plaintiff should be penalized under Rule 57.05(1), as claim against Frank Lachman tied to claims against Rajpatty Lachman, within the jurisdiction of this court, and he was a necessary party. Similarly, the cost penalty in Rule 76.13(3) should not be applied in the circumstances for the same reasons.

Air France v. Ogbeide, 2005 CarswellOnt 1222 (Ont. Div. Ct.), O'Driscoll, J. Sections 6(1) and 6(2) of the *Judicial Review Procedure Act*, R.S.O. 1990, c. J-1 are discretionary. No reason shown why matter should not proceed to trial. Application dismissed.

Kent v. Conquest Vacations Co., 2005 CarswellOnt 1312 (Ont. Div. Ct.), Lane, J. On February 1, 2005, reasons released dismissing the defendant, appellant's appeals in each of two actions heard together. Submissions as to costs considered.

Only minor differences in positions of husband and wife, arising largely from fact only wife gave evidence. The major point was legal one: had the plaintiffs split one case into two to avoid the limit on claims in the Small Claims Court, or were they two parties with separate causes of action?.

Respondents sought a premium over the docket amount of their costs. They referred to *Dube v. Penlon Ltd.*, 1992 CarswellOnt 3359, 10 O.R. (3d) 190 (Ont. Gen. Div.) where Zuber, J. awarded substantial indemnity costs. This case not similar to *Dube*. Costs to respondents fixed at $4,500 for each appeal for a total of $9,000.

Liu Estate v. Chau, 2004 CarswellOnt 442, 69 O.R. (3d) 756, 236 D.L.R. (4th) 711, 182 O.A.C. 366 (Ont. C.A.). Trial judge directing female defendant to leave courtroom while her husband was testifying because credibility was in issue. Direction contrary to Rule 52.06(2) of *Rules of Civil Procedure*. Party's inherent right to be present at trial may be curtailed only in exceptional circumstances which did not exist here. Breach of Rule 52.06(2) not entitling defendants to new trial as order did not occasion substantial wrong or miscarriage of justice. See *Changoo v. Changoo*, [1999] O.J. No. 865, 1999 CarswellOnt 831, 45 R.F.L. (4th) 194, 33 C.P.C. (4th) 86 (Ont. Gen. Div.) and *Baywood Paper Products Ltd. v. Paymaster Cheque-Writer (Canada) Ltd.*, 1986 CarswellOnt 465, [1986] O.J. No. 2076, 13 C.P.C. (2d) 204, 57 O.R. (2d) 229 (Ont. Dist. Ct.) at p. 239 O.R.

R. v. Ricci, 2004 CarswellOnt 4136, 190 O.A.C. 375, [2005] 1 C.T.C. 40 (Ont. C.A.). Appellant complaining that pre-trial judge failed to advise appellant of distinction between agent and lawyer. Appellant made informed choice to be represented by agent. No miscarriage of justice occurred.

R. v. Snow, [2004] O.J. No. 4309, 2004 CarswellOnt 4287, 191 O.A.C. 212, 190 C.C.C. (3d) 317, 73 O.R. (3d) 40 (Ont. C.A.) per Doherty, J.A. A trial judge is not a mere observer who must sit by passively allowing counsel to conduct the proceedings in any manner they choose. It is well recognized that a trial judge is entitled to manage the trial and control the procedure to ensure that the trial is effective, efficient and fair to both sides.

Defence counsel frequently refused to abide by rulings and this understandably provoked further interventions from the trial judge.

Bruvels v. Miller, 2004 CarswellOnt 1180 (Ont. Div. Ct.), Desmarais, J. Appeal from judgment of Justice T.C. Tierney of the Ontario Court of Justice (Small Claims) in Ottawa. Appellant sought new trial in part with respect whether there was a mediated agreement that both parties were bound by.

Jurisdiction to hear appeal based on s. 31 of the *Courts of Justice Act*. Standard of review for appeals from the order of judge whether judge was "clearly wrong"? Standard applies both to findings of fact and to the application of legal principles.

Even when no oral evidence heard, and a judge's findings not based on credibility, still entitled to deference from an Appellate Court. See *Equity Waste Management of Canada Corp. v. Halton Hills (Town)* (1997), 35 O.R. (3d) 321, 1997 CarswellOnt 3270, [1997] O.J. No. 3921, 40 M.P.L.R. (2d) 107, 103 O.A.C. 324 (Ont. C.A.) per Laskin, J.A. and *Schwartz v. R.*, 1996 CarswellNat 422F, 1996 CarswellNat 2940, 17 C.C.E.L. (2d) 141, (sub nom. *Minister of National Revenue v. Schwartz*) 193 N.R. 241, (sub nom. *Schwartz v. Canada*) 133 D.L.R. (4th) 289, 96 D.T.C. 6103, 10 C.C.P.B. 213, [1996] 1 C.T.C. 303, (sub nom. *Schwartz v. Canada*) [1996] 1 S.C.R. 254 (S.C.C.) at 303-6 (D.L.R.).

Appeal dismissed. Learned judge's original award was for $11,600. Deducting the $2,000 award for punitive damages, the final award and judgment $9,600 with interest. Not a proper case for costs.

Bechaalani v. Hostar Realty Ltd., 2004 CarswellOnt 2153, 187 O.A.C. 268 (Ont. Div. Ct.), Madam Justice C.D. Aitken. Appeal from Deputy Judge A. Doyle of the Ottawa Small Claims Court. Rule 7.01(2) of the *Small Claims Court Rules*, O. Reg. 258/98 sets out the requirement of what plaintiff's Claim is to contain.

Fundamental principle of civil litigation that parties entitled to have dispute between them resolved on basis of the issues joined in the pleadings. (*Rules of Civil Procedure*, R.R.O.

1990, Reg. 194, *Kalkinis (Litigation Guardian of) v. Allstate Insurance Co. of Canada*, 1998 CarswellOnt 4255, [1998] O.J. No. 4466, 41 O.R. (3d) 528, (sub nom. *Kalkinis v. Allstate Insurance Co. of Canada)* 117 O.A.C. 193 (Ont. C.A.) at 533-534 (O.R.); *460635 Ontario Ltd. v. 1002953 Ontario Inc.*, 1999 CarswellOnt 3428, [1999] O.J. No. 4071, 127 O.A.C. 48 (Ont. C.A.) at para. 9; *Rodaro v. Royal Bank*, 2002 CarswellOnt 1047, [2002] O.J. No. 1365, 22 B.L.R. (3d) 274, 157 O.A.C. 203, 49 R.P.R. (3d) 227, 59 O.R. (3d) 74 (Ont. C.A.) at para. 60.).

Procedure in Small Claims Court matters is simplified. There is no formal discovery process. The defendant's knowledge of the case to be met comes from the pleadings and from the mandatory pre-trial conference. Had there been any uncertainty on the part of Hostar as to what was being referenced in the Claim, a Demand for Particulars could have been served, or the issue could have been canvassed at the pre-trial conference. Hostar chose neither.

Standard of appellate review regarding findings of fact explained by Laskin, J.A. in *Equity Waste Management of Canada Corp. v. Halton Hills (Town)* (1997), 35 O.R. (3d) 321, 1997 CarswellOnt 3270, [1997] O.J. No. 3921, 40 M.P.L.R. (2d) 107, 103 O.A.C. 324 (Ont. C.A.) at 333 (O.R.). See also *Canada (Director of Investigation & Research) v. Southam Inc.*, [1997] 1 S.C.R. 748, 1997 CarswellNat 368, 1997 CarswellNat 369, 144 D.L.R. (4th) 1, 71 C.P.R. (3d) 417, 209 N.R. 20, 50 Admin. L.R. (2d) 199 (S.C.C.). Appeal dismissed.

2304606 Nova Scotia Ltd. v. Taylor, 2004 CarswellNS 456, 2004 NSSC 218 (N.S. S.C.), Arthur J. Leblanc, J. Applicant sought extension of time to file notice of appeal from decision of Small Claims Court. The applicant defendant in matter heard in Smalls Claims Court.

See *Spence v. Nantucket Investor Group*, 1998 CarswellNS 224, [1998] N.S.J. No. 258, 169 N.S.R. (2d) 176, 508 A.P.R. 176 (N.S. C.A. [In Chambers]); *Tibbetts v. Tibbetts*, 1992 CarswellNS 517, 90 D.L.R. (4th) 719, 112 N.S.R. (2d) 173, 307 A.P.R. 173 (N.S. C.A.) and *Briand v. Coachman Insurance*, 2003 NSCA 39, 2003 CarswellNS 124, [2003] N.S.J. No. 116 (N.S. C.A.) at para. 10.

Does justice require discretion be exercised in favour of granting the application (*Hanna v. Maritime Life Assurance Co.*, 1995 CarswellNS 284, 150 N.S.R. (2d) 34, 436 A.P.R. 34 (N.S. C.A. [In Chambers]) at para. 17)?.

Application granted to extend time to file the Notice of Appeal.

Palmer v. Van Keulen, 2005 CarswellAlta 399, 2005 ABQB 239 (Alta. Q.B.), Justice R.P. Marceau. Appeal by Van Keulen from decision of Provincial Court Judge.

The *Provincial Court Act*, R.S.A. 2000, c. P-31 ("Act"), Section 53, permits a party to appeal a decision from a Provincial Court Judge. The decision of the Court of Queen's Bench is final and cannot be further appealed.

Section 51 of the Act stipulates that an appeal from Provincial Court is an appeal on the record unless a party applies to have the matter heard *pro novo*. The parties have made no such application.

Standard of review applied by a civil appellate court outlined by Wittmann J.A., as he then was, in *Schoff v. Royal Insurance Co. of Canada*, 2004 CarswellAlta 687, 348 A.R. 366, 321 W.A.C. 366, 3 M.V.R. (5th) 69, 27 Alta. L.R. (4th) 208, [2004] I.L.R. I-4313, 13 C.C.L.I. (4th) 237, [2004] 10 W.W.R. 32, 2004 ABCA 180 (Alta. C.A.).

The standard of review that applies to factual inferences is palpable and overriding error: See *Housen v. Nikolaisen*, REJB 2002-29758, 2002 CarswellSask 178, [2002] S.C.J. No. 31, 2002 SCC 33, 286 N.R. 1, 10 C.C.L.T. (3d) 157, 211 D.L.R. (4th) 577, [2002] 7 W.W.R. 1, 219 Sask. R. 1, 272 W.A.C. 1, 30 M.P.L.R. (3d) 1, [2002] 2 S.C.R. 235 (S.C.C.) at para. 25.

Was Palmer's pleading at trial so deficient that no finding of fraud could have been made by trial judge?.

Pleading of Palmer was a Civil Claim filed in Provincial Court and not a Statement of Claim filed before Court of Queen's Bench. As a general rule, parties to a Provincial Court civil action are "confined to the particulars set out in the civil claim and dispute note": s. 34(1) of the Act. However, a Provincial Court trial judge is also granted a significant degree of discretion in determining how a particular claim will be heard. Specifically, see section 8 of the Act.

Litigants in Provincial Court are largely self-represented, and unfamiliar with the law and intricacies of our courts' practice and procedure. As such self-represented litigant pleadings. See *Deyell v. Siroccos Hair Co.*, 1999 CarswellAlta 378, 245 A.R. 294 (Alta. Q.B.) at para. 18.

Pleadings sufficient to support the allegation of fraud. Appeal dismissed.

Chuang v. Royal College of Dental Surgeons (Ontario), 2005 CarswellOnt 3707, 77 O.R. (3d) 280 (Ont. Div. Ct.), Carnwath, J. For Dr. Chuang to obtain an extension of time to perfect his appeal, he must satisfy the Court of the "justice of the case". In considering the "justice of the case," the Court examines the following:

(a)   the existence of a *bona fide* intention to appeal with the time period;.

(b)   the length of the appellant's delay in pursuing the appeal; and,.

(c)   the merits of the appeal. See *Miller Manufacturing and Development Co. v. Alden*, 1979 CarswellOnt 461, [1979] O.J. No. 3109, 13 C.P.C. 63 (Ont. C.A.).

If there is no merit to the appeal, inquiry ends. Lack of merit, in itself, sufficient to deny the extension of time (*Miller, supra*).

Court will not grant security for costs of an appeal simply because the appellant has not paid the costs awarded by the order under appeal. See *Toronto Dominion Bank v. Szilagyi Farms Ltd.*, 1988 CarswellOnt 429, [1988] O.J. No. 1223, 28 C.P.C. (2d) 231, 65 O.R. (2d) 433, 29 O.A.C. 357 (Ont. C.A. [In Chambers]).

Dr. Chuang has until 4:30 in the afternoon on Monday, September 19, 2005, to perfect his appeal.

967686 Ontario Ltd. v. Burlington (City), 2005 CanLII 9334 (Ont. Div. Ct.), MacKenzie J. Appeal by Corporation of City of Burlington (the appellant) from the judgment of Deputy Judge King, Burlington Small Claims Court.

The Supreme Court of Canada in *Housen v. Nikolaisen*, REJB 2002-29758, 2002 Carswell-Sask 178, [2002] S.C.J. No. 31, 2002 SCC 33, 286 N.R. 1, 10 C.C.L.T. (3d) 157, 211 D.L.R. (4th) 577, [2002] 7 W.W.R. 1, 219 Sask. R. 1, 272 W.A.C. 1, 30 M.P.L.R. (3d) 1, [2002] 2 S.C.R. 235 (S.C.C.), set out the standard of appellate review.

Appeal against liability dismissed. Appeal as to the damages award is allowed, in part.

Liu v. Toronto Police Services Board, 2005 CarswellOnt 2492 (Ont. Div. Ct.), O'Driscoll J. The Appellant/Plaintiff appeals under s. 31 of the *Courts of Justice Act*, from judgment of Deputy Judge M. Wolfe, in the Small Claims Court at Toronto, granting Respondents' motion for non-suit.

Standard of review as to whether or not non-suit should or should not have been granted by trial judge is a question of law, standard is one of correctness: See *Mallet v. Alberta (Administrator of the Motor Vehicle Accident Claims Act)*, 2002 CarswellAlta 1623, [2002] A.J. No. 1551, 39 M.V.R. (4th) 228, 330 A.R. 1, 299 W.A.C. 1, 15 Alta. L.R. (4th) 319, 2002 ABCA 297, [2003] 8 W.W.R. 271 (Alta. C.A.), at para. [35]; *Ontario v. O.P.S.E.U.*, 1990 CarswellOnt 711, [1990] O.J. No. 635 pp. 10-11, 37 O.A.C. 218 (Ont.. Div. Ct.); and

Hall v. Pemberton, 1974 CarswellOnt 873, 5 O.R. (2d) 438, 50 D.L.R. (3d) 518 (Ont. C.A.). See s. 134(6) of the *Courts of Justice Act*:

> A court to which an appeal is taken shall not direct a new trial unless some substantial wrong or miscarriage of justice has occurred.

No substantial wrong or miscarriage of justice in this case.

Findlay v. Sand, 2005 CarswellOnt 2402 (Ont. Div. Ct.), O'Driscoll J. Appeal from Order of Deputy Judge Libman, of Small Claims Court. The Order was an interim order that defendant pay money to satisfy a judgment during the adjourned period of a contempt of court show cause hearing.

Section 31 of the *Courts of Justice Act*, R.S.O. 1990 c. C.43 (CJA) governs appeals from the Small Claims Court. It does *not* provide for an appeal of an interlocutory order. By Notice of Abandonment the appellant/defendant "abandoned" her appeal. The plaintiff/respondent seeking costs on abandoned appeal. Plaintiff, Findlay, awarded costs of abandoned "appeal" at $1,687.57, plus costs of attending, fixed at $300.

Lacambra v. Richtree Markets Inc., 2005 CarswellOnt 4380 (Ont. Div. Ct.), Swinton J. Lacambra appeals from decision of Deputy Judge Levine in which he dismissed claim for two weeks' pay in lieu of notice. See *Minott v. O'Shanter Development Co.*, 1999 CarswellOnt 1, [1999] O.J. No. 5, 99 C.L.L.C. 210-013, 40 C.C.E.L. (2d) 1, 168 D.L.R. (4th) 270, 117 O.A.C. 1, 42 O.R. (3d) 321 (Ont. C.A.), where Laskin J.A. discussed concept of issue estoppel in context of wrongful dismissal action, where Board of Referees had already determined employee dismissed for misconduct.

Deputy Judge failed to properly apply principles relating to issue *estoppel*, appeal is allowed, decision is set aside. Matter referred back to the Small Claims Court for determination.

Mak v. TD Waterhouse Canada, 2005 CarswellOnt 1909 (Ont. Div. Ct.), Molloy J. Appeal from decision of Deputy Judge Wolfe dismissing plaintiff's claim.

Both plaintiff and defendant were unrepresented at trial. Main argument of Mrs. Mak that she was denied a fair trial. I agree.

Trial Judge faced with difficult situation. The plaintiff has no legal knowledge and very limited ability to communicate in English. Where both parties unrepresented, common, and often necessary, for trial judge to intervene. See *Garry v. Pohlmann*, 2001 CarswellBC 1893, [2001] B.C.J. No. 1804, 2001 BCSC 1234, 12 C.P.C. (5th) 107 (B.C. S.C.) and cases referred to therein; *E. Manoni Construction Ltd. v. Kalu*, [1997] O.J. No. 5880 (Ont. Gen. Div.). Intervention by trial judge went beyond what was necessary. He virtually took over the examination of witnesses.

Trial judge also unduly antagonistic towards Mr. Moore, agent for Mrs. Mak.

The trial judge never properly explained the process to Mr. Moore. Had trial been conducted in the Superior Court of Justice clear right to cross-examine witnesses. See Rule 53.07(4) and Rule 53.07(5). Trial judge committed fundamental error in declaring a non-suit on his own motion without giving plaintiff an opportunity to make submissions: *Felker v. Felker*, 1946 CarswellOnt 172, [1946] O.W.N. 368 (Ont. C.A.); *Carrier v. Cameron*, [1985] O.J. No. 1357, 1985 CarswellOnt 637, 6 C.P.C. (2d) 208, 11 O.A.C. 369 (Ont. Div. Ct.).

Appeal allowed, the decision of the trial judge is set aside and a new trial is directed. The plaintiff entitled to reasonable costs for this appeal. Moore sought costs of $1,500.

If plaintiff successful in her second trial, she shall be entitled to costs from the first trial as well.

Palmer v. Van Keulen, 2005 CarswellAlta 399, 2005 ABQB 239 (Alta. Q.B.), R.P. Marceau J. Appeal from decision of Provincial Court Judge.

The *Provincial Court Act*, R.S.A. 2000, c. P-31 ("Act") permits a party to appeal a decision from a Provincial Court Judge. Section 53 of the Act reads:

> 53. **Hearing of appeal** — (1) The Court of Queen's Bench shall
>
> (a) hear and determine an appeal,
>
> (b) give its judgment, and
>
> (c) make an order awarding costs, if any, to the parties, including costs of all proceedings previous to the appeal.
>
> (2) The decision of the Court of Queen's Bench is final and cannot be further appealed.

Section 51 of the Act stipulates that an appeal from Provincial Court is an appeal on the record unless a party applies to have the matter heard *de novo*. No such application in this case.

The standard of review that applies to factual inferences is palpable and overriding error: *Housen v. Nikolaisen*, REJB 2002-29758, 2002 CarswellSask 178, [2002] S.C.J. No. 31, 2002 SCC 33, 286 N.R. 1, 10 C.C.L.T. (3d) 157, 211 D.L.R. (4th) 577, [2002] 7 W.W.R. 1, 219 Sask. R. 1, 272 W.A.C. 1, 30 M.P.L.R. (3d) 1, [2002] 2 S.C.R. 235 (S.C.C.) at para. 25. An appellate court may intervene where the inference made by the trial judge is not supported by the evidence.

Was Palmer's pleading at trial so deficient that no finding of fraud could have been made by the trial judge?.

The Alberta *Rules of Court*, A.R. 390-68, *inter alia*, govern the content and form of pleadings in this Province.

> 115. In all cases in which the party pleading relies on any misrepresentation, fraud, breach of trust, wilful default or undue influence, particulars (with dates and items, if necessary) shall be stated in the pleading.

A self-represented litigant, as Mr. Palmer was during trial, is generally granted a greater degree of latitude with their pleadings. This approach is consistent with the purpose of our Provincial Court System. See *Deyell v. Siroccos Hair Co.*, 1999 CarswellAlta 378, 245 A.R. 294 (Alta. Q.B.) at para. 18.

Appeal dismissed.

Legrady v. Custom House Currency Exchange Ltd., 2005 CarswellBC 1305, 2005 BCSC 802 (B.C. S.C.), S.R. Romilly J. Appeal from judgment of the Provincial Court of B.C., Small Claims Division. Appeal dismissed.

Applicable standard of review found in judgment of Supreme Court of Canada in *Housen v. Nikolaisen*, REJB 2002-29758, 2002 CarswellSask 178, [2002] S.C.J. No. 31, 2002 SCC 33, 286 N.R. 1, 10 C.C.L.T. (3d) 157, 211 D.L.R. (4th) 577, [2002] 7 W.W.R. 1, 219 Sask. R. 1, 272 W.A.C. 1, 30 M.P.L.R. (3d) 1, [2002] 2 S.C.R. 235 (S.C.C.). See also standard applied in *R. v. Clark*, EYB 2005-83102, 2005 CarswellBC 137, 2005 CarswellBC 138, [2005] S.C.J. No. 4, [2005] 1 S.C.R. 6, 2005 SCC 2, 25 C.R. (6th) 197, 329 N.R. 10, 193 C.C.C. (3d) 289, 249 D.L.R. (4th) 257, 208 B.C.A.C. 6, 344 W.A.C. 6, 8 M.P.L.R. (4th) 289 (S.C.C.). Judgment does *not* provide a detailed analysis of the evidence in question however, this type of analysis is not necessary nor prudent in an oral judgment. See *Garda v. Osborne*, 1996 CarswellBC 418, [1996] B.C.J. No. 442, 72 B.C.A.C. 101, 119 W.A.C. 101 (B.C. C.A.) where at para. 31, Goldie J.A. stated:

> One does not expect to find in oral reasons the depth of analysis displayed in a reserved judgement. This does not mean that evidence was overlooked or misunderstood. For there to be such an error, its presence must be demonstrated with particularity.

In civil cases, not fundamental to the integrity of process that a party be present at trial or be fully aware of the evidence being presented provided that the party is represented by counsel. That is not the rule in criminal cases. Where a party to a civil action is present, is represented by counsel, and makes no complaint about his inability to hear the evidence at the time of the trial, he cannot be heard to argue on appeal that his inability to hear the evidence somehow invalidates the proceeding in the trial court.

Stockbrugger v. Spark, 2005 CarswellSask 247, 2005 SKQB 183 (Sask. Q.B.), Sandomirsky J. Appeal from Judge of Provincial Court of Saskatchewan.

Jurisdiction of Court described by former Justice Halvorson in decision *Estevan Motors Ltd. v. Anderson*, 1995 CarswellSask 132, 129 Sask. R. 70 (Sask. Q.B.). See paragraphs 4 and 5:

> [4] There is no uncertainty in the law respecting small claims appeals. Section 40 of the *Small Claims Act*, S.S. 1988-89, c. S-50.1, permits the Court, among other remedies to ". . . give the judgment that the judge who made the judgment which is appealed should have given. . .". This seemingly broad discretion has been circumscribed however, by case law. The appeal court will not retry the case, but will confine itself to correcting errors of law and reversing unreasonable findings of fact (see *Ruth Hartridge v. Tri-Fanta Industries*, Sask. Q.B. No. 1695/90, J.C. Saskatoon, September 25, 1990, Baynton, J. (unreported); *Coleman v. Saskatoon Car Town Ltd.*, 1986 CarswellSask 536, 45 Sask. R. 308 (Sask. Q.B.); and *Kitzul v. Ungar*, 1991 CarswellSask 485, 90 Sask. R. 239 (Sask. Q.B.)).

> [5] When this Court reviews evidence to determine the appropriateness of the findings by the trial judge, an approach is taken which is similar to that in summary conviction appeals. Where the findings are not supported by the evidence they may be reversed. Likewise, where the conclusions reached by the trial judge are so clearly wrong as to make the decision unreasonable, the judgment may be varied.

Appellant wishes to raise on appeal issues not raised at small claims trial conducted. Appeal dismissed.

Er-Conn Development Inc. v. Shaw Cablesystems Ltd., 2005 CarswellBC 740, 2005 BCSC 478 (B.C. S.C.), Johnston J. ("Shaw") appeals from decision of judge of Provincial Court Small Claims Division. Shaw also applies for leave to adduce new evidence on the appeal.

The first question is whether there is jurisdiction to receive new evidence on an appeal from a Small Claims decision.

Application to lead new evidence does not amount to a collateral attack on the order denying a new trial.

Bidart v. MacLeod, 2005 CarswellNS 288, 2005 NSSC 100, 234 N.S.R. (2d) 20, 745 A.P.R. 20 (N.S. S.C.), Frank Edwards J. Appeal from decision by Adjudicator of Small Claims Court.

Parties unrepresented.

Procedural fairness must be assessed in the context of the *Small Claims Court Act* which provides that claims are to be ". . . adjudicated informally and inexpensively but in accordance with established principles of law and natural justice." (S. 2) Adjudicator is required to maintain fairness and appearance of fairness at hearing.

Court does *not* have transcript of Small Claims Court hearing. Quality of party's right of appeal dependent upon content of Summary Report and written decision.

Appeal allowed, new hearing before different Adjudicator.

Hodgson v. Walker, 2005 CarswellBC 2952, 2005 BCSC 1658 (B.C. Master), Master Patterson. Application brought by plaintiff for costs in Supreme Court proceeding.

Counsel for the plaintiff argued costs in Supreme Court, from date of commencement, up to and including the application to transfer to Provincial Court.

Plaintiff found to be 50 per cent at fault, damages $1,500, total recovery of $1,800, the low end of Court scale limit of $10,000.

Onus on plaintiff to show, or justify, decision to proceed in Supreme Court. See *Garcia v. Bernath*, 2003 CarswellBC 1903, 18 B.C.L.R. (4th) 389, 2003 BCSC 1163 (B.C. Master).

Object of rule of 57(10) is to encourage actions to be brought in proper forum. Where limited expectation of any monetary recovery, appropriate it be done in the Provincial Court.

Application dismissed.

Classic Super Seamless Exteriors (1988) Ltd. v. Kaushik, 2005 CarswellSask 754, 2005 SKQB 457, 48 C.L.R. (3d) 101 (Sask. Q.B.), Wilson J. Classic appeals small claims judgment alleging trial judge not impartial and that decisions respecting report and invoice.

Appeal matter brought pursuant to s. 39(1) of the *Small Claims Act, 1997*. Pursuant to s. 42 of the Act, a judge of the Court of Queen's Bench, on hearing an appeal pursuant to s. 39, can do one of three things, as follows:

42 . . .

(a) allow the appeal and give the judgment that the trial judge should have given;

(b) dismiss the appeal; or

(c) order that the action be returned to the court for a new trial.

As regards counterclaims, s. 12 of the Act is relevant. Pursuant to s. 40, an appeal under the Act is to take form of an appeal on the record.

The trial judge should have allowed Mryglod to proceed with his counterclaim upon oral request as litigants are entitled to do. Mryglod believed he was entitled to transcripts of evidence of prior testimony before proceeding with his case. Litigants do not have a right to receive transcripts which was explained by the trial judge. If Mr. Mryglod wanted immediate transcripts he could have arranged for his own court reporter to be present to transcribe the evidence.

Trial judge not unfair throughout.

Many of the arguments resulted from Mryglod not being familiar with the law and rules of evidence. Trial judge empowered to make rulings throughout a trial. Litigants must respect rulings when made and continue on. Appeal dismissed.

Myrowsky v. Smith, 2005 CarswellSask 246, 12 C.P.C. (6th) 85, 2005 SKQB 177 (Sask. Q.B.), Dawson J. Appeals from judgment under the *Small Claims Act, 1997*, S.S. 1997, c. S-50.11, as amended.

Court has no power to rehear or retry a case; it is limited to correcting errors of law and reversing unreasonable findings of fact. Trial judge is in privileged position as trier of fact because he has the benefit of seeing and hearing the witnesses: *Lensen v. Lensen*, 1987 CarswellSask 391, 1987 CarswellSask 520, 23 C.P.C. (2d) 33, [1987] 2 S.C.R. 672, 44 D.L.R. (4th) 1, 79 N.R. 334, [1988] 1 W.W.R. 481, 64 Sask. R. 6 (S.C.C.).

See also *Housen v. Nikolaisen*, REJB 2002-29758, 2002 CarswellSask 178, [2002] S.C.J. No. 31, 2002 SCC 33, 286 N.R. 1, 10 C.C.L.T. (3d) 157, 211 D.L.R. (4th) 577, [2002] 7 W.W.R. 1, 219 Sask. R. 1, 272 W.A.C. 1, 30 M.P.L.R. (3d) 1, [2002] 2 S.C.R. 235 (S.C.C.).

Appeal dismissed.

Manji v. Ashton, 2005 CarswellBC 1409, 2005 BCSC 832 (B.C. S.C.), Williams J. Manji appealed to B.C. Supreme Court.

Decision final and conclusive.

Manji filed a notice of motion setting out the relief sought inter alia, that the hearing of this matter be re-opened to admit fresh evidence and an error of law and to consider the facts and the claim in light thereof.

Criteria for the admission of fresh evidence well settled: See *R. v. Palmer*, 1979 CarswellBC 533, 1979 CarswellBC 541, [1980] 1 S.C.R. 759, 30 N.R. 181, 14 C.R. (3d) 22, 17 C.R. (3d)

34 (Fr.), 50 C.C.C. (2d) 193, 106 D.L.R. (3d) 212 (S.C.C.); *H. (C.R.) v. H. (B.A.),* 2005 CarswellBC 1174, [2005] B.C.J. No. 1121, 13 R.F.L. (6th) 302, 42 B.C.L.R. (4th) 230, 212 B.C.A.C. 262, 350 W.A.C. 262, 2005 BCCA 277 (B.C. C.A.). Those four criteria are, in short, that:

(a)   the evidence is credible in the sense that it is reasonably capable of belief;.

(b)   the evidence could not have been obtained by the exercise of due diligence prior to trial;.

(c)   the evidence must be relevant in the sense that it bears upon a decisive or potentially decisive issue; and.

(d)   it must be such that if believed it could reasonably, when taken with the other evidence adduced, be expected to have affected the result.

New evidence proffered by Manji did not meet the test for admission. Not received.

Smith v. Krieger, 2005 CarswellSask 500, 2005 SKQB 308 (Sask. Q.B.), Allbright J. Trial judge dismissed the plaintiff's action and plaintiff appealed.

At the commencement of trial, the judge indicated the following:

> I have a problem here. I just realized that I know Mr. Krieger on a sort of collegial basis. We both used to work for the city of Saskatoon. And while I don't think I'm prejudice in any way, you have the right to object to me hearing this case.

Court familiar with Krieger and at the outset of proceedings brought this to attention of the parties. Parties had a right to object to him hearing the case. Both agreed that it would be appropriate for him to hear case.

Appeal dismissed.

Anderson v. Excel Collection Services Ltd., 2005 CarswellOnt 4829, 260 D.L.R. (4th) 367, 204 O.A.C. 43 (Ont. Div. Ct.), Swinton J. Appeal from 135 A.C.W.S. (3d) 761.

Collection agency appealed judgment against it for damages for mental suffering arising from harassment of putative debtor, who was not in debt to putative creditor. Court below did not err in finding that agency's actions were contrary to *Collection Agencies Act,* R.S.O. 1990, c. C.14 and regulations and therefore fell below standard of reasonable care. However, court erred in awarding damages for mental distress where there was no evidence of psychiatric or medical problems.

Appeal allowed but with no costs, in light of actions of collection agency and public interest in bringing case forward.

Corral v. Aquarium Services Warehouse Outlets, 2006 CarswellOnt 15 (Ont. S.C.J.), Tulloch, J. Appeal by plaintiff of decision by Deputy Judge McCabe sitting as a Small Claims Court judge.

Plaintiff had sought to enter Internet document as evidence. The request was refused on the grounds plaintiff failed to give notice to defendant until very day of trial. Issue whether learned trial judge erred in law as to application of the balance of probability test and he failed to allow plaintiff to file a document from the Internet on Koi disease even when that information was public knowledge and available to defendant. Appeal dismissed. Judge did adjourn case at which time Internet document filed as exhibit. Solely within purview of trial judge's discretion to determine appropriate amount of weight to give to document. Reasoning legally correct. Deference should be given to findings of fact.

Ron Robinson Ltd. v. Canadian Indemnity Co., 1984 CarswellOnt 1354, 45 O.R. (2d) 124, 2 O.A.C. 359 (Ont. Div. Ct.). Small Claims Court dismissing action on basis of *res judicata.* Plaintiff's appeal dismissed. Divisional Court having no jurisdiction to hear appeal. S. 108 of

Act not providing for appeal from order made *before* trial even if determinative of issue. *Small Claims Courts Act*, R.S.O. 1980, c. 476, s. 108.

Gelber v. Allstate Insurance Co. of Canada, 1983 CarswellOnt 457, 41 O.R. (2d) 318, 35 C.P.C. 324 (Ont. Div. Ct.). Interlocutory order made prior to trial postponing trial date. Divisional Court without jurisdiction to entertain appeal. *Small Claims Courts Act*, R.S.O. 1980, c. 476, s. 108.

Morton v. Harper Gray Easton, 1995 CarswellBC 306, [1995] B.C.J. No. 1356, 8 B.C.L.R. (3d) 53 (B.C. S.C.). The conduct of trial on appeal governed by the Rules of the Small Claims Court. Section 3(1)(a) of the Act empowered the Supreme Court, on appeal, to make any order which could have been made in the small claims court.

Since plaintiff could not have pursued her claim for punitive damages in Small Claims Court, she could not claim them on appeal. Neither could factual information in plaintiff's written argument be received in Small Claims Court, as all oral evidence had to be given under oath or affirmation.

Matlin v. Crane Canada Inc., 2004 CarswellOnt 3648 (Ont. S.C.J.). Defendant in Small Claims Court action moved before Superior Court of Justice to stay action on ground that Small Claims Court lacked jurisdiction over subject matter of action. Motion dismissed. Appeal of final order of Small Claims Court is to single judge of Divisional Court pursuant to s. 31 of *Courts of Justice Act*. Superior court judge had no inherent appellate jurisdiction in case.

Er-Conn Development Inc. v. Shaw Cablesystems Ltd., 2005 CarswellBC 740, 2005 BCSC 478 (B.C. S.C.); reversing 2004 CarswellBC 2449 (B.C. Prov. Ct.). Judge concerned with lack of jurisdiction to hear appeal since more than 40 days had elapsed between time judgment signed and when appeal filed, contrary to s. 6 of *Small Claims Act*. Tenant granted extension of time for filing notice of appeal pursuant to s. 15 of the Act.

Lambert v. Clarke (1904), 7 O.L.R. 130 (Ont. C.A.). Where the jurisdiction of an appellate court is dependent upon a certain sum in dispute, it is the amount recovered in the court below and not the amount of the original claim which must be relied upon to give jurisdiction.

Affordable Car Co. v. McCarthy, 2006 CanLII 5129 (N.B. C.A.) 2006-02-20.

Affordable seeks leave to appeal decision of judge of Court of Queen's Bench dismissing an application under *Small Claims Act*.

Application sought to have judgment against Affordable set aside on grounds Affordable had not been named as a party to the small claims action, had not been given notice of the proceedings and had not had an opportunity to be heard.

Nothing in either the *Small Claims Act* or *Regulation* to empower judge of Court of Appeal to grant leave to appeal a decision made under the *Small Claims Act* or *Regulation* other than decision made by judge of Court of Queen's Bench following a trial *de novo*.

Leave dismissed. As interpreted in *Naderi v. Strong*, [2005] N.B.J. No. 67, 2005 CarswellNB 89, 2005 CarswellNB 90, 280 N.B.R. (2d) 379, 734 A.P.R. 379, 2005 NBCA 10 (N.B. C.A.), no award of costs.

Levy v. Sherman Hines Photographic Ltd., 2006 CarswellNS 102, 2006 NSSC 77 (N.S. S.C.) 2006-03-13.

Small Claims Court awarded claimant judgment and costs totalling $6,537.50. The respondent (defendant) appealed the decision partially on basis of failures by adjudicator to follow requirements of natural justice.

See *Laura M. Cochrane Trucking Ltd. v. Canadian General Insurance Co.*, 1995 CarswellNS 270, 148 N.S.R. (2d) 200, 429 A.P.R. 200 (N.S. S.C.), at para. 3:

> Indeed, the Small Claims Court is not a court of record and there is no record of the evidence presented at the hearing or trial. No transcript of the evidence for the appeal court to examine or review. Appeal court obliged to accept as fact, without question, the findings of fact made by the Adjudicator as set out in the stated case.

See also *Brett Motors Leasing Ltd. v. Welsford* (1999), 181 N.S.R. (2d) 76, 560 A.P.R. 76, 1999 CarswellNS 410 (N.S. S.C.).

Appeal dismissed.

Nelson v. Stebbings, 2006 CarswellNB 236, 2006 CarswellNB 237, 2006 NBCA 44 (N.B. C.A.) 2006-05-04.

Pursuant to s. 19 of *Act*, S.N.B. 1997, c. S-9.1, a party can appeal an adjudicator's decision to Court of Queen's Bench; section 35(2) of *New Brunswick Regulation 98-84* under the *Small Claims Act* provides that such an appeal is by trial *de novo* and that a request for appeal must be filed within 30 days after the date the adjudicator's decision is filed. Application for extension of time by judge of Court of Queen's Bench dismissed. See *Atlantic Pressure Treating Ltd. v. Bay Chaleur Construction (1981) Ltd.*, 1987 CarswellNB 29, [1987] N.B.J. No. 528, 65 C.B.R. (N.S.) 122, 81 N.B.R. (2d) 165, 205 A.P.R. 165 (N.B. C.A.), Ryan J.A. at para. 7. Appeal allowed. Application judge failed to consider all the relevant factors.

Appeal allowed.

Duke v. King, 2006 CarswellNfld 79, 2006 NLTD 41 (N.L. T.D.) 2006-03-03.

Duke appealed Small Claims Court decision to award damages to King for breach of contract. Duke took no steps to perfect his appeal for almost 18 months. Application allowed. Appeal had no merit.

R. v. Alessi-Severini, 2006 CarswellMan 75, 2006 MBCA 31 (Man. C.A. [In Chambers]) 2006-03-02.

Applicant seeks leave to appeal decision of Queen's Bench judge, made in a small claims matter. Leave to appeal granted only on a question of law. See Iacobucci J. in *Canada (Director of Investigation & Research) v. Southam Inc.*, [1997] 1 S.C.R. 748, 1997 CarswellNat 368, 1997 CarswellNat 369, 144 D.L.R. (4th) 1, 71 C.P.R. (3d) 417, 209 N.R. 20, 50 Admin. L.R. (2d) 199 (S.C.C.) (at para. 35).

Under s. 3(1) of the Act a claim may be filed for an amount of money not exceeding $7,500. The judge awarded almost $1,000 over that amount. The applicant asserts that the judge exceeded his jurisdiction, and in doing so committed an error in law. Leave granted to the applicant to appeal the decision of judge on the following question: Did the judge err in law in awarding an amount in excess of $7,500?.

Bentley v. Humboldt Society for Aid to the Handicapped, 2006 CarswellSask 164, 2006 SKQB 125 (Sask. Q.B.) 2006-03-20.

Appellant appeals judgment. Standard of appellate review found in *Housen v. Nikolaisen*, REJB 2002-29758, 2002 CarswellSask 178, [2002] S.C.J. No. 31, 2002 SCC 33, 286 N.R. 1, 10 C.C.L.T. (3d) 157, 211 D.L.R. (4th) 577, [2002] 7 W.W.R. 1, 219 Sask. R. 1, 272 W.A.C. 1, 30 M.P.L.R. (3d) 1, [2002] 2 S.C.R. 235 (S.C.C.).

Jurisdiction of appellate court, acting under provisions of the *Small Claims Act, 1997*, is not to retry the case or rehear the case. Judgment reflects findings of fact. There was evidence before the trial judge upon which she could reach the conclusions she did. Appeal dismissed.

Pearce v. UPI Inc., [2006] O.J. No. 1836 (Ont. Div. Ct.) 2006-05-08.

Appellant ("UPI") appeals Master Beaudoin's order.

UPI's appeal of the Master's order refusing to dismiss Plaintiff's claim not proper before a single judge of the Divisional Court under s. 19(1)(c) of the *Courts of Justice Act*, because order interlocutory; see *V.K. Mason Construction Ltd. v. Canadian General Insurance Group Ltd./Groupe d'assurance canadienne generale Ltée*, 1998 CarswellOnt 4909, [1998] O.J. No. 5291, 42 C.L.R. (2d) 241, *(sub nom. Mason (V.K.) Construction Ltd. v. Canadian General Insurance Group Ltd.)* 116 O.A.C. 272, *(sub nom. V.K. Mason Construction Ltd. v. Canadian General Insurance Group Ltd.)* 42 O.R. (3d) 618 (Ont. C.A.). Appeal should have been brought under s. 17(a) of the *Courts of Justice Act* before a Superior Court judge, as required by Rule 62.01. The Master's order also dismissed UPI's third party claim against Kemar, a final order which is properly before this court. Because a third party claim is not technically part of the same "proceeding" as the main action, s. 19(2) of the *Courts of Justice Act* does *not* confer jurisdiction to transfer the interlocutory appeal to the Divisional Court to be heard together with the appeal from the Master's final order.

Appeal dismissed against the Master's order whereby he refused the Appellant UPI's motion for summary judgment dismissing the Plaintiffs' claim. Appeal allowed and the Master's order is set aside to the extent that he granted summary judgment to the Respondent Kemar, dismissing UPI's third party claim against Kemar.

Sepe v. Monteleone, 2006 CarswellOnt 234, 262 D.L.R. (4th) 105, 78 O.R. (3d) 676, 207 O.A.C. 38, 22 C.P.C. (6th) 323 (Ont. C.A.) 2006-01-18.

Plaintiff appealing both dismissal of claim and award of judgment on defendant's counter-claim. Each amount under $25,000 but total amount over $25,000. Appeal falling within monetary jurisdiction of Divisional Court. Word "or" in s. 19(1)(a) of *Courts of Justice Act* to be given its ordinary disjunctive meaning. *Courts of Justice Act*, R.S.O. 1990, c. C.43, s. 19(1)(a).

Kaur v. Deopaul, 2006 CarswellOnt 6388, 216 O.A.C. 247 (Ont. Div. Ct.), Cameron J.

Deputy Judge Iacono dismissed Plaintiff's action as being statute barred.

Plaintiff appealed that judgment be set aside and matter set down for trial.

Three issues in appeal:

1. Is motion for summary judgment permissible in the Small Claims Court?.

2. When did the limitation period start to run?.

3. Did the Defendant waive the limitation period?.

There is no rule in the *Small Claims Court Rules* that allows a motion for summary judgment.

See *Clayton v. Zorn*, Claim No. T96340/04, a medical malpractice action, commenced 20 months after expiry of the limitation period. The court said:

> There is no provision in the Rules of the Small Claims Court to bring a motion for summary judgment. See *Wolf v. Goldenberg*, [2003] O.J. No. 3067, Maefs, Deputy Judge set out the interrelationship between Rules 1.03(2) and 12.02(2) of the Rules of the Small Claim Court and Rule 21.01(1) dismissing an action on a point of law.

> Defendant should be able to bring a motion for summary judgment similar to Rule 20.01(3) of the *Rules of Civil Procedure* for summary judgment.

Jurisdiction in Small Claims Court to dismiss the action, notwithstanding the absence of a specific provision, if the limitation period has clearly expired.

Small Claims Court action out of time. No waiver or estoppel. Claim dismissed.

Elliott v. Chiarelli, 2006 CarswellOnt 6261, 83 O.R. (3d) 226 (Ont. S.C.J.), 2006-10-06, Baltman J.

Appeal from judgment of Deputy Judge dismissing appellant's malpractice claim against the respondent. The appellant "hired" respondent, Vince Chiarelli, a paralegal. Claim in Small Claims Court against Chiarelli to recover money paid him, based on professional negligence and breach of contract. Appeal allowed.

Issue of standard of care applicable to a paralegal: see *West v. Eisner*, 1999 CarswellOnt 4017, [1999] O.J. No. 4705, 48 C.C.L.T. (2d) 274, 41 C.P.C. (4th) 378 (Ont. S.C.J.), Stinson J.; and *ter Neuzen v. Korn*, 1995 CarswellBC 593, 1995 CarswellBC 1146, [1995] S.C.J. No. 79, EYB 1995-67069, [1995] 10 W.W.R. 1, 64 B.C.A.C. 241, 105 W.A.C. 241, 188 N.R. 161, 11 B.C.L.R. (3d) 201, [1995] 3 S.C.R. 674, 127 D.L.R. (4th) 577 (S.C.C.).

Standard of review is palpable and overriding error. Deputy Judge erred in construing relationship between parties and contract too narrowly. Standard based on common sense and ordinary understanding appropriate. Respondent's advice clearly wrong. Respondent misled appellant. Respondent acted unconscionably.

Bird v. Ireland, 2005 CarswellOnt 6945, [2005] O.J. No. 5125, 205 O.A.C. 1 (Ont. Div. Ct.), Clark J.

Plaintiff successfully sued to recover commission. Defendant appealed. Appeal allowed. Plaintiff not entitled to claim commission. Trial judge's findings based on misapprehension of evidence. Costs award set aside. Costs awarded exceeded maximum permitted by *Small Claims Court Rules* (Ont.) and s. 29 of *Courts of Justice Act* (Ont.). Section 29 of Act was to limit powers of Small Claims Court to award costs, not to increase it.

Dunbar v. Helicon Properties Ltd., 2006 CarswellOnt 4580, [2006] O.J. No. 2992, 213 O.A.C. 296 (Ont. Div. Ct.), 2006-07-25, McIsaac J.

Appellants allege trial judge made two errors in assessment of damages for breach of contract.

Appellants argue that because monetary jurisdiction of the Small Claims Court is $10,000, the trial judge should have deducted the amounts set off in their favour from that amount instead of the total damages alleged by the respondent, an amount found to exceed $15,000. Appellants failed to satisfy appeal court that trial judge exceeded monetary limit of the Small Claims Court. He awarded the respondent $10,000, which complied with the applicable regulation: see O. Reg. 626/00.

Trial judge awarded respondent costs of $750 inclusive of approximately $250 in disbursements. The appellants argue that this $500 costs award exceeds the maximum provided for by way of counsel fee pursuant to R. 19.04 by $200. However, this provision has been interpreted as a daily counsel fee award: see *Bird v. Ireland*, 2005 CarswellOnt 6945, [2005] O.J. No. 5125, 205 O.A.C. 1 (Ont. Div. Ct.).

Appeal dismissed. Respondent awarded costs in fixed amount of $3,000.

Boyle, Re, 2006 CarswellAlta 1004, 2006 ABQB 585, 24 C.B.R. (5th) 252 (Alta. Q.B.), J.B. Veit J.

Judge presided over bankruptcy proceedings and contempt hearings. Debtor brought application for removal of judge for bias. Application dismissed. Reasonable observer would not find likelihood of bias.

Ghalamzan v. Aslani, 2006 CarswellBC 2938, 2006 BCSC 1778 (B.C. S.C.), 2006-12-01, Sigurdson J.

Appeal and a cross-appeal from the decision of Honourable Judge Bagnall of the Provincial Court of British Columbia of July 18, 2006.

Section 12 of the *Small Claims Act*, R.S.B.C. 1996, c. 430 reads:

An appeal to the Supreme Court under this Act

(a) may be brought to review the order under appeal on questions of fact and on questions of law, and

(b) must not be heard as a new trial unless the Supreme Court orders that the appeal be heard in that court as a new trial.

The appropriate standard of review in *King v. Holker*, 2000 BCSC 64, 2000 CarswellBC 1435 (B.C. S.C.). On an appeal (which is not an appeal by way of trial *de novo*) to this court from judgment of Small Claims Division of Provincial Court, issue must be decided same basis and same criteria as appeal to Court of Appeal from a judgment of this court in a civil action (see *Stewart v. Strutt*, 1998 CarswellBC 565, [1998] B.C.J. No. 636 (B.C. S.C.) at para. 10). See also *Gomes v. Insurance Corp. of British Columbia*, [1998] B.C.J. No. 280, 1998 CarswellBC 164, 33 M.V.R. (3d) 110, 45 B.C.L.R. (3d) 206 (B.C. C.A.).

No error of fact or law. Appeal and the cross-appeal dismissed.

Canadian Kawasaki Motors Inc. v. Freedom Cycle Inc., 2006 CarswellNS 512, 2006 NSSC 347, (sub nom. *Freedom Cycle Inc. v. Canadian Kawasaki Motors Inc.*) 792 A.P.R. 268, (sub nom. *Freedom Cycle Inc. v. Canadian Kawasaki Motors Inc.*) 249 N.S.R. (2d) 268 (N.S. S.C.), 2006-11-21, M. Heather Robertson J.

Appeal from findings of Small Claims Court adjudicator who found appellant Canadian Kawasaki Motors Inc. liable in negligence.

Appellant relied on *Stein v. "Kathy K." (The)*, 1975 CarswellNat 385, 1975 CarswellNat 385F, [1976] 1 Lloyd's Rep. 153, 6 N.R. 359, 62 D.L.R. (3d) 1, [1976] 2 S.C.R. 802 (S.C.C.). In *Stein*, the court was a court of record. In Small Claims Court there is no transcript of the proceeding. Incumbent on adjudicator to expressly state findings of fact and basis for findings.

With respect to alternate pleadings the appellants rely on *Malloy v. Atton*, [2004] N.S.J. No. 217, 2004 CarswellNS 218, 50 C.P.C. (5th) 176, 2004 NSSC 110, 225 N.S.R. (2d) 201, 713 A.P.R. 201 (N.S. S.C.) in which Murphy J. found that in the absence of *Small Claims Court Rules* the *Civil Procedure Rules* may be consulted for guidance. They also rely on *R. Llewellyn Building Supplies Ltd. v. Nevitt*, 1987 CarswellNS 319, [1987] N.S.J. No. 262, 80 N.S.R. (2d) 415, 200 A.P.R. 415 (N.S. Co. Ct.) where the court found that *CPRs'* 14.20 and 16 could inform s. 25 of the *Small Claims Act*, with respect to the adjudicator's authority to "order the counterclaim to be excluded or tried separately." A pleading in the alternative can be supported.

Appeal dismissed.

Sussex Insurance Agency.Com Inc. v. Insurance Corp. of British Columbia, 2006 CarswellBC 2074, 60 B.C.L.R. (4th) 230, 2006 BCSC 1269 (B.C. S.C.), N. Garson J.

Issue as to appropriate test determining whether to reopen civil trial based on new evidence. Defendants asserted binding authority recent Supreme Court of Canada judgment in civil matter (civil case) which states that trial can only be reopened if new evidence would probably change result. Plaintiff relied on judgment of Supreme Court of Canada in criminal matter (criminal case) where Court adopted two-part test for reopening trial which only requires that there be "reasonable possibility" that verdict would be different. Civil case binding authority. See *R. c. Taillefer*, [2003] S.C.J. No. 75, 2003 CarswellQue 2765, 2003 CarswellQue 2766, (sub nom. *R. v. Taillefer*) [2003] 3 S.C.R. 307, (sub nom. *R. v. Taillefer*) 114 C.R.R. (2d) 60, (sub nom. *R. v. Taillefer*) 179 C.C.C. (3d) 353, (sub nom. *R. v. Taillefer*) 233 D.L.R. (4th) 227, (sub nom. *R. v. Taillefer*) 313 N.R. 1, 2003 SCC 70, 17 C.R. (6th) 57 (S.C.C.) in which the court adopted a two-part test derived from another criminal case, *R. v. McQuaid*,

[1997] N.S.J. No. 20, 1997 CarswellNS 129, (sub nom. *R. v. Dixon)* 156 N.S.R. (2d) 81, (sub nom. *R. v. Dixon)* 461 A.P.R. 81 (N.S. C.A.).

Two years before *Taillefer* was decided, the Supreme Court of Canada considered this issue in the context of a civil case in *671122 Ontario Ltd. v. Sagaz Industries Canada Inc.* (2001), 150 O.A.C. 12, 2001 CarswellOnt 3357, 2001 CarswellOnt 3358, [2001] S.C.J. No. 61, 2001 SCC 59, 11 C.C.E.L. (3d) 1, [2001] 4 C.T.C. 139, 204 D.L.R. (4th) 542, 274 N.R. 366, 17 B.L.R. (3d) 1, 55 O.R. (3d) 782 (headnote only), 12 C.P.C. (5th) 1, 8 C.C.L.T. (3d) 60, [2001] 2 S.C.R. 983, 2002 C.L.L.C. 210-013 (S.C.C.). *Sagaz* followed.

Edwards Dean & Co. v. University of Kings College, 2006 CarswellNS 507, 2006 NSSC 341, (sub nom. *University of Kings College v. Edwards Dean & Co.)* 249 N.S.R. (2d) 222, (sub nom. *University of Kings College v. Edwards Dean & Co.)* 792 A.P.R. 222 (N.S. S.C.), 2006-11-17, Arthur W.D. Pickup J.

Appeal by University of Kings College from an order made by adjudicator of Small Claims Court. No transcript of proceedings. Must be a palpable and overriding error. See *Brett Motors Leasing Ltd. v. Welsford* (1999), 181 N.S.R. (2d) 76, 560 A.P.R. 76, 1999 CarswellNS 410 (N.S. S.C.). Adjudicator committed an error of law. Remitted back for hearing before another adjudicator.

Rébéré v. Van Horlick, 2006 CarswellSask 20, 2006 SKQB 20, 274 Sask. R. 212 (Sask. Q.B.), Gerein J.

Trial judge denied appellant opportunity to call witnesses from church mediation where agreement was allegedly reached. By denying appellant opportunity to call witnesses, trial judge committed error in law. Appellant should be afforded opportunity to have court hear issue of whether agreement was reached and effect of agreement.

Gidda v. Malik Law Office, 2006 CarswellOnt 6506, (sub nom. *Gidda v. Malik)* 216 O.A.C. 241 (Ont. Div. Ct.), Sproat J.

Appeal from decision of Deputy Judge McCrea dated March 7, 2005 dismissing plaintiff's claim.

The Deputy Judge suggested to parties that case proceed on an agreed statement of facts.

Appeal dismissed. Trial judge found negligence and then proceeded to find that the action should be dismissed as damages not proven. As such, he did not address causation. On agreed facts, plaintiff has not established that the negligence of the law firm caused his damage.

Cosentino v. Roiatti, 2006 CarswellOnt 7944, 219 O.A.C. 66 (Ont. Div. Ct.), 2006-12-13, DiTomaso J.

Dispute over payment of solicitor's account issued November 6, 1998. Deputy Judge accepted the evidence of both Roiattis over that of Cosentino.

Judge not required to demonstrate that he or she knows the law and that he or she has considered all aspects of the evidence. If judge states his or her conclusions and conclusions supported by evidence, judgment should not be overturned. See *R. v. Sheppard*, 2002 SCC 26, [2002] S.C.J. No. 30, 2002 CarswellNfld 74, 2002 CarswellNfld 75, 162 C.C.C. (3d) 298, 210 D.L.R. (4th) 608, 50 C.R. (5th) 68, 284 N.R. 342, 211 Nfld. & P.E.I.R. 50, 633 A.P.R. 50, [2002] 1 S.C.R. 869 (S.C.C.) para. 32.

Appeal dismissed.

Meyknecht-Lischer Contractors Ltd. v. Stanford, 2006 CarswellOnt 6806, 57 C.L.R. (3d) 145 (Ont. Div. Ct.), 2006-10-16, Madam Justice M. Linhares de Sousa.

Appeal from judgment of Deputy Judge. *Housen v. Nikolaisen*, REJB 2002-29758, 2002 CarswellSask 178, [2002] S.C.J. No. 31, 2002 SCC 33, 286 N.R. 1, 10 C.C.L.T. (3d) 157, 211 D.L.R. (4th) 577, [2002] 7 W.W.R. 1, 219 Sask. R. 1, 272 W.A.C. 1, 30 M.P.L.R. (3d)

1, [2002] 2 S.C.R. 235 (S.C.C.) referred to. Standard of review for questions of law that of correctness; for findings of fact that of palpable and overriding error. The standard of palpable and overriding error also applies to the inference of fact drawn by the trial judge. Issues raised in appeal of mixed fact and law.

Appeal dismissed on all grounds.

Brown v. Edwards, 2006 CarswellOnt 5472 (Ont. Div. Ct.), 2006-09-06, Justice T.D. Little.

Appeal proceeded on sole grounds that Deputy Judge, while acknowledging the correct standard of care, applied a higher standard in his specific findings.

Correct standard to apply to defendant was that of a simple bailee. Deputy Judge's fact-findings must not be disturbed. He was correct in finding that ordinary standard of care applicable to bailees applied.

Appeal allowed, action dismissed.

Antra Electric (1998) Ltd. v. Faema Corp. 2000 Ltd., 2006 CarswellOnt 1190 (Ont. Div. Ct.), Epstein J.

F unrepresented at trial and plaintiff was represented by paralegal. F's principal called as witness by plaintiff and was cross-examined by plaintiff and judge before putting his case in. Trial judge made no effort to assist him with court process. F not fluent in English. Trial judge ruled that F's only witness could not give evidence. Trial conducted in unfair manner which justified setting judgment aside. Appeal allowed.

Routhier v. Borris, 2006 CarswellOnt 7458 (Ont. Div. Ct.), 2006-11-21, R.J. Smith J.

Appellants appealed from decision of Deputy Judge Houle. They alleged he erred by finding that the words "new roof in 2002" constituted a misrepresentation. Deputy Judge made a finding of mixed fact and law, and according to *Housen v. Nikolaisen*, REJB 2002-29758, 2002 CarswellSask 178, [2002] S.C.J. No. 31, 2002 SCC 33, 286 N.R. 1, 10 C.C.L.T. (3d) 157, 211 D.L.R. (4th) 577, [2002] 7 W.W.R. 1, 219 Sask. R. 1, 272 W.A.C. 1, 30 M.P.L.R. (3d) 1, [2002] 2 S.C.R. 235 (S.C.C.), should be given great deference.

Findings of Deputy Judge required for responsibility for a negligent misrepresentation as set out in *Queen v. Cognos Inc.*, 1993 CarswellOnt 801, 1993 CarswellOnt 972, EYB 1993-67486, [1993] S.C.J. No. 3, 45 C.C.E.L. 153, 93 C.L.L.C. 14,019, 99 D.L.R. (4th) 626, 60 O.A.C. 1, 14 C.C.L.T. (2d) 113, [1993] 1 S.C.R. 87, 147 N.R. 169 (S.C.C.) are mixed findings of fact and law and therefore entitled to great deference.

Appeal dismissed.

Carreau v. Turpie, 2006 CarswellOnt 6513 (Ont. Div. Ct.), 2006-10-20, M. Linhares de Sousa J.

Appeal from judgment of Deputy Judge Houlahan, Ottawa Small Claims, February 9, 2006.

Trial judge did not misapprehend the evidence.

Trial judge stated correctly the legal definition of "fraudulent misrepresentation" as stated by Leitch J. in *Morlani v. McCormack*, 1999 CarswellOnt 1430, [1999] O.J. No. 1697 (Ont. Gen. Div.), and as approved by the Supreme Court of Canada in *Nesbitt v. Redican*, 1923 CarswellOnt 92, [1923] S.C.J. No. 47, [1924] 1 W.W.R. 305, [1924] S.C.R. 135, [1924] 1 D.L.R. 536 (S.C.C.).

Appeal dismissed.

Oberoi v. R., 2005 CarswellNat 5588, 2005 CarswellNat 5849, 2006 TCC 293, 2006 D.T.C. 3110 (Eng.), [2006] 4 C.T.C. 2316, 2006 CCI 293 (T.C.C.), Lamarre Proulx J.T.C.C.

Counsel for both parties signed out-of-court settlement. No evidence appellant forced to sign. No ground to annul out-of-court settlement.

Drzemczewska v. Grigorescu, 2006 CarswellOnt 5720, 216 O.A.C. 119 (Ont. Div. Ct.), 2006-09-22, R. Smith J.

Appeal from decision of Deputy Judge denying claim and granting counterclaim. Appellants allege words or actions of presiding judge give rise to a reasonable apprehension of bias. Hodson also alleges that the fact that he is hearing impaired was a factor which coloured the progress of the trial.

The test for finding a reasonable apprehension of bias set out by Cory J. in *R. v. S. (R.D.)*, 1997 CarswellNS 301, 1997 CarswellNS 302, [1997] S.C.J. No. 84, 151 D.L.R. (4th) 193, 118 C.C.C. (3d) 353, 10 C.R. (5th) 1, 218 N.R. 1, 161 N.S.R. (2d) 241, 477 A.P.R. 241, [1997] 3 S.C.R. 484, 1 Admin. L.R. (3d) 74 (S.C.C.). See also *Sorger v. Bank of Nova Scotia*, 1998 CarswellOnt 2108, 109 O.A.C. 130, 160 D.L.R. (4th) 66, 39 O.R. (3d) 1 (Ont. C.A.).

In the case of *Garry v. Pohlmann*, 2001 CarswellBC 1893, [2001] B.C.J. No. 1804, 2001 BCSC 1234, 12 C.P.C. (5th) 107 (B.C. S.C.), cited in *Auto Trim Shop v. Preston*, 2005 CarswellOnt 577 (Ont. S.C.J.), the Court stated that, "appellate courts have recognized that the role of trial judges in Small Claims Court is often, by necessity, more interventionist." An appellate court must consider interventions in context of the Small Claims Court proceedings and in this case, with fact neither party legally represented. No evidence of any inappropriate conduct or remarks related to the appellant's hearing impairment.

Three contextual factors that must be considered by an appeal court are:

    (a)   The fact that this is a Small Claims Court proceeding and proceedings are more informal;.

    (b)   The parties were self represented and appeared to be unaware of how to enter evidence, exhibits, prove damages, etc.; and.

    (c)   The nature of the case, namely a fact-based construction dispute involving what work was done, was it done properly or not, and the value of the work performed.

Appeal dismissed.

R. v. Shiwram, 2006 CarswellOnt 8424, [2006] O.J. No. 4206 (Ont. C.J.), Knazan J.

Unrepresented defendant not given fair opportunity to cross-examine officer. Trial justice interrupted defendant, then asked him questions which went to the heart of his defence and did not allow him to finish his response. Trial was not fair or had the appearance of fairness to objective observer.

Bhaduria v. National Post, 2005 CarswellOnt 827, [2005] O.J. No. 809 (Ont. C.A.).

Appellant appealed from summary judgment dismissing his claim that respondents defamed him.

A Small Claims Court judge had made a finding that the appellant "did acknowledge that he had said that he had a LL.B. when he did not." Appellant did not file transcripts to support assertion nor evidence that he had attempted to obtain such transcripts. Appeal dismissed.

Esbin Realty Corp. v. Dauson Properties Ltd. & Noik Group of Cos., 2006 CanLII 20089 (Ont. Div. Ct.), 2006-06-14, Epstein J.

Dauson Properties Ltd. & Noik Group of Companies appeals from judgment of Justice D. Godfrey dated June 30, 2005. Ordered Dauson to pay plaintiff $9,223.40 plus interest and costs.

Appeal involved interpretation of listing agreement.

No reason to interfere with trial judge's determination that plaintiff entitled to its commission.

Appeal dismissed.

Pleasant Developments Inc. v. Iyer, 2006 CanLII 10223 (Ont. Div. Ct.), 2006-04-05, Brown J.

Appeal by Pleasant from judgment of Deputy Judge Kilian of Small Claims Court awarding the Respondents refund of $9,300 of deposit of $10,000.

Trial judge erred in awarding Respondents relief from forfeiture of deposit.

Appeal allowed.

Ferguson v. Birchmount Boarding Kennels Ltd., 2006 CarswellOnt 399, 207 O.A.C. 98, 79 O.R. (3d) 681 (Ont. Div. Ct.), 2006-01-27, Chapnik J.

Plaintiffs sued defendants for damages relating to loss of their dog. After trial in Small Claims Court, Deputy Judge awarded plaintiffs $2,527.42 in damages plus prejudgment interest and costs. The court dismissed the plaintiff's claim as against two named defendants.

Applicable standard of review on question of law that of correctness. Factual findings not to be reversed unless it can be established that trial judge made a palpable and overriding error: see *Housen v. Nikolaisen*, REJB 2002-29758, 2002 CarswellSask 178, [2002] S.C.J. No. 31, 2002 SCC 33, 286 N.R. 1, 10 C.C.L.T. (3d) 157, 211 D.L.R. (4th) 577, [2002] 7 W.W.R. 1, 219 Sask. R. 1, 272 W.A.C. 1, 30 M.P.L.R. (3d) 1, [2002] 2 S.C.R. 235 (S.C.C.).

Decision well supported by evidence.

Appeal dismissed.

Piacente v. Zeppieri & Associates, 2006 CarswellOnt 3097 (Ont. Div. Ct.), 2006-05-17, Justice Swinton.

Appellant, Zeppieri & Associates, appealed from judgment of Deputy Judge Skolnik in which he ordered appellant to pay damages to plaintiff, Piacente, of $6,000.

Issue whether Deputy Judge made palpable and overriding error.

Deputy Judge made findings with respect to credibility of all the witnesses.

Appeal dismissed.

Brown v. Godfrey, 2006 CarswellOnt 3091, 210 O.A.C. 156 (Ont. Div. Ct.), 2006-05-18, Swinton J.

Appeal from decision of Tierney J. in which he awarded damages to Brown, $8,723.07, and costs of $150.

Trial judge erred in awarding damages for mental distress. No reference in the claim for such damages. Plaintiff cannot recover for claims not pleaded, since defendants did not have proper notice of issue to be able to respond adequately. See *Rodaro v. Royal Bank*, 2002 CarswellOnt 1047, [2002] O.J. No. 1365, 22 B.L.R. (3d) 274, 157 O.A.C. 203, 49 R.P.R. (3d) 227, 59 O.R. (3d) 74 (Ont. C.A.).

Such damages rarely awarded for breach of contract. Not an appropriate case to award them. See also *Turczinski Estate v. Dupont Heating & Air Conditioning Ltd.*, 2004 CarswellOnt 4532, (sub nom. *Turczinski v. Dupont Heating & Air Conditioning Ltd.)* 191 O.A.C. 350, 38 C.L.R. (3d) 123, 246 D.L.R. (4th) 95 (Ont. C.A.).

Trial judge erred in awarding damages for costs incurred in contemplation of litigation. The costs recoverable matter of procedural law governed by the *Small Claims Court Rules* and the *Courts of Justice Act*, R.S.O. 1990, c. C.43.

Pursuant to s. 134(1) of the *Courts of Justice Act*, Appellate court may make any order or decision that ought to or could have been made by the court appealed from.

Appeal allowed. Award of $8,723.07 set aside, order to go awarding the respondent $5,000.

Stebbings v. Nelson, 2006 CarswellNB 314, 2006 NBQB 195 (N.B. Q.B.).

Defendant brought application to extend time to file appeal for a trial *de novo*. Notes taken by defendant after asking questions on appeal process to person at clerk's office established intention to appeal from time defendant received decision. Defendant understood that clerk's office would send necessary form for appeal. Defendant received demand for payment from plaintiffs. Defendant went to clerk's office to inquire about status of appeal and learned of time-limit. In the interests of justice to grant application to extend time for filing request to appeal.

Wan v. Wan, 2005 CarswellOnt 5637 (Ont. Div. Ct.), Lane J.

Deputy Judge erred in setting aside default judgment granted to plaintiff. Deputy Judge noted that there were number of actions in Small Claims Court between same parties and became concerned about monetary jurisdiction of that court because claims could not be divided to come within $10,000 limit. However, no motion existed to set aside default judgment. Plaintiff had no notice that her judgment was at risk. Order made without jurisdiction. Appeal allowed.

936464 Ontario Ltd. v. Mungo Bear Ltd., [2003] O.J. No. 3795, 2003 CarswellOnt 8091, 74 O.R. (3d) 45, 258 D.L.R. (4th) 754 (Ont. Div. Ct.), Heeney J.

On appeal of small claims court judgment, appellant asserted judge lacked jurisdiction to award damages on *quantum meruit* basis because *Courts of Justice Act* (Ont.) s. 96(3) provided equitable remedies to be available in Superior Court of Justice. Word "court" in s. 96(1) not defined and hence includes small claims court and court's jurisdiction over monetary amounts of $10,000 or less also contemplated equitable remedies.

Dhillon v. Dhillon, 2005 CarswellBC 2541, 28 C.P.C. (6th) 308, 2005 BCCA 529 (B.C. C.A. [In Chambers]), Southing J.A.

Appellant appealed for leave to forgo the filing of transcript of the trial or at least some part of it. The respondent did not agree. *Held*: Application dismissed. Section 10(2) of the *Court of Appeal Act*, R.S.B.C. 1996, c. 77, of sufficient breadth that a judge of the court may dispense with a transcript if he or she thought interests of justice required it.

Union des producteurs agricoles c. Rocheleau, EYB 2005-92512, 2005 CarswellQue 4703, 2005 QCCA 666 (Que. C.A.). Reasons in French.

Certain comments made in course of proceeding that R should obtain legal counsel were made in interest of justice and did not reflect biased attitude. Application dismissed.

CAA Insurance Co. v. Botsis, 2006 CarswellOnt 5087, 214 O.A.C. 323, 82 O.R. (3d) 379, [2006] I.L.R. I-4535 (Ont. Div. Ct.), 2006-08-09, Loukidelis J.

CAA appealed from decision of Deputy Judge Winer granting judgment to respondent in sum of $8,075.

Deputy Judge held appellant estopped from relying on the one-year limitation period.

See *Maddix v. White*, [2002] O.J. No. 230, 2002 CarswellOnt 309 (Ont. C.A.).

Test for promissory estoppel set out in *Maracle v. Travellers Indemnity Co. of Canada*, [1991] S.C.J. No. 43, 1991 CarswellOnt 450, 1991 CarswellOnt 1019, EYB 1991-67614, [1991] I.L.R. 1-2728, 125 N.R. 294, 80 D.L.R. (4th) 652, 47 O.A.C. 333, (sub nom. *Travellers Indemnity Co. of Canada v. Maracle*) [1991] 2 S.C.R. 50, 50 C.P.C. (2d) 213, 3 C.C.L.I. (2d) 186, 3 O.R. (3d) 510 (note) (S.C.C.).

Appeal allowed. Judgment in favour of respondent set aside. Action dismissed.

Bourbonnais c. Canada (Procureur général), 2006 CarswellNat 1030, 2006 CarswellNat 318, (sub nom. *Bourbonnais v. Canada (Attorney General)*) 348 N.R. 28, 2006 FCA 62, [2006] 4 F.C.R. 170, 2006 CAF 62, (sub nom. *Bourbonnais v. Canada (Attorney General)*) 267 D.L.R. (4th) 120, 46 Admin. L.R. (4th) 70 (F.C.A.).

Former member asked IRB to assume responsibility for the legal costs incurred in defending himself. The IRB refused to do so, stating that the member had not established, as required by art. 7.2 of the Treasury Board's *Policy on the Indemnification of and Legal Assistance for Crown Servants*, that he had "acted honestly and without malice within his . . . scope of duties or employment and [had] met reasonable departmental expectations.".

No reasonable and informed person would perceive that judicial independence was compromised because Superior Court judges had to bear the legal costs of their defence against such charges unless there is evidence that the government attempting to punish particular judge.

Walters v. Walters, 2006 CarswellOnt 4137, 212 O.A.C. 77 (Ont. C.A.).

Parties were unrepresented.

Court of Appeal allowed husband's appeal and ordered new trial. Because husband was unrepresented, unfair to discourage him from preparing proper documents and to require him to proceed without prior formal notice of, and without an explicit statement of, the wife's claims. Proceeding to trial amounted to denial of natural justice.

Somerleigh v. Polhill, [2005] O.J. No. 4367, 2005 CarswellOnt 5005, 203 O.A.C. 1 (Ont. Div. Ct.).

Divisional Court had no jurisdiction to hear appeal except as provided for by statute. Appeal from final order of Superior Court Judge to be heard by Court of Appeal. Party sought to appeal order dismissing motion to set aside certificate of costs of $6,908. Appeal not in respect of single payment or not more than $25,000. Appeal ordered transferred to Ontario Court of Appeal.

Ellis v. MacPherson, 2006 CarswellPEI 7, 21 C.P.C. (6th) 258, 2006 PESCAD 3, 253 Nfld. & P.E.I.R. 345, 759 A.P.R. 345, 40 R.P.R. (4th) 246 (P.E.I. C.A.).

Appeal Court reconsidered its reasons for judgment with respect to award of costs to appellant. Formal order not taken out. Appellant's claim for counsel fee on hearing of appeal accidentally overlooked. Fee ordered paid by respondent to appellant together with other costs awarded to her by reasons for judgment.

Lipcsei v. Trafalgar Insurance Canada, 2006 CarswellOnt 1104, (sub nom. *Lipcsei v. Trafalgar Insurance Co. of Canada*) 207 O.A.C. 387, 36 C.C.L.I. (4th) 288 (Ont. Div. Ct.).

Lipcseis sued insurer and contractor. Deputy judge dismissed claim. Lipcseis appealed. They argued oral reasons of deputy judge so brief as to be inadequate under the circumstances. The Divisional Court, per Greer J., allowed the appeal. Reasons two and one half pages in length. Judges owed an obligation to all parties to give reasons for their decision. The deputy judge had not followed that reasoning.

R. v. Alessi-Severini, 2006 CarswellMan 75, 2006 MBCA 31 (Man. C.A. [In Chambers]).

Small claims court judge found that applicant terminated her employment prior to agreement being signed, requiring her to return $8,497 Recruitment/Retention Allowance. Small claims court's monetary jurisdiction of $7,500. Leave to appeal was granted on question of whether judge erred in law in awarding amount in excess of $7,500.

Pirner v. Pirner, 2005 CarswellOnt 6878, 22 R.F.L. (6th) 291, 208 O.A.C. 147 (Ont. C.A.).

Trial judge asked party to call certain witness but withdrew his request when he realized that he should have left the conduct of the trial to counsel. Court of Appeal held that trial judge's intervention did not amount to an impermissible usurpation of the function of counsel nor did it raise a reasonable apprehension of partiality.

Thompson v. Consolidated Fastfrate Inc., 2006 CarswellSask 416, [2006] 9 W.W.R. 414, 378 W.A.C. 1, 285 Sask. R. 1, 2006 SKCA 75 (Sask. C.A.).

New trial ordered. Corporation did not receive fair trial. Employee failed to show that counsel's misconduct did not affect jury verdict. Several comments of employee's counsel inappropriate and intended to invite and encourage jury to make its determination based on irrelevant considerations including emotion and sympathy for employee instead of evidence.

Liu Estate v. Chau, 2004 CarswellOnt 442, 69 O.R. (3d) 756, 236 D.L.R. (4th) 711, 182 O.A.C. 366 (Ont. C.A.).

Trial judge directing female defendant to leave courtroom while husband testifying. Direction contrary to rule 52.06(2) of *Rules of Civil Procedure*. Party's inherent right to be present at trial to be curtailed only in exceptional circumstances. See *Baywood Paper Products Ltd. v. Paymaster Cheque-Writer (Canada) Ltd.*, 1986 CarswellOnt 465, [1986] O.J. No. 2076, 13 C.P.C. (2d) 204, 57 O.R. (2d) 229 (Ont. Dist. Ct.) at p. 239 O.R., "[t]he presence of a party at the examination for discovery, like the presence of a party at trial, is consistent with due process and the right to protect his or her interests by observing the conduct of the examination.".

Thiessen v. British Columbia (Attorney General), 2006 CarswellBC 2194, 2006 BCCA 388, 230 B.C.A.C. 199, 380 W.A.C. 199 (B.C. C.A. [In Chambers]).

Thiessen applied for indigent status and for an extension of time for bringing an appeal. Not the court's practice to make an order granting such status if the judge concluded that the proposed appeal had no possibility of success. No possibility of success. Therefore, not appropriate to grant indigent status.

Peart v. Peel Regional Police Services Board, [2006] O.J. No. 4457, 2006 CarswellOnt 6912, 39 M.V.R. (5th) 123, 43 C.R. (6th) 175, 217 O.A.C. 269 (Ont. C.A.).

Trial judges are not required to vet each and every step in their fact-finding analysis with counsel. Counsel cannot reasonably claim to be taken by surprise when a trial judge factors the failure to produce potentially supportive evidence into his or her consideration of the weight to be assigned to certain evidence offered at trial.

Walford v. Stone & Webster Canada LP, 2006 CarswellOnt 6873, 217 O.A.C. 166 (Ont. S.C.J.).

Plaintiff appealed dismissal of his action and subsequent costs. Divisional Court, per Power J., held that Rule 61.03(7) of the *Rules of Civil Procedure* applied, request for leave to appeal costs award must be included in notice of appeal respecting the dismissal of the action or supplementary notice of appeal. Issue as to whether leave to appeal should be granted under s. 133(b) of the *Courts of Justice Act* not subject to criteria for leave to appeal in Rule 62.02.

Matthews v. Royal & SunAlliance Canada, 2007 CarswellNfld 30, 2007 NLTD 11, 45 C.C.L.I. (4th) 138, (sub nom. *Matthews v. Royal & Sun Alliance Insurance*) 798 A.P.R. 255, (sub nom. *Matthews v. Royal & Sun Alliance Insurance*) 263 Nfld. & P.E.I.R. 255 (N.L. T.D.) (N.L. T.D.), 2007-01-18, James P. Adams J.

Appeal of decision of Provincial Court denying request for postponement to retain counsel. No error committed.

Appeal also on ground trial judge did not exclude respondent's only witness from court during appellant's testimony. There had been no request for exclusion.

Judge's decisions discretionary in nature.

Trial judge noted that it was usual that parties in Small Claims Court are not represented by counsel, appellant had represented himself throughout the proceedings and that he had drafted his own documents in an adequate manner.

Ibrahim v. Kadhim (2007), 2007 CarswellOnt 6 (Ont. S.C.J.); additional reasons at (2007), 2007 CarswellOnt 5606, 86 O.R. (3d) 728 (Ont. S.C.J.), 2007-01-02, Tulloch J.

Appeal by plaintiffs, defendants by counterclaim, from judgment of Deputy Judge. Deputy Judge dismissed Kadhim's and granted Ibrahim's (the "respondent") counterclaim.

Interventions did not result in unfair trial or created reasonable apprehension of bias. Nature of Small Claims Court proceedings by necessity results in trial judges being more interventionist. See *Garry v. Pohlmann*, 2001 CarswellBC 1893, [2001] B.C.J. No. 1804, 2001 BCSC 1234, 12 C.P.C. (5th) 107 (B.C. S.C.), at page 12 and *Wil v. Burdman*, [1998] O.J. No. 2533, 1998 CarswellOnt 2541 (Ont. Div. Ct.). Appeal dismissed.

Levy v. Sherman Hines Photographic Ltd., 2006 CarswellNS 102, 2006 NSSC 77 (N.S. S.C.), Warner J.

Defendant appealed judgment against it rendered by adjudicator of small claims court. No record transcribed and appeal limited to summary report prepared by adjudicator. Appellate court required to accept facts related therein as true. None of defendant's grounds of appeal which related to procedural fairness borne out by summary report. Appeal denied.

Cymbalski v. Alcorn, 2006 CarswellOnt 1498, 209 O.A.C. 47 (Ont. Div. Ct.).

Ontario Housing Rental Tribunal allowed landlord's application to terminate a tenancy. The tenants appealed. No transcript or tape recording was available for the proceedings due to a mechanical malfunctioning of recording equipment.

In the absence of transcript, the court could not determine issues raised on the appeal. Court allowed appeal, set aside the decision, and directed that matter be remitted to Tribunal.

Gemmell v. Reddicopp, 2005 CarswellBC 3041, 48 B.C.L.R. (4th) 349, 2005 BCCA 628, 220 B.C.A.C. 219, 362 W.A.C. 219 (B.C. C.A.).

Reasonable apprehension of bias. King represented Gemmell. During cross-examination, trial judge made comments to King regarding legal education and King's conduct.

Court of Appeal dismissed appeal. Trial judge's interjections might have been intemperate but had not risen to level necessary to establish reasonable apprehension of bias. The trial obviously difficult. Objective observer would not have considered judge to be biased.

Armstrong v. McCall, 2006 CarswellOnt 3134, [2006] O.J. No. 2055, 28 C.P.C. (6th) 12, 213 O.A.C. 229 (Ont. C.A.).

Physicians successfully brought third motion to dismiss action for delay or for failure to comply with court orders and were awarded $13,500 for costs of action and motion to dismiss. Plaintiff appealed. Appeal allowed. Although there was considerable delay, plaintiff rebutted presumption of prejudice and physicians failed to provide convincing evidence of prejudice that they would be unable to have fair trial.

Royal Bank v. Goebel, 2006 CarswellAlta 612, 30 C.P.C. (6th) 141, 2006 ABQB 369 (Alta. Q.B.).

Defendants brought application in June 2000 and application was adjourned on consent until May 2006. Application granted. Defendants failed to move promptly almost six years ago. Since consent adjournment there were three cross-examinations on male defendant's affidavit and undertakings, scheduling delays, and delays of 12 months and 15 months regarding undertakings. Delay had been wilful or that defendants failed to move promptly.

2878852 Canada Inc. v. Jones Heward Investment Counsel Inc., 2007 CarswellOnt 90, [2007] O.J. No. 78, 2007 ONCA 14 (Ont. C.A.).

Trial judge's decision to incorporate parts of parties' written argument into reasons ill-advised and unfortunate. Reasons should be comprehensive on their own. Nevertheless, trial judge adequately explained his credibility finds.

Appeal dismissed. Reasons sufficient to meet test in *R. v. Sheppard*, 2002 SCC 26, [2002] S.C.J. No. 30, 2002 CarswellNfld 74, 2002 CarswellNfld 75, 162 C.C.C. (3d) 298, 210 D.L.R. (4th) 608, 50 C.R. (5th) 68, 284 N.R. 342, 211 Nfld. & P.E.I.R. 50, 633 A.P.R. 50, [2002] 1 S.C.R. 869 (S.C.C.), as discussed in a civil context in *Canadian Broadcasting Corp. Pension Plan v. BF Realty Holdings Ltd.*, [2002] O.J. No. 2125, 2002 CarswellOnt

1759, 214 D.L.R. (4th) 121, 26 B.L.R. (3d) 180, 35 C.B.R. (4th) 197, *(*sub nom. *MacDonald v. BF Realty Holdings Ltd.)* 160 O.A.C. 72 (Ont. C.A.).

Keays v. Honda Canada Inc., 2006 CarswellOnt 5885, [2006] O.J. No. 3891, 216 O.A.C. 3, 82 O.R. (3d) 161, 274 D.L.R. (4th) 107, 2006 C.L.L.C. 230-030, 52 C.C.E.L. (3d) 165 (Ont. C.A.).

Trial judge used several colourful metaphors. However, evidence sustained findings of bad faith and outrageous and high-handed conduct, some strong judicial language could not be avoided. Nor could it be said to reflect a want of fairness or impartiality in coming to those conclusions.

This ground of appeal failed.

P. (M.N.) (Next Friend of) v. Whitecourt General Hospital, 2006 CarswellAlta 1071, [2006] 12 W.W.R. 397, 397 A.R. 333, 384 W.A.C. 333, 2006 ABCA 245, 64 Alta. L.R. (4th) 1 (Alta. C.A.).

Appellant denied opportunity to test on cross-examination or rebut with evidence the proposition advanced by the trial judge. Issue did not arise during course of evidentiary portion of trial.

See *Rodaro v. Royal Bank*, 2002 CarswellOnt 1047, [2002] O.J. No. 1365, 22 B.L.R. (3d) 274, 157 O.A.C. 203, 49 R.P.R. (3d) 227, 59 O.R. (3d) 74 (Ont. C.A.) at 93:

> It is fundamental to the litigation process that lawsuits be decided within the boundaries of the pleadings. As Labrosse J.A. said in *460635 Ontario Ltd. v. 1002953 Ontario Inc.*, 1999 CarswellOnt 3428, [1999] O.J. No. 4071, 127 O.A.C. 48 (Ont. C.A.) at para. 9:
>
> > . . . The parties to a legal suit are entitled to have a resolution of their differences on the basis of the issues joined in the pleadings. A finding of liability and resulting damages against the defendant on a basis that was not pleaded in the statement of claim cannot stand. It deprives the defendant of the opportunity to address that issue in the evidence at trial. . . .

New trial confined to theory of causation not tested at first trial.

R. v. Ertmoed, 2006 CarswellBC 2253, 2006 BCCA 365, 229 B.C.A.C. 168, 379 W.A.C. 168, 211 C.C.C. (3d) 49 (B.C. C.A.).

Accused appealed his conviction, submitting 1) that his lawyer was incompetent and rendered ineffective assistance at trial and 2) right to a fair trial prejudiced by trial judge's disparagement of defence counsel and defence advanced by him. Appeal dismissed.

Judge has duty to control trial process and to protect witnesses from repetitious and irrelevant questions. Judge's patience sorely tried, but nothing he said, either in isolation or collectively, could reasonably be said to have prejudiced a fair trial.

Baltruweit v. Rubin, 2006 CarswellOnt 3886 (Ont. C.A.), Cronk, Blair JJ.A. and Then J. (ad hoc). Appeal from 2005 CarswellOnt 3017 (Ont. S.C.J.) dismissed.

Trial judge producing outcome unfavourable to appellant did not mean trial judge biased against him or that he chose to disbelieve appellant based on prohibited stereotypical reasoning.

Atlantic Chemex Ltd. v. B. & D. Welders & Auto Repairs Ltd., 2006 CarswellNS 286, 2006 NSSC 198 (N.S. S.C.), LeBlanc J.

On appeal from decision of Small Claims Court adjudicator, inadequate record made it impossible for court to make determination as to whether there was error of law. Reasons brief and no transcript of proceedings. New hearing before new adjudicator was ordered.

Rando Drugs Ltd. v. Scott, 2007 CarswellOnt 4888, [2007] O.J. No. 2999, 42 C.P.C. (6th) 23, 2007 ONCA 553, 284 D.L.R. (4th) 756, 229 O.A.C. 1, 86 O.R. (3d) 641, *(*sub nom.

Rando Drugs Ltd. c. Scott) 86 O.R. (3d) 653 (Ont. C.A.); leave to appeal refused (2008), 2008 CarswellOnt 353, 2008 CarswellOnt 354, 384 N.R. 398 (note), 249 O.A.C. 39 (S.C.C.).

The issue is whether circumstances give rise to reasonable apprehension of bias because of prior involvement of trial judge's former firm in litigation. Test to be applied set out in the Supreme Court of Canada. *Committee for Justice & Liberty v. Canada (National Energy Board)*, 1976 CarswellNat 434, 1976 CarswellNat 434F, [1978] 1 S.C.R. 369, 68 D.L.R. (3d) 716, 9 N.R. 115 (S.C.C.), *R. v. S. (R.D.)*, 1997 CarswellNS 301, 1997 CarswellNS 302, [1997] S.C.J. No. 84, 151 D.L.R. (4th) 193, 118 C.C.C. (3d) 353, 10 C.R. (5th) 1, 218 N.R. 1, 161 N.S.R. (2d) 241, 477 A.P.R. 241, [1997] 3 S.C.R. 484, 1 Admin. L.R. (3d) 74 (S.C.C.) and *Roberts v. R.* (2003), 2003 SCC 45, (sub nom. *Wewaykum Indian Band v. Canada)* [2003] S.C.J. No. 50, 2003 CarswellNat 2822, 2003 CarswellNat 2823, 231 D.L.R. (4th) 1, 19 B.C.L.R. (4th) 195, (sub nom. *Wewayakum Indian Band v. Canada)* 309 N.R. 201, [2004] 2 W.W.R. 1, (sub nom. *Wewayakum Indian Band v. Canada)* [2003] 2 S.C.R. 259, 40 C.P.C. (5th) 1, 7 Admin. L.R. (4th) 1, (sub nom. *Wewaykum Indian Band v. Canada)* [2004] 1 C.N.L.R. 342 (S.C.C.).

The accepted test for reasonable apprehension of bias is found at pp. 394-95 S.C.R. of de Grandpré J.'s dissenting reasons in *Committee for Justice & Liberty*:

> ... the apprehension of bias must be a reasonable one, held by reasonable and right minded persons, applying themselves to the question and obtaining thereon the required information. ... that test is 'what would an informed person, viewing the matter realistically and practically — and having thought the matter through — conclude. Would he think that it is more likely than not that [the decision-maker], whether consciously or unconsciously, would not decide fairly.'

> . . . . .

> The grounds for this apprehension must, however, be substantial and I ... [refuse] to accept the suggestion that the test be related to the 'very sensitive or scrupulous conscience.'

In *Locabail (U.K.) Ltd. v. Bayfield Properties Ltd.*, [1999] E.W.J. No. 5918, [2000] Q.B. 451, [2000] 1 All E.R. 65 (Eng. C.A.), the court held, at para. 58, that there is no inflexible rule governing the disqualification of a judge and that, "[e]verything depends on the circumstances.".

Diamond Auto Collision Inc. v. Economical Insurance Group, 2007 CarswellOnt 4196, [2007] O.J. No. 2551, 2007 ONCA 487, 50 C.C.L.I. (4th) 213, 227 O.A.C. 51 (Ont. C.A.), Weiler, Simmons and LaForme, JJ.A.

Appeal dismissed. The standard for measuring the adequacy of reasons derived from *R. v. Sheppard*, 2002 SCC 26, [2002] S.C.J. No. 30, 2002 CarswellNfld 74, 2002 CarswellNfld 75, 162 C.C.C. (3d) 298, 210 D.L.R. (4th) 608, 50 C.R. (5th) 68, 284 N.R. 342, 211 Nfld. & P.E.I.R. 50, 633 A.P.R. 50, [2002] 1 S.C.R. 869 (S.C.C.). The three functions of reasons for judgment at trial are: (1) explaining to the losing party why he or she lost; (2) enabling informed consideration as to whether to appeal; and (3) enabling interested members of the public to see whether justice has been done. Reasons that fulfill functional requirements are, in short, reasons that permit meaningful appellate review.

Standing alone, the trial judge's reasons make meaningful appellate review difficult. In the result, however, even if the appellants are correct in their submission that the trial judge's reasons do not fulfill the functional requirement of reasons as they ought to, having regard to the record, the basis for her rejection is patent and the appellants have been told why they lost.

FL Receivables Trust 2002-A (Administrator of) v. Cobrand Foods Ltd., 2007 CarswellOnt 3697, 2007 ONCA 425, 85 O.R. (3d) 561, 46 C.P.C. (6th) 23, [2007] O.J. No. 2297 (Ont. C.A.), Laskin, Borins and Feldman JJ.A.

No miscarriage of justice even though party denied opportunity to make closing argument where party has fully argued case. Principle of appellate deference to trial judge's fact-finding and inference-drawing applies even when entire trial record is in writing. Trial judge must dismiss motion if plaintiff puts forward some evidence on all elements of its claim. Appeal dismissed.

The principle of appellate deference to a trial judge's fact-finding and inference-drawing applies even when the entire trial record is in writing. The principle of deference applies to the trial judge's finding that Prudential failed to establish that the transfers were fraudulent. That finding was based on inferences that the trial judge drew from the factual record.

Saylor v. Madsen Estate, [2007] S.C.J. No. 18, 2007 CarswellOnt 2754, 2007 CarswellOnt 2755, (sub nom. *Saylor v. Brooks*) 360 N.R. 327, 42 C.P.C. (6th) 1, 2007 SCC 18, 32 E.T.R. (3d) 61, (sub nom. *Saylor v. Brooks*) 224 O.A.C. 382, 279 D.L.R. (4th) 547, (sub nom. *Madsen Estate v. Saylor*) [2007] 1 S.C.R. 838 (S.C.C.).

Powers of appellate court. Trial judge failing to consider all evidence. Matter outstanding for nine years and amount in issue relatively small. Interests of justice for appellate court to consider evidence and make final determination rather than send matter back for new trial.

Roeder v. Lang Michener Lawrence & Shaw, [2007] B.C.J. No. 501, 2007 CarswellBC 544, 238 B.C.A.C. 164, 393 W.A.C. 164, 2007 BCCA 152, [2007] 7 W.W.R. 639, 67 B.C.L.R. (4th) 301, 280 D.L.R. (4th) 294 (B.C. C.A.).

Appeal untenable because there is no action in law for damages for breach of duty of fairness. Remedy for such a breach lies in administrative law by way of judicial review. Typically, remedy is a rehearing, but the court has right to refuse relief if no substantial wrong or miscarriage of justice has occurred. Plaintiff conceded on appeal that the result of the 1994 proceedings would have been the same without the alleged misconduct on the part of the lawyers.

Wiseman's Sales & Services Ltd. v. Atlantic Insurance Co., 2007 CarswellNfld 82, 45 C.C.L.I. (4th) 192, 264 Nfld. & P.E.I.R. 86, 801 A.P.R. 86, 2007 NLCA 15, [2007] I.L.R. I-4585, 280 D.L.R. (4th) 47 (N.L. C.A.).

Appeal allowed. On appeal, the court can consider new issue of law if it can do so without procedural prejudice to other party and if refusal to do so would lead to an injustice. The application for an order permitting it to adduce further evidence dismissed. No credible and relevant evidence that could reasonably be expected to have affected the result at trial, had it been adduced there.

Hanna v. Abbott, 2006 CarswellOnt 4937, (sub nom. *W.H. v. H.C.A.*) [2006] O.J. No. 3283, 82 O.R. (3d) 215, 219 O.A.C. 73, (sub nom. *Hanna (Litigation Guardian of) v. Abbott*) 272 D.L.R. (4th) 621, 31 C.P.C. (6th) 207 (Ont. C.A.).

Trial judge held, although father's convictions were *prima facie* proof of alleged abuse, that the father's evidence (sons' testimony) rebutted that proof. The Ontario Court of Appeal allowed the plaintiff's appeal. The doctrine of abuse of process ought to have precluded the father from contesting the underlying facts of his convictions.

Cosentino v. Roiatti, 2006 CarswellOnt 7944, 219 O.A.C. 66 (Ont. Div. Ct.).

A lawyer commenced a small claims action against former clients for payment of his outstanding account. Deputy judge dismissed the action based the parties' agreement, estoppel and the lawyer's unreasonable delay in bringing the action. The lawyer appealed. The Ontario Divisional Court dismissed the appeal. The judge's finding respecting the parties' agreement left only the lawyer's equitable claim (*quantum meruit*) for the further fees. The evidence supported the conclusion that the lawyer's delay in initiating the action for almost six years (just before limitation period expired) caused the clients to not proceed with their application to assess the lawyer's account and permitted a situation to arise which would be unjust to disturb in the circumstances.

Niagara North Condominium Corp. No. 125 v. Waddington, [2007] O.J. No. 936, 2007 CarswellOnt 1486, 222 O.A.C. 66, 52 R.P.R. (4th) 230, 2007 ONCA 184 (Ont. C.A.).

Application dismissed by Superior Court of Justice not appealed. Another Superior Court judge dismissed the application on the ground that it was an abuse of process, where the same facts and issues were involved, and a corporation employee had even sworn the affidavit in the original application. The corporation appealed. The Court of Appeal dismissed the appeal.

Steward v. Berezan, 2007 CarswellBC 542, 238 B.C.A.C. 159, 393 W.A.C. 159, 2007 BCCA 150, 64 B.C.L.R. (4th) 152, [2007] B.C.J. No. 499 (B.C. C.A.); additional reasons at 2009 CarswellBC 3136, 2009 BCCA 524, 99 B.C.L.R. (4th) 156 (B.C. C.A.).

Duty of appellate court where trial judge fails to give or gives inadequate reasons for judgment. The failure to discuss a relevant factor in depth, or even at all not itself a sufficient basis for an appellate court to reconsider the evidence. The omission only a "material error" if it gave rise to the "reasoned belief that the trial judge must have forgotten, ignored or misconceived the evidence in a way that affect [the] conclusion.".

Walford v. Stone & Webster Canada LP, 2006 CarswellOnt 6873, 217 O.A.C. 166 (Ont. S.C.J.), Power J.

Small Claims Court judge dismissed employee's action for wrongful dismissal and awarded costs in favour of employer fixed at $1,500 plus disbursements of $1,299.33. Employee appealed and subsequently amended notice of appeal to include appeal from costs award. Appeal dismissed. Pursuant to s. 31 of *Courts of Justice Act*, because employee claimed damages in excess of $10,000, he had to appeal as of right to Divisional Court with respect to dismissal of his action. Section 31 of Act silent as to appeal from costs applied and therefore leave to appeal costs award should have been included in notice of appeal or supplementary notice of appeal. Leave to appeal granted. However, appeal dismissed as award was reasonable for two-day trial with extensive documentation which was followed by written submissions.

Strudwick v. Lee, 2007 CarswellSask 43, [2007] S.J. No. 25, 2007 SKCA 11, 382 W.A.C. 269, 289 Sask. R. 269 (Sask. C.A.); leave to appeal refused (2007), 2007 CarswellSask 371, 2007 CarswellSask 372, 375 N.R. 393 (note), 314 Sask. R. 319 (note), 435 W.A.C. 319 (note) (S.C.C.).

Chambers judge's description of defendant as "self-styled advocate" and her comments such as "he purportedly received," "he relishes an opportunity," did not indicate that she was biased in fact; nor did they in any way raise reasonable apprehension of bias.

Gallop v. Jaegar (2007), 2007 CarswellOnt 6292 (Ont. Div. Ct.), 2007-10-02, Archibald J.

What is the obligation of a Small Claims Court judge to provide reasons in dismissing a plaintiff's statement of claim and in granting the defendant's counterclaim? The Supreme Court's ruling in *R. v. Shepherd* is clear that a modicum level of analysis should be provided. Both parties desire additional time to amend their factums. A new date will be set by the Registrar once the parties have addressed the issue of the adequacy of the reasons.

Brooker v. Silver (2007), 2007 CarswellOnt 7790, 232 O.A.C. 83, 67 C.L.R. (3d) 306 (Ont. Div. Ct.), 2007-12-03, Carnwath J.

Pursuant to s. 134(1) of the *Courts of Justice Act*, the court may make any order or decision that ought to or could have been made by the court appealed from or order a new trial. Pursuant to s. 134(4) of the *Courts of Justice Act*, the court may, in a proper case, draw inferences of fact from the evidence. Appeal granted. Independence Way Inc. ordered to return deposit in the sum of $10,000, recognizing the limit of the Small Claims Court jurisdiction. Brookers entitled to disbursements, including court costs for appeal and cost of transcript.

Bookman v. U-Haul Co. (Canada) Ltd. (2007), 2007 CarswellOnt 5714, 229 O.A.C. 194 (Ont. Div. Ct.); additional reasons at (2007), 2007 CarswellOnt 6275 (Ont. Div. Ct.), 2007-09-13, Fedak J.

The appellant, U-Haul Co. (Canada) Ltd., appeals from the judgment of Deputy Judge at the Superior Court of Justice (Small Claims Court) in Hamilton, Ontario dated November 28, 2006.

Clear from reasons Deputy Judge did not consider either depreciation or betterment in the award of damages. Neither counsel for the plaintiffs nor defendants raised the issue with her. The law clear that depreciation or betterment is a necessary factor to consider in awarding damages. Accordingly Deputy Judge erred. Judgment of Deputy Judge set aside and judgment granted in the amount of $4,951.18. Original costs awarded of $750 remain unchanged. Disbursements of $259.84 inclusive of GST remain the same.

Elliott v. Ritins International Inc. (2007), 2007 CarswellOnt 4640 (Ont. Div. Ct.), 2007-07-18, Lax J.

Motion for order directing Registrar not to dismiss the appellant's appeal until 60 days after transcripts completed. Appellant attempted to obtain the consent of respondent to an extension of time to perfect appeal to 30 days after the transcripts prepared. Respondent did not consent, motion brought.

No prejudice to respondent who had benefit of judgment and prejudgment interest. To dismiss the appeal would cause serious prejudice to the appellant. Court satisfied appellant has demonstrated a firm intention to appeal and provided a reasonable explanation for failing to observe time limits. Principles for granting relief satisfied. See *Frey v. MacDonald*, [1989] O.J. No. 236, 1989 CarswellOnt 343, 33 C.P.C. (2d) 13 (Ont. C.A.) and *Langer v. Yorkton Securities Inc.*, 1986 CarswellOnt 479, 14 C.P.C. (2d) 134, 57 O.R. (2d) 555, 19 O.A.C. 394 (Ont. C.A.).

Motion should have been consented to or at least unopposed. Reasonable explanation offered for failure to perfect appeal within applicable time limits.

Lowry v. Kushnir (2007), 2007 CarswellOnt 3214 (Ont. S.C.J.); additional reasons at (2007), 2007 CarswellOnt 5655 (Ont. S.C.J.), Turnbull J.

Applicant sought leave to appeal to the Divisional Court from order of case conference judge who ordered action be stayed until significant legal costs awarded in earlier matrimonial litigation between the same parties paid by applicant to respondent.

Rule 2(4) of the *Family Law Rules* specifically states that the primary objective of the Rules is to allow each case to be determined justly.

Test to grant leave to appeal has been met and applicant granted leave to appeal the order of the presiding judge at the case conference to the Divisional Court.

Petti v. George Coppel Jewellers Ltd. (2008), 2008 CarswellOnt 1324, 234 O.A.C. 85 (Ont. Div. Ct.), J.W. Quinn J.

Plaintiff appealed final order of deputy judge of Small Claims Court dismissing his claim at trial.

Appeal raised propriety of relying on polygraph evidence in legal proceedings. At opening of appeal, court confirmed Coppel had not filed responding materials. He requested adjournment for that purpose. Court declined request on the basis that his failure fell within the minimal level of self-education required of self-represented litigants.

Trial judge intervened during trial. "Let us adjourn this and why do you not do a lie detector test? . . . because the credibility issue now is 50-50 and, my goodness, if we have a chance to have this resolved by this scientific or quasi-scientific means, why not do it?".

The trial judge referred to the polygraph test results.

Some authority making this narrowly relevant, in both criminal and civil cases, the fact that a litigant volunteered to take a polygraph test. See *R. v. B. (S.C.)*, 1997 CarswellOnt 3907, [1997] O.J. No. 4183, 10 C.R. (5th) 302, 119 C.C.C. (3d) 530, 36 O.R. (3d) 516, 104 O.A.C. 81 (Ont. C.A.), a criminal case at para. 29 and *Whiten v. Pilot Insurance Co.*, [1999] O.J. No. 237, 1999 CarswellOnt 269, [1999] I.L.R. I-3659, 42 O.R. (3d) 641, 170 D.L.R. (4th) 280, 117 O.A.C. 201, 58 O.R. (3d) 480 (note), 32 C.P.C. (4th) 3 (Ont. C.A.). *Whiten* was reversed by the Supreme Court of Canada at 2002 CarswellOnt 537, 2002 CarswellOnt 538, [2002] S.C.J. No. 19, 2002 SCC 18, [2002] I.L.R. I-4048, 20 B.L.R. (3d) 165, 209 D.L.R. (4th) 257, 283 N.R. 1, 35 C.C.L.I. (3d) 1, 156 O.A.C. 201, [2002] 1 S.C.R. 595 (S.C.C.) on the issue of punitive damages but, as to the polygraph, the court stated, uncritically, at para. 24:

> [24] . . . the Whitens, in an attempt to satisfy Pilot that they did not set the fire, offered to take a polygraph test administered by an expert selected by Pilot. This was apparently accepted by the jury as a good faith offer made to allay Pilot's suspicions. Pilot refused, without giving any reasons.

Trial judge relied on results of polygraph tests, at least in part, when reaching his decision to dismiss claim. Results used to help decide truth of the facts in dispute, reversible error even though parties consented to tests. The court should not delegate its jurisdiction, even on consent. Appeal allowed and, pursuant to s. 134(1)(b) of the *Courts of Justice Act*, R.S.O. 1990, c. C.43, new trial ordered.

Abdallah v. Snopek (2008), 2008 CarswellOnt 997, 290 D.L.R. (4th) 234, 234 O.A.C. 15, 63 C.C.L.I. (4th) 266, 89 O.R. (3d) 771 (Ont. Div. Ct.), Molloy J. (for the majority).

Action dismissed. The plaintiff appealed from dismissal, arguing that defence counsel's address to jury so improper and inflammatory that to allow the verdict to stand could result in a substantial miscarriage of justice.

Three mistakes made at trial: the first by defence counsel, when he included in his address comments that were inflammatory, irrelevant and improper; the second by plaintiff's counsel, when he failed to immediately object to opposing counsel's address; the third mistake was by the trial judge, when he failed to intervene to prevent an injustice. This court ought not to compound those mistakes by denying a new trial because of the failure of counsel to object (compounding the second mistake) or by deferring to the discretion of the trial judge (compounding the third mistake). "The appellant now asks this court to correct these mistakes made at the first by ordering a new trial. In my opinion, such a disposition is the only way to achieve justice for the appellant." Appeal allowed and new trial ordered. Gans J. (dissenting).

Rando Drugs Ltd. v. Scott, 2007 CarswellOnt 4888, [2007] O.J. No. 2999, 42 C.P.C. (6th) 23, 2007 ONCA 553, 284 D.L.R. (4th) 756, 229 O.A.C. 1, 86 O.R. (3d) 641, (sub nom. *Rando Drugs Ltd. c. Scott)* 86 O.R. (3d) 653 (Ont. C.A.); leave to appeal refused (2008), 2008 CarswellOnt 353, 2008 CarswellOnt 354, 384 N.R. 398 (note), 249 O.A.C. 39 (S.C.C.).

Appeal from judgment of Justice Patterson of the Superior Court of Justice, dated September 27, 2005, dismissing counterclaim of plaintiff by counterclaim, Lena B.D. Scott, with costs, and further order of Justice Patterson, dated June 30, 2006, refusing to set aside his judgment of September 27, 2005 and not restoring action to trial list, with costs.

Allegations of bias against judge. More than 10 years before trial, trial judge, Justice Patterson, was partner of firm that had once represented one of the defendants by counterclaim.

Test to be applied explained in several cases from the Supreme Court of Canada, most notably, *Committee for Justice & Liberty v. Canada (National Energy Board)*, 1976 CarswellNat 434, 1976 CarswellNat 434F, [1978] 1 S.C.R. 369, 68 D.L.R. (3d) 716, 9 N.R. 115 (S.C.C.); *R. v. S. (R.D.)*, 1997 CarswellNS 301, 1997 CarswellNS 302, [1997] S.C.J. No. 84, 151 D.L.R. (4th) 193, 118 C.C.C. (3d) 353, 10 C.R. (5th) 1, 218 N.R. 1, 161 N.S.R. (2d) 241, 477 A.P.R. 241, [1997] 3 S.C.R. 484, 1 Admin. L.R. (3d) 74 (S.C.C.); and *Roberts v. R.* (2003), 2003 SCC 45, (sub nom. *Wewaykum Indian Band v. Canada)* [2003] S.C.J. No. 50, 2003 CarswellNat 2822, 2003 CarswellNat 2823, 231 D.L.R. (4th) 1, 19 B.C.L.R. (4th) 195, (sub nom. *Wewaykum Indian Band v. Canada)* 309 N.R. 201, [2004] 2 W.W.R. 1, (sub nom. *Wewaykum Indian Band v. Canada)* [2003] 2 S.C.R. 259, 40 C.P.C. (5th) 1, 7 Admin. L.R. (4th) 1, (sub nom. *Wewaykum Indian Band v. Canada)* [2004] 1 C.N.L.R. 342 (S.C.C.).

It would have been better for the appellant to have accepted the ruling, presented case and, if she lost, to have raised issue on appeal. See David Mullan's statement of law in *Administrative Law* (Toronto: Irwin Law, 2001) at 348 to be correct:

> . . . the party [who raised the bias issue] need not abandon the proceeding in the sense of refusing to take part. Indeed, not only does the law not require this but it is also very dangerous . . ..

The peril Mullan cautions against occurred here. By withdrawing from the courtroom, the appellant abandoned her case. She cannot rely on an unknown fact that might have affected the course of the proceedings had she remained.

Appeals dismissed with costs.

Volzhenin v. Haile, 2007 CarswellBC 1272, 243 B.C.A.C. 108, 70 B.C.L.R. (4th) 15, 401 W.A.C. 108, 2007 BCCA 317 (B.C. C.A.); leave to appeal refused (2008), 2008 CarswellBC 317, 2008 CarswellBC 318, 454 W.A.C. 319 (note), 270 B.C.A.C. 319 (note), 385 N.R. 391 (note) (S.C.C.).

Plaintiff appealed, arguing trial judge failed to ensure that plaintiff had a fair trial, that excessive interventions by the trial judge gave rise to a reasonable apprehension of bias, that trial judge made numerous factual errors, trial judge erred in finding regarding the plaintiff's credibility, and trial judge failed to correctly apply *Athey v. Leonati* (S.C.C.). Appeal dismissed.

Vuong v. Toronto East General & Orthopaedic Hospital (November 4, 2002), Doc. CA C38078 (Ont. C.A.).

The plaintiffs appealed the decision of the trial judge dismissing the appellants' statement of claim by acceding to the defendant's motion without providing any reasons. Plaintiff appealed. Appeal allowed. Litigants are entitled to know the reasons why a judge has allowed a motion and dismissed an entire statement of claim.

MacEwan v. Henderson, 2003 CarswellNS 424, 2003 NSCA 133, 219 N.S.R. (2d) 183, 692 A.P.R. 183 (N.S. C.A.).

Appellant appealed the dismissal of her motion by the judge of the Supreme Court of Nova Scotia based on apprehension of bias. Nova Scotia Court of Appeal dismissed the appeal and held that the apprehension of bias must be a reasonable one, held by reasonable and right-minded persons, applying themselves to the question and obtaining thereon the required information. The test contains a two-fold objective element: the person considering the alleged bias must be reasonable, and the apprehension of bias itself must also be reasonable in the circumstances of the case. (See *Bertram, supra*, at pp. 54-55; *Gushman, supra*, at para. 31).

Further the reasonable person must be an *informed* person, with knowledge of all the relevant circumstances, including "the traditions of integrity and impartiality that form a part of the background and apprised also of the fact that impartiality is one of the duties the judges swear to uphold." The reasonable person should also be taken to be aware of the social reality that forms the background to a particular case, such as societal awareness and acknowledgement of the prevalence of racism or gender bias in a particular community.

Seminatore v. Banks (July 5, 2006), Doc. 53/06/CA (N.B. C.A.).

Appellant appealed the decision of trial judge on the ground that he was not allowed to cross-examine the party-witness. Appeal allowed as trial judge failed to discharge duty to provide a fair and impartial process when she invited one of the self-represented parties to cross-examine the other party, but did not reciprocate with such an invitation when the party-witness roles were reversed.

Naderi v. Strong, 2005 CarswellNB 89, 2005 CarswellNB 90, [2005] N.B.J. No. 67, 2005 NBCA 10, 280 N.B.R. (2d) 379, 734 A.P.R. 379 (N.B. C.A.).

Appeal concerning the factors to be considered by a trial judge of the Court of Queen's Bench when assessing an application to extend the time for an appeal by trial *de novo*.

The basic rule to be followed in dealing with an application to extend time for appeal is that leave should be granted if justice requires that it be given. Thus, factors to be considered include: (a) an intention to appeal within the time prescribed; (b) explanation given by the proposed appellant for missing the limitation period; (c) evidence of actual prejudice the delay would cause to the other party; (d) whether or not there is a serious issue to be appealed by trial *de novo*; or (e) the matter is frivolous or vexatious.

Appeal allowed as the application judge erred when he refused to receive any information that would have enabled him to determine if the proposed appeal by trial *de novo* raised a serious issue or whether it was frivolous or vexatious.

Appellant appealed the decision of trial judge on the ground that he was not allowed to cross-examine the party-witness. Appeal allowed as trial judge failed to discharge duty to provide a fair and impartial process when she invited one of the self-represented parties to cross-examine the other party, but did not reciprocate with such an invitation when the party-witness roles were reversed.

Polgrain Estate v. Toronto East General Hospital (2007), 2007 CarswellOnt 6280, 47 C.P.C. (6th) 186, 87 O.R. (3d) 55, 286 D.L.R. (4th) 265 (Ont. S.C.J.); reversed 2008 CarswellOnt 3103, 293 D.L.R. (4th) 266, 90 O.R. (3d) 630, 60 C.R. (6th) 67, 2008 ONCA 427, 53 C.P.C. (6th) 297, 238 O.A.C. 1 (Ont. C.A.).

Plaintiff sought to relitigate the facts underlying an acquittal for sexual assault. The motion judge dismissed the action and concluded that it would be an abuse of process to allow the relitigation of the determination that the assaults did not occur. Plaintiff appealed. Appeal allowed.

Criminal acquittal of the respondent's staff member on sexual assault charge meant the staff member was legally, not factually, innocent. Appellant had no right of appeal from verdict in criminal proceedings. However, civil action against the respondent was not an abuse of process.

Volzhenin v. Haile, 2007 CarswellBC 1272, 243 B.C.A.C. 108, 70 B.C.L.R. (4th) 15, 401 W.A.C. 108, 2007 BCCA 317 (B.C. C.A.), (2008), 2008 CarswellBC 317, 2008 CarswellBC 318, 454 W.A.C. 319 (note), 270 B.C.A.C. 319 (note), 385 N.R. 391 (note) (S.C.C.).

The trial judge declined to award certain damages to the plaintiff. The plaintiff appealed arguing that excessive interventions by the trial judge destroyed the impression of a hearing before a disinterested and impartial court.

Appeal dismissed as the British Columbia Court of Appeal Court of did not find an "inappropriate crossing of the line" with respect to the trial judge's interventions. While one interjection had the appearance of counseling the lawyer for the defendants, in the context of the case it did not reflect bias, or give the appearance of bias such as to render the trial unfair.

Language difficulties, or cultural differences, did not render the trial unfair or fatally undermine the trial judge's assessment of the appellant's credibility and the findings of fact.

Baradaran v. Taberner (2008), 2008 CarswellOnt 4413 (Ont. Div. Ct.).

Appellant raised claim in *quantum meruit* for the first time on appeal. Ontario Divisional
Court dismissing the appeal assumed that it was "appropriate for this Court to entertain this
claim which was neither pleaded nor argued at trial," but found that there was no evidence
raised to support the claim.

Beard v. Suite Collections Canada Inc. (2008), 2008 CarswellOnt 4222, 68 C.C.E.L. (3d)
310 (Ont. Div. Ct.).

The general rule is that where the issue on appeal involves a question of mixed fact and law
and the trial judge's interpretation of the evidence as a whole, it should not be overturned
absent palpable and overriding error.

The appellant asked, in effect, to retry the case. On appeal to the Divisional Court no palpable or overriding error in the judge's findings of fact, and no error in principle or in her
application of the law was found. Appeal dismissed as the trial judge's decision was well-
reasoned and amply supported by the evidence.

Beitel v. Simone (2008), 2008 CarswellOnt 1678 (Ont. Div. Ct.).

Appeal related to the validity of the retainer, raised for the first time on the appeal dismissed.
Appeals to the Ontario Divisional Court should not be devoid of merit.

Black v. Mastrachuk, 2008 CarswellSask 339, 2008 SKQB 225, (sub nom. *Mastrachuk v.
Black)* 316 Sask. R. 95 (Sask. Q.B.).

Appellant appealed decision of trial judge who allegedly accepted the evidence of the plaintiff every time when there was any disagreement between parties in relation to evidence.
Appellate court should not interfere with factual findings of the trial judge absent some
clearly demonstrated factual error. Findings of fact may be appealed if they are not reasonably supported by the evidence or if there is a palpable or overriding error. Here, the appellant
could not demonstrated a basis to set aside such findings and conclusions, where there was
clearly evidence before the trial judge such as to enable her to come to reach such
conclusions.

Blattgerste v. Heringa, 2008 CarswellBC 856, [2008] 11 W.W.R. 47, 2008 BCCA 186, 254
B.C.A.C. 292, 426 W.A.C. 292, 82 B.C.L.R. (4th) 62 (B.C. C.A.).

Appeal by defendant from order winding up two companies allowed. Order set aside and
matter remitted to trial court for new hearing. Judge who heard matter died before signing
reasons for judgment he prepared. Reasons ultimately released by Chief Justice. Reasons for
judgment are not final and complete unless signed by judge who wrote them. Until reasons
were signed they were a work in progress subject to being revised or abandoned. As judge
had not signed reasons it could not be said that he had completed his judicial consideration
of matter.

Boone v. Advantage Car & Truck Rentals Ltd (2008), 2008 CarswellOnt 6234 (Ont. Div.
Ct.).

Extension of time to serve the Notice of Appeal and file the appeal. Extension of time may
be granted under Rule 3.02(1) and (3)1 on just terms. It was held that such factors as defendant's clear intention to appeal, the attempt to serve the Notice of Appeal within time, the
good faith filing of the appeal, the payment and ordering of the transcript, the delay was a
matter of days, due to inadvertence, and the plaintiff was not prejudiced by the delay allowed
to extend the time to serve the Notice of Appeal.

Brunt v. Yen (2008), 2008 CarswellOnt 3832, 239 O.A.C. 289 (Ont. Div. Ct.); additional
reasons at (2008), 2008 CarswellOnt 5952 (Ont. Div. Ct.).

Plaintiff sent bank draft to solicitors for purchase of shares in corporate client. Action dismissed. Plaintiff appealed. Appeal dismissed. No basis existed for interfering with trial judge's factual findings that plaintiff did not communicate with solicitors to establish role protecting interests and that solicitors did not receive funds subject to any conditions.

Standard of review: On a pure question of law, the trial judge is required to be correct. However, findings of fact are not to be reversed unless it can be established that the trial judge made a "palpable and overriding error." In particular, findings of credibility made by a trial judge are entitled to considerable deference.

There is a functional distinction between a trial and appellate tribunal, namely the trial court's responsibility is to find facts. Given that the trial judge has had the advantage of seeing and hearing the witnesses and assessing demeanour, the appellate courts traditionally treat all findings of fact made by the trial judge with deference.

Channan v. Hamilton (City) (2008), 2008 CarswellOnt 1260, 234 O.A.C. 81 (Ont. Div. Ct.); additional reasons at (2008), 2008 CarswellOnt 5452 (Ont. Div. Ct.).

The deference on the trial judge's *findings of fact* stays unless the appellate court is satisfied that a finding was the result of "a palpable and overriding error." A palpable error is one that is obvious, plain to see or clear. (See The Supreme Court of Canada in *H.L. v Canada (Attorney General)*, 2005 SCC 25 (CanLII), [2005] 1 S.C.R. 401 at para. 55);.

With respect to a *question of law*, the standard is "correctness." A decision will be incorrect if it is based on an erroneous interpretation of a statute or an erroneous application of a legal principle.

For questions of *mixed fact and law*, the same standard applies as to questions of fact; namely "palpable and overriding error" unless the trial judge made an inextricable error in principle with respect to the characterization of a standard or its application, in which case the error may amount to an error in law. (See *Ontario (Ministry of Labour) v. Modern Niagara Toronto Inc.*, [2006] O.J. 3684 at para. 20, citing to *Housen v. Nikolaisen*, 2002 SCC 33 (CanLII), [2002] 2 S.C.R. 235).

Cogliano v. Patel (2008), 2008 CarswellOnt 5630 (Ont. Div. Ct.).

The appellant submitted that the trial judge made findings of credibility and findings of fact not supported by the evidence. Appeal dismissed. Ontario Divisional Court found that trial judge was alive to the inconsistencies in the evidence and had the opportunity to observe the witnesses. "Findings of credibility are within the purview of the trial judge, and in our view, there was evidence to support her findings of fact." No palpable or overriding error was committed by the trial judge.

Dias v. RD Group International (2008), 2008 CarswellOnt 2473 (Ont. Div. Ct.).

Trial Judge committed palpable and overriding error in assuming that the Respondent's new company was a successor of BH Company, which was in breach of contractual obligations before the appellant. There was no evidence whatsoever that the Respondent's company was a successor to BH, nor that it had bound itself to the contracts of BH.

Emmanuel v. Capparelli (2008), 2008 CarswellOnt 5191 (Ont. Div. Ct.).

Appellant claimed that trial judge made erroneous findings of fact. Appeal dismissed. It is not the role of an appellate court to reconsider the evidence and substitute its own opinion for that of the trial judge. The trial judge weighed the evidence on a balance of probabilities and made no error that could be described as being clearly wrong.

Flegel v. Wirachowsky, 2008 CarswellSask 251, 2008 SKQB 189 (Sask. Q.B.).

On appeal, the appellant claimed that the other party failed to provide him a witness list before trial and also he got no notice of expert. Appeal dismissed. No notice of expert is required for the Small Claims Court.

If appellant was unprepared to deal with an expert, he should have indicated that to the trial judge and an adjournment may have been considered. Appellant was aware that adjournments were possible. Each party must come prepared for the possibility that an expert may testify or to speak.

Freedland v. Polten & Hodder (2008), 2008 CarswellOnt 6036 (Ont. Div. Ct.).

Moving party brought a motion alleging that a court reporter or a Deputy Judge excised portions of transcript that were evidencing a reasonable apprehension of bias against him. Based on this allegation it requested for extension of time to perfect his appeal.

Motion dismissed as: (1) there was no good reason to doubt accuracy of the transcript as required under s. 48(2) of the *Evidence Act*, R.S.O. 1990, c. E23; (2) comments that allegedly were made by the Deputy Judge, but not transcribed, would not support allegations of reasonable apprehension of bias; (3) the alleged comments were irrelevant to the trial judge's behavior towards the moving party; (4) some comments were made during submissions and submissions are not transcribed routinely in civil cases.

Henderson v. Canada (2008), 2008 CarswellOnt 2279, 238 O.A.C. 65, 37 C.E.L.R. (3d) 306, 292 D.L.R. (4th) 114 (Ont. Div. Ct.).

Respondent sought leave to appeal the trial judge's award of costs, and if leave be given, sought costs of the trial at a higher amount than was fixed by the trial judge. Defendant at trial level had not been asked for submissions as to costs. On appeal, the court found that the defendant was entitled to be heard on this issue. Failing to give him that opportunity was a breach of natural justice and fairness. Defendant entitled to recover the full amount of his disbursements, and as he had done an extraordinary amount of work to prepare his case, was entitled to increase the costs from $175 to $645.

Holden v. ACE Aviation Holdings Inc. (2008), 2008 CarswellOnt 4748, 296 D.L.R. (4th) 233, (sub nom. *ACE Aviation Holdings Inc. v. Holden)* 240 O.A.C. 184 (Ont. Div.Ct.).

Appeal related to the interpretation of the word "passenger" in Article 22 of the Montreal Convention. In construing the meaning of the word "passenger" in Article 22 of the Montreal Convention, recourse must be made to the canons of interpretation of international treaties and to the *Vienna Convention on the Law of Treaties*: regard should be had for the grammatical meaning, the logical interpretation, the teleological interpretation, and the historic context of the provision.

Appeal allowed as the construction of the word "passenger" advanced by the appellant was consonant with the purposes of uniformity, certainty and predictability and avoid the potential for exposure to an uncertain quantum of liability and exposure to an uncertain number of claimants.

Kissell v. Milosevic (2008), 2008 CarswellOnt 3300 (Ont. Div. Ct.).

Appeal involving two decisions of the Ontario Rental Housing Tribunal. The Tribunal failed to make the necessary finding in fact and erred in law. The decision of the Tribunal was set aside, and the application is remitted to the Tribunal for a rehearing, should the party seek to pursue the application.

Leader Media Productions Ltd. v. Sentinel Hill Alliance Atlantis Equicap Ltd. Partnership, 2008 CarswellOnt 3475, 2008 ONCA 463, 237 O.A.C. 81, 90 O.R. (3d) 561 (Ont. C.A.); leave to appeal refused (2008), 2008 CarswellOnt 7205, 2008 CarswellOnt 7206, 392 N.R. 391 (note) (S.C.C.).

Oral arguments:.

The defendants appealed a judgment against them, arguing that the trial judge did not hear oral argument before releasing his decision. The defendants also sought to introduce fresh evidence showing that the trial judge fell asleep at times during the trial. Appeal dismissed.

Trial judge's failure to give counsel opportunity to make oral submissions before releasing judgment not resulting in any substantial wrong or miscarriage of justice where counsel had opportunity to submit full written submissions.

The fresh evidence related to the validity of the trial process can be admitted on appeal level. However, in this case counsel was obliged to bring trial judge's inattention home to him at time. Not having done so and deciding to wait and see what happened, they could not later raise inattention for first time as ground of appeal on either substantive or contextual basis.

Leonard v. Dunn (2008), 2008 CarswellOnt 3085 (Ont. Div. Ct.).

Appeal involving assessment of special damages for dental work in personal injury case. The defendant argued that the plaintiff's witness did not have the expertise to opine as to the nature, scope and cost of future dental work. Ontario Divisional court found that the witness had been a dentist for ten years at the time she testified and had the expertise necessary to give opinion evidence in the area of post, core and crown restoration, the basis upon which damages were calculated. The fact that rest of the restorative work is yet to be done is irrelevant.

McGowan v. Toronto (City), 2008 CarswellOnt 2175, 45 M.P.L.R. (4th) 128 (Ont. Div. Ct.); reversed [2010] O.J. No. 2029, 2010 ONCA 362, 2010 CarswellOnt 3224, 70 M.P.L.R. (4th) 193 (Ont. C.A.).

Motion judge dismissed action commenced by the Plaintiff against city and police services as an abuse of process and as attempt at re-litigation. Plaintiff appealed. Appeal allowed. Ontario Divisional Court found that Deputy judge erred in his determination that plaintiff sought to re-litigate when Plaintiff's allegation was that he should not have been charged. "Plaintiff was not attempting to set aside any convictions" or "a judicial finding, which is the essence of abuse of process.".

Other issues:

- Whether the deputy judge erred in his finding that there was no reasonable cause of action against Toronto Police Services Board. Deputy judge found that, because pre-requisite of *proximity* was not met, it was *plain and obvious* that direct liability claim against board could not succeed. Kiteley J found that in making conclusions regarding proximity, Deputy judge drew inference of fact and law that was not warranted. However, while motion judge's reasoning was incorrect, conclusion was correct.

Mehta v. Natt (2008), 2008 CarswellOnt 3112 (Ont. Div. Ct.).

The appellant/tenant, appeals from the order of the Landlord and Tenant Board dismissing the tenant's application for a rent reduction. An appeal related to question of law alone. The standard of review on a question of law alone is correctness. The findings by the Landlord and Tenant Board represent a misapprehension of the evidence. It is a palpable and overriding error and as such constitutes an error in law.

Monks v. ING Insurance Co. of Canada, [2008] O.J. No. 1371, 2008 CarswellOnt 2036, 2008 ONCA 269, [2008] I.L.R. I-4694, 90 O.R. (3d) 689, 235 O.A.C. 1, 61 C.C.L.I. (4th) 1, 66 M.V.R. (5th) 38 (Ont. C.A.).

Successful plaintiff was awarded aggravated damages of $50,000, interest and costs while her counsel was awarded a $75,000 risk premium. On appeal defendant claimed that there was judicial bias in favour of the plaintiff. Appeal allowed in part.

The risk premium awarded to plaintiff's counsel was set aside because of subsequent Supreme Court of Canada decisions concluding risk premiums could not be passed on to unsuccessful defendants as part of a costs award. However, there was no evidence of judicial bias.

Although the judge used harsh language in expressing his findings, he was justified in doing so, and his comments did not constitute judicial bias.

Toshi Enterprises Ltd. v. Coffee Time Donuts Inc. (2008), 2008 CarswellOnt 7954, *(sub nom. Coffee Time Donuts Inc. v. Toshi Enterprises Ltd.)* 246 O.A.C. 17 (Ont. Div. Ct.).

Appeal by defendant from order granting judgment to plaintiff in amount of $4,378 allowed. Defendant found vicariously liable for fire found to have been started through the negligence in one of its franchises. Trial judge erred in making erroneous inference of negligence from franchisee's absence at trial when there was no evidence to otherwise support a finding that the franchisee had been negligent.

Walsh v. 1124660 Ontario Ltd., 2008 CarswellOnt 3809, 2008 ONCA 522 (Ont. C.A.).

Respondents entirely successful at trial. The trial judge made no order as to costs given the appellant's impecuniousity. The respondents, to their credit, did not challenge that exercise of the trial judge's discretion. The appellant chose to pursue an appeal. Once again, the respondents were totally successful. The respondents incurred further legal costs. They should not be deprived of their costs a second time.

Welwood v. Ecclesiastical Insurance Office Plc. (2008), 2008 CarswellOnt 1132 (Ont. Div. Ct.).

Moving party brought a motion for leave to appeal the order of the deputy judge striking the party's claim for failing to provide material facts and particulars in respect of bald allegations. Appeal dismissed as there was no good reason to doubt correctness of motions judge's order. In addition, proposed appeal did not involve matters of such importance that leave to appeal should have been granted.

Respondent sought costs on substantial indemnity. Appellant's motion came perilously close to being frivolous and devoid of any merit such that costs might arguably have been awarded on a substantial indemnity basis. Ontario Divisional court held that this was not an exceptional case for awarding substantial indemnity costs. Employee's current unemployment and principle of access to justice did not provide basis for deferring payment of costs until after trial.

Young v. Ewatski, 2008 CarswellMan 267, [2008] 11 W.W.R. 332, 56 C.P.C. (6th) 376, 2008 MBQB 148, 56 C.C.L.T. (3d) 111, 177 C.R.R. (2d) 167, 234 Man. R. (2d) 293 (Man. Q.B.); affirmed (2008), 2008 CarswellMan 621, 2008 MBCA 150, [2009] 1 W.W.R. 385, 62 C.P.C. (6th) 246 (Man. C.A.).

Plaintiff argued that, since the master sustained the pleading at the first hearing, the defendant is estopped from raising essentially the same issue on summary judgment. Assuming, without deciding, that issue estoppel may be applied to interlocutory orders, for the doctrine to apply, the issues would have to be identical, not almost identical. The motion to strike could not bar a trial on the merits whether on *viva voca* evidence or by affidavit evidence. Equally, it cannot bar a motion for summary judgment.

1541094 Ontario Inc. v. Crangle (2008), 2008 CarswellOnt 2069 (Ont. S.C.J.) (Ont. S.C.J.).

The moving party sought an extension of the time for filing a Notice of Appeal with respect to the decision of Deputy Judge. Motion dismissed.

Moving party argued that although he brought (unsuccessfully) a motion in the Small Claims Court for a new trial, he always had reserved his right to appeal.

The Court after consideration of argument (including claims that his counsel was confused and didn't appreciate the significance of an appeal versus a new trial motion) found that the moving party did not satisfy the test enunciated in *Frey v. MacDonald*, [1990] O.J. No. 280.

Jeffrys v. Veenstra, 2004 CarswellMan 393, 2004 MBCA 150 (Man. C.A.), Huband J.A.

Application for leave to appeal dismissed. Defendant intentionally attempting to evade service and, therefore, had no excuse for failing to appear at initial hearing. Wilful delay on part of defendant.

Friesen v. Hepworth, 2008 MBCA 69, 2008 CarswellMan 291 (Man. C.A.), Steel J.A.

Appellants appealed unsuccessful motion for extension of time to file motion for leave to appeal small claims matter. Appeal dismissed because appellants failed to show chambers judge committed any error. Appellants didn't point out any question of law arising from factual dispute, nor provide court with any good reason for not complying with court-mandated deadlines which would justify granting extension of time.

Jimenez v. Azizbaigi, 2008 BCSC 1465, 2008 CarswellBC 2302 (B.C. S.C. [In Chambers]); affirming 2008 CarswellBC 189, 2008 BCPC 12 (B.C. Prov. Ct.).

Plaintiff commenced action, in which he succeeded in claim for payment of debt owed for work performed. Defendant succeeded in her counterclaim for damages. Claims set off and defendant awarded $1,698. Plaintiff appealed and sought order for retrial on basis of trial unfairness. Appeal dismissed. Plaintiff failed to demonstrate palpable and overriding errors in trial judge's finding of fact. Plaintiff could not meet burden on party seeking to introduce new evidence. No basis for allegation that trial judge was biased against plaintiff as self-represented litigant. Interventions were for the purpose of ensuring both trial efficiency and trial fairness. Trial judge's interventions within permissible limit.

Cleeve v. Gregerson, 445 W.A.C. 184, 264 B.C.A.C. 184, [2009] 5 W.W.R. 28, 89 B.C.L.R. (4th) 67, 2009 CarswellBC 11, 2009 BCCA 2, 65 C.P.C. (6th) 303 (B.C. C.A.); additional reasons at (2009), [2010] 2 W.W.R. 103, 98 B.C.L.R. (4th) 260, 77 C.P.C. (6th) 17, 2009 BCCA 545, 2009 CarswellBC 3233 (B.C. C.A.); additional reasons at 67 C.P.C. (6th) 378, 2009 CarswellBC 1098, 2009 BCCA 190, 90 B.C.L.R. (4th) 296 (B.C. C.A.).

Judge gave judgment for plaintiff. Defendant's appeal allowed. New trial ordered. Submissions of counsel had not been recorded and affidavits of counsel differed on what words had been used. Decision to remove case from jury must be exercised judicially. Applicant for mistrial bears heavy onus to prove prejudice that cannot be remedied by court. None of impugned submissions amounted to misstatements of evidence. Any misstatement could have been remedied by direction from trial judge of clarification from defence counsel.

Grainger v. Windsor-Essex Children's Aid Society (2009), 96 O.R. (3d) 711, 2009 CarswellOnt 4000, [2009] O.J. No. 2872 (Ont. S.C.J.), Granger J.

Motion by defendant for summary judgment dismissing a Small Claims Court action dismissed on grounds that there was a genuine issue for trial. Leave to appeal that decision to the Divisional Court was granted by a judge of the Superior Court of Justice. Appeal should be quashed.

No right of appeal from an interlocutory order of a Small Claims Court judge. Section 31 of the *Courts of Justice Act*, R.S.O. 1990, c. C.43, dealing with appeals to the Divisional Court from Small Claims Court orders, applies only to final orders. No basis for looking outside s. 31 to find alternative means of appealing an interlocutory order of the Small Claims Court. Section 31 only section that governs appeals from the Small Claims Court.

See also *Matlin v. Crane Canada Inc.* (2004), [2004] O.J. No. 3497, 2004 CarswellOnt 3648 (Ont. S.C.J.), at para. 6, Hockin J. stated, "There is no inherent appellate jurisdiction. A right to appeal can only be provided by statute or regulation" and *Kourtessis v. Minister of National Revenue*, EYB 1993-67101, [1993] 1 C.T.C. 301, 1993 CarswellBC 1213, [1993] S.C.J. No. 45, 1993 CarswellBC 1259, 20 C.R. (4th) 104, [1993] 4 W.W.R. 225, 45 W.A.C. 81, 27 B.C.A.C. 81, 14 C.R.R. (2d) 193, 78 B.C.L.R. (2d) 257, 81 C.C.C. (3d) 286, 102 D.L.R. (4th) 456, [1993] 2 S.C.R. 53, 153 N.R. 1, 93 D.T.C. 5137 at paras. 15-16 (S.C.C.),

La Forest J. See also, *Gelber v. Allstate Insurance Co. of Canada* (1983), 1983 CarswellOnt 457, 35 C.P.C. 324, 41 O.R. (2d) 318 (Ont. Div. Ct.).

Moskaleva v. Laurie, 459 W.A.C. 164, 272 B.C.A.C. 164, 2009 CarswellBC 1489, 2009 BCCA 260, [2009] 8 W.W.R. 205, 94 B.C.L.R. (4th) 58, 79 M.V.R. (5th) 28 (B.C. C.A.).

Trial judge's questions did not restrict direct examination. Trial judge's questions and interjections during testimony of economists were directed at understanding their evidence and did not carry negative connotations suggested by defendant.

Papadopoulos v. Borg, 2009 ABCA 201, 2009 CarswellAlta 770 (Alta. C.A.).

Plaintiff's action dismissed on basis that plaintiff failed to call any evidence. Plaintiff appealed. Appeal dismissed. Plaintiff given every opportunity to present his case, and was treated fairly throughout. Trial judge discharged responsibility to assist self-represented litigant. Plaintiff advised well before trial that it would be prudent to retain counsel.

Pavlis v. HSBC Bank Canada, 2009 CarswellBC 1727, 2009 BCCA 309 (B.C. C.A. [In Chambers]), Kirkpatrick J.; affirmed (2009), 2009 CarswellBC 2775, 98 B.C.L.R. (4th) 72, [2010] 1 W.W.R. 208, 2009 BCCA 450, 469 W.A.C. 105, 277 B.C.A.C. 105 (B.C. C.A.).

Appellant brought motion for extension of time to file notice of appeal, declaration of indigent status and directions with respect to ordering of trial transcripts. Motion granted in part. Factors for indigent status established. Application for order that Supreme Court order transcripts of trial dismissed. Indigent status did not relieve appellant from costs of putting together appeal materials.

Park v. Lee, 98 O.R. (3d) 520, 2009 ONCA 651, 254 O.A.C. 52, 2009 CarswellOnt 5293 (Ont. C.A.).

Appellant, acting in person at trial, advanced claims in three actions. Appellant ill-prepared for trial. Appellant refused trial judge's offer to adjourn case. Trial judge on his own motion dismissed all three actions. He found appellant's evidence incoherent and incapable of proving case on balance of probabilities.

The trial judge should have adopted course suggested by counsel after trial judge indicated that he was considering the dismissal of the claim. Counsel stated:

> It appears that there is no choice but to let Mr. Park complete his case and then proceed with cross-examination of him and then for us to call Dr. Lee and Mr. Belitz as witnesses.

Failure to take this course amounted to denial of appellant's right to a fair trial.

Appeal allowed, new trial ordered.

Winter v. Chao, 2010 CarswellOnt 407, 2010 ONSC 464 (Ont. Div. Ct.), Molloy J.

Appeal by defendants from the decision of Godfrey J. of the Small Claims Court dated March 3, 2009. Godfrey J. awarded judgment to plaintiff in amount of $5,209.00 plus costs and interest based on her evidence at trial.

Significant gaps in evidence at trial. Appropriate remedy, new trial. Defendants entitled to recover $400.00 interpreter fee as a disbursement. Additional costs of $1,000.00 of appeal. Reduced counsel fee appropriate. Court took into account equities between parties and overall allocation of costs.

944936 Ontario Inc. v. Nanji (2010), 2010 ONSC 771, 2010 CarswellOnt 724 (Ont. Div. Ct.).

Appeal from trial decision. Appeal attempt to re-litigate matter. Trial judge's findings of fact entitled to deference on appeals. See *MacLeod v. MacLeod* (2003), 2003 CarswellOnt 4501, [2003] O.J. No. 4331 (Ont. C.A.).

Trial judge's reasons for judgment adequately explain his conclusions, and provide sufficient basis for meaningful appellate review. See *Chippewas of Mnjikaning First Nation v. On-*

tario, 2010 CarswellOnt 273, [2010] O.J. No. 212, 2010 ONCA 47, *(sub nom. Chippewas of Mnjikaning First Nation v. Ontario (Minister Responsible for Native Affairs))* [2010] 2 C.N.L.R. 18, 265 O.A.C. 247 (Ont. C.A.); additional reasons at 2010 ONCA 408, 2010 CarswellOnt 3730 (Ont. C.A.); leave to appeal refused 2010 CarswellOnt 4919, 2010 CarswellOnt 4920, [2010] S.C.C.A. No. 91, *(sub nom. Chippewas v. Mnjikaning First Nation v. Ontario (Minister Responsible for Native Affairs))* 276 O.A.C. 398 (note), *(sub nom. Chippewas of Mnjikaning First Nation v. Ontario (Minister Responsible for Native Affairs))* 409 N.R. 396 (note) (S.C.C.); *R. v. Sheppard*, 2002 CarswellNfld 74, 2002 CarswellNfld 75, [2002] S.C.J. No. 30, REJB 2002-29516, 50 C.R. (5th) 68, 211 Nfld. & P.E.I.R. 50, 633 A.P.R. 50, 210 D.L.R. (4th) 608, 284 N.R. 342, [2002] 1 S.C.R. 869, 2002 SCC 26, 162 C.C.C. (3d) 298 at para. 55 (S.C.C.); *R. v. Braich*, REJB 2002-29528, [2002] 1 S.C.R. 903, 285 N.R. 162, 162 C.C.C. (3d) 324, 2002 CarswellBC 552, 2002 CarswellBC 551, 2002 SCC 27, 268 W.A.C. 1, 164 B.C.A.C. 1, 210 D.L.R. (4th) 635, [2002] S.C.J. No. 29, 50 C.R. (5th) 92 at paras. 40-41 (S.C.C.); *R. v. M. (R.E.)*, 260 B.C.A.C. 40, 439 W.A.C. 40, [2008] S.C.J. No. 52, 380 N.R. 47, 297 D.L.R. (4th) 577, 60 C.R. (6th) 1, 235 C.C.C. (3d) 290, 2008 SCC 51, 2008 CarswellBC 2038, 2008 CarswellBC 2037, [2008] 3 S.C.R. 3, 83 B.C.L.R. (4th) 44, [2008] 11 W.W.R. 383 at paras. 52-57 (S.C.C.). Appeal dismissed.

Stoneforest International Canada Inc. v. Chan (2010), 2010 CarswellOnt 1770, 2010 ONSC 1715 (Ont. Div. Ct.).

Respondents moved for security for costs of appeal on grounds appeal frivolous and vexatious and appellant company has insufficient assets in Ontario to pay the respondent's costs.

Appellant succeeded at trial but awarded only $536.55 plus $175.00 costs by Deputy Judge. Appellant appeals on ground Deputy Judge should have awarded higher damages.

Appeal not frivolous.

No evidence amount of costs will be anything but modest in any event. No evidence appellant company has no assets of any kind to cover costs of respondents. Motion dismissed.

Action Auto Leasing & Gallery Inc. v. Robillard, 2011 ONSC 3264, 2011 CarswellOnt 4105, 106 O.R. (3d) 281, 22 C.P.C. (7th) 414, 335 D.L.R. (4th) 439, 278 O.A.C. 293, [2011] O.J. No. 2453 (Ont. Div. Ct.), Heeney J.; *Action Auto Leasing & Gallery Inc. v. Robillard*, 2011 ONSC 3264, 2011 CarswellOnt 4105, 106 O.R. (3d) 281, 22 C.P.C. (7th) 414, 335 D.L.R. (4th) 439, 278 O.A.C. 293, [2011] O.J. No. 2453 (Ont. Div. Ct.).

Appeals from Small Claims Court. Section 31(a) of the *Courts of Justice Act (Ont.)* provided that "An appeal lies to the Divisional Court from a final order of the Small Claims Court in an action, (a) for the payment of money in excess of the prescribed amount." The "prescribed amount" was defined in Regulation 244/10 as follows: "2. A final order of the Small Claims Court may be appealed to the Divisional Court if the order is for, (a) the payment of money in excess of $2,500." Judgment granted for $1,500. The plaintiff sought judgment for the full amount of $7,551.12. Divisional Court, *per* Heeney, J., held that no leave to appeal was necessary. There was a conflict between section 31 of the *Act* and section 2 of the Regulation. Statute prevailed (presumption of coherence). Since $7,551.12 was more than the prescribed amount of $2,500, the plaintiff had a right of appeal from the final order.

The motion was granted.

Martinek v. Dojc, 2011 ONSC 3795, 2011 CarswellOnt 5616, 282 O.A.C. 305 (Ont. Div. Ct.), J. Wilson J.

The appellant, on appeal, argued that the deputy judge had erred by exceeding his role as an impartial arbiter in raising the defence of qualified privilege, which was not pleaded by the respondent or raised during the trial by either party. The appellant submits that the deputy judge made unreasonable assumptions on the evidence, and that he incorrectly applied the test of qualified privilege.

The opportunity for parties to adduce evidence and make submissions in respect of an issue is fundamental to the right to be heard. A denial of natural justice may occur if such an opportunity is not afforded to the parties: See e.g. *Canadian Imperial Bank of Commerce v. Prasad*, 2010 ONSC 320, 2010 CarswellOnt 108 at para. 10 (Ont. S.C.J.).

See *Brighton Heating & Air Conditioning Ltd. v. Savoia*, 2006 CarswellOnt 340, [2006] O.J. No. 250, 79 O.R. (3d) 386, 49 C.L.R. (3d) 235, 207 O.A.C. 1 (Ont. Div. Ct.), where Quinn J. concluded that the trial judge had unfairly awarded a form of relief that had not been pleaded.

Justice Quinn made the following observations at para. 40:

> I agree with the proposition that, in Small Claims Court, a liberal, non-technical approach should be taken to pleadings. Therefore, unpled relief may be granted (and an unpled defence allowed) so long as supporting evidence is not needed beyond what was adduced at trial, or what reasonably should have been adduced, in support of the relief (or defence) that was pled; and, of course, provided that, in all of the circumstances, it is not unfair to grant such relief (or allow such a defence).

The appellant had no opportunity to call evidence of malice to rebut the defence, if it in fact applied. The appropriate remedy was to have the matter sent back for a new trial pursuant to sections 134(1)(b) and 134(6) of the *Courts of Justice Act*, R.S.O. 1990, c. C.43.

The matter is to be sent back for a new trial before a different judge. The trial judge decided the matter on the basis of a defence not pleaded, an unfairness that is a substantial wrong or miscarriage of justice.

Lum v. Jiang, 2011 ONSC 3608, 2011 CarswellOnt 4724, 3 C.L.R. (4th) 160 (Ont. S.C.J.), J. Mackinnon J.

The appeal from the judgment of Small Claims Court Deputy Judge Gilbert dated June 28, 2009, was dismissed.

The standard of review set out in *Plan Group v. Bell Canada*, 2009 ONCA 548, 2009 CarswellOnt 3807, [2009] O.J. No. 2829, (sub nom. *Bell Canada v. The Plan Group)* 96 O.R. (3d) 81, 81 C.L.R. (3d) 9, 62 B.L.R. (4th) 157, 252 O.A.C. 71 (Ont. C.A.) at para. 129 states:

> As my colleague noted, historically, interpretation of a contract was treated as a question of law, reviewable on a standard of correctness. However, *Housen v. Nikolaisen*, [2002] 2 S.C.R. 235, [2002] S.C.J. No. 31 dictates that a more nuanced approach be taken by reviewing courts. Questions of fact are reviewable on a standard of palpable and overriding error, or the "functional equivalents" of "clearly wrong," "unreasonable" or "not reasonably supported by the evidence": *H.L. v. Canada (Attorney General)*, [2005] 1 S.C.R. 401, [2005] S.C.J. No. 24 at para. 110. Questions of mixed law and fact, however, lie along a spectrum, with some questions being more akin to questions of law and others being more akin to questions of fact.

Fazari v. Simpson, 2011 ONSC 5953, 2011 CarswellOnt 10738 (Ont. Div. Ct.); additional reasons at 2011 ONSC 6948, 2011 CarswellOnt 13328 (Ont. Div. Ct.), Eberhard, J.

The deputy judge conducted a trial, demonstrated by the transcript, in a manner showing patience and considerable skill in instructing the litigants as to procedure, accommodating their lack of experience, maintaining an unbiased and impartial attitude, and explaining his reasons as required.

Perfect justice is unlikely to arise from an imperfect presentation.

Chaos accounts for an error in the deputy judge's comments on the evidence in his Reasons for Judgment. The trial judge's reasons were incomplete but not incorrect.

An appeal was granted. The judgment was set aside and replaced with a judgment for the plaintiff (respondent herein) against the defendant (appellant herein), Silvano Fazari, in the amount of $1,480, with costs of $400.

Ha v. Arista Homes (Boxgrove) Inc., 2011 ONSC 4561, 2011 CarswellOnt 9084, 10 R.P.R. (5th) 202, 285 O.A.C. 89 (Ont. Div. Ct.), Lauwers J.

The deputy judge awarded the plaintiffs $2,147.64.

The applicable standard of review on an appeal was expressed by Swinton J. in *Fresco v. Canadian Imperial Bank of Commerce*, 2010 ONSC 4724, 2010 CarswellOnt 6695, [2010] O.J. No. 3762, 103 O.R. (3d) 659, 267 O.A.C. 317, 85 C.C.E.L. (3d) 9, 90 C.P.C. (6th) 281, 323 D.L.R. (4th) 376, 2010 C.L.L.C. 210-049 (Ont. Div. Ct.); reversed 2012 ONCA 444, 2012 CarswellOnt 7956, 111 O.R. (3d) 501, 100 C.C.E.L. (3d) 81, 21 C.P.C. (7th) 223, 2012 C.L.L.C. 210-040, 293 O.A.C. 248 (Ont. C.A.); leave to appeal refused 2013 CarswellOnt 3154, 2013 CarswellOnt 3155, 452 N.R. 394 (note), 314 O.A.C. 402 (note), [2012] S.C.C.A. No. 379 (S.C.C.):

> [36] On appeal, the standard of review on a question of law is correctness. The standard of review for findings of fact is palpable and overriding error, while questions of mixed fact and law are on a spectrum. If a legal question can be separated out, it will be reviewed on s standard of correctness. Otherwise, questions of mixed fact and law will not be overturned absent palpable and overriding error (*Housen v. Nikolaisen*, [2002] 2 S.C.R. 235, [2002] S.C.J. No. 31 at paras. 8, 10 and 36-37).

This standard also applies to appeals from the decision of a deputy judge of the Small Claims Court: *Meyknecht-Lischer Contractors Ltd. v. Stanford*, 2006 CarswellOnt 6806, [2006] O.J. No. 4360, 57 C.L.R. (3d) 145 at para. 17 (Ont. Div. Ct.); additional reasons at 2006 CarswellOnt 8329 (Ont. Div. Ct.); *Kaur v. Deopaul*, 2006 CarswellOnt 6388, [2006] O.J. No. 4170, 216 O.A.C. 247 at para. 24 (Ont. Div. Ct.).

A party is bound by its pleading. See *Allison v. Street Imports Ltd.* (May 14, 2009), Doc. 03 DV 000953, [2009] O.J. No. 1979 at para. 13 (Ont. Div. Ct.), *Atlas Construction Inc. v. Brownstones Ltd.*, 1996 CarswellOnt 611, [1996] O.J. No. 616, 27 O.R. (3d) 711, 26 C.L.R. (2d) 97 at paras. 82-83 (Ont. Gen. Div.), *Lubrizol Corp. v. Imperial Oil Ltd.*, 1996 CarswellNat 2572, 1996 CarswellNat 651, [1996] F.C.J. No. 454, 112 F.T.R. 264 (note), [1996] 3 F.C. 40, 67 C.P.R. (3d) 1, 197 N.R. 241 at paras. 18-19 (Fed. C.A.).

The court found that the plaintiffs were relying on representations by the appellant's agents.

An overly-technical approach to the rules is not to be taken by the court, as noted in section 23 of the *Courts of Justice Act*, and by rule 2.01 of the *Small Claims Court Rules*. The plaintiffs were awarded $6,750.50 in reimbursement of fees paid.

Jogendra v. Campbell, 2011 ONSC 3324, 2011 CarswellOnt 4955 (Ont. Div. Ct.), J. Wilson J.

The respondent submitted that the Divisional Court had no jurisdiction to hear this matter. The court agreed.

Ferrier J. dismissed the appeal of Mr. Jogendra from two final decisions of deputy judges of the Small Claims Court. The decisions of Ferrier J. and the appellant's own documents make it clear that Ferrier J. was hearing two appeals, not any motion.

The only available route of appeal from Ferrier J.'s decision was pursuant to section 6(1)(a) of the *Courts of Justice Act*, that is, to the Court of Appeal with leave. Section 21(5) of the *Courts of Justice Act* has no application as Ferrier J. clearly was not hearing a motion. There was no inherent jurisdiction to hear the matter. The matter was dismissed without a determination on the merits.

O'Brien v. Ottawa Hospital, 2011 ONSC 231, 2011 CarswellOnt 88, [2011] O.J. No. 66 (Ont. Div. Ct.), J. Mackinnon J.

An appeal from the decision of Tierney J. dated October 2, 2009, dismissing action against the respondents pursuant to r. 20.01(3) of the *Rules of Civil Procedure*, R.R.O. 1990 Reg. 194, was submitted on the basis that there was no genuine issue for trial. The doctors moved under r. 20.01, and the Hospital moved under that rule and under *Rules of the Small Claims Court*, O. Reg. 258/98, r. 1 and r. 12 and the *Courts of Justice Act*, R.S.O. 1990, c. C.43, s. 25. The motion judge reached the correct decision on a motion brought pursuant to r. 20.01 of the *Rules of Civil Procedure*.

Kipiniak v. Dubiel, 2011 ONSC 825, 2011 CarswellOnt 766, 274 O.A.C. 249 (Ont. Div. Ct.), Molloy J.

Kipiniak appealed from two orders made by Small Claims Court Judge Thompson, both dated June 15, 2010. In one of the orders Kipiniak was the plaintiff and Ewa Dubiel was the defendant; in the other order (similar in its terms), made in action, Kipiniak was the plaintiff and Kinga Dubiel was the defendant. The Orders dismissed Kipiniak's actions and prohibited him from commencing any further proceedings related to their subject matter in any Small Claims Court in Ontario.

The Orders were made by a judge on her own initiative, in the absence of any motion before the court, without a proper evidentiary foundation, without notice to Kipiniak, and without providing him with any meaningful opportunity to be heard. The Orders were made without jurisdiction and in breach of principles of procedural fairness and natural justice. The Orders were set aside.

Both Orders made reference to a hearing on June 9, 2010. That hearing was a "to be spoken to" attendance, in respect to the action against Kinga Dubiel relating to hydro expenses.

Kipiniak submitted that the Small Claims Court judge erred in law by granting summary judgment and dismissing the two actions in the absence of a motion by the defendants.

Section 31 of the *Courts of Justice Act* provides that an appeal lies to the Divisional Court from a "final order of the Small Claims Court *in an action* for the payment of money in excess of $500, excluding costs." Both of the subject actions were for the payment of money in excess of $20,000.

The June 15, 2010 orders were final orders by which the Small Claims Court judge purported to dismiss the subject actions.

No authority was cited for the proposition that an action can be dismissed at a settlement conference without notice and without an opportunity to be heard. A judge presiding over a settlement conference has no special powers to dispose of actions over the objection of the parties. Jurisdiction to make such an order at a settlement conference is more circumscribed than on a motion.

Kipiniak was wholly successful on appeal. He was self-represented and retired from work and therefore sought only his disbursements. He had documented his out-of-pocket expenses in relation to the appeals at $1,600.63. Costs of $1,600 were awarded.

Tosti v. Society of the Madonna Di Canneto of Windsor Inc., 2011 ONSC 339, 2011 CarswellOnt 454, 275 O.A.C. 108 (Ont. Div. Ct.), Nolan, J.

A Small Claims Court judge determined that three plaintiffs had made donations to the defendant society rather than loans that had to be repaid, as alleged by the plaintiffs. The Divisional Court allowed the plaintiffs' appeals, ordering a new trial. The court rejected the plaintiffs' allegation of a reasonable apprehension of bias in that the trial judge, *inter alia*, had failed to control the conduct of counsel for the society and had assisted the society's counsel by doing his own cross-examination of some of the plaintiffs' witnesses. While the trial judge's interventionist approach at times appeared to assist the society, the conduct did not rise to the level required for a finding of bias. The court concluded by commenting on the role of the trial judge in permitting the society's counsel to call an individual who had no independent knowledge of profit boards. The trial judge had an obligation to act as a "gatekeeper" in the interests of ensuring a fair trial by holding a *voir dire* on the evidence that the society was attempting to elicit from this person. As the only reason that he was called was to give an opinion, he had to be qualified as an expert by way of a *voir dire*. If he could not be so qualified, the trial judge should not have allowed him to testify.

It is not the role of an appellate court to retry a case or to substitute its views for those of the trial judge.

See *R. v. Sheppard*, 2002 SCC 26, 2002 CarswellNfld 74, 2002 CarswellNfld 75, REJB 2002-29516, [2002] S.C.J. No. 30, [2002] 1 S.C.R. 869, 211 Nfld. & P.E.I.R. 50, 50 C.R. (5th) 68, 633 A.P.R. 50, 210 D.L.R. (4th) 608, 284 N.R. 342, 162 C.C.C. (3d) 298 (S.C.C.), the Supreme Court of Canada held that parties are entitled to be given sufficient reasons for a decision from a trial court so that the decision can be reviewed by an appellate court and the reasons are sufficient to inform the losing party as well as the community of the basis for the decision. One must apply a functional interpretation of the reasons, articulated by the Court of Appeal in both *R. v. Ahmed*, 2002 CarswellOnt 4075, [2002] O.J. No. 4597, 7 C.R. (6th) 308, 166 O.A.C. 254, 170 C.C.C. (3d) 27 (Ont. C.A.) and *R. v. Stewart*, 2003 CarswellOnt 283, [2003] O.J. No. 347 (Ont. C.A.).

Appeals were granted, and a new trial was ordered.

The deputy judge *inter alia* failed to explain how he considered Exhibit 1 to be hearsay and inadmissible, yet he made it an exhibit at the trial.

The deputy judge did not appreciate the evidentiary rule related to spoliation of evidence, or address the issue of the rebuttable presumption.

During the period of adjournment, the Society's counsel obtained an expert report from a handwriting expert. Rule 18.02 in the rules of Small Claims Court provide that such reports are to be served at least *30 days before the trial date* "unless the trial judge orders otherwise." [Emphasis added.].

The deputy judge should have offered an adjournment to the plaintiffs. I find that this is an error of law and requires that the decision of the deputy judge be set aside.

The deputy judge refused to permit the plaintiffs to call a reply witness.

The deputy judge had the obligation to act as "gatekeeper" in the interests of ensuring a fair trial and to hold a *voir dire* on the evidence.

In *R. v. Isiah*, 1999 CarswellOnt 1150, [1999] O.J. No. 1192, (sub nom. *R. v. J.I.)* 119 O.A.C. 165 (Ont. C.A.), Justice Rosenberg ordered a new trial on other grounds, however, at para. 27, the court emphasized that the expert evidence should not have been admitted without proper scrutiny at a *voir dire* (David M. Paciocco, "*Context, Culture and the Law of Expert Evidence*", (2001) 24 *Advocates' Quarterly*, 42 at p. 45). The trial judge remains the gatekeeper, responsible for determining admissibility.

Willmot v. Benton, 2011 ONCA 104, 2011 CarswellOnt 523, 11 C.P.C. (7th) 219 (Ont. C.A.).

A motion was made to quash an appeal. The respondents submitted that the court lacks jurisdiction to entertain the appeal because the order in question was interlocutory in that it did not finally dispose of the issues between the parties. The motion judge made an order that provided that the plaintiff appoint a litigation guardian and then that the plaintiff's litigation guardian appoint counsel to represent her.

The primary aspect of this order did not finally resolve an issue that went to the merit or substance of the litigation that asserts claims.

One specific aspect of the order was the subject of additional submissions. It reads as follows:

> This court further orders that the plaintiff's litigation guardian shall appoint counsel in the action, the application and the small claims action within 30 days of the date of the order failing which the Conservation Authority or any other defendant in the action or respondent to

the application may move without further notice pursuant to rule 21.01 of the *Rules of Civil Procedure* to strike out the plaintiff's pleadings and seek dismissal on the ground that the plaintiff's pleadings disclose no reasonable cause of action and are frivolous, vexatious and an abuse of the court's process.

The term did not render the order final. The order was interlocutory. The motion to quash was granted, and the appeal was quashed without prejudice to the respondent's ability to seek leave to appeal to the Divisional Court.

Farrell v. TD Waterhouse Canada Inc., 2011 BCCA 61, 2011 CarswellBC 198, [2011] B.C.J. No. 201 (B.C. C.A.); affirming 2010 BCSC 1930, 2010 CarswellBC 3762, [2010] B.C.J. No. 2770 (B.C. S.C.), Greyell J.

The plaintiff brought an action against the bank in Small Claims Court. The parties reached a settlement which stated the bank would return share certificates and the alleged debt of the plaintiff would be forgiven. The parties disagreed over the form of release. The plaintiff's petition for judicial review was dismissed. The plaintiff appealed. The appeal was dismissed. The trial judge properly concluded that the payment order could be cancelled. There was no merit in the plaintiff's appeal. Any non-compliance with the settlement was on the part of the plaintiff.

McNevan v. Agrico Canada Ltd., 2011 ONSC 2035, 2011 CarswellOnt 2253 (Ont. S.C.J.), Roccamo J.; affirmed 2011 ONCA 720, 2011 CarswellOnt 13239 (Ont. C.A.).

The vendor brought an action in Small Claims Court against the buyer to recover outstanding accounts. The buyer counterclaimed for damages greater than $50,000. The vendor brought a motion for summary judgment. The motion was granted. The vendor relied on an affidavit of its employee. The buyer furnished no evidence to preclude the inference to be drawn from the lab and veterinarian reports.

Issasi v. Rosenzweig, 2011 ONCA 112, 2011 CarswellOnt 637, [2011] O.J. No. 520, 95 R.F.L. (6th) 45, 277 O.A.C. 391 (Ont. C.A. [In Chambers]).

The appellant brought a motion for an order granting leave to extend the time to the day following the determination of the motion so that he could perfect his appeal. Rule 3.02(1) of the Ontario *Rules of Civil Procedure* provides that court might extend the time prescribed by the Rules on such terms as is just. The Court of Appeal stated that "[a]lthough this motion involves a request for leave to extend the time to perfect an appeal, it is useful to consider the factors that apply when determining whether to exercise discretion to extend the time for filing a notice of appeal . . . They are: (1) whether the appellant formed an intention to appeal within the relevant period; (2) the length of the delay and explanation for the delay; (3) any prejudice to the respondent; (4) the merits of the appeal; and (5) whether the justice of the case' requires it.".

Boghossian Legal Profession Corp. v. Permacharts Inc., 2011 ONSC 3783, 2011 Carswell-Ont 5833, 282 O.A.C. 330 (Ont. Div. Ct.), Aston J.

Permacharts Inc. and Carmine Bellow appealed to a Small Claims Court judgment dated October 30, 2009, which awarded the plaintiff $4,355 plus pre-judgment interest and costs.

The appellants sought to introduce fresh evidence on the appeal. The motion was dismissed.

Proposed fresh evidence otherwise must meet the test in *R. v. Palmer* (1979), 1979 CarswellBC 533, 1979 CarswellBC 541, [1979] S.C.J. No. 126, [1980] 1 S.C.R. 759, 30 N.R. 181, 14 C.R. (3d) 22, 17 C.R. (3d) 34 (Fr.), 50 C.C.C. (2d) 193, 106 D.L.R. (3d) 212 (S.C.C.) at p. 13 [S.C.R.]. the issue on appeal was not what the trial judge should have done or might have done on different evidence. An appeal is limited to the trial record. The standard of review is articulated in *Housen v. Nikolaisen*, 2002 SCC 33, 2002 CarswellSask 178, 2002 CarswellSask 179, REJB 2002-29758, [2002] S.C.J. No. 31, [2002] 2 S.C.R. 235, 10

C.C.L.T. (3d) 157, 211 D.L.R. (4th) 577, 286 N.R. 1, [2002] 7 W.W.R. 1, 30 M.P.L.R. (3d) 1, 219 Sask. R. 1, 272 W.A.C. 1 (S.C.C.).

There was no error of law or error in legal principle. There was also no palpable and overriding error in finding of facts or mixed fact and law.

The costs of appeal included the motion to introduce fresh evidence staggering in relation to the amount of money in issue. There were allegations that the plaintiff, a lawyer, obtained the judgment by perjury and fraud. The claim was for costs of almost $20,000 on a partial indemnity basis.

The plaintiff's evidence at the trial was careless and inaccurate.

The plaintiff was entitled to the costs of appeal. The amount of money at issue would probably cap those costs at $4,000 to $5,000. The plaintiff was entitled to more than that because of the allegations of fraud and perjury. The appellants were to pay costs fixed at $10,000 all inclusive.

Mehedi v. Canadian Imperial Bank of Commerce, 2011 ONSC 3635, 2011 CarswellOnt 5986 (Ont. Div. Ct.), Lederer J.

The appellant sued for a return of $2,765 to a G.I.C. A Small Claims Court judge found that the Bank was entitled to the set-off. The appellant exhausted the appeals available to him.

The appellant served a Statement of Defence, largely struck out by the order of Quigley J. What remained was struck out by the decision of Sproat J. who also granted default judgment to the Bank.

The appellant attempted to appeal from the decision of Sproat J. and set aside the default judgment he granted. There was no error in the decision or reasons; the appeal was dismissed.

The Statement of Defence was based on the allegations that were made, or could have been made, in Small Claims Court. It was subject to *res judicata* and cause of action estoppels. Principles provide that issues the Court has decided, or which properly could have been raised, cannot be litigated or re-litigated.

Bernard v. New Brunswick, 2006 NBCA 57, 2006 CarswellNB 277, 2006 CarswellNB 278, [2006] N.B.J. No. 216, 299 N.B.R. (2d) 198, 778 A.P.R. 198 (N.B. C.A.).

The appellant, Bernard, appealed the decision of a judge of the Court of Queen's Bench that dismissed his small claims action against the respondent, New Brunswick. Bernard sought to obtain the deductions the Province made to his monthly social assistance payments, represented by the amount of a monthly annuity payment he received as a pension from his former employer. The decision was appealed and reported at 2004 NBQB 3, 2004 CarswellNB 1, [2004] N.B.J. No. 1, 270 N.B.R. (2d) 83, 48 C.P.C. (5th) 228, 710 A.P.R. 83 (N.B. Q.B.); affirmed 2006 NBCA 57, 2006 CarswellNB 277, 2006 CarswellNB 278, [2006] N.B.J. No. 216, 299 N.B.R. (2d) 198, 778 A.P.R. 198 (N.B. C.A.).

Having failed to establish there was a debt or any damages due to him from the Province under the appeal process referred to above, the Court of Queen's Bench judge decided as follows at para. 22:

> In effect, Mr. Bernard is asking the Small Claims Court to review the Appeals Board's decision but the *Small Claims Act* does not give the Small Claims Court jurisdiction to do that. Its jurisdiction is limited to actions for debt, damages or the recovery of personal property and this claim does not fall into any of those categories.

The Court of Queen's Bench judge was correct in his conclusions and decision to dismiss the small claims action. The appeal was without merit.

Gulati v. Husain, 2011 ONSC 706, 2011 CarswellOnt 407, [2011] O.J. No. 384 (Ont. S.C.J.), D.L. Corbett J.

The applicant sought certiorari respecting an order from the learned deputy judge of Small Claims Court: (a) denying an adjournment of the motion to set aside default judgment; (b) staying enforcement of the default judgment; (c) setting aside the default judgment; and (d) costs of $300.

The Order to set aside the default judgment and costs order was set aside. The case was remitted back to a different deputy judge of the Small Claims Court to hear and decide the motion to set aside the default judgment. No costs below for the appearance from the decision reversed, and costs of this application, if not agreed, shall be addressed in writing.

It is inusual to refuse a request to accommodate the counsel's schedule reasonably on a first appearance. And it is not a proper basis to refuse an adjournment that the court believes counsel is unlikely to succeed on the substantive issue. In this case, whatever view the motions judge may have had about the merits of the motion to set aside the default judgment, he had an obligation to accord the respondents a reasonable time to file responding materials and to be heard in argument on the merits.

The deputy judge gave no reason for refusing the adjournment. The refusal to accord the applicant a reasonable opportunity to file materials and make argument required some reasons.

The motion to set aside the default judgment without hearing submissions from either side was a failure to accord procedural fairness to both sides, and cannot stand.

Rudy Hetu Logging Ltd. v. Greyback Logging Ltd., 2012 ABQB 15, 2012 CarswellAlta 29 (Alta. Q.B.).

Rudy Hetu applied for an order directing that an appeal from the decision of Ingram P.C.J. be by way of a trial *de novo*.

Under section 51 of the *Provincial Court Act*, R.S.A. 2000, Ch. P-20, ". . . appeal to be heard as appeal on record unless, on the application of party, Court of Queen's Bench orders appeal to be heard as a trial *de novo* . . .".

Where new evidence is basis for application, the *fresh evidence* rule should at a minimum be considered, following *Gill v. Sandhu*, 1999 ABQB 209, 1999 CarswellAlta 221 (Alta. Q.B. [In Chambers]).

The application for a direction of trial *de novo* was dismissed.

Most of the information the appellant wanted to put forward was available at the time of trial. All of the new information relates to the credibility of Soukup. None of it is on the key point.

In *Janzen v. Alberta (Minister of Infrastructure)*, 2002 ABCA 278, 2002 CarswellAlta 1486, 317 A.R. 228, 284 W.A.C. 228 (Alta. C.A.), the Court of Appeal stated at para. 16 "there should not be a new trial to let the Appellant reshape her case and find different evidence.".

Davison v. Canadian Artists Syndicate Inc., 2011 NSSM 28, 2011 CarswellNS 293, 303 N.S.R. (2d) 63, 957 A.P.R. 63 (N.S. Small Cl. Ct.).

An Execution Order named Davison as the judgment debtor. Davison applied for relief from that Execution Order. Davison wanted to pay $100 a month until the debt to the Canadian Artists Syndicate was paid off.

In *Smith's Field Manor Development Ltd. v. Campbell*, 2010 NSSC 63, 2010 CarswellNS 103 (N.S. S.C.) at para. 6, Justice Moir held that Rule 79.22 in the *Civil Procedure Rules* "continues the power to stay execution orders without any substantive change" from the old Rule 53.13 in the *Civil Procedure Rules* (1972). Court does possess the jurisdiction to grant relief from execution orders issued pursuant to judgments rendered in Court.

See, e.g., *Scaraveilli & Associates v. Quinlan*, 2005 NSSM 7, 2005 CarswellNS 616, [2005] N.S.J. No. 575, 241 N.S.R. (2d) 64, 767 A.P.R. 64 (N.S. Small Cl. Ct.) and *Wickwire Holm v. Wilkes*, 2005 NSSM 3, 2005 CarswellNS 439, [2005] N.S.J. No. 406, 237 N.S.R. (2d) 197, 754 A.P.R. 197, 28 C.P.C. (6th) 338 (N.S. Small Cl. Ct.), both decisions of the Small Claims Court in which the Adjudicators held that the Small Claims Court could direct a judgment debtor (pursuant to an order of the Small Claims Court) to attend a discovery in aid of execution.

It is reasonable to conclude that mechanisms of enforcement can and should be dealt with in the Small Claims Court in respect of Orders of the Small Claims Court (exclusive of *ex facie* contempt issues).

The interest of litigants in the Small Claims Court, many of whom are self-represented (as they are in the case before me), in accessing an informal and inexpensive court process applies not only to the adjudication of issues but also in the enforcement of Small Claims Court Orders that flow from that adjudication process.

There was no reason why the request that the application of the Execution Order be stayed, conditional upon payment of $100 a month, should be granted. The Application was denied.

Graham v. Vandersloot, 2012 ONCA 60, 2012 CarswellOnt 815, 108 O.R. (3d) 641, 6 C.C.L.I. (5th) 171, 346 D.L.R. (4th) 266, 288 O.A.C. 342, [2012] O.J. No. 353 (Ont. C.A.).

The appellant sought to set aside two orders of the Superior Court of Justice: (i) the order dated September 7, 2010, denying the appellant's request for an adjournment of the trial of this action, and (ii) the order dismissing the action.

Adjournment decisions are highly discretionary and appellate courts are rightly reluctant to interfere with them. Laskin J.A. succinctly summarized the operative legal principles in *Khimji v. Dhanani*, 2004 CarswellOnt 525, [2004] O.J. No. 320, 69 O.R. (3d) 790, 44 C.P.C. (5th) 56, 182 O.A.C. 142 (Ont. C.A.). Although he was in dissent, the majority accepted his articulation of the statement of principles. See paras. 14 and 18 in particular. See also *Ariston Realty Corp. v. Elcarim Inc.*, 2007 CarswellOnt 2371 at paras. 33, 36 and 38, [2007] O.J. No. 1497, 51 C.P.C. (6th) 326 (Ont. S.C.J.).

The motion judge gave undue weight to the appellant's lawyer's failure. As Hambley J. noted when granting leave to appeal to the Divisional Court in this matter, "the often applied principle that the sins of the lawyer should not be visited upon the client applies in this case." This principle was enunciated by this Court in *Halton Community Credit Union Ltd. v. ICL Computers Canada Ltd.*, 1985 CarswellOnt 357 at para. 11, [1985] O.J. No. 101, 8 O.A.C. 369, 1 C.P.C. (2d) 24 (Ont. C.A.):

> Undoubtedly counsel is the agent of the client for many purposes ... but it is a principle of very long standing that the client is not to be placed irrevocably in jeopardy by reason of the neglect or inattention of his solicitor, if relief to the client can be given on terms that protect his innocent adversary as to costs thrown away and as to the security of the legal position he has gained. There may be cases where the plaintiff has so changed his position that this is impossible.

It is the overall interests of justice that, at the end of the day, must govern. See *Ariston Realty Corp.*, at para. 38.

The interests of justice favour the appellant's having her day in court to put forward her claim for damages on the merits.

Theofylatos v. Plechac, 2012 ONSC 601, 2012 CarswellOnt 1252 (Ont. Div. Ct.).

The defendant sought to extend the time for appealing an order of a Small Claims Court judge pronounced September 24, 2010.

Under Rule 3.02, the defendant must show:

(i) He had, within the time fixed for an appeal, formed an intention to appeal;

(ii) He had a good explanation for the delay;

(iii) The proposed appeal has merit; and

(iv) There will be no prejudice to the plaintiff if leave is granted.

The appeal was dismissed.

Hodgins v. Grover, 2011 ONCA 72, 2011 CarswellOnt 336, [2011] O.J. No. 310, *(*sub nom. *Grover v. Hodgins)* 103 O.R. (3d) 721, *(*sub nom. *Grover v. Hodgins)* 275 O.A.C. 96, *(*sub nom. *Grover v. Hodgins)* 330 D.L.R. (4th) 712, 5 C.P.C. (7th) 33 (Ont. C.A.); leave to appeal refused 2012 CarswellOnt 825, 2012 CarswellOnt 826, 432 N.R. 392 (note), *(*sub nom. *Grover v. Hodgins)* 295 O.A.C. 398 (note), [2011] S.C.C.A. No. 142 (S.C.C.).

A deputy judge of the Small Claims Court granted judgment in favour of the plaintiffs. The deputy judge's order was for a portion of the legal fees that the defendants and other plaintiffs in the lawsuit paid to prosecute an action relating to a condominium complex in which they were all owners. The defendants appealed, challenging unjust enrichment analysis, and the plaintiffs cross-appealed. The appeal was allowed and the cross-appeal was dismissed. The deputy judge overlooked the fact that there was no evidence that the defendants requested that the plaintiffs subsidize their contribution to legal services.

Boghossian Legal Profession Corp. v. Permacharts Inc., 2011 ONSC 3783, 2011 CarswellOnt 5833, 282 O.A.C. 330 (Ont. Div. Ct.), Aston J.

Practice on appeal. The plaintiff lawyer was awarded a judgment of $4,355 for unpaid account. The defendant appealed. The appeal was dismissed. The defendant failed to demonstrate a palpable and overriding error in the judge's findings of fact. The plaintiff's evidence was hardly challenged on cross-examination. The judge accepted the testimony of the plaintiff and preferred it over that of the defendant. The judge found that the plaintiff's hourly rate was reasonable and accepted the plaintiff's unchallenged evidence on hours spent.

Janicek v. OC Transpo, 2011 ONSC 2601, 2011 CarswellOnt 8110 (Ont. Div. Ct.), Toscano Roccamo J.

The plaintiff appealed an Order dated June 12, 2009, dismissing without costs an action dated June 28, 2003. The applicable standard of review requires a measure of deference to the Court of the first instance, and only permits interference in the event of palpable and overriding errors in a decision rendering it clearly wrong. See *Woodheath Developments Ltd. v. Goldman*, 2003 CarswellOnt 3310, [2003] O.J. No. 3440, 66 O.R. (3d) 731, 38 C.P.C. (5th) 80, 175 O.A.C. 259 (Ont. Div. Ct.); leave to appeal refused 2004 CarswellOnt 1354, [2004] O.J. No. 1021, 44 C.P.C. (5th) 101 (Ont. C.A.); additional reasons at 2004 CarswellOnt 3922, 5 C.P.C. (6th) 36 (Ont. Div. Ct.). The appeal to the Court of Appeal was dismissed, 2004 CarswellOnt 1354, [2004] O.J. No. 1021, 44 C.P.C. (5th) 101 (Ont. C.A.). The limitation period prescribed by section 206 of the *Highway Traffic Act*, R.S.O. 1990, C. H-8 expired by the second anniversary dates of both accidents. The appeal was dismissed with costs against the plaintiff.

Labatt Brewing Co. v. NHL Enterprises Canada L.P., 2011 ONCA 511, 2011 CarswellOnt 6140, 106 O.R. (3d) 677, 86 B.L.R. (4th) 226, 282 O.A.C. 151 (Ont. C.A.).

The application judge's conclusion was not anchored in the pleadings, evidence, positions, or submissions of any of the parties. As NHL and Molson were not given an opportunity to address the ultimate conclusion reached by the application judge, they were denied procedural fairness. See *Rodaro v. Royal Bank*, 2002 CarswellOnt 1047, [2002] O.J. No. 1365, 59 O.R. (3d) 74, 49 R.P.R. (3d) 227, 157 O.A.C. 203, 22 B.L.R. (3d) 274 (Ont. C.A.). Doherty J.A. held that it is both fundamentally unfair and inherently unreliable for a trial judge to make findings against a defendant on the basis of a theory of legal liability not advanced by the claimant.

See also *A-C-H International Inc. v. Royal Bank*, 2005 CarswellOnt 2043, [2005] O.J. No. 2048, 6 B.L.R. (4th) 33, 197 O.A.C. 227, 254 D.L.R. (4th) 327 (Ont. C.A.), Blair J.A.; *Grass (Litigation Guardian of) v. Women's College Hospital*, 2005 CarswellOnt 1401, [2005] O.J. No. 1403, 75 O.R. (3d) 85, 30 C.C.L.T. (3d) 100, 196 O.A.C. 201 (Ont. C.A.); additional reasons at 2005 CarswellOnt 1701, [2005] O.J. No. 1719 (Ont. C.A.); leave to appeal refused 2005 CarswellOnt 5329, 2005 CarswellOnt 5330, [2005] S.C.C.A. No. 310, (sub nom. *Grass v. Women's College Hospital*) 348 N.R. 197 (note), (sub nom. *Grass v. Women's College Hospital*) 215 O.A.C. 393 (note) (S.C.C.), Cronk J.A.; *Garfin v. Mirkopoulos*, 2009 ONCA 421, 2009 CarswellOnt 2818, 71 C.P.C. (6th) 210, 250 O.A.C. 168 (Ont. C.A.), Sharpe J.A.; *Suddaby v. 864226 Ontario Inc.*, 2004 CarswellOnt 2512 at paras. 6-9, [2004] O.J. No. 2536 (Ont. C.A.); and *TSP-Intl Ltd. v. Mills*, 2006 CarswellOnt 4037, [2006] O.J. No. 2702, 81 O.R. (3d) 266, 19 B.L.R. (4th) 21, 212 O.A.C. 66 (Ont. C.A.).

Orders on contempt

A custodial term was imposed recently because of "utter disregard and contempt" for the court's authority. "It is necessary in the circumstances of this case to bring home to the gravity of misconduct." See *Uyj Air Inc. v. Barnes*; *Ogilvy Renault v. Barnes*.

The Ontario Court of Appeal upheld a 14-month sentence against Barry Landen in *Langston v. Landen* for not complying with numerous court orders in an alleged multi-million-dollar estates fraud. The appeal court also concluded in the contempt case of *Chiang (Re)* in 2009 that sentences of eight and 12 months for a couple who breached numerous orders requiring them to disclose assets weren't excessive.

In *Chiang*, one of several cases cited by Roberts, the Court of Appeal described civil contempt as a necessary "coercive" power to try to obtain compliance with court orders.

The Court of Appeal ruled that people serving sentences for contempt aren't eligible for parole and that the release date is within the jurisdiction of the court, not corrections officials.

Gligorevic v. McMaster, 2012 ONCA 115, 2012 CarswellOnt 2155, 109 O.R. (3d) 321, 347 D.L.R. (4th) 17, 254 C.R.R. (2d) 241, 287 O.A.C. 302 (Ont. C.A.).

The appellant, Zeljko Gligorevic, was detained at the CAMH (the Hospital) in Toronto by order of the Ontario Review Board (the ORB).

Gligorevic appealed the Board's decision. He argued that the assistance of counsel at the review hearing was ineffective. The appeal was allowed.

The right to advance an ineffective assistance claim on a criminal appeal is well-established. In *R. v. B. (G.D.)*, 2000 SCC 22, 2000 CarswellAlta 348, 2000 CarswellAlta 349, [2000] S.C.J. No. 22, [2000] 1 S.C.R. 520, 261 A.R. 1, [2000] 8 W.W.R. 193, 81 Alta. L.R. (3d) 1, 143 C.C.C. (3d) 289, 224 W.A.C. 1, 32 C.R. (5th) 207, 184 D.L.R. (4th) 577, 253 N.R. 201 (S.C.C.), the Supreme Court confirmed that the right to effective assistance of counsel extends to all accused persons. Justice Major, writing for the court, explained at para. 24: "In Canada that right is seen as a principle of fundamental justice. It is derived from the evolution of the common law, section 650(3) of the *Criminal Code of Canada* and sections 7 and 11(d) of the [*Charter*]." See also *R. v. Archer*, 2005 CarswellOnt 4964 at para. 118, [2005] O.J. No. 4348, 34 C.R. (6th) 271, (sub nom. *R. v. R.W.A.*) 203 O.A.C. 56, 202 C.C.C. (3d) 60 (Ont. C.A.); *Joanisse*, at pp. 56–58.

Nonetheless, this court has left open the possibility of an ineffective assistance argument as a ground of appeal in a civil case, on an exceptional basis, especially where the interests of vulnerable people are engaged. In *D.W.*, Catzman J.A. of this court stated, at para. 55:

> I would not be prepared to close the door to the viability of ineffective assistance of counsel as a ground for a new trial in a civil action. But, also like Grange J.A. [in *Dominion Readers' Service Ltd. v. Brant* (1982), 41 O.R. (2d) 1 (Ont. C.A.)], *I would limit the availability of that*

ground of appeal to the rarest of cases, such as (and these are by way of example only) cases involving some overriding public interest or cases engaging the interests of vulnerable persons like children or persons under mental disability. [Emphasis added.].

At common law, a patient's right of self-determination with respect to medical treatment is recognized and protected, absent emergency circumstances.

When a claim of ineffective assistance is raised, the appellant must demonstrate: (1) where the claim is based on contested facts, the facts that underpin the claim; (2) the incompetence of the assistance provided (the performance component); and (3) that the ineffective assistance caused a miscarriage of justice (the prejudice component): *Archer*, at paras. 119-120. See also *R. v. G. (D.M.)*, 2011 ONCA 343 at para. 100, 2011 CarswellOnt 2825, [2011] O.J. No. 1966, 105 O.R. (3d) 481, 84 C.R. (6th) 420, 281 O.A.C. 85, 275 C.C.C. (3d) 295 (Ont. C.A.); *Joanisse*, at p. 59; *R. v. DiPalma* (2002), 2002 CarswellOnt 6032 at para. 36, [2002] O.J. No. 2684, [2005] 2 C.T.C. 132 (Ont. C.A.).

R. v. Ryan, 2012 NLCA 9, 2012 CarswellNfld 53, 318 Nfld. & P.E.I.R. 15, 281 C.C.C. (3d) 352, 989 A.P.R. 15, 253 C.R.R. (2d) 258, [2012] N.J. No. 55 (N.L. C.A.).

A common theme running through all of the submissions on appeal is that Mr. Ryan, a man with limited formal education and representing himself, was, although he did not fully appreciate it, in the words of his counsel "out of his depth" and could not properly conduct his own defence.

The *Charter*, sections 7 and 11(d), guarantees an accused the right to a fair trial which includes the right to present full answer and defence. It is a fundamental underpinning of our criminal justice system. As stated by Carthy J.A. in *R. v. Clement*, 1995 CarswellOnt 549, 25 O.R. (3d) 230, 42 C.R. (4th) 40, 100 C.C.C. (3d) 103, 83 O.A.C. 226, 31 C.R.R. (2d) 17 (Ont. C.A.) at p. 239 [O.R.]; affirmed 1996 CarswellOnt 2842, 1996 CarswellOnt 2843, EYB 1996-67698, [1996] 2 S.C.R. 289, 28 O.R. (3d) 639, 107 C.C.C. (3d) 52, 198 N.R. 234, 92 O.A.C. 81, 1 C.R. (5th) 393, 41 C.R.R. (2d) 186 (S.C.C.), ". . . a fair trial is at the root of the administration of justice and an unfair trial cannot be condoned, no matter what the other circumstances may be.".

The right to a fair trial does not, of course, mean that the accused is entitled to a perfect trial or even the most advantageous trial from his point of view. See *R. v. Harrer*, 1995 CarswellBC 651, 1995 CarswellBC 1144, EYB 1995-67068, [1995] S.C.J. No. 81, [1995] 3 S.C.R. 562, 42 C.R. (4th) 269, 101 C.C.C. (3d) 193, 128 D.L.R. (4th) 98, 186 N.R. 329, 64 B.C.A.C. 161, 105 W.A.C. 161, 32 C.R.R. (2d) 273 (S.C.C.), McLachlin J.

As a society, we expect to be governed by a system that treats its citizens fairly and does not result in persons being convicted and punished for something they did not do. See *R. v. Bjelland*, 2009 SCC 38, 2009 CarswellAlta 1110, 2009 CarswellAlta 1111, [2009] S.C.J. No. 38, [2009] 2 S.C.R. 651, 460 A.R. 230, 194 C.R.R. (2d) 148, 67 C.R. (6th) 201, 462 W.A.C. 230, 391 N.R. 202, 246 C.C.C. (3d) 129, 10 Alta. L.R. (5th) 1, 309 D.L.R. (4th) 257, [2009] 10 W.W.R. 387 (S.C.C.), Rothstein, J.

A guilty plea of an accused will not be accepted and acted upon until, following a screening of the facts by the trial judge, it is concluded by the court that there is a factual basis for conviction. It also underpins the "innocence at stake" exceptions that justify piercing informer (*R. v. Leipert*, 1997 CarswellBC 101, 1997 CarswellBC 102, [1997] S.C.J. No. 14, [1997] 1 S.C.R. 281, 112 C.C.C. (3d) 385, 41 C.R.R. (2d) 266, 85 B.C.A.C. 162, 138 W.A.C. 162, 143 D.L.R. (4th) 38, 207 N.R. 145, 4 C.R. (5th) 259, [1997] 3 W.W.R. 457 (S.C.C.)) and solicitor-client privileges (*R. v. McClure*, 2001 SCC 14, 2001 CarswellOnt 496, 2001 CarswellOnt 497, REJB 2001-22807, [2001] S.C.J. No. 13, [2001] 1 S.C.R. 445, 40 C.R. (5th) 1, 195 D.L.R. (4th) 513, 151 C.C.C. (3d) 321, 142 O.A.C. 201, 80 C.R.R. (2d) 217, 266 N.R. 275 (S.C.C.)) in favour of ensuring full answer and defence: "Our system will not tolerate conviction of the innocent" (per Major J. in *McClure* at para. 40).

Sir James Fitzjames Stephen wrote in his *History of the Criminal Law of England*, Vol. 1 (London, U.K: MacMillan, 1883) p. 442: "when a prisoner is undefended, his position is often pitiable, even if he has a good case.".

The courts have said on more than one occasion that the court cannot "force counsel upon an unwilling accused": *Cunningham v. Lilles*, 2010 SCC 10, 2010 CarswellYukon 21, 2010 CarswellYukon 22, [2010] S.C.J. No. 10, (sub nom. *R. v. Cunningham)* [2010] 1 S.C.R. 331, 480 W.A.C. 280, 283 B.C.A.C. 280, (sub nom. *R. v. Cunningham)* 317 D.L.R. (4th) 1, (sub nom. *R. v. Cunningham)* 254 C.C.C. (3d) 1, 73 C.R. (6th) 1, 399 N.R. 326 (S.C.C.) at para. 9, per Rothstein J.; see also *R. v. Vescio*, 1948 CarswellMan 1, [1949] S.C.R. 139, 6 C.R. 433, 92 C.C.C. 161, [1949] 1 D.L.R. 720 (S.C.C.) at para. 144, per Taschereau J.; and *R. v. Fleming* (1999), 171 Nfld. & P.E.I.R. 183 (Nfld. C.A.) at para. 197, per Marshall J.A.. This position is reflective of "respect for individual autonomy within an adversarial system": per Lamer C.J.C. in *R. v. Swain*, 1991 CarswellOnt 1016, 1991 CarswellOnt 93, EYB 1991-67605, [1991] S.C.J. No. 32, [1991] 1 S.C.R. 933, 4 O.R. (3d) 383, 63 C.C.C. (3d) 481, 125 N.R. 1, 3 C.R.R. (2d) 1, 47 O.A.C. 81, 5 C.R. (4th) 253, 83 D.L.R. (4th) 193 (S.C.C.) at p. 972 [S.C.R.].

Canadian criminal law recognizes an accused's right to the effective assistance of counsel, once engaged. It is seen as a principle of fundamental justice under the Chapter: *R. v. B. (G.D.)*, 2000 SCC 22 at para. 24, 2000 CarswellAlta 348, 2000 CarswellAlta 349, [2000] S.C.J. No. 22, [2000] 1 S.C.R. 520, 261 A.R. 1, [2000] 8 W.W.R. 193, 81 Alta. L.R. (3d) 1, 143 C.C.C. (3d) 289, 224 W.A.C. 1, 32 C.R. (5th) 207, 184 D.L.R. (4th) 577, 253 N.R. 201 (S.C.C.). In *G.D.B.*, Major J.

The fundamental duty of a trial judge to see that an accused receives a fair trial means that the judge must take steps to provide assistance to an unrepresented accused to enable his or her defence, or any defence that proceeding may reasonably disclose, is brought to the attention of the jury with full force and effect: *R. v. Darlyn* (1946), 1946 CarswellBC 117, 3 C.R. 13, 88 C.C.C. 269, [1947] 1 W.W.R. 449, 63 B.C.R. 428, [1947] 3 D.L.R. 480 (B.C. C.A.) at para. 7, per O'Halleran J.A.; *R. v. McGibbon*, per Griffiths J.A. at p. 347; *R. v. Tran*, 2001 CarswellOnt 2706, [2001] O.J. No. 3056, 55 O.R. (3d) 161, 156 C.C.C. (3d) 1, 14 M.V.R. (4th) 1, 149 O.A.C. 120, 44 C.R. (5th) 12 (Ont. C.A.) at para. 22, per Borins J.A.; *R. v. Assoun*, 2006 NSCA 47, 2006 CarswellNS 155, [2006] N.S.J. No. 154, 244 N.S.R. (2d) 96, 774 A.P.R. 96, 207 C.C.C. (3d) 372 (N.S. C.A.); leave to appeal refused 2006 CarswellNS 400, 2006 CarswellNS 401, [2006] S.C.C.A. No. 233, [2006] 2 S.C.R. iv (note), 258 N.S.R. (2d) 400 (note), 359 N.R. 392 (note), 824 A.P.R. 400 (note) (S.C.C.) *per curiam* at paras. 259–263.

It cannot be said that a verdict of guilty is one a properly instructed jury, acting judicially, could not reasonably have rendered, within the meaning of such cases as *R. v. Yebes*, 1987 CarswellBC 243, 1987 CarswellBC 705, [1987] S.C.J. No. 51, [1987] 2 S.C.R. 168, [1987] 6 W.W.R. 97, (sub nom. *Yebes v. R.)* 43 D.L.R. (4th) 424, 78 N.R. 351, 17 B.C.L.R. (2d) 1, 36 C.C.C. (3d) 417, 59 C.R. (3d) 108 (S.C.C.) and *R. v. Biniaris* (2000), 2000 SCC 15, 2000 CarswellBC 753, 2000 CarswellBC 754, [1998] S.C.C.A. No. 164, [2000] S.C.J. No. 16, [2000] 1 S.C.R. 381, 134 B.C.A.C. 161, 219 W.A.C. 161, 32 C.R. (5th) 1, 184 D.L.R. (4th) 193, 143 C.C.C. (3d) 1, 252 N.R. 204 (S.C.C.).

I would allow the appeal and order a new trial.

In *Save Guana Cay Reef Association v. Queen, The*, [2009] UKPC 44, the reasonable apprehension of bias which was alleged arose out of the judge being appointed on a temporary basis:

> . . . it is said that he [the trial judge] was an acting judge appointed on a temporary basis (that is on a six-month renewable contract) and that the Government of the Bahamas was at the time in default in failing to review judges' salaries. Miss Jordan added, in reinforcement of those main

grounds, that the acting judge has been a senator in the governing party, and that the judicial review proceedings were of particular political sensitivity.

The Privy Council did not see this as raising a reasonable apprehension of bias. It indicated that there is no single test that is decisive.

In *Gedge v. Newfoundland & Labrador (Hearing Aid Practitioner Board)*, 2011 NLCA 50, 2011 CarswellNfld 231, 310 Nfld. & P.E.I.R. 199, 30 Admin. L.R. (5th) 162, 337 D.L.R. (4th) 359, 963 A.P.R. 199 (N.L. C.A.), it was held that "a reasonable apprehension of bias must be raised at the first possible opportunity. The basis for this rule is waiver: a party cannot ask for a remedy from a tribunal and afterwards claim reasonable apprehension of bias." However, the Court of Appeal also pointed out that "the waiver rule can only apply if the person alleging a reasonable apprehension of bias had a prior opportunity to raise the issue. The apprehension must be raised at the first possible opportunity." In *White v. Conception Bay South (Town)*, 2013 NLCA 10, 2013 CarswellNfld 50, 334 Nfld. & P.E.I.R. 325, 1037 A.P.R. 325 (N.L. C.A.), the Court of Appeal noted that "a recusal motion must generally be made before or during the hearing in respect of which the judge is being asked to recuse himself or herself."

Grainger v. Windsor-Essex Children's Aid Society, 2009 CarswellOnt 4000, 96 O.R. (3d) 711 (Ont. S.C.J.).

Judge of Superior Court of Justice erroneously granting leave to appeal order of Small Claims Court judge dismissing defendant's motion for summary judgment. No appeal lying from interlocutory order of Small Claims Court judge. Judge of Divisional Court having authority to quash order erroneously made by judge of Superior Court of Justice.

Motion by defendant for summary judgment dismissing a Small Claims Court action dismissed on grounds that there was a genuine issue for trial. Leave to appeal that decision to the Divisional Court was granted by a judge of the Superior Court of Justice. The appeal should be quashed.

Section 31 of the *Courts of Justice Act* provides for an appeal to this court from a "final order of the Small Claims Court".

The test of whether an order is final or interlocutory is set forth in *Hendrickson v. Kallio*, 1932 CarswellOnt 148, [1932] O.R. 675, [1932] 4 D.L.R. 580, [1932] O.J. No. 380 (Ont. C.A.), the leading case on the issue.

Accordingly, the order of the Deputy Judge was interlocutory, and, as it was made in the Small Claims Court, there is no appeal from such order. As a result, the order made by Gates J. was in error as he had no jurisdiction to grant leave to appeal.

National Service Dog Training Centre Inc. v. Hall, 2013 CarswellOnt 9429, [2013] O.J. No. 3216 (Ont. S.C.J.).

This case involves a dispute over the ownership and possession of a dog currently in the custody of the defendant.

At the opening of trial on April 29, 2013, the plaintiff brought two motions; one requesting an inspection of the dog which would require time and therefore an adjournment of the two-day trial, and the other requesting that the defendant's medical/behavioural evidence about the dog be excluded from trial.

Appeals are made to the Divisional Court and are only available for final orders. There is no appeal of an interim order. See *Cudini v. 1704405 Ontario Inc.*, 2012 ONSC 6645, 2012 CarswellOnt 15146, [2012] O.J. No. 5620 (Ont. Div. Ct.) *Ron Robinson Ltd. v. Canadian Indemnity Co.*, 1984 CarswellOnt 1354, 45 O.R. (2d) 124, 2 O.A.C. 359 (Ont. Div. Ct.); additional reasons 1984 CarswellOnt 1771 (Ont. Div. Ct.), *Gelber v. Allstate Insurance Co. of Canada*, 1983 CarswellOnt 457, 41 O.R. (2d) 318, 35 C.P.C. 324 (Ont. Div. Ct.).

There may be a right to judicial review of an interlocutory order. Such a review is also done by the Divisional Court and not by a deputy judge, and is described in the following excerpt from Ontario Small Claims Court Practice 2013 by Justice Marvin Zuker:

> The plaintiff may take temporary possession of the dog on six separate occasions, one for a veterinary assessment and up to five other six hour assessments during which the dog may be observed by one expert assessor of the plaintiff's choice. None of the assessments shall involve overnight stays. During the inspections, the dog shall remain in the care and control of the plaintiff at all times. The dog will be returned to the defendant at the conclusion of each occasion. All assessments are to be at the plaintiff's expense and completed within the next forty-five days.

2146100 Ontario Ltd. v. 2052750 Ontario Inc., 2013 ONSC 2483, 2013 CarswellOnt 5148, 115 O.R. (3d) 636, 308 O.A.C. 8, Boswell, J. (Ont. Div. Ct.)

The presiding Deputy Judge gave judgment in favour of the respondents (defendants) for $21,538.85. The appellant asserts that in the process of doing so, he exceeded the monetary jurisdiction of the Court.

The appellant argues that the trial judge's decision effectively adjudicated the appellant's claim at $21,538.85, and adjudicated the respondents' separate claim at $42,633.57, thereby exceeding the monetary jurisdiction of the court.

Subsection 111(3) expressly provides that if the court finds that a larger sum is due from the plaintiff to the defendant, than is found due from the defendant to the plaintiff, the defendant is entitled to judgment for the balance. Courts in Ontario now have the jurisdiction to calculate set offs whether or not the parties assent.

In *Burkhardt*, the plaintiffs sued for $20,000 in damages arising from a fatal car accident involving a pedestrian. The jury assessed damages at $26,000 but found the deceased to have been 50% at fault. In dispute was whether the plaintiffs were limited to 50% of the amount claimed — in other words half of $20,000 — or whether they were entitled to judgment for 50% of $26,000 (the damages assessed by the jury).

Cartwright J. found that the plaintiffs were entitled to half of the damages assessed by the jury.

At the end of the day it is the net judgment that matters. Here, the amount awarded was within the monetary jurisdiction of the Small Claims Court and did not exceed the amount claimed in the Defendants' Claim.

Appeal dismissed.

Stewart v. Toronto Standard Condominium Corp. No. 1591, 2014 ONSC 795, 2014 CarswellOnt 1377, Nordheimer, J. (Ont. Div. Ct.) — Stewart sought a judicial review of the decision of the Deputy Judge who, in dismissing Stewart's claim, ordered him to pay $2000 in costs. The jurisdiction set out in *ThyssenKrupp Elevator (Canada) Ltd. v. 1147335 Ontario Inc.*, 2012 ONSC 4139, 2012 CarswellOnt 9698, 43 Admin. L.R. (5th) 61, 18 C.L.R. (4th) 82, 295 O.A.C. 71, [2012] O.J. No. 3674 (Ont. Div. Ct.) is a "limited and narrow" one that will generally arise only in exceptional circumstances such as bias, breach of principles of natural justice, or an excess of jurisdiction. The conduct of the Deputy Judge did not rise to the level required to find a reasonable apprehension of bias. There was no breach of natural justice or breach of procedural fairness. Evidentiary rulings, right or wrong, do not constitute such a breach. There was no apparent unfairness in not acceding to an adjournment. Rule 19.06, when it refers to "otherwise acting unreasonably", must be interpreted as referring to the conduct of a party within the proceeding. The rule is not intended to give broad and unfettered discretion to make awards of compensation regarding conduct of party unrelated to the matter over which the Court has jurisdiction. Consistent with wording of s. 29 of the *Courts of Justice Act*. The Deputy Judge erred in penalizing the applicant in costs for conduct related to his dealings with his condominium corporation and not with respect to how he conducted himself within the proceeding.

Application allowed. Award of costs reduced to $150 under provisions of rule 14.07 (given the unaccepted offer to settle) plus disbursements of $500.

Shuster v. Ontario (Attorney General), 2013 HRTO 1158 (Ont. H.R.T.) — An application was filed under s. 34 of the Human Rights Code alleging discrimination with respect to services because of a disability. The application was dismissed. The applicant was the defendant in actions brought in a Small Claims Court. Judgment was granted to the plaintiffs. The applicant was advised of the cost to obtain transcripts. He refused to pay for them. The order granted that if the Court Reporter consent to request, the applicant could listen to recordings of the transcript. The Reporter advised the applicant that he needed to order the transcripts and that he could listen to the tapes after he had paid for the transcripts. The applicant allegee he has a hearing impediment. He never requested accommodation prior to filing Application. See *Dabic v. Windsor Police Service*, 2010 HRTO 1994, [2010] O.H.R.T.D. No. 1988 (Ont. Human Rights Trib.), paras. 8 and 9.

The application had no reasonable prospect of success. The application was dismissed.

Arnone v. Amelio, 2013 ONSC 6536, 2013 CarswellOnt 17340, Siegel, J. (Ont. Div. Ct.) — Appellant ("Amelio") appealed order of Deuputy Judge granting judgment favour of plaintiffs for $25,000. Amelio says trial judge became active participant in trial and lost her impartiality. Legal principles for assessing whether intervention of the trial judge gives rise to a claim of bias in *Chippewas of Mnjikaning First Nation v. Ontario*, 2010 ONCA 47, 2010 CarswellOnt 273, (sub nom. *Chippewas of Mnjikaning First Nation v. Ontario (Minister Responsible for Native Affairs))* [2010] 2 C.N.L.R. 18, 265 O.A.C. 247, [2010] O.J. No. 212 (Ont. C.A.); additional reasons 2010 ONCA 408, 2010 CarswellOnt 3730 (Ont. C.A.); leave to appeal refused 2010 CarswellOnt 4919, 2010 CarswellOnt 4920, (sub nom. *Chippewas of Mnjikaning First Nation v. Ontario (Minister Responsible for Native Affairs))* 409 N.R. 396 (note), (sub nom. *Chippewas v. Mnjikaning First Nation v. Ontario (Minister Responsible for Native Affairs))* 276 O.A.C. 398 (note), [2010] S.C.C.A. No. 91 (S.C.C.), at paras. 230-231. At para. 243 Court of Appeal expressed view that strong presumption exists that trial judges conduct themselves fairly and impartially. Given the absence of examinations-for-discovery prior to a trial in the Small Claims Court, courts have recognized that judicial involvement may be necessary to assist parties. Appeal dismissed.

Hatfield v. Child, 2013 ONSC 7801, (CanLII), M.A. Sanderson, J. — Appeal by Hatfield from decision of Deputy Judge. Factual findings of a trial Judge should not be overturned on appeal in the absence of palpable and overriding errors. *Housen v. Nikolaisen*, 2002 SCC 33, 2002 CarswellSask 179, 2002 CarswellSask 178, REJB 2002-29758, [2002] 2 S.C.R. 235, 10 C.C.L.T. (3d) 157, 211 D.L.R. (4th) 577, 30 M.P.L.R. (3d) 1, [2002] 7 W.W.R. 1, 286 N.R. 1, 219 Sask. R. 1, 272 W.A.C. 1, [2002] S.C.J. No. 31 (S.C.C.). Section 27 of the *Court of Justice Act* permits documentary and oral hearsay evidence in Small Claims Court trials. While Trial Judge made some minor errors of fact, he had sufficient basis to reach the factual conclusions he did. No reversible error of law. Appeal dismissed.

Aljamal v. Bell Canada, 2013 ONSC 5225, 2013 CarswellOnt 12452, A.W. Bryant, J. (Ont. S.C.J.) — The appellant, Aljamal, issued a claim in the Small Claims Court for $5000 which was subsequently amended to $2500. "For the purposes of clause 31(a) of the Act, the prescribed amount is $2500". In *Action Auto Leasing & Gallery Inc. v. Robillard*, 2011 ONSC 3264, 2011 CarswellOnt 4105, 106 O.R. (3d) 281, 22 C.P.C. (7th) 414, 335 D.L.R. (4th) 439, 278 O.A.C. 293, [2011] O.J. No. 2453 (Ont. Div. Ct.), at para. 36, Heeney J. held that the matter in dispute is the amount claimed in the action. Appeal and cross-appeal dismissed without costs.

Ibrahim v. Kadhim, 2007 CarswellOnt 6 (Ont. S.C.J.); additional reasons 2007 CarswellOnt 5606, 86 O.R. (3d) 728, Tulloch, J. (Ont. S.C.J.)

Appeal by plaintiffs, defendants by counterclaim from judgment of Deputy Judge. Court satisfied trial judge's conduct during trial was such to deny appellant right to a fair trial and gave rise to a reasonable apprehension of bias. Transcripts show trial judge's involvement in extensive and frequent ways, and the tone of the interventions raised some concerns. Interventions did not result in an unfair trail or create a reasonable apprehension of bias. The nature of Small Claims Court proceedings are of such that, by necessity, trial judges tend to be more interventionist.

See *Garry v. Pohlmann*, 2001 BCSC 1234, 2001 CarswellBC 1893, 12 C.P.C. (5th) 107, [2001] B.C.J. No. 1804 (B.C. S.C.) at page 12 and Farley J. in *Wil v. Burdman*, 1998 CarswellOnt 2541, [1998] O.J. No. 2533 (Ont. Div. Ct.):

> Given the nature of small claims proceedings, appellate courts have recognized that the role of trial judges in small claims court is often, by necessity, more interventionist.

As noted by Farley, J. in *Wil v. Burdman*:

> . . ., the task of a small claims judge in, in general, difficult and it is not inappropriate for a trial judge to attempt to focus and assist the parties by indicating an area of concern to the court. An appellate court must therefore look at the impugned interventions of the trial judge in the context of the overall nature of small claims proceedings when determining if the intervention rendered the trial unfair or created a reasonable apprehension of bias. The term "reasonable apprehension of bias" has been authoritatively defined in *R. v. R.D.S.*, [1997] 3. S.C.R. 484 at 530. Cory J. adopted the test proposed by de Grandpre J. in *Committee for Justice and Liberty v. National Energy Board*, [2978] 1 S.C.R. 369 as follows:
>
>> The apprehension of bias must be a reasonable one, held by reasonable and right-minded persons, applying themselves to the question and obtaining thereon the required information . . . [T]he test is "what would an informed person, viewing the matter realistically and practically . . . and having thought the matter through . . . conclude.

Appeal dismissed.

Cojocaru (Guardian ad litem of) v. British Columbia Women's Hospital & Health Center, 2013 SCC 30, 2013 CarswellBC 1400, 2013 CarswellBC 1401, (sub nom. *Cojocaru v. British Columbia Women's Hospital and Health Centre*) [2013] 2 S.C.R. 357, 51 Admin. L.R. (5th) 1, 44 B.C.L.R. (5th) 1, 1 C.C.L.T. (4th) 1, 357 D.L.R. (4th) 585, [2013] 7 W.W.R. 211, (sub nom. *Cojocaru v. British Columbia Women's Hospital and Health Center*) 336 B.C.A.C. 1, 445 N.R. 138, 574 W.A.C. 1, [2013] S.C.J. No. 30 (S.C.C.)

Despite extensive copying of the plaintiff's submissions, the defendants' arguments did not rebut the presumption of judicial integrity and impartiality. The fact that the trial judge rejected some of the plaintiffs' key submissions showed that he considered issues independently and impartially. The fact that large portions of reasons were copied from the plaintiffs' submissions did not displace presumption that trial judge engaged with issues and decided them in accordance with law. The judgment should not be set aside on the grounds that the trial judge incorporated large parts of the plaintiffs' submissions in his reasons.

Kay v. Caverson, 2013 ONCA 220, 2013 CarswellOnt 3900, 19 C.L.R. (4th) 213 (Ont. C.A.).

The plaintiff appealed, partly on grounds that the trial judge was biased. The appeal was dismissed.

Transcript references showed nothing more than the trial judge curtailing frequent, and largely inappropriate, interruptions of the plaintiff. There was nothing wrong with the way the trial judge dealt with an improper letter sent by the plaintiff to the trial judge during the course of the trial.

32. (1) Deputy judges — **A regional senior judge of the Superior Court of Justice may, with the approval of the Attorney General, appoint a lawyer to act as a deputy judge of the Small Claims Court.**

Commentary: The Small Claims Court is a branch of the Superior Court of Justice. It is presided over by deputy judges who are appointed by a regional senior judge with the approval of the Attorney General for a term, subject to renewal.

The *Ethical Principles for Judges* apply to deputy judges, with necessary modifications to reflect their part-time status as judges, as set out in the statement of the Deputy Judges Council dated August 1, 2012.

The Chief Justice of the Superior Court, with the approval of the Deputy Judges Council, established standards of conduct for Deputy Judges of the Small Claims Court entitled *Ethical Principles for Deputy Judges of the Small Claims Court*. The Principles refer to the Canadian Judicial Council's *Ethical Principles for Judges*. The *Ethical Principles for Judges* were established by the Canadian Judicial Council to provide ethical guidance for federally appointed judges. These Principles are: Judicial Independence, Integrity, Diligence, Equality, and Impartiality. The Principles as published have Commentaries on each of the Principles. Section 55 of the *Judges Act*, R.S.C. 1985, c.J-1, requires that federally appointed judges shall not engage in any occupation or business other than their judicial duties, but shall devote themselves exclusively to their judicial duties. In Ontario, the Small Claims Court is a branch of the Superior Court of Justice. It is presided over by Deputy Judges who are appointed by a regional senior judge with the approval of the Attorney General for a term, subject to renewal.

The Deputy Judges of the Small Claims Court are lawyers who are actively engaged in the practice of law, or retired lawyers or judges. They are members of the Law Society of Upper Canada and are subject to the Law Society Rules of Professional Conduct. They preside in court on a part-time basis. They are remunerated on the basis of sitting days.

The purpose of this statement is to affirm that the *Ethical Principles for Judges* apply to Deputy Judges of the Small Claims Court in all respects, subject to the fact that certain of the Commentaries which form part of the Principles should be interpreted to reflect that the Deputy Judges do not preside full-time and do not have tenure.

Case Law: *Ferster v. Bowerman*, [1986] S.J. 195, No. 1390 of 1985 J.C.P.A. (Sask. Q.B.) — Applicant sought judicial review to prohibit Provincial Court from continuing a small claims trial on the basis of apprehension of bias. The judge was "old friend" and "acquaintance" of the plaintiffs. The application was granted.

Therrien c. Québec (Ministre de la justice), REJB 2001-24493, 2001 CarswellQue 1013, 2001 CarswellQue 1014, [2001] S.C.J. No. 36, (sub nom. *Therrien, Re*) 155 C.C.C. (3d) 1, 2001 SCC 35, (sub nom. *Therrien, Re*) 200 D.L.R. (4th) 1, 43 C.R. (5th) 1, (sub nom. *Québec (Ministre de la Justice) v. Therrien*) 270 N.R. 1, 30 Admin. L.R. (3d) 171, (sub nom. *Therrien, Re*) 84 C.R.R. (2d) 1, (sub nom. *Therrien, Re*) [2001] 2 S.C.R. 3 (S.C.C.); affirming [1998] A.Q. No. 1666, 1998 CarswellQue 393, (sub nom. *Québec (Ministre de la justice) c. Thérrien*) [1998] R.J.Q. 1392 (Que. C.A.); affirming 1998 CarswellQue 1066, [1998] A.Q. No. 3105, 21 C.R. (5th) 296, [1998] R.J.Q. 2956 (Que. C.A.); reversing 1998 CarswellQue 3598, (sub nom. *Therrien c. Québec (Procureur général)*) [1998] Q.J. No. 180 (Que. S.C.). The process of selecting persons qualified for appointment of judges is so closely related to the exercise of the judicial function that they cannot be dissociated. The candidate's failure to reveal that he had been in trouble with the law was relevant to a selection committee charged with assessing a candidate's aptitude and qualification for judicial appointment.

Ontario Deputy Judges Assn. v. Ontario, 2006 CarswellOnt 3137, 80 O.R. (3d) 481, 28 C.P.C. (6th) 1, 268 D.L.R. (4th) 86, (sub nom. *Ontario Deputy Judges' Assn. v. Ontario (Attorney General))* 141 C.R.R. (2d) 238, 210 O.A.C. 94, [2006] O.J. No. 2057 (Ont. C.A.).

Deputy judges of the Small Claims Court, although they only preside part-time, fully assume the judicial role when presiding. The constitutional requirement for judicial independence applies to all judges of the Small Claims Court and requires the establishment of an independent body to address their remuneration.

Ontario Deputy Judges Assn. v. Ontario (Attorney General), 2012 ONCA 437, 2012 CarswellOnt 7932, 23 C.P.C. (7th) 1, [2012] O.J. No. 2865 (Ont. C.A.).

The need for the Small Claims Court and its deputy judges to be independent was re-affirmed. The process for initial appointment of deputy judges by the Regional Senior Justices, with the approval of the Attorney General, for a three year term, subject to renewals at the sole discretion of the Regional Senior Justices, does not offend the constitutional requirement for judicial independence.

(2) Term of appointment — **The appointment of a deputy judge is for a term of three years, subject to subsections (3) and (7).**

Case Law: *Rai v. Métivier*, 2005 CarswellOnt 3477, 201 O.A.C. 87, 76 O.R. (3d) 641, 258 D.L.R. (4th) 151 (Ont. Div. Ct.), Matlow J. Application for judicial review dismissed. The applicant is a lawyer who served as a Deputy Judge of the Small Claims Court in Ottawa. Respondent is the Senior Regional Judge of the East Region of the Court in Ottawa.

Section 32(2) of the *Courts of Justice Act* ("the Act") confers the authority on a Regional Senior Justice to renew the appointment of a Deputy Judge.

Applicant took issue with the respondent's expressed intention to apply retirement age, 75.

The applicant submits appropriate standard of review is correctness. The respondent and the intervenor submit that it is patent unreasonableness. See *Pushpanathan v. Canada (Minister of Employment & Immigration)*, [1998] S.C.J. No. 46, 1998 CarswellNat 830, 1998 CarswellNat 831, 226 N.R. 201, (sub nom. *Pushpanathan v. Canada (Minister of Citizenship & Immigration))* 160 D.L.R. (4th) 193, (sub nom. *Pushpanathan v. Canada (Minister of Citizenship & Immigration))* [1998] 1 S.C.R. 982, 43 Imm. L.R. (2d) 117, 11 Admin. L.R. (3d) 1, 6 B.H.R.C. 387, [1999] I.N.L.R. 36 (S.C.C.).

Standard of review is patent unreasonableness.

Decision of the respondent not the requisite standard.

McKenzie v. British Columbia (Minister of Public Safety), 2006 CarswellBC 2262, 2006 BCSC 1372, [2006] 12 W.W.R. 404, 145 C.R.R. (2d) 192, 272 D.L.R. (4th) 455, 52 C.C.E.L. (3d) 191, 61 B.C.L.R. (4th) 57 (B.C. S.C.).

Residential tenancies arbitrators. Appointment fixed, renewable, five-year term. Mid-term termination of appointment without cause unconstitutional. Arbitrator appointed to adjudicate litigious disputes between private parties, independent of government, entitled to security of tenure under unwritten constitutional principle of judicial independence. Termination of petitioner without cause raised spectre of Crown interference in conduct of private litigation, violation of principle of independence.

Saylor v. Madsen Estate, [2007] 1 S.C.R. 838, 279 D.L.R. (4th) 547, 224 O.A.C. 382, 32 E.T.R. (3d) 61, 2007 SCC 18, 2007 CarswellOnt 2755, 2007 CarswellOnt 2754, 42 C.P.C. (6th) 1, [2007] S.C.J. No. 18, 360 N.R. 327 (S.C.C.).

The trial judge failed to consider all evidence. A matter outstanding for nine years and amount in issue was relatively small. In interests of justice appellate court considered evidence and made final determination rather than send matter back for new trial. Where the circumstances warrant, appellate courts have jurisdiction to make a fresh assessment of the evidence on the record: see *Hollis v. Birch* (1995), [1995] S.C.J. No. 104, 26 B.L.R. (2d) 169, 27 C.C.L.T. (2d) 1, 14 B.C.L.R. (3d) 1, [1996] 2 W.W.R. 77, 111 W.A.C. 1, 67 B.C.A.C. 1, 190 N.R. 241, 129 D.L.R. (4th) 609, [1995] 4 S.C.R. 634, EYB 1995-67074, 1995 CarswellBC 1152, 1995 CarswellBC 967 (S.C.C.) and *Prudential Trust Co. v. Forseth* (1959), 21 D.L.R. (2d) 587, 30 W.W.R. 241, [1960] S.C.R. 210, 1959 CarswellSask 50 (S.C.C.).

Brown v. Newton, 2009 NSSC 388, 2009 CarswellNS 721, [2009] N.S.J. No. 621, 285 N.S.R. (2d) 228, 905 A.P.R. 228, 85 C.P.C. (6th) 90 (N.S. S.C.).

At a hearing in Small Claims Court, the plaintiff closed his case after giving his evidence. Counsel for the defendant elected not to call evidence, which surprised the plaintiff, who expected the defendant to testify in his own defence, therefore providing the plaintiff the opportunity to cross examine. Adjudicator dismissed plaintiff's claim without costs. Plaintiff appealed. Appeal allowed. By not exploring further reasons for plaintiff's surprise when he learned that defendant decided not to call evidence and by failing to provide additional information that might have alerted plaintiff to possibility of calling defendant and to cross examine him as part of case-in-chief, plaintiff denied natural justice.

See *R. v. H. (B.C.)*, 1990 CarswellMan 294, 58 C.C.C. (3d) 16 (Man. C.A.), at p. 22, where Justice Twaddle stated:

> The legal system in Canada is mainly adversarial. It works best when each side is represented by a qualified advocate. Inevitably, a litigant in person is at a disadvantage. In strict theory, this should not be so, but it is a fact and there is no use denying it.

As Justice McLachlin (as she then was) said, in *R. v. Harrer*, [1995] S.C.J. No. 81, [1995] 3 S.C.R. 562, 32 C.R.R. (2d) 273, 105 W.A.C. 161, 64 B.C.A.C. 161, 186 N.R. 329, 128 D.L.R. (4th) 98, 101 C.C.C. (3d) 193, 42 C.R. (4th) 269, EYB 1995-67068, 1995 CarswellBC 1144, 1995 CarswellBC 651 (S.C.C.), at para. 45:

> At base, a fair trial is a trial that appears fair, both from the perspective of the accused and the perspective of the community. A fair trial must not be confused with the most advantageous trial possible from the accused's point of view. . . . Nor must it be conflated with the perfect trial; in the real world, perfection is seldom attained. A fair trial is one which satisfies the public interest in getting at the truth, while preserving basic procedural fairness to the accused.

See "Statement of Principles on Self-Represented Litigants and Accused Persons" adopted by the Canadian Judicial Council in September 2006. Under the sub-heading, "For the Judiciary," the following four principles are listed:

1. Judges have a responsibility to inquire whether self-represented persons are aware of their procedural options, and to direct them to available information if they are not. Depending on the circumstances and nature of the case, judges may explain the relevant law in the case and its implications, before the self-represented person makes critical choices.

2. In appropriate circumstances, judges should consider providing self-represented persons with information to assist them in understanding and asserting their rights, or to raise arguments before the court.

3. Judges should ensure that procedural and evidentiary rules are not used unjustly to hinder the legal interests of self-represented persons.

4. The judiciary should engage in dialogues with legal professional associations, court administrators, government and legal aid organizations in an effort to design and provide for programs to assist self-represented persons.

Heald v. Campbell, [2008] O.J. No. 251, 2008 ONCA 59, 2008 CarswellOnt 295 (Ont. C.A.).

Would the result have been different if the solicitor had *not* been negligent? See *Folland v. Reardon*, 2005 CarswellOnt 232, [2005] O.J. No. 216, 74 O.R. (3d) 688, 28 C.C.L.T. (3d) 1, 194 O.A.C. 201, 249 D.L.R. (4th) 167 (Ont. C.A.); *Wernikowski v. Kirkland, Murphy & Ain*, 41 C.P.C. (4th) 261, 50 O.R. (3d) 124, 48 C.C.L.T. (2d) 233, 128 O.A.C. 33, 181 D.L.R. (4th) 625, 31 C.R. (5th) 99, 141 C.C.C. (3d) 403, [1999] O.J. No. 4812, 1999 CarswellOnt 4139 (Ont. C.A.); additional reasons at [2000] O.J. No. 469, 2000 CarswellOnt 464, 181 D.L.R. (4th) 625 at 642, 141 C.C.C. (3d) 403 at 420 (Ont. C.A.); leave to appeal refused 264 N.R. 196 (note), 145 O.A.C. 398 (note), [2000] S.C.C.A. No. 98, 2000 CarswellOnt 4191, 2000 CarswellOnt 4190 (S.C.C.). No justification for measuring a barrister's conduct by the more forgiving standard of "egregious error." See Krever, J. in *Demarco v. Ungaro*, 27 Chitty's L.J. 23, 95 D.L.R. (3d) 385, 8 C.C.L.T. 207, 21 O.R. (2d) 673, 1979 CarswellOnt 671 (Ont. H.C.). Counsel may be negligent for failing to call a witness whose evidence was necessary to establish the client's case. See, e.g., *Demarco v. Ungaro, Wong v. Thomson, Rogers*, 1992 CarswellOnt 3001, [1992] O.J. No. 1120 (Ont. Gen. Div.); affirmed 1994 CarswellOnt 2925, [1994] O.J. No. 1318 (Ont. C.A.); *Heald v. Campbell*, [2008] O.J. No. 251, 2008 ONCA 59, 2008 CarswellOnt 295 (Ont. C.A.); *Bartolovic v. Bennett*, [1996] O.J. No. 961, 1996 CarswellOnt 1123 (Ont. Gen. Div.); additional reasons at 1996 CarswellOnt 1290 (Ont. Gen. Div.); *Danyliw v. Mark*, 2001 CarswellOnt 2409, [2001] O.J. No. 2783, 55 O.R. (3d) 129, 9 C.P.C. (5th) 163 (Ont. S.C.J.) *Van Duzen v. Lecovin*, 2004 CarswellBC 2462, 2004 BCSC 1333, [2004] B.C.J. No. 2206 (B.C. S.C.).

Wawanesa Mutual Insurance Co. v. Weare, 2009 NSSC 395, 2009 CarswellNS 722, 285 N.S.R. (2d) 162, 87 C.P.C. (6th) 72, 905 A.P.R. 162 (N.S. S.C.), Nova Scotia Supreme Court, McDougall, J.

The appellant alleged it was denied natural justice by the adjudicator of Small Claims Court, who denied request by non-lawyer agent for adjournment to retrieve proof of claim. The appellant also alleged the adjudicator demonstrated bias against agent. Appeal allowed. Matters discussed or comments made in Small Claims Court *not recorded*. There was no transcript of proceeding and therefore what was said could not be reproduced with certainty nor was entire record available to provide context. The adjudicator's decision gave rise to injustice and was error of law resulting in denial of natural justice. In the words of Cromwell J.A. (as he then was) in the case of *Moore v. Economical Mutual Insurance Co.*, 542 A.P.R. 269, 177 N.S.R. (2d) 269, 1999 CarswellNS 218, [1999] N.S.J. No. 250 (N.S. C.A.):

> An appellate court should not substitute its judgment for that of the presiding judge but should limit its review to determining whether the judge applied a wrong principle or the decision gave rise to an injustice. [Emphasis added.].

Beard Winter LLP v. Shekhdar, 255 O.A.C. 245, 2008 CarswellOnt 6433 (Ont. S.C.J.); leave to appeal refused 2009 CarswellOnt 6325 (Ont. Div. Ct.); additional reasons at 2009 CarswellOnt 9148 (Ont. Div. Ct.).

On October 30, 2008, in Shekhdar's absence, Campbell J., dismissed Shekhdar's appeal from an order of Master exercising a case management function. Costs reserved. On April 20, 2009, Campbell J., determined costs issues. The parties could not agree on the order's form. The issue went back to Campbell J. On June 12, 2009, Campbell J., signed a formal order with written reasons. Shekhdar moved for leave to appeal. The Divisional Court, per Aston J., denied leave to appeal. The court rejected Shekhdar's argument that Campbell J., had erred in hearing and determining the matter in that he considered all of the material filed by Shekhdar. Campbell J., had not dismissed the appeal just because Shekhdar failed to make any oral submissions. Shekhdar's non-participation appeared to have been a conscious and strategic choice.

Pavlis v. HSBC Bank Canada (2009), 2009 CarswellBC 2775, 98 B.C.L.R. (4th) 72, [2010] 1 W.W.R. 208, 2009 BCCA 450, 277 B.C.A.C. 105, 469 W.A.C. 105 (B.C. C.A.).

The chambers judge ruled court does not have jurisdiction to order Crown to pay for transcripts on behalf of an appellant, citing *Jong v. Jong*, 2002 CarswellBC 1104, 2002 BCCA 322 (B.C. C.A. [In Chambers]) and *Barbeau-Lafacci v. Holmgren*, 283 W.A.C. 280, 173 B.C.A.C. 280, 2002 CarswellBC 2343, 2002 BCCA 553, [2002] B.C.J. No. 2295 (B.C. C.A. [In Chambers]); additional reasons at 2003 BCCA 549, 2003 CarswellBC 2533 (B.C. C.A. [In Chambers]).

No authority in Canada supporting a general right to access to justice (see *Christie v. British Columbia (Attorney General)*, 155 C.R.R. (2d) 366, [2007] 1 S.C.R. 873, [2007] 8 W.W.R. 64, 280 D.L.R. (4th) 528, 2007 CarswellBC 1118, 2007 CarswellBC 1117, 2007 SCC 21, [2007] S.C.J. No. 21, 2007 G.T.C. 1488 (Eng.), 361 N.R. 322, 66 B.C.L.R. (4th) 1, 2007 G.T.C. 1493 (Fr.), 398 W.A.C. 1, 240 B.C.A.C. 1, 2007 D.T.C. 5229 (Fr.), 2007 D.T.C. 5525 (Eng.) (S.C.C.)) that extends to transcripts. Transcripts free of charge were not a matter of right, not a "benefit" given by law. No stereotypical distinction (see *Corbiere v. Canada (Minister of Indian & Northern Affairs)*, [1999] 2 S.C.R. 203, [1999] 3 C.N.L.R. 19, 239 N.R. 1, 173 D.L.R. (4th) 1, [1999] S.C.J. No. 24, 61 C.R.R. (2d) 189, 1999 CarswellNat 664, 1999 CarswellNat 663, 163 F.T.R. 284 (note) (S.C.C.) at para. 7; reconsideration refused 2000 CarswellNat 2394, 2000 CarswellNat 2393 (S.C.C.)), or attribute stereotypical characteristics to any person or group (see *Eaton v. Brant (County) Board of Education* (1996), [1996] S.C.J. No. 98, [1997] 1 S.C.R. 241, 97 O.A.C. 161, 207 N.R. 171, 142 D.L.R. (4th) 385, 41 C.R.R. (2d) 240, 31 O.R. (3d) 574 (note), 1996 CarswellOnt 5036, 1996 CarswellOnt 5035 (S.C.C.) at paras. 66-7).

There must be state interference having a profound effect on a person's "psychological integrity," see *New Brunswick (Minister of Health & Community Services) v. G. (J.)*, 26 C.R. (5th) 203, [1999] S.C.J. No. 47, 177 D.L.R. (4th) 124, 244 N.R. 276, 1999 CarswellNB 306, 1999 CarswellNB 305, REJB 1999-14250, 7 B.H.R.C. 615, [1999] 3 S.C.R. 46, 552 A.P.R. 25, 216 N.B.R. (2d) 25, 50 R.F.L. (4th) 63, 66 C.R.R. (2d) 267 (S.C.C.), before deprivation may be found.

Where self-represented defendant declared intention to walk out of courtroom at start of trial, judge cautioned her that her absence and non-participation would effectively mean that court would, without challenge, receive plaintiff's evidence, which would be sole evidentiary basis upon which court would make its decision. Trial judge carried on with uncontested trial and gave judgment in plaintiff's favour. Court of Appeal dismissed defendant's appeal, finding no error in trial judge's decision to proceed with trial after defendant left. See *Berry v. Hall*, 2010 ONCA 546, 2010 CarswellOnt 5800 (Ont. C.A.); affirming 2009 CarswellOnt 9316 (Ont. S.C.J.), *per* Justice Alan C.R. Whitten.

The Ontario Court of Appeal upheld the trial judge's decision to carry on, saying:

> [1] The appellant founds her appeal on the trial judge having proceeded with the trial in her absence, not having inquired into why she acted as she did by leaving the courtroom. In our view, the trial judge was faced with a litigant saying she could not go through a trial, was without resources to retain a lawyer and felt the proceedings were a charade. She had decided therefore to leave. In the circumstances, we can see no error in the trial judge's proceeding with the trial after the appellant left.

No further obligation on trial judge to try to persuade party to remain and to take part in proceedings. Whether there is an obligation on the trial judge to probe into the party's reasons for the walk-out is not clear, although it would not seem wrong to do so.

An order is final, as opposed to interlocutory, if it finally disposes of the substantive issue between the parties. A decision that declines to stay an action, but rather directs that it should proceed to a trial on its merits, is the classic example of an interlocutory order.

VFC Inc. v. MacLean, 2009 NSSC 314, 2009 CarswellNS 570, 283 N.S.R. (2d) 32, 82 C.P.C. (6th) 372, 79 C.P.C. (6th) 105 (N.S. S.C.).

The defendant agreed to pay 130 bi-weekly payments for $24,671.40. The defendant failed to make all payments. VFC Inc. brought action in Small Claims Court. Small Claims Court dismissed claim on basis it did not have jurisdiction as VFC Inc. was not original party to contract as required by section 5(1) of *Small Claims Court Act*. VFC Inc. appealed. Appeal allowed. VFC Inc. was actually party to contract even though it did not sign contract, as it was worded so that the defendant must have known VFC Inc. was providing funds for purchase of car.

Park v. Lee, 98 O.R. (3d) 520, 2009 ONCA 651, 254 O.A.C. 52, 2009 CarswellOnt 5293 (Ont. C.A.).

Park, acting in person at trial, advanced claims in three actions for damages for personal injury. Apart from himself, he had no witnesses and failed to make his medical reports admissible. Defendants had undertaken to call evidence, including the defendant, Belitz. Park refused trial judge's offer to adjourn. Park made opening statement and took the stand. After two hours of Park's evidence in chief, the trial judge on his own motion dismissed all three actions on basis that Park's evidence was incoherent and incapable of proving the case. Two of the actions subsequently settled. Park appealed from dismissal of third. New trial ordered. Park denied fair trial. Inherent jurisdiction to control own process did not extend to dismissing cases without hearing the available evidence and submissions. Trial judge erred by interrupting Park before he had completed his evidence, before he had been given the full opportunity to present his case and before the defendants had honoured their undertaking to call Belitz.

Reid v. R.L. Johnston Masonry Inc., 252 O.A.C. 13, 80 C.L.R. (3d) 164, 2009 CarswellOnt 3428 (Ont. Div. Ct.).

Reid entered into oral contract with R.L. Johnston Masonry Inc. (Johnston) for repair of a water leak. Repairs completed. Reid commenced a small claims action. Action dismissed. The Divisional Court, per Glass J., stated trial judge erred in dismissing several heads of damages peremptorily as being trivial. Heads of damage ought to have been analyzed with a determination of whether they were proven claims.

Cicciarella v. Cicciarella, 252 O.A.C. 156, 72 R.F.L. (6th) 319, [2009] O.J. No. 2906, 2009 CarswellOnt 3972 (Ont. Div. Ct.).

The Divisional Court, referencing the Canadian Judicial Council's advisory "Statement of Principles on Self-represented Litigants and Accused Persons," discussed responsibilities of judges to conduct a fair and impartial proceeding when one party before the court was not self-represented.

Parkway Collision Ltd. v. Ryan, 2009 CarswellOnt 6266, 255 O.A.C. 74 (Ont. Div. Ct.).

Parkway Collision awarded judgment for a towing bill paid on behalf of Ryan and charges for storage of vehicle for $1,298.50. Ryan appealed, arguing trial judge erred in rejecting the evidence of bylaw tow rates in surrounding areas because bylaw not produced. Divisional Court, per Stong J., stated that: "In rejecting oral evidence of By-laws of other municipalities, which By-laws were not in fact presented to the court, the trial judge rejecting collateral and hearsay evidence the acceptance of which would have been simply opinion of a third party and not subject to cross-examination.".

Dew Point Insulation Systems Inc. v. JV Mechanical Ltd., 259 O.A.C. 179, 84 C.P.C. (6th) 297, 2009 CarswellOnt 8064, [2009] O.J. No. 5446, 87 C.L.R. (3d) 138 (Ont. Div. Ct.), at paras. 26–40.

Unrepresented defendants in action under the *Construction Liens Act (Ont.)* failed to comply with a Master's order for production of an affidavit of documents. The Master struck statement of defence. Divisional Court, per Bellamy J., quashed the decision where the Master did not extend procedural fairness to the defendants. Defendants did not appear to appreciate the significance of court procedures. The Master had not informed the defendants of the finality of the motion to strike. She did not provide them with an opportunity to make submissions. No evidence of prejudice to the plaintiff.

Garten v. Kruk, 2009 CarswellOnt 6477, 257 O.A.C. 59 (Ont. Div. Ct.).

Some six months after initial court appearance, without notifying the defendant, plaintiff's counsel had defendant noted in default. Six months later, the plaintiff's lawyer notified the defendant's lawyer of the noting in default. The defendant moved to set aside the noting of default. Master dismissed motion. Divisional Court, per Wilson, J., allowed appeal. The defendant demonstrated intent to defend. She had immediately obtained counsel. The fact that she appeared before Master and was now before Divisional Court spoke volumes of her desire to defend. Defendant should not be punished for her lawyer's errors. Her lawyer's affidavit clearly stated that his office inadvertently failed to deliver the statement of defence. Master did not accept the lawyer's sworn statement. Master's order reinforced sharp practice.

Gryphon Building Solutions Inc. v. Danforth Estates Management Inc., 253 O.A.C. 10, 2009 CarswellOnt 4741 (Ont. Div. Ct.).

Plaintiffs, Gryphon Building Solutions Inc. and Ontario Roofing, sought costs of appeal of $10,900 and $7,098, respectively, on basis they were successful both on jurisdictional issue and merits. Divisional Court found, on a partial indemnity basis, $4,000, all inclusive, as appropriate quantum of costs in relation to the jurisdictional issue. Jurisdictional issue not complex. Appeal unnecessary (the proper forum to challenge the Master's decision was a motion under r. 54.09). Court ordered the defendant to pay costs of $12,500, all inclusive, to Gryphon, and costs of $1,500, all inclusive, to Ontario Roofing.

McCormick v. Greater Sudbury Police Service, 2010 CarswellOnt 1871, 2010 ONSC 270, 259 O.A.C. 226, 6 Admin. L.R. (5th) 79 (Ont. Div. Ct.).

The hearing officer erred in law in purporting to take judicial notice that combined effects of consumption of alcohol and percocets would negatively impact on an individual's ability to perceive and recall experienced events. Subject was neither notorious nor within any specialized knowledge of tribunal, and properly the subject of expert evidence.

Sazant v. McKay, 2010 ONSC 4273, 2010 CarswellOnt 5903, 271 O.A.C. 63 (Ont. Div. Ct.).

Party's former lawyer now acting for opposite party. Court of Appeal effectively adopted respondent's submissions that lawyers owe duty of loyalty to former clients who must be able to speak to their lawyers frankly and without fear of exposure of their legal concerns. Clients must be confident that their lawyers will not in future become their adversaries' lawyers in course of same dispute. Lawyer's obligation, whether described as duty of loyalty owed to former client, or as professional obligation to promote public confidence in legal profession and administration of justice dictated that AL could not act on this appeal against his former client.

Consulate Ventures Inc. v. Amico Contracting & Engineering (1992) Inc., 270 O.A.C. 182, [2010] O.J. No. 4996, 2010 ONCA 788, 2010 CarswellOnt 8797, 97 C.P.C. (6th) 16 (Ont. C.A.).

The defendants brought motion for leave to appeal. Motion dismissed. Leave to appeal could be granted on question of law only. Leave to appeal could not be granted on questions of fact or questions of mixed fact and law. At best, issues raised by defendants were questions of mixed fact and law, not of law alone. See *Schultz v. Kopp Farms*, 2010 CarswellMan 75, 2010 MBCA 30 (Man. C.A. [In Chambers]).

Delano v. Craig, 2010 CarswellNS 264, 2010 NSSC 60 (N.S. S.C.).

The plaintiff brought claim in Small Claims Court concerning dispute over lawn mower. The adjudicator gave reasons why he preferred evidence of defendants over that of the plaintiff.

The claim was dismissed. Appeal dismissed. The adjudicator's reasons do not have to be exhaustive, but adequate to support findings of fact and demonstrate appreciation and proper application of law based on those facts.

Bulut v. Walker-Fairen, (sub nom. *Walker-Fairen v. Bulut)* 259 O.A.C. 15, 2010 ONSC 706, 2010 CarswellOnt 482 (Ont. Div. Ct.).

Trial judge reserved judgment, following seven-week trial. He did not ask for submissions as to costs and none were made. He awarded substantial indemnity costs to plaintiff throughout. Reasons respecting costs set out in the final paragraph of the reasons as follows: "I am not asking for submissions on costs ... Costs go to the plaintiff payable by all the defendants jointly and severally on a substantial indemnity basis throughout." Divisional Court held that, in the absence of submissions and unsupported by reasons, the trial judge's costs ruling was breach of procedural fairness and natural justice and could not stand. This was an extraordinary costs award, both respecting the scale of costs, the parties liable for the costs and the quantum of costs. Absence of meaningful reasons for award made appellate review impossible.

Link v. Venture Steel Inc., 69 B.L.R. (4th) 161, 79 C.C.E.L. (3d) 201, 259 O.A.C. 199, 2010 ONCA 144, 2010 CarswellOnt 1049, 2010 C.L.L.C. 210-017, [2010] O.J. No. 779 (Ont. C.A.).

The Ontario Court of Appeal stated that "[i]t is well accepted that the parties to an action are entitled to have a resolution of their differences based on the pleadings. Trial judge cannot make a finding of liability and award damages against a defendant on a basis not pleaded in the statement of claim because it deprives the defendant of the opportunity to address that issue." Pleadings included the critical mattes that underlay the plaintiff's claim. The defendant not misled or prejudiced as a result of general pleadings.

Cosentino v. S. Cosentino Leasing Ltd., 96 C.P.C. (6th) 372, 2010 ONSC 2611, 2010 CarswellOnt 2745, 261 O.A.C. 131, [2010] O.J. No. 1838 (Ont. Div. Ct.).

Cosentino, a lawyer, was retained in 1994 by defendant (his uncle's company) with respect to a civil action. Action was settled in 1999, on basis of nominal payment by defendant. Settlement funds paid June 16, 1999. The uncle died on August 17, 1999. Out of respect, Cosentino put file away and did not submit an account for legal services until August 3, 2002. The account was not paid. On July 30, 2008, the plaintiff sued the defendant in Small Claims Court on his account for legal services. Deputy judge found that cause of action arose when work completed and work was completed on June 16, 1999. Accordingly, claim barred under s. 45(1)(g) of the former *Limitations Act,* as the six-year limitation period had expired. Cosentino appealed. Divisional Court dismissed appeal. No palpable and overriding error in conclusion that retainer was at an end when Cosentino paid settlement funds on behalf of company.

R. v. Wang, 95 M.V.R. (5th) 80, 2010 CarswellOnt 3857, 2010 ONCA 435, 78 C.R. (6th) 134, [2010] O.J. No. 2490, 320 D.L.R. (4th) 680, 263 O.A.C. 194, 256 C.C.C. (3d) 225 (Ont. C.A.).

Court of Appeal stated that If unforeseen circumstances arise such that, after delivery of reasons that were meant to be final, a trial judge wishes to correct or supplement the reasons that were already delivered, various options are available. Issuance of an addendum, providing supplementary reasons or, when the original reasons were oral, subsequently issuing a set of amended reasons, written or oral. Candour and transparency are essential. Where changes or additions are made to the reasons, counsel as well as any reviewing court should have a clear record of what occurred and be in a position to opine as to the legal effect, if any, of the changes or additions made by the judge.".

Global Agriculture Trans-Loading Inc. v. (IRS) Industrial Repair Services, 2010 Car-swellBC 1470, 2010 BCCA 234, 288 B.C.A.C. 88, 488 W.A.C. 88 (B.C. C.A.).

Appellant defendant in action brought in Small Claims Court. It appealed order on basis plaintiff as named in proceedings not a legal entity. It also sought an order for payment out of court of monies attached post-judgment by garnishing order. Judgment had been obtained in default of appearance at mandated settlement conference but was later set aside.

Respondent a sole proprietorship but when the default judgment obtained, "Ltd." was added to its name in style of cause. That addition did not appear in garnishing order.

Litigants should not be burdened with legal technicality. If there is either a factual or a legal problem with the description of the respondent in the style of cause in that court, that is a matter that should be addressed in that court. The use and withdrawal of the designation "Ltd." does not go to the jurisdiction of the court. Appeal dismissed with costs.

Roskam v. Jacoby-Hawkins, 2010 ONSC 4439, 2010 CarswellOnt 7132 (Ont. S.C.J.), Boswell J.

Judgment delivered by deputy judge on February 12, 2010.

Roskam served a Notice of Appeal of the Small Claims Court Judgment on March 18, 2010, more than 30 days after Judgment released. Jacoby-Hawkins moved to strike out the Notice of Appeal.

Jacoby-Hawkins sought additional relief that Roskam be required to post security for costs of the appeal, that he be declared a vexatious litigant and that Roskam be required to remove all references he has authored about Jacoby-Hawkins and his counsel from the internet.

Section 31 of the *Courts of Justice Act*, R.S.O. 1990 c. C.43, provides that an appeal lies to the Divisional Court from a final order of the Small Claims Court in an action for the payment of money in excess of $500.00. Rule 61.04 of the *Rules of Civil Procedure* provides that any such appeal must be commenced within 30 days after the making of the order. The time for appeal usually runs from the date of pronouncement of a judgment: see *Permanent Investment Corp. v. Ops & Graham (Township)*, 1967 CarswellOnt 90, 62 D.L.R. (2d) 258, [1967] 2 O.R. 13 (Ont. C.A.).

Rule 3.02 deals with extensions of time generally. Rule 3.02 provides court with discretion to extend the time in which to file the Notice of Appeal, which was delivered four days late. *Bona fide* intention to pursue appeal. No prejudice to respondent as a result of late service.

Justice requires extension of time to file Notice of Appeal. See *Rizzi v. Mavros*, 2007 ONCA 350, 2007 CarswellOnt 2841, [2007] O.J. No. 1783, 85 O.R. (3d) 401, 224 O.A.C. 293 (Ont. C.A. [In Chambers]). Basis for security grounded in r. 56.01(1)(c) incorporated by reference in r. 61.06(1)(b). Request for security for costs not made out. Rationale underlying s. 140 discussed by Blair, J.A. in *Foy v. Foy (No. 2)*, [1979] O.J. No. 4386, 102 D.L.R. (3d) 342, 12 C.P.C. 188, 26 O.R. (2d) 220, 1979 CarswellOnt 458 (Ont. C.A.); leave to appeal refused 102 D.L.R. (3d) 342 (note), [1979] 2 S.C.R. vii, 12 C.P.C. 188n, 26 O.R. (2d) 220n, 31 N.R. 120 (S.C.C.).

The control of vexatious proceedings was necessary to protect integrity of the judicial system. The purpose of section to prevent people from using system for improper purposes, such as harassment or oppression. See *Dale Streiman & Kurz LLP v. De Teresi*, 2007 CarswellOnt 485, [2007] O.J. No. 255, 84 O.R. (3d) 383 (Ont. S.C.J.). Accordingly, a litigant's behaviour both inside and outside of the court is relevant. See *Canada Post Corp. v. Varma*, [2000] F.C.J. No. 851, 2000 CarswellNat 1183, 192 F.T.R. 278 (Fed. T.D.).

Section 140 of the *Courts of Justice Act* gives the court the authority to declare a party a vexatious litigant, thereby restricting his or her access to the courts of Ontario. It is a remedy that should be used very sparingly because the ability to have one's grievances addressed by the courts is fundamental to a free and just society. At the same time, the court must be wary of its processes being used for vexatious purposes.

Given Roskam's behaviour, appropriate case to make an order declaring Roskam to be a vexatious litigant.

Bérubé v. Rational Entertainment Ltd., 2010 ONSC 5545, 2010 CarswellOnt 7623, 324 D.L.R. (4th) 527, 80 B.L.R. (4th) 6, 271 O.A.C. 151 (Ont. Div. Ct.).

On October 16, 2009, Small Claims Court Justice made order dismissing appellant's claim for lack of jurisdiction. On November 17, 2009, appellant served a Notice of Appeal. On December 18, 2009, respondent brought a motion before Power J. sitting as a single judge of the Divisional Court, and requested order that the appeal be quashed pursuant to section 134(3) of the *Courts of Justice Act*. The provisions of sections 31 and 21 of the *Courts of Justice Act* make it clear that Power J. had jurisdiction to hear the respondent's motion on December 18, 2009, sitting as a single judge. Section 134(3) of the *Courts of Justice Act* provides that a court to which an appeal is taken may, in a proper case, quash the appeal when the appeal is manifestly devoid of merit. Rule 61.06 of the *Rules of Civil Procedure* provides for an order for security for costs if it appears that there is good reason to believe that the appeal is frivolous and vexatious and that the appellant has insufficient assets in Ontario to pay the costs of the appeal. Rule 56.01(e) contains a similar test. Appeal dismissed.

Cameron v. Nanaimo (Regional District), 2010 CarswellBC 705, 2010 BCCA 73, 317 D.L.R. (4th) 572, 482 W.A.C. 10, 285 B.C.A.C. 10 (B.C. C.A.).

There was sufficient evidence to support the appeal judge's conclusion that respondent's absence from the courtroom was not of her own informed choosing and that trial fairness was negatively affected as a result. The right of a party to a proceeding is to be present and to see and hear the evidence that could affect his or her interests fundamental under the law.

Chippewas of Mnjikaning First Nation v. Ontario, 2010 ONCA 47, 2010 CarswellOnt 273, [2010] O.J. No. 212, (sub nom. *Chippewas of Mnjikaning First Nation v. Ontario (Minister Responsible of Native Affairs))* [2010] 2 C.N.L.R. 18, 265 O.A.C. 247 (Ont. C.A.); additional reasons at 2010 ONCA 408, 2010 CarswellOnt 3730 (Ont. C.A.); leave to appeal refused 2010 CarswellOnt 4919, 2010 CarswellOnt 4920, [2010] S.C.C.A. No. 91, (sub nom. *Chippewas v. Mnjikaning First Nation v. Ontario (Minister Responsible for Native Affairs))* 276 O.A.C. 398 (note), (sub nom. *Chippewas of Mnjikaning First Nation v. Ontario (Minister Responsible for Native Affairs))* 409 N.R. 396 (note) (S.C.C.).

The trial judge's reasons were careful, thorough, and analytical. Reasons provided ample clarity and transparency to facilitate meaningful appellate review.

Interventions did not create an apprehension of bias. Experienced trial counsel did *not* object that trial judge was too interventionist at trial. The trial judge's interventions during closing arguments did not create an apprehension of bias. See de Grandpré J.'s dissenting opinion in *Committee for Justice & Liberty v. Canada (National Energy Board)* (1976), [1976] A.C.S. No. 118, [1976] S.C.J. No. 118, 1976 CarswellNat 434F, 1976 CarswellNat 434, 9 N.R. 115, 68 D.L.R. (3d) 716, [1978] 1 S.C.R. 369 (S.C.C.).

Canadian Imperial Bank of Commerce v. Houlahan, 2011 ONSC 558, 2011 CarswellOnt 291, 73 C.B.R. (5th) 223, 273 O.A.C. 140 (Ont. Div. Ct.).

Appeal from a final order of a Small Claims Court. Leave sought to admit fresh evidence.

"On a pure question of law, the basic rule with respect to the review of a trial judge's findings is that an appellate court is free to replace the opinion of the trial judge with its own. Thus the standard of review on a question of law is that of correctness," see *Housen v. Nikolaisen*, [2002] 2 S.C.R. 235 at para. 8.

The "traditional test for the admission of fresh evidence on appeal" summarized in *Public School Boards' Assn. of Alberta v. Alberta (Attorney General)*, [2000] 1 S.C.R. 44 at para. 6. A "court to which an appeal is taken may order a new trial," see the *Courts of Justice Act*, R.S.O. 1990, c. C.43, s. 134(1)(b). A new trial shall not be directed "unless some substantial wrong or miscarriage of justice has occurred," see the *Courts of Justice Act*, s. 134(6). "Where some substantial wrong or miscarriage of justice has occurred but it affects only part of an order or decision . . . a new trial may be ordered in respect of only that part . . .," see the *Courts of Justice Act*, s. 134(7). Appeal allowed in part and new trial ordered.

Gulati v. Husain, 2011 CarswellOnt 407, 2011 ONSC 706, [2011] O.J. No. 384 (Ont. S.C.J.).

The applicant sought *certiorari* respecting an order from deputy judge of the Small Claims Court (a) denying an adjournment of the motion to set aside default judgment; (b) staying enforcement of the default judgment; (c) setting aside the default judgment; and (d) costs of $300. Order setting aside default judgment, and costs order set aside.

The court has the discretion to refuse a consent adjournment. But this discretion should be exercised sparingly. It is unusual to refuse a request to accommodate counsel's schedule reasonably on a first appearance.

Deputy judge gave no reason for refusing adjournment. Deputy judge then decided the motion to set aside the default judgment without hearing submissions from either side.

Tosti v. Society of the Madonna Di Canneto of Windsor Inc., 2011 CarswellOnt 454, 2011 ONSC 339, 275 O.A.C. 108 (Ont. Div. Ct.).

Three appeals from judgment of deputy judge after four claims heard together in Windsor Small Claims Court over a five-day period in 2009. Written judgment released December 17, 2009.

In *R. v. Sheppard*, 2002 SCC 26, 2002 CarswellNfld 74, 2002 CarswellNfld 75, REJB 2002-29516, [2002] S.C.J. No. 30, [2002] 1 S.C.R. 869, 211 Nfld. & P.E.I.R. 50, 50 C.R. (5th) 68, 633 A.P.R. 50, 210 D.L.R. (4th) 608, 284 N.R. 342, 162 C.C.C. (3d) 298 (S.C.C.), the Supreme Court held that parties are entitled to be given sufficient reasons for a decision from a trial court so that the decision can be reviewed by an appellate court and the reasons are sufficient to inform the losing party as well as the community of the basis for the decision. At the same time, deficiencies in a trial judge's reasons do not automatically constitute a reversible error. Rather, one must apply a functional interpretation of the reasons. This functional approach articulated by the Court of Appeal in *R. v. Ahmed*, 170 C.C.C. (3d) 27, [2002] O.J. No. 4597, 166 O.A.C. 254, 7 C.R. (6th) 308, 2002 CarswellOnt 4075 (Ont. C.A.) and *R. v. Stewart*, [2003] O.J. No. 347, 2003 CarswellOnt 283 (Ont. C.A.).

Appeals were granted and new trial was ordered.

Significant errors of law and fact identified in the decision and the deputy judge's "they said, they said" simplistic approach to what were complicated factual and legal issues.

While the interventionist approach taken by the deputy judge appeared at times to assist the defendants, for example, when he conducted his own cross-examination of a number of the witnesses for the plaintiffs after he or she had been cross-examined by counsel for the Society and had been re-examined by counsel for the plaintiffs, conduct did not rise to the level required to find bias based on the test for such a finding set out in *Authorson (Litigation Guardian of) v. Canada (Attorney General)*, 2002 CarswellOnt 1724, [2002] O.J. No. 2050, 32 C.P.C. (5th) 357, 161 O.A.C. 1 (Ont. Div. Ct.); additional reasons at 2002 CarswellOnt 2939 (Ont. Div. Ct.). Judges must play "gatekeeper" role in relation to the admission of evidence. See David M. Paciocco, *"Context, Culture and the Law of Expert Evidence,"* (2001) 24 Advocates' Quarterly, 42 at p. 45. The trial judge remains the gatekeeper, responsible for determining admissibility.

Elsegood v. Cambridge Spring Service 2001 Ltd., 2011 CarswellOnt 652, 2011 ONSC 534 (Ont. Div. Ct.); affirmed 2011 ONCA 831, 2011 CarswellOnt 14782, 109 O.R. (3d) 143, 99 C.C.E.L. (3d) 327, 346 D.L.R. (4th) 353, 2012 C.L.L.C. 210-008, 287 O.A.C. 32, [2011] O.J. No. 6095 (Ont. C.A.).

An appeal of decision of deputy judge. The argument that respondent's pleadings at trial were not in accord with basis upon which the trial judge found liability. Flaws, or alleged flaws, in pleadings have not been fatal for several decades, especially true in a Small Claims Court setting.

Anand v. Sunfresh Organics, 2011 CarswellOnt 757, 2011 ONSC 776 (Ont. Div. Ct.); additional reasons at 2011 ONSC 1263, 2011 CarswellOnt 1101 (Ont. Div. Ct.).

The appeal by defendant from deputy judge. The appellant argued that trial judge ought to have granted adjournment request and that any prejudice to respondent could be compensated by a cost order. Within Court's jurisdiction to govern its own process and given the facts, trial judge's decision reasonable. The appellant argued the learned judge erred in allowing the plaintiff to reference a document which had not been disclosed to the defendant in accordance with the *Rules of Civil Procedure*. Reference to it not error in judgment or law by trial judge.

The appellant argued the judge allowed as evidence a letter in which an offer of settlement was made and which ought not to have been evidence as it was privileged. This is not a ground for appeal. There was a great deal of other evidence upon which the trial judge could rely to reach his decision. Appeal dismissed.

Saylor v. Madsen Estate, [2007] 1 S.C.R. 838, 279 D.L.R. (4th) 547, 224 O.A.C. 382, 32 E.T.R. (3d) 61, 2007 SCC 18, 2007 CarswellOnt 2755, 2007 CarswellOnt 2754, 42 C.P.C. (6th) 1, [2007] S.C.J. No. 18, 360 N.R. 327 (S.C.C.).

The trial judge failed to consider all evidence. A matter outstanding for nine years and amount in issue was relatively small. In interests of justice appellate court considered evidence and made final determination rather than send matter back for new trial. Where the circumstances warrant, appellate courts have jurisdiction to make a fresh assessment of the evidence on the record: see *Hollis v. Birch* (1995), [1995] S.C.J. No. 104, 26 B.L.R. (2d) 169, 27 C.C.L.T. (2d) 1, 14 B.C.L.R. (3d) 1, [1996] 2 W.W.R. 77, 111 W.A.C. 1, 67 B.C.A.C. 1, 190 N.R. 241, 129 D.L.R. (4th) 609, [1995] 4 S.C.R. 634, EYB 1995-67074, 1995 CarswellBC 1152, 1995 CarswellBC 967 (S.C.C.) and *Prudential Trust Co. v. Forseth* (1959), 21 D.L.R. (2d) 587, 30 W.W.R. 241, [1960] S.C.R. 210, 1959 CarswellSask 50 (S.C.C.).

Brown v. Newton, 2009 NSSC 388, 2009 CarswellNS 721, [2009] N.S.J. No. 621, 285 N.S.R. (2d) 228, 905 A.P.R. 228, 85 C.P.C. (6th) 90 (N.S. S.C.).

At a hearing in Small Claims Court, the plaintiff closed his case after giving his evidence. Counsel for the defendant elected not to call evidence, which surprised the plaintiff, who expected the defendant to testify in his own defence, therefore providing the plaintiff the opportunity to cross examine. Adjudicator dismissed plaintiff's claim without costs. Plaintiff appealed. Appeal allowed. By not exploring further reasons for plaintiff's surprise when he learned that defendant decided not to call evidence and by failing to provide additional information that might have alerted plaintiff to possibility of calling defendant and to cross examine him as part of case-in-chief, plaintiff denied natural justice.

See *R. v. H. (B.C.)*, 1990 CarswellMan 294, 58 C.C.C. (3d) 16 (Man. C.A.), at p. 22, where Justice Twaddle stated:

> The legal system in Canada is mainly adversarial. It works best when each side is represented by a qualified advocate. Inevitably, a litigant in person is at a disadvantage. In strict theory, this should not be so, but it is a fact and there is no use denying it.

As Justice McLachlin (as she then was) said, in *R. v. Harrer*, [1995] S.C.J. No. 81, [1995] 3 S.C.R. 562, 32 C.R.R. (2d) 273, 105 W.A.C. 161, 64 B.C.A.C. 161, 186 N.R. 329, 128 D.L.R. (4th) 98, 101 C.C.C. (3d) 193, 42 C.R. (4th) 269, EYB 1995-67068, 1995 CarswellBC 1144, 1995 CarswellBC 651 (S.C.C.), at para. 45:

> At base, a fair trial is a trial that appears fair, both from the perspective of the accused and the perspective of the community. A fair trial must not be confused with the most advantageous trial possible from the accused's point of view. . . . Nor must it be conflated with the perfect trial; in the real world, perfection is seldom attained. A fair trial is one which satisfies the public interest in getting at the truth, while preserving basic procedural fairness to the accused.

See "Statement of Principles on Self-Represented Litigants and Accused Persons" adopted by the Canadian Judicial Council in September 2006. Under the sub-heading, "For the Judiciary," the following four principles are listed:

1. Judges have a responsibility to inquire whether self-represented persons are aware of their procedural options, and to direct them to available information if they are not. Depending on the circumstances and nature of the case, judges may explain the relevant law in the case and its implications, before the self-represented person makes critical choices.

2. In appropriate circumstances, judges should consider providing self-represented persons with information to assist them in understanding and asserting their rights, or to raise arguments before the court.

3. Judges should ensure that procedural and evidentiary rules are not used unjustly to hinder the legal interests of self-represented persons.

4. The judiciary should engage in dialogues with legal professional associations, court administrators, government and legal aid organizations in an effort to design and provide for programs to assist self-represented persons.

Heald v. Campbell, [2008] O.J. No. 251, 2008 ONCA 59, 2008 CarswellOnt 295 (Ont. C.A.).

Would the result have been different if the solicitor had *not* been negligent? See *Folland v. Reardon*, 2005 CarswellOnt 232, [2005] O.J. No. 216, 74 O.R. (3d) 688, 28 C.C.L.T. (3d) 1, 194 O.A.C. 201, 249 D.L.R. (4th) 167 (Ont. C.A.); *Wernikowski v. Kirkland, Murphy & Ain*, 41 C.P.C. (4th) 261, 50 O.R. (3d) 124, 48 C.C.L.T. (2d) 233, 128 O.A.C. 33, 181 D.L.R. (4th) 625, 31 C.R. (5th) 99, 141 C.C.C. (3d) 403, [1999] O.J. No. 4812, 1999 CarswellOnt 4139 (Ont. C.A.); additional reasons at [2000] O.J. No. 469, 2000 CarswellOnt 464, 181 D.L.R. (4th) 625 at 642, 141 C.C.C. (3d) 403 at 420 (Ont. C.A.); leave to appeal refused 264 N.R. 196 (note), 145 O.A.C. 398 (note), [2000] S.C.C.A. No. 98, 2000 CarswellOnt 4191, 2000 CarswellOnt 4190 (S.C.C.). No justification for measuring a barrister's conduct by the more forgiving standard of "egregious error." See Krever, J. in *Demarco v. Ungaro*, 27 Chitty's L.J. 23, 95 D.L.R. (3d) 385, 8 C.C.L.T. 207, 21 O.R. (2d) 673, 1979 CarswellOnt 671 (Ont. H.C.). Counsel may be negligent for failing to call a witness whose evidence was necessary to establish the client's case. See, e.g., *Demarco v. Ungaro, Wong v. Thomson, Rogers*, 1992 CarswellOnt 3001, [1992] O.J. No. 1120 (Ont. Gen. Div.); affirmed 1994 CarswellOnt 2925, [1994] O.J. No. 1318 (Ont. C.A.); *Heald v. Campbell*, [2008] O.J. No. 251, 2008 ONCA 59, 2008 CarswellOnt 295 (Ont. C.A.); *Bartolovic v. Bennett*, [1996] O.J. No. 961, 1996 CarswellOnt 1123 (Ont. Gen. Div.); additional reasons at 1996 CarswellOnt 1290 (Ont. Gen. Div.); *Danyliw v. Mark*, 2001 CarswellOnt 2409, [2001] O.J. No. 2783, 55 O.R. (3d) 129, 9 C.P.C. (5th) 163 (Ont. S.C.J.) *Van Duzen v. Lecovin*, 2004 CarswellBC 2462, 2004 BCSC 1333, [2004] B.C.J. No. 2206 (B.C. S.C.).

Wawanesa Mutual Insurance Co. v. Weare, 2009 NSSC 395, 2009 CarswellNS 722, 285 N.S.R. (2d) 162, 87 C.P.C. (6th) 72, 905 A.P.R. 162 (N.S. S.C.), Nova Scotia Supreme Court, McDougall, J.

The appellant alleged it was denied natural justice by the adjudicator of Small Claims Court, who denied request by non-lawyer agent for adjournment to retrieve proof of claim. The appellant also alleged the adjudicator demonstrated bias against agent. Appeal allowed. Matters discussed or comments made in Small Claims Court *not recorded*. There was no transcript of proceeding and therefore what was said could not be reproduced with certainty nor was entire record available to provide context. The adjudicator's decision gave rise to injustice and was error of law resulting in denial of natural justice. In the words of Cromwell J.A. (as he then was) in the case of *Moore v. Economical Mutual Insurance Co.*, 542 A.P.R. 269, 177 N.S.R. (2d) 269, 1999 CarswellNS 218, [1999] N.S.J. No. 250 (N.S. C.A.)]:

> *An appellate court should not substitute its judgment for that of the presiding judge but should limit its review to determining whether the judge applied a wrong principle or the decision gave rise to an injustice.* [Emphasis added.].

Beard Winter LLP v. Shekhdar, 255 O.A.C. 245, 2008 CarswellOnt 6433 (Ont. S.C.J.); leave to appeal refused 2009 CarswellOnt 6325 (Ont. Div. Ct.); additional reasons at 2009 CarswellOnt 9148 (Ont. Div. Ct.).

On October 30, 2008, in Shekhdar's absence, Campbell J., dismissed Shekhdar's appeal from an order of Master exercising a case management function. Costs reserved. On April 20, 2009, Campbell J., determined costs issues. The parties could not agree on the order's form. The issue went back to Campbell J. On June 12, 2009, Campbell J., signed a formal order with written reasons. Shekhdar moved for leave to appeal. The Divisional Court, per Aston J., denied leave to appeal. The court rejected Shekhdar's argument that Campbell J., had erred in hearing and determining the matter in that he considered all of the material filed by Shekhdar. Campbell J., had not dismissed the appeal just because Shekhdar failed to make any oral submissions. Shekhdar's non-participation appeared to have been a conscious and strategic choice.

Pavlis v. HSBC Bank Canada (2009), 2009 CarswellBC 2775, 98 B.C.L.R. (4th) 72, [2010] 1 W.W.R. 208, 2009 BCCA 450, 277 B.C.A.C. 105, 469 W.A.C. 105 (B.C. C.A.).

The chambers judge ruled court does not have jurisdiction to order Crown to pay for transcripts on behalf of an appellant, citing *Jong v. Jong*, 2002 CarswellBC 1104, 2002 BCCA 322 (B.C. C.A. [In Chambers]) and *Barbeau-Lafacci v. Holmgren*, 283 W.A.C. 280, 173 B.C.A.C. 280, 2002 CarswellBC 2343, 2002 BCCA 553, [2002] B.C.J. No. 2295 (B.C. C.A. [In Chambers]); additional reasons at 2003 BCCA 549, 2003 CarswellBC 2533 (B.C. C.A. [In Chambers]).

No authority in Canada supporting a general right to access to justice (see *Christie v. British Columbia (Attorney General)*, 155 C.R.R. (2d) 366, [2007] 1 S.C.R. 873, [2007] 8 W.W.R. 64, 280 D.L.R. (4th) 528, 2007 CarswellBC 1118, 2007 CarswellBC 1117, 2007 SCC 21, [2007] S.C.J. No. 21, 2007 G.T.C. 1488 (Eng.), 361 N.R. 322, 66 B.C.L.R. (4th) 1, 2007 G.T.C. 1493 (Fr.), 398 W.A.C. 1, 240 B.C.A.C. 1, 2007 D.T.C. 5229 (Fr.), 2007 D.T.C. 5525 (Eng.) (S.C.C.)) that extends to transcripts. Transcripts free of charge were not a matter of right, not a "benefit" given by law. No stereotypical distinction (see *Corbiere v. Canada (Minister of Indian & Northern Affairs)*, [1999] 2 S.C.R. 203, [1999] 3 C.N.L.R. 19, 239 N.R. 1, 173 D.L.R. (4th) 1, [1999] S.C.J. No. 24, 61 C.R.R. (2d) 189, 1999 CarswellNat 664, 1999 CarswellNat 663, 163 F.T.R. 284 (note) at para. 7 (S.C.C.); reconsideration refused 2000 CarswellNat 2394, 2000 CarswellNat 2393 (S.C.C.)), or attribute stereotypical characteristics to any person or group (see *Eaton v. Brant (County) Board of Education* (1996), [1996] S.C.J. No. 98, [1997] 1 S.C.R. 241, 97 O.A.C. 161, 207 N.R. 171, 142 D.L.R. (4th)

385, 41 C.R.R. (2d) 240, 31 O.R. (3d) 574 (note), 1996 CarswellOnt 5036, 1996 Carswell-Ont 5035 at paras. 66-7 (S.C.C.)).

There must be state interference having a profound effect on a person's "psychological integrity," see *New Brunswick (Minister of Health & Community Services) v. G. (J.)*, 26 C.R. (5th) 203, [1999] S.C.J. No. 47, 177 D.L.R. (4th) 124, 244 N.R. 276, 1999 CarswellNB 306, 1999 CarswellNB 305, REJB 1999-14250, 7 B.H.R.C. 615, [1999] 3 S.C.R. 46, 552 A.P.R. 25, 216 N.B.R. (2d) 25, 50 R.F.L. (4th) 63, 66 C.R.R. (2d) 267 (S.C.C.), before deprivation may be found.

Where self-represented defendant declared intention to walk out of courtroom at start of trial, judge cautioned her that her absence and non-participation would effectively mean that court would, without challenge, receive plaintiff's evidence, which would be sole evidentiary basis upon which court would make its decision. Trial judge carried on with uncontested trial and gave judgment in plaintiff's favour. Court of Appeal dismissed defendant's appeal, finding no error in trial judge's decision to proceed with trial after defendant left. See *Berry v. Hall*, 2010 ONCA 546, 2010 CarswellOnt 5800 (Ont. C.A.); affirming 2009 CarswellOnt 9316 (Ont. S.C.J.), *per* Justice Alan C.R. Whitten.

The Ontario Court of Appeal upheld the trial judge's decision to carry on, saying:

> [1] The appellant founds her appeal on the trial judge having proceeded with the trial in her absence, not having inquired into why she acted as she did by leaving the courtroom. In our view, the trial judge was faced with a litigant saying she could not go through a trial, was without resources to retain a lawyer and felt the proceedings were a charade. She had decided therefore to leave. In the circumstances, we can see no error in the trial judge's proceeding with the trial after the appellant left.

No further obligation on trial judge to try to persuade party to remain and to take part in proceedings. Whether there is an obligation on the trial judge to probe into the party's reasons for the walk-out is not clear, although it would not seem wrong to do so.

An order is final, as opposed to interlocutory, if it finally disposes of the substantive issue between the parties. A decision that declines to stay an action, but rather directs that it should proceed to a trial on its merits, is the classic example of an interlocutory order.

VFC Inc. v. MacLean, 2009 NSSC 314, 2009 CarswellNS 570, 283 N.S.R. (2d) 32, 82 C.P.C. (6th) 372, 79 C.P.C. (6th) 105 (N.S. S.C.).

The defendant agreed to pay 130 bi-weekly payments for $24,671.40. The defendant failed to make all payments. VFC Inc. brought action in Small Claims Court. Small Claims Court dismissed claim on basis it did not have jurisdiction as VFC Inc. was not original party to contract as required by section 5(1) of *Small Claims Court Act*. VFC Inc. appealed. Appeal allowed. VFC Inc. was actually party to contract even though it did not sign contract, as it was worded so that the defendant must have known VFC Inc. was providing funds for purchase of car.

Park v. Lee, 98 O.R. (3d) 520, 2009 ONCA 651, 254 O.A.C. 52, 2009 CarswellOnt 5293 (Ont. C.A.).

Park, acting in person at trial, advanced claims in three actions for damages for personal injury. Apart from himself, he had no witnesses and failed to make his medical reports admissible. Defendants had undertaken to call evidence, including the defendant, Belitz. Park refused trial judge's offer to adjourn. Park made opening statement and took the stand. After two hours of Park's evidence in chief, the trial judge on his own motion dismissed all three actions on basis that Park's evidence was incoherent and incapable of proving the case. Two of the actions subsequently settled. Park appealed from dismissal of third. New trial ordered. Park denied fair trial. Inherent jurisdiction to control own process did not extend to dismissing cases without hearing the available evidence and submissions. Trial judge erred by interrupting Park before he had completed his evidence, before he had been given the full opportunity to present his case and before the defendants had honoured their undertaking to call Belitz.

Reid v. R.L. Johnston Masonry Inc., 252 O.A.C. 13, 80 C.L.R. (3d) 164, 2009 CarswellOnt 3428 (Ont. Div. Ct.).

Reid entered into oral contract with R.L. Johnston Masonry Inc. (Johnston) for repair of a water leak. Repairs completed. Reid commenced a small claims action. Action dismissed. The Divisional Court, per Glass J., stated trial judge erred in dismissing several heads of damages peremptorily as being trivial. Heads of damage ought to have been analyzed with a determination of whether they were proven claims.

Cicciarella v. Cicciarella, 252 O.A.C. 156, 72 R.F.L. (6th) 319, [2009] O.J. No. 2906, 2009 CarswellOnt 3972 (Ont. Div. Ct.).

The Divisional Court, referencing the Canadian Judicial Council's advisory "Statement of Principles on Self-represented Litigants and Accused Persons," discussed responsibilities of judges to conduct a fair and impartial proceeding when one party before the court was not self-represented.

Parkway Collision Ltd. v. Ryan, 2009 CarswellOnt 6266, 255 O.A.C. 74 (Ont. Div. Ct.).

Parkway Collision awarded judgment for a towing bill paid on behalf of Ryan and charges for storage of vehicle for $1,298.50. Ryan appealed, arguing trial judge erred in rejecting the evidence of bylaw tow rates in surrounding areas because bylaw not produced. Divisional Court, per Stong J., stated that: "In rejecting oral evidence of By-laws of other municipalities, which By-laws were not in fact presented to the court, the trial judge rejecting collateral and hearsay evidence the acceptance of which would have been simply opinion of a third party and not subject to cross-examination.".

Dew Point Insulation Systems Inc. v. JV Mechanical Ltd., 259 O.A.C. 179, 84 C.P.C. (6th) 297, 2009 CarswellOnt 8064, [2009] O.J. No. 5446, 87 C.L.R. (3d) 138 at paras. 26-40 (Ont. Div. Ct.).

Unrepresented defendants in action under the *Construction Liens Act (Ont.)* failed to comply with a Master's order for production of an affidavit of documents. The Master struck statement of defence. Divisional Court, per Bellamy J., quashed the decision where the Master did not extend procedural fairness to the defendants. Defendants did not appear to appreciate the significance of court procedures. The Master had not informed the defendants of the finality of the motion to strike. She did not provide them with an opportunity to make submissions. No evidence of prejudice to the plaintiff.

Garten v. Kruk, 2009 CarswellOnt 6477, 257 O.A.C. 59 (Ont. Div. Ct.).

Some six months after initial court appearance, without notifying the defendant, plaintiff's counsel had defendant noted in default. Six months later, the plaintiff's lawyer notified the defendant's lawyer of the noting in default. The defendant moved to set aside the noting of default. Master dismissed motion. Divisional Court, per Wilson, J., allowed appeal. The defendant demonstrated intent to defend. She had immediately obtained counsel. The fact that she appeared before Master and was now before Divisional Court spoke volumes of her desire to defend. Defendant should not be punished for her lawyer's errors. Her lawyer's affidavit clearly stated that his office inadvertently failed to deliver the statement of defence. Master did not accept the lawyer's sworn statement. Master's order reinforced sharp practice.

Gryphon Building Solutions Inc. v. Danforth Estates Management Inc., 253 O.A.C. 10, 2009 CarswellOnt 4741 (Ont. Div. Ct.).

Plaintiffs, Gryphon Building Solutions Inc. and Ontario Roofing, sought costs of appeal of $10,900 and $7,098, respectively, on basis they were successful both on jurisdictional issue and merits. Divisional Court found, on a partial indemnity basis, $4,000, all inclusive, as appropriate quantum of costs in relation to the jurisdictional issue. Jurisdictional issue not complex. Appeal unnecessary (the proper forum to challenge the Master's decision was a motion under r. 54.09). Court ordered the defendant to pay costs of $12,500, all inclusive, to Gryphon, and costs of $1,500, all inclusive, to Ontario Roofing.

McCormick v. Greater Sudbury Police Service, 2010 CarswellOnt 1871, 2010 ONSC 270, 259 O.A.C. 226, 6 Admin. L.R. (5th) 79 (Ont. Div. Ct.).

The hearing officer erred in law in purporting to take judicial notice that combined effects of consumption of alcohol and percocets would negatively impact on an individual's ability to perceive and recall experienced events. Subject was neither notorious nor within any specialized knowledge of tribunal, and properly the subject of expert evidence.

Sazant v. McKay, 2010 ONSC 4273, 2010 CarswellOnt 5903, 271 O.A.C. 63 (Ont. Div. Ct.).

Party's former lawyer now acting for opposite party. Court of Appeal effectively adopted respondent's submissions that lawyers owe duty of loyalty to former clients who must be able to speak to their lawyers frankly and without fear of exposure of their legal concerns. Clients must be confident that their lawyers will not in future become their adversaries' lawyers in course of same dispute. Lawyer's obligation, whether described as duty of loyalty owed to former client, or as professional obligation to promote public confidence in legal profession and administration of justice dictated that AL could not act on this appeal against his former client.

Consulate Ventures Inc. v. Amico Contracting & Engineering (1992) Inc., 270 O.A.C. 182, [2010] O.J. No. 4996, 2010 ONCA 788, 2010 CarswellOnt 8797, 97 C.P.C. (6th) 16 (Ont. C.A.).

The defendants brought motion for leave to appeal. Motion dismissed. Leave to appeal could be granted on question of law only. Leave to appeal could not be granted on questions of fact or questions of mixed fact and law. At best, issues raised by defendants were questions of mixed fact and law, not of law alone. See *Schultz v. Kopp Farms*, 2010 CarswellMan 75, 2010 MBCA 30 (Man. C.A. [In Chambers]).

Delano v. Craig, 2010 CarswellNS 264, 2010 NSSC 60 (N.S. S.C.).

The plaintiff brought claim in Small Claims Court concerning dispute over lawn mower. The adjudicator gave reasons why he preferred evidence of defendants over that of the plaintiff. The claim was dismissed. Appeal dismissed. The adjudicator's reasons do not have to be exhaustive, but adequate to support findings of fact and demonstrate appreciation and proper application of law based on those facts.

Bulut v. Walker-Fairen, (sub nom. *Walker-Fairen v. Bulut*) 259 O.A.C. 15, 2010 ONSC 706, 2010 CarswellOnt 482 (Ont. Div. Ct.).

Trial judge reserved judgment, following seven-week trial. He did not ask for submissions as to costs and none were made. He awarded substantial indemnity costs to plaintiff throughout. Reasons respecting costs set out in the final paragraph of the reasons as follows: "I am not asking for submissions on costs . . . Costs go to the plaintiff payable by all the defendants jointly and severally on a substantial indemnity basis throughout." Divisional Court held that, in the absence of submissions and unsupported by reasons, the trial judge's costs ruling was breach of procedural fairness and natural justice and could not stand. This was an extraordinary costs award, both respecting the scale of costs, the parties liable for the costs and the quantum of costs. Absence of meaningful reasons for award made appellate review impossible.

Link v. Venture Steel Inc., 69 B.L.R. (4th) 161, 79 C.C.E.L. (3d) 201, 259 O.A.C. 199, 2010 ONCA 144, 2010 CarswellOnt 1049, 2010 C.L.L.C. 210-017, [2010] O.J. No. 779 (Ont. C.A.).

The Ontario Court of Appeal stated that "[i]t is well accepted that the parties to an action are entitled to have a resolution of their differences based on the pleadings. Trial judge cannot make a finding of liability and award damages against a defendant on a basis not pleaded in the statement of claim because it deprives the defendant of the opportunity to address that issue." Pleadings included the critical mattes that underlay the plaintiff's claim. The defendant not misled or prejudiced as a result of general pleadings.

Cosentino v. S. Cosentino Leasing Ltd., 96 C.P.C. (6th) 372, 2010 ONSC 2611, 2010 CarswellOnt 2745, 261 O.A.C. 131, [2010] O.J. No. 1838 (Ont. Div. Ct.).

Cosentino, a lawyer, was retained in 1994 by defendant (his uncle's company) with respect to a civil action. Action was settled in 1999, on basis of nominal payment by defendant. Settlement funds paid June 16, 1999. The uncle died on August 17, 1999. Out of respect, Cosentino put file away and did not submit an account for legal services until August 3, 2002. The account was not paid. On July 30, 2008, the plaintiff sued the defendant in Small Claims Court on his account for legal services. Deputy judge found that cause of action arose when work completed and work was completed on June 16, 1999. Accordingly, claim barred under s. 45(1)(g) of the former *Limitations Act*, as the six-year limitation period had expired. Cosentino appealed. Divisional Court dismissed appeal. No palpable and overriding error in conclusion that retainer was at an end when Cosentino paid settlement funds on behalf of company.

R. v. Wang, 95 M.V.R. (5th) 80, 2010 CarswellOnt 3857, 2010 ONCA 435, 78 C.R. (6th) 134, [2010] O.J. No. 2490, 320 D.L.R. (4th) 680, 263 O.A.C. 194, 256 C.C.C. (3d) 225 (Ont. C.A.).

Court of Appeal stated that If unforeseen circumstances arise such that, after delivery of reasons that were meant to be final, a trial judge wishes to correct or supplement the reasons that were already delivered, various options are available. Issuance of an addendum, providing supplementary reasons or, when the original reasons were oral, subsequently issuing a set of amended reasons, written or oral. Candour and transparency are essential. Where changes or additions are made to the reasons, counsel as well as any reviewing court should have a clear record of what occurred and be in a position to opine as to the legal effect, if any, of the changes or additions made by the judge.".

Global Agriculture Trans-Loading Inc. v. (IRS) Industrial Repair Services, 2010 CarswellBC 1470, 2010 BCCA 234, 288 B.C.A.C. 88, 488 W.A.C. 88 (B.C. C.A.).

Appellant defendant in action brought in Small Claims Court. It appealed order on basis plaintiff as named in proceedings not a legal entity. It also sought an order for payment out of court of monies attached post-judgment by garnishing order. Judgment had been obtained in default of appearance at mandated settlement conference but was later set aside.

Respondent a sole proprietorship but when the default judgment obtained, "Ltd." was added to its name in style of cause. That addition did not appear in garnishing order.

Litigants should not be burdened with legal technicality. If there is either a factual or a legal problem with the description of the respondent in the style of cause in that court, that is a matter that should be addressed in that court. The use and withdrawal of the designation "Ltd." does not go to the jurisdiction of the court. Appeal dismissed with costs.

Roskam v. Jacoby-Hawkins, 2010 ONSC 4439, 2010 CarswellOnt 7132 (Ont. S.C.J.), Boswell J.

Judgment delivered by deputy judge on February 12, 2010.

Roskam served a Notice of Appeal of the Small Claims Court Judgment on March 18, 2010, more than 30 days after Judgment released. Jacoby-Hawkins moved to strike out the Notice of Appeal.

Jacoby-Hawkins sought additional relief that Roskam be required to post security for costs of the appeal, that he be declared a vexatious litigant and that Roskam be required to remove all references he has authored about Jacoby-Hawkins and his counsel from the internet.

Section 31 of the *Courts of Justice Act*, R.S.O. 1990 c. C.43, provides that an appeal lies to the Divisional Court from a final order of the Small Claims Court in an action for the payment of money in excess of $500.00. Rule 61.04 of the *Rules of Civil Procedure* provides that any such appeal must be commenced within 30 days after the making of the order. The time for appeal usually runs from the date of pronouncement of a judgment: see *Permanent Investment Corp. v. Ops & Graham (Township)*, 1967 CarswellOnt 90, 62 D.L.R. (2d) 258, [1967] 2 O.R. 13 (Ont. C.A.).

Rule 3.02 deals with extensions of time generally. Rule 3.02 provides court with discretion to extend the time in which to file the Notice of Appeal, which was delivered four days late. *Bona fide* intention to pursue appeal. No prejudice to respondent as a result of late service.

Justice requires extension of time to file Notice of Appeal. See *Rizzi v. Mavros*, 2007 ONCA 350, 2007 CarswellOnt 2841, [2007] O.J. No. 1783, 85 O.R. (3d) 401, 224 O.A.C. 293 (Ont. C.A. [In Chambers]). Basis for security grounded in r. 56.01(1)(c) incorporated by reference in r. 61.06(1)(b). Request for security for costs not made out. Rationale underlying s. 140 discussed by Blair, J.A. in *Foy v. Foy (No. 2)*, [1979] O.J. No. 4386, 102 D.L.R. (3d) 342, 12 C.P.C. 188, 26 O.R. (2d) 220, 1979 CarswellOnt 458 (Ont. C.A.); leave to appeal refused 102 D.L.R. (3d) 342 (note), [1979] 2 S.C.R. vii, 12 C.P.C. 188n, 26 O.R. (2d) 220n, 31 N.R. 120 (S.C.C.).

The control of vexatious proceedings was necessary to protect integrity of the judicial system. The purpose of section to prevent people from using system for improper purposes, such as harassment or oppression. See *Dale Streiman & Kurz LLP v. De Teresi*, 2007 CarswellOnt 485, [2007] O.J. No. 255, 84 O.R. (3d) 383 (Ont. S.C.J.). Accordingly, a litigant's behaviour both inside and outside of the court is relevant. See *Canada Post Corp. v. Varma*, [2000] F.C.J. No. 851, 2000 CarswellNat 1183, 192 F.T.R. 278 (Fed. T.D.).

Section 140 of the *Courts of Justice Act* gives the court the authority to declare a party a vexatious litigant, thereby restricting his or her access to the courts of Ontario. It is a remedy that should be used very sparingly because the ability to have one's grievances addressed by the courts is fundamental to a free and just society. At the same time, the court must be wary of its processes being used for vexatious purposes.

Given Roskam's behaviour, appropriate case to make an order declaring Roskam to be a vexatious litigant.

Bérubé v. Rational Entertainment Ltd., 2010 ONSC 5545, 2010 CarswellOnt 7623, 324 D.L.R. (4th) 527, 80 B.L.R. (4th) 6, 271 O.A.C. 151 (Ont. Div. Ct.).

On October 16, 2009, Small Claims Court Justice made order dismissing appellant's claim for lack of jurisdiction. On November 17, 2009, appellant served a Notice of Appeal. On December 18, 2009, respondent brought a motion before Power J. sitting as a single judge of the Divisional Court, and requested order that the appeal be quashed pursuant to section 134(3) of the *Courts of Justice Act*. The provisions of sections 31 and 21 of the *Courts of Justice Act* make it clear that Power J. had jurisdiction to hear the respondent's motion on December 18, 2009, sitting as a single judge. Section 134(3) of the *Courts of Justice Act* provides that a court to which an appeal is taken may, in a proper case, quash the appeal when the appeal is manifestly devoid of merit. Rule 61.06 of the *Rules of Civil Procedure* provides for an order for security for costs if it appears that there is good reason to believe that the appeal is frivolous and vexatious and that the appellant has insufficient assets in Ontario to pay the costs of the appeal. Rule 56.01(e) contains a similar test. Appeal dismissed.

Cameron v. Nanaimo (Regional District), 2010 CarswellBC 705, 2010 BCCA 73, 317 D.L.R. (4th) 572, 482 W.A.C. 10, 285 B.C.A.C. 10 (B.C. C.A.).

There was sufficient evidence to support the appeal judge's conclusion that respondent's absence from the courtroom was not of her own informed choosing and that trial fairness was negatively affected as a result. The right of a party to a proceeding is to be present and to see and hear the evidence that could affect his or her interests fundamental under the law.

Chippewas of Mnjikaning First Nation v. Ontario, 2010 ONCA 47, 2010 CarswellOnt 273, [2010] O.J. No. 212, *(sub nom. Chippewas of Mnjikaning First Nation v. Ontario (Minister Responsible for Native Affairs))* [2010] 2 C.N.L.R. 18, 265 O.A.C. 247 (Ont. C.A.); additional reasons at 2010 ONCA 408, 2010 CarswellOnt 3730 (Ont. C.A.); leave to appeal refused 2010 CarswellOnt 4919, 2010 CarswellOnt 4920, [2010] S.C.C.A. No. 91, *(sub nom. Chippewas of Mnjikaning First Nation v. Ontario (Minister Responsible for Native Affairs))* 276 O.A.C. 398 (note), *(sub nom. Chippewas of Mnjikaning First Nation v. Ontario (Minister Responsible for Native Affairs))* 409 N.R. 396 (note) (S.C.C.).

The trial judge's reasons were careful, thorough, and analytical. Reasons provided ample clarity and transparency to facilitate meaningful appellate review.

Interventions did not create an apprehension of bias. Experienced trial counsel did *not* object that trial judge was too interventionist at trial. The trial judge's interventions during closing arguments did not create an apprehension of bias. See de Grandpré J.'s dissenting opinion in *Committee for Justice & Liberty v. Canada (National Energy Board)* (1976), [1976] A.C.S. No. 118, [1976] S.C.J. No. 118, 1976 CarswellNat 434F, 1976 CarswellNat 434, 9 N.R. 115, 68 D.L.R. (3d) 716, [1978] 1 S.C.R. 369 (S.C.C.).

Canadian Imperial Bank of Commerce v. Houlahan, 2011 ONSC 558, 2011 CarswellOnt 291, 73 C.B.R. (5th) 223, 273 O.A.C. 140 (Ont. Div. Ct.).

Appeal from a final order of a Small Claims Court. Leave sought to admit fresh evidence.

"On a pure question of law, the basic rule with respect to the review of a trial judge's findings is that an appellate court is free to replace the opinion of the trial judge with its own. Thus the standard of review on a question of law is that of correctness," see *Housen v. Nikolaisen*, [2002] 2 S.C.R. 235 at para. 8.

The "traditional test for the admission of fresh evidence on appeal" summarized in *Public School Boards' Assn. of Alberta v. Alberta (Attorney General)*, [2000] 1 S.C.R. 44 at para. 6.

A "court to which an appeal is taken may order a new trial," see the *Courts of Justice Act*, R.S.O. 1990, c. C.43, s. 134(1)(b). A new trial shall not be directed "unless some substantial wrong or miscarriage of justice has occurred," see the *Courts of Justice Act*, s. 134(6). "Where some substantial wrong or miscarriage of justice has occurred but it affects only part of an order or decision . . . a new trial may be ordered in respect of only that part . . .," see the *Courts of Justice Act*, s. 134(7). Appeal allowed in part and new trial ordered.

Gulati v. Husain, 2011 CarswellOnt 407, 2011 ONSC 706, [2011] O.J. No. 384 (Ont. S.C.J.).

The applicant sought *certiorari* respecting an order from deputy judge of the Small Claims Court (a) denying an adjournment of the motion to set aside default judgment; (b) staying enforcement of the default judgment; (c) setting aside the default judgment; and (d) costs of $300. Order setting aside default judgment, and costs order set aside.

The court has the discretion to refuse a consent adjournment. But this discretion should be exercised sparingly. It is unusual to refuse a request to accommodate counsel's schedule reasonably on a first appearance.

Deputy judge gave no reason for refusing adjournment. Deputy judge then decided the motion to set aside the default judgment without hearing submissions from either side.

Tosti v. Society of the Madonna Di Canneto of Windsor Inc., 2011 CarswellOnt 454, 2011 ONSC 339, 275 O.A.C. 108 (Ont. Div. Ct.).

Three appeals from judgment of deputy judge after four claims heard together in Windsor Small Claims Court over a five-day period in 2009. Written judgment released December 17, 2009.

In *R. v. Sheppard*, 2002 SCC 26, 2002 CarswellNfld 74, 2002 CarswellNfld 75, REJB 2002-29516, [2002] S.C.J. No. 30, [2002] 1 S.C.R. 869, 211 Nfld. & P.E.I.R. 50, 50 C.R. (5th) 68, 633 A.P.R. 50, 210 D.L.R. (4th) 608, 284 N.R. 342, 162 C.C.C. (3d) 298 (S.C.C.), the Supreme Court held that parties are entitled to be given sufficient reasons for a decision from a trial court so that the decision can be reviewed by an appellate court and the reasons are sufficient to inform the losing party as well as the community of the basis for the decision. At the same time, deficiencies in a trial judge's reasons do not automatically constitute a reversible error. Rather, one must apply a functional interpretation of the reasons. This functional approach articulated by the Court of Appeal in *R. v. Ahmed*, 170 C.C.C. (3d) 27, [2002] O.J. No. 4597, 166 O.A.C. 254, 7 C.R. (6th) 308, 2002 CarswellOnt 4075 (Ont. C.A.) and *R. v. Stewart*, [2003] O.J. No. 347, 2003 CarswellOnt 283 (Ont. C.A.).

Appeals were granted and new trial was ordered.

Significant errors of law and fact identified in the decision and the deputy judge's "they said, they said" simplistic approach to what were complicated factual and legal issues.

While the interventionist approach taken by the deputy judge appeared at times to assist the defendants, for example, when he conducted his own cross-examination of a number of the witnesses for the plaintiffs after he or she had been cross-examined by counsel for the Society and had been re-examined by counsel for the plaintiffs, conduct did not rise to the level required to find bias based on the test for such a finding set out in *Authorson (Litigation Guardian of) v. Canada (Attorney General)*, 2002 CarswellOnt 1724, [2002] O.J. No. 2050, 32 C.P.C. (5th) 357, 161 O.A.C. 1 (Ont. Div. Ct.); additional reasons at 2002 CarswellOnt 2939 (Ont. Div. Ct.). Judges must play "gatekeeper" role in relation to the admission of evidence. See David M. Paciocco, *"Context, Culture and the Law of Expert Evidence,"* (2001) 24 Advocates' Quarterly, 42 at p. 45. The trial judge remains the gatekeeper, responsible for determining admissibility.

Elsegood v. Cambridge Spring Service 2001 Ltd., 2011 CarswellOnt 652, 2011 ONSC 534 (Ont. Div. Ct.); affirmed 2011 ONCA 831, 2011 CarswellOnt 14782, 109 O.R. (3d) 143, 99 C.C.E.L. (3d) 327, 346 D.L.R. (4th) 353, 2012 C.L.L.C. 210-008, 287 O.A.C. 32, [2011] O.J. No. 6095 (Ont. C.A.).

An appeal of decision of deputy judge. The argument that respondent's pleadings at trial were not in accord with basis upon which the trial judge found liability. Flaws, or alleged flaws, in pleadings have not been fatal for several decades, especially true in a Small Claims Court setting.

Anand v. Sunfresh Organics, 2011 CarswellOnt 757, 2011 ONSC 776 (Ont. Div. Ct.); additional reasons at 2011 ONSC 1263, 2011 CarswellOnt 1101 (Ont. Div. Ct.).

The appeal by defendant from deputy judge. The appellant argued that trial judge ought to have granted adjournment request and that any prejudice to respondent could be compensated by a cost order. Within Court's jurisdiction to govern its own process and given the facts, trial judge's decision reasonable. The appellant argued the learned judge erred in allowing the plaintiff to reference a document which had not been disclosed to the defendant in accordance with the *Rules of Civil Procedure*. Reference to it not error in judgment or law by trial judge.

The appellant argued the judge allowed as evidence a letter in which an offer of settlement was made and which ought not to have been evidence as it was privileged. This is not a ground for appeal. There was a great deal of other evidence upon which the trial judge could rely to reach his decision. Appeal dismissed.

(3) Annual appointment if 65 or older — If the deputy judge is 65 years of age or older and under 75 years of age, the appointment shall be for a term of one year, subject to subsection (8).

(4) Renewal before age 65 — The appointment of a deputy judge who is under 65 years of age may be renewed by a regional senior judge of the Superior Court of Justice for a term of three years, subject to subsection (7).

(5) Annual renewal if 65 or older — The appointment of a deputy judge who is 65 years of age or older and under 75 years of age may be renewed by a regional senior judge of the Superior Court of Justice for a term of one year, subject to subsection (8).

(6) No limit, renewals — Subject to subsections (7) to (9), there is no limit to the number of times the appointment of a deputy judge can be renewed under subsection (4) or (5).

(7) Expiry of term at age 65 — If the deputy judge is 63 years of age or older and under 65 years of age, an appointment under subsection (2) or a renewal under subsection (4) shall provide for a term that expires when he or she reaches 65 years of age.

(8) Expiry of term at age 75 — If the deputy judge is 74 years of age, an appointment under subsection (3) or a renewal under subsection (5) shall provide for a term that expires when he or she reaches 75 years of age.

(9) Age limit — No person shall be appointed as a deputy judge, or have an appointment renewed, once he or she reaches 75 years of age.

(10) Current appointments — For greater certainty, nothing in this section shortens or otherwise affects an appointment or renewed appointment that is in effect immediately before the day subsection 20(11) of Schedule 2 to the *Good Government Act, 2009* comes into force, but any renewals of the appointment on and after that day are subject to this section.

1994, c. 12, s. 12; 1996, c. 25, s. 9(17); 2009, c. 33, Sched. 2, s. 20(11)

Case Law: *Ontario Deputy Judges Assn. v. Ontario (Attorney General)*, 2012 ONCA 437, 2012 CarswellOnt 7932, 23 C.P.C. (7th) 1, [2012] O.J. No. 2865 (Ont. C.A.).

The process for renewing the appointments of Deputy Judges of the Small Claims Court ("Deputy Judges") does not infringe the principles of judicial independence.

Pursuant to s.32(1) of the *Courts of Justice Act*, R.S.O. 1990, c. C-43, as amended (the "*CJA*"), a Regional Senior Judge of the Superior Court may, with the approval of the Attorney General, appoint a lawyer to act as a Deputy Judge of the Small Claims Court for a period of three years.

Having regard to the nature of the jurisdiction of the Small Claims Court and the presumption that a Regional Senior Judge will act in the best interest of the administration of justice, that a reasonable and well informed observer would conclude that the Deputy Judges and the Ontario Small Claims Court are sufficiently independent so as to satisfy constitutional requirements.

We also endorse the application judge's comment as follows (at para. 62):

> Without doubt, the [Small Claims Court] plays an important and unique role in the justice system. It is absolutely essential that the [Small Claims Court] institutionally and the [Deputy Judges] personally, be regarded as independent.

System for renewal of the appointments of Deputy Judges does not undermine this independence.

Appeal dismissed.

33. (1) Deputy Judges Council — A council known as the Deputy Judges Council in English and as Conseil des juges suppléants in French is established.

(2) Composition — The Deputy Judges Council is composed of,

(a) the Chief Justice of the Superior Court of Justice, or another judge of the Superior Court of Justice designated by the Chief Justice;

(b) a regional senior judge of the Superior Court of Justice, appointed by the Chief Justice;

(c) a judge of the Superior Court of Justice, appointed by the Chief Justice;

(d) a provincial judge who was assigned to the Provincial Court (Civil Division) immediately before September 1, 1990, or a deputy judge, appointed by the Chief Justice;

(e) three persons who are neither judges nor lawyers, appointed by the Lieutenant Governor in Council on the Attorney General's recommendation.

(3) Criteria — In the appointment of members under clause (2)(e), the importance of reflecting, in the composition of the Council as a whole, Ontario's linguistic duality and the diversity of its population and ensuring overall gender balance shall be recognized.

(4) Chair — The Chief Justice of the Superior Court of Justice, or his or her designate, shall chair the meetings of the Deputy Judges Council.

(5) Same — The chair is entitled to vote, and may cast a second deciding vote if there is a tie.

(6) Functions — The functions of the Deputy Judges Council are,

(a) to review and approve standards of conduct for deputy judges as established by the Chief Justice;

(b) to review and approve a plan for the continuing education of deputy judges as established by the Chief Justice; and

(c) to make recommendations on matters affecting deputy judges.

(7) Duty of Chief Justice — The Chief Justice shall ensure that any standards of conduct are made available to the public, in English and French, when they have been approved by the Deputy Judges Council.

1994, c. 12, s. 13; 1996, c. 25, s. 9(14), (17); 2006, c. 21, Sched. A, s. 4

33.1 (1) Complaint — Any person may make a complaint alleging misconduct by a deputy judge, by writing to the judge of the Superior Court of Justice designated by the regional senior judge in the region where the deputy judge sits.

Commentary: New s. 33 establishes the Deputy Judges Council and its composition. The Council deals with the education of Small Claims Court deputy judges and makes recommendations on any other matters affecting them. Section 33.1 establishes a new procedure for complaints of alleged misconduct by deputy judges.

(2) Dismissal — The judge shall review the complaint and may dismiss it without further investigation if, in his or her opinion, it falls outside the jurisdiction of the regional senior judge, is frivolous or an abuse of process, or concerns a minor matter to which an appropriate response has already been given.

(3) **Notice of dismissal** — The judge shall notify the regional senior judge, the complainant and the deputy judge in writing of a dismissal under subsection (2), giving brief reasons for it.

(4) **Committee** — If the complaint is not dismissed, the judge shall refer it to a committee consisting of three persons chosen by the regional senior judge.

(5) **Same** — The three persons shall be a judge of the Superior Court of Justice, a deputy judge and a person who is neither a judge nor a lawyer, all of whom reside or work in the region where the deputy judge who is the subject of the complaint sits.

(6) **Investigation** — The committee shall investigate the complaint in the manner it considers appropriate, and the complainant and deputy judge shall be given an opportunity to make representations to the committee, in writing or, at the committee's option, orally.

(7) **Recommendation** — The committee shall make a report to the regional senior judge, recommending a disposition in accordance with subsections (8), (9) and (10).

(8) **Disposition** — The regional senior judge may dismiss the complaint, with or without a finding that it is unfounded, or, if he or she concludes that the deputy judge's conduct presents grounds for imposing a sanction, may,

    (a) warn the deputy judge;

    (b) reprimand the deputy judge;

    (c) order the deputy judge to apologize to the complainant or to any other person;

    (d) order that the deputy judge take specified measures, such as receiving education or treatment, as a condition of continuing to sit as a deputy judge;

    (e) suspend the deputy judge for a period of up to 30 days;

    (f) inform the deputy judge that his or her appointment will not be renewed under subsection 32(2);

    (g) direct that no judicial duties or only specified judicial duties be assigned to the deputy judge; or

    (h) remove the deputy judge from office.

(9) **Same** — The regional senior judge may adopt any combination of the dispositions set out in clauses (8)(a) to (g).

(10) **Disability** — If the regional senior judge finds that the deputy judge is unable, because of a disability, to perform the essential duties of the office, but would be able to perform them if his or her needs were accommodated, the regional senior judge shall order that the deputy judge's needs be accommodated to the extent necessary to enable him or her to perform those duties.

(11) **Application of subs. (10)** — Subsection (10) applies if,

    (a) the effect of the disability on the deputy judge's performance of the essential duties of the office was a factor in the complaint; and

    (b) the regional senior judge dismisses the complaint or makes a disposition under clauses (8)(a), (b), (c), (d), (e) or (g).

(12) Undue hardship — Subsection (10) does not apply if the regional senior judge is satisfied that making an order would impose undue hardship on the person responsible for accommodating the judge's needs, considering the cost, outside sources of funding, if any, and health and safety requirements, if any.

(13) Opportunity to participate — The regional senior judge shall not make an order under subsection (10) against a person without ensuring that the person has had an opportunity to participate and make submissions.

(14) Crown bound — An order made under subsection (10) binds the Crown.

(15) Compensation — The regional senior judge shall consider whether the deputy judge should be compensated for all or part of his or her costs for legal services incurred in connection with all the steps taken under this section in relation to the complaint.

(16) Recommendation — If the regional senior judge is of the opinion that the deputy judge should be compensated, he or she shall make a recommendation to the Attorney General to that effect, indicating the amount of compensation.

(17) Same — If the complaint is dismissed with a finding that it is unfounded, the regional senior judge shall recommend to the Attorney General that the deputy judge be compensated for his or her costs for legal services and shall indicate the amount of compensation.

(18) Maximum — The amount of compensation recommended under subsection (16) or (17) shall be based on a rate for legal services that does not exceed the maximum rate normally paid by the Government of Ontario for similar legal services.

(19) Payment — The Attorney General shall pay compensation to the judge in accordance with the recommendation.

(20) Non-application of *SPPA* — The *Statutory Powers Procedure Act* does not apply to a judge, regional senior judge or member of a committee acting under this section.

(21) Personal liability — No action or other proceeding for damages shall be instituted against a judge, regional senior judge or member of a committee for any act done in good faith in the execution or intended execution of the person's duty under this section.

1994, c. 12, s. 13; 1996, c. 25, s. 9(17)

Ontario Court of Justice

34. Ontario Court of Justice — The Ontario Court (Provincial Division) is continued as a court of record under the name Ontario Court of Justice in English and Cour de justice de l'Ontario in French.

1996, c. 25, s. 9(5)

35. Composition of Ontario Court of Justice — The Ontario Court of Justice shall consist of,

> (a) the Chief Justice of the Ontario Court of Justice appointed under subsection 42(3), who shall be president of the Ontario Court of Justice;

(a.1) the Associate Chief Justice and the Associate Chief Justice — Co-ordinator of Justices of the Peace of the Ontario Court of Justice appointed under subsections 42(4) and (5);

(b) a regional senior judge of the Ontario Court of Justice appointed under subsection 42(6) for each region;

(c) such provincial judges as are appointed under subsection 42(1); and

(d) such provincial judges as were assigned to the Provincial Court (Criminal Division) or the Provincial Court (Family Division) on the 31st day of December, 1989.

1994, c. 12, s. 14; 1996, c. 25, s. 9(18), (20)

36. (1) Powers and duties of Chief Justice of Ontario Court of Justice — The Chief Justice of the Ontario Court of Justice shall direct and supervise the sittings of the Ontario Court of Justice and the assignment of its judicial duties.

(2) Regional senior judges, Ontario Court of Justice — A regional senior judge of the Ontario Court of Justice shall, subject to the authority of the Chief Justice of the Ontario Court of Justice, exercise the powers and perform the duties of the Chief Justice of the Ontario Court of Justice in his or her region.

(3) Delegation — A regional senior judge of the Ontario Court of Justice may delegate to a judge of the Ontario Court of Justice in his or her region the authority to exercise specified functions.

(4) Absence of Chief Justice of Ontario Court of Justice — If the Chief Justice of the Ontario Court of Justice is absent from Ontario or is for any reason unable to act, his or her powers and duties shall be exercised and performed by an associate chief justice of the Ontario Court of Justice designated by the Chief Justice of the Ontario Court of Justice.

(5) Absence of regional senior judge of Ontario Court of Justice — The powers and duties of a regional senior judge of the Ontario Court of Justice who is absent from Ontario or is for any reason unable to act shall be exercised and performed by a judge of the Ontario Court of Justice designated by the Chief Justice of the Ontario Court of Justice.

(6) Meetings with regional senior judges — The Chief Justice of the Ontario Court of Justice may hold meetings with the regional senior judges of the Ontario Court of Justice in order to consider any matters concerning sittings of the Ontario Court of Justice and the assignment of its judicial duties.

1994, c. 12, s. 15; 1996, c. 25, s. 9(16), (18), (20)

37. (1) Judges assigned to regions — The Chief Justice of the Ontario Court of Justice shall assign every provincial judge to a region and may re-assign a judge from one region to another.

(2) Idem — Subsection (1) does not prevent the temporary assignment of a provincial judge to a location anywhere in Ontario.

1996, c. 25, s. 9(18), (20)

38. (1) Criminal jurisdiction — A provincial judge has the power and authority of two or more justices of the peace when sitting in the Ontario Court of Justice and shall exercise the powers and perform the duties that any Act of the Parliament of Canada confers on a provincial court judge when sitting in the Ontario Court of Justice.

(2) **Provincial offences and family jurisdiction** — The Ontario Court of Justice shall perform any function assigned to it by or under the *Provincial Offences Act*, the *Family Law Act*, the *Children's Law Reform Act*, the *Child and Family Services Act* or any other Act.

(3) **Youth court and youth justice court** — The Ontario Court of Justice is a youth court for the purposes of the *Young Offenders Act* (Canada) and a youth justice court for the purposes of the *Youth Criminal Justice Act* (Canada).

1996, c. 25, s. 9(18); 2006, c. 19, Sched. D, s. 5(1)

39. (1) Judge to preside — A proceeding in the Ontario Court of Justice shall be heard and determined by one judge of the Ontario Court of Justice.

(2) **Justice of the peace may preside** — A justice of the peace may preside over the Ontario Court of Justice in a proceeding under the *Provincial Offences Act*.

1996, c. 25, s. 9(18)

40. (1) Appeals — If no provision is made concerning an appeal from an order of the Ontario Court of Justice, an appeal lies to the Superior Court of Justice.

(2) **Exception** — Subsection (1) does not apply to a proceeding under the *Criminal Code* (Canada) or the *Provincial Offences Act*.

1996, c. 25, s. 9(17), (18)

41. Penalty for disturbance outside courtroom — Any person who knowingly disturbs or interferes with a proceeding in the Ontario Court of Justice without reasonable justification while outside the courtroom is guilty of an offence and on conviction is liable to a fine of not more than $1,000 or to imprisonment for a term of not more than thirty days, or to both.

1996, c. 25, s. 9(18)

Provincial Judges

42. (1) Appointment of provincial judges — The Lieutenant Governor in Council, on the recommendation of the Attorney General, may appoint such provincial judges as are considered necessary.

(2) **Qualification** — No person shall be appointed as a provincial judge unless he or she,

    (a) has been a member of the bar of one of the provinces or territories of Canada for at least 10 years; or

    (b) has, for an aggregate of at least 10 years,

        (i) been a member of a bar mentioned in clause (a), and

        (ii) after becoming a member of such a bar, exercised powers and performed duties of a judicial nature on a full-time basis in respect to a position held under a law of Canada or of one of its provinces or territories.

(3) **Chief Justice** — The Lieutenant Governor in Council may, on the recommendation of the Attorney General, appoint a provincial judge as Chief Justice of the Ontario Court of Justice.

(4) **Associate chief justices** — The Lieutenant Governor in Council may, on the recommendation of the Attorney General, appoint two provincial judges as associate chief justices of the Ontario Court of Justice.

(5) **Same** — One of the associate chief justices shall be appointed to the office of Associate Chief Justice — Co-ordinator of Justices of the Peace, which is created for the purposes of the *Justices of the Peace Act*.

(6) **Regional senior judges** — The Lieutenant Governor in Council may, on the recommendation of the Attorney General, appoint a provincial judge to be the regional senior judge of the Ontario Court of Justice for each region.

(6.1) **Same** — Before making a recommendation referred to in subsection (4) or (6), the Attorney General shall consult with the Chief Justice of the Ontario Court of Justice.

(7) **Terms of office** — The associate chief justices each hold office for six years, and regional senior judges each hold office for three years.

(7.1) **Same** — The Chief Justice holds office for eight years from the time of his or her appointment. If a successor has not yet been appointed on the day the term expires, the Chief Justice continues in office until a successor is appointed, but shall not hold office for more than nine years in any event.

(8) **Reappointment** — The Chief Justice and associate chief justices shall not be reappointed.

(9) **Same** — A regional senior judge may be reappointed once, for a further three years, on the Chief Justice's recommendation; if the Chief Justice so recommends, the Lieutenant Governor in Council shall reappoint the regional senior judge.

(10) **Salary at end of term** — A Chief Justice, associate chief justice or regional senior judge whose term expires continues to be a provincial judge and is entitled to receive the greater of the current annual salary of a provincial judge and the annual salary he or she received immediately before the expiry.

(11) **Transition** — The following applies to the Chief Judge and regional senior judges who are in office on the day section 16 of the *Courts of Justice Statute Law Amendment Act, 1994* comes into force:

    1. The Chief Judge holds office for eight years from the time of his or her appointment. If a successor has not yet been appointed on the day the term expires, the Chief Judge continues in office until a successor is appointed, but shall not hold office for more than nine years in any event.

    2. A regional senior judge holds office for five years from the time of his or her appointment, and may be reappointed once, for a further three years, on the Chief Judge's recommendation. If the Chief Judge so recommends, the Lieutenant Governor in Council shall reappoint the regional senior judge.

          1994, c. 12, s. 16; 1996, c. 25, ss. 1, 9(18), (20); 2006, c. 21, Sched. A, s. 5

43. (1) Judicial Appointments Advisory Committee — A committee known as the Judicial Appointments Advisory Committee in English and as Comité consultatif sur les nominations à la magistrature in French is established.

(2) Composition — The Committee is composed of,

(a) two provincial judges, appointed by the Chief Justice of the Ontario Court of Justice;

(b) three lawyers, one appointed by The Law Society of Upper Canada, one by the Canadian Bar Association — Ontario and one by the County and District Law Presidents' Association;

(c) seven persons who are neither judges nor lawyers, appointed by the Attorney General;

(d) a member of the Judicial Council, appointed by it.

(3) Criteria — In the appointment of members under clauses (2)(b) and (c), the importance of reflecting, in the composition of the Committee as a whole, Ontario's linguistic duality and the diversity of its population and ensuring overall gender balance shall be recognized.

(4) Term of office — The members hold office for three-year terms and may be reappointed.

(5) Staggered terms — Despite subsection (4), the following applies to the first appointments made under subsection (2):

1. One of the provincial judges holds office for a two-year term.

2. The lawyer appointed by the Canadian Bar Association — Ontario holds office for a two-year term and the lawyer appointed by the County and District Law Presidents' Association holds office for a one-year term.

3. Two of the persons who are neither judges nor lawyers hold office for two-year terms and two hold office for one-year terms.

(6) Chair — The Attorney General shall designate one of the members to chair the Committee for a three-year term.

(7) Term of office — The same person may serve as chair for two or more terms.

(8) Function — The function of the Committee is to make recommendations to the Attorney General for the appointment of provincial judges.

(9) Manner of operating — The Committee shall perform its function in the following manner:

1. When a judicial vacancy occurs and the Attorney General asks the Committee to make a recommendation, it shall advertise the vacancy and review all applications.

2. For every judicial vacancy with respect to which a recommendation is requested, the Committee shall give the Attorney General a ranked list of at least two candidates whom it recommends, with brief supporting reasons.

3. The Committee shall conduct the advertising and review process in accordance with criteria established by the Committee, including assessment of the professional excellence, community awareness and personal characteristics of candidates and recognition of the desirability of reflecting the diversity of Ontario society in judicial appointments.

4. The Committee may make recommendations from among candidates interviewed within the preceding year, if there is not enough time for a fresh advertising and review process.

(10) **Qualification** — A candidate shall not be considered by the Committee unless he or she has been a member of the bar of one of the provinces or territories of Canada for at least ten years or, for an aggregate of at least ten years, has been a member of such a bar or served as a judge anywhere in Canada after being a member of such a bar.

(11) **Recommendation by Attorney General** — The Attorney General shall recommend to the Lieutenant Governor in Council for appointment to fill a judicial vacancy only a candidate who has been recommended for that vacancy by the Committee under this section.

(12) **Rejection of list** — The Attorney General may reject the Committee's recommendations and require it to provide a fresh list.

(13) **Annual report** — The Committee shall submit to the Attorney General an annual report of its activities.

(14) **Tabling** — The Attorney General shall submit the annual report to the Lieutenant Governor in Council and shall then table the report in the Assembly.

1994, c. 12, s. 16; 1996, c. 25, s. 9(18), (20)

44. (1) **Full and part-time service** — A provincial judge may, at his or her option and with the Chief Justice's consent, change from full-time to part-time service or the reverse, or increase or decrease the amount of part-time service.

(2) **Part-time judges** — The Chief Justice, with the Attorney General's consent, may designate a former provincial judge who has retired from office to serve as a provincial judge on a part-time basis, not to exceed 50 per cent of full-time service in a calendar year.

(3) **Same** — A person designated under subsection (2) is a provincial judge and a member of the Ontario Court of Justice.

(4) **Same** — A judge who is serving on a part-time basis under subsection (1) or (2) shall not engage in any other remunerative occupation.

1994, c. 12, s. 16; 1996, c. 25, s. 9(18), (20)

45. (1) **Application for order that needs be accommodated** — A provincial judge who believes that he or she is unable, because of a disability, to perform the essential duties of the office unless his or her needs are accommodated may apply to the Judicial Council for an order under subsection (2).

(2) **Duty of Judicial Council** — If the Judicial Council finds that the judge is unable, because of a disability, to perform the essential duties of the office unless his or her needs are accommodated, it shall order that the judge's needs be accommodated to the extent necessary to enable him or her to perform those duties.

(3) **Undue hardship** — Subsection (2) does not apply if the Judicial Council is satisfied that making an order would impose undue hardship on the person responsible for accommodating the judge's needs, considering the cost, outside sources of funding, if any, and health and safety requirements, if any.

(4) Guidelines and rules of procedure — In dealing with applications under this section, the Judicial Council shall follow its guidelines and rules of procedure established under subsection 51.1(1).

(5) Opportunity to participate — The Judicial Council shall not make an order under subsection (2) against a person without ensuring that the person has had an opportunity to participate and make submissions.

(6) Crown bound — The order binds the Crown.

1994, c. 12, s. 16

46. (1) Outside activities — A provincial judge may act as commissioner, arbitrator, adjudicator, referee, conciliator or mediator only if expressly authorized by an Act of the Parliament of Canada or the Legislature or appointed or authorized by the Governor in Council or Lieutenant Governor in Council.

(2) Same — A judge who, before January 1, 1985, had the consent of the Attorney General to act as an arbitrator or conciliator may continue to do so.

(3) Remuneration — A judge acting under subsection (1) shall not receive remuneration but shall be reimbursed for reasonable travelling and other expenses incurred while so acting.

1994, c. 12, s. 16

47. (1) Retirement — Every provincial judge shall retire upon attaining the age of sixty-five years.

(2) Same — Despite subsection (1), a judge appointed as a full-time magistrate, judge of a juvenile and family court or master before December 2, 1968 shall retire upon attaining the age of seventy years.

(3) Continuation of judges in office — A judge who has attained retirement age may, subject to the annual approval of the Chief Justice of the Ontario Court of Justice, continue in office as a full-time or part-time judge until he or she attains the age of seventy-five years.

(4) Same, regional senior judges — A regional senior judge of the Ontario Court of Justice who is in office at the time of attaining retirement age may, subject to the annual approval of the Chief Justice, continue in that office until his or her term (including any renewal under subsection 42(9)) expires, or until he or she attains the age of seventy-five years, whichever comes first.

(5) Same, Chief Justice and associate chief justice — A Chief Justice or associate chief justice of the Ontario Court of Justice who is in office at the time of attaining retirement age may, subject to the annual approval of the Judicial Council, continue in that office until his or her term expires, or until he or she attains the age of seventy-five years, whichever comes first.

(6) Same — If the Judicial Council does not approve a Chief Justice's or associate chief justice's continuation in that office under subsection (5), his or her continuation in the office of provincial judge is subject to the approval of the Judicial Council and not as set out in subsection (3).

(7) Criteria — Decisions under subsections (3), (4), (5) and (6) shall be made in accordance with criteria developed by the Chief Justice and approved by the Judicial Council.

(8) **Transition** — If the date of retirement under subsections (1) to (5) falls earlier in the calendar year than the day section 16 of the *Courts of Justice Statute Law Amendment Act, 1994* comes into force and the annual approval is outstanding on that day, the judge's continuation in office shall be dealt with in accordance with section 44 of this Act as it read immediately before that day.

1994, c. 12, s. 16; 1996, c. 25, s. 9(18), (20)

48. (1) **Resignation of judge** — A provincial judge may at any time resign from his or her office by delivering a signed letter of resignation to the Attorney General.

(2) **Resignation as Chief Justice, etc.** — A Chief Justice, an associate chief judge or a regional senior judge may, before the expiry of his or her term of office under section 42, elect to hold the office of a provincial judge only, by delivering a signed letter to that effect to the Attorney General.

(3) **Former Co-ordinator of Justices of the Peace** — The former Co-ordinator of Justices of the Peace holds the office of a provincial judge, and is entitled to an annual salary equal to the greater of the current annual salary of a provincial judge or the annual salary he or she received immediately before ceasing to be Co-ordinator.

(4) **Effective date** — A resignation or election under this section takes effect on the day the letter is delivered to the Attorney General or, if the letter specifies a later day, on that day.

(5) **Repeal** — [Subsection (3) was repealed and replaced by the current subsection (3) on September 1, 1995.]

1994, c. 12, s. 16; 1996, c. 25, s. 9(20)

Ontario Judicial Council

49. (1) **Judicial Council** — The Ontario Judicial Council is continued under the name Ontario Judicial Council in English and Conseil de la magistrature de l'Ontario in French.

(2) **Composition** — The Judicial Council is composed of,

(a) the Chief Justice of Ontario, or another judge of the Court of Appeal designated by the Chief Justice;

(b) the Chief Justice of the Ontario Court of Justice, or another judge of that court designated by the Chief Justice, and the Associate Chief Justice of the Ontario Court of Justice;

(c) a regional senior judge of the Ontario Court of Justice, appointed by the Lieutenant Governor in Council on the Attorney General's recommendation;

(d) two judges of the Ontario Court of Justice, appointed by the Chief Justice;

(e) the Treasurer of The Law Society of Upper Canada, or another bencher of the Law Society who is a lawyer, designated by the Treasurer;

(f) a lawyer who is not a bencher of The Law Society of Upper Canada, appointed by the Law Society;

(g) four persons who are neither judges nor lawyers, appointed by the Lieutenant Governor in Council on the Attorney General's recommendation.

(3) **Temporary members** — The Chief Justice of the Ontario Court of Justice may appoint a judge of that court to be a temporary member of the Judicial Council in the place of another provincial judge, for the purposes of dealing with a complaint, if the requirements of subsections (13), (15), (17), (19) and (20) cannot otherwise be met.

(4) **Criteria** — In the appointment of members under clauses (2)(d), (f) and (g), the importance of reflecting, in the composition of the Judicial Council as a whole, Ontario's linguistic duality and the diversity of its population and ensuring overall gender balance shall be recognized.

(5) **Term of office** — The regional senior judge who is appointed under clause (2)(c) remains a member of the Judicial Council until he or she ceases to hold office as a regional senior judge.

(6) **Same** — The members who are appointed under clauses (2)(d), (f) and (g) hold office for four-year terms and shall not be reappointed.

(7) **Staggered terms** — Despite subsection (6), one of the members first appointed under clause (2)(d) and two of the members first appointed under clause (2)(g) shall be appointed to hold office for six-year terms.

(8) **Chair** — The Chief Justice of Ontario, or another judge of the Court of Appeal designated by the Chief Justice, shall chair the meetings and hearings of the Judicial Council that deal with complaints against particular judges and its meetings held for the purposes of section 45 and subsection 47(5).

(9) **Same** — The Chief Justice of the Ontario Court of Justice, or another judge of that court designated by the Chief Justice, shall chair all other meetings and hearings of the Judicial Council.

(10) **Same** — The chair is entitled to vote, and may cast a second deciding vote if there is a tie.

(11) **Open and closed hearings and meetings** — The Judicial Council's hearings and meetings under sections 51.6 and 51.7 shall be open to the public, unless subsection 51.6(7) applies; its other hearings and meetings may be conducted in private, unless this Act provides otherwise.

(12) **Vacancies** — Where a vacancy occurs among the members appointed under clause (2)(d), (f) or (g), a new member similarly qualified may be appointed for the remainder of the term.

(13) **Quorum** — The following quorum rules apply, subject to subsections (15) and (17):

   1. Eight members, including the chair, consistute a quorum.

   2. At least half the members present must be judges and at least four must be persons who are not judges.

(14) **Review panels** — The Judicial Council may establish a panel for the purpose of dealing with a complaint under subsection 51.4(17) or (18) or subsection 51.5(8) or (10) and considering the question of compensation under section 51.7, and the panel has all the powers of the Judicial Council for that purpose.

(15) **Same** — The following rules apply to a panel established under subsection (14):

   1. The panel shall consist of two provincial judges other than the Chief Justice, a lawyer and a person who is neither a judge nor a lawyer.

2. One of the judges, as designated by the Judicial Council, shall chair the panel.

3. Four members constitute a quorum.

(16) **Hearing panels** — The Judicial Council may establish a panel for the purpose of holding a hearing under section 51.6 and considering the question of compensation under section 51.7, and the panel has all the powers of the Judicial Council for that purpose.

(17) **Same** — The following rules apply to a panel established under subsection (16):

1. Half the members of the panel, including the chair, must be judges, and half must be persons who are not judges.

2. At least one member must be a person who is neither a judge nor a lawyer.

3. The Chief Justice of Ontario, or another judge of the Court of Appeal designated by the Chief Justice, shall chair the panel.

4. Subject to paragraphs 1, 2 and 3, the Judicial Council may determine the size and composition of the panel.

5. All the members of the panel constitute a quorum.

(18) **Chair** — The chair of a panel established under subsection (14) or (16) is entitled to vote, and may cast a second deciding vote if there is a tie.

(19) **Participation in stages of process** — The members of the subcommittee that investigated a complaint shall not,

(a) deal with the complaint under subsection 51.4(17) or (18) or subsection 51.5(8) or (10); or

(b) participate in a hearing of the complaint under section 51.6.

(20) **Same** — The members of the Judicial Council who dealt with a complaint under subsection 51.4(17) or (18) or subsection 51.5(8) or (10) shall not participate in a hearing of the complaint under section 51.6.

(21) **Expert assistance** — The Judicial Council may engage persons, including counsel, to assist it.

(22) **Support services** — The Judicial Council shall provide support services, including initial orientation and continuing education, to enable its members to participate effectively, devoting particular attention to the needs of the members who are neither judges nor lawyers and administering a part of its budget for support services separately for that purpose.

(23) **Same** — The Judicial Council shall administer a part of its budget for support services separately for the purpose of accommodating the needs of any members who have disabilities.

(24) **Confidential records** — The Judicial Council or a subcommittee may order that any information or documents relating to a mediation or a Council meeting or hearing that was not held in public are confidential and shall not be disclosed or made public.

(25) **Same** — Subsection (24) applies whether the information or documents are in the possession of the Judicial Council, the Attorney General or any other person.

(26) **Exceptions** — Subsection (24) does not apply to information and documents,

(a) that this Act requires the Judicial Council to disclose; or

(b) that have not been treated as confidential and were not prepared exclusively for the purposes of the mediation or Council meeting or hearing.

(27) **Personal liability** — No action or other proceeding for damages shall be instituted against the Judicial Council, any of its members or employees or any person acting under its authority for any act done in good faith in the execution or intended execution of the Council's or person's duty.

(28) **Remuneration** — The members who are appointed under clause (2)(g) are entitled to receive the daily remuneration that is fixed by the Lieutenant Governor in Council.

1994, c. 12, s. 16; 1996, c. 25, s. 9(15), (18), (20)

Case Law: *Kipiniak v. Ontario Judicial Council*, 2012 ONSC 5866, 2012 CarswellOnt 14214, 298 O.A.C. 389, [2012] O.J. No. 5299 (Ont. Div. Ct.), Lax, J. — Application for judicial review of decision of the Ontario Judicial Council (OJC). Court has no authority to order an inquiry into the OJC's conduct or to substitute opinion for that of the OJC. Jurisdiction flows from the *Judicial Review Procedure Act*. Application for judicial review dismissed. Costs to Kipiniak in any event in the amount of $382 representing the filing fee of $181 for the judicial review application and fee of $201 for perfecting application.

50. (1) Complaint against Chief Justice of the Ontario Court of Justice —
If the Chief Justice of the Ontario Court of Justice is the subject of a complaint,

(a) the Chief Justice of Ontario shall appoint another judge of the Ontario Court of Justice to be a member of the Judicial Council instead of the Chief Justice of the Ontario Court of Justice, until the complaint is finally disposed of;

(b) the Associate Chief Justice of the Ontario Court of Justice shall chair meetings and hearings of the Council instead of the Chief Justice of the Ontario Court of Justice, and make appointments under subsection 49(3) instead of the Chief Justice, until the complaint is finally disposed of; and

(c) any reference of the complaint that would otherwise be made to the Chief Justice of the Ontario court of Justice under clause 51.4(13)(b) and 51.4(18)(c), subclause 51.5(8)(b)(ii) or clause 51.5(10)(b) shall be made to the Chief Justice of the Superior Court of Justice instead of to the Chief Justice of the Ontario Court of Justice.

(2) **Suspension of Chief Justice** — If the Chief Justice of the Ontario Court of Justice is suspended under subsection 51.4(12),

(a) complaints that would otherwise be referred to the Chief Justice of the Ontario Court of Justice under clauses 51.4(13)(b) and 51.4(18)(c), subclause 51.5(8)(b)(ii) and 51.5(10)(b) shall be referred to the Associate Chief Justice of the Ontario Court of Justice, until the complaint is finally disposed of; and

(b) annual approvals that would otherwise be granted or refused by the Chief Justice of the Ontario Court of Justice shall be granted or refused by the Associate Chief Justice of the Ontario Court of Justice, until the complaint is finally disposed of.

(3) **Complaint against Associate Chief Justice or regional senior judge** — If the Associate Chief Justice of the Ontario Court of Justice or the regional senior judge appointed under clause 49(2)(c) is the subject of a complaint, the Chief Justice of the Ontario Court of Justice shall appoint another judge of the Ontario Court of Justice to be a member of the Judicial Council instead of the Associate Chief

Justice or regional senior judge, as the case may be, until the complaint is finally disposed of.

1994, c. 12, s. 16; 1996, c. 25, s. 9(6)

51. (1) Provision of information to public — The Judicial Council shall provide, in courthouses and elsewhere, information about itself and about the justice system, including information about how members of the public may obtain assistance in making complaints.

(2) Same — In providing information, the Judicial Council shall emphasize the elimination of cultural and linguistic barriers and the accommodation of the needs of persons with disabilities.

(3) Assistance to public — Where necessary, the Judicial Council shall arrange for the provision of assistance to members of the public in the preparation of documents for making complaints.

(4) Telephone access — The Judicial Council shall provide province-wide free telephone access, including telephone access for the deaf, to information about itself and its role in the justice system.

(5) Persons with disabilities — To enable persons with disabilities to participate effectively in the complaints process, the Judicial Council shall ensure that their needs are accommodated, at the Council's expense, unless it would impose undue hardship on the Council to do so, considering the cost, outside sources of funding, if any, and health and safety requirements, if any.

(6) Annual report — After the end of each year, the Judicial Council shall make an annual report to the Attorney General on its affairs, in English and French, including, with respect to all complaints received or dealt with during the year, a summary of the complaint, the findings and a statement of the disposition, but the report shall not include information that might identify the judge or the complainant.

(7) Tabling — The Attorney General shall submit the annual report to the Lieutenant Governor in Council and shall then table the report in the Assembly.

1994, c. 12, s. 16

51.1 (1) Rules — The Judicial Council shall establish and make public rules governing its own procedures, including the following:

    1. Guidelines and rules of procedure for the purpose of section 45.

    2. Guidelines and rules of procedure for the purpose of subsection 51.4(21).

    3. Guidelines and rules of procedure for the purpose of subsection 51.4(22).

    4. If applicable, criteria for the purpose of subsection 51.5(2).

    5. If applicable, guidelines and rules of procedure for the purpose of subsection 51.5(13).

    6. Rules of procedure for the purpose of subsection 51.6(3).

    7. Criteria for the purpose of subsection 51.6(7).

    8. Criteria for the purpose of subsection 51.6(8).

    9. Criteria for the purpose of subsection 51.6(10).

(2) **Part III (Regulations) of the *Legislation Act, 2006*** — Part III (Regulations) of the *Legislation Act, 2006* does not apply to rules, guidelines or criteria established by the Judicial Council.

(3) **Sections 28, 29 and 33 of *SPPA*** — Sections 28, 29 and 33 of the *Statutory Powers Procedure Act* do not apply to the Judicial Council.

1994, c. 12, s. 16; 2006, c. 21, Sched. F, s. 136(1), Table 1

51.2 (1) Use of official languages of courts — The information provided under subsections 51(1), (3) and (4) and the matters made public under subsection 51.1(1) shall be made available in English and French.

(2) **Same** — Complaints against provincial judges may be made in English or French.

(3) **Same** — A hearing under section 51.6 shall be conducted in English, but a complainant or witness who speaks French or a judge who is the subject of a complaint and who speaks French is entitled, on request,

(a) to be given, before the hearing, French translations of documents that are written in English and are to be considered at the hearing;

(b) to be provided with the assistance of an interpreter at the hearing; and

(c) to be provided with simultaneous interpretation into French of the English portions of the hearing.

(4) **Same** — Subsection (3) also applies to mediations conducted under section 51.5 and to the Judicial Council's consideration of the question of compensation under section 51.7, if subsection 51.7(2) applies.

(5) **Bilingual hearing or mediation** — The Judicial Council may direct that a hearing or mediation to which subsection (3) applies be conducted bilingually, if the Council is of the opinion that it can be properly conducted in that manner.

(6) **Part of hearing or mediation** — A directive under subsection (5) may apply to a part of the hearing or mediation, and in that case subsections (7) and (8) apply with necessary modifications.

(7) **Same** — In a bilingual hearing or mediation,

(a) oral evidence and submissions may be given or made in English or French, and shall be recorded in the language in which they are given or made;

(b) documents may be filed in either language;

(c) in the case of a mediation, discussions may take place in either language;

(d) the reasons for a decision or the mediator's report, as the case may be, may be written in either language.

(8) **Same** — In a bilingual hearing or mediation, if the complainant or the judge who is the subject of the complaint does not speak both languages, he or she is entitled, on request, to have simultaneous interpretation of any evidence, submissions or discussions spoken in the other language and translation of any document filed or reasons or report written in the other language.

1994, c. 12, s. 16

51.3 (1) Complaints — Any person may make a complaint to the Judicial Council alleging misconduct by a provincial judge.

(2) Same — If an allegation of misconduct against a provincial judge is made to a member of the Judicial Council, it shall be treated as a complaint made to the Judicial Council.

(3) Same — If an allegation of misconduct against a provincial judge is made to any other judge or to the Attorney General, the other judge, or the Attorney General, asthe case may be, shall provide the person making the allegation with information about the Judicial Council's role in the justice system and about how a complaint may be made, and shall refer the person to the Judicial Council.

(4) Carriage of matter — Once a complaint has been made to the Judicial Council, the Council has carriage of the matter.

(5) Information re complaint — At any person's request, the Judicial Council may confirm or deny that a particular complaint has been made to it.

1994, c. 12, s. 16

51.4 (1) Review by subcommittee — A complaint received by the Judicial Council shall be reviewed by a subcommittee of the Council consisting of a provincial judge other than the Chief Justice and a person who is neither a judge nor a lawyer.

(2) Rotation of members — The eligible members of the Judicial Council shall all serve on the subcommittee on a rotating basis.

(3) Dismissal — The subcommittee shall dismiss the complaint without further investigation if, in the subcommittee's opinion, it falls outside the Judicial Council's jurisdiction or is frivolous or an abuse of process.

(4) Investigation — If the complaint is not dismissed under subsection (3), the subcommittee shall conduct such investigation as it considers appropriate.

(5) Expert assistance — The subcommittee may engage persons, including counsel, to assist it in its investigation.

(6) Investigation private — The investigation shall be conducted in private.

(7) Non-application of *SPPA* — The *Statutory Powers Procedure Act* does not apply to the subcommittee's activities.

(8) Interim recommendations — The subcommittee may recommend to a regional senior judge the suspension, with pay, of the judge who is the subject of the complaint, or the judge's reassignment to a different location, until the complaint is finally disposed of.

(9) Same — The recommendation shall be made to the regional senior judge appointed for the region to which the judge is assigned, unless that regional senior judge is a member of the Judicial Council, in which case the recommendation shall be made to another regional senior judge.

(10) Power of regional senior judge — The regional senior judge may suspend or reassign the judge as the subcommittee recommends.

(11) Discretion — The regional senior judge's discretion to accept or reject the subcommittee's recommendation is not subject to the direction and supervision of the Chief Justice.

(12) Exception: complaints against certain judges — If the complaint is against the Chief Justice of the Ontario Court of Justice, an associate chief justice of the Ontario Court of Justice or the regional senior judge who is a member of the Judicial Council, any recommendation under subsection (8) in connection with the complaint shall be made to the Chief Justice of the Superior Court of Justice, who may suspend or reassign the judge as the subcommittee recommends.

(13) Subcommittee's decision — When its investigation is complete, the subcommittee shall,

(a) dismiss the complaint;

(b) refer the complaint to the Chief Justice;

(c) refer the complaint to a mediator in accordance with section 51.5; or

(d) refer the complaint to the Judicial Council, with or without recommending that it hold a hearing under section 51.6.

(14) Same — The subcommittee may dismiss the complaint or refer it to the Chief Justice or to a mediator only if both members agree; otherwise, the complaint shall be referred to the Judicial Council.

(15) Conditions, reference to Chief Justice — The subcommittee may, if the judge who is the subject of the complaint agrees, impose conditions on a decision to refer the complaint to the Chief Justice.

(16) Report — The subcommittee shall report to the Judicial Council, without identifying the complainant or the judge who is the subject of the complaint, its disposition of any complaint that is dismissed or referred to the Chief Justice or to a mediator.

(17) Power of Judicial Council — The Judicial Council shall consider the report, in private, and may approve the subcommittee's disposition or may require the subcommittee to refer the complaint to the Council.

(18) Same — The Judicial Council shall consider, in private, every complaint referred to it by the subcommittee, and may,

(a) hold a hearing under section 51.6;

(b) dismiss the complaint;

(c) refer the complaint to the Chief Justice, with or without imposing conditions as referred to in subsection (15); or

(d) refer the complaint to a mediator in accordance with section 51.5.

(19) Non-application of *SPPA* — The *Statutory Powers Procedure Act* does not apply to the Judicial Council's activities under subsections (17) and (18).

(20) Notice to judge and complainant — After making its decision under subsection (17) or (18), the Judicial Council shall communicate it to the judge and the complainant, giving brief reasons in the case of a dismissal.

(21) Guidelines and rules of procedure — In conducting investigations, in making recommendations under subsection (8) and in making decisions under subsections (13) and (15), the subcommittee shall follow the Judicial Council's guidelines and rules of procedure established under subsection 51.1(1).

(22) **Same** — In considering reports and complaints and making decisions under subsections (17) and (18), the Judicial Council shall follow its guidelines and rules of procedure established under subsection 51.1(1).

1994, c. 12, s. 16; 1996, c. 25, s. 9(7), (20)

51.5 (1) Mediation — The Judicial Council may establish a mediation process for complainants and for judges who are the subject of complaints.

(2) **Criteria** — If the Judicial Council establishes a mediation process, it must also establish criteria to exclude from the process complaints that are inappropriate for mediation.

(3) **Same** — Without limiting the generality of subsection (2), the criteria must ensure that complaints are excluded from the mediation process in the following circumstances:

1. There is a significant power imbalance between the complainant and the judge, or there is such a significant disparity between the complainant's and the judge's accounts of the event with which the complaint is concerned that mediation would be unworkable.

2. The complaint involves an allegation of sexual misconduct or an allegation of discrimination or harassment because of a prohibited ground of discrimination or harassment referred to in any provision of the *Human Rights Code*.

3. The public interest requires a hearing of the complaint.

(4) **Legal advice** — A complaint may be referred to a mediator only if the complainant and the judge consent to the referral, are able to obtain independent legal advice and have had an opportunity to do so.

(5) **Trained mediator** — The mediator shall be a person who has been trained in mediation and who is not a judge, and if the mediation is conducted by two or more persons acting together, at least one of them must meet those requirements.

(6) **Impartiality** — The mediator shall be impartial.

(7) **Exclusion** — No member of the subcommittee that investigated the complaint and no member of the Judicial Council who dealt with the complaint under subsection 51.4(17) or (18) shall participate in the mediation.

(8) **Review by Council** — The mediator shall report the results of the mediation, without identifying the complainant or the judge who is the subject of the complaint, to the Judicial Council, which shall review the report, in private, and may,

(a) approve the disposition of the complaint; or

(b) if the mediation does not result in a disposition or if the Council is of the opinion that the disposition is not in the public interest,

(i) dismiss the complaint,

(ii) refer the complaint to the Chief Justice, with or without imposing conditions as referred to in subsection 51.4(15), or

(iii) hold a hearing under section 51.6.

(9) **Report** — If the Judicial Council approves the disposition of the complaint, it may make the results of the mediation public, providing a summary of the complaint but not identifying the complainant or the judge.

(10) Referral to Council — At any time during or after the mediation, the complainant or the judge may refer the complaint to the Judicial Council, which shall consider the matter, in private, and may,

(a) dismiss the complaint;

(b) refer the complaint to the Chief Justice, with or without imposing conditions as referred to in subsection 51.4(15); or

(c) hold a hearing under section 51.6.

(11) Non-application of *SPPA* — The *Statutory Powers Procedure Act* does not apply to the Judicial Council's activities under subsections (8) and (10).

(12) Notice to judge and complainant — After making its decision under subsection (8) or (10), the Judicial Council shall communicate it to the judge and the complainant, giving brief reasons in the case of a dismissal.

(13) Guidelines and rules of procedure — In reviewing reports, considering matters and making decisions under subsections (8) and (10), the Judicial Council shall follow its guidelines and rules of procedure established under subsection 51.1(1).

1994, c. 12, s. 16; 1996, c. 25, s. 9(20)

51.6 (1) Adjudication by Council — When the Judicial Council decides to hold a hearing, it shall do so in accordance with this section.

(2) Application of *SPPA* — The *Statutory Powers Procedure Act*, except section 4 and subsection 9(1), applies to the hearing.

(3) Rules of procedure — The Judicial Council's rules of procedure established under subsection 51.1(1) apply to the hearing.

(4) Communication re subject-matter of hearing — The members of the Judicial Council participating in the hearing shall not communicate directly or indirectly in relation to the subject-matter of the hearing with any person, unless all the parties and the persons representing the parties under the authority of the *Law Society Act* receive notice and have an opportunity to participate.

(5) Exception — Subsection (4) does not preclude the Judicial Council from engaging counsel to assist it in accordance with subsection 49(21), and in that case the nature of the advice given by counsel shall be communicated to the parties so that they may make submissions as to the law.

(6) Parties — The Judicial Council shall determine who are the parties to the hearing.

(7) Exception, closed hearing — In exceptional circumstances, if the Judicial Council determines, in accordance with the criteria established under subsection 51.1(1), that the desirability of holding open hearings is outweighed by the desirability of maintaining confidentiality, it may hold all or part of the hearing in private.

(8) Disclosure in exceptional circumstances — If the hearing was held in private, the Judicial Council shall, unless it determines in accordance with the criteria established under subsection 51.1(1) that there are exceptional circumstances, order that the judge's name not be disclosed or made public.

(9) Orders prohibiting publication — If the complaint involves allegations of sexual misconduct or sexual harassment, the Judicial Council shall, at the request of a complainant or of another witness who testifies to having been the victim of similar conduct by the judge, prohibit the publication of information that might identify the complainant or witness, as the case may be.

(10) **Publication ban** — In exceptional circumstances and in accordance with the criteria established under subsection 51.1(1), the Judicial Council may make an order prohibiting, pending the disposition of a complaint, the publication of information that might identify the judge who is the subject of the complaint.

(11) **Dispositions** — After completing the hearing, the Judicial Council may dismiss the complaint, with or without a finding that is unfounded or, if it finds that there has been misconduct by the judge, may,

(a) warn the judge;

(b) reprimand the judge;

(c) order the judge to apologize to the complainant or to any other person;

(d) order that the judge take specified measures, such as receiving education or treatment, as a condition of continuing to sit as a judge;

(e) suspend the judge with pay, for any period;

(f) suspend the judge without pay, but with benefits, for a period up to thirty days; or

(g) recommend to the Attorney General that the judge be removed from office in accordance with section 51.8.

(12) **Same** — The Judicial Council may adopt any combination of the dispositions set out in clauses (11)(a) to (f).

(13) **Disability** — If the Judicial Council finds that the judge is unable, because of a disability, to perform the essential duties of the office, but would be able to perform them if his or her needs were accommodated, the Council shall order that the judge's needs be accommodated to the extent necessary to enable him or her to perform those duties.

(14) **Application of subs. (13)** — Subsection (13) applies if,

(a) the effect of the disability on the judge's performance of the essential duties of the office was a factor in the complaint; and

(b) the Judicial Council dismisses the complaint or makes a disposition under clauses (11)(a) to (f).

(15) **Undue hardship** — Subsection (13) does not apply if the Judicial Council is satisfied that making an order would impose undue hardship on the person responsible for accommodating the judge's needs, considering the cost, outside sources of funding, if any, and health and safety requirements, if any.

(16) **Opportunity to participate** — The Judicial Council shall not make an order under subsection (13) against a person without ensuring that the person has had an opportunity to participate and make submissions.

(17) **Crown bound** — An order made under subsection (13) binds the Crown.

(18) **Report to Attorney General** — The Judicial Council may make a report to the Attorney General about the complaint, investigation, hearing and disposition, subject to any order made under subsection 49(24), and the Attorney General may make the report public if of the opinion that this would be in the public interest.

(19) Non-identification of persons — The following persons shall not be identified in the report:

> 1. A complainant or witness at whose request an order was made under subsection (9).
>
> 2. The judge, if the hearing was conducted in private, unless the Judicial Council orders that the judge's name be disclosed.

(20) Continuing publication ban — If an order was made under subsection (10) and the Judicial Council dismisses the complaint with a finding that it was unfounded, the judge shall not be identified in the report without his or her consent and the Council shall order that information that relates to the complaint and might identify the judge shall never be made public without his or her consent.

1994, c. 12, s. 16; 2006, c. 21, Sched. C, s. 105(3)

51.7 (1) Compensation — When the Judicial Council has dealt with a complaint against a provincial judge, it shall consider whether the judge should be compensated for his or her costs for legal services incurred in connection with all the steps taken under sections 51.4, 51.5 and 51.6 and this section in relation to the complaint.

(2) Consideration of question combined with hearing — If the Judicial Council holds a hearing into the complaint, its consideration of the question of compensation shall be combined with the hearing.

(3) Public or private consideration of question — The Judicial Council's consideration of the question of compensation shall take place in public if there was a public hearing into the complaint, and otherwise shall take place in private.

(4) Recommendation — If the Judicial Council is of the opinion that the judge should be compensated, it shall make a recommendation to the Attorney General to that effect, indicating the amount of compensation.

(5) Same — If the complaint is dismissed after a hearing, the Judicial Council shall recommend to the Attorney General that the judge be compensated for his or her costs for legal services and shall indicate the amount.

(6) Disclosure of name — The Judicial Council's recommendation to the Attorney General shall name the judge, but the Attorney General shall not disclose the name unless there was a public hearing into the complaint or the Council has otherwise made the judge's name public.

(7) Amount of compensation — The amount of compensation recommended under subsection (4) or (5) may relate to all or part of the judge's costs for legal services, and shall be based on a rate for legal services that does not exceed the maximum rate normally paid by the Government of Ontario for similar services.

(8) Payment — The Attorney General shall pay compensation to the judge in accordance with the recommendation.

1994, c. 12, s. 16

51.8 (1) Removal for cause — A provincial judge may be removed from office only if,

> (a) a complaint about the judge has been made to the Judicial Council; and
>
> (b) the Judicial Council, after a hearing under section 51.6, recommends to the Attorney General that the judge be removed on the ground that he or she has

390

become incapacitated or disabled from the due execution of his or her office by reason of,

> (i) inability, because of a disability, to perform the essential duties of his or her office (if an order to accommodate the judge's needs would not remedy the inability or could not be made because it would impose undue hardship on the person responsible for meeting those needs, or was made but did not remedy the inability),

> (ii) conduct that is incompatible with the due execution of his or her office, or

> (iii) failure to perform the duties of his or her office.

(2) **Tabling of recommendation** — The Attorney General shall table the recommendation in the Assembly if it is in session or, if not, within fifteen days after the commencement of the next session.

(3) **Order for removal** — An order removing a provincial judge from office under this section may be made by the Lieutenant Governor on the address of the Assembly.

(4) **Application** — This section applies to provincial judges who have not yet attained retirement age and to provincial judges whose continuation in office after attaining retirement age has been approved under subsection 47(3), (4) or (5).

(5) **Transition** — A complaint against a provincial judge that is made to the Judicial Council before the day section 16 of the *Courts of Justice Statute Law Amendment Act, 1994* comes into force, and considered at a meeting of the Judicial Council before that day, shall be dealt with by the Judicial Council as it was constituted immediately before that day and in accordance with section 49 of this Act as it read immediately before that day.

1994, c. 12, s. 16

51.9 (1) Standards of conduct — The Chief Justice of the Ontario Court of Justice may establish standards of conduct for provincial judges, including a plan for bringing the standards into effect, and may implement the standards and plan when they have been reviewed and approved by the Judicial Council.

(2) **Duty of Chief Justice** — The Chief Justice shall ensure that any standards of conduct are made available to the public, in English and French, when they have been approved by the Judicial Council.

(3) **Goals** — The following are among the goals that the Chief Justice may seek to achieve by implementing standards of conduct for judges:

1. Recognizing the independence of the judiciary.

2. Maintaining the high quality of the justice system and ensuring the efficient administration of justice.

3. Enhancing equality and a sense of inclusiveness in the justice system.

4. Ensuring that judges' conduct is consistent with the respect accorded to them.

5. Emphasizing the need to ensure the professional and personal development of judges and the growth of their social awareness through continuing education.

1994, c. 12, s. 16; 1996, c. 25, s. 9(18), (20); 2006, c. 21, Sched. A, s. 6

51.10 (1) Continuing education — The Chief Justice of the Ontario Court of Justice shall establish a plan for the continuing education of provincial judges, and shall implement the plan when it has been reviewed and approved by the Judicial Council.

(2) **Duty of Chief Justice** — The Chief Justice shall ensure that the plan for contin-uing education is made available to the public, in English and French, when it has been approved by the Judicial Council.

(3) **Goals** — Continuing education of judges has the following goals:

1. Maintaining and developing professional competence.

2. Maintaining and developing social awareness.

3. Encouraging personal growth.

1994, c. 12, s. 16; 1996, c. 25, s. 9(18), (20)

51.11 (1) Performance evaluation — The Chief Justice of the Ontario Court of Justice may establish a program of performance evaluation for provincial judges, and may implement the program when it has been reviewed and approved by the Judicial Council.

(2) **Duty of Chief Justice** — The Chief Justice shall make the existence of the pro-gram of performance evaluation public when it has been approved by the Judicial Council.

(3) **Goals** — The following are among the goals that the Chief Justice may seek to achieve by establishing a program of performance evaluation for judges:

1. Enhancing the performance of individual judges and of judges in general.

2. Identifying continuing education needs.

3. Assisting in the assignment of judges.

4. Identifying potential for professional development.

(4) **Scope of evaluation** — In a judge's performance evaluation, a decision made in a particular case shall not be considered.

(5) **Confidentiality** — A judge's performance evaluation is confidential and shall be disclosed only to the judge, his or her regional senior judge, and the person or persons conducting the evaluation.

(6) **Inadmissibility, exception** — A judge's performance evaluation shall not be admitted in evidence before the Judicial Council or any court or other tribunal unless the judge consents.

(7) **Application of subss. (5), (6)** — Subsections (5) and (6) apply to everything contained in a judge's performance evaluation and to all information collected in con-nection with the evaluation.

1994, c. 12, s. 16; 1996, c. 25, s. 9(18), (20)

51.12 Consultation — In establishing standards of conduct under section 51.9, a plan for continuing education under section 51.10 and a program of performance eval-uation under section 51.11, the Chief Justice of the Ontario Court of Justice shall con-sult with judges of that court and with such other persons as he or she considers appropriate.

1994, c. 12, s. 16; 1996, c. 25, s. 9(15), (18), (20)

Provincial Judges' Remuneration

51.13 (1) Provincial Judges Remuneration Commission — The committee known as the Provincial Judges Remuneration Commission in English and as Commission de rémunération des juges provinciaux in French is continued.

(2) Composition and functions — The composition and functions of the Commission are set out in Appendix A of the framework agreement set out in the Schedule to this Act.

(3) Framework agreement — The framework agreement forms part of this Act.

(4) Same — The reference in paragraph 11 of the framework agreement to public servants as defined in the *Public Service Act* is deemed to be a reference to public servants employed under Part III of the *Public Service of Ontario Act, 2006.*

1994, c. 12, s. 16; 2006, c. 35, Sched. C, s. 20(1)

Miscellaneous

52. (1) Meeting of Superior Court of Justice judges — The judges of the Superior Court of Justice shall meet at least once in each year, on a day fixed by the Chief Justice of the Superior Court of Justice, in order to consider this Act, the rules of court and the administration of justice generally.

(2) Same, Family Court — The judges of the Family Court shall meet at least once in each year, on a day fixed by the Chief Justice of the Superior Court of Justice, in order to consider this Act, the rules of court and the administration of justice generally.

(2.1) Same, Ontario Court of Justice — The judges of the Ontario Court of Justice shall meet at least once in each year, on a day fixed by the Chief Justice of that court, in order to consider this Act, the rules of court and the administration of justice generally.

Proposed Repeal — 52(2.1)

(2.1) [Repealed 2009, c. 33, Sched. 2, s. 20(12). Not in force at date of publication.]

(2.2) Same, regional senior judges, Superior Court of Justice — The regional senior judges of the Superior Court of Justice and the Senior Judge of the Family Court shall meet at least once in each year with the Chief Justice and the Associate Chief Justice of the Superior Court of Justice, on a day fixed by the Chief Justice, in order to consider this Act, the rules of court and the administration of justice generally.

(3) Same, Ontario Court of Justice — The regional senior judges of the Ontario Court of Justice shall meet at least once in each year with the Chief Justice of the Ontario Court of Justice, on a day fixed by the Chief Judge, in order to consider this Act, the rules of court and the administration of justice generally.

Proposed Repeal — 52(3)

(3) [Repealed 2009, c. 33, Sched. 2, s. 20(13). Not in force at date of publication.]

(4) Regional meeting of judges — The judges of the Court of Ontario in each region shall meet at least once in each year in order to consider this Act, the rules of court and the administration of justice in the region generally, on a day fixed jointly by the regional senior judge of the Superior Court of Justice and the regional senior judge of the Ontario Court of Justice.

(5) Report of recommendations — The judges meeting under this section shall report their recommendations to the Attorney General.

Proposed Repeal — 52(5)

(5) [Repealed 2009, c. 33, Sched. 2, s. 20(14). Not in force at date of publication.]

1994, c. 12, s. 17; 1996, c. 25, s. 9(8), (14), (15), (17), (18), (20); 1998, c. 20, Sched. A, s. 22(9), (10); 2006, c. 21, Sched. A, s. 7

53. (1) Regulations — The Lieutenant Governor in Council may make regulations,

(a) fixing the number of judges of the Superior Court of Justice for the purpose of clause 12(1)(e);

(a.1) fixing the number of judges of the Superior Court of Justice who are members of the Family Court appointed under clause 21.2(1)(e);

(a.2) fixing the remuneration of provincial judges;

(a.3) providing for the benefits to which provincial judges are entitled, including benefits respecting,

(i) leave of absence and vacations,

(ii) sick leave credits and payments in respect of those credits, and

(iii) pension benefits for provincial judges and their surviving spouses and children.

(b) fixing the remuneration of case management masters and providing for the benefits to which they are entitled;

(b.1) fixing the remuneration of deputy judges of the Small Claims Court;

(c) prescribing a period of time for the purposes of subsection 86.1(2);

(d) [Repealed 2006, c. 21, Sched. A, s. 8.]

(e) prescribing the maximum amount of a claim in the Small Claims Court for the purposes of subsection 23(1);

(f) prescribing the maximum amount of a claim over which a deputy judge may preside for the purposes of subsection 24(3);

(g) prescribing the minimum amount of a claim that may be appealed to the Divisional Court for the purposes of section 31;

(h) [Repealed 1994, c. 12, s. 18(4).]

(i) prescribing for each region the minimum number of judges of the Superior Court of Justice and of the Ontario Court of Justice who are to be assigned to that region;

(j) prescribing for each region the minimum number of judges of the Superior Court of Justice who are members of the Family Court and to be assigned to that region.

(2) Idem — A reduction in the number of judges of the Superior Court of Justice under clause (1)(a) does not affect appointments existing at the time of the reduction.

(3) Idem — If there is a conflict between a regulation made under clause (1)(a.2) or (a.3) and the Framework Agreement set out in the Schedule, the Framework Agreement prevails.

(4) Application of regulations — A regulation made under subsection (1) may be general or particular in its application.

(5) Definitions — In clause (1)(a.3),

"same-sex partner" [Repealed 2005, c. 5, s. 17(3).]

"spouse" means,

(a) a spouse as defined in section 1 of the *Family Law Act*, or

(b) either of two persons who live together in a conjugal relationship outside marriage.

1994, c. 12, s. 18; 1996, c. 25, ss. 1(8), 9(17), (18); 1998, c. 20, s. 2, Sched. A, ss. 11, 22(11); 1999, c. 6, s. 18(2), (3); 2002, c. 18, Sched. A, s. 4(1); 2005, c. 5, s. 17(2)–(4); 2006, c. 21, Sched. A, s. 8; 2009, c. 33, Sched. 2, s. 20(15)

PART III — UNIFIED FAMILY COURT

54. [Repealed 1994, c. 12, s. 19.]

55. [Repealed 1994, c. 12, s. 19.]

56. [Repealed 1994, c. 12, s. 19.]

57. [Repealed 1994, c. 12, s. 19.]

58. [Repealed 1994, c. 12, s. 19.]

59. [Repealed 1994, c. 12, s. 19.]

60. [Repealed 1994, c. 12, s. 19.]

61. [Repealed 1994, c. 12, s. 19.]

62. [Repealed 1994, c. 12, s. 19.]

63. [Repealed 1994, c. 12, s. 19.]

64. [Repealed 1994, c. 12, s. 19.]

PART IV — RULES OF COURT

65. (1) Civil Rules Committee — The committee known as the Civil Rules Committee is continued under the name Civil Rules Committee in English and Comité des règles en matière civile in French.

(2) Composition — The Civil Rules Committee shall be composed of,

(a) the Chief Justice and Associate Chief Justice of Ontario;

(a.1) the Chief Justice and associate chief justice of the Superior Court of Justice;

(a.2) the Chief Justice of the Ontario Court of Justice, or another judge of that court designated by the Chief Justice;

(b) **two judges of the Court of Appeal, who shall be appointed by the Chief Justice of Ontario;**

(c) **eight judges of the Superior Court of Justice, who shall be appointed by the Chief Justice of the Superior Court of Justice;**

(d) **one judge who was assigned to the Provincial Court (Civil Division) on the 1st day of October, 1989, who shall be appointed by the Chief Justice of the Superior Court of Justice;**

(e) **the Attorney General or a person designated by the Attorney General;**

(f) **one law officer of the Crown, who shall be appointed by the Attorney General;**

(g) **two persons employed in the administration of the courts, who shall be appointed by the Attorney General;**

(h) **four lawyers, who shall be appointed by The Law Society of Upper Canada;**

(i) **one lawyer, who shall be appointed by the Chief Justice of Ontario;**

(j) **four lawyers, who shall be appointed by the Chief Justice of the Superior Court of Justice.**

(3) **Idem** — The Chief Justice of Ontario shall preside over the Civil Rules Committee but, if the Chief Justice of Ontario is absent or so requests, another member designated by the Chief Justice of Ontario shall preside.

(4) **Tenure of office** — Each of the members of the Civil Rules Committee appointed under clauses (2)(b), (c), (f), (g), (h), (i) and (j) shall hold office for a period of three years and is eligible for reappointment.

(5) **Vacancies** — Where a vacancy occurs among the members appointed under clause (2)(b), (c), (f), (g), (h), (i) or (j), a new member similarly qualified may be appointed for the remainder of the unexpired term.

(6) **Quorum** — One-third of the members of the Civil Rules Committee constitutes a quorum.

1994, c. 12, s. 20; 1996, c. 25, s. 9(14), (17), (18), (20); 1998, c. 20, Sched. A, s. 12; 2006, c. 21, Sched. A, s. 9

66. (1) **Civil rules** — Subject to the approval of the Attorney General, the Civil Rules Committee may make rules for the Court of Appeal and the Superior Court of Justice in relation to the practice and procedure of those courts in all civil proceedings, except for proceedings in relation to which the Family Rules Committee may make rules under section 68.

(2) **Idem** — The Civil Rules Committee may make rules under subsection (1), even though they alter or conform to the substantive law, in relation to,

(a) conduct of proceedings in the courts;

(b) joinder of claims and parties, settlement of claims by or against persons under disability, whether or not a proceeding has been commenced in respect of the claim, the binding effect of orders and representation of parties;

(c) commencement of proceedings, representation of parties and service of process in or outside Ontario;

(d) disposition of proceedings without a hearing and its effect and authorizing the Court of Appeal to determine in the first instance a special case arising in a proceeding commenced in the Superior Court of Justice;

(e) pleadings;

(f) discovery and other forms of disclosure before hearing, including their scope and the admissibility and use of that discovery and disclosure in a proceeding;

(g) examination of witnesses in or out of court;

(h) jurisdiction of masters and case management masters, including the conferral on masters and case management masters of any jurisdiction of the Superior Court of Justice, including jurisdiction under an Act, but not including the trial of actions or jurisdiction conferred by an Act on a judge;

(i) jurisdiction and duties of officers;

(j) motions and applications, including the hearing of motions and applications in the absence of the public and prohibiting a party from making motions without leave;

(k) preservation of rights of parties pending the outcome of litigation, including sale, recovery of possession or preservation of property;

(l) interpleader;

(m) preparation for trial and offers to settle and their legal consequences;

(n) the mode and conduct of trials;

(o) the appointment by the court of independent experts, their remuneration and the admissibility and use of their reports;

(p) the discount rate to be used in determining the amount of an award in respect of future pecuniary damages;

(q) references of proceedings or issues in a proceeding and the powers of a person conducting a reference;

(r) costs of proceedings, including security for costs and, in the case of a person representing a party or other person, the representative's liability for, or disentitlement to, costs;

(s) enforcement of orders and process or obligations under the rules;

(t) the time for and procedure on appeals and stays pending appeal;

(u) payment into and out of court;

(v) the method of calculating the amount to be included in an award of damages to offset any liability for income tax on income from investment of the award;

(w) the prejudgment interest rate with respect to the rate of interest on damages for non-pecuniary loss;

(w.1) the issuance, service, filing and storage of documents by electronic means, including methods of completing and signing documents for those purposes.

(x) any matter that is referred to in an Act as provided for by rules of court.

(3) Same — Nothing in subsection (1) or (2) authorizes the making of rules that conflict with an Act, but rules may be made under subsection (1) supplementing the provisions of an Act in respect of practice and procedure.

(4) Same — Rules made under subsection (1) in relation to the matters described in clauses (2)(p), (v) and (w) shall be reviewed at least once in every four-year period.

(5) Application — A rule made under this section may be general or particular in its application.
1994, c. 12, s. 21; 1996, c. 25, ss. 1(9), 9(17); 1998, c. 18, Sched. B, s. 5(1); 2006, c. 21, Sched. A, s. 10, Sched. C, s. 105(4)

67. (1) Family Rules Committee — The committee known as the Family Rules Committee is continued under the name Family Rules Committee in English and Comité des règles en matière de droit de la famille in French.

(2) Composition — The Family Rules Committee is composed of,

    (a) the Chief Justice and Associate Chief Justice of Ontario;

    (b) the Chief Justice and Associate Chief Justice of the Superior Court of Justice;

    (c) the Senior Judge of the Family Court;

    (d) the Chief Justice of the Ontario Court of Justice or, an associate chief justice designated by the Chief Justice;

    (e) one judge of the Court of Appeal, who shall be appointed by the Chief Justice of Ontario;

    (f) four judges of the Superior Court of Justice appointed by the Chief Justice of the Superior Court of Justice appointed by the Chief Justice of the Superior Court of Justice, at least two of whom shall be judges of the Family Court referred to in clause 21.2(1)(d) or (e);

    (g) two judges of the Ontario Court of Justice, who shall be appointed by the Chief Justice of the Ontario Court of Justice;

    (h) the Attorney General or a person designated by the Attorney General;

    (i) one law officer of the Crown, who shall be appointed by the Attorney General;

    (j) two persons employed in the administration of the courts, who shall be appointed by the Attorney General;

    (k) four lawyers, who shall be appointed by The Law Society of Upper Canada;

    (l) four lawyers, who shall be appointed by the Chief Justice of the Superior Court of Justice; and

    (m) two lawyers, who shall be appointed by the Chief Justice of the Ontario Court of Justice.

(3) Who shall preside — The Chief Justice of Ontario shall preside over the Family Rules Committee but, if the Chief Justice of Ontario is absent or so requests, another member designated by the Chief Justice shall preside.

(4) Tenure of office — Each of the members of the Family Rules Committee appointed under clauses (2)(e), (f), (g), (i), (j), (k), (l) and (m) shall hold office for a period of three years and is eligible for reappointment.

(5) Vacancies — Where a vacancy occurs among the members appointed under clause (2)(e), (f), (g), (i), (j), (k), (l) or (m), a new member similarly qualified may be appointed for the remainder of the unexpired term.

(6) Quorum — One-third of the members of the Family Rules Committee constitutes a quorum.

1994, c. 12, s. 22; 1996, c. 25, ss. 1(10), (11), 9(17), (18); 1998, c. 20, Sched. A, ss. 13(2), 22(12); 2006, c. 21, Sched. A, s. 11

68. (1) Family rules — Subject to the approval of the Attorney General, the Family Rules Committee may make rules for the Court of Appeal, the Superior Court of Justice and the Ontario Court of Justice in relation to the practice and procedure of those courts in the proceedings referred to in the Schedule to section 21.8.

(2) **Same** — Subsections 66(2), (3) and (5) apply with necessary modifications to the Family Rules Committee making rules under subsection (1).

(3) [Repealed 2006, c. 21, Sched. A, s. 12.]

(4) [Repealed 2006, c. 19, Sched. D, s. 5(2).]

(5) [Repealed 2009, c. 11, s. 20.]

1996, c. 25, s. 9(17), (18); 1998, c. 20, Sched. A, s. 22(13); 2006, c. 19, Sched. D, s. 5(2); 2006, c. 21, Sched. A, s. 12; 2009, c. 11, s. 20

69. (1) **Criminal Rules Committee** — The committee known as the Criminal Rules Committee is continued under the name Criminal Rules Committee in English and Comité des règles en matière criminelle in French.

(2) **Idem** — The Criminal Rules Committee shall be composed of,

(a) the Chief Justice and Associate Chief Justice of Ontario, the Chief Justice and Associate Chief Justice of the Superior Court of Justice and the Chief Justice and associate chief justices of the Ontario Court of Justice;

(b) one judge of the Court of Appeal, who shall be appointed by the Chief Justice of Ontario;

(c) three judges of the Superior Court of Justice, who shall be appointed by the Chief Justice of the Superior Court of Justice;

(d) four judges of the Ontario Court of Justice, who shall be appointed by the Chief Justice of the Ontario Court of Justice;

(e) [Repealed 1994, c. 12, s. 23(2).]

(f) the Attorney General or a person designated by the Attorney General;

(g) one law officer of the Crown, who shall be appointed by the Attorney General;

(h) four Crown attorneys, deputy Crown attorneys or assistant Crown attorneys, who shall be appointed by the Attorney General;

(i) two persons employed in court administration, who shall be appointed by the Attorney General;

(j) two lawyers, who shall be appointed by The Law Society of Upper Canada;

(k) one lawyer, who shall be appointed by the Chief Justice of Ontario;

(l) one lawyer, who shall be appointed by the Chief Justice of the Superior Court of Justice; and

(m) two lawyers, who shall be appointed by the Chief Justice of the Ontario Court of Justice.

(3) **Idem** — The Chief Justice of Ontario shall preside over the Criminal Rules Committee but, if the Chief Justice of Ontario is absent or so requests, another member designated by the Chief Justice of Ontario shall preside.

(4) **Tenure of office** — Each of the members of the Criminal Rules Committee appointed under clauses (2)(b), (c), (d), (e), (g), (h), (i), (j), (k), (l) and (m) shall hold office for a period of three years and is eligible for reappointment.

(5) **Vacancies** — Where a vacancy occurs among the members appointed under clause (2)(b), (c), (d), (e), (g), (h), (i), (j), (k), (l) or (m), a new member similarly qualified may be appointed for the remainder of the unexpired term.

(6) Quorum — One-third of the members of the Criminal Rules Committee constitutes a quorum.

1994, c. 12, s. 23; 1996, c. 25, s. 9(14), (17), (18), (20)

70. (1) Criminal rules — At the request of the Court of Appeal, the Superior Court of Justice or the Ontario Court of Justice, the Criminal Rules Committee may prepare rules for the purposes of section 482 of the *Criminal Code* (Canada) for consideration by the relevant court.

(2) Provincial offences rules — Subject to the approval of the Attorney General, the Criminal Rules Committee may make rules for the Court of Appeal, the Superior Court of Justice and the Ontario Court of Justice in relation to the practice and procedure of those courts in proceedings under the *Provincial Offences Act*.

(3) Idem — The Criminal Rules Committee may make rules under subsection (2),

(a) regulating any matters relating to the practice and procedure of proceedings under the *Provincial Offences Act*;

(b) prescribing forms;

(c) regulating the duties of the employees of the courts;

(c.1) regulating the duties of municipal employees and other persons who act under the authority of agreements made under Part X of the *Provincial Offences Act*.

(d) prescribing and regulating the procedures under any Act that confers jurisdiction under the *Provincial Offences Act* on the Ontario Court of Justice or a judge or justice of the peace sitting in it;

(e) prescribing any matter relating to proceedings under the *Provincial Offences Act* that is referred to in an Act as provided for by the rules of court.

1994, c. 12, s. 24; 1996, c. 25, s. 9(17), (18); 1998, c. 4, s. 2; 2006, c. 21, Sched. A, s. 13

Part V — Administration of the Courts

[Heading amended 2006, c. 21, Sched. A, s. 14.]

71. Goals — The administration of the courts shall be carried on so as to,

(a) maintain the independence of the judiciary as a separate branch of government;

(b) recognize the respective roles and responsibilities of the Attorney General and the judiciary in the administration of justice;

(c) encourage public access to the courts and public confidence in the administration of justice;

(d) further the provision of high-quality services to the public; and

(e) promote the efficient use of public resources.

2006, c. 21, Sched. A, s. 14

Commentary: This provision expresses the Attorney General's responsibility for the administration of the courts. It represents a specific aspect of the Attorney General's responsibilities under s. 5(c) of the *Ministry of the Attorney General Act*, R.S.O. 1990, c. M.17.

72. Role of Attorney General — The Attorney General shall superintend all matters connected with the administration of the courts, other than the following:

1. Matters that are assigned by law to the judiciary, including authority to direct and supervise the sittings and the assignment of the judicial duties of the court.

2. Matters related to the education, conduct and discipline of judges and justices of the peace, which are governed by other provisions of this Act, the *Justices of the Peace Act* and Acts of the Parliament of Canada.

3. Matters assigned to the judiciary by a memorandum of understanding under section 77.

1994, c. 12, s. 25; 1996, c. 25, s. 9(17), (18), (20); 1998, c. 20, Sched. A, s. 22(14); 2006, c. 21, Sched. A, s. 14

73. Court officers and staff — (1) **Appointment** — Registrars, sheriffs, court clerks, assessment officers and any other administrative officers and employees that are considered necessary for the administration of the courts in Ontario may be appointed under Part III of the *Public Service of Ontario Act, 2006*.

(2) **Exercise of powers** — A power or duty given to a registrar, sheriff, court clerk, bailiff, assessment officer, Small Claims Court referee or official examiner under an Act, regulation or rule of court may be exercised or performed by a person or class of persons to whom the power or duty has been assigned by the Deputy Attorney General or a person designated by the Deputy Attorney General.

(3) **Same** — Subsection (2) applies in respect of an Act, regulation or rule of court made under the authority of the Legislature or of the Parliament of Canada.

(4) [Repealed 2006, c. 21, Sched. A, s. 14.]

1994, c. 12, s. 26; 1996, c. 25, s. 9(18); 1998, c. 20, Sched. A, s. 22(15); 2006, c. 21, Sched. A, s. 14; 2006, c. 35, Sched. C, s. 20(2)

74. Destruction of documents — Documents and other materials that are no longer required in a court office shall be disposed of in accordance with the directions of the Deputy Attorney General, subject to the approval of,

(a) in the Court of Appeal, the Chief Justice of Ontario;

(b) in the Superior Court of Justice, the Chief Justice of the Superior Court of Justice;

(c) in the Ontario Court of Justice, the Chief Justice of the Ontario Court of Justice.

1994, c. 12, s. 27; 2006, c. 21, Sched. A, s. 14

75. (1) Powers of chief or regional senior judge — The powers and duties of a judge who has authority to direct and supervise the sittings and the assignment of the judicial duties of his or her court include the following:

1. Determining the sittings of the court.

2. Assigning judges to the sittings.

3. Assigning cases and other judicial duties to individual judges.

4. Determining the sitting schedules and places of sittings for individual judges.

5. Determining the total annual, monthly and weekly workload of individual judges.

6. Preparing trial lists and assigning courtrooms, to the extent necessary to control the determination of who is assigned to hear particular cases.

(2) Powers re masters, case management masters — Subsection (1) applies, with necessary modifications, in respect of directing and supervising the sittings and assigning the judicial duties of masters and case management masters.

(3) [Repealed 2006, c. 21, Sched. A, s. 14.]

(4) [Repealed 2006, c. 21, Sched. A, s. 14.]

1994, c. 12, s. 28; 1996, c. 25, ss. 1(12), 9(17), (18); 1998, c. 20, Sched. A, s. 22(16); 2006, c. 21, Sched. A, s. 14

76. (1) Direction of court staff — In matters that are assigned by law to the judiciary, registrars, court clerks, court reporters, interpreters and other court staff shall act at the direction of the chief justice of the court.

(2) Same — Court personnel referred to in subsection (1) who are assigned to and present in a courtroom shall act at the direction of the presiding judge, justice of the peace, master or case management master while the court is in session.

1996, c. 25, ss. 1(13), 9(20); 2006, c. 21, Sched. A, s. 14; 2009, c. 33, Sched. 2, s. 20(16)

77. Memoranda of understanding between Attorney General and Chief Justices — (1) **Court of Appeal** — The Attorney General and the Chief Justice of Ontario may enter into a memorandum of understanding governing any matter relating to the administration of the Court of Appeal.

(2) Superior Court of Justice — The Attorney General and the Chief Justice of the Superior Court of Justice may enter into a memorandum of understanding governing any matter relating to the administration of that court.

Commentary: This section is amended to include Small Claims Court referee (after assessment officer). The powers and duties given to a Small Claims Court referee under an Act, regulation, or rule of court can now be assigned to courts administration staff under this section.

(3) Ontario Court of Justice — The Attorney General and the Chief Justice of the Ontario Court of Justice may enter into a memorandum of understanding governing any matter relating to the administration of that court.

(4) Scope — A memorandum of understanding under this section may deal with the respective roles and responsibilities of the Attorney General and the judiciary in the administration of justice, but shall not deal with any matter assigned by law to the judiciary.

(5) Publication — The Attorney General shall ensure that each memorandum of understanding entered into under this section is made available to the public, in English and French.

1994, c. 12, s. 29; 2006, c. 21, Sched. A, s. 14; 2006, c. 35, Sched. C, s. 20(4)

78. (1) Ontario Courts Advisory Council — The council known as the Ontario Courts Advisory Council is continued under the name Ontario Courts Advisory Council in English and Conseil consultatif des tribunaux de l'Ontario in French.

(2) Same — The Ontario Courts Advisory Council is composed of,

(a) the Chief Justice of Ontario, who shall preside, and the Associate Chief Justice of Ontario;

(b) the Chief Justice and the Associate Chief Justice of the Superior Court of Justice and the Senior Judge of the Family Court;

(c) the Chief Justice and the associate chief justices of the Ontario Court of Justice; and

(d) the regional senior judges of the Superior Court of Justice and of the Ontario Court of Justice.

Commentary: The provision requires court staff assigned to and present in the courtroom to act at the direction of the presiding judge or master while the court is in session.

(3) Mandate — The Ontario Courts Advisory Council shall meet to consider any matter relating to the administration of the courts that is referred to it by the Attorney General or that it considers appropriate on its own initiative, and shall make recommendations on the matter to the Attorney General and to its members.

1996, c. 25, ss. 1(14), 9(9); 2006, c. 21, Sched. A, s. 14

79. (1) Ontario Courts Management Advisory Committee — The committee known as the Ontario Courts Management Advisory Committee is continued under the name Ontario Courts Management Advisory Committee in English and Comité consultatif de gestion des tribunaux de l'Ontario in French.

(2) Same — The Ontario Courts Management Advisory Committee is composed of,

(a) the Chief Justice and Associate Chief Justice of Ontario, the Chief Justice and Associate Chief Justice of the Superior Court of Justice, the Senior Judge of the Family Court and the Chief Justice and associate chief justices of the Ontario Court of Justice;

(b) the Attorney General, the Deputy Attorney General, the Assistant Deputy Attorney General responsible for courts administration, the Assistant Deputy Attorney General responsible for criminal law and two other public servants chosen by the Attorney General;

(c) three lawyers appointed by The Law Society of Upper Canada and three lawyers appointed by the County and District Law Presidents' Association; and

(d) not more than six other persons, appointed by the Attorney General with the concurrence of the judges mentioned in clause (a) and the lawyers appointed under clause (c).

(3) Who presides — The following persons shall preside over meetings of the Committee, by rotation at intervals fixed by the Committee:

1. A judge mentioned in clause (2)(a), selected by the judges mentioned in that clause.

2. The Attorney General, or a person mentioned in clause (2)(b) and designated by the Attorney General.

3. A lawyer appointed under clause (2)(c), selected by the lawyers appointed under that clause.

4. A person appointed under clause (2)(d), selected by the persons appointed under that clause.

(4) Function of Committee — The function of the Committee is to consider and recommend to the relevant bodies or authorities policies and procedures to promote the better administration of justice and the effective use of human and other resources in the public interest.

1996, c. 25, s. 9(14), (17), (18), (20); 1998, c. 20, Sched. A, s. 18; 2006, c. 21, Sched. A, s. 14

79.1 (1) Regions — For administrative purposes related to the administration of justice in the province, Ontario is divided into the regions prescribed under subsection (2).

(2) Regulations — The Lieutenant Governor in Council may make regulations prescribing regions for the purposes of this Act.

2006, c. 21, Sched. A, s. 14

79.2 (1) Regional Courts Management Advisory Committee — The committee in each region known as the Regional Courts Management Advisory Committee is continued under the name Regional Courts Management Advisory Committee in English and Comité consultatif régional de gestion des tribunaux in French, and is composed of,

(a) the regional senior judge of the Superior Court of Justice, the regional senior judge of the Ontario Court of Justice and, in a region where the Family Court has jurisdiction, a judge chosen by the Chief Justice of the Superior Court of Justice;

(b) the regional director of courts administration for the Ministry of the Attorney General and the regional director of Crown attorneys;

(c) two lawyers appointed jointly by the presidents of the county and district law associations in the region; and

(d) not more than two other persons, appointed by the Attorney General with the concurrence of the judges mentioned in clause (a) and the lawyers appointed under clause (c).

(2) Who presides — The following persons shall preside over meetings of the Committee, by rotation at intervals fixed by the Committee:

1. A judge mentioned in clause (1)(a), selected by the judges mentioned in that clause.

2. An official mentioned in clause (1)(b), selected by the officials mentioned in that clause.

3. A lawyer appointed under clause (1)(c), selected by the lawyers appointed under that clause.

4. A person appointed under clause (1)(d), selected by the persons appointed under that clause.

(3) Function of Committee — The function of the Committee is to consider and recommend to the relevant bodies or authorities policies and procedures for the region to promote the better administration of justice and the effective use of human and other resources in the public interest.

(4) Frequency of meetings — The Committee shall meet at least once each year.

2006, c. 21, Sched. A, s. 14

79.3 (1) Annual report on administration of courts — Within six months after the end of every fiscal year, the Attorney General shall cause a report to be prepared on the administration of the courts during that fiscal year, in consultation with the

Chief Justice of Ontario, the Chief Justice of the Superior Court of Justice and the Chief Justice of the Ontario Court of Justice.

(2) **Same** — The annual report shall provide information about progress in meeting the goals set out in section 71 and shall be made available to the public in English and French.

(3) **Inclusion in Ministry's annual report** — The Attorney General may cause all or part of the annual report on the administration of the courts to be incorporated into the corresponding annual report referred to in the *Ministry of the Attorney General Act*.

2006, c. 21, Sched. A, s. 14

PART VI — JUDGES AND OFFICERS

80. Oath of office — Every judge or officer of a court in Ontario, including a deputy judge of the Small Claims Court, shall, before entering on the duties of office, take and sign the following oath or affirmation in either the English or French language:

> I solemnly swear (affirm) that I will faithfully, impartially and to the best of my skill and knowledge execute the duties of ....
>
> So help me God. (*Omit this line in an affirmation*)

1994, c. 12, s. 30

81. Persona designata abolished — Where an adjudicative function is given by an Act to a judge or officer of a court in Ontario, the jurisdiction shall be deemed to be given to the court.

Commentary: Provincial statutes often gave jurisdiction to "a judge of the county or district court" or "a judge of the Supreme Court," instead of simply referring to "the court." This form of language arose particularly frequently in statutes that can be traced to the latter part of the 19th century. Over the years, provisions giving jurisdiction to "a judge" instead of "a court" generated a great deal of litigation on the issue of whether the judge was to act as the court or as a *persona designata*. In many cases, it was decided that the judge was acting as *persona designata*.

Where a judge acted as *persona designata*, several consequences followed. Since the judge was not acting as the court, the rules of court did not apply, the powers of the court did not apply and no appeal could be taken. These consequences resulted in considerable confusion. Some of the most serious drawbacks of the *persona designata* concept were dealt with in the *Judges' Orders Enforcement Act*, R.S.O. 1980, c. 222. That Act provided for enforcement of the orders of a judge acting as *persona designata*, for the judge to have jurisdiction to award costs, and for an appeal from the judge's order.

82. Liability of judges and other officers — The following persons have the same immunity from liability as judges of the Superior Court of Justice:

1. Judges of all courts in Ontario, including judges in the Small Claims Court and deputy judges of that court.

2. Masters.

3. Case management masters.

1994, c. 12, s. 32; 1996, c. 25, ss. 1(15), 9(17)

Commentary: Every judge of a court in Ontario has absolute immunity from civil liability for any acts related to or in connection with his or her judicial capacity. Judicial immunity is an essential component of judicial independence permitting judges to act impartially, without fear of personal liability, and independently. The law in this area is well established and numerous courts have struck out actions on motions on the basis of judicial immunity. See *Tsai v. Klug* (2005), [2005] O.J. No. 2277, 2005 CarswellOnt 2359 at paras. 4-9, 15 and 17-18 (Ont. S.C.J.); additional reasons at (2005), [2005] O.J. No. 2889, 2005 CarswellOnt 2914 (Ont. S.C.J.); affirmed (2006), [2006] O.J. No. 665, 2006 CarswellOnt 1020, 207 O.A.C. 225 at para. 2 (Ont. C.A.); leave to appeal denied (2006), [2006] S.C.C.A. No. 169, 2006 CarswellOnt 5001, 2006 CarswellOnt 5002, 225 O.A.C. 399 (note), 358 N.R. 391 (note) (S.C.C.); *Kopyto v. Ontario Court of Justice (Provincial Division)* (February 28, 1995), Doc. T 2861/1994, [1995] O.J. No. 601 at paras. 32-46 (Ont. Gen. Div.); *Rivard c. Morier*, 1985 CarswellQue 92, [1985] S.C.J. No. 81, 1985 CarswellQue 115, 64 N.R. 46, 17 Admin. L.R. 230, [1985] 2 S.C.R. 716, 23 D.L.R. (4th) 1 at paras. 67-81 and 85-113 (S.C.C.); *K. (L.M.) v. Ontario (Ministry of Community & Social Services)* (1996), 1996 CarswellOnt 1297, [1996] O.J. No. 812 at para. 21 (Ont. Gen. Div.); *Baryluk v. Campbell*, 2008 CarswellOnt 6355, 61 C.C.L.T. (3d) 292, [2008] O.J. No. 4279 (Ont. S.C.J.); additional reasons at 2009 CarswellOnt 3900, 66 C.C.L.T. (3d) 160 (Ont. S.C.J.) at paras. 19–32; *Dyce v. Ontario* (2007), [2007] O.J. No. 2142, 2007 CarswellOnt 3437 at para. 23 (Ont. S.C.J.).

The principle of judicial immunity was reviewed by Karakatsanis J. in *Tsai, supra*, affirmed on appeal, with leave to appeal to the Supreme Court of Canada denied (at paras. 4–7):

Judicial Immunity

The Plaintiff takes the position that any protection or immunity to judges in the exercise of their judicial functions cannot encompass an illegal act. By definition, the plaintiff argues, an illegal act would clearly be beyond the scope of their judicial capacity.

Section 82 of the *Courts of Justice Act* states that a Deputy Small Claims Court Judge has the same immunity as a Judge of the Superior Court. Similar provisions have been found to provide absolute civil immunity for commissioners of inquiries and justices of the peace in the execution of their judicial function.

In *Morier and Boiley v. Rivard*, [1985] 2 S.C.R. 716 (S.C.C.) at pp. 737 ff, the Supreme Court of Canada considered whether judicial immunity extended to acts that may be without or in excess of jurisdiction. The Supreme Court of Canada held that the civil immunity of Superior Court Judges in Ontario and Quebec was absolute. *While the immunity does not extend to purely personal acts, judges are however immune for any acts done in the course of or in connection with their legal duties, even if the acts are malicious or mal fides.* The Court cites with approval a number of old English cases. At page 737:

In *Fray v. Blackburn* (1863), 3 B. & S. 576, it states at p. 578: It is a principle of our law that no action will lie against a Judge of one of the superior Courts for a judicial act, though it be alleged to have been done maliciously and corruptly ... The public are deeply interested in this rule, which, indeed, exists for their benefit, and was established in order to secure the independence of the Judges and prevent their being harassed by vexatious actions. [Emphasis added.]

In *Tsai, supra*, the Court dismissed the claim on the basis of judicial immunity in respect of conduct claimed to be unlawful and not part of the defendants' judicial duties. That alleged conduct was as follows: (at paras. 2 and 17-18):

The pleadings against Deputy Judge Libman allege that he turned a blind eye to Mr. Tsai's representation, he collaborated with Mr. Klug to fraudulently set aside the plaintiff's default judgment in violation of the rules; that he was in breach of trust by not sending his decision to Mr. Tsai; that he dealt with the motion without a transcript; and that he was the leader of an organized team in Toronto Small Claims Court to collaborate with Mr. Klug to rig and manipulate the justice system to create social injustice. The pleadings allege fraud misrepresentation, breach of trust and malice against Deputy Judge Winer for hearing and dismissing a non-existent claim and phantom defence in breach of trust. They allege that he allowed Ms. Tsai to move to re-instate the claim thereby imposing on the plaintiff to pursue the claim so that Mr. Klug would reap the costs; that he illegally acquired documents during the hearing from Mr.

Klug; and that he forged reasons for judgment as the non-certified transcript, without indicating Mr. Tsai's appearance; and that he was a member of Deputy Judge Libman's team to rig and manipulate the justice system.

The Court in *Kopyto*, *supra*, similarly dismissed the claim on the basis of judicial immunity in similar circumstances to the present action. In that action, Mr. Kopyto alleged that the judge wrongly denied his right to act for his client, falsely advised his client that he could not act, and implied that he was incompetent. Mr. Kopyto claimed that such conduct was malicious and for the purpose of causing him financial harm and that he suffered financial harm because he could not act for the client. Mr. Kopyto claimed in injurious falsehood and breaches of ss. 11 and 24 of the *Charter of Rights and Freedoms*. In dismissing the action the court stated as follows (at paras. 36–40):

> It is a principle of our law that no action will lie against a judge of one of the superior courts for a judicial act, even if it be alleged to have been done maliciously or corruptly...
>
> Immunity from suit is not for the sake of the judges but for the sake of the public who must be assured that justice is being administered with freedom of thought and independence of judgment.
>
> Even though a Judge of a superior court goes outside her jurisdiction, the judge is not liable as long as acting judicially. [Emphasis added.]
>
> [*Kopyto v. Ontario Court of Justice (Provincial Division)*, O.J. No. 601 at paras. 36-40 (Ont S.C.J.).]

In *Morier*, the Supreme Court of Canada applied judicial immunity to immunize the defendants from liability in respect of the following wide range of allegations (at para. 6):

> 4. As will be explained below, defendants acted without jurisdiction and/or exceeded the jurisdiction they claimed to have, in particular in that:
>
> 4.1 they contravened the Act and the *audi alteram partem* rule of natural justice;
>
> 4.2 defendants failed to comply with s. 34.3 of the *Police Act* where plaintiff is concerned;
>
> 4.3 defendants acted in a discriminatory manner toward plaintiff;
>
> 4.4 defendants contravened the provisions of the Charter of Human Rights and Freedoms;
>
> 4.5 defendant Gilbert Morier could not sign the report relating to plaintiff and Terreau & Racine Ltée, since he did not hear the evidence;
>
> 4.6 the quorum of two in the matter of Terreau & Racine Ltée, as required by the Act, was not observed by defendant Gilbert Morier;
>
> 4.7 defendants knowingly committed a fraud on the law;
>
> [*Morier v. Rivard*, [1985] S.C.J. 81 at para. 6.]

The Supreme Court of Canada dismissed the claim, finding (at para. 110):

> It is possible that they exceeded their jurisdiction by doing or failing to do the acts mentioned in the statement of claim. It is possible that they contravened the rules of natural justice, that they did not inform respondent of the facts alleged against him or that they did not give him an opportunity to be heard. It is possible that they contravened the *Charter of Human Rights and Freedoms* ... in my opinion these are not allegations which may be used as the basis for an action in damages.
>
> [*Morier v. Rivard*, [1985] S.C.J. 81 at para. 110.]

In *Hamalengwa*, judicial immunity was even applied to the writing of a letter to the Law Society of Upper Canada. Furthermore, in *Pispidikis*, the court found that the judge was judicially immune in respect of his extra-jurisdictional sentence of one year of imprisonment for a charge that had a maximum six-month sentence. See *Hamalengwa v. Duncan* (2005), 2005 CarswellOnt 8201, [2005] O.J. No. 851 at para. 28 (Ont. S.C.J.); affirmed (2005), 2005 CarswellOnt 4451, [2005] O.J. No. 3993, 202 O.A.C. 233, 135 C.R.R. (2d) 251 at paras. 10-

11 (Ont. C.A.); leave to appeal denied (2006), [2005] S.C.C.A. No. 508, 2006 CarswellOnt 928, 2006 CarswellOnt 929, 221 O.A.C. 399 (note), 352 N.R. 196 (note) (S.C.C.); *Pispidikis v. Ontario (Justice of the Peace)* (2002), 2002 CarswellOnt 4508, [2002] O.J. No. 5081, (sub nom. *Pispidikis v. Scroggie)* 62 O.R. (3d) 596 (Ont. S.C.J.); additional reasons at (2003), 2003 CarswellOnt 1357 at paras. 37-39 (Ont. S.C.J.); affirmed (2003), [2003] O.J. No. 4830, 2003 CarswellOnt 4957, (sub nom. *Pispidikis v. Scroggie)* 68 O.R. (3d) 665, (sub nom. *Pispidikis v. Scroggie)* 180 O.A.C. 45 (Ont. C.A.).

Case Law: *Mayer v. Zuker* (2009), 2009 CarswellOnt 1781, 249 O.A.C. 1 (Ont. Div. Ct.), Low J.

The respondent was a judge who had presided over the appellant's family law action. The appellants alleged the negative decision of respondent judge was motivated by malice. The appellant then appealed the decision of the respondent judge and obtained a transcript of the proceedings which had been edited by the respondent, thereby delaying the appeal. The allegations that the respondent has fabricated evidence and obstructed justice did not give rise to a civil cause of action even if true. As there was no allegation in the appellants' pleading concerning the conduct of the respondent that did not fall within the ambit of activities either directly related or ancillary to judicial functions, the respondent was absolutely insulated from civil action by the principle of judicial immunity.

Bérubé v. Ontario Court of Justice, 2010 ONSC 1677, 2010 CarswellOnt 1930, [2010] O.J. No. 1271 (Ont. S.C.J.).

Motion by defendants, Mr. Justice R. Lajoie and her Majesty the Queen in right of Ontario to set aside a noting in default, and dismiss the action pursuant to r. 21 of the *Rules of Civil Procedure*, R.R.O. 1990, Reg. 194.

Citing *Hunt v. T & N plc*, 1990 CarswellBC 216, 1990 CarswellBC 759, EYB 1990-67014, (sub nom. *Hunt v. Carey Canada Inc.)* [1990] S.C.J. No. 93, [1990] 2 S.C.R. 959, 43 C.P.C. (2d) 105, 117 N.R. 321, 4 C.O.H.S.C. 173 (headnote only), (sub nom. *Hunt v. Carey Canada Inc.)* [1990] 6 W.W.R. 385, 49 B.C.L.R. (2d) 273, (sub nom. *Hunt v. Carey Canada Inc.)* 74 D.L.R. (4th) 321, 4 C.C.L.T. (2d) 1 (S.C.C.), counsel for the moving parties set out the legal principles applicable on a r. 21 motion to dismiss an action as follows:

> a) The allegations of fact in the statement of claim, unless patently ridiculous or incapable of proof, must be accepted as proven;
>
> b) The moving party, in order to succeed, must show that it is plain, obvious and beyond doubt that the Plaintiff could not succeed;
>
> c) A claim will not be dismissed simply because it is novel; and
>
> d) The Statement of Claim must be read generously with allowance for inadequacies due to drafting deficiencies.

Defendants argued that justices judicially immune from civil liability for any acts related to or ancillary to their judicial capacity.

Section 82 of the *Courts of Justice Act* states that a Deputy Small Claims Court Judge has the same immunity as a Judge of the Superior Court. Similar provisions have been found to provide absolute civil immunity for commissioners of inquiries and justices of the peace in the execution of their judicial function.

See *Rivard c. Morier*, 23 D.L.R. (4th) 1, [1985] 2 S.C.R. 716, 1985 CarswellQue 115, [1985] S.C.J. No. 81, 1985 CarswellQue 92, 17 Admin. L.R. 230, 64 N.R. 46 (S.C.C.) where the Supreme Court of Canada considered whether judicial immunity extended to acts that may be without or in excess of jurisdiction. It held that the civil immunity of Superior Court judges in Ontario and Quebec absolute. While the immunity does not extend to purely personal acts, judges are, however, immune for any acts done in the course of or in connection with their legal duties, even if the acts are malicious or *mal fides*.

The judges in the Province of Ontario are not agents and servants of the Crown. The Attorney General of Ontario cannot tell a judge how to decide his case. His or her role is to protect challenges on the constitutionality and legality of provincial laws. Le Dain J. in *R. v. Valente (No. 2)* (1985), 1985 CarswellOnt 948, 19 C.R.R. 354, 23 C.C.C. (3d) 193, 14 O.A.C. 79, 64 N.R. 1, 37 M.V.R. 9, [1985] 2 S.C.R. 673, 49 C.R. (3d) 97, 24 D.L.R. (4th) 161, [1985] S.C.J. No. 77, 1985 CarswellOnt 129, [1986] D.L.Q. 85, 52 O.R. (2d) 779 (S.C.C.) at 708 [S.C.R.] states:

> The third essential condition of judicial independence for purposes of s. 11(d) [*Charter of Rights and Freedoms*] is, in my opinion, the institutional independence of the tribunal with respect to matters of administration bearing directly on the exercise of its judicial function. . . .

There is ample authority for an award of full indemnity costs where unsubstantiated allegations of dishonesty, illegality, and conspiracy are advanced without merit. Allegations made or conduct by a party that are "reprehensible, scandalous, or outrageous" fall within the ambit of an award of full indemnity costs, see *Schreiber v. Mulroney*, 2007 CarswellOnt 5267, [2007] O.J. No. 3191 (Ont. S.C.J.); leave to appeal refused 2007 CarswellOnt 7184 (Ont. Div. Ct.); *Penney v. Penney*, 2006 CarswellOnt 7605, [2006] O.J. No. 4802 (Ont. S.C.J.); *Donmor Industries Ltd. v. Kremlin Canada Inc.*, 1992 CarswellOnt 1728, 6 O.R. (3d) 506, [1992] O.J. No. 4055 (Ont. Gen. Div.); and *Apotex Inc. v. Egis Pharmaceuticals*, 37 C.P.R. (3d) 335, 4 O.R. (3d) 321, 1991 CarswellOnt 3149, [1991] O.J. No. 1232 (Ont. S.C.J.).

Collins v. R. (2010), 2010 ONSC 6542, 2010 CarswellOnt 9265, 223 C.R.R. (2d) 370, [2011] 3 C.T.C. 211, [2010] O.J. No. 5210 (Ont. S.C.J.); affirmed 2011 ONCA 461, 2011 CarswellOnt 4984 (Ont. C.A.); leave to appeal refused 2012 CarswellOnt 251, 2012 CarswellOnt 252, (sub nom. *Collins v. Canada*) 432 N.R. 390 (note), (sub nom. *Collins v. Canada*) 294 O.A.C. 396 (note) (S.C.C.).

Defendant, Justice Elizabeth Heneghan, moved to have claim struck insofar as it asserts a claim against her.

For the purpose of motion under r. 21.01(1)(b) of the *Rules of Civil Procedure* facts pleaded must be accepted and are capable of being proven.

The law respecting judicial immunity was reviewed by Karakatsanis J. in *Tsai v. Klug*, 2005 CarswellOnt 2359, [2005] O.J. No. 2277, [2005] O.T.C. 480 (Ont. S.C.J.); additional reasons at [2005] O.J. No. 2889, 2005 CarswellOnt 2914 (Ont. S.C.J.); leave to appeal refused 2006 CarswellOnt 1020, [2006] O.J. No. 665, 207 O.A.C. 225 (Ont. C.A.); leave to appeal refused 2006 CarswellOnt 5001, 2006 CarswellOnt 5002, [2006] S.C.C.A. No. 169, 225 O.A.C. 399 (note), 358 N.R. 391 (note) (S.C.C.). The plaintiffs alleged that two Deputy Small Claims Court judges acted fraudulently, unlawfully and unconstitutionally. Karakatsanis J. struck the claim, and dismissed the action.

The Court of Appeal in *Tsai* expressed agreement with the reasons of Karakatsanis J.

See *Baryluk v. Campbell*, 2008 CarswellOnt 6355, [2008] O.J. No. 4279, 61 C.C.L.T. (3d) 292 (Ont. S.C.J.); additional reasons at 2009 CarswellOnt 3900, [2009] O.J. No. 2772, 66 C.C.L.T. (3d) 160 (Ont. S.C.J.), Hackland J., referring to *Tsai*, stated:

> [31] Like Karakatsanis J., I specifically reject the argument that a pleading of bad faith or deliberate excess of jurisdiction can defeat the principle of judicial immunity. If it were otherwise, mere allegations in pleadings could place judges in the position of having to defend the manner in which they have discharged their judicial duties in subsequent legal proceedings commenced by disaffected litigants. To place judges in this position would be seriously to undermine the principle of judicial independence.

See also *Taylor v. Canada (Attorney General)*, 2000 CarswellNat 3253, 253 N.R. 252, 184 D.L.R. (4th) 706, [2000] F.C.J. No. 268, 2000 CarswellNat 354, 37 C.H.R.R. D/368, 44

C.P.C. (4th) 1, [2000] 3 F.C. 298, 21 Admin. L.R. (3d) 27 (Fed. C.A.); leave to appeal refused 263 N.R. 399 (note), [2000] S.C.C.A. No. 213, 2000 CarswellNat 2567, 2000 CarswellNat 2566 (S.C.C.) the Federal Court of Appeal concluded, contrary to the Ontario authorities cited, that there is an exception to judicial immunity in the event that a judge knowingly acts beyond jurisdiction. The claim against Heneghan J. discloses no reasonable cause of action.

The plaintiff to file a fresh as amended Statement of Claim.

Kipiniak v. Superior Court of Justice Small Claims Court, 2011 HRTO 793 (Ont. Human Rights Trib.).

An Application was submitted under section 34 of the *Human Rights Code*, R.S.O. 1990, c. H.19 ("Code"), as amended. The applicant alleged that the respondent discriminated against him with respect to services because of a disability. First, he said, a deputy judge did not permit him to make an audio recording of a Small Claims Court hearing using his own personal recorder. Second, he alleges that during a mediation at the Small Claims Court, the mediator did not permit him to make an audio recording. According to the applicant, because of a disability he is unable to take notes and he requires the recording as an accommodation.

The Tribunal issued a Notice of Intent to Dismiss, seeking submissions from the applicant on whether the Application falls outside its jurisdiction as a result of the doctrine of judicial immunity. See *Cartier v. Nairn*, 2009 HRTO 2208, 2009 CarswellOnt 9111, 8 Admin. L.R. (5th) 150 (Ont. Human Rights Trib.) and *Hazel v. Ainsworth Engineered Corp.*, 2009 HRTO 2180, 2009 CarswellOnt 9730 (Ont. Human Rights Trib.).

The applicant argued the Application was filed against the Court and not an individual judge.

It is plain and obvious that the actions fell within the concept of judicial immunity and are therefore outside the Tribunal's jurisdiction (power) to decide.

The principle of judicial immunity has been applied to protect judicial actors from human rights complaints. See *Taylor v. Canada (Attorney General)*, 2000 CarswellNat 354, 2000 CarswellNat 3253, [2000] F.C.J. No. 268, [2000] 3 F.C. 298, 21 Admin. L.R. (3d) 27, 44 C.P.C. (4th) 1, 37 C.H.R.R. D/368, 184 D.L.R. (4th) 706, 253 N.R. 252 (Fed. C.A.); leave to appeal refused 2000 CarswellNat 2566, 2000 CarswellNat 2567, [2000] S.C.C.A. No. 213, 263 N.R. 399 (note) (S.C.C.).

In *Gonzalez v. British Columbia (Ministry of Attorney General)*, 2009 BCSC 639, 2009 CarswellBC 1274, 67 C.H.R.R. D/268, 95 B.C.L.R. (4th) 185, 97 Admin. L.R. (4th) 195, [2009] 11 W.W.R. 132 (B.C. S.C.), the Supreme Court of B.C. upheld a decision of the British Columbia Human Rights Tribunal in which it found that it lacked jurisdiction to deal with part of a complaint alleging discrimination by a provincial court judge on the basis of disability in respect of employment and services.

As Lord Bridge of Harwich said in *McC v. Mullan* (1984), [1984] 3 All E.R. 908, [1985] A.C. 528 (U.K. H.L.) at p. 916 [All E.R.]

> The principle underlying this rule is clear. If one judge in a thousand acts dishonestly within his jurisdiction to the detriment of a party before him, it is less harmful to the health of society to leave that party without a remedy than that nine hundred and ninety-nine honest judges should be harassed by vexatious litigation alleging malice in the exercise of their proper jurisdiction.

Judicial independence, protected in the Constitution, includes the ability of the judge to make determinations about *how* a case is conducted. See *R. v. Beauregard*, 1986 CarswellNat 1004, 1986 CarswellNat 737, EYB 1986-67283, [1986] S.C.J. No. 50, (sub nom. *Beauregard v. Canada*) [1986] 2 S.C.R. 56, 70 N.R. 1, 30 D.L.R. (4th) 481, 26 C.R.R. 59 (S.C.C.) at para. 21. The Superior Court, like the judge, benefits from this protection and this portion of the Application was dismissed.

At this stage it is not plain and obvious that the actions of the mediator, which may not be protected by the principles of judicial independence, are subject to immunity. Accordingly, the Application will be delivered to the respondent, which need only respond to the portions of it that relate to mediation.

Mennes v. Burgess, 2011 ONSC 3711, 2011 CarswellOnt 9691 (Ont. S.C.J.); additional reasons at 2011 ONSC 5515, 2011 CarswellOnt 10570 (Ont. S.C.J.).

An Application was brought by Mennes pursuant to Rule 14.05(3)(g) of the *Rules of Civil Procedure*, R.R.O. 194. The Application was for interpretation of section 24(2)(b) of the *Courts of Justice Act*, R.S.O. 1990, c. C.43, which concerns the appointment of small claims and deputy judges.

The applicant was entitled to have a matter heard in any court, including Small Claims Court, by an impartial and unbiased member of the judiciary. See *R. v. Curragh Inc.*, 1997 CarswellNS 88, 1997 CarswellNS 89, [1997] S.C.J. No. 33, [1997] 1 S.C.R. 537, 159 N.S.R. (2d) 1, 113 C.C.C. (3d) 481, 144 D.L.R. (4th) 614, 468 A.P.R. 1, 5 C.R. (5th) 291, 209 N.R. 252 (S.C.C.), "when a court of appeal determines that the trial judge was biased or demonstrated a reasonable apprehension of bias, that finding retroactively renders all the decisions and orders made during the trial void and without effect.".

Issues of recusal for bias have often been dealt with in the context of an appeal; see *Curragh, supra, Roskam v. Rogers Cable*, 2008 CarswellOnt 2958, [2008] O.J. No. 2049, *(sub nom. Roskam v. Rogers Cable (A Business))* 173 C.R.R. (2d) 157 (Ont. Div. Ct.) and *Rando Drugs Ltd. v. Scott*, 2007 ONCA 553, 2007 CarswellOnt 4888, [2007] O.J. No. 2999, 86 O.R. (3d) 641, *(sub nom. Rando Drugs Ltd. c. Scott)* 86 O.R. (3d) 653, 42 C.P.C. (6th) 23, 284 D.L.R. (4th) 756, 229 O.A.C. 1 (Ont. C.A.); leave to appeal refused 2008 CarswellOnt 353, 2008 CarswellOnt 354, 384 N.R. 398 (note), 249 O.A.C. 399 (note) (S.C.C.).

This was, in reality, an appeal from the deputy judge.

The proper forum for dealing with a complaint about a decision of a justice is the process of appeal; see *Moreau-Bérubé c. Nouveau-Brunswick*, 2002 SCC 11, 2002 CarswellNB 46, 2002 CarswellNB 47, REJB 2002-27816, [2002] S.C.J. No. 9, [2002] 1 S.C.R. 249, *(sub nom. Conseil de la magistrature (N.-B.) v. Moreau-Bérubé)* 245 N.B.R. (2d) 201, *(sub nom. Conseil de la magistrature (N.-B.) v. Moreau-Bérubé)* 636 A.P.R. 201, 36 Admin. L.R. (3d) 1, *(sub nom. Nouveau-Brunswick (Conseil de la magistrature) v. Moreau-Bérubé)* 281 N.R. 201, *(sub nom. Moreau-Bérubé v. New Brunswick (Judicial Council))* 209 D.L.R. (4th) 1 (S.C.C.). It is not through litigation brought against a justice personally and such an action will be dismissed: see *Mayer v. Zuker*, 2009 CarswellOnt 1781, [2009] O.J. No. 1354, 249 O.A.C. 1 (Ont. Div. Ct.), *Dyce v. Ontario*, [2007] O.J. No. 2142, 2007 CarswellOnt 3437 (Ont. S.C.J.) and *Tsai v. Klug*, 2005 CarswellOnt 2359, [2005] O.J. No. 2277, [2005] O.T.C. 480 (Ont. S.C.J.); additional reasons at [2005] O.J. No. 2889, 2005 CarswellOnt 2914 (Ont. S.C.J.); leave to appeal refused 2006 CarswellOnt 1020, [2006] O.J. No. 665, 207 O.A.C. 225 (Ont. C.A.); leave to appeal refused 2006 CarswellOnt 5001, 2006 CarswellOnt 5002, [2006] S.C.C.A. No. 169, 225 O.A.C. 399 (note), 358 N.R. 391 (note) (S.C.C.)). This matter was a civil matter for a declaration concerning a judicial officer carrying out his duties as a deputy judge of the Small Claims Court. There was a personal claim against the judge being pursued in this matter which created liability, if only to appear and defend his actions. This application offended the principles of judicial immunity as codified for the respondent in section 82 of the *Courts of Justice Act*. The Application was dismissed.

Tao v. Small Claims Court of Toronto, 2013 HRTO 25 (Ont. Human Rights Trib.).

The applicant states that an unnamed judge of the Small Claims Court of Toronto rendered an unfair decision in a matter before the Small Claims Court. The tribunal has stated that it has no jurisdiction to hear applications against courts and tribunals based on the execution of adjudicative duties or decision making because of the doctrine of judicial or adjudicative immunity. The tribunal directed the applicant to provide written submissions regarding jurisdiction issue by December 19, 2012. The applicant filed very limited submissions on December 10, 2012 opposing dismissal. In *Cartier v. Nairn*, 2009 HRTO 2208 (Ont. Human Rights Trib.), the Tribunal described the doctrine of judicial immunity. The principle of judicial immunity has been applied to protect judicial actors from human rights complaints. See *Taylor v. Canada (Attorney General)*, 2000 CarswellNat 354, 2000 CarswellNat 3253, [2000] 3 F.C. 298, 21 Admin. L.R. (3d) 27, 44 C.P.C. (4th) 1, 184 D.L.R. (4th) 706, 37 C.H.R.R. D/368, 253 N.R. 252, [2000] F.C.J. No. 268 (Fed. C.A.); leave to appeal refused 2000 CarswellNat 2566, 2000 CarswellNat 2567, 263 N.R. 399 (note), [2000] S.C.C.A. No. 213 (S.C.C.). See also *Gonzalez v. British Columbia (Ministry of Attorney General)*, 2009 BCSC 639, 2009 CarswellBC 1274, 97 Admin. L.R. (4th) 195, 95 B.C.L.R. (4th) 185, [2009] 11 W.W.R. 132, 67 C.H.R.R. D/268 (B.C. S.C.).

Application dismissed.

83. [Repealed 1996, c. 25, s. 1(16).]

84. (1) **Extra-judicial services** — A judge of the Court of Appeal or the Superior Court of Justice may act as a commissioner, arbitrator, adjudicator, referee, conciliator or mediator or on a commission of inquiry under an Act of the Legislature or under an agreement made under any such Act.

(2) **Remuneration** — A judge acting under subsection (1) shall not receive any remuneration but shall be reimbursed for reasonable travelling and other expenses incurred while so acting.

1996, c. 25, ss. 1(17), 9(17)

85. **Judges' gowns** — The Lieutenant Governor in Council may make regulations respecting the form of the gown to be worn in court by all judges appointed after the 1st day of September, 1990.

86. (1) **How certain judges to be addressed** — Every judge of the Court of Ontario may be addressed as "Your Honour" or as "(*Mr. or Madam*) Justice (*naming the judge*)" in English or as "Votre Honneur" ou "(M. ou Mme) le/la Juge (*nom de juge*)" in French.

(2) **Idem** — A judge appointed to the High Court of Justice before the 1st day of September, 1990 may elect to be addressed according to the practice in existence before that day.

(3) [Repealed 1996, c. 25, s. 9(11).]

(4) [Repealed 1998, c. 20, Sched. A, s. 19(2).]

1994, c. 12, s. 33; 1996, c. 25, s. 9(10), (11); 1998, c. 20, Sched. A, s. 19

86.1 (1) **Appointment of case management masters** — The Lieutenant Governor in Council, on the recommendation of the Attorney General, may appoint such case management masters as are considered necessary.

(2) **Qualification** — No person shall be appointed as a case management master unless he or she has been a member of the bar of one of the provinces or territories of Canada for at least the period of time prescribed in the regulations or, for an aggregate of at least that period, has been a member of such a bar or served as a judge anywhere in Canada after being a member of such a bar.

(3) **Term of office** — A case management master holds office for seven years.

(4) **Reappointment** — Subject to subsections (5) and (5.1), a case management master shall be reappointed for an additional seven-year term at the expiry of his or her intial seven-year term and each subsequent seven-year term.

(5) **Expiry of term at age of 65** — If the case management master is 58 years of age or older, the reappointment under subsection (4) shall provide for a term that expires when he or she reaches the age of 65.

(5.1) **Resignation or removal from office** — Subsection (4) does not apply if,

(a) the case management master has resigned under section 48; or

(b) the Chief Justice has decided to remove the case management master from office under clause 86.2(8)(g) and,

(i) the time for an appeal from the decision has expired without an appeal being filed, or

(ii) any appeal has been finally disposed of and the Chief Justice's decision has been confirmed.

(5.2) **Annual reappointments until age of 75** — A case management master who has reached the age of 65 may be reappointed by the Lieutenant Governor in Council, on the joint recommendation of the Attorney General and the Chief Justice, for a one-year term, subject to subsection (5.3); if the Attorney General and the Chief Justice so recommend, the Lieutenat Governor in Council shall reappoint the case management master.

(5.3) **Expiry of term at age of 75** — If the case management master is 74 years of age or older, the reappointment under subsection (5.2) shall provide for a term that expires when he or she reaches the age of 75.

(5.4) **No limit** — Subject to subsections (5) and (5.3), there is no limit to the number of times a case management master can be reappointed under subsection (4) and subsection (5.2).

(6) **Jurisdiction** — A case management master has,

(a) the jurisdiction of a master conferred by the rules of court; and

(b) the case management jurisdiction conferred by the rules of court.

(7) **Application of ss. 46 to 48** — Sections 46 to 48, except subsection 47(3), apply to case management masters, with necessary modifications, in the same manner as to provincial judges.

(8) **Same** — Section 46 does not apply in circumstances in which the rules of court require participation in alternative dispute resolution.

(9) **Standards of conduct** — The Chief Justice may establish standards of conduct for case management masters.

(10) **Duty of Chief Justice** — The Chief Justice shall ensure that any standards of conduct are made available to the public, in English and French.

1996, c. 25, ss. 1(18), 9(14); 2002, c. 18, Sched. A, s. 4(2); 2006, c. 21, Sched. A, s. 15

86.2 (1) Complaint — Any person may make a complaint alleging misconduct by a case management master, by writing to the Chief Justice of the Superior Court of Justice.

(2) Dismissal — The Chief Justice shall review the complaint and may dismiss it without further investigation if, in his or her opinion, it is frivolous or an abuse of process, or concerns a minor matter to which an appropriate response has already been given.

(3) Notice of dismissal — The Chief Justice shall notify the complainant and the case management master in writing of a dismissal under subsection (2), giving brief reasons for it.

(4) Committee — If the complaint is not dismissed, the Chief Justice shall refer it to a committee consisting of three persons chosen by him or her.

(5) Same — The three persons shall be a judge of the Superior Court of Justice, a case management master and a person who is neither a judge nor a lawyer.

(6) Investigation — The committee shall investigate the complaint in the manner it considers appropriate, and the complainant and the case management master shall be given an opportunity to make representations to the committee, in writing or, at the committee's option, orally.

(7) Recommendation — The committee shall make a report to the Chief Justice, recommending a disposition in accordance with subsections (8), (9) and (10).

(8) Disposition — The Chief Justice may dismiss the complaint, with or without a finding that it is unfounded, or, if he or she concludes that the case management master's conduct presents grounds for imposing a sanction, may,

(a) warn the case management master;

(b) reprimand the case management master;

(c) order the case management master to apologize to the complainant or to any other person;

(d) order that the case management master take specified measures, such as receiving education or treatment, as a condition of continuing to sit as a case management master;

(e) suspend the case management master for a period of up to 30 days;

(f) direct that no judicial duties or only specified judicial duties be assigned to the case management master; or

(g) remove the case management master from office.

(9) Same — The Chief Justice may adopt any combination of the dispositions set out in clauses (8)(a) to (f).

(9.1) Appeal — The Chief Justice's decision may be appealed to the Court of Appeal,

(a) by the case management master, as of right; or

(b) by the complainant, with leave of the Court of Appeal.

(9.2) Parties — The case management master and the complainant are parties to any appeal and the Attorney General is the respondent.

(9.3) Power of Court of Appeal — The Court of Appeal may substitute its opinion for that of the Chief Justice on all questions of fact and law.

(9.4) **Time for appeal** — The notice of appeal or motion for leave to appeal shall be filed within 30 days after the date of the Chief Justice's decision.

(9.5) **Stay** — On the filing of a notice of appeal, the imposition of any sanction is stayed until the final disposition of the appeal.

(10) **Compensation** — The Chief Justice shall consider whether the case management master should be compensated for all or part of his or her costs for legal services incurred in connection with the steps taken under this section in relation to the complaint.

(11) **Recommendation** — If the Chief Justice is of the opinion that the case management master should be compensated, he or she shall make a recommendation to the Attorney General to that effect, indicating the amount of compensation.

(12) **Same** — If the complaint is dismissed with a finding that it is unfounded, the Chief Justice shall recommend to the Attorney General that the case management master be compensated for his or her costs for legal services and shall indicate the amount of compensation.

(12.1) **Compensation** — When there is an appeal or motion for leave to appeal under subsection (9.1), the Court of Appeal shall consider whether the case management master should be compensated for all or part of his or her costs for legal services incurred in connection with the appeal or motion.

(12.2) **Recommendation** — If the Court of Appeal is of the opinion that the case management master should be compensated, it shall make a recommendation to the Attorney General to that effect, indicating the amount of compensation.

(12.3) **Same** — If a complainant's motion for leave to appeal is dismissed, the Court of Appeal shall recommend to the Attorney General that the case management master be compensated for his or her costs for legal services and shall indicate the amount of compensation.

(13) **Maximum** — The amount of compensation recommended under subsection (11), (12), (12.2) or (12.3) shall be based on a rate for legal services that does not exceed the maximum rate normally paid by the Government of Ontario for similar legal services.

(14) **Payment** — The Attorney General shall pay compensation to the case management master in accordance with the recommendation.

(15) **Confidential records** — The committee may order that any information or documents relating to a complaint that was not dealt with in a manner that was open to the public are confidential and shall not be disclosed or made public.

(16) **Same** — Subsection (15) applies whether the information or documents are in the possession of the committee, the Chief Justice, the Attorney General or any other person.

(17) **Limitation** — Subsection (15) applies only to information and documents that have been treated as confidential or were prepared exclusively for the committee, or for submission to the committee, in relation to its investigation.

(18) **Non-application of *SPPA*** — The *Statutory Powers Procedure Act* does not apply to a judge, case management master or member of a committee acting under this section.

(19) Personal liability — No action or other proceeding for damages shall be instituted against a judge, case management master or member of a committee for any act done in good faith in the execution or intended execution of the person's duty under this section.

1996, c. 25, ss. 1(18), 9(14), (17); 2002, c. 18, Sched. A, s. 4(3)–(5)

87. (1) Masters — Every person who was a master of the Supreme Court before the 1st day of September, 1990 is a master of the Superior Court of Justice.

(2) Jurisdiction — Every master has the jurisdiction conferred by the rules of court in proceedings in the Superior Court of Justice.

(3) Application of ss. 44 to 51.12 — Sections 44 to 51.12 apply to masters, with necessary modifications, in the same manner as to provincial judges.

(4) Exception — The power of the Chief Justice of the Ontario Court of Justice referred to in subsections 44(1) and (2) shall be exercised by the Chief Justice of the Superior Court of Justice with respect to masters.

(5) Same — The right of a master to continue in office under subsection 47(3) is subject to the approval of the Chief Justice of the Superior Court of Justice, who shall make the decision according to criteria developed by himself or herself and approved by the Judicial Council.

(6) Same — When the Judicial Council deals with a complaint against a master, the following special provisions apply:

    1. One of the members of the Judicial Council who is a provincial judge shall be replaced by a master. The Chief Justice of the Ontario Court of Justice shall determine which judge is to be replaced and the Chief Justice of the Superior Court of Justice shall designate the master who is to replace the judge.

    2. Complaints shall be referred to the Chief Justice of the Superior Court of Justice rather than to the Chief Justice of the Ontario Court of Justice.

    3. Subcommittee recommendations with respect to interim suspension shall be made to the appropriate regional senior judge of the Superior Court of Justice, to whom subsections 51.4(10) and (11) apply with necessary modifications.

(7) Same — Section 51.9, which deals with standards of conduct for provincial judges, section 51.10, which deals with their continuing education, and section 51.11, which deals with evaluation of their performance, apply to masters only if the Chief Justice of the Superior Court of Justice consents.

(8) Compensation — Masters shall receive the same salaries, pension benefits, other benefits and allowances as provincial judges receive under the framework agreement set out in the Schedule to this Act.

1994, c. 12, s. 34; 1996, c. 25, s. 9(14), (17), (18), (20)

87.1 (1) Small Claims Court judges — This section applies to provincial judges who were assigned to the Provincial Court (Civil Division) immediately before September 1, 1990.

(2) Full and part-time service — The power of the Chief Justice of the Ontario Court of Justice referred to in subsections 44(1) and (2) shall be exercised by the Chief Justice of the Superior Court of Justice with respect to provincial judges to whom this section applies.

(3) **Continuation in office** — The right of a provincial judge to whom this section applies to continue in office under subsection 47(3) is subject to the approval of the Chief Justice of the Superior Court of Justice, who shall make the decision according to criteria developed by himself or herself and approved by the Judicial Council.

(4) **Complaints** — When the Judicial Council deals with a complaint against a provincial judge to whom this section applies, the following special provisions apply:

1. One of the members of the Judicial Council who is a provincial judge shall be replaced by a provincial judge who was assigned to the Provincial Court (Civil Division) immediately before September 1, 1990. The Chief Justice of the Ontario Court of Justice shall determine which judge is to be replaced and the Chief Justice of the Superior Court of Justice shall designate the judge who is to replace that judge.

2. Complaints shall be referred to the Chief Justice of the Superior Court of Justice rather than to the Chief Justice of the Ontario Court of Justice.

3. Subcommittee recommendations with respect to interim suspension shall be made to the appropriate regional senior judge of the Superior Court of Justice, to whom subsections 51.4(10) and (11) apply with necessary modifications.

(5) **Application of ss. 51.9, 51.10, 51.11** — Section 51.9, which deals with standards of conduct for provincial judges, section 51.10, which deals with their continuing education, and section 51.11, which deals with evaluation of their performance, apply to provincial judges to whom this section applies only if the Chief Justice of the Superior Court of Justice consents.

1994, c. 12, s. 35; 1996, c. 25, s. 9(14), (17), (18), (20)

88. (1) **Regulations** — The Lieutenant Governor in Council may make regulations,

(a) prescribing the officer or employee to whom money paid into the Superior Court of Justice shall be paid and providing for the vesting of that money and any securities in which that money is invested in that officer or employee;

(b) governing the management and investment of money paid into a court;

(c) providing for the payment of interest on money paid into a court and fixing the rate of interest so paid;

(d) prescribing the officer or employee in whose name mortgages and other securities taken under an order of the Superior Court of Justice and instruments taken as security in respect of a proceeding in the Superior Court of Justice shall be taken;

(e) respecting the deposit of the mortgages, securities and instruments and the duty or obligation, if any, in respect of them of the officer or employee in whose name they are taken.

(2) **Regulations under *Public Guardian and Trustee Act*** — With respect to all functions performed by the Public Guardian and Trustee in his or her capacity as Accountant of the Superior Court of Justice, the *Public Guardian and Trustee Act* and the regulations made under that Act prevail over subsection (1) and the regulations made under it.

1996, c. 25, s. 9(12), (17); 1997, c. 23, s. 5; 2000, c. 26, Sched. A, s. 5

89. (1) **Children's Lawyer** — The Lieutenant Governor in Council, on the recommendation of the Attorney General, may appoint a Children's Lawyer for Ontario.

(2) Qualification — No person shall be appointed as Children's Lawyer unless he or she has been a member of the bar of one of the provinces or territories of Canada for at least ten years or, for an aggregate of at least ten years, has been a member of such a bar or served as a judge anywhere in Canada after being a member of such a bar.

(3) Duties — Where required to do so by an Act or the rules of court, the Children's Lawyer shall act as litigation guardian of a minor or other person who is a party to a proceeding.

(3.1) Same — At the request of a court, the Children's Lawyer may act as the legal representative of a minor or other person who is not a party to a proceeding.

(4) Costs — The same costs as are payable to litigation guardians are payable to the Children's Lawyer and costs recovered by the Children's Lawyer shall be paid into the Consolidated Revenue Fund.

(5) Security for costs — The Children's Lawyer shall not be required to give security for costs in any proceeding.

(6) Mortgages held by Accountant — Where a person for whom the Children's Lawyer has acted is interested in a mortgage held by the Accountant of the Superior Court of Justice, the Children's Lawyer shall take reasonable care to ensure that,

    (a) money payable on the mortgage is promptly paid;

    (b) the mortgaged property is kept properly insured; and

    (c) taxes on the mortgaged property are promptly paid.

(7) Payment into court — Money received by the Children's Lawyer on behalf of a person for whom he or she acts shall, unless the court orders otherwise, be paid into court to the credit of the person entitled.

(8) Assessment of costs — Where the amount payable into court under subsection (7) is to be ascertained by the deduction of unassessed costs from a fund, the Children's Lawyer may require the costs to be assessed forthwith.

(9) Audit — The Auditor General shall examine and report on the accounts and financial transactions of the Children's Lawyer.

1994, c. 12, s. 37; 1994, c. 27, s. 43; 1996, c. 25, s. 9(13); 1999, c. 12, Sched. B, s. 4(1); 2004, c. 17, s. 32, Table

90. (1) Assessment officers — The Lieutenant Governor in Council, on the recommendation of the Attorney General, may appoint assessment officers.

(2) Idem — Every master is an assessment officer.

(3) Jurisdiction — Every assessment officer has jurisdiction to assess costs in a proceeding in any court.

(4) Appeal from assessment of costs before tribunal — Where costs of a proceeding before a tribunal other than a court are to be assessed by an assessment officer,

    (a) the rules of court governing the procedure on an assessment of costs apply with necessary modifications; and

(b) an appeal lies to the Superior Court of Justice from a certificate of assessment of the costs if an objection was served in respect of the issue appealed in accordance with the rules of court.

1996, c. 25, s. 9(17)

91. Officers of court — Every official examiner and deputy official examiner is an officer of every court in Ontario.

92. Administration of oaths — Every officer of a court has, for the purposes of any matter before him or her, power to administer oaths and affirmations and to examine parties and witnesses.

93. Money held by officer of court — Money or property vested in or held by an officer of a court shall be deemed to be vested in the officer in trust for Her Majesty, subject to being disposed of in accordance with any Act, rule of court or order.

94. (1) **Disposition of court fees** — All fees payable to a salaried officer of a court in respect of a proceeding in the court shall be paid into the Consolidated Revenue Fund.

(2) **Exception** — Subsection (1) does not apply to fees payable to court reporters under the *Administration of Justice Act*.

PART VII — COURT PROCEEDINGS

95. (1) **Application of Part** — This Part applies to civil proceedings in courts of Ontario.

(2) **Application to criminal proceedings** — Sections 109 (constitutional questions) and 123 (giving decisions), section 125 and subsection 126(5) (language of proceedings) and sections 132 (judge sitting on appeal), 136 (prohibition against photography at court hearing) and 146 (where procedures not provided) also apply to proceedings under the *Criminal Code* (Canada), except in so far as they are inconsistent with that Act.

(3) **Application to provincial offences** — Sections 109 (constitutional questions), 125, 126 (language of proceedings), 132 (judge sitting on appeal), 136 (prohibition against photography at court hearings), 144 (arrest and committal warrants enforceable by police) and 146 (where procedures not provided) also apply to proceedings under the *Provincial Offences Act* and, for the purpose, a reference in one of those sections to a judge includes a justice of the peace presiding in the Ontario Court of Justice.

1996, c. 25, s. 9(18)

Common Law And Equity

96. (1) **Rules of law and equity** — Courts shall administer concurrently all rules of equity and the common law.

(2) **Rules of equity to prevail** — Where a rule of equity conflicts with a rule of the common law, the rule of equity prevails.

(3) Jurisdiction for equitable relief — Only the Court of Appeal and the Superior Court of Justice, exclusive of the Small Claims Court, may grant equitable relief, unless otherwise provided.

1994, c. 12, s. 38; 1996, c. 25, s. 9(17)

Commentary: The Court of Appeal for Ontario provided a detailed review of the jurisdiction of the Small Claims Court over rules and relief originating in equity, in *Hodgins v. Grover*, 2011 ONCA 72, 2011 CarswellOnt 336, (sub nom. *Grover v. Hodgins*) 103 O.R. (3d) 721, 5 C.P.C. (7th) 33, (sub nom. *Grover v. Hodgins*) 330 D.L.R. (4th) 712, (sub nom. *Grover v. Hodgins*) 275 O.A.C. 96, [2011] O.J. No. 310 (Ont. C.A.); leave to appeal refused (2012), 2012 CarswellOnt 825, 2012 CarswellOnt 826, 432 N.R. 392 (note), (sub nom. *Grover v. Hodgins*) 295 O.A.C. 398 (note), [2011] S.C.C.A. No. 142 (S.C.C.). There the court held that the Small Claims Court does have jurisdiction to apply equitable rules and grant equitable relief provided that the relief claimed is otherwise within the jurisdiction of that court. The question is not whether a rule or remedy raised by a party originated in equity rather than at common law. The question is whether the relief sought falls within the court's jurisdiction: i.e. a monetary claim not exceeding the maximum $25,000 limit, or a claim for recovery of possession of personal property where the value of the property does not exceed that same limit. The court's jurisdiction over a claim for damages for restitution or unjust enrichment was upheld.

Case Law: *Bemjapipatkul v. Rungruangwong* (January 13, 2014), Doc. SC-12-16636-0000, [2014] O.J. No. 119 (Ont. Small Cl. Ct.)

The Small Claims Court has no jurisdiction to order an accounting of income and profits of a corporation.

Brander v. Backstage Bar & Grill Inc. (January 28, 2014), Doc. 12-21, 12-22, 12-22 D1, [2014] O.J. No. 370 (Ont. S.C.J.)

The Small Claims Court has no jurisdiction over claims by unsecured creditors or minority shareholders of a corporation for an oppression remedy.

Moore v. Cdn. Newspapers Co. Ltd. (1989), 69 O.R. (2d) 262, 37 C.P.C. (2d) 189, 60 D.L.R. (4th) 113, 34 O.A.C. 328 (Ont. Div. Ct.) — The order to publish an apology and retraction was an equitable remedy because it refused the performance of a specified act. The provincial court has no jurisdiction to grant equitable relief. Query present wording of subsection deleting specific exclusion of the Small Claims Court.

McKay v. Toronto (City) (1991), 2 W.D.C.P. (2d) 422 (Ont. Sm. Cl. Ct.) — The plaintiff sought either to close a strip of land known as "The Belt Line" or to have constructed solid fences or buildings. The Small Claims Court had no jurisdiction to grant declaratory relief.

Ford Motor Co. of Canada Ltd. and Facchinato, Re (1978), 18 O.R. (2d) 581 (Ont. Div. Ct.) — A Small Claims Court cannot hear an action arising out of the interpretation, application, administration or alleged violation of a collective agreement.

Domtar Commercial Roofing & Insulation v. Exeter Roofing & Sheet Metal Co. Ltd. (1993), 13 C.L.R. (2d) 63, 109 D.L.R. (4th) 443 (Ont. Gen. Div.) — A declaratory claim dealing with trust funds, here pursuant to the *Construction Lien Act*, R.S.O. 1990, c. C.30 would ordinarily be decided by federally appointed Judges who are members of the General Division. The three Small Claims Court actions were therefore stayed pursuant to section 107 of the *Courts of Justice Act* since a similar one had already been commenced in the General Division.

McLean v. Compon Agro Inc. (1993), 90 Man. R. (2d) 59 (Q.B.) — The Small Claims Court in Manitoba, "the Small Claims Act", R.S.M. 1987, c. C285 does not have jurisdiction to grant declaratory relief under s. 232 or 234 of the *Corporations Act*, R.S.M. 1987, c. C 225.

American Home Assurance Co. v. Brett Pontiac Buick GMC. Ltd. (1991), 105 N.S.R. (2d) 425, 284 A.P.R. 425 — Action not transferred from superior court to the Small Claims Court since action included claim for declaratory and injunctive relief.

Vinet v. Campbellton (Ville) (January 16, 1991), Doc. 176/90/CA (N.B. C.A.) — The Small Claims Court was not competent to deal with a request for a mandatory injunction.

Manitoba Public Insurance Corp. v. Sundstrom, [1998] I.L.R. I-3529, 16 C.P.C. (4th) 353, 125 Man. R. (2d) 268, 2 C.C.L.I. (3d) 167 (Man. Q.B.) — Stay of proceedings granted. A claim for declaratory relief was outside the jurisdiction of Small Claims Court. The respondent's (Jain's) claim was premature because the regulations required the appraisal process to determine the quantum of loss.

Prtenjaca v. Fox (2001), 2001 CarswellOnt 1729, 9 C.L.R. (3d) 141 (Ont. Sm. Cl. Ct.) — Although Ontario Small Claims Court did not have jurisdiction to grant equitable "relief" pursuant to s. 96 of Ontario Courts of *Justice Act*, R.S.O. 1990, c. C.43, it had jurisdiction to administer "rules of equity," and could therefore consider claim of unjust enrichment and order monetary compensation.

Szeib v. Team Truck Centres-Freightliner (2001), 2001 CarswellOnt 2026 (Ont. Sm. Cl. Ct.) — Plaintiff claimed he gave defendant deposit pursuant to conditional sale contract. Plaintiff cancelled order before delivery. Defendant's motion for order that Small Claims Court without jurisdiction because claim equitable relief dismissed. Section 96(3) of *Courts of Justice Act*, R.S.O. 1990, c. C.43 did not prevail over s. 23(1)(b).

MacIntyre v. Ontario (Ministry of Community & Social Services) (2003), 68 O.R. (3d) 236, 2003 CarswellOnt 3847, 47 C.B.R. (4th) 52 (Ont. S.C.J.); affirmed (2004), 2004 CarswellOnt 956 (Ont. C.A.). Ministry of Community and Social Services defrauded of funds paid for social assistance. Ministry granted restitution order. Ministry obtained writ of seizure and sale. Ministry entitled to set-off of its claim against funds being paid by Motor Vehicle Accident Claim Fund, *Financial Administration Act*, R.S.O. 1990, c. F.12.

936464 Ontario Ltd. v. Mungo Bear Ltd., [2003] O.J. No. 3795, 2003 CarswellOnt 8091, 74 O.R. (3d) 45, 258 D.L.R. (4th) 754 (Ont. Div. Ct.).

Deputy Judge not lacking jurisdiction to award damages based on *quantum meruit*, common law rather than equitable remedy. Small Claims Court specifically empowered to grant equitable relief in forms of orders for payment of money and orders for recovery of possession of personal property. See *Courts of Justice Act*, R.S.O. 1990, c. C.43, ss. 23(1), 96(1), (3).

Courts authorized under s. 96(1) to concurrently administer all rules of equity and the common law. Small Claims Court not empowered to grant any forms of equitable relief, such as injunctions, declarations and specific performance (unless, perhaps, the performance involves nothing beyond the payment of money or the delivery of possession of personal property, within the applicable limits).

Mullin v. R - M & E Pharmacy, 2005 CarswellOnt 203, 74 O.R. (3d) 378 (Ont. S.C.J.).

Garnishment is an equitable remedy. Court has jurisdiction to declare moneys payable on account of personal injury damages for pain and suffering to be exempt from garnishment. Law of Ontario that damages awarded for pain and suffering exempt from a bankrupt's trustee. See *Holley v. Gifford Smith Ltd.*, 1986 CarswellOnt 178, [1986] O.J. No. 165, 14 O.A.C. 65, (sub nom. *Holley, Re)* 54 O.R. (2d) 225, (sub nom. *Holley, Re)* 26 D.L.R. (4th) 230, (sub nom. *Holley, Re)* 59 C.B.R. (N.S.) 17, 12 C.C.E.L. 161 (Ont. C.A.). Plaintiff in personal injury claim cannot assign his cause of action. If all proceeds were to be scooped up by creditors, plaintiffs would not pursue legitimate claims.

Grillo v. D'Angela (2009), [2009] O.J. No. 7, 2009 CarswellOnt 11, 306 D.L.R. (4th) 370 (Ont. S.C.J.); additional reasons at (2009), 2009 CarswellOnt 455.

Plaintiff — a principal of a law firm — commenced an action for a mandatory order requiring the Defendants — former associates of Plaintiff's law firm, to return 250 clients' files taken by the Defendants without Plaintiff's knowledge and permission when leaving his law firm.

The test for interlocutory injunctive relief is set out in *RJR-MacDonald Inc. v. Canada (A.G.)*, [1994] 1 S.C.R. 311:

    (a) is there a serious question to be tried?;

    (b) will the moving party suffer irreparable harm if the injunction is not granted?; and

    (c) where does the balance of convenience lie?

Plaintiff must establish a strong *prima facie* case: there must be a "higher degree of assurance" in the case of interlocutory mandatory orders and the case must be "unusually sharp and clear": See *Ticketnet Corporation v. Air Canada* (1987), 21 C.P.C. (2d) 38 (Ont. H.C.J.).

Hodgins v. Grover, 2011 ONCA 72, 2011 CarswellOnt 336, [2011] O.J. No. 310, (sub nom. *Grover v. Hodgins*) 103 O.R. (3d) 721, (sub nom. *Grover v. Hodgins*) 275 O.A.C. 96, (sub nom. *Grover v. Hodgins*) 330 D.L.R. (4th) 712, 5 C.P.C. (7th) 33 (Ont. C.A.); leave to appeal refused 2012 CarswellOnt 825, 2012 CarswellOnt 826, 432 N.R. 392 (note), (sub nom. *Grover v. Hodgins*) 295 O.A.C. 398 (note), [2011] S.C.C.A. No. 142 (S.C.C.).

Section 23 of the *Courts of Justice Act (Ont.)* sets out the jurisdiction of the Small Claims Court, while section 96 deals with the equitable jurisdiction of all courts. The Court of Appeal held that section 23 was a wide grant of jurisdiction. The wording "any action" was sufficiently broad enough to include the jurisdiction to grant equitable remedies. Sections 23, 96(1) and 96(3) are to be read as a "coherent package." Section 23 was broad enough to allow the Small Claims Court to deal with claims in common law and equity. Under section 96(1), the courts, including the Small Claims Court, is authorized to concurrently administer all rules of equity and the common law.

This court has been operating on the basis that it has jurisdiction to consider claims for equitable relief and, in appropriate cases, to grant it.

See *Szeib v. Team Truck Centres — Freightliner*, [2001] O.T.C. 439, [2001] O.J. No. 2208, 2001 CarswellOnt 2026 (Ont. Small Cl. Ct.), Searle Deputy, J., specifically considered the jurisdictional issue and held that the Small Claims Court has jurisdiction to grant relief from forfeiture, a form of equitable relief. See *Rizzo & Rizzo Shoes Ltd., Re*, 1998 CarswellOnt 1 at para. 21, 1998 CarswellOnt 2, [1998] S.C.J. No. 2, [1998] 1 S.C.R. 27, 36 O.R. (3d) 418 (headnote only), 50 C.B.R. (3d) 163, 33 C.C.E.L. (2d) 173, 154 D.L.R. (4th) 193, (sub nom. *Rizzo & Rizzo Shoes Ltd. (Bankrupt), Re*) 221 N.R. 241, (sub nom. *Rizzo & Rizzo Shoes Ltd. (Bankrupt), Re*) 106 O.A.C. 1, (sub nom. *Adrien v. Ontario Ministry of Labour*) 98 C.L.L.C. 210-006 (S.C.C.). Analysis must focus on the words of the relevant statutory provisions, read in their entire context and interpreted harmoniously with the scheme and the object of the *Act* and with the legislature's intention.

Kourtessis v. Minister of National Revenue, 1993 CarswellBC 1259, 1993 CarswellBC 1213, EYB 1993-67101, [1993] 2 S.C.R. 53, 78 B.C.L.R. (2d) 257, 81 C.C.C. (3d) 286, 20 C.R. (4th) 104, [1993] 1 C.T.C. 301, 102 D.L.R. (4th) 456, [1993] 4 W.W.R. 225, 27 B.C.A.C. 81, 14 C.R.R. (2d) 193, 93 D.T.C. 5137, 153 N.R. 1, 45 W.A.C. 81, [1993] S.C.J. No. 45 (S.C.C.).

Court pled provincial legislation which conferred admiralty jurisdiction on a small claims court; Court relied on a number of authorities which upheld provincial jurisdiction in [. . .] The superior court, and would therefore have jurisdiction to entertain an action for a declaration seeking this kind of relief but subject to the same discretion to refuse to exercise it.

Hodgins v. Grover, 2011 ONCA 72, 2011 CarswellOnt 336, (sub nom. *Grover v. Hodgins*) 103 O.R. (3d) 721, 5 C.P.C. (7th) 33, (sub nom. *Grover v. Hodgins*) 330 D.L.R. (4th) 712, (sub nom. *Grover v. Hodgins*) 275 O.A.C. 96, [2011] O.J. No. 310 (Ont. C.A.); leave to appeal refused (2012), 2012 CarswellOnt 825, 2012 CarswellOnt 826, 432 N.R. 392 (note), (sub nom. *Grover v. Hodgins*) 295 O.A.C. 398 (note), [2011] S.C.C.A. No. 142 (S.C.C.)

The Small Claims Court has jurisdiction to grant equitable relief when an order involves the return of personal property or monetary payment within the limits of the Small Claims Court. The Court is a statutory court that derives its jurisdiction solely through the *Courts of Justice Act*, R.S.O. 1990, c. C.43. Section 23 is of primary relevance in this appeal, while s. 96 is also informative to the analysis. The Court having jurisdiction to grant equitable relief is the decision of the Divisional Court in *936464 Ontario Ltd. v. Mungo Bear Ltd.*, 2003 CarswellOnt 8091, 74 O.R. (3d) 45, 258 D.L.R. (4th) 754, [2003] O.J. No. 3795 (Ont. Div. Ct.), in which a remedy based on quantum merit was in issue. Heeney J., at paras. 12–15, concluded that notwithstanding that quantum merit is part of the restitutionary group of remedies, its origins can be found in the common law and therefore the court does not need equitable jurisdiction to award it. Heeney J. noted [at para. 9] that while s. 96(3) specifically excludes the Small Claims Court from the list of courts able to grant equitable relief, it does so with the proviso found in the words "unless otherwise provided".

In *Moore v. Canadian Newspapers Co.*, 1989 CarswellOnt 423, 69 O.R. (2d) 262, 37 C.P.C. (2d) 189, 60 D.L.R. (4th) 113, 34 O.A.C. 328 (Ont. Div. Ct.), Rosenberg J. analyzed the jurisdiction of the Small Claims Court to award equitable relief and determined that there was none. However, this case was decided before the legislative changes in 1989 and 1994 (discussed below). Also, the remedy at issue in Moore was injunctive relief, not a monetary payment.

Matteau v. Johnson, 2012 ONSC 1179, 2012 CarswellOnt 2216, [2012] O.J. No. 763, Wilcox, J. (Ont. S.C.J.)

The Respondent appealed from order of Deputy Judge.

The claim was for payment of moneys allegedly owed by the Appellant to the Respondent under an oral agreement between them, together with some living expense debts. The Appellant's defence was based solely on procedural grounds.

In *Hodgins v. Grover*, 2011 ONCA 72, 2011 CarswellOnt 336, (sub nom. *Grover v. Hodgins*) 103 O.R. (3d) 721, 5 C.P.C. (7th) 33, (sub nom. *Grover v. Hodgins*) 330 D.L.R. (4th) 712, (sub nom. *Grover v. Hodgins*) 275 O.A.C. 96, [2011] O.J. No. 310 (Ont. C.A.); leave to appeal refused (2012), 2012 CarswellOnt 825, 2012 CarswellOnt 826, 432 N.R. 392 (note), (sub nom. *Grover v. Hodgins*) 295 O.A.C. 398 (note), [2011] S.C.C.A. No. 142 (S.C.C.), a decision of the Court of Appeal for Ontario dated January 27, 2011, Epstein J. A., writing for the court, after a lengthy analysis concluded that the Small Claims Court does have jurisdiction to award legal or equitable relief where the relief requested is a monetary payment under the limit of $25,000 or the return of personal property valued within that limit. The claim discloses a common law cause of action. The claim could be characterized as one based in contract for the repayment of moneys lent. The Respondent appears to have waived the excess in order to bring the claim within the monetary jurisdiction of the Small Claims Court. The appeal is dismissed.

97. Declaratory orders — The Court of Appeal and the Superior Court of Justice, exclusive of the Small Claims Court, may make binding declarations of right whether or not any consequential relief is or could be claimed.

1994, c. 12, s. 39; 1996, c. 25, s. 9(17)

Commentary: The Small Claims Court has no jurisdiction to grant declaratory relief: *Giannaris v. Toronto (City)*, 2012 ONSC 5183, 2012 CarswellOnt 11747, [2012] O.J. No. 4460 (Ont. Div. Ct.); *Hradecky v. Hydro One Networks Inc.*, 2014 CarswellOnt 3316, [2014] O.J. No. 1249 (Ont. Sm. Cl. Ct.).

Case Law: *Kelman v. Stibor* (1998), 55 C.R.R. (2d) 165 (Ont. Prov. Div.) — Only superior court can make in rem declaratory judgment, binding on other courts. Declaration of constitutional validity made by Provincial Division was *in personam* judgment, applicable to this particular case only.

Green v. Canada (Attorney General), 2011 ONSC 4778, 2011 CarswellOnt 8299, 91 C.C.P.B. 126 (Ont. S.C.J.), Kane J.; additional reasons at 2011 ONSC 5750, 2011 Carswell-Ont 10573, 93 C.C.P.B. 149 (Ont. S.C.J.).

The plaintiff commenced action by a Statement of Claim under the simplified procedure provided in Rule 76 of the *Rules of Civil Procedure*, R.R.O. 1990, Reg. 194. The relief sought was limited to declaratory relief.

The defendants sought an order:

(a) Striking out the Statement of Claim.

Section 97 of the *Courts of Justice Act* states:

> The Court of Appeal and the Superior Court of Justice, exclusive of the Small Claims Court, may make *binding declarations of right whether or not* any *consequential relief* is or could be claimed. [Emphasis added.]

The phrase "cause of action" is not a defined term under the *Rules of Civil Procedure* or the *Courts of Justice Act*.

It is unreasonable to interpret a "cause of action" under Rule 21.01(1)(b) as excluding an action which seeks a declaration only. To do so interprets a rule of procedure as defeating a right granted to parties under section 97 of the *Courts of Justice Act*. The phrase "cause of action," as it appears in Rule 21.01(1)(b), must include an action which claims nothing more than a declaration.

The test to be applied on a motion under Rule 21, assuming the allegations pleaded can be proved, is to ask "is it plain, obvious, and beyond doubt that the plaintiff could not succeed?" See *L. (A.) v. Ontario (Minister of Community & Social Services)*, 2006 CarswellOnt 7393 at para. 17, [2006] O.J. No. 4673, 83 O.R. (3d) 512, 274 D.L.R. (4th) 431, 35 R.F.L. (6th) 56, 218 O.A.C. 150, 36 C.P.C. (6th) 265, 45 C.C.L.T. (3d) 207 (Ont. C.A.); leave to appeal refused 2007 CarswellOnt 3059, 2007 CarswellOnt 3060, [2007] S.C.C.A. No. 36, 372 N.R. 390 (note), 239 O.A.C. 198 (note) (S.C.C.)).

Failure to obtain the declaration sought is not certain, and the granting of a declaration, being a discretionary matter, cannot be pronounced upon without first hearing evidence and conducting a trial. (See *Horton Bay Holdings Ltd. v. Wilks*, 1991 CarswellBC 584, [1991] B.C.J. No. 3481, 3 C.P.C. (3d) 112, 8 B.C.A.C. 68, 17 W.A.C. 68 (B.C. C.A.)).

See *Solosky v. R.* (1970), 1979 CarswellNat 4, 1979 CarswellNat 630, [1979] S.C.J. No. 130, [1980] 1 S.C.R. 821, 105 D.L.R. (3d) 745, 16 C.R. (3d) 294, 30 N.R. 380, 50 C.C.C. (2d) 495 (S.C.C.), setting out the principles which guide the Court in exercising its jurisdiction to grant declarations as including the following:

(a) The question must be real and not theoretical.

(b) There must be good reason for the court to exercise its discretion to resolve a point in issue by declaration.

As to whether the issue raised in the pleading is hypothetical or abstract, the Supreme Court in *Borowski v. Canada (Attorney General)*, 1989 CarswellSask 241, 1989 CarswellSask 465, [1989] S.C.J. No. 14, [1989] 1 S.C.R. 342, [1989] 3 W.W.R. 97, 57 D.L.R. (4th) 231, 92 N.R. 110, 75 Sask. R. 82, 47 C.C.C. (3d) 1, 33 C.P.C. (2d) 105, 38 C.R.R. 232 (S.C.C.) at para. 15 in dealing with the doctrine of mootness states that:

> 15 The doctrine of mootness is an aspect of a general policy or practice that a court may decline to decide a case which raises merely a hypothetical or abstract question.

An Order was made striking out the Statement of Claim, subject to the plaintiff's right for 60 days, to amend such pleading so as to place before the Court all constituent elements in action for negligent misrepresentation. Alternatively, if the action was struck because the Statement of Claim was not amended, that would be without prejudice to the right of the plaintiff to bring a properly constituted action on this or similar grounds in the future.

Green v. Canada (Attorney General), 2011 ONSC 4778, 2011 CarswellOnt 8299, 91 C.C.P.B. 126 at para. 17 (Ont. S.C.J.), Kane J.; additional reasons at 2011 ONSC 5750, 2011 CarswellOnt 10573, 93 C.C.P.B. 149 (Ont. S.C.J.).

It is not reasonable to interpret a "cause of action" under Rule 21.01(1)(b) [of the *Rules of Civil Procedure*, R.R.O. 1990, Reg. 194] as excluding an action which seeks a declaration only. To do so interprets a rule of procedure as defeating a right granted to parties under section 97 of the *Courts of Justice Act* [R.S.O. 1990, c. C.43].

98. Relief against penalties — A court may grant relief against penalties and forfeitures, on such terms as to compensation or otherwise as are considered just.

99. Damages in substitution for injunction or specific performance — A court that has jurisdiction to grant an injunction or order specific performance may award damages in addition to, or in substitution for, the injunction or specific performance.

100. Vesting orders — A court may by order vest in any person an interest in real or personal property that the court has authority to order be disposed of, encumbered or conveyed.

Interlocutory Orders

101. (1) Injunctions and receivers — In the Superior Court of Justice, an interlocutory injunction or mandatory order may be granted or a receiver or receiver and manager may be appointed by an interlocutory order, where it appears to a judge of the court to be just or convenient to do so.

(2) Terms — An order under subsection (1) may include such terms as are considered just.

1994, c. 12, s. 40; 1996, c. 25, s. 9(17)

102. Injunction in labour dispute — **(1) Definition** — In this section,

"labour dispute" means a dispute or difference concerning terms, tenure or conditions of employment or concerning the association or representation of persons in negotiating, fixing, maintaining, changing or seeking to arrange terms or conditions of employment, regardless of whether the disputants stand in the proximate relation of employer and employee.

(2) Notice — Subject to subsection (8), no injunction to restrain a person from an act in connection with a labour dispute shall be granted without notice.

(3) Steps before injunction proceeding — In a motion or proceeding for an injunction to restrain a person from an act in connection with a labour dispute, the court must be satisfied that reasonable efforts to obtain police assistance, protection and action to prevent or remove any alleged danger of damage to property, injury to persons, obstruction of or interference with lawful entry or exit from the premises in question or breach of the peace have been unsuccessful.

(4) **Evidence** — Subject to subsection (8), affidavit evidence in support of a motion for an injunction to restrain a person from an act in connection with a labour dispute shall be confined to statements of facts within the knowledge of the deponent, but any party may by notice to the party filing such affidavit, and payment of the proper attendance money, require the attendance of the deponent to be cross-examined at the hearing.

(5) **Interim injunction** — An interim injunction to restrain a person from an act in connection with a labour dispute may be granted for a period of not longer than four days.

(6) **Notice** — Subject to subsection (8), at least two days notice of a motion for an interim injunction to restrain a person from any act in connection with a labour dispute shall be given to the responding party and to any other person affected thereby but not named in the notice of motion.

(7) **Idem** — Notice required by subsection (6) to persons other than the responding party may be given,

    (a) where such persons are members of a labour organization, by personal service on an officer or agent of the labour organization; and

    (b) where such persons are not members of a labour organization, by posting the notice in a conspicuous place at the location of the activity sought to be restrained where it can be read by any persons affected,

and service and posting under this subsection shall be deemed to be sufficient notice to all such persons.

(8) **Interim injunction without notice** — Where notice as required by subsection (6) is not given, the court may grant an interim injunction where,

    (a) the case is otherwise a proper one for the granting of an interim injunction;

    (b) notice as required by subsection (6) could not be given because the delay necessary to do so would result in irreparable damage or injury, a breach of the peace or an interruption in an essential public service;

    (c) reasonable notification, by telephone or otherwise, has been given to the persons to be affected or, where any of such persons are members of a labour organization, to an officer of that labour organization or to the person authorized under section 89 of the *Labour Relations Act* to accept service of process under that Act on behalf of that labour organization or trade union, or where it is shown that such notice could not have been given; and

    (d) proof of all material facts for the purpose of clauses (a), (b) and (c) is established by oral evidence.

(9) **Misrepresentation as contempt of court** — The misrepresentation of any fact or the withholding of any qualifying relevant matter, directly or indirectly, in a proceeding for an injunction under this section, constitutes a contempt of court.

(10) **Appeal** — An appeal from an order under this section lies to the Court of Appeal without leave.

103. (1) **Certificate of pending litigation** — The commencement of a proceeding in which an interest in land is in question is not notice of the proceeding to a person

who is not a party until a certificate of pending litigation is issued by the court and the certificate is registered in the proper land registry office under subsection (2).

(2) **Registration** — Where a certificate of pending litigation is issued under subsection (1) it may be registered whether the land is registered under the *Land Titles Act* or the *Registry Act*.

(3) **Exception** — Subsections (1) and (2) do not apply to a proceeding for foreclosure or sale on a registered mortgage or to enforce a lien under the *Construction Lien Act*.

(4) **Liability where no reasonable claim** — A party who registers a certificate under subsection (2) without a reasonable claim to an interest in the land is liable for any damages sustained by any person as a result of its registration.

(5) **Recovery of damages** — The liability for damages under subsection (4) and the amount thereof may be determined in the proceeding in respect of which the certificate was registered or in a separate proceeding.

(6) **Order discharging certificate** — The court may make an order discharging a certificate,

(a) where the party at whose instance it was issued,

(i) claims a sum of money in place of or as an alternative to the interest in the land claimed,

(ii) does not have a reasonable claim to the interest in the land claimed, or

(iii) does not prosecute the proceeding with reasonable diligence;

(b) where the interests of the party at whose instance it was issued can be adequately protected by another form of security; or

(c) on any other ground that is considered just,

and the court may, in making the order, impose such terms as to the giving of security or otherwise as the court considers just.

(7) **Effect** — Where a certificate is discharged, any person may deal with the land as fully as if the certificate had not been registered.

104. (1) **Interim order for recovery of personal property** — In an action in which the recovery of possession of personal property is claimed and it is alleged that the property,

(a) was unlawfully taken from the possession of the plaintiff; or

(b) is unlawfully detained by the defendant,

the court, on motion, may make an interim order for recovery of possession of the property.

Case Law: *Peters v. Skyline Motor* (1988), 9 A.C.W.S. (3d) 134 (Alta. Q.B.) — A replevin application pursuant to Rule 428(b), related to parts supplied to the plaintiff's truck at the request of the plaintiff and that the defendant had not been paid. If the plaintiff wanted possession, he would have to pay off the defendant's claim and pursue any claim he thought he might have against the defendant in another action.

Abel Noser Corp. v. C.P.M.S. Computerized Portfolio Mgmt. Services Inc. (1987), 58 O.R. (2d) 633 (Ont. H.C.) — Where the plaintiff was never in possession of personal property and cannot identify that personal property, the conditions required for a replevin order have not been satisfied.

(2) Damages — A person who obtains possession of personal property by obtaining or setting aside an interim order under subsection (1) is liable for any loss suffered by the person ultimately found to be entitled to possession of the property.

Commentary: There are conflicting authorities from the Small Claims Court on whether that court has jurisdiction to make an order for interim recovery of personal property: see *Ever Fresh Direct Foods Inc. v. Schindler* (August 11, 2011), Doc. 315/11, [2011] O.J. No. 3634 (Ont. Sm. Cl. Ct.), where the applicable rules and authorities are reviewed. In any event, as was pointed out in *Gunn v. Gunn*, 2013 CarswellOnt 235, [2013] O.J. No. 30 (Ont. Sm. Cl. Ct.), even if such a jurisdiction existed, the moving party would bear the onus to prove among other things that there are substantial grounds for the claim to possession.

105. Physical or mental examination — (1) Definition — In this section,

"health practitioner" means a person licensed to practise medicine or dentistry in Ontario or any other jurisdiction, a member of the College of Psychologists of Ontario or a person certified or registered as a psychologist by another jurisdiction.

(2) Order — Where the physical or mental condition of a party to a proceeding is in question, the court, on motion, may order the party to undergo a physical or mental examination by one or more health practitioners.

(3) Idem — Where the question of a party's physical or mental condition is first raised by another party, an order under this section shall not be made unless the allegation is relevant to a material issue in the proceeding and there is good reason to believe that there is substance to the allegation.

(4) Further examinations — The court may, on motion, order further physical or mental examinations.

(5) Examiner may ask questions — Where an order is made under this section, the party examined shall answer the questions of the examining health practitioner relevant to the examination and the answers given are admissible in evidence.

1998, c. 18, Sched. G, s. 48

106. Stay of proceedings — A court, on its own initiative or on motion by any person, whether or not a party, may stay any proceeding in the court on such terms as are considered just.

Case Law: *Galtaco Redlaw Castings Corp. v. Brunswick Industrial Supply Co.* (1989), 69 O.R. (2d) 478 (Ont. H.C.) — The proper test to be applied when determining whether to stay an action between competing jurisdictions is:

> 1. the party seeking a stay must satisfy the court that there is another forum to whose jurisdiction it is amenable in which justice can be done between the parties at substantially less inconvenience or expense; and

> 2. if that is established, the responding party must then establish that the stay will deprive it of a legitimate personal or juridical advantage.

As part of the first step described above, the applicant for a stay must satisfy the court that the foreign jurisdiction is the convenient forum. Convenient forum means that the applicant must establish that the foreign jurisdiction is the most appropriate natural forum to try the action in the sense that the foreign jurisdiction has the most real and substantial connection with a lawsuit.

The action in Ohio was only for the price of goods sold. The Ontario action was more comprehensive. There may be a serious question as to the proper law contract. The defendant failed to demonstrate that justice could be done in Ohio at substantially less inconvenience or expense. The plaintiffs have satisfied whatever onus rests on them.

Kelman v. MacInnis (1993), 4 W.D.C.P. (2d) 136 (Ont. Gen. Div.) — A stay of a Small Claims Court action was granted for one year pending resolution of a similar action in the Ontario Court (General Division) involving the same defendants. A request for an order striking the claim was dismissed. The Court did *not* determine the issue of the equitable jurisdiction of a Small Claims Court Judge.

Simpkin v. Holoday (1997), 14 C.P.C. (4th) (Ont. Gen. Div.) — Motion to stay civil action set for trial in face of criminal charges against defendant dismissed. Defendant failed to demonstrate extraordinary or exceptional circumstances which was test. Stay would greatly prejudice plaintiffs who commenced action three years before and who were not complainants in criminal proceedings.

Stoney Band v. Stoney Band Council (1996), (sub nom. *Powderface v. Baptist)* 118 F.T.R. 118 (Fed. T.D.) — Two actions against Crown alleged breach of fiduciary duty. Crown moved to strike out or stay second action on ground that there were duplicate proceedings. Where pleadings were not identical, there were insufficient grounds to strike. However, second action stayed where there were serious issues to be tried, and Crown could suffer irreparable harm if contradictory judgments made. Balance of convenience weighed in favour of Crown.

1085178 Ontario Ltd. v. Henderson (December 3, 1997), Doc. 97-CV-1704, 100, 208/96 (Ont. Gen. Div.) — Second action, commenced dealing with many of same occurrences as first, stayed until first action was completed, pursuant to Rule 21.01(3) of *Rules of Civil Procedure*, R.R.O. 194, and s. 106 of *Courts of Justice Act*, R.S.O. 1990, c. C.43. Continuance of second action would be abuse of court process and stay would not cause any injustice to plaintiffs in second action.

Piper v. Scott Properties Ltd. (May 5, 1997), Doc. Saskatoon Q.B. 2291/96 (Sask. Q.B.) — Appellant's appeal to Queen's Bench was to protect his interests respecting his counterclaim which was in excess of jurisdiction of Small Claims Court. Appellant should have applied for stay of small claims matter pending resolution by Queen's Bench. Instead he forced small claims judge to determine issues relevant to counterclaim without benefit of hearing counterclaim. As trial judge did not commit error, appeal dismissed.

Catic-Pacus Investment Corp. v. Noble China Inc. (November 20, 1998), Doc. 98-CL-2991 (Ont. Gen. Div. [Commercial List]) — Motion by Noble China to stay application pursuant to Rules 21.01(3) and 25.11 of the *Rules of Civil Procedure*, R.R.O. 1990, Reg. 194 and section 106 of the *Courts of Justice Act*, R.S.O. 1990, c. C43. This application and application bearing Court File No. B105/97 was between the same parties. Court adopted approach by Morin J. in *Sportmart Inc. v. Toronto Hospital Foundation* (1995), 62 C.P.R. (3d) 129 (Ont. Gen. Div.). Fairest to stay application, without prejudice to amending the first application to enlarge the relief sought.

Dominion of Canada General Insurance Co. v. Lee (1998), 8 C.C.L.I. (3d) 152 (Ont. Gen. Div.) — A motion by defendant for order staying this action pending disposition of an application for arbitration. See the *Courts of Justice Act*, R.S.O. 1990 c. C.43, sections 106 and 138. Arbitration is not a proceeding in the court. Arbitration under the *Insurance Act* is an elective process. This action (98-CV-5676) stayed until final determination of application for arbitration.

Hudson's Bay Co. c. Sklar (20 juillet 2000), no C.A. Montréal 500-09-009804-006 (Que. C.A.) — In order to justify stay of civil proceedings, the applicant was required to show that without a stay, the right to a full and fair defence was compromised. No such grounds were established. No basis for leave to appeal made out.

Dimitrov v. Summit Square Strata Corp., 2005 CarswellBC 2490, 2005 BCSC 1469 (B.C. S.C.), Halfyard J. Applicant Dimitrov seeks declaration she is an indigent person, and an order she not be required to pay court fees in respect of appeal from order in small claims court.

She further seeks order pursuant to s. 8(6) of the *Small Claims Act* which would exempt her from requirements to deposit $200 security for costs, and the amount of the judgment ($725), when she files her notice of appeal.

She is unemployed, current net monthly income is $1,060.92, source of her income is social assistance, child support and government child tax benefits. The child tax benefits have been cancelled. She owns strata property jointly with her husband which she values at approximately $43,000, but mortgage balance is more than $34,000. Her household goods have an approximate value of $5,000. She is a person possessed of some means, but such scanty means that she is needy and poor. She is an indigent person. (See *Munro v. Stewart*, 1988 CarswellBC 353, 31 B.C.L.R. (2d) 164 (B.C. S.C.).).

Leading case of *Hunt v. T & N plc*, 1990 CarswellBC 759, 1990 CarswellBC 216, (sub nom. *Hunt v. Carey Canada Inc.*) [1990] S.C.J. No. 93, 4 C.C.L.T. (2d) 1, 43 C.P.C. (2d) 105, 117 N.R. 321, 4 C.O.H.S.C. 173 (headnote only), (sub nom. *Hunt v. Carey Canada Inc.*) [1990] 6 W.W.R. 385, 49 B.C.L.R. (2d) 273, (sub nom. *Hunt v. Carey Canada Inc.*) 74 D.L.R. (4th) 321, [1990] 2 S.C.R. 959 (S.C.C.). The test is: Assuming the facts asserted in the notice of appeal are true, is it plain and obvious that the appeal is certain to fail?.

Appellant should be required to show there is at least a reasonable possibility that the appeal will succeed. Words "reasonable prospect of success" also convey appropriate test.

Amount required to be deposited by Ms. Dimitroy when filing her notice of appeal, reduced from $925 to $200.

Bryant v. City Dairy Co. (1921), 50 O.L.R. 40, 37 C.C.C. 405, 64 D.L.R. 283 (Ont. C.A.). Where civil action brought in a Division Court within the jurisdiction of court, Judge has full authority to order a stay of proceedings based on the same transaction, and such judicial discretion may not be interfered with by way of prohibition.

Clarke v. Our Neighbourhood Living Society, 2004 CarswellNS 669, 258 N.S.R. (2d) 1, 824 A.P.R. 1, 48 C.P.C. (6th) 56, 2004 NSSM 32 (N.S. Small Cl. Ct.).

Plaintiff commenced an action in both small claims court and Supreme Court against same defendants and some issues were same. Defendant brought counterclaim in small claims court. Court ruled that counterclaim in small claims court action should be served. Defendant's counterclaim dealt with separate matter and it could be severed from plaintiff's claim. Defendant was not prejudiced since it could raise matters in its counterclaim by amending its pleadings in Supreme Court action to make these claims.

107. (1) Consolidation of proceedings in different courts — Where two or more proceedings are pending in two or more different courts, and the proceedings,

(a) have a question of law or fact in common;

(b) claim relief arising out of the same transaction or occurrence or series of transactions or occurrences; or

(c) for any other reason ought to be the subject of an order under this section,

an order may, on motion, be made,

(d) transferring any of the proceedings to another court and requiring the proceedings to be consolidated, or to be heard at the same time, or one immediately after the other; or

(e) **requiring any of the proceedings to be,**

   (i) **stayed until after the determination of any other of them, or**

   (ii) **asserted by way of counterclaim in any other of them.**

Case Law: *Shouldice v. Stewart* (November 20, 1996), Doc. 96-CU-98520CM (Ont. Gen. Div.) — Cause of action in second action was debt for $135,500, representing three advances. First action was against S. personally and second one was against corporation. Relief claimed did not arise out of same transaction. There was no application of "any other reason" provision in r. 6.01 of *Rules of Civil Procedure* (Ont.). Motion for consolidation denied.

Foote v. Mutual of Omaha Insurance Co. (1997), 157 Nfld. & P.E.I.R. 252, 486 A.P.R. 252 (Nfld. T.D.) — Order granted for trial together, not for consolidation of two actions. Actions had little in common except they had roots in same insurance policy. Insurer raised real and substantial defences to claim which militated against consolidation.

Rosenthal v. Burchell (March 9, 1999), Doc. Vancouver 97034165 (B.C. Prov. Ct.) — Application by Rosenthal to have his action transferred from the Small Claims Court to the Supreme Court. Application allowed. Rosenthal proved that the monetary outcome of the claim might exceed $10,000. Although Rosenthal's award might have been reduced by a finding of contributory negligence, this was not a sufficiently compelling argument in this inquiry.

Roberts v. S-G. Transport Ltd. (1998), 160 Nfld. & P.E.I.R. 128, 494 A.P.R. 128, 26 C.P.C. (4th) 339, 1998 CarswellPEI 49 (P.E.I. T.D. [In Chambers]) — Two plaintiffs filed a total of 25 claims against the defendant in Small Claims Court on the same day. The defendant successfully applied to have noting in default in all claims set aside and moved for a consolidation of claims. The consolidation required matters to be moved from Small Claims to General Division and the defendant was given an opportunity to file defences. The plaintiffs' filing fees for 25 notices were ordered refunded less the filing fee in General Division.

Ram Western Express Ltd. v. Baskin, 2004 CarswellOnt 3363 (Ont. S.C.J.), J.E. Ferguson, J. — Motion by Ram for order for directions as to how three actions should proceed.

Third action commenced in the Brampton Small Claims Court for liquidated damages. That claim similar to another claim. Rule 6.01 of the *Rules of Civil Procedure* and Section 107(1) of the *Courts of Justice Act* relevant to the relief being sought. Prerequisite conditions set out in Rule 6.01 and Section 107(1) not met. No common questions of law or fact. See *Rae-Dawn Construction Ltd. v. Edmonton (City)*, 1992 CarswellAlta 333, 3 C.L.R. (2d) 190, 10 C.P.C. (3d) 356, (sub nom. *Ellis-Don Management Services v. Rae-Dawn Construction Ltd.*) 131 A.R. 190, (sub nom. *Ellis-Don Management Services v. Rae-Dawn Construction Ltd.*) 25 W.A.C. 190 (Alta C.A.).

Under section 107(2) of the *CJA* a proceeding in Small Claims Court shall not be transferred under clause (1)(d) to the Superior Court of Justice without consent of plaintiff in proceeding in the Small Claims Court. Banting did consent on behalf of 1124396. *Vigna v. Toronto Stock Exchange*, 1998 CarswellOnt 4560, [1998] O.J. No. 4924, 115 O.A.C. 393, 28 C.P.C. (4th) 318 (Ont. Div. Ct.) distinguished. Motion dismissed.

1029822 Ontario Inc. v. Smith, 2005 CarswellOnt 906 (Ont. C.A.).

Appeal from Justice Power's dismissal of Superior Court action. Dismissal determined that action abuse of process because it raised the same *lis* that had already been determined in earlier Small Claims Court action.

In Small Claims Court action, appellant swore that issues in the two separate actions "dealt with the exact same issues." In the Superior Court action, the appellant swore that his earlier statement was in error and that the two actions raised different legal issues.

Actions not identical.

Superior Court action should *not* have been dismissed. Appeal allowed. Dismissal of Superior Court action set aside.

Domjan Investments Inc. v. D.J. Wagner Investments Inc., 2005 CarswellOnt 7750, 79 O.R. (3d) 150 (Ont. S.C.J.).

Partnership action and action for payment of personal loan ordered consolidated. Actions having question of fact or law in common. Relief claimed in both actions arising out of same transaction or occurrence.

Clarke v. Our Neighbourhood Living Society, 2004 CarswellNS 669, 258 N.S.R. (2d) 1, 824 A.P.R. 1, 48 C.P.C. (6th) 56, 2004 NSSM 32 (N.S. Small Cl. Ct.).

Plaintiff commenced actions in both Small Claims Court and Supreme Court against same defendants and some of issues were same. Society brought counterclaim in Small Claims Court relating to monies allegedly owing by plaintiff to society in respect of clients who were under written contract for plaintiff's services at different location. Court ruled that counterclaim in Small Claims Court action should be severed. Defendant's counterclaim dealt with separate matter which was written contract for plaintiff's services at O home and it could be severed from plaintiff's claim. Society not prejudiced since it could raise matters in its counterclaim by amending its pleadings in Supreme Court action to make these claims.

Haines, Miller & Associates Inc. v. Foss, 1996 CarswellNS 301, 153 N.S.R. (2d) 53, 450 A.P.R. 53, 3 C.P.C. (4th) 349 (N.S. S.C. [In Chambers]) and *R. Llewellyn Building Supplies Ltd. v. Nevitt*, 1987 CarswellNS 319, [1987] N.S.J. No. 262, 80 N.S.R. (2d) 415, 200 A.P.R. 415 (N.S. Co. Ct.) provided authority for the Small Claims Court severing the counterclaim or set off from the main claim.

Gulamani v. Chandra, 2008 CarswellBC 271, 80 B.C.L.R. (4th) 382, 2008 BCSC 179 (B.C. S.C.).

Application brought by the defendants to have two actions commenced by the plaintiff tried together. The applicants, as defendants in the first action, submitted that it was in the interests of justice that the proceedings be heard together given identical allegations of injuries, losses, and damages. The court found that it was too early in the evolution of the second action to meaningfully assess common issues and the risk of inconsistent findings. Further delay was highly prejudicial to the plaintiff. Application dismissed.

Wood v. Farr Ford Ltd. (2008), 2008 CarswellOnt 6116, 67 C.P.C. (6th) 23 (Ont. S.C.J.).

Motion brought by the plaintiff to have his action and the action against him brought by the defendants to be consolidated into once action. Defendants were represented by different counsels in the actions and opposed consolidation due to possible loss of its counsel of choice in its action against plaintiff. Motion allowed. There was no reason that defendants would not be able to continue to have their present counsel represent them with their counsel of choice serving as co-counsel. Consolidation would provide great time and costs savings.

Cunning v. Whitehorse (City), 2009 CarswellYukon 90, 2009 YKSC 48, 74 C.P.C. (6th) 141 (Y.T. S.C.).

Plaintiff and other homeowners brought action in Supreme Court. Plaintiff brought concurrent action in Small Claims Court, making same allegations. Action stayed in Small Claims Court until plaintiff discontinued action in Supreme Court. Trial judge came to correct conclusion that Small Claims Court had jurisdiction to hear dispute. Since plaintiff only sought damages, it did not matter that litigation peripherally involved land. Litigation would likely involve some analysis of easement agreement but only in context of what city should have done as prudent municipality.

Farlow v. Hospital for Sick Children, 2009 CarswellOnt 7124, [2009] O.J. No. 4847, 100 O.R. (3d) 213, 83 C.P.C. (6th) 290 (Ont. S.C.J.).

The plaintiffs brought a medical malpractice action in Small Claims Court against hospital and doctors for the death of their infant daughter. The defendants brought the motion to transfer action to Superior Court and exempt it from simplified procedure, and plaintiffs sought order immunizing them from costs in Superior Court. Motion granted. The action was exempted from simplified procedure. Costs immunity not granted. The claim raised complex issues requiring evidence from number of experts. Given reasons for transferring, particularly the need for discovery and expert witnesses, it was preferable to exempt case from simplified procedure.

A judge of a superior court has the inherent power to transfer a matter from the Small Claims Court to the Superior Court in appropriate circumstances (*Vigna v. Toronto Stock Exchange*, 28 C.P.C. (4th) 318, [1998] O.J. No. 4924, 115 O.A.C. 393, 1998 CarswellOnt 4560 (Ont. Div. Ct.) at para. 7). It is, however, a discretion that should be rarely exercised (*Crane Canada Co. v. Montis Sorgic Associates Inc.*, 2006 CarswellOnt 3051, [2006] O.J. No. 1999 (Ont. C.A.)).

Given the reasons for transferring this case to the Superior Court, that is, the complexity and seriousness of the allegations, the need for discovery and the number of potential expert witnesses, it is preferable to exempt the case from simplified procedure.

Court's Jurisdiction to Grant Costs Immunity

The courts' broad discretion to order costs has long been recognized (*British Columbia (Minister of Forests) v. Okanagan Indian Band* (2003), 21 B.C.L.R. (4th) 209, 309 W.A.C. 161, 189 B.C.A.C. 161, [2004] 1 C.N.L.R. 7, 233 D.L.R. (4th) 577, 2003 CarswellBC 3041, 2003 CarswellBC 3040, 2003 SCC 71, [2003] 3 S.C.R. 371, 313 N.R. 84, [2004] 2 W.W.R. 252, 114 C.R.R. (2d) 108, [2003] S.C.J. No. 76, 43 C.P.C. (5th) 1 (S.C.C.)). In Ontario, this discretion is recognized in section 131(1) of the *Courts of Justice Act* and r. 57.01 of the *Rules of Civil Procedure*.

There have been several exceptions to the general rule that costs follow the cause and that costs can only be determined at the conclusion of the proceeding. A losing party that raises a serious legal issue of public importance will not necessarily bear the other party's costs. In exceptional cases, the successful party may have to pay the costs of the losing party (*B. (R.) v. Children's Aid Society of Metropolitan Toronto* (1995), [1994] S.C.J. No. 24, EYB 1995-67419, 1995 CarswellOnt 515, 1995 CarswellOnt 105, 78 O.A.C. 1, 176 N.R. 161, 26 C.R.R. (2d) 202, [1995] 1 S.C.R. 315, 122 D.L.R. (4th) 1, 21 O.R. (3d) 479 (note), 9 R.F.L. (4th) 157 (S.C.C.)). Interim or advance costs may be awarded prior to the conclusion of the proceeding. Access to justice may be a factor to be taken into consideration.

A costs immunity order raises the risk that the party that has been immunized from a costs order may fail to be accountable for the time and money expended on the case. However, this risk could be addressed by requiring that the litigant relinquish some control over the litigation process. The action should be transferred. Given the nature of the case, it should be exempted from the simplified procedure.

Craig-Smith v. John Doe, [2009] I.L.R. I-4889, 2009 CarswellOnt 5827 (Ont. S.C.J.), Hourigan J.

The plaintiff brought motion for order that actions be consolidated or tried together. Motion granted. Actions had overlapping facts, evidence and legal issues and were sufficiently similar. This was not one of the clearest of cases where actions should be separated. The defendant did not establish any prejudice if motion granted.

Atkins v. Joyce, 2010 BCPC 147, 2010 CarswellBC 1867 (B.C. Prov. Ct.).

Two applications heard:

1) Application by claimant, Atkins, for an order consolidating action with actions no. 0509789 and 0509790 to the Supreme Court. If consolidation not granted, the claimant sought order for Action No. 0509789 to be transferred to Supreme Court.

2) Application by defendants, Joyce and Ishida, for order to enforce settlement agreement reached at pre-trial conference and stay of proceedings.

Was there a concluded settlement to enforce? See *Gerald Walsh Recruitment Services Inc. v. Fraser*, 2002 NSSC 105, 2002 CarswellNS 179, [2002] N.S.J. No. 204 (N.S. S.C.).

See *Radhakrishnan v. University of Calgary Faculty Assn.* (2002), 2002 ABCA 182, 2002 CarswellAlta 943, [2002] A.J. No. 961, 312 A.R. 143, [2003] 1 W.W.R. 244, 5 Alta. L.R. (4th) 1, 215 D.L.R. (4th) 624, 45 Admin. L.R. (3d) 77, 281 W.A.C. 143 (Alta. C.A.)

43 Each party to a settlement makes concessions and assumes some risk, in favour of bringing the dispute to an end. Interests of finality prevail, unless there are contractual problems such as fraud, misrepresentation, duress, undue influence, unconscionability, or mutual or unilateral mistake.

45 The public interest in finality is noticed in *Christiansen v. Bachul* (2001), 284 A.R. 196: "There is a well-established policy in favour of finality of litigation. To accede to this application would undermine that policy." The principle of finality was emphasized where it precluded interference with settlement of even an infant's claim made on incomplete and erroneous fact assumptions: see *Tsaoussis v. Baetz*, 1998 CanLII 5454 (ON C.A.).

49 Whether or not that is correct, the strong policy of the law is to let parties negotiate their own settlements: *Amoco Can. Petro. Co. v. Propak Systems*, 2001 ABCA 110 (CanLII), 2001 ABCA 110. Absent material inducement by misrepresentation, fraud, duress or undue influence, the courts steadfastly refuse to look at the adequacy of consideration.

Based on sections 2(1) and (2) of the *Small Claims Act* and *Rules* as well as following policy in favour of finality of litigation, application to consolidate three files to the Supreme Court denied as well as the application to transfer Action No. 0509789 to the Supreme Court made by the claimant.

(2) Transfer from Small Claims Court — A proceeding in the Small Claims Court shall not be transferred under clause (1)(d) to the Superior Court of Justice without the consent of the plaintiff in the proceeding in the Small Claims Court.

Case Law: *CAD-FM Micro Systems v. Coldmatic Refrigeration of Canada Ltd.* (1994), 71 O.A.C. 348 (Ont. Gen. Div.) — Defendant brought motion transferring trial to the General Division since counterclaim exceeded monetary jurisdiction of the Court. Any action is limited in the Small Claims Court to its monetary jurisdiction. The action cannot be transferred to the General Division. The plaintiff by counterclaim could commence a separate action in the General Division and apply s. 107 of the *Courts of Justice Act*.

MacMaster v. Insurance Corp. of British Columbia (1994), 24 C.P.C. (3d) 288 (B.C. C.A.) — The appellant sought a transfer of action from the Small Claims Court to the Supreme Court. The plaintiff brought an action on the last day of the limitation period and later discovered that the damages exceeded the limit of the Small Claims Court. There was no statutory authority to transfer the case. Appeal from 35 A.C.W.S. (3d) 194 was dismissed.

Rathjen v. Clippingdale (January 29, 1997), Doc. Nelson 5548 (B.C. S.C. [In Chambers]) — Plaintiff initiated several actions in Small Claims Court before commencing action in Supreme Court. Small Claims judge stayed actions pending trial in Supreme Court. Defendant sought to set aside stay. Court held that Small Claims judge had no jurisdiction to adjourn actions *sine die*. Actions could proceed.

Vigna v. Toronto Stock Exchange, 1998 CarswellOnt 4560, [1998] O.J. No. 4924, 115 O.A.C. 393, 28 C.P.C. (4th) 318 (Ont. Div. Ct.) — Motions judge declined to transfer matter, absent Vigna's consent to the transfer. The Toronto Stock Exchange appealed. Divisional Court allowed the appeal. The procedures of the Small Claims Court inadequate to deal with the complex nature of issues. Additional parties would have to participate, *viva voce* and documentary evidence would be required and expert opinion would be necessary. Section 138 of the *Courts of Justice Act*, R.S.O. 1990, c. C.43, provides that, as far as possible, a multiplicity of legal proceedings shall be avoided. Section 107(1)(d) is applicable here. Judge had the necessary jurisdiction inherent to his powers as a Superior Court judge to control the process of the courts. Rule 76 of the *Rules of Civil Procedure*, R.R.O. 1990, Reg. 194, appropriate here, does not contain any provision for the transfer of a case from Small Claims Court.

Hayes v. Maritime Life Assurance Co. (2000), 45 C.P.C. (4th) 333, 225 N.B.R. (2d) 133, 578 A.P.R. 133, 2000 CarswellNB 163 (N.B. Q.B.) — The plaintiff brought an action in Small Claims Court for a maximum $6,000. The insurance company applied to transfer the matter to the Court of Queen's Bench. The application was granted. The transfer was due to the complexity and the possibility of multiplicity of actions. The potential for payment under the policy continued until the plaintiff reached age 65. The potential existed for a $6,000 action in Small Claims Court every time the amount should have been paid and was not. No provision existed in small claims actions for discovery procedures or medical examination of the plaintiff prior to trial.

Cunningham v. Millard, 2005 CarswellBC 1890, 2005 BCPC 343 (B.C. Prov. Ct.), Judge D.E. Moss. Ruling on a Transfer Application to Supreme Court involving Provincial Court Small Claims.

Position that Provincial Court's $10,000 monetary limit insufficient to satisfy their claim, even with the Court's enhanced jurisdiction to $25,000 as of September 1, 2005, monetary award they seek will exceed.

Appropriate to transfer case to Supreme Court of British Columbia for all purposes. Should the plaintiff's claim prove to be successful but have a value of under $25,000, claimant ought to be visited with costs as it was clearly open to proceed within the Provincial Court.

Griffioen v. Liao, 2003 CarswellOnt 5290, 68 O.R. (3d) 535 (Ont. S.C.J.).

Former "rule of thumb" that defamation actions should not be tried with other actions no longer applying. Two defamation actions and counterclaim arising out of dispute between two doctors over ten-month period. Consolidation of actions appropriate. See Rule 1.04(1) of the *Rules of Civil Procedure*. Consolidating claims and counterclaim more likely to promote pre-trail settlement and resolution.

Layland v. Roberts & Associates (2007), 2007 CarswellOnt 4847 (Ont. S.C.J.), B.A. Allen J.

Motion pursuant to s. 107 of the *Courts of Justice Act*, R.S.O. 1990, c. C.43 for order to have action commenced in Small Claims Court in Richmond Hill transferred and continued as an action before Superior Court in Toronto.

Layland further sought order allowing her to amend statement of claim pursuant to Rule 26 of the *Rules of Civil Procedure*. She sought under Rule 76 to proceed under the court's simplified Procedure.

Respondents brought cross-motion under Rule 21.01(3)(d) for order dismissing claim as frivolous and vexatious or abuse of process.

Layland cited case authorities to support position to amend pleadings. See *Denton v. Jones (No. 2)*, 1976 CarswellOnt 363, 14 O.R. (2d) 382, 73 D.L.R. (3d) 636, 3 C.P.C. 137 (Ont. H.C.) and *Atlantic Steel Industries Inc. v. CIGNA Insurance Co. of Canada*, [1997] O.J. No.

1278, 1997 CarswellOnt 913, 33 O.R. (3d) 12, (sub nom. *Atlantic Steel Industries Inc. v. Cigna Insurance Co. of Canada)* 31 O.T.C. 184 (Ont. Gen. Div.).

See also *Mrzlecki v. Kusztos*, 1987 CarswellOnt 850, [1987] O.J. No. 325, 59 O.R. (2d) 301 (Ont. H.C.) and *Williams (Litigation Guardian of) v. Barnett*, 2000 CarswellOnt 3681, [2000] O.J. No. 3815, 11 C.P.C. (5th) 224 (Ont. S.C.J.) as to new evidence to support increase in claim for damages..

Request for order to transfer Small Claims action to the Superior Court premature. No new evidence, medical or otherwise, that warranted a claim for higher damages. Court ordered Layland's motion under s. 107 of the *Courts of Justice Act*, R.S.O. 1990, c. C.43 dismissed. Motion under Rule 26 dismissed, cross-motion dismissed.

Shaughnessy v. Roth, 2006 CarswellBC 2963, 61 B.C.L.R. (4th) 268, 2006 BCCA 547, 386 W.A.C. 212, 233 B.C.A.C. 212 (B.C. C.A.).

Claimant filed claim with Small Claims Court for damages against defendant, who filed counterclaim. Defendant also commenced action in Supreme Court. Defendant successfully applied for transfer of claim and counterclaim to Supreme Court. Provincial Court judge stated that two hearings in two different courts could result in conflicting judicial findings, and there was potential for damages that would exceed jurisdiction of court. Claimant's application for judicial review was granted in part. Provincial Court directed to determine whether claim had monetary outcome that might exceed $25,000, and if so, whether claimant chose to abandon amount over $25,000. Defendant appealed. Appeal dismissed. For purposes of r. 71, court must consider monetary values of claim and counterclaim separately.

Country Cottage Living Inc. v. Heath (2008), 2008 CarswellOnt 2766, 72 C.L.R. (3d) 301 (Ont. S.C.J.).

Trial judge consolidated Small Claims Action with the Construction Lien Action. The counsel for the defendant submits that s. 107(2) of the *Courts of Justice Act* is inconsistent with the general consolidation power provided for in s. 59(2) of the *Construction Lien Act*. Argument rejected by the court. The wording of s. 107(2) of the *Courts of Justice Act* is clear and unambiguous and the consolidation power under s. 59(2) of the *CLA* is limited to lien actions and does not apply to "regular" actions.

Farlow v. Hospital for Sick Children, 2009 CarswellOnt 7124, 83 C.P.C. (6th) 290, [2009] O.J. No. 4847, 100 O.R. (3d) 213 (Ont. S.C.J.), Herman, J.

Plaintiffs brought a complex medical malpractice case to Small Claims Court. Defendants moved successfully for order transferring action to Superior Court *and* exempting it from simplified procedure. Plaintiffs' request for immunity from costs dismissed. Court having discretion to grant such order in exceptional circumstances. Plaintiffs failed to establish they would be denied access to justice. Plaintiffs not immunized from costs. Facts were complex and expert evidence was required.

Lau v. Rai, 2009 CarswellBC 1390, 2009 BCSC 696, [2009] B.C.J. No. 1037, 72 C.P.C. (6th) 112 (B.C. S.C.); affirmed 2010 BCCA 26, 2010 CarswellBC 99, 2 B.C.L.R. (5th) 119, [2010] 5 W.W.R. 18 (B.C. C.A.), R.E. Powers J.; additional reasons 2010 BCCA 194, 2010 CarswellBC 944, 282 B.C.A.C. 110, 476 W.A.C. 110 (B.C. C.A.); additional reasons to 2007 CarswellBC 2888, 2007 BCSC 1746 (B.C. S.C.), R.E. Powers J.

The plaintiff brought action in Small Claims Court. Plaintiff successfully applied to have proceedings transferred to Supreme Court. Defendants contended that any costs allowed to plaintiff should be limited by r. 57(10) of *Rules of Court*, 1990. Rule states that the plaintiff recovering sum within jurisdiction of Provincial Court under *Small Claims Act* is not entitled to costs, other than disbursements, unless court finds there was sufficient reason to bring action in Supreme Court, and so orders. The plaintiff had sufficient reason for brings proceedings to Supreme Court when it was initially transferred from Provincial Court.

376101 Alberta Ltd. v. Westvillage Condominiums Ltd., 2009 ABPC 329, 2009 CarswellAlta 2231, 483 A.R. 304 (Alta. Prov. Ct.), B.K. O'Ferrall Prov. J.

The plaintiff brought action in Provincial Court against the developers of a condominium. Application dismissed. Superior Court had jurisdiction over alternative claim for relief under *Business Corporations Act*. Fact there were 45 other actions against defendants for damages totalling $750,000 was not ground for transferring this action. Claim did not bring title to land into question.

Gradek v. DaimlerChrysler Financial Services Canada Inc./Services Financiers DaimlerChrysler Canada Inc., 2010 CarswellBC 665, 2010 BCSC 356, 95 C.P.C. (6th) 375 (B.C. S.C. [In Chambers]); affirmed 2011 BCCA 136, 2011 CarswellBC 588, 100 C.P.C. (6th) 12, (sub nom. *Gradek v. DaimlerChrysler Financial Services Canada Inc.)* 307 B.C.A.C. 7, (sub nom. *Gradek v. DaimlerChrysler Financial Services Canada Inc.)* 519 W.A.C. 7 (B.C. C.A.); additional reasons to 2009 BCSC 1572, 2009 CarswellBC 3297, [2009] B.C.J. No. 2432 (B.C. S.C.).

The defendant argued the plaintiff should receive costs only if action was in accordance with r. 57(10) of *Rules of Court*, 1990, which states that the plaintiff who recovers sum in jurisdiction of Provincial Court under *Small Claims Act* is not entitled to costs unless the court finds there was sufficient reasons for bringing action in Supreme Court. The plaintiff was from Poland and spoke little English. The plaintiff would have had extraordinary difficulty presenting case on his own. The defendant submitted that in Provincial Court it would have been represented by the adjuster, but Court held that the plaintiff still would have been outmatched.

1000728 Ontario Ltd. v. Kakish, 2010 ONSC 538, 2010 CarswellOnt 599, 88 C.P.C. (6th) 108 (Ont. S.C.J.).

The consignee brought motion to transfer action from Small Claims Court to Superior Court of Justice. Motion granted. Case complex and expert evidence required to assess interrelationship of invoices, purchase orders, bills of lading and other documents as well as their legal relationship. Small Claims Court lacked procedure for exchange of expert reports prior to trial. Full discovery was required.

Cases may be moved from the Small Claims Court on a motion and with the order of a Superior Court judge. See *Alexandrov v. Csanyi*, 247 O.A.C. 228, 2009 CarswellOnt 1325 (Ont. Div. Ct.); *Csanyi v. Alexandrov*, 2009 CarswellOnt 5446 (Ont. S.C.J.), and *Haines, Miller & Associates Inc. v. Foss*, 1996 CarswellNS 301, 3 C.P.C. (4th) 349, 450 A.P.R. 53, 153 N.S.R. (2d) 53 (N.S. S.C. [In Chambers]); additional reasons at 1996 CarswellNS 304, 466 A.P.R. 389, 158 N.S.R. (2d) 389 (N.S. S.C. [In Chambers]).

In *Alexandrov*, the Court stated that the jurisprudence on transfer is that a plaintiff may be forced, in very exceptional cases, into the Superior Court against the actual wishes of the plaintiff. In *Farlow v. Hospital for Sick Children*, 2009 CarswellOnt 7124, 83 C.P.C. (6th) 290, [2009] O.J. No. 4847, 100 O.R. (3d) 213 (Ont. S.C.J.), Court held that on a motion to transfer an action from Small Claims Court to the Superior Court of Justice, there must be a balancing of the various factors enumerated in that decision.

The Small Claims Court does *not* have procedural framework similar to rr. 53.03 and 76.10(4) of the *Rules of Civil Procedure*, R.R.O. 1990, Reg. 194 for the timely exchange of expert reports in advance of the trial. In *Crane Canada Co. v. Montis Sorgic Associates Inc.*, 2005 CarswellOnt 9989, [2005] O.J. No. 6247 (Ont. S.C.J.); affirmed 2006 CarswellOnt 3051, [2006] O.J. No. 1999 (Ont. C.A.), the Court found that expert evidence would be central to the determination of the claims and that such evidence would likely be complex, and decided accordingly that claims would be more appropriately dealt with in the Superior Court.

Capano v. Rahm, 2010 CarswellOnt 4760, 2010 ONSC 3241, [2010] O.J. No. 2866 (Ont. S.C.J.); additional reasons at 2010 ONSC 4131, 2010 CarswellOnt 6013 (Ont. S.C.J.); leave to appeal refused 2010 CarswellOnt 7425 (Ont. Div. Ct.), Pitt J.

The motion was brought pursuant to the rr. 1.04(1), (1.1) and 48.04(1) of the *Rules of Civil Procedure*, R.R.O. 1990, Reg. 194, and sections 23(2) and 110 of the *Courts of Justice Act*, R.S.O. 1990, c. C.43 by the plaintiffs, for order moving matter *to* the Small Claims Court, in light of the increase in the Small Claims Court's monetary jurisdiction to $25,000 from $10,000 as of January 1, 2010.

Section 23(2) of the *Courts of Justice Act* makes it clear that an action in the Superior Court of Justice may be transferred to the Small Claims Court before the trial commences only on the consent of *all* parties. The defendant refused to consent.

Court may draw on its inherent powers over its own process to transfer an action from one judicial forum to another: see *Vigna v. Toronto Stock Exchange* (1998), 28 C.P.C. (4th) 318, [1998] O.J. No. 4924, 115 O.A.C. 393, 1998 CarswellOnt 4560 (Ont. Div. Ct.) at para. 7. However, particular facts of this case do not warrant its exercise.

Master has jurisdiction to decide whether to move an action in the Superior Court to the Small Claims Court. Section 107(4) of the *Courts of Justice Act* states that where there are two or more proceedings pending in two or more different courts, a request to transfer must be made to a judge of the Superior Court. In other words, judges of the Superior Court have the exclusive jurisdiction to hear motions for consolidation, hearing together, or hearing one after the other of *existing* proceedings. By implication, requests for transfer *simpliciter* can be dealt with by either a judge or a master.

On February 22, 2010, pretrial adjourned to a date after August 1, 2010. Plaintiffs had benefit of mediation, two motions and the assessment of Master Haberman. Pretrial to proceed without need for expert evidence. It was too late to transfer case to another court. Motion dismissed.

Sioux Lookout (Municipality) v. Goodfellow, 2010 ONSC 1812, 2010 CarswellOnt 2349 (Ont. S.C.J.); additional reasons at 2010 ONSC 2875, 2010 CarswellOnt 4195, [2010] O.J. No. 2564 (Ont. S.C.J.), Justice D.C. Shaw.

The municipality of Sioux Lookout was the plaintiff in this action in the Superior Court. Goodfellow was the sole defendant; Goodfellow was the plaintiff in 10 actions in the Small Claims Court at Dryden.

A motion was made to strike Goodfellow's defence and counterclaim, in a Superior Court action, with leave to file a fresh claim and counterclaim to include claims made by Goodfellow as the plaintiff in the 10 Small Claims Court actions, and to stay or dismiss the Small Claims Court actions. In the alternative, the municipality sought to have the 10 Small Claims Court actions consolidated with the Superior Court of Justice action.

All 10 Small Claims Court actions should be transferred to the Superior Court of Justice.

See *Vigna v. Toronto Stock Exchange*, 1998 CarswellOnt 4560, [1998] O.J. No. 4924, 115 O.A.C. 393, 28 C.P.C. (4th) 318 (Ont. Div. Ct.). It is part of the jurisdiction of the Superior Court to transfer a matter from the Small Claims Court to the Superior Court in appropriate circumstances, without the consent of the plaintiff in the Small Claims Court proceedings.

It was inappropriate for Goodfellow to split what was, in essence, one cause of action into separate causes of action so that they could proceed in the Small Claims Court. See Rule 6.02 of the *Small Claims Court Rules*.

Goodfellow agreed to transfer the two Small Claims Court actions relating to the costs of his claim to the Superior Court of Justice, leaving the remaining eight Small Claims Court actions, totalling $21,418.44, within recently increased monetary jurisdiction of the Small

Claims Court of $25,000. All ten Small Claims Court actions were essentially one cause of action.

The transfer of the actions was consistent with the policy objective of the *Rules of Civil Procedure* as set out in rule 1.04(1):

> These rules shall be liberally construed to secure the just, most expeditious and least expensive determination of every civil proceeding on its merits.

Rule 6.03(1) of the *Small Claims Court Rules* is to similar effect:

> These rules shall be liberally construed to secure the just, most expeditious and least expensive determination of every proceeding on its merits in accordance with section 25 of the *Courts of Justice Act*.

Once a Small Claims Court action is transferred to the Superior Court, the question becomes whether the court should order consolidation, or whether it should order the hearing of the proceedings together or one after the other.

Particulars for pleading are only to be ordered when they are not within the knowledge of the party demanding them and they are necessary to enable the other party to plead. The onus to satisfy the court that these two criteria have been met rests on the party requesting the particulars. See *Obonsawin v. Canada*, 2001 CarswellOnt 306, [2001] O.J. No. 369, [2001] 2 C.T.C. 96, [2001] G.S.T.C. 26 (Ont. S.C.J.) *per* Epstein J. (as she was then) and *Cutajar v. Frasca*, 2009 CarswellOnt 7476, [2009] O.J. No. 5126 (Ont. Master), *per* Master Muir.

Vista Sudbury Hotel Inc. v. Double T Earth Moving Ltd., 2011 ONSC 3454, 2011 CarswellOnt 4890 (Ont. S.C.J.), R.D. Gordon J.

"Double T" brought an action against Vista in the Small Claims Court for payment of unpaid invoices. Vista filed a defence to that action.

Vista subsequently brought an action in the Superior Court of Justice against Double T for a breach of contact. Vista brought a motion for an order traversing Sudbury Small Claims Court file to the Ontario Superior Court of Justice.

The actions in the Small Claims Court and the Superior Court of Justice involved the same parties and arose out of the same set of facts. Common questions of law and fact were discussed.

The motion was governed by section 107 of the *Courts of Justice Act*.

Three issues arose: (1) Whether the plaintiff was requesting an order under section 107(1)(d); (2) If so, whether there was jurisdiction in the Court to make the requested order; and (3) If so, whether that order ought to be granted in the circumstances of the case.

Section 107(3) of the *Courts of Justice Act* provides that a proceeding in a Small Claims Court shall not be required under subclause (1)(e)(ii) to be asserted by way of counterclaim in a proceeding in the Superior Court of Justice without the consent of the plaintiff in the proceeding in the Small Claims Court.

Section 107(2) provides that a proceeding in the Small Claims Court *shall not* be transferred under clause (1)(d) to the Superior Court of Justice without the consent of the plaintiff in the proceeding in the Small Claims Court. Double T, the plaintiff, had *not* consented.

Vista relied on the case of *Vigna v. Toronto Stock Exchange*, 1998 CarswellOnt 4560, [1998] O.J. No. 4924, 115 O.A.C. 393, 28 C.P.C. (4th) 318 (Ont. Div. Ct.), where the Divisional Court held that it is open to a judge of the Superior Court to transfer a matter from the Small Claims Court to the General Division in appropriate circumstances without the consent of the plaintiff in the Small Claims proceeding. The case was distinguishable because the Divisional Court specifically found that the relief claimed it did not fall under section 107(1)(d) and the consent of the plaintiff was not required.

Section 107 clearly contemplates coincident actions in the Small Claims Court and the Superior Court of Justice that may involve common parties, common issues of fact, and common issues of law.

Where the effect of the requested order is to force the plaintiff in the Small Claims Court action to adjudicate his or her claims in the Superior Court in concert with another Superior Court action, or as a counterclaim in a Superior Court action, the consent of the plaintiff is a precondition to transfer.

The motion was dismissed.

Resort Country Realty Inc. v. Tanglewood (Sierra Homes) Inc., 2013 ONSC 1120, 2013 CarswellOnt 1770 (Ont. S.C.J.); additional reasons 2013 ONSC 1650, 2013 CarswellOnt 3372 (Ont. S.C.J.), M.P. Eberhard J.

The Respondent moves for leave to appeal the order of McCarthy J. dated October 3, 2012 which granted the Plaintiff's motion to consolidate and transfer Small Claims Court actions to the Superior Court of Justice and which dismissed the Defendant's motion to strike the claims for abuse of process.

It is conceded that but for the issues arising from the earlier proceeding in the Superior Court of Justice the consolidation and transfer of the several Small Claims Court actions to this court would be proper.

In the present case there wereco-existing claims in three courts. The consent dismissal was silent as to these other cases. The correspondence referred to discontinuance, then dismissal, of the case in the Superior Court of Justice and the consent and resulting order referred to it by number. No one, not either lawyer, chose to be specific about the co-existing cases.

There is no prejudice that cannot be remedied by applying the same principles to bring the counterclaim back before the court or by costs for the steps generated by the plaintiff blundering into the Small Claims Court.

Motion dismissed.

Singh v. McHatten, 2012 BCCA 286, 2012 CarswellBC 1878, 33 B.C.L.R. (5th) 251, [2012] 10 W.W.R. 280, 323 B.C.A.C. 314, 550 W.A.C. 314 (B.C. C.A.).

The respondent brought two separate actions for claims arising from a single motor vehicle accident; the first was in the Small Claims Court and the second in Supreme Court.

The appellants in the Supreme Court action pleaded *res judicata* and moved to dismiss the action. On 11 August 2011, a summary trial judge dismissed the application: 2011 BCSC 1093, 2011 CarswellBC 2098 (B.C. S.C.); reversed 2012 BCCA 286, 2012 CarswellBC 1878, 33 B.C.L.R. (5th) 251, [2012] 10 W.W.R. 280, 323 B.C.A.C. 314, 550 W.A.C. 314 (B.C. C.A.). The appellants appeal from that decision.

The appellants say the judge erred in confusing the respondent's motivation for bringing the first proceeding with the cause of action supporting it and in failing to identify any valid special circumstance justifying the refusal to give effect to cause of action estoppel.

Innes v. Bui, is not similar to the case at bar. The Small Claims action in this case is not framed in terms of contract or breach of statutory duty against ICBC but in negligence against alleged tortfeasors.

Appeal allowed, action dismissed.

Vista Sudbury Hotel Inc. v. Double T Earth Moving Ltd., 2011 ONSC 3454, 2011 Carswell-Ont 4890, R. D. Gordon J. (Ont. S.C.J.)

The actions in the Small Claims Court and the Superior Court of Justice involve the same parties and arise out of the same set of facts. The two actions will involve common questions of law and fact.

Vista's motion was governed by provisions of section 107 of the *Courts of Justice Act.*

Three issues arise from this section: (1) Whether the plaintiff is requesting an order under section 107(1)(d); (2) If so, whether there is jurisdiction in the Court to make the requested order; and (3) If so, whether that order ought to be granted in the circumstances of this case.

Section 107 clearly contemplates coincident actions in the Small Claims Court and the Superior Court of Justice that may involve common parties, common issues of fact, and common issues of law. Where the effect of the requested order is to force the plaintiff in the Small Claims Court action to adjudicate his or her claim in the Superior Court in concert with another Superior Court action, or as a counterclaim in a Superior Court action, the consent of the plaintiff is a precondition to transfer. Absent Double T's consent in this instance, the Court was unable to make the requested order. Should court be mistaken, however, this is not the type of rare case referred to by the court in *Vigna v. Toronto Stock Exchange* that would warrant a transfer to the Superior Court.

Vista's motion is dismissed.

Sioux Lookout (Municipality) v. Goodfellow, 2010 ONSC 1812, 2010 CarswellOnt 2349, Mr. Justice D.C. Shaw (Ont. S.C.J.); additional reasons 2010 ONSC 2875, 2010 CarswellOnt 4195, [2010] O.J. No. 2564 (Ont. S.C.J.).

Goodfellow is the plaintiff in 10 actions in the Small Claims Court at Dryden. The Municipality is the sole defendant in 9 of the 10 actions. The Municipality, Stan Nissley, and Perron Contracting 917260 Ont. Inc. are the defendants in one of the 10 actions. All 10 Small Claims Court actions should be transferred to the Superior Court of Justice.

Based on *Vigna v. Toronto Stock Exchange*, 1998 CarswellOnt 4560, 28 C.P.C. (4th) 318, 115 O.A.C. 393, [1998] O.J. No. 4924 (Ont. Div. Ct.), it is within the jurisdiction of the Superior Court of Justice to transfer a matter from the Small Claims Court to the Superior Court of Justice in appropriate circumstances, without the consent of the plaintiff in the Small Claims Court proceeding.

It was inappropriate for Goodfellow to split one cause of action into separate causes of action so that they could proceed in the Small Claims Court. Rule 6.02 of the *Small Claims Court Rules* prohibits a cause of action from being divided into two or more actions for the purpose of bringing it within the court's jurisdiction. All 10 Small Claims Court actions are essentially one cause of action.

Transfer of actions consistent with the policy objective of the *Rules of Civil Procedure* as set out in rule 1.04(1):

> These rules shall be liberally construed to secure the just, most expeditious and least expensive determination of every civil proceeding on its merits.

Rule 6.03(1) of the *Small Claims Court Rules* is to similar effect:

> These rules shall be liberally construed to secure the just, most expeditious and least expensive determination of every proceeding on its merits in accordance with section 25 of the *Courts of Justice Act.*

1000728 Ontario Ltd. v. Kakish, 2010 ONSC 538, 2010 CarswellOnt 599, 88 C.P.C. (6th) 108, Spence, J. (Ont. S.C.J.)

Motion by defendant, ("Access"), for an order transferring Small Claims Court Claim (the "Action") to the Superior Court of Justice. Baron pleads it is entitled to recover from Access unpaid invoices by reason of Access being a consignee of goods under a bill of lading for purposes of the *Mercantile Law Amendment Act*, R.S.O. 1990, c. M.10.

Cases may be moved from the Small Claims Court on a motion and with the order of a Superior Court judge. (See: *Alexandrov v. Csanyi*, 2009 CarswellOnt 1325, 247 O.A.C. 228 (Ont. Div. Ct.); *Csanyi v. Alexandrov*, 2009 CarswellOnt 5446 (Ont. S.C.J.); *Haines, Miller & Associates Inc. v. Foss*, 1996 CarswellNS 301, 153 N.S.R. (2d) 53, 3 C.P.C. (4th) 349,

450 A.P.R. 53 (N.S. S.C. [In Chambers]); additional reasons 1996 CarswellNS 304, 158 N.S.R. (2d) 389, 466 A.P.R. 389 (N.S. S.C. [In Chambers]).

In *Farlow v. Hospital for Sick Children*, 2009 CarswellOnt 7124, 100 O.R. (3d) 213, 83 C.P.C. (6th) 290, [2009] O.J. No. 4847 (Ont. S.C.J.) at para. 18, Court held that on a motion to transfer an action from Small Claims Court to the Superior Court of Justice, there must be a balancing of the various factors enumerated in that decision.

Expert evidence will be necessary for determination of issues are to be tried. Expert evidence can be given in the Small Claims Court. However, it is not contested that the Small Claims Court does not have procedural framework similar to Rules 53.03 and 76.10(4) of the *Rules of Civil Procedure*, R.R.O. 1990, Reg. 194 for the timely exchange of expert reports in advance of the trial.

See *Crane Canada Co. v. Montis Sorgic Associates Inc.*, 2005 CarswellOnt 9989, [2005] O.J. No. 6247 (Ont. S.C.J.); affirmed 2006 CarswellOnt 3051, [2006] O.J. No. 1999 (Ont. C.A.). The Small Claims Court is not in a position to provide consecutive trial dates, which is a standard procedure in the Superior Court of Justice. Motion granted.

(3) Idem — A proceeding in the Small Claims Court shall not be required under subclause (1)(e)(ii) to be asserted by way of counterclaim in a proceeding in the Superior Court of Justice without the consent of the plaintiff in the proceeding in the Small Claims Court.

Case Law: *Miller v. Walters*, 2008 CarswellBC 2190, 2008 BCPC 292 (B.C. Prov. Ct.), K.D. Skilnick Prov. J.

Claimants brought application for order transferring claim to Supreme Court. Application dismissed. Claimants did not show, on balance of probabilities, prima facie case that monetary outcome of claim would exceed $25,000. Claimants offered no evidence supporting their assertion.

Csanyi v. Alexandrov (2009), [2009] O.J. No. 3829, 2009 CarswellOnt 5446 (Ont. S.C.J.), Pattillo J.

Circumstances necessary to enable court to exercise its discretion to transfer Small Claims action to Superior Court not present. Issues in Small Claims action not complex. Simple claim within monetary jurisdiction of the Small Claims Court could be easily resolved within Small Claims Court procedure. Allowing the Small Claims action to proceed would not cause any injustice to any of the parties in either the Small Claims action or the Superior Court action.

Farlow v. Hospital for Sick Children (2009), 2009 CarswellOnt 7124, [2009] O.J. No. 4847 (Ont. S.C.J.), Herman J.

Defendants sought order transferring small claims action by plaintiffs to the Superior Court and for exemption from simplified procedure. The court allowed motion because nature and complexity of issues warranted transfer to Superior Court and exemption from simplified procedure to facilitate discovery of several experts.

However, circumstances did not warrant exceptional remedy of order granting plaintiffs immunity from a future award of costs. Insufficient evidence of plaintiffs' finances to determine whether denial of access to justice would occur if case transferred. No costs immunity or interim costs were awarded. Impact of such an order on the defendants, as private litigants and a public sector institution, uncertain. Public interest did not support award for costs immunity, as claim in its current form sought a monetary remedy.

Rabbit Hill Recreations Inc. v. Stelter, 2009 ABQB 329, 2009 CarswellAlta 795, 82 R.P.R. (4th) 238, 9 Alta. L.R. (5th) 106 (Alta. Q.B.), D. Lee J.

Statements of claim in two actions virtually identical. Also, third party notices in each action were extremely similar. Parties also similar. Accordingly, actions could be consolidated and it was further ordered that trials be heard together by same judge and all evidence admissible in one action to be admissible in other.

(4) **Motions** — The motion shall be made to a judge of the Superior Court of Justice.

(5) **Directions** — An order under subsection (1) may impose such terms and give such directions as are considered just, including dispensing with service of a notice of readiness or listing for trial and abridging the time for placing an action on the trial list.

(6) **Transfer** — A proceeding that is transferred to another court under clause (1)(d) shall be titled in the court to which it is transferred and shall be continued as if it had been commenced in that court.

(7) **Discretion at hearing** — Where an order has been made that proceedings be heard either at the same time or one immediately after the other, the judge presiding at the hearing nevertheless has discretion to order otherwise.

1996, c. 25, s. 9(17)

Procedural Matters

108. (1) **Jury trials** — In an action in the Superior Court of Justice that is not in the Small Claims Court, a party may require that the issues of fact be tried or the damages assessed, or both, by a jury, unless otherwise provided.

(2) **Trials without jury** — The issues of fact and the assessment of damages in an action shall be tried without a jury in respect of a claim for any of the following kinds of relief:

1. Injunction or mandatory order.

2. Partition or sale of real property.

3. Relief in proceedings referred to in the Schedule to section 21.8.

4. Dissolution of a partnership or taking of partnership or other accounts.

5. Foreclosure or redemption of a mortgage.

6. Sale and distribution of the proceeds of property subject to any lien or charge.

7. Execution of a trust.

8. Rectification, setting aside or cancellation of a deed or other written instrument.

9. Specific performance of a contract.

10. Declaratory relief.

11. Other equitable relief.

12. Relief against a municipality.

Commentary: Section 108(2) has been amended so that a jury is only prohibited in respect of the claim of one of the enumerated kinds of relief (e.g. equitable relief). A jury may therefore still determine the issues of fact with respect to other claims in an action.

(3) **Idem** — On motion, the court may order that issues of fact be tried or damages assessed, or both, without a jury.

(4) Composition of jury — Where a proceeding is tried with a jury, the jury shall be composed of six persons selected in accordance with the *Juries Act*.

(5) Verdicts or questions — Where a proceeding is tried with a jury,

(a) the judge may require the jury to give a general verdict or to answer specific questions, subject to section 15 of the *Libel and Slander Act*; and

(b) judgment may be entered in accordance with the verdict or the answers to the questions.

(6) Idem — It is sufficient if five of the jurors agree on the verdict or the answer to a question, and where more than one question is submitted, it is not necessary that the same five jurors agree to every answer.

(7) Discharge of juror at trial — The judge presiding at a trial may discharge a juror on the ground of illness, hardship, partiality or other sufficient cause.

(8) Continuation with five jurors — Where a juror dies or is discharged, the judge may direct that the trial proceed with five jurors, in which case the verdict or answers to questions must be unanimous.

(9) Specifying negligent acts — Where a proceeding to which subsection 193(1) of the *Highway Traffic Act* applies is tried with a jury, the judge may direct the jury to specify negligent acts or omissions that caused the damages or injuries in respect of which the proceeding is brought.

(10) Malicious prosecution — In an action for malicious prosecution, the trier of fact shall determine whether or not there was reasonable and probable cause for instituting the prosecution.

1996, c. 25, s. 9(17); 2006, c. 21, Sched. A, s. 16

109. (1) Notice of constitutional question — Notice of a constitutional question shall be served on the Attorney General of Canada and the Attorney General of Ontario in the following circumstances:

1. The constitutional validity or constitutional applicability of an Act of the Parliament of Canada or the Legislature, of a regulation or by-law made under such an Act or of a rule of common law is in question.

2. A remedy is claimed under subsection 24(1) of the *Canadian Charter of Rights and Freedoms* in relation to an act or omission of the Government of Canada or the Government of Ontario.

(2) Failure to give notice — If a party fails to give notice in accordance with this section, the Act, regulation, by-law or rule of common law shall not be adjudged to be invalid or inapplicable, or the remedy shall not be granted, as the case may be.

(2.1) Form of notice — The notice shall be in the form provided for by the rules of court or, in the case of a proceeding before a board or tribunal, in a substantially similar form.

(2.2) Time of notice — The notice shall be served as soon as the circumstances requiring it become known and, in any event, at least fifteen days before the day on which the question is to be argued, unless the court orders otherwise.

(3) **Notice of appeal** — Where the Attorney General of Canada and the Attorney General of Ontario are entitled to notice under subsection (1), they are entitled to notice of any appeal in respect of the constitutional question.

(4) **Right of Attorneys General to be heard** — Where the Attorney General of Canada or the Attorney General of Ontario is entitled to notice under this section, he or she is entitled to adduce evidence and make submissions to the court in respect of the constitutional question.

(5) **Right of Attorneys General to appeal** — Where the Attorney General of Canada or the Attorney General of Ontario makes submissions under subsection (4), he or she shall be deemed to be a party to the proceedings for the purpose of any appeal in respect of the constitutional question.

(6) **Boards and tribunals** — This section applies to proceedings before boards and tribunals as well as to court proceedings.

1994, c. 12, s. 42

Case Law: *Paluska v. Cava*, 2002 CarswellOnt 1457, 59 O.R. (3d) 469, 18 C.P.C. (5th) 290, 212 D.L.R. (4th) 226, 94 C.R.R. (2d) 169, 158 O.A.C. 319, [2002] O.J. No. 1767 (Ont. C.A.).

The requirement for notice of a constitutional question is mandatory. Where notice was not provided, the resulting decision by a motions judge was invalid and not merely voidable.

110. (1) Proceeding in wrong forum — Where a proceeding or a step in a proceeding is brought or taken before the wrong court, judge or officer, it may be transferred or adjourned to the proper court, judge or officer.

Case Law: *Armstrong Manufacturing Co. v. Keyser* (1987), 9 W.D.C.P. 193 (Ont. Prov. Ct.) — The court has jurisdiction to transfer both a claim and/or a counterclaim to the Supreme Court of Ontario. In this case, the counterclaim of $250,000 and pleadings relating thereto were inappropriate for transfer. The counterclaim was therefore dismissed as being in excess of the monetary jurisdiction of the court.

Graves v. Avis Rent A Car System Inc. (1993), 21 C.P.C. (3d) 391 (Ont. Gen. Div.) — This Court has inherent jurisdiction to govern its own process. Pursuant to section 23(2) of the *Courts of Justice Act* the defendants refused to consent to transfer the action to the Small Claims Court. Rule 1.04 to be applied, case transferee. Jury Notice of no effect. Section 110(1) also not available because the proceeding was not commenced in the wrong court.

Castle v. Toronto Harbour Commissioners, 1987 CarswellOnt 464, 20 C.P.C. (2d) 266 (Ont. Prov. Ct.) — There was no jurisdiction in court to hear the plaintiff's claim since the matter related to the admiralty jurisdiction. The action was transferred to the Supreme Court of Ontario.

Mrzlecki v. Kusztos, 1987 CarswellOnt 850, [1987] O.J. No. 325, 59 O.R. (2d) 301 (Ont. H.C.) — A judge of the Supreme Court has an inherent jurisdiction associated with a power of certiorari to move matters from a lower court into a superior court of jurisdiction.

Tawfik v. Baker (1992), 10 C.P.C. (3d) 239 (Ont. Gen. Div.) — The fact that a personal injury action was brought in the Small Claims Court for an amount exceeding the monetary jurisdiction limit of the Court did not render the Small Claims Court the "wrong court" within the meaning of s. 110. However, there was authority to transfer the action to the General Division.

Sahota v. Beauchamp (1994), 5 W.D.C.P. (2d) 168, [1994] O.J. No. 466, 1994 CarswellOnt 4413 (Ont. Gen. Div.) — Section 110 of the *Courts of Justice Act* cannot be invoked for the purpose of transferring actions to the General Division. The number of defendants does not increase the number of causes of action having regard to Rule 6.02.

Buchanan v. Singh (1994), 51 A.C.W.S. (3d) 633 (B.C. S.C.) — An application to transfer a matter to Small Claims Court was dismissed. The defendant relied on the plaintiff having the matter set down so that jury notice could be filed. The plaintiff was refused order transferring the action to Small Claims Court. Although the plaintiff was prepared to reduce the monetary claim to Small Claims limit, the defendant should not be deprived of an opportunity for jury trial. The defendant was awarded costs in any event.

Grisé v. Sebestyen (1994), 26 C.P.C. (3d) 339 (B.C. Master); reversed (1994), 30 C.P.C. (3d) 51 (B.C. S.C.) — In an action for damages, the plaintiff determined that the damages were in the jurisdiction of the Small Claims Court and sought a transfer from the Supreme Court. As the defendant had not delivered trial and jury notices when the application to re-elect was brought, it could not be said that the action was set for jury trial before the motion was brought. Appeal from 48 A.C.W.S. (3d) 554.

In an action for damages, the plaintiff determined that the most likely award of damages was within the Small Claims Court jurisdiction and sought to transfer from the Supreme Court. After the defendant was advised of the plaintiff's request for consent to transfer, the defendant served jury notice prior to the motion for transfer. Held, on appeal, unless granted by statute, the Judge did not have unfettered discretion to override the party's election for trial by jury. As the defendant had actual notice of the plaintiff's concession that claim fell within the monetary jurisdiction of the Small Claims Court and that the plaintiff had bona fide intention tore-elect jurisdiction, as the defendant had not delivered notice of trial and jury when the plaintiff's application to re-elect was brought. It could not be said that the action was set for jury trial before the motion was brought. The case was transferred to the Small Claims Court. The appeal was allowed.

Juker v. Keith (1994), 29 C.P.C. (3d) 253, 99 B.C.L.R. (2d) 262 (B.C. S.C.) — The plaintiff had been injured in a motor vehicle accident. Counsel for the defendant informed the plaintiff's counsel that he intended to set the matter down for jury trial. The plaintiff's counsel had determined by this time that damages would be in $10,000 range and before the defendant had confirmed any trial dates, the plaintiff brought his application for transfer to the Small Claims Court. The defendant objected to this transfer. Held, the balance of convenience was overwhelmingly in favour of the plaintiff's application. It is not reasonable to compel 8 citizens to put their lives on hold for couple of days to accommodate the defendant's insurers' policy. Application to transfer action to the Small Claims Court was allowed.

Long v. Insurance Corp. of British Columbia (1994), 45 A.C.W.S.(3d) 865 (B.C. S.C.) — An application to transfer action for damages from the Supreme Court to the Small Claims Court was allowed. Quantum was agreed to be set at the Small Claims Court level. No real costs had been incurred by the defence. The plaintiff's costs were limited to disbursements for commencement of proceedings and service.

Long v. Jackson, 1994 CarswellBC 110, [1994] B.C.J. No. 258, 88 B.C.L.R. (2d) 46, 24 C.P.C. (3d) 323, [1994] B.C.W.L.D. 573, 45 A.C.W.S. (3d) 864 (B.C. Master) — An application to transfer action for damages from the Supreme Court to the Small Claims Court was allowed. Liability was not in issue and quantum was now agreed to be at the Small Claims Court level. A simple accident did not justify a five-day judge and jury trial. Costs incurred prior to transfer would be paid at the Supreme Court tariff.

Long v. Jackson, 1994 CarswellBC 137, 89 B.C.L.R. (2d) 106, 24 C.P.C. (3d) 331, [1994] B.C.W.L.D. 934 (B.C. S.C.) — A transfer of action from the Supreme Court to the Small Claims Court would deprive the defendant, who had elected trial by jury, of right to a jury trial. S. 13.1 of *Supreme Court Act*, R.S.B.C. 1979, does not apply to jury trials. Appeal of decision at 45 A.C.W.S. (3d) 864 was allowed.

Pachini v. Pietramala, 1995 CarswellBC 294, 7 B.C.L.R. (3d) 266, 38 C.P.C. (3d) 122, 54 A.C.W.S. (3d) 19 (B.C. S.C.) — Plaintiff entitled to costs at Supreme Court level even though recovery at Small Claims Court level. Onus on plaintiff satisfied that it was reasonable and that there was sufficient cause to continue in Supreme Court after discoveries.

McGinty v. Toronto Transit Commission (1996), 7 W.D.C.P. (2d) 101 (Ont. Div. Ct.) — Pre-trial judge, on his own motion, decided to transfer action from the General Division to the Small Claims Court. If it were clear that the plaintiff's claim was for $6,000 or less, then under s. 23(2) of the *Courts of Justice Act* with consent of all parties, the action could have been transferred to the Small Claims Court. If it were also clear that the plaintiff's claim was for $6,000 or less, even without a motion made by a party the pre-trial judge could exercise his inherent jurisdiction and, without necessary recourse to either s. 23(2) or s. 110(1), could have made an order transferring the action to the Small Claims Court. See *Shoppers Trust Co. v. Mann Taxi Management Ltd.* (1993), 16 O.R. (3d) 192 (Gen. Div.), just as an action brought in the Small Claims Court could be transferred to the General Division where the value of the claim exceeds that of the Small Claims Court. See *Tawfik v. Baker* (1992), 10 O.R. (3d) 569 (Gen. Div.). Jurisprudence governing pre-trials followed in *Essa (Township) v. Guergis* (1993), 15 O.R. (3d) 573 (Div. Ct.).

Leblanc v. Parry (1998), 3 C.C.L.I. (3d) 45 (Ont. Gen. Div.) — The plaintiff sustained injuries when her vehicle was struck by the dislodged wheel of the defendant's vehicle. She originally commenced an action in Small Claims Court. At the pre-trial, the plaintiff was unrepresented, and the defendant was represented by a student-at-law. The defendant's representative told her that her claim should be filed with her insurer and based upon this and other statements made to her by the defendant's representative, the plaintiff agreed to sign a dismissal of the Small Claims Court proceeding. Approximately 10 months later, the plaintiff commenced an action in General Division based on the same facts. The Court held that a judgment by consent is the same as a judgment after the trial of an action. In this case, however, the Court found that the plaintff's consent was not informed consent because it was based on advice given by the opposing party, advice upon which the consent to dismissal was obtained and executed. There was no abuse of process.

Siebert v. Tse (September 3, 1998), Doc. Toronto CP-05375/97, CP-05376/97 (Ont. Small Cl. Ct.) — At the pre-trial of these matters, the Deputy Judge ordered that any party "may move the Court as to the matter of jurisdiction within 15 days". The Plaintiff has brought a motion to determine whether these two claims can proceed as separate causes of action or whether they should be consolidated into one action for $6,000. It is not within the authority of this court to consolidate the two actions for the sum of $12,000 and then traverse to the General Division: Sections 107 and 110, *Courts of Justice Act*, R.S.O. 1990, c. C43; *Tawfik v. Baker* (1992), 10 O.R. (3d) 569 (Ont. Gen. Div.).

Fantasy Construction Ltd. v. Condominium Plan No. 9121612, 1998 CarswellAlta 1007, 26 C.P.C. (4th) 311, (sub nom. *Owners-Condominium Plan No. 9121612 v. Fantasy Construction Ltd.)* 235 A.R. 147 (Alta. Q.B.) — A construction company sued in Provincial Court in the sum of $5,665 for damages. The construction company applied to have action transferred to the Court of Queen's Bench. The provincial judge granted an adjournment on the condition that the company pays $5,665 into court within 15 days. The *Provincial Court Act* (Alberta.), s. 70, did not disclose a statutory authority for the judge to impose such a condition as that appealed from. The effect of the order was to take away the individual's right to defend the action unless the individual could pay into court the amount for which the individual was being sued.

Pappin v. Continental Insurance Co., 1999 CarswellBC 2996 (B.C. Master) — The defendant moved to have a matter transferred to Small Claims Court. There was no evidence that the plaintiff would succeed on a claim exceeding the sum of $10,000. There were no other compelling reasons to keep the matter in the Supreme Court. Motion allowed.

Livingston v. Ould, 1976 CarswellOnt 321, 2 C.P.C. 41 (Ont. H.C.). Issues of general importance seriously raising novel and complicated questions of law. Small claims courts are Courts of equity and good conscience. They are too pressed by their case loads and too informal in nature to deal with such matters. When plaintiffs are not without financial means, such a case may be transferred to the Supreme Court pursuant to the wide discretion conferred under s. 62 of the Act, without any special order as to costs. This was an action for $25 damages based upon a contested claim for a declaration.

Davis v. Ojibway Windsor Realty Co. (1923), 24 O.W.N. 242 (Ont. H.C.). Where plaintiff's cause of action was within Division Court jurisdiction, but the defence involved matters beyond the competence of the Division Court, but defendant made no application for a transfer of the action under s. 71, prohibition could not be granted.

McGregor v. Union Life Insurance Co., 1906 CarswellOnt 170, 7 O.W.R. 423 (Ont. H.C.). Where a plaintiff's cause of action is within the competence of a Division Court, a defendant who applies for an order of removal to the High Court should establish good, substantial reason for involving plaintiff in a much more expensive, complicated, and lengthened controversy in another court. He has to make out that case "ought" to be tried there, and "more fit" to be tried there than in an inferior court.

Qualico Developments Ltd. v. Doherty, 1985 CarswellAlta 256, 41 Alta. L.R. (2d) 380, 23 D.L.R. (4th) 605, 67 A.R. 334 (Alta. Q.B.). Provincial Court Judge transferring matter in its entirety to Court of Queen's Bench. Plaintiff appealing. Appeal dismissed. Transfer to Court of Queen's Bench appropriate since claim and counterclaim containing similar facts and issues.

Ottawa-Carleton Regional Transit Commission v. Banister, 1973 CarswellOnt 407, [1973] 2 O.R. 152 (Ont. H.C.). Where action commenced in Small Claims Court and counterclaim by defendant exceeds monetary jurisdiction of that Court, defendant may be granted order transferring whole matter to the County Court. The combined effect of ss. 1(1)(a), 54(a), 61(1) and 190(1) of the Act and R. 117 is that the word "action" in ss. 1(1)(a) and 61(1) includes the word, "counterclaim." No reason why s. 61(1) should be available only to a plaintiff.

Markwart v. Blaine Lake No. 434 (Rural Municipality), 2005 CarswellSask 548, 2005 SKQB 356 (Sask. Q.B. [In Chambers]), Baynton J.

Trial judge declined to hear case because he concluded that claim was in substance a judicial review application and not a damage claim. Application dismissed. Section 11 of the Act provided that a small claims matter commenced in Provincial Court may be transferred to the Court of Queen's Bench if the Provincial Court Judge made a transfer order with the consent of the parties or if the Provincial Court Judge made a transfer order because he or she concluded that the matter was one to which the Act did not apply. Once a s. 11 transfer order had been made action deemed to have been commenced in the Court of Queen's Bench. The Provincial Court file should not have been sent to Court of Queen's Bench without a s. 11 transfer order of a Provincial Court Judge.

Leus v. Laidman, 2008 CarswellBC 2931, 2008 BCSC 1819, 65 C.P.C. (6th) 327 (B.C. S.C.).

Plaintiff commenced action for injuries sustained in motor vehicle accident. Defendants made formal offer to settle under now repealed R. 37 of Rules of Court, 1990, for $16,000 plus costs, which was rejected. Plaintiff awarded $12,748.48 at trial. No costs awarded. Plaintiff had sufficient reason to bring action in Supreme Court rather than pursuant to Small

Claims rules, so R. 57(10) irrelevant. Depriving plaintiff of costs sufficient to meet objectives of Rule. Size of award, fact that it was less than $4,000 lower than offer, and impact of costs decision on what plaintiff will actually receive, were particularly considered.

Alexandrov v. Csanyi (2009), [2009] O.J. No. 1030, 2009 CarswellOnt 1325, 247 O.A.C. 228 (Ont. Div. Ct.), Low J.

The plaintiff commenced a small claims action for unpaid wages. The defendants brought their own claim for $10,000, alleging $1 million in damages were caused by the plaintiff's negligence. The defendants unsuccessfully moved for consolidation and to transfer both claims into the Superior Court. The court found that the fact that the defendants commenced an action alleging damages of $1 million did not make the Small Claims Court the "wrong court" as contemplated in is. 110 of the *Courts of Justice Act*, R.S.O. 1990, c. C 43. There was no basis to transfer plaintiff's claim from the Small Claims to the Superior Courts court. Plaintiff had right to choose his forum. Nothing complex about the case.

Cunning v. Whitehorse (City), 2009 CarswellYukon 90, 2009 YKSC 48, 74 C.P.C. (6th) 141 (Y.T. S.C.).

Plaintiff and other homeowners brought action in Supreme Court against city. Plaintiff brought concurrent action in Small Claims Court. City brought motion to dismiss claim for lack of jurisdiction. Plaintiff abandoned all claims other than monetary damages. Action stayed in small Claims Court until plaintiff discontinued action in Supreme Court. Trial judge came to correct conclusion that Small Claims Court had jurisdiction to hear dispute. In s. 2(2)(a) of *Small Claims Court Act*, phrase "recovery of land" limited and coloured more general limitation on jurisdiction excluding cases involving "interest in land." Litigation would likely involve some analysis of easement agreement but only in context of what city should have done as prudent municipality.

Howard v. Madill, 2009 CarswellBC 3265, 2009 BCPC 355 (B.C. Prov. Ct.), K.D. Skilnick Prov. J.

Matter involved three separate court files.

Nothing which prevents parties from litigating some issues in the Supreme Court and litigating other issues in Small Claims Court, assuming that the subjects of the litigation fall within the jurisdiction of the respective courts. Dismissal of a Claim prior to trial is a remedy which must be exercised cautiously. See *Cecil v. Holt Renfrew & Co.*, 2001 BCPC 54, 2001 CarswellBC 583, [2001] B.C.J. No. 789 at para. 7 (B.C. Prov. Ct.).

Abuse of process has been defined by *Toronto (City) v. C.U.P.E. Local 79*, 31 C.C.E.L. (3d) 216, 120 L.A.C. (4th) 225, 179 O.A.C. 291, 2003 C.L.L.C. 220-071, REJB 2003-49439, 311 N.R. 201, 2003 CarswellOnt 4329, 2003 CarswellOnt 4328, 2003 SCC 63, 17 C.R. (6th) 276, [2003] 3 S.C.R. 77, 9 Admin. L.R. (4th) 161, 232 D.L.R. (4th) 385, [2003] S.C.J. No. 64 (S.C.C.), at para. 35, as proceedings which are unfair to the point that they are contrary to interests of justice. See also *Shaughnessy v. Roth*, [2006] B.C.J. No. 3125, 2006 CarswellBC 2963, 61 B.C.L.R. (4th) 268, 2006 BCCA 547, 386 W.A.C. 212, 233 B.C.A.C. 212 (B.C. C.A.).

K.N. Umlah Insurance Agency Ltd. v. Christie, 2009 CarswellNS 286, 278 N.S.R. (2d) 285, 886 A.P.R. 285, 2009 NSSM 15 (N.S. Small Cl. Ct.), Adjudicator W.A. Richardson.

The case started in the Supreme Court of Nova Scotia and was transferred to the Small Claims Court. Successful party claimed costs incurred in the Supreme Court prior to the transfer to the Small Claims Court. Section 15(1) of *Small Claims Court Forms and Procedures Regulations* specifies cost award that may be made by adjudicator to successful party. The word "costs" in s. 15(1)(e) was found to mean only the costs incurred in the Supreme Court prior to transfer in nature of disbursements and did not include the costs of retaining a lawyer.

Lau v. Rai, 2009 CarswellBC 1390, 72 C.P.C. (6th) 112, 2009 BCSC 696, [2009] B.C.J. No. 1037 (B.C. S.C.); additional reasons to 2007 CarswellBC 2888, 2007 BCSC 1746 (B.C. S.C.); affirmed 2010 CarswellBC 99, 2010 BCCA 26, 2 B.C.L.R. (5th) 119, [2010] 5 W.W.R. 18 (B.C. C.A.); additional reasons 2010 BCCA 194, 2010 CarswellBC 944, 282 B.C.A.C. 110, 476 W.A.C. 110 (B.C. C.A.).

Plaintiff's claim totalled $8,071.30. Plaintiff successfully applied to have proceedings transferred to Supreme Court. At trial, plaintiff was awarded damages of $9,243.12, including $7,243.12. Defendant contended any costs allowed to plaintiff should be limited, that plaintiff who recovers sum within jurisdiction of Provincial Court under *Small Claims Act* is not entitled to costs, other than disbursements, unless court finds there was sufficient reason to bring action in Supreme Court. Plaintiff entitled to costs throughout. Court of Appeal had concluded that only time to consider whether plaintiff had sufficient reason to bring proceeding in Supreme Court was time of initiation of action. Plaintiff had sufficient reason for bringing proceedings to Supreme Court when it was initially transferred from Provincial Court.

Ostovic v. Foggin, 2009 BCSC 58, 2009 CarswellBC 114 (B.C. S.C.).

Parties acknowledged matter fell within jurisdiction of Small Claims Court. Position of defendant justified plaintiff pursuing case in Supreme Court where pre-trial discovery available. Had plaintiff taken action in Provincial Court, he would not have been able to recover costs of counsel that he would have required to face institutional defendant. Plaintiff entitled to costs under circumstances.

Williams v. Kameka (2009), 2009 NSCA 107, 2009 CarswellNS 553, 77 C.P.C. (6th) 218, 282 N.S.R. (2d) 376, 85 M.V.R. (5th) 157, 895 A.P.R. 376 (N.S. C.A.).

Williams sued Kameka in Small Claims Court and obtained a judgment against Kameka for $6,257.68. Williams sued Kameka in the Nova Scotia Supreme Court. Defendants sought dismissal of the claim on the basis of *res judicata*. Application was dismissed. Defendants appealed.

See *Cox v. Robert Simpson Co.* (1973), 1973 CarswellOnt 888, 40 D.L.R. (3d) 213, 1 O.R. (2d) 333 (Ont. C.A.), where plaintiff advanced claim for cost of repairs to his vehicle under the *Division Courts Act* (subsequently renamed the *Small Claims Court Act*). The defendant paid the monies claimed into court and the plaintiff accepted the payment. He then sued in County Court alleging personal injuries, seeking special and general damages. His claim was dismissed due to his earlier claim. Arnup, J.A., for the court, concluded that the plaintiff's cause of action could not be split. He wrote:

> "The factual situation" which gave the plaintiff a cause of action was the negligence of the defendant which caused the plaintiff to suffer damage. This single cause of action cannot be split to be made the subject of several causes of action.

If not a court of competent jurisdiction, the doctrine of *res judicata* would have no application whatsoever. Remedy respondent sought in Supreme Court action in fact available in Small Claims Court. See further *Comeau v. Breau* (1994), [1994] N.B.J. No. 74, 1994 CarswellNB 256, 372 A.P.R. 329, 145 N.B.R. (2d) 329 (N.B. C.A.) and *Ontario v. National Hard Chrome Plating Co.* (1996), [1996] O.J. No. 93, 1996 CarswellOnt 119 (Ont. Gen. Div.).

Chambers judge erred in law. Williams had one cause of action against Kameka. Having obtained judgment in the Small Claims Court, cause of action merged into that judgment. Appeal allowed with costs.

Cunning v. Whitehorse (City), 2008 YKSM 3, 2008 CarswellYukon 84 (Y.T. Small Cl. Ct.).

Some 74 current owners of properties in question commenced an action in the Supreme Court of Yukon. Cunning, one of the 74 plaintiffs in the Supreme Court action, sued the City in the Small Claims Court. Allegations of fact, and relief claimed, were identical to those contained in the Supreme Court action, except that the damage claim in the small Claims Court action was limited to $25,000.

The City of Whitehorse moved to have the Supreme Court either dismiss or stay Cunning's Small Claims Court action on two grounds. City said the award of a declaration or an injunction was beyond the jurisdiction of the Small Claims Court. The City argued that the plaintiff must elect to proceed in one court or the other.

The Small Claims Court is a statutory court and, in consequence, has only the powers expressly given to it by statute, subject to the implied power to control its own process.

The Court has no power to grant equitable relief. Decisions from other courts supported the City's contention that the court cannot grant injunctive or declaratory relief. (See, for e.g., *Icecorp International Cargo Express Corp. v. Nicolaus*, 2007 BCCA 97, 2007 CarswellBC 444, 236 B.C.A.C. 294, 390 W.A.C. 294, 38 C.P.C. (6th) 26 (B.C. C.A.), *Hellman v. Crane Canada Co.*, 2007 BCPC 133, 2007 CarswellBC 1067 (B.C. Prov. Ct.).).

The plaintiff abandoned her claim for a declaration and an injunction, but insisted the claim for damages could proceed despite the existence of the action in the Supreme Court.

The plaintiff refused to elect. Counsel for the plaintiff stated that if he pursued the Small Claims action, and obtained a judgment in Cunning's favour, he might then continue the Supreme Court action in an attempt to obtain the declaration and/or injunction.

The plaintiff could not divide her claim in that way.

Even where no *forum conveniens* issue arises, and two courts have clear concurrent jurisdiction over a matter, law is clear that you cannot maintain concurrent suits in both courts where the parties, the object, and the cause are the same in both cases. See *Dominion Ready Mix Inc. c. Rocois Construction Inc.*, 1990 CarswellQue 105, 1990 CarswellQue 105F, (sub nom. *Rocois Construction Inc. v. Québec Ready Mix Inc.*) [1990] 2 S.C.R. 440, 112 N.R. 241, 31 Q.A.C. 241 (S.C.C.); *ABN Amro Bank Canada v. Wackett*, 1997 CarswellNS 370, (sub nom. *ABN AMRO Bank Canada v. Collins Barrow*) 161 N.S.R. (2d) 48, 477 A.P.R. 48 (N.S. C.A.).

Cunning was required to elect which court she would proceed in, and that her action in the Small Claims Court ought to be stayed unless and until her action in the Supreme Court was discontinued.

The British Columbia Court of Appeal in *Shaughnessy v. Roth*, 2006 BCCA 547, 2006 CarswellBC 2963, [2006] B.C.J. No. 3125, 61 B.C.L.R. (4th) 268, 386 W.A.C. 212, 233 B.C.A.C. 212 (B.C. C.A.) held that subsection 92 provides the only statutory basis for transferring a claim to the Supreme Court had acted without jurisdiction in transferring a claim on the basis that there were concurrent, related proceedings in the Supreme Court.

Provided that a claimant is prepared to abandon any claim in excess of the Small Claims Court's jurisdiction, their choice to proceed in that court should be respected.

Cunning's claim in the Small Claims court stayed until such time as she provided proof of the discontinuance of her Supreme Court action relating to the same matter. Should she elect to discontinue the Supreme Court action, the Small Claims Court action may proceed. If the plaintiff so elects, the decision of this court will finally determine the dispute between the parties. The plaintiff will not retain the right to sue for additional relief in the Supreme Court.

(2) **Continuation of proceeding** — A proceeding that is transferred to another court under subsection (1) shall be titled in the court to which it is transferred and shall be continued as if it had been commenced in that court.

Commentary: This provision permits a proceeding, or a step in a proceeding, brought or taken before the wrong court, judge or officer, to be transferred or adjourned to the proper court, judge or officer. Without this provision, a person who mistakenly chooses the wrong forum may find that he has missed a time period and is too late to start again.

111. (1) Set off — **In an action for payment of a debt, the defendant may, by way of defence, claim the right to set off against the plaintiff's claim a debt owed by the plaintiff to the defendant.**

(2) Idem — **Mutual debts may be set off against each other, even if they are of a different nature.**

Commentary: This provision was derived from former s. 135(1) of the *Judicature Act*, R.S.O. 1980, c. 223, which did not contain a reference to setting off debts owed in a personal capacity against debts owed in another capacity. This has now been connected.

(3) Judgment for defendant — **Where, on a defence of set off, a larger sum is found to be due from the plaintiff to the defendant than is found to be due from the defendant to the plaintiff, the defendant is entitled to judgment for the balance.**

Case Law: *2146100 Ontario Ltd. v. 2052750 Ontario Inc.*, 2013 ONSC 2483, 2013 CarswellOnt 5148, 115 O.R. (3d) 636, 308 O.A.C. 8, Boswell, J. (Ont. Div. Ct.)

The presiding Deputy Judge gave judgment in favour of the respondents (defendants) for $21,538.85. The appellant asserts that in the process of doing so, he exceeded the monetary jurisdiction of the Court.

The appellant argues that the trial judge's decision effectively adjudicated the appellant's claim at $21,538.85, and adjudicated the respondents' separate claim at $42,633.57, thereby exceeding the monetary jurisdiction of the court.

Subsection 111(3) expressly provides that if the court finds that a larger sum is due from the plaintiff to the defendant, than is found due from the defendant to the plaintiff, the defendant is entitled to judgment for the balance. Courts in Ontario now have the jurisdiction to calculate set offs whether or not the parties assent.

In *Burkhardt*, the plaintiffs sued for $20,000 in damages arising from a fatal car accident involving a pedestrian. The jury assessed damages at $26,000 but found the deceased to have been 50% at fault. In dispute was whether the plaintiffs were limited to 50% of the amount claimed — in other words half of $20,000 — or whether they were entitled to judgment for 50% of $26,000 (the damages assessed by the jury).

Cartwright J. found that the plaintiffs were entitled to half of the damages assessed by the jury.

At the end of the day it is the net judgment that matters. Here, the amount awarded was within the monetary jurisdiction of the Small Claims Court and did not exceed the amount claimed in the Defendants' Claim.

Appeal dismissed.

112. (1) Investigation and report of Children's Lawyer — **In a proceeding under the *Divorce Act* (Canada) or the *Children's Law Reform Act* in which a question concerning custody of or access to a child is before the court, the Children's Lawyer may cause an investigation to be made and may report and make recommendations to the court on all matters concerning custody of or access to the child and the child's support and education.**

(2) **Idem** — The Children's Lawyer may act under subsection (1) on his or her own initiative, at the request of a court or at the request of any person.

(3) **Report as evidence** — An affidavit of the person making the investigation, verifying the report as to facts that are within the person's knowledge and setting out the source of the person's information and belief as to other facts, with the report attached as an exhibit thereto, shall be served on the parties and filed and on being filed shall form part of the evidence at the hearing of the proceeding.

(4) **Attendance on report** — Where a party to the proceeding disputes the facts set out in the report, the Children's Lawyer shall if directed by the court, and may when not so directed, attend the hearing on behalf of the child and cause the person who made the investigation to attend as a witness.

1994, c. 27, s. 43(2)

113. Agreement preventing third party claim or crossclaim — Rules of court permitting a defendant to make a third party claim or crossclaim apply despite any agreement that provides that no action may be brought until after judgment against the defendant.

114. Agreement as to place of hearing — Where a party moves to change the place of hearing in a proceeding, an agreement as to the place of hearing is not binding, but may be taken into account.

115. Security — Where a person is required to give security in respect of a proceeding in a court, a bond of an insurer licensed under the *Insurance Act* to write surety and fidelity insurance is sufficient, unless the court orders otherwise.

1997, c. 19, s. 32

Commentary: Section 115 of the *Courts of Justice Act*, R.S.O. 1990, c. C.43 permits guarantee companies (to which the *Guarantee Companies Security Act*, R.S.O. 1990, c. G.11 applies), to give security by bond, policy, or guarantee contract in court proceedings. Previously, such companies were listed in a regulation made under the *Guarantee Companies Security Act*. Regulation 541, R.R.O. 1990 has been revoked and the list of approved companies is not maintained by Order-in-Council. Some of the proceedings to which security by bond may apply are: an interim order for recovery of personal property under the *Rules of Civil Procedure*; matters under the *Construction Lien Act* and the *Repair and Storage Liens Act*; and estates matters.

The corporations currently approved as guarantee companies were approved by Order-in-Council 1266/94 made on May 11, 1994.

The list of corporations was amended by Order-in-Council No. 2569/94 which was approved and ordered on October 7, 1994.

The depositing of security with a court pursuant to s. 24 of the *Repair and Storage Liens Act* is another procedure which is new to the Small Claims Courts. The deposits can only be in the form of an Irrevocable Letter of Credit (Form 10) or a Financial Guarantee Bond (Form 11) and these forms are issued directly to the applicant by the financial institution involved for filing with the court. These documents are retained by the court and if the respondent accepts the monies offered in settlement under s. 24 the documents are returned to the applicant for cancellation by him. If, or course, the respondent does not accept the monies offered in settlement the court will retain the documents pending receipt of a court order setting out their disposition.

116. (1) Periodic payment and review of damages — In a proceeding where damages are claimed for personal injuries or under Part V of the *Family Law Act* for loss resulting from the injury to or death of a person, the court,

(a) if all affected parties consent, may order the defendant to pay all or part of the award for damages periodically on such terms as the court considers just; and

(b) if the plaintiff requests that an amount be included in the award to offset any liability for income tax on income from the investment of the award, shall order the defendant to pay all or part of the award periodically on such terms as the court considers just.

(2) No order — An order under clause (1)(b) shall not be made if the parties otherwise consent or if the court is of the opinion that the order would not be in the best interest of the plaintiff, having regard to all the circumstances of the case.

(3) Best interests — In considering the best interests of the plaintiff, the court shall take into account,

(a) whether the defendant has sufficient means to fund an adequate scheme of periodic payments;

(b) whether the plaintiff has a plan or a method of payment that is better able to meet the interests of the plaintiff than periodic payments by the defendant; and

(c) whether a scheme of periodic payments is practicable having regard to all the circumstances of the case.

(4) Future review — In an order made under this section, the court may, with the consent of all the affected parties, order that the award be subject to future review and revision in such circumstances and on such terms as the court considers just.

(5) Amount to offset liability for income tax — If the court does not make an order for periodic payment under subsection (1), it shall make an award for damages that shall include an amount to offset liability for income tax on income from investment of the award.

1996, c. 25, s. 1(20)

116.1 (1) Periodic payment, medical malpractice actions — Despite section 116, in a medical malpractice action where the court determines that the award for the future care costs of the plaintiff exceeds the prescribed amount, the court shall, on a motion by the plaintiff or a defendant that is liable to pay the plaintiff's future care costs, order that the damages for the future care costs of the plaintiff be satisfied by way of periodic payments.

(2) The order — If the court makes an order under subsection (1), the court shall determine the amount and frequency of the periodic payments without regard to inflation and shall order the defendant to provide security for those payments in the form of an annuity contract that satisfies the criteria set out in subsection (3).

(3) Form of security — The annuity contract shall satisfy the following criteria:

1. The annuity contract must be issued by a life insurer.

2. The annuity must be designed to generate payments in respect of which the beneficiary is not required to pay income taxes.

3. The annuity must include protection from inflation to a degree reasonably available in the market for such annuities.

(4) **Directions from the court** — If the parties are unable to agree on the terms of the annuity, either party may seek directions from the court about the terms.

(5) **Filing and approval of plan** — Unless the court orders otherwise, a proposed plan to provide security required by an order under subsection (2) shall be filed with the court within 30 days of the judgment or within another period that the court may specify, and the court may approve the proposed plan, with or without modifications.

(6) **Effect of providing security** — If security is provided in accordance with a plan approved by the court, the defendant by whom or on whose behalf the security is provided is discharged from all liability to the plaintiff in respect of damages that are to be paid by periodic payments, but the owner of the security remains liable for the periodic payments until they are paid.

(7) **Effect of not providing security** — If a proposed plan is not filed in accordance with subsection (5) or is not approved by the court, the court shall, at the request of any party to the proceeding, vacate the portions of the judgment in which periodic payments are awarded and substitute a lump sum award.

(8) **Application for lump sum** — The court may order that the future care costs be paid in whole or in part by way of a lump sum payment to the extent that the plaintiff satisfies the court that a periodic payment award is unjust, having regard to the capacity of the periodic payment award to meet the needs for which the damages award for future care costs is intended to provide compensation.

(9) **Amount to offset liability for income tax** — If the court does not make an order for periodic payments under subsection (1) or makes an order for a lump sum payment under subsection (7) or (8), the court shall make an award for damages that shall include an amount to offset liability for income tax on income from investment of the award except to the extent that the evidence shows that the plaintiff will not derive taxable income from investing the award.

(10) **Periodic payments exempt from garnishment, etc.** — Periodic payments of damages for future care costs are exempt from seizure or garnishment to the same extent that wages are exempt under section 7 of the *Wages Act*, unless the seizure or garnishment is made by a provider of care to the plaintiff and the seizure or garnishment is to pay for the costs of products, services or accommodations or any one of them with respect to the plaintiff.

(11) **Future review** — In an order made under this section, the court may, with the consent of all the affected parties, order that the award be subject to future review and revision in such circumstances and on such terms as the court considers just.

(12) **Regulations** — The Lieutenant Governor in Council may make regulations prescribing or calculating the amount of future care costs for the purpose of subsection (1).

(13) **Definitions** — In this section,

"future care costs" means the cost of medical care or treatment, rehabilitation services or other care, treatment, services, products or accommodations that is incurred at a time after judgment;

"medical malpractice action" means an action for personal injuries alleged to have arisen from negligence or malpractice in respect of professional services requested of, or rendered by, a health professional who is a member of a health profession as defined in the *Regulated Health Professions Act, 1991* or an employee of the health professional or for which a hospital as defined in the *Public Hospitals Act* is held liable;

"prescribed amount" means $250,000 or such greater amount as may be prescribed by regulation, calculated as a present value at the time of judgment in accordance with the *Rules of Civil Procedure.*

(14) **Transition** — This section applies to all proceedings in which a final judgment at trial or final settlement has not been made on the day the *Access to Justice Act, 2006* receives Royal Assent.

2006, c. 21, Sched. A, s. 17

117. Assessment of damages — Where damages are to be assessed in respect of,

(a) a continuing cause of action;

(b) repeated breaches of a recurring obligation; or

(c) intermittent breaches of a continuing obligation,

the damages, including damages for breaches occurring after the commencement of the proceeding, shall be assessed down to the time of the assessment.

Case Law: *Wright (Richard) v. Bell Canada* (September 22, 1988), Doc. No. 680/87 (Ont. Div. Ct.) — The costing refusal of the defendant to provide the plaintiff with a 666 number was not a continuing cause of action and therefore the judgment was set aside as the matter was *res judicata.*

118. Guidance and submissions — In an action for damages for personal injury, the court may give guidance to the jury on the amount of damages and the parties may make submissions to the jury on the amount of damages.

119. Power of court on appeal — On an appeal from an award for damages for personal injury, the court may, if it considers it just, substitute its own assessment of the damages.

Commentary: This new section allows an appeal court to substitute its assessment of damages for that of a jury.

120. (1) **Advance payments** — If a defendant makes a payment to a plaintiff who is or alleges to be entitled to recover from the defendant, the payment constitutes, to the extent of the payment, a release by the plaintiff or the plaintiff's personal representative of any claim that the plaintiff or the plaintiff's personal representative or any person claiming through or under the plaintiff or by virtue of Part V of the *Family Law Act* may have against the defendant.

(2) **Idem** — Nothing in this section precludes the defendant making the payment from demanding, as a condition precedent to such payment, a release from the plaintiff or the plaintiff's personal representative or any other person to the extent of such payment.

(3) **Payment to be taken into account** — The court shall adjudicate upon the matter first without reference to the payment but, in giving judgment, the payment shall be taken into account and the plaintiff shall only be entitled to judgment for the net amount, if any.

(4) Disclosure — The fact of any payment shall not be disclosed to the judge or jury until after judgment but shall be disclosed before formal entry thereof.

121. (1) Foreign money obligations — Subject to subsections (3) and (4), where a person obtains an order to enforce an obligation in a foreign currency, the order shall require payment of an amount in Canadian currency sufficient to purchase the amount of the obligation in the foreign currency at a bank in Ontario listed in Schedule I to the *Bank Act* (Canada) at the close of business on the first day on which the bank quotes a Canadian dollar rate for purchase of the foreign currency before the day payment of the obligation is received by the creditor.

(2) Multiple payments — Where more than one payment is made under an order referred to in subsection (1), the rate of conversion shall be the rate determined as provided in subsection (1) for each payment.

(3) Discretion of court — Subject to subsection (4), where, in a proceeding to enforce an obligation in a foreign currency, the court is satisfied that conversion of the amount of the obligation to Canadian currency as provided in subsection (1) would be inequitable to any party, the order may require payment of an amount in Canadian currency sufficient to purchase the amount of the obligation in the foreign currency at a bank in Ontario on such other day as the court considers equitable in the circumstances.

(4) Other obligations that include conversion — Where an obligation enforceable in Ontario provides for a manner of conversion to Canadian currency of an amount in a foreign currency, the court shall give effect to the manner of conversion in the obligation.

(5) Enforcement by seizure or garnishment — Where a writ of seizure and sale or notice of garnishment is issued under an order to enforce an obligation in a foreign currency, the day the sheriff, bailiff or clerk of the court receives money under the writ or notice shall be deemed, for the purposes of this section and any obligation referred to in subsection (4), to be the day payment is received by the creditor.

122. (1) Actions for accounting — Where an action for an accounting could have been brought against a person, the action may be brought against the person's personal representative.

(2) Idem — An action for an accounting may be brought by a joint tenant or tenant in common, or his or her personal representative, against a co-tenant for receiving more than the co-tenant's just share.

123. (1) Definitions — In this section,

"chief judge" means a person having authority to assign duties to the judge;

"judge" includes a master and a case management master.

(2) Decision after retirement, etc. — A judge may, within ninety days of,

    (a) reaching retirement age;

    (b) resigning; or

    (c) being appointed to another court,

give a decision or participate in the giving of a decision in any matter previously tried or heard before the judge.

(3) **Inability to give decision; panel of judges** — Where a judge has commenced a hearing together with other judges and,

(a) dies before the decision is given;

(b) is for any reason unable to participate in the giving of the decision; or

(c) does not participate in the giving of the decision under subsection (2),

the remaining judges may complete the hearing and give the decision of the court but, if the remaining judges are equally divided, a party may make a motion to the chief judge for an order that the matter be reheard.

(4) **Inability to give decision; sitting alone** — Where a judge has commenced hearing a matter sitting alone and,

(a) dies without giving a decision;

(b) is for any reason unable to make a decision; or

(c) does not give a decision under subsection (2),

a party may make a motion to the chief judge for an order that the matter be reheard.

(5) **Failure to give decision** — Where a judge has heard a matter and fails to give a decision,

(a) in the case of a judgment, within six months; or

(b) in any other case, within three months,

the chief judge may extend the time in which the decision may be given and, if necessary, relieve the judge of his or her other duties until the decision is given.

(6) **Continued failure** — Where time has been extended under subsection (5) but the judge fails to give the decision within that time, unless the chief judge grants a further extension,

(a) the chief judge shall report the failure and the surrounding circumstances to the appropriate judicial council; and

(b) a party may make a motion to the chief judge for an order that the matter be reheard.

(7) **Rehearing** — Where an order is made under subsection (3), (4) or (6) for the rehearing of a matter, the chief judge may,

(a) dispose of the costs of the original hearing or refer the question of those costs to the judge or judges presiding at the rehearing;

(b) direct that the rehearing be conducted on the transcript of evidence taken at the original hearing, subject to the discretion of the court at the rehearing to recall a witness or require further evidence; and

(c) give such other directions as are considered just.

1996, c. 25, s. 1(21)

124. [Repealed 2009, c. 33, Sched. 2, s. 20(17).]

Language

125. (1) Official languages of the courts — The official languages of the courts of Ontario are English and French.

(2) Proceedings in English unless otherwise provided — Except as otherwise provided with respect to the use of the French language,

(a) hearings in courts shall be conducted in the English language and evidence adduced in a language other than English shall be interpreted into the English language; and

(b) documents filed in courts shall be in the English language or shall be accompanied by a translation of the document into the English language certified by affidavit of the translator.

Commentary: English and French are the official languages of the courts in Ontario. You have the right to a bilingual court proceeding for all criminal and non-jury civil cases held in the Ontario Court of Justice, the Superior Court of Justice and the Court of Appeal for Ontario. The right to a bilingual proceeding extends to all other hearings associated with the proceeding, such as procedural motions, pre-trial hearings, and hearings to assess costs. You may address the court directly in French. Witnesses testify in the language in which they feel most comfortable and the court provides interpreters as needed.

You may exercise your right to a bilingual proceeding by:

- Filing or issuing your first document in French

- Filing a requisition form requesting a bilingual proceeding

- Filing a written statement with the court requesting a bilingual proceeding

- Making an oral statement to the court during an appearance in the proceeding that expresses the desire that the proceeding be conducted as a bilingual proceeding

Legal Resources Available to French-speaking Residents of Ontario

The Law Society of Upper Canada

The Law Society of Upper Canada operates a bilingual referral service that can provide the names of French-speaking lawyers in your area. For further information, contact:

> Lawyer Referral Services
>
> Osgoode Hall, 1230 Queen Street West
>
> Toronto, Ontario M5H 2N6
>
> Telephone: (905) 565-4577
>
> Web site: <http://www.lsuc.on.ca/en>

The Ontario Bar Association

The Ontario Bar Association offers bilingual information on locating and working with a lawyer. You can access this information by visiting their web site at <http://www.oba.org> or by calling the association, toll-free, at 1-800-668-8900.

Legal Aid

Legal Aid is available to people who cannot afford the services of a lawyer. If you qualify for legal aid, you will be given a legal aid lawyer certificate. This certificate is a guarantee of payment from Legal Aid Ontario to the private lawyer of your choice, subject to the rates and limitations set out in the legal aid tariff. For further information, contact:

> Legal Aid Ontario

375 University Avenue, Suite 404

Toronto, ON M5G 2G1

Toll free: 1-800-668-8258

Web site: http://www.legalaid.on.ca

Case Law: *Mutual Tech Canada Inc. v. Law* (2000), 189 D.L.R. (4th) 325, 76 C.R.R. (2d) 64, 2 C.P.C. (5th) 143, 2000 CarswellOnt 2088 (Ont. S.C.J.) — Motion for interpreter granted. Attempt by counsel to restate answers compromised opposite counsel's right to cross-examine. Witness was unable to understand English language; interpreter ordered.

Wittenberg v. Fred Geisweiller/Locomotive Investments Inc. (1999), 44 O.R. (3d) 626, (sub nom. *Wittenberg v. Geisweiller)* 123 O.A.C. 139, 41 C.P.C. (4th) 358, 1999 CarswellOnt 1888 (Ont. S.C.J.) — Presiding judge erred in not offering the defendant bilingual proceeding. The denial of right to bilingual proceeding under s. 126 of *Courts of Justice Act* constituted a substantial wrong.

Chiasson c. Chiasson (1999), 222 N.B.R. (2d) 233, 570 A.P.R. 233, 44 C.P.C. (4th) 276, 1999 CarswellNB 599, 1999 CarswellNB 600 (N.B. C.A.) — The defendant appealed a small claims judgment on the ground of being denied the right to testify in English. The appeal was allowed and a new trial was ordered. The defendant was francophone but informed the court that he intended to testify in English. The defendant had the fundamental right to testify in either official language. The trial judge erred in commenting on the defendant's choice of language.

Upper Canada District School Board v. Conseil de District des Écoles Publiques de Langue Française No. 59 (2002), 2002 CarswellOnt 1161, [2002] O.J. No. 1525 (Ont. S.C.J.); additional reasons at (2002), 2002 CarswellOnt 1470 (Ont. S.C.J.) — Defendant exercised right to plead in French under section 126(1) of *Courts of Justice Act* (Ontario). Costs awarded against defendant should not include costs of translation for Anglophone counsel for plaintiff. Award would improperly penalize defendant for exercising its right.

Kilrich Industries Ltd. v. Halotier, 2007 CarswellYukon 50, 2007 CarswellYukon 51, 406 W.A.C. 159, 246 B.C.A.C. 159, 161 C.R.R. (2d) 331, 2007 YKCA 12 (Y.T. C.A.).

A French-speaking defendant appealed an order allowing the plaintiff's action in debt after a summary trial on the ground that the defendant did not have a fair opportunity to present his defence because the Rules of Court were not available to him in French. Appeal allowed, decision set aside and matter remitted to trial court to have a new trial. The defendant was denied a fundamental right accorded him by the *Languages Act*. The failure to print and publish the Rules of Court in French seriously impaired the defendant's ability to engage in the Court's processes.

Kilrich Industries Ltd. v. Halotier, 2008 CarswellYukon 16, 261 B.C.A.C. 301, 440 W.A.C. 301, 2008 YKCA 4, 56 C.P.C. (6th) 214 (Y.T. C.A.).

This case involves assessment of costs to be paid by an intervenor, Minister of Justice in this case, in appeal concerning scope of French language rights in Yukon courts. Yukon Court of Appeal held that because of systemic failure caused unnecessary expenses to parties, the Minister of Justice should pay special costs of both parties for trial and appeal.

Ndem v. Patel, 2008 CarswellOnt 1271, 2008 CarswellOnt 1272, 2008 ONCA 148, (sub nom. *Belende v. Patel)* 290 D.L.R. (4th) 490, (sub nom. *Belende v. Patel)* 89 O.R. (3d) 494, (sub nom. *Belende c. Patel)* 89 O.R. (3d) 502 (Ont. C.A.).

Plaintiff did not attend motion for dismissal of his claim on grounds that bilingual judge was not provided for him pursuant to s. 126 of *Court of Justice Act*. His counsel brought unsuccessful motion for adjournment. The motion judge held that in his opinion the plaintiff was attempting to manipulate the bilingual obligation of provincial laws to his own purpose in order to delay the proceedings and granted summary judgment against the Plaintiff. Plaintiff appealed. Appeal allowed.

The motion judge's failure to adjourn the proceeding and refer the matter to a bilingual judge violated the plaintiff's rights under s. 126 of the Act. Language rights under s. 126 of the Act are quasi-constitutional in nature, and violation of those rights constitutes material prejudice to the linguistic minority.

Toronto Dominion Bank c. Ndem, 2008 CarswellOnt 1065, 2008 ONCA 146 (Ont. C.A.); leave to appeal refused (2008), [2008] S.C.C.A. No. 125, 2008 CarswellOnt 3797, 2008 CarswellOnt 3798, *(sub nom. Toronto-Dominion Bank v. Ndem)* 387 N.R. 400 (note) (S.C.C.).

The defendant appealed judgment at trial on basis that trial judge had not been bilingual. At hearing, lawyer appeared and indicated that she represented a third party on appeal. Defendant objected to lawyers presence on basis that her client was not part of appeal. Appeal allowed. Defendant has right to trial before bilingual judge. Lawyer client had no interest in appeal as his own application to extend time limits had been dismissed.

Bajikijaie v. Mbuyi (2009), 2009 CarswellOnt 3318, 2009 CarswellOnt 3319, 252 O.A.C. 304 (Ont. Div. Ct.), J.M. Wilson J..

Appeal by plaintiff from costs order. Plaintiff commenced action by filing a statement of claim in French. The case management Master was not bilingual and ordered the action to be discontinued on consent and fixed costs in favour of the defendants. Pursuant to s. 3(1) of Regulation for Bilingual Proceedings, the plaintiff deemed to have exercised his right to have all proceedings presided over by a bilingual judge or officer. The deeming provisions that required all future hearings in the proceeding to be presided over by a bilingual person had been breached.

Sandhu v. British Columbia (Provincial Court Judge), 2012 BCSC 1064, 2012 CarswellBC 2278, 44 Admin. L.R. (5th) 92, [2012] B.C.J. No. 1502 (B.C. S.C.); affirmed 2013 BCCA 88, 2013 CarswellBC 457, 52 Admin. L.R. (5th) 326, 42 B.C.L.R. (5th) 1, 359 D.L.R. (4th) 329, *(sub nom. Sandhu v. McKinnon)* 334 B.C.A.C. 173, *(sub nom. Sandhu v. McKinnon)* 572 W.A.C. 173, [2013] B.C.J. No. 327, Justice Gropper (B.C. C.A.).

Sandhu applies under the provisions of the *Judicial Review Procedure Act*, R.S.B.C. 1996, c. 241 (JRPA) seeking judicial review of the May 16, 2011, decision of Provincial Court Judge Jane McKinnon. Sandhu challenges McKinnon P.C.J.'s decision that he could not act as an interpreter to a party in a small claims action.

The role of counsel for a tribunal whose decision is impugned is thoroughly canvassed in the jurisprudence. In *Legal Services Society (British Columbia) v. Brahan*, 1983 CarswellBC 175, 46 B.C.L.R. 32, 5 C.C.C. (3d) 404, 148 D.L.R. (3d) 692 (B.C. S.C.), the court expressed the view that it was not appropriate for counsel on behalf of a Provincial Court Judge to appear on judicial review and make submissions in favour of upholding an order by the judge: at 38.

The applicable standard of review is reasonableness. As noted in *Farrell v. TD Waterhouse Canada Inc.*, 2010 BCSC 1930, 2010 CarswellBC 3762, [2010] B.C.J. No. 2770 (B.C. S.C.); affirmed 2011 BCCA 61, 2011 CarswellBC 198, [2011] B.C.J. No. 201 (B.C. C.A.), the appropriate standard of review to be applied to an interlocutory decision of the Small Claims Court is reasonableness: at paras. 22 to 25.

Mr. Nahal required an interpreter from the list maintained by the registry falls within a range of possible, acceptable outcomes which are defensible in respect of the facts. It is also a reasonable decision in law.

There is nothing in the *Small Claims Act* or *Small Claims Rules* which requires a Provincial Court Judge to certify interpreters. McKinnon P.C.J. was required to decide the case before her. She was not required to consider Mr. Sandhu's application to act as an interpreter. Nonetheless, she adopted a reasonable basis upon which to exercise discretion.

Mr. Sandhu did not have a right to be heard or owed a duty of fairness. Neither he, nor Mr. Hara on his behalf, was entitled to make submissions or present evidence. The transcript demonstrates that McKinnon P.C.J. attempted to explain to Mr. Nahal her practice of requiring that interpreters be on the list of court-certified interpreters. She allowed Mr. Sandhu an opportunity to investigate why he was not on the list and whether that was an error.

The petition is dismissed.

Solarcan Portes et fenêtres Corp. c. Bruce, 2012 QCCQ 2254 (Que. Small Cl. Ct.), Michel A. Pinsonnault, J.C.Q.

Under our Constitution, the official languages of Canada (English and French) can be used in the Courts of law of Québec. The parties and witnesses may address the Court in the official language of their choosing. In Montreal, Justices sitting in the Small Claims Court Division are versed in the two official languages.

The Ministère de la Justice has issued Directive A-6 dealing with interpretation services and payment of costs relating thereto.

Section B of Directive A-6 entitled *"In Civil Matters"* stipulates:

> B) — In Civil Matters
>
> i) Court of Québec, Civil Division and Superior Court.
>
> A party must request interpretation services on his own and will assume the related costs, where he or the witness he has assigned does not understand the language used at the hearing.
>
> ii) Court of Québec, Civil Division, Small Claims Division.
>
> Where a judge does not understand the language used by one of the parties or one of the witnesses, interpretation services are provided at the hearing on his request, then the costs are at the expense of the *Ministère de la Justice*. Otherwise, a party makes his own request for interpretation services and assumes the related costs.
>
> [Emphasis added].
>
> [An excerpt of the Directive is attached to the present judgment to form part hereof as if recited at length herein].

Based on the foregoing, while the Court is sympathetic to Mrs. Bruce's request, it cannot accede to her request, under the present circumstances. If Mrs. Bruce feels that the services of an interpreter are nevertheless warranted, she will have to make the arrangements herself and assume all costs related thereto.

For those reasons, the court dismisses the motion to appoint a French/English interpreter.

Wittenberg v. Fred Geisweiller / Locomotive Investments Inc., 1999 CarswellOnt 1888, 44 O.R. (3d) 626, 41 C.P.C. (4th) 358, (sub nom. *Wittenberg v. Geisweiller)* 123 O.A.C. 139, Rivard, J. (Ont. S.C.J.)

The trial judge rejected the defendant's request that the Small Claims Court case be heard in French on the grounds that the judge not bilingual. The defendant's right to a bilingual proceeding is conferred by s. 126(1) of the *Courts of Justice Act* and is a substantive right which cannot be overridden by the direction in s. 25 to Small Claims Court judges to keep procedures simple and costs low. The denial of the defendant's right to a bilingual proceeding constituted a substantial wrong. An appeal was allowed; a new trial was ordered. The defendant did not waive his right to a bilingual proceeding under s. 126. The waiver of such a right must be clear and informed. A reading of the transcript does not satisfy it was clear or informed.

Sera v. Amboise, 2013 ONSC 7067, 2013 CarswellOnt 15619, 40 R.F.L. (7th) 425 (Ont. S.C.J.); leave to appeal refused 2014 ONSC 2981, 2014 CarswellOnt 6162, C.A. Gilmore, J. (Ont. S.C.J.)

Respondent mother brought motion to adjourn trial. She requested that the trial be heard as a bilingual matter. She sought to set aside all previous interim orders on grounds that her right to a bilingual hearing had been breached.

The father opposed the filing of documents in French. He argued that section 126(2) parts 6 and 7 of the *Courts of Justice Act* specify that documents may only be filed in French (except with the consent of the parties) in designated Schedule 2 areas. Newmarket is not a designated Schedule 2 area.

The court declined to adjourn the trial of this matter. The father does not consent to documents being filed in French as he does not speak French nor does his lawyer. That rule pertains to the Superior Court of Justice, and any so called exception in section 126(4) of the *Courts of Justice Act* does not apply as it would otherwise completely contradict the intention of section 126(2) and (6) of the *Courts of Justice Act*. While Newmarket is not a designated schedule 2 area, it does not mean that section 126(4) of the *Courts of Justice Act* can be ignored. The mother has the right to file future documents in French. Upon the request of the father, documents may be translated into English.

126. (1) Bilingual proceedings — A party to a proceeding who speaks French has the right to require that it be conducted as a bilingual proceeding.

(2) Idem — The following rules apply to a proceeding that is conducted as a bilingual proceeding:

1. The hearings that the party specifies shall be presided over by a judge or officer who speaks English and French.

2. If a hearing that the party has specified is held before a judge and jury in an area named in Schedule 1, the jury shall consist of persons who speak English and French.

3. If a hearing that the party has specified is held without a jury, or with a jury in an area named in Schedule 1, evidence given and submissions made in English or French shall be received, recorded and transcribed in the language in which they are given.

4. Any other part of the hearing may be conducted in French if, in the opinion of the presiding judge or officer, it can be so conducted.

5. Oral evidence given in English or French at an examination out of court shall be received, recorded and transcribed in the language in which it is given.

6. In an area named in Schedule 2, a party may file pleadings and other documents written in French.

7. Elsewhere in Ontario, a party may file pleadings and other documents written in French if the other parties consent.

8. The reasons for a decision may be written in English or French.

9. On the request of a party or counsel who speaks English or French but not both, the court shall provide interpretation of anything given orally in the other language at hearings referred to in paragraphs 2 and 3 and at examinations out of court, and translation of reasons for a decision written in the other language.

(2.1) Prosecutions — When a prosecution under the *Provincial Offences Act* by the Crown in right of Ontario is being conducted as a bilingual proceeding, the prosecutor assigned to the case must be a person who speaks English and French.

(3) Appeals — When an appeal is taken in a proceeding that is being conducted as a bilingual proceeding, a party who speaks French has the right to require that the appeal be heard by a judge or judges who speak English and French; in that case subsection (2) applies to the appeal, with necessary modifications.

(4) Documents — A document filed by a party before a hearing in a proceeding in the Family Court of the Superior Court of Justice, the Ontario Court of Justice or the Small Claims Court may be written in French.

Commentary: A document filed by a party before a hearing in a proceeding in the Ontario Court of Justice or the Small Claims Court may be written in French.

Case Law: Case Law: *Ndem v. Patel*, 2008 ONCA 148, 2008 CarswellOnt 1271, 2008 CarswellOnt 1272, (sub nom. *Belende v. Patel*) 89 O.R. (3d) 494, (sub nom. *Belende c. Patel*) 89 O.R. (3d) 502, (sub nom. *Belende v. Patel*) 290 D.L.R. (4th) 490 (Ont. C.A.).

The right to bilingual proceeding under section 126 of *Courts of Justice Act* is *not* qualified by judicial discretion. The Court is able to control process and prevent abuse without violating litigant's statutory right to bilingual proceeding.

Before hearing, appellant notified bilingual judge would not be available. Appellant's request for adjournment denied and motion judge, who was not bilingual, dismissal action. Appeal allowed. Right to a bilingual hearing a particular kind of right. Violation of the right, which was quasi-constitutional in nature, constituted material prejudice to the linguistic minority. Order was set aside and matter referred back to the court below.

See also *R. v. Beaulac*, [1999] S.C.J. No. 25, [1999] 1 S.C.R. 768, 62 C.R.R. (2d) 133, 173 D.L.R. (4th) 193, 134 C.C.C. (3d) 481, 198 W.A.C. 227, 121 B.C.A.C. 227, 238 N.R. 131, 1999 CarswellBC 1026, 1999 CarswellBC 1025 (S.C.C.), at para. 41:

> Language rights have a totally distinct origin and role [when compared with the right to a fair trial]. They are meant to protect official language minorities in this country and to insure the equality of status of French and English.

In *Greenspoon v. Belende*, [2004] O.J. No. 3269, 2004 CarswellOnt 3247, 2004 CarswellOnt 3241, 189 O.A.C. 140 (Ont. C.A.); leave to appeal refused 2004 CarswellOnt 5203, 2004 CarswellOnt 5202, 338 N.R. 195 (note) (S.C.C.) at para. 15, court stated:

> Where, as in this case, the appellant has met the procedural requirements to trigger a right to a bilingual hearing, this right is more than purely procedural, it is substantive and the appropriate remedy is to set aside the order.

Sera v. Amboise, 2013 ONSC 7067, 2013 CarswellOnt 15619 (Ont. S.C.J.) — In the Ontario Court of Justice, Small Claims Court, or the Family Court of the Superior Court of Justice, an originating process and documents may be written in French.

(5) Process — A process issued in or giving rise to a criminal proceeding or a proceeding in the Family Court of the Superior Court of Justice or the Ontario Court of Justice may be written in French.

(6) Translation — On a party's request, the court shall provide translation into English or French of a document or process referred to in subsection (4) or (5) that is written in the other language.

(7) Interpretation — At a hearing to which paragraph 3 of subsection (2) does not apply, if a party acting in person makes submissions in French or a witness gives oral evidence in French, the court shall provide interpretation of the submissions or evidence into English.

(8) Parties who are not natural persons — A corporation, partnership or sole proprietorship may exercise the rights conferred by this section in the same way as a natural person, unless the court orders otherwise.

(9) Regulations — The Lieutenant Governor in Council may make regulations,

(a) prescribing procedures for the purpose of this section;

(b) adding areas to Schedule 1 or 2.

Appendix 1 — Bilingual Juries
Paragraphs 2 and 3 of subsection 126(2)

The following counties:

    Essex

    Middlesex

    Prescott and Russell

    Renfrew

    Simcoe

    Stormont, Dundas and Glengarry

The following territorial districts:

    Algoma

    Cochrane

    Kenora

    Nipissing

    Sudbury

    Thunder Bay

    Timiskaming

The area of the County of Welland as it existed on December 31, 1969.

The Municipality of Chatham Kent.

The City of Hamilton.

The City of Ottawa.

The Regional Municipality of Peel.

The City of Greater Sudbury.

The City of Toronto.

    O. Reg. 922/93, s. 1 [Amended O. Reg. 441/97, s. 1.]; 1994, c. 12, s. 43(3); 1997, c. 26, Sched.; 2002, c. 17, Sched. F, s. 1

Appendix 2 — Bilingual Documents
Paragraph 6 of subsection 126(2)

The following counties:

    Essex

    Middlesex

Prescott and Russell

Renfrew

Simcoe

Stormont, Dundas and Glengarry

The following territorial districts:

Algoma

Cochrane

Kenora

Nipissing

Sudbury

Thunder Bay

Timiskaming

The area of the County of Welland as it existed on December 31, 1969.

The Municipality of Chatham Kent.

The City of Hamilton.

The City of Ottawa.

The Regional Municipality of Peel.

The City of Greater Sudbury.

The City of Toronto.

O. Reg. 922/93, s. 2 [Amended O. Reg. 441/97, s. 2.]; 1994, c. 12, s. 43(3); 1997, c. 26, Sched.;
2002, c. 17, Sched. F, s. 1
1994, c. 12, s. 43; 1996, c. 25, s. 9(17), (18)

Commentary: Additional areas where a party may file pleadings and other documents in French were added by O. Reg. 922/93 which came into force on December 17, 1993. This amendment is to include those changes in the *Courts of Justice Act*.

The following French language court proceedings apply to all courts:

A party who speaks the French language has the right to:

(a) file documents in French;

(b) a pre-trial hearing before a bilingual referee;

(c) a trial before a bilingual judge;

(d) subsequent examinations before a bilingual judge.

This can also include a corporation, partnership or sole proprietorship unless the court orders otherwise.

Requests for such services can be made in many ways:

1. By filing a claim or defence in French. (This automatically means that a request has been made);

2. By making an oral statement to the court during an appearance in the proceeding;

3. By filing a written statement with the clerk where the proceeding was commenced;

4. By filing a requisition on Form 1.

The request should be made before the notice of trial is sent. A request can be made subsequently with the leave of the court.

If a party who speaks the French language as not requested a trial before a bilingual court, no interpreter is provided. Where parties do not speak the French language and therefore are not entitled to a bilingual trial, but such parties wish to call a witness or witnesses who wish to testify in French, the court will provide an interpreter. Parties should advise the court of this requirement in writing at least 10 days before the hearing.

NOTE: The following is available for use in the courts:

Form 1 — Requisition — Bilingual Proceeding

Courts of Justice Act, 1984

Claim Number:...................................

       PLAINTIFF:..................................

       DEFENDANT:................................

       COURT:.......... Small Claims Court

...................................(name of party), a party who speaks the French language, requires that (check (1) or (2) below):

       ....(1) The hearing be conducted before a judge/referee who speaks both the English and French languages.

       ....(2) The hearing of the appeal be conducted before a judge (or judges) who speaks both the English and French languages.

Date: ....

Name, address and telephone number or solicitor filing requisition:

       ....

       ....

       ....

Ontario Regulation 806/84, Form 1

The following Small Claims Courts (County/District in brackets) arerequired to provide services in French when requested:

       ALEXANDRIA (Stormont, Dundas & Glengarry)
       AMHERSTBURG (Essex)
       BELLEVILLE (Hastings)
       BLIND RIVER (Algoma)
       BRAMPTON (Peel)
       BURLINGTON (Halton)
       CAMBRIDGE (Waterloo)
       CHAPLEAU (Sudbury)
       CHATHAM (Kent)
       COCHRANE (Cochrane)
       CORNWALL (Stormont, Dundas & Glengarry)
       ELLIOT LAKE (Algoma)
       ENGLEHART (Timiskaming)
       ESPANOLA (Sudbury)
       ETOBICOKE (Metro Toronto)
       HAILEYBURY (Timiskaming)
       HAMILTON (Hamilton-Wentworth)
       HAWKESBURY (Prescott & Russell)
       IROQUOIS (Stormont, Dundas & Glengarry)
       IROQUOIS FALLS (Cochrane)
       KAPUSKASING (Cochrane)
       KILLALOE STATION (Renfrew)
       KINGSTON (Frontenac)
       KINGSVILLE (Essex)
       KIRKLAND LAKE (Timiskaming)
       KITCHENER (Waterloo)

LONDON (Middlesex)
MIDLAND (Simcoe)
MILTON (Halton)
NEWMARKET (York Region)
NIAGARA FALLS (Niagara South)
NORTH BAY (Nipissing)
NORTH YORK (Metro Toronto)
OAKVILLE (Halton)
OSHAWA (Durham)
OTTAWA (Ottawa-Carleton)
PEMBROKE (Renfrew)
RENFREW (Renfrew)
RECLINED (Prescott & Russell)
ST. CATHARINES (Niagara North)
SARNIA (Lambton)
SAULT STE. MARIE (Algoma)
SCARBOROUGH (Metro Toronto)
STURGEON FALLS (Nipissing)
SUDBURY (Sudbury)
THESSALON (Algoma)
TIMMINS (Cochrane)
TORONTO (Metro Toronto)
WAWA (Algoma)
WELLAND (Niagara South)

WHITBY (Durham)
WINCHESTER (Stormont, Dundas & Glengarry)
WINDSOR (Essex)

Interest and Costs

127. (1) Definitions — In this section and in sections 128 and 129,

"bank rate" means the bank rate established by the Bank of Canada as the minimum rate at which the Bank of Canada makes short-term advances to the banks listed in Schedule I to the *Bank Act (Canada)*;

"date of the order" means the date the order is made, even if the order is not entered or enforceable on that date, or that the order is varied on appeal, and in the case of an order directing a reference, the date the report on the reference is confirmed;

"postjudgment interest rate" means the bank rate at the end of the first day of the last month of the quarter preceding the quarter in which the date of the order falls, rounded to the next higher whole number where the bank rate includes a fraction, plus 1 per cent;

"prejudgment interest rate" means the bank rate at the end of the first day of the last month of the quarter preceding the quarter in which the proceeding was commenced, rounded to the nearest tenth of a percentage point;

"quarter" means the three-month period ending with the 31st day of March, 30th day of June, 30th day of September or 31st day of December.

(2) Calculation and publication of interest rates — After the first day of the last month of each quarter, a person designated by the Deputy Attorney General shall forthwith,

    (a) determine the prejudgment and postjudgment interest rate for the next quarter; and

    (b) publish in the prescribed manner a table showing the rate determined under clause (a) for the next quarter and the rates determined under clause (a) or under a predecessor of that clause for all the previous quarters during the preceding 10 years.

Commentary: NOTE: It appears that causes of action arising on or before October 23, 1989 are governed by the former s. 137(1)(d). As a result of the amendment (s. 127(1) "prejudgment interest rate"), the prejudgment and postjudgment interests are now to be calculated differently.

Pre- and Post-Interest Calculations

If judgment is awarded in court and the judge sets an interest rate for pre-, that rate applies to pre-, not postjudgment interest.

If the judge awards pre-interest and states from what date the interest is to be awarded from but does not set an interest rate, the rate is determined by the month the claim was originally filed.

If the judge awards pre-interest but does not indicate a date, then the number of days are to be determined from the date of the claim or if stated in the claim from the date stated.

If judgment is by default and there is a date stated in the claim as to when the monies were owing the number of days is calculated from this date at the rate of the month when the claim was filed.

If judgment is by default and there is an interest rate mentioned with supporting documentation, both pre- and post- are calculated at this amount from the date when the monies were owing, or if not stated, from the date of the claim.

If judgment is by default and the claim mentions no date from when the monies were owing or an interest rate then the days are calculated from the date the claim is filed and the rate the month when the claim was filed.

Post-interest is calculated at the rate of month the judgment was awarded by default, or at the interest rate the judge has awarded, or at the rate of the month the judgment was awarded by the judge.

Formula to calculate prejudgment interest:

    Principal Judgment Amount

        × prejudgment interest rate %

        × number of days from date the claim arose (or the claim was issued) to date of judgment

    divided by 365 days

Formula to calculate postjudgment interest:

        × postjudgment interest rate %

        × number of days from date of judgment to date of enforcement process (or payment received)

divided by 365 days

Note: Calculation of interest is always on the amount owing from time to time as payments are received. This is true for both prejudgment and postjudgment interest.

Courts of Justice Act

Postjudgment and Prejudgment Interest Rates

Please note that effective October 1, 2007, postjudgment and prejudgment interest rates are published on the Ministry's website pursuant to O. Reg. 339/07.

1. Postjudgment interest rates (and prejudgment interest rates for causes of action arising on or before October 23, 1989) are as follows:

	1st Quarter	2nd Quarter	3rd Quarter	4th Quarter
1985	12%	13%	11%	11%
1986	11%	13%	10%	10%
1987	10%	9%	10%	11%
1988	10%	10%	11%	12%
1989	13%	13%	14%	14%
1990	14%	15%	15%	14%
1991	14%	11%	11%	10%
1992	9%	9%	8%	7%
1993	10%	8%	7%	6%
1994	6%	6%	8%	7%
1995	8%	10%	9%	8%
1996	8%	7%	6%	6%
1997	5%	5%	5%	5%
1998	5%	6%	6%	7%
1999	7%	7%	6%	6%
2000	6%	7%	7%	7%
2001	7%	7%	6%	6%
2002	4%	4%	4%	4%
2003	4%	4%	5%	5%
2004	4%	4%	4%	4%
2005	4%	4%	4%	4%
2006	5%	5%	6%	6%
2007	6%	6%	6%	6%
2008	6%	6%	5%	5%
2009	4%	3%	2%	2%
2010	2%	2%	2%	2%
2011	3.0%	3.0%	3.0%	3.0%
2012	3.0%	3.0%	3.0%	3.0%
2013	3.0%	3.0%	3.0%	3.0%
2014	3.0%	3.0%	3.0%	

Notes: *Example 74,00000 × NS = 962 + 74000·00* [handwritten]

This table shows the postjudgment interest rates for orders made in the quarters indicated. This table also shows the prejudgment interest rates for actions commenced in the quarters indicated in respect of causes of action arising on or before October 23, 1989.

For proceedings commenced before January 1, 1985, the postjudgment interest rate is the prime bank rate, which is published in the Bank of Canada Review. The rate can be found from either the back copies of the Bank of Canada Review or by calling the Bank of Canada.

2. Prejudgment interest rates for causes of action arising after October 23, 1989 are as follows:

	1st Quarter	2nd Quarter	3rd Quarter	4th Quarter
1989				12.4%
1990	12.5%	13.5%	13.9%	12.9%
1991	12.3%	10.0%	9.1%	8.8%
1992	7.7%	7.5%	6.3%	5.1%
1993	8.3%	6.1%	5.1%	5.0%
1994	4.3%	4.1%	6.6%	5.6%
1995	6.0%	8.0%	7.6%	6.6%
1996	6.1%	5.6%	5.0%	4.3%
1997	3.3%	3.3%	3.3%	3.5%
1998	4.0%	5.0%	5.0%	6.0%
1999	5.3%	5.3%	4.8%	4.8%
2000	5.0%	5.3%	6.0%	6.0%
2001	6.0%	5.8%	4.8%	4.3%
2002	2.5%	2.3%	2.5%	3.0%
2003	3.0%	3.0%	3.5%	3.3%
2004	3.0%	2.8%	2.3%	2.3%
2005	2.8%	2.8%	2.8%	2.8%
2006	3.3%	3.8%	4.5%	4.5%
2007	4.5%	4.5%	4.5%	4.8%
2008	4.8%	4.3%	3.3%	3.3%
2009	2.5%	1.3%	0.5%	0.5%
2010	0.5%	0.5%	0.5%	1.0%
2011	1.3%	1.3%	1.3%	1.3%
2012	1.3%	1.3%	1.3%	1.3%
2013	1.3%	1.3%	1.3%	1.3%
2014	1.3%	1.3%	1.3%	

[Handwritten margin notes: "if it's the percentage is less than 10 then you put it as 0.01, 0.02 etc."; "12.5% = 0.125"; "7.7% = 0.077"; "5.0% = 0.05"; "1.3% = 0.013"; "1.3% = 0.013"; "0.01.3%"]

Notes:

This table shows the prejudgment interest rates for actions commenced in the quarters indicated in respect of causes of action arising after October 23, 1989.

(3) Regulations — The Attorney General may, by regulation, prescribe the manner in which the table described in clause (2)(b) is to be published.

2006, c. 21, Sched. A, s. 18

128. (1) Prejudgment interest — A person who is entitled to an order for the payment of money is entitled to claim and have included in the order an award of interest thereon at the prejudgment interest rate, calculated from the date the cause of action arose to the date of the order.

(2) Exception for non-pecuniary loss on personal injury — Despite subsection (1), the rate of interest on damages for non-pecuniary loss in an action for personal injury shall be the rate determined by the rules of court under clause 66(2)(w).

Commentary: The amendment deletes the discount rate determined by the rules of court as the rate of interest on damages for non-pecuniary loss in a personal injury action and substitutes the prejudgment interest rate [see section 21(2) amendment to clause 66(2)(w)].

(3) Special damages — **If the order includes an amount for past pecuniary loss, the interest calculated under subsection (1) shall be calculated on the total past pecuniary loss at the end of each six-month period and at the date of the order.**

(4) Exclusion — **Interest shall not be awarded under subsection (1),**

    (a) on exemplary or punitive damages;

    (b) on interest accruing under this section;

    (c) on an award of costs in the proceeding;

    (d) on that part of the order that represents pecuniary loss arising after the date of the order and that is identified by a finding of the court;

    (e) with respect to the amount of any advance payment that has been made towards settlement of the claim, for the period after the advance payment has been made;

    (f) where the order is made on consent, except by consent of the debtor; or

    (g) where interest is payable by a right other than under this section.

1994, c. 12, s. 44

Commentary: The *Courts of Justice Act* (the "Act") (Section 128) provides for an order of prejudgment interest.

Prejudgment interest rate is defined in the *Courts of Justice Act* (s. 127(1)). These rates posted quarterly in the Ontario Gazette.

It is the responsibility of the claimant to seek prejudgment interest in the claim and insert the full amount of interest on the requisition and default judgment filed (principal judgment amount × prejudgment interest rate % × number of days from the date the claim arose (or the claim was issued) to date of judgment / 365 days).

In general, the Act states that a person is entitled to claim prejudgment interest calculated from the date the action arose to the date the order for payment of money was made. The order is to reflect the prejudgment interest rate.

However, the Act states that prejudgment interest will not be awarded on the following [s. 128(3), *CJA*]:

Interest accruing under this section:

- An award of costs in the proceeding;
- For any advance payment that has already been made, from the date the payment was made;
- Where the order is made on consent, except by consent of the debtor; and/or
- Where interest is payable by a right (e.g. contractual right) other than under Section 128, *Courts of Justice Act*.

What happens if the date the cause of action arose is not set out in the claim and the claimant does not specify in the claim a date from which interest is to commence, yet prejudgment interest is claimed? In that case, interest would be calculated from the date that the claim was filed, issued and at the rate applicable at that time.

How are claimants to determine the date of judgment for the purpose of calculating prejudgment interest when the default judgment is mailed in? Claimants electing to submit notices of default judgment by mail must accept and calculate prejudgment interest by using the date of mailing as the date of judgment.

Recovery Of Legal Fees

Where a solicitor has commenced an action to recover unpaid legal fees, the right to prejudgment interest is governed by s. 33 of the *Solicitors Act*, R.S.O. 1990, c. S.15. Pursuant to subsection 33(4) of the Act, there is no entitlement to prejudgment interest if the rate of interest is not shown on the account delivered to the defendant(s).

In the case of postjudgment interest, a solicitor who has obtained a judgment for unpaid legal fees is entitled to postjudgment interest pursuant to subsection 129(1) of the *Courts of Justice Act* even if there is no mention of it in the account delivered to the defendant(s).

The precise rate of interest must be stated on the account delivered to the defendant. A copy of the account as delivered showing the actual rate of interest must be filed with the court before judgment is entered.

The applicable rate of interest shall be the rate shown on the account as long as it does not exceed the rate permitted by the *Courts of Justice Act*. Where the account contains a rate which is higher than that permitted under the *Courts of Justice Act*, it is the statutory rate which applies. The statutory rate is the rate in effect on the date that the account was delivered to the defendant by the solicitor. Interest runs from one month after the account is delivered to the date of judgment.

If no precise interest rate is stated on the account as delivered, the plaintiff is not entitled to any prejudgment interest. It is not sufficient to state "interest in accordance with Section 33 of the Solicitors Act."

Postjudgment interest is applicable to all judgments even where no rate has been stated or where the original account contains no reference to postjudgment interest. The interest rate is the statutory rate in effect on the date that judgment was entered. If the parties have agreed to a contractual rate, the contractual rate will apply.

Section 25 — Prejudgment Interest and Postjudgment Interest.

Case Law: *Danforth Roofing Supply Ltd. v. Smith* (1987), 9 W.D.C.P. 62 (Ont. Prov. Ct.) — Merely putting an interest amount on an invoice does not create a right pursuant to s. 138 of the *Courts of Justice Act*, 1984. The plaintiff would have received interest at a compound interest rate.

Alderson v. Callaghan (March 2, 1995), Doc. 300257/87 (Ont. Gen. Div.) — Plaintiff's claim for no-fault benefits in November, 1985 did not constitute "notice" of a claim for prejudgment interest as required by s. 138 of *Courts of Justice Act* [now s. 128(1)]. Now allowed from when cause of action arose.

Dell Holdings Ltd. v. Toronto Area Transit Operating Authority (2000), 193 D.L.R. (4th) 762, 71 L.C.R. 161, 2000 CarswellOnt 3957 (Ont. S.C.J.) — Endorsement — The party who was successful before the Supreme Court of Canada on expropriation matter sought payment of interest on costs award. At the time of the hearing no interest was payable on costs award, but the law changed. Applicability of current state of law should be raised in the court that made the costs award and not before the Superior Court of Justice.

Plester v. Wawanesa Mutual Insurance Co., 2006 CarswellOnt 5536, 215 O.A.C. 187, 41 C.C.L.I. (4th) 15, 275 D.L.R. (4th) 552 (Ont. C.A.).

After release of appellate decision, counsel for plaintiffs brought application for prejudgment interest on award of aggravated damages. Insurer argued plaintiffs had not requested prejudgment interest earlier, nor raised the issue by way of cross-appeal. Application for prejudgment interest dismissed. Finality to litigation was one of the hallmarks of a just result.

Capital One Bank v. Matovska (2007), 2007 CarswellOnt 5661, 230 O.A.C. 1 (Ont. Div. Ct.); additional reasons at (2007), [2007] O.J. No. 3368, 2007 CarswellOnt 5605 (Ont. Div. Ct.), MacKenzie J.

Bank obtained default judgment against three credit card customers for the balance debt. Trial judge refused to award bank prejudgment or postjudgment interest at rate stipulated in credit card agreements or pre-proceeding collection expenses paid to legal counsel. The bank appealed. Appeal allowed.

Bank entitled to prejudgment and postjudgment interest at the rate stipulated in the credit card agreement. It was also entitled to the pre-proceeding collection expenses, as they constituted a claim for a liquidated demand for money.

Pre-proceeding collection expenses claimed in the credit card agreement claim for a liquidated demand for money, within the meaning of the Small Claims Court Rules 11.10(1) and 11.02(1). See *Holden Day Wilson v. Ashton* (1993), 14 O.R. (3d) 306, 104 D.L.R. (4th) 266, 64 O.A.C. 4 (Div. Ct.). See also *Cantalia Sod Co. v. Patrick Harrison & Co.*, 1967 Carswell-Ont 176, [1968] 1 O.R. 169 (Ont. H.C.).

The *Courts of Justice Act*, R.S.O. 1990, c. C.43, as amended, sets out the rules respecting an award of prejudgment interest (s. 128) and postjudgment interest (s. 129), subject to the overriding discretion of the court.

In *Bank of America Canada v. Mutual Trust Co.*, [2002] S.C.J. No. 44, 2002 CarswellOnt 1114, 2002 CarswellOnt 1115, REJB 2002-30907, 287 N.R. 171, 211 D.L.R. (4th) 385, 49 R.P.R. (3d) 1, 159 O.A.C. 1, 2002 SCC 43, [2002] 2 S.C.R. 601 (S.C.C.), the Supreme Court of Canada interpreted the above sections of the *Courts of Justice Act*.

129. (1) Postjudgment interest — Money owing under an order, including costs to be assessed or costs fixed by the court, bears interest at the postjudgment interest rate, calculated from the date of the order.

(2) Interest on periodic payments — Where an order provides for periodic payments, each payment in default shall bear interest only from the date of default.

(3) Interest on orders originating outside Ontario — Where an order is based on an order given outside Ontario or an order of a court outside Ontario is filed with a court in Ontario for the purpose of enforcement, money owing under the order bears interest at the rate, if any, applicable to the order given outside Ontario by the law of the place where it was given.

(4) Costs assessed without order — Where costs are assessed without an order, the costs bear interest at the postjudgment interest rate in the same manner as if an order were made for the payment of costs on the date the person to whom the costs are payable became entitled to the costs.

(5) Other provision for interest — Interest shall not be awarded under this section where interest is payable by a right other than under this section.

Commentary

Post-judgment Interest

Section 129 of the *Courts of Justice Act* provides that money owing under an order, including any cost award, bears interest at the post-judgment interest rate calculated from the date of the order.

Unlike prejudgment interest, a creditor does not have to claim post-judgment interest to be entitled to it. Moneys owing under an order, including costs, bear post-judgment interest according to the CJA from the date of the order, or, if there is no order, from the date the person to whom costs are payable became entitled to them.

The post-judgment interest rate is defined within section 127(1) of the *Courts of Justice Act*.

Interest will not be awarded in accordance with section 127(1) of the *Courts of Justice Act* where there is a right to receive post-judgment interest at a different rate. For example, a contract or lease might specify a different post-judgment interest rate that the parties agreed to.

Unless otherwise directed by the court in its judgment, post-judgment interest is to be calculated from the date of the order. This applies where the court makes an order or judgment, but releases reasons on a later date. However, if the judgment is reserved, the interest is calculated from the date the judgment is released.

"Date of the order" means the date the order is made even if the order is not issued or enforceable on the date [s. 127(1), CJA].

Post-judgment interest is calculated on the total amount of the order including prejudgment interest and costs. Post-judgment interest is payable on prejudgment interest included in the judgment because the prejudgment interest is "money owing under an order."

130. (1) Discretion of court — **The court may, where it considers it just to do so, in respect of the whole or any part of the amount on which interest is payable under section 128 or 129,**

   (a) disallow interest under either section;

   (b) allow interest at a rate higher or lower than that provided in either section;

   (c) allow interest for a period other than that provided in either section.

Case Law: *Agribrands Purina Canada Inc. v. Kasamekas*, 2011 ONCA 460, 2011 CarswellOnt 5034, 106 O.R. (3d) 427, 87 B.L.R. (4th) 1, 86 C.C.L.T. (3d) 179, 334 D.L.R. (4th) 714, 278 O.A.C. 363, [2011] O.J. No. 2786 (Ont. C.A.); additional reasons 2011 ONCA 581, 2011 CarswellOnt 9210, 86 C.C.L.T. (3d) 206 (Ont. C.A.)

The prejudgment interest rate prescribed under s. 128 for the quarter when the claim was issued is the applicable rate unless the court finds special circumstances to justify departing from it. Here the trial judge erred by applying a rate based on the average interest rate for the year in which the cause of action arose, rather than applying the statutory rate for the quarter in which the claim was commenced.

Niagara Air Bus Inc. v. Camerman (1991), 3 O.R. (3d) 108 (Ont. C.A.) — An action was brought on a number of promissory notes maturing in 1986 and 1987, in which the stated rate of interest was 2% per month. Upon maturity, principal and interest merged to become a simple debt due at that date. Interest was payable therefore within the exercise of discretion under s. 140 [now s. 130], in this case an annual effective rate of interest of 24% was allowed and not restricted to interest at 5% pursuant to s. 4 of the federal *Interest Act*.

Murano v. Bank of Montreal (1998), [1998] O.J. No. 2897, 1998 CarswellOnt 2841, 111 O.A.C. 242, 163 D.L.R. (4th) 21, 22 C.P.C. (4th) 235, 41 B.L.R. (2d) 10, 41 O.R. (3d) 222, 5 C.B.R. (4th) 57 (Ont. C.A.) — An unsuccessful litigant asserted on appeal that the trial judge erred in awarding prejudgment interest at the average rate of 7 per cent per annum rather than 10 per cent. The Ontario Court of Appeal stated that the components of a prejudgment interest award were, to some extent, a matter of discretion. The court referred to the requirement for courts to take changes in interest rates into account pursuant to s. 130(2)(a) of the Act.

Bank of America Canada v. Mutual Trust Co. (2000), 30 R.P.R. (3d) 167, 184 D.L.R. (4th) 1, 130 O.A.C. 149, 2000 CarswellOnt 654 (Ont. C.A.); leave to appeal allowed (2000), 261

N.R. 398 (note), 2000 CarswellOnt 3824, 2000 CarswellOnt 3825 (S.C.C.) — The trial judge erred in law in finding that he had jurisdiction under s. 130 of the *Courts of Justice Act* to award compound interest. Section 130 cannot be read to empower the court to override clear legislative insert found in ss. 128 and 129 that both prejudgment and postjudgment interest is awarded on simple, not compounded, basis.

Allen v. McLean, Budden Ltd. (2000), 128 O.A.C. 138, 2000 CarswellOnt 118 (Ont. C.A.) — Postjudgment interest payable according to rate prescribed by s. 127(1) of the *Courts of Justice Act*. Date of judgment effectively determined as date of court's reasons.

Mullins v. Levy, 2006 CarswellBC 2869, 38 C.P.C. (6th) 82, 2006 BCSC 1723, 276 D.L.R. (4th) 251 (B.C. S.C.), Holmes J.

Plaintiff awarded general damages for assault and wrongful detention. General damages non-pecuniary damages arising from personal injury. Plaintiff entitled to interest on general damages awarded for non-pecuniary damages arising from personal injury.

Prince Albert Co-operative Assn. Ltd. v. Rybka, 2006 CarswellSask 793, 2006 SKCA 136, 24 B.L.R. (4th) 256, [2007] 4 W.W.R. 23, 382 W.A.C. 92, 289 Sask. R. 92 (Sask. C.A.).

Creditor brought application for summary judgment allowing action in debt, including interest of 24 per cent per annum. Application granted in part. Creditor ordered to account to debtor for principal owed together with interest rate of 5 per cent. Trial judge found creditor had made unilateral changes to frequency of interest calculation and rate of interest charged. Appeal allowed. Debtor was entitled to principal owed with interest thereon at rate of 24 per cent per annum. Trial judge made error of fact in finding that interest provisions of invoices supplanted interest terms of credit agreement.

Capital One Bank v. Matovska, [2007] O.J. No. 3368, 2007 CarswellOnt 5605 (Ont. Div. Ct.), 2007-09-04, MacKenzie J.

In each case, the plaintiff sought recovery of a debt pursuant to a written credit card agreement for outstanding principal, interest and pre-proceeding collection expenses. Although the defendants each failed to deliver defences and were noted in default, the Small Claims Court clerk did not sign default judgment on requisition and matter went to trial on an uncontested basis. The trial judge declined to award any amount for interest as stipulated in the credit card agreement nor for any pre-proceeding collection expenses of the plaintiff pursuant to terms of the credit card agreement.

Appeals based on alleged error by the trial judges in failing to find that pre-proceeding collection expenses claimed by the plaintiff were a liquidated demand for money and in failing to make an award for pre- and postjudgment interest at a rate stipulated in the credit card agreement.

Pre-proceeding collection expenses claimed in the credit card agreement are a claim for liquidated demand for money, within the meaning of the *Small Claims Court Rules* 11.10(1) and 11.02(1). See *Holden Day Wilson v. Ashton* (1993), 14 O.R. (3d) 306, 104 D.L.R. (4th) 266, 64 O.A.C. 4 (Div. Ct.). See also *Cantalia Sod Co. v. Patrick Harrison & Co.*, 1967 CarswellOnt 176, [1968] 1 O.R. 169 (Ont. H.C.).

The claim for pre-proceeding collection expenses charged by the plaintiff's counsel pursuant to a retainer agreement providing for a fixed percentage of the outstanding indebtedness is a "liquidated demand for money" and by necessary implication enforceable as a liquidated demand for money by the plaintiff against the defendants.

The *Courts of Justice Act*, R.S.O. 1990, c. C.43, as amended, sets out the rules respecting an award of prejudgment interest (s. 128) and postjudgment interest (s. 129), subject to the overriding discretion of the court to, among other things, disallow interest under either s. 128 or 129 or to allow interest at a rate higher or lower than that provided in either of those sections: see s. 130(1)(a) and (b). In *Bank of America Canada v. Mutual Trust Co.*, [2002]

S.C.J. No. 44, 2002 CarswellOnt 1114, 2002 CarswellOnt 1115, REJB 2002-30907, 287 N.R. 171, 211 D.L.R. (4th) 385, 49 R.P.R. (3d) 1, 159 O.A.C. 1, 2002 SCC 43, [2002] 2 S.C.R. 601 (S.C.C.), the Supreme Court of Canada interpreted the above sections of the *Courts of Justice Act*. Unless the terms respecting interest rates in the credit card agreement are vague or unclear or unless the interest rate derived from the written agreement infringes a statutory provision such as the *Interest Act*, effect should be given to the contractual rate for the determination of both pre- and postjudgment interest.

Brown v. Newton, 293 N.S.R. (2d) 27, 928 A.P.R. 27, 2010 CarswellNS 256, 2010 NSSM 33 (N.S. Small Cl. Ct.).

The defendant is a lawyer; the claimant his client. The claimant sought pre-judgment interest from November 2, 2004. At issue was trial judge's reduction in the period through which pre-judgment interest would be paid from approximately six years to four years. It took the claimant some 3-1/2 years to commence claim against the defendant. Pre-judgment interest awarded from November 2, 2004, through to and including November 2, 2007.

(2) Idem — **For the purpose of subsection (1), the court shall take into account,**

    (a) changes in market interest rates;

    (b) the circumstances of the case;

    (c) the fact that an advance payment was made;

    (d) the circumstances of medical disclosure by the plaintiff;

    (e) the amount claimed and the amount recovered in the proceeding;

    (f) the conduct of any party that tended to shorten or to lengthen unnecessarily the duration of the proceeding; and

    (g) any other relevant consideration.

131. (1) Costs — **Subject to the provisions of an Act or rules of court, the costs of and incidental to a proceeding or a step in a proceeding are in the discretion of the court, and the court may determine by whom and to what extent the costs shall be paid.**

Case Law: *Miller v. York Downs Craft & Garden Centre Ltd.* (1987), 17 C.P.C. (2d) 142 (Ont. Prov. Ct.) — The court has discretion under s. 141 of the Courts of Justice Act, 1984 to award disbursements where they were reasonable and necessary to the proceedings. The disbursements were assessed at $1,160.90 including the attendance and report of experts' throughout the three day trial. Certain disbursements were not allowed as they could not be assessed by the clerk in the absence of specific court direction. See also Rule 20.

Tanner v. Clark (2002), 164 O.A.C. 228, 2002 CarswellOnt 3177, 24 C.P.C. (5th) 68 (Ont. Div. Ct.); leave to appeal refused (2003), 2003 CarswellOnt 594, 34 M.V.R. (4th) 23, 30 C.P.C. (5th) 103, [2003] O.J. No. 677, 63 O.R. (3d) 508, 169 O.A.C. 152, 224 D.L.R. (4th) 635 (Ont. C.A.); leave to appeal refused (2003), CarswellOnt 4377, 2003 CarswellOnt 4378 (S.C.C.) — The Ontario Divisional Court stated at para. 7, "In fixing costs, the Court acts under the discretion afforded by section 131 of the *Courts of Justice Act* and Rule 57.01. The latter gives a useful reminder of the elements to be examined in the exercise of the discretion. They include the result, complexity, importance of the issues, conduct, improper or unnecessary steps and any other matter that is relevant to the costs. The court is given the opportunity to craft a costs order that fits the case.".

(2) Crown costs — **In a proceeding to which Her Majesty is a party, costs awarded to Her Majesty shall not be disallowed or reduced on assessment merely because they relate to a lawyer who is a salaried officer of the Crown, and costs recovered on behalf of Her Majesty shall be paid into the Consolidated Revenue Fund.**

1994, c. 12, s. 45

Appeals

132. Judge not to hear appeal from own decision — A judge shall not sit as a member of a court hearing an appeal from his or her own decision.

133. Leave to appeal required — No appeal lies without leave of the court to which the appeal is to be taken,

    (a) from an order made with the consent of the parties; or

    (b) where the appeal is only as to costs that are in the discretion of the court that made the order for costs.

134. (1) Powers on appeal — Unless otherwise provided, a court to which an appeal is taken may,

    (a) make any order or decision that ought to or could have been made by the court or tribunal appealed from;

    (b) order a new trial;

    (c) make any other order or decision that is considered just.

(2) Interim orders — On motion, a court to which a motion for leave to appeal is made or to which an appeal is taken may make any interim order that is considered just to prevent prejudice to a party pending the appeal.

(3) Power to quash — On motion, a court to which an appeal is taken may, in a proper case, quash the appeal.

(4) Determination of fact — Unless otherwise provided, a court to which an appeal is taken may, in a proper case,

    (a) draw inferences of fact from the evidence, except that no inference shall be drawn that is inconsistent with a finding that has not been set aside;

    (b) receive further evidence by affidavit, transcript of oral examination, oral examination before the court or in such other manner as the court directs; and

    (c) direct a reference or the trial of an issue,

to enable the court to determine the appeal.

(5) Scope of decisions — The powers conferred by this section may be exercised even if the appeal is as to part only of an order or decision, and may be exercised in favour of a party even though the party did not appeal.

(6) New trial — A court to which an appeal is taken shall not direct a new trial unless some substantial wrong or miscarriage of justice has occurred.

(7) Idem — Where some substantial wrong or miscarriage of justice has occurred but it affects only part of an order or decision or some of the parties, a new trial may be ordered in respect of only that part or those parties.

1999, c. 12, Sched. B, s. 4(3)

Case Law: *Aim Business Furnishings & Filing Systems Inc. v. Alterior-Designs*, 2013 ONSC 377, 2013 CarswellOnt 428 (Ont. S.C.J.), Healey J.

The standard of review of an appellate court with respect to alleged errors in consideration of the evidence by the trial judge requires the appellant to show that a palpable and overriding error was committed: *Housen v. Nikolaisen*, 2002 SCC 33, 2002 CarswellSask 178, 2002

CarswellSask 179, REJB 2002-29758, [2002] 2 S.C.R. 235, 10 C.C.L.T. (3d) 157, 211 D.L.R. (4th) 577, 30 M.P.L.R. (3d) 1, [2002] 7 W.W.R. 1, 286 N.R. 1, 219 Sask. R. 1, 272 W.A.C. 1, [2002] S.C.J. No. 31 (S.C.C.). Absent such an error, the evaluation of the evidence and findings made by a trial judge are to be given considerable deference by a reviewing court.

As there were no errors made by the trial judge, the appeal is dismissed with costs to the respondent.

Wiles Welding Ltd. v. Solutions Smith Engineering Inc., 2012 NSSC 255, 2012 CarswellNS 511, 318 N.S.R. (2d) 396, 1005 A.P.R. 396, [2012] N.S.J. No. 379 (N.S. S.C.), Justice Arthur W.D. Pickup.

Appeal by Wile's Welding Limited from an order made by an adjudicator of the Small Claims Court on September 28, 2011.

The appellant submits that in allowing Mr. Crane to testify, the adjudicator relied on Mr. Crane's evidence which reduced the actual impact of Mr. Doucette's statement.

The standard of review, where a ground of appeal raises an error of law, is correctness. The second ground of appeal, which is failure to follow requirements of natural justice, does not engage the standard of review analysis in the traditional sense (*Sackville Trenching Ltd. v. Nova Scotia (Occupational Health & Safety Appeal Panel*, 2012 NSCA 39, 2012 CarswellNS 252, (sub nom. *Sackville Trenching Ltd. v. Healthy & Safety)* 315 N.S.R. (2d) 308, 998 A.P.R. 308 (N.S. C.A.)). The burden for the court is to determine if the process was fair to the claimant.

Did the adjudicator fail to follow the requirements of natural justice? Was the process fair to the claimant?.

While the failure to follow the requirements of natural justice does not engage a standard of review analysis, the court is tasked with determining if the process was fair to the respective parties. The requirements of natural justice are complicated by the fact that the appellant was self-represented.

In *Earthcraft Landscape Ltd. v. Clayton*, 2002 NSSC 259, 2002 CarswellNS 497, 210 N.S.R. (2d) 101, 659 A.P.R. 101, [2002] N.S.J. No. 516 (N.S. S.C.), Justice LeBlanc allowed an appeal from the Small Claims Court on the grounds that the adjudicator had failed to follow the requirements of natural justice.

Appeal allowed and remitted back to the Small Claims Court for a new trial before a different adjudicator.

Doyle v. Topshee Housing Co-operative Ltd., 2012 NSSC 371, 2012 CarswellNS 773, [2012] N.S.J. No. 570 (N.S. S.C.), Justice J. E. Scanlan.

The Court asked to consider issue whether Appellant should be entitled to admit fresh evidence on the hearing of a Small Claims Court appeal.

The *Small Claims Court Act* and regulations do not contemplate an appeal by way of trial de novo. Appeals are to be based on the record. See *Killam Properties Inc. v. Patriquin*, 2011 NSSC 338, 2011 CarswellNS 647, 307 N.S.R. (2d) 170, 975 A.P.R. 170, [2011] N.S.J. No. 502 (N.S. S.C.) at para. 8 by Justice MacDougall.

Tests for the introduction of new evidence was stated in the Supreme Court in *R. v. Nielsen*, 1988 CarswellMan 112, 1988 CarswellMan 257, EYB 1988-67144, (sub nom. *R. v. Stolar)* [1988] 1 S.C.R. 480, (sub nom. *R. v. Stolar)* 40 C.C.C. (3d) 1, (sub nom. *R. v. Stolar)* 62 C.R. (3d) 313, [1988] 3 W.W.R. 193, 52 Man. R. (2d) 46, (sub nom. *R. v. Stolar)* 82 N.R. 280, [1988] S.C.J. No. 20 (S.C.C.).

Litigants in the Small Claims Court are not required to provide the Court with applicable legislation although it is helpful. The Adjudicator in this case was required to take judicial notice of applicable legislation.

To require litigants in Small Claims Court to produce copies of legislation would be an error at law and that appears to be what occurred during the Small Claims Court proceedings. In addition, if the bylaws were not before the Small Claims Court one must ask how the Adjudicator could determine the issue of whether the bylaws were complied with?.

Respondent to decide if it will continue in asserting its resistance to the appeal and that issue will be decided on the final hearing of this appeal.

Young v. Refinements-Renovations and Construction Developments Inc., 2013 NSSC 52, 2013 CarswellNS 96 (N.S. S.C.), Justice Gerald R. P. Moir.

The *Small Claims Court Forms and Procedure Regulations* provide that an appeal is commenced not only by filing the notice of appeal before a deadline, but also by serving a copy of the notice on the respondent before the deadline.

Did the approach adopted by the adjudicator exceed the monetary limit for Small Claims Court?.

There was a *bona fide* intention to appeal and there is a reasonable excuse for the delay, but the notice of appeal does not present grounds of sufficient merit because it is clear that Adjudicator Parker had to do as he did: subtract the assessed amount of the lower claim over which he had jurisdiction from the assessed amount of the higher claim over which he had separate jurisdiction.

Motion dismissed.

Leighton v. Stewiacke Home Hardware Building Center, 2012 NSSC 184, 2012 CarswellNS 300, 316 N.S.R. (2d) 315, 28 C.P.C. (7th) 285 (N.S. S.C.), Justice Peter P. Rosinski.

Leighton requested that the Small Claims adjudicator reconsider the hearing outcome, by application made pursuant to s. 23 of the *Small Claims Court Act* RSNS 1989 c. 430 as amended.

The appropriate standards of review canvassed by Justice Saunders in *Mor-Town Developments Ltd. v. MacDonald*, 2012 NSCA 35, 2012 CarswellNS 225, 316 N.S.R. (2d) 183, 19 C.P.C. (7th) 227, 349 D.L.R. (4th) 161 (N.S. C.A.) at paras. 19 and 51.

Although "within Canada, defendants are presumed to know the law of the jurisdiction seized with any action against them" [per Major, J. for the Majority at para. 68 *Beals v. Saldanha*, 2003 SCC 72, 2003 CarswellOnt 5101, 2003 CarswellOnt 5102, REJB 2003-51513, [2003] 3 S.C.R. 416, 70 O.R. (3d) 94 (note), 39 B.L.R. (3d) 1, 39 C.P.C. (5th) 1, 234 D.L.R. (4th) 1, 113 C.R.R. (2d) 189, 314 N.R. 209, 182 O.A.C. 201, [2003] S.C.J. No. 77 (S.C.C.)], here the applicable sections of the *Small Claims Court Act* and its Regulations are patently so poorly drafted that they are rendered unintelligible to the average person; those for whom the Act is intended to create a simple and understandable procedure to make or contest "small claims".

New hearing of the claim take place before a different adjudicator and Defendant to file a Defence by 30 days from the release of these written reasons.

Public Access

Case Law: *Massoudinia v. Volfson*, 2013 ONCA 29, 2013 CarswellOnt 256 (Ont. C.A. [In Chambers]).

Motion for leave to appeal and to extend the time within which to appeal.

Appeal has no merit. The moving party now seeks leave to appeal to this court on a question that is not a question of fact alone. The Divisional Court judge adopted the functional approach mandated by the Supreme Court of Canada in *R. v. Sheppard*, 2002 SCC 26, 2002 CarswellNfld 74, 2002 CarswellNfld 75, REJB 2002-29516, [2002] 1 S.C.R. 869, 211 Nfld. & P.E.I.R. 50, 162 C.C.C. (3d) 298, 50 C.R. (5th) 68, 210 D.L.R. (4th) 608, 633 A.P.R. 50, 284 N.R. 342, [2002] S.C.J. No. 30 (S.C.C.), in assessing the reasons.

As Binnie J. held in *Sheppard*, at para. 53, inadequate reasons do not alone give "a free-standing right of appeal" or "entitlement to appellate intervention".

Appellate courts recognize that oral reasons ordinarily cannot be as thorough and detailed as written reasons. As Carthy J.A. said, in *R. v. Richardson*, 1992 CarswellOnt 830, 9 O.R. (3d) 194, 74 C.C.C. (3d) 15, 57 O.A.C. 54, [1992] O.J. No. 1498 (Ont. C.A.) at para. 13, "[i]n moving under pressure from case to case it is expected that oral judgments will contain much less than the complete line of reasoning leading to the result."

Where the parties have already had one appeal, a court deciding whether or not to grant leave should also consider the significance of the legal issues raised to the general administration of justice. See *Canada Mortgage & Housing Corp. v. Iness*, 2002 CarswellOnt 3879, (sub nom. *Iness v. Canada Mortgage & Housing Corp.*) 62 O.R. (3d) 255, 220 D.L.R. (4th) 682, (sub nom. *Iness v. Canada Mortgage & Housing Corp.*) 166 O.A.C. 38 (Ont. C.A. [In Chambers]). While the moving party in this case framed the question in such a manner as to raise an issue of importance to the administration of justice, it is plain from the record that this case has no general significance.

Motion dismissed.

Canadian Imperial Bank of Commerce v. Houlahan, 2011 ONSC 558, 2011 CarswellOnt 291, 73 C.B.R. (5th) 223, 273 O.A.C. 140 (Ont. Div. Ct.), J.W. Quinn J.

An action was made in Small Claims Court against the appellant ("Houlahan"), for unpaid student loans. Houlahan did not testify or call witnesses. The argument presented on his behalf at trial related only to the statute-barred defence. Documents filed at trial did not mention the *Canada Student Loans Act*. A "court to which an appeal is taken may order a new trial": see the *Courts of Justice Act*, R.S.O. 1990, c. C.43, s. 134(1)(b). A new trial shall not be directed "unless some substantial wrong or miscarriage of justice has occurred": see the *Courts of Justice Act*, s. 134(6).

"Where some substantial wrong or miscarriage of justice has occurred but it affects only part of an order or decision . . . a new trial may be ordered in respect of only that part . . .": see the *Courts of Justice Act*, s. 134(7).

An appeal was allowed in part, and a new trial was ordered.

135. (1) Public hearings — **Subject to subsection (2) and rules of court, all court hearings shall be open to the public.**

(2) Exception — **The court may order the public to be excluded from a hearing where the possibility of serious harm or injustice to any person justifies a departure from the general principle that court hearings should be open to the public.**

(3) Disclosure of information — **Where a proceeding is heard in the absence of the public, disclosure of information relating to the proceeding is not contempt of court unless the court expressly prohibited the disclosure of the information.**

Case Law: *Case Law: Jane Doe v. D'Amelio*, 2009 CarswellOnt 5842, 98 O.R. (3d) 387, 83 C.P.C. (6th) 67 (Ont. S.C.J.).

The plaintiff brought a motion for various relief, including an order permitting her to commence action against defendants by way of pseudonym. Motion dismissed. Rule 14.06 of

Rules of Civil Procedure did not provide automatic exclusion for civil cases involving allegations of sexual assault. The onus was on the person seeking exemption from that rule to provide compelling evidence on which the court could exercise its discretion to grant relief sought, and it must be something more than plaintiff's own assessment of her own vulnerability. The Supreme Court has confirmed that openness of the courts is a fundamental aspect of Canadian democracy. See *MacIntyre v. Nova Scotia (Attorney General)*, 1982 CarswellNS 110, 65 C.C.C. (2d) 129, 132 D.L.R. (3d) 385, 96 A.P.R. 609, 26 C.R. (3d) 193, 1982 CarswellNS 21, 40 N.R. 181, 49 N.S.R. (2d) 609, [1982] 1 S.C.R. 175 (S.C.C.); *Dagenais v. Canadian Broadcasting Corp.*, [1994] S.C.J. No. 104, 1994 CarswellOnt 112, 25 C.R.R. (2d) 1, 76 O.A.C. 81, 94 C.C.C. (3d) 289, 175 N.R. 1, 120 D.L.R. (4th) 12, [1994] 3 S.C.R. 835, 20 O.R. (3d) 816 (note), 34 C.R. (4th) 269, EYB 1994-67668, 1994 SCC 102, 1994 CarswellOnt 1168 (S.C.C.); *Sierra Club of Canada v. Canada (Minister of Finance)*, REJB 2002-30902, [2002] 2 S.C.R. 522, [2002] S.C.J. No. 42, 93 C.R.R. (2d) 219, 2002 CarswellNat 823, 2002 CarswellNat 822, 2002 SCC 41, 40 Admin. L.R. (3d) 1, 20 C.P.C. (5th) 1, 223 F.T.R. 137 (note), 211 D.L.R. (4th) 193, 44 C.E.L.R. (N.S.) 161, 18 C.P.R. (4th) 1, 287 N.R. 203 (S.C.C.); and *Toronto Star Newspapers Ltd. v. Ontario*, 132 C.R.R. (2d) 178, 200 O.A.C. 348, 335 N.R. 201, [2005] S.C.J. No. 41, 76 O.R. (3d) 320 (note), 2005 CarswellOnt 2614, 2005 CarswellOnt 2613, 2005 SCC 41, [2005] 2 S.C.R. 188, EYB 2005-92055, 197 C.C.C. (3d) 1, 29 C.R. (6th) 251, 253 D.L.R. (4th) 577 (S.C.C.).

Palkowski v. Ivancic, 2009 ONCA 705, 2009 CarswellOnt 5950, 100 O.R. (3d) 89, 76 C.P.C. (6th) 204, 312 D.L.R. (4th) 329, 258 O.A.C. 55, 84 R.P.R. (4th) 226 (Ont. C.A.).

The defendant brought motion to determine whether, or to what extent, amended statement of claim complied with motion judge's order. Counsel asked to join motion judge in anteroom adjacent to courtroom. Motion judge advised counsel that she had prepared endorsements which included copy of proposed amended statement of claim with extensive revisions. The plaintiffs appealed motion decision. Appeal allowed on other grounds. Nothing in record contrary to section 135(1) of *Courts of Justice Act*, which provides that, subject to subsection 2 and rules of court, all court hearings shall be open to public. No one requested that plaintiffs personally be permitted to attend on motion judge with their counsel. Where counsel in the court below is of the view that the judge is exhibiting bias, they have the obligation to raise it with that judge below at the time. The words "open to the public" should be given the ordinary grammatical sense that best accords with the statutory purpose of section 135. The phrase "Open to the public" when interpreted to foster its enormously important purposes must be taken to mean a forum where the public understands it is free to enter without specifically requesting admission.

136. (1) Prohibition against photography, etc., at court hearing — Subject to subsections (2) and (3), no person shall,

    (a) take or attempt to take a photograph, motion picture, audio recording or other record capable of producing visual or aural representations by electronic means or otherwise,

        (i) at a court hearing,

        (ii) of any person entering or leaving the room in which a court hearing is to be or has been convened, or

        (iii) of any person in the building in which a court hearing is to be or has been convened where there is reasonable ground for believing that the person is there for the purpose of attending or leaving the hearing; or

    (b) publish, broadcast, reproduce or otherwise disseminate a photograph, motion picture, audio recording or record taken in contravention of clause (a); or

    (c) broadcast or reproduce an audio recording made as described in clause (2)(b).

(2) Exceptions — Nothing in subsection (1),

(a) prohibits a person from unobtrusively making handwritten notes or sketches at a court hearing; or

(b) prohibits a lawyer, a party acting in person or a journalist from unobtrusively making an audio recording at a court hearing, in the manner that has been approved by the judge, for the sole purpose of supplementing or replacing handwritten notes.

(3) Exceptions — Subsection (1) does not apply to a photograph, motion picture, audio recording or record made with authorization of the judge,

(a) where required for the presentation of evidence or the making of a record or for any other purpose of the court hearing;

(b) in connection with any investitive, naturalization, ceremonial or other similar proceeding; or

(c) with the consent of the parties and witnesses, for such educational or instructional purposes as the judge approves.

(4) Offence — Every person who contravenes this section is guilty of an offence and on conviction is liable to a fine of not more than $25,000 or to imprisonment for a term of not more than six months, or to both.

1996, c. 25, s. 1(22)

Commentary

Access to Digital Court Recording in the Superior Court of Justice and Ontario Court of Justice

The Superior Court of Justice and the Ontario Court of Justice have developed new policies for access to digital court recordings, effective April 15, 2013. These policies do not apply to Small Claims Court proceedings.

The new access to audio policy does not apply to Small Claims Court proceedings. Parties requesting access to these recordings must obtain a court order from the presiding judicial official or the Regional Senior Judge or Local Administrative Judge (or their designate) where the presiding judicial is not available.

Parties should review section 136 of the *Courts of Justice Act*. Two request forms and undertakings have been developed. There is a request form/undertaking for counsel/paralegal of record licensed by the Law Society of Upper Canada and a request form/undertaking for other persons.

Recording the Proceedings

Courts of Record.

The Superior Court of Justice (including Divisional Court and Small Claims Court) are courts of record. Proceedings in these courts must always be recorded if they involve the presentation of evidence to the court, unless there is clear judicial direction to the contrary on record.

Recordings of the *Parental Responsibility Act* for reasons of confidentiality are recorded, annotated, and stored separately.

Ontario Regulation 158/03 (as amended by Ontario Regulation 109/11) under the *Evidence Act*, requires that the court reporter prepare a Form 1 certifying that they were in charge of the audio recording device and that the recording is the evidence and proceedings. The Form 1 provides assurance that the audio recording is a reliable, accurate, and complete record of the referenced proceedings.

137. (1) Documents public — On payment of the prescribed fee, a person is entitled to see any document filed in a civil proceeding in a court, unless an Act or an order of the court provides otherwise.

(2) Sealing documents — A court may order that any document filed in a civil proceeding before it be treated as confidential, sealed and not form part of the public record.

(3) Court lists public — On payment of the prescribed fee, a person is entitled to see any list maintained by a court of civil proceedings commenced or judgments entered.

(4) Copies — On payment of the prescribed fee, a person is entitled to a copy of any document the person is entitled to see.

Miscellaneous

138. Multiplicity of proceedings — As far as possible, multiplicity of legal proceedings shall be avoided.

139. (1) Joint liability not affected by judgment or release — Where two or more persons are jointly liable in respect of the same cause of action, a judgment against or release of one of them does not preclude judgment against any other in the same or a separate proceeding.

(2) Two proceedings in respect of same damage — Where a person who has suffered damage brings two or more proceedings in respect of the damage, the person is not entitled to costs in any of the proceedings, except the first proceeding in which judgment is obtained, unless the court is of the opinion that there were reasonable grounds for bringing more than one proceeding.

140. (1) Vexatious proceedings — Where a judge of the Superior Court of Justice is satisfied, on application, that a person has persistently and without reasonable grounds,

    (a) instituted vexatious proceedings in any court; or

    (b) conducted a proceeding in any court in a vexatious manner,

the judge may order that,

    (c) no further proceeding be instituted by the person in any court; or

    (d) a proceeding previously instituted by the person in any court not be continued,

except by leave of a judge of the Superior Court of Justice.

Commentary: Section 140(1) of the *Courts of Justice Act* provides that an application may be made to a judge of the Superior Court of Justice for an order against a vexatious litigant who has persistently, and without reasonable grounds, brought vexatious proceedings in any court, or conducted a proceeding in a vexatious manner. This application process is referred to as a vexatious proceeding.

When the court is satisfied that there are grounds on which an order may be made against the vexatious litigant, the judge may:

• Order that the person not institute any further proceeding in any court;

OR

• Order that a proceeding instituted by the person not continue, without leave of a judge of the Superior Court of Justice.

The particulars of vexatious proceedings orders vary. Prior to refusing any process from a person listed on the Index of Vexatious Proceedings Orders, the Small Claims Court must refer to the relevant vexatious proceedings order itself to confirm the exact direction given in a vexatious proceedings order.

Jurisprudence establishes that Canadian courts of superior jurisdiction maintain a general inherent jurisdiction, which includes the discretion to control their own process.

In the words of English procedural law authority I.H. Jacob, "the juridical basis of this jurisdiction is therefore the authority of the judiciary to uphold, to protect and to fulfill the judicial function of administering justice according to law in a regular, orderly and effective measure." [I.H. Jacob, "The Inherent Jurisdiction of the Court" (1970) 23 *Current Legal Problems* 23 at 27-28.]

Vexatious litigant provisions have their roots in England, which enacted its first vexatious litigants statute in 1896. See *Vexatious Actions Act*, 1896 (U.K.) 59 & 60 Vict., c. 51. This statute was primarily meant to protect public bodies or officers from vexatious litigation: see Simon Smith, "Vexatious Litigants and Their Judicial Control — The Victorian Experience" (1989) 15 *Monash U.L. Rev.* 48 at 57. The 1925 English statute, 1925 (15 & 16 *Geo.* 5), c. 49, s. 51, provided the model for an equivalent 1930 Ontario statute, referring to a person who "has habitually and persistently and without any reasonable ground instituted vexatious legal proceedings . . ."

Vexatious proceedings legislation does not take away an individual's right to redress. Rather it provides that if an order is made against that individual under the legislation, he/she cannot seek redress until he/she has satisfied the proper authority that the proposed legal proceedings are not an abuse of process of the Court and there is *prima facie* ground for them. See *Foy v. Foy (No. 2)*, 1979 CarswellOnt 458, [1979] O.J. No. 4386, 26 O.R. (2d) 220, 12 C.P.C. 188, 102 D.L.R. (3d) 342 (Ont. C.A.) at 225 (O.R.).

Case Law: *Godding v. Berg's Cartage & Storage Ltd.*, [1995] B.C.W.L.D. 2662 (B.C. S.C.) as of July, 1998, no listing of B.C. C.A. decision — Order precluding petitioner from bringing further actions against respondents was made. Special costs were awarded to respondents on ground that petitioner circumvented spirit of order by reconstituting small claims action under different guise and causing respondents under stress. Inflammatory statements made against respondents and their lawyer was reprehensible conduct deserving of award of special costs.

Canada Post Corp. v. Varma (February 19, 1998), Doc. 98-CV-141125 (Ont. Gen. Div.) — Respondent had commenced 16 actions of which 12 were dismissed. Actions found to comprise harassment and oppression of other parties, repeating of previous actions. Respondent had persistently, and without reasonable grounds, instituted vexatious proceedings. Costs orders against respondent remained unpaid. Order under s. 140(1) of *Courts of Justice Act*, R.S.O. 1990, c. 43 made prohibiting further proceedings without leave.

Warren v. Pollitt (March 11, 1999), Doc. 98-FA-7046 (Ont. Gen. Div.) — Request by applicant for Order prohibiting respondent from instituting any further proceedings. Several cases deal with vexatious proceedings. *Foy v. Foy (No. 2)*, 1979 CarswellOnt 458, [1979] O.J. No. 4386, 26 O.R. (2d) 220, 12 C.P.C. 188, 102 D.L.R. (3d) 342 (Ont. C.A.); *Kitchener-Waterloo Record Ltd. v. Weber* (1986), 53 O.R. (2d) 687 (Ont. H.C.); and *Law Society of Upper Canada v. Zikov* (1984), 47 C.P.C. 42 (Ont. H.C.), were reviewed by Henry J. in *Lang Michener Lash Johnston v. Fabian*, 1987 CarswellOnt 378, [1987] O.J. No. 355, 16 C.P.C. (2d) 93, 59 O.R. (2d) 353, 37 D.L.R. (4th) 685 (Ont. H.C.). Respondent has failed to pay costs of prior unsuccessful proceedings and the Respondent's conduct as a litigant fell within the principles enunciated in case law. For these reasons application granted.

Law Society of Upper Canada v. Chavali (1998), 21 C.P.C. (4th) 20 (Ont. Gen. Div.); affirmed (December 21, 1998), Doc. CA C29428 (Ont. C.A.) — Respondents had commenced 19 actions since 1989. Order under s. 140 of *Courts of Justice Act*, R.S.O. 1990, c. C.43, prohibiting further proceedings without leave justified.

1066087 Ontario Inc. v. Church of the First Born Apostolic Inc. (2002), 23 C.P.C. (5th) 297, 2002 CarswellOnt 2648 (Ont. Master) — Defendants brought motion pursuant to Rule 56.01(e) of RCP for order for security for costs on basis action frivolous and vexatious. Motion granted. Conjunctive test under Rule 56.01(e) required both good reason to believe that action is frivolous and vexatious and that plaintiff has insufficient assets to pay costs. While defendants established that plaintiff had insufficient assets, they failed to establish that action was frivolous and vexatious. Given defendants' solicitors' respective experience, fact that solicitors charging reduced rate based on church's charitable status represented partial indemnity scale, complete indemnity not appropriate. Security for costs was awarded to defendants in amount of $65,000.

Ebrahim v. Ebrahim, 2003 CarswellBC 363, [2003] B.C.J. No. 338, 2003 BCCA 94 (B.C. C.A.) — Husband commenced action for malicious prosecution against wife arising out of fact that he was found in contempt of court in family law proceedings. Contempt order set aside on grounds of lack of notice. Wife's application to strike out claim allowed on grounds action was vexatious. No error in striking out claim. Appeal from 2002 CarswellBC 694, [2002] B.C.J. No. 638, 2002 BCSC 466 (B.C. S.C.) dismissed.

Sinclair v. Elwood & Pensa (2001), 2001 CarswellOnt 4886 (Ont. S.C.J.) — Claim was attempt to re-litigate issued raised in earlier actions. Claim dismissed as frivolous and vexatious. No further proceeding to be instituted by plaintiff in any court and any proceeding previously instituted by him in any court not to continue.

R. v. Wu, 2003 SCC 73, 2003 CarswellOnt 5099, 2003 CarswellOnt 5100, [2003] S.C.J. No. 78, [2003] 3 S.C.R. 530, 180 C.C.C. (3d) 97, 16 C.R. (6th) 289, 234 D.L.R. (4th) 87, 182 O.A.C. 6, 313 N.R. 201 (S.C.C.). Genuine inability to pay a fine is not a proper basis for imprisonment. A conditional sentence is a form of imprisonment. Unless, in the terms of s. 734.7(1), the Crown can establish that such a defaulter has "without reasonable excuse, refused to pay", a warrant of committal should not be issued.

McTeague v. Kalevar, 2005 CarswellOnt 337 (Ont. S.C.J.), Ferrier, J. — Kalevar has sued for damages in at least 13 proceedings involving nine parties. Nine of these proceedings have been dismissed. Order under s. 140 to go.

Dempsey v. Peart, 2004 CarswellBC 1611, 2004 BCCA 395 (B.C. C.A.) — Dempsey brought appeal from orders dismissing three actions, Supreme Court of British Columbia barring him, pursuant to s. 18 of the *Supreme Court Act*, R.S.B.C. 1996, c. 443, from bringing any further action or application without leave of the court against any of the defendants, *inter alia*. Appeal dismissed.

Griffiths v. Hughes, 2006 CarswellOnt 3369 (Ont. S.C.J.) 2006-06-05.

Motion by the defendant. Griffiths requested an adjournment. Court denied the adjournment. Action dismissed as an abuse of process. Hughes seeks an order under s. 140 of the *Courts of Justice Act*. Griffiths has instituted vexatious proceedings. Griffiths shall not commence any further proceeding against Peter Norman Hughes in any court governed by the *Courts of Justice Act* without first obtaining leave from a judge of the Superior Court of Justice.

Kalevar v. McTeague (September 16, 2005) (Ont. C.A.).

Kalevar appealled order declaring him a vexatious litigant. Kalevar under impression that before he can be declared a vexatious litigant first necessary for the multiple other proceedings he has instituted to be concluded. That is wrong. Appeals without merit, and dismissed. Order of Ferrier J. confirmed.

Barrie (City) v. Predie, 2006 CarswellOnt 2309 (Ont. S.C.J.), D.S. Ferguson J.

Respondent had history of litigating matters and seeking adjournments and failed to pay costs on many other cases. Respondent had commenced vexatious proceedings and was barred from bringing any further proceedings or appeals.

Kalaba v. Bylykbashi, [2006] O.J. No. 545, 2006 CarswellOnt 749, *(sub nom. Kallaba v. Bylykbashi)* 265 D.L.R. (4th) 320, 23 R.F.L. (6th) 235, 207 O.A.C. 60 (Ont. C.A.).

Vexatious litigant order is a final order for the purpose of s. 6(1) of the *CJA* because it constituted a final determination of right to engage in further litigation. Accordingly, right to appeal from that order. While the order's wording appeared to limit statutory right of appeal, no order under s. 140(1) of the *CJA* could operate that broadly. Motion judge's order should be read down so as not to apply to an appeal from this order.

Dale Streiman & Kurz LLP v. De Teresi (2007), [2007] O.J. No. 255, 2007 CarswellOnt 485, 84 O.R. (3d) 383 (Ont. S.C.J.), Wein J.

The applicant lawyer sued by the respondent paralegal. Applicant brought application to have respondent declared a vexatious litigant. Application granted. See s. 140 of the *Courts of Justice Act*, R.S.O. 1990, c. C.43 ("*CJA*").

The term "vexatious proceedings" was defined by Chief Justice Howland in *Foy v. Foy*, in the context of the *Vexatious Proceedings Act*, R.S.O. 1970, c. 481, the predecessor to *CJA* s. 140, as follows:

> The word 'vexatious' has not been clearly defined. Under the Act the legal proceedings must be vexatious and must also have been instituted without reasonable ground. In many of the reported decisions the legal proceedings have been held to be vexatious because they were instituted without any reasonable ground. As a result the proceedings were found to constitute an abuse of the process of the Court. An example of such proceedings is the bringing of one or more actions to determine an issue which has already been determined by a Court of competent jurisdiction.

Foy v. Foy (No. 2), 1979 CarswellOnt 458, [1979] O.J. No. 4386, 26 O.R. (2d) 220, 12 C.P.C. 188, 102 D.L.R. (3d) 342 (Ont. C.A.), at p. 226 (O.R.) as cited by Sedgwick J. in *National Bank of Canada v. Filzmaier*, 2000 CarswellOnt 474, [2000] O.J. No. 567, [2000] O.T.C. 19 (Ont. S.C.J.). See also *Lang Michener Lash Johnston v. Fabian*, 1987 CarswellOnt 378, [1987] O.J. No. 355, 16 C.P.C. (2d) 93, 59 O.R. (2d) 353, 37 D.L.R. (4th) 685 (Ont. H.C.), at pp. 358-59 (O.R.).

R. v. Deutsch (2007), 2007 CarswellOnt 7400, [2007] O.J. No. 4411 (Ont. S.C.J.) 2007-11-15, T. Ducharme J.

The judge convicted Mr. Deutsch of one count of perjury. The count related to a civil case, *Fleet Rent-A-Car Ltd. v. Vadim Bidnyk*, heard by Justice Thomson of the same court.

Ducharme J. stated:

> Having considered Mr. Deutsch's criminal record, I can do no better here than adopt Justice Moldaver's description of Mr. Deutsch in *R. v. Deutsch*, 2005 CarswellOnt 7455, [2005] O.J. No. 5542, 205 O.A.C. 272, 204 C.C.C. (3d) 361 (Ont. C.A.) at 379 in dismissing his appeal from the fraud conviction.

> The appellant is a life-long fraud artist. He is incorrigible and he is a menace to society. In his case, I see virtually no hope of reformation.

> . . . . .

> The fact that Mr. Deutsch has been declared a vexatious litigant does not make any of these principles less applicable to the determination of the appropriate sentence in this case.

Appropriate sentence 14 months.

British Columbia (Attorney General) v. Lindsay, 2007 CarswellBC 600, [2007] B.C.J. No. 565, 393 W.A.C. 254, 238 B.C.A.C. 254, 2007 BCCA 165 (B.C. C.A.); leave to appeal refused (2007), 2007 CarswellBC 2730, 2007 CarswellBC 2731, 381 N.R. 400 (note), 445 W.A.C. 320 (note), 264 B.C.A.C. 320 (note) (S.C.C.).

Appellant challenged order declaring Appellant a vexatious litigant and ordering that he "must not, without leave of the court, institute or commence legal proceedings in any British Columbia court, nor file applications in any existing legal proceedings in any British Columbia court without leave of the court . . .".

Leave required for instituting proceedings in either the Provincial or Supreme Court, and the Court of Appeal added itself to the list that Appellant obtain leave of a justice before commencing a proceeding in the Court of Appeal, as "Mr. Lindsay's litigation conduct before this Court has been as fruitless and vexatious as it has been in the Provincial and Supreme Courts.".

Bono General Construction Ltd. v. Susin, 2006 CarswellOnt 4476 (Ont. C.A.).

Respondents' application for order under s. 140 of *Courts of Justice Act* granted. Applicant barred from commencing or continuing proceedings against respondents without leave. Appeal dismissed. Respondents did not lack status to bring application on basis that they were undischarged bankrupts. Relief sought by respondents did not deal with property but was personal in nature.

Henson v. Berkowits, 2005 CarswellMan 144, 2005 MBQB 32, 193 Man. R. (2d) 170 (Man. Q.B.); affirmed 2006 CarswellMan 301, 2006 MBCA 102, 208 Man. R. (2d) 42, 383 W.A.C. 42 (Man. C.A.).

Plaintiff brought separate actions against individual defendants in Small Claims Court. Defendants brought application for order to prohibit plaintiff from instituting proceedings without leave of court. Application granted. Present actions were brought with view to harass individual defendants and to oppress board. Order made pursuant to s. 73 of *Court of Queen's Bench Act*.

Nelson v. Canada (Customs & Revenue Agency), 2006 CarswellBC 2444, 2006 BCCA 442 (B.C. C.A.).

Plaintiff declared vexatious litigant under provincial *Supreme Court Act* in 1981. At that time, chief justice made order prohibiting plaintiff from bringing any court proceeding without leave. Paragraph of order forbidding plaintiff from filing any application for leave to commence proceedings until plaintiff paid costs award set aside. Paragraph imposed condition that might undermine plaintiff's access to courts should he have reasonably founded or arguable case unrelated to frivolous and vexatious claims disclosed on four applications he already brought before provincial Supreme Court.

Sauvé v. Merovitz, [2006] O.J. No. 4266, 2006 CarswellOnt 6601 (Ont. S.C.J.); additional reasons at 2006 CarswellOnt 8132 (Ont. S.C.J.), R. Smith J.

Application under s. 140 of *Courts of Justice Act* seeking order that no further proceedings be instituted or continued by man except by leave of judge of Superior Court of Justice. Application granted.

Vrooman v. Taylor (2007), 2007 CarswellOnt 495 (Ont. S.C.J.), B.H. Matheson J.

Frivolous or vexatious pleadings. Because of conduct of plaintiff, action should be struck on grounds that it is frivolous and vexatious.

O'Neill v. Deacons, [2007] A.J. No. 1397, 2007 CarswellAlta 1695, 83 Alta. L.R. (4th) 152, 49 C.P.C. (6th) 130, 441 A.R. 60, 2007 ABQB 754 (Alta. Q.B.).

Defendants brought an application to bar plaintiff from instituting or continuing any proceedings without leave of court on the grounds that plaintiff had mislead or attempted to mislead court on several occasions. Application allowed.

Plaintiff was found to be a vexatious litigant since persistently abused processes of courts for improper purposes. Plaintiff's failure to pay costs of numerous failed applications, her persistence in bringing such applications, and her attempts to mislead court were incidences of conduct of a vexatious litigant.

Benson v. Manitoba (Workers' Compensation Board), [2008] M.J. No. 88, 2008 CarswellMan 120, 2008 MBCA 32, [2008] 5 W.W.R. 420, 53 C.P.C. (6th) 269, 228 Man. R. (2d) 46, 427 W.A.C. 46 (Man. C.A.).

Appellant challenged dismissal of application for judicial review of Workers Compensation Board's denial of benefits for alleged injuries arising from anxiety attack. Motions judge found the injury was not a result of an accident causing a disability within the meaning of the *Workers Compensation Act* and therefore did not give rise to a claim against the Board. Appeal dismissed. Benson did not demonstrate that motions judge made any error in principle or any palpable and overriding error.

Intervener employer brought motion for order declaring employee to be vexatious litigant and be prevented from instituting further proceedings without leave. Motion granted. Employer as added party can request vexatious litigant declaration and order prohibiting further proceedings.

McIntyre v. Connolly (2008), 2008 CarswellOnt 1604, [2008] O.J. No. 1097 (Ont. S.C.J.), Himel J.

Defendants brought motions to dismiss or strike out plaintiff's claim, and to have plaintiff declared vexatious litigant. Motions granted. Plaintiff vexatious litigant. Plaintiff's action brought in circumstances where same issues had already been determined by Superior Court, Small Claims Court and labour arbitrator.

Roskam v. Jacoby-Hawkins, 2010 ONSC 4439, 2010 CarswellOnt 7132 (Ont. S.C.J.), Boswell J..

Judgment delivered by deputy judge on February 12, 2010.

Roskam served a Notice of Appeal of the Small Claims Court Judgment on March 18, 2010, more than 30 days after Judgment released. Jacoby-Hawkins moved to strike out the Notice of Appeal.

Jacoby-Hawkins sought additional relief that Roskam be required to post security for costs of the appeal, that he be declared a vexatious litigant and that Roskam be required to remove all references he has authored about Jacoby-Hawkins and his counsel from the internet.

Section 31 of the *Courts of Justice Act*, R.S.O. 1990 c. C.43, provides that an appeal lies to the Divisional Court from a final order of the Small Claims Court in an action for the payment of money in excess of $500.00. Rule 61.04 of the *Rules of Civil Procedure* provides that any such appeal must be commenced within 30 days after the making of the order. The time for appeal usually runs from the date of pronouncement of a judgment: see *Permanent Investment Corp. v. Ops & Graham (Township)*, 1967 CarswellOnt 90, 62 D.L.R. (2d) 258, [1967] 2 O.R. 13 (Ont. C.A.).

Rule 3.02 deals with extensions of time generally. Rule 3.02 provides court with discretion to extend the time in which to file the Notice of Appeal, which was delivered four days late. *Bona fide* intention to pursue appeal. No prejudice to respondent as a result of late service.

Justice requires extension of time to file Notice of Appeal. See *Rizzi v. Mavros*, 2007 ONCA 350, 2007 CarswellOnt 2841, [2007] O.J. No. 1783, 85 O.R. (3d) 401, 224 O.A.C. 293 (Ont. C.A. [In Chambers]). Basis for security grounded in r. 56.01(1)(c) incorporated by reference in r. 61.06(1)(b). Request for security for costs not made out. Rationale underlying s. 140 discussed by Blair, J.A. in *Foy v. Foy (No. 2)*, [1979] O.J. No. 4386, 102 D.L.R. (3d) 342, 12 C.P.C. 188, 26 O.R. (2d) 220, 1979 CarswellOnt 458 (Ont. C.A.); leave to appeal refused 102 D.L.R. (3d) 342 (note), [1979] 2 S.C.R. vii, 12 C.P.C. 188n, 26 O.R. (2d) 220n, 31 N.R. 120 (S.C.C.).

The control of vexatious proceedings was necessary to protect integrity of the judicial system. The purpose of section to prevent people from using system for improper purposes, such as harassment or oppression. See *Dale Streiman & Kurz LLP v. De Teresi*, 2007 CarswellOnt 485, [2007] O.J. No. 255, 84 O.R. (3d) 383 (Ont. S.C.J.). Accordingly, a litigant's behaviour both inside and outside of the court is relevant. See *Canada Post Corp. v. Varma*, [2000] F.C.J. No. 851, 2000 CarswellNat 1183, 192 F.T.R. 278 (Fed. T.D.).

Section 140 of the *Courts of Justice Act* gives the court the authority to declare a party a vexatious litigant, thereby restricting his or her access to the courts of Ontario. It is a remedy that should be used very sparingly because the ability to have one's grievances addressed by the courts is fundamental to a free and just society. At the same time, the court must be wary of its processes being used for vexatious purposes.

Given Roskam's behaviour, appropriate case to make an order declaring Roskam to be a vexatious litigant.

Petrykowski v. 553562 Ontario Ltd., 2011 ONSC 6711, 2011 CarswellOnt 12895 (Ont. S.C.J.), Milanetti J.

This motion is the latest in a long line of procedural missteps by Petrykowski. Petrykowski filed a claim in the Small Claims Court. He revived the claim against him in the Superior Court.

The justice of the case considered the governing principle in determining whether to grant leave to extend the time for an appeal (Laskin J.A. in *Bratti v. Wabco Standard Trane Inc.*, 1994 CarswellOnt 267, [1994] O.J. No. 855, 25 C.B.R. (3d) 1 (Ont. C.A.)).

In circumstances where the court finds that an appeal is without merit, the court should not be required to assist in bringing it forward. In such cases, the justice of the case should compel a court to bring closure to the proceeding instead (*Petrykowski v. 553562 Ontario Ltd.*, 2011 ONSC 1101, 2011 CarswellOnt 1014, [2011] O.J. No. 734 (Ont. Div. Ct.)). Petrykowski's overly-litigious conduct was well documented. The motion to extend the time to appeal was dismissed.

Houweling Nurseries Ltd. v. Houweling, 2010 BCCA 315, 2010 CarswellBC 1511, 321 D.L.R. (4th) 317, 289 B.C.A.C. 121, 489 W.A.C. 121 (B.C. C.A.).

Vexatious litigant orders were made against the appellant. The Orders were to be used sparingly and only in the clearest of cases. This is one of those cases. The appellant precluded from filing any further documents in the Court of Appeal in connection with the subject matter of litigation. The court has an inherent jurisdiction to control its own process from being abused. This was clearly a case where the court should act on its own motion.

Dyce v. Lyons-Batstone, 2012 ONSC 490, 2012 CarswellOnt 568 (Ont. S.C.J.); affirmed 2012 ONCA 553, 2012 CarswellOnt 10390 (Ont. C.A.); affirmed 2012 ONCA 626, 2012 CarswellOnt 17231 (Ont. C.A.).

Since 2007, there has been a plethora of litigation between Wayne Dyce and Megan Hubbard.

Allegations in statement of claim were very similar in nature to the allegations Wayne Dyce made in the actions before Cunningham A.C.J.S.C.J. and therefore should be struck.

Pleading shows complete absence of material facts. It is frivolous and vexatious and should be struck as being scandalous: see *Aristocrat Restaurants Ltd. v. Ontario*, 2003 CarswellOnt 5574, [2003] O.J. No. 5331 (Ont. S.C.J.).

Accordingly, pursuant to rules 21.01(1)(b), 21.01(3)(d) and 25.11 of the *Rules of Civil Procedure*, the claim was struck and the action dismissed.

This would be a case in which security for costs would be appropriate, pursuant to rule 56.01(1)(c) and (e), of the *Rules of Civil Procedure*.

The Court was unable to grant such an order at this time since the defendants had not filed a statement of defence.

Section 140 of the *Courts of Justice Act* provided the jurisdiction to a judge of the superior court to deem a person to be a vexatious litigant.

In *Roskam v. Jacoby-Hawkins*, 2010 ONSC 4439, 2010 CarswellOnt 7132 (Ont. S.C.J.), Boswell J. set out the rationale of section 140.

See also Henry J., in *Lang Michener Lash Johnston v. Fabian*, 1987 CarswellOnt 378, [1987] O.J. No. 355, 59 O.R. (2d) 353, 16 C.P.C. (2d) 93, 37 D.L.R. (4th) 685 at para. 19 (Ont. H.C.). The behaviour of a litigant was also considered in the decision of Dawson J. in *Canada Post Corp. v. Varma*, 2000 CarswellNat 1183, [2000] F.C.J. No. 851, 192 F.T.R. 278 at para. 23 (Fed. T.D.).

The Court of Appeal for Ontario has made it clear that orders requiring a litigant to seek leave prior to continuing with "any such proceeding previously instituted . . . in any court" include appeals to their court. Only the order declaring the litigant to be vexatious is appealable as of right pursuant to section 6(1)(b) of the *Courts of Justice Act*: see *Kallaba v. Bylykbashi*. Furthermore, this order can include the staying of actions until outstanding costs orders are paid: see *Landmark Vehicle Leasing Corp. v. Marino*, 2011 ONSC 1671, 2011 CarswellOnt 1771 (Ont. S.C.J.); additional reasons at 2011 ONSC 8028, 2011 CarswellOnt 5858 (Ont. S.C.J.).

V.I. Fabrikant v. Eisenberg, 2011 QCCA 1560, 2011 CarswellQue 9346, EYB 2011-195209 (Que. C.A.); leave to appeal refused 2012 CarswellQue 501, 2012 CarswellQue 502, 432 N.R. 396 (note) (S.C.C.).

Fabrikant, the applicant, has been serving a life sentence since 1992. He was declared a vexatious litigant. On April 3, 2011, he initially sought authorization to institute an action in damages against the respondents (the "doctors"), via an application dated April 3, 2011. The Application for authorization to institute an action was brought under Rule 84 and following of the *Rules of Practice* of the Superior Court of Québec, since the Applicant can no longer institute any proceedings before the Courts of Québec without prior authorization. The Application for leave to appeal to the Supreme Court of Canada was dismissed with costs.

Szpakowsky v. Kramar, 2012 ONCA 77, 2012 CarswellOnt 1320, 19 C.P.C. (7th) 274, [2012] O.J. No. 446 (Ont. C.A.); additional reasons at 2012 ONCA 136, 2012 CarswellOnt 2087 (Ont. C.A.).

This case contains security for costs, as the case may be a waste of time or nuisance. The Court does not need to be satisfied that a case is without merit and frivolous, vexatious, or otherwise an abuse of the court's process. The Court needs only to have "good reason to believe" that a case has those characteristics. The appellant's history of re-litigating this case brought it within those characteristics. For this and other grounds, the appeal court ordered the appellant to pay $15,000 into the court as security for the costs of appeal.

With respect to the second arm of the test in clause 61.06(1)(a) of *Rules of Civil Procedure*, the appellant conceded that she was impecunious. Impecunious litigants are not entitled to litigate with impunity, causing their opponents to run up significant costs and without having to face normal consequences of costs if they (impecunious litigants) were unsuccessful. The

Court was unwilling to make an order for security for costs of more than $43,000 and instead settled upon a sum of $15,000 as security for costs. The appeal has been stayed pending the appellant's compliance with this order.

Liu v. Tangirala, 2010 ABCA 383, 2010 CarswellAlta 2441, 493 A.R. 378, 502 W.A.C. 378, 2 C.P.C. (7th) 426 (Alta. C.A.); leave to appeal refused 2011 CarswellAlta 1123, 2011 CarswellAlta 1124, 522 A.R. 408 (note), 426 N.R. 389 (note), 544 W.A.C. 408 (note) (S.C.C.).

The plaintiff brought an action against the defendant. The plaintiff had brought at least 24 applications, and commenced or sought leave to commence at least seven appeals. The decision to declare the plaintiff a vexatious litigant was a discretionary decision. From the plaintiff's conduct and statements, there was a real risk that he would continue to commence actions.

Hudgins v. Hudgins, 2012 ONSC 2133, 2012 CarswellOnt 4130 (Ont. S.C.J.), Shaughnessy J.

The Respondent, Hudgins brings a motion for an order declaring that the Applicant is a vexatious litigant and from further instituting or continuing any proceedings instituted in any court in Ontario, except with leave of the Regional Senior Judge of the Superior Court of Justice or his/her designate pursuant to s. 140(1)(a) to (d) and s. 140(3) of the *Courts of Justice Act R.S.O. 1990, c. C. 43* and the *Family Law Rules*, 2(2), 2(3), and 14(21) O.Reg. 114/99, as amended. See *Lang Michener Lash Johnston v. Fabian*, 1987 CarswellOnt 378, 59 O.R. (2d) 353, 16 C.P.C. (2d) 93, 37 D.L.R. (4th) 685, [1987] O.J. No. 355 (Ont. H.C.) at para. 19, where Justice Henry considered a number of judicial decisions and summarized the principles relating to vexatious proceedings.

The Court has a broad jurisdiction under s. 140 of the *Courts of Justice Act*. The Court of Appeal has stated that orders requiring a litigant to seek leave to continue with proceedings or to institute new proceedings in any court includes appeals to their court. Only the order declaring the litigant to be vexatious is appealable as of right pursuant to s. 6(1)(b) of the *Courts of Justice Act*. (*Kalaba v. Bylykbashi*, 2006 CarswellOnt 749, (sub nom. *Kallaba v. Bylykbashi*) 265 D.L.R. (4th) 320, 23 R.F.L. (6th) 235, 207 O.A.C. 60, [2006] O.J. No. 545 (Ont. C.A.); leave to appeal refused 2006 CarswellOnt 5138, 2006 CarswellOnt 5139, [2006] 2 S.C.R. ix (note), 358 N.R. 394 (note), 227 O.A.C. 394 (note), [2006] S.C.C.A. No. 144 (S.C.C.). Order of vexatious litigant can include the staying of actions, whether by way of further motion, appeals or other steps, until outstanding cost orders are paid. (*Landmark Vehicle Leasing Corp. v. Marino*, 2011 ONSC 1671, 2011 CarswellOnt 1771 (Ont. S.C.J.) at para. 47; ; additional reasons 2011 ONSC 8028, 2011 CarswellOnt 5858 (Ont. S.C.J.)).

Appropriate to make an order declaring Hudgins a vexatious litigant and to impose terms on him.

Ontario v. Jogendra, 2012 ONSC 3303, 2012 CarswellOnt 7960, [2012] O.J. No. 2899 (Ont. S.C.J.); affirmed 2012 ONCA 834, 2012 CarswellOnt 15025, [2012] O.J. No. 5605 (Ont. C.A.); leave to appeal refused 2013 CarswellOnt 4862, 2013 CarswellOnt 4863 (S.C.C.), Hainey J.

Regis Jogendra is a former Justice of the Peace who has instituted a myriad of civil, administrative, regulatory and private criminal proceedings against the Crown and its employees, judicial officials and other adjudicators, and many of the lawyers who represent them.

The Applicant seeks orders declaring Mr. Jogendra a vexatious litigant, and prohibiting him from instituting or continuing any civil or private criminal proceedings without obtaining leave of a judge of this court.

Court may consider all of the proceedings in which he has been a party and may also consider his conduct as a litigant within those proceedings: *Dale Streiman & Kurz LLP v. De Teresi*, 2007 CarswellOnt 485, 84 O.R. (3d) 383, [2007] O.J. No. 255 (Ont. S.C.J.).

Order Jogendra obtain leave of a judge of the Superior Court of Justice prior to instituting or continuing any civil proceedings in any court, and that any such application for leave made pursuant to section 140(3) of the *Courts of Justice Act* shall be made on at least ten days written notice to the Attorney General of Ontario.

Bank of Montreal v. Cudini, 2013 ONSC 482, 2013 CarswellOnt 525 (Ont. S.C.J.), Gray, J. — Application under s. 140 of the *Court of Justice Act*, to declare respondent vexatious litigant. Application granted. Applicant relies on *Lang Michener Lash Johnston v. Fabian*, 1987 CarswellOnt 378, 59 O.R. (2d) 353, 16 C.P.C. (2d) 93, 37 D.L.R. (4th) 685, [1987] O.J. No. 355 (Ont. H.C.); *Law Society of Upper Canada v. Chavali*, 1998 CarswellOnt 1581, 21 C.P.C. (4th) 20, [1998] O.J. No. 5890 (Ont. Gen. Div.); affirmed 1998 CarswellOnt 4982, 31 C.P.C. (4th) 221, [1998] O.J. No. 5344 (Ont. C.A.); *Ontario v. Coote*, 2011 ONSC 858, 2011 CarswellOnt 989, [2011] O.J. No. 697 (Ont. S.C.J.); affirmed 2011 ONCA 562, 2011 CarswellOnt 8624 (Ont. C.A.); and *Hainsworth v. Canada (Attorney General)*, 2011 ONSC 2642, 2011 CarswellOnt 3844, [2011] O.J. No. 2408 (Ont. S.C.J.). Conduct of Cudini vexatious within s. 140 of the *Act*. Order similar to van Rensburg J. in *Coote*. Order will include a form of "screening" that will require an *ex parte* written application before a judge before a responding party is required to respond to a motion for leave.

See also Norheimer J. in *Chavali v. Law Society of Upper Canada*, 2006 CarswellOnt 3122, [2006] O.J. No. 2036 (Ont. S.C.J.) at paras. 20–22.

(2) [Repealed 1998, c. 18, Sched. B, s. 5(2).]

(3) Application for leave to proceed — **Where a person against whom an order under subsection (1) has been made seeks leave to institute or continue a proceeding, the person shall do so by way of an application in the Superior Court of Justice.**

(4) Leave to proceed — **Where an application for leave is made under subsection (3),**

> **(a) leave shall be granted only if the court is satisfied that the proceeding sought to be instituted or continued is not an abuse of process and that there are reasonable grounds for the proceeding;**

> **(b) the person making the application for leave may seek the recission of the order made under subsection (1) but may not seek any other relief on the application;**

> **(c) the court may rescind the order made under subsection (1);**

> **(d) the Attorney General is entitled to be heard on the application; and**

> **(e) no appeal lies from a refusal to grant relief to the applicant.**

(5) Abuse of process — **Nothing in this section limits the authority of a court to stay or dismiss a proceeding as an abuse of process or on any other ground.**

1996, c. 25, s. 9(17); 1998, c. 18, Sched. B, s. 5(2)

Case Law: *Hoban v. Draymon* (December 9, 1996) (B.C. S.C. [In Chambers]) — Plaintiff had been placed on probation for violation of court order. Plaintiff had ulterior desire to use court to espouse his scheme involving company and was using litigation for collateral and improper purposes. Claims were struck out as abuse of process. As plaintiff had habitually, persistently instituted vexatious proceedings, he was declared vexatious litigant.

Mayes v. Beland (November 17, 1997) (Sask. Prov. Ct.) — Employer laid criminal charges for theft by former bookkeeper. Charges were dismissed. President of employer not party to criminal matter, and different standard of proof applied. Action by employer did not constitute abuse of process and should not be struck.

Minott v. Danbury Sales Inc. (January 21, 1998), Doc. 98-CV-139018 (Ont. Gen. Div.) — Plaintiff commenced action relating to purchase of goods at auction conducted by one of defendants. Defendants sought to dismiss proceeding on basis that it was virtually identical to earlier claim which had been dismissed. Parties in two actions were same but for addition of two plaintiffs and five defendants. Issues, claims and relief sought were identical. Court dismissed action as abuse of process of court.

Varma v. Rozenberg (October 21, 1998), Doc. CA C27230, C28110, C28550, C28548, C28549, C28201, C28202 (Ont. C.A.); leave to appeal refused (1999), 246 N.R. 396 (note), 127 O.A.C. 398 (note) (S.C.C.) — The case involved an appeal of seven orders striking out the appellant's statements of claim in seven actions as disclosing no reasonable cause of action. The appellant sought to appeal from the order, which declared the appellant to be a vexatious litigant, pursuant to s. 140 of *Courts of Justice Act*, R.S.O. 1990, c. C.43. The appeals were stayed pending leave being obtained to continue them, or until such time as a s. 140 order was set aside, reversed, rescinded, or stayed under s. 7(5) of Act.

Toronto Hospital v. Nourhaghighi (2000), [1999] S.C.C.A. No. 382, 254 N.R. 398 (note), 134 O.A.C. 398 (note), 2000 CarswellOnt 915, 2000 CarswellOnt 916 (S.C.C.) — The applicant brought several actions raising condominium law issues and made allegations of police torture, etc. The applicant was found to be a vexatious litigant.

Kalevar v. McTeague, 2005 CarswellOnt 1958 (Ont. S.C.J.), DiTomaso J. Applicant (Kalevar) brought application for leave to continue Small Claims Court actions. Actions previously joined for trial together in Whitby Small Claims Court.

Issue whether Kalevar should be granted leave to continue the three Small Claims Court actions pursuant to s. 140(3) of the *Courts of Justice Act*.

Section 140 of the *Courts of Justice Act* deals with the subject of vexatious proceedings:

> (3) Application for leave to proceed — Where a person against whom an order subsection (1) has been made seeks leave to institute or continue a proceeding, the person shall do so by way of an application in the Superior Court of Justice.

Leave sought very same leave to continue sought by his counsel and denied by Justice Ferrier.

For issue *estoppel* see, *Danyluk v. Ainsworth Technologies Inc.*, REJB 2001-25003, 2001 CarswellOnt 2434, 2001 CarswellOnt 2435, [2001] S.C.J. No. 46, 2001 SCC 44, 54 O.R. (3d) 214 (headnote only), 201 D.L.R. (4th) 193, 10 C.C.E.L. (3d) 1, 7 C.P.C. (5th) 199, 272 N.R. 1, 149 O.A.C. 1, 2001 C.L.L.C. 210-033, 34 Admin. L.R. (3d) 163, [2001] 2 S.C.R. 460 (S.C.C.). Issue *estoppel* has been successfully invoked by the respondents. See also *R. v. Scott*, EYB 1990-67596, 1990 CarswellOnt 65, 1990 CarswellOnt 1012, [1990] S.C.J. No. 132, 116 N.R. 361, 1 C.R.R. (2d) 82, 43 O.A.C. 277, 2 C.R. (4th) 153, 61 C.C.C. (3d) 300, [1990] 3 S.C.R. 979 (S.C.C.), p. 1007 re abuse of process.

Multiplicity of proceedings indicative of vexatiousness. Application dismissed with costs.

Jensen v. Jackman, 496 W.A.C. 225, 293 B.C.A.C. 225, 2010 CarswellBC 9, 2010 BCCA 6 (B.C. C.A. [In Chambers]).

The applicant was required by prior court order to get leave to commence any legal proceeding as she had history of starting vexatious proceedings. Application dismissed. The applicant could not show her appeal was not without merit or that her proposed claim against defendants was reasonably founded or arguable.

Ontario v. Coote, 2011 ONCA 562, 2011 CarswellOnt 8624 (Ont. C.A.); affirming 2011 ONSC 858, 2011 CarswellOnt 989, [2011] O.J. No. 697 (Ont. S.C.J.). Vexatious proceedings and abuse of process.

141. (1) Civil orders directed to sheriffs — Unless the Act provides otherwise, orders of a court arising out of a civil proceeding and enforceable in Ontario shall be directed to a sheriff for enforcement.

Commentary: The *Sheriffs Act*, R.S.O. 1980, c. 470 has been repealed and replaced in part by this section.

This removes the former appointment process of Small Claims Court clerks, bailiffs, and referees, as well as deputy clerks and deputy bailiffs. The powers and duties given to clerks, bailiffs and referees are now assigned, by Regional Directors, to court office staff under s. 77(2) of the Act. When s. 13 of Bill 136 came into force, the Order in Council appointments of all Small Claims Court clerks, bailiffs, and referees was repealed.

With the repeal of s. 30 of the *Courts of Justice Act* which provided that Small Claims Court orders were to be directed to a bailiff for enforcement, effective February 28, 1995, all orders arising out of a civil proceeding in Ontario are to be directed to a sheriff for enforcement in accordance with s. 141(1) of the Act.

Section 30 was repealed, effective February 28, 1995, by s. 11 of the *Courts of Justice Statute Law Amendment Act, 1994*, S.O. 1994, c. 12. The effect of the repeal of s. 30 is that s. 141 of the *Courts of Justice Act* now applies to orders of the Small Claims Court. Subsection 141(1) states:

> Unless an Act provides otherwise, orders of a court arising out of a civil proceeding and enforceable in Ontario shall be directed to a sheriff for enforcement.

Presumably, the repeal of s. 30 and the new application of s. 141 to orders of the Small Claims Court reflects the increasing amalgamation of all enforcement measures for both the Superior Court of Justice and the Small Claims Court into one office in each region. In this connection, public servants who act as court enforcement officers have been assigned the duties of both sheriffs and bailiffs by the Deputy Attorney General pursuant to s-s. 77(2) of the *Courts of Justice Act*.

It can be argued that s. 141(1) (and the former s. 30 of the *Courts of Justice Act*) is not intended to apply to notices of garnishment. The reason for this is that the nature of garnishment as a remedy and the manner of enforcing a notice of garnishment are fundamentally different from a court order such as a writ of seizure and sale.

The rules of the Small Claims Court would then permit service of a notice of garnishment by someone other than the bailiff and, specifically, by a creditor.

Enforcement necessarily includes service of the enforcement document. Accordingly, a creditor's right to enforce a notice of garnishment necessarily includes the right to serve the notice.

(2) Police to assist sheriff — A sheriff who believes that the execution of an order may give rise to a breach of the peace may require a police officer to accompany the sheriff and assist in the execution of the order.

142. Protection for acting under court order — A person is not liable for any act done in good faith in accordance with an order or process of a court in Ontario.

143. (1) Enforcement of bonds and recognizances — A bond or recognizance arising out of a civil proceeding may be enforced in the same manner as an order for the payment of money by leave of a judge on motion by the Attorney General or any other person entitled to enforcement.

(2) Enforcement of fines for contempt — A fine for contempt of court may be enforced by the Attorney General in the same manner as an order for the payment of money or in any other manner permitted by law.

(3) Enforcement by sheriff — The sheriff to whom a writ obtained under subsection (1) or (2) is directed shall proceed immediately to carry out the writ without a direction to enforce.

Commentary: The *Criminal Code*, R.S.C. 1985, c. C-46, and the *Provincial Offences Act*, R.S.O. 1990, c. P.33, contain specific provisions dealing with the enforcement of fines and recognizances under those Acts. However, there is a small category of fines and recognizances that are not dealt with by those Acts. For example, a fine imposed for contempt is not enforceable under the *Criminal Code* or the *Provincial Offences Act*. These fines are enforced under the *Escheats Act*, R.S.O. 1990, c. E.20, an archaic statute that is not widely known. This provision replaces the *Escheats Act* and provides a straightforward method of enforcing fines, bonds and recognizances that are not enforced under other statutes.

143.1 [Repealed 1999, c. 12, Sched. B, s. 4(4).]

144. Orders enforceable by police — Warrants of committal, warrants for arrest and any other orders requiring persons to be apprehended or taken into custody shall be directed to police officers for enforcement.

Commentary: This was added to provide for the police to enforce the apprehension or taking into custody of persons as set out.

145. Consul as official representative — Where a person who is ordinarily resident in a foreign country is entitled to money or property that is in the hands of a court or an executor or administrator, and if the foreign country has a consul in Canada who is authorized to act as the person's official representative, the money or property may be paid or delivered to the consul.

146. Where procedures not provided — Jurisdiction conferred on a court, a judge or a justice of the peace shall, in the absence of express provision for procedures for its exercise in any Act, regulation or rule, be exercised in any manner consistent with the due administration of justice.

147. (1) Seal of court — The courts shall have such seals as are approved by the Attorney General.

(2) Idem — Every document issued out of a court in a civil proceeding shall bear the seal of the court.

148. Jurisdiction of Federal Court — The Federal Court of Canada has jurisdiction,

    (a) in controversies between Canada and Ontario;

    (b) in controversies between Ontario and any other province in which an enactment similar to this section is in force,

in accordance with section 19 of the *Federal Court Act* (Canada).

PART VIII — MISCELLANEOUS

149. (1) [Repealed 1994, c. 12, s. 47(2).]

(2) **Repeal** — Subsection (1) is repealed on January 1, 1996.

1994, c. 12, s. 47

150. Renewal of writs of execution issued before January 1, 1985 — A writ of execution that was issued before the 1st day of January, 1985 may be renewed in the same manner and with the same effect as a writ of execution issued on or after that day.

151. (1) **References to counties for judicial purposes** — A reference in this Act or any other Act, rule or regulation to a county or district for judicial purposes is deemed to be a reference to the corresponding area that, for municipal or territorial purposes, comprises the county, district, union of counties or regional, district or metropolitan municipality.

(2) **Separated municipalities** — For the purpose of subsection (1), every city, town and other municipality is united to and forms part of the county in which it is situate.

(3) **Exceptions** — Subsection (1) is subject to the following:

1. A reference in an Act or regulation to a county or district for judicial purposes is, in the case of The Regional Municipality of Haldimand-Norfolk, deemed to be a reference to the following areas:

   i. All the area of the County of Haldimand as it existed on the 31st day of March, 1974.

   ii. All the area of the County of Norfolk as it existed on the 31st day of March, 1974.

2. A reference in an Act or regulation to a county or district for judicial purposes is, in the case of The Regional Municipality of Niagara, deemed to be a reference to the following areas:

   i. All the area of the County of Lincoln as it existed on the 31st day of December, 1969.

   ii. All the area of the County of Welland as it existed on the 31st day of December, 1969.

3. A reference in an Act or regulation to a county or district for judicial purposes is, in the case of The Regional Municipality of Sudbury and the Territorial District of Sudbury, deemed to be a reference to all the area in The Regional Municipality of Sudbury and in the Territorial District of Sudbury.

4. A reference in an Act or regulation to a county or district for judicial purposes is, in the case of an area described below, deemed to be a reference to all the area in the areas described below:

   i. All the area in the County of Victoria.

   ii. All the area in the County of Haliburton.

   iii. All the area in any part of the townships of Sherborne, McClintock, Livingstone, Lawrence and Nightingale located in Algonquin Park, so long as the part remains part of Algonquin Park.

151.1 Meaning unchanged — Despite the repeal of the *Municipal Act*, for the purposes of this Act and any provision of another Act or regulation that relates to the operation of the courts or the administration of justice, the terms "county", "district", "union of counties", "regional municipality" and "district municipality" have the same meaning as they did on December 31, 2002, unless the context otherwise requires.

2002, c. 17, Sched. F

SCHEDULE [1]

The number in square brackets has been editorially added by Carswell.

Appendix A to Framework Agreement

BETWEEN:

Her Majesty the Queen in right of the Province of Ontario represented by the Chair of Management Board

("the Minister")

and

the Judges of the Ontario Court (Provincial Division) and the former Provincial Court (Civil Division) represented by the respective Presidents of The Ontario Judges Association, The Ontario Family Law Judges Association, and the Ontario Provincial Court (Civil Division) Judges' Association

("the Judges")

These are the terms to which the Minister and the Judges agree:

Definitions

1. In this agreement,

"Commission" means the Provincial Judges' Remuneration Commission;

"Crown" means Her Majesty the Queen in right of the Province of Ontario;

"judges' associations" means the associations representing the Judges of the Ontario Court (Provincial Division) and the former Provincial Court (Civil Division);

"parties" means the Crown and the judges' associations.

Introduction

2. The purpose of this agreement is to establish a framework for the regulation of certain aspects of the relationship between the executive branch of the government and the Judges, including a binding process for the determination of Judges' compensation. It is intended that both the process of decision-making and the decisions made by the Commission shall contribute to securing and maintaining the independence of the Provincial Judges. Further, the agreement is intended to promote co-operation between the executive branch of the government and the judiciary and the efforts of both to develop a justice system which is both efficient and effective, while ensuring the dispensation of independent and impartial justice.

3. It is the intention of the parties that the binding process created by this document will take effect with respect to the 1995 Provincial Judges Remuneration Commission, and thereafter.

4. The Minister or the Judges may designate one or more persons to act on their behalf under this agreement.

Commission And Appointments

5. The parties agree that the Provincial Judges Remuneration Commission is continued.

6. The parties agree that the Commission shall consist of the following three members:

1. One appointed jointly by the associations representing provincial judges.

2. One appointed by the Lieutenant Governor in Council.

3. One, who shall head the Commission, appointed jointly by the parties referred to in paragraphs 1 and 2.

7. The parties agree that the members of the Commission shall serve for a term of three years beginning on the first day of July in the year their inquiry under paragraph 13 is to be conducted.

8. The parties agree that the term of office of the persons who are members of the Commission on May 1, 1991 shall expire on June 30, 1995.

9. The parties agree that the members of the Commission may be reappointed when their term of office expires.

10. The parties agree that if a vacancy occurs on the Commission, a replacement may be appointed for the unexpired part of the term.

11. The parties agree that judges and public servants, as defined in the *Public Service Act*, shall not be members of the Commission.

12. The parties agree that the members of the Commission shall be paid the remuneration fixed by the Management Board of Cabinet and, subject to Management Board's approval, the reasonable expenses actually incurred in carrying out their duties.

Scope

13. The parties agree that in 1995, and in every third year after 1995, the Commission shall conduct an inquiry respecting:

(a) the appropriate base level of salaries,

(b) the appropriate design and level of pension benefits, and

(c) the appropriate level of and kind of benefits and allowances of provincial judges.

14. The parties agree that in addition to the inquiry referred to in paragraph 13, the Commission may, in its discretion, conduct any further inquiries into any matter relating to salary levels, allowances and benefits of provincial judges that are mutually agreed by the judges and the Government of Ontario.

15. The parties agree that the Commission whose term begins July 1, 1995 and all subsequent Commissions shall begin their inquiry under paragraph 13 immediately after their term begins and shall, on or before the thirty-first day of December in the year the inquiry began, present recommendations and a report to the Chair of the Management Board of Cabinet.

16. The parties agree that the Commission shall make an annual report of its activities to the Chair of Management Board and the Chair shall table the report in the Legislature.

Powers And Procedures

17. The parties agree that the Commission may retain support services and professional services, including the services of counsel, as it considers necessary, subject to the approval of the Management Board.

18. The parties agree that the representatives of the Judges and the Lieutenant Governor in Council may confer prior to, during or following the conduct of an inquiry and may file such agreements with the Commission as they may be advised.

19. The parties agree that the Commission may participate in joint working committees with the judges and the government on specific items related to the inquiry of the Commission mentioned in paragraphs 13 and 14.

20. The parties agree that in conducting its inquiries, the Commission shall consider written and oral submissions made by provincial judges' associations and by the Government of Ontario.

21. The parties agree that the following rules govern the presentation to the Commission of submissions by provincial judges' associations and by the Government of Ontario, and their consideration by the Commission:

1. Each judges' association is entitled to receive advance disclosure of written submissions by the Government of Ontario and is entitled to make a written submission in reply.

2. The Government of Ontario is likewise entitled to receive advance disclosure of written submissions by provincial judges' associations and is entitled to make a written submission in reply.

3. When a representative of the Government of Ontario or of a judges' association makes an oral submission, the Commission may exclude from the hearing all persons except representatives of the Government of Ontario and of the judges' associations.

4. The representatives of the Government of Ontario and of the judges' associations are entitled to reply to each other's oral submissions.

5. If people have been excluded from the hearing under paragraph 3, the submissions of the Government of Ontario and of the judges' associations shall not be made public except to the extent that they are mentioned in the Commission's report.

22. The parties agree that the Commission may hold hearings, and may consider written and oral submissions from other interested persons and groups.

23. The parties agree that the Government of Ontario and the provincial judges' associations are entitled to be present when other persons make oral submissions to the Commission and are entitled to receive copies of other persons' written submissions.

24. Despite the repeal of the *Public Inquiries Act*, in connection with, and for the purposes of, any inquiry, the Commission or any member thereof has the powers of a commission under that Act.

2009, c. 33, Sched. 6, s. 50

Criteria

25. The parties agree that the Commission in making its recommendation on provincial judges' compensation shall give every consideration to, but not limited to, the following criteria, recognizing the purposes of this agreement as set out in paragraph 2:

(a) the laws of Ontario,

(b) the need to provide fair and reasonable compensation for judges in light of prevailing economic conditions in the province and the overall state of the provincial economy,

(c) the growth or decline in real per capital income,

(d) the parameters set by any joint working committees established by the parties,

(e) that the Government may not reduce the salaries, pensions or benefits of Judges, individually or collectively, without infringing the principle of judicial independence,

(f) any other factor which it considers relevant to the matters in issue.

Report

26. The parties agree that they may jointly submit a letter to the Commission requesting that it attempt, in the course of its deliberations under paragraph 13, to produce a unanimous report, but in the event that the Commission cannot deliver a majority report, the Report of the Chair shall be the Report of the Commission for the purpose of paragraphs 13 and 14.

Binding And Implementation

27. The recommendations of the Commission under paragraph 13, except those related to pensions, shall come into effect on the first day of April in the year following the year the Commission began its inquiry, except in the case of salary recommendations which shall come into effect on the first of April in the year in which the Commission began its inquiry and shall have the same force and effect as if enacted by the Legislature and are in substitution for the provisions of any schedule made pursuant to this Agreement and shall be implemented by the Lieutenant Governor in Council by order-in-council within sixty days of the delivery of the Commission's report pursuant to paragraph 15.

28. The parties agree that the Commission may, within thirty days, upon application by the Crown or the judges' associations made within ten days after the delivery of its recommendations and report pursuant to paragraph 15, subject to affording the Crown and the judges' associations the opportunity to make representations thereupon to the Commission, amend, alter or vary its recommendations and report where it is shown to the satisfaction of the Commission that it has failed to deal with any matter properly arising from the inquiry under paragraph 13 or that an error relating to a matter properly under paragraph 13 is apparent on the report, and such decision is final and binding on the Crown and the judges' associations, except those related to pensions.

29. Where a difference arises between the Crown and the judges' associations relating to the implementation of recommendations properly within the scope of issues set out in paragraph 13, except those related to pensions, the difference shall be referred to the Commission and, subject to affording the Crown and the judges' associations the opportunity to make representation thereupon to the Commission, its decision is final and binding on the Crown and the judges' associations.

30. The parties agree that the recommendations with respect to pensions, or any reconsideration under paragraph 28 of a matter relating to pensions, shall be presented to the Management Board of Cabinet for consideration.

31. The parties agree the recommendations and report of the Commission following a discretionary inquiry pursuant to paragraph 14 shall be presented to the Chair of Management Board of Cabinet.

32. The parties agree that the recommendations of the Commission in consequence of an inquiry pursuant to paragraph 14 shall be given every consideration by Management Board of Cabinet, but shall not have the same force and effect as recommendations referred to in paragraph 13.

33. The parties agree that if the Management Board of Cabinet endorses recommendations referenced in paragraph 30 or 31, or some variation of those recommendations, the Chair of Management Board shall make every effort to implement them at the earliest possible date, following subsequent approval from Cabinet.

Disputes

34. The parties agree that if disputes arise as to whether a recommendation is properly the subject of an inquiry referenced in paragraph 13, or whether the recommendation falls within the parameters of paragraph 27 or 30, or with respect to the process, either party may require the Commission to consider the matter further.

35. The parties agree that requests by either party, made under paragraph 34, shall be presented to the Commission for consideration within one month of the presentation of the report to the Chair of Management Board.

36. The parties agree that the Commission, upon receiving notice from either party as set out in paragraph 34, shall present to the Chair of Management Board a decision with respect to the said matter, within one month of receiving such notice.

37. The parties may, during the course of the Commission's inquiry set out in paragraph 34, present either written or oral positions to the Commission for consideration on the said matter, which shall be disclosed to either party.

38. The parties agree that the decision of the Commission, as set out in paragraph 36, shall be given every consideration and very great weight by the Management Board of Cabinet.

39. Neither party can utilize the dispute clauses to limit, or to narrow, the scope of the Commission's review as set out under paragraph 13, or the binding effect of recommendations within its scope as set out under paragraphs 27 and 28.

40. The parties agree that in the event that an item(s) is referred to the Commission under paragraph 34, the Minister will proceed to implement the other recommendations of the Commission as set out in paragraphs 27, 28 and 33, except where the matter in dispute under paragraph 34 directly impacts the remaining items.

Review

41. The parties agree that either party may, at any time, request the other party to meet and discuss improvements to the process.

42. The parties agree that any amendments agreed to by the parties in paragraph 41 shall have the same force and effect as if enacted by the Legislature and are in substitution for the provisions of this Act or any schedule made pursuant to this Act.

Communication

43. The parties agree that all provincial judges should be made aware of any changes to their compensation package as a result of recommendations of the Commission.

44. The parties agree that all provincial judges should receive updated copies of legislation, regulations or schedules as necessary, related to compensation changes.

Salaries And Indexing

45. The parties agree that effective on the first day of April in every year after 1995, the annual salaries for full-time provincial judges shall be adjusted as follows:

1. Determine the Industrial Aggregate for the twelve-month period that most recently precedes the first day of April of the year for which the salaries are to be calculated.

2. Determine the Industrial Aggregate for the twelve-month period immediately preceding the period referred to in paragraph 1.

3. Calculate the percentage that the Industrial Aggregate under paragraph 1 is of the Industrial Aggregate under paragraph 2.

4. If the percentage calculated under paragraph 3 exceeds 100 per cent, the salaries are to be calculated by multiplying the appropriate salaries for the year preceding the year for which the salaries are to be calculated by the lesser of that percentage and 107 per cent.

5. If the percentage calculated under paragraph 3 does not exceed 100 per cent, the salaries shall remain unchanged.

46. In paragraph 45, "Industrial Aggregate" for a twelve-month period is the average for the twelve-month period of the weekly wages and salaries of the Industrial Aggregate in Canada as published by Statistics Canada under the authority of the *Statistics Act* (Canada).

47. The salaries, allowances and benefits of provincial judges shall be paid out of the Consolidated Revenue Fund.

Additional Provisions

48. This agreement shall be binding upon and enure to the benefit of the parties hereto and their respective successors and assigns.

Appendix B of Framework Agreement
Judicial Salaries

Date	Formula
April 1, 1991	$124,250
April 1, 1992	0%
April 1, 1993	AIW*
April 1, 1994	AIW*

Notes:

* See paragraph 45 of Appendix "A". 1994, c. 12, s. 48

Public Access to Court Files and Documents
Access to Court Records

Anyone can order a transcript of a proceeding or copies of court documents, providing there is no legislative or other legal barrier in place (see e.g. *Youth Criminal Justice Act*, Part IV (young persons), *Provincial Offences Act*, public excluded during the proceeding, s. 486 publication bans, set out in the *Criminal Code*).

Court records are defined as anything containing information that is created or kept by a court or submitted to the court for the purpose of a proceeding. In general, court records are a matter of public record unless a legislative provision or court order restricts public access. Generally court hearings are open to the public, including the media. Therefore court records may be accessible.

For the purpose of access there are *certain exceptions to this general rule*. Thus, criminal court records have been categorized as either accessible or non-accessible documents to the general public. Records deemed non-accessible require a judge's order to be released.

Publication bans can be made under a number of sections of the *Criminal Code* (e.g. ss. 276.3, 486, 517, 539, 631, 648, etc.) as well as by common law. With the exception of s. 486, in general, when a publication ban is imposed, the court record may be made available for inspection or reproduction to any requesting member of the public.

Public Access to Exhibits

If the exhibit was attached to an affidavit and filed with the court, it is a document filed in a proceeding and is publicly accessible under section 137 of the *Courts of Justice Act* unless a statutory provision, common law rule or court order restricts access. If an exhibit is referred to in an affidavit as being produced and shown to the deponent, the party does not attach the exhibit in the affidavit. Instead, the party leaves the exhibit with the registrar for the court's use. In this case, the exhibit is not "filed" with the court and is not accessible under section 137 of the *Courts of Justice Act*.

Fees to Access Civil and Enforcement Documents

Ontario Court of Justice

There are no charges to access court documents in the Ontario Court of Justice.

Superior Court of Justice

There are no charges to access court documents in:

- The Family Court branch of the Superior Court of Justice
- Family cases heard by the Superior Court of Justice that are not appeals

The following chart summarizes the prescribed fees under the *Administration of Justice Act* to access court documents in the Superior Court of Justice, including Small Claims Court and the Enforcement Office.

	Superior Court of Justice and Court of Appeal (excluding family cases that are not appeals) (O. Reg. 293/92)	**Small Claims Court (O. Reg. 432/93)**	**Enforcement Office (O. Reg. 294/92)**
To inspect a court file (per file)			
By a solicitor* or party in the proceeding	no charge	no charge	n/a
By a person who has entered into an agreement with the Attorney General for the bulk inspection of court files	$4.00	$1.00	n/a
By any other person	$10.00	$10.00	n/a
For the retrieval from storage of a court file	$61.00	n/a	n/a
For a search for writs (per name searched)	n/a	n/a	$11.00
For a report showing the details of a writ, lien or order (per report)	n/a	n/a	$6.00 (maximum $60.00 per name)

Notes:

n/a   Fee schedule used by court staff does not include this service.

*   Note: Refers to a solicitor for a party in the proceedings, not any solicitor in general

Parties may apply to enter into an agreement with the Ministry of the Attorney General for bulk file inspection of civil and Small Claims Court files at the rate of $4.00 per file. The party must pay for all relevant court files on a province wide basis for all court locations, regardless of whether or not they choose to inspect the files at every court location. For example, a person who wishes to inspect civil judgment files at Newmarket and Brampton only does not meet this criteria.

The following chart summarizes copy fees prescribed under the *Administration of Justice Act* for each level of court.

	Certified (per page)	**Non-certified (per page)**
Superior Court of Justice and Court of Appeal O. Reg. 293/92	$4.00	$1.00
Superior Court of Justice and Court of Appeal (Family cases that are not appeals) O. Reg. 293/92	$3.50	$1.00
Family Court O. Reg. 417/95	$3.50	$1.00
Small Claims Court O. Reg. 432/93	$3.50	$1.00
Ontario Court of Justice O. Reg. 210/07	$3.50	$1.00
Sheriff's Office O. Reg. 294/92	$3.50*	$2.00*

Notes:

*   For documents other than writs of execution, orders and certificates of lien. See section above for fees for copies of a report showing the details of a writ, lien or order.

Contingency Fees

Contingency fee arrangements allow lawyers and their clients to agree that the lawyer will be paid only in the event of success.

On December 9, 2002, Bill 213, the *Justice Statute Law Amendment Act, 2002*, received Royal Assent. Schedule A of this legislation amended the *Solicitors Act* to regulate contingency fee agreements. It contains broad regulation-making power relating to contingency fees, and includes the following regulatory controls:

- Requires all contingency fee agreements to be made in writing;
- Prohibits contingency fees in criminal, quasi-criminal and family law matters;
- Precludes lawyers from collecting both the pre-determined contingency fee and legal costs, unless approved by a judge;
- Allows clients to collect full payment for an award of costs, even if it exceeds the amount payable under a contingency fee agreement, if the award is used to pay the client's solicitor;
- Authorizes the LGIC to prescribe a maximum percentage that can be charged as a contingency fee; and
- Allows the courts to review contingency fee contracts and to endorse negotiated fees above the prescribed standards where it is fair to do so.

ONT. REG. 258/98 — RULES OF THE SMALL CLAIMS COURT

made under the *Courts of Justice Act*

O. Reg. 258/98, as am. O. Reg. 295/99; 461/01 [ss. 1(2), 4(2), 7(4), 8(2), (4), 9(2), 10(3), 12(2), (4), 13(5), 14(3), 17(2), 19(3), 20(3), 22(2), 23(2) revoked O. Reg. 330/02, ss. 1(2), 3(2), 4(2), 5(2), (4), 6(2), 7(2), 8(2), (4), 9(2), 10(2), 11(2), 12(2), 13(3), 14(3), 15(2), respectively.]; 330/02, ss. 1(1), 2, 3(1), 4(1), (3), 5(1), (3), 6(1), 7(1), 8(1), (3), 9(1), 10(1), 11(1), 12(1), 13(1), (2), 14(1), (2), 15(1); 440/03; 78/06; 574/07; 56/08; 393/09, ss. 1–13, 14(1)–(3), (4) (Fr.), (5) (Fr.), (6), 15 (Fr.), 16–25; 505/09; 440/10; 56/12; 400/12; 230/13; 44/14.

Commentary: The procedural rules of the Small Claims Court are known as the *Small Claims Court Rules*. Subject to the provisions of the *Courts of Justice Act* applicable to the Small Claims Court, the *Small Claims Court Rules* establish the basic framework for practice and procedure in that court.

The most basic elements of Small Claims Court practice are pleadings, settlement conference and trial.

Pleadings consist of Plaintiff's Claims (see Rule 7), Defences (see Rule 9) and Defendant's Claims (see Rule 10). Service of court documents including pleadings is addressed by Rule 8 and venue or in other words the appropriate court office where a claim must be commenced, is addressed by Rule 6.

Undefended claims may be the subject of default proceedings which are addressed by Rule 11. Stagnant claims may be dismissed for delay by the clerk, pursuant to Rule 11.1.

Settlement conferences are mandatory in defended cases and are addressed by Rule 13. Matters which are not settled may then be set down for trial by any party.

Trials are scheduled pursuant to Rule 16. Trial procedure is addressed by Rule 17 and evidence at trial is addressed by Rule 18. Costs are addressed by Rule 19.

Enforcement of orders, where required, may be accomplished through a series of methods set out in Rule 20.

Court documents in the Small Claims Court are as set out in the Forms.

Rule 1 — General

[Heading amended O. Reg. 78/06, s. 1.]

1.01 Citation — These rules may be cited as the Small Claims Court Rules.

History [1.01]: Formerly 1.01(2).

1.02 (1) Definitions — In these rules,

"court" means the Small Claims Court;

"disability", where used in respect of a person or party, means that the person or party is,

(a) a minor,

(b) mentally incapable within the meaning of section 6 or 45 of the *Substitute Decisions Act, 1992* in respect of an issue in the proceeding, whether the person or party has a guardian or not, or

(c) an absentee within the meaning of the *Absentees Act*;

"document" includes data and information in electronic form;

"electronic" includes created, recorded, transmitted or stored in digital form in other intangible form by electronic, magnetic or optical means or by any other means that has capabilities for creation, recording, transmission or storage similar to those means, and "electronically" has a corresponding meaning;

"holiday" means,

(a) any Saturday or Sunday,

(b) New Year's Day,

(b.1) Family Day,

(c) Good Friday,

(d) Easter Monday,

(e) Victoria Day,

(f) Canada Day,

(g) Civic Holiday,

(h) Labour Day,

(i) Thanksgiving Day,

(j) Remembrance Day,

(k) Christmas Day,

(l) Boxing Day, and

(m) any special holiday proclaimed by the Governor General or the Lieutenant Governor,

and if New Year's Day, Canada Day or Remembrance Day falls on a Saturday or Sunday, the following Monday is a holiday, and if Christmas Day falls on a Saturday or Sunday, the following Monday and Tuesday are holidays, and if Christmas Day falls on a Friday, the following Monday is a holiday;

"information technology" [Repealed O. Reg. 78/06, s. 2(1).]

"order" includes a judgment;

"paralegal" means a person licensed under the *Law Society Act* to provide legal services in Ontario;

"proof of service" means, with respect to a document, proof of service of the document in accordance with rule 8.06; (*"preuve de la signification"*)

"representative" means the lawyer, paralegal or other person representing a person in a proceeding under these rules;

"self-represented", when used in reference to a person, means that the person is not represented by a representative;

"territorial division" means,

    (a) a county, a district or a regional municipality, and

    (b) each of the following, as they existed on December 31, 2002:

        (i) The combined area of County of Brant and City of Brantford.

        (ii) Municipality of Chatham-Kent.

        (iii) Haldimand County.

        (iv) City of Hamilton.

        (v) City of Kawartha Lakes.

        (vi) Norfolk County.

        (vii) City of Ottawa.

        (viii) County of Prince Edward.

        (ix) City of Toronto.

(2) [Repealed O. Reg. 78/06, s. 2(3).]

    O. Reg. 461/01, s. 1 [s. 1(2) revoked O. Reg. 330/02, s. 1(2).]; 330/02, s. 1(1); 440/03, s. 5, item 1; 78/06, s. 2; 574/07, s. 1; 393/09, s. 1; 230/13, s. 1; 44/14, s. 1

History [R. 1.02]: Formerly 1.01(1); clause (b) under the definition of "disability" changed to link the determination of mental competency and capacity to the criteria in the *Substitute Decisions Act.*

Case Law: *Wo-Built Inc. v. Sangster*, 2011 ONSC 3554, 2011 CarswellOnt 5213, 4 C.L.R. (4th) 286 at para. 9 (Ont. Master), Julian Polika.

A "hearing" is defined in rule 1.03(1) of the *Rules of Civil Procedure*, R.R.O. 1990, Reg. 194, as "the hearing of an application, motion, reference, appeal or assessment of costs, or a trial."

TD Financing Services Inc. v. McInnis, 2012 NSSC 52, 2012 CarswellNS 59, 313 N.S.R. (2d) 89, 100 B.L.R. (4th) 157, 25 C.P.C. (7th) 188, 990 A.P.R. 89, [2012] N.S.J. No. 60 (N.S. S.C.)

There was an appeal, pursuant to section 32(1) of the *Small Claims Court Act*, RSNS 1989, c. 430, of an order or determination made by an adjudicator of the Small Claims Court, who determined that the appellant was not an "original party" to the contract and dismissed its claim on the basis of section 5(1) of the *Small Claims Court Act*. The appeal was allowed.

The proper definition of "original party" in section 5(1) of the *Small Claims Court Act* is a question of statutory interpretation, which is a question of law, reviewable on the correctness standard (*Royal & Sun Alliance v. Baltzer* (2009), 2009 NSCA 110, 2009 CarswellNS 592, 283 N.S.R. (2d) 344, [2010] I.L.R. I-4902 at para. 12 (N.S. C.A.)). The question of whether the appellant met the definition of "original party" is a question of mixed fact and law, normally reviewable on the more deferential palpable and overriding standard (*McPhee v. Gwynne-Timothy*, 2005 NSCA 80, 2005 CarswellNS 191, [2005] N.S.J. No. 170, 232 N.S.R. (2d) 175, 737 A.P.R. 175, 44 C.L.R. (3d) 32 at para. 33 (N.S. C.A.)). Rule qualified in *R. v. W. (R.E.)*, 2011 NSCA 18, 2011 CarswellNS 96, [2011] N.S.J. No. 81, 298 N.S.R. (2d) 154, 945 A.P.R. 154, 268 C.C.C. (3d) 557, 230 C.R.R. (2d) 266 (N.S. C.A.) where the court said:

> However, if a trial judge, in the course of making findings of fact or mixed law and fact, seriously misapprehends important evidence or ignores relevant evidence, deference evaporates since these kinds of errors are errors of law on their own, although they frequently underlie findings that are found to be errors that are palpable and overriding.

A corporate "name is merely a means of identification and a change of name does not affect the identity of the company nor its continued existence as the original body corporate"

(*Alliance Securities Ltd. v. Posnekoff*, 1922 CarswellSask 227, 16 Sask. L.R. 214, [1922] 3 W.W.R. 1201 at para. 2 (Sask. K.B.)). Just as changing a human person's family name has no bearing on that person's debt obligations or assets, so too does changing a corporate person's name have no bearing on the corporation's legal obligations or entitlements (*Provincial Insurance Co. v. Cameron*, 1881 CarswellOnt 146, 31 U.C.C.P. 523 (Ont. C.P.); affirmed (1883), 9 O.A.R. 56 (Ont. C.A.)).

"Original" modifies "parties." If the Legislature were only concerned with barring debts assigned to collections agencies or subrogated tort claims by insurance companies, it would have been unnecessary to add the word "original."

1.03 (1) General Principle — These rules shall be liberally construed to secure the just, most expeditious and least expensive determination of every proceeding on its merits in accordance with section 25 of the *Courts of Justice Act*.

History [R. 1.03]: Formerly 1.02.

Commentary: NOTE: Section 25 of the *Courts of Justice Act* provides:

> The Small Claims Court shall hear and determine in a summary way all questions of law and fact and may make such order as is considered just and agreeable to good conscience.

Case Law: *Absolute Bailiffs Inc. v. Wangensteen* (November 27, 1998), Doc. New Westminster S0-47110 (B.C. S.C. [In Chambers]) — One issue was effect of respondent's failure to raise the validity of repairer's lien in pleadings. *Cappos v. Zurich Canada* (1996), 12 C.C.L.I. (3d) 9, 1996 CarswellBC 2929 (B.C. Prov. Ct.). In *Lovrich v. Insurance Corp. of British Columbia* (August 10, 1994), Doc. Vancouver 93-1081 (B.C. Prov. Ct.), Burdett P.C.J. considered whether necessary to specifically plead fraud as a defence in Small Claims Court pleadings. Pleadings may be informal to conclude matters in a "just, speedy, inexpensive and simple manner"(at paragraph 13). However, a party is entitled to have proper notice of the claims being made against it. It is inappropriate, and perhaps unjust and unfair, to try an issue that has not been properly raised in the pleadings.

DeFehr v. De Fehr, 156 B.C.A.C. 240, 2001 CarswellBC 1716, 2001 BCCA 485, 255 W.A.C. 240, 11 C.P.C. (5th) 195 (B.C. C.A. [In Chambers]) — Husband applied for indigent status. The term "indigent" is not defined in the Rules of Court, but its meaning has been considered in a number of cases. Indigent status ought to be granted to the applicant.

D. (M.J.) v. D. (J.P.), 149 B.C.A.C. 153, 2001 CarswellBC 395, 2001 BCCA 155, 244 W.A.C. 153 (B.C. C.A. [In Chambers]) — The husband/father was an unemployed mechanical engineer. The British Columbia Court of Appeal, per Ryan, JA., held that although in financial difficulties, the husband/father was not truly indigent. The Court refused his application to be relieved from paying the fees associated with his intended appeal.

Volzhenin v. Insurance Corp. of British Columbia, 2003 BCCA 59, 2003 CarswellBC 154 (B.C. C.A. [In Chambers]); affirmed 2003 CarswellBC 1383, 2003 BCCA 334 (B.C. C.A.) — Application for indigent status pursuant to Rule 56 dismissed. Materials provided to court set out number of assertions unsupported by explanation or documentation.

Gardiner v. Mulder (2007), 2007 CarswellOnt 1411, 221 O.A.C. 200 (Ont. Div. Ct.); additional reasons at (2007), 2007 CarswellOnt 2829, 224 O.A.C. 156 (Ont. Div. Ct.), March 9, 2007, Cusinato J.

Appeal by Plaintiff from a Small Claims Court judgment arising from dismissal of Plaintiffs' claims against the Defendants collectively for breach of contract and damages.

Although these are not proceedings where parties not totally self-represented, see s. 25 of the *Courts of Justice Act*, R.S.O. 1990, c. C.43, which applies to both represented and unrepresented parties. See Heeney J. in *936464 Ontario Ltd. v. Mungo Bear Ltd.*, [2003] O.J. No. 3795, 2003 CarswellOnt 8091, 74 O.R. (3d) 45, 258 D.L.R. (4th) 754 (Ont. Div. Ct.) in reference to precise pleadings relative to claimed relief. See *Popular Shoe Store Ltd. v. Simoni*, 1998 CarswellNfld 48, [1998] N.J. No. 57, 163 Nfld. & P.E.I.R. 100, 503 A.P.R. 100, 24 C.P.C. (4th) 10 (Nfld. C.A.) at 106 (Nfld. & P.E.I.R.).

Even where there is a failure of the Plaintiff to properly plead and frame claim, it is for the court "to make such order as is considered just and agreeable to good conscience" and the evidence. This principle is subject, however, to the considerations of fairness, surprise and amendment if required.

Appeal allowed in part for damages relative to the hot tub. Issue of costs awarded to the Defendants set aside.

Anand v. Sunfresh Organics, 2011 CarswellOnt 757, 2011 ONSC 776 (Ont. Div. Ct.); additional reasons at 2011 ONSC 1263, 2011 CarswellOnt 1101 (Ont. Div. Ct.)

The appeal by defendant from deputy judge. The appellant argued that trial judge ought to have granted adjournment request and that any prejudice to respondent could be compensated by a cost order. Within Court's jurisdiction to govern its own process and given the facts, trial judge's decision reasonable. The appellant argued the learned judge erred in allowing the plaintiff to reference a document which had not been disclosed to the defendant in accordance with the *Rules of Civil Procedure*. Reference to it not error in judgment or law by trial judge.

The appellant argued the judge allowed as evidence a letter in which an offer of settlement was made and which ought not to have been evidence as it was privileged. This is not a ground for appeal. There was a great deal of other evidence upon which the trial judge could rely to reach his decision. Appeal dismissed.

(2) Matters Not Covered in Rules — If these rules do not cover a matter adequately, the court may give directions and make any order that is just, and the practice shall be decided by analogy to these rules, by reference to the *Courts of Justice Act* and the Act governing the action and, if the court considers it appropriate, by reference to the *Rules of Civil Procedure*.

O. Reg. 78/06, s. 3

Commentary: The *intent* of this subrule is that if matters are not provided for in these rules, the practice shall be determined by analogy to them *and*, *if* necessary, by analogy to the *Rules of Civil Procedure*.

Case Law: *Danson v. Ontario (Attorney General)* (1987), 60 O.R. (2d) 676 (Ont. C.A.); affirmed (1990), 74 O.R. (2d) 763 (note), 43 C.P.C. (2d) 165, 73 D.L.R. (4th) 686, [1990] 2 S.C.R. 1086, 50 C.R.R. 59, 41 O.A.C. 250, 112 N.R. 362, 1990 CarswellOnt 366, 1990 CarswellOnt 1004 (S.C.C.) — The possibility of judicial abuse of a rule of civil procedure, without some adequate facts cannot provide a proper foundation for using an application seeking a declaratory judgment to challenge the constitutional validity of various rules of the *Rules of Civil Procedure*.

Chalupiak v. Gunner Industries Ltd. (1990), 89 Sask. R. 76 (Sask. Q.B.) — The trial judge added party during trial. Intent of legislation to leave the process to the court. In all cases of tribunals, conducting hearings in the absence of prescribed rules, the criterian is fairness.

523090 Ontario Ltd. v. Argiris & Associates (December 22, 1997), Doc. Toronto T0364197 (Ont. Sm. Cl. Ct.) — Small Claims Court was not governed by *Rules of Civil Procedure* (Ont.) and Small Claims Court Rules (Ont.) do not have similar rule relating to counterclaims. Small Claims Court Rules viewed "action" as meaning all pleadings and issues. Word "action" meant litigation and defendant adopted this word. Consent to settle, by using word "action," encompassed both claim and counterclaim.

Kuntz v. British Columbia (Workers' Compensation Board), 2002 CarswellBC 2033, 2002 BCSC 1278 (B.C. S.C.) — The plaintiff self-represented. Defendants sought application dismissing the action against them. Application granted. In a case involving litigant who did not have counsel and who attempted to prosecute claim, issue for presiding judge whether latitude should be extended to that litigant and to what extent. The plaintiff incapable or unwilling to deal with issues in application. No basis on which defendants should be denied relief.

Kaur v. Deopaul, 2006 CarswellOnt 6388, 216 O.A.C. 247 (Ont. Div. Ct.), Cameron J.

Plaintiff commenced action in Small Claims Court against former lawyer for alleged negligence. Defendant moved for summary judgment dismissing action as statute barred. Deputy Judge allowed motion and dismissed action. Plaintiff appealed to Divisional Court.

Appeal dismissed.

No rule in Small Claims Court Rules that allows for summary judgment. Rule 1.03 provides that for matters not covered in the rules the Small Claims Court may make any order that is just and the practice shall be decided by, *inter alia*, reference to the *Courts of Justice Act*. Section 25 of the *Courts of Justice Act* provides Small Claims Court shall determine all questions of fact and law in summary way.

Van de Vrande v. Butkowsky, 319 D.L.R. (4th) 132, 2010 CarswellOnt 1777, 2010 ONCA 230, 99 O.R. (3d) 641, 99 O.R. (3d) 648, [2010] O.J. No. 1239, 260 O.A.C. 323, 85 C.P.C. (6th) 205 (Ont. C.A.); additional reasons at 2010 CarswellOnt 3629, 2010 ONCA 400, 85 C.P.C. (6th) 212 (Ont. C.A.)

See rr. 1.03(2) and 1.03(1), and 25 CJA: "not a gap, but a deliberate omission."

Rule 12.02 of the *Small Claims Court Rules*, O. Reg. 258/98 allows a party to bring a motion to strike out or amend a document. Pursuant to this rule, the appellant, Butkowsky, brought a motion for summary judgment. The trial judge granted the motion, finding that the appellant was immune from suit and action brought beyond applicable limitation period. The Divisional Court set aside the order, finding the trial judge had erred by making findings of fact on the motion.

The procedure of a motion for summary judgment is *not* available under the *Small Claims Court Rules* but the motion judge's decision is nonetheless sustainable under r. 12.02.

The failure to provide for summary judgment motions is not a gap in the *Small Claims Court Rules*, but rather a deliberate omission. Not up to the court to read in such a provision, particularly in light of the fact that r. 12.02 specifically addresses the ability to bring a motion in the nature of those contemplated by rr. 20, 21 and 76 of the *Rules of Civil Procedure*.

Rule 12.02 of the *Small Claims Court Rules* allows a party to bring a motion to strike a document, including a claim, before trial. It is therefore more akin to a r. 21 motion than a r. 20 motion. It is, however, worded differently than rr. 20, 21, or 76 of the *Rules of Civil Procedure*.

There are several important differences between r. 21.01 of the *Rules of Civil Procedure* and r. 12.02 of the *Small Claims Court Rules*. A r. 12.02 motion can be brought to strike any document. Second, the prohibition on admitting evidence contained in r. 21.01(2) is absent from r. 12.02. Third, where r. 21.01(3) allows an action to be struck on the very narrow grounds of it being frivolous, vexatious or an abuse of process, r. 12.02(1)(c) adds the criteria of inflammatory, waste of time and nuisance.

Further, r. 12.02 applies in a somewhat different context than the *Rules of Civil Procedure*. Section 25 of the *Courts of Justice Act* provides that, in Small Claims Court proceedings, the court is to "hear and determine in a summary way all questions of law and fact." The court can make "such order as is considered just and agreeable to good conscience." In addition, r. 1.03(1) of the *Small Claims Court Rules* provides that the rules shall be "liberally construed to secure the just, most expeditious and least expensive determination of every proceeding on its merit in accordance with s. 25 of the *Courts of Justice Act*."

Although the motion judge did not indicate the specific provision of r. 12.02(1) that she was applying, it is apparent that, after making her findings, the claim could properly be viewed as a "waste of time" and struck pursuant to r. 12.02(1)(c).

Appeal allowed and motion judge's dismissal of claim reinstated.

1286342 Ontario Inc. v. Dennis, 2010 ONSC 5575, 2010 CarswellOnt 7696 (Ont. S.C.J.)

Motion brought by plaintiff ("Desnoyers"):

1. To allow Desnoyers to represent 1286342 Ontario Inc. o/a Yachtware Marine Services ("Yachtware");

2. To add party defendants; and

3. To vary the Statement of Claim.

Named defendants brought cross-motions for:

1. An order dismissing the action of Desnoyers;

2. An order that the plaintiff Yachtware appoint a solicitor pursuant to r. 15.01(2) of the *Rules of Civil Procedure* within 30 days of this order;

3. Yachtware post security for costs within 30 days of this order; and

4. Costs.

Desnoyers represented himself and Yachtware. He has *not* attempted to co-operate with counsel.

See statement of former Justice Donald Ferguson made in his book *Ontario Courtroom Procedure* at page 69: "Self-represented litigants may be held to the standard of civility expected of lawyers and a proper remand for failure to do so is an award of costs on a substantial indemnity basis."

Rule 15.01(2) states: "A party to a proceeding that is a corporation shall be represented by a lawyer, except with leave of the court."

See *Lamond v. Smith*, 2004 CarswellOnt 3213, [2004] O.J. No. 3255, 11 C.P.C. (6th) 104 (Ont. S.C.J.), at paras. 13 and 15:

> Mr. DeLorenzo submits that it has not been suggested that the corporate defendant is unable to pay for a lawyer. This is correct. Impecuniosity may be one reason why leave should be granted in a motion under subrule 15.01(2), but it is not a necessary reason. Frankly, I do not see shy the ability or inability to afford a lawyer should be a relevant factor. Some people and companies may think that they have better things to do with their money than to pay lawyers. They may be right; they may be wrong.
>
>   . . . . .
>
> The historical reluctance of trial courts to grant leave to a corporation to be represented by a non-lawyer has little merit in the case of a small, one-man company. Therefore, I exercise my discretion in favour of the moving party and grant leave for 1198827 Ontario Inc. to be represented by Mr. Smith.

Desnoyers allowed to represent Yachtware in this litigation.

Rule 56.01 deals with the issue of security for costs.

See *Willets v. Colalillo*, [2007] O.J. No. 4623, 2007 CarswellOnt 7616 (Ont. Master).

The court in *Zeitoun v. Economical Insurance Group*, 2008 CarswellOnt 2576, [2008] O.J. No. 1771, 91 O.R. (3d) 131, 236 O.A.C. 76, 64 C.C.L.I. (4th) 52, 53 C.P.C. (6th) 308, 292 D.L.R. (4th) 313 (Ont. Div. Ct.); additional reasons at 2008 CarswellOnt 3734, 56 C.P.C. (6th) 191, 64 C.C.L.I. (4th) 68 (Ont. Div. Ct.); affirmed 2009 ONCA 415, 2009 CarswellOnt

2665, [2009] O.J. No. 2003, 96 O.R. (3d) 639, 73 C.C.L.I. (4th) 255, 257 O.A.C. 29, 73 C.P.C. (6th) 8, 307 D.L.R. (4th) 218 (Ont. C.A.), at paras. 48–50 stated that:

> ... There is a difference in the quality of the evidence required depending on whether or not the plaintiff is able to show impecuniosity.

> Where impecuniosity is shown, the plaintiff needs only to demonstrate that the claim is not plainly devoid of merit. (See *John Wink Ltd. v. Sico Inc.* (1987), 57 O.R. (2d) 705 (H.C.J.)). That is a very low evidentiary threshold.

Where impecuniosity has not been shown, however, a closer scrutiny of the merits of the case is warranted; in those cases there is no compelling argument that there is a danger that poverty of the plaintiff will cause an injustice by impeding pursuit of a claim that otherwise would have been permitted to be tried. Where impecuniosity has not been shown, a legitimate factor in deciding whether or not it would be just to require security for costs is whether the claim has a good chance of success.

Order to go for security for costs.

Caprio v. Caprio, 2009 CarswellOnt 8270, 97 O.R. (3d) 312 (Ont. Sm. Cl. Ct.)

There is a difference between not covering a matter adequately and a procedure not being provided for at all. If Rule 20 summary judgment motions could be made available in Small Claims Court "by analogy", other procedures from the *Rules of Civil Procedure* such as cross-examinations on affidavits, affidavits of documents and examinations for discovery could equally be made applicable in Small Claims Court. The analogy rule cannot be applied in such a broad manner.

Fountain v. Ford, 2009 CarswellOnt 705, [2009] O.J. No. 562 (Ont. Sm. Cl. Ct.)

The analogy rule cannot be employed to introduce into Small Claims Court practice procedures which are entirely alien to the summary procedures of that court.

Lemont v. State Farm Mutual Automobile Insurance Co., 2011 CarswellOnt 15743, 9 C.C.L.I. (5th) 318, [2011] O.J. No. 4601 (Ont. Sm. Cl. Ct.)

The analogy rule can only be applied where the *Small Claims Court Rules* fail to cover a matter adequately. Since it appears plain that discovery has been deliberately omitted from the summary procedures of the Small Claims Court, the court did not have jurisdiction to make a non-party production order "by analogy" to rule 30.10 of the *Rules of Civil Procedure*, which rules expressly state that they do not apply in Small Claims Court.

Frothingham v. Regional Health Authority B, 2012 NBQB 155, 2012 CarswellNB 249, 388 N.B.R. (2d) 204, 34 C.P.C. (7th) 200, 1006 A.P.R. 204 (N.B. Q.B.), Justice Peter S. Glennie.

Each of the defendants seeks security for costs from the plaintiff, Dr. Elizabeth Frothingham, a citizen and resident of the United States of America.

The defendants have each filed a motion for security for costs pursuant to subrule 58.01(a) of the *Rules of Court*. The first issue to be determined is whether Rule 58, the Security for Cost Rule, applies to Rule 80 actions. Rule 80, which is the simplified procedure rule for certain claims not exceeding $30,000 came into force on July 15th, 2010 as a replacement for the now repealed *Small Claims Act*. The purpose of Rule 80 is to provide litigants with a simplified litigation process for specific matters involving claims up to $30,000. Dr. Frothingham is claiming $30,000.00 against the defendants in this action.

In *Dugas, Re*, 2003 CarswellNB 270, (sub nom. *Dugas Estate (Bankrupt), Re*) 261 N.B.R. (2d) 99, 43 C.B.R. (4th) 127, (sub nom. *Dugas Estate (Bankrupt), Re*) 685 A.P.R. 99, [2003] N.B.J. No. 230 (N.B. C.A.), Chief Justice Drapeau concluded that an order for security for costs may only issue when it is in the interest of justice.

Security for costs will be ordered where the defendant has satisfied all requirements established by the courts in the absence of any evidence that the plaintiff may be unable to pursue the action if such an order were made. See *Isabelle v. Campbellton Regional Hospital and Arseneau, supra*.

Dr. Frothingham is not an impecunious plaintiff.

If the defendants are successful in this litigation they may nevertheless be put to considerable expense in recovering their costs outside of the Province of New Brunswick against the plaintiff's real property assets in Nova Scotia.

In the result, the plaintiff shall pay $1,000 by cash or certified cheque as security for costs in trust to each of the law firms of the defendants' solicitors by June 26, 2012. The Plaintiff's action is accordingly stayed until such payments for security for costs are made by the Plaintiff and received by counsel for the defendants.

1.04 Orders on Terms — When making an order under these rules, the court may impose such terms and give such directions as are just.

History [R. 1.04]: Formerly 1.03.

Case Law: *Canadian Imperial Bank of Commerce v. Prasad*, 2010 ONSC 320, 2010 CarswellOnt 108 (Ont. S.C.J.), D.L. Corbett J.

Routine credit card collections action concerning alleged debt of $16,258.47. Bank moved for summary judgment. Motions judge, on his own initiative, raised two issues at the motion for summary judgment.

During the period of time the reasons under reserve, Bank asked to be permitted to provide evidence addressing points raised by motions judge at hearing of motion. Request denied. It is not for the court to tease out issues that have not been raised by the parties, except, perhaps, where the court is concerned that it lacks jurisdiction or that the order it is being asked to make is illegal (i.e., cannot be reconciled with binding authority), unconstitutional, unfairly affects a person not before the court, is an abuse of process.

Where issue arises that has not been addressed in evidence by parties, court should give both sides a reasonable opportunity to adduce evidence in respect to the issue.

The decision of the motions judge is binding authority in the Small Claims Court and before the Master. A great many credit card collections cases are brought in those courts.

The goal of civil litigation, as embodied in R. 1.04(1), is to secure the just, most expeditious and least expensive determination of every civil proceeding on its merits.

Leave to appeal granted.

Van de Vrande v. Butkowsky (2010), 2010 ONCA 230, 2010 CarswellOnt 1777, [2010] O.J. No. 1239, 99 O.R. (3d) 648, 99 O.R. (3d) 641, 85 C.P.C. (6th) 205, 260 O.A.C. 323, 319 D.L.R. (4th) 132 (Ont. C.A.); additional reasons at 2010 ONCA 400, 2010 CarswellOnt 3629, 85 C.P.C. (6th) 212 (Ont. C.A.)

Pursuant to Rule 12.02 of the *Small Claims Court Rules*, O. Reg. 258/98, the appellant, Butkowsky, brought a motion for summary judgment. The trial judge granted the motion. The Divisional Court set aside the order, finding that the trial judge erred by making findings of fact on the motion.

Summary judgment not available under the *Small Claims Court Rules* but the motion judge's decision sustainable under r. 12.02.

Motion had been granted pursuant to rr. 1.03(2) and 12.02 of the *Small Claims Court Rules*.

The Divisional Court set aside the motion judge's order based on Rule 20 of the *Rules of Civil Procedure*, R.R.O. 1990, Reg. 194.

Failure to provide for summary judgment motions in the *Small Claims Court Rules* deliberate omission. Rule 12.02 of the *Small Claims Court Rules* is more akin to a r.21 motion than a r. 20 motion.

Rule 12.02 applies in a different context than the *Rules of Civil Procedure*. Section 25 of the *Courts of Justice Act*, provides that the court is to "hear and determine in a summary way all questions of law and fact." The court can make "such order as is considered just and agreeable to good conscience." In addition, r. 1.03(1) of the *Small Claims Court Rules*, provides that the rules shall be "liberally construed to secure the just, most expeditions and least expensive determination of every proceeding on its merit in accordance with s. 25".

Appeal allowed. Motion judge's dismissal of claim reinstated.

Indcondo Building Corp. v. Sloan, 2012 ONCA 83, 2012 CarswellOnt 1742, 18 C.P.C. (7th) 223, 347 D.L.R. (4th) 119 (Ont. C.A. [In Chambers]); affirmed 2012 ONCA 502, 2012 CarswellOnt 9030, 91 C.B.R. (5th) 324, 22 C.P.C. (7th) 22, 352 D.L.R. (4th) 235, 293 O.A.C. 392 (Ont. C.A.); additional reasons 2012 ONCA 619, 2012 CarswellOnt 11697 (Ont. C.A.); leave to appeal refused 2013 CarswellOnt 8, 2013 CarswellOnt 9, 446 N.R. 391 (note), 309 O.A.C. 399 (note) (S.C.C.)

The respondents sought an order requiring the law firm for the appellant to pay into court security for the costs of an action, which was dismissed as an abuse of process, and to pay into court security for costs of the appeal.

The appellant corporation and its principal were impecunious. The appellant had insufficient assets in Ontario to pay the costs below and the costs of appeal. The appellant's law firm was retained on a contingency basis.

The issue was addressed by Nordheimer J. in *Intellibox Concepts Inc. v. Intermec Technologies Canada Ltd.*, 2005 CarswellOnt 1603, [2005] O.J. No. 1087, [2005] O.T.C. 310, 14 C.P.C. (6th) 339 at para. 12 (Ont. S.C.J.):

> As I have noted, the logical extension of ordering security for costs to be posted by an impecunious corporate plaintiff by reason of the fact that its solicitors are operating on a contingency fee basis is, in effect, to require those solicitors to provide the security. Solicitors who make legal services available based on contingency fee arrangements with clients, who could not otherwise afford to litigate a claim, assume the risk that they may not be paid for their work unless a favourable result is achieved. To require those solicitors to assume the additional burden of posting security for costs, with the concomitant risk of losing those funds (in addition to going unpaid for their own services), would impose a significant disincentive to contingency fee arrangements and would run contrary to the very rationale by which they are permitted. In my view, it would be incongruous to interpret the *Rules of Civil Procedure* in such a fashion.

It may be that in some future case, a basis will be established upon which such an order is justified. That said, I do not see this as such a case. The motion was dismissed without costs.

2066209 Ontario Inc. v. Tannis, 2012 ONSC 6665, 2012 CarswellOnt 14837, 299 O.A.C. 190 (Ont. Div. Ct.); additional reasons 2013 ONSC 97, 2013 CarswellOnt 1262 (Ont. Div. Ct.), Aitken J.

This is an appeal from the decision of Deputy judge of the Small Claims Court.

Tannis appeals on the grounds that the trial judge erred in finding that Tannis was personally liable to the Plaintiff. Tannis argues that the trial judge erred in the following ways: (1) in deciding that he did not need to pierce the corporate veil when he found Tannis personally liable, and (2) in finding personal liability on Tannis' part in the absence of evidence that the Plaintiff ever considered Tannis personally liable.

The courts have to manage their own resources in a way that is consistent with the provisions in, and the spirit of, the *Rules*. See Rule 1.04(1). See also Rule 1.04(2)

See *Montreal Trust Co. of Canada v. ScotiaMcLeod Inc.*, 1995 CarswellOnt 1203, *(*sub nom. *ScotiaMcLeod Inc. v. Peoples Jewellers Ltd.)* 26 O.R. (3d) 481, 23 B.L.R. (2d) 165, 129 D.L.R. (4th) 711, 9 C.C.L.S. 97, 87 O.A.C. 129, [1995] O.J. No. 3556 (Ont. C.A.) at para. 25; ; leave to appeal refused 1996 CarswellOnt 6010, 1996 CarswellOnt 6011, [1996] 3 S.C.R. viii (note), 137 D.L.R. (4th) vi (note), 205 N.R. 314 (note), 95 O.A.C. 399 (note), [1996] S.C.C.A. No. 40 (S.C.C.), of circumstances under which corporate veil can be pierced to render directors and officers of a company liable.

Judgment of trial judge against Tannis personally set aside and replaced by a judgment in the same amount and on the same terms against 6681875 Canada Inc. (c.o.b. as Fat Albert's and Ralph's).

1.05 Standards for Documents — A document in a proceeding shall be printed, typewritten, written or reproduced legibly.

O. Reg. 78/06, s. 4

History [R. 1.05]: Formerly 1.04.

1.05.1 (1) Electronic Filing, Issuance of Documents — If these rules permit or require a document to be filed electronically, the software authorized by the Ministry of the Attorney General for the purpose shall be used for the filing.

(2) If these rules permit or require a document to be issued electronically, the software authorized by the Ministry of the Attorney General for the purpose shall be used for the issuance.

(3) A document issued using the authorized software is deemed to have been issued by the Small Claims Court.

(4) Requirement for Signature — If a document is filed or issued electronically, a requirement in these rules that the document contain a person's signature is satisfied if the authorized software indicates on the document that the document has been electronically filed or issued, as the case may be.

(5) Date of Filing, Issuance — The date on which a document that is filed or issued electronically is considered to have been filed or issued, as the case may be, is the date indicated for the document by the authorized software.

(6) Filing, Issuance Outside of Business Hours — A document that is filed or issued electronically outside of regular business hours is deemed to have been filed or issued, as the case may be, on the next day that is not a holiday.

(7) Requirement to Keep Original — A person who electronically files an affidavit or other signed or certified document in accordance with these rules shall,

    (a) keep the original document until the third anniversary of the electronic filing, until the clerk requests that the original document be filed or until these rules require that the original document be filed, whichever is earliest; and

    (b) file the original document on the clerk's request.

(8) Limit on Application of Rule — Despite subrules (1) and (2) and anything to the contrary in these rules, a rule permitting or requiring a document to be filed or issued electronically does not apply unless the Ministry of the Attorney General has authorized software to be used for the purpose for the court location at which the proceeding to which the document relates was or is to be commenced or to which it was transferred.

O. Reg. 44/14, s. 2

Commentary: Starting July 1, 2014, electronic filing and issuance of certain court documents in Small Claims Court will become available on a gradual basis, starting with certain larger centers on a pilot project basis. To determine whether e-filing is available in a particular court office, that office should be contacted.

1.06 (1) Forms — The forms prescribed by these rules shall be used where applicable and with such variations as the circumstances require.

(2) Table of Forms — In these rules, when a form is referred to by number, the reference is to the form with that number that is described in the Table of Forms at the end of these rules and is available on the Internet through *www.ontariocourtforms.on.ca*.

(3) Additional Parties — If a form does not have sufficient space to list all of the parties to the action on the first page, the remaining parties shall be listed in Form 1A, which shall be appended to the form immediately following the first page.

(4) Additional Debtors — If any of the following forms do not have sufficient space to list all of the debtors in respect of which the form applies, the remaining debtors shall be listed in Form 1A.1, which shall be appended to the form:

1. Certificate of judgment (Form 20A).
2. Writ of seizure and sale of personal property (Form 20C).
3. Writ of seizure and sale of land (Form 20D).
4. Direction to enforce writ of seizure and sale of personal property (Form 20O).

(5) Affidavit — If these rules permit or require the use of an affidavit, Form 15B may be used for the purpose unless another form is specified.

(6) [Repealed O. Reg. 78/06, s. 4.]

(7) [Repealed O. Reg. 78/06, s. 4.]

(8) [Repealed O. Reg. 78/06, s. 4.]

(9) [Repealed O. Reg. 78/06, s. 4.]

(10) [Repealed O. Reg. 78/06, s. 4.]

(11) [Repealed O. Reg. 78/06, s. 4.]

(12) [Repealed O. Reg. 78/06, s. 4.]

(13) [Repealed O. Reg. 78/06, s. 4.]

(14) [Repealed O. Reg. 78/06, s. 4.]

(15) [Repealed O. Reg. 78/06, s. 4.]

(16) [Repealed O. Reg. 78/06, s. 4.]

(17) [Revoked O. Reg. 440/03, s. 1.]

(18) [Revoked O. Reg. 440/03, s. 1.]

(19) [Revoked O. Reg. 440/03, s. 1.]

O. Reg. 461/01, s. 2; 330/02, s. 2; 440/03, s. 1; 78/06, s. 4; 393/09, s. 2

1.07 (1) Telephone and Video Conferences — Where Available — If facilities for a telephone or video conference are available at the court, all or part of any of the following may be heard or conducted by telephone or video conference as permitted by subrules (2) and (3):

1. A settlement conference.

2. A motion.

Commentary: Before submitting a request to appear by telephone or videoconference, if facilities are available, the requesting party should determine whether the other parties consent to the request.

The request form should set out whether it is made on consent and precisely who needs to appear by conference (i.e. counsel or paralegal only, or client only or both, etc.). Contact numbers must be provided in the request form and if the request is granted the party must be available from the applicable start time (i.e. 10 a.m.) until the case is reached. There are usually multiple cases on a given day's list and the fact that a conference attendance may have been permitted does not necessarily push that case to the top of the list.

(1.1) If facilities for a video conference are available at the court, all or part of an examination of a debtor or other person under rule 20.10 may be conducted by video conference as permitted by subrules (2) and (3).

(2) Request to be Made — A settlement conference or motion may be heard or conducted by telephone or video conference or all or part of an examination under rule 20.10 may be conducted by video conference if a party files a request for the conference (Form 1B), indicating the reasons for the request, and the court grants the request.

(3) Balance of Convenience — In deciding whether to direct a telephone or video conference, the judge shall consider,

(a) the balance of convenience between the party that wants the telephone or video conference and any party that opposes it; and

(b) any other relevant matter.

(4) Arrangements for Conference — If an order directing a telephone or video conference is made, the court shall make the necessary arrangements for the conference and notify the parties of them.

(5) Setting Aside or Varying Order — A judge presiding at a proceeding or step in a proceeding may set aside or vary an order directing a telephone or video conference.

O. Reg. 78/06, s. 4; 393/09, s. 3

1.08 Representation — For greater certainty, nothing in these rules permits or authorizes the court to permit a person to act as a representative if that person is not authorized to do so under the *Law Society Act*.

O. Reg. 230/13, s. 2

Commentary: This rule is intended to prevent or discourage the appearance of representatives in Small Claims Court who are neither licensees of the Law Society nor exempted persons under By-Law 4. For further reference, see the commentary on pp. 1186 to 187 under Courts of Justice Act s. 26.

Rule 2 — Non-Compliance With The Rules

2.01 Effect of Non-Compliance — A failure to comply with these rules is an irregularity and does not render a proceeding or a step, document or order in a proceeding a nullity, and the court may grant all necessary amendments or other relief, on such terms as are just, to secure the just determination of the real matters in dispute.

Commentary: In general, the court staff should not refuse to accept a document for filing and/or issuing for any other reason than the party's failure to submit to the clerk the required fee(s) in accordance with the SCC Schedule of Fees. A document cannot be refused on the basis that it is illegible or has been brought in the wrong forum. However, there are some situations where the Rules or a court order may specifically require staff to refuse a document. A party may attend the court office to file and/or issue a court document that does not comply with the *Rules of the Small Claims Court*. Sometimes, an issued document may subsequently be found to contain one or more errors made by court staff.

For example:

- The date on the endorsement is not the same as it appears on the issued document;

- An order is issued and then found to have incorrect content (e.g. the spelling or order of names is not exactly the same as the originating or amended process document);

- A paragraph in the judge's endorsement is missing from the issued order; or

- A standard paragraph required by legislation or judicial direction is missing from the issued order.

Since such errors are purely 'clerical' in nature, they may be corrected by the assigned court staff to reflect the correct information which is contained in the court record(s).

Case Law: *Tummillo v. Prouty* (1990), 42 C.P.C. (2d) 308 (Ont. Dist. Ct.) — A statement of claim was brought to the Kenora Local Registrar's office and simply left for issuance as was the local practice. It was issued some six days later, after the expiration of a limitation period. The plaintiff's motion for an order amending the date of issuance of the claim nunc pro tunc was granted, the delay being attributable to the court officials.

Global Agriculture Trans-Loading Inc. v. (IRS) Industrial Repair Services, 2010 CarswellBC 1470, 2010 BCCA 234, 288 B.C.A.C. 88, 488 W.A.C. 88 (B.C. C.A.)

Appellant defendant in action brought in Small Claims Court. It appealed order on basis plaintiff as named in proceedings not a legal entity. It also sought an order for payment out of court of monies attached post-judgment by garnishing order. Judgment had been obtained in default of appearance at mandated settlement conference but was later set aside.

Respondent a sole proprietorship but when the default judgment obtained, "Ltd." was added to its name in style of cause. That addition did not appear in garnishing order.

Litigants should not be burdened with legal technicality. If there is either a factual or a legal problem with the description of the respondent in the style of cause in that court, that is a matter that should be addressed in that court. The use and withdrawal of the designation "Ltd." does not go to the jurisdiction of the court. Appeal dismissed with costs.

Roskam v. Jacoby-Hawkins, 2010 ONSC 4439, 2010 CarswellOnt 7132 (Ont. S.C.J.), Boswell J.

Judgment delivered by deputy judge on February 12, 2010.

Roskam served a Notice of Appeal of the Small Claims Court Judgment on March 18, 2010, more than 30 days after Judgment released. Jacoby-Hawkins moved to strike out the Notice of Appeal.

Jacoby-Hawkins sought additional relief that Roskam be required to post security for costs of the appeal, that he be declared a vexatious litigant and that Roskam be required to remove all references he has authored about Jacoby-Hawkins and his counsel from the internet.

Section 31 of the *Courts of Justice Act*, R.S.O. 1990 c. C.43, provides that an appeal lies to the Divisional Court from a final order of the Small Claims Court in an action for the payment of money in excess of $500.00. Rule 61.04 of the *Rules of Civil Procedure* provides that any such appeal must be commenced within 30 days after the making of the order. The time for appeal usually runs from the date of pronouncement of a judgment: see *Permanent Investment Corp. v. Ops & Graham (Township)*, 1967 CarswellOnt 90, 62 D.L.R. (2d) 258, [1967] 2 O.R. 13 (Ont. C.A.).

Rule 3.02 deals with extensions of time generally. Rule 3.02 provides court with discretion to extend the time in which to file the Notice of Appeal, which was delivered four days late. *Bona fide* intention to pursue appeal. No prejudice to respondent as a result of late service.

Justice requires extension of time to file Notice of Appeal. See *Rizzi v. Mavros*, 2007 ONCA 350, 2007 CarswellOnt 2841, [2007] O.J. No. 1783, 85 O.R. (3d) 401, 224 O.A.C. 293 (Ont. C.A. [In Chambers]). Basis for security grounded in r. 56.01(1)(c) incorporated by reference in r. 61.06(1)(b). Request for security for costs not made out. Rationale underlying s. 140 discussed by Blair, J.A. in *Foy v. Foy (No. 2)*, [1979] O.J. No. 4386, 102 D.L.R. (3d) 342, 12 C.P.C. 188, 26 O.R. (2d) 220, 1979 CarswellOnt 458 (Ont. C.A.); leave to appeal refused 102 D.L.R. (3d) 342 (note), [1979] 2 S.C.R. vii, 12 C.P.C. 188n, 26 O.R. (2d) 220n, 31 N.R. 120 (S.C.C.).

The control of vexatious proceedings was necessary to protect integrity of the judicial system. The purpose of section to prevent people from using system for improper purposes, such as harassment or oppression. See *Dale Streiman & Kurz LLP v. De Teresi*, 2007 CarswellOnt 485, [2007] O.J. No. 255, 84 O.R. (3d) 383 (Ont. S.C.J.). Accordingly, a litigant's behaviour both inside and outside of the court is relevant. See *Canada Post Corp. v. Varma*, [2000] F.C.J. No. 851, 2000 CarswellNat 1183, 192 F.T.R. 278 (Fed. T.D.).

Section 140 of the *Courts of Justice Act* gives the court the authority to declare a party a vexatious litigant, thereby restricting his or her access to the courts of Ontario. It is a remedy that should be used very sparingly because the ability to have one's grievances addressed by the courts is fundamental to a free and just society. At the same time, the court must be wary of its processes being used for vexatious purposes.

Given Roskam's behaviour, appropriate case to make an order declaring Roskam to be a vexatious litigant.

Elsegood v. Cambridge Spring Service 2001 Ltd., 2011 CarswellOnt 652, 2011 ONSC 534 (Ont. Div. Ct.); affirmed (2001), 2011 ONCA 831, 2011 CarswellOnt 14782, 109 O.R. (3d) 143, 99 C.C.E.L. (3d) 327, 346 D.L.R. (4th) 353, 2012 C.L.L.C. 210-008, 287 O.A.C. 32, [2011] O.J. No. 6095 (Ont. C.A.)

An appeal of decision of deputy judge. The argument that respondent's pleadings at trial were not in accord with basis upon which the trial judge found liability. Flaws, or alleged flaws, in pleadings have not been fatal for several decades, especially true in a Small Claims Court setting.

Citroen v. Ontario (Minister of Transportation), 2012 ONSC 975, 2012 CarswellOnt 1361, 27 C.P.C. (7th) 339, 29 M.V.R. (6th) 288, [2012] O.J. No. 533 (Ont. S.C.J.).

The plaintiffs seek an order that the trial of action take place in Hamilton, where the plaintiffs instituted these proceedings. The position of the defendant is that, pursuant to subsection 33(9) of the *Public Transportation and Highway Improvement Act (the Act)* R.S.O. 1990, c. P.50, the trial take place in Peterborough County.

Analysis requires Rule 13.1 of the *Rules of Civil Procedure* and subsection 33(9) of the *Public Transportation and Highway Improvement Act* R.S.O. 1990, c. P.50 (*the Act*).

Under Rule 2, non compliance with the Rules is an irregularity, not a nullity. Rule 2.03 permits the court to dispense with compliance with any rule in the interest of justice.

This test requires a fact-specific analysis in which all of the factors listed in Rule 13.1.02(2)(b) are weighed to determine what trial venue will be "in the interests of justice." *Wilcox v. Flintstone Glass & Mirror Ltd.*, 2009 CarswellOnt 8217, 85 C.P.C. (6th) 394, 79 C.C.E.L. (3d) 80 at paras. 12-19 (Ont. Master); *Paul's Hauling Ltd. v. Ontario (Minister of Transportation)*, 2011 ONSC 3970, 2011 CarswellOnt 7229, [2011] O.J. No. 3447, 106 O.R. (3d) 590 at paras. 17-22 (Ont. S.C.J.). The interests of justice warrant the court to deviate from the presumption that the trial take place in Peterborough. The most expeditious and least expensive determination of the proceeding on its merits favours the trial of this matter taking place in the City of Hamilton.

2.02 Court May Dispense With Compliance — If necessary in the interest of justice, the court may dispense with compliance with any rule at any time.

History [R. 2.02]: Plain language changes.

Rule 3 — Time

3.01 Computation — If these rules or an order of the court prescribe a period of time for the taking of a step in a proceeding, the time shall be counted by excluding the first day and including the last day of the period; if the last day of the period of time falls on a holiday, the period ends on the next day that is not a holiday.

History [R. 3.01]: Plain language changes.

Commentary: If the Rules or an order of the court prescribe a period of time for the taking of a step in a proceeding, the time is counted by excluding the first day, and including the last day, of the period; if the last day of the period of time falls on a holiday, the period ends on the next day that is not a holiday [r. 3.01]. "Holiday" is defined in r. 1.02.

Case Law: *Dyce v. Aquarius Management Inc.* (1995), 65 B.C.A.C. 316, 106 W.A.C. 316 (C.A.) — Proceedings in the Small Claims Division are intended for an inexpensive, expeditious disposition of judicial remedies and the rules of the court permit the extension of time where appropriate.

3.02 (1) Powers of Court — The court may lengthen or shorten any time prescribed by these rules or an order, on such terms as are just.

(2) Consent — A time prescribed by these rules for serving or filing a document may be lengthened or shortened by filing the consent of the parties.

O. Reg. 461/01, s. 3

Case Law: *Malatesta v. 2088675 Ontario Inc.*, 2014 ONSC 1793, 2014 CarswellOnt 3532 (Ont. S.C.J.)

The court denied an extension of time to serve the statement of claim where the delay of two years after issuance of the claim was not satisfactorily explained and there would be prejudice to the defendants if the extens13ion was granted.

William MacDonald Motors Ltd. v. Bragg, 1975 CarswellOnt 324, 8 O.R. (2d) 123 (Ont. Sm. Cl. Ct.) — Action in this section includes a counterclaim and the court has jurisdiction to transfer a claim within the monetary jurisdiction and a counterclaim above the monetary jurisdiction of the Small Claims Court to the District Court.

Flatt v. Brent, [1973] 1 O.R. 282 (Ont. H.C.) — An application *ex parte* under this subsection to transfer an action to a County Court without an amendment being made to the claim may be granted where it is supported by an affidavit showing that the amount involved is in excess of $400.

Further, the judge has jurisdiction to require the plaintiff to serve a new statement of claim within a certain number of days.

Ottawa-Carleton Regional Transit Commission v. Banister, 1973 CarswellOnt 407, [1973] 2 O.R. 152 (Ont. H.C.) — The word "action" includes a counterclaim.

Ontario (Attorney General) v. Palmer (1980), 28 O.R. (2d) 35, 15 C.P.C. 125, 108 D.L.R. (3d) 349 (Ont. C.A.) — Section 11 of the *Public Authorities Protection Act*, R.S.O. 1970, c. 374 provides in part that "no action ... shall be instituted ... unless it is commenced within six months next after the act ..." The court held a counterclaim was an action as defined in s. 1(a) of the *Judicature Act*, R.S.O. 1980, c. 223, as amended, being a "civil proceeding commenced by writ or in such other manner as prescribed by the Rules." On the facts of this case, the snow plough operator and the Crown were persons who were engaged in a public duty and were therefore entitled to protection under the *Public Authorities Protection Act*.

Rajakaruna v. Air France (1979), 24 O.R. (2d) 156 (Ont. H.C.) — Plaintiffs should be permitted, save in exceptional circumstances, to take their claims to the small claims court when the claims lie within the jurisdiction of that court. Four small claims court actions by different plaintiffs were commenced against the same two defendants. There is a limited jurisdiction for such actions to be transferred to County Court pursuant to s. 61(1) of the *Small Claims Court Act*. The policy underlying the *Small Claims Court Act* is to allow access to the small claims courts by plaintiffs. Discretion to transfer actions from the small claims court will be exercised otherwise in only exceptional circumstances. The complexity of the legal and factual issues and the desirability of examinations for discovery do not necessarily create exceptional circumstances.

Livingston v. Ould, 1976 CarswellOnt 321, 2 C.P.C. 41 (Ont. H.C.) — Action for $25 damages based upon a contested claim for a declaration re constitution, rules and by-laws of a union. Issues of general importance seriously raising novel and complicated questions of law and also requiring a careful investigation of facts cannot be conveniently or appropriately tried in small claims courts, which are courts of equity and good conscience and too pressed by their caseloads and too informal in nature to deal with such matters. When the plaintiffs are not without financial means, such a case may be transferred to the Supreme Court pursuant to the wide discretion conferred under s. 62 of the *Small Claims Courts Act*, without any special order as to costs.

Re Can. Training & Dev. Group Inc. and Air Can. and Schweyer (May 19, 1983) (Ont. H.C.), Hughes J. — Application to transfer case to the Supreme Court of Ontario refused. *Livingston v. Ould*, 1976 CarswellOnt 321, 2 C.P.C. 41 (Ont. H.C.) distinguished: "I would be hesitant to reach similar conclusions about a project recently embarked upon for the improvement of the administration of justice, implying as they may that the judges of that court are in some way incompetent."

Agnew v. Sault Ste. Marie Bd. of Educ. (1976), 2 C.P.C. 273 (Ont. H.C.) — Combines claims by 365 separate individuals for individual salary arrears in respect of which each individual claim is within the monetary jurisdiction of the small claims court must be asserted in higher courts if cumulatively the claims exceed $800.

Hutley v. Great West Life Assur. Co. (1982), 40 O.R. (2d) 34 (Ont. H.C.) — In an action for breach of a contract of insurance, the defendant brought an application for an order transferring the small claims court action to the Supreme Court on the grounds that it was fit to be tried in the Supreme Court and that the claim, in effect, exceeded the monetary jurisdiction of the lower court by reason of a claim for a declaration of total disablement which would have an ongoing effect, entitling the plaintiff to payments in excess of $3000. The fact that an action is fit to be tried in the Supreme Court does not mean it ought to be tried there if it is also fit to be tried in the court where is was commenced. The claim did not exceed the monetary jurisdiction of the court as the declaration would not have an ongoing effect since the plaintiff alleged disablement at a given point in time and the declaration would be limited to that point in time and not have a prospective operation.

Merill & Hennessey Realty Ltd. v. Williams (1983), 57 N.S.R. (2d) 38 (N.S. S.C.) — Here there was concurrent jurisdiction in the amount of the claim of the respondent and the plaintiff in the small claims court action for the amount of $1000. If the respondent solicitor's position is acceded to there would, of necessity, be two trials. It is not in the interest of justice that there should be two proceedings. It is not in the interest of the parties that part of the claim should be litigated in one court and the remainder litigated in another court. Where there is concurrent jurisdiction respecting at least part of the matters in issue and the superior court decides to exercise its jurisdiction, certainly the inferior court must give way.

Qualico Developments Ltd. v. Doherty, 1985 CarswellAlta 256, 41 Alta. L.R. (2d) 380, 23 D.L.R. (4th) 605, 67 A.R. 334 (Alta. Q.B.) — In an action brought in the provincial court for an amount within that court's jurisdiction, the defendant counterclaimed for $25,000. The provincial court judge transferred both the claim and the counterclaim to the Court of Queen's Bench. Where the counterclaim raises an independent action, an order transferring the counterclaim but retaining jurisdiction over the claim itself is appropriate. Otherwise, a claimant would be denied the benefit of a swift and inexpensive trial in provincial court merely because a counterclaim had been brought. However, where the claim and counterclaim are closely related, both matters should be transferred to avoid trials on the same issue in two different courts.

Guillemette v. Dube (1974), 6 O.R. (2d) 663 (Ont. Div. Ct.) — Where, in a small claims court action for damages to a motor vehicle, no dispute as to the amount of damages is raised in the pleadings or at trial, the plaintiff may prove his damages by testifying to the amount paid for repairs and by filing another estimate as an exhibit. He need not incur the considerable expense of calling a mechanic to prove the account because the allowance for witness fees in small claims court is minimal while the hourly charges for a mechanic are substantial.

MacDonald v. Weather Products Corp. Ltd. (1982), 32 C.P.C. 58 (N.S. Co. Ct.) — The intent of the legislation is to provide an informal forum where disputes can be settled quickly and justly with a minimum of formality. Thus, an adjudicator should hear the parties and allow them to fully present their respective cases before ruling on a limitation period.

Thompson v. Butkus (1980), 28 O.R. (2d) 368 (Ont. Div. Ct.) — It is desirable for judges to give meaningful reasons, however short, in all cases where judgment is rendered following the hearing of *viva voce* evidence. However, where the sole issue is one of credibility between the plaintiff and the defendant, the appellate court may reasonably conclude in the absence of reasons that, in dismissing the action, the trial judge either disbelieved the plaintiff or concluded on the conflicting evidence that the plaintiff had not met the burden of proof, and a new trial need not be ordered.

Malamas v. Paraskevopoulos (1980), 23 C.P.C. 60 (Ont. Div. Ct.) — A person who does not file a dispute to a counterclaim has not lost the right to represent himself and cross-examine.

Travel Machine Ltd. v. Madore, 1983 CarswellOnt 901, 143 D.L.R. (3d) 94 (Ont. H.C.) — A trial judge cannot simply, on the basis of "equity and good conscience", ignore statutory law.

Smith v. Galin, [1956] O.W.N. 432 (Ont. C.A.) — The section does not entitle the judge to disregard general principles of law. The Court may have jurisdiction to disregard technical defects which would defeat the justice of the claim.

A.G. Can. v. Khimani (1985), 50 O.R. (2d) 476 (Ont. Div. Ct.) — The defendant gave a penal bond to secure performance of the conditions upon which a visitor was admitted to Canada. The conditions were not fulfilled and the Attorney-General brought an action in the small claims court to enforce the bond. The action was dismissed on the basis of "equity and good conscience." By s. 57 of the *Small Claims Court Act*, R.S.O. 1980, c. 476, the judge may make such an order or judgment as appears "just and agreeable to equity and good conscience".

On appeal to the Divisional Court, allowing the appeal, it was held that the bond was valid and enforceable. The sum, though called penal, was liquidated damages, and the agreement was not unreasonable or extravagant. Section 57 did not give judges equitable jurisdiction to make a decision contrary to law and legal principles.

Valley Credits Ltd. v. Key, [1977] 2 W.W.R. 422 (B.C. Prov. Ct.) — A collection agency that makes assignments of claims and brings actions on them in return for a fee based on a percentage of the amount recovered is engaging in the practice of law. Actions brought by a collection agency in such circumstances are contemptuous and the court has power to prevent abuse of its process by dismissing them.

A.G.B.C. v. Varcoe (1979), 10 B.C.L.R. 13 (B.C. S.C.) — Upon the return day of a judgment summons issued to collect a fine imposed in criminal proceedings, an employee of the Department of the Attorney General of British Columbia, who was the court administrator and also a justice of the peace, appeared for the Crown. A provincial court judge, sitting in small claims court, has a discretion to decide what persons could appear before the court as agents, and such discretion was rightfully exercised against permitting a person to appear as agent who was also a judicial officer of the same court.

B.C. Telephone Co. v. Rueben, [1982] 5 W.W.R. 428 (B.C. S.C.) — There is a discretionary power to grant a privilege of audience to persons other than lawyers, but that discretion should be exercised rarely and with caution. While a corporation may be represented by an officer, a paralegal employed by the corporation has no right of audience to represent the corporation before a small claims court, and a judge does not err in refusing to exercise his discretion in favour of allowing the employee to so appear.

Nissan Auto Co. v. Pelletier, [1981] 1 S.C.R. 67 (S.C.C.); affirming (1978), 97 D.L.R. (3d) 277 (Que. C.A.) — Articles 966, 956 and 985 of the Quebec Code of Civil Procedure, S.Q. 1965, c. 80 [en. 1971, c. 86, s. 1], which prohibit representation of a party by counsel before the Provincial Court, Small Claims Division, are *intra vires* the Quebec Legislature, at least to the extent that the substance of the problem dealt with in a particular case is within provincial competence. There is no Canadian constitutional statute that clearly sanctions the right to representation by counsel before the courts. Subsection 5(3) of the Canadian Bill of Rights extends only to "matters coming within the legislative authority of the Parliament of Canada." Provincial legislatures can legislate with respect to the right to representation by counsel before civil courts where the substance of the problem falls within its constitutional competence.

Stapelton v. Sears Ltd. (1982), 141 D.L.R. (3d) 130 (Ont. H.C.) — Although s. 57 of the *Judicature Act*, R.S.O. 1980, c. 223, provides that an action for false arrest and false imprisonment shall be tried by a jury unless waived, where the amount claimed is within the jurisdiction of the small claims court, that court has jurisdiction without consent of the parties. The action is not expressly excluded from the court's jurisdiction by the *Small Claims Courts Act*, R.S.O. 1980, c. 476, and the general provisions of the *Judicature Act* must yield to the provisions of the special Act. Where the claim is within the monetary limit of the *Small Claims Court Act*, a summary determination of the issue is most appropriate. Where allegations of serious infringement of rights are involved, there is a mechanism in the *Small Claims Courts Act* to permit removal of the action to the Supreme Court.

Teitel v. Theriault, 1983 CarswellOnt 866, 44 O.R. (2d) 127 (Ont. Div. Ct.) — There is no exclusion of false arrest and false imprisonment from the jurisdiction of this court.

The two most important Rules may well be Rules 1.02 and 2. Rule 1.02 articulates the overriding purpose of all the Rules and really the Court itself, *i.e.*, the securing of "the just, most expeditious and least expensive determination" of the proceeding on its merits.

Rule 2.01 provides that non-compliance with the Rules constitutes an irregularity, not a nullity, and empowers the court to grant amendments, on terms, to correct all non-compliance problems. Rule 2.02 goes further and allows the court to dispense with rule compliance at any time in the interests of justice. These Rules maybe a salvation for those who, at trial, or at an earlier stage of the action, run into difficulties with problems in their pleadings or who have failed to comply with various notice requirements.

If the rules are silent, the practice shall be determined by analogy to the rules and the court may make any appropriate and "just" order at any stage: Rule 1.02(2).

The court may lengthen or shorten any prescribed times, at any time,or it may be done on the consent of the parties: Rule 3.02(1). If the period of time is prescribed, the first day is excluded and the last day is included, but if the last day is on a holiday or Saturday, you would move forward to the next day.

National Bank of Greece (Canada) v. Kremidas (November 12, 2002), Doc. C.S. Montréal 500-05-068044-013, 500-05-068045-010 (Que. S.C.) — Motion on November 7, 2002 to reopen hearing. File active since October 2001. Procedure established in Small Claims Court is derogation from the non-inquisitorial role of the courts. Assistance may be given to an unrepresented party with the greatest caution in order not to appear to favour that party as opposed to the one who has benefit of legal representation. Improper to proceed by motion to re-open hearing rather than wait for judgment on merits and decide then on the opportunity of filing an appeal. The necessary criteria for the re-opening of a hearing not met.

Rule 4 — Parties Under Disability

4.01 (1) Plaintiff's Litigation Guardian — An action by a person under disability shall be commenced or continued by a litigation guardian, subject to subrule (2).

(2) Exception — A minor may sue for any sum not exceeding $500 as if he or she were of full age.

(3) Consent — A plaintiff's litigation guardian shall, at the time of filing a claim or as soon as possible afterwards, file with the clerk a consent (Form 4A) in which the litigation guardian,

(a) states the nature of the disability;

(b) in the case of a minor, states the minor's birth date;

History [R. 4.01(3)(b)]: New.

(c) sets out his or her relationship, if any, to the person under disability;

History [R. 4.01(3)(c)]: Formerly 4.01(3)(b).

(d) states that he or she has no interest in the proceeding contrary to that of the person under disability;

History [R. 4.01(3)(d)]: Formerly 4.01(3)(c).

(e) acknowledges that he or she is aware of his or her liability to pay personally any costs awarded against him or her or against the person under disability; and

History [R. 4.01(3)(e)]: Formerly 4.01(3)(d).

(f) states whether he or she is represented by a representative and, if so, gives that person's name and confirms that the person has written authority to act in the proceeding.

History [R. 4.01(3)(f)]: New.

O. Reg. 230/13, s. 3

Commentary: An action by a person under disability shall be commenced or continued by a litigation guardian [r. 4.01(1)], but a minor (a person under the age of 18) may sue for any sum up to $500 as if he or she were of full age [r. 4.01(2)].

If a litigation guardian is required, the general heading should be set out as follows:

> (Name of person under disability), a person under disability (or a minor) by his/her litigation guardian (name of litigation guardian).

Where the Children's Lawyer or Public Guardian and Trustee acts as litigation guardian, a consent is not required [r. 4.04(2)].

A request to remove or replace the plaintiff's litigation guardian may be commenced by notice of motion, or a judge may make such an order without notice.

A party may attend the court office and/or make a written inquiry (without any completed forms) to have a consent to act as plaintiff's litigation guardian filed.

Once a party attends the court office with completed forms, whereby a person under disability commences an action, at the time of issuing the plaintiff's claim or after issuing the claim, a party may file a completed consent to act as plaintiff's litigation guardian (Form 4A).

An action against a person under disability must be defended by a litigation guardian [r. 4.02(1)]. A defendant's litigation guardian shall file, with the Defence (Form 9A), a Consent to Act as Defendant's Litigation Guardian (Form 4B) [r. 4.02(2)].

The Rules set out who may be a litigation guardian [r. 4.03] and the duties of the litigation guardian [r. 4.04]. The Rules provide for the court's appointment of a litigation guardian where a defendant under disability does not have one [r. 4.02(3)].

A request to remove or replace the defendant's litigation guardian may be commenced by notice of motion, or a judge may make such an order without notice.

A party may attend the court office and/or make a written inquiry (without any completed forms) to have a consent to act as defendant's litigation guardian filed.

Where a claim is commenced by a person under disability, default should be noted against any defendant, who has failed to file a defence within the required time and, who is not a person under disability. Monies payable to a person under disability pursuant to an order or settlement shall be paid into court unless otherwise ordered by a judge. Where monies are paid into court and no order for disposition has been given, the matter will be listed for hearing before a judge. The monies will not be paid out without a judge's order. No settlement of a claim made by a person under disability is binding on the person without the approval of the court.

Failure to appoint a litigation guardian is an irregularity that may be cured by the appointment of a litigation guardian even after a limitation period has expired (see *Crossett v. Labraceur*, [1958] O.W.N. 29 (Ont. H.C.) and *Doyle v. Garden of the Gulf Security & Investigation Inc.* (1979), 24 Nfld. & P.E.I.R. 123, 65 A.P.R. 123, 12 C.P.C. 127 (P.E.I. S.C.)). If an action is commenced without a litigation guardian, the solicitor commencing the action may be liable to the defendant for his or her costs even if the solicitor was unaware of the legal disability of the plaintiff. (See *Geilinger v. Gibbs*, [1897] 1 Ch. 479 (Eng. Ch. Div.); but see *Marley-King Line Construction Ltd. v. Marley*, [1962] O.W.N. 253 (Ont.

Master).) If an action on behalf of a partnership is brought in the firm name, the minor partners need not be represented by litigation guardian, if the partnership is duly registered (see *British Products Unlimited v. Tenenbaum*, [1949] O.W.N. 240 (Ont. Master)).

Unless there is some other person willing to act as litigation guardian, the court shall appoint the Children's Lawyer where the person under disability is a minor. Likewise, the court will appoint the Public Guardian and Trustee where the person is mentally incapable within the meaning of the *Substitute Decisions Act* in respect of an issue in the proceeding and there is no guardian or attorney under a power of attorney with authority to act as litigation guardian. Where a person is both a minor and mentally incapable, the court may appoint either the Children's Lawyer or the Public Guardian and Trustee: see *Cameron v. Louden* (1998), 24 C.P.C. (4th) 50 (Ont. Master).

A litigation guardian is an officer of the court, is not a party to the action, is not *dominus litis* (master of the suit), and represents the party under disability only in a limited sense (see *B. (L.) v. Manitoba Public Insurance Corp.*, [1983] 4 W.W.R. 749 (Man. C.A.): *Poulin v. Nadon*, [1950] O.R. 219, [1950] O.W.N. 163, [1950] 2 D.L.R. 303 (Ont. C.A.)).

If you are not in a financial position to retain the services of a lawyer, you may wish to contact the Legal Aid Ontario office closest to you to see if you qualify for legal aid. For more information you may visit Legal Aid Ontario's website at www.legalaid.on.ca.

Parties under a disability and parties acting in a representative capacity must be represented by a lawyer. A party under a disability is defined in the *Rules of Civil Procedures* as a minor, or a person who is mentally incapable within the meaning of the *Substitute Decisions Act, 1992*, whether he or she has a guardian or not, or an absentee within the meaning of the *Absentee Act*.

Case Law: *Cameron v. Louden* (1998), 24 C.P.C. (4th) 50 (Ont. Master) — Motion by defendants for order appointing a litigation guardian for plaintiff on basis plaintiff is a party under disability. In the alternative, the defendants seek an order for a medical examination of the plaintiff pursuant to s. 105 of the *Courts of Justice Act* to determine if she is a party under disability. *Bilek v. Constitution Insurance* (1990), 49 C.P.C. (2d) 304 (Ont. Dist. Ct.) and *Kirby v. Leather*, [1965] 2 All E.R. 441 (Eng. C.A.) referred to. Evidence satisfied definition of "disability" as is found in Rule 1.03 of the *Rules of Civil Procedure* of a party under disability and the incorporated references to ss. 6 and 45 of the *Substitute Decisions Act, 1992*, S.O. 1992, c. 30. Order to issue appointing a litigation guardian for plaintiff.

Limbani (Litigation Guardian of) v. Limbani (1999), 29 C.P.C. (4th) 33 (Ont. Gen. Div.) — The plaintiff mother did not speak English. The sons brought an application to have the litigation guardian removed pursuant to Rule 7.01(1) of the *Rules of Civil Procedure*. The application was granted. The mother was not disabled under s. 6 or s. 45 of the *Substitute Decisions Act, 1992* or under Rule 1.03, as required for the appointment of a litigation guardian.

Bisoukis v. Brampton (City) (1999), 180 D.L.R. (4th) 577, 127 O.A.C. 107, 46 O.R. (3d) 417, 7 M.P.L.R. (3d) 1, 41 C.P.C. (4th) 33, 1 M.V.R. (4th) 42, 1999 CarswellOnt 3949 (Ont. C.A.); leave to appeal refused (2000), 261 N.R. 200 (note), 2000 CarswellOnt 3008, 2000 CarswellOnt 3009 (S.C.C.) — Three-month limitation period set out in s. 284(2) of *Municipal Act*, R.S.O. 1990, c. M.45 did not commence to run against an adult plaintiff who was found to be of unsound mind. Person of unsound mind for the purposes of the *Limitations Act* is incapable of managing his/her affairs in relation to an accident as would a reasonable person.

Musgrove v. Nielsen, 20 C.P.C. (5th) 94, 2000 CarswellAlta 1660, 2000 ABPC 12, (sub nom. *Musgrove v. J.J.N.)* 316 A.R. 155 (Alta. Prov. Ct.) — At trial, liability and quantum determined. Defendants' status as infants was not disclosed to Court until conclusion of trial, at which time Court questioned whether each defendant should have had guardian *ad litem* for services and to defend action. Parties made submissions as to whether lack of service upon litigation guardian rendered proceedings nullity. Non-compliance with Rules constituted irregularity. Defendants were represented by solicitors, who did not disclose their status in pleadings, nor orally at pre-trial conference or at commencement of trial. Such conduct amounted to waiver by defendants. Plaintiff's conduct was not so devoid of fairness and did not bring administration of justice into disrepute.

Morgan v. Toronto (Municipality) Police Services Board, 2003 CarswellOnt 1105, 169 O.A.C. 390, 34 C.P.C. (5th) 46 (Ont. C.A.) — Appeal allowed from order dismissing motion to set aside default judgment. Focus on Rule 7.07(1), *Rules of Civil Procedure*, relating to a party under disability (Rule 1.03(b)). *Karas v. Gegios* (2001), [2001] O.J. 732, 2001 CarswellOnt 577 (Ont. S.C.J.) referred to. Motion judge should have exercised his discretion under Rule 19.08(2).

Bannon v. Thunder Bay (City) (2002), 156 O.A.C. 307, 2002 CarswellOnt 549, 2002 CarswellOnt 550, [2002] S.C.J. No. 18, 2002 SCC 20, 27 M.P.L.R. (3d) 31, 210 D.L.R. (4th) 62, 284 N.R. 190, [2002] 1 S.C.R. 716 (S.C.C.) — The Ontario Court (General Division), in a decision reported at (1998), 73 O.T.C. 210, 1998 CarswellOnt 3460, 47 M.P.L.R. (2d) 170 (Ont. Gen. Div.), held that the plaintiff's action was not statute barred because she was physically and mentally incapable of complying with the section 284(5), notice requirements during the first seven days after the accident. The Court held that failing to respond to the request to admit should not be taken as a deemed admission of the facts contained in the request. The Supreme Court of Canada allowed the appeal and restored the trial judge's decision. The Ontario Court of Appeal had overturned the appeal, holding that the plaintiff failed to discharge her onus of demonstrating she was incapable on account of her mental condition, of giving the requisite notice (*Limitation Act*, s. 47). The Supreme Court of Canada restored the trial judge's decision, holding that the Court of Appeal wrongly interfered with his findings of fact respecting the plaintiff's incapacity.

Weidenfeld, Re (November 15, 2007)(2007), 2007 CarswellOnt 7457, 53 C.P.C. (6th) 97, 162 C.R.R. (2d) 359 (Ont. S.C.J.); leave to appeal refused (2008), 2008 CarswellOnt 3367 (Ont. Div. Ct.); leave to appeal refused (2008), 2008 CarswellOnt 5373, 60 C.P.C. (6th) 324 (Ont. Div. Ct.); affirmed (2008), 2008 CarswellOnt 6534 (Ont. C.A.); leave to appeal refused (2009), 2009 CarswellOnt 4364, 2009 CarswellOnt 4365 (S.C.C.).

Robert Weidenfeld, in his personal capacity, and Joel Weidenfeld, a minor, by his litigation guardian Robert Weidenfeld (herein collectively the "Plaintiffs") commenced action.

Mr. Weidenfeld entitled to represent himself in action, but in his capacity as the litigation guardian he must be represented by a solicitor, as required by Rule 7.05(3). A litigation guardian is liable to pay costs and must look after the minor's interest (*Poulin v. Nadon*, [1950] O.R. 219, [1950] O.W.N. 163, [1950] 2 D.L.R. 303 (Ont. C.A.); *Salamon v. Alberta (Minister of Education)*, 1991 CarswellAlta 199, [1991] A.J. No. 922, 1 C.P.C. (3d) 193, 120 A.R. 298, 8 W.A.C. 298, 83 Alta. L.R. (2d) 275 (Alta. C.A.) at p. 2).

Rule 7.05(3) protects persons under a disability from unscrupulous representatives, as well as from friends and family members who mistakenly believe they are acting in the best interests of a minor. The Supreme Court of Canada in *Fortin c. Chretien* recognized that permitting non-lawyers to act for litigants may be adverse to the litigant's own interests. In addition to their lack of training and experience, non-lawyers do not have a code of ethics or carry liability insurance for negligence (*Fortin c. Chrétien*, 2001 CarswellQue 1395, 2001 CarswellQue 1396, REJB 2001-25001, (sub nom. *Fortin v. Chrétien*) 201 D.L.R. (4th) 223, (sub nom. *Fortin v. Barreau du Québec*) 272 N.R. 359, 2001 SCC 45, [2001] 2 S.C.R. 500 (S.C.C.), at paras. 48-49). As well, there is no solicitor-client privilege protecting confidential communications (*Stone v. Stone*, [2000] O.J. No. 570, 2000 CarswellOnt 486, [2000] O.T.C. 87, 5 R.F.L. (5th) 151 (Ont. S.C.J.), at para. 4).

Plaintiffs failed to satisfy court that Rule 7.05(3) violated their human dignity or freedom by reason of one of the characteristics named in s. 15 or any analogous characteristic.

Philion (Litigation Guardian of) v. Lemieux Estate, 2007 CarswellOnt 2185, [2007] O.J. No. 1405, 2007 ONCA 281, 46 C.P.C. (6th) 203, (sub nom. *Philion (Litigation Guardian of) v. Lemieux (Estate of))* 85 O.R. (3d) 1, (sub nom. *Philion v. Lemieux Estate)* 223 O.A.C. 267 (Ont. C.A.).

Minor's claim arose before s. 9 of the 2002 *Limitations Act* came into force on January 1, 2004. Section 9 entitled a potential defendant to have a litigation guardian appointed for a potential minor plaintiff, which could cause the limitation period to commence running immediately. If s. 9 was not available to a claim arising before January 1, 2004, then s. 47 of the 1990 *Limitations Act* applied and the limitation period would not commence running until the minor reached the age of majority and would permit the minor two years to commence an action. The Court of Appeal allowed the appeal and set aside the appointment of the litigation guardian. Pursuant to s. 24(5) of the 2002 *Limitations Act*, the 1990 *Limitations Act* continued to govern.

British Columbia (Public Guardian & Trustee) v. Ralston (Guardian ad litem of), 2007 CarswellBC 1158, 241 B.C.A.C. 224, 399 W.A.C. 224, 2007 BCCA 282 (B.C. C.A. [In Chambers]).

The Public Guardian and Trustee of British Columbia (the Public Guardian) applied to be named appellant in their proposed appeal against a chambers judge's order that approved a contingency fee agreement based legal fee payable to the minor plaintiff's lawyer. The British Columbia Court of Appeal allowed the application. A litigation guardian for a minor plaintiff had a contingency fee agreement with the plaintiff's lawyer. The plaintiff's claim was settled and the lawyer's fees had to be judicially approved.

Weidenfeld, Re (2007), 2007 CarswellOnt 7457, 53 C.P.C. (6th) 97, 162 C.R.R. (2d) 359 (Ont. S.C.J.); leave to appeal refused (2008), 2008 CarswellOnt 3367 (Ont. Div. Ct.); leave to appeal refused (2008), 2008 CarswellOnt 5373, 60 C.P.C. (6th) 324 (Ont. Div. Ct.); affirmed (2008), 2008 CarswellOnt 6534 (Ont. C.A.); leave to appeal refused (2009), 2009 CarswellOnt 4364, 2009 CarswellOnt 4365 (S.C.C.)

The plaintiffs, a minor's father who wished to represent the son, sought a declaration that Rule 7.05(3) which requires minor plaintiff's litigation guardian be represented by a solicitor was of no force or effect. The motion dismissed as the court found that the subject litigation was complex and difficult, and the father lacked the necessary experience and legal training to litigate this case on behalf of his son. These vulnerable persons were in need of protection and the rule was in furtherance of the government's *parens patriae* jurisdiction.

Speerin v. North Bay (City) (1991), 1991 CarswellOnt 454, 5 O.R. (3d) 492, 85 D.L.R. (4th) 365, 5 C.P.C. (3d) 6, 8 C.R.R. (2d) 335, 7 M.P.L.R. (2d) 308 (Ont. Gen. Div.)

Any limitation period to a right of action which fails to provide consideration for those people unable to comply with its terms because of physical disability offends s. 15(1) and is not sustainable under s. 1 of the *Charter*. Real prejudice could result to the defendant if early notification not given. However, when compared with prejudice faced by physically disabled claimant who cannot comply with the notice requirement, proportionality dictates, as a minimum, that municipality obligated to demonstrate actual prejudice, which it has not done.

Wilmot v. Benton, 2010 ONSC 5610, 2010 CarswellOnt 10721 (Ont. S.C.J.), Ray J.; leave to appeal refused 2011 ONSC 2531, 2011 CarswellOnt 2646 (Ont. S.C.J.)

The plaintiff represented herself in the unusual position of having put forward her disability in very strong terms, and then attempting to discount it. She failed to understand and appreciate the risks and consequences of litigation. She was ordered to appoint a litigation guardian, failing which the defendant could move to strike out the plaintiff's pleadings.

4.02 (1) Defendant's Litigation Guardian — An action against a person under disability shall be defended by a litigation guardian.

(2) A defendant's litigation guardian shall file with the defence a consent (Form 4A) in which the litigation guardian,

    (a) states the nature of the disability;

    (b) in the case of a minor, states the minor's birth date;

    (c) sets out his or her relationship, if any, to the person under disability;

    (d) states that he or she has no interest in the proceeding contrary to that of the person under disability; and

History [R. 4.02(2)(d)]: Formerly 4.02(2)(c).

    (e) states whether he or she is represented by a representative and, if so, gives that person's name and confirms that the person has written authority to act in the proceeding.

History [R. 4.02(2)]: Plain language changes.

(3) If it appears to the court that a defendant is a person under disability and the defendant does not have a litigation guardian the court may, after notice to the proposed litigation guardian, appoint as litigation guardian for the defendant any person who has no interest in the action contrary to that of the defendant.

O. Reg. 78/06, s. 5; 230/13, s. 4

History [R. 4.02(3)]: Plain language changes.

Commentary: NOTE: A claim against a person under disability shall be defended by a litigation guardian (formerly guardian ad litem).

The defendant in the claim should be described as follows:

    A.B. — A person under disability.

    A copy of the claim should be served:

        (a) On a minor, by leaving a copy of claim with the minor and where the minor resides with a parent or other person having the care or lawful custody of the minor, by leaving another copy of the document with the parent or other person.

        (b) On all other persons under disability, as set out in subrules 8.03(h) and 8.03(j).

The plaintiff should also serve the parent or any other person having the care or lawful custody of the person under disability if the party is a minor. The demand may be served with the claim or at a later date. It is the responsibility of the plaintiff to serve the demand if it is served other than with the claim. If the demand is not served with the claim, service may be made by mail.

A person may act as litigation guardian by filing a consent with the defence.

Where the defendant fails to have a litigation guardian appointed, the plaintiff should proceed by notice of motion to have the Official Guardian or Public Trustee appointed. The Official Guardian or Public Trustee should be served with a copy of the notice of motion as well as the person under disability.

4.03 (1) Who May Be Litigation Guardian — Any person who is not under disability may be a plaintiff's or defendant's litigation guardian, subject to subrule (2).

(2) If the plaintiff or defendant,

    (a) is a minor, in a proceeding to which subrule 4.01(2) does not apply,

        (i) the parent or person with lawful custody or another suitable person shall be the litigation guardian, or

        (ii) if no such person is available and able to act, the Children's Lawyer shall be the litigation guardian;

    (b) is mentally incapable and has a guardian with authority to act as litigation guardian in the proceeding, the guardian shall be the litigation guardian;

    (c) is mentally incapable and does not have a guardian with authority to act as litigation guardian in the proceeding, but has an attorney under a power of attorney with that authority, the attorney shall be the litigation guardian;

    (d) is mentally incapable and has neither a guardian with authority to act as litigation guardian in the proceeding nor an attorney under a power of attorney with that power,

        (i) a suitable person who has no interest contrary to that of the incapable person may be the litigation guardian, or

        (ii) if no such person is available and able to act, the Public Guardian and Trustee shall be the litigation guardian;

    (e) is an absentee,

        (i) the committee of his or her estate appointed under the *Absentees Act* shall be the litigation guardian,

        (ii) if there is no such committee, a suitable person who has no interest contrary to that of the absentee may be the litigation guardian, or

        (iii) if no such person is available and able to act, the Public Guardian and Trustee shall be the litigation guardian;

    (f) is a person in respect of whom an order was made under subsection 72(1) or (2) of the *Mental Health Act* as it read before April 3, 1995, the Public Guardian and Trustee shall be the litigation guardian.

History [R. 4.03]: New provision, explaining who may be a litigation guardian. This rule is an abbreviated version of *Rules of Civil Procedure* Rules 7.02(1) and (1.1) and 7.03(2.1).

4.04 (1) Duties of Litigation Guardian — A litigation guardian shall diligently attend to the interests of the person under disability and take all steps reasonably necessary for the protection of those interests, including the commencement and conduct of a defendant's claim.

History [R. 4.04(1)]: Formerly 4.03(1); references to counterclaim and third party claim changed to "defendant's claim."

(2) Public Guardian and Trustee, Children's Lawyer — The Public Guardian and Trustee or the Children's Lawyer may act as litigation guardian without filing the consent required by subrule 4.01(3) or 4.02(2).

History [R. 4.04(2)]: Formerly 4.03(2); terminology changes to correspond with the *Substitute Decisions Act.*

4.05 Power of Court — The court may remove or replace a litigation guardian at any time.

History [R. 4.05]: Formerly 4.04.

4.06 Setting Aside Judgment, etc. — **If an action has been brought against a person under disability and the action has not been defended by a litigation guardian, the court may set aside the noting of default or any judgment against the person under disability on such terms as are just, and may set aside any step that has been taken to enforce the judgment.**

History [R. 4.06]: Formerly 4.05; plain language changes.

4.07 Settlement Requires Court's Approval — **No settlement of a claim made by or against a person under disability is binding on the person without the approval of the court.**

History [R. 4.07]: Formerly 4.06.

Commentary: Without the approval of a judge, a settlement of a claim by or against a minor is not binding and may not prevent further litigation of the same dispute. There is the misapprehension that without a commenced proceeding no court approval is required for a settlement, which is obviously erroneous. Similarly, any money payable to a child must be paid into court unless a judge orders otherwise.

A motion or application to a judge for settlement of a minor's claim does not have to be served on the Children's Lawyer. A motion or application is needed only where a judge directs that the materials be referred to the Children's Lawyer and shall be forwarded to the Children's Lawyer. Within two weeks of receipt of the materials, which should not provide for a return date, the Children's Lawyer shall contact the child's representative to advise whether the Children's Lawyer has objection to the proposed settlement and give a time frame for the Children's Lawyer's oral or written report to the court.

In practice the procedure for obtaining judicial approval of an infant settlement and the materials required in support of such a request are essentially the same as under rule 7.08 of the *Rules of Civil Procedure*.

Case Law: *Woolner v. D'Abreau* (2009), 2009 CarswellOnt 664, 70 C.P.C. (6th) 290, 50 E.T.R. (3d) 59, [2009] O.J. No. 1746 (Ont. S.C.J.), Brown J.; reversed (2009), 2009 CarswellOnt 6479, 53 E.T.R. (3d) 18 (Ont. Div. Ct.).

This case involves consideration of jurisdiction of court to direct independent representation of a person whose capacity was in issue. The *parens patriae* jurisdiction of the court well-established, based on court's power to protect the vulnerable. Section 3(1) of the *Substitute Decisions Act*, 1992 authorizes the court to direct the Public Guardian and Trustee to arrange for independent representation of a person whose capacity is in issue in a proceeding. While not applicable to a Rule 57.07 hearing, that section provides an appropriate analogy upon which this court can draw in deciding to direct the appointment of independent counsel, through the Public Guardian and Trustee.

4.08 (1) Money to be Paid into Court — **Any money payable to a person under disability under an order or a settlement shall be paid into court, unless the court orders otherwise, and shall afterwards be paid out or otherwise disposed of as ordered by the court.**

(2) If money is payable to a person under disability under an order or settlement, the court may order that the money shall be paid directly to the person, and payment made under the order discharges the obligation to the extent of the amount paid.

History [R. 4.08]: Formerly 4.07; plain language changes.

Commentary: Forms associated with Rule 4 are drafted in the simplest way possible. Form 4A is used for a litigation guardian for a plaintiff and Form 4B is used for a litigation guardian for a defendant.

A person under disability may sue for any amount not exceeding $500 as if he were of full age. For any other claim, the action shall be commenced by a litigation guardian (formerly next friend). Rule 4 provides that a person under a disability shall commence the action or continue the action with a litigation guardian. The exception to this rule is an action to proceed without a litigation guardian if the sum sought does not exceed $500. This monetary sum is the same as the provision as to appeals. There can be no appeal from a decision of the Small Claims Court if the amount claimed does *not* exceed $2,500, exclusive of costs. This does not preclude applying for a new trial if warranted.

Rule 4.01(3) indicates in clear language the steps that need to be taken in connection with the Form 4A.

The same principle applies to Form 4B and the defendant's litigation guardian with the exception that the defendant's litigation guardian is not required to acknowledge liability for costs. If it is found that a defendant does not have a litigation guardian, Rule 4.02(3) gives the court the power to appoint a person to be a litigation guardian. The duties as set forth are the same as those found in the *Rules of Civil Procedure*, Rule 7.05(2).

The litigation guardian shall file with the court a "consent" at the time the claim is filed or as soon thereafter as possible. There the Children's Lawyer or Public Trustee acts as litigation guardian, a consent is not required

If the litigation guardian has incurred out of pocket expenses on behalf of the person under disability, and wishes to recover same, the style of cause should be set out naming the person under disability by his or her litigation guardian and the said litigation guardian personally. The rule further provides for the Children's Lawyer or the Public Trustee to act in the capacity of a litigation guardian without the consent as contemplated by Rules 4.01(2) or 4.02(2).

The court on motion or otherwise may at any time remove or replace a litigation guardian.

Monies payable to a person under disability pursuant to an order or settlement shall be paid into court unless otherwise ordered by a judge. The monies will be distributed in accordance with the judge's order. Where monies are paid into court and no order for disposition has been given, the matter may be listed for hearing before a judge. The monies will not be paid out without a judges' order.

Rules 4.04 and 4.05 give the court power to remove or change a litigation guardian who may no longer be required or to give relief where the action has not been properly defended due to the absence of a litigation guardian.

No settlement of a claim made by a person under disability is binding on the person without the approval of the court.

A claim against a person under disability shall be defended by a litigation guardian (formerly guardian *ad litem*). A copy of the claim should be served on both the person under disability and the parent or person having care or custody of the person under disability. The plaintiff should also serve the person under disability and the parent or person having care or custody of the person under disability with a demand. The demand may be served with the claim or at a later date. A person may act as litigation guardian by filing a consent with the defence.

Where the defendant fails to have a litigation guardian appointed, the plaintiff should file a notice of motion to have the Children's Lawyer or Public Trustee appointed and the Children's Lawyer or Public Trustee should be served with a copy of the notice of motion.

If monies are paid into court by someone under disability, same will not be released to the plaintiff without a judge's order. Also, of course, no settlement of a claim against a person under disability is binding without the approval of the court.

As previously stated, the approval of a settlement of any claim involving a person under disability must be made by the court itself. Rule 4.08 provides for both payment into and payment out of court. This rule allows the clerk to act pursuant to a court order. The rule provides for an order for direct payment to a person under a disability. If the payment is made pursuant to an order given in that regard, then there is no further liability on the person who has paid the amount provided for in the order.

RULE 4: PARTIES UNDER DISABILITY

DEMAND

ONTARIO COURT (SUPERIOR COURT OF JUSTICE)
_____SMALL CLAIMS COURT

BETWEEN:

BUD BLACK
and   Plaintiff

BILL BROWN, a party under disability
Defendant

DEMAND

TAKE NOTICE that as Arthur Black, the above-named defendant, is a party under disability (a minor under the age of eighteen years or as the case may be) he/she must defend this action by litigation guardian appointed for such purpose.

AND TAKE FURTHER NOTICE that unless within twenty (20) days from the receipt hereof action is taken to have the defendant's father, mother or other suitable adult appointed as litigation guardian for the defendant an application will be made without further notification to you to have the Childrens' Lawyer (or Public Guardian and Trustee as the case may be) appointed litigation guardian for the purpose of this action.

DATED at   this day of   , A.D.20__.

_____
(name)

_____
(address)

_____
(plaintiff/solicitor/agent)

TO:
The above-named defendant
Bill Brown
Toronto, Ontario
AND TO:
Mr. Brown, Senior
(Father of Bill Brown)
Toronto, Ontario

(3) Supporting Affidavit — A motion for an order under this rule shall be supported by an affidavit in Form 4B rather than an affidavit in Form 15A.

(4) Costs — In making an order under this rule, the court may order that costs payable to the moving party be paid out of the money in court directly to the moving party's representative.

O. Reg. 400/12, s. 1; 230/13, s. 5

Rule 5 — Partnerships And Sole Proprietorships

5.01 Partnerships — **A proceeding by or against two or more persons as partners may be commenced using the firm name of the partnership.**

Commentary: A proceeding by or against two or more persons as partners may be commenced using the firm name of the partnership [r. 5.01]. The proper title in commencing an action against a partnership is either:

(a) A and B carrying on business (or cob/c.o.b.) as C; or

(b) C

In a proceeding against a partnership using the partnership's name, a plaintiff who seeks an order that would be enforceable personally against a person as a partner may also serve the person with the claim, together with a Notice to Alleged Partner (Form 5A) [r. 5.03(1)]. When proof of service of the claim is filed, the affidavit of service may indicate that the notice to alleged partner was served at the same time.

If a person carries on business in a business name other than his or her own name, a proceeding may be commenced by or against the person using the business name [r. 5.06(1)]. The proper title in commencing an action against a sole proprietorship is either:

(a) A carrying on business (or cob/c.o.b.) as B; or

(b) B

Rules 5.01 to 5.05 (partnerships) apply, with the necessary modifications, to a proceeding commenced by or against a sole proprietor using a business name, as though the sole proprietor were a partner and the business name were the firm name of a partnership [r. 5.06(2)].

Case Law: *Suzanne Street Properties Ltd. v. Manhold Development Corp.* (1998), *(*sub nom. *Street (Suzanne) Properties Ltd. v. Manhold Development Corp.)* 106 O.A.C. 311, 37 O.R. (3d) 797 (Ont. C.A.) — Plaintiff, general partner of limited partnership, found to have capacity to sue defendant. Defendant argued only limited partnership had capacity to sue. Evidence showed general partner was owner of property in question as well as contracting party to all relevant agreements in issue.

Kucor Construction & Developments & Associates v. Canada Life Assurance Co., 1998 CarswellOnt 4423, 41 O.R. (3d) 577, 43 B.L.R. (2d) 136, 167 D.L.R. (4th) 272, 21 R.P.R. (3d) 187, 114 O.A.C. 201, [1998] O.J. No. 4733 (Ont. C.A.)

The procedural option to sue using the partnership's name addresses the problems where there are a large number of partners. The alternative is to sue some or all of the individual partners. However it is improper to sue both the partnership and the individual partners.

Downtown Eatery (1993) Ltd. v. Ontario (2002), 2002 CarswellOnt 246, 2002 CarswellOnt 247, [2001] S.C.C.A. No. 397, 289 N.R. 195 (note), 163 O.A.C. 397 (note) (S.C.C.) — Plaintiff suing corporation that issued salary cheques for wrongful dismissal. Considering, but deciding not to sue principals. Not considering suing related corporations on basis of common employer doctrine. Estopped from suing principals. Not estopped from suing related corporations.

Domjan Investments Inc. v. D.J. Wagner Investments Inc., 2005 CarswellOnt 7750, 79 O.R. (3d) 150 (Ont. S.C.J.).

Partnership action and action for payment of personal loan ordered consolidated. Actions having question of fact or law in common. Relief claimed in both actions arising out of same transaction or occurrence.

Coulombe v. Sabatier, 2006 CarswellAlta 1108, 66 Alta. L.R. (4th) 17, 2006 ABQB 618, 24 B.L.R. (4th) 1 (Alta. Q.B.), at paras. 120 and 123, Watson J.

Even though participants at liberty to conduct independent business affairs either separately or jointly for unrelated purposes, the output of the use of the shared land and assets, together with the shared work connected with it, was understood to be partnership property. They created a sort of partnership of a flexible form.

Parties understood they were entering into something in the nature of a partnership with mutual rights and obligations in furtherance of a common business for a shared ability to profit by the business.

Point on the Bow Development Ltd. v. William Kelly & Sons Plumbing Contractors Ltd., 2007 CarswellAlta 809, 2007 ABCA 204, 78 Alta. L.R. (4th) 16, [2007] 11 W.W.R. 46, 410 W.A.C. 191, 417 A.R. 191, 45 C.P.C. (6th) 5 (Alta. C.A.)

Appeal by plaintiff from finding that it was in contempt of court and dismissed. Evidence demonstrated that plaintiff failed to comply with court orders requiring information to be provided by certain dates and that it failed to demonstrate any reasonable excuse for its non-compliance. Failure to act was intentional and not accidental and contempt must was proved beyond reasonable doubt. Sanctions not overly severe or disproportionate to the harm caused.

Cross-appeal brought by defendant from decision that partners and former partners of plaintiff were entitled to file their own statements of defence was also dismissed. The Court found that *Partnership Act* did not take away entitlement of partners and former partners to defend themselves separate and apart from whatever the managing partner might have done.

All Canadian Mechanical & Electrical Inc. v. Henderson, 2011 CarswellOnt 15950, [2011] O.J. No. 1456 (Ont. Sm. Cl. Ct.)

Instead of following the procedure set out in rule 5.01, the plaintiff named two partners as a single defendant carrying on business as the partnership name, then served only one of the two partners and sought to enforce the resulting default judgment against the other partner who had not been served. The court found the default judgment to have been irregularly-obtained and it was set aside.

5.02 If a proceeding is commenced against a partnership using the firm name, the partnership's defence shall be delivered in the firm name and no person who admits being a partner at any material time may defend the proceeding separately, except with leave of the court.

History [R. 5.02]: Plain language changes.

5.03 (1) Notice to Alleged Partner — **In a proceeding against a partnership using the firm name, a plaintiff who seeks an order that would be enforceable personally against a person as a partner may serve the person with the claim, together with a notice to alleged partner (Form 5A).**

(2) A person served as provided in subrule (1) is deemed to have been a partner at the material time, unless the person defends the proceeding separately denying having been a partner at the material time.

History [R. 5.03]: Plain language changes.

Commentary: Where, after an order has been made against a partnership using the firm name, the creditor claims to be entitled to enforce it against any person who has not been served with a notice as provided in Rule 5.03, the party must make a motion to the court for leave to do so. This also applies where a judgment has been obtained against a sole proprietorship in the business name.

Where a claim is commenced against a partnership using the firm name there is only one defendant. However, if the plaintiff wishes notices (Form 5A) served on alleged partners the plaintiff is required to file sufficient additional copies of the claim with the court. Two copies for each alleged partner if they are to be served at their residences or, one additional copy if they are to be served at the business address.

Where a claim has been issued against a partnership using the firm name and service is to be made on more than one person (i.e. alleged partners), the clerk is only entitled to charge the appropriate filing fee for a claim against one defendant.

Where a notice to alleged partner has been served by the plaintiff, the person served then has 20 days (25 days if service was made on an adult member of the same household where the person to be served resides, 40 days from the date the claim was mailed where service was made under subrule 8.03(7)) to enter a defence denying that he or she was a partner at the material time. The plaintiff should file an affidavit of service with the court. Where a partnership has been sued in the firm name and has been noted in default, default judgment should not be signed until all persons who have been served with a notice under Rule 5.03 have had an opportunity to file a defence.

Where a person has been served with a notice to alleged partner under Rule 5.03 and fails to defend the proceeding separately, denying that he or she was a partner at the material time, the clerk should when signing default judgment include in the order that it is enforceable against that alleged partner. If this is not done at the time of signing judgment, a party wishing to enforce the order against any person who was served with a notice as provided under Rule 5.03 must apply to a judge by way of a notice of motion for leave to do so.

The same rules (5.01 to 5.05) apply, with necessary modifications, to a sole proprietorship sued in the business name.

5.04 (1) Disclosure of Partners — If a proceeding is commenced by or against a partnership using the firm name, any other party may serve a notice requiring the partnership to disclose immediately in writing the names and addresses of all partners constituting the partnership at a time specified in the notice; if a partner's present address is unknown, the partnership shall disclose the last known address.

(1.1) [Repealed O. Reg. 78/06, s. 6.]

(1.1.1) [Repealed O. Reg. 78/06, s. 6.]

(2) If a partnership fails to comply with a notice under subrule (1), its claim may be dismissed or the proceeding stayed or its defence may be struck out.
O. Reg. 461/01, s. 4 [s. 4(2) revoked O. Reg. 330/02, s. 3(2).]; 330/02, s. 3(1); 440/03, s. 5, item 2; 78/06, s. 6

History [R. 5.04]: Plain language changes.

5.05 (1) Enforcement of Order — An order against a partnership using the firm name may be enforced against the partnership's property.

History [R. 5.05(1)]: Plain language changes.

Commentary: Where, after an order has been made against a partnership using the firm name, a creditor claims to be entitled to enforce it against any person who has not been served with a notice as provided in Rule 5.03, the party must bring a motion to the court for leave to do so. This also applies where a judgment has been obtained against a sole proprietorship in the business name.

Where a claim is commenced against a partnership using the firm name there is only one defendant. If the plaintiff wishes notices (Form 5A) served on alleged partners, the plaintiff is required to file sufficient additional copies of the claim with the court. Two copies for each alleged partner if they are to be served at their residences or, one additional copy if they are to be served at the business address.

Rule 5.03(1) allows a plaintiff to serve an alleged partner with a copy of the claim, together with a notice to the alleged partner.

(2) An order against a partnership using the firm name may also be enforced, if the order or a subsequent order so provides, against any person who was served as provided in rule 5.03 and who,

> **(a) under that rule, is deemed to have been a partner at the material time;**
>
> **(b) has admitted being a partner at that time; or**
>
> **(c) has been adjudged to have been a partner at that time.**

(3) Against Person not Served as Alleged Partner — If, **after an order has been made against a partnership using the firm name, the party obtaining it claims to be entitled to enforce it against any person alleged to be a partner other than a person who was served as provided in rule 5.03, the party may make a motion for leave to do so; the judge may grant leave if the person's liability as a partner is not disputed or, if disputed, after the liability has been determined in such manner as the judge directs.**

O. Reg. 78/06, s. 7

Commentary: The change to subrule (3) clarifies the right of a creditor who wishes to enforce an order against individual partners or a proprietor although the claim was issued against only the firm. Where a person has been served with a notice to an alleged partner along with the statement of claim and fails to file a defence denying that he or she was a partner or proprietor at the material time specified in the notice, the order may be enforced against both the individual and the firm. A judge's order is not required to permit enforcement against the individual. If no notice was served with the claim, the order is only enforceable against the firm. However, the creditor can proceed by way of a notice of motion to seek an order against the individual partner or proprietor.

5.06 (1) Sole Proprietorships — If **a person carries on business in a business name other than his or her own name, a proceeding may be commenced by or against the person using the business name.**

(2) Rules 5.01 to 5.05 apply, with necessary modifications, to a proceeding by or against a sole proprietor using a business name, as though the sole proprietor were a partner and the business name were the firm name of a partnership.

History [R. 5.06(2)]: Plain language changes.

Commentary: Normally an action is simply commenced by or against an individual or a corporation without regard or concern as to the status of the litigant.

It was deemed advisable that the disability issues and partnerships and sole proprietorships be the subject of specific rules.

Rule 5.01 makes it clear that the firm name of the partnership may be used where there is an action by or against two or more persons who are partners. Rule 5.02 requires the partnership, when it is a defendant, to deliver the defence in the firm name and prevents separate defences unless leave of the court is obtained.

In the event the plaintiff seeks to enforce a judgment against one person as a partner personally, the plaintiff must proceed with notice to the alleged partner utilizing Form 5A. Jf partner does not respond to the notice, Rule 5.03(2) provides that the partner shall be to have been a partner unless he or she defends the proceedings separately.

is required to file sufficient additional copies of the claim with the court. Two copies for each alleged partner if they are to be served at their residences or, one additional copy if they are to be served at the business address.

Rule 5.03(1) allows a plaintiff to serve an alleged partner with a copy of the claim, together with a notice to the alleged partner.

(2) An order against a partnership using the firm name may also be enforced, if the order or a subsequent order so provides, against any person who was served as provided in rule 5.03 and who,

    (a) under that rule, is deemed to have been a partner at the material time;

    (b) has admitted being a partner at that time; or

    (c) has been adjudged to have been a partner at that time.

(3) Against Person not Served as Alleged Partner — **If, after an order has been made against a partnership using the firm name, the party obtaining it claims to be entitled to enforce it against any person alleged to be a partner other than a person who was served as provided in rule 5.03, the party may make a motion for leave to do so; the judge may grant leave if the person's liability as a partner is not disputed or, if disputed, after the liability has been determined in such manner as the judge directs.**

O. Reg. 78/06, s. 7

Commentary: The change to subrule (3) clarifies the right of a creditor who wishes to enforce an order against individual partners or a proprietor although the claim was issued against only the firm. Where a person has been served with a notice to an alleged partner along with the statement of claim and fails to file a defence denying that he or she was a partner or proprietor at the material time specified in the notice, the order may be enforced against both the individual and the firm. A judge's order is not required to permit enforcement against the individual. If no notice was served with the claim, the order is only enforceable against the firm. However, the creditor can proceed by way of a notice of motion to seek an order against the individual partner or proprietor.

5.06 (1) Sole Proprietorships — If a person carries on business in a business name other than his or her own name, a proceeding may be commenced by or against the person using the business name.

(2) Rules 5.01 to 5.05 apply, with necessary modifications, to a proceeding by or against a sole proprietor using a business name, as though the sole proprietor were a partner and the business name were the firm name of a partnership.

History [R. 5.06(2)]: Plain language changes.

Commentary: Normally an action is simply commenced by or against an individual or a corporation without regard or concern as to the status of the litigant.

It was deemed advisable that the disability issues and partnerships and sole proprietorships be the subject of specific rules.

Rule 5.01 makes it clear that the firm name of the partnership may be used where there is an action by or against two or more persons who are partners. Rule 5.02 requires the partnership, when it is a defendant, to deliver the defence in the firm name and prevents separate defences unless leave of the court is obtained.

In the event the plaintiff seeks to enforce a judgment against one person as a partner personally, the plaintiff must proceed with notice to the alleged partner utilizing Form 5A. If that partner does not respond to the notice, Rule 5.03(2) provides that the partner shall be deemed to have been a partner unless he or she defends the proceedings separately.

The essential question of disclosure is dealt with in Rule 5.04(1). There is a sanction in Rule 5.04(2) which may cause the claim to be dismissed, the proceedings stayed or the defendant struck out if disclosure is not made.

Rule 5.05(1) and (2) provide enforcement or an order. Rule 5.05(3) gives assistance to a plaintiff for a subsequent order against an individual person as well as a partnership subject to adjudication in the manner described by the court.

Sole proprietorships are dealt with in a similar fashion as partnerships, pursuant to Rule 5.06. This rule allows a person who carries on business in a name other than his or her own name to commence proceedings in the business name. Rule 5.06(2) provides that the preceding Rules 5.01 to 5.05 inclusive apply with the necessary modifications to sole proprietorship situations.

Case Law: *Elliott v. Ritins International Inc.* (April 8, 2008), Doc. 316/06 (Ont. Div. Ct.) — Ritins should not have been held personally liable because he ceased to be a party to the action when his companies replaced him as parties to the action. Joint and several liability should not have been imposed on the two companies, as one ceased to exist when the other commenced operations. Judge erred in law in imposing liability on Andrejs Ritins personally in his Addendum to Judgment.

Rule 6 — Forum And Jurisdiction

6.01 Place of Commencement and Trial — **(1) An action shall be commenced,**

> **(a) in the territorial division,**

>> **(i) in which the cause of action arose, or**

>> **(ii) in which the defendant or, if there are several defendants, in which any one of them resides or carries on business; or**

> **(b) at the court's place of sitting that is nearest to the place where the defendant or, if there are several defendants, where any one of them resides or carries on business.**

(2) An action shall be tried in the place where it is commenced, but if the court is satisfied that the balance of convenience substantially favours holding the trial at another place than those described in subrule (1), the court may order that the action be tried at that other place.

Case Law: *Pizza Pizza Ltd. v. Boyack* (1995), 38 C.P.C. (3d) 306 (Ont. Gen. Div.) — Onus on moving party (Rule 46.03) (the defendant) that the balance of convenience for trial was Peterborough and not Toronto. Financial considerations not established. See also *Ridley v. Ridley* (1989), 37 C.P.C. (2d) 167 (Ont. H.C.).

Murray v. Stokes (1996), (sub nom. *Stokes v. Murray)* 157 N.S.R. (2d) 55, 462 A.P.R. 55 (N.S. S.C.) — Buyer of horse which was found to be diseased and had to be destroyed. Claim for damages. Action commenced in county in which animal died and not in county where sale was made. Adjudicator had jurisdiction to hear claim as cause of action arose in county in which death occurred. Jurisdiction not lost by delay by adjudicator in preparation of summary of decision for appeal.

Assie Industries Ltd. v. SMB Agri Service Ltd. (1995), [1996] 1 W.W.R. 219, 136 Sask. R. 215 (Q.B.) — The plaintiff sued the defendant corporation for goods it delivered to the defendant. The plaintiff's action omitted part of the defendant's name. The plaintiff brought the action at the judicial centre nearest to where the contract was made and where payment was to be made. The defendant was registered and carried on business in another judicial centre, and it proposed to call witnesses from that centre.

Seine River Resources Inc. v. PenSa Inc. (1998), 25 C.P.C. (4th) 360 (B.C. S.C.) — The plaintiff company incorporated in British Columbia and the defendant company was a Colorado corporation. The parties joined in an oil and gas development venture in Guatemala. The defendants argued that B.C. was not an appropriate jurisdiction. The parties knew the transaction was subject to regulatory approval in B.C. The parties contemplated that B.C. law would govern translation. Real and substantial connection existed between alleged tort and B.C. as jurisdiction *simpliciter*.

Backtrax Roadhouse Inc. v. Scott (1998), 233 A.R. 390 (Alta. Master) — Action ordered transferred from Edmonton to Calgary. The cause of action arose in Calgary and majority of witnesses was there. The action was commenced in Edmonton only because the president of company lived closer to Edmonton than to Calgary. The balance of convenience favoured Calgary.

3212041 Canada Inc. v. C.M. Hydraulique Inc. (17 septembre 1999), no C.A Montréal 500-09-007957-996 (Que. C.A.) — The plaintiff made offer for sale of its building in Montreal, and sent a signed contract to the defendant in the second judicial district. The defendant accepted the offer and returned acceptance to Montreal by telecopier. The plaintiff was entitled to bring the action in Montreal. The contract was formed where the acceptance was received. The appeal by the plaintiff from dismissal of action for lack of jurisdiction was allowed.

Lions Gate Films Corp. v. EAX Worldwide (September 2, 1999), Doc. Toronto CP- 1568299 (Ont. Sm. Cl. Ct.) — The plaintiff brought an Ontario action for non-delivery of equipment valued at $1,900. The shipping document provided that lawsuits had to be brought in California, where the defendant had its head office. The plaintiff did not have notice of clause relegating disputes to California. The business was conducted in Ontario. The defendant's motion to dismiss was dismissed.

Town Shoes Ltd. v. Panalpina Inc. (1999), 169 F.T.R. 267 (Fed. T.D.) — A contract specified that trials of disputes between parties were to be litigated in Germany. Canada was a more appropriate forum than Germany. Evidence was more readily available in Canada, and Canadian law governed key issues.

The defendant moved for a change of venue under Rule 6.01(2) as well as Rule 6.01(1)(a)(i). The plaintiff, in Toronto, communicated with the defendants with respect to leasing a cottage near Bracebridge. The defendants faxed a signed lease to the plaintiff, who then signed it and faxed it back to the defendant in Muskoka. *Eastern Power Ltd. v. Azienda Comunale Energia & Ambiente*, 1999 CarswellOnt 2807, [1999] O.J. No. 3275, 178 D.L.R. (4th) 409, (sub nom. *Eastern Power Ltd. v. Azienda Communale Energia & Ambiente*) 125 O.A.C. 54, 50 B.L.R. (2d) 33, 39 C.P.C. (4th) 160 (Ont. C.A.) makes it clear that normal rules of contact law apply. The contract is made in the location where offerors [defendants] receive notification of offeree's [plaintiff's] acceptance. Under Rule 6.01(2), the balance of convenience is dictated by which court is the most appropriate and has the closest connection, not only to the parties, but to the action. Considering issues, and probability that there are no non- party witnesses of the plaintiff, Bracebridge is the most appropriate forum for this matter to go ahead: see *Pizza Pizza Ltd. v. Boyack* (1995), 38 C.P.C. (3d) 306 (Ont. Gen. Div.). The case was transferred to Bracebridge Small Claims Court. *Livingstone v. Tomen* (2000), 2000 CarswellOnt 1436 (Ont. Sm. Cl. Ct.).

Abick v. Continental Insurance Co. of Canada (2000), 24 C.C.L.I. (3d) 281, [2001] I.L.R. I-3931, 2000 CarswellOnt 4963 (Ont. Master) — The defendants moved for and order changing place of trial to Toronto from Thunder Bay on grounds of balance of convenience. The plaintiff carried on a practice in Toronto. Proposed witnesses had closer connection to Thunder Bay than to Toronto. The action itself had substantial connection to Thunder Bay. The trial would be reached sooner if it were in Toronto. The motion was dismissed.

Braegen Group Inc. v. Fame Information Services Inc. (2000), 2000 CarswellOnt 4270 (Ont. Div. Ct.) — The existence of a more appropriate forum must be clearly established to displace forum selected by the plaintiff. See *Amchem Products Inc. v. British Columbia (Workers' Compensation Board)*, [1993] 1 S.C.R. 897, 1993 CarswellBC 47, 1993 CarswellBC 1257, [1993] 3 W.W.R. 441, 14 C.P.C. (3d) 1, 150 N.R. 321, 23 B.C.A.C. 1, 39 W.A.C. 1, 102 D.L.R. (4th) 96, 77 B.C.L.R. (2d) 62, [1993] I.L.Pr. 689 (S.C.C.) at 104 and 111 [D.L.R.]. The determination of the factors essentially a question of fact.

Oreck Corp. v. Bissell Ltd. (1998), 26 C.P.C. (4th) 212, 1998 CarswellOnt 3693 (Ont. Gen. Div.) — No evidence indicating the plaintiff owed a debt to the Canadian subsidiary. Laws of the United States had no application to replevin action instituted in Ontario for recovery of equipment situated in Ontario. Defendant ordered to return equipment to plaintiff.

Teskey v. Peraan (1999), 34 C.P.C. (4th) 333, 1999 CarswellOnt 1316 (Ont. Master) — Service of claim effected by mail under Rule 16.03(4) of Rules in 1992. Default judgment was obtained later that year. The plaintiff moved in 1998 to set aside judgment. The motion was granted. The service is only effective if acknowledgement of receipt card or post office receipt bearing signature purporting to be that of person served is returned. Signature on post office receipt was that of the defendant's common-law spouse and not that of the defendant.

VitaPharm Canada Ltd. v. F. Hoffman-LaRoche Ltd. (2000), 48 O.R. (3d) 21, 186 D.L.R. (4th) 549, 46 C.P.C. (4th) 156, 2000 CarswellOnt 1323 (Ont. S.C.J.) — An order with respect to venue of assigned case management judge superceded all prior orders with respect to venue. Overall balance of convenience, including subject matter location of parties, counsel and witnesses and issues of expedition favoured Toronto rather than Windsor.

Livingstone v. Tomen (2000), 2000 CarswellOnt 1436 (Ont. Small Cl. Ct.) — The plaintiff commenced an action in Toronto for damages for alleged infestation of cottage rented by him in Muskoka. The plaintiff was not likely to call non-party witnesses. The action should be transferred to Bracebridge as the judicial district for Muskoka.

Prebushewski v. Dodge City Auto (1984) Ltd. (1999), 187 Sask. R. 76, 1999 CarswellSask 772 (Sask. Q.B.) — A motion by the plaintiff was made to transfer action against the vendor of a motor vehicle located in Saskatoon to Yorkton where she resided. It was inappropriate to apply principles of cases of negligent manufacture of goods outside of the province.

Djukic v. Canada (Attorney General) (2000), 52 O.R. (3d) 348, 2000 CarswellOnt 4872, 4 C.P.C. (5th) 205 (Ont. C.A.) — Plaintiff brought action for damages for interference by Government of Canada with plaintiff's immigration consulting business in Vienna, Bonn, and Sarajevo. See s. 21(1) of *Crown Liability and Proceedings Act*, R.S.C. 1985, c. C-50. Appeal allowed. As claims advanced did not arise in Ontario, Superior Court of Ontario lacked jurisdiction to hear them.

Lemmex v. Bernard (2001), 55 O.R. (3d) 657, 2001 CarswellOnt 2925, [2001] O.J. No. 3023, 6 C.C.L.T. (3d) 286, 204 D.L.R. (4th) 192, 149 O.A.C. 343, 12 C.P.C. (5th) 169 (Ont. Div. Ct.); reversed 2002 CarswellOnt 1812, [2002] O.J. No. 2131, 213 D.L.R. (4th) 627, 160 O.A.C. 31, 60 O.R. (3d) 54, 13 C.C.L.T. (3d) 203, 26 C.P.C. (5th) 259 (Ont. C.A.); additional reasons at *Muscutt v. Courcelles* (2002), 2002 CarswellOnt 2313, 213 D.L.R. (4th) 661, 162 O.A.C. 122, 13 C.C.L.T. (3d) 238, 26 C.P.C. (5th) 203 (Ont. C.A.) — Ontario plaintiff purchased package holiday organized by Canadian company which included sea cruise operated by Florida corporation. Cruise operator had entered into arrangement for provision of shore tours by independent Grenadian company. Plaintiff allegedly suffered carbon monoxide poising in vehicle operated by Grenadian resident while on shore trip organized by Grenadian company. Real and substantial connection existed between Ontario and subject matter of action. Motions judge entitled to conclude that Ontario had jurisdiction and that Ontario most convenient forum.

Leufkens v. Alba Tours International Inc. (2001), 53 O.R. (3d) 112, 2001 CarswellOnt 590, [2001] O.J. No. 644, 4 C.C.L.T. (3d) 300 (Ont. S.C.J.); affirmed (2002), 2002 CarswellOnt 1811, [2002] O.J. No. 2129, 213 D.L.R. (4th) 614, 160 O.A.C. 43, 60 O.R. (3d) 84, 13 C.C.L.T. (3d) 217, 26 C.P.C. (5th) 247 (Ont. C.A.); additional reasons at *Muscutt v. Courcelles* (2002), 2002 CarswellOnt 2313, 213 D.L.R. (4th) 661, 162 O.A.C. 122, 13 C.C.L.T. (3d) 238, 26 C.P.C. (5th) 203 (Ont. C.A.) — Plaintiff brought action in Ontario against Costa Rican company for damages for injuries suffered while on holiday in Costa Rica. Alleged negligence and damages occurred in Costa Rica. No real and substantial connection existed between subject matter of action against Costa Rican company and Ontario. Actions stayed on ground that Ontario court lacked jurisdiction.

Morriss v. British Columbia (2001), 152 B.C.A.C. 217, 2001 CarswellBC 963, 2001 BCCA 344, 250 W.A.C. 217, 74 L.C.R. 13 (B.C. C.A.) — What constitutes a cause of action? The British Columbia Court of Appeal held that bare promises could not found an action for breach of contract. In order for a promise to be actionable, there must be some legal obligation on the part of the promisor to the promisee, to perform the promise.

Ontario is not the appropriate forum for an action to set aside agreements relating to a Florida trust where circumstances related to events that occurred in Florida. The agreements and trust provided that Florida law governed, and the defendants agreed to submit to Florida law and courts. The burden is on the plaintiff to justify the choice of domestic forum in a case of service *ex juris. Frymer v. Brettschneider* (1994), 19 O.R. (3d) 60, 28 C.P.C. (3d) 84, 72 O.A.C. 360, 1994 CarswellOnt 538, [1994] O.J. No. 1411, 115 D.L.R. (4th) 744, [1996] I.L.Pr. 138 (Ont. C.A.).

Enterprise Excellence Corp. v. Royal Bank (2000), 19 C.P.C. (5th) 393, 2000 CarswellOnt 585, [2000] O.J. No. 665 (Ont. S.C.J.) — Plaintiff's action set for trial in Kitchener. Defendant proposed to call eight witnesses, most of who resided or worked in Toronto area. Plaintiff proposed to call five witnesses, all of whom resided or had accommodation in Kitchener area. Defendant raised concerns about cost and inconvenience of bringing its witnesses from Toronto to Kitchener to testify. Defendant brought motion to change place of trial from Kitchener to Toronto. Motion dismissed. Defendant did not establish that balance of convenience substantially favoured holding trial in Toronto. Trial could be set in Kitchener at least as expeditiously as in Toronto and there was no evidence to contrary.

Elliott v. Healey (2002), 2002 CarswellOnt 2451, [2002] O.J. No. 2887 (Ont. S.C.J.) — Place of trial. Venue changed from Sudbury to Barrie. Parties and all potential witnesses resided in and around Barrie area. Cause of action arose in Barrie and timing of trial similar to what it would be in Sudbury. No rational logic why Sudbury or any other jurisdiction other than Barrie ought to be place of trial.

Hodnett v. Taylor Manufacturing Industries Inc. (2002), 2002 CarswellOnt 2328, [2002] O.J. No. 2281, 18 C.C.E.L. (3d) 297, 22 C.P.C. (5th) 360 (Ont. S.C.J.); additional reasons at (2002), 2002 CarswellOnt 2316, [2002] O.J. No. 2692, 18 C.C.E.L. (3d) 293 (Ont. S.C.J.) — Plaintiff brought wrongful dismissal action in Ontario as result of termination of his employment in Atlanta, Georgia. Sufficient connection between Ontario and events giving rise to situation, satisfied real and substantial connection test. Loss of juridical advantage if plaintiff compelled to litigate in Georgia. Ontario more appropriate forum. Defendants' motion for stay dismissed.

Procon Mining & Tunnelling Ltd. v. Waddy Lake Resources Ltd., 2002 BCSC 129, 2002 CarswellBC 275, [2002] B.C.J. No. 157, 16 C.P.C. (5th) 30 (B.C. S.C. [In Chambers]) — Application by defendants to set aside service *ex juris* of writ/claim. Excellent review and analysis by Her Lordship of "Jurisdiction Simpliciter" and "Forum Conveniens."

Mathers v. Bruce, 2002 BCSC 210, 2002 CarswellBC 364 (B.C. Master) — Detailed discussion of service of documents abroad pursuant to Rules 13(11)(12)(13) of B.C. S.C., particularly "Convention" on Service Abroad of Judicial and Extra-Judicial Documents in Civil or Commercial Matters, signed at the Hague on November 15, 1965.

Sidlofsky v. Crown Eagle Ltd. (2002), 2002 CarswellOnt 3620, [2002] O.J. No. 4152 (Ont. S.C.J.) — Plaintiffs purchased vacation package in Ontario from defendant S, Ontario corporation. Accommodation was at Holiday Inn in Jamaica. Holiday Inn was Tennessee corporation. Plaintiff fell and was injured at hotel. Ontario had both jurisdiction and was *forum conveniens*.

Johnson v. Hogarth, 2004 BCPC 32, 2004 CarswellBC 364 (B.C. Prov. Ct.). Defendant sought to have the trial transferred to Victoria on Vancouver Island. Only connection anyone had to North Vancouver was that defendant Hogarth's solicitor there. Counsel for Plaintiff had business in Vancouver. Under *The Small Claims Act* (2.1) R.S.B.C. 1996 c. 430, the intent is to have claims resolved in as just and speedy and inexpensive manner as reasonable. This includes determination on "balance of convenience" where trial will be heard.

Fair to all parties to conduct litigation nearest event that resulted in the claim, i.e., the closest Court Registry to Sidney, British Columbia. File transferred to Victoria for trial.

Load Runner Logistics Ltd. v. Transport Seblac Inc., 2003 MBQB 15, 2003 CarswellMan 38, 30 C.P.C. (5th) 176, 171 Man. R. (2d) 214, [2003] 7 W.W.R. 158 (Man. Q.B.).

Appeal by Plaintiff (*Appellant*) under *The Court of Queen's Bench Small Claims Practices Act*, R.S.M. 1987 c. C285 (the Act) from decision of Court Officer of Small Claims Court holding that he had no jurisdiction to hear the Plaintiff's claim.

Appeal allowed in that the Small Claims Court of the Queen's Bench under the Act had jurisdiction and that the Small Claims Court is a *forum conveniens* to adjudicate the claim. See *Muscutt v. Courcelles* (2002), 60 O.R. (3d) 20, 2002 CarswellOnt 1756, [2002] O.J. No. 2128, 213 D.L.R. (4th) 577, 160 O.A.C. 1, 13 C.C.L.T. (3d) 161, 26 C.P.C. (5th) 206 (Ont. C.A.); additional reasons at (2002), 2002 CarswellOnt 2313, 213 D.L.R. (4th) 661, 162 O.A.C. 122, 13 C.C.L.T. (3d) 238, 26 C.P.C. (5th) 203 (Ont. C.A.), *Amchem Products Inc. v. British Columbia (Workers' Compensation Board)*, [1993] 1 S.C.R. 897, 1993 CarswellBC 47, 1993 CarswellBC 1257, [1993] 3 W.W.R. 441, 14 C.P.C. (3d) 1, 150 N.R. 321, 23 B.C.A.C. 1, 39 W.A.C. 1, 102 D.L.R. (4th) 96, 77 B.C.L.R. (2d) 62, [1993] I.L.Pr. 689 (S.C.C.), and *Morguard Investments Ltd. v. DeSavoye*, EYB 1990-67027, 1990 CarswellBC 283, 1990 CarswellBC 767, [1990] S.C.J. No. 135, 46 C.P.C. (2d) 1, 15 R.P.R. (2d) 1, 76 D.L.R. (4th) 256, 122 N.R. 81, [1991] 2 W.W.R. 217, 52 B.C.L.R. (2d) 160, [1990] 3 S.C.R. 1077 (S.C.C.).

Samson v. Hooks Industrial Inc. (2003), 2003 CarswellOnt 4094, 42 C.P.C. (5th) 312 (Ont. S.C.J.). Plaintiff sought costs on motion. Plaintiff self-employed. For Plaintiff, as for lawyer, time was money. Successful Plaintiff should be at least partially indemnified. Costs of $400.

Limoges v. Investors Group Financial Services Inc., 2003 CarswellAlta 1268, 2003 ABQB 757 (Alta. Q.B.). Trial judge made critical findings of fact before the Defendant could present its evidence or cross-examine the Plaintiff or her witnesses. The trial judge used the premature and poorly conceived findings to threaten the Defendant into settling. New trial ordered.

B.C. Marine Industry Standard Welfare Plan (Trustees of) v. Dizdarevich, 2003 CarswellBC 2082, 36 C.P.C. (5th) 97, 2003 BCSC 1314 (B.C. S.C.). Plaintiff applying to registrar default judgment. Application rejected on basis defence already filed but *after* required time. Plaintiff applying to master for default judgment. Application dismissed. Defendant clearly wishing to defend proceeding. Inappropriate to grant default judgment.

Momen v. Insurance Corp. of British Columbia, 2003 CarswellBC 1232, [2003] B.C.J. No. 1174, 2003 BCSC 788 (B.C. S.C.). Plaintiff awarded $8,589. Plaintiff seeking costs. Defendant opposing on grounds that matter within jurisdiction of Small Claims Court. Costs not awarded. Public policy of *Rule 57(1)* to encourage matters to be resolved in provincial court. Policy thwarted if costs awarded in borderline cases.

Fast Trac Bobcat & Excavating Service v. Riverfront Corp. Centre Ltd., 2002 CarswellBC 2469, [2002] B.C.J. No. 2356, 2002 BCSC 1399 (B.C. S.C.); affirmed 2004 CarswellBC 1093, 2004 BCCA 279 (B.C. C.A.). AC previously disbarred. Law Society of British Columbia and AC entered into consent order where AC agreed not to engage in practice of law until he became member in good standing. Law Society alleged that AC held himself out to be solicitor and sought order that prevented him from appearing in trial courts. Application granted.

Denys v. Shirkey, 2004 CarswellSask 532, 2004 SKPC 47, 252 Sask. R. 269, 7 C.P.C. (6th) 270 (Sask. Prov. Ct.), Halderman, P.C.J. Claim cannot be said to have arisen in Regina. The claim arose at Porcupine Plain where the defendant failed to make the payment allegedly required.

See also *J & S Hardware Ltd. v. Ed Penner Construction Ltd.*, 1989 CarswellSask 530, [1989] S.J. No. 569, 81 Sask. R. 38 (Sask. Q.B.).

Johnson v. Hogarth, 2004 BCPC 32, 2004 CarswellBC 364 (B.C. Prov. Ct.), D.E. Moss, J. Test generally based on "Balance of Convenience." Discretionary order of Provincial Court based on balancing relevant factors. To have trial held closest to the accident location would not work any particular hardship on either party or potential witnesses.

The plaintiff does not have an unfettered right to commence and/or maintain an action wherever he/she pleases. Court's discretion should not be invoked lightly or unreasonably. File transferred to Victoria Provincial Court for trial.

M.J. Jones Inc. v. Kingsway General Insurance Co., [2004] O.J. No. 1087, 2004 Carswell-Ont 1022, 185 O.A.C. 113 (Ont. C.A.), Sharpe, J.A. Appeal from order that Superior Court Justice has jurisdiction over claim and, further, that Ontario is the *forum conveniens* for dispute.

Section 106 of the *Courts of Justice Act*, R.S.O. 1990, c. C.43 permits court to stay any proceeding on such terms as are considered just. Principles enunciated initially by Supreme Court of Canada in *Morguard Investments Ltd. v. DeSavoye*, EYB 1990-67027, 1990 CarswellBC 283, 1990 CarswellBC 767, [1990] S.C.J. No. 135, 46 C.P.C. (2d) 1, 15 R.P.R. (2d) 1, 76 D.L.R. (4th) 256, 122 N.R. 81, [1991] 2 W.W.R. 217, 52 B.C.L.R. (2d) 160, [1990] 3 S.C.R. 1077 (S.C.C.), and *Hunt v. T & N plc*, 1993 CarswellBC 1271, 1993 CarswellBC 294, [1993] S.C.J. No. 125, [1994] 1 W.W.R. 129, 21 C.P.C. (3d) 269, (sub nom. *Hunt v. Lac d'Amiante du Québec Ltée*) 37 B.C.A.C. 161, (sub nom. *Hunt v. Lac d'Amiante du Québec Ltée*) 60 W.A.C. 161, (sub nom. *Hunt v. T&N plc*) 109 D.L.R. (4th) 16, 85 B.C.L.R. (2d) 1, (sub nom. *Hunt v. Lac d'Amiante du Québec Ltée*) 161 N.R. 81, (sub nom. *Hunt v. T&N plc*) [1993] 4 S.C.R. 289 (S.C.C.). See also *Muscutt v. Courcelles* (2002), 60 O.R. (3d) 20, 2002 CarswellOnt 1756, [2002] O.J. No. 2128, 213 D.L.R. (4th) 577, 160 O.A.C. 1, 13 C.C.L.T. (3d) 161, 26 C.P.C. (5th) 206 (Ont. C.A.). In action with multiple defendants and multiple claims, some of which have an extra-territorial dimension, claims must be assessed as a whole, for purposes of the jurisdictional analysis, without treating the claim against the foreign defendant as a separate action: *McNichol Estate v. Woldnik*, 2001 CarswellOnt 3342, [2001] O.J. No. 3731, 150 O.A.C. 68, 13 C.P.C. (5th) 61 (Ont. C.A.); *Muscutt, supra*, at paras. 67-68; *Incorporated Broadcasters Ltd. v. Canwest Global Communications Corp.*, 2003 CarswellOnt 601, [2003] O.J. No. 560, 223 D.L.R. (4th) 627, 31 B.L.R. (3d) 161, 63 O.R. (3d) 431, 30 C.P.C. (5th) 282, 169 O.A.C. 1 (Ont. C.A.) at para. 38. Appeal dismissed.

Marandu v. Bernaroch, 2004 CanLII 7790 (Ont. C.A.), Rosenberg, J.A. Appeal from orders made on motions by respondents to stay the action. Motions were properly granted, appeal dismissed. Ontario courts do not have jurisdiction over this action. *Muscutt v. Courcelles*, 2002 CarswellOnt 1756, [2002] O.J. No. 2128, 213 D.L.R. (4th) 577, 160 O.A.C. 1, 60 O.R.

(3d) 20, 13 C.C.L.T. (3d) 161, 26 C.P.C. (5th) 206 (Ont. C.A.) and the companion cases referred to. *Oakley v. Barry*, 1998 CarswellNS 140, [1998] N.S.J. No. 122, 158 D.L.R. (4th) 679, 166 N.S.R. (2d) 282, 498 A.P.R. 282, 25 C.P.C. (4th) 286 (N.S. C.A.); leave to appeal to the Supreme Court of Canada dismissed [1998] S.C.C.A. No. 282, 233 N.R. 397 (note), 175 N.S.R. (2d) 400 (note), 534 A.P.R. 400 (note) (S.C.C.) distinguished. See also MacPherson, J.A. in *Eastern Power Ltd. v. Azienda Comunale Energia & Ambiente*, 1999 CarswellOnt 2807, [1999] O.J. No. 3275, 178 D.L.R. (4th) 409, (sub nom. *Eastern Power Ltd. v. Azienda Communale Energia & Ambiente*) 125 O.A.C. 54, 50 B.L.R. (2d) 33, 39 C.P.C. (4th) 160 (Ont. C.A.); application for leave to appeal to the Supreme Court of Canada dismissed 2000 CarswellOnt 2212, 2000 CarswellOnt 2213, [1999] S.C.C.A. No. 542, 259 N.R. 198 (note), 139 O.A.C. 397 (note) (S.C.C.), at paras. 19 and 20.

Bangoura v. Washington Post, 2005 CarswellOnt 4343, [2005] O.J. No. 3849, 17 C.P.C. (6th) 30, 258 D.L.R. (4th) 341, 202 O.A.C. 76 (Ont. C.A.), Armstrong J.A. The motion judge analysis of jurisdiction issue articulated by Sharpe J.A. in *Muscutt v. Courcelles*, 2002 CarswellOnt 1756, [2002] O.J. No. 2128, 213 D.L.R. (4th) 577, 160 O.A.C. 1, 60 O.R. (3d) 20, 13 C.C.L.T. (3d) 161, 26 C.P.C. (5th) 206 (Ont. C.A.). Real and substantial connection test developed by Supreme Court of Canada in *Morguard Investments Ltd. v. DeSavoye*, EYB 1990-67027, 1990 CarswellBC 283, 1990 CarswellBC 767, [1990] S.C.J. No. 135, 46 C.P.C. (2d) 1, 15 R.P.R. (2d) 1, 76 D.L.R. (4th) 256, 122 N.R. 81, [1991] 2 W.W.R. 217, 52 B.C.L.R. (2d) 160, [1990] 3 S.C.R. 1077 (S.C.C.).

Judgment of S.C.C. in *Beals v. Saldanha*, 2003 CarswellOnt 5101, 2003 CarswellOnt 5102, REJB 2003-51513, [2003] S.C.J. No. 77, 2003 SCC 72, 113 C.R.R. (2d) 189, 70 O.R. (3d) 94 (note), 39 B.L.R. (3d) 1, 39 C.P.C. (5th) 1, 234 D.L.R. (4th) 1, [2003] 3 S.C.R. 416, 314 N.R. 209, 182 O.A.C. 201 (S.C.C.) made it clear that real and substantial connection test applies to international cases.

Sharpe J.A. in *Leufkens* cautioned that if an Ontario court assumes jurisdiction against a foreign defendant, it would require Ontario courts to enforce foreign judgments pronounced on the same jurisdictional basis against Ontario defendants. See *Leufkens v. Alba Tours International Inc*, 2002 CarswellOnt 1811, [2002] O.J. No. 2129, 213 D.L.R. (4th) 614, 160 O.A.C. 43, 60 O.R. (3d) 84, 13 C.C.L.T. (3d) 217, 26 C.P.C. (5th) 247 (Ont. C.A.); *Lemmex v. Bernard*, 2002 CarswellOnt 1812, [2002] O.J. No. 2131, 213 D.L.R. (4th) 627, 160 O.A.C. 31, 60 O.R. (3d) 54, 13 C.C.L.T. (3d) 203, 26 C.P.C. (5th) 259 (Ont. C.A.); *Sinclair v. Cracker Barrel Old Country Store Inc.*, 2002 CarswellOnt 1755, 213 D.L.R. (4th) 643, 160 O.A.C. 54, 60 O.R. (3d) 76, 13 C.C.L.T. (3d) 230, 26 C.P.C. (5th) 239 (Ont. C.A.); *Gajraj v. DeBernardo*, 2002 CarswellOnt 1766, [2002] O.J. No. 2130, 213 D.L.R. (4th) 651, 160 O.A.C. 60, 60 O.R. (3d) 68, 28 M.V.R. (4th) 10, 40 C.C.L.I. (3d) 163, 24 C.P.C. (5th) 258, 13 C.C.L.T. (3d) 194 (Ont. C.A.).

No real and substantial connection between this action and Ontario.

Coldmatic Refrigeration of Canada Ltd. v. Leveltek Processing LLC, 2004 CarswellOnt 1382, 70 O.R. (3d) 758, 47 C.P.C. (5th) 139 (Ont. S.C.J.). Conflict of laws Forum convenience. Plaintiff sending coils from Ontario to West Virginia for processing by defendant. Plaintiff bringing action in Ontario for breach of contract and negligence and serving defendant in West Virginia. Stay of proceedings granted. West Virginia more convenient forum than Ontario.

Appeal of judgment to Court of Appeal dismissed, with appeal with respect to costs allowed, on January 24, 2005. See 2005 CarswellOnt 189, [2005] O.J. No. 160, 5 C.P.C. (6th) 258, 75 O.R. (3d) 638 (Ont. C.A.).

Motion judge erred in principle in awarding $36,000 for counsel fee. See *Boucher v. Public Accountants Council (Ontario)*, 2004 CarswellOnt 2521, [2004] O.J. No. 2634, (sub nom. *Boucher v. Public Accountants Council for the Province of Ontario*) 71 O.R. (3d) 291, 48

C.P.C. (5th) 56, 188 O.A.C. 201 (Ont. C.A.) and *Moon v. Sher*, [2004] O.J. No. 4651, 2004 CarswellOnt 4702, 246 D.L.R. (4th) 440, 192 O.A.C. 222 (Ont. C.A.), which emphasize "the overriding principle of reasonableness." The issue not what respondent's counsel entitled to charge his or her own client, but rather what amount was reasonable to impose on the loser.

Eveready Industrial Services Corp. v. Jacques Daoust Coatings Management Inc., 2005 CarswellOnt 2331, 76 O.R. (3d) 390, 15 C.P.C. (6th) 330 (Ont. S.C.J.), Stinson J. Plaintiff commencing action in Toronto arising out of contract to wash bridges in Sarnia. Defendant moving under rule 13.1.02(2) to transfer action from Toronto to either Kitchener or Sarnia. Master failed to weigh and consider each factor enumerated in rule 13.1.02(2)(b).

Transfer of action from Toronto to Sarnia desirable in interests of justice.

See *B. (A.) v. Stubbs*, 1999 CarswellOnt 1936, 175 D.L.R. (4th) 370, 44 O.R. (3d) 391, 36 C.P.C. (4th) 175 (Ont. S.C.J.), "litigation that directly affects a community should be heard in a court that serves the community." *Chippewas of Sarnia Band v. Canada (Attorney General)*, 1996 CarswellOnt 792, [1996] O.J. No. 627, 45 C.P.C. (3d) 216 (Ont. Gen. Div.), *First Real Properties Ltd. v. Hamilton (City)*, 2002 CarswellOnt 1524, 59 O.R. (3d) 477, 21 C.P.C. (5th) 93, 29 M.P.L.R. (3d) 314 (Ont. Div. Ct.), *Laurin v Favot*, 1996 CarswellOnt 793, [1996] O.J. No. 628, 45 C.P.C. (3d) 203, 28 O.R. (3d) 114 (Ont. Gen. Div.), Borins J. reviewed authorities on change of venue and compares language of Rule 46 to the old Rule 245 from former Rules of Practice.

Towne Meadow Development Corp v. Israel Development Bank, 2005 CarswellOnt 571 (Ont. S.C.J.). Canadian construction companies carried on business in Israel. Israel far more convenient forum for litigation to proceed than Ontario. All loans and transactions to projects undertaken in Israel. Most witnesses material to issue were located in Israel.

Wood v. Sharp, 2006 CarswellOnt 2962 (Ont. S.C.J.) 2006-06-12.

Applicant Sharp requests proceedings in Ontario be stayed and action transferred to Michigan.

Plaintiff Wood visitor on vacation in Michigan, and passenger in motor vehicle owned and operated by the defendant Sharp.

Plaintiff Ontario resident.

Defendant attorned to and consented to the jurisdiction; see *Muscutt v. Courcelles* (2002), 60 O.R. (3d) 20, 2002 CarswellOnt 1756, [2002] O.J. No. 2128, 213 D.L.R. (4th) 577, 160 O.A.C. 1, 13 C.C.L.T. (3d) 161, 26 C.P.C. (5th) 206 (Ont. C.A.), at para. 19, where Sharpe J.A. held: "Consent-based jurisdiction permits jurisdiction over an extra-provincial defendant who consents, whether by voluntary submission, attornment by appearance and defence, or prior agreement to submit disputes to the jurisdiction of the domestic court."

Defendant did *not* object to the jurisdiction of the Ontario courts pursuant to rule 17.06(1) before filing a notice to defend or a statement of defence.

Defendant attorned to the jurisdiction of the Ontario courts by filing a notice to defend and a statement of defence and by conducting an examination for discovery of the plaintiff in Ontario pursuant to *Rules of Civil Procedure*. Defendant consented to the jurisdiction of the Ontario courts (*M.J. Jones Inc. v. Kingsway General Insurance Co.*, [2004] O.J. No. 3286, 2004 CarswellOnt 3244, 72 O.R. (3d) 68, 6 C.P.C. (6th) 121, 242 D.L.R. (4th) 139, 189 O.A.C. 272 (Ont. C.A. [In Chambers]), at para. 24).

Plaintiff has also satisfied the jurisdiction *simpliciter* test that there is a real and substantial connection between the litigation and Ontario and that the requirement of fairness has been established.

Plaintiff Ontario resident examined by medical health practitioners in Ontario and has received treatment by specialists in Ontario.

There is a real and substantial connection between the damages suffered and jurisdiction of Ontario. There is a real and substantial connection between the accident and the state of Michigan. The relationship of the plaintiff to the defendant prior to and independent of the accident lessens the strength of this factor favouring the plaintiff (*Doiron v. Bugge*, 2005 CarswellOnt 4930, [2005] O.J. No. 4285, 258 D.L.R. (4th) 716, 204 O.A.C. 30, 20 C.P.C. (6th) 213 (Ont. C.A.), at para. 11).

The question of jurisdiction is a question of fact but the matter of foreign *non conveniens* is a matter of judicial discretion.

Crown Resources Corp. S.A. v. National Iranian Oil Co., [2006] O.J. No. 3345, 2006 CarswellOnt 5053, 273 D.L.R. (4th) 65 (Ont. C.A.).

Domestic corporation entering contract with foreign corporation. Contract negotiated and signed in foreign jurisdiction. Domestic corporation having offices in foreign jurisdiction. Breach occurring in foreign jurisdiction. No real and substantial connection with domestic jurisdiction. Action for breach of contract stayed.

Red Seal Tours Inc. v. Occidental Hotels Management B.V., 2007 CarswellOnt 5604, 228 O.A.C. 290, 47 C.P.C. (6th) 1, 284 D.L.R. (4th) 702, 37 B.L.R. (4th) 236, 2007 ONCA 620, [2007] O.J. No. 3397 (Ont. C.A.).

Plaintiff Ontario company offered discount travel packages. Plaintiff negotiated guarantee agreements with defendant hotel chain through its Ontario agent. Guarantee agreements did not contain choice of forum clauses. Guarantee agreement could not be read as stand-alone agreement as it was labelled as "addendum." Guarantee agreement independent from tour operator agreements not supportable. Deference owed to forum selection clauses and no strong cause existed to displace forum chosen by parties in tour operator agreements. Motions judge's order set aside and substituted with order permanently staying action. See *Z.I. Pompey Industrie v. ECU-Line N.V.*, 2003 CarswellNat 1031, 2003 CarswellNat 1032, REJB 2003-40815, [2003] S.C.J. No. 23, 2003 SCC 27, 2003 A.M.C. 1280, (sub nom. *Pompey (Z.I.) Industrie v. Ecu-Line N.V.)* 303 N.R. 201, 30 C.P.C. (5th) 1, [2003] 1 S.C.R. 450, 240 F.T.R. 318 (note), 224 D.L.R. (4th) 577 (S.C.C.) at para. 20 (S.C.R.): "[i]t is essential that the courts give full weight to the desirability of holding contracting parties to their agreements."

Visic v. University of Windsor (2007), 2007 CarswellOnt 3593, 227 O.A.C. 129 (Ont. Div. Ct.); additional reasons at (2007), 2007 CarswellOnt 5106, 228 O.A.C. 224 (Ont. Div. Ct.); affirmed 2008 CarswellOnt 6345, 2008 ONCA 731 (Ont. C.A.); leave to appeal refused (2009), 2009 CarswellOnt 1636, 2009 CarswellOnt 1637, 396 N.R. 385 (note) (S.C.C.).

Plaintiff, resident of Toronto, sued University of Windsor and others. Defendants moved for a transfer to Windsor.

Superior Court, in decision reported 2006 CarswellOnt 5627, ordered transfer, conditional upon defendants undertaking, in any event of the cause, to pay plaintiff's reasonable transportation and accommodation expenses if her presence was required in Windsor for the court proceeding or discovery. The defendants appealed against the conditions. The plaintiff cross-appealed against transfer order.

Divisional Court allowed defendants' appeal in part. The court altered condition imposed on the University to require a written undertaking from it that it would pay plaintiff's reasonable transportation and accommodation costs. Court dismissed the cross-appeal.

Bevo Farms Ltd. v. Veg Gro Inc., 2007 CarswellBC 870, 2007 BCSC 570 (B.C. S.C.); affirmed 2008 CarswellBC 254, 2008 BCCA 66, 42 B.L.R. (4th) 210 (B.C. C.A.)

The plaintiff, a British Columbia corporation, sued the defendant, an Ontario corporation for unpaid invoices. Defendant, made an application for stay of action due to lack of jurisdiction. Application dismissed. British Columbia was *forum conveniens* as breach of contract occurred in British Columbia. The defendant could not plead *forum non conveniens* once it attorned to jurisdiction. There were no juridical advantages or disadvantages given the similarity of the governing legislation.

Fleet v. Jim Penney Ltd., 2007 CarswellNfld 345, 2007 NLTD 194, 272 Nfld. & P.E.I.R. 330, 830 A.P.R. 330, 50 C.P.C. (6th) 349 (N.L. T.D.)

Motion was brought by plaintiff for order that matter be transferred to St. John's from Gander. Plaintiff now lived in St. John's where she received majority of medical treatments. Counsel for both parties resided in St. John's. Motion allowed. It would be more convenient to majority of witnesses and considerably less costly in terms of travel time, travel and accommodation expenses incurred by her counsel and her witnesses if venue changed to St. John's.

Nutech Brands Inc. v. Air Canada (2007), 2007 CarswellOnt 8464, [2007] O.J. No. 5031, 57 C.P.C. (6th) 242, 88 O.R. (3d) 768 (Ont. S.C.J.)

Motion by defendants for transfer of proposed class action from London, Ontario to Toronto was denied.

It was held that defendants failed to demonstrate that it was in interests of justice to transfer proposed class action proceeding. Neither London nor Toronto was more expeditious or convenient in relation to documentation review. Although it seemed more than likely that a substantial part of the damages were sustained outside of London, the connection to Toronto was not as strong as that asserted by the moving defendants. The extent of any inconvenience posed by having witnesses and defense counsel travel to London was given little weight given the international context of the action.

Schreiber v. Mulroney (2007), 2007 CarswellOnt 8274, [2007] O.J. No. 4997, 88 O.R. (3d) 605, 288 D.L.R. (4th) 661 (Ont. S.C.J.)

The plaintiff commenced an action against the defendant for breach of contract involving an agreement for services allegedly made in Ontario. The defendant moved for orders setting aside service of the amended statement of claim and dismissing or staying the proceedings. Motion granted and action dismissed.

It was assumed that the contract between parties involved an agreement for services. Valid service was not by itself sufficient to establish jurisdiction. The evidence didn't establish that the agreement was made in Ontario, that the defendant was to perform services in Ontario, or that damages would have been sustained in Ontario.

Klotz v. Kitchener (City) (2008), 2008 CarswellOnt 2557, 46 M.P.L.R. (4th) 149, 57 C.P.C. (6th) 388, [2008] O.J. No. 1757 (Ont. S.C.J.)

Motion by the defendant city to transfer action from Brampton to Kitchener dismissed. The plaintiff, a resident of Brampton, slipped and broke his ankle on a Kitchener sidewalk. The plaintiff brought the action there in Brampton. The factors which determined whether a transfer of venue was in the interests of justice were closely balanced between the cities and the factors favoring Kitchener were not so compelling as to require transferring the action.

Attornment is when a person appears as a defendant in a court that would not ordinarily have personal jurisdiction over the respondent and pleads to the merits of an applicant's case. The appearance and pleading on the merits taken as a waiver of any objection to the court's personal jurisdiction over defendant. A party who attorns is still *not* prevented from raising the issue of the proper forum: *Follwell v. Holmes*, [2006] O.J. No. 4387, 2006 CarswellOnt 6776 (Ont. S.C.J.), where the court found Nicaragua (a non-reciprocating jurisdiction) to be a more appropriate jurisdiction to hear case than Ontario, and stayed the Ontario case.

Meunier-MacKay v. Psyllias, 2009 CarswellOnt 3365, 82 C.P.C. (6th) 69 (Ont. Master)

The location of national office of union where plaintiff worked was in Ottawa. The plaintiff did not provide evidence that she would be inconvenienced by going to Toronto and acknowledged that discovery would take place there. Convenience of parties, witnesses, and court favoured Toronto. The concept of "attornment" has no application in determining which court site an action should be assigned to. The Superior Court of Justice is a single court that sits throughout Ontario. Attornment applies when a foreign litigant submits to the jurisdiction of a domestic court. Jurisdiction is not in issue in deciding which geographic location within the court is the most appropriate for the conduct of the litigation.

Northern Sawmills Inc. v. Northwest Installations Inc. (2009), 2009 CarswellOnt 5396, 82 C.P.C. (6th) 317 (Ont. Master).

The plaintiff commenced an action in connection with a fire that occurred in Thunder Bay. The statement of claim indicated plaintiff wanted trial to be held in Toronto. Certain defendants retained Toronto counsel. The plaintiff brought a motion for order changing place of trial from Toronto to Thunder Bay. Motion granted. Most, if not all, key witnesses lived in Thunder Bay area. Scheduling witnesses would be easier if the trial was held in their community. Since the current limitation period was shorter than it used to be, the plaintiffs should not be held as strictly to their initial choice of place of trial.

Wilcox v. Flintstone Glass & Mirror Ltd., 2009 CarswellOnt 8217, 85 C.P.C. (6th) 394, 79 C.C.E.L. (3d) 80 (Ont. Master), Ontario Master.

MW brought action in Toronto against F Ltd., BW and FW for wrongful dismissal. Defendants brought motion to transfer action to Brampton. Motion was dismissed. Transfer of venue was not desirable in interest of justice. Given close proximity of locations the added burden of travelling to Toronto negligible, and convenience of court and court facilities available were neutral factors. Mandatory mediation and potential for civil case management in Toronto real benefits, and such benefits were not available in Brampton.

History of the "change of venue" rules and jurisprudence thoroughly reviewed by Stinson J. in *Eveready Industrial Services Corp. v. Jacques Daoust Coatings Management Inc.*, [2005] O.J. No. 2285, 15 C.P.C. (6th) 330, 2005 CarswellOnt 2331, 76 O.R. (3d) 390 (Ont. S.C.J.). The approach under current r. 13.102(2) is "to weigh and consider each of the factors enumerated in r. 13.1.01(2)(b) in order to determine whether a transfer of the action was desirable in the interest of justice." See also D.M. Brown J. in *Hallman v. Pure Spousal Trust (Trustee of)*, 80 C.P.C. (6th) 139, 52 E.T.R. (3d) 29, [2009] O.J. No. 4001, 2009 CarswellOnt 5795 (Ont. S.C.J.). See further *Siemens Canada Ltd. v. Ottawa (City)*, [2008] O.J. No. 3740, 73 C.L.R. (3d) 201, 2008 CarswellOnt 5650, 93 O.R. (3d) 220, 49 M.P.L.R. (4th) 258 (Ont. S.C.J.).

Skidmore v. Carleton University, 2009 CarswellOnt 2667, [2009] O.J. No. 2010, 79 C.P.C. (6th) 301 (Ont. Master); affirmed 2009 CarswellOnt 2448, [2009] O.J. No. 1854, 79 C.P.C. (6th) 306 (Ont. S.C.J.)

The defendant brought motion under r. 13.1.02(2)(b) of *Rules of Civil Procedure* to transfer action to Ottawa. Motion dismissed. The rational connection between Toronto and the venue was chosen by the plaintiff. The plaintiff resided in Toronto. Most if not all of identifiable witnesses on issue of damages lived in Toronto. Plaintiff has *prima facie* right to select the venue and onus on the moving defendant to establish requested transfer is in the interest of justice. See *Siemens Canada Ltd. v. Ottawa (City)*, 2008 CarswellOnt 5650, [2008] O.J. No. 3740, 93 O.R. (3d) 220, 49 M.P.L.R. (4th) 258, 73 C.L.R. (3d) 201 (Ont. S.C.J.). Plaintiff's right to select the venue for the action is not to be abrogated lightly. See *Joseph v. Lefaivre Investments (Ottawa) Ltd.*, [2005] O.J. No. 2324, 2005 CarswellOnt 2301 (Ont. S.C.J.); leave to appeal refused 2005 CarswellOnt 3635 (Ont. S.C.J.). The moving defendant must demonstrate transfer desirable in the interests of justice, having regard to the factors listed in r. 13.1.02(2)(b).

Dilkas v. Red Seal Tours Inc., 94 C.P.C. (6th) 76, 267 O.A.C. 363, 325 D.L.R. (4th) 301, 2010 ONCA 634, 2010 CarswellOnt 7384, 104 O.R. (3d) 221 (Ont. C.A.)

Best Day challenged both the jurisdiction of the Ontario court and the convenience of the Ontario forum. When serving Best Day in Mexico, the plaintiffs relied on rr. 17.02(h), (o) and (f) (contracts made in Ontario). Reference to r. 17.02(f) presumably based on theory of case where Best Day a foreign agent of Sunwing, and contract between plaintiffs and Sunwing entered into in Ontario. This would not trigger a jurisdictional presumption. In *Van Breda*, Sharpe J.A. held jurisdictional presumption under r. 17.02(f) did not arise regarding the foreign agent of the Ontario defendants, even though the foreign agent was involved in the promotion and execution of the Ontario contract: *Van Breda v. Village Resorts Ltd.*, 2010 ONCA 84, 2010 CarswellOnt 549, [2010] O.J. No. 402, 98 O.R. (3d) 721, 71 C.C.L.T. (3d) 161, 81 C.P.C. (6th) 219, 316 D.L.R. (4th) 201, 77 R.F.L. (6th) 1, 264 O.A.C. 1 (Ont. C.A.) at para. 113; additional reasons at 2010 ONCA 232, 2010 CarswellOnt 1751, [2010] O.J. No. 1220, 81 C.P.C. (6th) 269, 77 R.F.L. (6th) 51, 72 C.C.L.T. (3d) 225 (Ont. C.A.); affirmed 2012 SCC 17, 2012 CarswellOnt 4268, 2012 CarswellOnt 4269, (sub nom. *Club Resorts Ltd. v. Van Breda*) [2012] 1 S.C.R. 572, (sub nom. *Charron Estate v. Village Resorts Ltd.*) 114 O.R. (3d) 79 (note), 91 C.C.L.T. (3d) 1, 17 C.P.C. (7th) 223, 343 D.L.R. (4th) 577, 10 R.F.L. (7th) 1, 429 N.R. 217, 291 O.A.C. 201, [2012] A.C.S. No. 17, [2012] S.C.J. No. 17 (S.C.C.). The decision on whether there is a more convenient and appropriate forum is an exercise of judicial discretion and subject to deference on appeal.

Paul's Hauling Ltd. v. Ontario (Minister of Transportation), 2011 ONSC 3970, 2011 CarswellOnt 7229, 106 O.R. (3d) 590, [2011] O.J. No. 3447 (Ont. S.C.J.), Pierce R.S.J.

The plaintiff commenced an action in the District of Kenora for damages arising from a motor vehicle accident in the District of Rainy River. The defendant's motion to transfer proceedings to the District of Thunder Bay or then District of Rainy River was dismissed. The plaintiff was prima facie entitled to name the place of trial. There is no pre-condition existing that the place of trial must have a rational connection to the cause of action. Kenora was reasonably proximate to the place of the accident and alleged loss, and to both parties' witnesses. The transfer of the trial was not desirable in the interest of justice.

Boldt v. Law Society of Upper Canada, 2010 ONSC 3568, 2010 CarswellOnt 4353 (Ont. S.C.J.)

On both a motion to dismiss or stay an action for want of jurisdiction and a motion to strike out an action as an abuse of the process of the court, the facts pleaded in the statement of claim are presumed to be true and provable. The court will strike out an action as an abuse of process *only* when it is plain and obvious or beyond doubt that the action must fail. This is a stringent test and is applicable even in respect of novel claims.

See *Odhavji Estate v. Woodhouse* (2003), 180 O.A.C. 201, 312 N.R. 305, 2003 CarswellOnt 4852, 2003 CarswellOnt 4851, 2003 SCC 69, 70 O.R. (3d) 253 (note), [2003] 3 S.C.R. 263, 11 Admin. L.R. (4th) 45, 233 D.L.R. (4th) 193, [2004] R.R.A. 1, [2003] S.C.J. No. 74, 19 C.C.L.T. (3d) 163 (S.C.C.), Iacobucci J. (at para. 15):

> . . . The test is a stringent one. The facts are to be taken as pleaded. When so taken, the question that must then be determined is whether there it is "plain and obvious" that the action must fail. It is only if the statement of claim is certain to fail because it contains a "radical defect" that the plaintiff should be driven from the judgment. See also *Attorney General of Canada v. Inuit Tapirisat of Canada*, [1980] 2 S.C.R. 735.

Motion to dismiss or stay for want of jurisdiction.

The Supreme Court of Canada, in *Bella v. Young*, [2006] R.R.A. 1, [2006] 1 S.C.R. 108, 37 C.C.L.T. (3d) 161, 764 A.P.R. 26, 254 Nfld. & P.E.I.R. 26, 261 D.L.R. (4th) 516, 21 C.P.C.

(6th) 1, 2006 CarswellNfld 20, 2006 CarswellNfld 19, 2006 SCC 3, 343 N.R. 360, [2006] S.C.J. No. 2 (S.C.C.), wrote (at para. 31):

> ... The relationship between the appellant and the University had a contractual foundation, giving rise to duties that sound in both contract and tort: *Central Trust Co. v. Rafuse*, [1986] 2 S.C.R. 147.

Based upon the evidence before her, Hennessy J. made the following finding:

> I, therefore, find that Maureen Boldt carried on the unauthorized practice of law in direct contravention to the clear and plain terms of the injunction. *It is regrettable that she thought she could ignore the injunction simply by changing the title on her document. This is a flagrant breach of the order of Bolan J.* [Emphasis added.]

Hennessy J.'s order was appealed by Boldt to the Court of Appeal which dismissed her appeal on February 16, 2007.

The Court of Appeal rejected Boldt's application, and delivered the following endorsement:

> The appellant seeks to introduce fresh evidence with a view to having her appeal, determined against her on February 16, 2007, re-opened for another hearing. The proposed fresh evidence relates to an affidavit from Mr. Sangster and the testimony of Ms. Labbé in a subsequent small claims proceeding, which, the appellant contends, conflicts with her testimony before the trial judge in this matter.
>
> We disagree.

Boldt issued a claim for damages for malicious prosecution, and other alleged wrongs arising from the same facts, against most of the defendants in this action in September 2008, in Court File CV-08-362049. All defendants in that suit moved to strike the claim.

The Court of Appeal stated in *Canam Enterprises v. Coles*:

> The principle of *res judicata* applies where a judgment rendered by a court of competent jurisdiction provides a conclusive disposition of the merits of the case and acts as an absolute bar to any subsequent proceedings involving the same claim, demand or cause of action. Issue estoppel is one aspect of *res judicata*. The oft-cited requirements of issue estoppels are attributed to Lord Guest in *Carl-Zeiss-Stiftung v. Rayner & Keeler Ltd. (No. 2)* (1966), [1967] 1 A.C. 853 (U.K. H.L.), at 935: (1) That the same question has been previously decided; (2) that the judicial decision which is said to create the estoppels was final; and, (3) that the parties to the judicial decision or their privies were the same persons as the parties to the proceedings in which the estoppel is raised or their privies.

Canam Enterprise Inc. v. Coles (2000), 51 O.R. (3d) 481 (C.A.); reversed on other grounds (2002), 220 D.L.R. (4th) 466, [2002] S.C.C. 63, at para. 19.

As between Boldt and the Law Society, all elements of *res judicata* were satisfied.

The Law Society is not liable for the erroneous exercise of its discretion so long as it acted *bona fide* and without malice: see *Calvert v. Law Society of Upper Canada*, 1981 Carswell-Ont 782, 121 D.L.R. (3d) 169, 32 O.R. (2d) 176 (Ont. H.C.) per Steele J., at paras. 20 and 21.

The jurisprudence clearly establishes a judicial immunity from negligence for the Law Society's discipline process, including the investigative function at the front end. The Law Society's disciplinary powers must respond to its statutory mandate and the requirements of due process, not to a private law duty of care: see *Edwards v. Law Society of Upper Canada*, 2001 SCC 80, 2001 CarswellOnt 3962, 2001 CarswellOnt 3963, REJB 2001-26863, [2001] S.C.J. No. 77, [2001] 3 S.C.R. 562, (sub nom. *Edwards v. Law Society of Upper Canada (No. 2)*) 56 O.R. (3d) 456 (headnote only), 34 Admin. L.R. (3d) 38, 8 C.C.L.T. (3d) 153, 13 C.P.C. (5th) 35, 206 D.L.R. (4th) 211, 277 N.R. 145, 153 O.A.C. 388 (S.C.C.); (2000).

It is not actionable for the Law Society to require a good character hearing in the context of Boldt's application to become a licensed paralegal. Equally, it is not actionable for the Law

Society to act in the public interest by restraining untrained, uninsured and unlicensed persons such as Boldt from practising law.

In *Brignolio v. Desmarais, Keenan* (1995), 1995 CarswellOnt 4761, [1995] O.J. No. 3499 (Ont. Gen. Div.), at paras. 7, 8, 15 to 17; affirmed (1996), 1996 CarswellOnt 5875, [1996] O.J. No. 4812 (Ont. C.A.); leave to appeal refused (1996), [1996] S.C.C.A. No. 326 (S.C.C.), Lane J., in a decision affirmed on appeal, held that an action in negligence against the solicitor for one's adversary in litigation is not tenable under the law of Ontario, because there is no duty of care, and because such an action is contrary to public policy. Further, Lane J. held that a party to litigation cannot bring an action against the adverse party's solicitor based upon alleged breaches of ethical duties since such duties are owed to the court and, in Ontario, to the Law Society, but not to the opposite party in the litigation.

Fabbian Homes Inc. v. Guelph (City), [2010] O.J. No. 2152, 2010 CarswellOnt 3499, 72 M.P.L.R. (4th) 314 (Ont. S.C.J.)

Plaintiff development company F Inc. sought refund from defendant municipality G for overpayment of development charges it paid for building permit. The municipality brought motion to dismiss action for lack of jurisdiction. Motion granted. Previous decision by Court of Appeal came to the conclusion that the court could in fact be intended to have concurrent jurisdiction with board or tribunal set up by legislature. The Court found no special circumstances that would encourage court to exercise its concurrent jurisdiction in advance of municipal board.

Richardson v. RxHousing Inc., 2010 NSSM 67, 2010 CarswellNS 780, 297 N.S.R. (2d) 254, 943 A.P.R. 254 (N.S. Small Cl. Ct.), O'Hara M., adjudicator.

Claim arising out of contract for rental of residential premises in West Hollywood, California. The claimant was a resident of Halifax, Nova Scotia. The defendant was a Texas-based corporation. Communications leading up to contract done through e-mail. Subsequently, the claimant had her agent view the apartment.

Defendant raised three issues to displace jurisdiction of Court:

> 1. The Nova Scotia Small Claims Court does not have territorial competence to hear this matter;
>
> 2. Even if the Court has territorial competence, the Court should decline to exercise jurisdiction on the basis of *forum non conveniens*;
>
> 3. Finally, even if the Court would otherwise have jurisdiction, the Nova Scotia *Residential Tenancies Act*, R.S.N.S. 1989, c. 430, would apply to the case, and under that *Act*, the Small Claims Court would not have originating jurisdiction.

Did the contract result from ". . . a solicitation of business in the Province by or on behalf of the seller"? See *Society of Composers, Authors & Music Publishers of Canada v. Canadian Assn. of Internet Providers*, REJB 2004-66511, 32 C.P.R. (4th) 1, [2004] 2 S.C.R. 427, 322 N.R. 306, 2004 CarswellNat 1920, 2004 CarswellNat 1919, 2004 SCC 45, [2004] S.C.J. No. 44, 240 D.L.R. (4th) 193 (S.C.C.). A solicitation that comes through the internet to a person situate in Nova Scotia is received in Nova Scotia. The presumption of real and substantial connection arises by virtue of section 11 of the *Court Jurisdiction and Transfer Act*. Nothing has been raised that rebuts the presumption.

Hagar v. Toronto Transit Commission, 2011 ONSC 4007, 2011 CarswellOnt 5582 (Ont. S.C.J.), T. Maddalena J.

Place of trial was set. An Application for a change of venue was put forth. The defendant, TTC, brought a motion for a change of venue from Welland to Toronto, Ontario. The judge dismissed the motion, finding that TTC had not proved that it was in the interest of justice to change venues. TTC brought a motion for a leave to appeal. The motion was dismissed. The judge did not raise any issue of prejudice or change relevant test.

Forum Non Conveniens

Counsel for the defendant cited *Z.I. Pompey Industrie v. ECU-Line N.V.*, 224 D.L.R. (4th) 577, 240 F.T.R. 318 (note), [2003] 1 S.C.R. 450, 30 C.P.C. (5th) 1, [2003] S.C.J. No. 23, REJB 2003-40815, 303 N.R. 201, 2003 A.M.C. 1280, 2003 CarswellNat 1032, 2003 CarswellNat 1031, 2003 SCC 27 (S.C.C.) as authority for the principle that where there is a choice of forum clause the plaintiff must show "strong cause" as to why a stay should not be granted. See *CKF Inc. v. Huhtamaki Americas Inc.*, 2009 NSSC 21, 2009 CarswellNS 72, 877 A.P.R. 67, 275 N.S.R. (2d) 67 (N.S. S.C.) at paras. 57-58.

In *Hayes v. Peer 1 Network Inc.*, 2007 CarswellOnt 105, 55 C.C.E.L. (3d) 132 (Ont. Master); reversed 2007 CarswellOnt 4093, [2007] O.J. No. 2476, 86 O.R. (3d) 475, 60 C.C.E.L. (3d) 153, 228 O.A.C. 348 (Ont. Div. Ct.); additional reasons at 2007 CarswellOnt 5072, 60 C.C.E.L. (3d) 157, 228 O.A.C. 348 at 352 (Ont. Div. Ct.), Master Glustein considered and ultimately concluded that the following clause was not an exclusive jurisdiction clause: "This Agreement is governed by the laws of the state of Washington and each party irrevocably attorns to the jurisdiction of the court system of the state of Washington."

In *Penny (Litigation Guardian of) v. Bouch*, 2009 NSCA 80, 2009 CarswellNS 414, [2009] N.S.J. No. 339, (sub nom. *Penny v. Bouch*) 281 N.S.R. (2d) 238, (sub nom. *Penny v. Bouch*) 893 A.P.R. 238, 310 D.L.R. (4th) 433, 67 C.C.L.T. (3d) 165, 74 C.P.C. (6th) 218 (N.S. C.A.); leave to appeal refused 2010 CarswellNS 174, 2010 CarswellNS 175, (sub nom. *Penny v. Bouch*) 406 N.R. 387 (note), (sub nom. *Penny v. Bouch*) 303 N.S.R. (2d) 400 (note), (sub nom. *Penny v. Bouch*) 957 A.P.R. 400 (note) (S.C.C.); reconsideration refused 2010 CarswellNS 773, 2010 CarswellNS 774 (S.C.C.), the Court of Appeal confirmed that the test remains that the competing jurisdiction (Harris County, Texas, in this case) must be shown to be clearly more appropriate (para. 62). The Small Claims Court does not have originating jurisdiction over matters falling under the *Residential Tenancies Act*. See *Reference re Act to Amend Chapter 401 of the Revised Statutes, 1989, the Residential Tenancies Act, S.N.S. 1992, c. 31*, 1996 CarswellNS 166F, 1996 CarswellNS 166, [1996] S.C.J. No. 13, [1996] 1 S.C.R. 186, 131 D.L.R. (4th) 609, 432 A.P.R. 1, 149 N.S.R. (2d) 1, 193 N.R. 1, 35 Admin. L.R. (2d) 169, 50 R.P.R. (2d) 137, EYB 1996-67373 (S.C.C.). The Small Claims Court has territorial jurisdiction over the subject matter of this claim.

Citroen v. Ontario (Minister of Transportation), 2012 ONSC 975, 2012 CarswellOnt 1361, 27 C.P.C. (7th) 339, 29 M.V.R. (6th) 288, [2012] O.J. No. 533 (Ont. S.C.J.)

The plaintiffs seek an order that the trial of action take place in Hamilton, where the plaintiffs instituted these proceedings. The position of the defendant is that, pursuant to subsection 33(9) of the *Public Transportation and Highway Improvement Act (the Act)* R.S.O. 1990, c. P.50, the trial take place in Peterborough County.

Analysis requires Rule 13.1 of the *Rules of Civil Procedure* and subsection 33(9) of the *Public Transportation and Highway Improvement Act* R.S.O. 1990, c. P.50 *(the Act)*.

Under Rule 2, non compliance with the Rules is an irregularity, not a nullity. Rule 2.03 permits the court to dispense with compliance with any rule in the interest of justice.

This test requires a fact-specific analysis in which all of the factors listed in Rule 13.1.02(2)(b) are weighed to determine what trial venue will be "in the interests of justice." *Wilcox v. Flintstone Glass & Mirror Ltd.*, 2009 CarswellOnt 8217, 85 C.P.C. (6th) 394, 79 C.C.E.L. (3d) 80 at paras. 12-19 (Ont. Master); *Paul's Hauling Ltd. v. Ontario (Minister of Transportation)*, 2011 ONSC 3970, 2011 CarswellOnt 7229, [2011] O.J. No. 3447, 106 O.R. (3d) 590 at paras. 17-22 (Ont. S.C.J.). The interests of justice warrant the court to deviate from the presumption that the trial take place in Peterborough. The most expeditious and least expensive determination of the proceeding on its merits favours the trial of this matter taking place in the City of Hamilton.

2055525 Ontario Ltd. v. Thirty Three Rosedale Holdings Inc., 2013 CarswellOnt 15959, [2013] O.J. No. 5350, Deputy Judge Winny (Ont. S.C.J.).

A motion for a change of venue from Kitchener to Toronto was granted. The plaintiff's office is in Cambridge. The defendants are both located in Toronto.

In this case, both of the defendants are located in Toronto. The cause of action is the alleged failure to close the mortgage pertaining to a Toronto property. There is no viable argument to support a conclusion that the cause of action occurred in the Regional Municipality of Waterloo.

Toronto is more closely connected to the case than Cambridge. The policy behind rule 6.01 is that convenience to plaintiffs is sacrificed in favour of convenience to defendants.

Ontario College of Pharmacists v. 1724665 Ontario Inc., 2013 ONCA 381, 2013 Carswell-Ont 7601, 363 D.L.R. (4th) 724, 308 O.A.C. 200 (Ont. C.A.); additional reasons 2013 ONCA 394, 2013 CarswellOnt 7709, 308 O.A.C. 200 at 215 (Ont. C.A.).

Respondent G. Inc., successor to Ontario corporation, had its corporate offices in Belize Respondent R Inc., owned by respondents P and S, operated a call centre in Ontario G Inc. and R Inc. sold pharmaceuticals purchases from India to customers located in the United States. Ontario College brought successful application for declaration it had statutory disciplinary jurisdiction over pharmaceutical-related business activities of G Inc. The respondents appealed. The appeal was dismissed. The respondents sold prescription drugs in Ontario. Without R Inc.'s staff at the call centre in Ontario, no prescription drugs would flow from G Inc. to its customers. Although G Inc. and R Inc. had separate legal identities, they did not operate separately, and that R Inc. served as G Inc.'s agent in matters relating to G Inc.'s business. College fulfilling its legislated duty to serve and protect public interest.

(3) If, when an action is called for trial or settlement conference, the judge finds that the place where the action was commenced is not the proper place of trial, the court may order that the action be tried in any other place where it could have been commenced under this rule.

O. Reg. 78/06, s. 8(1)

Commentary

Jurisdiction

When can a Canadian court assume jurisdiction over a law suit whose genesis originates in a foreign jurisdiction?

See *Club Resorts Ltd. v. Van Breda*.

A plaintiff, in a tort action in Ontario, must demonstrate the presence of a "presumptive connecting factor" that links the subject matter of the litigation to Ontario. The Court identified four "presumptive connecting factors" (at para. 90):

    i. The defendant is domiciled or resident in the province;

    ii. The defendant carries on business in the province;

    iii. The tort was committed in the province; and

    iv. A contract connected with the dispute was made in the province.

This list is not exhaustive and it is open to a plaintiff to demonstrate an analogous ground to establish a real and substantial connection.

If a presumptive connecting factor is present, then the onus is on the defendant to rebut the presumption. If the defendant cannot rebut the presumption then the court must assume jurisdiction over the case. The Supreme Court of Canada gave several examples of situations in which the presumption could be rebutted.

The Supreme Court found in *Van Breda* that the contract between Club Resorts Ltd. and Viktor Berg was made in Ontario and, thus, a presumptive connecting factor was made out which Club Resorts Ltd. did not rebut.

The Small Claims Court has its own particular rule on venue or where a case must be started and tried. The general rule is that the case must proceed in the court office in the territorial division where the defendant resides or carries on business, or where there are several defendants, where at least one of them resides or carries on business. In effect the rule favours the convenience of defendants over the convenience of plaintiffs. See *Xerox Canada Inc. v. Neary*, 1984 CarswellOnt 385, 47 O.R. (2d) 776, 43 C.P.C. 274 (Ont. Prov. Ct.); *Canada Trust Mastercard v. Nowick*, 1981 CarswellOnt 445, 27 C.P.C. 183 (Ont. Small Cl. Ct.); *McNeilly v. Bennet*, 1915 CarswellOnt 226, 25 D.L.R. 785, 34 O.L.R. 400 (Ont. H.C.).

The most common exception to that general rule is where the cause of action arose elsewhere than where the defendant resides or carries on business. In such cases the plaintiff may elect to start the case where the cause of action arose. However care should be taken to avoid misunderstanding the concept of where a cause of action arises. For example, in a negligence case the cause of action generally arises where the accident occurred. However in simple debt cases the cause of action arises from non-payment (the cause of action arises from the breach of contract not its formation). In such cases the location where the contract was signed or entered into is not a proper venue if the defendants reside or carry on business elsewhere: see *Action Auto Leasing & Gallery Inc. v. Braun*, 2009 CarswellOnt 8666, [2009] O.J. No. 1003 (Ont. Sm. Cl. Ct.).

In any case where all the defendants have been served outside the court's territorial division, default cannot be noted until the plaintiff establishes that the action was properly brought in that territorial division: rule 11.01(3). An Affidavit for Jurisdiction (Form 11A) is generally sufficient for that purpose. If however the court is not satisfied that the claim has been brought in the proper territorial division, the case may be transferred to the proper venue, with appropriate terms.

The court may order a change of venue on motion under rule 6.01(2), but the moving party must establish that the balance of convenience substantially favours the proposed venue over the existing venue. Caselaw developed under Rule 13.1 of the *Rules of Civil Procedure* should be read with care given the materially different wording of that rule.

The court may also make an order for a change of venue where the proceeding was commenced in the wrong venue, even if the substantial balance of convenience test is not satisfied: *2055525 Ontario Ltd. v. Thirty Three Rosedale Holdings Inc.*, 2013 CarswellOnt 15959, [2013] O.J. No. 5350 (Ont. S.C.J.).

Case Law: *Kambulow v. Toronto Airport Christian Fellowship* (2008), 2008 CarswellOnt 1288, 60 C.P.C. (6th) 38 (Ont. Div. Ct.)

Reasonable interpretation of s. 20 of *Court of Justice Act* R.S.O. 1990, c.C.43 ("CJA"), and Rule 61.03 of the *Rules of Civil Procedure*, R.R.O. 1990, Reg.194 is that motion for leave to appeal to Divisional Court from interlocutory order of Superior Court of Justice must be filed and heard in region where the appeal was to be heard.

Transfer of action to Toronto from Brampton did not result in appeal being heard in Toronto. Appeal was to be heard in Brampton despite change of venue. Court was to ensure appeals were heard in the same jurisdiction as originating proceedings in order to avoid impractical results.

6.02 A cause of action shall not be divided into two or more actions for the purpose of bringing it within the court's jurisdiction.

Commentary: If your claim is beyond the monetary jurisdiction of the court your claim should provide that "The plaintiff has agreed to reduce the claim to (the monetary limit) to bring it within the monetary jurisdiction of the court". A plaintiff has several options at any time up to the trial date:

(a) Discontinue the Small Claims Court action and start a new action in the Superior Court of Justice [formerly Ontario Court (General Division)].

(b) Bring a motion to a judge to have the action transferred to the Superior Court of Justice [formerly Ontario Court (General Division)] under section 110 of the *Courts of Justice Act*.

(c) Reduce the claim to the court's limit and request that default judgment be signed for the maximum.

Case Law: *Dorman Estate v. Korean Air Lines Co.* (June 15, 1995), Doc. 5510/85, 5513/85, 5557/85 (Ont. Div. Ct.) — Leave to appeal granted relating to decision which held that the Ontario courts had jurisdiction on the basis that the defendant had an office in Toronto through which sales of airline tickets were affected.

Tope v. Stratford (City) (1994), 52 A.C.W.S. (3d) 783 (Ont. Sm. Cl. Ct.) — Two actions arose out of personal injury suffered by the female plaintiff. The claim of the male plaintiff was a derivative claim pursuant to the *Family Law Act*, R.S.O. 1990, c. F.3. Each claim was at the maximum monetary limit of the Small Claims Court. Although claims had been ordered and tried together, claims were separate causes of action in that each involved a substantive claim in its own right. The plaintiffs had not split a single cause of action to avoid monetary ceiling of the Small Claims Court.

R. Llewellyn Building Supplies Ltd. v. Nevitt, 1987 CarswellNS 319, [1987] N.S.J. No. 262, 80 N.S.R. (2d) 415, 200 A.P.R. 415 (N.S. Co. Ct.) — Where the claims of two parties are arising form the same set off acts, it is ordinarily advisable to consolidate the two matters and hear them as one, even if the effect is to remove the combined proceedings from the jurisdiction of the Small Claims Court.

Ingersoll Press Automation & Machinery Inc. v. Tom Saab Industries (1994), 46 A.C.W.S. (3d) 153 (Ont. Sm. Cl. Ct.) — Rule 6.01(1)(a) prescribes that where the cause of action did notarise in the territorial division favoured by the plaintiff, the action must be brought in the territorial division in which the defendant resides or carries on business. Since *Canada Trust Master Card v. Nowick* (1982), 27 C.P.C. 183, it has been the law that a plaintiff may have a claim entered and tried in its home division only if the entire cause of action arose there.

W.B. Knox & Son Ltd. v. St. Amand (1986), 5 W.D.C.P. 333 (Ont. Prov. Ct.) — Although the cause of action did not arise in the jurisdiction where the action commenced, it was the proper forum since the corporate defendant's head office was located in that jurisdiction.

Ruffolo v. Mulroney (1988), 12 W.D.C.P. 313 (Ont. Prov. Ct.) — Although no reasonable cause of action was established, the action would have to be transferred to Ottawa since those named in a representative capacity were all resident in Ottawa.

Elguindy v. Core Laboratories Can. Ltd. (1987), 21 C.P.C. (2d) 281 (Ont. Div. Ct.) — The plaintiff employed in Ontario was discharged as a result of a telephone call from Alberta. The cause of action arose in Ontario. Convenience, however, favors the holding of the trial in Alberta.

Can. Trust Mastercard v. Nowick (1982), 27 C.P.C. 183 (Ont. Sm. Cl. Ct.) — The plaintiff, with its head office in London, wished to sign default judgment against the defendant, a resident of Oshawa. The clerk of the court refused to sign judgment saying the Middlesex court had no jurisdiction. The defendant's credit card application originated in Oshawa and she resided there at all material times. The plaintiff's cause of action originated in Middlesex. The court found that the whole cause of action did not originate there. The plaintiff sought to prove the jurisdiction of the Middlesex court. The action was transferred to the court where the defendant resided. The clerk was correct in referring the jurisdiction to a judge when the affidavit filed by the plaintiff failed to establish the jurisdiction of the court.

Interamerican Transport Systems Inc. v. Grand Trunk Western Railroad (1985), 51 O.R. (2d) 568 (Ont. Div. Ct.) — Where a foreign railway company employs a sales manager who maintains an office within the jurisdiction and whose duties include solicitation of freight and calling on prospective customers, the corporation is subject to the jurisdiction of the small claims court pursuant to s. 66 of the *Small Claims Courts Act*, R.S.O. 1980, c. 476, even though the sales manager had no capacity to sign or enter contracts on behalf of his employer.

Lysiak v. Re/Max Cataract City Ltd. (1989), 15 W.D.C.P. 202 (Ont. Prov. Ct.) — There were five actions for commissions owing on two separate real estate transactions and for mortgage placements made upon referrals from the plaintiffs. There was a contract of employment for each transaction.

The realtor moved for an order consolidating the actions and transferring them to District Court on the grounds that the plaintiffs divided the cause of action into two or more actions for the purposes of bringing the cause within the monetary jurisdiction of the Small Claims Court. The actions were stayed.

The employment agreements were subject at all times to periodic and regular accountings between the parties as to amounts due to them and amounts for which the employer had the right to deduct. The real cause of action was for a final accounting between the parties after the termination of the agreements.

The combined actions of each plaintiff were still in excess of the monetary jurisdiction of the Court if each action arose out of the same cause of action. The cause of action was divided contrary to Rule 6.02. The jurisdiction to transfer the actions was provided by section 123 of the *Courts of Justice Act, 1984*, S.O. 1984, c. 11 rather than section 120(2), (3). The actions were stayed pending an election by the plaintiffs to proceed in the Small Claims Courts and abandon the excess of their claim over $1,000. Failing such election, the actions would be transferred to the District Court.

Cox v. Robert Simpson Co. (1973), 1 O.R. (2d) 333 (Ont. C.A.) — A cause of action cannot be split. Consequently, when a plaintiff accepts sum in full satisfaction of his claim, he cannot later commence a County Court action on the same cause of action.

Aitchison v. Nordson Canada Ltd. (1990), 1 W.D.C.P. (2d) 3 (Ont. Prov. Ct.) — Where an employee brought three actions for damages for breach of contract, claiming payment for overtime worked, and where the amount claimed in each action did not exceed $3,000 but the total claimed was $4,723.12, the actions were ordered consolidated and the plaintiff was granted 30 days to reduce his claim to $3,000 failing which the proceedings would be stayed.

Qualico Developments Ltd. v. Doherty, 1985 CarswellAlta 256, 41 Alta. L.R. (2d) 380, 23 D.L.R. (4th) 605, 67 A.R. 334 (Alta. Q.B.) — If a claim is filed within the monetary jurisdiction but defendant's counterclaim exceeds jurisdiction and does not appear to have any bearing on claim, but merely raises independent action against the plaintiff, then the provincial court judge would properly exercise his discretion by transferring counterclaim to Court of Queen's Bench and proceeding to determine claim. However, where the counterclaim raises issues connected with the claim which would be raised in defence, then the provincial court judge properly exercises his discretion by transferring both claim and counterclaim to Queen's Bench to avoid duplication of trials.

Canadian Overnite Courier (1983) Ltd. v. Jasper Printing Group Ltd. (Jan. 14, 1985) (Alta. Q.B.), Master Funduk — An action that contained a counterclaim exceeding the jurisdiction of the Provincial Court was removed to the Court of Queen's Bench. When the Queen's Bench struck out the counterclaim, the action was referred back to Provincial Court.

Plante v. Dalgleish (Nov. 1, 1984) (Man. Q.B.), Kennedy J. — An action commenced in Small Claims Court was transferred to the Court of Queen's Bench. Small Claims Court was established for uncomplicated cases, and this case involved witnesses requiring an interpreter, a counterclaim exceeding jurisdiction of Small Claims Court and the possibility of appeal.

Jackson v. Houle, [1991] 3 W.W.R. 756 (Sask. Q.B.) — The plaintiff lost a Small Claims Court action against the defendant arising from a car accident. The plaintiff brought a second action against the same defendant for damages in the Court of Queen's Bench. *Res judicata* was applied.

McGraw v. Merchant Retail Services Ltd. (1989), 92 N.S.R. (2d) 240 (N.S. Co. Ct.) — Section 5 of the Nova Scotia *Small Claims Court Act* precludes a corporation or partnership from claiming on a contract under the Act unless it was one of the original parties to the contract.

Joan Balcom Sales Inc. v. Poirier (1991), 49 C.P.C. (2d) 180 (N.S. Co. Ct.) — The defendants did not reside in either Kings County or Annapolis County in Nova Scotia. The location and ownership of the property were irrelevant to the locus of the cause of action. The action was for a simple contract to pay a sales commission.

Royal Bank v. Metcalfe (1985), 3 C.P.C. (2d) 228 (Ont. Dist. Ct.) — This case defines the phrase "cause of action" as being all facts that give rise to a claim. It was the location of the parties and the place where the contract was formalized and/or breached which affected the place where the action ought to have been properly taken. The applicable law was the law of Nova Scotia, not Ontario.

Bernier v. LFD Industries Ltd. (1994), 48 A.C.W.S. (3d) 80 (B.C.S.C.) — The plaintiff claimed $7,983 in respect of funds held back from a share purchase agreement. The plaintiff brought a second claim for $9,871 for payments due under the agreement. The plaintiff should not have been required to pursue a single claim and abandon excess. The matters were distinct and could be heard separately, although originating in same agreement. An appeal from setting aside claims was allowed.

Traditional Air Systems Inc. v. Custom Gas Heating Ltd. (1995), 86 O.A.C. 72 (Div. Ct.) — Small Claims Court Rule 6.02 provides that a cause of action shall *not* be divided into two or more actions for the purpose of bringing it within the court's jurisdiction. The trial judge had no jurisdiction to proceed with the trials.

Bartor Developments Inc. v. Leon's Furniture Ltd. (1997), 103 O.A.C. 314 (Ont. C.A.) — Principle of *res judicata* did not apply to prohibit plaintiff from making claim on running account where default had continued to accrue between date of last claim and motion for summary judgment. To require plaintiff to continually update claim would defeat summary nature of proceedings.

Maple Lodge Farms Ltd. v. Penny Lane Fruit Market Inc., [1997] O.J. No. 4401, 1997 CarswellOnt 4306 (Ont. Gen. Div.) — Plaintiff broke up claim for unpaid invoices into eight Small Claims Court proceedings. On consent, actions transferred to General Division. Plaintiff was in breach of action-splitting rule of Small Claims Court. Court had no jurisdiction to effect transfer. Nor did consent of parties create jurisdiction. However, General Division was entitled to exercise inherent jurisdiction and did so in light of size of claim, simple nature of claim and fact of consent.

Warwaruk v. LeBoutillier (1997), 117 Man. R. (2d) 221 (Man. Master) — Mechanic's latest Small Claims Court action for repair costs was not abuse of process. Settlement of Queen's Bench action did not address issue of mechanics repair account.

Schmalfuss v. Feldman (May 20, 1998), Doc. 527/97 (Ont. Gen. Div.) — The parties settled two actions for a total of $11,000. When the plaintiff stopped making the required payments, the respondent obtained judgment for $5,500 in each action. Appeal dismissed. There was no substantial wrong or miscarriage of justice.

Roberts v. S-G. Transport Ltd. (1998), 160 Nfld. & P.E.I.R. 128, 494 A.P.R. 128, 26 C.P.C. (4th) 339, 1998 CarswellPEI 49 (P.E.I. T.D. [In Chambers]) — Motion to set aside a notice of default. Two plaintiffs filed various notices of claim against S-G Transport in Small Claims Court. S-G Transport then sought to strike the pleadings as an abuse of process. At issue was whether the noting in default should be set aside and whether the claims should be consolidated. Motion granted. The failure to defend was as a result of inadvertence. The notices of default were set aside. The 25 claims had common questions of law or fact. The claims of both plaintiffs were consolidated into two claims and ordered to be heard together at trial.

Duncan v. Coceancic (January 15, 1999), Doc. Thunder Bay 98-0088, 98-0089, 98-0090 (Ont. Sm. Cl. Ct.) — Rule 6.02 precluded division of cause of action. The plaintiff commenced three actions on the same day, arising from the same transaction, and for a total of more than twice the amount of jurisdiction. Default judgments obtained were nullity and were set aside.

Tyo Law Corp. v. White (1999), 1 C.P.C. (5th) 323, 1999 CarswellBC 1569 (B.C. S.C.) — Two accounts that were subject to settlement within Small Claims Court proceedings were not subject to review. The correct entity to defend accounts was the solicitor and not the firm. Where several accounts were all related to retainer for single purpose, each account should be treated as interim, and all accounts except for two within terms of settlement were subject to review.

The motion was to stay claim on the basis that the plaintiff is potentially splitting his action. He claims that the failure of the defendant to keep him informed "is costing [him] nearly $3,100 per year." The clear value of the plaintiff's damages far exceeds the jurisdiction of Court.

To allow action to continue would encourage the plaintiff to pursue his claim on a piecemeal basis. This matter should be heard in the Superior Court: *Imperial Life Financial v. Langille* (1997), 166 N.S.R. (2d) 46, 498 A.P.R. 46, 2 C.C.L.I. (3d) 117, 21 C.P.C. (4th) 170 (N.S. S.C. [In chambers]); *Paul Revere Life Insurance Co. v. Herbin*, 1996 CarswellNS 101, [1996] N.S.J. No. 88, 149 N.S.R. (2d) 200, 432 A.P.R. 200, [1996] I.L.R. 1-3321 (N.S. S.C.). Allegation of breach of fiduciary duty is serious and parties ought to be given full range of production and discovery. The claim is stayed. *Baslik v. O.T.F.* (2000), 24 C.C.P.B. 28, 2000 CarswellOnt 1469 (Ont. Sm. Cl. Ct.).

Celik v. St. Paul Insurance Co. (2000), 2000 CarswellOnt 1623 (Ont. C.A.); leave to appeal refused (2001), 267 N.R. 192 (note), (sub nom. *Oxford Building Maintenance v. Ontario*) 146 O.A.C. 200 (note), 2001 CarswellOnt 29, 2001 CarswellOnt 30 (S.C.C.) — Two separate actions were found to be a clear attempt to relitigate prior decisions in which the plaintiff was unsuccessful.

Nitsopolous v. Marriott Corp. Canada (2000), 138 O.A.C. 136, 2000 CarswellOnt 3867 (Ont. C.A.) — The plaintiff previously commenced similar action, which was dismissed for delay and not appealed. A new claim of abuse of process was presented. Earlier decision not to appeal could not be viewed in isolation from institution of new action. It was unnecessary to consider *res judicata*.

Canada (Attorney General) v. David (2000), 5 C.P.C. (5th) 401, 2000 CarswellOnt 5014 (Ont. S.C.J.) — Prior federal action had been dismissed. Ontario action based on the same facts was vexatious.

Baslik v. O.T.F. (2000), 24 C.C.P.B. 28, 2000 CarswellOnt 1469 (Ont. Sm. Cl. Ct.) — The plaintiff claimed for reduction of pension. The claim was for one year of artificial splitting of action where the claim could be renewed. Damages far exceeded jurisdiction. The claim should be heard in Superior Court and was stayed.

Morrison v. Rosser (Rural Municipality), 2001 CarswellMan 293, [2001] M.J. No. 290, 2001 MBCA 108 (Man. C.A. [In Chambers]); additional reasons at 2001 CarswellMan 443, 2001 MBCA 149 (Man. C.A. [In Chambers]); additional reasons at 2002 CarswellMan 97, 2002 MBQB 26 (Man. C.A. [In Chambers]) — Plaintiff brought two small claims actions. Defendant denied stay. Hearing officer dismissed claims because amount exceeded jurisdiction. On appeal claims consolidated and recovery limited. Leave to appeal. Plaintiff entitled to know manner Court decided whether claims distinct.

434438 B.C. Ltd. v. R.S. & D. Contracting Ltd., 171 B.C.A.C. 111, 2002 CarswellBC 1563, 2002 BCCA 423, 280 W.A.C. 111 (B.C. C.A.); additional reasons at 2002 CarswellBC 3128, 2002 BCCA 650 (B.C. C.A.) — Multiple documents entered into by plaintiffs and defendant concerning the subdivision and sale of property. At issue was which of these instruments was binding on the parties. To that end two actions were "consolidated" by consent. The B.C. Court of Appeal stated that a defendant who claimed relief should counterclaim as well as defend. It was technically not possible to "consolidate" actions in which the plaintiff in one was the defendant in the other. The solution was for one of the actions to be discontinued and the plaintiff to assert its rights by counterclaim. If neither party would yield, the proper order was that the actions be tried together.

Walter Construction (Canada) Ltd. v. Greater Vancouver Sewerage & Drainage District, 2002 CarswellBC 1872, 2002 BCSC 1193 (B.C. S.C.) — Applicant head contractor on construction development. A large number of lawsuits commenced. Eight lawsuits resolved but seven that remained scheduled to be tried at the same time. The applicant commenced action for damages and sought order that action be tried at the same time as other seven trials. Application allowed. The issue regarding the adequacy of the design drawings and their on work major issue, common to the action.

James v. Dietitians of Canada (2002), 2002 CarswellOnt 2172 (Ont. S.C.J.) — Plaintiff involved in litigation with defendant on two previous occasions. Plaintiff's claim here referred to exactly the same facts as stated in previous two actions. Action dismissed. Matter previously decided.

B & S Publications Inc. v. Gaulin, 2002 CarswellAlta 1227, 2002 ABCA 238, 317 A.R. 397, 284 W.A.C. 397 (Alta. C.A.) — Order consolidated two actions. Appellant argued that consolidation unfairly retarded progress of first action. Appeal dismissed. Separate trial would result in duplication of related parties, arose from same series of transactions and had common questions of fact. Inconsistent verdicts to be avoided.

Stan v. Gene's Machine & Repair Shop Ltd., 2004 SKPC 21, 2004 CarswellSask 26, 246 Sask. R. 10 (Sask. Prov. Ct.). The Plaintiff purchased rebuilt engine from Defendant. Return of purchase price. He also claims cost of installing engine as well as certain damages. Plaintiff commenced two actions.

Sections 5(1) of *The Small Claims Act, 1997*, Statutes of Saskatchewan, 1997, c. S-50.11 ("the Act") provides that a person shall not divide a claim that exceeds the monetary limit into more than one claim. A single claim cannot exceed the sum of $5,000. Since both actions related, must be dealt with as one action.

Plaintiff entitled to judgment against Defendant in sum of $5,000 and interest, not damages of $5,916.28.

Trevor Nicholas Construction Co. v. Canada (Minister for Public Works), 2003 CarswellNat 1883, 2003 CarswellNat 2553, 26 C.L.R. (3d) 1, 242 F.T.R. 317 (note), 2003 FCA 277, 2003

CAF 277 (Fed. C.A.); leave to appeal refused (2004), 2004 CarswellNat 4, 2004 CarswellNat 5 (S.C.C.). Trial judge's requests to appellant to clarify his responses did not support allegation of bias. Appellant had raised no objection to admissibility of any of Respondent's evidence.

Davis v. Davidson, 2003 CarswellAlta 550, 2003 ABPC 81, 42 C.B.R. (4th) 8 (Alta. Prov. Ct.). Creditor entitled to claim for debt incurred *after* bankruptcy. Provincial Court had jurisdiction where debt amount within monetary jurisdiction.

Dynamic Oil Tools Inc. v. Dynamic Petroleum Services Inc., 2002 CarswellAlta 1276, 2002 ABQB 894, 6 Alta. L.R. (4th) 248, 27 C.P.C. (5th) 68, 333 A.R. 201 (Alta. Master). Claim sent to Defendant's solicitor. Defendant sought to set aside noted in default on grounds claim not served on Defendant. Under *Rule 16* solicitor must show his or her acceptance to acknowledge agency and must give undertaking. Admission of service not acceptance of service. Service not good service.

Kent v. Conquest Vacations Co., 2005 CarswellOnt 335, [2005] O.J. No. 312, 194 O.A.C. 302 (Ont. Div. Ct.), Lane, J. Conquest argues that Small Claims Court did not have jurisdiction to hear actions because there should have been only one action since contract was for two adults and one child to take a vacation together, "it was not in any way separated by individuals." Issue of breach of Rule 6.02 of the *Rules of the Small Claims Court*, Ontario Regulation 258/98?

Rule 5 of *Rules of the Superior Court*, although not directly applicable to the Small Claims Court, instructive. It provides that two or more plaintiffs, if represented by the same solicitor, "may" join as the plaintiffs in the same proceeding where their claims arise out of the same transaction. The joinder is voluntary. The Kents have not split their case, as prohibited by Rule 6.02. No error in assessment of damages by trial judge. Appeal dismissed with costs.

Van Der Beke v. Halford Estate, 2005 CarswellBC 453, 2005 BCSC 270 (B.C. Master), Master Keighley. Proceedings may be consolidated at any time by order of the court or may be ordered to be tried at the same time or on the same day.

Do common claims disputes and relationships exist between the parties? Are the two actions so interwoven as to make separate trials at different times before different judges undesirable and fraught with problems and expense?

While the Court must concern itself with the possibility of inconsistent findings on identical issues, the chance of that occurring seems relatively slight in this case. Courts unable to find claims are "so interwoven as to make separate trials at different times before different judges undesirable and fraught with problems and economic expense." Application dismissed.

626125 Saskatchewan Ltd. v. Pritchard, 2005 CarswellSask 391, 2005 SKQB 224, 267 Sask. R. 66 (Sask. Q.B.), Hunter J. Plaintiff applied for summary judgment against defendant for $8,500.

Claim for an alleged debt and *other* causes of action.

Rule 129 should not be used to piecemeal the claim and obtain judgment on single issues when there are triable issues in the same proceeding (See the *Queen's Bench Act, 1998*, S.S. 1998, c. Q-1.01, s. 29). The issue of the initial debt should be litigated in the context of all the issues.

Application for summary judgment dismissed.

KNP Headwear Inc. v. Levinson, 2005 CarswellOnt 7346, 205 O.A.C. 291 (Ont. Div. Ct.), Then J. Appeal from judgment of Deputy Judge Bedard wherein Plaintiff awarded $5,248.15 for unpaid invoices and from judgment of Deputy Judge Bedard where Plaintiff awarded $10,000 for unpaid invoices addressed to Millenitex Inc. (Actions #2 and #3). All three related actions heard at same time.

No written demand made on guarantees. Issues raised on appeal are: (i) Was there an improprer splitting of claims in order to remain within monetary jurisdiction of the Small Claims Court; (ii) was the Guarantee enforceable where there was not a prior written demand delivered to Defendant before commencement of actions? Defendant relied on case law interpreting rule 6.02 which characterizes a cause of action as "the factual circumstances which give rise to a right to sue." See *Sahota v. Beauchamp* (1994), 5 W.D.C.P. (2d) 168, [1994] O.J. No. 466, 1994 CarswellOnt 4413 (Ont. Gen. Div.).

Plaintiff relied on decision of Lane J. in *Kent v. Conquest Vacations Co.*, 2005 CarswellOnt 335, [2005] O.J. No. 312, 194 O.A.C. 302 (Ont. Div. Ct.). Lane J. held that each of the Kents had a cause of action against the defendant and were not obliged to sue as joint plaintiffs. Reasoning in *Kent* preferred over that of *Sahota*.

Defendant relied on decision of Russell J. of the Newfoundland Supreme Court in *TSC Shannock Corp. v. Dial-A-Video Ltd.*, 1992 CarswellNfld 284, [1992] N.J. No. 123, 99 Nfld. & P.E.I.R. 326, 315 A.P.R. 326 (Nfld. T.D.). See also *Brown's Estate, Re*, [1893] 2 Ch. 300 (Eng. Ch. Div.), per Chitty J. at pp. 304-5.

That case also held that the issuance of the statement of claim itself could not be construed as a sufficient demand.

A guarantor is entitled to insist upon rigid adherence by the creditor to the terms of the guarantee and a guarantee must be construed strictly.

Appeals allowed. Decision set aside and actions on each of the guarantees dismissed.

Artero v. Huntley, 2005 CarswellOnt 7935 (Ont. S.C.J.), Connolly D.J.

Defendants contended that plaintiffs attempting to bring claim of $20,000 by dividing it into two actions disguised by naming of different defendants. Plaintiffs contended that each claim issued separate cause of action founded, in this case, in negligence, and in other in breach of contract against builder. Claims ordered stayed until plaintiffs elected to either issue amended claim limited to $10,000 or proceed as consolidated action for total claim of $10,000.

Angle v. Minister of National Revenue (1974), [1974] S.C.J. No. 95, 2 N.R. 397, 47 D.L.R. (3d) 544, [1975] 2 S.C.R. 248, 1974 CarswellNat 375F, 28 D.T.C. 6278, 1974 CarswellNat 375 (S.C.C.) considered issue estoppels as compared to "cause of action estoppels."

Defendant's Application to have second Claim dismissed on the basis of *res judicata* established. Claim dismissed.

519080 Alberta Ltd. v. Turtle Mountain Tire & Battery, [2002] A.J. No. 1316, 355 A.R. 14, 2002 CarswellAlta 1312, 2002 ABPC 108 (Alta. Prov. Ct.), Jacobson Prov. J.

Plaintiff commenced three separate actions against defendant respecting unpaid account in attempt to bring itself within jurisdiction of provincial court. Plaintiff not permitted to proceed with three separate actions arising out of one indebtedness. A single cause of action arising out of one factual situation cannot be split to be the subject of several transactions. Best interests of the administration of justice to hear all the evidence, to raise all the issues, and hear all submissions in a single action and trial.

Critch v. Ceda-Reactor Ltd., 883 A.P.R. 281, 72 C.C.E.L. (3d) 222, 286 Nfld. & P.E.I.R. 281, [2009] N.J. No. 78, 69 C.P.C. (6th) 335, 2009 NLTD 41, 2009 CarswellNfld 74 (N.L. T.D.)

Employee lived in Newfoundland and Labrador ("NL") and worked for employer located in Alberta. Employee dismissed. Employee brought action in NL. Employer brought application to stay action on grounds that NL was *forum non conveniens*. Application dismissed. Situs of evidence favoured employee as he had to provide details of employment relationship and had to address decision to dismiss him. Employee would be prejudiced if action stayed as he would have to start action over in Alberta, it would be cost-prohibitive, and it would create access to justice issue. Employer did not establish that NL was *forum non conveniens*.

Ezekiel v. Macaulay, 2009 CarswellBC 3407, 2009 BCPC 372 (B.C. Prov. Ct.), Phillips Prov. J.

Counsel for Defendant filed affidavits in support of application to dismiss plaintiff's second claim on basis matter *res judicata*. See *Cahoon v. Franks* (1967), 63 D.L.R. (2d) 274, 60 W.W.R. 684, 1967 CarswellAlta 48, [1967] S.C.R. 455 (S.C.C.), where the court decided that negligence arising out of a motor-vehicle accident gives one cause of action only against a particular defendant. This single cause of action cannot be split to be made the subject of several causes of action depending on damages claimed. See also *Lehndorff Management Ltd. v. L.R.S. Development Enterprises Ltd.*, 1980 CarswellBC 19, [1980] B.C.J. No. 2, [1980] 5 W.W.R. 14, 19 B.C.L.R. 59, 16 C.P.C. 1, 109 D.L.R. (3d) 729 (B.C. C.A.) (at pages 734-35) [D.L.R.]:

> The maxim *res judicata* . . . also applied not only to points on which the Court in the first action was actually required by the parties to form an opinion and pronounce a judgment, but to every point which properly belonged to the subject of the first litigation and which the parties, exercising reasonable diligence, might have brought forward at the time . . . .

Nicolazzo v. Princess Cruises (2009), 2009 CarswellOnt 3185, 250 O.A.C. 4, (sub nom. *Princess Cruises v. Nicolazzo*) 97 O.R. (3d) 630 (Ont. Div. Ct.), J.A. Ramsay J.

The appellant Princess Cruises appealed order of the Small Claims Court dismissing its motion for summary judgment. Appellant claimed court lacked territorial jurisdiction over the action. The motion judge discovered through his own Internet research that the appellant was owned by another corporation that had places of business in Canada. Appeal allowed. Plain and obvious that appellant had no place of business in Canada. Finding that Princess Cruises was a cruise brand of another corporation was not supported by the evidence.

Patry v. Sudbury Regional Hospital (2009), [2009] O.J. No. 1060, 69 C.P.C. (6th) 385, 2009 CarswellOnt 1462 (Ont. S.C.J.)

Plaintiffs brought two related actions for medical negligence against number of defendants. Actions brought in Newmarket. All five plaintiffs resided in Sudbury area. Defendants brought motion for order transferring actions to Sudbury pursuant to Rules of Civil Procedure. Motion granted. All events that gave rise to actions occurred in Sudbury, all damages sustained in Sudbury. Subject matter of actions located in Sudbury, majority of witnesses located in Sudbury.

Skidmore v. Carleton University (2009), 2009 CarswellOnt 2448, [2009] O.J. No. 1854, 79 C.P.C. (6th) 306 (Ont. S.C.J.), G.R. Strathy J.; affirming (2009), [2009] O.J. No. 2010, 2009 CarswellOnt 2667, 79 C.P.C. (6th) 301 (Ont. Master), Master Graham.

Plaintiff brought action in Toronto against defendant university. Defendant brought unsuccessful motion under R. 13.1.02(2)(b) of Rules of Civil Procedure to transfer action from Toronto to Ottawa. Master found that evidence favoured two possible venues equally and therefore was unable to conclude Ottawa substantially better venue for action, as such defendant did not meet its onus. Defendant appealed. Appeal dismissed.

Van Breda v. Village Resorts Ltd., 2010 ONCA 84, 2010 CarswellOnt 549, [2010] O.J. No. 402, 98 O.R. (3d) 721, 71 C.C.L.T. (3d) 161, 81 C.P.C. (6th) 219, 316 D.L.R. (4th) 201, 77 R.F.L. (6th) 1, 264 O.A.C. 1 (Ont. C.A.); additional reasons at 2010 ONCA 232, 2010 CarswellOnt 1751, [2010] O.J. No. 1220, 81 C.P.C. (6th) 269, 77 R.F.L. (6th) 51, 72 C.C.L.T. (3d) 225 (Ont. C.A.); affirmed 2012 SCC 17, 2012 CarswellOnt 4268, 2012 CarswellOnt 4269, (sub nom. *Club Resorts Ltd. v. Van Breda*) [2012] 1 S.C.R. 572, (sub nom. *Charron Estate v. Village Resorts Ltd.*) 114 O.R. (3d) 79 (note), 91 C.C.L.T. (3d) 1, 17 C.P.C. (7th) 223, 343 D.L.R. (4th) 577, 10 R.F.L. (7th) 1, 429 N.R. 217, 291 O.A.C. 201, [2012] A.C.S. No. 17, [2012] S.C.J. No. 17 (S.C.C.)

Issue when Ontario courts should assume jurisdiction over out-of-province defendants. Claims for personal injury damages as a result of accidents suffered by Canadian tourists at resorts in Cuba. Test for assumed jurisdiction laid down in *"Muscutt* quintet." See *Muscutt v. Courcelles* (2002), 13 C.C.L.T. (3d) 161, 26 C.P.C. (5th) 206, 60 O.R. (3d) 20, 160 O.A.C. 1, 2002 CarswellOnt 1756, [2002] O.J. No. 2128, 213 D.L.R. (4th) 577 (Ont. C.A.); additional reasons at (2002), 13 C.C.L.T. (3d) 238, 26 C.P.C. (5th) 203, 213 D.L.R. (4th) 661, 162 O.A.C. 122, 2002 CarswellOnt 2313 (Ont. C.A.); *Leufkens v. Alba Tours International Inc.* (2002), 13 C.C.L.T. (3d) 217, 26 C.P.C. (5th) 247, 60 O.R. (3d) 84, 160 O.A.C. 43, [2002] O.J. No. 2129, 213 D.L.R. (4th) 614, 2002 CarswellOnt 1811 (Ont. C.A.); additional reasons at (2002), 13 C.C.L.T. (3d) 238, 26 C.P.C. (5th) 203, 213 D.L.R. (4th) 661, 162 O.A.C. 122, 2002 CarswellOnt 2313 (Ont. C.A.); *Lemmex v. Bernard* (2002), 13 C.C.L.T. (3d) 203, 26 C.P.C. (5th) 259, 60 O.R. (3d) 54, 160 O.A.C. 31, [2002] O.J. No. 2131, 213 D.L.R. (4th) 627, 2002 CarswellOnt 1812 (Ont. C.A.); additional reasons at (2002), 13 C.C.L.T. (3d) 238, 26 C.P.C. (5th) 203, 213 D.L.R. (4th) 661, 162 O.A.C. 122, 2002 CarswellOnt 2313 (Ont. C.A.); *Sinclair v. Cracker Barrel Old Country Store Inc.* (2002), 13 C.C.L.T. (3d) 230, 26 C.P.C. (5th) 239, 60 O.R. (3d) 76, 160 O.A.C. 54, 2002 CarswellOnt 1755, [2002] O.J. No. 2127, 213 D.L.R. (4th) 643 (Ont. C.A.); additional reasons at (2002), 13 C.C.L.T. (3d) 238, 26 C.P.C. (5th) 203, 213 D.L.R. (4th) 661, 162 O.A.C. 122, 2002 CarswellOnt 2313 (Ont. C.A.); *Gajraj v. DeBernardo* (2002), 13 C.C.L.T. (3d) 194, 60 O.R. (3d) 68, 160 O.A.C. 60, 2002 CarswellOnt 1766, 24 C.P.C. (5th) 258, 40 C.C.L.I. (3d) 163, 213 D.L.R. (4th) 651, [2002] O.J. No. 2130, 28 M.V.R. (4th) 10 (Ont. C.A.); additional reasons at (2002), 13 C.C.L.T. (3d) 238, 26 C.P.C. (5th) 203, 213 D.L.R. (4th) 661, 162 O.A.C. 122, 2002 CarswellOnt 2313 (Ont. C.A.)

Principles of order and fairness set out by the Supreme Court of Canada in *Hunt v. T & N plc* (1993), [1993] S.C.J. No. 125, (sub nom. *Hunt v. Lac d'Amiante du Québec Ltée)* 161 N.R. 81, 85 B.C.L.R. (2d) 1, (sub nom. *Hunt v. T&N plc)* 109 D.L.R. (4th) 16, (sub nom. *Hunt v. Lac d'Amiante du Québec Ltée)* 60 W.A.C. 161, (sub nom. *Hunt v. Lac d'Amiante du Québec Ltée)* 37 B.C.A.C. 161, 21 C.P.C. (3d) 269, [1994] 1 W.W.R. 129, EYB 1993-68597, (sub nom. *Hunt v. T&N plc)* [1993] 4 S.C.R. 289, 1993 CarswellBC 294, 1993 CarswellBC 1271 (S.C.C.).

Morguard Investments Ltd. v. De Savoye (1990), [1990] S.C.J. No. 135, 1990 CarswellBC 767, 1990 CarswellBC 283, [1990] 3 S.C.R. 1077, 52 B.C.L.R. (2d) 160, [1991] 2 W.W.R. 217, 122 N.R. 81, 76 D.L.R. (4th) 256, 15 R.P.R. (2d) 1, 46 C.P.C. (2d) 1, EYB 1990-67027 (S.C.C.), and *Hunt* laid down common law test for assumed jurisdiction and enforcement of foreign judgements based on the idea of "real and substantial connection" and respect for the principles of "order and fairness." *Muscutt* test should be clarified and reformulated.

Tevonian c. 9134-7849 Québec Inc. (Fringe Coiffure), 2010 QCCQ 11156 (C.Q.)

Two claims based on same cause of action between the same parties acting in the same qualities. Tevonian divided claim of $11,314 into two claims of $7,000 each in order to remain within the jurisdiction of the Small Claims Division. Article 955 of the *Code of Civil Procedure* prevents a claimant from dividing its claim into two distinct proceedings. Court joined the two actions but limited claim to maximum of $7,000.

Atkins v. Joyce, 2010 BCPC 147, 2010 CarswellBC 1867 (B.C. Prov. Ct.)

Two applications heard:

> 3) Application by claimant, Atkins, for an order consolidating action with actions no. 0509789 and 0509790 to the Supreme Court. If consolidation not granted, the claimant sought order for Action No. 0509789 to be transferred to Supreme Court.

> 4) Application by defendants, Joyce and Ishida, for order to enforce settlement agreement reached at pre-trial conference and stay of proceedings.

Was there a concluded settlement to enforce? See *Gerald Walsh Recruitment Services Inc. v. Fraser*, 2002 NSSC 105, 2002 CarswellNS 179, [2002] N.S.J. No. 204 (N.S. S.C.).

See *Radhakrishnan v. University of Calgary Faculty Assn.* (2002), 2002 ABCA 182, 2002 CarswellAlta 943, [2002] A.J. No. 961, 312 A.R. 143, [2003] 1 W.W.R. 244, 5 Alta. L.R. (4th) 1, 215 D.L.R. (4th) 624, 45 Admin. L.R. (3d) 77, 281 W.A.C. 143 (Alta. C.A.)

> 43 Each party to a settlement makes concessions and assumes some risk, in favour of bringing the dispute to an end. Interests of finality prevail, unless there are contractual problems such as fraud, misrepresentation, duress, undue influence, unconscionability, or mutual or unilateral mistake.
>
> 45 The public interest in finality is noticed in *Christiansen v. Bachul* (2001), 284 A.R. 196: "There is a well-established policy in favour of finality of litigation. To accede to this application would undermine that policy." The principle of finality was emphasized where it precluded interference with settlement of even an infant's claim made on incomplete and erroneous fact assumptions: see *Tsaoussis v. Baetz*, 1998 CanLII 5454 (ON C.A.).
>
> 49 Whether or not that is correct, the strong policy of the law is to let parties negotiate their own settlements: *Amoco Can. Petro. Co. v. Propak Systems*, 2001 ABCA 110 (CanLII), 2001 ABCA 110. Absent material inducement by misrepresentation, fraud, duress or undue influence, the courts steadfastly refuse to look at the adequacy of consideration.

Based on sections 2(1) and (2) of the *Small Claims Act* and *Rules* as well as following policy in favour of finality of litigation, application to consolidate three files to the Supreme Court denied as well as the application to transfer Action No. 0509789 to the Supreme Court made by the claimant.

Lock v. Waterloo (Regional Municipality), 2011 CarswellOnt 15974, [2011] O.J. No. 4898 (Ont. Sm. Cl. Ct.)

Discussion of several aspects of the limits of the monetary jurisdiction of the court. Several plaintiffs may sue jointly each claiming up to the monetary limit and are not limited to sharing that limit between them. Plaintiffs may allege and prove damages in excess of the monetary limit but cannot claim and the court cannot award more than that limit. The damages claimed up to the monetary limit may be claimed on a net basis after consideration of any statutory deductible or contributory negligence factors.

Sioux Lookout (Municipality) v. Goodfellow, 2010 ONSC 1812, 2010 CarswellOnt 2349, Mr. Justice D.C. Shaw (Ont. S.C.J.); additional reasons 2010 ONSC 2875, 2010 CarswellOnt 4195, [2010] O.J. No. 2564 (Ont. S.C.J.).

Goodfellow is the plaintiff in 10 actions in the Small Claims Court at Dryden. The Municipality is the sole defendant in 9 of the 10 actions. The Municipality, Stan Nissley, and Perron Contracting 917260 Ont. Inc. are the defendants in one of the 10 actions. All 10 Small Claims Court actions should be transferred to the Superior Court of Justice.

Based on *Vigna v. Toronto Stock Exchange*, 1998 CarswellOnt 4560, 28 C.P.C. (4th) 318, 115 O.A.C. 393, [1998] O.J. No. 4924 (Ont. Div. Ct.), it is within the jurisdiction of the Superior Court of Justice to transfer a matter from the Small Claims Court to the Superior Court of Justice in appropriate circumstances, without the consent of the plaintiff in the Small Claims Court proceeding.

It was inappropriate for Goodfellow to split one cause of action into separate causes of action so that they could proceed in the Small Claims Court. Rule 6.02 of the *Small Claims Court Rules* prohibits a cause of action from being divided into two or more actions for the purpose of bringing it within the court's jurisdiction. All 10 Small Claims Court actions are essentially one cause of action.

Transfer of actions consistent with the policy objective of the *Rules of Civil Procedure* as set out in rule 1.04(1):

> These rules shall be liberally construed to secure the just, most expeditious and least expensive determination of every civil proceeding on its merits.

Rule 6.03(1) of the *Small Claims Court Rules* is to similar effect:

> These rules shall be liberally construed to secure the just, most expeditious and least expensive determination of every proceeding on its merits in accordance with section 25 of the *Courts of Justice Act*.

6.03 [Repealed O. Reg. 78/06, s. 8(2).]

History [R. 6.03]: Formerly 18.01(4).

Rule 7 — Commencement Of Proceedings

7.01 (1) Plaintiff's Claim — **An action shall be commenced by filing a plaintiff's claim (Form 7A) with the clerk, together with a copy of the claim for each defendant.**

History [R. 7.01(1)]: Clarifies that the rule refers to the plaintiff's claim only.

(2) Contents of Claim, Attachments — **The following requirements apply to the claim:**

> **1. It shall contain the following information, in concise and non-technical language:**
>
> > **i. The full names of the parties to the proceeding and, if relevant, the capacity in which they sue or are sued.**
> >
> > **ii. The nature of the claim, with reasonable certainty and detail, including the date, place and nature of the occurences on which the claim is based.**
> >
> > **iii. The amount of the claim and the relief requested.**
> >
> > **iv. The name, address, telephone number, fax number if any, and Law Society of Upper Canada registration number if any, of the representative representing the plaintiff or, if the plaintiff is self-represented, the plaintiff's address, telephone number and fax number if any.**
> >
> > **v. The address where the plaintiff believes the defendant may be served.**
>
> **2. If the plaintiff's claim is based in whole or in part on a document, a copy of the document shall be attached to each copy of the claim, unless it is unavailable, in which case the claim shall state the reason why the document is not attached.**

History [R. 7.01(2)]: Fax numbers required; plain language changes.

Commentary: A claim cannot be divided into two or more actions for the purpose of bringing it within the court's jurisdiction [r. 6.02]. A claim in excess of $25,000 can be reduced to comply with the monetary jurisdiction of the court.

If a claim exceeds $25,000, the party may be advised that the claim exceeds the prescribed monetary limit of the court.

Where a plaintiff files more than one claim against the same defendant, the total of which exceeds the monetary jurisdiction of the Small Claims Court, while default will be noted against a defendant who fails to file a Defence (Form 9A), default judgment will NOT be entered. The claims should both be placed on a trial list before a judge for adjudication.

Where a party makes a claim in a foreign currency (e.g. U.S. dollars), conversion of the amount to Canadian dollars takes place when the enforcement and execution of a judgment takes place.

A liquidates claim is a claim for a sum of money due under an express agreement where the amount is fixed and does not depend on any subsequent evaluation by the court. Examples of liquidated claims are as follows:

- unpaid accounts for goods or services sold and delivered;

- unpaid loans;

- unpaid rent;

- NSF cheques.

A claim dealing with solicitors' accountsfor fees is a liquidated claim if the following criteria are met:

- the demand must be based upon only the claim itself and other material appended to the claim, which should, as a general rule, include the legal account;

- the claim and/or appended material must indicate that:

  - the solicitor was retained;

  - the legal account is capable of mathematical calculation based upon an hourly rate and number of hours worked; and

  - an hourly fee was agreed upon in advance;

  OR

  - the legal account is a fixed amount or fixed estimated amount and that the amount was agreed upon in advance.

In determining whether or not the claim is liquidated, it is not relevant whether the defendant has paid part of the solicitor's account, has not filed a defence, or has not applied for an assessment under the *Solicitor's Act*.

An unliquidated claim is a claim where the amount in dispute is not fixed and the court must determine the amount that the plaintiff is entitled to receive. Examples of unliquidated claims (i.e., damages) are as follows:

- property damage;

- clothes damaged by a dry cleaner;

- personal injuries;

- breach of contract (written or verbal).

See also Rule 11.03 dealing with Default Judgment. Frequent claimant fees are set by regulation under the *Administration of Justice Act*.

A frequent claimant is a party (not the claimant's agent) who issues ten or more plaintiff's claims per calendar year in the same Small Claims Court location. Once a claimant has issued the tenth claim, that claimant becomes a frequent claimant in that court location and is required to pay the frequent claimant rate for all subsequent steps in all actions where a frequent claimant rate applies, whether or not a frequent claimant rate was paid when the action was commenced.

Proceedings initiated in a Small Claims Court office for enforcement do not count towards determining frequent/infrequent status of that claimant.

The *Rules of the Small Claims Court* do not limit the time period within which a claim may be issued. Issues relating to limitations periods are legal matters to be determined by the courts.

Plaintiff's Claim

There are some cases where both the company and the proprietor of the company would be defendants. These are cases where the proprietor has something to do with the case, beyond just being the proprietor of the company.

For information on how to search a corporation or registered business name, there is the Companies Helpline at the Ministry of Government Services, Companies and Personal Property Security Branch. There is a fee for the search and the search will not be conducted over the phone. The Helpline can be reached at (416) 314-8880 or toll-free in Ontario at 1-800-361-3223. If the business you are suing is not incorporated (for example, a sole proprietorship or partnership), you will need the correct name of the business and the address for service. You may also wish to name the proprietor(s) or partner(s) as parties if you wish to obtain a judgment against them as well.

You can use "c.o.b." as a short form for "carrying on business" if you wish.

Case Law: *2066209 Ontario Inc. v. Tannis*, 2012 ONSC 6665, 2012 CarswellOnt 14837, 299 O.A.C. 190 (Ont. Div. Ct.); additional reasons 2013 ONSC 97, 2013 CarswellOnt 1262 (Ont. Div. Ct.)

A judgment was set aside as against the director of a corporation where no basis for personal liability was presented through the pleadings and the evidence.

Zanzibar Tavern Inc. v. Nikolakis, 2013 ONSC 4896, 2013 CarswellOnt 11054, [2013] O.J. No. 3516 (Ont. Div. Ct.)

At trial, judgment was granted against the director but not the corporation, on the basis that because the corporation was dissolved he was the only "viable defendant". On appeal that decision was reversed and judgment granted against the corporation only. An action can be maintained against a dissolved corporation. There was no evidence the director was personally a party to the contract in question.

Versailles Convention Centre Inc. v. Gilmour, 2013 ONCA 674, 2013 CarswellOnt 15223, 312 O.A.C. 394 (Ont. C.A.)

Appeal of dismissal of application for assessment of the accounts of the respondent, Gilmour, a lawyer. The *Limitations Act* does *not* apply to the review of a solicitor's account. In *Guillemette v. Doucet*, 2007 ONCA 743, 2007 CarswellOnt 7034, 88 O.R. (3d) 90, 48 C.P.C. (6th) 17, (sub nom. *Doucet v. Guillemette*) 287 D.L.R. (4th) 522, 230 O.A.C. 202, [2007] O.J. No. 4172 (Ont. C.A.) at paras. 35-36, this court found: No absolute time bar against Application for the assessment of lawyers' accounts . . . Time alone will not . . . preclude the examination of the suitability of a lawyer's accounts where other circumstances compel a review of those accounts." Appeal allowed. Appellants' request for the assessment of the accounts of Gilmour dated January 25, 2010, February 22, 2010, and April 1, 2010 granted with direction to the assessment officer, to determine what amount should have been properly paid to Gilmour under the terms of paragraph 43 of the supervision order.

Wakeford v. Canada (Attorney General) (2001), 156 O.A.C. 385, 2001 CarswellOnt 4368 (Ont. C.A.); leave to appeal refused (2002), 2002 CarswellOnt 1097, 2002 CarswellOnt 1098, 300 N.R. 197 (note), 169 O.A.C. 196 (note) (S.C.C.) — Constitutionality of assisted suicide prohibition. Defendant brought motion to strike out statements of claim, as there was Supreme Court case law squarely on point. Appeal dismissed.

Hughes v. Sunbeam Corp. (Canada) Ltd. (2000), 2 C.P.C. (5th) 335, 2000 CarswellOnt 4614, [2000] O.J. No. 4595, 11 B.L.R. (3d) 236 (Ont. S.C.J.) — Defendants brought motion to strike out statement of claim as disclosing no reasonable cause of action. Motion granted.

Statement of claim contained insufficient facts as to any alleged misrepresentations. Statement of claim did not allege existence of special relationship giving rise to duty of care with respect to any representations made.

Sable Offshore Energy Inc. v. Bingley, 2003 NSSC 20, 2003 CarswellNS 46, 211 N.S.R. (2d) 15, 662 A.P.R. 15, [2003] N.S.J. No. 33 (N.S. S.C.) — Rehearing granted before new adjudicator. Nova Scotia Civil Procedure Rule 21 states that for admissions to be made, must be made in writing to court. They cannot be implied. Rule 14.14(a) states that a defendant must specifically admit every fact not contested by the defendant and those not admitted shall be deemed to be denied. This is in contrast to provincial jurisdictions, such as Ontario, where facts not denied may be deemed to be admitted. Proceeding in Small Claims Court has air of informality. Pleadings not required to be as detailed in a court of record in order to allow parties to proceed unrepresented. Duty owed by Adjudicator to examine pleadings and determine whether a cause of action exists. See *Oasis Motor Home Rentals Ltd. v. Thomas*, [2001] N.S.J. No. 112, 2001 CarswellNS 113, 2001 NSSC 45 (N.S. S.C.), Gruchy J. As parties are often unrepresented and untrained in the law, pleadings might not properly describe the appropriate cause of action. Liberal approach ought to be taken to pleadings that are presented to ensure that access to proper adjudication of claims not prevented on a technicality. A Small Claims judge has a duty, on being presented with facts that fall broadly within the umbrella of the circumstances described in the claim, to determine whether those facts constitute a cause of action known to the law.

Bakaluk v. McGregor, 2003 SKQB 386, 2003 CarswellSask 689, 46 C.P.C. (5th) 69, 45 M.V.R. (4th) 96, 239 Sask. R. 185 (Sask. Q.B.). A judge may refuse to issue a summons if judge considers it is not in the interest of one or more of the parties to proceed with the claim pursuant to *The Small Claims Act*, 1997. Where a judge refuses to issue a summons, that refusal does not prevent a Plaintiff from proceeding in the Court of Queen's Bench or in any other manner authorized by law.

Cotton v. Cotton, 2004 CarswellOnt 793 (Ont. S.C.J.), J.D. Searle, Deputy Judge. Plaintiff an undischarged bankrupt. Plaintiff has no status or authority to maintain proceeding, see s. 71(2) of the *Bankruptcy and Insolvency Act*, R.S.C. 1985, c. B-3 (as renamed by 1992, c. 27); *Hall-Chem Inc. v. Vulcan Packaging Inc.*, 1994 CarswellOnt 309, 28 C.B.R. (3d) 161, 75 O.A.C. 74, 120 D.L.R. (4th) 552, 21 O.R. (3d) 89, 33 C.P.C. (3d) 361 (Ont. C.A.); *Sier Bath Deck Gear Corp. v. Polymotion Ltd.* (1996), 30 O.R. (3d) 736, 1996 CarswellOnt 3873, 42 C.B.R. (3d) 1, 15 O.T.C. 323 (Ont. Gen. Div.). See also Rule 11 of the *Rules of Civil Procedure*.

McNutt v. Canada (Attorney General), 2004 CarswellBC 1905, 2004 BCSC 1113 (B.C. S.C.), Allen, Madam Justice. Defendant Maley applied for Order pursuant to Rule 19(24), striking plaintiff's Further Amended Statement of Claim and dismissing the claims against her. Test for striking pleadings for failing to disclose a cause of action is whether it is "plain and obvious" that the claim is bound to fail. Facts in pleading are assumed to be true and no evidence is permissible on such an application. The fact that claim is novel or difficult one is not sufficient ground to strike the claim: *Hunt v. T & N plc*, 1990 CarswellBC 759, 1990 CarswellBC 216, (sub nom. *Hunt v. Carey Canada Inc.*) [1990] S.C.J. No. 93, 4 C.C.L.T. (2d) 1, 43 C.P.C. (2d) 105, 117 N.R. 321, 4 C.O.H.S.C. 173 (headnote only), (sub nom. *Hunt v. Carey Canada Inc.*) [1990] 6 W.W.R. 385, 49 B.C.L.R. (2d) 273, (sub nom. *Hunt v. Carey Canada Inc.*) 74 D.L.R. (4th) 321, [1990] 2 S.C.R. 959 (S.C.C.).

Amended statement of claim not a model of linguistic perfection, but adequately sets out elements of torts of abuse of public office and conspiracy. See *Folland v. Ontario*, 2003 CarswellOnt 1087, [2003] O.J. No. 1048, 104 C.R.R. (2d) 244, 17 C.C.L.T. (3d) 271, 170 O.A.C. 17, 225 D.L.R. (4th) 50, 64 O.R. (3d) 89 (Ont. C.A.); leave to appeal to S.C.C. refused [2003] S.C.C.A. No. 249, 2003 CarswellOnt 3811, 2003 CarswellOnt 3812, 325 N.R. 391 (note), 194 O.A.C. 200 (note) (S.C.C.). Inappropriate to strike out claims at that stage of the proceedings. A pleading is embarrassing if it does not state the real issue in an intelligible form. Plaintiff's particulars sufficient.

Trizec Properties Inc. v. Citygroup Markets Inc., 2004 CanLII 1548 (Ont. S.C.J.), Carnwath, J. Defendants move to strike the pleadings that allege negligence and breach of the *Competition Act*, as disclosing no reasonable cause of action.

Test to be applied on a Rule 21.01(1)(b) Motion to Strike?

As in England, if there is a change plaintiff might succeed, then plaintiff should *not* be "driven from the judgment seat." Neither length and complexity of the issues, novelty of cause of action, nor potential for defendant to present a strong defence should prevent plaintiff from proceeding with his or her case. See *Haskett v. Trans Union of Canada Inc.*, 2003 CarswellOnt 692, [2003] O.J. No. 771, 169 O.A.C. 201, 224 D.L.R. (4th) 419, 15 C.C.L.T. (3d) 194, 63 O.R. (3d) 577 (Ont. C.A.) But see *Kripps v. Touche Ross & Co.*, 1992 CarswellBC 191, 69 B.C.L.R. (2d) 62, 94 D.L.R. (4th) 284, 15 B.C.A.C. 184, 27 W.A.C. 184, [1992] B.C.J. No. 1550 at p. 5 (B.C. C.A.); leave to appeal dismissed (1993), 78 B.C.L.R. (2d) xxxiv, [1993] 2 S.C.R. viii (note), 101 D.L.R. (4th) vii (note) (S.C.C.).

Paragraphs 58-51 inclusive and paragraphs 54-61, inclusive, struck from Fresh as Amended Statement of Claim.

S. 46 of the *Small Claims Act*, 1997, provides a mechanism whereby a party may extend the time limitation for claims arising out of a motor vehicle accident for one year where the person files a notice in the prescribed manner before the expiry of any limitation period and serves the notice on the proposed defendant. The process of commencing an action under the *Small Claims Act*, 1997, is different from the procedure in the Court of Queen's Bench.

Watt v. Beallor Beallor Burns Inc., 2004 CarswellOnt 429, 1 C.B.R. (5th) 141 (Ont. S.C.J.), Farley J.

Plaintiff brought action against law firm of which he was member prior to disbarment. Defendant brought motion to strike out statement of claim. Motion granted.

Hunt v. T & N plc, 1990 CarswellBC 759, 1990 CarswellBC 216, (sub nom. *Hunt v. Carey Canada Inc.*) [1990] S.C.J. No. 93, 4 C.C.L.T. (2d) 1, 43 C.P.C. (2d) 105, 117 N.R. 321, 4 C.O.H.S.C. 173 (headnote only), (sub nom. *Hunt v. Carey Canada Inc.*) [1990] 6 W.W.R. 385, 49 B.C.L.R. (2d) 273, (sub nom. *Hunt v. Carey Canada Inc.*) 74 D.L.R. (4th) 321, [1990] 2 S.C.R. 959 (S.C.C.) provides that Court must assume facts as stated in the pleading can be proven, unless they are patently ridiculous or incapable of proof. The test is whether it is plain and obvious or beyond a reasonable doubt that the Statement of Claim discloses no reasonable cause of action.

Pleadings do not come close to adhering to the standard required under the Rules. See *Balanyk v. University of Toronto*, 1999 CarswellOnt 1786, [1999] O.J. No. 2162, 1 C.P.R. (4th) 300 (Ont. S.C.J.); *National Trust Co. v. Furbacher*, [1994] O.J. No. 2385 (Ont. Gen. Div. [Commercial List]).

An abuse of process exists if issues raised in action are *res judicata*: See *Danyluk v. Ainsworth Technologies Inc.*, REJB 2001-25003, 2001 CarswellOnt 2434, 2001 CarswellOnt 2435, [2001] S.C.J. No. 46, 2001 SCC 44, 54 O.R. (3d) 214 (headnote only), 201 D.L.R. (4th) 193, 10 C.C.E.L. (3d) 1, 7 C.P.C. (5th) 199, 272 N.R. 1, 149 O.A.C. 1, 2001 C.L.L.C. 210-033, 34 Admin. L.R. (3d) 163, [2001] 2 S.C.R. 460 (S.C.C.).

The court has power to dismiss action if plaintiff engaging in abuse of process of the court. See *Pizza Pizza Ltd. v. Toronto Star Newspapers Ltd.*, 2002 CarswellOnt 163, [2002] O.J. No. 184 (Ont. S.C.J.); leave to appeal refused 2002 CarswellOnt 1615, [2002] O.J. No. 1858 (Ont. Div. Ct.); *Toronto (City) v. C.U.P.E., Local 79*, REJB 2003-49439, 2003 CarswellOnt 4328, 2003 CarswellOnt 4329, [2003] S.C.J. No. 64, 2003 SCC 63, 2003 C.L.L.C. 220-071,

232 D.L.R. (4th) 385, 31 C.C.E.L. (3d) 216, 9 Admin. L.R. (4th) 161, 311 N.R. 201, 120 L.A.C. (4th) 225, 179 O.A.C. 291, [2003] 3 S.C.R. 77, 17 C.R. (6th) 276 (S.C.C.).

Milano Computer Systems Inc. o/a Milano Systems v. 1450676 Ontario Inc. o/a Tresses aka MT Investments (November 7, 2006) (Ont. Small Cl. Ct.), Pamela A. Thomson J.

Motion to dismiss claim.

Plaintiff discovered that "MT Investments" was a limited company called "MT Investments Inc." Action taken by plaintiff against "MT Investments Inc. operating as Tresses," default judgment issued in 2003.

When the sheriff went to execute on judgment it was discovered that vendor's permit was in the name of "1450676 Ontario Inc. operating as Tresses." This was improper because the business name was not registered to that corporation.

Who is to be the defendant must be decided before action, not after judgment

Claim dismissed on basis set out in the following cases: *Westar Aluminum & Glass Ltd. v. Brenner*, 1993 CarswellOnt 415, [1993] O.J. No. 699, 17 C.P.C. (3d) 228 (Ont. Gen. Div.); *CFGM 1320 Radio Broadcasting Ltd. v. Doyle*, 1987 CarswellOnt 406, [1987] O.J. No. 1430, 17 C.P.C. (2d) 65 (Ont. Dist. Ct.); *CPU Options Inc. v. Milton*, 2006 CarswellOnt 341, [2006] O.J. No. 253, 79 O.R. (3d) 365 (Ont. S.C.J.); *Esprit de Corp (1980) Ltd. v. Papadimitriou*, 1995 CarswellOnt 854, 23 O.R. (3d) 733 (Ont. Gen. Div.).

Searchlight Systems Ltd. v. Liu, 2006 CarswellBC 499, 2006 BCSC 349, 27 C.P.C. (6th) 157 (B.C. S.C.), Ehrcke J.

Plaintiff suing by writ only. Defendant applying to strike claim. Application allowed. Writ not giving a concise statement of the nature of the claim and relief required. Plaintiff only able to say that it is investigating claim. Purpose of writ to notify plaintiff of claim and not that a claim might be brought against it.

McInnes Cooper v. Canus Fisheries Ltd., 2006 CarswellNS 190, 27 C.P.C. (6th) 397, 2006 NSSM 9 (N.S. Sm. Cl. Ct.).

Cause of action for purposes of legal accounts S. 41 of *Judicature Act* did not arise until accounts were assessed and certified as reasonable since law firm's accounts subject to independent review by court. Law firm estopped from asserting any claim for interest including claim under *Judicature Act* prior to date of certification because it failed to advise client at beginning of retainer that it would make claim on outstanding accounts.

Young v. Borzoni, 2007 CarswellBC 119, [2007] B.C.J. No. 105, 2007 BCCA 16, 388 W.A.C. 220, 277 D.L.R. (4th) 685, 235 B.C.A.C. 220, 64 B.C.L.R. (4th) 157 (B.C. C.A.).

Judge entitled in circumstances to subject allegations to sceptical analysis. Allegations based on speculation and assumptions and incapable of proof. Statement of claim failed to plead necessary material facts to ground claims. Plaintiffs did not plead facts establishing solicitor owed duty of care or visible and provable illness caused by actions.

Shaughnessy v. Roth, 2006 CarswellBC 2963, 61 B.C.L.R. (4th) 268, 2006 BCCA 547, 386 W.A.C. 212, 233 B.C.A.C. 212 (B.C. C.A.).

A union organizer sued a floor-layer in Small Claims Court. The floor-layer applied to have both the claim and counterclaim transferred to the Supreme Court citing the existence of a related lawsuit that had been commenced by him in Supreme Court. The British Columbia Provincial Court allowed the application and transferred the claim and counterclaim to the Supreme Court. The union organizer applied for judicial review.

The chambers judge held that Provincial Court judge lacked jurisdiction to make order transferring union organizer's claim to the Supreme Court and therefore the standard of correctness applied to the review of that statutory power of decision. The chambers judge held that the word "claim" in the *Small Claims Act* had to be applied separately to a claim and a counterclaim (i.e., each had to be considered in the context of the Provincial Court's monetary jurisdiction and the Provincial Court judge appeared to have considered them cumulatively). The British Columbia Court of Appeal dismissed the appeal.

Section 3 of the *Small Claims Act* provided that the Provincial Court had jurisdiction if the amount claimed was equal to or less than $10,000 (now $25,000). Rule 7.1 of the *Small Claims Rules* provided that the court must transfer a claim to the Supreme Court if the court was satisfied that "the monetary outcome of a claim may exceed $25,000." The British Columbia Court of Appeal discussed the meaning of the word "claim" as used in r. 7.1.

Solomon v. Education Fund Services Inc., 2006 CarswellOnt 7579, [2006] O.J. No. 4773, 26 C.B.R. (5th) 266, 56 C.C.E.L. (3d) 296 (Ont. S.C.J.), Lederman J.; leave to appeal refused (2007), 2007 CarswellOnt 8395 (Ont. S.C.J.).

In 1997, plaintiff commenced action against employer and personal defendants. Plaintiff had not disclosed claims to trustee. Defendants brought motion to dismiss action as nullity. Motion granted. Plaintiff did not have authority or legal capacity to commence or continue action. Claims vested in trustee. Once property vests in trustee, it does not revert back to bankrupt on discharge. Limitation period had passed and any transfer of claims by trustee to plaintiff would not revive action.

Podgornaja v. Maccione (2007), 2007 CarswellOnt 2896 (Ont. S.C.J.); leave to appeal refused (2007), 2007 CarswellOnt 8395 (Ont. S.C.J.).

Striking out claim for absences of reasonable cause of action. General principles.

D. (B.) v. Children's Aid Society of Halton (Region), 2007 CarswellOnt 4789, 2007 CarswellOnt 4790, (sub nom. *Syl Apps Secure Treatment Centre v. D. (B.)*) [2007] S.C.J. No. 38, 39 R.F.L. (6th) 245, 49 C.C.L.T. (3d) 1, 284 D.L.R. (4th) 682, 2007 SCC 38, 365 N.R. 302, 227 O.A.C. 161, (sub nom. *Syl Apps Secure Treatment Centre v. D. (B.)*) [2007] 3 S.C.R. 83, 86 O.R. (3d) 720 (note) (S.C.C.).

Striking out of claim absence of reasonable cause of action. *Child and Family Services Act* ("Act") gives primacy to child's best interests, not those of family. Nothing in Act detracted from Act's overall emphasis on protection and promotion of child's best interests. No legal duty of care was owed by STC and social worker to parents, no reasonable cause of action against them disclosed in statement of claim.

Allen v. Thorne, 2007 CarswellNS 324, [2007] N.S.J. No. 310, 2007 NSSM 31 (N.S. Sm. Cl. Ct.), D.T.R. Parker Adjud.

Matter heard in the Small Claims Court at Truro, Nova Scotia, on February 26, 2007, and May 14, 2007.

No specific pleading that there was a fraudulent or negligent misrepresentation. Within context of the Supreme Court of Nova Scotia claimant not able to proceed successfully without specifically pleading allegations. However, Small Claims Court not bound by these restrictions. See, e.g., *Popular Shoe Store Ltd. v. Simoni*, 1998 CarswellNfld 48, [1998] N.J. No. 57, 163 Nfld. & P.E.I.R. 100, 503 A.P.R. 100, 24 C.P.C. (4th) 10 (Nfld. C.A.), per Justice Green of the Newfoundland Court of Appeal.

A Small Claims Court judge has a duty, on being presented with facts that fall broadly within the umbrella of the circumstances described in claim, to determine whether those facts constitute a cause of action known to the law, regardless of whether claimant, as a matter of pleading, has asserted that or any other particular cause of action. Subject to considerations of fairness and surprise to the other side, if cause of action established, appropriate remedy, within the subject-matter jurisdiction of court, ought to be granted. See also *Touche Ross Ltd. v. McCardle*, 1987 CarswellPEI 81, [1987] P.E.I.J. No. 90, 66 Nfld. & P.E.I.R. 257, 204 A.P.R. 257 (P.E.I. S.C.), McQuaid J.

Open to party to apply to amend pleadings throughout a proceeding. Here the plaintiff did not apply to amend her pleadings even though issue was raised on a number of occasions. Claim based on facts therefore dismissed.

Elguindy v. Koren (2008), [2008] O.J. No. 764, 2008 CarswellOnt 1081 (Ont. S.C.J.), M.G.J. Quigley J.

Motion by defendants striking pleadings of plaintiffs owing to their failure to deliver particulars as demanded by the defendants, or alternatively, an order requiring that particulars be delivered within a short specified time period.

Defendants asked court to strike plaintiffs' pleadings as an abuse of process, and as a scandalous, frivolous and vexatious claim which reveals no cause of action. See *Currie v. Halton Regional Police Services Board* (2003), 179 O.A.C. 67, 2003 CarswellOnt 4674, [2003] O.J. No. 4516, 233 D.L.R. (4th) 657 (Ont. C.A.). Referring to *Black's Law Dictionary*, Armstrong J.A. noted that "frivolous" means lacking a legal basis or legal merit. It refers to something that is not serious or not reasonably purposeful. "Vexatious" is a word similar but not identical in meaning. In *Foy v. Foy (No. 2)*, 1979 CarswellOnt 458, [1979] O.J. No. 4386, 26 O.R. (2d) 220, 12 C.P.C. 188, 102 D.L.R. (3d) 342 (Ont. C.A.) at page 226 (O.R.), Chief Justice Howland considered the meaning of "vexatious" under the *Vexatious Proceedings Act*, R.S.O. 1970, c. 481.

In *Canam Enterprises Inc. v. Coles*, 2000 CarswellOnt 4739, [2000] O.J. No. 4607, 139 O.A.C. 1, 5 C.P.C. (5th) 218, 51 O.R. (3d) 481, 194 D.L.R. (4th) 648 (Ont. C.A.); reversed on other grounds [2002] S.C.J. No. 64, 2002 CarswellOnt 3261, 2002 CarswellOnt 3262, REJB 2002-34843, 167 O.A.C. 1, 24 C.P.C. (5th) 1, 61 O.R. (3d) 416 (note), [2002] 3 S.C.R. 307, 2002 SCC 63, 220 D.L.R. (4th) 466, 296 N.R. 257 (S.C.C.), at paragraph 31, Finlayson J.A. stated that apart from the power given to the court under Rule 21.01 to strike pleadings, the court can still utilize the broader doctrine of abuse of process.

Gross miscarriage of justice to require defendants continue to incur costs. See *Warren Industrial Feldspar Co. v. Union Carbide Canada Ltd.*, 1986 CarswellOnt 552, [1986] O.J. No. 2364, 8 C.P.C. (2d) 1, 54 O.R. (2d) 213 (Ont. H.C.) per Trainor J. and *Hallum v. Canadian Memorial Chiropractic College*, [1989] O.J. No. 1399, 1989 CarswellOnt 896, 70 O.R. (2d) 119 (Ont. H.C.). Such a miscarriage of justice cannot be permitted to continue. The plaintiff's Statement of Claim shall be struck and the action permanently stayed.

Order striking claim of plaintiffs.

Seeliger v. Eagle Ridge Hospital, 2007 CarswellBC 2815, 74 B.C.L.R. (4th) 229, 50 C.P.C. (6th) 119, 2007 BCCA 582, 248 B.C.A.C. 297, 412 W.A.C. 297 (B.C. C.A.)

Plaintiff appealed the dismissal of his application to renew a writ of summons. The application to renew came to the appellant's solicitor's attention within 8 days of its expiry and the application to renew was brought promptly. Appeal allowed. The relevant period was so short that it could not have reasonably have prejudiced the respondents. The chambers judge erred when he considered the period before the writ expired as relevant to delay and his decision was flawed on that ground.

Alexis v. Darnley, 2009 CarswellOnt 7518, 2009 ONCA 847, 79 C.P.C. (6th) 10, 259 O.A.C. 148, [2009] O.J. No. 5170, 100 O.R. (3d) 232 (Ont. C.A.); leave to appeal refused 407 N.R. 397 (note), 2010 CarswellOnt 2638, 2010 CarswellOnt 2637, 271 O.A.C. 399 (note) (S.C.C.)

The plaintiff sent an email to the Premier of Ontario in October 2005 in which she expressed suicidal thoughts. Police officers forced their way into her home. In March 2008, the plaintiff sued, claiming damages under s. 24(1) of the *Canadian Charter of Rights and Freedoms*. The defendants brought a motion to dismiss the claim as statute-barred by the two-year limitation period in the *Limitations Act*. Motion granted. With respect to establishing liability for a constitutional tort and obtaining relief under s. 24(1) of the *Charter*, there must be proof of wilfulness or *male fides* in the creation of a risk or course of conduct that leads to damages. Proof of simple negligence is not sufficient for an award in damages in an action under the *Charter*. See *McGillivary v. New Brunswick* (1994), [1994] N.B.J. No. 265, 1994 CarswellNB 343, 116 D.L.R. (4th) 104, 92 C.C.C. (3d) 187, 149 N.B.R. (2d) 311, 381 A.P.R. 311 (N.B. C.A.); leave to appeal refused (1995), [1994] S.C.C.A. No. 408, 120 D.L.R. (4th) vii (note), 95 C.C.C. (3d) vi (note), 188 N.R. 319 (note), 164 N.B.R. (2d) 317 (note), 421 A.P.R. 317 (note) (S.C.C.).

TD Financing Services Inc. v. McInnis, 2012 NSSC 52, 2012 CarswellNS 59, 313 N.S.R. (2d) 89, 100 B.L.R. (4th) 157, 25 C.P.C. (7th) 188, 990 A.P.R. 89, [2012] N.S.J. No. 60 (N.S. S.C.)

There was an appeal, pursuant to section 32(1) of the *Small Claims Court Act*, RSNS 1989, c. 430, of an order or determination made by an adjudicator of the Small Claims Court, who determined that the appellant was not an "original party" to the contract and dismissed its claim on the basis of section 5(1) of the *Small Claims Court Act*. The appeal was allowed.

The proper definition of "original party" in section 5(1) of the *Small Claims Court Act* is a question of statutory interpretation, which is a question of law, reviewable on the correctness standard (*Royal & Sun Alliance v. Baltzer* (2009), 2009 NSCA 110, 2009 CarswellNS 592, 283 N.S.R. (2d) 344, [2010] I.L.R. I-4902 at para. 12 (N.S. C.A.)). The question of whether the appellant met the definition of "original party" is a question of mixed fact and law, normally reviewable on the more deferential palpable and overriding standard (*McPhee v. Gwynne-Timothy*, 2005 NSCA 80, 2005 CarswellNS 191, [2005] N.S.J. No. 170, 232 N.S.R. (2d) 175, 737 A.P.R. 175, 44 C.L.R. (3d) 32 at para. 33 (N.S. C.A.)). Rule qualified in *R. v. W. (R.E.)*, 2011 NSCA 18, 2011 CarswellNS 96, [2011] N.S.J. No. 81, 298 N.S.R. (2d) 154, 945 A.P.R. 154, 268 C.C.C. (3d) 557, 230 C.R.R. (2d) 266 (N.S. C.A.) where the court said:

> However, if a trial judge, in the course of making findings of fact or mixed law and fact, seriously misapprehends important evidence or ignores relevant evidence, deference evaporates since these kinds of errors are errors of law on their own, although they frequently underlie findings that are found to be errors that are palpable and overriding.

A corporate "name is merely a means of identification and a change of name does not affect the identity of the company nor its continued existence as the original body corporate" (*Alliance Securities Ltd. v. Posnekoff*, 1922 CarswellSask 227, 16 Sask. L.R. 214, [1922] 3 W.W.R. 1201 at para. 2 (Sask. K.B.)). Just as changing a human person's family name has no bearing on that person's debt obligations or assets, so too does changing a corporate person's name have no bearing on the corporation's legal obligations or entitlements (*Provincial Insurance Co. v. Cameron*, 1881 CarswellOnt 146, 31 U.C.C.P. 523 (Ont. C.P.); affirmed (1883), 9 O.A.R. 56 (Ont. C.A.)).

"Original" modifies "parties." If the Legislature were only concerned with barring debts assigned to collections agencies or subrogated tort claims by insurance companies, it would have been unnecessary to add the word "original."

Britton v. Manitoba (2011), 2011 MBCA 77, 2011 CarswellMan 476, [2012] 1 W.W.R. 421, 87 C.C.L.T. (3d) 104, 21 C.P.C. (7th) 321, 2011 C.E.B. & P.G.R. 8457, 270 Man. R. (2d) 43, 524 W.A.C. 43, 341 D.L.R. (4th) 448 at para. 35 (Man. C.A.), Hamilton J.A.

A cause of action is a "set of facts that provides the basis for an action in court" (see *Markevich v. Canada*, 2003 SCC 9, 2003 CarswellNat 446, 2003 CarswellNat 447, REJB 2003-38213, [2003] S.C.J. No. 8, [2003] 1 S.C.R. 94, (sub nom. *Markevich v. Minister of National Revenue*) 239 F.T.R. 159 (note), 223 D.L.R. (4th) 17, [2003] 2 C.T.C. 83, (sub nom. *Markevich v. Minister of National Revenue*) 300 N.R. 321, (sub nom. *R. v. Markevich*) 2003 D.T.C. 5185 at para. 27 (S.C.C.)). A claim for punitive damages does not, in and of itself, determine whether the claim is an independent cause of action, as was expressed in *J-Sons Inc. v. N.M. Paterson & Sons Ltd.* (2009), 2009 MBQB 263, 2009 CarswellMan 493,

246 Man. R. (2d) 176, 85 C.L.R. (3d) 126, [2010] 5 W.W.R. 750 at para. 49 (Man. Q.B.); affirmed 2010 MBCA 67, 2010 CarswellMan 297, [2010] 9 W.W.R. 52, 255 Man. R. (2d) 149, 486 W.A.C. 149, 91 C.L.R. (3d) 1 (Man. C.A.) and relied on by Manitoba.

Green v. Canada (Attorney General), 2011 ONSC 4778, 2011 CarswellOnt 8299, 91 C.C.P.B. 126 at para. 17 (Ont. S.C.J.), Kane J.; additional reasons at 2011 ONSC 5750, 2011 CarswellOnt 10573, 93 C.C.P.B. 149 (Ont. S.C.J.).

It is not reasonable to interpret a "cause of action" under Rule 21.01(1)(b) [of the *Rules of Civil Procedure*, R.R.O. 1990, Reg. 194] as excluding an action which seeks a declaration only. To do so interprets a rule of procedure as defeating a right granted to parties under section 97 of the *Courts of Justice Act* [R.S.O. 1990, c. C.43].

Capital One Bank v. Wright, 2013 ONSC 5440, 313 ONSC 5440, 2013 CarswellOnt 12424, (sub nom. *Capital One Bank v. Toogood)* 313 O.A.C. 49, [2013] O.J. No. 4023, Edwards, J. (Ont. Div. Ct.)

At issue on appeal was whether deputy judge erred in ruling that a claim for a credit card debt, set out on an invoice and owing pursuant to a written credit card agreement, was not a liquidated demand for money. The appeal also dealt with the issue of contractual rate of interest and whether the contractual rate of interest applies after the breach of the contract. Dealing with the issue of what is a liquidated debt, Ferguson J. stated in *Cantalia Sod Co. v. Patrick Harrison & Co.* (1967), 1967 CarswellOnt 176, [1968] 1 O.R. 169 (Ont. H.C.) at para. 3, as follows:

> . . . whether the amount to which the plaintiff is entitled (if he is entitled to anything) can be ascertained from the contract itself or by calculation or fixed by a scale of charges agreed upon by the contract or implied by it. In *Holden Day Wilson v. Ashton*, 1993 CarswellOnt 1834, 14 O.R. (3d) 306, 104 D.L.R. (4th) 266, 64 O.A.C. 4, [1993] O.J. No. 1195 (Ont. Div. Ct.), White J. for the Divisional Court undertook a lengthy review of the meaning of "liquidated demand". In *Capital One Bank v. Matovska*, 2007 CarswellOnt 5605, [2007] O.J. No. 3368 (Ont. Div. Ct.), the Divisional Court considered whether a claim for pre-proceeding collection expenses provided for in a credit card agreement was a claim for a liquidated demand for money. Divisional Court relying on *Holden, supra*, determined that such a claim was a liquidated demand and stated: Pre-proceeding collection expenses claimed in the credit card agreement are a claim for a liquidated demand for money, within the meaning of the *Small Claims Court Rules* 11.10(1) and 11.02(1). In *Canadian Imperial Bank of Commerce v. Prasad*, 2010 ONSC 320, 2010 CarswellOnt 108 (Ont. S.C.J.), Corbett J. offered the following comments on the general approach which should be taken on credit card debt collection cases, in the context of a summary judgment motion:

In *Gyimah v. Bank of Nova Scotia*, 2013 ONCA 252, 2013 CarswellOnt 4712, 305 O.A.C. 198, [2013] O.J. No. 1832 (Ont. C.A.), the Ontario Court of Appeal found no error on the part of the motion judge in accepting the bank's sworn testimony as to the amount outstanding in a claim for the amount owing on a line of credit and a credit card. While the decision of the motions court judge in *Gyimah* was not published, it seems fundamentally clear that the approach adopted by the deputy Small Claims Court judge is at odds with the prevailing caselaw.

Plaintiff's appeal allowed.

(3) [Repealed O. Reg. 78/06, s. 9(2).]

O. Reg. 461/01, s. 5; 78/06, s. 9; 56/08, s. 1; 230/13, s. 6

7.02 (1) Electronic Filing of Claim — **A plaintiff's claim may be filed with the clerk electronically in accordance with this rule, if the following conditions are satisfied:**

1. The claim is for a debt or liquidated demand in money, including any interest.

2. Any interest payable in relation to the claim is no greater than 35 per cent per year.

3. The defendant is not a person under disability.

4. The claim is one that may, under subrule 6.01(1), be filed in a court location for which the software authorized by the Ministry of the Attorney General for the purpose may be used, as indicated by the Ministry.

(2) The plaintiff's claim shall specify at which court location referred to in paragraph 4 of subrule (1) the action is being commenced, and that court location is deemed to be the place at which the action is commenced.

(3) An email address at which the plaintiff agrees to accept service of documents from the court must be specified when filing the plaintiff's claim.

(4) If a plaintiff's claim is filed electronically, the requirement in subrule 7.01(1) to also file a copy of the claim for each defendant does not apply.

(5) **Requirement to File in Paper Format** — A plaintiff's claim that has been filed and issued electronically shall be filed with the clerk, with proof of service, in the following circumstances and in accordance with the following rules:

1. If a defence is filed disputing all or part of the claim, the documents shall be filed at least 14 days before the date of the settlement conference, for the purposes of subrule 13.03(2).

2. If the plaintiff files a request to clerk under subrule 9.03(3) for a terms of payment hearing, the documents shall be filed together with the request.

3. If default judgment has been obtained against a defendant under Rule 11 and a motion to set aside the default judgment is filed, the documents shall be filed at least three days before the hearing date.

4. If the plaintiff files a request to clerk under clause 11.03(2)(b) for an assessment hearing, the documents shall be filed together with the request.

O. Reg. 44/14, s. 3

History [R. 7.02]: Plain language changes.

7.03 (1) **Issuing Claim** — On receiving the plaintiff's claim, the clerk shall immediately issue it by dating, signing and sealing it and assigning it a court file number.

(2) The original of the claim shall remain in the court file and the copies shall be given to the plaintiff for service on the defendant.

History [R. 7.03]: Clarifies that the rule refers to the plaintiff's claim only.

Commentary

The Frequent Claimant

A frequent claimant is a party (not the claimant's agent) who files 10 or more claims per calendar year in a Small Claims Court in the same location. Once a claimant has filed the 10th claim in a single Small Claims Court location, that claimant becomes a frequent claimant in that court location and is required to pay the frequent claimant rate for all subsequent steps in all actions where a frequent claimant rate applies, whether or not a frequent claimant rate was paid when the action was commenced.

Q. Can an agent/lawyer filing on behalf of a client be a frequent claimant?

A. No. An agent Pro-Server, files a total of 22 claims:

5 claims for Bank of "X";

2 claims for Your Dental Office;

12 claims for Sears; and

3 claims for Next-Door-Window Cleaners

(a) If no previous claims were filed by any of the plaintiffs in the current calendar year, the only frequent claimant is Sears and it would pay the frequent claimant fee on 2 claims. All other claimants would pay the infrequent claimant fees for their filings.

(b) If Bank of"X" had previously filed 8 claims, it would pay the frequent claimant fee on 3 out of the 5 claims being filed. After the 10th claim is issued, the frequent user fee must be charged for all subsequent activities to which a frequent user fee applies; for example, signing default judgments or fixing a date for trial for previously issued claims.

The court staff cannot refuse to accept or issue a claim for any reason, except insufficient funds. This includes no right to refuse because of illegible writing/printing and/or wrong forum. The reason is that the refusal to accept a claim could deprive a party of a right to which the court may subsequently determine the party has an entitlement. This is considered to be a judicial function which is beyond the authority of court staff.

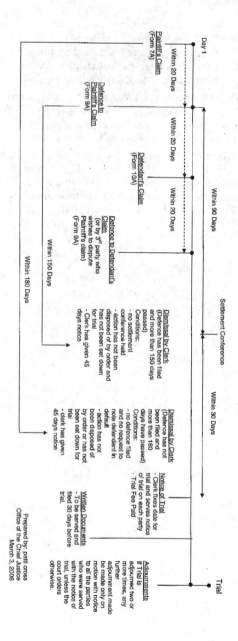

A SMALL CLAIMS COURT CASE - 2006 (Amended Rules)
FROM CLAIM TO TRIAL
A Case Flow Chart

7.04 Electronic Issuance of Claim — **(1)** A plaintiff's claim that is filed electroni-cally under rule 7.02 shall be issued electronically.

(2) If a plaintiff's claim is issued electronically, subrule 7.03(2) does not apply. Instead, the claim shall be retained electronically, and a copy shall be placed into the court file by the clerk only if a request is made by a person in accordance with section 137 of the *Courts of Justice Act* to see the claim.

O. Reg. 44/14, s. 3

Rule 8 — Service

[Handwritten: personal Service → Alternative to personal Service.]

8.01 (1) Service of Particular Documents — Plaintiff's or Defendant's Claim — A plaintiff's claim or defendant's claim (Form 7A or 10A) <u>shall</u> be served personally as provided in rule 8.02 or by an alternative to personal service as provided in rule 8.03. *[Handwritten: Shall = MusT]*

History [R. 8.01(1)]: References to forms added; clarifies that the section refers to both plaintiff's and defendant's claims; numbering of references to other sections changed.

Commentary: There is no restriction as to who may be named as a defendant in the defendant's claim. The defendant should be referred to as the "Plaintiff by Defendant's Claim."

If the defendant of the defendant's claim is an incorporated company, the name of the com-pany must be exact. This information may be obtained from the Ministry of Government Services, Companies and Personal Property Security Branch. The help line may be reached at 416-314-8880, or toll free at 1-800-361-3223.

The address of any party to an action should contain a postal code for mailing purposes. The party may use the Canada Post — Postal Code Lookup (<http://www.canadapost.ca/tools/pcl/bin/advanced-e.asp>) to find a postal code. If the plaintiff is represented by a lawyer or agent the form should include the address, telephone number, fax number and, in the case of a lawyer or licensed paralegal, the LSUC number.

Service of Claims and Notices of Examination

In a court case, everyone involved must receive the key documents they need. "Serving" documents means giving copies to all the other parties. Generally speaking, this must be done at each step in the case. The plaintiff must serve a copy of the claim form on the defendant.

Changes to the Rules regarding service of claims and notices of examination include the following:

1. — Removal of the option to serve a claim to the last known address of an individual, as an alternative to personal service

A Claim can be served by personal service or by an alternative to personal service. One type of an alternative to personal service allowed a plaintiff to mail the claim to the defendant's last-known address using regular letter mail, and then wait for the expiration of a 20-day period following the date the document was mailed. If the mail was not returned to the sender within that 20-day period, it was deemed to have been served on the defendant.

The new rule provides for service of a claim by an alternative to personal service, by regis-tered mail or courier with verification (by Canada Post or the courier company) that the document was received, rather than by service to last-known address by regular letter mail.

For service to be effective under this option, the defendant is required to sign the verification of receipt document provided by Canada Post or the courier company. If the verification is not received, the plaintiff may proceed to serve the claim by personal service (under rule

8.02), another alternative to personal service (under rule 8.03), or request an order allowing substituted service.

2. — *Personal Service of the Notice of Examination*

Under the Rules, if a person who owes money under a court order (the "debtor") fails to pay, the creditor can ask the court to hold an examination hearing. At the hearing, the creditor can ask the debtor or other person questions about:

- why the debtor did not pay,

- the debtor's income or property,

- debts owed to and by the debtor, and

- whether the debtor intends to obey the court order or has any reason for not doing so.

The creditor begins the examination process by serving a notice of examination on the debtor or other person to be examined. In the past, this notice could be sent by regular letter mail.

Now, the notice of examination form has to be served by personal service (under rule 8.02) or by an alternative to personal service (under rule 8.03). In addition, the creditor must file at the court the notice of examination together with an affidavit of service at least three days prior to the examination hearing date.

Case Law: *Butler v. Roberts* (1995), [1996] 3 W.W.R. 198 (Sask. Q.B.) — The plaintiff obtained default judgment in Small Claims Court. The defendant applied to set aside the judgment. She alleged a counterclaim or set off. She also swore that as the plaintiff had not served her with the small claims summons she had not known of the action. The plaintiff swore that he had served the defendant personally. Where there is an issue as to service and one party has sworn a false affidavit, the court should not make an order that would ignore the issue. Here either the plaintiff or the defendant swore a false affidavit as to service. The defendant was entitled to proceed to the trial of the issue as to whether service was properly effected.

Teskey v. Ricciardella (July 27, 1999), Doc. Toronto 93-CT-023447, Brampton C23447/93 (Ont. Master) — The defendant was served by alternate to personal service, upon his brother, at his place of residence. The defendant failed to explain why statement of claim did not come to his knowledge until almost one year later. The defendant did not deny that it was his place of residence at relevant time. He asserted the existence of the agreement and limitation period defence, without further particular. Motion denied.

Kraft v. Kraft (1999), 121 O.A.C. 331, 48 R.F.L. (4th) 132, 1999 CarswellOnt 1620, [1999] O.J. No. 1995 (Ont. C.A.) — The husband served the wife a divorce petition by service on the son. The son stated by affidavit that he did not advise the wife of the documents. The Court of Appeal allowed the wife's appeal on terms and ordered a trial on equalization payment issue. The material before the motions judge reflected issue that ought to be tried to avoid miscarriage of justice.

Chiarelli v. Wiens (1999), 122 O.A.C. 147, 34 C.P.C. (4th) 227, 1999 CarswellOnt 1168, [1999] O.J. No. 1456 (Ont. Div. Ct.); reversed (2000), 46 O.R. (3d) 780, (sub nom. *Chiarelli v. Weins*) 129 O.A.C. 129, 43 C.P.C. (4th) 19, 2000 CarswellOnt 280 (Ont. C.A.) — The plaintiffs applied for an extension of time to serve a claim in action for damages. The claim was not served on time because of the plaintiffs' lawyer's delay. The Divisional Court allowed the appeal and dismissed the motion for an extension of time for service.

Long v. Carl (2000), 2000 CarswellOnt 1004 (Ont. S.C.J.) — The defendant failed to rebut evidence as to service upon him filed by process server by way of explanation as to where he was living at the time.

Farrell v. Hewitt (2001), 2001 CarswellOnt 3248 (Ont. S.C.J.) — Plaintiff sought to extend time to serve co-defendant estate of spouse of main defendant who was now also deceased. Only witness was main defendant, who was now dead, such that estate was prejudiced. No explanation for failure to estate was given. Motion to extend time refused.

P.I.I.M. Canada Corp. v. Poetry in Motion (Canada) Inc. (2000), 1 C.P.C. (5th) 339, 2000 CarswellOnt 962 (Ont. S.C.J.) — Plaintiff unable to effect personal service on defendant. Served claim on adult who identified himself as living at defendant's address. Defendant failed to file statement of defence. Plaintiff obtained default judgment. Motion granted. Defendant's evidence indicated he never resided there and that address incorrect in any event.

Goodkey v. Dynamic Concrete Pumping Inc., 2003 CarswellBC 1025, 2003 BCSC 546 (B.C. S.C.). Employment standards regime not overriding ability of Courts to deal with severance pay in alleged wrongful dismissal action. Leading decision on whether a determination of an issue by an administrative tribunal will bind a Court in civil litigation is *Danyluk v. Ainsworth Technologies Inc.*, REJB 2001-25003, 2001 CarswellOnt 2434, 2001 CarswellOnt 2435, [2001] S.C.J. No. 46, 2001 SCC 44, 54 O.R. (3d) 214 (headnote only), 201 D.L.R. (4th) 193, 10 C.C.E.L. (3d) 1, 7 C.P.C. (5th) 199, 272 N.R. 1, 149 O.A.C. 1, 2001 C.L.L.C. 210-033, 34 Admin. L.R. (3d) 163, [2001] 2 S.C.R. 460 (S.C.C.).

Bank of Nova Scotia v. Baker (2003), 2003 CarswellOnt 1616 (Ont. S.C.J.); affirmed (2004), 2004 CarswellOnt 2954 (Ont. C.A.). Credit line granted to spouses in 1990 provided for increases by written notice to either spouse. Statements provided only to husband, and increase made in 1994 arranged by him. Spouses separated in 1999. Husband declared bankruptcy. Wife remained liable pursuant to terms of loan.

Belsar Corp. v. Simonin (2003), 2003 CarswellOnt 1566, [2003] O.J. No. 1601 (Ont. S.C.J.). Plaintiff obtained default judgment after service on defendant through service on sister of Defendant. Such service did not constitute effective alternative to personal service to rely on default judgment. Plaintiff did not comply with *Rule of Civil Procedure* (Ont.), Rule 16.03(5)(a), and (b) regarding sealed envelope and mailing of claim. Default judgment set aside.

Peel Financial Holdings Ltd. v. Western Delta Lands Partnership, 2003 CarswellBC 1205, 37 C.P.C. (5th) 115, 2003 BCSC 784 (B.C. S.C.). Plaintiffs in two actions were identical. Defendants in two actions almost identical. The lawsuits arose out of contractual disputes between the parties. The Defendants applied to have both actions tried together. Application granted.

Ontario v. Deutsch (2004), [2004] O.J. No. 535, 2004 CarswellOnt 482 (Ont. S.C.J.). Order pursuant to section 140 of the CJA, R.S.O. c. C.43, "no further proceedings may be instituted . . . continued . . . by 1(i), the Respondent Melvyn Philip Deutsch. He cannot appear" . . . as a representative or in any court . . . either directly . . . or indirectly. See also *Ontario (Attorney General) v. Fleet Rent-A-Car Ltd.*, 2002 CarswellOnt 4286, 29 C.P.C. (5th) 315, [2002] O.J. No. 4693 (Ont. S.C.J.) where Her Honour made a similar decision in a very lengthy, well-reasoned judgment.

Matton v. Yarlasky (2007), 2007 CarswellOnt 1137 (Ont. C.A.); affirming (2007), 2006 CarswellOnt 2821 (Ont. S.C.J.), Hennessy J.

Plaintiff sent defendant statement of claim by regular mail with receipt. Receipt not returned. No personal service effected and no order for substitutional service obtained. Plaintiff brought motion to validate service, which was dismissed. Plaintiff appealed. Appeal dismissed.

(2) Time for Service of Claim — A claim shall be served within six months after the date it is issued, but the court may extend the time for service, before or after the six months has elapsed.

History [R. 8.01(2)]: Formerly 8.02; plain language changes.

Commentary: A claim shall be served within six months after the date it is issued. The court may extend the time for service (by way of motion) before or after the six months has elapsed [r. 8.01(2)].

Effective December 15, 2009 section 124 of the *Courts of Justice Act* has been repealed. Section 124 previously stated: "*No document shall be served and no order shall be executed on Sunday, except with leave of the court*". Therefore, litigants may now serve court documents on Sunday.

If a document is to be served by mail under these rules, it shall be sent, by regular lettermail or registered mail, to the last address of the person or of the person's representative that is:

　　a) on file with the court, if the document is to be served by the clerk;

　　b) known to the sender, if the document is to be served to any other person. O. Reg. 258/98 r. 8.07(1).

If the last address on file with the court or known to the sender is the place of employment, then the document can be served by mail at the place of employment.

(3) [Repealed O. Reg. 44/14, s. 4(1).

History [R. 8.01(3)]: New provision that largely repeats 9.01(2) — placed here as well to keep all service information together; option of service by fax added.

(3.1) [Repealed O. Reg. 78/06, s. 10.]

(4) Default Judgment — A default judgment (Form 11B) shall be served by the clerk, by mail or by fax, on all parties named in the claim.

History [R. 8.01(4)]: Formerly 10.02(4) — placed here as well to keep all service information together.

(4.1) Despite subrule (4), if a plaintiff's claim was issued electronically under rule 7.04, the clerk may serve the default judgment on the plaintiff by email to the email address provided by the plaintiff for the purpose, if these rules permit it.

(4.1.1) [Repealed O. Reg. 78/06, s. 10.]

(5) Assessment Order — An order made on a motion in writing for an assessment of damages under subrule 11.03(2) shall be served by the clerk to the moving party if the party provides a stamped, self-addressed envelope with the notice of motion and supporting affidavit.

History [R. 8.01(5)]: Formerly 19.03(2), placed here to keep all service information together; notes that the party who requires the presence of the witness must serve the witness; refers to the appropriate form, now Form 18A, formerly Form 19A.

(6) Settlement Conference Order — An order made at a settlement conference shall be served by the clerk by mail or by fax, on all parties that did not attend the settlement conference.

History [R. 8.01(6)]: Formerly 21.08(4), placed here to keep all service information together; allows service on the garnishee to be made by regular mail instead of registered mail; refers to the appropriate form, now Form 20E, formerly Form 21E.

(7) Summons to Witness — A summons to witness (Form 18A) shall be served personally by the party who requires the presence of the witness, or by the party's representative, at least 10 days before the trial date; at the time of service, attendance

money calculated in accordance with the regulations made under the *Administration of Justice Act* shall be paid or tendered to the witness.

History [R. 8.01(7)]: Part of former 21.10(3), placed here to keep all service information together; allows service by mail, as well as personal service; refers to the appropriate form, now Form 20F, formerly Form 21F.

(8) Notice of Garnishment — A notice of garnishment (Form 20E) shall be served by the creditor,

    (a) together with a sworn affidavit for enforcement request (Form 20P), on the debtor, by mail, by courier, personally as provided in rule 8.02 or by an alternative to personal service as provided in rule 8.03; and

    (b) together with a garnishee's statement (Form 20F), on the garnishee, by mail, by courier, personally as provided in rule 8.02 or by an alternative to personal service as provided in rule 8.03.

History [R. 8.01(8)]: Part of former 21.10(3), placed here to keep all service information together; service is required within 30 days, instead of 14 days.

Note that it is only a "Notice of Judgement Debtor Examination" that has to be served 30 days before the date fixed for the examination. This 30-day rule does not apply to a "Notice of Contempt Hearing." See Rules 8.01(7), (8) and (9).

(9) Notice of Garnishment Hearing — A notice of garnishment hearing (Form 20Q) shall be served by the person requesting the hearing on the creditor, debtor, garnishee and co-owner of the debt, if any, and any other interested persons by mail, by courier, personally as provided in rule 8.02 or by an alternative to personal services as provided in rule 8.03.

History [R. 8.01(9)]: Formerly 21.10(11), placed here to keep all service information together; service may no longer be made by mail; refers to the appropriate form, now Form 20G, formerly Form 21G.

(10) Notice of Examination — A notice of examination (Form 20H) shall be served by the creditor on the debtor or person to be examined, personally as provided in rule 8.02 or by an alternative to personal service as provided in rule 8.03.

History [R. 8.01(10)]: Formerly 8.01(2) and (3), with plain language changes; service may be by fax instead of mail; provision added that the court may require different service than is required by this section.

Case Law: *Clarke v. P.F. Collier & Son Ltd.* (1993), 23 C.P.C. (3d) 397 (N.S.S.C.) — The appellant had served a notice of appeal of default judgment by fax. The *Small Claims Court Act* (N.S.) did not allow for service of a notice of appeal by fax. The appellant had not filed an affidavit of service. The appeal was premature in that he could have brought an application in Small Claims Court to set aside the default judgment but had not done so. The appeal was dismissed.

Kryzanowksi v. Sadlowski (1996), 149 Sask. R. 261 (Q.B.); affirmed (1997), 152 Sask. R. 242, 140 W.A.C. 242 (C.A.) — Respondent had attempted unsuccessfully to serve applicant at his parents' house. Registered mail returned. Respondent obtained order to effect substituted service by sending summons by regular mail and by serving applicant's father. Father did not give summons to son and mailed summons was apparently not received by him. However, where applicant knew of possibility of litigation, yet did not check to see whether registered mail related to litigation, he had simply avoided litigation. Application dismissed.

Toronto Dominion Bank v. Machado (1998), 28 C.P.C. (4th) 289, 1998 CarswellOnt 4659 (Ont. Master) — Process server served claim on the wife by serving the husband and completing service by sending a copy by mail next day. The default judgment against the wife was set aside. The wife was not properly served. The husband was properly served. *Laframboise v. Woodward* (2002), 2002 CarswellOnt 1448, 59 O.R. (3d) 338 (Ont. S.C.J.) — Plaintiff's motion without notice for subservice on automobile insurer granted. Counsel had to show unable to effect prompt personal service. "Impractical" in Rule 16.04(1) of *Rules of Civil Procedure* (Ontario) meant "unable to be carried out or done." Difficulty in serving defendant personally not sufficient. All reasonable steps must be taken to locate party and to personally serve party.

(11) Financial Statement — If the person to be examined is the debtor and the debtor is an individual, the creditor shall serve the notice of examination on the debtor together with a blank financial information form (Form 20I).

(12) The notice of examination,

(a) shall be served, together with the financial information form if applicable, at least 30 days before the date fixed for the examination; and

(b) shall be filed, with proof of service, at least three days before the date fixed for the examination.

(13) Notice of Contempt Hearing — A notice of a contempt hearing shall be served by the creditor on the debtor or person to be examined personally as provided in rule 8.02.

(14) Defence and Other Documents — The following documents may be served by mail, by courier, by fax, personally as provided in rule 8.02 or by an alternative to personal service as provided in rule 8.03, unless the court orders otherwise:

1. A defence.

2. Any other document not referred to in subrules (1) to (13).

O. Reg. 461/01, s. 7 [s. 7(4) repealed O. Reg. 330/02, s. 4(2).]; 330/02, s. 4(1), (3); 440/03, s. 5, item 3; 78/06, s. 10; 393/09, s. 4; 230/13, s. 7; 44/14, s. 4

Must have an affidavit of services to file Defence.

8.02 Personal Service — If a document is to be served personally, service shall be made,

(a) **Individual** — on an individual, other than a person under disability, by leaving a copy of the document with him or her;

Commentary: If a place of residence is not known for an individual, can they be served with any court document at their place of employment without a court order and would this employment address be the address listed on the court documents? If they can be served at place of employment, please confirm type of service.

If a document is to be served personally on an individual pursuant to subrule 8.02(a), the document can be served by leaving a copy with the individual, unless the individual is under a disability. A person can be served with the document at their place of employment. If a document is to be served by mail, see Rule 8.07(1). If a document is to be served by courier, see Rule 8.07.1(1).

If there is an admission of *all* of the plaintiff's claim and a proposal of terms of payment under subrule 9.03(1), then there would not be a settlement conference. However, if there were only a partial admission of liability and a proposal of terms of payment, they would schedule a settlement conference for the part of the claim the defendant does not admit.

Case Law: *Darlind Construction Inc. v. Rooflifters LLC* (2009), 2009 CarswellOnt 1618, 76 C.P.C. (6th) 339, 84 C.L.R. (3d) 299 (Ont. S.C.J.)

Plaintiff's process server left claim at defendant's premises with receptionist who actually worked for a company sharing premises. Claim came to defendant's attention following day. Plaintiff obtained default judgment 21 days after claim given to receptionist, on same day that defendant attempted to file notice of intent to defend. Plaintiff issued notices of garnishment to satisfy judgment. Defendant brought motion to set aside default judgment and notices of garnishment. Motion granted. Plaintiff did not complete service under R. 16.02(1)(c) of Rules of Civil Procedure. R. 16.07 provided for setting aside consequences of default where document did not come to person's notice. Plaintiff attempting to take advantage of technical error or misunderstanding. Since other defendants in lawsuit had filed defence, appropriate that actions proceed together.

(b) Municipality — on a municipal corporation, by leaving a copy of the document with the chair, mayor, warden or reeve of the municipality, with the clerk or deputy clerk of the municipality or with a lawyer for the municipality;

(c) Corporation — on any other corporation, by leaving a copy of the document with, *4 would serve the Headquarters not the store.*

(i) an officer, a director or another person authorized to act on behalf of the corporation, or

(ii) a person at any place of business of the corporation who appears to be in control or management of the place of business;

Case Law: *Firestone Tire Co. v. Douglas*, [1940] O.W.N. 143 (Ont. H.C.) — A corporation resides where its head office is situated. See also *Miles Transport Co. v. Mail Printing Co.*, [1935] O.W.N. 541 (Ont. H.C.).

Dana Classic Fragrances Inc. v. Consolidated Group of Cos., 2009 CarswellOnt 6957 (Ont. Sm. Cl. Ct.), Pamela A. Thomson J.

A corporation is served by leaving a copy of the Claim or document. Mail not an option. If the corporation cannot be found, then Claim can be mailed to the last known address, in which case it must also be mailed to the directors. Service on a corporation can be made by delivery (Rule 8.02(c)); by mail on last registered address and all directors (Rule 8.03(3)); or on a lawyer (Rule 8.03(5)).

(d) Board or Commission — on a board or commission, by leaving a copy of the document with a member or officer of the board or commission;

(e) Person Outside Ontario Carrying on Business in Ontario — on a person outside Ontario who carries on business in Ontario, by leaving a copy of the document with anyone carrying on business in Ontario for the person;

(f) Crown in Right of Canada — on Her Majesty the Queen in right of Canada, in accordance with subsection 23(2) of the *Crown Liability and Proceedings Act* (Canada);

Case Law: *Luo v. Canada (Attorney General)*, 1996 CarswellOnt 3936 (Ont. Small Cl. Ct.) — Rule 8.03(f) contemplates that Small Claims Court has jurisdiction to hear cases pursuant to the *Crown Liability and Proceedings Act*.

(g) Crown in Right of Ontario — on Her Majesty the Queen in right of Ontario, in accordance with section 10 of the *Proceedings Against the Crown Act*;

(h) Absentee — on an absentee, by leaving a copy of the document with the absentee's committee, if one has been appointed or, if not, with the Publ___ ___. ian and Trustee;

(i) Minor — on a minor, by leaving a copy of the document with the m' the minor resides with a parent or other person having his or her ca custody, by leaving another copy of the document with the parent or (

(j) Mentally Incapable Person — on a mentally incapable person,

    (i) if there is a guardian or an attorney acting under a validated power of attorney for personal care with authority to act in the proceeding, by leaving a copy of the document with the guardian or attorney,

    (ii) if there is no guardian or attorney acting under a validated power of attorney for personal care with authority to act in the proceeding but there is an attorney under a power of attorney with authority to act in the proceeding, by leaving a copy of the document with the attorney and leaving an additional copy with the person,

    (iii) if there is neither a guardian nor an attorney with authority to act in the proceeding, by leaving a copy of the document bearing the person's name and address with the Public Guardian and Trustee and leaving an additional copy with the person;

(k) Partnership — on a partnership, by leaving a copy of the document with,

    (i) any one or more of the partners, or

    (ii) a person at the principal place of business of the partnership who appears to be in control or management of the place of business; and

(l) Sole Proprietorship — on a sole proprietorship, by leaving a copy of the document with,

    (i) the sole proprietor, or

    (ii) a person at the principal place of business of the sole proprietorship who appears to be in control or management of the place of business.

History [R. 8.02(l)]: Formerly 8.03.

(a)–(g) Plain language changes.

(h) Terminology changed to correspond with the *Substitute Decisions Act*.

(i) Plain language changes.

(j) Merges former 8.03(j) and (k); terminology changed to correspond with the *Substitute Decisions Act*.

(k)–(l) Formerly 8.03(l) and (m), respectively.

Case Law: *Medd v. Farm No. One Ltd.* (1987), 62 O.R. (2d) 170 (Ont. Div. Ct.) — An order was made for service of a statement of claim by ordinary mail. Two defendants were additionally served personally. Rule 16.03(1) of the *Rules of Civil Procedure* is similar to Rule 8.03 and Rule 16.01(1) is similar to Rule 8.01. Since the primary method of service contemplated by the rules is personal service, the time for filing the statement of defence runs from the date of personal service.

Action Auto Leasing & Gallery Inc. v. Boulding, 2009 CarswellOnt 8657, [2009] O.J. No. 1768, 88 C.P.C. (6th) 91 (Ont. Sm. Cl. Ct.)

The plaintiff commenced claim in Small Claims Court. The plaintiff purported to serve claim on defendants by mail. No defence filed. The plaintiff had defendants noted in default and obtained default judgment. The defendants denied receipt of claim and learned of lawsuit after garnishments effected. Motion granted. The plaintiff could not establish valid service by mail pursuant to r. 8.03 of *Small Claims Court Rules*. Affidavits of service failed to indicate requirements of r. 8.03(8). If requirements of rr. 8.03(7) and (8) were not satisfied, then default judgment was irregularly obtained and had to be set aside as of right. It was unnecessary to determine whether defendants had arguable defence on merits. Motion was brought as soon as reasonably possible.

The defendants moved, pursuant to r. 11.06 of the *Small Claims Court Rules*, O. Reg. 258/98 ("SCCR"), to set aside the clerk's default judgment.

Recent authorities for proposition that irregularly-obtained default judgment must be set aside automatically, or as of right, without terms, are *Royal Trust Corp. of Canada v. Dunn*, [1991] O.J. No. 2231, 1991 CarswellOnt 468, 6 O.R. (3d) 468, 6 C.P.C. (3d) 351, 86 D.L.R. (4th) 490 (Ont. Gen. Div.), and *Benlolo v. Barzakay*, 169 O.A.C. 39, 2003 CarswellOnt 658, [2003] O.J. No. 602 (Ont. Div. Ct.); additional reasons at 170 O.A.C. 115, 2003 CarswellOnt 1260 (Ont. Div. Ct.). In such cases, there is no requirement on moving party to show, as there is in cases of regularly-obtained judgments, that he or she has an arguable defence on the merits. That is because irregularly-obtained judgments must be set aside *ex bebito justitiae* (for the sake of justice).

Onus to prove valid service is on the party asserting that proper service was effected: *Ivan's Films Inc. v. Kostelac*, 29 C.P.C. (2d) 20, 1988 CarswellOnt 441 (Ont. Master); leave to appeal refused (1988), 30 C.P.C. (2d) lv (Ont. H.C.); *Don Bodkin Leasing Ltd. v. Rayzak*, [1993] O.J. No. 503, 1993 CarswellOnt 4016 (Ont. Gen. Div.); reversed 1994 CarswellOnt 2220, [1994] O.J. No. 280 (Ont. Gen. Div.) at para. 10; and *Ryan (In Trust) v. Kaukab*, [2004] O.J. No. 5656, 2004 CarswellOnt 5898 (Ont. S.C.J.); additional reasons at [2005] O.J. No. 603, 2005 CarswellOnt 643 (Ont. S.C.J.); additional reasons at 2005 CarswellOnt 644 (Ont. S.C.J.); leave to appeal refused 2005 CarswellOnt 653 (Ont. Div. Ct.) at para. 9.

O. Reg. 56/12, s. 1; 230/13, s. 8

8.03 (1) Alternatives to Personal Service — If a document is to be served by an alternative to personal service, service shall be made in accordance with subrule (2), (3) or (5); in the case of a plaintiff's claim or defendant's claim served on an individual, service may also be made in accordance with subrule (7).

History [R. 8.03(1)]: Formerly 8.04(1); references to the appropriate subrules is provided; plain language changes. *Have to say youve attempted more than once*

(2) At Place of Residence — If an attempt is made to effect personal service at an individual's place of residence and for any reason personal service cannot be effected, the document may be served by,

(a) leaving a copy in a sealed envelope addressed to the individual at the place of residence with anyone who appears to be an adult member of the same household; and

(b) on the same day or the following day, mailing or sending by courier another copy of the document to the individual at the place of residence.

History [R. 8.03(2)]: Formerly part of 8.04(2); effective date separated out into another subrule (8.03(4)); plain language changes.

(3) Corporation — If the head office or principal place of business of a corporation or, in the case of an extra-provincial corporation, the attorney for service in Ontario cannot be found at the last address recorded with the Ministry of Government Services, service may be made on the corporation,

(a) by mailing or sending by courier a copy of the document to the corporation or to the attorney for service in Ontario, as the case may be, at that address; and

(b) by mailing or sending by courier a copy of the document to each director of the corporation as recorded with the Ministry of Government Services, at the director's address as recorded with that Ministry.

History [R. 8.03(3)]: Clarifies effective date 8.03(4).

(4) When Effective — **Service made under subrule (2) or (3) is effective on the fifth day after the document is mailed or verified by courier that it was delivered.**

History [R. 8.03(4)]: Formerly part of 8.04(2); plain language changes.

fifth day after document has been served.

(5) Acceptance of Service by Lawyer or Paralegal — **Service on a party who is represented by a lawyer or paralegal may be made by leaving a copy of the document with the lawyer or paralegal, or with an employee in the lawyer's or paralegal's office, but service under this subrule is effective only if the lawyer, paralegal or employee endorses on the document or a copy of it an acceptance of service and the date of the acceptance.**

History [R. 8.03(5)]: Formerly 8.04(4); plain language changes.

(6) By accepting service, the lawyer or paralegal is deemed to represent to the court that he or she has the client's authority to accept service.

History [R. 8.03(6)]: Formerly 8.04(5); plain language changes.

(7) Service of Claim — **Service of a plaintiff's claim or defendant's claim on an individual against whom the claim is made may be made by sending a copy of the claim by registered mail or by courier to the individual's place of residence, if the signature of the individual or any person who appears to be a member of the same household, verifying receipt of the copy, is obtained.**

History [R. 8.03(7)]: Formerly 8.04(6); this section now only applies to a "claim," not any document.

Commentary: Service by mail on corporations, sole proprietorships and partnerships is an acceptable form of service for the purposes of signing default judgment. Therefore, service is deemed to have been effected on the 20th day after the date of mailing.

(8) Service under subrule (7) is effective on the date on which receipt of the copy of the claim is verified by signature, as shown in a delivery confirmation provided by or obtained from Canada Post or the commercial courier, as the case may be.

History [R. 8.03(8)]: Formerly part of 8.04(7); the part about completion of service separated out into another subrule (8.03(9)); plain language changes.

(9) [Repealed O. Reg. 393/09, s. 5(4).]

O. Reg. 78/06, s. 11; 393/09, s. 5; 440/10, s. 1; 230/13, s. 9

History [R. 8.03(9)]: Contains completion of service part from former 8.04(7).

8.04 Substituted Service — **If it is shown that it is impractical to effect prompt service of a claim personally or by an alternative to personal service, the court may allow substituted service.**

History [R. 8.04]: Formerly 8.05; plain language changes.

Commentary: Substituted service is the exception and should not be necessary in most cases, particularly given the flexible methods of alternative service available as of right where personal service is impractical or problematic.

If substituted service is desired the plaintiff must bring a motion and obtain leave of the court. The specific method of service, the place or address for service, and the effective date of such service must be addressed in such an order. The motion must be supported by an affidavit which contains sufficient evidence to satisfy the motions judge that prompt personal or alternative service is impractical and that the proposed method of substituted service is likely to bring the claim to the defendant's attention: see *Laframboise v. Woodward*, 2002 CarswellOnt 1448, 59 O.R. (3d) 338, [2002] O.J. No. 1590 (Ont. S.C.J.). Plaintiffs bringing such a motion should also consider whether an extension of the time for service under rule 8.01(2) and/or an extension of the time for automatic dismissal under rule 11.1 is also required and if so, address those issues in the motion materials.

In *Malatesta v. 2088675 Ontario Inc.*, 2014 ONSC 1793, 2014 CarswellOnt 3532 (Ont. S.C.J.), substituted service was denied where the two-year delay was unexplained, the defendants would be prejudiced, and if any real effort had been made the defendants could have been located and served in time.

Note that substituted service is not applicable in situations where the plaintiff simply does not know where the defendant resides or carries on business. If the defendant's location for service is unknown, any proposed method of substituted service will not be likely to bring the claim to the defendant's attention. The usual bottom line for such situations is that the plaintiff must either pursue further investigation to determine where the defendant may be served, or consider abandonment of the claim. Possibly in highly unusual cases, service could be dispensed with under rule 2.02, in which case the authorities under rule 16.04 of the *Rules of Civil Procedure* might be considered.

8.05 Service Outside Ontario — If the defendant is outside Ontario, the court may award as costs of the action the costs reasonably incurred in effecting service of the claim on the defendant there.

O. Reg. 78/06, s. 12

History [R. 8.05]: Formerly 8.06; plain language changes.

8.06 Proof of Service — An affidavit of service (Form 8A) made by the person effecting the service constitutes proof of service of a document.

O. Reg. 461/01, s. 8 [s. 8(2) revoked O. Reg. 330/02, s. 5(2); s. 8(4) revoked 330/02, s. 5(4).]; 330/02, s. 5(1), (3); 440/03, s. 5, item 4; 78/06, s. 13

History [R. 8.06]: Formerly 8.09; plain language changes.

8.07 (1) Service by Mail — If a document is to be served by mail under these rules, it shall be sent, by regular lettermail or registered mail, to the last address of the person or of the person's representative that is,

(a) on file with the court, if the document is to be served by the clerk;

(b) known to the sender, if the document is to be served by any other person.

History [R. 8.07(1)]: Formerly part of 8.07; includes a new provision that the document is to be sent to the last address known to the sender, or, if the sender is the clerk, to the last address on file with the court; the effective date of service is separated out into another subrule (8.07(2)); plain language changes.

(2) When Effective — Service of a document by mail is deemed to be effective on the fifth day following the date of mailing. 5th day after Served.

History [R. 8.07(2)]: Contains effective date from former 8.07.

(3) Exception — This rule does not apply when a claim is served by registered mail under subrule 8.03(7).

O. Reg. 78/06, s. 14; 393/09, s. 6; 230/13, s. 10

8.07.1 (1) Service by Courier — If a document is to be served by courier under these rules, it shall be sent by means of a commercial courier to the last address of the

person or of the person's representative that is on file with the court or known to the sender.

(2) When Effective — Service of a document sent by courier is deemed to be effective on the fifth day following the date on which the courier verifies to the sender that the document was delivered.

(3) Exception — This rule does not apply when a claim is served by courier under subrule 8.03(7).

O. Reg. 78/06, s. 15; 393/09, s. 7; 230/13, s. 11

8.08 (1) Service by Fax — Service of a document by fax is deemed to be effective,

(a) on the day of transmission, if transmission takes place before 5 p.m. on a day that is not a holiday;

(b) on the next day that is not a holiday, in any other case.

(2) A document containing 16 or more pages, including the cover page, may be served by fax only between 5 p.m. and 8 a.m. the following day, unless the party to be served consents in advance.

O. Reg. 393/09, s. 8

History [R. 8.08]: New provision providing effective date for service by fax, based on *Rules of Civil Procedure* 16.05(1).

8.09 Notice of Change of Address — **(1)** A party whose address for service changes shall serve notice of the change on the court and other parties within seven days after the change takes place.

(2) Service of the notice may be proved by affidavit if the court orders that proof of service is required.

(3) [Repealed O. Reg. 78/06, s. 16.]

(4) [Repealed O. Reg. 78/06, s. 16.]

(5) [Repealed O. Reg. 78/06, s. 16.]

O. Reg. 461/01, s. 9 [s. 9(2) revoked O. Reg. 330/02, s. 6(2).]; 330/02, s. 6(1); 440/03, s. 5, item 5;
78/06, s. 16

History [R. 8.09]: Formerly 8.08; plain language changes.

Commentary: A party whose address for service changes during a proceeding is responsible to notify the other parties and the court office. In the absence of such notice, communications remain directed to the existing contact information on the court file. Failure to notify the other parties and the court of a change of address may result in that party not receiving notice of further proceedings including notice of trial and such proceedings could then occur without notice in fact to the party who has failed to update his or her contact information.

Document and Service Rule(s)	Who Serves*	How Service May be Made	Time for Service
Plaintiff's Claim (Form 7A) Defendant's Claim (Form 10A) r. 8.01(1), (2) r. 10.02	Party	• Personal service [r. 8.02] • Alternative to personal service (including registered mail, courier and other methods) [r. 8.03] • Substituted service (with leave of court) [r. 8.04]	Within 6 months after date issued (or longer with leave of court)
Summons to Witness (Form 18A) r. 8.01(7)	Party	Personal service [r. 8.02]	
Notice of Garnishment (Form 20E) r. 8.01(8) r. 20.08(6) and Notice of Renewal of Garnishment (Form 20E.1)	Creditor	On the debtor together with a sworn Affidavit for Enforcement Request (Form 20P) On the garnishee together with a Garnishee's Statement (Form 20F) by: • Personal service [r. 8.02] • Alternative to personal service [r. 8.03] • Mail [r. 8.07] • Courier [r. 8.07.1]	On the debtor within 5 days of service on the garnishee
Garnishee's Statement Form 20F r. 20.08(13)	Garnishee	On creditor and debtor	
Notice of Garnishment Hearing (Form 20Q) r. 8.01(9) r. 20.08(15.1)	Party	On creditor, debtor, garnishee, co-owner of debt (if any) and any other interested persons by: • Personal service [r. 8.02] • Alternative to personal service [r. 8.03] • Mail [r. 8.07] • Courier [r. 8.07.1]	
Notice of Contempt Hearing (not a prescribed form) r. 8.01(13); r. 20.11(3).(6)	Creditor	On debtor by: •Personal service [r. 8.02]	Affidavit of Service filed at least 7 days before the date of the hearing.
Notice of Examination (Form 20H) r. 8.01(10), (11), (12) r. 20.10(3)	Creditor	On debtor together with a blank Financial Information Form [Form 20I] by: • Personal service [r. 8.02] • Alternative to personal service [r. 8.03]	At least 30 days before the date fixed for the examination and filed, with proof of service, at least 3 days before the date fixed for the examination
Completed Financial Information Form (Form 20I) (for an examination hearing) r. 20.10(4.1)(b)(i)	Person served with a Notice of Examination where the debtor is an individual	On the creditor requesting the examination hearing by: •Personal service [r. 8.02] •Alternative to personal service [r. 8.03] •Mail [r. 8.07] •Courier [r. 8.07.1] •Fax [r. 8.08]	
"Amended" claim or defence	Party making amendment	On all parties including parties noted in default by:	Filing and service at least 30 days before

Document and Service Rule(s)	Who Serves*	How Service May be Made	Time for Service
r. 8.01(14) r. 12.01(2)		• Personal service [r. 8.02] • Alternative to personal service [r. 8.03] • Mail [r. 8.07] • Courier [r. 8.07.1] • Fax [r. 8.08]	the originally scheduled trial date unless the court, on motion, allows a shorter notice period or a clerk's order permitting the amendment is obtained under subrule 11.2.01 (1)
Notice to Co-owner of Debt (Form 20G) r. 20.08(14) r. 8.01(14)	Creditor	On co-owners of the debt by: • Personal service [r. 8.02] • Alternative to personal service [r. 8.03] • Mail [r. 8.07] • Courier [r. 8.07.1] • Fax [r. 8.08]	
Notice of Motion (Form 15A) r. 15.01(3), (6) r. 8.01(14)	Party filing motion	Prior to Judgment: On every party who has filed a claim and any defendant who has not been noted in default, or After Judgment: On all parties, including those noted in default, by: • Personal service [r. 8.02] • Alternative to personal service [r. 8.03] • Mail [r. 8.07] • Courier [r. 8.07.1] • Fax [r. 8.08]	At least 7 days before the hearing Filed with proof of service at least 3 days before the hearing date.
Order on Motion made without Notice r. 15.03(2) r. 8.01(14)	Party obtaining order on motion without notice	On co-owners of the debt by: • Personal service [r. 8.02] • Alternative to personal service [r. 8.03] • Mail [r. 8.07] • Courier [r. 8.07.1] • Fax [r. 8.08]	Within 5 days after order signed
Other Documents r. 8.01(14)	Party	• Personal service [r. 8.02] • Alternative to personal service [r. 8.03] • Mail [r. 8.07] • Courier [r. 8.07.1] • Fax [r. 8.08]	
Notice of Discontinued Claim (Form 11.3A)	Plaintiff	•Personal service [r. 8.02] •Alternative to personal service [r. 8.03] •Mail [r. 8.07] •Courier [r. 8.07.1] •Fax [r. 8.08]	After time for filing defence has elapsed (and no defence is filed)
Request to Clerk	Plaintiff	To defendant by:	Within 20 days after

Document and Service Rule(s)	Who Serves*	How Service May be Made	Time for Service
(Form 9B) (for a terms of payment hearing) r. 8.01(14) r. 9.03(3)		• Personal service [r. 8.02] • Alternative to personal service [r. 8.03] • Mail [r. 8.07] • Courier [r. 8.07.1] • Fax [r. 8.08]	service of the defence

Notes:

*   Service by the party includes service by his or her lawyer or agent.

Commentary

The court staff does not decide whether service of a claim at the address of the defendant's employer is proper service on the defendant. It is up to the defendant to challenge the method of service. If a document is to be served personally on an individual pursuant to subrule 8.02(a), the document can be served by leaving a copy with the individual, unless the individual is under a disability. A person can be served with the document at their place of employment. According to subrule *8.01(8)*, a notice of garnishment is to be served by mail, by courier, personally, or by an alternative to personal service.

A claim can be served on a sole proprietor under subrules 8.03(2), (5), and (7). Along with personal service pursuant to rule 8.02, subrules 8.03(2), (5), and (7) provide options for service of a claim on a sole proprietor.

Barring judicial direction, subrules 8.03(5) and (6) do not apply to paralegals, as there is no reference in the subrules to "agent." A party may wish to seek an order for such substituted service pursuant to subrule 8.04.

Service Chart

Document and Service Rule(s)	Who Serves	How Service May be Made	Time for Service
Defence to a Plaintiff's Claim (Form 9A) r. 9.01(1) r. 8.01(3)	Staff	On all plaintiffs named in the claim by: • Mail [r. 8.07] • Fax [r. 8.08]	
Defence to a Defendant's Claim (Form 9A) r. 10.03(1), (2) r. 8.01(3)	Staff	On all parties named in the claim by: • Mail [r. 8.07] • Fax [r. 8.08]	
Default Judgment (Form 11B) r. 11.02(3) r. 8.01(4)	Staff	On all parties named in the claim by: • Mail [r. 8.07] • Fax [r. 8.08]	
Notice of Assessment Hearing (not a prescribed form, generated by the system) r. 11.03(4) r. 8.01(14)	Staff	On plaintiffs who requested the Assessment Hearing by: • Mail [r. 8.07] • Fax [r. 8.08] • Courier [r. 8.07.1]	
Assessment Order set out in (Endorsement Record/Order of the Court) (not a prescribed form, generated by the system)	Staff	On the moving party if the party provides a stamped, self-addressed envelope with the notice of motion and supporting affidavit.	

Document and Service Rule(s)	Who Serves	How Service May be Made	Time for Service
r. 11.03(6) r. 8.01(5)			
Notice of Terms of Payment Hearing (not a prescribed form, generated by the system) r. 9.03(4) r. 9.03(4.1)	Staff	On all parties by: • Mail [r. 8.07] • Fax [r. 8.08]	Reasonable notice period after the date the request is served
Financial Information Form (Form 20I) r. 9.03(4.2) r. 9.03(4.1) The clerk shall serve on the defendant, together with the notice of terms of payment hearing, if the defendant is an individual	Staff	On the defendant(s) by: • Mail [r. 8.07] • Fax [r. 8.08] (Debtor to also serve on creditor before hearing [r. 9.03(4.3)])	
Dismissal Notice(s) r. 11.1.01(1) 4 r. 11.1.01(2) 4 r. 8.01(14)	Staff	For undefended actions on the plaintiffs by: • Mail [r. 8.07] • Fax [r. 8.08] • Courier [r. 8.07.1] For defended actions on all parties by: • Mail [r. 8.07] • Fax [r. 8.08] • Courier [r. 8.07.1]	More than 135 days have passed since the date the claim was issued More than 105 days have passed since the date the first defence was filed
Dismissal Order(s) r. 11.1.01(1)1 r. 11.1.01(2)1 r. 8.01(14)	Staff	For undefended actions on the plaintiffs by: • Mail [r. 8.07] • Fax [r. 8.08] • Courier [r. 8.07.1] For defended actions on all parties by: • Mail [r. 8.07] • Fax [r. 8.08] • Courier [r. 8.07.1]	More than 180 days have passed since the date the claim was issued More than 150 days have passed since the date the first defence was filed
Notice of Settlement Conference (not a prescribed form, generated by the system) r. 13.01(2) r. 13.02(4) r. 8.01(14)	Staff	On all parties by: • Mail [r. 8.07] • Fax [r. 8.08] • Courier [r. 8.07.1]	
List of Proposed Witnesses (Form 13A) r. 13.01(2) r. 8.01(14)	Staff	On all parties by: • Mail [r. 8.07] • Fax [r. 8.08] • Courier [r. 8.07.1]	List of proposed witnesses to be served with settlement conference notice [r 13.01(2)]

Document and Service Rule(s)	Who Serves	How Service May be Made	Time for Service
Request for Clerk's Order (Form 11.2A) r. 11.2.01(2) r. 11.2.01(3) r. 8.01(14)	Staff	If granted on the party that requests it and provides a stamped self-addressed envelope by: • Mail [r. 8.07] • Fax [r. 8.08] • Courier [r. 8.07.1] If refused on all parties by: • Mail [r. 8.07] • Fax [r. 8.08] • Courier [r. 8.07.1]	
Notice to Set Action Down for Trial (not a prescribed form, generated by the system) r. 13.07 r. 8.01(14)	Staff	On all parties by: •Provide to all parties at or after the settlement conference together with the Settlement Conference Order (Endorsement Record/order of the Court) • Mail [r. 8.07] • Fax [r. 8.08] • Courier [r. 8.07.1]	
Notice of Trial (not a prescribed form, generated by the system) r. 16.01(1) r. 16.01(2)	Staff	On each party who has filed a claim or defence by: • Mail [r. 8.07] • Fax [r. 8.08]	After a settlement conference has been held and a party has requested that the clerk fix a date for trial and has paid the required fee
Termination of consolidation order (not a prescribed form, generated by the system) r. 20.09(11.1)	Staff	On creditors named in consolidation order by: • Mail [r. 8.07] • Fax [r. 8.08]	
Warrant of Committal (Form 20J) r. 20.11(8)(b)	Staff	Forwarded to Police Services for execution of Warrant	
Settlement Conference Order (Settlement Conference Endorsement Record) (not a prescribed form, generated by the system) r. 13.05(5) r. 8.01(6)	Staff	Provide to all parties at settlement conference, or mail or fax to all parties immediately after settlement conference • Mail [r. 8.07] • Fax [r. 8.08]	At or after settlement conference

8.10 Failure to Receive Document — A person who has been served or who is deemed to have been served with a document in accordance with these rules is nevertheless entitled to show, on a motion to set aside the consequences of default, on a motion for an extension of time or in support of a request for an adjournment, that the document,

(a) did not come to the person's notice; or

597

(b) came to the person's notice only at some time later than when it was served or is deemed to have been served.

O. Reg. 461/01, s. 9(1)

Rule 9 — Defence

9.01 (1) Defence — A defendant who wishes to dispute a plaintiff's claim shall, within 20 days of being served with the claim,

(a) serve on every other party a defence (Form 9A); and

(b) file the defence, with proof of service, with the clerk.

O. Reg. 461/01, s. 10 [s. 10(3) revoked O. Reg. 330/02, s. 7(2).]; 330/02, s. 7(1); 440/03, ss. 2, 5,
item 6; 78/06, s. 17; 440/10, s. 2; 44/14, s. 5

Commentary: Effective July 1, 2014, defendants are required to serve their defence before filing it with proof of service. A defence may be served by mail, courier, fax, personally or by alternative service: rule 8.01(14).

[handwritten: 20 days to file defence, on 21st day can not in default]

9.02 (1) Contents of Defence, Attachments — The following requirements apply to the defence:

[handwritten: Include weekends — Don't include the 1st day]

1. It shall contain the following information:

   i. The reasons why the defendant disputes the plaintiff's claim, expressed in concise non-technical language with a reasonable amount of detail.

   ii. If the defendant is self-represented, the defendant's name, address and telephone number, and fax number if any.

   iii. If the defendant is represented by a representative, that person's name, address and telephone number, fax number if any, and Law Society of Upper Canada registration number if any.

2. If the defence is based in whole or in part on a document, a copy of the document shall be attached to each copy of the defence, unless it is unavailable, in which case the defence shall state the reason why the document is not attached.

History [R. 9.02(1)]: Formerly 9.02; requires the lawyer, the agent and defendant's fax number, if any, and an address for service.

NOTE: Neither this subrule, nor subrules 7.01(2) and 10.01(4), provide for either explaining the failure to attach documents nor what is to happen when you do not comply.

(2) [Repealed O. Reg. 78/06, s. 19.]

O. Reg. 461/01, s. 11; 78/06, ss. 18, 19; 56/12, s. 2; 230/13, s. 12

History [R. 9.02(2)]: New provision, corresponding to Rule 7.02 for plaintiff's claim.

Case Law: *Patym Holdings Ltd. v. Michalakis*, 2006 CarswellBC 936, 51 B.C.L.R. (4th) 254, 2006 BCCA 192, 32 C.P.C. (6th) 218, 224 B.C.A.C. 157, 370 W.A.C. 157 (B.C. C.A.).

Statement of defence stated defendant denied "each and every allegation of fact contained in plaintiff's statement of claim." Master struck statement of defence.

Appeal allowed.

Although defendant entitled to rely on terse form of specific denial he used in defence, preferable to limit that form to introductory averments in statement of claim. Use of that form of specific denial contrary to spirit of the Rules "to secure the just, speedy and inexpensive determination of every proceeding on its merits."

Patym Holdings Ltd. v. Michalakis, 2005 CarswellBC 3045, 48 B.C.L.R. (4th) 73, 2005 BCCA 636, 21 C.P.C. (6th) 279, 220 B.C.A.C. 230, 362 W.A.C. 230 (B.C. C.A.).

No indication defendant trying to be intentionally evasive. Pleadings not improper. Statement of defence was one paragraph that generally denied allegations. Master struck statement of defence. Defendant appealed to a judge. Appeal dismissed. The defendant appealed to the Court of Appeal. Appeal allowed.

Canadian Imperial Bank of Commerce v. Murphy, 2006 CarswellNB 108, 294 N.B.R. (2d) 194, 765 A.P.R. 194, 2006 NBQB 69 (N.B. Q.B.).

Application by plaintiff to strike out defence as not disclosing a reasonable defence and for judgment allowed. Defendants did not deny they owed money to plaintiff. Fact that they did not have money not a defence and was insufficient to deny the plaintiff judgment. Plain and obvious that the defence did not disclose a reasonable defence.

De Shazo v. Nations Energy Co., 2006 CarswellAlta 1716, 2006 ABCA 400, 401 A.R. 142, 391 W.A.C. 142, 36 C.P.C. (6th) 190, 68 Alta. L.R. (4th) 57, 276 D.L.R. (4th) 559 (Alta. C.A.).

One of the defendants brought application for summary judgment dismissing action. Before application heard, plaintiff filed discontinuance of action. Application judge held that plaintiff's right to discontinue action subject to overriding fairness to all parties, which the court can police under its inherent jurisdiction. Court granted summary judgment. The plaintiff appealed. Appeal dismissed.

9.03 (1) Admission of Liability and Proposal of Terms of Payment — A defendant who admits liability for all or part of the plaintiff's claim but wishes to arrange terms of payment may in the defence admit liability and propose terms of payment.

History [R. 9.03(1)]: Formerly 9.04(1).

(2) Where No Dispute — If the plaintiff does not dispute the proposal within the 20-day period referred to in subsection (3),

    (a) the defendant shall make payment in accordance with the proposal as if it were a court order;

    (b) the plaintiff may serve a notice of default of payment (Form 20L) on the defendant if the defendant fails to make payment in accordance with the proposal; and

    (c) the clerk shall sign judgment for the unpaid balance of the undisputed amount on the filing of an affidavit of default of payment (Form 20M) by the plaintiff swearing,

        (i) that the defendant failed to make payment in accordance with the proposal,

        (ii) to the amount paid by the defendant and the unpaid balance, and

        (iii) that 15 days have passed since the defendant was served with a notice of default of payment.

History [R. 9.03(2)]: Incorporates part of former 9.04(6); states that the subsection only applies where the plaintiff does not dispute the proposal; states that the defendant shall make payments as though the proposal were a court order.

Commentary: If a Defence (Form 9A) has been filed for a debt or liquidated demand in money, the clerk may sign Default Judgment (Form 11B) on the undefended part of the liquidated claim.

If a defence has been filed in which the defendant makes a proposal of terms of payment (and the plaintiff did not dispute the proposal), and if the defendant fails to make payment in accordance with the proposal, then the plaintiff will file an Affidavit of Default of Payment(Form 20M) indicating that the Notice of Default of Payment (Form 20L) was served on the defendant.

The plaintiff may file a copy of the notice of default of payment but is not required to do so.

The clerk will sign default judgment for the unpaid balance of the undisputed amount as long as:

- The affidavit of default of payment indicates that the defendant failed to make payment in accordance with the proposal;

- 15 days have passed since the defendant was served with the notice of default of payment;

- The amount paid by the defendant and the unpaid balance [r. 9.03(2)(c)]; and

- The parties have not filed a written consent to waive the default of payment.

If a defence has been filed admitting liability, but failing to set out the proposed terms of payment, default judgment should not be issued. Rather, the plaintiff may request that the matter be listed for a Terms of Payment hearing [r. 9.03(3)].

Where a partnership has been sued in the firm name and has been noted in default, default judgment should not be signed until the time has expired for the filing of a defence by all persons who have been served under r. 5.03 as alleged partners.

(3) Dispute — The plaintiff may dispute the proposal within 20 days after service of the defence by filing with the clerk and serving on the defendant a request to clerk (Form 9B) for a terms of payment hearing before a referee or other person appointed by the court.

History [R. 9.03(3)]: Formerly 9.04(2); provision added that the court shall fix a time for the hearing; plain language changes.

(4) The clerk shall fix a time for the hearing, allowing for a reasonable notice period after the date the request is served, and serve a notice of hearing on the parties.

(4.1) Manner of Service — The notice of hearing shall be served by mail or fax.

(4.2) Financial Information Form, Defendant an Individual — The clerk shall serve a financial information form (Form 20I) on the defendant, together with the notice of hearing, if the defendant is an individual.

(4.3) Where a defendant receives a financial information form under subrule (4.2), he or she shall complete it and serve it on the creditor before the hearing, but shall not file it with the court.

(5) Order — On the hearing, the referee or other person may make an order as to terms of payment by the defendant.

History [R. 9.03(5)]: Formerly 9.04(3); form number change to Form 11A from Form 10A.

(6) Failure to Appear, Default Judgment — If the defendant does not appear at the hearing, the clerk may sign default judgment against the defendant for the part of the claim that has been admitted and shall serve a default judgment (Form 11B) on the defendant in accordance with subrule 8.01(4).

History [R. 9.03(6)]: Formerly 9.04(4).

Commentary: The plaintiff may attend the court office and/or make a written inquiry to indicate that the defendant has failed to make a payment in accordance with either a proposal of terms of payment or court-ordered terms of payment. If the defendant fails to make payments in accordance with an order for payments made at a terms of payment hearing, the plaintiff may file an Affidavit of Default of Payment (Form 20M) in support of a request that the clerk issue a default judgment. Before a defendant(s) is noted in default, the plaintiff must provide an affidavit to support the noting in default [r. 9.03(7)]. Here, the affidavit refers to an Affidavit of Default of Payment (Form 20M).

(6.1) [Repealed O. Reg. 78/06, s. 20(5).]

(7) Failure to Make Payments — Unless the referee or other person specifies otherwise in the order as to terms of payment, if the defendant fails to make payment in accordance with the order, the clerk shall sign judgment for the unpaid balance on the filing of an affidavit by the plaintiff swearing to the default and stating the amount paid and the unpaid balance.

　　O. Reg. 461/01, s. 12 [s. 12(2) revoked O. Reg. 330/02, s. 8(2); s. 12(4) revoked 330/02, s. 8(4).];
　　　　　　　　　　　　　　330/02, s. 8(1), (3); 440/03, s. 5, item 7; 78/06, s. 20

History [R. 9.03(7)]: Formerly 9.04(5).

NOTE: Authority of the referee/mediator under this subrule. See also subrule 21.01(2).

Rule 10 — Defendant's Claim

History [R. 10]: The defendant's claim must now be filed within 20 days of the defence being filed. Otherwise, leave of the court is needed. A defendant to a defendant's claim cannot defend the defendant's liability to the plaintiff in the main action unless such a defence is filed. Subrule 11.04 clarifies that an undefended defendant's claim cannot result in judgment without a motion or a trial in the main action.

10.01 (1) Defendant's Claim — A defendant may make a claim,

　　(a) against the plaintiff;

　　(b) against any other person,

　　　　(i) arising out of the transaction or occurrence relied upon by the plaintiff, or

　　　　(ii) related to the plaintiff's claim; or

　　(c) against the plaintiff and against another person in accordance with clause (b).

History [R. 10.01(1)]: Basic provision allowing defendant's claim; incorporates parts of former 12.01 (Third Party Claim) and 9.03 (Counterclaim).

Rule 10: Defendant's Claim

The address of any party to an action should contain a postal code for mailing purposes. The party may use the Canada Post — Postal Code Lookup to find a postal code. If the Plaintiff is represented by a representative the form should include the address, telephone number, fax number and, in the case of a lawyer or a licensed paralegal, the LSUC number.

Commentary: A defendant may attend the court office and/or make a written inquiry (without any completed forms) to commence an action in the Small Claims Court, arising out of the occurrence relied upon/related to the Plaintiff's Claim.

The defendant will:

　　1.　Provide at least two copies of a completed defendant's claim.

2.   Where applicable, provide a completed Consent to Act as Defendant's Litigation Guardian (Form 4B).

3.   Pay the required fee for issuing of a defendant's claim in accordance with the SCC Schedule of Fees.

There is no restriction as to who may be named as a defendant in the defendant's claim. The defendant should now be referred to as the plaintiff of the defendant's claim.

If the defendant of the defendant's claim is an incorporated company, the name of the company must be exact. This information may be obtained from the Ministry of Consumer and Business Services, Companies and Personal Property Security Branch. The help line may be reached at 416-314-8880, or toll free at 1-800-361-3223. The address of any party to an action should contain a postal code for mailing purposes.

Case Law: *Wellisch v. Duerrschnabel* (1988), 14 W.D.C.P. 222 (Ont. Prov. Ct.) — An action for $2,802.72 was transferred to the Ottawa Small Claims Court without notice to the third party. The third party objected, by motion, to exposure to a damage claim having a potential of $2800 when the monetary jurisdictional limit in Ottawa was $1,000. The court declined jurisdiction in both the main action and the third party claim.

London Motor Products Ltd. v. Smith (1993), 4 W.D.C.P. (2d) 460 (Ont. Sm. Cl. Ct.) — The Small Claims Court rules do not require a defendant that wishes to add a third party to establish that the addition of the third party will resolve an issue between the plaintiff and the defendant.

To Optimize The Environment Inc. v. Canada Cart Inc. (January 9, 1998), Doc. 94-CU-77754 (Ont. Gen. Div.) — Leave to issue third party proceedings not granted where trial was imminent, and plaintiff would be prejudiced by delay. Defendant aware of nature of third party's involvement at examinations for discovery two years before.

Métivier v. Toulon Development Corp., 2002 CarswellNB 110, 2002 NBBR 89 (N.B. Q.B.) — Defendant granted extension for filing third party notice. Plaintiff should not be prejudiced as to trial date. Third party proceedings could only be heard together with main action if ready for trial on date already set for main action.

Pilot Pacific Developments Inc. v. Albion Securities Co., 2002 CarswellBC 648, 2002 BCSC 372 (B.C. S.C.) — Defendants in this action were plaintiffs in first action. Defendants claimed equitable set-off against first action on Promissory Note. Equitable claim related to merits of first action. Court ordered stay of further proceedings pursuant to counterclaim pending determination of trial of other issues raised in two proceedings.

Poche v. Henkel, 2004 CarswellSask 858, 2004 SKPC 127 (Sask. Prov. Ct.), E. Kalenith, P.C.J. — Tort of abuse of process requires defendant to have used legal process for collateral or illicit purpose. See *Norman v. Soule*, 1991 CarswellBC 801, 7 C.C.L.T. (2d) 16 (B.C. S.C.). Judgment to Henkel. Claim dismissed.

Wilkings v. Velocity Group Inc. (2008), 2008 CarswellOnt 1665, 55 C.P.C. (6th) 321, 235 O.A.C. 30, 89 O.R. (3d) 751 (Ont. Div. Ct.)

The appellant defendants brought a motion for an order compelling the corporate plaintiffs to post security for costs of the underlying action on the basis that they had insufficient assets in Ontario. Appeal allowed.

The existence of a counterclaim raising the same issues as the defence to the initiating plaintiff's claim is a relevant fact to be considered in the exercise of discretion when considering whether to order security for costs against the plaintiff by counterclaim. However, the fact of a counterclaim should not be a relevant factor for consideration by the court in exercising discretion in respect of a motion for security for costs against an initiating plaintiff in the main action. The motion judge erred in relying on the fact that the defence to the counterclaim was closely related to the statement of claim in the main action. Assuming that such a close relationship did, in fact, exist, it was not a relevant factor in determining whether or not the initiating plaintiffs should post security for costs.

(2) The defendant's claim shall be in Form 10A and may be issued,

(a) within 20 days after the day on which the defence is filed; or

(b) after the time described in clause (a) but before trial or default judgment, with leave of the court.

Case Law: *Jones v. Craig* (June 8, 2009), Doc. 712/08, 712D1/08 and 1337/08, [2009] O.J. No. 2365 (Ont. Sm. Cl. Ct.)

While the point may not be free from doubt, rule 10.01(2)(b) does not appear to contemplate leave to issue a defendant's claim being granted after a trial has started but before it is completed. In this case leave was requested on the third day of trial, and was denied.

(3) Copies — The defendant shall provide a copy of the defendant's claim to the court.

(4) Contents of Defendant's Claim, Attachments — The following requirements apply to the defendant's claim:

1. It shall contain the following information:

i. The full names of the parties to the defendant's claim and, if relevant, the capacity in which they sue or are sued.

ii. The nature of the claim, expressed in concise non-technical language with a reasonable amount of detail, including the date, place and nature of the occurrences on which the claim is based.

iii. The amount of the claim and the relief requested.

iv. If the defendant is self-represented, the defendant's name, address and telephone number, and fax number if any.

v. If the defendant is represented by a representative, that person's name, address and telephone number, fax number if any, and Law Society of Upper Canada registration number if any.

vi. The address where the defendant believes each person against whom the claim is made may be served.

vii. The court file number assigned to the plaintiff's claim.

2. If the defendant's claim is based in whole or in part on a document, a copy of the document shall be attached to each copy of the claim, unless it is unavailable, in which case the claim shall state the reason why the document is not attached.

(5) [Repealed O. Reg. 78/06, s. 21(4).]

(6) Issuance — On receiving the defendant's claim, the clerk shall immediately issue it by dating, signing and sealing it, shall assign it the same court file number as the plaintiff's claim and shall place the original in the court file.

(7) [Repealed O. Reg. 78/06, s. 21(4).]

(8) [Repealed O. Reg. 78/06, s. 21(4).]

O. Reg. 461/01, s. 13 [s. 13(5) revoked O. Reg. 330/02, s. 9(2).]; 330/02, s. 9(1); 440/ ?·
78/06, s. 21; 56/12, s. 3; 230/

10.02 Service — A defendant's claim shall be served by the defendant on every person against whom it is made, in accordance with subrules 8.01(1) and (2).

10.03 A party who wishes to dispute the defendant's claim or a third party who wishes to dispute the plaintiff's claim shall, within 20 days after service of the defendant's claim,

> (a) serve on every other party a defence (Form 9A); and
>
> (b) file the defence, with proof of service, with the clerk.

O. Reg. 461/01, s. 14 [s. 14(3) revoked O. Reg. 330/02, s. 10(2).]; 330/02, s. 10(1); 440/03, ss. 4, 5, item 8; 78/06, s. 22; 44/14, s. 6

History [R. 10.03]: Essentially former 12.03; refers to service provisions under rule 8.

10.04 (1) Defendant's Claim to be Tried with Main Action — A defendant's claim shall be tried and disposed of at the trial of the action, unless the court orders otherwise.

(2) Exception — If it appears that a defendant's claim may unduly complicate or delay the trial of the action or cause undue prejudice to a party, the court may order separate trials or direct that the defendant's claim proceed as a separate action.

(3) Rights of Third Party — If the defendant alleges, in a defendant's claim, that a third party is liable to the defendant for all or part of the plaintiff's claim in the action, the third party may at the trial contest the defendant's liability to the plaintiff but only if the third party has filed a defence in accordance with subrule 10.03(1).

O. Reg. 78/06, s. 23

Case Law: *Seaside Chevrolet Oldsmobile Ltd. v. VFC Inc.*, 2005 CarswellNB 397, 2005 NBQB 233, 22 C.P.C. (6th) 374, 761 A.P.R. 61, 292 N.B.R. (2d) 61 (N.B. Q.B.), McIntyre J.

Clerk of Small Claims Court refused to allow a third party (Seaside) to file a fourth-party claim. The parties agreed case not complex. Seaside applied to transfer action to Court of Queen's Bench.

Court denied application, matter with the addition of a fourth-party claim within the jurisdiction of the Small Claims Court.

Zurich Insurance Co. v. Precision Surfacing Ltd., 2007 CarswellAlta 503, 2007 ABQB 252, 73 Alta. L.R. (4th) 326 (Alta. Q.B.).

Application to set aside third-party notice. Triable issue existed as whether third party owed defendant duty to inform during dispute resolution. No prejudice which was not compensable in costs to plaintiff or third party would be triggered by inclusion of third-party claim.

Cameron v. Equineox Technologies Ltd., 2009 BCSC 221, 66 C.P.C. (6th) 361, 2009 CarswellBC 436 (B.C. S.C. [In Chambers])

Defendant brought third party claim against company. Company applied for order striking out third party notice. Application dismissed. Third party claim did not lie against company for allegation of negligent supervision, which could be raised directly against plaintiff as contributory negligence.

Strata Plan LMS 3851 v. Homer Street Development Ltd. Partnership, 2011 BCSC 1127, 2011 CarswellBC 2167, 8 C.L.R. (4th) 186 (B.C. S.C.), Truscott J.

Third party procedure. The proposed amendments to amended third party notice were insufficient to set out a reasonable claim against any of the third parties with respect to defects, and the amendments in present form on that issue were denied.

History [R. 10.04]: Essentially former 12.04.

10.05 (1) Application of Rules to Defendant's Claim — These rules apply, with necessary modifications, to a defendant's claim as if it were a plaintiff's claim, and to a defence to a defendant's claim as if it were a defence to a plaintiff's claim.

History [R. 10.05(1)]: Essentially part of former 12.05; the part about default separated out into another subrule (10.05(2)).

(2) Exception — However, when a person against whom a defendant's claim is made is noted in default, judgment against that person may be obtained only in accordance with rule 11.04.

History [R. 10.05(2)]: Essentially part of former 12.05; wording changed to refer to new rule 11.03, rather than stating directly that default judgment may only be obtained at trial or on motion.

Small Claims Court — Process Defence

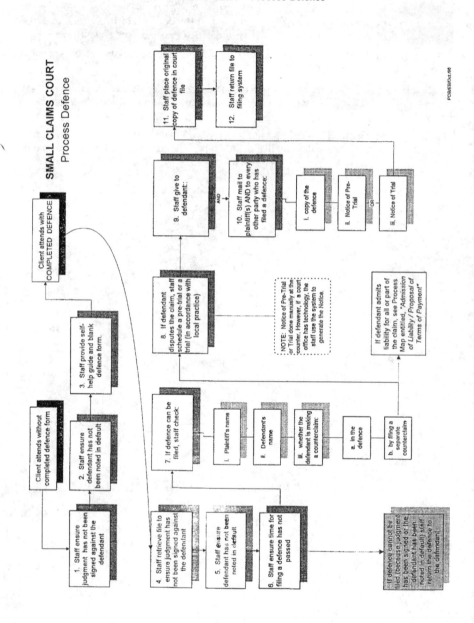

(3) Exception, Electronic Filing, Issuance — Subrule (1) does not apply to rule 7.02 (electronic filing of claim) or rule 7.04 (electronic issuance of claim).

O. Reg. 56/08, s. 2; 44/14, s. 7

Rule 11 — Default Proceedings

11.01 (1) Noting Defendant in Default — If a defendant to a plaintiff's claim or a defendant's claim fails to file a defence to all or part of the claim with the clerk within the prescribed time, the clerk may, when proof is filed that the claim was served within the territorial division, note the defendant in default.

(1.1) Electronic Filing — In the case of a plaintiff's claim that was issued electronically under rule 7.04, the plaintiff may file the proof referred to in subrule (1) electronically.

(2) Leave Required for Person under Disability — A person under disability may not be noted in default under subrule (1), except with leave of the court.

History [R. 11.01(2)]: Formerly 10.01, plain language changes.

Commentary: The provisions with respect to defaults are contained in rule 11. See also subrules 8.09, 8.10, 9.03, 17.01(4) and (5), and 20.02(2), (3), (4). The clerk notes a party in default once an Affidavit of Service is filed, with or without the Affidavit of Jurisdiction as appropriate (Form 11A). A plaintiff is only entitled to interest on a Default Judgment for a liquidated amount if that interest has been claimed (subrule 11.02(1)).

Once there is a noting in default, a plaintiff may request an assessment of Damages only if all defendants have been served. Pursuant to subrules 11.03(1) and (7), if even one defence is filed there can be no assessment. Assessment of damages will be exparte with an Affidavit (Form 15B) together with all attachments necessary to prove damages. The plaintiff can request and pay for an Assessment Hearing rather than file an exparte motion.

A further affidavit, with or without attachments, can be ordered, or the matter can be sent on to an Assessment Hearing by a duty judge. Damages will be assessed and judgment endorsed on the Endorsement Record.

An Assessment Hearing, like a garnishment hearing, is a trial, not a motion, as is made clear in subrule 11.03(4) where there is a specific reference to rule 17.

A defendant in default is not entitled to notice of any step in the proceeding or to be served except to receive the default judgment, to be served with an amended claim or an amended defence, or to be served with any process or motion after judgment (subrule 11.05(3)).

See subrule 11.06 for the noting of default and setting aside default judgment. These parameters apply to motions brought under subrule 8.10. If a defence has been filed, these would not apply to a set aside motion brought under subrule 17.01(4). Subrule 11.1.01(3)1 provides that the rules apply to all actions as of July 1, 2006.

A request for a Clerk's Order on Consent (Form 11.2A) may be filed where the relief sought is of a technical nature. Pleadings, defaults, order and unfinished enforcements may be set aside or amended; claims and motions may be dismissed. The consent of an added or deleted party must be filed.

If a party has been noted in default, staff will refuse to file any further documents except as ordered by the court or with the consent of the plaintiff [r. 11.05(1)].

A plaintiff to a Plaintiff's Claim (Form 7A) or to a Defendant's Claim (Form 10A) may attend the court office and/or make a written request (without any completed forms) to note a defendant in default.

Where a file consists of a plaintiff's claim and a defendant's claim, and the plaintiff's claim has been dismissed for delay, the defendant's claim would not be dismissed.

The Rules of the Small Claims Court currently do not provide guidance regarding dismissing defendant's claims for delay.

If the party to be noted in default is the Crown in Right of Ontario s. 10, *Proceedings Against the Crown Act*, service on the Crown must be made through the office of:

> Crown Law Office — Civil
> 8th Floor, 720 Bay Street
> Toronto, ON
> M7A 2S9

If the party to be noted in default is Her Majesty in Right of Canada s. 23, *Crown Liability and Proceedings Act*,], service on the Crown in respect of proceedings in the Province of Ontario must be made through the Toronto Regional Office of the Deputy Attorney General:

> Department of Justice Canada
> 130 King Street West,
> P.O. Box 36, Suite 3400
> Toronto, ON M5X 1K6
>
> OR
>
> through the office of the Deputy Attorney General
> in Ottawa:
> Deputy Minister of Justice and
> Deputy Attorney General of Canada
> 284 Wellington Street
> Ottawa, ON K1A 0H8
>
> OR

service on the chief executive officer of the agency in whose name the proceedings are taken, as the case may be.

Pursuant to section 5(1) of the *Crown Liability and Proceedings (Provincial Court) Regulations*, the Federal Attorney General may file a defence to originating proceedings, including a defendant's claim, within 30 days after service of the originating process or the time provided by or under the Rules, whichever is greater, or within such further time as may be allowed by the court.

Interest

The *Courts of Justice Act* (the "Act") (section 128) provides for an order of prejudgment interest.

Prejudgment interest rate is defined in the *Courts of Justice Act* (s. 127(1)). These rates are posted quarterly in the Ontario Gazette and on the Ministry's website.

- It is the responsibility of the claimant to indicate prejudgment interest to the date the claim was prepared. Prejudgment interest may be claimed in accordance with the *Courts of Justice Act* or payable by the agreement.

The Act states that prejudgment interest will not be awarded on the following [s. 128(3), CJA]:

- an award of costs in the proceeding;
- an advance payment that has already been made, from the date the payment was made;
- an order made on consent, except by consent of the debtor; and/or

- where interest is payable by a right (e.g., contractual right) other than under section 128, *Courts of Justice Act.*

Type of Service of Claim	When Deemed Served	Time to File Defence	When Defendant May Be Noted in Default*	Rule
Personal Service	Day of Service	20 days	20 clear calendar days from date of service (on the 21st day)	*r. 9.01(1);* *r. 10.03(1)*
Alternative to Personal Service at place of residence (leaving a copy with adult, then mailing a copy)	5 days after mailing	20 days	25 clear calendar days from date of mailing or sending by courier (on the 26th day)	*r. 9.01(1)* *r. 8.03(1)* *r. 8.03(2)* *r. 10.03(1)*
Service by Registered Mail or Courier to Individual's Place of Residence	Service effective on date on which the individual verifies receipt of the copy of the claim by signature, as shown in a delivery confirmation provided by or obtained from Canada Post or the commercial courier	20 days	20 clear calendar days from date of verification of receipt of the copy of the claim (on the 21st day)	*r. 9.01(1)* *r. 8.03(8)* *r. 10.03(1)*
Service on a Corporation at Last Known Address If the head office or principal place of business or attorney for service cannot be found at the last address recorded by Ministry of Government Services.	5 days after mailing	20 days	25 clear calendar days from date of mailing or verified by courier that it was delivered (on the 26th day)	*r. 8.03(3)* *r. 8.03(4)* *r. 9.01(1)* *r. 10.03(1)*
Acceptance of Service by Lawyer	Date acceptance signed	20 days	20 clear calendar days from date of acceptance (on the 21st day)	*r. 8.03(5)* *r. 9.01(1)* *r. 10.03(1)*

Notes:

*   The Federal Crown has 30 clear calendar days from date of service (on the 31st day).

(3) Service Outside Territorial Division — **If all the defendants have been served outside the court's territorial division, the clerk shall not note any defendant in default until it is proved by an affidavit for jurisdiction (Form 11A) submitted to the clerk, or by evidence presented before a judge, that the action was properly brought in that territorial division.**

(4) Electronic Filing — **In the case of a plaintiff's claim that was issued electronically under rule 7.04, the plaintiff may file the affidavit for jurisdiction electronically.**

O. Reg. 78/06, s. 24; 44/14, s. 8

11.02 (1) Default Judgment, Plaintiff's Claim, Debt or Liquidated Demand — **If a defendant has been noted in default, the clerk may sign default judgment (Form 11B) in respect of the claim or any part of the claim to which the default applies that is for a debt or liquidated demand in money, including interest if claimed.**

History [R. 11.02(1)]: Formerly 10.02(1); plain language changes.

Commentary: *Solicitor's Accounts*: If a claim involves an action to recover unpaid legal fees, the right to prejudgment interest is governed by section 33 of the *Solicitors Act*.

- A solicitor has no entitlement to prejudgment interest if the rate of interest is not shown on the account delivered to the defendant. It is not sufficient to state "interest in accordance with section 33 of the *Solicitors Act*";

- Where a rate is shown on the account, it will be the applicable rate of prejudgment interest as long as it does not exceed the rate permitted by the *Courts of Justice Act*;

- The rate of prejudgment interest is the rate in effect on the date that the account was delivered to the defendant by the solicitor; and

- If the parties have agreed to a contractual rate, the contractual rate will apply.

It is the responsibility of the claimant to seek prejudgment interest in the claim and insert the full amount of interest. It is the responsibility of the claimant to calculate the amount of post-judgment interest owing.

A solicitor who has obtained a judgment for unpaid legal fees is entitled to post-judgment interest pursuant to section 129 of the *Courts of Justice Act*, even if there is no mention of it in the account delivered to the defendant(s).

Where the plaintiff seeks to obtain a default judgment in the Superior Court of Justice on a claim that is within the monetary jurisdiction of the Small Claims Court, the registrar shall assess costs in accordance with that court's tariff [r. 57.05(03)].

Default Judgment Scenarios

In each, assume that:

a. it is not against a party under disability (or leave of a judge has been obtained);

b. it is not against a defendant to a cross-claim who has been noted in default;

c. it is not against a third party claim in a third party claim who has been noted in default;

d. no Defence is filed;

e. Affidavit of Service filed complies with applicable rules of service;

f. the defendant has been noted in default;

g. The Crown in right of Ontario is not a party (or leave of the court has been obtained); and

h. Her Majesty the Queen in right of Canada is not a party (or leave of the court has been obtained).

The clerk can sign default judgment because the claim is for:

- a debt or liquidated demand in money, including interest if claimed in the statement of claim;

- recovery of possession of land;

- recovery of possession of personal property; or

- foreclosure, sale or redemption of a mortgage.

A liquidated claim is a claim for a sum of money due under an express agreement where the amount is fixed and does not depend on any subsequent evaluation by the court. An unliquidated claim is a claim where the amount in dispute is not fixed and the court must determine the amount that the plaintiff is entitled to receive.

SCENARIO 1: Person A makes a verbal agreement with Person B for the restoration of an automobile for $30,000. The automobile is restored. Person B sends to Person A an invoice for $30,000 which is not paid and subsequently Person B makes a claim for $30,000, attaching a copy of the invoice.

A: This is a liquidated claim. Person A obligated himself to pay Person B a specific sum of money for the restoration of the automobile. Person A neither paid for the restoration nor filed a defence denying that the repairs were made.

SCENARIO 2: Person A makes a verbal agreement with Person B to repair a motorcycle. Person B makes the repairs and is paid $12,000 by Person A. Person A makes a claim stating that the repairs are faulty and seeks the full return of his payment.

A: This is an unliquidated claim. The court must assess the value of the repairs done in order to arrive at a final figure owing to the plaintiff.

SCENARIO 3: Person A rents a house to Person B for $3,500 per week. There is no lease or other written agreement. For six months the cash payments are made each Friday. Person B does not make the payment for 3 weeks (although he promises he will do so) and then vacates the house. Person A subsequently makes a claim for the unpaid rental amount of $10,500. No supporting documentation is attached to the claim.

A: This is a liquidated claim. Person B obligated himself to pay Person A for rental of the house pursuant to a verbal agreement. The amount of the claim is capable of being ascertained as a simple arithmetical calculation (i.e. $3,500 x 3 weeks). There is no general requirement to attach supporting documentation to a claim unless the claim is specifically based on a document.

SCENARIO 4: Person A sees Person B's son throwing garbage into Person A's well. Person B offers to repair the well. Person A repairs it herself and pursues a claim against Person B for the cost of materials plus hourly rate for performing the repairs.

A: This is an unliquidated claim. Person B did not obligate himself to pay a specific sum of money for the repairs of the well. A judge would be required to determine whether the amount claimed for the repairs was reasonable in the circumstances.

SCENARIO 5: Person A repairs person B's car under a verbal agreement. Person B pays for the cost of the repairs by cheque, which is dishonoured and returned by the bank marked "NSF." Person A makes a claim for recovery of the amount of the NSF cheque and associated bank charges and attaches a copy of the returned cheque including the statement of charges.

A: This is a liquidated claim. The amount of the claim is fixed and verified by the returned cheque and statement of charges.

SCENARIO 6: Lawyer A files a claim against Person B for an unpaid legal account.

A: Lawyers' accounts can be considered liquidated claims, and default judgment can be signed if the claim or appended material indicates that:

- the legal account is for a fixed amount or fixed estimated amount and that the amount was agreed upon in advance; *OR*

- the legal account is capable of mathematical calculation based upon an hourly rate and number of hours worked, and the hourly rate was agreed to in advance.

It is not sufficient for the claim to simply state that the lawyer was retained and to append an account; the claim and appended material (if any) must show how the account was arrived at. If insufficient information were available to determine the fixed amount owing, or to make a mathematical calculation, the plaintiff would be required to make a motion to a judge to obtain judgment.

SCENARIO 9: Person A paid Person B in advance to renovate his kitchen. A signed contract with details of the work agreed upon to be done is attached to the claim. Person A makes a claim against Person B for failing to renovate Person A's home according to the terms of the contract.

A: This is an unliquidated claim. The amount of the claim would depend on a subsequent valuation by the court. Evidence would be required to determine the value of the renovations completed.

Case Law: *Eades v. Kootnikoff* (1995), 13 B.C.L.R. (3d) 182 (S.C.) — Whether a claim can be identified as a "liquidated demand" such that, upon default of appearance, final judgment may be taken for the amount of the claim depends upon whether the amount to which the plaintiff is entitled can be ascertained from the contract itself or by calculation or fixed by a scale of charges agreed upon by the contract or implied by it. Some lawyers' accounts for legal services may be liquidated demands and others may not. Where the pleadings do not claim that there was an agreement as to the amount the lawyer was to be paid or as to the method of calculation of the lawyer's fee, a lawyer's claim for legal services is not a liquidated demand. *Holden Day Wilson v. Ashton* (1993), 14 O.R. (3d) 306, 104 D.L.R. (4th) 266, 64 O.A.C. 4 (Div. Ct.) applied.

Rule 19.02(1) of the *Rules of Civil Procedure* provide that a defendant who has been noted in default is deemed to admit the truth of all allegations of fact made in the claim. In default hearings, facts going to liability deemed to be true but facts going to damages must be proven. Judgment amended to read that the wife and brother were jointly and severally liable to plaintiff for the damages suffered. *Umlauf v. Umlauf* (2001), 197 D.L.R. (4th) 715, 53 O.R. (3d) 355, 142 O.A.C. 328, 9 C.P.C. (5th) 93, 2001 CarswellOnt 851, [2001] O.J. No. 1054 (Ont. C.A.), *per* Finlayson J.A. (O'Connor and MacPherson JJ.A. concurring).

Benesch v. Fairmont Hotels Inc. (2001), 2001 CarswellOnt 1916 (Ont. S.C.J.) — Plaintiff acting in person noted individual defendant in default before time limit. Plaintiff obtained default judgment against other defendants in breach of agreement to notify before taking steps. Plaintiff made intimidating communications to represented parties and counsel. Judgment set aside and restraining order granted.

David Wilson Consulting v. Cesar Pedro TV Productions (2001), 2001 CarswellOnt 3157 (Ont. C.A.) — No basis for interference with decision of motions judge. Plaintiff's claim was liquidated demand in money and had complied with Rule 19.04(1)(a) of the *Rules of Civil Procedure*. Appellant had not explained circumstances which led to default and did not present a triable defence on the merits.

Beaucage v. Grand & Toy Ltd. (2001), 2001 CarswellOnt 4568, 19 B.L.R. (3d) 196, 17 C.P.R. (4th) 125, [2001] O.J. No. 5128 (Ont. S.C.J.); additional reasons at (2002), 2002 CarswellOnt 49 (Ont. S.C.J.) — To withstand motion to strike out pleading, there must be sufficient particulars in statement of claim to enable defendant to know specifically what facts plaintiffs relied on in their claims.

Temple v. Riley, 6 C.P.C. (5th) 116, 2001 CarswellNS 64, 2001 NSCA 36, 191 N.S.R. (2d) 87, 596 A.P.R. 87, [2001] N.S.J. No. 66 (N.S. C.A.) — Applicant seeking to set aside default judgment must show both defence on merits and reasonable excuse for delay in filing defence. Defendant provided ample evidence of arguable defence on merits, and reasonable explanation for delay in applying to set aside orders. Default judgment entered without notice to insurer or it's insured. Neither received notice of intended assessment of damages.

Sonnenschein v. Kramchynski, 8 C.P.C. (5th) 80, 2000 CarswellSask 329, 2000 SKQB 181, 192 Sask. R. 279 (Sask. Q.B.) — Plaintiff lawyer brought action against defendant clients for payment of account. Lawyer's account not taxed. Clients noted in default and brought application to set aside default judgment. Application dismissed. Judgment should not be set aside as matter of public policy merely because it represents account for solicitor's fees and disbursements.

P.I.I.M. Canada Corp. v. Poetry in Motion (Canada) Inc. (2000), 1 C.P.C. (5th) 339, 2000 CarswellOnt 962 (Ont. S.C.J.) — Plaintiff unable to effect personal service on defendant. Served claim on adult who identified himself as living at defendant's address. Defendant failed to file statement of defence. Plaintiff obtained default judgment. Motion granted. Defendant's evidence indicated he never resided there and that address incorrect in any event.

Tyo Law Corp. v. White (1999), 1 C.P.C. (5th) 323, 1999 CarswellBC 1569 (B.C. S.C.) — Solicitor accepted $1,000 from client in payment of outstanding accounts. Solicitor released file contents to client and filed notice of withdrawal of Small Claims action concerning outstanding accounts. Client filed application to review accounts. Application dismissed. Solicitor entitled to accord and satisfaction as client bargained with solicitor and settled matter. Client estopped by his conduct regarding outstanding accounts. Retainer agreement should be construed *contra proferentum*. Mutual intent of solicitor and client was that accounts represented payment on account of fees or disbursements in respect of entire contract.

Protect-A-Home Services Inc. v. Heber (2001), 2001 CarswellMan 530, [2001] M.J. No. 466, 2001 MBCA 171, [2002] 3 W.W.R. 281, 160 Man. R. (2d) 100, 262 W.A.C. 100 (Man. C.A.) — Plaintiff noted defendant in default after giving notice of its intention to do so if defence not served, and after defendant failed to comply with interim order obtained by plaintiff restraining defendant from infringing plaintiff's exclusive right to use business name and related relief. Where defendant flouted interim orders lack of defence on merits was fatal.

Halow Estate v. Halow (2002), 2002 CarswellOnt 1062, 158 O.A.C. 125, 59 O.R. (3d) 211 (Ont. C.A.) — Appellant noted in default under Rule 19.01(2) of *Rules of Civil Procedure* (Ontario) and sought to appeal to Court of Appeal. No jurisdiction lay in appeal court as appellant had to set aside default judgment under Rule 19.08. Default was not final judgment pursuant to section 6.(1)(b) of *Courts of Justice Act* (Ontario).

Kaplin v. Gottdenker (2003), 2003 CarswellOnt 1831 (Ont. S.C.J.). Self-represented Plaintiff provided post office box address and no address for personal service. Defendant's motion to strike statement of claim was sent to incorrect postal code and was not served. Claim defective but not entirely devoid of merit. Order striking claim was set aside, on terms.

Suwinski v. Porcupine (Rural Municipality) No. 395, 2002 CarswellSask 824, 2002 SKPC 113, 229 Sask. R. 293 (Sask. Prov. Ct.). After failure of Plaintiff to attend court on day of trial, he applied to revive original summons requiring Defendant to appear in Court. Trial struck from docket constituted dismissal of action. Such dismissal was without prejudice to

Plaintiff's right to recommence proceedings by having new summons issued. Not appropriate to simply adjourn matter to new date. Plaintiff required to issue and serve new summons if he wished to pursue claim.

B & S Publications Inc. v. Gaulin, 2002 CarswellAlta 1227, 2002 ABCA 238, 317 A.R. 397, 284 W.A.C. 397 (Alta. C.A.). Order consolidated two actions. Appeal dismissed. Separate trial would result in duplication of process because likely same witnesses would testify. Inconsistent verdicts were to be avoided.

Van Moorsel v. Tomaszeski, 2002 CarswellAlta 1258, 2002 ABQB 905 (Alta. Q.B.). Trial judge found in favour of Respondent. Respondent did not appear on appeal. Appellants attempted to pay judgment but registered letter containing cheque was returned to them. Respondent gave false address to Court. Appeal dismissed.

Burchell Hayman Parish v. Sirena Canada Inc., 2006 CarswellNS 520, 2006 NSSM 28 (N.S. Sm. Cl. Ct.), 2006-11-21, W. Augustus Richardson, Adjudicator.

Taxation of legal fees.

Time spent as set out in two accounts totalled 44.1 hours, too high for work done. Reason lawyer spent so much time is that, as a young lawyer just starting out, she lacked the knowledge, experience and confidence of a more senior lawyer.

Client should not be required to pay for the learning experience of a junior: see *Goodman & Carr v. Tempra Management Ltd.* (1991), 25 A.C.W.S. (3d) 169 (Ont Assess. O.), and *Canada Trustco Mortgage Co. v. Homburg*, 1999 CarswellNS 354, [1999] N.S.J. No. 382, 44 C.P.C. (4th) 103, 180 N.S.R. (2d) 258, 557 A.P.R. 258 (N.S. S.C.) at paras. 17-18. Test simply whether charge for a new lawyer's time is "fair and reasonable and stand the test of taxation, if requested": *Toulany v. McInnes, Cooper & Robertson*, [1989] N.S.J. No. 99, 1989 CarswellNS 298, 90 N.S.R. (2d) 256, 230 A.P.R. 256, (sub nom. *Toulany, Re)* 57 D.L.R. (4th) 649 (N.S. T.D.) at p. 4.

Witten LLP v. Arsenault, 2006 CarswellAlta 132, 393 A.R. 216, 2006 ABPC 29, 27 C.P.C. (6th) 174 (Alta. Prov. Ct.).

Plaintiff solicitors brought action for payment of their account. Defendant sought referral of solicitor's account for taxation. Taxation of solicitor's account directed. Line of cases that held Provincial Court judge not bound by R. 626 of *Alberta Rules of Court*, which prohibited default judgment with respect to solicitor's accounts, was unsound. Public policy, basis of R. 626, should be same in Provincial Court as in Court of Queen's Bench. R. 626 should apply to all accounts between lawyers and their clients both in Court of Queen's Bench and in Provincial Court.

Ford v. Thorold (City), 2006 CarswellOnt 4129 (Ont. S.C.J.), J.W. Quinn J.

Plaintiff's solicitor not able to obtain instructions from plaintiff and was removed from record. Plaintiff did not appoint new solicitor or serve notice of intention to act in person. Facts did not show active interest of plaintiff to prosecute action. Order to dismiss action was to issue after filing of affidavit of service. Costs were fixed at $750 plus GST.

D & S Developments Inc. v. Gamble, 329 Sask. R. 247, 2009 SKQB 187, 81 C.L.R. (3d) 134, 2009 CarswellSask 339 (Sask. Q.B.); leave to appeal refused 337 Sask. R. 114, 464 W.A.C. 114, 81 C.L.R. (3d) 149, 2009 CarswellSask 456, 2009 SKCA 82 (Sask. C.A. [In Chambers]), Lane J.A.

Third party brought application to set aside noting of default of August 19, 2004, and judgment granted by Court on February 18, 2009, and to grant third party leave to defend third party claim. Application granted. Court not satisfied that setting aside judgment will seriously prejudice plaintiff that cannot be compensated to her by way of adequate costs security. There was no suggestion delay in participating in this litigation has resulted in loss of witness availability or evidence.

Coinage Distribution Inc. v. Royal Canadian Mint, 2011 BCSC 352, 2011 CarswellBC 646 (B.C. S.C.), Gropper J.; leave to appeal refused 2011 BCCA 296, 2011 CarswellBC 1549, 307 B.C.A.C. 296, 519 W.A.C. 296, 21 B.C.L.R. (5th) 4 (B.C. C.A. [In Chambers]); affirming on reconsideration 2010 BCSC 1245, 2010 CarswellBC 2342 (B.C. S.C. [In Chambers]); affirming on reconsideration 2010 BCSC 1244, 2010 CarswellBC 2341 (B.C. S.C. [In Chambers]), Gropper J.

The defendant advised the plaintiff that requirements of section 25 *Crown Liability and Proceedings Act* prevented his obtaining of a default judgment. The defendant gave notice of intention to set a stay motion down at the same time as an anticipated motion for leave to obtain default judgment. The defendant applied for a stay of proceedings and an order setting aside a default judgment. The applications were granted and the plaintiff was ordered to pay special costs to the defendant. The plaintiff applied to set aside the orders. The application was dismissed. The obtaining of a default judgment without notice deserves a rebuke. The plaintiff's counsel had not provided an explanation. Special costs were payable by the plaintiff to the defendant.

(2) The fact that default judgment has been signed under subrule (1) does not affect the plaintiff's right to proceed on the remainder of the claim or against any other defendant for all or part of the claim.

History [R. 11.02(2)]: Formerly 10.02(2), adds that the clerk may note the party in default.

(3) Manner of Service of Default Judgment — A default judgment (Form 11B) shall be served in accordance with subrule 8.01(4) and, if applicable, subrule 8.01(4.1).

(4) [Repealed O. Reg. 78/06, s. 24.]

O. Reg. 78/06, s. 24; 44/14, s. 9

History [R. 11.02(4)]: Formerly 10.02(4).

Commentary: If the claim is for a debt or liquidated claim and a defence is received for part of the claim only, the clerk may note the defendant in default and sign default judgment on the undefended part of the claim. (The undefended part is the admitted debt.)

11.03 (1) Default Judgment, Plaintiff's Claim, Unliquidated Demand — If all defendants have been noted in default, the plaintiff may obtain judgment against a defendant noted in default with respect to any part of the claim to which rule 11.02 does not apply.

History [R. 11.04(1)]: Formerly 10.03(1), refers to claims other than those under subrule 11.02(1), which was formerly 10.02(1); refers to Form 16A, formerly Form 17A; plain language changes.

(2) To obtain judgment, the plaintiff may,

(a) file a notice of motion and supporting affidavit (Form 15A) requesting a motion in writing for an assessment of damages, setting out the reasons why the motion should be granted and attaching any relevant documents; or

(b) file a request to clerk (Form 9B) requesting that an assessment hearing be arranged.

History [R. 11.04(2)]: Formerly 10.03(2); plain language changes.

(3) Inadequate Supporting Affidavit — On a motion in writing for an assessment of damages under clause (2)(a), a judge who finds the plaintiff's affidavit inadequate or unsatisfactory may order that,

(a) a further affidavit be provided; or

(b) an assessment hearing be held.

(4) Assessment Hearing — If an assessment hearing is to be held under clause (2)(b) or (3)(b), the clerk shall fix a date for the hearing and send a notice of hearing to the plaintiff, and the assessment hearing shall proceed as a trial in accordance with rule 17.

(5) Matters to be Proved — On a motion in writing for an assessment of damages or at an assessment hearing, the plaintiff is not required to prove liability against a defendant noted in default, but is required to prove the amount of the claim.

(6) Service of Order — An order made on a motion in writing for an assessment of damages shall be served by the clerk in accordance with subrule 8.01(5).

(7) No Assessment where Defence Filed — If one or more defendants have filed a defence, a plaintiff requiring an assessment of damages against a defendant noted in default shall proceed to a settlement conference under rule 13 and, if necessary, a trial in accordance with rule 17.

O. Reg. 78/06, s. 24; 393/09, s. 9

History [R. 11.03]: New provision, stating that default judgment on a defendant's claim may only be obtained at trial or on motion.

Commentary: Default judgment for unliquidated claims is only available where all defendants have been noted in default, as indicated by rule 11.03(1). If a defence has been filed the matter should proceed to a single trial of both the defended and undefended claims: see *Belair Insurance Co. v. Dias*, 2013 CarswellOnt 1806, 47 C.P.C. (7th) 160 (Ont. S.C.J.).

If a Defence (Form 9A) has been filed for a part of a debt or liquidated demand in money, the clerk may sign default judgment and issue a Notice of Default Judgment (Form 11A) on the undefended part of the liquidated claim.

If a defence has been filed, whereby the defendant has offered a proposal of terms of payment (and the plaintiff did not dispute the proposal), and there is a failure to make payment in accordance with the proposal, the clerk will sign default judgment and issue a notice of default judgment for the unpaid balance of the undisputed amount on the filing of an Affidavit (Form 15B). It is unnecessary to review the Plaintiff's Claim (Form 7A) to determine whether the amount for which the defendant has admitted liability is for a liquidated or unliquidated claim [r. 9.03(2)(b)].

If a defence has been filed admitting liability, but failing to set out the proposed terms of payment, a notice of default judgment is not issued. The matter should be listed for a hearing in accordance with local practice.

Where a partnership has been sued in the firm name and has been noted in default, default judgment should not be signed until the time has expired for the filing of a statement of defence by all persons who have been served under r. 5.03 as alleged partners.

A default judgment also may not be issued in the following circumstances:

1. In a Defendant's Claim (Form 10A), where the plaintiff in the defendant's claim wishes to obtain judgment against a defendant who has been noted in default with re-

spect to a defendant's claim, judgment may only be obtained at trial or on motion to a judge [r. 11.04];

2. In an action in which the Crown in Right of Ontario is a party, leave of the court is required before default judgment may be issued [section 18, *Proceedings Against the Crown Act*];

3. In an action in which Her Majesty in right of Canada is a party, leave of the court is required before default judgment may be issued [section 25, *Crown Liability and Proceedings Act*]; and

4. In an action in which the defendant is a person under disability, *unless* leave of the court has been given to note the defendant in default [r. 11.01(2)].

If a party files a default judgment and pays the prescribed fee, staff may note the other party in default and then proceed to sign the default judgment.

Once a default judgment has been issued, the plaintiff and/or creditor may request the issuance of any of the following:

- Certificate of judgment;

- Writ of seizure and sale of personal property;

- Writ of seizure and sale of land;

- Notice of garnishment;

- Notice of examination;

- Writ of delivery (once an order of the court directing the return of goods to the rightful owner has been made).

A notice of examination and a notice of garnishment may only be issued from the court where the debtor resides or carries on business. A certificate of judgment may only be issued from the court where judgment was obtained.

The fee for default judgment is payable for the act of issuing a default judgment. In situations of a default judgment against more than one defendant in the same action at the same time, only one fee would be payable. In situations where default judgment is refused on more than one occasion relating to the same file, a fee would be payable in each instance where judgment is issued.

If a deputy judge at a settlement conference orders "that the defendant pay costs of $100 before a specific date or the defence will be struck," unless the order indicates otherwise, if the defendant fails to pay costs as ordered, the plaintiff could proceed as if the defence had not been filed. The plaintiff must file an affidavit indicating that the payment of costs was not made. If the claim was for a liquidated amount, the plaintiff can request default judgment. If the claim amount was not liquidated, the plaintiff can request an assessment hearing or file a motion in writing for an assessment of damages.

Can a Clerk Sign Default Judgment Because the Claim is for a Liquidated Amount?

SCENARIO 1: Person A makes a verbal agreement with Person B for the repair of a broken window for $300. The window is repaired. Person B sends Person A an invoice for $300 which is not paid and, subsequently, Person B makes a claim for $300, attaching a copy of the invoice. Would the clerk sign default judgment?

A: This is a liquidated claim. Person A obligated himself to pay Person B a specific sum of money for the repair of the window. Person a neither paid for the repairs nor filed a defence denying that the repairs were made. The clerk would sign default judgment.

SCENARIO 2: Person A makes a verbal agreement with Person B to repair a motorcycle. Person B makes the repairs and is paid $2,000 by Person A. Person A makes a claim stating that the repairs are faulty and seeks the full return of his payment. Would the clerk sign default judgment?

A: This is an unliquidated claim. The clerk would not sign default judgment. The court must assess the value of the repairs done in order to arrive at a final figure owing to the plaintiff.

SCENARIO 3: Person A rents a car to Person B for $250 per week. There is no lease or other written agreement. For six months the cash payments are made each Friday. Person B does not make the payment for 3 weeks (although he promises he will do so) and then returns the car. Person a subsequently makes a claim for the unpaid rental amount of $750. No supporting documentation is attached to the claim. Would the clerk sign default judgment?

A: This is a liquidated claim. The clerk would sign default judgment. Person B obligated himself to pay Person A for rental of the car pursuant to a verbal agreement. The amount of the claim is capable of being ascertained as a simple arithmetical calculation (i.e. $250 × 3 weeks). There is no general requirement to attach supporting documentation to a claim unless the claim is specifically based on a document.

SCENARIO 4: Person A sees Person B's son throw a rock through Person A's basement window. Person B offers to repair the window. Person A repairs it herself and pursues a claim against Person B for the cost of materials plus hourly rate for performing the repairs. Would the clerk sign default judgment?

A: This is an unliquidated claim. The clerk would not sign default judgment. Person B did not obligate himself to pay a specific sum of money for the repairs of the window. A judge would be required to determine whether the amount claimed for the repairs was reasonable in the circumstances.

SCENARIO 5: Person A makes a written agreement with person B to loan him the amount of $900 at an interest rate of 30% per annum. Person B makes only two loan payments of $100 each. Person A subsequently makes a claim for recovery of the $700 owing plus interest at the rate of 30% per annum and attaches a copy of the agreement. Would the clerk sign default judgment?

A: This is a liquidated claim. The clerk would sign default judgment. The amount owing can be ascertained from the loan amount and the interest rate agreed on by the parties set out in their agreement. The rate of interest charged is of no concern to the clerk unless it exceeds 60% per annum. It is an offence under s. 347 of the *Criminal Code* for anyone who enters into an agreement or arrangement to receive interest at the criminal rate, or to actually receive an interest payment that exceeds the annual criminal rate of 60%. If the interest rate claimed exceeds 60%, the plaintiff would be required to seek an assessment of damages before a judge.

SCENARIO 6: Solicitor A files a claim against Person B for an unpaid legal account. Would the clerk sign default judgment?

A: Solicitors' accounts can be considered liquidated claims, and default judgment can be signed if the claim or appended material indicates that:

- The legal account is for a fixed amount or fixed estimated amount and that the amount was agreed upon in advance; or

- The legal account is capable of mathematical calculation based upon an hourly rate and number of hours worked and the hourly rate was agreed to in advance.

It is not sufficient for the claim to simply state that the solicitor was retained and to append an account; the claim and appended material (if any) must show how the account was arrived at. If insufficient information were available to determine the fixed amount owing, or to make a mathematical calculation, the plaintiff would be required to seek an assessment of damages before a judge.

SCENARIO 7: A car dealership sold a car to Person A. Person A defaulted on the loan payments to the dealership with $8,000 still owing. The contract signed by Person A indicated that in the event of default, the vehicle would be repossessed and sold at auction and any outstanding balance would remain payable. The dealership had the car repossessed and sold it for $3,000 at auction. The dealership claims $6,000 from Person A, which is the amount of the debt remaining of $5,000 plus $1,000 in expenses for the repossession and auctioneer. The dealership provides documentation of the original sales contract, the repossession fee of $500, the auctioneer fee of $500 and the final bill of sale for $3,000. The dealership asks the clerk to sign default after filing the affidavit of service. Would the clerk sign default judgment?

A: This is a liquidated claim. The clerk would sign default judgment. A claim based on a contractual obligation that resulted in a monetary deficiency in the resale of the car is a liquidated claim. The dealership had a duty to sell the vehicle at a fair price. This duty does not prevent the claim from being a liquidated claim. No valuation by the court is necessary. The expenses, incurred in accordance with the contractual provisions for default on loan payments, are supported by documentation and are fixed.

Commentary: Caselaw dealing with Rule 19 of the *Rules of Civil Procedure* should be read with caution, given the different legislation applicable in the Small Claims Court. In addition, the current state of the authorities from the Court of Appeal dealing with what must be proved at an undefended hearing is unsatisfactory, essentially because of *Umlauf v. Umlauf*, *infra*. It is submitted that the Court of Appeal's earlier decision in *Segraves v. Fralick*, *infra*, and its subsequent decision in *Canadian-Automatic Data Processing Services Ltd. v. CEEI Safety & Security Inc.*, *infra*, more accurately state the law. It is submitted that the first instance decisions from the Superior Court of Justice in *Englefield v. Wolfe*, *infra*, *Plouffe v. Roy*, *infra*, and *Nikore v. Jarmain Investment Management Inc.*, *infra*, correctly state the law under the *Rules of Civil Procedure*. Fundamentally it is impractical in many cases to treat liability and damages as watertight compartments, for example given the need for a causal link between them. The different procedural rules of the Small Claims Court may or may not mean that those authorities can safely be applied in this court.

Case Law: *Segraves v. Fralick* (1951), 1951 CarswellOnt 88, [1951] O.R. 871, [1952] 1 D.L.R. 544, [1951] O.W.N. 917 (Ont. C.A.)

It was held that a default judgment declaring a marriage null and void, which was premised on deemed admissions resulting from the defendant's noting in default, had to be set aside. The fact of a prior marriage ought to have been strictly proved by evidence at trial. There is no magic in the default rules which would compel the court to act on allegations made by a plaintiff which become deemed admissions.

Umlauf v. Umlauf, 2001 CarswellOnt 851, 53 O.R. (3d) 355, 9 C.P.C. (5th) 93, 197 D.L.R. (4th) 715, 142 O.A.C. 328, [2001] O.J. No. 1054 (Ont. C.A.)

At an undefended trial, the action was dismissed on the ground that no basis for liability in negligence was established. On appeal, that decision was reversed and judgment granted for the plaintiff. It was held that in default hearings, facts going to liability are deemed to be true but facts going to damages must be proved, and that the trial judge was wrong to enter into an inquiry as to liability.

Canadian-Automatic Data Processing Services Ltd. v. CEEI Safety & Security Inc., 2004 CarswellOnt 4993, 50 B.L.R. (3d) 31, 246 D.L.R. (4th) 400, 192 O.A.C. 152, [2004] O.J. No. 4879 (Ont. C.A.)

On a motion for default judgment, Carnwath J. dismissed the plaintiff's claim for unjust enrichment on the basis that no such unjust enrichment was proved. The Court of Appeal agreed and the appeal was dismissed.

Englefield v. Wolf, 2005 CarswellOnt 6609, 33 B.L.R. (4th) 267, 20 C.P.C. (6th) 157, [2005] O.J. No. 4895 (Ont. S.C.J.); additional reasons 2006 CarswellOnt 1962, 33 B.L.R. (4th) 288, 26 C.P.C. (6th) 103 (Ont. S.C.J.); additional reasons 2006 CarswellOnt 4983, 33 B.L.R. (4th) 294, 31 C.P.C. (6th) 174 (Ont. S.C.J.)

The default judgment procedure under Rule 19 of the *Rules of Civil Procedure* does not require the court to accept a legally-untenable theory of liability on a motion for judgment. If liability is pleaded on the basis of facts that would not constitute a cause of action known to law, the plaintiff is not entitled to a default judgment.

Plouffe v. Roy, 2007 CarswellOnt 5739, 50 C.C.L.T. (3d) 137, [2007] O.J. No. 3453 (Ont. S.C.J.)

An undefended trial is not merely an assessment of damages, even if the defendant is deemed to have admitted the allegations of fact made in the statement of claim. The court is not obliged to accept that ludicrous or erroneous allegations of fact are true. The court is not relegated to the role of a rubber stamp. While the defendant's absence means that there is no one to attack or challenge the plaintiff's evidence, the plaintiff still has to prove that he or she is entitled to the judgment sought as a matter of fact and law.

Viola v. Hornstein, 2009 CarswellOnt 1963, [2009] O.J. No. 1486 (Ont. S.C.J.)

At an undefended trial, the trial judge not only must consider the deemed admissions flowing from the default, but should also perform the general tasks of considering credibility, weighing the evidence and making findings of fact, in order to determine whether the plaintiff is entitled to judgment. If the trial judge concludes that the plaintiff has proved liability, the trial judge can proceed to assess damages on the evidence adduced.

Nikore v. Jarmain Investment Management Inc., 2009 CarswellOnt 5258, 97 O.R. (3d) 132 (Ont. S.C.J.)

An undefended trial is not limited to an assessment of damages. The fact that allegations of law or mixed fact and law are not defended does not bind the court. It is for the court to determine whether the evidence is sufficient to entitle a plaintiff to judgment, whether on the basis of deemed admissions or when considered together with all the other evidence.

Cobean v. Jannit Developments Inc. (April 26, 2010), Doc. 67/10, [2010] O.J. No. 1705 (Ont. Sm. Cl. Ct.)

On an assessment hearing, the plaintiff is required to satisfy the court that he or she is entitled to judgment as a matter of fact and law.

Barber-Collins Security Services Ltd. v. Vranki Family Holdings Ltd., 2011 CarswellOnt 16002, [2011] O.J. No. 1268 (Ont. Sm. Cl. Ct.)

Where the plaintiff's evidence and pleading established a contract with a party other than the defendant against who default judgment was sought, the claim was dismissed.

Grand River Natural Stone Ltd. v. Armour Masonry, 2011 CarswellOnt 15934, [2011] O.J. No. 5707 (Ont. Sm. Cl. Ct.)

Plaintiff sought default judgment against a company and an alleged guarantor. The court held that there was no separate guarantee and dismissed the claim as against that defendant. Discussion of authorities relating to default judgment in the Small Claims Court.

627220 Ontario Inc. v. Waterloo North Hydro Inc., 2007 CarswellOnt 6666, [2007] O.J. No. 4109 (Ont. Sm. Cl. Ct.)

At this assessment hearing, the claim was dismissed. The Plaintiff's Claim contained no allegations of negligence or particulars of negligence and failed to disclose a reasonable cause of action. The affidavit filed in an attempt to prove damages was found to affirmatively prove that no damages were sustained. When default judgment is requested, the court's duty is to examine the material before it and determine whether the plaintiff has established a legally-tenable claim and a proper evidentiary foundation for its undefended request. Discussion of legislation applicable to requests for default judgment in the Small Claims Court.

Capitol Hill I v. Stieler (August 31, 2009), Doc. 850/09, [2009] O.J. No. 3562 (Ont. Sm. Cl. Ct.)

The plaintiff's supporting affidavit was not in proper form, attaching an unsworn statement to an empty affidavit stating only "See attached Schedule 'A'". The substance of the statement was a bald assertion that the former tenant "left damages beyond normal wear and tear to the premises." There was a request for rent arrears which was not pleaded in the Plaintiff's Claim, and supporting documentation was lacking. The court found that no damages were proved and the claim was dismissed.

Bennett Leasing Ltd. v. Jennings (October 23, 2009), Doc. 927/09, [2009] O.J. No. 4418 (Ont. Sm. Cl. Ct.)

The assessment hearing was previously adjourned at the plaintiff's request, to permit better affidavit evidence to be filed, but none was filed. The sole affidavit was so poorly drafted and unintelligible as to leave considerable doubt whether the deponent could possibly have read and understood its content before signing. No supporting documentation was attached as exhibits to the affidavit in support of an unparticularized figure representing the alleged net arrears on a motor vehicle lease. No evidence of what the plaintiff's position would have been but for the alleged breach of contract was provided, nor was the disposition of the vehicle disclosed. The claim was dismissed.

Orangehen.com v. Collins (December 2, 2009), Doc. 1027/09, [2009] O.J. No. 5160 (Ont. Sm. Cl. Ct.)

At an assessment hearing, the plaintiff is required to satisfy the court that it is entitled to judgment as a matter of fact and law. The court granted, in part, a default judgment but declined to allow several charges which were found to constitute illegal interest charges contrary to s. 347 of the *Criminal Code*, R.S.C. 1985, c. C-46.

Panza v. Bayaty (October 6, 2009), Doc. 78072/08, [2009] O.J. No. 4163 (Ont. Sm. Cl. Ct.)

On a motion for default judgment, the court found that the claim was commenced after expiry of the applicable limitation period. However, a limitation defence must be pleaded by the defendant. Since the defendant had entered no defence, judgment was granted for the plaintiff.

11.04 Default Judgment, Defendant's Claim — If a party against whom a defendant's claim is made has been noted in default, judgment may be obtained against the party only at trial or on motion.

O. Reg. 78/06, s. 24

Commentary: Where a claim is for an unliquidated amount (i.e., where the claim is not for a debt or a liquidated demand in money), and the defendant has been noted in default, the plaintiff shall proceed to trial (also known as an assessment of damages or trial in default) to prove the amount of the claim. The clerk cannot issue a notice of default judgment. The clerk will fix a trial date and send a Notice of Trial (Form 16A) to the plaintiff and any defendant who has filed a defence [r. 11.04(1)].

11.05 Consequences of Noting in Default — (1) A defendant who has been noted in default shall not file a defence or take any other step in the proceeding, except making a motion under rule 11.06, without leave of the court or the plaintiff's consent.

History [R. 11.05(1)]: Formerly 10.04(1); refers to a motion under subrule 11.06(1), which was formerly 10.05(1); plain language changes.

(2) Any step in the proceeding may be taken without the consent of a defendant who has been noted in default.

History [R. 11.05(2)]: Formerly 10.04(2); plain language changes.

(3) A defendant who has been noted in default is not entitled to notice of any step in the proceeding and need not be served with any other document, except the following:

　　1. Subrule 11.02(3) (service of default judgment).

　　2. Rule 12.01 (amendment of claim or defence).

　　3. Subrule 15.01(6) (motion after judgment).

　　4. Postjudgment proceedings against a debtor under rule 20.

O. Reg. 78/06, s. 24

Commentary: If a party has been noted in default, staff will refuse to file any further documents from the party noted in default except as ordered by the court or with the consent of the plaintiff [r. 11.05(1)].

If one defendant is served within the territorial division where the claim was issued, the plaintiff is not required to establish that the claim was filed in the appropriate territorial division. However, if all defendants were served outside the territorial division, prior to having any party noted in default, the plaintiff must establish that the action was brought in the proper territorial division by filing an affidavit for jurisdiction before staff may note a defendant in default [r. 11.01(3)].

Affidavit(s) of service must provide that:

- Service has been made and the time set out in the Rules for filing a defence has elapsed.

　　a. When service is deemed to have been made under the service Rules [r. 8];

　　b. That a defendant is to file a defence within 20 days of being served with the claim [r. 9.01(1)] and [r. 10.03(1)]; and

　　c. Whether a delay may be associated with a requirement for French/English translation.

Regular mail includes postal services provided by Canada Post, including Priority Courier and Xpresspost, unless otherwise ordered by a judge. Although the service provided by Canada Post is called "Priority Courier," it is not courier service for the purposes of this Rule. It is considered to be regular mail service.

11.06 Setting Aside Noting of Default by Court on Motion — The court may set aside the noting in default or default judgment against a party and any step that has been taken to enforce the judgment, on such terms as are just, if the party makes a motion to set aside and the court is satisfied that,

　　(a) the party has a meritorious defence and a reasonable explanation for the default; and

　　(b) the motion is made as soon as is reasonably possible in all the circumstances.

O. Reg. 461/01, s. 15; 78/06, s. 24

History [R. 11.06]: Former subsec. (2) previously 10.05; plain language changes.

Commentary: If a defendant fails to file a defence (see Rule 9.03(6)), default may be noted. This deals with service in the same territorial division.

NOTE: Is there a conflict between subrule 11.06(1), 17.01(4) and 17.04(3)2 concerning the non-attendance at trial?

Subrule 11.01(2) has been amended to make it clear that default only applies where all the defendants in an action have been served outside the court's territorial division. In that situation, the clerk shall not note any defendant in default until it is proved by an affidavit of jurisdiction with the clerk or by evidence presented in court that the action was brought in the proper court.

After noting a default (a defence has not been received) for a debt or liquidated demand in money, the clerk may sign default judgment for the amount claimed, including court costs and interest, if claimed in the claim. Where a defendant has filed a defence in respect of part of the claim, the clerk may sign default judgment for the balance of the claim, provided no request has been made for payment under Rule 9.03. The claim must be listed for trial for the amount in dispute. Immediately on entering judgment under this rule, the clerk shall mail a Notice of Default Judgment (Form 11A) to the plaintiff and to the defendant at the address at which the claim was served.

Where in an action two defendants are named, but only one defendant has been served and has been noted in default, the clerk may enter judgment and forward notices of default judgment to the plaintiff and the defendant who has been served (Form 11A). On the motion of a party in default (Rule 11.06(1)), the court may set aside the noting of default or any judgment against the party on such terms as are just. Where default judgment has been signed and the defendant wishes to have the judgment set aside, he must file a Notice of Motion (Form 15A) and an Affidavit (Form 15B). Where the written consent of the parties is filed, the clerk may set aside the noting of default or the entry of a default judgment. Where a defendant has not filed a defence within the prescribed time *and* default judgment has been signed, the clerk, upon receiving the written consent of all parties, may set aside the noting of default and default judgment and accept a defence or otherwise as directed by the parties.

Case Law: *Mountain View Farms Ltd. v. McQueen*, 2014 ONCA 194, 2014 CarswellOnt 3011 (Ont. C.A.)

A motions judge declined to set aside a default judgment but varied the interest rate from a contractual rate of 24% to 5%. On appeal that variation of the judgment was set aside and the defendant was granted leave to file a defence to the claim for contractual interest at 24%. The motions judge erred by setting aside the interest provision of the default judgment and substituting a final determination on that issue in the defendant's favour. If the issue was arguable, a final determination was inappropriate and the issue should proceed to trial.

Toronto Dominion Bank v. Nawab, 2014 ONCA 152, 2014 CarswellOnt 2301 (Ont. C.A.)

The court declined to set aside a default judgment signed before the 20-day period to file a defence had elapsed. The defendant was not prejudiced by the irregularity and it was not in the interests of justice to set aside the default judgment as of right.

Bank of Nova Scotia v. Kostuchuk, 2002 CarswellMan 230, 2002 MBQB 134, [2002] 8 W.W.R. 173, 164 Man. R. (2d) 295 (Man. Q.B.); reversed 2003 CarswellMan 169, 2003 MBCA 66, 173 Man. R. (2d) 262, 293 W.A.C. 262, [2003] 8 W.W.R. 589, 34 C.P.C. (5th) 210 (Man. C.A.) — Defendant took two bank loans on behalf of a friend who later defaulted. Bank obtained default judgment against defendant in two actions, for $2,762 and $3,505. Defendant aware of judgments and paid in full. Bank later realized error in second action, which should have been for $26,285. Bank failed to show defendant should have been aware of error. Bank's application to set aside judgment dismissed.

Kemp v. Prescesky, [2006] N.S.J. No. 174, 2006 CarswellNS 175, 244 N.S.R. (2d) 67, 744 A.P.R. 67, 28 C.P.C. (6th) 361, 2006 NSSC 122 (N.S. S.C.) 2006-03-21.

Issue whether rules in Small Claims Court for filing defences, setting down hearings, and setting aside default judgments, fail to meet the requirements of natural justice.

Small Claims Court created by Act of Nova Scotia Legislature in 1980. It came into effect on January 1, 1981. The monetary jurisdiction at that time was $3,000.

The Legislature passed a law to increase the limit to $25,000. That monetary limit came into effect on April 1, 2006. While s. 3(1) of the *Small Claims Court Act* says the Small Claims Court is a court of law and of record, there is no recording of the proceedings. The only record is the summary report of the Adjudicator, prepared only in response to an appeal of his or her decision.

It is a breach of the requirements of natural justice *not* to have a mechanism in Small Claims Court whereby, if a defendant does not file a defence or appear at a hearing by mistake, but can show that he or she has an arguable defence that should be heard on its merits, and he or she has a reasonable excuse for defaulting and is not just stalling, and there is no prejudice to the claimant's ability to prove its case, the judgment cannot be set aside.

The requirements for natural justice in the Small Claims Court system have increased with the increase in the monetary jurisdiction of the court.

Decision of Adjudicator set aside.

Small Claims Court does not have a system for costs. New hearing ordered.

620369 Ontario Inc. v. Kreuzer, 2006 CarswellOnt 2261 (Ont. Div. Ct.) 2006-04-13.

Appeal from judgment of Deputy Judge dismissing a motion to set aside a default judgment. Kreuzer filed an affidavit indicating when he received claim and understood he had 20 days to defend. Both counsel on appeal were not counsel in the court below. There the plaintiff was represented by an agent and the defendants were self-represented by Mr. Kreuzer. Appeal allowed. The fact Kreuzer was never properly served is itself reason to set aside default judgment against him.

Sinnadurai v. Laredo Construction Inc., 2005 CarswellOnt 7305, [2005] O.J. No. 5429, 38 R.P.R. (4th) 7, 20 C.P.C. (6th) 234, 78 O.R. (3d) 321, 206 O.A.C. 235 (Ont. C.A.) 2005-12-19.

Appeal from order dismissing motion to set aside a default judgment with added issue of jurisdiction.

Motions judge addressed the three-part test for setting aside a default judgment. See *Morgan v. Toronto (Municipality) Police Services Board*, 2003 CarswellOnt 1105, 169 O.A.C. 390, 34 C.P.C. (5th) 46 (Ont. C.A.) at para. 19.

Section 19(1)(a)(i) of the *Courts of Justice Act*, R.S.O. 1990, c. C.43, provides that an appeal lies to the Divisional Court from a final order of a judge of the Superior Court "for a single payment of *not more* than $25,000, exclusive of costs."

Appeal within the jurisdiction of the Divisional Court, but Court of Appeal not prepared to send the matter back.

The factors governing the setting aside of a default judgment are not to be applied rigidly: see *Chitel v. Rothbart*, 1988 CarswellOnt 451, [1988] O.J. No. 1197, 29 C.P.C. (2d) 136 (Ont. C.A.). There have been cases where the explanation for the default has been given less weight because the defence had merit: see *441612 Ontario Ltd. v. Albert*, 1995 CarswellOnt 135, [1995] O.J. No. 271, 36 C.P.C. (3d) 198 (Ont. Gen. Div.) at para. 48 and *D.R. McKay Financial Group Inc. v. Klad Enterprises Ltd.*, [2004] O.J. No. 4288, 2004 CarswellOnt 4261, 193 O.A.C. 281 (Ont. Div. Ct.).

See also *Janssen-Ortho Inc. v. Novopharm Ltd.*, [2005] S.C.C.A. No. 189, 2005 CarswellNat 2110, 2005 CarswellNat 2111, 2005 SCC 33, 42 C.P.R. (4th) 385, [2005] 1 S.C.R. 776, 345 N.R. 174 (S.C.C.), where LeBel J. refused an application to extend the time of an application for leave to appeal to the Supreme Court of Canada.

The decision to set aside a default judgment is a discretionary one. See Rule 19.08(1) of the *Rules of Civil Procedure*.

A judgment against a defendant who has been noted in default that is signed by the registrar or granted by the court on motion under rule 19.04 may be set aside or varied by the court on such terms as are just. See *Bottan v. Vroom*, 2002 CarswellOnt 1044, [2002] O.J. No. 1383 (Ont. C.A.).

Appeal dismissed.

Wan v. Wan, 2005 CarswellOnt 5637 (Ont. Div. Ct.), Lane J.

Deputy Judge erred in setting aside default judgment granted to plaintiff. Deputy Judge noted that there were number of actions in Small Claims Court between same parties and became concerned about monetary jurisdiction of that court because claims could not be divided to come within $10,000 limit. However, no motion existed to set aside default judgment. Plaintiff had no notice that her judgment was at risk. Order made without jurisdiction. Appeal allowed.

620369 Ontario Inc. v. Kreuzer, 2006 CarswellOnt 2261 (Ont. Div. Ct.), Sproat J.

Appeal from judgment of Deputy Judge H.C. Adams on April 18, 2005 dismissing motion to set aside a default judgment granted April 4, 2005.

In all but very clear cases best strategy for plaintiff is to agree to set aside a default judgment on terms and to have the matter decided on merits.

Appeal allowed.

Service defective in relation to Kreuzer in that it purports to serve the claim on him by serving "Manny Grewbalt — person in charge."

TD Meloche Monnex / Security National Insurance Co. v. Donavan, 2006 CarswellNB 389, 2006 NBQB 251, 306 N.B.R. (2d) 90, 793 A.P.R. 90 (N.B. Q.B.), L.A. LaVigne J.

Four months after claim served on defendant, plaintiff noted defendant in default. Defendant unsuccessfully tried to file statement of defence one week after being noted in default. Defendant brought motion to set aside noting in default. Motion granted. Defendant clearly illustrated ongoing intention to defend action, immediately retained services of solicitor, expert witness and filed notice of intent to defend. Defendant provided justifiable explanation for default.

Lukenda v. Campbell, [2003] O.J. No. 5022, 2003 CarswellOnt 4787, 67 O.R. (3d) 688, 48 C.P.C. (5th) 372 (Ont. S.C.J.).

Registrar signing default judgment against defendant in July 1988. Defendant moving in 2003 to set aside default judgment. Defendant not moving as soon as possible and not adequately explaining circumstances giving rise to default. No defence on merits. Motion dismissed.

Rangi v. Rangi, 2006 CarswellBC 1541, 2006 BCSC 947, 33 C.P.C. (6th) 347, 57 B.C.L.R. (4th) 171 (B.C. S.C.).

KSR brought application to set aside orders made despite failure to appear at hearings, application granted. KSR not guilty of wilful delay or default because he was not aware of application for judgment. Service of application ineffective. KSR provided reasonable explanation for delay, wife was diagnosed with cancer. Defence worthy of investigation.

Burzan v. Burzan (August 9, 2005) (B.C. C.A.).

While there was a defence worthy of investigation, the chambers judge had been correct in dismissing claim on grounds that father deliberately failed to file a defence, and had no good explanation for applying to set aside the judgment in a timely way. Further, with respect to the defence issue, matter of quantum had been referred to the trial list, so matters of causation and damages would be determined at that stage.

Lariviere v. Clarke, [2005] O.J. No. 4024, 2005 CarswellOnt 4549 (Ont. S.C.J.), Morawetz J.

Defendant moved to set aside judgment while plaintiff moved to enforce judgment. Defendant alleged he had not been served despite process server's affidavit. Defendant failed to discharge onus of rebutting plaintiff's evidence of service. Defendant's motion dismissed.

Sinnadurai v. Laredo Construction Inc., 2005 CarswellOnt 7305, [2005] O.J. No. 5429, 38 R.P.R. (4th) 7, 20 C.P.C. (6th) 234, 78 O.R. (3d) 321, 206 O.A.C. 235 (Ont. C.A.).

Company unsuccessfully brought motion to set aside default judgment. Motion judge found that company's affidavit supporting motion was insufficient to set aside default judgment. It provided no explanation. Motion judge found that affidavit merely suggesting that company was not certain it had received claim was feeble evidence. Company appealed. Appeal dismissed.

Vuu v. Andrade, 2005 CarswellOnt 7235 (Ont. S.C.J.), Matlow J.

Defendant illiterate. Defendant sought to set aside default judgment. Defendant's affidavit deposing defendant illiterate did not have attachment indicating that affidavit was explained to defendant. No weight was given to affidavit. Motion dismissed. Affidavits containing conflicting evidence as to when defendant first learned of action caused court to doubt reliability of everything asserted by defendant.

Larry Penner Enterprises Inc. v. Lake St. Martin First Nation, 2006 CarswellMan 53, [2006] 2 C.N.L.R. 93, 202 Man. R. (2d) 213, 2006 MBQB 30 (Man. Master), Master Harrison.

Plaintiffs moved *ex parte* on default judgment to garnish moneys allegedly owed by Province to defendants. Claim for continuing garnishing order dismissed. Subject moneys owed by Province were tax rebates from goods sold on reservation. Money payable by Province to defendants subject to Crown immunity.

Gill v. Szalay, 2006 CarswellOnt 3807 (Ont. S.C.J.), Stewart J.

Self-represented defendant applied to set aside default judgment. Defendant at all times intended to defend action and had arguable case. Defendant claimed not to have been advised by trial coordinator of date on which trial was to commence. Circumstances appropriate to set aside judgment but on terms. Defendant ordered to pay judgment amount into plaintiffs' solicitor's trust account pending new trial plus $5,000 in costs to be held in trust.

Royal Bank v. Goebel, 2006 CarswellAlta 612, 30 C.P.C. (6th) 141, 2006 ABQB 369 (Alta. Q.B.), Smith J.

Statement of claim alleged defendants issued Visa card and that they jointly and severally owed $26,205. Plaintiff obtained default judgment against both defendants who disputed liability. Accumulation of defects, both procedural and ethical, that favoured setting aside default judgment. Default judgment set aside.

Okanagan Aggregates Ltd. v. Boake, 2006 CarswellBC 718, 2006 BCSC 466 (B.C. S.C. [In Chambers]), Blair J.

Application to set aside a default judgment not granted because party duly served intentionally refrained from appearing.

Phan v. Jevco Insurance Co., 2006 CarswellOnt 3937, [2006] O.J. No. 2614, 39 C.C.L.I. (4th) 293 (Ont. S.C.J.), Shaw J.

Motion for default judgment heard on December 12 and plaintiff granted judgment on December 22, 2005. Application by defendant to set aside noting of default and default judgment dismissed. Defendant did not prove it had valid reason for default. Only explanation was that through inadvertence its adjuster failed to assign counsel to defend matter. Not a particularly compelling explanation and not adequate.

Peterbilt of Ontario Inc. v. 1565627 Ontario Ltd., [2007] O.J. No. 1685, 2007 CarswellOnt 2713, 41 C.P.C. (6th) 316, 87 O.R. (3d) 479, 2007 ONCA 333 (Ont. C.A.).

Appeal allowed. Motion judge ultimately determines whether interests of justice favour order setting aside default judgment, having regard to potential prejudice to parties and effect on overall integrity of administration of justice. Affidavit of defendants, while perhaps deficient, sufficient to put detailed defence set out in statement of defence "in play" on motion to set aside default judgment. Statement of defence had been served and filed in timely fashion and contained detailed and full defences to claims. Prejudice to defendants in refusal of motion was obvious. Defendants were denied any opportunity to present defence on merits.

Heaps Estate v. Jesson, 2007 CarswellOnt 2322, 47 C.C.L.I. (4th) 271, 42 C.P.C. (6th) 334 (Ont. S.C.J.), Dunn J.

Motion granted. Extension would advance just resolution of serious dispute. Claim involving fatal injuries not to be discarded lightly. Plaintiffs should not be unduly penalized for counsel's inadvertence in not serving statement of claim. Despite lengthy delay, defendants would not suffer undue prejudice in having to defend action. Defendants would have access to expert report which would help facilitate defence. Defendants made well aware of particulars of plaintiffs' claim by own insurer and well within any limitation period.

Nobosoft Corp. v. No Borders Inc., 2007 CarswellOnt 3903, 2007 ONCA 444, 43 C.P.C. (6th) 36, 225 O.A.C. 36, [2007] O.J. No. 2378 (Ont. C.A.).

Appeal allowed, noting in default set aside. Motions judge erred by only inquiring as to whether B Inc. had intent to defend prior to expiry of time for delivery of its defence. No evidence that B Inc. formed intent to defend within requisite period. No evidence that B Inc. sought to flout or abuse Rules. B Inc. moved relatively promptly to set aside noting in default, and at very least, its delay in seeking relief was not inordinate.

British Columbia v. Ismail, 2007 CarswellBC 172, 235 B.C.A.C. 299, 388 W.A.C. 299, 2007 BCCA 55 (B.C. C.A. [In Chambers]).

Wilson J. set aside judgment for a liquidated amount entered by plaintiff in default of appearance by defendants. The plaintiff sought directions as to whether leave to appeal from that order was required and if leave was required, sought leave. Leave required. Leave to appeal dismissed. A decision setting aside a default judgment was an interlocutory order and leave to appeal such order required.

Ravnyshyn v. Drys, 2007 CarswellBC 1731, 33 E.T.R. (3d) 189, 2007 BCCA 400, 44 C.P.C. (6th) 64, 405 W.A.C. 127, 245 B.C.A.C. 127 (B.C. C.A.); leave to appeal refused (2008), 2008 CarswellBC 94, 2008 CarswellBC 95, [2007] S.C.C.A. No. 485, 384 N.R. 393 (note), 452 W.A.C. 317 (note), 268 B.C.A.C. 317 (note) (S.C.C.).

R informed court she might be late for hearing of motion. Judge did not receive message and dismissed motion on basis that no one was there to pursue it. Application to set aside order granted. Unjust to allow order to stand because of administrative error. Had judge received message that she would be arriving late, she would have set down application so that it could be heard on merits.

Srdoc v. Ayres, 2006 CarswellOnt 7740 (Ont. Div. Ct.), Carnwath J.

Lack of reasons for motion judge's decision not to set aside default judgment.

Canadian Imperial Bank of Commerce v. Csorba, 2007 CarswellOnt 1687, [2007] O.J. No. 1081, 2007 ONCA 211 (Ont. C.A.).

Application to set aside default judgment. Discretion of court.

Altman v. St. Gelais, 2006 CarswellSask 757, 38 C.P.C. (6th) 120, 2006 SKQB 495, 290 Sask. R. 156 (Sask. Q.B.), Currie J., November 16, 2006.

Plaintiff in Small Claims Court action failed to attend for case management conference. Judge dismissed claim for want of prosecution. Plaintiff appealed. Appeal dismissed for want of jurisdiction. Provincial Court had jurisdiction to set aside its own default judgments whether made at trial or case management conference. Legislature failed to make consequential amendment after introduction of conferences. Reference in section to "any party" gave plaintiff right to apply despite further reference to having "valid defence." Section was not well drafted. No logical reason to exclude plaintiff from operation of section.

See *Trull v. Midwest Driveways Ltd.*, 2004 CarswellSask 857, [2004] S.J. No. 800, 2004 SKQB 528, 4 C.P.C. (6th) 324, 256 Sask. R. 314 (Sask. Q.B.). On that appeal, Mr. Justice Baynton reviewed the purpose and effect of s. 37 of the *Small Claims Act, 1997*. At paras. 10-12 he concluded that: a) where a party failed to appear for a small claims trial in Provincial Court, and then wished to set aside the judgment granted in his or her absence, that party effectively was asking to set aside a default judgment. Court of Queen's Bench does not have jurisdiction to hear appeal. Altman's remedy is under s. 37 of *the Small Claims Act, 1997*, asking the Provincial Court to consider setting aside the judgment that was granted in his absence. Appeal dismissed.

100578 P.E.I. Inc. v. Label Construction Ltd., 2008 CarswellPEI 16, 2008 PESCTD 15, 274 Nfld. & P.E.I.R. 292, 837 A.P.R. 292 (P.E.I. T.D.), B.B. Taylor J. (February 20, 2008).

Motion by defendant ("Label") for order setting aside default judgment by plaintiff on July 4, 2007. Motion allowed, but with costs to plaintiff on a full indemnity basis.

Rule 19.08(3) states:

> (3) On setting aside a judgment under subrule (1) or (2) the court or judge may also set aside the noting of default under Rule 19.03.

See *Jorand Holdings Inc. v. Pecoskie*, 2007 CarswellPEI 78, 2007 PESCTD 17, 285 Nfld. & P.E.I.R. 243, 879 A.P.R. 243 (P.E.I. T.D.) and *Bank of Montreal v. Dockendorff*, 2003 CarswellPEI 23, 2003 PESCTD 19, 224 Nfld. & P.E.I.R. 4, 669 A.P.R. 4 (P.E.I. T.D.).

Inadvertence may be a plausible explanation for failure to file a defence on time. Plaintiff's evidence strong, but not up to court to weigh competing evidence. An "arguable" case is a low threshold.

Jay v. DHL Express (Canada) Ltd./DHL Express (Canada) Ltée, 2008 CarswellPEI 15, 2008 PESCTD 13, 277 Nfld. & P.E.I.R. 210, 52 C.P.C. (6th) 166, (sub nom. *Jay v. DHL Express (Canada) Ltd.)* 850 A.P.R. 210 (P.E.I. T.D.); reversed 2009 CarswellPEI 5, 2009 PECA 2, 283 Nfld. & P.E.I.R. 1, 65 C.P.C. (6th) 58, (sub nom. *Jay v. DHL Express (Canada) Ltd.)* 873 A.P.R. 1 (P.E.I. C.A.), K.R. MacDonald J.; additional reasons at 2009 PECA 11, 2009 CarswellPEI 24, 284 Nfld. & P.E.I.R. 348, 875 A.P.R. 348, 67 C.P.C. (6th) 400 (P.E.I. C.A.).

Plaintiff sought relief under Rule 30.08 and Rule 60 of the *Rules of Court*.

Rule 30.08(2) reads:

> (2) Where a party fails to serve an affidavit of documents or produce a document for inspection in compliance with these rules or fails to comply with an order of the court under Rule 30.08(2) to 30.11, the court may,
>
> . . .
>
> (b) dismiss the action, if the party is a plaintiff, or strike out the statement of defence, if the party is a defendant; . . .

Rule 60 deals in part with contempt orders.

Defendant DHL either saw the task of producing documents too time consuming or could not produce documents. See *MacDougall v. Mutual Life Assurance Co. of Canada*, 2004 CarswellPEI 78, (sub nom. *MacDougall v. Mutual Life Assurance Co.)* 241 Nfld. & P.E.I.R. 92, (sub nom. *MacDougall v. Mutual Life Assurance Co.)* 716 A.P.R. 92, 2004 PESCTD 61 (P.E.I. T.D.), where court dismissed claim because of plaintiff's delay in production of documents and the delay from the time of the undertaking, to the time of the motion to dismiss four and one-half years.

Cases where the "too hard to get" defence considered time and costs have been put forth as a defence to production. See *Anderson Preece & Associates Inc. v. Dominium Appraisal Group Inc.*, [2000] A.J. No. 459, 2000 CarswellAlta 1494, 2000 ABQB 254, 264 A.R. 177 (Alta. Q.B.), Veit J. See also *L.M. Harding Medical Supplies Ltd. v. Patriquen*, 2005 CarswellNS 129, [2005] N.S.J. No. 113, 232 N.S.R. (2d) 111, 737 A.P.R. 111, 11 C.P.C. (6th) 315, 2005 NSCA 48 (N.S. C.A.), MacDonald, C.J.N.S.; *Andrei v. Regina (City)*, 1993 CarswellSask 279, 117 Sask. R. 161 (Sask. Q.B.), Hrabinsky J.; and *Ivey v. Canada Trust Co.*, [1962] O.W.N. 62 (Ont. Master) (referred to in *Choate on Discovery*, 2nd P.3-84.14) per Senior Master.

If excuses were allowed, justice would be seriously compromised. Losing documents, misplacing documents, inadvertently destroying documents and other more ingenious excuses would all be brought out as a reason for not producing the documents. Defence dismissed. Procedure comparable to noting a defendant in default.

Whitehorse Wholesale Auto Centre Ltd. v. Clark, 2007 CarswellYukon 63, 2007 YKSM 2 (Y.T. Small Cl. Ct.), Overend J.

Section 53 of the *Consumers Protection Act*, R.S.Y. 2002, c. 40, s. 53(1) states, in part:

... if a seller under a time sale repossesses the goods comprised in the time sale, ... no action is thereafter maintainable by the seller to recover the balance or any part thereof.

Whitehorse Wholesale Auto Centre's claim for amount owing under *Consumers Protection Act* barred by statute.

Claimant had recovered default judgment. Matter was set down only for assessment of damages. However, where on assessment hearing claim unfounded in law, abuse of process of court to allow action to continue. Court could on its own motion set aside judgment. Claimant has suffered no damages. Damages fixed at zero.

Webster v. Stewart, 2008 CarswellNB 335, 332 N.B.R. (2d) 288, 2008 NBQB 232, 852 A.P.R. 288, 73 C.L.R. (3d) 270 (N.B. Q.B.)

Motion by defendants to set aside default judgment. Defendants moved to set aside noting of default as soon as it came to their attention. Court satisfied that there was a good and valid defence or triable issue with respect to the slander of title action brought against them. There was a reasonable excuse for the default, namely their solicitor's inadvertence. Their actions showed an intention to defend the action throughout, and no prejudice arose to the plaintiff from the delay.

Stoughton Trailers Canada Corp. v. James Expedite Transport Inc., 2008 ONCA 817, 2008 CarswellOnt 7214 (Ont. C.A.); reversing (2008), 2008 CarswellOnt 7344 (Ont. S.C.J.)

Plaintiff brought motion for default judgment. Default judgment awarded and defendants brought motion to set aside default judgment. Defendants sought to adjourn motion. Motion adjourned on consent order. Defendants brought motion to vary or set aside consent adjournment order. Motion allowed. As moneys in issue had been paid, proper to adjourn motion to set aside to time fixed on consent of parties.

Daum v. Elko (2009), 2009 CarswellBC 834, 2009 BCSC 349 (B.C. S.C. [In Chambers]), Barrow J.

Defendant applied to set aside default judgment. Application granted. Defendant applied as soon as reasonably possible after learning of default judgment. Defendant did not wilfully or deliberately fail to file statement of defence. Failure to file statement of defence could give rise to inference of ignoring action, but this was not the case in view of steps taken by defendant prior to deadline.

Garten v. Kruk (2009), 2009 CarswellOnt 2285 (Ont. Master), Master R. Dash.; additional reasons at (2009), 2009 CarswellOnt 2961 (Ont. Master); reversed (2009), 2009 CarswellOnt 6477 (Ont. Div. Ct.)

Parties made submissions as to costs. No costs awarded to either party. Plaintiff had not warned defendant of his intention to note defendant in default and then failed to advise defendant that he had noted her in default for six months. Highly unprofessional of plaintiff's counsel not to warn. If costs were to be awarded to plaintiff, it would not only be rewarding unprofessional conduct of plaintiff for failing to warn, but might also encourage plaintiff's counsel and other counsel to engage in similar conduct in other actions. Failure to warn grounds in itself to deny costs of motion to plaintiff.

Coombs v. Curran (2010), 2010 CarswellOnt 1175, 2010 ONSC 1312, 100 O.R. (3d) 554 (Ont. Div. Ct.), Quinn, J.

Appeals of Small Claims Court judge dismissing motion defendant sought to set aside default judgment.

Three-part test for setting aside a default judgment set out in *HSBC Securities (Canada) Inc. v. Firestar Capital Management Corp.*, 2008 ONCA 894, 2008 CarswellOnt 7956, [2008] O.J. No. 5345, 245 O.A.C. 47 (Ont. C.A.), at para. 21, leave to appeal refused (2009), 2009 CarswellOnt 3642, 2009 CarswellOnt 3641, 262 O.A.C. 398 (note), 399 N.R. 398 (note) (S.C.C.), citing *Morgan v. Toronto (Municipality) Police Services Board* (2003), 169 O.A.C. 390, [2003] O.J. No. 1106, 34 C.P.C. (5th) 46, 2003 CarswellOnt 1105 (Ont. C.A.), at para. 19, the Court of Appeal described the test in these words:

> a) Whether the motion was brought without delay after the defendant learned of the default judgment;
>
> b) Whether the circumstances giving rise to the default were adequately explained; and
>
> c) Whether the defendant has an arguable defence on the merits.

Setting aside default judgment is discretionary judicial power.

A court is a world of words, and is subject to the polar pull of precision and precedent. It cannot be ascertained whether motion judge regarded "meritorious" to be synonymous with "arguable." Proper test not applied. Error in law made. Appeal allowed and default judgment set aside.

Royal Bank v. Sheikh (2010), 2010 CarswellOnt 97, 2010 ONSC 131 (Ont. S.C.J. [Commercial List])

Defendant/appellant ("Biela"), appeals decision of Small Claims Court judge dismissing motion she sought to set aside default judgment.

The three-part test for setting aside a default judgment. See *HSBC Securities (Canada) Inc. v. Firestar Capital Management Corp.*, 245 O.A.C. 47, 2008 CarswellOnt 7956, 2008 ONCA 894 (Ont. C.A.) at para. 21; leave to appeal refused 262 O.A.C. 398 (note), 399 N.R. 398 (note), 2009 CarswellOnt 3642, 2009 CarswellOnt 3641 (S.C.C.), citing *Morgan v. Toronto (City) Police Services Board* (2003), 34 C.P.C. 95th 46 (Ont. C.A.), at para. 19, the Court of Appeal described the test in these words:

> (a)   Whether the motion was brought without delay after the defendant learned of the default judgment;

(b)   Whether the circumstances giving rise to the default were adequately explained; and

(c)   Whether the defendant has an arguable defence on the merits.

Setting aside default judgment exercise of a discretionary judicial power.

Motion judge said that, in addition to giving "a reasonable explanation for the default" and bringing motion "as soon as reasonably possible," Biela also "must show that there is a meritorious defence." "Meritorious" represents a higher threshold than "arguable."

Appeal allowed; default judgment set aside.

Healey v. Robert McIntosh Family Trust, 2009 CarswellOnt 4597 (Ont. S.C.J.), Hoy J.

The lawyer commenced action to collect legal fees from defendants, who were formerly husband and wife, and their family trust. Default judgment granted after defendants' statement of defence struck for failure to serve their affidavit of documents and to reply to demands for particulars. They did not appeal. Motion dismissed. Wife knew about judgment for at least two years before bringing motion. None of the principles governing the exercise of discretion to set aside default judgment satisfied and interests of justice did not favour setting it aside.

Action Auto Leasing & Gallery Inc. v. Boulding, 2009 CarswellOnt 8657, [2009] O.J. No. 1768, 88 C.P.C. (6th) 91 (Ont. Sm. Cl. Ct.)

The plaintiff commenced claim in Small Claims Court. The plaintiff purported to serve claim on defendants by mail. No defence filed. The plaintiff had defendants noted in default and obtained default judgment. The defendants denied receipt of claim and learned of lawsuit after garnishments effected. Motion granted. The plaintiff could not establish valid service by mail pursuant to r. 8.03 of *Small Claims Court Rules*. Affidavits of service failed to indicate requirements of r. 8.03(8). If requirements of rr. 8.03(7) and (8) were not satisfied, then default judgment was irregularly obtained and had to be set aside as of right. It was unnecessary to determine whether defendants had arguable defence on merits. Motion was brought as soon as reasonably possible.

The defendants moved, pursuant to r. 11.06 of the *Small Claims Court Rules*, O. Reg. 258/98 ("SCCR"), to set aside the clerk's default judgment.

Recent authorities for proposition that irregularly-obtained default judgment must be set aside automatically, or as of right, without terms, are *Royal Trust Corp. of Canada v. Dunn*, [1991] O.J. No. 2231, 1991 CarswellOnt 468, 6 O.R. (3d) 468, 6 C.P.C. (3d) 351, 86 D.L.R. (4th) 490 (Ont. Gen. Div.), and *Benlolo v. Barzakay*, 169 O.A.C. 39, 2003 CarswellOnt 658, [2003] O.J. No. 602 (Ont. Div. Ct.); additional reasons at 170 O.A.C. 115, 2003 CarswellOnt 1260 (Ont. Div. Ct.). In such cases, there is no requirement on moving party to show, as there is in cases of regularly-obtained judgments, that he or she has an arguable defence on the merits. That is because irregularly-obtained judgments must be set aside *ex bebito justitiae* (for the sake of justice).

Onus to prove valid service is on the party asserting that proper service was effected: *Ivan's Films Inc. v. Kostelac*, 29 C.P.C. (2d) 20, 1988 CarswellOnt 441 (Ont. Master); leave to appeal refused (1988), 30 C.P.C. (2d) lv (Ont. H.C.); *Don Bodkin Leasing Ltd. v. Rayzak*, [1993] O.J. No. 503, 1993 CarswellOnt 4016 (Ont. Gen. Div.); reversed 1994 CarswellOnt 2220, [1994] O.J. No. 280 (Ont. Gen. Div.) at para. 10; and *Ryan (In Trust) v. Kaukab*, [2004] O.J. No. 5656, 2004 CarswellOnt 5898 (Ont. S.C.J.); additional reasons at [2005] O.J. No. 603, 2005 CarswellOnt 643 (Ont. S.C.J.); additional reasons at 2005 CarswellOnt 644 (Ont. S.C.J.); leave to appeal refused 2005 CarswellOnt 653 (Ont. Div. Ct.) at para. 9.

Garten v. Kruk, 2009 CarswellOnt 6477, 257 O.A.C. 59 (Ont. Div. Ct.)

Some six months after initial court appearance, without notifying the defendant, plaintiff's counsel had defendant noted in default. Six months later, the plaintiff's lawyer notified the defendant's lawyer of the noting in default. The defendant moved to set aside the noting of default. Master dismissed motion. Divisional Court, per Wilson, J., allowed appeal. The defendant demonstrated intent to defend. She had immediately obtained counsel. The fact that she appeared before Master and was now before Divisional Court spoke volumes of her desire to defend. Defendant should not be punished for her lawyer's errors. Her lawyer's affidavit clearly stated that his office inadvertently failed to deliver the statement of defence. Master did not accept the lawyer's sworn statement. Master's order reinforced sharp practice.

Zammit Semple LLP v. Attar, [2009] O.J. No. 5044, 2009 CarswellOnt 7369 (Ont. S.C.J.)

The plaintiff obtained default judgment against the defendant. The defendant brought the motion to set aside default judgment. Motion dismissed. The plaintiff waited over one-and-a-half years. The circumstances were not obstacle to granting the defendant relief sought. The defendant met test, being whether motion brought forthwith after default judgment came to the defendant's attention. The defendant failed, however, to meet branch of test, whether the defendant could present viable defence on merits.

Canadian Imperial Bank of Commerce v. Darmantchev, 2010 BCCA 247, 2010 CarswellBC 1523, 488 W.A.C. 100, 288 B.C.A.C. 100 (B.C. C.A.)

The defendants unsuccessfully applied to set aside default judgments in favour of plaintiff bank. The defendants appealed. Appeal dismissed. The defendants gave up right to challenge claim when they did not file defences which application judge found was intentional. Beyond bare assertion that the application judge failed to account for fact that they were laypersons, the defendants offered no basis upon which this could be said and how they were prejudiced.

George L. Mitchell Electrical v. Rouvalis, 2010 NSSC 203, 2010 CarswellNS 398, 10 C.P.C. (7th) 316 (N.S. S.C.), Arthur J. LeBlanc J.

The defendants had reasonable excuse for failing to file defence within required time. The plaintiff appealed. Appeal allowed. Order for default judgment reinstated. The defendants offered no ancillary reason for failure to file defence beyond fact that they did not read claim. Adjudicator erred in law.

Wagner v. East Coast Paving Ltd., 2010 NSSM 63, 2010 CarswellNS 699 (N.S. Sm. Cl. Ct.)

The application was pursuant to section 23(2) of the Nova Scotia *Small Claims Court Act* to set aside a *quick* judgment. Notice of claim filed on July 20, 2010, and served on July 27, 2010. It indicated hearing of claim set for August 31, 2010. Reference to 10 days on the form was in fact incorrect. Application for quick judgment filed August 17 and, on August 18, a quick judgment granted on basis of written material filed with application. The application to set aside quick judgment was filed on August 24, 2010.

The defendant argued that evidence showed defendant was a self-represented litigant who simply did not understand that she was required to file a document defending the matter. Her clear evidence was that she intended to defend and to be present on August 31.

The defendant must provide some evidence showing it had a reasonable excuse for not filing a defence. Not *any* excuse but a *reasonable* excuse. The issue is whether there is shown to be a reasonable excuse for not filing a defence. The evidence does not satisfy requirement that there be a reasonable excuse for failing to file a defence. The application was dismissed pursuant to section 23.

1000728 Ontario Ltd. v. Kakish, 2010 ONSC 538, 2010 CarswellOnt 599, 88 C.P.C. (6th) 108 (Ont. S.C.J.), Spence J.

Finance company relied on provisions of *Mercantile Amendment Act* to sue the consignee. The consignee brought motion to transfer action from Small Claims Court to Superior Court. Motion granted. Case was complex. Small Claims Court could not provide consecutive trial dates and it was reasonable to expect trial to last more than one day.

See also *Alexandrov v. Csanyi*, 247 O.A.C. 228, 2009 CarswellOnt 1325 (Ont. Div. Ct.); *Csanyi v. Alexandrov*, 2009 CarswellOnt 5446 (Ont. S.C.J.); *Haines, Miller & Associates Inc. v. Foss*, 1996 CarswellNS 301, 153 N.S.R. (2d) 53, 450 A.P.R. 53, 3 C.P.C. (4th) 349 (N.S. S.C. [In Chambers]); additional reasons at 1996 CarswellNS 304, 158 N.S.R. (2d) 389, 466 A.P.R. 389 (N.S. S.C. [In Chambers]).

In *Alexandrov*, Court said that the jurisprudence on transfer is that a plaintiff may be forced, in very exceptional cases, into the Superior Court against the wishes of the plaintiff.

In *Farlow v. Hospital for Sick Children*, 2009 CarswellOnt 7124, [2009] O.J. No. 4847, 100 O.R. (3d) 213, 83 C.P.C. (6th) 290 (Ont. S.C.J.), Court held that on a motion to transfer an action from Small Claims Court to the Superior Court, there must be a balancing of the various factors enumerated in that decision.

Expert evidence necessary to determine issues to be tried. Expert evidence can be given in the Small Claims Court. The Small Claims Court does *not* have procedural framework similar to rr. 53.03 and 76.10(4) of the *Rules of Civil Procedure*, R.R.O. 1990, Reg. 194 for the timely exchange of expert reports in advance of the trial.

In *Crane Canada Co. v. Montis Sorgic Associates Inc.*, 2005 CarswellOnt 9989, [2005] O.J. No. 6247 (Ont. S.C.J.); affirmed 2006 CarswellOnt 3051, [2006] O.J. No. 1999 (Ont. C.A.), the Court found that expert evidence would be central to the determination of the claims and that such evidence would likely be complex, and decided accordingly that claims would be more appropriately dealt with in the Superior Court.

Infolink Technologies Ltd. v. IVP Technology Corp., 2011 ONSC 2781, 2011 CarswellOnt 6371 (Ont. S.C.J.), Cumming J.; additional reasons at 2011 ONSC 5425, 2011 CarswellOnt 9452 (Ont. S.C.J.).

Default proceedings. Judgment following default. By motion for judgment. General principles. Action allowed. Rule 19.02(1)(a) of *Rules of Civil procedure* was provided as a consequence of having been noted in default, as T deemed to admit the truth of all allegations of fact made in the claim. Therefore, judgment was granted pursuant to r. 19.05 of rules against T as to the issue of liability.

Rifici v. Sitebrand Inc., 2011 ONSC 4049, 2011 CarswellOnt 5745 (Ont. S.C.J.), Aitken J.

The employer terminated the employee without cause. The employee agreed to the payment terms for amounts owing under the employment agreement. The employer only made one payment. The employee commenced an action for the amount owing. The employee noted that the employer was in default and obtained a default judgment. The employer brought a motion for an order setting aside the default judgment. The motion was dismissed. The employer waited 5 1/2 months before bringing the motion and had not provided an adequate explanation for the delay. The employer failed to explain why the defence was not filed in a timely manner, and failed to establish arguable defence on merits. The employer had not committed to pursue particular defences, and even the employer's purported possible defences had no merit.

Misir v. Baichulall, 2012 ONSC 893, 2012 CarswellOnt 1449 (Ont. S.C.J.)

This action proceeded as an undefended trial because all of the defendants were noted to be in default. Conway J. ordered that the plaintiff's trial proceed pursuant to Rule 19 of the *Rules of Civil Procedure*.

The plaintiff submitted that because it was an undefended trial and the defendants were noted as in default, it was not open to enter into an inquiry about the liability of the defendants. See decision in *Umlauf v. Umlauf*, 2001 CarswellOnt 851, [2001] O.J. No. 1054, 53 O.R. (3d) 355, 142 O.A.C. 328, 9 C.P.C. (5th) 93, 197 D.L.R. (4th) 715 (Ont. C.A.). D.M. Brown J. considered this issue in *Viola v. Hornstein*, 2009 CarswellOnt 1963 (Ont. S.C.J.). The approach set out in *Plouffe* and *Fuda* gives effect to Rule 19.06. Findings were based on deemed admissions arising as a result of Rule 19.02(1)(a). For the reasons outlined above, the plaintiff was awarded damages of $5,000 and costs in the amount of $1,500 against all of the defendants.

Canadian Imperial Bank of Commerce v. Petten, 2010 ONSC 6726, 2010 CarswellOnt 9126, 6 C.P.C. (7th) 429 (Ont. S.C.J.)

The defendants did not defend the action. Summary judgment was issued in the plaintiff's favour. The defendants brought a motion to set aside the judgement almost five months later. The motion was dismissed. The defendants chose to ignore the proceeding until it was too late and then attempted to manipulate the system in their favour. The defence on merits was weak, but the matter turned on the triable issue of credibility.

Aguas v. Rivard Estate, 2011 ONCA 494, 2011 CarswellOnt 5822, [2011] O.J. No. 3108, 107 O.R. (3d) 142, 335 D.L.R. (4th) 365, 7 C.P.C. (7th) 16, 282 O.A.C. 39 (Ont. C.A.)

There were sufficient grounds for setting the order aside. The plaintiff's motion to set aside the order by the registrar pursuant to R. 48.14 of *Rules of Civil Procedure* was dismissed. The plaintiff appealed. The appeal was allowed. The motion judge placed unreasonable emphasis on prejudice. The defendant's counsel's lack of display of any sense of urgency undercut the claim of actual prejudice.

Royal Bank of Canada v. US Distribution Services Inc., 2012 ONSC 7261, 2012 CarswellOnt 16817 (Ont. S.C.J.), Hourigan J.

Motion to set aside a default judgment brought by the defendant, Linda Earle-Barron.

A motions judge must ultimately determine whether the interests of justice favour the granting of the order (see *Peterbilt of Ontario Inc. v. 1565627 Ontario Ltd.*, 2007 ONCA 333, 2007 CarswellOnt 2713, 87 O.R. (3d) 479, 41 C.P.C. (6th) 316, [2007] O.J. No. 1685 (Ont. C.A.) and *HSBC Securities (Canada) Inc. v. Firestar Capital Management Corp.*, 2008 ONCA 894, 2008 CarswellOnt 7956, 245 O.A.C. 47, [2008] O.J. No. 5345 (Ont. C.A.); leave to appeal refused 2009 CarswellOnt 3641, 2009 CarswellOnt 3642, 399 N.R. 398 (note), 262 O.A.C. 398 (note) (S.C.C.)).

The judgment obtained against Ms. Earle-Barron was only $14,537.46. However, the overall judgment was $49,830.63. That amount is well in excess of the Small Claims Court's maximum jurisdiction of $25,000. Rule 57.05(3) has no application as the default judgment is for a total amount in excess of the Small Claims Court's jurisdiction. Ms. Earle-Barron simply did not defend the action because she was busy with other matters, specifically waiting for a court decision. Motion dismissed.

1775323 Ontario Inc. v. AAH Gas Inc., 2012 ONSC 6735, 2012 CarswellOnt 14854 (Ont. C.J.), Justice Robert B. Reid.

The plaintiff secured a default judgment against defendant Mohammad Asghar. That judgment flowed from an order striking the Statement of Defence. The defendant was then noted in default and the default judgment was issued.

Rule 37.14(1)(b) allows a party to move to set aside an order on a motion when the person has failed to appear on the motion through accident, mistake or insufficient notice. In this case, Court satisfied that there was a mistake or accident and that Mr. Asghar, if properly advised and fully aware of the legal process, would have attended on January 6.

Rule 19.03(1) allows the court to set aside the noting of default on such terms as are just.

The discretion to award costs is found under section 131 of the *Courts of Justice Act*, and the provisions of rule 57.01 list a variety of factors to be considered in exercising that discretion.

Costs order in favour of the plaintiff against the defendant Mohammad Asghar fixed in the amount of $7,500 inclusive of HST and disbursements.

William Hannah Heating and Cooling Inc. v. Evans Estate, 2013 ONSC 517, 2013 Carswell-Ont 524 (Ont. S.C.J.), Master MacLeod.

This is a lien proceeding for an amount that would otherwise be well within the jurisdiction of the Small Claims Court. Motion to set aside a default judgment.

If leave is required to bring motion under s. 67(2) of the Act meets test of a necessary step if the defendant can show that refusing to set aside the default judgment is unjust. That is the moving party must show the motion was brought promptly, that there is a reasonable explanation for the failure to defend, and there exists a genuine defence. The latter should be set out in a proposed statement of defence compliant with subrules 25.06 and 25.07. But in a lien action the defendant must also meet the test for setting aside the noting of default under s. 54 of the Act. That requires the court to be satisfied that the proposed defence is supported by actual evidence. See *Metaldoor Hardware & Installations Ltd. v. York Region District School Board*, 2012 ONSC 3067, 2012 CarswellOnt 7143, 25 C.L.R. (4th) 21 (Ont. S.C.J.)

There is little prejudice to the plaintiff in setting aside the judgment because the full amount of the lien plus 25% for security for costs has been paid into court.

Always an intent to defend and that was known to the plaintiff. Default judgment set aside as will the noting of default, defendants have 15 days to file their defence.

Stealth Web Designs Inc. v. Wildman, 2012 SKPC 73, 2012 CarswellSask 344, 397 Sask. R. 17 (Sask. Prov. Ct.)

The applicant (defendant) Melanie Wildman applies to set aside a judgment in favour of the respondent (plaintiff) Stealth Web Designs Inc.

Section 7.1 of *The Small Claims Act* gives authority to a judge to make any appropriate order or give judgment against a party who does not attend a case management conference.

At the case management conference on October 27, 2011, pursuant to section 7.1, this Court awarded judgment in favour of the respondent in the amount of $6,017.83, along with pre-judgment interest in the amount of $63.36 and costs of issuing and serving the claim in the amount of $230.00, for a total of $6,311.19.

Section 37(2) of *The Small Claims Act* provides that after the expiry of 90 days from the date of judgment, the Court may allow an application to be made to set aside the judgment, in exceptional circumstances. The term "exceptional" is defined in the *Canadian Oxford Dictionary (2d ed.)* as: "(1) forming an exception; (2) unusual; not typical (exceptional circumstances)."

The business-related reasons cannot be characterized as unusual or atypical. It is the Court's view that they would not be sufficient to meet the test of "exceptional circumstances" as required by section 37(2). Something more or different must be demonstrated to allow an application to proceed after 90 days has expired.

Once the Court has allowed the application to proceed, the applicant must satisfy the Court that she had a reasonable excuse for failing to attend the case management conference and that she has a valid defence to the respondent's claim.

The Court is of the view that the defence is valid, in that it discloses a triable issue and is not without reasonable grounds, frivolous, vexatious or an abuse of the court's process.

The applicant had a reasonable excuse for not attending the case management conference and has a valid defence.

Fundamental to our system of justice is the principle that parties to a dispute have the opportunity to be heard. However, the Court recognizes the hardship that further delay of these proceedings poses to the respondent, a small, fledgling business.

Having found the applicant had a reasonable excuse for not attending the case management conference and has a valid defence, judgment set aside, and new case management conference to be scheduled.

Mayo v. Veenstra, 2003 CarswellOnt 9, 63 O.R. (3d) 194, Belch J. (Ont. S.C.J.)

The defendant in a Small Claims Court action moved to set aside noting in default. The defendant was ordered to submit to cross-examination or motion to be dismissed. The order was made in error; there was no authority to order cross-examinations prior to judgment in Small Claims Court.

2272546 Ontario Inc. v. Garnett, 2013 CarswellOnt 5765 (Ont. S.C.J.)

Motion to set aside order striking statement of defence and subsequent order granting judgment. Defence struck at settlement conference and judgment granted after assessment of damages. Defendant relies upon Rule 11.06 on motion. Proper remedy in the Superior Court of Justice is to move under Rule 19.08 before the same court. See *Halow Estate v. Halow*, 2002 CarswellOnt 1062, (sub nom. *Halow Estate v. Halow, Sr.*) 59 O.R. (3d) 211, 158 O.A.C. 125, [2002] O.J. No. 1446 (Ont. C.A.). Rule 11.06 is to preclude appeals to the Divisional Court from the multitude of default judgments. A defendant in the Small Claims Court must exhaust the setting aside remedies of the Small Claims Court before an appeal lies to the Divisional Court. See also *Ketelaars v. Ketelaars*, 2011 ONCA 349, 2011 CarswellOnt 2887, 2 R.F.L. (7th) 296, [2011] O.J. No. 2009 (Ont. C.A.) at para. 5. See also *Maly v. Hanniman* (October 26, 2012), Doc. No. SC-11-116748, [2012] O.J. No. 5130 (Ont. Small Cl. Ct.).

When a defence is struck for whatever reason and judgment thereafter obtained *ex parte*, the judgment in the nature of a default judgment.

Under Rule 11.06, the defendant must satisfy the court that he has a reasonable explanation for his default. The defendant must also show that a meritorious defence to put forward.

Tests governing the setting aside of default judgments are not to be applied rigidly. See *Chitel v. Rothbart*, 1988 CarswellOnt 451, 29 C.P.C. (2d) 136, [1988] O.J. No. 1197 (Ont. C.A.); leave to appeal refused (1989), 98 N.R. 132 (note), (sub nom. *Rothbart v. Chitel*) 34 O.A.C. 399 (note), [1988] S.C.C.A. No. 427 (S.C.C.), at para. 1. In *Peterbilt of Ontario Inc. v. 1565627 Ontario Ltd.*, 2007 ONCA 333, 2007 CarswellOnt 2713, 87 O.R. (3d) 479, 41 C.P.C. (6th) 316, [2007] O.J. No. 1685 (Ont. C.A.), at para. 2, the court held that tests are a guide and that governing principle whether interests of justice favour or do not favour setting aside default judgment.

The motion was dismissed with costs to the plaintiff.

Ward v. Landmark Inn Limited Partnership (April 17, 2013), Doc. No. SC-12-1031, Deputy Judge Cleghorn, K. (Ont. Small Cl. Ct.)

Motion to set aside noting in default and permission to file a defence.

See Rule 11.06 of the *Small Claims Court Rules*. A motion was brought as soon as reasonably possible.

I do not equate the word "meritorious" with "arguable". See J.W. Quinn, J. in *Coombs v. Curran*, 2010 ONSC 1312, 2010 CarswellOnt 1175, [2010] O.J. No. 815, 100 O.R. (3d) 554 (Ont. Div. Ct.), quoting the New Shorter Oxford English Dictionary, "meritorious" is defined as "entitling a person to reward; well-deserving, meriting commendation, having merit" (at para. 30).

Rule 1.03(1) of the *Rules of the Small Claims Court* provides:

> 1.03(1) These rules shall be liberally construed to secure the just, most expeditious and least expensive determination of every proceeding on its merits in accordance with section 25 of the *Courts of Justice Act*. O. Reg. 258/98, r. 1.03(1).

This is a matter of judicial discretion. Motion granted. Noting of default set aside and defendants have permission to file their defence.

Rule 11.1 — Dismissal by Clerk

11.1.01 (1) Dismissal — Undefended Actions — The clerk shall make an order dismissing an action as abandoned if the following conditions are satisfied, unless the court orders otherwise:

1. More than 180 days have passed since the date the claim was issued or an order was made extending the time for service of the claim under subrule 8.01(2).

2. No defence has been filed.

3. The action has not been disposed of by order and has not been set down for trial.

4. The clerk has given 45 days notice to the plaintiff that the action will be dismissed as abandoned.

(2) Dismissal — Defended Actions — The clerk shall make an order dismissing an action as abandoned if the following conditions are satisfied, unless the court orders otherwise:

1. More than 150 days have passed since the date the first defence was filed.

2. All settlement conferences required under Rule 13 have been held.

3. The action has not been disposed of by order and has not been set down for trial.

4. The clerk has given 45 days notice to all parties to the action that the action will be dismissed as abandoned.

(3) Transition — If an action was started before July 1, 2006, the following applies:

1. The action or a step in the action shall be carried on under these rules on or after July 1, 2006.

2. Despite paragraph 1, if a step in the action is taken on or after July 1, 2006, the timetable set out in subrules (1) and (2) shall apply as if the action started on the date on which the step was taken.

(4) Same — If an action was commenced before July 1, 2006 and no step is taken in the action on or after that date, the clerk may make an order dismissing it as abandoned if,

(a) where an action is undefended, more than two years have passed since the date the claim was issued and the conditions set out in paragraphs 2, 3 and 4 of subrule (1) are satisfied; or

(b) more than two years have passed since the date the first defence was filed and the conditions set out in paragraphs 3 and 4 of subrule (2) are satisfied.

(5) Exception Where Terms of Settlement Signed — Subrules (1), (2) and (4) do not apply if terms of settlement (Form 14D) signed by all parties have been filed.

(6) Exception Where Admission of Liability — Subrule (2) and clause (4)(b) do not apply if the defence contains an admission of liability for the plaintiff's claim and a proposal of terms of payment under subrule 9.03(1).

Commentary: The *Small Claims Court Rules* were amended in 2006 to provide that cases which have been stagnant for a certain period of time will be automatically dismissed by the court clerk. This means that plaintiffs must move their cases along or face dismissal under Rule 11.1.

The requirements for automatic dismissal for delay are slightly different for undefended actions and defended actions, under rules 11.1.01(1) and 11.1.01(2), respectively. The key deadlines are 180 days after issuance of a claim in undefended actions, and 150 days after filing of the first defence in defended actions. Among other things, this means that despite the six-month time for service of a claim under rule 8.01(2), it is better to serve a claim as soon as possible after issuance because time under Rule 11.1 runs from issuance of a claim.

Prior to making an automatic dismissal order, the clerk must give 45 days' notice of the pending dismissal. Such notices are given in writing and sent by regular mail.

A plaintiff who receives a Notice of Pending Dismissal must take certain steps within the 45 days or face automatic dismissal.

If the claim has been served on all defendants and they have all filed defences, the only step that is required is to set the action down for trial. A settlement conference is required before setting down, but in the normal course of events should already have occurred by the time a Notice of Pending Dismissal is issued.

In cases where defences have not been filed by all defendants, or not all the defendants have been served with the claim, the plaintiff may have several options and the best choice will depend on the circumstances. For example, if a defendant has not been served and has been evading service or his or her whereabouts are unknown, the plaintiff might want to bring a motion for substituted service or to extend the times for service under Rule 11.1. Sometimes a plaintiff who has sued several defendants but has been unable to find or serve one of them may elect to abandon the claim against that defendant once the Notice of Pending Dismissal is issued.

Regardless of what may be the most desirable step for a plaintiff in the particular case, the plaintiff needs to do something within 45 days after a Notice of Pending Dismissal is issued. If nothing is done, the clerk will dismiss the action after the 45 days have expired.

Once an action has been dismissed under Rule 11.1, the case is over unless the plaintiff brings a motion to a judge to set aside the clerk's automatic dismissal order. There is no specific rule under the *Small Claims Court Rules* which provides for such a motion, but the practice contemplates such motions nonetheless.

A motion to set aside a dismissal order obviously affects the interests of the defendant, and must be brought on notice. See also rule 15.01(6), which requires notice of a motion made after judgment even on defendants who have been noted in default.

There has been an abundance of recent caselaw from the Court of Appeal dealing with the considerations which apply to a motion to set aside a clerk's automatic dismissal for delay order. Although arising under the *Rules of Civil Procedure* and not from the *Small Claims Court Rules*, the principles apply in Small Claims Court.

In the leading case of *Scaini v. Prochnicki*, 2007 ONCA 63, 2007 CarswellOnt 408, [2007] O.J. No. 299, 85 O.R. (3d) 179, 39 C.P.C. (6th) 1, 219 O.A.C. 317 (Ont. C.A.), the court held that the overriding consideration was the justice of the case, which should be assessed contextually. Four criteria may be considered in making that contextual assessment: (i) explanation of the litigation delay; (ii) inadvertence in missing the deadline; (iii) the motion is brought promptly; and (iv) no prejudice to the defendant. In that case, the action was reinstated.

In *Marché d'Alimentation Denis Thériault Ltée v. Giant Tiger Stores Ltd.*, 2007 ONCA 695, 2007 CarswellOnt 6522, [2007] O.J. No. 3872, 87 O.R. (3d) 660, 47 C.P.C. (6th) 233, 247 O.A.C. 22, 286 D.L.R. (4th) 487 (Ont. C.A.), those principles were applied and in that case the action was not reinstated. It was held that the plaintiff's delay was inordinate, the interest of the administration of justice in finality was a proper part of the contextual analysis, and the plaintiff could pursue a negligence claim against its lawyer if the action were dismissed for delay. The action was not reinstated.

The panel in *Finlay v. Van Paassen*, 2010 ONCA 204, 2010 CarswellOnt 1543, [2010] O.J. No. 1097, 101 O.R. (3d) 390, 266 O.A.C. 239, 318 D.L.R. (4th) 686 (Ont. C.A.), found that speculation about whether a plaintiff has a potential negligence claim against his or her representative is unhelpful and should not inform the decision whether to set aside an automatic dismissal for delay order. Other recent decisions of the Court of Appeal include *Wellwood v. Ontario Provincial Police*, 2010 ONCA 386, 2010 CarswellOnt 3521, [2010] O.J. No. 2225, 102 O.R. (3d) 555, 319 D.L.R. (4th) 412, 262 O.A.C. 349, 90 C.P.C. (6th) 101 (Ont. C.A.); additional reasons at 2010 ONCA 513, 2010 CarswellOnt 5182, 88 C.P.C. (6th) 206 (Ont. C.A.); *Hamilton (City) v. Svedas Koyanagi Architects Inc.*, 2010 ONCA 887, 2010 Carswell-Ont 9774, [2010] O.J. No. 5572, 104 O.R. (3d) 689, 97 C.L.R. (3d) 1, 271 O.A.C. 205, 328 D.L.R. (4th) 540, 2 C.P.C. (7th) 114 (Ont. C.A.); *Aguas v. Rivard Estate*, 2011 ONCA 494, 2011 CarswellOnt 5822, [2011] O.J. No. 3108, 107 O.R. (3d) 142, 335 D.L.R. (4th) 365, 7 C.P.C. (7th) 16, 282 O.A.C. 39 (Ont. C.A.).

An excellent discussion of these principles as applicable in the Small Claims Court is provided by Deputy Judge Abraham Davis in *Cozzi v. Cordeiro* (August 21, 2008), Doc. 48211/07, [2008] O.J. No. 3199 (Ont. Sm. Cl. Ct.), extension of time to appeal denied *Cozzi v. Cordeiro*, 2009 CarswellOnt 5648, [2009] O.J. No. 3914 (Ont. Div. Ct.). See also *Groscki v. Bell Mobility* (October 31, 2011), Doc. SC-10-00007592-0000, [2011] O.J. No. 5317 (Ont. Sm. Cl. Ct.).

Evans v. Triserve Management Inc., 2013 CarswellOnt 7648, [2013] O.J. No. 2651, Deputy Judge Winny (Ont. Sm. Cl. Ct.).

The plaintiffs moved to set aside the clerk's order dismissing the claim as abandoned dated April 23, 2013. Motion granted. Whether a notice and subsequent dismissal order under Rule 11.1 of the *Small Claims Court Rules*, O.Reg. 258/98, when issued only under the court file number of the plaintiff's claim, also affect a defendant's claim? In this case, the clerk issued a notice under rule 11.1(2) in the plaintiff's claim only, and subsequently issued a dismissal order using that same court file number only. It is unfair to interpret Rule 11.1 in a manner that would fail to give due notice to defendants who have issued defendants claims that their claims are in jeopardy of dismissal for delay.

The order was set aside dismissing the plaintiff's claim as abandoned and directed that they set the action down for trial within ten days.

The best practice for plaintiffs is to plan ahead for the 180-day deadline after issuance of their claims, and to take steps to avoid the deadlines under Rule 11.1. If a 45-day Notice of Pending Dismissal is issued by the court clerk, steps should be taken immediately to avoid issuance of the clerk's dismissal order, which may require a motion. If the dismissal order is issued the remedy is a motion to a judge to set it aside, but as the caselaw indicates, the judge's discretion may result in a denial of reinstatement of the action.

An action that has been automatically dismissed for delay does not necessarily preclude a fresh action for the same cause of action; however, if a limitation period has expired in the meantime, the fresh action may be precluded by virtue of that fact.

A clerk's automatic dismissal order under Rule 11.1 is a dismissal without costs.

In *Dewan v. Burdet (In Trust)*, 2013 ONSC 793, 2013 CarswellOnt 4115, [2013] O.J. No. 1668 (Ont. S.C.J.), it was held that a claim and a counterclaim are independent actions and where a registrar's order purported to dismiss the action, it did not dismiss both proceedings. The order was set aside. In Small Claims Court, a defendant's claim has a slightly different court file number than the associated plaintiff's claim. Where a clerk's notice of pending dismissal and dismissal order referenced only the plaintiff's claim, it was held that they had no effect on and did not dismiss the defendant's claim. The order dismissing only the plaintiff's claim for delay was set aside: *Evans v. Triserve Management Inc.*, 2013 CarswellOnt 7648, [2013] O.J. No. 2651 (Ont. Sm. Cl. Ct.).

Triggering Timelines

Triggering Code	Data Definition	Result	Explanation
NOBR — Notice of Bankruptcy	When a trustee in bankruptcy provides written notice to the court or enforcement staff of a stay of proceedings against a particular debtor under the *Bankruptcy and Insolvency Act*. Written notice of the stay may be received in a notice of intention to make a proposal; a proposal; a consumer proposal; a receiving order; an assignment in bankruptcy.	Timeline cancelled.	When notice of stay is filed, the case has been stayed against a particular debtor and all timelines are cancelled. See *Bankruptcy and Insolvency Act*.
TS — Terms of Settlement	When a Terms of Settlement (Form 14D) is filed indicating the claim, and any Defendant's Claim, is withdrawn.	Timeline cancelled.	Where the Plaintiff's Claim, and any Defendant's Claim, is withdrawn, there is no need to track timelines any longer.
Event Result/Order Detail Code			
JU — Judgment	When a court has rendered final judgment in an action, disposing of the claim(s) against all parties.	Timeline cancelled.	Where judgment has been obtained, all timelines are cancelled since the matter has been disposed of against all parties. See r. 11.1.01(2)3.

Triggering Code	Data Definition	Result	Explanation
JUC — Judgment on Consent	When a court has rendered final judgment in an action, disposing of the claim(s) against all parties, on consent of all parties.	Timeline cancelled.	Where judgment has been obtained, all timelines are cancelled since the matter has been disposed of against all parties. See r. 11.1.01(2)3.
Judgment default (against all defendants)	When a clerk has issued default judgment against all defendants in an action.	Timeline cancelled.	Where a default judgment has been obtained, all timelines are cancelled since the matter has been disposed of against all parties. See r. 11.1.01(2)3.
Judgment reserved	When a court has reserved issuing its judgment after the hearing of a motion or trial.	Timeline cancelled.	Where judgment has been obtained, all timelines are cancelled since the matter has been disposed of against all parties. See r. 11.1.01(2)3.
Order Dismissing Claim (On Consent)	When a judge or clerk makes an order dismissing a claim on consent of all parties.	Timeline cancelled.	Where a final order is made dismissing a claim on consent, all timelines are cancelled. See r. 11.1.01(2)3.
Order Dismissing Claim	When a judge makes an order dismissing a claim of all parties.	Timeline cancelled.	Where a final order is made dismissing a claim, all timelines are cancelled. See r. 11.1.01(2)3.

Order stay of proceeding	When an order to stay a proceeding is made.	Timeline cancelled.	Where a claim has been stayed, it has effectively been disposed of against all parties and there is no need to track timelines any longer. See r. 11.1.01(2)3.

(7) Service of Orders — **The clerk shall serve a copy of an order made under subrule (1) or clause (4)(a) on the plaintiff and a copy of an order made under subrule (2) or clause (4)(b) on all parties to the action.**

O. Reg. 78/06, s. 24; 56/08, s. 3; 393/09, s. 10; 56/12, s. 4

Case Law: *Ohayon v. Airlift Limousine Service Ltd.* (November 8, 2007) (Ont. Sm. Cl. Ct.), P.A. Thomson J.

Plaintiff issued claim in May 1996. The defendant's claim, with a reply and defence to defendant's claim were all filed in 1997. The amended claim was filed January 1998 and the trial was adjourned in July, October and December 1998, with a further adjournment in April 1999 "*sine die.*" Negotiations occurred sporadically in May 1999 and late 2005 and 2006.

Claim never struck. Not put on trial list due to a court error. Delay in noticing court's delay not intentional.

The defendant, in the absence of complaint, condoned the delay and court error by not bringing motion to dismiss earlier or by requesting defendant's claim be placed on trial list.

Claim and defendant's claim against to be placed on trial list. Plaintiff's right to interest under the *Courts of Justice Act* is abrogated by the delay during the years 2002 to 2007 inclusive.

Marché d'Alimentation Denis Thériault Ltée v. Giant Tiger Stores Ltd., 2007 CarswellOnt 6522, [2007] O.J. No. 3872, 2007 ONCA 695, 47 C.P.C. (6th) 233, 286 D.L.R. (4th) 487, 87 O.R. (3d) 660 (Ont. C.A.).

Dismissal for delay. Excusing delay risked undermining public confidence and overlooking lawyer's conduct risked legal system being seen as protecting its own. As five years had passed since dismissal, defendants entitled to assurance that judicial system had finally disposed of plaintiff's action. As years passed, defendants' interest in finality had to trump plaintiff's plea for indulgence, especially since plaintiffs had another remedy, and even though order was not on merits.

The Court has the authority to dismiss action or defence as a sanction for default of court orders and failure to comply with case management timetables. The decision to strike claim or defence one of discretion, must be exercised on proper principles: *Starland Contracting Inc. v. 1581518 Ontario Ltd.*, 252 O.A.C. 19, 83 C.L.R. (3d) 1, [2009] O.J. No. 2480, 2009 CarswellOnt 3431 (Ont. Div. Ct.).

Brandon Forest Products Ltd. v. 2121645 Ontario Inc. (April 10, 2012), Doc. SC-10-00001961-0000, [2012] O.J. No. 2337 (Ont. Sm. Cl. Ct.)

Effect should be given to dismissal orders under Rule 11.1 unless otherwise indicated. Where the cause of action arise five years earlier and the motion to set aside the dismissal order was not brought until one year after it was issued and was based on poor quality affidavit evidence, the motion to set it aside was dismissed.

Cozzi v. Cordeiro (August 21, 2008), Doc. Whitby 48211/07, [2008] O.J. No. 3199 (Ont. Sm. Cl. Ct.); extension of time to appeal denied 2009 CarswellOnt 5648, [2009] O.J. No. 3914 (Ont. Div. Ct.)

A motion to set aside an automatic dismissal order, which was brought about one year after the dismissal order, was dismissed. The plaintiff's affidavit evidence failed to satisfactorily explain the delay leading up to the dismissal order, and the motion was brought after further unexplained delay. Applying a contextual analysis, the appropriate order was to dismiss the motion.

Contact Resource Services Inc. v. Rampersad (November 27, 2009), Doc. 843/08, [2009] O.J. No. 5893 (Ont. Sm. Cl. Ct.)

An *ex parte* motion to set aside an automatic dismissal order was dismissed. Orders setting aside automatic dismissal orders may be granted in appropriate cases but they are not granted automatically. The motion was heard 17 months after the action was started and the claim had not yet been served on the defendant. The plaintiff did not request the necessary extension of the time for service. The applicable limitation period had expired. The supporting affidavit failed to provide any meaningful explanation for the delay, the motion was launched 9 months after the automatic dismissal order was issued, and was brought without notice to the defendant. For 17 months to have elapsed in a Small Claims Court action without even accomplishing service of the claim on the defendant could hardly be described as summary proceedings.

FCT Insurance Co. v. Knibb (October 28, 2009), Doc. 52/09, [2009] O.J. No. 4486 (Ont. Sm. Cl. Ct.)

A motion to set aside an automatic dismissal order was dismissed. The supporting affidavit provided no evidence of any steps taken following receipt of the clerk's 45-day notice, but contained a vague reference to oversight on the part of the plaintiff's lawyer. In addition the motion ought to have been brought on notice to the defendant.

LTP Tracer Corp. v. Newhook (August 25, 2009), Doc. 1374/08, [2009] O.J. No. 3524 (Ont. Sm. Cl. Ct.)

An *ex parte* motion to set aside an automatic dismissal order was dismissed. The supporting affidavit indicated that the plaintiff did nothing to move the action forward from issuance of the claim until after the dismissal order. The plaintiff claimed to have mailed the claim in to the court office for issuance, but never received it back. There was no evidence the plaintiff did not receive the clerk's 45-day notice prior to dismissal, or that the plaintiff took any steps in response to that notice. The plaintiff needed but did not request extensions of the time for service under rule 5.01(2) and under rule 11.1.01, and the motion ought to have been brought on notice to the defendant.

Multan v. 381713 B.C. Ltd., 2012 BCSC 1743, 2012 CarswellBC 3737 (B.C. S.C.), Justice Barrow.

There are two applications before the court in relation to this Small Claims appeal. The respondent seeks to have the appeal dismissed for want of prosecution. The appellants seek an order that the appeal be heard as a new trial.

At the conclusion of the trial judge's reasons, he invited the parties to make submissions on whether he ought to impose a penalty under Rule 20(5) of the *Small Claims Rules*. That Rule permits the judge to order a party to pay up to 10 percent of the amount claimed if the proceeding was carried through trial with no reasonable basis and no reasonable prospect of success.

Test to be applied on an application for dismissal of an appeal for want of prosecution is the same as that which is to be applied on an application made in the first instance, that is, an application to dismiss an action for want of prosecution.

A delay of two-and-a-half years is inordinate.

The next issue involves an assessment of the reasons for the delay and, based on that assessment, a determination of whether the delay is excusable.

Court not persuaded that justice requires that, provided clear conditions are imposed which will result in the matter being brought to a conclusion in the reasonably near future.

Krauck v. Shoppers Drug Mart, 2014 CarswellOnt 672, [2014] O.J. No. 343 (Ont. S.C.J.)

The court dismissed a motion to set aside the clerk's dismissal order. The action was 2.5 years old, the delay was unexplained, and the motion was not brought promptly. In addition, the claim failed to disclose a reasonable cause of action.

Evans v. Triserve Management Inc., 2013 CarswellOnt 7648, [2013] O.J. No. 2651 (Ont. Sm. Cl. Ct.)

A notice of approaching dismissal and clerk's dismissal order were issued in the plaintiff's claim. It was held that since no notice and order were issued in the defendant's claim, that claim was unaffected by the dismissal of the plaintiff's claim.

Rule 11.2 — Request for Clerk's Order on Consent

11.2.01 (1) Consent Order — The clerk shall, on the filing of a request for clerk's order on consent (Form 11.2A), make an order granting the relief sought, including costs, if the following conditions are satisfied:

1. The relief sought is,

    i. amending a claim or defence less than 30 days before the originally scheduled trial date,

    ii. adding, deleting or substituting a party less than 30 days before the originally scheduled trial date,

    iii. setting aside the noting in default or default judgment against a party and any specified step to enforce the judgment that has not yet been completed,

    iv. restoring a matter that was dismissed under rule 11.1 to the list,

    v. noting that payment has been made in full satisfaction of a judgment or terms of settlement, or

    vi. dismissing an action.

2. The request is signed by all parties (including any party to be added, deleted or substituted) and states,

    i. that each party has received a copy of the request, and

    ii. that no party that would be affected by the order is under disability.

3. [Repealed O. Reg. 393/09, s. 11(3).]

4. [Repealed O. Reg. 393/09, s. 11(3).]

(2) Service of order — The clerk shall serve a copy of an order made under subrule (1) in accordance with subrule 8.01(14) on a party that requests it and provides a stamped, self-addressed envelope.

(3) Same, Refusal to Make Order — Where the clerk refuses to make an order, the clerk shall serve a copy of the request for clerk's order on consent (Form 11.2A), with reasons for the refusal, on all the parties.

Commentary: Rule 11.2.01 regarding clerk's orders on consent now clearly states that parties only need a clerk's order when they wish to amend a claim or defence within 30 days of the originally scheduled trial date. Amendments to a claim or defence made more than 30 days before the originally scheduled trial date can be filed without a clerk's order under Rule 12.

(4) Notice of Setting Aside of Enforcement Step — Where an order is made setting aside a specified step to enforce a judgment under subparagraph 1 iii of subrule (1), a party shall file a copy of the order at each court location where the enforcement step has been requested.

O. Reg. 78/06, s. 24; 393/09, s. 11

Commentary: Small Claims Court clerks can make orders only in the specific circumstances set out in the Rules. These orders can only be made if the written consent of all parties has been provided to the clerk. The clerk makes the order based on the Request for Clerk's Order on Consent [Form 11.2A] filed with the court. No hearing is required.

The consent form must state that no party who would be affected by the order is under legal disability, and that all parties to the action have received a copy of the request for clerk's order on consent form.

The clerk can make an order for the following:

- amending a claim or defence where the originally scheduled trial date is less than 30 days away (otherwise see rule 12 for amendments);

- adding, deleting or substituting a party where the originally scheduled trial date is less than 30 days away;

- setting aside a noting in default or default judgment against a party, and any specified step to enforce the judgment that has not yet been completed;

- restoring a matter that was dismissed under rule 11.1 to the list;

- noting payment is made in full satisfaction of a judgment or terms of settlement; or

- dismissing an action.

See rule 11.2 of the Rules.

The Request for Clerk's Order on Consent [Form 11.2A] will indicate which order you are seeking.

Each party must sign the request for clerk's order on consent form in the presence of a witness. If a party is being added or substituted, the signature of that new party is also required. If a party is being deleted, that party must also sign. If all parties do not consent, the clerk cannot make the order requested. If a party has been noted in default, his or her consent is not required.

The form states that each party has received a copy of the form, and no party who would be affected by the order is under legal disability.

The clerk will review the documents and, if the legal requirements of the Rules are met, the clerk will sign the order. The clerk will mail a copy of the order to a party who requested it if a stamped self-addressed envelope was provided.

The clerk may refuse to make a clerk's order if:

- the criteria set out in rule 11.2 (discussed above) are not met;

- the consent of all parties is not obtained; or

- the form is incomplete.

When the clerk refuses to sign an order, the clerk will serve a copy of the request for clerk's order, with reasons for the refusal, on all parties.

Case Law: *Robb-Simm v. RE/MAX Real Estate Centre Inc.*, 2012 CarswellOnt 13437, [2012] O.J. No. 5232 (Ont. Sm. Cl. Ct.)

The clerk's powers to grant consent orders to not include any jurisdiction to grant adjournments of trials. In this case the parties had filed a Request to Clerk asking for consent adjournment of a full-day trial, and then failed to show up on the day of trial. The court dismissed the plaintiff's claim. Discussion on scheduling of trials in the Small Claims Court.

Rule 11.3 — Discontinuance

[Heading added O. Reg. 393/09, s. 12.]

11.3.01 Discontinuance by Plaintiff in Undefended Action — (1) A plaintiff may discontinue his or her claim against a defendant who fails to file a defence to all or part of the claim with the clerk within the prescribed time by,

(a) serving a notice of discontinued claim (Form 11.3A) on all defendants who were served with the claim; and

(b) filing the notice with proof of service.

(2) A claim may not be discontinued by or against a person under disability, except with leave of the court.

(3) **Electronic Filing** — If the plaintiff's claim was issued electronically under rule 7.04, the plaintiff may file the notice of discontinued claim, with proof of service, electronically.

O. Reg. 393/09, s. 12; 44/14, s. 10

11.3.02 Effect of Discontinuance on Subsequent Action — The discontinuance of a claim is not a defence to a subsequent action on the matter, unless an order granting leave to discontinue provides otherwise.

O. Reg. 393/09, s. 12

Commentary: Now a plaintiff can file a Notice of Discontinued Claim (Form 11.3A) if he or she no longer wishes to proceed with the claim. However, this can only be used to discontinue a claim against a defendant who has failed to file a defence in the case.

Once a defence has been filed, the parties still can agree amongst themselves to settle the action and then notify the court in writing. If they can't come to a settlement agreement, the parties would then attend the settlement conference.

Rule 12 — Amendment, Striking out, Stay and Dismissal

12.01 (1) Right to Amend — A plaintiff's or defendant's claim and a defence to a plaintiff's or defendant's claim may be amended by filing with the clerk a copy that is marked "Amended", in which any additions are underlined and any other changes are identified.

History [R. 12.01(1)]: This section now allows a party to amend a claim or defence without obtaining the court's permission at any time up to 30 days before the trial. The amended document must be served on all other parties and filed with the court. Amendments should be made no later than 30 days before trial is scheduled, rather than last minute adjournments.

New provision allowing amendment by filing an amended copy with the clerk.

Commentary: A party may amend a claim or defence, without obtaining an order from the court to do so, as long as it is filed and served 30 days before the trial. A party will file with the clerk a copy that is marked "AMENDED" and with any additions underlined and any other changes identified of the amended pleadings [r. 12.01(1)]. No fee is required to file an amended claim and/or defence.

Affidavit(s) of service relating to amended documents must provide that:

(1) It was served on all parties, including any parties in default [r. 12.01(2)];

(2) It was served and filed at least 30 days before the originally scheduled trial date by reviewing the proof of service (the court may grant a shorter time period or the parties may consent to a clerk's order allowing the amendment within 30 days of trial) [r. 12.01(3)] and [r.11.2.01(1)(i)]; and

(3) It was served according to r. 8.01(1) on any person that is added as a party to action through the amendment of the document [r. 12.01(4)].

If a party needs to amend a claim or defence less than 30 days before the originally scheduled trial date, a party may file a Request for a Clerk's Order on Consent or file a motion to obtain such an order from the court.

A newly added party that has not been previously served with the originally issued claim must be served personally or by an alternative to personal service [r. 8.01(1)].

The *Rules of the Small Claims Court* do not speak to whether amending documents must be filed together with or without proof of service. The Rules indicate that "filing and service of the amended document shall take place at least 30 days before the originally scheduled trial date . . ." Proof of service is required to comply with the Rules.

Sloan v. Sauve Heating Ltd., 2011 ONCA 91, 2011 CarswellOnt 515, [2011] O.J. No. 402 (Ont. C.A.)

The Court of Appeal held that the plaintiff's application to add the independent contractor and truck driver should be dismissed. The only step the plaintiff took was to question Sauve Heating Ltd. on discovery. The plaintiff failed to provide a reasonable explanation as to why proposed defendants were not identifiable and therefore not named prior to the expiry of the *Limitations Act, 2002.*

A party has the right to amend a pleading until 30 days before the originally scheduled trial date (subrule 12.01(3)). The parties do not have to file an amended pleading when served with an amendment (subrule 12.01(5)). Within the 30 days before trial, amendments may only be filed with leave of the Court, or on consent pursuant to a request to the clerk under rule 11.2.

Any amendments to an opposing party's pleadings or filings must be by motion under subrule 12.02.

The grounds upon which a pleading or a document will be struck are set out in subrule 12.02(1): delay, absence of a reasonable cause of action or defence, or being "inflammatory, a waste of time, a nuisance or an abuse of process."

A party may amend a claim or defence, without obtaining an order from the court to do so, as long as it is filed and served 30 days before the originally scheduled trial date. A party will file with the clerk a copy that is marked "AMENDED" and with any additions underlined and any other changes identified on the amended pleadings [r. 12.01(1)]. No fee is required to file an amended claim and/or defence.

An amended document shall be served by the party making the amendment on all parties, including any parties in default, by mail, courier or fax, personally, or by an alternative to personal service [r. 12.01(2), 11.05(3)] unless the court orders otherwise. Filing and service of the amended document shall take place at least 30 days before the originally scheduled trial date, unless:

- the clerk makes an order (on filing of request for clerk's order) on consent within 30 days of the scheduled trial date [r. 11.2.01(1)Ii]; or

- the court, on motion, allows a shorter notice period [r. 12.01(3)].

A party may amend a Plaintiff's Claim (Form 7A), a Defendant's Claim (Form 10A), at least 30 days before the originally scheduled trial date (unless otherwise ordered by the court or by a clerk's order or consent).

Case Law: *1760357 Ontario Ltd. v. 1789316 Ontario Ltd.*, 2013 CarswellOnt 7863, [2013] O.J. No. 2748 (Ont. Sm. Cl. Ct.)

In Small Claims Court, leave is required where a defendant seeks to advance at trial an unpleaded position which is inconsistent with an admission pleaded in its defence.

Decoration J.M. Laflamme Inc. v. Arra Chemicals Inc. (1993), 44 A.C.W.S. (3d) 226 (Ont. Div. Ct.) — The defendant had brought a motion to amend the defence and it was denied. Pursuant to Rule 11.01(1) of the Small Claims Court Rules, absent prejudice to the plaintiff that could not be compensated for in costs, the court must grant leave to amend the defence. In this case, any prejudice to the plaintiff could have been compensated for in costs and the amendment should have been granted.

The defendant sought an order extending time to deliver a notice of appeal. The defendant proceeded expeditiously in attempting to have the matter heard by way of appeal. The applicant had a bona fide intention to appeal and the length of delay in not doing so would be explained and was not such as to cause prejudice to the plaintiff. Merits of appeal also militated in favour of the defendant.

Tkachuk v. Janzen (1996), 191 A.R. 275, 204 A.R. 386, 51 Alta. L.R. (3d) 34 (Master); affirmed [1997] 7 W.W.R. 672 (Alta. Q.B.) — Application by plaintiff to amend statement of claim for second time. Defendant argued against amendment as over two years had passed since accident. Court allowed amendment based on functional approach for amendment following expiration of limitation period. Defendant was not prejudiced.

Hanlan v. Sernesky (1996), 37 C.C.L.I. (2d) 262, 1 C.P.C. (4th) 1 (Ont. Gen. Div.); reversed (1996), 39 C.C.L.I. (2d) 107, 95 O.A.C. 297, 3 C.P.C. (4th) 20 (C.A.) — Motions judge refused amendment to statement of defence to plead law of place where tort occurred, as result of recent Supreme Court of Canada decision in *Tolofson v. Jensen*, 120 D.L.R. (4th) 289. There was no prejudice resulting from amendment.

Ragno Excavating Ltd. v. Granville Constructors Ltd. (December 16, 1997), Doc. 97-CV-130613-CM (Ont. Gen. Div.) — Amendment to statement of claim permitted plaintiff to argue at trial that company was known by another name. Amendment was relevant in light of changes of corporations' names.

Gajic v. Wolverton Securities Ltd., [1996] B.C.W.L.D. 2490 (B.C. S.C.) — Unrepresented and allegedly impecunious plaintiff claimed damages for substantial losses from stockbroker. Plaintiff should have final opportunity to file adequate pleadings, on same terms as to security as imposed by previous judge.

Vigna v. Toronto Stock Exchange, 1998 CarswellOnt 4560, [1998] O.J. No. 4924, 115 O.A.C. 393, 28 C.P.C. (4th) 318 (Ont. Div. Ct.) — In statement of defence, Honda Canada denied designing or manufacturing the vehicle in question. Through inadvertence, the plaintiff's solicitor did not notice the denial until several months later. Reasonable inference could be drawn that Honda Canada had advised the other companies of the claim and that they were not prejudiced. Plaintiff permitted to add the other companies as defendants after the limitation period had expired.

Cowsill v. Strohmeyer (April 23, 1999), Doc. Welland 8886/97 (Ont. S.C.J.) — The plaintiffs sought to amend pleadings. The defendants sought an expedited trial and an order requiring the plaintiffs to pay all outstanding arrears on mortgage at issue. The plaintiffs were stalling. The plaintiffs were allowed to amend pleadings. No payments were required up to March 1, 1999 until the main action was heard. The payments were to restart as of April 1, 1999. Expedited trial ordered.

White v. Atlantic Home Improvement Ltd. (1999), 211 N.B.R. (2d) 182, 539 A.P.R. 182 (N.B. Q.B.) — The Rules of Court allowed discretion to amend pleadings unless prejudice will result that cannot be compensated for by costs or adjournment. The plaintiff was permitted to amend the statement of claim to conform to the evidence.

Smith v. Sliwa (August 23, 1999), Doc. 96-CU-108908 (Ont. S.C.J.); leave to appeal refused (November 24, 1999), Doc. Toronto 617/99 (Ont. S.C.J.) — An order dismissing the plaintiff's action for delay was set aside based on new facts. The plaintiff relied upon improper advice of his agent. The plaintiff did not become aware that he was given wrong advice until some time later. The delay in bringing the motion was not the plaintiff's fault. Had the Master been aware of all circumstances, the decision would have been different.

Strata Plan NW 580 v. Canada Mortgage & Housing Corp., 2000 BCCA 507, 144 B.C.A.C. 161, 236 W.A.C. 161, 2000 CarswellBC 1906 (B.C. C.A.) — Defendant applying to strike out claim on grounds of no cause of action. The application was granted. Plaintiff successfully appealing that defects could be cured by amendments.

Bruno v. Canada (Customs & Revenue Agency), 2000 BCSC 1255, [2000] 4 C.T.C. 57, 2000 CarswellBC 1734 (B.C. S.C.); affirmed 2002 BCCA 47, [2002] 2 C.T.C. 142, 162 B.C.A.C. 293, 264 W.A.C. 293, 2002 CarswellBC 208 (B.C. C.A.) — The claim had already been dismissed. The plaintiff was applying to amend the claim. The application was dismissed; cannot amend claim after dismissal.

Andersen Consulting Ltd. v. Canada (Attorney General) (2001), 150 O.A.C. 177, 2001 CarswellOnt 3139, 13 C.P.C. (5th) 251, [2001] O.J. No. 3576 (Ont. C.A.) — Well-established rule that amendments should be presumptively approved unless they would occasion prejudice that could not be compensated by costs or an adjournment. They were shown to be scandalous, frivolous, vexatious or an abuse of the court's process, or they displaced no reasonable cause of action.

G.C. Rentals Ltd. v. Falco Steel Fabricators Inc. (2000), 132 O.A.C. 70, 2000 CarswellOnt 1040 (Ont. Div. Ct.) — G.C. Rentals Ltd. was the plaintiff lien claimant in two actions. The plaintiff sought order amending its name to "G.C. Rentals & Repairs" and to make the appropriate and necessary amendments to the statements of claim. The Ontario Divisional Court ordered that the plaintiff substitute "G.C. Rentals & Repairs" wherever "G.C. Rentals Ltd." appeared. The Divisional Court stated that it was not prepared to say that a defective affidavit of verification respecting a construction lien necessarily invalidated a claim for lien, which claim for lien might otherwise be validated by the curative provisions of s. 6 of the *Construction Lien Act*, R.S.O. 1990, c. C.30.

Graham v. Moore Estate, 2002 CarswellBC 1676, 2002 BCSC 637, [2002] B.C.J. No. 1660 (B.C. S.C.) — Party amending pleading. Amendment causing other parts of pleading to be inconsistent. Party required to amend inconsistent parts.

Perkins-Aboagye v. Chadwick, 2002 CarswellOnt 1084, [2002] O.J. No. 1248, [2002] O.T.C. 244 (Ont. S.C.J.) — Second action brought by unrepresented plaintiff nothing more than attempt to collaterally attack decision of judge on defendant bank's motion in first action. Second action dismissed. Plaintiff granted 20 days to serve amended statement of claim in first action.

Corlett v. Matheson, 2001 CarswellAlta 1723, 2001 ABQB 963, 302 A.R. 139 (Alta. Q.B.) — Plaintiff having default judgment sought to amend statement of claim without re-opening default judgment. Application dismissed.

Mazzuca v. Silvercreek Pharmacy Ltd. (2001), 2001 CarswellOnt 4133, [2001] O.J. No. 4567, 207 D.L.R. (4th) 492, 56 O.R. (3d) 768, 152 O.A.C. 201, 15 C.P.C. (5th) 235 (Ont. C.A.) — Appeal from decision permitting amendment to change identity of plaintiff from individual party to corporate entity after expiry of limitation period dismissed. Amendment properly allowed as no prejudice to defendant by reason of name change.

Ager v. Canjex Publishing Ltd., 2003 CarswellBC 430, [2003] B.C.J. No. 431, 2003 BCSC 305 (B.C. S.C.) — Defendant sought to amend defence five weeks before trial. Application was dismissed as proposed amendment would not substantially change evidence to be given at trial.

Hilton v. Norampac Inc. (2003), 176 O.A.C. 309, 2003 CarswellOnt 3111, 26 C.C.E.L. (3d) 179, 2004 C.L.L.C. 210-030 (Ont. C.A.); leave to appeal refused (2004), 2004 CarswellOnt 1608, 2004 CarswellOnt 1609 (S.C.C.). Before Plaintiff cross-examined, the trial judge gave parties "some comments" on what he had heard so far. Comments would have been far better left unsaid but they did *not* show he had prejudged the case. Views tentative and he had *not* closed his mind to the employer's position.

Seaside Chevrolet Oldsmobile Ltd. v. VFC Inc., 2005 CarswellNB 397, 2005 NBQB 233, 22 C.P.C. (6th) 374, 761 A.P.R. 61, 292 N.B.R. (2d) 61 (N.B. Q.B.). Place of trial. Fourth party claims in Small Claims Court. No provisions comparable to R. 30.13 of Rules of Court, but Small Claims Court has jurisdiction to hear fourth or subsequent party claims. Amount of Claim was within jurisdiction of Small Claims Court. Parties agreed that action was not complex and was not rendered complex by participation of counsel and addition of fourth party.

Samson v. Insurance Corp. of British Columbia, 2006 CarswellBC 678, 2006 BCPC 99 (B.C. Prov. Ct.) 2006-03-20.

Claimant made application to increase amount claimed from $10,000 to $15,000 on grounds that when claim filed monetary jurisdiction of Small Claims Court limited to $10,000, but as of September 1, 2005 jurisdiction increased to $25,000.

Claimant's application made *after* completion of trial, judgment reserved and not yet delivered.

No cases where an amendment of pleadings was allowed after trial.

Nowhere there any reference to amendments to pleadings after trial or after judgment.

Under *Small Claims Rule* as compared to the *Supreme Court Rule*, not permissible because *Small Claims Rule* specifically calls for filing and serving of amended document, and option for Reply to be filed.

Application dismissed.

Leonard v. Labrador City (Town), 2006 CarswellNfld 150, 2006 NLTD 82 (N.L. T.D.) 2006-05-16.

What is being asked is that the court permit an amendment to the most recent Statement of Claim allowing Plaintiffs to add "reinstatement" to their former employment positions as a potential remedy.

See *Rees v. Royal Canadian Mounted Police*, [2004] N.J. No. 59, 2004 CarswellNfld 41, 2004 NLSCTD 32 (N.L. T.D.) and *Petten v. E.Y.E. Marine Consultants*, 1994 CarswellNfld 358, 120 Nfld. & P.E.I.R. 313, 373 A.P.R. 313 (N.L. T.D.) at paragraphs 85 to 100.

Test to be met before an amendment is permitted is that the amendment: (1) Must not cause injustice to the other side; (2) Must raise a triable issue; (3) Must not be embarrassing; and (4) Must be pleaded with particularity.

An amendment should be allowed if it does not do an injustice to the other party which cannot be compensated in costs.

The court, before allowing an amendment, ought to be satisfied that the presence of the amendment could not lead to a successful application by other parties.

The party proposing an amendment must pass the threshold requirement of being able to show that the amendment discloses a reasonable cause of action. The court must not try the merits of the claim. The threshold test is a low one.

There is no potential injustice that cannot be compensated for in costs and the amendment to the Statement of Claim is permitted.

Dempsey v. Envision Credit Union, 2006 CarswellBC 1172, 2006 BCSC 750 (B.C. S.C.) 2006-05-11.

Applications made to dismiss some of the actions and in others to strike out and dismiss counterclaims.

Where it is "plain and obvious" that the claims, as pleaded, or as they might be amended, disclose no reasonable claim, the court has the discretion to dismiss the claim. Any doubt is to be resolved in favour of allowing the pleadings to stand (see *Hunt v. T & N plc*, 1990 CarswellBC 759, 1990 CarswellBC 216, (sub nom. *Hunt v. Carey Canada Inc.*) [1990] S.C.J. No. 93, 4 C.C.L.T. (2d) 1, 43 C.P.C. (2d) 105, 117 N.R. 321, 4 C.O.H.S.C. 173 (head-note only), (sub nom. *Hunt v. Carey Canada Inc.*) [1990] 6 W.W.R. 385, 49 B.C.L.R. (2d) 273, (sub nom. *Hunt v. Carey Canada Inc.*) 74 D.L.R. (4th) 321, [1990] 2 S.C.R. 959 (S.C.C.) at p. 980).

Pleadings will be struck out if they abuse the process of the court. (See *Toronto (City) v. C.U.P.E., Local 79*, REJB 2003-49439, 2003 CarswellOnt 4328, 2003 CarswellOnt 4329, [2003] S.C.J. No. 64, 2003 SCC 63, 2003 C.L.L.C. 220-071, 232 D.L.R. (4th) 385, 31 C.C.E.L. (3d) 216, 9 Admin. L.R. (4th) 161, 311 N.R. 201, 120 L.A.C. (4th) 225, 179 O.A.C. 291, [2003] 3 S.C.R. 77, 17 C.R. (6th) 276 (S.C.C.) at para. 37.)

One way in which these principles are violated is where parties make allegations in subsequent proceedings that are *res judicata*.

See *Henderson v. Henderson* (1843), 67 E.R. 313, 3 Hare 100, [1843-60] All E.R. Rep. 378 (Eng. V.-C.), 114 to 115 (Hare).

James v. British Columbia, 2006 CarswellBC 1395, 2006 BCSC 873 (B.C. S.C.) 2006-06-06.

In the statement of defence to the plaintiff's statement of claim, the defendant pleaded:

> 7. In the further alternative and in further answer to the whole of the Statement of Claim, the issues giving rise to this action were resolved in Supreme Court of British Columbia and the Crown says matter *res judicata* and an abuse of process. In the alternative, the Crown says plaintiff, is estopped from bringing this claim as a result of the resolution of the action in Action No. S012533.

There are three pre-conditions which must be satisfied to establish the necessary and sufficient condition for estoppel:

  i)   the cause of action in both proceedings must be identical;

  ii)   the judgment which is said to create the estoppel must be final; and

  iii) the parties to that judgment or their privies are the same persons as the parties to the proceedings in which the estoppel is raised or their privies.

Although the parties are not the same, their privies are the same.

In *Cahoon v. Franks*, [1967] S.C.R. 455, 1967 CarswellAlta 48, 60 W.W.R. 684, 63 D.L.R. (2d) 274 (S.C.C.), all damages arising out of the same negligent act must be asserted by the claimant in one action, and any subsequent action was barred by the doctrine of *res judicata*.

Taken cumulatively, the factors identified by the plaintiff do not bring this case within any of the precedents in which the court has *declined* to prevent relitigation notwithstanding the preconditions of estoppel, either action or issue, have been established. The plaintiff has not discharged the burden imposed upon him. Accordingly, the defendant's application is allowed. The action is dismissed.

Chudzik v. Fehr, 2006 CarswellOnt 4, 20 C.P.C. (6th) 38, 79 O.R. (3d) 205 (Ont. S.C.J.).

Plaintiffs brought motion for leave to amend statement of claim to correct name of defendant. Motion granted. Presumption of prejudice had been rebutted. S Ltd. was aware of accident from outset, and commenced investigation and shared information with B Ltd., which was a related sister company.

Garth v. Halifax (Regional Municipality), [2006] N.S.J. No. 300, 2006 CarswellNS 316, 271 D.L.R. (4th) 470, 2006 NSCA 89, 31 C.P.C. (6th) 124, 245 N.S.R. (2d) 108, 777 A.P.R. 108 (N.S. C.A.).

Plaintiff sought amendment to add party after expiry of limitation period. Overriding general power to allow amendment not limited by specific instances in rules. Broad general discretionary power not limited by specific instances where amendment permitted after a limitation period had expired.

1225145 Ontario Inc. v. Kelly (2007), 2007 CarswellOnt 97 (Ont. C.A.).

Appeal from order denying application by appellant to amend pleadings. Appellant sought to amend counterclaim by adding a claim for specific performance. No reference made to Rule 26.01 of the *Rules of Civil Procedure*. Respondents did not make out case for prejudice sufficient to provide a basis to deny amendment. Appeal allowed.

Burtch v. Barnes Estate, [2006] O.J. No. 1621, 2006 CarswellOnt 2423, 27 C.P.C. (6th) 199, 80 O.R. (3d) 365, 20 M.P.L.R. (4th) 160, 209 O.A.C. 219 (Ont. C.A.).

Discoverability and reasonable diligence. Plaintiff injured in car accident. Plaintiff issued notice of action naming several defendants. Motion judge exercised discretion reasonably in granting plaintiffs leave to amend statement of claim to add M as defendant. Order appropriate, as plaintiffs put forward some evidence of their diligence.

Ryan (In Trust) v. Kaukab, 2005 CarswellOnt 6806 (Ont. Master), Master Egan.

Plaintiff's motion for leave to amend statement of claim to add plaintiff allowed. Concern that proposed defendant would be required to be witness too hypothetical. Plaintiff's claims arose out of same series of transactions, had common factual issues and balance of convenience favoured plaintiff.

Riddell v. Pasini, 2005 CarswellOnt 7939 (Ont. Sm. Cl. Ct.), Mungovan D.J.

In having clerk of Small Claims Court issue amended claim, plaintiff simply retaliating to criminal charges laid less than month before plaintiff's pleading was amended. Plaintiff could amend his pleading as a result of criminal charges laid against him so long as no intention to use civil process to undermine criminal process. Doctrine of abuse of process did not apply. Civil proceedings ordered stayed, albeit on temporary basis, until criminal proceedings came to an end or until court ordered otherwise.

Sicard v. Sendziak, 2006 CarswellAlta 1358, 2006 ABQB 725, 34 C.P.C. (6th) 320 (Alta. Q.B.), M.C. Erb J.

Plaintiff ordered to amend his pleadings to include better particulars of his claim only as raised by expert reports and within scope of existing pleadings. *Limitations Act* did not prevent plaintiff from amending his pleadings since no new cause of action was contemplated and Act permitted amendments that were related to events in original pleadings.

Sable Offshore Energy Inc. v. Ameron International Corp., [2006] N.S.J. No. 442, 2006 CarswellNS 496, 2006 NSSC 332, 57 C.L.R. (3d) 163, 792 A.P.R. 122, 249 N.S.R. (2d) 122 (N.S. S.C.), Hood J.

Application to strike dismissed. Jurisprudence in Canada with respect to recovery for economic loss is in continuing state of evolution and development. There were facts pleaded that could lead trial judge to conclude that there was such proximity so that defendants could reasonably contemplate that carelessness of their part was likely to cause damage to plaintiffs.

Reynolds v. Smith, [2007] O.J. No. 2161, 2007 CarswellOnt 3133, (sub nom. *Reynolds v. Kingston Police Services Board)* 225 O.A.C. 112, (sub nom. *Reynolds v. Kingston (Police Services Board))* 86 O.R. (3d) 43, 2007 ONCA 375, 47 C.C.L.T. (3d) 200 (Ont. C.A.); additional reasons to 2007 CarswellOnt 1424, (sub nom. *Reynolds v. Kingston Police Services Board)* 221 O.A.C. 216, 2007 ONCA 166, 45 C.C.L.T. (3d) 19, (sub nom. *Reynolds v. Kingston (City) Police Services Board)* 84 O.R. (3d) 738, (sub nom. *Reynolds v. Kingston (City) Police Services Board)* 280 D.L.R. (4th) 311 (Ont. C.A.); reversing [2006] O.J. No. 2039, 2006 CarswellOnt 3105, (sub nom. *Reynolds v. Kingston (City) Police Services Board)* 267 D.L.R. (4th) 409, (sub nom. *Reynolds v. Kingston Police Services Board)* 212 O.A.C. 299, 39 C.C.L.T. (3d) 257 (Ont. Div. Ct.); reversing 2002 CarswellOnt 7809 (Ont. S.C.J.), Coo J.; reversing 2005 CarswellOnt 3781 (Ont. Master), Master Egan.

Given permissive right to amend pleadings in r. 26.01 of *Rules of Civil Procedure*, Divisional Court erred in reversing order to amend pleadings. Claim for misfeasance of public office should be allowed to proceed to trial to be fully considered on basis of proper factual record and in light of other claims asserted by plaintiff. It was not plain and obvious that action for misfeasance of public office would fail.

Ross v. Charlottetown (City), 2006 CarswellPEI 51, 2006 PESCAD 24, 790 A.P.R. 316, 261 Nfld. & P.E.I.R. 316 (P.E.I. C.A.).

Motions judge correctly cited law with respect to application of rules and noted that amendment to pleadings is mandatory unless prejudice is found. Motions judge was not patently wrong in his conclusion that proposed amendments would cause undue delay and prejudice to city that could not be compensated for by costs or adjournment.

CT Comm Edmonton Ltd. v. Shaw Communications Inc., 2007 CarswellAlta 971, 2007 ABQB 482 (Alta. Q.B.).

Plaintiff's application to amend pleadings and defendants' application to strike portions of the statement of claim was allowed in part. It is not permitted to bring new causes of action outside of the limitation period that are not related to the initial claim, or pleadings that constitute an opinion, is an attempt to plead evidence or that merely repeated the relief sought in the statement of claim. The plaintiff is permitted to make amendments that enlarged and particularized allegations in the initial claim.

Canadian Bar Assn. v. British Columbia, 2008 CarswellBC 379, 290 D.L.R. (4th) 617, 422 W.A.C. 76, 252 B.C.A.C. 76, 2008 BCCA 92, 167 C.R.R. (2d) 161, 76 B.C.L.R. (4th) 48, [2008] 6 W.W.R. 262 (B.C. C.A.); leave to appeal refused [2008] S.C.C.A. No. 185, 2008 CarswellBC 1610, 2008 CarswellBC 1611, 180 C.R.R. 372 (note), 390 N.R. 381 (note), 463 W.A.C. 319 (note), 274 B.C.A.C. 319 (note) (S.C.C.)

The appellant challenged the legal aid system in British Columbia. On a preliminary motion, the action was dismissed on the dual basis that the Association lacked standing to bring the claims and that the statement of claim should be struck under Rule 19(24) of the Rules of Court as disclosing no reasonable claim.

The Court of Appeal dismissed the Association's appeal. The pleadings were too general to permit the relief sought. The broadly-directed pleadings of a systematic problem violating unwritten constitutional principles did not raise a reasonable claim. The court cannot resolve appellants standing to bring the action absent to a reasonable statement of claim.

Club Pro Adult Entertainment Inc. v. Ontario, 2008 CarswellOnt 1106, [2008] O.J. No. 777, 233 O.A.C. 355, 2008 ONCA 158, 42 B.L.R. (4th) 47 (Ont. C.A.); leave to appeal refused 2008 CarswellOnt 5426, 2008 CarswellOnt 5427, 390 N.R. 390 (note) (S.C.C.)

Plaintiffs sought damages under several private law causes and challenged constitutionality of the *Smoke-Free Ontario Act*. The judge found the claims disclosed no tenable cause of action, however allowed the Plaintiff to amend the pleadings to argue breach of contract and did not strike the claim the Act was *ultra vires*. The plaintiffs appealed the orders striking the majority of their claims against Ontario. Appeal dismissed. There was no uncertainty in the jurisprudence, either with respect to the private law claims or the appellants' constitutional arguments. There was no error in motion's judge decision to strike claims she did.

Frohlick v. Pinkerton Canada Ltd., 2008 CarswellOnt 66, [2008] O.J. No. 17, 2008 ONCA 3, 62 C.C.E.L. (3d) 161, 49 C.P.C. (6th) 209, 232 O.A.C. 146, 88 O.R. (3d) 401, 289 D.L.R. (4th) 639 (Ont. C.A.)

The Appellant sought to amend her claim against the respondent. The motion judge refused to allow the amendments on the basis that they advanced a new and unrelated claim and that this new claim was statute-barred. Appeal dismissed. Rule 26.01 did not contemplate the addition of unrelated statute-barred claims by way of amendment to an existing statement of claim. Appellant failed to show the existence of special circumstances that rebutted the presumption that the defendant would suffer prejudice from the loss of a limitation defence.

Miller v. Squires, 2008 CarswellNfld 43, 2008 NLTD 25 (N.L. T.D.)

The plaintiff commenced an action for defamatory statements made by the two defendants. The plaintiff amended the statement of claim to include the third and fourth defendant. Statement was struck down as there was no connection between the first defendant's alleged defamatory statements and his directorships of the third and fourth defendant companies. However, the court held that although the pleadings failed to state alleged defamatory statements these deficiencies were not necessarily fatal to the action and demonstrate more than a skeleton or a ghost of a chance of success. Plaintiff was invited to amend the statement of claim.

Moore v. Bertuzzi (2008), [2008] O.J. No. 347, 2008 CarswellOnt 422 (Ont. Master); additional reasons at (2008), 2008 CarswellOnt 2590 (Ont. Master)

Motion by plaintiffs to amend pleadings allowed. Plaintiff a professional hockey player who suffered serious injury as result of conduct of opposing team player. Based on discovery evidence, the plaintiffs sought to plead direct liability on the part of the corporate defendants that owned the opposing team. Defendants objected to certain of the proposed amendments as prolix, repetitive, pleaded evidence, scandalous, vexatious, inflammatory and an abuse of process. The court found that the proposed amendments were relevant to the cause of action respecting the alleged tortious conduct and were not legally scandalous or vexatious. No evidence amendments sought for an improper purpose. No abuse of process.

Peardon v. Long, 2008 CarswellPEI 40, 2008 PESCAD 13, 279 Nfld. & P.E.I.R. 32, 856 A.P.R. 32 (P.E.I. C.A.)

Appellant's submission is that the motions judge made an error of law by failing to provide appropriate compensation for the prejudice incurred by the appellant as a result of the amendment of pleadings by the respondents after oral discovery of a respondent.

Appeal dismissed. Pursuant to R. 26.01 of Rules of Civil Procedure, the motion judge had discretion to grant leave to amend pleading "on such terms as are just." The standard of review of the exercise of discretion is reasonableness, which means that a reviewing court would only interfere if the motions judge exercised his discretion on a wrong principle or misapprehended the facts, which is the same as saying he was clearly wrong.

The motions judge did not make error in principle when he determined that defendant's revelations were within scope of original examination, and that plaintiff had opportunity to examine on them.

Pinsky v. Julien (2008), 2008 CarswellOnt 1024 (Ont. Div. Ct.)

Applicant, a practicing lawyer representing himself, brought a motion for declaration that settlement did not preclude examination of further witnesses. Motion granted.

The settlement was confined to the examination of parties and did not affect the applicant's right to examine non-parties. The applicant was awarded costs of the motion. As he is a practising lawyer he is entitled to an allowance for those costs which he has incurred by acting as his own counsel, but not for the time and expense which any litigant incurs as litigant. The costs should be moderate and it is appropriate for the motion judge to fix them as he is in the best position to do so.

Rare Charitable Research Reserve v. Chaplin (2008), 2008 CarswellOnt 5658, [2008] O.J. No. 3764, 241 O.A.C. 208 (Ont. Div. Ct.)

Application for leave to appeal the decision to add two solicitors and their law firms as parties with the right to intervene, dismissed.

In private, as opposed to public litigation, the discretion to add parties should be exercised sparingly or rarely, depending upon the facts of this case. The "bench mark of caution" test with respect to adding parties in the context of private litigation should apply, yet the court should be concerned with maximizing efficiency and avoiding multiplicity of proceedings.

The motions court judge concluded that the facts of this case met the test for the exercise of his discretion under Rule 13.01(1) of the *Rules of Civil Procedure*, having regard to the principle of the "bench mark of caution." Thus, the lawyers were not only participating, but were legally bound by any factual and legal conclusions reached in these applications.

Spirito Estate v. Trillium Health Centre (2007), [2007] O.J. No. 3832, 2007 CarswellOnt 6366 (Ont. S.C.J.), van Rensburg J.; affirmed 246 O.A.C. 150, 302 D.L.R. (4th) 654, [2008] O.J. No. 4524, 69 C.P.C. (6th) 36, 2008 ONCA 762, 2008 CarswellOnt 6684 (Ont. C.A.)

Test for determining whether amendment new defendant is whether the "litigating finger" pointed at proposed defendant in Claim. Would a person having knowledge of the facts be aware of the true identity of a misnamed party by reading the Statement of Claim? Here motion by plaintiff for leave to amend claim in medical malpractice action to substitute defendant doctors for unnamed doctors allowed. Statement of claim issued December 4, 2004, included description of four defendant doctors without naming them. No prejudice demonstrated where the defendant doctors had the same counsel as doctors who were involved with action from its commencement.

Collins v. R. (2010), 2010 ONSC 6542, 2010 CarswellOnt 9265, 223 C.R.R. (2d) 370, [2011] 3 C.T.C. 211, [2010] O.J. No. 5210 (Ont. S.C.J.); affirmed 2011 ONCA 461, 2011 CarswellOnt 4984 (Ont. C.A.); leave to appeal refused 2012 CarswellOnt 251, 2012 CarswellOnt 252, (sub nom. *Collins v. Canada*) 432 N.R. 390 (note), (sub nom. *Collins v. Canada*) 294 O.A.C. 396 (note) (S.C.C.)

Defendant, Justice Elizabeth Heneghan, moved to have claim struck insofar as it asserts a claim against her.

For the purpose of motion under r. 21.01(1)(b) of the *Rules of Civil Procedure* facts pleaded must be accepted and are capable of being proven.

The law respecting judicial immunity was reviewed by Karakatsanis J. in *Tsai v. Klug*, 2005 CarswellOnt 2359, [2005] O.J. No. 2277, [2005] O.T.C. 480 (Ont. S.C.J.); additional reasons at [2005] O.J. No. 2889, 2005 CarswellOnt 2914 (Ont. S.C.J.); leave to appeal refused 2006 CarswellOnt 1020, [2006] O.J. No. 665, 207 O.A.C. 225 (Ont. C.A.); leave to appeal refused 2006 CarswellOnt 5001, 2006 CarswellOnt 5002, [2006] S.C.C.A. No. 169, 225 O.A.C. 399 (note), 358 N.R. 391 (note) (S.C.C.). The plaintiffs alleged that two Deputy Small Claims Court judges acted fraudulently, unlawfully and unconstitutionally. Karakatsanis J. struck the claim, and dismissed the action.

The Court of Appeal in *Tsai* expressed agreement with the reasons of Karakatsanis J.

See *Baryluk v. Campbell*, 2008 CarswellOnt 6355, [2008] O.J. No. 4279, 61 C.C.L.T. (3d) 292 (Ont. S.C.J.); additional reasons at 2009 CarswellOnt 3900, [2009] O.J. No. 2772, 66 C.C.L.T. (3d) 160 (Ont. S.C.J.), Hackland J., referring to *Tsai*, stated:

> [31] Like Karakatsanis J., I specifically reject the argument that a pleading of bad faith or deliberate excess of jurisdiction can defeat the principle of judicial immunity. If it were otherwise, mere allegations in pleadings could place judges in the position of having to defend the manner in which they have discharged their judicial duties in subsequent legal proceedings commenced by disaffected litigants. To place judges in this position would be seriously to undermine the principle of judicial independence.

See also *Taylor v. Canada (Attorney General)*, 2000 CarswellNat 3253, 253 N.R. 252, 184 D.L.R. (4th) 706, [2000] F.C.J. No. 268, 2000 CarswellNat 354, 37 C.H.R.R. D/368, 44 C.P.C. (4th) 1, [2000] 3 F.C. 298, 21 Admin. L.R. (3d) 27 (Fed. C.A.); leave to appeal refused 263 N.R. 399 (note), [2000] S.C.C.A. No. 213, 2000 CarswellNat 2567, 2000 CarswellNat 2566 (S.C.C.) the Federal Court of Appeal concluded, contrary to the Ontario authorities cited, that there is an exception to judicial immunity in the event that a judge knowingly acts beyond jurisdiction. The claim against Heneghan J. discloses no reasonable cause of action.

The plaintiff to file a fresh as amended Statement of Claim.

Butera v. Fragale, 2010 ONSC 3702, 2010 CarswellOnt 4669 (Ont. S.C.J.), Turnbull J.

Defendants move to strike out Statement of Claim and the Reply to Statement of Defence without leave to amend for failing to disclose a reasonable cause of action pursuant to r. 21.01(1)(b) of the *Rules of Civil Procedure*.

Party may move under r. 21.01(3)(d) to dismiss an action on basis action frivolous or vexatious or is otherwise an abuse of the process. Court will only dismiss or stay action as being frivolous, vexatious or abusive in the "clearest of cases where, on the face of the action and circumstances, it is plain and obvious that the case cannot succeed." See *Butera v. Fragale*, 2010 ONSC 3702, 2010 CarswellOnt 4669 (Ont. S.C.J.).

A party may also move under r. 25.11(b) and (c) to strike out or expunge all or part of a pleading with or without leave to amend on ground that the pleading is scandalous, frivolous, vexatious or an abuse of process of the court. See *Currie v. Halton Regional Police Services Board*, 233 D.L.R. (4th) 657, 2003 CarswellOnt 4674, 179 O.A.C. 67, [2003] O.J. No. 4516 (Ont. C.A.). See also, *Canam Enterprises Inc. v. Coles*, [2000] O.J. No. 4607, 194 D.L.R. (4th) 648, 51 O.R. (3d) 481, 2000 CarswellOnt 4739, 5 C.P.C. (5th) 218, 139 O.A.C. 1 (Ont. C.A.); leave to appeal allowed 202 D.L.R. (4th) vi, 155 O.A.C. 200 (note), 276 N.R. 394 (note), [2001] S.C.C.A. No. 50, 2001 CarswellOnt 3074, 2001 CarswellOnt 3073 (S.C.C.); reversed REJB 2002-34843 296 N.R. 257, 220 D.L.R. (4th) 466, 2002 CarswellOnt 3262, 2002 CarswellOnt 3261, 2002 SCC 63, [2002] 3 S.C.R. 307, 61 O.R. (3d) 416 (note), [2002] S.C.J. No. 64, 24 C.P.C. (5th) 1, 167 O.A.C. 1 (S.C.C.).

Attempting to re-litigate actions or determine issues which have already been determined by a court of competent jurisdiction constitute vexatious proceedings and are an abuse of process. See *Baryluk v. Campbell*, 61 C.C.L.T. (3d) 292, 2008 CarswellOnt 6355, [2008] O.J. No. 4279 (Ont. S.C.J.); additional reasons at [2009] O.J. No. 2772, 66 C.C.L.T. (3d) 160, 2009 CarswellOnt 3900 (Ont. S.C.J.). See also *Canadian National Railway v. Brant*, 96 O.R.

(3d) 734, [2009] O.J. No. 2661, [2009] 4 C.N.L.R. 47, 2009 CarswellOnt 3720 (Ont. S.C.J.); additional reasons at 2009 CarswellOnt 5106 (Ont. S.C.J.).

The issues had already been determined by the Ontario Labour Relations Board and the Small Claims Court. Consequently, action vexatious and abuse of process.

In *Lehan v. St. Catharines (City)*, 2009 CarswellOnt 6794, [2009] O.J. No. 4643 (Ont. S.C.J.) at para. 17 summarized the established body of law relating to amending pleadings:

> . . . It was well established that Amendments . . . should be presumptively approved unless they would occasion prejudice that cannot be compensated by costs or an adjournment; they are shown to be scandalous, frivolous, vexatious or an abuse of the court's process or they disclose no reasonable cause of action.

Leave not granted to plaintiff to amend pleadings. The plaintiff's action dismissed.

Callinan Mines Ltd. v. Hudson Bay Mining & Smelting Co., 2011 MBQB 159, 2011 CarswellMan 341, 8 C.P.C. (7th) 100, 266 Man. R. (2d) 214, [2011] 11 W.W.R. 537 (Man. Q.B.)

C Ltd. brought an Application for leave to amend its statement of claim. The Application was granted. The nature of the amendments would not cause any prejudice to H Ltd. The amendments sought did not preclude a meaningful response. There was no obvious delay. The amendments raised a valid and arguable point that went to the central issue in the matter.

Gordon v. Krieg, 2011 BCSC 916, 2011 CarswellBC 1825 (B.C. Master), Master R.W. McDiarmid; reversed 2011 BCSC 1248, 2011 CarswellBC 2461 (B.C. S.C.); additional reasons to 2011 BCSC 882, 2011 CarswellBC 1704 (B.C. Master), Master McDiarmid.

This case dealt with adding or substituting parties and general principles. The defendants WK and KK brought an Application for leave to file a third party notice. All applications were dismissed. As events involving I Ltd. happened 22 years ago, two months was not sufficient time to prepare. It would have been prejudicial to I Ltd. to force it to trial. If any third parties were added, the trial would have to be adjourned. If the trial was adjourned, it would be highly prejudicial to the plaintiff.

Boisvert v. Korczynski, 2011 ONSC 4423, 2011 CarswellOnt 7210 (Ont. S.C.J.), D.C. Shaw J.

The plaintiffs brought a motion to amend their statement of claim seeking to delete the words "inherently dangerous." The motion was granted. Rule 26.01 of the *Rules of Civil Procedure* is mandatory and amendments must be allowed unless the responding party can demonstrate a prejudice that cannot be compensated by costs. Prejudice must arise from the amendment. The defendants did not demonstrate prejudice would result from the proposed amendment.

Streamline Foods Ltd. v. Jantz Canada Corp., 2011 ONSC 1630, 2011 CarswellOnt 1674, 280 O.A.C. 152, 6 C.P.C. (7th) 399 (Ont. Div. Ct.)

Where a limitation period has expired, a party's name can only be changed if there is a misnomer. A new party cannot be added. Principles which have been articulated in cases prior to the *Limitations Act, 2002*, are to be treated with caution. It is no longer possible to add parties after the expiry of a limitation period even in the face of special circumstances. The correct test was applied.

The *Limitations Act, 2002*, came into effect on January 1, 2004. See *Joseph v. Paramount Canada's Wonderland*, 2008 ONCA 469, 2008 CarswellOnt 3495, [2008] O.J. No. 2339, 90 O.R. (3d) 401, 294 D.L.R. (4th) 141, 56 C.P.C. (6th) 14, 241 O.A.C. 29 (Ont. C.A.). This case did not involve a misnomer. The plaintiff's counsel failed to issue a statement of claim within the limitation period. The case involved section 21 of the *Act* and the doctrine of special circumstances. An appeal was allowed.

Marks v. Ottawa (City), 2011 ONCA 248, 2011 CarswellOnt 2165, [2011] O.J. No. 1445, 81 M.P.L.R. (4th) 161, 280 O.A.C. 251 (Ont. C.A.)

The Court of Appeal found that, although general rule amendments to pleadings were presumptively approved, there was no absolute right to amend the pleadings. The Court has a residual right to deny amendments where appropriate. An amendment should be allowed unless it would cause an injustice not compensable in costs. A proposed amendment has to be shown to be an issue worthy of trial and prima facie meritorious. No amendment should be allowed which, if originally pleaded, would have been struck. The proposed amendment has to contain sufficient particulars. See also *Daniele v. Johnson*, 1999 CarswellOnt 2096, [1999] O.J. No. 2562, 45 O.R. (3d) 498, 90 O.T.C. 240 (note), 123 O.A.C. 186 at paras. 11-15 (Ont. Div. Ct.).

Transwest Roofing Ltd. v. Isle of Mann Construction Ltd., 2012 BCPC 136, 2012 CarswellBC 1434 (B.C. Prov. Ct.), Judge M. B. Hicks.

Defendant seeks to file amended reply and counterclaim. The Claimant opposes the application. Rule 8(1) of the Provincial Court Small Claims Rules requires leave of the Court for this to occur if a settlement conference has taken place which is the case here.

No prejudice to Claimant in now confronting an argument from the only party with whom it says a contract existed that there never was a contract formed.

There is no suggestion that memories have so dimmed or that the number or identity of witnesses is so complicated that the Claimant would be greatly prejudiced by the amendment. There is no evidence that substantial additional documents would be required to now address this issue.

The interest of justice is best served by granting leave to the Defendant to file and serve an amended Reply and Counterclaim in the form proposed.

Dee Ferraro Ltd. v. Pellizzari, 2012 ONCA 55, 2012 CarswellOnt 816, 346 D.L.R. (4th) 624, [2012] O.J. No. 355 (Ont. C.A.); reversing 2011 ONSC 3995, 2011 CarswellOnt 8211 (Ont. S.C.J.)

This judgment illustrates the difference between amending a statement of claim to allege a new cause of action (impermissible if the new claim is stature barred), and amending the statement of claim to add new remedies or heads of damages (permissible), provided there is no non-compensable prejudice.

The original pleading contained all the facts necessary to support the amendments. The amendments simply claimed additional forms of relief, or clarified the relief sought, based on the same facts as originally pleaded. The Court relied on *Canadian National Railway v. Canadian Industries Ltd.*, 1940 CarswellOnt 213, [1940] 4 D.L.R. 629, 52 C.R.T.C. 31, [1940] O.W.N. 452, [1940] O.J. No. 266 (Ont. C.A.); affirmed 1941 CarswellOnt 84, [1941] S.C.R. 591, [1941] 4 D.L.R. 561, 53 C.R.T.C. 162 (S.C.C.), and distinguished *Frohlick v. Pinkerton Canada Ltd.*, 2008 ONCA 3, 2008 CarswellOnt 66, 88 O.R. (3d) 401, 62 C.C.E.L. (3d) 161, 49 C.P.C. (6th) 209, 289 D.L.R. (4th) 639, 232 O.A.C. 146, [2008] O.J. No. 17 (Ont. C.A.).

This was not a case in which new and unrelated causes of action were being asserted based on new facts. The claims flow directly from the facts previously pleaded. Therefore, the claims were not statute-barred and the amendments should have been permitted, since there was no evidence of non-compensable prejudice.

Streamline Foods Ltd. v. Jantz Canada Corp., 2012 ONCA 174, 2012 CarswellOnt 3333, [2012] O.J. No. 1213 (Ont. C.A.); affirming 2011 ONSC 1630, 2011 CarswellOnt 1674, 6 C.P.C. (7th) 399, 280 O.A.C. 152 (Ont. Div. Ct.); affirming 2010 ONSC 6393, 2010 CarswellOnt 8790, [2010] O.J. No. 4988 (Ont. Master) .

This judgment establishes that s. 21(1) of the *Limitations Act, 2002 does* apply to plaintiffs (as opposed, as some have argued, only to defendants). The Court refused to allow for the plaintiff's parent corporation to be added as a party plaintiff after the limitation period had expired.

This was not a misnomer. The plaintiffs sought to add the parent corporation of the original plaintiff because it was the parent corporation which incurred certain losses, not the original plaintiff. The plaintiffs were not seeking to correct the name of a party; rather, they were seeking to add a party and to pursue that party's claims.

Livingston v. Williamson, 2011 ONSC 3849, 2011 CarswellOnt 5872, 107 O.R. (3d) 75, 99 C.C.L.I. (4th) 331 (Ont. Master)

The plaintiff sued the TTC in its capacity as owner of the bus, employer of the driver, and provider of uninsured motorist coverage.

The TTC was not the insurer. The plaintiff was unaware that TTC Insurance was a separate company. The plaintiff brought a motion to correct the name of the insurer by adding TTC Insurance as a party defendant. TTC Insurance took the position that this was a motion to add a party after the limitation period had expired. Motion allowed both the TTC legal department and TTC Insurance operated from the same building, had identical postal codes and were represented by the same lawyer on the argument of the motion. Master Hawkins found that a representative of the TTC Insurance would have known immediately that insofar as unidentified motorist coverage was concerned, TTC Insurance was intended. Neither TTC nor TTC Insurance suffered any actual prejudice.

Stekel v. Toyota Canada Inc., 2011 ONSC 6507, 2011 CarswellOnt 11971, 107 O.R. (3d) 431 (Ont. S.C.J.); leave to appeal refused 2012 ONSC 2572, 2012 CarswellOnt 5718 (Ont. Div. Ct.); affirming 2011 ONSC 2211, 2011 CarswellOnt 2378, [2011] O.J. No. 1591 (Ont. Master)

Plaintiff injured due to an apparent mechanical malfunction in Lexus vehicle she was driving. She sued Toyota Canada Inc., believing it was both the distributor and manufacturer of the vehicle. More than two years after the accident, the plaintiff learned that the vehicle was in fact manufactured by Toyota Motors Canada. She moved to add Toyota Manufacturers Canada (TMC) as a party defendant in the action.

While the limitation period in respect of the plaintiff's claim against TMS has expired, s. 21(2) of the *Limitations Act 2002* permitted the plaintiffs to correct their "misnomer" with respect to the manufacturer of their vehicle and add TMC as a defendant to the litigation. The plaintiffs had always intended to include the manufacturer of the vehicle as a defendant in their action. Equally importantly, TMC knew that the plaintiffs were pointing at the manufacturer of the vehicle, even though they had misnamed the manufacturer.

(2) Service — **The amended document shall be served by the party making the amendment on all parties, including any parties in default, in accordance with subrule 8.01(14).**

History [R. 12.01(2)]: New provision on service of amended documents.

Commentary: An amended document shall be served by the party making the amendment on all parties, including any parties in default, by mail, courier, or fax, personally, or by an alternative to personal service [r. 12.01(2), 11.05(3)] unless the court orders otherwise. Filing and service of the amended document shall take place at least 30 days before the originally scheduled trial date, unless:

- The clerk makes an order (on filing of request for clerk's order) on consent within 30 days of the scheduled trial date [r. 11.2.01(1)l i]; or

- The court, on motion, allows a shorter notice period [r. 12.01(3)].

A party who is served with an amended document is not required to amend the party's defence or claim, e.g. where a plaintiff files and serves an amended claim, the defendant is not required to file another defence if there is already one on file respecting the original claim, pursuant to rule 12.01(5). The defendant may file an amended defence if he or she wishes to do so, pursuant to rule 12.01(1).

(3) Time — Filing and service of the amended document shall take place at least 30 days before the originally scheduled trial date, unless,

 (a) the court, on motion, allows a shorter notice period; or

 (b) a clerk's order permitting the amendment is obtained under subrule 11.2.01(1).

History [R. 12.01(3)]: New provision requiring amendment and service to take place at least 30 days before trial.

Commentary: A party may amend a Plaintiff's Claim (Form 7A), a Defendant's Claim (Form 10A), and a Defence (Form 9A), at least 30 days before the originally scheduled trial date (unless otherwise ordered by the court or by a clerk's order or consent). The party requesting such a substitution must amend the party's pleading in accordance with rule 12.01. A party who takes issue with the procedure may make a motion to a judge for direction.

(4) Service on Added Party — A person added as a party shall be served with the claim as amended, except that if the person is added as a party at trial, the court may dispense with service of the claim.

History [R. 12.01(4)]: Formerly 11.01(2); plain language changes.

(5) No Amendment Required in Response — A party who is served with an amended document is not required to amend the party's defence or claim.

O. Reg. 78/06, s. 25; 393/09, s. 13

Commentary: While amendment of a pleading in response to amendment of the opponent's pleading is not mandatory, it may be desirable in some cases. If an unpleaded defence to an issue pleaded by amendment to a claim is advanced at trial, it could give rise to objection, prejudice, potential adjournment with costs, or theoretically even a mistrial. Any party who faces an amended pleading from the opponent should consider whether it is desirable to amend their own pleading even if such amendment, by virtue of rule 12.01(5), is not mandatory.

12.02 Motion to Strike out or Amend a Document — (1) The court may, on motion, strike out or amend all or part of any document that,

 (a) discloses no reasonable cause of action or defence;

 (b) may delay or make it difficult to have a fair trial; or

 (c) is inflammatory, a waste of time, a nuisance or an abuse of the court's process.

History [R. 12.02(1)]: Formerly part of 11.02; court's power to stay or dismiss action separated into another subrule (12.02(2)); plain language changes.

(2) In connection with an order striking out or amending a document under subrule (1), the court may do one or more of the following:

 1. In the case of a claim, order that the action be stayed or dismissed.

 2. In the case of a defence, strike out the defence and grant judgment.

 2.1 In the case of a motion, order that the motion be stayed or dismissed.

3. Impose such terms as are just.

History [R. 12.02(2)]: Contains court's power to stay or dismiss action from former 11.02.

Commentary: Rule 12.02 provides for motions to strike all or part of a claim or defence, whether on the basis of pleadings law or based on factual merit. If compared to similar provisions under the *Rules of Civil Procedure*, it is like an amalgam of rules 20.04, 21.01 and 25.11 under those rules.

In *Van de Vrande v. Butkowsky*, 2010 ONCA 230, 2010 CarswellOnt 1777, 99 O.R. (3d) 648, 99 O.R. (3d) 641, 85 C.P.C. (6th) 205, 319 D.L.R. (4th) 132, 260 O.A.C. 323, [2010] O.J. No. 1239 (Ont. C.A.); additional reasons 2010 ONCA 400, 2010 CarswellOnt 3629, 85 C.P.C. (6th) 212 (Ont. C.A.), the court held that rule 12.02 must be interpreted within the specific context of Small Claims Court procedure and that the terminology and caselaw developed under Rules 20 and 21 of the *Rules of Civil Procedure* should not be applied to rule 12.02 motions. It was held that rule 12.02 is conceptually somewhere in between a pleadings motion and a summary judgment motion under Rules 21 and 20 of the Rules of Civil Procedure. In that case, the dismissal of a claim based on limitation and absolute immunity defences by a motions judge was restored.

In *O'Brien v. Ottawa Hospital*, 2011 ONSC 231, 2011 CarswellOnt 88, [2011] O.J. No. 66 (Ont. Div. Ct.), the court upheld the dismissal of a claim based on there being "no meaningful chance of success at trial." It was a medical malpractice claim in which the motions judge had found that the plaintiff had no supportive expert evidence and could not succeed on liability. See also *Vuong v. Toronto East General & Orthopaedic Hospital*, 2010 ONSC 6827, 2010 CarswellOnt 10206, 328 D.L.R. (4th) 759 (Ont. Div. Ct.); *Diler v. Uppal* (May 7, 2010), Doc. 110/10, [2010] O.J. No. 1903 (Ont. Sm. Cl. Ct.); *Dougherty v. Goad & Goad Barristers & Solicitors*, 2011 CarswellOnt 15742, [2011] O.J. No. 2423 (Ont. Sm. Cl. Ct.).

The pleading must contain sufficient detail so that the parties and the Court can ascertain the exact nature of the questions to be tried and so the opposing party can meet the charge and respond accordingly. (See *Copland v. Commodore Business Machines Ltd.* (1985), 1985 CarswellOnt 410, 3 C.P.C. (2d) 77, 52 O.R. (2d) 586 (Ont. Master); affirmed (1985), 3 C.P.C. (2d) 77n, 52 O.R. (2d) 586n (Ont. H.C.)).

The pleadings may be challenged "because it has failed to allege the necessary elements of a claim that, if properly pleaded, would constitute a reasonable cause of action." (See *Dawson v. Rexcraft Storage & Warehouse Inc.* (1998), 20 R.P.R. (3d) 207, 1998 CarswellOnt 3202, 164 D.L.R. (4th) 257, 111 O.A.C. 201, [1998] O.J. No. 3240, 26 C.P.C. (4th) 1 at para. 10 (Ont. C.A.).).

Case Law: *Tuka v. Butt*, 2014 CarswellOnt 2035, [2014] O.J. No. 852 (Ont. Sm. Cl. Ct.) The defendant's claim was dismissed under rule 12.02. The court held that the claim fell within the exclusive jurisdiction of the Landlord and Tenant Board, which had heard several prior applications between these parties. Her claims for an abatement of rent and for damages for personal property left on the premises when she was evicted were dismissed for want of jurisdiction, and her claim for personal property was also dismissed as barred by s. 41 of the *Residential Tenancies Act, 2006.*

Camm v. Kirkpatrick (August 19, 2013), Doc. 13-SC-125385, [2013] O.J. No. 3830 (Ont. Sm. Cl. Ct.)

A debt claim was dismissed under rule 12.02 based on the limitation defence. The court held that despite some complexity in the limitations law relating to demand obligations, no further or different evidence could be expected if a trial was held. The claim had no meaningful chance of success at trial.

W.J. Realty Mgmt. Ltd. v. Price (1973), 1 O.R. (2d) 501 (Ont. C.A.) — Where an original plaintiff has no cause of action, a new plaintiff who is alleged to have a cause of action cannot be substituted for the original plaintiff under this section.

Turgeon v. Border Supply (EMO) Ltd. (1977), 16 O.R. (2d) 43 (Ont. Div. Ct.) — Where an action is brought in the name of a partnership which had been dissolved prior to the commencement of the action and the chose in action assigned, the original plaintiff had no cause of action and an order cannot be made adding the assignee as plaintiff at the trial of the small claims court action. Griffiths J. (dissenting) stated,

> It could not be said that the action was a nullity in that the plaintiffs had legal status to sue. While the original plaintiffs may not have had a cause of action, denial of the amendment adding the assignee as plaintiff would defeat the very spirit and purpose of the small claims procedure.

Grimshaw v. Grimshaw (1983), 32 C.P.C. 11 (Ont. H.C.) — Plaintiff brought action as an administratrix. Plaintiff allowed to amend style of cause to substitute herself as a next friend. *Bona fide* mistake and not a case where a new plaintiff was being substituted for the original plaintiff.

Frobisher Ltd. v. Can. Pipelines & Petroleums Ltd. (1957), 10 D.L.R. (2d) 338 (Sask. C.A.); sustained [1960] S.C.R. 126 (S.C.C.) — If there are no injustices to the other side and if it can be compensated in costs, amendments can be allowed after all evidence is in, but before argument.

Amer. Express Can. Inc. v. Engel (1983), 39 O.R. (2d) 600 (Ont. Div. Ct.) — The defence did not comply with Rule 26 of the Provincial Court (Civil Division) Project Regulations, R.R.O. 1980, Reg. 806, because no reasons why the dispute was put forward were included and accordingly, no true defence had been filed. A claim for harassment was not a defence to a claim for debt. (See also *Gillman v. Vic Tanny*.)

Joly v. Pelletier (May 16, 1999), Doc. 99-CV-166273, 99-CV-167339 (Ont. S.C.J.) — Motion to strike out the plaintiff Rene Joly's Statements of Claim and thereby dismiss the actions (Rule 21.01(3) (b) or Rule 25.11, *Rules of Civil Procedure*, R.R.O. 1990, Reg. 194). Joly's claim asserts that he is not a human being, but a martian. The Court must accept the facts alleged in the Claim as proven unless patently ridiculous and incapable of proof and must read these generously in the Statement of Claim with allowance for inadequacies due to drafting deficiencies. See *Falloncrest Financial Corp. v. Ontario* (1995), (*sub nom. Nash v. Ontario*) 27 O.R. (3d) 1 (Ont. C.A.) and *Hunt v. T & N plc* (1990), (*sub nom. Hunt v. Carey Canada Inc.*) 74 D.L.R. (4th) 321 (S.C.C.) and *Steiner v. R.* (1996), (*sub nom. Steiner v. Canada*) 122 F.T.R. 187 (Fed. T.D.). Actions patently ridiculous. Statements of Claim in both actions are struck and the actions are dismissed.

Skolnik v. Arviv (2000), 2000 CarswellOnt 3880 (Ont. C.A.) — Appeal by defendants from decision that struck out their statement of defence and counterclaim on grounds that it alleged that the main action was brought maliciously and in abuse of process. The defendants' pleading adequately pleaded elements of causes of action it asserted.

Zeus v. Spick (2000), 2000 CarswellOnt 3623 (Ont. S.C.J.); affirmed (2001), 2001 CarswellOnt 2470 (Ont. C.A.) — Endorsement — The plaintiff uttered death threats against the landlord. The plaintiff pleaded guilty and subsequently brought an action against the landlord and police officer for damages for wrongful arrest and conviction. Cause of action was not properly pleaded; the claim was frivolous and vexatious and struck out.

Wakeford v. Canada (Attorney General) (2001), 81 C.R.R. (2d) 342, 2001 CarswellOnt 352 (Ont. S.C.J.); affirmed (2001), 156 O.A.C. 385, 2001 CarswellOnt 4368 (Ont. C.A.); leave to appeal refused (2002), 2002 CarswellOnt 1097, 2002 CarswellOnt 1098, 300 N.R. 197 (note), 169 O.A.C. 196 (note) (S.C.C.) — The defendant brought a motion to strike out claim, as there was Supreme Court case law squarely on point. The plaintiff was unable to show realistic possibility that the earlier case would be overruled.

C. (V.) v. Edwards (2001), 2001 CarswellOnt 2362 (Ont. Master) — Motion to strike out paragraph in claim alleging that Criminal Injuries Compensation Board found defendant guilty of sexual assault. Board neither criminal nor quasi-criminal tribunal.

Mills v. Gibbs, 2003 CarswellSask 383, 2003 SKQB 245 (Sask. Q.B.). Defendants sought Order striking the claim against each of them pursuant to *Rule 173* of The Queen's Bench Rules. Principles clearly set out in *Collins v. McMahon*, 2002 SKQB 201, [2002] S.J. No. 318, 2002 CarswellSask 342 (Sask. Q.B.) paragraphs 11 to 13.

The jurisdiction to strike a claim should only be exercised in plain and obvious cases where the matter is beyond doubt. *Milgaard v. Kujawa*, 123 Sask. R. 164, 1994 CarswellSask 243, [1994] 9 W.W.R. 305, 118 D.L.R. (4th) 653, 74 W.A.C. 164, 28 C.P.C. (3d) 137 (Sask. C.A.); leave to appeal refused (1995), [1994] S.C.C.A. No. 458, 32 C.P.C. (3d) 101 (note), [1995] 2 W.W.R. lxiv (note), 119 D.L.R. (4th) vi (note), 186 N.R. 77 (note), 134 Sask. R. 320 (note), 101 W.A.C. 320 (note) (S.C.C.).

The Plaintiff must state sufficient facts to establish the requisite legal elements for a cause of action. (See *Sandy Ridge Sawing Ltd. v. Norrish*, 140 Sask. R. 146, 1996 CarswellSask 72, [1996] 4 W.W.R. 528, 28 C.C.L.T. (2d) 113, 46 C.P.C. (3d) 316 (Sask. Q.B.)).

The proper course of action here to allow to amend claim further to properly defind the cause or causes of action.

Benoit v. Akert, 2003 CarswellSask 558, 2003 SKPC 113 (Sask. Prov. Ct.). The Plaintiff brought action under *The Small Claims Act* against Defendant, with respect to damages done to rental property pursuant to agreement for sale which was not concluded.

Subs. 3(1) and subs. 3(1.1) of the *Land Contract (Actions) Act* states:

> "No action shall be commenced except by leave of the Court granted upon application under this section."

Section 11 of *The Small Claims Act* provides that a judge may order that matter be transferred to the Court of Queen's Bench. Proceedings of Court to the Court of Queen's Bench.

Furlong v. Avalon Bookkeeping Services Ltd., 2003 NLSCTD 140, 2003 CarswellNfld 230, 231 Nfld. & P.E.I.R. 68, 686 A.P.R. 68, 42 C.P.C. (5th) 315 (N.L. T.D.); reversed 2004 CarswellNfld 237, 2004 NLCA 46, 243 D.L.R. (4th) 153, 49 C.P.C. (5th) 225, 6 M.V.R. (5th) 79, 239 Nfld. & P.E.I.R. 197, 709 A.P.R. 197 (N.L. C.A.). Small Claims action was an adjustication of only the vehicle owner's claim for property damages, injured Plaintiff not a necessary party to Small Claims action. Claim not adjudicated on by Small Claiims Court — *res judicata* not made out. Issue estoppel found against the Defendants. Summary judgment entered for Plaintiff with damages to be assessed.

Six and a half years elapsed since collision. Claim of prejudice purely speculative.

Charlottetown (City) v. MacIsaac, 2003 CarswellPEI 9, 2003 PESCTD 7, 35 M.P.L.R. (3d) 271, 223 Nfld. & P.E.I.R. 95, 666 A.P.R. 95 (P.E.I. T.D.). City pleads, *inter alia*, that the Plaintiff's claim should be struck as it discloses no cause of action. City moved for Order pursuant to *Rule 74.01(4)(b)* to have *Rule 20*, the summary judgment Rule, and *Rule 21.01(1)(b)*, apply in this case.

A municipal council is a trustee of municipal property, including funds, for all inhabitants of the municipality. Statement of claim is struck out.

Allen v. College of Dental Surgeons (British Columbia), 2005 CarswellBC 1382, 2005 BCSC 842, 31 Admin. L.R. (4th) 118, 32 C.C.L.T. (3d) 256 (B.C. S.C.), Ehrcke J. Defendant College applied under Rule 19(24) of the *Rules of Court* to strike out plaintiff's writ of summons and amended statement of claim as disclosing no reasonable cause of action.

Test whether, assuming facts set out in pleadings could be proven, it is plain and obvious that claim as it reads or as it may reasonably be amended discloses no reasonable claim. See *Hunt v. T & N plc*, 1990 CarswellBC 759, 1990 CarswellBC 216, (sub nom. *Hunt v. Carey Canada Inc.)* [1990] S.C.J. No. 93, 4 C.C.L.T. (2d) 1, 43 C.P.C. (2d) 105, 117 N.R. 321, 4 C.O.H.S.C. 173 (headnote only), (sub nom. *Hunt v. Carey Canada Inc.)* [1990] 6 W.W.R. 385, 49 B.C.L.R. (2d) 273, (sub nom. *Hunt v. Carey Canada Inc.)* 74 D.L.R. (4th) 321, [1990] 2 S.C.R. 959 (S.C.C.). See also *Rogers v. Faught*, 2002 CarswellOnt 1068, [2002] O.J. No. 1451, 212 D.L.R. (4th) 366, 159 O.A.C. 79, 93 C.R.R. (2d) 329 (Ont. C.A.). Court concluded that the governing body of dentists did not owe a private law duty of care to individual patients of dentists.

Plaintiff has no reasonable claim against the College in negligence, that aspect of her pleadings struck out.

Plaintiff's claim in libel discloses no reasonable cause of action against College, that claim struck out.

D'Andrea v. Schmidt, 2005 CarswellSask 304, 2005 SKQB 201, 263 Sask. R. 290, 130 C.R.R. (2d) 282, [2006] 2 W.W.R. 251, 20 R.F.L. (6th) 246 (Sask. Q.B.), Currie J. Defendant applied for order striking out part of claim of former fiancé, Troy D'Andrea, for return of engagement ring.

In England Parliament abolished actions for breach of promise of marriage in the discretely named *Law Reform (Miscellaneous Provisions) Act, 1970*, (U.K.) 1970, c. 33, s. 1. The Legislature of New Brunswick has not yet formally abolished it.

See *Iliopoulos v. Gettas*, 1981 CarswellOnt 1224, 32 O.R. (2d) 636 (Ont. Co. Ct.) relating to the giving of an engagement ring in contemplation of marriage.

If cause of action can be modified to conform with underlying values, then court has jurisdiction to make that incremental change to the common law. See *Hill v. Church of Scientology of Toronto*, EYB 1995-68609, 1995 CarswellOnt 396, 1995 CarswellOnt 534, [1995] S.C.J. No. 64, 25 C.C.L.T. (2d) 89, 184 N.R. 1, (sub nom. *Manning v. Hill)* 126 D.L.R. (4th) 129, 24 O.R. (3d) 865 (note), 84 O.A.C. 1, [1995] 2 S.C.R. 1130, (sub nom. *Hill v. Church of Scientology)* 30 C.R.R. (2d) 189, 1995 SCC 67 (S.C.C.).

Very different where two private parties are involved in a civil suit. See also the comments of Mr. Justice Iacobucci in *R. v. Salituro*, EYB 1991-67635, 1991 CarswellOnt 124, 1991 CarswellOnt 1031, 9 C.R. (4th) 324, 8 C.R.R. (2d) 173, 50 O.A.C. 125, [1991] 3 S.C.R. 654 at 670, 131 N.R. 161, 68 C.C.C. (3d) 289 (S.C.C.):

> . . . Judges can and should adapt the common law to reflect the changing social, moral and economic fabric of the country. Judges should not be quick to perpetuate rules whose social foundation has long since disappeared. Nonetheless, there are significant constraints on the power of the judiciary to change the law. As McLachlin J. indicated in *Walkins [v. Olafson*, 1989 CanLII 36 (S.C.C.), [1989] 2 S.C.R. 750], in a constitutional democracy such as ours it is the legislature, not the courts which has the major responsibility for law reform. Judiciary should confine itself to those incremental changes which are necessary to keep the common law in step with the dynamic and evolving fabric of our society.

Application to strike out claim dismissed.

Fitzpatrick v. Durham Regional Police Services Board, 2005 CarswellOnt 2155, [2005] O.J. No. 2161, 76 O.R. (3d) 290 (Ont. S.C.J.), MacDougall J. No cause of action for negligent prosecution. Pleadings containing only bald assertions of malice. Malice not to be inferred from fact Crown continued prosecution following recantation by complainant. Damages for Charter breach depending on finding of malicious prosecution. Application granted, statement of claim struck.

Motion under rule 21.01(1) to strike claim.

Rule 25.06(8) provides that where malice is alleged, the pleadings shall contain full particulars.

Legal framework in motion to strike pleadings for failure to disclose reasonable cause of action summarized by Epstein J. in *Aristrocrat Restaurants Ltd. (c.o.b. Tony's East) v. Ontario*, 2003 CarswellOnt 5574, [2003] O.J. No. 5331 (Ont. S.C.J.).

Allegations in the nature of assumptions and speculations not to be taken as true (*Holland v. Ontario (Ministry of the Attorney General)*, 2000 CarswellOnt 542, [2000] O.J. No. 566 (Ont. S.C.J.)).

No cause of action in law exists for negligent prosecution. Even "gross negligence" not sufficient to ground malicious prosecution claim against a Crown Attorney. See *Proulx c. Québec (Procureur général)*, REJB 2001-26159, 2001 CarswellQue 2187, 2001 CarswellQue 2188, [2001] S.C.J. No. 65, 2001 SCC 66, 46 C.R. (5th) 1, 7 C.C.L.T. (3d) 157, (sub nom. *Proulx v. Quebec (Attorney General)*) 206 D.L.R. (4th) 1, (sub nom. *Proulx v. Quebec (Attorney General)*) 159 C.C.C. (3d) 225, (sub nom. *Proulx v. Québec (Procureur général)*) 276 N.R. 201, (sub nom. *Proulx v. Quebec (Attorney General)*) [2001] 3 S.C.R. 9 (S.C.C.). See also *Nelles v. Ontario*, EYB 1989-67463, 1989 CarswellOnt 963, 1989 CarswellOnt 415, [1989] S.C.J. No. 86, 69 O.R. (2d) 448 (note), [1989] 2 S.C.R. 170, 60 D.L.R. (4th) 609, 98 N.R. 321, 35 O.A.C. 161, 41 Admin. L.R. 1, 49 C.C.L.T. 217, 37 C.P.C. (2d) 1, 71 C.R. (3d) 358, 42 C.R.R. 1 (S.C.C.), where Lamer J., as he then was, reviewed law as to what is required for plaintiff to succeed in action for malicious prosecution.

Spillane v. United Parcel Service Canada Ltd., 2006 CarswellBC 1150, 2006 BCSC 687 (B.C. S.C. [In Chambers]) 2006-04-28.

Defendants applied to have plaintiff's action dismissed as against all defendants, alternatively defendants sought dismissal of action as against the personal defendants.

The test for striking a claim is whether, assuming that the facts set out in the statement of claim can be proved, it is plain and obvious that the plaintiff's statement of claim discloses no reasonable cause of action; see *Hunt v. T & N plc*, 1990 CarswellBC 759, 1990 CarswellBC 216, (sub nom. *Hunt v. Carey Canada Inc.*) [1990] S.C.J. No. 93, 4 C.C.L.T. (2d) 1, 43 C.P.C. (2d) 105, 117 N.R. 321, 4 C.O.H.S.C. 173 (headnote only), (sub nom. *Hunt v. Carey Canada Inc.*) [1990] 6 W.W.R. 385, 49 B.C.L.R. (2d) 273, (sub nom. *Hunt v. Carey Canada Inc.*) 74 D.L.R. (4th) 321, [1990] 2 S.C.R. 959 (S.C.C.) at 979. The test in *Hunt* must be applied after the claims have been carefully considered and analyzed in the context of the applicable law. Where the pleadings disclose a "triable issue," either as they are, or as they may be amended, they should not be struck out: see *Citizens for Foreign Aid Reform Inc. v. Canadian Jewish Congress*, 1999 CarswellBC 2111, [1999] B.C.J. No. 2160, 36 C.P.C. (4th) 266 (B.C. S.C. [In Chambers]) at para. 34; *Minnes v. Minnes*, 1962 CarswellBC 78, 39 W.W.R. 112, 34 D.L.R. (2d) 497 (B.C. C.A.). Certain passages of writ and statement of claim struck.

Kaukinen v. Sonntag, 2006 CarswellSask 281, 2006 SKQB 199 (Sask. Q.B.) 2006-04-26.

Defendants apply for an order striking plaintiff's claims against them as disclosing no reasonable cause of action. Test set out in *Sagon v. Royal Bank*, 1992 CarswellSask 439, [1992] S.J. No. 197, 105 Sask. R. 133, 32 W.A.C. 133 (Sask. C.A.) at 139. The defendants should not be in a position of having to guess as to what the cause or causes of action are. "Pleading" means stating material facts which are the constituent elements of the cause of action. Rather than strike statement of claim, Court prepared to grant a period of time within which to file proper pleadings.

Wolker v. Ogilvie Realty Ltd., 2006 CarswellOnt 512, 23 C.P.C. (6th) 154 (Ont. S.C.J.).

Plaintiff brought motion pursuant to R. 25.11 of *Rules of Civil Procedure* to strike out reference to store as being scandalous, inserted for colour and to embarrass plaintiff. Motion granted. Actual identification of store had no probative value and not relevant to issues. Location of slip and fall could be readily established without reference to name of store.

Young v. Borzoni, 2007 CarswellBC 119, [2007] B.C.J. No. 105, 2007 BCCA 16, 388 W.A.C. 220, 277 D.L.R. (4th) 685, 235 B.C.A.C. 220, 64 B.C.L.R. (4th) 157 (B.C. C.A.).

Plaintiffs losing protracted litigation against housing corporation. Bringing action against barrister and solicitor who represented housing corporation. Defendant moved to dismiss action. Action unnecessary, scandalous, frivolous, vexatious, and abuse of process. Action dismissed. There was no relationship of proximity.

Englund v. Pfizer Canada Inc., 2007 CarswellSask 288, 2007 SKCA 62, [2007] 9 W.W.R. 434, 43 C.P.C. (6th) 296, 408 W.A.C. 298, 299 Sask. R. 298, 284 D.L.R. (4th) 94, [2007] S.J. No. 273 (Sask. C.A.).

Well established that commencement of more than one action in the same jurisdiction against defendant in relation to same matter is an abuse of process. The same concerns may apply where multiple actions have been commenced in two or more jurisdictions. Although the status of a Saskatchewan proceeding which has an extra-jurisdictional counterpart is normally resolved through the application of the *Court Jurisdiction and Proceedings Transfer Act*, S.S. 1997, c. C-41.1, the doctrine of abuse of process may still be engaged in appropriate circumstances. Both actions sought the certification of a national class and sought certification in respect of the same individuals. The respondents might have avoided the problem if the Ontario action had been brought by different proposed representative plaintiffs. Appeal allowed.

Reynolds v. Smith, [2007] O.J. No. 2161, 2007 CarswellOnt 3133, *(sub nom. Reynolds v. Kingston Police Services Board)* 225 O.A.C. 112, *(sub nom. Reynolds v. Kingston (Police Services Board))* 86 O.R. (3d) 43, 2007 ONCA 375, 47 C.C.L.T. (3d) 200 (Ont. C.A.); additional reasons to 2007 CarswellOnt 1424, *(sub nom. Reynolds v. Kingston Police Services Board)* 221 O.A.C. 216, 2007 ONCA 166, 45 C.C.L.T. (3d) 19, *(sub nom. Reynolds v. Kingston (City) Police Services Board)* 84 O.R. (3d) 738, *(sub nom. Reynolds v. Kingston (City) Police Services Board)* 280 D.L.R. (4th) 311, [2007] O.J. No. 2161 (Ont. C.A.).

Pathologist moved under rule 21.02(1)(b) of the *Rules of Civil Procedure* to strike mother's statement of claim for failure to disclose a reasonable cause of action. Ontario Court of Appeal restored Masters' decisions allowing the mother's motion and dismissing the pathologist's. It was not plain and obvious that the mother's claims would fail. Issue for trial respecting ambit of both the witness immunity rule and the "constantly evolving" tort of misfeasance in public office. Claims should be allowed to proceed to trial for resolution on basis of a complete factual record.

Marcoccia v. Marcoccia, 2008 CarswellOnt 7783, 60 R.F.L. (6th) 1, 2008 ONCA 866 (Ont. C.A.)

Appeal by husband from order striking answer to wife's support and equalization claim allowed. Husband's failure to fully disclose information about the sale of his business was not so egregious as to warrant striking the pleadings. He acted under an understandable, although erroneous assumption that the wife had received the required disclosure. Wife would not have had sufficient information to stop the sale in any event. A remedy striking a pleading is a serious one and should only be used in unusual cases. Husband was ordered to pay costs because he could have been more forthcoming with information.

Johnston v. Charlottetown Area Development Corp., 2005 CarswellPEI 76, 20 C.P.C. (6th) 30, 2005 PESCTD 40 (P.E.I. T.D.), Taylor, J.

Motions by the defendants in two separate but related actions to strike out the statements of claim of plaintiff for 1) failure to disclose a reasonable cause of action, and 2) because the statement of claim is frivolous, vexatious and an abuse of the process of the court, and 3) plaintiff failed to conform with *Prince Edward Island Rules of Civil Procedure* respecting pleadings.

See *Patterson & Hidson v. Livingstone et al.*, [1930] S.C.J. No. 75, at paragraph two, whether ". . . enough can be collected from the statement of claim to make it impossible to affirm, at this stage of the proceedings, that there are no facts alleged which entitle the plaintiffs to call upon the defendants for their defence . . .."

See also *Hunt v. T & N plc*, 1990 CarswellBC 216, 1990 CarswellBC 759, *(sub nom. Hunt v. Carey Canada Inc.)* [1990] S.C.J. No. 93, EYB 1990-67014, 43 C.P.C. (2d) 105, 117 N.R. 321, 4 C.O.H.S.C. 173 (headnote only), *(sub nom. Hunt v. Carey Canada Inc.)* [1990] 6 W.W.R. 385, 49 B.C.L.R. (2d) 273, *(sub nom. Hunt v. Carey Canada Inc.)* 74 D.L.R. (4th) 321, [1990] 2 S.C.R. 959, 4 C.C.L.T. (2d) 1 (S.C.C.), at para. 30, [Wilson J.], for the Court, confirmed the "plain and obvious" test described by Estey J. in *Inuit Tapirisat of Canada v. Canada (Attorney General)*, 1980 CarswellNat 633, 1980 CarswellNat 633F, [1980] 2 F.C.R. 735, [1980] 2 S.C.R. 735, 115 D.L.R. (3d) 1, 33 N.R. 304 (S.C.C.), at page 740 [S.C.R.].

Vicarious liability not specified in pleadings, but should be.

Where plaintiff claims *Charter* violation but does not specify both the section(s) of the *Charter* and particulars of how section(s) was/were violated, that part of claim should be struck as disclosing no cause of action. Nothing in claim suggest[s] plaintiff not in possession of any of the material facts necessary to found a claim within the limitation period . . .". See *Central & Eastern Trust Co. v. Rafuse*, 1986 CarswellNS 40, 1986 CarswellNS 135, EYB 1986-67369, [1986] S.C.J. No. 52, 37 C.C.L.T. 117, *(sub nom. Central Trust Co. v. Rafuse)* 186 A.P.R. 109, 42 R.P.R. 161, 34 B.L.R. 187, *(sub nom. Central Trust Co. c. Cordon)* [1986] R.R.A. 527 (headnote only), *(sub nom. Central Trust Co. v. Rafuse)* [1986] 2 S.C.R. 147, *(sub nom. Central Trust Co. v. Rafuse)* 31 D.L.R. (4th) 481, *(sub nom. Central Trust Co. v. Rafuse)* 69 N.R. 321, *(sub nom. Central Trust Co. v. Rafuse)* 75 N.S.R. (2d) 109 at para. 77 (S.C.C.).

Not plain and obvious statements of claim do not disclose a reasonable cause of action. Plaintiff to amend both statements of claim.

Hubbard v. Acheson (2009), 458 W.A.C. 215, 271 B.C.A.C. 215, 2009 BCCA 251, 2009 CarswellBC 1439, 93 B.C.L.R. (4th) 315 (B.C. C.A.).

Appeal from order of Supreme Court of British Columbia granting the petitioner Hubbard's application for judicial review of proceedings in the Provincial Court of British Columbia, and remitting it back to the Provincial Court for a rehearing.

Court to assess decision of Provincial Court Judge in light of correct standard of review. See *Q. v. College of Physicians & Surgeons (British Columbia)*, [2003] 5 W.W.R. 1, *(sub nom. Dr. Q., Re)* 295 W.A.C. 170, *(sub nom. Dr. Q., Re)* 179 B.C.A.C. 170, *(sub nom. Dr. Q. v. College of Physicians & Surgeons of British Columbia)* [2003] 1 S.C.R. 226, *(sub nom. Dr. Q., Re)* 302 N.R. 34, 48 Admin. L.R. (3d) 1, 223 D.L.R. (4th) 599, REJB 2003-39403, 11 B.C.L.R. (4th) 1, 2003 CarswellBC 743, 2003 CarswellBC 713, 2003 SCC 19, [2003] S.C.J. No. 18 at para. 43 (S.C.C.) and *Housen v. Nikolaisen*, REJB 2002-29758, [2002] S.C.J. No. 31, [2002] 2 S.C.R. 235, 272 W.A.C. 1, 219 Sask. R. 1, 30 M.P.L.R. (3d) 1, 2002 SCC 33, 2002 CarswellSask 179, 2002 CarswellSask 178, [2002] 7 W.W.R. 1, 286 N.R. 1, 211 D.L.R. (4th) 577, 10 C.C.L.T. (3d) 157 (S.C.C.); *New Brunswick (Board of Management) v. Dunsmuir*, 2008 SCC 9, *(sub nom. Dunsmuir v. New Brunswick)* 95 L.C.R. 65, 64 C.C.E.L. (3d) 1, 2008 CarswellNB 125, 2008 CarswellNB 124, *(sub nom. Dunsmuir v. New Brunswick)* 291 D.L.R. (4th) 577, *(sub nom. Dunsmuir v. New Brunswick)* 170 L.A.C. (4th) 1, 329 N.B.R. (2d) 1, [2008] A.C.S. No. 9, [2008] S.C.J. No. 9, D.T.E. 2008T-223, *(sub nom. Dunsmuir v. New Brunswick)* 2008 C.L.L.C. 220-020, 844 A.P.R. 1, *(sub nom. Dunsmuir v. New Brunswick)* [2008] 1 S.C.R. 190, 69 Imm. L.R. (3d) 1, 69 Admin. L.R. (4th) 1, 372

N.R. 1 (S.C.C.) and *Delmas v. Vancouver Stock Exchange* (1995), [1995] B.C.J. No. 2449, 1995 CarswellBC 1011, 108 W.A.C. 200, 66 B.C.A.C. 200, 34 Admin. L.R. (2d) 313, 130 D.L.R. (4th) 461, [1996] 4 W.W.R. 293, 42 C.P.C. (3d) 167, 15 B.C.L.R. (3d) 136, 9 C.C.L.S. 1 (B.C. C.A.).

Hubbard applied in provincial Court to set aside default judgment. Provincial Court Judge palmer dismissed the application to set aside the default judgment. Respondent had failed to establish that she had not wilfully or deliberately failed to enter her appearance or reply, and respondent had failed to establish that she had a meritorious defence to appellants' claim.

Supreme Court judge did not err in holding that it was unreasonable for the Provincial Court judge to rule that there was no defence worthy of investigation.

Appeal dismissed. Case remitted to Provincial Court for a rehearing on the application to set aside the default judgment.

Loojune v. Bailey (2009), 2009 CarswellOnt 6254 (Ont. S.C.J.), Lemon J.

Appeal by plaintiff allowed from an order of motions judge striking his claim as disclosing no reasonable cause of action and dismissing claim. Motions judge erred in applying the test for the summary judgment motion rather than the motion to strike and made findings of credibility of the plaintiff which should have been left to trial judge. Not plain and obvious that plaintiff's claim raised no reasonable cause of action.

Vollant c. R., (sub nom. *Vollant v. Canada*) 393 N.R. 183, 2009 CarswellNat 1900, 2009 CAF 185, 2009 CarswellNat 1622, 2009 FCA 185 (F.C.A.); reversing 2008 CarswellNat 1799, 2008 CarswellNat 2675, 2008 CF 729, 2008 FC 729 (F.C.), J.K. Hugessen J.

Motion judge struck out amended claim in its entirety without leave to amend. Plaintiffs appealed. Appeal allowed. Federal Court had jurisdiction to hear claims for declarations made against federal Crown. Court had no jurisdiction to make declarations against provincial Crown. Decisions of motion judge set aside. Motion to strike dismissed and stay of proceedings ordered.

McLellan v. Martin, 2009 ONCA 657, 2009 CarswellOnt 5437 (Ont. C.A.); leave to appeal refused (2010), 2010 CarswellOnt 430, 2010 CarswellOnt 429, [2009] S.C.C.A. No. 443, 270 O.A.C. 393 (note), 404 N.R. 397 (note) (S.C.C.).

Motion judge did not err by dismissing the action as being frivolous, vexatious and abuse of process. Second action brought by appellants against respondent, their former employee, for statements she made as to alleged irregularities in the appellants' affairs. First action settled and the appellants provided the respondent with a broadly worded release. Action brought for an improper purpose, namely, "to harass her and suborn her testimony in the oppression proceeding."

Toronto District School Board v. Molson Breweries Properties Ltd. (2009), 2009 CarswellOnt 3661 (Ont. S.C.J.)

West Harbour refused to pay costs on a substantial indemnity basis to the School Boards and Molson. Court inclined to make punitive award because substantial costs may be awarded where a party has behaved in an abusive manner bringing proceedings devoid of merit and running up the costs of the litigations: *Standard Life Assurance Co. v. Elliott* (2007), 86 O.R. (3d) 221 (S.C.J.). Motions to strike under rule 21 went beyond proper resort to that rule because it was plain and obvious that it was not plain and obvious that the School Boards' claims and Molson's crossclaims were bound to fail and West Harbour's motions were singularly unproductive in advancing the litigation. Order made pursuant to rule 20.06(1).

Elgammal v. Toronto French School, 2010 CarswellOnt 1298, 2010 ONSC 1435 (Ont. Master), Master Glustein.

Motion to strike paragraphs of Amended Amended Statement of Claim for failure to comply with Rules 25.06 and 25.11 of the *Rules of Civil Procedure*. Impugned Paragraphs not to be struck.

See *Quizno's Canada Restaurant Corp. v. Kileel Developments Ltd.*, 241 O.A.C. 148, 92 O.R. (3d) 347, 2008 CarswellOnt 5525, 2008 ONCA 644, [2008] O.J. No. 3674 (Ont. C.A.) ("Quizno's") at para. 14; *Canadian National Railway v. Brant*, 96 O.R. (3d) 734, [2009] O.J. No. 2661, [2009] 4 C.N.L.R. 47, 2009 CarswellOnt 3720 at para. 27 (Ont. S.C.J.); additional reasons at 2009 CarswellOnt 5106 (Ont. S.C.J.) ("CNR").

If the allegations in question are relevant and material, the court should exercise this power with "considerable caution": *Quizno's*, at para. 15; *C.N.R.*, at para. 30; and *Wolker v. Ogilvie Realty Ltd.* (2006), [2006] O.J. No. 381, [2006] O.T.C. 102, 2006 CarswellOnt 512, 23 C.P.C. (6th) 154 (Ont. S.C.J.) ("Walker") at para. 10.

Every pleading shall contain a concise statement of the material facts on which the party relies for the claim or defence, but not the evidence by which those facts are to be proved. A material fact is a fact that is necessary for a complete cause of action. Material facts include facts that establish the constituent elements of the claim or defence.

Mercier v. Summerside Police Department, 2010 CarswellPEI 1, 2010 PESC 1 (P.E.I. S.C.), Taylor J.

Motion by defendant to dismiss or strike out claim of plaintiff. Claim struck out, with leave to plaintiff to re-file. Claim not presented chronologically, not in any apparent sequence, rambling and unreadable. Claim full of completely irrelevant evidence and evidence which ought not to be in claim. Claim sought "unspecified (punitive) damages," but does not specify amount claimed.

Limitation period should always be considered in deciding whether to strike, or order amendments.

Van de Vrande v. Butkowsky, 2010 ONCA 230, 2010 CarswellOnt 1777, [2010] O.J. No. 1239, 99 O.R. (3d) 648, 99 O.R. (3d) 641, 85 C.P.C. (6th) 205, 260 O.A.C. 323, 319 D.L.R. (4th) 132 (Ont. C.A.); additional reasons at 2010 ONCA 400, 2010 CarswellOnt 3629, 85 C.P.C. (6th) 212 (Ont. C.A.)

Pursuant to Rule 12.02 of the *Small Claims Court Rules*, O. Reg. 258/98, the appellant, Butkowsky, brought a motion for summary judgment. The trial judge granted the motion. The Divisional Court set aside the order, finding that the trial judge erred by making findings of fact on the motion.

Summary judgment not available under the *Small Claims Court Rules* but the motion judge's decision sustainable under r. 12.02.

Motion had been granted pursuant to rr. 1.03(2) and 12.02 of the *Small Claims Court Rules*.

The Divisional Court set aside the motion judge's order based on Rule 20 of the *Rules of Civil Procedure*, R.R.O. 1990, Reg. 194.

Failure to provide for summary judgment motions in the *Small Claims Court Rules* deliberate omission. Rule 12.02 of the *Small Claims Court Rules* is more akin to a r.21 motion than a r. 20 motion.

Rule 12.02 applies in a different context than the *Rules of Civil Procedure*. Section 25 of the *Courts of Justice Act*, provides that the court is to "hear and determine in a summary way all questions of law and fact." The court can make "such order as is considered just and agreeable to good conscience." In addition, r. 1.03(1) of the *Small Claims Court Rules*, provides that the rules shall be "liberally construed to secure the just, most expeditions and least expensive determination of every proceeding on its merit in accordance with s. 25".

Appeal allowed. Motion judge's dismissal of claim reinstated.

Garth v. Halifax (Regional Municipality), 777 A.P.R. 108, 245 N.S.R. (2d) 108, 31 C.P.C. (6th) 124, 2006 CarswellNS 316, 2006 NSCA 89, [2006] N.S.J. No. 300, 271 D.L.R. (4th) 470 (N.S. C.A.)

Plaintiff seeking amendment to add party after expiry of limitation period. Overriding general power to allow amendment not limited by specific instances in rules.

Both rr. 5.04 and 15 are relevant. Rule 5.04(2)(b) permits the court to order any party who ought to have been joined to be added. It provides:

> 5.04 . . .
>
> (2) At any stage of a proceeding the court may, on such terms as it thinks just and either of its own motion or on application . . .
>
>> (b) order an person, who ought to have been joined as a party or whose participation in the proceeding is necessary to ensure that all matters in the proceeding may be effectually adjudicated upon, be added as a party;

The discretion to amend must be exercised judicially in order to do justice between the parties. Generally amendments should be granted if they do not occasion prejudice which cannot be compensated in costs.

Nothing in a pleading can be scandalous if it is relevant: *Quizno's Canada Restaurant Corp. v. Kileel Developments Ltd.*, 241 O.A.C. 148, 92 O.R. (3d) 347, 2008 CarswellOnt 5525, 2008 ONCA 644, [2008] O.J. No. 3674 (Ont. C.A.) (*"Quizno's"*) at para. 14. See also *Canadian National Railway v. Brant*, 96 O.R. (3d) 734, [2009] O.J. No. 2661, [2009] 4 C.N.L.R. 47, 2009 CarswellOnt 3720 (Ont. S.C.J.); additional reasons at 2009 CarswellOnt 5106 (Ont. S.C.J.) (*"CNR"*) at para. 27.

The court must balance the rights of the parties on the particular facts of the case and must consider carefully the extent to which the particulars attacked are necessary to enable the party to prove its case and their probative value in establishing that case. If allegations in question are relevant and material, the court should exercise this power with "considerable caution": *Quizno's*, at para. 15; *CNR*, at para. 30; *Wolker v. Ogilvie Realty Ltd.*, [2006] O.J. No. 381, [2006] O.T.C. 102, 2006 CarswellOnt 512, 23 C.P.C. (6th) 154 (Ont. S.C.J.); *"Wolker"* at para. 10.

Every pleading shall contain concise statement of material facts on which party relies for the claim or defence, but not the evidence by which those facts are to be proved (see r. 25.06(1) and see *Cavanaugh v. Grenville Christian College*, [2009] O.J. No. 875, 2009 CarswellOnt 1127 (Ont. S.C.J.); reversed 2009 CarswellOnt 6606, 2009 ONCA 753, [2009] O.J. No. 4502 (Ont. C.A.) (*"Cavanaugh"*), at para. 21).

Coote v. Ontario (Human Rights Commission), [2009] O.J. No. 4264, 2009 CarswellOnt 6165 (Ont. S.C.J.), Daley J; additional reasons at 2009 CarswellOnt 9410 (Ont. S.C.J.); leave to appeal refused 2010 ONCA 460, 2010 CarswellOnt 4324 (Ont. C.A.)

Two statements of claim were struck entirely. Causes of action asserted unsustainable at law, inconsistent with notion of justice to grant leave to amend, as no amount of improved drafting would cure deficiencies. All actions were dismissed against Commission. It was plain and obvious and beyond doubt that employee could not succeed.

Veerella v. Khan, 2009 CarswellOnt 5658 (Ont. Div. Ct.); additional reasons at 2009 CarswellOnt 5980 (Ont. Div. Ct.), Jennings J.; affirming 2009 CarswellOnt 8624 (Ont. Master), Master Sproat.

The plaintiff brought motion to amend statement of claim by substituting V Inc. as the plaintiff in place of himself. Motion was dismissed. The Master found that motion was to replace one party with another and did not involve misnomer. Appeal dismissed. The plaintiff put no evidence before Master regarding his intentions in bringing claim in his name. The choice of plaintiff was a conscious decision, not error.

Rose v. British Columbia, 2009 CarswellBC 2157, 2009 BCSC 1116 (B.C. S.C.), Halfyard J.

Facts pleaded were unlikely to be proven. Applications granted; actions dismissed. All main allegations in actions were substantially same and about same subject matter as those made in previous action. Finding in previous action that no reasonable claim was disclosed applied as estoppel in these two subsequent actions with respect to common defendants. No cause of action was disclosed against other defendants.

Jaffer v. York University, 268 O.A.C. 338, [2010] O.J. No. 4252, 326 D.L.R. (4th) 148, 2010 CarswellOnt 7531, 2010 ONCA 654 (Ont. C.A.); leave to appeal refused 2011 CarswellOnt 1270, 2011 CarswellOnt 1269, 418 N.R. 395 (note), 284 O.A.C. 399 (note), [2010] S.C.C.A. No. 402 (S.C.C.)

The motion judge concluded there was no jurisdiction to hear action, both because the complaint was academic in nature and because it belonged before the OHRC. A r. 21 motion must be based upon the facts alleged in the Statement of Claim unless they are patently ridiculous or incapable of proof: see e.g., *Morneau Sobeco Ltd. Partnership v. Aon Consulting Inc.*, 2008 ONCA 196, 2008 CarswellOnt 1427, (sub nom. *Morneau Sobeco Ltd. Partnership v. AON Consulting Inc.)* 237 O.A.C. 267, 65 C.C.L.I. (4th) 159, 40 C.B.R. (5th) 172, 65 C.C.P.B. 293, (sub nom. *Slater Steel Inc. (Re))* 2008 C.E.B. & P.G.R. 8285, 291 D.L.R. (4th) 314 (Ont. C.A.), at para. 22; additional reasons at 2008 ONCA 347, 2008 CarswellOnt 2471, 66 C.C.P.B. 315, 65 C.C.L.I. (4th) 171 (Ont. C.A.); leave to appeal refused 2008 CarswellOnt 5185, 2008 CarswellOnt 5186, [2008] S.C.C.A. No. 230, (sub nom. *Morneau Sobeco Limited Partnership v. AON Consulting Inc.)* 257 O.A.C. 396 (note), 390 N.R. 387 (note) (S.C.C.) . A pleading should only be struck under r. 21 where it is "plain and obvious" that the claim has no chance of success: *Freeman-Maloy v. York University*, 267 D.L.R. (4th) 37, [2006] O.J. No. 1228, 79 O.R. (3d) 401, 208 O.A.C. 307, 2006 CarswellOnt 1888 (Ont. C.A.), at para. 18; leave to appeal refused [2006] 2 S.C.R. ix (note), [2006] S.C.C.A. No. 201, 227 O.A.C. 396 (note), 359 N.R. 391 (note), 267 D.L.R. (4th) ix (note), 2006 CarswellOnt 5559, 2006 CarswellOnt 5558 (S.C.C.), citing *Hunt v. T & N plc*, 1990 CarswellBC 216, 1990 CarswellBC 759, EYB 1990-67014, (sub nom. *Hunt v. Carey Canada Inc.)* [1990] S.C.J. No. 93, [1990] 2 S.C.R. 959, 43 C.P.C. (2d) 105, 117 N.R. 321, 4 C.O.H.S.C. 173 (headnote only), (sub nom. *Hunt v. Carey Canada Inc.)* [1990] 6 W.W.R. 385, 49 B.C.L.R. (2d) 273, (sub nom. *Hunt v. Carey Canada Inc.)* 74 D.L.R. (4th) 321, 4 C.C.L.T. (2d) 1 (S.C.C.). Appeal allowed in part. Pleadings struck but Jaffer permitted to amend Statement of Claim in accordance with reasons.

Boldt v. Law Society of Upper Canada, 2010 ONSC 3568, 2010 CarswellOnt 4353 (Ont. S.C.J.)

On both a motion to dismiss or stay an action for want of jurisdiction and a motion to strike out an action as an abuse of the process of the court, the facts pleaded in the statement of claim are presumed to be true and provable. The court will strike out an action as an abuse of process *only* when it is plain and obvious or beyond doubt that the action must fail. This is a stringent test and is applicable even in respect of novel claims.

See *Odhavji Estate v. Woodhouse* (2003), 180 O.A.C. 201, 312 N.R. 305, 2003 CarswellOnt 4852, 2003 CarswellOnt 4851, 2003 SCC 69, 70 O.R. (3d) 253 (note), [2003] 3 S.C.R. 263, 11 Admin. L.R. (4th) 45, 233 D.L.R. (4th) 193, [2004] R.R.A. 1, [2003] S.C.J. No. 74, 19 C.C.L.T. (3d) 163 (S.C.C.), Iacobucci J. (at para. 15):

> ... The test is a stringent one. The facts are to be taken as pleaded. When so taken, the question that must then be determined is whether there it is "plain and obvious" that the action must fail. It is only if the statement of claim is certain to fail because it contains a "radical defect" that the plaintiff should be driven from the judgment. See also *Attorney General of Canada v. Inuit Tapirisat of Canada*, [1980] 2 S.C.R. 735.

Motion to dismiss or stay for want of jurisdiction.

The Supreme Court of Canada, in *Bella v. Young*, [2006] R.R.A. 1, [2006] 1 S.C.R. 108, 37 C.C.L.T. (3d) 161, 764 A.P.R. 26, 254 Nfld. & P.E.I.R. 26, 261 D.L.R. (4th) 516, 21 C.P.C. (6th) 1, 2006 CarswellNfld 20, 2006 CarswellNfld 19, 2006 SCC 3, 343 N.R. 360, [2006] S.C.J. No. 2 (S.C.C.), wrote (at para. 31):

> . . . The relationship between the appellant and the University had a contractual foundation, giving rise to duties that sound in both contract and tort: *Central Trust Co. v. Rafuse*, [1986] 2 S.C.R. 147.

Based upon the evidence before her, Hennessy J. made the following finding:

> I, therefore, find that Maureen Boldt carried on the unauthorized practice of law in direct contravention to the clear and plain terms of the injunction. *It is regrettable that she thought she could ignore the injunction simply by changing the title on her document. This is a flagrant breach of the order of Bolan J.* [Emphasis added.]

Hennessy J.'s order was appealed by Boldt to the Court of Appeal which dismissed her appeal on February 16, 2007.

The Court of Appeal rejected Boldt's application, and delivered the following endorsement:

> The appellant seeks to introduce fresh evidence with a view to having her appeal, determined against her on February 16, 2007, re-opened for another hearing. The proposed fresh evidence relates to an affidavit from Mr. Sangster and the testimony of Ms. Labbé in a subsequent small claims proceeding, which, the appellant contends, conflicts with her testimony before the trial judge in this matter.

We disagree.

Boldt issued a claim for damages for malicious prosecution, and other alleged wrongs arising from the same facts, against most of the defendants in this action in September 2008, in Court File CV-08-362049. All defendants in that suit moved to strike the claim.

The Court of Appeal stated in *Canam Enterprises v. Coles*:

> The principle of *res judicata* applies where a judgment rendered by a court of competent jurisdiction provides a conclusive disposition of the merits of the case and acts as an absolute bar to any subsequent proceedings involving the same claim, demand or cause of action. Issue estoppel is one aspect of *res judicata*. The oft-cited requirements of issue estoppels are attributed to Lord Guest in *Carl-Zeiss-Stiftung v. Rayner & Keeler Ltd. (No. 2)* (1966), [1967] 1 A.C. 853 at 935 (U.K. H.L.): (1) That the same question has been previously decided; (2) that the judicial decision which is said to create the estoppels was final; and, (3) that the parties to the judicial decision or their privies were the same persons as the parties to the proceedings in which the estoppel is raised or their privies.

Canam Enterprise Inc. v. Coles (2000), 51 O.R. (3d) 481 (C.A.); reversed on other grounds (2002), 220 D.L.R. (4th) 466, [2002] S.C.C. 63, at para. 19.

As between Boldt and the Law Society, all elements of *res judicata* were satisfied.

The Law Society is not liable for the erroneous exercise of its discretion so long as it acted *bona fide* and without malice: see *Calvert v. Law Society of Upper Canada*, 1981 Carswell-Ont 782, 121 D.L.R. (3d) 169, 32 O.R. (2d) 176 (Ont. H.C.) per Steele J., at paras. 20 and 21.

The jurisprudence clearly establishes a judicial immunity from negligence for the Law Society's discipline process, including the investigative function at the front end. The Law Society's disciplinary powers must respond to its statutory mandate and the requirements of due process, not to a private law duty of care: see *Edwards v. Law Society of Upper Canada*, 2001 SCC 80, 2001 CarswellOnt 3962, 2001 CarswellOnt 3963, REJB 2001-26863, [2001] S.C.J. No. 77, [2001] 3 S.C.R. 562, (sub nom. *Edwards v. Law Society of Upper Canada (No. 2)*) 56 O.R. (3d) 456 (headnote only), 34 Admin. L.R. (3d) 38, 8 C.C.L.T. (3d) 153, 13 C.P.C. (5th) 35, 206 D.L.R. (4th) 211, 277 N.R. 145, 153 O.A.C. 388 (S.C.C.); (2000).

It is not actionable for the Law Society to require a good character hearing in the context of Boldt's application to become a licensed paralegal. Equally, it is not actionable for the Law Society to act in the public interest by restraining untrained, uninsured and unlicensed persons such as Boldt from practising law.

In *Brignolio v. Desmarais, Keenan* (1995), 1995 CarswellOnt 4761, [1995] O.J. No. 3499 (Ont. Gen. Div.), at paras. 7, 8, 15 to 17; affirmed (1996), 1996 CarswellOnt 5875, [1996] O.J. No. 4812 (Ont. C.A.); leave to appeal refused (1996), [1996] S.C.C.A. No. 326 (S.C.C.), Lane J., in a decision affirmed on appeal, held that an action in negligence against the solicitor for one's adversary in litigation is not tenable under the law of Ontario, because there is no duty of care, and because such an action is contrary to public policy. Further, Lane J. held that a party to litigation cannot bring an action against the adverse party's solicitor based upon alleged breaches of ethical duties since such duties are owed to the court and, in Ontario, to the Law Society, but not to the opposite party in the litigation.

Tiwana v. Sandhu, 2010 ONCA 592, 2010 CarswellOnt 6822, [2010] O.J. No. 3862 (Ont. C.A.)

Husband was ordered on three different occasions before three different judges to make financial disclosure. Motion judge gave husband one last chance but he failed again to do so. Motion to strike pleadings was heard *ex parte* and was successful. Court of Appeal stated that the decision to strike pleadings and determine the parameters of trial participation was discretionary that deserved deference on appeal when exercised on proper principles. Ordinarily, striking any pleadings on *ex parte* basis where that party purports to have made required disclosure was practice that Court of Appeal could not endorse, preferring that striking order be on notice to affected party so that he or she could explain or assert compliance with prior disclosure order. Compare with *Stephens v. Stephens*, 2010 ONCA 586, [2010] O.J. No. 3765, 2010 CarswellOnt 6690, 89 R.F.L. (6th) 260, 324 D.L.R. (4th) 169 (Ont. C.A.)

O'Brien v. Ottawa Hospital, 2011 CarswellOnt 88, 2011 ONSC 231, [2011] O.J. No. 66 (Ont. Div. Ct.)

Appeals from decision dismissing action against Respondents pursuant to r. 20.01(3) of the *Rules of Civil Procedure*, R.R.O. 1990 Reg. 194, on basis of no genuine issue for trial.

The court held, in *Van de Vrande v. Butkowsky*, 2010 ONCA 230, 2010 CarswellOnt 1777, [2010] O.J. No. 1239, 99 O.R. (3d) 648, 99 O.R. (3d) 641, 85 C.P.C. (6th) 205, 260 O.A.C. 323, 319 D.L.R. (4th) 132 (Ont. C.A.); additional reasons at 2010 ONCA 400, 2010 CarswellOnt 3629, 85 C.P.C. (6th) 212 (Ont. C.A.), that the procedure of a motion for summary judgment is *not* available under the *Rules of the Small Claims Court*. In that case, the motion had actually been brought under r. 1.03(2) and 12.02 of the *Rules of the Small Claims Court*.

MacNeil v. Humber River Regional Hospital, 2011 ONSC 2094, 2011 CarswellOnt 4011 (Ont. Master), Master Thomas R. Hawkins; reversed in part 2011 ONSC 6691, 2011 CarswellOnt 12141 (Ont. S.C.J.).

Case contained general principles relating to amending an application.

Abrahim v. Sliwin, 2011 ONCA 754, 2011 CarswellOnt 13237, [2011] O.J. No. 5324 (Ont. C.A.); affirming 2011 ONSC 1905, 2011 CarswellOnt 2039, [2011] O.J. No. 1370 (Ont. S.C.J.), *per* Justice Douglas K. Gray.

The affected party failed to appear through accident or inadequate notice. The defendant in this civil claim chose the litigation strategy of wearing the plaintiff down with delaying and stonewalling. When the defendant's lawyer failed to appear on the day of the initial motion, the judge struck out the defendant's statement of defence. The rules of the court would allow a re-instatement of pleadings if the affected party could show that the lawyer's failure to appear on the critical day was due to "mistake or accident." Misguided litigation strategy did not qualify as a "mistake or accident." The motion for re-instatement was dismissed.

A. (D.K.) v. H. (T.), 2011 YKCA 5, 2011 CarswellYukon 74, 309 B.C.A.C. 277, 523 W.A.C. 277 (Y.T. C.A.); affirming 2010 YKSC 63, 2010 CarswellYukon 172 (Y.T. S.C.).

Pleadings. Statement of claim. Striking out for absence of reasonable cause of action. Cause not known in law. Although the application of this tort to the case at the bar was novel, the court should not strike out a statement of claim simply based on novelty alone. However, the employee did not plead sufficient facts to support this allegation; there were no facts relating to economic harm. Wilful incitement of hatred is not a recognized tort in Canada. Regarding defamation, the employee only appeared to take issue with the alleged comment that he was physically black.

Alessandro v. Smith, 2013 ONSC 6471, 2013 CarswellOnt 15039 (Ont. Div. Ct.), Pardu, J. — The defendants brought a motion to strike out the claim pursuant to Rule 12.02(1) of the Rules of the Small Claims Court. Communications which take place during, incidental to or in furtherance of judicial proceedings are absolutely privileged. (See *Fraleigh v. RBC Dominion Securities Inc.*, 2009 CarswellOnt 9155, 99 O.R. (3d) 290, [2009] O.J. No. 5120 (Ont. S.C.J. [Commercial List]). This privilege extends to all of the causes of action pleaded by the plaintiff. (See *Web Offset Publications Ltd. v. Vickery*, 1998 CarswellOnt 5379, 40 O.R. (3d) 526, 34 C.P.C. (4th) 343, [1998] O.J. No. 6478 (Ont. Gen. Div.); affirmed 1999 CarswellOnt 2270, 43 O.R. (3d) 802, 123 O.A.C. 235, [1999] O.J. No. 2760 (Ont. C.A.); leave to appeal refused 2000 CarswellOnt 1808, 2000 CarswellOnt 1809, 43 O.R. (3d) 802 (note), 256 N.R. 200 (note), 136 O.A.C. 199 (note), [1999] S.C.C.A. No. 460 (S.C.C.).) This was a sufficient basis to dismiss the claim. Appeal dismissed.

Camm v. Kirkpatrick (July 12, 2013), Doc. No. 13-SC-125385 (Ont. Sm. Cl. Ct.), Deputy Judge P. Lepsoe — The defendant moved for a dismissal of the plaintiff's claim on the basis that the limitation period had expired before the claim was commenced. An application of Rule 12 of the *Small Claims Court Rules* regarding possible dismissal of claim by motion. Applicable test for dismissal under Rule 12.02(1) is: no meaningful chance of success at trial": *O'Brien v. Ottawa Hospital*, 2011 ONSC 231, 2011 CarswellOnt 88, [2011] O.J. No. 66 (Ont. Div. Ct.). In *Metcalfe v. Khanna*, 2012 CarswellOnt 4737, [2012] O.J. No. 34 (Ont. Sm. Cl. Ct.), Deputy Judge Winny dismissed the claim under Rule 12.02 on the basis of the *Act* where it was "inescapable" on what date the cause of action became known to the plaintiff. Similarly, in *1528590 Ontario Ltd. v. Ferrera Concrete Ltd.*, 2011 CarswellOnt 15745, [2011] O.J. No. 4845 (Ont. Sm. Cl. Ct.), a claim was dismissed by Deputy Judge Koprowski under Rule 12.02 on the basis of the *Act* where the date on which the limitation began to run was readily determinable on the basis of material filed. The defendant's motion was granted, and the claim was dismissed.

(3) General Power to Stay, Dismiss Action — The court may, on its own initiative, make the order referred to in paragraph 1 of subrule (2) staying or dismissing an action, if the action appears on its face to be inflammatory, a waste of time, a nuisance or an abuse of the court's process.

(4) Unless the court orders otherwise, an order under subrule (3) shall be made on the basis of written submissions in accordance with the following procedures:

    1. The court shall direct the clerk to send notice by mail to the plaintiff that the court is considering making the order.

    2. The plaintiff may, within 20 days after receiving the notice, file with the court a written submission, no more than four pages in length, responding to the notice.

3. If the plaintiff does not file a written submission that complies with pa]
2, the court may make the order without any further notice to the plaint
any other party.

4. If the plaintiff files a written submission that complies with paragraph 2, the
court may direct the clerk to send a copy of the submission by mail to any other
party.

5. A party who receives a copy of the plaintiff's submission may, within 10 days
after receiving the copy, file with the court a written submission, no more than
four pages in length, responding to the plaintiff's submission, and shall send a
copy of the responding submission by mail to the plaintiff, and, on the request of
any other party, to that party.

(5) The clerk shall send a copy of an order made under subrule (1) by mail to all the
parties as soon as possible after the order is made.

(6) A document required under this rule to be sent by mail shall be mailed in the manner described in subrule 8.07(1), and is deemed to have been received on the fifth day
after it is mailed.

(7) **General Power to Stay, Dismiss Motion** — The court may, on its own initiative, make the order referred to in paragraph 2.1 of subrule (2) staying or dismissing a
motion, if the motion appears on its face to be inflammatory, a waste of time, a nuisance or an abuse of the court's process.

(8) Subrules (4) to (6) apply, with necessary modifications, to the stay or dismissal of a
motion under subrule (7) and, for the purpose, a reference to the plaintiff shall be read
as a reference to the moving party.

(9) **Clerk to Notify Court** — If the clerk becomes aware that an action could be the
subject of an order under subrule (3), or that a motion could be the subject of an order
under subrule (7), the clerk shall notify the court.

O. Reg. 78/06, s. 26; 44/14, s. 11(2), (3)

12.03 (1) Stay or Dismissal if No Leave under *Courts of Justice Act* — If
the court determines that a person who is subject to an order under subsection 140(1)
of the *Courts of Justice Act* has instituted or continued an action without the order
having been rescinded or leave granted for the action to be instituted or continued, the
court shall make an order staying or dismissing the action.

(2) **Request for Order** — Any party to the action may file with the clerk a written
request for an order under subrule (1).

(3) **Service of Order** — An order under subrule (1) may be made without notice, but
the clerk shall send a copy of the order by mail, in the manner described in subrule
8.07(1), to every party to the action as soon as possible after the order is made.

O. Reg. 44/14, s. 11(4)

Rule 13 — Settlement Conferences

[Heading amended O. Reg. 78/06, s. 27.]

13.01 (1) Settlement Conference Required in Defended Action — A settlement conference shall be held in every defended action.

History [R. 13.01(1)]: Formerly 14.01(1); refers to Form 13A, formerly Form 14A; plain language changes.

Commentary: Rule 13.01(2) states that the clerk serves the Notice of Settlement Conference and List of Proposed Witnesses "on the parties." There is an exception in r. 11.05(3), which allows the clerk to *not* serve any party who was noted in default with the Notice of Settlement Conference and List of proposed Witnesses. However, clerks are required to serve all defendants who have *not* been noted in default.

Clerks do not have the authority to adjourn matters. Scheduling is a judicial matter and SCC staff responsible for scheduling will act under the direction of the Regional Senior Judge or his or her designate.

If there is an admission of *all* of the plaintiff's claim and a proposal of terms of payment under r. 9.03(1) then staff would not schedule a settlement conference. However, if there were only a partial admission of liability and a proposal of terms of payment, the clerk would schedule a settlement conference for the part of the claim the defendant does not admit.

(2) Duty of Clerk — The clerk shall fix a time, date and place for the settlement conference and serve a notice of settlement conference, together with a list of proposed witnesses (Form 13A), on the parties.

History [R. 13.01(2)]: Formerly part of 14.01(2); clerk's duties are separated out into another subrule (13.01(3)).

(3) Timing — The settlement conference shall be held within 90 days after the first defence is filed.

History [R. 13.01(3)]: Contains the clerk's duties from former 14.01(2).

Commentary: If the defendant files a defence, the parties will receive a notice of settlement conference in the mail from the court office indicating the date, time and location of the settlement conference. A settlement conference should be held within 90 days after the first defence is filed.

If there is going to be a trial, the settlement conference is also an opportunity to get prepared for the trial. The judge may make recommendations and there are a number of orders the judge might make.

At the end of the settlement conference, if the parties do not settle the case, the Rules provide that the judge will give the clerk a memorandum listing the issues remaining in dispute, matters agreed on, and information related to scheduling. The memorandum will be provided to the trial judge. The judge who conducts your settlement conference will not preside at the trial.

After the settlement conference, the clerk will provide the parties with a copy of the Endorsement Record/Order of the Court, either in person, by mail or by fax. The Endorsement Record/Order of the Court contains any orders that the judge made at the settlement conference.

The people who attend must have the authority to settle the case.

A settlement conference can be heard or conducted by telephone or video conference if the facilities are available at the court. A party can file a Request for Telephone or Video Conference [Form 1B].

If all parties agree on a final settlement, the judge may make an order that disposes of the case and you will not need to go to trial. If a settlement is not reached, the settlement conference is an opportunity to try to resolve some issues before the trial and to assist in preparing for the trial.

The Endorsement Record/Order of the Court will include a Notice to Set Action Down for Trial that states that one of the parties must request a trial date and pay the fee for setting the action down for trial. Failure to set the action down for trial will result in the clerk eventually sending you a notice of approaching dismissal.

If the claim is for $2,500 or less ($2,500 is the minimum claim that can be appealed under the *Courts of Justice Act*), there is a special procedure available to parties who consent to it. The parties can file a signed Consent [Form 13B] (before the settlement conference) indicating that they wish to have final judgment at the settlement conference. If the parties do not reach a settlement, the judge can then make a final judgment at the settlement conference. If you consent to this procedure, this will be the final judgment in your case and you will not have to attend again for a trial, or pay the trial fee.

(4) Exception — **Subrules (1) to (3) do not apply if the defence contains an admission of liability for all of the plaintiff's claim and a proposal of terms of payment under subrule 9.03(1).**

History [R. 13.01(4)]: Formerly 14.01(3).

(5) [Repealed O. Reg. 78/06, s. 27.]

History [R. 13.01(5)]: Formerly 14.01(4); plain language changes.

(6) [Repealed O. Reg. 78/06, s. 27.]

History [R. 13.01(6)]: Formerly 14.01(5); refers to subrules (4) and (5), formerly subrules (3) and (4), respectively.

(7) [Repealed O. Reg. 78/06, s. 27.]

O. Reg. 78/06, s. 27

History [R. 13.01(7)]: Formerly 14.01(6); refers to Form 16A, formerly Form 17A; plain language changes.

13.02 (1) Attendance — **A party and the party's representative, if any, shall, unless the court orders otherwise, participate in the settlement conference,**

　　(a) by personal attendance; or

　　(b) by telephone or video conference in accordance with rule 1.07.

History [R. 13.02(1)]: Formerly 14.02(1).

(2) Authority to Settle — **A party who requires another person's approval before agreeing to a settlement shall, before the settlement conference, arrange to have ready telephone access to the other person throughout the conference, whether it takes place during or after regular business hours.**

History [R. 13.02(2)]: Formerly part of 14.02(2); restrictions on disclosure separated out into another subrule (13.02(3)).

(3) Additional Settlement Conferences — **The court may order the parties to attend an additional settlement conference.**

History [R. 13.02(3)]: Contains restrictions on disclosure from former 14.02(2).

Commentary: There is nothing to prevent a pre-trial judge from setting out for unrepresented litigants a schedule of time limits within which they must begin or complete certain steps or to deliver certain documents. See *Charlebois v. Leadbeater* (1993), 4 W.D.C.P. (2d) 195 (Ont. Gen. Div.), per Justice E. Stach. Nor is there any prohibition on a judge's scheduling or arranging of preliminary issues (such as statutory bars or limitation periods) at the outset, so that the litigants know exactly where they stand before they commit themselves to the expense and risk of trial; see *Newlove v. Petrie* (June 29, 1995), Doc. Toronto 39122/89 (Ont. Gen. Div.), per Justice J. Wilkins.

One of the purposes of a pre-trial conference as set out in subrule 13.02(1) is to facilitate settlement of the action. Where the parties agree to settle, the practice in Metropolitan Toronto is to have the parties sign minutes of settlement which state that, in the event of default, judgment may be signed by the clerk. If default subsequently occurs, judgment is entered by the clerk on the filing of an affidavit from the party requesting judgment. The minutes of settlement do not have to be approved by a judge as required by subrule 13.03(4). When minutes of settlement are prepared as a result of a hearing before a judge in Toronto, the court record may be endorsed as being settled in accordance with the minutes of settlement. Again, the minutes contain a proviso that judgment will only be issued by the clerk on the filing of an affidavit from the party requesting judgment.

The practice is not consistent throughout the province. In some locations minutes of settlement arising from a pre-trial conference presided over by the referee are subject to approval by a judge in all cases. In nearly all instances, minutes of settlement are approved by a judge without comment. There may be nothing to preclude conducting pre-trials by way of video conferencing. Certainly case memoranda in one form or another may be a good idea.

(4) The clerk shall fix a time and place for any additional settlement conference and serve a notice of settlement conference, together with a list of proposed witnesses (Form 13A) on the parties.

(5) Failure to Attend — If a party who has received a notice of settlement conference fails to attend the conference, the court may,

    (a) impose appropriate sanctions, by way of costs or otherwise; and

    (b) order that an additional settlement conference be held, if necessary.

(6) If a defendant fails to attend a first settlement conference, receives notice of an additional settlement conference and fails to attend the additional settlement conference, the court may,

    (a) strike out the defence and dismiss the defendant's claim, if any, and allow the plaintiff to prove the plaintiff's claim; or

    (b) make such other order as is just.

(7) Inadequate Preparation, Failure to File Material — The court may award costs against a person who attends a settlement conference if,

    (a) in the opinion of the court, the person is so inadequately prepared as to frustrate the purposes of the conference;

    (b) the person fails to file the material required by subrule 13.03(2).

O. Reg. 78/06, s. 27; 230/13, s. 14

13.03 (1) Purposes of Settlement Conference — The purposes of a settlement conference are,

    (a) to resolve or narrow the issues in the action;

    (b) to expedite the disposition of the action;

    (c) to encourage settlement of the action;

    (d) to assist the parties in effective preparation for trial; and

    (e) to provide full disclosure between the parties of the relevant facts and evidence.

History [R. 13.03(1)]: Formerly 14.03(1); plain language changes.

(2) Disclosure — At least 14 days before the date of the settlement conference, each party shall serve on every other party and file with the court,

(a) a copy of any document to be relied on at the trial, including an expert report, not attached to the party's claim or defence; and

(b) a list of proposed witnesses (Form 13A) and of other persons with knowledge of the matters in dispute in the action.

History [R. 13.03(2)]: Formerly part of 14.03(2); the types of orders that a judge may make are separated out into another subrule (13.03(3)); clarifies that the orders a judge may make are interlocutory orders; plain language changes.

(3) At the settlement conference, the parties or their representatives shall openly and frankly discuss the issues involved in the action.

Commentary: A hearing panel of the Law Society, in a decision, *Law Society of Upper Canada v. Ernest Guiste*, 2011 ONLSHP 24, ruled that lawyers' conduct during the mediation process is subject to the Rules of Professional Conduct. The panel found that the provisions of confidentiality contained in an agreement to mediate was for the benefit of the parties and was not intended to protect lawyers from allegations of misconduct.

The lawyer, who was the subject of findings of professional misconduct, was alleged to have committed six acts of professional misconduct.

The allegation with respect to the conduct during mediation is:

1. On June 21, 2007, during a mediation in the matter of *D.L. v. N. Ltd. et al.*, the respondent failed to be courteous, civil, and act in good faith by using sexually explicit, rude, and profane language, and raising his voice at a mediation session, contrary to Rule 4.01(6) of the *Rules of Professional Conduct*:

(6) A lawyer shall be courteous, civil, and act in good faith to the tribunal and with all persons with whom the lawyer has dealings in the course of litigation.

Case Law: *Shannon v. Shannon* (1995), 6 W.D.C.P. (2d) 534 (Ont. Gen. Div.) — At a pre-trial, a provincial judge ordered that a psychiatric assessment be conducted by the Clarke Institute and that the husband pay to the wife costs of $150 in the absence of the consent of the parties. The pre-trial rule only authorizes the judge to resolve or to narrow the issues or to settle the procedure at trial and is confined to procedural matters in the interest of expediting the trial process. It cannot be expanded to include substantive matters affecting parties' rights. The Ontario Court (Prov. Division) is a statutory court and can act only under statutory authority. Although it does have some inherent jurisdiction to control its own process, such jurisdiction cannot be extended to include matters affecting parties' rights.

McGinty v. Toronto Transit Commission (1996), 7 W.D.C.P. (2d) 101 (Ont. Div. Ct.) — The pre-trial judge, on his own motion, ordered action transferred to the Small Claims Court. The endorsement transferring the action allowed for the possibility that the plaintiff's damages could exceed the Small Claims Court limit. In granting motion, the court found that there was reason to doubt the correctness of the pre-trial judge's decision. Neither ss. 23(2) or 110(1) of the *Courts of Justice Act*, R.S.O. 1990, c. C.43 nor the judge's inherent jurisdiction afforded authority for ordering the transfer of the action under those terms. Pre-trial judges were not to make significant, contentious rulings without clear notice and an opportunity to respond. The court also found that the matter transcended the interests of the particular litigants.

Kamloops Dental Centre v. McMillan (1997), 68 A.C.W.S. 270 (B.C. S.C.) — The plaintiff had brought an action in small claims court against the defendants for money owed. At a settlement conference, the plaintiff sent a person who the provincial court judge found did not have authority to enter into a settlement. The judge consequently dismissed the claim. The plaintiff appealed. Held, the appeal was allowed. Under R. 7(14) of the Small Claims Rules a judge can only dismiss a claim after discussing the merits of the case and finding that there is no reasonable claim. It did not appear that the judge had heard evidence or discussed the merits of the claim.

The Law Society has published the *Articling Handbook for Principals and Students* (the "handbook") which sets out in detail the objectives of the bar admission course and the authority of articled students-at-law to appear before courts and tribunals.

Wei Estate v. Dales (1998), 37 O.R. (3d) 548, 16 C.P.C. (4th) 29 (Ont. Gen. Div.) — The issue was whether there was a reasonable apprehension of bias of the judge who was to hear the trial because the judge had been improperly informed by plaintiff's counsel of the pre-trial judge's views as to liability. The judge held that there was no statutory restriction prohibiting him from hearing the trial and further, he could not see how knowing of the pre-trial judge's views on liability would preclude him from conducting the trial of the action in an entirely impartial manner. See Rules 50.03 and 50.04 of the *Rules of Civil Procedure* (Pre-trials), and the problems of correspondence being sent by counsel to judges in advance of the trial or after the trial and before the final decision has been reached.

Rumbaua v. Byrne (January 11, 1999), Doc. Vancouver 96-30864 (B.C. Prov. Ct.) — Application by Rumbaua to dismiss the defence and enter a default judgment. Application dismissed. There was no express or implied authority to grant a default judgment at settlement conference. The consequences for failure to be prepared were limited to an order for costs. The defendants were ordered to pay costs of $300 to Rumbaua.

Webb v. Stewart (January 19, 1998), Doc. Vancouver A970068 (B.C. S.C.), Lysyk J. — Appeal of a dismissal of an action. The appeal was granted. Webb was told to disclose the documents to Stewart and the others before the settlement conference. He complied with the strict wording of the order. The presiding judge was restricted in her jurisdiction to dismiss Webb's action at the settlement conference. Webb had a reasonable claim. Liability and damages were triable issues.

M.R.S. Trust Co. v. 835099 Ontario Ltd. (November 18, 1998), Doc. St. J. 2393/93 (Nfld. T.D.) — The court ruled it was premature to award costs of a pretrial hearing to the defendants, who were successful in having claims. Relevance of evidence taken and documents produced at a pretrial hearing should be determined at the conclusion of the proceeding.

Baird v. Taylor (2000), 2000 CarswellOnt 3804 (Ont. S.C.J.) — A lawyer refused to attend a settlement conference after the judge refused his request to proceed by way of telephone conference. The judge had jurisdiction to award costs of abortive conference against the lawyer.

Giza v. Eastwood & Co., 2001 BCSC 199, 2001 CarswellBC 476, [2001] B.C.J. No. 192 (B.C. S.C.) — The defendant was unwilling to settle. The judge ordered a $100 penalty, which exceeded jurisdiction. A default judgment was ordered against the defendant. The defendant misunderstood the procedure but made no effort to follow up or to clarify what was going on. The judgment was upheld.

Wood v. Siwak, 2000 BCSC 397, 21 Admin. L.R. (3d) 310, 2000 CarswellBC 559 (B.C. S.C. [In Chambers]) — There is general obligation on a settlement conference judge to facilitate a settlement process and ensure that all legal issues are properly canvassed and that parties are dealt with fairly. The settlement conference judge must make all reasonable inquiries to determine the validity of the claim and consider all relevant facts and issues before summarily dismissing the claim.

To v. Toronto (City) Board of Education (2001), 55 O.R. (3d) 641, 2001 CarswellOnt 3048, 204 D.L.R. (4th) 704, 150 O.A.C. 54 (Ont. C.A.); additional reasons at (2001), 2001 CarswellOnt 3727 (Ont. C.A.) — Failure to respond meaningfully to request to admit might constitute relevant factor if it prolonged trial or otherwise added to trial costs. Defendant's appeal from costs order allowed. Plaintiffs awarded party-and-party costs throughout subject to direction to assessment officer to assess solicitor-and-client costs for any time that trial extended because of defendant's failure to respond appropriately to request to admit.

Yannacoulias v. Yannacoulias, 17 C.P.C. (5th) 260, 2002 CarswellSask 219, 2002 SKQB 163, 34 C.B.R. (4th) 145, 218 Sask. R. 251 (Sask. Q.B.) — Y made assignment in bankruptcy, and was not yet discharged. Y's former partners G and T brought several actions against Y. Y refused to participate in pre-trial conference. G and T brought application for order setting pre-trial conference. Application granted. Not all claims against Y were provable in bankruptcy. Focus of pre-trial conferences had become settlement and issues best dealt with if all litigants were present.

Comrie v. Comrie, 2001 CarswellSask 130, [2001] S.J. No. 136, [2001] 7 W.W.R. 294, 2001 SKCA 33, 197 D.L.R. (4th) 223, 203 Sask. R. 164, 240 W.A.C. 164, 17 R.F.L. (5th) 271 (Sask. C.A.) — Following pre-trial conferences, husband and wife agreed to consent judgment. Five years later, husband applied to end spousal support. Rules provided that communications in pre-trial conferences privileged and inadmissible in all proceedings. Trial judge not allowing husband to adduce evidence. Appeal allowed. Evidence relevant and admissible, related to factors and objectives taken into account in fixing spousal support. Procedural rules such as Queen's Bench (Saskatchewan) Rule 191(14), (15), cannot change substantive law (i.e., material change in circumstances).

Scheuneman v. R., 2003 CarswellNat 88, 2003 CarswellNat 4763, 2003 FCT 37, 2003 CFPI 37 (Fed. T.D.); affirmed 2003 CarswellNat 3741, 2003 CarswellNat 4624, 2003 FCA 440, 2003 CAF 440 (F.C.A.); leave to appeal refused (2004), 2004 CarswellNat 378, 2004 CarswellNat 379 (S.C.C.) — Self-represented plaintiff sought to be relieved from obligation of attending pre-trial conference in person because of alleged disability. Plaintiff incapable of representing himself. Plaintiff directed to appoint solicitor. Such solicitor ordered to file further pre-trial conference memorandum in conformity with Rules.

Pete v. Lanouette, 2002 BCSC 75, 2002 CarswellBC 98 (B.C. Master) — Disclosure of documents relating to "any matter in question in the action." Public interest may trump any privilege if wrongdoing may result from the failure to disclose.

519080 Alberta Ltd. v. Turtle Mountain Tire & Battery, 2002 ABPC 108, 2002 CarswellAlta 1312, [2002] A.J. No. 1316 (Alta. Prov. Ct.) — Pre-trial conference ruling dealing with issue of taking a single cause of action arising out of one factual situation and splitting same to be the subject of several actions. Choices provided to the plaintiff. *Cahoon v. Franks*, [1967] S.C.R. 455, 1967 CarswellAlta 48, 60 W.W.R. 684, 63 D.L.R. (2d) 274 (S.C.C.); *Maple Lodge Farms Ltd. v. Penny Lane Fruit Market Inc.*, [1997] O.J. No. 4401, 1997 CarswellOnt 4306 (Ont. Gen. Div.); *Malcolm v. Carr*, [1997] 7 W.W.R. 371, 1997 CarswellAlta 481, [1997] A.J. No. 485, 200 A.R. 53, 146 W.A.C. 53, 51 Alta. L.R. (3d) 66 (Alta. C.A.); and *Wah Loong Ltd. v. Fortune Garden Restaurant (Richmond) Ltd.*, [2000] B.C.J. No. 1581, 2000 BCPC 163, 2000 CarswellBC 2838 (B.C. Prov. Ct.) referred to.

OBP Realty (Pickering Centre) Inc. v. Ladowsky (2003), 2003 CarswellOnt 1877 (Ont. S.C.J.). Defendant brought motion to set aside default judgment that was entered against him as a result of his failure to pay costs. Motion dismissed. Defendant did not suffer from hardship, and because he was consulting with solicitor, he understood consequences of his failure to pay.

Homewood Enterprises Ltd. v. 147486 Canada Ltd., 2003 CarswellNS 70, 2003 NSSC 24, 212 N.S.R. (2d) 390, 665 A.P.R. 390 (N.S. S.C.). Plaintiff discontinued one week before trial. Defendant had completed trial preparation. Defendant awarded costs of $1,700. Plaintiff prohibited from commencing fresh action until costs paid.

Lowe v. Redding, 2003 CarswellBC 778, 2003 BCSC 356, 14 B.C.L.R. (4th) 192 (B.C. S.C. [In Chambers]). Plaintiff suing for defamation. Defendant making offer to settle for zero dollars and costs. Plaintiff seeking award of costs. Application allowed. While amount within jurisdiction of Small Claims Court, action for defamation not permitted in Small Claims Court.

Eco-Tourism 2010 Society v. Vancouver 2010 Bid Corp., 2005 CarswellBC 245, 2005 BCPC 23, [2005] B.C.J. No. 203 (B.C. Prov. Ct.), K.D. Skilnick, P.C.J. Dismissal of claim at a settlement conference is a remedy to be used sparingly and only in clear cases. When it is clear the court has no jurisdiction to hear the claim brought, appropriate to dismiss the claim at this stage. The facts supporting the jurisdictional claim must be "plain and obvious." See *Hunt v. T & N plc*, 1990 CarswellBC 759, 1990 CarswellBC 216, (sub nom. *Hunt v. Carey Canada Inc.*) [1990] S.C.J. No. 93, 4 C.C.L.T. (2d) 1, 43 C.P.C. (2d) 105, 117 N.R. 321, 4 C.O.H.S.C. 173 (headnote only), (sub nom. *Hunt v. Carey Canada Inc.*) [1990] 6 W.W.R. 385, 49 B.C.L.R. (2d) 273, (sub nom. *Hunt v. Carey Canada Inc.*) 74 D.L.R. (4th) 321, [1990] 2 S.C.R. 959 (S.C.C.); the party against whom the application is made, particularly an unrepresented party, ought to be given a reasonable opportunity to obtain legal advice, and a reasonable explanation as to the argument and caselaw the other side will be relying on. The Court must be satisfied generally that there is no purpose to be served by proceeding to a settlement conference. Appropriate case to make order under Rule 7(14)(i) dismissing claim brought by Claimant.

Halsey v. Milton Keynes General NHS Trust, [2004] E.W.C.A. Civ. 576 (C.A.). The refusal of a party to participate in mediation can result in costs being awarded against that party even if that party is ultimately successful at trial, according to the Court of Appeal (Civil Division) of the English Supreme Court of Judicature.

Halsey ultimately unsuccessful at trial and costs were awarded to the Hospital. Halsey argued that Hospital acted unreasonably in refusing to agree to attend mediation and, for that reason, trial judge wrong to award Hospital its costs. Scope for court to deprive party ultimately successful in action, of some or all of its costs on the ground that it refused to agree to ADR. This is important where parties ask Court to consider the implications of an offer to settle (Rule 49). Given current requirement that parties attend mandatory mediation in case managed actions, this case of relevance in actions where the quantum of damages is less than $50,000 or in non-case managed actions.

Hagel v. Giles, 2006 CarswellOnt 805, 80 O.R. (3d) 170 (Ont. S.C.J.) 2006-02-14.

Defendants seek judgment in accordance with alleged settlement of proceeding which, they say, was reached at a mediation. They say parties agreed to an order or judgment dismissing this action on a without costs basis and upon delivery by the Plaintiff of a written full and final release of the Defendants.

The purpose of mandatory mediation is to "reduce cost and delay in litigation and facilitate the early and fair resolution of disputes." (See r. 24.1.01.) The mediator's role is to "act as a neutral third party to facilitate communication among the parties to a dispute, to assist them in reaching a mutually acceptable resolution." (See r. 24.1.02.) See *Rogacki v. Belz*, [2003] O.J. No. 3809, 2003 CarswellOnt 3717, 232 D.L.R. (4th) 523, 177 O.A.C. 133, 67 O.R. (3d) 330, 41 C.P.C. (5th) 78 (Ont. C.A.), Borins J.A. at para. 18.

See also Lederman J. in *Rudd v. Trossacs Investments Inc.*, [2004] O.J. No. 2918, 2004 CarswellOnt 2863, 244 D.L.R. (4th) 758, 72 O.R. (3d) 62, 7 C.P.C. (6th) 1 (Ont. S.C.J.).

There is a large body of common law precedent permitting a court to enforce an oral settlement under r. 20 and r. 49.09, as well as beyond the scope of these two rules.

Second thoughts do not constitute a valid reason for refusing to enforce agreements. (See, e.g., *Belanger v. Southwestern Insulation Contractors Ltd.*, 1993 CarswellOnt 507, [1993]

O.J. No. 3095, 16 O.R. (3d) 457, 32 C.P.C. (3d) 256 (Ont. Gen. Div.); *Stoewner v. Hanneson*, [1992] O.J. No. 697, 1992 CarswellOnt 3695 (Ont. Gen. Div.); and *Trembath v. Trembath*, [1993] O.J. No. 202, 1993 CarswellOnt 3974 (Ont. Gen. Div.).)

Defendants entitled to judgment in accordance with the settlement effected between the parties. Action dismissed without costs and Plaintiff to execute a full and final release of the Defendants.

McRandall v. Burzic, 2006 CarswellOnt 5321 (Ont. Sm. Cl. Ct.), September 1, 2006, J.D. Searle D.J.

Motion by plaintiff that order made on June 16, 2006 by Deputy Judge MacKenzie be set aside. During pre-trial Deputy Judge MacKenzie struck plaintiff's claim for disclosing no reasonable cause of action.

The matter pre-tried by Deputy Judge Lepine who ordered particulars.

Case came before Deputy Judge MacKenzie for a third pre-trial or a second resumption of the pre-trial or what some call a "reference."

Question whether relief sought in motion properly before this court or be before the appeal court.

Court reluctant to pass judgment on Deputy Judge Little or Deputy Judge MacKenzie. Unacceptable that any judge be put in position of passing judgment on other judges of the same rank.

394705 Ont. Ltd. v. Moerenhout, 1983 CarswellOnt 452, 35 C.P.C. 258, 41 O.R. (2d) 637 (Ont. Co. Ct.) (Salhany J.) referred to.

Section 31 of the *Courts of Justice Act* grants a right of appeal to the Divisional Court "from a final order of the Small Claims Court." Order of Deputy Judge MacKenzie is a final order because it disposes of a substantive right of a party. See *Bachmann Trust Co. v. Singer*, [2005] O.J. No. 612, 2005 CarswellOnt 9183 (Ont. Div. Ct.).

Motion dismissed. Costs in the cause.

Greeley v. Town Council for Conception Bay South (Town), 2006 CarswellNfld 194, 2006 NLTD 109, 779 A.P.R. 254, 258 Nfld. & P.E.I.R. 254, 36 C.P.C. (6th) 280 (N.L. T.D.), Halley J.

Powers of settlement conference judge. Settlement conference judge dismissed appellant's claim against respondent on basis limitation period expired. Judge did not have power to dismiss without considering evidence and arguments of parties which could only take place during trial. Dismissal set aside and matter remitted to Provincial Court for trial.

Moudry v. Moudry, 2006 CarswellOnt 6010, 216 O.A.C. 84, 33 R.F.L. (6th) 52 (Ont. C.A.).

Mother appealed regarding custody and contempt. Court of Appeal allowed appeal, set aside the portions of the trial judge's decision dealing with custody and contempt. Although mother clearly had an obligation to attend mini pre-trial, her failure to do so should not have resulted in her losing the right to be present at the trial. The mother was denied the right to be heard as she could not participate at the trial or give evidence.

Appellant denied right to be heard, fundamental to our justice system, as she could not participate at the trial or give evidence. See *Supermarchés Jean Labrecque Inc. v. Québec (Tribunal du travail)*, EYB 1987-67731, 1987 CarswellQue 89, 1987 CarswellQue 94, 43 D.L.R. (4th) 1, 78 N.R. 201, [1987] 2 S.C.R. 219, 28 Admin. L.R. 239, 9 Q.A.C. 161, 87 C.L.L.C. 14,045 (S.C.C.), at para. 46.

Enns v. Caithcart, 2006 CarswellSask 131, [2006] S.J. No. 145, 2006 SKQB 102, 277 Sask. R. 1, 30 C.P.C. (6th) 135 (Sask. Q.B.).

Pre-trial conference respecting two actions between parties held and agreement respecting all outstanding issues negotiated and signed by parties. Party brought application for summary judgment based on agreement reached at pre-trial conference. Application dismissed with leave to bring further application. Since party did not seek resumption of pre-trial conference but sought instead judicial ruling respecting agreement, judge presiding over reconvened pre-trial conference had no jurisdiction to make any judicial rulings that were binding on parties except those of trial management nature.

IPL Inc. c. Hofmann Plastics Canada Inc., 2006 CarswellNat 3648, 2006 CF 1343 (F.C.), Morneau Prothonotary.

Pre-trial procedures. Motion dismissed. Court may try issues separately where it is of opinion that doing so will lead to just result in most expeditious and economical way. Court could not draw conclusion at this stage of proceedings that patent was invalid.

Brar v. Trevren Enterprises Ltd., 2008 CarswellBC 290, 2008 BCPC 18 (B.C. Prov. Ct.), J. Auxier Prov. J.

At settlement conference to be held on November 15, 2007 neither of named claimants attended, nor did anyone attend on behalf of corporate claimant. Claim dismissed.

Failure of claimants to appear at settlement conference not wilful, but inadvertent. They acted promptly in taking steps to set the order aside.

Applicant must also satisfy court claim worthy of investigation. Claimants would not succeed in action for return of deposit. Application to set aside dismissal order dismissed.

Canada (Attorney General) v. Ketenjian (2007), 2008 CarswellOnt 1356 (Ont. Div. Ct.), Cumming J.

Respondent Attorney General of Canada awarded judgment in Small Claims Court against appellant Ketenjian (self represented on this appeal), for $3,167.82, plus postjudgment interest for monies owing for an outstanding Canada-Ontario integrated student loan issued January 7, 2005.

Judgment given by Deputy Judge by endorsement at a settlement conference. She also struck Mr. Ketenjian's defence and claim without leave to amend at that time, pursuant to Rule 13.05(1) and (2) of the *Small Claims Court Rules*. No real defence to the Attorney General of Canada's claim. Deputy Judge had jurisdiction to make endorsement she made.

Appeal dismissed.

Oz Merchandising Inc. v. Lianos (2007), 2007 CarswellOnt 2463, 49 C.P.C. (6th) 158, [2007] O.J. No. 1565 (Ont. S.C.J.)

Plaintiff sought to set aside a prior order by a case management master dismissing its action for failure to file a settlement conference memorandum, which was not filed due to change of plaintiff's solicitors. The default judgment was set aside.

There was no real prejudice to defendant apart from loosing benefit that accrued from default. Justice could not be achieved where one party seeks to take advantage of an honest mistake of the other, particularly where the party who enjoys the benefit of a default judgment resulting from something as simple as the failure to file a settlement conference memorandum.

Jacobs v. Ottawa Police Services Board (2008), 2008 CarswellOnt 1635, 234 O.A.C. 140 (Ont. Div. Ct.)

The plaintiff appealed a decision of a Small Claims Court judge in which he dismissed her claim as disclosing no cause of action at a settlement conference. Appeal allowed. A judge conducting a settlement conference may make any order relating to the conduct of the action that the court could make. The word "conduct" suggests that such orders be limited to procedural issues, not substantive issues unless on consent. In the absence of the consent of the parties at the settlement conference the trial judge exceeded his jurisdiction.

R. v. Gregoire, 2008 CarswellOnt 3377, 2008 ONCA 459, [2008] O.J. No. 2261 (Ont. C.A.); leave to appeal refused (2009), [2008] S.C.C.A. No. 489, 2009 CarswellOnt 436, 2009 CarswellOnt 437, 395 N.R. 383 (note) (S.C.C.)

Judges who conduct pre-trials should avoid conducting the trial. However, it is not per se reversible error to do so. It is possible for a pre-trial judge to preside over the trial where there is the absence of any clear objection from counsel and prejudice.

R. v. Li (2008), 2008 CarswellOnt 1568, 231 C.C.C. (3d) 563 (Ont. S.C.J.)

As part of the application, the accused sought the notes of the judges who presided at the two pre-trials. The accused submitted that the records would shed some light on why a second pre-trial was necessary. Application dismissed. The actions of a pre-trial judge, including note-taking, enjoyed complete immunity. This was not a case where there was no other extrinsic evidence to establish the pre-trial information, and neither was this an exceptional case where privilege must give way to ensure confidence in the administration of justice.

Sabo v. Clément, 2008 CarswellYukon 44, 2008 YKCA 6, 436 W.A.C. 7, 259 B.C.A.C. 7 (Y.T. C.A.)

Plaintiff brought action against various government officials in relation to alleged meteorite found by plaintiff. Case management judge who presided over ten case management conferences refused to become involved in plaintiff' allegations at last conference. Plaintiff applied to have case management judge recuse himself from case on grounds of bias or reasonable apprehension of bias. Case management judge dismissed plaintiff's recusal motion and plaintiff appealed. Appeal dismissed.

Informed person would not conclude that it was more likely that case management judge would not decide case fairly. Judge explained his refusal to become involved in plaintiff's allegations of misconduct on basis that cases could be sidetracked by such allegations. Judge made every effort to explain process and rules to plaintiff; if plaintiff misunderstood judge's comments, it could not be laid at court's feet. Although case management judge did not err in restricting his consideration to last conference, there was no basis for allegations of bias in transcripts of earlier conferences either.

Landmark Realty Corp. v. 0763486 B.C. Ltd., 2009 BCSC 810, 2009 CarswellBC 1606 (B.C. S.C.), Fisher, J.

Petitioner sought judicial review of order made by a Provincial Court judge during a mandatory Small Claims settlement conference conducted under Rule 7 of the *Small Claims Rules*. Petitioner contended settlement conference judge exceeded his jurisdiction by making a final order granting judgment in favour of Respondent in the absence of notice, evidence and submissions.

Judge dismissed Reply and awarded judgment in favour of Landmark for $6,477.41 plus costs. He did so under the authority of Rule 7(14)(i) of the *Small Claims Rules*:

(14) At a settlement conference, a judge may do one or more of the following: . . .

(i) dismiss a claim, counterclaim, reply or third party notice if, after discussion with the parties and reviewing the filed documents, a judge determines that it

(i) is without reasonable grounds,

(ii) discloses no triable issue, or

(iii) is frivolous or an abuse of the court's process; . . .

Provincial Court judge is entitled to deference in the exercise of his or her discretion.

Appropriate standard of review in this case is reasonableness.

Proceedings in Small Claims Court are designed to be relatively simple and affordable, recognizing that many litigants are self-represented but are still governed by substantive law and the *Small Claims Act* and *Rules*.

Obligation on settlement conference judge to facilitate the settlement process, ensure that all legal issues are properly canvassed and treat all parties fairly, particularly where a litigant is self-represented.

Judge made order on his own motion, after discussing the case with the parties.

Rule 7(14) does not permit a settlement conference judge to dismiss a claim against a party where there is a factual dispute which must be determined through the receipt of evidence.

Decision by settlement conference judge to dismiss the Developer's Replay not "within a range of possible, acceptable outcomes which are defensible in respect of the facts and law" (see *Dunsmuir* New Brunswick, 2008 SCC 9 at para. 47), and is therefore unreasonable. Decision quashed and the matter remitted back to the Provincial Court for trial.

Aronowicz v. EMTWO Properties Inc., 64 B.L.R. (4th) 163, 2010 ONCA 96, 2010 Carswell-Ont 598, (sub nom. *Aronowicz v. Emto Properties Inc.*) 316 D.L.R. (4th) 621, (sub nom. *Aronowicz v. Emto Properties Inc.*) 258 O.A.C. 222, [2010] O.J. No. 475, 98 O.R. (3d) 641 (Ont. C.A.).

Proper test for summary judgment, as articulated in *Irving Ungerman Ltd. v. Galanis* (1991), 1991 CarswellOnt 370, 83 D.L.R. (4th) 734, 20 R.P.R. (2d) 49 (note), 1 C.P.C. (3d) 248, (sub nom. *Ungerman (Irving) Ltd. v. Galanis)* 50 O.A.C. 176, 4 O.R. (3d) 545, [1991] O.J. No. 1478 (Ont. C.A.), at pp. 550-551, is whether there is a genuine issue of material fact that requires a trial for its resolution. See also *Aguonie v. Galion Solid Waste Material Inc.* (1998), [1998] O.J. No. 459, 156 D.L.R. (4th) 222, 17 C.P.C. (4th) 219, 1998 CarswellOnt 417, 107 O.A.C. 114, 38 O.R. (3d) 161 (Ont. C.A.) and *Dawson v. Rexcraft Storage & Warehouse Inc.* (1998), 20 R.P.R. (3d) 207, 1998 CarswellOnt 3202, 164 D.L.R. (4th) 257, 111 O.A.C. 201, [1998] O.J. No. 3240, 26 C.P.C. (4th) 1 (Ont. C.A.).

See *Papaschase Indian Band No. 136 v. Canada (Attorney General)*, 2008 CarswellAlta 398, 2008 CarswellAlta 399, [2008] S.C.J. No. 14, (sub nom. *Lameman v. Canada (Attorney General))* 372 N.R. 239, [2008] 5 W.W.R. 195, 2008 SCC 14, [2008] 2 C.N.L.R. 295, 68 R.P.R. (4th) 59, 292 D.L.R. (4th) 49, (sub nom. *Canada (Attorney General) v. Lameman)* [2008] 1 S.C.R. 372, (sub nom. *Lameman v. Canada (Attorney General))* 429 A.R. 26, (sub nom. *Lameman v. Canada (Attorney General))* 421 W.A.C. 26, 86 Alta. L.R. (4th) 1 (S.C.C.) and *Guarantee Co. of North America v. Gordon Capital Corp.* (1999), 39 C.P.C. (4th) 100, 1999 CarswellOnt 3172, 1999 CarswellOnt 3171, [1999] S.C.J. No. 60, 178 D.L.R. (4th) 1, 15 C.C.L.I. (3d) 1, [1999] 3 S.C.R. 423, 49 B.L.R. (2d) 68, 247 N.R. 97, 126 O.A.C. 1, [2000] I.L.R. I-3741 (S.C.C.). Defendants moved for summary judgment under rule 20.04 and for the determination of a question of law under rule 21.01(1)(a).

Generally courts reluctant to determine unsettled matters of law at a pre-trial stage — including on motions for summary judgment, on theory new or important questions of law should not be determined on an incomplete factual records. See e.g., *Romano v. D'Onofrio* (2005), 262 D.L.R. (4th) 181, [2005] O.J. No. 4969, 77 O.R. (3d) 583, 2005 CarswellOnt 6725 at para. 7 (Ont. C.A.) and *Bendix Foreign Exchange Corp. v. Integrated Payment Systems Canada Inc.* (2005), [2005] O.J. No. 2241, 2005 CarswellOnt 2224, 18 C.P.C. (6th) 15 at para. 6 (Ont. C.A.).

Court may determine question of law on motion for summary judgment if it has the necessary undisputed factual record before it, is in just as good a position as the trial judge would be to do so, and is satisfied the only genuine issue is a question of law. See e.g., *Bader v. Rennie* (2007), [2007] O.J. No. 3441, 2007 CarswellOnt 5778, 229 O.A.C. 320 at para. 22 (Ont. Div. Ct.); additional reasons at (2008), 2008 CarswellOnt 700, 233 O.A.C. 390 (Ont.

Div. Ct.); *Robinson v. Ottawa (City)* (2009), 2009 CarswellOnt 280, 55 M.P.L.R. (4th) 283 at paras. 63-64 (Ont. S.C.J.); additional reasons at (2009), 2009 CarswellOnt 2669 (Ont. S.C.J.); *Alexis v. Darnley*, 79 C.P.C. (6th) 10, 2009 ONCA 847, 2009 CarswellOnt 7518, 259 O.A.C. 148, [2009] O.J. No. 5170, 100 O.R. (3d) 232 (Ont. C.A.) at para. 19, leave to appeal refused 407 N.R. 397 (note), 2010 CarswellOnt 2638, 2010 CarswellOnt 2637, 271 O.A.C. 399 (note) (S.C.C.).

Attornment is when a person appears as a defendant in a court that would not ordinarily have personal jurisdiction over the respondent and pleads to the merits of an applicant's case. The appearance and pleading on the merits taken as a waiver of any objection to the court's personal jurisdiction over defendant. A party who attorns is still *not* prevented from raising the issue of the proper forum: *Follwell v. Holmes*, [2006] O.J. No. 4387, 2006 CarswellOnt 6776 (Ont. S.C.J.), where the court found Nicaragua (a non-reciprocating jurisdiction) to be a more appropriate jurisdiction to hear case than Ontario, and stayed the Ontario case.

Tiwana v. Sandhu, 2010 ONCA 592, 2010 CarswellOnt 6822, [2010] O.J. No. 3862 (Ont. C.A.)

Husband was ordered on three different occasions before three different judges to make financial disclosure. Motion judge gave husband one last chance but he failed again to do so. Motion to strike pleadings was heard *ex parte* and was successful. Court of Appeal stated that the decision to strike pleadings and determine the parameters of trial participation was discretionary that deserved deference on appeal when exercised on proper principles. Ordinarily, striking any pleadings on *ex parte* basis where that party purports to have made required disclosure was practice that Court of Appeal could not endorse, preferring that striking order be on notice to affected party so that he or she could explain or assert compliance with prior disclosure order. Compare with *Stephens v. Stephens*, 2010 ONCA 586, [2010] O.J. No. 3765, 2010 CarswellOnt 6690, 89 R.F.L. (6th) 260, 324 D.L.R. (4th) 169 (Ont. C.A.).

Watch Lake North Green Lake Volunteer Fire Department Society v. Haskins, 2010 CarswellBC 1605, 2010 BCPC 114, 71 B.L.R. (4th) 101 (B.C. Prov. Ct.).

Former directors acted in good faith and within scope of their authority. The Court had jurisdiction to hear application to dismiss proceedings. Rule 16(6)(o) of B.C. *Small Claims Rules* gave authority to dismiss proceedings. Fact that application brought prior to settlement conference not fatal.

Elliott v. Turbitt, 2011 ONSC 3637, 2011 CarswellOnt 6117, [2011] O.J. No. 3116 (Ont. Master), Master Joan M. Haberman.

Pre-trial procedures. Severance. Of actions. The defendants brought a motion for the severance of a counterclaim from the main action. The motion was granted. This was a rare case in which the relief claimed was appropriate. The plaintiffs were guilty of excessive delay and did not appear to be serious about pursuing the action. The result of the counterclaim might resolve the main action.

A recent decision from the U.S. District Court of Montana examines when a court can compel settlement after a party settles in principle but then reconsiders before executing a written agreement. See *U.S. Fid. & Guar. Co. and Cont'l Ins. Co. v. Soco W., Inc.* The decision also highlights the problems that occur when clients and their counsel fail to clearly communicate about the details of settlement agreements. A party is bound to a settlement agreement if he or she manifested assent to the terms and did not manifest an intent not to be bound. The district court stated, "It is presumed that an attorney-of-record who enters into a settlement agreement had authority to do so."

(4) Further Disclosure Restricted — Except as otherwise provided or with the consent of the parties (Form 13B), the matters discussed at the settlement conference shall not be disclosed to others until after the action has been disposed of.

History [R. 13.03(4)]: Formerly 14.03(3); plain language changes.

(5) [Repealed O. Reg. 78/06, s. 27.]

History [R. 13.03(5)]: Formerly part of 14.03(4), except more detailed; lists the information that may be provided in the pre-trial conference memorandum; clerk's duties separated out into another subrule (13.03(6)).

(6) [Repealed O. Reg. 78/06, s. 27.]

O. Reg. 78/06, s. 27

History [R. 13.03(6)]: Contains clerk's duties from former 14.03(4); provision added that the clerk shall provide copies to the trial judge.

13.04 Recommendations to Parties — The court may make recommendations to the parties on any matter relating to the conduct of the action, in order to fulfil the purposes of a settlement conference, including recommendations as to,

    (a) the clarification and simplification of issues in the action;

    (b) the elimination of claims or defences that appear to be unsupported; and

    (c) the admission of facts or documents without further proof.

O. Reg. 78/06, s. 27

History [R. 13.04]: Formerly 14.04.

Commentary: *Lucy v. Kitchener (City)*, 2013 CarswellOnt 381, 6 M.P.L.R. (5th) 285 (Ont. Sm. Cl. Ct.)

Disclosure of settlement conference discussions during costs submissions to the trial judge, even on consent, is prohibited.

Filippova v. Arvato Digital Services Canada Inc. (August 1, 2012), Doc. 1212/11, [2012] O.J. No. 3623 (Ont. Sm. Cl. Ct.)

A settlement conference judge's comments about the merits of the case cannot be disclosed to the trial judge during costs submissions. The parties are responsible for their own assessments of the merits of the case.

Mandatory attendance is prescribed. Both the representative and party must be present personally at the settlement conference. Telephone conference under subrule 1.07 can also ensure personal presence.

If the person to approve a settlement is not present, that person must be available by "ready telephone access."

If a party fails to attend, the sanctions include costs and ordering an "Additional Settlement Conference." Failure by the defendant to attend the additional settlement conference can result in the striking of the defence and an order dismissing the defendant's claim. The plaintiff may be allowed to prove their claim for a liquidated amount, and obtain judgment. The powers to make orders under subrule 13.05(2)(a)(v) will be invoked with respect to dismissing the claim or striking the defence to a defendant's claim.

Since July 1, 2006 for matters up to $2,500, the parties may file written consent in advance of the settlement conference date to have a mediator grant Judgment, should a settlement not be reached (subrule 13.05(4)).

The mediator cannot be the trial judge even on consent. Matters "discussed" may not be disclosed until the action is disposed of (subrule 13.02(4)).

A claim may not be withdrawn after a settlement conference unless there is consent or an order is made at a motion.

The settlement conference judge can make recommendations on the Settlement Conference Memorandum (subrule 13.06). They can endorse various Orders (subrules 13.05(1), (2) and (4)) on the Endorsement Record.

Notice with respect to setting the matter down and paying the trial fee is contained in the Settlement Conference Endorsement Record. The clerk only sends the Endorsement Record to absent parties.

The costs sanction at each settlement conference is $100 exclusive of disbursements. Disbursements might include accommodation expenses in addition to court fees and parking or travel expenses.

Section 29 of the *Courts of Justice Act* only applies if there is a further "need" to penalize someone. The limit of 15 per cent of the amount claimed applies to each costs award.

The $100 can be increased where "the court orders otherwise because there are special circumstances." A costs award under rules 13 or 15 is not considered part of the 15 per cent limit set by section 29 in an award of costs after trial.

It is worthwhile considering the purposes of the former rule for Discovery process since in many ways the pre-trial process in the Small Claims Court serves the same purposes:

1. to enable the examining party to know the case to be met;

2. to enable the procuring of admissions which will dispense with other formal proof of the case;

3. to procure admissions that will destroy an opponent's case;

4. to facilitate settlement, pre-trials and trials;

5. to eliminate or narrow issues;

6. to avoid surprises at trial; and

7. to request parties to provide witness lists within specified time.

See *Modriski v. Arnold*, [1947] O.W.N. 483 (Ont. C.A.) and *Malofy v. Andrew Merrilees Ltd.* (1982), 37 O.R. (2d) 711 (Ont. Div. Ct.).

At or after the pre-trial conference, the clerk must provide a Notice to the pre-trial parties stating that the parties must request a trial date if the action is not disposed of within 30 days after the pre-trial conference, and pay the fee required for setting the action down for trial. At the end of the pre-trial, the judge or designated person may file with the clerk a memorandum summarizing the pre-trial conference. A copy of the memorandum must be given to the trial judge. This document is public record.

Green v. Green (August 19, 2008), Doc. Toronto 110/08 (Ont. Div. Ct.)

The motion to adjourn to obtain a transcript of the trial management conference was denied. The presence of the court reporter at the conference is a practice adopted when a litigant is unrepresented. The transcript cannot be ordered without the permission of the conference judge. To grant an adjournment based on the hope that the permission would be granted makes no sense.

Rule 38.15 of the *Rules of Civil Procedure* does not assist. It contemplates a transcript of oral evidence — nothing more. No one gave oral evidence at the case management conference.

Neddow v. Weidemann, 2008 CarswellAlta 886, 2008 ABQB 378, 56 C.P.C. (6th) 193, 92 Alta. L.R. (4th) 331 (Alta. Q.B.)

Defendant's lawyer drafted order which plaintiff's lawyer refused to sign. Defendant brought an application for advice and directions on signing court order resulting from conference. Application granted. Plaintiff's lawyer had professional obligation to sign the court order as there were no circumstances, such as fraud, lack of capacity or the form of order being inaccurate, which required fresh instructions from the client.

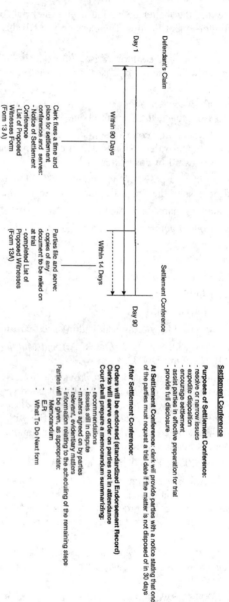

A SMALL CLAIMS COURT CLAIM - 2006 (Amended Rules)
MANDATORY SETTLEMENT CONFERENCES - Rule 13
A Case Flow Chart

Settlement Conference

Purposes of Settlement Conference:
- resolve or narrow issues
- expedite disposition
- encourage settlement
- assist parties in effective preparation for trial
- provide full disclosure

At Settlement Conference: clerk will provide parties with a notice stating that one of the parties must request a trial date if the matter is not disposed of in 30 days

After Settlement Conference:

Orders will be endorsed (standardized Endorsement Record)
Clerks will serve order on parties not in attendance
Court shall prepare a memorandum summarizing:
- recommendations
- issues still in dispute
- matters agreed on by parties
- relevant, evidentiary matters
- information relating to the scheduling of the remaining steps

Parties will be given, as appropriate:
- Memorandum
- E.R.
- What To Do Next form

Defendant's Claim

Day 1

Within 90 Days

Within 14 Days

Day 90

Settlement Conference

Clerk fixes a time and place for settlement conference and serves:
- Notice of Settlement Conference
- List of Proposed Witnesses Form (Form 13.A)

Parties file and serve:
- copies of any document to be relied on at trial
- completed List of Proposed Witnesses (Form 13A)

Prepared by: patti cross
Office of the Chief Justice
March 2, 2006

690

Case Law: *Marcon Custom Metals Inc. v. Arlat Environmental Inc.* (2001), 2001 CarswellOnt 2928 (Ont. S.C.J.) — At pre-trial for debt action defendants sought to amend defence and counterclaim and add new parties. Plaintiffs failed to show prejudice not compensable in costs. Amendment allowed on terms including immediate payment of solicitor-client costs of joinder and amendment.

Ryan v. Charters Estate (2001), 2001 CarswellOnt 4347 (Ont. S.C.J.) — Trial judge dismissed motion to set aside his judgment on basis he had conducted pretrial conference. Whether meeting between trial judge and counsel and clients was pretrial conference and, if so, whether new trial should be ordered were issues to be addressed on appeal.

Cridge v. Turner, 2006 CarswellBC 578, 2006 BCSC 407 (B.C. S.C.) 2006-03-13.

In 2004, Cridge brought action in Small Claims Court for return of alleged $1,000 retainer held by Turner, a lawyer. Turner pled the $1,000 was provided as security for legal fees of Cridge's previous lawyer. At a second settlement conference, Challenger J. dismissed the action. Cridge asserted Challenger J. held a bias against her as a "lay litigant" and that she should therefore disqualify herself.

Test to be applied in determining whether or not a reasonable apprehension of bias exists was set out by the Supreme Court of Canada in *Committee for Justice & Liberty v. Canada (National Energy Board)*, 1976 CarswellNat 434, 1976 CarswellNat 434F, [1978] 1 S.C.R. 369, 68 D.L.R. (3d) 716, 9 N.R. 115 (S.C.C.) at para. 40. The test has subsequently been affirmed in a number of cases, including *R. v. S. (R.D.)*, 1997 CarswellNS 301, 1997 CarswellNS 302, [1997] S.C.J. No. 84, 151 D.L.R. (4th) 193, 118 C.C.C. (3d) 353, 10 C.R. (5th) 1, 218 N.R. 1, 161 N.S.R. (2d) 241, 477 A.P.R. 241, [1997] 3 S.C.R. 484, 1 Admin. L.R. (3d) 74 (S.C.C.).

Standard to be applied when reviewing preliminary dismissal of claim by a Provincial Court judge at a settlement conference is that of "patent unreasonableness." *Markel Insurance Co. of Canada v. Kamloops Freightliner Ltd.*, 1997 CarswellBC 1094 (B.C. S.C.); *Atlas Van Lines (Canada) Ltd. v. Strachan*, 1996 CarswellBC 709 (B.C. S.C.).

Decision of judge not patently unreasonable. Relief sought denied.

Kee v. MacDonald, 2006 CarswellPEI 32, 2006 PESCTD 35, 781 A.P.R. 202, 259 Nfld. & P.E.I.R. 202 (P.E.I. T.D.), Matheson J.

Pre-trial procedures. Consolidation or hearing together. Hearing together or sequentially. Government brought motion to consolidate actions. Motion granted.

Jamani v. Encore Promotions Ltd., 2005 CarswellBC 2032, 2005 BCSC 1211 (B.C. S.C.), Crawford J.

Claim against corporation dismissed at settlement conference. Claimant unrepresented at time and appealing dismissal. Appeal adjourned. Small claims court having jurisdiction to dismiss claim. Issue whether claimant properly advised of arguments of corporation prior to settlement conference. Appeal adjourned for further evidence on this issue.

Greeley v. Town Council for Conception Bay South (Town), 2006 CarswellNfld 194, 2006 NLTD 109, 779 A.P.R. 254, 258 Nfld. & P.E.I.R. 254, 36 C.P.C. (6th) 280 (N.L. T.D.), R.J. Halley J.

Plaintiff commenced action in Small Claims Division of Provincial Court. Judge presiding at settlement conference dismissed action on ground that limitation period expired. Plaintiff disputed jurisdiction to dismiss claim. Plaintiff appealed. Appeal allowed. Matter remitted for trial. Object and purpose of settlement conference is to attempt to reach settlement of as many issues as possible with aid of judge. Judge did not have power to dismiss claim without considering evidence and arguments which could only take place during trial of action.

Hawkes v. Aliant Telecom/Island Tel, 2004 CarswellPEI 29, 2004 PESCAD 5 (P.E.I. C.A.)

Appeal of decision of Prothonotary striking out a Statement of Claim on the ground that it discloses no reasonable cause of action. Appeal allowed. The decision of the Prothonotary to strike out the Plaintiff's claim was a quasi-judicial function performed within a required step in the proceeding. While the impugned act of the Prothonotary occurred within a pre-trial conference as contemplated by the Small Claims Section Rules, and as such there was no record, there should be a record regarding this kind of matter. This was a substantive decision that terminated the Plaintiff's claim. A hearing and decision regarding that portion of a pre-trial conference should be recorded.

Wood v. Wong, 2011 BCSC 794, 2011 CarswellBC 1507 (B.C. S.C.), Mr. Justice Greyell.

There was an appeal from the Provincial Court of British Columbia (Civil Claims Division). The judge dismissed the appellant's application to cancel Order for Seizure and Sale and to set aside an Affidavit of Non-Compliance. The case proceeded to mediation. The parties entered into a Mediation Agreement. Wong filed an Affidavit of Non-Compliance with the Provincial Court deposing he had not received payment.

Wood brought an application to cancel the Order.

The application was dismissed. The judge accepted that Wood was in breach of the Mediation Agreement.

13.05 (1) Orders at Settlement Conference — A judge conducting a settlement conference may make any order relating to the conduct of the action that the court could make.

(2) Without limiting the generality of subrule (1), the judge may,

   (a) make an order,

      (i) adding or deleting parties,

      (ii) consolidating actions,

      (iii) with written reasons, staying or dismissing the action,

      (iv) amending or striking out a claim or defence under subrule 12.02(1),

      (v) [Repealed O. Reg. 44/14, s. 12(3).

      (vi) directing production of documents,

      (vii) changing the place of trial under rule 6.01,

      (viii) directing an additional settlement conference under subrule 13.02(3), and

      (ix) ordering costs; and

   (b) at an additional settlement conference, order judgment under subrule 13.02(6).

Commentary: A deputy judge at a settlement conference orders "that the defendant pay costs of $100 before a specific date or the defence will be struck." Can the plaintiff proceed with default judgment if the defendant does not make the payment by the specified date?

Unless the deputy judge's order indicates otherwise, if the defendant fails to pay costs as ordered at a settlement conference, a plaintiff can proceed as if the defence had not been filed. The plaintiff would first file an affidavit indicating that the payment of costs was not made. If the claim was for a liquidated amount, the plaintiff could request default judgment. If the claim amount was not liquidated, the plaintiff could request an assessment hearing or file a motion in writing for an assessment of damages.

Jogendra v. Campbell, 2011 ONSC 272, 2011 CarswellOnt 433, [2011] O.J. No. 356, 275 O.A.C. 130, Ferrier J. (Ont. Div. Ct.)

Appeal of two decisions of deputy judges in the Toronto Small Claims Court:

(i) The decision of Deputy Judge Lévesque dated January 14, 2009, dismissing the appellant's action against the respondent Kenneth Campbell, and

(ii) The decision of Deputy Judge Winer, dated February 23, 2010, dismissing the appellant's motion to set aside the above decision of Deputy Judge Lévesque.

In 1999 the plaintiff, then a Justice of the Peace (JP), was charged with sexual assault. The plaintiff requested reimbursement for his legal expenses. In 2008, the plaintiff commenced a Small Claims action against the defendant, an AG staff member, alleging, *inter alia*, negligence. The claim was identical to a 2007 human rights complaint that had been dismissed. The defendant moved to have the action dismissed. Lévesque, D.J., granted the motion. Winer, D.J., denied the plaintiff's motion to set aside the decision. The Divisional Court, *per* Ferrier, J., dismissed the plaintiff's appeal. As Lévesque, D.J.'s order was a final order, the plaintiff's motion was, in effect, an appeal. Winer, D.J., had no jurisdiction to hear such an appeal. His order to deny the motion was correct. The plaintiff's action was clearly an abuse of process and was frivolous and vexatious. None of the claims had any legal basis or merit. For the plaintiff to suggest that he was protected by judicial immunity was "simply specious." Finally, as the cause of action arose in 1999, it was out of time. Lévesque, D.J.'s order was correct.

The appellant argued that Rule 13.05(2)(b) of the Small Claims Court Rules limits the kinds of orders that can be made at "an additional settlement conference." The court disagreed.

Rule 13.05(2)(b) does not *limit* the powers of the judge, rather, it expands those powers to permit a judge to grant judgment in favour of a plaintiff when a defendant fails to attend two settlement conferences.

This action was an abuse of process and was frivolous and vexatious. The Claim discloses no reasonable cause of action.

Defence was available, though not pleaded in a statement of defence because the statement of claim was such that it was clear that the limitation period had expired. See *Greatrek Trust S.A./Inc. v. Aurelian Resources Inc.*, [2009] O.J. No. 611, 2009 CarswellOnt 748 at para. 10 (Ont. S.C.J.). The appeal was dismissed.

Roskam v. Rogers Cable, 2008 CarswellOnt 2958, (sub nom. *Roskam v. Rogers Cable (A Business)*) 173 C.R.R. (2d) 157, [2008] O.J. No. 2049 (Ont. Div. Ct.)

The court upheld a settlement conference judge's dismissal of a claim based on there being no reasonable cause of action and no provable damages. Authority for dismissal of a claim by a settlement conference judge is specifically provided in rule 13.05(2)(a)(v).

Jacobs v. Ottawa Police Services Board, 2008 CarswellOnt 1635, 234 O.A.C. 140 (Ont. Div. Ct.)

The court held that a settlement conference judge has no jurisdiction to dismiss a claim as disclosing no reasonable cause of action, unless on consent.

Bank of Montreal v. McConnell, 2008 CarswellOnt 5187, [2008] O.J. No. 3464 (Ont. Sm. Cl. Ct.)

The court found that *Roskam v. Rogers Cable, supra*, and *Jacobs v. Ottawa Police Services Board, supra*, were directly conflicting authorities. The court noted that there was no reference to rule 13.05 in *Jacobs*, and preferred to follow *Roskam*.

Case Law: *Kedzior v. Pond*, 2014 ONSC 1561, 2014 CarswellOnt 3155 (Ont. S.C.J.)

After the settlement conference judge dismissed the claim under rule 13.05(2)(a)(v), the plaintiff brought a motion to set aside that order. The motions judge ruled that he had no jurisdiction to hear such a motion because it was in substance an appeal from a final order. On appeal from the motions judge's order, Justice MacKenzie agreed that the settlement conference judge had made a final order which could have been appealed but which the motions judge had no jurisdiction to set aside. The appeal was dismissed.

(3) Recommendations to Judge — If the settlement conference is conducted by a referee, a judge may, on the referee's recommendation, make any order that may be made under subrules (1) and (2).

(4) Consent to Final Judgment — A judge may order final judgment at a settlement conference where the matter in dispute is for an amount under the appealable limit and a party files a consent (Form 13B) signed by all parties before the settlement conference indicating that they wish to obtain final determination of the matter at the settlement conference if a mediated settlement is not reached.

(5) Service of Order — Within 10 days after the judge signs an order made at a settlement conference, the clerk shall serve the order on the parties that were not present at the settlement conference in accordance with subrule 8.01(6).

O. Reg. 78/06, s. 27; 44/14, s. 12

13.06 Memorandum — (1) At the end of the settlement conference, the court shall prepare a memorandum summarizing,

> (a) recommendations made under rule 13.04;

> (b) the issues remaining in dispute;

> (c) the matters agreed on by the parties;

> (d) any evidentiary matters that are considered relevant; and

> (e) information relating to the scheduling of the remaining steps in the proceeding.

(2) The memorandum shall be filed with the clerk, who shall give a copy to the trial judge.

O. Reg. 78/06, s. 27

13.07 Notice of Trial — At or after the settlement conference, the clerk shall provide the parties with a notice stating that one of the parties must request a trial date if the action is not disposed of within 30 days after the settlement conference, and pay the fee required for setting the action down for trial.

O. Reg. 78/06, s. 27

Commentary: Parties are encouraged to make further attempts to settle after the settlement conference if settlement at the conference is not accomplished. There is no fixed time period for any potential further settlement discussions. The reference to a 30-day period in rule 13.07 does not prevent a party from setting the action down for trial during those 30 days, but simply encourages parties to consider a 30-day period for further potential settlement discussions after the settlement conference. If no party sets the action down for trial, the action may be eligible for a clerk's dismissal order under Rule 11.1.01(2).

13.08 Judge Not To Preside At Trial — A judge who conducts a settlement conference in an action shall not preside at the trial of the action.

O. Reg. 78/06, s. 27

13.09 Withdrawal of Claim — After a settlement conference has been held, a claim against a party who is not in default shall not be withdrawn or discontinued by the party who brought the claim without,

> (a) the written consent of the party against whom the claim is brought; or

(b) leave of the court.

O. Reg. 78/06, s. 27

Case Law: *Tuka v. Butt*, 2014 CarswellOnt 2035, [2014] O.J. No. 852 (Ont. Sm. Cl. Ct.)

On motion, the plaintiff was granted leave to discontinue her claim, without costs. The defendant was self-represented and the potential costs award would have been perhaps $100.

Ever Fresh Direct Foods Inc. v. Schindler, 2012 CarswellOnt 9843, [2012] O.J. No. 3673 (Ont. Sm. Cl. Ct.)

The plaintiff made an oral motion for leave to discontinue its claim in Small Claims Court after it issued a related claim in the Superior Court of Justice. The motion was made on the morning of the third scheduled trial date, and after the plaintiff itself had caused the two prior adjournments before retaining counsel who issued the new claim in the Superior Court of Justice. There had also been a settlement conference and a significant motion. The motion to discontinue was denied. Review of applicable caselaw.

Vance v. Bartlett, 2012 BCPC 266, 2012 CarswellBC 2350 (B.C. Prov. Ct.), Judge J.D. Cowling.

This is an application pursuant to Rule 8(6) of the *Small Claims Rules*, to set aside a notice of withdrawal filed in this proceeding. The notice of withdrawal was part of the settlement of a disputed claim between Mr. and Mrs. Vance and the defendant solicitor and his corporate entity.

The decisions in *Northwest Waste Systems Inc. v. Szeto*, 2003 BCPC 431, 2003 CarswellBC 3093 (B.C. Prov. Ct.), Dhillon J. and *Wilson v. Regoci*, 2009 BCPC 170, 2009 CarswellBC 1468 (B.C. Prov. Ct.), Romilly J., confirm the jurisdiction of this Court to set aside the notice of withdrawal.

On the balance of the material there are sufficient grounds in the particular context of this case to exercise my discretion to grant permission to the claimants to proceed pursuant to Rule 8(6).

Order requesting transfer of claim to the Supreme Court of British Columbia.

13.10 Costs — The costs of a settlement conference, exclusive of disbursements, shall not exceed $100 unless the court orders otherwise because there are special circumstances.

O. Reg. 78/06, s. 27

Superior Court of Justice, Small Claims Court Branch — Important Information about Your Settlement Conference

1. Parties and their representatives (if any) **must** attend the settlement conference on the date indicated in the Notice of Settlement Conference.

2. A settlement conference is an informal, confidential meeting between the parties in the presence of a judicial officer (a judge or deputy judge). The judicial officer at your settlement conference will **not** be the judge at your trial.

3. At a settlement conference, you do not need to stand up when you address the judicial officer; you need only do so in court. You should address a judge or deputy judge as "Your Honour".

4. The purpose of your settlement conference is to:

    a) Resolve some or all of the issues in the action.

    b) Encourage settlement of the action.

    c) Help you get ready for trial.

d) Provide full disclosure among the parties of all the relevant facts and evidence.

5. You may feel free to discuss your case openly at your settlement conference. What you say **cannot** be repeated at trial. Your discussions at a settlement conference are strictly confidential, and will remain so. Unless you consent, the matters discussed at the settlement conference, and during any negotiations, shall not be disclosed to anyone. You must *never* mention the settlement conference during the actual trial.

6. The role of the judicial officer at a settlement conference is to listen to your story, to deal with any procedural problems, and to give you his or her opinion of how your case will likely be decided if it goes to trial. That opinion will be based on their experience as a lawyer, judge or deputy judge. You have the right to know what that opinion is, and you also have the right to ignore that opinion. However, you should carefully consider what they say because their opinion is based upon years of experience.

7. There are many good reasons why parties should try to settle their dispute before going to trial:

a) It saves time;

b) It saves money;

c) It avoids the stresses of a trial; and

d) It gives you the power to resolve your dispute on your own, rather than have a stranger resolve it for you.

8. There is no obligation to settle. However, you owe it to yourselves to think about it. A good settlement is one where both parties have engaged in a fair compromise.

9. Before you appear at your settlement conference, you are encouraged to talk to the other side, to see if you can settle all or any part of your dispute, or if you can agree on any facts.

Osgoode Hall, June 21, 2012
Superior Court of Justice, Office of the Chief
Justice

Caselaw: *Hasselsjo v. CBI Home Health Care*, 2013 ONSC 2684, 2013 CarswellOnt 5630, [2013] O.J. No. 2064 (Ont. S.C.J.)

A settlement conference judge consolidated and then dismissed two claims for $25,000 each, on the basis that the plaintiff had improperly split a claim which exceeded the court's monetary jurisdiction. Costs of $1,000 all-inclusive were awarded to the defendant and the plaintiff sought leave to appeal that costs order. Leave to appeal was denied. The costs order was discretionary and an effective award of about $400 plus disbursements and HST for each action was not clearly wrong.

Rule 14 — Offer To Settle

14.01 A party may serve on any other party an offer to settle a claim on the terms specified in the offer.

History [R. 14.01]: Formerly 15.01.

Commentary: An "Offer to Settle" is the name given to a formal written offer made by one party to the other party. Either party can make a written offer to settle to the other party at any time until a judge disposes of the case. The party may use the Offer to Settle [Form 14A] or may write a letter setting out the terms of the offer.

If you have made or received an offer to settle and it has not been accepted you must not mention the offer to settle or any negotiations relating to it to the judge during the trial until a final disposition has been made of all issues of liability and relief, except for costs.

If a party fails to comply with the terms of an accepted offer, the other party may move for judgment under the terms of the accepted offer, or continue the proceeding as if there had been no accepted offer. If such a motion is brought, the judge "may grant judgment accordingly". On such a motion, evidence will be put before the court by both parties, and the court must decide whether the parties have settled the case. Sometimes the affidavit evidence will be contradictory, and there will be issues of credibility; in such case the court may be unable to make findings of fact on the motion, and instead will order the trial of an issue on the settlement.

Regarding the authority of a lawyer, the normal rule is that a solicitor may bind his or her client in a settlement unless the client has given limited authority and the opposing side has knowledge of the limitation: *Belanger v. Southwestern Insulation Contractors Ltd.*, 1993 CarswellOnt 507, [1993] O.J. No. 3095, 16 O.R. (3d) 457, 32 C.P.C. (3d) 256 (Ont. Gen. Div.). However, if there is clear and uncontradicted evidence that the solicitor did not have authority, the court will not grant judgment pursuant to Rule 49.09(1)(a) even though opposing counsel had no knowledge of the lack of authority: *Smith v. Robinson* (1992), 7 O.R. (3d) 550, 4 C.P.C. (3d) 262, 87 D.L.R. (4th) 360 (Ont. Gen. Div.). Where an offer to settle has been accepted based on a solicitor's misconception of the offer and where the offeror will suffer no prejudice, it would be inequitable to allow the moving party to take advantage of the mistake: *Draper v. Sisson* (1991), 50 C.P.C. (2d) 171 (Ont. Gen. Div.); *Milios v. Zagas*, 1996 CarswellOnt 2951, 3 C.P.C. (4th) 149, 11 O.T.C. 398 (Ont. Gen. Div); reversed 1998 CarswellOnt 810, [1998] O.J. No. 812, 38 O.R. (3d) 218, 108 O.A.C. 224, 18 C.P.C. (4th) 13 (Ont. C.A.).

In performing the vital exercise of determining whether the judgment at trial is as favourable as or more favourable than the offer to settle, the court must consider the matter of accruing prejudgment interest. This is because the amount of the damage award at trial (which will include both a principal and an interest component) is being compared with an offer that in many cases will have been made many months, or even years, before. The interest component of the offer to settle will probably be less than the amount of interest awarded at trial, not because the interest component of the offer was unreasonably low, but because the interest to which the plaintiff is entitled increases with the passage of time. See *Orsini v. Sherri* (1987), 16 C.P.C. (2d) 194 (Ont. H.C.); *Mathur v. Commercial Union Assurance Co. of Canada* (1988), 24 C.P.C. (2d) 225, 28 O.A.C. 55 (Ont. Div. Ct.); *Merrill Lynch Canada Inc. v. Cassina* (1992), 15 C.P.C. (3d) 264 (Ont. Gen. Div.); *Emery v. Royal Oak Mines Inc.* (1995), 26 O.R. (3d) 216, 15 C.C.E.L. (2d) 49 (Ont. Gen. Div.).

Case Law: *Parente v. Van Holland* (1988), 8 A.C.W.S. (3d) 200 (Ont. Dist. Ct.) — Having regard to Rule 16.08 of the Rules of Practice, service by the defendant of an offer to settle with the plaintiff by means of a telecopier or fax machine was validated as a proper service even though the rules do not specifically allow such service. It was also recommended that a confirming letter follow such procedure.

Merrill v. Royal Bank of Canada (October 30, 1997), Doc. Toronto T24613/96 (Ont. Small Claims Ct.) — Defendant made offer for dismissal without costs. Offer made within context of threat to bring motion for dismissal on basis of want of prosecution, for failure to transfer action to another jurisdiction. Plaintiff's transferral was, by its nature, rejection of offer. Further, offer was for immediate consent to dismissal. Consent to dismissal 14 months later was not one given immediately. There was no offer open for acceptance.

Sea Vision Marine Products Ltd. v. McKitrick (June 9, 1999), Doc. Thunder Bay 97-0736 (Ont. S.C.J.) — The Court ruled that the defendant's "without prejudice" letter of November 4, 1998, which suggested possibility of settling at lower figure, was not an offer to settle capable of acceptance by the plaintiff in the manner in which it was submitted, thus it in no way affected the validity of the March 27, 1998 offer, which complied with Rule 49.01(1).

Rosero v. Huang (1999), 44 O.R. (3d) 669 (Ont. S.C.J.) — The defendant offered to settle an action with "costs to be assessed or agreed upon." The offer was expressly stated to be in accordance with *Rules of Civil Procedure* (Ontario). The issue was whether the plaintiff was entitled to costs of action up to the date of the offer or the date of the acceptance. The ambiguity was to be resolved in manner consonant with Rule 49.07(5). The plaintiff was entitled to costs up to the date of the offer.

Shelanu Inc. v. Print Three Franchising Corp. (2000), 11 B.L.R. (3d) 100, 2000 Carswell-Ont 4407 (Ont. S.C.J.) — The plaintiff recovered judgment more favourable than an offer to settle. The plaintiff was awarded party-and-party costs up to September 7, 2000, and solicitor-and-client costs thereafter.

Scanlon v. Standish (2002), 2002 CarswellOnt 128, [2002] O.J. No. 194, 155 O.A.C. 96, 57 O.R. (3d) 767, 24 R.F.L. (5th) 179 (Ont. C.A.) — Prior to commencement of litigation, wife making offer to settle and husband making counter-offer. Pre-litigation offer was not Rule 49 offer. Delivery of counter-offer destroyed power to accept wife's original offer.

Blanchard v. Canada Life Assurance Co. (2001), 7 C.P.C. (5th) 98, 2001 CarswellNB 45, [2001] N.B.J. No. 42, 235 N.B.R. (2d) 153, 607 A.P.R. 153 (N.B. Q.B.) — Defendant moved for order that plaintiff's claim be dismissed for failure to comply with terms of settlement or alternatively that terms of settlement be adopted by Court. Motion granted. Plaintiff bound by settlement. While plaintiff denied having accepted offer and her former solicitor did not testify nor was his affidavit filed, former solicitor had retainer and had accepted offer on behalf of his client in course of retainer.

Catalanotto v. Nina D'Aversa Bakery Ltd. (2001), 2001 CarswellOnt 4058 (Ont. S.C.J.) — Issues at trial not complex and matter ultimately within jurisdiction of Small Claims Court. Plaintiff acted unreasonably in not offering settlement. Failure of plaintiff to continue proceeding under simplified rules in Ontario justified that plaintiff pay defendant's party-and-party costs.

Low v. North Shore Taxi (1996) Ltd., 2005 CarswellBC 117, 2005 BCPC 7 (B.C. Prov. Ct.), W.J. Rodgers, J. — Application brought by defendants for judgment to be granted to the claimant for full amount set out in the Claim. Defendants filed Offer to Settle for a total of $10,216 "in full and final settlement under the jurisdiction of the Provincial Court of British Columbia, Small Claims Division." Order to go.

Icecorp International Cargo Express Corp. v. Nicolaus, 2006 CarswellBC 15, 2006 BCSC 25, 30 C.P.C. (6th) 396 (B.C. S.C.), Pitfield J. Offer to settle made October 15, 2002, but not accepted until October 27, 2004. Rule 37(37) amended effective July 1, 2003.

Plaintiff claims Rule 37(37) in force at time offer was accepted governs. Form of the Rule that existed at time of acceptance must prevail. Rule 37 complete code in respect of offers to settle, and actual consequences associated with offer defined by acceptance. See *Brown v. Lowe*, 2002 CarswellBC 72, [2002] B.C.J. No. 76, 2002 BCCA 7, 97 B.C.L.R. (3d) 246, 14 C.P.C. (5th) 13, 162 B.C.A.C. 203, 264 W.A.C. 203 (B.C. C.A.).

These applications highlight benefit to be derived from use of transitional rules when the Rules of Court are amended in a manner that will alter or have an effect on pre-existing facts or circumstances.

Effect of accepted settlement offer upon such pre-trial orders considered by Low J., as he then was, in *Tomkin v. Tingey*, 2000 CarswellBC 1573, 2000 BCSC 1133, 2 C.P.C. (5th) 56 (B.C. S.C. [In Chambers]). Plaintiff entitled to costs and disbursements to October 15, 2004.

Reischer v. Insurance Corp. of British Columbia, 2006 CarswellBC 270, [2006] B.C.J. No. 235, 2006 BCSC 198 (B.C. S.C. [In Chambers]) 2006-02-03.

Plaintiff appeals final order of Master dismissing her claim to entitlement to costs other than disbursements having accepted Offer to Settle for an amount, including interest, within monetary jurisdiction of the Small Claims Court.

Until July 2003, Rule 37(37) read as follows:

> 37. (37) Notwithstanding subrule (22), if an offer is accepted for a sum within the jurisdiction of the Provincial Court under the *Small Claims Act*, the plaintiff is not entitled to costs other than disbursements.

Appeal dismissed.

Menduk v. Ashcroft, 2006 CarswellBC 380, 2006 BCSC 274 (B.C. S.C.) 2006-02-16.

How does the September 1, 2005 increase in the monetary jurisdiction of the Provincial Court from $10,000 to $25,000 affect the application of Rule 37(37) of the Rules of Court, where an action was commenced in Supreme Court before the change took effect, but an offer of settlement was accepted after the change?

On September 1, 2005, the monetary jurisdiction of the Provincial Court in civil matters was increased to $25,000 by *B.C. Reg.* 179/2005.

On November 7, 2005, the defendant delivered to the plaintiff a formal offer to settle for $24,100. On December 9, 2005, the plaintiff accepted the defendant's offer to settle.

Where an offer is accepted that is within the jurisdiction of the Provincial Court, Rule 37(37) may apply to deprive the plaintiff of its costs other than disbursements, even if it would normally have been entitled to those costs under Rule 37(22). The plaintiff's claim is one which could not appropriately have been brought in Provincial Court. Plaintiff *not* disentitled to his costs by reason of Rule 37(37).

Wood v. Kabaroff, 2006 CarswellBC 2345, 2006 BCSC 1391, 59 B.C.L.R. (4th) 69, 36 C.P.C. (6th) 308 (B.C. S.C.), B. Fisher J.

Issue whether sum of an offer to settle was within the jurisdiction of the Provincial Court under the *Small Claims Act*. If it was, plaintiff not entitled to costs under Rule 37.

Offer to settle was for $26,000. Amount of the accepted offer was for a sum not within the jurisdiction of the Provincial Court. Case whether the monetary jurisdiction was $10,000 or $25,000.

Chytros v. Standard Life Assurance Co., 2006 CarswellOnt 6289, 83 O.R. (3d) 237 (Ont. S.C.J.), Kent J.

Counsel for both parties informed trial judge just before trial commenced that settlement reached. Plaintiff subsequently taking position that she had not given her counsel authority to enter into settlement. Any limitation on ostensible authority of counsel for plaintiff should have been made known to trial judge and was not. Settlement held enforceable.

Counsel who are retained by and represent a party in an action have ostensible authority to conduct all matters in the action. See *Scherer v. Paletta*, 1966 CarswellOnt 119, [1966] 2 O.R. 524, 57 D.L.R. (2d) 532, [1966] O.J. No. 1017 (Ont. C.A.). If there are limitations on the authority of counsel they are only effective against an opposing party if they are made known to that opposing party. Any dispute between a client and counsel is an issue only between those parties. See *Sign-O-Lite v. Bugeja*, 1994 CarswellOnt 4796, [1994] O.J. No. 1381 (Ont. Gen. Div.).

Counsel who agrees to a settlement on behalf of a client and has no specific authority with respect to the client but believes, however, that his recommendation to the client will be accepted has made a settlement binding on his client. See *Fabian v. Bud Mervyn Construction Ltd.*, 1981 CarswellOnt 395, 35 O.R. (2d) 132, 23 C.P.C. 140, 127 D.L.R. (3d) 119, [1981] O.J. No. 3205 (Ont. Div. Ct.).

Even when a party alleges that it was not fully advised of the proceedings by its counsel and that counsel did not have authority to settle the case, the courts have held that such breach of duty or lack of authority is an issue only between the party and its counsel. See *Dos Santos v. Waite*, 1995 CarswellOnt 3384, [1995] O.J. No. 1803 (Ont. Gen. Div.), at para. 9.

Love v. News Datacom Ltd., [2006] M.J. No. 360, 2006 CarswellMan 277, [2006] 9 W.W.R. 729, (sub nom. *Love v. Bell ExpressVu Ltd. Partnership)* 383 W.A.C. 24, (sub nom. *Love v. Bell ExpressVu Ltd. Partnership)* 208 Man. R. (2d) 24, 2006 MBCA 92, (sub nom. *Kudelski, S.A. v. Love)* 273 D.L.R. (4th) 761 (Man. C.A.).

With respect to first appeal, the settlement agreement, consent to judgment arising out of it, and all the court proceedings intertwined. Defendants had to rely on pleadings, affidavits and other material filed in the original proceedings for the Anton Piller injunction. Defendant not entitled to rely upon material and evidence from the earlier proceedings due to the doctrine of absolute privilege.

St. Louis-Lalonde v. Carleton Condominium Corp. No. 12, 2005 CarswellOnt 4709, [2005] O.J. No. 4164 (Ont. S.C.J.); additional reasons to 2005 CarswellOnt 2731 (Ont. S.C.J.), Lalonde J.; affirmed 2007 CarswellOnt 836 (Ont. C.A.).

After three-day trial, action dismissed. Rule 49.10 of *Rules of Civil Procedure* sets out cost consequences of failing to accept offer but has no application where plaintiff fails to recover any judgment at all. In such situations, courts rely on their discretion under s. 131 of *Courts of Justice Act*. Combination of both partial and substantial indemnity costs more appropriate.

363066 Ontario Ltd. v. Gullo, 2007 CarswellOnt 7374, 88 O.R. (3d) 170, 2007 ONCA 785 (Ont. C.A.).

Rule 49.04(1) expressly provides that an offer to settle may be withdrawn at any time before it is accepted. 2004 offer not accepted at time that 2006 offer made and 2006 offer complied with requirements of rule 49.04(1); the appellants were entitled to withdraw the 2004 offer despite the fact that it was stated to be irrevocable.

Downey v. St. Paul's Hospital, 2007 CarswellBC 1080, 47 C.C.L.T. (3d) 112, 2007 BCSC 695, 71 B.C.L.R. (4th) 232, [2007] 12 W.W.R. 154 (B.C. S.C.).

Pursuant to r. 37(24), if plaintiff's claim dismissed, defendant who has made offer to settle claim that has not expired or been withdrawn or accepted is entitled to costs assessed to date offer was delivered and to double costs assessed thereafter. See *Rules of Court, 1990*, B.C. Reg. 221/90.

Sidorsky v. Lowry, 2009 CarswellAlta 567, 2009 ABQB 197, 73 C.P.C. (6th) 58, 463 A.R. 183 (Alta. Q.B.)

Defendant offered to settle with plaintiff for $75,000 plus costs but offer only open until start of trial. Plaintiff awarded $2,265.41 plus costs. Plaintiff awarded costs up to date of offer while defendant was awarded costs for steps taken after date of offer. Rule 169(1) permitted service of offer any time before trial. Rule 169(2) stipulated offer could only be accepted before start of trial. Fact that R. 169(3) precluded withdrawal of offer within 45 days of service except with leave of court not relevant.

Smagh v. Bumbrah, 2009 CarswellBC 1226, 2009 BCSC 623, 73 C.P.C. (6th) 70 (B.C. S.C.).

Application by defendant for costs. Defendant made an offer to settle. Jury awarded substantially less than the offer. Plaintiff in difficult financial circumstances. See *Radke v. Parry*, 90 B.C.L.R. (4th) 132, [2008] B.C.J. No. 1991, 2008 BCSC 1397, 2008 CarswellBC 2204, 64 C.P.C. (6th) 176 (B.C. S.C.), where Madam Justice Boyd made note of the "substantial disparity in financial circumstances between the parties": at para. 42. Circumstances militate against an award of double costs.

Bomhof v. Eunoia Inc., 2012 ONSC 4091, 2012 CarswellOnt 8765 (Ont. S.C.J.), D.A. Broad J.

The lack of an element of compromise in the Offer to Settle militates against the exercise of a discretion in favour of substantial indemnity costs (see *Data General (Canada) Ltd. v. Molnar Systems Group Inc.*, 1991 CarswellOnt 402, 6 O.R. (3d) 409, 3 C.P.C. (3d) 180, 85 D.L.R. (4th) 392, 52 O.A.C. 212, [1991] O.J. No. 1857 (Ont. C.A.); *Walker Estate v. York-Finch General Hospital*, 1999 CarswellOnt 667, 43 O.R. (3d) 461, 44 C.C.L.T. (2d) 205, 31 C.P.C. (4th) 24, 169 D.L.R. (4th) 689, 118 O.A.C. 217, [1999] O.J. No. 644 (Ont. C.A.); affirmed 2001 SCC 23, 2001 CarswellOnt 1209, 2001 CarswellOnt 1210, [2001] 1 S.C.R. 647, 6 C.C.L.T. (3d) 1, 5 C.P.C. (5th) 1, 198 D.L.R. (4th) 193, 268 N.R. 68, 145 O.A.C. 302, [2001] S.C.J. No. 24 (S.C.C.)).

Fair and appropriate to permit trial judge to rule on question of the costs of motion in the context of a global costs consideration following trial. Such a consideration could encompass the effect of the possibility that the plaintiff's recovery may not exceed the Small Claims Court limit.

Issue of costs of motion for summary judgment reserved to the trial judge.

2964376 Canada Inc. v. Bisaillon, 2012 ONSC 4447, 2012 CarswellOnt 9372 (Ont. S.C.J.), Métivier J.

The plaintiff was successful in its action for defamation against the defendant. The defendant's cross-claim was dismissed.

The plaintiff submits that it is entitled to substantial indemnity costs, and puts these at $39,795.49. The defendant submits that the substantial indemnity rate inappropriate. It was not granted aggravated damages. Award of costs on a substantial indemnity basis appropriate. The offer made by plaintiff reasonable, that by the defendant not. Malice found.

Evans v. Complex Services Inc., 2013 ONSC 120, 2013 CarswellOnt 144, 10 C.C.E.L. (4th) 73, Kent J. (Ont. S.C.J.)

The plaintiff, who was dismissed by the defendant without cause, obtained judgment awarding her damages. Although the claim was commenced using ordinary procedure and rules, the damages award was well within the ambit of the Simplified Procedure rules. The quantum of damages was only slightly more than the maximum permitted in a Small Claims Court action.

Counsel for the defendant points out that the damages award obtained by the plaintiff is not very significantly more than the rule 49 offer of the defendant. Nevertheless, the plaintiff had a modest success and should not be deprived of costs. A partial indemnity claim for costs in the amount of $43,700 for less and $2,253.66 for disbursement, however, is excessive and disproportionate. The plaintiff's judgment is for $30,360.20.

Costs awarded to plaintiff, fixed at $17,500.

14.01.1 (1) Written Documents — An offer to settle, an acceptance of an offer to settle and a notice of withdrawal of an offer to settle shall be in writing.

(2) Use of Forms — An offer to settle may be in Form 14A, an acceptance of an offer to settle may be in Form 14B and a notice of withdrawal of an offer to settle may be in Form 14C.

(3) Terms of Settlement — The terms of an accepted offer to settle may be set out in terms of settlement (Form 14D).

O. Reg. 78/06, s. 28

14.02 (1) Time for Making Offer — An offer to settle may be made at any time.

(2) Costs Consequences — The costs consequences referred to in rule 14.07 apply only if the offer to settle is served on the party to whom it is made at least seven days before the trial commences.

O. Reg. 78/06, s. 29

History [R. 14.02]: Formerly 15.02; refers to rule 14.07, formerly 15.07.

14.03 (1) Withdrawal — An offer to settle may be withdrawn at any time before it is accepted, by serving a notice of withdrawal of an offer to settle on the party to whom it was made.

History [R. 14.03(1)]: Formerly 15.03(1); plain language changes.

(2) Deemed Withdrawal — If an offer to settle specifies a date after which it is no longer available for acceptance, and has not been accepted on or before that date, the offer shall be deemed to have been withdrawn on the day after that date.

History [R. 14.03(2)]: Formerly 15.03(2).

(3) Expiry When Court Disposes of Claim — An offer may not be accepted after the court disposes of the claim in respect of which the offer is made.

O. Reg. 461/01, s. 16; 78/06, s. 29

14.04 No Disclosure to Trial Judge — If an offer to settle is not accepted, no communication about it or any related negotiations shall be made to the trial judge until all questions of liability and the relief to be granted, other than costs, have been determined.

O. Reg. 78/06, s. 29

History [R. 14.04]: Formerly 15.04; plain language changes.

14.05 (1) Acceptance of an Offer to Settle — An offer to settle may be accepted by serving an acceptance of an offer to settle on the party who made it, at any time before it is withdrawn or before the court disposes of the claim in respect of which it is made.

History [R. 14.05(1)]: Formerly 15.05(1).

(2) Payment Into Court As Condition — An offer by a plaintiff to settle a claim in return for the payment of money by a defendant may include a term that the defendant pay the money into court; in that case, the defendant may accept the offer only by paying the money into court and notifying the plaintiff of the payment.

History [R. 14.05(2)]: Formerly 15.05(2); plain language changes.

(3) If a defendant offers to pay money to a plaintiff in settlement of a claim, the plaintiff may accept the offer with the condition that the defendant pay the money into court; if the offer is so accepted and the defendant fails to pay the money into court, the plaintiff may proceed as provided in rule 14.06.

History [R. 14.05(3)]: Formerly 15.05(3); plain language changes; refers to rule 14.06, formerly 15.06.

(4) Costs — If an accepted offer to settle does not deal with costs, the plaintiff is entitled,

(a) in the case of an offer made by the defendant, to the plaintiff's disbursements assessed to the date the plaintiff was served with the offer;

(b) in the case of an offer made by the plaintiff, to the plaintiff's disbursements assessed to the date that the notice of acceptance was served.

O. Reg. 78/06, s. 30

History [R. 14.05(4)]: Formerly 15.05(4); correction of "defendant's disbursements" in clause (a) to "plaintiff's disbursements"; plain language changes.

14.06 Failure to Comply With Accepted Offer — If a party to an accepted offer to settle fails to comply with the terms of the offer, the other party may,

(a) make a motion to the court for judgment in the terms of the accepted offer; or

(b) continue the proceeding as if there had been no offer to settle.

History [R. 14.06]: Formerly 15.06.

Case Law: *Srebot v. Srebot Farms Ltd.*, 2013 ONCA 84, 2013 CarswellOnt 1376 (Ont. C.A.)

The discretion not to enforce a concluded settlement should be reserved for those rare cases where compelling circumstances establish that the enforcement of the settlement would not be in the interests of justice.

All Canadian Mechanical & Electrical Inc. v. Henderson, 2011 CarswellOnt 15950, [2011] O.J. No. 1456 (Ont. Sm. Cl. Ct.); further proceedings (2011), 218 A.C.W.S. (3d) 85, 2011 CarswellOnt 15906, [2011] O.J. No. 3252 (Ont. Sm. Cl. Ct.); affirmed 2012 ONSC 1370, 2012 CarswellOnt 2953 (Ont. S.C.J.); affirmed 2012 ONSC 5620, 222 A.C.W.S. (3d) 344, 2012 CarswellOnt 12786, [2012] O.J. No. 4761 (Ont. Div. Ct.)

The court rejected the plaintiff's contention that several related actions had been settled through correspondence between counsel. Even where an accepted settlement offer is established, the court has a discretion to decline to enforce the resulting settlement. Review of relevant authorities.

14.07 (1) Costs Consequences of Failure to Accept — When a plaintiff makes an offer to settle that is not accepted by the defendant, the court may award the plaintiff an amount not exceeding twice the costs of the action, if the following conditions are met:

1. The plaintiff obtains a judgment as favourable as or more favourable than the terms of the offer.

2. The offer was made at least seven days before the trial.

3. The offer was not withdrawn and did not expire before the trial.

History [R. 14.07(1)]: Formerly 15.07.

Case Law: *Diefenbacher v. Young* (1995), 22 O.R. (3d) 641 (C.A.) — A decreasing offer to settle by a plaintiff, and an increasing offer by a defendant without reference to an earlier offer, is by implication a withdrawal of the earlier offer.

Sona Computer Inc. v. Carnegie (March 7, 1995), Doc. Ottawa 596/94 (Ont. Gen. Div.) — Defendant failed to make payment as directed by the pre-trial judge. No error in law by trial judge in awarding judgment of on-half plaintiff's claim (recommended at pre-trial).

(2) When a defendant makes an offer to settle that is not accepted by the plaintiff, the court may award the defendant an amount not exceeding twice the costs awardable to a successful party, from the date the offer was served, if the following conditions are met:

1. The plaintiff obtains a judgment as favourable as or less favourable than the terms of the offer.

2. The offer was made at least seven days before the trial.

3. The offer was not withdrawn and did not expire before the trial.

Case Law: *King v. Royal Insurance Co.* (1987), 10 W.D.C.P. 126 (Ont. Prov. Ct.) — Although the defendant's offer to settle for $750 was not accepted and the plaintiff's action was dismissed at trial, the fact that the plaintiff attempted to negotiate at the pretrial mitigated against the court awarding double costs to the defendant. Although the defendant used its own process server it could only recover the same costs as if the service had been by the court. See also Rule 20.03.

Niagara Structural Steel (St. Catharines) Ltd. v. W.D. LaFlamme Ltd. (1987), 1987 CarswellOnt 440, [1987] O.J. No. 2239, 58 O.R. (2d) 773, 19 O.A.C. 142, 19 C.P.C. (2d) 163 (Ont. C.A.) — Rule 49.10 (similar to Rule 15.07) of the Rules of Practice does not apply to cases pending appeal. Exceptions to the normal cost consequences with respect to offers to settle should only be made where it appears the interests of justice requires a departure.

Roberts v. Dresser Industries Can. Inc. (1988), 9 A.C.W.S. (3d) 290 (Ont. Dist. Ct.) — An award at trial exceeded the offer of settlement by only $78.12. Pursuant to rule 49.10(1) of the Rules of Practice, (compare with Civil Division Rule 15), the plaintiff in question was entitled to costs on a solicitor and client basis. It is the rule itself that draws the line where "minimal" becomes "sufficient."

Shah v. Mohr (September 14, 1998), Doc. Kitchener 2148/94 (Ont. Gen. Div.) — The claim and the counterclaim were dismissed. The defendant was granted costs on party-and-party basis in main action to date of second offer and solicitor-and-clients costs thereafter. The second offer revoked the first offer. Failure to award costs to the successful defendant would encourage unmeritorious litigation.

Kenny v. Summerside (City), 2000 PESCTD 31, 45 C.P.C. (4th) 258, 2000 CarswellPEI 31 (P.E.I. T.D.) — The plaintiff brought an action for damages in the amount of $100,000. The plaintiff was awarded $3,500 in damages. Within court's discretion to accept offer to settle was not made within time limits. The plaintiff was awarded party-and-party costs until point of $5,000 offer and the city was awarded party-and-party costs after that point.

Soulis v. Samaras (2000), 2000 CarswellOnt 314 (Ont. S.C.J.) — Prior to trial, the plaintiff had made an offer of settlement, which the defendant did not accept. The defendant fared less well. The plaintiff was entitled to solicitor-client costs on *prima facie* application of Rule 49.10.

978011 Ontario Ltd. v. Cornell Engineering Co. (2001), 2001 CarswellOnt 2749, 148 O.A.C. 250 (Ont. C.A.) — Plaintiff entitled to party-and-party costs to date of offer and solicitor-and-client costs after date of offer which expired ten minutes after trial commenced. Fact that costs component not ascertainable not fatal to offer being effective as offer capable of acceptance. Fact some relief obtained by defendant's voluntary payment just prior to trial did not affect success of offer.

George v. Imagineering Ltd. (2001), 2001 CarswellOnt 3832 (Ont. S.C.J.). Costs awarded to plaintiff on party-and-party basis. Assessment officer directed to assess reasonable articling student fees in preparation for trial itself.

Schaer v. Barrie Yacht Club, 2003 CarswellOnt 2531, [2003] O.J. No. 2673 (Ont. S.C.J.). Appeal of matters originating in the Small Claims Court where cost recovery is restricted. Where a party has escalated the expense of litigation so disproportional to modest claims, he cannot then be heard to complain that he should have the benefit of limitations. The Appellant/Plaintiff resoundingly impolite. Worst example of a litigator demanding the time, attention and tolerance. Self-represented litigants may be held to the standards of civility expected of lawyers. A proper reprimand for failure to do so is award of costs on a substantial indemnity basis. Costs fixed against the Appellant/Plaintiff at $10,000.

Martin v. Martin, 2003 CarswellNB 573, 2003 NBQB 464, 50 C.B.R. (4th) 120 (N.B. Q.B.). Claims which survive discharge from bankruptcy. Section 178(1)(a.1)(i) exempted judgment in respect of bodily harm intentionally inflicted. Application that judgment not released by discharge dismissed.

Vandenelsen v. Merkley (2003), [2003] O.J. No. 3577, 2003 CarswellOnt 3483 (Ont. C.A.). After decision refusing to waive court administrative fees, for lack of jurisdiction, that ground was held unconstitutional in another case. Decision was also based on lack of evidence that refusal of waiver would frustrate ability to proceed with appeal. Appeal from refusal dismissed.

Seymour v. Jenkins, 2003 CarswellNS 69, 2003 NSSC 23 (N.S. S.C.). Adjudicator's omission of reasons for finding in favour of claimant constituted error of law. Matter ordered returned to Small Claims Court for rehearing.

Morrell v. Boulton, 2006 CarswellOnt 7940, 39 C.P.C. (6th) 203 (Ont. S.C.J.), B.H. Matheson J.

Defendants brought motion for costs on substantial indemnity basis and submitted two detailed bills of costs. Motion granted. Defendants awarded costs on substantial indemnity basis of $17,000 for main action and $11,500 for motion to dismiss. Plaintiffs claimed $90,000, which was substantial amount, and recovered nothing. Plaintiffs' claim not complex. They were responsible for outlandish delays while defendants acted in proper and sensible manner. Defendants made five offers to consent to dismissal without costs but plaintiffs accepted none. Plaintiffs' solicitor gave little response to defendants' solicitor's many letters.

Reischer v. Insurance Corp. of British Columbia, 2006 CarswellBC 270, [2006] B.C.J. No. 235, 62 B.C.L.R. (4th) 353, 2006 BCSC 198, 34 C.P.C. (6th) 83 (B.C. S.C. [In Chambers]).

Plaintiff brought action against insurer in Supreme Court. Plaintiff accepted offer to settle action for amount within monetary jurisdiction of Provincial Court. Under r. 37(37) of *Rules of Court, 1990*, plaintiff not entitled to costs other than disbursements if offer is accepted for sum within jurisdiction of Provincial Court and proceeding could appropriately have been brought in Provincial Court. Intent of rule to avoid unfairness that could arise where party had no choice of forum in which to bring claim, yet would be subject to costs consequences for accepting offer within monetary jurisdiction of Provincial Court. Whether plaintiff had sufficient reason to bring action in Supreme Court was irrelevant.

Wood v. Kabaroff, 2006 CarswellBC 2345, 2006 BCSC 1391, 59 B.C.L.R. (4th) 69, 36 C.P.C. (6th) 308 (B.C. S.C.), B. Fisher J.

Registrar determined that advance payment of $1,000 placed offer to settle at $26,000, properly within jurisdiction of Supreme Court. He allowed units for costs including unit for negotiations. Monetary jurisdiction of provincial court was $10,000 for purposes of r. 37(37) since this was jurisdiction at time when plaintiff commenced his action. Registrar erred in principle by allowing costs under r. 37(22)(b) for negotiations until time offer was delivered to plaintiff since no evidence existed that settlement was result of any negotiations up to time offer was accepted by plaintiff.

Authorson (Litigation Guardian of) v. Canada (Attorney General), 2007 CarswellOnt 4221, 2007 ONCA 501, 86 O.R. (3d) 321, 60 C.C.P.B. 280, 41 C.P.C. (6th) 114, (sub nom. *Authorson (Litigation Administrator of) v. Canada (Attorney General))* 283 D.L.R. (4th) 341, (sub nom. *Authorson v. Canada (Attorney General))* 226 O.A.C. 4 (Ont. C.A.); additional reasons at 2007 CarswellOnt 5501, 61 C.C.P.B. 319, 43 C.P.C. (6th) 253, 2007 ONCA 599 (Ont. C.A.); leave to appeal refused 2008 CarswellOnt 179, 2008 CarswellOnt 180, (sub nom. *Authorson v. Canada (Attorney General))* 384 N.R. 391 (note), (sub nom. *Authorson v. Canada (Attorney General))* 249 O.A.C. 399 (note), [2008] 1 S.C.R. v (note) (S.C.C.).

Decision that statutory bar to damages claim operable. Statutory bar applying to entire damages claim. Judgment constituting final judgment. "General acceptance" not sufficient to ground judicial notice where dispute amongst reasonable persons on subject. Application for leave to appeal to Supreme Court of Canada filed on September 26, 2007 (Court File No. 32262).

Baliwalla v. York Condominium Corp. No. 438, 2007 CarswellOnt 4096, 63 C.L.R. (3d) 169, 226 O.A.C. 66, [2007] O.J. No. 2484 (Ont. Div. Ct.).

Deputy Small Claims Court Judge allowed the action and awarded Baliwalla damages of $5,350.29. The condominium corporation appealed.

The Ontario Divisional Court, per Greer J., in a decision reported at 224 O.A.C. 192, allowed the appeal and dismissed Baliwalla's action. The condominium corporation sought costs of $52,943.48 on a substantial indemnity basis or $46,830.98 on a partial indemnity basis. The court fixed the condominium corporation's total costs at $7,452.73 for the action and appeal.

Appellant had made an offer to settle under r. 49 of the *Rules of Civil Procedure*. Relying on the decision in *Niagara Structural Steel (St. Catharines) Ltd. v. W.D. LaFlamme Ltd.* (Ont. C.A.), the respondent argued that r. 49.10 did not apply to offers to settle made pending an appeal. The rule speaks to obtaining "a judgment" by a plaintiff in the operation of the rule, and these terms do not apply to appeals.

"The amount in question fell within the jurisdiction of the Small Claims Court. Appellant entitled to the full amount of disbursements and GST of $1,014.21 expended on the appeal. Weighing the factors in this case and applying the principles set down by the Court of Appeal, I award the appellant the sum of $3,000 for the appeal."

Anderson v. Routbard, 2007 CarswellBC 647, [2007] B.C.J. No. 627, 2007 BCCA 193, 396 W.A.C. 98, 239 B.C.A.C. 98, 41 C.P.C. (6th) 95, 67 B.C.L.R. (4th) 66 (B.C. C.A.).

Trial judge found offer did not afford plaintiff meaningful opportunity to assess amount he would receive if offer accepted as he could not know at time of offer what pt. 7 benefits, if any, would be subject of dispute. Plaintiff appealed. Appeal allowed. Costs increased to $8,640. Despite difficulties in calculating actual amount offered, agreement was not vague. Settlement proposal was not uncertain, based on objective standard which takes legal context into account. Offer to settle under r. 37 constitutes circumstances in which discretion can be used to depart from fixed costs as set out in r. 66(29). As matter was one of general importance to profession, no costs awarded on appeal.

Icecorp International Cargo Express Corp. v. Nicolaus, 2007 CarswellBC 444, 236 B.C.A.C. 294, 390 W.A.C. 294, 38 C.P.C. (6th) 26, 2007 BCCA 97 (B.C. C.A.).

Defendants made offer to settle plaintiff's action October 15, 2002 for "$100 and costs in accordance with rule 37(22)." Rule 37(37) provided that plaintiff not entitled to costs other than disbursements, on accepting an offer made by the defendant, if (a) the offer was accepted for a sum within the jurisdiction of the Provincial Court under the *Small Claims Act*, and (b) the proceeding in which the offer was made could appropriately have been brought in the Provincial Court. The plaintiff claimed its costs and disbursements to the date of the offer, arguing that the action could not appropriately have been brought in Provincial Court. The British Columbia Supreme Court, in a decision reported at 2006 CarswellBC 15, agreed with plaintiff. The defendants sought leave to appeal. Appeal dismissed.

Kolasa v. 1408803 Ontario Ltd. (2007), 2007 CarswellOnt 2968 (Ont. Div. Ct.); additional reasons at (2007), 2007 CarswellOnt 4060 (Ont. Div. Ct.).

Leave granted to appeal award of costs. Appellant submits that he erred as damages recovered within the monetary jurisdiction of the Small Claims Court. It successfully defended most of the substantive claims against it and made an offer to settle for $7,000 all-inclusive.

Section 134(1)(a) of the *Courts of Justice Act*, R.S.O. 1990, c. C.43 provides that an appeal court may make any order that ought to have been made by the court appealed from. See *340812 Ontario Ltd. v. Canadian National Railway*, 1997 CarswellOnt 2743, 102 O.A.C. 230, 149 D.L.R. (4th) 575 (Ont. C.A.).

Given that appellant's offer to settle included costs, court unable to determine whether the respondent received amount at trial that was as favourable or less favourable than the offer, as required by Rule 49.10.

Costs fixed at $5,000 all-inclusive. Appeal allowed in part. Paragraph 1 of judgment varied to substitute an order for damages of $4,996.75. Paragraph 2 varied to substitute an order of costs to the respondent in amount of $5,000.

Gardiner v. Mulder (2007), 2007 CarswellOnt 2829, 224 O.A.C. 156 (Ont. Div. Ct.), 2007-04-30, Cusinato J.

An offer to settle a claim in Small Claims Court does not continue to remain open after disposition, even if not withdrawn.

In the wording of Rule 14.03(3) of the *Small Claims Court Rules*, it provides the following:

> (3) **Expiry when court disposes of claim** — An offer may not be accepted after the court disposes of the claim in respect of which the offer is made.

See *The Law of Costs*, 2nd ed. (Ontario: Canada Law Book, 2005) at pp. 8-16, Orkin, in respect of costs in appeals where the party is partly successful:

> **Costs where divided success**
>
> The general rule is that an appellant is entitled to costs where he or she has substantially succeeded on the appeal, but where the appellant succeeds only partially, or success is divided, no costs should be allowed.

Delco Projects Ltd. v. Young, 2008 CarswellBC 291, 2008 BCPC 19 (B.C. Prov. Ct.), J. Auxier Prov. J.

If claimant made offer to settle pursuant to Rule 10.1 of *Small Claims Rules* and served on defendants and rejected by them, the defendants might face a penalty of up to 20 per cent of the amount of the offer to settle. If such offer made, claimant to file offer to settle and proof of service of offer on the defendant. Court would then deal with the issue of whether penalty appropriate and how much it should be.

Rigitano Estate v. Western Assurance Co., 2007 CarswellOnt 6412, 54 C.C.L.I. (4th) 163, (sub nom. *Western Assurance Co. v. Rigitano Estate*) 229 O.A.C. 351 (Ont. Div. Ct.), Fedak J.

Small Claims Court allowed action and awarded judgment to estate of $3,500 plus prejudgment and postjudgment interest. Western Assurance appealed. The estate cross-appealed interest award. Fedak J. dismissed appeal and allowed cross-appeal.

The deputy judge gave adequate reasons for finding offer to settle valid. Even though the deputy judge did not expressly refer to the issue of consensus, he wrote: "[Western Assurance] intended to settle all claims, past, present and future, and did so with the lawful representative for their insured namely, his Estate Trustee."

Qubti v. Reprodux Ltd., 2010 CarswellOnt 2192, 2010 ONSC 2200 (Ont. S.C.J.)

The employee's offer to settle that remained open at trial far exceeded amount awarded and was therefore outside boundaries of r. 49.10 of *Rules of Civil Procedure*. Costs awarded ought to be proportionate to degree of success achieved. The employee recovered 4 percent of amount claimed. Court awarded $40,000 in costs plus $11,360 in disbursements.

Melara-Lopez v. Richarz, 2009 CarswellOnt 6333, 255 O.A.C. 160 (Ont. Div. Ct.).

The employee's offer to settle that remained open at trial far exceeded amount awarded and was therefore outside boundaries of r. 49.10 of *Rules of Civil Procedure*. Costs awarded ought to be proportionate to degree of success achieved. The employee recovered 4 percent of amount claimed. Court awarded $40,000 in costs plus $11,360 in disbursements.

The appellants sued respondent solicitor for negligence. They recovered $1,393.53 plus pre-judgment and post-judgment interest. The respondent had made offer before litigation began to settle action for $2,000, and then subsequent to litigation, he offered to settle for $3,000. Trial judge applied r. 14.07 of the *Small Claims Court Rules*. He concluded that both offers would have surpassed the appellants' recovery at trial and awarded respondent costs fixed at $3,298.88. The appellants appealed costs award. Divisional Court dismissed appeal. Small Claims Court r. 14.02.1 specified that an offer to settle could be made at any time. No prohibition on offers made before start of litigation. No over-arching principle costs must follow the event. Early offers to settle were to be encouraged. The trial judge determined that failure to accept reasonable and timely offer constituted unreasonable behaviour and crafted a costs award accordingly.

Qubti v. Reprodux Ltd., 2010 CarswellOnt 2192, 2010 ONSC 2200 (Ont. S.C.J.)

The employee's offer to settle that remained open at trial far exceeded amount awarded and was therefore outside boundaries of r. 49.10 of *Rules of Civil Procedure*. Costs awarded ought to be proportionate to degree of success achieved. The employee recovered 4 percent of amount claimed. Court awarded $40,000 in costs plus $11,360 in disbursements.

Habib v. Jack, 2011 BCSC 1294, 2011 CarswellBC 2621, 25 B.C.L.R. (5th) 162 (B.C. S.C.), Ross J.; additional reasons to 2011 BCSC 399, 2011 CarswellBC 731, 19 B.C.L.R. (5th) 207 (B.C. S.C.), Ross J.

Offers to settle. Failure to accept offer. The plaintiff brought an action for damages against the defendants. The defendants offered to settle for $1,000, six weeks before the trial. The plaintiff refused. The action was dismissed. The trial judge ordered costs to the defendants. Double costs were not appropriate. At the time of the offer, it was clear that the plaintiff had suffered an injury and there was dispute related to liability. The offer was nominal given the extent of the plaintiff's injury. It could not be said that the offer should have been accepted, as it was not clear that the action had little chance of success.

Cairns v. Gill, 2011 BCSC 420, 2011 CarswellBC 787, 8 C.P.C. (7th) 240 (B.C. S.C.)

The defendants made an offer to settle, which was refused by the plaintiff. The matter proceeded to trial. The plaintiff was the successful party at trial, but was awarded less than the defendants had offered in their offer to settle. The defendants brought an Application for payment of their costs and disbursements from the date of their offer to settle. The Application was dismissed. There were sufficient reasons for the plaintiff to proceed in Supreme Court.

The plaintiff would not have obtained much, if any, benefit from the offer at the time it was made or afterward, because of the costs component. Although the jury awarded an amount roughly two-thirds of defendants' offer, the size of the offer was so small that any amount awarded would have represented a significant portion. The defendants were in a better financial position to cover their costs of litigation.

Until recently, the funding of litigation costs by an insurer, as a matter of the relative financial circumstances of the parties under 9-1(6)(c) of the B.C. Rules, was not a proper consideration in relation to costs. This is no longer the case. See *Smith v. Tedford*, 2010 BCCA 302, 2010 CarswellBC 1527, [2010] B.C.J. No. 1236, [2010] I.L.R. I-5009, 488 W.A.C. 227, 288 B.C.A.C. 227, 7 B.C.L.R. (5th) 246, 88 C.P.C. (6th) 199 (B.C. C.A.).

Hayes v. Silva, 2011 ONSC 3109, 2011 CarswellOnt 3575, 6 C.L.R. (4th) 156 (Ont. Master), Master Albert.

Hayes was successful in obtaining judgment for $14,272.90 and defending against the counterclaim of $37,000.

As a general principle, costs in a proceeding under the *Construction Lien Act* are in the absolute discretion of the court. The court must consider the facts and circumstances of the particular case; it is not a mechanical exercise. The court must be fair and reasonable in exercising its discretion to award costs.

Rule 57.01(1) describes factors for the court to consider when fixing costs. The list is non-exhaustive. Proportionality must also be considered. Costs should be proportionate to the importance and complexity of the issues and to the amount involved in the proceeding. See Rule 1.04.

The court disagreed with submissions of Silva's counsel that a paralegal could have represented the plaintiff because quantum was within jurisdiction of Small Claims Court. Having regard to the *Construction Lien Act*, section 67(5), the *Law Society Act*, and the regulations thereunder, paralegals have no standing in trials in the Superior Court of Justice under the *Construction Lien Act*. In any event, it is not unreasonable for a plaintiff to choose to be represented by a lawyer rather than by a paralegal in a construction lien claim that goes to trial.

The plaintiff served an offer to settle.

Silva submitted that cost consequences of rule 49 should not apply because the quantum of the claim was within the monetary jurisdiction of the Small Claims Court. That argument ignored the requirement under the *Construction Lien Act* that a claimant who seeks the remedies *only available* under that *Act must* bring the claim in the Superior Court of Justice.

The plaintiff successfully defended the counterclaim for an amount greater than the Small Claims Court limit. The Rules applied except where inconsistent with the *Construction Lien Act*. Rule 1.04, as recently amended, provides:

> 1.04 (1.1) In applying these rules, the court shall make orders and give directions that are proportionate to the importance and complexity of the issues, and to the amount involved, in the proceeding.

Costs were fixed at $10,750.

Cairns v. Gill, 2011 BCSC 420, 2011 CarswellBC 787, 8 C.P.C. (7th) 240 (B.C. S.C.), Justice E.A. Arnold-Bailey.

The plaintiff declined to accept the defendants' offer to settle her claim for $1,292 (the "offer to settle") plus costs, and proceeded to a three-day trial before a judge and jury. The plaintiff, although successful at trial, received a total award of $851.

See McLachlin J.A., as she then was, in *Houweling Nurseries Ltd. v. Fisons Western Corp.*, 1988 CarswellBC 471, [1988] B.C.J. No. 306, 29 C.P.C. (2d) 168, 49 D.L.R. (4th) 205, 37 B.C.L.R. (2d) 2 (B.C. C.A.) at p. 25 [B.C.L.R.]; leave to appeal refused [1988] S.C.C.A. No. 200, [1988] 1 S.C.R. ix (note), 37 B.C.L.R. (2d) 2 (note), 30 C.P.C. (2d) lv (note), 89 N.R. 398 (note) (S.C.C.):

> Costs in our system of litigation serve the purpose, not only of indemnifying the successful litigant to a greater or lesser degree, but indemnifying the successful litigant to a greater or lesser degree, but of deterring frivolous actions or defences. Parties, in calculating the risks of proceeding with a particular action or defence, should be able to forecast with some degree of precision what penalty they face should they be unsuccessful. Moreover, there is a sound reason for keeping costs within relatively modest limits. The possibility of high costs may unduly deter a party from bringing an uncertain but meritorious claim or defence.

The defendant's offer to settle cannot be ignored. The plaintiff cannot avoid some consequences.

Pursuant to Rule 7.1(1) of the *Small Claims Rules*, B.C. Reg. 261/93, a judge, on an application at any time or on their own motion, if satisfied that the monetary outcome of a claim may exceed $25,000, not including interest and expenses, must transfer a claim to the Supreme Court. The defendants' claim for costs after the date of offer to settle was dismissed.

There was sufficient reason, at the commencement of the action, to proceed in Supreme Court. The plaintiff denied all of her disbursements incurred after the date of the offer to settle. Each party was to bear its own costs.

(3) If an amount is awarded under subrule (1) or (2) to a self-represented party, the court may also award the party an amount not exceeding $500 as compensation for inconvenience and expense.

O. Reg. 78/06, s. 31

Commentary: Since July 1, 2006 all offers must be in writing to affect the cost consequences pursuant to subrule 14.07. There are also optional forms now available that may be used for offers, acceptance, and withdrawal. Further subrule 14.04 has been expanded to include communications relating to on-going negotiations until liability is determined and relief granted.

No communication of an offer, if it is not accepted, may be made to the trial judge until after the decision on the merits. Acceptance of an offer must be served before it is withdrawn or is disposed of. A plaintiff's offer may include a condition that the defendant pay money into court and, if so, the defendant must pay in and advise the plaintiff.

The party initiating the offer is responsible for service either personally at least seven days before the hearing or by mail at least twelve days in advance. Where monies are paid into court as a condition, they will not be paid out unless there is a judge's order or written consent of all the parties. The clerk will also ensure that any reference to the offer to settle will be removed from the file before the action proceeds to trial.

If the defendant's offer includes money, the plaintiff may accept on the condition of payment into court and, if the defendant defaults,the plaintiff may move under Rule 15.06 for judgment or to continue the action.

If the accepted offer is silent, and if the plaintiff makes the offer,he is entitled to his disbursements to the date of acceptance; and if the defendant makes the offer, the plaintiff is entitled to disbursements to date of offer.

If there is any default under the accepted offer, the other party may move for judgment on the offer or proceed with the action as if no offer had been made.

Where an amount is awarded under subrule 14.07(1) or 14.07(2) to a party who is not represented by another person, the court may also award the party an amount not exceeding $500 as compensation for expense and inconvenience.

Rules 13 and 15 provide for costs to be awarded when pre-trials and motions, respectively, frustrate the process. They also place a limit of $100 plus disbursements on the award. It is proposed that those limits be removed and the court decide the amount.

Rule 14 deals with cost and compensation consequences of a failure to accept an offer to settle. It is proposed that the basis for calculating an award of costs and compensation in the case of unrepresented parties from an amount up to double the costs be changed to a more generic wording which would allow the court to impose costs or compensation sanctions for the failure to accept a reasonable settlement offer. The compensation clause, 14.07(3), will then become unnecessary.

Case Law: *Brockman v. Sinclair* (1979), 26 O.R. (2d) 276 (Ont. Small Cl. Ct.); affirmed (1980), 31 O.R. (2d) 436 (Ont. Div. Ct.) — The provisions of the *Small Claims Courts Act*, R.S.O. 1970, c. 439, s. 83, requiring a plaintiff to pay to the defendant costs in the event that the plaintiff recovers judgment for less than the amount of money paid into court by the defendant are mandatory. Accordingly, although the trial judge awarded judgment to the plaintiff and costs, where the amount of such judgment was for less than the amount the defendants paid into court, by virtue of the statute, the defendants are entitled to tax their costs after the date of payment.

Gibson v. McAdams (July 13, 1998), Doc. CA C21575 (Ont. C.A.) — The offer to settle contained in the pretrial memorandum was held to constitute an offer to settle under Rule 49 of the *Rules of Civil Procedure* (Ontario). The plaintiffs obtained more than that offered in the pretrial memorandum at trial. The order for solicitor-and-client costs was affirmed.

Ron's Electric Ltd. v. Harder Burke, 13 C.P.C. (5th) 328, 2000 CarswellAlta 1269, 2000 ABPC 172 (Alta. Prov. Ct.) — Contractor brought action against homeowner for payment under contract. Action allowed in amount of $3,332.08 and counterclaim allowed in amount of $4,204.24. Contractor ordered to pay to difference of $872.16 plus costs of $600. Contractor offered to settle counterclaim for $1,500, two days prior to commencement of trial, with offer specified to be withdrawn upon commencement of trial if not accepted. No appropriate to apply Rule 174 of Alberta Rules of Court, by way of section 19.1 of *Provincial Court Act*. Existing costs award was fair and reasonable in circumstances.

Jama v. Bobolo, 2002 CarswellAlta 435, 2002 ABQB 216, [2002] 7 W.W.R. 523, 19 C.P.C. (5th) 284, 2 Alta. L.R. (4th) 186, 311 A.R. 362, [2002] A.J. No. 398 (Alta. Q.B.) — Plaintiffs brought action against defendants with respect to personal injuries arising out of motor vehicle accident, dismissed by jury with costs to defendants. Defendants filed offer to settle for one dollar, inclusive of all damages, prejudgment interest, and costs. Defendants applied for double costs. Defendants' offer of settlement was *bona fide* offer.

Rooney (Litigation Guardian of) v. Graham, 2001 CarswellOnt 887, [2001] O.J. No. 1055, 198 D.L.R. (4th) 1, (sub nom. *Rooney v. Graham*) 144 O.A.C. 240, 9 C.P.C. (5th) 50, 53 O.R. (3d) 685 (Ont. C.A.) — Plaintiff bringing successful action against defendant driver. Plaintiff's offer seeking party-and-party costs to date of offer and solicitor-and-client costs thereafter. Damages awarded at trial exceeding offer. Offer to settle fell within Rule 49. Uncertainty of provision for ongoing costs did not deprive party of benefits of rule. Costs payable on solicitor-and-client scale. *Rules of Civil Procedure*, R.R.O. 1990, Reg. 194, Rule 49.

Corporate Cars v. Parlee (2002), 2002 CarswellOnt 3170 (Ont. S.C.J.) — Plaintiff made formal offer to settle. Judgment more favourable than terms of offer. Issues not complex. Claim was for $12,339. Costs fixed at $6,000 plus $993 for disbursements. Counsel could not expect to receive same remuneration for smaller amounts under simplified rules as for litigation of larger amounts with much greater complexity.

Kuzyk v. Fireman LoFranco, 2005 CanLII 25771 (Ont. S.C.J.), Archibald J. — For cost consequences of Rule 49 to be invoked, Offer to Settle must be clear and unambiguous. Offer to Settle proposed dismissal of plaintiff's action without costs to any party. An Offer to Settle that offers a dismissal of a plaintiff's claim, is not a formal offer engaging the cost consequences of rule 49: see *Rooney (Litigation Guardian of) v. Graham*, 2001 CarswellOnt 887, [2001] O.J. No. 1055, 198 D.L.R. (4th) 1, (sub nom. *Rooney v. Graham*) 144 O.A.C. 240, 9 C.P.C. (5th) 50, 53 O.R. (3d) 685 (Ont. C.A.).

Relevant factors under rule 57 reviewed.

With regard to disbursements, see *3664902 Canada Inc. v. Hudson's Bay Co.*, 2003 CarswellOnt 869, 169 O.A.C. 283, [2003] O.J. No. 950 (Ont. C.A.), at para. 17. Disbursements are to be assessed "upon the basis of what was actually spent, reduced if appropriate to what is reasonably spent."

Sharpe v. Brokerhouse Distributors Inc., 2005 CarswellBC 1020, 12 C.P.C. (6th) 370, 2005 BCSC 629 (B.C. S.C. [In Chambers]), Madam Justice Garson. Application by plaintiff for costs of action concluded by the plaintiff's acceptance of a formal offer to settle, pursuant to Rule 37 of the *Rules of Court* for $5,000. Defendant argued amount of settlement jurisdiction of the Small Claims Court and therefore plaintiff not entitled to costs other than disbursements.

Defendant contends offer and acceptance resolved *only* the plaintiff's claim against the defendant and *not* counterclaims. See *Charest Construction Ltd. v. McKay (c.o.b. Ken McKay Enterprises)*, 1985 CarswellBC 599, [1985] B.C.J. No. 90, 6 C.P.C. (2d) 61 (B.C. Co. Ct.) (cited to C.P.C.) when Provenzano Co. Ct. J. found that it was "conceivable and reasonable" in the circumstances for the plaintiff to assume that the payments into court were made in regard to the claim and not the counterclaim.

In *Immocreek Corp. v. Pretiosa Enterprises Ltd.*, 1996 CarswellOnt 4044, (sub nom. *Immo Creek Corp. v. Pretiosa Enterprises Ltd.)* 14 O.T.C. 391, [1996] O.J. No. 3436 (Ont. Gen. Div.), the Ontario Court, General Division, reached the opposite conclusion to that in *Charest*. In *Immocreek*, the court found that the plaintiff's offer to settle "all outstanding issues in this action" amounted to an offer to settle both the claim and the counterclaim.

See also *Demitri v. Niemann*, 1981 CarswellBC 92, 22 C.P.C. 112, 28 B.C.L.R. 74 (B.C. S.C.) where Locke J. found that where offer to settle not specific on which aspects of the claim it aimed at settling, the defendant "had no means of knowing to what claim the offer was directed" and therefore the plaintiff could not benefit from a rule which otherwise would have allowed her double costs. The defendant in *Demitri* did not accept the plaintiff's offer.

In this case the style of cause refers to the counterclaim. The offer refers to "this proceeding," which language generally connotes the whole proceeding.

Defendant's offer ambiguous and such ambiguity should be resolved against it as the author of the "ambiguous" document. Ambiguity results in imperfect compliance with Rule 37.

Plaintiff's application for costs as assessed allowed.

Clark v. Sidhu, 2005 CarswellBC 1488, [2005] B.C.J. No. 1373, 51 B.C.L.R. (4th) 119, 2005 BCSC 914, 18 C.P.C. (6th) 66 (B.C. S.C.).

Defendant claimed double costs after offer to settle. Trial judge ordered double costs not appropriate. Offers to settle must be reasonable as policy. Defendant's offer not reasonable as there was some evidence of injury, albeit slight injury, to plaintiff.

Bader v. Rennie (2008), 2008 CarswellOnt 700, 233 O.A.C. 390 (Ont. Div. Ct.).

Defendant moved for summary judgment and lost. Leave to appeal allowed. Court asked for submissions as to costs. Rule 49 does not apply to offers to settle appeals. See *Jones v. Kansa General Insurance Co.*, [1992] O.J. No. 1597, 1992 CarswellOnt 664, 93 D.L.R. (4th) 481, 57 O.A.C. 213, 11 C.C.L.I. (2d) 194, 10 O.R. (3d) 56 (Ont. C.A.) at paragraph 58; *Douglas Hamilton Design Inc. v. Mark*, [1993] O.J. No. 1856, 1993 CarswellOnt 459, 20 C.P.C. (3d) 224, 66 O.A.C. 44 (Ont. C.A.).

At the end of the day, what is the total for fees and disbursements that would be a fair and reasonable amount to be paid by unsuccessful parties in the particular circumstances of case?

The Queen v. Henderson, 292 D.L.R. (4th).

The matter of costs was considered *de novo* since there was a complete absence of any submissions on the issues of costs before trial judge. The court declined to increase costs due to plaintiff's settlement offer because Crown reasonable in its approach and offer not a substantial compromise of plaintiff's claim. Important points of principle involved and issues related to liability. Costs of trial fixed at $645.50.

The trial judge awarded costs to Henderson in amount of $175.00. He did not ask for submissions. Henderson was entitled to be heard. Failing to give him that opportunity was breach of natural justice and fairness and warrants granting leave to appeal on issue of costs.

The trial judge had further discretion under the *Rules of the Small Claims Court*, O. Reg. 258/98, to award Henderson up to $500.00 as compensation for inconvenience and expense and a further $50.00 as a fee for preparation of pleadings. Henderson made settlement offer re section 14.07 of the *Rules of Small Claims Court*. Total amount recoverable for costs, however, is capped at 15% of the judgment recovered.

Appeal by Her Majesty the Queen dismissed. Leave granted to Henderson to appeal costs award and judgment of trial judge varied to increase the costs award to $645.50.

Rule 15 — Motions

15.01 (1) Notice of Motion and Supporting Affidavit — A motion shall be made by a notice of motion and supporting affidavit (Form 15A).

History [R. 15.01(1)]: Formerly part of 16.01(1); refers to forms 15A and 15B, formerly 16A and 16B, respectively; eliminates exception for motions made at trial.

(2) The moving party shall obtain a hearing date from the clerk before serving the notice of motion and supporting affidavit under subrule (3).

History [R. 15.01(2)]: Formerly 16.01(2).

Motions [R. 15.01(2)]: A motion can be heard or conducted by telephone or video conference (if facilities for a telephone or video conference are available and the court permits it). A party can file a Request for Telephone or Video Conference (Form 1B), indicating the reasons for the request.

Motion schedules are established in each court location. A party may obtain a motion date from staff in advance of completing a Notice of Motion and Supporting Affidavit (Form 15A). The date must be obtained by a party at least 7 days before the date set for the hearing, since all documents must be served at least 7 days before the hearing. In providing the hearing date, consideration must be given to the type of service the person making the motion intends to use. For example, if the motion will be served on a party by mail, an additional 5 days should be added for service of the materials.

The motion shall be served on every party who has filed a claim and any defendant who has not been noted in default at least 7 days before the hearing date [r. 15.01(3)].

The motion date may need to be changed if the notice of motion and supporting affidavit was not served in time or was served by an inappropriate method.

If the nature of circumstances of the motion make notice unnecessary or not reasonably possible [r. 15.03(1)], a party may make motion without notice. In such circumstances a party will not file an affidavit of service when filing the motion materials. However, a party who obtains an order on motion without notice shall serve the order on every affected party, together with a copy of the notice of motion and supporting affidavit used on the motion, within 5 days after the order is signed.

The supporting affidavit in response to the motion shall be served on every party who has filed a claim and any defendant who has not been noted in default, and file it, with proof of service, at least two days before the hearing date [r. 15.01(03)].

An affidavit is a voluntary declaration of facts written down and sworn to by the declarant before an officer authorized to administer oaths, such as a Small Claims Court clerk, lawyer or notary public. The declarant is also known as the deponent of affirmant. Like other court documents, an affidavit cannot be amended once it is filed. A further affidavit may be filed to qualify information in the original affidavit.

(3) The notice of motion and supporting affidavit,

    (a) shall be served on every party who has filed a claim and any defendant who has not been noted in default, at least seven days before the hearing date; and

    (b) shall be filed, with proof of service, at least three days before the hearing date.

(4) Supporting Affidavit in Response — A party who prepares an affidavit **(Form 15B) in response to the moving party's notice of motion and supporting affidavit shall serve it on every party who has filed a claim or defence and file it, with proof of service, at least two days before the hearing date.**

(5) Supplementary Affidavit — The moving party may serve a supplementary affidavit on every party who has filed a claim or defence and file it, with proof of service, at least two days before the hearing date.**

(6) Motion After Judgment Signed — A motion that is made after judgment has been signed shall be served on all parties, including those who have been noted in default.**

O. Reg. 78/06, s. 32; 393/09, s. 14(1)–(3), (6)

Commentary: The U.S. Supreme Court in *Bell Atlantic v. Twombly*, 550 U.S. 544, 127 S.Ct. 1955 (U.S. Sup. Ct., 2007) discarded the oft-cited "no set of facts" standard. See also the Court's recent decision in *Ashcroft v. Iqbal*, 129 S.Ct. 1937 (U.S. Sup. Ct., 2009).

Iqbal differs from *Twombly* in another important way. Even after dividing the allegations in the complaint into allegations of law and fact, disregarding the former and parsing the latter, the Court could not say that, taken as true, the factual allegations failed to set forth the basis for a claim. So under the guise of explaining the concept of "plausibility" first announced in *Twombly*, the Court imposed a gatekeeper-type duty on the district court that applies even if the allegations of the complaint are well pleaded and thus assumed to be true.

Motions

Write short, cogent sentences in clear and precise language. Make your argument, cite the law, and tell the court what you want. Be direct. Don't assume that the judge knows the facts and/or the cases. Spell it out. Don't force the judge to search through every page. Make it easy. With many motions on her desk, she's not reading every word.

Provide evidence through the exhibits and make them easy to access. Make the complicated simple. Judges handle hundreds of cases.

Know the judge. What are her rules and procedures? Some are sticklers for adhering to how and when you serve and file. Does he give adjournments? How many? For how long?

Look the part. If you look like a slob, with a stained suit and scuffed shoes, you may be discounted. Serious lawyers look the part. Spit out your gum.

Know the facts and law better than your adversary. Who knows what the judge will ask? Be prepared for everything. But if you don't know, tell the judge.

Organize your argument and your file. Write an outline of the points you wish to emphasize. Consult it. In the heat of battle, you may forget an issue.

Speak to the judge. Answer inquiries directly. Provide reasoning and legal support. Be professional. Don't go off on a tangent. Don't go on and on. When you have completed your presentation, thank the court and sit down.

Motions in Writing

There is one type of motion that can be made "in writing." It is called a "motion in writing for assessment of damages," which can be made by the plaintiff when all defendants have failed to file a defence and have been noted in default. For a motion in writing, the plaintiff does not have to attend court for a hearing. Instead, the documents filed at the court should provide the court with everything the judge needs to make a decision.

If all defendants have been noted in default and your claim is an "unliquidated" claim, then you can ask for an order from a judge for an assessment of damages. To get this order, you can either file a motion in writing for an assessment of damages or request an assessment hearing before a judge.

You may make a motion in writing for an assessment of damages where:

- all defendants in the claim have been served with the claim;

- no defendants have filed a defence; and

- all defendants have been noted in default.

If one or more defendants have not been served with the claim, you cannot obtain an assessment of damages against any defendants who have been served, because all defendants must be noted in default. The clerk will not note a defendant in default if he or she has not been served with the claim. If one or more defendants has filed a defence, you cannot obtain an assessment of damages against the other defendants. You will need to attend a settlement conference and, if necessary, a trial.

What if I am Noted in Default?

Setting aside the noting in default or a default judgment, there are two ways under the *Rules*:

1. A motion to set aside the noting in default or default judgment. The *Rules* provide that the defendant should bring a motion to set aside a default judgment "as soon as is reasonably possible in the circumstances." The *Rules* also outline the test to meet. Rule 11.06 sets out all the requirements.

2. You may also file a Request for Clerk's Order on Consent [Form 11.2A], in which all parties consent to set aside the noting in default and default judgment.

If the noting in default and/or default judgment is set aside, you will need to complete and file a Defence [Form 9A].

A motion can be heard or conducted by telephone or video conference (if facilities for a telephone or video conference are available and the court permits it). A party can file a Request for Telephone or Video Conference [Form 1B], indicating the reasons for the request. If the judge grants the request, the court will make the necessary arrangements and notify the parties.

Motion schedules are established in each court location. A party may obtain a motion date from staff in advance of completing a Notice of Motion and Supporting Affidavit [Form 15A]. The date must be obtained by a party at least seven days before the date set for the hearing, since all documents must be served at least seven days before the hearing.

A motion may only be *adjourned* or *withdrawn* before the hearing date where the written consent of all parties is filed when the request is made, unless the court orders otherwise [rules 15.05, 15.06].

Parties request a transcript of the reasons for judgment and any other portion of the proceeding that is relevant, so that proof of the request may be served with the notice of motion and supporting affidavit requesting a new trial. It is the party's responsibility to pay the required fee directly to the court reporter. In such cases, the motion material must be submitted within 30 days after a final order is made [rule 17.04(1)].

A Notice of Motion and Supporting Affidavit may be filed for a motion in writing for an assessment of damages [rule15.02(c)]. The plaintiff does not have to attend the motion (because it is in writing) nor does he or she have to serve the motion materials on the defendant who has been noted in default. However, a date and time for hearing the motion must be scheduled.

Rule 15.03(1) and (2) describes:

- when a party may make a motion without notice to the other party; and

- how the order must be served on every affected party within 5 days after the order is signed.

Rule 15.03(3) provides that a party who is affected by an order obtained on motion without notice may make a motion to set aside or vary the order, within 30 days after being served with the order.

Examples of Motions	Rule
Lengthen or shorten any time prescribed by the rules	3.02(1)
Substituted service	8.04
Default judgment, defendant's claim	11.04
Set aside noting in default or default judgment or enforcement measures	11.06
Amend claim or defence less than 30 days before trial	12.01(3)(a)
Judgment in the terms of an accepted offer when party fails to comply	14.06
For a new trial	17.04(1)
Order directing delivery of property other than property referred to in a writ of delivery (if that property cannot be found or taken)	20.05(2)
Order consolidating 2 or more unsatisfied orders for payment of money	20.09(1)

The Powers of the Court

Does the court have *any* inherent jurisdiction?

Yes, the right to control our own process.

- The right to determine who can address the court ("the right of audience")

- The right to control the use of interpreters: *Horvath v. Lakatos* (2004), 9 R.F.L. (6th) 116, 2004 CarswellOnt 4440, 73 O.R. (3d) 277, 6 C.P.C. (6th) 394 (Ont. S.C.J.) (Any court of record has the inherent power to control the use of interpreters; where the court finds that an interpreter's translations have been inaccurate and misleading, the court may bar a person from acting as a court interpreter until a proper authority has reviewed the person's credentials)

- The right to dismiss any case for delay:

  Any court of record has the discretionary power to dismiss a case for delay: *Housser v. Savin Canada Inc.* (2005), [2005] O.J. No. 4217, 19 C.P.C. (6th) 156, 77 O.R. (3d) 251, 2005 CarswellOnt 4819 (Ont. S.C.J.). The test is whether the delay has caused such prejudice to the other party that he or she cannot get a fair trial: *Vrban v. Manias* (2003), [2003] O.J. No. 3705, 2003 CarswellOnt 3619 (Ont. C.J.), per Karswick J., reversed (2004), 2004 CarswellOnt 3904, [2004] O.J. No. 3941 (Ont. S.C.J.) (four-year delay during which a material witness on the issue of whether the respondent had treated the child as his own, had died; case dismissed for delay).

- The right to set aside our own orders:

Any court of record has this inherent jurisdiction: *Brown v. Fairchild* (1998), 38 R.F.L. (4th) 214, 1998 CarswellOnt 696, [1998] O.J. No. 609 (Ont. Prov. Div.) per Katarynych J.

Failure to Obey Order Made on Motion

Can you strike a party's pleadings if he or she doesn't show up in court?

Yes: *Kelly v. Mitts*, [2008] O.J. No. 476, 2008 CarswellOnt 668, 50 R.F.L. (6th) 407 (Ont. S.C.J.); additional reasons at 2008 CarswellOnt 2100 (Ont. S.C.J.); further additional reasons at (2008), 2008 CarswellOnt 2101 (Ont. S.C.J.) (note: in that case, the offending party didn't show up at a settlement conference *and* was also in breach of a disclosure order).

Harry v. Singh, 2007 CarswellOnt 4627, 40 R.F.L. (6th) 293, 2007 ONCJ 326 (Ont. C.J.) per Bovard J.: pleadings struck when party walked out of the courtroom in the middle of the case conference because she didn't like what the judge was saying (note: the party was also in breach of a disclosure order).

Consequences of an order striking pleadings

A party whose pleadings have been struck is not entitled to participate further in the case: *Caldwell v. Caldwell* (2006), 2006 CarswellOnt 2248, [2006] O.J. No. 1469 (Ont. C.A.).

If a party's pleadings have been struck, he or she cannot commence another proceeding on the same issue: *Halow Estate v. Halow* (2004), 2004 CarswellOnt 1742 (Ont. C.A.).

Once you have struck a party's pleadings, you have the authority to reinstate them (on motion), and to impose appropriate conditions (i.e., provide the required disclosure by a fixed date, pay costs, etc.): *Costabile v. Costabile* (2005), 2005 CarswellOnt 6909, [2005] O.J. No. 5129 (Ont. C.A.); *Caldwell v. Caldwell* (2007), 2007 CarswellOnt 433, [2007] O.J. No. 332, 51 R.F.L. (6th) 399 (Ont. S.C.J.); additional reasons at (2007), 2007 CarswellOnt 1681, 51 R.F.L. (6th) 417 (Ont. S.C.J.) (pleadings reinstated on motion by party whose pleadings were struck; he established that the court had been misled by the other party, who had omitted key facts from her affidavit in support of the motion to strike the pleadings).

The court should not make a "frivolous and vexatious" order on its own motion without first giving the parties an opportunity to make submissions.

Self-represented litigant kept bringing motions, with rambling, incomprehensible materials; there was no main application before the court, but she kept bringing motions; Timms J. of the Ontario Superior Court made order prohibiting the party from commencing any proceedings without a judge's permission; held, order upheld: *Spears v. Haugen*, 2007 ONCA 568, 2007 CarswellOnt 5213 (Ont. C.A.).

Orders prohibiting a party from commencing a proceeding or taking any further steps in a proceeding until an existing order is complied with.

General Stay Power

Section 106 of the *Courts of Justice Act* states:

> A court, on its own initiative or on motion by any person, whether or not a party, may stay a proceeding in the court on such terms as are considered just.

Using the stay power to prohibit a party from proceeding with his or her case until a prior costs order (or some other condition) has been satisfied.

A stay can be imposed until the costs have been paid: *Susin v. Chapman* (2004), [2004] O.J. No. 123, 2004 CarswellOnt 143 (Ont. C.A.); *Laue v. Laue* (1996), 10 O.F.L.R. 133, [1996] O.J. No. 4224, 1996 CarswellOnt 4672 (Ont. Prov. Div.) per Katarynych J.; *Amediku v. Amediku* (2003), [2003] O.J. No. 3016, 2003 CarswellOnt 2947 (Ont. C.J.) per Dunn J.

Case Law: *Green v. Green* (2008), 2008 CarswellOnt 4885 (Ont. Div. Ct.)

Appeal related to the denial by the trial judge of the leave to bring a motion to remove appellants as a party to the proceeding.

The history of the proceeding led trial judge to make an order that no one could bring a motion without her leave. It was entirely within the jurisdiction of the trial judge to make such an order because of the manner in which parties choose to litigate their disputes.

It was held that "it is apparent from trial judge's decision that the reasons that led her to add the appellant originally as a party were still extant" and thus, there was no reason to interfere with that conclusion.

15.02 Method of Hearing — (1) A motion may be heard,

(a) in person;

(b) by telephone or video conference in accordance with paragraph 2 of subrule 1.07(1);

(c) by a judge in writing under clause 11.03(2)(a);

(d) by any other method that the judge determines is fair and reasonable.

(2) The attendance of the parties is not required if the motion is in writing under clause (1)(c).

O. Reg. 78/06, s. 32

History [R. 15.02]: Formerly 16.02; plain language changes.

Commentary: Given the Small Claims Court is a statutory court, it does not have any general or inherent power to make orders, on motion or otherwise, merely because they are desired by one or more parties. The court's jurisdiction to deal with a particular motion issue and to grant specific orders must be conferred by the applicable legislation, whether expressly or by necessary implication.

What follows is a review of several motion issues which arise from time to time in Small Claims Court and raise questions of jurisdiction.

1. — Motions for Judgment

Under the *Rules of Civil Procedure*, an action in the Superior Court of Justice can be determined on the merits by final judgment without a trial, under either Rule 20 or Rule 21. Rule 21 is essentially a pleadings motion in which the court is asked to decide, before a trial has occurred, whether a claim or defence is fatally flawed as a matter of law. Rule 20 provides for an assessment of affidavit evidence, so that the court may determine whether a claim or defence presents any factual issue which requires a trial for its resolution.

It was recently determined by the Court of Appeal that there is no such thing in the Small Claims Court as a summary judgment motion akin to the procedure in Rule 20 of the *Rules of Civil Procedure*: see *Van de Vrande v. Butkowsky*, 2010 ONCA 230, 2010 CarswellOnt 1777, [2010] O.J. No. 1239, 99 O.R. (3d) 648, 99 O.R. (3d) 641, 85 C.P.C. (6th) 205, 260 O.A.C. 323, 319 D.L.R. (4th) 132 (Ont. C.A.); additional reasons at 2010 ONCA 400, 2010 CarswellOnt 3629, 85 C.P.C. (6th) 212 (Ont. C.A.). Rather, there is rule 12.02 of the *Small Claims Court Rules*, which contemplates a motion that is conceptually situated between Rules 20 and 21 of the *Rules of Civil Procedure* but which is more akin to Rule 21 than to Rule 20. The Court of Appeal cautioned against importing into the Small Claims Court the jurisprudence generated under Rule 20 and 21 of the *Rules of Civil Procedure*. Terms such as "summary judgment motion" and "genuine issue for trial" should be avoided. A motions under rule 12.02 is more appropriately described as a motion for judgment, motion to strike, or rule 12.02 motion. The court in *Van de Vrande* provided little guidance on the circumstances in which it is appropriate to grant judgment on a rule 12.02 motion, effectively leaving that issue to be developed by the Small Claims Court and Divisional Court.

Van de Vrande was first considered by the Divisional Court in *Vuong v. Toronto East General & Orthopaedic Hospital*, 2010 ONSC 6827, 2010 CarswellOnt 10206, 328 D.L.R. (4th) 759 (Ont. Div. Ct.). In that case the dismissal of a claim under rule 12.02 was upheld by the appeal court, based on abuse of process and limitation defences.

In *O'Brien v. Ottawa Hospital*, 2011 ONSC 231, 2011 CarswellOnt 88, [2011] O.J. No. 66 (Ont. Div. Ct.), the appeal judge upheld the dismissal under rule 12.02 of a claim for medical malpractice, on the basis that the claim had "no meaningful chance of success at trial." The defence expert evidence indicated that the standard of care was met, and the plaintiff had no expert evidence to the contrary.

A dental malpractice claim was dismissed under rule 12.02 in *Diler v. Uppal* (May 7, 2010), Doc. 110/10, [2010] O.J. No. 1903 (Ont. Sm. Cl. Ct.), where it was held that the claim was barred by expiry of the limitation period, disclosed no reasonable cause of action, was unsupported by expert evidence, and had "no meaningful chance of success at trial." See also *1690422 Ontario Inc. v. Altagas Holdings No. 2*, [2011] O.J. No. 1115, 2011 CarswellOnt 1792 (Ont. Sm. Cl. Ct.); *Dougherty v. Goad & Goad* (June 1, 2011), [2011] O.J. No. 2423 (Ont. Sm. Cl. Ct.); *1528590 Ontario Ltd. v. Ferrera Concrete Ltd.* (September 14, 2011), Doc. 368/10, [2011] O.J. No. 4845 (Ont. Sm. Cl. Ct.); *Metcalfe v. Khanna* (January 8, 2012), Doc. 1859/11, [2012] O.J. No. 34 (Ont. Sm. Cl. Ct.), where claims were dismissed under rule 12.02 based on limitations defences and other grounds.

In light of the Court of Appeal's decision in *Van de Vrande, supra*, the authorities dealing with motions for judgment in the Small Claims Court which pre-date that case are unlikely to be of further assistance.

2. — Document Discovery Motions

Some parties attempt to compel production of documents from opposing parties, or even non-parties, by way of motion before trial. However there is no discovery in the Small Claims Court: *Phillips v. Dis-Management*, 1995 CarswellOnt 865, 24 O.R. (3d) 435 (Ont. Gen. Div.). As the Court of Appeal confirmed in *Van de Vrande v. Butkowsky*, 2010 ONCA 230, 2010 CarswellOnt 1777, [2010] O.J. No. 1239, 99 O.R. (3d) 648, 99 O.R. (3d) 641, 85 C.P.C. (6th) 205, 260 O.A.C. 323, 319 D.L.R. (4th) 132 (Ont. C.A.); additional reasons at 2010 ONCA 400, 2010 CarswellOnt 3629, 85 C.P.C. (6th) 212 (Ont. C.A.), motion procedure in the Small Claims Court is governed by the *Small Claims Court Rules* and not the *Rules of Civil Procedure*.

To some extent, disclosure of documents between parties occurs through the practice of attaching significant documents the parties rely upon to their respective pleadings (see rules 7.01(2)at para. 2 and 9.02(1) at para. 2), and in preparation for a settlement conference (rule 13.03(2)(a)). Those provisions mandate disclosure of documents each party relies on rather than all relevant documents. Such disclosure is substantially more limited than document discovery under Rule 30 of the *Rules of Civil Procedure*, which requires production of all relevant documents even if the party does not intend to rely on them at trial.

A settlement conference judge may make an order for the production of documents between the parties (rule 13.05(2)(a)(vi)). That power may be exercised based on relevance rather than reliance, and is therefore somewhat broader than the previously-mentioned rules; however, it has been held that there is no jurisdiction for a motions judge to entertain requests for the production of documents: *Norquay Developments Ltd. v. Oxford County Housing Corp.*, 2010 CarswellOnt 366, [2010] O.J. No. 274 (Ont. Sm. Cl. Ct.); *Petrykowski v. 553562 Ontario Ltd.* (March 16, 2010), Doc. 886/09, [2010] O.J. No. 1048 (Ont. Sm. Cl. Ct.). In other words, requests for documents can be made at a settlement conference, but motions for production of documents are not part of the Small Claims Court procedure. There have, however, been cases where such orders have been made: see for example *Frederick v. Osborn*, 2003 CarswellOnt 2181, [2003] O.J. No. 2215 (Ont. Sm. Cl. Ct.). It is submitted that the better view is that document discovery motions, like other forms of discovery comparable to Rules 30 to 35 of the *Rules of Civil Procedure*, are not contemplated by the *Small Claims Court Rules*.

On a related subject, it has been held that the Small Claims Court has no jurisdiction to compel production of documents by non-parties before trial: *Polymer Distribution Inc. v. Rasmussen* (March 25, 2011), Doc. 1513/10, [2011] O.J. No. 1281 (Ont. Sm. Cl. Ct.); *Lemont v. State Farm Mutual Automobile Ins. Co.*, 2011 CarswellOnt 15743, 9 C.C.L.I. (5th) 318, [2011] O.J. No. 4601 (Ont. Sm. Cl. Ct.). The *Small Claims Court Rules* contain no equivalent to rule 30.10 of the *Rules of Civil Procedure*.

3. — Motions for Interim Possession

There are conflicting cases over the availability, in cases where the recovery of possession of personal property is claimed, of motions before trial dealing with interim possession of property.

The Small Claims Court has no jurisdiction to grant an injunction or mandatory order; however, its monetary jurisdiction includes both the jurisdiction to hear claims for damages within the monetary jurisdiction, and claims for recovery of personal property where the value of the property does not exceed the monetary jurisdiction: see s. 23(1) of the *Courts of Justice Act*. Sometimes plaintiffs claiming recovery of possession of personal property are not willing to wait for a trial to obtain recovery of the property. The question is whether the court can grant relief before trial in those situations.

In *Easy Home v. Rogalski*, 2004 CarswellOnt 475, 46 C.P.C. (5th) 318 (Ont. Sm. Cl. Ct.), the plaintiff sought the return of personal property by way of a motion, but had not commenced an action. Justice J. Wright, sitting as a judge of the Small Claims Court, held that the court had no jurisdiction to issue a writ of delivery on a motion brought in that fashion. Rather the plaintiff had to commence an action and obtain a judgment, either by default or otherwise. The writ of delivery (Form 20B) was a mechanism for the enforcement of an order, and was not available to a plaintiff who did not first obtain an order for the delivery of personal property in the normal course.

In *Easyhome Ltd. v. Geveart*, 2007 CarswellOnt 3237, [2007] O.J. No. 2025 (Ont. Sm. Cl. Ct.), a claim had been issued but not served when the plaintiff brought an *ex parte* motion for a writ of delivery. Deputy Judge Searle dismissed the motion, holding that there was no jurisdiction to issue a writ of delivery before a judgment had been obtained after service of the claim on the defendant. See also *N.C.R. Leasing, Inc. v. Michano* (June 12, 2008), Doc. 08-0396, [2008] O.J. No. 2351 (Ont. Sm. Cl. Ct.).

In *E-Zee Rent-To-Own Inc. v. Hopkins*, 2009 CarswellOnt 1480 (Ont. Sm. Cl. Ct.), however, an *ex parte* motion for interim recovery of personal property was granted. The judge applied Rule 44 of the *Rules of Civil Procedure*, "by analogy," finding that the power of "the court" to award interim recovery of personal property under section 104 of the *Courts of Justice Act* extended to the Small Claims Court. No caselaw was cited.

In *Coulthard v. Lawrence* (November 29, 2011), Doc. SC-11-90801-00, [2011] O.J. No. 6207 (Ont. Sm. Cl. Ct.), the court granted a motion for interim recovery of possession of two dogs. The deputy judge found that he had jurisdiction to make that order, but lacked jurisdiction to order an expedited trial.

There appears to be no binding authority directly on point. The best that can be said is that (i) in *Van de Vrande, supra*, the Court of Appeal confirmed the general proposition that procedure in the Small Claims Court is governed by the *Small Claims Court Rules* — which contain no reference to a motion for interim recovery of possession of personal property; and

(ii) at present the weight of authorities from the Small Claims Court is against the existence of a jurisdiction to make such an order.

Examples of Motions	Rule
Lengthen or shorten any time prescribed by the rules	3.02(1)
Substituted service	8.04
Default judgment, defendant's claim	11.04
Set aside noting in default or default judgment	11.06
Amend claim or defence less than 30 days before trial	12.01(3)
Judgment in the terms of an accepted offer when party fails to comply	14.06
For a new trial	17.04(1)
Order directing delivery of property other than property referred to in a writ of delivery (if that property cannot be found or taken)	20.05(2)
Order consolidating 2 or more unsatisfied orders for payment of money	20.09(1)

If a claim and defence are filed in Small Claims Court and the parties file minutes of settlement and a draft judgment for the judge's signature, is this considered an *ex parte* motion?

If a date was not yet fixed for trial and the trial fee has not yet been paid, then this should be treated as an *ex parte* motion and a motion fee would be payable. A party may attend the court office and/or make a written inquiry (without any completed documents) to obtain an order of the court by way of a motion.

Q. A plaintiff fixes a date for an Assessment of Damages in SCC and pays the $100 fee to do so and subsequently judgment is granted in favour of the plaintiff. The defendant then brings a motion to set aside the judgment. The motion is granted and the matter is now in a position to proceed to trial (this would constitute fixing a second trial). Is there a fee to fix a date for trial?

A. The $100 fee would *not* have to be paid to fix a date for trial again. The plaintiff would have paid the $100 fee in the first instance and should not be expected to pay it again in this situation.

Q. The defendant files a defence and the plaintiff pays the $100 to fix a date for trial. The defendant fails to attend the trial (*e.g.*, hospitalized) and the trial is held in the defendant's absence. The defendant subsequently makes a motion to have the matter brought back on the list for trial. The motion is granted. Is there a fee to fix a date for trial again?

A. The $100 fee would *not* have to be paid to fix a date for trial again.

Q. A plaintiff pays the $100 fee to set a matter down for trial. The trial is held, and then one of the parties makes a motion to the court for a new trial within 30 days after the original trial. Is there a fee to have the matter set down?

A. The $100 fee *would have to be paid again.*

Summary Judgment Motions

Some Small Claims Courts allow summary judgment motions: see *Om v. Insurance Corp. of British Columbia*, [1999] B.C.J. No. 3077 (B.C. Prov. Ct.); *Anton, Campion, MacDonald & Phillips v. Rowat*, [1996] Y.J. No. 130, 1996 CarswellYukon 84 (Y.T. Terr. Ct.); *N.A.P.E. v. Drake*, [1996] N.J. No. 170 (Nfld. Prov. Ct.). The rules contain no provision for a summary judgment motion because the Small Claims Court Rules were themselves intended to provide for "... the summary disposition after a trial of small claims, with a minimum of pre-trial proceedings": *Ron Robinson Ltd. v. Canadian Indemnity Co.*, 1984 CarswellOnt 1354, 45 O.R. (2d) 124, 2 O.A.C. 359 (Ont. Div. Ct.). See also *Santesso Bros. Iron Works Ltd. v. Forte Construction Corp.*, [1999] O.J. No. 5365 (Ont. Small Cl. Ct.).

Costs Sanctions in Small Claims Court

A Small Claims Court may consider it necessary in the interests of justice to penalize a party, counsel or agent for unreasonable behaviour in the proceedings. Illustrations of unreasonable behaviour are:

1. False and hurtful allegations, in particular:

     a) a "bizarre and ridiculous" claim by the plaintiff containing "false and vicious" allegations the defendant was dishonest and had committed a fraud: *Molnar v. Langille*, [2003] O.J. No. 846, 2003 CarswellOnt 783 (Ont. S.C.J.) at paras. 25, 36 and 34.

     b) in a claim the plaintiff brought ". . . to punish and make life unpleasant for his enemies rather than to obtain compensation for a wrong," the plaintiff falsely alleged criminal misappropriation against one defendant: *Biggins v. Bovan*, [2005] O.J. No. 1000 (Ont. S.C.J.) at para. 20.

2. Failure to accept a reasonable offer: *Jones v. LTL Contracting Ltd.*, [1995] O.J. No. 4927 (Ont. Sm. Cl. Ct.); affirmed [1995] O.J. No. 4928 (Ont. Gen. Div.); *Kakamin v. Hasan*, 2005 CarswellOnt 4066, [2005] O.J. No. 2778 (Ont. Sm. Cl. Ct.) at para. 10.

Case Law: *Ivan's Films Inc. v. Kostelac* (1988), A.C.W.S. (3d) 260 (Ont. Master) — The onus with respect to the proper service of a statement of claim on the defendant remains with the plaintiff. A motion granted to set aside default judgment where the affidavit of service was by an officer of the plaintiff was not sworn until months after the service, and was not acted upon until months after the affidavit was sworn.

James Sturino Realty Ltd. v. Andrew Michaels Group Ltd. (1988), 64 O.R. (2d) 410 (Ont. Div. Ct.) — In setting aside a default judgment, parties should not be placed in jeopardy by reason of the neglect or inadvertence of their solicitors. Additionally, however, a court exercising its discretion must consider how soon the motion was brought, the explanation of the default and the defence to the action on the merits.

Weber c. Paramount Paving Inc. (January 16, 1998), Doc. 500-22-013321-974 (Qué Civ. Div.), Renaud J. — The defendant's motion was made on the basis of *res judicata* in that the plaintiff previously brought a similar action in the Small Claims Court, which resulted in a settlement. Motion was dismissed. Although the parties were the same in the two actions, the subject-matter was different. The first action was brought on the basis of the defective work; whereas, this action was strictly on the basis of the breach of the settlement agreement.

Ellis v. GeoPremiere Developments Ltd. (November 3, 1998), Doc. 97-CT-045786 (Ont. Gen. Div.) — Motion by the defendants for judgment dismissing the plaintiff's action or for partial judgment. The plaintiffs commenced a Small Claims Court action for $6,000 in damages in relation to the club's special assessment. That claim was currently pending before the court. Motion dismissed. The plaintiffs raised a genuine issue for trial in respect of repudiation. The test for repudiation was an objective one, and a trial judge was required to hear all of the evidence in respect of the suggestion of repudiation to determine whether it met the objective test.

Karanikas v. Jewell (January 7, 1999), Doc. 90-CQ-047217 (Ont. Master) — The defendant solicitor brought a motion to dismiss action against him for delay. The defendant argued that pursuant to inherent jurisdiction of court and s. 106 of *Courts of Justice Act*, the court had jurisdiction to dismiss the action. The action was dismissed. Rule 24.01 of *Rules of Civil*

Procedure (Ontario) is not exhaustive of the mechanisms available to the defendant who claims to be prejudiced by delay.

Holmes Foundry Ltd. v. Point Edward (Village), [1963] 2 O.R. 404, 39 D.L.R. (2d) 621 (Ont. C.A.) — An order may be withdrawn, altered, or modified by a judge either on his or her own initiative or on the application of a party until such time as the order has been drawn up, passed, and entered.

A consent order is a contract and can only be varied by subsequent consent or on any ground which would invalidate a contract: *Chitel v. Rothbart* (1984), 42 C.P.C. 217 (Ont. Master); affirmed (1985), 2 C.P.C. (2d) xlix (Ont. Div. Ct.); leave to appeal refused (1985), 15 C.P.C. (2d) xlviii (Ont. C.A.).

Lee v. Canadian Tire Corp. (2000), 2000 CarswellOnt 1470 (Ont. Sm. Cl. Ct.) — The defendants were entitled to costs of motion required to compel the plaintiffs to comply with previous court orders. An amount of $50 for pleading and a counsel fee of $300 as well as costs thrown away for disbursements relating to the motion in amount of $110 was awarded.

Pinuela v. Ellis (1999), 1999 CarswellOnt 4745 (Ont. S.C.J.) — The plaintiff (NP) was unrepresented and submissions were unintelligible. The costs of motion imposed entirely upon NP. Costs of $1,000 were in favour of the defendant (CE) and $1,250 was in favour of the defendant OE.

Borealis Exploration Ltd. v. Manitoba, 2001 CarswellMan 505, 2001 MBCA 165, 160 Man. R. (2d) 61, 262 W.A.C. 61, 14 C.P.C. (5th) 1 (Man. C.A.) — Sheriff and provincial Crown appealed dismissal of their motion to dismiss plaintiff's claim that they acted negligently in manner in which seizure of plaintiff's goods was effected. Findings of bad faith would negative statutory immunity in respect of sheriff's and Crown's actions. Appeal from 2001 CarswellMan 9, 6 C.P.C. (5th) 342, 2000 MBQB 239, 152 Man. R. (2d) 311 dismissed.

British Columbia v. Sherbaniuk, 2000 CarswellBC 2750, 2000 BCSC 1875 (B.C. S.C. [In Chambers]) — Respondent unrepresented. Petitioner sought to regulate respondent's conduct. Respondent ordered to deliver material in timely fashion and refrain from making allegations of impropriety against solicitor's firm and process server.

Armstrong v. West Vancouver (District), 2002 BCSC 135, 2002 CarswellBC 279, 26 M.P.L.R. (3d) 129, [2002] B.C.J. No. 254 (B.C. S.C.); affirmed 2003 CarswellBC 264, 2003 BCCA 73, 10 B.C.L.R. (4th) 305, 35 M.P.L.R. (3d) 108, 223 D.L.R. (4th) 102, 178 B.C.A.C. 233, 292 W.A.C. 233, [2003] B.C.J. No. 303 (B.C. C.A.) — Application to dismiss plaintiff's claim prior to trial. Issue of B.C. Limitations Act, in particular section 6(5)(c) ". . . knowledge of or means of knowledge of any previous owner is attributed to any subsequent owner. . ." Action dismissed.

Goudie v. Ottawa (City), 2003 SCC 14, 2003 CarswellOnt 862, 2003 CarswellOnt 863, [2003] S.C.J. No. 12, 2003 C.L.L.C. 220-028, [2003] 1 S.C.R. 141, 223 D.L.R. (4th) 395, 30 C.P.C. (5th) 207, 301 N.R. 201, 170 O.A.C. 201, 23 C.C.E.L. (3d) 1 (S.C.C.) — If a pre-employment agreement was made as alleged, a claim for its enforcement cannot arise from the interpretation, application, administration or violation of the collective agreement.

Clayton et al. v. Dr. M.L.T. Zorn (Ont. Sm. Cl. Ct.), J.R. Connolly, D.J., SC-04-096340-00, December 3, 2004 — No evidence to support any claim of a negligent act. No provision in *Rules of Small Claims Court* to hear motion for summary judgment. In *Wolf v. Goldenberg*, [2003] O.J. No. 3067, Maefs Deputy J., set out relationship between Rules 1.03(2) and 12.02(2) of the *Rules of the Small Claims Court* and Rule 21.01(1) in dismissing an action as a point of law.

Defendant should be able to bring a motion for summary judgment similar to Rule 20.01(3) of the *Rules of Civil Procedure*. See also *Gutierrez v. Tropic International Ltd.*, 2002 CarswellOnt 2599, [2002] O.J. No. 3079, 162 O.A.C. 247, 63 O.R. (3d) 63, 33 B.L.R. (3d) 18 (Ont. C.A.). Action dismissed.

Wakelin v. Gourley, 2005 CarswellOnt 2808, 76 O.R. (3d) 272, 19 C.P.C. (6th) 13 (Ont. Master), Master Dash. Plaintiff moving to add third parties as defendants after limitation period. Claimed he did not know and could not with reasonable diligence have known names of proposed defendants.

Defendants usually added with leave to plead limitation defence where plaintiff puts in evidence as to steps taken to ascertain identity of tortfeasors and gives reasonable explanation as to why such information not obtainable with due diligence. Plaintiff not meeting low threshold. Motion dismissed. See also *Wong v. Adler*, [2004] O.J. No. 1575, 2004 CarswellOnt 1522, 70 O.R. (3d) 460, 5 M.V.R. (5th) 142, 2 C.P.C. (6th) 175 (Ont. Master); affirmed 2005 CarswellOnt 4221, 76 O.R. (3d) 237, 17 C.P.C. (6th) 65 (Ont. Div. Ct.), *Parlette v. Sokkia Inc.*, [2004] O.T.C. 995 (Ont. S.C.J.); affirmed [2005] O.J. No. 318, 2005 CarswellOnt 343, 194 O.A.C. 22 (Ont. Div. Ct.).

Finlayson v. GMAC Leaseco Ltd./GMAC Location Ltée, 2007 CarswellOnt 900, 84 O.R. (3d) 680, 40 C.P.C. (6th) 332, [2007] O.J. No. 597 (Ont. S.C.J.), J.W. Quinn J.

Motion granted. Court could add solicitor as party via inherent jurisdiction. Court had inherent jurisdiction to control its own process and such jurisdiction included determining whether particular person could intervene as added party to proceeding. Solicitor in position to be adversely affected by judgment in defendant's motion. Several questions of law and fact existed between solicitor and other parties to defendant's motion.

Leeuw v. Arrow Transportation Systems Inc., 2007 CarswellBC 2587, 47 C.P.C. (6th) 388, 2007 BCSC 1590, 55 C.C.L.I. (4th) 216 (B.C. S.C.), Smart J.

Parties disagreed on interpretation of offer to settle accepted by defendant. Plaintiff's motion to enforce her interpretation of offer granted. Prior to decision, defendant rejected plaintiff's offer to settle motion for $5,900. Plaintiff awarded $5,947.06. Plaintiff applied for double costs. Application dismissed. Rule 37(23) of *Rules of Court, 1990* applies to offer to settle "claim." Motion was not claim within meaning of Rule. Motion not cause of action but interlocutory incident of litigation.

A "cause of action" defined by Diplock LJ in *Letang v. Cooper*, [1965] 1 Q.B. 232, [1964] 2 All E.R. 929, [1964] Lloyd's Rep. 339 (Eng. C.A.) at 242-43 (Q.B.) and adopted in *Consumers Glass Co. v. Foundation Co. of Canada/Cie fondation du Canada*, 1985 CarswellOnt 143, 51 O.R. (2d) 385, 20 D.L.R. (4th) 126, 9 O.A.C. 193, 30 B.L.R. 87, 33 C.C.L.T. 104, 13 C.L.R. 149, 1 C.P.C. (2d) 208 (Ont. C.A.) at 131 (D.L.R.) as "a factual situation, the existence of which entitles one person to obtain from the court a remedy against another."

Reddy v. Oshawa Flying Club (1992), [1992] O.J. No. 1337, 1992 CarswellOnt 349, 11 C.P.C. (3d) 154 (Ont. Gen. Div.)

Three separate actions in which the proposed plaintiff was a party had been dismissed on consent. Actions dismissed. The issues raised in the current action were virtually identical to those raised in the earlier actions.

The doctrine of abuse of process is somewhat similar to the doctrine of res judicata in that it also seeks to prevent a multiplicity of proceedings or the re-litigation of an issue determined in earlier proceedings or which might have been raised in earlier proceedings but the party now raising the issue before the court chose not to do so.

Canam Enterprises Inc. v. Coles (2000), 2000 CarswellOnt 562, 47 O.R. (3d) 446 (Ont. S.C.J.)

Plaintiff was unsuccessful in his action against the defendant. Plaintiff then commenced an action against own solicitor for negligence. The solicitor denying negligence and brought third party claims against the defendants. Solicitor's claim was dismissed. The Court of Appeal held that doctrine of abuse of process is used to bar proceedings inconsistent with objectives of public policy, and can be relied upon by persons who were not parties to prior litigation but who should have been sued in that litigation.

Abuse of process is not limited to the application of issue estoppel. Abuse of process is a discretionary principle that is not limited by any set number of categories. The doctrine can be relied upon by persons who were not parties to the previous litigation but who claim that if they were going to be sued they should have been sued in the previous litigation.

Alvi v. Misir (2004), 2004 CarswellOnt 5302, [2004] O.J. No. 5088, 50 B.L.R. (3d) 175, 73 O.R. (3d) 566 (Ont. S.C.J. [Commercial List])

Defendants successfully brought a motion for order dismissing or staying action on ground that it was frivolous, vexatious and abuse of process of court. The court ruled that it clearly has jurisdiction to control its own process and to prevent abuse of process.

Abuse of process: The doctrine of abuse of process is a flexible doctrine which engages the inherent power of the court to prevent misuse of its procedure in a way that would be manifestly unfair to a party to the litigation before it or would in some other way attack the integrity of the adjudicative process and bring the administration of justice into disrepute.

Kramer Ltd. v. Dallas Contracting Ltd., 2007 CarswellSask 86, 292 Sask. R. 187, 47 C.P.C. (6th) 332, 2007 SKQB 24 (Sask. Q.B.)

The plaintiffs sought the production of the defendants' representatives' file and minute books in relation to its allegations. Although the defendants were willing to produce the documents, its' representatives asserted a solicitor's lien. The defendants' representatives were ordered to produce the files and minute books held in their possession for the purpose of the discovery process. The defendants' obligation to produce the files superseded the representatives' right to retain them under a solicitor's lien.

MCAP Service Corp. v. McLaren (2008), 2008 CarswellOnt 1376 (Ont. Div. Ct.); reversing (2007), 2007 CarswellOnt 9063 (Ont. S.C.J.); refusing leave to appeal (2007), 2007 CarswellOnt 944 (Ont. S.C.J.)

Fundamental to administration of justice that litigants entitled to have reasons delivered by Court in disposing of matters. Failure to give reasons and circumstances of case gave rise to real concern that motions judge failed to deal with motion for leave on its merits. Motion for leave to be reheard, before another judge.

Bagaco v. Union Energy Ltd. Partnership (2009), [2009] O.J. No. 673, 2009 CarswellOnt 900, 76 C.P.C. (6th) 314 (Ont. S.C.J.)

Thirty-five plaintiffs brought action for negligence and breach of contract. Defendant brought motion for order severing plaintiffs' claims. Motion granted. Claims were improperly joined. Twenty-seven claims within Small Claims Court jurisdiction, so could be conducted pursuant to summary procedures.

Bryfogle v. Smit, 2009 CarswellBC 1442, 2009 BCCA 256, [2009] B.C.J. No. 1117 (B.C. C.A.).

Bryfogle appealed order of Meiklem, J., made 2 April 2007, dismissing Bryfogle's action against defendants and enjoining him from instituting "any legal proceedings in any court" without leave of the court. Reasons for judgment indexed as 2007 BCSC 457. Hallmarks of vexatious conduct of legal proceedings set out by Henry J. in *Lang Michener Lash Johnston v. Fabian* (1987), [1987] O.J. No. 355, 1987 CarswellOnt 378, 16 C.P.C. (2d) 93, 59 O.R. (2d) 353, 37 D.L.R. (4th) 685 at para. 62 (Ont. H.C.). No reviewable error. Appeal dismissed.

Donaghy v. Scotia Capital Inc./Scotia Capitaux Inc., 2009 CarswellOnt 168, 93 O.R. (3d) 776, 2009 ONCA 40, 73 C.P.C. (6th) 1 (Ont. C.A.); leave to appeal refused, 398 N.R. 391 (note), 262 O.A.C. 394 (note), 2009 CarswellOnt 4362, 2009 CarswellOnt 4363 (S.C.C.)

Motion for summary judgment to enforce settlement under R. 49.09 applies to settlements reached after litigation commenced and that R. 20 was appropriate rule to enforce settlement. Motion dismissed since court did not make jurisdictional error in granting summary judgment order. Even if court was in error in applying R.49.09, it was irregularity not nullity pursuant to R. 2.01(1). Outcome would not have been different under R. 20. Appeal dismissed.

Fountain v. Ford (2009), 2009 CarswellOnt 705, [2009] O.J. No. 562 (Ont. Sm. Cl. Ct.), Searle D.J.

Motion for summary judgment dismissed. Summary judgment procedure alien to Small Claims Court as examinations for discovery and cross-examination on affidavits for use on return of motion. What was sought was not recourse to provisions of R. 1.03(2) of Small Claims Court Rules to resolve difficulty that arose when rules of Small Claims Court "do not cover matter adequately," but rather recourse to this sub-rule to introduce alien procedure. Motion not brought pursuant to R. 12.02, being rule that permits court to strike out or amend all or any part of document that discloses no reasonable cause of action.

Grant v. McKnight, 2009 CarswellNB 8, 2009 CarswellNB 9, 75 R.P.R. (4th) 182, 306 D.L.R. (4th) 357, 56 B.L.R. (4th) 60, 2009 NBCA 4, 73 C.P.C. (6th) 43, 340 N.B.R. (2d) 386, 871 A.P.R. 386 (N.B. C.A.)

Plaintiff brought motion to enforce settlement. Motion granted. Defendants appealed. Appeal dismissed. Motion judge did not err in concluding oral agreement to settle lawsuit was binding as it fell outside of ambit of s. 1 of Statute of Frauds.

Hamilton (City) v. Svedas Koyanagi Architects (2009), 79 C.L.R. (3d) 91, 2009 CarswellOnt 1327 (Ont. S.C.J.)

City brought motion to amend its statement of claim to add H Ltd. and HC Ltd. as defendants to existing action. Motion dismissed. No attempt made on motion to lead evidence as to attempts made by city to discover identity of H Ltd. and HC Ltd. Inference drawn nothing had been done. No triable issue with respect to discoverability to leave trial judge or judge hearing motion for summary judgment.

Taylor v. Canada (Attorney General) (2009), (sub nom. *Taylor v. Canada (Minister of Health)*) 309 D.L.R. (4th) 400, [2009] O.J. No. 2490, 95 O.R. (3d) 561, 2009 ONCA 487, 2009 CarswellOnt 3443 (Ont. C.A.); affirming (2008), 2008 CarswellOnt 1882 (Ont. S.C.J.)

Third parties brought motion to strike pleading and dismiss third party claim. Motion granted. Plaintiff's amendments to her statement of claim rendered third party claim untenable.

MCAP Service Corp. v. McLaren (2008), 2008 CarswellOnt 1376 (Ont. Div. Ct.); reversing (2007), 2007 CarswellOnt 9063 (Ont. S.C.J.); refusing leave to appeal (2007), 2007 CarswellOnt 944 (Ont. S.C.J.)

Fundamental to administration of justice that litigants entitled to have reasons delivered by Court in disposing of matters. Failure to give reasons and circumstances of case gave rise to real concern that motions judge failed to deal with motion for leave on its merits. Motion for leave to be reheard, before another judge

Zhang v. 1606238 Ontario Inc., 2010 CarswellOnt 760, 2010 ONSC 973 (Ont. S.C.J.).

Plaintiff moved to stay Defendant's Small Claims Court action, arguing that a multiplicity of proceedings should be avoided and that the Plaintiff may be prejudiced in these proceedings by any ruling in the Small Claims Court by operation of the principle of issue estoppel.

Starland Contracting Inc. v. 1581518 Ontario Ltd., 252 O.A.C. 19, 83 C.L.R. (3d) 1, [2009] O.J. No. 2480, 2009 CarswellOnt 3431 (Ont. Div. Ct.)

The Court has the authority to dismiss action or defence as a sanction for default of court orders and failure to comply with case management timetables. The decision to strike claim or defence one of discretion, must be exercised on proper principles.

Watch Lake North Green Lake Volunteer Fire Department Society v. Haskins, 2010 CarswellBC 1605, 2010 BCPC 114, 71 B.L.R. (4th) 101 (B.C. Prov. Ct.)

Former directors acted in good faith and within scope of their authority. The Court had jurisdiction to hear application to dismiss proceedings. Rule 16(6)(o) of B.C. *Small Claims Rules* gave authority to dismiss proceedings. Fact that application brought prior to settlement conference not fatal.

Fritsch v. Magee, 2012 ONSC 2755, 2012 CarswellOnt 5791, 40 C.P.C. (7th) 320, Baltman, J. (Ont. S.C.J.); additional reasons 2012 ONSC 4301, 2012 CarswellOnt 9116 (Ont. S.C.J.).

The defendant brought a motion at the outset of the trial to have the plaintiff's action dismissed as statute barred. The alleged assault occurred on May 13, 2006. The plaintiff issued a claim in Small Claims Court on July 17, 2007, well within that period.

The plaintiff's counsel asked to have the Small Claims Court action "stayed" on consent on July 31, 2008, when the matter was scheduled to be spoken to. On July 30, 2008, the plaintiff's counsel issued a statement of claim in the Superior Court. In these circumstances it was grossly unfair to preclude the plaintiff from proceeding.

See *Waymark v. Barnes*, 1995 CarswellBC 61, 3 B.C.L.R. (3d) 354, 57 B.C.A.C. 249, 94 W.A.C. 249, [1995] B.C.J. No. 658 (B.C. C.A. [In Chambers]), where Taylor J.A. on behalf of the British Columbia Court of Appeal (in chambers) commented at para. 7 that:

> . . . it seems that once the limitation period has expired a claim cannot be moved from that court to the Supreme Court: see also *MacMaster v. Insurance Corp. of British Columbia*, 1994 CarswellBC 206, 91 B.C.L.R. (2d) 276, 24 C.P.C. (3d) 288, 41 B.C.A.C. 306, 66 W.A.C. 306 (B.C. C.A.). In direct contrast, Ontario's *Courts of Justice Act* expressly provides in s. 107 for a transfer from small claims court to Superior Court. And s. 107(6) states that a proceeding that is transferred "shall be continued as if it had been commenced in that court."

The defendant's motion was dismissed.

15.03 (1) Motion Without Notice — Despite rule 15.01, a motion may be made without notice if the nature or circumstances of the motion make notice unnecessary or not reasonably possible.

(2) Service of Order — A party who obtains an order on motion without notice shall serve it on every affected party, together with a copy of the notice of motion and supporting affidavit used on the motion, within five days after the order is signed.

(3) Motion to Set Aside or Vary Motion Made Without Notice — A party who is affected by an order obtained on motion without notice may make a motion to set aside or vary the order, within 30 days after being served with the order.

O. Reg. 78/06, s. 32

15.04 No Further Motions Without Leave — If the court is satisfied that a party has tried to delay the action, add to its costs or otherwise abuse the court's process by making numerous motions without merit, the court may, on motion, make an order prohibiting the party from making any further motions in the action without leave of the court.

O. Reg. 78/06, s. 32

15.05 Adjournment of Motion — A motion shall not be adjourned at a party's request before the hearing date unless the written consent of all parties is filed when the request is made, unless the court orders otherwise.

O. Reg. 78/06, s. 32

15.06 Withdrawal of Motion — A motion shall not be withdrawn without,

    (a) the written consent of all the parties; or

    (b) leave of the court.

O. Reg. 78/06, s. 32

15.07 Costs — The costs of a motion, exclusive of disbursements, shall not exceed $100 unless the court orders otherwise because there are special circumstances.

O. Reg. 78/06, s. 32

Commentary:

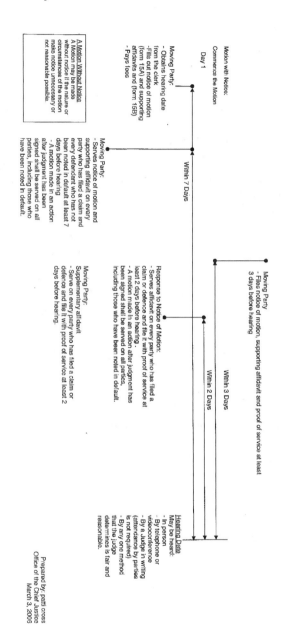

A SMALL CLAIMS COURT CASE - 2006 (Amended Rules)

MOTIONS

A Case Flow Chart

Motion with Notice:
Commence the Motion

Day 1

Moving Party:
- Obtains hearing date from the clerk
- Fills out notice of motion (form 15A) and supporting affidavits and (form 15B)
- Pays fees

Within 7 Days

A Motion Without Notice
A Motion may be made without notice if the nature or circumstances of the motion make notice unnecessary or not reasonable possible.

Moving Party:
- Serves notice of motion and supporting affidavit on every party who has filed a claim and every defendant who has not been noted in default at least 7 days before hearing.
- A motion made in an action after judgment has been signed shall be served on all parties, including those who have been noted in default.

Moving Party
- Files notice of motion, supporting affidavit and proof of service at least 3 days before hearing

Within 3 Days

Within 2 Days

Response to Notice of Motion:
- Serves affidavit on every party who has filed a claim or defence and file it with proof of service at least 2 days before hearing.
- A motion made in an action after judgment has been signed shall be served on all parties, including those who have been noted in default.

Moving Party:
Supplementary affidavit
- Serve on every party who has filed a claim or defence and file it with proof of service at least 2 days before hearing.

Hearing Date
May be heard:
- In person
- By telephone or videoconference
- By a Judge in writing (attendance by parties is not required)
- By any one method that the judge determines is fair and reasonable.

Prepared by: patti cross
Office of the Chief Justice
March 3, 2006

Case Law: *Kirwan v. Silver Brooke Golf Course Inc.*, 2006 CarswellOnt 2382, [2006] O.J. No. 1571, 46 R.P.R. (4th) 104 (Ont. S.C.J.), Weekes J.

Plaintiffs contended that any award of costs should be payable at end of trial since to order costs to be paid now when plaintiffs could not afford to do so would deny plaintiffs access to justice. Impecuniosity of plaintiff irrelevant. Litigants without means cannot ignore rules of court. Costs of motion ordered to be paid within 30 days.

2301072 Nova Scotia Ltd. v. Lienaux, 2007 CarswellNS 236, 42 C.P.C. (6th) 308, 2007 NSCA 66, 255 N.S.R. (2d) 114, 814 A.P.R. 114 (N.S. C.A.); leave to appeal refused (2007), 2007 CarswellNS 515, 2007 CarswellNS 516, 383 N.R. 385 (note), 867 A.P.R. 400 (note), 271 N.S.R. (2d) 400 (note) (S.C.C.).

MacDonald C.J.N.S. found Appellants had "abysmal failure to honour previous court orders for costs" to be special circumstances that would justify the relief requested. Appellants claimed motion judge should not consider the merits before ordering costs. See *Turner-Lienaux v. Campbell*, 2001 CarswellNS 291, [2001] N.S.J. No. 333, 2001 NSCA 122, (sub nom. *Campbell v. Lienaux)* 196 N.S.R. (2d) 364, (sub nom. *Campbell v. Lienaux)* 613 A.P.R. 364 (N.S. C.A. [In Chambers]) and *Wall v. Horn Abbot Ltd.*, [1999] N.S.J. No. 124, 1999 CarswellNS 120, (sub nom. *Wall v. 679927 Ontario Ltd.)* 176 N.S.R. (2d) 96, (sub nom. *Wall v. 679927 Ontario Ltd.)* 538 A.P.R. 96, 29 C.P.C. (4th) 204 (N.S. C.A.).

United Rentals of Canada Inc. v. H.E. Bent Services Ltd., 2007 CarswellNB 204, 2007 CarswellNB 205, 2007 NBCA 29, (sub nom. *Bent (H.E.) Services Ltd. v. United Rentals of Canada Inc.)* 809 A.P.R. 335, (sub nom. *Bent (H.E.) Services Ltd. v. United Rentals of Canada Inc.)* 313 N.B.R. (2d) 335, 50 C.P.C. (6th) 297 (N.B. C.A.)

Appellant failed to appear at trial, and argued it did not receive notice of date by prepaid registered or certified mail or prepaid courier, as required for extra-provincial corporations. Court held that rules concerning service only applied to documents that were required to be "served." "Service" of notice of resumption of trial was not required, and notice by ordinary mail sufficed.

Rule 16 — Notice of Trial

16.01 (1) Clerk Fixes Date and Serves Notice — **The clerk shall fix a date for trial and serve a notice of trial on each party who has filed a claim or defence if,**

   (a) a settlement conference has been held; and

   (b) a party has requested that the clerk fix a date for trial and has paid the required fee.

History [R. 16.01(1)]: Formerly part of 17.01; exception for cases involving pre-trial conferences separated out into another subrule (16.01(2)); refers to Form 16A, formerly Form 17A; plain languages changes.

Commentary

Setting Action Down for Trial

Setting an action down for trial simply means having it put on the list of cases that are ready for trial. That cannot be done until after a settlement conference has been held. It is accomplished by filing a Request to Clerk (Form 9B) and paying the required fee (currently $100). Any party can do so, although in practice it is usually the plaintiff.

Estimated Trial Time

Orderly trial scheduling is easier if an estimate of the time needed for trial is provided to the court office. The best way to do this is to ask the settlement conference judge to include a time estimate in the settlement conference endorsement or memorandum. Failing such a notation, the parties are at liberty to provide their own estimate to the court office. Without accurate trial estimates, it is more difficult for the court staff to avoid overbooking trial dates, and there is a greater risk in the event of overbooking that the parties and their witnesses may attend the trial date only to find that there isn't enough time and they must return at some later date.

Trial Dates

As provided in rule 16.01(1), it is the court clerk who schedules trial dates; however, the parties are at liberty to provide the court office with a list of available dates or, alternatively, a list of dates which are problematic, when the action is set down but before a notice of trial has been issued. The court staff will generally be able to work with that information to select a trial date that is convenient to the parties. The simple step of communicating with the court office before a trial date is set can avoid the wasted time and money which results if a trial date is fixed and turns out to be problematic for any reason.

Once a trial date has been set, it is expected to proceed on that date: see *Holtzman v. Suite Collections Canada Inc.*, 2013 ONSC 4240, 2013 CarswellOnt 9010, 310 O.A.C. 243 (Ont. Div. Ct.).

Adjournments

Sometimes adjournments are required even though the parties are present and ready to proceed with their trial. This can occur if the trial list simply has more cases on it than the court can hear in one day. Trial lists are often overbooked on purpose, to some extent, based on the usual expectation that some cases will be settled.

Other circumstances may lead a party to request an adjournment. An adjournment request must be made known to the other parties immediately so as to determine if the adjournment will be agreed or contested. The court should also be advised once the need for an adjournment request is identified. The later an adjournment request is left before it is made known to the other party or the court, the greater the risk that it may result in wasted time and money, and that the adjournment may be denied.

Rule 17.02 deals with adjournment requests and provides that the court "may" adjourn. Rule 17.02(2) suggests that after two adjournments, any further adjournment request is less likely to be granted.

If an adjournment is granted by the court, terms such as payment of costs by the requesting party to the other party may be imposed. Particularly for last-minute adjournment requests, there will often been some wasted costs to the other party if the adjournment is granted. A party requesting adjournment runs the risk of paying costs as the price of adjournment.

A court's decision to grant or deny an adjournment request is highly discretionary. It involves a balancing of the interests of the plaintiff, the interests of the defendant, and the interests of the administration of justice.

The highly discretionary nature of the court's power to grant or deny an adjournment request is reflected in two decisions of the Court of Appeal, both of which produced a majority ruling with a strong dissent.

O'Brien v. Griffin, 2006 CarswellOnt 96, [2006] O.J. No. 88, 263 D.L.R. (4th) 412, 22 R.F.L. (6th) 134, (sub nom. *Griffin v. O'Brien*) 206 O.A.C. 121 (Ont. C.A.) was a family law proceeding. At an earlier trial the applicant had been criticized by the trial judge for his failure to present documentation in affidavit form. At a subsequent trial, he presented key information in the form of a notarized letter rather than an affidavit. The trial judge ruled the letter inadmissible and drew an adverse inference from the applicant's failure to call a witness from the company which had produced the letter. On appeal, the majority ordered a new trial, based on their finding that the applicant thought he was responding to the criticism of the first trial judge by presenting the notarized letter. In the view of the majority, it was incumbent on the second trial judge, in the particular circumstances, to adjourn the trial to allow a reasonable opportunity to secure the attendance of the witness. In dissent, Lang J.A. held that the exclusion of the letter resulted in no substantive prejudice to the applicant. She held at para. 53:

> 53. A trial judge has the discretion to adjourn a trial. That discretion must be exercised judicially, balancing the interests of the parties with a view to providing an expeditious and fair hearing. This applies in both the civil and family context and whether dealing with litigants represented by counsel or with self-represented litigants. [citations omitted]

In *Khimji v. Dhanani*, 2004 CarswellOnt 525, [2004] O.J. No. 320, 69 O.R. (3d) 790, 44 C.P.C. (5th) 56, 182 O.A.C. 142 (Ont. C.A.), the trial had been adjourned for the second time, for approximately five weeks, to permit the plaintiff to retain counsel. At the new trial date, a third adjournment request was denied and the plaintiff's claim was dismissed. He had done nothing to retain counsel during the first two weeks of the five-week adjournment, and he had failed to pay the costs of the adjournment. At the new trial date, he had secured the agreement of a lawyer to appear at trial, but only if the trial was adjourned once more. On appeal, the majority found no basis to interfere with the trial judge's decision to deny a third adjournment in the circumstances. In dissent, Laskin J.A. held that the third adjournment request was reasonable and should have been granted. He said at para. 14:

> 14. A trial judge enjoys wide latitude in deciding whether to grant or refuse the adjournment of a scheduled civil trial. The decision is discretionary and the scope for appellate intervention is correspondingly limited. In exercising this discretion, however, the trial judge should balance the interests of the plaintiff, the interests of the defendant and the interests of the administration of justice in the orderly processing of civil trials on their merits. In any particular case, several considerations may bear on these interests. A trial judge who fails to take account of relevant considerations may exercise his or her discretion unreasonably and if, as a result, the decision is contrary to the interests of justice, an appellate court is justified in intervening. In my opinion, that is the case here.

The fact that judges of the Court of Appeal can disagree over whether an adjournment should have been granted in a particular case illustrates the subjectivity of a decision to grant or deny an adjournment request.

There have been a number of cases in which the Divisional Court has upheld decisions by Small Claims Court judges to deny adjournment requests. In *Toste v. Baker*, 2007 CarswellOnt 1368, [2007] O.J. No. 835 (Ont. Div. Ct.), the defendant requested adjournment based on a medical procedure, but produced no supporting medical documentation. The judgment was upheld on appeal. In *Vallières c. Samson*, 2009 CarswellOnt 4539, (sub nom. *Vallières v. Samson*) 97 O.R. (3d) 761, 97 O.R. (3d) 770, (sub nom. *Vallières v. Samson*) 252 O.A.C. 253 (Ont. Div. Ct.), the trial judge's decision to adjourn the trial, but for only one day, was upheld on appeal. The plaintiff bore the duty to be prepared for trial, which had been scheduled long in advance. In *Susman v. Zafir*, 2007 CarswellOnt 6865, 230 O.A.C. 197 (Ont. Div. Ct.); additional reasons at 2008 CarswellOnt 49 (Ont. Div. Ct.), the self-represented defendant decided two days before trial that he needed to retain counsel. The adjournment was denied and judgment granted for the plaintiff. An appeal by the defendant was dismissed.

Even if an adjournment is denied and the appeal court is persuaded that the adjournment should have been granted, the appeal judge may decide to deprive the successful appellant of appeal costs and require payment by the appellant of costs of the first trial: see *Sprostranov v. State Farm Mutual Automobile Insurance Co.*, 2009 CarswellOnt 1217, [2009] O.J. No. 923 (Ont. Div. Ct.).

Particularly for full-day trials, last-minute adjournment requests may be looked on with disfavour by the court, given the waste of valuable judicial resources which results from such adjournments. Adjournment requests may be denied even if made on consent: see *Steckley v.*

Haid (March 20, 2009), Doc. 1494/07, [2009] O.J. No. 1167 (Ont. Sm. Cl. Ct.); *Petrykowski v. 553562 Ontario Ltd.* (June 16, 2010), Doc. 886/09, [2010] O.J. No. 2574 (Ont. Sm. Cl. Ct.); motion for new trial dismissed (July 21, 2010), Doc. 886/09, [2010] O.J. No. 3129 (Ont. Sm. Cl. Ct.); extension of time to appeal denied *2011 ONSC 1101*, 2011 CarswellOnt 1014, [2011] O.J. No. 734 (Ont. Div. Ct.). The best way to avoid such difficulties is for the parties to seek a workable trial date before a date is scheduled by the court clerk, and in cases in which a scheduling problem only develops after a trial date is fixed, to identify the problem and make it known to the other parties and to court as soon as possible. The reality is that most scheduling problems can be readily avoided simply by addressing the situation sooner rather than later.

(1.1) [Repealed O. Reg. 78/06, s. 32.]

(1.2) [Repealed O. Reg. 78/06, s. 32.]

(1.3) [Repealed O. Reg. 78/06, s. 32.]

(2) Manner of Service — The notice of trial shall be served by mail or fax.
    O. Reg. 461/01, s. 17 [s. 17(2) revoked O. Reg. 330/02, s. 11(2).]; 330/02, s. 11(1); 440/03, s. 5, item 9; 78/06, s. 32

History [R. 16.01(2)]: Contains the exception for cases involving pre-trial conferences from former 17.01; refers to rule 13, formerly rule 14; clarifies that subrule 13.01(7) applies rather than subrule 16.01(1).

Commentary: The following was prepared by a Special Committee of the Superior Court of Justice.

General Suggestions for Judges Applicable to any Civil Proceeding Involving a Self-Represented Litigant

- Ensure through a court officer that the self-represented litigant understands the basic requirements of decorum and conduct in the courtroom;

- As in any other case, consider any possible security risk and take unobtrusive measures for the safety of the courtroom where suggested or required. Keep in mind the safety of all persons in the courtroom;

- Verify that proper service has been made, particularly where a self-represented litigant fails to appear;

- Scrutinize any consent submitted to the court in a case where the self-represented litigant fails to appear. If present, ensure the self-represented litigant understands the meaning of the consent;

- Explain the nature of the proceeding and how it is to be conducted. While doing so, take the opportunity to put the self-represented litigant at ease, and assure him/her that you will, within the limits of the law, assist as is appropriate;

- Ensure the presence of a court reporter. If prepared to preside without one, tape record the proceedings or take complete notes;

- As with any litigant, represented or not, be scrupulously polite;

- Use simple language avoiding jargon or legalese;

- Take a recess whenever feelings run high; and

- Apply the same legal principles, rules of evidence, and standards of procedure to both sides. Ins doing so, take the extra time to explain to the self-represented litigant the reasons for any ruling.

Additional Suggestions for a Motion or Application

- At the outset, describe how the motion will be conducted and make clear the self-represented litigant will be given a full opportunity to speak at the appropriate time in the proceeding;

- Keep the represented party's presentation as focused and brief as possible, so as not to invite the self-represented litigant to be prolix;

- Avoid dialogue with counsel which might be mistakenly interpreted to reflect some personal relationship or friendship;

- As in any case, avoid humour;

- State what you understand to be the self-represented litigant's position to avoid any misunderstanding;

- Give a decision at the end of the motion, unless there are emotional or security reasons for not doing so;

- If the self-represented litigant is unsuccessful regarding the motion, explain the implication of costs. Consider ordering an assessment to avoid any suggestion of hasty or punitive measures; and

- Where the successful side is represented by counsel, consider the endorsement specifying that the order may be submitted to you for signature without the approval of the unsuccessful party.

Settlement, Case Management and Trial Management Conferences

- As far as possible, hold such conferences in court on the record. Avoid having the self-represented litigant in your chambers. If you are prepared to do so, have a reporter present or tape the proceeding;

- While it is proper for a judge to encourage settlement and express an opinion, avoid any action which could be interpreted as unduly pressuring the self-represented litigant to settle; and

- As in every case, do not see or speak separately with either side in the absence of the opposing party. Where necessary, use the conference as an opportunity to explain what the self-represented litigant must do in preparation for the next stage.

Conference Calls

- Avoid conducting a conference call with a self-represented litigant.

The Trial

- Do not allow another lay person to speak and act for a self-represented litigant, except where permitted by law;

- Avoid asking counsel "what the case is all about", thereby giving the impression that a biased consultative process is already underway. Ask each party to give a brief opening statement;

- Ensure that counsel is fair to the self-represented litigant;

- Warn counsel against the use of complex, incomprehensible, or flowery language;

- Consider assisting the self-represented party in presenting the evidence. Then ask if there is anything else that needs to be added, emphasizing you need to hear everything the litigant wishes you to know;

- Explain to the self-represented litigant, before the commencement of the first cross-examination, the distinction between asking relevant questions of opposing witnesses as opposed to giving evidence or making argument. Stop any inappropriate conduct immediately, emphasizing that the opportunity to testify either will come or has passed, and that argument takes place after all the evidence has been heard;

- Explain the purpose of submissions and point out there is no necessity to repeat earlier testimony when submitting argument;

- Remind counsel for the represented party of counsel's obligation to the court to ensure that all relevant legal principles are canvassed and that, consistent with counsel's duty to the client, counsel's duty is to ensure the judge has all the help to which the judge is entitled;

- As with a motion, consider reserving your decision where the self-represented litigant is unsuccessful. A reserve is appropriate where feelings are high or where there is a security risk; and

- Be no more active in the conduct of the trial than is necessary to do justice to the parties.

Communications Directly from the Self-Represented Litigant with or without a Copy Sent to the Opposing Counsel

- Avoid a personal response. Have either your secretary or a senior administrative official respond with a brief comment about any impropriety in such communication. The language of the communication should be yours or approved by you;

- In a case where the other side has not received a copy of the communication, send it to that counsel (or that self-represented litigant, should that be the case), together with a copy of the reply sent at your direction; and

- Should there be a telephone call, cut it short and indicate that, just as the caller would be upset if he/she came to know that you had been talking to opposing counsel about the case, so it is wrong for you to talk to the self-represented litigant about the case. Say you are confident no impropriety was intended.

Adjournments

Settlement conferences can be adjourned or continued under subrules 13.02(3) and (5), and motions are adjourned under subrule 15.05. Trials adjourned on such terms are just, including payment of compensation for inconvenience and expense (subrule 17.02(1)). Section 29 of the *Courts of Justice Act* governs, of course. From July 1, 2006, trials cannot be adjourned a *third* time without leave given at a motion with notice to all parties (subrule 17.02(2)).

Rule 18 adds two additional grounds for adjourning a trial. A trial will be adjourned with costs if a party does not send all other parties a copy of any served summons (subrule 18.02(5) to (7)) or if a party has not provided for an interpreter for any summoned witness (subrule 18.03(5.2)).

Facing the Unrepresented Litigant

Most lawyers hate to try a case against an unrepresented litigant. Unfortunately, the number of cases in which one or the other party is not represented by counsel is forever increasing.

The primary cause for this increase may be the perception that lawyers' hourly rates are exorbitant, at least, that's what those unrepresented often suggest. Many jurisdictions such as Ontario provide small claims courts, where unrepresented litigants can tell their story to the judge often unfettered by many technical considerations.

In theory, statutes, prevailing case law, and the rules of court apply to all litigants equally. In practice, this does not always happen. The lawyer is held to the standards that the court knows the lawyer is aware of, while frequently the unrepresented litigant may not be held to any standards at all.

All lawyers know that certain consequences flow from the failure to follow the rules and procedures. Most unrepresented litigants are not even aware that there are rules and procedures, let alone that there are consequences for the failure to follow them. These are the seeds of a double standard seen by some to be applied by our courts.

How does a lawyer deal with an unrepresented opponent? Very carefully! The potential for ethical problems abounds when a lawyer discusses a case with an unrepresented litigant. Some lawyers refuse to talk to an unrepresented litigant. Other lawyers who meet with unrepresented litigants attempt to put settlement discussions in writing. Lawyers who do so religiously will be prepared for that special occasion where six months after a settlement, an unrepresented litigant decides that the settlement was not favourable to him/her, and that you misled them. At least you have the paperwork documenting the negotiations and how ethical you were in your approach.

Whenever you settle a case with an unrepresented during litigation or a settlement conference, ask the judge to put it on the record and question the unrepresented party about whether he is satisfied with and understands the terms of the agreement. Also ask the judge to confirm on the record that the unrepresented litigant is satisfied that you treated him fairly.

Any trial against an unrepresented litigant can create difficult problems. It is helpful if you know the judge. You need to protect the record. If you object to everything that is objectionable, you will annoy everybody. The better choice is to selectively object to inadmissible testimony that has the potential to be damaging to your case. Letting the unrepresented litigant babble on about irrelevant things makes the problem the judge's, not yours. It also makes you seem rather reasonable, both to the court and to the unrepresented litigant.

Employ a rolling analysis of when to make an objection: Based on what has already happened in the case, is the answer to the unrepresented litigant's question going to help me, hurt me, or be neutral?

There are some don'ts. Don't do anything to cause the unrepresented party to turn the thing about which he/she is angry into an all-consuming cause. If you do that, you may never get rid of them. Don't talk down. Even if they don't have a clue, treat them as your equal. Treat them with respect; kill them with kindness. Surprisingly, good behaviour is frequently reciprocated. Make a brief opening statement outlining the areas where procedural or evidentiary problems could arise. Alert the court to the applicable statute, court rule, or case law. That puts everyone on notice of problem areas. It also reminds the court that you want your case handled just like any other case, i.e., by the rules.

This is Nothing New

William Penn (founder of Pennsylvania), who never obtained an academic degree, represented himself in Bushel's Case (1670) which "established the independence of the jury beyond question in English jurisprudence." "At his trial in the Old Bailey on Sept. 1, 1670 he skilfully exposed the unconstitutionality of the proceedings and inspired the jury to withstand the brutal pressure of the judges for a verdict of guilty." (21 *Encyclopedia Americana* (c. 1992) s.v. "Penn, William").

Lawyers were actually banned outright or faced tight restrictions in many U.S. colonies for much of the 18th century. . . . The "Body of Liberties" adopted by the Massachusetts Bay Colony in 1641 expressed the typical attitudes of the time: "Every man that findeth himselfe unfit to plead to his own cause in any court shall have libertie to employ any man. . ., provided he give him noe fee or reward for his pain. . . ."

In the U.S., the strong tradition that each American should be able to master the laws probably peaked in the years between . . . 1825 and . . . 1865. Most states enforced few if any restrictions on non-lawyers appearing in court on behalf of others, as Lincoln himself did before he talked a judge into granting him attorney status. . . . the American Bar Association convinced states to pass "unauthorized practice of law" statutes in the 1920s and 1930s, which effectively gave lawyers a monopoly over the sale of legal information. . . .

As well as many Canadian cases cited in this publication, there are at least four relatively recent U.S. federal decisions which offer support to the unrepresented litigant.

Picking v. Pennsylvania Railway, 151 F.2d 240, Third Circuit Court of Appeals. In *Picking*, the plaintiffs civil rights was 150 pages and described by a federal judge as "inept." Nevertheless, it was held:

> Where a plaintiff pleads pro-se in a suit for protection of civil rights, the court should endeavor to construe plaintiffs pleading without regard to technicalities.

In *Walter Process Equipment v. Food Machinery*, 382 U.S. 172 (1965) it was held that in a "motion to dismiss, the material allegations of the complaint are taken as admitied (*sic*)." From this vantage point, courts are reluctant to dismiss complaints unless it appears the plaintiff can prove no set of facts in support of his claim which would entitle him to relief (see *Conley v. Gibson*, 355 U.S. 41 (1957)).

In *Puckett v. Cox*, it was held that a *pro-se* complaint requires a less stringent reading than one drafted by a lawyer (456 F.2d 233 (1972 Sixth Circuit USCA)). Said Justice Black in *Conley v. Gibson*, 355 U.S. 41 at 48 (1957): "The Federal Rules rejects the approach that pleading is a game of skill in which one misstep by counsel may be decisive to the outcome and accept the principle that the purpose of pleading is to facilitate a proper decision on the merits." According to rule 8(f) FRCP all pleadings shall be construed to do substantial justice. The Court also cited Rule 8(f) FRCP, which holds that "all pleadings shall be construed to do substantial justice."

Courts have long held that non-lawyers generally should not be held accountable for all of the procedural nuances of the law.

> When a litigant chooses to represent himself, it is the duty of the trial court to insure fairness, allowing reasonable accommodations for the pro se litigant so long as no harm is done an adverse party. . . . Most importantly, the trial court must strive to insure that no person's cause of defense is defeated solely by reason of their unfamiliarity with procedural or evidentiary rules.

State ex rel. Dillon v. Egnor, 188 W.Va. 221 227423 S.E.2d 624 630 (1992)

> Of course, the court must not overlook the rules of the prejudice of any party. The court should strive, however, to ensure that the diligent pro se party does not forfeit any substantial rights by inadvertent omission or mistake. Cases should be decided on the merits, and to that end, justice is served by reasonably accommodating all parties, whether represented by counsel or not.

Blair v. Maynard, 174 W.Va. 247 253324 S.E.2d 391 396 (1984).

For Myself 36 Years and Counting

From my and our court staffs' perspective to be aware of:

- lack of understanding of rules of procedure, rules of evidence, and courtroom protocol by self-represented litigants

- papers not complete or correct causing delay

- litigants have difficulty presenting their position without getting emotionally involved

- difficulty in remaining fair and impartial when one party is represented by counsel and the other is not

- discomfort after ruling against an unrepresented litigant due to procedural failures

- the use of court staff time

- difficulty in drawing the line between giving legal information and giving legal advice.

From the lawyer's perspective:

- waiting in court with a lengthy docket while another unrepresented litigant in another case wastes everyone's time and my client's money

- difficulty in knowing how to conduct myself when the other party is unrepresented. If I raise all objections, the process goes nowhere, yet, I have a duty to represent my client

- danger that the unrepresented litigant thinks I represent him or her too

- worry over future problems that might arise at a later date and be harder and more expensive to resolve if matters are not correctly resolved at the trial.

From the self-represented litigant's perspective:

- lack of information and the inability to get the right forms or information for what I need to do

- confusion and intimidation

- fear to move forward with my case

- belief that they cannot afford a lawyer

- lack of respect from judges, court staff, and opposing counsel.

Training on the handling of self-represented litigants should become a standard part of the orientation for all judges. This training needs to address the ethical issues that trouble judges in adopting the more engaged judicial role required to effectively handle these cases. It should equip judges with specific techniques they can use in cases involving two unrepresented parties and in the more difficult situation in which one party is represented and the other is not.

For examples of such techniques, see Albrecht, Greacen, Hough & Zorza, "Judicial Techniques for Cases Involving Self-Represented Litigants," 42/1 Judges', J. 16 (Winter 2003). See also Richard Zorza, "The Disconnect Between the Requirements of Judicial Neutrality of Those of the Appearance of Neutrality and Those of the Appearance of Neutrality When Parties Appear Pro Se: Causes, Solutions, Recommendations, and Implications," 17 GEO.J.LEGAL ETHICS 423 (2004). See also, e.g., "Conference of State Court Administrators, Position Paper on Self-Represented Litigation" (August 2000), available at www.cosca.ncsc.dni.us; "Conference of Chief Justices and Conference of State Court Administrators, Report of the Joint Task Force on Pro Se Litigation" (July 2002), available at www.cosca.ncsc.dni.us.

Rule 17 — Trial

17.01 (1) Failure to Attend — If an action is called for trial and all the parties fail to attend, the trial judge may strike the action off the trial list.

History [R. 17.01(1)]: Formerly 18.01(1); plain language changes.

(2) If an action is called for trial and a party fails to attend, the trial judge may,

(a) proceed with the trial in the party's absence;

(b) if the plaintiff attends and the defendant fails to do so, strike out the defence and dismiss the defendant's claim, if any, and allow the plaintiff to prove the plaintiff's claim, subject to subrule (3);

(c) if the defendant attends and the plaintiff fails to do so, dismiss the action and allow the defendant to prove the defendant's claim, if any; or

(d) make such other order as is just.

History [R. 17.01(2)]: Formerly 18.01(2); plain language changes.

(2.1) In the case described in clause (2)(b) or (c), the person with the claim is not required to prove liability against the party who has failed to attend but is required to prove the amount of the claim.

(3) In the case described in clause (2)(b), if an issue as to the proper place of trial under subrule 6.01(1) is raised in the defence, the trial judge shall consider it and make a finding.

Commentary

Trial

1) Ask each party to outline the issues to be determined and their position as to each issue. What order will they ask the court to make?

2) Ask the parties if there are any issues of law, evidentiary issues or scheduling issues. If you are alerted to legal and evidentiary issues, you may be able to outline for a self-represented litigant problems he or she may face during the trial. This also gives the individual an opportunity to think about how to handle the difficulties, e.g., if there are experts being tendered for whom no report has been served or filed. Some, if not all, of these issues should have been dealt with at the Settlement Conference but at times the self-represented party appears for trial still completely unfocused.

3) The procedure of the trial must be explained. This should include:

* Opening addresses

* Plaintiff's case in chief

* Cross-examination

* Difference between questioning and giving evidence or submissions

* Re-examination and scope of it

* Defendant's case in chief

* Reply evidence

* Closing addresses

* Decision

* costs

Adjournments

One of the most common scenarios at trial is the request for an adjournment made by the self-represented litigant. The court will consider various factors but the focus is often on the recalcitrance of the party making the request.

Self-represented litigants may have a hidden agenda or ulterior motive in pursuing litigation. It is not uncommon for them to try and "drag" out a case in the hope of wearing down the other party's endurance or jacking up their legal costs. Habitually, these tactics will include:

* frequent adjournment requests, often under the guise of "wanting to retain counsel"

* wasted court appearances where nothing has been done since the last adjournment was granted at the self-rep's request

- bullying, intimidating, trying to manipulate or constantly interrupting the opposing party or counsel in court

- acting confrontational, evasive or non-responsive with the judge.

Experienced counsel understand that the self-represented people may be entitled to some leeway at the front end of an action, especially in respect to compliance with filing requirements and deadlines pursuant to the Rules and in respect of disclosure. Reasonable lawyers will generally consent to a first adjournment request for this reason. Judges may be vocal to unreasonable counsel who do not agree to such adjournment requests and waste the court's time.

The Rules apply to all litigants, whether represented by counsel or not. A lawyer and a party are entitled to know the case that they have to meet and should not have to be continually blindsided by verbal allegations or inadmissible statements made in court. The interests of fairness and natural justice require that a proper record is before the court, especially in the event of an appeal. The Rules specifically contemplate the avoidance of litigation drift and the judge must be ever mindful of this objective, as drift is not fair to the party seeking judicial intervention.

While it is not appropriate for opposing counsel to give legal advice to a self-represented litigants, if is acceptable, in the absence of available duty counsel, for a judge to simply explain basic procedural requirements to them and, if necessary, ask opposing counsel to reiterate this advice out in the hall.

The Rules of Professional Conduct of the Law Society of Upper Canada mandate lawyers to treat self-represented people courteously and professionally, regardless of how difficult they may be.

Smart lawyers will only communicate with self-represented people outside of the courthouse in writing, so as to preserve a written record of what was disseminated, a very necessary precaution to protect a lawyer from spurious complaints by self-represented people to the law society. If is not uncommon for self-represented litigants to make such a complaint as a tactic to try and force the removal of a solicitor for the opposing party.

If self-represented people pose a genuine physical danger to a retained counsel or the opposing party, lawyers are within their rights to request the assistance of court security, including in the courtroom. From counsel's perspective, it is better if the court clerk notifies the judge that a problem has arisen, so as not to prejudice anyone by having the fact that security is required put on the record, unless absolutely necessary.

Judges should expect lawyers to act ethically in dealing with self-represented people and, in particular, ensure that lawyers do not take unfair advantage of procedural "blunders" by them. Judges should not hesitate to call to task a lawyer who tries to take advantage of these situations. Such conduct by a lawyer is akin to "sharp practice" were it to occur between two counsel rather than a lawyer and a self-represented person.

Counsel have a duty to explore settlement options at every juncture in a proceeding. Counsel may loathe to do so with self-represented people. Judges need to be clear in stating their opinions in plain language vis-à-vis settlement options and in expecting counsel to address those suggestions with the self-rep.

Self-represented litigants will often blurt out the contents of confidential settlement discussions that may have previously taken place with counsel. Sometimes they will try to produce counsel's written offer to settle. They do not understand the nature of "privilege" in settlement context. In such situations, even if it is not a settlement conference, it can be helpful to counsel to let confidential settlement information in and accord it the weight the judge feels it is worth, especially if the judge endorses all or the essence of the proposal reasonable. Doing this can lead to creative dispute resolution.

Opening Statements

The judge peers over her glasses, mumbles your name and other words you don't hear because your mind is racing, hands trembling. You jerk your head from your notes, breathe deeply, and suddenly you're focused. You stand, thank the court, nod at your adversary, stride to the podium, place your papers, and pause.

It's time to tell your story. Be thorough and logical, detail the facts, touch on the law.

The opening is what you've been anticipating. An opportunity to teach, explain, introduce your client and case.

A polished opening that no one understands is worthless. Years ago, a trial practice guru actually tried a case and kept using the phrase "red herring" in his opening. There was only one problem: no one knew its meaning.

We watch the Super Bowl and *American Idol, Oprah*, and *Dancing with the Stars*; we read tabloids and *People*; we obsess over Angelina and Brad. So save the Shakespearean references, the vocabulary words learned while cramming for the SATs. And no one believes that you really love the History Channel while knowing everything about the latest *Project Runway* episode.

"Show Them the Truck"

It doesn't matter how smart you are if the judge can't hear you. The irreducible minimum of effective courtroom delivery is to be understood, one hopes; to persuade, if at all possible; but, above all, to be *heard*.

The first fundamental of courtroom delivery is orientation. Stage actors learn to speak in the direction of the audience, even when addressing another actor on the stage. Not only is the audience more likely to *hear* a line spoken in their direction, but also they will better understand the line while seeing the actor's facial expression, posture, and other non-verbal clues.

The beginning of proper orientation in the courtroom is a pre-trial visit to the courtroom to see where you will be sitting. If there is any pre-trial jockeying for position to be done, this is the time for it, as well as a first-rate opportunity to acquaint yourself with the clerks, the court reporter, and even the judge. The object of this planning is to orient yourself and your client so that speaking in the direction of the judge and witness will be easy and natural.

The second fundamental is, collectively, projection, enunciation, and pace. Without attention to these three elements of courtroom delivery, any lawyer is in danger of being unheard, misunderstood, and ultimately ignored. *Projection* — as opposed to sheer volume — is the ability to make oneself heard even from across a courtroom with less-than-optimal acoustics. *Enunciation* is the accurate pronunciation and articulation of words so that none are lost on the audience. Pace is the optimal speed and rhythm of the spoken word, neither dizzyingly fast nor ponderously slow.

Enunciation is nothing more or less than speaking your words clearly and distinctly: think Professor Henry Higgins in *My Fair Lady*. Even young lawyers seem to have little trouble with this concept as they are well ready, correctly pronounce words, and have considerable public-speaking experience behind them in trial advocacy or debate.

Speech is a trial lawyer's stock-in-trade. Let's revisit our starting point: It doesn't matter how smart you are if the judge can't hear you.

We are pre-conditioned to speak too fast. We know the case so well that our mouths struggle to keep up with our minds. We're nervous or, at the very least, "adrenalized." We, like high school debaters of yore, are determined to spread the record thick with facts, some repeated many times. Finally, we feel the judge's eyes upon us, urging "Hurry up, hurry up." Who wouldn't talk too fast?

Here are two suggestions for slowing down the pace that many lawyers lapse into in the courtroom. First, when questioning a witness, look at him while listening — really listening — to his answer, even if you know what it's going to be. Don't have your next question spring-loaded for the moment the witness finishes speaking. Second, when preparing your remarks to the judge, plan to talk at a leisurely pace about the few important points rather than racing through every witness, every exhibit, and every red herring your opponent throws out. If you aren't sure what those few important points are, you still have some deep thinking to do about your case.

The use of concise, grammatical sentences, built upon everyday words and consistent terminology. Think Hemingway, not Faulkner. It is difficult, even for an engaged listener, to follow a complex question, then the answer, then make sense of how both fit into the case on trial. So speak in active voice, not passive, and impose a word limit on your questions and statements. (Hint: If a question can't be asked in 15 words or fewer, it may be more than one question.)

Consistent terminology means calling the same thing by the same name every time, or as close to it as humanly possible. If you're talking about a letter you've chosen to characterize as an agreement, refer to it as an agreement every time, not as an "agreement" the first time and a "contract" the next.

Another fundamental is courtesy. Courtesy may seem out of place in a discussion of courtroom delivery, but courtesy is not only important to effective advocacy, it is *essential*. A genuinely courteous lawyer can make up for shortcomings in her style of speaking, but a lawyer perceived to be discourteous to the judge, opposing counsel, or courtroom staff is doomed. I don't think courtesy can be faked, at least not the kind that favourably disposes a judge to you and your case.

Courtesy was the bedrock of the legal profession until the end of the twentieth century, when it was eroded by the red tide of Rambo litigators. Courtesy then became legislated by bar associations and courts across our country. Everyone understands we should be courteous to judges as a matter of base self-interest, and we are required to cooperate at least grudgingly with opposing counsel or face the court's wrath. What more is there to say about courtesy in the courtroom and its effect on how we are understood by the court?

There are many explanations as to why a lawyer behaves discourteously: I'm tired from preparation; I'm stressed because my client's fate (and, in some respects, my own) hangs in the balance; the judge keeps ruling incorrectly (i.e., against me); the witness isn't cooperating; and opposing counsel is determined to make me look like a fool. Good reasons all, but at least one reason to remain courteous to witnesses and opposing counsel is the judge will turn you off if he or she thinks you are rude.

Some of us grew up watching movies and shows where lying witnesses were broken down by blistering cross-examination, and a lawyer's righteous indignation carried the day. (Atticus Finch in *To Kill a Mockingbird* was a noteworthy exception of steady, chivalrous courtroom demeanour under the most trying circumstances.) But the reality is that it's uncomfortable to be in a room with people who are quarrelling, no matter which side of the quarrel you favour. When your temper rises with a witness or you find yourself bickering with opposing counsel, take a deep breath, count to ten, go to your "happy place," or do anything else you need to do to regain your composure.

Another fundamental of courtroom delivery is humour. Effective humour in the courtroom is almost never the result of planning. Deliberately injecting levity into a court proceeding is a tricky business, and only those with a deft touch should try it. Just as they respond to respect and courtesy, however, a judge may be grateful for an occasional humorous interlude in a tedious trial. These welcome moments of levity should arise naturally from courtroom events, such as an unintentionally funny answer by a witness or a bit of bumbling with a demonstrative exhibit, but never from inserting a joke or "funny" anecdote into a jury argument. That might work for Seinfeld, but you and I are not Seinfeld. And even if you think you have a sure-fire zinger, you run the risk of treading on the hidden sensitivities of the judge or, worst of all, being perceived by the judge as a buffoon rather than a serious advocate for your client's cause.

"This trial is serious business, and I'm serious about my client's case, but I don't take myself too seriously." Self-deprecation, or the willingness to allow a laugh at your own expense, is part and parcel of the humility that underlies proper respect for the trial process itself. I would encourage a young lawyer not to *try* to be funny, but to be ready to smile and shrug his shoulders when he suffers one of the countless indignities coming his way in the courtroom. Above all, be natural.

There is also the use of demonstrative exhibits, or "show them the truck." For example, in a defective pickup truck case, you put on witness after witness to describe the mechanical shortcomings of the pickup truck your client had been sold. After a couple of hours of this, think: "Show them the truck!" meaning a photograph of the truck in question. A truck's defects are not outwardly visible, so the photos really don't demonstrate anything relevant to the case. But there is a natural curiosity to see the truck being talked about so the judge could mentally file away that image — "red, F-150, long-bed" — and listen to the rest of the evidence.

The value of models, drawings, and other demonstrative exhibits is beyond dispute because there often is a tangible or at least representable object, device, or invention at issue. Commercial cases tend to hinge on documents, which ordinarily don't convert to compelling demonstrative exhibits. But the signature page of a lengthy contract can be quite compelling if you've been arguing that your opponent should be bound by the agreement he signed. And can you try a real estate case without showing the judge a picture or at least a map of the property?

We all relapse into bad habits (or even develop new ones). Thinking about these simple yet sometimes elusive fundamentals enables all of us to sweep away the mental clutter, draw a deep breath, look directly at the judge . . . and *communicate*.

Role of the Judge

Judges have an important role to play as mediators in keeping the parties on track and moving in a principled way towards resolution in all resolvable cases. The back-and-forth, the "negotiation dance," can be difficult and it can also result in very unfair resolution.

When parties simply split the difference in the amount, this usually rewards the most unreasonable or maybe even a dishonest party. We all know that the judge must intervene to balance the inequity between counsel. Nudging the agents/lawyers/parties towards an objective evaluation will promote justice and maybe even a civil relationship between the parties and respect for the deputy judge conducting the settlement conference.

Another way to keep the parties on course is to move them off positional haggling and move them towards not just *objective criteria* but a focus on their *interests*. This can be done by asking them how strong or weak their case is. Do they really want to go to trial? Can they win? Will they aggravate their client's cause by dragging everyone through the trial process?

A trial is sometimes referred to as the Best Alternative To a Negotiated Agreement (BATNA) but is, in fact, the only alternative. By focusing on their BATNA, you quite often will have them realistically consider settlement because of the financial and other costs involved in going to trial.

Another important area to focus on is *authority*. What authority do the parties have? Is the client there as additional authority referred in order to settle the matter? Nothing is more unfair and frustrating than to spend that 45 precious minutes at a settlement conference with the following scenario: the defendant's lawyer has worked his opponent down from $20,000 to $5,000 as a possible settlement figure. However, when Minutes of Settlement are about to be signed, the defendant's lawyer now claims no authority to settle and must check with the client, principal, or their partner.

If judges conduct themselves fairly, firmly and honestly, there will never be any question of their authority.

What about the *relationship* of the parties and the relationship between counsel and the judge? Some counsel/agents do not realize that their reputation is a key building block of relationship. If they are not trusted, they will have a very hard time getting a proper resolution of their cases. Judges, most of whom are human (I think), will react adversely towards parties who are unfair, untrustworthy or even deceitful.

You can do many things to build and maintain proper relationships between the parties. Give lawyers, agents, time to chat together before they enter the discussions. They may not have opened their files for weeks. A face-to-face chat with the other side can do wonders. This pause in proceeding may allow the parties to iron out differences, get to the settlement range and narrow the issues, before the judge even becomes involved.

The two C's of negotiation settlement are: *communication* and *commitment*. They are both important elements in the final stage of any successful case resolution. Commitments cannot be made without the authority to do so. Commitment will not come without a trusting relationship between the parties.

Likewise if the settlement is not properly recorded by the settlement conference judge and then communicated to the parties in an understandable process, the entire procedure can lead to capitulation and confusion that can end any settlement and positive relationship of the parties.

Valerie McNaughton suggests that judges should learn to listen in a manner that will result in better understanding. She offers some suggestions on how to be "active" listeners:

- Resist the impulse to control the pace or content of comments made in the formal courtroom settling.

- Resist the urge to interpret what parties say as a challenge to your authority.

- Ask for clarification of any remarks made that you are not sure you understand.

- Neutrally (non-judgmentally) rephrase parties' statements to test and demonstrate your understanding.

- Give the parties an opportunity to talk about their underlying concerns and to put themselves in the other party's shoes. See Valerie McNaughton, "Active Listening: Applying Mediation Skills in the Courtroom," 38(2) Judges J. 23 (1999).

It is recognized that the Small Claims Court deals routinely with high case volumes and that judges hearing cases do not routinely have the benefit of the arguments of learned counsel. Nevertheless, those circumstances do not negate the general duty to give to the litigants, and in particular to the losing party, some indication, however concise, of why the result went as it did, why they lost (unless, of course, they have already run out of the room/courtroom).

The Small Claims Court has always been intended as an accessible forum for the public. Where orders are made that are not made intelligible to the litigants, the court may fail to discharge one of its central duties and the objectives of economy and speed are thwarted. The absence of reasons itself may provide an impetus to appeal regardless of the result where the presence of reasons, however brief, may have informed a decision to accept the result. See Bellamy J. in *Vuong v. Toronto East General & Orthopaedic Hospital* (2009), 2009 CarswellOnt 597, [2009] O.J. No. 472 (Ont. Div. Ct.). In *Vuong*, the deputy judge dismissed the plaintiffs' claim without giving reasons. The defendant in the action sought dismissal on the ground of res judicata and on the ground that the action was frivolous or vexatious or otherwise an abuse of the court. Bellamy J. held that appellate review was not possible in the absence of reasons and remitted the matter to the Small Claims Court for a rehearing of the motion before a different judge.

Subrule 17.01 has not been changed other than adding subrule 2.1 providing that where a claim or defence is struck, the person with the claim is not required to prove liability but is required to prove the amount of the claim. See also the assessment hearing provision in subrule 11.03(5).

A defendant, who is sued in a division where he or she does not reside or carry on business and who specifically alleges in the defence that the court sitting in that territorial division is not the proper place of trial, is permitted to have an opportunity to have the defence as to forum considered by the judge even where the defendant is unable to show up at the trial because of the distance involved.

If an issue as to the proper place of trial is raised in the defence,the trial judge shall consider that issue and make a finding notwithstanding that clause 17.01(2)(b) would otherwise authorize the judge to dismiss the defence on the basis of the non-appearance of the defendant. If the judge finds that the territorial division where the judge is sitting is not the proper place of trial, then the rule provides that, automatically, the action must be tried either where the defendant resides or carries on business or in the court's place of sitting that is nearest to the place where the defendant resides or carries on business. The power of the trial judge to order the trial to be held somewhere else on a balance of convenience is preserved.

The effect of the rule is to give defendants who are unable to travel a long distance to attend personally in court an opportunity to dispute the territorial jurisdiction of the division where the action has been brought and if successful, to require that the action be tried in the place where the defendant resides or carries on business.

Case Law: *Wright v. Bell Can.* (1988), 13 W.D.C.P. 228 (Ont. Div. Ct.) — Facts with respect to the cause of action were known at the time of the first action. Since the factors alleged to render the action a continuous cause of action were determinable at the first trial and therefore could have been sought as a remedy at that time, the second judgment was set aside as the matter was *res judicata.*

Hasenclever v. Hoskins (1988), 14 W.D.C.P. 171 (Ont. Div. Ct.) — The plaintiff's action did not support a claim for general damages. The plaintiff did not request an adjournment at trial to amend his pleadings. Since the plaintiff failed to plead the requisite elements, his appeal failed.

Bird v. Kehrig (1990), 43 C.P.C. (2d) 97 (Sask. Q.B.) — The defendant appeared at trial but the plaintiff did not. The Small Claims Court Judge simply endorsed the file "no action taken". The failure of the Judge to give judgment, grant an adjournment or dismiss the claim rendered the first summons a nullity and caused the Court to lose jurisdiction of the first proceeding.

St. Mary's Credit Union Ltd. v. General Doors (1991), 42 C.P.C. (2d) 115 (Sask. Q.B.) — Evidence at trial was not given under oath, and there was no cross-examination. Oral evidence is to be given under oath, and the opposite party is to be given the opportunity to cross-examine on the evidence. There was no proper trial of the issues.

DiMenna v. Colborne Auctions (1993), 4 W.D.C.P. (2d) 137 (Ont. Sm. Cl. Ct.) — Rule 18.04 was designed to cure mishaps such as the inadvertent non-appearance of a party. To stretch the rule to the point where apart-time Deputy Judge is passing judgment on the conduct of another part-time Deputy Judge or even a Judge of the General Division sitting in Small Claims Court would not be appropriate.

British Columbia (Ministry of Transportation & Highways) v. L. Steinke & Sons Logging Ltd. (October 22, 1998), Doc. Quesnel 8720 (B.C. Prov. Ct.) — Application by the plaintiff for default judgment against the defendant, L. Steinke & Sons. The Ministry also sought to have the hearing heard by telephone. Steinke was an Alberta company and it was not registered extraprovincially under the *Company Act*, R.S.B.C. 1996, c. 62. Application dismissed. The action against Steinke could not proceed. The court only had jurisdiction over foreign companies registered as an extraprovincial company. Steinke was not registered in this manner. Steinke never attorned to the jurisdiction. Steinke not properly served. Service upon a company could not be effected against its lawyer or the lawyer's office. A default hearing could not be conducted by telephone where *viva voce* evidence was involved.

O'Krane v. Braich (1999), 126 B.C.A.C. 262, 206 W.A.C. 262 (B.C. C.A.) — The appellants failed to attend at trial and a default judgment allowing claim and dismissing the counterclaim was obtained. Motion to set aside the judgment on the claim was dismissed. The dismissal of counterclaim was set aside on the condition that the appellants pay costs. Judge had jurisdiction to impose conditions for setting aside the dismissal. The appeal of refusal to set aside the judgment on claim and costs condition on counterclaim was dismissed.

Prince v. Boulevard Four Fashion (1996) (May 5, 1999), Doc. AI 99-30-04068 (Man. C.A. [In Chambers]) — The plaintiffs failed to appear at a Small Claims Court trial but succeeded on appeal, at which the defendant failed to appear. The defendant alleged that non-attendance was inadvertent and sought leave to appeal. The proper remedy for the defendant was to seek rescission or variation under Queen's Bench Rule 37.11(1) (Manitoba). Leave to appeal not granted.

Spoor v. Nicholls, 2001 CarswellBC 1279, 2001 BCCA 426, 90 B.C.L.R. (3d) 88 (B.C. C.A.); additional reasons at 2002 CarswellBC 337, 2002 BCCA 119 (B.C. C.A.); was additional reasons to (1999), 45 C.L.R. (2d) 95, 1999 CarswellBC 711 (B.C. S.C.) — Once defence evidence concluded at trial, there was evidence upon which trial judge could have assessed damages. By allowing defendant opportunity to present new evidence at subsequent hearing, trial judge had permitted defendant to split case. That was improper.

Mosher v. Ontario (2001), 2001 CarswellOnt 2897 (Ont. S.C.J.) — Unrepresented plaintiff brought motion under Rule 52.01(3) of *Rules of Civil Procedure* to set aside judgment obtained by defendant after plaintiff failed to appear for trial. Court had proposed relocating trial, then denied plaintiff's request for adjournment. Plaintiff attended at proposed new location for trial. After plaintiff left courtroom, Court did not in fact relocate trial. Judgment set aside. Plaintiff under genuine belief trial had been relocated.

Steele v. Campbell, 2001 CarswellNB 298, 2001 NBQB 122 (N.B. Q.B.) — Appellant claimed he believed date of hearing was February 7, when in fact it was February 5. Failed to provide any supporting evidence. No supporting medical evidence adduced. Appeal dismissed.

Emery Customs Brokerage Ltd. v. K. (D.) (2001), 2001 CarswellOnt 4423 (Ont. Master) — Stay of proceedings. Concurrent criminal proceedings. Defendant failed to discharge onus on her to demonstrate exceptional or extraordinary circumstances sufficient to warrant stay of civil proceeding. The mere fact that a defendant at discovery may be required to disclose her defence in a criminal proceeding was not necessarily exceptional.

671122 Ontario Ltd. v. Sagaz Industries Canada Inc. (2001), 150 O.A.C. 12, 2001 CarswellOnt 3357, 2001 CarswellOnt 3358, [2001] S.C.J. No. 61, 2001 SCC 59, 11 C.C.E.L. (3d) 1, [2001] 4 C.T.C. 139, 204 D.L.R. (4th) 542, 274 N.R. 366, 17 B.L.R. (3d) 1, 55 O.R. (3d) 782 (headnote only), 12 C.P.C. (5th) 1, 8 C.C.L.T. (3d) 60, [2001] 2 S.C.R. 983, 2002 C.L.L.C. 210-013 (S.C.C.); reconsideration refused (2001), 2001 CarswellOnt 4155, 2001 CarswellOnt 4156, 55 O.R. (3d) 782 (headnote only), 18 B.L.R. (3d) 159, 10 C.C.L.T. (3d) 292 (S.C.C.) — Trial judge refused plaintiff's motion to reopen the trial to hear the owner's evidence on the ground that the evidence available at trial and the plaintiff made a tactical decision not to call the owner. The Supreme Court of Canada allowed the appeal and restored the trial judge's decision.

Frampton v. Williams, Roebothan, McKay & Marshall (2002), 2002 CarswellNfld 90, 213 Nfld. & P.E.I.R. 299, 640 A.P.R. 299 (Nfld. T.D.) — Small Claims Court decision set aside where party having work and child care responsibilities given only one clear day's notice of hearing date and had requested teleconference to consider postponement request. Small Claims Rules, Rule 19(4). Fundamental tenet of our justice system that litigants be afforded full opportunity to present evidence and argument in court. If because of practical difficulties litigant prevented from so exercising that right, the right itself becomes illusory.

Earthcraft Landscape Ltd. v. Clayton, 2002 CarswellNS 497, [2002] N.S.J. No. 516, 2002 NSSC 259, 210 N.S.R. (2d) 101, 659 A.P.R. 101 (N.S. S.C.). Duty to assist unrepresented litigant. Adjudicator failing to advised unrepresented party that letter tendered in evidence would have less weight than oral testimony and that party had right to secure attendance of letter writer to provide oral evidence. Failure to advise constituted denial of natural justice.

Predie v. Paul Sadlon Motors Inc., 2005 CarswellOnt 801 (Ont. S.C.J.), Howden, J. Notice of Discontinuance as served dated day before case conference. Rule 23.05 of the *Civil Rules of Procedure* sets out consequence of discontinuing an action, Rule 23.05(a).

The Motion by plaintiff for leave to appeal an order made by management judge refusing leave to bring a further motion in this action after he had discontinued it, based on pre-abandonment conduct. Rule 63.01 does not provide an automatic stay in the case of a motion for leave to appeal. All claims have been either discontinued or dismissed and no costs have been awarded on a final basis, subject only to rights of appeal. No further interlocutory proceedings may be brought.

Lariviere v. Bertrand, 2006 CarswellMan 159, 2006 MBQB 104, 27 C.P.C. (6th) 231 (Man. Q.B.).

Section 11(1) of *Court of Queen's Bench Small Claims Practices Act* provides that where defendant fails to appear at Small Claims hearing, judge or court officer is entitled both to give default judgment against defendant and dismiss any counterclaim by defendant but defendant can apply for leave to appeal and have second chance at trial *de novo* with respect to plaintiff's claim and its own counterclaim. Statute does not give defendant right to appeal or move to set aside order when he/she fails to appear at hearing of appeal. In contrast, plaintiff not given second chance under statute after inadvertently failing to attend at scheduled hearing. *Queen's Bench Rules*, except R. 76.01, do not apply to Small Claims hearing nor to Small Claims appeal unless ordered by judge.

Plaintiff should not be punished for delay attributable to his lawyer. Delay not wilful nor did it result in irreparable harm to defendant. Affidavit set out circumstances of his claim and defence on merits.

Haché v. Canada (Minister of Fisheries & Oceans), 2006 CarswellNat 1005, 2006 CarswellNat 3574, 2006 FC 434, 2006 CF 434 (F.C.), de Montigny J.

Various plaintiffs brought action against Ministry of Fisheries before judge who had previously worked for Department of Justice as chief of staff.

Plaintiffs brought motion for recusal of judge at opening of trial. Motion dismissed. Automatic disqualification of judge solely for having been associated with such organization has been rejected in Canada. No actual bias or reasonable apprehension of bias arose.

Alpha-Mar Navigation Inc. v. Prestige International Inc., 2007 CarswellNat 1625, 2007 FC 620 (F.C.), M. Beaudry J. Time of trial. Discretion of trial judge.

X. v. Y., 2004 CarswellYukon 74, 13 C.P.C. (6th) 161, 2004 YKSC 45 (Y.T. S.C.)

Plaintiff brought an application for permission to use initials to describe plaintiff and two defendants, to seal court file or, alternatively, for publication ban on actual initials in connection with sexual allegations. Application allowed in part.

Use of initials was widely accepted in sexual assault cases where reputations of both parties can be adversely affected merely by filing claim. Publication ban was only appropriate where it was necessary to prevent risk to the proper administration of justice and where the benefit of the ban outweighed the negative effects on the open court principle. Use of initials and publication ban was appropriate in this case. However, this was not an appropriate case for sealing the court file.

Shearer v. Hood, 2007 CarswellMan 216, 2007 MBQB 117, 216 Man. R. (2d) 217, 49 C.P.C. (6th) 355 (Man. Master); additional reasons at [2007] M.J. No. 335, 2007 CarswellMan 364, 2007 MBQB 214 (Man. Master)

Moving party brought a motion to for order expunging affidavit of the other party's solicitor from court file. Motion granted. Affidavit from solicitor acting as advocate never should have been filed. Courts developed practice of not allowing solicitors to rely on their own evidence while acting as advocates.

Reilly v. British Columbia (Attorney General), 2008 CarswellBC 768, 77 B.C.L.R. (4th) 230, 2008 BCCA 167, 55 C.C.L.T. (3d) 174, [2008] 10 W.W.R. 287, 254 B.C.A.C. 161, 426 W.A.C. 161 (B.C. C.A.)

Appeal by the plaintiff and cross-appeal by the defendants from a summary trial decision. Plaintiff sued defendant for malicious prosecution and negligence as a result of a criminal investigation by defendant resulting in criminal charges against plaintiff. Plaintiff commenced action within two-year limitation period after his acquittal. Defendants cross appealed decision finding negligence claim against defendant police officer was not statute barred.

Appeal allowed. Claim for malicious prosecution could not be determined at summary trial. It was unfair to decide the issue of reasonable and probable grounds without the available circumstantial evidence, when it was known to exist or to be obtainable.

Cross-appeal dismissed. Negligence claim was not statute barred as cause of action did not arise until plaintiff's acquittal.

Doucet v. Spielo Manufacturing Inc., 2008 CarswellNB 612, 69 C.P.C. (6th) 252, 2008 NBQB 413, 340 N.B.R. (2d) 198, 871 A.P.R. 198 (N.B. Q.B.)

After close of defence, plaintiff's counsel applied to call plaintiff in reply. Application dismissed. Plaintiff had full opportunity to adduce proposed evidence during his case. Plaintiff's counsel chose not to ask him any questions on re-direct. Reply was improper notwithstanding defendant bore onus of proof on issue of cause. Plaintiff bound to present all his evidence on issue. A plaintiff cannot "split" his or her case. "As a general rule, all matters which are properly part of the plaintiff's case in chief are to be excluded from reply evidence."

See Schroeder, J.A. in *Allcock, Laight & Westwood Ltd. v. Patten* (1966), 1966 CarswellOnt 151, [1967] 1 O.R. 18, [1966] O.J. No. 1067 (Ont. C.A.) at pg. 21 [O.R.].

Canadian National Railway v. Huntingdon Real Estate Investment Trust (2009), 2009 MBQB 232, 2009 CarswellMan 435, 88 C.P.C. (6th) 230, [2010] 1 W.W.R. 307 (Man. Q.B.)

The plaintiff brought action against the defendants. The plaintiff refused to provide witness list at pre-trial disclosure but did provide names and contact information for 77 people. The plaintiff pared down the list to 23, and stated that unspecified 15 would be called as witnesses. The defendants brought motion for order directing that plaintiff provide witness list at least 45 days prior to commencement of trial. Motion dismissed. Disclosure of witness list is not required and there is no specific statutory provision.

See *Canada Deposit Insurance Corp. v. Commonwealth Trust Co.*, 1993 CarswellBC 565, [1993] B.C.J. No. 1804, 22 C.B.R. (3d) 113, 49 W.A.C. 248, 30 B.C.A.C. 248, 83 B.C.L.R. (2d) 49 (B.C. C.A.):

> 64 At common law, there is no power in the court to require a litigant to reveal in advance who the witnesses for his side will be. To that general rule, the *Evidence Act* provides an exception in the case of expert witnesses.

See also Sopinka J. for the court in *R. v. Stinchcombe* (1991), [1991] S.C.J. No. 83, 8 C.R. (4th) 277, 120 A.R. 161, 83 Alta. L.R. (2d) 193, 130 N.R. 277, [1991] 3 S.C.R. 326, [1992] 1 W.W.R. 97, 1991 CarswellAlta 192, 1991 CarswellAlta 559, EYB 1991-66887, 8 W.A.C. 161, 68 C.C.C. (3d) 1, 18 C.R.R. (2d) 210 (S.C.C.), at 6.

Trial efficiency arguments to be made in support of requiring the disclosure of a witness list, but are also risks in so doing described in *Fidelis Fisheries Ltd. v. Thorden*, 12 F.R.D. 179, 1952 U.S. Dist. LEXIS 3601 (U.S. Dist. Ct. S.D. N.Y., 1952).

The nature of a court's inherent jurisdiction considered in *Montreal Trust Co. v. Churchill Forest Industries (Manitoba) Ltd.*, 21 D.L.R. (3d) 75, 1971 CarswellMan 42, [1971] 4 W.W.R. 542, [1971] M.J. No. 38 (Man. C.A.), wherein Freedman C.J.M., speaking for the court adopted quote from p. 51 of an article by Master I.H. Jacob entitled "The Inherent Jurisdiction of the Court," published in *Current Legal Problems*, vol. 23 (London: Stevens & Sons, 1970):

In this light, the jurisdiction of the court may be defined as being the reserve or fund of powers, a residual source of powers, which the court may draw upon as necessary whenever it is just or equitable to do so, and in particular to ensure the observance of the due process of law, to prevent improper vexation or oppression to do justice between the parties and to secure a fair trial between them.

(4) Setting Aside or Variation of Judgment — The court may set aside or vary, on such terms as are just, a judgment obtained against a party who failed to attend at the trial.

History [R. 17.01(4)]: Formerly 18.01(5).

Case Law: *G. Richard Watson v. Crystal Mountain Resources Ltd.* (1988), 9 A.C.W.S. (3d) 238 (B.C. C.A.) — Setting aside a default judgement and the imposition of terms is a discretionary matter and, provided there is material capable of supporting the order made by the judge, the appeal court will not legally interfere. The sum of $142,900 was required to be paid into court as a condition of the order.

H.C. Sanders & Sons Ltd. v. Collins (1988), 10 A.C.W.S. (3d) 159 (N.S. Co. Ct.) — This action was dismissed without costs to either party as neither party appeared at trial. By way of stated case, the appeal was allowed. A defendant who attends without the plaintiff would suffer a prejudice if the action is merely adjourned. The defendant is entitled to a dismissal. If neither party attends, the defendant suffers no prejudice upon the adjournment. The "better" way is to strike the matter off the list with proper notice to be given to the defendant.

Mount Royal Painting & Decorating Inc. v. Central Interiors Inc., [1996] 7 W.D.C.P. (2d) 18 (Ont. Sm. Cl. Ct.) — Court considered "failure to attend at trial" under subrule 18.01(5). In this case, the defendant should not be denied relief (an adjournment) sought because a representative of the defendant attended trial to request an adjournment.

Chernick v. Spodek (1997), 37 O.R. (3d) 422 (Ont. Gen. Div.) — Scheduling problem arose in trial. It was incumbent upon counsel to ensure they had reliable staff to keep counsel up to date. Counsel's failure to notify court in timely manner regarding scheduling problem, failure to properly list his three offices in at least one legal directory and failure to advise court of change in address are sufficient to cause counsel to fall into "other default" under *Rules of Civil Procedure*, Rule 57.07(1).

Wilbee v. Baldinelli (1997), 45 O.T.C. 297, 1997 CarswellOnt 3582 (Ont. Gen. Div.) — Automobile insurer which paid claim brought Small Claims Court action for property damage against second driver. Default judgment entered against second driver, who made monthly payments on judgment. Plaintiff obtained order setting aside Small Claims Court judgment, which would have operated as bar to personal injury claim, and withdrew action. Broker not affected by order setting aside judgment, but by payments made on judgment which resulted in denial of coverage by broker's liability insurers. Order setting aside judgment made within jurisdiction.

Caverly v. Popoff (1997), 159 Sask. R. 75, 14 C.P.C. (4th) 265 (Sask. Q.B.) — Application to set aside Small Claims Court judgment obtained by default against defendant who claimed not to have been notified of service of process on wife. Service properly effected upon wife of defendant who signed on his behalf. No other discretion available by statute respecting setting aside of Small Claims Court judgments. Safeguards contained in Queen's Bench Rules (Sask.). Not available to such judgments.

Markel Insurance Co. of Canada v. Kamloops Freightliner Ltd., 1997 CarswellBC 1094 (B.C. S.C.) — Petitioner failed to attend settlement conference as provided by *Small Claims Act* (B.C.). Provincial Court judge refused to set aside default judgment granted to respondent, pursuant to s. 17(2) of Act, on basis that petitioner did not have meritorious defence. There were no grounds for concluding that judge exercised his discretion either wrongly or in breach of rules of natural justice.

Richard v. J & K General (October 28, 1998), Doc. Whitehorse 98-S0070 (Y.T. Terr. Ct.) — Application to set aside a default judgment. Application dismissed. Lavidas had notice of the claim and did not reply. He had notice of the default judgment on September 28. He failed to justify reopening the case.

Skendos v. Igbinosun (1999), 117 O.A.C. 125 (Ont. Div. Ct.) — Rule 19.08(1) of the *Rules of Civil Procedure*, R.R.O. 1990, Reg. 194, "confers a broad discretion to set aside a default judgment 'on such terms as are just'"(at 126).

Ridings Financial Services Inc. v. Singh (September 19, 1998), Doc. C28136/94 (Ont. Master) — Motion to set aside a default judgment signed on December 18, 1995. The grounds are that statement of claim was never served and did not come to the attention of defendant until February 19, 1998 when defendant was faced with garnishee proceedings. Plaintiff produced evidence that on that date, statement of claim served at 2770 Aquitaine Avenue, Apartment 302, in Mississauga, Ontario, while he, Mr. Singh, was actually located at 1034 Haig Blvd., in Mississauga. Corroborated by income tax forms and driver's licence records (kept by the Provincial Government) filed on the motion. Court found that statement of claim was never served on defendant.

Skendos v. Igbinosun (1999), 117 O.A.C. 125 (Ont. Div. Ct.) — The appeal against conditions to setting aside default judgment was dismissed. The *Rules of Civil Procedure* (Ontario), Rule 19.08(1), conferred upon the judge broad discretion to set aside judgment on such terms as are just. Lengthy delay and lack of credibility of defendant as to impecuniosity permitted the judge to make a finding of special circumstances. Costs to the respondent fixed at $1,500.

National Bank v. Royal Bank (1999), 121 O.A.C. 304, 44 O.R. (3d) 533 (Ont. C.A.) — Due to a remedy in Rule 19.08 for setting aside default judgment, a default judgment is not a final order for the purposes of appeal to the Court of Appeal. The default judgment is not a final judgment until a remedy has been sought and refused.

Teskey v. Peraan (1999), 34 C.P.C. (4th) 333, 1999 CarswellOnt 1316 (Ont. Master) — A default judgment on a claim served by registered mail was set aside where the signature of the person receiving the registered mail was not that of the defendant. Had the registrar been aware that the signature was not that of the defendant, the default judgment would not have been signed without an order under Rule 16.08 of Ontario's *Rules of Civil Procedure*.

Lewis v. General Accident Assurance Co. (1997), 36 O.R. (3d) 604, 29 C.P.C. (4th) 357 (Ont. Master) — The plaintiffs submitted a requisition to note the defendant in default and for default judgment. On same day, the defendant was noted in default and the default judgment was signed. The defendant brought a motion returnable two days before the actual entry of the judgment to set aside the noting of default and the default judgment. The motion was adjourned. The judgment was entered two days after the original date for the return of the motion. No proceedings can be taken until an order is entered. Until a default judgment is entered, there is no formal judgment. The defendant met the requisite test. The defendant intended to defend the action. The failure to defend was the result of solicitors' inadvertence. The defendant moved promptly to set aside the noting of default.

The court dismissed a motion to set aside a judgment where it was not shown that the fresh evidence could not have been obtained by reasonable diligence prior to judgment. Judgment in the case of a minor should be given the same force and effect as any other judgment: *Tsaoussis (Litigation Guardian of) v. Baetz* (1998), (sub nom. *Tsaoussis v. Baetz)* 112 O.A.C. 78, 165 D.L.R. (4th) 268, 41 O.R. (3d) 257, 27 C.P.C. (4th) 223 (Ont. C.A.); leave to appeal refused (1999), (sub nom. *Tsaoussis v. Baetz)* 236 N.R. 189 (note), (sub nom. *Tsaoussis v. Baetz)* 122 O.A.C. 199 (note) (S.C.C.).

Schill & Beninger Plumbing & Heating Ltd. v. Gallagher Estate (Litigation Administrator of) (2000), 2000 CarswellOnt 1985 (Ont. S.C.J.); reversed in part (2001), 140 O.A.C. 353, 6 C.P.C. (5th) 80, 2001 CarswellOnt 188, [2001] O.J. No. 260 (Ont. C.A.) — The executor lawyer and the estate solicitor made deliberate informed decision not to defend despite urging of the plaintiff. Default not accidental. Judgment was not set aside.

Hunter Douglas Canada Inc. v. Skyline Interiors Corp. (2000), 2000 CarswellOnt 3300 (Ont. S.C.J.) — The plaintiff caused the defendant to be noted in default only six days after service. The defendants were not afforded minimum time to respond. The default judgment was set aside: *Rules of Civil Procedure* (Ontario), Rule 18.01.

Baltson v. AT&T Canada Inc. (2000), 2000 CarswellOnt 3481 (Ont. Div. Ct.) — The plaintiff was unrepresented throughout, moved before Divisional Court for order setting aside two orders to which he had consented. There was no evidence or basis to set aside consent orders.

Isofab Insulation Inc. v. RSG Mechanical Inc. (2000), 2000 CarswellOnt 4239 (Ont. S.C.J.) — Default judgment was set aside and moneys garnisheed and held by Sheriff were returned to the defendant. Default was without notice after a period of negotiations. Amount in dispute was $1,500. The whole procedure was unnecessary, expensive and over-lawyered. The matter was transferred to Small Claims Court.

Osowsky v. General Refrigeration & Air Conditioning Inc. (1999), 1999 CarswellSask 799 (Sask. Q.B.) — A trial date was set for January 25. The plaintiffs attended. The clerk unsuccessfully attempted to find a telephone number for the defendant. The plaintiffs failed to inform the court and proceeded to obtain default judgment. The defendant showed intent to defend, acted promptly after learning of judgment, and showed meritorious defence. The judgment was set aside and a new trial ordered.

Koffski v. Ashworth, 2001 CarswellBC 2521, 2001 BCSC 1469 (B.C. S.C.) — Defendant had default judgment entered against him and failed to have it set aside. Defendant sought to participate in assessment of damages hearing. Defendant waived right to participate in hearing.

Gehring v. Prairie Co-operative Ltd., 2001 CarswellSask 476, 2001 SKQB 320, 209 Sask. R. 285 (Sask. Q.B.) — Appellant argued it was not served and did not understand that he had been served. Judge refused to set aside default judgment. This was an appeal.

Grinnell Supply Sales Co. v. Heger Contracting Ltd., 2001 CarswellBC 1744, 2001 BCSC 1105 (B.C. S.C.) — Evidence of defendants provided nothing more than statement that proceeding did not come to their attention until June 23, 1999. No explanation as to why the substitutional service did not come to their attention. Their son had been served; no explanation as to why son had not brought the matter to their attention. Dismissed.

Canadian Shareholders Assn. v. Osiel (2001), 2001 CarswellOnt 3226 (Ont. S.C.J.) — Motion to set aside noting of default and default judgment brought within one month. There was arguable defence on several factual and legal matters. Judgment and noting of default set aside.

Watts, Griffis, & McOuat Ltd. v. Harrison Group of Cos. (2001), 2001 CarswellOnt 3377, 18 C.P.C. (5th) 117 (Ont. S.C.J.) — Plaintiff obtained summary judgment for balance of fees against one of several defendants. That defendant sought to adduce fresh evidence from accounting files produced by plaintiff after judgment. Materials available earlier with due diligence, and would not have affected decision. Application dismissed.

Carnegie-Mellon Financial Group Inc. v. Adirondack Technologies Inc. (2001), 2001 CarswellOnt 3818 (Ont. S.C.J.) — Defendant business had failed to file statement of defence through inadvertence. Business appeared to have valid defence and counter-claim. Default judgment set aside.

Corlett v. Matheson, 2001 CarswellAlta 1723, 2001 ABQB 963, 302 A.R. 139 (Alta. Q.B.) — Plaintiff having default judgment sought to amend statement of claim without reopening default judgment. Application dismissed.

Mills v. Scarborough General Hospital (2001), 2001 CarswellOnt 3517 (Ont. C.A. [In Chambers]) — Self-represented appellant aware from February 2000 that order refusing to set aside dismissal of action was final and not interlocutory, and that she was in wrong court in filing in Divisional Court. Failure to file in Court of Appeal until March 2001 insufficiently explained. Extension of time refused.

Huggins v. Nicholson (2001), 156 O.A.C. 158, 2001 CarswellOnt 4845 (Ont. Div. Ct.) — Deputy Judge Barron gave judgment to the plaintiffs in the absence of defendant for $6,000 plus costs and prejudgment interest. The defendant had filed a defence. Notice of trial had never been received by defendant's counsel. Defendant's counsel moved to set aside default judgment. The Divisional Court, per Sills J., allowed the appeal, set aside the judgment, and remitted matter to the Small Claims Court for a new trial date. The Court stated that Rule 19 (default proceedings) ought not to have been invoked until an order had been made striking out the defence and then inviting a motion for default judgment.

Atkin v. Clarfield (2002), 2002 CarswellOnt 971 (Ont. S.C.J.) — Defendant brought motion to set aside default judgment. Defendant author of own misfortune by changing addresses and assuming that proceeding had been resolved. Substantial prejudice would accrue to plaintiff. Default not set aside.

Michalakis v. Nikolitsas, 2002 CarswellBC 3258, 2002 BCSC 1708 (B.C. S.C.) — Respondent issued small claims writ against petitioner. Petitioner filed reply. Settlement conference was to take place, petitioner ill, rescheduled. Petitioner did not attend rescheduled settlement conference because he did not receive notice of it. Settlement judge noted petitioner in default. Petitioner applied to set aside default judgment. The chambers judge erred in distinguishing a default judgment obtained without service of originating process from a default judgment obtained without service of notice of an interlocutory proceeding. Natural justice required that a party not be found in default of a proceeding he did not know about. It was patently unreasonable to confirm judgment against him. The result, denial of natural justice.

Credit Union Atlantic Ltd. v. McAvoy, 2002 CarswellNS 481, 2002 NSCA 145, 210 N.S.R. (2d) 207, 659 A.P.R. 207 (N.S. C.A.) — Defendant unable to pay for legal advice and unaware that she could defend on own behalf. Later found counsel on affordable terms. Chambers judge erred in refusing to set aside judgment. Test not whether defendant had decided not to defend, but whether she had reasonable excuse for failure. Appeal allowed and judgment set aside.

Maurice's Service Centre Ltd. v. Ryan, 2005 CanLII 1484 (N.L. Prov. Ct.), Howe, P.C.J. — Defendants sought default judgment to set aside. Rule 20 of the *Small Claims Rules* (NLR 52/97) essentially codification of existing caselaw. For instance, in *Langor v. Spurrell*, 1997 CarswellNfld 238, [1997] N.J. No. 264, 157 Nfld. & P.E.I.R. 301, 486 A.P.R. 301, 17 C.P.C. (4th) 1 (Nfld. C.A.), Green, J.A.

"This notion of judicial discretion necessarily imports the concept of power of free decision or latitude of choice within reasonable legal parameters." (Marshall, J.A. writing for the majority in *House of Haynes (Restaurant) Ltd. v. Snook*, 1995 CarswellNfld 16, 13 C.C.E.L. (2d) 149, (sub nom. *Newfoundland Human Rights Commission v. House of Haynes*) 95 C.L.L.C. 230-032, 134 Nfld. & P.E.I.R. 23, 417 A.P.R. 23, (sub nom. *House of Haynes (Restaurant) Ltd. v. Halleran*) 24 C.H.R.R. D/278, [1995] N.J. No. 292 (Nfld. C.A.) at paragraph 19.) Default Judgment set aside.

Trenders Inc. v. Krygier, 2005 CarswellSask 478, 2005 SKPC 66 (Sask. Prov. Ct.), S.C. Carter, PCJ. Application by Trenders Inc. to set aside default judgment of Bekolay, P.C.J.

Section 37 of the *Small Claims Act, 1997*, governs the application. See *Gehring v. Prairie Co-operative Ltd.*, 2001 CarswellSask 476, 2001 SKQB 320, 209 Sask. R. 285 (Sask. Q.B.).

Reasonableness of applicant's excuse for not being aware of the small claims action doubtful. No reasonable excuse for failing to attend.

First Citizens Mortgage Corp. v. Felger, 2006 CarswellBC 108, 2006 BCPC 1 (B.C. Prov. Ct.), Judge K.D. Skilnick. On each occasion when Defendant failed to attend court (i.e., the settlement conference, the trial date, and the last application to set aside default judgment), representative for Claimant (Williams) appeared. Williams requested order that Claimant pay costs on a solicitor-client basis. Rule 20(6) of the *Small Claims Act Rules* provides that "A judge may order a party or witness whose conduct causes another party or witness to incur expenses to pay all or part of those expenses."

In *Weeks v. Ford Credit Canada Ltd.* (April 28, 1994), Doc. Vancouver C9303264 (B.C. Prov. Ct.), Judge Baird-Ellan held that "expenses" as that term used in this rule, refers to money actually spent.

Rule 17(4) provides: "In making an order under these rules, a judge may impose any conditions or given any direction that the judge thinks is fair."

Order that Defendant not make any further applications until monies deposited with court registry to be held as security. In event Defendant successful in setting aside default judgment and defending claim, $5,000 to be returned to him.

Lariviere v. Bertrand, 2006 CarswellMan 159, 2006 MBQB 104, 27 C.P.C. (6th) 231 (Man. Q.B.) 2006-05-06.

Plaintiff moved to set aside decision of Suche J. who dismissed Plaintiff's claim against Defendant and awarded costs against Plaintiff.

Originally Plaintiff successful in obtaining a judgment against Defendant after a hearing before Hearing Officer. That decision was appealed by Defendant and a date for hearing set for November 28, 2005. Plaintiff failed to attend resulting in Suche J. dismissing Plaintiff's claim.

Ultimately wherever possible, parties should be given the opportunity to litigate their claims and have matters resolved on the basis of evidence.

Decision set aside.

Astral Media Radio Atlantic Inc. v. Brewer, 2007 CarswellNB 247, 2007 NBQB 198, 51 C.P.C. (6th) 85 (N.B. Q.B.)

Appeal by defendant from adjudicator's decision refusing to set aside default judgment. Appellant failed to appear at trial and argued he did not receive notice of trial date. The notice was sent by registered mail, but the appellant never picked up registered mail from post office. Although appellant acted unreasonably, notice of hearing date was not required to be sent by registered mail, therefore appealed allowed.

Matthes v. Manufacturers Life Insurance Co., 2008 CarswellBC 7, 52 C.P.C. (6th) 1, 2008 BCSC 6 (B.C. S.C. [In Chambers])

Application brought by the defendants to set aside a default judgment and for a reassessment of damages was dismissed. The defendant and her companies were served by substituted service which they denied. The court found the defendant could not rely on her own refusal to accept registered mail to explain her lack of a timely response to the judgment. Such refusal was deliberate and willful and thus the explanation for the delay was unreasonable.

McFaull v. Palchinski, 2008 CarswellSask 92, 2008 SKPC 23, 315 Sask. R. 156, [2008] S.J. No. 92 (Sask. Prov. Ct.)

Plaintiff was granted a judgment in absence of the defendant. Defendant brought application to set aside judgment granted against him. Application granted. Judgment was set aside due to appellant's reasonable excuse for not appearing and his defence that can only be sorted out at new trial. New trial was granted in order to attempt to balance interests of both parties. It was fundamental to system of justice that parties to dispute have opportunity to be heard, however when party has not availed himself of that opportunity, other parties should not be prejudiced or put to additional expense.

Sharma v. Giffen LLP, 2012 CarswellOnt 15430, [2012] O.J. No. 5800 (Ont. Sm. Cl. Ct.)

The plaintiff had failed to show up for this two-day trial, having expected it to be adjourned on consent, and his claim was dismissed. He brought a motion to set aside that dismissal. The court held that the test was the same as that to set aside a default judgment under rule 11.06. It was held that the plaintiff's failure to appear for his trial date was not satisfactorily explained, and more importantly, on the merits his claim was doomed to failure on several grounds. The motion was dismissed.

(5) Conditions to Making of Order under Subrule (4) — The court may make an order under subrule (4) only if,

> (a) the party who failed to attend makes a motion for the order within 30 days after becoming aware of the judgment; or

> (b) the party who failed to attend makes a motion for an extension of the 30-day period mentioned in clause (a) and the court is satisfied that there are special circumstances that justify the extension.

O. Reg. 78/06, s. 33

Commentary: When there is a motion to set aside a judgment given after a trial, and involving matters in excess of $500 exclusive of costs, some judges insist that a copy of a transcript of the reasons for judgment be served with the motion papers and filed with the court. If this is the case, the applicant should be referred to the appropriate court reporter for the transcript. (It is the applicant's responsibility to pay the required fee directly to the court reporter). In these circumstances the notice of motion and supporting affidavit should be filed with the court within 30 days of the trial date (Rule 17.04) and the date of hearing scheduled to allow sufficient time for the transcript to be obtained and served with the other motion papers within the necessary time limits. The applicant should not attempt service until the transcript is obtained. The bringing of a motion does not stay any other proceedings, including enforcement proceedings taken on a judgment, or prevent the commencement of any other proceedings unless the court has ordered otherwise. Moneys standing in court or moneys received after a motion has been filed to set aside a judgment should be held pending the outcome of the motion or an order for their release. Where a judgment is set aside and no order is made as to the disposition of the moneys, staff should continue to hold the moneys pending the outcome of any subsequent trial or an order for their release.

Where a judgment has been transferred to a second small claims court for enforcement, an application may be brought in the home court by the defendant to have the judgment set aside. The usual practice has been to have the home court notify the second court that a notice of motion has been commenced and notify them of the outcome. Once the notice has been received any monies held by the court are not released until the motion has been dealt with. If the application is successful, the second court often holds the funds in its possession until there is a court order authorizing the release of the funds.

Any suitor funds that are received are returned to the home court once judgment has been set aside until a judge orders otherwise. If a second judgment is awarded in the favour of the plaintiff and a balance remains after the funds are disbursed, then a new certificate of judgment should be issued by the home court before any further enforcement proceedings are brought.

Once a judgment is set aside, the clerk of the home court is responsible for the particular file and the distribution of any funds. No action will be taken by the clerk of the second court until a further certificate of judgment is received and the latter reflects the date and particulars of the new judgment.

17.02 Adjournment — (1) The court may postpone or adjourn a trial on such terms as are just, including the payment by one party to another of an amount as compensation for inconvenience and expense.

(2) If the trial of an action has been adjourned two or more times, any further adjournment may be made only on motion with notice to all the parties who were served with the notice of trial, unless the court orders otherwise.

O. Reg. 78/06, s. 34

History [R. 17.02(2)]: Formerly 18.02; plain language changes.

Commentary: The power to adjourn a trial is given to "the court" — which means a judge of the court. The court clerk has no jurisdiction to adjourn a trial: see *Robb-Simm v. RE/MAX Real Estate Centre Inc.*, 2012 CarswellOnt 13437, [2012] O.J. No. 5232 (Ont. Sm. Cl. Ct.). For more detailed commentary on adjournments see the discussion on that subject above in the commentary under rule 16.01.

Case Law: *Holtzman v. Suite Collections Canada Inc.*, 2013 ONSC 4240, 2013 Carswell-Ont 9010, 310 O.A.C. 243 (Ont. Div. Ct.)

Once a trial date has been set in the Small Claims Court, the trial is expected to proceed on that date. The Practice Direction as to Trial Dates and Adjournments dated June 9, 1999, applies to the Small Claims Court. In this case when the matter was called for a trial which had been set months earlier, the defendant requested an adjournment on the basis it had retained a lawyer just four days earlier despite knowing he was not available for the trial.

The deputy judge denied the adjournment and proceeded with the trial. An appeal from the denied adjournment was dismissed.

Bond v. Deeb, 2013 CarswellOnt 696, [2013] O.J. No. 287 (Ont. Sm. Cl. Ct.); further proceedings 2013 CarswellOnt 3769, [2013] O.J. No. 1524 (Ont. Sm. Cl. Ct.)

The trial had been adjourned three times before and the last adjournment was made peremptory on all parties. At the peremptory fourth trial date, the plaintiff failed to attend court but left messages stating that she could not attend trial because her mother was in hospital. The action was dismissed. A subsequent motion by the plaintiff to set aside that order was dismissed. The court found that her failure to attend trial was not satisfactorily explained, her claim was doomed to failure and the justice of the case did not favour setting aside the dismissal order.

Oberbichler v. State Farm Mutual Automobile Insurance Co., 2013 CarswellOnt 11871, [2013] I.L.R. I-5481 (Ont. Sm. Cl. Ct.)

The Small Claims Court has a discretion to adjourn a trial and direct that it be heard together with another related action between the same parties. In this case there were two pending actions both involving claims by the same plaintiff against the same insurer for statutory accident benefits arising from the same motor vehicle accident. On motion the court adjourned the trial of one action for hearing together with the trial of the second action.

Campbell v. Maritime Engine Specialists (October 11, 1995), Doc. AD-0607 (P.E.I. C.A.) — If a plaintiff is taken by surprise at trial and needs an adjournment, he should advise the trial judge of that fact. Although proceedings in Small Claims Court are informal, this does not extend to the trial judge conducting the case for the parties.

Strosberg v. Wahl (1994), 6 W.D.C.P. (2d) 86 (Ont. Sm. Cl. Ct.) — A motion for leave to discontinue an action for the purposes of bringing another action in a more senior court was granted where the court found that the responding party would not suffer substantial prejudice if the motion was granted.

In granting the motion, the court found that the abandonment of an excess of a claim or counterclaim was merely a procedural step and was not irreversible. No prejudice to the respondents had been demonstrated other than the inconvenience of having less speedy and costly proceedings, but which could be compensated for by an order of costs. There was no evidence of prejudice substantially disabling the respondents from presenting their defence and counterclaim in any other court proceedings.

R. v. Gregoire (November 18, 1994) (Ont. Prov. Div.), Allen J. — Client, charged with an offence under the *Highway Traffic Act*, was represented in Provincial Court by HK, a former lawyer who had been disbarred for dishonesty. On behalf of HK, client's mother appeared before the court requesting an adjournment, as HK was not available on the date set for appeal. The judge refused to entertain the application for an adjournment, stating the client was free to be represented by any type of agent, but that he would not allow an appearance by HK in his court. The appeal was to go ahead as scheduled unless another basis for adjournment could be found.

Direk v. Dixon (1999), 236 N.R. 196 (note) (S.C.C.); refusing leave to appeal from (1998), 111 O.A.C. 137 (Ont. C.A.) — On trial date, the plaintiff's new counsel requested an adjournment to allow him to prepare and amend statement of claim. The judge granted the request and fixed a peremptory trial date. Plaintiff failed to amend his pleadings by the new trial date. He sought another adjournment. The trial judge dismissed the motion.Court of Appeal affirmed ruling. Trial judges had responsibility to control the process that was before them. Trial judge's conclusion in respect of unfairness entirely justified in light of history of matter.

Brydon v. Hoskin (November 20, 1998), Doc. Vancouver CA024036 (B.C. C.A) — Appeal by Brydon from the dismissal of his application for judicial review. Attorney General had not been notified as required under s. 16(1) of the *Judicial Review Procedures Act*, R.S.B.C. 1996, c. 244, either with respect to the application for judicial review or the appeal. Appeal dismissed. This was not an appropriate case to exercise the discretion to grant an adjournment.

Mazzobel v. Liebman (May 6, 1998), Doc. 677/97 (Ont. Div. Ct.) — This was an appeal by Mazzobel against the dismissal of a Small Claims Court action. The action was dismissed. The judge held that Mazzobel had no intention of proceeding and the request for adjournment was only a delaying tactic. The appeal was allowed. The trial judge erred in principle when she concluded that the adjournment request was for an improper motive. Any prejudice to Liebman could have been overcome by giving him costs.

Widjojo v. Clifford (1998), 112 B.C.A.C. 254, 182 W.A.C. 254 (B.C. C.A.) — The appellant granted adjournments twice to change solicitors. The subsequent application to adjourn, to submit complete medical records, and to retain new counsel, was refused. The appellant appealed and brought a motion to introduce new evidence. The appeal and the motion were dismissed. The trial judge exercised discretionary jurisdiction properly in declining to adjourn the trial.

Technologie Labtronix inc. c. Technologie Micro Contrôle inc. (24 août 1998), no C.A. Montréal 500-09-004365-979 (Que. C.A.) — The Court erred in ordering a visit to the site on its own motion. A better course of action would have been for the Court to make a suggestion and then receive submissions. The Court exceeded discretion in taking the initiative, which had the effect of transforming the process from an adversarial to an inquisitorial process, which was not contemplated under Code.

Smith v. Garbutt (October 14, 1998), Doc. Vancouver CA023231 (B.C. C.A.) — A motion for non-suit at end of the plaintiff's case resulted in a motion to amend statement of claim. The trial judge did not err in granting an amendment on the basis of conforming to evidence that had been given at trial to date. The amendment did not prejudice the appellant defendants.

Strata Plan VR 2000 v. Shaw (January 8, 1999), Doc. Vancouver C946094 (B.C. S.C.) — The defendants applied for an adjournment of trial. The plaintiff argued that the case was ready for trial. The plaintiff was entitled to have the case heard unless the adjournment accorded with interests of justice. It was reasonable to assume that any adjournment would be for more than a year. This was prejudicial to all parties and to the judicial system.

Banman v. Weipert (1999), 179 D.L.R. (4th) 487, 129 B.C.A.C. 300, 210 W.A.C. 300 (B.C. C.A.) — The appeal was from an order that granted adjournment of trial upon the request of the defendants, who retained new counsel. This was a case where intervention was called for. Prejudice to the appellant far outweighed whatever prejudice the defendants would suffer. Where a discretionary order is clearly created injustice, it was open to the court to set it aside. The trial was directed to proceed at the earliest date.

Bio-Med Waste Disposal System Ltd. v. Disco General Repair Ltd. (April 7, 1998), Doc. 406/97, Corbett, J. — The defendant was not ready to proceed and requested an amendment to the defence. The trial judge disallowed the motion on the ground of undue delay and undue prejudice. At trial, the prejudice referred to by the trial judge could have been compensated for by costs and an adjournment. The trial judge therefore erred in not permitting an adjournment on terms.

Mist Management Information Security Tempest International Inc. v. Standard Trust Co. (Liquidator of) (2000), 131 O.A.C. 83, 2000 CarswellOnt 532 (Ont. C.A.) — The judge acted judicially in exercising discretion in refusing to grant an adjournment and did not err in dismissing the appeal for want of prosecution.

McCready v. McCready, 2001 CarswellBC 2034, 2001 BCCA 539 (B.C. C.A.) — Appellant firing counsel prior to hearing and seeking adjournment. No indication action done to delay appeal. Appeal proceeding expeditiously. Adjournment granted.

Holderness v. Gettings, 2002 CarswellBC 226, 2002 BCCA 92, 163 B.C.A.C. 84, 267 W.A.C. 84 (B.C. C.A. [In Chambers]) — Plaintiff served with new expert report just prior to trial. Plaintiff requesting adjournment. Adjournment granted and defendant ordered to pay advance to plaintiff. Defendant seeking leave to appeal. Application dismissed.

Mills v. Scarborough General Hospital (2001), 2001 CarswellOnt 2276 (Ont. Div. Ct.) — Adjournment due to medical condition of unrepresented plaintiff appellant. Leave to appeal had been delayed to considerable future time. Plaintiff given one final chance. Matters adjourned peremptory to plaintiff to set date on terms.

Marbach v. Marbach, 158 B.C.A.C. 219, 2001 CarswellBC 2043, 2001 BCCA 570, 258 W.A.C. 219 (B.C. C.A.) — At a pre-trial conference shortly before the March date, husband assured trial judge that his new solicitor would be available for the March date. When trial opened, the husband sought an adjournment. The Court of Appeal affirmed trial judge was correct in refusing the adjournment.

Prefontaine v. Gosman, 2002 CarswellAlta 846, 2002 ABCA 166 (Alta. C.A.) — Hearing date for May 2002 set in October 2001. Medical information stating inability of two appellants to argue, based respectively on agitated mental state and depression, not sufficient to justify adjournment. Application denied and appeal should proceed.

Canada Photofax Ltd. v. Cuddeback, 2003 CarswellBC 40, 2003 BCSC 51 (B.C. S.C.) — Claimant sued respondent in Small Claims Court. Respondent not appearing and telephoned by trial judge. Respondent requesting adjournment. Trial judge proceeding with trial and claimant awarded judgment. Respondent appealed. Appeal dismissed. Trial judge exercising discretion in refusing to grant adjournment.

Holderness v. Gettings, 2002 CarswellBC 226, 2002 BCCA 92, 163 B.C.A.C. 84, 267 W.A.C. 84 (B.C. C.A. [In Chambers]) — Plaintiff served with new expert report just prior to trial. Plaintiff requesting adjournment. Adjournment granted and defendant ordered to pay advance to plaintiff. Defendant seeking leave to appeal. Application dismissed.

1162994 Ontario Inc. v. Bakker (2004), 184 O.A.C. 157, 2004 CarswellOnt 869 (Ont. C.A.) Tenant Protection Act did not articulate procedure to be followed on appeal and the *Rules of Civil Procedure* therefore applied to appeals originating from the Ontario Rental Housing Tribunal. Conduct of an appeal not governed exclusively by *Rule 61 of Civil Rules*.

Moss v. NN Life Insurance Co. of Canada/Transamerica Life Canada, 2004 CarswellMan 28, 2004 MBCA 10, [2004] 7 W.W.R. 211, 180 Man. R. (2d) 253, 310 W.A.C. 253, 42 C.P.C. (5th) 19, 235 D.L.R. (4th) 735 (Man. C.A.). Appeal by Plaintiff from decision her spouse who was not lawyer not authorized to act on her behalf at trial of her action against insurer. Right being asserted similar to representation by lawyer, which was prohibited. Appeal dismissed.

1335333 Ontario Ltd. v. Residences of Victoria Gardens Inc. (2004), 2004 CarswellOnt 103 (Ont. S.C.J.). Respondent knowingly and deliberately failed to comply with Order for provision of information and documents, but later purged contempt. Incarceration should only be imposed in extreme circumstances. Respondent ordered to pay funds into Court on receipt, and pay costs on substantial indemnity basis.

Garcia v. Bernath, 2003 CarswellBC 1903, 18 B.C.L.R. (4th) 389, 2003 BCSC 1163 (B.C. Master). Action for personal injuries commenced in Supreme Court, then transferred to Small Claims Court after examinations for discovery. Plaintiff recovered total of $4,173 and now sought costs on party-and-party basis up to date of transfer. Plaintiff had good reason to commence action in Supreme Court particularly given Defendant's insistence that no injury was sustained, awarded costs up to date of discovery at Scale 3.

Protect-A-Home Services Inc. v. Heber, 2003 CarswellMan 332, 178 Man. R. (2d) 150, 2003 MBQB 181 (Man. Q.B.). Plaintiff issued garnishing orders to recover its costs. Defendant misnamed in garnishing order. No evidence anyone misled by misname and garnishing order should not be set aside for this reason.

Bank of Nova Scotia v. Johnston, 2002 CarswellNB 305, 2002 CarswellNB 306, 2002 NBCA 57, 251 N.B.R. (2d) 280, 654 A.P.R. 280 (N.B. C.A.). Trial judge granted four previous adjournments, refused to grant another. Defendant argued that trial judge erred in failing to accommodate defendant's physical ailments and that there was apprehension of bias. Appeal dismissed. Trial judge did not err in refusing further adjournment.

MacNeil v. MacNeil (2002), 2002 CarswellNS 552, 2003 NSSC 44, 212 N.S.R. (2d) 380, 665 A.P.R. 380 (N.S. S.C.). *Small Claims Court Act (N.S.)*, s. 29(1) provided that adjudicator "may" make Order on claim no later than 60 days after hearing. Provision permissive. Order made 66 days after, not valid. Decision that Defendant was liable based on credibility. Appeal dismissed.

Canada Photofax Ltd. v. Cuddeback, 2003 CarswellBC 40, 2003 BCSC 51 (B.C. S.C.). Respondent not appearing and telephoned by trial Judge. Respondent requesting adjournment. Trial Judge proceeding with trial and claimant awarded judgment. Respondent appealing. Appeal dismissed.

Scheuneman v. R., 2003 CarswellNat 88, 2003 CarswellNat 4763, 2003 FCT 37, 2003 CFPI 37 (Fed. T.D.); affirmed 2003 CarswellNat 3741, 2003 CarswellNat 4624, 2003 FCA 440, 2003 CAF 440 (F.C.A.); leave to appeal refused (2004), 2004 CarswellNat 378, 2004 CarswellNat 379 (S.C.C.). Self-represented Plaintiff sought to be relieved from obligation of attending pretrial conference in person because of alleged disability. Plaintiff incapable of representing himself. Plaintiff was directed to appoint solicitor. Such solicitor was ordered to file further pretrial conference memorandum in conformity with Rules.

Charlottetown (City) v. MacIsaac, 2003 CarswellPEI 9, 2003 PESCTD 7, 35 M.P.L.R. (3d) 271, 223 Nfld. & P.E.I.R. 95, 666 A.P.R. 95 (P.E.I. T.D.). Plaintiff brought small claims action for return of portion of property taxes for garbage collection. No cause of action shown.

Khimji v. Dhanani, 2004 CarswellOnt 525, [2004] O.J. No. 320, 69 O.R. (3d) 790, 44 C.P.C. (5th) 56, 182 O.A.C. 142 (Ont. C.A.). Trial judge granting adjournment but making matter peremptory and ordering plaintiff to pay defendants' costs thrown away by new trial date. Plaintiff appearing unrepresented on trial date and seeking another adjournment. Trial judge justified in refusing adjournment and dismissing action in light of plaintiff's failure to take reasonable steps to be prepared for trial and to comply with costs order.

Appellant legally blind and not fluent in English language. Neither relevant to the reasonableness of the trial judge's refusal to grant an adjournment. No suggestion that the appellant's physical disability or his difficulties with the English language interfered in any way with his ability to retain and instruct counsel.

The option of dismissal must be available to the trial court to ensure ongoing effective operation of trial lists and to preserve the integrity of court orders. Strong deference due to decisions of those in trial courts who are responsible for the day-to-day maintenance of an efficient and just system of civil trials. The trial court is in a much better position to balance the competing interests than is the appeal court.

O'Brien v. Griffin, 2006 CarswellOnt 96, 22 R.F.L. (6th) 134, (sub nom. *Griffin v. O'Brien*) 206 O.A.C. 121, 263 D.L.R. (4th) 412 (Ont. C.A.) 2006-01-13.

Appeal by Griffin from judgment of Metivier J. of the Superior Court in which application of Griffin to vary divorce judgment was dismissed. Griffin not a lawyer and acted on his own behalf.

Griffin requested adjournment to permit him to call proposed witness either in person or by way of videoconference. The request was denied.

It was incumbent on the trial judge, in the particular circumstances, to assist Griffin by granting an adjournment for a reasonable period of time to permit him to secure the personal attendance of the witness. This is particularly so in view of the fact that the trial judge drew an adverse inference from his failure to call witness. Appeal allowed and new trial is ordered.

Lang J.A. (dissenting) refers to *Khimji v. Dhanani*, 2004 CarswellOnt 525, [2004] O.J. No. 320, 69 O.R. (3d) 790, 44 C.P.C. (5th) 56, 182 O.A.C. 142 (Ont. C.A.), which sets out the degree of deference paid to the exercise of discretion on the part of a trial judge.

> A trial judge has the discretion to adjourn a trial. That discretion must be exercised judicially, balancing the interests of the parties with a view to providing an expeditious and fair hearing. This applies in both the civil and family context and whether dealing with litigants represented by counsel or with self-represented litigants. See *McLeod v. Castlepoint Development Corp.*, 1997 CarswellOnt 174, [1997] O.J. No. 386, 97 O.A.C. 123, 31 O.R. (3d) 737, 8 R.P.R. (3d) 97, 25 C.P.C. (4th) 256 (Ont. C.A.); leave to appeal refused [1997] S.C.C.A. No. 191, 105 O.A.C. 160 (note), 223 N.R. 394 (note), 34 O.R. (3d) xv (S.C.C.), *Cornfield v. Cornfield*, [2001] O.J. No. 5733 (Ont. C.A.), and *Appiah v. Appiah*, [1999] O.J. No. 500, 1999 CarswellOnt 481, 118 O.A.C. 189, 45 R.F.L. (4th) 172 (Ont. C.A.).

> In my view (dissenting), the trial judge did *not* err in exercising her discretion to refuse the adjournment.

Matthews v. Royal & SunAlliance Canada, 2007 CarswellNfld 30, 2007 NLTD 11, 45 C.C.L.I. (4th) 138, (sub nom. *Matthews v. Royal & Sun Alliance Insurance*) 798 A.P.R. 255, (sub nom. *Matthews v. Royal & Sun Alliance Insurance*) 263 Nfld. & P.E.I.R. 255 (N.L. T.D.) (N.L. T.D.), 2007-01-18, James P. Adams J.

Appeal of decision of Provincial Court denying request for postponement to retain counsel. No error committed.

Appeal also on ground trial judge did not exclude respondent's only witness from court during appellant's testimony. There had been no request for exclusion.

Judge's decisions discretionary in nature.

Trial judge noted that it was usual that parties in Small Claims Court are not represented by counsel, appellant had represented himself throughout the proceedings and that he had drafted his own documents in an adequate manner.

Westcoast Landfill Diversion Corp. v. Cowichan Valley (Regional District), 2006 CarswellBC 487, 2006 BCSC 273 (B.C. S.C.), Shabbits J.

Defendant seeking adjournment of trial close to trial date. Application allowed. Plaintiff having very large claim. Defendant forced to take on new counsel as a result of prior counsel withdrawing. Defendant entitled to brief period to allow new counsel to get up to speed on issues. Prejudice to defendant of trial going ahead far outweighing prejudice to plaintiff of trial not proceeding.

Toste v. Baker (2007), 2007 CarswellOnt 1368 (Ont. Div. Ct.), March 7, 2007, Cumming J.

Appeal of Small Claims Court decision of Deputy Judge's refusal to grant an adjournment at defendants' request at hearing such that the decision at the conclusion of the ensuing trial is properly to be set aside.

No medical evidence was presented at the hearing to support the defendant's assertion that the defendant Baker could not attend because of medical problems. Mr. Baker's counsel simply made an oral submission that there was a medical problem as the reason for his absence.

Onus on defendants to establish basis for requested exceptional relief of overturning on appeal a refused request for adjournment by the trial judge. See generally *Thunderstone Quarries Ltd. v. Three Sisters Resorts Inc.*, 2004 CarswellAlta 232, [2004] A.J. No. 232, 2004 ABCA 47 (Alta. C.A.).

No good reason to interfere with discretion exercised by Deputy Judge in refusing the adjournment. Appeal dismissed.

Ramlall v. Salvation Army, 2006 CarswellOnt 1149 (Ont. Div. Ct.), Epstein J.

Respondent advised of hearing date. Respondent made last minute request for adjournment. Respondent self represented. Matter adjourned to specified date on terms. Costs fix at $500 awarded to moving party.

Oudeerkirk v. Clarry, 2005 CarswellOnt 6767 (Ont. S.C.J.), Sachs J.

Defendant sought second adjournment of trial on ground plaintiff had not produced all relevant medical information and this information could impact liability, damages and plaintiff's credibility. Not in interests of justice to proceed with trial and force jury to reach conclusions about issues in absence of potentially significant information which was available about those issues. Adjournment granted.

Kaplun v. Kaplun (2007), 2007 CarswellOnt 5889, 45 R.F.L. (6th) 115 (Ont. S.C.J.), Brown J.

Adjournment requests should be communicated to opposing counsel well in advance of hearing date.

Request for adjournment of motion by former solicitor of husband relating to costs of motion to remove him as solicitor of record. Wife also sought adjournment. Motions granted.

Ochnik v. Ontario (Securities Commission) (2007), 2007 CarswellOnt 2759, 224 O.A.C. 99 (Ont. Div. Ct.); additional reasons at (2007), 2007 CarswellOnt 3383 (Ont. Div. Ct.).

The Ontario Securities Commission found that Ochnik and 1464210 had traded while unregistered and without a prospectus. Divisional Court awarded Commission costs of $4,000. Although its partial indemnity costs amounted to $12,875, the Commission sought an award of $4,000, indicating that it did not wish to inhibit self-represented parties, such as Ochnik, by seeking prohibitive costs awards.

Ochnik and 1464210 submitting, *inter alia*, that because 1464210 under bankruptcy protection and Ochnik was an undeclared bankrupt at the time of the proceeding, there was a statutory stay. The Divisional Court dismissed appeal. Ochnik asserted that the Commission erred in refusing to grant an adjournment. The decision to grant an adjournment was best made by the tribunal. Ochnik had ample time to retain counsel and to review disclosure. The panel adapted the hearing to recognize that Ochnik was unrepresented and provided him with assistance.The conclusion that an adjournment was not warranted was reasonable.

Stocker v. Linley, 2007 CarswellOnt 4100 (Ont. S.C.J.), Walters J. Adjournment. General principles.

M.C.M. Contracting Ltd. v. Canada (Attorney General), [2002] Y.J. No. 108, 2002 CarswellYukon 112, 2002 YKSC 47 (Y.T. S.C.)

An action was commenced on behalf of corporation which was dissolved on November 3, 2000. Plaintiff's application was adjourned for 14 days at the request of the Plaintiff in order to allow the Plaintiff's company to successfully restore its registration. Plaintiff took no steps to restore itself to the register. Application was made by the Plaintiff for further adjournment. Application for an adjournment dismissed. The delay by the Plaintiff mitigated against the granting of an adjournment, which was also justified by the strength of the defendant's position. An action commenced on behalf of a corporation that had been dissolved was a nullity and not an irregularity that could be cured.

Zynik Capital Corp. v. Faris, 2004 CarswellBC 1784, 41 B.C.L.R. (4th) 190, 2004 BCSC 1032 (B.C. S.C.)

The defendants apply to dismiss the action on the basis that it was commenced in the name of a corporation that had been voluntarily dissolved. Plaintiff lacked capacity to bring action as it was dissolved. It is common ground that an action commenced on behalf of a corporation that has been dissolved is a nullity, unless the corporation has been revived before the action was commenced. Action was nullity and could not be cured by amendment of statement of claim pleading facts of corporate reorganization.

Tulloch v. AmeriSpec Home Inspection Services, 2006 CarswellNS 623, 2006 NSSM 48, 47 C.P.C. (6th) 337, 253 N.S.R. (2d) 37, 807 A.P.R. 37 (N.S. Sm. Cl. Ct.)

Claimant brought action on contract in Small Claims Court. Arbitration clause in contract provided exclusion of jurisdiction of the Small Claims Court. It was held that arbitration clause was void as pursuant to s. 14(1)(a) of *Small Claims Court Act*, provision in agreement excluding, limiting or varying jurisdiction of Small Claims Court is void. There is no jurisdiction in the Small Claims Court to stay claims, although the Court may grant an adjournment in some situations.

Canadian Equipment Rentals Ltd. v. G.A.P. Contracting Ltd., 2008 CarswellBC 1977, 2008 BCCA 360, 259 B.C.A.C. 200, 436 W.A.C. 200 (B.C. C.A. [In Chambers])

Solicitor for defendant unsuccessfully requested adjournment due to absence of principal defendant. Provincial Court judge ruled defendant failed to attend and allowed plaintiff's claim without requiring it to prove its damages. Defendant unsuccessfully appealed to Supreme Court. Defendant commenced second appeal to Supreme Court and brought application for stay of execution pending appeal. Application dismissed. Supreme Court did not have jurisdiction to entertain application as no appeal was available from prior judgment of Supreme Court. Defendant had exercised right of appeal from Provincial Court judgment pursuant to s. 5 of *Small Claims Act*.

Toronto-Dominion Bank v. Transfer Realty Inc., 2010 ONCA 166, 2010 CarswellOnt 1195 (Ont. C.A.).

TD Bank moved for judgment to enforce Minutes of Settlement. Appellants requested adjournment to obtain alternate legal counsel. The motion judge denied appellants' request and granted judgment in favour of TD Bank. Decision to grant adjournment is discretionary. Accordingly, scope for appellate intervention is limited: see *Khimji v. Dhanani* (2004), [2004] O.J. No. 320, 182 O.A.C. 142, 44 C.P.C. (5th) 56, 69 O.R. (3d) 790, 2004 Carswell-Ont 525 (Ont. C.A.). Appellants have not demonstrated refusal to grant adjournment contrary to the interests of justice. Appeal dismissed.

Gulati v. Husain, 2011 CarswellOnt 407, 2011 ONSC 706, [2011] O.J. No. 384 (Ont. S.C.J.)

The applicant sought *certiorari* respecting an order from deputy judge of the Small Claims Court (a) denying an adjournment of the motion to set aside default judgment; (b) staying enforcement of the default judgment; (c) setting aside the default judgment; and (d) costs of $300. Order setting aside default judgment, and costs order set aside.

The court has the discretion to refuse a consent adjournment. But this discretion should be exercised sparingly. It is unusual to refuse a request to accommodate counsel's schedule reasonably on a first appearance.

Deputy judge gave no reason for refusing adjournment. Deputy judge then decided the motion to set aside the default judgment without hearing submissions from either side.

Maryland's highest court has held that a trial court abused its discretion by refusing to suspend a civil trial despite a litigant's planned absence during two days of the trial for religious reasons. *Neustadter v. Holy Cross Hosp. of Silver Spring, Inc.* The plaintiff asserted that the scheduled trial partially conflicted with an Orthodox Jewish holiday that would occur during two days in the middle of trial. The plaintiff argued that, when he was observing the holiday, he was prohibited from working or relying on agents to work on his behalf. The court held that the trial court's concerns about a negative impact on jurors, judicial resources, and the trial court's docket should not be "unreasonably juxtaposed" against the plaintiff's request for a religious accommodation.

Reland Development Ltd. v. Whitby (Town), 2011 ONCA 661, 2011 CarswellOnt 11771 (Ont. C.A.)

A trial judge enjoys a wide latitude in deciding whether to grant adjournment of scheduled civil trial: see *Khimji v. Dhanani*, 2004 CarswellOnt 525, [2004] O.J. No. 320, 69 O.R. (3d) 790, 44 C.P.C. (5th) 56, 182 O.A.C. 142 (Ont. C.A.). Decision entitled to considerable deference: see *Murphy v. Werry Estate*, 2005 CarswellOnt 313, [2005] O.J. No. 280, *(sub nom. Murphy v. Werry)* 193 O.A.C. 356 (Ont. C.A.). The appellant had been granted two adjournments totalling a year and had not secured counsel. He had also applied for, and was denied, additional extensions, including once just two weeks before the trial. Fresh evidence was not admitted. The appellant failed to satisfy the criteria of diligence, relevance, and likelihood of affecting the outcome of the adjournment motion.

Appeal dismissed with costs to the respondent fixed at $9,000.

Leigh v. Belfast Mini-Mills Ltd., 2011 NSSC 23, 2011 CarswellNS 144, 303 N.S.R. (2d) 1, 957 A.P.R. 1, [2011] N.S.J. No. 118, Arthur J. LeBlanc J. (N.S. S.C.)

The defendants were entitled to costs under R. 77.05(2) of Civil Procedure Rules since the motion was abandoned and the defendants were not responsible for the adjournment. The plaintiffs were self-represented, and unable to understand and comply with rules. The adjournment caused unnecessary delay, and thus lost effort and increased work for defendants. Costs were awarded against plaintiffs in the amount of $1,000 payable in any event of cause and at the end of the proceeding.

Graham v. Vandersloot, 2012 ONCA 60, 2012 CarswellOnt 815, 108 O.R. (3d) 641, 6 C.C.L.I. (5th) 171, 346 D.L.R. (4th) 266, 288 O.A.C. 342, [2012] O.J. No. 353 (Ont. C.A.)

The appellant sought to set aside two orders of the Superior Court of Justice: (i) the order dated September 7, 2010, denying the appellant's request for an adjournment of the trial of this action, and (ii) the order dismissing the action.

Adjournment decisions are highly discretionary and appellate courts are rightly reluctant to interfere with them. Laskin J.A. succinctly summarized the operative legal principles in *Khimji v. Dhanani*, 2004 CarswellOnt 525, [2004] O.J. No. 320, 69 O.R. (3d) 790, 44 C.P.C. (5th) 56, 182 O.A.C. 142 (Ont. C.A.). Although he was in dissent, the majority accepted his articulation of the statement of principles. See paras. 14 and 18 in particular. See also *Ariston Realty Corp. v. Elcarim Inc.*, 2007 CarswellOnt 2371, [2007] O.J. No. 1497, 51 C.P.C. (6th) 326 at paras. 33, 36 and 38 (Ont. S.C.J.).

The motion judge gave undue weight to the appellant's lawyer's failure. As Hambley J. noted when granting leave to appeal to the Divisional Court in this matter, "the often applied principle that the sins of the lawyer should not be visited upon the client applies in this case." This principle was enunciated by this Court in *Halton Community Credit Union Ltd. v. ICL Computers Canada Ltd.*, 1985 CarswellOnt 357, [1985] O.J. No. 101, 8 O.A.C. 369, 1 C.P.C. (2d) 24 at para. 11 (Ont. C.A.):

> Undoubtedly counsel is the agent of the client for many purposes . . . but it is a principle of very long standing that the client is not to be placed irrevocably in jeopardy by reason of the

neglect or inattention of his solicitor, if relief to the client can be given on terms that protect his innocent adversary as to costs thrown away and as to the security of the legal position he has gained. There may be cases where the plaintiff has so changed his position that this is impossible.

It is the overall interests of justice that, at the end of the day, must govern. See *Ariston Realty Corp.*, at para. 38.

The interests of justice favour the appellant's having her day in court to put forward her claim for damages on the merits.

Kaycan Ltée/Kaycan Ltd. v. R.P.M. Rollforming Ltd., 2011 ONSC 1454, 2011 CarswellOnt 1466 (Ont. S.C.J.), Perell, J.; additional reasons at 2011 ONSC 2040, 2011 CarswellOnt 2195 (Ont. S.C.J.)

A motion was made for a summary judgment for payment of the price of goods sold and delivered. The defendant, ("R.P.M."), asked for an adjournment of the motion, which the court declined to grant. Factors for a court to consider in deciding to grant or refuse an adjournment were set out in *Ariston Realty Corp. v. Elcarim Inc.*, 2007 CarswellOnt 2371, [2007] O.J. No. 1497, 51 C.P.C. (6th) 326 (Ont. S.C.J.). Adjournments are not a given right. There was no violation of the principles of natural justice by refusing the adjournment. R.P.M. had been given the right to put its evidence before the court, and it had exercised that right. R.P.M.'s lawyer had been on the case throughout, and he was or ought to have been ready to argue the case with or without a factum.

Fritsch v. Magee, 2012 ONSC 2755, 2012 CarswellOnt 5791, 40 C.P.C. (7th) 320, Baltman, J. (Ont. S.C.J.); additional reasons 2012 ONSC 4301, 2012 CarswellOnt 9116 (Ont. S.C.J.).

The defendant brought a motion at the outset of the trial to have the plaintiff's action dismissed as statute barred. The alleged assault occurred on May 13, 2006. The plaintiff issued a claim in Small Claims Court on July 17, 2007, well within that period.

The plaintiff's counsel asked to have the Small Claims Court action "stayed" on consent on July 31, 2008, when the matter was scheduled to be spoken to. On July 30, 2008, the plaintiff's counsel issued a statement of claim in the Superior Court. In these circumstances it was grossly unfair to preclude the plaintiff from proceeding.

See *Waymark v. Barnes*, 1995 CarswellBC 61, 3 B.C.L.R. (3d) 354, 57 B.C.A.C. 249, 94 W.A.C. 249, [1995] B.C.J. No. 658 (B.C. C.A. [In Chambers]), where Taylor J.A. on behalf of the British Columbia Court of Appeal (in chambers) commented at para. 7 that:

> ... it seems that once the limitation period has expired a claim cannot be moved from that court to the Supreme Court: see also *MacMaster v. Insurance Corp. of British Columbia*, 1994 CarswellBC 206, 91 B.C.L.R. (2d) 276, 24 C.P.C. (3d) 288, 41 B.C.A.C. 306, 66 W.A.C. 306 (B.C. C.A.). In direct contrast, Ontario's *Courts of Justice Act* expressly provides in s. 107 for a transfer from small claims court to Superior Court. And s. 107(6) states that a proceeding that is transferred "shall be continued as if it had been commenced in that court."

The defendant's motion was dismissed.

Holtzman v. Suite Collections Canada Inc., 2013 ONSC 4240, 2013 CarswellOnt 9010, 310 O.A.C. 243, Grace, J. (Ont. Div. Ct.) — Holtzman commenced Small Claims Court action. She alleged that "all of the defendants have been reckless and negligent in their actions" and had breached a regulation made pursuant to the *Collection Agencies Act*, R.S.O. 2990, c. C. 14.

Deputy Judge rejected adjournment request by the defendants. The appellants relied on *Khimji v. Dhanani*, 2004 CarswellOnt 525, 69 O.R. (3d) 790, 44 C.P.C. (5th) 56, 182 O.A.C. 142, [2004] O.J. No. 320 (Ont. C.A.). Rule 17.02 of the *Small Claims Court Rules* addresses adjournments. The decision to proceed with the trail was amply supported. The Practice Direction as to trial dates and adjournments dated June 9, 1999 applies to the Small Claims Court as well. Paragraph 1(1) reads:

> Where a date for trial . . . of a matter has been set by the Superior Court of Justice . . . the trial . . . is expected to take place on that date.

The Practice Direction outlines its three objectives:

i. To ensure that trial lists are respected;

ii. To reduce court delays, the waste of court resources and the unnecessary expense and inconvenience to the public that adjournments cause — especially those requested late; and

iv. To assist parties in having adequate representation by a lawyer acceptable by them.

See J. W. Quinn, J. in *Brighton Heating & Air Conditioning Ltd. v. Savoia*, 2006 Carswell-Ont 340, 79 O.R. (3d) 386, 49 C.L.R. (3d) 235, 207 O.A.C. 1, [2006] O.J. No. 250 (Ont. Div. Ct.) at para. 40:

> . . . in the Small Claims Court, a liberal, non-technical approach should be taken to pleadings. Therefore, unpled relief may be granted . . . so long as supporting evidence is not needed beyond what was adduced at trial . . . provided that, in all circumstances, it is not unfair to grant such relief . . . Appeal allowed in part. Award of punitive or exemplary damages set aside. General damages reduced to $565.

17.03 Inspection — The trial judge may, in the presence of the parties or their representatives, inspect any real or personal property concerning which a question arises in the action.

History [R. 17.03]: Formerly 18.03; plain language changes.

Commentary: This procedure was formerly known as "taking a view" and involves the judge along with the parties, their representatives and the necessary court staff taking an excursion to look at the property in question. Taking a view is exceptionally rare even in the Superior Court of Justice in cases involving very large stakes, given the ready availability of photographic and video evidence and the relative expense and inconvenience of taking a view. It is difficult to imagine a scenario in which the taking of a view by the Small Claims Court would be appropriate, but the rule remains in place.

17.04 (1) Motion for New Trial — A party may make a motion for a new trial within 30 days after a final order is made.

Case Law: *George v. Wagenhoffer* (1995), 129 Sask. R. 214 (Q.B.) — New trial ordered where trial judge descended into the arena. Trial judge became counsel to the plaintiff and brought out facts material to the plaintiff's claim.

Shoppers Mortgage & Loan Corp. v. Health First Wellington Square Ltd. (1995), 38 C.P.C. (3d) 8 (Ont. C.A.) — During examination-in-chief and cross-examination of witnesses, the trial judge intervened on numerous occasions, adopting an adversarial position inimical to the co-defendant and his counsel. The trial judge refused to hear evidence on the agency issue and refused to hear evidence from expert witnesses on the issue of mitigation, admonishing defence counsel for "wasting my time" and "clutching at straws." A reasonable litigant in the co-defendant's position or any reasonable observer would have had some apprehension as to whether the agency and mitigation issues had been prejudged and rejected before all the evidence was in. The test was not prejudice to the co-defendant's case, but whether the image of impartiality, the absence of which deprived the court of jurisdiciton, was destroyed.

Saldanha v. Eastville Hldgs. Ltd. (1985), 2 W.D.C.P. 221 (Ont. Prov. Ct.) — Questions of law, in this case the failure to permit an amendment of a claim at trial, are the proper subject matter of an appeal, not the granting of a new trial. Grounds for granting new trials are discussed.

Svajlenko v. Appco Paving Ltd. (1985), 3 W.D.C.P. 34 (Ont. Prov. Ct.) — Where there has been a trial on the merits, in that both parties have the opportunity to present their own witnesses and to give evidence, and where there has been an adjudication on the merits, then a new trial is in appropriate unless there was such lack of jurisdiction.

Porter v. MacDonald (1993), 20 C.P.C. (3d) 355 (N.S. S.C.) — En route to trial, the appellant's car broke down and he could not get to the trial. What is the proper procedure in the Small Claims Court when a defence has been filed and the defendant does not appear at the time of the hearing? Appeal by the defendant from default judgment was allowed; the judgment was set aside and the matter was set down for rehearing. Refers to s. 23(3) of *Small Claims Court Act*, R.S.N.S. 1989, c. 430. Where a defence has been filed, an adjudicator is obliged to hear evidence before making an order in favour of the claimant.

Sears Canada Inc. v. Scott (1994), 51 A.C.W.S. (3d) 1232 (Ont. Sm. Cl. Ct.) — The plaintiff moved for a new trial pursuant to r. 18.04, Rules of Small Claims Court (Ont.). Jurisdiction to order a new trial pursuant to that rule only arose in instances where there was no trial on merits such that both parties had opportunity to present their evidence and there was adjudication on merits. Here, there had been trial as merits and appeal should be launched pursuant to s. 31 of *Courts of Justice Act* (Ont.).

Safty v. Carey (December 20, 1996), Doc. Vancouver C936887, C963488, C963448 (B.C. S.C.) — Plaintiff represented himself in three actions and was on sabbatical leave outside Canada for year. Plaintiff returned but alleged inability to attend trial by reason of illness, filing statement from doctor not specifying reason. Defendants had given adequate notice. Trial should proceed.

Falso v. De Stefanis, [1996] B.C.W.L.D. 2775 (B.C. C.A.); leave to appeal refused (1997), 87 B.C.A.C. 80 (note), 143 W.A.C. 80 (note) (S.C.C.) — Trial judge directed that plaintiff was to obtain transcript of evidence heard up to time of adjournment, and to provide transcript of evidence when trial continued. Plaintiff failed to obtain transcript. Order set aside order striking out appeal, but required plaintiff to produce transcript. Plaintiff sought adjournment. Court held it was not in interests of justice to grant plaintiff further extension to produce transcript.

Baziuk v. BDO Dunwoody Ward Mallette (1997), 13 C.P.C. (4th) 156, 34 O.T.C. 53, 1997 CarswellOnt 2507 (Ont. Gen. Div.) — Courts must deal with the issue of fairness with respect to unrepresented parties; however, a sense of fairness and understanding granted to unrepresented parties could not apply to the degree that the courts did not give effect to existing law. Inaddition, the issue of fairness to an unrepresented party could not override the rights of the other litigant. Therefore, while B did not raise certain issues in the first action, she could not be allowed to relitigate an issue that was originally in question between the parties. See also *Jones v. LTL Contracting* (July 4, 1995), Doc. Thunder Bay D94-95 (Ont. Gen. Div.).

Best Value Ltd. v. Subway Sandwiches & Salads (1998), 21 C.P.C. (4th) 14 (Ont. Sm. Cl. Ct.) — Plaintiff moved for a new trial under Rule 18.04(1) of the Rules of Small Claims Court, R.R.O. 1990, Reg. 201 (now Rule 17.04(1)), on ground the presiding deputy judge was not impartial. After the trial, plaintiff learned the deputy judge appeared in the Small Claims Court as counsel for a person sued by the plaintiff in an earlier unrelated action. See *R. v. S. (R.D.)*, 1997 CarswellNS 301, 1997 CarswellNS 302, [1997] S.C.J. No. 84, 151 D.L.R. (4th) 193, 118 C.C.C. (3d) 353, 10 C.R. (5th) 1, 218 N.R. 1, 161 N.S.R. (2d) 241, 477 A.P.R. 241, [1997] 3 S.C.R. 484, 1 Admin. L.R. (3d) 74 (S.C.C.) as to the test to be applied when it is alleged a judge is not impartial. The deputy judge recognized the risk of a reasonable apprehension of bias because he disclosed he had a relationship with the defendant. In the face of this disclosure, the plaintiff consented to proceed with the trial. The consent was not an informed consent. Motion allowed without costs.

K.W. Robb & Associates Ltd. v. Wilson (1998), 169 N.S.R. (2d) 201 (N.S. C.A.) — The fact that the trial judge did not advise the unrepresented appellant of possible ramifications of not testifying did not warrant a new trial. The trial judge was not required to, and ought not to, act as counsel for an unrepresented litigant.

637568 Alberta Ltd. v. Lyman (March 16, 1999), Doc. Grande Prairie 9904-00062 (Alta. Q.B.) — The provincial court judge did not allow the defendant to call evidence and granted judgment against him. The defendant appealed. The judge erred in law, and therefore lost jurisdiction.

Gill v. Sandhu (March 18, 1999), Doc. Edmonton 9803-07701 (Alta. Q.B. [In Chambers]). The plaintiff awarded judgment in a small claims action. The defendant appealed. The trial was unsatisfactory and rushed. The interpretation of the witnesses' testimony was below standard expected at trial. Documentary evidence at trial was not determinative, and not properly explored at trial. New evidence proffered by the defendant at the new trial could be conclusive of the matter.

Kochan v. Chuback (1999), 182 Sask. R. 5 (Sask. Q.B.) — The plaintiff appealed the dismissal of his Small Claims Court claim for want of prosecution. The matter had been set for August 6, 1998. The Court gave the plaintiff a note saying the hearing would be on August 7, 1998. The plaintiff did not appear for the hearing on August 6, hence the dismissal. The defendant refused to consent to an order directing a new trial. The plaintiff should not be denied his day in court because of an institutional scheduling error. Appeal was allowed.

Laverty v. Bhiro (September 16, 1999), Doc. CA C30353 (Ont. C.A.) — The trial judge's decision to proceed with trial was based on insufficient information and resulted in the appellant being unable to present his counterclaim properly. Nevertheless, the appellant was not prejudiced by the judgment granted against him in the main action since no realistic defence was advanced. A new trial was ordered only with respect to the counterclaim. The judgment was ordered stayed pending determination of counterclaim. Appeal was varied.

Freshair Enterprises Ltd. v. Kotrla (June 10, 1999), Doc. Regina Q.B.G. 227/99 (Sask. Q.B.) — A new trial was ordered because only the trial judge could determine whether the performance of services was sufficient satisfaction of debt owed to the plaintiff. A new trial seemed unrealistic because of the small amount of the claim, so the court suggested the defendant pay the plaintiff $267, one-half the amount of the claim as form of summary resolution. The suggestion was not binding.

Moore v. Economical Mutual Insurance Co. (1999), 177 N.S.R. (2d) 269, 542 A.P.R. 269 (N.S. C.A.) — Broad discretion under Rule 62.23 and s. 38(3) of the *Judicature Act* (N.S.) permitted the court to order a new trial. Given the strength of the case of fraud against the appellant and that nothing was advanced that materially weakened or created doubt, denial of adjournment did not result in substantial injustice.

Williams (Litigation Guardian of) v. Barnett, 2000 CarswellOnt 3681, [2000] O.J. No. 3815, 11 C.P.C. (5th) 224 (Ont. S.C.J.); additional reasons at (2001), 2001 CarswellOnt 92 (Ont. S.C.J.) — Excessive interference by the trial judge resulted in a new trial being ordered.

Hinton v. Alberta Heirloom House Ltd. (1999), 246 A.R. 397 (Alta. Q.B.) — The trial judge did not exceed his jurisdiction by participating in questioning during the course of trial. The trial judge was required to assess credibility, which he did after a lengthy hearing.

Androutsos v. Noram Interiors Ltd. (July 27, 1999), Doc. 97-CU-122263CM (Ont. S.C.J.) — The appellant's counterclaim pursuant to motion for summary judgment dismissed. The Court of Appeal permitted the appellant an opportunity to present evidence. Counsel for the respondent sent letters to the Master and the Master endorsed further order. Counsel's contact with the Master was improper. Nothing in Case Management Rules foreclosed the right to be heard before a decision is made. Order of the Master was set aside.

R. v. M. (M.) (1999), 122 O.A.C. 387 (Ont. C.A.) — An accused alleged that there was a reasonable apprehension of bias arising from the fact that the trial judge had presided over the pretrial where there was an early guilty plea. Three years elapsed before the accused raised this ground of appeal. Apprehension of bias requires a demonstration that the grounds for this apprehension must be substantial, that a real likelihood of bias exists and that a mere suspicion is not enough: *R. v. S. (R.D.)*, 1997 CarswellNS 301, 1997 CarswellNS 302, [1997] S.C.J. No. 84, 151 D.L.R. (4th) 193, 118 C.C.C. (3d) 353, 10 C.R. (5th) 1, 218 N.R. 1, 161 N.S.R. (2d) 241, 477 A.P.R. 241, [1997] 3 S.C.R. 484, 1 Admin. L.R. (3d) 74 (S.C.C.).

Creedan Valley Nursing Home Ltd. v. van Klaveren (1999), 126 O.A.C. 163 (Ont. Div. Ct.) — The plaintiffs appealed dismissal of action, arguing that the trial judge intervened to such an extent that he became *de facto* counsel for the unrepresented defendant. Interventions did not go significantly beyond the necessary role of a trial judge where there were complicated legal and evidentiary matters and where one party was unrepresented.

Davids v. Davids (1999), 125 O.A.C. 375, 1999 CarswellOnt 3304, [1999] O.J. No. 3930 (Ont. C.A.) — The husband appealed the divorce judgment. He argued that the trial was a miscarriage of justice. He argued that he could not represent himself effectively in a complex litigation. The Court of Appeal rejected the argument. The trial was adjourned part way through but the husband continued to represent himself after the four-week adjournment. There was no cause to doubt the reliability of the result.

The Royal "R" Co. v. The Bank of Nova Scotia (March 11, 1996), Court File No. 274/95 (Div. Ct.), MacPherson, J. — The appeal was allowed. Even allowing for the summary nature of proceedings in Small Claims Court, the deputy judge was wrong to cut off the right to cross-examine only witness produced by the bank after only three questions.

Wil v. Burdman, [1998] O.J. No. 2533, 1998 CarswellOnt 2541 (Ont. Div. Ct.) — While there may be some criticism that could be justifiable, when one looks at the proceedings overall, far from there being a miscarriage of justice in the conduct of the trial, as discussed in *Jones v. National Coal Board*, [1957] 2 All E.R. 155, [1957] 2 Q.B. 55 (Eng. C.A.) and John Sopinka: The Trial of an Action (Markham: Butterworths Canada, 1981 at 115-124), the Deputy Judge was attempting to have focus and assist the parties. The appeal was dismissed.

Inzola Construction (1976) Ltd. v. Sirro Brothers Ltd. (November 12, 1998), Doc. 326/96, MacFarland, J. — While the trial judge was only trying to help an unrepresented litigant, he went beyond the limit to which a trial judge should go. The trial judge took over the examination in chief of the main witness on behalf of the plaintiff and essentially examined him in chief. The judge must be vigilant and never appear to be helping one party to the necessary detriment of the other. The appeal was allowed and a new trial was ordered.

At the pretrial conference in a small claims action in August 1998, settlement was not reached and trial date was set for January 25, 1999. The plaintiffs attended on that date. The clerk unsuccessfully attempted to find the telephone number for the defendant. The plaintiffs were aware of the number but failed to inform the court, and proceeded to obtain a default judgment. The defendant sought to set aside the judgment on the ground that he had been informed that the trial date was January 29. The defendant showed intent to defend, acted promptly after learning of judgment, and showed meritorious defence. The judgment was set aside and a new trial was ordered, conditional on payment of judgment amount into court by the defendant. *Osowsky v. General Refrigeration & Air Conditioning Inc.* (1999), 1999 CarswellSask 799 (Sask. Q.B.).

Although the trial judge's involvement in cross-examination went beyond mere clarification, the questions were not designed to bolster one side of case. They were primarily designed to assist in understanding what occurred. The trial judge did not unduly interfere with the flow of cross-examination, nor did he give rise to reasonable apprehension of bias. The trial judge's requests were based on the use of time and continuity of proceedings and his prompt delivery of judgment did not raise reasonable apprehension of bias. Appeal dismissed. *Matthews v. Accent Lines (1988) Ltd.* (1999), 250 A.R. 29, 213 W.A.C. 29 (Alta. C.A.).

Benedict v. Ontario (2000), 136 O.A.C. 259, 48 C.P.C. (4th) 1, 51 O.R. (3d) 147, 193 D.L.R. (4th) 329, 2000 CarswellOnt 3747 (Ont. C.A.) — Where a judge perceives potential self-interest, especially where circumstances not known to litigants, he or she should withdraw from case or raise potential problems and make full disclosure of the proceedings. Where any party takes the position reasonable apprehension of bias exists, judge must carefully weigh submission and in doubt should disqualify himself or herself.

Harris Floors Ltd. v. Eversen Enterprise Ltd., 2001 CarswellAlta 1602, 2001 ABQB 1013 (Alta. Q.B.) — Trial judge awarded plaintiff judgment on invoices. The defendant appealed. Appeal allowed. New trial ordered. As this appeal was a trial de novo defendant provided some new evidence. Defendant satisfied Court her evidence might have been inadvertently overlooked or not fully understood by trial judge.

Berube v. Wingrowich, 2001 CarswellAlta 1494, 2001 ABQB 1000 (Alta. Q.B.) — Defendants applied to ask Court to reconsider decision. Absent exceptional circumstances, rehearings should not be granted. Proper remedy for defendants' complaints was appeal.

Rudd v. Hayward, 91 B.C.L.R. (3d) 227, 2001 CarswellBC 1463, 2001 BCCA 454, 12 M.V.R. (4th) 200, 156 B.C.A.C. 27, 255 W.A.C. 27 (B.C. C.A.) — Plaintiff's case did not require expert evidence, but it was logical and appropriate to allow him to call expert to reply to defendant's expert. Trial judge's decision to deny defendant opportunity to call second expert following testimony of plaintiff's expert was within his discretion. Restrictions on questioning represented proper enforcement of usual rule regarding evidence in reply.

Whitehorn v. Wallden, 90 B.C.L.R. (3d) 275, 2001 CarswellBC 1278, 2001 BCCA 419, 156 B.C.A.C. 317, 255 W.A.C. 317 (B.C. C.A.) — Defendant conceded that trial judge had erred in law by limiting plaintiff's ability to question expert witness. Properly instructed jury in possession of excluded evidence could have reached different verdict.

Lennox v. Arbor Memorial Services Inc. (2001), 56 O.R. (3d) 795, 2001 CarswellOnt 4248, 151 O.A.C. 297, 16 C.C.E.L. (3d) 157 (Ont. C.A.) — Both the nature and the extent of the interventions of the trial judge crossed the line and created the appearance of possible injustice. Moreover, the interventions were only directed at AMS Inc. and created an appearance of unfairness. Where errors are made by the trial judge in the conduct of the trial, a new trial is required.

Marchand (Litigation Guardian of) v. Public General Hospital Society of Chatham (2000), 138 O.A.C. 201, 2000 CarswellOnt 4362, [2000] O.J. No. 4428, 51 O.R. (3d) 97 (Ont. C.A.); leave to appeal refused 2001 CarswellOnt 3412, 2001 CarswellOnt 3413, [2001] S.C.C.A. No. 66, 282 N.R. 397 (note), (sub nom. *Marchand v. Public General Hospital Society of Chatham*) 156 O.A.C. 358 (note) (S.C.C.) — Informed and reasonable observer looking realistically at trial would not have apprehended bias or unfair adjudication. Experts may not testify about new matters not touched on in expert's report delivered before trial. *Rules of Civil Procedure*, Rules 31.09, 53.03(1).

Lennox v. Arbor Memorial Services Inc. (2001), 56 O.R. (3d) 795, 2001 CarswellOnt 4248, 151 O.A.C. 297, 16 C.C.E.L. (3d) 157 (Ont. C.A.) — Trial judge's conduct of the trial created an appearance of unfairness. Trial judge appeared to assist the respondent in the following:

- redirected lines of questioning which respondent's counsel sought to pursue and which the trial judge viewed as unhelpful to the respondent and strategically ill-advised;

- engaged in extensive cross-examination of two of Arbor's witnesses and challenged their credibility;

- required production of the appellant's policy manual, not part of the pleadings or productions, and therefore not part of the case before the Court as prepared and conducted by counsel; and

- sought more than an explanation or clarification of evidence brought out by counsel, by questioning two witnesses extensively about the policy manual.

Baker v. Smith, 2002 CarswellNS 323, 2002 NSCA 98, 207 N.S.R. (2d) 63, 649 A.P.R. 63 (N.S. C.A.) — Plaintiff claimed he could not hear parts of trial and that new trial should be ordered. Plaintiff aware for some time of his difficulty with hearing. Plaintiff did not raise problem with his counsel during or immediately after trial. Fresh evidence as to plaintiff's difficulty with hearing not received.

Minister of National Revenue v. Mathers (2001), 2001 CarswellNat 305, 2001 CarswellNat 3334, 2001 CFPI 104, 2001 D.T.C. 5197 (Fr.), 2001 FCT 104, [2002] 3 C.T.C. 582 (Fed. T.D.); affirmed 2001 CarswellNat 558, 2001 CarswellNat 1695, 2001 CFPI 241, [2001] 4 C.T.C. 16, 206 F.T.R. 162 (Fed. T.D.) — Judgment creditor garnished moneys from objector. Objector claimed reasonable apprehension of bias and brought motion for prothonotary to disqualify himself because his spouse worked in same department as counsel for judgment creditor. Counsel for objector filed affidavit in support of motion. Motion dismissed. Reasonable and well-informed person would not conclude there was reasonable apprehension of bias.

Von Felix v. Direct Protect (2002), 2002 CarswellOnt 2242 (Ont. S.C.J.) — Moving party sought to have new trial, claiming funds owed to her due to cancellation of her insurance policy. On review of evidence, no funds found to be owing. Motion dismissed.

Diamond v. Maidment, 2006 CarswellNfld 70, 2006 NLTD 40 (N.L. T.D.) 2006-03-03.

Appellant wished to call witness who came with him to court but left to babysit her child. Diamond wishes court to hear her evidence. Neither party represented by counsel. On March 2, 2006 court heard evidence of Connie Nalden, a witness called by the Appellant Scott Diamond. Appeal dismissed.

Midway Garden Restaurant v. Pye, 2006 CarswellNfld 38, 2006 NLTD 23 (N.L. T.D.) 2006-02-03.

Where the Court fails to permit counsel to present argument and summations at the end of a trial, the trial is incomplete and the resulting decision of the court cannot stand. Appeal from decision of Provincial Court of Newfoundland and Labrador, Small Claims Division. Trial continued without affording parties the opportunity to present further evidence and without providing any opportunity to the parties to make their oral arguments on the evidence and the law. Principal of fundamental justice that both sides in a trial be given an opportunity to summarize their positions and to argue the facts and evidence of a particular case and the law relating to those facts and evidence. New trial ordered.

Liu Estate v. Chau, 2004 CarswellOnt 442, 69 O.R. (3d) 756, 236 D.L.R. (4th) 711, 182 O.A.C. 366 (Ont. C.A.).

Trial judge directing female defendant to leave courtroom while husband testifying. Direction contrary to rule 52.06(2) of *Rules of Civil Procedure*. Party's inherent right to be present at trial to be curtailed only in exceptional circumstances. See *Baywood Paper Products Ltd. v. Paymaster Cheque-Writer (Canada) Ltd.*, 1986 CarswellOnt 465, [1986] O.J. No. 2076, 13 C.P.C. (2d) 204, 57 O.R. (2d) 229 (Ont. Dist. Ct.) at p. 239 O.R., "[t]he presence of a party at the examination for discovery, like the presence of a party at trial, is consistent with due process and the right to protect his or her interests by observing the conduct of the examination."

Canada Trustco Mortgage Co. v. Renard, 2007 CarswellBC 812, 2007 BCSC 523, 39 C.P.C. (6th) 211, 55 R.P.R. (4th) 104, [2008] 2 W.W.R. 279, 71 B.C.L.R. (4th) 305 (B.C. S.C.)

Defendants applied for order that trial be reopened to admit new evidence. Application dismissed. The applicant did not establish that a miscarriage of justice would occur if the trial was not reopened and that the evidence or arguments they wished to present would probably change the result of the trial. Reopening of the trial would have amounted to an abuse of process and an improper prolonging of the litigation.

Kelly v. Palazzo, 2008 CarswellOnt 564, 2008 ONCA 82, 233 O.A.C. 160, 290 D.L.R. (4th) 315, 89 O.R. (3d) 111, 168 C.R.R. (2d) 256 (Ont. C.A.); leave to appeal refused 2008 CarswellOnt 3741, 2008 CarswellOnt 3742, 387 N.R. 397 (note) (S.C.C.)

The trial judge dismissed the action of the plaintiff concluding that there was no reasonable basis to infer that the defendants racially profiled the plaintiff. After the trial judge released her reasons the appellant applied to reopen the trial for the purposes of amending his pleadings to include a claim based on violation of s. 98(3) of the *Customs Act*, R.S.C. 1985. Trial judge refused to reopen the case. The plaintiff appealed on the ground that the trial judge's conduct demonstrated a reasonable apprehension of bias. Appeal dismissed as there was no violation of s. 98(3).

Rejection of the racial profiling claim by the judge would not necessarily result in a presumption of bias against that judge.

Ring v. Canada (Attorney General), 2010 NLCA 20, 2010 CarswellNfld 86, [2010] N.J. No. 107, 297 Nfld. & P.E.I.R. 86, 918 A.P.R. 86, 86 C.P.C. (6th) 8, 72 C.C.L.T. (3d) 161 (N.L. C.A.); leave to appeal refused 2010 CarswellNfld 304, 2010 CarswellNfld 305, 410 N.R. 399 (note), 309 Nfld. & P.E.I.R. 362 (note), 962 A.P.R. 362 (note) (S.C.C.)

The application judge admitted affidavit of plaintiff's expert. Appeal allowed. It was error in law to admit affidavit of plaintiff's expert for purpose of proof of content of published texts or papers discussed by her. All such papers and texts remained inadmissible hearsay in absence of author of work or expert in proper field who was prepared to adopt work. Findings could not be made on basis of published scientific treatises discovered on research of judge or bibliographer.

Covriga v. Covriga, 2011 ONCA 769, 2011 CarswellOnt 13682, 4 R.F.L. (7th) 247 (Ont. C.A.); affirming 2009 CarswellOnt 4718, [2009] O.J. No. 3359, 73 R.F.L. (6th) 78 (Ont. S.C.J.), *per* Justice Carolyn J. Horkins.

This appeal was based on the competence of a lawyer. In the appeal, the mother argued that it was apparent to the trial judge that the mother's lawyer was poorly versed in family law and that the trial judge should have declared mistrial. The Court of Appeal rejected the mother's position, pointing out that the mother had made no motion for a mistrial in the course of the 14-day trial, for which she was represented by her lawyer throughout. There was no basis for the trial judge, on her own initiative, to declare a mistrial under the circumstances of this case.

Franks v. Wade, 2010 SKQB 204, 2010 CarswellSask 421, 4 C.P.C. (7th) 421, 357 Sask. R. 125 (Sask. Q.B.)

New trial; the grounds for granting included interference by the trial judge. The plaintiff's action was dismissed. The trial judge found the claim barred under *Limitations Act*. The plaintiff appealed, and the appeal was allowed. The trial judge erred in the application of the *Act*. By trying to help parties focus on issues for argument, the court gave the impression that negligence was not an issue for argument, except with respect to negligent misrepresentation.

Yukon Territory (Director of Occupational Health & Safety) v. Yukon, 2011 YKSC 50, 2011 CarswellYukon 53 (Y.T. S.C.), L.F. Gower J.

The government brought an application to have an appeal determined by way of a new trial on the ground of fresh evidence. The Application was dismissed. The proposed fresh evidence did not support new trial. It was not in the interests of justice to allow the minister's evidence on appeal. The government did not establish any special grounds for admission of the minister's evidence.

Rourke v. Toronto (City), 2012 ONSC 2563, 2012 CarswellOnt 5325, [2012] O.J. No. 1896 (Ont. Div. Ct.), Moore J.

Rourke brings two appeals arising from two orders made by judges in an action in the Small Claims Court.

Ashby DJ was asked to order a new trial for Rourke and his authority to do that arose from the provisions of Rule 17.04(1) of the *Small Claims Court Rules*. The rule is restrictive and specific. It provides that a party may make a motion for a new trial within 30 days after a final order is made. There is no doubt but that the order made by Kilian DJ dismissing Rourke's action was a final order.

The Rule permits the motions judge to grant a new trial only if the moving party demonstrates that there was a purely mathematical error in the determination of the amount of damages awarded, a criterion that does not apply in this case, or that there is relevant evidence that was not available to the party at the time of the original trial and could not reasonably have been expected to be available at that time.

A party has the right to be represented at trial or to present the case without representation.

Requests made by Kilian DJ of Rourke to introduce his evidence in a cordial manner were fair and necessary in order to allow the determination of the case before the court.

Intervention by trial judge during Rourke's testimony made necessary by fact that Rourke insisted on providing his testimony from a prepared speech addressing issues that the judge had deemed to be irrelevant. The text and its delivery were inflammatory and addressed matters that had been struck from the pleadings and constituted argument rather than oral evidence.

Appeals dismissed.

Green v. Ferma Construction Co. (February 24, 1998), Doc. Toronto T23135/93 (Ont. Small Cl. Ct.) — Motion by the plaintiff for clarification of the trial judgment. The formal judgment overrode the words and numbers in the reasons for judgment.

Harvie v. Schiller (January 22, 1998), Doc. Vancouver 95-13052 (B.C. Prov. Ct.) — This was an application for an amendment to a judgment. The application was granted in part. A portion of the expenses were allowed over and above the expenses granted at trial.

Bendell Bursaries Ltd. v. White (September 20, 1990), Doc. 78/90/CA (N.B. C.A.)

Appellant challenged the decision of the trial judge based on mandatory provision requiring the administration of oaths to the witnesses in small claims actions which was apparently overlooked by the trial judge. Appeal allowed since the witnesses who answered the Judge's questions were neither sworn nor did they affirm or declare as required by the Rule 75.12(4).

Caber Distributors Inc. v. Gill, 2008 CarswellBC 404, 2008 BCPC 42 (B.C. Prov. Ct.)

If both parties are willing to proceed, the same judge who made dismissal order can hear application for order canceling dismissal order.

The issue arose whether dismissal order by court was final or interlocutory. The Provincial Court of British Columbia held that there is nothing in the Rules indicating that dismissal orders made in presence of parties affected by them should, unlike dismissal orders made in parties' absence, be immune from cancellation in proper cases. Thus, R. 17(2) should be read liberally to permit court to cancel dismissal order made in presence of affected party.

(2) **Transcript** — In addition to serving and filing the notice of motion and supporting affidavit (Form 15A) required under rule 15.01, the moving party shall serve and file proof that a request has been made for a transcript of,

    (a) the reasons for judgment; and

    (b) any other portion of the proceeding that is relevant.

Commentary: In general, a party who is dissatisfied with the judgment rendered at trial is limited to the potential right of appeal to Divisional Court under s. 31 of the *Courts of Justice Act*. There are however two narrow grounds on which a dissatisfied litigant may instead bring a motion to the trial court for a new trial under rule 17.04.

As set out in rule 17.04(5), the only conditions which support a motion under rule 17.04 are either that there was a purely arithmetical error in the determination of the amount of damages awarded, or there is relevant evidence that was not available to the party at the time of the original trial and could not reasonably have been expected to be available at that time. The rule is restrictive and specific: *Rourke v. Toronto (City)*, 2012 ONSC 2563, 2012 CarswellOnt 5325, [2012] O.J. No. 1896 (Ont. Div. Ct.). These limited grounds are not intended as a substitute for appeal or to permit re-argument of the issues decided at the original trial: *Haig v. Ottawa-Carleton Regional Transit Commission* (January 9, 1995), Doc. OT21343/93, [1995] O.J. No. 4801 (Ont. Sm. Cl. Ct.); *Petrykowski v. 553562 Ontario Ltd.*, 2010 CarswellOnt 11114, [2010] O.J. No. 3129 (Ont. Sm. Cl. Ct.).

The practice is that wherever possible the motion for a new trial will be scheduled before the judge who presided over the original trial: *Christie Mechanical Contracting v. Magine Contracting*, 1997 CarswellOnt 1875, 10 C.P.C. (4th) 330, 101 O.A.C. 316 (Ont. Gen. Div.); *394705 Ontario Ltd. v. Moerenhout*, 1983 CarswellOnt 452, 41 O.R. (2d) 637, 35 C.P.C. 258 (Ont. Co. Ct.).

(3) **Service and Filing of Transcript** — If available, a copy of the transcript shall, at least three days before the hearing date,

    (a) be served on all parties who were served with the original notice of trial; and

    (b) be filed, with proof of service.

History [R. 17.04(3)]: Conditions added to specify grounds for a new trial. The grounds provided are broader than *Rules of Civil Procedure* subrules 59.06(1) and (2).

(4) **Powers of Court on Motion** — On the hearing of the motion, the court may,

    (a) if the party demonstrates that a condition referred to in subrule (5) is satisfied,

        (i) grant a new trial, or

        (ii) pronounce the judgment that ought to have been given at trial and order judgment accordingly; or

    (b) dismiss the motion.

(5) **Conditions** — The conditions referred to in clause (4)(a) are:

1. There was a purely arithmetical error in the determination of the amount of damages awarded.

2. There is relevant evidence that was not available to the party at the time of the original trial and could not reasonably have been expected to be available at that time.

O. Reg. 78/06, s. 35; 393/09, s. 16

Commentary:

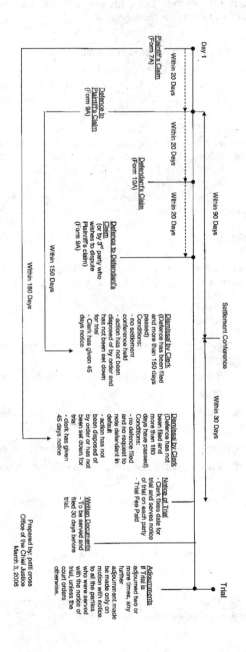

A SMALL CLAIMS COURT CASE - 2006 (Amended Rules)
FROM CLAIM TO TRIAL
A Case Flow Chart

History [R. 17.04]: Formerly 18.04.

Rule 18 — Evidence At Trial

18.01 Affidavit — **At the trial of an undefended action, the plaintiff's case may be proved by affidavit, unless the trial judge orders otherwise.**

History [R. 18.01]: Formerly 19.01.

Commentary: The party calling a witness should generally use open-ended as opposed to leading questions. "Leading questions are questions that suggest an answer or assume a state of facts that it is in dispute." See *R. v. W. (E.M.)*, 2011 SCC 31, 2011 CarswellNS 392, 2011 CarswellNS 393, [2011] 2 S.C.R. 542, 305 N.S.R. (2d) 1, 270 C.C.C. (3d) 464, 335 D.L.R. (4th) 89, 966 A.P.R. 1, 417 N.R. 171, [2011] S.C.J. No. 31 (S.C.C.). The first kind of leading questions — those that suggest an answer — are easy to identify. They either directly or by implication invite the witness to testify in a way that affirms a proposition suggested in the question by the examiner. These kinds of question are sometimes permitted. The second kind of leading question described in E.M.W. is more subtle, and never permissible. These kinds of leading questions presuppose the existence of a controversial fact not already testified to by the witness. They often contain, buried within the question, a proposition of fact on which the witness is not invited to comment.

Although the answers to leading questions are not inadmissible, the fact that they were obtained by leading questions may affect their weight. As indicated, there are numerous situations where the first kind of leading question is appropriate. These include:

- introductory or undisputed matters;
- the identification of persons or things;
- the contradiction of statements made by another;
- complicated or technical matters;
- where leave has been obtained to cross-examine a witness as adverse or hostile;
- where the witness is having difficulty answering the question and leave has been obtained to lead the witness; and
- where the question will refresh the memory of a witness and leave has been obtained to lead the witness, and any other case where leave has been obtained to lead the witness, in the interests of justice.

Real evidence refers to tangible items exhibited to the judge. This evidence may be directly linked to the occurrence or may be "demonstrative evidence," which refers to aids used to help witnesses better illustrate or explain their evidence. The evidence is admissible provided it is properly authenticated. The trial judge must be satisfied that there is a sufficient basis to support the identification of the exhibit, its continuity, and its integrity.

Real evidence may also be excluded where its potential to arouse undue prejudice outweighs its probative value.

In what way can a document be authenticated?

Documents may be authenticated in a variety of ways:

- by calling the writer;
- by calling a witness who saw the document signed;
- by calling a witness who is familiar with the writer's handwriting;

- by comparison of the writing in dispute with a written specimen proved to the satisfaction of the court to be genuine;

- by the calling of experts; or

- through an admission by the opposing party.

Circumstantial evidence may also point to the genuineness of the document. For example, letters received in reply to an earlier correspondence are accepted as being made by the sender; *Stevenson v. Dandy*, 1920 CarswellAlta 128, [1920] 2 W.W.R. 643 (Alta. C.A.). A second example is that of ancient documents, generally more than thirty years old, which are admissible provided the circumstances raise no suspicions and the documents are produced from a source that would normally have custody of them.

The admissibility of photographs or videotapes depends upon:

a) their accuracy in truly representing the facts;

b) their fairness and absence of any intention to mislead; and

c) their verification on oath by a person capable of doing so. *R. v. Creemer* (1967), 1967 CarswellNS 1, [1968] 1 C.C.C. 14, 1 C.R.N.S. 146, 53 M.P.R. 1, 4 N.S.R. 1965–69 546 (N.S. C.A.) at p. 22 [C.C.C.]. See also: *R. v. Adams*, 2011 NSCA 54, 2011 CarswellNS 363, 303 N.S.R. (2d) 356, 274 C.C.C. (3d) 502, 957 A.P.R. 356, (sub nom. *R. v. Murphy)* [2011] N.S.J. No. 302 (N.S. C.A.)

The person verifying the authenticity of the photographs or videotapes need not be the photographer. And eye-witness of the scene or events may confirm that the photograph or videotape is a fair and accurate reproduction. This is true even if the photograph of the scene is taken well after the events, as long as a witness testifies that it is a fair and accurate reproduction of the scene as it looked at the time of the incident.

Case Law: *Les Freeman Farms Ltd. v. R.G.M. Holdings Ltd.* (1998), 171 Sask. R. 287 (Sask. Q.B.) — Affidavit evidence properly rejected by the trial judge. The transcript disclosed that upon learning affidavit evidence would not be admissible, the Appellant took no steps to request an adjournment or additional time to have the witness attend in person. In any event, all facts were entered into evidence through *viva voce* testimony. Real problem was that witness who swore affidavit may have been of assistance in providing additional facts to the court. However, none of this factual information was contained in the rejected affidavit.

Ewaskiw v. Zellers Inc. (1998), 165 D.L.R. (4th) 346, 40 O.R. (3d) 795, 27 C.P.C. (4th) 347 (Ont. Gen. Div.) — The defendants asserted that the plaintiffs had not shown damages arising from the purchase of window blinds that contained lead, and brought a motion to dismiss the proposed class action. The defendants' refund policy allowed the plaintiffs to recover the costs of blinds. There was no evidence of any injury arising from using the blinds. The action was dismissed.

Robb Estate v. St. Joseph's Health Care Centre (May 17, 1999), Doc. 92-CU-54356, 92-CU-59486, 98-CV-139060 (Ont. Gen. Div.) — The case involved multiple defendants and order of presentation. The convention was that the defendants proceeded in order they appeared. Title of proceedings is subject to judicial discretion. The pleadings suggested that deviation from the general rule was appropriate.

Praxair Canada Inc. v. City Centre Plaza Ltd. (2000), 2000 CarswellOnt 4280 (Ont. S.C.J.) — Tenants claimed it was improper for the Court to raise an issue not specifically leaded by the landlord. It is always open for the judge to raise legal argument or cause of action arising from facts.

Ontario Federation of Anglers & Hunters v. Ontario (Ministry of Natural Resources) (2001), 4 C.P.C. (5th) 288, 2001 CarswellOnt 76, [2001] O.J. No. 86, 196 D.L.R. (4th) 367, 142 O.A.C. 231 (Ont. Div. Ct.); reversed (2002), 2002 CarswellOnt 1061, 211 D.L.R. (4th) 741, 158 O.A.C. 255, 93 C.R.R. (2d) 1, [2002] O.J. No. 1445 (Ont. C.A.); leave to appeal refused (2003), 2003 CarswellOnt 1067, 2003 CarswellOnt 1068, 313 N.R. 198 (note), 101 C.R.R. (2d) 376 (note), 181 O.A.C. 198 (note) (S.C.C.) — Although characterized as contextual framework evidence, introduction of newspaper articles amounted to hearsay. Newspaper articles represented opinion of authors who could not be cross-examined, contained controversial material and did not constitute legislative fact. Evidence not new and could have been readily put before motions judge.

Koffski v. Ashworth, 2001 CarswellBC 2521, 2001 BCSC 1469 (B.C. S.C.) — Defendant had default judgment entered against him and failed to have it set aside. Defendant sought to participate in assessment of damages hearing. Defendant waived right to participate in hearing.

Bain v. Rodrigue, 2004 CarswellBC 1752, 2004 BCPC 259 (B.C. Prov. Ct.), Judge J. Gedye — Defendant applied for disclosure of a list of documents in preparation of civil claim. Claimant opposed disclosure of his criminal record. Defendant off-duty Vancouver police officer. Issue one of relevance. It is unusual for a party in a civil trial to request such a record. However unusual such a record is compellable and Provincial Court Judge has the jurisdiction to order production. I am making that Order, decision of trial judge if evidence contained in record is admissible, what use can be made of the contents of the record if it is admitted and what weight if any can be attached to it.

Gardner (Litigation Guardian of) v. Hann, 2011 ONSC 41052011 CarswellOnt 6236 (Ont. S.C.J.), D.A. Wilson J.

The plaintiff sought to call a neuroradiologist, C, as an expert witness. The defendant took the position that C lacked the necessary impartiality to provide an expert opinion. The defendant relied in part on an article authored by C about the role of a neuroradiologist as an expert (impugned article). The impugned article appeared in the journal of Ontario Trial Lawyers Association, which comprised lawyers who acted for plaintiffs exclusively. The defendant brought a motion for an order that C not be permitted to testify on the basis of bias. The motion was dismissed. C's participation in seminars organized by associations whose membership might comprise lawyers acting for one party or another did not compromise his ability to offer an unbiased opinion.

18.02 (1) Written Statements, Documents and Records — A document or written statement or an audio or visual record that has been served, at least 30 days before the trial date, on all parties who were served with the notice of trial, shall be received in evidence, unless the trial judge orders otherwise.

(2) Subrule (1) applies to the following written statements and documents:

1. The signed written statement of any witness, including the written report of an expert, to the extent that the statement relates to facts and opinions to which the witness would be permitted to testify in person.

2. Any other document, including but not limited to a hospital record or medical report made in the course of care and treatment, a financial record, a receipt, a bill, documentary evidence of loss of income or property damage, and a repair estimate.

(3) Details about Witness or Author — A party who serves on another party a written statement or document described in subrule (2) shall append to or include in the statement or document,

    (a) the name, telephone number and address for service of the witness or author; and

    (b) if the witness or author is to give expert evidence, a summary of his or her qualifications.

(4) A party who has been served with a written statement or document described in subrule (2) and who wishes to cross-examine the witness or author may summon him or her as a witness under subrule 18.03(1).

Commentary [S. 18.02(4)]

The Calling of Witnesses

Our trial system is based on the calling of witnesses and, as a general rule, the court is entitled to hear every person's evidence, provided the person is competent to testify. At common law, many potentially valuable witnesses were rendered incompetent to testify. The common law judges were concerned about the giving of inaccurate or perjured testimony. Therefore, at common law people were precluded from testifying on grounds of interest, infamy (should the witness have a criminal history), infancy, insanity, disbelief in a Supreme Being, and marriage. Fortunately, most of the common law rules barring certain persons from testifying have been swept aside by statute.

Today, for the most part, all potential witnesses are allowed to testify — warts and all; their frailties are left as a matter of credibility for the trier of fact to assess. However, vestiges of the common law remain with respect to children and with respect to the calling of spouses of accursed persons.

The Competency of Witnesses

In general terms, what does "competency" entail?

Competency involves two aspects: capacity and responsibility.

- The witness must have the capacity to observe, recollect, and communicate.

- The witness must also accept and be aware of the responsibility to testify in a truthful manner.

The applicable statutory provisions reflect these dual themes of capacity and responsibility. They address issues of capacity and responsibility by establishing tests to determine whether witnesses are entitled to give testimony under oath or affirmation, or by way of a promise. Should a witness fail to qualify under these tests, the witness will be held incompetent to testify.

See e.g., Ontario, *Evidence Act*, R.S. O. 1990, c. E. 23, s. 18.2.

The *Ontario Evidence Act*, R.S.O. 1990, c. E. 23 goes further than the *Canada Evidence Act*, R.S.C. 1985, c. C 5 by providing an option in those cases where the *Act* applies. It enables unsworn evidence to be given without a promise to tell the truth: subsection 18.1(3). Those witnesses who can communicate the evidence but who do not understand what it means to speak the truth can still testify, provided the trial judge concludes, as a matter of discretion, that the evidence is "sufficiently reliable" to receive.

In 2005, the *Canada Evidence Act* was amended once again. (See Bill C-2 enacted as S.C. 2005, C.32.) The new legislation, now found in 16.1 of the *Canada Evidence Act*, markedly changed the test for determining the competence of a child witness.

R. 18.02(4)

Examination-in-Chief

How should you question your own witnesses?

The party calling a witness should generally use open-ended, as opposed to leading questions. Although the answers to leading questions are not inadmissible, the fact that they were obtained by leading questions may affect their weight. There are two kinds of leading questions. The first kind suggests the answer to the witness. The second kind presupposes the existence of a fact not presented by that witness in evidence. This second kind of leading question is never permissible unless the presupposed matter is not contested. There are numerous situations where the first kind of leading question is appropriate. These include:

- Introductory or undisputed matters,

- The identification of persons or things,

- The contradiction of statements made by another,

- Complicated or technical matters,

- Where leave has been obtained to cross-examine a witness as adverse or hostile,

- Where the witness is having difficulty answering the question and leave has been obtained to lead the witness,

- Where the question will refresh the memory of a witness and leave has been obtained to lead the witness, and any other case where leave has been obtained to lead the witness, in the interests of justice.

The rules of court may allow leading questions to be used if "a witness appears unwilling or unable to give responsive answers." See e.g. Ontario, *Rules of Civil Procedure*, r. 53.01(4).

Refreshing Memory

What means can be used by witnesses to refresh their memory prior to trial?

As a general rule, witnesses are free to use whatever means they choose to refresh their memories prior to trial, although the means used can affect the weight that is given to their evidence.

By what means can witnesses refresh their memory during the course of their testimony?

If a witness testifies to or demonstrates an inability to recall, where certain prerequisites are met, a rule known generally as "past recollection recorded" permits witnesses to use, in court, documents (such as business records, or memoranda of events) or electronic recordings, to assist them while giving their testimony.

1. The past recollection must have been recorded in some reliable way.

2. At the time the witness made or reviewed the record, his memory must have been sufficiently fresh and vivid to be probably accurate.

3. The witness must be able now to assert that the record accurately represented his knowledge and recollection at the time he reviewed it. The usual phrase requires the witness to affirm that he "knew it to be true at the time."

Once a witness has reviewed a document that contains "past recollection recorded," the witness may incorporate the contents of the record into their testimony. The document is not simply read into the record. Instead, the witness refers to it as a source of information when answering questions.

It is also settled that a court may allow witnesses who cannot recall matters they have previously testified about to be shown transcripts of their earlier testimony or their depositions. These transcripts are not subject to the contemporaneity requirement for past recollection recorded. Nor is there a need for the witness to have read over the transcript and to have verified that it accurately recorded her testimony.

Challenging the Credibility of Your Own Witness

When is a party entitled to challenge the credibility of its own witness?

A witness is "hostile" when he does not wish to tell the truth because of a motive to harm the party who has called him, or to assist the opposing party. A witness is "adverse" if the evidence he gives is unfavourable, or opposed in interest, to the party who has called him.

With the leave of the court, a party can cross-examine his own witness at large about the evidence in the case; if the judge declares the witness "hostile", it can be admitted as proof of the truth of its contents.

Cross-Examination

The Purpose of Cross-Examination

The use of leading questions in cross-examination is permitted; however, the use of leading questions becomes improper where the witness proves partisan to the cross-examiner's side.

Each witness who takes the stand puts his or her credibility into issue, and counsel in cross-examination are free to discredit or to "impeach" the witness's credibility.

Cross-examination designed to impeach a witness may focus on a number of areas:

- By showing bias, prejudice, interest, or corruption;

- By attacking the character of the witness through raising prior convictions, prior bad acts, or poor reputation;

- By contradicting the witness through previous inconsistent statements;

- By challenging the witness's capacity to observe, recall, and communicate accurately;

- By putting contrary evidence to the witness; and

- By showing that the witness's evidence is contrary to common experience.

In general, when a cross-examiner asks a question relating purely to credibility, the witness's answer is final. This practice is called the collateral fact rule, which prohibits the presenting of evidence to contradict a witness on a collateral matter.

What is the purpose of cross-examination?

The opportunity to cross-examine in order to test or to challenge a witness's evidence is an absolutely vital part of the adversary process. Cross-examination has two basic goals: (1) eliciting favourable testimony from the witness and (2) discrediting the testimony of the witness. The practice in Canada is to follow the "English Rule," which allows the cross-examiner to inquire into any relevant matter, in contrast to the "American Rule," where cross-examination is limited to subjects or topics that were covered in examination-in-chief and to matters relating to the witness's credibility.

The "right of cross-examination" is neither unlimited nor absolute. The scope of cross-examination is by necessity contextual. Relevancy and materiality are fixed concepts, but are fluid and change with the issues at hand and the type of hearing involved. In certain circumstances, limits may be placed on the "right of cross-examination."

"A trial judge is not a mere observer who must sit by passively allowing counsel to conduct the proceedings in any manner they choose. A trial judge is entitled to manage the trial and control the procedure to ensure that the trial is effective, efficient, and fair to both sides."

Real Evidence

Real evidence refers to tangible items exhibited to the judge. This evidence may be directly linked to the occurrence or may be "demonstrative evidence," which refers to aids used to help witnesses better illustrate or explain their evidence. The evidence is admissible provided it is properly authenticated. The trial judge must be satisfied that there is a sufficient basis to support the identification of the exhibit, its continuity, and its integrity.

Real evidence may also be excluded where its potential to arouse undue prejudice outweighs its probative value.

Documents may be authenticated in a variety of ways:

- By calling the writer;

- By calling a witness who saw the document signed;

- By calling a witness who is familiar with the writer's handwriting;

- By comparison of the writing in dispute with a written specimen proved to the satisfactions of the court to be genuine;

- By the calling of experts; or

- Through an admission by the opposing party.

Must the original document be presented in all cases?

The best evidence rule, or perhaps better stated, "the original documents" rule, requires that the original of a document be tendered when a party seeks to prove the contents of that document. Secondary evidence, by way of copies or the testimony of witnesses, is inadmissible. The rule, as it exists today, is confined to cases where a party has the original document and could produce it, but does not. The party may satisfy the court that the original is lost, destroyed, or is otherwise in the possession of another and cannot be obtained.

The admissibility of photographs or videotapes depends upon:

1. Their accuracy in truly representing the facts;

2. Their fairness and absence of any intention to mislead; and

3. Their verification on oath by a person capable of doing so.

The person verifying the authenticity of the photographs or videotapes need not be the photographer. An eye-witness of the scene or events may confirm that the photograph or videotape is a fair and accurate reproduction. This is true even if the photograph of the scene is taken well after the events, as long as a witness testifies that it is a fair and accurate reproduction of the scene *as it looked at the time of the incident.*

Judicial Notice

Judicial notice is the acceptance by a court, without the requirement of proof, of any fact or matter that is so generally known and accepted in the community that it cannot be reasonably questioned, or any fact or matter that can be readily determined or verified by resort to sources whose accuracy cannot reasonably be questioned.

Judicial notice dispenses with the need for proof of facts that are clearly uncontroversial or beyond reasonable dispute. Facts judicially noticed are not proved by evidence under oath. Nor are they tested by cross-examination. Therefore, the threshold for judicial notice is strict. A court may properly take judicial notice of facts that are either:

1. So notorious or generally accepted as not to be the subject of debate among reasonable persons; or

2. Capable of immediate and accurate demonstration by resort to readily accessible sources of indisputable accuracy.

It is important to distinguish between taking judicial notice of "adjudicative facts" and legislative facts. "Adjudicative facts" are the facts to be determined in the particular case. Judicial notice, as outlined, applies to *adjudicative facts*, which are facts to be determined in the litigation between the parties.

Legislative facts are also admitted without the need for proof. However, legislative facts are those that have relevance to legal reasoning and the law-making process and involve broad considerations of policy. Legislative facts assist in determining questions of law and are not intended to assist in resolving questions of fact.

In recent years, *social framework facts* have emerged as a third form of judicial notice. These facts are really a hybrid of adjudicative and legislative facts. They "refer to social science research that is used to construct a frame of reference or background context for deciding factual issues crucial to the resolution of a particular case." C. L'Heureux-Dubé, "Re-examining the Doctrine of Judicial Notice in the Family Law Context" (1994) 26 Ottawa L. Rev. 551 to 556.

Social framework facts are not "facts" in the true sense of the word; rather, they are general explanations about society or human behaviour. Usually experts are called to explain the relevant social condition.

The test for accepting judicial notice of adjudicative facts is strict — there is need for notoriety or acceptance by an indisputable source. If the criteria are not satisfied, then the adjudicative fact will *not* be judicially recognized. It is as simple as that.

In-Court Observations

When a judge intends to treat courtroom behaviour he or she observes as circumstantial evidence that affects the credibility of the witness or the accused (such as "signalling" between the witness and the accused). Timely disclosure of the observation should be made to the parties so that they have a fair opportunity to address the significance of the judge's observations, either by calling evidence or making appropriate submissions. Where the observation is merely of the ordinary testimonial demeanour of the witness, however, the preferred practice is to avoid commenting in order to avoid creating the appearance of having prejudged the witness's credibility.

Turner v. Rogers

The U.S. Supreme Court's June 2011 decision in *Turner v. Rogers* may greatly influence the judicial handling of civil self-represented litigation. Behind the changed judicial environment is the Court's effective endorsement of judicial engagement as helping ensure fairness and accuracy, and to meet the requirements of due process.

In *Turner*, a custodial maternal grandparent asked the court to penalize the father for failure to pay child support. Neither party had counsel, nor was the state a party. The judge imposed a 12-month civil contempt order, upheld on appeal to the South Carolina Supreme Court. At the urging of the United States, as *amicus curiae*, Justice Stephen Breyer's majority opinion reversed on the ground that in the absence of counsel, the judge's failure to provide procedural safeguards *sua sponte* constituted a violation of the father's due process rights.

The duty imposed on judges takes the place of the far more expensive and constitutionally complicated alternative of requiring counsel for the parties in all such proceedings.

Research into self-represented cases has shown that

- Judicial engagement and questioning are necessary,

- Judges have broad discretion in how they do this, and

- There are plenty of easy and tested techniques for doing so.

Procedural rules and appellate court decisions permit judges to take into account the representation status of the parties in deciding how the rules are to be applied. This is just what happened in *Turner*, in which extensive discussion of the lack of counsel on both sides shaped the Court's due process views as to the appropriate procedure.

The simple approaches include, but are not limited to, the notice and questioning that are the focus of *Turner*. Many of these approaches apply in almost all self-represented cases, especially those in which neither side has a lawyer. The application of those approaches in more difficult situations, as where one party is represented or there is a jury, will be discussed at another time.

One overriding principle informs many of these "best practices" — that is, the desirability of transparency. If judges explain what they are doing, and why they are doing it, litigants will generally give them the benefit of the doubt even when the judge rules against them. Litigants want to trust the process and the judge. Nothing enhances trust like transparency. Thus, explanation of questions, descriptions of procedure and of the law, and clarifications of what will happen next are all cherished by the self-represented.

Recommended Techniques

1. Introduce the parties and explain the procedural context of the hearing.

2. Make sure the parties understand what is to be decided at the current hearing.

3. Outline the procedure to be followed at the hearing.

4. Indicate the time available for the hearing.

5. Explain, if needed, the governing law.

6. Use simple language and invite questions.

7. Clarify that the judge's questions and interruptions have no purpose other than getting to the facts.

Managing Evidence

1. Consider dividing the hearing into small blocks for an individual decision on the facts.

2. Permit narrative testimony.

3. Allow parties to adopt their pleadings as their sworn testimony.

4. Ask questions to get to evidence.

5. Ask questions to establish the foundation of evidence.

6. Probe for detail.

7. Give verbal and nonverbal cues to encourage the giving of testimony.

8. Shift back from one side to the other during questioning.

9. Maintain control of the courtroom.

10. Help litigants stay focused on matters that are relevant to the judge's ultimate decision.

11. Clarify the relevance of testimony when it is uncertain.

12. In assessing evidence, remember that judges can deem evidence objected to, can admit un-objected-to evidence for all purposes, and can give evidence the weight they see fit.

13. Consider telling litigants when they have failed to establish an important element, and then provide an opportunity to fill the gap.

14. Provide a final opportunity for litigants to add to the testimony.

15. If you are unable to do what a litigant asks because of neutrality concerns, explain the reasons.

Managing a Decision and Beyond

1. Consider discussing potential decisions to find the most practicable for the parties.

2. Announce the decision, if possible, from the bench, taking the opportunity to encourage the litigants to explain any problems they might have complying.

3. Explain the decision and consider acknowledging the positions and strengths of both sides.

4. Make sure that the litigants understand the decision and what is expected of them, while making sure that they know you expect compliance with the ultimate decision.

5. Where relevant, inform the litigants of what will be happening next in the case and what is expected of them.

6. Make sure that the decision is given in written or printed form to the litigants.

7. Thank the parties for their participation and acknowledge their efforts.

Case Law: *MBK Services Inc. v. PowerForward Inc.*, 2013 ONSC 4506, 2013 Carswell-Ont 9211, [2013] O.J. No. 3115 (Ont. Div. Ct.)

Documents which may be qualified for admission under rule 18.02 (i.e. served at least 30 days before trial and containing the required witness information) may nevertheless be excluded where appropriate grounds for exclusion exist. The rule gives the court a discretion to admit eligible documents without formal identification evidence from a live witness, but does not require the court to accept all such documents as evidence.

Suganthan v. Calexico Holdings Inc. (August 30, 2012), Doc. SC-11-88015-00, [2012] O.J. No. 6612 (Ont. S.C.J.)

Digital video recordings on DVD may be admitted into evidence in the same way as traditional photographic and video evidence. Modern methods of storage of electronic video and photographic data such as memory sticks, USB drives, etc., can all be admitted as evidence subject to the traditional criteria of accuracy, fairness, and absence of any intention to mislead, and verification under oath by a person capable to do so.

Birch Paving & Excavating Co., Inc. v. Clark (March 31, 2014), Doc. 13-015178 (Ont. S.C.J.)

Rule 18.02 may be applied to admit a document or statement whose author is outside Ontario or in another country. The party who is served with such a statement may take steps to summons an out-of-province witness and should not assume that the statement will be inadmissible under rule 18.02 merely because the author is not located in Ontario.

Trento Motors v. McKinney (1992), 39 M.V.R. (2d) 142, 54 O.A.C. 190 (Div. Ct.) — Compliance with s. 5 of the *Motor Vehicle Repair Act*, R.S.O. 1990, c. M.43 in that information referred by the section was recorded on the mechanic's copy of the invoice. The Act did not apply to towing charges.

Nagle v. Rosman (1986), 6 W.D.C.P. 58 (Ont. Prov. Ct.) — The defendant's motion to set aside a default judgment was dismissed since the key witness for the plaintiff, present at the original trial for assessment of damages, would no longer be available, the transcript not admitted, and, therefore, it would be prejudicial to the plaintiff.

Minto Management Ltd. v. Solomonescu (1986), 5 W.D.C.P. 262 (Ont. Prov. Ct.) — The plaintiff served the defendant with a written statement of a witness pursuant to Rule 19.02(1). The statement was admitted into evidence. Rather than cross-examine the author under Rule 19.02(4), the defendant was permitted, through his own witness, to report something said to her by the author of the statement.

O'Connell v. Custom Kitchen & Vanity (1986), 56 O.R. (2d) 57 (Ont. Div. Ct.) — Documents do not have to be served on all parties 14 days before trial to be admitted. Even if Rule

19.02 was prohibitory, s. 80 of the *Courts of Justice Act* superseded Rule 19.02(1) and permits judicial discretion to allow hearsay. The defendant did not object until the completion of the evidence.

Kapoor, Selnes, Klimm & Brown v. Mitchell (January 11, 1999) (Sask. Prov. Ct.), Diehl Prov. J. — Action in debt for fees for professional services rendered by a firm of solicitors. What standard of proof of costs is acceptable under the *Small Claims Act*? The main purpose of the *Small Claims Act* stated in *Burkhart v. Popoff*, [1983], 6 W.W.R. 669 (Sask Q.B.). Party litigants, be they lawyers or not, do not have to prove service fees by affidavit, declaration, certificate or other evidence under oath in uncontested actions. There should be, as there was here, some documentary evidence filed about which discretion may be exercised by the presiding judge as to stated facts.

Mitchell v. Noakes (2003), 2003 CarswellOnt 143, 167 O.A.C. 347 (Ont. Div. Ct.) — Evidence at trial concluded May 22, 2001. Written submissions requested (no time frame indicated). Plaintiff, alone, delivered written submissions September 25, 2001. No substantial wrong or miscarriage of justice. Appeal dismissed. *Carrier v. Cameron*, [1985] O.J. No. 1357, 1985 CarswellOnt 637, 6 C.P.C. (2d) 208, 11 O.A.C. 369 (Ont. Div. Ct.) referred to as well as section 25 of the CJA.

P. (D.) v. Wagg, [2004] O.J. No. 2053, 2004 CarswellOnt 1983, 239 D.L.R. (4th) 501, 120 C.R.R. (2d) 52, 184 C.C.C. (3d) 321, 187 O.A.C. 26, 71 O.R. (3d) 229, 46 C.P.C. (5th) 13 (Ont. C.A.) — Statements made to police and ruled inadmissible in criminal trial may be produced in a civil discovery process, but a screening process must be followed to obtain disclosure of the remainder of the Crown brief.

Court of Appeal emphasized "society has an interest in seeing that justice is done in civil cases as well as criminal cases, and generally speaking that will occur when parties have opportunity to put all relevant evidence before the court." It is a fundamental principle that an accused is not required to assist the state in making out its case. There is, however, no such principle in the civil context.

Farzam v. Canada (Minister of Citizenship & Immigration), [2005] F.C.J. No. 1776, 2005 CarswellNat 3452, 2005 CarswellNat 5863, 282 F.T.R. 238, 2005 FC 1453, 2005 CF 1453 (F.C.), Martineau J.

Shortly before commencement of trial, plaintiff sought court order to allow him to introduce evidence of Iranian witnesses at trial through use of teleconferencing. Court not satisfied that issuance of order that evidence of Iranian witnesses be taken by telephone was in interest of justice. Motion dismissed.

Vointsev v. Irina International Tours Ltd. (2007), 2007 CarswellOnt 6015, 52 C.P.C. (6th) 281 (Ont. S.C.J.)

The issue in this case was whether, in the event of a conflict, Rule 19 of the *Rules of Procedure*, which stated that a party noted in default need not be given notice of any step in the action, prevailed over the requirements of the *Evidence Act*, which required a party seeking to rely on medical records to give notice of an intention to do so. The court held that mandatory provisions of Act requiring notice of intention to introduce medical reports or business records prevail over Rules of Civil Procedure. In addition, plaintiff's documents should not be considered as "medical records", but business records, because the doctor that issued them was not licensed or registered to practice in Canada.

1465778 Ontario Inc. v. 1122077 Ontario Ltd., [2006] O.J. No. 4248, 82 O.R. (3d) 757, 275 D.L.R. (4th) 321, 2006 CarswellOnt 6582, 38 C.P.C. (6th) 1, 216 O.A.C. 339 (Ont. C.A.)

Plaintiffs' counsel was acting *pro bono* and sought costs from losing party. The defendants argued lawyers acting *pro bono* in commercial matters should not be awarded costs. The purpose of costs awards should include access to justice. There is no prohibition on award of costs to *pro bono* counsel in appropriate cases. Costs awarded. Costs could serve purposes other than indemnity, including the objectives of encouraging settlement, preventing frivolous or vexatious litigation, and discouraging unnecessary steps. In this case, plaintiffs impecunious, and it was because they were unable to pay a costs order that the case initially dismissed. No reason why the losing party should not be ordered to pay costs of the appeal.

See Major J. in a speech titled "Lawyers' Obligation to Provide Legal Services" delivered to the National Conference on the Legal Profession and Professional Ethics at the University of Calgary in 1994 (33 Alta. L. Rev. 719) where he said:

> It has long been part of the duty and tradition of the legal profession to provide services gratuitously for those who require them but cannot afford them. The profession, recognizing its commitment to the larger principle of justice, has traditionally not let such cases go unanswered merely because the individual is impecunious. Instead, the profession has collectively accepted the burden of such cases, thereby championing the cause of justice while at the same time sharing the cost that such cases entail. This is a tradition which dates to the very inception of the profession in medieval Europe in the thirteenth century.

Costs have been awarded in cases where the litigant was self-represented (*Skidmore v. Blackmore*, 122 D.L.R. (4th) 330, 35 C.P.C. (3d) 28, 90 W.A.C. 191, 55 B.C.A.C. 191, 27 C.R.R. (2d) 77, [1995] 4 W.W.R. 524, 2 B.C.L.R. (3d) 201, [1995] B.C.J. No. 305, 1995 CarswellBC 23 (B.C. C.A.)); where the winning party was a law firm represented by one of its partners who was not charging fees (*Fellowes, McNeil*); where counsel was salaried (*Solicitors Act*, R.S.O. 1990, c. S.15, s. 36); and, where the responsibility for a party's legal fees was undertaken by a third party (*Lavigne v. O.P.S.E.U.*, 1987 CarswellOnt 1074, 41 D.L.R. (4th) 86, 60 O.R. (2d) 486, 87 C.L.L.C. 14,044 (Ont. H.C.)).

Costs have also been awarded to counsel acting *pro bono* in *Charter* or public interest cases. See *Rogers v. Greater Sudbury (City) Administrator of Ontario Works*, 57 O.R. (3d) 467, [2001] O.J. No. 3346, 2001 CarswellOnt 2934 (Ont. S.C.J.).

In non-public interest cases, see e.g. *Mackay Homes v. North Bay (City)*, [2005] O.J. No. 3263, 2005 CarswellOnt 3367 (Ont. S.C.J.), *Spatone v. Banks*, [2002] O.J. No. 4647, 2002 CarswellOnt 4143 (Ont. S.C.J.), and *Jacks v. Victoria Amateur Swimming Club*, [2005] B.C.J. No. 2086, 2005 CarswellBC 2300, 2005 BCSC 1378 (B.C. S.C. [In Chambers]). In *Ontario (Human Rights Commission) v. Brockie*, 2004 CarswellOnt 1231, 185 O.A.C. 366 (Ont. C.A.), court reversed a decision of the Divisional Court that denied costs to *pro bono* counsel, holding that "[s]uch a policy would act as a severe penalty to lawyers acting in the public interest by making it possible for litigants of modest means to access the courts."

VFC Inc. v. Balchand, 291 D.L.R. (4th) 367, 233 O.A.C. 359, 2008 CarswellOnt 909 (Ont. Div. Ct.)

Defendant appealed judgment of Small Claims Court finding her liable under a bill of sale and conditional sales contract for purchase of motor vehicle. The only witness called by plaintiff was the supervisor of the legal department, not present when bill of sale and conditional sales contract signed but saw documents when forwarded to plaintiff.

Trial judge dismissed defendant's motion for a non-suit, bill of sale and conditional sales contract bearing apparent signature of defendant, in the absence of evidence to the contrary, established defendant was a party to the contract and liable for the amount owing. Appeal dismissed.

Nothing in the *Evidence Act*, R.S.O. 1990, c. E.23, calls into question the admissibility of hearsay at a Small Claims Court trial, even when the hearsay is contained in business records. Section 35 of the *Evidence Act* provides a statutory mechanism for the admission of business records into evidence and section 27(1) of the *Courts of Justice Act*, R.S.O. 1990, c. C.43, permits hearsay evidence to be admitted into evidence. A consideration of these provisions leads to the conclusion that the trial judge did *not* err in law in admitting into evidence the oral and documentary hearsay of the plaintiff's witness. See *Central Burner Service Inc. v. Texaco Canada Inc.*, 1989 CarswellOnt 1427, 36 O.A.C. 239 (Ont. Div. Ct.). Section 27(1) permits the Small Claims Court to admit as evidence at a hearing and act upon any oral testimony and any document or other thing, so long as the evidence is relevant. In *Central Burner*, Steele J. concluded that section 80(1) of the *Courts of justice Act, 1984*, S.O. 1984, c. 11, the predecessor of section 27(1), allows relevant hearsay evidence to be admitted and relied upon in a Small Claims Court trial even in relation to a critical issue. See also *Sathaseevan v. Suvara Travel Canada Inc.*, [1998] O.J. No. 1055, 1998 CarswellOnt 880 (Ont. Div. Ct.).

Section 27(1) is, by its terms, subject to subsections (3) and (4). Section 2 of the *Ontario Evidence Act*, R.S.O. 1990, c. E.23, provides, "This Act applies to all actions and other matters whatsoever respecting which the Legislature has jurisdiction."

Section 35 of the *Evidence Act* deals with business records.

If a party to any proceeding governed by the *Ontario Evidence Act* proposes that a business record be received in evidence pursuant to section 35(2), the proponent of the evidence must comply with the section. The record must be made in the usual and ordinary course of business as described in section 35(2), and notice must be given in accordance with section 35(3).

Prior to the liberalizing impact of the decision in *Ares v. Venner*, 14 D.L.R. (3d) 4, 73 W.W.R. 347, 12 C.R.N.S. 349, [1970] S.C.R. 608, 1970 CarswellAlta 142, [1970] S.C.J. No. 26, 1970 CarswellAlta 80 (S.C.C.), the common law rules governing the admissibility of business records were widely felt to be completely out of line with the every-increasing complexity of business organizations.

The object of section 80(1) of the *Courts of Justice Act*, the predecessor of section 27(1) of the *Act*, was remedial. As stated in *Central Burner*, "The object of s. 80 is to avoid technical procedures and the additional cost of calling extra witnesses in cases involving small claims."

Jones v. Meinema, 2011 SKQB 130, 2011 CarswellSask 225, 100 C.L.R. (3d) 311, 21 C.P.C. (7th) 205 (Sask. Q.B.), A.R. Rothery J.; affirming 2010 SKPC 126, 2010 CarswellSask 576, [2010] S.J. No. 522 (Sask. Prov. Ct.), Q.D. Agnew Prov. J.

The trial judge allowed the contractor's action for payment owing, and allowed in part the homeowners' counterclaim to remedy deficiencies. The trial judge awarded the contractor $7,547.25, and the homeowners $2,000, although they had counterclaimed for $17,000. The trial judge declined to qualify ET as an expert witness to give opinion evidence on the cost to remedy the deficiencies, but accepted the opinion evidence of the building inspector RS. The homeowners appealed. The appeal was dismissed. The trial judge's decision on qualifications of ET did not affect the outcome of trial. Whether qualified as an expert or not, ET had very little to add to the evidence and conceded he did not even prepare an estimate of the costs of repairs.

(5) Where Witness or Author is Summoned — **A party who serves a summons to witness on a witness or author referred to in subrule (3) shall, at the time the summons is served, serve a copy of the summons on every other party.**

(6) Service of a summons and the payment or tender of attendance money under this rule may be proved by affidavit (Form 8A).

(7) Adjournment — **A party who is not served with a copy of the summons in accordance with subrule (5) may request an adjournment of the trial, with costs.**

O. Reg. 78/06, s. 36

Commentary [S. 18.02(7)]: Some examples of evidence to be brought to court to support a case are:

- contract, letters, invoices, statements, drawings, written expert opinions;
- quotations (at least two) for repair work;
- witnesses (any person who is able to support your case);
- photographs that may help the court understand the reason for the claim or defence;
- where a claim is being made against a parent under the *Parental Responsibility Act, 2000* for property damage, loss or destruction caused by a child under 18 years of age who has been found guilty and sentenced for the offence in Youth Court, you *may* file an order of disposition, should you choose to do so, obtained from the office of the Youth Court where the child was found guilty and sentenced for the offence. To obtain the order of disposition, you *must* file with the Youth Court office, a completed request for a copy of the disposition for the purposes of the *Parental Responsibility Act, 2000* form to support your request for a copy of the order of disposition. A blank request form, which includes an affidavit, may be obtained from a Small Claims Court office or Youth Court office; and
- should you obtain an order of disposition from the Youth Court, and intend to file and rely upon it in the Small Claims Court, you *must* also file with the Small Claims Court the completed notice about evidence obtained. This pre-printed form may be obtained from the Small Claims Court office.

If you serve on another party a written statement or document described in subrule 18.02(2) of the Rules, you must include:

- the name, telephone number and address for service of the witness or author; and
- if the witness or author is to give expert evidence, you must also include a summary of his or her qualifications.

If you want to ask questions of the author of another party's written report or document, you can summons the author as described below in the discussion about witnesses. You must also serve a copy of your summons to witness form on all parties in the case. If you do not, a party who has not been served may request an adjournment of the trial and, if granted, you may be ordered to pay costs.

You should bring the original documents and at least three copies of each document to the trial. The original may be entered by the court as an exhibit. The copies are for the judge, the other party (or parties) and yourself.

Check with the court office prior to the scheduled trial date to ensure that any equipment you may require is available in the courtroom (e.g., a television and VCR, if you have footage that you would like to show the judge). You may be required to bring the necessary equipment with you.

You may be required to file an Affidavit of Service [Form 8A] to prove service of the summons and attendance money.

If the witness fails to attend trial after being properly served with a summons to witness and attendance money, the trial judge may issue a warrant for his or her arrest. If the court finds a party has abused the power to summons a witness, the judge may order the party to pay money to the witness to compensate him or her for inconvenience and expense. If a witness who is summoned requires an interpreter, the court will provide an interpreter from English to French or French to English or visual language interpretation.

History [R. 18.02]: Formerly 19.02; plain language changes; refers to subrule 18.03(1), formerly 19.03(1).

18.03 (1) Summons to Witness — **A party who requires the attendance of a person in Ontario as a witness at a trial may serve the person with a summons to witness (Form 18A) requiring him or her to attend the trial at the time and place stated in the summons.**

History [R. 18.03(1)]: Formerly part of 19.03(1); provision respecting the requirement to produce documents or things separated out into another subrule (18.03(2)).

Commentary: You will have to request the clerk to issue a notice (summons to witness) requiring them to attend. This will also be proof to an employer, who must allow an employee to attend court during work hours.

(2) The summons may also require the witness to produce at the trial the documents or other things in his or her possession, control or power relating to the matters in question in the action that are specified in the summons.

History [R. 18.03(2)]: Contains provision respecting the requirement to produce documents or things.

(3) A summons to witness (Form 18A) shall be served in accordance with subrule 8.01(7).

History [R. 18.03(3)]: Formerly 19.03(2); refers to subrule 8.01(5), rather than describing the type of service required; plain language changes.

(4) Service of a summons and the payment or tender of attendance money may be proved by affidavit (Form 8A).

History [R. 18.03(4)]: Formerly 19.03(3).

(5) A summons to witness continues to have effect until the attendance of the witness is no longer required.

History [R. 18.03(5)]: Formerly 19.03(4).

(5.1) Interpreter — **If a party serves a summons on a witness who requires an interpreter, the party shall arrange for a qualified interpreter to attend at the trial unless the interpretation is from English to French or French to English and an interpreter is provided by the Ministry of the Attorney General.**

(5.2) If a party does not comply with subrule (5.1), every other party is entitled to request an adjournment of the trial, with costs.

(6) Failure to Attend or Remain in Attendance — **If a witness whose evidence is material to the conduct of an action fails to attend at the trial or to remain in attendance in accordance with the requirements of a summons to witness served on him or her, the trial judge may, by warrant (Form 18B) directed to all police officers in Ontario, cause the witness to be apprehended anywhere within Ontario and promptly brought before the court.**

History [R. 18.03(6)]: Formerly 19.03(5); refers to Form 18B, formerly Form 19B; no longer refers to bailiffs and peace officers, instead referring to police officers to conform with *Courts of Justice Act* s. 144; plain language changes.

(6.1) Identification Form — **The party who served the summons on the witness may file with the clerk an identification form (Form 20K) to assist the police in apprehending the witness.**

(7) On being apprehended, the witness may be detained in custody until his or her presence is no longer required or released on such terms as are just, and may be ordered to pay the costs arising out of the failure to attend or remain in attendance.

History [R. 18.03(7)]: Formerly 19.03(6); plain language changes.

(8) Abuse of Power to Summon Witness — If satisfied that a party has abused the power to summon a witness under this rule, the court may order that the party pay directly to the witness an amount as compensation for inconvenience and expense.

O. Reg. 78/06, s. 37

History [R. 18.03(8)]: Formerly 19.03(7); plain language changes.

Commentary: Rule 18 should be read having regard to section 27 of the *Courts of Justice Act*.

Productions have been expanded to include not only documents or written statements and expert reports, but also to audio and visual records.

Service of productions is now made thirty (30) days in advance of the trial date. The trial judge may refuse to admit documents served under subrule 18.02(1).

If a written statement contains the opinion of an expert, a summary of the qualifications of the expert must also be served.

Provided is a copy of a summons to witness on a witness or author to be served on all parties so they know who is coming (subrule 18.02(5)). A summons must be served at least 10 days in advance (subrule 8.01(7)).

There is a new obligation on a party who serves a summons to find out whether the witness requires an interpreter. See subrule 18.03(5.1). If a "bench warrant" is issued under subrule 18.03(6), the party is encouraged to file an Identification Form (Form 20K) to assist the police in executing the order.

In *Gass v. Childs* (1959), 43 M.P.R. 87, Mr. Justice Ritchie of the New Brunswick Court of Appeal indicated that, when dealing with repair estimates, evidence to prove damages for repairs of any nature should be definite. Testimony as to the amount paid for repairs is not sufficient. This case was commented upon in *Guillemette v. Dube* (1974), 6 O.R. (2d) 663 (Ont. Div. Ct.), a decision of Mr. Justice Holden in the Ontario Divisional Court. Mr. Justice Holden indicated that if no dispute had been raised either in the pleadings or at trial as to the amount of special damages, there is no reason why the plaintiff should be required to incur the considerable expense of calling a mechanic to prove the account. The allowance for witness fees in Small Claims Court is minimal, whereas the hourly charges for a mechanic are substantial.

Rule 19.02(4) is to encourage everyone to utilize Rule 19.02 and to provide a disincentive for parties routinely requesting the presence of witnesses as opposed to relying upon their written statements or documents.

Rule 18.03 provides that the trial judge may, in the presence of parties, inspect any place or property concerning which a question arises in the action. It is likely that, given the monetary jurisdiction of the court, inspection will rarely take place, but it does preserve the option for the trial judge to exercise in his discretion consistent with a summary procedure.

Rule 19.03(7) provides for the payment to a witness of an amount as compensation for inconvenience and expense in cases where there has been an abuse of the power to summon a witness. This is consistent with the purpose of the Rules to try and limit the issues in contention, thus insuring that, through document and written statement, the most expeditious resolution of matters is achieved and that penalties are provided where real inconvenience to parties or witnesses has occurred.

Section 25 of the *Courts of Justice Act* provides for hearings in a summary way of all questions of fact and law. To interpret that section it is important to make reference to *Re Lounsbury Realty Ltd. and Shekter* (1978), 23 O.R. (2d) 309, a County Court decision. The court was faced with a motion in an application under Part IV of the *Landlord and Tenant Act* to include procedures by reference from the Civil Rules of Procedure.

At common law a party to an action could not put into evidence a medical report by itself. The *Evidence Act* altered the common law by permitting a party to file any report by a "legally qualified medical practitioner". In order to encourage parties to avoid unnecessarily calling medical experts to testify, section 52(4) of the act imposed cost sanctions for calling *vive voce* evidence which could have been adduced as effectively by way of a medical report. Unfortunately, the simplified procedure could only be used with respect to doctors. Recent amendments to the *Evidence Act* [now R.S.O. 1990, c. E.23] recognized the same need for other health care givers as with doctors. "Practitioner" is defined by s. 52 of the *Evidence Act* as:

1. *Health Disciplines Act*, R.S.O. 1990, c. H.4: medical doctors, dentists, nurses, optometrists and pharmacists;

2. *Drugless Practitioners Act*, R.S.O. 1990, c. D.18: chiropractors, physiotherapists, naturopaths, osteopaths and massage therapists;

3. *Psychologists Registration Act*, R.S.O. 1990, c. P.36: registered psychologists; and

4. Any person licensed or registered to practice in another part of Canada under an Act similar to the Acts referred to above.

Clauses (a) and (c) to (f) repealed and the following cls. (a) and (c) substituted 1998, c. 18, Sched. G, s. 50:

(a) a member of a College as defined in subsection 1(1) of the *Regulated Health Professions Act, 1991*,

(b) a person licensed or registered to practise in another part of Canada under an Act that is similar to an Act referred to in clause (a) or (b).

The purpose of this section is to permit filing of medical reports in lieu of calling viva voce evidence, and not to permit both, but the other side had the option of cross-examining witnesses.

As a result of the amendments all the health professionals listed above need not be called to give evidence at trial, but rather their reports may be put into evidence without adducing the evidence *viva voce*.

Case Law: *Micheli v. Zuppetti* (October 19, 1984) (Ont. Div. Ct.), Galligan J. — Any tribunal has inherent power unless specifically restricted by statute to impose reasonable terms for granting adjournments. Payment into court of $1,000 as a term of adjournment is not considered unreasonable.

York v. T.V. Guide Inc. (1984), 5 O.A.C. 330 (Ont. Div. Ct.) — It is incumbent upon the trial judge to proceed and the plaintiff to call evidence pursuant to subrule 51(92)(1) where the defendant seeks an adjournment and the court cannot simply grant judgment to the plaintiff without calling evidence.

MacInnes v. Leaman (1976), 8 N.R. 297 (S.C.C.) — Adjournments are within the discretionary powers of the trial judge.

Svajlenko v. Appco Paving Ltd. (1985), 3 W.D.C.P. 34 (Ont. Prov. Ct.) — A motion by defendant to set aside judgment pursuant to Rule 18.04 was based on fact that defendant, representing itself, failed to introduce proper evidence. It was held that where there was a total failure to have a trial on merits, because one party was completely incapable of proceeding or because one party failed to attend, this type of motion was proper. However, where there was something that could fairly be described as a trial on the merits, in that both parties had an opportunity to present their own witnesses and give evidence, and where there could be no suggestion that the judge failed to make adjudication on merits, this type of motion was not proper unless it was clear from face of record that there was some lack of jurisdiction. *Johanson v. Williamson* (1977), 18 O.R. (2d) 585 (Ont. Sm. Cl. Ct.) — The addition of this section to the Act is an amendment which is procedural in nature and, accordingly, the section may be invoked in an action which was commenced before the amendment took effect. The section is to be read as overriding the procedural aspects of the *Evidence Act* of Ontario.

Howard v. Canadian National Express (1980), 23 C.P.C. 77 (Ont. Dist. Ct.) — Two letters, although hearsay and although opposing counsel were not provided with copies before trial, were admitted in evidence given the purposes of the Small Claims Court, section 96a and the expense of calling the writers of the letters as witnesses.

Borden Ladner Gervais LLP v. Cohen, 2005 CarswellOnt 2444, 199 O.A.C. 8 (Ont. Div. Ct.). Rodney Cohen appeals judgment of Herman J. dated June 23, 2004, granting summary judgment against him of $19,058.15 plus interest, costs and dismissing his counterclaim in which he sought referral of the plaintiffs' claim for unpaid legal fees to an assessment. BLG acted for the appellant in two actions, the POI action and the Amati action.

At pre-trial in October 2001 judge suggested transferring action to the Small Claims Court and this was finally done on February 1, 2002 upon terms that after judgment in the Small Claims Court, either party could apply to the Superior Court to deal with costs. Right of a client to have solicitor's account assessed is an important right and emphasized by the Commentary to Rule 2.08 of the Rules of Professional Conduct.

Motion judge erred in granting summary judgment when fairness of accounts not conceded and not considered.

Judgment in appeal set aside, bills referred to Assessment Officer for assessment.

Resch v. Canadian Tire Corp., 2006 CarswellOnt 3822 (Ont. S.C.J.), February 8, 2006, Spies J.

Application to determine order for cross-examination of witnesses to be called by the Defendant MR. Counsel for other defendants sought to cross-examine first. Court deviated from the usual order for cross-examination and granted the request. Unfair to allow plaintiffs to cross-examine last based on the alliance that existed between the plaintiffs and MR.

Rule 19 — Costs

19.01 (1) Disbursements — A successful party is entitled to have the party's reasonable disbursements, including any costs of effecting service or preparing a plaintiff's or defendant's claim or a defence and expenses for travel, accommodation, photocopying and experts' reports, paid by the unsuccessful party, unless the court orders otherwise.

History [R. 19.01(1)]: Formerly 20.01(1); deletes phrase "as assessed by the clerk," for clarity; plain language changes.

Commentary [S. 19.01(1)]

See R. 19.01(1).

Provided that a receipt or invoice is submitted, the clerk shall assess disbursements made in accordance with the regulations made under the *Administration of Justice Act*, any receipted disbursement for effecting service (which shall not exceed $60 for each person served unless the court orders otherwise) or preparing a plaintiff's or defendant's claim or defence (which shall not exceed $100 for each plaintiff's or defendant's claim or defence prepared). The clerk's assessment is subject to review by the court [r. 19.01(2)].

According to Rule 19.01, the court may order costs if requested to do so. The endorsement record/order of the court will indicate if the court has ordered costs. The clerk may also award up to $100 for each plaintiff's or defendant's claim or defence prepared where a receipt or invoice is provided [r. 19.01(4)].

Where a party wishes to recover costs (i.e. disbursements and expenses) of an amount in excess of the amount allowed under the Rules or the SCC Schedule of Fees, a party may make a motion to review the clerk's assessment of costs.

The clerk can only award up to $200 for the preparation of the plaintiff's claim and the defence to a defendant's claim. A receipt or an invoice must be provided. In-house legal service providers can provide services to their employers without being licensed by the Law Society of Upper Canada, and as such, a company/business may issue a receipt or invoice for the preparation of pleadings.

(1.1) For greater certainty, subrule (1) includes costs associated with the electronic filing or issuance of documents under these rules.

(2) The clerk shall assess the disbursements in accordance with the regulations made under the *Administration of Justice Act* and in accordance with subrules (3) and (4); the assessment is subject to review by the court.

History [R. 19.01(2)]: Formerly 20.01(2); explicitly requires clerk to assess disbursements; plain language changes.

(3) The amount of disbursements assessed for effecting service shall not exceed $60 for each person served unless the court is of the opinion that there are special circumstances that justify assessing a greater amount.

History [R. 19.01(3)]: New provision, limiting the amount of disbursements to $60.

Commentary: A successful party is entitled to have the party's disbursements, including any costs of effecting service, paid by the unsuccessful party, unless the court orders otherwise. The clerk shall assess disbursements in accordance with the regulations made under the *Administration of Justice Act*. The amount of disbursements assessed for effecting service shall not exceed $60 for each person served, unless there are special circumstances. The assessment is subject to review by the court [r. 19.01].

If costs are not included in the claim, does that mean that the successful party is not reimbursed for any costs?

No. According to Rule 19.01, the court may order costs.

Where a party wishes to recover costs of an amount in excess of the SCC Schedule of Fees, a hearing to review the clerk's assessment of costs should be scheduled before a judge [r. 19.01(2)], according to local practice.

Where a solicitor has commenced an action to recover unpaid legal fees, the right to prejudgment interest is governed by s. 33 of the *Solicitors Act*. Pursuant to s. 33(4) of the Act, there is no entitlement to prejudgment interest if the rate of interest is not shown on the account delivered to the defendant(s). In the case of postjudgment interest, a solicitor who has obtained a judgment for unpaid legal fees is entitled to postjudgment interest pursuant to s. 129(1) of the *Courts of Justice Act* even if there is no mention of it in the account delivered to the defendant(s). The applicable rate of interest shall be the rate shown on the account as long as it does not exceed the rate permitted by the *Courts of Justice Act*. Where the account contains a rate which is higher than that permitted under the *Courts of Justice Act*, it is the statutory rate which applies. The statutory rate is the rate in effect on the date that the account was delivered to the defendant by the solicitor. Interest runs from one month after the account is delivered to the date of judgment. If no precise interest rate is stated on the account as delivered, the plaintiff is not entitled to any prejudgment interest. It is not sufficient to state "interest in accordance with Section 33 of the *Solicitors Act*."

Subsection 23(3) of the *Courts of Justice Act* provides that once an action has been transferred to the Small Claims Court "it shall be titled and continued as if it had been commenced in that court."

Provided that a receipt or invoice is submitted, the clerk shall assess disbursements made in accordance with the regulations made under the *Administration of Justice Act* (some fees relevant to Small Claims Court matters are set out in the Guide to Fee Schedules) any receipted disbursement for effecting service (which shall not exceed $60 for each person served unless the court orders otherwise) or preparing a plaintiff's or defendant's claim or defence (which shall not exceed $100 for each plaintiff's or defendant's claim or defence prepared). The clerk's assessment is subject to review by the court [r. 19.01(2)].

According to r. 19.01, the court may order costs if requested to do so.

The clerk may award up to $60.00 for each person served if the party provides receipts or invoices showing the amount paid to effect service [r. 19.01(3)]. The clerk may also award up to $100 for each plaintiff's or defendant's claim or defence prepared where a receipt or invoice is provided [r. 19.01(4)].

Where a party wishes to recover costs (i.e., disbursements and expenses) of an amount in excess of the amount allowed under the Rules or the SCC Schedule of Fees, a party may make a motion to review the clerk's assessment of costs. It should be scheduled before a judge [r. 19.01(2)], according to local practice. Refer to r. 15 of this manual regarding the process for motions.

The clerk can only award up to $100 for the preparation of a plaintiff's or defendant's claim or defence once. If the party wishes to recover more, they may bring a motion to review the clerk's assessment of costs (see note above).

The clerk can only award up to $200 for the preparation of the plaintiff's claim and the defence to a defendant's claim.

To support the clerk in assessing the amount of disbursements paid for the preparation of the plaintiff's claim and the defence to a defendant's claim, a receipt or an invoice must be provided.

1. *Disbursements Recoverable by a Successful Party* — Where the litigant serves the document, the cost of mailing the document where service is made by mail alone is recoverable with the provision of a post office receipt to verify the amount. Where the document is served by someone other than the litigant, recoverable entitlements include any amount that exceeds the amount permitted under the tariff and/or rules, any amount other than the actual postage cost where service is made by mail only and where an invoice from the person serving the document is not filed with the court office. Where the document is served by someone other than the litigant, a successful party may also recover costs paid to someone else to serve the document by personal service, or by an alternative to personal service (excluding service by mail only) provided the amount does not exceed the amount payable to a bailiff under the tariff and/or rules.

2. *Disbursements Not Recoverable by a Successful Party* — Where the litigant serves the document, any disbursements, other than the actual costs of mailing, where service is made by mail only (*e.g.*, travel to a post office, etc.) are not recoverable by a successful party. Additionally, there is no provision to allow for the cost of mailing where a post office receipt cannot be produced, or for any disbursements (*e.g.*, gasoline, taxi fare, etc.) incurred by a litigant in serving a document by a method other than mail only.

Case Law: *Beverly Hills Aluminium Sales v. Kenny* (1987), 10 W.D.C.P. 102 (Ont. Prov. Ct.) — A claim for reimbursement of moneys deducted from the defendant employees wages was not statute barred and thus should not be struck out.

Schmidt v. Faryna (1994), 46 A.C.W.S. (3d) 830 (B.C. S.C.) — Plaintiff sought to escape the effects of a rule limiting costs to disbursements if award was less than monetary jurisdiction of the Provincial Small Claims Division (B.C.). The adjuster advised the plaintiff, who was injured in a car accident, that no offer would be made. Writ was issued less than three months after the accident. The plaintiff was symptom-free within four months. Issuance of writ could have waited until full recovery. There was never any indication that the expected compensation would exceed monetary jurisdiction of the Small Claims Court. Application was dismissed.

Shibley v. Harris, [1995] B.C.W.L.D. 2724 (B.C. S.C.) — Offer to settle in Supreme Court rejected by plaintiff. Damages awarded of $4,400. Plaintiff *only* entitled to disbursements up to date offer made. Defendant entitled to costs and disbursements thereafter.

Bemar Construction (Ontario) Inc. v. Toronto Transit Commission (2000), 1 C.L.R. (3d) 137, 2000 CarswellOnt 451, [2000] O.J. No. 647 (Ont. Master) — An unrepresented plaintiff sought costs calculated on solicitor-client basis. The requirement was that conduct be egregious, devoid of ethical conduct or intentional misuse of process. Costs awarded on party-and-party basis.

Brown v. Lowe, 85 B.C.L.R. (3d) 162, 2001 CarswellBC 114, [2001] B.C.J. No. 127, 2001 BCSC 105 (B.C. S.C.) — Photocopying necessary to send material to consultants and for making copies of numerous documents for court and jury. Counsel did not produce client ledger printout or any other means of verifying number of photocopies made. While production of printout is not necessary in all cases, it was specifically requested by letter and should have been provided, if available. Reasonable number of copies estimated based on examples of books of documents prepared for trial. Disbursement for medical consultant disallowed. Fact that no written report made did not disable defendant from proving reasonableness of fee by describing work done and advice given. Affidavit of justification did not provide information to enable assessment of reasonableness of fee. Mere proof of date and amount of disbursement and name of person not sufficient.

Kha v. Salhab, 11 C.P.C. (5th) 150, 2001 CarswellAlta 53, 2001 ABQB 44, 282 A.R. 324 (Alta. Q.B.) — Non-native English-speaking plaintiffs retained translators provided prior to commencement of action to assist them in pursing action. Plaintiffs appealed order of taxing officer on taxation of bill of costs disallowing disbursements for translation services incurred prior to commencement of action. Appeal dismissed. Alberta Rules of Court do not contemplate award of costs in relation to disbursements for interpretation services incurred prior to commencement of action.

Kelly v. Lam, 2006 CarswellBC 677, 2006 BCPC 98 (B.C. Prov. Ct.) 2006-03-15.

Defendants apply for order pursuant to Rule 20(2) that Claimant pay the Defendants disbursements of $2,537.25.

Rule 20(2) states as follows:

> An unsuccessful party must pay to the successful party the following expenses, unless a judge or registrar orders otherwise:
>
> (a) any fees the party paid for filing any documents
>
> (b) reasonable amounts the party paid for serving any documents
>
> (c) any other reasonable charges or expenses that the judge or registrar considers directly related to the conduct of the proceeding

Agents' fees would fall under subsection (c), being reasonable expenses that directly relate to the conduct of the proceeding. See *Gaudet v. Mair*, [1996] B.C.J. No. 2547 (B.C. Prov.

Ct.) where court ruled that reasonable disbursements for agents' fees are recoverable, defendant claiming agents' fees of $534.

Service fee reasonable. Claim for clinical records in the amount of $1,102.05. Amount claimed for photocopies reasonable.

Claimant suggests she should not have to pay expenses because she does not have financial resources.

Persons of modest means with legitimate claims should not be denied the opportunity to pursue them. However, such persons must be mindful of fact that there is a cost to defend claims, and that persons who are required to spend sums of money in order to do so should not be left without some recourse to recover those costs.

Euteneier v. Lee, 2005 CarswellOnt 6906, 260 D.L.R. (4th) 145, 204 O.A.C. 287, 139 C.R.R. (2d) 55 (Ont. C.A.) 2005-12-01.

On appeal from the order of Divisional Court, dated November 10, 2003, reported at 2003 CarswellOnt 5557, [2003] O.J. No. 4239, 113 C.R.R. (2d) 44 (Ont. Div. Ct.). Appellants wholly successful before court.

Appellants prepared to accept costs in the total amount of $150,000.

Particular facts and context of case warrant departure from application of usual costs rule and that *no costs* should be made. Issues raised by respondent in her action concerned her interests in maintaining her dignity and privacy while she was detailed in police custody and her constitutional rights under ss. 7 and 12 of the *Charter of Rights and Freedoms*.

Respondent's financial interest clearly modest in comparison to the overall costs of the proceedings.

Respondent and her disabled daughter exist on monthly child support totaling $850.

Parties to bear their own costs.

Murray v. Murray, 2005 CarswellOnt 7278, 205 O.A.C. 107, 79 O.R. (3d) 147 (Ont. C.A.) 2005-12-15.

Each side should bear their own costs.

Wife impecunious, and costs award would have a devastating effect on her. Moreover, her claim was not dismissed outright; the trial judge's analysis was flawed, but the wife might succeed in a second trial. Appropriate order at trial and on appeal was that each side should bear their own costs.

Pierlot Family Farm Ltd. v. Polstra, 2006 CarswellPEI 27, 2006 PESCAD 13, 271 D.L.R. (4th) 525, 766 A.P.R. 169, 257 Nfld. & P.E.I.R. 169 (P.E.I. C.A.).

Plaintiff, self represented, was successful at trial. The defendant appealed unsuccessfully to the Prince Edward Island Court of Appeal. Plaintiff submitted a bill of costs in excess of $14,000.

Plaintiff entitled to recover costs of $800, plus disbursements.

Costs should only be awarded to self-represented lay litigants who can demonstrate they devoted time and effort to do the work ordinarily done by a lawyer retained to conduct remunerative activity. Costs should only reflect provision of material and argument of assistance to the court, not compensate for excessive time spent while litigant was learning the process.

Marshall RVR (2000) Ltd. v. Gorman, 2007 CarswellAlta 1567, 2007 ABPC 313, 48 C.P.C. (6th) 385 (Alta. Prov. Ct.)

Plaintiff brought an application for costs after the plaintiff's action was dismissed and unspecified costs were awarded to the defendant. The plaintiff argued that the court ought to exercise its discretion not to award costs against him as an award of costs at this point is punitive and would impose further hardship upon him.

The plaintiff was awarded $2,308 in costs. Where lawyers chose to utilize electronic means of research, they were to do so at their own expense.

Arabi v. Toronto Dominion Bank (2008), 2008 CarswellOnt 3579, 59 C.P.C. (6th) 235, 239 O.A.C. 293 (Ont. Div. Ct.)

Appeal related to the issue of costs. In class action proceedings class members are liable for costs with respect to determination of their own individual claims. "Special weight" in disposition of costs in class proceedings must be given to the factors whether the class proceedings were a "test case", raised a novel point of law or involved a matter of public interest. This case involved individual contracts and thus, cannot be treated as novel point of law or one of public interest.

Kailey v. Kellner, 2008 CarswellBC 343, 56 C.P.C. (6th) 40, 2008 BCSC 224 (B.C. S.C.)

The parties were agreed that the plaintiff was entitled to his costs and disbursements up to the date of delivery of the defendants' offers to settle and the defendants were entitled to their costs and disbursements thereafter, as the offers were more favourable to the plaintiff than the result at trial. The issue was how those costs would be assessed, either in accordance with the limits set forth in Rule 66 or by reference to the usual tariff in Appendix B, and certain disbursements the plaintiff submitted ought to be disallowed.

Ross v. Henriques, 2008 CarswellBC 1336, 257 B.C.A.C. 131, 432 W.A.C. 131, 2008 BCCA 282 (B.C. C.A. [In Chambers])

Application brought by lawyer for leave to appeal. Trial judge decided to order lawyer to pay portion of costs on motion concerning document disclosure. The judge found that the list of documents was inadequate, that the lawyer failed to meet his professional responsibilities in the preparation of the list and thus, caused the costs to be incurred without reasonable cause. Motion dismissed. Appeal was significant to lawyer but was not of significance to practice or action. There was no error in principle in judge's determination of the facts concerning motion for document disclosure or his exercise of discretion in ordering lawyer to pay part of costs associated with it. Appeal not prima facie meritorious.

S. (J.A.) v. S. (N.J.), 2008 CarswellBC 20, [2008] B.C.J. No. 21, 77 B.C.L.R. (4th) 66, 2008 BCCA 5, 250 B.C.A.C. 101, [2008] 9 W.W.R. 483, 48 R.F.L. (6th) 41, 289 D.L.R. (4th) 315, 416 W.A.C. 101 (B.C. C.A.); leave to appeal refused (2008), 2008 CarswellBC 1278, 2008 CarswellBC 1279, 387 N.R. 395 (note), 461 W.A.C. 319 (note), 273 B.C.A.C. 319 (note) (S.C.C.)

Trial judge held that the appellant, a third party in dispute between B. and J.A.S., was liable for special costs of the J.A.S and of all future proceedings to assess costs as a result of appellant's reprehensible behavior. The appellant challenged the costs orders.

The Court of Appeal held that it was open to trial judge to make findings on costs against individuals who were not parties to the litigation. In making his decision, trial judge made every effort to ensure that the process he followed was fair to all the parties. The effect of appellant's misconduct was to increase the length and complexity of any assessment of costs that might ensue, thus, there was no basis for interfering with the trial judge's order.

681638 Ontario Ltd. v. UGT Ltd., 252 O.A.C. 285, 2009 CarswellOnt 4477 (Ont. Div. Ct.); additional reasons at 2009 CarswellOnt 6473 (Ont. Div. Ct.); additional reasons at 2009 CarswellOnt 8141 (Ont. Div. Ct.)

The plaintiff applied for leave to appeal costs awarded to three defendants against which the plaintiff had discontinued small claims action. The Divisional Court noted that trial judge made no reference to either of the two relevant statutory provisions, specifically, section 29 of the *Courts of Justice Act*, and r. 19.04(1) of the *Small Claims Court Rules*. Section 29 provided an award of costs, other than disbursements, was not to exceed 15 per cent of the amount claimed unless it was "necessary in the interests of justice to penalize a party . . . for unreasonable behaviour in the proceeding." The trial judge made no finding "of unreasonable behaviour" on the part of the plaintiff. Section 29, in the context of this case, limited any single award of costs to any one of the defendants to 15 percent of $1,000, namely, $1,500. That interpretation was supported by the use of "award" (singular) in section 29 and by public policy. There was a separate issue of costs between the plaintiff and each of the defendants. The trial judge required to consider each one separately and make a separate award to *each* defendant. If a judge invoked the "unreasonable behaviour" sanction against one of several unsuccessful defendants, that should affect only the additional amount for costs that could be awarded against only that defendant. However, if unsuccessful plaintiff engaged in "unreasonable behaviour," it might be that more than one of the successful defendants could be found to be entitled to costs in excess of 15 percent maximum.

Cunning v. Doucet, 2009 NSSM 35, 2009 CarswellNS 493, 79 C.P.C. (6th) 293 (N.S. Small Cl. Ct.)

The parties settled with disbursements to be agreed upon or taxed. The defendant paid $9,605.66 without protest for photocopies, faxes, postage, unspecified disbursements, and physician's booking fee. The plaintiff's counsel charged $0.40 per photocopy. The plaintiff denied further amount for photocopies. Prior authorities limited photocopy charges to $0.25 or less. Performing legal research was part of the solicitor's job. The ability to do online research was convenience to solicitors that was now available for minimal cost.

The plaintiff denied her solicitor's travel and meal expenses. Travel expenses were not appropriate disbursements on party and party basis. The rule of thumb client was responsible to get his or her solicitor to courthouse. Principle was the same for activities apart from trial. Principle was extended to include meals.

West End Tree Service Inc. v. Stabryla, 2010 CarswellOnt 12, 2010 ONSC 68, 257 O.A.C. 265, [2010] O.J. No. 7 (Ont. Div. Ct.)

The defendant in small claims action paid money into court pursuant to notice of garnishment. The plaintiff obtained default judgment. The defendant obtained order setting aside judgment, but garnished money had already been paid out to the plaintiff. The endorsement stated, "Provided the defendant complies with my order, then, on or before 15 February 2008, the plaintiff is ordered to return the monies to the court to be held pending trial." When trial commenced, the plaintiff had not paid the money into court. Trial judge dismissed action and awarded defendant $1,500 in costs, where the plaintiff had neither paid the money into court nor undertaken to do so. Divisional Court allowed appeal. The court stated that had it not allowed the appeal on the merits, it would have set aside the costs order. Contrary to the judge's finding, the plaintiff had indicated at the outset of trial that if it had to pay, it would do so that day. Order required payment by February 15, 2008, but not sent to the plaintiff's lawyer until February 22, 2008. Even if unreasonable behaviour, judge gave no explanation as to how he arrived at $1,500. Costs pursuant to section 29 should logically bear some relationship to costs incurred by recipient as a result of other party's unreasonable behaviour. Costs would have been $375. Even if elevated costs warranted, no principled basis to arrive at $1,500.

Transport Training Centres of Canada v. Wilson, 2010 ONSC 2099, 2010 CarswellOnt 2155, (sub nom. *Wilson v. Transport Training Centres of Canada*) 261 O.A.C. 301 (Ont. Div. Ct.); additional reasons at 2010 ONSC 2714, 2010 CarswellOnt 3549, (sub nom. *Wilson v. Transport Training Centres of Canada*) 263 O.A.C. 226 (Ont. Div. Ct.)

The plaintiff employed by defendant for 16 months. She sued for wrongful dismissal. At trial, plaintiff claimed general damages of $1,000 for undue mental distress caused by the termination and punitive damages of $7,000. Small Claims Court found dismissal without cause, but with appropriate pay in lieu of notice. He dismissed claim for punitive damages, but awarded $7,000 in general damages for undue mental distress, instead of claimed amount of $1,000, and amended her claim accordingly. Defendant appealed. Divisional Court set aside award of $7,000 for general damages for undue mental distress because it was unsupported by evidence. Rule 19.04(2) stated that "In the case of a student-at-law or an agent, the representation fee shall not exceed half of the maximum costs that may be awarded under section 29 of the *Courts of Justice Act*." If the defendant had not been successful on appeal, trial costs should have been fixed at 15% of $7,000, an amount of $1,050 divided by 2, for total costs of $525. Both r. 19.04(2) and section 29 mandatory because they used the word "shall." These provisions could not be ignored. No evidence of "unreasonable behaviour in the proceeding."

Ward (Next Friend of) v. Ward, 2011 ABQB 465, 2011 CarswellAlta 1224, (sub nom. *Ward v. Ward)* 516 A.R. 192 (Alta. Q.B.), A.B. Moen J.; additional reasons to 2010 ABQB 654, 2010 CarswellAlta 2053, (sub nom. *Ward v. Ward)* 496 A.R. 42 (Alta. Q.B.), A.B. Moen J.

Costs. Particular items of costs. Disbursements. Travelling expenses. Where two actions were heard together, the plaintiff in one action may only claim costs for travel for the one day in which he appeared as a witness but may not claim it for those days in which he sat in at the trial as the plaintiff.

Moore v. Brazeau Seller LLP, 2011 CarswellOnt 15740, [2011] O.J. No. 3171 (Ont. Sm. Cl. Ct.)

In this professional malpractice case involving expert witnesses, the successful defendant was awarded disbursements fixed at $13,581.

(4) The amount of disbursements assessed for preparing a plaintiff's or defendant's claim or a defence shall not exceed $100.

O. Reg. 78/06, s. 38; 440/10, s. 3; 44/14, s. 13

19.02 Limit — **Any power under this rule to award costs is subject to section 29 of the** *Courts of Justice Act*, **which limits the amount of costs that may be awarded.**

O. Reg. 78/06, s. 39

History [R. 19.02]: New.

Case Law: *Coutu v. Fraser*, 2012 ONSC 3997, 2012 CarswellOnt 8470 (Ont. S.C.J.), Wilcox J.

The Respondent successfully sued the Appellant in Small Claims Court and was awarded the maximum available at the time of $10,000 plus $500 in costs. Both parties self-represented at trial.

S. 131(1) of the *Courts of Justice Act* leaves the costs incidental to a proceeding or a step in a proceeding in the discretion of the court, subject to the provisions of an Act or the rules of the court.

Rule 19 of the Small Claims Court Rules deals with costs. Rule 19.02 says that, "Any power under this rule to award costs is subject to s. 29 of the *Courts of Justice Act*, which limits the amount of costs that may be awarded."

That would apply to trial proceedings in the Small Claims Court. Without deciding whether it is directly applicable to the appeal of Small Claims Court matters, it provides guidance in the approach to take in determining costs in an appeal.

Costs of the appeal and motion $2,500.

19.03 [Repealed O. Reg. 440/10, s. 4.]

History [R. 19.03]: Formerly 20.02; amount that may be allowed raised to $50.

19.04 Representation Fee — **If a successful party is represented by a lawyer, student-at-law or paralegal, the court may award the party a reasonable representation fee at trial or at an assessment hearing.**

O. Reg. 78/06, s. 39; 440/10, s. 5; 230/13, s. 15

History [R. 19.04]: Formerly 20.03(1) and (2), restructured for clarity.

Commentary

Articled Student-at-Law Rights to Appear Before Courts and Tribunals

Articled Students-at-law are permitted to appear on the civil law matters:

i. Consent motions and matters before Ontario Court of Justice and the Superior Court of Justice, and before the masters and registrars of the Superior Court of Justice and the registrars of the Court of Appeal for Ontario, including references and assessments of costs.

ii. Matters brought without notice to the opposing party before the Ontario Court of Justice and the Superior Court of Justice, and before the masters and registrars of the Superior Court of Justice, provided no substantial rights will be affected.

iii. Simple contested interlocutory motions before the Ontario Court of Justice and the Superior Court of Justice and before the masters and registrars of the Superior Court of Justice, unless the result of such interlocutory motion could be to finally dispose of a party's substantive rights by determining the subject matter in dispute.

iv. Subject to the discretion of a judge of the Superior Court of Justice, on the passing of accounts in estate matters.

v. Examinations for discovery, examinations in aid of execution, examinations of witnesses on pending motions and cross-examinations on affidavits in support of interlocutory motion.

vi. Assignment court matters in both the Superior Court of Justice and the Ontario Court of Justice.

vii. Status hearings in the Superior Court of Justice.

viii. Applications in the Ontario Court of Justice. Students-at-law may not appear on contested Crown Wardship Applications.

ix. Proceedings before administrative tribunals in appropriate matters and the Small Claims Court.

Explanatory Notes

The *Criminal Code* provides for a number of offences where the Crown may elect to proceed either by way of summary conviction or by way of indictment. In terms of classification, the offence is an indictable offence until the Crown elects to proceed by summary conviction. Authority for this position is to be found in the *Interpretation Act*, R.S.C. 1985, c. 1–21, s. 34(1), which provides:

Where an enactment creates an offence,

(a) The offence shall be deemed to be an indictable offence if the enactment provides that the offender may be prosecuted for the offence by indictment.

Section C.(ii) should not be interpreted to confer upon a student-at-law the unrestricted right to appear on a summary conviction trial in all instances. The articling principal is responsible for providing effective supervision to the student-at-law according to all the circumstances of the situation, including the complexity of the matter. This includes consideration of the possible consequences to the accused.

Articled student-at-law rights to appear in Youth Court are guided by the same rules as for criminal matters heard in other courts. Therefore, articled students-at-law may appear on summary conviction matters in Youth Court subject to the qualifications in note 6 above. They may, however, appear only on remands in indictable offence matters.

Articled students-at-law may appear in the Ontario Court of Justice under the *Provincial Offences Act*. Articled students-at-law may appear at pre-trial conferences in Small Claims Court.

Students-at-law may extend their rights of appearance beyond the conclusion of their articles up until their call to the bar by executing an Agreement and Confirmation of Supervision form with their supervising lawyer and filing it with the Office of the Registrar.

Legal Services for P1 Licensees

The new regulatory scheme set out in the Law Society's By-Law 4 permits paralegals to practice in what are already permitted areas of practice. Subsection 6(2) authorizes licensed paralegals to represent someone:

- in Small Claims Court;

- in the Ontario Court of Justice under the *Provincial Offences Act*;

- on summary conviction offices where the maximum penalty does not exceed six months' imprisonment;

- before administrative tribunals, including the Financial Services Commission of Ontario.

A person with a paralegal licence can do the following in the course of representing a client in any of the above-mentioned proceedings:

- give legal advice concerning legal interests, rights, or responsibilities with respect to a proceeding or the subject matter of a proceeding;

- draft or assist with drafting documents for use in a proceeding;

- negotiate on behalf of a person who is a party to a proceeding.

Anyone in Ontario who provides legal services requires a licence, unless the *Law Society Act* or a by-law of the Law Society says that a licence is not required. The *Law Society Act* gives the Law Society the authority to issue licences and to specify the scope of practice for each licence:

> A person provides legal services if the person engages in conduct that involves the application of legal principles and judgment with regards to the circumstances or objectives of a person [s. 1(5) of the *Law Society Act*].

The Canadian Society of Immigration Consultants (CSIC) is responsible for regulating the activities of immigration consultants who are CSIC members and provide immigration advice for a fee. They do not require a licence under Bill 14.

Staff of collection agencies, who work to collect debts owing to clients of their agencies, need a licence to appear in Small Claims Court. Under the *Law Society Act*, a person who is acting in the normal course of carrying on a profession or occupation governed by another Act of the Legislature that regulates specifically the activities of persons engaged in that profession or occupation, does not require a licence. Under the *Law Society Act*, staff of collection agencies working to collect debts owing to clients of their agencies who do *not* use the Small Claims Court to do so do not need a licence to carry on that work.

People who "merely" serve documents are not providing legal services. Process servers who serve documents for their employers can continue to do so without obtaining a paralegal licence, as long as they do not decide what documents to serve, how to serve the documents, and on whom to serve the documents. People who perform these actions are providing legal services and require a licence.

The Law Society's model for the regulation of paralegals governs everyone who does advocacy work, i.e. appear in front of a court or tribunal. Individuals who do non-advocacy work under the supervision of a lawyer do not require a licence. These include law clerks in law firms, independent contractors, document preparers and title searchers whose only clients are lawyers. The circumstances of persons whose work is supervised by a lawyer are governed by rule 5.01(2) of the lawyers' *Rules of Professional Conduct*. Non-lawyers appearing in court or before a tribunal need a licence, even if they are supervised by a lawyer, unless they are appearing on behalf of a lawyer on a scheduling or other related routine administrative matter.

The criteria for applicants applying after October 31, 2007, and prior to July 2010 are as follows:

> Paralegal applicants are not able to provide legal services until they are licensed, but are eligible to apply to become licensed as paralegals if they have graduated within three years prior to the application, from a legal services program, approved by the Ministry of Training, Colleges and Universities at the time they graduated.

After June 30, 2010, all applicants must have graduated from an accredited legal services program.

Case Law: *Garson v. Braithwaite* (1994), 5 W.D.C.P. (2d) 424 (Ont. Gen. Div.) — The landlord represented himself and the defendant tenant was represented by an agent who was neither a student-at-law, nor a law clerk operating under the supervision of a solicitor. The defendant was successful and moved for an award of party-and-party costs at the level as if his agent was a solicitor. Should costs be awarded where a party is represented by an agent who is neither a law clerk nor a student-at-law? Costs were not awarded. Under s. 131(1) of the *Courts of Justice Act*, costs could only be awarded in connection with the services of solicitors, students-at-law, or law clerks operating under the supervision of a solicitor.

Skidmore v. Blackmore, 122 D.L.R. (4th) 330, 1995 CarswellBC 23, [1995] B.C.J. No. 305, 2 B.C.L.R. (3d) 201, [1995] 4 W.W.R. 524, 27 C.R.R. (2d) 77, 55 B.C.A.C. 191, 90 W.A.C. 191, 35 C.P.C. (3d) 28 (B.C. C.A.) — An action was successfully conducted by one of the plaintiffs who was a former member of the Law Society, but no longer held a practising certificate. The trial judge held there was a binding precedent that unless a litigant is a practising lawyer, no costs may be awarded, only disbursements may be recovered. Can costs be awarded to a self-represented litigant, who is a non-lawyer? "The view that costs are awarded solely to indemnify the successful litigant for legal fees and disbursements incurred is now outdated. Party-and-party costs serve many functions. They partially indemnify the successful litigant, deter frivolous actions and defences, encourage reasonable offers to settle, and discourage improper or unnecessary steps in the litigation."

Weiss v. Prentice Hall Canada Inc. (1995), 1995 CarswellOnt 729, [1995] O.J. No. 4188, 66 C.P.R. (3d) 417, 7 W.D.C.P. (2d) 99 (Ont. Small Cl. Ct.) — There is concurrent jurisdiction of provincial courts and the Federal Court: s. 37 of the *Copyright Act*. That Act of the Federal Parliament makes every provincial court a *curia designata* to enforce civil remedies provided by that Act. The application of Rule 20.03 of the Small Claims Court Rules with its maximum counsel fee $300 is inconsistent with the discretion in s. 25 of the *Courts of Justice Act*. The court referred to s. 29 of the *Courts of Justice Act*. Section 29 is in conflict with Rule 20.03 of the Small Claims Rules. Any conflict must be resolved in favour of the *Act*.

Fellowes, McNeil v. Kansa General International Insurance Co. (1997), 37 O.R. (3d) 464, 1997 CarswellOnt 5013, 17 C.P.C. (4th) 400 (Ont. Gen. Div.) — Plaintiff law firm was successful in action. Since one of the partners acted in person on plaintiff's behalf, plaintiff asked the court for a direction under Rule 57.02 that partner's bill of costs be treated the same as that of a represented litigant. Partner submitted that such a direction was needed because there was a body of "judge made law" that established the principle that unrepresented litigants did not get full costs. Defendant argued that costs awards were footed on the principle of indemnification, and that no counsel fees were incurred by plaintiff with the result that no counsel fees should be fixed in its favour. Here, a partner should be compensated for his party and party costs because while he did not pay costs to third parties as counsel to the firm in this action, he deprived his partners and himself of income that would otherwise have been available had he been able to serve other clients. The principle of indemnity which footed the old concepts that had been followed by the courts in dealing with the issue (distinguishing between three classes of litigants) was now outdated because costs were to serve many functions.

Martin v. East Coast Lumber Ltd. (1998), 166 Nfld. & P.E.I.R. 295, 511 A.P.R. 295 (P.E.I. T.D.) — Application by defendant for costs. Application dismissed. Given the divided success of the action, and the aim of small claims litigation to keep the procedure simple and to maximize self-representation, it was inappropriate to require the plaintiff to pay costs to the defendant.

Skovberg v. Lampimaki (1998), 227 A.R. 278 (Alta. Q.B.), Lee J. — Motion by appellant, Lampimaki, for costs of an appeal from a Small Claims Court judgment in action by Skovberg against Lampimaki. The amount of the original claim was only $283 plus $131 in costs. The legal costs of the appeal were considerably higher. Motion allowed and Column One costs ordered. While the small amount of monies involved in the case was definitely a factor, it was not the overriding factor.

Lavigne v. Canada (Human Resources Development) (1998), (sub nom. *Lavigne v. Canada (Minister of Human Resources Development))* 229 N.R. 205 (Fed. C.A.) — The motions judge confirmed that lay litigants cannot receive counsel's fees under the Federal Court Rules when they have successfully represented themselves. Under Tariff B of those Rules, a service cannot be rendered by a litigant to himself. The Courts, be it the Trial Division or the Court of Appeal, are not at liberty to change what is legislation. Does the Rule breach rights protected by the *Charter*, especially those covered by ss. 7 and 15? Answer is no as found by the Court in *Rubin v. Canada (Attorney General),* [1990] 3 F.C. 642 (Fed. T.D.).

Insch v. Geary (June 22, 1999), Doc. Winnipeg Centre CI 99-01-12460 (Man. Master) — A lawyer represented a client in a Small Claims Court action arising out of a motor vehicle accident. The lawyer estimated cost at $1,000 to defend action. A fee of $1,500 was charged. The hearing was, at most, one hour longer than anticipated. A fair and reasonable fee should not exceed $1,000 plus actual out-of-pocket disbursements plus GST.

Duca Community Credit Union Ltd. v. Giovannoli (2000), 2000 CarswellOnt 4814 (Ont. S.C.J.) — Unrepresented defendant. No rule denying recovery of costs by self-represented litigants.

Tran v. Financial Debt Recovery Ltd. (2000), 193 D.L.R. (4th) 168, 2 C.C.L.T. (3d) 270, 2000 CarswellOnt 4219 (Ont. S.C.J.) — The defendant collection agency was harassing the plaintiff for loan repayment by repeatedly making abusive telephone calls to workplace, contrary to statute. Unrepresented party. The litigant in person is entitled to compensation for time spent in preparation, but not time in court.

George v. Imagineering Ltd. (2001), 2001 CarswellOnt 3832 (Ont. S.C.J.) — Costs awarded to plaintiff on party-and-party basis. Assessment officer directed to assess reasonable articling student fees in preparation for trial itself.

In Ontario there are only two types of costs: party-and-party and solicitor-and-client. The factors set out in Rule 57 provide sufficient flexibility under either category so that there is no need to create a hybrid scale of "enhanced" party-and-party costs. *Vanek v. Great Atlantic & Pacific Co. of Canada* (1999), 180 D.L.R. (4th) 748, 48 O.R. (3d) 228, 127 O.A.C. 286,

1999 CarswellOnt 4036 (Ont. C.A.); leave to appeal refused (2000), 193 D.L.R. (4th) vii, 2000 CarswellOnt 4184, 2000 CarswellOnt 4185, 264 N.R. 191 (note), 145 O.A.C. 200 (note) (S.C.C.); reconsideration refused (2001), 2001 CarswellOnt 958, 2001 CarswellOnt 959 (S.C.C.).

Dechant v. Stevens, 2001 CarswellAlta 356, 2001 ABCA 81, [2001] 5 W.W.R. 448, (sub nom. *Dechant v. Law Society of Alberta*) 277 A.R. 333, (sub nom. *Dechant v. Law Society of Alberta*) 242 W.A.C. 333, 89 Alta. L.R. (3d) 289, (sub nom. *Dechant v. Law Society of Alberta*) 203 D.L.R. (4th) 157, [2001] A.J. No. 373 (Alta. C.A.); leave to appeal refused (2001), 2001 CarswellAlta 1211, 2001 CarswellAlta 1212, 283 N.R. 394 (note), (sub nom. *Dechant v. Law Society of Alberta*) 299 A.R. 177 (note), (sub nom. *Dechant v. Law Society of Alberta*) 266 W.A.C. 177 (note) (S.C.C.) — Non-practicing lawyer self-represented. Appellant appealed ruling of Chambers Judge awarding costs solely for disbursements. It was appropriate to make award beyond that of disbursements to compensate for lost opportunity.

Metrin Mechanical v. Big H (2001), 10 C.P.C. (5th) 302, 2001 CarswellOnt 605 (Ont. Master) — Court terminated relationship between solicitors and clients on basis of alleged conflict raised by another party to action. Solicitors purported to exercise solicitor's lien in respect of clients' files. Motion granted. Case management master had jurisdiction to hear motion. Rationale behind solicitor's lien is to prevent party from lawyer shopping mid-way through after running up account. Focus should be on whether or not client voluntarily initiated change of counsel. Clients in this case did not initiate that process; accordingly solicitor's lien not available.

Morris Rose Ledgett LLP. v. Crisolago (2001), 2001 CarswellOnt 5065 (Ont. S.C.J.) — In action for recovery of legal fees from client, Court ordered assessment to be carried out. Retainer not disputed as client had paid initial account in amount of $3,194 and was only disputing two subsequent bills. At assessment client could object to specific items not being authorized. No party had applied for assessment pursuant to *Solicitors Act*, R.S.O. 1990, c. S.15, but Court had inherent jurisdiction over solicitors as officers of court to refer matter to assessment. Order for assessment would permit justice between parties to be done as type of inquiry was one in which assessment officer was particularly qualified.

Korhani v. Bank of Montreal (2002), 2002 CarswellOnt 4223, [2002] O.J. No. 4785 (Ont. S.C.J.) — Claim against self-represented defendant dismissed as part of settlement of action by other parties. Defendant not employed and not entitled to compensation for her time spent, or that of husband who assisted her. However, defendant entitled to generous disbursements of $6,990 including fees paid to solicitors who assisted, travel costs for obtaining documents, and child care costs for attendance times, payable jointly by plaintiff and other defendant.

Schaer v. Barrie Yacht Club (2003), 2003 CarswellOnt 5233, 108 O.A.C. 95 (Ont. Div. Ct.); leave to appeal refused (2004), 2004 CarswellOnt 3007 (Ont. C.A.) Appeal of judgment of Deputy Judge in two Small Claims Court actions. "Vandalism Action." "Lien Action."

Trespass actionable without proof of damage.

Appellants argued trial judge erred pursuant to ss. 96, 97, 106, 107 of *The Courts of Justice Act* to stay the Small Claims Court proceedings until determination in action B2743 in the Superior Court. I disagree. That outstanding action, dealt with equitable relief not unavailable in the Small Claims Court. *Repair and Storage Liens Act* applied.

Respondents represented by counsel, accordingly, *Rule 19.04* of *The Small Claims Court Rules* applicable. Section 29 of *The Courts of Justice Act* cannot be used to circumvent the inapplicability of *Rule 19.05* to compensate the successful defendant at trial when there was no finding of unreasonable behaviour against the unsuccessful Plaintiff at trial.

Verchere v. Greenpeace Canada, 2003 CarswellBC 2539, 2003 BCSC 1571 (B.C. S.C.). Plaintiffs having sufficient reason to bring claim in Supreme Court. Appropriate to award Plaintiffs costs notwithstanding fact that judgment not exceeding $10,000.

1467736 Ontario Ltd. v. Galli (2003), 2003 CarswellOnt 4070, 48 C.B.R. (4th) 147 (Ont. Master). Plaintiff declared bankrupt. Plaintiff's claim vested in trustee. No Order to continue applied for. Defendant argued entire action was stayed not just that of bankrupt Plaintiff. Motion for stay allowed. Wording of Rule 11 of *Rules of Civil Procedure* (Ont.) clear.

Williams v. Babb (July 11, 2003), Doc. St. J. 2541/98, 2542/98 (N.L. T.D.), Master, Sinclair. Plaintiff argued Babb not entitled to allowance for personal time as self-represented litigant. Self-represented lay-litigant was not entitled to allowance for any amount in nature of counsel fees. Trial judge's discretionary authority did not extend to granting such allowance. Court was bound by doctrine of *stare decisis*.

Belanger v. McGrade Estate (2003), [2003] O.J. No. 2853, 2003 CarswellOnt 2682, (sub nom. *McGrade Estate, Re)* 65 O.R. (3d) 829 (Ont. S.C.J.). Superior Court Judge has jurisdiction to hear appeal of contempt finding and punishment made by another Superior Court Judge. The grammatical and ordinary sense of *Rule 57.07(1)* did not require proof of bad faith on part of lawyer before he was ordered to pay costs personally.

Concrete Restorations Ltd. v. 784169 Alberta Ltd., 2003 CarswellAlta 786, 37 C.P.C. (5th) 225, 345 A.R. 387, 2003 ABPC 99 (Alta. Prov. Ct.). Registered office of corporation was residential address, having community postal box. Postal service delivered notification of registered mail to box, but corporation failed to claim mail. Default judgment not set aside.

Schaffran v. Alseaidy (2003), 2003 CarswellOnt 1571 (Ont. Div. Ct.). Claim sent by registered mail, signed for, but later returned to sender as unknown. Business address shared by unrelated corporations. Defendant's evidence that signatory was not employee or known to it was uncontested. Default judgment set aside for lack of proper service.

Bains v. Mattu, 2002 CarswellBC 2397, 2002 BCSC 1437 (B.C. S.C.). Plaintiff succeeded on claim on loan for $15,000 and defendant succeeded on claim for $6,250 on promissory note. Transactions found to be separate. Two separate judgments should issue, and claim of Plaintiff should be reduced to $10,000 monetary jurisdiction limit *before* set-off of claim of Defendant.

Guindon v. Ontario (Minister of Natural Resources), 2006 CarswellOnt 3173, 212 O.A.C. 207 (Ont. Div. Ct.).

Divisional Court rejected applicant's assertion that no costs be awarded given the public interest nature of the litigation. Applicants had not acted solely as public interest litigants. Nevertheless, the amount fixed should be fair and reasonable and within applicants' reasonable expectations.

Dunbar v. Helicon Properties Ltd., 2006 CarswellOnt 4580, [2006] O.J. No. 2992, 213 O.A.C. 296 (Ont. Div. Ct.).

Appellants argued that because monetary jurisdiction of Small Claims Court is $10,000, trial judge should have deducted the amounts set off in their favour from amount instead of the total damages alleged by respondent, an amount over $15,000. Trial judge awarded the respondent $10,000, which complied with the applicable regulation: see O. Reg. 626/00.

Appellants argued $500 costs award exceeded maximum provided for by way of counsel fee pursuant to R. 19.04 by $200. However, this provision has been interpreted as a daily counsel fee award: see *Bird v. Ireland*, 2005 CarswellOnt 6945, [2005] O.J. No. 5125, 205 O.A.C. 1 (Ont. Div. Ct.).

Pierlot Family Farm Ltd. v. Polstra, 2006 CarswellPEI 27, 2006 PESCAD 13, 271 D.L.R. (4th) 525, 766 A.P.R. 169, 257 Nfld. & P.E.I.R. 169 (P.E.I. C.A.).

Plaintiff, a self-represented litigant, was successful at trial. The defendant appealed unsuccessfully. Plaintiff awarded partial indemnity costs. He submitted a bill of costs in excess of $14,000. Plaintiff entitled to recover costs of $800, plus disbursements.

Costs should only be awarded to self-represented lay litigants who can demonstrate that they devoted time and effort to do the work ordinarily done by a lawyer retained to conduct the litigation, and that as a result, they incurred an opportunity cost by foregoing remunerative activity. GST and PST were not included. Plaintiff entitled to recover costs of $800, based on 40 hours at a rate of $20 per hour.

Costs are now accepted as payable to a lay litigant (see *Prince Edward Island (Attorney General) v. Ayangma*, 2004 CarswellPEI 85, (sub nom. *Ayangma v. Prince Edward Island (Attorney General)*) 242 Nfld. & P.E.I.R. 77, (sub nom. *Ayangma v. Prince Edward Island (Attorney General)*) 719 A.P.R. 77, 4 C.P.C. (6th) 66, 2004 PESCAD 22 (P.E.I. C.A.); *Fong v. Chan* (1999), 46 O.R. (3d) 330, 1999 CarswellOnt 3955, [1999] O.J. No. 4600, 181 D.L.R. (4th) 614, 128 O.A.C. 2 (Ont. C.A.)).

Kennedy v. Kiss, [2006] B.C.J. No. 404, 2006 CarswellBC 453, 54 B.C.L.R. (4th) 151, 2006 BCSC 296 (B.C. S.C.), February 21, 2006, Williams J.

Plaintiff self-represented lawyer in fast-track personal injury litigation. Plaintiff made offer to settle in amount of $26,000 in July 2005. Plaintiff recovered judgment at trial in October 2005 in amount of $30,007.64. Parties made submissions on costs. Plaintiff awarded double costs capped at $7,200. As self-represented lawyer, plaintiff was entitled to costs. As well, plaintiff did bring counsel to lead his evidence and that was substantial component of evidence. Trial almost one-and-one-half days and should be treated as two-day trial for purpose of assessing costs.

Caselaw supports contention that self-represented lawyers may be awarded costs: *London Scottish Benefit Society v. Chorley* (1884), 13 Q.B.D. 872, [1881-1885] All E.R. 1111, 53 L.J.Q.B. 551, 51 L.T. 100, (sub nom. *London Permanent Building Society v. Thorley*) 32 W.R. 781 (Eng. C.A.). See *Fong v. Chan* (1999), 46 O.R. (3d) 330, 1999 CarswellOnt 3955, [1999] O.J. No. 4600, 181 D.L.R. (4th) 614, 128 O.A.C. 2 (Ont. C.A.).

Phillips v. Cedar Springs Motorsports Ltd., 2006 CarswellOnt 8899, [2006] O.J. No. 5505 (Ont. S.C.J.); additional reasons to 2006 CarswellOnt 5609 (Ont. S.C.J.), D.J. Lange D.J.

Plaintiff awarded costs of $1,500 and A Inc. awarded costs of $500. Rule 19.04(1) of *Small Claims Court Rules* regarding representation fee applied even though trial took place just three weeks after new rules came into force. Section 29 of *Courts of Justice Act* limited amount recoverable in costs to no more than 15 per cent of amount claimed. Trial lengthy by Small Claims Court standards and had legal issues of some complexity which were important to all parties.

King v. K-W Homes Ltd., 2006 CarswellOnt 8358 (Ont. S.C.J.); additional reasons to 2006 CarswellOnt 6834 (Ont. Sm. Cl. Ct.), N.B. Pickell D.J.

Defendant represented by lawyer, C, with 17 years' litigation experience. After three-day trial, plaintiff's claim dismissed and defendant's claim allowed in amount of $4,964.99. Defendant awarded costs of $2,600, legal representation fee of $2,400. $2,400 fair given amounts sought in both claims, relative success of parties, length of trial, C's experience, and fact that C's cross-examination of plaintiff was necessary to bring out all facts. Representation fee not subject to $300 limit under r. 19.04 of *Rules of Small Claims Court* as it existed before amendment. Amendment to r. 19.04 removing $300 limit became effective July 1, 2006, which was after two days of evidence but before last day of trial. New Rules applied as of July 1, 2006 regardless of whether action was commenced prior to that date. Defendant also awarded $125 for disbursements and $75 for preparation and filing of pleadings.

CT Comm Edmonton Ltd. v. Shaw Communications Inc., 2007 CarswellAlta 937, 2007 ABQB 473, 423 A.R. 338 (Alta. Q.B.); additional reasons at 2007 CarswellAlta 971, 2007 ABQB 482 (Alta. Q.B.)

Defendants to action by self-represented company awarded party and party costs for each of three applications in which defendants largely succeeded. Defendants should not to bear costs of unnecessary applications due to failure of plaintiff to retain counsel. A trial judge have a duty to provide basic information to unrepresented litigants, but must be careful not to allow assistance given to effect its duty to provide both parties equally with fair hearing.

R. v. Moran (2008), 2008 CarswellOnt 3404, 69 M.V.R. (5th) 228 (Ont. S.C.J.)

Defendant appealed his conviction on the basis trial judge erred in law by denying standing to his representative, an articled student-at-law. Furthermore, the defendant asserted that he was effectively denied the opportunity to be heard on the merits of his application which gave rise to a reasonable apprehension of bias. Appeal allowed.

The decision to deny standing to the appellant's representative, an articled student-at-law, was in error as an articled student-at-law had a prima facie right to appear at a summary conviction trial. The inquiry should be limited to whether the defendant was making an informed choice to be represented by a student.

The trial judge's statement that the Crown's factum was correct in law and application would be dismissed subject to anything new being raised considered as denial the natural justice to the defendant. This raised a reasonable apprehension of bias.

Transport Training Centres of Canada v. Wilson, 2010 ONSC 2099, 2010 CarswellOnt 2155, (sub nom. *Wilson v. Transport Training Centres of Canada*) 261 O.A.C. 301 (Ont. Div. Ct.); additional reasons at 2010 ONSC 2714, 2010 CarswellOnt 3549, (sub nom. *Wilson v. Transport Training Centres of Canada*) 263 O.A.C. 226 (Ont. Div. Ct.).

The trial judge awarded employee $7,000 in general damages for undue mental distress instead of claimed amount of $1,000, amending her statement of claim accordingly, and fixing her costs at $1,500. The employer appealed. Appeal allowed. The trial judge erred in awarding damages to employee. Interaction of r. 19.04(2) of *Small Claims Court Rules* and section 29 of *Courts of Justice Act* meant that award of costs with respect to employee's agent could not exceed half of statutory maximum of 15 percent of amount claimed. No evidence of unreasonable behaviour by employer, so as to justify under section 29 of *Act* amount exceeding statutory maximum amount. Costs award exceeded trial judge's discretion and was set aside.

Vigna v. Levant, 2011 CarswellOnt 357, 2011 ONSC 629, 2011 CarswellOnt 2592 (Ont. S.C.J.)

Factors to be considered when fixing costs set out in r. 57 of the *Rules of Civil Procedure* and include, in addition to success, the amount claimed and recovered, the complexity and importance of the matter and the principle of proportionality, the conduct of any party which unduly lengthened the proceeding, whether any step was improper, vexatious or unnecessary, or taken through negligence, mistake or excessive caution, a party's denial or refusal to admit anything, any offer to settle, the principle of indemnity, scale of costs, hourly rate claimed in relation to the partial indemnity rate set out in the Information to the Profession effective July 1, 2005, the time spent, and the amount that a losing party would reasonably expect to pay.

The plaintiff claims substantial indemnity costs for the law firm of Heenan Blaikie of $26,434.54. The plaintiff claims substantial indemnity fees in the amount of $68,250 for himself as a self-represented lawyer.

Vigna is a lawyer who was called to the Bar of Québec in 1992. Vigna is not engaged in private practice and has no overhead expenses.

In *Fong v. Chan*, 1999 CarswellOnt 3955, [1999] O.J. No. 4600, 46 O.R. (3d) 330, 181 D.L.R. (4th) 614, 128 O.A.C. 2 (Ont. C.A.), the court held that the issue the right to recover award costs to a self-represented litigant remains within the discretion of the trial judge. The Court of Appeal held that self-represented litigants, whether legally trained or not, are not entitled to costs on the same basis as those of a litigant retaining private counsel. Losing party would reasonably expect to pay the sum of $30,000 plus disbursement in costs.

Ernst v. Royal Mutual Funds Inc., 2011 CarswellOnt 15933, 80 E.T.R. (3d) 39 (Ont. S.C.J.) The successful defendant's representation fee for this one-day trial was fixed at $1,500. The primary costs rules, apart from rule 14.07, are the items in Rule 19. Once costs are fixed, the result must be measured against the *prima facie* limit under *Courts of Justice Act* s. 29 to determine if the award would exceed that limit and if so, whether a penalty costs order is warranted.

19.05 Compensation for Inconvenience and Expense — The court may order an unsuccessful party to pay to a successful party who is self-represented an amount not exceeding $500 as compensation for inconvenience and expense.

O. Reg. 78/06, s. 39; 440/10, s. 5

History [R. 19.05]: Formerly 20.04, restructured for clarity.

Case Law: *Trudel v. Virta*, [1972] 2 O.R. 761 (Ont. Dist. Ct.) — Costs are limited to disbursements established by the tariff and to costs allowed under other provisions of the Small Claims Courts Act.

DeCorte v. Methot (1981), 11 A.C.W.S. (2d) 101 (Ont. Sm. Cl. Ct.) — There is no provision in the *Small Claims Courts Act* to award costs on a motion for a Contempt of Court order. See also *Trudel v. Virta, supra*, and *Breen v. Corkum, infra*.

Breen v. Corkum, [1973] 3 O.R. 660 (Ont. C.A.) — A student-at-law is not a "counsel" within the meaning of this section. Section amended subsequent to decision.

Apparel Original Ltd. v. Falus (1980), 23 C.P.C. 49 (Ont. Sm. Cl. Ct.) — County Court action for less than $1,000 commenced September 1976. Transferred to the Provincial Court (Civil Division) July 1980, Prejudgment interest as of November 25, 1977. Costs awarded pursuant to Rule 64. Note, cf. with section 38 of the *Judicature Amendment Act, 1977*, S.O. 1977, c. 51, s. 3(1), (2).

Re Lachowski and Federated Mut. Ins. Co. (1980), 29 O.R. (2d) 273 (Ont. Div. Ct.) — "Trial judge awarded $200 by way of costs. Any award of costs must be based upon the provisions of the *Small Claims Court Act* and the Tariff of that Court. Examples of the types of costs which may be awarded as conditions of adjournments (see also Section 94) are the costs of transportation, babysitters and reimbursement for loss of pay", per Cory J.

Fanaken v. Bell, Temple (1985), 49 C.P.C. 212 (Ont. Assess. Ct.) — A law firm recovered costs after successfully defending (after appeals to the Divisions Court and Court of Appeal) an action for damages by a former clerk dismissed by the firm. Where a law firm defends itself through the use of an employee or partner, no counsel fee should be allowed on assessment of costs. The member of the firm who appears on its behalf is not in court as counsel but as litigant, in the assessment of counsel fees the money must be disbursed in payment of the fees as a condition precedent. A barrister, who is also a litigant or part of the litigant, cannot pay money or be liable to himself.

Lamont v. Nieuwenhuis (1988), 12 W.D.C.P. 23 (Ont. Prov. Ct.) — A plaintiff's action for malicious prosecution was dismissed with costs to the defendant. The defendant was awarded $200 and costs of subpoenas for inconvenience and expense. As well, the proceedings were unduly complicated or lengthened by the plaintiff.

Fossil Fuel Development Ltd. v. Tudex Petroleum Ltd. (1987), 6 A.C.W.S. (3d) 66 (Sask. C.A.) — Costs are, of course, discretionary and, barring the unusual, they follow the event. Even though the counterclaim, which was dismissed, occupied a secondary position at trial, the trial judge should have granted costs with respect to the counterclaim.

Caringi v. Porco (1989), 17 W.D.C.P. 21 (Ont. Prov. Ct.) — The defendant was awarded $450 with respect to the costs of an expert although not provided for in the Rules. However, analogy was made to the Tariff under the Provincial Court (Family Division) Rules, Tariff Part II, Items 19, 20 and 22.

Khokhar v. Blackburn (1994), 20 C.P.C. (3d) 313 (Alta. Q.B.) — An appeal Court could award costs to successful unrepresented litigant for time and effort expended in preparation for and arguing appeal. Costs were not compensation for respondent's lost wages.

Maza Electric Ltd. v. Metropolitan Toronto Housing Co. (1994), 47 A.C.W.S. (3d) 1163 (Ont. Gen. Div.) — The plaintiff recovered $4,250 plus interest of $1,155. Costs should not be on the Small Claims Court's scale since the construction lien remedy was not available in that court and it did not prolong the trial. It was appropriate to consider the amount recovered and the fact that the defendant made no offer to pay holdback. Since the amount recovered was about one-half of $10,000, the fees of $2,650 claimed were reduced to $850 and the counsel fees were reduced from $6,875 to $2,250. Considering the amount recovered it would have been foolish to allow amount claimed for counsel fee without reduction.

Agricultural Credit Corp. of Saskatchewan v. Crush, [1991] 5 W.W.R. 221, 2 C.P.C. (3d) 183, 96 Sask. R. 248 (Q.B.) — The plaintiff abandoned a frivolous motion. Since costs may be used to deter frivolous actions, the unrepresented defendant is entitled to costs. Such circumstances are an exception to the principle that costs are for indemnification.

Vance v. Regina Motor Products (1970) Ltd. (1990), 87 Sask. R. 59 (Sask. Q.B.) — The plaintiff sued to recover in the Court of Queen's Bench. The plaintiff was awarded $500 and should have sued in the Small Claims Court. Costs were awarded in any event at the Queen's Bench level.

San Francisco Pizza Ltd. v. Granata (1995), 6 W.D.C.P. (2d) 245 (Ont. Gen. Div.) — Request for cost award against solicitor personally dismissed where Court found solicitor did not act outside his client's authority or that his conduct was outrageous.

Fuss v. Fidelity Electronics of Canada Ltd. (1996), 7 W.D.C.P. (2d) 66 (Ont. Gen. Div.) — The Court found that there was no basis for allowing a party, who was a solicitor, costs on his own time and preparation when the personal preparation costs were denied to all other non-solicitor litigants. A barrister-litigant who acted as his/her own counsel could not recover a counsel fee any more than a lay person who pleaded his/her own cause. The Court also found that although the defendant's counsel had conferred from time to time with the defendant during the course of argument, the defendant did not materially participate in argument on the motion.

Pachini v. Pietramala, 1995 CarswellBC 294, 7 B.C.L.R. (3d) 266, 38 C.P.C. (3d) 122, 54 A.C.W.S. (3d) 19 (B.C. S.C.) — Plaintiff entitled to costs at Supreme Court level even though recovery at Small Claims Court level. Onus on plaintiff satisfied that it was reasonable and that there was sufficient cause to continue in Supreme Court after discoveries.

32262 B.C. Ltd. v. 271617 B.C. Ltd., [1995] B.C.W.L.D. 1674 (B.C. S.C.) — Plaintiff brought motion for summary judgment. Defendant brought two motions. Judgment awarded but court did *not* award costs, commenting that judgment could have been obtained and maybe more cheaply in the Small Claims Court.

Mohsen v. Watson, 1995 CarswellOnt 2198 (Ont. Gen. Div.) — Plaintiff recovered $1,600 at trial where original claim was $13,587.97. Plaintiff awarded one-half party and party costs fixed at $5,061.45. Defendant made no offer to settle and neither party applied to transfer case to Small Claims Court. Rule 57.05(1) of *Rules of Civil Procedure* applied.

Purcell v. Taylor (1994), 120 D.L.R. (4th) 161 (Ont. Gen. Div.) — Monetary recovery of $2,500 within jurisdiction of Small Claims Court, trial in General Division. Rule 57.05(1) of *Rules of Civil Procedure* did not apply re default judgment against dog owner, costs assessed pursuant to Rule 57.05(3) and Small Claims Court tariff. Successful defendant home owner awarded costs of $2,000. Plaintiff should have transferred case down to Small Claims Court.

Stewart v. Manitoba Opera Assn. Inc. (1995), 104 Man. R. (2d) 159 (Q.B.) — Amount awarded at trial in Queen's Bench within jurisdiciton of Small Claims Court. Court awarded costs of $1,500, not $100 set out in Small Claims tariff. Discoveries had been held prior to trial.

32262 B.C. Ltd. v. Trans Western Express Inc. (1995), 38 C.P.C. (3d) 201 (B.C. S.C.) — Section 13 of the *Small Claims Act* (B.C.) allowed the Supreme Court of British Columbia to award costs to any party to an appeal, in accordance with the rules of court. A party who failed on an appeal should be subject to an award of costs from the appeal. A defendant who succeeded on an appeal had a moral claim to costs of the appeal, having been brought into litigation at the instance of the plaintiff. A plaintiff who has rightly chosen the Provincial Court as the proper forum for his claim but has been denied victory wrongly should, succeeding on appeal, ordinarily be entitled to an award of costs. That general rule was subject to the recognized exception where the case was won in the Supreme Court on the basis of evidence or a submission not presented in the Provincial Court.

Perret v. Pappas (1995), 13 B.C.L.R. (3d) 166 (Master) — The plaintiff sued for damages. After pleadings were filed, documents exchanged, discovery completed and motion heard, the plaintiff applied successfully to transfer action to Provincial Court-Small Claims Division. The defendant applied for costs of proceedings in the Supreme Court. The plaintiff had availed himself of procedures, such as examinations for discovery, not available in the Provincial Court. Defendant entitled to costs, including disbursements of $1,800.

Yee v. Tight Spot Rentals Ltd. (1995), 11 B.C.L.R. (3d) 291 (S.C.) — The plaintiff sued for damages for a mild injury. Despite liability being clear, the defendants disputed it and delivered a notice requiring trial by jury. Plaintiff awarded non-pecuniary damages of $1,000. The defendants applied for an order limiting the costs recoverable by the plaintiff to those available in the Provincial Court-Small Claims Division. The application was dismissed on the basis that the plaintiff was prevented from transferring his action to the Provincial Court by the defendants' insistence on a jury trial. The view that costs are awarded solely to indemnify a successful litigant for legal fees and disbursements is outdated.

Manufacturer's Life v. Molyneux (January 9, 1995), Doc. 868/94 (Ont. Div. Ct.) — Application pursuant to s. 114 of the *Landlord and Tenant Act* dismissed. Successful landlord, respondent on appeal represented by agent. Costs awarded in the sum of $250. See also *Bonshaw-Estates Inc. and Indrakumaran et al.*, unreported, File No. 421/92 where agent awarded $750 in costs (Ont. Div. Ct.).

Guest v. Sailaway Enterprises Ltd. (1996), 78 B.C.A.C. 187, 128 W.A.C. 187 (C.A.) — Costs of $5,300 awarded by trial judge to self-represented lay litigants upheld on appeal.

Gunning Estate v. Abrams (February 21, 1997), Doc. 642/95, 643/95 (Ont. Div. Ct.) — It is appropriate to award costs to a self-represented litigant who is a lawyer. Rate fixed at $90 per hour. Costs fixed at $360.

Day v. Wilson (1996), 4 C.P.C. (4th) 251 (B.C. Master) — The plaintiff commenced an action in Supreme Court. The defendant issued a notice of trial and jury notice. To settle the issue of costs before the matter was heard would require a determination as to whether the plaintiff had sufficient reasons to commence the action in Supreme Court. The defendant was entitled to the costs thrown away in setting the matter down for trial in any event of the cause.

Phosy v. Island Pacific Transport Ltd. (May 2, 1996), Doc. Victoria 95/1123 (B.C. S.C.) — The plaintiff's action arose out of a minor collision. They were awarded $4,200 and $7,300 respectively, for whiplash-type injuries. The defendant applied for an order that the plaintiffs' costs be limited to disbursements only, on the ground that they should have sued in Provincial Court. The action arose out of one transaction. An amount greater than the Provincial Court limit was awarded. In the circumstances, the plaintiffs were entitled to one set of costs at the usual scale.

Owen Bird v. Nanaimo Shipyards Ltd., 1996 CarswellBC 2742 (B.C. S.C.) — The Provincial Court did not have jurisdiction to make an award of costs arising out of the Supreme Court action, although it did have jurisdiction to award damages for breach of contract. However, it was the litigation from which the legal expenses flowed, and not the breach of contract of retainer. The claim made in the Provincial Court as damages could not be characterized as damages but rather was for costs of the litigation in the Supreme Court and the Provincial Court, acted without jurisdiction.

Myers v. Metropolitan Toronto (Municipality) Police Force, 1995 CarswellOnt 152, [1995] O.J. No. 1321, 37 C.P.C. (3d) 349, (sub nom. *Myers v. Metropolitan Toronto (Municipality) Chief of Police*) 125 D.L.R. (4th) 184, (sub nom. *Myers v. Metropolitan Toronto Chief of Police*) 84 O.A.C. 232 (Ont. Div. Ct.) — The plaintiff moved to amend the statement of claim. The motion was granted on terms that the plaintiff pay costs of $9,000 within 15 days, failing which the action was to be dismissed. The judge was aware of the plaintiff's impecuniosity at the time of making the order. The plaintiff appealed that portion of the order which dismissed the action for failure to pay costs within 15 days. The general rule is that costs are in the discretion of the court. It is important to avoid a situation in which litigants without means can ignore the rules of the court with impunity and it is distasteful to create a rule which is incapable of consistent application.

Abrams v. Wentworth Condominium Corp. No. 93 (1997), 103 O.A.C. 388 (Ont. Div. Ct.); additional reasons at (1997), 103 O.A.C. 395 (Ont. Div. Ct.) — Appeal from Deputy Judge's award of $745.18. Judgment of appeal greater than original award. Court has discretion to deprive a successful party of costs "in a proper case" under Rule 57.01(2). Appellant Abrams awarded $1,500 for costs relating to preparation, attendance at appeal and written submissions and all out-of-pocket expenses of $1,200.45.

Saxton v. Aloha Pools Ltd. (July 6, 1998), Doc. Vancouver A970668 (B.C. S.C. [In Chambers]); was additional reasons to (1998), 47 B.C.L.R. (3d) 51 (B.C. S.C.) — Issue whether appellant should pay costs. Appellant was sued in Small Claims Court and lost. She appealed to the Supreme Court of British Columbia and lost her appeal. Justice Fraser in *32262 B.C. Ltd. v. Trans Western Express Inc.* (1995), 38 C.P.C. (3d) 201 (B.C. S.C.) stated at 203: "A plaintiff or defendant who has been unsuccessful in the Small Claims Division and who unsuccessfully appeals should be subject to an award of costs from the appeal ... [A]ppellant may be seen as having used up at the initial level the generosity of the system." Appellant required to pay costs.

Church v. Myers (August 6, 1998), Doc. Vancouver B971219 (B.C. S.C.); varying (July 22, 1998), Doc. Vancouver B971219 (B.C. S.C.) — A plaintiff who recovers a sum within the jurisdiction of the Provincial Court under the *Small Claims Act* is not entitled to costs, other than disbursements, unless the court finds that there was sufficient reason for bringing the proceedings in the Supreme Court and so orders (B.C. Reg. 221/90, Rule 57(10)). In cases of personal injury, a plaintiff will not necessarily know that the damage award will be $10,000 or less, particularly when the claim is for an amount greater than $10,000. There was sufficient reason for the plaintiff in her claim for damages for personal injury to bring the proceedings in Supreme Court. No reason to deprive the plaintiff of costs.

Peacock v. Choi (June 16, 1998), Doc. 54/98 (Ont. Gen. Div.) — Small Claims Court appeal allowed to extent of reducing costs from $1500 to $960. There was no support found for increasing costs in consequence of any misconduct envisaged by wording of s. 29 of the *Courts of Justice Act*, R.S.O. 1990, c. C.43. Interpretive approach set forth in such cases as *Trudel v. Virta*, [1972] 2 O.R. 761 (Ont. Dist. Ct.), *Lachowski v. Federated Mutual Insurance Co.* (1980), 29 O.R. (2d) 273 (Ont. Div. Ct.) and *Miller v. York Downs Craft & Garden Centre Ltd.* (1987), 17 C.P.C. 142 (Ont. Prov. Ct.) ought to apply. Section 25 of the *Courts of Justice Act* should not be read to provide open door for free exercise of discretion. Rule 18.02 (now Rule 17.02, O. Reg 258/98) of the Rules of The Small Claims Court does not provide authority to grant costs, but rather to deal in monetary terms with "compensation for inconvenience and expense", a phrase used in that rule and also Rule 20.04 (now Rule 19.04, O. Reg. 258/98), to deal with expenses as opposed to costs.

Barke v. Calgary (City) (August 31, 1998), Doc. Calgary 9301-20045 (Alta. Q.B.) — The plaintiff argued that he should receive costs from August 1995, even though he was an unrepresented litigant. He argued that costs should be used as a sword to punish the defendant. The defendant argued it should receive costs from its offer. Costs were awarded to the plaintiff. The Court awarded costs of $500 to indemnify plaintiff for vacation time he used up during trial.

Marcjan v. Ma (December 29, 1998), Doc. Vancouver B964311 (B.C. S.C.) — The plaintiff was awarded $500 by a jury. The defendants wasted costs at trial. The plaintiff had a lawyer until a short time before trial, which he conducted himself. The plaintiff was person of little means and was 75 years old. The defendant made no offer to settle. It would create injustice to award the defendants their costs; that would completely dwarf the meager award obtained by the plaintiff. It was not patently evident that a lawsuit should not have been started, and the method of trial was dictated by the defendants who chose a jury trial.

Petten v. E.Y.E. Marine Consultants, a division of CSE Marine Services Inc. (1998), 180 Nfld. & P.E.I.R. 1, 548 A.P.R. 1 (Nfld. T.D.) — The individual plaintiffs who were largely successful at trial, but were unrepresented for parts due to financial and other constraints, were entitled to party-and-party costs for portions where they were represented. The corporate plaintiff could not claim costs to extend that it was unrepresented and its costs were also limited to periods in trial when counsel appeared.

Pritchard v. Fitchett (April 29, 1999), Doc. 12905/92, 12905C/98 (Ont. S.C.J.) — The lay litigant was awarded $1,200 plus disbursements in representing himself, his son, and his companies. Costs were in discretion of the court to be assessed in accordance with tariffs under Rule 58 of Ontario's *Rules of Civil Procedure*.

Churchland v. Gore Mutual Insurance Co. (September 23, 1999), Doc. New Westminster S0-9912 (B.C. S.C.) — The plaintiff was unsuccessful at trial. The plaintiff claimed that costs should not follow event, on grounds of hardship and relative economic strength. Sympathy and financial hardship were not sufficient grounds. The general rule should apply.

Kelley v. R., [1999] 4 C.T.C. 2274, 99 D.T.C. 1018 (T.C.C. [General Procedure]) — Party-and-party costs are to be those that are essential for the conduct of the proceeding. No evidence was presented to explain why transcript was necessary. Expense was disallowed. The respondent sought to recover for hotel bills for witnesses at rate of $81 per night. Hotel rates were not exorbitant; amount claimed allowed.

The court allowed reasonably incurred costs for expert witnesses, including the costs of travel, accommodation, and meals, and reasonable fees for investigation, reporting, and assisting counsel with their evidence and the evidence of others: *Ligate v. Abick* (1992), 2 C.P.C. (3d) 216, 8 O.R. (3d) 49 (Ont. Gen. Div.); additional reasons to (1991), 2 C.P.C. (3d)

209, [1992] G.S.T.C. 4, 5 O.R. (3d) 332, 5 T.C.T. 4067 (Ont. Gen. Div.); further additional reasons to (July 3, 1991), Doc. Thunder Bay 1093/87 (Ont. Gen. Div.); affirmed on other grounds 28 O.R. (3d) 1, 89 O.A.C. 355, 134 D.L.R. (4th) 538, 20 M.V.R. (3d) 75, [1996] G.S.T.C. 30, 4 G.T.C. 6131 (Ont. C.A.).

Johnson & Johnson Inc. v. Bristol-Myers Squibb Canada Inc. (1996), 71 C.P.R. (3d) 24 (Ont. Gen. Div.) — The court disallowed a photocopy expense where its description was not sufficiently clear to determine whether the charge was paid to an outside business or was an expense incurred within the defendant counsel's firm.

Grinshpun v. University of British Columbia (2000), 2000 CarswellNat 1942 (Fed. T.D.) — The self-represented plaintiff was unsuccessful in a copyright infringement action. The fact that the plaintiff included irrelevant matters relating to parallel dispute with defendant did not justify increased costs.

Nowak v. Nowak, 2000 BCSC 1243, 2000 CarswellBC 1708 (B.C. S.C.) — An unrepresented party was successful at trial. The Court ordered the plaintiff to "have costs of this action." The registrar could not go behind the order of the Court and question whether unrepresented party merited costs.

Nesbitt Aggregates Ltd. v. Smiths Construction Co. (Arnprior) Ltd. (2000), 36 C.E.L.R. (N.S.) 60, 2000 CarswellOnt 3177 (Ont. S.C.J.) — It is the discretion of the trial judge to fix costs where one party objects. An offer to settle is only one factor. Expert fees allowed, even though not called at trial. The issues were complex and the defence had to be prepared.

Simai v. University Health Network (2001), 2001 CarswellOnt 3106, 14 C.P.C. (5th) 320 (Ont. Master) — Plaintiff sought interim disbursements to file own expert report. Plaintiff failed to show grounds for order merely by being student and on legal aid. Motion dismissed.

To v. Toronto (City) Board of Education (2001), 55 O.R. (3d) 641, 2001 CarswellOnt 3048, 204 D.L.R. (4th) 704, 150 O.A.C. 54 (Ont. C.A.); additional reasons at (2001), 2001 CarswellOnt 3727 (Ont. C.A.) — Defendant's appeal from costs order allowed. Plaintiffs awarded party-and-party costs throughout subject to direction to assessment officer to assess solicitor-and-client costs for any time that trial extended because of defendant's failure to respond appropriately to request to admit.

McIntyre Estate v. Ontario (Attorney General), 2002 CarswellOnt 2880, [2002] O.J. No. 3417, 23 C.P.C. (5th) 59, 218 D.L.R. (4th) 193, 61 O.R. (3d) 257, 164 O.A.C. 37 (Ont. C.A.) — Declaration granted not contrary to public policy to enter into contingency fee agreement and that arrangement must be governed by principle of what is fair and reasonable to be determined at conclusion of action. Although lawyers' contingency fee agreements are not prohibited by Act, it must be determined whether the lawyer had improper motive in entering into allegedly champertous agreement. In assessing motive, consideration should be given to fairness and reasonableness of fee structure in contingency fee agreement.

Carleton Condominium Corp. No. 21 v. Minto Construction Ltd. (2002), 21 C.P.C. (5th) 308, 2002 CarswellOnt 1515, [2002] O.J. No. 948 (Ont. S.C.J.); additional reasons at (2002), 2002 CarswellOnt 1731 (Ont. S.C.J.) — In December 2001, trial judge allowed action and awarded damages to owner. In January 2002, new costs regime became effective. Amended Rule 57 changed type of costs available to plaintiff. New regime had substantial indemnity scale instead of solicitor and client scale. Applying new regime would have retroactive effect. Legislation contained no clear indication that retroactive effect was intended.

Clarke v. Scrannage, 21 C.P.C. (5th) 125, 2002 CarswellBC 1707, 2002 BCSC 1008, 40 C.C.L.I. (3d) 138 (B.C. S.C.) — Jury awarded plaintiff $1,350 for damages from motor vehicle accident and found plaintiff 10 per cent responsible for accident. Government insurer was third party and had made offer to settle action for $13,668.75. Upon motion for judgment, argument raised whether costs of plaintiff should be fixed at disbursements only pursuant to

Rule 57(10) of Rules of Court, 1990. For defendant or third party to be faced with paying 90 per cent of plaintiff's costs throughout whole of proceeding, including trial, would have been patently unfair.

Clarke, Re, 2002 CarswellBC 1335, 2002 BCSC 809, 35 C.B.R. (4th) 73 (B.C. S.C.) — Plaintiff suing employer for wrongful dismissal. Action dismissed and costs awarded in favour of employer. Plaintiff subsequently declaring bankruptcy. Employer seeking order that costs survive bankruptcy. Application dismissed. Award of costs not arising as a result of fraud.

Izzard v. Goldreich (2002), 2002 CarswellOnt 1533, 159 O.A.C. 365 (Ont. Div. Ct.); additional reasons at (2002), (sub nom. *Izzard v. Friedberg*) [2002] O.J. No. 2931, 2002 CarswellOnt 4780 (Ont. Div. Ct.) — Appeal from Mungovan J. (Small Claims Court), File No. T15616/99. Appeal dismissed. No unreasonable findings of fact. *Bryars Estate v. Toronto General Hospital* (1997), 152 D.L.R. (4th) 243, 1997 CarswellOnt 3269, 103 O.A.C. 53 (Ont. C.A.) referred to. Costs can be made to unrepresented party. *Fong v. Chan* (1999), 46 O.R. (3d) 330, 1999 CarswellOnt 3955, [1999] O.J. No. 4600, 181 D.L.R. (4th) 614, 128 O.A.C. 2 (Ont. C.A.) referred to.

Dickinson v. Brown Dryer Karol (April 10, 2002), Doc. No. 58801 (Ont. Div. Ct.), Lane J. — Appeal from Deputy, Small Claims Court, awarding respondent law firm full payment. Evidence of client and solicitor not equally balanced. *Gorin v. Flinn Merrick* (1994), 30 C.P.C. (3d) 260, 1994 CarswellNS 95, 131 N.S.R. (2d) 55, 371 A.P.R. 55 (N.S. S.C.) referred to.

Jeff (Guardian ad litem of) v. Kozak, 2002 BCSC 103, 2002 CarswellBC 108 (B.C. S.C.) — Issue of payment of disbursements, in particular expert's report, whether in fact an expert, unnecessary travel expenses, fee to "deliver protocols," courier and faxing expenses disallowed in part. Quicklaw Research disallowed.

Lunn v. Martin, 2003 SKPC 109, 2003 CarswellSask 497 (Sask. Prov. Ct.). The Plaintiffs allege the Defendant backed her vehicle into their vehicle causing damage. Plaintiffs' claim dismissed.

The Defendant filed a counterclaim for loss of income due to time spend in court and for preparation of case. The Defendant presented no evidence upon which the Plaintiffs could be found liable. The damages set out were in fact costs of appearing in court and did not fall within the costs allowed by section 31 of *The Small Claims Act*, 1997. Counterclaim also dismissed.

Kraft Canada Inc. v. 1319895 Ontario Inc. (2003), 2003 CarswellOnt 3510 (Ont. S.C.J.). Motion for Summary Judgment pursuant to Rule 76.07(9)(a) and (b) of the *Rules of Civil Procedure*. These Rules govern simplified procedure cases.

Plaintiff's claim against the personal Defendant allowed in the amount of $9,442.93, plus interest.

Assuming no Rule 49 offers, the Plaintiff entitled to costs $500. Court taking into account action should have been in Small Claims Court.

Lawrence v. Toronto Humane Society, 2005 CarswellOnt 3860 (Ont. S.C.J.), August 24, 2005, Speigel J.

New costs regime applied since costs award was post June 2005. Successful charitable Society made no offer to settle. No reason for substantial indemnity. Outcome was important to both litigants, but 85 hours of lawyers' time excessive. Considering also Rule 47.01 (Ont.) and principles of proportionality, costs fixed at $18,000 including disbursements and GST.

Pierlot Family Farm Ltd. v. Polstra, 2006 CarswellPEI 27, 2006 PESCAD 13, 271 D.L.R. (4th) 525, 766 A.P.R. 169, 257 Nfld. & P.E.I.R. 169 (P.E.I. C.A.).

Lay litigant entitled to costs taking into account only lost opportunity, not actual hours spent, and at lower rate than counsel. Costs of trial and appeal claimed at over $14,000. Some evidence was led at trial from which one could infer that litigant lost business income by reason of his involvement in acting as counsel. On partial indemnity basis, 40 hours of preparation reasonable, at $20 per hour, for total preparation fee of $800, plus disbursements, for total of $2,486.

Walker v. Ritchie, 2006 CarswellOnt 6185, 2006 CarswellOnt 6186, [2006] S.C.J. No. 45, 2006 SCC 45, 353 N.R. 265, 33 C.P.C. (6th) 1, 43 C.C.L.I. (4th) 161, 43 C.C.L.T. (3d) 1, 273 D.L.R. (4th) 240, 217 O.A.C. 374, [2006] 2 S.C.R. 428 (S.C.C.).

Counsel successfully representing impecunious plaintiffs in contested litigation. Plaintiffs awarded substantial indemnity costs. Trial judge awarding additional amount for risk premium. Risk premium set aside. See *Rules of Civil Procedure*, R.R.O. 1990, Reg. 194, rules 49, 57.01(1). Risk premiums and contingency fees payable by the plaintiff already encouraged counsel to take on cases of impecunious plaintiffs.

1465778 Ontario Inc. v. 1122077 Ontario Ltd., 2006 CarswellOnt 6582, [2006] O.J. No. 4248, 216 O.A.C. 339, 38 C.P.C. (6th) 1, 275 D.L.R. (4th) 321, 82 O.R. (3d) 757 (Ont. C.A.).

A lawyer who successfully represented party in appeal was entitled to modest costs as claimed, which, in this case, were substantially less than costs on partial-indemnity basis. Cost awards to *pro bono* lawyers would encourage more lawyers to volunteer their services, thus increasing access to justice but still ensuring that fear of costs sanction would guard against reckless litigation by some parties.

Ayangma v. Prince Edward Island (Human Rights Commission), 2005 CarswellPEI 58, 2005 PESCAD 23, 33 Admin. L.R. (4th) 204 (P.E.I. C.A.).

Board ordered to pay costs to appellant. Appellant was lay litigant seeking $21,868 as disbursements related to application and appeal. Respondent sought to have costs disallowed. Costs awarded at trial were $1,000. Court noted in decision that grounds raised by appellant dealt with in other proceedings, some grounds not supported by facts and some grounds dealt with previously decided matters. Respondent was ordered to pay $2,000 as disbursements for legal fees for application and $2,000 for appeal plus GST and PST on fees. Attendance fees claimed not allowed because there was no evidence of loss of income. Disbursements for travel from Halifax allowed. Disbursements for photocopying and binding allowed at 40 per cent. Prejudgment interest not allowed. Total costs were $6,241.

National Bank Financial Ltd. v. Potter, 2005 CarswellNS 418, 237 N.S.R. (2d) 48, 754 A.P.R. 48, 2005 NSSC 264, 17 C.P.C. (6th) 84 (N.S. S.C.).

Successful unrepresented litigant entitled to costs but not at same rate as litigant who has retained solicitor. Award represented substantial partial indemnity and took into account unique circumstances of case. DP carried substantial portion of load in filing briefs, submissions, examination and cross-examination of witnesses. Issues complex and went to very essence of proper administration of justice.

St. James' Preservation Society v. Toronto (City), 2006 CarswellOnt 4103, [2006] O.J. No. 2726, 24 M.P.L.R. (4th) 226, 272 D.L.R. (4th) 149 (Ont. S.C.J.), T. Ducharme J.

Applicant was not entitled to costs, since it was unsuccessful save in minor respects. This was a case in which costs should be awarded against a non-party, namely two of the applicant's directors in addition to the applicant.

Park v. Perrier, 2006 CarswellOnt 5525, 35 C.P.C. (6th) 209 (Ont. Div. Ct.).

Unrepresented client appealed unsuccessfully from officer's report. Client successfully appealed to Superior Court of Justice. Court found officer had no jurisdiction to proceed where there was conflict respecting evidence concerning retainer which required findings of credibility in order to resolve. Client not entitled to recover vast majority of sums claimed, in particular claims for cash advances, pocket money, labour charges, fees for attendance at court, and interest on everything claimed at rate of 19.5 per cent.

Philipps c. Canada (Bibliothécaire & archiviste), 2007 CarswellNat 3100, 2007 CarswellNat 1377, 2007 FC 526, 2007 CF 526 (F.C.), Perrier Assess. O.

Plaintiff, self represented, filed bill of costs in amount of $2,276.15. Plaintiff entitled to costs in amount of $397.01. Self-represented party not permitted counsel fee. Plaintiff not entitled to transportation, parking, office supplies or meals because these were ordinary expenses incurred in litigation. Plaintiff was awarded photocopy costs, filing fees.

Veysey v. Ontario (Superintendent of Maplehurst Correctional Complex) (2007), 2007 CarswellOnt 361, 220 O.A.C. 96 (Ont. Div. Ct.).

The Ontario Divisional Court ordered that the parties bear their own costs. Awarding costs against the inmate would be a "brutal deterrent" to future inmates seeking to protect or further inmates' rights in Ontario. Voluntary reduction by the institution did not matter. Even $7,000 meant that prisoners were not welcome. It was not in the public interest to create such a barrier to justice for some of the community's most unfortunate members. Where, as here, litigation by such a citizen raised bona fide issues of law or procedural fairness of importance to the community, it was appropriate to exercise discretion respecting costs. See also, *Canadian Foundation for Children, Youth & the Law v. Canada (Attorney General)*, 2004 CarswellOnt 252, 2004 CarswellOnt 253, [2004] S.C.J. No. 6, REJB 2004-53164, 2004 SCC 4, 315 N.R. 201, 183 O.A.C. 1, 70 O.R. (3d) 94 (note), (sub nom. *Canadian Foundation for Children v. Canada)* [2004] 1 S.C.R. 76, 115 C.R.R. (2d) 88, 16 C.R. (6th) 203, 46 R.F.L. (5th) 1, 234 D.L.R. (4th) 257, 180 C.C.C. (3d) 353 (S.C.C.).

Braithwaite v. Duncan Summer Swim Club, 2008 CarswellBC 487, 2008 BCPC 68, [2008] B.C.J. No. 442 (B.C. Prov. Ct.)

Mr. Braithwaite, who was not party but witness for claimant and main instigator and promoter of vexatious action, was ordered under R. 20(6) to pay defendants' disbursements. Notwithstanding that claimant was not instigator of action, penalty was warranted since action should not have been started.

Provincial Court of British Columbia held that "the justice system must not be employed solely to create stress, inconvenience or unnecessary expense. Those who ignore this caution do so at their peril and, where they persist even in the face of warnings, they must be prepared to compensate those from whom they seek to extract concessions, financial or otherwise."

Geremia v. Harb (2008), 2008 CarswellOnt 2483, 90 O.R. (3d) 185, [2008] O.J. No. 1716, 54 R.F.L. (6th) 274 (Ont. S.C.J.)

Self-represented lay litigants may be awarded costs and such costs may include allowances for counsel fees. A self-represented litigant does not have "an automatic right to recover costs. The matter remains fully within the discretion of the trial judge." Self represented litigants, be they legally trained or not, are not entitled to costs calculated on the same basis as those of the litigant who retains counsel.

The court noted that all litigants suffer loss of time by their involvement in legal process and thus, self-represented litigant should not recover costs for time and effort that any litigant would have to devote to case. Self-represented litigants should recover costs for lost financial opportunities only if they show that that they devoted time and effort to do work ordinarily done by lawyer hired to conduct litigation. A self-represented lay litigant should receive only a 'moderate' or 'reasonable' allowance for the loss of time devoted to preparing and presenting the case. This excludes routine awards on a *per diem* basis to litigants who would ordinarily be in attendance at court in any event.

In this case the plaintiff did enormous amount of preparation for his case but it was done outside of court hours and there was no satisfactory proof that, during those hours, the plaintiff lost income-earning opportunities.

Guillemette v. Doucet, 2007 CarswellOnt 7034, 88 O.R. (3d) 90, 230 O.A.C. 202, 2007 ONCA 743, *(sub nom. Doucet v. Guillemette)* 287 D.L.R. (4th) 522, 48 C.P.C. (6th) 17 (Ont. C.A.)

Appeal by solicitor from order that his accounts rendered to client be assessed. Solicitor claimed that two-year limitation period set out in section 4 of the *Limitations Act* applied and client's application was out of time.

Appeal dismissed. Client demonstrated special circumstances which justifies extension of two-year limitation period. Client's medical issues represented legitimate barrier to launch of assessment. Superior court has an inherit jurisdiction to review lawyers' accounts entirely apart from any statutory authority and not subject to a time limit.

Prince Edward Island School Board, Regional Administrative Unit No. 3 v. Morin, 2008 CarswellPEI 4, *(sub nom. Morin v. Board of Education of Regional Administrative Unit No. 3)* 833 A.P.R. 65, *(sub nom. Morin v. Board of Education of Regional Administrative Unit No. 3)* 273 Nfld. & P.E.I.R. 65, 2008 PESCTD 2 (P.E.I. T.D.); varied 2009 CarswellPEI 41, 2009 PECA 18, *(sub nom. Morin v. Prince Edward Island Regional Administrative Unit No. 3)* 288 Nfld. & P.E.I.R. 85, *(sub nom. Morin v. Prince Edward Island Regional Administrative Unit No. 3)* 888 A.P.R. 85, 74 C.P.C. (6th) 8 (P.E.I. C.A.); additional reasons at 2009 CarswellPEI 45, 2009 PECA 20 (P.E.I. C.A.); leave to appeal refused 2010 CarswellPEI 7, 2010 CarswellPEI 8, *(sub nom. Morin v. Board of Education of Regional Unit No. 3)* 298 Nfld. & P.E.I.R. 287 (note), *(sub nom. Morin v. Board of Education of Regional Unit No. 3)* 921 A.P.R. 287 (note), *(sub nom. Morin v. Prince Edward Island Regional Administrative Unit No. 3)* 405 N.R. 394 (note) (S.C.C.)

The respondent, a self-represented litigant, was awarded costs of $174,835. The appellate court reduced the award to $76,622. A self-represented litigant who is unemployed, underemployed, or loses employment for reasons other than required attendance for his law suit (not as a party) is not entitled to opportunity costs. The plaintiff did not establish that his inability to find work was due to his work as a self-represented litigant.

Mustang Investigations Inc. v. Ironside, 2010 ONSC 3444, 2010 CarswellOnt 5398, 103 O.R. (3d) 633, 321 D.L.R. (4th) 357, 267 O.A.C. 302, 98 C.P.C. (6th) 105, [2010] O.J. No. 3184 (Ont. Div. Ct.); reversing 2009 CarswellOnt 5563, 82 C.P.C. (6th) 80 (Ont. S.C.J.)

The plaintiff moved for leave to discontinue action. One of the defendants (Ironside), who was self-represented, opposed motion on the ground that he required his day in court in order to vindicate his reputation. The motions judge allowed the motion on the condition that the plaintiff pay Ironside $20,000 for counsel fee on a partial indemnity basis plus disbursements of $1,051.40. Divisional Court affirmed the award for disbursements of $1,051.40, but set aside the $20,000 award. The costs should only be awarded to self-represented litigants who demonstrated that they devoted time and effort to the work ordinarily done by a lawyer retained and that as a result they incurred an opportunity cost by foregoing remunerative activity. A self-represented litigant should only receive a moderate or reasonable allowance for the loss of time devoted to preparing and presenting the case.

Leading authority on costs to be awarded to unrepresented litigants, in *Fong v. Chan*, 46 O.R. (3d) 330, 128 O.A.C. 2, 181 D.L.R. (4th) 614, [1999] O.J. No. 4600, 1999 CarswellOnt 3955 (Ont. C.A.). *Fong* followed in *Izzard v. Goldreich*, 2002 CarswellOnt 1533, 159 O.A.C. 365 (Ont. Div. Ct.); additional reasons at [2002] O.J. No. 2931, 2002 CarswellOnt 4780 (Ont. Div. Ct.) (para. 3). *Fong* applied in *Logtenberg v. ING Insurance Co.*, 2008 CarswellOnt 2930 (Ont. S.C.J.).

See *White v. Ritchie*, 2009 CarswellOnt 3268, [2009] O.J. No. 2360 (Ont. S.C.J. [Commercial List]), Newbould, J. re *Fong*, at paragraph 15 that "Mr. White has not shown that he has a current job or other income sources that he has had to forego in order to spend time preparing his case. He has not worked for some considerable period of time."

In *Henderson v. Pearlman*, 2010 ONSC 149, 2010 CarswellOnt 75 (Ont. S.C.J.), Hennessy J., after alluding to *Fong*, agreed with Newbould J., in *White v. Ritchie* and without making reference to whether or not lost opportunity costs established, awarded unrepresented litigant 120 hours of time spent at $20 per hour.

1286342 Ontario Inc. v. Dennis, 2010 ONSC 5575, 2010 CarswellOnt 7696 (Ont. S.C.J.)

Motion brought by plaintiff ("Desnoyers"):

4. To allow Desnoyers to represent 1286342 Ontario Inc. o/a Yachtware Marine Services ("Yachtware");

5. To add party defendants; and

6. To vary the Statement of Claim.

Named defendants brought cross-motions for:

5. An order dismissing the action of Desnoyers;

6. An order that the plaintiff Yachtware appoint a solicitor pursuant to r. 15.01(2) of the *Rules of Civil Procedure* within 30 days of this order;

7. Yachtware post security for costs within 30 days of this order; and

8. Costs.

Desnoyers represented himself and Yachtware. He has *not* attempted to co-operate with counsel.

See statement of former Justice Donald Ferguson made in his book *Ontario Courtroom Procedure* at page 69: "Self-represented litigants may be held to the standard of civility expected of lawyers and a proper remand for failure to do so is an award of costs on a substantial indemnity basis."

Rule 15.01(2) states: "A party to a proceeding that is a corporation shall be represented by a lawyer, except with leave of the court."

See *Lamond v. Smith*, 2004 CarswellOnt 3213, [2004] O.J. No. 3255, 11 C.P.C. (6th) 104 (Ont. S.C.J.), at paras. 13 and 15:

> Mr. DeLorenzo submits that it has not been suggested that the corporate defendant is unable to pay for a lawyer. This is correct. Impecuniosity may be one reason why leave should be granted in a motion under subrule 15.01(2), but it is not a necessary reason. Frankly, I do not see shy the ability or inability to afford a lawyer should be a relevant factor. Some people and companies may think that they have better things to do with their money than to pay lawyers. They may be right; they may be wrong.
>
> . . . . .
>
> The historical reluctance of trial courts to grant leave to a corporation to be represented by a non-lawyer has little merit in the case of a small, one-man company. Therefore, I exercise my discretion in favour of the moving party and grant leave for 1198827 Ontario Inc. to be represented by Mr. Smith.

Desnoyers allowed to represent Yachtware in this litigation.

Rule 56.01 deals with the issue of security for costs.

See *Willets v. Colalillo*, [2007] O.J. No. 4623, 2007 CarswellOnt 7616 (Ont. Master).

The court in *Zeitoun v. Economical Insurance Group*, 2008 CarswellOnt 2576, [2008] O.J. No. 1771, 91 O.R. (3d) 131, 236 O.A.C. 76, 64 C.C.L.I. (4th) 52, 53 C.P.C. (6th) 308, 292 D.L.R. (4th) 313 (Ont. Div. Ct.); additional reasons at 2008 CarswellOnt 3734, 56 C.P.C.

(6th) 191, 64 C.C.L.I. (4th) 68 (Ont. Div. Ct.); affirmed 2009 ONCA 415, 2009 CarswellOnt 2665, [2009] O.J. No. 2003, 96 O.R. (3d) 639, 73 C.C.L.I. (4th) 255, 257 O.A.C. 29, 73 C.P.C. (6th) 8, 307 D.L.R. (4th) 218 (Ont. C.A.), at paras. 48–50 stated that:

> ... There is a difference in the quality of the evidence required depending on whether or not the plaintiff is able to show impecuniosity.
>
> Where impecuniosity is shown, the plaintiff needs only to demonstrate that the claim is not plainly devoid of merit. (See *John Wink Ltd. v. Sico Inc.* (1987), 57 O.R. (2d) 705 (H.C.J.)). That is a very low evidentiary threshold.

Where impecuniosity has not been shown, however, a closer scrutiny of the merits of the case is warranted; in those cases there is no compelling argument that there is a danger that poverty of the plaintiff will cause an injustice by impeding pursuit of a claim that otherwise would have been permitted to be tried. Where impecuniosity has not been shown, a legitimate factor in deciding whether or not it would be just to require security for costs is whether the claim has a good chance of success.

Order to go for security for costs.

The Queen v. Henderson, 292 D.L.R. (4th).

The matter of costs was considered *de novo* since there was a complete absence of any submissions on the issues of costs before trial judge. The court declined to increase costs due to plaintiff's settlement offer because Crown reasonable in its approach and offer not a substantial compromise of plaintiff's claim. Important points of principle involved and issues related to liability. Costs of trial fixed at $645.50.

The trial judge awarded costs to Henderson in amount of $175.00. He did not ask for submissions. Henderson was entitled to be heard. Failing to give him that opportunity was breach of natural justice and fairness and warrants granting leave to appeal on issue of costs.

The trial judge had further discretion under the *Rules of the Small Claims Court*, O. Reg. 258/98, to award Henderson up to $500.00 as compensation for inconvenience and expense and a further $50.00 as a fee for preparation of pleadings. Henderson made settlement offer re section 14.07 of the *Rules of Small Claims Court*. Total amount recoverable for costs, however, is capped at 15% of the judgment recovered.

Appeal by Her Majesty the Queen dismissed. Leave granted to Henderson to appeal costs award and judgment of trial judge varied to increase the costs award to $645.50.

Aya Kitchens & Bath Ltd. v. Blue Forest Homes Inc., 2012 ONSC 2871, 2012 CarswellOnt 5943 (Ont. S.C.J.), Justice J.A. Milanetti

The plaintiff asked for costs of $10,000 on a partial indemnity basis.

Decision awarded plaintiffs $3,801.79. The plaintiff's claim originally for $61,827.09. The plaintiff could not possibly be recipient of costs as such would ignore the consequences set out in Rules 57 and 76 entirely.

The poor legal behaviour of plaintiff attenuated by their failure to admit any of the facts or documents set out in the defence formal Request to Admit.

Request for enhanced costs from date of offer denied.

Defendant entitled to partial indemnity fees of $15,000.00 plus HST plus disbursements of $1,806.46.

Brumley v. Bonilla, 2013 ONSC 897, 2013 CarswellOnt 1233, [2013] O.J. No. 543 (Ont. S.C.J.), Stinson J.

Although the amount claimed and awarded was less than $25,000, at the time the proceeding was commenced the monetary limit for Small Claims Court was $10,000. As a result, the action was properly brought in the Superior Court and rule 57.05(1) does not apply. In any event, the counterclaim sought more than $90,000 and thus the action had to be tried in the Superior Court.

No reason to depart from standard approach that successful party should be awarded costs against the unsuccessful party. The plaintiffs therefore entitled to costs as against the defendant.

19.06 Penalty — If the court is satisfied that a party has unduly complicated or prolonged an action or has otherwise acted unreasonably, the court may order the party to pay an amount as compensation to another party.

O. Reg. 78/06, s. 39

Commentary: Awards under rules 19.05 and 19.06 are not routinely made but are reserved for unusual cases. Self-represented parties do not have an automatic entitlement to recover costs as compensation for the time they devoted to the litigation, but recovery may be permitted where they performed work normally performed by a lawyer: *Fong v. Chan*, 1999 CarswellOnt 3955, 46 O.R. (3d) 330, 181 D.L.R. (4th) 614, 128 O.A.C. 2, [1999] O.J. No. 4600 (Ont. C.A.); *Mustang Investigations Inc. v. Ironside*, 2010 ONSC 3444, 2010 CarswellOnt 5398, 103 O.R. (3d) 633, 98 C.P.C. (6th) 105, 321 D.L.R. (4th) 357, 267 O.A.C. 302, [2010] O.J. No. 3184 (Ont. Div. Ct.).

Courts have the inherent jurisdiction to award or refuse to award costs, and to use the cost sanction to control their process and to prevent abuse of that process. See *Young v. Young*, EYB 1993-67111, [1993] S.C.J. No. 112, 1993 CarswellBC 264, 1993 CarswellBC 1269, [1993] 8 W.W.R. 513, 108 D.L.R. (4th) 193, 18 C.R.R. (2d) 41, [1993] 4 S.C.R. 3, 84 B.C.L.R. (2d) 1, 160 N.R. 1, 49 R.F.L. (3d) 117, 34 B.C.A.C. 161, 56 W.A.C. 161, [1993] R.D.F. 703 (S.C.C.). This discretionary authority is supplemented by the provisions of the *Courts of Justice Act*, s. 131. See also Rule 57 of the *Rules of Civil Procedure*. Where the rules of the Small Claims Court are silent as to costs, a discretion is conferred on the court. (see Rule 1.02(3)).

The traditional view that unrepresented litigants do not merit awards of costs is heavily under siege and may even be in retreat. In *McBeth v. Governors of Dalhousie College and University* (1986), 72 N.S.R. (2d) 224, 26 D.L.R. (4th) 321, 10 C.P.C. (2d) 69 (N.S. App. Div.), the Court found that common law rule that discriminated against unrepresented litigants offended ss. 7 and 15 of the *Canadian Charter of Rights and Freedoms*, and could not be saved by the "resonableness test" in s. 1. But see *contra, Law Society of Prince Edward Island v. Johnson*, 1988 CarswellPEI 106, [1988] P.E.I.J. No. 118, 54 D.L.R. (4th) 18, [1988] 2 P.E.I.R. B28, 73 Nfld. & P.E.I.R. 239, 229 A.P.R. 239 (P.E.I. C.A.).

Other courts have preferred less drastic ways of effecting change, such as the natural evolution and progression of common law concepts. See *Canada Life Assurance Co. v. Stewart* (1994), 132 N.S.R. (2d) 324, 118 D.L.R. (4th) 67 (N.S. App. Div.).

The section deals with "the costs of a proceeding or a step in a proceeding" and, therefore, must be considered with respect to any aspect of an action in the Small Claims Court. The section confers a discretion on the court to determine not only by whom costs shall be paid, but also to what extent costs shall be paid, subject to the provisions of the Rules.

The philosophy of the Rules of the Small Claims Court and, therefore, by inference, of the Committee which drafted them, is reflected in Rule 1.02(1).

The Rules of the Small Claims Court deal with costs, both expressly and by implication. Where the Rules deal with the question of costs by implication, the words, "such terms as are just" are normally found. While these words are not limited to the imposition of costs, they will probably give rise to their consideration. The phrase quoted above is found in Rule 1.03, which deals generally with orders made under the Rules and confers on the court a general discretion to "impose such terms ... as are just." Similarly, in Rule 2.01, where the court is granted a broad discretion to relieve against non-compliance with the Rules, it may again do soon "such terms as are just" (see also Rule 3.02(1)). See the decision of Henry J. in *Apotex Inc. v. Egis Pharmaceuticals* (1991), [1991] O.J. No. 1232, 4 O.R. (3d) 321, 37 C.P.R. (3d) 335 (Ont. Gen. Div.), at pp. 324–328 [O.R.], for a general description of the principles underlying the awarding and fixing of costs.

Rule 19 is the general costs rule in the Small Claims Court. The Rule addresses disbursements, fees for pleadings, counsel fees and an amount for compensation for inconvenience and expenses which can be awarded to a party who is not represented by another person.

Rule 19.04 deals with counsel fee. The Rule is applicable only to a successful party represented by a solicitor or a student-at-law. Rule 19.05 deals with the costs of a successful party who is not represented by another person. It does not apply to corporate litigants or to those represented by agents. As with Rule 19.04, Rule 19.05 applies where the amount claimed exceeds $500, exclusive of interest and costs. The court must be satisfied that the proceeding (not the trial) was unduly complicated or prolonged by an unsuccessful party. A discretion is conferred to order an unsuccessful party to pay a successful party an amount not exceeding $300 "as compensation for inconvenience and expense."

Rule 13.01(4) confers a discretion on the court to impose costs on a party who has received notice of a pre-trial conference but does not attend. Similarly, Rule 13.01(5) confers a discretion on the court to impose costs where a person attends a pre-trial conference but is "so inadequately prepared as to frustrate the purposes of the pre-trial conference" (enumerated in Rule 13.02(1)). Rule 13.01(6) limits the costs to be awarded to $50 unless there are "special circumstances." Rule 13.01(5) speaks of "a person," not a party. Where a solicitor, student-at-law, or agent attends a pre-trial conference and is so inadequately prepared as to frustrate the purposes of the pre-trial conference, the costs may be awarded against the solicitor, student-at-law or agent. If the pre-trial is conducted by a referee, the referee may make recommendations for costs.

The costs sanctions referred to in rule 13.01(4) and (5) can only be imposed by a judge of the court. This follows from Rule 14.03(2).

The cost consequences of Offers to Settle are significant.

Rule 14 encompasses the situation where a defendant offers to settle and is found liable, but for an amount less than the amount for which the defendant offered to settle. The court can still award an amount not exceeding twice the amount which would otherwise be payable to the defendant as a successful party.

Resort to Rule 14.07 is discretionary. The drafting of Rule 14 can be compared to Rule 49 of the *Rules of Civil Procedure*. The cost consequences provided for in Rule 49 of the *Rules of Civil Procedure* are stated to be mandatory unless the court orders otherwise.

Rule 14.04 prohibits communication of the making of an offer to the trial judge until all questions of liability and the relief to be granted have been determined, other than relief by way of costs.

Rule 15 is a general rule for motions' practice. Rule 15.02(1) provides that no costs shall normally be awarded on a motion. The court has the discretion to order that the costs awarded on a motion be paid immediately. This provision, read together with Rule 1.03, referred to above, clearly gives the court discretion to stay further proceedings in an action where a motion has been brought until the costs of the motion have been paid where the circumstances warrant such an order.

If you have lost your motion and are asked by the judge to speak to costs, offer to pay costs in a reasonable amount at a reasonable time. You might even suggest "in the cause". If the point was arguable, you might suggest no costs. If you have won your motion, you should be reasonable.

In exercising its discretion under s. 131 of the *Courts of Justice Act* to award costs, the court may consider, in addition to the result of the proceeding and any offer to settle made in writing,

    1. the amount claimed and the amount recovered in the proceeding;

    2. the apportionment of liability;

    3. the complexity of the proceeding;

    4. the importance of the issue;

    5. the conduct of any party that tended to shorten or to lengthen unnecessarily the duration of the proceeding;

    6. whether any step in the proceeding was,

        (a) improper, vexatious or unnecessary, or

        (b) taken through negligence, mistake or excessive caution;

    7. a party's denial of or refusal to admit anything that should have been admitted; or

    8. any other matter relevant to the question of costs.

Paralegal Rules of Conduct

Adopted by Convocation on March 29, 2007

In Effect: May 1, 2007

Amended: May 25, 2007, January 24, 2008, April 24, 2008, October 30, 2008, November 27, 2008, January 29, 2009, January 28, 2010, February 25, 2010, May 27, 2010, November 25, 2010, January 27, 2011, April 28, 2011, September 22, 2011, January 23, 2014

Paralegal Rules of Conduct: Contents

Rule 1: — Citation and Interpretation

Definitions for key terms used throughout the Rules and guidelines for interpretation of the Rules.

Rule 2: — Professionalism

Rules on issues related to professionalism, such as integrity and civility, undertakings, harassment, and discrimination.

Rule 3: — Duty to Clients

Rules on client-related issues, such as competence, confidentiality, conflict of interest, client property, and withdrawal from representation.

Rule 4: — Advocacy

Rules related to advocacy such as duty to clients, tribunals and others, disclosure of documents, interviewing witnesses, communication with witnesses giving testimony, the paralegal as witness and dealing with unrepresented persons.

Rule 5: — Fees and Retainers

Rules on fee issues including contingency fees, joint retainers, fee splitting, and referral fees.

Rule 6: — Duty to the Administration of Justice

Rules relating to the paralegal's duty to the administration of justice and the courts, including security of court facilities, public appearances and statements, and unauthorized practice.

Rule 7: — Duty to Licensees and Others

Rules governing a paralegal's conduct toward licensees and other including the duty to act with courtesy and good faith.

Rule 8: — Practice Management

Rules on issues related to practice management including general obligations, advertising, insurance, and firm names, letterhead, and signs.

Rule 9: — Responsibility to the Law Society

Rules covering a paralegal's duty to the Law Society including communications from the Law Society, duties to report, professional misconduct, and conduct unbecoming a paralegal.

Traditionally, the awards of costs on a motion are as follows:

1. *"Costs in the cause"* — such an order entitles the party that eventually is awarded the costs of the proceeding as a whole to receive the costs of the motion. The "cause" referred to in this order is not the cause of action on which the proceeding is based, but rather the "cause" of costs in the main proceeding. A plaintiff is awarded damages at the trial of the action, but for some reason is denied the costs of the action, the plaintiff will not receive the costs of any motion in which costs were awarded "in the cause."

2. *"Costs to a specified party in the cause"* (*e.g.* "costs to the plaintiff in the cause," or "costs to the third party in the cause") — Such an order means that the named party is entitled to receive the costs of the motion if that party succeeds as to costs in the proceeding.

3. *"Costs to a party in any event of the cause"* (*e.g.*, "costs to the plaintiff in any event of the cause") — Such an order entitles the named party to receive the costs of the motion no matter what order (if any) is made as to costs of the proceeding, no matter what the outcome of the proceeding.

4. *"Costs fixed in the amount of $X"* — The party awarded costs is entitled to have the deputy judge or judge fix the amount of the costs award immediately following the hearing of the motion.

5. *"Costs payable forthwith after assessment thereof"* — This is an order entitling the party to immediate assessment and payment of the costs after the motion.

6. *"Costs reserved to the trial judge"* — By this order, the costs of the motion are reserved for disposition by the trial judge. Unless the trial judge specifically disposes of the costs of the motion, no party will be entitled to receive the costs of the motion.

7. *"No costs"* — This means that no costs of the motion are to be paid by or to any party.

On January 1, 2002, the *Rules of Civil Procedure* was amended in a number of respects, by *O. Reg. 284/01*. One of the amendments changed the terminology respecting the scale of costs. The former term "party and party" costs was replaced with the term "partial indemnity" costs, and the term "solicitor-client" costs was replaced with the term "substantial indemnity" costs.

In *Niagara Structural Steel (St. Catharines) Ltd. v. W.D. LaFlamme Ltd.* (1987), 1987 CarswellOnt 440, [1987] O.J. No. 2239, 58 O.R. (2d) 773, 19 O.A.C. 142, 19 C.P.C. (2d) 163 (Ont. C.A.), the Ontario Court of Appeal held that courts should depart from those prima facie cost consequences only where, after giving due weight to the Rule and the importance of the necessity of reasonable predictability and the even application of the Rule, the interests of justice require such a departure. In effect, the rule provisions must be applied unless there is a compelling reason not to do so.

Rule 15.02(2) imposes a limit of $50 on the costs to be awarded on a motion unless there are special circumstances. This rule is similar to Rule 13.01(6).

Rule 17 is the general Rule for trial practice. Rule 17.02 is the significant provision with respect to courts. The words "as compensation for inconvenience and expense" are similar to the word used in Rule 19.05. Rule 19.05 only applies to parties who are not represented by another person. No similar limitation applies with respect to Rule 17.02. The "inconvenience and expense" compensated for, with respect to a postponement or adjournment of the trial of a proceeding, can include an amount as compensation for the inconvenience and expense of a solicitor, articling student or agent.

The right to your day in court does not always mean the right to everyone else's day in court as well. Costs sanctions will be granted where appropriate. See *Singh v. Singh* (1992), 10 C.P.C. (3d) 42 (Ont. Gen. Div.).

Rule 4 provides that parties under disability shall be represented by a litigation guardian. Rule 4.01(3)(e) provides that a litigation guardian who seeks to act for a plaintiff must file a consent, with the clerk of the court, in which he acknowledges that he is liable to pay personally any costs awarded against him or against the person under disability for whom he acts. See also new subrule 4.01(3)(f), effective September 1, 1998. Rule 8.05 provides that the court may allow costs reasonably incurred to serve a defendant, who is outside of Ontario, as costs in the proceeding. These costs are not limited.

Rule 11.06(1) specifically deals with a motion to set aside default. The court may do so on "such terms as are just." As noted above, the Rule should be read in conjunction with Rule 15.02.

Rule 12.02, which confers a discretion on the court to strike out a claim or defence or any part thereof, or dismiss an action, specifically provides that in doing so, the court may impose "such terms as are just." Rule 20 deals with enforcement of orders. There are several situations calling for cost orders under this Rule.

In a proceeding where the amount claimed does not exceed $500, exclusive of interests and costs, costs should not be a significant feature of the proceeding. No counsel fee or inconvenience fee at trial is provided for. Costs of interlocutory proceedings and postponement or adjournment of trial may, however, be awarded. Those costs may be doubled under Rule 14.07 in appropriate circumstances.

In proceedings where the amount claimed exceeds $500, exclusive of interest and costs, costs are a significant consideration.

1465778 Ontario Inc. v. 1122077 Ontario Ltd., 2006 CarswellOnt 6582, [2006] O.J. No. 4248, 216 O.A.C. 339, 38 C.P.C. (6th) 1, 275 D.L.R. (4th) 321, 82 O.R. (3d) 757 (Ont. C.A.).

There should be no prohibition on an award of costs in favour of *pro bono* counsel in appropriate cases. The law now recognizes that costs awards may serve purposes other than indemnity. Allowing *pro bono* parties to be subject to the ordinary costs consequences that apply to other parties has two positive consequences.

"There are provisions in the [Civil Procedure Rules] that can be used to level the playing field when costs are awarded to a *pro bono* party." See, e.g., Rule 57.03(2) and Rule 57.01(4)(b).

Costs

There are five kinds of costs in this court:

1. "reasonable disbursements" (19.01);
2. "an amount not exceeding $50 for preparation and filing" (19.03);
3. "a reasonable representation fee" (19.04); or
4. "an amount not exceeding $500 for inconvenience and expense" (19.05); and
5. "a penalty" (19.06 and s. 29 *CJA*).

All costs awards, except disbursements, are subject to the limits and parameters of section 29 *Courts of Justice Act* (subrule 19.02).

Disbursements under subrule 19.01(1) must be reasonable and now include "expenses for travel, accommodation, photocopying and experts reports." Although 19.01(2) provides that the clerk shall assess the disbursements, the trial judge should handle disbursements where receipts should be filed. Service can cost more than $20.

Subrule 19.01(3) has been amended to allow the court to assess a greater amount in "special circumstances."

At trial, there is no longer a "counsel fee" but, rather, a "representation fee." Representation fees and compensation for inconvenience only apply to matters over the appealable limit. For matters under $500 the parties are limited to disbursements, the preparation and filing fee, and any penalty under s. 29.

The compensation available to successful self-represented litigants for inconvenience and expense has been increased to $500 (subrule 19.05).

The new rule on penalty costs allows the court to sanction unreasonable behaviour or unduly complicating or delaying the action (subrule 19.06). The amount of the penalty assessed under subrule 19.06 must be such that the penalty plus any costs awarded at the time as representation fee or compensation for inconvenience add up to no more than 15 per cent. If a penalty is awarded under section 29, the 15 per cent cap may be exceeded.

The Ontario Court of Appeal case of *Harper Jaskot LLP v. Bosanac* (2002), 2002 Carswell-Ont 4307, 167 O.A.C. 157, 62 O.R. (3d) 635, 30 C.P.C. (5th) 57 (Ont. C.A.) deals with applicability of the doctrine of issue estoppel where a solicitor's costs have been fixed by the court at the conclusion of litigation and the client then seeks to have the lawyer's bill taxed. According to the Court of Appeal, a lawyer's bill can be taxed even after costs have been awarded and fixed. The *Solicitors Act* has never been clear when it came to what accounts are allowed to be assessed. See *Lang, Michener, Cranson, Farquharson & Wright v. Newell* (January 11, 1985), [1985] O.J. No. 272 (Ont. H.C.); affirmed (January 27, 1986), [1986] O.J. No. 2459 (Ont. C.A.); *Minkarious v. Abraham, Duggan* (1995), 1995 CarswellOnt 1341, 129 D.L.R. (4th) 311, 44 C.P.C. (3d) 210, 27 O.R. (3d) 26 (Ont. Gen. Div.); and *Enterprise Rent-A-Car Co. v. Shapiro, Cohen, Andrews, Finlayson*, 1998 CarswellOnt 707, [1998] O.J. No. 727, 157 D.L.R. (4th) 322, (sub nom. *Shapiro, Cohen, Andrews, Finlayson v. Enterprise Rent-A-Car Co.)* 107 O.A.C. 209, 38 O.R. (3d) 257, 80 C.P.R. (3d) 214, 18 C.P.C. (4th) 20 (Ont. C.A.). Along with the Ontario Court of Appeal decision of *Price v. Sonsini* (2002), 2002 CarswellOnt 2255, [2002] O.J. No. 2607, 215 D.L.R. (4th) 376, 22 C.P.C. (5th) 1, 60 O.R. (3d) 257, 162 O.A.C. 85 (Ont. C.A.), Jaskot makes it clear that the right of the client to assess a solicitor's account must be jealously guarded.

Costs Against a Solicitor

An order as to costs against the solicitor is made by the court in the exercise of its inherent jurisdiction to control the conduct of its officers. In some cases the courts have held that a solicitor should not be ordered to pay costs where the solicitor is guilty merely of a mistake, an error in judgment, or negligence: *931473 Ontario Ltd. v. Coldwell Banker Canada Inc.* (1992), 5 C.P.C. (3d) 271 (Ont. Gen. Div.). Nevertheless, there are instances where the solicitors have been personally ordered to pay costs because they failed to exercise reasonable competence. For example, in *Lico v. Griffith* (1996), 7 C.P.C. (4th) 131, 38 C.C.L.I. (2d) 240, 12 O.T.C. 201 (Ont. Gen. Div.) the court ordered the plaintiff's former solicitor to pay costs of a motion to extend time for service where he negligently failed to serve and file the statement of claim. The rationale behind the court's jurisdiction to order costs against a solicitor personally was explained in the decision of the House of Lords in *Myers v. Elman* (1939), [1940] A.C. 282, [1939] 4 All E.R. 484 (U.K. H.L.).

Standard Life Assurance Co. v. Elliott, [2007] O.J. No. 2031, 2007 CarswellOnt 3236, 50 C.C.L.I. (4th) 288, 86 O.R. (3d) 221 (Ont. S.C.J.).

Costs awarded against solicitor personally. Defendant issuing third-party claim against every employee of plaintiff who had ever handled her file. Third-party claim struck as abusive.

Costs Regime

Costs awards to successful parties are an integral part our civil courts system. In Ontario, the new costs regime that came into force in 2002 was meant to attempt to save time and clients' money by having costs fixed within certain criteria, thus avoiding the delay and expense of a full assessment.

In *Toronto (City) v. First Ontario Realty Corp.* (2002), [2002] O.J. No. 2519, 59 O.R. (3d) 568 (Ont. S.C.J.), Justice Matlow made a judicial assessment of the successful respondent First Ontario's bill of costs under the new costs regime. (The respondent had successfully defended against the city's motion for leave to appeal a decision of the Ontario Municipal Board.) Justice Matlow analyzed the new cost regime in subrules 57.01(1), (3), (4) of the *Rules of Civil Procedure*, the new Grid, as well as the enabling section 131(1) of the *Court of Justice Act*. He found that even though some of these subrules list specific factors for the court's consideration, the framework leaves the court with a very broad discretion and entitles it to consider anything that is "relevant to the question of costs" to "determine by whom and to what extent the costs shall be paid," including a discretion as to what hourly rates are to be applied.

Justice Matlow's reasonable expectation test is consistent with that of Morden A.C.J.O. in *Murano v. Bank of Montreal* (1998), [1998] O.J. No. 2897, 1998 CarswellOnt 2841, 111 O.A.C. 242, 163 D.L.R. (4th) 21, 22 C.P.C. (4th) 235, 41 B.L.R. (2d) 10, 41 O.R. (3d) 222, 5 C.B.R. (4th) 57 (Ont. C.A.), where he held that the fixing of costs by a judge is not an assessment, item by item, according to the tariffs, as would be performed by an assessment officer. The judge must conduct a critical examination of the work undertaken in order to determine that the costs claimed have been reasonably incurred and reflect what the court considers proper and appropriate in the circumstances having regard to given the complexity and significance of the proceeding (he quotes with approval Henry J. in *Apotex Inc. v. Egis Pharmaceuticals* (1991), [1991] O.J. No. 1232, 4 O.R. (3d) 321, 37 C.P.R. (3d) 335 (Ont. Gen. Div.) at 322 [O.R.]); see also *Haines J., in Worsley Estate v. Lichong* (March 1, 1994), [1994] O.J. No. 614, Doc. 1069, 16422 (Ont. Gen. Div.).

By amendment of S.O. 2002, chapter 24, section 26, Parts II and III of the *Limitations Act* (R.S.O. 1990, chapter L.15) were repealed. The remaining portion of the Act (the definitions and Part I) dealt exclusively with real property limitation. The Act was renamed the *Real Property Limitations Act*. A new Act, the *Limitations Act, 2002*, was enacted to deal with limitation periods other than those affecting real property. The *Limitations Act* (R.S.O. 1990), as it now reads before the amendment by S.O. 2002, chapter 24, came into force on January 1, 2004.

Note in part and in particular sections 4, 5, 6, 10 and 19:

> 4. Unless this Act provides otherwise, a proceeding shall not be commenced in respect of a claim after the second anniversary of the day on which the claim was discovered.
>
> 2002, c. 24, Sched. B, s. 4
>
> 5. (1) Discovery — A claim is discovered on the earlier of,
>
> > (a) the day on which the person with the claim first knew,
> >
> > > (i) that the injury, loss or damage had occurred,
> > >
> > > (ii) that the injury, loss or damage was caused by or contributed to by an act or omission,
> > >
> > > (ii) that the act or omission was that of the person against whom the claim is made, and

(iv) that, having regard to the nature of the injury, loss or damage, a proceeding would be an appropriate means to seek to remedy it; and

(b) the day on which a reasonable person with the abilities and in the circumstances of the person with the claim first ought to have known of the matters referred to in clause (a).

2002, c. 24, Sched. B, s. 5(1)

(2) **Presumption** — A person with a claim shall be presumed to have known of the matters referred to in clause (1)(a) on the day the act or omission on which the claim is based took place, unless the contrary is proved.

2002, c. 24, Sched. B, s. 5(2)

6. **Minors** — The limitation period established by section 4 does not run during any time in which the person with the claim,

(a) is a minor; and

(b) is not represented by a litigation guardian in relation to the claim.

2002, c. 24, Sched. B, s. 6

. . . . .

10. (1) The limitation period established by section 4 does not run in respect of a claim based on assault or sexual assault during any time in which the person with the claim is incapable of commencing the proceeding because of his or her physical, mental or psychological condition.

2002, c. 24, Sched. B, s. 10(1)

(2) **Presumption** — Unless the contrary is proved, a person with a claim based on an assault shall be presumed to have been incapable of commencing the proceeding earlier than it was commenced if at the time of the assault one of the parties to the assault had an intimate relationship with the person or was someone on whom the person was dependent, whether financially or otherwise.

2002, c. 24, Sched. B, s. 10(2)

(3) **Same** — Unless the contrary is proved, a person with a claim based on a sexual assault shall be presumed to have been incapable of commencing the proceeding earlier than it was commenced.

2002, c. 24, Sched. B, s. 10(3)

. . . . .

19. (1) A limitation period set out in or under another Act that applies to a claim to which the Act applies is of no effect unless,

(a) the provision establishing it is listed in the Schedule of this Act; or

(b) the provision establishing it,

(i) is in existence on the day this Act comes into force, and

(ii) incorporates by reference a provision listed in the Schedule of this Act.

2002, c. 24, Sched. B, s. 19(1)

Rule 20 — Enforcement Of Orders

20.01 Definitions — In rules 20.02 to 20.12,

"creditor" means a person who is entitled to enforce an order for the payment or recovery of money;

"debtor" means a person against whom an order for the payment or recovery of money may be enforced.

O. Reg. 78/06, s. 40

History [R. 20.01]: Formerly 21.01.

Commentary: The Rules of the *Small Claims Court* provide for a number of enforcement options for parties who are in possession of a judgment or order that has not been complied with.

The enforcement options available to a party with an enforceable order will vary and will likely be determined by a number of factors including:

- the type of order requiring enforcement;

- where the order originated;

- the creditor's knowledge about the whereabouts of the debtor(s); and/or

- the creditor's knowledge about the debtor(s) assets.

IMPORTANT: Section 29 of the *Crown Liability and Proceedings Act* (Federal) and section 21 of the *Proceedings Against the Crown Act* prohibit the issuance of executions against the Crown (Federal or Provincial).

Where a creditor requests the issuance of an execution against "Her Majesty the Queen in Right of Ontario," "Sa Majesté du chef de l'Ontario," or the Attorney General of Canada, they must be advised that the court is expressly prohibited from doing so in accordance with the applicable *Act* (above).

Proceedings against the Federal Crown may also include agencies of the Crown where an Act of Parliament authorizes proceedings to be taken in the name of the agency.

The *Rules of the Small Claims Court* do not limit the time period within which the following methods of enforcement may be issued:

- Certificate of Judgment;

- Writ of Delivery; or

- Notice of Examination.

If more than six years have elapsed since the judgment was made, the clerk shall *not* issue:

- a writ of seizure and sale of land [r. 20.07(2)],

- a writ of seizure and sale of personal property [r. 20.06(1.1)], or

- a Notice of Garnishment [r. 20.08(2.1)].

In these cases, the creditor would be required to obtain leave of the court in order to have the garnishment or writ(s) issued.

Service of Enforcement Documents at a Place of Employment

If a document is to be served personally on an individual pursuant to subrule 8.02(a), the document can be served by leaving a copy with the individual, unless the individual is under a disability. A person can be served with the document at their place of employment.

If a document is to be served by mail, Rule 8.07(1) states:

> 8.07 (1) If a document is to be served by mail under these rules, it shall be sent, by regular lettermail or registered mail, to the last address of the person or of the person's lawyer or agent that is,
>
> a. on file with the court, if the document is to be served by the clerk;
>
> b. know to the sender, if the document is to be served by any other person. O.Reg. 258–98, r. 8.07(1).

If the last address on file with the court or known to the sender is the place of employment, then the document can be served by mail at the place of employment.

If a document is to be served by courier, Rule 8.07.1(1) states:

> 8.07.1 (1) If a document is to be served by courier under these rules, it shall be sent by means of a commercial courier to the last address of the person or of the person's lawyer or agent that is on file with the court or known to the sender. O. Reg. 78/06, s. 15.

If the last address on file with the court or known to the sender is the place of employment, the document can be served by courier at the place of employment.

On occasion, litigants may inquire about the enforcement of multiple judgments that have been awarded on a single claim. For example, it is possible that a creditor may have received a default judgment with respect to an admitted portion of a claim (where the defendant defaulted on their payment terms) and a second judgment with respect to a portion of the claim that was disputed and awarded at trial.

Depending upon how a party obtained judgment, the affidavit for enforcement request may be the first time that the creditor is attending to the process of calculating pre-judgment or post-judgment interest or thinking about the post-judgment costs that they may be entitled to.

When a creditor obtains a judgment, their award may have included costs. These costs form part of the overall judgment and are subject to post-judgment interest.

Post-judgment interest does not accrue on subsequent costs unless they are assessed or fixed by the court. Where costs are assessed or fixed by the court, they may accrue interest from the date they are assessed or fixed.

Some of the fees or expenses that might be claimed by a creditor include:

- fees paid to issue a certificate of judgment, examination, garnishment, or writ;

- fees paid to the enforcement office for the filing of a writ; and

- costs associated with the service of a document.

Examples of costs or expenses that cannot be claimed by a creditor include, but are not limited to:

- costs associated with conducting searches or obtaining certificates (e.g. Used Vehicle Information Packages, PPSA or RSLA searches, etc.);

- costs of obtaining appraisals of debtor property; and

cost of credit bureau searches.

Orders or Judgments for Filing and Enforcement

There are a variety of orders or judgments issued by agencies, boards, tribunals, other levels of court in Ontario, or other jurisdictions that may be filed and subsequently enforced in the Small Claims Court.

Certificate of Judgment from another Small Claims Court location

Where a Certificate of Judgment (Form 20A) is issued by the clerk of the originating court and filed with the clerk of another court, either a garnishment or examination of the debtor can be issued in the receiving court. Only the originating court can issue a certificate of judgment when requested to do so by the creditor.

A creditor may attend the court office and/or make a written inquiry to enforce a judgment by garnishment or through examination of the debtor. Where the debtor lives or carries on business outside of the jurisdiction of the originating court, the creditor *must* obtain a certificate of judgment from the originating court and file it at the court in the jurisdiction where the debtor lives or carries on business.

Restitution Orders under the *Criminal Code* of Canada

Pursuant to the *Criminal Code of Canada*, the Ontario Court of Justice or the Superior Court of Justice may make an order naming a person(s) entitled to recover monetary restitution pursuant to:

- A restitution order under section 738 or 739

- A condition of probation under section 732.1

- A condition of a conditional sentence under section 742.3

Where an amount that is ordered to be paid under sections 732.1, 738, 739 or 742.3 is not paid without delay, the person to whom the amount was ordered to be paid may, by filing the order, enter as a judgment the amount ordered to be paid in any civil court that has jurisdiction to enter a judgment for that amount. That judgment is enforceable against the offender in the same manner as if it were a judgment rendered against the offender in that court in civil proceedings [s. 741(1) *CCC*].

Restitution Order under sections 738 or 739

The offender and the victim are each provided with a copy of the restitution order. The order may be filed at any time *after* the date it is issued by the originating criminal court. The order may be filed for enforcement in any civil court of appropriate monetary jurisdiction, either the Superior Court of Justice or the Small Claims Court. Upon filing, it is entered as a judgment of the court and is then enforceable in the same manner as a civil judgment of the court.

Orders under sections 732.1 or 742.3

Where an amount that is ordered to be paid as a condition of a probation or conditional sentence order under sections 732.1 or 742.3 is not paid within the time given by the criminal court judge, *only* then may the order be filed for enforcement. If a victim wishes to enforce an order for restitution that is a condition of a probation/conditional sentence order that remains unpaid on the expiry of the time allowed for payment, he/she must attend at the criminal court office where the original probation/conditional sentence order was issued to obtain a copy of the relevant order.

Monetary restitution orders will usually be filed in the county/district in which the court ordering the restitution is located.

A restitution order or the probation/conditional sentence order in which a condition provides for restitution may be accepted for filing at any court location provided that it falls within the proper monetary jurisdiction of the court. To issue a notice of garnishment or notice of examination, the order must be filed in the territorial division where the debtor resides or carries on business [r. 20.08(3), 20.10(1)].

The general guideline concerning Small Claims Court territorial divisions where these orders may be filed are:

- "reside" — the offender may be considered to reside, where he/she is incarcerated, or his/her usual residence prior to conviction and to where the offender may return;

- "cause of action" — may be considered to be the location where the offence was committed or where the restitution order was made.

The restitution order or the probation/conditional sentence order in which a condition provides for restitution bears post-judgment interest calculated from the date the order is filed as a judgment in the civil court. The rate is governed by the *Courts of Justice Act* and is the rate in effect on the date the order was made by the criminal court.

Where a restitution order or a probation/conditional sentence order in which a condition provides for restitution is made in a Canadian court outside Ontario, and it is filed with a court in Ontario for the purpose of enforcement, money owing under the order bears post-judgment interest at the rate, if any, applicable to the order given outside Ontario by the law of the place where it was given [s.129(3) CJA].

No fees are payable for the filing of a restitution order or the issuance of enforcement processes. However, any out-of-pocket expenses incurred as a result of enforcement activity conducted (e.g. costs of towing a seized vehicle) will be required to be paid to the enforcement office in advance of enforcement activity.

Where monetary restitution is ordered pursuant to a restitution order, or as a condition of a probation/conditional sentence order, and the amount is not paid, a victim/creditor may:

1. File three copies of the order of restitution

It is not necessary for the victim/creditor to file certified copies of the restitution order or the probation/conditional sentence order in which a condition provides for restitution, in the civil court.

The filed order automatically becomes a judgment enforceable in the same manner as if it were rendered in a civil proceeding against the offender. All payments must be made to the civil court where the order was filed. Payments cannot be made to the criminal court where the order was issued after filing in the civil court.

Statutory Powers Procedure Act

Tribunals are, in effect, the adjudicative units that preside over individual cases, and their roles, powers, and responsibilities are referred to in both the *Statutory Powers Procedures Act* (SPPA) and the parent legislation governing a regulatory scheme (e.g. *Residential Tenancies Act* is the parent legislation governing the Landlord and Tenant Board). The SPPA sets out basic procedural rules for most (but not all) of Ontario's tribunals, and also sets out where a Tribunal may itself make rules governing its proceedings.

In addition to the provisions of the SPPA, the "parent" statute of a tribunal (which establishes its existence and function) may establish procedural provisions effecting the tribunal and may also stipulate that some proceedings (usually minor ones) of a tribunal are exempted from the SPPA, either because those proceedings do not involve a statutory power of decision or because the parent statute specifically exempts those proceedings from the SPPA's application.

Neither the SPPA nor any specific administrative law regime has its own separate enforcement procedures. Most decisions and orders of tribunals that are not complied with must be enforced through the civil courts.

The most commonly filed orders authorized to be filed under section 19 of the SPPA are Landlord and Tenant Board orders issued under the *Residential Tenancies Act* and Orders to Pay issued under the *Employment Standards Act*.

Other statutes that provide for the issuance of an order that might be filed with a civil court of competent jurisdiction include, inter alia:

- *Mining Act*;

- *Human Rights Code*;

- Ontario *Works Act, 1997*; and

- Ontario *Disability Support Program Act, 1997*.

In accordance with the *Statutory Powers Procedures Act*, a certified copy of a tribunal's decision or order in a proceeding may be filed in the Superior Court of Justice by the tribunal or by a party, and on filing shall be deemed to be an order of that court and once entered is enforceable as such.

The *Landlord and Tenant Board* (LTB) is a tribunal, created under the *Residential Tenancies Act, 2006* (RTA).

Landlord and Tenant Board Orders (Board Orders) that include awards for monetary compensation may be enforced by filing a Board-certified copy of the Board Order with the Small Claims Court [s.19(1), SPPA].

The party is not required to file the order where the debtor resides or carries on business, but as a practical matter should try to file the order in the appropriate territorial division to avoid having to obtain a Certificate of Judgment to permit enforcement by way of examination or garnishment in another jurisdiction.

The monetary jurisdiction of the Landlord and Tenant Board (LTB) is limited to the jurisdiction of the Small Claims Court and increased from $10,000.00 to $25,000.00 on January 1, 2010.

Board Orders are usually issued where a tenant is in arrears with respect to rent and/or required to compensate a landlord for damages to a rental unit. The landlord may seek compensation, termination of a tenancy agreement, and eviction of a tenant from premises. A tenant may also make applications to the LTB for compensation.

The Small Claims Court may proceed with processing/managing the filing and enforcement of a Board Order before, during, or after the enforcement office has carried out enforcement of the eviction portion of the Board Order.

If a creditor seeks to issue a Notice of Garnishment, the Landlord and Tenant Board Order would ideally be filed in the Small Claims Court where the debtor resides. Otherwise, the creditor would be required to request the issuance of a certificate of judgment directed to the clerk of the appropriate court location to facilitate issuance of the garnishment.

At the time of filing the Board Order, the creditor must also provide the name, address, and telephone numbers of the creditor, creditor representatives, and the debtor (if known). If the Board Order included per diem values, or multiple awards (rent plus compensation for damages), the creditor must set out the amount owing under the award and to set out the form of calculation used.

The LTB, tenants, or other interested parties may file documents (such as a Notice of Appeal, Notice of Void Order, etc.) with the Small Claims Court and possibly the enforcement office (re: evictions) that may have the effect of suspending or staying further enforcement of an order.

Section 74(4) of the RTA provides that a tenant debtor may avoid enforcement of the eviction portion of a Board Order at any time after the Board Order is issued but before the eviction portion of the Board Order is effective (enforceable), upon payment of amounts specified within the order to the LTB and/or the landlord/agent.

If the tenant debtor pays the amount specified in the order to the LTB, the staff of the LTB will issue a notice to the landlord and tenant acknowledging that the order is void (Notice of Void Order). The tenant or the LTB may submit a copy of this order to the court/enforcement office.

If the tenant debtor pays the amount specified to the landlord or part to the landlord and part to the LTB, the tenant debtor may file a motion with the LTB, without notice to the landlord, asking for the LTB to issue an order determining that the tenant debtor has paid the full amount due and confirming that the order is void. Such an order will be made without holding a hearing (Ex-parte Board Order).

A landlord may seek an order of the LTB to determine that the setting aside/ex parte ceases to apply and enforcement may proceed [s.74(10), *RTA*].

Stay or Suspension of Order Pending Appeal

Any person affected by a Board Order can appeal the order to the Divisional Court.

An appeal to Divisional Court must be filed within 30 days of the date the order was issued.

When an appeal of an order is filed with the Divisional Court, the order is automatically stayed in accordance with section 25 of the *Statutory Powers Procedure Act* and r. 63.01(3) of the *Rules of Civil Procedure* and cannot be enforced until the disposition of the appeal, unless the Divisional Court lifts (or removes) the stay at the request of a party.

The debtor or their representative may deliver a copy of a Notice of Appeal with the Divisional court file number (to establish proof of filing with the Divisional Court) to the court office at any time [r. 63.01(1) — Ontario *Rules of Civil Procedure*].

Section 21.2 of the *Statutory Powers Procedures Act* authorizes a tribunal (which adopts rules of practice) to review its own orders. The scope of and procedures for such reviews are set out in the LTB Rules of Practice.

A person affected by an order may request a review if they believe the Member (adjudicator) made a serious error, such as an error of procedure or fact or an unreasonable application of discretion. The Board can issue a stay under Rule 28.9 of the LTB Rules of Practice related to a request to amend an order. Once the stay is issued, the landlord cannot enforce the original order. As soon as the tenant receives the order (staying proceedings) from the Board, they are responsible for taking a copy of the order to the court/enforcement office.

A copy of the Stay of Order Pending Review is sufficient for the court/enforcement office to suspend all enforcement activity.

The Ministry of Labour administers the *Employment Standards Act* (Act) and conducts investigations into a variety of complaints made by employees in Ontario, including complaints with respect to unpaid wages.

In accordance with section 126(1) of the Act, the Director of Employment Standards (Director) may choose to seek enforcement of the Order to Pay by filing a copy of the order (certified by the Director to be a true copy) with a court of competent jurisdiction. Upon filing, the order is deemed to be an order of the court in which it was filed and may be enforced as if it was a judgment or order of the court.

The Order to Pay is an electronically generated document. Employment Standards Officers will sign statements to certify the document as a true copy in accordance with s.126 of the *Employment Standards Act*.

The certificate of true copy should include information that will enable staff to confirm that it attaches to the Order to Pay, such as reference to:

- Order Number,
- Date Order Issued,
- Amount (Total Amount of Order), and
- Name of Debtor(s), including address details (if any).

Recent developments in the administration of these orders at MOL have resulted in amendments to the *Act* that permit MOL to authorize a "collector" to exercise the powers of the Director specified in the authorization to collect amounts owing under this *Act*.

MOL obtains the services of one or more collection agents/agencies to assist them in the collection of monetary awards under the *Act*. In accordance with OPS procurement policies, MOL must undergo the request for proposal process in order to identify viable collection service providers.

As stated above, in accordance with s. 127(1) of the *Employment Standards Act*, the Director of Employment Standards may authorize a collector to exercise specified powers under sections 125, 126, 130 and 135(3) in the collection of amounts owing under these sections of the Act or under an order made by a reciprocating state.

Reciprocal Enforcement of Judgments Act

An order originating from another Canadian province or territory (*other than Quebec*) may be filed in accordance with the *Reciprocal Enforcement of Judgments Act*, R.S.O. 1990, c. R.5., and may then be enforced. Creditors must obtain the permission of the court before the order may be filed in Ontario and accepted as an enforceable judgment.

Creditors may make the request for permission to file the order with the court in Ontario by filing a Notice of Motion and Supporting Affidavit [Form 15A] along with a certified copy of the order that the creditor wishes to file in Ontario at the Small Claims Court office where the creditor wants to have the order filed.

Within motion materials, the creditor must provide an explanation as to why they wish to file the order for enforcement in Ontario. Details about how the matter proceeded through the court in the other province or territory, including how and when the debtor was served with any documentation and if they defended themselves in the original matter, should also be provided by the creditor. The creditor is not required to attend at the motion, but may do so if they wish. In the event that the court grants the creditor the relief requested within their motion, the creditor will be notified by mail.

An order originating from an Ontario court may be filed and enforced in another Canadian province or territory (*other than Quebec*). About half of the provinces in Canada (Alberta, British Columbia, Manitoba, Newfoundland, Prince Edward Island, and Yukon) require the creditor to file a certificate to register an out-of-province order. The certificate is required if the application is being made without notice or ex parte and places the onus on the creditor to prove that the judgment should be registered. In provinces or territories where there is no certificate required, the onus is on the debtor to show to the court that the judgment should not be registered.

The requirements of each province are set out in the applicable legislation:

> *Alberta* — *Reciprocal Enforcement of Judgments Act*, RSA c. R-6 (s.2(3));
>
> *British Columbia* — *BC Court Order Enforcement Act, 1996*, c. 78 (s.29(3));
>
> *Manitoba* — *Reciprocal Enforcement of Judgments Act, 1987*, CCSM c.J20;
>
> *New Brunswick* — *Reciprocal Enforcement of Judgments Act*, c.R-3 (s.2(3));
>
> *Nova Scotia* — *Reciprocal Enforcement of Judgments Act, 1989*, c.338 (s.3(4));
>
> *Newfoundland* — *Reciprocal Enforcement of Judgments Act*, RSNL 1990 C.R-4 (s.3(3));
>
> *Nunavut* — *Reciprocal Enforcement of Judgments Act*, R.S.N.W.T. 1988, R-1 amended by S. Nu. 2002, c. 26, s. 47 and S. Nu. 2006 c.10, s.6 (s.2(5));
>
> *Northwest Territories* — *Reciprocal Enforcement of Judgments Act*, R.S.N.W.T. 1988, R-1 (s.2(5));
>
> *Prince Edward Island* — *Reciprocal Enforcement of Judgments Act*, R-6 (s.2(3));
>
> *Yukon* — *Reciprocal Enforcement of Judgments Act, 2002*, c. 189. (s.2(3)); and
>
> *Saskatchewan* — *Reciprocal Enforcement of Judgments Act, 1996*. C. R-3.1 (s.3(5)).

Note: Some provinces may require a certified copy of the court order to accompany the original certificate. Where the creditor wishes to file and enforce an Ontario court order in another Canadian province or territory which requires the creditor to file a certificate to register an out-of-province order, *the creditor will*:

1. Attend the court office and/or make a written request to have a certificate issued.
2. Provide two copies of a completed certificate.
3. Pay the required fee in accordance with the SCC Schedule of Fees.

Noël et Associés, s.e.n.c.r.l. v. Sincennes, 2012 ONSC 3770, 2012 CarswellOnt 9810, (sub nom. *Noël et Associés, S.E.N.C.R.L. v. Sincennes)* 112 O.R. (3d) 138, 41 C.P.C. (7th) 175, Kane J. (Ont. S.C.J.)

A holder of foreign judgment from a non-reciprocating state for payment of money should be brought in Small Claims Court rather than in Superior Court of Justice where foreign judgment is for payment of money in an amount within monetary jurisdiction of Small Claims Court.

The Supreme Court in *Morguard Investments Ltd. v. De Savoye* (1990), 1990 CarswellBC 283, 1990 CarswellBC 767, EYB 1990-67027, [1990] 3 S.C.R. 1077, 52 B.C.L.R. (2d) 160, 46 C.P.C. (2d) 1, 76 D.L.R. (4th) 256, 15 R.P.R. (2d) 1, [1991] 2 W.W.R. 217, 122 N.R. 81, [1990] S.C.J. No. 135 (S.C.C.) held that the courts in one province should give full faith and credit to the judgments given in another province or territory as long as that court has appropriately exercised jurisdiction in the action. The Supreme Court rejected the argument that a foreign judgment may not be enforced in another province unless the defendant had attorned to the jurisdiction of the foreign court.

The Court of Appeal in *Lax v. Lax*, 2004 CarswellOnt 1633, 70 O.R. (3d) 520, 50 C.P.C. (5th) 266, 239 D.L.R. (4th) 683, 3 R.F.L. (6th) 387, 186 O.A.C. 20, [2004] O.J. No. 1700 (Ont. C.A.); additional reasons 2004 CarswellOnt 5343, 75 O.R. (3d) 482, 4 C.P.C. (6th) 194, 247 D.L.R. (4th) 1, 12 R.F.L. (6th) 112, [2004] O.J. No. 5146 (Ont. C.A.) dealt with the applicability of a limitation period and the enforcement of a foreign judgment. In considering that issue, the court considered the nature of an action to enforce a judgment debt for the payment of money. I will return to this decision below.

Quebec is not a reciprocating state. A Quebec judgment may not be registered in and enforced here as if obtained in Ontario. The holder of that Quebec judgment must commence an Ontario proceeding.

Proceedings in Ontario for debt owing in the amount of $25,000 or less, based on a foreign judgment from a non- reciprocating state, should be brought by action in the Small Claims Court.

Line Fences Act

The purpose of the *Line Fences Act* is to provide a procedure for the resolution of line fence disputes between the owners of adjoining properties. Line fences are fences that mark the boundary between properties; they are often referred to as boundary or division fences as well. The Act does not deal with disputes about fences that are not on a boundary line.

Owners of properties who are unable to reach agreement about a fence line may apply to their local municipality to have the dispute arbitrated by three fence-viewers who are appointed by municipal council or, in areas where appropriate municipal organization does not exist, the ministry of municipal affairs and housing will provide assistance.

Proceedings Under Section 68 of the *Provincial Offences Act*

Under the provisions of the *Provincial Offences Act*, when an unpaid fine imposed under the *Act* is in default it may be collected by means of civil enforcement. The *Act* further provides that enforcement may be carried out in a court of competent jurisdiction.

Multiple fines against the same person can either be issued on separate certificates, or on one certificate with an attached schedule indicating the different fines.

Effective December 15, 2009 section 68(2) of the *Provincial Offences Act* has been repealed. Section 68(2) previously stated: *"A certificate shall not be filed under subsection (1) after two years after the default in respect of which it is issued."* Therefore, the 2 year limitation period for filing POA Certificates of Defaults under section 68(2) of the POA has been repealed.

> 68. (3) Where a certificate has been filed under subsection (1) and the fine is fully paid, the clerk shall file a certificate of payment upon which the certificate of default is discharged and, where a writ of execution has been filed with the sheriff, the clerk shall file a certificate of payment with the sheriff, upon which the writ is cancelled.

Provincial Offences Act above is the clerk of the Ontario Court of Justice (POA court).

Section 70 of the *Provincial Offences Act*

> 70. (1) Where the payment of a fine is in default and the time for payment is not extended or further extended under subsection 66(6), the defendant shall pay the administrative fee prescribed by the regulations.
>
> (2) For the purpose of making and enforcing payment, a fee payable under this section shall be deemed to be part of the fine that is in default.

Section 68 of the *Provincial Offences Act* permits the filing of the certificate "in a court of competent jurisdiction." Provided the amount owing does not exceed the monetary jurisdiction of the Small Claims Court, the certificate would be filed in the territorial division where the defendant resides or carries on business [r 6.01(1)]. The certificate could, however, be filed in the territorial division where the Ontario Court of Justice is situated if the only enforcement process to issue was a writ of seizure and sale of lands.

All funds recovered pursuant to the Certificate are payable to the creditor Municipal Partner and should be paid over to that Municipal Partner (at the address on the Certificate of Default). See sections 165(4) and 165.1(2) and (3) of the *Provincial Offences Act*.

The Certificate of Default does not become a court order until it is filed in the court of competent jurisdiction, therefore, the Affidavit for Enforcement Request should list the Small Claims Court location as the location where the order was made (section 2 on Form 20P).

Jurisdiction

The initial filing of the Certificate of Default must take place in the court having jurisdiction where the land affected by the award is located. Once the initial filing takes place, the creditor may then request the issuance of a Certificate of Judgment and file it in the small claims court location where the debtor resides and carries on business for the purpose of having any Notices of Garnishment or Notices of Examination issued.

The amounts awarded within the Certificate of Default bear post-judgment interest at a rate established according to the provisions of the *Municipal Act* (Section 412). The filing party should have the municipal clerk endorse the applicable rate of interest on the certificate.

Enforcement of Orders

Section 29 of the *Crown Liability and Proceedings Act* (Federal) and section 21 of the *Proceedings Against the Crown Act* prohibit the issuance of executions against the Crown (Federal or Provincial). Proceedings against the Federal Crown may also include agencies of the Crown where an Act of Parliament authorizes proceedings to be taken in the name of the agency.

Issuing a Warrant of Committal — Small Claims Court proceeding

The only time that a warrant of committal will be issued in Small Claims Court proceedings by Superior Court of Justice staff will be when the summoned person attends the contempt hearing heard by a Superior Court judge and the judge orders a warrant of committal. A warrant of committal would then be required immediately to take the person to a correctional institution.

If the judge orders a warrant of committal when the person is not in attendance, the warrant is not immediately required by police services. In this case, the file will be returned to the originating Small Claims Court and the required paperwork will be prepared and distributed from that office.

Issuing a Warrant for Arrest (Contempt) — Small Claims Court proceeding

If a Superior Court judge presiding over a Small Claims Court contempt hearing orders a Warrant for Arrest (Contempt), the Superior Court of Justice courtroom registrar will prepare the Warrant for Arrest and present it to the Superior Court of Justice judge for signature. The original signed warrant, the corresponding endorsement record and the file will then be returned to the originating Small Claims Court office for distribution in accordance with usual practice.

The court where the judgment is made is called the originating court. Sometimes, the debtor lives or carries on business within the area of a court other than the originating court. In this case, before the creditor can get either a notice of garnishment or notice of examination from the court in that jurisdiction, a Certificate of Judgment [Form 20A] is required. The creditor may also request the issuance of a certificate of judgment if they wish to have it for their records or, where required, as proof of judgment (e.g., may be required by sheriff as proof of judgment where sale of land is requested). The certificate of judgment must be requested and issued by the originating court and filed in the court office where the judgment will be enforced. There is a fee for issuing each certificate of judgment.

If you are the creditor, it is your responsibility to contact the court to advise that the debt has been paid in full and to stop or withdraw any enforcement steps. If the debt is paid in full under a notice of garnishment, you must immediately serve a Notice of Termination of Garnishment [Form 20R] on the garnishee and on the clerk.

If you are the debtor, once you have paid all you owe to the creditor under the judgment, you can fill out a Request for Clerk's Order on Consent [Form 11.2A]. Each party must sign the form in the presence of his or her witness.

If the creditor is unavailable or unwilling to complete the notice of termination of garnishment form or sign the Request for Clerk's Order on Consent [Form 11.2A], you can bring a motion for an order stating that payment has been made in full satisfaction of the debt.

A creditor can request an examination hearing if there is a default under an order for the payment or recovery of money.

At the hearing, the debtor or other person should be prepared to answer questions about the debtor's employment, any property the debtor owns such as motor vehicles or land, and about all bank branches where the debtor has an account, including accounts which may be held jointly with another person.

A judge may also make orders at an examination, such as an order as to payment.

The creditor and the person to be examined (usually the debtor) *must* attend the examination. Lawyers or agents may also attend. The examination will be conducted under oath. The public will not be allowed to attend unless the court orders otherwise.

The creditor can begin the examination process by filing a Notice of Examination [Form 20H] indicating the person to be examined (usually the debtor). If the debtor is a company, name the person who has the information you need, an officer or director of the corporation, a partner in the partnership or the sole proprietor.

An Affidavit for Enforcement Request [Form 20P] is necessary in support of a request for a notice of examination.

The notice of examination is served on the debtor or other person to be examined at least 30 days before the hearing. If the debtor to be examined is an individual, you will also need to serve a blank Financial Information Form [Form 20I]. If the debtor is a business, no financial information form is required.

The Affidavit of Service [Form 8A] is necessary to prove service on the debtor or person to be examined. The notice of examination must be served by personal service or an alternative to personal service.

The debtor (or other person) can be examined in relation to:

- the reason for non-payment;

- the debtor's income and property;

- the debts owed to and by the debtor;

- the disposal the debtor has made of any property either before or after the order was made;

- the debtor's present, past and future means to satisfy the order;

- whether the debtor intends to obey the order or has any reason for not doing so; and

- any other matter pertinent to the enforcement of the order.

A debtor who is an individual must fill out the Financial Information Form [Form 20I] and serve it on the creditor before the hearing. A financial information form provides a snapshot of the debtor's income, expenses, debts and assets. The form is *not* filed with the court.

If, at the examination, the court orders a periodic payment schedule, the debtor must make the payments in the amounts and on the dates ordered in the schedule. As long as those periodic payments are made, the creditor cannot do anything else to enforce the judgment, other than issue a writ of seizure and sale of land.

If the debtor fails to make a payment or makes only a partial payment, you can serve on the debtor and file with the court a Notice of Default of Payment [Form 20L] and an Affidavit of Default of Payment [Form 20M]. An order for periodic payment terminates 15 days after you serve the debtor with the notice of default of payment, unless a Consent [Form 13B] in which you waive the default, is filed with the court within the 15-day period.

If the debtor or other person attends the examination but refuses to produce documents or answer questions, the judge may order a contempt hearing before a judge of the Small Claims Court.

The creditor must serve the notice on the debtor or other person who has been ordered to attend the contempt hearing by means of sworn (or affirmed) and filed with the Small Claims Court at least seven days in advance of the hearing date.

The creditor and the debtor (or other person) must attend the contempt hearing.

If the debtor (or other person) does not attend the examination hearing, the judge may order the person to attend a contempt hearing to determine whether he or she is in contempt of court. The contempt hearing will take place before a judge of the Superior Court of Justice.

At the contempt hearing, you will be given an opportunity to explain your actions and any reasons for them. The judge may order you to attend an examination hearing. The judge may also make an order that you are to be jailed for up to 40 days for contempt of court. If you do not attend the contempt hearing, orders may be made against you or a warrant for your arrest may be issued.

If the judge orders the debtor or other person to be jailed for contempt of court, the clerk will issue a Warrant of Committal [Form 20J] directed to the police. The warrant authorizes the police to take the individual named in the warrant to the nearest correctional institution and hold him or her there for the time specified in the warrant.

Limitation Period for Enforcement

The *Rules of the Small Claims Court* do not limit the time period within which the following methods of enforcement may be issued:

- Certificate of Judgment;

- Writ of Delivery; or

- Notice of Examination.

If more than six years have elapsed since the judgment was made, the clerk shall *not* issue:

- a writ of seizure and sale of land [r. 20.07(2)],

- a writ of seizure and sale of personal property [r. 20.06(1.1)], or

- a Notice of Garnishment [r 20.08(2.1)].

The creditor is required to obtain leave of the court in order to have the garnishment or writ(s) issued. The creditor must file a motion to make this request and is required to attend at a motion hearing and advise the court as to why there has been no enforcement within six years of obtaining judgment.

The court will make a determination as to how or if the creditor will be allowed to proceed with enforcement of their judgment or order.

Multiple Judgments

A creditor may have received a default judgment with respect to an admitted portion of a claim (where the defendant defaulted on their payment terms) and a second judgment with respect to a portion of the claim that was disputed and awarded at trial.

The prescribed forms do not contemplate the enforcement of multiple judgments within one form. In the event that multiple judgments are included within an Affidavit for Enforcement Request (Form 20P), the creditor should provide a copy of the affidavit for enforcement and/or attached pages along with the writ of seizure and sale of land or personal property when filing with the enforcement office.

Costs, Interest and Calculations

Depending upon how a party obtained judgment, the affidavit for enforcement request must calculate pre-judgment or post-judgment interest or thinking about the post-judgment costs that they may be entitled to.

Costs — Subsequent Costs

When a creditor obtains a judgment, the award may have included costs. These costs form part of the overall judgment and are subject to post-judgment interest.

The post-judgment interest rate is defined within section 127(1) of the *Courts of Justice Act*. Interest may not be awarded in accordance with section 127(1) of the *Courts of Justice Act* where there may be a right to receive post-judgment interest at a different rate.

Calculation of Post-judgment Interest

Unless otherwise directed by the court in its judgment, post-judgment interest must be calculated from the date of the order. This applies where the court makes an order or judgment, but releases reasons on a later date. If the judgment is reserved, the interest is calculated from the date the judgment is released.

"Date of the order" means the date the order is made even if the order is not issued or enforceable on the date [s.127(1), CJA].

Post-judgment interest is calculated on the total amount of the order including prejudgment interest and costs. Post-judgment interest is payable on prejudgment interest included in the judgment because the prejudgment interest is "money owing under an order."

Interest continues to accrue until the judgment is paid but is to be calculated and recalculated (as the case may be) on the value of the judgment, pre-judgment interest, and costs awarded at the time of judgment as payments are made by the debtor.

Notice of Garnishment

In this process, an affidavit refers to an Affidavit for Enforcement Request (Form 20P).

Where a debtor does not pay a debt pursuant to a judgment, in order to make a demand of money owed to the debtor by someone else (e.g. garnishment of bank accounts, wages or money owed through a contract), a creditor must obtain a notice of garnishment in the jurisdiction where the debtor resides or carries on business. The person or company to whom the notice is sent is the garnishee.

A Notice of Garnishment (Form 20E) remains in force for six years from the date of its issue and for a further six years from each renewal [r.20.08(5.1)].

The creditor may first have to obtain a certificate of judgment in the originating court and file it in the court in the jurisdiction where the debtor resides or carries on business.

If a creditor is considering the garnishment of wages or amounts owing to a debtor by the Canadian Armed Forces, or the Federal/Provincial Crown, there are special time limits and additional steps that the creditor will be required to take.

The garnishee is liable to pay to the clerk any monies he or she owes to the debtor, up to the amount shown in the notice of garnishment, within 10 days after service of the notice on the garnishee or 10 days after the debt becomes payable, whichever is later [r. 20.08(7)]. A debt the garnishee owes to the debtor includes:

- a debt payable at the time the notice of garnishment is served;

- a debt payable (whether absolutely or on the fulfilment of a condition) within six years after the notice is served and within six years after it is issued [r. 20.08(8)].

A garnishee who admits owing a debt to the debtor shall pay it to the clerk in the manner prescribed by the notice of garnishment, subject to section 7 of the *Wages Act* [r. 20.08(9)]. The amounts paid into court shall not exceed the portion of the debtor's wages that are subject to garnishment under section 7 of the *Wages Act*. Interpretation and compliance with the *Wages Act* is the responsibility of the garnishee.

If more than six years have elapsed since the judgment was made, the clerk shall not issue a notice of garnishment [r. 20.08(2.1)]. The party requires leave of the court in order to have the writ issued.

Where a notice of garnishment is requested following the filing of a certificate of default under the *Provincial Offences Act*, the clerk shall not issue the garnishment if more than six years have elapsed since the date of the earliest date of the default for which the certificate was issued. The party requires leave of the court in order to have the garnishment issued.

Where a notice of garnishment is requested following the filing of a tribunal order under the *Residential Tenancies Act* or the *Employment Standards Act*, the clerk shall not issue the garnishment if more than six years have elapsed since the date tribunal order is effective. The party requires leave of the court in order to have the garnishment issued.

In the event that an order granting leave to issue is made, the notice of garnishment must be issued within one year after the date of the order, otherwise the order granting leave ceases to have effect and the creditor must obtain another order from the court by way of a subsequent motion [r. 20.08(2.2.)].

Garnishing the Wages of Federal/Provincial Employees

There are specific time limits and extra steps that must be taken if a creditor intends to garnish the wages of an employee of the federal government, a member of the Canadian Armed Forces, or an employee of the provincial government.

Garnishing the wages of an employee of the Federal Government:

The federal government requires information in addition to the basic information provided within the notice of garnishment before they will honour a garnishment request.

The creditor must obtain and complete a form called an "Application to Garnishee." The Application to Garnishee form is available online at http://laws.justice.gc.ca/eng/SOR-83-212/page-4.html#anchorsc:1, or by contacting the Garnishment Registry at the address provided below.

The creditor must serve the certified copy of their order or judgment, the issued notice of garnishment, and the completed Application to Garnishee on the federal government at the Garnishment Registry Office, which is located in the Department of Justice Canada — Ontario Regional Office, The Exchange Tower, 130 King St. West, Suite 3400, Box 36, Toronto, Ontario M5X 1K6.

The creditor must serve the aforementioned documents on the federal government within 30 days of the notice of garnishment being issued by the clerk of the Small Claims Court, otherwise the federal government may consider the garnishment invalid in accordance with the *Garnishment, Attachment and Pension Diversion Act*, section 6(2).

In accordance with the *Garnishment, Attachment and Pension Diversion Act*, section 10, the federal government has a minimum of 15 days to respond to the notice of garnishment.

For more information about the process of garnishing the wages of a federal government employee, see http://www.tbs-sct.gc.ca/pol/doc-eng.aspx?id=12138.

Garnishing the wages of a member of the Canadian Armed Forces:

The creditor must give the debtor's commanding officer notice of their intention to issue a garnishment at least 30 days before serving the notice of garnishment. If the creditor does not know the identity of the debtor's commanding officer, the creditor should be advised to contact the Office of the Judge Advocate General — National Defence Headquarters for instructions (613) 992-6420.

A commanding officer has a minimum of 30 days from the date that they are served with the notice of garnishment to respond.

For more information about garnishing the wages of a member of the Canadian Armed Forces, see http://www.admfincs.forces.gc.ca/qro-orf/vol-03/doc/chapter-chapitre-207.pdf.

Garnishing the wages of an employee of the provincial government (Ontario):

The *Proceedings Against the Crown Act*, R.R.O 1990, Reg. 940, requires that a Statement of Particulars must be served along with the issued notice of garnishment.

> 2. The creditor would proceed to have their notice of garnishment issued by the clerk of the court in the usual way.

> 3. The creditor must complete a form called a "Statement of Particulars." This regulated form is contained within the *Proceedings Against the Crown Act*, R.R.O 1990, Reg. 940.

In accordance with the *Proceedings Against the Crown Act*, R.R.O 1990, Reg.940, section 2, the province had 30 days from the date that service is effective, in which to respond to the notice of garnishment.

Writ of Seizure and Sale of Personal Property

If the debtor has been ordered by the court to pay the creditor money but he or she has not paid, the creditor can ask the enforcement office to take specific personal possessions belonging to the debtor and sell them at public auction so that the money can be used to pay the judgment debt. The costs of this procedure can be relatively high. The creditor risks paying these costs with no chance of recovery if the debtor does not have any goods worth seizing and selling, and the other enforcement remedies fail.

Under the *Execution Act*, a debtor is entitled to certain exemptions from seizure of personal property such as:

- Clothing (up to a certain amount);

- Household furniture, utensils, equipment, food and fuel (up to a certain amount);

- Tools and instruments used in the debtor's business (other than tillage of the soil or farming)(up to a certain amount);

- Tools, books and instruments used for the tillage of the soil or farming and livestock, fowl, bees and seed (up to a certain amount); and

- One motor vehicle worth less than the specified amount.

The debtor has a right to choose the goods that make up the exemptions.

If the creditor is requesting that a motor vehicle, snowmobile or boat be seized, he or she must also provide the court with proof that the following searches have been made:

> *Personal Property Security Act* search and *Repair and Storage Liens Act* search to show whether there are any liens or other securities registered against the vehicle, the amounts of the liens or securities, and whether there is enough equity in the vehicle for it to be seized and sold.

The writ will expire six years from the date it is issued, unless it is renewed for an additional six-year period.

Writ of Seizure and Sale of Land

A creditor can file a writ of seizure and sale of land against a debtor in any county or district where the debtor may own land (including a house). The writ would encumber any land presently owned or land which may be purchased in the future by the debtor in the county(ies) or district(s) where the writ is filed. If you wish to enforce the writ in more than one location, you must issue a separate writ for each location and file it there.

If another creditor has a writ filed in the same enforcement office against the same debtor and is actively enforcing it, everyone will share, on a pro-rata basis (divided on a proportionate basis depending on the amount of each debt), in any money paid into the enforcement office (sheriff) from any enforcement activity taken against the debtor.

The creditor does not have to wait for the debtor to decide to sell the land. Four months after filing the writ with the enforcement office, someone may direct the enforcement office (sheriff) to seize and sell the land, but the actual sale cannot proceed until the writ has been on file for six months. The enforcement office can only sell the portion of the land that the debtor actually owns. Mortgages, liens, and encumbrances may reduce the value of the property that is available to be seized and sold by the enforcement office. Creditors should determine, before proceeding with this process, that the debtor actually has equity (difference between what a property is worth and what the owner owes against that property) available to be sold. The writ will expire six years from the date it is issued, unless you renew it for an additional six-year period. There is a fee to file and renew a writ.

Writ of Delivery

When a person or business has personal property that does not belong to him or her and refuses to return it to the rightful owner, the owner can request a court order for a writ of delivery. This writ authorizes enforcement staff to take the specific items and return them.

The court requires a full description of the personal property, i.e., serial numbers, make, model, photographs (if available), the exact location where the items can be found and proof of ownership, where applicable.

Once the judge grants the order for a writ of delivery, an Affidavit for Enforcement Request [Form 20P] and Writ of Delivery [Form 20B] must be filled out.

If the personal property referred to in a writ of delivery cannot be found or taken by an enforcement officer, a notice of motion can request an order directing an enforcement officer to seize any other personal property owned by the debtor.

Consolidation Order

This order would combine the judgment debts and set up a schedule of repayments for all creditors named in the order. As long as payments are made as ordered, no other enforcement measures can be taken to collect the debts included in the order, except each creditor could seek issuance of a Writ of Seizure and Sale of Land [Form 20D] and file it with the enforcement office (sheriff).

A Notice of Motion and Supporting Affidavit [Form 15A] listing the judgments, debts, income from all sources and any family support obligations is the process for this order. The notice of motion and affidavit must be served on each creditor at least seven days before the scheduled motion date.

A judge will hear evidence about income and expenses and may make an order combining debts and order payments to be made in installments.

A consolidation order will terminate immediately if:

- an order for payment of money is obtained against you for a debt incurred after the date of the consolidation order; or

- if you are in default under the terms of the order for 21 days.

If the order is terminated, no further consolidation order can be made until a year has passed from the date of the termination.

Enforcement Improvements

If you are the plaintiff and you win the case, the court may order the defendant to pay you money. The defendant (often referred to as the "debtor" after judgment) may pay right away, or you may give the debtor more time to pay. If the debtor does not pay, there are steps the creditor can take to get the money. This is called enforcing the judgment.

Changes to the rules for enforcing a judgment include the following:

1. — Writ of Seizure and Sale of Personal Property — Holding Period

When a debtor has been ordered by the court to pay the creditor money, but fails to do so, the creditor may ask the clerk of the court to issue a writ of seizure and sale of personal property. The creditor can then take the writ to the enforcement office.

The enforcement office may enforce the writ by taking personal possessions belonging to the debtor and selling them at public auction. The money from the sale would be used to pay the judgment debt owed to the creditor and any costs associated with the enforcement steps taken. The process governing the writ of seizure and sale of personal property is set out in rule 20.06.

Before, subrule 20.06(6) required the enforcement office to hold seized personal property for at least 30 days before it could be sold. Now, under the amended subrule 20.06(6), the holding period has been reduced to ten days. This reduces the holding costs charged by the enforcement office.

Order for a Contempt Hearing

Examination Hearing

A creditor can request an examination hearing if there is a default under an order for the payment of recovery of money. See r. 20.10.

An examination of the debtor gives both the court and the creditor information about the debtor's financial situation. It may be that the creditor wants to enforce an order though garnishment and needs to know where the debtor works or banks. The examination may give the creditor the information needed to request a garnishment. The creditor can also examine a person other than the debtor to get information about the debtor's assets.

The creditor and the person to be examined (usually the debtor) *must* attend the examination. Lawyers or agents may also attend. The examination will be conducted under oath. The public will not be allowed to attend unless the court orders otherwise.

The debtor or any other person to be examined should be prepared to answer questions and provide documents in relation to the examination.

A debtor who is an individual (i.e. not a corporation) must fill out the Financial Information Form [Form 20I] and serve it on the creditor before the hearing. The debtor must also bring a copy of the completed form to the hearing and give it to the judge. A financial information form provides a snapshot of the debtor's income, expenses, debts and assets. The form is *not* filed with the court. The debtor must also bring to the hearing documents that support the information given in the form.

If, at the examination, the court orders a periodic payment schedule, the debtor must make the payments in the amounts and on the dates ordered in the schedule. As long as those periodic payments are made, the creditor cannot do anything else to enforce the judgment, other than issue a writ of seizure and sale of land.

What Can a Creditor Do if the Debtor Fails to Make a Payment Under a Periodic Payment Order or Makes a Partial Payment?

If the debtor fails to make a payment or makes only a partial payment, you can serve on the debtor and file with the court a Notice of Default of Payment [Form 20L] and an Affidavit of Default of Payment [Form 20M]. An order for periodic payment terminates 15 days after you serve the debtor with the notice of default of payment, unless a Consent [Form 13B] in which you waive the default, is filed with the court within the 15-day period. You can then proceed with another method of enforcement.

If the debtor or other person attends the examination but refuses to produce documents or answer questions, the judge may order the person to attend a contempt hearing to determine whether the person is in contempt of court.

If the debtor (or other person) does not attend the examination hearing, the judge may order the person to attend a contempt hearing to determine whether the person is in contempt of court.

If the judge orders the debtor or other person to be jailed for contempt of court, the clerk will issue a Warrant of Committal [Form 20J] directed to the police. The warrant authorizes the police to take the individual named in the warrant to the nearest correctional institution and hold him or her there for the time specified in the warrant.

If you are found in contempt of court at the contempt hearing and a warrant of committal is issued, you or your representative may ask the court to set aside the warrant and the finding of contempt by filing a Notice of Motion and supporting Affidavit [Form 15A] at the Small Claims Court office. In your supporting affidavit and at the motion hearing, explain to the judge the reasons why the contempt order should be set aside.

Contempt Hearings for Wilful Failure to Attend an Examination

Previously, a contempt hearing for wilful failure to attend an examination in Small Claims Court was required to be heard before a judge of the Superior Court of Justice. As of January 1, 2011, these hearings may also be heard by a deputy judge or provincial civil judge.

Also, as of January 1, 2011, where the court finds a person in contempt of court for wilful failure to attend an examination, the maximum penalty has been reduced from 40 days to 5 days in jail.

Execution Act

The *Execution Act* is the primary legislation in Ontario affecting the seizure and sale of assets. Key sections of the *Execution Act* Include:

Categories of Exemption from Seizure	Section 2 sets out six categories of chattels that are exempt from seizure under any writ issued out of any court. Exemptions from seizure generally exist to permit debtors to carry on the basics of daily life and to engage in their business in order to continue to earn income. (See Section 5: Exemptions From Seizure)
Sale and Refund of Amount of Exemption	Section 3 sets out circumstances in which certain chattels against which the debtor claims an exemption may nonetheless be seized. In those cases a refund of the exemption amount will be paid to the debtor from the sale proceeds. (See Section 5.1.3: Tools of Trade and Section 5.1.4: Livestock and Farm Tools)
No Exemption for Corporate Debtor	Section 7(4) provides that the exemptions in the *Execution Act* are not available to a corporate debtor.
Disputes	Section 8(1) provides for debtors or creditors to apply to the Superior Court of Justice to determine whether a chattel is eligible for exemption from seizure, or whether chattels claimed to be exempt exceed the value of the exemption. Section 8(2) provides that a sheriff may apply to the Superior Court of Justice for direction on matters arising from exemptions under the *Execution Act*.
Seizure and Sale of Land	Section 9 allows for the seizure and sale of the lands of the execution debtor, including land held in trust for the debtor, and including any interest of the debtor in lands held in joint tenancy.
Seizure and Sale of Shares or Dividends	Section 14 contains provisions for the seizure and sale of shares or dividends. (See Section 10.26: Seizure Of Specific Goods — Shares and Dividends and Section 20.8: Sale of Shares and Dividends)
Seizure and Sale of Rights in Chattels	Section 18 provides for the seizure and sale of the debtor's interests in chattels. The sale conveys the debtor's interest as of the time the execution was delivered to the sheriff (or for Small Claims court at the time of seizure).

| Mortgages | Section 19 provides for the seizure of money and securities. Sections 23 and 24 contain specific procedures for the seizure and sale of mortgages. (See Section 10.19: Seizure — Specific Assets — Mortgages and Section 20.5: Sale of Mortgage) |
| Reasonable Force | Section 20 sets out the circumstances for using reasonable force during a seizure. |

Repair and Storage Liens Act

The *Repair and Storage Liens Act* deals with the resolution of disputed amounts for the repair or storage of tangible articles other than fixtures. The enforcement office is required to seize an article subject to a repair and storage lien in two circumstances:

- After a non-possessory lien claimant registers the claim under the *Personal Property Security Act*, he or she may give the enforcement office a direction to seize the article to which the lien applies; or

- Where the owner of the article or other lawful applicant has paid the disputed amount into court (or posted security) and the lien claimant does not return the article, the applicant may obtain a writ of seizure from the clerk of the court and file it with the enforcement office.

Key sections of the *Repair and Storage Liens Act* include:

Direction to Seize	Section 14(1) provides for a non-possessory registered lien claimant to deliver to the sheriff a direction to seize the article. (See Section 11.5.9: Enforcement of Non-Possessory Liens — Direction to Seize)
Requirement to Seize	Section 14(2) requires the sheriff to seize the article and deliver it to the lien claimant after receiving a copy of the registered claim for lien and a direction to seize.
Costs of Seizure	Section 16(1) provides that where a lien claimant has sold an article, part of the proceeds go to the costs of seizure.
Payment of Sale Proceeds Into Court	Section 16(2) provides for a lien claimant to pay sale proceeds into court where there is a question about the right of any person to share in the proceeds.
Application to Determine Questions	Section 23(1) states that any person may apply to court to determine questions about seizure, sale by the lien claimant, the distribution of proceeds, the amount of the lien, the right to a lien, or other matters. (See Section 11.7.1: Application to Determine Questions)
Application to Resolve Dispute and Return Article	Section 24 provides for the owner or other lawfully entitled person to apply to the court to recover possession of the article, and for the payment of funds into court or posting security. (See Section 11.7.2: Application to Resolve Dispute and Return Article)
Writ of Seizure	Section 24(9) provides for an applicant to obtain a writ of seizure where the respondent does not release an article as required. (See Section 11.7.2: Application for Return of Articles — Writ of Seizure for Non-Return of Article)
Reasonable Force	Section 31(1) sets out the circumstances for using reasonable force in enforcing a direction to seize or a writ of seizure under the *Repair and Storage Liens Act*.

Wages Act

Section 7 of the *Wages Act* puts limits on the amount of a debtor's wages that can be seized from an employer.

Bail Act

Section 1 of the *Bail Act* provides for the Crown Attorney to transmit a certificate of lien to the sheriff in cases where a person has been committed for trial and admitted to bail. The certificate of lien contains information about the surety for bail for the appearance of the individual in court.

Land Titles Act

Section 138 of the *Land Titles Act* states that the seizure of a mortgage or charge or lease-hold land registered under the Act does not take effect until the sheriff's certificate is lodged with the land registrar. This section does not apply where the sheriff has provided the land registrar with a notice under Section 23 of the *Execution Act*.

Mining Act

Under section 64 of the *Mining Act*, a copy of a writ of seizure and sale may be filed with the mining recorder and recorded on a mining claim held by the judgment debtor. The sheriff may then treat the judgment debtor's mining interest as if it were goods and chattels subject to a writ of seizure and sale.

Absconding Debtors Act

Section 2 of the *Absconding Debtors Act* provides for the court to make an "order of attachment" to seize the non-exempt real or personal property from an Ontario resident who departs from Ontario to defraud creditors or to avoid being arrested or served with process. The Act sets out specific procedures for the sheriff to follow in enforcing orders of attachment.

Federal Statutes

Bankruptcy and Insolvency Act

Section 69.3(1) of the federal *Bankruptcy and Insolvency Act* states that on the bankruptcy of a debtor, no creditor has any remedy against the debtor or the debtor's property or shall continue execution or proceedings until the trustee has been discharged. Section 69.4 provides for creditors to seek a court declaration in connection with a stay of proceeding.

Bank Act

Schedule I and II of the *Bank Act* list banks from which seizure and sale of shares and dividends can take place.

Indian Act

Section 89 of the *Indian Act* provides that, with few exceptions, the real and personal property of an Indian or band situated on a reserve cannot be seized except at the instance of another Indian or band.

Canada Shipping Act

Under section 629 of the *Canada Shipping Act*, the Admiralty Court may require the arrest of a ship found in Canadian waters in order to enforce an order for money owed for work done in connection with the ship.

Other statutes that provide for the issuance of an order that might be filed with a civil court of competent jurisdiction include, but are not limited to:

- *Mining Act*;
- *Human Rights Code*;
- *Ontario Works Act, 1997*; and

- *Ontario Disability Support Program Act, 1997.*

The Landlord and Tenant Board (LTB) is a tribunal, created under the *Residential Tenancies Act, 2006* (RTA).

The RTA came into effect on January 31, 2007 and sets out the rules for most residential rental housing in Ontario. The previous legislation, known as the *Tenant Protection Act*, is no longer in effect.

Landlord and Tenant Board Orders (Board Orders) that include awards for monetary compensation may be enforced by filing a Board-certified copy of the Board Order with the Small Claims Court [s.19(1), SPPA].

The Ministry of Labour administers the *Employment Standards Act* (Act) and conducts investigations into a variety of complaints made by employees in Ontario, including complaints with respect to unpaid wages.

As a result of these investigations, an Order to Pay may be issued by the Ministry of Labour against an employer.

In accordance with section 126(1) of the Act, the Director of Employment Standards (Director) may choose to seek enforcement of the Order to Pay by filing a copy of the order (certified by the Director to be a true copy) with a court of competent jurisdiction. Upon filing, the order is deemed to be an order of the court in which it was filed and may be enforced as if it was a judgment or order of the court.

In accordance with s. 127(1) of the *Employment Standards Act*, the Director of Employment Standards may authorize a collector to exercise specified powers under sections 125, 126, 130 and 135(3) in the collection of amounts owing under these sections of the Act or under an order made by a reciprocating state.

Section 127(3) of the Act allows the Director of Employment Standards to authorize the collector to collect a reasonable fee or reasonable disbursements or both from each person from whom the collector seeks to collect amounts owing under this Act. Under section 127(4) of the Act, the Director may also set limitations on the amount that a collector is entitled to collect (such limitations would be required to be explicitly stated, in writing).

Case Law: *McIntosh v. Lalonde* (1998), 165 D.L.R. (4th) 178 (Ont. Div. Ct.) — To what extent is a welfare recipient protected against seizure, by creditors, of funds received under a provincial welfare disability allowance? When a family benefits disability allowance is deposited electronically into a bank account, and the allowance is the sole source of the funds in the account, are the funds in the bank account immune from seizure under s. 5(1)(b) of the *Family Benefits Act*, R.S.O. 1990, c. F.2? Case governed by s. 5(1)(b) of the *Family Benefits Act*. See O'Brien J. in *Metropolitan Toronto (Municipality) v. O'Brien* (1995), 23 O.R. (3d) 543 (Ont. Gen. Div.). Protection from creditors continues after the benefit is paid into a bank account provided that the bank account's purpose is to receive the benefit. Use of bank account and electronic deposits is an administratively convenient and secure way to make welfare payment. Any other interpretation would also undermine the underlying social purpose of welfare legislation like the *Family Benefits Act*.

Ladies' Dress & Sportswear Industry Advisory Committee v. 1265122 Ontario Ltd. (November 9, 1999), Doc. Toronto CP-12682-98 (Ont. Small Cl. Ct.) — The corporation was operated by the same individual, as an alter ego, working for the same clients. The plaintiff was entitled to enforce judgment against the second corporation, which was a sham.

R. v. Devgan (1999), 121 O.A.C. 265, 44 O.R. (3d) 161, 136 C.C.C. (3d) 238, 26 C.R. (5th) 307, 1999 CarswellOnt 1534 (Ont. C.A.); leave to appeal refused (2000), 254 N.R. 393 (note), 134 O.A.C. 396 (note), 2000 CarswellOnt 911, 2000 CarswellOnt 912 (S.C.C.) — Civil judgment against the accused not precluding granting of compensation order. Compensation order may not be granted for legal fees, disbursements or interest: *Criminal Code*, R.S.C. 1985, c. C-46, s. 725(1).

Superior Propane Inc. v. Veer Preet Petro Products Canada Inc. (2002), 2002 CarswellOnt 2150, 23 C.P.C. (5th) 303, [2002] O.J. No. 2660 (Ont. Master) — Default judgment against corporate defendant not stayed. No explanation for default given. No genuine issue for trial as against corporate defendant. Default judgment would stand but enforcement of judgment was stayed pending final determination of counterclaim on terms that corporate defendant pay into court portion of judgment as security.

Adekunte v. 1211531 Ontario Ltd. (2002), 2002 CarswellOnt 2166 (Ont. S.C.J.) — Inconclusive as to whether or not claim reached corporate defendant. Default judgment set aside and all future enforcement proceedings stayed on condition that corporate defendant file defence to defendant's claim and counterclaim.

Credit Union Atlantic Ltd. v. McAvoy, 2002 CarswellNS 481, 2002 NSCA 145, 210 N.S.R. (2d) 207, 659 A.P.R. 207 (N.S. C.A.). Defendant unable to pay for legal advice and unaware that she could defend on own behalf. Later found counsel on affordable terms. Chambers judge erred in refusal to set aside judgment. Test was not whether Defendant had decided not to defend, but whether she had reasonable excuse for failure. Appeal allowed and judgment set aside.

MacKay v. Dauphinee, 2007 CarswellNS 178, 254 N.S.R. (2d) 127, 810 A.P.R. 127, 47 C.P.C. (6th) 380, 2007 NSSM 11 (N.S. Small Cl. Ct.); reversed 2008 CarswellNS 312, 2008 NSSC 190, 44 C.B.R. (5th) 205, 61 C.P.C. (6th) 395, 266 N.S.R. (2d) 92, 851 A.P.R. 92 (N.S. S.C.)

Applicant sought to enforce judgment in small claims court and brought an action for order granting leave to sell interests in land of judgment debtor. Application dismissed. The adjudicator determined that the Small Claims Court did not have jurisdiction, due to s. 10(a) of the *Small Claims Court Act* which states that no claim could be made under Act for recovery of land or estate or interest therein.

MacKay v. Dauphinee, 2008 CarswellNS 312, 2008 NSSC 190, 44 C.B.R. (5th) 205, 61 C.P.C. (6th) 395, 266 N.S.R. (2d) 92, 851 A.P.R. 92 (N.S. S.C.)

Plaintiff brought unsuccessful application in the Small Claims Court for order granting leave to sell interests in debtor's land free of prior judgments. The adjudicator determined that the Small Claims Court did not have jurisdiction, due to *s. 10(a)* of the *Small Claims Court Act* which states that no claim could be made under Act for recovery of land or estate or interest therein. The plaintiff appealed. Appeal allowed.

The Supreme Court of Nova Scotia held that an execution order issued to enforce payment of a judgment which has the result of forcing a sale a real property is not a claim for the recovery of land or an interest or an estate in land. An execution order issued by the court is simply a recognition by the court that the claimant is entitled to recover on its judgment. As such, the appellant is entitled to the order sought before the Small Claims Court, granting him leave to sell the judgment debtor's land free of the encumbrances of the prior judgments.

R. v. Castro, [2010] O.J. No. 4573, 261 C.C.C. (3d) 304, 2010 ONCA 718, 2010 CarswellOnt 8120, 270 O.A.C. 140, 102 O.R. (3d) 609 (Ont. C.A.)

The appellant ordered to make restitution pursuant to s. 738(1) of the *Criminal Code*, R.S.C. 1985. The appellant sought to have restitution portion of his sentence set aside or reduced.

Trial judge ordered restitution in the amount of $141,752.

Section 738(1)(a) governs the making of restitution orders when money has been taken. It gives the court discretion to order the offender to make restitution by paying the victim "an amount not exceeding the replacement value of the property as of the date the order is imposed, less the value of any part of the property that is returned. . . where the amount is readily ascertainable."

Appellate court will only interfere with the sentencing judge's exercise of discretion on the basis of error in principle or if the order is excessive or inadequate. See *R. v. Devgan*, 26 C.R. (5th) 307, 136 C.C.C. (3d) 238, 44 O.R. (3d) 161, [1999] O.J. No. 1825, 121 O.A.C. 265, 1999 CarswellOnt 1534 (Ont. C.A.); leave to appeal refused 254 N.R. 393 (note), 134 O.A.C. 396 (note), 2000 CarswellOnt 912, 2000 CarswellOnt 911, [1999] S.C.C.A. No. 518 (S.C.C.). Discretion in making restitution order found in in *R. v. Zelensky*, [1978] 3 W.W.R. 693, 41 C.C.C. (2d) 97, 21 N.R. 372, 86 D.L.R. (3d) 179, 2 C.R. (3d) 107, [1978] 2 S.C.R. 940, 1978 CarswellMan 121, 1978 CarswellMan 51 (S.C.C.).

See further *R. v. Fitzgibbon*, 1990 CarswellOnt 996, 1990 CarswellOnt 172, 76 C.R. (3d) 378, 55 C.C.C. (3d) 449, 78 C.B.R. (N.S.) 193, 40 O.A.C. 81, 107 N.R. 281, [1990] 1 S.C.R. 1005, EYB 1990-67542 at pp. 1012–14 (S.C.C.); *London Life Insurance Co. v. Zavitz*, 1992 CarswellBC 63, [1992] B.C.J. No. 400, 22 W.A.C. 164, 11 B.C.A.C. 164, 12 C.R. (4th) 267, 65 B.C.L.R. (2d) 140, 5 C.P.C. (3d) 14 (B.C. C.A.), at p. 270 [C.R.]; *R. v. Scherer*, 1984 CarswellOnt 79, 42 C.R. (3d) 376, 5 O.A.C. 297, [1984] O.J. No. 156, 16 C.C.C. (3d) 30 (Ont. C.A.); leave to appeal refused [1984] 2 S.C.R. x (note), [1984] S.C.C.A. No. 29, 58 N.R. 80n, 16 C.C.C. (3d) 30 (note) at pp. 37-38 (S.C.C.) *R. v. Salituro*, 1990 CarswellOnt 101, 56 C.C.C. (3d) 350, 78 C.R. (3d) 68, 38 O.A.C. 241 (Ont. C.A.), at pp. 372-73 [C.C.C.], affirmed 1991 CarswellOnt 124, 1991 CarswellOnt 1031, [1991] S.C.J. No. 97, 68 C.C.C. (3d) 289, 131 N.R. 161, [1991] 3 S.C.R. 654, 50 O.A.C. 125, 8 C.R.R. (2d) 173, 9 C.R. (4th) 324, EYB 1991-67635 (S.C.C.); *R. v. Horne* (1996), 34 O.R. (3d) 142, 1996 CarswellOnt 5479 (Ont. Gen. Div.), at pp. 148-49 [O.R.]; and *R. v. Carter*, 1990 CarswellOnt 1032, [1990] O.J. No. 3140, 9 C.C.L.S. 69 (Ont. Gen. Div.), at pp. 75-76 [C.C.L.S.], varied 1991 CarswellOnt 1080, 9 C.C.L.S. 82 (Ont. C.A.); leave to appeal refused 55 O.A.C. 390 (note), 137 N.R. 400 (note), 9 C.C.L.S. 82n (S.C.C.).

Imposition of restitution order proper exercise of trial judge's discretion. Appeal dismissed and restitution order upheld.

R. v. Popert, 251 C.C.C. (3d) 30, 258 O.A.C. 163, 2010 CarswellOnt 535, 2010 ONCA 89 (Ont. C.A.)

Generally speaking, an insurance company that has paid out a claim on a house that was subject of arson can obtain a compensation order in the course of the sentencing proceedings concerning the person who committed the arson, either on the basis of subrogation or on the basis that it is a person who has suffered "the loss . . . of . . . property . . . as a result of the commission of the offence" within the meaning of s. 738(1)(a) of the *Code*. The fact that the person to whose rights the insurance company is subrogated hired the arsonist does not bar a claim for the order.

20.02 (1) **Power of Court** — The court may,

(a) **stay the enforcement of an order of the court, for such time and on such terms as are just; and**

(b) **vary the times and proportions in which money payable under an order of the court shall be paid, if it is satisfied that the debtor's circumstances have changed.**

History [R. 20.02(1)]: Formerly 21.02; plain language changes.

Commentary: Where a stay of execution is ordered by the court pursuant to Rule 20.02, all enforcement proceedings, including the necessity for a garnishee to make payments, cease. Where a Notice of Garnishment was previously issued, the garnishee company should be advised by the court of the stay and directed to cease further remittances until the stay has expired or a subsequent order of the court states otherwise. Monies received under a Notice of Garnishment after a stay is issued will be returned to the garnishee, unless the terms of the order direct otherwise.

Stay of Proceedings

Rule 63.01 of the *Rules of Civil Procedure* states that the delivery of a notice of appeal from an interlocutory or final order stays, until the disposition of the appeal, any provision of the order for the payment of money, except a provision that awards support or enforces a support order. If the writ was issued in accordance with the *Rules of Civil Procedure* or the *Rules of the Small Claims Court*, a copy of the filed notice of appeal is sufficient proof of the appeal and would stay any further enforcement proceedings until the appeal is disposed of.

Writs issued under other rules or legislation will likely require the filing of a Certificate of Stay issued by the registrar in accordance with r. 63.02 of the *Rules of Civil Procedure*, which indicates that an interlocutory or final order may be stayed on such terms as are just,

(a) By an order of the court whose decision is to be appealed; or

(b) By an order of a judge of the court to which a motion for leave to appeal has been made or to which an appeal has been taken. O. Reg. 465/93, s. 8

The Certificate of Stay (Form 63A) is issued by the registrar on request of a party in accordance with r. 63.03(4) of the *Rules of Civil Procedure*.

Where an order is stayed, no steps may be taken under the order or for its enforcement, except by order of a judge of the court to which a motion for leave to appeal has been made or an appeal has been taken. A stay does not prevent the issue of a writ of execution or filing of the writ in the sheriff's office [r. 63.03(3)], *Rules of Civil Procedure*.

Stay Due to Bankruptcy

As a general rule, the commencement of bankruptcy proceedings under the *Bankruptcy and Insolvency Act* gives rise to a stay of proceedings, including enforcement activity, against the debtor.

Written notice of the stay may be received in:

• A Notice of Intention to Make a Proposal

• A proposal

• A consumer proposal

• A receiving order

• An assignment in bankruptcy

If a party to the proceedings wants to take steps against the debtor, the party should apply to Bankruptcy Court for leave to do so, or for an order that the stay does not apply. If there is a dispute about the stay, the party should take the matter to the Bankruptcy Court for resolution.

A stay of proceedings due to bankruptcy must be applied to all writs that exist for the debtor(s) named within the document/notice. The application of notice of a stay of proceedings is applied to all of the debtor's writs in an effort to ensure that no further enforcement activity will occur, until further notice is received from the court or Trustee in Bankruptcy.

Since an order setting aside default judgment is an interlocutory order (as per *Laurentian Plaza v. Martin* (1992), 7 O.R. (3d) 111 (C.A.), no appeal of that interlocutory order is possible). Thus, an interlocutory order of the Small Claims Court directing payment of funds to a party must be obeyed.

Under s. 3(5) of the *Creditors' Relief Act*, where the enforcement office has a writ against a debtor, at the request of a creditor, the enforcement office may provide a demand, in writing, for any garnishment funds being held in Small Claims Court in connection with that same debtor.

The demand procedure under the *CRA* applies where the sheriff's writ names the same debtor as the debtor named in the SCC Notice of Garnishment (Form 20E). The sheriff is entitled to take those garnished funds and distribute them under the *CRA*.

Where a judgment creditor in the Superior Court of Justice wishes to obtain funds held by the Small Claims Court, the creditor should file a Writ of Seizure and Sale and a Direction to enforce with the sheriff. Depending on the origins of the money held by the Small Claims Court, the sheriff will then take the appropriate action. There are three possible types of funds in this scenario: funds received by the Small Claims Court by way of garnishment, funds held by the Small Claims Court bailiff as a result of a seizure under an execution, and funds paid in to the Small Claims Court pending the outcome of a proceeding. If funds are in the hands of the Small Claims Court as a result of garnishment, the sheriff is authorised to demand and receive them pursuant to subsection 3(5) of the *Creditors' Relief Act*, R.S.O. 1990, c. C.45.

Pursuant to subsection 25(1) of the *Creditors' Relief Act*, funds or other property held by the Small Claims Court bailiff as a result of a seizure under a writ of seizure and sale may be demanded and obtained by the sheriff only if the sheriff has first been unable to find sufficient other property or monies of the judgment debtor to satisfy the writ that is in the sheriff's hands. Thus, funds should not be released unless the Registrar or court clerk is provided with some evidence that the sheriff has taken steps to locate other monies or property of the debtor.

Funds paid into the Small Claims Court pending the outcome of a proceeding cannot be attached or seized until a determination has been made as to entitlement to those funds. Once it has been determined that a person who is a judgment debtor is entitled to the funds, a sheriff or other interested party may make an application to the Small Claims Court for those funds pursuant to s. 23 of the *Creditors' Relief Act*.

It is not possible to garnishee funds held by the Small Claims Court. The funds, in accordance with s. 93 of the *Courts of Justice Act* are held by Her Majesty the Queen and subsection 21(1) of the *Proceedings Against the Crown Act*, R.S.O. 1990, c. P.27 reads as follows:

> Subject to subsections (2) and (3), no execution or attachment or process in the nature thereof shall be issued out of any court against the Crown.

Subsection 21(1) clearly prohibits any execution or attachment to be issued against the Crown. Subsection 21(2) states that a garnishment that is otherwise valid may issue against the Crown for the payment of money owing or accruing as remuneration payable by the Crown for goods or services. Thus, subsection 21(1) refers not only to execution or attachment processes in which the Crown is the debtor but also refers to situations where the Crown is the garnishee. Subsection 21(3) states that a garnishment may issue against the Crown for an amount owing or accruing under an order for support or maintenance. Thus, the Crown can only be named as a garnishee when the Crown owes money as remuneration for services or goods to a debtor or when the debtor who is owed money by the Crown owes money for support or maintenance.

The Supreme Court of Canada has ruled on the criteria that should be applied in determining whether an order should be stayed pending appeal. See *RJR-MacDonald Inc. v. Canada (Attorney General)*, [1994] 1 S.C.R. 311, 1994 CarswellQue 120F, 1994 CarswellQue 120, [1994] S.C.J. No. 17, 54 C.P.R. (3d) 114, (sub nom. *RJR-MacDonald Inc. c. Canada (Procureur général)*) 164 N.R. 1, (sub nom. *RJR-MacDonald Inc. c. Canada (Procureur général)*) 60 Q.A.C. 241, 111 D.L.R. (4th) 385, (sub nom. *RJR-Macdonald Inc. c. Canada (Procureur général)*) 171 N.R. 402 (note) (S.C.C.) and *Metropolitan Stores (MTS) Ltd. v. Manitoba Food & Commercial Workers, Local 832*, (sub nom. *Manitoba (Attorney General) v. Metropolitan Stores Ltd.)* [1987] 1 S.C.R. 110, 1987 CarswellMan 176, 1987 CarswellMan 272, [1987] S.C.J. No. 6, *(sub nom. Manitoba (Attorney General) v. Metropolitan Stores (M.T.S.) Ltd.)* 38 D.L.R. (4th) 321, 73 N.R. 341, 46 Man. R. (2d) 241, *(sub nom. Manitoba (Attorney General) v. Metropolitan Stores (M.T.S.) Ltd.)* 87 C.L.L.C. 14,015, 18 C.P.C. (2d) 273, *(sub nom. Manitoba (Attorney General) v. Metropolitan Stores (M.T.S.) Ltd.)* 25 Admin. L.R. 20, [1987] D.L.Q. 235, *(sub nom. Manitoba (Attorney General) v. Metropolitan Stores (M.T.S.) Ltd.)* [1987] 3 W.W.R. 1 (S.C.C.). A three-part test is involved. In the case of a motion for a stay, the court must first undertake a preliminary assessment of the merits to ensure that there is a serious question to be determined on the appeal itself. Second, it must be determined whether the appellant who is seeking the stay would suffer irreparable harm (that is, harm not readily compensable in money damages) if the stay were not granted. Third, a comparison must be made as to which of the parties would suffer the greater harm from the granting or refusing of the stay sought (this is often referred to as the "balance of convenience" or, in the words of Ontario courts from time to time, the "balance of inconvenience" test).

The *Execution Act*, R.S.O. 1990, c. E.24 states in part:

> 10. (1) Subject to the *Land Titles Act* and to section 11, a writ of execution binds the goods and lands against which it is issued from the time it has been received for execution and recorded by the sheriff.
>
> R.S.O. 1990, c. E.24, s. 10(1)
>
> . . . . .
>
> (4) Subsection (1) does not apply to an execution against goods issued out of the Small Claims Court, swhich binds only from the time of the seizure.
>
> R.S.O. 1990, c. E.24, s. 10(4)
>
> 11. (1) **Writ not to bind lands unless name of debtor sufficient** — Where the name of an execution debtor set out in a writ of execution is not that of a corporation or the firm name of a partnership, the writ does not bind the lands of the execution debtor unless,
>
> > (a) the name of the execution debtor set out in the writ includes at least one given name in full; or
> >
> > (b) a statutory declaration of the execution creditor or execution creditor's solicitor is filed with the sheriff identifying the execution debtor by at least one given name in full.
> >
> > R.S.O. 1990, c. E.24, s. 11(1)

See the *Reciprocal Enforcement of Judgments (U.K.) Act*, R.S.O. 1990, Chapter R.6 as to the reciprocal recognition and enforcement of judgments in Ontario courts, in particular Part IV, Article VI.

Case Law: *Han v. Re/Max Town & Country Realty Inc.* (1996), 97 O.A.C. 228, 4 C.P.C. (4th) 203 (C.A.); amended (1997), 7 C.P.C. (4th) 187 (Ont. C.A. [In Chambers]) — Appellants sought order lifting automatic stay. Court had ordered accounting. Certain consumers were beneficiaries of statutory trust created by *Real Estate and Business Brokers Act*, R.S.O. 1990, c. s. 20. There was no basis for continuing stay as it affected consumers and accountant as they were entitled to be paid in priority to all other claimants. Stay not lifted with respect to agents.

Desautels Creative Printing Papers Inc. v. Printcrafters Inc. (1999), 138 Man. R. (2d) 309, 202 W.A.C. 309 (Man. C.A.) — The defendant claimed summary judgment should be stayed pending determination of its counterclaim. The defendant had not shown that it would be manifestly unjust to allow the plaintiff to enforce payment of its judgment. The test pending appeal was stated in *American Cyanamid Co. v. Ethicon Ltd.*, [1975] 1 All E.R. 504 (H.L.). The defendant was not able to demonstrate irreparable harm or that the balance of convenience was in its favour. The trial judged erred in staying summary judgment.

The plaintiff moved for removal of a stay. The stay was not one granted by the Courts of Justice Act, but created by s. 69(1) of the *Bankruptcy and Insolvency Act*, R.S.C. 1992, c. 27, as amended. The defendant was an undischarged bankrupt. Only a superior court sitting in bankruptcy has authority to lift a stay and grant leave to proceed: *Bankruptcy and Insolvency Act* s. 183. Execution of the default judgment may only proceed with leave of the bankruptcy court: *382231 Ontario Ltd. v. Wilanson Resources Ltd.* (1982), 43 C.B.R. (N.S.) 153 (Ont. S.C.).

Once a defendant is discharged, the plaintiff may seek leave from the Small Claims Court to continue, subject to s. 178(1) of the *Bankruptcy and Insolvency Act*, giving credit for the security: *Re Bouchard* (1939), 21 C.B.R. 8; *Franklin v. Shultz*, [1967] 2 O.R. 149, 10 C.B.R. (N.S.) 29, 62 D.L.R. (2d) 643 (Ont. C.A.); *Ladanyi v. Malcolm* (1990), 3 C.B.R. (3d) 216; *Associates Financial Services of Canada Ltd. v. Campbell* (1998), 8 C.B.R. (4th) 187, 1998 CarswellOnt 5089 (Ont. Sm. Cl. Ct.).

Chan v. Bernlor Enterprises Inc., 2001 CarswellAlta 1106, 2001 ABCA 210 (Alta. C.A.) — Plaintiffs each got judgment of $2,500 plus costs. Defendants applied for stay of enforcement and also for order including transcript of proceedings before Chambers Judge in appeal book. Presumption with money judgment was that it should be enforced and grave harm would not result to defendants if enforcement levied. Transcript was included as no real harm caused.

Knodell v. Blackburn (2002), 2002 CarswellOnt 1124 (Ont. S.C.J.) — Applicant was landlord who had order to evict tenant from Rental Housing Tribunal. Labour strike prevented enforcement of order. Applicant then sought order of Superior Court. Inherent jurisdiction existed to issue order at Superior Court. Section 85 of *Tenant Protection Act* (Ontario) stated order of Tribunal was to be enforced on same basis as orders from Superior Court. Order issued.

R. v. Bullen, 2001 YKTC 504, 2001 CarswellYukon 91, 48 C.R. (5th) 110 (Y.T. Terr. Ct.) — Interesting and lengthy discussion of compensation and the role of the victim in any joint sentencing submission. Restitution covered by section 738(1) of the *Criminal Code*. 1995 amendments to Code clarified that restitution can be a stand-alone remedy enforceable in civil courts. It also does not affect subsequent civil actions, except, perhaps, as a set-off.

Odhavji Estate v. Woodhouse, 2003 SCC 69, 2003 CarswellOnt 4851, 2003 CarswellOnt 4852, [2003] S.C.J. No. 74, 19 C.C.L.T. (3d) 163, [2003] 3 S.C.R. 263, 11 Admin. L.R. (4th) 45, 233 D.L.R. (4th) 193, 312 N.R. 305, 180 O.A.C. 201 (S.C.C.). Plaintiffs submitting that they are public interest litigants and should not have been required to pay costs. Actions involving public authorities and raising issues of public interest insufficient to alter essential nature of litigation. Plaintiffs not falling within definition of public interest litigants. No clear and compelling reasons to interfere with Court of Appeal's decision to award costs in accordance with usual rule that successful party is entitled to costs.

Wickwire Holm v. Wilkes, [2005] N.S.J. No. 406, 2005 CarswellNS 439, 237 N.S.R. (2d) 197, 754 A.P.R. 197, 28 C.P.C. (6th) 338 (N.S. Small Cl. Ct.).

Section 31 of *Small Claims Court Act* of Nova Scotia provides that order of Small Claims Court may be enforced in same manner as order of Supreme Court. Small Claims Court has, within its own statutory limits, jurisdiction concurrent with Supreme Court. Under s. 31 of *Act*, Small Claims Court has jurisdiction to issue order for discovery in aid of execution.

R. v. Popert, 251 C.C.C. (3d) 30, 2010 CarswellOnt 535, 2010 ONCA 89, 258 O.A.C. 163 (Ont. C.A.).

Does the court have the power to make a restitution order in favour of an insurance company under s. 738(1)(a) of the *Criminal Code*? Power to make a restitution order comes from s. 738(1). See *R. v. Fitzgibbon*, 1990 CarswellOnt 996, 1990 CarswellOnt 172, 76 C.R. (3d)

378, 55 C.C.C. (3d) 449, 78 C.B.R. (N.S.) 193, 40 O.A.C. 81, 107 N.R. 281, [1990] 1 S.C.R. 1005, EYB 1990-67542 (S.C.C.), where the Supreme Court of Canada found that the Law Society of Upper Canada was a "person aggrieved" and, therefore, was entitled to a restitution order under s. 653(1) of the *Criminal Code*, despite the fact that the Law Society had made compensation to the victims of the offences.

Restitution orders are not a substitute for civil proceedings nor are they intended to displace the civil remedies necessary to ensure full compensation to victims. *R. v. Zelensky*, [1978] 3 W.W.R. 693, 41 C.C.C. (2d) 97, 21 N.R. 372, 86 D.L.R. (3d) 179, 2 C.R. (3d) 107, [1978] 2 S.C.R. 940, 1978 CarswellMan 121, 1978 CarswellMan 51 (S.C.C.). Rather, restitution orders are one factor to be considered when deciding the total sentence to be imposed on an offender.

(2) Enforcement Limited While Periodic Payment Order in Force — While an order for periodic payment is in force, no step to enforce the judgment may be taken or continued against the debtor by a creditor named in the order, except issuing a writ of seizure and sale of land and filing it with the sheriff.

History [R. 20.02(2)]: New provision, prohibiting the creditor from taking steps to enforce a judgment except by issue of a writ of seizure and sale of land. This change extends the protection that a debtor currently receives.

(3) Service of Notice of Default of Payment — The creditor may serve the debtor with a notice of default of payment (Form 20L) in accordance with subrule 8.01(14) and file a copy of it, together with an affidavit of default of payment (Form 20M), if the debtor fails to make payments under an order for periodic payment.

History [R. 20.02(3)]: New provision, indicating the point at which the order for periodic payment terminates, thereby allowing the creditor to take further steps to enforce the order.

(4) Termination on Default — An order for periodic payment terminates on the day that is 15 days after the creditor serves the debtor with the notice of default of payment, unless a consent (Form 13B) in which the creditor waives the default is filed within the 15-day period.

O. Reg. 78/06, s. 41

20.03 General — In addition to any other method of enforcement provided by law,

(a) an order for the payment or recovery of money may be enforced by,

(i) a writ of seizure and sale of personal property (Form 20C) under rule 20.06;

(ii) a writ of seizure and sale of land (Form 20D) under rule 20.07; and

(iii) garnishment under rule 20.08; and,

(b) a further order as to payment may be made under subrule 20.10(7).

History [R. 20.03]: Formerly 21.03, restructured for clarity; refers to forms 20C and 20D, formerly 21C and 21D, respectively; refers to Rules 20.06, 20.07, 20.08, and 20.10, formerly 21.06, 21.07, 21.08, and 21.10, respectively.

20.04 (1) Certificate of Judgment — If there is default under an order for the payment or recovery of money, the clerk shall, at the creditor's request, supported by an affidavit for enforcement request (Form 20P) stating the amount still owing, issue a certificate of judgment (Form 20A) to the clerk at the court location specified by the creditor.

History [R. 20.04(1)]: Formerly 21.04(1); now requires an affidavit from the creditor, rather than a "written statement"; refers to Form 20A, formerly 21A; plain language changes.

Commentary: Where a debtor lives or carries on business outside of the jurisdiction of the court and the creditor wants to enforce the judgment by:

- garnishment; and/or

- holding an examination of the debtor or other person;

the creditor may request that the originating court (where the original judgment was made) to issue Certificate(s) of Judgment (Form 20A), which can be filed in other court location(s) as specified by the creditor [Rule 20.04(1)].

Section 29 of the *Crown Liability and Proceedings Act* (Federal) and section 21 of the *Proceedings Against the Crown Act* prohibit the issuance of executions against the Crown (Federal or Provincial).

Where a creditor requests the issuance of an execution against "Her Majesty the Queen in Right of Ontario", "Sa Majesté du chef de l'Ontario", or the Attorney General of Canada, they must be advised that the court is expressly prohibited from doing so in accordance with the applicable Act (above).

Proceedings against the Federal Crown may also include agencies of the Crown where an Act of Parliament authorizes proceedings to be taken in the name of the agency.

A certificate of judgment may also be issued to a party to an action (creditor) for:

- personal records or to forward a copy to another party.

- filing with the Ministry of Transportation in claims involving motor vehicle damages for the purpose of revoking the debtor's licence.

- proving the filing of an order of a board, tribunal, agency, or other court as a judgment of the court in which it is filed. However, if the order is from another Small Claims Court, the originating court (where the order of the board, tribunal, agency or other court was first filed) must issue the certificate.

- enforcement purposes, such as proof of judgment as required by a sheriff before proceeding with the sale of lands under the *Rules of Civil Procedure.*

If a creditor finds that a debtor has moved or returned to the originating court's jurisdiction, the creditor may return to the originating court to pursue enforcement, or alternatively request the issuance of a certificate of judgment directed to another court location.

(2) The certificate of judgment shall state,

   (a) the date of the order and the amount awarded;

   (b) the rate of postjudgment interest payable; and

   (c) the amount owing, including postjudgment interest.

O. Reg. 393/09, s. 17

History [R. 20.04(2)]: Formerly 21.04(2).

20.05 (1) Delivery of Personal Property — An order for the delivery of personal property may be enforced by a writ of delivery (Form 20B) issued by the clerk to a bailiff, on the request of the person in whose favour the order was made, supported by an affidavit of that person or someone acting on that person's authority stating that the property has not been delivered.

History [R. 20.05(1)]: Formerly 21.05(1); refers to Form 21B, formerly 20B.

Commentary: In this process, an affidavit refers to an Affidavit for Enforcement Request(s) or an Affidavit in Form 15B.

For the return of personal property, a party must file a Plaintiff's Claim (Form 7A) and a Notice of Motion (Form 15A) and an Affidavit (Form 15B).

An enforcement officer acting under a writ of seizure and sale, a writ of delivery or a writ of sequestration cannot use force to enter a dwelling unless the court order specifically authorizes the use of force. The court may make such an order where, in the opinion of the court, there is reasonable and probable grounds to believe there is property on the premises may be taken under the writ [s. 20(2) *Execution Act*].

The party should have had a plaintiff's claim issued or obtained either an interim order [s. 104 *CJA*] or an order of the court for the return of personal property [r. 20.05(1)].

Case Law: *Easy Home v. Rogalski*, 2004 CarswellOnt 475, 46 C.P.C. (5th) 318 (Ont. Sm. Cl. Ct.), J. deP. Wright, Justice. Procedure to be followed in obtaining Writ of Delivery for return of personal property in Small Claims Court. Plaintiff must first commence action by issuing a claim for return of goods in question. Plaintiff must then obtain judgment either by default or otherwise for return of goods. Only when that judgment or order not complied with Plaintiff may file affidavit setting out non-compliance and obtain a Writ of Delivery for the forcible return of the goods. See also S. 104 of the *Courts of Justice Act* and Rule 44 of the *Rules of Civil Procedure*. Motions improperly constituted and dismissed.

Lease Truck Inc. v. Serbinek (2008), 2008 CarswellOnt 6960, 67 C.C.L.I. (4th) 247 (Ont. S.C.J.)

Motion by garnishee for an order determining its liability on the Notice of Garnishment to pay the creditor some or all of the statutory accident benefits accruing to debtor. Section 65(1) of the SABS prohibits "assignment" of benefits due under that Act, whereas r. 60.09(1) provides for enforcement of an order for the payment of money by garnishment of debts payable to the debtor by other persons. Issue complicated by fact that at least part of benefits payable substitute lost wages.

Motion allowed.

Garnishee must pay *Statutory accident Benefits Schedule* monies payable to debtor until amount claimed is satisfied, but is to pay 80% of any income replacement benefits directly to the debtor. "Assignment" is not defined in the *SABS*. There is no conflict between the prohibition on assigning a benefit under s. 65(1) of the *SABS* and the seizure or attachment of a debt pursuant to rule 60.09(1). Because income replacement benefits are deemed in s. 7(1.1) of the Wages act to be wages for the purposes of s. 7, and 80% of a person's wages are exempted from seizure or garnishment under s. 7(2), the aforementioned amounts should be excluded from garnishment.

(2) Seizure of Other Personal Property — If the property referred to in a writ of delivery cannot be found or taken by the bailiff, the person in whose favour the order was made may make a motion to the court for an order directing the bailiff to seize any other personal property of the person against whom the order was made.

History [R. 20.05(2)]: Formerly 21.05(2).

Case Law: *Brydon v. Berrigan* (2003), 2003 CarswellOnt 651 (Ont. S.C.J.). Garnishment hearing pursuant to *Rule 20.08(15)* of the *Rules of Court*.

Does *inter alia* restitution order made under Section 738 of the *Criminal Code of Canada* and entered as a judgment in the Small Claims Court attract postjudgment interest pursuant to the *Courts of Justice Act*?

Section 741 of *Criminal Code* permits amount awarded in restitution order to be entered as a judgment for enforcement. Unlike prejudgment interest, postjudgment interest attaches by operation of law and does not depend on an Order of Court.

(3) Unless the court orders otherwise the bailiff shall keep personal property seized under subrule (2) until the court makes a further order for its disposition.

History [R. 20.05(3)]: Formerly 21.05(3); plain language changes.

(4) Storage Costs — The person in whose favour the order is made shall pay the bailiff's storage costs, in advance and from time to time; if the person fails to do so, the seizure shall be deemed to be abandoned.

O. Reg. 78/06, s. 42; 230/13, s. 16

Commentary: The process of recovery of possession of personal property unlawfully taken from, or unlawfully detained by, another person has been made less complicated and less expensive through the use of a writ of delivery.

Section 104 of the *Courts of Justice Act* authorizes the obtaining of an interim order (prior to judgment) for delivery of possession of personal property upon motion to a judge. The writ of delivery would then be served along with the claim. The *Courts of Justice Act* also provides that a person who improperly obtains a writ of delivery is liable for any loss suffered by a person who is ultimately found to be entitled to possession of the property.

Rule 20.05(1) of the rules of the Small Claims Court deals with enforcement by a writ of delivery and section 20 of the *Execution Act*, R.S.O. 1990, c. E.24 controls the use of force which the bailiff can apply in executing a writ of delivery. Section 20 of the *Execution Act* provides that the bailiff may use reasonable force to effect seizure if the property in in *other than a dwelling*. If the property is located in a dwelling, the bailiff must apply to the court for an order to use reasonable force.

Unlike a writ of seizure and sale of personal property, where goods seized by the bailiff must be stored and sold by public auction, a writ of delivery requires the seizure and delivery of the personal property to the applicant. It is also important to note that a "sheriff" as defined in section 1, includes a bailiff who is acting on a writ of delivery.

If property to be seized is a vehicle, the creditor must provide an up-to-date *Personal Property Security Act* ("PPSA") search at the time of issuing the Writ of Seizure and Sale of Property. The PPSA search is to be no older than 48 hours when filed. To allow a writ to be renewed, a request for renewal must be received before the writ has expired. The writ is renewed six months from the day of issuance or renewal. A writ of seizure and sale of personal property cannot be renewed after it has expired.

Case Law: *Voulgarakis v. 730048 Ontario Ltd.* (1999), 40 C.P.C. (4th) 288, 1999 CarswellOnt 3648 (Ont. Master) — The defendants repossessed a truck, alleging breach of payment provisions in lease agreement allegedly executed by both parties. The defendants were entitled to retain possession on condition of posting bond for twice the amount already invested in truck by plaintiff. The plaintiff was entitled to regain possession on posting bond for twice the amount of value less amount already invested, and on terms.

20.06 (1) Writ of Seizure and Sale of Personal Property — If there is default under an order for the payment or recovery of money, the clerk shall, at the creditor's request, supported by an affidavit for enforcement request (Form 20P) stating the amount still owing, issue to a bailiff a writ of seizure and sale of personal property (Form 20C), and the bailiff shall enforce the writ for the amount owing, postjudgment interest and the bailiff's fees and expenses.

History [R. 20.06(1)]: Formerly 21.06(1); now requires an affidavit from the creditor, rather than a "written statement"; refers to Form 20C, formerly 21C; plain language changes.

Commentary: Where a debtor does not pay a debt pursuant to a court order, in order to have the debtor's property seized and sold to satisfy the judgment, the creditor must obtain a writ of seizure and sale of personal property in the court where judgment was rendered (or where a Certificate of Judgment (Form 20A) is filed).

The *Rules of the Small Claims Court* do not limit the time period within which methods of enforcement may be issued.

A creditor may attend the court office and/or in writing make an inquiry to have a Writ of Seizure and Sale of Personal Property (Form 20C) issued.

Rule 20.06(1) provides that the bailiff shall enforce a writ of seizure and sale of personal property, including post judgment interest, the bailiff's fees and the bailiff's expenses. This would include the reasonable costs of a private bailiff or auctioneer used to carry out the sale.

If a debtor does not pay a court order to meet his or her debt, the creditor can act to have the debtor's property seized and sold to satisfy the judgment.

Before the court can issue a writ of seizure and sale of personal property the court must receive written instructions and a completed writ of seizure and sale of personal property from the creditor and a statement of the balance of money owing. The writ can then be enforced and the property of the debtor seized and held for auction.

Before the debtor's property can be seized and/or sold, the following must occur:

- the creditor must give specific instructions to take possession of the property;
- the creditor should ensure that the items to be seized are owned solely by the debtor; and
- the creditor must deposit enough funds with the court office to cover the costs of removing and storing the items to be seized as well as the cost of publishing notice of the seizure. These costs will be added to the amount owing by the debtor.

Goods or property seized have to be sold at public auction, and it is easier to sell items that are free of any other legal claims (liens or security interests). Certain goods cannot be seized. These include clothing, furniture, utensils, tools and home implements.

At any time up to the sale of the seized items, the debtor can prevent the sale by paying the amount of the judgment, plus costs and interest. The debtor can also ask the court to have the seizure postponed or to pay the judgment in installments.

Burns v. Ontario Society for the Prevention of Cruelty to Animals, 2012 ONSC 339, 2012 CarswellOnt 513, 27 C.P.C. (7th) 192 (Ont. S.C.J.)

A motion was brought by the Society to issue a new alias Writ of Seizure and Sale referable to the Order of the Honourable Justice Cosgrove dated February 18, 2002, pursuant to rule 60.07(2) of the *Rules of Civil Procedure*.

The writ expired on July 19, 2010, six years after it was issued. Due to an oversight, the Writ not renewed pursuant to Rule 60.07(6) and (8). The reason for non-renewal was because neither the Society nor the law firm acting for them at the time received notice from the Sheriff that the Writ was expiring. The motion was adjourned at least twice. It was heard on January 5, 2012.

Shmegilsky v. Slobodzian, 1964 CarswellOnt 473, [1964] 1 O.R. 633 (Ont. Master), *McLay v. Molock*, 1993 CarswellOnt 471, 21 C.P.C. (3d) 189 (Ont. Gen. Div.) and *Colombe v. Caughell*, 1985 CarswellOnt 647, 52 O.R. (2d) 767, 6 C.P.C. (2d) 314 (Ont. Dist. Ct.) cited for the proposition that a court can grant leave to issue an alias Writ after the expiration of the original Writ of Seizure and Sale. See also *Canada (Attorney General) v. Palmer-Virgo*, 2002 CarswellOnt 5003, 31 C.P.C. (5th) 143 (Ont. S.C.J.); additional reasons at 2003 Cars- wellOnt 1409, [2003] O.J. No. 1238 (Ont. S.C.J.) which allowed for leave to issue alias Writs of Seizure and Sale.

It is incongruous that a judgment can remain in effect for 20 years, while a Writ of Seizure and Sale to enforce it cannot be renewed or issued after it has expired even though judgment to be enforced is still in effect. Leave was granted for the Society to issue an alias Writ of Seizure and Sale to take effect the day that it was issued out of the Sheriff's office. The original Writ was not renewed *nunc pro tunc*. This is to protect any intervening rights which may have accrued to the parties from the date of expiry of the original Writ to the date of issuance of the alias Writ. No interest was permitted to accrue from the date of expiry of the original Writ to the date of issuance of the alias Writ. There was no order as to costs.

(1.1) If more than six years have passed since the order was made, a writ of seizure and sale of personal property may be issued only with leave of the court.

(1.2) If a writ of seizure and sale of personal property is not issued within one year after the date on which an order granting leave to issue it is made,

(a) the order granting leave ceases to have effect; and

(b) a writ of seizure and sale of personal property may be issued only with leave of the court on a subsequent motion.

(1.3) A writ of seizure and sale of personal property shall show the creditor's name, address and telephone number and the name, address and telephone number of the creditor's representative, if any.

(2) Duration of Writ — A writ of seizure and sale of personal property remains in force for six years after the date of its issue and for a further six years after each renewal.

History [R. 20.06(2)]: Formerly 21.06(2).

Commentary: A Writ of Seizure and Sale of Personal Property (Form 20C) remains in force for six years from the date of issue and for a further six years from each renewal [r. 20.06(2)].

A writ of seizure and sale of personal property may be renewed before its expiration by filing a Request to Renew a Writ of Seizure and Sale of Personal Property (Form 20N), with the bailiff (enforcement office) [r. 20.06(3)].

An oversight in rule 20.06(3) required that litigants file renewal requests with the clerk. On January 1, 2010, this oversight was corrected and litigants are now instructed within the rules to file renewal requests with the bailiff (enforcement office).

Sale of Personal Property

Personal property seized shall not be sold by the bailiff unless a notice of the time and place of sale has been:

- Mailed to the creditor or the creditor's lawyer and to the debtor at least 14 days before the sale,

- Advertised in a manner that is likely to bring it to the attention of the public [r. 20.06(6)].

(3) Renewal of Writ — A writ of seizure and sale of personal property may be re- newed before its expiration by filing a request to renew a writ of seizure and sale (Form 20N) with the bailiff.

History [R. 20.06(3)]: Formerly 21.06(3); plain language changes.

(4) Direction to Enforce — The creditor may request enforcement of a writ of seizure and sale of personal property by filing a direction to enforce writ of seizure and sale of personal property (Form 20O) with the bailiff.

History [R. 20.06(4)]: Formerly 21.06(4); plain language changes.

(5) Inventory of Property Seized — Within a reasonable time after a request is made by someone acting on the debtor's authority, the bailiff shall deliver an inventory of personal property seized under a writ of seizure and sale of personal property.

History [R. 20.06(5)]: Formerly 21.06(5); plain language changes.

(6) Sale of Personal Property — Personal property seized under a writ of seizure and sale of personal property shall not be sold by the bailiff unless notice of the time and place of sale has been,

   (a) mailed, at least 10 days before the sale,

   (i) to the creditor at the address shown on the writ, or to the creditor's representative, and

   (ii) to the debtor at the debtor's last known address; and

   (b) advertised in a manner that is likely to bring it to the attention of the public.

O. Reg. 78/06, s. 43; 393/09, s. 18; 230/13, s. 17

History [R. 20.06(6)]: Formerly 21.06(6); plain language changes.

Commentary: If a debtor does not pay a debt pursuant to a judgment, in order to place a lien against the debtor's land or have the debtor's land seized and sold to satisfy the judgment, a creditor must obtain a Writ of Seizure and Sale of Land (Form 20D) in the court where judgment was rendered (or the court where a certificate of judgment was filed). If more than six years or more have elapsed since the judgment was made, the clerk shall not issue a writ of seizure and sale of land [r. 20.07(2)]. In that case, the party requires a court order prior to the issue of the writ. Enforcement fees must be paid at the enforcement office where the writ is to be filed.

Subsection 25(1) of the *Creditors' Relief Act*, R.S.O. 1990, c. C.45, provides that a sheriff who has knowledge of funds or property in the hands of a bailiff pursuant to a writ of seizure and sale of personal property, shall demand the funds or property from the bailiff for distribution under that Act. Similarly, subsection 3(5) permits a sheriff to demand and receive from a clerk, monies paid into the Small Claims Court as a result of garnishment proceedings.

The sheriff distributes money pursuant to s. 5(2) of the Act. This basically includes Writs of Seizure and Sale, Writs of Fieri Facias, Certificates issued under this Act or Orders of the Court filed in the sheriff's office. Section 4(6) makes one exception, in the case of Garnishment Proceedings: the *attaching creditor* under whose garnishment funds are collected may also share with the Execution Creditors.

Where a sheriff is aware that a Small Claims Court or Family Court has garnishment funds in court relating to a debtor in respect of whom the sheriff has a writ of execution on file, the sheriff shall, upon written request of the creditor, demand from the clerk/administrator, that the funds be paid over to him/her. [s. 3(5) *Creditors' Relief Act*]

Where monies belonging to a judgment debtor, or to which a judgment debtor is entitled are held in court, a sheriff or any person interested, may make application in writing to have the monies paid over to the sheriff, and it shall be deemed to be monies levied under an execution. [s. 23 *Creditors' Relief Act*]

Where monies are held by a bailiff under an execution or attachment against the debtor, the sheriff shall, on written request of the creditor, demand the funds from the bailiff. [s. 25(1) *Creditors' Relief Act*];

Where monies are paid to a sheriff in whose hands there is no execution against the property of the debtor, a sheriff who has a filed execution (or a creditor of the debtor) may make application for receipt of the funds for distribution, and the court shall fix compensation for the sheriff who received the funds from the garnishee. [s. 3(4) *Creditors' Relief Act*]

As a general rule, funds recovered through garnishment of the seizure and sale of property in the Small Claims Court are not governed by the *Creditors' Relief Act*. However, s. 3(5) provides an exception to this general rule, stating:

> Where money recovered by garnishment is paid into the Small Claims Court, the Ontario Court (Provincial Division) or the Unified Family Court, the sheriff is entitled to demand and receive it from the clerk of the court for the purpose of distributing it under this Act, except in so far as the priority created by subsection 4(1) applies to the money.

In other words, where the sheriff is aware that there are garnishment funds being held by the Small Claims Court with respect to a debtor and the sheriff has an execution on hand against the same debtor, the sheriff may demand that the Small Claims Court funds be handed over for the purpose of distribution under the Act. Subsection 3(6) then provides that the attaching Small Claims Court creditor is entitled to share in the sheriff's distribution.

Subsection 3(8) goes on to provide:

> The clerk of the Small Claims Court, the Ontario Court (Provincial Division) or the Unified Family Court is not liable for making payment to the creditor unless, at the time of the payment, the clerk has notice that there is an execution against the property of the debtor in the sheriff's hands.

"Notice" is not defined in s. 3(8) of the *Execution Act* or elsewhere in the *Act*, nor is it defined in the *Interpretation Act*, R.S.O. 1990, c. I.11.

"Notice" in s. 3(8) of the *Execution Act* may simply be the equivalent to knowledge.

Personal property seized *shall not be* sold by the bailiff unless a notice of the time and place of sale has been:

- mailed to the creditor or the creditor's lawyer and to the debtor at least 30 days before the sale;

advertised in a manner that is likely to bring it to the attention of the public [r. 20.06(6)].

20.07 (1) Writ of Seizure and Sale of Land — If an order for the payment or recovery of money is unsatisfied, the clerk shall at the creditor's request, supported by an affidavit for enforcement request (Form 20P) stating the amount still owing, issue to the sheriff specified by the creditor a writ of seizure and sale of land (Form 20D).

History [R. 20.07(1)]: Formerly 21.07(1); now requires an affidavit from the creditor, rather than a "written statement"; refers to Form 20D, formerly 21D; plain language changes.

(1.1) If more than six years have passed since the order was made, a writ of seizure and sale of land may be issued only with leave of the court.

(1.2) If a writ of seizure and sale of land is not issued within one year after the date on which an order granting leave to issue it is made,

(a) the order granting leave ceases to have effect; and

(b) a writ of seizure and sale of land may be issued only with leave of the court on a subsequent motion.

(1.3) **Electronic Filing, Issuance** — The following persons may electronically file a request under subrule (1) for a writ of seizure and sale of land, without the supporting affidavit for enforcement request:

1. A lawyer or a paralegal.

2. A person who has filed a requisition with the clerk to provide for the electronic filing and issuance of documents in relation to the enforcement of an order.

(1.4) If the request is filed electronically, the writ of seizure and sale of land shall be issued electronically.

(1.5) Subrule 1.05.1(6) does not apply to an electronically filed request or an electronically issued writ.

(2) **Application of *Rules of Civil Procedure* to Issued Writ** — Subject to subrules (3) and (4), the *Rules of Civil Procedure* apply for all purposes instead of these rules to an issued writ of seizure and sale of land, as if the writ were a writ of seizure and sale issued under rule 60.07 of those Rules.

History [R. 20.07(2)]: Formerly 21.07(2).

Commentary: In this process, an affidavit refers to an Affidavit for Writ of Seizure and Sale of Land (Form 20O).

If a debtor does not pay a debt pursuant to a judgment, in order to place a lien against the debtor's land or have the debtor's land seized and sold to satisfy the judgment, a creditor must obtain a Writ of Seizure and Sale of Land (Form 20D) in the court where judgment was rendered.

If more than six years have elapsed since the judgment was made, the clerk shall not issue a writ of seizure and sale of land [r. 20.07(2)]. The party requires leave of the court in order to have the writ issued.

The writ must be filed with the enforcement officer four months before he or she can direct the enforcement office (sheriff) to seize and sell the property. The actual sale cannot proceed until the writ has been on file for six months. The sale of land is a complicated and costly process and is rarely used to enforce a Small Claims Court judgment.

The enforcement office has a general duty to act reasonably and in good faith towards all parties. The enforcement office can refuse to act if the estimated costs of executing the writ of seizure and sale are greater than the debtor's equity in the property to be seized.

A Writ of Seizure and Sale of Land (Form 20D) remains in force for six years from the date of its issue and for a further six years from each renewal [r. 20.07(3)].

- If more than six years have elapsed since the judgment was made, the court shall not issue a writ of seizure and sale of land [r. 20.07(1.1)]. The party requires leave of the court to have the writ issued.

- Where a writ of seizure and sale of land is requested following the filing of a certificate of default under the *Provincial Offences Act*, the court shall not issue the writ if more than six years have elapsed since the date of the earliest date of the default for which the certificate was issued. A party requires leave of the court in order to have the writ issued.

- Where a writ of seizure and sale of land is requested following the filing of a tribunal order under the residential *Tenancies Act* or the *Employment Standards Act*, the court shall not issue the writ if more than six years have elapsed since the date tribunal order is effective. Leave of the court is required in order to have the writ issued.

If an order granting leave to issue is made, the writ of seizure and sale of land must be issued within one year after the date of the order, otherwise the order granting leave ceases to have effect and the creditor must obtain another order from the court by way of a subsequent motion [r. 20.07(1.2)].

A Request to Renew Writ of Seizure and Sale (Form 20N) must be filed with the enforcement office before the expiration of the writ of seizure and sale of land.

(3) Duration of Writ — A writ of seizure and sale of land remains in force for six years after the date of its issue and for a further six years after each renewal.

(4) Alternative Method of Renewal — Instead of being renewed under the *Rules of Civil Procedure* in accordance with subrule (2), a writ of seizure and sale of land may be renewed before its expiration by filing a request to renew a writ of seizure and sale (Form 20N) with the sheriff.

O. Reg. 78/06, s. 44; 393/09, s. 19; 44/14, s. 14

Commentary: The *Rules of the Small Claims Court* do not limit the time period within which the following methods of enforcement may be issued:

- Certificate of Judgment

- Writ of Delivery

- Notice of Garnishment

- Notice of Examination

If more than six years have elapsed since the judgment was made, the clerk shall *not* issue a writ of seizure and sale of land [r. 20.07(2)] or a writ of seizure and sale of personal property [r. 20.06(1.1)]. In both cases, the creditor requires leave of the court in order to have the writ issued.

Failure to Renew Writ of Execution

Kovachis v. Dunn, 2011 ONSC 4174, 2011 CarswellOnt 6738, 38 C.P.C. (7th) 206, 71 E.T.R. (3d) 28 (Ont. S.C.J.) confirms that failure to renew a writ of *fieri facias* (also referred to as a writ of seizure and sale or writ of execution) within the 20-year limitation period under the old *Limitations Act* R.S.O. 1990, c.L 15 (the old Act) results in a time-bar of the enforcement of the underlying judgment under the transition provisions of the *Limitations Act 2002* S.O. 2002, c 24. Sch. B, (the new Act). Citing *Lax v. Lax*, 2004 CarswellOnt 1633, 70 O.R. (3d) 520, 50 C.P.C. (5th) 266, 239 D.L.R. (4th) 683, 3 R.F.L. (6th) 387, 186 O.A.C. 20, [2004] O.J. No. 1700 (Ont. C.A.); additional reasons 2004 CarswellOnt 5343, 75 O.R. (3d) 482, 4 C.P.C. (6th) 194, 247 D.L.R. (4th) 1, 12 R.F.L. (6th) 112, [2004] O.J. No. 5146 (Ont. C.A.), Justice Corrick notes that "[w]rits extend limitation periods. A judgment can be enforced indefinitely be renewing a writ of seizure and sale: Failure to renew a writ required an application for leave to issue an execution under rule 60.07(2) of the *Rules of Civil Procedure.*" (at para 16). The court was bound by the Ontario Court of Appeal's decision in *Joseph v. Paramount Canada's Wonderland*, 2008 ONCA 469, 2008 CarswellOnt 3495, 90 O.R. (3d) 401, 56 C.P.C. (6th) 14, 294 D.L.R. (4th) 141, 241 O.A.C. 29, [2008] O.J. No. 2339 (Ont. C.A.) which held that the doctrine of special circumstances enables a court to amend or add a claim to an existing action, but does not give a "court the power to allow the commencement of an action after the expiry of a limitation period. Ms. Dunn's application for leave to issue an execution must be denied." (at para. 22).

20.08 (1) Garnishment — A creditor may enforce an order for the payment or recovery of money by garnishment of debts payable to the debtor by other persons.

History [R. 20.08(1)]: Formerly 21.08(1).

Commentary: If a debtor has not paid a debt pursuant to a court order, the creditor can make demand for money owed to the debtor by someone else by issuing a notice of garnishment, (for example, garnishment of bank accounts, wages, or money owed on some contract). Service on garnishee — by mail, personal service as per Rule 8.02 or by an alternative to personal service as per Rule 8.03. Service on debtor — by mail, personal service as per Rule 8.02 or by an alternative to personal service as per Rule 8.03. A Notice of Garnishment is effective for a term of two years from the date of service on the garnishee (Subrules 20.08 (7), (8)).

Payment obligations made pursuant to orders of the Workplace Safety and Insurance Board may be enforced in the Small Claims Court. Sections 139 and 140 of the *Workplace and Insurance Act, 1997*, S.O. 1997, c. 16, Sched. A provide:

139. (1) If a person does not pay amounts owing under this Act when they become due, the Board may issue a certificate stating that the person is in default under this Act and setting out the amount owed and the person to whom it is owed.

1997, c. 16, Sched. A, s. 139(1)

(2) The Board may file the certificate with the Superior Court of Justice or with the Small Claims Court and it shall be entered in the same way as an order of that court and is enforceable as such. Despite any other rule of the court, the Board may file the certificate by mail and personal attendance at the court is not required.

1997, c. 16, Sched. A, s. 139(2); 2000, c. 26, Sched. I, s. 1(17)

140. (1) **Enforcement through municipal tax rolls** — If an employer does not pay amounts owing under this Act within 30 days after they become due, the Board may issue a certificate setting out the employer's status under this Act and the address of the employer's establishment, stating that the employer is more than 30 days in default under this Act and setting out the amount owed.

In accordance with the *Bankruptcy and Insolvency Act* (Canada), where a debtor is bankrupt, the bankruptcy affects a stay of proceedings against the bankrupt/debtor. Written notice of the debtor's bankruptcy must be received from the trustee in bankruptcy. Generally, the garnishment is stayed until the bankruptcy is discharged. The question of whether the stay affects the running of the six-year lifetime of the garnishment is up to the parties to determine or dispute.

For example, should the garnishee believe that the six-year period continues to run during the bankruptcy, and the bankrupt debtor is discharged after the six-year period expires, the garnishee will not send any more money into court. In this case, it is up to the creditor to challenge the garnishee's decision.

Note that the debt that is owed by the bankrupt debtor may or may not be discharged by the bankruptcy. A garnishee may, therefore, send money into court believing that the debt has not been discharged.

Garnishment — Rule 20.08

Section 7 of the *Wages Act* restricts the amount of wages that can be garnished. Some exemptions from garnishment are employment insurance, social assistance, and pension payments, even if the funds have been deposited into an account at a financial institution.

Most other kinds of debts owing to the debtor are 100% garnishable

Case Law: *Take-a-Break Coffee Service v. Raymond* (1987), 26 C.P.C. (2d) 184 (Ont. Prov. Ct.) — There was an outstanding debt owed by the Federal Crown to the judgment debtor when the garnishment of the provincial court had been received. Once a competing Quebec garnishment claim had been satisfied payments were required to be remitted and continued during the ensuing six month period or until the government was fully retained.

Frangeskaki v. Director of Support and Custody Enforcement (1990), 31 R.F.L. (3d) 110 (Ont. Gen. Div.) — The debtor unsuccessfully challenged the jurisdiction of the provincially appointed Director to garnish the wages of an employee of a federal corporation. The relevant provincial statute was of general application and it did not attempt to regulate the very nature of the undertaking.

667801 Ontario Ltd. v. Moir (1990), 1 W.D.C.P. (2d) 266 (Ont. Prov. Ct.) — Commission due from the garnishee to the judgment debtor was a debt payable within the meaning of Rule 21.08. The garnishment in favour of the judgment creditor and notice of garnishee took precedence over the advances of loans to the judgment debtor by the garnishee.

Director of Support & Custody Enforcement v. Jones (1992), 3 C.P.C. (2d) 206 (Ont. Div. Ct.) — At common law, a joint bank account could not be garnished to satisfy a debt owing by a garnishee to a judgment debtor. To permit this would oblige a court to ascertain the exact extent of the judgment debtor's ownership of the funds in the joint account, and would implicitly authorize the court to re-write the joint account agreement.

Jantunen v. Ross (1991), 5 O.R. (3d) 433 (Ont. Div. Ct.) — Tips paid to a waiter (by credit card) were not exempt from the protection of s. 7(2) of the *Wages Act*. "Wages" included salary payable by "time or by the job or piece or otherwise" and credit card tips fell under "otherwise".

Canada Mortgage & Housing Corp. v. Apostolou (1995), 22 O.R. (3d) 190 (Gen. Div.) — Issue on motion was question of priority between garnishment issued and served by creditor, and earlier assignment of wages by debtor to other creditor, financing statement for which was registered subsequent to service of notice of garnishment. Serving notice of garnishment placed direct influence and restrictions upon garnishee. Liability of garnishee took effect at that time, and no further steps were required. Notice of garnishment stood in priority to wage assignment. Section 145 of the *Small Claims Court Act*, R.S.O. 1980, c. 476 had been repealed. *Bank of Montreal v. Osborne* (1983), 3 P.P.S.A.C. 227 (Ont. Div. Ct.) no longer applicable.

Dacon Corp. v. Treats Ontario Inc., [1995] 6 W.D.C.P. (2d) 174 (Ont. Gen. Div.) — Rents payable under a sublease were a garnishable debt owing to the sublessor by the sublessee. Sublessee, once served with a notice of garnishment, had to comply and pay rent to the sheriff, not sublessor. See Rule 60.08(19) of *Rules of Civil Procedure*.

Cadillac Fairview Corp. v. Grandma Lee's Ontario Inc. (1995), 6 W.D.C.P. (2d) 432 (Ont. Gen. Div.) — Rent money not attachable (garnishable) because it was owed jointly by both the garnishee/subtenant and the debtor/tenant to the creditor/landlord.

Crich Holdings & Buildings Ltd. and David Hall; Eugene Madore o/a Absolute Office Furniture Services, Garnishee, (December 20, 1994), File # 633/94 Searle, Dep. J., Woodstock (Ont. Sm. Cl. Ct.) — The issue is whether an employer who is served as a garnishee with a notice of garnishment is liable to remit even if the judgment debtor does not become employed by the garnishee until after the notice is served. The creditor sought order against the garnishee for payment/pursuant to the Small Claims Court Rule 21.08, (5), (6). Rule 60.08 of the *Rules of Civil Procedure* referred to. Court held no valid agreement unless employer/employee relationship at time. Notice of garnishment served.

Toronto Dominion Bank v. Cooper, Sandler, West & Skurka (1998), 157 D.L.R. (4th) 515, 37 O.R. (3d) 729 (Ont. Div. Ct.) — Client deposited $15,000 with solicitors, held in trust as retainer for defence on criminal charges of fraud and breach of trust. Relationship not debtor-creditor relationship. Funds held as true retainer were not debt to client and thus not subject to garnishment.

Whalley v. Harris Steel Ltd. (1997), 46 C.C.L.I. (2d) 250 (Ont. C.A.) — Trial judge properly held that annuity policies and payments were exempt by s. 196(2) of *Insurance Act*, R.S.O.

1990, c. I.8, provided that designation of specified persons was in effect, even if moneys were not payable to designated beneficiary. Exemption does not apply to funds resulting from collapse of plan.

Waldteufel v. Fiducie Desjardins (1995), 95 D.T.C. 5183, 9 C.C.P.B. 78, (sub nom. *Ministre du Revenu national v. Waldteufel*) 118 F.T.R. 133 (Fed. T.D.) — Crown sought garnishment of R.R.S.P. owned by debtor and administered by garnishee. Investment non-garnishable under Act respecting trust companies and savings companies (Que.) as it was fixed-term annuity that was exempt from seizure but any annuity ultimately paid to debtor could be garnished.

Baskind v. Lauzen (1998), 43 B.L.R. (2d) 83 (Ont. Gen. Div.) — Defendant organized financial affairs entirely through corporation which he owned. Court found moneys paid to defendant were in form of "salary" and were properly subject to garnishment.

1066232 Ontario Ltd. v. Anbor Corp. (1998), 27 C.P.C. (4th) 279 (Ont. Gen. Div.) — Subrule 68.01(11) of the *Rules of Civil Procedure*, R.R.O. 1990, Reg. 194, sets out the limits of the garnishee's obligation to the sheriff and the time within which there must be compliance. Subrule 68.01(12) sets out those debts which are subject to garnishment. Is there a debt owing by the garnishee to the debtor, as contemplated under Rule 68.08 of the Rules of Civil Procedure? Amount of security deposit not a debt within the meaning of Rule 68.08.

Arnot v. Ermine (1999), 33 C.P.C. (4th) 374, 181 Sask. R. 161 (Sask. Q.B.) — A law firm applied for an order appointing the chief of S Band as the proper officer to be examined in aide of execution. The application was granted. The defect in describing the corporate garnishee and, subsequently, the party against whom judgment was obtained represented irregularity and did not nullify proceedings. S Band was not prejudiced by misdescription, as error did not mislead either Band officers or their solicitors as to the identity of the judgment debtor.

Lifescan Canada Ltd. v. Hogg (1999), 174 D.L.R. (4th) 187, 24 R.P.R. (3d) 224, 44 O.R. (3d) 593, 10 C.B.R. (4th) 180 (Ont. S.C.J.) — As result of a motion brought by garnishees pursuant to Rules of Civil Procedure (Ontario), Rule 60.08(16), the Court ordered moneys paid under Notices of Garnishment be released to the judgment creditor and that all subsequent moneys should be paid to S.L. Garnishees awarded solicitor-and-client costs fixed at $3,900, as conduct of S.L throughout proceedings was appalling and egregious. The garnishees were forced to bring the motion after being locked out from the property without notice.

Tremblay c. Bourbeau, [1999] R.J.Q. 1601 (C.A.) — The court below erred in finding that garnishment proceedings were not execution proceedings and therefore did not fall within traditional common-law Crown immunity. Garnishment proceedings imposed certain legal obligations upon the garnishee, which were subject to sanction if ignored.

General Motors Acceptance Corp. of Canada Ltd. v. McClintock (2000), 49 C.P.C. (4th) 215, 138 O.A.C. 138, 2000 CarswellOnt 4414, [2000] O.J. No. 3836 (Ont. C.A.) — Appeal from (1999), 37 C.P.C. (4th) 25 dismissed. — A partnership bank account was debt payable to the partnership and not to the individual partners. The debtor partner had no independent right to deal with the funds in the account. Share of debtor was not subject to garnishment.

Statute making "cheques, bills of exchange, promissory notes, bonds, specialties or other securities for money" exigible. Registered retirement savings plans are not other security for money. Not exigible: *Memorials and Executions Act*, R.S.N.B. 1973, c. M-9, s. 26(1).

Hayes Debeck Stewart & Little v. Nikka Developments Ltd. (1996), 41 C.P.C. (4th) 364, 1996 CarswellBC 2628 (B.C. Master) — A claim was made by accountants for professional services. The debt was for a definite amount. The claim was for a liquidated amount. Cause of action in debt. Services rendered and payment demanded by way of invoice.

Horne v. Canada (Attorney General) (1996), 149 Nfld. & P.E.I.R. 46, 467 A.P.R. 46, 42 C.P.C. (4th) 325, 1996 CarswellPEI 126 (P.E.I. T.D. [In Chambers]) — A solicitor obtained an order for payment into court. A garnishee against the solicitor was set aside. The solicitor not owing debt; the Crown subject to garnishment. The applicant failed to garnishee Crown, which was the debtor according to the settlement. Garnishee set aside: *Garnishment, Attachment and Pension Diversion Act*, R.S.C. 1985, c. G-2, s. 3.

Alessandro v. Ontario (Provincial Court Justice of the Peace) (2000), 2000 CarswellOnt 1331 (Ont. S.C.J.) — Effect of s. 5 of Act to make provincial garnishment law applicable to Federal Crown employees: *Garnishment, Attachment and Pension Diversion Act*, R.S.C. 1985, c. G-2, s. 5.

Ferguson Gifford v. Lax Kw'Alaams Indian Band, 2000 BCSC 273, 72 B.C.L.R. (3d) 363, [2000] 2 C.N.L.R. 30, 2000 CarswellBC 333, [2000] B.C.J. No. 317 (B.C. S.C. [In Chambers]); leave to appeal allowed 2000 BCCA 280, 2000 CarswellBC 907 (B.C. C.A. [In Chambers]) — *Indian Act*, R.S.C. 1985, c. I-5, s. 89 prohibited moneys belonging to Indian band from seizure. Bank garnished moneys and placed moneys into court. Status Indian who was assignee was not permitted release of moneys.

Royal Bank v. Calonego (1999), 1999 CarswellOnt 4377 (Ont. S.C.J.) — A bank was entitled to proceed against both or either of the husband and wife who were joint debtors on a line of credit. A covenant not to sue the wife after payment of sum did not amount to a release by the husband.

Noble China Inc. v. Lei (1999), 1999 CarswellOnt 4244, [1999] O.J. No. 5030 (Ont. S.C.J.) — None of the money garnished from a joint bank account belonged to the debtor. The only information about the account was received in discovery process in another action and was protected by deemed undertaking not to use for any purposes outside action. Garnishment ordered was set aside.

720659 Ontario Inc. v. Wells (2001), 2001 CarswellOnt 3247 (Ont. S.C.J.) — Judgment debtor had gone bankrupt before garnishee hearing. Garnishment set aside. All proceedings had been stayed under ss. 69(1) and 70 of *Bankruptcy and Insolvency Act*, R.S.C. 1985, c. B-3.

Davidson & Co. v. MacAdam (2001), 2001 CarswellBC 2285, 2001 BCSC 1393, 95 B.C.L.R. (3d) 320, [2002] 1 W.W.R. 760, C.E.B. & P.G.R. 8392 (note) (B.C. S.C.) — Plaintiff law firm successfully acted for defendant in claim for disability benefits provided by solicitor's lien. Solicitor's lien was charge on benefit and was void by s. 65(1) of *Canada Pension Plan*, R.S.C. 1985, c. C-8.

20 Toronto Street Holdings Ltd. v. Coffee, Tea or Me Bakeries Inc. (2001), 53 O.R. (3d) 360, 2001 CarswellOnt 593, 4 C.P.C. (5th) 393 (Ont. S.C.J.) — Subtenant agreeing to be bound by the terms of the head lease. Subtenant paying its rent directly to the head landlord. Subtenant's payment of rent to head landlord extinguishing subtenant's debt to the tenant. Subtenant's rent not subject to garnishment by creditor of tenant.

Cina v. Ultratech Tool & Gauge Inc. (2001), 2001 CarswellOnt 4023, 56 O.R. (3d) 338, 15 C.P.C. (5th) 71 (Ont. S.C.J.) — Notice of Garnishment served upon garnishee described as TD Canada Trust not invalid. It was name under which five entities carried on retail banking business. Service as effected was effective to constitute service on all five corporations. Order jointly and severally to pay to sheriff amount in question.

Minister of National Revenue v. Hypnat Ltée, 2001 CarswellNat 789, 2001 CarswellNat 2161, 2001 CFPI 285, 2001 D.T.C. 5288 (Fr.), [2001] 4 C.T.C. 201 (Fed. T.D.) — Judgment creditor obtained provisional order of garnishment against account receivable owed to garnishee by judgment debtor. Judgment creditor then obtained final order. Debt not prescribed. Garnishee's financial statements and worksheets indicated that debt existed between garnishee and judgment debtor. Transactions were admission of existence of debt regularly renewed by garnishee, which constituted interruption of prescription by debt recognition.

Schmutz v. Parsons (2003), 2003 CarswellOnt 2832 (Ont. Master), Case Management Master, Hawkins. Plaintiff brought motion to change place of trial from Toronto to Whitby. Defendant brought motion to change place of trial from Toronto to Fort Frances. Plaintiff's medical witnesses were from Toronto. Plaintiff's motion allowed.

Citifinancial Canada Inc. v. Sherven, 2005 CarswellSask 812, 2005 SKQB 485 (Sask. Q.B.), Rothery J. *Ex parte* application for payment out of funds to the plaintiff under provisions of the *Attachment of Debts Act*, R.S.S. 1978, c. A-32. Application for payment out includes claim for costs payable to plaintiff in priority to satisfaction of judgment. Counsel seeks order for solicitor-client costs for $1,100 plus disbursements of $470.01. Total draft bill of costs $1,756.91, almost $300 more than the funds paid into court by garnishee. Costs of garnishment proceedings entirely in court's discretion. If plaintiff seeks costs in garnishment proceedings, defendant must be served with Motion.

RCT Sales Ltd. v. Hamilton, 2005 CarswellBC 2280, 2005 BCPC 400 (B.C. Prov. Ct.). Garnishment. Nature and extent. General principles.

Mullin v. R - M & E Pharmacy, 2005 CarswellOnt 203, 74 O.R. (3d) 378 (Ont. S.C.J.).

Garnishment is an equitable remedy. Court has jurisdiction to declare moneys payable on account of personal injury damages for pain and suffering to be exempt from garnishment. Law of Ontario that damages awarded for pain and suffering exempt from a bankrupt's trustee. See *Holley v. Gifford Smith Ltd.*, 1986 CarswellOnt 178, [1986] O.J. No. 165, 14 O.A.C. 65, (sub nom. *Holley, Re)* 54 O.R. (2d) 225, (sub nom. *Holley, Re)* 26 D.L.R. (4th) 230, (sub nom. *Holley, Re)* 59 C.B.R. (N.S.) 17, 12 C.C.E.L. 161 (Ont. C.A.). Plaintiff in personal injury claim cannot assign his cause of action. If all proceeds were to be scooped up by creditors, plaintiffs would not pursue legitimate claims.

Larry Penner Enterprises Inc. v. Lake St. Martin First Nation, 2006 CarswellMan 53, [2006] 2 C.N.L.R. 93, 202 Man. R. (2d) 213, 2006 MBQB 30 (Man. Master), Master Harrison.

Plaintiffs moved *ex parte* on default judgment to garnish moneys allegedly owed by Province to defendants. Claim for continuing garnishing order dismissed. Subject moneys owed by Province were tax rebates from goods sold on reservation. Money payable by Province to defendants subject to Crown immunity.

Trick v. Trick, 2006 CarswellOnt 4139, 271 D.L.R. (4th) 700, 213 O.A.C. 105, 54 C.C.P.B. 242, 31 R.F.L. (6th) 237, 81 O.R. (3d) 241, 83 O.R. (3d) 55 (Ont. C.A.); leave to appeal refused 2007 CarswellOnt 575, 2007 CarswellOnt 576 (S.C.C.).

Payor in receipt of Canada Pension Plan and Old Age Security benefits falling in arrears under support order. Provincial law capping garnishment at 50 per cent where provincial agency seeking enforcement. Appeal allowed. Court had discretion to set amount of garnishment. Discretion to be exercised in light of legislative policy to preserve one-half of benefits for payor.

The *Pension Benefits Act* ("PBA"), s. 66(1), exempts money payable under a pension plan from "execution, seizure or attachment." There is no authority to increase the 50 per cent exemption. Section 65(3) of the *PBA* cannot provide relief from the s. 65(1) general prohibition against pension assignment.

Univar Canada Ltd. v. PCL Packaging Corp., 2007 CarswellBC 2894, 2007 BCSC 1737, 76 B.C.L.R. (4th) 196 (B.C. S.C. [In Chambers])

Appeal by plaintiff from dismissal of its application for pre-judgment garnishing order and order for service *ex juris* allowed. B.C. plaintiff sought garnishment of bank account at Ontario branch of TD Canada Trust. Master erred in finding branch was not in jurisdiction of court as TD Canada Trust operated branches in B.C. and was in jurisdiction of court. However, pursuant to *Bank Act*, plaintiff was required to serve branch where funds were located, so plaintiff was required to obtain leave to serve garnishing order *ex juris*.

(2) Joint Debts Garnishable — **If a debt is payable to the debtor and to one or more co-owners, one-half of the indebtedness or a greater or lesser amount specified in an order made under subrule (15) may be garnished.**

History [R. 20.08(2)]: New. Conforms to *Rules of Civil Procedure*. See Rule 60.08(1.1).

Commentary: As of September 1, 1998 joint debts are garnishable. You will be able to garnish up to 50 per cent of the joint debt. The garnishee is required to identify the co-owners of the debt to the creditor and the court. The creditor must notify the co-owner of the joint debt about the garnishment. The co-owner of the debt can dispute the amount of money payable for the joint debt. To do so, the co-owner of the debt must make a motion to the court. Before a notice of garnishment is issued, you as the creditor first have to file a sworn statement (affidavit re: garnishment) with the court where the debtor lives or carries on business.

Case Law: *Maxine's Ladies Wear v. Veltri* (May 26, 1998), Doc. 1114/97 (Ont. Gen. Div.) — Motion by the Garnishee for return of $664.39 remitted to the Small Claims Court. In *Director of Support & Custody Enforcement (Ontario) v. Jones* (1991), 5 O.R. (3d) 499 (Ont. Div. Ct.), the Divisional Court held that joint bank accounts in the name of a judgment debtor and another person are not garnishable because the bank is indebted to both joint account holders and not solely the judgment debtor. Motion therefore allowed.

A bank was entitled to pursue both or either of husband and wife who were joint debtors on a line of credit. A covenant not to sue the wife after payment of the sum did not amount to the husband's release. Both M.C. and the wife were principal debtors, joint and several and the bank was entitled to proceed against either or both. M.C.'s argument that his rights as guarantor under the mortgage were impaired by material variation in terms between the bank and his wife failed. *Royal Bank of Canada v. Calonego* (December 2, 1999), Doc. 98-0886 (Ont. S.C.J.).

(2.1) Where Leave Required — **If more than six years have passed since the order was made, or if its enforcement is subject to a condition, a notice of garnishment may be issued only with leave of the court.**

(2.2) If a notice of garnishment is not issued within one year after the date on which an order granting leave to issue it is made,

   (a) the order granting leave ceases to have effect; and

   (b) a notice of garnishment may be issued only with leave of the court on a subsequent motion.

(2.3) A notice of renewal of garnishment may be issued under subrule (5.3) without leave of the court before the original notice of garnishment or any subsequent notice of renewal of garnishment expires.

(3) Obtaining Notice of Garnishment — **A creditor who seeks to enforce an order by garnishment shall file with the clerk of a court in the territorial division in which the debtor resides or carries on business,**

   (a) an affidavit for enforcement request (Form 20P) naming one debtor and one garnishee and stating,

      (i) the date of the order and the amount awarded,

      (ii) the territorial division in which the order was made,

      (iii) the rate of postjudgment interest payable,

(iv) the total amount of any payments received since the order was granted,

(v) the amount owing, including postjudgment interest,

(vi) the name and address of the named garnishee to whom a notice of garnishment is to be directed,

(vii) the creditor's belief that the named garnishee is or will become indebted to the debtor, and the grounds for the belief, and

(viii) any particulars of the debts that are known to the creditor; and

(b) a certificate of judgment (Form 20A), if the order was made in another territorial division.

History [R. 20.08(3)]: Formerly 21.08(2); refers to Form 20A, formerly Form 21A.

Commentary: Where a debtor does not pay a debt pursuant to a judgment, in order to make a demand of money owed to the debtor by someone else (e.g., garnishment of bank accounts, wages or money owed through a contract), a creditor must obtain a notice of garnishment in the jurisdiction where the debtor resides or carries on business. The person or company to whom the notice is sent is the garnishee.

The creditor may first have to obtain a certificate of judgment in the originating court and file it in the court in the jurisdiction where the debtor resides or carries on business.

A Notice of Garnishment (Form 20E) is effective for six years from the date of service on the garnishee. Notices of garnishment, unlike writs, cannot be renewed. Therefore, a new affidavit and a new notice of garnishment must be completed and filed to obtain a new notice of garnishment [r. 20.08(8)].

The garnishee is liable to pay to the clerk any monies he or she owes to the debtor, up to the amount shown in the notice of garnishment, within 10 days after service of the notice on the garnishee or 10 days after the debt becomes payable, whichever is later [r. 20.08(7)]. A debt the garnishee owes to the debtor includes:

- a debt payable at the time the notice of garnishment is served;
- a debt payable (whether absolutely or on the fulfilment of a condition) within six years after the notice is served [r. 20.08(8)].

A garnishee who admits owing a debt to the debtor shall pay it to the clerk in the manner prescribed by the notice of garnishment, subject to s. 7 of the *Wages Act* [r. 20.08(9)]. The amounts paid into court shall not exceed the portion of the debtor's wages that are subject to garnishment under s. 7 of the *Wages Act*. Interpretation and compliance with the *Wages Act* is the responsibility of the garnishee. The *Rules of the Small Claims Court* do not limit the time period within which garnishments may be issued.

According to subrule 8.01(8), a notice of garnishment is to be served by mail, by courier, personally, or by an alternative to personal service.

Within 10 days of being served with a Notice of Garnishment (Form 20E), a garnishee who wishes to dispute the garnishment, or pay to the clerk less than the amount set out in the notice of garnishment, is responsible for filing a Garnishee's Statement (Form 20F).

A creditor may be informed by the garnishee that the debtor has a co-owner of debt.

- Serving a Notice to Co-Owner of Debt (Form 20G) together with a copy of the Garnishee's Statement (Form 20F) to any co-owners of debt.
  - The co-owner of debt has 30 days from the date of service of the notice of co-owner of debt to request a garnishment hearing [r. 2.08(16)].

- If the 30-day time period for requesting a garnishment hearing has expired, within 30 days afterwards the creditor may file with the clerk [r. 20.08(21)]:

  - An Affidavit of Service (Form 8A) of the notice to co-owner of debt [r. 8.06];

  - An affidavit (Form 15B) stating he or she believes that no co-owner of the debt is a person under disability and the grounds for the belief [r. 20.08(21)].

Case Law: *Smith v. Schaffner*, 2007 CarswellNS 306, 2007 NSSC 210, 34 C.B.R. (5th) 316, 43 C.P.C. (6th) 358, 820 A.P.R. 58, 257 N.S.R. (2d) 58 (N.S. S.C.).

Mother brought application for enforcement of execution order against joint account. Application granted. Mother established on balance of probabilities that father's contribution to joint account was at least 45 per cent of amounts deposited. Bank ordered to apply execution order to 45 per cent of any monies in joint account. No reason existed to deny creditor's entitlement to have sheriff attach execution to debtor's interest in joint property if interest of execution debtor in such property was established. See *Penney v. Canadian Imperial Bank of Commerce*, 1996 CarswellNfld 238, 145 Nfld. & P.E.I.R. 355, 453 A.P.R. 355 (Nfld. T.D.).

(4) On the filing of the documents required by subrule (3), the clerk shall issue a notice of garnishment (Form 20E) naming as garnishee the person named in the affidavit.

History [R. 20.08(4)]: Formerly 21.08(3).

(5) A notice of garnishment issued under subrule (4) shall name only one debtor and only one garnishee.

History [R. 20.08(5)]: New. See R. 60.08(6.1) *Rules of Civil Procedure* O. Reg. 534/95.

(5.1) Duration and Renewal — A notice of garnishment remains in force for six years from the date of its issue and for a further six years from each renewal.

Commentary: Section 29 of the *Crown Liability and Proceedings Act* (Federal) and section 21 of the *Proceedings Against the Crown Act* prohibit the issuance of executions against the Crown (Federal or Provincial).

Where a creditor requests the issuance of an execution against "Her Majesty the Queen in Right of Ontario", "Sa Majesté du chef de l'Ontario", or the Attorney General of Canada, they must be advised that the court is expressly prohibited from doing so in accordance with the applicable Act (above).

Proceedings against the Federal Crown may also include agencies of the Crown where an Act of Parliament authorizes proceedings to be taken in the name of the agency.

The garnishee is liable to pay to the clerk any monies he or she owes to the debtor, up to the amount shown in the notice of garnishment, within 10 days after service of the notice on the garnishee or 10 days after the debt becomes payable, whichever is later [r. 20.08(7)]. A debt the garnishee owes to the debtor includes:

- a debt payable at the time the notice of garnishment is served;

- a debt payable (whether absolutely or on the fulfilment of a condition) within six years after the notice is served and within six years after it is issued [r. 20.08(8)].

A garnishee who admits owing a debt to the debtor shall pay it to the clerk in the manner prescribed by the notice of garnishment, subject to section 7 of the *Wages Act* [r. 20.08(9)]. The amounts paid into court shall not exceed the portion of the debtor's wages that are subject to garnishment under section 7 of the *Wages Act*. Interpretation and compliance with the *Wages Act* is the responsibility of the garnishee. Issues relating to the *Wages Act* are legal matters and the garnishee should seek legal advice.

Garnishing the Wages of Federal/Provincial Employees

There are specific time limits and extra steps that must be taken if a creditor intends to garnish the wages of an employee of the federal government, a member of the Canadian Armed Forces, or an employee of the provincial government.

Garnishing the wages of an employee of the Federal Government:

The federal government requires information in addition to the basic information provided within the notice of garnishment before they will honour a garnishment request.

1. The creditor would proceed to have their notice of garnishment issued by the clerk of the court in the usual way.

2. The creditor must also obtain a certified copy of their order or judgment or a certificate of judgment.

3. The creditor must obtain and complete a form called an "Application to Garnishee". The Application to Garnishee form is available online at http://laws.justice.gc.ca/eng/SOR-83-212/page-4.html#anchorsc:1, or by contacting the Garnishment Registry at the address provided below.

4. The creditor must serve the certified copy of their order or judgment, the issued notice of garnishment and the completed Application to Garnishee on the federal government. Pursuant to s.4(1)(f) of the *Garnishment and Attachment Regulations*, if the garnishment is issued by one of the following locations:

  a) District of Algoma;

  b) District of Cochrane;

  c) County of Frontenac;

  d) District of Kenora;

  e) County of Lanark;

  f) Counties of Leeds and Grenville;

  g) Counties of Lennox and Addington;

  h) District of Manitoulin;

  i) District of Nipissing;

  j) Judicial District of Ottawa-Carleton;

  k) District of Parry Sound;

  l) Counties of Prescott and Russell;

  m) County of Prince Edward;

  n) District of Rainy River;

  o) County of Renfrew;

  p) Counties of Stormont, Dundas and Glengarry;

  q) District of Sudbury;

  r) District of Temiskaming; and

  s) District of Thunder Bay

service must be effected at the Garnishment Registry in Ottawa at the following address:

Department of Justice

Justice Building

P.O. Box 2730, Station D

Ottawa, Ontario

K1P 5W7

Attention: Garnishment Registry

If the garnishment is issued by a court location in Ontario other than the counties, districts, or locations listed above (s. 4(1)(g)), service must be effected at:

Department of Justice

Toronto Regional Office

2 First Canadian Place

Box 36

Toronto, Ontario

M5X 1K6

Attention: Garnishment Registry

Note: The creditor must serve the aforementioned documents on the federal government within 30 days of the notice of garnishment being issued by the clerk of the Small Claims Court, otherwise the federal government may consider the garnishment invalid in accordance with the *Garnishment Attachment and Pension Diversion Act*, s. 6(2).

In accordance with the *Garnishment Attachment and Pension Diversion Act*, s.10, the federal government has a minimum of 15 days to respond to the notice of garnishment.

The creditor must serve the aforementioned documents on the federal government within 30 days of the notice of garnishment being issued by the clerk of the Small Claims Court, otherwise the federal government may consider the garnishment invalid in accordance with the *Garnishment, Attachment and Pension Diversion Act*, section 6(2).

In accordance with the *Garnishment, Attachment and Pension Diversion Act*, section 10, the federal government has a minimum of 15 days to respond to the notice of garnishment.

Garnishing the wages of a member of the Canadian Armed Forces:

The creditor must give the debtor's commanding officer notice of their intention to issue a garnishment at least 30 days before serving the notice of garnishment. If the creditor does not know the identity of the debtor's commanding officer, the creditor should be advised to contact the Office of the Judge Advocate General — National Defence Headquarters for instructions, at (613) 992-6420.

In this process, an affidavit refers to an Affidavit for Enforcement Request (Form 20P).

If there is a default in payment of a debt pursuant to a judgment, the creditor may require the debtor or other person to be examined for the purposes of assessing the debtor's assets which may be available for satisfying the judgment.

Section 29 of the *Crown Liability and Proceedings Act* (Federal) and section 21 of the *Proceedings Against the Crown Act* prohibit the issuance of executions against the Crown (Federal or Provincial).

Where a creditor requests the issuance of an execution against "Her Majesty the Queen in Right of Ontario," "Sa Majesté du chef de l'Ontario," or the Attorney General of Canada, they must be advised that the court is expressly prohibited from doing so in accordance with the applicable *Act* (above).

Proceedings against the Federal Crown may also include agencies of the Crown where an Act of Parliament authorizes proceedings to be taken in the name of the agency.

A Notice of Examination (Form 20H) is issued by the clerk in the jurisdiction where the debtor or other person resides or carries on business. The creditor may first have to obtain a certificate of judgment in the originating court and file it in the court in the jurisdiction where the debtor or other person resides or carries on business.

A separate notice of examination must be completed for each person examined and a fee must be submitted for each notice of examination.

"Examination days" on which examinations are scheduled may be established in each court. A creditor may attend the court office and/or make a written request to obtain a date, time, and place for the hearing of the examination.

Rule 1.07(1.1) grants parties the ability to request that all or part of an examination be conducted by *videoconference only* where facilities exist by filing a Request for Telephone or Video Conference (Form 1B), indicating the reasons for the request. If the request is granted, the court will make the necessary arrangements and notify the parties.

Financial Information Form

In the case of a debtor who is an individual, they will be served with the Financial Information form (Form 20I) along with the notice of examination. In accordance with r. 20.10(4.1)(b), the debtor must complete the financial information form and serve a copy on the creditor, and provide a copy to the judge at the examination hearing. In accordance with r. 20.10(4.2), the debtor must also bring documents to the examination hearing to support the information provided in the financial information form.

(5.2) A notice of garnishment may be renewed before its expiration by filing with the clerk of the court in which the notice of garnishment was issued a notice of renewal of garnishment (Form 20E.1), together with an affidavit for enforcement request (Form 20P).

(5.3) On the filing of the notice and affidavit required by subrule (5.2), the clerk shall issue the notice of renewal of garnishment (Form 20E.1) naming as garnishee the person named in the affidavit.

(5.4) The provisions of these rules that apply with respect to notices of garnishment also apply with respect to notices of renewal of garnishment.

(6) Service of Notice of Garnishment — The notice of garnishment (Form 20E) **shall be served by the creditor in accordance with subrule 8.01(8).**

History [R. 20.08(6)]: Essentially former 21.08(4); refers to subrule 8.01(6) rather than describing the type of service required.

Commentary: Where the garnishee is a bank, trust company, loan corporation, credit union, or the Province of Ontario Savings Office, the Notice of Garnishment should be served at the branch where the debt to the payor is payable.

Section 212 of the federal *Bank Act*, R.S.C. 1985, c. B-1, limits the effect of any writ or process to the branch where it was served.

Once issued, the creditor is required in accordance with rule 20.08(6) to serve both the debtor and the garnishee with a copy of the Notice of Garnishment together with a copy of the sworn Affidavit for Enforcement Request.

The debtor must be served with a copy of the garnishment within five days of serving it on the garnishee.

The rule of service that applies with respect to garnishments is rule 8.01(8).

Service on:	Documents Requiring Service:	Acceptable Methods of Service:	Timelines for Service:
Debtor	• Notice of Garnishment, and • Affidavit for Enforcement Request.	• Personally (8.02) • Alternative to Personal Service (8.03) • Mail (8.07) • Courier (8.07.1)	Within 5 days of effecting service on garnishee.
Garnishee	• Notice of Garnishment, and • Garnishee Statement.	• Personally (8.02) • Alternative to Personal Service (8.03) • Mail (8.07) • Courier (8.07.1)	

It is acceptable for a debtor to be served with a Notice of Garnishment at the debtor's place of employment.

(6.1) The creditor shall serve the notice of garnishment on the debtor within five days of serving it on the garnishee.

(6.2) Financial Institution — If the garnishee is a financial institution, the notice of garnishment and all further notices required to be served under this rule shall be served at the branch at which the debt is payable.

(6.3) Proof of Service — Service of the notice of garnishment may be proved by affidavit.

(7) Garnishee Liable From Time of Service — The garnishee is liable to pay to the clerk any debt of the garnishee to the debtor, up to the amount shown in the notice of garnishment, within 10 days after service of the notice on the garnishee or 10 days after the debt becomes payable, whichever is later.

History [R. 20.08(7)]: Formerly 21.08(5).

(8) For the purpose of subrule (7), a debt of the garnishee to the debtor includes,

(a) a debt payable at the time the notice of garnishment is served; and

(b) a debt payable (whether absolutely or on the fulfilment of a condition) after the notice is served and within six years after it is issued.

History [R. 20.08(8)]: Formerly 21.08(6), restructured for clarity.

Commentary: A garnishment remains in force for 24 months from the date of service [Rule 20.08(8)]. A debt of the garnishee to the debtor includes a debt payable at the time the Notice of Garnishment is served and a debt payable within 24 months after the notice is served or payable on the fulfilment of a term or condition with 24 months after the notice is served. Where the full amount of the order has not been paid within the 24 month period, the creditor/agent must file a new affidavit.

(9) Payment by Garnishee — A garnishee who admits owing a debt to the debtor shall pay it to the clerk in the manner prescribed by the notice of garnishment, and the

amounts paid into court shall not exceed the portion of the debtor's wages that are subject to seizure or garnishment under section 7 of the *Wages Act.*

History [R. 20.08(9)]: Formerly 21.08(7); plain language changes.

Commentary: Effective April 17, 2000, cheques for garnished funds received by Small Claims Court should be issued payable to the creditor, unless there is a letter of direction from the creditor instructing otherwise. They may be mailed either care of the agent/lawyer's address or to the creditor, as directed. The Small Claims Court Form #SCR 20.08-20E "Notice of Garnishment" has been amended to reflect this change with the following note: *"Note: Any garnished funds received by the court will be made payable to the judgment creditor in all instances, unless an irrevocable letter of direction is received from the judgment creditor directing otherwise."*

(10) Equal Distribution Among Creditors — If the clerk has issued notices of garnishment in respect of a debtor at the request of more than one creditor and receives payment under any of the notices of garnishment, he or she shall distribute the payment equally among the creditors who have filed a request for garnishment and have not been paid in full.

History [R. 20.08(10)]: Formerly 21.08(8); plain language changes.

Commentary: Where a judgment creditor requests issuance of a garnishment after the funds have been received even though they may not have been distributed, the creditor is not entitled to a share of the funds standing in court. The judgment creditor will be entitled to a share of any funds received after the request for garnishment has been filed with the court. A judgment creditor who has filed a request for garnishment in another territorial division is *not* entitled to share in any distribution of funds. Only judgment creditors who have filed requests for garnishment in the territorial division where the funds are being received are entitled to share in any distribution.

Suppose creditor "A" issues a Notice of Garnishment against a debtor's bank account, and creditor "B" issues a notice of garnishment against the same debtor's employer. They would each share equally in any moneys paid into court by either garnishee. If additional notices of garnishment are subsequently issued against the same debtor naming the same or other garnishees, those creditors would share equally in any distribution of moneys received from any of the garnishees.

(11) Disputing Garnishment — A garnishee referred to in subrule (12) shall, within 10 days after service of the notice of garnishment, file with the court a statement (Form 20F) setting out the particulars.

History [R. 20.08(11)]: Formerly 21.08(9); plain language changes; Form 20F new.

(12) Subrule (11) applies to a garnishee who,

   (a) wishes to dispute the garnishment for any reason; or

   (b) pays to the clerk less than the amount set out in the notice of garnishment as owing by the garnishee to the debtor, because the debt is owed to the debtor and to one or more co-owners of the debt or for any other reason.

History [R. 20.08(12)]: New — required because of 20.08(2).

Commentary: A garnishee can dispute a garnishment within 10 days after it was served with the Notice of Garnishment by sending a statement to the court setting out the particulars of the dispute [Rule 20.08(11)]. Distribution of garnishment monies received must be made equally among all creditors who filed a garnishment, regardless of the garnishee named. The garnishee is responsible to identify if the debt is owed to the debtor and one or more co-owners. He/she must serve a copy of the statement on the creditor and the debtor, and file with the court, a copy of the garnishee's statement indicating that the debt is owed to the debtor and one or more co-owners (see Subrules 20.08 (13) and (14)). A garnishment hearing may be requested by a creditor, debtor, garnishee, co-owner of the debt and any other interested person.

Within 10 days of being served with a Notice of Garnishment (Form 20E), a garnishee who wishes to dispute the garnishment, or pay to the clerk less than the amount set out in the notice of garnishment, is responsible for filing a Garnishee's Statement (Form 20F).

A dispute filed under this rule could include any one or more of the following reasons:

1. That, at the time of being served with the Notice of Garnishment the payor owed the recipient no money, either,

   (a) because the amount claimed by the recipient was paid up in full; or

   (b) because the amount claimed by the recipient was calculated for an order that, by its own wording, is no longer effective or that has been suspended or found no longer to be effective by an appropriate court.

2. That, at the time of being served with the Notice of Garnishment declaration for indexed support, the payor owed less than the amount claimed by the recipient, either,

   (a) because some of the amount was paid; or

   (b) because some of the amount was calculated for an order that, by its own wording, is suspended or no longer effective or that has been suspended or found no longer effective by an appropriate court.

3. That, at the time of being served with the Notice of Garnishment,the garnishee did not owe the payor any money and that the garnishee does not now owe and does not expect in the future to owe the payor any money.

4. That the garnishee owes or will owe the payor money, but that this money is protected from garnishment by a legal exemption, the details of which must be set out in the dispute.

5. That the garnishee has a right of set-off against the payor, the details of which must be set out in the dispute.

6. That the amount being garnisheed is greater than what is allowed,

   (a) under section 7 of the *Wages Act*;

   (b) in an order made under section 7 of the *Wages Act*;

   (c) in an order made under section 68 of the *Bankruptcy and Insolvency Act* (Canada); or

   (d) under any other law, the details of which must be set out in the dispute.

7. That the money owed by the garnishee to the payor is not a wage under the Wages Act, that the amount being garnisheed is causing a serious financial hardship for the payor and that the payor is asking for a change in the amount being garnished. The case of *Gavitz v. Brock* (1974), 3 O.R. (2d) 58 (C.A.) determined that wages includes a salesperson's commission.

Case Law: *Shaffer v. Greenberg* (1994), 26 C.P.C. (3d) 331 (Man. Q.B.) — The defendant moved to vary or suspend the notice of garnishment because the plaintiff breached an agreement not to take action before February 24 and did not use his best efforts to collect funds from the co-defendant. The notice of garnishment was set aside. The plaintiff by obtaining the notice of garnishment against the co-defendant and attempting to sustain the order against him fulfilled his obligation, therefore, the plaintiff may properly proceed with efforts to collect from the defendant.

Cina v. Ultratech Tool & Gauge Inc. (2001), 2001 CarswellOnt 4023, 56 O.R. (3d) 338, 15 C.P.C. (5th) 71 (Ont. S.C.J.) — Notice of Garnishment served upon garnishee described as TD Canada Trust not invalid. It was name under which five entities carried on retail banking business. Service as effected was effective to constitute service on all five corporations. Order jointly and severally to pay to sheriff amount in question.

Stoneworth Ltd. v. Applegate (Ont. Sm. Cl. Ct.), Thomson J.

Motion to set aside judgment against garnishee.

Garnishee did not file statement of garnishment, was not present at hearing and had not informed either Court or the plaintiff of proper names of the defendant's employer. Court gave judgment against garnishee for wages paid in the period of time between service of garnishment and defendant's consumer proposal.

Judgment against garnishee set aside. Costs payable by the garnishee to the plaintiff.

Garnishee took position in motion that it was under restraint to inform either Court or plaintiff of correct name of the employer of the defendant. The legal employer of the defendant is a management company with different officers and shareholders. It supplies Applegate's services to Robins Appleby. This is a normal configuration for law firms.

(13) Service on Creditor and Debtor — The garnishee shall serve a copy of the garnishee's statement on the creditor and the debtor.

History [R. 20.08(13)]: New — see 20.08(2).

(14) Notice to Co-owner of Debt — A creditor who is served with a garnishee's statement under subrule (13) shall forthwith send to any co-owners of the debt, in accordance with subrule 8.01(14), a notice to co-owner of debt (Form 20G) and a copy of the garnishee's statement.

History [R. 20.08(14)]: New — see 20.08(2).

(15) Garnishment Hearing — At the request of a creditor, debtor, garnishee, co-owner of the debt or any other interested person, the clerk shall fix a time and place for a garnishment hearing.

History [R. 20.08(15)]: Formerly 21.08(10); now refers to co-owners.

Case Law: *Cotton v. Cotton*, 2004 CarswellOnt 793 (Ont. S.C.J.). Does Plaintiff have status to maintain proceeding given now an undischarged bankrupt? Plaintiff has no status or authority to maintain proceeding, based on a consideration of section 71(2) of *The Bankruptcy and Insolvency Act*, R.S.C. 1985, c. B-3, *Hall-Chem Inc. v. Vulcan Packaging Inc.*, 1994 CarswellOnt 309, 28 C.B.R. (3d) 161, 75 O.A.C. 74, 120 D.L.R. (4th) 552, 21 O.R. (3d) 89, 33 C.P.C. (3d) 361 (Ont. C.A.), *Sier Bath Deck Gear Corp. v. Polymotion Ltd.* (1996), 30 O.R. (3d) 736, 1996 CarswellOnt 3873, 42 C.B.R. (3d) 1, 15 O.T.C. 323 (Ont. Gen. Div.), a decision of the Ontario Court (General Division) on appeal from the Small Claims Court. See also *Rule 11* of the *Ontario Rules of Civil Procedure*. Action stayed.

(15.1) Service of Notice of Garnishment Hearing — After having obtained a hearing date from the clerk, the party requesting the garnishment hearing shall serve the notice of garnishment hearing (Form 20Q) in accordance with subrule 8.01(9).

(15.2) Powers of Court at Hearing — At the garnishment hearing, the court may,

(a) if it is alleged that the garnishee's debt to the debtor has been assigned or encumbered, order the assignee or encumbrancer to appear and state the nature and particulars of the claim;

(b) determine the rights and liabilities of the garnishee, any co-owner of the debt, the debtor and any assignee or encumbrancer;

(c) vary or suspend periodic payments under a notice of garnishment; or

(d) determine any other matter in relation to a notice of garnishment.

(16) **Time to Request Hearing** — A person who has been served with a notice to co-owner of debt is not entitled to dispute the enforcement of the creditor's order for the payment or recovery of money or a payment made by the clerk unless the person requests a garnishment hearing within 30 days after the notice is sent.

History [R. 20.08(16)]: New — see 20.08(2).

(17) **Enforcement Against Garnishee** — If the garnishee does not pay to the clerk the amount set out in the notice of garnishment and does not send a garnishee's statement, the creditor is entitled to an order against the garnishee for payment of the amount set out in the notice, unless the court orders otherwise.

History [R. 20.08(17)]: Formerly 21.08(11).

(18) **Payment to Person other than Clerk** — If, after service of a notice of garnishment, the garnishee pays a debt attached by the notice to a person other than the clerk, the garnishee remains liable to pay the debt in accordance with the notice.

History [R. 20.08(18)]: Formerly 21.08(12).

(19) **Effect of Payment to Clerk** — Payment of a debt by a garnishee in accordance with a notice of garnishment is a valid discharge of the debt as between the garnishee and the debtor and any co-owner of the debt, to the extent of the payment.

History [R. 20.08(19)]: Formerly 21.08(13); includes co-owners.

(20) **Distribution of Payments** — When proof is filed that the notice of garnishment was served on the debtor, the clerk shall distribute a payment received under a notice of garnishment to a creditor in accordance with subrule (20.1), unless,

(a) a hearing has been requested under subrule (15);

(b) a notice of motion and supporting affidavit (Form 15A) has been filed under rule 8.10, 11.06 or 17.04; or

(c) a request for clerk's order on consent (Form 11.2A) has been filed seeking the relief described in subparagraph 1 iii of subrule 11.2.01(1).

History [R. 20.08(20)]: Formerly 21.08(14).

Commentary: Is the 24-month lifetime of a garnishment suspended where notice is received from a trustee in bankruptcy stating that the debtor is bankrupt?

In accordance with the *Bankruptcy and Insolvency Act* (Canada) where a debtor is bankrupt, the bankruptcy effects a stay of proceedings against the bankrupt/debtor. Generally, the garnishment is stayed until the bankrupt debtor is discharged. Written notice of the debtor's bankruptcy must be received from the trustee in bankruptcy. The question of whether the stay affects the running of the 24-month lifetime of the garnishment is up to the parties to determine or dispute.

For example, should the garnishee believe that the 24-month period continues to run during the bankruptcy, and the bankrupt debtor is discharged after the 24-month period expires, the garnishee will not send any more money into court. In this case, it is up to the creditor to challenge the garnishee's decision.

Should the garnishee believe that the 24-month lifetime of the garnishment is suspended until the bankruptcy is discharged and that the garnishment is revived after the discharge, and the garnishee sends money in to court, court staff should process it as garnishment money and leave it to the debtor to dispute.

Note that the debt that is owed by the bankrupt debtor may or may not be discharged by the bankruptcy. A garnishee may, therefore, send money into court believing that the debt has not been discharged. As is the usual practice where money is received, court staff should process it as garnishment money and leave it to the party/garnishee to dispute.

Under s. 3(5) of the *Creditors' Relief Act*, where the enforcement office has a writ against a debtor, the enforcement office may provide a demand, in writing, for any garnishment funds being held in Small Claims Court in connection with that same debtor.

The demand procedure under the *CRA* applies where the sheriff's writ names the same debtor as the debtor named in the SCC Notice of Garnishment (Form 20E). The sheriff is entitled to take those garnished funds and distribute them under the *CRA*.

Case Law: *Bazar McBean LLP v. 1464294 Ontario Ltd.* (2009), 2009 CarswellOnt 5934, [2009] O.J. No. 4088 (Ont. Div. Ct.), Richetti J.

The plaintiff garnished $2,544 from the individual defendants. All the parties then reached a settlement for $1,000 and paid the monies. The individual defendants then learned monies had already been garnished from them. To permit the plaintiff to keep the garnished funds and the settlement funds would be inequitable. It was not viable to set aside the settlement instead of the garnishment as it was impossible to believe the plaintiff really thought it was entitled to a windfall.

(20.1) The clerk shall distribute the payment,

   (a) in the case of the first payment under the notice of garnishment, 30 days after the date it is received; and

   (b) in the case of every subsequent payment under the notice of garnishment, as they are received.

(20.2) Notice Once Order Satisfied — Once the amount owing under an order that is enforced by garnishment is paid, the creditor shall immediately serve a notice of termination of garnishment (Form 20R) on the garnishee and on the clerk.

(21) Payment if Debt Jointly Owned — If a payment of a debt owed to the debtor and one or more co-owners has been made to the clerk, no request for a garnishment hearing is made and the time for doing so under subrule (16) has expired, the creditor may file with the clerk, within 30 days after that expiry,

   (a) proof of service of the notice to co-owner; and

   (b) an affidavit stating that the creditor believes that no co-owner of the debt is a person under disability, and the grounds for the belief.

History [R. 20.08(21)]: New — see 20.08(2).

(22) The affidavit required by subrule (21) may contain statements of the deponent's information and belief, if the source of the information and the fact of the belief are specified in the affidavit.

(23) If the creditor does not file the material referred to in subrule (21) the clerk shall return the money to the garnishee.

O. Reg. 461/01, s. 18; 78/06, s. 45; 393/09, s. 20

Commentary: A creditor may be informed by the garnishee that the debtor has a co-owner of debt.

The creditor is responsible for:

1.   Serving a Notice to Co-Owner of Debt (Form 20G) together with a copy of the Garnishee's Statement (Form 20F) to any co-owners of debt.

The co-owner of debt has 30 days from the date of service of the notice of co-owner of debt to request a garnishment hearing [r. 2.08(16)].

2.   If the 30-day time period for requesting a garnishment hearing has expired, within 30 days afterwards the creditor may file with the clerk [r. 20.08(21)]

- An Affidavit of Service (Form 8A) of the notice to co-owner of debt [r. 8.06];

- An affidavit (Form 15B) stating he or she believes that no co-owner of the debt is a person under disability and the grounds for the belief [r. 20.08(21)].

If the creditor does not file proof of service of the notice to co-owner and an affidavit stating that the creditor believes that no co-owner of the debt is a person under disability, and the grounds for the belief, the clerk shall return any received money back to the garnishee [r. 20.08(23)].

20.09 (1) Consolidation Order — A debtor against whom there are two or more unsatisfied orders for the payment of money may make a motion to the court for a consolidation order.

History [R. 20.09(1)]: Formerly 21.09(1).

(2) The debtor's notice of motion and supporting affidavit (Form 15A) shall set out, in the affidavit portion,

(a) the names and addresses of the creditors who have obtained an order for the payment of money against the debtor;

(b) the amount owed to each creditor;

(c) the amount of the debtor's income from all sources, identifying them; and

(d) the debtor's current financial obligations and any other relevant facts.

History [R. 20.09(2)]: Formerly 21.09(2).

(3) For the purposes of clause 15.01(3)(a), the notice of motion and supporting affidavit shall be served on each of the creditors mentioned in it at least seven days before the hearing date.

History [R. 20.09(3)]: Formerly 21.09(3); deletes description of types of service available.

Commentary: If a debtor has more than one outstanding Small Claims Court judgment against him or her, the debtor can apply to the Small Claims Court in the jurisdiction where he or she lives or carries on business for a consolidation order. The requested order would combine the judgment debts and set up a schedule of repayments for all creditors named in the order. While the consolidation order is in force, no step to enforce the judgment may be taken or continued against the debtor by a creditor named in the order, except issuing a writ of seizure and sale of land and filing it with the sheriff [r. 20.09(8)].

At the hearing, a judge will hear evidence about the debtor's income and expenses and may make an order combining the debts and order payments to be made in instalments.

"Motion days" are established in each court. A party may obtain a motion date from staff in advance of completing a Notice of Motion (Form 15A). The date must be obtained by a party at least seven days before the date set for the hearing since all documents must be served at least seven days before the hearing.

A motion can be heard or conducted by telephone or video conference if facilities are available and the court grants the request. A party can file a *Request for Telephone or Video Conference* [Form 1B], indicating the reasons for the request. If the request is granted, the court will make the necessary arrangements and notify the parties.

When the debtor has obtained an order of the court for consolidation, a creditor may attend the court office and/or make a written request to be added to a consolidation order (provided that the creditor obtained the order for the payment of money against the debtor after the date of the consolidation order, for debt incurred before the date of the consolidation order). [r. 20.09(7)]

A creditor may attend the court office and/or make a written request to terminate a consolidation order if an order for the payment of money is obtained against the debtor for a debt incurred after the date of the consolidation order.

A consolidation order terminates immediately if:

- an order for payment of money is obtained against the debtor for a debt incurred after the date of the consolidation order; or
- if the debtor is in default under the terms of the order for 21 days [r. 20.09(8), (10)].

If the order is terminated, no further consolidation order can be made until a year has passed from the date of the termination [r. 20.09(9)].

A party may attend the court office and/or make a written request to terminate a consolidation order.

A creditor may attend the court office and/or make a written request to terminate a consolidation order in default.

A consolidation order terminates immediately if:

- an order for payment of money is obtained against the debtor for a debt incurred after the date of the consolidation order; or
- if the debtor is in default under the terms of the order for 21 days.

If the order is terminated, no further consolidation order can be made until a year has passed from the date of the termination.

A party may attend the court office and/or make a written request to terminate a consolidation order.

(4) Contents of Consolidation Order — At the hearing of the motion, the court may make a consolidation order setting out,

    (a) a list of unsatisfied orders for the payment of money against the debtor, indicating in each case the date, court and amount and the amount unpaid;

    (b) the amounts to be paid into court by the debtor under the consolidation order; and

    (c) the times of the payments.

History [R. 20.09(4)]: Formerly 21.09(4); plain language changes.

(5) The total of the amounts to be paid into court by the debtor under a consolidation order shall not exceed the portion of the debtor's wages that are subject to seizure or garnishment under section 7 of the *Wages Act*.

History [R. 20.09(5)]: Formerly 21.09(5).

(6) Creditor May Make Submissions — At the hearing of the motion, a creditor may make submissions as to the amount and times of payment.

History [R. 20.09(6)]: Formerly 21.09(6).

(7) Further Orders Obtained After Consolidation Order — If an order for the payment of money is obtained against the debtor after the date of the consolidation order for a debt incurred before the date of the consolidation order, the creditor may file with the clerk a certified copy of the order; the creditor shall be added to the consolidation order and shall share in the distribution under it from that time.

History [R. 20.09(7)]: Formerly 21.09(7); plain language changes.

(8) A consolidation order terminates immediately if an order for the payment of money is obtained against the debtor for a debt incurred after the date of the consolidation order.

History [R. 20.09(8)]: Formerly 21.09(8); deletes requirement that the order for payment of money be after the date of the consolidation order, as obvious.

(9) Enforcement Limited While Consolidation Order in Force — While the consolidation order is in force, no step to enforce the judgment may be taken or continued against the debtor by a creditor named in the order, except issuing a writ of seizure and sale of land and filing it with the sheriff.

History [R. 20.09(9)]: Formerly 21.09(9); plain language changes.

(10) Termination on Default — A consolidation order terminates immediately if the debtor is in default under it for 21 days.

History [R. 20.09(10)]: Formerly 21.09(10); plain language changes.

(11) Effect of Termination — If a consolidation order terminates under subrule (8) or (10), the clerk shall notify the creditors named in the consolidation order, and no further consolidation order shall be made in respect of the debtor for one year after the date of termination.

History [R. 20.09(11)]: Formerly 21.09(11); plain language changes.

(11.1) Manner of Sending Notice — The notice that the consolidation order is terminated shall be served by mail or fax.

(11.2) [Repealed O. Reg. 78/06, s. 46(2).]

(11.3) [Repealed O. Reg. 78/06, s. 46(2).]

(12) Equal Distribution Among Creditors — All payments into a consolidation account belong to the creditors named in the consolidation order who shall share equally in the distribution of the money.

History [R. 20.09(12)]: Formerly 21.09(12).

(13) The clerk shall distribute the money paid into the consolidation account at least once every six months.

O. Reg. 461/01, s. 19 [s. 19(3) revoked O. Reg. 330/02, s. 12(2).]; 330/02, s. 12(1); 440/03, s. 5, item 10; 78/06, s. 46; 393/09, s. 21

History [R. 20.09(13)]: Formerly 21.09(13).

Commentary:

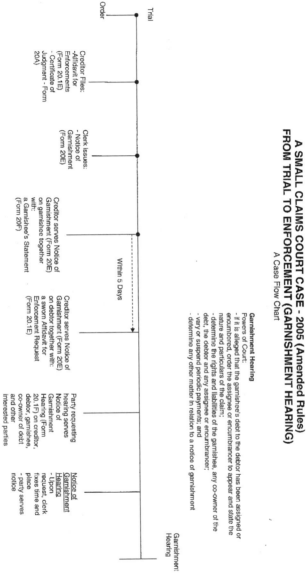

20.10 (1) Examination of Debtor or Other Person — If there is default under an order for the payment or recovery of money, the clerk of a court in the territorial division in which the debtor or other person to be examined resides or carries on business shall, at the creditor's request, issue a notice of examination (Form 20H) directed to the debtor or other person.

History [R. 20.10(1)]: Formerly 21.10(1); term "debtor" changed to "debtor or other person to be examined," to include a representative of a corporation or business; refers to Form 20F, formerly Form 21F; plain language changes.

Commentary: In this process, an affidavit refers to an Affidavit for Enforcement Request (Form 20P).

If there is a default in payment of a debt pursuant to a judgment, the creditor may require the debtor or other person to be examined for the purposes of assessing the debtor's assets which may be available for satisfying the judgment. A Notice of Examination (Form 20H) is issued by the clerk in the jurisdiction where the debtor or other person resides or carries on business. Thus, the creditor may first have to obtain a certificate of judgment in the originating court and file it in the court in the jurisdiction where the debtor or other person resides or carries on business.

A separate notice of examination must be completed for each person examined and a fee must be submitted for each notice of examination.

"Examination days" on which examinations are scheduled may be established in each court. A creditor may attend the court office and/or make a written request to obtain a date, time and place for the hearing of the examination.

Case Law: *Bank of America National Trust & Savings Assn. v. Shefsky* (1997), 4 C.B.R. (4th) 32, 24 C.P.C. (4th) 135 (Ont. Gen. Div.) — An inability to collect on a judgment because of a lack of funds constituted "difficulty in enforcement," which justified examination of the third party. Information sought was relevant and critical to enforcing the judgment. Questions relating to the debtor's income and to the debtor's present, past and future means of satisfying judgment were to be answered.

Advance Magazine Publishers Inc. v. Fleming, 2002 CarswellBC 1571, 2002 BCSC 995 (B.C. Master) — Spouse of judgment debtor required to attend to answer questions of judgment creditor. Questions confined to debtor's ability to satisfy judgment.

(2) The creditor's request shall be accompanied by,

    (a) an affidavit for enforcement request (Form 20P) setting out,

        (i) the date of the order and the amount awarded,

        (ii) the territorial division in which the order was made,

        (iii) the rate of postjudgment interest payable,

        (iv) the total amount of any payments received since the order was granted, and

        (v) the amount owing, including postjudgment interest; and

    (b) a certificate of judgment (Form 20A), if the order was made in another territorial jurisdiction.

History [R. 20.10(2)]: Formerly 21.10(2); refers to Form 20F, formerly Form 21F; plain language changes.

(3) Service of Notice of Examination — The notice of examination shall be served in accordance with subrules 8.01(10), (11) and (12).

History [R. 20.10(3)]: Formerly 21.10(3); refers to subrules 8.01(7) and (8), rather than describing the types of service available.

(4) The debtor, any other persons to be examined and any witnesses whose evidence the court considers necessary may be examined in relation to,

(a) **the reason for nonpayment;**

(b) **the debtor's income and property;**

(c) **the debts owed to and by the debtor;**

(d) **the disposal the debtor has made of any property either before or after the order was made;**

(e) **the debtor's present, past and future means to satisfy the order;**

(f) **whether the debtor intends to obey the order or has any reason for not doing so; and**

(g) **any other matter pertinent to the enforcement of the order.**

History [R. 20.10(4)]: Formerly 21.10(4); plain language changes.

Commentary: The creditor is responsible for serving the debtor with the Notice of Examination (Form 20H) and, if the debtor is an individual, a blank Financial Information Form (Form 20I).

Once the creditor has effected service, the creditor may attend the court office and/or make a written inquiry to prove service of a notice of examination.

Case Law: *Teskey v. Peraan* (September 29, 1998), Doc. 92-CU-50498 (Ont. Master) — An affidavit sworn in support of a judgment debtor's motion to set aside a default judgment. The plaintiff creditor sought an adjournment to permit cross-examination. The adjournment was refused. The affidavit set out a good defence at law. Cross-examination would serve no useful purpose.

Zeppieri & Associates v. Jabbari, 2014 ONSC 818, 2014 CarswellOnt 1414, Nordheimer, J. (Ont. Div. Ct.) — The applicant sought a judicial review of the decision of a Deputy Judge who refused to allow the applicant to proceed with an examination of the respondent/debtor under rule 20.10. The Deputy Judge advised counsel he could not proceed "because she's on public assistance . . . if she's on welfare, we do not proceed with enforcements." The issue could have been avoided had the debtor completed the financial information form required under rule 20.10(4.1) or had the Deputy Judge acceded to request for an adjournment so the debtor could provide further information to the creditor. Application allowed. The order of the Deputy Judge was set aside and the application was ordered to go for a further examination before a different Deputy Judge.

(4.1) Duties of Person to be Examined — A person who is served with a notice of examination shall,

(a) **inform himself or herself about the matters mentioned in subrule (4) and be prepared to answer questions about them; and**

(b) **in the case of an examination of a debtor who is an individual, complete a financial information form (Form 20I) and,**

(i) **serve it on the creditor requesting the examination, but not file it with the court, and**

(ii) **provide a copy of it to the judge presiding at the examination hearing.**

(4.2) A debtor required under clause (4.1)(b) to complete a financial information form (Form 20I) shall bring such documents to the examination hearing as are necessary to support the information that he or she provides in the financial information form.

(5) **Who May Be Examined** — An officer or director of a corporate debtor, or, in the case of a debtor that is a partnership or sole proprietorship, the sole proprietor or any partner, may be examined on the debtor's behalf in relation to the matters set out in subrule (4).

History [R. 20.10(5)]: Formerly 21.10(5); plain language changes.

(5.1) **Attendance** — A person required to attend an examination may attend,

   (a) in person; or

   (b) by video conference in accordance with rule 1.07.

(6) **Examinations Private, Under Oath and Recorded** — The examination shall be,

   (a) held in the absence of the public, unless the court orders otherwise;

   (b) conducted under oath; and

   (c) recorded.

History [R. 20.10(6)]: Formerly 21.10(6).

(7) **Order As To Payment** — After the examination or if the debtor's consent is filed, the court may make an order as to payment.

History [R. 20.10(7)]: Formerly 21.10(7).

Commentary: A notice of examination must be issued in the territorial division where the debtor resides or carries on business. The debtor, an officer or director of a corporate debtor, a partner or sole proprietor and any witnesses whose evidence the court considers necessary may be examined (see subrules 21.10(4) and 21.10(5)). The examination shall be held in the absence of the public unless the court orders otherwise (subrule 21.10(6)). After the examination or with the debtor's written consent, the court may make an order as to payment (subrule 21.10(7)).

(8) **Enforcement Limited while Order as to Payment in Force** — While an order as to payment is in force, no step to enforce the judgment may be taken or continued against the debtor by a creditor named in the order, except issuing a writ of seizure and sale of land and filing it with the sheriff.

History [R. 20.10(8)]: New provision, prohibiting the creditor from taking steps to enforce a judgment except by issue of a writ of seizure and sale of land. This change extends the protection that a debtor currently enjoys under a consolidation order to other types of enforcement proceedings. This provision is party of the B.C. Small Claims Court Rules.

(9) [Repealed O. Reg. 78/06, s. 47(5).]

History [R. 20.10(9)]: Based on former 21.10(8); changes the reference to the "debtor" to "a person on whom a notice of examination has been served" to include a representative of a corporation or business; removes the power of the court to order the person committed to a correctional institution, replacing it with the power to find the person in contempt and order the person to appear before the court for a hearing.

Case Law: *Burgoyne Holdings Inc. v. Magda*, 2005 CarswellOnt 537, 74 O.R. (3d) 417 (Ont. S.C.J.). Contempt of court. Nature of offence. Civil and criminal contempt defined.

(10) [Repealed O. Reg. 78/06, s. 47(5).]

History [R. 20.10(10)]: New provision, based in part on former 21.10(10) and (11).

(10.1) [Repealed O. Reg. 78/06, s. 47(5).]

(11) [Repealed O. Reg. 78/06, s. 47(5).]

History [R. 20.10(11)]: Based on former 21.10(12); deletes reference to the warrant of committal; allows the court to order the person jailed.

Case Law: *Canadian Imperial Bank of Commerce v. Teh*, 2003 CarswellAlta 1822, 2003 ABQB 1052 (Alta. Master). Application by Defendant to open up default judgment against her for $8,462 granted. Defendant failed to respond to Claim when served. Full and complete defence to Plaintiff's claim. No real prejudice to Plaintiff provided they were compensated for their costs.

Benoit v. Akert, 2003 CarswellSask 558, 2003 SKPC 113 (Sask. Prov. Ct.), Robinson J. Action dismissed. *The Land Contract (Actions) Act* applied to Plaintiff's claim. Action related to an agreement for the sale of land. Plaintiff required consent of Court of Queen's Bench to proceed.

Abegweit Potatoes Ltd. v. J.B. Read Marketing Inc., 2003 CarswellPEI 84, 36 C.P.C. (5th) 203, 2003 PESCAD 24, 227 Nfld. & P.E.I.R. 151, 677 A.P.R. 151 (P.E.I. C.A.). Respondent suing appellant for unpaid potatoes. Appellant suing shipper for negligence and breach of contract. Actions consolidated as involving common issue.

Martin v. Universal Cleaning Equipment Inc., 2005 CarswellBC 1440, 2005 BCPC 234 (B.C. Prov. Ct.), J.P. Gordon J. Application brought by Martin, the judgment creditor, to have a warrant for the arrest of Mohns, one of the judgment debtors issued, result of Mohns's failure to attend scheduled payment hearing.

Question whether to issue warrant inasmuch as he was served substitutionally. Warrant to issue.

In the case of *Ho v. Porter* (January 21, 1994), Doc. C92-04018 (B.C. Prov. Ct.), decided at Vancouver, jurisdiction for court to make order of substitutional service, but that before doing so, the judge should be satisfied, one, that there is an overwhelming likelihood that the debtor who is avoiding process of the court will receive *de facto* notice of the payment hearing and that such a notice includes advice that should the judgment debtor fail to attend, as required, he may be arrested.

Provisions to Rule 14(1) of the *Small Claims Rules* provide that:

> If a warrant of arrest is issued under Section 12(15) . . .
>
> [And that is the one that I have just dealt with.]
>
> . . . the registrar must serve the person named in the warrant with a notice of arrest.

The warrant of arrest should contain the recommendation that the judgment debtor only be released upon posting security.

Orphan v. Roulston, 2000 CarswellBC 1472, 2000 BCSC 1062 (B.C. S.C.). Defendant refused to answer questions on examination for discovery. Plaintiff obtained order requiring defendant to answer. Defendant continued to refuse, then gave false answers. Where no outstanding order exists which requires defendant's compliance, court has no power to punish for civil contempt, in absence of some important public purpose. Most appropriate means of addressing defendant's conduct would have been to request special costs at trial.

McDonald v. Lancaster Separate School Board (1916), 35 O.L.R. 614, 29 D.L.R. 731 (Ont. H.C.). Per Masten J., quoting Oswald on *Contempt of Court*, 3rd ed., p. 1: "Contempt, in the legal acceptance of the term, primarily signified disrespect to that which is entitled to legal regard. . . . In its origin, all legal contempt will be found to consist in an offence more or less direct against the Sovereign himself as the fountain-head of law and justice."

(12) [Repealed O. Reg. 78/06, s. 47(5).]

History [R. 20.10(12)]: Based on part of former 21.10(9); refers to power of court under clause 20.10(11)(c), rather than former subrule 20.10(8); refers to Form 20J, formerly Form 21G; directs that the warrant shall be issued to police officers rather than the bailiff, to comply with *Courts of Justice Act* s. 144; the provision in former 21.10(9) requiring delivery to the institution referred to in the warrant is separated out into another subrule (20.10(3)).

Commentary: The court may order a debtor or other person on whom a notice of examination has been properly served under rule 20.10 to attend a contempt hearing. There are two possible scenarios which may happen at the examination hearing in the Small Claims Court which may lead to contempt proceedings:

1. If the person attends the examination but refuses to answer questions or to produce documents or records, the contempt hearing will be scheduled before a judge or deputy judge of the Small Claims Court or

2. If the person fails to attend the examination, the contempt hearing will be scheduled before a judge of the Superior Court of Justice.

A person who has been ordered to attend a contempt hearing before a Superior Court Judge may make a motion to a judge of the Small Claims Court to set aside the order, before or after receiving the notice of contempt hearing. This motion must be heard before the date of the contempt hearing.

A warrant remains in force for 12 months after its date of issue, subject to an order of the court [r. 20.11(10)].

Where a contempt hearing has been held, the presiding judge of the Small Claims Court or judge of the Superior Court of Justice may order a warrant of committal to issue stating that the debtor or other person be jailed for a period not exceeding 40 days. A creditor *may* provide a completed Identification Form (Form 20K).

See Flow Chart also.

(13) [Repealed O. Reg. 78/06, s. 47(5).]

History [R. 20.10(13)]: Contains provision requiring delivery to the nearest institution; refers to police officers instead of the bailiff to comply with *Courts of Justice Act* s. 144.

Case Law: *Roberts v. R.* (2003), 2003 SCC 45, (sub nom. *Wewaykum Indian Band v. Canada)* [2003] S.C.J. No. 50, 2003 CarswellNat 2822, 2003 CarswellNat 2823, 231 D.L.R. (4th) 1, 19 B.C.L.R. (4th) 195, (sub nom. *Wewayakum Indian Band v. Canada)* 309 N.R. 201, [2004] 2 W.W.R. 1, (sub nom. *Wewayakum Indian Band v. Canada)* [2003] 2 S.C.R. 259, 40 C.P.C. (5th) 1, 7 Admin. L.R. (4th) 1, (sub nom. *Wewayakum Indian Band v. Canada)* [2004] 1 C.N.L.R. 342 (S.C.C.). A judge's impartiality is presumed and a party arguing for disqualification must establish that the circumstances justify a finding that the judge must be disqualified. The criterion of disqualification is the reasonable apprehension of bias. The question is what would an informed, reasonable and right-minded person, viewing the matter realistically and practically, and having thought the matter through, conclude.

(14) [Repealed O. Reg. 78/06, s. 47(5).]

History [R. 20.10(14)]: Formerly 21.10(13); period the warrant is in force changed from six months to 12 months.

Commentary: A warrant of committal now remains in force for 12 months from the date of its issue and may be renewed by order of the court. The method of renewal may vary from division to division depending on the requirements of both the local police force and the judiciary. The renewal should take place prior to the expiry date of the warrant. It is the responsibility of the creditor to arrange for the renewal.

Subrule 20.10(1) allows the issue of a notice of examination "directed to the debtor" *only*. Form 20H (notice of examination) can only be used in respect of summoning the debtor. (Rule 20.10(1)).

Subrule 20.10(13) requires delivery to the nearest institution and refers to police officers, not bailiffs. Not all counties or districts have correctional institutions within their boundaries and these courts are directing incarceration in adjoining counties or districts. In addition, not all counties or districts have correctional institutions that will accommodate women.

Subrule 20.10(12) requires the clerk to immediately issue a warrant of committal when an order is made.

Case Law: *Consumers' Gas Co. v. Ferreira* (1990), 1 W.D.C.P. (2d) 259 (Ont. Prov. Ct.) — The claim, notice of default judgment, and notice of examination of the judgment debtor were all served by mail. A notice of show caused was mailed to the debtor who failed to appear. The Court was not satisfied that the debtor refused to attend. A renewal should not be granted where the Court was not satisfied that the debtor had notice of the claim, the default judgment and the warrant.

Ontario (Attorney General) v. Rae (1984), 44 O.R. (2d) 493 (Ont. H.C.) — A judge can proceed to enforce a maintenance order made by another province, though the creditor is not present and is unrepresented.

(15) [Repealed O. Reg. 78/06, s. 47(5).]
O. Reg. 461/01, s. 20 [s. 20(3) revoked O. Reg. 330/02, s. 13(3).]; 330/02, s. 13(1), (2); 440/03, s. 5, item 11; 78/06, s. 47; 393/09, s. 22; 440/10, s. 6

History [R. 20.10(15)]: Formerly 21.10(14), restructured for clarity; refers to the "person" instead of the "debtor" to include a representative of a corporation or business.

Commentary: There are two types of warrants in Small Claims Court: a Warrant of Committal (Form 20J) and a Warrant for Arrest of Defaulting Witness (Form 18B).

Rule 20 deals with the enforcement of orders. Note that in Rule 1 "order" is defined to include a judgment. The Small Claims Court has the power to make orders that are not judgments, for example, an order of costs at a pre-trial conference (see Rule 14.01(4)) and an order for the payment of compensation directly to a witness where the power to summon a witness has been abused (see Rule 19.01(7)). These orders can be enforced under Rule 20 in the same manner as a default judgment or a judgment after trial.

Section 28 of the *Courts of Justice Act* provides that the Small Claims Court may order the times and the proportions in which money payable under an order of the court shall be paid. Rule 20.02(1)(b) says that the court may vary the times and proportions in which money payable under an order of the court shall be paid if it is satisfied that the debtor's circumstances have changed. Another general power of the court is Rule 20.02(1)(a), which provides that the court may stay proceedings to enforce an order of the court for such time and on such terms as are just. There is no automatic stay of enforcement proceedings pending an appeal.

There are several ways in which an order or judgment may be enforced. Enforcement is initiated by means of a written request or an affidavit. These forms are available from any court office. No action to enforce an order or judgment will be taken by the court without the creditor's instructions and payment of the required fee. Enforcement proceedings (with the exception of writs of seizure and sale against lands) in Small Claims Courts are normally issued in the territorial division in which the debtor resides or carries on business. It may, therefore, be necessary to transfer the judgment from one court to another before enforcement can take place. All enforcements must be carried out by a Small Claims Court bailiff.

Any request or affidavit required by the Small Claims Court Rules to initiate enforcement action must provide a breakdown of the outstanding amount. It is the responsibility of the creditor or his or her representative to calculate the amount to be recovered and include this in the request or affidavit. If it is not included, the enforcement process will issue only for the amount shown. This may result in further enforcement proceedings having to be taken or the possible loss of these monies.

A certificate of judgment will be completed by the original court and forwarded directly to the receiving court. Once a certificate of judgment has been issued no enforcement proceedings can be commenced in the original court. It is the responsibility of the creditor or the creditor's representative to determine that the certificate has been received before submitting the request for enforcement to the receiving court.

Section 23 of the *Courts of Justice Act* provides that the Small Claims Court has jurisdiction in an action for the recovery of possession of personal property where the value of the property does not exceed the prescribed amount, e.g., $10,000. The court may make an order for the recovery of personal property in one of two ways.

The court may make an interim order for the recovery of possession of personal property under s. 104 of the *Courts of Justice Act*. An order for the interim recovery of possession of property can be obtained on motion to the court after an action has been commenced. The court can impose conditions on the granting of the order. In addition, a person who obtains possession of personal property as a result of an interim order is liable for any loss that is suffered by the person who is ultimately found to be entitled to possession of the property. Where no order has been made by a Judge for the issuance of a writ of delivery, anyone who wishes to obtain a unit of delivery is required to commence an action by filing a claim along with the ex parte notice of motion requesting the issuance of a writ of delivery. If the enforcement proceeding is commenced by way of an ex parte notice of motion, the claim will normally be served at the same time as the writ of delivery is executed.

An order for the recovery of property may also be made after trial in the form of a judgment of the court. The default judgment procedure is not available where the claim is for the recovery of personal property, and accordingly, the action must go before a judge.

Where a creditor has obtained a final order of the court requiring a debtor to return personal property, it may be enforced by filing with the clerk a request and an affidavit stating that the property has not been returned. The clerk will issue a writ of delivery and direct it to the bailiff for enforcement. Where the property is recovered, the bailiff will turn it over to the creditor or his or her representative. If the property cannot be found or delivered, the creditor or his or her representative may proceed by way of a notice of motion and supporting affidavit for an order to seize other personal property of the debtor. Any property subsequently recovered will be held by the bailiff pending an order of the court for its release.

It is also possible to obtain an interim order for the return of personal property. The application is commenced by means of a notice of motion and supporting affidavit which is filed with the court at the same time as the statement of claim. The clerk should be consulted to determine if the local practice requires service of a copy of the notice of motion and supporting affidavit on the defendant. After the goods have been recovered, the bailiff will serve a copy of the claim on the defendant. Unless the court has ordered otherwise, the property will be turned over to the plaintiff for his or her representative.

Where the personal property of a debtor is located in the territorial division where judgment was recovered, the creditor may request in writing that a writ of seizure and sale of personal property be issued by the Court. If the debtor resides in another territorial division it will be necessary to transfer the judgment before enforcement.

A written request should indicate (a) the style of cause and the action number; (b) the amount remaining unsatisfied; and (c) description of the goods including serial numbers.

With regards to a car, the creditor should also provide to the court a copy of the Ministry of Transportation vehicle search, indicating that the registered owner and the judgment debtor are the same.

Bank Accounts, Guaranteed Investments Certificates, Bonds, Registered Retirement Savings Plans, other financial instruments, contents of safe deposit boxes, and contents of cash registers can also be seized.

In addition to the filing fees, the court may request a deposit against the costs involved in seizing the items requested. With automobiles, this deposit will be applied to towing and storage charges.

Goods seized under a writ of seizure and sale of personal property will not be sold by the bailiff until notice of the time and place of the sale have been advertised in a manner likely to bring the sale to the public's attention and, of course, both the creditor and debtor have been advised. If the notice is delivered personally, fourteen clear days are required before the sale can take place. If the notice is sent by regular mail then an additional five days notice is required.

Note the exemptions set out in section 2 of the *Execution Act*, R.S.O. 1990, c. E.24.

The *Creditors' Relief Act*, R.S.O. 1990, c. C.45 provides in part:

> 3. (5) Where money recovered by garnishment is paid into the Small Claims Court, the Ontario Court of Justice or the Family Court of the Superior Court of Justice, the sheriff is entitled to demand and receive it from the clerk of the court for the purpose of distributing it under this Act, except insofar as the priority created by subsection 4(1) applies to the money.
>
> R.S.O. 1990, c. C.45, s. 3(5); 2006, c. 19, Sched. C, s. 1(2), (4)
>
> . . . . .
>
> (8) The clerk of the Small Claims Court, the Ontario Court of Justice or the Family Court of the Superior Court of Justice is not liable for making payment to the creditor unless, at the time of payment, the clerk has notice that there is an execution against the property of the debtor in the sheriff's hands.
>
> R.S.O. 1990, c. C.45, s. 3(8); 2006, c. 19, Sched. C, s. 1(2), (4)
>
> . . . . .
>
> 25. (1) If the sheriff does not find property of a debtor leviable under the executions and certificates in his or her hands sufficient to pay the same in full, but finds property or the proceeds thereof in the hands of a bailiff of the Small Claims Court under an execution or attachment against the debtor, the sheriff shall demand and obtain them from the bailiff, who shall forthwith deliver them to the sheriff with a copy of every execution and attachment in his or her hands against the debtor and a memorandum showing the amount to be levied under the execution, including the bailiff's fees, and the date upon which each execution or attachment was received by the bailiff.
>
> (2) **Penalty for default** — If the bailiff fails to deliver any of such property or the proceeds thereof, the bailiff shall pay double the value of that which is retained, which may be recovered by the sheriff from him or her with costs of suit, and shall be accounted for by the sheriff as part of the estate of the debtor.
>
> (3) **Costs** — The costs and disbursements of the bailiff are a first charge upon such property or the proceeds thereof and shall be paid by the sheriff to the bailiff upon demand after being assessed by the Small Claims Court clerk.
>
> (4) The sheriff shall distribute the proceeds among the creditors entitled to share in the distribution, and the Small Claims Court execution creditors are entitled without further proof to stand in the same position as creditors whose executions are in the sheriff's hands.
>
> R.S.O. 1990, c. C.45, s. 25

One of the major changes as provided by Rule 20, enforcement of orders, pertains to garnishments: a Notice of Garnishment must be issued where the debtor resides or carries on business; a Notice of Garnishment remains in force for a period of twelve moths, or until such time as the order is paid, or the garnishment is withdrawn; and where there is more than one Notice of Garnishment issued by various plaintiffs against one debtor, each plaintiff shares equally in the proceeds.

A creditor may enforce an order for the payment or recovery of money by garnishment of debts payable to the debtor by other persons.

The creditor must file with the clerk in the territorial division in which the debtor resides or carries on business and affidavit stating the details of the judgment, the name and address of the garnishee and the basis for believing that the garnishee is or will become indebted to the judgment debtor. If the territorial division in which the debtor resides is different from the one in which the judgment was obtained, the creditor must also arrange for a certificate of judgment to be transferred and filed in the territorial division in which the debtor resides or carries on business.

Where an order is obtained in a court against a debtor who resides in the territorial division of another court, the plaintiff must be advised that, if a garnishment is to be issued, it must be transferred to the court in which the debtor resides. For example, a claim (cause of action took place in Metropolitan Toronto) is filed in the Toronto Small Claims Court and the debtor resides in Brampton. After an order is obtained (either by default judgment or after a hearing) in the Toronto Small Claims Court, and the plaintiff or agent wishes to garnish the wages of the debtor who is employed in Toronto, or any other county where the debtor is employed, the claim must be transferred to the Brampton Small Claims Court.

Funds received by the court are normally held for fourteen days prior to their release to the appropriate party. However, the funds will not be disbursed if a garnishment hearing has been requested or if either an appeal or an application to set aside the judgment has been commenced. In these cases, the funds will continue to be held by the court office pending an order for their release.

An administration fee will be deducted by the court office from each payment received from the garnishee with the exception of the initial payment. The remaining funds will be released to the creditor or the creditor's representative unless the court office has issued notices of garnishment at the request of more than one creditor. It is always possible that a garnishment may expire before the full amount is paid. The creditor should always monitor the proceedings to determine if a further garnishment will be required.

If the garnishee fails to comply with the Notice of Garnishment the creditor may apply to a judge for an order for payment against the garnishee. On receipt of a written request for a hearing, the court office will forward a notice of hearing to the creditor or the creditor's representative, the debtor and the garnishee.

Rule 20.10 of the Rules of the Small Claims Court provides that, where there is default under an order for payment of recovery of money, the clerk of the territorial division where the debtor resides or carries on business shall, at the creditor's request, issue a notice of examination directed to the debtor or other person to be examined. The purpose of the examination is to examine the person as to his or her assets and ability to satisfy the judgment. The creditor's request must be accompanied by an affidavit setting out the particulars of the judgment and the outstanding balance, including postjudgment interest. The Notice of Examination is served pursuant to subrule 20.10(3). A notice of the hearing date will be sent to the creditor or the creditor's representative who must be prepared to attend the examination hearing.

A warrant remains in force for 12 months from its date of issue and may be renewed by order of a judge. It is the responsibility of the creditor or the creditor's representative to arrange for the renewal.The court office should be contacted to determine the appropriate renewal procedure.

A judgment creditor who seeks to enforce an order by garnishment shall file, with the clerk in the territorial division in which the debtor resides or carries on business: (1) the appropriate fee; (2) an affidavit stating the date of the order and the amount awarded, the territorial division in which the order was made, the rate of postjudgment interest payable, the date and amount of any payment received since the order was granted, the amount owing (including postjudgment interest), the name and address of each person to whom a notice of garnishment is to be directed and to whom the creditor believes are or will become indebted to the debtor, the grounds for the belief (and such particulars of the debts as are known to the creditor); and (3) a certificate of judgment (Form 20A).

The certificate of judgment issued to a plaintiff and the one issued to another court to transfer a judgment from one division to another are identical. However, if a plaintiff attempts to file a certificate along with an enforcement request in a court other than the one where the judgment was given, it would be refused. The practice has been to have the court issue a certificate of judgment directed to the forwarding court. The plaintiff would then forward a request for enforcement to the second court.

On the filing of the material required by subrule (2), the clerk shall issue notices of garnishment (Form 20E), naming as garnishee the persons named in the affidavit. On the filing of the request for garnishment, the clerk shall issue notices of garnishment. The garnishments are served on the garnishee by registered mail, on the debtor by regular mail or, if requested, on either party by personal service (see Rules of Services).

Rule 20.08(10) provides that where the clerk has issued notices of garnishment in respect of a debtor at the request of more than one creditor, and the clerk receives payment under any of the notices of garnishment, the clerk shall distribute the payment equally among the creditors who have filed a request for garnishment and have not been paid in full.

A plaintiff must request that a Notice of Garnishment be issued in order to share in the payments received.

A Notice of Garnishment remains in force for twelve months following service on the garnishee and where wages are being attached, will likely result in multiple payments from the garnishee. Creditors should always maintain contact with the court office to ensure that payments are being received regularly.

A debtor against whom there are two or more unsatisfied orders for the payment of money may make a motion to the court for a consolidation order.

In terms of the garnishment of wage, note the *Wages Act*, R.S.O. 1990, c. W.1, in particular sections 1 and 7 in part:

1.

"wages" means wages or salary whether the employment in respect of which the same is payable is by time or by the job or piece or otherwise.

R.S.O. 1990, c. W.1, s. 1

. . . . .

7. (1) For the purposes of this section,

"wages" does not include an amount that an employer is required by law to deduct from wages.

R.S.O. 1990, c. W.1, s. 7(1)

(1.1) For the purposes of this section, payments from an insurance or indemnity scheme that are intended to replace income lost because of disability shall be deemed to be wages, whether the scheme is administered by the employer or another person.

1999, c. 12, Sched. B, s. 18

(2) Subject to subsection (3), 80 per cent of a person's wages are exempt from seizure or garnishment.

R.S.O. 1990, c. W.1, s. 7(2)

(3) Fifty per cent of a person's wages are exempt from seizure or garnishment in the enforcement of an order for support or maintenance enforceable in Ontario.

R.S.O. 1990, c. W.1, s. 7(3)

(4) A judge of the court in which a writ of execution or notice of garnishment enforceable against a person's wages is issued may, on motion by the creditor on notice to the person, order that the exemption set out in subsection (2) or (3) be decreased, if the judge is satisfied that it is just to do so, having regard to the nature of the debt owed to the creditor, the person's financial circumstances and any other matter the judge considers relevant.

R.S.O. 1990, c. W.1, s. 7(4)

(5) A judge of the court in which a writ of execution or notice of garnishment enforceable against a person's wages is issued may, on motion by the person on notice to the creditor, order that the exemption set out in subsection (2) or (3) be increased, if the judge is satisfied that it is just to do so, having regard to the person's financial circumstances and any other matter the judge considers relevant.

R.S.O. 1990, c. W.1, s. 7(5)

(6) Where an employer receives notice of a motion under subsection (4) or (5), the employer may pay into court the part of the person's wages that is not exempt from seizure or garnishment under subsection (2) or (3), as the case may be, and the judge on the hearing of the motion may make such order for payment out of court as is just.

R.S.O. 1990, c. W.1, s. 7(6)

(7) Subject to subsection (8), an assignment of wages or any part of them to secure payment of a debt is invalid.

R.S.O. 1990, c. W.1, s. 7(7)

(8) A person may assign to a credit union to which the *Credit Unions and Caisses Populaires Act* applies the part of the person's wages that does not exceed the part that may be seized or garnished under this section.

R.S.O. 1990, c. W.1, s. 7(8)

The garnishee, the debtor, the creditor or any other interested person may request that the clerk set down a dispute to the garnishment for hearing by a judge. At the hearing, the judge may determine the rights and liabilities of the parties and of any assignee or encumbrancer or may determine nay other matter in relation to the notice of garnishment. The purpose of the examination is to examine the debtor with respect to his or her assets and their ability to pay.

Where more than one creditor has issued a Notice of Garnishment in respect of the same debtor and the clerk receives payment under any of the notices of garnishment, the clerk must distribute the payments he receives equally among all the creditors who have filed a request for garnishment and are not paid in full.

A notice of examination will be issued at the creditor's request in the territorial division where the debtor resides or carries on business (Rule 20.10(1)). The clerk is entitled to deduct an administrative fee from each payment submitted by a garnishee and will remit the balance to the creditor or his or her representative. However, if more than one Notice of Garnishment has been issued against the same defendant, any funds received from a garnishee (after deducting the administrative fee) will be distributed equally among the creditors who have issued notices. The clerk is not required to notify the creditor or its representative of the receipt of monies. If no monies will be forthcoming, the garnishee must advise the clerk and a copy of their response will usually be sent to the creditor or his or her representative. The creditor should also be aware of the expiry date of the Notice of Garnishment as there could still be an outstanding balance. In such cases, a new affidavit should be filed with the court if enforcement is to continue.

Should the garnishee fail to comply with the Notice of Garnishment, the creditor or his or her representative can apply to the court for an order against the garnishee to pay the amount set out in the notice. A written request to place the matter on the court list should be filed with the clerk. In addition, the clerk should be consulted regarding the need to subpoena the books and records of the garnishee as some judges are reluctant to grant an order in the absence of service of a subpoena. The creditor, debtor, garnishee or any other interested party may request a hearing to determine any matter relating to the Notice of Garnishment.

Examinations shall be held in the absence of the public unless the court orders otherwise. Subrule 20.10(4) provides that the debtor may be examined in relation to the following matters: (a) the reason for nonpayment; (b) the debtor's income and property; (c) the debts owed to and by the debtor; (d) the disposal the debtor has made of any property either before or after the making of the order; (e) the debtor's present, past and future means to satisfy the order; (f) whether the debtor intends to obey the order or has reason for not doing so; and (g) any other matter relevant to the enforcement of the order.

Section 28 of the *Courts of Justice Act* allows the court to order that a judgment be paid in instalments. Rule 21.02(b) allows the court to vary the times and amounts of the instalments.

Section 7(5) of the *Wages Act* provides for an increase to the exempt portion of the wages of a judgment debtor that may be attached by garnishment proceedings. A request for an increase in the exempt amount must be made by motion supported by affidavit, by the debtor on notice to the creditor.

Consolidation orders are available to a debtor against whom there are two or more unsatisfied orders of the Small Claims Court. The debtor may apply for a consolidation order by way of a notice of motion to the court. With the notice of motion, the debtor must file an affidavit which sets out his or her creditors, the amount owed to each creditor, details of the debtor's income and a statement of the debtor's current financial obligations.

Where a debtor has two or more unsatisfied orders and wishes to obtain a consolidation order, the clerk shall assist the debtor in the preparation of a notice of motion and affidavit applying for a consolidation order. The affidavit shall contain the information set out in Rule 20.09(2). The debtor is responsible for the services of the notices of motion and affidavits, either by registered mail or by personal service on each creditor or their representative. The clerk shall prepare a consolidation order setting out the information contained in Rule 20.09(4). After the consolidation of order is obtained, a creditor shall file with the clerk a certified copy of judgment from the court in which a judgment has been obtained. Upon filing the certified copy of an order, the creditor shall be added to the consolidation order.

All payments into a consolidation order shall be distributed every six months. The funds in court will be divided equally among the creditors named in the consolidation order.

Where an order (judgment) is obtained against a debtor for a debt incurred after the date on which a consolidation order is obtained and where a debtor is in default for 21 days under the order, the consolidation order will be immediately terminated by the clerk.

The debtor and any witnesses whose evidence the court considers necessary may be examined; see Rule 20.10(4) and Rule 20.10(5) as to who may be examined. The examination shall be held in the absence of the public unless the court orders otherwise (Rule 20.10(6)). After the examination, or with the debtors' written consent, the court may make an order as to payment (Rule 20.10(7)).

A notice of examination must be issued in the territorial division where the debtor resides or carries on business. Where an order has been obtained in another court, the order must be transferred to the proper court. The creditor must request that a notice of examination (Form 20H) be issued, and file an affidavit setting out the information contained in Rule 20.10(2). The clerk shall issue a notice of examination, setting out the date of examination, and deliver the notice to the bailiff for service.

Rule 20.09(5) provides that the total of the amount to be paid into court under a consolidation order shall not exceed the portion of the debtor's income that is subject to seizure or garnishment under s. 7 of the *Wages Act*, namely 20 per cent of net wages. The creditor is entitled to make submissions at the consolidation order hearing.

As long as the consolidation order is in force, no enforcement proceedings, may be taken. The one exception to this stay of proceedings is that a writ of seizure and sale of land may be issued by the clerk and filed with a sheriff.

An order may be enforced by Notice of Garnishment, Writ of Delivery, Writ of Seizure and Sale of Personal Property, Writ of Seizure and Sale of Land, or examination of debtor immediately after an order has been obtained, either upon the signing of default judgment or after a court hearing where judgment is given.

To issue an enforcement process (garnishment, writ of seizure and sale of personal property, examination of a debtor) against a debtor who does not reside in, or has moved out of, the jurisdiction in which an order has been obtained, it is necessary that the order be transferred to the court in which the debtor resides.

The plaintiff or agent must request in writing that the order be transferred. The plaintiff or agent shall advise the clerk of the amount still owing (principal plus prejudgment interest). The clerk shall prepare and send a certificate of judgment (Form 20A) to the clerk of the court specified by the creditor.

Where an order has been obtained against two or more defendants, a creditor may request that a Notice of Garnishment be issued against one debtor and a writ of seizure and sale of personal property be issued against the other debtor, or one of the other debtors. Proceedings can take place to enforce a judgment indifferent territorial divisions at the same time. Any request to transfer must be directed to the original court only.

Where there are two or more defendants, it is not necessary that an order be transferred as is the process for one defendant. For example, there are two defendants and an order is obtained against both in Court "A." One of the defendants resides in the court where the order was obtained ("A" Court), and the other defendant resides or has personal property in another territorial division ("B" Court). The creditor requests that a Notice of Garnishment be issued against the defendant in Court "A" and a writ of seizure and sale of personal property be issued against the other defendant in Court "B."

Where defences have been received from either or both debtors, the clerk must ensure that only the proper amount of judgment, costs and interest (prejudgment and postjudgment) are remitted to the plaintiff or his agent or solicitor. Any surplus funds should be returned to the proper debtor.

Effective January 1, 1989, amendments to the *Proceedings Against the Crown Act*, S.O. 1988, c. 29 [now R.S.O. 1990, c. P.27], permit a creditor to attach monies owing by the Crown in Right of Ontario through a notice of garnishment. This includes wages owing to a provincial Crown employee as well as monies that may be owing to an independent contractor for goods or services supplied to the Crown.

The *Garnishment, Attachment and Pension Diversion Act*, R.S.C. 1985, c. G-2, as amended 1992, c. 1, s. 141 and 1997, c. 1, ss. 24–40, in force May 1, 1997.

Part I — Garnishment and Attachment Proceedings

Part II — Diversion of Pension Benefits to Satisfy Financial Support Orders

Part I of the Act relates specifically to the process to issue a garnishment attaching the salary of all persons as defined in Part I — Division 1 — Section 4 (Salary Means) and Section 6, where a judgment or order against the debtor has been obtained.

General Information

1. Under the provisions of the Act and the Regulations thereto, it is now possible to garnish or attach the salary or remuneration of all persons, who are paid out of federal funds, as defined in Part 1 — Division 1 — see section 4.

2. Before the issuance of a garnishment or attachment, a notice of intention to garnishee, together with an affidavit for notice of intention to garnishee must be served on Her Majesty, at a place specified by the Regulations (see item 7 below).

3. Her Majesty has 30 days from the time of service to the notice of intention to garnishee. (Where service is effected by registered mail, the document shall be deemed to be served on the day of it receipt by Her Majesty.) Where no response is received within that period, a creditor or agent is required to issue a garnishee within the next thirty days after the date of service. If a garnishee is not issued within this time frame, it will be necessary to repeat the process described in 2. Please review amendment to Act.

Schedule I — Appendix 1 — Notice Of Intention To Garnishee Her Majesty

(Subsection 3(1))

Under Part 1 of the *Garnishment, Attachment and Pension Diversion Act* (Canada).

This notice must be served at the place specified in the *Garnishment and Attachment Regulations*. See SOR/97-177, April 8, 1997.

Address of place of service:

. . . .

. . . .

. . . .

ATTENTION: Garnishment Registry

TAKE NOTICE that the undersigned intends to serve a garnishee summons on Her Majesty within the next 30 to 60 days after service of this notice to garnishee or attach the salary or remuneration payable by Her Majesty to the debtor.

1. Full name of debtor: . . . .

2. Latest known address of debtor: . . . .

3. Name of employer (Department or Crown corporation):

. . . .

4. Is the debtor a member of the senate? (yes/no) . . . .

House of Commons? (yes/no) . . . .

5. Is the debtor a judge to whom the *Judge's Act* applies? (yes/no) . . . .

If yes, the name of the court to which the debtor is appointed . . . . and the location of that court . . . .

6. Debtor's place of employment: . . . .

7. Is the unpaid debt under the judgment or order attached hereto a maintenance, support or other debt? . . . .

8. The amount of the debt remaining unpaid or to be paid periodically is . . . .

9. The name and location of the court that has issued or will be issuing the garnishee summons: (name of court) . . . . and (location of court) .

10. Does the garnishee summons have or will the garnishee summons have continuing effect? (yes/no) . . . .

11. The following information may be provided:

    (1) Is the money which is payable to the debtor payable as:

        (a) salary? (yes/no) . . . .

        (b) remuneration? (yes/no) . . . .

If yes, is the money payable in respect of the performance of service? (yes/no) . . .

    (2) Occupation, profession, job classification or title of the debtor: . . . .

    (3) Telephone number of the debtor at the debtor's place of residence and the debtor's place of employment:

        residence . . . .

        employment . . . .

    (4) Section, division or branch of department on behalf of which or the Crown corporation by which salary or remuneration is payable to the debtor: . . . .

    (5) Street address of the debtor's place of employment:

        . . . .

Date: . . . .

Address of undersigned: . . . .

. . . .

Signature . . . .

Schedule II — Appendix 2 — Affidavit For Notice Of Intention To Garnishee

(Subsection 3(3))

IN THE

BETWEEN: Creditor (By Judgment or Order)

— and —

                                       Debtor (by Judgment or Order)

AFFIDAVIT

I, ... the above-named Creditor (or solicitor or agent acting for the above-named Creditor), make oath and say as follows:

1. By a (Judgment or Order) of . . . . Court made in this action and dated . . . . , 19. . . . . , it was (adjudged or ordered) that the above-named Creditor should recover against the above-named Debtor the sum of $. . . . . and also interest thereon at the rate of . . . .% per annum from . . . . , 20. . . . . , and $. . . . . for cost taxed together with interest at the rate of . . . .% per annum thereon from . . . . , 20. . . . .

2. The sum of $. . . . . of the said (Judgment or Order) (remains unpaid or is the amount to be paid periodically) on or as of . . . . and is justly due and owing to me.

3. Her Majesty, (name of Department or Crown Corporation) . . . . located at . . . . is indebted to the Debtor in a sum which I am unable to name.

SWORN OR DECLARED before me at the . . . . of . . . . in the . . . . of . . . . , this . . . . day of . . . . A.D. 20. . . . .

(A Commissioner, Justice of the Peace, Notary Public etc.) of ....

  (i) Where the Notice of Garnishment is issued or will be issued by a court located in

    (1) the following counties, districts, or Regional Municipalities of Ontario, namely,

      (A) District of Algoma,

      (B) District of Cochrane,

      (C) County of Frontenac,

      (D) District of Kenora,

      (E) County of Lanark,

      (F) United Counties of Leeds and Grenville,

      (G) Counties of Lennox and Addington,

      (H) District of Manitoulin,

      (I) District of Nipissing,

      (J) Regional Municipality of Ottawa-Carleton,

      (K) District of Parry Sound,

      (L) United Counties of Prescott and Russell,

      (M) County of Prince Edward,

      (N) District of Rainy River,

      (O) County of Renfrew,

      (P) Counties of Stormont, Dundas and Glengarry,

      (Q) District of Sudbury,

      (R) District of Timiskaming, and

      (S) District of Thunder Bay, or

  (ii) that part of the National Capital Region located in Quebec,

    Garnishment Registry
    Department of Justice,
    Montreal Regional Office,
    9th Floor, East Tower,
    200 Rene Levesque Blvd. West,
    Montreal, Quebec
    H2Z 1X4
    (514) 283-4934

(iii) Where the Notice of Garnishment is issued or will be issued by a court located in Ontario, other than the counties districts or regional municipality referred to above,

    Garnishment Registry
    Department of Justice,

    Toronto Regional Office,

    First Canadian Place, Box 16
    Toronto, Ontario

    M5X 1K6

    (416) 973-3036

The Notice of Garnishment binds only those debts payable to a judgment debtor by the garnishee named in the Notice of Garnishment. Where a creditor has named the wrong Ministry, a new Notice of Garnishment showing the proper Ministry must be issued and the preceding steps must be repeated.

Note section 12(9) of the *Line Fences Act*, R.S.O. 1990, c. L.17, which states in relation to an award by fence-views:

> 12. (9) **Levy of amount against goods and chattels** — Instead of having the amount certified placed upon the collector's roll, or instead of applying for that amount or a portion thereof under a by-law passed under subsection (6), the owner entitled to receive the amount may file a copy of the certificate and of the award in respect of which the certificate was made, certified by the clerk in accordance with this Act, with the clerk of the Small Claims Court of the division in which any part of the land affected by the award is situate, and upon being so filed, the amount may be levied against the goods and chattels and land of the adjoining owner in the same manner of a judgment of the Small claims Court may be levied.
>
> R.S.O. 1990, c. L.17, s. 12(9)

Note also the *Municipal Statute Law Amendment Act*, 2006, c. 32, Sched. C, s. 30 and Sched. D, s. 6.

It is possible that a debtor to the award may reside or carry on business in the jurisdiction of a Small Claims Court other than where the land affected by the award is situate. If this is the case, the initial filing will still have to take place in the court having jurisdiction where the land is situate. The proceedings will then have to be transferred to the court having jurisdiction where the debtor resides or carries on business.

An Order to Pay unpaid wages issued by an employment standards officer against an employer, which remains wholly or partially unpaid, can been forced under the provisions of the *Employment Standards Act*, S.O. 2000, c. 41 as amended, upon the issuance and filing of a copy of the order certified by the Director in a court of competent jurisdiction. See section 103(4) as to the maximum order of $10,000 for wages, payment in trust, sections 104(3)(4) and section 126.

The certificate bears postjudgment interest from the date of issue at the "postjudgment interest rate" prescribed by section 127 of the *Courts of Justice Act*.

Under the provisions of the *Provincial Offences Act*, R.S.O. 1990, c. P.33, as amended, where a fine imposed by a Provincial Offences Court is in default it may be collected by means of civil enforcement. The Act further provides that enforcement may be carried out in a court of competent jurisdiction. Subsections 68(1) to (5) of the *Provincial Offences Act* state:

> 68 (1) **Civil enforcement of fines** — When the payment of a fine is in default, the clerk of the court may complete a certificate in the prescribed form as to the imposition of the fine and the amount remaining unpaid and file the certificate in a court of competent jurisdiction and upon filing, the certificate shall be deemed to be an order or judgment of that court for the purposes of enforcement.
>
> (2) **Limitation** — A certificate shall not be filed under subsection (1) after two years after the default in respect of which it is issued.
>
> (3) **Certificate of discharge** — Where a certificate has been filed under subsection (1) and the fine is fully paid, the clerk shall file a certificate of payment upon which the certificate of default is discharged and, where a writ of execution has been filed with the sheriff, the clerk shall file a certificate of payment with the sheriff, upon which the writ is cancelled.
>
> (4) **Costs of enforcement** — Costs incurred in enforcing the deemed court order or judgment shall be added to the order or judgment and form part of it.
>
> (5) **More than one fine** — The clerk may complete and file one certificate under this section in respect of two or more fines imposed on the same person.

Section 68 permits the filing of the certificate "in a court of competent jurisdiction". Provided the amount owing does not exceed the monetary jurisdiction of the Small Claims

Court, the certificate would be filed in the jurisdiction where the defendant resides or carries on business. The certificate could be filed in the jurisdiction where the Ontario Court of Justice [formerly Ontario Court (Provincial Division)] is situated if the only enforcement process to issue was a writ of seizure and sale of lands. In this case, should any other enforcement process be requested, the proceeding would have to be transferred to the jurisdiction where the defendant resides or carries on business.

See also section 161, orders under Statutes, 2000, c. 26, Sched. A, s. 13(b).

A creditor is entitled to post judgment interest from the date that the certificate is filed with the Small Claims Court, at the rate prescribed by the *Courts of Justice Act* in effect on the date of the filing of the certificate.

Sample Debtor Examination — Individuals[20]

Date..........

Full name.................................. Date of Birth..................................

Address.................................. Postal Code.......... Phone..........

Employment

Employer's name & address..................................

....

How long?.......... Type of work..................................

Gross income $..........wk/mth/yr. Net income $..........wk/mth/yr.

Income from all other sources (pension, family allowances, rental income, etc.) List below

.... $..........

.... $..........

.... $..........

Marital Status

Married?.......... Divorced?.......... Separated?.......... Single?..........

If married

Name of Spouse.................................. Earnings $..........wk/mth/yr.

Any dependents?.......... How many?.......... Ages..................................

Home

Own?.......... Rent?.......... Mortgage/Rent payment $..................................wk/mth

Name & address of owner/mortgagee..................................

....

If owned, how registered?.................................. Value $..................................

Amount of Mortgages 1st $.......... payments $..........wk/mth

2nd $.......... payments $..........wk/mth

Own or have interest in any other property?

Location..................................

.... Value $..........

Mortgage?.......... Amount $.................................. payments $..........wk/mth

---

[20]Samples reproduced with the permission of the Ministry of the Attorney General.

Motor Vehicles

Own?.......... Lease?.......... Co-owner?.......... if so, with whom?................................

List all vehicles including that of spouse

	year	make	model	licence #	amount of lien	lienholder
#1						
#2						

List all Bank, Trust or Credit Union Accounts including spouse's

	Name	Address	Type of Account
#1			
#2			
#3			

Stocks, Bonds, G.I.C.'s, etc. Identify and indicate value and where located. Include those owned by spouse.

....

....

Any money owing to debtor or spouse from any source? If so, list...................................

....

Other Debts List

	Creditor	Amount	Payments?
#1		$	
#2		$	
#3		$	
#4		$	
#5		$	

Results:

Sample Debtor Examination — Proprietorships and Partnerships

Date ....

Proper Company Name..................................

Address..................................

Postal Code.......... Phone..........

Is company registered?.......... Proprietorship?.......... Partnership?................................

Bank Accounts

Name	Address	Status (overdraft, ect.)

Assets List & Value. State if encumbered, and if so, to whom?

For motor vehicles give make, model & licence no...................................

....

....
....
....
....

Receivables List below. Are they assigned to the bank?

Name	Address	Amount
		$
		$
		$
		$
		$
		$
		$

List Creditors

Name	Address	Amount	Payments
		$	
		$	
		$	
		$	
		$	
		$	
		$	
		$	

PROPRIETORSHIP Give proper name and address of proprietor

Name................................ Phone #..........

Address................................ Postal Code..........

PARTNERSHIPS List Names and Addresses of *ALL* Partners

1. Name................................ Phone #................................

Address................................ Postal Code................................

2. Name................................ Phone #................................

Address................................ Postal Code................................

3. Name................................ Phone #................................

Address................................ Postal Code................................

4. Name................................ Phone #................................

Address................................ Postal Code................................

Proprietors and partners to answer all questions in individual capacity.

If proprietorship or partnership is owned in whole or part by a limited company refer to form respecting limited company examinations.

Sample Debtor Examination — Limited Companies

Date..........

Proper name of company....................................

Address.................................

Postal Code.......... Phone #..........

Name & Position of person examined.................................

Does company operate under any other name? If so, list below

....

....

Bank Accounts

	Name	Address	position — overdraft, etc.
#1			
#2			

Is company indebted to Bank? If so, explain. Amount $.................................

How secured?.................................

Receivables List below Are they assigned to the Bank?

Name	Address		Amount
		$	
		$	
		$	
		$	
		$	
		$	
		$	
		$	
		$	
		$	

Assets Lists & Value State if encumbered and by whom.

For motor vehicles give make, model and licence #.

....

....

....

....

....

....

....

....

Any loans to shareholders by the company? If so, list names, addresses & amounts

....

Any outstanding shares? Give details ....

List names and addresses of all officers and directors.

....

....

....

....

List Creditors

Name	Address		Amount	Payments
		$		
		$		
		$		
		$		
		$		

Personal Property Security Act ("PPSA") Search

Consider also doing a PPSA search. You may also find out which bank the debtor uses, and you may get some indication of what he or she will say on examination when asked about liabilities. An execution search will tell you if there are any other judgments outstanding against the debtor. If there is a substantial writ already, you will not want to spend the money going after the debtor just so somebody else will get paid. Once a debtor has been located and it is time to conduct an examination, be specific and thorough in questioning. Debtors are not particularly forthcoming with information. Ask what the debtor previously owned, and consider the possibility of conveyances and preferences. If you know the debtor's name, you can search through the rolls to find the legal description of property he may own. You can also do a subsearch of the property to determine who owns it and if there are any encumbrances. Also check court files. Searching these sometimes uncovers judgments and/or cost awards in favour of the debtor that you may be able to garnish. Something else to consider are estate files. The debtor may be the beneficiary of a will that can be garnished.

Case Law: *Pioneer Communications Ltd. v. Broadcast Services Ltd.*, [1979] 1 W.W.R. 8 (Sask. Dist. Ct.) — The plaintiff was awarded judgment in the sum of $500. The defendant did not file any defence or counterclaim. Thereafter the defendant sued the plaintiff and was allowed the $500 as a set-off. This subsequent action was defended by the plaintiff. The defendant was denied a stay of execution of the $500 since its action was not commenced until after the first judgment was granted, and since it had not defended the first action. Also, the sum in question, $500, was not so large as to prejudice the defendant.

MacKinnon v. MacKinnon (1979), 14 C.P.C. 94 (Ont. Div. Ct.) — A *decree nisi* providing for maintenance, issued by the court of another province and registered pursuant to section 15 of the *Divorce Act* (Canada) and Rule 813 of the Rules of Practice, is a judgment which can be filed in a small claims court and upon which a direction to garnishee wages can therefore issue.

Bonus Finance Ltd. v. Smith, [1971] 3 O.R. 732 (Ont. H.C.) — Moneys payable under a registered pension plan are made immune from attachment by s. 24 of the *Pension Benefits Act*, R.S.O. 1970, c. 342.

Avco Financial Services Can. Ltd. v. Bowe (1979), 23 O.R. (2d) 264 (Ont. Div. Ct.) — An employee who is paid regularly in advance is entitled to payment at the beginning of each pay period and, accordingly, the moneys then owing may be the subject of garnishment proceedings.

Trans-Can. Credit Corp. v. Rogers Moving (1977), 26 C.B.R. (N.S.) 187 (Ont. Div. Ct.) — The affidavit filed in support of a direction to garnishee was defective, and the small claims court judge failed to hold a judicial hearing with respect to the garnishee proceedings.

Bain v. Rosen (1984), 45 O.R. (2d) 672 (Ont. Div. Ct.) — What is the debt due or accruing. The employer deducted 30 per cent from the net wage under s. 224(1) of the *Income Tax Act*. You must begin with the gross wage due, and then deduct the statutorily mandated deductions under the *Income Tax Act*, the *Unemployment Insurance Act* and the *Canada Pension Act*.

Re Landry (1973), 1 O.R. (2d) 107 (Ont. Sm. Cl. Ct.) — A judgment of a Superior, County or District Court filed with a small claims court under s. 130(3) of this Act is not a small claims court judgment but remains a judgment of the court in which it was made. Consequently, this section does not apply to a debtor against whom there is one unsatisfied small claims court judgment and a number of District Court judgments.

Re Young (1973), 4 O.R. (2d) 390 (Ont. Sm. Cl. Ct.) — A consolidation order was refused where one of the creditors was a divorced wife who has filed a Supreme Court order for maintenance of the children of the marriage with the small claims court. The order was refused in view of the public interest in the maintenance of the children, and the complexity involved in determining the amount due at any particular time under an order for continuing maintenance.

Dainard v. Dainard (1981), 22 C.P.C. 283 (Ont. Prov. Ct.) — A support order cannot be included in a consolidation order of the small claims court; support order and variation is to be effected only by recourse to s. 37 of the *Family Law Act, 1986* (Ontario), S.O. 1986, c. 4.

Once garnishment is instituted a creditor is required to wait until it is completed before pursuing alternate collection procedures; however, where, as in this case, the garnishment has been completed, the small claims court does not retain exclusive jurisdiction to deal with the arrears merely because the support order remains filed at the small claims court. Accordingly, the Provincial Court (Family Division) (now the Ontario Court (Provincial Division)) could enter in the wife's enforcement proceeding.

Texaco Can. v. Deganais (1983), 40 C.P.C. 64 (Ont. Div. Ct.) — For the purposes of this section, the "sum of dispute" was the amount of the judgment appealed against, where the "sum in dispute" excluded $500. Upon an appeal in garnishee proceedings, the amount was determined by reference to the actual amount of the judgment in the garnishee proceedings, not to the debt itself.

Nunez-do-Cela v. May Co. (1973), 1 O.R. (2d) 217 (Ont. C.A.) — A judgment against a defendant in a trade name may be enforced against the defendant himself without any additional order.

T. Eaton Co. Ltd. v. Higgins (1984), 7 C.P.C. (2d) 277 (Ont. Prov. Ct.) — In a Small Claims Court action, the judgment debtor was a recipient of welfare benefits under s. 7(1) of the *General Welfare Assistance Act*, R.S.O. 1980, c. 188. The sum of $410 was standing to the credit of the judgment debtor in an account with the garnishee bank. Once the welfare assistance was paid to the judgment debtor and he in turn deposited the moneys into his bank account, a debtor-creditor relationship was established between the garnishee bank and the judgment debtor making the account subject to attachment by garnishee.

Bank of Nova Scotia v. Cameron Inco Ltd. (1985), 1 C.P.C (2d) 18 (Ont. Prov. Ct.) — An employer received three notices of garnishment issued out of three different Small Claims Courts and one Notice of Garnishment issued by the District Court purporting to garnishee the wages of its employee. Correspondence with the courts as to the proper procedure for distributing the funds garnished did not produce a satisfactory response. It was held that the effect of the Rules of Civil Procedure and of the Provincial Court Rules, 1985 was to require that the Notice of Garnishment be dealt with in priority of their receipt and not on a *pro rata* basis. When the first creditor had been satisfied, subsequent garnishments should be honoured by the garnishee.

20.11 (1) Contempt Hearing — If a person on whom a notice of examination has been served under rule 20.10 attends the examination but refuses to answer questions or to produce records or documents, the court may order the person to attend before it for a contempt hearing.

(2) Same — If a person on whom a notice of examination has been served under rule 20.10 fails to attend the examination, the court may order the person to attend before it for a contempt hearing under subsection 30(1) of the *Courts of Justice Act*.

(3) If the court makes an order for a contempt hearing,

(a) the clerk shall provide the creditor with a notice of contempt hearing setting out the time, date and place of the hearing; and

(b) the creditor shall serve the notice of contempt hearing on the debtor or other person in accordance with subrule 8.01(13) and file the affidavit of service at least seven days before the hearing.

(4) Setting Aside Order for Contempt Hearing — A person who has been ordered to attend a contempt hearing under subsection 30(1) of the *Courts of Justice Act* may make a motion to set aside the order, before or after receiving the notice of contempt hearing but before the date of the hearing and, on the motion, the court may set aside the order and order that the person attend another examination under rule 20.10.

(5) Finding of Contempt of Court — At a contempt hearing held under subrule (1), the court may find the person to be in contempt of court if the person fails to show cause why the person should not be held in contempt for refusing to answer questions or produce records or documents.

Commentary: When a Deputy Judge presides over a contempt hearing and a debtor fails to appear, the Deputy Judge may refer the matter to a Superior Court Judge for possible issuance of a warrant for arrest. Where a debtor has failed to attend a contempt hearing and a Deputy Judge has referred the matter to a Superior Court judge to consider the issuance Warrant for Arrest (Contempt), the Notice to Debtor form will be mailed to the debtor along with a copy of the endorsement record. The Notice to Debtor provides the debtor with 30 days from the date of the contempt hearing to bring a motion to explain his or her failure to attend the hearing and to convene a judgment debtor examination.

(6) Same — The finding of contempt at a hearing held under subsection 30(1) of the *Courts of Justice Act* is subject to subsection 30(2) of that Act.

Commentary: The court may order a debtor or other person on whom a notice of examination has been properly served under rule 20.10 to attend a contempt hearing.

From July 1, 2006 to December 31, 2010, only a Superior Court Judge could preside over a hearing in Small Claims Court for contempt of court for a debtor's wilful failure to attend an examination hearing. The Rules of the Small Claims Court and the *Courts of Justice Act* have been changed to also give deputy judges and provincial civil judges jurisdiction to preside over these contempt hearings as of January 1, 2011 (r. 20.11(2); new *Courts of Justice Act*, s. 30).

A person who has been ordered to attend a contempt hearing for wilful failure to attend an examination hearing under section 30(1) of the *Courts of Justice Act* may make a motion to a judge of the Small Claims Court to set aside the order, before or after receiving the notice of contempt hearing [r. 20.11(4)].

This motion must be heard before the date of the contempt hearing [r. 20.11(2)].

Where the Small Claims Court presiding judge orders a contempt hearing, the creditor will attend at the Small Claims Court to request that a contempt hearing be scheduled.

Where the Small Claims Court presiding judge orders that a contempt hearing be referred to the Regional Senior Justice for scheduling before a Superior Court Judge, the creditor will attend at the Small Claims Court to request that a contempt hearing be scheduled.

Under the *Rules*, a warrant remains in force for 12 months after its date of issue, subject to an order of the court [r. 20.11(10)].

Where a contempt hearing has been held, the presiding judge of the Small Claims Court or judge of the Superior Court of Justice may order a warrant of committal to issue stating that the debtor or other person be jailed. Where the presiding judge is a judge of the Small Claims Court, an order may be made ordering a warrant of committal to issue stating that the debtor or other person be jailed for a period *of not more than 5 days*. A creditor *may* provide a completed Identification Form (20K).

The police require the individual's date of birth or age in order to enter the Warrant of Committal on CPIC. A creditor *may* provide a completed Identification Form (20K).

If a Superior Court judge presiding over a contempt hearing orders a Warrant for Arrest (Contempt) the Superior Court courtroom registrar will prepare the Warrant for Arrest and present it to the SCJ judge for signature.

A Warrant of Committal (Form 20J) shall only be renewed by order of the court, on the creditor's motion.

Subject to judicial direction, a warrant of committal that is issued pursuant to an order of a presiding judge of the Small Claims Court can be renewed by a presiding judge of the Small Claims Court.

Subject to judicial direction, a warrant of committal that is issued pursuant to an order of a judge of the Superior Court of Justice may only be renewed by a judge of the Superior Court of Justice.

This Rule provides mechanisms for the enforcement of various types of orders. Enforcement mechanisms include, among others, a writ of seizure of sale, a notice of garnishment, a writ of sequestration, and a writ of possession.

In addition, a monetary tribunal order can be filed at any time following the date set out in the tribunal order for payment of any money. Tribunal monetary orders can be enforced as provided by any of the enforcement processes available in the court where the tribunal order is filed.

Criminal Code of Canada monetary restitution orders may also be filed for enforcement.

The tribunal order or monetary restitution is treated in the same manner as an order or judgment originating in the court where the tribunal order is filed. Unless ordered by the tribunal or the Criminal Court, the order does not expire. The creditor may choose the court in which to file the order. There is no minimum that can be claimed and there are no restrictions as to the territorial jurisdiction in the Superior Court of Justice.

A tribunal order that orders both an eviction and a monetary award can be taken to both the sheriff and also filed with the court of appropriate monetary jurisdiction for enforcement of the monetary portion. The creditor will file a certified copy the order in each location.

The only time that a warrant of committal will be issued in Small Claims Court proceedings by Superior Court of Justice staff will be when the summoned person attends the contempt hearing heard by a Superior Court judge and the judge orders a warrant of committal. A warrant of committal would then be required immediately to take the person to a correctional institution.

If a Superior Court judge presiding over a Small Claims Court contempt hearing orders a Warrant for Arrest (Contempt), the Superior Court of Justice courtroom registrar will prepare the Warrant for Arrest and present it to the Superior Court of Justice judge for signature. The original signed warrant, the corresponding endorsement record, and the file will then be returned to the originating Small Claims Court office for distribution in accordance with usual practice.

Enforcement of a Divisional Court order, which arises as a result of an appeal from a lower court order, is issued by the originating/lower court where the proceeding was commenced; see Rule 60.04(1), Rule 60.07(1), and Rule 60.08(4). An order of the Divisional Court shall also be entered in the originating/lower court, in accordance with Rule 59.05(3).

Pursuant to the *Criminal Code of Canada*, the Ontario Court of Justice or the Superior Court of Justice may make an order naming a person(s) entitled to recover monetary restitution pursuant to:

- A restitution order under section 738 or 739;

- A condition of probation under section 732.1; and

- A condition of a conditional sentence under section 742.3.

Where an amount that is ordered to be paid under sections 732.1, 738, 739, or 742.3 is not paid without delay, the person to whom the amount was ordered to be paid may, by filing the order, enter as a judgment the amount ordered to be paid in any civil court in Canada that has jurisdiction to enter a judgment for that amount. That judgment is enforceable against the offender in the same manner as if it were a judgment rendered against the offender in that court in civil proceedings [s. 741(1), CCC].

The offender and the victim are each provided with a copy of the restitution order. The order may be filed at any time after the date it is issued by the originating criminal court. The order may be filed for enforcement in any civil court of appropriate monetary jurisdiction of the Superior Court of Justice. Upon filing, it is entered as a judgment of the court and it then becomes enforceable in the same manner as a civil judgment of the court.

Where an amount that is ordered to be paid as a condition of a probation or conditional sentence order under sections 732.1 or 742.3 is not paid within the time given by the criminal court judge, only then may the order be filed for enforcement. Criminal court staff do not routinely provide a victim with a copy of the probation or conditional sentence order. If the victim wishes to enforce an order for restitution that is a condition of a probation/conditional sentence order that remains unpaid on the expiry of the time allowed for payment, he/she would be required to attend at the criminal court office where the original probation/conditional sentence order was issued to obtain a copy of the relevant order.

Monetary restitution orders will usually be filed in the county/district in which the court ordering the restitution is located.

In the Superior Court of Justice (SCJ), the restitution order or the probation/conditional sentence order in which a condition provides for restitution may be enforced in the same manner as any other judgment of the Court for the payment or recovery of money. The rules applicable to the enforcement method requested, such as the issuance of a writ of seizure and sale and/or notice of garnishment, apply. The enforcement process must be issued from the court location where the restitution order was filed.

The Nature of Contempt

Contempt involves a breach or arguably a disobedience of a lawful order of a court of competent jurisdiction. Disobedience of a prohibitory order is civil contempt: See *Canadian Transport (U.K.) Ltd. v. Alsbury*, 1953 CarswellBC 3, (sub nom. *Poje v. British Columbia (Attorney General)*) 17 C.R. 176, (sub nom. *Poje v. British Columbia (Attorney General)*)

[1953] 1 S.C.R. 516, 105 C.C.C. 311, [1953] 2 D.L.R. 785, 53 C.L.L.C. 15,055 (S.C.C.). Disobedience of a prohibitory order may also constitute criminal contempt: See *Poje, supra,* at p. 519 [S.C.R.], and *U.N.A. v. Alberta (Attorney General),* EYB 1992-66869, 1992 CarswellAlta 10, 1992 CarswellAlta 465, [1992] S.C.J. No. 37, [1992] 3 W.W.R. 481, 89 D.L.R. (4th) 609, 71 C.C.C. (3d) 225, 135 N.R. 321, 92 C.L.L.C. 14,023, 1 Alta. L.R. (3d) 129, 13 C.R. (4th) 1, 125 A.R. 241, 14 W.A.C. 241, [1992] 1 S.C.R. 901, 9 C.R.R. (2d) 29, [1992] Alta. L.R.B.R. 137 (S.C.C.), at pp. 931-32 S.C.R.

The principal distinguishing feature between civil and criminal contempt is the element of public defiance of the court's process in a way calculated to lessen societal respect for the courts: *United Nurses, supra,* at pp. 931-32 [S.C.R]; *Poje,* at p. 527 [S.C.R.].

Contempt, whether civil or criminal, requires proof that the alleged contemnor had actual knowledge of the order that was the subject of the contempt proceedings: see *Bhatnager v. Canada (Minister of Employment & Immigration),* 43 C.P.C. (2d) 213, 12 Imm. L.R. (2d) 81, 111 N.R. 185, [1990] 2 S.C.R. 217, 71 D.L.R. (4th) 84, 44 Admin. L.R. 1, 1990 CarswellNat 737, 36 F.T.R. 91 (note), 1990 CarswellNat 73, EYB 1990-67238 at para. 17 (S.C.C.). The standard of proof required in contempt proceedings, again regardless of whether the contempt is civil or criminal, is proof beyond a reasonable doubt.

A director, for example, may also be found liable for the conduct of a corporate contemnor. See O'Leary J. in *Canada Metal Co. v. Canadian Broadcasting Corp. (No. 2)* (1974), 1974 CarswellOnt 894, 19 C.C.C. (2d) 218, 48 D.L.R. (3d) 641, 4 O.R. (2d) 585 (Ont. H.C.); varied (1975), 1975 CarswellOnt 921, 8 O.R. (2d) 375, 59 D.L.R. (3d) 430, 23 C.C.C. (2d) 445 (Ont. C.A.); affirmed (1975), 1975 CarswellOnt 810, 65 D.L.R. (3d) 231, 29 C.C.C. (2d) 325, 11 O.R. (2d) 167 (Ont. C.A.).

The failure of the judge to expressly articulate the precise standard of proof applied does not vitiate the finding, so long as the evidence proves contempt beyond a reasonable doubt. See *Kopyto v. Clarfield* (1999), 30 C.P.C. (4th) 241, [1999] O.J. No. 672, 118 O.A.C. 130, 43 O.R. (3d) 435, 1999 CarswellOnt 644 at para. 19 (Ont. C.A.), and *Ali v. Triple 3 Holdings Inc.* (2002), [2002] O.J. No. 4405, 2002 CarswellOnt 3986 at paras. 4-5 (Ont. C.A.).

Notice of Contempt Hearing before a judge of the Superior Court of Justice

From July 1, 2006 to December 31, 2010, only a Superior Court Judge could preside over a hearing in Small Claims Court for contempt of court for a debtor's wilful failure to attend an examination hearing. The Rules of the Small Claims Court and the *Courts of Justice Act* were changed to also give deputy judges and provincial civil judges jurisdiction to preside over these contempt hearings as of January 1, 2011 (r. 20.11(2); new *Courts of Justice Act,* section 30).

A person who has been ordered to attend a contempt hearing for wilful failure to attend an examination hearing under section 30(1) of the *Courts of Justice Act* may make a motion to a judge of the Small Claims Court to set aside the order, before or after receiving the notice of contempt hearing [r. 20.11(4)]. This motion must be heard before the date of the contempt hearing [rule 20.11(2)]. If not, the person must attend the contempt hearing.

Where the Small Claims Court presiding judge orders that a contempt hearing be referred to the Regional Senior Justice for scheduling before a Superior Court Judge, the creditor will attend at the Small Claims Court to request that a contempt hearing be scheduled.

A person who has been ordered to attend a contempt hearing for wilful failure to attend an examination hearing under section 30(1) of the *Courts of Justice Act* to be scheduled before a Superior Court Judge may make a motion to a judge of the Small Claims Court to set aside the order, before or after receiving the notice of contempt hearing.

This motion must be heard before the date of the contempt hearing [r. 20.11(4)]. If not, the person must attend the contempt hearing.

Case Law: *Mercedes-Benz Financial v. Kovacevic* (2009), 2009 CarswellOnt 1142, [2009] O.J. No. 888, 308 D.L.R. (4th) 562, 74 C.P.C. (6th) 326 (Ont. S.C.J.)

Six months after obtaining court order requiring K to deliver up car, dealership brought motion for civil contempt. Motion granted. K found guilty of contempt, sentenced to five days' imprisonment. Filings under *Personal Property Security Act* demonstrated that K's refusal to return car was result of deliberate plan to avoid obligations to dealership by splitting persons. K's defiance of Canadian law was palpable, unrepentant and unremitting. See also *777829 Ontario Ltd. v. McNally* (1991), 1991 CarswellOnt 476, [1991] O.J. No. 3458, 9 C.P.C. (3d) 257 (Ont. Gen. Div.), *Niagara Regional Police Services Board v. Curran* (2002), [2002] O.J. No. 179, (sub nom. *Niagara (Municipality) (Police Services Board) v. Curran*) 57 O.R. (3d) 631, 16 C.P.C. (5th) 139, 2002 CarswellOnt 137 (Ont. S.C.J.), *Sussex Group Ltd. v. Sylvester* (2002), 62 O.R. (3d) 123, [2002] O.J. No. 4350, 32 C.P.C. (5th) 308, 2002 CarswellOnt 3893 (Ont. S.C.J. [Commercial List]), *Sussex Group Ltd. v. 3933938 Canada Inc.*, [2003] O.J. No. 2952, 2003 CarswellOnt 2908, [2003] O.T.C. 683 (Ont. S.C.J. [Commercial List]), and *Milligan v. Lech* (2006), 2006 CarswellOnt 7415, [2006] O.J. No. 4700 (Ont. C.A.).

Telehop Communications Inc. v. Chamberlain (2009), 2009 CarswellOnt 4780 (Ont. S.C.J.).

Defendant found in contempt for failing to attend examination as a judgment debtor and for failing to attend the within contempt proceeding. In 2005, the plaintiff obtained a small claims default judgment against the defendant. The defendant subsequently ignored several Notices of Examination and the Notice of Contempt Hearing requiring his attendance. Court found defendant in contempt and issued a warrant for his committal to jail for up to seven days or until payment of the judgment plus outstanding costs was made.

Korea Data Systems Co. v. Chiang, 2009 ONCA 3, 2009 CarswellOnt 28, [2009] O.J. No. 41, (sub nom. *Chiang (Trustee of) v. Chiang*) 93 O.R. (3d) 483, 49 C.B.R. (5th) 1, (sub nom. *Chiang (Trustee of) v. Chiang*) 305 D.L.R. (4th) 655, (sub nom. *Mendlowitz & Associates Inc. v. Chiang*) 257 O.A.C. 64, 78 C.P.C. (6th) 110 (Ont. C.A.); additional reasons at 2009 ONCA 153, 2009 CarswellOnt 769, 50 C.B.R. (5th) 13, 68 C.P.C. (6th) 32 (Ont. C.A.); additional reasons at 2010 ONCA 67, 2010 CarswellOnt 345, 63 C.B.R. (5th) 201 (Ont. C.A.)

The defendants frustrated plaintiffs' efforts to collect debt for 15 years. In 2003, the defendants consented to finding they were in contempt of court orders and were given opportunity to purge their contempt. The trial judge found that the defendants failed to fully comply with undertakings. The defendants sentenced to imprisonment. Defendants appealed. The appeal should be heard, and was allowed in part. The sentence varied to substitute sentence of seven days' imprisonment for each defendant. The consent order addressed court's sanctions if defendants failed to fulfil undertakings.

The Ontario Court of Appeal reviewed the law of contempt. "Our law has distinguished between civil and criminal contempt of court. A person who breaches a court order, other than an order for payment of money, commits civil contempt of court . . . Where breach accompanied by element of public defiance or public depreciation of the court's authority, contempt becomes criminal . . . The distinction between civil and criminal contempt is not always clear-cut. Civil contempt must be made out to the criminal standard of proof beyond a reasonable doubt. A person found in civil contempt of court may be committed to jail or face any other sanction available for a criminal offence, such as a fine or community service."

Maple Villa Long Term Care Centre v. Bourgoin Estate, 2010 ONSC 5095, 2010 CarswellOnt 6946, 62 E.T.R. (3d) 110 (Ont. S.C.J. [In Chambers]), Michael G. Quigley J.

A nursing home obtained judgment against an estate in Small Claims Court for unpaid care fees. The applicant estate trustee had not complied with numerous Small Claims Court orders and faced contempt hearing. The estate trustee brought application for advice and directions pursuant to section 60 of *Trustee Act* regarding legitimacy of Small Claims Court orders. Application dismissed. Application brought without notice and in improper form. Public guardian and trustee was appointed as estate trustee's litigation guardian. Estate trustee had disability. Estate trustee faced jail time for failing to comply with court orders. Estate trustee had need for assistance of litigation guardian to prosecute and defend matters on her behalf.

Alberta (Director, Child, Youth & Family Enhancement Act) v. M. (B.), 2010 ABCA 240, 2010 CarswellAlta 1487, 482 A.R. 273, 490 W.A.C. 273, 8 Admin. L.R. (5th) 1, 30 Alta. L.R. (5th) 42, 86 R.F.L. (6th) 1, [2010] 12 W.W.R. 232, 323 D.L.R. (4th) 745, 259 C.C.C. (3d) 154 (Alta. C.A.); and *Alberta (Director, Child, Youth & Family Enhancement Act) v. M. (B.)*, 246 C.C.C. (3d) 170, 460 A.R. 188, 94 Admin. L.R. (4th) 295, 462 W.A.C. 188, 9 Alta. L.R. (5th) 225, 70 R.F.L. (6th) 32, [2009] 11 W.W.R. 450, 2009 CarswellAlta 1103, 2009 ABCA 258, [2009] A.J. No. 773 (Alta. C.A.); reversed 2010 ABCA 240, 2010 CarswellAlta 1487, 259 C.C.C. (3d) 154, 323 D.L.R. (4th) 745, [2010] 12 W.W.R. 232, 86 R.F.L. (6th) 1, 30 Alta. L.R. (5th) 42, 8 Admin. L.R. (5th) 1, 482 A.R. 273, 490 W.A.C. 273 (Alta. C.A.)

In appropriate circumstances, a government official can be held personally liable in civil contempt proceedings that arise from the failure of his or her department to comply with a court order.

Uyj Air Inc. v. Barnes; *Ogilvy Renault v. Barnes*

A custodial term was imposed on an order for contempt because of "utter disregard and contempt" for the court's authority. "It is necessary in the circumstances of this case to bring home to the gravity of misconduct."

The Ontario Court of Appeal upheld a 14-month sentence against Barry Landen in *Langston v. Landen* for not complying with numerous court orders in an alleged multi-million-dollar estates fraud. It concluded in the contempt case of *Chiang (Re)* in 2009 that sentences of eight and 12 months for a couple who breached numerous orders requiring them to disclose assets were not excessive.

In *Chiang*, the Court of Appeal described civil contempt as a necessary "coercive" power to try to obtain compliance with court orders. People serving sentences for contempt are not eligible for parole, and the release date is within the jurisdiction of the court, not correction officials.

(7) Other Powers of Court at Contempt Hearing — At a contempt hearing, the court may order that the person,

(a) attend an examination under rule 20.10;

(b) be jailed for a period of not more than five days.

(c) attend an additional contempt hearing under subrule (1) or subsection 30(1) of the *Courts of Justice Act*, as the case may be; or

(d) comply with any other order that the judge considers necessary or just.

Commentary: If a Superior Court judge presiding over a contempt hearing orders a Warrant for Arrest (Contempt), the Superior Court courtroom registrar will prepare the Warrant for Arrest and present it to the SCJ judge for signature. The original Warrant, the endorsement record and the file will then be returned to the originating SCC office.

A Warrant of Committal (Form 20J) shall only be renewed by order of the court, on the creditor's motion.

A warrant of committal that is issued pursuant to an order of a judge of the Superior Court of Justice shall only be renewed by a judge of the Superior Court of Justice.

If the motion is to be scheduled before a judge of the Superior Court of Justice, Small Claims Court staff will advise the person that he/she must attend before a judge of the Superior Court of Justice and will contact the Superior Court of Justice on his/her behalf to obtain a motion date.

(8) Warrant of Committal — If a committal is ordered under clause (7)(b),

(a) the creditor may complete and file with the clerk an identification form (Form 20K) to assist the police in apprehending the person named in the warrant of committal; and

(b) the clerk shall issue a warrant of committal (Form 20J), accompanied by the identification form, if any, directed to all police officers in Ontario to apprehend the person named in the warrant anywhere in Ontario and promptly bring the person to the nearest correctional institution.

Warrant of Committal

Under the *Rules*, a warrant remains in force for 12 months after its date of issue, subject to an order of the court [r. 20.11(10)].

Where a contempt hearing has been held, the presiding judge of the Small Claims Court or judge of the Superior Court of Justice may order a warrant of committal to issue stating that the debtor or other person be jailed. Where the presiding judge is a judge of the Small Claims Court, an order may be made ordering a warrant of committal to issue stating that the debtor or other person be jailed for a period *of not more than 5 days*.

(9) Discharge — A person in custody under a warrant issued under this rule shall be discharged from custody on the order of the court or when the time prescribed in the warrant expires, whichever is earlier.

(10) Duration and Renewal of Warrant of Committal — A warrant issued under this rule remains in force for 12 months after the date of issue and may be renewed by order of the court on a motion made by the creditor for 12 months at each renewal, unless the court orders otherwise.

(11) [Repealed O. Reg. 440/10, s. 7(11).]

O. Reg. 78/06, s. 48; 440/10, s. 7

Commentary: The court may order a debtor or other person on whom a notice of examination has been properly served under rule 20.10 to attend a contempt hearing. There are two possible scenarios which may happen at the examination hearing in the Small Claims Court which may lead to contempt proceedings:

1. If the person attends the examination but refuses to answer questions or to produce documents or records, the contempt hearing will be scheduled before a judge or deputy judge of the Small Claims Court. This process is set out in section 20.20 below; or

2. If the person fails to attend the examination, the contempt hearing will be scheduled before a judge of the Superior Court of Justice. This process is set out in section 20.21.

A person who has been ordered to attend a contempt hearing before a Superior Court judge may make a motion to a judge of the Small Claims Court to set aside the order, before or after receiving the notice of contempt hearing. This motion must be heard before the date of the contempt hearing [rule 20.11(2)]. If not, the person must attend the contempt hearing.

Small Claims Court forms and fees apply to any process under the contempt process except for the Warrant for Arrest (Contempt) Form 60K.

Where the Small Claims Court presiding judge orders a contempt hearing, the creditor will attend at the Small Claims Court to request that a contempt hearing be scheduled.

The creditor is responsible for ensuring that there are sufficient true copies of the notice of contempt hearing for service on the person named in the notice. The notice of contempt must be served personally [r. 8.01(13), 20.11(3)(b)].

The creditor must file the affidavit of service of the notice of contempt hearing at least seven days before the hearing date.

If the notice was served but was filed late and the judge refused to allow the matter to proceed, the creditor must contact the debtor to indicate that the matter will not proceed on the original date.

A new Notice of Contempt Hearing can be issued or the date on the original Notice of Contempt Hearing can be changed by putting a line through the original date and inserting the new date.

Where the Small Claims Court presiding judge orders a contempt hearing before a Superior Court judge, the creditor will attend at the Small Claims Court to request that a contempt hearing be scheduled.

A person who has been ordered to attend a contempt hearing before a Superior Court judge may make a motion to a judge of the Small Claims Court to set aside the order, before or after receiving the notice of contempt hearing. This motion must be heard before the date of the contempt hearing [rule 20.11(2)]. If not, the person must attend the contempt hearing.

Renewing a Warrant of Committal

A Warrant of Committal (Form 20J) shall only be renewed by order of the court, on the creditor's motion.

Subject to judicial direction, a warrant of committal that is issued pursuant to an order of a presiding judge of the Small Claims Court can be renewed by a presiding judge of the Small Claims Court.

Subject to judicial direction, a warrant of committal that is issued pursuant to an order of a judge of the Superior Court of Justice may only be renewed by a judge of the Superior Court of Justice.

Failure to notify police services of the court-ordered renewal means that the warrant will be removed from the police information system after 12 months. The warrant will be treated as expired and returned to the clerk of the issuing Small Claims Court.

A warrant shall only be rescinded by order of the court, on motion. A warrant issued pursuant to an order of a presiding judge of the Small Claims Court can be rescinded by a presiding judge of the Small Claims Court. Subject to judicial direction, a warrant that is issued pursuant to an order of a judge of the Superior Court of Justice may only be rescinded by a judge of the Superior Court of Justice.

Case Law: *Intrans-Corp v. Environmental Cleaning Systems Inc.*, 2006 CarswellOnt 4335, 23 C.B.R. (5th) 227 (Ont. Sm. Cl. Ct.), P. Thomson J.

Creditor served notice of examination on debtor. Debtor did not show up for examination. In similar situations, other justices had exercised discretion to send matter immediately back for second examination. Hearing held to determine whether to proceed to contempt hearing or send matter back for second examination. Matter would proceed directly to contempt hearing and notice to be served personally on debtor. Court disagreed with discretion exercised by other judges. Second examination was appropriate only in exceptional circumstances. An innocent creditor who had properly served and paid for notice of examination should not have to expend further time and expense mandated by second examination. Second notice would be in same form as first and therefore would wastefully repeat initial service. Proceeding to contempt hearing put onus on debtor to move or not move with respect to setting aside contempt hearing and restoring matter to judgment debtor list.

Rules 20.10(2), 20.11(3)–(7) as amended referred to.

Boyle, Re, 2006 CarswellAlta 1004, 2006 ABQB 585, 24 C.B.R. (5th) 252 (Alta. Q.B.).

Judge presided over bankruptcy proceedings and contempt hearings. Debtor brought application for removal of judge for bias. Application dismissed. Reasonable observer would not find likelihood of bias. *Roberts v. R.* (2003), 2003 SCC 45, (sub nom. *Wewaykum Indian Band v. Canada)* [2003] S.C.J. No. 50, 2003 CarswellNat 2822, 2003 CarswellNat 2823, 231 D.L.R. (4th) 1, 19 B.C.L.R. (4th) 195, (sub nom. *Wewayakum Indian Band v. Canada)* 309 N.R. 201, [2004] 2 W.W.R. 1, (sub nom. *Wewayakum Indian Band v. Canada)* [2003] 2 S.C.R. 259, 40 C.P.C. (5th) 1, 7 Admin. L.R. (4th) 1, (sub nom. *Wewaykum Indian Band v. Canada)* [2004] 1 C.N.L.R. 342 (S.C.C.) followed.

Milligan v. Lech, 2006 CarswellOnt 7415 (Ont. C.A.).

Throughout case, defendant had repeatedly broken his promises to court and showed deliberate and flagrant disregard for court orders. He was imprisoned for 12 months for contempt in failing to disclose documents, to answer questions on discovery and to attend in court. Nine months later, he was incarcerated for another 15 months on second contempt order made for same reasons. Two years later when he still refused to comply, third contempt order yielded him further 15 months in prison, which he appealed. Appeal court found that this was not case of punishing him for same refusal but rather for fresh, discrete and wilful refusal to comply with existing obligation. No error in motion judge's decision to commit defendant for third contempt.

Dickie v. Dickie, 2007 CarswellOnt 606, 2007 CarswellOnt 607, [2007] S.C.J. No. 8, 221 O.A.C. 394, 43 C.P.C. (6th) 1, 84 O.R. (3d) 799 (note), 2007 SCC 8, 357 N.R. 196, [2007] 1 S.C.R. 346, 279 D.L.R. (4th) 625, 39 R.F.L. (6th) 30 (S.C.C.).

Payor appealed to Ontario Court of Appeal where he was confronted by motion made by mother that challenged his right to be heard until he first purged his contempt. Majority exercised discretion in favour of allowing payor to present argument because his appeal concerned the legality of contempt proceeding itself and not the validity of underlying support orders. Finding of contempt set aside on appeal.

Mother appealed to Supreme Court of Canada. The full court chose not to interfere with discretionary conclusion of majority in Court of Appeal whereby payor allowed right of audience without first having to purge his contempt (although it said that it could find no fault with the discretionary disposition of the dissenting Appeals Justice John I. Laskin, who would have adjourned the payor's appeal until he complied with the securing orders).

Supreme Court agreed with dissenting judgment that securing orders did not create a fixed debt obligation requiring payor to make payments to mother. Securing orders not orders for the payment of money within meaning of subrule 60.11(1) of the *Rules of Civil Procedure*, R.R.O. 1990, Reg. 194, as amended.

Baumung v. 8 & 10 Cattle Co-operative Ltd., [2005] S.J. No. 530, 2005 CarswellSask 574, 2005 SKCA 108, 259 D.L.R. (4th) 292, 269 Sask. R. 190, 357 W.A.C. 190 (Sask. C.A.).

To be found in contempt of court, the alleged contemnor must intentionally act contrary to the order in question. While it had to be shown only that the act contravening the order was itself done intentionally, the contemnor had to have notice of the terms of the order. In order to ground a contempt finding, a court order must be clear.

No proof that order formally served on the plaintiff.

Anthes v. Wilson Estate, 2005 CarswellOnt 1742, 197 O.A.C. 110, 25 C.P.C. (6th) 216 (Ont. C.A.).

Court's own motion for contempt poses particular procedural problems. Contempt process, even civil contempt process, is criminal in nature and requires proof of contemptuous conduct beyond reasonable doubt. Conduct must be wilful, deliberate and of contumacious and egregious nature. Trial judge did not address issue of burden of proof. Nothing on record that could justify finding of contempt.

Johnson v. Schwalm, 2006 CarswellOnt 2620 (Ont. S.C.J.), Spence J.

Respondent found in contempt. On return of motion, submissions made regarding penalty and costs. Respondent ordered to pay fine of $750. Impossible to tell whether contempt had been purged. Respondent's assertion that he was unable to understand terms of court order preposterous. Respondent ordered to pay costs related to previous and current contempt proceedings in amount of $16,750. Respondent ordered imprisoned for period of seven days, to be permanently stayed if fine and costs paid within 45 days.

Brian Mallard Insurance Services Ltd. v. Shirley, 2005 CarswellAlta 1750, 2005 ABQB 858, 20 C.P.C. (6th) 1, 385 A.R. 249 (Alta. Q.B.).

K wrote to trial judge in other action in which he was defendant that judge who granted Anton Piller Order participated in felony. Plaintiffs brought motion to find K in contempt. Motion granted on other grounds. K's actions not in face of court not calculated to scandalize court. Law of contempt designed to protect dignity and authority of court. Personal abuse of judge not contempt.

Directv Inc. v. Boudreau, 2005 CarswellOnt 6630, 42 C.P.R. (4th) 388 (Ont. C.A. [In Chambers]).

Defendant committed for civil contempt and sentenced to imprisonment for nine months. Defendant appealed sentence. Defendant's motion to stay sentence pending disposition of appeal allowed. Defendant's arguments raised serious question. Defendant would suffer irreparable harm. Balance of convenience favoured defendant.

Taylor v. Taylor, [2005] O.J. No. 4593, 2005 CarswellOnt 5264, 21 R.F.L. (6th) 449 (Ont. S.C.J.), Corbett J.

Disobedience of court order. Husband flagrantly breached court orders in family law proceeding and caused his former wife untold stress. Resentful spouse not above the law. Breaches serious and warranted sanction beyond declaration. Husband offered no reasonable explanation for his misconduct. In view of his apparent means, systematic and ongoing contempt for his wife's interests, fine must be substantial. Husband ordered to pay fine of $25,000 to wife.

Dickie v. Dickie, 2007 CarswellOnt 606, 2007 CarswellOnt 607, [2007] S.C.J. No. 8, 221 O.A.C. 394, 43 C.P.C. (6th) 1, 84 O.R. (3d) 799 (note), 2007 SCC 8, 357 N.R. 196, [2007] 1 S.C.R. 346, 279 D.L.R. (4th) 625, 39 R.F.L. (6th) 30 (S.C.C.).

The Court of Appeal dismissed the ex-wife's preliminary motion. In dissent, Justice Laskin reasoned that court should exercise its discretion not to entertain ex-husband's appeal because he had wilfully and continuously refused to obey court orders. Justice Laskin also found that the purpose of exception in rule 60.11(1) was to ensure that a person could not be imprisoned for failure to pay an ordinary civil debt and that the security orders did not create fixed debts. Appeal allowed. Mrs. Dickie should be awarded her costs before the Supreme Court of Canada on a solicitor and client basis and in the Court of Appeal on a substantial indemnity basis.

Blais v. Belanger, 2007 CarswellOnt 2421, 54 R.P.R. (4th) 9, 2007 ONCA 310, 282 D.L.R. (4th) 98, 224 O.A.C. 1, [2007] O.J. No. 1512 (Ont. C.A.).

The applicants brought motion for contempt. Gordon J. ordered that access be restored and the parties agreed to adjourn the contempt matter until after the trial respecting the declaration. The Court of Appeal held that Belanger's disregard of the court's authority was properly found to be contemptuous. He was not entitled to disregard their orders because he believed the court would ultimately decide the issue in his favour.

Point on the Bow Development Ltd. v. William Kelly & Sons Plumbing Contractors Ltd., 2006 CarswellAlta 1396, 68 Alta. L.R. (4th) 308, [2007] 3 W.W.R. 731, 405 A.R. 1, 2006 ABQB 775 (Alta. Q.B.).

Breach of court order, plus delay and lack of cooperation, more than sufficient to establish finding of contempt. Proceeding in disregard or ignorance of order is, *prima facie*, contempt. While merely civil, act or failure to act must be intentional and accidental, and contempt must be proved beyond reasonable doubt. Contempt is a very serious matter and ought to be invoked in only most extreme circumstances. Contempt is affront to whole administration of justice and aggrieved party should seek remedy in timely fashion and not accumulate grievances for later application. Contempt is not contempt inter parties, but contempt of court.

Wickwire Holm v. Nova Scotia (Attorney General), 2007 CarswellNS 428, 2007 NSSC 287, 285 D.L.R. (4th) 439, 824 A.P.R. 259, 258 N.S.R. (2d) 259, 56 C.P.C. (6th) 324 (N.S. S.C.), 2007-10-04, G.M. Warner J.

The text of the original decision corrected on October 12, 2007.

The applicant seeks "(a) a declaratory order that any order issued by an Adjudicator of the Nova Scotia Small Claims Court shall be enforced according to the terms of the order, (b) another order to be issued by Adjudicator Casey requiring the Sheriff of Halifax County to cause Peter Wilkes to appear before the Small Claims Court on specified dates to show cause why he should not be held in contempt, and (c) costs." The respondent states that the first issue to be decided is whether the Small Claims Court has *ex facie* civil contempt jurisdiction.

The inherent common law jurisdiction of superior courts continues to be available to those statutory courts and tribunals which are intended to have the protection of contempt proceedings to enforce the orders of those statutory courts and tribunals. The nature of proceedings in the Small Claims Court are judicial, not administrative, and are therefore of the type for which *ex facie* civil contempt is intended to be available.

The jurisdiction of the Supreme Court to deal with *ex facie* civil contempt of the Small Claims Court continues to exist. No provision of the Act attempts to oust the inherent jurisdiction of the Supreme Court to deal with contempt of inferior tribunals or statutory courts.

The fact that the Supreme Court retains jurisdiction to enforce orders and proceedings in the Small Claims Court by civil contempt does not, by itself, mean that the Small Claims Court does not have *ex facie* civil contempt jurisdiction.

The Small Claims Court of Nova Scotia does not have *ex facie* civil contempt jurisdiction, based on the Supreme Court of Canada's decisions in *Canadian Broadcasting Corp. v. Quebec (Police Commission)*, 1979 CarswellQue 98, 1979 CarswellQue 163, [1979] 2 S.C.R. 618, 28 N.R. 541, 14 C.P.C. 60, 48 C.C.C. (2d) 289, (sub nom. *Canadian Broadcasting Corp. v. Cordeau)* 101 D.L.R. (3d) 24 (S.C.C.), and *Chrysler Canada Ltd. v. Canada (Competition Tribunal)*, EYB 1992-67219, 1992 CarswellNat 4, 1992 CarswellNat 657, 42 C.P.R. (3d) 353, 138 N.R. 321, 92 D.L.R. (4th) 609, [1992] 2 S.C.R. 394, 7 B.L.R. (2d) 1, 12 Admin. L.R. (2d) 1 (S.C.C.).

Some jurisdictions have legislatively set out the enforcement jurisdiction and procedures of Small Claims Courts; for example, Rule 20 of the *Rules of the Small Claims Court*, being Ontario Regulation 258/98, made pursuant to the *Courts of Justice Act*, R.S.O. 1990, Chapter C.43, provides for examination of debtors (Rule 20.10), and for contempt hearings before a judge of the Superior Court of Justice if the debtor fails to attend (Rule 20.11), and section 13 of the *Statutory Powers Procedure Act*, R.S.O. 1990, Chapter S.22, sets out the jurisdiction and procedure for the Divisional Court to hear contempt in respect of tribunals.

Kassay v. Kassay (2000), 2000 CarswellOnt 3262, [2000] O.J. No. 3373, 11 R.F.L. (5th) 308 (Ont. S.C.J.)

Motion by the husband for a finding of contempt against the wife regarding a denial of access to child. Motion allowed. The court held that there are two types of civil contempt: contempt in the face of the court (in facie) and contempt not in the face of the court (ex facie). An order requiring a person to do an act other than the payment of money, or to abstain from doing an act, may be enforced against the person refusing or neglecting to obey the order by a contempt order. However, it must be established that he or she deliberately or willfully or knowingly did some act which was designed to result in the breach of a court order. The wife willfully breached an access order and thus, was found in contempt.

Pro Swing Inc. v. ELTA Golf Inc., [2006] S.C.J. No. 52, 2006 CarswellOnt 7203, 2006 CarswellOnt 7204, 52 C.P.R. (4th) 321, [2006] 2 S.C.R. 612, 2006 SCC 52, 354 N.R. 201, 218 O.A.C. 339, 273 D.L.R. (4th) 663, 41 C.P.C. (6th) 1 (S.C.C.)

Successful foreign plaintiff brought a motion to the Ontario Superior Court of Justice for recognition and enforcement of the contempt order against the Ontario based defendant. The motions judge held that non-money foreign judgments can be enforced in Ontario. The Court of Appeal set aside the motions judge's decision. The plaintiff appealed.

Supreme Court of Canada dismissed the appeal. The contempt order is quasi-criminal in nature, and a Canadian court will not enforce a foreign penal order, either directly or indirectly. Receiving courts should use their discretion to refrain from enforcing orders that subject Canadian litigants to unforeseen obligations.

Wickwire Holm v. Nova Scotia (Attorney General), 2007 CarswellNS 428, 2007 NSSC 287, 285 D.L.R. (4th) 439, 824 A.P.R. 259, 258 N.S.R. (2d) 259, 56 C.P.C. (6th) 324 (N.S. S.C.)

Adjudicator issued order that Sheriff cause debtor to appear at show cause hearing after debtor failed to appear. Provincial department advised adjudicator that sheriff could not enforce the order because of departmental directive. Application brought by creditor for declaration that order of the Small Claims Court requiring Sheriff to cause debtor to appear at show cause hearing shall be enforced and for order directing Small Claims adjudicator to reissue order Application granted in part.

Although respondent obligated to obey court order or have it stayed or overturned, Small Claims Court had no ex facie civil contempt jurisdiction. Respondent had no authority to direct a Sheriff not to enforce a court order and Sheriff had no authority to refuse to enforce a court order.

College of Optometrists (Ontario) v. SHS Optical Ltd., [2008] O.J. No. 3933, 2008 CarswellOnt 6073, 300 D.L.R. (4th) 548, 241 O.A.C. 225, 2008 ONCA 685, 93 O.R. (3d) 139 (Ont. C.A.); leave to appeal refused 2009 CarswellOnt 3393, 2009 CarswellOnt 3394 (S.C.C.)

Appeal by the appellant from a decision finding the appellants in contempt of an order of the Superior Court of Justice. The appellant claimed that the Notice of Application submitted by the respondents when they brought contempt proceedings against the appellant was inadequately particular. Appeal dismissed. Appellants did not apply for particulars or complain of any insufficiency of detail in the notice. No basis for finding of unfair hearing as the application judge assisted the applicant whenever he asked for help; applicant was self-represented by choice, had no language difficulties and was experienced business person.

St. Elizabeth Home Society v. Hamilton (City), 2008 CarswellOnt 1381, 52 C.P.C. (6th) 48, 237 O.A.C. 25, 230 C.C.C. (3d) 199, 2008 ONCA 182, 89 O.R. (3d) 81, 291 D.L.R. (4th) 338, [2008] O.J. No. 983 (Ont. C.A.)

Appellant, a newspaper reporter, appealed a decision finding him in contempt of court. Appellant was subpoenaed to testify at trial but refused to disclose identity of one source claiming that to do so would lead to the identification of a confidential source. The source eventually revealed himself before conclusion of trial. Appeal allowed.

Citations for contempt should be used as a last resort and this is particularly apt where journalist-informant confidentiality was at stake. Even if appellant's claim of privilege had failed the court should have first explored other means of proceeding that would be less intrusive to journalist-informant relationship of confidentiality.

York (Regional Municipality) v. Schmidt (October 20, 2008), Doc. CV-07083917 (Ont. S.C.J.)

Applicant made an application for a finding that the defendant was in contempt of a court order. Application allowed. The applicant satisfied the court beyond a reasonable doubt that Schmidt was in contempt of the order. The order was clear and it was breached. The evidence showed that the breach was deliberate.

Dickie v. Dickie, 39 R.F.L. (6th) 30, 279 D.L.R. (4th) 625, [2007] 1 S.C.R. 346, 357 N.R. 196, 2007 SCC 8, 84 O.R. (3d) 799 (note), [2007] S.C.J. No. 8, 2007 CarswellOnt 607, 2007 CarswellOnt 606, 43 C.P.C. (6th) 1, 221 O.A.C. 394 (S.C.C.).

Ex-husband did not comply with new orders. *Rules of Civil Procedure* precluding contempt proceedings to enforce orders require "payment of money." Contempt proceedings available. Orders not within exception and did not create fixed debts. See *Rules of Civil Procedure*, R.R.O. 1990, Reg. 194, r. 60.11(1).

The motion judge found ex-husband in contempt. Husband sought to appeal contempt order while in non-compliance with underlying orders. Appellate court had discretion to refuse to entertain appeal; see *Courts of Justice Act*, R.S.O. 1990, c. C.43, s. 140(5).

In dissent, Laskin J. reasoned that court should exercise its discretion not to entertain the ex-husband's appeal because he had wilfully and continuously refused to obey court orders. He would have adjourned proceedings until the ex-husband complied with security orders. He also found ex-husband's appeal failed on merits. Purpose of exception in r. 60.11(1) was to ensure that a person could not be imprisoned for failure to pay an ordinary, civil debt, and that the security orders did not create fixed debts. Rather, they required provision of security and so did not fall within exception. Finally, he found that ex-husband had received a fair hearing.

Held, on ex-wife's appeal, appeal should be allowed.

Wickwire Holm v. Nova Scotia (Attorney General), 56 C.P.C. (6th) 324, 258 N.S.R. (2d) 259, 824 A.P.R. 259, 285 D.L.R. (4th) 439, 2007 NSSC 287, 2007 CarswellNS 428 (N.S. S.C.)

The applicant law firm obtained default judgment and execution order in Small Claims against client debtor. The debtor failed to appear for discovery in aid of execution. Small Claims Court of Nova Scotia did not have *ex facie* civil contempt jurisdiction.

Applicant sought order requiring sheriff to cause debtor to appear before Small Claims Court to show cause why he should not be held in contempt. Application granted. Department of Justice had no authority, statutorily or constitutionally, to direct sheriff *not* to enforce court order. Sheriff had no authority to refuse to enforce court order. Department of Justice and sheriff were required to carry out orders of Small Claims Court unless court of competent jurisdiction stayed order or otherwise released them from obligation to enforce it.

Supreme Court jurisdiction to deal with *ex facie* civil contempt of the Small Claims Court continued to exist. Supreme Court had inherent jurisdiction to deal with *ex facie* contempt of orders and proceedings in the Small Claims Court. Common law presumption was against statutory courts and inferior tribunals having *ex facie* civil contempt jurisdiction unless granted by statute and in clear and unambiguous language.

Granting of declaratory judgment discretionary. Small Claims Court entitled to have its orders respected in same manner as other courts and tribunals unless its orders stayed, reversed by appeal, judicial review, prerogative writ or by an equally effective order to the effect that its order need not be obeyed.

Cellupica v. Di Giulio, 2010 ONSC 5839, 2010 CarswellOnt 8573, [2010] O.J. No. 4844, 5 C.P.C. (7th) 371 (Ont. S.C.J.).

The plaintiffs brought a motion for an order of contempt. The motion was granted. Two missed examination dates and unfulfilled undertaking were not properly specified in the notice, and so could not be relied on for contempt. The defendant raised reasonable doubt about the first missed court hearing, and was given a move to a different courtroom. The defendant failed to explain the non-attendance at the ordered examination, or the failure to obtain bank records. The defendant deliberately and wilfully failed to perform the obligations imposed on him by the court order, and was in contempt of court. The defendant would not be given any further time to purge contempt, as he had repeatedly toyed with plaintiffs and breached court orders.

Elements required to find a person in contempt of court are referred to in *Hobbs v. Hobbs*, 2008 ONCA 598, 2008 CarswellOnt 5037, [2008] O.J. No. 3312, 240 O.A.C. 202, 54 R.F.L. (6th) 1 at para. 26 (Ont. C.A.).

On a motion seeking to find a defendant in contempt of a court order, the moving party must prove that the defendant was aware of the terms of the order: *College of Optometrists (Ontario) v. SHS Optical Ltd.*, 2008 ONCA 685, 2008 CarswellOnt 6073, [2008] O.J. No. 3933, 93 O.R. (3d) 139, 300 D.L.R. (4th) 548, 241 O.A.C. 225 at para. 71 (Ont. C.A.); leave to appeal refused 2009 CarswellOnt 3393, 2009 CarswellOnt 3394, 262 O.A.C. 396 (note), 398 N.R. 400 (note) (S.C.C.). Generally, a copy of the order must be served on the person affected by it in sufficient time to enable the defendant to perform the ordered act: See Donald Ferguson, *Ontario Courtroom Procedure*, 2009, pp. 540-541.

Where an alleged contemnor testifies at a contempt hearing, a court should assess the evidence in accordance with the principles laid down by the Supreme Court of Canada in *R. v. W. (D.)*, 1991 CarswellOnt 1015, 1991 CarswellOnt 80, EYB 1991-67602, [1991] S.C.J. No. 26, [1991] 1 S.C.R. 742, 3 C.R. (4th) 302, 63 C.C.C. (3d) 397, 122 N.R. 277, 46 O.A.C. 352 (S.C.C.).

Once a person is found in civil contempt of court, the court will usually afford a contemnor an opportunity to purge his contempt before the penalty or punishment phase of the proceeding begins: *College of Optometrists (Ontario)*, supra, para. 73. If, after being found in contempt of court, a party purges his contempt by subsequently complying with the court order, compliance may be taken into account as a mitigating factor on the sentence. See *Korea Data Systems Co. v. Chiang*, 2009 ONCA 3, 2009 CarswellOnt 28, [2009] O.J. No. 41, (sub nom. *Chiang (Trustee of) v. Chiang)* 93 O.R. (3d) 483, 49 C.B.R. (5th) 1, (sub nom. *Chiang (Trustee of) v. Chiang)* 305 D.L.R. (4th) 655, (sub nom. *Mendlowitz & Associates Inc. v. Chiang)* 257 O.A.C. 64, 78 C.P.C. (6th) 110 at paras. 50 to 52 (Ont. C.A.); additional reasons at 2009 ONCA 153, 2009 CarswellOnt 769, 50 C.B.R. (5th) 13, 68 C.P.C. (6th) 32 (Ont. C.A.); additional reasons at 2010 ONCA 67, 2010 CarswellOnt 345, 63 C.B.R. (5th) 201 (Ont. C.A.).

2076280 Ontario Inc. v. TransCanada Inc., 2011 ONSC 799, 2011 CarswellOnt 691 (Ont. S.C.J.), Sproat J.

Surinderjit Singh Gill, owner of TransCanada Inc., failed to attend a judgment debtor exam on October 19, 2010. He was personally served with a Notice of Contempt Hearing and did attend in the Superior Court of Justice on November 23, 2010. At that time he was ordered to attend an examination in Small Claims Court on January 28, 2011, and the contempt motion was adjourned to February 1, 2011.

He did not attend January 28, 2011. He also did not attend on February 1, 2011 although paged three times. Form 60K warrant was signed to issue for his arrest. A Copy of Endorsement was mailed to him. An arrest warrant was issued immediately.

World Assurances Inc. v. Al Imam, 2011 QCCS 5792, 2011 CarswellQue 12070, EYB 2011-197842 (Que. S.C.), Peacock, J.S.C.

Jurisprudence has developed sentencing objectives for civil contempt as well as factors to be considered. These factors are: (a) extenuating and aggravating circumstances; (b) the particular situation of the defendant; and (c) harmonization of sanctions. The Court of Appeal has confirmed the objectives of sentencing (See *Bellemare c. Abaziou*, 2009 QCCA 210, 2009 CarswellQue 570, EYB 2009-153875, [2009] R.J.Q. 276 at para. 22 (Que. C.A.)) in civil contempt, which were originally established in the Superior Court case of *Syndicat des travailleurs(euses) des épiciers unis Métro-Richelieu (CSN) v. E. Chèvrefils & Fils Inc.*, [1998] R.J.Q. 2838, 227 N.R. 280 (note) (S.C.C.).

The defendant did not have the right to opt out of the system when he decided the Court order did not suit him. He did not have the right to destroy data that an impartial tribunal was entitled to analyze — and decide whether relevant or not — in the main civil dispute between he and the plaintiff.

A fundamental precept of our Canadian justice system is that once a judgment has become final, it must be respected by all parties, including the losing party. This provides certainty and finality. It allows the parties, for better or worse, to move on.

There is a procedure to follow for a losing party who disagrees with a judgment: they can seek to appeal to a higher court. What they cannot do is take justice into their own hands and ignore a judgment, fairly and independently given, by acting intentionally in contravention of that judgment. If this were to be allowed there would be no rule of law, and there would be no fair and free system of justice.

Punishment for civil contempt of court has an objective to ensure respect for our entire system of justice, which includes respect for the judges and their role in ensuring respect for the rule of law.

The appropriate fine should be $10,500. The fine must have sufficient consequence that it cannot simply be dismissed as a "licence fee" and part of "the costs of doing business."

Nashid v. Michael, 2012 ONSC 675, 2012 CarswellOnt 1001, 18 R.F.L. (7th) 417, [2012] O.J. No. 459 (Ont. S.C.J.)

The applicant, Dr. Nashid, was found in contempt. Nashid was provided with the opportunity to purge her contempt.

Michael submitted Nashid's pleadings should be struck for her failure to comply with court orders, her failure to purge her contempt, and her failure to pay four outstanding cost orders.

The authority to strike a pleading for non-compliance with orders is provided for in *Family Law Rules* 1(8) and 14(23). In addition, Rule 13(17) provides that the court may dismiss the party's case if the party does not obey an order to serve and file a financial statement, including an updated financial statement.

See *Purcaru v. Purcaru*, 2010 ONCA 92, 2010 CarswellOnt 563, [2010] O.J. No. 427, 265 O.A.C. 121, 75 R.F.L. (6th) 33 (Ont. C.A.), where Lang J.A. noted, at para. 50, that the decision to strike pleadings and to determine the parameters of trial participation was a discretionary one. She cited *Sleiman v. Sleiman*, 2002 CarswellOnt 1595, [2002] O.J. No. 1887, 28 R.F.L. (5th) 447 (Ont. C.A.), a case involving a refusal of financial disclosure in which the motion judge determined that the party had demonstrated a "blatant disregard for the process and the orders of the court."

She also cited the decision of the Divisional Court in *Vacca v. Banks*, 2005 CarswellOnt 146, [2005] O.J. No. 147, 6 C.P.C. (6th) 22 (Ont. Div. Ct.) in which the plaintiff had repeatedly failed to comply with orders related to the discovery and the progress of litigation. In that case, Ferrier J. noted that the master's remedy of the dismissal of the action may be an appropriate sanction to recognize the court's "responsibility for the administration of justice."

In *Horzempa v. Ablett*, 2011 ONCA 633, 2011 CarswellOnt 11184, [2011] O.J. No. 4391 (Ont. C.A.), the Court of Appeal heard an appeal from an order striking the appellant's pleadings and dismissing the appellant's motion to change a final order for spousal support. The court indicated, at paragraph 7, that striking a pleading and denying a party the right to be heard on a motion is a "drastic remedy of last resort." The Court of Appeal dismissed the appeal, noting, "The record demonstrates a consistent and unyielding pattern of noncompliance with court orders and a total disregard for the process of the court" and that, by his refusal to follow rules or obey orders, the appellant had chosen not to avail himself of "the numerous opportunities for meaningful participation that the ordinary process provides."

The pleadings of Nashid were therefore struck. Michael has leave to proceed with an undefended trial after March 31, 2012.

It is appropriate that Michael receive full recovery for the contempt motion.

If a party seeks a postponement of the payment of costs on the basis of an inability to pay, the onus is on that party to provide evidence. There was no such evidence in this case.

Culligan Canada Ltd. v. Fettes, 2010 SKCA 151, 2010 CarswellSask 802, [2011] 7 W.W.R. 726, 2 C.P.C. (7th) 79, 326 D.L.R. (4th) 463, 506 W.A.C. 24, 366 Sask. R. 24 (Sask. C.A.)

Disobedience of court. A court order sought to be enforced by contempt applications incorporated overly broad and unclear language. External circumstances exacerbated the order's lack of clarity. The order was sufficiently ambiguous to preclude a finding of contempt. The ambiguity of the order made the application of order to facts problematic for the reviewing court. There was no distinct legal issue, regarding the use of mass mailing devices, which could be decided without considering what it meant to "serve." A lack of clarity was fatal to the application.

Commentary

A Small Claims Court Case — 2006 (Amended Rules) Contempt — Rule 20.11

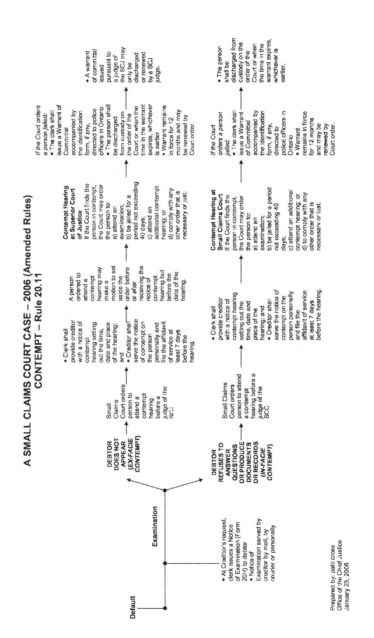

A SMALL CLAIMS COURT CASE – 2006 (Amended Rules) CONTEMPT – Rule 20.11

Default

Examination

- At Creditor's request, clerk issues a Notice of Examination (Form 20H) to debtor
- Notice of Examination served by creditor by mail, by courier or personally

DEBTOR DOES NOT APPEAR (EX-FACIE CONTEMPT)

Small Claims Court orders person to attend a contempt hearing before a judge of the SCJ

- Clerk shall provide creditor with a notice of contempt hearing setting out the time, date and place of the hearing; and
- Creditor shall serve the notice of contempt on the person personally and file the affidavit of service at least 7 days before the hearing.

A person ordered to attend a contempt hearing may make a motion to set aside the order before or after receiving the notice of contempt hearing but before the date of the hearing.

Contempt Hearing at Superior Court of Justice

If the Court finds the person in contempt, the Court may order the person to:
a) attend an examination;
b) be jailed for a period not exceeding 40 days;
c) attend an additional contempt hearing; or
d) comply with any other order that is necessary or just.

If the Court orders a person jailed:
- The clerk shall issue a Warrant of Committal accompanied by the identification form, if any, directed to police officers in Ontario
- The person shall be discharged from custody on the order of the Court or when the time in the warrant expires, whichever is earlier
- Warrant remains in force for 12 months and may be renewed by Court order.

- A warrant of committal issued pursuant to a judge of the SCJ may only be discharged or renewed by a SCJ judge.

DEBTOR REFUSES TO ANSWER QUESTIONS OR PRODUCE DOCUMENTS OR RECORDS (IN-FACIE CONTEMPT)

Small Claims Court orders person to attend a contempt hearing before a judge of the SCC

- Clerk shall provide creditor with a notice of contempt hearing setting out the time, date and place of the hearing; and
- Creditor shall serve the notice of contempt on the person personally and file the affidavit of service at least 7 days before the hearing.

Contempt Hearing at Small Claims Court

If the Court finds the person in contempt, the Court may order the person to:
a) attend an examination;
b) be jailed for a period not exceeding 40 days;
c) attend an additional contempt hearing; or
d) comply with any other order that is necessary or just.

If the Court orders a person jailed:
- The clerk shall issue a Warrant of Committal accompanied by the identification form, if any, directed to police officers in Ontario
- Warrant remains in force for 12 months and may be renewed by Court order.

- The person shall be discharged from custody on the order of the Court or when the time in the warrant expires, whichever is earlier.

Prepared by: patti cross
Office of the Chief Justice
January 23, 2006

925

20.12 Satisfaction of Order — If payment is made in full satisfaction of an order,

(a) where all parties consent, a party may file a request for clerk's order on consent (Form 11.2A) indicating that payment has been made in full satisfaction of the order or terms of settlement; or

(b) the debtor may make a motion for an order confirming that payment has been made in full satisfaction of the order or terms of settlement.

O. Reg. 78/06, s. 48; 393/09, s. 23

Commentary

Satisfaction of Orders

The creditor who proceeds with enforcement of a judgment/order under the Rules of the Small Claims Court must ensure that the court and the enforcement office (where applicable) is advised that the judgment or order has been satisfied in full and to stop or withdraw any enforcement steps.

If a debt is paid in full under a notice of garnishment, the creditor must immediately serve a Notice of Termination of Garnishment [Form 20R] on the garnishee and on the clerk in accordance with r. 20.08920.2.

Where all the parties consent, a party may file a Request for Clerk's Order on consent [Form 11.2A], in accordance with r. 11.2.01(1).

If the creditor is unavailable or unwilling to complete the notice of termination of garnishment form or sign the Request for Clerk's Order on Consent [Form 11.2A], the debtor may bring a motion before the court seeking an order of the court stating that payment has been made in full satisfaction of the debt.

Rule 21 — Referee

21.01 (1) A person assigned the powers and duties of a referee under subsection 73(2) of the *Courts of Justice Act* may, if directed by the regional senior justice or his or her designate,

(a) hear disputes of proposals of terms of payment under rule 9.03;

(b) conduct settlement conferences under rule 13;

(c) hear motions for consolidation orders under rule 20.09; and

(d) assess receipted disbursements for fees paid to the court, a court reporter or a sheriff under the regulations made under the *Administration of Justice Act.*

History [R. 21.01(1)]: Part of former 22.01(1); the reference to pre-trial conferences and examinations is separated out into another subrule 21.01(2); plain language changes.

Commentary: Pursuant to Rule 21.01(1), a referee designated under subsection 77(2) of the *Courts of Justice Act* may, if directed by the regional senior justice or his or her designate:

- hear disputes of proposals of terms of payment under rule 9.03
- conduct settlement conferences under rule 13
- hear motions for consolidation orders under rule 20.09
- assess receipted disbursements for fees paid to the court, a court reporter, or a sheriff under the regulations under the *Administration of Justice Act.*

The Rules do not provide for assessment officers presiding in Small Claims Courts matters.

(2) Except under subrule **9.03(5)** **(order as to terms of payment)**, a referee shall not make a final decision in any matter referred to him or her but shall report his or her findings and recommendations to the court.

History [R. 21.01(2)]: Contains the reference to pre-trial conferences and examinations from former 22.01(1); refers to rule 13, rather than describing pre-trial examinations; refers to rule 21.10, formerly 21.10.

(3) **[Repealed O. Reg. 78/06, s. 49.]**

O. Reg. 78/06, s. 49; 393/09, s. 24

History [R. 21.01(3)]: Formerly 22.01(2); referred to subrule 9.03(3), formerly 9.04(3).

Commentary: A referee is someone designated under section 77(2) of the *Courts of Justice Act* and is directed by the Regional Senior Justice or the local Administrative Justice to hear matters under the *Small Claims Court Rules*. Referees hear terms of payment disputes under subrule 9.03, conduct settlement conferences under rule 13, make consolidation orders under subrule 20.09, and can assist the clerk in assessing disbursements. The latter authority is new as of July 1, 2006.

Case Law: *Bussineau v. Roberts* (1982), 15 A.C.W.S. (2d) 367 (Ont. Sm. Cl. Ct.) — The duties of a pre-trial referee in Small Claims Court (see R.R.O. 1980, Reg. 917, ss. 68(1) and (2)) do *not* include conducting a trial by hearing evidence from the parties and their witnesses. The referee cannot dismiss the claim for failure of the plaintiff to attend or to give judgment of the plaintiff for failure to the defendant to attend a hearing.

Lagadin v. King (1985), 2 W.D.C.P. 259 (Ont. Prov. Ct.) — At a resolution hearing, with the plaintiffs appearing, the defendant absent and no defence entered, the referee exceeded the jurisdiction by recommending judgment with respect of an unliquidated claim. This cannot be done without the written consent to same by all parties.

Rule 22 — Payment Into and Out of Court

[Heading amended O. Reg. 400/12, s. 2.]

22. [Repealed O. Reg. 400/12, s. 2.]

Payment Into and Out of Court

Rules of the Small Claims Court

The Rules of the Small Claims Court will include a new Rule 22 (Payment into and out of court).

A party can obtain a payment out from funds that are held by the Accountant with a court order by filing required documentation with the Accountant. A new Form 4B has been made for use in motions to seek payment out of court for persons under disability under Rule 4.08 of the Rules of the Small Claims Court.

A Ministry form has been posted on the Ontario Court Forms website entitled "Request to pay money into or out of court" for use by parties seeking to pay money into or out of court.

The new rule applies to money paid into court after January 1, 2013. Transition rules have been made for money that was paid into local courts before January 1, 2013. Money that will continue to be held locally will continue to be handled in accordance with local practice.

A party may be required to pay money into court for the following reasons:

- A judge has ordered the party to pay money into court,

- A statute or court rule may require a party to pay money into court (for example, in applications under the *Repair and Storage Liens Act*),

- Where a party is "under disability" (e.g. a minor or a mentally incapable person), Rule 4.08 requires that any money to be paid to that party must be paid into court.

Rule 22 does not apply to money paid or to be paid into court,

- Under an order or proposal for payment made under [r. 9.03];

- Under an offer to settle a claim in return for the payment of money; or

- For the enforcement of an order for the payment or recovery of money under Rule 20 including enforcement by garnishment.

As of October 1, 2012, court staff will;

- Print the information sheet double-sided to ensure both the French and the English versions are printed on a single page.

- Mail the information sheet to all parties, or their representatives, in a Small Claims Court action together with the Notice of Settlement Conference.

- Post the information sheet in a conspicuous location such as small claims court public waiting areas, with both languages prominently displayed.

22.01 Definitions — In this Rule,

"**Accountant**" means the Accountant of the Superior Court of Justice;

"**clerk**" means the clerk in the location where the proceeding was commenced.

O. Reg. 400/12, s. 2

22.02 Non-Application of Rule — This Rule does not apply to money paid or to be paid into court,

(a) under an order or proposal for payment made under rule 9.03;

(b) under an offer to settle a claim in return for the payment of money; or

(c) for the enforcement of an order for the payment or recovery of money under Rule 20, including enforcement by garnishment.

O. Reg. 400/12, s. 2

22.03 (1) Payment into Court — Subject to subrule (7), a party who is required to pay money into court shall do so in accordance with subrules (2) to (6).

(2) **Filing with Clerk or Accountant** — The party shall file the following documents with the clerk or the Accountant:

1. If the payment into court is under a statutory provision or rule, a written request for payment into court that refers to that provision or rule.

2. If the payment into court is under an order, a written request for payment into court and a copy of the order that bears the court's seal.

(3) **Direction** — On receiving the documents required to be filed under subrule (2), the clerk or Accountant shall give the party a direction to receive the money, addressed to a bank listed in Schedule I or II to the *Bank Act* (Canada) and specifying the account in the Accountant's name into which the money is to be paid.

(4) **Clerk to Forward Documents** — If the documents are filed with the clerk, the clerk shall forward the documents to the Accountant.

(5) Payment — On receiving the direction referred to in subrule (3), the party shall pay the money into the specified bank account in accordance with the direction.

(6) Bank's Duties — On receiving the money, the bank shall give a receipt to the party paying the money and immediately send a copy of the receipt to the Accountant.

(7) Payment to Accountant by Mail — A party may pay money into court by mailing to the Accountant the applicable documents referred to in subrule (2), together with the money that is payable; the written request for payment into court referred to in that subrule shall include the party's name and mailing address.

(8) Accountant to Provide Receipt — On receiving money under subrule (7), the Accountant shall send a receipt to the party paying the money.

(9) Proof of Payment — A party who pays money into court shall, immediately after receiving a receipt from the bank under subrule (6) or from the Accountant under subrule (8), as the case may be, send to every other party a copy of the receipt and file a copy of the receipt with the court.

O. Reg. 400/12, s. 2

22.04 (1) Payment Out of Court — Money may only be paid out of court under an order.

(2) Documents to be Filed — A person who seeks payment of money out of court shall file with the Accountant,

   (a) a written request for payment out and supporting affidavit, in the form provided by the Ministry; and

   (b) a copy of the order for payment out that bears the court's seal.

(3) Payment Out, Children's Lawyer or Public Guardian and Trustee — If the person seeking payment out is the Children's Lawyer or the Public Guardian and Trustee,

   (a) the written request need not be in the form provided by the Ministry and a supporting affidavit is not required; and

   (b) a single written request that deals with more than one proceeding may be filed.

(4) Payment Out, Minor Attaining Age of Majority — Despite subrule (2), money in court to which a party is entitled under an order once the party attains the age of majority may be paid out to the party on filing with the Accountant, in the forms provided by the Accountant,

   (a) a written request for payment out; and

   (b) an affidavit proving the identity of the party and that the party has attained the age of majority.

(5) Accountant's Duties — If the requirements of subrule (2) or (4), as the case may be, are met, the Accountant shall pay the money to the person named in the order for payment out, and the payment shall include any accrued interest, unless a court orders otherwise.

O. Reg. 400/12, s. 2

22.05 Transition — This Rule applies to the payment into and out of court of money paid into court on and after the day on which Ontario Regulation 400/12 comes into force.

O. Reg. 400/12, s. 2

Rule 23

23. This Regulation comes into force on September 1, 1998.

4 — Court Fees

Ont. Reg. 432/93 — Small Claims Court — Fees And Allowances

made under the *Administration of Justice Act*

O. Reg. 432/93, as am. O. Reg. 139/94 (Fr.); 214/97; 488/98; 17/00; 11/05; 271/05; 363/06; CTR 21 NO 11 – 1; 248/12.

1. (1) The fees set out in Schedule 1 are payable to clerks of the Small Claims Court.

(2) In this section and Schedule 1,

"claim" does not include a defendant's claim;

"claimant" includes an individual, a sole proprietorship, a partnership, an unincorporated organization and a corporation.

(3) For the purposes of Schedule 1, a claimant who files a claim in a Small Claims Court office on or after January 1 in any calendar year and who has already filed 10 or more claims in the same office in that calendar year is a frequent claimant.

(4) For the purposes of Schedule 1, a claimant who is not a frequent claimant under subsection (3) is an infrequent claimant.

O. Reg. 214/97, s. 1; 488/98, s. 1

2. The fees and allowances set out in Schedule 2 are payable to bailiffs of the Small Claims Court.

3. The fees and allowances set out in Schedule 3 are payable to witnesses appearing before the Small Claims Court.

4. Ontario Regulations 585/91, 297/92 and 367/92 are revoked.

Schedule 1 — Clerk's Fees

Item		Amount
1.	Filing of a claim by an infrequent claimant	$ 75.00
2.	Filing of a claim by a frequent claimant	$ 145.00
3.	Filing of a defendant's claim	$ 75.00
4.	Filing a notice of motion served on another party, a notice of motion without notice or a notice of motion for a consent order (except a notice of motion under the *Wages Act*	$ 40.00
5.	Filing a defence	$ 40.00

Item		Amount
6.	Issuing a summons to a witness	$ 19.00
7.	Receiving for enforcement a process from the Ontario Court of Justice or an order or judgment as provided by statute	$ 25.00
8.	Issuing a certificate of judgment	$ 19.00
9.	Issuing a writ of delivery, a writ of seizure and sale or a notice of examination	$ 35.00
10.	Issuing a notice of garnishment	$ 100.00
11.	Preparing and filing a consolidation order	$ 75.00
12.	Forwarding a court file to Divisional Court for appeal	$ 20.00
13.	Issuing a certified copy of a judgment or other document, per page	$ 3.50
14.	Transmitting a document other than by mail Cost of transmission	
15.	For the inspection of a court file,	
	i. by a solicitor or party in the proceeding	no charge
	ii. by a person who has entered into an agreement with the Attorney General for the bulk inspection of court files, per file	$ 1.00
	iii. by any other person, per file	$ 10.00
16.	Making a photocopy of a document not requiring certification, per page	$ 1.00
17.	For a copy on compact disc (CD) of a digital recording of a court hearing in respect of a case, if such a recording exists and a copy is available:	
	i. For a single day's recording	22.00
	Ii For each additional day's recording, if the request is made at the same time as a request under subitem i	10.50
18.	In an application under the *Repair and Storage Liens Act*;	
	i. on the filing of,	
	A. an application	$ 100.00
	B. a notice of objection	$ 35.00
	C. a waiver of further claim and a receipt	no charge
	ii. on the issuing of,	
	A. an initial certificate	$ 35.00
	B. a final certificate	$ 35.00
	C. a writ of seizure	$ 35.00
19.	Fixing of a date for a trial or an assessment hearing by an infrequent claimant	$ 100.00
20.	Fixing of a date for a trial or an assessment hearing by a frequent claimant	$ 130.00
21.	Entering of a default judgment by an infrequent claimant	$ 35.00
22.	Entering of a default judgment by a frequent claimant	$ 50.00

O. Reg. 214/97, s. 2; 488/98, s. 2; 17/00, s. 1; 11/05, s. 1; 271/05, s. 1; 363/06, s. 1; CTR 21 NO 11 – 1; 248/12, s. 1

SCHEDULE 2 — BAILIFF'S FEES

1.	[Repealed O. Reg. 363/06, s. 2.]	
2.	For each attempt, whether successful or not, to enforce a writ of delivery	36.00
3.	For each attempt, whether successful or not, to enforce a writ of seizure and sale of personal property,	
	i. where no sale is necessary	36.00
	ii. where a sale is necessary	60.00
4.	For each attempt, whether successful or not, to enforce a writ of seizure under the *Repair and Storage Liens Act*	36.00
5.	Enforcing a writ of delivery or a writ of seizure and sale of personal property, removing property seized, advertising the sale of personal property, including obtaining assistance in seizing, securing or retaining property	Reasonable disbursements necessarily incurred, including appraisers' fees

O. Reg. 11/05, s. 2; 363/06, s. 2

SCHEDULE 3 — FEES AND ALLOWANCES TO WITNESSES

1.	For attendance in court, unless item 2 applies, per day	$ 6.00
2.	For attendance in court by a barrister, solicitor, physician, surgeon, engineer or veterinary surgeon who is not a party to the action, to give evidence of a professional service rendered or to give a professional opinion, per day	$ 15.00
3.	For travel to courtReasonable travelling expenses actually incurred, but not exceeding the kilometre allowance set out in Regulation 11 of the Revised Regulations of Ontario, 1990	

Notes:

A frequent claimant is a party who issues more than 10 claims per calendar year in a Small Claims Court in the same location. Enquiries should be made by e-mail at scc.frequent.users@jus.gov.on.ca.

Commentary: You must pay a fee to file a claim in Small Claims Court and for most steps in a proceeding such as filing a motion, requesting a trial date and taking steps to enforce a judgment.

Court fees are set out in regulations made under the *Administration of Justice Act*. If you need to take steps to enforce your judgment, you may need to pay some of the fees listed in the *Sheriffs — Fees* regulation. If you wish to appeal the judge's decision at trial, you will need to pay fees listed in the *Court Reporter's and Court Monitor's Fees* regulation for preparing the transcript of your case, as well as a fee for filing your appeal. Remember, you should always refer to the actual regulations. The current regulations are available at the Ontario government's e-laws website at *www.e-laws.gov.on.ca*.

What court fees will I have to pay if I make a claim in Small Claims Court?

The fees that must be paid in a proceeding vary from case to case depending on what steps you take.

Example 1

Jill sues Jack for a debt he owes to her.

Jill wins at trial but Jack still does not pay.

Jill files a Notice of Garnishment in the same Court location to have his wages garnished.

In this situation, the total fees that Jill would pay are as follows:

Plaintiff's claim	$ 75
Filing a request for trial date	$100
Notice of garnishment	$100
Total Fees	$275

If you summon a witness to attend your trial, you must pay the witness an attendance fee and travel allowance.

What if I cannot afford to pay the fees?

If you cannot afford to pay court and enforcement fees, you may request a fee waiver; see page 1034. The fee waiver applies to most fees in Small Claims Court proceedings. See also *www.attorneygeneral.jus.gov.on.ca.*

What is a frequent claimant?

A frequent claimant is a party who files 10 or more claims in a calendar year in Small Claims Court. Frequent claimants pay higher fees to file a claim, to file a default judgment and to fix a trial date. Once a party has filed his or her tenth claim, that party is required to pay the frequent claimant rate for all new actions and for new steps in current actions.

Case Law: *R. v. Lord Chancellor*, [1997] 2 All E.R. 781, [1998] Q.B. 575, [1998] 2 W.L.R. 849 (Eng. Q.B.) — Applicant wished to bring proceedings in the court but could not afford to pay the applicable court fees. He applied for judicial review, asking for a declaration that the Act which set forth the fee schedule was *ultra vires* and unlawful on the ground that it breached the implied limitation in that section that fees could not be prescribed in such a way as to deprive a citizen of his constitutional right of access to the courts. Court held that a citizen's right of access to the courts is a common law constitutional right which could only be abrogated by specific statutory authority which specifically conferred the power to abrogate that right. In this instance, the effect was to bar many persons from seeking justice in the courts, and as such the provision was held to be unlawful.

Breeze v. Ontario (Attorney General) (December 10, 1997) (Ont. Gen. Div.), Southey J. — The Court held that the Lieutenant Governor in Council, pursuant to the *Administration of Justice Act* and its regulations, has the power to make regulations requiring the payment of fees in respect of proceedings in any court and to prescribe the amount thereof. For this reason, the applicant's argument that a filing fee of $75 to file a motion in Landlord and Tenant Court should not be required was rejected.

Polewsky v. Bank of Montreal (April 6, 1999), Doc. 433-97 (Ont. Sm. Cl. Ct.) — At issue, the validity of Rule 13.01(7) and the Small Claims Court Tariff on grounds, among others, that is violates s. 15(1) of the *Charter*. Plaintiff seeking Order waiving his fee to file the matter for Trial and for an Order to bring this case to Trial. Right of certain individuals to access the Court system? *Pleau v. Nova Scotia*, [1998] N.S.J. 526 followed. *B.C.G.E.U., Re*, EYB 1988-67021, 1988 CarswellBC 762, 1988 CarswellBC 363, [1988] S.C.J. No. 76, (sub nom. *B.C.G.E.U. v. British Columbia (Attorney General)*) [1988] 6 W.W.R. 577, 30 C.P.C. (2d) 221, [1988] 2 S.C.R. 214, 220 A.P.R. 93, 53 D.L.R. (4th) 1, 87 N.R. 241, 31 B.C.L.R.

(2d) 273, 71 Nfld. & P.E.I.R. 93, 44 C.C.C. (3d) 289, 88 C.L.L.C. 14,047 (S.C.C.) followed. Plaintiff of limited means, with less than $900 per month in income. Order granted requiring the Clerk of this Court to set this case for trial without fee.

Polewsky v. Home Hardware Stores Ltd., [1999] O.T.C. 109, 1999 CarswellOnt 3500, [1999] O.J. No. 4151, 68 C.R.R. (2d) 330, 40 C.P.C. (4th) 330 (Ont. S.C.J.) — The plaintiff argued that tariff fees charged in Small Claims Court were unconstitutional as discriminating against poor persons. The Rules and parent legislation failed to provide discretion to waive fees, so no discretion existed. Fees are not based on presumed characteristics of poor. The fees did not offend s. 15 of the *Charter*. The motions were dismissed.

Polewsky v. Home Hardware Stores Ltd. (2000), 71 C.R.R. (2d) 330, 2000 CarswellOnt 72 (Ont. S.C.J.), allowing leave to appeal from case cited above — The *Administration of Justice Act*, R.S.O. 1990, c. A.6 authorizes the Lieutenant Governor in Council to make regulations providing for the payment of fees as a prerequisite for the use of the courts. The Small Claims Court requires a payment in full and in advance of $50 before a claim may be issued, and a fee of $100 to set the claim on a list for trial. There is no statutory provision contained in the *Courts of Justice Act*, R.S.O. 1990, c. C.43, the *Administration of Justice Act*, or in the *Small Claims Court Rules* that grants a discretion to reduce or to waive the prescribed fees because of poverty. However, leave to appeal granted. Pursuant to Rule 62.02(1)(b) of the *Rules of Civil Procedure* where there is good reason to doubt the correctness of the order and where the proposed appeal involves a matter of such importance that leave should be granted. Do the fees deny access to a significant number of citizens? In essence, a deprivation of the benefit of the rule of law?

Boddie v. Connecticut (1971), 401 U.S. 371 — In view of the basic position of the marriage relationship in our society and the state monopolization of the means for dissolving that relationship, due process of law prohibits a State from denying, solely because of inability to pay court fees and costs, access to its courts to indigents who, in good faith, seek judicial dissolution of their marriage.

Ryder v. Ryder, 2000 BCSC 554, 2000 CarswellBC 1982 (B.C. S.C.) — The plaintiff applied for status as an indigent person in order to be excused from paying court fees. Most relief sought by the plaintiff was available at no expense and no urgency to divorce. The term "indigent" does not mean a "pauper" or person without any means, but a person possessed of such scant means that he or she is needy or poor. The application was dismissed.

Hawkes v. Aliant Telecom/Island Tel, 2004 CarswellPEI 29, 2004 PESCAD 5 (P.E.I. C.A.) — Appellant, because of her indigent circumstances, should be provided with a CD recording of the motion hearing free of charge. We have easy access to the audio recording if it is necessary that we listen to some parts of it in relation to the grounds of appeal alleging lack of due process and bias on the part of the motion Judge.

Lawrence v. British Columbia (Attorney General), 2003 CarswellBC 1574, 2003 BCCA 379, 184 B.C.A.C. 26, 302 W.A.C. 26, 109 C.R.R. (2d) 93 (B.C. C.A. [In Chambers]), Ryan J.A.

Application by plaintiff for declaration she was entitled to a legal counsel and the legal fees to be paid for by defendant Attorney General dismissed. The *Canadian Charter of Rights and Freedoms* did not apply. Plaintiff's action is a civil dispute between private litigants. The right of access to justice does not include a right to state-funded legal fees.

Christie v. British Columbia (Attorney General), (sub nom. *British Columbia (Attorney General) v. Christie*) 155 C.R.R. (2d) 366, (sub nom. *British Columbia (Attorney General) v. Christie*) [2007] 1 S.C.R. 873, 280 D.L.R. (4th) 528, 2007 CarswellBC 1118, 2007 CarswellBC 1117, 2007 SCC 21, [2007] S.C.J. No. 21, (sub nom. *British Columbia (Attorney General) v. Christie*) 2007 G.T.C. 1488 (Eng.), 361 N.R. 322, 66 B.C.L.R. (4th) 1, (sub nom. *British Columbia (Attorney General) v. Christie*) 2007 G.T.C. 1493 (Fr.), 398 W.A.C. 1, 240 B.C.A.C. 1, (sub nom. *British Columbia (Attorney General) v. Christie*) 2007 D.T.C. 5229

(Fr.), (sub nom. *British Columbia (Attorney General) v. Christie)* 2007 D.T.C. 5525 (Eng.) (S.C.C.)

There is no general constitutional right to counsel in proceedings before courts and tribunals dealing with rights and obligations. The right to access the courts is not absolute and a legislature has the power under s. 92(14) of the *Constitution Act, 1867* to impose at least some conditions on how and when people have a right to access the courts. General access to legal services is also not a currently recognized aspect of, or a precondition to, the rule of law. If the reference to the rule of law implied the right to counsel in relation to all proceedings where rights an obligations are at stake, then s. 10(b) of the *Canadian Charter of Rights and freedoms*, which provides for a right to retain and instruct counsel and to be informed of that right "on arrest or detention," would be redundant. The fact that s. 10(b) does not exclude a finding of a constitutional right to legal assistance in other situations, notably under s. 7 of the *Charter*, does not support a general right to legal assistance whenever a matter of rights and obligations is before a court or tribunal. The right to counsel outside the s. 10(b) context is a case-specific multi-factored enquiry.

General access to legal services is not a currently recognized aspect of the rule of law. Our Courts have emphasized the important role that lawyers play in ensuring access to justice and upholding the rule of law: *Andrews v. Law Society (British Columbia)*, [1989] S.C.J. No. 6, 1989 CarswellBC 701, 1989 CarswellBC 16, [1989] 1 S.C.R. 143, 36 C.R.R. 193, 25 C.C.E.L. 255, 34 B.C.L.R. (2d) 273, 91 N.R. 255, 56 D.L.R. (4th) 1, [1989] 2 W.W.R. 289, 10 C.H.R.R. D/5719, EYB 1989-66977 (S.C.C.); *MacDonald Estate v. Martin* (1990), 1990 CarswellMan 384, [1990] S.C.J. No. 41, 1990 CarswellMan 233, EYB 1990-68602, [1991] 1 W.W.R. 705, 77 D.L.R. (4th) 249, 121 N.R. 1, (sub nom. *Martin v. Gray)* [1990] 3 S.C.R. 1235, 48 C.P.C. (2d) 113, 70 Man. R. (2d) 241, 285 W.A.C. 241 (S.C.C.) at p. 1265 [S.C.R.]; *Fortin c. Chrétien*, REJB 2001-25001, [2001] 2 S.C.R. 500, 2001 SCC 45, 2001 CarswellQue 1396, 2001 CarswellQue 1395, (sub nom. *Fortin v. Barreau du Québec)* 272 N.R. 359, (sub nom. *Fortin v. Chrétien)* 201 D.L.R. (4th) 223 at para. 49 (S.C.C.); *Law Society (British Columbia) v. Mangat*, REJB 2001-26158, [2001] 3 S.C.R. 113, 96 B.C.L.R. (3d) 1, [2002] 2 W.W.R. 201, 276 N.R. 339, 2001 CarswellBC 2169, 2001 CarswellBC 2168, 2001 SCC 67, 205 D.L.R. (4th) 577, 16 Imm. L.R. (3d) 1, 256 W.A.C. 161, 157 B.C.A.C. 161, [2001] S.C.J. No. 66 at para. 43 (S.C.C.); *R. v. Lavallee, Rackel & Heintz*, REJB 2002-33795, (sub nom. *Lavallee, Rackel & Heintz v. Canada (Attorney General))* 651 A.P.R. 183, (sub nom. *Lavallee, Rackel & Heintz v. Canada (Attorney General))* 217 Nfld. & P.E.I.R. 183, 281 W.A.C. 201, 312 A.R. 201, (sub nom. *Lavallee, Rackel & Heintz v. Canada (Attorney General))* 292 N.R. 296, [2002] 4 C.T.C. 143, 3 C.R. (6th) 209, 2002 D.T.C. 7287 (Fr.), 2002 D.T.C. 7267 (Eng.), (sub nom. *Lavallee, Rackel & Heintz v. Canada (Attorney General))* [2002] 3 S.C.R. 209, [2002] 11 W.W.R. 191, (sub nom. *Lavallee, Rackel & Heintz v. Canada (Attorney General))* 96 C.R.R. (2d) 189, 2002 SCC 61, (sub nom. *Lavallee, Rackel & Heintz v. Canada (Attorney General))* 164 O.A.C. 280, 2002 CarswellAlta 1819, 2002 CarswellAlta 1818, 4 Alta. L.R. (4th) 1, (sub nom. *Lavallee, Rackel & Heintz v. Canada (Attorney General))* 167 C.C.C. (3d) 1, 216 D.L.R. (4th) 257, [2002] S.C.J. No. 61 (S.C.C.) at paras. 64–68, per LeBel J. (dissenting in part but not on this point.)

Pavlis v. HSBC Bank Canada (2009), 2009 BCCA 450, [2010] 1 W.W.R. 208, 98 B.C.L.R. (4th) 72, 2009 CarswellBC 2775, 469 W.A.C. 105, 277 B.C.A.C. 105 (B.C. C.A.), Newbury J.A.

Application by appellant for order that she be provided trial transcripts free of charge in her appeal dismissed. No one entitled to require that transcripts be prepared free of charge as a matter of right. This is not a "benefit" provided by law. No basis for appellant's argument that the requirement that she provide court with transcripts engaged her right to the equal protection and equal benefit of the law. Section 7 of the *Charter* not intended to extend to obligations of this kind.

Shuster v. Ontario (Attorney General), **2013 HRTO 1158 (Ont. H.R.T.) — An application was filed under s. 34 of the Human Rights Code alleging discrimination with respect to services because of a disability. The application was dismissed. The applicant was the defendant in actions brought in a Small Claims Court. Judgment was granted to the plaintiffs. The applicant was advised of the cost to obtain transcripts. He refused to pay for them. The order granted that if the Court Reporter consent to request, the applicant could listen to recordings of the transcript. The Reporter advised the applicant that he needed to order the transcripts and that he could listen to the tapes after he had paid for the transcripts. The applicant allegee he has a hearing impediment. He never requested accommodation prior to filing Application. See *Dabic v. Windsor Police Service*, 2010 HRTO 1994, [2010] O.H.R.T.D. No. 1988 (Ont. Human Rights Trib.), paras. 8 and 9.**

The application had no reasonable prospect of success. The application was dismissed.

ONT. REG. 293/92 — SUPERIOR COURT OF JUSTICE AND COURT OF APPEAL — FEES

made under the *Administration of Justice Act*

O. Reg. 293/92, as am. O. Reg. 136/94 (Fr.); 272/94; 359/94; 802/94; 212/97; 248/97 (Fr.); 403/98; 329/99; 14/00; 136/04; 10/05; 272/05; 169/07; 247/12.

[Note: The title of this Regulation was changed from "Ontario Court (General Division) and Court of Appeal — Fees" to "Superior Court of Justice and Court of Appeal — Fees" by O. Reg. 14/00, s. 1.]

1. The following fees are payable, except in respect of proceedings to which section 1.2 applies:

1.	On the issue of,	
	i. a statement of claim or notice of action	$181.00
	ii. a notice of application	181.00
	iii. a third or subsequent party claim	181.00
	iv. a statement of defence and counterclaim adding a party	181.00
	v. a summons to a witness	22.00
	vi. a certificate, other than a certificate of a search by the registrar required on an application for a certificate of appointment of estate trustee, and not more than five pages of copies of the Court document annexed	22.00
	for each additional page	2.00
	vii. a commission	44.00
	viii. a writ of execution	55.00
	ix. a notice of garnishment (including the filing of the notice with the sheriff)	115.00
2.	On the signing of,	
	i. an order directing a reference, except an order on requisition directing the assessment of a bill under the *Solicitors Act*	235.00
	ii. an order on requisition directing the assessment of a bill under the *Solicitors Act*	
	A. if obtained by a client	75.00
	B. if obtained by a solicitor	144.00
	iii. a notice of appointment for the assessment of costs under the Rules of Civil Procedure	104.00
3.	On the filing of,	
	i. a notice of intent to defend	144.00

ii. if no notice of intent to defend has been filed by the same party, a statement of defence, a defence to counterclaim, a defence to crossclaim or a third party defence		144.00
iii. a notice of appearance		102.00
iv. a notice of motion served on another party, a notice of motion without notice, a notice of motion for a consent order or a notice of motion for leave to appeal, other than a notice of motion in a family law appeal		127.00
v. a notice of return of motion, other than a notice of return of motion in a family law appeal		127.00
vi. in a family law appeal, a notice of motion served on another party, a notice of motion without notice, a notice of motion for a consent order or a notice of return of motion		90.00
vii. a notice of motion for leave to appeal in a family law case		90.00
viii. a requisition for signing of default judgment by registrar		127.00
ix. a trial record, for the first time only		337.00
x. a notice of appeal or cross-appeal from an interlocutory order		181.00
xi. a notice of appeal or cross-appeal to an appellate court of a final order of the Small Claims Court		104.00
xii. a notice of appeal or cross-appeal to an appellate court of a final order of any court or tribunal, other than the Small Claims Court or the Consent and Capacity Board		259.00
xiii. a request to redeem or request for sale		104.00
xiv. an affidavit under section 11 of the *Bulk Sales Act*		75.00
xv. a jury notice in a civil proceeding		104.00
4.	For obtaining an appointment with a registrar for settlement of an order	104.00
5.	For perfecting an appeal or judicial review application	201.00
6.	For the making up and forwarding of papers, documents and exhibits	75.00 and the transportation costs
7.	For making copies of documents,	
	i. not requiring certification, per page	1.00
	ii. requiring certification, per page	4.00
8.	For the inspection of a court file,	
	i. by a solicitor or party in the proceeding	No charge
	ii. by a person who has entered into an agreement with the Attorney General for the bulk inspection of court files, per file	4.00
	iii. by any other person, per file	10.00
9.	For the retrieval from storage of a court file	61.00

10.	For the taking of an affidavit or declaration by a commissioner for taking affidavits	13.00
11.	For a settlement conference under rule 77.14 of the Rules of Civil Procedure	127.00
12.	For a copy on compact disc (CD) of a digital recording of a court hearing in respect of a case, if such a recording exists and a copy is available:	
	i. For a single day's recording	22.00
	ii. For each additional day's recording, if the request is made at the same time as a request under subitem i	10.50

O. Reg. 359/94, s. 1; 212/97, s. 1; 248/97, s. 1; 403/98, s. 1; 329/99, s. 1; 14/00, s. 2; 136/04, s. 1; 10/05, s. 1; 272/05, s. 1; 169/07, s. 1; 247/12, s. 1

1.1 (1) If a minor or other person under disability is entitled to receive a payment or payments under a multi-provincial/territorial assistance program agreement between Ontario and a person who has been infected with the human immunodeficiency virus through the receipt by transfusion of blood or a blood product, no fee is payable for the issue of a notice of application under Rule 7.08 of the Rules of Civil Procedure on behalf of the minor or other person under disability, and subparagraph ii of paragraph 1 of section 1 does not apply.

(2) Where before the coming into force of this Regulation an applicant on behalf of a minor or other person under disability has paid a fee for the issue of a notice of application referred to in subsection (1), the fee shall be refunded to the applicant.

O. Reg. 272/94; 136/04, s. 2

1.2 (1) The following fees are payable in respect of proceedings that are governed by Ontario Regulation 114/99 (*Family Law Rules*), except for proceedings under rule 38 (appeals), to which section 1 applies:

1.	On the filing of an application	**$157.00**
2.	On the filing of an answer, other than an answer referred to in item 3	125.00
3.	On the filing of an answer where the answer includes a request for a divorce by a respondent	157.00
4.	On the placing of an application on the list for hearing	280.00
5.	On the issue of a summons to a witness	19.00
6.	On the issue of a certificate with not more than five pages of copies of the Court document annexed	19.00
	For each additional page	2.00
7.	For making copies of documents,	
	i not requiring certification, per page	1.00
	ii requiring certification, per page	3.50
8.	For making up and forwarding papers, documents and exhibits	65.00 and the transportation costs
9.	For a copy on compact disc (CD) of a digital recording of a court hearing in respect of a case, if such a recording exists and a copy is available:	

| i | For a single day's recording . . . . | 22.00 |
| ii | For each additional day's recording, if the request is made at the same time as a request under subitem i . . . | 10.50 |

(2) Despite subsection (1), no fees are payable for the filing of an application, the filing of an answer or the placing of an application on the list for hearing in respect of,

(a) proceedings under the *Children's Law Reform Act*, the *Family Law Act* (except Parts I and II), the *Family Responsibility and Support Arrears Enforcement Act, 1996*, the *Marriage Act* or the *Interjurisdictional Support Orders Act, 2002*; or

(b) proceedings to enforce an order for support, custody or access made under any of these Acts.

O. Reg. 136/04, s. 3; 169/07, s. 2; 247/12, s. 2

2. (1) The following fees are payable in estate matters:

1.	For a certificate of succeeding estate trustee or a certificate of estate trustee during litigation	$75.00
2.	For an application of an estate trustee to pass accounts, including all services in connection with it	322.00
3.	For a notice of objection to accounts	69.00
4.	For an application other than an application to pass accounts, including an application for proof of lost or destroyed will, a revocation of a certificate of appointment, an application for directions or the filing of a claim and notice of contestation	173.00
5.	For a notice of objection other than a notice of objection to accounts, including the filing of a notice of appearance	69.00
6.	For a request for notice of commencement of proceedings	69.00
7.	For the deposit of a will or codicil for safekeeping	20.00
8.	For an assessment of costs, including the certificate	46.00

(2) The fees set out in section 1 are payable in estate matters in addition to the fees set out in subsection (1).

O. Reg. 293/92, s. 2; 802/94; 14/00, s. 3; 10/05, s. 2

3. (1) The following fees are payable in an action under the *Construction Lien Act*:

1.	Where the claim, crossclaim, counterclaim or third party claim does not exceed $6,000,	
	i. on the issuing of a statement of claim, crossclaim, counterclaim or third party claim	$75.00
2.	Where the claim, crossclaim, counterclaim or third party claim exceeds $6,000,	
	i. on the issuing of a statement of claim, crossclaim, counterclaim or third party claim	181.00
	ii. on the filing of a statement of defence	104.00
	iii. on the issuing of a certificate of action	104.00
	iv. on the filing of a trial record	339.00

(2) The fees set out in section 1, except those in paragraphs 1, 2 and 3 of that section, are payable in an action under the *Construction Lien Act* in addition to the fees set out in subsection (1).

O. Reg. 359/94, s. 2; 212/97, s. 2; 14/00, s. 4; 10/05, s. 3

4. (1) The following fees are payable in respect of an application under the *Repair and Storage Liens Act*:

1.	On the filing of,	
	i. an application	$184.00
	ii. a notice of objection	104.00
	iii. a waiver of further claim and a receipt	no charge
2.	On the issuing of,	
	i. an initial certificate	104.00
	ii. a final certificate	104.00
	iii. a writ of seizure	55.00

(2) The fees set out in section 1, except those in paragraphs 1, 2 and 3 of that section, are payable in an action under the *Repair and Storage Liens Act* in addition to the fees set out in subsection (1).

O. Reg. 359/94, s. 3; 212/97, s. 3; 14/00, s. 5; 10/05, s. 4

5. (1) The following fees are payable to an official examiner:

1. For the appointment, for each person examined $9.50

2. For the provision of facilities, for the first two hours or part 32.00

For each additional hour or part 16.00

3. For a reporter's attendance, for the first two hours or part 40.00

For each additional hour or part 20.00

4. For the transcript of an examination, per page, regardless of the party ordering,

    i. for one copy of the first transcript ordered 4.00

    ii. for one copy of each transcript ordered after the reporter has satisfied the order for a transcript described in subparagraph i 3.40

    iii. for each additional copy ordered before the reporter has satisfied the order for a transcript described in subparagraph i or ii 0.80

5. For handling costs, per invoice 5.50

6. For cancellation of or failure to keep an appointment, with less than three working days notice,

    i. for the cancellation or failure to attend 11.50

    ii. for the first two hours or part reserved for the appointment 72.00

    iii. for each additional hour or part reserved for the appointment ....
.... 36.00

(2) The official examiner shall be paid, in addition to the fees set out in subsection (1), a travelling allowance in accordance with Ontario Regulation 283/82, for attendance out of the office.

(3) If a party requires a transcript within five working days of placing the order for the transcript, the party shall pay the official examiner 75 cents per page, in addition to the fee set out in paragraph iv of subsection (1).

(4) If a party requires a transcript within two working days of placing the order for the transcript, the party shall pay the official examiner $1.50 per page, in addition to the fee set out in paragraph iv of subsection (1).

(5) If more than one party requires a transcript as described in subsection (3) or (4), only the first party to place the order shall be required to pay the additional fee.

Note: A solicitor who is charged more than the amounts provided in section 5 of this Regulation or who receives a transcript that does not substantially conform with Rule 4.09 of the Rules of Civil Procedure should notify the Assistant Deputy Minister, Courts Administration Division, Ministry of the Attorney General, in writing

O. Reg. 359/94, s. 4; 212/97, s. 4

6. Ontario Regulations 158/83, 405/84, 605/85, 171/90 and 393/90 are revoked.

ONT. REG. 294/92 — SHERIFFS — FEES

made under the *Administration of Justice Act*

O. Reg. 294/92, as am. O. Reg. 431/93; 137/94 (Fr.); 358/94; 213/97; 404/98; 4/99; 330/99; 217/00; 508/10; 12/11 (Fr.).

1. (1) The following fees are payable to a sheriff:

1. For up to three attempts, whether or not successful, to serve a document, for each person to be served **$100.00**

2. For filing or renewing a writ of execution or order which a sheriff is liable or required to enforce and for delivering a copy of the writ or order or a renewal of it to the land registrar of a land titles division 100.00

3. For filing or renewing a writ of execution or order which a sheriff is liable or required to enforce and which is not required to be delivered to a land registrar of a land titles division... 75.00

4. For filing a writ of seizure or a direction to seize under the *Repair and Storage Liens Act* 115.00

5. For each attempt, whether or not successful, to enforce,

    i. a writ of delivery,

    ii. a writ of sequestration,

    iii. an order for interim recovery of personal property,

    iv. an order for interim preservation of personal property, or

    v. a writ of seizure or direction to seize under the *Repair and Storage Liens Act* 400.00

6. For each attempt, whether or not successful, to enforce a writ of seizure and sale or an order directing a sale 240.00

7. For each attempt, whether or not successful, to enforce any other writ of execution or order 240.00

8. For a search for writs, per name searched ..... 11.00 before November 2, 2015 and, on and after that date, the amount determined under subsection (4)

9. For each report showing the details of a writ, lien or order or for a copy of a writ, lien or order .... 6.00 before November 2, 2015 and, on and after that date, the amount determined under subsection (4), to a maximum fee of $60.00 for each name searched before November 2, 2015 and, on and after that date, to a maximum fee of the amount determined under subsection (5)

10. For preparing a schedule of distribution under the *Creditors' Relief Act*, per writ or notice of garnishment listed on the schedule .... 45.00 to a maximum of an amount equal to 20 per cent of the money received

11. For a calculation for satisfaction of writs and garnishments, per writ or notice of garnishment 45.00

12. For any service or act ordered by a court for which no fee is provided, for each hour or part of an hour spent performing the service or doing the act ....
.... 55.00

13. For making copies of documents (other than writs of execution, orders and certificates of lien),

    i. not requiring certification, per page 2.00

    ii. requiring certification, per page 3.50

(2) In addition to the fees set out in paragraphs 5, 6, 7 and 12 of subsection (1), the person who requests the service shall pay the sheriff his or her reasonable and necessary disbursements in carrying out the services described in those paragraphs.

(3) In subsections (4) to (8),

"actual fee" means, for a specified year, the fee that is payable on the annual effective date in the specified year;

"actual maximum fee" means, for a specified year, the maximum fee that is payable on the annual effective date in the specified year;

"annual effective date" means the first Monday in November;

"Consumer Price Index" means the Consumer Price Index for Canada, all-items, not seasonally adjusted (2002=100), as published by Statistics Canada in Table 5 of *The Consumer Price Index* (Catalogue no. 62-001-X).

(4) For the purposes of paragraphs 8 and 9 of subsection (1), the following is the amount of the fee that is payable on and after November 2, 2015:

1. The fee payable on and after November 2, 2015 and before the annual effective date in 2016 is the amount determined in accordance with the following rules:

    i. Calculate the notional fee for 2015 using the formula,

$$(A \times B \times 0.5) + A$$

in which,

"A" is the actual fee payable for 2014, and

"B" is the indexation factor for 2015, as determined in accordance with subsection (6).

    ii. Choose the amount that is the higher of the notional fee for 2015 and the actual fee for 2014.

    iii. The amount chosen, as rounded to the nearest multiple of five cents, is the amount of the fee payable on and after November 2, 2015 and before the annual effective date in 2016.

2. The fee payable on and after the annual effective date in a specified year after 2015 and before the annual effective date in the following year is the amount determined in accordance with the following rules:

    i. Calculate the notional fee for the year using the formula,

$$(C \times D \times 0.5) + C$$

in which,

"C" is the notional fee for the preceding year, and

"D" is the indexation factor for the specified year, as determined in accordance with subsection (7).

    ii. Choose the amount that is the higher of the notional fee for the year and the actual fee for the preceding year.

    iii. The amount chosen, as rounded to the nearest multiple of five cents, is the amount of the fee payable on and after the annual effective date in the specified year and before the annual effective date in the following year.

(5) For the purposes of paragraph 9 of subsection (1), the applicable maximum fee payable on and after November 2, 2015 is determined in accordance with the rules set out in subsection (4), with necessary modifications, to be read as if each reference to "fee", "notional fee" or "actual fee" in that subsection were a reference to "maximum fee", "notional maximum fee" or "actual maximum fee", respectively.

(6) The indexation factor for 2015 is the percentage, rounded to the nearest one-thousandth, that is calculated using the formula,

$$[(1 + E) \times (1 + F) \times (1 + G) \times (1 + H) \times (1 + J)] - 1$$

in which,

"E" is the Consumer Price Index percentage change, for June 2011, from the corresponding month of the previous year,

"F" is the Consumer Price Index percentage change, for June 2012, from the corresponding month of the previous year,

"G" is the Consumer Price Index percentage change, for June 2013, from the corresponding month of the previous year,

"H" is the Consumer Price Index percentage change, for June 2014, from the corresponding month of the previous year, and

"J" is the Consumer Price Index percentage change, for June 2015, from the corresponding month of the previous year.

(7) The indexation factor for a specified year after 2015 is the Consumer Price Index percentage change, for June of the specified year, from the corresponding month of the previous year.

(8) A reference in subsection (6) or (7) to the Consumer Price Index percentage change, for a month, from the corresponding month of the previous year is a reference to the percentage change published by Statistics Canada in Table 5 of *The Consumer Price Index* (Catalogue no. 62-001-X).

    O. Reg. 213/97, s. 1; 404/98, s. 1; 4/99, s. 1; 330/99, s. 1; 217/00, s. 1; 508/10, s. 1

2. In addition to the fees and disbursements set out in section 1, the person who requests the service shall pay the sheriff a travel allowance as set out in [R.R.O. 1990, Reg. 11] for the distance he or she necessarily travels, both ways, between the court house and the place where the sheriff,

    (a) [Revoked O. Reg. 431/93, s. 2.]

    (b) enforces or attempts to enforce a writ or order; or

    (c) performs or attempts to perform any other service directed by a court.

    O. Reg. 431/93, s. 2

3. Ontario Regulation 392/90 is revoked.

ONT. REG. 2/05 — FEE WAIVER

made under the *Administration of Justice Act*

O. Reg. 2/05, as am. O. Reg. 671/05; 95/14.

1. Definitions — (1) In this Regulation,

"child" includes a person whom a person has demonstrated a settled intention to treat as a child of his or her family, except under an arrangement where the child is placed for valuable consideration in a foster home by a person having lawful custody;

"dependent child" means a child who,

(a) is a minor or is enrolled in a full time program of education, and

(b) if 16 years of age or more, has not withdrawn from parental control;

"gross monthly household income", when used with respect to a person, means the gross amount of all regular payments of any kind received by the members of the person's household during a month;

"household" means a person and his or her spouse and dependent children;

"household liquid assets", when used with respect to a person, means all assets owned by the members of the person's household that are money or can readily be converted into money;

"household net worth", when used with respect to a person, means the difference between,

(a) the value of all assets owned by the members of the person's household, and

(b) the value of all debts and other financial liabilities of the members of the person's household;

"spouse" means spouse as defined in Part III of the *Family Law Act*.

(2) Two persons are not spouses for the purpose of this section if they are living separate and apart as a result of a breakdown of their relationship.

O. Reg. 671/05, s. 1

2. Prescribed conditions — A person meets the prescribed conditions referred to in subsections 4.3(4), 4.5(2) and 4.6(2) of the Act if,

(a) the primary source of the person's gross monthly household income is one or more of,

(i) income assistance under the *Ontario Works Act, 1997*, income support under the *Ontario Disability Support Program Act, 1997* or an allowance under the *Family Benefits Act*,

(ii) a pension, together with a guaranteed income supplement, under the *Old Age Security Act* (Canada),

(iii) a benefit paid under the *Canada Pension Plan*, or

(iv) an allowance paid under the *War Veterans Allowance Act* (Canada); or

(b) each of the following is less than the corresponding amount shown in the Table:

(i) the person's gross monthly household income,

(ii) the value of the person's household liquid assets, and

(iii) the person's household net worth.

3. **Exempted fees** — Sections 4.3 to 4.9 of the Act do not apply to the following fees:

1. Fees under Ontario Regulation 94/14 (*Fees for Court Transcripts*) made under the Act.

2. Fees and travelling allowances under section 5 of Ontario Regulation 293/92 (*Superior Court of Justice and Court of Appeal — Fees*) made under the Act.

3. Fees under the regulation described in paragraph 2 with respect to proceedings relating to offences under Acts of the Parliament of Canada.

4. Fees under the regulation described in paragraph 2 with respect to appeals under the *Provincial Offences Act*.

5. Disbursements under subsection 1(2) and travel allowances under section 2 of Ontario Regulation 294/92 (*Sheriffs — Fees*) made under the Act, except in relation to the enforcement of an order made under subsection 35(3) of the *Tenant Protection Act, 1997*.

6. Disbursements under item 5 of Schedule 2 (Bailiff's Fees) to Ontario Regulation 432/93 (*Small Claims Court — Fees and Allowances*) made under the Act.

7. Fees and travel allowances under Schedule 3 (Fees and Allowances to Witnesses) to the regulation described in paragraph 6.

8. Fees under Ontario Regulation 451/98 (*Mediators' Fees (Rule 24.1, Rules of Civil Procedure)*) made under the Act.

8.1 Fees under Ontario Regulation 43/05 (*Mediators' Fees (Rule 75.1, Rules of Civil Procedure)*) made under the Act.

9. Fees under Ontario Regulation 210/07 (*Ontario Court of Justice — Fees*) made under the Act, except with respect to proceedings that are governed by Ontario Regulation 114/99 (*Family Law Rules*) made under the *Courts of Justice Act*.

O. Reg. 671/05, s. 2; 95/14, s. 1

4. **Exempted persons** — Sections 4.3 to 4.9 of the Act do not apply to a person if, in connection with the proceeding in respect of which the fee is payable,

(a) the person's fees are being paid under the *Legal Aid Services Act, 1998*;

(b) the person has been appointed a representative party under the *Class Proceedings Act, 1992* and has entered into an agreement providing for payment of disbursements only in the event of success, as described in section 33 of that Act; or

(c) the person is a party to a contingency fee agreement made under the *Solicitors Act* under which the person's lawyer is responsible for the payment of disbursements during the course of the proceeding.

5. **Requests under ss. 4.3 and 4.4 of Act** — A request for a fee waiver that is made under section 4.3 or 4.4 of the Act shall be submitted,

(a) in the case of a request to the Registrar of the Court of Appeal or to a judge of that court, to the office of the Registrar;

(b) in any other case, to the office of the court in the county, municipality or territorial division, as the case may be,

(i) where the proceeding is or would be commenced, or

(ii) to which the proceeding has been transferred.

6. Requests under s. 4.7 of Act — A request for a fee waiver that is made under section 4.7 of the Act shall be submitted to the office of the court in the county, municipality or territorial division, as the case may be, where the tribunal order is to be enforced.

TABLE

Number of persons in household	Gross monthly household income
1	**$1,500**
2	**2,250**
3	**2,583**
4	**3,083**
5 or more	**3,583**
Household liquid assets: $1,500	
Household net worth: $6,000	

7. Litigation guardian or representative — (1) This section applies to a person who is,

(a) under a "disability" as defined in subrule 1.03(1) of Regulation 194 of the Revised Regulations of Ontario, 1990 (*Rules of Civil Procedure*) made under the *Courts of Justice Act*;

(b) under a "disability" as defined in subrule 1.02(1) of Ontario Regulation 258/98 (*Rules of the Small Claims Court*) made under that Act;

(c) a "special party" as defined in subrule 2(1) of Ontario Regulation 114/99 (*Family Law Rules*) made under that Act.

(2) Where a person to whom this section applies seeks to obtain a fee waiver certificate, and the proceeding in respect of which the fee waiver is sought is one in which the person has or will have a,

(a) litigation guardian under Rule 7 of Regulation 194 of the Revised Regulations of Ontario, 1990 (*Rules of Civil Procedure*) made under the *Courts of Justice Act*;

(b) litigation guardian under Rule 4 of Ontario Regulation 258/98 (*Rules of the Small Claims Court*) made under that Act; or

(c) special party representative under Rule 4 of Ontario Regulation 114/99 (*Family Law Rules*) made under that Act,

any fee waiver request made under the *Administration of Justice Act* shall be completed by the litigation guardian or representative, or by the person who intends to become the litigation guardian or representative.

O. Reg. 671/05, s. 3

Commentary: Fees for Small Claims Court cases, appeals, and for enforcement of a court or tribunal order are prescribed by regulation under the *Administration of Justice Act*.

The Act was amended and a new regulation [O. Reg. 2/05] came into effect on January 28, 2005. The amended Act provides a fee waiver mechanism to promote access to justice for persons who might otherwise be denied access due to their financial circumstances to be excused from paying fees.

Per s. 3 of O. Reg. 2/05, the fee waiver does not apply to disbursements made to the sheriff for the enforcement of orders (except for the enforcement of an order made under sub. 35(3) of the *Tenant Protection Act, 1997*).

In addition, the fee waiver does not apply to fees that are not payable under the *Administration of Justice Act*, including fees for the service of documents and costs ordered to be paid to another party.

Fee Waiver

In addition, fee waiver does not apply to fees that are not payable under the *Administration of Justice Act*, including:

- fees for bankruptcy proceedings under the *Bankruptcy and Insolvency Act*;
- fees for service of documents;
- fees to mediators for family mediation services;
- costs ordered to be paid to another party;
- federal Central Registry of Divorce Proceedings fee; and
- lawyers' fees.

Section 4 of O. Reg. 2/05 describes persons not eligible for fee waiver and includes:

- a person whose court and/or enforcement fees are being paid by Legal Aid Ontario; and
- a party whose court and/or enforcement fees are being paid by a lawyer under a contingency fee agreement.

A fee waiver request may only be made by an individual, not a business or organization. To request a fee waiver, a person must be:

- a party in a case;
- a person who intends to be a party in a case; or
- a party who will enforce a court of tribunal order.

The individual who is seeking to file a document where a fee is required must either pay the fee or request the fee waiver. Only the individual (i.e. the individual who would normally pay the fee) seeking to file the one document would fill out the request for fee waiver. For example, in the circumstance where there are multiple plaintiffs filing a claim, not all plaintiffs would need to fill out a fee waiver form; only the one plaintiff seeking to file the claim would fill out the request.

If the requestor has or will have:

- a litigation guardian under the *Rules of Civil Procedure* or the *Rules of the Small Claims Court;* or
- a special party representative under the *Family Law Rules*

A person may request a fee waiver:

- before a case has started;
- at any time after it has started; or
- at the enforcement stage.

A person may request a fee waiver in two ways, by completing:

- fee waiver request to registrar, clerk or sheriff (form #FW-A 3 or form #FW-A 6); or

- fee waiver to court (form #FW-A 4 or form #FW-A 7)

A person who has completed a fee waiver request to staff (registrar, clerk or sheriff) must swear to or affirm the information provided in the request.

A person making a request to the court must swear to or affirm an affidavit, which forms part of the fee waiver request to court form.

The fee waiver request may be submitted in person, by the individual or their representative, or by mail. A person may contact the court or enforcement office to ask about other methods to submit a request that may be available (e.g. by fax).

If a fee waiver request relates to a court case, a person will:

- submit the request to staff or a request to the court office in the county, municipality or territorial division where the case was or will be started, or to which the case has been transferred.

If a fee waiver request relates to enforcement of a court order, a person will:

- submit a request to staff of:
  - the office of the court that made the order; or
  - an enforcement office that will enforce the order, depending on where the fee would be paid;

OR

- submit a request to the court to:
  - the office of the court that made the order.

If a fee waiver request is to enforce a tribunal order for an amount within the monetary jurisdiction of the Small Claims Court, a person will:

- submit a request to staff to:
  - an enforcement office that will enforce the order;

OR

- submit a request to the court to:
  - the Small Claims Court office in the county, municipality or territorial division where the tribunal order is to be enforced.

If a fee waiver request is to enforce any other tribunal order, including one that does not order the payment of money, a person will:

- submit a request to staff to:
  - to an enforcement office that will enforce the order;

OR

- submit a request to the court to:
  - the Superior Court of Justice office in the county, municipality or territorial division where the tribunal order is to be enforced.

If a fee waiver request is *to enforce a tribunal order for an amount within the monetary jurisdiction of the Small Claims Court*, a person will:

- Submit a request to staff to:
  - An enforcement office that will enforce the order; or

- Submit a request to the court to:
  - The Small Claims Court office in the county, municipality or territorial division where the tribunal order is to be enforced.

If a fee waiver request is *to enforce any other tribunal order*, including one that does not order the payment of money, a person will:

- Submit a request to staff:
    - To an enforcement office that will enforce the order;

Or

- Submit a request to the court to:
    - The superior Court of Justice office in the county, municipality or territorial division where the tribunal order is to be enforced.

Fee Waiver and Court Interpreter Fees

Court interpreters in civil, family, and Small Claims Court cases will be provided to individuals who have been given a Fee Waiver Certificate and who indicate the need for an interpreter for either themselves or for their witness(es), for all court appearances at which a judicial official presides. The presence and use of the court interpreter in the courtroom remains at the discretion of the presiding judicial official.

Fee Waiver Requests by Persons under Disability and Special Parties, or Minors

If the requestor has or will have:

- A litigation guardian under the *Rules of Civil Procedure* or the *Rules of the Small Claims Court,*

Or

- a special party representative under the *Family Law Rules*

for the proceeding or case for which he or she is seeking fee waiver, his or her request must be completed by that person. If the requestor does not yet have a litigation guardian or special party representative, his or her request must be completed by a person who intends to act as a litigation guardian/special party representative.

What are the Financial Eligibility Criteria?

The financial eligibility criteria are:

1. Your primary source of household income is one or more of:

- income assistance from Ontario Works;
- income support from the Ontario Disability Support Program;
- *Family Benefits Act* allowance;
- Old Age Security Pension together with the Guaranteed Income Supplement;
- War Veterans Allowance; or
- Canada Pension Plan benefits.

OR

2. Your household income and assets are below the following cut-offs:

Number of people in household	Gross monthly household income
1	$1,500
2	$2,250
3	$2,583
4	$3,083
5 or more	$3,583
Household liquid assets:	$1,500

Number of people in household	Gross monthly household income
Household net worth:	$6,000

Those covered by Legal Aid Ontario or who have a contingency-fee agreement with their lawyers are exempt from the fee waiver.

Fee Waiver Criteria on a Request to Staff

A registrar, clerk or sheriff CANNOT give a person a fee waiver certificate if the requestor has checked

"yes" to paragraph 8.

A registrar, clerk or sheriff SHALL give a person a fee waiver certificate if the requestor has checked

"no" to paragraph 8 and

"yes" to paragraph 9.

A registrar, clerk or sheriff SHALL give a person a fee waiver certificate if the requestor has checked

"no" to paragraph 8 and

"no" to paragraph 9; and

- persons in the household is 1 and gross monthly income is less than $1,500
- persons in the household is 2 and gross monthly income is less than $2,250
- persons in the household is 3 and gross monthly income is less than $2,583
- persons in the household is 4 and gross monthly income is less than $3,083
- persons in the household is 5 or more gross monthly income is less than $3,583.

and he or she has checked

"yes" to paragraph 12 and

"yes" to paragraph 13.

Fee Waiver Criteria on a Request to Court

A registrar, clerk or sheriff CANNOT give a person a fee waiver certificate if the requestor has checked

"yes" to paragraph 4.

A registrar, clerk or sheriff SHALL give a person a fee waiver certificate if the requestor has checked

"no" to paragraph 4 and

"yes" to paragraph 5.

A registrar, clerk or sheriff SHALL give a person a fee waiver certificate if the requestor has checked

"no" to paragraph 4 and

"no" to paragraph 5; and

- persons in the household is 1 and gross monthly income is less than $1,500
- persons in the household is 2 and gross monthly income is less than $2,250
- persons in the household is 3 and gross monthly income is less than $2,583
- persons in the household is 4 and gross monthly income is less than $3,083
- persons in the household is 5 or more gross monthly income is less than $3,583.

and he or she has checked

"yes" to paragraph 8 and

"yes" to paragraph 9.

Where is a fee waiver request to be submitted?

If a fee waiver request relates to a court case, a person will:

Submit the request to staff or a request to the county, municipality or territorial division where the case is to be started, or to which the case has been transferred.

If a fee waiver request relates to enforcement of a court order, the person will:

Submit a request to staff to

- the office of the court that made the order,

or

- an enforcement office that will enforce the order, depending on where the fee would be paid;

OR

- submit a request to the court to

— the office of the court that made the order.

If a fee waiver request is to enforce a tribunal order for an amount within the monetary jurisdiction of the Superior Court of Justice, a person will:

Submit a request to staff to

- an enforcement office that will enforce the order;

OR

Submit a request to the court to

- the Superior Court of Justice office in the county, municipality or territorial division where the tribunal order is to be enforced.

If a fee waiver request is to enforce any other tribunal order, including one that does not order the payment of money, a person will:

Submit a request to staff to

- an enforcement office that will enforce the order;

OR

Submit a request to the court to

- the Superior Court of Justice office in the county, municipality or territorial division where the tribunal order is to be enforced.

Effective September 15th, 2005, court interpreters in Small Claims Court cases will be provided for those who have been given a Fee Waiver Certificate and who indicate the need for an interpreter either themselves or for their witness(es), for all court appearances.

Amendments to Fee Waiver Regulation

Amendments to the *Administration of Justice Act* Fee Waiver regulation (O. Reg. 2/05) came into effect December 28, 2005.

For the proceeding or case for which he or she is seeking fee waiver request must be completed by that person. If the requestor does have a litigation guardian or special party representative, his or her request may be completed by a person who intends to act as a litigation guardian or special party representative.

The rule of law was addressed by the B.C. Court of Appeal in *Christie v. British Columbia (Attorney General)*, [2005] B.C.J. No. 2745, 2005 CarswellBC 3040, 48 B.C.L.R. (4th) 267,

[2006] 2 W.W.R. 610, 136 C.R.R. (2d) 323, 2005 BCCA 631, 262 D.L.R. (4th) 51, 220 B.C.A.C. 165, 362 W.A.C. 165 (B.C. C.A.); additional reasons 2006 CarswellBC 286, 48 B.C.L.R. (4th) 322, 263 D.L.R. (4th) 582, [2006] 3 W.W.R. 437, 2006 BCCA 59, 222 B.C.A.C. 150, 368 W.A.C. 150 (B.C. C.A.). The court struck down the *Social Services Tax Amendment Act (No. 2)*, 1993, S.B.C. c. 24, which imposed a 7 per cent tax on fees billed for legal services. The basis for the decision was that the legislation offended the principle of access to justice as an element of the rule of law. The court held that the tax impeded all persons trying to access legal assistance. To the extent that the legislation purported to tax these services, it was held to be unconstitutional. Contrast with *British Columbia v. Imperial Tobacco Canada Ltd.*, EYB 2005-95296, 2005 CarswellBC 2207, 2005 CarswellBC 2208, [2004] S.C.C.A. No. 302, 45 B.C.L.R. (4th) 1, [2005] 2 S.C.R. 473, 134 C.R.R. (2d) 46, 2005 SCC 49, 257 D.L.R. (4th) 193, [2006] 1 W.W.R. 201, 218 B.C.A.C. 1, 359 W.A.C. 1, 339 N.R. 129, 27 C.P.C. (6th) 13 (S.C.C.). Major J. considered it difficult to conceive that the rule of law could ever be used to invalidate legislation.

Christie was subsequently reversed by the Supreme Court of Canada: [2007] S.C.J. No. 21, 2007 CarswellBC 1117, 2007 CarswellBC 1118, (sub nom. *British Columbia (Attorney General) v. Christie*) 2007 D.T.C. 5525 (Eng.), (sub nom. *British Columbia (Attorney General) v. Christie*) 2007 D.T.C. 5229 (Fr.), 240 B.C.A.C. 1, 398 W.A.C. 1, (sub nom. *British Columbia (Attorney General) v. Christie*) 2007 G.T.C. 1493 (Fr.), 66 B.C.L.R. (4th) 1, 361 N.R. 322, (sub nom. *British Columbia (Attorney General) v. Christie*) 2007 G.T.C. 1488 (Eng.), 2007 SCC 21, 280 D.L.R. (4th) 528, [2007] 8 W.W.R. 64, (sub nom. *British Columbia (Attorney General) v. Christie*) [2007] 1 S.C.R. 873, (sub nom. *British Columbia (Attorney General) v. Christie*) 155 C.R.R. (2d) 366 (S.C.C.).

In *Murphy v. Wynne*, 2007 CarswellBC 603, 2007 BCCA 156 (B.C. C.A.), proceedings in *forma pauperis*.

Case Law: *Joubarne v. Loodu*, 2005 CarswellBC 2222, 2005 BCSC 1340 (B.C. S.C.), Madam Justice Arnold-Bailey. Standard of review applicable to small claims appeal. See *IBI Group v. LeFevre & Co. Property Agents Ltd.*, [2004] B.C.J. No. 433, 2004 CarswellBC 506, 33 C.L.R. (3d) 302, 2004 BCSC 298 (B.C. S.C.), at para. 16:

> The test applied on an appeal from Provincial Court pursuant to s. 12 of the *Small Claims Act* is whether trial judge was "clearly wrong" on the facts or law. It is akin to standard applied by Court of Appeal, which provides that findings of fact made at trial, though not immutable, are not to be reversed unless it can be established that trial judge made some palpable and overriding error which affected his or her assessment of facts. Duty to re-examine evidence in order to be satisfied that no such error occurred, but not to substitute own assessment on balance of probabilities.

Appeal allowed against respondent company and respondent, Sital Loodu, in his personal capacity.

Mackay Homes v. North Bay (City), 2005 CarswellOnt 910, 6 M.P.L.R. (4th) 44 (Ont. S.C.J.) at para. 15, Bolan J. [For the purposes of s. 3(1) para. 12 of the *Assessment Act*, R.S.O. 1990, c. A.31 . . .] the term "poor" is a relative term and that, while the persons who benefit need not be destitute there must be an element of economic deprivation or need, the relief from which is a part of the purpose of the institution claiming the exemption. "Relief of the poor" must be read in the concept of our complex, multicultural society and current concerns about relieving poverty.

Baird v. R., 2006 CarswellNat 1729, 2006 CarswellNat 3599, 2006 FCA 183, 2006 CAF 183 (F.C.A.), J.D.D. Pelletier J.A.

Motion for order for financial aid for self-represented impecunious litigant. Impecuniosity and belief in justness of cause not sufficient grounds.

Kuntz v. Canadian Medical Protective Assn., 2006 CarswellBC 933, 2006 BCCA 188 (B.C. C.A. [In Chambers]), Lowry J.A.

Physician applied for order granting him indigent status. Application dismissed. Material filed in support of application scant and disclosed little more than that physician had been unemployed for 20 years and had pension of $321 monthly, but had expenses of $1,900 monthly. Although physician appeared impecunious, he also appeared able to find financial assistance on which to live and to litigate. It could not be said that informed person, viewing position of judge realistically and practically, could reasonably conclude that application would not be decided fairly.

Burrell v. Peel (Regional Municipality) Police Services Board, [2007] O.J. No. 4232, 2007 CarswellOnt 6992, 48 C.P.C. (6th) 349 (Ont. Master), Master R. Dash; additional reasons at (2007), 2007 CarswellOnt 7767 (Ont. Master); affirmed (2008), 2008 CarswellOnt 8173, 66 C.P.C. (6th) 223 (Ont. S.C.J.); leave to appeal refused (2008), 2008 CarswellOnt 8050 (Ont. Div. Ct.); affirmed (2008), 2008 CarswellOnt 8173, 66 C.P.C. (6th) 223 (Ont. S.C.J.).

Motion by defendants to dismiss, or alternatively stay, the action for failure to pay two costs orders pursuant to Rules 57.03(2) and 60.12. Plaintiff impecunious and raises issues of access to justice.

See *Baksh v. Sun Media (Toronto) Corp.*, 2003 CarswellOnt 24, [2003] O.J. No. 68, 63 O.R. (3d) 51 (Ont. Master) at para. 19. Quoted with approval of *Schaer v. Barrie Yacht Club*, [2003] O.J. No. 4171, 2003 CarswellOnt 4009 (Ont. S.C.J.); *R. v. Briggs*, [2001] O.J. No. 685, 2001 CarswellOnt 536, 53 O.R. (3d) 124, 142 O.A.C. 41 (Ont. C.A.) at p. 126 (O.R.); *Household Trust Co. v. Golden Horse Farms Inc.*, 1992 CarswellBC 83, 65 B.C.L.R. (2d) 355, 13 B.C.A.C. 302, 24 W.A.C. 302 (B.C. C.A.) at p. 362 (B.C.L.R.); *Bottan v. Vroom*, 2001 CarswellOnt 2382, [2001] O.J. No. 2737 (Ont. S.C.J.); affirmed 2002 CarswellOnt 1044, [2002] O.J. No. 1383 (Ont. C.A.); *Myers v. Metropolitan Toronto (Municipality) Police Force*, 1995 CarswellOnt 152, [1995] O.J. No. 1321, 37 C.P.C. (3d) 349, (sub nom. *Myers v. Metropolitan Toronto (Municipality) Chief of Police*) 125 D.L.R. (4th) 184, (sub nom. *Myers v. Metropolitan Toronto Chief of Police*) 84 O.A.C. 232 (Ont. Div. Ct.) (headnote); *Heu v. Forder Estate*, [2004] O.J. No. 705, 2004 CarswellOnt 729 (Ont. Master) at paras. 19, 20, 22; *Mugenzi v. R.*, 2006 CarswellOnt 6720, [2006] O.J. No. 4355 (Ont. Master) at para. 11; *Abbott v. Reuter-Stokes Canada Ltd.*, 1988 CarswellOnt 520, 32 C.P.C. (2d) 161 (Ont. H.C.) at para. 162; *Burrell v. Peel (Regional Municipality) Police Services Board*, supra, at para. 8; *Myers v. Metropolitan Toronto (Municipality) Police Force*, supra, paras. 9 and 22.

Action stayed on conditions. If the stay is not lifted within six months of the date endorsement released, the defendants may move to dismiss the action.

Jakob v. Jakob, 2007 CarswellBC 1372, 2007 BCCA 332 (B.C. C.A. [In Chambers]), Chiasson J.A.

Husband brought application for indigent status in protracted and bitter matrimonial dispute. Application dismissed. Jurisprudence showed that criteria for application were likelihood of success of appeal and financial position of husband and that application would be refused if no reasonable prospect of appeal's success existed.

Zeitoun v. Economical Insurance Group (2008), [2008] O.J. No. 1771, 2008 CarswellOnt 2576, 236 O.A.C. 76, 64 C.C.L.I. (4th) 52, 53 C.P.C. (6th) 308, 292 D.L.R. (4th) 313, 91 O.R. (3d) 131 (Ont. Div. Ct.); additional reasons at (2008), 2008 CarswellOnt 3734, 56 C.P.C. (6th) 191, 64 C.C.L.I. (4th) 68 (Ont. Div. Ct.); affirmed [2009] O.J. No. 2003, 2009 CarswellOnt 2665, 73 C.C.L.I. (4th) 255, 2009 ONCA 415, 73 C.P.C. (6th) 8, 307 D.L.R. (4th) 218, 96 O.R. (3d) 639 (Ont. C.A.).

On appeal, the motions judge treated the appeal from order of master as a de novo hearing and set aside the order for security for costs made by master. The defendant appealed. Appeal allowed.

The decision of master should only be interfered with if master made error of law or exercised his or her discretion on wrong principles or misapprehended evidence such that there was palpable and overriding error. The motions judge erred in substituting his view of the evidence for that of the master.

Where impecuniosity has not been shown, a legitimate factor in deciding whether or not it would be just to require security for costs is whether the claim has a good chance of success. The master's exercise of discretion to order security for costs was supportable on the evidence and based on correct principles.

B.C.G.E.U., Re, [1988] S.C.J. No. 76, 1988 CarswellBC 762, 1988 CarswellBC 363, EYB 1988-67021, (sub nom. *B.C.G.E.U. v. British Columbia (Attorney General))* [1988] 6 W.W.R. 577, 30 C.P.C. (2d) 221, [1988] 2 S.C.R. 214, 220 A.P.R. 93, 53 D.L.R. (4th) 1, 87 N.R. 241, 31 B.C.L.R. (2d) 273, 71 Nfld. & P.E.I.R. 93, 44 C.C.C. (3d) 289, 88 C.L.L.C. 14,047 (S.C.C.) at 229-230 [S.C.R.].

The right of access to justice is protected by the rule of law, an unwritten principle of Canada's constitution. See also *Canadian Council of Churches v. R.* (1992), 49 F.T.R. 160 (note), 1992 CarswellNat 25, EYB 1992-67212, [1992] S.C.J. No. 5, 1992 CarswellNat 650, (sub nom. *Canadian Council of Churches v. Canada (Minister of Employment & Immigration))* [1992] 1 S.C.R. 236, (sub nom. *Canadian Council of Churches v. Canada (Minister of Employment & Immigration))* 8 C.R.R. (2d) 145, 16 Imm. L.R. (2d) 161, (sub nom. *Canadian Council of Churches v. Canada)* 88 D.L.R. (4th) 193, 2 Admin. L.R. (2d) 229, 5 C.P.C. (3d) 20, (sub nom. *Canadian Council of Churches v. Canada)* 132 N.R. 241 (S.C.C.), where the Supreme Court of Canada described (in the context of a decision on public interest standing) at para. 35 that "[i]t is essential that a balance be struck between ensuring access to the courts and preserving judicial resources. It would be disastrous if the courts were allowed to become hopelessly overburdened as a result of the unnecessary proliferation of marginal or redundant suits."

John Carten Personal Law Corp. v. British Columbia (Attorney General) (1997), 98 G.T.C. 6053, 161 W.A.C. 1, 98 B.C.A.C. 1, 48 C.R.R. (2d) 12, 40 B.C.L.R. (3d) 181, [1998] 3 W.W.R. 571, [1997] B.C.J. No. 2460, 153 D.L.R. (4th) 460, 1997 CarswellBC 2290 (B.C. C.A.); leave to appeal refused 196 W.A.C. 121 (note), 120 B.C.A.C. 121 (note), 55 C.R.R. (2d) 375 (note), 232 N.R. 198 (note), [1998] S.C.C.A. No. 205, [1998] 2 S.C.R. viii (note) (S.C.C.)

Applicant applied for declaration that imposition of seven-percent tax on legal services unconstitutional. Petition dismissed. Applicant appealed. Appeal dismissed. Applicant's *Charter* arguments could not be sustained because of lack of proof that rights of access to the courts, to justice or to legal services have been denied by the tax. What was required would be proof that people who would have been able to exercise the legal rights in question if the tax were not in effect were prevented by the tax from exercising those rights.

Hawkes v. Prince Edward Island (Human Rights Commission), 794 A.P.R. 115, 262 Nfld. & P.E.I.R. 115, 151 C.R.R. (2d) 243, 2007 PESCAD 1, 2007 CarswellPEI 1 (P.E.I. C.A.); leave to appeal refused (2007), 156 C.R.R. (2d) 374 (note), 856 A.P.R. 44 (note), 279 Nfld. & P.E.I.R. 44 (note), 374 N.R. 400 (note), 2007 CarswellPEI 42, 2007 CarswellPEI 41 (S.C.C.)

Applicant applied unsuccessfully for order appointing state-funded counsel to assist her in her application for judicial review of decision of the Prince Edward Island Human Rights Commission. Applicant appealed. Appeal dismissed. Denial of state-funded counsel did not threaten her rights under s. 7 of the *Canadian Charter of Rights and Freedoms*. Leave to appeal to the S.C.C., dated January 4, 2007, dismissed, No. 31900, July 5, 2007, Bastarache, LeBel and Fish JJ.

See also *New Brunswick (Minister of Health & Community Services) v. G. (J.)*, 26 C.R. (5th) 203, [1999] S.C.J. No. 47, 177 D.L.R. (4th) 124, 244 N.R. 276, 1999 CarswellNB 306, 1999 CarswellNB 305, REJB 1999-14250, 7 B.H.R.C. 615, [1999] 3 S.C.R. 46, 552 A.P.R. 25, 216 N.B.R. (2d) 25, 50 R.F.L. (4th) 63, 66 C.R.R. (2d) 267 (S.C.C.). Appellant did not establish required criteria for right to state-funded counsel according to the *G.(J.)* case.

D. (P.) v. British Columbia, 210 C.R.R. (2d) 1, 2010 CarswellBC 571, 2010 BCSC 290, 82 R.F.L. (6th) 180, 7 B.C.L.R. (5th) 312, [2010] B.C.J. No. 405 (B.C. S.C.)

No general right to state-funded counsel. See *Christie v. British Columbia (Attorney General)*, 155 C.R.R. (2d) 366, [2007] 1 S.C.R. 873, [2007] 8 W.W.R. 64, 280 D.L.R. (4th) 528, 2007 CarswellBC 1118, 2007 CarswellBC 1117, 2007 SCC 21, [2007] S.C.J. No. 21, 2007 G.T.C. 1488 (Eng.), 361 N.R. 322, 66 B.C.L.R. (4th) 1, 2007 G.T.C. 1493 (Fr.), 398 W.A.C. 1, 240 B.C.A.C. 1, 2007 D.T.C. 5229 (Fr.), 2007 D.T.C. 5525 (Eng.) (S.C.C.). Trial process is stressful for most self-represented litigants. See *Blencoe v. British Columbia (Human Rights Commission)*, [2000] 2 S.C.R. 307, 231 W.A.C. 161, 141 B.C.A.C. 161, 77 C.R.R. (2d) 189, REJB 2000-20288, 260 N.R. 1, 2000 C.L.L.C. 230-040, 23 Admin. L.R. (3d) 175, [2000] S.C.J. No. 43, [2000] 10 W.W.R. 567, 190 D.L.R. (4th) 513, 81 B.C.L.R. (3d) 1, 38 C.H.R.R. D/153, 3 C.C.E.L. (3d) 165, 2000 CarswellBC 1861, 2000 CarswellBC 1860, 2000 SCC 44 (S.C.C.) and *Barrett v. Layton*, [2003] O.J. No. 5572, 69 O.R. (3d) 384, 2003 CarswellOnt 5602 (Ont. S.C.J.) at pp. 391-2.

Toronto Dominion Bank v. Beaton, 2012 ABQB 125, 2012 CarswellAlta 369, 534 A.R. 132, 23 C.P.C. (7th) 303 (Alta. Q.B.), Madam Justice J.B. Veit.

Asserting that he is impecunious, and relying on the fact that other judges of this court have given him an order of the same type that he is requesting today, Mr. Beaton asks the court to order the Transcript Service of the Alberta Government to provide him with a free transcript of court proceedings.

The court concluded it does have jurisdiction to make an order of the type requested: a procedure to obtain waiver of court fees which does not take into account the merits of the underlying application in addition to the applicant's financial circumstances breaches the applicant's constitutional right to access to justice.

Assuming that it does have the authority to make the order requested, and assuming that Mr. Beaton is impecunious. The court concludes that this is not an appropriate situation in which to exercise its discretion: in the court's opinion, Mr. Beaton does not have a meritorious appeal to the Supreme Court of Canada from a decision of our Court of Appeal.

See *Polewsky v. Home Hardware Stores Ltd.*, 2003 CarswellOnt 2755, 66 O.R. (3d) 600, 34 C.P.C. (5th) 334, 229 D.L.R. (4th) 308, 109 C.R.R. (2d) 189, 174 O.A.C. 358, [2003] O.J. No. 2908 (Ont. Div. Ct.); leave to appeal allowed 2004 CarswellOnt 763, [2004] O.J. No. 954 (Ont. C.A.); *Purtle v. Novak* (October 18, 2010), Doc. 1091/10, 1129/10, 1090/10, 1111/10, [2010] O.J. No. 4401 (Ont. S.C.J.); *British Columbia (Minister of Forests) v. Okanagan Indian Band* (2003), 2003 SCC 71, 2003 CarswellBC 3040, 2003 CarswellBC 3041, [2003] 3 S.C.R. 371, 21 B.C.L.R. (4th) 209, 43 C.P.C. (5th) 1, 233 D.L.R. (4th) 577, [2004] 2 W.W.R. 252, 189 B.C.A.C. 161, [2004] 1 C.N.L.R. 7, 114 C.R.R. (2d) 108, 313 N.R. 84, 309 W.A.C. 161, [2003] S.C.J. No. 76 (S.C.C.)

In other words, *Polewski* makes a very strong argument that, in some situations, the common law historically, and the Charter today, makes access to justice a constitutional right.

Somewhat similar comments to those in *Polewski* concerning the necessity for proof of a meritorious claim were made in *Purtle*:

> The last substantive issue is the question of the Fee Waiver which Mr. Purtle obtained from the court clerk pursuant to rule 4.3 of the *Administration of Justice Act*, R.S.O. 1990, c. A.6. Mr. Purtle conceded that if these actions were dismissed, there was no purpose in maintaining his Fee Waiver. Accordingly I struck out the fee waiver.
>
> I observe that there is an unfortunate distinction under that Act, as between requests for Fee Waiver which are determined by the court staff, and requests which are determined by a judge. When a request is made to a judge, the request may be denied, among other grounds, if the judge is not satisfied, under s. 4.4(7) para. 2, that:
>
>> Commencing, defending, continuing or intervening in the proceeding, as the case may be, is not frivolous, vexatious or otherwise an abuse of the process of the court.

Application to have the court waive the court fees applying to transcripts denied.

R. v. W. (J.), 2013 ONCA 723, 2013 CarswellOnt 16201, [2013] O.J. No. 5451 (Ont. C.A.)

Applicant, J.W., sought order that court reporter, produce transcripts at the rate of $0.55 per page for the purposes of perfecting appeal. Request on fact that complete transcripts already produced at trial, and at the time of production rates of $3.20 per page for original transcripts and $0.55 per page for copies were paid to the reporter.

This application involves the interpretation of O. Reg. 587/91, made under the *Administration of Justice Act*, R.S.O. 1990, c. A.6, which deals with the fees payable to court reporters and court monitors for a simple copy of a transcript of evidence for the purpose of reproduction in an appeal to the Court of Appeal. One of the objectives of the justice system is to be accessible to litigants who are before the courts. The most effective way of achieving this goal is for the justice system to allow parties to litigate issues at a reasonable cost. See Simmons J.A. in *R. v. Papadopoulos*, 2004 CarswellOnt 4564, 73 O.R. (3d) 258, 190 C.C.C. (3d) 359, 191 O.A.C. 341, [2004] O.J. No. 4546 (Ont. C.A. [In Chambers]) at para. 21:

> For transcripts prepared for the Court of Appeal, the court reporter is entitled to and shall be paid a fee of $3.75 per original page. However, if the transcript has previously been transcribed and produced at the lower court level for any reason, the reporter is entitled to charge, for an appeal, $0.55 per page per copy for portions previously transcribed, and $3.75 per page for any portions not previously transcribed. If the transcript has already been typed but requires substantial changes, the reporter may charge the one-time fee of $3.75 per page for pages requiring substantial changes.

ONT. REG. 94/14 — FEES FOR COURT TRANSCRIPTS

made under the *Administration of Justice Act*

O. Reg. 94/14

1. Definitions — In this Regulation,

"authorized court transcriptionist" means a member of a class of persons authorized by the Attorney General to transcribe recordings;

"recording" means a recording made under subsection 5(1) of the *Evidence Act* of a court proceeding or of evidence in a court proceeding.

2. Fees for court transcripts — The following fees are payable to an authorized court transcriptionist:

TABLE

Item	Service	Fee
1.	To transcribe all or part of a recording and produce a first certified copy of a transcript	$4.30 per page or $20.00, whichever is greater
2.	To transcribe all or part of a recording and produce a first certified copy of a transcript, to be provided within five business days	$6.00 per page or $20.00, whichever is greater
3.	To transcribe all or part of a recording and produce a first certified copy of a transcript, to be provided within 24 hours	$8.00 per page or $20.00, whichever is greater
4.	For any additional certified copy of the transcript, in printed format	$.55 per page or $20.00, whichever is greater
5.	For an electronic copy of the transcript, requested at the same time as a request for item 1, 2, 3 or 4	No charge
6.	For an electronic copy of the transcript, requested at any other time	$20.00

3. Transcripts for judges — Fees payable under section 2 for transcripts requested by a judge for the judge's own use shall be paid by the Province of Ontario.

4. Revocation — Ontario Regulation 587/91 is revoked.

5. Commencement — This Regulation comes into force on the later of May 1, 2014 and the day it is filed.

5 — COURT FORMS IN SMALL CLAIMS COURT

SCHEDULE 1 — FORMS

Note that publicly-available electronic versions of all the Small Claims Court Forms are available in both PDF and Word format at www.ontariocourtforms.on.ca and may be downloaded free of charge.

Table of Forms

See Sched. 1.

Form Number	Form Title	Date of Form
1A	Additional Parties	June 1, 2009
1A.1	Additional Debtors	June 1, 2009
1B	Request for Telephone or Video Conference	September 1, 2010
4A	Consent to Act as Litigation Guardian	June 1, 2013
5A	Notice to Alleged Partner	June 1, 2009
7A	Plaintiff's Claim	January 7, 2014
8A	Affidavit of Service	June 1, 2013
9A	Defence	January 7, 2014
9B	Request to Clerk	June 1, 2009
10A	Defendant's Claim	January 7, 2014
11A	Affidavit for Jurisdiction	June 1, 2009
11B	Default Judgment	September 1, 2010
11.2A	Request for Clerk's Order on Consent	June 1, 2009
11.3A	Notice of Discontinued Claim	September 1, 2010
13A	List of Proposed Witnesses	June 1, 2009
13B	Consent	September 1, 2010
14A	Offer to Settle	June 1, 2009
14B	Acceptance of Offer to Settle	June 1, 2009
14C	Notice of Withdrawal of Offer to Settle	June 1, 2009
14D	Terms of Settlement	June 1, 2009
15A	Notice of Motion and Supporting Affidavit	September 1, 2010
15B	Affidavit	June 1, 2009
18A	Summons to Witness	June 1, 2009

Form Number	Form Title	Date of Form
18B	Warrant for Arrest of Defaulting Witness	June 1, 2009
20A	Certificate of Judgment	September 1, 2010
20B	Writ of Delivery	June 1, 2009
20C	Writ of Seizure and Sale of Personal Property	June 1, 2009
20D	Writ of Seizure and Sale of Land	June 1, 2009
20E	Notice of Garnishment	September 1, 2010
20E.1	Notice of Renewal of Garnishment	September 1, 2010
20F	Garnishee's Statement	April 11, 2012
20G	Notice to Co-owner of Debt	September 1, 2010
20H	Notice of Examination	April 11, 2012
20I	Financial Information Form	April 11, 2012
20J	Warrant of Committal	September 1, 2010
20K	Identification Form	June 1, 2009
20L	Notice of Default of Payment	June 1, 2009
20M	Affidavit of Default of Payment	April 11, 2012
20N	Request to Renew Writ of Seizure and Sale	June 1, 2009
20O	Direction to Enforce Writ of Seizure and Sale of Personal Property	June 1, 2009
20P	Affidavit for Enforcement Request	June 1, 2009
20Q	Notice of Garnishment Hearing	September 1, 2010
20R	Notice of Termination of Garnishment	September 1, 2010

Non-Prescribed Forms — Computer Generated (not publicly available)

Form Title
Notice of Approaching Dismissal (2 years)
Notice of Approaching Dismissal (Defended)
Notice of Approaching Dismissal (Undefended)
Notice of Assessment Hearing
Notice of Contempt Hearing
Notice of Contempt Hearing before a Superior Court Judge
Notice of Settlement Conference
Notice of Terms of Payment Hearing
Notice of Trial
Notice to set Action Down for trial
Order Dismissing Claim as Abandoned (2 years)
Order Dismissing Claim as Abandoned (Defended)
Order Dismissing Claim as Abandoned (Undefended)

Form Title
Request to Pay Money into or out of Court
Termination of Consolidation Order
Settlement Conference Memorandum
Endorsement Record/Order of the Court

ONTARIO
Superior Court of Justice
Cour supérieure de justice

PAGE 1A

Additional Parties
Parties additionnelles
Form / Formule 1A Ont. Reg. No. / Régl. de l'Ont. : 258/98

Claim No. / Nº de la demande _____

☐ **Plaintiff No. / *Demandeur nº*** _____ ☐ **Defendant No. / *Défendeur nº*** _____

Last name, or name of company / Nom de famille ou nom de la compagnie		
First name / Premier prénom	Second name / Deuxième prénom	Also known as / Également connu(e) sous le nom de
Address (street number, apt., unit) / Adresse (numéro et rue, app., unité)		
City/Town / Cité/ville	Province	Phone no. / Nº de téléphone
Postal code / Code postal		Fax no. / Nº de télécopieur
Representative / Représentant(e)		LSUC # / Nº du BHC
Address (street number, apt., unit) / Adresse (numéro et rue, app., unité)		
City/Town / Cité/ville	Province	Phone no. / Nº de téléphone
Postal code / Code postal		Fax no. / Nº de télécopieur

☐ **Plaintiff No. / *Demandeur nº*** _____ ☐ **Defendant No. / *Défendeur nº*** _____

Last name, or name of company / Nom de famille ou nom de la compagnie		
First name / Premier prénom	Second name / Deuxième prénom	Also known as / Également connu(e) sous le nom de
Address (street number, apt., unit) / Adresse (numéro et rue, app., unité)		
City/Town / Cité/ville	Province	Phone no. / Nº de téléphone
Postal code / Code postal		Fax no. / Nº de télécopieur
Representative / Représentant(e)		LSUC # / Nº du BHC
Address (street number, apt., unit) / Adresse (numéro et rue, app., unité)		
City/Town / Cité/ville	Province	Phone no. / Nº de téléphone
Postal code / Code postal		Fax no. / Nº de télécopieur

☐ **Plaintiff No. / *Demandeur nº*** _____ ☐ **Defendant No. / *Défendeur nº*** _____

Last name, or name of company / Nom de famille ou nom de la compagnie		
First name / Premier prénom	Second name / Deuxième prénom	Also known as / Également connu(e) sous le nom de
Address (street number, apt., unit) / Adresse (numéro et rue, app., unité)		
City/Town / Cité/ville	Province	Phone no. / Nº de téléphone
Postal code / Code postal		Fax no. / Nº de télécopieur
Representative / Représentant(e)		LSUC # / Nº du BHC
Address (street number, apt., unit) / Adresse (numéro et rue, app., unité)		
City/Town / Cité/ville	Province	Phone no. / Nº de téléphone
Postal code / Code postal		Fax no. / Nº de télécopieur

SCR 1.05-1A (June 1, 2009 / 1ᵉʳ juin 2009) CSD

ONTARIO
Superior Court of Justice
Cour supérieure de justice

Additional Debtors
Débiteurs additionnels
Form / Formule 1A.1 Ont. Reg. No. / Régl. de l'Ont. : 258/98

Claim No. / N° de la demande

If a debtor has "also known as names", list each also known as name in a separate set of boxes below. / *Si un débiteur a d'autres noms sous lesquels il est également connu, indiquez chacun de ces noms ci-dessous dans un ensemble séparé de cases.*

Last name of debtor, or name of company / Nom de famille du débiteur/de la débitrice ou nom de la compagnie		
First name / Premier prénom	Second name / Deuxième prénom	Third name / Troisième prénom

Last name of debtor, or name of company / Nom de famille du débiteur/de la débitrice ou nom de la compagnie		
First name / Premier prénom	Second name / Deuxième prénom	Third name / Troisième prénom

Last name of debtor, or name of company / Nom de famille du débiteur/de la débitrice ou nom de la compagnie		
First name / Premier prénom	Second name / Deuxième prénom	Third name / Troisième prénom

Last name of debtor, or name of company / Nom de famille du débiteur/de la débitrice ou nom de la compagnie		
First name / Premier prénom	Second name / Deuxième prénom	Third name / Troisième prénom

Last name of debtor, or name of company / Nom de famille du débiteur/de la débitrice ou nom de la compagnie		
First name / Premier prénom	Second name / Deuxième prénom	Third name / Troisième prénom

Last name of debtor, or name of company / Nom de famille du débiteur/de la débitrice ou nom de la compagnie		
First name / Premier prénom	Second name / Deuxième prénom	Third name / Troisième prénom

Last name of debtor, or name of company / Nom de famille du débiteur/de la débitrice ou nom de la compagnie		
First name / Premier prénom	Second name / Deuxième prénom	Third name / Troisième prénom

SCR 1A.1 (June 1, 2009 / 1er juin 2009) CSD

ONTARIO

Superior Court of Justice
Cour supérieure de justice

Request for Telephone or Video Conference
Demande de conférence téléphonique ou de vidéoconférence
Form / Formule 1B Ont. Reg. No. / Règl. de l'Ont. : 258/98

Small Claims Court / Cour des petites créances de

Claim No. / N° de la demande

Address / Adresse

Phone number / Numéro de téléphone

BETWEEN / ENTRE

Plaintiff(s) / Demandeur(s)/demanderesse(s)

and / et

Defendant(s) / Défendeur(s)/défenderesse(s)

TO THE CLERK OF THE_____ **SMALL CLAIMS COURT:**
AU GREFFIER DE LA COUR (Name of Small Claims Court location / Emplacement de la Cour
DES PETITES CRÉANCES DE des petites créances)

My name is_____ **and I request the court schedule the:**
Je m'appelle (Name of requesting party / Nom de la partie requérante) *et je demande au tribunal de tenir :*

(Check appropriate box(es). /
Cochez la ou les cases appropriées.)

☐ settlement conference
   la conférence en vue d'une transaction

☐ motion
   l'audition de la motion

☐ examination of a debtor or other person *(examination of a debtor or other person
   cannot be conducted by telephone conference)*
   l'interrogatoire d'un débiteur ou d'une autre personne (l'interrogatoire d'un
   débiteur ou d'une autre personne ne peut être mené par conférence téléphonique)

in this case to be heard by
dans la présente cause par

☐ telephone conference
   conférence téléphonique

☐ video conference
   vidéoconférence

where facilities are available and the court permits it.
si des installations sont disponibles et que le tribunal le permet.

My current telephone number is_____
Mon numéro de téléphone actuel est le (Telephone number with area code / Numéro de téléphone avec l'indicatif régional)

Where a judge directs a telephone or video conference, the clerk will make the necessary arrangements and
notify the parties of them [R. 1.07(5)].
*Lorsqu'un juge ordonne la tenue d'une conférence téléphonique ou d'une vidéoconférence, le greffier prend les
dispositions nécessaires à cette fin et en avise les parties [par. 1.07 (5)].*

SCR 1.07-1B (September 1, 2010 / 1er septembre 2010) CSD

FORM / *FORMULE* 1B   PAGE 2

Claim No. / *N° de la demande*

The reasons for my request are as follows:
Les motifs de ma demande sont les suivants :

_____
_____
_____
_____
_____
_____
_____

_____ , 20 ____

(Signature of party or representative / *Signature de la partie/du (de la)*
représentant(e))

NOTE: If you are requesting that a motion be heard by telephone or video conference, file this request together with your Notice of Motion and Supporting Affidavit (Form 15A) OR together with a copy of the Notice of Motion and Supporting Affidavit served on you by the opposing party.

REMARQUE :   *Si vous demandez qu'une motion soit entendue par conférence téléphonique ou par vidéoconférence, déposez la présente demande conjointement avec votre avis de motion et affidavit à l'appui (formule 15A) OU conjointement avec une copie de l'avis de motion et affidavit à l'appui qui vous a été signifié par la partie qui s'y oppose.*

DISPOSITION: *(The judge will complete this section. / Partie à remplir par le juge.)*
DÉCISION :

Order to go as follows:
Ordonnance de procéder comme suit :

_____
_____
_____
_____
_____
_____
_____
_____
_____
_____
_____
_____
_____
_____
_____

_____ , 20 ____

(Signature of judge / *Signature du juge*)

SCR 1.07-1B (September 1, 2010 / *1ᵉʳ septembre 2010*) CSD

ONTARIO

Superior Court of Justice
Cour supérieure de justice

Consent to Act as Litigation Guardian
Consentement pour agir en qualité de tuteur à l'instance
Form / Formule 4A Ont. Reg. No. / Régl. de l'Ont. : 258/98

Small Claims Court / *Cour des petites créances de*

Claim No. / *N° de la demande*

Address / *Adresse*

Phone number / *Numéro de téléphone*

BETWEEN / ENTRE

Plaintiff(s) / *Demandeur(s)/demanderesse(s)*

and / et

Defendant(s) / *Défendeur(s)/défenderesse(s)*

My name is **Je m'appelle**	Name / *Nom*
And I live at **et j'habite à**	Street and number / *Numéro et rue*
	City, province, postal code / *Ville, province, code postal*
	Phone number and fax number / *Numéro de téléphone et numéro de télécopieur*

1. I consent to act as litigation guardian in this action for the
   Je consens à agir à titre de tuteur à l'instance dans la présente action au nom du

   ☐ plaintiff, named
   demandeur suivant : _____ (Name of plaintiff / *Nom du demandeur/de la demanderesse*)

(Check one box only. / *Cochez une seule case.*)

   and I acknowledge that I may be personally responsible for any costs awarded against me or against this person.
   et je reconnais que je peux être tenu(e) personnellement responsable des dépens auxquels moi-même ou cette personne pourrions être condamné(e)s.

   ☐ defendant, named
   défendeur suivant : _____ (Name of defendant / *Nom du défendeur/de la défenderesse*)

2. The above-named person is under the following disability:
   La personne susmentionnée est incapable parce qu'elle est :

   ☐ a minor whose birth date is _____
   un mineur dont la date de naissance est le (State date of birth of minor / *Indiquez la date de naissance du mineur*)

(Check appropriate box(es). / *Cochez la ou les cases appropriées.*)

   ☐ mentally incapable within the meaning of Section 6 or Section 45 of the *Substitute Decisions Act, 1992* in respect of an issue in a proceeding.
   mentalement incapable au sens de l'article 6 ou 45 de la Loi de 1992 sur la prise de décisions au nom d'autrui à l'égard d'une question dans une instance.

   ☐ an absentee within the meaning of the *Absentees Act.*
   une personne absente au sens de la Loi sur les absents.

SCR 4.01-4.02-4A (June 1, 2009 / 1er juin 2009) CSD

Court Forms in Small Claims Court

Claim No. / *N° de la demande*

3. My relationship to the person under disability is:
   Mon lien de parenté avec l'incapable est le suivant :
   (State your relationship to the person under disability. / Indiquez votre lien de parenté avec l'incapable.)

_____
_____
_____
_____
_____
_____
_____
_____

4. I have no interest in this action contrary to that of the person under disability.
   Je n'ai dans la présente action aucun intérêt opposé à celui de l'incapable.

5. I am
   Je

(Check one
box only. /
Cochez une
seule case.)

☐ represented and have given written authority to _____
    suis représenté(e) et j'ai autorisé par écrit :   (Name of lawyer/agent with authority to act in this
                                        proceeding / *Nom de l'avocat/du mandataire autorisé à*
                                             agir dans la présente instance)

    of _____
    de   (Address for service / *Adresse aux fins de signification)*

    _____
    (Phone number and fax number / *Numéro de téléphone et numéro de télécopieur)*

    to act in this proceeding.
    à agir dans la présente instance.

☐ not represented by a lawyer/agent.
    ne suis pas représenté(e) par un avocat/un mandataire.

_____ , 20 _____

_____
(Signature of litigation guardian consenting / *Signature du*
tuteur à l'instance qui consent)

_____
(Signature of witness / *Signature du témoin)*

_____
(Name of witness / *Nom du témoin)*

NOTE:	Within seven (7) calendar days of changing your address for service, notify the court and all other parties in writing.
REMARQUE :	*Dans les sept (7) jours civils qui suivent tout changement de votre adresse aux fins de signification, veuillez en aviser par écrit le tribunal et les autres parties.*

SCR 4.01-4.02-4A (June 1, 2009 / 1ᵉʳ juin 2009) CSD

ONTARIO
Superior Court of Justice
Cour supérieure de justice

Affidavit (Motion for Payment Out of Court)
Affidavit (Motion en vue du versement d'une somme d'argent consignée)

Form / Formule 4B Ont. Reg. No. / Régl. de l'Ont. 258/98

Small Claims Court / Cour des petites créances de

Claim No. / N° de la demande

Address / Adresse

Phone number / Numéro de téléphone

BETWEEN / ENTRE

Plaintiff(s)/Creditor(s) / Demandeur(s)/débiteur(s)/créancier(s)/créancière(s)

and / et

Defendant(s)/Debtor(s) / Défendeur(s)/défenderesse(s)/débiteur(s)/débitrice(s)

My name is
Je m'appelle

(Full name / Nom et prénoms)

I live in
J'habite à

(Municipality & province / Municipalité et province)

I make this affidavit to support my motion for payment out of court of money belonging to
Je fais le présent affidavit à l'appui d'une motion en vue du versement d'une somme d'argent consignée qui appartient à

(Name of person under disability / Nom de l'incapable)

of
de

(Address / Adresse)

who is
qui est

(State the nature of the disability / Indiquez la nature de l'incapacité)

and who was born on
et qui est né(e) le

(Date)

I am
Je suis

(State your connection with the person under disability / Indiquez votre rapport avec l'incapable)

The Accountant has informed me that $
Le comptable m'a informé(e) que la somme de

, including interest accrued to
$, y compris les intérêts courus au

, is in court.
est consignée au tribunal.

(Date)

There has been previously paid out the sum of $
Il a déjà été versé sur ce montant la somme de

on
$ le

(Date)

I propose that the sum of $
Je propose que la somme de

should be paid out of court to
soit versée à

(Name of person / Nom du personne)

for the following purpose: (Set out what the person you named will do with the money.)
aux fins de (Précisez ce que la personne que vous avez nommée fera de l'argent.)

SCR 4 (848) (November 1, 2012 / 1ᵉʳ novembre 2012) CSD

Continued on next page / Suite à la page suivante

FORM / *FORMULE* 4B   PAGE 2

I believe that this money should be paid out of court for the following reasons:
J'estime que cet argent doit être versé pour les raisons suivantes :

Set out your reasons in numbered paragraphs.
Indiquez vos raisons sous forme de dispositions numérotées.

....

....

....

....

....

....

....

....

....

....

....

....

....

....

....

....

....

....

If more space is required, attach and initial extra pages. / *Si vous avez besoin de plus d'espace, annexez une ou des feuilles supplémentaires et paraphez-les.*

Sworn/Affirmed before me at _____ *Déclaré sous serment/Affirmé* *solennellement devant moi à* (Municipality / *municipalité*) in _____ *en/à/au* (Province, state or country / *province, État ou pays*) on _____ , 20 _____ *le* Commissioner for taking affidavits *Commissaire aux affidavits* (Type or print name below if signature is illegible.) *(Dactylographiez le nom ou écrivez-le en caractères d'imprimerie ci-dessous si la signature est illisible.)*	_____ Signature (This form is to be signed in front of a lawyer, justice of the peace, notary public or commissioner for taking affidavits.) *(La présente formule doit être signée en présence d'un avocat, d'un juge de paix, d'un notaire ou d'un commissaire aux affidavits.)*

WARNING: IT IS AN OFFENCE UNDER THE *CRIMINAL CODE* TO KNOWINGLY SWEAR OR AFFIRM A FALSE AFFIDAVIT.

AVERTISSEMENT : FAIRE SCIEMMENT UN FAUX AFFIDAVIT CONSTITUE UNE INFRACTION AU CODE CRIMINEL.

SCR 4.08-4B (November 1, 2012 / *1ᵉʳ novembre 2012*) CSD

ONTARIO
Superior Court of Justice
Cour supérieure de justice

Notice to Alleged Partner
Avis au prétendu associé
Form / Formule 5A Ont. Reg. No. / Régl. de l'Ont. : 258/98

Small Claims Court / Cour des petites créances de _____

Claim No. / N° de la demande _____

Address / Adresse _____

Phone number / Numéro de téléphone _____

BETWEEN / ENTRE

_____

Plaintiff(s) / Demandeur(s)/demanderesse(s)

and / et

_____

Defendant(s) / Défendeur(s)/défenderesse(s)

TO:
DESTINATAIRE :

| Name of alleged partner / Nom du (de la) prétendu(e) associé(e) |
| Street and number / Numéro et rue |
| City, province, postal code / Ville, province, code postal |

YOU ARE ALLEGED TO HAVE BEEN A PARTNER on _____ , 20 ____
IL EST ALLÉGUÉ QUE VOUS ÉTIEZ UN(E) ASSOCIÉ(E) le

(or during the period) _____ , 20 ____ to _____ , 20 ____
(ou pendant la période du) *au*

in the partnership/business of _____
de la société en nom collectif/l'entreprise de (Firm name / Raison sociale)

a party named in this proceeding.
désignée comme partie à l'instance.

IF YOU WISH TO DENY THAT YOU WERE A PARTNER at any material time, you must defend this proceeding separately from the partnership, denying that you were a partner at the material time. If you fail to do so, you will be deemed to have been a partner on the date (or during the period) set out above.
SI VOUS SOUHAITEZ NIER QUE VOUS ÉTIEZ UN(E) ASSOCIÉ(E) à l'époque en cause, vous devez présenter dans l'instance une défense distincte de celle de la société en nom collectif, selon laquelle vous niez avoir été un(e) associé(e) à cette époque. À défaut de ce faire, vous serez réputé(e) avoir été une(e) associé(e) à la date (ou pendant la période) susmentionnée.

| **CAUTION:** | **AN ORDER AGAINST THE PARTNERSHIP MAY BE ENFORCED AGAINST YOU PERSONALLY** if you are deemed to have been a partner, if you admit that you were, or if the court finds that you were at the material time. |
| **AVERTISSEMENT :** | *UNE ORDONNANCE CONTRE LA SOCIÉTÉ EN NOM COLLECTIF PEUT ÊTRE EXÉCUTÉE CONTRE VOUS PERSONNELLEMENT si vous êtes réputé(e) avoir été un(e) associé(e), si vous admettez ce fait ou si le tribunal conclut que vous étiez un(e) associé(e) à l'époque en cause.* |

_____ , 20 ____

_____
(Signature of plaintiff or representative / Signature du demandeur/de la demanderesse ou du/de la représentant(e))

SCR 5.03-5A (June 1, 2009 / 1er juin 2009) CSD

Court Forms in Small Claims Court

Instructions for Making a Claim

Step 1: COMPLETE the <u>Plaintiff's Claim</u> form. Be sure to get the defendant's name right. Explain what happened in detail. Include dates and places. State how much money you want or what goods you want returned. Attach copies of any documents that help your case. Examples are contracts, repair bills and photographs of damaged goods. If you want interest on money you are claiming, ask for it on the claim form. You and the defendant may have a contract that sets an annual interest rate. If so, use that rate. If not, claim the *Courts of Justice Act* interest rate posted on the Ministry of the Attorney General website at www.attorneygeneral.jus.gov.on.ca.

If there is more than one plaintiff or defendant, complete an **Additional Parties** form (Form 1A) and put it right behind page one of your plaintiff's claim form. You can get the additional parties form from the court office or at the following website: www.ontariocourtforms.on.ca.

Step 2: FILE the plaintiff's claim and related documents by taking it or mailing it to the Small Claims Court office. You must also file a copy for every defendant. There is a fee. Cheques or money orders are payable to the Minister of Finance. The fees are listed at the court office and online at: www.attorneygeneral.jus.gov.on.ca. The clerk will return stamped copies of the plaintiff's claim to you.

Step 3 – SERVE. You must deliver a copy of the filed claim and your documents to each defendant. This is called "serving" the defendants. There are rules about how this must be done. See the Small Claims Court **"Guide to Serving Documents"** at the court office or online at www.attorneygeneral.jus.gov.on.ca.

Is it worth it? It is important to consider whether the person or company you are claiming from is likely to be able to pay. If they:

- are unemployed;
- are bankrupt;
- have no money of their own;
- have no personal property and have nothing else of value belonging to them (such as a car) which is not subject to a lease agreement;
- have ceased to carry on business; or
- have other debts to pay,

the court may not be able to help you get your money. However, you may be able to get your money if you are prepared to accept small instalments over a period of time. See the Small Claims Court **"After Judgment – Guide to Getting Results"** at the court office or online at www.attorneygeneral.jus.gov.on.ca.

DO NOT FILE THIS PAGE.

SCR 7.01 7A (September 1, 2010 / 1ᵉʳ septembre 2010) CED

Instructions pour présenter une demande

Étape 1 : REMPLISSEZ la formule <u>Demande du demandeur</u>. Assurez-vous d'indiquer le nom du défendeur correctement. Expliquez ce qui s'est passé en détail. Précisez les dates et les lieux. Indiquez la somme d'argent demandée ou les biens dont vous demandez la restitution. Joignez des copies des documents à l'appui de votre cause. Par exemple, des contrats, des factures de réparation et des photographies des biens endommagés. Si vous voulez des intérêts sur la somme demandée, demandez-les sur la formule de demande. Si vous et le défendeur avez conclu un contrat fixant un taux d'intérêt annuel, utilisez ce taux. Sinon, demandez le taux d'intérêt visé par la Loi sur les tribunaux judiciaires qui est affiché sur le site Web du ministère du Procureur général à l'adresse www.attorneygeneral.jus.gov.on.ca.

S'il y a plus d'un demandeur ou d'un défendeur, remplissez la formule **Parties additionnelles** (formule 1A) que vous placerez après la première page de votre formule de demande du demandeur. Vous pouvez obtenir la formule sur les parties additionnelles au greffe ou sur le site Web suivant : www.ontariocourtforms.on.ca.

Étape 2 : DÉPOSEZ la demande du demandeur et les documents qui y sont associés en les remettant en personne ou par la poste au bureau de la Cour des petites créances. Vous devez aussi remettre une copie pour chaque défendeur. Cela coûte quelque chose. Les chèques ou mandats doivent être faits à l'ordre du ministre des Finances. Les frais sont publiés au bureau de la Cour des petites créances et en ligne à l'adresse www.attorneygeneral.jus.gov.on.ca. Le greffier vous remettra des copies officialisées de la demande du demandeur.

Étape 3 — SIGNIFIEZ. Vous devez remettre une copie de la demande déposée et de vos documents à chacun des défendeurs. C'est ce qui s'appelle la «signification» aux défendeurs. Il existe des règles sur la façon de signifier. Consultez le **«Guide sur la signification des documents»** de la Cour des petites créances au greffe ou en ligne à l'adresse www.attorneygeneral.jus.gov.on.ca.

Votre demande en vaut-elle la peine? Il est important de se demander si la personne ou la compagnie à laquelle vous demandez une somme est vraisemblablement en mesure de payer. Si, selon le cas :

- elle est sans emploi;
- elle a fait faillite;
- elle n'a pas d'argent à son nom;
- elle n'a pas de biens meubles et n'a aucune autre possession de valeur (telle qu'une automobile) qui ne fait pas l'objet d'un contrat de location;
- elle a cessé ses activités;
- elle a d'autres dettes à payer,

le tribunal ne sera peut-être pas capable de vous aider à obtenir votre argent. Cependant, vous pourrez peut-être l'obtenir si vous êtes disposé(e) à accepter des petits versements échelonnés. Consultez le **«Guide sur la façon d'obtenir des résultats après le jugement»** de la Cour des petites créances au greffe ou en ligne à l'adresse www.attorneygeneral.jus.gov.on.ca.

NE DÉPOSEZ PAS LA PRÉSENTE PAGE.

Form 7A — Plaintiff's Claim

Ont. Reg. No. 258/98

[Repealed O. Reg. 78/06, s. 51.]

[Editor's Note: Forms 1A to 20Q of the Rules of the Small Claims Court have been repealed by O. Reg. 78/06, effective July 1, 2006. Pursuant to Rule of the Small Claims Court 1.06, when a form is referred to by number, the reference is to the form with that number that is described in the Table of Forms at the end of these rules and which is available on the Internet through www.ontariocourtforms.on.ca. For your convenience, the government form as published on this website is reproduced below.]

ONTARIO

Superior Court of Justice

	....	....
	Small Claims Court	Claim No.
Seal	....	
	....	
	Address	
	....	
	Phone number	

Plaintiff No. 1 ❑ Additional plaintiff(s) listed on attached Form 1A. ❑ Under 18 years of age.

Last name, or name of company		
First name	Second name	Also known as
Address (street number, apt., unit)		
City/Town	Province	Phone no.
Postal code		Fax no.
Representative		LSUC #

Address (street number, apt., unit)		
City/Town Province	Phone no.	
Postal code	Fax no.	

Defendant No. 1 ❑ Additional defendant(s) listed on attached Form 1A. ❑ Under 18 years of age.

Last name, or name of company		
First name	Second name	Also known as
Address (street number, apt., unit)		
City/Town Province	Phone no.	
Postal code	Fax no.	
Representative	LSUC #	
Address (street number, apt., unit)		
City/Town Province	Phone no.	
Postal code	Fax no.	

Reasons for Claim and Details

Explain what happened, including where and when. Then explain how much money you are claiming or what goods you want returned.

If you are relying on any documents, you *MUST* attach copies to the claim. If evidence is lost or unavailable, you *MUST* explain why it is not attached.

What happened? ....

Where? ....

When? ....

....

....

....

....

....

....

....

....

....

....

....

....

....

....

....

....

....

....

....

....

....

....

....

....

....

....

....

....

....

....

....

....

....

....

....

....

....

....

How much? $ .... (Principal amount claimed)

❑ *ADDITIONAL PAGES ARE ATTACHED BECAUSE MORE ROOM WAS NEEDED.*

The plaintiff also claims pre-judgment interest from .... *(Date) under:*

(Check only one box)

    ❑ *the* Courts of Justice Act

    ❑ *an agreement at the rate of* ....*% per year*

and post-judgment interest, and court costs.

Prepared on:	..............................., 20..........

....

(Signature of plaintiff or representative)

Issued on:	..............................., 20..........

....

(Signature of clerk)

CAUTION TO DEFENDANT: IF YOU DO NOT FILE A DEFENCE (Form 9A) and an Affidavit of Service (Form 8A) with the court within twenty (20) calendar days after you have been served with this Plaintiff's Claim, judgment may be obtained without notice and enforced against you. Forms and self-help materials are available at the Small Claims Court and on the following website: *www.ontariocourtforms.on.ca.*

January 7, 2014

Court Forms in Small Claims Court

ONTARIO

Superior Court of Justice
Cour supérieure de justice

Affidavit of Service
Affidavit de signification
Form / Formule 8A Ont. Reg. No. / Régl. de l'Ont. : 258/98

Small Claims Court / Cour des petites créances de

Claim No. / N° de la demande

Address / Adresse

Phone number / Numéro de téléphone

BETWEEN / ENTRE

Plaintiff(s) / Demandeur(s)/demanderesse(s)

and / et

Defendant(s) / Défendeur(s)/défenderesse(s)

My name is
Je m'appelle

(Full name / Nom et prénoms)

I live in
J'habite à

(Municipality & province / Municipalité et province)

and I swear/affirm that the following is true:
et je déclare sous serment/j'affirme solennellement que les renseignements suivants sont véridiques :

1. **I served**
   J'ai signifié à   (Full name of person/corporation served / Nom et prénoms   , **on** _____ , 20 ___ ,
   de la personne/nom au complet de la personne morale   , ***le*** _____ (Date)
   qui a reçu la signification)

   at
   au   (Address (street and number, unit, municipality, province) / Adresse (numéro et rue, unité, municipalité, province))

   which is   ☐ the address of the person's home
   soit   l'adresse du domicile de la personne

   ☐ the address of the corporation's place of business
   l'adresse du lieu de travail de l'établissement de la personne morale

   ☐ the address of the person's or corporation's representative on record with the court
   l'adresse du/de la représentant(e) de la personne ou de la personne morale figurant au
   dossier du tribunal

   ☐ the address on the document most recently filed in court by the party
   l'adresse figurant sur le document déposé le plus récemment au tribunal par la partie

   ☐ the address of the corporation's attorney for service in Ontario
   l'adresse du fondé de pouvoir de la personne morale aux fins de signification en Ontario

   ☐ other address:
   autre adresse :   (Specify. / Précisez.)

   with
   ce qui suit :   (Name(s) of document(s) served / Titre(s) du ou des documents signifiés)

SCR 8.06-8A (September 1, 2010 / 1er septembre 2010) CSD

FORM / FORMULE 8A   **PAGE 2**

2. I served the document(s) referred to in paragraph one by the following method:
J'ai signifié le ou les documents mentionnés au numéro un de la façon suivante :
(Tell how service took place by checking appropriate box(es).)
(Indiquez la façon dont la signification a été effectuée en cochant la ou les cases appropriées.)

Personal service / Significa-tion à personne

☐ leaving a copy with the person.
en laissant une copie à la personne.

☐ leaving a copy with the _____ of the corporation.
en laissant une copie au/à la   *(Office or position / Charge ou poste)*   *de la personne morale.*

☐ leaving a copy with: _____
en laissant une copie à :   *(Specify person's name and office or position. / Indiquez le nom de la personne ainsi que sa charge ou son poste.)*

Service at place of residence / Significa-tion au domicile

☐ leaving a copy in a sealed envelope addressed to the person at the person's place of residence with a person who appeared to be an adult member of the same household, and sending another copy of the same document(s) to the person's place of residence on the same day or the following day by:
en laissant une copie au domicile de la personne, dans une enveloppe scellée adressée à celle-ci, auprès d'une personne habitant sous le même toit qui semblait majeure et en envoyant une autre copie du ou des mêmes documents au domicile de la personne le même jour ou le jour suivant :

  ☐ regular lettermail.
  par courrier ordinaire.

  ☐ registered mail.
  par courrier recommandé.

  ☐ courier.
  par messagerie.

Service by registered mail / Significa-tion par courrier recom-mandé

☐ registered mail.
par courrier recommandé.
(If a copy of a plaintiff's claim or defendant's claim was served by registered mail, attach a copy of the Canada Post delivery confirmation, showing the signature verifying delivery, to this affidavit.)
(Si une copie de la demande du demandeur ou de la demande du défendeur a été signifiée par courrier recommandé, annexez au présent affidavit une copie de la confirmation de livraison remise par Postes Canada sur laquelle figure une signature qui confirme la livraison.)

Service by courier / Significa-tion par messa-gerie

☐ courier.
par messagerie.
(If a copy of a plaintiff's claim or defendant's claim was served by courier, attach a copy of the courier's delivery confirmation, showing the signature verifying delivery, to this affidavit.)
(Si une copie de la demande du demandeur ou de la demande du défendeur a été signifiée par messagerie, annexez au présent affidavit une copie de la confirmation de livraison remise par le service de messagerie sur laquelle figure la signature du destinataire de la signification.)

Service on lawyer / Significa-tion à l'avocat

☐ leaving a copy with a lawyer who accepted service on the person's behalf.
en laissant une copie avec l'avocat qui a accepté la signification au nom de la personne.
(Attach a copy of the document endorsed with the lawyer's acceptance of service.)
(Annexez une copie du document, sur lequel l'avocat a inscrit qu'il a accepté la signification.)

Service by regular lettermail / Significa-tion par courrier ordinaire

☐ regular lettermail.
par courrier ordinaire.

SCR 8.06-8A (September 1, 2010 / 1er septembre 2010) CSD   Continued on next page / Suite à la page suivante

Court Forms in Small Claims Court

FORM / FORMULE 8A   PAGE 3

Service by fax / Signification par télécopie
☐ fax sent at _____ at the following fax number: _____
par télécopie (Time / heure) *au numéro de télécopieur* (Fax number / numéro de
envoyée à *suivant :* télécopieur)

Service to last known address of corporation or attorney for service, and to the directors / Signification à la dernière adresse connue de la personne morale ou de son fondé de pouvoir aux fins de signification et aux administrateurs
☐ mail/courier to corporation or attorney for service at last known address recorded with the Ministry of Government Services, and
d'une part, par la poste/par messagerie à la personne morale ou à son fondé de pouvoir aux fins de signification, à la dernière adresse connue figurant dans les dossiers du ministère des Services gouvernementaux;

mail/courier to each director, as recorded with the Ministry of Government Services, as set out below:
d'autre part, par la poste/par messagerie à chaque administrateur mentionné dans les dossiers du ministère des Services gouvernementaux et dont le nom et l'adresse sont indiqués ci-dessous :

Name of director / Nom de l'administrateur	Director's address as recorded with the Ministry of Government Services (street & number, unit, municipality, province) / Adresse de l'administrateur figurant dans les dossiers du ministère des Services gouvernementaux (numéro et rue, unité, municipalité, province)

(Attach separate sheet for additional names if necessary. /
Joignez au besoin une feuille séparée s'il y a d'autres noms à ajouter.)

Substituted service / Signification indirecte
☐ substituted service as ordered by the court on _____ , 20 ___
par signification indirecte ordonnée par le tribunal le (Date)

as follows: (Give details.)
comme suit ; (Précisez.)

Sworn/Affirmed before me at _____
Déclaré sous serment/Affirmé (Municipality / municipalité)
solennellement devant moi à

in _____
en/à/au (Province, state, or country / province, État ou pays)

on _____ , 20 ___
le

Commissioner for taking affidavits
Commissaire aux affidavits
(Type or print name below if signature is illegible.)
(Dactylographiez le nom ou écrivez-le en caractères d'imprimerie ci-dessous si la signature est illisible.)

Signature
(This form is to be signed in front of a lawyer, justice of the peace, notary public or commissioner for taking affidavits.)
(La présente formule doit être signée en présence d'un avocat, d'un juge de paix, d'un notaire ou d'un commissaire aux affidavits.)

SCR 8.06-8A (September 1, 2010 / 1er septembre 2010) CSD

Court Forms in Small Claims Court

Instructions for Filing a Defence to a Claim

Step 1: COMPLETE a **Defence** form. Make sure your name and address are right so you will receive documents about the case. State what you disagree with and why, and if there is anything you agree with. Attach copies of any documents that help your case. If you want to pay all or part of the amount owing, state how much you will pay and when you will pay.

If there is more than one plaintiff or defendant, complete an **Additional Parties** form (Form 1A) and put it right behind page one of your defence form. You can get the additional parties form and other forms at the court office or online at www.ontariocourtforms.on.ca.

Step 2: FILE your defence form. Take the completed form and related documents to the court office where the plaintiff filed the claim. You must file a copy for every party. You must do this within 20 days after you received the claim. If you miss the 20 day deadline, you can still file the defence as long as the plaintiff has not yet asked the court to have you noted in default, or with leave of the court if you have been noted in default. Pay the court filing fee. Cheques and money orders are payable to the Minister of Finance. The fees are listed at the court office and online at www.attorneygeneral.jus.gov.on.ca. The court office will deliver a copy of your defence to each of the other parties.

If you have been noted in default, you must take additional steps if you wish to file a defence. See the Small Claims Court **"Guide to Replying to a Claim"** referenced below for more information.

If your Defence contains a proposal of terms of payment and you fail to make payment in accordance with your proposal, judgment for the unpaid balance may be ordered against you.

What if the plaintiff owes me money or someone else is responsible for the loss?

If you wish to file a **Defendant's Claim** form (Form 10A) against the plaintiff or other person, you must file it no later than 20 days after you file your defence. If you miss this deadline, you can ask the court on motion for permission to file it later. There is a filing fee.

For more information about replying to a claim or making a defendant's claim, see the Small Claims Court **"Guide to Replying to a Claim"** available at the court office and online at www.attorneygeneral.jus.gov.on.ca. Also see the **Defendant's Claim** form online at www.ontariocourtforms.on.ca.

DO NOT FILE THIS PAGE.

SCR 9.01 10.03 9A (September 1, 2010 / 1er septembre 2010) CSD

Instructions pour déposer une défense à une demande

Étape 1 : REMPLISSEZ la formule **Défense**. Assurez-vous que vos nom et adresse soient indiqués correctement pour pouvoir recevoir les documents se rapportant à votre cause. Indiquez les points sur lesquels vous n'êtes pas d'accord et pourquoi et ceux sur lesquels vous êtes d'accord. Joignez des copies des documents à l'appui de votre cause. Si vous voulez payer la totalité ou une partie de la somme due, indiquez le montant du paiement et quand vous effectuerez ce paiement.

S'il y a plus d'un demandeur ou d'un défendeur, remplissez la formule **Parties additionnelles** (formule 1A) que vous placerez après la première page de votre formule de défense. Vous pouvez obtenir la formule sur les parties additionnelles et d'autres formules au greffe ou en ligne à l'adresse www.ontariocourtforms.on.ca.

Étape 2 : DÉPOSEZ votre formule de défense. Allez porter la formule dûment remplie et les documents qui s'y rapportent au greffe où le demandeur a déposé sa demande. Vous devez en déposer une copie à l'intention de chaque partie. Vous avez 20 jours pour le faire après que vous avez reçu la demande. Si vous ne le faites pas dans ce délai de 20 jours, vous pouvez toujours déposer la défense pourvu que le demandeur n'ait pas encore demandé au tribunal de constater votre défaut, ou avec l'autorisation du tribunal si vous avez été constaté(e) en défaut. Acquittez les frais de dépôt. Les chèques et mandats doivent être faits à l'ordre du ministre des Finances. Les frais sont publiés au greffe et en ligne au site www.attorneygeneral.jus.gov.on.ca. Le greffe remettra une copie de votre défense à chacune des autres parties.

Si vous avez été constaté(e) en défaut, vous devez prendre des mesures supplémentaires si vous désirez déposer une défense. Consultez le **«Guide sur la réponse à la demande»** de la Cour des petites créances mentionné ci-dessous pour de plus amples renseignements.

Si votre défense comprend une proposition à l'égard des modalités de paiement et que vous n'effectuez pas vos paiements conformément aux modalités que vous proposez, un jugement à l'égard du solde impayé peut être obtenu contre vous.

Que dois-je faire si le demandeur me doit de l'argent ou que quelqu'un d'autre est responsable de la perte?

Si vous voulez déposer la formule **Demande du défendeur** (formule 10A) contre le demandeur ou une autre personne, vous devez le déposer au plus tard 20 jours après avoir déposé votre défense. Si vous ne le faites pas avant la fin de ce délai, vous pouvez demander au tribunal, sur motion, la permission de le déposer plus tard. Des frais de dépôt sont exigés.

Pour de plus amples renseignements sur la réponse à une demande ou la présentation d'une demande du défendeur, consultez le **«Guide sur la réponse à la demande»** de la Cour des petites créances qui est disponible au greffe et en ligne à l'adresse www.attorneygeneral.jus.gov.on.ca. Vous pouvez également consulter la formule **Demande du défendeur** en ligne à l'adresse www.ontariocourtforms.on.ca.

NE DÉPOSEZ PAS LA PRÉSENTE PAGE.

ONTARIO

Superior Court of Justice
Cour supérieure de justice

Defence / *Défense*

Form / *Formule* 9A Ont. Reg. No. / *Régl. de l'Ont.* : 258/98

Small Claims Court / *Cour des petites créances de*

Claim No. / *N° de la demande*

Address / *Adresse*

Phone number / *Numéro de téléphone*

Plaintiff No. 1 / *Demandeur n° 1*

☐ Additional plaintiff(s) listed on attached Form 1A.
Le ou les demandeurs additionnels sont mentionnés sur la formule 1A ci-jointe.

☐ Under 18 years of age.
Moins de 18 ans.

Last name, or name of company / *Nom de famille ou nom de la compagnie*		
First name / *Premier prénom*	Second name / *Deuxième prénom*	Also known as / *Également connu(e) sous le nom de*
Address (street number, apt., unit) / *Adresse (numéro et rue, app., unité)*		
City/Town / *Cité/Ville*	Province	Phone no. / *N° de téléphone*
Postal code / *Code postal*		Fax no. / *N° de télécopieur*
Representative / *Représentant(e)*		LSUC # / *N° du BHC*
Address (street number, apt., unit) / *Adresse (numéro et rue, app., unité)*		
City/Town / *Cité/Ville*	Province	Phone no. / *N° de téléphone*
Postal code / *Code postal*		Fax no. / *N° de télécopieur*

Defendant No. 1 / *Défendeur n° 1*

☐ Additional defendant(s) listed on attached Form 1A.
Le ou les défendeurs additionnels sont mentionnés sur la formule 1A ci-jointe.

☐ Under 18 years of age.
Moins de 18 ans.

Last name, or name of company / *Nom de famille ou nom de la compagnie*		
First name / *Premier prénom*	Second name / *Deuxième prénom*	Also known as / *Également connu(e) sous le nom de*
Address (street number, apt., unit) / *Adresse (numéro et rue, app., unité)*		
City/Town / *Cité/Ville*	Province	Phone no. / *N° de téléphone*
Postal code / *Code postal*		Fax no. / *N° de télécopieur*
Representative / *Représentant(e)*		LSUC # / *N° du BHC*
Address (street number, apt., unit) / *Adresse (numéro et rue, app., unité)*		
City/Town / *Cité/Ville*	Province	Phone no. / *N° de téléphone*
Postal code / *Code postal*		Fax no. / *N° de télécopieur*

SCR 9.01-10.03-9A (September 1, 2010 / *1er septembre 2010*) CSD

Court Forms in Small Claims Court

THIS DEFENCE IS BEING FILED ON BEHALF OF: (Name(s) of defendant(s))
LA PRÉSENTE DÉFENSE EST DÉPOSÉE AU NOM DE : (Nom du/de la ou des défendeur(s)/défenderesse(s))

and I/we: (Check as many as apply)
et je/nous : (Cochez la ou les cases qui s'appliquent)

☐   Dispute the claim made against me/us.
    conteste/contestons la demande présentée contre moi/nous.

☐   Admit the full claim and propose the following terms of payment:
    reconnais/reconnaissons être redevable(s) de la totalité de la demande et propose/proposons les
    modalités de paiement suivantes :

    $ _____ per _____ commencing _____ , 20 ____ .
    (Amount / *Montant*)   *$ par* (Week/month / *semaine/mois*)   *à compter du*

☐   Admit part of the claim in the amount of $_____ and propose the following terms of payment:
    reconnais/reconnaissons être redevable(s) (Amount / *Montant*)   *$ et propose/proposons les modalités de*
    d'une partie de la demande, soit   *paiement suivantes :*

    $ _____ per _____ commencing _____ , 20 ____ .
    (Amount / *Montant*)   *$ par* (Week/month / *semaine/mois*)   *à compter du*

REASONS FOR DISPUTING THE CLAIM AND DETAILS:
MOTIFS DE CONTESTATION DE LA DEMANDE ET PRÉCISIONS :

Explain what happened, including where and when. Explain why you do not agree with the claim made against you.
Expliquez ce qui s'est passé, en précisant où et quand. Expliquez pourquoi vous contestez la demande
présentée contre vous.

If you are relying on any documents, you **MUST** attach copies to the Defence. If evidence is lost or unavailable,
you **MUST** explain why it is not attached. *Si vous vous appuyez sur des documents, vous **DEVEZ** en annexer des copies à la défense. Si une preuve est*
*perdue ou n'est pas disponible, vous **DEVEZ** expliquer pourquoi elle n'est pas annexée.*

What happened?
Where?
When?
Que s'est-il
passé?
Où?
Quand?

FORM / *FORMULE* 9A   PAGE 3

Claim No. / *N° de la demande*

Why I/we disagree with all or part of the claim: /

Je conteste/Nous contestons la totalité ou une partie de la demande pour les motifs suivants :

☐ ADDITIONAL PAGES ARE ATTACHED BECAUSE MORE ROOM WAS NEEDED.
DES FEUILLES SUPPLÉMENTAIRES SONT ANNEXÉES EN RAISON DU MANQUE D'ESPACE.

Prepared on: _____ , 20 ____
Fait le :

                        (Signature of defendant or representative /
Signature du défendeur/de la défenderesse ou du/de la représentant(e))

NOTE:	Within seven (7) calendar days of changing your address for service, notify the court and all other parties in writing.
REMARQUE :	*Dans les sept (7) jours civils qui suivent tout changement de votre adresse aux fins de signification, veuillez en aviser par écrit le tribunal et les autres parties.*

CAUTION TO PLAINTIFF(S):	If this Defence contains a proposal of terms of payment, you are deemed to have accepted the terms **unless** you file with the clerk and serve on the defendant(s) a Request to Clerk (Form 9B) for a terms of payment hearing **WITHIN TWENTY (20) CALENDAR DAYS** of service of this Defence [R. 9.03(3)].
AVERTISSEMENT AU(X) DEMANDEUR(S) :	*Si la présente défense comprend une proposition à l'égard des modalités de paiement, vous êtes réputé(e)(s) les avoir acceptées, **sauf** si vous déposez auprès du greffier et signifiez au(x) défendeur(s) une demande au greffier (formule 9B) pour la tenue d'une audience relative aux modalités de paiement **DANS LES VINGT (20) JOURS CIVILS** de la signification de la présente défense [par. 9.03 (3)].*

SCR 9.01-10.03-9A (September 1, 2010 / 1er septembre 2010) CSD

ONTARIO

Superior Court of Justice
Cour supérieure de justice

Request to Clerk
Demande au greffier
Form / *Formule* 9B Ont. Reg. No. / *Régl. de l'Ont.* : 258/98

Small Claims Court / *Cour des petites créances de*   Claim No. / *N° de la demande*

Address / *Adresse*

Phone number / *Numéro de téléphone*

BETWEEN / ENTRE

Plaintiff(s) / *Demandeur(s)/demanderesse(s)*

and / et

Defendant(s) / *Défendeur(s)/défenderesse(s)*

TO THE CLERK OF THE _____ **SMALL CLAIMS COURT:**
AU GREFFIER DE LA COUR   (Name of Small Claims Court location / *Emplacement de la*
DES PETITES CRÉANCES DE   *Cour des petites créances*) :

My name is _____   **and I request that the clerk of the court:**
Je m'appelle   (Name of party/representative / *Nom de la partie ou du/de la*   *et je demande au greffier du tribunal*
     représentant(e))   *de faire ce qui suit :*

(Check appropriate box(es). / Cochez la ou les cases appropriées.)

☐   note defendant(s)
   constater le ou les défendeurs   (Name of defendant(s) / *Nom du/de la/des défendeur(s)/défenderesse(s)*)

   in default for failing to file a Defence (Form 9A) within the prescribed time period [R. 11.01(1)].
   en défaut pour n'avoir pas déposé de défense (formule 9A) dans le délai prescrit [par. 11.01 (1)].

☐   schedule an assessment hearing (all defendants have been noted in default) [R. 11.03(2)(b)].
   fixer la date d'une audience d'évaluation (tous les défendeurs ont été constatés en défaut) [alinéa
   11.03 (2) b)].

☐   schedule a terms of payment hearing because I dispute the defendant's proposed terms of payment
   contained in the Defence (Form 9A) [R. 9.03(3)].
   fixer la date d'une audience relative aux modalités de paiement parce que je conteste les modalités de
   paiement proposées par le défendeur dans la défense (formule 9A) [par. 9.03 (3)].

☐   schedule a trial [R. 16.01(1)(b)].
   fixer une date de procès [alinéa 16.01 (1) b)].

☐   accept payment in the amount of $ _____   into court according to an order of the court, dated
   accepter que le paiement de   (Amount / *Montant*) $ *soit consigné au tribunal, conformément à une*
                                          ordonnance du tribunal datée du

_____ , 20 _____

FORM / *FORMULE* 9B   **PAGE 2**

☐ accept payment in the amount of $ _____ into court for a person under disability according to
accepter que le paiement de _(Amount / Montant)_ $ *soit consigné au tribunal au nom d'un incapable,*
conformément

an order or settlement dated _____ , 20 ____ [R. 4.08(1)].
à une ordonnance ou à une transaction datée du *[par. 4.08 (1)].*

☐ accept payment in the amount of $ _____ into court pursuant to the attached written offer to
accepter que le paiement de _(Amount / Montant)_ $ *soit consigné au tribunal aux termes de l'offre de*
transaction écrite ci-jointe

settle, dated _____ , 20 ____ [R. 14.05(2)].
datée du *[par. 14.05 (2)].*

☐ accept payment in the amount of $ _____ into court according to the following legislation:
accepter que le paiement de _(Amount / Montant)_ $ *soit consigné au tribunal conformément à la*
disposition législative suivante :

_____
(Name of statute or regulation and section / *Titre de la loi ou du règlement et mention de l'article*)

☐ Other: _____
Autre :   (Specify / *Précisez.*)

_____ , 20 ____
                                          (Signature of party or representative / *Signature de la partie ou du/de la*
                                          représentant(e))

CAUTION:	To obtain an assessment of damages, all defendants must be noted in default. If one or more defendants has filed a defence, the matter must proceed to a settlement conference and, if necessary, trial. To bring a motion in writing for an assessment of damages, file a Notice of Motion and Supporting Affidavit (Form 15A). You can get forms at court offices or online at www.ontariocourtforms.on.ca.
AVERTISSEMENT :	*Pour obtenir une évaluation des dommages-intérêts, tous les défendeurs doivent être constatés en défaut. Si un ou plusieurs défendeurs ont déposé une défense, l'affaire doit passer à l'étape de la conférence en vue d'une transaction et, si cela est nécessaire, au procès. Pour présenter une motion par écrit en vue d'une évaluation des dommages-intérêts, déposez un avis de motion et affidavit à l'appui (formule 15A). Vous pouvez obtenir les formules aux greffes des tribunaux ou en ligne à l'adresse www.ontariocourtforms.on.ca*

©CR 4.0-11-14-16-0B (June 1, 2000 / *1er juin 2000*) CSD

Instructions for Making a Defendant's Claim

As a defendant, you can also make a claim of your own against the plaintiff or someone else. This is called a **defendant's claim**. For example, the plaintiff may owe you money. Or you may believe someone else caused the plaintiff's loss and that person should have to pay. To make your claim against the plaintiff or another party take the following steps:

Step 1: COMPLETE the **Defendant's Claim** form. Fill in the claim number from the Plaintiff's Claim form in the top right hand corner. You are the "plaintiff by defendant's claim." Explain what happened in detail. Include dates and places. State how much money you want or what goods you want returned. Attach copies of any documents that help your case. Examples are contracts, repair bills and photographs of damaged goods. If you want interest on money you are claiming, ask for it on the claim form. You and the defendant may have a contract that sets an annual interest rate. If so, use that rate. If not, claim the *Courts of Justice Act* interest rate posted on the Ministry of the Attorney General website at www.attorneygeneral.jus.gov.on.ca.

If there is more than one plaintiff or defendant, complete an **Additional Parties** form (Form 1A) and put it right behind page one of your defendant's claim form. You can get the additional parties form from the court office or at the following website: www.ontariocourtforms.on.ca.

Step 2: FILE the defendant's claim form and related documents with the court office where the plaintiff's claim was filed. You must file your claim no later than 20 days after you file your defence, unless you have leave of the court. There is a filing fee. The clerk will return a stamped copy of the defendant's claim form and documents to you.

Step 3: SERVE the defendant's claim. You must deliver a copy of the filed defendant's claim and your documents to each of the persons you are claiming against. This is "serving" your claim. There are rules about how this must be done. See the Small Claims Court **"Guide to Serving Documents"** at the court office or online at www.attorneygeneral.jus.gov.on.ca. Each party will have 20 days to file a defence to your claim after receiving it.

DO NOT FILE THIS PAGE.

SCR 10.01 10A (June 1, 2000 / 1er juin 2000) CSD

Instructions pour présenter une demande du défendeur

En tant que défendeur, vous pouvez également présenter votre propre demande contre le demandeur ou quelqu'un d'autre. C'est ce qui s'appelle la **demande du défendeur**. Par exemple, le demandeur vous doit peut-être de l'argent. Ou vous croyez peut-être qu'une autre personne est responsable de la perte du demandeur et que celle-ci devrait payer. Pour présenter votre demande contre le demandeur ou une autre partie, vous devez suivre les étapes suivantes :

Étape 1 : REMPLISSEZ la formule **Demande du défendeur**. Indiquez le numéro de la demande figurant sur la formule de demande du demandeur dans le coin supérieur droit. Vous êtes le «demandeur dans la demande du défendeur». Expliquez ce qui s'est passé en détail. Précisez les dates et les lieux. Indiquez la somme d'argent demandée ou les biens dont vous demandez la restitution. Joignez des copies des documents à l'appui de votre cause. Par exemple, des contrats, des factures de réparation et des photographies des biens endommagés. Si vous voulez des intérêts sur la somme demandée, demandez-les sur la formule de demande. Si vous et le défendeur avez conclu un contrat fixant un taux d'intérêt annuel, utilisez ce taux. Sinon, demandez le taux d'intérêt visé par la *Loi sur les tribunaux judiciaires* qui est affiché sur le site Web du ministère du Procureur général à l'adresse www.attorneygeneral.jus.gov.on.ca.

S'il y a plus d'un demandeur ou d'un défendeur, remplissez la formule **Parties additionnelles** (formule 1A) que vous placerez après la première page de votre formule de demande du défendeur. Vous pouvez obtenir la formule sur les parties additionnelles au greffe ou sur le site Web suivant : www.ontariocourtforms.on.ca.

Étape 2 : DÉPOSEZ la formule de demande du défendeur et les documents qui s'y rapportent au greffe où la demande du demandeur a été déposée. Vous devez déposer votre demande au plus tard 20 jours après avoir déposé votre défense, à moins que vous n'ayez l'autorisation du tribunal. Des frais de dépôt sont exigés. Le greffier vous rendra une copie cachetée de la formule de demande du défendeur et les documents.

Étape 3 — SIGNIFIEZ la demande du défendeur. Vous devez remettre une copie de la demande du défendeur déposée et de vos documents à chacune des personnes contre qui vous présentez votre demande. C'est ce qui s'appelle «signifier» votre demande. Il existe des règles sur la façon de signifier. Consultez le **«Guide sur la signification des documents»** de la Cour des petites créances au greffe ou en ligne à l'adresse www.attorneygeneral.jus.gov.on.ca. Chaque partie aura 20 jours pour déposer une défense à votre demande après l'avoir reçue.

NE DÉPOSEZ PAS LA PRÉSENTE PAGE.

Form 10A — Defendant's Claim

Ont. Reg. No. 258/98

[Repealed O. Reg. 78/06, s. 51.]

[Editor's Note: Forms 1A to 20Q of the Rules of the Small Claims Court have been repealed by O. Reg. 78/06, effective July 1, 2006. Pursuant to Rule of the Small Claims Court 1.06, when a form is referred to by number, the reference is to the form with that number that is described in the Table of Forms at the end of these rules and which is available on the Internet through www.ontariocourtforms.on.ca. For your convenience, the government form as published on this website is reproduced below.]

ONTARIO

Superior Court of Justice

Seal

....

Small Claims Court

....

....

Address

....

Phone number

....

Claim No.

Plaintiff by Defendant's Claim No. 1 ❑ Additional plaintiff(s) listed on attached Form 1A. ❑ Under 18 years of age.

Last name, or name of company		
First name	Second name	Also known as
Address (street number, apt., unit)		
City/Town Province		Phone no.
Postal code		Fax no.
Representative		LSUC #

Address (street number, apt., unit)		
City/Town	Province	Phone no.
Postal code		Fax no.

Defendant by Defendant's Claim No. 1 ❏ Additional defendant(s) listed on attached Form 1A. ❏ Under 18 years of age.

Last name, or name of company		
First name	Second name	Also known as
Address (street number, apt., unit)		
City/Town	Province	Phone no.
Postal code		Fax no.
Representative		LSUC #
Address (street number, apt., unit)		
City/Town	Province	Phone no.
Postal code		Fax no.

Reasons for Claim and Details

Explain what happened, including where and when. Then explain how much money you are claiming or what goods you want returned.

If you are relying on any documents, you *MUST* attach copies to the claim. If evidence is lost or unavailable, you *MUST* explain why it is not attached.

What happened? ....

Where? ....

When? ....
....
....
....
....
....
....
....
....
....
....
....
....
....
....
....
....
....
....
....
....
....
....
....
....
....
....
....
....
....
....
....
....
....

....

....

....

....

....

....

....

How much? $ .... (Principal amount claimed)

❏ *ADDITIONAL PAGES ARE ATTACHED BECAUSE MORE ROOM WAS NEEDED.*

The plaintiff by defendant's claim also claims pre-judgment interest from .... (Date) under:

(Check only one box)

      ❏ *the* Courts of Justice Act

      ❏ *an agreement at the rate of* ....% *per year*

and post-judgment interest, and court costs.

Prepared on:	.............................., 20..........	....
		(Signature of plaintiff or representative)

Issued on:	.............................., 20..........	....
		(Signature of clerk)

CAUTION TO DEFENDANT BY DEFENDANT'S CLAIM: IF YOU DO NOT FILE A DEFENCE (Form 9A) and an Affidavit of Service (Form 8A) with the court within twenty (20) calendar days after you have been served with this Defendant's Claim, judgment may be obtained by Defendant's Claim without notice and enforced against you. Forms and self-help materials are available at the Small Claims Court and on the following website: *www.ontariocourtforms.on.ca.*

                                                  January 7, 2014

ONTARIO

Superior Court of Justice
Cour supérieure de justice

Affidavit for Jurisdiction
Affidavit établissant la compétence
Form / *Formule* 11A Ont. Reg. No. / *Régl. de l'Ont.* : 258/98

Small Claims Court / *Cour des petites créances de*

Claim No. / *N° de la demande*

Address / *Adresse*

Phone number / *Numéro de téléphone*

BETWEEN / ENTRE

Plaintiff(s) / *Demandeur(s)/demanderesse(s)*

and / et

Defendant(s) / *Défendeur(s)/défenderesse(s)*

My name is _____
Je m'appelle   (Full name / *Nom et prénoms*)

I live in _____
J'habite à   (Municipality & province / *Municipalité et province*)

and I swear/affirm that the following is true:
et je déclare sous serment/j'affirme solennellement que les renseignements suivants sont véridiques :

1. In this action, I am the
    Dans la présente action, je suis le/la

    ☐ plaintiff
       demandeur/demanderesse

    ☐ representative of the plaintiff(s) _____
       représentant(e) du/de la/des   (Name of plaintiff(s) / *Nom du/de la/des demandeur(s)/demanderesse(s)*)
       demandeur(s)/demanderesse(s)

2. I make this affidavit in support of the plaintiff's request to note the defendant(s) in default, where all the defendants have been or will be served outside the court's territorial division [R. 11.01 (3)].
    Je fais le présent affidavit à l'appui de la demande du demandeur de faire constater le ou les défendeurs en défaut étant donné que tous les défendeurs ont reçu ou recevront la signification en dehors de la division territoriale du tribunal [par. 11.01 (3)].

SCR 11.01-11A (June 1, 2009 / *1er juin 2009*) CSD

Court Forms in Small Claims Court

3. The plaintiff is entitled to proceed with this action in this territorial division because this is:
   Le demandeur a le droit de poursuivre cette action dans cette division territoriale parce que :

   ☐ where the event (cause of action) took place.
   l'événement (cause d'action) a eu lieu dans cette division territoriale.

   ☐ where the defendant lives or carries on business.
   le défendeur réside dans cette division territoriale ou y exploite une entreprise.

   ☐ the court nearest to the place where the defendant lives or carries on business [R. 6.01].
   c'est dans cette division territoriale que se trouve le greffe du tribunal qui est le plus près de l'endroit où le défendeur réside ou exploite une entreprise. [règle 6.01].

Sworn/Affirmed before me at _____
Déclaré sous serment/Affirmé   (Municipality : *municipalité*)
solennellement devant moi à

in _____
en/à/au   (Province, state or country / *province, État ou pays*)

on _____ , 20 ____
le

Commissioner for taking affidavits
Commissaire aux affidavits
(Type or print name below if signature is illegible.)
(Dactylographiez le nom ou écrivez-le en caractères d'imprimerie ci-dessous si la signature est illisible.)

_____
Signature
(This form is to be signed in front of a lawyer, justice of the peace, notary public or commissioner for taking affidavits.)
(La présente formule doit être signée en présence d'un avocat, d'un juge de paix, d'un notaire ou d'un commissaire aux affidavits.)

WARNING:	IT IS AN OFFENCE UNDER THE *CRIMINAL CODE* TO KNOWINGLY SWEAR OR AFFIRM A FALSE AFFIDAVIT.
AVERTISSEMENT :	*FAIRE SCIEMMENT UN FAUX AFFIDAVIT CONSTITUE UNE INFRACTION AU CODE CRIMINEL.*

Court Forms in Small Claims Court

Instructions for Getting Default Judgment

Step 1: NOTE the defendant in default. If you have filed a claim and the defendant has not filed a defence within 20 days after you served it on him or her, ask the court clerk to find or "note" the defendant in default. You can do this by bringing or mailing a completed **Request to Clerk** form (Form 9B) to the court office.

If there is more than one plaintiff or defendant, complete an **Additional Parties** form (Form 1A) and put it right behind page one of your default judgment form. You can get the additional parties form from the court office or online at www.ontariocourtforms.on.ca.

Step 2: You can ask the court to order the defendant to pay money in one of two ways:

- if your claim is for a specified sum of money, ask the court clerk to sign a default judgment; or
- if your claim is for damages, ask a judge to make a judgment and assess your damages.

Court fees must be paid to take these steps.

How to ask a court clerk to sign default judgment

The court clerk can sign a default judgment in cases where the amount in dispute is stated under an agreement. The agreement does not have to be in writing. Examples include:

- unpaid accounts for goods or services sold and delivered
- unpaid loans
- back rent

To ask a clerk to sign a default judgment, you must fill out and file a **Default Judgment** form.

How to ask a judge to make a judgment and assess damages

A judge can make a judgment and assess damages in cases where the amount in dispute is not spelled out under an agreement. Examples include cases where your property has been damaged or you have been physically injured.

You can ask a judge to make a judgment and assess damages in one of two ways:

1. Make a written request, called a "motion in writing". To do this, you file a **Notice of Motion and Supporting Affidavit** form (Form 15A). In the affidavit you state the reasons why the motion should be granted. Attach all relevant documents. You do not have to go to court to speak to the judge. The judge will read all the documents and then decide the case.

2. Ask for an **assessment hearing** before a judge. To do this, fill out a **Request to Clerk** form (Form 9D) and file it with the court. A hearing is like a trial, except that the defendant is not in court. You and your witnesses are the only people who will be present before the judge. You must prove the amount that the defendant should pay. You can call witnesses and present evidence such as photos of damaged goods and receipts for repairs. The judge will then make a decision about the case.

See the following Small Claims Court guides at the court office or online at www.attorneygeneral.jus.gov.on.ca:

- for default judgments, see the **"Guide to Making a Claim"**
- for a motion in writing, see the **"Guide to Motions and Clerk's Orders"**
- for assessment hearings, see the **"Guide to Getting Ready for Court"**

DO NOT FILE THIS PAGE.

SCR 11.02.11B (September 1, 2010 / 1er septembre 2010) CSD

Instructions pour obtenir un jugement par défaut

Étape 1 : CONSTATATION du défendeur en défaut. Si vous avez déposé une demande et que le défendeur n'a pas déposé de défense au plus tard 20 jours après que vous lui avez signifié la demande, demandez au greffier de déclarer ou de «constater» le défendeur en défaut. Vous pouvez accomplir cette démarche en allant porter ou en envoyant par la poste au greffe la formule **Demande au greffier** (formule 9B) dûment remplie.

S'il y a plus d'un demandeur ou d'un défendeur, remplissez la formule **Parties additionnelles** (formule 1A) que vous placerez après la première page de votre formule de jugement par défaut. Vous pouvez obtenir la formule sur les parties additionnelles au greffe ou en ligne à l'adresse www.ontariocourtforms.on.ca.

Étape 2 : Vous pouvez demander au tribunal d'ordonner au défendeur de payer une somme d'argent de l'une ou l'autre des façons suivantes :

- si vous demandez une somme précisée, demandez au greffier de signer un jugement par défaut;
- si vous demandez des dommages-intérêts, demandez au juge de rendre un jugement et d'évaluer les dommages-intérêts.

Des frais judiciaires doivent être acquittés pour prendre ces mesures.

Comment demander au greffier de signer un jugement par défaut

Le greffier peut signer un jugement par défaut dans les cas où la somme en litige est indiquée dans un accord. Cet accord n'a pas besoin d'être par écrit. Par exemple :

- des factures impayées pour des biens ou des services vendus et livrés;
- des prêts non remboursés;
- un arriéré de loyer.

Pour demander au greffier de signer un jugement par défaut, vous devez remplir et déposer la formule **Jugement par défaut**.

Comment demander à un juge de rendre un jugement et d'évaluer les dommages-intérêts

Un juge peut rendre un jugement et évaluer les dommages-intérêts dans les cas où la somme en litige n'est pas précisée dans un accord. Par exemple, les cas où vos biens ont été endommagés ou vous avez été blessé(e).

Vous pouvez demander au juge de rendre un jugement et d'évaluer les dommages-intérêts de l'une ou l'autre des façons suivantes :

1. En présentant une demande écrite, appelée «motion écrite». Pour ce faire, vous devez déposer la formule **Avis de motion et affidavit à l'appui** (formule 15A). Dans l'affidavit, indiquez les motifs pour lesquels la motion devrait être accordée. Joignez tous les documents pertinents. Vous n'avez pas besoin de vous présenter au tribunal pour parler au juge. Le juge lira tous les documents et rendra ensuite une décision sur la cause.

2. En demandant la tenue d'une **audience d'évaluation** devant un juge. Pour ce faire, remplissez la formule **Demande au greffier** (formule 9D) et déposez-la au tribunal. Une audience est semblable à un procès, sauf que le défendeur ne se présente pas au tribunal. Vous et vos témoins serez les seules personnes présentes devant le juge. Vous devez prouver la somme que le défendeur devrait payer. Vous devez appeler des témoins et présenter des preuves telles que des photos de biens endommagés et des reçus pour des réparations. Le juge rendra ensuite une décision sur la cause.

Consultez les guides suivants de la Cour des petites créances au greffe ou en ligne à l'adresse www.attorneygeneral.jus.gov.on.ca :

- pour les jugements par défaut, le **«Guide sur le dépôt de la demande»**
- pour les motions écrites, le **«Guide sur les motions et les ordonnances du greffier»**
- pour les audiences d'évaluation, le **«Guide sur la procédure judiciaire»**

NE DÉPOSEZ PAS LA PRÉSENTE PAGE.

ONTARIO

Superior Court of Justice
Cour supérieure de justice

Default Judgment
Jugement par défaut

Form / Formule 11B Ont. Reg. No. / Régl. de l'Ont. : 258/98

Small Claims Court / *Cour des petites créances de*   Claim No. / *N° de la demande*

Seal / *Sceau*

Address / *Adresse*

Phone number / *Numéro de téléphone*

Plaintiff No. 1 / *Demandeur n° 1* ☐ Additional plaintiff(s) listed on attached Form 1A.
Le ou les demandeurs additionnels sont mentionnés sur la formule 1A ci-jointe.

Last name, or name of company / *Nom de famille ou nom de la compagnie*		
First name / *Premier prénom*	Second name / *Deuxième prénom*	Also known as / *Également connu(e) sous le nom de*
Address (street number, apt., unit) / *Adresse (numéro et rue, app., unité)*		
City/Town / *Cité/Ville*	Province	Phone no. / *N° de téléphone*
Postal code / *Code postal*		Fax no. / *N° de télécopieur*
Representative / *Représentant(e)*		LSUC # / *N° du BHC*
Address (street number, apt., unit) / *Adresse (numéro et rue, app., unité)*		
City/Town / *Cité/Ville*	Province	Phone no. / *N° de téléphone*
Postal code / *Code postal*		Fax no. / *N° de télécopieur*

Defendant No. 1 / *Défendeur n° 1* ☐ Additional defendant(s) listed on attached Form 1A.
Le ou les défendeurs additionnels sont mentionnés sur la formule 1A ci-jointe.

Last name, or name of company / *Nom de famille ou nom de la compagnie*		
First name / *Premier prénom*	Second name / *Deuxième prénom*	Also known as / *Également connu(e) sous le nom de*
Address (street number, apt., unit) / *Adresse (numéro et rue, app., unité)*		
City/Town / *Cité/Ville*	Province	Phone no. / *N° de téléphone*
Postal code / *Code postal*		Fax no. / *N° de télécopieur*
Representative / *Représentant(e)*		LSUC # / *N° du BHC*
Address (street number, apt., unit) / *Adresse (numéro et rue, app., unité)*		
City/Town / *Cité/Ville*	Province	Phone no. / *N° de téléphone*
Postal code / *Code postal*		Fax no. / *N° de télécopieur*

SCR 11.02-11B (September 1, 2010 / *1er septembre 2010*) CSD

FORM / *FORMULE* 11B   PAGE 2

NOTICE TO THE DEFENDANT(S):
AVIS AU(X) DÉFENDEUR(S) :

(Check one box only. / *Cochez une seule case.*)

☐ You have been noted in default according to Rule 11.01.
   vous avez été constaté(e) en défaut aux termes de la règle 11.01.

☐ You have defaulted in your payment according to Rule 9.03(2)(b), pursuant to
   vous n'avez pas effectué vos paiements aux termes de l'alinéa 9.03 (2) b), conformément à/au

_____ dated _____ , 20 _____ ,
        (Name of document / *Titre du document*)   *daté(e) du*

and 15 days have passed since you were served with a Notice of Default of Payment (Form 20L).
et 15 jours se sont écoulés depuis qu'un avis de défaut de paiement vous a été signifié (formule 20L).

DEFAULT JUDGMENT IS GIVEN against the following defendant(s):
UN JUGEMENT PAR DÉFAUT EST RENDU contre le ou les défendeurs suivants :

Last name, or name of company / *Nom de famille ou nom de la compagnie*			
First name / *Premier prénom*	Second name / *Deuxième prénom*		Also known as / *Également connu(e) sous le nom de*

Last name, or name of company / *Nom de famille ou nom de la compagnie*			
First name / *Premier prénom*	Second name / *Deuxième prénom*		Also known as / *Également connu(e) sous le nom de*

Last name, or name of company / *Nom de famille ou nom de la compagnie*			
First name / *Premier prénom*	Second name / *Deuxième prénom*		Also known as / *Également connu(e) sous le nom de*

☐ Additional defendant(s) listed on attached page (*list in same format*).
   Défendeur(s) additionnei(s) mentionné(s) sur une feuille annexée (énumérez-les en suivant le même format).

THE DEFENDANT(S) MUST PAY to the plaintiff(s) the following sums:
LE OU LES DÉFENDEURS DOIVENT VERSER au(x) demandeur(s) les sommes suivantes :

(A) **DEBT** (principal amount claimed minus any payments received since the plaintiff's
    claim was issued) $ _____
    LA CRÉANCE (somme demandée moins tout paiement reçu depuis la délivrance $
    de la demande du demandeur)

(B) **PRE-JUDGMENT INTEREST** calculated
    LES INTÉRÊTS ANTÉRIEURS AU JUGEMENT calculés

    on the sum of $ _____ at the rate of _____ %
    sur la somme de   *$ au taux de*   *pour cent*

    per annum from _____ , 20 ____ , to _____ , 20 ____ ,
    par an du   *au*

    being _____ days. $ _____
    soit   *jours.* $

FORM / *FORMULE* 11B   PAGE 3

_____
Claim No. / *N° de la demande*

(C) **COSTS** to date (including the cost of issuing this judgment) $ _____
LES DÉPENS à ce jour (dont les frais afférents à la prononciation $
du présent jugement)

                                                TOTAL $ _____
                                                           $

This judgment bears post-judgment interest at _____ % per annum commencing this date.
Le présent jugement porte des intérêts postérieurs   *pour cent à partir de la date du présent jugement.*
au jugement calculés au taux annuel de

_____ , 20 ____   _____
                                                      (Signature of clerk / *Signature du greffier*)

CAUTION TO DEFENDANT:	**YOU MUST PAY THE AMOUNT OF THIS JUDGMENT DIRECTLY TO THE PLAINTIFF(S) IMMEDIATELY.** Failure to do so may result in additional post-judgment interest and enforcement costs.
AVERTISSEMENT AU DÉFENDEUR :	*VOUS DEVEZ VERSER DIRECTEMENT AU(X) DEMANDEUR(S) LE MONTANT DÛ AUX TERMES DU PRÉSENT JUGEMENT IMMÉDIATEMENT, à défaut de quoi d'autres intérêts postérieurs au jugement et dépens de l'exécution forcée pourront vous être imputés.*

SCR 11.02-11B (September 1, 2010 / *1ᵉʳ septembre 2010*) CSD

ONTARIO
Superior Court of Justice
Cour supérieure de justice

Request for Clerk's Order on Consent
Demande d'ordonnance du greffier sur consentement
Form / Formule 11.2A Ont. Reg. No. / Régl. de l'Ont. : 258/98

Small Claims Court / *Cour des petites créances de*

Claim No. / *N° de la demande*

Address / *Adresse*

Phone number / *Numéro de téléphone*

Plaintiff No. 1 / *Demandeur n° 1*

☐ Additional plaintiff(s) listed on attached Form 1A.
Le ou les demandeurs additionnels sont mentionnés sur la formule 1A ci-jointe.

Last name, or name of company / *Nom de famille ou nom de la compagnie*		
First name / *Premier prénom*	Second name / *Deuxième prénom*	Also known as / *Également connu(e) sous le nom de*
Address (street number, apt., unit) / *Adresse (numéro et rue, app., unité)*		
City/Town / *Cité/ville*	Province	Phone no. / *N° de téléphone*
Postal code / *Code postal*		Fax no. / *N° de télécopieur*
Representative / *Représentant(e)*		LSUC # / *N° du BHC*
Address (street number, apt., unit) / *Adresse (numéro et rue, app., unité)*		
City/Town / *Cité/ville*	Province	Phone no. / *N° de téléphone*
Postal code / *Code postal*		Fax no. / *N° de télécopieur*

Defendant No. 1 / *Défendeur n° 1*

☐ Additional defendant(s) listed on attached Form 1A.
Le ou les défendeurs additionnels sont mentionnés sur la formule 1A ci-jointe.

Last name, or name of company / *Nom de famille ou nom de la compagnie*		
First name / *Premier prénom*	Second name / *Deuxième prénom*	Also known as / *Également connu(e) sous le nom de*
Address (street number, apt., unit) / *Adresse (numéro et rue, app., unité)*		
City/Town / *Cité/ville*	Province	Phone no. / *N° de téléphone*
Postal code / *Code postal*		Fax no. / *N° de télécopieur*
Representative / *Représentant(e)*		LSUC # / *N° du BHC*
Address (street number, apt., unit) / *Adresse (numéro et rue, app., unité)*		
City/Town / *Cité/ville*	Province	Phone no. / *N° de téléphone*
Postal code / *Code postal*		Fax no. / *N° de télécopieur*

NOTE: This request must be signed by all parties and anyone being added, deleted or substituted.
REMARQUE : *La présente demande doit être signée par toutes les parties et par toute personne qui est jointe, radiée ou substituée.*

SCR 11.2.01-11.2A (June 1, 2009 / 1er juin 2009) CSD

FORM / *FORMULE* 11.2A

PAGE 2

Claim No. / *N° de la demande*

TO THE PARTIES:
AUX PARTIES :

THIS REQUEST IS FILED BY: _____
LA PRÉSENTE DEMANDE EST DÉPOSÉE PAR :

(Name of party / *Nom de la partie*)

I state that:
Je déclare que :

☐ Each party has received a copy of this form.
Chaque partie a reçu une copie de la présente formule.

☐ No party that would be affected by the order is under disability.
Aucune partie sur laquelle l'ordonnance aurait une incidence n'est incapable.

☐ This form has been signed and consented to by all parties, including any parties to be added, deleted or substituted.
Toutes les parties, y compris celles qui doivent être jointes, radiées ou substituées, ont signé la présente formule et y ont consenti.

I request that the clerk make the following order(s) on the consent of all parties:
Je demande au greffier de rendre l'ordonnance ou les ordonnances suivantes sur consentement de toutes les parties :
(Check appropriate boxes. / *Cochez les cases appropriées.*)

☐ set aside the noting in default of _____
l'annulation de la constatation du défaut de

(Name of defendant(s) / *Nom du/de la/des défendeur(s)/défenderesse(s)*)

☐ set aside Default Judgment against _____
l'annulation du jugement par défaut prononcé contre

(Name of defendant(s) / *Nom du/de la/des défendeur(s)/défenderesse(s)*)

☐ restore to the list the following matter that was dismissed under Rule 11.1: _____
la réinscription au rôle de l'affaire suivante qui a été rejetée aux termes de la règle 11.1 :

(Specify / *Précisez.*)

☐ cancel the examination hearing regarding _____
l'annulation de l'interrogatoire concernant

(Name of person to be examined / *Nom de la personne qui doit être interrogée*)

☐ with respect to the following step(s) taken to enforce the default judgment that are not yet completed:
à l'égard de la ou des mesures suivantes qui ont été prises pour exécuter le jugement par défaut et qui ne sont pas encore menées à terme :

☐ withdraw the Writ of Seizure and Sale of Land issued against:
le retrait du bref de saisie-exécution de biens-fonds délivré contre :

(Name of debtor(s) / *Nom du/de la/des débiteur(s)/débitrice(s)*)

and directed to the sheriff of the _____ :
et adressé au shérif de

(Name of county/region in which the sheriff/enforcement office) is located / *Nom du comté/de la région où se trouve le shérif (bureau de l'exécution)*)

(Provide instructions about what is to be done with any proceeds held or property seized by the sheriff. / *Donnez des instructions sur ce qu'il faut faire de tout produit de la vente détenu ou bien saisi par le shérif.*)

_____
_____
_____

SCR 11.2.01-11.2A (June 1, 2009 / *1er juin 2009*) CSD

Continued on next page / *Suite à la page suivante*

FORM / FORMULE 11.2A   **PAGE 3**

Claim No. / N° de la demande _____

☐ withdraw the Writ of Seizure and Sale of Personal Property issued against:
le retrait du bref de saisie-exécution de biens meubles délivré contre :   (Name of debtor(s) / Nom du/de la/des débiteur(s)/débitrice(s))

and directed to the bailiff of the _____ :
et adressé à l'huissier de   (Small Claims Court location / Emplacement de la Cour des petites créances)

(Provide instructions about what is to be done with any proceeds held by the clerk of the court or property that has been seized by the bailiff. / Donnez des instructions sur ce qu'il faut faire de tout produit de la vente détenu par le greffier du tribunal ou de tout bien saisi par l'huissier.)

_____

_____

☐ terminate the Notice of Garnishment or Notice of Renewal of Garnishment issued against:
la fin de l'avis de saisie-arrêt ou de l'avis de renouvellement de la saisie-arrêt délivré contre :

(Name of debtor(s) / Nom du/de la/des débiteur(s)/débitrice(s))

and directed to _____ :
et adressé à   (Name of garnishee / Nom du tiers saisi)

(Provide instructions about what is to be done with any money held by the clerk of the court. / Donnez des instructions sur ce qu'il faut faire de toute somme d'argent détenue par le greffier du tribunal.)

_____

_____

☐ note that payment has been made in full satisfaction of an order or terms of settlement
le constat qu'un paiement intégral a été effectué en exécution d'une ordonnance ou des conditions de la transaction

☐ dismiss the: ☐ Plaintiff's Claim   ☐ Defendant's Claim
le rejet de la :   demande du demandeur   demande du défendeur

☐ costs in the amount of $ _____ , to be paid to _____
le versement de   (Amount / Montant) $ au titre des dépens à   (Name of party(ies) / Nom de la ou des parties)

_____ by _____
                                                par   (Name of party(ies) / Nom de la ou des parties)

The originally scheduled trial date is less than 30 days away and I request that the clerk make the following order(s) on the consent of all parties and any person to be added or substituted :
La date du procès fixée à l'origine tombe dans moins de 30 jours et je demande au greffier de rendre l'ordonnance ou les ordonnances suivantes sur consentement de toutes les parties et de toute personne qui doit être jointe ou substituée :
(Check appropriate boxes. / Cochez les cases appropriées.)

☐ amend a Plaintiff's Claim issued on _____ , 20 _____ .
la modification de la demande d'un demandeur délivrée le
(Attach two (2) copies of the amended Plaintiff's Claim. / Annexez deux (2) copies de la demande du demandeur modifiée.)

☐ amend a Defence filed on _____ , 20 _____ .
la modification d'une défense déposée le
(Attach two (2) copies of the amended Defence. / Annexez deux (2) copies de la défense modifiée.)

FORM / *FORMULE* 11.2A　　　　　　　　**PAGE 4**

Claim No. / *N° de la demande*

☐ amend a Defendant's Claim issued on _____ , 20 _____ .
la modification de la demande d'un défendeur délivrée le
(Attach two (2) copies of the amended Defendant's Claim. / *Annexez deux (2) copies de la demande du défendeur modifiée.*)

☐ add _____
la jonction de　　　　　　　　　　　　(Name of party / *Nom de la partie*)

to the	☐ Plaintiff's Claim	☐ Defendant's Claim
à la	*demande du demandeur*	*demande du défendeur*
as a	☐ defendant	☐ Plaintiff
à titre de	*défendeur/défenderesse*	*demandeur/demanderesse*

☐ delete _____
la radiation de　　　　　　　　　　　(Name of party / *Nom de la partie*)

| from the | ☐ Plaintiff's Claim | ☐ Defendant's Claim |
| *de la* | *demande du demandeur* | *demande du défendeur* |

☐ substitute _____
la substitution à　　　　　　　　　　(Name of party / *Nom de la partie*)

with _____
de　　　　　　　　　　　　　　　　(Name of party / *Nom de la partie*)

| in the | ☐ Plaintiff's Claim | ☐ Defendant's Claim |
| *dans la* | *demande du demandeur* | *demande du défendeur* |

_____ , 20 _____　　　　　　_____ , 20 _____

(Signature of party consenting / *Signature de la partie qui consent*)　　(Signature of party consenting / *Signature de la partie qui consent*)

(Name of party consenting / *Nom de la partie qui consent*)　　(Name of party consenting / *Nom de la partie qui consent*)

(Signature of witness / *Signature du témoin*)　　(Signature of witness / *Signature du témoin*)

(Name of witness / *Nom du témoin*)　　(Name of witness / *Nom du témoin*)

_____ , 20 _____　　　　　　_____ , 20 _____

(Signature of party consenting / *Signature de la partie qui consent*)　　(Signature of party consenting / *Signature de la partie qui consent*)

(Name of party consenting / *Nom de la partie qui consent*)　　(Name of party consenting / *Nom de la partie qui consent*)

(Signature of witness / *Signature du témoin*)　　(Signature of witness / *Signature du témoin*)

(Name of witness / *Nom du témoin*)　　(Name of witness / *Nom du témoin*)

SCR 11.2.01-11.2A (June 1, 2009 / *1er juin 2009*) CSD

Continued on next page / *Suite à la page suivante*

FORM / *FORMULE* 11.2A   **PAGE 5**

Claim No. / *N° de la demande*

DISPOSITION: *The clerk of the court will complete this section.*
DÉCISION :   *Le greffier du tribunal remplit cette partie.*

☐   order to go as asked
    ordonnance de procéder comme il a été demandé

☐   order refused because:
    ordonnance refusée pour les motifs suivants :

_____

_____

_____

_____

_____

_____

_____

_____

_____

_____

_____ , 20 _____   _____

                                                 (Signature of clerk / *Signature du greffier*)

SCR 11.2.01-11.2A (June 1, 2009 / *1er juin 2009*) CSD

ONTARIO
Superior Court of Justice
Cour supérieure de justice

Notice of Discontinued Claim
Avis de désistement de demande
Form / Formule 11.3A Ont. Reg. No. / Régl. de l'Ont. 258/98

Small Claims Court / *Cour des petites créances de*

Claim No. / *N° de la demande*

Address / *Adresse*

Phone number / *Numéro de téléphone*

BETWEEN / ENTRE

Plaintiff(s) / *Demandeur(s)/demanderesse(s)*

and / et

Defendant(s) / *Défendeur(s)/défenderesse(s)*

TAKE NOTICE that the plaintiff discontinues the claim against the following defendant(s) who did not file a defence:
PRENEZ ACTE que le demandeur se désiste de la demande contre le ou les défendeurs suivants, lesquels n'ont pas présenté de défense :

Last name, or name of company / *Nom de famille ou nom de la compagnie*

First name / *Premier prénom* | Second name / *Deuxième prénom* | Also known as / *Également connu(e) sous le nom de*

Last name, or name of company / *Nom de famille ou nom de la compagnie*

First name / *Premier prénom* | Second name / *Deuxième prénom* | Also known as / *Également connu(e) sous le nom de*

Last name, or name of company / *Nom de famille ou nom de la compagnie*

First name / *Premier prénom* | Second name / *Deuxième prénom* | Also known as / *Également connu(e) sous le nom de*

☐ Additional defendant(s) listed in attached page *(list in same format)*.
Défendeur(s) additionnel(s) mentionné(s) sur une feuille annexée (énumérez-les en suivant le même format).

, 20

(Signature of plaintiff or representative / *Signature du demandeur/de la demanderesse ou du/de la représentant(e)*)

(Name, address and phone number of party or representative / *Nom, adresse et numéro de téléphone de la partie ou du/de la représentant(e)*)

NOTE: **THIS NOTICE** must be served on all defendants who were served with the claim, and filed with the court with proof of service. A claim may not be discontinued by or against a person under disability, except with leave of the court.
REMARQUE : **LE PRÉSENT AVIS** doit être signifié à tous les défendeurs auxquels la demande a été signifiée et déposé auprès du tribunal avec preuve de la signification. Une demande ne peut faire l'objet d'un désistement par un incapable ou contre lui sans l'autorisation du tribunal.

SCR 11.3-11.3A (September 1, 2010 / *1er septembre 2010*) CSD

ONTARIO
Superior Court of Justice
Cour supérieure de justice

List of Proposed Witnesses
Liste des témoins proposés
Form / Formule 13A Ont. Reg. No. / Régl. de l'Ont. : 258/98

Small Claims Court / *Cour des petites créances de*

Claim No. / *N° de la demande*

Address / *Adresse*

Phone number / *Numéro de téléphone*

BETWEEN / ENTRE

Plaintiff(s) / *Demandeur(s)/demanderesse(s)*

and / et

Defendant(s) / *Défendeur(s)/défenderesse(s)*

My name is _____
Je m'appelle
(Name of party/representative / *Nom de la partie ou du/de la représentant(e)*)

The following is my list of proposed witnesses in this case:
La liste suivante constitue ma liste des témoins proposés dans la présente cause :

Name of witness / *Nom du témoin*	Address, phone and fax numbers / *Adresse, numéros de téléphone et de télécopieur*
1.	
2.	
3.	

SCR 13.01-13A (June 1, 2009 / *1er juin 2009*) CSD

Court Forms in Small Claims Court

PAGE 2

_____
Claim No. / N° de la demande

4. _____   _____
                               _____
                               _____
                               _____
                               _____
                               _____

5. _____   _____
                               _____
                               _____
                               _____
                               _____
                               _____

The following is my list of other persons with knowledge of the matter in dispute in this case:
La liste suivante constitue ma liste des autres personnes qui ont connaissance des questions en litige dans la présente cause :

Name of person / *Nom de la personne*   Address, phone and fax numbers / *Adresse, numéros de téléphone et de télécopieur*

1. _____   _____
                               _____
                               _____
                               _____
                               _____

2. _____   _____
                               _____
                               _____
                               _____
                               _____

(Attach a separate sheet in the above format for additional witnesses or other persons.)
(En cas de témoins ou de personnes additionnels, annexez une autre feuille reproduisant le format ci-dessus.)

_____, 20 _____   _____
                                         (Signature of party or representative / *Signature de la partie ou du/de la représentant(e)*)

                                         _____
                                         _____
                                         (Name, address and phone number of party or representative / *Nom, adresse et numéro de téléphone de la partie ou du/de la représentant(e)*)

NOTE: **EACH PARTY MUST SERVE THIS LIST** on all other parties and file it with the court at least fourteen (14) days before the settlement conference [R. 13.03(2)(b)].

REMARQUE : *CHAQUE PARTIE DOIT SIGNIFIER LA PRÉSENTE LISTE à toutes les autres parties et la déposer auprès du tribunal au moins quatorze (14) jours avant la tenue de la conférence en vue d'une transaction [alinéa 13.03 (2) b)].*

SCR 13.01-13A (June 1, 2009 / 1er juin 2009) CSD

ONTARIO
Superior Court of Justice
Cour supérieure de justice

Consent
Consentement

Form / *Formule* 13B Ont. Reg. No. / *Règl. de l'Ont.* : 258/98

Small Claims Court / *Cour des petites créances de*

Claim No. / *N° de la demande*

Address / *Adresse*

Phone number / *Numéro de téléphone*

BETWEEN / ENTRE

_____
Plaintiff(s) / *Demandeur(s)/demanderesse(s)*

and / et

_____
Defendant(s) / *Défendeur(s)/défenderesse(s)*

I/We, _____
Je/Nous soussigné(e)(s),
(Name of party(ies) / *Nom de la ou des parties*)

consent to the following:
consens/consentons à ce qui suit :

_____
_____
_____
_____
_____
_____
_____
_____
_____
_____

The parties do not need to sign this consent on the same day, but each must sign in the presence of his or her witness who signs a moment later. (For additional parties' signatures, attach a separate sheet in the format below.)
Les parties ne sont pas tenues de signer le présent consentement le même jour, mais chacune doit le signer en présence de son témoin, qui le signe à son tour aussitôt après. (S'il y a lieu, annexez une autre feuille portant la signature des parties additionnelles présentée selon le format suivant.)

_____, 20 _____

(Signature of party consenting / *Signature de la partie qui consent*)

_____

(Name of party consenting / *Nom de la partie qui consent*)

_____

(Signature of witness / *Signature du témoin*)

_____

(Name of witness / *Nom du témoin*)

_____, 20 _____

(Signature of party consenting / *Signature de la partie qui consent*)

_____

(Name of party consenting / *Nom de la partie qui consent*)

_____

(Signature of witness / *Signature du témoin*)

_____

(Name of witness / *Nom du témoin*)

SCR 3-8-11-14-20-13B (September 1, 2010 / *1er septembre 2010*) CSD

ONTARIO

Superior Court of Justice
Cour supérieure de justice

Offer to Settle
Offre de transaction

Form / *Formule* 14A Ont. Reg. No. / *Régl. de l'Ont.* : 258/98

Small Claims Court / *Cour des petites créances de*	Claim No. / *N° de la demande*

Address / *Adresse*

Phone number / *Numéro de téléphone*

BETWEEN / *ENTRE*

Plaintiff(s) / *Demandeur(s)/demanderesse(s)*

and / *et*

Defendant(s) / *Défendeur(s)/défenderesse(s)*

My name is
Je m'appelle

(Full name / *Nom et prénoms*)

1. In this action, I am the
   Dans la présente action, je suis le/la

   ☐ Plaintiff
   demandeur/demanderesse

   ☐ Defendant
   défendeur/défenderesse

   ☐ representative of
   représentant(e) de
   (Name of party(ies) / *Nom de la ou des parties*)

2. I offer to settle this action against
   Je présente une offre de transaction dans cette action contre
   (Name of party(ies) / *Nom de la ou des parties*)

   on the following terms: *(Set out terms in numbered paragraphs, or on an attached sheet.)*
   selon les conditions suivantes : *(Indiquez les conditions sous forme de paragraphes numérotés ou sur une feuille annexée.)*

SCR 14.01.1-14A (June 1, 2009 / *1er juin 2009*) CSD

FORM / FORMULE 14A   PAGE 2

Claim No. / N° de la demande

_____

_____

_____

_____

_____

_____

_____

_____

_____

_____

3.   This offer to settle is available for acceptance until _____ , 20 ____ .
     L'acceptation de la présente offre de transaction peut se faire jusqu'au

This offer to settle may be accepted by serving an acceptance of offer to settle (Form 14B may be used) on the
party who made it, at any time before it is withdrawn or before the court disposes of the claim to which the offer
applies [R. 14.05(1)]. You can get forms at court offices or online at www.ontariocourtforms.on.ca.
La présente offre de transaction peut être acceptée en signifiant une acceptation de l'offre de transaction (la
formule 14B peut être utilisée) à la partie qui l'a faite, avant que l'offre ne soit retirée ou avant que le tribunal ne
décide la demande qui en fait l'objet [par. 14.05 (1)]. Vous pouvez obtenir des formules aux greffes des
tribunaux ou en ligne à l'adresse www.ontariocourtforms.on.ca.

_____ , 20 ____

(Signature of party or representative making offer / Signature de la partie ou
du/de la représentant(e))

_____

(Name, address and phone number of party or representative / Nom,
adresse et numéro de téléphone de la partie ou du/de la représentant(e))

NOTE:	**IF YOU ACCEPT AN OFFER TO SETTLE, THEN FAIL TO COMPLY WITH ITS TERMS,** judgment in the terms of the accepted offer may be obtained against you on motion to the court, or the action may continue as if there has been no offer to settle [R. 14.06].
REMARQUE :	**SI VOUS ACCEPTEZ UNE OFFRE DE TRANSACTION MAIS QU'ENSUITE VOUS N'EN OBSERVEZ PAS LES CONDITIONS,** un jugement suivant les conditions de l'offre acceptée peut être obtenu contre vous sur présentation d'une motion au tribunal ou l'action peut continuer comme s'il n'y avait jamais eu d'offre de transaction [règle 14.06].

NOTE:	**IF THIS OFFER TO SETTLE IS NOT ACCEPTED, IT SHALL NOT BE FILED WITH THE COURT OR DISCLOSED** to the trial judge until all questions of liability and relief (other than costs) have been determined [R. 14.04].
REMARQUE :	**SI LA PRÉSENTE OFFRE DE TRANSACTION N'EST PAS ACCEPTÉE, ELLE NE DOIT PAS ÊTRE DÉPOSÉE AUPRÈS DU TRIBUNAL NI DIVULGUÉE** au juge du procès tant que toutes les questions relatives à la responsabilité et aux mesures de redressement (à l'exclusion des dépens) n'ont pas été décidées [règle 14.04].

SCR 14.01.1-14A (June 1, 2009 / 1er juin 2009) CSD

ONTARIO
Superior Court of Justice
Cour supérieure de justice

Acceptance of Offer to Settle
Acceptation de l'offre de transaction
Form / Formule 14B Ont. Reg. No. / Régl. de l'Ont. : 258/98

Small Claims Court / Cour des petites créances de

Claim No. / N° de la demande

Address / Adresse

Phone number / Numéro de téléphone

BETWEEN / ENTRE

Plaintiff(s) / Demandeur(s)/demanderesse(s)

and / et

Defendant(s) / Défendeur(s)/défenderesse(s)

My name is _____
Je m'appelle   (Full name / Nom et prénoms)

1. In this action, I am the
    Dans la présente action, je suis le/la

    ☐ plaintiff
       demandeur/demanderesse

    ☐ defendant
       défendeur/défenderesse

    ☐ representative of _____
       représentant(e) de   (Name of party(ies) / Nom de la ou des parties)

2. I accept the offer to settle from _____
    J'accepte l'offre de transaction faite par   (Name of party(ies) / Nom de la ou des parties)

    dated _____ , 20 _____ .
    et datée du

3. This offer to settle has not expired and has not been withdrawn.
    Cette offre de transaction n'est pas expirée et n'a pas été retirée.

    _____ , 20 _____

    (Signature of party or representative accepting offer / Signature de la partie
    ou du/de la représentant(e) qui accepte l'offre)

    (Name, address and phone number of party or representative / Nom, adresse
    et numéro de téléphone de la partie ou du/de la représentant(e))

CAUTION:	IF YOU ACCEPT AN OFFER TO SETTLE, THEN FAIL TO COMPLY WITH ITS TERMS, judgment in the terms of the accepted offer may be obtained against you on motion to the Court, or this action may continue as if there has been no offer to settle [R. 14.06].
AVERTISSEMENT :	SI VOUS ACCEPTEZ UNE OFFRE DE TRANSACTION MAIS QU'ENSUITE VOUS N'EN OBSERVEZ PAS LES CONDITIONS, un jugement suivant les conditions de l'offre acceptée peut être obtenu contre vous sur présentation d'une motion au tribunal ou la présente action peut continuer comme s'il n'y avait jamais eu d'offre de transaction [règle 14.06].

SCR 14.01.1-14B (June 1, 2009 / 1er juin 2009) CSD

ONTARIO
Superior Court of Justice
Cour supérieure de justice

Notice of Withdrawal of Offer to Settle
Avis de retrait de l'offre de transaction
Form / Formule 14C Ont. Reg. No. / Règl. de l'Ont. : 258/98

Small Claims Court / Cour des petites créances de	Claim No. / N° de la demande

Address / Adresse

Phone number / Numéro de téléphone

BETWEEN / ENTRE

_____
Plaintiff(s) / Demandeur(s)/demanderesse(s)

and / et

_____
Defendant(s) / Défendeur(s)/défenderesse(s)

My name is _____
Je m'appelle
(Full name / Nom et prénoms)

1. In this action, I am the
   Dans la présente action, je suis le/la

   ☐ plaintiff
     demandeur/demanderesse

   ☐ defendant
     défendeur/défenderesse

   ☐ representative of _____
     représentant(e) de
     (Name of party(ies) / Nom de la ou des parties)

2. I withdraw the offer to settle provided to _____
   Je retire l'offre de transaction faite à
   (Name of party(ies) / Nom de la ou des parties)

   dated _____ , 20 _____ , which has not been accepted.
   et datée du , *laquelle n'a pas été acceptée.*

   _____ , 20 _____

   _____
   (Signature of party or representative withdrawing offer / Signature de la
   partie ou du/de la représentant(e) qui retire l'offre)

   _____

   (Name, address and phone number of party or representative / Nom,
   adresse et numéro de téléphone de la partie ou du/de la représentant(e))

SCR 14.01.1-14C (June 1, 2009 / 1er juin 2009) CSD

ONTARIO

Superior Court of Justice
Cour supérieure de justice

Terms of Settlement
Conditions de la transaction

Form / *Formule* 14D Ont. Reg. No. / *Règl. de l'Ont.* : 258/98

Small Claims Court / *Cour des petites créances de*

Claim No. / *N° de la demande*

Address / *Adresse*

Phone number / *Numéro de téléphone*

BETWEEN / ENTRE

Plaintiff(s) / *Demandeur(s)/demanderesse(s)*

and / et

Defendant(s) / *Défendeur(s)/défenderesse(s)*

We have agreed to settle this action on the following terms:
Nous avons convenu de régler la présente action selon les conditions suivantes :

1.

_____ shall pay to
Name of party(ies) / *Nom de la ou des parties*   verse à

the sum of
Name of party(ies) / *Nom de la ou des parties*   la somme de

$ _____ as follows as full and final settlement of the claim, inclusive of interest and costs:
$ comme suit, à titre de transaction complète et définitive sur la demande, y compris les intérêts et les dépens :

(Provide terms of payment such as start date, frequency, amount and duration.)
(Indiquez les modalités de paiement telles que la date de début des versements ainsi que leur fréquence, leur montant et leur durée.)

Put a line through any blank space and initial.
Tracez une ligne en travers de tout espace laissé en blanc et apposez vos initiales.

SCR 14D (June 1, 2009 / *1ᵉʳ juin 2009*) CSD

FORM / *FORMULE* 14D   PAGE 2

2.   This claim (and Defendant's Claim, if any) is withdrawn.
     Cette demande (et celle du défendeur, le cas échéant) est retirée (sont retirées).

3.   If a party to these terms of settlement fails to comply, judgment in the terms of settlement may be obtained
     against that party on motion to the court or this action may continue as if there has been no settlement.
     *Si une partie aux présentes conditions de la transaction n'en observe pas les conditions, un jugement
     suivant les conditions de la transaction peut être obtenu contre cette partie sur présentation d'une motion
     au tribunal ou la présente action peut continuer comme s'il n'y avait jamais eu de transaction.*

4.   Provided that the terms of settlement are complied with, the parties above fully and finally release one
     another from all claims related to the facts and issues raised in this action.
     *Pourvu que les conditions de la transaction soient observées, les parties susmentionnées se dégagent
     l'une et l'autre complètement et définitivement de toutes demandes liées aux faits et questions en litige
     soulevés dans la présente action.*

The parties do not need to sign terms of settlement on the same day, but each must sign in the presence of his or her witness who signs a
moment later. (For additional parties' signatures, attach a separate sheet in the below format.)
*Les parties ne sont pas tenues de signer les conditions de la transaction le même jour, mais chacune doit les signer en présence de son
témoin, qui les signe à son tour aussitôt après. (S'il y a lieu, annexez une autre feuille portant la signature des parties additionnelles
présentée selon le format indiqué ci-dessous.)*

_____ , 20 ____   _____ , 20 ____

(Signature of party / *Signature de la partie*)   (Signature of party / *Signature de la partie*)

(Name of party / *Nom de la partie*)   (Name of party / *Nom de la partie*)

(Signature of witness / *Signature du témoin*)   (Signature of witness / *Signature du témoin*)

(Name of witness / *Nom du témoin*)   (Name of witness / *Nom du témoin*)

_____ , 20 ____   _____ , 20 ____

(Signature of party / *Signature de la partie*)   (Signature of party / *Signature de la partie*)

(Name of party / *Nom de la partie*)   (Name of party / *Nom de la partie*)

(Signature of witness / *Signature du témoin*)   (Signature of witness / *Signature du témoin*)

(Name of witness / *Nom du témoin*)   (Name of witness / *Nom du témoin*)

SCR 14D (June 1, 2009 / *1er juin 2009*) CSD

Instructions for Making a Motion in Small Claims Court

A motion is a request to a judge to make an order about a case. For example, a defendant could ask the court for more time to send in a defence or a defendant's claim. Or either party could ask for more time to serve documents.

Motions can help the parties in a case. They can also make the case take longer and cost more money. If the judge grants your motion, you can ask the judge to make the other party pay some of your costs. These costs can include court filing fees, lawyer or agent fees, and expenses for witnesses, photocopying, faxing and delivery of documents.

Step 1: **EXPLAIN** what you are asking the judge to do and why. This is done by filling out a **Notice of Motion and Supporting Affidavit** form. Contact the clerk of the court to choose a time and date when the court could hear the motion. The clerk of the court will provide a hearing date and time. Put the date and time on the form.

Step 2: **SERVE.** The form must then be served on the other parties at least 7 days before the hearing date. There are rules about how this must be done. See the Small Claims Court **"Guide to Serving Documents"** at the court office or online at www.attorneygeneral.jus.gov.on.ca. Copies of documents attached to the form must also be served.

Step 3: **FILE** the **Notice of Motion and Supporting Affidavit** form at the court at least 3 days before the hearing date. There is a filing fee. Also file an **Affidavit of Service** (Form 8A) proving that the other parties were served.

Motion in Writing for an Assessment of Damages

If all defendants have been noted in default after failing to file a defence, you can bring a motion in writing for an assessment of damages. You do not have to attend the motion. The judge will make a decision based on the documents that you filed. If the judge thinks the documents you filed are inadequate, the court may order you to provide a further affidavit or to attend an assessment hearing. You can also request an assessment hearing.

For more information, see the **"Guide to Motions and Clerk's Orders"** at the court office or online at www.attorneygeneral.jus.gov.on.ca

DO NOT FILE THIS PAGE.

SCR 15.01 15A (September 1, 2010 / 1ᵉʳ septembre 2010) CSD

Instructions pour présenter une motion à la Cour des petites créances

Une motion est une demande présentée à un juge pour qu'il rende une ordonnance au sujet d'une cause. Par exemple, un défendeur pourrait demander au tribunal plus de temps pour envoyer une défense ou une demande du défendeur. Ou encore, l'une ou l'autre des parties pourrait demander plus de temps pour signifier des documents.

Les motions peuvent aider les parties dans une cause. Elles peuvent aussi prolonger la durée de la cause et coûter plus d'argent. Si le juge accorde votre motion, vous pouvez lui demander d'ordonner à l'autre partie de payer une partie de vos dépens. Ces dépens peuvent comprendre les frais de dépôt de documents au tribunal, les honoraires d'avocat ou de mandataire ainsi que les frais des témoins, de photocopie, de télécopie et de délivrance des documents.

Étape 1 : ***EXPLIQUEZ*** ce que vous demandez au juge de faire et pourquoi. Cette démarche est accomplie en remplissant la formule ***Avis de motion et affidavit à l'appui***. Communiquez avec le greffier du tribunal pour choisir la date et l'heure de l'audition de la motion par le tribunal. Le greffier vous donnera une date et une heure d'audience. Inscrivez-les sur la formule.

Étape 2 : ***SIGNIFIEZ.*** La formule doit ensuite être signifiée aux autres parties au moins 7 jours avant la date de l'audience. Il existe des règles sur la façon de signifier. Consultez le «***Guide sur la signification des documents***» de la Cour des petites créances au greffe ou en ligne à l'adresse www.attorneygeneral.jus.gov.on.ca. Des copies des documents joints à la formule doivent également être signifiées.

Étape 3 : ***DÉPOSEZ*** la formule ***Avis de motion et affidavit à l'appui*** au tribunal au moins 3 jours avant la date de l'audience. Des frais de dépôt sont exigés. Déposez aussi un ***Affidavit de signification*** (formule 8A) prouvant que la signification aux autres parties a été effectuée.

Motion par écrit en vue d'une évaluation des dommages-intérêts

Si tous les défendeurs ont été constatés en défaut parce qu'ils n'ont pas déposé de défense, vous pouvez présenter une motion par écrit en vue d'une évaluation des dommages-intérêts. Vous n'avez pas besoin d'être présent(e) à l'audition de la motion. Le juge rendra une décision en se fondant sur les documents que vous avez déposés. S'il estime qu'ils ne sont pas suffisants, le tribunal peut vous ordonner de remettre un autre affidavit ou de vous présenter à une audience d'évaluation. Vous pouvez aussi demander la tenue d'une audience d'évaluation.

Pour de plus amples renseignements, consultez le «***Guide sur les motions et les ordonnances du greffier***» au greffe ou en ligne à l'adresse www.attorneygeneral.jus.gov.on.ca

NE DÉPOSEZ PAS LA PRÉSENTE PAGE.

ONTARIO

Superior Court of Justice
Cour supérieure de justice

Notice of Motion and Supporting Affidavit
Avis de motion et affidavit à l'appui
Form / *Formule* 15A Ont. Reg. No. / *Régl. de l'Ont.* : 258/98

Small Claims Court / *Cour des petites créances de*	Claim No. / *N° de la demande*

Address / *Adresse*

Phone number / *Numéro de téléphone*

Plaintiff No. 1 / *Demandeur n° 1* ☐ Additional plaintiff(s) listed on attached Form 1A.
Le ou les demandeurs additionnels sont mentionnés sur la formule 1A ci-jointe.

Last name, or name of company / *Nom de famille ou nom de la compagnie*		
First name / *Premier prénom*	Second name / *Deuxième prénom*	Also known as / *Également connu(e) sous le nom de*
Address (street number, apt., unit) / *Adresse (numéro et rue, app., unité)*		
City/Town / *Cité/ville* Province		Phone no. / *N° de téléphone*
Postal code / *Code postal*		Fax no. / *N° de télécopieur*
Representative / *Représentant(e)*		LSUC # / *N° du BHC*
Address (street number, apt., unit) / *Adresse (numéro et rue, app., unité)*		
City/Town / *Cité/ville* Province		Phone no. / *N° de téléphone*
Postal code / *Code postal*		Fax no. / *N° de télécopieur*

Defendant No. 1 / *Défendeur n° 1* ☐ Additional defendant(s) listed on attached Form 1A.
Le ou les défendeurs additionnels sont mentionnés sur la formule 1A ci-jointe.

Last name, or name of company / *Nom de famille ou nom de la compagnie*		
First name / *Premier prénom*	Second name / *Deuxième prénom*	Also known as / *Également connu(e) sous le nom de*
Address (street number, apt., unit) / *Adresse (numéro et rue, app., unité)*		
City/Town / *Cité/ville* Province		Phone no. / *N° de téléphone*
Postal code / *Code postal*		Fax no. / *N° de télécopieur*
Representative / *Représentant(e)*		LSUC # / *N° du BHC*
Address (street number, apt., unit) / *Adresse (numéro et rue, app., unité)*		
City/Town / *Cité/ville* Province		Phone no. / *N° de téléphone*
Postal code / *Code postal*		Fax no. / *N° de télécopieur*

SCR 15.01-15A (September 1, 2010 / *1er septembre 2010*) CSD

Court Forms in Small Claims Court

Claim No. / N° de la demande

THIS COURT WILL HEAR A MOTION on _____ , 20 ____ , at _____ ,
LE TRIBUNAL PRÉCITÉ ENTENDRA UNE MOTION le   , à   (Time / heure)

or as soon as possible after that time, at _____
ou dès que possible par la suite à/au   (Address of court location and courtroom number / *Adresse du tribunal et numéro de la salle d'audience*)

Complete Part A or Part B below, then complete the affidavit in support of motion on page 3. / *Remplissez la partie A ou la partie B ci-dessous. Remplissez ensuite l'affidavit à l'appui de la motion à la page 3.*

A.   This motion will be made in person by _____ ,
    La motion sera présentée en personne par :   (Name of party / *Nom de la partie*)

    for the following order : / *en vue d'obtenir l'ordonnance suivante :*

     ☐   the court's permission to extend time to (Specify)
         l'autorisation du tribunal de proroger le délai pour *(Précisez)*

     ☐   set aside default judgment and noting in default.
         l'annulation du jugement par défaut et la constatation du défaut.

     ☐   set aside noting in default.
         l'annulation de la constatation du défaut.

     ☐   permission to file a Defence.
         l'autorisation de déposer une défense.

     ☐   permission to file a Defendant's Claim.
         l'autorisation de déposer une demande du défendeur.

     ☐   set aside order dismissing claim as abandoned.
         l'annulation d'une demande pour cause de renonciation

     ☐   terminate garnishment and/or withdraw writ(s).
         la mainlevée de la saisie-arrêt ou le retrait d'un ou de plusieurs brefs, ou les deux.

     ☐   Other: _____
         Autre : _____

    ☐   ADDITIONAL PAGES ARE ATTACHED BECAUSE MORE ROOM WAS NEEDED.
        DES FEUILLES SUPPLÉMENTAIRES SONT ANNEXÉES EN RAISON DU MANQUE D'ESPACE.

    ☐   DOCUMENTS ARE ATTACHED.
        PIÈCES JOINTES.

NOTE: IF YOU FAIL TO ATTEND AN IN-PERSON MOTION, an order may be made against you, with costs, in your absence. If you want to attend the motion by telephone or video conference, complete and file a Request for Telephone or Video Conference (Form 1B). If the court permits it, the clerk will make the necessary arrangements and notify the parties [R. 1.07(5)].

REMARQUE :   *SI VOUS NE VOUS PRÉSENTEZ PAS EN PERSONNE À L'AUDITION DE LA MOTION, une ordonnance peut être rendue contre vous en votre absence, avec dépens. Si vous voulez assister à l'audition de la motion par conférence téléphonique ou vidéoconférence, remplissez et déposez la Demande de conférence téléphonique ou vidéoconférence (formule 1B). Si le tribunal l'autorise, le greffier prendra les dispositions nécessaires et en avisera les parties [par. 1.07 (5)]*

Claim No. / *N° de la demande*

B. **This motion in writing for an assessment of damages is made by**
La présente motion par écrit en vue d'une évaluation des dommages-intérêts est présentée par

_____

(Name of plaintiff / *Nom du demandeur/de la demanderesse*)

who asks the court for an order assessing damages against
qui demande au tribunal de rendre une ordonnance d'évaluation des dommages-intérêts contre

_____

(Name of defendant(s) / *Nom du/de la/des défendeur(s)/défenderesse(s)*)

who have/has been noted in default.
qui a/ont été constaté(e)(s) en défaut.

AFFIDAVIT IN SUPPORT OF MOTION / *AFFIDAVIT À L'APPUI DE LA MOTION*

My name is _____
Je m'appelle
(Full name / *Nom et prénoms*)

I live in _____
J'habite à
(Municipality & province / *Municipalité et province*)

I swear/affirm that the following is true:
Je déclare sous serment/j'affirme solennellement que les renseignements suivants sont véridiques :

Set out the facts in numbered paragraphs. If you learned a fact from someone else, you must give that person's name and state that you believe that fact to be true.
Indiquez les faits sous forme de dispositions numérotées. Si vous avez pris connaissance d'un fait par l'entremise d'une autre personne, vous devez indiquer le nom de cette personne et déclarer que vous croyez que ce fait est véridique.

_____
_____
_____
_____
_____
_____
_____
_____
_____
_____
_____
_____
_____
_____
_____
_____
_____
_____
_____
_____

SCR 15.01-15A (September 1, 2010 / *1er septembre 2010*) CSD

Continued on next page / *Suite à la page suivante*

FORM / *FORMULE* 15A   PAGE 4

Claim No. / *N° de la demande*

AFFIDAVIT IN SUPPORT OF MOTION, continued / *AFFIDAVIT À L'APPUI DE LA MOTION, suite*

_____
_____
_____
_____
_____
_____
_____
_____
_____
_____
_____
_____
_____
_____
_____
_____
_____
_____
_____
_____
_____
_____
_____
_____
_____
_____

If more space is required, attach and initial extra pages. / Si vous avez besoin de plus d'espace, annexez une ou des feuilles supplémentaires et paraphez-les.

Sworn/Affirmed before me at _____
Déclaré sous serment/Affirmé   (Municipality / *municipalité*)
solennellement devant moi à

in _____
en/à/au   (Province, state or country / *province, État ou pays*)

on _____ , 20 ____   _____
le   Commissioner for taking affidavits
                              Commissaire aux affidavits
                 (Type or print name below if signature is illegible.)
                 *(Dactylographiez le nom ou écrivez-le en
                 caractères d'imprimerie ci-dessous si la
                 signature est illisible.)*

_____
Signature
(This form is to be signed in front of a
lawyer, justice of the peace, notary public
or commissioner for taking affidavits.)
*(La présente formule doit être signée en
présence d'un avocat, d'un juge de paix,
d'un notaire ou d'un commissaire aux
affidavits.)*

WARNING: IT IS AN OFFENCE UNDER THE *CRIMINAL CODE* TO KNOWINGLY SWEAR OR
                AFFIRM A FALSE AFFIDAVIT.
*AVERTISSEMENT : FAIRE SCIEMMENT UN FAUX AFFIDAVIT CONSTITUE UNE INFRACTION AU CODE
                CRIMINEL.*

SCR 15.01-15A (September 1, 2010 / *1er septembre 2010*) CSD

ONTARIO

Superior Court of Justice
Cour supérieure de justice

Affidavit
Affidavit

Form / *Formule* 15B Ont. Reg. No. / *Règl. de l'Ont.* : 258/98

Small Claims Court / *Cour des petites créances de*　　Claim No. / *N° de la demande*

Address / *Adresse*

Phone number / *Numéro de téléphone*

BETWEEN / ENTRE

Plaintiff(s)/Creditor(s) / *Demandeur(s)/demanderesse(s)/créancier(s)/créancière(s)*

and / et

Defendant(s)/Debtor(s) / *Défendeur(s)/défenderesse(s)/débiteur(s)/débitrice(s)*

My name is
Je m'appelle

(Full name / *Nom et prénoms*)

I live in
J'habite à

(Municipality & province / *Municipalité et province*)

I make this affidavit in relation to:
Je fais le présent affidavit relativement à : (Specify why the affidavit is being filed with the court. / *Précisez les raisons pour lesquelles l'affidavit est déposé auprès du tribunal.*)

and I swear/affirm that the following is true:
et je déclare sous serment/j'affirme solennellement que les renseignements suivants sont véridiques :
Set out the facts in numbered paragraphs. If you learned a fact from someone else, you must give that person's name and state that you believe that fact to be true.
Indiquez les faits sous forme de dispositions numérotées. Si vous avez pris connaissance d'un fait par l'entremise d'une autre personne, vous devez indiquer le nom de cette personne et déclarer que vous croyez que ce fait est véridique.

SCR 15.01-15B (June 1, 2009 / *1er juin 2009*) CSD

FORM / *FORMULE* 15B   PAGE 2

Claim No. / *N° de la demande*

_____

_____

_____

_____

_____

_____

_____

_____

_____

_____

_____

_____

_____

_____

_____

_____

_____

_____

_____

_____

_____

_____

_____

_____

If more space is required, attach and initial extra pages. / *Si vous avez besoin de plus d'espace, annexez une ou des feuilles supplémentaires et paraphez-les.*

Sworn/Affirmed before me at _____
Déclaré sous serment/Affirmé   (Municipality / *municipalité*)
solennellement devant moi à

in _____
en/à/au   (Province, state or country / *province, État ou pays*)

on _____ , 20 _____   _____
le   Commissioner for taking affidavits
                                      Commissaire aux affidavits
                                      (Type or print name below if signature is illegible.)
                                      (Dactylographiez le nom ou écrivez-le en
                                      caractères d'imprimerie ci-dessous si la
                                      signature est illisible.)

_____
Signature
(This form is to be signed in front of a
lawyer, justice of the peace, notary public
or commissioner for taking affidavits.)
(La présente formule doit être signée en
présence d'un avocat, d'un juge de paix,
d'un notaire ou d'un commissaire aux
affidavits.)

WARNING:	IT IS AN OFFENCE UNDER THE *CRIMINAL CODE* TO KNOWINGLY SWEAR OR AFFIRM A FALSE AFFIDAVIT.
AVERTISSEMENT :	*FAIRE SCIEMMENT UN FAUX AFFIDAVIT CONSTITUE UNE INFRACTION AU CODE CRIMINEL.*

Court Forms in Small Claims Court

ONTARIO

Superior Court of Justice
Cour supérieure de justice

Summons to Witness
Assignation de témoin

Form / *Formule* 18A Ont. Reg. No. / *Régl. de l'Ont.* : 258/98

Small Claims Court / *Cour des petites créances de*

Claim No. / *N° de la demande*

Seal / *Sceau*

Address / *Adresse*

Phone number / *Numéro de téléphone*

BETWEEN / *ENTRE*

Plaintiff(s) / *Demandeur(s)/demanderesse(s)*

and / *et*

Defendant(s) / *Défendeur(s)/défenderesse(s)*

TO:
DESTINATAIRE :

(Name of witness / *Nom du témoin*)

YOU ARE REQUIRED TO ATTEND AND TO GIVE EVIDENCE IN COURT at the trial of this action on
*VOUS ÊTES REQUIS(E) DE VOUS PRÉSENTER DEVANT LE TRIBUNAL POUR TÉMOIGNER à l'instruction
de cette action le*

, 20 _____ **at**
à   (Time / *heure*)   , at
à/au

(Address of court location / *Adresse du tribunal*)

and to remain until your attendance is no longer required. You may be required to return to court from time to time.
*et d'y demeurer jusqu'à ce que votre présence ne soit plus requise. Vous pourriez être requis(e) de vous
présenter à nouveau devant le tribunal à l'occasion.*

YOU ARE ALSO REQUIRED TO BRING WITH YOU AND PRODUCE AT THE TRIAL the following documents
or other things in your possession, control or power:
*VOUS ÊTES EN OUTRE REQUIS(E) D'APPORTER AVEC VOUS ET DE PRODUIRE LORS DE
L'INSTRUCTION les documents ou autres objets suivants dont vous avez la garde, la possession ou le contrôle :*

(Identify and describe particular documents and other things required / *Indiquez et décrivez les documents et autres objets particuliers qui sont requis*)

SCR 18.03-18A (June 1, 2009 / *1er juin* 2009) CSD

1020

Court Forms in Small Claims Court

Claim No. / N° de la demande _____

_____

_____

_____

_____

_____

_____

_____

_____

_____

_____

_____

_____

_____

_____

_____

_____

_____

and all other documents or other things in your possession, control or power relating to the action.
ainsi que tous les autres documents ou autres objets dont vous avez la garde, la possession ou le contrôle et qui se rapportent à l'action.

_____   has requested the clerk to issue this summons.
(Name of party / *Nom de la partie*)   *a demandé au greffier de délivrer la présente assignation.*

_____ , 20 _____   _____
(Signature of clerk / *Signature du greffier*)

NOTE:	THIS SUMMONS MUST BE SERVED personally, at least 10 days before the trial date, on the person to be summoned together with attendance money calculated in accordance with the Small Claims Court Schedule of Fees, which is a regulation under the *Administration of Justice Act*. To obtain a copy of the regulation, attend the nearest Small Claims Court or access the following website: www.e-laws.gov.on.ca
REMARQUE :	*LA PRÉSENTE ASSIGNATION DOIT ÊTRE SIGNIFIÉE à personne, au moins 10 jours avant la date du procès, à la personne devant être assignée, avec l'indemnité de présence calculée conformément au barème des honoraires et frais de la Cour des petites créances qui constitue un règlement pris en application de la Loi sur l'administration de la justice. Vous pouvez obtenir un exemplaire du règlement auprès de la Cour des petites créances de votre localité ou en consultant le site Web suivant : www.lois-en-ligne.gouv.on.ca.*

CAUTION:	IF YOU FAIL TO ATTEND OR REMAIN IN ATTENDANCE AS REQUIRED BY THIS SUMMONS, A WARRANT MAY BE ISSUED FOR YOUR ARREST.
AVERTISSEMENT :	*SI VOUS NE VOUS PRÉSENTEZ PAS OU SI VOUS NE DEMEUREZ PAS PRÉSENT(E) COMME L'EXIGE LA PRÉSENTE ASSIGNATION, UN MANDAT D'ARRÊT PEUT ÊTRE DÉLIVRÉ CONTRE VOUS.*

SCR 18.03-18A (June 1, 2005 / 1ᵉʳ juin 2005) CSD

ONTARIO
Superior Court of Justice
Cour supérieure de justice

Warrant for Arrest of Defaulting Witness
Mandat d'arrêt d'un témoin défaillant
Form / Formule 18B Ont. Reg. No. / Régl. de l'Ont. : 258/98

Seal / Sceau

Small Claims Court / *Cour des petites créances de*

Claim No. / *N° de la demande*

Address / *Adresse*

Phone number / *Numéro de téléphone*

BETWEEN / ENTRE

Plaintiff(s) / *Demandeur(s)/demanderesse(s)*

and / et

Defendant(s) / *Défendeur(s)/défenderesse(s)*

TO ALL POLICE OFFICERS IN ONTARIO AND TO THE OFFICERS OF ALL CORRECTIONAL INSTITUTIONS IN ONTARIO:
À TOUS LES AGENTS DE POLICE DE L'ONTARIO ET AUX AGENTS DE TOUS LES ÉTABLISSEMENTS CORRECTIONNELS DE L'ONTARIO :

The witness
Le témoin

(Name / *Nom*)

of
de

(Address / *Adresse*)

was served with a Summons to Witness (Form 18A) to give evidence at the trial of this action, and the prescribed attendance money was paid or tendered.
a reçu signification d'une assignation de témoin (formule 18A) pour témoigner à l'instruction de la présente action, et l'indemnité de présence prescrite lui a été versée ou offerte.

The witness failed to attend or to remain in attendance at the trial, and I am satisfied that the evidence of this witness is material to this proceeding.
Le témoin ne s'est pas présenté ou n'est pas demeuré présent au procès, et je suis convaincu(e) que son témoignage est essentiel à l'instance.

YOU ARE ORDERED TO ARREST AND BRING this person before the court to give evidence in this action, and if the court is not then sitting or if the person cannot be brought before the court immediately, to deliver the person to a provincial correctional institution or other secure facility, to be admitted and detained there until the person can be brought before the court.
JE VOUS ORDONNE D'ARRÊTER CETTE PERSONNE ET DE L'AMENER devant le tribunal afin qu'elle témoigne dans l'action et, si le tribunal ne siège pas ou si la personne ne peut être amenée devant le tribunal immédiatement, de la livrer à un établissement correctionnel provincial ou à un autre établissement de garde en milieu fermé, afin qu'elle y soit admise et détenue jusqu'à ce qu'elle puisse être amenée devant le tribunal.

I FURTHER ORDER YOU TO HOLD this person in custody and to detain him/her only so long as necessary to bring this person before a court as ordered above.
JE VOUS ORDONNE EN OUTRE DE MAINTENIR cette personne sous garde et de la détenir tant et aussi longtemps qu'il sera nécessaire pour l'amener devant un tribunal, comme il est ordonné ci-dessus.

, 20

(Signature of judge / *Signature du juge*)

SCR 18.03-20.11-18B (June 1, 2009 / *1er juin 2009*) CSD

ONTARIO
Superior Court of Justice
Cour supérieure de justice

Certificate of Judgment
Certificat de jugement
Form / Formule 20A Ont. Reg. No. / Règl. de l'Ont. : 258/98

Seal / Sceau

Small Claims Court / Cour des petites créances de

Claim No. / N° de la demande

Address / Adresse

Phone number / Numéro de téléphone

BETWEEN / ENTRE

Creditor(s) / Créancier(s)/créancière(s)

and / et

Debtor(s) / Débiteur(s)/débitrice(s)

A judgment was made in this action on _____ , 20 _____ , **in the**
Un jugement a été rendu dans la présente action le , *à la*

(Name of court where judgment was made / Nom de la cour où le jugement a été rendu)

against / contre

Last name of debtor, or name of company / Nom de famille du débiteur/de la débitrice ou nom de la compagnie		
First name / Premier prénom	Second name / Deuxième prénom	Third name / Troisième prénom
Address / Adresse		

Last name of debtor, or name of company / Nom de famille du débiteur/de la débitrice ou nom de la compagnie		
First name / Premier prénom	Second name / Deuxième prénom	Third name / Troisième prénom
Address / Adresse		

Last name of debtor, or name of company / Nom de famille du débiteur/de la débitrice ou nom de la compagnie		
First name / Premier prénom	Second name / Deuxième prénom	Third name / Troisième prénom
Address / Adresse		

☐ Additional debtor(s) and also known as names are listed on attached Form 1A.1.
Le ou les débiteur(s) additionnel(s) et le ou les noms sous lesquels les débiteurs sont également connus sont mentionnés sur la formule 1A.1 ci-jointe.

SCR 20.04-20A (September 1, 2010 / 1ᵉʳ septembre 2010) CSD

FORM / FORMULE 20A   PAGE 2

Claim No. / N° de la demande

Judgment was made for the following sums:
Un jugement a été rendu à l'égard des sommes suivantes :

(A) **AMOUNT OF JUDGMENT** (debt and pre-judgment interest) $ _____
    LE MONTANT DU JUGEMENT (créance et intérêts antérieurs au jugement) $

(B) **COSTS** to date of judgment $ _____
    LES DÉPENS à la date du jugement $

    Post-judgment interest continues to accrue at _____ % per annum.
    Les intérêts postérieurs au jugement continuent   (Interest rate /   % par an.
    à courir au taux de   *Taux d'intérêt)*

    _____ , 20 ____   _____
                                        (Signature of clerk / *Signature du greffier*)

TO THE CLERK OF THE _____
AU GREFFIER DE LA COUR DES PETITES   (Name of court to where the judgment is to be filed   **SMALL CLAIMS COURT:**
CRÉANCES DE   / *Nom du tribunal où le jugement doit être déposé*)

The person requesting this certificate is _____
La personne qui demande le présent certificat est   (Name of party requesting certificate / *Nom de la partie qui demande le certificat*)

_____
                    (Address of party requesting certificate / *Adresse de la partie qui demande le certificat*)
_____

SCR 20.04-20A (September 1, 2010 / *1er septembre 2010*) CSD

ONTARIO
Superior Court of Justice
Cour supérieure de justice

Writ of Delivery
Bref de délaissement
Form / Formule 20B Ont. Reg. No. / Régl. de l'Ont. . 258/98

Seal / Sceau

Small Claims Court / Cour des petites créances de   Claim No. / N° de la demande

Address / Adresse

Phone number / Numéro de téléphone

BETWEEN / ENTRE

Plaintiff(s) / Demandeur(s)/demanderesse(s)

and / et

Defendant(s) / Défendeur(s)/défenderesse(s)

TO THE BAILIFF OF   **SMALL CLAIMS COURT:**
À L'HUISSIER DE LA COUR   (Name of Small Claims Court location / Emplacement de la Cour
DES PETITES CRÉANCES DE   des petites créances)

Under an order of this court made on _____ , 20 _____
En vertu d'une ordonnance rendue par le tribunal précité le

YOU ARE DIRECTED to seize from _____
NOUS VOUS ENJOIGNONS de saisir auprès de   (Name of person against whom the order was made / Nom de la personne
                                                                  contre qui l'ordonnance a été rendue)

and to deliver without delay to | Name of person in whose favour the order was made / Nom de la personne en faveur de qui
et de remettre sans retard à | l'ordonnance a été rendue
| Street and number / Numéro et rue
| City, province, postal code / Ville, province, code postal
| Phone number and fax number, if any / Numéro de téléphone et numéro de télécopieur, le cas échéant

possession of the following personal property:
la possession des biens meubles suivants :
(According to the court order, set out a description of the property to be delivered. Identify any marks or serial numbers. If the order refers to items set out in the issued claim, attach a copy of the issued claim.)
(Conformément à l'ordonnance du tribunal, donnez la description des biens qui doivent être remis. Indiquez toute marque d'identification ou tout numéro de série y figurant. Si l'ordonnance vise des articles énoncés dans la demande délivrée, annexez une copie de la demande délivrée.)

SCR 20.05-20B (June 1, 2009 / 1er juin 2009) CSD

FORM / *FORMULE* 20B   PAGE 2

Claim No. / *N° de la demande*

_____

_____

_____

_____

_____

_____

_____

_____

_____

_____

_____

_____

_____

_____

_____

The above personal property is located at: _____
Les biens meubles susmentionnés se trouvent à/au :
                                          (Address / *Adresse*)

If the address provided does not clearly identify where the items are located, please attach a detailed map that shows the nearest intersection.
Si l'adresse fournie n'indique pas clairement l'emplacement des articles, veuillez annexer un plan détaillé qui montre l'intersection la plus rapprochée.

(To be completed by the clerk of the court. / Section à remplir par le greffier du tribunal.)   ☐ **THE COURT HAS EXPRESSLY ORDERED** that you are authorized to use reasonable force to enter a private dwelling to execute this writ of delivery, if necessary [*Execution Act*, s. 20(2)]. A copy of the court's order on the endorsement record is attached.
EN VERTU D'UNE ORDONNANCE EXPRESSE DU TRIBUNAL, *vous êtes autorisé(e) à avoir recours à la force raisonnable pour pénétrer dans un logement privé pour exécuter le présent bref de délaissement, si cela est nécessaire [Loi sur l'exécution forcée, par. 20 (2)]. Une copie de l'ordonnance du tribunal qui figure au dossier des inscriptions est annexée.*

_____, 20 _____   _____
                                                  (Signature of clerk / *Signature du greffier*)

SCR 20.05-20B (June 1, 2009 / *1er juin 2009*) CSD

ONTARIO

Superior Court of Justice
Cour supérieure de justice

Writ of Seizure and Sale of Personal Property
Bref de saisie-exécution de biens meubles
Form / Formule 20C Ont. Reg. No. / Régl. de l'Ont. : 258/98

Seal / Sceau

Small Claims Court / Cour des petites créances de

Claim No. / N° de la demande

Address / Adresse

Phone number / Numéro de téléphone

Creditor No. 1 / Créancier n° 1

☐ Additional party(ies) listed on attached Form 1A.
La ou les parties additionnelles sont mentionnées sur la formule 1A ci-jointe.

Last name, or name of company / Nom de famille ou nom de la compagnie		
First name / Premier prénom	Second name / Deuxième prénom	Also known as / Également connu(e) sous le nom de
Address (street number, apt., unit) / Adresse (numéro et rue, app., unité)		
City/Town / Cité/ville	Province	Phone no. / N° de téléphone
Postal code / Code postal		Fax no. / N° de télécopieur
Representative / Représentant(e)		LSUC # / N° du BHC
Address (street number, apt., unit) / Adresse (numéro et rue, app., unité)		
City/Town / Cité/ville	Province	Phone no. / N° de téléphone
Postal code / Code postal		Fax no. / N° de télécopieur

Debtor No. 1 / Débiteur n° 1

☐ Additional party(ies) listed on attached Form 1A.
La ou les parties additionnelles sont mentionnées sur la formule 1A ci-jointe.

Last name, or name of company / Nom de famille ou nom de la compagnie		
First name / Premier prénom	Second name / Deuxième prénom	Also known as / Également connu(e) sous le nom de
Address (street number, apt., unit) / Adresse (numéro et rue, app., unité)		
City/Town / Cité/ville	Province	Phone no. / N° de téléphone
Postal code / Code postal		Fax no. / N° de télécopieur
Representative / Représentant(e)		LSUC # / N° du BHC
Address (street number, apt., unit) / Adresse (numéro et rue, app., unité)		
City/Town / Cité/ville	Province	Phone no. / N° de téléphone
Postal code / Code postal		Fax no. / N° de télécopieur

SCR 20.06-20C (June 1, 2009 / 1er juin 2009) CSD

FORM / *FORMULE* 20C   **PAGE 2**

Claim No. / *N° de la demande*

TO THE BAILIFF OF THE _____ **SMALL CLAIMS COURT:**
À L'HUISSIER DE LA COUR   (Small Claims Court location / *Emplacement de la Cour des*
DES PETITES CRÉANCES DE   *petites créances*)

Under an order of this court made on _____ , 20 _____ , in favour of
En vertu d'une ordonnance rendue par ce tribunal le   *, en faveur de*

(Name of creditor(s) / *Nom du/de la/des créancier(s)/créancière(s)*)

YOU ARE DIRECTED to seize and sell the personal property of
NOUS VOUS ENJOIGNONS *de saisir les biens meubles de*

Last name, or name of company / *Nom de famille ou nom de la compagnie*		
First name / *Premier prénom*	Second name / *Deuxième prénom*	Third name / *Troisième prénom*

☐ Additional debtor(s) and also known as names listed on attached Form 1A.1.
   Le ou les débiteurs additionnels et le ou les noms sous lesquels ils sont également connus sont mentionnés
   sur la formule 1A.1 ci-jointe.

situated within your jurisdiction and to realize from the seizure and sale the following sums:
qui se trouvent dans votre ressort et de procéder à leur vente pour réaliser les sommes suivantes :

(A) **AMOUNT OF JUDGMENT** (debt and pre-judgment interest) $ _____
    LE MONTANT DU JUGEMENT *(créance et intérêts antérieurs au jugement)* $

(B) **COSTS** to date of judgment $ _____
    LES DÉPENS *à la date du jugement* $

(C) **TOTAL AMOUNT OF PAYMENTS RECEIVED FROM DEBTOR** after
    judgment (if any) $ _____
    LE MONTANT TOTAL DES PAIEMENTS REÇUS DU DÉBITEUR *après le* $
    jugement (le cas échéant)

    Post-judgment interest continues to accrue
    Les intérêts postérieurs au jugement continuent à courir

    at the rate of _____ % per annum from _____ , 20 _____ .
    au taux de   *% par an à compter du*

(D) **SUBSEQUENT COSTS** incurred after judgment (including the cost of issuing this writ) $ _____
    LES DÉPENS SUBSÉQUENTS *engagés après le jugement (y compris le coût* $
    de délivrance du présent bref)

(E) Your fees and expenses in enforcing this writ.
    Les honoraires et frais qui vous sont dus pour l'exécution forcée du présent bref.

SCR 20.06-20C (June 1, 2009 / *1ᵉʳ juin 2009*) CSD   Continued on next page / *Suite à la page suivante*

FORM / *FORMULE* 20C   PAGE 3

YOU ARE DIRECTED to calculate the amount owing at the time of enforcement and to pay the proceeds over to the clerk of this court for the creditor.
ET NOUS VOUS ENJOIGNONS de calculer la somme due au moment de l'exécution forcée et de verser le produit de la vente au greffier du tribunal précité pour le compte du créancier.

_____ , 20 _____   _____

(Signature of clerk / *Signature du greffier*)

Reasonable disbursements necessarily incurred to enforce this writ	$
Débours raisonnables qui ont dû être engagés pour exécuter le présent bref	(filled in and initialled by the enforcement office / $
(Bailiff (enforcement office) fees and expenses / *Honoraires et frais de l'huissier (bureau de l'exécution)*)	*à remplir et à parapher par le bureau de l'exécution*)

NOTE:	**THIS WRIT REMAINS IN FORCE FOR SIX YEARS** after the date of its issue and for a further six years after each renewal. The writ may be renewed before it expires by filing a Request to Renew a Writ of Seizure and Sale (Form 20N) with the bailiff (enforcement office).
REMARQUE :	*LE PRÉSENT BREF RESTE EN VIGUEUR PENDANT SIX ANS après la date de sa délivrance ou après chaque renouvellement. Le bref peut être renouvelé avant qu'il n'expire en déposant une demande de renouvellement du bref de saisie-exécution (formule 20N) auprès de l'huissier (bureau de l'exécution).*

ONTARIO
Superior Court of Justice
Cour supérieure de justice

Writ of Seizure and Sale of Land
Bref de saisie-exécution de biens-fonds
Form / Formule 20D Ont. Reg. No. / Régl. de l'Ont. : 258/98

Small Claims Court / Cour des petites créances de	Claim No. / N° de la demande

Seal / Sceau

Address / Adresse

Phone number / Numéro de téléphone

☐ Additional party(ies) listed on attached Form 1A.
La ou les parties additionnelles sont mentionnées sur la formule 1A ci-jointe.

Creditor No. 1 / Créancier n° 1

Last name, or name of company / Nom de famille ou nom de la compagnie		
First name / Premier prénom	Second name / Deuxième prénom	Also known as / Également connu(e) sous le nom de
Address (street number, apt., unit) / Adresse (numéro et rue, app., unité)		
City/Town / Cité/ville	Province	Phone no. / N° de téléphone
Postal code / Code postal		Fax no. / N° de télécopieur
Representative / Représentant(e)		LSUC # / N° du BHC
Address (street number, apt., unit) / Adresse (numéro et rue, app., unité)		
City/Town / Cité/ville	Province	Phone no. / N° de téléphone
Postal code / Code postal		Fax no. / N° de télécopieur

☐ Additional party(ies) listed on attached Form 1A.
La ou les parties additionnelles sont mentionnées sur la formule 1A ci-jointe.

Debtor No. 1 / Débiteur n° 1

Last name, or name of company / Nom de famille ou nom de la compagnie		
First name / Premier prénom	Second name / Deuxième prénom	Also known as / Également connu(e) sous le nom de
Address (street number, apt., unit) / Adresse (numéro et rue, app., unité)		
City/Town / Cité/ville	Province	Phone no. / N° de téléphone
Postal code / Code postal		Fax no. / N° de télécopieur
Representative / Représentant(e)		LSUC # / N° du BHC
Address (street number, apt., unit) / Adresse (numéro et rue, app., unité)		
City/Town / Cité/ville	Province	Phone no. / N° de téléphone
Postal code / Code postal		Fax no. / N° de télécopieur

NOTE:	**THIS WRIT REMAINS IN FORCE FOR SIX YEARS** after the date of its issue and for a further six years after each renewal. The writ may be renewed before it expires by filing a Request to Renew a Writ of Seizure and Sale (Form 20N) with the sheriff (enforcement office.)
REMARQUE :	*LE PRÉSENT BREF RESTE EN VIGUEUR PENDANT SIX ANS après la date de sa délivrance ou après chaque renouvellement. Le bref peut être renouvelé avant qu'il n'expire en déposant une demande de renouvellement du bref de saisie-exécution (formule 20N) auprès du shérif (bureau de l'exécution).*

SCR 20.07-20D (June 1, 2009 / 1er juin 2009) CSD

Court Forms in Small Claims Court

Claim No. / *N° de la demande*

TO THE SHERIFF OF _____ :
AU SHÉRIF DE   (Name of county/region in which the enforcement office is located / *Nom du comté/de la région où est situé le bureau de l'exécution*)

Under an order of this court made on _____ , 20 _____ , in favour of
En vertu d'une ordonnance rendue par ce tribunal le   , *en faveur de*

_____
(Name of creditor(s) / *Nom du/de la/des créancier(s)/créancière(s)*)

YOU ARE DIRECTED to seize and sell the real property of
NOUS VOUS ENJOIGNONS *de saisir les biens immeubles de*

Last name, or name of company / *Nom de famille ou nom de la compagnie*		
First name / *Premier prénom*	Second name / *Deuxième prénom*	Third name / *Troisième prénom*

☐ Additional debtor(s) and also known as names listed on attached Form 1A.1.
Le ou les débiteurs additionnels et le ou les noms sous lesquels ils sont également connus sont mentionnés sur la formule 1A.1 ci-jointe.

situated within your jurisdiction and to realize from the seizure and sale the following sums:
qui se trouvent dans votre ressort et de procéder à leur vente pour réaliser les sommes suivantes :

(A) **AMOUNT OF JUDGMENT** (debt and pre-judgment interest) $ _____
      MONTANT DU JUGEMENT *(créance et intérêts antérieurs au jugement)* $

(B) **COSTS** to date of judgment $ _____
      LES DÉPENS *à la date du jugement* $

(C) **TOTAL AMOUNT OF PAYMENTS RECEIVED FROM DEBTOR** after
      judgment (if any) $ _____
      LE MONTANT TOTAL DES PAIEMENTS REÇUS DU DÉBITEUR *après le* $
      jugement (le cas échéant)

      Post-judgment interest continues to accrue
      Les intérêts postérieurs au jugement continuent à courir

      at the rate of _____ % per annum from _____ , 20 _____ .
      au taux de   % *par an à compter du*

(D) **SUBSEQUENT COSTS** incurred after judgment (including the cost of issuing this writ) $ _____
      LES DÉPENS SUBSÉQUENTS *engagés après le jugement (y compris le coût* $
      de délivrance du présent bref)

(E) Your fees and expenses in enforcing this writ.
      Les honoraires et frais qui vous sont dus pour l'exécution forcée du présent bref.

YOU ARE DIRECTED to calculate the amount owing at the time of enforcement and pay out the proceeds
according to law and to report on the execution of this writ if required by a party who filed this writ.
*ET NOUS VOUS ENJOIGNONS de calculer la somme due au moment de l'exécution forcée et de verser le
produit de la vente conformément à la loi et de faire un rapport sur l'exécution forcée du présent bref si la partie
qui l'a déposé l'exige.*

_____ , 20 _____   _____
                                                  (Signature of clerk / *Signature du greffier*)

SCR 20.07-20D (June 1, 2009 / *1ᵉʳ juin 2009*) CSD

Instructions for Enforcing a Judgment using Garnishment

If you are the plaintiff and you win the case, the court may order the defendant to pay you money. If the defendant is ordered to pay you money, the defendant (called the "debtor" after judgment, and you are called the "creditor") may pay right away, or you may give the debtor more time to pay. If the debtor does not pay, there are steps you can take to get the money. This is called **enforcing** the judgment. There are fees for these steps.

If someone else owes the debtor money, you can ask the court to order that person to send the money to the court office. The court will then pay you. This is called garnishment. For example, if you know where the debtor has a bank account or where the debtor works, you can ask the court to have the debtor's bank or employer pay money to the court.

Step 1: COMPLETE and FILE a **Notice of Garnishment** form and an **Affidavit for Enforcement Request** (Form 20P) with the court office. The clerk will stamp the notice. There is a fee.

Step 2: SERVE. You then serve a copy of the stamped notice of garnishment and a blank **Garnishee's Statement** form (Form 20F) on the person or business that has the money (the "garnishee") owed to the debtor. You also serve a copy of the stamped notice and the affidavit on the debtor. There are rules about how this must be done. See the Small Claims Court **"Guide to Serving Documents"** at the court office or online at www.attorneygeneral.jus.gov.on.ca. You can get copies of forms at the court office or online at www.ontariocourtforms.on.ca.

Step 3: TERMINATE. Once the judgment has been paid in full, the rules of the court require you to serve a **Notice of Termination of Garnishment** (Form 20R) on the garnishee and the court clerk. There are rules about how this must be done. See the Small Claims Court **"Guide to Serving Documents"** at the court office or online at www.attorneygeneral.jus.gov.on.ca. There is no fee.

For more information about enforcing a judgment, see the Small Claims Court **"After Judgment – Guide to Getting Results"** at the court office or online at www.attorneygeneral.jus.gov.on.ca.

DO NOT FILE THIS PAGE.

SCR 20.08.20E (September 1, 2010 / 1ᵉʳ septembre 2010) CSD

Instructions pour l'exécution forcée d'un jugement par voie de saisie-arrêt

Si vous êtes le demandeur et que vous avez gain de cause, le tribunal peut ordonner au défendeur de vous verser une somme d'argent. S'il est ordonné au défendeur de vous verser une somme d'argent, le défendeur (après le jugement ce dernier est appelé «débiteur» et vous, «créancier») peut payer immédiatement ou vous pouvez lui donner plus de temps pour payer. Si le débiteur ne paie pas, vous pouvez prendre certaines mesures pour obtenir votre argent. C'est ce qui s'appelle l'**exécution forcée** du jugement. Des frais sont exigés relativement à ces mesures.

Si une autre personne doit une somme d'argent au débiteur, vous pouvez demander au tribunal d'ordonner à cette personne d'envoyer l'argent au greffe. Le tribunal vous paiera ensuite. C'est ce qui s'appelle la saisie-arrêt. Par exemple, si vous savez dans quelle banque le débiteur a un compte ou à quel endroit il travaille, vous pouvez demander au tribunal d'ordonner à la banque ou à l'employeur du débiteur de verser l'argent au tribunal.

Étape 1 : REMPLISSEZ et DÉPOSEZ au greffe la formule **Avis de saisie-arrêt** et un **Affidavit relatif à une demande d'exécution forcée** (formule 20P). Le greffier apposera un cachet sur l'avis. Des frais sont exigés.

Étape 2 : SIGNIFIEZ. Vous signifiez ensuite une copie de l'avis de saisie-arrêt, marqué du cachet du tribunal, et une formule en blanc de **Déclaration du tiers saisi** (formule 20F) à la personne ou à l'entreprise qui a la somme d'argent (le «tiers saisi») due au débiteur. Vous signifiez aussi au débiteur une copie de l'avis marqué du cachet du tribunal et l'affidavit. Il existe des règles sur la façon de signifier. Consultez le **Guide sur la signification des documents»** de la Cour des petites créances au greffe ou en ligne à l'adresse www.attorneygeneral.jus.gov.on.ca. Vous pouvez obtenir des exemplaires des formules au greffe ou en ligne à l'adresse www.ontariocourtforms.on.ca.

Étape 3 : MAINLEVÉE. Une fois que le montant accordé dans le jugement a été acquitté intégralement, les règles de procédure exigent que vous signifiez un **Avis de mainlevée de la saisie-arrêt** (formule 20R) au tiers saisi et au greffier du tribunal. Il existe des règles sur la façon de signifier. Consultez le **«Guide sur la signification des documents»** de la Cour des petites créances au greffe ou en ligne à l'adresse www.attorneygeneral.jus.gov.on.ca. Il n'y a pas de frais à acquitter.

Pour de plus amples renseignements sur l'exécution forcée d'un jugement, consultez le **«Guide sur la façon d'obtenir des résultats après le jugement»** de la Cour des petites créances au greffe ou en ligne à l'adresse www.attorneygeneral.jus.gov.on.ca.

NE DÉPOSEZ PAS LA PRÉSENTE PAGE.

ONTARIO
Superior Court of Justice
Cour supérieure de justice

Notice of Garnishment
Avis de saisie-arrêt
Form / Formule 20E Ont. Reg. No. / Règt. de l'Ont. : 258/98

(Seal / Sceau)

Small Claims Court / *Cour des petites créances de*

Claim No. / *N° de la demande*

Address / *Adresse*

Phone number / *Numéro de téléphone*

☐ Additional creditor(s) listed on the attached Form 1A.
Le ou les créanciers additionnels sont mentionnés sur la formule 1A ci-jointe.

Creditor / *Créancier*

Last name, or name of company / *Nom de famille ou nom de la compagnie*		
First name / *Premier prénom*	Second name / *Deuxième prénom*	Also known as / *Également connu(e) sous le nom de*
Address (street number, apt., unit) / *Adresse (numéro et rue, app., unité)*		
City/Town / *Cité/ville*	Province	Phone no. / *N° de téléphone*
Postal code / *Code postal*		Fax no. / *N° de télécopieur*
Representative / *Représentant(e)*		LSUC # / *N° du BHC*
Address (street number, apt., unit) / *Adresse (numéro et rue, app., unité)*		
City/Town / *Cité/ville*	Province	Phone no. / *N° de téléphone*
Postal code / *Code postal*		Fax no. / *N° de télécopieur*

Debtor / *Débiteur*

Last name, or name of company / *Nom de famille ou nom de la compagnie*		
First name / *Premier prénom*	Second name / *Deuxième prénom*	Also known as / *Également connu(e) sous le nom de*
Address (street number, apt., unit) / *Adresse (numéro et rue, app., unité)*		
City/Town / *Cité/ville*	Province	Phone no. / *N° de téléphone*
Postal code / *Code postal*		Fax no. / *N° de télécopieur*

Garnishee / *Tiers saisi*

Last name, or name of company / *Nom de famille ou nom de la compagnie*		
First name / *Premier prénom*	Second name / *Deuxième prénom*	Also known as / *Également connu(e) sous le nom de*
Address (street number, apt., unit) / *Adresse (numéro et rue, app., unité)*		
City/Town / *Cité/ville*	Province	Phone no. / *N° de téléphone*
Postal code / *Code postal*		Fax no. / *N° de télécopieur*

NOTE:	**THE CREDITOR SHALL SERVE THIS NOTICE** on the debtor with an Affidavit for Enforcement Request (Form 20P) and serve on the garnishee this notice with a blank Garnishee's Statement (Form 20F).
REMARQUE :	*LE CRÉANCIER SIGNIFIE LE PRÉSENT AVIS au débiteur conjointement avec un affidavit en vue d'une demande d'exécution (formule 20P) et signifie au tiers saisi le présent avis avec une déclaration du tiers saisi (formule 20F) en blanc.*

SCR 20.08-20E (September 1, 2010 / *1ᵉʳ septembre 2010*) CSD

FORM / *FORMULE* 20E   PAGE 2

Claim No. / *N° de la demande*

TO THE GARNISHEE:
AU TIERS SAISI :

The creditor has obtained a court order against the debtor. The creditor claims that you owe or will owe the debtor a debt in the form of wages, salary, pension payments, rent, annuity or other debt that you pay out in a lump-sum, periodically or by instalments. (A debt to the debtor includes both a debt payable to the debtor alone and a joint debt payable to the debtor and one or more co-owners.)
Le créancier a obtenu une ordonnance du tribunal contre le débiteur. Le créancier prétend que vous êtes ou serez redevable au débiteur d'une dette sous forme de salaire, de prestations de retraite, de loyer, de rente ou autre que vous payez par somme forfaitaire, périodiquement ou par versements échelonnés. (Une dette envers le débiteur comprend à la fois une dette payable au débiteur seul et une dette payable conjointement au débiteur et à un ou plusieurs autres cotitulaires de la créance.)

YOU ARE REQUIRED TO PAY to the clerk of the _____ Small Claims Court
VOUS ÊTES REQUIS(E) DE PAYER au greffier (Garnishment issuing court / *Tribunal qui prononce la*
de la Cour des petites créances de   *saisie-arrêt)*

(a)   all debts now payable by you to the debtor, **within 10 days** after this notice is served on you; **and**
        d'une part, toutes les dettes dont vous êtes maintenant redevable au débiteur, dans les 10 jours qui suivent la signification du présent avis;

(b)   all debts that become payable by you to the debtor after this notice is served on you and **within 6 years** after this notice is issued, **within 10 days** after they become payable.
        d'autre part, toutes les dettes dont vous deviendrez redevable au débiteur après la signification du présent avis et dans les 6 années qui suivent sa délivrance, dans les 10 jours qui suivent la date à laquelle elles deviennent exigibles.

The total amount of all your payments to the clerk is not to exceed $ _____ .
La totalité des paiements que vous ferez au greffier ne doit pas dépasser (Amount unsatisfied / **$.**
                                                                              Montant impayé)

THIS NOTICE IS LEGALLY BINDING ON YOU until it expires or is changed, renewed, terminated or satisfied. If you do not pay the total amount or such lesser amount as you are liable to pay, you must serve a Garnishee's Statement (Form 20F) on the creditor and debtor, and file it with the clerk within 10 days after this notice is served on you.
LE PRÉSENT AVIS VOUS LIE LÉGALEMENT jusqu'à ce qu'il expire ou qu'il soit modifié, renouvelé ou résilié, ou qu'il y soit satisfait. Si vous ne payez pas le montant total ou le montant moindre dont vous êtes redevable, vous devez signifier une déclaration du tiers saisi (formule 20F) au créancier et au débiteur et la déposer auprès du greffier dans les 10 jours qui suivent la signification du présent avis.

EACH PAYMENT, payable to the Minister of Finance, **MUST BE SENT** with a copy of the attached garnishee's payment notice to the clerk at the above court address.
CHAQUE PAIEMENT, libellé à l'ordre du ministre des Finances, DOIT ÊTRE ENVOYÉ au greffier, à l'adresse du tribunal indiquée ci-dessus, avec une copie de l'avis de paiement du tiers saisi ci-joint.

If your debt is jointly owed to the debtor and to one or more co-owners, you must pay the debtor's appropriate share of the amount now payable, or which becomes payable, or such a percentage as the court may order.
Si votre dette est payable conjointement au débiteur et à un ou plusieurs autres cotitulaires de la créance, vous devez payer la quote-part appropriée du débiteur du montant dont vous êtes maintenant redevable, ou qui devient redevable, ou le pourcentage que le tribunal ordonne.

FORM / *FORMULE* 20E   PAGE 3

The amounts paid into court shall not exceed the portion of the debtor's wages that are subject to seizure or garnishment under Section 7 of the *Wages Act* (information available at: www.attorneygeneral.jus.gov.on.ca and www.e-laws.gov.on.ca). The portion of wages that can be garnished may be increased or decreased only by order of the court. If such a court order is attached to this notice or is served on you, you must follow the direction in that court order.

Les montants consignés au tribunal ne doivent pas dépasser la partie du salaire du débiteur qui peut faire l'objet d'une saisie ou d'une saisie-arrêt aux termes de l'article 7 de la Loi sur les salaires (pour de plus amples renseignements, reportez-vous aux adresses : www.attorneygeneral.jus.gov.on.ca et www.lois-en-ligne.gouv.on.ca). La partie saisissable du salaire ne peut être augmentée ou réduite que sur ordonnance du tribunal. Si une telle ordonnance du tribunal est annexée au présent avis ou vous est signifiée, vous devez vous conformer à la directive qui y est énoncée.

...., 20 ....

....

(Signature of clerk / *Signature du greffier*)

CAUTION TO GARNISHEE:	**IF YOU FAIL TO PAY** to the clerk the amount set out in this notice and do not file a Garnishee's Statement (Form 20F) disputing garnishment, **JUDGMENT MAY BE OBTAINED AGAINST YOU BY THE CREDITOR** for payment of the amount set out above, plus costs. If you make a payment to anyone other than the clerk of the court, you may be liable to pay again [R. 20.08(17) and (18)].
AVERTISSEMENT AU TIERS SAISI :	*SI VOUS NE VERSEZ PAS au greffier le montant précisé dans le présent avis et ne déposez pas la déclaration du tiers saisi (formule 20F) contestant la saisie-arrêt, **LE CRÉANCIER PEUT OBTENIR CONTRE VOUS UN JUGEMENT** ordonnant le paiement du montant précisé ci-dessus et des dépens. Si vous effectuez un paiement à une personne qui n'est pas le greffier du tribunal, vous pouvez être tenu(e) de payer de nouveau [par. 20.08 (17) et (18)].*

NOTE:	Any party or interested person may complete and serve a Notice of Garnishment Hearing (Form 20Q) to determine any matter related to this notice. To obtain forms and self-help materials, attend the nearest Small Claims Court or access the following website: www.ontariocourtforms.on.ca.
REMARQUE :	*Toute partie ou personne intéressée peut remplir et signifier un avis d'audience sur la saisie-arrêt (formule 20Q) en vue de décider une question relative au présent avis. Vous pouvez obtenir les formules et la documentation à l'usage du client auprès de la Cour des petites créances de votre localité ou en consultant le site Web suivant : www.ontariocourtforms.on.ca.*

FORM / *FORMULE* 20E   PAGE 4

Claim No. / *N° de la demande*

The top portion of the garnishee's payment notice, below, is to be completed by the creditor before the Notice of Garnishment is issued. Where it is anticipated that more than one payment will be made by the garnishee, the creditor should supply extra copies of the garnishee's payment notice. Additional copies of the garnishee's payment notice are available at court offices or online at www.ontariocourtforms.on.ca (see Form 20E or 20E.1). *Le créancier doit remplir la partie supérieure de l'avis de paiement du tiers saisi figurant ci-dessous avant la délivrance de l'avis de saisie-arrêt. S'il est prévu que le tiers saisi fera plus d'un paiement, le créancier doit fournir des exemplaires supplémentaires de l'avis de paiement du tiers saisi. Vous pouvez obtenir des exemplaires supplémentaires de l'avis de paiement du tiers saisi aux greffes des tribunaux ou en ligne à l'adresse www.ontariocourtforms.on.ca (consultez la formule 20E ou 20E.1).*

GARNISHEE'S PAYMENT NOTICE / *AVIS DE PAIEMENT DU TIERS SAISI*

Make payment by cheque or money order payable to the Minister of Finance and send it, along with this payment notice to the clerk of the court at the following address. *Effectuez le paiement par chèque ou mandat-poste à l'ordre du ministre des Finances et envoyez-le, avec une copie du présent avis de paiement, au greffier du tribunal à l'adresse suivante :*

Court address: _____
Adresse du tribunal :

Claim No.: _____
N° de la demande :

Creditor: _____
Créancier/créancière :

Debtor: _____
Débiteur/débitrice :

Garnishee: _____
Tiers saisi :

TO BE COMPLETED BY GARNISHEE FOR EACH PAYMENT
À REMPLIR PAR LE TIERS SAISI LORS DE CHAQUE PAIEMENT

Date of payment: _____ , 20 _____
Date du paiement :

Amount enclosed: $ _____
Montant inclus : $

SCR 20.08 20E (September 1, 2010 / *1ᵉʳ septembre 2010*) CSD

Instructions for Renewing a Notice of Garnishment

Your garnishment will expire 6 years after it is issued. If the amount owed to you has not been paid in full, you may wish to have the garnishment renewed to ensure that the garnishee will continue to make payments. This must be done before the garnishment expires.

Step 1: COMPLETE and FILE a **Notice of Renewal of Garnishment** form and an **Affidavit for Enforcement Request** (Form 20P) with the court office. The clerk will stamp the notice.

Step 2: SERVE. You then serve a copy of the stamped notice of renewal of garnishment and a blank **Garnishee's Statement** form (Form 20F) on the original garnishee. You also serve a copy of the stamped notice and the affidavit on the debtor. There are rules about how this must be done. See the Small Claims Court **"Guide to Serving Documents"** at the court office or online at www.attorneygeneral.jus.gov.on.ca. You can get copies of forms at the court office or online at www.ontariocourtforms.on.ca.

Step 3: TERMINATE. Once the judgment has been paid in full, the rules of the court require you to serve a **Notice of Termination of Garnishment** (Form 20R) on the garnishee and the court clerk. There are rules about how this must be done. See the Small Claims Court **"Guide to Serving Documents"** at the court office or online at www.attorneygeneral.jus.gov.on.ca .

For more information about enforcing a judgment, see the Small Claims Court **"After Judgment – Guide to Getting Results"** at the court office or online at www.attorneygeneral.jus.gov.on.ca

DO NOT FILE THIS PAGE.

Instructions pour renouveler un avis de saisie-arrêt

Votre saisie-arrêt expirera 6 ans après sa délivrance. Si la somme qui vous est due n'a pas été payée au complet, vous voudrez peut-être renouveler la saisie-arrêt pour garantir que le tiers saisi continue de faire les paiements. La saisie-arrêt doit être renouvelée avant son expiration.

*Étape 1 : REMPLISSEZ et DÉPOSEZ au greffe la formule **Avis de renouvellement de la saisie-arrêt** et un **Affidavit relatif à une demande d'exécution forcée** (formule 20P). Le greffier apposera un cachet sur l'avis.*

*Étape 2 : SIGNIFIEZ. Vous signifiez ensuite au tiers saisi originaire une copie de l'avis de renouvellement de la saisie-arrêt, marqué du cachet du tribunal, et une formule en blanc de **Déclaration du tiers saisi** (formule 20F). Vous signifiez aussi au débiteur une copie de l'avis marqué du cachet du tribunal et l'affidavit. Il existe des règles sur la façon de signifier. Consultez le **«Guide sur la signification des documents»** de la Cour des petites créances au greffe ou en ligne à l'adresse www.attorneygeneral.jus.gov.on.ca. Vous pouvez obtenir des exemplaires des formules au greffe ou en ligne à l'adresse www.ontariocourtforms.on.ca.*

*Étape 3 : MAINLEVÉE. Une fois que le montant accordé dans le jugement a été acquitté intégralement, les règles de procédure exigent que vous signifiez un **Avis de mainlevée de la saisie-arrêt** (formule 20R) au tiers saisi et au greffier du tribunal. Il existe des règles sur la façon de signifier. Consultez le **«Guide sur la signification des documents»** de la Cour des petites créances au greffe ou en ligne à l'adresse www.attorneygeneral.jus.gov.on.ca.*

*Pour de plus amples renseignements sur l'exécution forcée d'un jugement, consultez le **«Guide sur la façon d'obtenir des résultats après le jugement»** de la Cour des petites créances au greffe ou en ligne à l'adresse www.attorneygeneral.jus.gov.on.ca.*

NE DÉPOSEZ PAS LA PRÉSENTE PAGE.

ONTARIO

Superior Court of Justice
Cour supérieure de justice

Notice of Renewal of Garnishment
Avis de renouvellement de la saisie-arrêt
Form / Formule 20E.1 Ont. Reg. No. / Régl. de l'Ont. : 258/98

(Seal / Sceau)

Small Claims Court / *Cour des petites créances de*

Claim No. / *N° de la demande*

Address / *Adresse*

Phone number / *Numéro de téléphone*

☐ Additional creditor(s) listed on the attached Form 1A.
Le ou les créanciers additionnels sont mentionnés sur la formule 1A ci-jointe.

Creditor / Créancier

Last name, or name of company / Nom de famille ou nom de la compagnie		
First name / Premier prénom	Second name / Deuxième prénom	Also known as / Également connu(e) sous le nom de
Address (street number, apt., unit) / Adresse (numéro et rue, app., unité)		
City/Town / Cité/ville	Province	Phone no. / N° de téléphone
Postal code / Code postal		Fax no. / N° de télécopieur
Representative / Représentant(e)		LSUC # / N° du BHC
Address (street number, apt., unit) / Adresse (numéro et rue, app., unité)		
City/Town / Cité/ville	Province	Phone no. / N° de téléphone
Postal code / Code postal		Fax no. / N° de télécopieur

Debtor / Débiteur

Last name, or name of company / Nom de famille ou nom de la compagnie		
First name / Premier prénom	Second name / Deuxième prénom	Also known as / Également connu(e) sous le nom de
Address (street number, apt., unit) / Adresse (numéro et rue, app., unité)		
City/Town / Cité/ville	Province	Phone no. / N° de téléphone
Postal code / Code postal		Fax no. / N° de télécopieur

Garnishee / Tiers saisi

Last name, or name of company / Nom de famille ou nom de la compagnie		
First name / Premier prénom	Second name / Deuxième prénom	Also known as / Également connu(e) sous le nom de
Address (street number, apt., unit) / Adresse (numéro et rue, app., unité)		
City/Town / Cité/ville	Province	Phone no. / N° de téléphone
Postal code / Code postal		Fax no. / N° de télécopieur

SCR 20.08-20E.1 (September 1, 2010 / 1er septembre 2010) CSD

FORM / *FORMULE* 20E.1   PAGE 2   _____

                                                                                       Claim No. / *N° de la demande*

TO THE GARNISHEE:
AU TIERS SAISI :

The creditor has renewed the garnishment issued or last renewed on _____ , 20 ____ ,
Le créancier a renouvelé la saisie-arrêt prononcée ou renouvelée   (Date)
la dernière fois le

against the debtor. The creditor claims that you owe or will owe the debtor a debt in the form of wages, salary, pension payments, rent, annuity or other debt that you pay out in a lump-sum, periodically or by instalments. (A debt to the debtor includes both a debt payable to the debtor alone and a joint debt payable to the debtor and one or more co-owners.)
contre le débiteur. *Le créancier prétend que vous êtes ou serez redevable au débiteur d'une dette sous forme de salaire, de prestations de retraite, de loyer, de rente ou autre que vous payez par somme forfaitaire, périodiquement ou par versements échelonnés. (Une dette envers le débiteur comprend à la fois une dette payable au débiteur seul et une dette payable conjointement au débiteur et à un ou plusieurs autres cotitulaires de la créance.)*

YOU ARE REQUIRED TO PAY to the clerk of the _____ Small Claims Court
VOUS ÊTES REQUIS(E) DE PAYER *au greffier*   (Garnishment issuing court / *Tribunal qui prononce la*
de la Cour des petites créances de   *saisie-arrêt)*

    (a)   all debts now payable by you to the debtor, **within 10 days** after this notice is served on you; **and**
             *d'une part, toutes les dettes dont vous êtes maintenant redevable au débiteur, **dans les 10 jours** qui suivent la signification du présent avis;*

    (b)   all debts that become payable by you to the debtor after this notice is served on you and **within 6 years** after this notice is issued, **within 10 days** after they become payable.
             *d'autre part, toutes les dettes dont vous deviendrez redevable au débiteur après la signification du présent avis et **dans les 6 années** qui suivent sa délivrance, **dans les 10 jours** qui suivent la date à laquelle elles deviennent exigibles.*

The total amount of all your payments to the clerk is not to exceed $ _____ .
La totalité des paiements que vous ferez au greffier ne doit pas dépasser   (Amount unsatisfied /   **$.**
                                                                     Montant impayé)

THIS NOTICE IS LEGALLY BINDING ON YOU until it expires or is changed, renewed, terminated or satisfied. If you do not pay the total amount or such lesser amount as you are liable to pay, you must serve a Garnishee's Statement (Form 20F) on the creditor and debtor, and file it with the clerk within 10 days after this notice is served on you.
LE PRÉSENT AVIS VOUS LIE LÉGALEMENT *jusqu'à ce qu'il expire ou qu'il soit modifié, renouvelé ou résilié, ou qu'il y soit satisfait. Si vous ne payez pas le montant total ou le montant moindre dont vous êtes redevable, vous devez signifier une déclaration du tiers saisi (formule 20F) au créancier et au débiteur et la déposer auprès du greffier dans les 10 jours qui suivent la signification du présent avis.*

EACH PAYMENT, payable to the Minister of Finance, **MUST BE SENT** with a copy of the attached garnishee's payment notice to the clerk at the above court address.
CHAQUE PAIEMENT, *libellé à l'ordre du ministre des Finances, **DOIT ÊTRE ENVOYÉ** au greffier, à l'adresse du tribunal indiquée ci-dessus, avec une copie de l'avis de paiement du tiers saisi ci-joint.*

If your debt is jointly owed to the debtor and to one or more co-owners, you must pay the debtor's appropriate share of the amount now payable, or which becomes payable, or such a percentage as the court may order.
Si votre dette est payable conjointement au débiteur et à un ou plusieurs autres cotitulaires de la créance, vous devez payer la quote-part appropriée du débiteur du montant dont vous êtes maintenant redevable, ou qui devient redevable, ou le pourcentage que le tribunal ordonne.

FORM / *FORMULE* 20E.1   PAGE 3

The amounts paid into court shall not exceed the portion of the debtor's wages that are subject to seizure or garnishment under Section 7 of the *Wages Act* (information available at: www.attorneygeneral.jus.gov.on.ca and www.e-laws.gov.on.ca). The portion of wages that can be garnished may be increased or decreased only by order of the court. If such a court order is attached to this notice or is served on you, you must follow the direction in that court order.

Les montants consignés au tribunal ne doivent pas dépasser la partie du salaire du débiteur qui peut faire l'objet d'une saisie ou d'une saisie-arrêt aux termes de l'article 7 de la Loi sur les salaires (pour de plus amples renseignements, reportez-vous aux adresses : www.attorneygeneral.jus.gov.on.ca et www.lois-en-ligne.gouv.on.ca). La partie saisissable du salaire ne peut être augmentée ou réduite que sur ordonnance du tribunal. Si une telle ordonnance du tribunal est annexée au présent avis ou vous est signifiée, vous devez vous conformer à la directive qui y est énoncée.

_____ , 20 _____   _____
(Signature of clerk / *Signature du greffier*)

CAUTION TO GARNISHEE:	**IF YOU FAIL TO PAY** to the clerk the amount set out in this notice and do not file a Garnishee's Statement (Form 20F) disputing garnishment, **JUDGMENT MAY BE OBTAINED AGAINST YOU BY THE CREDITOR** for payment of the amount set out above, plus costs. If you make a payment to anyone other than the clerk of the court, you may be liable to pay again [R. 20.08(17) and (18)].
AVERTISSEMENT AU TIERS SAISI :	*SI VOUS NE VERSEZ PAS au greffier le montant précisé dans le présent avis et ne déposez pas la déclaration du tiers saisi (formule 20F) contestant la saisie-arrêt, LE CRÉANCIER PEUT OBTENIR CONTRE VOUS UN JUGEMENT ordonnant le paiement du montant précisé ci-dessus et des dépens. Si vous effectuez un paiement à une personne qui n'est pas le greffier du tribunal, vous pouvez être tenu(e) de payer de nouveau [par. 20.08 (17) et (18)].*

NOTE:	Any party or interested person may complete and serve a Notice of Garnishment Hearing (Form 20Q) to determine any matter related to this notice. To obtain forms and self-help materials, attend the nearest Small Claims Court or access the following website: www.ontariocourtforms.on.ca.
REMARQUE :	*Toute partie ou personne intéressée peut remplir et signifier un avis d'audience sur la saisie-arrêt (formule 20Q) en vue de décider une question relative au présent avis. Vous pouvez obtenir les formules et la documentation à l'usage du client auprès de la Cour des petites créances de votre localité ou en consultant le site Web suivant : www.ontariocourtforms.on.ca.*

SCR 20.08 20E.1 (September 1, 2010 / 1ᵉʳ septembre 2010) CSD

Continued on next page / *Suite à la page suivante*

FORM / FORMULE 20E.1   PAGE 4

Claim No. / N° de la demande

The top portion of the garnishee's payment notice, below, is to be completed by the creditor before the Notice of Renewal of Garnishment (Form 20E.1) is issued. Where it is anticipated that more than one payment will be made by the garnishee, the creditor should supply extra copies of the garnishee's payment notice. Additional copies of the garnishee's payment notice are available at court offices or online at www.ontariocourtforms.on.ca (see Form 20E or 20E.1).

Le créancier doit remplir la partie supérieure de l'avis de paiement du tiers saisi figurant ci-dessous avant la délivrance de l'avis de renouvellement de la saisie-arrêt (formule 20E.1). S'il est prévu que le tiers saisi fera plus d'un paiement, le créancier doit fournir des exemplaires supplémentaires de l'avis de paiement du tiers saisi. Vous pouvez obtenir des exemplaires supplémentaires de l'avis de paiement du tiers saisi aux greffes des tribunaux ou en ligne à l'adresse www.ontariocourtforms.on.ca (consultez la formule 20E ou 20E.1).

GARNISHEE'S PAYMENT NOTICE / *AVIS DE PAIEMENT DU TIERS SAISI*

Make payment by cheque or money order payable to the Minister of Finance and send it, along with this payment notice to the clerk of the court at the following address:

Effectuez le paiement par chèque ou mandat-poste à l'ordre du ministre des Finances et envoyez-le, avec une copie du présent avis de paiement, au greffier du tribunal à l'adresse suivante :

Court address: _____
Adresse du tribunal :

Claim No.: _____
N° de la demande :

Creditor: _____
Créancier/créancière :

Debtor: _____
Débiteur/débitrice :

Garnishee: _____
Tiers saisi :

TO BE COMPLETED BY GARNISHEE FOR EACH PAYMENT
À REMPLIR PAR LE TIERS SAISI LORS DE CHAQUE PAIEMENT

Date of payment: _____ , 20 _____
Date du paiement :

Amount enclosed: $ _____
Montant inclus : $

SCR 20.08 20E.1 (September 1, 2010 / 1er septembre 2010) CSD

ONTARIO
Superior Court of Justice
Cour supérieure de justice

Garnishee's Statement
Déclaration du tiers saisi
Form / *Formule* 20F Ont. Reg. No. / *Régl. de l'Ont.* : 258/98

Small Claims Court / *Cour des petites créances de* _____ Claim No. / *N° de la demande* _____

Address / *Adresse* _____

Phone number / *Numéro de téléphone* _____

BETWEEN / *ENTRE*

_____
Creditor(s) / *Créancier(s)/créancière(s)*
and / *et*

_____
Debtor(s) / *Débiteur(s)/débitrice(s)*

Name of Garnishee
Nom du tiers saisi _____
(Full legal name of garnishee / *Nom et prénoms officiels du tiers saisi*)

A Notice of Garnishment was issued on _____ , 20 _____ , naming me/us as garnishee
Un avis de saisie-arrêt a été délivré le , *me/nous désignant comme tiers saisi(s)*

in relation to the debtor _____ .
en rapport avec le débiteur
(Name of debtor / *Nom du/de la débiteur/débitrice*)

☐ **I/WE DO NOT OWE** and do not expect to owe to the debtor the amount set out in the Notice of Garnishment for the following reason(s):
JE NE SUIS/NOUS NE SOMMES PAS REDEVABLE(S) *et je ne m'attends/nous ne nous attendons pas à être redevable(s) au débiteur du montant énoncé dans l'avis de saisie-arrêt pour le ou les motifs suivants :*

_____

_____

_____

☐ **I/WE OWE OR WILL OWE** the debtor (or the debtor and one or more co-owners), wages or periodic payments based on the terms explained below:
JE SUIS OU SERAI/NOUS SOMMES OU SERONS REDEVABLE(S) *au débiteur (ou au débiteur et à un ou plusieurs autres cotitulaires de la créance) des montants suivants exigibles à titre de salaire ou de versements périodiques et selon les modalités suivantes :*

(State the amount(s) and how often the debtor is paid. If the debtor is paid wages, state the gross amount of the debtor's wages before any deductions required by law and the net amount after those deductions, and attach a copy of a pay slip. If you owe or will owe the debtor a lump sum, state when and how much will be paid.)
(*Indiquez le ou les montants et la fréquence des paiements faits au débiteur. Si le débiteur touche un salaire, indiquez son salaire brut avant les retenues que vous êtes tenu(e)(s) de déduire, selon la loi, ainsi que le montant net après les retenues, et annexez une copie d'un bordereau de paie. Si vous êtes ou serez redevable(s) d'une somme forfaitaire au débiteur, indiquez-en le montant et à quel moment sera effectué le paiement.*)

_____

_____

_____

_____

SCR 20.08-20F (April 11, 2012 / *11 avril 2012*) CSD

Continued on next page / *Suite à la page suivante*

Court Forms in Small Claims Court

Claim No. / *N° de la demande*

☐ **I/We are making payment of less than** the amount stated because the debt is owed to the debtor and to one or more co-owners, or for another reason explained below:
J'effectue/Nous effectuons un paiement inférieur au montant indiqué parce qu'il s'agit d'une dette envers le débiteur et envers un ou plusieurs autres cotitulaires de la créance, ou pour un autre motif indiqué ci-dessous :

(Identify the amount(s) and percentage owed to the debtor and each co-owner / *Précisez le ou les montants et le pourcentage redevable au débiteur et à chaque autre cotitulaire de la créance*)

Co-owner(s) of the debt:
Cotitulaire(s) de la créance :   (Full legal name(s) / *Nom et prénoms officiels*)

(Address (street & number, unit, municipality, province) / *Adresse (numéro et rue, unité, municipalité, province)*)

☐ **I/We are not making a payment at this time or are making a payment of less than the amount stated** because I/we have been served with other notice(s) of garnishment against the debtor. (Provide details below.)
Je n'effectue/Nous n'effectuons aucun paiement présentement ou j'effectue/nous effectuons un paiement inférieur au montant indiqué parce que j'ai/nous avons reçu signification d'un ou de plusieurs autres avis de saisie-arrêt contre le débiteur. (Donnez-en les détails ci-dessous.)

Name of creditor *Nom du créancier*	Name of issuing court *Nom du tribunal délivreur*	Location of court or Sheriff's Office where payment is currently being made *Emplacement du tribunal ou bureau du shérif où le paiement est actuellement effectué*	Date Notice of Garnishment received *Date de réception de l'avis de saisie-arrêt*

☐ **I/We will dispute the garnishment** by completing and serving a Notice of Garnishment Hearing (Form 20Q) on the creditor, debtor and co-owner(s) of the debt (if any) and any other interested person, and filing it with the clerk of the court.
Je contesterai/Nous contesterons la saisie-arrêt en remplissant et en signifiant un avis d'audience sur la saisie-arrêt (formule 20Q) au créancier, au débiteur et au(x) cotitulaire(s) de la créance (le cas échéant) et à tout autre intéressé et en le déposant auprès du greffier du tribunal.

_____ , 20 _____

(Signature of garnishee or representative / *Signature du tiers saisi ou du/de la représentant(e)*)

(Address, phone and fax number of garnishee or representative / *Adresse, numéro de téléphone et de télécopieur du tiers saisi ou du/de la représentant(e)*)

NOTE TO GARNISHEE: *REMARQUE AU TIERS SAISI :*	The garnishee must serve a copy of the Garnishee's Statement on the creditor and the debtor and file it with the court. You can get an electronic version of this form online at www.ontariocourtforms.on.ca. *Le tiers saisi doit signifier une copie de la déclaration du tiers saisi au créancier et au débiteur et la déposer auprès du tribunal. Vous pouvez obtenir une version électronique de la présente formule en ligne à l'adresse www.ontariocourtforms.on.ca.*

NOTE TO CREDITOR: *REMARQUE AU CRÉANCIER :*	A creditor who is served with a Garnishee's Statement must send it to the co-owners of the debt, if any, together with a Notice to Co-owner of Debt (Form 20G). You can get forms at court offices or online at www.ontariocourtforms.on.ca. *Le créancier qui reçoit signification de la déclaration du tiers saisi doit la faire parvenir aux cotitulaires de la créance, le cas échéant, avec l'avis au cotitulaire d'une créance (formule 20G). Vous pouvez obtenir des formules aux greffes des tribunaux ou en ligne à l'adresse www.ontariocourtforms.on.ca.*

SCR 20.08-20F (April 11, 2012 / *11 avril 2012*) CSD

ONTARIO
Superior Court of Justice
Cour supérieure de justice

Notice to Co-owner of Debt
Avis au cotitulaire d'une créance
Form / *Formule* 20G Ont. Reg. No. / *Régl. de l'Ont.* : 258/98

Small Claims Court / *Cour des petites créances de*	Claim No. / *N° de la demande*

Address / *Adresse*

Phone number / *Numéro de téléphone*

☐ Additional creditor(s) listed on the attached Form 1A.
Le ou les créanciers additionnels sont mentionnés sur la formule 1A ci-jointe.

Creditor / *Créancier*

Last name, or name of company / *Nom de famille ou nom de la compagnie*		
First name / *Premier prénom*	Second name / *Deuxième prénom*	Also known as / *Également connu(e) sous le nom de*
Address (street number, apt., unit) / *Adresse (numéro et rue, app., unité)*		
City/Town / *Cité/ville*	Province	Phone no. / *N° de téléphone*
Postal code / *Code postal*		Fax no. / *N° de télécopieur*
Representative / *Représentant(e)*		LSUC # / *N° du BHC*
Address (street number, apt., unit) / *Adresse (numéro et rue, app., unité)*		
City/Town / *Cité/ville*	Province	Phone no. / *N° de téléphone*
Postal code / *Code postal*		Fax no. / *N° de télécopieur*

Debtor / *Débiteur*

Last name, or name of company / *Nom de famille ou nom de la compagnie*		
First name / *Premier prénom*	Second name / *Deuxième prénom*	Also known as / *Également connu(e) sous le nom de*
Address (street number, apt., unit) / *Adresse (numéro et rue, app., unité)*		
City/Town / *Cité/ville*	Province	Phone no. / *N° de téléphone*
Postal code / *Code postal*		Fax no. / *N° de télécopieur*

Garnishee / *Tiers saisi*

Last name, or name of company / *Nom de famille ou nom de la compagnie*		
First name / *Premier prénom*	Second name / *Deuxième prénom*	Also known as / *Également connu(e) sous le nom de*
Address (street number, apt., unit) / *Adresse (numéro et rue, app., unité)*		
City/Town / *Cité/ville*	Province	Phone no. / *N° de téléphone*
Postal code / *Code postal*		Fax no. / *N° de télécopieur*

NOTE: **THIS NOTICE SHALL BE SERVED BY THE CREDITOR** on each co-owner of debt together with a copy of the Garnishee's Statement (Form 20F) received from the garnishee.
REMARQUE : LE CRÉANCIER SIGNIFIE LE PRÉSENT AVIS à chaque cotitulaire d'une créance conjointement avec une copie de la déclaration du tiers saisi (formule 20F) qu'il reçoit du tiers saisi

SCR 20.08-20G (September 1, 2010 / *1er septembre 2010*) CSD

1044

FORM / FORMULE 20G   **PAGE 2**

Claim No. / N° de la demande _____

TO: **DESTINATAIRE :** *(Attach a separate sheet, in the same format, for additional co-owners of debt. / Annexez une autre feuille, présentée selon le même format, en cas d'autres cotitulaires de la créance.)*	Name of co-owner(s) of debt / Nom du ou des cotitulaires de la créance Street and number / Numéro et rue City, province, postal code / Ville, province, code postal

The creditor has obtained a court order against the debtor. The creditor has served a Notice of Garnishment
Le créancier a obtenu une ordonnance du tribunal contre le débiteur. Le créancier a signifié un avis de saisie-arrêt

(Form 20E), dated _____ , 20 ____ , on _____
(formule 20E), daté du   *à*   (Name of garnishee / Nom du tiers saisi)

claiming that the garnishee owes or will owe the debtor a debt in the form of wages, salary, pension payments, rent, annuity, or other debt that the garnishee pays out in a lump-sum, periodically or by instalments. (A debt to the debtor includes both a debt payable to the debtor alone and a joint debt payable to the debtor and one or more co-owners.)
dans lequel il prétend que le tiers saisi est ou sera redevable au débiteur d'une dette sous forme de salaire, de prestations de retraite, de loyer, de rente ou autre que le tiers saisi paie par somme forfaitaire, périodiquement ou par versements échelonnés. (Une dette envers le débiteur comprend à la fois une dette payable au débiteur seul et une dette payable conjointement au débiteur et à un ou plusieurs autres cotitulaires de la créance.)

The garnishee has set out in the attached Garnishee's Statement (Form 20F) that you are a co-owner of debt. Under the Notice of Garnishment, the garnishee has paid or will pay to the clerk of the Small Claims Court the appropriate share of the amount payable or such a percentage as the court may order.
Le tiers saisi a indiqué dans la déclaration du tiers saisi annexée (formule 20F) que vous êtes un cotitulaire de la créance. Aux termes de l'avis de saisie-arrêt, le tiers saisi a payé ou paiera au greffier de la Cour des petites créances la quote-part appropriée du montant redevable ou le pourcentage que le tribunal ordonne.

IF YOU HAVE A CLAIM to the money being paid to the clerk of the Small Claims Court by the garnishee, you have 30 days from service of this notice to request a garnishment hearing by completing and serving a Notice of Garnishment Hearing (Form 20Q) on the creditor, debtor and garnishee, and filing it with the clerk. If you fail to do so, you are not entitled to dispute the enforcement of the creditor's order for the payment or recovery of money and the funds may be paid out to the creditor unless the court orders otherwise.
SI VOUS PRÉTENDEZ AVOIR UN DROIT sur l'argent que le tiers saisi verse au greffier de la Cour des petites créances, vous disposez de 30 jours à compter de la signification du présent avis pour demander une audience sur la saisie-arrêt en remplissant et en signifiant un avis d'audience sur la saisie-arrêt (formule 20Q) au créancier, au débiteur et au tiers saisi, et en le déposant auprès du greffier. Si vous ne le faites pas, vous n'aurez pas le droit par la suite de contester l'exécution forcée de l'ordonnance obtenue par le créancier en vue du paiement ou du recouvrement de sommes d'argent et ces sommes pourront être remises au créancier, sauf ordonnance contraire du tribunal.

To obtain forms and self-help materials, attend the nearest Small Claims Court or access the following website: www.ontariocourtforms.on.ca.
Vous pouvez obtenir les formules et la documentation à l'usage du client auprès de la Cour des petites créances de votre localité ou en consultant le site Web suivant : www.ontariocourtforms.on.ca.

_____ , 20 ____

        (Signature of creditor or representative / Signature du créancier/de la
        créancière ou du/de la représentant(e))

NOTE:	Within seven (7) calendar days of changing your address for service, notify the court and all other parties in writing.
REMARQUE :	Dans les sept (7) jours civils qui suivent tout changement de votre adresse aux fins de signification, veuillez en aviser par écrit le tribunal et les autres parties.

SCR 20.00-20G (September 1, 2010 / 1er septembre 2010) CSD

Instructions for Getting an Examination Hearing

If you are the plaintiff and you win the case, the court may order the defendant to pay you money. The defendant (called the "debtor" after judgment, and you are called the "creditor") may pay right away, or you may give the debtor more time to pay. If the debtor does not pay, there are steps you can take to get the money. This is called **enforcing** the judgment. There are fees for these steps.

For example, you can ask the court to hold a hearing on the defendant's finances so that you can get more information about the debtor. This is called an examination.

Step 1: FILE a **Notice of Examination** form at the court office. Also file an **Affidavit for Enforcement Request** (Form 20P) with details of the debt. You must contact the clerk of the court to choose a time and date when the court could hold this examination. The court clerk will fill in the hearing date and time and sign the notice of examination.

Step 2: SERVE. This notice must be served by the creditor on the debtor or person to be examined at least 30 days before the hearing date. If a debtor to be examined is an individual, serve the notice together with a blank **Financial Information Form (Form 20I)**. There are rules about service. See the Small Claims Court **"Guide to Serving Documents"** at the court office or online at www.attorneygeneral.jus.gov.on.ca. You can get forms at the court office or online at www.ontariocourtforms.on.ca.

Step 3: FILE the **Notice of Examination** form at the court at least 3 days before the hearing date. Also file an **Affidavit of Service** (Form 8A) proving service.

Step 4: ATTEND the examination hearing and ask questions. See the Financial Information Form for ideas about what to ask. At the hearing, the debtor (or other person) will have to give information about his or her job, income, property, bank accounts, debts, expenses and reasons for not paying. Based on this information, the judge may order the debtor to make payments on certain dates, or you may want to take other enforcement steps.

If the debtor does not make the payments ordered, you can choose another step to try to get the money such as garnishment or seizure and sale of personal property or of land.

For more information about enforcing a judgment, see the Small Claims Court **"After Judgment – Guide to Getting Results"** at the court office or online at www.attorneygeneral.jus.gov.on.ca.

DO NOT FILE THIS PAGE.

SCR 20.10-20H (April 11, 2012 / 11 avril 2012) CSD

Instructions pour obtenir la tenue d'un interrogatoire

Si vous êtes le demandeur et que vous avez gain de cause, le tribunal peut ordonner au défendeur de vous verser une somme d'argent. Le défendeur (après le jugement ce dernier est appelé «débiteur» et vous, «créancier») peut payer immédiatement ou vous pouvez lui donner plus de temps pour payer. Si le débiteur ne paie pas, vous pouvez prendre certaines mesures pour obtenir votre argent. C'est ce qui s'appelle l'**exécution forcée** du jugement. Des frais sont exigés relativement à ces mesures.

Par exemple, vous pouvez demander au tribunal de tenir une audience sur la situation financière du défendeur pour obtenir plus de renseignements au sujet du débiteur. C'est ce qui s'appelle un interrogatoire.

Étape 1 : DÉPOSEZ au greffe la formule **Avis d'interrogatoire**. Déposez aussi un **Affidavit relatif à une demande d'exécution forcée** (formule 20P) avec des précisions sur la créance. Vous devez communiquer avec le greffier du tribunal pour choisir la date et l'heure où le tribunal pourrait tenir l'interrogatoire. Le greffier inscrira la date et l'heure de l'audience et signera l'avis d'interrogatoire.

Étape 2 : SIGNIFIEZ. Le présent avis doit être signifié par le créancier au débiteur ou à la personne qui doit être interrogée au moins 30 jours avant la date de l'interrogatoire. Si le débiteur qui doit être interrogé est un particulier, signifiez l'avis avec la **Formule de renseignements financiers** (formule 20I) en blanc. Il existe des règles relatives à la signification. Consultez le **«Guide sur la signification des documents»** de la Cour des petites créances au greffe ou en ligne à l'adresse www.attorneygeneral.jus.gov.on.ca. Vous pouvez obtenir les formules au greffe ou en ligne à l'adresse www.ontariocourtforms.on.ca.

Étape 3 : DÉPOSEZ au greffe la formule **Avis d'interrogatoire** au moins 3 jours avant la date de l'interrogatoire. Déposez aussi un **Affidavit de signification** (formule 8A) qui sert de preuve de la signification.

Étape 4 : PRÉSENTEZ-VOUS à l'interrogatoire et posez des questions. Consultez la Formule de renseignements financiers pour avoir une idée des questions à poser. À l'interrogatoire, le débiteur (ou l'autre personne) devra donner des renseignements sur son emploi, ses revenus, ses biens, ses comptes bancaires, ses dettes, ses dépenses et les motifs pour lesquels il ne paie pas. En se fondant sur ces renseignements, le juge peut ordonner au débiteur de faire des paiements à certaines dates ou vous voudrez peut-être prendre d'autres mesures d'exécution forcée.

Si le débiteur ne fait pas les paiements ordonnés, vous pouvez opter pour une autre mesure pour essayer d'obtenir l'argent, telle que la saisie-arrêt ou la saisie-exécution de biens meubles ou de biens-fonds.

Pour de plus amples renseignements sur l'exécution forcée d'un jugement, consultez le **«Guide sur la façon d'obtenir des résultats après le jugement»** de la Cour des petites créances au greffe ou en ligne à l'adresse www.attorneygeneral.jus.gov.on.ca.

NE DÉPOSEZ PAS LA PRÉSENTE PAGE.

ONTARIO
Superior Court of Justice
Cour supérieure de justice

Notice of Examination
Avis d'interrogatoire
Form / Formule 20H Ont. Reg. No. / Règl. de l'Ont. : 258/98

(Seal / Sceau)

Small Claims Court / *Cour des petites créances de*

Claim No. / *N° de la demande*

Address / *Adresse*

Phone number / *Numéro de téléphone*

BETWEEN / ENTRE

Creditor(s) / *Créancier(s)/créancière(s)*

and / et

Debtor(s) / *Débiteur(s)/débitrice(s)*

TO:
DESTINATAIRE : (Name of person to be examined / Nom de la personne qui doit être interrogée)

of
de/du (Address of person to be examined / Adresse de la personne qui doit être interrogée)

The creditor _____ of
Le créancier (Name of creditor / Nom du/de la créancier/créancière) *de* (Address of creditor / Adresse du/de la créancier/créancière)

has obtained a judgment against _____ on _____ ,
a obtenu un jugement contre (Name of debtor / Nom du débiteur/de la débitrice) *le*

20 _____ , in the _____ Small Claims Court.
à la Cour des petites créances de (Name of court where judgment was made / Nom du tribunal où le jugement a été rendu)

According to the supporting affidavit filed by the creditor, the total due on the judgment is
Selon l'affidavit à l'appui déposé par le créancier, le solde somme due aux termes du jugement s'élève à

$ _____ . (This amount must match the total amount identified in the supporting affidavit.)
(Total) **$.** (Ce montant doit correspondre au montant total énoncé dans l'affidavit à l'appui.)

This total due takes into account all money received, accrued post-judgment interest and costs to
Ce solde somme due tient compte de toutes les sommes reçues, des intérêts postérieurs au jugement courus et des dépens

this date: _____ , 20 _____ . (This date must match the date of the supporting affidavit.)
à cette date : (Cette date doit correspondre à celle de l'affidavit à l'appui.)

YOU ARE REQUIRED TO ATTEND AN EXAMINATION HEARING to explain how the debtor will pay this judgment and if there are any reasons for not doing so.
VOUS ÊTES REQUIS(E) DE VOUS PRÉSENTER À UN INTERROGATOIRE pour expliquer de quelle façon le débiteur acquittera la somme due aux termes de ce jugement et s'il existe quelque motif que ce soit de ne pas le faire.

Continued on next page / *Suite à la page suivante*

FORM / *FORMULE* 20H   PAGE 2

THIS COURT WILL HOLD AN EXAMINATION HEARING
LE TRIBUNAL PRÉCITÉ TIENDRA UN INTERROGATOIRE

on _____ , 20 _____ , at _____ or as soon as possible after that time, at
le _____ , *à* _____ (Time / *heure*) *ou dès que possible par la suite à/au*

_____

(Address of court location / *Adresse du tribunal*)

_____

(Courtroom number / *Numéro de la salle d'audience*)

_____ , 20 _____   _____

(Signature of clerk / *Signature du greffier*)

CAUTION TO PERSON BEING EXAMINED: *AVERTISSEMENT À LA PERSONNE QUI EST INTERROGÉE :*	If you fail to attend the examination hearing or attend and refuse to answer questions or produce documents, you may be ordered to attend a contempt hearing. At the contempt hearing, you may be found in contempt of court and the court may order you to be jailed. *Si vous ne vous présentez pas à l'interrogatoire ou si vous vous présentez mais que vous refusez de répondre aux questions ou de produire des documents, le tribunal peut ordonner que vous vous présentiez à une audience pour outrage. Lors de l'audience pour outrage, vous pouvez être reconnu(e) coupable d'outrage au tribunal et le tribunal peut ordonner que vous soyez incarcéré(e).*

NOTE TO DEBTOR: *REMARQUE AU DÉBITEUR :*	A debtor who is an individual must serve on the creditor a completed Financial Information Form (Form 20I) prior to the hearing. This form must **not** be filed with the court. The debtor must provide a completed copy of this form to the judge at the examination hearing. The debtor must also bring to the hearing documents that support the information given in this form. *Le débiteur qui est un particulier doit signifier au créancier une formule de renseignements financiers remplie (formule 20I) avant l'interrogatoire. Cette formule ne doit **pas** être déposée auprès du tribunal. Le débiteur doit remettre la formule dûment remplie au juge chargé de l'audience. Le débiteur doit aussi apporter à l'audience les documents qui appuient l'information donnée sur cette formule.*

SCR 20.10-20H (April 11, 2012 / *11 avril 2012*) CSD

FINANCIAL INFORMATION FORM
FORMULE DE RENSEIGNEMENTS FINANCIERS
Form / Formule 20I Ont. Reg. No. / Règl. de l'Ont. : 258/98

This form is to be completed by the debtor and served on the creditor.
La présente formule doit être remplie par le débiteur et signifiée au créancier.

This form is not to be filed at the court office. The debtor must provide a completed copy of this form to the judge at the examination hearing. The debtor must also bring to the hearing documents that support the information given in this form.
Cette formule ne doit pas être déposée au bureau du tribunal. Le débiteur doit remettre la formule dûment remplie au juge chargé de l'audience. Le débiteur doit aussi apporter à l'audience les documents qui appuient l'information donnée sur cette formule.

MONTHLY INCOME / *REVENU MENSUEL*			MONTHLY EXPENSES / *DÉPENSES MENSUELLES*		
Employer(s) / *Employeur(s)*			Rent/Mortgage / *Loyer/Hypothèque*	$	$
Employer(s) / *Employeur(s)*			Maintenance/Support Payments / *Versements d'aliments*	$	$
Net salary / *Salaire net*	$	$	Property taxes / *Impôts fonciers*	$	$
Commissions / *Commissions*	$	$	Utilities (heat, water & light) / *Services d'utilité publique (chauffage, eau et éclairage)*	$	$
Tips and gratuities / *Pourboires et gratifications*	$	$	Phone / *Téléphone*	$	$
Employment insurance / *Prestations d'assurance-emploi*	$	$	Cable / *Câblodistribution*	$	$
Pension income / *Revenu de pension*	$	$	House/Tenant insurance / *Assurance-habitation /assurance de responsabilité locative*	$	$
Investment income / *Revenu de placements*	$	$	Life insurance / *Assurance-vie*	$	$
Rental income / *Revenu de location*	$	$	Food / *Nourriture*	$	$
Business income / *Revenu tiré d'une entreprise*	$	$	Childcare/Babysitting / *Garderie/gardiennage d'enfants*	$	$
Child tax benefit / *Prestation fiscale pour enfants*	$	$	Motor vehicle (lease or loan) / *Véhicule automobile (location à bail ou prêt)*	$	$
Maintenance (if any) / *Aliments (le cas échéant)*	$	$	(licence, insurance, fuel & maintenance) / *(permis, assurance, essence et entretien)*	$	$
Monthly income of other adult household members / *Revenu mensuel des autres membres adultes du ménage*	$	$	Transportation (public) / *Transports (en commun)*	$	$
Other / *Autre*	$	$			
Income assistance / *Aide au revenu*	$	$			
INCOME TOTAL / *REVENU TOTAL*	$	$	EXPENSES TOTAL / *DÉPENSES TOTALES*	$	$

SCR 9.03-20.10-20I (April 11, 2012 / *11 avril 2012*) CSD

Continued on next page / *Suite à la page suivante*

MONTHLY DEBTS / *DETTES MENSUELLES*		VALUE OF ASSETS / *VALEUR DES AVOIRS*		
Credit card(s) payments *(please specify):* Paiements de carte(s) de crédit *(Veuillez préciser.)*		Real estate equity *Valeur nette réelle des biens immobiliers*	$	$
_____	$ $	Market value *Valeur marchande*	$ $	
_____	$ $	Mortgage balance $ *Solde de l'hypothèque* $		
_____	$ $	Automobile equity *Valeur nette réelle des véhicules automobiles*	$	$
Bank or finance company loan payments *(please specify):* Remboursement de prêt(s) d'une banque ou d'une compagnie de financement *(Veuillez préciser.)*		Make and year *Marque et année* _____		
		Loan balance $ *Solde du/des prêts* $		
_____	$ $	Bank or other account balance(s) *(include RRSPs) Solde de compte(s) bancaire(s) ou autre(s) compte(s) (Incluez les REÉR.)*	$	$
_____	$ $			
Department store(s) payments *(please specify):* Versements à un ou des grands magasins *(Veuillez préciser.)*		Stocks & bonds *Actions et obligations*	$	$
_____	$ $	Life insurance (cash value) *Assurance-vie (valeur de rachat)*	$	$
_____	$ $	Money owing to you *Sommes qui vous sont dues*	$	$
		Name of debtor *Nom du débiteur/de la débitrice* _____		
DEBTS TOTAL $ *DETTES TOTALES* $		Personal property *Biens meubles*	$	$
		Cash *Argent comptant*	$	$
		Other *Autre*	$	$
		TOTAL VALUE OF ASSETS $ *VALEUR TOTALE DES AVOIRS*		$

_____   _____

(Name / *Nom*)   (Signature)

SCR 9.03-20.10-20I (April 11, 2012 / *11 avril 2012*) CSD

ONTARIO

Superior Court of Justice
Cour supérieure de justice

Warrant of Committal
Mandat de dépôt

Form / *Formule* 20J Ont. Reg. No. / *Règl. de l'Ont.* : 258/98

Small Claims Court / *Cour des petites créances de*	Claim No. / *N° de la demande*

Seal / *Sceau*

Address / *Adresse*

Phone number / *Numéro de téléphone*

BETWEEN / *ENTRE*

Plaintiff(s) / *Demandeur(s)/demanderesse(s)*

and / *et*

Defendant(s) / *Défendeur(s)/défenderesse(s)*

TO ALL POLICE OFFICERS IN ONTARIO AND TO THE OFFICERS OF ALL CORRECTIONAL INSTITUTIONS IN ONTARIO:
À TOUS LES AGENTS DE POLICE DE L'ONTARIO ET AUX AGENTS DE TOUS LES ÉTABLISSEMENTS CORRECTIONNELS DE L'ONTARIO :

THIS WARRANT IS FOR THE COMMITTAL OF / *LE PRÉSENT MANDAT EST DÉCERNÉ POUR L'INCARCÉRATION DE*

Last name / *Nom de famille*		
First name / *Premier prénom*	Second name / *Deuxième prénom*	Also known as / *Également connu(e) sous le nom de*
Address (street number, apt., unit) / *Adresse (numéro et rue, app., unité)*		
City/Town / *Cité/ville*	Province	Phone no. / *N° de téléphone*
Postal code / *Code postal*		Fax no. / *N° de télécopieur*

A Notice of Contempt Hearing was issued from this court which required
Un avis d'audience pour outrage a été délivré par le tribunal précité ordonnant à

(Name of person required to attend contempt hearing / *Nom de la personne tenue de se présenter à l'audience pour outrage*)

to attend the sittings of this court at _____ on _____ , 20 ____ .
de se présenter aux séances du tribunal à (Time / *Heure*) *le* (Date)

At the contempt hearing, it was duly proven that the Notice of Contempt Hearing was properly served, and
Lors de l'audience pour outrage, il a été dûment prouvé que l'avis d'audience pour outrage a été signifié en bonne et due forme et

SCR 20.11-20J (September 1, 2010 / *1er septembre 2010*) CSD

1051

FORM / *FORMULE* 20J   **PAGE 2**

this court found this person to be in contempt of court because he/she:
d'autre part, le tribunal a reconnu la personne susmentionnée coupable d'outrage au tribunal pour l'un des motifs suivants :

(Check appropriate box. / Cochez la case appropriée.)

☐ wilfully failed to attend an examination hearing as required by a Notice of Examination (Form 20H), which was properly served.
elle a délibérément omis de se présenter à un interrogatoire comme l'exigeait un avis d'interrogatoire (formule 20H), qui a été signifié en bonne et due forme.

☐ attended the examination hearing, refused to answer questions or produce documents or records, and failed to show cause why he/she should not be held in contempt for refusing to answer questions or produce documents or records.
elle s'est présentée à l'interrogatoire mais a refusé de répondre aux questions ou de produire des documents ou des dossiers et a omis de justifier pourquoi elle ne devrait pas être accusée pour outrage pour avoir refusé de répondre aux questions ou de produire des documents ou des dossiers.

At the contempt hearing, a judge of this court ordered this person to be committed.
Lors de l'audience pour outrage, un juge du tribunal a ordonné l'incarcération de la personne susmentionnée.

YOU ARE ORDERED to take the person named above to the nearest correctional institution and admit and
IL VOUS EST ORDONNÉ *d'amener la personne susmentionnée à l'établissement correctionnel le plus proche*

detain him or her there for _____ days.
et de l'y admettre et l'y détenir pendant _____ *jours.*

This warrant expires twelve (12) months from the date of issue, unless renewed by court order. If renewed, the warrant expires twelve (12) months from the date of the renewal.
Le présent mandat expire douze (12) mois à compter de la date de sa délivrance, sauf si le tribunal le renouvelle par ordonnance. S'il est renouvelé, le mandat expire douze (12) mois à compter de la date du renouvellement.

_____ , 20 _____   _____

(Signature of clerk / *Signature du greffier*)

ONTARIO

Superior Court of Justice
Cour supérieure de justice

Identification Form
Formule de renseignements signalétiques
Form / Formule 20K Ont. Reg. No. / Regl. de l'Ont. : 258/98

Small Claims Court / *Cour des petites créances de*

Claim No. / *N° de la demande*

Address / *Adresse*

Phone number / *Numéro de téléphone*

BETWEEN / ENTRE

Plaintiff(s)/Creditor(s) / *Demandeur(s)/demanderesse(s)/Créancier(s)/créancère(s)*

and / et

Defendant(s)/Debtor(s) / *Défendeur(s)/défenderesse(s)/Débiteur(s)/débitrice(s)*

TO HELP PROCESS A CIVIL WARRANT FOR COMMITTAL, the following information, or **as much information as is reasonably available should be provided.** This is necessary for the police to identify the person to be arrested. Without this information it will be difficult to enforce the warrant.
POUR FACILITER LA DÉLIVRANCE D'UN MANDAT DE DÉPÔT AU CIVIL, les renseignements suivants ou autant de renseignements qui sont raisonnablement disponibles devraient être fournis. Ces renseignements sont nécessaires pour que la police puisse identifier la personne à arrêter. Sans ces renseignements, il sera difficile d'exécuter le mandat.

1. Name
   Nom (Last name of individual / *Nom de famille du particulier*)   (First name / *Premier prénom*)   (Second name / *Deuxième prénom*)

2. Also known as names (if any)
   Nom(s) sous lequel/lesquels la personne est également connue (le cas échéant)

3. Last known address and telephone number
   Dernière adresse connue et dernier numéro de téléphone connu

4. (a) Date of birth (d, m, y)
   Date de naissance (j, m, a)

5. Physical description
   Description physique

   (a) Gender   (b) Height   (c) Weight   (d) Build
       Sexe   *Taille*   *Poids*   *Corpulence*

   (e) Colour of eyes   (f) Hair colour   (g) Complexion
       Couleur des yeux   *Couleur des cheveux*   *Teint*

   (h) Clean-shaven   (i) Wears glasses
       Rasé de près   *Porte des lunettes*

   (j) Clothing habits and tastes
       Habitudes et goûts vestimentaires

SCR 20 11-20K (June 1, 2009 / *1er juin 2009*) CSD

Court Forms in Small Claims Court

PAGE 2

Claim No. / *N° de la demande*

(k) Distinguishing marks, scars, tattoos, etc.
   Marques distinctives, cicatrices, tatouages, etc.

(l) Other
   Autre   (Specify / *Précisez.*)

6. Usual occupation
   Profession habituelle

7. Last known place of employment
   Dernier lieu de travail connu

8. Vehicle description
   Description du véhicule

   (a) Make, model and year   (b) Colour
      Marque, modèle et année   *Couleur*

   (c) Licence plate number   Province or state
      Numéro de la plaque d'immatriculation   *Province ou État*

   (d) Driver's licence number   Province or state
      Numéro du permis de conduire   *Province ou État*

   (e) Distinguishing features on the vehicle (dents, car stereo, etc.)
      Caractéristiques distinctives du véhicule (bosses, autoradio, etc.)

9. Other information
   Autres renseignements

10. Photograph of the person provided in the box below, if available.
   Une photographie de la personne figure dans la case ci-dessous, si elle est disponible.

The information supplied above is true to the best of my knowledge and belief.
Au mieux de ma connaissance et de ce que je tiens pour véridique, les renseignements ci-dessus sont exacts.

_____
(Signature of party / *Signature de la partie*)

_____
(Name of party / *Nom de la partie*)

_____ , 20 _____

ONTARIO

Superior Court of Justice
Cour supérieure de justice

Notice of Default of Payment
Avis de défaut de paiement
Form / Formule 20L Ont. Reg. No. / Régl. de l'Ont. : 258/98

Small Claims Court / Cour des petites créances de

Claim No. / N° de la demande

Address / Adresse

Phone number / Numéro de téléphone

BETWEEN / ENTRE

Plaintiff(s)/Creditor(s) / Demandeur(s)/demanderesse(s)/Créancier(s)/créancière(s)

and / et

Defendant(s)/Debtor(s) / Défendeur(s)/défenderesse(s)/Débiteur(s)/débitrice(s)

TO:
DESTINATAIRE(S) :   (Name of defendant(s)/debtor(s) / Nom du/de la/des défendeur(s)/défenderesse(s)/débiteur(s)/débitrice(s))

TAKE NOTICE that you defaulted in your payment(s) to
VEUILLEZ PRENDRE NOTE que vous n'avez pas effectué le ou les paiements que vous deviez verser à

(Name of plaintiff(s)/creditor(s) / Nom du/de la/des demandeur(s)/demanderesse(s)/créancier(s)/créancière(s))

(Check appropriate box. / Cochez la case appropriée.)

☐ under an order for periodic payment, dated _____ , 20 ____ .
en vertu d'une ordonnance prescrivant des versements périodiques datée du

According to Rule 20.02(4) of the *Rules of the Small Claims Court*, the order for periodic payment terminates on the day that is 15 days after the creditor serves the debtor with this notice, unless before that date, a Consent (Form 13B) is filed in which the creditor waives the default.
Conformément au paragraphe 20.02 (4) des Règles de la Cour des petites créances, l'ordonnance prescrivant des versements périodiques prend fin le 15e jour qui suit la signification par le créancier au débiteur du présent avis, sauf si, avant cette date, le créancier dépose le consentement (formule 13B) dans lequel il renonce à la constatation du défaut.

☐ under a proposal of terms of payment in the Defence (Form 9A) dated _____ , 20 ____ .
en vertu d'une proposition à l'égard des modalités de paiement dans la défense (formule 9A) datée du

According to Rule 9.03(2)(c) the clerk may sign judgment for the unpaid balance of the undisputed amount on the day that is 15 days after the plaintiff serves the defendant with this notice.
Conformément à l'alinéa 9.03 (2) c), le greffier peut consigner un jugement relativement au solde impayé de la somme non contestée le 15e jour qui suit la signification par le demandeur au défendeur du présent avis.

SCR 20.02-20L (June 1, 2000 / 1er juin 2000) CCD

1055

FORM / *FORMULE* 20L   PAGE 2

Claim No. / *N° de la demande*

You can get forms and self-help materials at the Small Claims Court or online at: www.ontariocourtforms.on.ca.
Vous pouvez obtenir les formules et la documentation à l'usage du client auprès de la Cour des petites créances ou en ligne à l'adresse : www.ontariocourtforms.on.ca.

NOTE TO DEFENDANT/DEBTOR: / *REMARQUE AU DÉFENDEUR/DÉBITEUR :*

If you / *Si, selon le cas :*

- failed to make payments but intend to do so; or
  vous n'avez pas effectué de paiements mais vous avez l'intention de le faire;

- made payments but the payments were not received by the creditor;
  vous avez effectué des paiements mais le créancier ne les a pas reçus;

contact the plaintiff/creditor to make payment arrangements or correct the reason for non-receipt of payments. You may obtain the plaintiff/creditor's written consent (Form 13B may be used) to waive the default and file it with the court within 15 days of being served with this notice. Failure to do so may result in the following:
communiquez avec le demandeur/créancier pour prendre les dispositions de paiement ou pour régler le motif de la non-réception des paiements. Vous pouvez obtenir le consentement écrit du demandeur/créancier (vous pouvez utiliser la formule 13B) pour renoncer à la constatation du défaut et le déposer au tribunal dans les 15 jours de la signification du présent avis. Si vous ne le faites pas, vous pourriez subir l'une ou l'autre des conséquences suivantes :

- in the case of default under a proposal of terms of payment in the Defence (Form 9A), the plaintiff may obtain default judgment for the unpaid balance of the undisputed amount; or
  si vous n'effectuez pas les paiements conformément aux modalités de paiement proposées dans la défense (formule 9A), le demandeur pourra obtenir un jugement par défaut relativement au solde impayé de la somme non contestée;

- in the case of default under an order for periodic payment, the order will terminate and the creditor may take other steps to enforce the order.
  si vous n'effectuez pas les paiements conformément à une ordonnance prescrivant des versements périodiques, l'ordonnance prendra fin et le créancier pourra prendre d'autres mesures en vue de l'exécution forcée de l'ordonnance.

_____ , 20 _____

(Signature of plaintiff/creditor or representative / *Signature du demandeur/de la demanderesse/du créancier/de la créancière ou du/de la représentant(e)*)

_____

_____

(Name, address and phone number of plaintiff/creditor or representative / *Nom, adresse et numéro de téléphone du demandeur/de la demanderesse/du créancier/de la créancière ou du/de la représentant(e)*)

SCR 20.02-20L (June 1, 2009 / *1er juin 2009*) CSD

Court Forms in Small Claims Court

ONTARIO
Superior Court of Justice
Cour supérieure de justice

Affidavit of Default of Payment
Affidavit de défaut de paiement
Form / Formule 20M Ont. Reg. No. / Règl. de l'Ont. : 258/98

Small Claims Court / *Cour des petites créances de*   Claim No. / *N° de la demande*

Address / *Adresse*

Phone number / *Numéro de téléphone*

BETWEEN / *ENTRE*

Plaintiff(s)/Creditor(s) / *Demandeur(s)/demanderesse(s)/Créancier(s)/créancière(s)*
and / *et*

Defendant(s)/Debtor(s) / *Défendeur(s)/défenderesse(s)/Débiteur(s)/débitrice(s)*

My name is _____
Je m'appelle   (Full name / *Nom et prénoms*)

I live in _____
J'habite à   (Municipality & province / *Municipalité et province*)

and I swear/affirm that the following is true:
et je déclare sous serment/j'affirme solennellement que les renseignements suivants sont véridiques :

1. In this action, I am the
   Dans la présente action, je suis le/la

   (Check one box only. / Cochez une seule case.)

   ☐ plaintiff/creditor.
   demandeur/demanderesse/créancier/créancière.

   ☐ representative of the
   plaintiff(s)/creditor(s) _____
   représentant(e) du/de la/des demandeur(s)/demanderesse(s)   (Name of plaintiff(s)/creditor(s) / *Nom du/de la/des*
   ou du/de la/des créancier(s)/créancière(s)   *demandeur(s)/demanderesse(s) ou du/de la/des*
   créancier(s)/créancière(s)

2. To date, I have received from the defendant(s)/debtor(s) $ _____ , the last payment being made
   À ce jour, j'ai reçu du ou des défendeurs/débiteurs   (Amount / *Montant*)   *$, soit le dernier paiement ayant*

   on or about _____ , 20 _____ .
   été effectué le ou vers le

3. I make this affidavit in support of a request that:
   Je fais le présent affidavit à l'appui d'une demande visant à :

   (Check appropriate box and complete paragraph. / Cochez la case appropriée et remplissez le point.)

   ☐ the clerk of the court issue a Default Judgment (Form 11B) [R. 9.03(2)(c)]. The defendant(s)
   enjoindre au greffier du tribunal de rendre un jugement par défaut (formule 11B) [alinéa 9.03 (2) c)].
   Le ou les défendeurs

   _____
   (Name(s) of defendant(s) / *Nom du/de la/des défendeur(s)/défenderesse(s)*)

   failed to make payment in accordance with the proposed terms of payment in the Defence
   n'ont pas effectué les paiements conformément aux modalités de paiement proposées dans la défense

   (Form 9A) dated _____ , 20 _____ and fifteen (15) days have passed since the
   (formule 9A) datée du   *et quinze (15) jours se sont écoulés depuis*

   defendant was served with a Notice of Default of Payment (Form 20L) at the following address(es):
   la signification de l'avis de défaut de paiement au défendeur (formule 20L) à l'adresse (aux adresses)
   suivante(s) :

   _____
   (Address(es) of defendant(s) / *Adresse(s) du/de la/des défendeur(s)/défenderesse(s)*)

SCR 9.03-20M (April 11, 2012 / *11 avril 2012*) CSD

FORM / FORMULE 20M PAGE 2

Claim No. / N° de la demande

☐ the clerk of the court issue a Default Judgment (Form 11B) [R. 9.03(7)]. The defendant(s)
*enjoindre au greffier du tribunal de rendre un jugement par défaut (formule 11B) [par. 9.03 (7)]. Le
ou les défendeurs*

(Name of defendant(s) / *Nom du/de la/des défendeur(s)/défenderesse(s)*)

*(Check appropriate box and complete paragraph. /
Cochez la case appropriée et remplissez le point.)*

failed to make payment in accordance with the terms of payment order
n'ont pas effectué les paiements conformément à l'ordonnance relative aux modalités de paiement

dated _____ , 20 _____ .
datée du

☐ I may enforce the judgment [R. 20.02(3)]. The debtor(s)
m'autoriser à exécuter le jugement [par. 20.02 (3)]. Le ou les débiteurs

(Name(s) of debtor(s) / *Nom du/de la/des débiteur(s)/débitrice(s)*)

failed to make payment in accordance with the order for periodic payment dated
*n'ont pas effectué les paiements conformément à l'ordonnance prescrivant des versements
périodiques datée du*

_____ , 20 _____ , and fifteen (15) days have passed since the debtor(s) has/have
et quinze (15) jours se sont écoulés depuis la signification de

been served with a Notice of Default of Payment (Form 20L) at the following address(es):
l'avis de défaut de paiement (formule 20L) au ou aux débiteurs à l'adresse (aux adresses) suivante(s) :

(Address(es) of debtor(s) / *Adresse(s) du/de la/des débiteur(s)/débitrice(s)*)

A Consent (Form 13B) in which the creditor waives the default has not been filed.
*Un consentement (formule 13B) dans lequel le créancier renonce à la constatation du défaut n'a
pas été déposé.*

4. The unpaid balance is calculated as follows:
Le solde impayé est calculé de la façon suivante :

(A) **DEBT**
   LA CRÉANCE $ _____

                                                                              $

(B) **PRE-JUDGMENT INTEREST** calculated
   LES INTÉRÊTS ANTÉRIEURS AU JUGEMENT *calculés*

on the sum of $ _____ at the rate of _____ %
sur la somme de $ au taux de   pour cent

per annum from _____ , 20 to _____ , 20 _____ ,
par an du   au

being _____ days.
soit   jours. $ _____

                                                                              $

NOTE:	Calculation of interest is always on the amount owing from time to time as payments are received. This is true for both pre-judgment and post-judgment interest. Attach a separate sheet setting out how you calculated the total amount of any pre/post-judgment interest.
REMARQUE :	*Les intérêts doivent toujours être calculés sur la somme due. Le calcul doit tenir compte des paiements reçus de temps à autre. Ceci s'applique autant aux intérêts antérieurs au jugement qu'aux intérêts postérieurs au jugement. Annexez une feuille distincte indiquant comment vous avez calculé le montant total des intérêts antérieurs et postérieurs au jugement.*

SUBTOTAL (amount of judgment) $ ························
TOTAL PARTIEL *(montant du jugement)* $

Continued on next page / *Suite à la page suivante*

FORM / *FORMULE* 20M   PAGE 3

Claim No. / *N° de la demande*

(C) **COSTS** to date of judgment
     LES DÉPENS à la date du jugement
     $ _____ $

(D) **TOTAL AMOUNT OF PAYMENTS RECEIVED FROM DEBTOR**
     after judgment (if any)   (minus) $ _____
     LE MONTANT TOTAL DES PAIEMENTS REÇUS DU DÉBITEUR   *(moins)* $
     après le jugement (le cas échéant)

(E) **POST-JUDGMENT INTEREST** to date calculated
     LES INTÉRÊTS POSTÉRIEURS AU JUGEMENT à ce jour, calculés

     on the sum of $ _____   at the rate of   ____ %
     sur la somme de $ *au taux de*   *pour cent*

     per annum from _____ , 20 ____ to _____ , 20 ____ ,
     par an du   *Au*

     being _____ days. $ _____
     soit   *jours.* $

(F) **SUBSEQUENT COSTS** incurred after judgment (including the cost of serving
     the Notice of Default of Payment (Form 20L)) $ _____
     LES DÉPENS SUBSÉQUENTS engagés après le jugement (y compris le coût de $
     signification de l'avis de défaut de paiement (formule 20L))

                     TOTAL DUE $ ....
                     SOLDE DÛ $

Sworn/Affirmed before me at _____
Déclaré sous serment/Affirmé   (Municipality / *municipalité*)
solennellement devant moi à

in _____
en/à/au   (Province, state, or county / *province, État ou pays*)

on _____ , 20 ____   Signature
le   Commissioner for taking affidavits   (This form is to be signed in front of a
         Commissaire aux affidavits   lawyer, justice of the peace, notary public
         (Type or print name below if signature is   or commissioner for taking affidavits.)
         illegible.)   (*La présente formule doit être signée en*
         (*Dactylographiez le nom ou écrivez-le en*   *présence d'un avocat, d'un juge de paix,*
         caractères d'imprimerie ci-dessous si la   *d'un notaire ou d'un commissaire aux*
         signature est illisible.)   *affidavits.*)

WARNING: **IT IS AN OFFENCE UNDER THE *CRIMINAL CODE* TO KNOWINGLY SWEAR OR**
              AFFIRM A FALSE AFFIDAVIT.
AVERTISSEMENT :   *FAIRE SCIEMMENT UN FAUX AFFIDAVIT CONSTITUE UNE INFRACTION AU CODE*
              CRIMINEL.

SCR 9.03-20M (April 11, 2012 / *11 avril 2012*) CSD

ONTARIO

Superior Court of Justice
Cour supérieure de justice

Request to Renew Writ of Seizure and Sale
Demande de renouvellement du bref de saisie-exécution
Form / Formule 20N Ont. Reg. No. / Règl. de l'Ont. : 258/98

Small Claims Court / *Cour des petites créances de*

Claim No. / *N° de la demande*

Address / *Adresse*

Phone number / *Numéro de téléphone*

BETWEEN / ENTRE

Creditor(s) / *Créancier(s)/créancière(s)*

and / et

Debtor(s) / *Débiteur(s)/débitrice(s)*

TO THE SHERIFF/BAILIFF OF
AU SHÉRIF/À L'HUISSIER DU/DE LA (Name of county/region and city/town in which the enforcement office is located / *Nom du comté/de la région et de la cité/ville où est situé le bureau de l'exécution*)

YOU ARE REQUESTED TO RENEW the
VOUS ÊTES PRIÉ(E) DE RENOUVELER le

☐ Writ of Seizure and Sale of Personal Property (Form 20C)
bref de saisie-exécution de biens meubles (formule 20C)

☐ Writ of Seizure and Sale of Land (Form 20D)
bref de saisie-exécution de biens-fonds (formule 20D)

issued on _____ , 20 _____ , in this proceeding and filed in your office for a period of
délivré le _____ , 20 _____ *dans la présente instance et déposé à votre bureau, pour*

six years from the date of renewal.
une période de six ans à compter de la date du renouvellement.

_____ , 20 _____

(Signature of creditor or representative / *Signature du créancier/de la créancière ou du/de la représentant(e)*)

(Name, address and phone number of creditor or representative / *Nom, adresse et numéro de téléphone du créancier/de la créancière ou du/de la représentant(e)*)

NOTE: **A WRIT OF SEIZURE AND SALE OF LAND OR OF PERSONAL PROPERTY** remains in force for six years after the date of its issue and for a further six years after each renewal.
REMARQUE : *LE BREF DE SAISIE-EXÉCUTION DE BIENS-FONDS OU DE BIENS MEUBLES reste en vigueur pendant six ans après la date de sa délivrance ou après chaque renouvellement.*

SCR 20.06-20.07-20N (June 1, 2009 / 1er juin 2009) CSD

ONTARIO

Superior Court of Justice
Cour supérieure de justice

Direction to Enforce Writ of Seizure and Sale of Personal Property
Ordre d'exécution d'un bref de saisie-exécution de biens meubles

Form / Formule 20O Ont. Reg. No. / Régl. de l'Ont. : 258/98

Small Claims Court / Cour des petites créances de

Claim No. / N° de la demande

Address / Adresse

Phone number / Numéro de téléphone

BETWEEN / ENTRE

Creditor(s) / Créancier(s)/créancière(s)

and / et

Debtor(s) / Débiteur(s)/débitrice(s)

My name is
Je m'appelle

(Full name / Nom et prénoms)

1. In this action, I am the
   Dans la présente action, je suis le/la

   (Check one box only. / Cochez une seule case.)

   ☐ creditor.
   créancier/créancière.

   ☐ representative of the creditor(s).
   représentant(e) du/de la/des créancier(s)/créancière(s).

   A Writ of Seizure and Sale of Personal Property (Form 20C) directed to the bailiff of the
   Un bref de saisie-exécution de biens meubles (formule 20C) adressé à l'huissier de la Cour des petites créances de

   Small Claims Court was issued on:
   a été délivré le :

   (Small Claims Court location / emplacement de la Cour des petites créances)

   _____ , 20 _____ , in favour of
   , *en faveur de*

   (Name of creditor / Nom du/de la créancier/créancière)

2. I am filing this direction to enforce the Writ of Seizure and Sale of Personal Property, and direct the bailiff to seize and sell (if required) the personal property belonging to the following debtor(s):
   Je dépose le présent ordre d'exécution du bref de saisie-exécution de biens meubles et ordonne à l'huissier de saisir et de vendre (s'il y a lieu) les biens meubles appartenant au(x) débiteur(s) suivant(s) :

Last name, or name of company / Nom de famille ou nom de la compagnie		
First name / Premier prénom	Second name / Deuxième prénom	Third given name (individual only) (if applicable) / Troisième prénom (particulier seulement) (s'il y a lieu)

   ☐ Additional debtor(s) and also known as names are listed on attached Form 1A.1.
   Le ou les débiteurs additionnels et le ou les noms sous lesquels les débiteurs sont également connus sont mentionnés sur la formule 1A.1 ci-jointe.

   Set out a description of the property to be seized. Identify any marks or serial numbers.
   Donnez la description des biens qui doivent être saisis. Indiquez toute marque d'identification ou tout numéro de série y figurant.

SCR 20 06-20O (June 1, 2009 / 1er juin 2009) CSD

FORM / *FORMULE* 200   PAGE 2

Claim No. / *N° de la demande*

3. The above personal property is located at: _____
   Les biens meubles susmentionnés se trouvent à/au :   (Address / *Adresse*)

If the address provided does not clearly identify where the property is located, please attach a detailed map showing the nearest intersection.
Si l'adresse fournie n'indique pas clairement l'emplacement des biens, veuillez annexer un plan détaillé qui montre l'intersection la plus rapprochée.

4. From the date that the Writ of Seizure and Sale of Personal Property was issued, the following payments
   have been received from the debtor and/or subsequent costs incurred by the creditor:
   Depuis la date de délivrance du bref de saisie-exécution de biens meubles, les paiements suivants ont été
   reçus du débiteur ou les dépens subséquents engagés par le créancier :

   (A) **PAYMENTS RECEIVED FROM DEBTOR**
       PAIEMENTS REÇUS DU DÉBITEUR

Date of Payment *Date du paiement*	Payment Amount *Montant du paiement*	
	$	$
	$	$
	$	$
	$	$

   ☐ List of additional payments attached
      Liste de paiements additionnels ci-jointe

   (B) **SUBSEQUENT COSTS** incurred since issuance of Writ of Seizure and Sale of Personal Property
       DÉPENS SUBSÉQUENTS *engagés depuis la délivrance du bref de saisie-exécution de biens meubles*

Reason cost was incurred *Raison pour laquelle les dépens ont été engagés*	Cost Amount *Montant des dépens*	
	$	$
	$	$
	$	$
	$	$

   ☐ List of additional costs attached
      Liste de dépens additionnels ci-jointe

The bailiff will calculate the amount owing based on the information provided within the Writ of Seizure and Sale
of Personal Property and the details provided above. This amount will include any reasonable disbursements
necessarily incurred to enforce this writ.
L'huissier calculera la somme due en fonction des renseignements donnés dans le bref de saisie-exécution de
biens meubles et des précisions données ci-dessus. Cette somme inclura les débours raisonnables qui ont dû
être engagés pour exécuter ce bref.

_____, 20____

(Signature of creditor or representative / *Signature du créancier/de la*
créancière ou du/de la représentant(e))

_____

(Name, address and phone number of creditor or representative / *Nom, adresse et*
numéro de téléphone du créancier/de la créancière ou du/de la représentant(e))

SCR 20.06-20O (June 1, 2009 / *1er juin 2009*) CSD

ONTARIO

Superior Court of Justice
Cour supérieure de justice

Affidavit for Enforcement Request
Affidavit relatif à une demande d'exécution forcée
Form / Formule 20P Ont. Reg. No. / Régl. de l'Ont. : 258/98

Small Claims Court / *Cour des petites créances de*   Claim No. / *N° de la demande*

Address / *Adresse*

Phone number / *Numéro de téléphone*

BETWEEN / ENTRE

Plaintiff(s)/Creditor(s) / *Demandeur(s)/demanderesse(s)/Créancier(s)/créancière(s)*

and / et

Defendant(s)/Debtor(s) / *Défendeur(s)/défenderesse(s)/Débiteur(s)/débitrice(s)*

My name is
Je m'appelle   (Full name / *Nom et prénoms*)

I live in
J'habite à   (Municipality & province / *Municipalité et province*)

and I swear/affirm that the following is true:
et je déclare sous serment/j'affirme solennellement que les renseignements suivants sont véridiques :

1. In this action, I am the
    Dans la présente action, je suis le/la

    (Check one   ☐ plaintiff/creditor.
    box only. /   *demandeur/demanderesse/créancier/créancière.*
    Cochez une
    seule case.)   ☐ representative of the plaintiff(s)/creditor(s).
                           représentant(e) du/de la/des demandeur(s)/demanderesse(s)/créancier(s)/créancière(s).

    I make this affidavit in support of a request that the clerk of the court issue the following enforcement process(es):
    Je fais le présent affidavit à l'appui d'une demande visant à enjoindre au greffier du tribunal de délivrer l'acte ou les actes de procédure portant exécution forcée suivants :

    ☐ Certificate of Judgment (Form 20A) to the clerk of the
        Certificat de jugement (formule 20A), au greffier   (Name of court where the judgment is to be filed / *Nom du tribunal*
        de la Cour des petites créances de   *où le jugement doit être déposé)*

        Small Claims Court.

    ☐ Writ of Seizure and Sale of Personal Property (Form 20C) directed to the bailiff of
        Bref de saisie-exécution de biens meubles (formule 20C) adressé à l'huissier de la Cour des petites créances de

                                                                                    Small Claims Court.
    _____
    (Name of court location / *Emplacement du tribunal*)

    ☐ Writ of Seizure and Sale of Land (Form 20D) directed to the sheriff of
        Bref de saisie-exécution de biens-fonds (formule 20D) adressé   (Name of county/region in which the
        au shérif du/de la   enforcement office is located / *Comté/région où*
                                                                                  est situé le bureau de l'exécution)

FORM / *FORMULE* 20P   **PAGE 2**

☐ Notice of Garnishment (Form 20E)/Notice of Renewal of Garnishment (Form 20E.1).
Avis de saisie-arrêt (formule 20E)/Avis de renouvellement de la saisie-arrêt (formule 20E.1).

I believe that the garnishee _____
Je crois que le tiers saisi   (Name of garnishee / *Nom du tiers saisi*)

at _____
à/au   (Address of garnishee / *Adresse du tiers saisi*)

is indebted to the debtor or will become indebted to the debtor for the following reasons:
est ou sera redevable d'une dette au débiteur pour les motifs suivants :

_____
_____
_____
_____

The Notice will be served on the debtor _____
L'avis sera signifié au débiteur,   (Name of debtor / *Nom du débiteur/de la débitrice*)

at _____
à/au   (Address of debtor for service / *Adresse du débiteur/de la débitrice aux fins de signification*)

within five days of serving it on the garnishee.
dans les cinq jours qui suivent sa signification au tiers saisi.

☐ Notice of Examination (Form 20H).
Avis d'interrogatoire (formule 20H).

☐ Writ of Delivery (Form 20B).
Bref de délaissement (formule 20B).

☐ Other (Set out the nature of your request):
Autre (Indiquez la nature de votre demande) :

_____
_____
_____

Complete this section if you are requesting a Writ of Delivery.
Remplissez la présente section si vous demandez un bref de délaissement.

2. An order for the delivery of the following personal property:
Une ordonnance de délaissement des biens meubles suivants :
(According to the court order, set out a description of the property to be delivered. Identify any marks or serial numbers. / *Selon l'ordonnance du tribunal, donnez la description des biens qui doivent être restitués. Indiquez toute marque d'identification ou tout numéro de série y figurant.*)

_____
_____
_____
_____
_____

Continued on next page / *Suite à la page suivante*

Court Forms in Small Claims Court

Claim No. / N° de la demande _____

was made in this action against: _____
a été rendue dans l'action contre :   (Name of person against whom the order was made / Nom de la personne contre qui l'ordonnance a été rendue)

on _____ , 20 _____ , in the _____
le   à la Cour des petites   (Name of court location where order was made / Emplacement
                créances de   du tribunal où l'ordonnance a été rendue)

Small Claims Court. Since the above listed personal property has not been delivered, I make this affidavit in support of a request that the clerk of the court issue a Writ of Delivery (Form 20B) to the bailiff of the
Étant donné que les biens meubles susmentionnés n'ont pas été restitués, je fais le présent affidavit à l'appui d'une demande visant à enjoindre au greffier du tribunal de délivrer un bref de délaissement (formule 20B) à l'huissier de la Cour des petites créances de

_____ Small Claims Court.

(Name of court location / Emplacement du tribunal)

Complete this section if you are requesting a Certificate of Judgment, Writ of Seizure and Sale of Personal Property, Writ of Seizure and Sale of Land, Notice of Garnishment, Notice of Renewal of Garnishment or Notice of Examination.
Remplissez la présente section si vous demandez un certificat de jugement, un bref de saisie-exécution de biens meubles, un bref de saisie-exécution de biens-fonds, un avis de saisie-arrêt, un avis de renouvellement de la saisie-arrêt ou un avis d'interrogatoire.

3. A judgment was made in this action against _____
    Un jugement a été rendu dans l'action contre   (Name of debtor(s) / Nom du/de la/des débiteur(s)/débitrice(s))

on _____ , 20 _____ in the _____
le   à la Cour des petites créances de

_____ Small Claims Court

(Name of court where judgment was made / Nom du tribunal où le jugement a été rendu)

for the following sums:
à l'égard des sommes suivantes :

(A) **DEBT** $ _____
     LA CRÉANCE $

(B) **PRE-JUDGMENT INTEREST** calculated
     LES INTÉRÊTS ANTÉRIEURS AU JUGEMENT *calculés*

     on the sum of $ _____   at the rate of _____ %
     sur la somme de $ *au taux de*   *pour cent*

     per annum from _____ , 20 ___ to _____ , 20 ___ ,
     par an du   *au*

     being _____ days. $ _____
     soit   *jours.* $

                                 SUBTOTAL (Amount of Judgment) $ _____
                                 TOTAL PARTIEL (montant du jugement) $

(C) **COSTS** to date of judgment $ _____
     LES DÉPENS *à la date du jugement* $

FORM / *FORMULE* 20P   PAGE 4

Claim No. / *N° de la demande*

(D) **TOTAL AMOUNT OF PAYMENTS RECEIVED FROM DEBTOR**
after judgment (if any)   (minus) $ _____
LE MONTANT TOTAL DES PAIEMENTS REÇUS DU   *(moins)* $ _____
DÉBITEUR après le jugement (le cas échéant)

(E) **POST-JUDGMENT INTEREST** to date calculated
LES INTÉRÊTS POSTÉRIEURS AU JUGEMENT à ce jour, calculés

on the sum of $ _____   at the rate of _____ %
sur la somme de $ *au taux de*   *pour cent*

per annum from _____ , 20 ___ to _____ , 20 ___ ,
par an du   *au*

being _____   days. $ _____
soit   *jours.* $ _____

> **NOTE:** Calculation of interest is always on the amount owing from time to time as payments are received. This is true for both pre-judgment and post-judgment interest. Attach a separate sheet setting out how you calculated the total amount of any pre/post-judgment interest.
> **REMARQUE :** *Les intérêts doivent toujours être calculés sur la somme due. Le calcul doit tenir compte des paiements reçus de temps à autre. Ceci s'applique autant aux intérêts antérieurs au jugement qu'aux intérêts postérieurs au jugement. Annexez une feuille distincte indiquant comment vous avez calculé le montant total des intérêts antérieurs et postérieurs au jugement.*

(F) **SUBSEQUENT COSTS** incurred after judgment (including the cost of issuing
the requested enforcement(s)) $ _____
LES DÉPENS SUBSÉQUENTS engagés après le jugement (y compris le $ _____
coût de la délivrance de la ou des mesures d'exécution forcée demandées)

TOTAL DUE $ _____
SOLDE DÛ $ _____

Sworn/Affirmed before me at _____
Déclaré sous serment/Affirmé   (Municipality / *municipalité*)
solennellement devant moi à

in _____
en/à/au   (Province, state or country / *province, État ou pays*)

on _____ , 20 ___
le   Commissioner for taking affidavits
                       Commissaire aux affidavits
                       (Type or print name below if signature is illegible.)
                       (Dactylographiez le nom ou écrivez-le en caractères
                       d'imprimerie ci-dessous si la signature est illisible.)

Signature
(This form is to be signed in front of a
lawyer, justice of the peace, notary public
or commissioner for taking affidavits.)
(La présente formule doit être signée en
présence d'un avocat, d'un juge de paix, d'un
notaire ou d'un commissaire aux affidavits.)

> **WARNING:** IT IS AN OFFENCE UNDER THE *CRIMINAL CODE* TO KNOWINGLY SWEAR OR AFFIRM A FALSE AFFIDAVIT.
> **AVERTISSEMENT :** *FAIRE SCIEMMENT UN FAUX AFFIDAVIT CONSTITUE UNE INFRACTION AU CODE CRIMINEL.*

SCR 20.04-10-20P (June 1, 2009 / *1er juin 2009*) CSD

ONTARIO

Superior Court of Justice
Cour supérieure de justice

Notice of Garnishment Hearing
Avis d'audience sur la saisie-arrêt

Form / Formule 20Q Ont. Reg. No. / Règl. de l'Ont. : 258/98

Small Claims Court / Cour des petites créances de

Claim No. / N° de la demande

Address / Adresse

Phone number / Numéro de téléphone

☐ Additional creditor(s) listed on the attached Form 1A.
Le ou les créanciers additionnels sont mentionnés sur la formule 1A ci-jointe.

Creditor / Créancier

Last name, or name of company / Nom de famille ou nom de la compagnie		
First name / Premier prénom	Second name / Deuxième prénom	Also known as / Également connu(e) sous le nom de
Address (street number, apt., unit) / Adresse (numéro et rue, app., unité)		
City/Town / Cité/ville	Province	Phone no. / N° de téléphone
Postal code / Code postal		Fax no. / N° de télécopieur
Representative / Représentant(e)		LSUC # / N° du BHC
Address (street number, apt., unit) / Adresse (numéro et rue, app., unité)		
City/Town / Cité/ville	Province	Phone no. / N° de téléphone
Postal code / Code postal		Fax no. / N° de télécopieur

Debtor / Débiteur

Last name, or name of company / Nom de famille ou nom de la compagnie		
First name / Premier prénom	Second name / Deuxième prénom	Also known as / Également connu(e) sous le nom de
Address (street number, apt., unit) / Adresse (numéro et rue, app., unité)		
City/Town / Cité/ville	Province	Phone no. / N° de téléphone
Postal code / Code postal		Fax no. / N° de télécopieur
Representative / Représentant(e)		LSUC # / N° du BHC
Address (street number, apt., unit) / Adresse (numéro et rue, app., unité)		
City/Town / Cité/ville	Province	Phone no. / N° de téléphone
Postal code / Code postal		Fax no. / N° de télécopieur

NOTE:	The Notice of Garnishment Hearing must be served by the person requesting the hearing on the creditor, debtor, garnishee, co-owner of debt, if any, and any other interested person [R. 8.01(9)].
REMARQUE :	L'avis d'audience sur la saisie-arrêt doit être signifié par la personne qui demande l'audience au créancier, au débiteur, au tiers saisi et au cotitulaire de la créance, le cas échéant, et à tout autre intéressé [par. 8.01 (9)].

SCR 20.08-20Q (September 1, 2010 / 1ᵉʳ septembre 2010) CSD

1067

FORM / FORMULE 20Q   **PAGE 2**

Garnishee / Tiers saisi

Last name, or name of company / Nom de famille ou nom de la compagnie		
First name / Premier prénom	Second name / Deuxième prénom	Also known as / Également connu(e) sous le nom de
Address (street number, apt., unit) / Adresse (numéro et rue, app., unité)		
City/Town / Cité/ville	Province	Phone no. / N° de téléphone
Postal code / Code postal		Fax no. / N° de télécopieur
Representative / Représentant(e)		LSUC # / N° du BHC
Address (street number, apt., unit) / Adresse (numéro et rue, app., unité)		
City/Town / Cité/ville	Province	Phone no. / N° de téléphone
Postal code / Code postal		Fax no. / N° de télécopieur

Co-Owner of Debt (if any) /
Cotitulaire d'une créance (le cas échéant)

☐ Additional co-owner(s) listed on attached Form 1A.
Le ou les cotitulaires additionnels sont mentionnés sur la formule 1A ci-jointe.

Last name, or name of company / Nom de famille ou nom de la compagnie		
First name / Premier prénom	Second name / Deuxième prénom	Also known as / Également connu(e) sous le nom de
Address (street number, apt., unit) / Adresse (numéro et rue, app., unité)		
City/Town / Cité/ville	Province	Phone no. / N° de téléphone
Postal code / Code postal		Fax no. / N° de télécopieur
Representative / Représentant(e)		LSUC # / N° du BHC
Address (street number, apt., unit) / Adresse (numéro et rue, app., unité)		
City/Town / Cité/ville	Province	Phone no. / N° de téléphone
Postal code / Code postal		Fax no. / N° de télécopieur

Other Interested Person (if any) /
Autre intéressé (le cas échéant)

☐ Additional interested person(s) listed on attached Form 1A.
Le ou les intéressés additionnels sont mentionnés sur la formule 1A ci-jointe.

Last name, or name of company / Nom de famille ou nom de la compagnie		
First name / Premier prénom	Second name / Deuxième prénom	Also known as / Également connu(e) sous le nom de
Address (street number, apt., unit) / Adresse (numéro et rue, app., unité)		
City/Town / Cité/ville	Province	Phone no. / N° de téléphone
Postal code / Code postal		Fax no. / N° de télécopieur
Representative / Représentant(e)		LSUC # / N° du BHC
Address (street number, apt., unit) / Adresse (numéro et rue, app., unité)		
City/Town / Cité/ville	Province	Phone no. / N° de téléphone
Postal code / Code postal		Fax no. / N° de télécopieur

SCR 20.08-20Q (September 1, 2010 / 1er septembre 2010) CSD   **Continued on next page / Suite à la page suivante**

Court Forms in Small Claims Court

Claim No. / N° de la demande

TO THE PARTIES:
AUX PARTIES :

(The person requesting this garnishment hearing or the person's representative must contact the clerk of the court to choose a time and date when the court could hold this garnishment hearing. / La personne qui demande l'audience sur la saisie-arrêt ou son représentant doit communiquer avec le greffier du tribunal pour choisir la date et l'heure où le tribunal pourrait tenir cette audience.)

THIS COURT WILL HOLD A GARNISHMENT HEARING on _____ , 20 ____ , at
LE TRIBUNAL PRÉCITÉ TIENDRA UNE AUDIENCE SUR LA SAISIE-ARRÊT le , à

_____ **, or as soon as possible after that time, at** (Address of court location and courtroom number)
(Time / heure)   **, ou dès que possible par la suite, à/au** (Adresse du tribunal et numéro de la salle d'audience)

_____

because (Check the appropriate box.)
parce que (Cochez la case appropriée.)

☐ the creditor   ☐ the debtor   ☐ the garnishee   ☐ the co-owner of debt
   le créancier   *le débiteur*   *le tiers saisi*   *le cotitulaire d'une créance*

☐ other interested person: _____
   une autre personne intéressée :   (Specify / Précisez.)

states the following: (In numbered paragraphs, provide details of your dispute and the order(s) requested.)
déclare ce qui suit : (Donnez, sous forme de paragraphes numérotés, le détail de votre contestation et l'ordonnance ou les ordonnances demandées.)

_____
_____
_____
_____
_____
_____
_____
_____
_____
_____
_____
_____
_____
_____

☐ **Additional pages are attached because more space was needed.**
Des feuilles supplémentaires sont annexées en raison du manque d'espace.

_____ , 20 ____

(Signature of party or representative / Signature de la partie ou du/de la représentant(e))

NOTE:	If you fail to attend this garnishment hearing, an order may be made in your absence and enforced against you.
REMARQUE :	Si vous ne vous présentez pas à cette audience sur la saisie-arrêt, une ordonnance peut être rendue en votre absence et être exécutée contre vous.

SCR 20.08-20Q (September 1, 2010 / 1er septembre 2010) CSD

ONTARIO

Superior Court of Justice
Cour supérieure de justice

Notice of Termination of Garnishment
Avis de mainlevée de la saisie-arrêt
Form / Formule 20R Ont. Reg. No. / Régl. de l'Ont. : 258/98

Small Claims Court / Cour des petites créances de

Claim No. / N° de la demande

Address / Adresse

Phone number / Numéro de téléphone

BETWEEN / ENTRE

Creditor(s) / Créancier(s)/créancière(s)

and / et

Debtor(s) / Débiteur(s)/débitrice(s)

TO
À

(Name of garnishee / Nom du tiers saisi)

AND TO the clerk of the
ET AU greffier de la Cour
des petites créances de

(Name of court location / Emplacement du tribunal)

Small Claims Court:

The Notice of Garnishment/Notice of
Renewal of Garnishment dated
L'avis de saisie-arrêt/l'avis de
renouvellement de la saisie-arrêt daté du

, 20

, served on you with respect to the debt of
qui vous a été signifié à l'égard de la
créance de :

Last name of debtor, or name of company / Nom de famille du débiteur/de la débitrice ou nom de la compagnie		
First name / Premier prénom	Second name / Deuxième prénom	Also known as / Également connu(e) sous le nom de
Address / Adresse		

is terminated and you are not to make any further payments under it.
prend fin et vous n'avez pas besoin de faire d'autres paiements aux termes de celui-ci.

, 20

(Signature of creditor or representative / Signature du créancier/de la
créancière ou du/de la représentant(e))

(Name, address and phone number of creditor or representative / Nom,
adresse et numéro de téléphone du créancier/de la créancière ou du/de la
représentant(e))

NOTE: The creditor must serve this notice on the garnishee and on the court clerk.
REMARQUE : Le créancier doit signifier le présent avis au tiers saisi et au greffier du tribunal.

SCR 20.08-20R (September 1, 2010 / 1er septembre 2010) CSD

6 — Small Claims Court Judges and Court Offices

Schedule 6

Small Claims Court Judges

The Small Claims Court is generally presided over by deputy judges appointed pursuant to *Courts of Justice Act* s. 24(2)(b). In addition, pursuant to *Courts of Justice Act* s.. 24(2)(a), there are currently two *per diem* justices of the former Provincial Court (Civil Division), both located in Toronto. Finally, although this occurs only in rare situations, the Small Claims Court may be presided over by judges of the Superior Court of Justice sitting as judges of the Small Claims Court pursuant to *Courts of Justice Act* s. 22(3).

The Honourable M. Donald Godfrey (Toronto Region)
The Honourable Pamela A. Thomson (Toronto Region)

Note: Every judge of the Superior Court of Justice is also a judge of the Small Claims Court. *Courts of Justice Act*, section 22(3).

Deputy Judges of the Small Claims Court

Toronto Region
Central East Region
Central South Region
Central West Region
East Region
North East Region
North West Region
South West Region

Toronto Region

Deputy Judge Deborah Anschell
Deputy Judge Christopher Ashby
Deputy Judge Michael Bay
Deputy Judge Lionel Berger
Deputy Judge Carla L. Bocci
Deputy Judge Nathalie Boutet
Deputy Judge Catherine M. Buie
Deputy Judge Jay J. D. Burnside
Deputy Judge Robert Caplan
Deputy Judge Licio E. Cengarle
Deputy Judge Joanna Chadwick
Deputy Judge Miray B. Cheskes-Granovsky
Deputy Judge Thomas H. Clemenhagen
Deputy Judge William C. De Lucia
Deputy Judge Thora H. Espinet
Deputy Judge Albert Ferranti
Deputy Judge Vincent Genova
Deputy Judge Kathleen A. Howes
Deputy Judge John C. F. Hunt
Deputy Judge Robert C. Kay
Deputy Judge Chris W. Kilian
Deputy Judge David G. Leitch
Deputy Judge Gerard Levesque
Deputy Judge Larry J. Levine
Deputy Judge Peter Libman
Deputy Judge Samuel S. Marr
Deputy Judge Paul J. Martial
Deputy Judge Paul J. McNeely
Deputy Judge Michael O. Mungovan
Deputy Judge Laura Ntoukas
Deputy Judge Gina Papageorgiou
Deputy Judge Harry Perlis
Deputy Judge Z. Jack C. Prattas
Deputy Judge Louie Reznick
Deputy Judge Lewis J. Richardson
Deputy Judge Rebecca Rosenberg
Deputy Judge Dr. Sashika Seevaratnam
Deputy Judge Lawrence N. Shapiro
Deputy Judge Jerald Shuman

Deputy Judge Steven H. Skolnik
Deputy Judge Burton B. C. Tait
Deputy Judge John Twohig
Deputy Judge Lynn Wheatley
Deputy Judge Winnie W. Wong
Deputy Judge Peter J. Zibarras

Central East Region

Deputy Judge James N. Aitchison
Deputy Judge Bernard Aron
Deputy Judge Stanley Baker
Deputy Judge Robert A. Besunder
Deputy Judge Catharine A. Blastorah
Deputy Judge Michael Boland
Deputy Judge Lorraine A. Bortolussi
Deputy Judge Jeffrey G. Brown
Deputy Judge W. Mark Burch
Deputy Judge Neil Burgess
Deputy Judge Jay Chauhan
Deputy Judge Abraham Davis
Deputy Judge Peter R. Deacon
Deputy Judge Alessandro M. Di Cecco
Deputy Judge Bruno Di Gregorio
Deputy Judge Dan Dooley
Deputy Judge Paul W. Dusome
Deputy Judge Brian Kenneth Evans
Deputy Judge Robert F. Evans
Deputy Judge Alan Fisher
Deputy Judge Boris G. Freesman
Deputy Judge Derek G. Friend
Deputy Judge Janet Gillespie
Deputy Judge Elliott Goldstein
Deputy Judge Paul Gollom
Deputy Judge DeeAnn M.P. Gonsalves
Deputy Judge Lionel Gray
Deputy Judge James B. Halls
Deputy Judge Deborah A. Hastings
Deputy Judge Carmine T. Iacono
Deputy Judge Chris W. Kilian
Deputy Judge Brian Kinnear
Deputy Judge Ching Y. Kitchen
Deputy Judge Gary G. Kitchen
Deputy Judge Teresa Kowalishin
Deputy Judge Mark Kowalsky
Deputy Judge Paul Kupferstein
Deputy Judge Jeffrey D. Lanctot
Deputy Judge Donald J. Lange
Deputy Judge William J. Leslie
Deputy Judge K. Joy Levison
Deputy Judge J. Michael Longworth
Deputy Judge Edward P. Mayhew
Deputy Judge Alan J. McMackin

Deputy Judge A. Scott McMichael
Deputy Judge Wendy Miller
Deputy Judge David A. Morin
Deputy Judge Charles S. Morison
Deputy Judge K. Julaine Palmer
Deputy Judge Mart A. Pikkov
Deputy Judge Stan Raphael
Deputy Judge Thérèse Reilly
Deputy Judge John F. L. Rose
Deputy Judge Rob Rossi
Deputy Judge Mark Scharf
Deputy Judge Howard Schneider
Deputy Judge Raymond G. Selbie
Deputy Judge Joel E. Shaw
Deputy Judge Martina Shaw
Deputy Judge Steven H. Skolnik
Deputy Judge Ronald G. Sparks
Deputy Judge Vincent Stabile
Deputy Judge Leonard Susman
Deputy Judge William P. Taws
Deputy Judge Judith Turner
Deputy Judge Victor L. Vandergust
Deputy Judge Shirley R. Wales
Deputy Judge Lawrence F. Wallach
Deputy Judge Barry A. Walters
Deputy Judge Jack Zwicker

Central South Region

Deputy Judge Ronald F. Adams
Deputy Judge James G. Battin
Deputy Judge James H. Bennett
Deputy Judge David W. Black
Deputy Judge David T. Bogdon
Deputy Judge Douglas C. Brown
Deputy Judge A. Douglas Burns
Deputy Judge Richard Campbell
Deputy Judge Michael E. Cobb
Deputy Judge Janis P. Criger
Deputy Judge Cindy Dickinson
Deputy Judge Deborah L. Ditchfield
Deputy Judge Daniel J. Fife
Deputy Judge Peter B. Forbes
Deputy Judge John B. Gallagher
Deputy Judge Sondra Gibbons
Deputy Judge Mark S. Grossman
Deputy Judge Kenneth N. Hagan
Deputy Judge D. Bryan Holub
Deputy Judge Keith M. Jones
Deputy Judge John Krawchenko
Deputy Judge Anthony G. Lados
Deputy Judge Michael D. Lannan
Deputy Judge Claude F. Leduc

Deputy Judge Robert J. Lefebvre
Deputy Judge Joan M. MacDonald
Deputy Judge James Marentette
Deputy Judge Brian K. Marotta
Deputy Judge Terry Marshall
Deputy Judge Cindy A. Martin-Hrycak
Deputy Judge C. Edward McCarthy
Deputy Judge Roderick H. McDowell
Deputy Judge Shelley M. McGill
Deputy Judge Paula McPherson
Deputy Judge Virginia S. Mendes da Costa
Deputy Judge Gerald E. Miller
Deputy Judge Marcel D. Mongeon
Deputy Judge Charles A. Morrison
Deputy Judge Joan M. Mouland
Deputy Judge Robert G. Nairn
Deputy Judge Paul Oddi
Deputy Judge Christopher Rous
Deputy Judge Deborah L. Scime
Deputy Judge R. Keith Simpson
Deputy Judge Joseph E. Sloniowski
Deputy Judge Andrew Spurgeon
Deputy Judge Oswald W. Stahl
Deputy Judge Jay State
Deputy Judge Paul M. Stillman
Deputy Judge Siona Sullivan
Deputy Judge David A. van der Woerd
Deputy Judge Jane Weary
Deputy Judge J. Sebastian Winny

Central West Region

Deputy Judge David W. Acri
Deputy Judge William S. Aird
Deputy Judge H. Robert Barlow
Deputy Judge George W. Barycky
Deputy Judge Judith A. Birchall
Deputy Judge Gordon Z. Bobesich
Deputy Judge L. Ruthanne Bowker
Deputy Judge Stephen B. Collinson
Deputy Judge Noel da Silva
Deputy Judge Andrew Drury
Deputy Judge Richard A. Fellman
Deputy Judge Robert A. Filkin
Deputy Judge Stewart C. E. Gillis
Deputy Judge Stuart W. Henderson
Deputy Judge D. Bryan Holub
Deputy Judge Todd Jenney
Deputy Judge Kenneth Kelertas
Deputy Judge Donald G. Kidd
Deputy Judge Martin E. Klein
Deputy Judge Marvin Kurz
Deputy Judge Ian K. Latimer

Deputy Judge Marek S. Malicki
Deputy Judge Beverley Martel
Deputy Judge Kenneth F. McCabe
Deputy Judge Warren McCrea
Deputy Judge Ross C. McLean
Deputy Judge J. Brian McNulty
Deputy Judge Eric Nadler
Deputy Judge John C. Noonan
Deputy Judge Laura E. Oliver
Deputy Judge Lois E. Payne
Deputy Judge Steven W. Pettipiere
Deputy Judge Sheri Richardson
Deputy Judge H. Jane Robertson
Deputy Judge Marlon Roefe
Deputy Judge Angelo A. Serafini
Deputy Judge Leslie J. Smith
Deputy Judge Karen A. Thompson
Deputy Judge Karen Thompson-Harry
Deputy Judge Ross H. Thomson
Deputy Judge Kim Twohig
Deputy Judge Edwin G. Upenieks
Deputy Judge Willa M. B. Voroney
Deputy Judge Frances M. Wood

East Region

Deputy Judge Leslie Ault
Deputy Judge Rohan G. Bansie
Deputy Judge Jean J. A. Bédard
Deputy Judge Katherine Cartwright
Deputy Judge Harry C. Clarke
Deputy Judge Gina L. Cockburn
Deputy Judge Roy B. Conacher
Deputy Judge Kenneth J. Conroy
Deputy Judge Catherine Coplea
Deputy Judge John R. Crouchman
Deputy Judge Kevin W. Doyle
Deputy Judge David Y. Dwoskin
Deputy Judge E. Susan Elliott
Deputy Judge Brian G. Evely
Deputy Judge Marie T. Fortier
Deputy Judge Lyon Gilbert
Deputy Judge A. Peter Girard
Deputy Judge Raymond H. Gouin
Deputy Judge Michael J. Houle
Deputy Judge Robert B. Howe
Deputy Judge David R. Hurley
Deputy Judge Joanne Hurley
Deputy Judge Patrick E. Hurley
Deputy Judge Douglas B. James
Deputy Judge Laurie E. Joe
Deputy Judge Robert G. Julien
Deputy Judge Edward J. Kafka

Deputy Judge Shane A. Kelford
Deputy Judge Robert R. Kennedy
Deputy Judge Christine M. LaCasse
Deputy Judge Bruce Leach
Deputy Judge Roger R. Leclaire
Deputy Judge Paul Lepsoe
Deputy Judge Tracy Lyle
Deputy Judge J. Bruce MacNaughton
Deputy Judge Terrance J. McCarthy
Deputy Judge Brooke McNabb
Deputy Judge George C. McNeely
Deputy Judge Harold McNeely
Deputy Judge Judith Millard
Deputy Judge Donald T. Mowat
Deputy Judge Elizabeth M. Osborne
Deputy Judge Jocelyne Paquette-Landry
Deputy Judge Andre G. Poirier
Deputy Judge J. Guy Potvin
Deputy Judge Harry R. Preston
Deputy Judge Michael J. Pretsell
Deputy Judge C. Roderick Rolston
Deputy Judge Michael V. Ross
Deputy Judge Rod Sauriol
Deputy Judge David R. Shelly
Deputy Judge John D. Simpson
Deputy Judge William G. Sirman
Deputy Judge Deborah H. Souder
Deputy Judge Ian R. Stauffer
Deputy Judge William W. Walker
Deputy Judge Donald J. White
Deputy Judge Ivan G. Whitehall

North East Region

Deputy Judge J. Roland H. Aube
Deputy Judge Pierre D. Brunelle
Deputy Judge Sylvano A. Carlesso
Deputy Judge Patricia L. Cassidy
Deputy Judge Wayne A. Chorney
Deputy Judge Kim Cogar
Deputy Judge Selma N. Colvin
Deputy Judge Douglas R. Grandy
Deputy Judge Gerard E. Guimond
Deputy Judge Romuald Kwolek
Deputy Judge Erin J. Lainevool
Deputy Judge Terence E. Land
Deputy Judge O. Kennedy Lawson
Deputy Judge Michelle C. Mailloux
Deputy Judge Gerard E. McAndrew
Deputy Judge Patricia Meehan
Deputy Judge Michael S. Mensour
Deputy Judge Judith L. Munn
Deputy Judge Nicola S. Munro

Deputy Judge George Olah
Deputy Judge Benjamin F. Pritchard
Deputy Judge J. J. Marc Remillard
Deputy Judge Wayne G. Stickland
Deputy Judge David G. Stone
Deputy Judge Victor F. Vere
Deputy Judge Barbara Morland Wellard
Deputy Judge Bruce Willson
Deputy Judge Donald W. Wood
Deputy Judge James M. Young

North West Region

Deputy Judge Brian Babcock
Deputy Judge Paul Brett
Deputy Judge Kevin W. Brothers
Deputy Judge Clare A. Brunetta
Deputy Judge Kristen L. Bucci
Deputy Judge Thomas J. Carten
Deputy Judge Kevin G. Cleghorn
Deputy Judge Wesley Derksen
Deputy Judge David J. Elliott
Deputy Judge Richard Halabisky
Deputy Judge Judith Jacob
Deputy Judge Jack Jamieson
Deputy Judge Steve Kovanchak
Deputy Judge Rick Lauder
Deputy Judge James L. Murray
Deputy Judge W. Randall Seller
Deputy Judge Walter C. Wieckowski
Deputy Judge Robert G. Zochodne

South West Region

Deputy Judge James G. Battin
Deputy Judge Geoffrey A. Beasley
Deputy Judge Joseph F. Belecky
Deputy Judge Bruce H. Blake
Deputy Judge James Branoff
Deputy Judge Kenneth J. Brooks
Deputy Judge J. Bernard Comiskey
Deputy Judge Theodore Crljenica
Deputy Judge Simon R. R. Davies
Deputy Judge Elena Dempsey
Deputy Judge Brian D'hondt
Deputy Judge Avril Farlam
Deputy Judge Alan Fisher
Deputy Judge James B. Gee
Deputy Judge Gerald F. Gillespie
Deputy Judge Kristen L. Hales
Deputy Judge Jeffrey J. Hewitt
Deputy Judge Kenneth W. Koprowski
Deputy Judge Peter Kuker

Deputy Judge Therese Landry
Deputy Judge Elisabeth N. Lella
Deputy Judge Paul L. Lepine
Deputy Judge Anthony H. Little
Deputy Judge J. Richard Lockwood
Deputy Judge Celia A. MacDonald
Deputy Judge Trudy Mauth
Deputy Judge Hugh D. McDonald
Deputy Judge David Miller
Deputy Judge A. Paul Parlee
Deputy Judge Judith R. Pascoe
Deputy Judge Norman B. Pickell
Deputy Judge Judith Potter
Deputy Judge David J. Reinhart
Deputy Judge Christine Riley
Deputy Judge Michael A. Robb
Deputy Judge Heather J. Ross
Deputy Judge Sheldon Schwartz
Deputy Judge James D. Searle
Deputy Judge Robert Stevens
Deputy Judge Robert B. Stewart
Deputy Judge Paul J. Trudell
Deputy Judge Helen R. Turner
Deputy Judge Despina S. Valassis
Deputy Judge Glenn C. Walker
Deputy Judge Byron P. Westfall
Deputy Judge Brenda L. Yeates

Last Updated: May 29, 2014

Courts Administration Directors of Court Operations

See Sched. 1.

See Chart on following page.

Superior Court of Justice and Ontario Court of Justice (Judicial Regions)

See Sched. 1.

Note: For the territorial divisions of the Small Claims Court, see O. Reg. 159/85 and R.R.O. 1990, Reg. 206, as am. O. Reg. 245/01, ss. 1, 2; repealed O. Reg. 448/09.

REGIONAL SENIOR JUSTICES OF THE SUPERIOR COURT OF JUSTICE	
CHIEF JUSTICE HEATHER FORSTER SMITH Osgoode Hall, 130 Queen Street West, Toronto, Ontario M5H 2N5	
(Northeast Region) Mr. Justice Robbie D. Gordon Regional Senior Justice Superior Court of Justice	(Southwest Region) Mr. Justice Thomas A. Heeney Regional Senior Justice Superior Court of Justice

Small Claims Court Judges and Court Offices

REGIONAL SENIOR JUSTICES OF THE SUPERIOR COURT OF JUSTICE	
Court House, 155 Elm Street 2nd Floor	Court House, 15th Floor, Unit G 80 Dundas Street
Sudbury, ON P3C 1T9 Tel: (705) 564-7814 Fax: (705) 564-7902 Justice M. Gregory Ellies Administrative Judge	London, ON N6A 6B3 Tel: (519) 660-2291 Fax: (519) 660-2294 Justice Scott K. Campbell Administrative Judge
(Central West Region) Madame Justice Francine E. Van Melle Regional Senior Justice Superior Court of Justice Court House, 7755 Hurontario Street Brampton, ON L6W 4T6 Tel: (905) 456-4837 Fax: (905) 456-4836 Justice Thomas A. Bielby Administrative Judge	(Toronto Region) Mr. Justice Geoffrey B. Morawetz Regional Senior Justice Superior Court of Justice Court House, 361 University Avenue, Toronto, ON M5G 1T3 Tel: (416) 327-5094 Fax: (416) 327-9931 Justice Alison Harvison Young Administrative Judge
(East Region) Mr. Justice James E. McNamara Regional Senior Justice Superior Court of Justice	(Central East Region) Madame Justice Michelle K. Fuerst Regional Senior Justice Superior Court of Justice
Court House, 161 Elgin Street Ottawa, ON K2P 2K1 Tel: (613) 239-1527 Fax: (613) 239-1507 Justice Charles T. Hackland Administrative Judge	Court House, 50 Eagle Street West Newmarket, ON L3Y 6B1 Tel: (905) 853-4827 Fax: (905) 853-4826 Justice John R. McCarthy Administrative Judge
(Central South Region) Mr. Justice R. H. Turnbull Regional Senior Justice Superior Court of Justice John Sopinka Courthouse, 45 Main Street East, Suite 721 Hamilton, ON L8N 2B7 Tel: (905) 645-5323 Fax: (905) 645-5374 Justice Peter B. Hambly Administrative Judge	(Northwest Region) Madame Justice Helen M. Pierce Regional Senior Justice Superior Court of Justice Court House, 277 Camelot Street Thunder Bay, ON P7A 4B3 Tel: (807) 343-2712 Fax: (807) 343-2713 Justice John F. McCartney Administrative Judge

Province of Ontario Small Claims Court Office Contact List

See Sched. 1.

Province of Ontario Small Claims Court Office Contact Information

Judicial Region	Location/District	Mailing Address/Telephone
Central East	Barrie SCC/ County of Simcoe	75 Mulcaster Street Barrie, ON L4M 3P2 705-739-6111
Central East	Bracebridge SCC/ District Municipality of Muskoka	3 Dominion Street North Bracebridge, On P1L 2E6 705-645-8793
Central East	Brighton SCC/ County of Northumberland	Municipal Building 35 Alice St. Brighton, ON K0K 1H0 905-372-3751
Central East	Campbellford SCC/ County of Northumberland	Masonic Temple 53 Front St. South Campbellford, ON K0L 1L0 905-372-3751
Central East	Cobourg SCC/ County of Northumberland	860 William Street Cobourg, ON K9A 3A9 905-372-3751
Central East	Collingwood/ County of Simcoe	49 Huron St. Collingwood, ON L9Y 1C5 705-445-9332
Central East	Huntsville SCC/ District Municipality of Muskoka	36 Chaffey Street Huntsville, ON P1H 1J4. 705-645-8793
Central East	Lindsay SCC/ City of Kawartha Lakes	440 Kent Street West Lindsay, ON K9V 6K2 705-324-1400
Central East	Midland SCC/ County of Simcoe	605 Yonge St. Midland, ON L4R 2E1

Judicial Region	Location/District	Mailing Address/Telephone
		705-526-0251
Central East	Minden SCC/ City of Kawartha Lakes	7 Milne St. Minden, ON K0M 2K0 705-324-1400
Central East	Newmarket SCC/ York Region	Newmarket Administration Office — Le Parc Office Tower 8500 Leslie St. Suite 395 Markham, ON L3T 7M8 905-853-4809 905-731-2664
Central East	Orillia SCC/ County of Simcoe	Orillia Courthouse 700 Memorial Avenue Cottage C, P.O. Box 218 Orillia, ON L3V 6J3 705-326-2671
Central East	Peterborough SCC/ Peterborough County	70 Simcoe Street Peterborough, ON K9H 7G9 705-876-3816
Central East	Port Hope SCC/ County of Northumberland	Town Hall, 56 Queen St. Port Hope, ON L1A 3Z9 905-372-3751
Central East	Richmond Hill SCC/ York Region	855 Major MacKenzie Drive Richmond Hill, ON L4B 4C6 905-737-4416
Central East	Oshawa SCC/ Durham Region	150 Bond Street East Oshawa, ON L1G 0A2 905-743-2630
Central West	Brampton SCC/ Peel	7755 Hurontario Street Brampton, ON L6W 4T1 905-456-4700
Central South	Brantford SCC/ County of Brant	70 Wellington Street Brantford, ON N3T 2L9

Judicial Region	Location/District	Mailing Address/Telephone
		519-752-7828
Central West	Burlington / Halton	2021 Plains Road East Burlington, ON L7R 4M3 905-637-4125
Central South	Cayuga SCC/ Haldimand	55 Munsee Street P.O. Box 70 Cayuga, ON N0A 1E0 905-772-3335
Central South	Hamilton SCC/ Hamilton / Wentworth	45 Main Street East Hamilton, ON L8N 2B7 905-645-5252
Central West	Milton SCC/ Halton	491 Steeles Avenue East Milton, ON L9T 1Y7 905-878-7285
Central West	Orangeville SCC / Dufferin	10 Louisa Street Orangeville, ON L9W 3P9 519-944-5802
Central South	Simcoe SCC/ Norfolk	50 Frederick Hobson VC Drive Simcoe, ON N3Y 4L5 519-426-6550
Central South	St. Catharines SCC/ Niagara North	59 Church Street, 1st Floor St. Catharines, ON L2R 7N8 905-988-6200
Central South	Welland SCC/ Niagara South	102 Main Street East, 1st Fl Welland, ON L3B 3W6 905-735-0010
East	Alexandria SCC/ Glengarry County	110 Main Street North, P.O. Box 699 Alexandria, ON K0C 1A0 613-525-4330
East	Arnprior SCC/ Renfrew County	Arnprior Public Library

Judicial Region	Location/District	Mailing Address/Telephone
		21 Madawaska St. Arnprior, ON K7S 1R6 613-432-3139
East	Bancroft SCC/ Hastings County	5 Fairway Blvd, RR # 5 Bancroft, ON K0L 1C0 613-962-9106
East	Belleville SCC/ Hastings and Prince Edward Counties	Belleville Courthouse c/o New Quinte Courthouse 15 Bridge Street West Belleville, ON K8P 0C7 613-962-9106
East	Brockville SCC/ County of Leeds & Grenville	41 Court House Square Brockville, On K6V 7N3 613-341-2800
East	Cornwall SCC/ Stormont, Dundas and Glengarry Counties	29 - 2nd Street West Cornwall, ON K6J 1G3 613-933-7500
East	Kingston SCC/ Frontenac County	5 Court Street Kingston, ON K7L 2N4 613-548-6811
East	Kaladar SCC/ County of Lennox & Addington	41 Dundas St. W. Kaladar, ON K7R 1Z5 613-354-3845
East	L'Orignal SCC/ County of Prescott and Russell	59 Court Street, 2nd Fl. L'Orignal, ON K0B 1K0 613-675-4567 1-800-666-0124
East	Morrisburg SCC/ Dundas County	8 - Fifth Street West Morrisburg, ON K0C 1X0 613-543-2193
East	Napanee SCC/ County of Lennox & Addington	41 Dundas Street West Napanee, ON K7R 1Z5 613-354-3845

Judicial Region	Location/District	Mailing Address/Telephone
East	Ottawa SCC/ City of Ottawa	161 Elgin Street, 2nd Floor Ottawa, ON K2P 2K1 613-239-1079
East	Pembroke SCC/ Renfrew County	297 Pembroke Street East Pembroke, ON K8A 3K2 613-732-8581
East	Perth SCC/ Lanark County	43 Drummond Street East Perth, ON K7H 1G1 613-267-2021
East	Picton SCC/ Prince Edward County	44 Union Street P.O. Box 680 Picton, ON K0K 2T0 613-476-6236
East	Renfrew SCC/ Renfrew County	315 Raglan Street South P.O. Box 386 Renfrew, ON K7V 1R6 613-432-3193
Southwest	Chatham SCC/ Waterloo/Municipality of Chatham-Kent	425 Grand Avenue West Chatham, ON N7M 6M8 519-355-2200
Southwest	Goderich SCC/ Huron County	1 Court House Square Goderich, ON N7A 1M2 519-524-7322
Central West	Guelph SCC/ Wellington County	74 Woolwich Street Guelph, ON N1H 3T9 519-824-1488
Central South	Kitchener SCC/ Regional Municipality of Waterloo	85 Frederick Street Kitchener, ON N2H 0A7 519-741-3270
Southwest	Leamington SCC/ Essex County	7 Clark St. W. Leamington, ON N8H 1E5 519-973-6620

Small Claims Court Judges and Court Offices

Judicial Region	Location/District	Mailing Address/Telephone
Southwest	London SCC / Middlesex County	80 Dundas Street, Unit A London, ON N6A 6A3 519-660-3000 x5000
Central West	Mount Forest SCC/ Wellington County	381 Main St. N. Mount Forest, ON N0G 2C0 519-824-4169
Central West	Owen Sound SCC/Grey County	611 - 9th Avenue East Owen Sound, ON N4K 6Z4 519-370-2430
Southwest	Sarnia SCC/Lambton County	700 North Christina Street Sarnia, ON N7V 3C2 519-333-2950
Southwest	SCC/Elgin County	145 Curtis Street, 2nd Fl. P.O. Box 310, Main Stn. St. Thomas, ON N5P 3Z7 519-631-3530 ext. 251
Southwest	Stratford SCC/Perth County	100 St. Patrick St. Stratford, ON N5A 7W1 519-271-9252
Southwest	Stratford SCC/Perth County	1 Huron Street Stratford, ON N5A 5S4 519-271-1850
Central West	Walkerton SCC/ Bruce County	207 Cayley Street P.O. Box 39 Walkerton, ON N0G 2V0 519-881-1772
Southwest	Windsor SCC/Essex County	245 Windsor Avenue Windsor, ON N9A 1J2 519-973-6620
Southwest	Woodstock SCC / Oxford County	415 Hunter Street P.O. Box 70 Woodstock, ON N4S 7W5

Judicial Region	Location/District	Mailing Address/Telephone
		519-539-6187 ext. 234
North	Blind River SCC / District of Algoma	15 Hudson St. Blind River, ON P0R 1B0 705-848-2383
North	Burks Falls/South River SCC/ Parry Sound Region	300 Ontario Street, Plaza 11, Hwy 11 P.O. Box 119 Burks Falls, ON P0A 1C0 705-382-2571
Northeast	Chapleau SCC/District of Cochrane	Chapleau Civic Centre P. O. Box 129 Chapleau, ON P0M 1K0 705-360-4231
Northeast	Cochrane SCC/District of Cochrane	149 - 4th Avenue P.O. Box 638 Cochrane, ON P0L 1C0 705-272-4256
Northeast	Elliott Lake SCC / District of Algoma	200 Ontario Avenue Elliot Lake, ON P5A 1Y5 705-848-2383
Northeast	Espanola / District of Sudbury	Town Hall 100 Tudhope St., 2nd Fl., Suite 3 Espanola, ON P5E 1S6 705-869-4334
Northeast	Gore Bay SCC/ District of Manitoulin	27 Philips Street Gore Bay, ON P0P 1H0 705-282-2461
Northeast	Haileybury SCC/District of Temiskaming	Court House 393 Main St., Box 609 Haileybury, ON P0J 1K0 705-672-3321

Judicial Region	Location/District	Mailing Address/Telephone
Northeast	Hearst SCC/District of Cochrane	925 Alexandra St. Hearst, ON P0N 1N0 705-337-1477
Northeast	Iroquois Falls SCC/District of Cochrane	Corporation of the Town of Iroquois Falls 253 Main St., P.O. Box 230 Iroquois Falls, ON P0M 1K0 705- 272-4256
Northeast	Kapuskasing SCC/District of Cochrane	Ontario Government Building 122 Government Road West Kapuskasing, ON P5N 2X8 705-337-1477
Northeast	Kapuskasing SCC/District of Cochrane	Courthouse — no documents go here 88 Riverside Drive Kapuskasing, ON P5N 1B3 705-337-1477
Northeast	Kirkland Lake SCC/District of Temiskaming	140 Government Road P.O. Box 730 Kirkland Lake, ON P2N 2G2 705-567-9381
Northeast	North Bay SCC/ District of Nipissing	360 Plouffe Street North Bay, ON P1B 9L5 705-495-8309
Northeast	Parry Sound SCC/District of Parry Sound	89 James Street Parry Sound, ON P2A 1T7 705-746-4237
Northeast	Sault Ste. Marie SCC/ District of Algoma	426 Queen Street East Sault Ste. Marie, ON P6A 6W2 705-945-8000 ext. 530
Northeast	Sturgeon Falls SCC/ Nipissing	201 River Rd., Royal Canadian Legion Sturgeon Falls, ON P2B 1T4 705-753-1090

Judicial Region	Location/District	Mailing Address/Telephone
Northeast	Sudbury SCC/ District of Sudbury	155 Elm Street Sudbury, ON P3C 1T9 705-564-7600
Northeast	Sundridge SCC / District of Parry Sound	Sundridge Strong and Joly Arena 14 Albert St. N. Sundridge, ON P0A 1Z0 705-746-4237
Northeast	Timmins SCC/District of Cochrane	48 Spruce Street North Timmins, ON P4N 6M7 705-360-4231
Northeast	Wawa SCC / District of Algoma	40 Broadway Avenue Wawa, ON P0S 1C2 705-945-8000
Northwest	Dryden SCC / District of Kenora	479 Government House Box 1 Dryden, ON P8N 3K9 807-223-2348
Northwest	Fort Frances SCC/ District of Rainy River	333 Church Street Fort Frances, ON P9A 1C9 807-274-5961
Northwest	Geraldton SCC/ District of Thunder Bay	209 Beamish St. Box 39 Geraldton, ON P0T 1M1 807-854-1488
Northwest	Kenora SCC/ District of Kenora	216 Water Street Kenora, ON P9N 1S4 807-468-2842
Northwest	Nipigon SCC/ Thunder Bay	5 Wadsworth Drive Nipigon, ON P0T 2J0 807-887-3829
Northwest	Red Lake SCC/ District of Kenora	115 Howey Street P.O. Box 1070 Red Lake, ON P0V 2M0

Judicial Region	Location/District	Mailing Address/Telephone
		807-727-2376
Northwest	Thunder Bay SCC/District of Thunder Bay/Kenora/Rainy River	1805 East Arthur Street - 2nd Floor Thunder Bay, ON P7E 5N7 807-343-2710
Toronto	Toronto SCC/ City of Toronto	47 Sheppard Avenue East 3rd Floor Toronto, ON M2N 5N1 416-326-3554
Toronto	Listowel Courthouse	330 Wallace Ave. Listowel, ON N4W 1L2 519-271-4940
Toronto	Attawapiskat Courthouse	Regional Louttit Sportsplex Attawapiskat, ON P0L 1A0 705-272-4256
Toronto	Sharbot Lake Courthouse	1107 Garrett Street Sharbot Lake, ON K0H 2P0 613-548-6811

Ontario Deputy Judges Association
Suite 374
3 - 35 Stone Church Road
Ancaster, Ontario L9K 1S4
w: www.odja.ca

Bilingual Proceedings

See Sched. 1.
See Chart on following page.

	How to obtain a Bilingual Proceeding: Former Regulation 185	How to obtain a Bilingual Proceeding: New Regulation O. Reg. 53/01 (in force June 1, 2001)	New Provisions
Civil, Family & Small Claims Court Proceedings *Ontario Court of Justice *Superior Court of Justice	- File a Requisition Form	1. File a Requisition Form [Form 1] 2. File a written statement with the registrar where the proceeding has begun 3. Make an oral statement to the Court during an appearance in the proceeding	Unless the court, on motion, orders otherwise, the requisition or statement: • Must be filed or made not later than 7 days before the date of the first hearing indicated in the requisition or statement [ss. 5(1)(a)(b); (3) and (7)] • Shall specify one or more future hearings shall be heard before a bilingual judge or officer, *and* may specify that all future hearings in the proceeding shall be heard by a bilingual judge or officer [ss. 5(2) and 7] • Where the proceeding is a trial of an action to be heard by a bilingual judge, the requisition or statement must be filed or made before the action is placed on the trial list [ss. 5(1)(a)(b); (4)(a) and (7)] • The requisition or written statement must be served on every other party in accordance with the rules of court [s. 5(8)]
		4. File or issue the first document in French	Unless the court, on motion, orders otherwise, the first document:

How to obtain a Bilingual Proceeding: Former Regulation 185	How to obtain a Bilingual Proceeding: New Regulation O. Reg. 53/01 (in force June 1, 2001)	New Provisions
		• Must be filed or issued no later than 7 days before the hearing; party deemed to have exercised the right to a bilingual proceeding under s. 126(1) of the *CJA*, and to have specified that all future hearings in the proceeding are to be heard by a bilingual judge or officer [ss. 3(1)(a)(b); (2); and (3)] • *Applies only to the areas listed in Schedule 2 to s. 126 of the Courts of Justice Act; or elsewhere in Ontario if the other parties consent* [s. 3(4)] [paras. 6 and 7 of s. 126(2) CJA] • Party must file consents or to make motion for leave, at the earliest possible opportunity [s. 6(1) and (2)]
	How to withdraw a request for bilingual hearing: • File consents of all other parties, or on motion, with leave of the Court	
• File a Requisition Form	• File a requisition form [Form 2] with registrar or clerk	Appellant to file at the time the notice of appeal is filed: Respondent to file within 10 days after the notice of appeal served; unless the court, on motion, allows otherwise [ss. 8(1)(a) and (b); and (2)] Requisition to be served on every other party to the appeal as provided in the applicable rules of court [s. 8(3)]
Appeals •All Courts Sitting as an Appeal Court		
	• The first document that is filed by a party to the appeal is written in French	Document to be filed no later than 7 days before the appeal hearing, unless the court on motion, allows otherwise [ss. 7(1), (2) and (3)]

How to obtain a Bilingual Proceeding: Former Regulation 185	How to obtain a Bilingual Proceeding: New Regulation O. Reg. 53/01 (in force June 1, 2001)	New Provisions
		Applies only to appeal documents filed in a Schedule 2 area* or elsewhere in Ontario if the other parties consent [Section 126(4)] and paras. 6 & 7 of section 126(2) Courts of Justice Act [ss. 7(1) and (4)]
	How to withdraw a Request for an appeal heard by bilingual judge or judges:	Party must file consents or make the motion at the earliest possible opportunity [ss. 9(1) and (2)]
	• File written consent of all other parties,	* The areas named in Schedule 2 are Essex; Chatham-Kent; Middlesex, Prescott and Russell; Renfrew; Simcoe; Stormont Dundas and Glengarry; Algoma; Cochrane; Kenora; Nipissing; Sudbury (formerly the Territorial District now included as the City of Greater Sudbury); Thunder Bay and Timiskaming; the area of the County of Welland as it existed on December 31, 1969 (otherwise referred to as Niagara South); the City of Hamilton; the City of Ottawa; the City of Greater Sudbury; the City of Toronto; the Regional Municipality of Peel

7 — APPEALS

7

Appeals

What is an Appeal?

An appeal is totally different than a trial. It is not a means to obtain a second opinion about a case. Rather, it is a review for specific types of error on the part of the trial judge.

Going into a trial, the trial judge makes no presumption about who is likely to win. All parties are entitled to the same right to a full and fair hearing. At the conclusion of a trial, the result is a judgment which usually means victory for one side and defeat for the other. Appeals aren't intended to change the reality that litigation produces successful and unsuccessful parties. Rather, appeals provide a means for quality control, to ensure that trial judges apply legal rules correctly and make findings of fact that are reasonably supported by the evidence.

Appeal courts apply a presumption that the trial judge made no reversible errors. Unless that presumption is rebutted, the appeal will be dismissed. An appellant bears the onus to satisfy the appeal court that some significant error was committed which affected the outcome. An unsuccessful litigant may be dissatisfied with the judgment at trial and may be convinced it is wrong, but may have no meaningful chance of winning an appeal from that judgment.

A trial involves a presentation of evidence and argument, after which the trial judge determines the necessary factual and legal issues and delivers a judgment. Civil trial judges find what facts are true based on the balance of probabilities standard, which requires only that a given fact be found to be more than 50% probable. Trial judges often face several possible choices in finding what the facts are, and several alternative findings may be reasonable based on the evidence. That is a significant reason why it is often said that going to trial is risky, while settlement is certain. Litigants, and particularly self-represented litigants, sometimes fail to appreciate the reality that however clear their own view of the truth may be, from the objective and impartial standpoint of a judge, it is unusual that only one specific outcome will be reasonable based on the evidence. The trial judge has the power to select just one outcome among as many outcomes as are reasonably supported by the evidence. In most cases, the unsuccessful litigant will be unable to successfully appeal from a trial judge's findings of fact.

There are three basic elements in assessing the prospects for successful appeal. First, is there a right of appeal? Second, what is the applicable standard of appellate review? Third, is the proposed appeal financially viable?

Is There a Right of Appeal?

An appeal is solely a creature of statute. For there to be a right of appeal, there must be a statute which says so.

There is a right of appeal from final orders of the Small Claims Court, subject to the minimum appealable limit prescribed under section 31 of the *Courts of Justice Act*. The right of appeal applies to a final order in an action for the payment of money in excess of $2,500, exclusive of costs, or in an action for the recovery of personal property, where the value of the property exceeds $2,500.

There is no appeal from interlocutory orders of the Small Claims Court. For examples of interlocutory orders which cannot be appealed, see the cases annotated under section 31 of the *Courts of Justice Act*. Examples of interlocutory orders are an order setting aside default judgment and an order adjourning a trial. Recent confirmation that there is no appeal from interlocutory orders of the Small Claims Court is found in *Grainger v. Windsor-Essex Children's Aid Society*, 2009 CarswellOnt 4000, 96 O.R. (3d) 711 (Ont. Div. Ct.).

The distinction between final and interlocutory orders has a history; the leading case is *Hendrickson v. Kallio*, 1932 CarswellOnt 148, [1932] O.R. 675, [1932] 4 D.L.R. 580 (Ont. C.A.). A final order is an order which finally determines who wins or loses the case or an issue in the case. An interlocutory order is merely an order made along the way towards a final order, but which leaves the issues in dispute between the parties for later determination. Final orders include a judgment at trial, an order striking out a pleading without leave to amend, and an order dismissing a motion to set aside default judgment.

Based on the language of *Courts of Justice Act* section 31, the amount of the minimum appealable limit in actions for damages includes the total of both the amount of damages the amount of prejudgment interest claimed: see *Medis Health & Pharmaceutical Services Inc. v. Belrose*, 1994 CarswellOnt 486, 17 O.R. (3d) 265, 23 C.P.C. (3d) 273, 72 O.A.C. 161 (Ont. C.A.); *Watson v. Boundy*, 2000 CarswellOnt 905, 49 O.R. (3d) 134, 130 O.A.C. 328 (Ont. C.A.). Therefore in some cases, it will be necessary to calculate the amount of prejudgment interest to determine whether the action (damages plus prejudgment interest) is for an amount which exceeds the minimum appealable limit and is subject to appeal.

If there is otherwise a right of appeal under section 31, then if the proposed appeal is from a consent order or a costs order, the proposed appeal requires leave to appeal: *Courts of Justice Act* section 133.

Standard of Appellate Review

The basic reality of appellate litigation is that most appeals are dismissed. Why? Because an appeal is an entirely different creature than a trial.

An appeal is not a mere request for a second opinion as to some theoretical single correct outcome, but a search for significant error which affected the outcome at trial. Based on a review of the documentary evidence and the transcript of the oral evidence given at trial, if the appeal judge can find no reversible error — if the outcome was reasonably supported by the evidence and untainted by legal error affecting the outcome — the appeal must be dismissed. Many appeals are dismissed even though the appeal judge might have decided the case differently if he or she had presided at trial. That is because an appeal is not a second trial before an appeal judge, but a focused review for specific types of error on the trial judge's part.

Before hearing the appeal, an appeal judge starts with the presumption that the trial judge made no errors of fact or law. The appellant must convince the appeal court that, in this particular case, that usual assumption is wrong and the trial judge did commit one or more reversible errors.

The standard of appellate review is the same for appeals from the Small Claims Court as for appeals from other courts: *Allison v. Street Imports Ltd.* (May 14, 2009), Doc. 03 DV 000953, [2009] O.J. No. 1979 (Ont. Div. Ct.); *Tang v. Jarrett*, 2009 CarswellOnt 1656, 251 O.A.C. 123, [2009] O.J. No. 1282 (Ont. Div. Ct.). See also *Zeitoun v. Economical Insurance Group*, 2008 CarswellOnt 2576, [2008] O.J. No. 1771, 91 O.R. (3d) 131, 236 O.A.C. 76, 64 C.C.L.I. (4th) 52, 53 C.P.C. (6th) 308, 292 D.L.R. (4th) 313 (Ont. Div. Ct.); additional reasons at 2008 CarswellOnt 3734, 56 C.P.C. (6th) 191, 64 C.C.L.I. (4th) 68 (Ont. Div. Ct.); affirmed 2009 ONCA 415, 2009 CarswellOnt 2665, [2009] O.J. No. 2003, 96 O.R. (3d) 639, 73 C.C.L.I. (4th) 255, 257 O.A.C. 29, 73 C.P.C. (6th) 8, 307 D.L.R. (4th) 218 (Ont. C.A.), where it was held that there was no principled reason to apply a different standard of appellate review to decisions by masters than applies to decisions by judges. The same reasoning applies to appeals from the Small Claims Court.

Factual findings are reviewed on a deferential standard and will not be interfered with on appeal unless they are the product of palpable and overriding error, are unreasonable or unsupported by the evidence, or are clearly wrong. Findings of pure law are reviewed for correctness: *Housen v. Nikolaisen*, 2002 SCC 33, 2002 CarswellSask 178, 2002 CarswellSask 179, REJB 2002-29758, [2002] S.C.J. No. 31, [2002] 2 S.C.R. 235, 10 C.C.L.T. (3d) 157, 211 D.L.R. (4th) 577, 286 N.R. 1, [2002] 7 W.W.R. 1, 30 M.P.L.R. (3d) 1, 219 Sask. R. 1, 272 W.A.C. 1 (S.C.C.); *L. (H.) v. Canada (Attorney General)*, 2005 SCC 25, 2005 Carswell-Sask 268, 2005 CarswellSask 273, REJB 2005-89538, EYB 2005-89538, [2005] S.C.J. No. 24, [2005] 1 S.C.R. 401, 333 N.R. 1, 8 C.P.C. (6th) 199, 24 Admin. L.R. (4th) 1, 262 Sask. R. 1, 347 W.A.C. 1, [2005] 8 W.W.R. 1, 29 C.C.L.T. (3d) 1, 251 D.L.R. (4th) 604 (S.C.C.). Particularly for fact-driven appeals, the appellant faces a difficult burden. Appeal courts show deference to the factual findings made by trial courts because the trial court had the benefit of seeing and hearing the evidence in person. This causes appellate courts to reject arguments that a trial judge ought to have weighed the evidence differently, or ought to have made different findings of fact merely because the appellant would have preferred a different outcome.

The powers of an appeal court are set out in *Courts of Justice Act* section 134. Generally, where appellate interference is warranted, an appeal court can make any order which the trial judge should have made: section 134(1)(a). A new trial shall not be ordered unless some substantial wrong or miscarriage of justice has occurred: section 134(6). That means that in some cases, the appellate court may find an error to have been committed by the trial judge, but may find it to be a "harmless error" which does not warrant appellate interference with the result.

The bottom line is that generally speaking, an appeal is an uphill battle for the appellant. According to the statistics found in the 2009 Annual Report of the Court of Appeal for Ontario, for example, the percentage of civil appeals (excluding family law) that were allowed during the years 2004 through 2009 varied from a high of 37% to a low of 27%: see www.ontariocourts.on.ca/coa/en/ps/annualreport/2009. While those statistics do no relate specifically to appeals from the Small Claims Court, they illustrate the simple fact that most appeals are dismissed.

Is the Proposed Appeal Financially Viable?

Most trial judgments are not appealed. Appeals from the Small Claims Court are launched less frequently than appeals from other courts, simply because the monetary value of disputes in the Small Claims Court is comparatively low and the cost of appeal is therefore comparatively high.

A party considering an appeal faces two costs which must be assessed to determine whether the appeal is financially viable.

The first cost which a potential appellant must be prepared to incur is that party's own cost of the appeal. That cost consists of the legal fees and disbursements which the potential appellant must pay to proceed with the appeal.

The largest cost on appeal is the cost of legal representation, which will depend on what particular lawyers may charge for appellate cases. Legal fees could involve $5,000 and up. In the appeal court, corporations must be represented by a lawyer (subject to leave under rule 15.01(2) of the *Rules of Civil Procedure*) and paralegals are not permitted to appear.

The disbursements required to appeal may be estimated at $1,000, including court fees and a full-day trial transcript, and more for the transcripts for longer trials. If desired, an estimate of the actual cost for the transcript may be obtained from the court reporter. The transcript cost is usually the largest disbursement for an appeal and varies depending on the length of the trial.

Based on those rough estimates, the potential appellant will in many cases have to commit at least $6,000 to pursue an appeal.

The second cost which a potential appellant faces is the potential costs liability to the respondent if the appeal is unsuccessful. The unsuccessful party on appeal is usually ordered to compensate the successful party for appeal costs on a partial indemnity scale. The amount of such costs is determined by the appeal judge, and is subject to significant potential variance. Awards of Small Claims Court appeal costs are most often in a range from $2,500 to $10,000, depending on the time required for the appeal, the complexity of the issues, the amount in dispute, and other factors including any offers to settle the appeal. For recent examples of appeal costs awards, see the annotations under section 31 of the *Courts of Justice Act*.

The financial reality is that many potential appeals are not financially viable, even if the appellant has an arguable appeal. The potential appellant must be prepared to accept the risk of not only the loss of that party's own cost of the appeal, but also liability for the other party's appeal costs.

On the other hand, if an appeal is successful, there are cost consequences for the respondent as well. That party will have paid the cost of its own participation in the appeal, and also faces liability for the appellant's appeal costs, in addition to the cost of reversal or variation of the trial judgment or possibly a new trial.

Where an appeal is launched, the parties are just as free to settle while the appeal is pending as they were while the trial was pending. However appeals tend to settle less frequently than trials.

Procedure on Appeal

An appeal from the Small Claims Court is to the Divisional Court, which is a branch of the Superior Court of Justice. Such appeals are heard by a single judge of the Divisional Court: *Courts of Justice Act* section 21(2)(b). The appeal proceeds in the county in which the Small Claims Court heard the case. Other Divisional Court appeals which are heard by three judges proceed in the designated regional center for each judicial region, but that practice does not apply to single-judge appeals, which are heard by the judges of the local Superior Court of Justice, sitting as Divisional Court judges.

The procedure for appeals is set out in Rule 61 of the *Rules of Civil Procedure*.

The time to initiate an appeal is within 30 days of the order appealed from. Within that time, the appellant must serve a notice of appeal (Form 61A) and appellant's certificate (Form 61C): rule 61.04(1). The notice of appeal must be filed with proof of service within 10 days after service: rule 61.04(4). The appeal is filed in the office of the Superior Court of Justice that is in the same court house, or the same county, as that where the Small Claims Court heard the case.

A respondent may serve the respondent's certificate respecting evidence (Form 61D), within 15 days after service of the appellant's certificate: rule 61.05(2). The parties may make an agreement respecting the evidence that is necessary for the appeal: rule 61.05(4).

A respondent may launch a cross-appeal within 15 days after service of the notice of appeal, by serving a notice of cross-appeal (Form 61E): rule 61.07(1). That notice must be filed within 10 days after service: rule 61.07(2).

The court fee for an appeal from a final order of the Small Claims Court is currently $104. That fee must be paid by the appellant to file the notice of appeal. A respondent who wishes to file a notice of cross-appeal must pay that same fee.

The appellant must order the transcripts of all oral evidence that the parties have not agreed to omit, and file proof of ordering: rule 61.05(5). The court reporters' office will produce a certificate of ordering transcript once the order is in place. The transcript preparation time will depend on a variety of factors, but should generally involve up to three months. The appellant must pay for the transcript (original and one copy for each set of parties). That cost varies with the length of transcript but may be estimated at $500 per day of trial, for one original and two copies of the transcript.

Once the transcript is completed, the appeal must be perfected — which means that the appellant has filed all of the material required by rule 61.09, and paid the court fee to perfect the appeal (currently $201). The materials required to perfect the appeal are as follows:

- appeal book and compendium (see rule 61.10)
- exhibit book (see rule 61.10.1)
- transcript (printed version, with electronic version if provided)
- appellant's factum (printed version, with electronic version) (see rule 61.11)
- book of authorities (may be filed after appeal is perfected)
- certificate of perfection (see rule 61.09(3)(c))

A respondent must serve and file, within 60 days after service of the appellant's materials, a respondent's factum and a respondent's compendium: rule 61.12.

Depending how long the court reporter needs to prepare the transcript, appeals can be expected to take 6 to 12 months from the date of the order appealed from.

Second Potential Appeal

A party who wishes to appeal further after the Divisional Court decides the appeal faces a limited prospect for further recourse. The only further appeal is for questions that are not questions of fact alone, and first requires that leave to appeal to the Court of Appeal be sought and granted, on motion: *Courts of Justice Act* section 6(1)(a). Such a motion for leave to appeal must be launched within 15 days after the date of the Divisional Court's decision: *Rules of Civil Procedure*, rule 61.03.1(3).

Leave for a second appeal is rarely granted. The strong general rule is that where there is a right of appeal, there is only one appeal. In practical terms, it is very rare for a Small Claims Court case to go to the Court of Appeal.

A decision by the Court of Appeal is usually the last word in any civil case. A potential further appeal to the Supreme Court of Canada requires that leave to appeal to that court first be granted, and such leave is granted in fewer than 1 in 20 civil cases in which leave is sought.

Judicial Review of Small Claims Court Decisions?

Judicial review under the *Judicial Review Procedure Act*, R.S.O. 1990, c. J.1, is generally used to review the decisions of administrative tribunals. Under that Act, the concept of what may be judicially reviewed is described as a "statutory power of decision." Section 1 defines that concept as including "the powers of an inferior court." Does judicial review lie from decisions of the Small Claims Court?

Recently it was held that interlocutory orders of the Small Claims Court could be the subject of judicial review, but only as to jurisdictional error or breach of natural justice.

In *Peck v. Residential Property Management Inc.*, 2009 CarswellOnt 4330, [2009] O.J. No. 3064 (Ont. Div. Ct.), it was held that orders of the Small Claims Court, including interlocutory orders of the court, could be the subject of judicial review under the *Judicial Review Procedure Act*. However, the court expressed its reluctance to interfere with an order of the Small Claims Court "unless it is an order made without jurisdiction or in breach of principles of natural justice." The court will decline to interfere with interlocutory orders where the application is in essence an appeal by a different name. In that case the application, which was to review a decision setting aside a default judgment, was dismissed. That decision was recently applied by a differently-constituted panel in *Pardar v. McKoy*, 2011 ONSC 2549, 2011 CarswellOnt 3059, [2011] O.J. No. 2092 (Ont. Div. Ct.).

The correctness of *Peck, supra*, may have been questionable in light of authorities holding that the Divisional Court cannot judicially review other branches or officers of the Superior Court of Justice: see *Connie Steel Products Ltd. v. Greater National Building Corp.*, 1977 CarswellOnt 231, 3 C.P.C. 327, [1977] O.J. No. 668 (Ont. Div. Ct.); *Canada Building Materials Co. v. London (City)*, 1978 CarswellOnt 365, 22 O.R. (2d) 98, 13 C.P.C. 184, 92 D.L.R. (3d) 249 (Ont. Div. Ct.); *Butcher v. Sun Media Corp.* (November 21, 2001), Doc. 01-DV-000608, [2001] O.J. No. 4702 (Ont. Div. Ct.); *Schorr v. Selkirk*, 1977 CarswellOnt 190, 15 O.R. (2d) 37, 13 C.P.C. 184, 2 C.P.C. 249 (Ont. Div. Ct.). None of those authorities appears to have been considered in *Peck, supra*, or *Pardar, supra*.

Those authorities were however addressed by Nordheimer J. writing for the panel in *Thyssenkrupp Elevator (Canada) Ltd. v. 1147335 Ontario Inc.*, 2012 ONSC 4139, 2012 CarswellOnt 9698, 43 Admin. L.R. (5th) 61, 18 C.L.R. (4th) 82, 295 O.A.C. 71, [2012] O.J. No. 3674 (Ont. Div. Ct.). The court's conclusion was that it did have jurisdiction to judicially review the interlocutory decision of a master, despite the absence of a statutory right of appeal, on the narrow grounds of jurisdictional error or natural justice. There appears to be no principled basis to hold that result inapplicable to the Small Claims Court context. While it will be rare for any Small Claims Court litigant to be willing to undertake judicial review proceedings, that remedy may be available based on jurisdictional error or natural justice grounds.

A separate but related question is whether orders of the Small Claims Court may be challenged by originating application to the Superior Court of Justice. There appear to be two cases in which such applications have been entertained.

In *Mayo v. Veenstra*, 2003 CarswellOnt 9, 63 O.R. (3d) 194 (Ont. S.C.J.), the applicant alleged jurisdictional error. A deputy judge hearing a motion to set aside a default judgment had ordered that the defendant submit to cross-examination on her motion affidavit, failing which her motion would be dismissed. The applications judge held that the deputy judge had no jurisdiction to order cross-examination, which is not part of the court's motion procedures. In *Gulati v. Husain*, 2011 ONSC 706, 2011 CarswellOnt 407, [2011] O.J. No. 384 (Ont. S.C.J.), the applicant alleged a breach of natural justice. A deputy judge had refused an adjournment of a motion to set aside default judgment, gave no reasons for refusing the adjournment, and granted the motion to set aside the default judgment without hearing submissions. The applications judge set aside the deputy judge's order and remitted the matter for hearing by a different deputy judge. The applications judge acknowledged but did not answer the question whether the matter ought to be heard by the Divisional Court.

The effect of the above-noted cases is that in exceptional circumstances involving jurisdictional error or breach of natural justice, decisions of the Small Claims Court, including interlocutory decisions, may be judicially reviewed by the Divisional Court.

GLOSSARY OF LEGAL TERMS

Glossary

absentee — A person who has disappeared or whose whereabouts are unknown.

accountant of the Superior Court of Justice — The person who has the authority to accept monies that are paid into the Superior Court, except for proceedings under the *Landlord and Tenant Act* or the *Repair and Storage Lien Act* or actions in Small Claims Court.

action — A legal proceeding in a civil case.

act of bankruptcy — An act committed by a debtor as defined under the *Bankruptcy and Insolvency Act*, e.g. a debtor ceases to meet his liabilities as they generally become due. A creditor with a provable claim of $1,000 and over may file a petition for a receiving order if the debtor has committed such an act within the six months preceding the filing of the petition.

actus reus — Proof that a criminal act has occurred, the requirement of a guilty mind.

ad hoc — For this (special) purpose.

ad idem — At one.

adjournment — court approved postponement of a hearing to a future date.

adjudication — Giving or pronouncing a judgment.

admissible — Evidence which can be legally and properly introduced at a trial.

adversary proceeding — One having opposing, contested parties.

adversary system — The trial method used based on the belief that truth can best be determined by giving opposing parties full opportunity to present and establish their evidence, and to test the evidence presented by cross-examination.

advocates — A lawyer, appearing in a court of law.

affidavit — A written statement or declaration of facts that are sworn or affirmed to be true.

affidavit for jurisdiction — a plaintiff's sworn or affirmed written statement that he or she filed the claim:

- In the territorial division where the cause of action arose (i.e. where the event took place or problem occurred);

- At the court in the territorial division in which the defendant lives or carries on business (if there are several defendants, then it can be the court in the territorial division in which any one of them lives or carries on business); or

- At the court's place of sitting that is nearest to the place where the defendant lives or carries on business (if there are several defendants, then it can be the court nearest to the place in which any one of them lives or carries on business).

(Court addresses and phone numbers can be found online at www.ontario.ca/attorneygeneral.)

affidavit of service — An affidavit certifying that a document has been served on a party.

affirmation — A solemn declaration made by a person to tell the truth. Lying in an affirmation is perjury, a criminal offence.

alternative dispute resolution — Resolving conflict through means other than going to court. Examples of alternative dispute resolution include: arbitration, mediation, and collaborative family law.

>*arbitration* — A process where a neutral third party, selected by the disputing parties, makes a decision on the issue in dispute.

>*collaborative family law* — A process where the parties and lawyers formally agree to negotiate a resolution of the issues in dispute through a series of meetings, without going to court.

>*mediation* — A process where a neutral third party (mediator), selected by the disputing parties, assists parties to reach agreement on issues in dispute.

amicus curiae — Latin for "friend of the court." A lawyer who assists the court during the course of a hearing, to represent a position of interest, usually at the court's request.

answer — A response to an allegation or an application.

appeal — A request by the losing party in a legal action that the order or judgment be reviewed by a higher court.

appeal period — The time limit within which one can appeal.

appellant — A person who brings an appeal. The word "appellant" may refer to either party from a "lower" proceeding (e.g. plaintiff or defendant, applicant, or respondent), depending on who appealed the decision.

application —

1. The commencement of a proceeding in a court by way of filing the appropriate court form.

2. A request made to the court.

arrears — Money that is owed to a party under a court order or agreement, but has not been paid.

assessment —

1. The determination of the rate or amount of something. For example, damages or a fine imposed.

2. In civil cases, a determination of the capacity of an individual to manage property, to make personal care decisions, or to properly retain and instruct counsel.

>*solicitor-client assessment* — A hearing where an assessment officer reviews the amount of a lawyer's bill.

>*capacity assessment* — A determination by a capacity assessor, or the court, as to a person's ability to manage property, make personal care decisions, or to properly retain and instruct counsel.

assignment in bankruptcy — A voluntary assignment by an insolvent person of all of his property to a trustee for the general benefit of creditors.

bench — The seat occupied by the judge or, more broadly, the court itself.

bona fide — In good faith.

burden of proof — In the law of evidence, the necessity or duty of proving facts in dispute raised between the parties in an action. The responsibility of proving a point. For example, in a civil case the burden of proof rests with the plaintiff, who establish his or her case by such standards of proof as on the balance of probabilities.

case law — Law based on previous decisions.

causa causans — Causing, cause.

cause of action — The fact or facts which give a person the legal right to begin a lawsuit.

certiorari — A means of getting an appellate court to review a lower court's decision. An order requiring the lower court to convey the record of the case to the appellate court and to certify it as accurate and complete. If an appellate court grants a writ of certiorari, it agrees to take the appeal.

citation — A reference to a source of legal authority.

civil action — Non-criminal cases in which one private individual or business sues another for redress of private or civil rights.

claim — Demand for money or personal property owing to the plaintiff by the defendant.

claim form — The form used by the party who is suing or making the claim to start the action. Form 7A.

claimant or plaintiff — Party who is suing or making the claim.

clerk — The court official to whom certain powers and duties are given by law. These powers and duties may be exercised or performed by one or more staff in the court office.

common law — Law arising from tradition and judicial decisions rather than from laws passed by legislatures. Also called case law.

compensation — A sum of money paid to provide for loss, breakage, hardship, inconvenience, or personal injury.

consensus (ad idem) — Agreement (in the same terms).

consolidation order — A process permitting a debtor against whom there is more than one Small Claims Court judgment to combine the judgments under one order which can be paid by installments.

contempt of court — An "offence" that can lead to a fine and even imprisonment because of a lack of respect or obedience by an individual in a court of law.

contra — Against.

contra proferentum — Against the proferror (*i.e.*, one who prepared a document).

contributory negligence — A legal doctrine that says that if the plaintiff in a civil action for negligence is also negligent, he or she cannot recover damages from the defendant for the defendant's negligence depending, of course, on degree.

corroborating evidence — Supplementary evidence that tends to strengthen or confirm the initial evidence.

court costs — The expenses of bringing or defending a lawsuit other than lawyer's fees. An amount of money may be awarded to the successful party (and recoverable from the losing party) as reimbursement for court costs.

creditor — One to whom a debt is owed, or in insolvency matters, a person having a claim provable under the *Bankruptcy and Insolvency Act*.

damages — Money awarded by a court to a person injured by the unlawful act or negligence of another.

debtor — Party against whom a judgment for the payment or recovery of money may be enforced.

decision — The judgment reached or given by a court of law.

de facto — In fact, that is, actually occurring although not officially sanctioned.

default — A failure to respond to a lawsuit within a specified time.

lt judgment — A document signed by a Clerk for relief claimed against a defendant) has not (1) replied to a claim, (2) disputed a claim, or (3) failed to maintain offered ,ments.

defence — A dispute or reply to the claim (in Small Claims Court, it may also mean a request for time to pay the debt).

defence form — The form used by the party who is being sued to dispute or reply to a claim. Form 9A.

defendant — Party who is being sued (the one against whom the claim is made).

defendant's claim — The process by which a defendant initiates a claim against a plaintiff or against any other person related to or arising from the plaintiff's claim. This claim is brought in the same file as the plaintiff's claim. Form 10A.

de jure — In law, that is, occurring as a result of official action.

de novo — Hearing or trying a matter anew, as if it had not been heard or tried previously.

deponent — A person making a statement under oath.

discovery — The pre-trial process by which one party discovers the evidence that will be relied upon in a trial by the opposing party.

dismissal — The termination of a lawsuit.

dissent — An appellate court's opinion of reasons setting forth the minority view and outlining the disagreement of one or more judges with the majority decision.

docket — A list of cases to be heard by a court.

due process — The right of all persons to receive the guarantees and safeguards of the law and the judicial process. Includes such requirements as adequate notice, the right to counsel, the right to remain silent, to a speedy and public trial, to an impartial jury, and to confront and secure witnesses.

eiusdem generis — Of the same class.

en banc All judges of a court sitting together. Often appellate courts hear cases in panels of three judges. If a case is heard by the full court, it is heard en banc.

endorsement record — a document on which a judge makes a written judgment or court order.

enforcement — The process available to the creditor to help in the collection of money or property owed to the creditor. For example, Writ of Seizure and Sale of Land or Personal Property, Garnishment, Notice of Examination.

equity — Generally, justice or fairness. Historically, equity refers to a separate body of law developed in England in reaction to the inability of the common-law courts, in their strict adherence to rigid writs and forms of action, to consider or provide a remedy for every injury. The principle of this jurisprudence is that equity will find a way to achieve a lawful result when legal procedure is inadequate.

et al — And others.

ex parte — On behalf only of one party without notice to any other party.

ex post facto — After the fact.

exhibit — A document or other article introduced as evidence during a trial or hearing.

factum — A bound document containing a concise summary of facts, the law, and the arguments made in support of, or in response to, an appeal.

garnishee — Party, named in the notice of garnishment, who the creditor believes owes a debt to the debtor, for example, a bank, employer or company who owes the debtor money.

garnishment — A legal process whereby a creditor requires a third party to turn over to the creditor a debtor's property such as wages or bank account.

gavel — A small mallet used to signal for attention. One of the most famous symbols of the judiciary, but ironically, not actually used in courtrooms.

grounds — The reasons or basis upon which the appellant claims the appeal should be allowed.

hearsay — A statement or document made by someone who is not in court.

hearing — Proceedings before a court.

ibid. — In the same place.

idem (or id.) — The same.

in camera — In chambers, or in private. A hearing in camera may take place in the judge's office outside of the presence of the jury and the public.

in loco parentis — In place of a parent, someone charged with the same rights, duties, and responsibilities.

in re — In the matter (of).

infra — Below, signifying a cross reference to a subsequent part of the document or chapter.

inter alia — Among other things.

inter alios — Among other persons.

inter vires — Within the powers.

injunction — An order of the court requiring a party to refrain or cease from doing a particular act or taking certain actions. A preliminary injunction may be granted provisionally, until a full hearing can be held to determine if it should be made permanent.

issue — The clerk dates and signs completed documents.

joint and several liability — The liability of more than one individual that may be enforced against them all by a joint action or against any one of them by an individual action.

judgment — A formal decision issued by a court on a matter under its consideration.

judicial review — Authority of a court to review the official actions of a court.

jurisdiction — The power of the court to hear a particular matter. The *Courts of Justice Act* provides for the appellate jurisdiction of the Divisional Court. However, provisions of other statutes governing particular litigation may modify the general provisions of the *Courts of Justice Act.*

justiciable — Issues and claims properly examined in court.

leading question — A question which suggests the answer desired of the witness. May be asked on cross-examination.

liable — Legally responsible for.

limitations — Statutes setting out times within which actions must be brought.

liquidated claim — a "liquidated" claim is a claim for a sum of money due under an express agreement where the amount is fixed and does not depend on an assessment by the court.

litigant — A party to a lawsuit.

litigation — A case, controversy, or lawsuit between two or more parties for the purpose of enforcing an alleged right or recovering money damages for a breach of duty.

litigation guardian — A person who acts on behalf of a minor or a mentally incompetent person in a lawsuit. Where the plaintiff or defendant is a minor, the litigation guardian will normally be a parent. However, the litigation guardian must have no interest in the lawsuit that conflicts with the interest of the person he or she represents.

mala fides — Bad faith.

mandamus — A writ issued by a court ordering or commending a public official to perform an act.

mediation — Process taking place outside a court to resolve a dispute.

mens rea — Guilty mind.

motion — A process used to make a request to a judge for an order.

mutatis mutandis — With necessary changes.

negligence — Failure to exercise that degree of care that a reasonable person would exercise under the same circumstances.

notice — Formal notification of a legal proceeding to the party that has been sued in a civil case.

notice of motion — Written notice by one party to the other party in a lawsuit about an intention to argue a particular issue before a judge.

notice of trial — A formal notice issued by the court to all parties in a claim stating the date, time and place at which trial or pre-trial is to take place.

novus actus interveniens — New act intervening (*i.e.*, to break a chain of causation).

nunc pro tunc — Now for then (*i.e.*, retroactively).

obiter — By the way.

obiter dictum — (plural dicta) Thing said by the way.

onus — Burden.

open court — The vast majority of hearings are held in open court, with members of the public free to enter the courtroom and observe proceedings. Some cases may be held "in camera," which means "in the chamber" or in private.

order — a written decision made by a judge during the course of a proceeding. An order made by a judge resolving the dispute is also called a judgment. Generally, the decision is documented on an endorsement record. You can ask for a copy of an endorsement record at the court office.

parens patriae — Father of the country.

pari passu — In equal step (*i.e.*, equally).

party — Any person, corporation, unincorporated organization, sole proprietorship or partnership named as a plaintiff or a defendant in a Small Claims Court action.

pendente lite — The lawsuit pending.

per — By.

per se — By itself.

person — Includes a natural person (human being), a partnership, and a corporation that is recognized by law as having the same rights and duties as a natural person.

plaintiff — The person who brings a claim against another person, company or organization.

plaintiff's claim — The process by which a plaintiff/claimant starts a suit against one or more defendants. Started by completing and filing Form 7A.

precedent — A previously decided case which may guide the decision of future cases.

pre-trial conference — An informal hearing held before a judge or designated court official, to attempt to settle the dispute before the actual trial.

pre-trial hearing — A meeting between the judge and parties or their lawyers involved in a lawsuit to narrow the issues, agree on what will be presented at the trial, and to make a further effort to settle the case without a trial.

prima facie — At first sight, fact presumed to be true unless disproved by evidence to the contrary.

privilege — The right of a party to refuse to disclose a document or produce a document or to refuse to answer questions on the ground of some special interest recognized by law.

proximate cause — The act which caused an event to occur. A person generally is liable only if an injury was proximately caused by his or her action or his or her failure to act when he or she had a duty to act.

ratio decidendi — Reason for deciding.

reasonable man — A phrase used to denote a hypothetical person who exercises qualities of attention, knowledge, intelligence, and judgment that society requires of its members for the protection of their own interest and the interests of others. Thus, the test of negligence is based on either a failure to do something that a reasonable person, guided by considerations that ordinarily regulate conduct, would do, or on the doing of something that a reasonable and prudent person would not do.

referee — Court official who may hear pre-trial hearings. In many cases, he/she assists in working out a scheme of debtor's payments to the creditor and may assist in the obtaining of consolidation orders.

Regina — Queen.

relief — What you are asking the court to do.

remedy — Legal or judicial means by which a right or privilege is enforced or the violation of a right or privilege is prevented,redressed, or compensated.

replevin — An action for the recovery of a possession that has been wrongfully taken.

res — Thing, matter, substance.

res gestae — Things done, facts surrounding an incident.

res judicata — Matter adjudicated.

respondent — A person who *responds* to an appeal. In an appeal, the word "respondent" may refer to either party from the lower proceeding (e.g. plaintiff of defendant, applicant or respondent), depending on who appealed the decision.

respondent superior — Theory whereby a master is held liable for the wrongful acts of his or her servant or employee if the servant or employee is acting within the scope of his or her employment.

Rex — King.

self defence — Claim that an act otherwise criminal was legally justifiable.

service/serving — Getting a document to another person in the way the rules of court require or allow.

set off — A debt the plaintiff owes the defendant which may be deducted from the amount the court finds the plaintiff is owed.

settlement — An agreement between the parties disposing of a lawsuit.

sine die — Without a day (*i.e.*, indefinitely).

sine qua non — Without which not (*i.e.*, essential).

stare decisis — The doctrine that courts will follow principles of law laid down in previous cases. To observe precedent.

status quo (ante) — The original state.

statutory law — Law enacted by legislatures as distinguished from case law or common law.

stay — An order of the court halting a judicial proceeding.

sub judice — Before the courts.

summons to witness — A legal document from the court requiring a witness to appear in court at a specific time.

supra — Above, signifying cross reference to an earlier part of the document or chapter.

tort — A theory of negligence involving an injury or wrong committed on the person or property of another. A tort is an infringement of the rights of an individual, not founded on contract. There must be a legal duty to the person harmed. There must be a breach of that duty and there must be damage to the person wronged as the proximate result of the breach.

uberrimae fidei — The utmost good faith.

ultra vires — Beyond the powers.

unliquidated..... — A nonspecific dollar amount which requires some form of proof to permit a judge to come to a decision, *e.g.*, repair of a motor vehicle.

verbatim — Word for word.

versus — Against.

viva voce — With living voice (*i.e.*, orally).

volenti non fit injuria — Voluntary assumption of risk of unjury.

writ — Written instructions to a court officer to enforce a court order.

Index

All references in this Index are to the Rules and Forms, unless preceeded by "s." or "ss." which indicates section number(s) of the *Courts of Justice Act* or by "p." or "pp." which indicates page number(s).

Default judgment - Pre judgment

1) Claim Amount: | $ 21,764.87
2) Date of Claim: | Sept 17 2014
| (205 days)
3) Date of filing:
4) Interest Amount: % 0.013 (1.3)

Formula (Days ÷ 365) x Tax Amount x Amount of Claim.

(205 ÷ 365) x 0.013 x $ 21,764.87

0.5616 x 0.013 x $ 21,764.87

0.0073637 x $ 21,764.87

= $ 158.91   Pg. 931 for Cost & fees   Can't Everyday

Default judgment

Cost of Claim - $ 75.00
Serve claim fee - $ 46.87
Legal fees $ 3000.0
(Teacher will give you) $421.87

* Must provide Reciept of costs.
on test Attached is the Reciept.

Grand Total:

Amount of Claim - $ 21,764.87
New Interest - $ 15.89
Amount of Default $ 421.87
judgment

$ 22,345.65

post Judgment - Day of start April 10/15

1) Claim Amount +   - $21,923.78
   Interest
   (21,764.87 + 158.91)

2) Default Judgment   - $421.87
   Cost

3) New Interest: - 2.0%

4) New Costs   - $35.00 ⎱ $54.00
   * Certificate of   - $19.00 ⎰
     Service
   * writ ⌃ from pg. 900

   * Any legal fees   - No in this Case.

Interest Calculations:
                            2015
Day of payment - April 30th (20 days)

Formula:

(20 days ÷ 365) × Amount of claim + Interest

= Post Judgment Interest Amount

= $ 24.03

Claim Amount: -$21,923.78
Re Judgment Amount: $421.87
Post Judgment Interest $24.03

Grand TOTAL $22,423.68

A write on test

: Attached is the bill of costs.